English 21

for Literature

academic.cengage.com/english21

Supporting students through every step of the writing process

More than just the largest compilation of online resources ever organized for literature courses, English21 supports students through every step of the writing process, from assignment to final draft. This complete support system weaves robust, self-paced instruction with interactive assignments to engage students as they become better prepared and more effective writers.

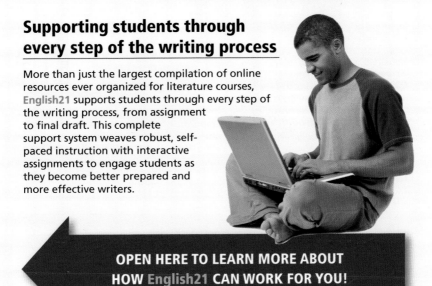

OPEN HERE TO LEARN MORE ABOUT HOW English21 CAN WORK FOR YOU!

[Legacies]

Fiction Poetry Drama Nonfiction

Fourth Edition

Jan Zlotnik Schmidt

SUNY New Paltz

Lynne Crockett

Sullivan County Community College

Carley Rees Bogarad

Late, SUNY New Paltz

WADSWORTH
CENGAGE Learning™

Australia • Brazil • Japan • Korea • Mexico • Singapore • Spain • United Kingdom • United States

WADSWORTH
CENGAGE Learning™

Legacies: Fiction, Poetry, Drama, Nonfiction, Fourth Edition
Jan Zlotnik Schmidt, Lynne Crockett, Carley Rees Bogarad

Publisher: Lyn Uhl

Development Editor: Cheryl Forman

Editorial Assistant: Lindsey Veautour

Technology Project Manager: Stephanie Gregoire

Executive Marketing Manager: Mandee Eckersley

Marketing Assistant: Kathleen Remsberg

Advertising Project Manager: Stacey Purviance

Senior Content Project Manager: Karen Stocz

Creative Director: Rob Hugel

Senior Art Director: Cate Barr

Manufacturing Manager: Marcia Locke

Print Buyer: Elizabeth Donaghey

Permissions Editor: Fred Courtright/Mardell Glinski-Schultz

Production Service: Newgen–Austin

Text Designer: Carrington Design

Photo Researcher: Fred Courtright

Copy Editor: Kathy Clayton

Cover Designer: Laurie Anderson

Cover Image: © 2007 Masterfile Corporation

For product information and technology assistance, contact us at
Cengage Learning Academic Resource Center,
1-800-423-0563

For permission to use material from this text or product, submit all requests online at
www.cengage.com/permissions.
Further permissions questions can be e-mailed to **permissionrequest@cengage.com**.

Library of Congress Control Number: 2007937851
ISBN-13: 978-1-4282-0629-8
ISBN-10: 1-4282-0629-9

Wadsworth Cengage Learning
25 Thomson Place
Boston, MA 02210
USA

Cengage Learning products are represented in Canada by Nelson Education, Ltd.

For your course and learning solutions, visit **academic.cengage.com.**

Purchase any of our products at your local college store or at our preferred online store **www.ichapters.com.**

Printed in the United States of America
2 3 4 5 6 7 12 11 10 09 08

[Dedication]

IN MEMORIUM
Dr. Carley Rees Bogarad
An Inspirational Teacher and Colleague

Brief Contents

Contents

Part 2   Thematic Anthology

Chapter 5   Identity and Rites of Passage   50

    Crossing the Genres: Identity and the Body

Part 3   Reading and Writing about the Genres

Additional Thematic Clusters that Cross the Genres

Contents by Genre

POETRY

DRAMA

NONFICTION

Preface

Legacies challenges students to enter the world of the twenty-first century, a culturally diverse place in which people's fates are crucially interconnected. It also introduces students to the analysis of literature, critical thinking and reading, and argument. The selections—fiction, poetry, drama, and nonfiction—represent complex and exciting traditions from 500 B.C. to the first decade of the twenty-first century. They include both global masterpieces and contemporary works, from Lao-tzu to Luisa Valenzuela, from Sophocles to August Wilson, from Rabindranath Tagore to Nadine Gordimer. As a thematic exploration of the individual in social, political, and cultural contexts, *Legacies* engages us in intellectual inquiry and provides the personal pleasures associated with the arts.

By reading and responding to fiction, poetry, drama, and nonfiction, we discover more about ourselves and others; we expand our thinking as conscious human beings. We develop moral imagination so that we can envision the views, experiences, and beliefs of others. Reading and writing about literature involves us in a process of critical analysis no different from the faculties we use in our everyday lives, but the process becomes directed, focused, and intensified. Interpretation of literary works encourages us to question, to observe keenly, to probe, and to critique—habits of mind central to a liberal education.

Organization

Because we agree with Wittgenstein's statement that "the limits of [our] language mean the limits of [our] world," we have written and edited this textbook with excellence and expansiveness as guiding principles. We divided the book into three major sections and four appendixes. In Part 1, Acts of Interpretation, the first chapter defines types of critical thinking and critical reading and then connects these ideas to the analysis of literature. Chapter 2 contains a discussion of forms of reader response to literature. Chapter 3 presents the process of writing about literary works and the forms of the essay. Chapter 4 introduces forms of argumentative thinking and relates it to writing about literary texts. Part 2, the Thematic Anthology, features readings organized by genre around five themes that progress from exploration of the self to larger issues: Identity and Rites of Passage; The Self and Beyond; Gender and Sexuality; Sites of Conflict; and Borderlands. We hope that each work will open and illuminate the others in order to inspire dynamic and complex inquiry and insight in every reader.

Part 3, Reading and Writing about the Genres, introduces forms and elements of fiction, poetry, drama, nonfiction, and visual texts. The appendixes include a full description of the research process and MLA documentation, analysis of visual texts, an overview of contemporary approaches to literary criticism, and author biographies.

The Anthology

Each anthology chapter of Part 2 has an introduction that articulates provocative ideas about the theme, selections, and connections among the texts. We intend our comments not as definitive interpretations but as starting points for discussion. The initial Crossing the Genres sections in the chapters combine works from the four literary genres to offer various possibilities for analysis, as do the suggested clusters in the Additional Thematic Clusters that Cross the Genres table of contents, which students can use to explore more themes on their own. In addition, clusters of thematically linked short stories, poems, and essays on controversial topics are included in every chapter. Exploratory questions, suggestions for reader response, and formal writing activities that connect the readings close each cluster. Extensive, process-oriented writing assignments appear at the end of each chapter.

Pedagogical Features

Legacies engages students in the indivisible activities of reading and writing and enlarges their capacities to develop ideas and to appreciate the richness and depth of responding to literature through the following important features:

- **Emphasis on Critical Thinking, the Reading and Writing Processes, and Argument.** Part 1: Acts of Interpretation, presents numerous examples of student responses, formal writing, a profile of one student's writing process: notes and initial and final drafts of an essay on Gloria Anzaldúa's "horse," and a comprehensive treatment of argument.
- **A Wide Variety of Readings from Traditional and Nontraditional Canons.** Selections in Part 2: Thematic Anthology, represent the best of new voices and of classic writers. These diverse readings, which prompt us to consider, among other things, issues of identity, family, gender and sexuality, ethnicity, class, terror and terrorism, and global and environmental concerns, embody our heritage, our literary legacies. Note the number of Nobel Prize laureates.
- **Juxtapositions of Readings within Themes.** In each chapter, an initial section entitled Crossing the Genres groups readings by theme across the genres. Additional suggestions for groupings across the genres are contained in the Additional Thematic Clusters that Cross the Genres table of contents. Within fiction, poetry, and nonfiction there also are clusters of readings organized by theme. Finally, these selections can also be studied by juxtaposing a number of works, according to subtopics of the major theme, gender of author, new and traditional voices, or regions of the world, to name only a few possibilities. This process leads naturally

to contrastive analysis, to questioning, and to examination of issues from multiple perspectives.

- **Thematic Clusters: Crossing the Genres.** These sets of suggested readings from each genre introduce each anthology chapter and exemplify the principle of juxtaposition. In each cluster, the poem may serve, for example, as motivation for discussion; the essay may provide a framework for analysis; and the fiction and/or drama may play against or complement each other. Together, these works can stimulate a dynamic process of critical inquiry.

- **Extensive Questions for Explorations of the Text.** These questions may be used for individual study, for guided class discussion, for lesson plans, or for collaborative (group) work. The questions begin with issues intrinsic to a given work (both textual and interpretive) and then consider thematic connections with other works. Questions have been field-tested: the number and nature of the exploratory questions represent the suggestions of students in classes.

- **Variety of Writing Activities.** Possibilities for reader response and ideas for writing follow each reading. They provide opportunities for personal reaction, creative expression, practice in various modes of exposition and argument, analysis, and interpretation of literature, and consideration of formal elements of the genres. Additional topics have been added to stimulate debate and argumentative writing.

- **Sample Student Essays.** Each anthology chapter offers a model student portfolio, illustrating a different form of the essay about literature, such as thematic analysis, comparison/contrast, critical analysis, explication, argument, cultural, historical or social analysis, and creative responses to literature.

- **Interesting and Ample Writing Assignments.** At the end of each anthology chapter, many of the assignments require a number of stages that encourage thorough exploration of topics; many others are traditional, and some contain directed research topics.

- **Extensive Treatment of the Forms and Features of Each Genre.** Part 3: Reading and Writing about the Genres, features comprehensive discussions of the genres with lively examples. The models of student writing in each chapter offer a wide range of approaches to all aspects of the reading and writing processes: reader response, explication, critical analysis, and evaluation.

- **Research, MLA Documentation, and Student Essay with Editorial Comments (Appendix A).** This appendix introduces a complete study of the research process and documentation, all major forms of MLA citation including online sources, and an example of a student paper with comments. No handbook should be necessary for the research process.

- **Visual Texts (Appendix B).** This new appendix introduces students to analyzing visual texts, including graphic literature.

- **Critical Theory (Appendix C).** *Legacies* presents a concise explanation of current approaches to literature and demonstrates these theories through multiple interpretations of Kate Chopin's "The Story of an Hour."

- **Author Biographies (Appendix D).** Brief biographies are included for every author represented in the book.
- **Extensive Definitions of Literary Terms.** Definitions of terms appear in the text as well as in the Glossary. Terms are printed in boldface type when they first appear in the text.
- **Comprehensive Instructor's Manual.** Our Instructor's Manual, based on materials tested and developed in the classroom, includes sample syllabi (with readings organized by theme or genre), answers to the "Explorations of the Text" for each selection, suggested further works and films to complement the readings in each chapter, and lesson plans.
- **Web Resources.** *On the Web* clusters and resources centered on such topics as fairy tales, gothic tales, modern love, protest songs, responses to 9/11, and the environment are included in every anthology chapter and links can be found on our companion website. Historical, social and cultural, and biographical and critical contexts can be found on the site as well.

New to the Fourth Edition

Increased Focus on Argumentative Thinking and Writing:

- New chapter on argumentative thinking and writing arguments about literature.
- New "Write an Argument" questions and writing assignments are included for most selections, giving students many opportunities to analyze arguments in the texts and to write their own persuasive essays.
- General expansion of argument coverage through the essay clusters and additional controversial essays in each anthology chapter.

Innovative Themes and New Genre-Specific Thematic Clusters

- Each anthology chapter explores a unique and engaging theme, three of which are new to this edition: Identity and Rites of Passage (Chapter 5), The Self and Beyond (Chapter 6), and Borderlands (Chapter 9).
- Students delve deeper into each theme in the Crossing the Genres clusters that open each anthology chapter. These clusters bring together readings in each of the four genres and cover innovative themes such as Identity and the Body, The Elusive Sexual Self, Terror and Terrorism, and The Human Animal.
- New genre-specific clusters ask students to make connections between works and include such themes as Free Will vs. Determinism/*Fiction* and Loss and Family/*Poetry*. All genre-specific clusters have been expanded from the previous edition and now include "Explorations of the Text," "The Reading/Writing Connection," and "Ideas for Writing" questions and writing assignments that help students explore each theme in depth.
- New clusters of essays grouped by controversial topics to stimulate argumentative thinking, writing, and debate. These include Pilgrimages, Es-

cape or Enlightenment?; The Nuclear Family Redefined?; Masculinities/
Femininities—Conditioned or Constructed?; and Visions of the Spirit.

Over Thirty Percent New Readings

- Addition of more authors from the traditional canon (such as Robert
  Browning, William Carlos Williams, Gabriela Mistral, Robert Frost) as
  well as new pieces by multicultural and global authors (such as Edwidge
  Danticat, Dagoberto Gilb, Naomi Shihab Nye, and Daniel Alarcón) and
  by new contemporary writers (such as Jonathan Lethem, Alison Bechdel,
  Mary Gaitskill, and Mark Doty).
- Expanded selection of classic and contemporary drama (i.e., William
  Shakespeare's *Othello,* Henrik Ibsen's *A Doll's House,* David Henry
  Hwang's *M Butterfly,* August Wilson's *The Piano Lesson,* and Paula
  Vogel's *How I Learned to Drive*).
- New essays that provide contexts for the readings (i.e., Bruno Bettelheim's
  "Introduction" to *The Uses of Enchantment,* Elie Wiesel's "Why I Write:
  Making No Become Yes," and Andrew Sullivan's "What's So Bad About
  Hate?").
- Expanded treatment of forms of creative nonfiction including such au-
  thors as Joan Didion, Gretel Ehrlich, Scott Russell Sanders, and David
  Sedaris.
- Inclusion of graphic literature by such authors as Marjane Satrapi, Lynda
  Barry, and Art Spiegelman.
- Inclusion of online works that expand the themes and add context to the
  selections.

New Appendix on Visual Rhetoric

- Discussions introduce visual forms and elements, analysis of visual texts,
  and a process for reading and writing about visual texts.
- Analysis of visual texts: a web page and a panel from Marjane Satrapi's
  graphic novel, *Persepolis.*

Eduardo Galeano suggests that "one writes out of a need to communicate and to commune with others. . . . One assumes that literature transmits knowledge and affects the
behavior and language of those who read, thus helping us to know ourselves better and
to save ourselves collectively." We hope that this book will prompt readers to "communicate and to commune." In large measure, we have based this volume on what our
students have told us that they want to "know." It reflects their choices of texts and
presents examples of their thoughts and writing. It is their book, their legacy.

Acknowledgments

Thanks must go to everyone who contributed to this fourth edition of *Legacies*. First, we thank our students for their cooperation and contributions to this project. We also acknowledge colleagues who contributed their insights and suggestions. At the State University of New York, New Paltz, Marissa Caston, Ernelle Fife, Penny Freel, Peggy Hach, Jason Letts, Vika Shock, Goretti Vianney-Benca, and Nicholas Wright.

At the State University of New York, New Paltz, several faculty members served as consultants for the anthology. Professors Laurence Carr and Anita Gonzalez offered extensive advice and suggestions about drama. Professor Pauline Uchmanowicz recommended several outstanding ethnic writers and selected texts as well as suggestions about graphic literature. As our Shakespeare consultant and scholar, Professor Thomas G. Olsen was particularly helpful in providing scholarly perspectives and a thorough and comprehensive apparatus for *Othello*. His assistance was invaluable. We learned a great deal from our colleagues and profited from their expertise.

More specifically, we want to acknowledge the efforts of those who contributed particular sections to this edition of *Legacies*:

- Robert Waugh, for his superb translation of Paul Celan's "Death Fugue"
- Carrie Holligan, for the apparatus for "How to Tell a True War Story"
- Rachel Rigolino, for her class project—the online assignment, student creative work, and discussion forum for "horse"
- Abigail Robin, for her suggestions for essays by Emma Goldman and the apparatus for "Minorities vs. Majorities"
- Fiona Paton and John Langan, for their collaboration on the second edition of *Legacies* and for their revision of Appendix B, Critical Approaches to Literature
- Aniko Berman, for her research on online magazines and selection of online texts
- Jennifer Sherman, for her recommendation of Alisa Quart's *Branded*
- Russell Dembin, Alyssa Moore, and Joe Whalen for their feedback about new works
- Dr. Thomas Lund, for his scholarly perspective concerning boys' development
- Christopher Cimino, for his lesson plan and research on *Persepolis*
- Mary Fakler, for her work on the student portfolio for *A Doll's House*

We are deeply indebted to Mark Bellomo for his extraordinary work creating the author biographies and composing the Instructor's Manual. His advice was central to the development of this edition. We also thank our colleagues at SUNY New Paltz who served as reviewers of the third edition and participated in a focus group that helped us determine the selection of readings: Donna Baumler, Tina Iraca, Jenica Lyons, Rachel Rigolino, and Abigail Robin. As long-time users of the book, they provided in-depth and productive feedback. This book truly was a collaborative effort.

Finally, and most importantly, we thank Harold A. Zlotnik—a consummate teacher, poet, and mentor—he provides a model of excellence in teaching that continues to inspire.

For her work on *Legacies,* for her commitment and dedication to this project, we also express our gratitude to Ethel Wesdorp. This volume could not have come to fruition without her dedicated efforts.

We also are grateful for the many productive suggestions and comments from the following reviewers, though, of course, any remaining shortcomings of the volume are our responsibility alone.

Ashley Bonds, *Copiah-Lincoln Community College*

Virginia Dumont-Poston, *Lander University*

Dwonna Goldstone, *Austin Peay State University*

Nate Gordon, *Kishwaukee College*

Kenneth Hawley, *Lubbock Christian University*

Elizabeth Keats, *College of Lake County*

Elizabeth Kleinfeld, *Red Rocks Community College*

Amy Lerman, *Mesa Community College*

Miles Mccrimmon, *J. Sargeant Reynolds Community College*

Jane Rosecrans, *J. Sargeant Reynolds Community College*

Martha Stoddard Holmes, *California State University San Marcos*

Allison Whittenberg, *Drexel University*

Robert Williams, *Radford University*

Roseann Wolak, *College of St. Benedict*

At Cengage Learning, we thank Aron Keesbury, a brilliant and imaginative acquisitions editor who has a passion for literature and who believed in this book, and Cheryl Forman, a supportive, energetic, and efficient developmental editor. We thank Fred Courtright for his relentless pursuit of permissions and Karen Stocz and Jamie Armstrong for turning our manuscript into a beautiful book.

Finally, we acknowledge friends and family who contributed their suggestions, insights, proofreading skills, and most importantly, their support: Barbara and Michael Adams, Arthur Cash, Judith Dorney, Phyllis R. Freeman, Mary Gordon, Patricia Phillips, Deborah Roth, Robert and Katherine Waugh. Most of all, we thank our families—Tom, Pat, Eran, and Coreen Crockett; Mary Gardeski and Pat Mitchell; John and Pamela Gardeski; Peter and Maggie Crockett; Donald and Rolf Gardeski; Marilyn Zlotnik, Peter Hultberg, Samantha and Gabriel; Adrienne Swezey, Jared, Dylan, and Mechelle; Gayle, Segev, and Yotam Guistizia; Philip and Reed Schmidt; and Mae and Harold Zlotnik—for their unending encouragement and unwavering love. They have been our best readers. We dedicate this book to them and to our students.

[Acts of Interpretation]

Critical Thinking and Critical Analysis of Literature

> [The mysterious] is the fundamental emotion which stands at the cradle of true art and science. He [she] who knows it not and can no longer wonder, no longer feels amazement, is as good as dead, a snuffed out candle.
>
> Albert Einstein

Two girls discover
the secret of life
in a sudden line of
poetry.

I who don't know the
secret wrote
the line. They
told me

(through a third person)
they had found it
but not what it was,
not even

what line it was. No doubt
by now, more than a week
later, they have forgotten
the secret,

the line, the name of
the poem. I love them
for finding what
I can't find

and for loving me
for the line I wrote

and for forgetting it
so that

a thousand times, til death
find them, they may
discover it again, in other
lines,

in other
happenings. And for
wanting to know it,
for

assuming there is
such a secret, yes
for that
most of all.

Denise Levertov, "The Secret"

As human beings, when we "read" the world around us, whether we realize it or not, we delve into the world's secrets. From our vantage point, we may look at a beautiful mountain scene and ask ourselves if a fog is on the mountain, what wildflowers would grow there, or whether a hiking path leads to the summit. Or we may take a bus ride, observe the passengers, and construct visions of their lives: An elderly woman in a dark housedress lives alone in a depressing New York apartment; a young boy with a base-ball cap is going to a little league game; a college student with a book bag is on her way to take a final exam that will determine whether she passes or fails a class. We observe, question, and construct visions of the "secrets" of a place and/or of a person. Then, as quickly as we create meanings, the scene disappears from view, and we may begin the process again to "discover" meanings "in other happenings." The ways in which we re-spond to the texts of our world are not qualitatively different from the ways in which we read literary works. When we read, we look more deeply, and we "discover" and con-struct a work's "secret[s]"—visions of experience—and share these mysteries with other readers. And then, as Denise Levertov suggests, we may forget our interpretations, reread a work, and discover new meanings. The study of literature gives us this vital process—opportunities to find "the secret of life" in a "sudden line of poetry."

The Critical Thinking Process

This ability to wonder, to be curious, to probe, to observe, to question, to look below the surface, to reflect, to discover, and to create meanings constitutes our capacity for critical thinking. As human beings, we constantly seek meaning from—and impose meaning upon—our experiences. In our desire to comprehend, we reflect on our per-ceptions, feelings, experiences, and ideas, and in the process, we create interpretations of our world.

The Critical Thinking/Critical Reading Connection

In critical analysis of literature, certain aspects of the thinking process that we use in daily life are heightened and intensified: reaction and response, analysis, interpretation, and evaluation and judgment. According to Ellin Oliver Keene and Susan Zimmerman in *Mosaics of Thought,* we read on several levels. We make **text-to-self, text-to-text,** and **text-to-world** connections. In **text-to-self** connections, we read a work, react, create associations between the work and our own lives, and explore our feelings and responses. We may ask how we respond to the world of the reading. For example, if we are reacting to a short story, we may analyze our responses to setting, to character, and to the plot. We may ask ourselves if we are involved in the world of the reading, if the experiences of the characters resonate with our own, if we come to realizations as a result of our reading, and if our own experiences are illuminated by the ideas represented in the literary work. We assess the impact of the work upon our inner lives, and we determine if the author's vision will enlarge or change our views of self and of the world. We wonder if the work's "secret[s]" will lead us to understand our own.

We also read, observe, and ask ourselves about the meaning and the effect of the words on the page. We create **text-to-text** connections to form an interpretation of the work. We look beneath the surface of the words to find implied meaning. We consider the ideas that are implicit in the words. In this process, we ask ourselves the following questions:

1. What is stated?
2. What exists beyond the surface level? What is implied?
3. What information do we need to make inferences?
4. What are our biases? How does our perspective shape our views?
5. How does the writer's perspective shape the work?
6. What conclusions do we form as to meaning?

We form conclusions about our inferences and develop patterns of meaning—**text-to-text** connections that constitute interpretations of a work. Our impressions often undergird our process of critical analysis—and, after we analyze, we may change or deepen our responses.

Finally we create **text-to-world** connections. We ask ourselves if, through reading, we will comprehend another world, another culture, or another time in history. We also make connections between ideas in the work and issues in our world and, consequently, gain insights about our own life and times. Extratextual material also includes biographical information, historical background, cultural and social contexts and issues, and critical views. All these perspectives expand our understanding of the "secret[s]" of a work, and they enlarge our own view of the world.

We also read to discern if the ideas presented in a work have value. We engage in an ongoing dialogue with a work, and we evaluate the language of the text, assess the words for evidence of a writer's bias and assumptions, and draw conclusions about a writer's attitude toward his or her subject and beliefs. We may compare the author's stance with our own beliefs. We may criticize, **argue** with, and debate the meanings and views of a text—accepting or rejecting its ideas and embracing or disdaining its author's point of view.

In addition, we may judge the language to determine its worth. If the text is an argument, we may ask if the writer is persuasive. If it is a descriptive piece, we may examine our involvement in the world of the reading. If it is a political speech, we may ask how the politician wants us to respond. We may wonder if we are being manipulated by the words of the speech; we may analyze the slant of the speaker, the use of evidence, and the logic of the approach. To determine the effectiveness of a literary work, we may focus intensively on a study of language and explore the effects of words: the **denotations** (dictionary definitions) and **connotations** (associations, suggested and implied meanings) of the words; the author's **tone** (attitude) and **point of view** (perspective) toward his or her subject; the **structure** (organization) of the work; **style** (detail, imagery, word choice); and the nature of the themes presented. Finally, we may ask ourselves if the work seems effective and worthwhile and determine its merits according to our standards of judgment.

Consider student responses during a class discussion of Lorna Dee Cervantes's poem "Refugee Ship" as an illustration of the critical thinking/critical reading connection.

Lorna Dee Cervantes

Refugee Ship

like wet cornstarch
I slide past mi abuelita's[1] eyes
bible placed by her side
she removes her glasses
the pudding thickens   5

mama raised me with no language
I am an orphan to my spanish name
the words are foreign, stumbling on my tongue
I stare at my reflection in the mirror
brown skin, black hair   10

I feel I am a captive
aboard the refugee ship
a ship that will never dock
a ship that will never dock

First the students made **text-to-self** connections. They reacted to the title and stated that the poem made them feel sad and that it invoked comparisons with the plight of the Vietnamese, with the predicament of other immigrant groups who came earlier to the United States, and with the tragedy of the Haitian boat people or other refugees. As they pondered the significance of the title in relation to the story of a grandmother

---

[1] **mi abuelita's eyes:** my grandmother's eyes.

and a granddaughter, they expressed feelings, discovered personal associations, and asked questions about the text.

They also realized that they needed to step back, to cast their personal associations aside, and to develop an interpretation of the work that focused on the relationship of the grandmother and her granddaughter and the speaker's connection to her heritage. They made **text-to-text** connections. They gathered information from the poem and focused first on understanding the grandmother's character through analyzing the objects associated with her: "glasses," "bible," and her gesture of taking off her spectacles. They concluded that she was a traditional Latina grandmother, unable to understand the speaker, her granddaughter. Some descriptive details (the images of "cornstarch" and "pudding [that] thickens") puzzled them. They wondered, "What is 'like wet cornstarch'?"; "What does the image have to do with the portrayal of the granddaughter?"; "What is the speaker like?" "Why is she described as an 'orphan' and as a 'captive'?" They began by making observations, and then they started analyzing the stated and implied meanings of the words and images of the poem.

The students concluded that the grandmother and granddaughter exist in separate worlds. The granddaughter, the speaker, cannot communicate with her grandmother because the latter cannot speak or understand English. The persona (the speaker in the poem) has learned "no language"; she has not learned Spanish and, therefore, she finds herself with "words [that] are foreign, stumbling on [her] tongue," her Spanish heritage lost. The granddaughter yearns to know Spanish, to communicate with her grandmother, and to learn more about her people. As the students began deciphering the meaning of the words and images, they realized that "wet cornstarch" is a necessary ingredient that "thick[ens]" a pudding; and that the "pudding" then suggests the emotional distance between grandmother and granddaughter, a distance that the speaker cannot dissolve or resolve.

Lastly they made **text-to-world** connections. As the students formed interpretations about the meaning of the work, they also realized that the speaker feels as if she lives like a "captive" on a "refugee ship/a ship that will never dock." One student exclaimed, "The movement of the ship—anxiety—never to be able to dock, to find stability, to understand her roots, to have a home"; and another reflected, "The repetition of the last line adds emphasis and sadness." Finally, a student concluded, "Both people are lost, not at home in America, and lost to each other."

The class discussion dynamically progressed from text-to-self, to text-to-text, to text-to-world connections. The students moved beyond their first impressions of the work and discovered multiple layers of implied meanings. They also evaluated the work and determined that each word, phrase, and image evoked vivid and significant ideas. A deceptively simple poem presented to them a compelling vision of loss of heritage, language, and connection with one's past.

Critical Analysis of Literature: A Classroom Experience

Examine this more expansive model of the critical reading process that emerged during a class discussion of Theodore Roethke's "My Papa's Waltz."

Theodore Roethke

My Papa's Waltz

The whiskey on your breath
Could make a small boy dizzy;
But I hung on like death:
Such waltzing was not easy.

We romped until the pans   5
Slid from the kitchen shelf;
My mother's countenance
Could not unfrown itself.

The hand that held my wrist
Was battered on one knuckle;   10
At every step you missed
My right ear scraped a buckle.

You beat time on my head
With a palm caked hard by dirt,
Then waltzed me off to bed   15
Still clinging to your shirt.

Text-to-Self Connections

The teacher asked students to record their initial responses to the poem in the form of a cluster that she put on the board:

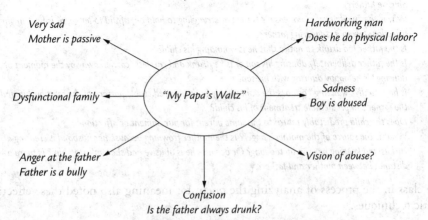

First Impressions
Emotional Responses and Associations

Very sad
Mother is passive

Hardworking man
Does he do physical labor?

Dysfunctional family   *"My Papa's Waltz"*   *Sadness*
Boy is abused

Anger at the father
Father is a bully

Vision of abuse?

Confusion
Is the father always drunk?

Text-to-Text Connections

Next she had students focus on key words and questions and group their observations into patterns of meaning. The students asked, for example, whether the waltz suggested a moment of closeness, albeit tainted, between father and son or a relationship between an abusive parent and child. Witness the next cluster that they formed and their list of several patterns of meaning.

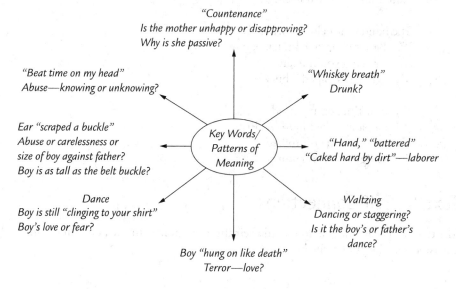

The basic facts: Drunken father, a dance between father and child
Scene: The kitchen—The dance creates a mess—pans fall down
Fun or Frenzy?

"Countenance"
Is the mother unhappy or disapproving?
Why is she passive?

"Beat time on my head"
Abuse—knowing or unknowing?

"Whiskey breath"
Drunk?

Ear "scraped a buckle"
Abuse or carelessness or
size of boy against father?
Boy is as tall as the belt buckle?

Key Words/
Patterns of
Meaning

"Hand," "battered"
"Caked hard by dirt"—laborer

Dance
Boy is still "clinging to your shirt"
Boy's love or fear?

Waltzing
Dancing or staggering?
Is it the boy's or father's
dance?

Boy "hung on like death"
Terror—love?

Patterns of Meaning/Questions and Interpretations

- Is the boy hoping that the dance will never end? (Is it a moment of closeness, or is the boy clinging to an abusive father?)
- Why is the "waltzing . . . not easy"? Is the boy struggling to hold on, afraid to let go, or is he "clinging" affectionately to a staggering father?
- Is the father too drunk to notice that he is wounding his child?
- Is the father deliberately abusing his son or is he drunk and careless, carried away by the moment of dancing? Is he happy dancing with his son?
- Is he actually "waltzing" or does the dance imply both the predictable pattern of the relationship and the father's unpredictable treatment of his child?
- Does the child predictably return to the same parent for punishment or affection?
- What is the source of the mother's anger? Is the mother frowning because her husband is creating a ruckus and keeping her son up too long? Or because he is abusive and she can't stop him? Is there a distance between mother and father?

The class in the process of analyzing the poem for meaning also noted these effective poetic techniques:

- The rhythm, rhyme, and four-line stanzas are unobtrusive and fit the waltzing motif.
- The images of the dance are powerful.
- The perspective of the child works.

Finally, the class formed interpretations of the poem. The class was divided in its analysis of the meaning of the work. Some students believed that the speaker was presenting a moment between an alcoholic father who was negligent and careless but who loved his child. This group of students thought that the poem depicts a moment of bonding between father and son, represented in the boy's "clinging" to the father's shirt as he was danced "off to bed." However, the other group of students determined that the father was abusive. They pointed to the images of cruelty in the poem: The boy's ear "scraped a buckle"; The father was "beat[ing] time on [the boy's] head" while the boy "hung on like death." Both groups examined the work carefully, dissecting word and image, constructing patterns of meaning and interpretations. "Who was right?" they asked. The teacher assured students that several interpretations of a work were valid as long as they returned to the text to test their evolving interpretation and to find evidence to support their ideas.

At this point she also suggested the possibility of turning to extra-textual materials (**text-to-world information**), of doing biographical research, or of reading criticism of the work. Although biographical information may be misleading, it also may illuminate a writer's choices: a portrayal of a character's dilemma, a plot element, or a symbolic motif. It is important to realize, the teacher suggested, that his poem is based on Roethke's memory of a "dance" with his father, that the poet's father was a florist and owned a greenhouse (hence, "the palm caked hard by dirt"), and, therefore, that the ambiguities in the poem may reflect the ambivalent response of a son to a father and the fuzziness of memory. The teacher also provided a sociological perspective, asking the class if the work presents a portrait of an abused child: What aspects of the persona's, the father's, or the mother's behavior could lead to an interpretation of the waltz as the "dance" of a dysfunctional family? In addition, the teacher challenged the students to consider a feminist, critical perspective by asking about the role of the mother in the scene: Does the mother try to stop the father? Is she silent? Why could her "countenance/. . . not unfrown itself"? What does her behavior suggest about her role in the family and her relationship with her husband? A lively discussion of the family dynamics deepened the students' critical interpretations of the work.

As the students examined their responses to "My Papa's Waltz," they began to understand the various processes involved in critical reading. Many of the analyses and evaluations they agreed upon. Then they uncovered disagreements. Ultimately, they decided that the poem had multiple layers of meaning and that they could entertain several points of view at once as they tested their conclusions against the words on the page, the words of others in the class, and critical sources. They learned that class discussion, dialogue, and research enhanced the critical reading process. Finally, in the course of discussion, they also discovered the wholeness of the process. In reading any text, we do not separate modes of feeling and thinking, but simultaneously engage in many critical acts of interpretation. We react, remember, associate, observe, infer from information, form conclusions, analyze, interpret, evaluate, argue, and judge. These processes lead to a deepened appreciation of the phenomena and texts of our world.

The Reading Process

Reader Response

To be frank, not every reading experience becomes a full, rich, interpretation of a text. Many times we read simply to garner information, as when we survey road signs, food labels, or sets of instructions. We may read newspapers, letters, and textbooks in our college classes; and the main aim may be solely to summarize information. At other times, we may wish to read a book on a level approaching pure emotional response and appreciation. Often, while we read, our minds are wandering, not concentrating on the work. However, the process of critical reading that we wish to emphasize is one in which the reader is fully involved, responding on many levels of feeling and thinking. We do not simply scan words on a page; we form emotional reactions, gather information, construct patterns of meaning, analyze, interpret, and evaluate a work to determine its effectiveness and its worth.

The Reading/Writing Connection

Writing helps develop the reading process, keeping it active and critical. Writing also inspires fuller **text-to-self, text-to-text,** and **text-to-world** connections. The following are some procedures for reading and reacting to a text, called *reader response strategies,* all of which involve writing. These procedures include *glossing* and *annotating, brainstorming* and *questioning, freewriting, journal writing, blogs, notetaking, "think" writings, arguments about literary texts,* and *creative responses to literature.*

Glossing and Annotating

Examine a series of reader responses written by students about Gloria Anzaldúa's poem, "horse," from her autobiography, *Borderlands: La Frontera—The New Mestiza.* You may react to this poem in many ways. Reading theorists suggest that you first preview the work by looking at the title and by scanning the poem to gain an overview of it. Then you read the passage again to learn content and to write notes about your reactions to the text. This process is called *glossing* and *annotating.* When you gloss a work, you read it to understand content; and you take notes, called *annotations,* as you read. You may make comments in the margins, underline the title and key words, and record reactions or questions. You create a map of the reading so that you know its structure and key points. You also discover your own questions, reactions, and initial responses. After you have completed your marginal annotations, you might make *end comments* that include the key ideas and describe the impact of the work on you. Analyze this annotation and end comment for "horse":

horse
(para la gente de Hargill, Texas[1])

Why the title?
Why small letters?
Is this a true story? What does the dedication mean?

Horse is free, powerful.

Great horse running in the fields
come thundering toward
the outstretched hands
nostrils flaring at the corn

Look at ing verbs: power-action

5 only it was knives in the hidden hands
can a horse smell tempered steel?

*Shift to death and destruction

Anoche[2] some kids cut up a horse
it was night and the pueblo[3] slept
the Mexicans mutter among themselves:

Key: hobbled crippled horse

10 they hobbled the two front legs
the two hind legs, kids aged sixteen
but they're gringos
and the sheriff won't do a thing
he'd just say boys will be boys

Contrast Spanish words vs. anglos Spanish gringo

15 just following their instincts.

Mexican World Narrative form Build up of story

Horse— Soul of people

But it's the mind that kills
the animal the mexicanos murmur
killing it would have been a mercy
black horse running in the dark

Horse— symbol of Mexican identity

20 came thundering toward
the outstretched hands
nostrils flaring at the smell
only it was knives in the hidden hands
did it pray all night for morning?

Repetition— Contrast Power of horse vs. crippling

Mexican people?

25 It was the owner came running
30.30 in his hand
put the caballo[4] out of its pain
the Chicanos shake their heads
turn away some rich father

A Mexican must put horse out of pain. Mexican people go home to die.

30 fished out his wallet
held out the folds of green

Strong images of blood. Graphic. Is the horse castrated?

as if green could staunch red
pools dripping from the ribbons
on the horse's flanks

Boys "get off." Money is power.

35 could cast up testicles
grow back the ears on the horse's head

What does the corn symbolize?

no ears of corn but sheaths
hiding blades of steel
earth drinking blood sun rusting it

Corn—symbol of sustenance, replaced by knives, death. Opposition.

40 in that small Texas town

---

[1] **para la gente de Hargill, Texas:** for the people of Hargill, Texas.   [2] **Anoche:** last night.   [3] **pueblo:** town or village.   [4] **caballo:** horse.

the mexicanos shuffle their feet
shut their faces stare at the ground.

Dead horse neighing in the night
come thundering toward the open faces
45 hooves iron-shod hurling lightning
only it is <u>red red</u> in the moonlight
in their sleep the gringos cry out
the mexicanos mumble if you're Mexican
you are born old.

Repetition of color

Gringos cry out—why?

Why are hooves hurling lightning? Is it anger at racism?

Cycle of racism?

End Comment: Does this poem use a true story of boys crippling and mutilating a horse to suggest the pain and suffering of Mexicans in Texas facing prejudice and racism?

Brainstorming and Questioning

Another notetaking process is *brainstorming,* a process in which you write down ideas and comments in any order without attention to sequence, logic, or sentence structure. Register as many of your reactions as you can as your mind "storms" through a work. Jot single words or phrases without worrying about creating coherent, grammatical sentences and without worrying about organization and development. This technique allows you to sketch the range of your responses; later you can select certain ideas to compose your essay. One focused form of brainstorming is generating a list of questions concerning the work. You may use the reporter's questions (Who? What? When? Where? Why? How?) to trigger your explorations. Examine Mark Greenberg's brainstorming exercise for "horse":

Who is the "great horse"? Symbol?
Who is the speaker?
Who has the knives?
Why are they hidden?
Why did they do it?
The sheriff is hateful.
How can he use such lame excuses—"boys will be boys?" I'm a man, and
     I would never participate in such a terrible act.
Why does the father cover for the son? My dad would kill me.
The dead horse can thunder, can hurl lightning?
Is this the poet's retelling of the story? Autobiographical?
The horse, in many images, has many meanings.
Social tensions—inequalities between gringos and Mexicans.
Finally something about race relations.
A true story?

In his exercise, Greenberg's questions focus on the events of the poem, on the cruelty, and on his reactions to the sheriff who excuses and to the father who covers for the barbaric actions of the "boys." His responses direct Greenberg to the beginning of an interpretation: this is a poem about "inequalities between gringos and Mexicans" and "race relations."

Freewriting

Another method to express your responses, reactions, questions, associations, and analysis of the work is to freewrite immediately after you finish reading. *Freewriting* is a process in which you give yourself a certain amount of time, say, five minutes, to compose sentences without stopping and without censoring your thoughts. Write without stopping, without worrying, and without rereading—just keep going. Do not worry about grammar, spelling, punctuation, or meaning. Freewriting is a way to unleash thoughts, to discover your own responses and ideas. It is a way to bypass the part of the writer's self who is the editor and critic, that part of the self that blocks and censors the process of discovery. Often it is helpful not only to freewrite immediately after a first reading, but also to freewrite after several readings. You can compose a first sample, then isolate one idea from that work, and draft another version based on that idea. This second activity is called *focused freewriting*. You may create a series of freewritings that prompt you to discover your full reactions and to develop your thoughts into an essay.

Here are two examples of freewriting about "horse":

horse
Frances Gonzalez

The poem presents a powerful set of contrasts between the soul of the Mexican people and what happens to people when there is racism. The horse is powerful, black, free. The "thundering" gives a feeling of strength and force. Then the horse is "hobbled"; racism cripples. The black horse "running" "thundering" is contrasted with the impotence of, the powerlessness of the Mexicans who "mumble" "shake their heads" "shuffle" "stare at the ground" and "mumble." They seem weak, yet there is some hope. For the "dead horse" in the night "comes thundering" "hurling lightning"—that "lightning" is "red red." Does that mean that the Mexicans will rebel against injustice—that eventually justice will be done? Is the poet "hurling lightning" hoping to cry out—hoping her words will be heard that people will learn and speak "from the mind" in a different way? Not a way that kills?

horse
Julie Miller

I love the feeling of freedom at the beginning of the poem. There are such powerful images of the horse—running, "thundering"—"nostrils flaring." The horse is powerful and alive—then I knew danger was coming in the image of the knives. Why did the boys cut up the horse? Why would anyone do anything that senseless? I thought that it was so brutal and cruel that the horse was mutilated. It was hard to read. What did the horse symbolize? Did it symbolize the Mexicans? The "gringos" just think nothing of cutting up the horse. In the same way the white world in Texas is stopping Mexicans from having opportunities. The poem is asking people to feel the way the Mexicans are treated unfairly. The way they are being oppressed. The white world wins—The "rich father" pays off the owner. The boys aren't punished. The gringos have power. I understand the lines "if you're Mexican/you are born old." You are born with the knowledge of prejudice. This poem makes a powerful plea for understanding injustice.

Journal Writing

You may chart your reading responses by keeping a journal: an informal record of your thoughts and impressions. Your instructor already may have asked you to write a personal journal. A *reader response journal* provides an opportunity for you to write informally about the works that you read and encourages an expansion of the process of personal writing. The methods previously discussed are appropriate for a reader response journal in which you may include glosses and annotations (if you include the works), brainstorming notes and questions, freewrites, and responses to texts. In your reader response journal, you may write significant ideas and quotations. You may focus on any one of the following subjects:

- Explication, analyses (explanations of the works)
- Personal response (feelings-reactions to the works)
- Likes/dislikes
- Associations with other characters, other works, other readings, themes, issues, current events, materials in other classes
- Associations with events in your life
- Responses to characters
- Responses to key events
- Responses to key passages or to quotations
- Responses to issues presented (social, political)
- Judgments of characters
- Arguments with the writer, with key ideas, with characters' views
- Arguments with positions presented in class discussion
- Creative writing (stories, poems, plays)
- Imitations of style
- Monologues in the voices of characters

Again, as in freewriting, you need not worry about grammar, punctuation, spelling, or logical presentation of subject matter. Follow your own responses, ideas, and questions; and let them take over. A journal entry, however, may be more developed and more structured than a freewrite. You may be asked to revise your reactions into developed paragraphs. Your journal may become the source of ideas for essays. In your journal, you may have a record not only of your reading responses, but also of your emotional and intellectual development.

In this entry about "horse," Mark Greenberg summarizes information, reacts to descriptive language, begins to respond to details in the poem, and ends with his feelings about the message of the work.

horse

The black horse "thundered" toward the boys because they beckoned it. How could they summon a "great horse," the Mexican, only to cut it to pieces with knives, knives hidden in their hands? They tortured the animal because they believed that they had a right to do so. The "red red" blood, the flaying, excited them. They expected their fathers to pay for their cruelty and the owner of the horse to kill it—to finish their game. They exercised rights which they believed came with the color of their skin, with their social and economic positions. Little did they know that the dark horse would invade their dreams and make them "cry out," the dead horse—"red red"—"hurling lightning" through their dreams forever.

Blogging

A *blog,* or *web log,* is an online journal where you can write on an ongoing basis as you would in a diary or journal, quickly posting thoughts or ideas. The difference between an online and a paper journal is that with a blog, in addition to the written text, you can post electronic images; create links to music, videos, or other websites; and share your entries with your friends or with an unlimited audience. The audience can respond to your entries, thus creating an online dialogue. A blog can be a place for private contemplation or a collaborative space where people can meet to discuss ideas and issues.

To begin your blog, find a blog website, such as LiveJournal.com or webblogger.com. At the blog website, you can create an account, label and determine the design of your space, and determine who your audience will be. You can control people's access to your space by limiting it to yourself; to a small community of friends; to a larger group, such as your class or a club of which you are a member; or you can choose unlimited access, so that anyone can read your entries. You, as a blog writer, may choose a username that is similar to your real name, or you may prefer to use a name that leaves your identity anonymous. Going to these types of websites also gives you the opportunity to read and comment on others' blogs. One benefit of blogging is that it may expand your personal, social, and intellectual universe and bring you into contact with many more enriching ideas and points of view.

Notetaking and the Double-Entry Notebook

Another method of becoming an active reader is to keep a *double-entry notebook,* a form of notetaking adapted from theorist Ann Berthoff, who contends that writing and reading processes involve us in continually "interpreting our interpretations." Berthoff suggests that readers sometimes recognize only one level of reaction to a text—summary of main information—and neglect other levels of thinking provoked by the words: reactions, associations, questionings, analysis, synthesis, and theorizing. The double-entry notebook, or *dialectical notebook* as Berthoff calls it, prompts readers to be aware of all acts of interpretation and creates what Berthoff calls "the continuing audit of meaning." The journal entries provide readers with records of what they think about their own thinking.

For a double-entry notebook, we recommend that you write on the left-hand page of a notebook the facts, key points, and main information from a work. On the right-hand page, write all of your other responses, feelings, associations, questions, comparisons with other ideas, and interpretations. The notes need to be recorded as the reading takes place so that you capture your mind in action. Alternate from the left-hand page to the right-hand page. Keep writing back and forth from fact to reaction, analysis, questions, and comments. The double-entry notebook results in a more complex and complete response to a work. You are, therefore, much better prepared to write an essay about the text.

Examine the beginning and the conclusion of Mark Greenberg's double-entry notebook concerning "horse":

horse
Gloria Anzaldúa

Title "horse"	*Symbolic. Why no caps?*
para la gente de Hargill	*I don't know Spanish, but I can guess that the words mean—"For the people of Hargill." Why does she dedicate the poem? Is it a true story?*

Great horse
  running
  thundering
  nostrils flaring
	The horse is powerful, beautiful, expectant. Progressives add power and action. Good parallel constructions.

Knives in hidden hands	*Why offer corn and hide knives? Who?*
Question about smelling steel	*Rhetorical? Good sounds. Does steel have a smell?*
"Anoche"	*"Night"? "Last night"? "The night before"? "At night"?*
The Mexicans slept, and boys cut up *a horse*	*The straight story. Incredible cruelty.* *A narrative poem.*
The Mexicans "mutter"	*They cannot protest aloud.*
The "gringos" hobbled the legs	*How did they conceive of such cruelty? The horse is like the Mexicans—hobbled.*
Sheriff "boys will be boys" following instincts	*The law does not apply to gringos. What is wrong with us? This racism is blatant.*
It's the mind that kills the animal	*This statement is like a thesis sentence. It clearly emphasizes the situation of the Mexicans.*
Mexicans "murmur"	*Again, they cannot speak loudly.*
Killing would have been mercy	*These boys feel no sadness, have no mercy. The suffering seems unbearable. The writer must want me to feel this pain.*

Repetition of images and event
  black horse thundering
  outstretched hands
  flaring nostrils
  corn—knives
	Now that I know about the knives, the repetition is incredibly effective. The horse represents everything and everyone who was ever destroyed by promises of kindness and who was nurtured only to be conquered, tortured, or killed. This poem is difficult to read, to face, and to accept. The horse symbolizes the Mexicans.

■ ■ ■

Dead horse neighing in night
  thundering hooves
  "iron-shod"
  hurling lightning
	Paradox—unravels in dreams Retribution for the knives.

"red red in moonlight"	The horse has turned red, transformation. Blood, anger, revenge?
"gringos" "cry out"	The horse enters their dreams; they are not absolved; they have not triumphed. They have received a life sentence of nightmares.
The Mexicanos "mumble" "If you're Mexican/you are born old."	They do not speak. They are not empowered by the horse which hurls lightning. They are born old in a corrupt and oppressive environment. I want racism to disappear. I want a world which includes everyone. I want it now.

Note the writer's questions, analysis of the portrait and the symbolism of the horse, and inferences about the knife and the central action of the poem. Notice also the judgments about the boys' behavior and about the effectiveness of the verbs and images. The double-entry exercise prompted the writer to engage in all aspects of critical thinking and analysis. Sometimes an instructor may ask you to create a third column to prompt you to focus on a particular approach to a text, for example, a particular critical perspective, such as a feminist or Marxist analysis (see Appendix C for discussions of these and other critical approaches to literature).

"Think" Writings

Your instructor may assign as homework informal paragraphs or mini-essays with designated topics or questions that relate to the readings. Some instructors prefer not to incorporate freewriting or journals in a course because they think that these forms of writing are too subjective and unstructured and will not necessarily provoke in-depth analysis of works. They concentrate, instead, on more objective and formal modes of response to the assigned works. These **"think" writings**, however, like the more personal forms of reaction, prompt you to explore your responses to a literary work, direct your thinking, prepare you for participating in class discussion and for writing the essay about literature, and stimulate analysis and reflection. The questions may focus on a particular issue or theme of the work or a specific literary technique (for example, the symbolism in "horse"). Your instructor may collect these writings on a weekly or monthly basis or may ask you to select several of them as part of a writing portfolio. In addition, your instructor may ask you to frame these "think" questions yourself, to become a class discussion leader, and to present these topics as the opening to class discussion or as the basis of collaborative work. Finally, your instructor may ask you to participate in an online discussion group and to respond to "think" questions as part of your work in the course. (See Chapter 8 for an example of an online exercise in response to "horse.")

Possibilities for "think" writing topics include the following:

- First and final impressions of a work
- In-depth analysis of a key passage
- Treatment of a literary technique
- Selection and response to a quotation

- Focus on a particular theme
- Debate with a position suggested by a reading
- Letter to an author or to a character

Note Esther Martinez's short paragraph written in response to this "think" question: "What does the poem suggest about the American dream?" Note how she connects the horse with the identity of Mexican Americans and then compares the mutilation of the horse with the destruction of the American dream for Mexican Americans.

> *This is a poem about racism. Whites against Mexicans. There are a lot of ways that the poet shows the "inferiority" of the Mexicans. "horse" is not capitalized. Although the horse is a powerful, passionate animal, "thundering," "nostrils flaring," the horse is treated as inferior. The description of the kids hacking away at the horse symbolizes the Mexicans being beaten down, harassed. The castration symbolizes the Mexicans' shame. Their culture, way of life, traditions are seen as less special, their lifestyle as inferior. Is it wrong just because gringos say it's wrong? Are they not entitled to opportunity? What happens to their dreams for themselves, for their lives?*

Arguments about Literary Texts

Another form of "think" writing is an argumentative response to the text. You may create positions about issues, ideas, themes, or characters in a work. What follows are argumentative responses by Erick Estrada and Jennifer Bernstein to "horse" based on the following prompts: Respond to the vision in "horse," either pro or con. Or argue whether you find the poem's portrayal of white people to be stereotypical.

"horse"
Erick Estrada

> *I thought the poem represented a good contrast between the way Mexican people were treated in comparison to the white people. The horse represents something neutral, that isn't looked upon in a positive or negative way. Once the words that included "knives" and "steel" came in the poem, something negative was going to happen. Once the boys cut up the horse, it was like cutting up the boundary that keeps racism hidden. It is easy to understand how the boys get away with the crime. When the boys cut the horse and the father pays them off, it means that they have power and the advantage to break the neutrality. On the other hand, Mexicans don't have power, hence not having power to break neutrality. This poem makes a good point on racism and power.*

"horse": The Portrayal of White People
Jennifer Bernstein

> *If you study American history there is a clear pattern showing Caucasians' tendency to oppress others: Native Americans, Africans, African Americans, and Mexicans. Although I would say the depiction of Whites in the poem, "horse," by Gloria Anzaldúa is stereotypical, it is not necessarily historically inaccurate.*
>
> *In the poem, Anzaldúa states that "kids aged sixteen/but they're gringos/and the sheriff won't do a thing." It is a generalized statement that the sheriff will not care because the kids are "gringos"; however, Whites have been able to get away with a lot of violent*

acts performed against people of color. To assume the white sheriff "wouldn't care" is a bit presumptuous, but then again, following historical precedent it is a realistic theory. White people created the slave trade; Caucasians massacred Native Americans and stole their land; the White race has been known to mistreat other human beings horribly based on the color of their skin with little, if any, consequences.

The poem also portrays the idea that people who have money can use it to buy themselves out of any situation, and it is a commonly used stereotype that White people have more money than minorities. "[T]he Chicanos shake their heads/ turn away some rich father/ fished out his wallet/ held out the folds of green/ as if green could staunch red." In recent days ancestors of slave-owning families have been paying reparations to organizations like the NAACP and to individual families. As if paying African Americans now could ever make up for the pain inflicted upon their ancestors by their White oppressors.

Creative Responses to Literature

Another way to write about a work is to respond imaginatively through creative writing exercises. Imaginative writing gives you a different perspective on a work. Some possible approaches include the following:

- Write a letter to a character.
- Write a prequel or a sequel to a story.
- Add a scene to a drama.
- Turn a scene from a short story or drama into a film script.
- Cast the characters in a work as if you were directing a film. Explain your choices.
- Compose another stanza to a poem.
- Create a parody or imitation of a poem.
- Create a response to a poem using a different voice.
- Create a dialogue between characters from different works.
- Create a talk show featuring characters from different works.
- Change the genre of a work—for example, turn a realistic story into a horror story.
- Add another character to a work, and tell the story from his or her perspective.
- Change the point of view of a work—for example, if it is told in first person, shift to third person.
- Change the narrative perspective—for example, tell the story from the point of view of a minor character in the text.
- Create a book cover, portrait of a character, or scene from a work.
- Create a new rhetorical situation for information in the text, such as a newspaper account, biography or obituary for a character, eyewitness report, or psychological case study.
- Create a poem, short story, or work of art in response to a work, and then evaluate your text, suggesting how it reveals your responses to the work and/or specific themes of the work.
- Choose several lines from a poem and create a new work. Then suggest how your poem highlights themes from the text.

What follows is a creative response to "horse," a last stanza to the poem written by Emily Kate Hertzberg:

memory like explosives in a feather pillow
hundreds of missing lines
horrible mouths torn from old
they melted the horse from their minds
like photographs taken by dead people with cameras without film
black out-of-tune notes playing a death dirge on a violin strung with barbwire
at a loss for a reason
surrounded by danger and uncertainty
hallucinating that the horse still rode in the night
breaking the mirror of silence
badly beaten by invisible things
water boiling underground
remember to remember
time to turn somebody in
it's now and never
never seen or heard from again

Critical analysis requires your active involvement in the process. These forms of reader response—glossing and annotating, brainstorming and questioning, freewriting, journal writing, blogs, keeping a double-entry notebook, "think" writings, arguments about literature, and creative responses—will help you become a more involved reader and lead to richer, fuller, more complex interpretations and judgments of literary works.

Some Final Considerations about the Reading Process

These methods of reader response enable us to discover ideas and to unpeel the layers of our reactions to a work. They also validate our approaches to literature. They remind us that the reading process is both objective and subjective—objective, because we interpret verifiable texts; subjective, because we are unique in our reactions to those texts. We create meanings as a result of our own perspectives, gender, ethnic and class backgrounds, cultural contexts, personalities, and values. Reading is an interactive process. The writer, who has a particular perspective, personality, and background and who is part of a particular culture at a specific time in history, creates a work and invests it with a set of meanings. The reader, who, likewise, is a product of individual traits and cultural influences at a particular point in history, brings ideas and values to the work and derives meaning from the work. The text acts on the reader; the reader creates a particular version (interpretation) of the text.

Certain aspects of literature, however, may be more widely comprehended. "Do Not Go Gentle into That Good Night" by Dylan Thomas (Chapter 9) generally will be considered a meditation on mortality. Yet each period's writers, each culture's writers, reinterpret these objective judgments, guided by emotional, personal, and social concerns. Each literary work, then, represents both a moment in history and in culture and a moment in an individual reader's and writer's life.

Would Harriet Beecher Stowe have written her antislavery novel, *Uncle Tom's Cabin,* if she had not been the daughter of an abolitionist minister, if she had not been driven by moral outrage and financial need, if she had not known the patterns of slave narratives, if she had not herself seen a place where runaway slaves had crossed the Ohio River to freedom? In each century, readers interpret Stowe's fiction differently. During her lifetime, readers in New England were moved by her novel to struggle to abolish slavery; her book was a bestseller. However, some present readers criticize her sentimentality and her depiction of the black slave.

Interpretations will vary, but some analyses of a work seem more valid than others. To justify our interpretations, we return continually to the work as the primary source, and we share our views with others in a community of readers in order to discuss and to compare ideas. In dialogue or collaboration with others, we may critique; and we may change our ideas and impressions. We may agree with an interpretation that differs from our original conclusion. We can enlarge our understanding of a work as we engage in the cyclic activities required by thinking, reading, and writing. Through these processes, which are *recursive,* to which we continuously return, we develop new perspectives on a work. For example, we may reread "Refugee Ship" (Chapter 1) and suddenly decide to study the poem from the point of view of the grandmother who cannot understand her granddaughter. The "glasses," the "bible," and the "pudding" assume new connotations as we shift attention from the speaker to the situation of another character in the work. In the process, we recognize that critical reading activities lead to a more comprehensive understanding of literature.

[3]

The Writing Process: Writing the Essay about Literature

When you approach the task of writing about literature, you may worry that you will not understand the text, that you will miss its secrets, and that you will not give the responses the instructor expects. You might believe that you have nothing to say. Such anxieties are natural—and groundless. Keep in mind that writing essays about literature evolves from the processes of critical thinking and reader response described in Chapters 1 and 2. These multifaceted activities provide no right or wrong answers.

You will not be asked to write papers that pose correct answers, although you will be expected to provide thoughtful interpretations supported by careful reading of a work. As you learn to trust your own thinking, you also will learn to trust your own acts of interpretation. Remember that you have valuable insights to contribute and that you will have opportunities to question, to test ideas with your peers and instructor, and to construct more developed interpretations that confirm, deny, or expand your initial views of a work.

Interrelated Stages of Writing

Writing essays about literature follows directly from procedures for reader response. You should realize, however, that an essay is not composed in a short burst of reader reaction or in moments of brilliant creative insights. Rather, the best essays result from many, many hours of thinking; and they take shape on paper in interrelated stages that include the following:

1. **Prewriting:** Discovering and planning ideas for writing.
2. **Shaping:** Organizing, outlining, and structuring ideas with an audience in mind.
3. **Drafting:** Composing and concentrating on organization, development, and fluency.
4. **Revising and Editing:** Sharpening wording, sentence structure, and style; re-arranging, deleting, and clarifying; checking for sentence variety and correct usage.
5. **Proofreading:** Correcting grammar, spelling, and punctuation.

These stages do not always occur in this sequential order; they vary from person to person and from writing task to writing task. Some people draft, edit, and proofread as they work. Others quickly write a first draft and check spelling, grammar, and punctuation later. Different writing situations dictate different processes: a laboratory report, a meditative essay, a journal, and a research paper all require distinct approaches to writing. Whatever your task, you will probably engage in many of these activities before you submit the final version of your essay. Consider each of these stages in detail:

Prewriting

Prewriting, the first stage of the process, takes place even before beginning a first draft and involves finding ideas for composing. As you prewrite, you discover subject matter, approach, and **point of view** (attitude toward the subject matter). Various prewriting strategies include these techniques—annotating, brainstorming, taking notes, listing, freewriting, clustering, mapping, journal writing, and talking with others. You also will select the form of your essay: think about the requirements of your assignment (page length and designated rhetorical mode—exposition, argument, research—for example). Then consider the purpose of your assignment; your main goal in writing. Some central purposes for writing are the following: to express yourself, to inform, to argue, or to create a literary work. You will begin to define your audience. In writing about literary subjects, you may assume that your audience is your instructor and your classmates—people who are familiar with the works that you discuss. Your instructor may designate such different audiences for your material as the campus newspaper or some group interested in the subject. Considerations of point of view, purpose, and audience constitute the **rhetorical situation** of a writing.

Shaping

The second stage of the writing process involves clear definition of focus, point of view, tone, tentative **thesis** (main idea), and topics for discussion. In terms of point of view and tone, you need to decide how you want your essay to sound to the reader. Will you write formally or informally? Will you sound sympathetic, involved, or angry? Will you be lyrical, meditative, or persuasive? These decisions fall into place as you determine your thesis, topics, method of organization, and relationship to audience. At this point, you assess your audience, determine the direction of thesis and topics, and develop and shape supporting evidence with your audience in mind. Then you map ideas, plan your writing, and create informal or formal outlines.

Drafting

The third stage of the writing process is drafting. In creating versions of essays, you consider not only purpose, requirements of the assignment, and audience, but also development and organization. You may recast your thesis, alter points, delete and add supporting information (quotations, facts, and specific paraphrased examples from the text), and sharpen language.

Revising and Editing

The fourth stage of the writing process involves revising and editing your essay. Consider your relationship with your audience, and ask yourself if you have organized and developed points with a particular audience in mind. Ask yourself if your tone and point of view are appropriate, if they are likely to interest your readers, and if they are convincing and strong. Examine your introduction to determine if it will capture your readers' attention and establish your purpose and thesis. Determine whether you have sufficiently developed your thesis and supporting points. Evaluate your conclusion and decide if it conveys the proper emphasis. Rewriting sometimes requires reviewing ideas and clarifying points—perhaps, even rethinking the entire piece—but it also involves fine tuning through editing, through changes in word choice, and through small alterations of order and structure.

Proofreading

Proofreading is the final stage of the writing process. Check your final draft for grammatical, punctuation, spelling, and typographical errors. For example, if you have trouble with sentence fragments, review sentence structure. If you tend to confuse "it's" and "its," reread your paper with this problem in mind. Examine the manuscript to ensure that it still follows the original requirements of the assignment.

Composing on a Computer

Many students compose directly on a computer. After jotting down some preliminary notes, they may draft immediately on the computer and embed the processes of prewriting, shaping, drafting, revising, and editing. If you work in this manner, here are some useful strategies to consider:

- Create a file folder for saving your prewriting (e.g., brainstorming, notes, and outlines). You may want to refer to this work later on in the process.
- Archive versions of your essay. Again, you don't want to lose important information that may not be contained in your final draft. You may want to refer to it later.
- If you work from a single paragraph exploratory draft and then use your cut-and-paste function to block out separate introductory, body, and concluding paragraphs, making sure these paragraphs and sentences within a paragraph proceed logically from point to point. Check the progression of ideas. As you rearrange and delete text, you should make sure your ideas still cohere. Check your transitional expressions; add transition words or sentences as necessary to create a fluid essay.
- As you expand and develop ideas, take the time to return to the text for further evidence. Note significant facts, quotes, and specifics in the margins of a draft. Then revise. It is difficult to draft and to find supporting evidence at the same time. (See Esther Martinez's work later in this chapter.)

- Leave time to evaluate a version of your essay. Print out a penultimate copy for review. It is crucial to see your work as a whole in order to assess it.
- And, of course, use your spell check and proofread thoroughly.
- Always save your work in a separate file.

Electronic Portfolio

Your teacher may want you to create an electronic portfolio of your essays for the class. This portfolio may contain a table of contents, a reflective letter assessing your progress as a writer, prewriting, and rough and final drafts of your work.

Summary

There are as many composing processes as there are students and writing situations. You need to work through the process in your own way; however, the omission of stages of composing can lead to weaknesses in your final draft. For example, if you do not spend enough time planning your writing, your essay may be disorganized and unconvincing. If you do not spend enough time prewriting and exploring ideas, you may submit a final draft that is lifeless and undeveloped. If you do not spend enough time editing and proofreading, you may create a work so riddled with distracting grammatical errors and spelling mistakes that your essay will fail to convince your readers of the merit of your ideas. Each stage of the writing process is necessary to the development of a strong essay.

The Writing Process: An Example

As an exercise in reading, responding, and writing, assume that your instructor has asked you to create a short essay, a literary analysis of a poem, building on one of your "think" writings. Esther Martinez chose to expand her treatment of "horse," concentrating on such specific literary techniques as symbolism, diction, and imagery.

Esther began her paper by doing the assigned "think" writing (presented in Chapter 2). She next jotted down some notes and observations and created a thesis and a mini-outline.

Notes on "horse"

What are the words for literary essays? Diction, word choice, irony, imagery.

Diction: Repetition

"Great horse"

"Thundering"

"Mexicans mutter"

Thesis: Through diction, repetition, imagery, the author clearly portrays the injustice experienced by Mexican Americans.

Diction

Repetition

Imagery

Symbolism

Additional Notes:

Tone changes from awe to disgust and frenzy

There is tension, craziness

Money is power

White man rules

Instead of killing the horse—they watch it suffer in a pool of blood

Description of kids works. Testicles—shame

Title—'horse'—lowercase

After jotting down these notes and developing a thesis, she wrote a short exploratory draft and noted details that she wanted to include. In her second draft, she more systematically focused on symbolism, diction, and imagery. Following her instructor's suggestions, she treated each technique in a separate paragraph and she developed the symbolism of the horse and compared it with the state of the Mexican Americans. In her third draft she more clearly organized and developed the essay, devoting a paragraph to each literary technique, and she included an historical reference that places the boys' actions within a particular historical context. This context explains and deepens the symbolic motif in the poem. The boys' actions not only represent the aberrant, violent, and racist behavior of adolescents, but they also mirror the prejudice directed at Mexican Americans and experienced by those who have been on the margins in this country from its inception. Perhaps what is most significant is that Esther's involvement with the work began with her own connection to her Mexican American heritage. Notice how her passion fuels her analysis, yet she retains the capacity to "stand back" and objectively analyze the work. What emerges is a complex and thoughtful treatment of a powerful poem.

Esther Martinez's First Exploratory
Draft and Notes (Written at Home)

In the poem entitled, "horse" by Gloria Anzaldúa, the poet describes a symbolic situation of teenage boys killing a horse and the consequences of their action.
imagery
Through the title, syntax, diction, and <u>immagry</u> and
symbolism   *poet*
foreshadowing the <u>peot</u> makes a statement about the power of money and the white man by showing the injustice shown to Mexicans.

Action

<u>Through diction</u>, the Mexican people are characterized along with their suffering. The "great horse" gallops and "some kids" follow as "Mexicans mutter among
(knowing)
themselves" in anticipation and knowing. This powerful horse racing through the field symbolizes the Mexican people and their culture. Great care is taken in describing the power of the horse as it races through the field symbolizing the Mexican people and their culture. On the other hand, the white teens are simply "some kids" showing the Mexican people are threatened and at-
because
tacked mentally and physically by the—it doesn't matter who killed the horse and their identity won't matter because whites don't get in trouble for lashing out at Mexicans. The Mexicans are aware of what is going on, but are unable to stop what is happening. The tension of the poem mounts . . . "Hidden hands" await the horse
connote
that "cast up testicles." The hidden hands conotate
Imagery
the . . . ? <u>Immagery</u> creates a powerful picture of the
helplessness of the
oppressed Mexican people and their reaction to the situation. The "mexicanos murmur" and "shuffle their feet" as their "faces stare at the ground." <u>The image</u> created <u>shows</u> the inferiority felt by the Mexicans who shuffle their feet in nervous anticipation and a desire to lash
allowed
out at their oppressor. However, they aren't <u>alowed</u> to speak out or act, so in shame and helplessness they

*The poem
can be
related to
all races*

*tempered
steel—
unbreakable,
unbendable,
powerful,
strong*

whisper

listen, wait, watch, <u>wisper</u>. The "folds of green" cover the stain of the "earth drinking blood."

Symbolism is used throughout the poem to help show the brutality of racism.

- boys pretending to feed horse
- weapon hidden in corn
- money
- can money replace/make all injury to Mexicans in the U.S. go away?

Second Draft
(Turned in to Instructor)

In the poem "horse" by Gloria Anzaldúa, the poet describes a symbolic situation of teenage boys killing a horse and the consequences of their action. Through symbolism, diction and imagery the poet makes a statement about the power of money and the white man by demonstrating the injustice shown to Mexicans.

Commas

Excellent opening

Excellent thesis

Solid topics

Symbolism is used throughout the poem to help show the brutality of racism. In the poem a "horse [runs]" toward open palms holding tempting "ears of corn," not knowing there is "tempered steel" hidden within. The situation symbolizes the characteristic injustice of whites that in past history have been known to befriend a foe and gain trust in order to defeat "the enemy." This tactic was used when the whites coaxed the Indians out of hiding by declaring peace and giving them land to live on. When the Native Americans settled, the Europeans slaughtered the people, burnt the village, and destroyed the corn. The tempered steel symbolizes, not only the weapons used to mutilate the horse, but also the Americans who are powerful, cold, and unjust.

Could you give more pointed historical information?

Vague—too general

You could expand with historical references and explanations.

Diction and imagery create a powerful picture of the oppressed Mexican people and their reaction to the situation in the poem. "Folds of green" sneak out of a father's wallet, money that is to correct the injustice performed on the "great horse" that "some kids" mutilated. Much care is taken in describing the "great horse" as it races through the field. There is a passion and power behind it's "thundering" gallop, "flaring" "nostrils" and "iron-shod" hooves. The white teens, however, are simply described as "some kids" — showing that the identity of the whites doesn't and won't matter, because whites don't get in trouble for racism. Money is used to resolve the situation, however, money isn't capable of wiping

Divide into two paragraphs— separate topics

its
it's = it is

comma splice

Excellent discussion of imagery of the horse

Good use of particular details from text

Excellent analysis of wording

Careful, no comma!

Solid focus on verbs to describe Mexicanos

away the pain, suffering, shame felt by the victims. The "<u>mexicanos</u> murmur" and "shuffle their feet" and "their faces stare at the ground." The images created show the inferiority felt by the Mexicans who desire to defend their lifestyle and culture. However, they aren't allowed to speak out or act, so <u>in shame</u> and helplessness they listen, <u>wait, watch, whisper</u>.

Excellent interpretation and portrayal of the Mexicanos

Solid parallelism in wording

Careful, format for including lines of poetry; use slash between lines

Excellent point

"If you're Mexican you are born old," the poem concludes. From birth, Mexicans must struggle for their lives—not only against the injustice of racism, but also against poverty. Their childhood is snatched away as quickly as it's given. The poem "horse" can be related to any race people ~~or~~ *with a particular* lifestyle suffering from persecution. The title itself—in all lowercase letters—signifies a people looked at as inferior.

Focus on closing image. How can the image of the "dead horse" contrast with the image of Mexicanos who are born old? Expand analysis of closing. Is this an emphatic closing sentence?

Instructor's Comments

I am impressed with your process of revision. You revise beautifully—what a difference between your initial "think" writing and drafts. This essay has a solid thesis, is well-organized, well-developed, and persuasive. Work on the concluding images in the poem and your conclusion.

Question

How does the image of the "dead horse" contrast with the image of Mexicanos who are "born old"? Develop your conclusion further.

Final Draft

In the poem "horse" by Gloria Anzaldúa the poet

Add comma

describes a symbolic situation of teenage boys' killing

a horse and the consequences of their action. Through

symbolism, diction and imagery the poet makes a state-

Careful, add commas!

Solid thesis

ment about the power of money and the white man by

demonstrating the injustice shown to Mexicans.

Symbolism is used throughout the poem to help

show the brutality of racism. In the poem, a "horse

[runs]" toward open palms holding tempting ears of

"corn," not knowing there is "tempered steel" hidden

within. The situation symbolizes the characteristic in-

justice of whites that in past history have been known

Excellent use of historical reference

to befriend a foe and gain trust in order to defeat "the

enemy." This tactic was used when the whites coaxed

the Indians out of hiding by declaring peace and giving

them land to live on. When the Native Americans settled,

the Europeans slaughtered the people, burnt the village,

and destroyed the corn. In <u>American Slavery, American</u>

Again add comma

<u>Freedom</u> Edmund Morgan wrote:

> Since the Indians were better woodsmen than
> the English and virtually impossible to track
> down, the method was to feign peaceful inten-
> tions, let them settle down and plant their corn
> wherever they chose, and then just before har-
> vest, fall upon them, killing as many as possible
> and burning the corn.

Excellent inclusion of a quote

(Zinn 13)

The tempered steel symbolizes not only the weapons

used to mutilate the horse, but also the Americans who

are powerful, cold, and unjust.

the spirit of the Mexicans,

Diction is used to reveal the arrogance of the

whites, and the cruelty shown to the Mexicans. The fa-

Again, add comma

ther "[fishes] out his wallet" intending to correct the in-

justice performed on the "great horse" that "some kids"

Transition needed.

However, that power doesn't protect the Mexicans. The teens have the power to destroy.

mutilated. Much care is taken in describing the "great horse" as it races through the field. There is a passion and power behind it's "thundering" gallop, "flaring" nos-trils, and "iron-shod" hooves. The white ~~teens, however,~~ *adolescents* are simply described as "some kids"—showing that the identity of the whites doesn't and won't matter, because whites don't get punished for racism. The father lightly and carelessly pulls out his wallet—confident that money will resolve the situation. Money, however, isn't capable of wiping away the pain, suffering, and shame felt by the victims.

its again!

No comma

Through imagery, a powerful picture is painted of the reactions of both the perpetrators and the oppressed Mexican people. The neighing horse hurtles toward the "open faces" of the sleeping gringos who "cry out" in des-peration. The reader can clearly see the white boys wak-ing up night after night—faces pale and clammy with perspiration, mouths open in shock and terror after having yet another nightmare. The whites are forever haunted by the images and brutality of their actions—an inadequate penance. With the *Because "mexicanos" is written in* <u>mexicanos</u> in lowercase and italicized, the reader feels compelled to whisper the phrase, and, in turn, to experience the same anxiety, tension, and anticipation felt by the tormented people. The image created also shows the inferiority felt by the Mexicans who desire to defend their lifestyle and cul-ture. However, they aren't allowed to speak out or act, so in shame and helplessness they listen, wait, watch, whisper.

Excellent expanded treatment

wording needs to be clearer

comma again

"If you're Mexican/you are born old," the poem con-cludes. From birth, Mexicans must struggle for their lives—not only against the injustice of racism, but also against poverty. Their childhood is snatched away as quickly as it's given. The phrase "dead horse neighing *, however,* in the night"—shows that although the Mexicans' voices

Change the order of sentences for greater emphasis in conclusion

are stifled, they will not give up in their struggle for equality and justice. The poem "horse" can be related to any race, people, or lifestyle suffering from persecution. [The title itself—in all lowercase letters—signifies a people viewed as inferior.]

Again—re-order closing sentences

Work Cited

Zinn, Howard. A People's History of the United States: 1492–Present. New York: Harper Perennial, 1995.

Instructor's Comments

A wonderful essay, Esther. You analyze the themes of the poem beautifully. Excellent added treatment of the imagery.

Work on:

- Transitions
- Progression of thought from sentence to sentence
- Commas

Student's Comments

I chose to analyze the poem "horse" because I was able to relate to the message. I felt anger and frustration as I read the poem and wanted to expose the truth of the poem. My family is Hispanic and has suffered because of racism and oppression, and because of the personal experience, I thought, with my emotions raging, I would be able to write an effective paper. I was also able to relate to the past suffering the Native Americans experienced. It was remarkable and horrifying to see the hatred and cruelty that hasn't died in America, but, instead, is thriving.

Peer Evaluation

Be aware that you may exchange early drafts of your essays with a peer for feedback if your instructor so desires, or your instructor may read and comment on drafts of your writing. Three levels of peer critique are helpful:

1. *Provide Initial Reaction.* A peer may give you an initial emotional response and react to specific sections of the work in terms of his or her feelings and thoughts about the work.
2. *Indicate Organizational Strengths and Weaknesses.* A peer reader can outline the work—pinpointing thesis, key points, and details—to check the progression and development of the writer's arguments. A peer editor also may single out examples that are most convincing and vivid and note areas that are confusing and/or need further development.
3. *Provide an Evaluative Response.* Your instructor or your peer reviewers can provide a detailed evaluation of your essay's focus, thesis, organization, paragraph development, logic, transitions, style, and sentence structure.

It is helpful to evaluate a draft with a set of questions in mind so that the critical responses might provide pointed, productive feedback. Here is a checklist for evaluating a draft of writing:

The Reading/Writing Connection

1. Have I used some form of reader response first to gain ideas?
2. What is the focus of my response? What is my purpose?

Content

3. What is my perspective? My point of view? Tone?
4. What is my main idea? My thesis? Who is my audience? Have I structured my thesis and topics with my audience in mind?
5. Do my major points follow from the thesis? Are they appropriate for the audience?

Organization

6. Are my major points arranged in a logical order? Do they build? Do I emphasize my most convincing point?
7. Does my essay have an introduction, middle paragraphs, and a conclusion?
8. Will my introduction interest a reader and give the reader a sense of the direction of my essay?
9. Does my conclusion end emphatically and reinforce my main idea and points? Do I leave the reader with something to consider?

Development

10. Have I included enough evidence (reasons, details, quotations, and examples) from the work to explain my points? Have I explained the examples sufficiently?
11. Have I included this evidence properly? Have I used proper quoting techniques and proper techniques for paraphrasing?

Grammar, Style, Sentence Sense

12. Have I written about the work in the present tense?
13. Have I maintained a consistent tone? (e.g., objective? personal? persuasive? meditative?)
14. Am I satisfied with wording, sentence structure, patterns of sentences (emphasis, variety)? Have I avoided repetitive wording and phrasing?
15. Have I created coherence by repeating key words, by creating transitions from point to point, and by using parallelism?
16. Have I shifted levels of diction?
17. Is my word choice specific, pointed, not vague?
18. Have I checked the final draft for grammar, punctuation, and spelling errors?

Special Requirements for Writing about Literature

Several special requirements for writing about literature are important to note. First, compose primarily in the present tense. Use the past tense to refer only to events in a text that clearly took place in the past. For example, in "horse," you would use the present tense to describe the horse's mythic running in the night, but you would use the past tense to describe the animal's mutilation because that event occurred before the speaker begins her story.

Another important feature of writing about literature is the inclusion of quotations from the work. When you quote, be careful to cite the exact quotation and to insert ellipses (. . .) for any information that you delete within a quotation; use four periods (. . . .) for any part of a sentence that you delete at the end of the quotation. Block and indent quotations of more than four lines of prose or three lines of poetry. You also must make the quotation consistent with the preceding discussion. Use brackets to insert any changes in wording so that the quotation fits content and presentation of ideas and so that it makes sense. For example, consider this sentence from Martinez's essay: "In the poem, a 'horse [runs]' toward open palms." The writer changed "ran" to "runs" to keep the tense consistent.

Select sufficient quotations from the work as evidence. Your writing will be more persuasive if you include specifics from the work. Remember the student's weaving of quotations into her discussion of "horse." Be aware, however, that it is disastrous to overload your analysis with unexplained or extensive quotations. This technique could lead a reader to assume that you have not understood the work fully.

Summary and Paraphrase

Two other important techniques you need to use when incorporating evidence from a text are **summary** and **paraphrase.** When you **summarize,** you give an overview of the major points, ideas, or events in a work. When you **paraphrase,** you recast the sentences in the original work into your own words as accurately as possible, keeping to the approximate length and tone of the original. When you do not use quotations from a work, you still want to support your points with descriptions and examples drawn from the text. This is when you need to summarize and paraphrase. Be careful to choose only your own words in a paraphrase; any of the original language from a work must be placed within quotation marks. Consider this additional example from Martinez's essay: "Much care is taken in describing the 'great horse' as it races through the field." Martinez describes the action of the horse as she also uses a direct quotation from the poem to add emphasis and to name the creature.

Forms of the Essay about Literature

In critical analysis of literature, you experience a complicated process of response. In writing about literature, you focus your energies on one aspect, one strand of your reading experience. Depending on your particular reading and on your goals in writing, you may then compose an essay in response to literature that may assume any of several different forms: response; explication; comparison/contrast; critical analysis; historical, social, or cultural analysis; review; multi-genre works; creative responses to literature; and research.

Response Essay

A response essay is an analysis of a reader's emotional response to a work. In this kind of paper, you explain both your reading experience and the parts of the work that evoke your reaction. For example, you might respond to Luisa Valenzuela's story "The Verb to Kill" (Chapter 8) by discussing your mounting horror and disgust at the characters' behavior. You may want to proceed sequentially through the story to discuss the stages and aspects of your response. Or you may focus on one main emotional reaction and explore its components: the elements of the story that provoke your reaction.

Explication Essay

Another form of response, explication, is a careful analysis of the work to examine its meaning. In this type of essay, the writer proceeds through the text methodically and analyzes those aspects of the work and the writer's technique that create the themes. Usually explications of meaning are done on short texts so that the work can be analyzed in depth and treated fully. For example, a student may explore a theme of Emily Dickinson's "I'm Nobody! Who Are You?" (Chapter 8) by carefully examining each line, each image, and each stanza and by finding the strands of connection revealed by this process. Such analysis demonstrates aspects of the poem (wording, imagery, figurative language, point of view, tone, rhythm, and rhyme) that develop Dickinson's message. You may organize the essay by treating each part of the text as a separate paragraph or by organizing in terms of poetic techniques; that is, have each technique serve as a topic for a middle paragraph.

Comparison/Contrast Essay

In this form of essay, you may compare and/or contrast two works to find similarities and differences. Then you may have to decide to concentrate on treatment of theme, character, style, or technique. Instructors often specify the subject of the comparison and ask students to compare two characters in two different stories, to evaluate two poems with similar themes, or to assess two plays to determine which treatment of character or theme seems more effective.

There are two major organizational patterns for a comparison/contrast essay. You may treat first one text and then the other in successive paragraphs: this format is labeled *block* or *side-by-side* organization. For example, you might devote several paragraphs to a given theme, such as coming of age in "The Stolen Party," followed immediately by several paragraphs on the same theme in "Flood" (Chapter 5). This type of pattern is sometimes not effective because it separates the discussion of the two works and confuses or loses the reader. The other pattern relies on *point-by-point* or *alternating* organization. In this form of the essay, each of the middle (body) paragraphs presents

• Patterns for Comparison/Contrast Essays •

Block or Side-by-Side		Point-by-Point	
Introduction—Thesis		Introduction—Thesis	
Middle Paragraphs		Middle Paragraphs	
Work A	"The Stolen Party"	**Topic 1**	Innocence of protagonist
Topic 1	Innocence of protagonist	**Work A**	"The Stolen Party"
Topic 2	Capacity for moral decisions	**Work B**	"Flood"
Work B	"Flood"	**Topic 2**	Capacity for moral decisions
Topic 1	Innocence of protagonist	**Work A**	"The Stolen Party"
Topic 2	Capacity for moral decisions	**Work B**	"Flood"
Conclusion		Conclusion	

the treatment of a key topic (point) in both of the works. For example, in a discussion of coming of age in "The Stolen Party" and in "Flood," one middle paragraph might focus on the innocence of the main protagonist. The next paragraph might explain each protagonist's capability for moral decision making as a prerequisite for growing beyond childhood. In every paragraph, the writer would consider first "The Stolen Party" and then "Flood." This method keeps the topics for comparison foremost in the reader's mind and allows the reader to weigh and compare the evidence from each story.

Critical Analysis Essay

In a *critical analysis,* you are asked to analyze a literary work according to a single principle: theme, character, style, or a particular technique of fiction, poetry, drama, or nonfiction. For example, you may be asked to explore one theme of "Hills Like White Elephants" (Chapter 7); or you might be asked to analyze the character of the woman in that story; your instructor may ask you to analyze Hemingway's style; or you might be asked to focus on the imagery of the hills or the symbolism of the title. In each case, you isolate one level of a work and explore its function and its impact. Critical analysis often leads to judgments of effectiveness. Is the theme treated compellingly? Is the character portrayal moving? Believable? Is the imagery powerful? Is Hemingway's style effective?

Historical, Social, or Cultural Analysis Essay

The *historical, social,* or *cultural analysis essay* involves a study of how the work reveals historical, social, or cultural realities or trends. In this essay, you concentrate on how the work mirrors, comments on, or critiques particular historical, social, or cultural phenomena. For example, Esther Martinez, in her essay about "horse," views the poem as a critical examination of the oppression faced by Mexicans in the United States and then relates the work to larger issues—the way "any race . . . or people . . . [suffer] from persecution." She locates the poem in a particular time and place, connects it to the past history of minorities in this country, and analyzes the social, political, and cultural forces portrayed in the work.

In another instance, in an historical analysis of Charlotte Gilman Perkins's "The Yellow Wallpaper," an autobiographically inspired work of fiction about a woman at the turn of the century who has a nervous breakdown after the birth of her child (Chapter 7), you may be asked to research the autobiographical roots of the work and learn more about the historical context and background of the work, particularly the treatment for postpartum depression. In a social analysis, you may evaluate how the work presents gender roles for men and women at the turn of the century; in a cultural analysis, you may consider if the work critiques such roles. In historical, social, or cultural analyses, your reading would extend beyond the text to encompass the author's biography, letters, or autobiography; historical background information; and other texts of the time, such as advertisements, documents, historical tracts, or other cultural artifacts. You would consider the relevance of such information to your reading of the work.

Evaluation and Review Essay

Evaluation and *review* are forms of critical analysis that focus on determining the effectiveness of a work. When you are asked to evaluate a text, you compare the text with chosen standards and come to conclusions about its worth and effectiveness. You might evaluate Henrik Ibsen's *A Doll's House* (Chapter 5), for example, and conclude that its characters, dialogue, conflict, and themes create a drama of great power.

A *review* is a particular form of evaluative response commonly used in both academic and journalistic prose. You may be asked to write a book, magazine, film, or theater review to demonstrate your ability to evaluate a work. Reviews often follow this set pattern:

Paragraph One: General assessment of a work. Relevant background information.
Paragraph Two: Summary of key features of the work.
                  (The reviewer assumes that the reader has not yet seen or read the work.)
Paragraph Three: Strengths
Paragraph Four: Weaknesses
Conclusion: A general recommendation

Creative Essay

The *creative essay* about literature presents an imaginative response to a literary work. The approaches explained in Chapter 2, "Creative Responses to Literature," may be used to develop this kind of essay. In addition, your instructor may ask you to analyze your creative work, concentrating on your composing process, an analysis of character or theme, or particular literary elements (e.g., use of figurative language or symbolism).

Note the extended online forum about "horse" presented in Chapter 8—the creative responses and comment on the works.

Multi-Genre Works

As new technologies emerge and develop, you have increased access to visual images, streaming video, podcasts, music, and other media and resources from the Internet. You also have the ability to easily create your own multimedia projects. Your instructor may ask you to create a nontraditional reaction to a work, a multi-genre text that incorporates a variety of media. For example, in a critical response essay about "horse," you might include a song of protest as a prelude to your discussion of the text or a photograph of horses galloping in a field juxtaposed with your analysis. Or you may even incorporate a video clip, a short dramatic scene you create about the poem, or an interview with friends about the work. In another instance, in an autobiographical essay, you may want to scan in photographs as part of your work. Technology not only offers the potential for more experimental approaches to composing essays, but these multi-genre works also create new senses of your voice and perspective as a writer, as well as possibilities for the reader to experience the work in new, nonlinear ways. The juxtaposition of image and word and the opening up of meditative spaces in the work through this juxtaposition can lead the audience to pursue more personal, reflective, and intellectual avenues of thought.

Research Essay

The *research essay* is a writing assignment that involves searching beyond the text to find information that expands your understanding of the work. Research opens the text to different interpretations and enriches the reading experience. Research may move in different directions. You may explore any one of the following areas:

- *Biographical research:* Research on the writer's life. Exploration of the connections between the writer's life and art.
- *Research on the historical, cultural, political, philosophical, or sociological background or context of the work.*
- *Reading of criticism that treats the work.* This reading of another's exploration of the text will help you understand it and, perhaps, explain aspects that are puzzling. Critics provide you with alternative interpretations.
- *Reading of specific forms of literary criticism.* These may include historical, cultural, social, formalist, feminist, deconstructive. (See Appendix C.) These particular schools of literary criticism will provide you with frameworks and theories that will help you read the work in particular ways and place it in new intellectual contexts.

In each instance, once you write about secondary sources, you must cite the sources of the information and give adequate documentation for the works that you quote or paraphrase. One accepted method of documenting information in essays about literature is MLA (Modern Language Association of America) citation form as recommended in the *MLA Handbook for Writers of Research Papers*. The MLA citation form involves two steps: citations of references in the work itself and a "Works Cited" page that contains all of your primary and secondary sources in alphabetical order by author's last name. The MLA citations within the discussion sections of your paper include two parts: author, page. If the author's name is presented in your essay, you only indicate page number. If an author has written two books, you should include an abbreviated title in the citation. Note the following excerpt from a research essay, "Literature as History" by Eric Schoonebeek, discussing literature as history and the representation of the Holocaust in Cynthia Ozick's "The Shawl" (Chapter 8). Note the correct form of MLA citation. You can find a complete discussion of MLA documentation and of this research essay in Appendix A.

> Documented history focuses on the awareness of the masses, and historical narrative sets its sights on the necessity of a created version of the past on a more personal level as to be easily identifiable. And, in the most basic function of imagination and memory, "we can only know the actual by contrasting it with the imaginable" (White 406), as to create our own valid consciousness. Historical narratives serve this purpose.

Summary

The recursive processes of critical thinking, reader response, and composing the essay about literature develop new capacities for understanding texts in different genres—fiction, poetry, drama, and nonfiction. As you read, analyze, and write about selections in the thematic anthology that follows, you not only will find yourself more interested in issues like those presented in Gloria Anzaldúa's poem, "horse," but you also will find your life enriched by the insights and ideas provided by the study of these works.

Arguments about Literature

You may wonder how argument and literary study are related. When you think of argumentative writing, you may first think of taking a stand on a controversial issue, such as capital punishment, gay marriage, or the war in Iraq. However, literary works also present arguments that you may respond to. For example, Gloria Anzaldúa's poem, "horse," portrays the discrimination experienced by Mexicans in this country. Esther Martinez in her essay not only critically analyzes the work, but also responds to that vision in the formulation of her thesis. Reading literature provokes a form of critical inquiry that may lead you to form a position or engage in a debate or dialogue with a text.

An argument essay presents your point of view, your opinion (position), reasons, and supporting evidence. For an argumentative paper on a literary work, you take a particular position regarding the text, and then you defend your position by providing reasons and supporting evidence. As in other forms of argument, you need to create a sound thesis, defend your thesis with logical reasoning, and provide sufficient evidence to prove your points and to convince the reader. In addition, you need to consider the opposing point of view, to evaluate and to analyze arguments in opposition to yours.

Generative Frames for Argument: Classical, Toulminian, and Rogerian Argument

There are various ways to structure argumentative essays about literature. In **classical argument,** you state your thesis (your main position), present reasons and evidence, acknowledge and refute opposition arguments, and then restate and emphasize your argumentative position. In **Toulmin logic,** you present the **claim:** the main argumentative position; and the **data:** reasons that support the position and evidence. You also need to take into account, in Toulmin's terms, the warrants: the underlying assumptions that link evidence and claim. It is important to evaluate the warrants to determine if your argument is valid and reasonable. In **Rogerian argument,** the emphasis is not on asserting your thesis and defeating the opposition; rather, the emphasis is on listening and being open to divergent points of view. In a Rogerian argument, you state an argumentative question, consider and evaluate reasons for one side of the controversial position and then the other, and finally come to a compromise position in your conclusion.

In all of these forms of argument, it is important to create a position, a claim that is actually arguable, that is not too general or obvious, and that can be supported with reasons and evidence from the text. Your claim or position should also be provocative and lead the reader to think more deeply about the story you are analyzing. For example, in Joyce Carol Oates's "Where Are You Going, Where Have You Been?"

(Chapter 5)—a story about a young teenager stalked by a possible serial killer—a weak claim would be that abducting teenage girls is bad. This claim is weak because it is not arguable; few people would actually disagree with it. However, overly general controversial claims also can be faulty. A paper that argued in favor of teaching young girls to beware of young men because many men are untrustworthy would be quite controversial and, indeed, could antagonize your readers. This claim is weak because it is too biased; it is more of an opinion than an objective stance. As such, it would be difficult to support with evidence. A better argument would be that most young women need the support of family and community in order to grow into healthy, successful adults. Evidence from within the story is available from the unrealistic expectations of Connie's mother (that Connie be like her sister June), the shallow relationship between Connie and her father, and the overall absence of supportive adults in the lives of Connie and her friends. The responsible adults in the story seem preoccupied with their own lives and are indifferent to those of Connie and her peers, who are too young and inexperienced to make the decisions necessary to protect themselves from older boys and men like Arnold Friend. This last position is more narrowly focused and complex than the other ones, and textual evidence is easily found to support it.

Consider this question about Connie in "Where Are You Going, Where Have You Been?": Does Connie's treatment by her parents contribute to her fate and render her vulnerable to Arnold Friend's advances? In responding to this question, you formulate an argumentative stance, a position about the role of parenting. Here are several thesis statements exemplifying different approaches to argument:

- *Classical Argument:* Because Connie's parents do not give her positive guidance and direction, she turns to other forms of self-affirmation used by teenagers to bolster their sense of self. She becomes concerned about her appearance and wants to be desired by the opposite sex.
- *Toulmin Logic:* Because Connie's parents do not provide guidance in the form of constructive advice and praise and are not involved in her life, Connie turns to other ways to develop a sense of self.
  - –Warrants (assumptions): Parents need to give teenagers direction and set limits for their behavior.
  - –Teenage girls are particularly susceptible to being concerned about body image, beauty, and popularity.

  Note: In Toulmin logic, it is important to evaluate the assumptions underlying your position and reasons and test their validity. Are these assumptions confirmed by your view of teenage life?
- *Rogerian Argument:* Is Connie's mother a good mother? Although Connie's mother does not seem to understand her daughter or provide her with direction, one can see that her mother is concerned about Connie because her daughter reminds her of her younger self. These arguments take into account the complexities of Connie's mother's response to her.

Proofs

As in other forms of argument, you will incorporate proof—evidence for your position—what Aristotle defined as the three major forms of appeals:

Pathos: an appeal to the emotions, attitudes, values, and experiences of the audience (the reader)

Ethos: an appeal based on the character of the speaker

Logos: an appeal based on the use of logic and evidence

For example, in discussing Connie's character, you may appeal to a college-level audience, a year out of high school, by viewing her as a representative adolescent. This view of her will provoke your readers' interest and evoke memories of high school, prompting them to connect to Connie and be interested in her life. In addition, as a writer, you also want to sound like an authority, appear to have thoroughly studied the work, and present a reasoned, well-informed argument based on your critical reading of the text. Finally, you also must argue in a reasoned way and present explanations and evidence, specifics from the work, which will lead readers to be convinced of your position and your analysis of the text.

Patterns of Development in Argumentative Thinking and Writing

Definition

Some arguments depend upon a **definition** of terms. In a **formal definition** of a word, you provide the general class the word belongs to and then differentiate it by describing the particular traits. For example, you might say about an adolescent that he or she is a person not yet fully grown who is confused about his or her state of identity. **An extended definition** is one where you provide your own explanations and understanding of a term, concept, idea, or abstraction. For example, if your teacher asks you to write an essay arguing about whether Connie is a typical adolescent, you first would need to define and explain what a typical adolescent is as part of your **claim.** Often definition writing includes narrative, examples, and contrasts (statements of difference) as part of the explanation.

Cause and Effect

Many arguments present a claim about **cause and effect;** that is, one would examine a phenomenon for the underlying causes and the effects, or results. It is important that a logical chain of reasoning from cause to effect is presented. An example of a cause-and-effect argument in a character analysis would be as follows: Because Connie is pretty she is attractive to men and will need to defend herself from unwanted attention. The logic within this statement lies within the assumption that pretty girls attract men and that these men may attempt to manipulate or coerce the girls to return their attention. The cause and effect lies within the logic: the "cause" is pretty girls, and the "effect" is the attraction of men. Sometimes effects are debatable; for example, one can examine the conclusion of "Where Are You Going, Where Have You Been?" and explore what happens to Connie. As you determine your position and write your essay, be aware of the cause-and-effect structure you are presenting. If the effect does not follow from the cause, your reader will not be convinced of your claim.

Evaluative Claims

Often when you present arguments, you probably do so as a way to **evaluate** something. Each time you argue with a friend about the superiority of one movie over another, you are presenting an **evaluative claim**, using evidence from the two movies to support your thesis. When you disagree with a friend about where to eat, the impetus is also evaluative: you prefer the food at restaurant A over that of restaurant B. Within an evaluative argument you recognize and choose criteria with which to value and judge the worth of one object over another. Examples of this type of evaluative claim can be found in reviews of music, restaurants, movies, and books, or in comparisons of works treated in different genres, such as a movie based on a book (see "Evaluation and Review Essay" in Chapter 3).

Another kind of assignment that incorporates evaluative claims is the comparison/contrast essay. For example, an instructor may ask you to argue pro or con: Arnold Friend is not as evil as Rappaccini ("Rappaccini's Daughter," Chapter 6). In this claim you are comparing two dangerous male characters, determining criteria for what constitutes evil, and then comparing and evaluating the two characters with these criteria in mind.

Logical Fallacies in Literary Arguments

When you construct literary arguments, some common logical fallacies are important to avoid, for they will weaken your presentation of ideas. Knowing these fallacies will help you to develop more effective, reasoned argumentative thesis statements and critical judgments about a work. What follows are illogical and then rephrased argumentative theses or critical comments for an essay about "Where Are You Going, Where Have You Been?" (Chapter 5).

Sweeping Generalization

Avoid overgeneralizing. Limit your argumentative thesis to a debatable point about the work.

Illogical Thesis:	In "Where Are You Going, Where Have You Been?" Connie, like all teenagers, has "two sides" to her nature.
Comment:	Do all teenagers have "two sides"? How could you prove this?
Rephrased Thesis:	Like many teenagers, Connie has "two sides" to her nature.

Hasty Generalization

Make sure your thesis is a claim supported by evidence throughout the work, not by one quotation or specific example.

Illogical Thesis:	Like many schizophrenics, Connie has a divided self.
Comment:	Other than the surreal dream sequence at the end of the story, is there evidence throughout the text to support the contention that Connie is schizophrenic? Are there any other reasons for this stylistic turn at the end of the work?
Rephrased Thesis:	Connie's divided self reaches its heightened state in her final interaction with Arnold Friend at the end of the story.

False Causal Relationships

Make sure that your argumentative points, your conclusion about motivations for a character's actions or a cause-and-effect relationship in the plot, can be supported by specifics from the text.

Illogical Thesis:	In "Where Are you Going, Where Have You Been?" Connie's downfall is caused by her "two sides."
Comment:	Are the "two sides" the actual cause of her demise? Or does her behavior outside of the house lead her to the fast-food place where Arnold spies her?
Rephrased Thesis:	Connie's two-sidedness is a contributing factor but not a direct cause of her downfall.

False Context

Be careful to examine the context of a work—its specific historical, cultural, social, and biographical frame of reference. Do not attribute characteristics or behavior to a character or present an explanation of a theme that is not consistent with these factors.

Illogical Thesis:	Connie is a flower child of the 1960s.
Comment:	The story was published in 1970 but set in the early 1960s, before the late 1960s youth culture.
Rephrased Thesis:	At the root of Connie's character is a restlessness that gets her into trouble.

Summary Rather than Critical Comment

Avoid an argumentative thesis that is a summary rather than a critical response, claim, or evaluation of a work.

Illogical Thesis:	Connie is threatened by Arnold Friend, who stalks her at her house.

Comment:	This is a one-sentence summary of part of the plot.
Rephrased Thesis:	Arnold Friend is symbolically portrayed as a demon lover, a figure that dominates European mythology.

The rephrased thesis presents an interpretation of Arnold Friend's symbolic character rather than plot details.

Checklist for Argumentative Writing

Here is a checklist for evaluating a draft of an argumentative essay:

1. Do I have a sound argumentative **position** or claim?
2. What is my **point of view** and **tone (ethos)** as a writer?
3. Have I established **authority** through a thorough reading of the work?
4. Have I considered my **audience (pathos)**?
5. Do my **reasons** follow from and support my **claim**?
6. Is my **organization** appropriate for the type of argument I am constructing?
7. What **pattern of development** am I using?
8. Have I checked my reasoning and explanations for **logical fallacies (logos)**?
9. Am I aware of my **warrants**, or assumptions?
10. Have I used enough **evidence from the text** to support my points?
11. Have I used enough **evidence from research** (biographical, historical, cultural, or critical information; see Chapter 3) to support my points?
12. Have I taken into account **opposing points of view**?
13. Do I have a satisfying **conclusion**?

Student Essay: Argument

Following is an example of an argument essay composed by Jennifer Bernstein for her in-class midterm. The germ of the essay was a homework assignment, a freewrite that served as a first exploratory response (see Chapter 2). Note her thesis statement in the first paragraph (that fear leads to oppression), her use of supporting reasons (her analysis of both the gringos' and Chicanos' actions), and the specific evidence that supports her claim.

Jennifer Bernstein
"horse"

The poem, "horse," by Gloria Anzaldúa, uses images

taken from nature to illustrate through symbolism a

deeper meaning in her work. She portrays the conflict

between white people, <u>gringos</u>, and Mexicans. Racism

evolves through fear. The white boys depicted in the

poem fear the Mexicans and this fear creates a need in the boys to oppress the Chicanos.

Throughout the poem Anzaldúa uses words connecting power and strength to describe the "horses," or Mexicans. The horses are described as "running," "thundering," and "great" (ll. 1-2); their hooves are "iron-shod hurling lightening" (l. 45).

The gringos in the poem sense the inner strength of the "horses"; that is why they try to oppress them, and they partially succeed. The white people are able to control the Mexicans by crippling them, or restricting their freedom: "the mexicanos murmur" (l. 17) and "the Mexicans mutter among themselves:/ they hobbled the two front legs/ the two hind legs" (ll. 9-11). The Mexicans cannot voice their opinions aloud.

The white boys attack the horse; however, their actions show great cowardice. They attack the horse at night, while "the pueblo slept" (l. 8) so there was no chance someone could catch the gringos in the act. The gringos use weapons, but the horse is defenseless. The boys also conceal their weapons, "sheaths/ hiding blades of steel" (ll. 37-38). Even more cowardly, the gringos attack a horse, or people who are already crippled, who cannot cry out. The boys would not have acted violently if they hadn't known that "the sheriff won't do a thing/ he'd just say boys will be boys/ just following their instincts" (ll. 13-15).

Although the gringos so badly injure the horse that its owner must put it "out of its pain" (l. 27), the gringos cannot oppress the Chicanos entirely: "it's the mind that kills" (l. 16). The Mexicans do not surrender their minds; they do not lose hope or their self-respect: "the Chicanos shake their heads/ turn away some rich father/ fished out his wallet/ held out the folds of green/ as if green could staunch red" (ll. 29–32). They are too proud to accept the blood money. The Mexicans know that money can never make up for the gringos' actions. The soul of the horse lives on: "Dead horse neighing in the night" (l. 43). "[I]n their sleep the gringos cry out" (l. 47), meaning the horse haunts their dreams. The memories of the violent acts the gringos commit will never be forgotten.

Fear cripples and eventually fear kills. The whites and the Mexicans in "horse" are both handicapped through racism. The gringos are narrow-minded, and because of their prejudice, they are plagued "in their sleep" by the "dead horse neighing in the night" (ll. 47, 43). The Mexicans are oppressed, and, therefore, handicapped because of the gringos' fear of the "horse's," or the Mexicans', power and inner strength.

[Thematic Anthology]

Identity and Rites of Passage

Introduction

I came to explore the wreck.
The words are purposes.
The words are maps.
I came to see the damage that was done
and the treasures that prevail.

Adrienne Rich, "Diving into the Wreck"

It is not possible to define the self without acts of consciousness, without surveying "the damage that was done/and the treasures that prevail." Similarly, it is not possible to grow without being challenged by experience and cultural mores. When we are young, we live in a seemingly idyllic world. As we mature, we experience those rites of passage that take away our innocence, that complicate our lives, and that provide the basis for growth and for the development of identity. These rites of passage also enrich us, endowing our lives with depth and greater meaning.

Adolescence is a time of great growth, challenge, and joy. One of the greatest challenges is dealing with the adolescent body and the physical, emotional, and intellectual changes that growth brings. Many works affirmatively portray the physical energy and vitality of adolescence. In some cases, the vitality of adolescence emerges from a drive to rebel. Members of ethnic groups who experience alienation in North American culture often use rebellion to gain an understanding of prejudice and to reject societal mores. Experiencing discrimination also can lead to an awareness of difference and to confusion about cultural heritage, as many of the works in this chapter illustrate. Should we aspire to assimilate or to embrace our cultural legacies, or are we caught between worlds? The process of coming of age differs for women and for men as well as from culture to culture.

One outcome of these challenges is the consolidation of identity—"the treasures that prevail": the movement from confusion to a surer, albeit not necessarily static, sense of the adult self. Certainly the development of selfhood is not solidified when we reach adulthood; rather, confusion and identity crises persist into our twenties, thirties, and forties. We continue to face experiences that challenge us to define and to redefine self, to examine our relationship with our past, and to find our place in the world.

As readers we are cognizant that acts of writing, acts of communication, are revelatory. Like Adrienne Rich, we know that words are the "purposes," the "maps," by which we come to know ourselves and to find our ways in the world.

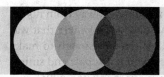

Crossing the Genres

Identity and the Body

Joyce Carol Oates   *(1938–   )*

Where Are You Going, Where Have You Been?   *1970*

To Bob Dylan

Her name was Connie. She was fifteen and she had a quick nervous giggling habit of craning her neck to glance into mirrors or checking other people's faces to make sure her own was all right. Her mother, who noticed everything and knew everything and who hadn't much reason any longer to look at her own face, always scolded Connie about it. "Stop gawking at yourself, who are you? You think you're so pretty?" she would say. Connie would raise her eyebrows at these familiar complaints and look right through her mother, into a shadowy vision of herself as she was right at that moment: she knew she was pretty and that was everything. Her mother had been pretty once too, if you could believe those old snapshots in the album, but now her looks were gone and that was why she was always after Connie. "Why don't you keep your room clean like your sister? How've you got your hair fixed—what the hell stinks? Hair spray? You don't see your sister using that junk."

Her sister June was twenty-four and still lived at home. She was a secretary in the high school Connie attended, and if that wasn't bad enough—with her in the same building—she was so plain and chunky and steady that Connie had to hear her praised all the time by her mother and her mother's sisters. June did this, June did that, she saved money and helped clean the house and cooked and Connie couldn't do a thing, her mind was all filled with trashy daydreams. Their father was away at work most of the time and when he came home he wanted supper and he read the newspaper at supper and after supper he went to bed. He didn't bother talking much to them, but around his bent head Connie's mother kept picking at her until Connie wished her mother were dead and she herself were dead and it were all over. "She makes me want to throw up sometimes," she complained to her friends. She had a high, breathless, amused voice which made everything she said sound a little forced, whether it was sincere or not.

There was one good thing: June went places with girlfriends of hers, girls who were just as plain and steady as she, and so when Connie wanted to do that her mother had no objections. The father of Connie's best girlfriend drove the girls the three miles to town and left them off at a shopping plaza, so that they could walk through the stores or go to a movie, and when he came to pick them up again at eleven he never bothered to ask what they had done.

They must have been familiar sights, walking around that shopping plaza in their shorts and flat ballerina slippers that always scuffed the sidewalk, with charm bracelets jingling on their thin wrists; they would lean together to whisper and laugh secretly if someone passed by who amused or interested them. Connie had long dark blond hair that drew anyone's eye to it, and she wore part of it pulled up on her head and puffed out and the rest of it she let fall down her back. She wore a pullover jersey blouse that looked one way when she was at home and another way when she was away from home. Everything about her had two sides to it, one for home and one for anywhere that was not home: her walk that could be childlike and bobbing, or languid enough to make anyone think she was hearing music in her head, her mouth which was pale and smirking most of the time, but bright and pink on these evenings out, her laugh which was cynical and drawling at home—"Ha, ha, very funny"—but high-pitched and nervous anywhere else, like the jingling of the charms on her bracelet.

Sometimes they did go shopping or to a movie, but sometimes they went across the highway, ducking fast across the busy road, to a drive-in restaurant where older kids hung out. The restaurant was shaped like a big bottle, though squatter than a real bottle, and on its cap was a revolving figure of a grinning boy who held a hamburger aloft. One night in midsummer they ran across, breathless with daring, and right away someone leaned out a car window and invited them over, but it was just a boy from high school they didn't like. It made them feel good to be able to ignore him. They went up through the maze of parked and cruising cars to the bright-lit, fly-infested restaurant, their faces pleased and expectant as if they were entering a sacred building that loomed out of the night to give them what haven and what blessing they yearned for. They sat at the counter and crossed their legs at the ankles, their thin shoulders rigid with excitement, and listened to the music that made everything so good: the music was always in the background like music at a church service, it was something to depend upon.

A boy named Eddie came in to talk with them. He sat backward on his stool, turning himself jerkily around in semicircles and then stopping and turning again, and after a while he asked Connie if she would like something to eat. She said she did and so she tapped her friend's arm on her way out—her friend pulled her face up into a brave droll look—and Connie said she would meet her at eleven, across the way. "I just hate to leave her like that," Connie said earnestly, but the boy said that she wouldn't be alone for long. So they went out to his car and on the way Connie couldn't help but let her eyes wander over the windshields and faces all around her, her face gleaming with a joy that had nothing to do with Eddie or even this place; it might have been the music. She drew her shoulders up and sucked in her breath with the pure pleasure of being alive, and just at that moment she happened to glance at a face just a few feet from hers. It was a boy with shaggy black hair, in a convertible jalopy painted gold. He stared at her and then his lips widened into a grin. Connie slit her eyes at him and turned away, but she couldn't help glancing back and there he was still watching her. He wagged a finger and laughed and said, "Gonna get you, baby," and Connie turned away again without Eddie noticing anything.

She spent three hours with him, at the restaurant where they ate hamburgers and drank Cokes in wax cups that were always sweating, and then down an alley a mile or so away, and when he left her off at five to eleven only the movie house was still open at the plaza. Her girlfriend was there, talking with a boy. When Connie came up and the two girls smiled at each other and Connie said, "How was the movie?" and the girl said, "*You* should know." They rode off with the girl's father, sleepy and pleased, and Connie couldn't help but look at the darkened shopping plaza with its big empty parking lot and its signs that were faded and ghostly now, and over at the drive-in restaurant where cars were still circling tirelessly. She couldn't hear the music at this distance.

Next morning June asked her how the movie was and Connie said, "So-so."

She and that girl and occasionally another girl went out several times a week that way, and the rest of the time Connie spent around the house—it was summer vacation—getting in her mother's way and thinking, dreaming, about the boys she met.

But all the boys fell back and dissolved into a single face that was not even a face, but an idea, a feeling, mixed up with the urgent insistent pounding of the music and the humid night air of July. Connie's mother kept dragging her back to the daylight by finding things for her to do or saying, suddenly, "What's this about the Pettinger girl?"

And Connie would say nervously, "Oh, her. That dope." She always drew thick clear lines between herself and such girls, and her mother was simple and kindly enough to believe her. Her mother was so simple, Connie thought, that it was maybe cruel to fool her so much. Her mother went scuffling around the house in old bedroom slippers and complained over the telephone to one sister about the other, then the other called up and the two of them complained about the third one. If June's name was mentioned her mother's tone was approving, and if Connie's name was mentioned it was disapproving. This did not really mean she disliked Connie and actually Connie thought that her mother preferred her to June because she was prettier, but the two of them kept up a pretense of exasperation, a sense that they were tugging and struggling over something of little value to either of them. Sometimes, over coffee, they were almost friends, but something would come up—some vexation that was like a fly buzzing suddenly around their heads—and their faces went hard with contempt.

One Sunday Connie got up at eleven—none of them bothered with church—and washed her hair so that it could dry all day long, in the sun. Her parents and sisters were going to a barbecue at an aunt's house and Connie said no, she wasn't interested, rolling her eyes to let her mother know just what she thought of it. "Stay home alone then," her mother said sharply. Connie sat out back in a lawn chair and watched them drive away, her father quiet and bald, hunched around so that he could back the car out, her mother with a look that was still angry and not at all softened through the windshield, and in the back seat poor old June all dressed up as if she didn't know what a barbecue was, with all the running yelling kids and the flies. Connie sat with her eyes closed in the sun, dreaming and dazed with the warmth about her as if this were a kind of love, the caresses of love, and her mind slipped over onto thoughts of the boy she had been with the night before and how nice he had been, how sweet it always was, not the way someone like June would suppose but sweet, gentle, the way it was in movies and promised in songs; and when she opened her eyes she hardly knew where she was, the back yard ran off into weeds and a fence line of trees and behind it the sky was perfectly blue and still. The asbestos "ranch house" that was now three years old startled her—it looked small. She shook her head as if to get awake.

It was too hot. She went inside the house and turned on the radio to drown out the quiet. She sat on the edge of her bed, barefoot, and listened for an hour and a half to a program called XYZ Sunday Jamboree, record after record of hard, fast, shrieking songs she sang along with, interspersed by exclamations from "Bobby King": "An' look here you girls at Napoleon's—Son and Charley want you to pay real close attention to this song coming up!"

And Connie paid close attention herself, bathed in a glow of slow-pulsed joy that seemed to rise mysteriously out of the music itself and lay languidly about the airless little room, breathed in and breathed out with each gentle rise and fall of her chest.

After a while she heard a car coming up the drive. She sat up at once, startled, because it couldn't be her father so soon. The gravel kept crunching all the way in from the road—the driveway was long—and Connie ran to the window. It was a car she didn't know. It was an open jalopy, painted a bright gold that caught the sunlight opaquely. Her heart began to pound and her fingers snatched at her hair, checking it, and she whispered "Christ, Christ," wondering how bad she looked. The car came to a stop at the side door and the horn sounded four short taps as if this were a signal Connie knew.

She went into the kitchen and approached the door slowly, then hung out the screen door, her bare toes curling down off the step. There were two boys in the car and now she recognized the driver: he had shaggy, shabby black hair that looked crazy as a wig and he was grinning at her.

"I ain't late, am I?" he said.

"Who the hell do you think you are?" Connie said.

"Toldja I'd be out, didn't I?"

"I don't even know who you are."

She spoke sullenly, careful to show no interest or pleasure, and he spoke in a fast bright monotone. Connie looked past him to the other boy, taking her time. He had fair brown hair, with a lock that fell onto his forehead. His sideburns gave him a fierce, embarrassed look, but so far he hadn't even bothered to glance at her. Both boys wore sunglasses. The driver's glasses were metallic and mirrored everything in miniature.

"You wanta come for a ride?" he said.

Connie smirked and let her hair fall loose over one shoulder.

"Don'tcha like my car? New paint job," he said. "Hey."

"What?"

"You're cute."

She pretended to fidget, chasing flies away from the door.

"Don'tcha believe me, or what?" he said.

"Look, I don't even know who you are," Connie said in disgust.

"Hey, Ellie's got a radio, see. Mine's broke down." He lifted his friend's arm and showed her the little transistor the boy was holding, and now Connie began to hear the music. It was the same program that was playing inside the house.

"Bobby King?" she said.

"I listen to him all the time. I think he's great."

"He's kind of great," Connie said reluctantly.

"Listen, that guy's *great*. He knows where the action is."

Connie blushed a little, because the glasses made it impossible for her to see just what this boy was looking at. She couldn't decide if she liked him or if he was just a jerk, and so she dawdled in the doorway and wouldn't come down or go back inside. She said, "What's all that stuff painted on your car?"

"Can'tcha read it?" He opened the door very carefully, as if he was afraid it might fall off. He slid out just as carefully, planting his feet firmly on the ground, the tiny metallic world in his glasses slowing down like gelatine hardening and in the midst of it Connie's bright green blouse. "This here is my name, to begin with," he said. ARNOLD FRIEND was written in tarlike black letters on the side, with a drawing of a round grinning face that reminded Connie of a pumpkin, except it wore sunglasses. "I wanta introduce myself, I'm Arnold Friend and that's my real name and I'm gonna be your friend, honey, and inside the car's Ellie Oscar, he's kinda shy." Ellie brought his transistor radio up to his shoulder and balanced it there. "Now these numbers are a secret code, honey," Arnold Friend explained. He read off the numbers 33, 19, 17 and raised his eyebrows at her to see what she thought of that, but she didn't think much of it. The left rear fender had been smashed and around it was written, on the gleaming gold background: DONE BY CRAZY WOMAN DRIVER. Connie had to laugh at that. Arnold Friend was pleased at her laughter and looked up at her. "Around the other side's a lot more—you wanta come and see them?"

"No."

"Why not?"

"Why should I?"

"Don'tcha wanta see what's on the car? Don'tcha wanta go for a ride?"

"I don't know."

"Why not?"

"I got things to do."

"Like what?"

"Things."

He laughed as if she had said something funny. He slapped his thighs. He was standing in a strange way, leaning back against the car as if he were balancing himself. He wasn't tall, only an inch or so taller than she would be if she came down to him. Connie liked the way he was dressed, which was the way all of them dressed: tight faded jeans stuffed into black, scuffed boots, a belt that pulled his waist in and showed how lean he was, and a white pullover shirt that was a little soiled and showed the hard small muscles of his arms and shoulders. He looked as if he probably did hard work, lifting and carrying things. Even his neck looked muscular. And his face was a familiar face, somehow: the jaw and chin and cheeks slightly darkened, because he hadn't shaved for a day or two, and the nose long and hawklike, sniffing as if she were a treat he was going to gobble up and it was all a joke.

"Connie, you ain't telling the truth. This is your day set aside for a ride with me and you know it," he said, still laughing. The way he straightened and recovered from his fit of laughing showed that it had been all fake.

"How do you know what my name is?" she said suspiciously.

"It's Connie."

"Maybe and maybe not."

"I know my Connie," he said, wagging his finger. Now she remembered him even better, back at the restaurant, and her cheeks warmed at the thought of how she sucked in her breath just at the moment she passed him—how she must have looked at him. And he had remembered her. "Ellie and I come out here especially for you," he said. "Ellie can sit in back. How about it?"

"Where?"

"Where what?"

"Where're we going?"

He looked at her. He took off the sunglasses and she saw how pale the skin around his eyes was, like holes that were not in shadow but instead in light. His eyes were like chips of broken glass that catch the light in an amiable way. He smiled. It was as if the idea of going for a ride somewhere, to some place, was a new idea to him.

"Just for a ride, Connie sweetheart."

"I never said my name was Connie," she said.

"But I know what it is. I know your name and all about you, lots of things," Arnold Friend said. He had not moved yet but stood still leaning back against the side of his jalopy. "I took a special interest in you, such a pretty girl, and found out all about you like I know your parents and sister are gone somewheres and I know where and how long they're going to be gone, and I know who you were with last night, and your best girlfriend's name is Betty. Right?"

He spoke in a simple lilting voice, exactly as if he were reciting the words to a song. His smile assured her that everything was fine. In the car Ellie turned up the volume on his radio and did not bother to look around at them.

"Ellie can sit in the back seat," Arnold Friend said. He indicated his friend with a casual jerk of his chin, as if Ellie did not count and she should not bother with him.

"How'd you find out all that stuff?" Connie said.   60

"Listen: Betty Schultz and Tony Fitch and Jimmy Pettinger and Nancy Pettinger," he said, in a chant. "Raymond Stanley and Bob Hutter—"

"Do you know all those kids?"

"I know everybody."

"Look, you're kidding. You're not from around here."

"Sure."   65

"But—how come we never saw you before?"

"Sure you saw me before," he said. He looked down at his boots, as if he were a little offended. "You just don't remember."

"I guess I'd remember you," Connie said.

"Yeah?" He looked up at this, beaming. He was pleased. He began to mark time with the music from Ellie's radio, tapping his fists lightly together. Connie looked away from his smile to the car, which was painted so bright it almost hurt her eyes to look at it. She looked at that name. ARNOLD FRIEND. And up at the front fender was an expression that was familiar—MAN THE FLYING SAUCERS. It was an expression kids had used the year before, but didn't use this year. She looked at it for a while as if the words meant something to her that she did not yet know.

"What're you thinking about? Huh?" Arnold Friend demanded. "Not worried   70
about your hair blowing around in the car, are you?"

"No."

"Think I maybe can't drive good?"

"How do I know?"

"You're a hard girl to handle. How come?" he said. "Don't you know I'm your friend? Didn't you see me put my sign in the air when you walked by?"

"What sign?"   75

"My sign." And he drew an X in the air, leaning out toward her. They were maybe ten feet apart. After his hand fell back to his side the X was still in the air, almost visible. Connie let the screen door close and stood perfectly still inside it, listening to the music from her radio and the boy's blend together. She stared at Arnold Friend. He stood there so stiffly relaxed, pretending to be relaxed, with one hand idly on the door handle as if he were keeping himself up that way and had no intention of ever moving again. She recognized most things about him, the tight jeans that showed his thighs and buttocks and the greasy leather boots and the tight shirt, and even that slippery friendly smile of his, that sleepy dreamy smile that all the boys used to get across ideas they didn't want to put into words. She recognized all this and also the singsong way he talked, slightly mocking, kidding, but serious and a little melancholy, and she recognized the way he tapped one fist against the other in homage of the perpetual music behind him. But all these things did not come together.

She said suddenly, "Hey, how old are you?"

His smile faded. She could see then that he wasn't a kid, he was much older—thirty, maybe more. At this knowledge her heart began to pound faster.

"That's a crazy thing to ask. Can'tcha see I'm your own age?"

"Like hell you are."   80

"Or maybe a coupla years older, I'm eighteen."

"Eighteen?" she said doubtfully.

He grinned to reassure her and lines appeared at the corners of his mouth. His teeth were big and white. He grinned so broadly his eyes became slits and she saw how thick the lashes were, thick and black as if painted with a black tarlike material. Then he seemed to become embarrassed, abruptly, and looked over his shoulder at Ellie. "*Him,* he's crazy," he said. "Ain't he a riot, he's a nut, a real character." Ellie was still listening to the music. His sunglasses told nothing about what he was thinking. He wore a bright orange shirt unbuttoned halfway to show his chest, which was a pale, bluish chest and not muscular like Arnold Friend's. His shirt collar was turned up all around and the very tips of the collar pointed out past his chin as if they were protecting him. He was pressing the transistor radio up against his ear and sat there in a kind of daze, right in the sun.

"He's kinda strange," Connie said.

"Hey, she says you're kinda strange! Kinda strange!" Arnold Friend cried. He 85 pounded on the car to get Ellie's attention. Ellie turned for the first time and Connie saw with shock that he wasn't a kid either—he had a fair, hairless face, cheeks reddened slightly as if the veins grew too close to the surface of his skin, the face of a forty-year-old baby. Connie felt a wave of dizziness rise in her at this sight and she stared at him as if waiting for something to change the shock of the moment, make it all right again. Ellie's lips kept shaping words, mumbling along with the words blasting in his ear.

"Maybe you two better go away," Connie said faintly.

"What? How come?" Arnold Friend cried. "We come out here to take you for a ride. It's Sunday." He had the voice of the man on the radio now. It was the same voice, Connie thought. "Don'tcha know it's Sunday all day and honey, no matter who you were with last night today you're with Arnold Friend and don't you forget it!—Maybe you better step out here," he said, and this last was in a different voice. It was a little flatter, as if the heat was finally getting to him.

"No. I got things to do."

"Hey."

"You two better leave." 90

"We ain't leaving until you come with us."

"Like hell I am—"

"Connie, don't fool around with me. I mean, I mean, don't fool *around*," he said, shaking his head. He laughed incredulously. He placed his sunglasses on top of his head, carefully, as if he were indeed wearing a wig, and brought the stems down behind his ears. Connie stared at him, another wave of dizziness and fear rising in her so that for a moment he wasn't even in focus but was just a blur, standing there against his gold car, and she had the idea that he had driven up the driveway all right but had come from nowhere before that and belonged nowhere and that everything about him and even about the music that was so familiar to her was only half real.

"If my father comes and sees you—"

"He ain't coming. He's at a barbecue." 95

"How do you know that?"

"Aunt Tillie's. Right now they're—uh—they're drinking. Sitting around," he said vaguely, squinting as if he were staring all the way to town and over to Aunt Tillie's back yard. Then the vision seemed to get clear and he nodded energetically. "Yeah. Sitting around. There's your sister in a blue dress, huh? And high heels, the poor sad bitch—nothing like you, sweetheart! And your mother's helping some fat woman with the corn, they're cleaning the corn—husking the corn—"

"What fat woman?" Connie cried.

"How do I know what fat woman, I don't know every goddam fat woman in the world!" Arnold laughed.

"Oh, that's Mrs. Hornby . . . Who invited her?" Connie said. She felt a little light- 100
headed. Her breath was coming quickly.

"She's too fat. I don't like them fat. I like them the way you are, honey," he said, smiling sleepily at her. They stared at each other for a while, through the screen door. He said softly, "Now what you're going to do is this: you're going to come out that door. You're going to sit up front with me and Ellie's going to sit in the back, the hell with Ellie, right? This isn't Ellie's date. You're my date. I'm your lover, honey."

"What? You're crazy—"

"Yes, I'm your lover. You don't know what that is, but you will," he said. "I know that too. I know all about you. But look: it's real nice and you couldn't ask for nobody better than me, or more polite. I always keep my word. I'll tell you how it is, I'm always nice at first, the first time. I'll hold you so tight you won't think you have to try to get away or pretend anything because you'll know you can't. And I'll come inside you where it's all secret and you'll give in to me and you'll love me—"

"Shut up! You're crazy!" Connie said. She backed away from the door. She put her hands against her ears as if she'd heard something terrible, something not meant for her. "People don't talk like that, you're crazy," she muttered. Her heart was almost too big now for her chest and its pumping made sweat break out all over her. She looked out to see Arnold Friend pause and then take a step toward the porch lurching. He almost fell. But, like a clever drunken man, he managed to catch his balance. He wobbled in his high boots and grabbed hold of one of the porch posts.

"Honey?" he said. "You still listening?" 105

"Get the hell out of here!"

"Be nice, honey. Listen."

"I'm going to call the police—"

He wobbled again and out of the side of his mouth came a fast spat curse, an aside not meant for her to hear. But even this "Christ!" sounded forced. Then he began to smile again. She watched this smile come, awkward as if he were smiling from inside a mask. His whole face was a mask, she thought wildly, tanned down onto his throat but then running out as if he had plastered makeup on his face but had forgotten about his throat.

"Honey—? Listen, here's how it is. I always tell the truth and I promise you this: I 110
ain't coming in that house after you."

"You better not! I'm going to call the police if you—if you don't—"

"Honey," he said, talking right through her voice, "honey, I'm not coming in there but you are coming out here. You know why?"

She was panting. The kitchen looked like a place she had never seen before, some rooms she had run inside but which wasn't good enough, wasn't going to help her. The kitchen window had never had a curtain, after three years, and there were dishes in the sink for her to do—probably—and if you ran your hand across the table you'd probably feel something sticky there.

"You listening, honey? Hey?"

"—going to call the police—" 115

"Soon as you touch the phone I don't need to keep my promise and can come inside. You won't want that."

She rushed forward and tried to lock the door. Her fingers were shaking. "But why lock it," Arnold Friend said gently, talking right into her face. "It's just a screen door.

It's just nothing." One of his boots was at a strange angle, as if his foot wasn't in it. It pointed out to the left, bent at the ankle. "I mean, anybody can break through a screen door and glass and wood and iron or anything else if he needs to, anybody at all and specially Arnold Friend. If the place got lit up with a fire honey you'd come runnin' out into my arms, right into my arms an' safe at home—like you knew I was your lover and'd stopped fooling around. I don't mind a nice shy girl but I don't like no fooling around." Part of those words were spoken with a slight rhythmic lilt, and Connie somehow recognized them—the echo of a song from last year, about a girl rushing into her boyfriend's arms and coming home again—

Connie stood barefoot on the linoleum floor, staring at him. "What do you want?" she whispered.

"I want you," he said.

"What?"   120

"Seen you that night and thought, that's the one, yes sir. I never needed to look any more."

"But my father's coming back. He's coming to get me. I had to wash my hair first—" She spoke in a dry, rapid voice, hardly raising it for him to hear.

"No, your Daddy is not coming and yes, you had to wash your hair and you washed it for me. It's nice and shining and all for me, I thank you, sweetheart," he said, with a mock bow, but again he almost lost his balance. He had to bend and adjust his boots. Evidently his feet did not go all the way down; the boots must have been stuffed with something so that he would seem taller. Connie stared out at him and behind him Ellie in the car, who seemed to be looking off toward Connie's right into nothing. This Ellie said, pulling the words out of the air one after another as if he were just discovering them, "You want me to pull out the phone?"

"Shut your mouth and keep it shut," Arnold Friend said, his face red from bending over or maybe from embarrassment because Connie had seen his boots. "This ain't none of your business."

"What—what are you doing? What do you want?" Connie said. "If I call the   125 police they'll get you, they'll arrest you—"

"Promise was not to come in unless you touch the phone, and I'll keep that promise," he said. He resumed his erect position and tried to force his shoulders back. He sounded like a hero in a movie, declaring something important. He spoke too loudly and it was as if he were speaking to someone behind Connie. "I ain't made plans for coming in that house where I don't belong but just for you to come out to me, the way you should. Don't you know who I am?"

"You're crazy," she whispered. She backed away from the door but did not want to go into another part of the house, as if this would give him permission to come through the door. "What do you . . . . You're crazy, you . . ."

"Huh? What're you saying, honey?"

Her eyes darted everywhere in the kitchen. She could not remember what it was, this room.

"This is how it is, honey; you come out and we'll drive away, have a nice ride. But   130 if you don't come out we're gonna wait till your people come home and then they're all going to get it."

"You want that telephone pulled out?" Ellie said. He held the radio away from his ear and grimaced, as if without the radio the air was too much for him.

"I toldja shut up, Ellie," Arnold Friend said, "you're deaf, get a hearing aid, right? Fix yourself up. This little girl's no trouble and's gonna be nice to me, so Ellie keep to yourself, this ain't your date—right? Don't hem in on me. Don't hog. Don't crush. Don't bird dog. Don't trail me," he said in a rapid meaningless voice, as if he were running through all the expressions he'd learned but was no longer sure which one of them was in style, then rushing on to new ones, making them up with his eyes closed, "Don't crawl under my fence, don't squeeze in my chipmunk hole, don't sniff my glue, suck my popsicle, keep your own greasy fingers on yourself!" He shaded his eyes and peered in at Connie, who was backed against the kitchen table. "Don't mind him honey he's just a creep. He's a dope. Right? I'm the boy for you and like I said you come out here nice like a lady and give me your hand, and nobody else gets hurt, I mean, your nice old bald-headed daddy and your mummy and your sister in her high heels. Because listen: why bring them in this?"

"Leave me alone," Connie whispered.

"Hey, you know that old woman down the road, the one with the chickens and stuff—you know her?"

"She's dead!"   135

"Dead? What? You know her?" Arnold Friend said.

"She's dead—"

"Don't you like her?"

"She dead—she's—she isn't there any more—"

"But don't you like her, I mean, you got something against her? Some grudge or   140
something?" Then his voice dipped as if he were conscious of a rudeness. He touched the sunglasses perched on top of his head as if to make sure they were still there. "Now you be a good girl."

"What are you going to do?"

"Just two things, or maybe three," Arnold Friend said. "But I promise it won't last long and you'll like me the way you get to like people you're close to. You will. It's all over for you here, so come on out. You don't want your people in any trouble, do you?"

She turned and bumped against a chair or something, hurting her leg, but she ran into the back room and picked up the telephone. Something roared in her ear, a tiny roaring, and she was so sick with fear that she could do nothing but listen to it—the telephone was clammy and very heavy and her fingers groped down to the dial but were too weak to touch it. She began to scream into the phone, into the roaring. She cried out, she cried for her mother, she felt her breath start jerking back and forth in her lungs as if it were something Arnold Friend were stabbing her with again and again with no tenderness. A noisy sorrowful wailing rose all about her and she was locked inside it the way she was locked inside this house.

After a while she could hear again. She was sitting on the floor with her wet back against the wall.

Arnold Friend was saying from the door, "That's a good girl. Put the phone back."   145

She kicked the phone away from her.

"No, honey. Pick it up. Put it back right."

She picked it up and put it back. The dial tone stopped.

"That's a good girl. Now you come outside."

She was hollow with what had been fear, but what was now just an emptiness. All   150
that screaming had blasted it out of her. She sat, one leg cramped under her, and deep inside her brain was something like a pinpoint of light that kept going and would not let her relax. She thought, I'm not going to see my mother again. She thought, I'm not going to sleep in my bed again. Her bright green blouse was all wet.

Arnold Friend said, in a gentle-loud voice that was like a stage voice, "The place where you came from ain't there any more, and where you had in mind to go is canceled out. This place you are now—inside your daddy's house—is nothing but a cardboard box I can knock down any time. You know that and always did know it. You hear me?"

She thought, I have got to think. I have to know what to do.

"We'll go out to a nice field, out in the country here where it smells so nice and it's sunny," Arnold Friend said. "I'll have my arms tight around you so you won't need to try to get away and I'll show you what love is like, what it does. The hell with this house! It looks solid all right," he said. He ran a fingernail down the screen and the noise did not make Connie shiver, as it would have the day before. "Now put your hand on your heart, honey. Feel that? That feels solid too, but we know better, be nice to me, be sweet like you can because what else is there for a girl like you but to be sweet and pretty and give in?—and get away before her people come back?"

She felt her pounding heart. Her hand seemed to enclose it. She thought for the first time in her life that it was nothing that was hers, that belonged to her, but just a pounding, living thing inside this body that wasn't really hers either.

"You don't want them to get hurt," Arnold Friend went on. "Now get up, honey. 155
Get up all by yourself."

She stood.

"Now turn this way. That's right. Come over here to me—Ellie, put that away, didn't I tell you? You dope. You miserable creepy dope," Arnold Friend said. His words were not angry but only part of an incantation. The incantation was kindly. "Now come out through the kitchen to me honey, and let's see a smile, try it, you're a brave sweet little girl and now they're eating corn and hot dogs cooked to bursting over an outdoor fire, and they don't know one thing about you and never did and honey you're better than them because not a one of them would have done this for you."

Connie felt the linoleum under her feet; it was cool. She brushed her hair back out of her eyes. Arnold Friend let go of the post tentatively and opened his arms for her, his elbows pointing in toward each other and his wrists limp, to show that this was an embarrassed embrace and a little mocking, he didn't want to make her self-conscious.

She put out her hand against the screen. She watched herself push the door slowly open as if she were safe back somewhere in the other doorway, watching this body and this head of long hair moving out into the sunlight where Arnold Friend waited.

"My sweet little blue-eyed girl," he said, in a half-sung sigh that had nothing to do 160
with her brown eyes but was taken up just the same by the vast sunlit reaches of the land behind him and on all sides of him, so much land that Connie had never seen before and did not recognize except to know that she was going to it. ●

Heinz Insu Fenkl *(1960–)*

"My Father's Hand . . . ."   *1996*
from *Memories of My Ghost Brother*

My father's hand arched out of the hot water like a knuckled fish, and he draped it in the dun-colored washcloth so it looked like the wet, textured hide of a land animal. It came up with a slurping sound as the water drained out, leaving a sucking pocket of air—*shuuuuurp!* "Badogaaaa!" he said. "Yongchoraaa!" and I leaned back and away from him in the round bathtub, laughing with fear and amusement. My father put the washcloth away, then ducked his head under the hot water and emerged again, sputtering.

"You're a big boy now," he said to me. "You used to be afraid of Yongchora and Badoga,[1] but now you're a big boy. Six years old. It's time for you to go to school and learn some English." He pulled me to his chest, which was matted with clumps of dark, reddish hair. "What do you say?"

"I no go school," I said. "I go school dey hit."

"Only if you're bad."

"I no bad. Good."   5

"Then you've got no problem. You don't want to grow up a heathen, do you?"

"Headen?"

My father lifted me high above his head, where the air was steamy hot, then unexpectedly cold. Drops of condensation from the ceiling dripped on my back and pierced my flesh.

"Next week you go to Sunday school, my little Booby."

I did not know what he was talking about. When he put me down and stood up,   10
towering out of the water like a golden-haired giant, I cowered back against the lip of the round tub.

Sunday school. I didn't know those words, but now for the first time in the many times I had bathed in the Japanese-style tub, I saw that it was the exact shape of the iron pots in which Emo[2] cooked our rice.

My father splashed out onto the tiles and began to dry himself with his too-small towel. "Next week, rain or shine," he said. "We're going to Sunday school, my little man."

He had appeared unexpectedly that day, still sweaty and disheveled from field maneuvers, with a whole case of C-rations. I had leapt up at him, shouting "Aboji, aboji!" grabbing onto his sleeves and counting his stripes to see if he had gotten any more. He had asked me where Mahmi was, and I had answered as I had been told: "Mahmi not home." Not asking where she might have gone, he had stoked the fire himself and prepared the hot bath.

When we emerged from the steaming room, wrapped in our towels, we saw Emo down in the kitchen, wiping her forehead on the dishtowel she carried.

"Ask Emo when Mommy will be home," my father said to me.   15

I translated for him and gave Emo's reply: "Emo say Mahmi come back eat nighttime."

"Where is she?"

I knew my mother was probably at the NCO Club or at the PX buying things for the black market. "Mahmi go friend," I said.

"Ask Emo."

"Emo," I said in Korean, "where did Mahmi go?"   20

Emo said quickly, "She's going to the club where she always goes, and then to Paekmajang. Tell your father she's gone to bring Country Aunt home with her." Country Aunt had gone out a little earlier to the market.

"Emo say Mahmi go get Country Emo. They come nighttime eat."

---

[1] **Yongchora and Badoga:** A reference to Yong chorri, a little boy character in a Korean elementary school reading book.   [2] **Emo:** Aunt.

"Well, Booby, then you and me are going to ASCOM[3] for lunch. How about that?"

"Okay!" I said.

"Tell Emo we'll be back by dinnertime. And you go put on some nice clothes."   25

"Emo," I said, "Aboji is taking me to the army post to eat lunch. We'll come back for dinner. Can you give me good clothes?"

Emo led me to the room and dressed me in the *Lederhosen* my grandmother had sent from Germany. Instead of my Korean rubber shoes, she made me wear brown leather shoes with clean white socks, and instead of my usual white T-shirt, she buttoned me into a short-sleeved shirt with a constricting collar. When she had me all dressed up, Emo combed my wet hair and flipped it to one side, parting it on the left the way my father preferred. "When you go through the gate, remember to ask one of the ladies in line to tell Mahmi to come home, *ungh?* Mahmi didn't know your father was coming today. On days he comes, she's supposed to be home."

"*Ungh,* Emo."

"Don't forget. It's an important matter."

"I won't forget."   30

Emo let me clomp across the *maru* in my leather shoes. I ran to my father and followed him out to the road to catch a taxi. We didn't have to wait very long for the dented blue cab to appear. It was the same one that had brought him to the house.

"ASCOM, main gate," my father said to the driver as we got into the back.

The skinny driver looked into the rearview mirror and saluted. "We go numbah one, sah-jing," he said, and drove off down the dirt road. I waved to Emo through the rear window and watched with wonder how quickly the rice paddies by the embankment receded from us. When we drew near the Catholic church that bordered the main road the taxi suddenly stopped bouncing—we had reached the blacktop to Inchon.

"Were you good while I was in the field?" said my father.

I nodded quickly. "I *too* good."   35

"Not *too* good. *Very* good."

"I *very* good."

"I *was* very good."

"I *was* very good," I said loudly.

"Boy-san undastan bery good," said the taxi driver, looking back at us. "Soon   40
sound like GI—no shit."

"That's right," said my father.

"I *talk* very good," I said to impress them.

My father and the taxi driver laughed. We continued the English lesson, the driver joining in to amuse us, until we reached the ASCOM gate where a dozen women were lined up waiting for GIs to take them in. This was where I had seen Gannan each time my mother brought me to ASCOM. Sometimes Gannan would still be waiting there in the hot sun, calling out to the passing GIs, when we came back hours later. If she had married a sergeant, she could have gone to the front of the line and the MP would have let her in without a word.

"Let's go," said my father, picking me up out of the backseat. "Where do you want to eat? You're getting heavy."

"Snack Bar," I said.   45

---

[3]**ASCOM:** Military acronym for Army Service Command, the processing center for all U.S. Army personnel coming into Korea.

"The Snack Bar it is." He put me down, paid the driver, and led me toward the gate.

A woman in line called, "Sah-jing, I give you one good time. You take me inside?" I didn't recognize her. She must have been new—none of the other women ever said anything to my father because they knew he was married to a Korean. Another woman, a friend of Gannan's, grabbed the new woman's arm and whispered something to her. "Sorry, sah-jing," said the new woman, smiling. My father ignored all of this, but I waved at the women I knew and they all said hello to me. One of Gannan's friends gave me a sympathetic look and patted my head.

"*Ajuma*," I said, "when you go in, tell my mother my father is here. Tell her to go home before dinnertime."

"All right," she said. "You go in and have fun with your father. I'll tell your mother."

I thanked her and ran in through the gate where my father waited with a dis- 50 pleased look. One of the things that always made him angry was when Mahmi stopped to talk to the other women.

"Hey, Insu," called the Korean MP, speaking half Korean and half English, "your *aboji* doesn't look too happy. Ask him if he wants to buy a good watch."

"Aboji, you want buy watchee? MP ask you."

"What kind?"

"Timex," said the MP, lifting his right arm. "Good watchee. I sell you five dallah. See, steel watcheeban look nice."

My father examined the watch and said, "Three dollars." 55

The MP was supposed to argue with him, but he surprised him instead by saying, "Okay, suree dallah."

"Fine," said my father. He pulled out his old wallet and handed the MP three MPC dollars. The MP unsnapped the watch and pulled it off, giving it to my father with a big smile and a bow.

"This watchee go long time," said the MP. "You makee watcheeban bigger and you wear. You watchee you give Insu when he know how time tell, okay?"

"Sure," said my father. "Heinz, you get my old watch when you start school. How about that?"

"Okay." 60

As we left, I turned to look back toward the gate. The MP waved to me. "I like new watchee," I said. "I can have old watchee today?"

"Not *watchee*. Say *watch*."

"*Watchy*."

"*Watch*. You stop right after the *ch*."

"*Waatch*." 65

"Good. Ten times now, after me. *Watch, watch. . . .*"

Even when I could say it properly, he wouldn't give me the old watch. He would probably give it to Hyongbu or his houseboy in Camp Casey, and when I started school, Mahmi would have to buy me one herself.

My father and I went first to the NCO Club, which was just inside the gate. He bought me a can of Coke and had a beer while he cooled off in the air-conditioned bar, sitting on the same stool the yellow-haired GI had been sitting on before he had met Gannan. We could have eaten there, too, but my father didn't like this NCO Club very much. Mahmi knew too many people there; she would talk to all the waitresses and see the manager about some business. Or she would play slot machines for hours. She didn't play very long when my father was with her, but he probably knew.

While my father drank his beer, I played with the can opener that was chained to the counter. If I pressed it properly I could make the can go *crack crack* and leave sharp, triangular teeth in a circle around the rim of the can. When I was done, the top of my Coke can looked like a face with a sharp-toothed smile along the bottom.

"Careful," said my father.

I drank the rest of the bubbly Coke through its dangerous smile. I would rather have drunk it outside on the grass like I did when Mahmi brought me to ASCOM, but my father liked to keep me near him. He only played slot machines with the change he had in his pocket and cursed when he lost. He hardly talked to anyone except other GIs he knew, and there weren't many of those in ASCOM because he was from Camp Casey. I wondered if he ever sang and danced like the Koreans. Every time Hyongbu drank Johnnie Walker or *makolli,* he would start to talk loudly and sing even if he was by himself, but my father sat quietly.

Now I remembered Rubberhand's mother singing the sad song on the night when Gannan died. I didn't remember any of the words, but I could almost hear it again, with the sound of the wind and rain, as the air conditioner buzzed in the background. I felt suddenly alone and very cold in the dark NCO Club bar.

"Aboji," I said.

"Hmmm?" My father looked down at me from his awful height, more frightening than comforting.

"Aboji," I said again. My mouth twisted into a funny shape and my eyes filled with tears. "Gannan die!" I said, bursting into tears. My father put me on his lap and held me while I cried.

"*Genug, mein Heinzchen, genug, genug,*" he said after a while. "*Wir mussen nicht—* we shouldn't get too sad." He rocked me back and forth, patting my back as if to make me burp. When I had calmed enough, my father made me tell him everything I could in the English words I knew, but it took a long time before I felt any better because, when I was done, he didn't have the proper words to comfort me.

Later, on our way to the Snack Bar, my father told me a story about how his grandmother had decided to die one evening before leaving her home in Czechoslovakia. She had simply gone upstairs to bed on the night before and died in her sleep.

"You burn you granma clothes, Aboji?"

"No. We were poor. We wore them and gave them to people."

"Ghost no come back?"

"No. Well, maybe it did, but we all had to leave the house to go to Germany."

"Why you go German?"

"Some bad people chased us out of our home." He was silent for a while.

We crested the hill and climbed up the stairs to where the PX, Foodland, the Snack Bar, and the Post Theatre were all lined up along the sidewalk. Here, many GIs trafficked back and forth between the PX and the Snack Bar. Korean shoeshine boys in their AAFES uniforms called out to them to buy magazines, newspapers, and *Playboy* calendars, or to get special spit shines. We passed through the business and went into the Snack Bar, and each time my father saluted or returned a salute along the way, I quickly imitated him. My father stopped in the Snack Bar foyer and bought a *Stars and Stripes.*

"Shoeshine?" said the Korean man.

"No."

"For boy-san maybe? He look just like you."

My father looked down at me. "How would you like a shoeshine?" he asked with a smile.

I nodded. The man lifted me up onto the shoeshine seat, and because my legs were too short to reach the foot rests, he pulled my shoes off. My father sat in the other seat and read the paper while I watched the man shine my shoes with rapid motions that reminded me of a wet dog shaking itself dry.

I could smell my father's perspiration, which had soaked the sides and back of his summer uniform shirt. His yellow-smell wasn't as strong as usual. Sometimes I could smell him in the room days after he went back to Camp Casey.

"Aboji," I said.

"Hmm?"

"Why you not come when Gannan dead?"

"I didn't know," he said. "I was up in the hills near the DMZ. I would have gotten emergency leave if I had known."

"What *emergen see?*"

"Emergency *leave.* I ask my CO if I can go home because a relative is sick or there's a funeral. Then he lets me go for a few days."

"Okay." I went back to watching the shoeshine boy buffing my shoes. My father folded the paper in half and read the back part with a frown.

I stepped cautiously down in my newly shined shoes while my father paid and tipped the shoeshine boy, and during my meal of hamburger and Coke, I was careful not to drip anything. My father ate a bowl of chili with lots of crackers and a huge glass of 7-Up.

In one corner of the Snack Bar a jukebox played the same two country & western songs over and over while in the other corner, two pinball machines made a clamorous racket as the GIs knocked them about and cursed at them. One Black GI stayed on a machine all by himself, tapping the sides to the music. When I became a GI I would do these things, too, until I was a sergeant like my father.

"What do you want to do now?" said my father.

"Ice cream."

"How about ice cream, then we go home?"

"Okay."

As we left the Snack Bar with our ice-cream cones, I saw a taxi coming from the direction of the Lower Four Club. It had stopped for a moment to let two GIs cross the street to the Post Office. The driver had taken off his driver's hat and was turned around, getting a light for his cigarette. In the backseat, next to the woman who held the lighter, sat my mother.

"Wait here," said my father. "I'll go get the cab to call us one." He tapped my shoulder and turned to go down the stairs. He hadn't seen Mahmi yet, but I knew that if he did, something bad would happen. I had heard him yelling at her for going on post to the clubs, and I knew how much she tried to keep it a secret. Mahmi had explained to me many times about how my father wasn't supposed to know about how she bought things and then sold them to the black market people.

My heart pounded fiercely as my father took the first steps toward the street. If he saw Mahmi they would argue all night and then she would be unhappy for a long time. I did not want her to be sad the way Gannan had been.

"*Aboji!*" I called.

"What is it?"

When he turned to look at me, I said, "I show some sing," and turning to a tall red-haired GI who had just come out of the Snack Bar with his friends, I did the thing Hyongbu had taught me many times. "Hwuk you!" I shouted. "Hwuk you, muddah-wukka! Hwuk you! Eat my shet!" I waved my ice cream in one hand and thrust the middle finger of my other hand into his crotch. I heard the GIs laughing and a loud "Hey!" from my father behind me. Then, before I quite knew what had happened, I was lifted into the air, my ice cream splattering on the sidewalk, and I felt a terrible, hot pain on my backside again and again. I heard the loud slaps of my father's giant palm against the thick leather seat of my pants and his tremendous voice, saying, "Don't you *ever* do that again, you son of a bitch!" and just before my vision blurred as I burst out crying over my father's shoulder, I saw Mahmi's taxi driving off down the street. ●

Marie Howe   (1950–)

The Attic   *1998*

Praise to my older brother, the seventeen-year-old boy, who lived
in the attic with me an exiled prince grown hard in his confinement,

bitter, bent to his evening task building the imaginary building
on the drawing board they'd given him in school. His tools gleam

under the desk lamp. He is as hard as the pencil he holds,   5
drawing the line straight along the ruler.

Tower prince, young king, praise to the boy
who has willed his blood to cool and his heart to slow. He's building

a structure with so many doors it's finally quiet,
so that when our father climbs heavily up the attic stairs, he doesn't   10

at first hear him pass down the narrow hall. My brother is rebuilding
the foundation. He lifts the clear plastic of one page

to look more closely at the plumbing,
—he barely hears the springs of my bed when my father sits down—   15

he's imagining where the boiler might go, because
where it is now isn't working. Not until I've slammed the door behind

the man stumbling down the stairs again
does my brother look up from where he's working. I know it hurts him

to rise, to knock on my door and come in. And when he draws his   20
    skinny arm
around my shaking shoulders,

I don't know if he knows he's building a world where I can one day
love a man—he sits there without saying anything.

Praise him.
I know he can hardly bear to touch me.

Rita Dove *(1952–)*

Adolescence—I
Adolescence—II
Adolescence—III *1980*

Adolescence–I

In water-heavy nights behind grandmother's porch
We knelt in the tickling grasses and whispered:
Linda's face hung before us, pale as a pecan,
And it grew wise as she said:
    "A boy's lips are soft,   5
     As soft as baby's skin."
The air closed over her words.
A firefly whirred near my ear, and in the distance
I could hear streetlamps ping
Into miniature suns   10
Against a feathery sky.

Adolescence–II

Although it is night, I sit in the bathroom, waiting.
Sweat prickles behind my knees, the baby-breasts are alert.
Venetian blinds slice up the moon; the tiles quiver in pale strips.

Then they come, the three seal men with eyes as round
As dinner plates and eyelashes like sharpened tines.   5
They bring the scent of licorice. One sits in the washbowl,
One on the bathtub edge; one leans against the door.
"Can you feel it yet?" they whisper.
I don't know what to say, again. They chuckle,

Patting their sleek bodies with their hands.   10
"Well, maybe next time." And they rise,
Glittering like pools of ink under moonlight,

And vanish. I clutch at the ragged holes
They leave behind, here at the edge of darkness.
Night rests like a ball of fur on my tongue.   15

Adolescence—III

> With Dad gone, Mom and I worked
> The dusky rows of tomatoes.
> As they glowed orange in sunlight
> And rotted in shadow, I too
> Grew orange and softer, swelling out   5
> Starched cotton slips.
>
> The texture of twilight made me think of
> Lengths of Dotted Swiss.[1] In my room
> I wrapped scarred knees in dresses
> That once went to big-band dances;   10
> I baptized my earlobes with rosewater.
> Along the window-sill, the lipstick stubs
> Glittered in their steel shells.
>
> Looking out at the rows of clay
> And chicken manure, I dreamed how it would happen: 15
> He would meet me by the blue spruce,
> A carnation over his heart, saying,
> "I have come for you, Madam;
> I have loved you in my dreams."
>
> At his touch, the scabs would fall away.   20
> Over his shoulder, I see my father coming toward us:
> He carries his tears in a bowl,
> And blood hangs in the pine-soaked air.

Alissa Quart

Body Branding: Cosmetic Surgery   *2003*
from *Branded: The Buying and Selling of Teenagers*

Carolyn, five feet two and 135 pounds, has blue eyes and platinum blonde hair. She lives in a wealthy suburb in the Mid West where kids with new money show it off by going to the salon regularly and being concerned about who made their pants and how much their jackets cost. Carolyn is like them in that she wears only posh brands such as Bebe and BCBG. Unlike her classmates, however, she lives modestly, with her divorced mother, a paralegal, in a two-story home; she works fifteen hours a week at a local upscale bakery so that she can buy her fancy clothes.

Carolyn is like many other middle-class teenagers today. But she is not like middle-class teenagers of a decade ago. Sure, she wants designer threads and, eventually, law school. What sets her apart from her teen predecessors is her most expensive dream: larger breasts. She has been obsessed with getting them since she was sixteen. Since then, not a day has gone by that she has not thought about her new, bigger

---

[1] **Dotted Swiss:** A muslin material with raised dots.

breasts. She is ready to buy them the month she graduates from high school. Like other girls in her school who talk about plastic surgery nonstop, she says, she is getting her enlarged mammary glands as a graduation present; the only difference is that she is giving the present to herself.

So for six months Carolyn has been consulting a surgeon and keeping a booklet of her fears and questions. Will they be too hard or look like grapefruit halves? Will they lose feeling? These worries, and the health risks associated with surgery, aren't enough to dissuade her. "I want breast implants as soon as possible," she says.

Carolyn is not alone. In only one year, from 2000 to 2001, the number of cosmetic surgeries on teens eighteen and under has jumped 21.8 percent, from 65,231 to 79,501. Almost 306,000 of the 7.4 million plastic surgeries performed in 2000 in the United States were alterations of teens and children. In 2000, according to the American Society of Plastic Surgeons (ASPS), breast augmentation was the third most popular surgery for people eighteen and under, when 3,682 girls underwent the surgery. The same year, 29,700 teen noses were reshaped, 23,000 teen ears were done, 95,097 teens were chemically peeled, another 74,154 young faces were microdermabraded, and 45,264 kids had hair removed by laser. It should be noted that while saline breast implants are approved by the Food and Drug Administration only for women eighteen years or older, it is not illegal for doctors to perform implant surgery on minors, nor is it difficult for minors to find doctors who will do the procedure.

Minors need only find a particularly permissive and accommodating doctor—and there are many—who might find their physical "imperfection" worthy of a "medical" procedure as opposed to a merely cosmetic one. Once they have found a willing surgeon, the kids have their parents sign consent forms for surgery to be performed. As Paul Weiss, M.D., a member of the ASPS, puts it, "A girl ought to have the right to decide whether she wants breast implants if she is an otherwise normal sixteen-year-old with little breast development." Other situations include those where one breast develops normally, says Weiss, and the other doesn't much or one breast is normal size and the other is very large. As for liposuction, Weiss says that "teenagers are small adults, with a small difference in their physiology: hypothetically, if I saw a sixteen-year-old with normal body habitus but extremely heavy thighs, I wouldn't turn my nose up at liposuction."

Teenagers now alter their bodies extremely and proudly. Among teens eighteen and under in 1994, only 392 had breast augmentations and 511 liposuction; in 2001 there were 2,596 augmentations and 2,755 liposuctions among that age group, a 562 percent increase. According to the ASPS, the rate of liposuction and breast augmentation for all age groups increased by 386 percent and 476 percent respectively between 1992 and 2000.

"It's totally common for people to have their eyes done, their chins implanted, their ears pinned back," says Mara, a seventeen-year-old swan of a girl from Miami Beach. Mara is now a freshman at a New York City women's college. She still bears the markings of her palmy origins: the heavy makeup, the half-head of blonde highlights, the superthin frame, the tight designer pants and designer clutch handbag. "My friend went to Argentina for the summer and got surgery done—it's cheaper there," Mara explains. "What can you say? Plastic surgery is more and more accepted, and people do it either in fifth grade or after high school, before college."

For Mara, and for the teens who now get plastic surgery, the procedures themselves are not a cause for shame. The real cause of embarrassment is having one's peers notice the change in appearance. That's why Jessica notes that the best time for the alteration is between middle school and junior high, junior high or high school, or high school and college, to lessen the chances of that sort of chagrin.

Manhattan-based facial plastic surgeon Phillip Miller, M.D., says that 30 percent of his practice consists of teens who get smaller noses or bigger lips—"luscious" mouths, in the argot of the beauty magazines. The plumping effect is produced through injections of collagen (good for five months) or by the permanent implants of fat that has been removed from other parts of the body. The girls present Miller with displays of fashion models from *Mademoiselle, Cosmo, Elle,* and *Allure,* and pictures of lippy movie stars such as Angelina Jolie and Julia Roberts. These women have lips that "make teens self-aware of what they may not have," as Miller puts it.

Growing up in a social context in which models' bodies are used to sell products   10 and lifestyles and atmospheres, teenagers feel significant pressure to purchase whatever it takes to become part of that role. This takes a psychic toll on Generation Y, and a financial one as well. To buy her $7,000 breast implants, Carolyn will spend part of a $100-a-week allowance, along with the money she makes at her job. Her aunt will throw in $2,000. The final $1,000 will be put on Carolyn's credit card, making her part of a new legion of teenagers carrying credit card debt. (According to Nellie Mae, students owed an average of $2,327 in credit card debt in 2001.)

The teenagers who now seek surgery can't imagine a time when there wasn't so much media coverage and salesmanship of these bodily correctives. When I speak to them, I remember my own adolescence, before the self-branding of the teen body really took. In 1985, at age thirteen, I, too, experienced intense physical self-loathing. I hid my mortifying "womanly" breasts under oversized boys' clothing because I hated them and what they meant. With the assurance that nothing could be done, I transformed this self-hatred into a hipster androgyny and became a creature of the mind—mostly a creature of my own mind. Perhaps this wasn't the best way. But at least when I and others like me left that visceral self-disgust behind at about sixteen, when we became happier in our own skins, our transformation was a result of character development and improving mental health, not a newly puffy mouth or surgically inflated breasts.

But it is different in the age of public flesh. If I were a teen today, I'm sure I would also be goaded by "abvertisements" (or ads that use sinewy abdomens to sell) in the magazines and would feel the urge to trawl the Web for beauty remedies. As so many girls do now, I might also trade my clumsy, inverted bookishness, body obscured under a plaid shirt that smells like patchouli and dust, and hair hanging blackly over my eyes for what would appear on the surface to be radiant, adult sexuality.

Julie, now a sweet-voiced, well-grounded business student of twenty-one, recalls the thinking that finally led her to get a $6,800 nose job. Growing up in North Hollywood, she recalls, she noticed girls in magazines with their perfect bodies and perfect facial features, and she became acutely aware of her flaws. "There are all these perfect things all around and you realize you don't look like that. In all the advertisements, there are no fat girls, no big-nosed girls," she says. "When I was younger, all the movie stars had surgery, which was comforting—all those people did it, went through it, why can't I?" she adds, her recognition that these stars used artificial means to achieve perfection consoling her that such alterations are both possible and commonplace enough among the celebrity class not to seem dangerous for an ordinary person. Julie then says that it became even more reasonable to her when "almost anyone" started to get nose jobs—the procedure seemed less vain and iconoclastic.

For Generation Y, liposuction is not just for Bel Air television producers' daughters but also for eighteen-year-old shop girls in Yonkers. First the province of the syphilitic and deformed, then of theater and movie stars, then of the rich, plastic surgery has become naturalized for the upper- and lower-middle classes.

In fact, Dr. Miller says he sees teens drawn to what he thinks is the remaining luxurious stigma of plastic surgery, the I-can't-believe-I-am-in-a-plastic surgeon's office frisson that excites both the young patient and the patient's parent. Like the other markers of affluence among an American middle class still anxious about its social position, a self-bettering beauty treatment is some proof that a girl has made it to the upper echelons, that her family no longer has necessities, only stylized tastes and desires. The sociologist Pierre Bourdieu has written that as the distance from necessity grows, some then mark this distance by "proving" their superiority to those who are ruled by needs, not wants. The girls who have plastic surgery use their improved bodies as proof of their supremacy to those who simply survive as they live out their days in fat, small-breasted, ordinary bodies that are destined more for laboring than for shopping.

Sociology aside, could the trend in youthful plastic surgery continue without an increase in advertising? Not likely. In fact, it was an antitrust court decision in the 1970s that deregulated medical advertising and ads for learned professional service. That decision cleared the way for the barrage of ads for the surgery we see today.

Slowly but inexorably, doctors began to advertise. As Deborah Sullivan writes in *Cosmetic Surgery: The Cutting Edge of Commercial Medicine in America,* there was a time when a plastic surgeon with a license plate that read "BOOBS" was state-of-the-art advertising for the industry. It took a decade for the paid ads for plastic surgery that appeared in the late 1970s to suffuse the backs of magazines, newspapers, and the yellow pages, all promising larger, firmer breasts, flatter tummies, tinier noses, stronger jaws. For today's teenagers, "breast augmentation" and "liposuction" are literally household words.

Still, it is the editorial media coverage of cosmetic surgery that really lures consumers, including teens. Plastic surgeons now pay up to $6,000 monthly to public relations representatives to ensure a client base. The fruits of these PR firms' labors are the stories appearing in women's magazines that showcase plastic surgery. In the 1960s, a scant 15 articles about plastic surgery appeared in the major women's magazines listed in the *Reader's Guide to Periodical Literature.* In the 1970s, the number rose to 55. In the 1980s, it nearly doubled to 107. Since the later 1980s, there has been a general rise in stories about breast augmentations—countless newspaper articles and television shows and even stories in general-interest magazines—and the *Reader's Guide* listed 39 articles on plastic surgery in the bigger women's magazines in 1999 alone. "Commercialism," Sullivan writes, "like Pandora's box, is full of problems for the medical profession's service ethic, occupational authority and autonomy."

Cosmetic surgeons and their new publicists are simply joining in the aggressive branding that has long characterized the industries competing for beauty consumers' dollars. And compete they do; if there was a time when doctors tried to maintain a special dignity in their marketing, that time has passed. On their Web sites, surgeons play ruthlessly on teenagers' desire for relief from their self-contempt. The Web site of Barry Davidson, M.D., for instance, offers up the profile of a fifteen-year-old as an inspiration to other girls with "weak" chins and "hook" noses. Incidentally, the ad copy echoes Jessica's thought on the timing of teen surgeries: "This patient elected to undergo rhinoplasty and chin implant during the summer vacation between high school and college," it reads. "This is a choice that is often made so that no explanations will be required to her new classmates."

Other cosmetic surgery sites are more subtle, but no less assured in their market- 20 ing agenda. While striking a temperate, caring medical stance—asking the potential clients seeking nose jobs about their emotional readiness, for example—they all the while note that new noses and chins boost "self-esteem" in the very young. The site of one cosmetic surgeon exhorts parents to "discuss with your teenager why he or she may feel insecure" and follows up with a promise of psychic happiness resulting from going under the knife: "One teenager suffered years of acne and was left with exten- sive scarring," it reads. "After he and his parents pursued scar revision surgery, the teen expressed that his biggest joy was not being teased about the scarring like he had been teased about the acne. Teens who pursue facial plastic or reconstructive surgery are looking to feel more confident and have a better self-image." Perhaps the most overt and unbecoming plea for teen beauty dollars appears on a surgery site that claims "suc- cessful plastic surgery may result in reversal of the social withdrawal that so often ac- companies teens who feel 'different.'"

The teen breast augmentation fetish has also been egged on by other advertise- ments in magazines such as *Teen Vogue* and *Seventeen*. The two mags have run ads (the ads were full-page in *Teen Vogue*) for Bloussant, an herbal breast enhancement tablet. Bloussant is, like all herbal supplements, unregulated by the FDA and costs $229 for an eight-week supply. The results are dubious at best, but these magazines—which have the trust of preteens and young teenagers—have carried advertisements for Bloussant, mixed in with the usual stories about boyfriends and makeup tips. The photo in the ad is of an ample young woman dripping out of her bathing suit; the text promises a "less invasive alternative to cosmetic surgery" resulting in increased cleavage, firmness, and fullness. *Seventeen* has unapologetically run the ad at least three times.

Perhaps it's no coincidence that in an October 2000 *Seventeen* magazine ques- tionnaire of readers from thirteen to twenty-two years old found that 25 percent had considered liposuction, tummy tucks, or breast augmentation, while 12 percent had considered nose jobs.

Some of the purveyors of these beauty fantasies, the plastic surgeons, don't seem money-mad at first blush, but rather sober and kindly. Nevertheless, they work from the assumption that for their patients, happiness will happen through physical cor- rection toward a normative mean. When I meet with a genial New York-based plastic surgeon named Brian Forley, M.D., for example, he tells me the story of how he aug- mented the breast of a fifteen-year-old with an asymmetrical bosom: "The girl limited her social engagements because of her deformity [the smaller breast]," he says. "She was looking for a way out. I found it medically appropriate to reconstruct."

Forley doesn't question why a girl with one smaller breast might consider the asym- metry a deformity, which seemed to me arguable. But it's common now for teenagers to consider lumpy thighs, a fleshy midriff, or small breasts to be horrific aberrations. Such is the price of viewing one too many teen catalog models. They imagine that becoming perfect will make them more and more socially acceptable. Obviously, that's the im- pulse behind the thousands and thousands of nose jobs teens have subjected themselves to over the past three decades.

Breast augmentation, on the other hand, speaks to a different and very current 25 impulse—the desire to redesign oneself into a being that one's social group agrees is sexualized. Girls who get breast augmentation are more interested in sexualizing them- selves than merely "normalizing" their faces. Teen girls who get the breast enhance- ments wish to be erotic objects of consumption, following the not-so-hidden currents in the general culture that both eroticizes teenage girls and punishes those who act on their libidinal impulses. On a teen Internet chat line, a girl writes that she wants breast augmentation because her 34B breasts are "a little on the saggy side." She adds, "I'd like them to be perky and fuller. The cost isn't an issue," her mind full of images of such "perfect" breasts from films and magazines, these breasts acting as a tacit competitor with her for sexual supremacy in social situations.

Happiness Through the Beautiful

That achieving physical normalcy or aesthetic perfection will bring about happiness is not a new idea. According to historian Joan Jacobs Brumberg, author of the *The Body Project: An Intimate History of American Girls,* Victorian-era girls were also taught to be most interested in their bodies. Their interests, however, followed different contours. Those girls were corseted and virginal at all costs, while their contemporary versions may starve, work out, wax, pierce, and tattoo their bodies, but nonchalantly relinquish their virginity.

But Brumberg also writes that girls today are much more bodily oriented. Nineteenth-century young women "had a very different orientation from those of girls today. . . . [before World War I] girls rarely mentioned their bodies in terms of strategies for self-improvement." In contrast, in this age of branded youth, the body is regarded as something to be processed, plucked, and subdued, refined through financial expenditure.

Sander Gilman, in his 1998 book *Creating Beauty to Cure the Soul: Race and Psychology in the Shaping of Aesthetic Surgery,* links the growth of cosmetic surgery to the relatively new prevalence of Prozac and an increased medicalization of psychological pain: If one kind of individual happiness is achievable through external medical means and is worth the price, by the same logic a saline intervention on a miserable and small-breasted girl may be just as worthwhile. "The idea of the cure of the psyche as central to the undertaking of aesthetic surgery postulates a 'patient' with a 'healthy' body but an 'unhappy soul,'" as Gilman puts it.

And like shopping at high-rent venues, this faith in surgical beautification and the consumption of luxury goods is often transmitted from parents to children as well. Both mothers and daughters may now view their bodies as plastic, moldable objects, constructed according to one's own will: All it takes to transform a mind or body is the money with which to purchase a new one. As the *Boston Globe* put it in March 2001, baby boomer enthusiasm has spilled over to other generations: "Many cosmetic surgeons say their teenage clientele has increased significantly in recent years. . . . Former patients transmit tips about surgery and surgeons to their children in a modern rite of passage. [Barry] Davidson [a plastic surgeon] says he routinely sees two generations of breast implants, and three generations is not uncommon. 'A daughter with the same build as her mother and grandmother sees what they had done and decides she can do something about it, too,' he explains."

The numbers confirm that Generation Y's parents are also getting surgery in record numbers; in 2000, 3.2 million people between the ages of thirty-five and fifty had cosmetic plastic surgery. Cosmetic surgery has become so commonplace that it has come to resemble the rest of the designer products mothers and daughters share.

Phillip Miller also sees a new acceptance of plastic surgery within families. "The mother had rhinoplasties at sixteen and seventeen," says Miller of the adolescent sur-

30

geries of thirty or so years ago, a more secretive practice that was more often tied up with a desire to assimilate out of one's ethnicity. "When they bring their daughters in for them, they feel camaraderie with their children," he says. "They say proudly, 'Now my daughters are getting it.'" A darker version of this scenario occurs, as well. "If the mother didn't have one, she may feel a little jealous—she wanted one as a child," says Miller. "By and large, these mothers also feel excitement that their daughters are getting something they couldn't have or afford for themselves when they were teenagers."

Carolyn grew up as part of this culture, seeing the upper-middle-class moms in their thirties, forties, and fifties with bust implants. These mothers, she says, offer them to their daughters. (Or are themselves plastic surgeons: the doctor who will operate on Carolyn is the father of a kid at her school.)

And affluent parents who refuse their children's requests for surgery no longer necessarily speak from a position of certitude or strength. They may be so confused and ambivalent about their daughters' pleas that they need the plastic surgeon not for the surgery itself but for the reinforcement in their efforts to discourage their daughters from going under the knife. With a sort of morose nonchalance, plastic surgeon Brian Forley tells me about the mothers who have visited his office with their daughters. When one sixteen-year-old girl visited him in tears and told him that she just had to have new breasts, her mother sat and listened, her face frozen. Forley conjectures that the parent thought of him as the last resort. "She hoped I would talk some sense into her daughter," he said. "I tried." (Of course, not all plastic surgeons try to dissuade young girls from nonmedical surgeries; it's likely that the girl would find someone else to do the surgery if one plastic surgeon wouldn't.)

Given the social climate, it is not surprising that Forley's patient did not come by her common sense on her own; she is, after all, very young. The branding of the flesh starts earlier than ever before, in the tween years. As one sixteen-year-old recently said before her breast augmentation surgery, "I was probably about thirteen when I started, you know, considering having surgery to correct my breasts."

Carolyn began to dream about larger breasts at that same age. "As long as I can remember, I never liked my breasts," she says. "Since I was thirteen, I was insecure when I was getting intimate with someone—I just don't like my body. I wanted augmentation when I was thirteen, and that was even before I had access to nude photos."

We may worry about these children's dented self-images and precocious, other-focused sexuality, but the truth of the matter is that our social order has created the double bind. Girls and women are actively encouraged to resemble the processed goods they consume. They wish to buy and then to become the perfect profiles of the media stars and movie heroines who are now themselves surgically altered and enhanced. They also dwell in the "after" side of the "before" and "after" surgical narrative, inspired by this primitive advertising technique or laudatory nonfiction accounts of the procedure. As Carolyn says, "I was watching something on HBO about a plastic surgery and decided to go for it."

Fake décolletage everywhere has an insalubrious effect on teenagers. One could argue that the manufacturing of this inadequacy is a sales strategy—a superior one, for it opens the door for the suggestion that the adolescent's physical inadequacy can be remedied by a purchase, be it thongs, jeans, or augmentation. (One plastic surgeon comments that teens now treat cosmetic alterations as if they were designer jeans.) It was the rumors of Britney Spears' breast implant surgery, doctors say, that spurred the latest and most intense interest in breast implant surgery among the very young. The girls who self-brand through plastic surgery do mention Spears and other media avatars of voluptuousness, such as actress Halle Berry.

Such ample women are also more likely to appear nearly undressed in public, revealing all their natural or newly acquired charms. Today's adolescents are surrounded by more exposed flesh than girls of previous generations, especially from the quasi-pornography of the laddie magazines *Maxim, FHM,* and *Gear.* Those magazines, no longer relegated to the pornographic brown wrappers of yore, display teen starlet cover girls, complete with their prerequisite, unnaturally firm bosoms, who smile meretriciously down at American girls from the windows of all magazine stores. None of these magazines existed a decade ago. Music videos have had a similar effect.

"Teenagers are more cognizant of the size of their breasts due to music videos," asserts Forley. "Prior to the expansion of MTV, girls had far less access to such constant imagery. Now they see them everywhere and they believe large breasts are the norm."

America's love affair with gigantism, the philosophy that bigger is better, also plays 40 a role in the new surgeries. Carolyn compares it with a giggle to supersizing. She says her desire for implants is similar to her taste for acrylic nails "that are longer and longer, so long they are ghetto fabulous." (She refers to the extremely long, often decorated talons preferred by some African American teenagers.) "I start with three-inch stiletto heels and I go to five-inch ones," she adds. "The desire for more and bigger just hits me all of a sudden."

The comparison is flip and Carolyn knows it. But she's not entirely kidding. Carolyn and the thousands of other girls getting implants have grown up watching giant films and their even more gargantuan sequels. They have played in theme parks that go on forever. They have eaten enormous bags of chips and great buckets of movie popcorn. Supersizing means that a Coca-Cola at Burger King now runs as big as 42 ounces, and a large order of French fries is double the size it was a few years ago. It's no wonder that kids are supersized, too: Obesity engulfs 17 percent of the teen population, a number they have grown into from kids and preteens—where one child in seven is obese. Today's generation of rampant teenage consumers have lived only in the era of supersizing; they know no other. They cannot distinguish the proper size of breasts, bank accounts, or cola portions.

Teens and tweens are perhaps more open to altering or branding their bodies than adults. The idea of a permanent change to the body—made practically overnight—appeals to adolescents, people who are by definition shifting identity daily. The more expensive, so much the better. Many teenage cosmetic surgeries emanate from self-aversion, camouflaged as an emblem of self-esteem and normalcy. The girl who chooses cosmetic surgery chooses obsession with the body and mastery over it rather than an attempt at the transcendence that means forgetting the body.

"Implants will make me much more confident," Carolyn says, not terribly convincingly. "Once I get them I will get used to them, and they will change the distorted perception of how my body is." ●

Explorations of the Text

1. How does social conditioning shape the different ways that the protagonists in these works view their bodies?

2. What bodily characteristics are coupled with gender roles, with predetermined masculine or feminine traits?

3. How do the protagonists in these works take control of their bodies? Do they create a new story for their bodies? How do gender stereotypes and images of beauty mark them?

4. How is body image linked to self-esteem, self-image, identity, individuality, conformity, and to rites of passage? Think of Connie's absorption in her looks in "Where Are You Going, Where Have You Been?" or the persona's obsession with her body in Rita Dove's "Adolescence I, II, III."

5. Outline the arguments presented in Alissa Quart's "Body Branding: Cosmetic Surgery" from *Branded*. Do you agree with Quart that the emphasis on body image and beauty for young women has intensified in the past several years? As a culture are we still just as consumed by images of beauty? Are there still rigid gender roles for men and women? Have cultural values changed? Is the emphasis on external markers of identity—on appearance, clothing, material possessions—as a means of self-definition still prevalent?

6. Compare and contrast the visions of masculine and feminine gender roles and sexual identity presented in the works in this cluster. Compare and contrast, for example, Heinz Insu Fenkl's reaction to his father's body with Rita Dove's views of her own changing, adolescent body in "Adolescence I, II, III." How do the personae's relationships with their bodies affect their attitudes, behavior, and self-image?

The Reading/Writing Connection

1. Freewrite: Write about or create a dialogue with some part of your body (for example, hair, hips, or eyes). Or write a poem about some part of your body. Or pick the aspect of your physical self that says that most about you (for example, your eyes). What does your appearance suggest about you?

2. **Write an Argument:** Agree or disagree with the following: "We are a beauty- and youth-obsessed culture."

3. Create a double-entry notebook for one section of "Body Branding: Cosmetic Surgery." What do you conclude? Do you agree with Quart's point of view?

Ideas for Writing

1. **Write an Argument:** Agree or disagree with the following statement from Alissa Quart's essay: "Teen girls who get the breast enhancements wish to be erotic objects of consumption, following the not-so-hidden currents in the general culture that both eroticizes teenage girls and punishes those who act on their libidinal impulses."

2. Alissa Quart states: "Teens and tweens are more open to altering or branding their bodies than adults. The idea of a permanent change to the body . . . appeals to adolescents, people who are by definition shifting identity daily. . . . Many teenage cosmetic surgeries emanate from self-aversion camouflaged as an emblem of self-esteem and normalcy." Do you agree with Quart's point of view? In what ways does transforming the body through surgery or medication substitute for other more internal or psychological modes of self-transformation?

3. **Write an Argument:** Does transforming appearance through tattooing, dress, or piercing become a statement of individuality? Argue pro or con.

FICTION

Wendi Kaufman   *(1964–   )*

Helen on Eighty-Sixth Street   *1997*

I hate Helen.[1] That's all I can say. I hate her. Helen McGuire is playing Helen, so Mr. Dodd says, because, out of the entire sixth grade, she most embodies Helen of Troy. Great. Helen McGuire had no idea who Helen of Troy even was! When she found out, well, you should have seen her—flirting with all the boys, really acting the part. And me? Well, I know who Helen was. I am pissed.

My mother doesn't understand. Not that I expected she would. When I told her the news, all she said was "Ah, the face that launched a thousand ships." She didn't even look up from her book. Later, at dinner, she apologized for quoting Marlowe. Marlowe is our cat.

At bedtime I told my mother, "You should have seen the way Helen acted at school. It was disgusting, flirting with the boys."

Mom tucked the sheets up close around my chin, so that only my head was showing, my body covered mummy style. "Vita," she said, "it sounds like she's perfect for the part."

So, I can't play Helen. But, to make it worse, Mr. Dodd said I have to be in 5 the horse. I can't believe it. The horse! I wanted to be one of the Trojan women— Andromache, Cassandra, or even Hecuba. I know all their names. I told Mr. Dodd this, and then I showed him I could act. I got really sad and cried out about the thought of the body of my husband, Hector, being dragged around the walls of my city. I wailed and beat my fist against my chest. "A regular Sarah Heartburn" was all he said.

"Well, at least you get to be on the winning team," my mother said when I told her about the horse. This didn't make me feel any better. "It's better than being Helen. It's better than being blamed for the war," she told me.

Mom was helping me make a shield for my costume. She said every soldier had a shield that was big enough to carry his body off the field. I told her I wasn't going to be a body on the field, that I was going to survive, return home.

"Bring the shield, just in case," she said. "It never hurts to have a little help."

Mom and I live on West Eighty-sixth Street. We have lived in the same building, in the same apartment, my entire life. My father has been gone for almost three years. The truth is that he got struck with the wanderlust—emphasis on "lust," my mother says—and we haven't heard from him since.

"Your father's on his own odyssey," my mother said. And now it's just me and 10 Mom and Marlowe and the Keatses, John and John, our parakeets, or "pair of Keats," as Mom says. When I was younger, when Dad first left and I still believed he was coming back, it made me happy that we still lived in the same building. I was happy be-

---

[1]**Helen:** According to Greek mythology, Helen was considered the most beautiful woman in the world and the indirect cause of the Trojan War.

cause he would always know where to find us. Now that I am older, I know the city is not that big. It is easy to be found and easy to stay lost.

And I also know not to ask about him. Sometimes Mom hears things through old friends—that he has travelled across the ocean, that he is living on an island in a commune with some people she called "the lotus eaters," that he misses us.

Once I heard Mr. Farfel, the man who's hanging around Mom now, ask why she stayed in this apartment after my father left. "The rent's stabilized," she told him, "even if the relationship wasn't."

At school, Helen McGuire was acting weird because I'm going to be in the horse with Tommy Aldridge. She wanted to know what it's like: "Is it really cramped in there? Do you have to sit real close together?"

I told her it's dark, and we must hold each other around the waist and walk to make the horse move forward. Her eyes grew wide at this description. "Lucky you," she said.

Lucky me? She gets to stand in the center of the stage alone, her white sheet barely 15 reaching the middle of her thighs, and say lines like "This destruction is all my fault" and "Paris, I do love you." She gets to cry. Why would she think I'm lucky? The other day at rehearsal, she was standing onstage waiting for her cue, and I heard Mrs. Reardon, the stage manager, whisper, "That Helen is as beautiful as a statue."

At home Old Farfel is visiting again. He has a chair in Mom's department. The way she describes it, a chair is a very good thing. Mom translates old books written in Greek and Latin. She is working on the longest graduate degree in the history of Columbia University. "I'll be dead before I finish," she always says.

Old Farfel has been coming around a lot lately, taking Mom and me to dinner at Italian places downtown. I don't like to be around when he's over.

"I'm going to Agamemnon's apartment to rehearse," I told Mom.

Old Farfel made a small laugh, one that gets caught in the back of the throat and never really makes it out whole. I want to tell him to relax, to let it out. He smells like those dark cough drops, the kind that make your eyes tear and your head feel like it's expanding. I don't know how she can stand him.

"Well, the play's the *thing*," Old Farfel said. "We're all just players strutting and 20 fretting our hour on the stage." Mom smiled at this, and it made me wish Old Farfel would strut his hours at his apartment and not at our place. I hate the way he's beginning to come around all the time.

When I get back from rehearsal, Mom is spinning Argus. It's what she does when she gets into one of her moods. Argus, our dog, died last summer when I was away at camp. My mother can't stand to part with anything, so she keeps Argus, at least his ashes, in a blue-and-white vase that sits on our mantel.

Once I looked into the vase. I'd expected to see gray stuff, like the ash at the end of a cigarette. Instead, there was black sand and big chunks of pink like shells, just like at the beach.

My mother had the vase down from the mantel and was twirling it in her hands. I watched the white figures on it turn, following each other, running in a race that never ends.

"Life is a cycle," my mother said. The spinning made me dizzy. I didn't want to talk about life. I wanted to talk about Helen.

"Helen, again with Helen. Always Helen," my mother said. "You want to know 25 about Helen?"

I nod my head.

"Well, her father was a swan and her mother was too young to have children. You don't want to be Helen. Be lucky you're a warrior. You're too smart to be ruled by your heart."

"And what about beauty? Wasn't she the most beautiful woman in the world?" I asked.

Mom looked at the Greek vase. "Beauty is truth, truth beauty—that is all ye need to know."

She is not always helpful.   30

"Manhattan is a rocky island," Mom said at dinner. "There is no proper beach, no shore." My mother grew up in the South, near the ocean, and there are times when she still misses the beach. Jones, Brighton, or even Coney Island beaches don't come close for her. I know when she starts talking about the water that she's getting restless. I hope this means that Old Farfel won't be hanging around too long.

Every night I write a letter to my father. I don't send them—I don't know where to send them—but, still, I write them. I keep the letters at the back of my closet in old shoeboxes. I am on my third box. It's getting so full that I have to keep the lid tied down with rubber bands.

I want to write, "Mom is talking about the water again. I think this means she is thinking of you. We are both thinking of you, though we don't mention your name. Are you thinking of us? Do you ever sit on the shore at night and wonder what we're doing, what we're thinking? Do you miss us as much as we miss you?"

But instead I write, "I am in a play about the Trojan War. I get to wear a short white tunic, and I ambush people from inside a big fake horse. Even though we win the war, it will be many, many years before I return home. Until I see my family again. In this way, we are the same. I will have many adventures. I will meet giants and witches and see strange lands. Is that what you are doing? I wish you could come to the play."

Old Farfel is going to a convention in Atlanta. He wants Mom to go with him.   35 From my bed, I can hear them talking about it in the living room. It would be good for her, he says. I know that Mom doesn't like to travel. She can't even go to school and back without worrying about the apartment—if she turned the gas off, if she fed the cat, if she left me enough money. She tells him that she'll think about it.

"You have to move on, Victoria," he tells her. "Let yourself go to new places."

"I'm still exploring the old places," she says.

He lets the conversation drop.

Mom said once that she travelled inside herself when Dad left. I didn't really understand, but it was one of the few times I saw her upset. She was sitting in her chair, at her desk, looking tired. "Mom, are you in there?" I waved my hand by her face.

"I'm not," she said. "I'm on new ground. It's a very different place."   40

"Are you thinking about Dad?"

"I was thinking how we all travel differently, Vita. Some of us don't even have to leave the house."

"Dad left the house."

"Sometimes it's easier to look outside than in," she said.

That night I dreamed about a swan. A swan that flies in circles over the ocean. This   45 is not the dark water that snakes along the West Side Highway and slaps against the banks of New Jersey but the real ocean. Open water. Salty, like tears.

■ ■ ■

At play practice, I watch the other girls dress up as goddesses and Trojan women. They wear gold scarves wound tight around their necks and foreheads. They all wear flowers in their hair and flat pink ballet slippers. I wear a white sheet taken from my bed. It is tied around the middle with plain white rope. I also wear white sneakers. I don't get to wear a gold scarf or flowers. Mr. Dodd wrote this play himself and is very picky about details. Tommy Aldridge, my partner in the horse, was sent home because his sheet had Ninja Turtles on it. "They did not have Ninja Turtles in ancient Greece," Mr. Dodd said.

Mr. Dodd helps Helen McGuire with her role. "You must understand," he tells her, "Helen is the star of the show. Men have travelled great distances just to fight for her. At the end, when you come onstage and look at all the damage you've caused, we must believe you're really upset by the thought that this is all your fault."

Helen nods and looks at him blankly.

"Well, at least try to think of something really sad."

Old Farfel is taking Mom out to dinner again. It's the third time this week. Mom says it is a very important dinner, and I am not invited. Not that I would want to go, but I wasn't even asked. Mom brought in takeout, some soup and a cheese sandwich, from the coffee shop on the corner.

I eat my soup, alone in the kitchen, from a blue-and-white paper cup. I remember once at a coffee shop Mom held the same type of cup out in front of me.

"See this building, Vita?" she said. She pointed to some columns that were drawn on the front of her cup. It wasn't really a building—more like a cartoon drawing. "It's the Parthenon," she said. "It's where the Greeks made sacrifices to Athena."

"How did they make sacrifices?" I asked.

"They burned offerings on an altar. They believed this would bring them what they wanted. Good things. Luck."

I finish my soup and look at the tiny building on the cup. In between the columns are the words "Our Pleasure to Serve You." I run my fingers across the flat lines of the Parthenon and trace the roof. I can almost imagine a tiny altar and the ceremonies that were performed there.

It is then that I get an idea. I find a pair of scissors on Mom's desk and cut through the thick white lip of the cup toward the lines of the little temple. I cut around the words "Our Pleasure to Serve You." Then I take the temple and the words and glue them to the back of my notebook. The blue-and-white lines show clearly against the cardboard backing. I get Argus's big metal water bowl from the kitchen and find some matches from a restaurant Old Farfel took us to for dinner.

In my room I put on my white sheet costume and get all my letters to Dad out from the back of the closet. I know that I must say something, to make this more like a ceremony. I think of any Greek words I know: *spanakopita, moussaka, gyro.* They're only food words, but it doesn't matter. I decide to say them anyway. I say them over and over out loud until they blur into a litany, my own incantation: "*Spanakopitamoussaka-andgyro, Spanakopitamoussakaandgyro, Spanakopitamoussakaandgyro.*"

As I say this, I burn handfuls of letters in the bowl. I think about what I want: to be Helen, to have my father come back. Everything I have ever heard says that wishes are granted in threes, so I throw in the hope of Old Farfel's leaving.

I watch as the words burn. Three years of letters go up in smoke and flame. I see blue-lined paper turn to black ashes; I see pages and pages, months and years, burn, crumble, and then disappear. The front of my white sheet has turned black from soot, and my eyes water and burn.

When I am done, I take the full bowl of ashes and hide it in the vase on the man- 60
tel, joining it with Argus. My black hands smudge the white figures on the vase, until
their tunics become as sooty as my own. I change my clothes and open all the windows, but still Mom asks, when she comes home, about the burning smell. I told her
I was cooking.

She looked surprised. Neither of us cooks much. "No more burnt offerings when
I'm not home," she said. She looked upset and distracted, and Old Farfel didn't give
that stifled laugh of his.

It's all my fault. Helen McGuire got chicken pox. Bad. She has been out of school for
almost two weeks. I know my burning ceremony did this. "The show must go on,"
Mr. Dodd said when Achilles threw up the Tater Tots or when Priam's beard got
caught in Athena's hair, but this is different. This is Helen. And it's my fault.

I know all her lines. Know them backward and forward. I have stood in our living
room, towel tied around my body, and acted out the entire play, saying every line for
my mother. When Mr. Dodd made the announcement about Helen at dress rehearsal,
I stood up, white bedsheet slipping from my shoulders, and said in a loud, clear voice,
"The gods must have envied me my beauty, for now my name is a curse. I have become
hated Helen, the scourge of Troy."

Mr. Dodd shook his head and looked very sad. "We'll see, Vita. She might still get
better," he said.

Helen McGuire recovered, but she didn't want to do the part because of all the 65
pockmarks that were left. Besides, she wanted to be inside the horse with Tommy
Aldridge. Mr. Dodd insisted that she still be Helen until her parents wrote that they
didn't want her to be pressured, they didn't want to *do any further damage,* whatever
that means. After that, the part was mine.

Tonight is the opening, and I am so excited. Mom is coming without Old Farfel. "He
wasn't what I wanted," she said. I don't think she'll be seeing him anymore.

"What is beautiful?" I ask Mom before the play begins.

"Why are you so worried all the time about beauty? Don't you know how beautiful you are to me?"

"Would Daddy think I was beautiful?"

"Oh, Vita, he *always* thought you were beautiful." 70

"Would he think I was like Helen?"

She looked me up and down, from the gold lanyard snaked through my thick hair
to my too tight pink ballet slippers.

"He would think you're more beautiful than Helen. I'm almost sorry he won't be
here to see it."

"*Almost* sorry?"

"Almost. At moments like this—you look so good those ancient gods are going to 75
come alive again with envy."

"What do you mean, come alive again? What are you saying about the gods?"

"Vita, Greek polytheism is an extinct belief," she said, and laughed. And then she
stopped and looked at me strangely. "When people stopped believing in the gods, they
no longer had power. They don't exist anymore. You must have known that."

Didn't I get the part of Helen? Didn't Old Farfel leave? I made all these things
happen with my offering. I know I did. I don't believe these gods disappeared. At least
not Athena.

"I don't believe you."

She looked at me, confused.

"You can't know for sure about the gods. And who knows? Maybe Daddy will even be here to see it."

"Sure," she said. "And maybe this time the Trojans will win the war."

I stand offstage with Mr. Dodd and wait for my final cue. The dry-ice machine has been turned on full blast and an incredible amount of fake smoke is making its way toward the painted backdrop of Troy. Hector's papier-mâché head has accidentally slipped from Achilles' hand and is now making a hollow sound as it rolls across the stage.

I peek around the thick red curtain, trying to see into the audience. The auditorium is packed, filled with parents and camcorders. I spot my mom sitting in the front row, alone. I try to scan the back wall, looking for a sign of him, a familiar shadow. Nothing.

Soon I will walk out on the ramparts, put my hand to my forehead, and give my last speech. "Are you sure you're ready?" Mr. Dodd asks. I think he's more nervous than I am. "Remember," he tells me, "this is Helen's big moment. Think loss." I nod, thinking nothing.

"Break a leg," he says, giving me a little push toward the stage. "And try not to trip over the head."

The lights are much brighter than I had expected, making me squint. I walk through the smoky fog toward center stage.

"It is I, the hated Helen, scourge of Troy."

With the light on me, the audience is in shadow, like a big pit, dark and endless. I bow before the altar, feeling my tunic rise. "Hear my supplication," I say, pulling down a bit on the back of my tunic.

"Do not envy me such beauty—it has wrought only pain and despair."

I can hear Mr. Dodd, offstage, loudly whispering each line along with me.

"For this destruction, I know I will be blamed."

I begin to recite Helen's wrongs—beauty, pride, the abdication of Sparta—careful to enunciate clearly. "Troy, I have come to ask you to forgive me."

I'm supposed to hit my fist against my chest, draw a hand across my forehead, and cry loudly. Mr. Dodd has shown me this gesture, practiced it with me in rehearsal a dozen times—the last line, my big finish. The audience is very quiet. In the stillness there is a hole, an empty pocket, an absence. Instead of kneeling, I stand up, straighten my tunic, look toward the audience, and speak the line softly: "And to say goodbye."

There is a prickly feeling up the back of my neck. And then applause. The noise surrounds me, filling me. I look into the darkened house and, for a second, I can hear the beating of a swan's wings, and, then, nothing at all. ●

Explorations of the Text

1. Analyze the relationship between Vita and her mother; between Vita and her father.

2. Discuss the first person point of view and the use of humor.

3. Analyze the mother's character and her relationship with her "lost" husband and Mr. Farfel.

4. Why is Vita writing letters to her father? Why does she burn the letters?

5. How do the allusions to Helen of Troy and to the Trojan War serve as a context for the story? Why does Vita want to play Helen? How does the play, as an element of the plot, develop the conflicts in the work?

6. Discuss Vita's reflections at the end of the work. What is the symbolic signifi-

cance of the final line of Helen's speech: "'And to say goodbye'"?

7. Compare Vita's coming of age with Connie's in "Where Are You Going, Where Have You Been?"

The Reading/Writing Connection

1. "Think" Topic: Compare the first-person perspective in this work with the narrative point of view in "The Stolen Party."

2. Freewrite: Write about an experience in your own life within the context of a myth.

3. Create one of the letters that Vita writes to her father.

Ideas for Writing

1. Research Helen of Troy and the Trojan War. How do these allusions develop character and themes of the work?

2. Discuss the humor in the work. Is it effective?

3. Compare ideas of "beauty" presented in this work with one of the works in

Crossing the Genres/Identity and the Body. Why do the characters desire beauty? What power will it give them? What will changing their appearance or image accomplish?

John Updike   *(1932–)*

A&P   *1961*

In walks these three girls in nothing but bathing suits. I'm in the third checkout slot, with my back to the door, so I don't see them until they're over by the bread. The one that caught my eye first was the one in the plaid green two-piece. She was a chunky kid, with a good tan and a sweet broad soft-looking can with those two crescents of white just under it, where the sun never seems to hit, at the top of the backs of her legs. I stood there with my hand on a box of HiHo crackers trying to remember if I rang it up or not. I ring it up again and the customer starts giving me hell. She's one of these cash-register-watchers, a witch about fifty with rouge on her cheekbones and no eyebrows, and I know it made her day to trip me up. She'd been watching cash registers forty years and probably never seen a mistake before.

By the time I got her feathers smoothed and her goodies into a bag—she gives me a little snort in passing, if she'd been born at the right time they would have burned her over in Salem—by the time I get her on her way the girls had circled around the bread and were coming back, without a pushcart, back my way along the counters, in the aisle between the check-outs and the Special bins. They didn't even have shoes on. There was this chunky one, with the two-piece—it was bright green and the seams on the bra were still sharp and her belly was still pretty pale so I guessed she just got it (the suit)—there was this one, with one of those chubby berry-faces, the lips all bunched together under her nose, this one, and a tall one, with black hair that hadn't quite frizzed right, and one of these sunburns right across under the eyes, and a chin that was too long—you know, the kind of girl other girls think is very "striking" and "attractive" but never quite makes it, as they very well know, which is why they like her so much—and then the third one, that wasn't quite so tall. She was the queen. She kind of led them, the other two peeking around and making their shoulders round. She didn't look around, not this queen, she just walked straight on slowly, on these long white prima-donna legs. She came down a little hard on her heels, as if she didn't walk in her bare feet that much, putting down her heels and then letting the weight move along to her toes as if she was testing the floor with every step, putting a little deliberate extra action into it. You never know for sure how girls' minds work (do you really think it's a mind in there or just a little buzz like a bee in a glass jar?) but you got the idea she had talked the other two into coming in here with her, and now she was showing them how to do it, walk slow and hold yourself straight.

She had on a kind of dirty-pink—beige maybe, I don't know—bathing suit with a little nubble all over it and, what got me, the straps were down. They were off her shoulders looped loose around the cool tops of her arms, and I guess as a result the suit had slipped a little on her, so all around the top of the cloth there was this shining rim. If it hadn't been there you wouldn't have known there could have been anything whiter than those shoulders. With the straps pushed off, there was nothing between the top of the suit and the top of her head except just *her,* this clean bare plane of the top of her chest down from the shoulder bones like a dented sheet of metal tilted in the light. I mean, it was more than pretty.

She had sort of oaky hair that the sun and salt had bleached, done up in a bun that was unravelling, and a kind of prim face. Walking into the A & P with your straps down, I suppose it's the only kind of face you *can* have. She held her head so high her neck, coming up out of those white shoulders, looked kind of stretched, but I didn't mind. The longer her neck was, the more of her there was.

She must have felt in the corner of her eye me and over my shoulder Stokesie in ⁵ the second slot watching, but she didn't tip. Not this queen. She kept her eyes moving across the racks, and stopped, and turned so slow it made my stomach rub the inside of my apron, and buzzed to the other two, who kind of huddled against her for relief, and they all three of them went up the cat-and-dog-food-breakfast-cereal-macaroni-rice-raisins-seasonings-spreads-spaghetti-soft-drinks-crackers-and-cookies aisle. From the third slot I look straight up this aisle to the meat counter, and I watched them all the way. The fat one with the tan sort of fumbled with the cookies, but on second thought she put the package back. The sheep pushing their carts down the aisle—the girls were walking against the usual traffic (not that we have one-way signs or anything)—were pretty hilarious. You could see them, when Queenie's white shoulders dawned on them, kind of jerk, or hop, or hiccup, but their eyes snapped back to their own baskets and on they pushed. I bet you could set off dynamite in an A & P and the people would by and large keep reaching and checking oatmeal off their lists and muttering "Let me see, there was a third thing, began with A, asparagus, no, ah, yes, applesauce!" or whatever it is they do mutter. But there was no doubt, this jiggled them. A few houseslaves in pin curlers even looked around after pushing their carts past to make sure what they had seen was correct.

You know, it's one thing to have a girl in a bathing suit down on the beach, where what with the glare nobody can look at each other much anyway, and another thing in the cool of the A & P, under the fluorescent lights, against all those stacked packages, with her feet paddling along naked over our checkerboard green-and-cream rubber-tile floor.

"Oh Daddy," Stokesie said beside me. "I feel so faint."

"Darling," I said. "Hold me tight." Stokesie's married, with two babies chalked up on his fuselage already, but as far as I can tell that's the only difference. He's twenty-two, and I was nineteen this April.

"Is it done?" he asks, the responsible married man finding his voice. I forgot to say he thinks he's going to be manager some sunny day, maybe in 1990 when it's called the Great Alexandrov and Petrooshki Tea Company or something.

What he meant was, our town is five miles from a beach, with a big summer colony 10
out on the Point, but we're right in the middle of town, and the women generally put on a shirt or shorts or something before they get out of the car into the street. And anyway these are usually women with six children and varicose veins mapping their legs and nobody, including them, could care less. As I say, we're right in the middle of town, and if you stand at our front doors you can see two banks and the Congregational church and the newspaper store and three real-estate offices and about twenty-seven old free-loaders tearing up Central Street because the sewer broke again. It's not as if we're on the Cape; we're north of Boston and there's people in this town haven't seen the ocean for twenty years.

The girls had reached the meat counter and were asking McMahon something. He pointed, they pointed, and they shuffled out of sight behind a pyramid of Diet Delight peaches. All that was left for us to see was old McMahon patting his mouth and looking after them sizing up their joints. Poor kids, I began to feel sorry for them, they couldn't help it.

Now here comes the sad part of the story, at least my family says it's sad, but I don't think it's so sad myself. The store's pretty empty, it being Thursday afternoon, so there was nothing much to do except lean on the register and wait for the girls to show up again. The whole store was like a pinball machine and I didn't know which tunnel they'd come out of. After a while they come around out of the far aisle, around the light bulbs, records at discount of the Caribbean Six or Tony Martin Sings or some such gunk you wonder they waste the wax on, sixpacks of candy bars, and plastic toys done up in cellophane that fall apart when a kid looks at them anyway. Around they come, Queenie still leading the way, and holding a little gray jar in her hand. Slots Three through Seven are unmanned and I could see her wondering between Stokes and me, but Stokesie with his usual luck draws an old party in baggy gray pants who stumbles up with four giant cans of pineapple juice (what do these bums *do* with all that pineapple juice? I've often asked myself) so the girls come to me. Queenie puts down the jar and I take it into my fingers icy cold. Kingfish Fancy Herring Snacks in Pure Sour Cream: 49¢. Now her hands are empty, not a ring or a bracelet, bare as God made them, and I wonder where the money's coming from. Still with that prim look she lifts a folded dollar bill out of the hollow at the center of her nubbled pink top. The jar went heavy in my hand. Really, I thought that was so cute.

Then everybody's luck begins to run out. Lengel comes in from haggling with a truck full of cabbages on the lot and is about to scuttle into that door marked MANAGER behind which he hides all day when the girls touch his eye. Lengel's pretty dreary, teaches Sunday school and the rest, but he doesn't miss that much. He comes over and says, "Girls, this isn't the beach."

Queenie blushes, though maybe it's just a brush of sunburn I was noticing for the first time, now that she was so close. "My mother asked me to pick up a jar of herring snacks." Her voice kind of startled me, the way voices do when you see the people first, coming out so flat and dumb yet kind of tony, too, the way it ticked over "pick up" and "snacks." All of a sudden I slid right down her voice into her living room. Her father and the other men were standing around in icecream coats and bow ties and the women were in sandals picking up herring snacks on toothpicks off a big plate and they were all holding drinks the color of water with olives and sprigs of mint in them. When my parents have somebody over they get lemonade and if it's a real racy affair Schlitz in tall glasses with "They'll Do It Every Time" cartoons stencilled on.

"That's all right," Lengel said. "But this isn't the beach." His repeating this struck   15
me as funny, as if it had just occurred to him, and he had been thinking all these years the A & P was a great big dune and he was the head lifeguard. He didn't like my smiling—as I say he doesn't miss much—but he concentrates on giving the girls that sad Sunday-school-superintendent stare.

Queenie's blush is no sunburn now, and the plump one in plaid, that I liked better from the back—a really sweet can—pipes up, "We weren't doing any shopping. We just came in for the one thing."

"That makes no difference," Lengel tells her, and I could see from the way his eyes went that he hadn't noticed she was wearing a two-piece before. "We want you decently dressed when you come in here."

"We *are* decent," Queenie says suddenly, her lower lip pushing, getting sore now that she remembers her place, a place from which the crowd that runs the A & P must look pretty crummy. Fancy Herring Snacks flashed in her very blue eyes.

"Girls, I don't want to argue with you. After this come in here with your shoulders covered. It's our policy." He turns his back. That's policy for you. Policy is what the kingpins want. What the others want is juvenile delinquency.

All this while, the customers had been showing up with their carts but, you know,   20
sheep, seeing a scene, they had all bunched up on Stokesie, who shook open a paper bag as gently as peeling a peach, not wanting to miss a word. I could feel in the silence everybody getting nervous, most of all Lengel, who asks me, "Sammy, have you rung up this purchase?"

I thought and said "No" but it wasn't about that I was thinking. I go through the punches, 4, 9, GROC, TOT—it's more complicated than you think, and after you do it often enough, it begins to make a little song, that you hear words to, in my case "Hello (*bing*) there, you (*gung*) happy *pee*-pul (*splat*)!"—the *splat* being the drawer flying out. I uncrease the bill, tenderly as you may imagine, it just having come from between the two smoothest scoops of vanilla I had ever known were there, and pass a half and a penny into her narrow pink palm, and nestle the herrings in a bag and twist its neck and hand it over, all the time thinking.

The girls, and who'd blame them, are in a hurry to get out, so I say "I quit" to Lengel quick enough for them to hear, hoping they'll stop and watch me, their unsuspected hero. They keep right on going, into the electric eye; the door flies open and they flicker across the lot to their car, Queenie and Plaid and Big Tall Goony-Goony (not that as raw material she was so bad), leaving me with Lengel and a kink in his eyebrow.

"Did you say something, Sammy?"

"I said I quit."

"I thought you did." 25

"You didn't have to embarrass them."

"It was they who were embarrassing us."

I started to say something that came out "Fiddle-de-doo." It's a saying of my grandmother's, and I know she would have been pleased.

"I don't think you know what you're saying," Lengel said.

"I know you don't," I said. "But I do." I pull the bow at the back of my apron and 30 start shrugging it off my shoulders. A couple customers that had been heading for my slot begin to knock against each other, like scared pigs in a chute.

Lengel sighs and begins to look very patient and old and gray. He's been a friend of my parents for years. "Sammy, you don't want to do this to your Mom and Dad," he tells me. It's true, I don't. But it seems to me that once you begin a gesture it's fatal not to go through with it. I fold the apron, "Sammy" stitched in red on the pocket, and put it on the counter, and drop the bow tie on top of it. The bow tie is theirs, if you've ever wondered. "You'll feel this for the rest of your life," Lengel says, and I know that's true, too, but remembering how he made that pretty girl blush makes me so scrunchy inside I punch the No Sale tab and the machine whirs "pee-pul" and the drawer splats out. One advantage to this scene taking place in summer, I can follow this up with a clean exit, there's no fumbling around getting your coat and galoshes, I just saunter into the electric eye in my white shirt that my mother ironed the night before, and the door heaves itself open, and outside the sunshine is skating around on the asphalt.

I look around for my girls, but they're gone, of course. There wasn't anybody but some young married screaming with her children about some candy they didn't get by the door of a powder-blue Falcon station wagon. Looking back in the big windows, over the bags of peat moss and aluminum lawn furniture stacked on the pavement, I could see Lengel in my place in the slot, checking the sheep through. His face was dark gray and his back stiff, as if he'd just had an injection of iron, and my stomach kind of fell as I felt how hard the world was going to be to me hereafter. •

Explorations of the Text

1. How does the point of view—Sammy's perspective—develop the narrative? How would the story change if it were told from Queenie's, Stokesie's, or Lengel's perspective or if there were an omniscient narrator?

2. Analyze Sammy's character. Consider his background, his attitudes, his values, and his interactions with the customers and with the girls. Compare and contrast his character with that of Stokesie, Lengel, or Queenie.

3. Why does Sammy quit?

4. Explore the significance of this statement: "I felt how hard the world was going to be to me hereafter." Discuss the significance of such word choices as "hard" and "to me" as opposed to "for me." Is the ending optimistic or pessimistic? Critics are divided on this point.

5. How does the setting enlarge the scope of the work? Explicate the imagery used to depict the store. What critique is Updike presenting of this early 1960s world?

6. Explore the class differences presented in the work. How do these differences explain the behavior of the characters?

The Reading/Writing Connection

1. Freewrite in response to this statement: "There's people in this town haven't seen the ocean for twenty years."
2. Write a monologue in Queenie's or one of the other girl's voices. Tell the story from her perspective. Or continue the narrative. What happens to Sammy?

Ideas for Writing

1. This story is set in the early 1960s. Is the story still relevant? How would it change if it were set in a supermarket today? Write a new version of the story, and then in a short essay, explain your changes.
2. In an earlier version of this story, Updike described what happens after Sammy quits his job. In the final version, Updike deleted this ending, later using it as the basis of another work, "Lifeguard." Find a copy of "Lifeguard," and compare the two stories, focusing on such elements of fiction as setting, character development, plot, and theme.

Liliana Heker   *(1943–)*

The Stolen Party   *1982*

As soon as she arrived she went straight to the kitchen to see if the monkey was there. It was: what a relief! She wouldn't have liked to admit that her mother had been right. *Monkeys at a birthday? Get away with you, believing any nonsense you're told!* She was cross, but not because of the monkey, the girl thought; it's just because of the party.

"I don't like you going," she told her. "It's a rich people's party."

"Rich people go to Heaven too," said the girl, who studied religion at school.

"Get away with Heaven," said the mother. "The problem with you, young lady, is that you like to fart higher than your ass."

The girl didn't approve of the way her mother spoke. She was barely nine, and one of the best in her class.   5

"I'm going because I've been invited," she said. "And I've been invited because Luciana is my friend. So there."

"Ah yes, your friend," her mother grumbled. She paused. "Listen, Rosaura," she said at last. "That one's not your friend. You know what you are to them? The maid's daughter, that's what."

Rosaura blinked hard: she wasn't going to cry. Then she yelled: "Shut up! You know nothing about being friends!"

Every afternoon she used to go to Luciana's house and they would both finish their homework while Rosaura's mother did the cleaning. They had their tea in the kitchen and they told each other secrets. Rosaura loved everything in the big house, and she also loved the people who lived there.

"I'm going because it will be the most lovely party in the whole world, Luciana told me it would. There will be a magician, and he will bring a monkey and everything." 10

The mother swung around to take a good look at her child, and pompously put her hands on her hips.

"Monkeys at a birthday?" she said. "Get away with you, believing any nonsense you're told!"

Rosaura was deeply offended. She thought it unfair of her mother to accuse other people of being liars simply because they were rich. Rosaura too wanted to be rich, of course. If one day she managed to live in a beautiful palace, would her mother stop loving her? She felt very sad. She wanted to go to that party more than anything else in the world.

"I'll die if I don't go," she whispered, almost without moving her lips.

And she wasn't sure whether she had been heard, but on the morning of the party 15 she discovered that her mother had starched her Christmas dress. And in the afternoon, after washing her hair, her mother rinsed it in apple vinegar so that it would be all nice and shiny. Before going out, Rosaura admired herself in the mirror, with her white dress and glossy hair, and thought she looked terribly pretty.

Señora Ines seemed to notice. As soon as she saw her, she said:

"How lovely you look today, Rosaura."

Rosaura gave her starched skirt a slight toss with her hands and walked into the party with a firm step. She said hello to Luciana and asked about the monkey. Luciana put on a secretive look and whispered into Rosaura's ear: "He's in the kitchen. But don't tell anyone, because it's a surprise."

Rosaura wanted to make sure. Carefully she entered the kitchen and there she saw it: deep in thought, inside its cage. It looked so funny that the girl stood there for while, watching it, and later, every so often, she would slip out of the party unseen and go and admire it. Rosaura was the only one allowed into the kitchen. Señora Ines had said: "You yes, but not the others, they're much too boisterous, they might break something." Rosaura had never broken anything. She even managed the jug of orange juice, carrying it from the kitchen into the dining room. She held it carefully and didn't spill a single drop. And Señora Ines had said: "Are you sure you can manage a jug as big as that?" Of course she could manage. She wasn't a butterfingers, like the others. Like that blonde girl with the bow in her hair. As soon as she saw Rosaura, the girl with the bow had said:

"And you? Who are you?" 20

"I'm a friend of Luciana," said Rosaura.

"No," said the girl with the bow, "you are not a friend of Luciana because I'm her cousin and I know all her friends. And I don't know you."

"So what," said Rosaura. "I come here every afternoon with my mother and we do our homework together."

"You and your mother do your homework together?" asked the girl, laughing.

"I and Luciana do our homework together," said Rosaura, very seriously. 25

The girl with the bow shrugged her shoulders.

"That's not being friends," she said. "Do you go to school together?"

"No."

"So where do you know her from?" said the girl, getting impatient.

Rosaura remembered her mother's words perfectly. She took a deep breath. 30

"I'm the daughter of the employee," she said.

Her mother had said very clearly: "If someone asks, you say you're the daughter of the employee; that's all." She also told her to add: "And proud of it." But Rosaura thought that never in her life would she dare say something of the sort.

"What employee?" said the girl with the bow. "Employee in a shop?"

"No," said Rosaura angrily. "My mother doesn't sell anything in any shop, so there."

"So how come she's an employee?" said the girl with the bow. 35

Just then Señora Ines arrived saying *shh shh,* and asked Rosaura if she wouldn't mind helping serve out the hotdogs, as she knew the house so much better than the others.

"See?" said Rosaura to the girl with the bow, and when no one was looking she kicked her in the shin.

Apart from the girl with the bow, all the others were delightful. The one she liked best was Luciana, with her golden birthday crown; and then the boys. Rosaura won the sack race, and nobody managed to catch her when they played tag. When they split into two teams to play charades, all the boys wanted her for their side. Rosaura felt she had never been so happy in all her life.

But the best was still to come. The best came after Luciana blew out the candles. First the cake. Señora Ines had asked her to help pass the cake around, and Rosaura had enjoyed the task immensely, because everyone called out to her, shouting "Me, me!" Rosaura remembered a story in which there was a queen who had the power of life or death over her subjects. She had always loved that, having the power of life or death. To Luciana and the boys she gave the largest pieces, and to the girl with the bow she gave a slice so thin one could see through it.

After the cake came the magician, tall and bony, with a fine red cape. A true ma- 40
gician: he could untie handkerchiefs by blowing on them and make a chain with links that had no openings. He could guess what cards were pulled out from a pack, and the monkey was his assistant. He called the monkey "partner." "Let's see here, partner," he would say, "turn over a card." And, "Don't run away, partner: time to work now."

The final trick was wonderful. One of the children had to hold the monkey in his arms and the magician said he would make him disappear.

"What, the boy?" they all shouted.

"No, the monkey!" shouted back the magician.

Rosaura thought that this was truly the most amusing party in the whole world.

The magician asked a small fat boy to come and help, but the small fat boy got 45
frightened almost at once and dropped the monkey on the floor. The magician picked him up carefully, whispered something in his ear, and the monkey nodded almost as if he understood.

"You mustn't be so unmanly, my friend," the magician said to the fat boy.

"What's unmanly?" said the fat boy.

The magician turned around as if to look for spies.

"A sissy," said the magician. "Go sit down."

Then he stared at all the faces, one by one. Rosaura felt her heart tremble. 50

"You, with the Spanish eyes," said the magician. And everyone saw that he was pointing at her.

She wasn't afraid. Neither holding the monkey, nor when the magician made him vanish; not even when, at the end, the magician flung his red cape over Rosaura's head and uttered a few magic words . . . and the monkey reappeared, chattering happily, in her arms. The children clapped furiously. And before Rosaura returned to her seat, the magician said:

"Thank you very much, my little countess."

She was so pleased with the compliment that a while later, when her mother came to fetch her, that was the first thing she told her.

"I helped the magician and he said to me, 'Thank you very much, my little 55 countess.'"

It was strange because up to then Rosaura had thought that she was angry with her mother. All along Rosaura had imagined that she would say to her: "See that the monkey wasn't a lie?" But instead she was so thrilled that she told her mother all about the wonderful magician.

Her mother tapped her on the head and said: "So now we're a countess!"

But one could see that she was beaming.

And now they both stood in the entrance, because a moment ago Señora Ines, smiling, had said: "Please wait here a second."

Her mother suddenly seemed worried. 60

"What is it?" she asked Rosaura.

"What is what?" said Rosaura. "It's nothing; she just wants to get the presents for those who are leaving, see?"

She pointed at the fat boy and at a girl with pigtails who were also waiting there, next to their mothers. And she explained about the presents. She knew, because she had been watching those who left before her. When one of the girls was about to leave, Señora Ines would give her a bracelet. When a boy left, Señora Ines gave him a yo-yo. Rosaura preferred the yo-yo because it sparkled, but she didn't mention that to her mother. Her mother might have said: "So why don't you ask for one, you blockhead?" That's what her mother was like. Rosaura didn't feel like explaining that she'd be horribly ashamed to be the odd one out. Instead she said:

"I was the best-behaved at the party."

And she said no more because Señora Ines came out into the hall with two bags, 65 one pink and one blue.

First she went up to the fat boy, gave him a yo-yo out of the blue bag, and the fat boy left with his mother. Then she went up to the girl and gave her a bracelet out of the pink bag, and the girl with the pigtails left as well.

Finally she came up to Rosaura and her mother. She had a big smile on her face and Rosaura liked that. Señora Ines looked down at her, then looked up at her mother, and then said something that made Rosaura proud:

"What a marvelous daughter you have, Herminia."

For an instant, Rosaura thought that she'd give her two presents: the bracelet and the yo-yo. Señora Ines bent down as if about to look for something. Rosaura also leaned forward, stretching out her arm. But she never completed the movement.

Señora Ines didn't look in the pink bag. Nor did she look in the blue bag. Instead 70 she rummaged in her purse. In her hand appeared two bills.

"You really and truly earned this," she said handing them over. "Thank you for all your help, my pet."

Rosaura felt her arms stiffen, stick close to her body, and then she noticed her mother's hand on her shoulder. Instinctively she pressed herself against her mother's body. That was all. Except her eyes. Rosaura's eyes had a cold, clear look that fixed itself on Señora Ines's face.

Señora Ines, motionless, stood there with her hand outstretched. As if she didn't dare draw it back. As if the slightest change might shatter an infinitely delicate balance. ●

Explorations of the Text

1. What is the central conflict between the mother and Rosaura?
2. What fantasies does Rosaura invent about herself and about her life?
3. How does Heker weave a subtle pattern of servitude into Rosaura's participation in the party?
4. In the episode with the monkey, what is the role of the fat boy? What does the incident symbolize?
5. Why does Señora Ines offer Rosaura money? What does Rosaura's "cold, clear look" suggest? What is the "infinitely delicate balance" at the end?
6. Two pairs of mothers and daughters appear in this story. What do you learn about the social status and world views of these characters?
7. How would you characterize the tone of this story? Why?
8. How do details contribute to the theme of the story? What can you learn about subtlety, about irony, and about organization from Liliana Heker?
9. Compare Rosaura's coming-of-age experience with Sammy's in "A&P."

The Reading/Writing Connection

1. Write a paragraph that continues the story.
2. "Think" Topic: What characterizes children's perceptions of prejudice or stereotyping in the works by Heker and by Countee Cullen?

Ideas for Writing

1. How does point of view contribute to the development of the themes in this work?

Barbara Kingsolver *(1955–   )*

Rose-Johnny   *1989*

Rose-Johnny wore a man's haircut and terrified little children, although I will never believe that was her intention. For her own part she inspired in us only curiosity. It was our mothers who took this fascination and wrung it, through daily admonitions, into the most irresistible kind of horror. She was like the old wells, covered with ancient rotting boards and overgrown with weeds, that waited behind the barns to swallow us down: our mothers warned us time and again not to go near them, and still were certain that we did.

My own mother was not one of those who had a great deal to say about her, but Walnut Knobs was a small enough town so that a person did not need to be told things directly. When I had my first good look at her, at close range, I was ten years old. I fully understood the importance of the encounter.

What mattered to me at the time, though, was that it was something my sister had not done before me. She was five years older, and as a consequence there was hardly an achievement in my life, nor even an article of clothing, that had not first been Mary Etta's. But, because of the circumstances of my meeting Rose-Johnny, I couldn't tell a living soul about it, and so for nearly a year I carried the secret torment of a great power that can't be used. My agitation was not relieved but made worse when I told the story to myself, over and over again.

She was not, as we always heard, half man and half woman, something akin to the pagan creatures whose naked torsos are inserted in various shocking ways into parts of animal bodies. In fact, I was astonished by her ordinariness. It is true that she wore Red Wing boots like my father. And also there was something not quite womanly in her face, but maybe any woman's face would look the same with that haircut. Her hair was coal black, cut flat across the top of her round head, so that when she looked down I could see a faint pale spot right on top where the scalp almost surfaced.

But the rest of her looked exactly like anybody's mother in a big flowered dress 5 without a waistline and with two faded spots in front, where her bosom rubbed over the counter when she reached across to make change or wipe away the dust.

People say there is a reason for every important thing that happens. I was sent to the feed store, where I spoke to Rose-Johnny and passed a quarter from my hand into hers, because it was haying time. And because I was small for my age. I was not too small to help with tobacco setting in the spring, in fact I was better at it than Mary Etta, who complained about the stains on her hands, but I was not yet big enough to throw a bale of hay onto the flatbed. It was the time of year when Daddy complained about not having boys. Mama said that at least he oughtn't to bother going into town for the chicken mash that day because Georgeann could do it on her way home from school.

Mama told me to ask Aunt Minnie to please ma'am give me a ride home. "Ask her nice to stop off at Lester Wall's store so you can run in with this quarter and get five pound of laying mash."[1]

I put the quarter in my pocket, keeping my eye out to make certain Mary Etta understood what I had been asked to do. Mary Etta had once told me that I was no better than the bugs that suck on potato vines, and that the family was going to starve to death because of my laziness. It was one of the summer days when we were on our knees in the garden picking off bugs and dropping them into cans of coal oil. She couldn't go into town with Aunt Minnie to look at dress patterns until we finished with the potato bugs. What she said, exactly, was that if I couldn't work any harder than that, then she might just as well throw *me* into a can of coal oil. Later she told me she hadn't meant it, but I intended to remember it nonetheless.

---

[1] **laying mash:** A type of boiled grain, bran, or meal, fed warm to horses, cattle, and chickens.

Aunt Minnie taught the first grade and had a 1951 Dodge. That is how she referred to her car whenever she spoke of it. It was the newest automobile belonging to anyone related to us, although some of the Wilcox cousins had once come down to visit from Knoxville in a Ford they were said to have bought the same year it was made. But I saw that car and did not find it nearly as impressive as Aunt Minnie's, which was white and immense and shone like glass. She paid a boy to polish it every other Saturday.

On the day she took me to Wall's, she waited in the car while I went inside with my fist tight around the quarter. I had never been in the store before, and although I had passed by it many times and knew what could be bought there, I had never imagined what a wonderful combination of warm, sweet smells of mash and animals and seed corn it would contain. The dust lay white and thin on everything like a bridal veil. Rose-Johnny was in the back with a water can, leaning over into one of the chick tubs. The steel rang with the sound of confined baby birds, and a light bulb shining up from inside the tub made her face glow white. Mr. Wall, Rose-Johnny's Pa, was in the front of the store talking to two men about a horse. He didn't notice me as I crept up to the counter. It was Rose-Johnny who came forward to the cash register.

"And what for you, missy?"

She is exactly like anybody's mama, was all I could think, and I wanted to reach and touch her flowered dress. The two men were looking at me.

"My mama needs five pound of laying mash and here's a quarter for it." I clicked the coin quickly onto the counter.

"Yes, ma'am." She smiled at me, but her boots made heavy, tired sounds on the floor. She made her way slowly, like a duck in water, over to the row of wooden bins that stood against the wall. She scooped the mash into a paper bag and weighed it, then shoved the scoop back into the bin. A little cloud of dust rose out of the mash up into the window. I watched her from the counter.

"Don't your mama know she's wasting good money on chicken mash? Any fool chicken will eat corn." I jumped when the man spoke. It was one of the two, and they were standing so close behind me I would have had to look right straight up to see their faces. Mr. Wall was gone.

"No sir, they need mash," I said to the man's boots.

"What's that?" It was the taller man doing the talking.

"They need mash," I said louder. "To lay good sturdy eggs for selling. A little mash mixed in with the corn. Mama says it's got oster shells in it."

"Is that a fact," he said. "Did you hear that, Rose-Johnny?" he called out. "This child says you put oster shells in that mash. Is that right?"

When Rose-Johnny came back to the cash register she was moon-eyed. She made quick motions with her hands and pushed the bag at me as if she didn't know how to talk.

"Do you catch them osters yourself, Rose-Johnny? Up at Jackson Crick?" The man was laughing. The other man was quiet.

Rose-Johnny looked all around and up at the ceiling. She scratched at her short hair, fast and hard, like a dog with ticks.

When the two men were gone I stood on my toes and leaned over the counter as far as I could. "Do you catch the osters yourself?"

She hooked her eyes right into mine, the way the bit goes into the mule's mouth and fits just so, one way and no other. Her eyes were the palest blue of any I had ever seen. Then she threw back her head and laughed so hard I could see the wide, flat bottoms of her back teeth, and I wasn't afraid of her.

When I left the store, the two men were still outside. Their boots scuffed on the front-porch floorboards, and the shorter one spoke.

"Child, how much did you pay that woman for the chicken mash?"

"A quarter," I told him.

He put a quarter in my hand. "You take this here, and go home and tell your daddy something. Tell him not never to send his little girls to Wall's feed store. Tell him to send his boys if he has to, but not his little girls." His hat was off, and his hair lay back in wet orange strips. A clean line separated the white top of his forehead from the red-burned hide of his face. In this way, it was like my father's face.

"No, sir, I can't tell him, because all my daddy's got is girls."

"That's George Bowles's child, Bud," the tall man said. "He's just got the two girls."

"Then tell him to come for hisself," Bud said. His eyes had the sun in them, and looked like a pair of new pennies.

Aunt Minnie didn't see the man give me the quarter because she was looking at herself in the side-view mirror of the Dodge. Aunt Minnie was older than Mama, but everyone mistook her for the younger because of the way she fixed herself up. And, of course, Mama was married. Mama said if Aunt Minnie ever found a man she would act her age.

When I climbed in the car she was pulling gray hairs out of her part. She said it was teaching school that caused them, but early gray ran in my mama's family.

She jumped when I slammed the car door. "All set?"

"Yes, ma'am," I said. She put her little purple hat back on her head and slowly pushed the long pin through it. I shuddered as she started up the car.

Aunt Minnie laughed. "Somebody walked over your grave."

"I don't have a grave," I said. "I'm not dead."

"No, you most certainly are not. That's just what they say when a person shivers like that." She smiled. I liked Aunt Minnie most of the time.

"I don't think they mean your real grave, with you in it," she said after a minute. "I think it means the place where your grave is going to be someday."

I thought about this for a while. I tried to picture the place, but could not. Then I thought about the two men outside Wall's store. I asked Aunt Minnie why it was all right for boys to do some things that girls couldn't.

"Oh, there's all kinds of reasons," she said. "Like what kinds of things, do you mean?"

"Like going into Wall's feed store."

"Who told you that?"

"Somebody."

Aunt Minnie didn't say anything.

Then I said, "It's because of Rose-Johnny, isn't it?"

Aunt Minnie raised her chin just a tiny bit. She might have been checking her lipstick in the mirror, or she might have been saying yes.

"Why?" I asked.

"Why what?"

"Why because of Rose-Johnny?"

"I can't tell you that, Georgeann."

"Why can't you tell me?" I whined. "Tell me."

The car rumbled over a cattle grate. When we came to the crossing, Aunt Minnie stepped on the brake so hard we both flopped forward. She looked at me. "Georgeann, Rose-Johnny is a Lebanese. That's all I'm going to tell you. You'll understand better when you're older."

When I got home I put the laying mash in the henhouse. The hens were already roosting high above my head, clucking softly into their feathers and shifting back and forth on their feet. I collected the eggs as I did every day, and took them into the house. I hadn't yet decided what to do about the quarter, and so I held on to it until dinnertime.

Mary Etta was late coming down, and even though she had washed and changed 55 she looked pale as a haunt from helping with the haying all day. She didn't speak and she hardly ate.

"Here, girls, both of you, eat up these potatoes," Mama said after a while. "There's not but just a little bit left. Something to grow on."

"I don't need none then," Mary Etta said. "I've done growed all I'm going to grow."

"Don't talk back to your mama," Daddy said.

"I'm not talking back. It's the truth." Mary Etta looked at Mama. "Well, it is."

"Eat a little bite, Mary Etta. Just because you're in the same dresses for a year don't 60 mean you're not going to grow no more."

"I'm as big as you are, Mama."

"All right then." Mama scraped the mashed potatoes onto my plate. "I expect now you'll be telling me you don't want to grow no more either," she said to me.

"No, ma'am, I won't," I said. But I was distressed, and looked sideways at the pink shirtwaist I had looked forward to inheriting along with the grown-up shape that would have to be worn inside it. Now it appeared that I was condemned to my present clothes and potato-shaped body; keeping these forever seemed to me far more likely than the possibility of having clothes that, like the Wilcox automobile, had never before been owned. I ate my potatoes quietly. Dinner was almost over when Daddy asked if I had remembered to get the laying mash.

"Yes, sir. I put it in the henhouse." I hesitated. "And here's the quarter back. Mr. Wall gave me the mash for nothing."

"Why did he do that?" Mama asked. 65

Mary Etta was staring like the dead. Even her hair looked tired, slumped over the back of her chair like a long black shadow.

"I helped him out," I said. "Rose-Johnny wasn't there, she was sick, and Mr. Wall said if I would help him clean out the bins and dust the shelves and water the chicks, then it wouldn't cost me for the laying mash."

"And Aunt Minnie waited while you did all that?"

"She didn't mind," I said. "She had some magazines to look at."

It was the first important lie I had told in my life, and I was thrilled with its power. 70 Every member of my family believed I had brought home the laying mash in exchange for honest work.

I was also astonished at how my story, once I had begun it, wouldn't finish. "He wants me to come back and help him again the next time we need something," I said.

"I don't reckon you let on like we couldn't pay for the mash?" Daddy asked sternly.

"No, sir. I put the quarter right up there on the counter. But he said he needed the help. Rose-Johnny's real sick."

He looked at me like he knew. Like he had found the hole in the coop where the black snake was getting in. But he just said, "All right. You can go, if Aunt Minnie don't mind waiting for you."

"You don't have to say a thing to her about it," I said. "I can walk home the same   75
as I do ever day. Five pound of mash isn't nothing to carry."

"We'll see," Mama said.

That night I believed I would burst. For a long time after Mary Etta fell asleep I twisted in my blankets and told the story over to myself, both the true and false versions. I talked to my doll, Miss Regina. She was a big doll, a birthday present from my Grandma and Grandpa Bowles, with a tiny wire crown and lovely long blond curls.

"Rose-Johnny isn't really sick," I told Miss Regina. "She's a Lebanese."

■ ■ ■

I looked up the word in Aunt Minnie's Bible dictionary after school. I pretended to be looking up St. John the Baptist but then turned over in a hurry to the *L*'s while she was washing her chalkboards. My heart thumped when I found it, but I read the passage quickly, several times over, and found it empty. It said the Lebanese were a seafaring people who built great ships from cedar trees. I couldn't believe that even when I was older I would be able, as Aunt Minnie promised, to connect this with what I had seen of Rose-Johnny. Nevertheless, I resolved to understand. The following week I went back to the store, confident that my lie would continue to carry its own weight.

Rose-Johnny recognized me. "Five pounds of laying mash," she said, and this time   80
I followed her to the feed bins. There were flecks of white dust in her hair.

"Is it true you come from over the sea?" I asked her quietly as she bent over with the scoop.

She laughed and rolled her eyes. "A lot of them says I come from the moon," she said, and I was afraid she was going to be struck dumb and animal-eyed as she was the time before. But, when she finished weighing the bag, she just said, "I was born in Slate Holler, and that's as far from here as I ever been or will be."

"Is that where you get the osters from?" I asked, looking into the mash and trying to pick out which of the colored flecks they might be.

Rose-Johnny looked at me for a long time, and then suddenly laughed her big laugh. "Why, honey child, don't you know? Osters comes from the sea."

She rang up twenty-five cents on the register, but I didn't look at her.   85

"That was all, wasn't it?"

I leaned over the counter and tried to put tears in my eyes, but they wouldn't come. "I can't pay," I said. "My daddy said to ask you if I could do some work for it. Clean up or something."

"Your daddy said to ask me that? Well, bless your heart," she said. "Let me see if we can't find something for you to do. Bless your little heart, child, what's your name?"

"Georgeann," I told her.

"I'm Rose-Johnny," she said, and I did not say that I knew it, that like every other   90
child I had known it since the first time I saw her in town, when I was five or six, and had to ask Mama if it was a man or a lady.

"Pleased to meet you," I said.

We kept it between the two of us: I came in every week to help with the pullets and the feed, and took home my mash. We did not tell Mr. Wall, although it seemed it would not have mattered one whit to him. Mr. Wall was in the store so seldom that he might not have known I was there. He kept to himself in the apartment at the back where he and Rose-Johnny lived.

It was she who ran the store, kept the accounts, and did the orders. She showed me how to feed and water the pullets and ducklings and pull out the sick ones. Later I learned how to weigh out packages of seed and to mix the different kinds of mash. There were lists nailed to the wall telling how much cracked corn and oats and grit to put in. I followed the recipes with enormous care, adding tiny amounts at a time to the bag on the hanging scales until the needle touched the right number. Although she was patient with me, I felt slow next to Rose-Johnny, who never had to look at the lists and used the scales only to check herself. It seemed to me she knew how to do more things than anyone I had ever known, woman or man.

She also knew the names of all the customers, although she rarely spoke to them. Sometimes such a change came over her when the men were there that it wasn't clear to me whether she was pretending or had really lost the capacity to speak. But afterward she would tell me their names and everything about them. Once she told me about Ed Charney, Sr. and Bud Mattox, the two men I had seen the first day I was in the store. According to Rose-Johnny, Ed had an old red mule he was in the habit of mis-treating. "But even so," she said, "Ed's mule don't have it as bad as Bud's wife." I never knew how she acquired this knowledge.

When she said "Bud Mattox," I remembered his penny-colored eyes and con- 95 nected him then with all the Mattox boys at school. It had never occurred to me that eyes could run in families, like early gray.

Occasionally a group of black-skinned children came to the store, always after hours. Rose-Johnny opened up for them. She called each child by name, and asked af-ter their families and the health of their mother's laying hens.

The oldest one, whose name was Cleota, was shaped like Mary Etta. Her hair was straight and pointed, and smelled to me like citronella candles. The younger girls had plaits that curved out from their heads like so many handles. Several of them wore dresses made from the same bolt of cloth, but they were not sisters. Rose-Johnny filled a separate order for each child.

I watched, but didn't speak. The skin on their heels and palms was creased, and as light as my own. Once, after they had left, I asked Rose-Johnny why they only came into the store when it was closed.

"People's got their ways," she said, stoking up the wood stove for the night. Then she told me all their names again, starting with Cleota and working down. She looked me in the eye. "When you see them in town, you speak. Do you hear? By *name*. I don't care who is watching."

■ ■ ■

I was allowed to spend half an hour or more with Rose-Johnny nearly every day after 100 school, so long as I did not neglect my chores at home. Sometimes on days that were rainy or cold Aunt Minnie would pick me up, but I preferred to walk. By myself, with-out Mary Etta to hurry me up.

As far as I know, my parents believed I was helping Mr. Wall because of Rose-Johnny's illness. They had no opportunity to learn otherwise, though I worried that someday Aunt Minnie would come inside the store to fetch me, instead of just honking, or that Daddy would have to go to Wall's for something and see for himself that Rose-Johnny was fit and well. Come springtime he would be needing to buy tobacco seed.

It was soon after Christmas when I became consumed with a desire to confess. I felt the lies down inside me like cold, dirty potatoes in a root cellar, beginning to sprout and crowd. At night I told Miss Regina of my dishonesty and the things that were likely to happen to me because of it. In so doing, there were several times I nearly confessed by accident to Mary Etta.

"Who's going to wring your neck?" she wanted to know, coming into the room one night when I thought she was downstairs washing the supper dishes.

"Nobody," I said, clutching Miss Regina to my pillow. I pretended to be asleep. I could hear Mary Etta starting to brush her hair. Every night before she went to bed she sat with her dress hiked up and her head hung over between her knees, brushing her hair all the way down to the floor. This improved the circulation to the hair, she told me, and would prevent it turning. Mary Etta was already beginning to get white hairs.

"Is it because Mama let you watch Daddy kill the cockerels? Did it scare you to see   105
them jump around like that with their necks broke?"

"I'm not scared," I murmured, but I wanted so badly to tell the truth that I started to cry. I knew, for certain, that something bad was going to happen. I believe I also knew it would happen to my sister, instead of me.

"Nobody's going to hurt you," Mary Etta said. She smoothed my bangs and laid my pigtails down flat on top of the quilt. "Give me Miss Regina and let me put her up for you now, so you won't get her hair all messed up."

I let her have the doll. "I'm not scared about the cockerels, Mary Etta. I promise." With my finger, under the covers, I traced a cross over my heart.

■ ■ ■

When Rose-Johnny fell ill I was sick with guilt. When I first saw Mr. Wall behind the counter instead of Rose-Johnny, so help me God, I prayed this would be the day Aunt Minnie would come inside to get me. Immediately after, I felt sure God would kill me for my wickedness. I pictured myself falling dead beside the oat bin. I begged Mr. Wall to let me see her.

"Go on back, littl'un. She told me you'd be coming in," he said.   110

I had never been in the apartment before. There was little in it beyond the necessary things and a few old photographs on the walls, all of the same woman. The rooms were cold and felt infused with sickness and an odor I incorrectly believed to be medicine. Because my father didn't drink, I had never before encountered the smell of whiskey.

Rose-Johnny was propped on the pillows in a lifeless flannel gown. Her face changed when she saw me, and I remembered the way her face was lit by the light bulb in the chick tub, the first time I saw her. With fresh guilt I threw myself on her bosom.

"I'm sorry. I could have paid for the mash. I didnt mean to make you sick." Through my sobs I heard accusing needly wheezing sounds in Rose-Johnny's chest. She breathed with a great pulling effort.

"Child, don't talk foolish."

■ ■ ■

As weeks passed and Rose-Johnny didn't improve, it became clear that my lie was pro-   115
phetic. Without Rose-Johnny to run the store, Mr. Wall badly needed my help. He seemed mystified by his inventory and was rendered helpless by any unusual demand

from a customer. It was March, the busiest time for the store. I had turned eleven, one week before Mary Etta turned sixteen. These seven days out of each year, during which she was only four years older, I considered to be God's greatest gifts to me.

The afternoon my father would come in to buy the vegetable garden and tobacco seed was an event I had rehearsed endlessly in my mind. When it finally did transpire, Mr. Wall's confusion gave such complete respectability to my long-standing lie that I didn't need to say a word myself in support of it. I waited on him with dignity, precisely weighing out his tobacco seed, and even recommended to him the white runner beans that Mr. Wall had accidentally overstocked, and which my father did not buy.

Later on that same afternoon, after the winter light had come slanting through the dusty windows and I was alone in the store cleaning up, Cleota and the other children came pecking at the glass. I let them in. When I had filled all the orders Cleota unwrapped their coins, knotted all together into a blue handkerchief. I counted, and counted again. It was not the right amount, not even half.

"That's what Miss Rose-Johnny ast us for it," Cleota said. "Same as always." The smaller children—Venise, Anita, Little-Roy, James—shuffled and elbowed each other like fighting cocks, paying no attention. Cleota gazed at me calmly, steadily. Her eyebrows were two perfect arches.

"I thank you very much," I said, and put the coins in their proper places in the cash drawer.

During that week I also discovered an epidemic of chick droop in the pullets. I 120 had to pull Mr. Wall over by the hand to make him look. There were more sick ones than well.

"It's because it's so cold in the store," I told him. "They can't keep warm. Can't we make it warmer in here?"

Mr. Wall shrugged at the wood stove, helpless. He could never keep a fire going for long, the way Rose-Johnny could.

"We have to try. The one light bulb isn't enough," I said. The chicks were huddled around the bulb just the way the men would collect around the stove in the mornings to say howdy-do to Mr. Wall and warm up their hands on the way to work. Except the chicks were more ruthless: they climbed and shoved, and the healthy ones pecked at the eyes and feet of the sick ones, making them bleed.

I had not noticed before what a very old man Mr. Wall was. As he stared down at the light, I saw that his eyes were covered with a film. "How do we fix them up?" he asked me.

"We can't. We've got to take the sick ones out so they won't all get it. Rose-Johnny 125 puts them in that tub over there. We give them water and keep them warm, but it don't do any good. They've got to die."

He looked so sad I stood and patted his old freckled hand.

I spent much more time than before at the store, but no longer enjoyed it particularly. Working in the shadow of Rose-Johnny's expertise, I had been a secret witness to a wondrous ritual of counting, weighing, and tending. Together we created little packages that sailed out like ships to all parts of the country, giving rise to gardens and barnyard life in places I had never even seen. I felt superior to my schoolmates, knowing that I had had a hand in the creation of their families' poultry flocks and their mothers' kitchen gardens. By contrast, Mr. Wall's bewilderment was pathetic and only increased my guilt. But each day I was able to spend a little time in the back rooms with Rose-Johnny.

There were rumors about her illness, both before and after the fact. It did not occur to me that I might have been the source of some of the earlier rumors. But, if I didn't think of this, it was because Walnut Knobs was overrun with tales of Rose-Johnny, and not because I didn't take notice of the stories. I did.

The tales that troubled me most were those about Rose-Johnny's daddy. I had heard many adults say that he was responsible for her misfortune, which I presumed to mean her short hair. But it was also said that he was a colored man, and this I knew to be untrue. Aunt Minnie, when I pressed her, would offer nothing more than that if it were up to her I wouldn't go near either one of them, advice which I ignored. I was coming to understand that I would not hear the truth about Rose-Johnny from Aunt Minnie or anyone else. I knew, in a manner that went beyond the meanings of words I could not understand, that she was no more masculine than my mother or aunt, and no more lesbian than Lebanese. Rose-Johnny was simply herself, and alone.

And yet she was such a capable woman that I couldn't believe she would be sick 130 for very long. But as the warm weather came she grew sluggish and pale. Her slow, difficult breathing frightened me. I brought my schoolbooks and read to her from the foot of the bed. Sometimes the rather ordinary adventures of the boy in my reader would make her laugh aloud until she choked. Other times she fell asleep while I read, but then would make me read those parts over again.

She worried about the store. Frequently she would ask about Mr. Wall and the customers, and how he was managing. "He does all right," I always said. But eventually my eagerness to avoid the burden of further lies, along with the considerable force of my pride, led me to confess that I had to tell him nearly everything. "He forgets something awful," I told her.

Rose-Johnny smiled. "He used to be as smart as anything, and taught me. Now I've done taught you, and you him again." She was lying back on the pillows with her eyes closed and her plump hands folded on her stomach.

"But he's a nice man," I said. I listened to her breathing. "He don't hurt you does he? Your pa?"

Nothing moved except her eyelids. They opened and let the blue eyes out at me. I looked down and traced my finger over the triangles of the flying-geese patch on the quilt. I whispered, "Does he make you cut off your hair?"

Rose-Johnny's eyes were so pale they were almost white, like ice with water run- 135 ning underneath. "He cuts it with a butcher knife. Sometimes he chases me all the way down to the river." She laughed a hissing laugh like a boy, and she had the same look the yearling calves get when they are cornered and jump the corral and run to the woods and won't be butchered. I understood then that Rose-Johnny, too, knew the power of a lie.

■ ■ ■

It was the youngest Mattox boy who started the fight at school on the Monday after Easter. He was older than me, and a boy, so nobody believed he would hit me, but when he started the name calling I called them right back, and he threw me down on the ground. The girls screamed and ran to get the teacher, but by the time she arrived I had a bloody nose and had bitten his arm wonderfully hard.

Miss Althea gave me her handkerchief for my nose and dragged Roy Mattox inside to see the principal. All the other children stood in a circle, looking at me.

"It isn't true, what he said," I told them. "And not about Rose-Johnny either. She isn't a pervert. I love her."

"Pervert," one of the boys said.

I marveled at the sight of my own blood soaking through the handkerchief. "I love   140
her," I said.

I did not get to see Rose-Johnny that day. The door of Wall's store was locked. I could see Mr. Wall through the window, though, so I banged on the glass with the flats of my hands until he came. He had the strong medicine smell on his breath.

"Not today, littl'un." The skin under his eyes was dark blue.

"I need to see Rose-Johnny." I was irritated with Mr. Wall, and did not consider him important enough to prevent me from seeing her. But evidently he was.

"Not today," he said. "We're closed." He shut the door and locked it.

I shouted at him through the glass. "Tell her I hit a boy and bit his arm, that was   145
calling her names. Tell her I fought with a boy, Mr. Wall."

The next day the door was open, but I didn't see him in the store. In the back, the apartment was dark except for the lamp by Rose-Johnny's bed. A small brown bottle and a glass stood just touching each other on the night table. Rose-Johnny looked asleep but made a snuffing sound when I climbed onto the bottom of the bed.

"Did your daddy tell you what I told him yesterday?"

She said nothing.

"Is your daddy sick?"

"My daddy's dead," she said suddenly, causing me to swallow a little gulp of air.   150
She opened her eyes, then closed them again. "Pa's all right, honey, just stepped out, I imagine." She stopped to breathe between every few words. "I didn't mean to give you a fright. Pa's not my daddy, he's my mama's daddy."

I was confused. "And your real daddy's dead?"

She nodded. "Long time."

"And your mama, what about her? Is she dead too?"

"Mm-hmm," she said, in the same lazy sort of way Mama would say it when she wasn't really listening.

"That her?" I pointed to the picture over the bed. The woman's shoulders were bare   155
except for a dark lace shawl. She was looking backward toward you, over her shoulder.

Rose-Johnny looked up at the picture, and said yes it was.

"She's pretty," I said.

"People used to say I looked just like her." Rose-Johnny laughed a wheezy laugh, and coughed.

"Why did she die?"

Rose-Johnny shook her head. "I can't tell you that."   160

"Can you when I'm older?"

She didn't answer.

"Well then, if Mr. Wall isn't your daddy, then the colored man is your daddy," I said mostly to myself.

She looked at me. "Is that what they say?"

I shrugged.   165

"Does no harm to me. Every man is some color," she said.

"Oh," I said.

"My daddy was white. After he died my mama loved another man and he was brown."

"What happened then?"

"What happened then," she said. "Then they had a sweet little baby Johnny." Her 170 voice was more like singing than talking, and her eyes were so peacefully closed I was afraid they might not open again. Every time she breathed there was the sound of a hundred tiny birds chirping inside her chest.

"Where's he?"

"Mama's Rose and sweet little baby Johnny," she sang it like an old song. "Not nothing bad going to happen to them, not nobody going to take her babies." A silvery moth flew into the lamp and clicked against the inside of the lampshade. Rose-Johnny stretched out her hand toward the night table. "I want you to pour me some of that bottle."

I lifted the bottle carefully and poured the glass half full. "That your medicine?" I asked. No answer. I feared this would be another story without an end, without meaning. "Did somebody take your mama's babies?" I persisted.

"Took her man, is what they did, and hung him up from a tree." She sat up slowly on her elbows, and looked straight at me. "Do you know what lynched is?"

"Yes, ma'am," I said, although until that moment I had not been sure. 175

"People will tell you there's never been no lynchings north of where the rivers don't freeze over. But they done it. Do you know where Jackson Crick is, up there by Floyd's Mill?" I nodded. "They lynched him up there, and drowned her baby Johnny in Jackson Crick, and it was as froze as you're ever going to see it. They had to break a hole in the ice to do it." She would not stop looking right into me. "In that river. Poor little baby in that cold river. Poor Mama, what they did to Mama. And said they would do to me, when I got old enough."

She didn't drink the medicine I poured for her, but let it sit. I was afraid to hear any more, and afraid to leave. I watched the moth crawl up the outside of the lampshade.

And then, out of the clear blue, she sat up and said, "But they didn't do a thing to me!" The way she said it, she sounded more like she ought to be weighing out bags of mash than sick in bed. "Do you want to know what Mama did?"

I didn't say.

"I'll tell you what she did. She took her scissors and cut my hair right off, every bit 180 of it. She said, 'From now on, I want you to be Rose and Johnny both.' And then she went down to the same hole in the crick where they put baby Johnny in."

I sat with Rose-Johnny for a long time. I patted the lump in the covers where her knees were, and wiped my nose on my sleeve. "You'd better drink your medicine, Rose-Johnny," I said. "Drink up and get better now," I told her. "It's all over now."

■ ■ ■

It was the last time I saw Rose-Johnny. The next time I saw the store, more than a month later, it was locked and boarded up. Later on, the Londroski brothers took it over. Some people said she had died. Others thought she and Mr. Wall had gone to live somewhere up in the Blue Ridge, and opened a store there. This is the story I believed. In the years since, when passing through that part of the country, I have never failed to notice the Plymouth Rocks and Rhode Islands scratching in the yards, and the tomato vines tied up around the back doors.

. . .

I would like to stop here and say no more, but there are enough half-true stories in my past. This one will have to be heard to the end.

Whatever became of Rose-Johnny and her grandfather, I am certain that their going away had something to do with what happened on that same evening to Mary Etta. And I knew this to be my fault.

It was late when I got home. As I walked I turned Rose-Johnny's story over and over, like Grandpa Bowles's Indian penny with the head on both sides. You never could stop turning it over.

When I caught sight of Mama standing like somebody's ghost in the front doorway I thought she was going to thrash me, but she didn't. Instead she ran out into the yard and picked me up like she used to when I was a little girl, and carried me into the house.

"Where's Daddy?" I asked. It was suppertime, but there was no supper.

"Daddy's gone looking for you in the truck. He'll be back directly, when he don't find you."

"Why's he looking for me? What did I do?"

"Georgeann, some men tried to hurt Mary Etta. We don't know why they done it, but we was afraid they might try to hurt you."

"No, ma'am, nobody hurt me," I said quietly. "Did they kill her?" I asked.

"Oh Lordy no," Mama said, and hugged me. "She's all right. You can go upstairs and see her, but don't bother her if she don't want to be bothered."

Our room was dark, and Mary Etta was in bed crying. "Can I turn on the little light?" I asked. I wanted to see Mary Etta. I was afraid that some part of her might be missing.

"If you want to."

She was all there: arms, legs, hair. Her face was swollen, and there were marks on her neck.

"Don't stare at me," she said.

"I'm sorry." I looked around the room. Her dress was hanging over the chair. It was her best dress, the solid green linen with covered buttons and attached petticoat that had taken her all winter to make. It was red with dirt and torn nearly in half at the bodice.

"I'll fix your dress, Mary Etta. I can't sew as good as you, but I can mend," I said.

"Can't be mended," she said, but then tried to smile with her swollen mouth. "You can help me make another one."

"Who was it that done it?" I asked.

"I don't know." She rolled over and faced the wallpaper. "Some men. Three or four of them. Some of them might have been boys, I couldn't tell for sure. They had things over their faces."

"What kind of things?"

"I don't know. Just bandanners and things." She spoke quietly to the wall. "You know how the Mattoxes have those funny-colored eyes? I think some of them might of been Mattoxes. Don't tell, Georgeann. Promise."

I remembered the feeling of Roy Mattox's muscle in my teeth. I did not promise.

"Did you hit them?"

"No. I screamed. Mr. Dorsey come along the road."

"What did they say, before you screamed?"

"Nothing. They just kept saying, 'Are you the Bowles girl, are you the Bowles girl?' And they said nasty things."

"It was me they was looking for," I said. And no matter what anyone said, I would not believe otherwise. I took to my bed and would not eat or speak to anyone. My convalescence was longer than Mary Etta's. It was during that time that I found my sister's sewing scissors and cut off all my hair and all of Miss Regina's. I said that my name was George-Etta, not Georgeann, and I called my doll Rose-Johnny.

For the most part, my family tolerated my distress. My mother retrimmed my hair   210 as neatly as she could, but there was little that could be done. Every time I looked in the mirror I was startled and secretly pleased to see that I looked exactly like a little boy. Mama said that when I went back to school I would have to do the explaining for myself. Aunt Minnie said I was going through a stage and oughtn't to be pampered.

But there was only a month left of school, and my father let Mary Etta and me stay home to help set tobacco. By the end of the summer my hair had grown out sufficiently so that no explanations were needed. Miss Regina's hair, of course, never grew back. ●

Explorations of the Text

1. Why do you think Georgeann tells the lie about the quarter?
2. Why does she want to work at the feed store? What attracts her to Rose-Johnny?
3. Characterize Rose-Johnny. What do you learn about her from her appearance, gestures, actions, dialogue?
4. What repetitions of plot occur in the story? Why do the men assault Mary Etta?
5. Why does Georgeann say her name is George-Etta?

6. What is the significance of the last line—of the doll's hair staying cut?
7. What is the narrative perspective? What are the aspects of a child's perspective? Of an adult looking back and recalling a child's experiences?
8. Compare Georgeann's coming of age with Li'l Bit's in *How I Learned to Drive* (appearing in this chapter). What do these characters learn about life and the world?

The Reading/Writing Connection

1. "Think" Topic: In an interview Barbara Kingsolver revealed that she "often [chose] to tell stories in the voices of fairly unsophisticated people. Children are . . . [a] good choice because they haven't lived long enough yet to get so-

phisticated." What is the impact of her point of view? Is it successful?
2. Journal Entry: Write about a moment when you felt different from others or when you observed or experienced prejudice.

Ideas for Writing

1. In that same interview, Kingsolver suggested that she "invented this story, which got wilder and wilder but had everything to do with prejudices of small towns in the South and how they rein

people in or cut them free." Discuss the theme of conformity in this work and in "Helen on Eighty-Sixth Street."
2. Analyze the character of Rose-Johnny or of Georgeann.

Daniel Alarcón   *(1977–   )*

Flood   *2005*

I was fourteen when the lagoon spilled again. It was up in the mountains, at the far edges of our district. Like everything beautiful around here, no one had ever seen it. There was no rain, only thick clouds to announce the coming flood. Then the water came running down the avenue, pavement glistening, taking trash and rock and mud with it through the city and toward the sea. It was the first flood since Lucas had been sent to the University, a year into a five-year bid for assault. The neighborhood went dark and we ran to the avenue to see it: a kind of miracle, a ribbon of gleaming water where the street should have been. A few old cars were lined up, their headlights shining. Street mutts raced around us, barking frantically at the water and the people and the circus of it. Everyone was out, even the gangsters, everyone barefoot and shirtless, moving earth with their hands, forming a dike of mud and rock to keep the water out. Across the avenue those kids from Siglo XX stared at us like they wanted something. They worked on their street and we worked on ours.

"Watch them," Renán said. He was my best friend, Lucas's younger brother. Over in Siglo XX they still had light. I could taste how much I hated them, like blood in my mouth. I would've liked to burn their whole neighborhood down. They had no respect for us without Lucas. They'd beat you with sticks and pipes. They'd shove sand in your mouth and make you sing the national anthem. The week before, Siglo XX had caught Renán waiting for a bus on the wrong side of the street. They'd taken his ball cap and his kicks, left his eye purple and swollen enough to squint through.

Buses grunted up the hill against the tide, honking violently. The men moved wooden boards and armloads of bricks and sandbags, but the water kept coming. Our power came on, a procession of lights dotting the long, sinking slope toward the city. Everyone stopped for a moment and listened to the humming water. The oily skin of the avenue shone orange, and someone raised a cheer.

In the half-light, Renán said he saw one of the kids that got him. He had just the one good eye to see through. "Are you sure?" I asked.

They were just silhouettes. The flood lapped at our ankles, and the work was fierce.   5
Renán was gritting his teeth. He had a rock in his hand. "Hold it," he said.

I felt its weight and passed it to Chochó. We all agreed it was a good rock.

Renán threw it high over the avenue. We watched it disappear, Renán whistling the sinking sound of a bomb falling from the sky. We laughed and didn't see it land.

Then Siglo XX tore across the avenue, a half dozen of them. They were badass kids. They went straight for our dike and wrecked it. It was a suicide mission. Our old men were beating them, then the gangsters too. Arms flailed in the dim lights, Siglo XX struggling to break free. Then their whole neighborhood came and then ours and we fell into the thick fight of it, that inexplicable rush, that drug. We spilled onto the avenue and fought like men, side by side with our fathers and our brothers against their fathers and their brothers. It was a carnival. My hands moved in closed fists and I was in awe of them. I pounded a kid while Chochó held him down. Renán swung his arms like helicopter blades, grinning the whole time, manic. We took some hits and gave some and swore inside we lived for this. If Lucas could have seen us! The water spilled over our broken dike but we didn't care. We couldn't care. We were blind with happiness.

■ ■ ■

We called it the University because it's where you went when you finished high school. There were two kinds of prisoners there: terrorists[1] and delinquents. The *terrucos* answered to clandestine communiqués and strange ideologies. They gathered in the yard each morning and did military stretches. They sang war songs all day and heckled the young guards. The war was more than ten years old. When news came of a successful attack somewhere in the city, they celebrated.

Lucas was more of a delinquent and so behaved in ways that were easier to com- 10 prehend. A kid from Siglo XX caught a bad one and someone said they saw Lucas running across the avenue back to our street. That was enough for five years. He hadn't even killed anyone. They lightened his sentence since he'd been in the army. Before he went in, he made us promise we'd join up when we were old enough. "Best thing I ever did," he said. We spoke idly of things we'd do when he got out, but our street was empty without him. People called us Diablos Jr. because we were just kids. Without Lucas, the gangsters hardly acknowledged us, except to run packages downtown, but that was only occasionally.

Only family was allowed to visit prisoners, but the first time, about a year before the flood, we went with Renán anyway. To keep him company, I suppose, or to gaze at those high walls. We had no older brothers except for Lucas, no one we respected the way we respected him. We thought of Renán as lucky. He could call Lucas blood.

The University was sunk between two dry burnt hills and surrounded by teeming shanties. The people there lived off smuggling weed and coke inside. Everyone knew this, which is why it was one of the safest parts of the city back then. Chochó and I waited outside and smoked cigarettes, looking up at the dull ashen sky. Every half hour or so a guard told us to move out a little farther. He looked uncomfortable with his gun, a little scared. Chochó saluted him, called him Captain.

We talked and smoked and the sky cleared, giving way to bright sun. The third time the guard shooed us away Chochó lit a smoke and offered it to him. Chochó was like that, friendly in his way, though he didn't look it. I knew him well enough to know silence made him nervous. "Come on, friend," Chochó said. "We're good kids."

The guard frowned. He checked the cigarette over suspiciously and then took a deep drag. He looked around to make sure no one had seen him.

Chochó cupped a hand over his eyes. "Our boy is in there visiting his older 15 brother," he said.

The guard nodded. His uniform looked like it could have been his father's: a drab, faded green, too big in the shoulders. "*Terruco?*" he asked.

"No," we said together.

"Those people don't deserve to live."

We nodded in agreement. It's what Lucas had always told us.

"We've got them by the balls," the guard said matter-of-factly. 20

"Really?" Chochó asked.

"Lucas was in the army," I offered. "Like you."

"And he's in there on some bullshit."

The guard shrugged. "What can you do?"

---

[1] terrorists: The rebels referred to in the story, set in Peru, are the Shining Path, a revolutionary Maoist guerilla group, active in Peru in the 1980s and 1990s.

We were quiet for a moment, then Chochó coughed. "That gun works?" he asked,   25
pointing at the guard's sidearm.

"Yeah," he muttered, blushing. It was clear he'd never used it.

"Tell a joke, Chochó," I said, so the guard wouldn't be embarrassed.

Chochó smiled, closed his eyes for a second. "Okay," he said, "but it's an old one."
He looked back and forth between us. "Listen: two soldiers downtown. Almost midnight, a few minutes before curfew and they see a man hurrying home. The first soldier
checks his watch. 'He's got five minutes', he says. The second soldier raises his gun and
shoots the man dead."

I felt a smile welling up inside me. In the sun, Chochó gleamed like a polished
black stone.

"'Why'd you shoot him?' the first soldier says. 'He had five minutes!' 'He lives on   30
my street,' the other one says. 'He won't make it in time.'"

Chochó laughed. Me too. The guard smiled. He stubbed out his smoke and
thanked us before going back to his post near the visitors' door. I'm sure he even told
us his name, but I don't remember it.

Renán came out awhile later looking beat. He didn't seem like he wanted to talk.
We wanted to know everything. The waiting had made us impatient.

"He asked if you were still the same pussies as before, but I lied."

"Thanks."

"No use making him feel bad. I mean, you were born this way."   35

"Whatever."

"You ask, I tell," Renán muttered.

"What's it like inside?" Chochó asked.

Renán lit a cigarette. "Crowded," he said.

We walked back to the bus in silence. Standing outside did no one any good. It   40
sapped my energy, made me feel helpless. Renán too. "My brother's bored," he said finally. "He's got five more years to go and he's already fucking bored."

"Sorry," I heard myself say.

"He says people start fights just to pass the time."

"Imagine," Chochó said.

Everywhere there was water and the muddy remains of the flood. The clouds broke
but the water stayed. A pestilent odor hung in the streets. Summer came on heavy.
Some people moved their furniture outside to dry, or set their dank carpets on the roof
to catch the sun. They were the unlucky ones. The adrenaline of that night was what
would stay, long after everything was dry and clean. My knuckles were still sore and
Renán had been hit in the eye again, but it didn't matter.

It was a couple days later when a cruiser pulled up to our street. Two cops got out   45
and asked for the Diablos Jr. There was a mother in the back, a gray-haired woman,
staring out the rolled-down window. She pointed at us.

"This punk?" one of the cops asked. He grabbed Renán by the wrist and twisted
his arm behind him. I watched my friend crumple. The veins at Renán's temples looked
as if they might pop, and tears gathered in the corners of his eyes. "Is this him? Are you
sure?" the cop said.

How could she be sure of anything?

"Any other Diablos?" the other cop yelled.

A crowd had gathered, but no one dared to speak.

Renán whimpered.

The cop fired a shot in the air. "Should I name names?" he yelled.

We rode in the back with the woman who had fingered Renán. The windows were up and the heat was a sickening thing. I was sweating against her, but she pulled away from me as if I were diseased. I folded my bruised knuckles into my lap and put on my nice guy voice. "Madam," I asked, "what did we do?"

"Shame," she hissed. She looked straight ahead.

They dropped her off in Siglo XX somewhere. She got out without saying a word. It made me happy to see her furniture was outdoors. One of her sons was seated on the drying couch, his feet up on a rotting wooden table. He snickered when he saw us and blew me a kiss. *Fuck you,* he mouthed silently.

We left Siglo XX and turned onto the avenue, down the hill toward the city. Our neighborhood faded. One of the cops smacked the grille that separated the front seat from the back. "Don't fall asleep back there," he growled. "We're going to the University."

I looked up. Renán snapped to attention. "What did we do?" he cried. It was an old tactic. They were trying to scare us.

"Don't ask me what you did. There's a dead boy in Siglo XX."

"What boy?"

"The dead one."

"You can't take us to the University," Renán said. "We're too young and we didn't do shit."

We screeched to a stop. One of the cops barreled out, and then our door was open and Renán was gone. I heard him get hit, but I didn't look: it was like the sound of wood cracking. They threw him back in, the side of his face swollen and red.

"Now shut the fuck up," the cop said. We drove.

I remembered the water and the beautiful street battle. The dogs barking and the headlights from passing cars. We'd returned victorious to our flooded streets. No one had died. Even in the harsh disorder of it, I knew no one had died. The cops were lying. We passed neighborhoods that all looked the same: half-built, unpainted houses, every construction a bleached tawny color. The carcasses of buses and cars lined the avenue, the dirt beneath them oily black. Kids played soccer barefoot on the damp side streets, their feet and ankles stained with mud.

When we were younger walking was all we did, along the ridges of the dry mountains, scavenging for things to steal in the streets below. It was safer then, before the war got out of control. Neighborhoods like these stretched on forever, all the way to the city. Once, we climbed the hills above the University and looked over its walls. The delinquents and the terrorists had separate wings. I remember the *terrucos* standing in formation, singing and chanting at the guards that watched them from the towers. Rifles poked out from the turrets. We picked off the prisoners with our fingers, whispering *bang bang,* and imagined them slumping to the ground: shot, bleeding, dead. Lucas had done a tour in the jungle. He'd come with us that day. "The *terrucos* are animals," he said. He blamed them for everything wrong with the country. We all did. It took a while to get used to killing them, he said, and he was scared at first. By the end he was a pro. He carved his name and rank in their backs. "Just cause," he said.

He had seven thin scars on his forearm, lines he'd cut himself, one for each kill. He hated the *terrucos,* but he loved the war. He came back home and was respected by everyone: by us, the gangsters, even Siglo XX. He wanted to start a business, he told us, and we would help him. We would own the neighborhood.

We sat in the hills while the *terrucos* sang in the prison courtyard, something incongruously melodic. "I'd kill them all if I could," Lucas said.

"Think of all those stripes," said Renan, holding out his forearm.

Now we turned off the avenue. "I'm thirsty," said Renán. He looked at me as if for support.

"So be thirsty," came a voice from up front.

They put us in a room stinking of urine and smoke. There were names and dates on 70
the walls. In places the stone was falling apart. It was hot. The *terrucos* had scratched slogans into the paint and I could hear them singing. A cop came in. He said that a boy had been hit by a rock. That the rock had broken his skull open and he was dead. "Think about that," the cop said. "He was a kid. Nine years old. How do you feel now?" He spat on the floor as he left. I swear I'd forgotten about the rock until that moment. The flood and then the fight—who could remember how it started?

"I knew it," Renán said.

"No one knows nothing," I told him.

He didn't have it in him to be a killer. If he was thinking about his brother, he didn't say it. I was. I wondered how close Lucas was to us in that moment. In the year since that first visit, I'd written him almost a dozen letters. I wrote about the neighborhood, about girls, and most enthusiastically about joining the army. It's what he might want to hear, I figured, and he would know I hadn't forgotten. It was easy to talk to people who couldn't respond. Renán said they wouldn't give Lucas pen and paper. I knew the truth, though. He'd never learned to write so well.

I put my arm around my friend. "Fuck Siglo XX," I said.

"Yeah," he said, but he sounded defeated. 75

"Chochó, tell us a joke," I said.

"Ain't nothing funny."

"Fuck you then," said Renán, and we were quiet.

I don't know how long we were there. Every hour or so, a voice would yell that they were bringing new prisoners in, that we should make room. We sat together in one corner, but the iron door never opened. The *terrucos* were chanting in the prison yard. Occasionally, a loudspeaker announcement would make threats, but these were ignored. The air was hot and dank and hard to breathe. We dozed against the dirty wall. Then a man in a suit came in, carrying a stool and a clipboard. He placed the stool in the center of the cell and sat with his hands on his thighs, leaning forward, looking as if he might fall. His black hair was shiny and slick. He introduced himself as Humboldt and asked for our real names. He scanned the papers on his clipboard and coughed loudly into his closed fist. "There are family members outside, you know," he said finally. "Family members of a young man who is dead. They're begging me to let you go so they can kill you themselves. What do you think about that?"

"Let them try," said Chochó. 80

"They'll tear you limb from limb, I promise you this. You want to go out there?"

"We're not scared," Renán said. "We have families too."

He looked at his notes. "Not so far away, eh?"

"My brother," Renán said, "was in the army."

"That's nice," said Humboldt, smiling. "How did he end up here?" 85

"He's innocent."

"Incredible. How many kills did he have?"

"Seven," said Renán.

"How many do you have?"

We stared at him, silent. 90

"Pathetic," Humboldt said. "I'll tell you. You have one between the three of you, that is, until I figure out who threw the rock that killed an innocent nine-year-old. Then I'm going to string you up. You want to know what he looked like? You want to know his name?"

We didn't want to know. Our inquisitor didn't blink.

I had the sickest, emptiest feeling in my stomach. I strained to feel innocent. I imagined a boy sprawled out, down as if struck by lightning, never having seen it or expected it or imagined it: the flood waters of the lagoon running over him, dead, dead, dead.

"You think you're neighborhood war heroes, don't you?"

"We didn't kill anyone," I said. 95

"What happened to your knuckles?"

I hid them between my legs. "I didn't kill anyone," I said.

Humboldt softened into something like pity. "Do you *know* that? Who threw the rock?"

"There was a fight," Chochó said.

"They came at us," said Renán. 100

"I know about the fight, and I know you throw rocks like cowards."

"That didn't happen," Renán said.

"You couldn't muster the strength to do it with your hands, like a man would." Humboldt coughed and looked up. "Just like your brother over there. The whore of Pavilion C."

Was he talking about Lucas?

"He's a veteran? What's his name? Your brother? Oh, you didn't know? No wonder 105 the war goes so well, with faggots carrying guns."

Renán tried to lunge at Humboldt, but we held him back. Lucas was a killer. He was brave and made of metal.

Humboldt watched impassively from his stool. "Young man," he said to Renán, "I'll explain something to you. They put common criminals in uniform and call them soldiers, but it never works out. They're only cut out for their little neighborhood scuffles. Men like me win wars."

"Don't listen to him, Renán. He's a suit," Chochó said. "A tool."

Renán glared.

Humboldt smiled coldly at Chochó. "I like you, fat boy. But you don't know 110 dick."

Then he left. "I'm going home to my family," Humboldt said before the iron door shut behind him. "If you ever want to do the same, you should start talking."

We were there a night and another day while our families came up with the bribes. I dreamed we were killers, assassins by chaos, murderers without design. Our city was built for dying. The *terrucos* Lucas fought in the jungle were descending on us. They were in the prison with us, singing their angry songs. We were surrounded. They had their own neighborhoods, places where the cops wouldn't go without the army, and beyond that, places the army wouldn't go at all. Bombs exploded in shopping centers, dynamite attacks assaulted the power grid. *Terrucos* robbed banks and kidnapped judges. Back then it was possible to imagine the war would never end.

Sometime in the middle of the night, Renán woke us up. He was sweating and held a piece of the crumbling wall in his hand.

"Look," he was saying. He ran the sharp edge of it against his forearm, the skin rising in red lines. "I'm going to tell them."

"Go to sleep," Chochó said.

There was no talking to Renán. "They can put me in with Lucas," he whispered. "They can all go to hell."

I wanted to say something, to offer my friend some part of me, but I didn't. My eyes shut on their own. I slept because I had to. The damp floor felt almost warm, and then it was morning.

Humboldt came back in to tell us about ourselves: how we were scum and all the slow and painful ways we deserved to die. He was angry and red-faced. "The human rights people expect me to defend this country with one hand tied behind my back!" he yelled. He said we'd be back when we were older, that he'd be there. Renán hadn't slept. He watched Humboldt, and I knew he was waiting for him to mention Lucas. And I knew if he did, Renán would kill him. Or try to.

But Humboldt seemed to have forgotten Lucas altogether. Somehow, this was even worse. Renán twisted on his haunches. Humboldt rambled on. He spat on the floor and called us names. Then he let us go.

Outside it was sunny, the sky a metallic blue. The earth had baked once again to dust. Our people were waiting for us, our mothers, our fathers, our brothers and sisters. They looked ill. They thought they'd never see us again. They smothered us with kisses and hugs and we pretended we'd never been afraid. And enough time passed for us to forget we had been. Renán took a few weeks off and then went back to see his brother like he had every Sunday for a year. I wrote Lucas a letter and said I was sorry we hadn't seen him, having been so close. I asked him if he knew Humboldt and which Pavilion he was in. Only four years left, I wrote hopefully, but I scratched that out before I sent it.

I didn't get a letter back.

The rumor around the neighborhood was that there'd been no dead boy that night. People said our rock had struck and killed a dog—a pure breed. It made sense. Two of our neighborhood dogs were poisoned, and then everything was normal again.

Four months passed and the riot started on a Thursday afternoon, on the terrorist side. It was the beginning of the end of the war. Chairs and tables from the cafeteria were set ablaze in the yard. The *terrucos* smoked the guards out of the watchtowers and took some administrators hostage. Weapons had been smuggled in. There was a shootout and black smoke and singing. The *terrucos* were resigned to die. Families gathered outside the University, praying it all ended well. We were there too, learning how to ask God for things we knew we didn't deserve. The *terrucos* burned everything they could and we imagined shooting them. They demanded food and water. The delinquents were starving too, the killers and the thieves and Lucas. They joined the rioting and there were more fires and the guards were killed one by one, their bodies tossed from the towers over the walls of the prison. The authorities surrounded the place. The city gathered on the hills to watch, the smoke twisting black knots in the sky. The *terrucos* hung the flag upside down and wore bandanas over their faces. Whenever anyone moved to retrieve a body, a *terruco* sniped them from the towers. It was on every television, on every radio and newspaper, and we saw it. We sat in the hills. Renán wore his brother's medals pinned to his threadbare T-shirt. His mother and father held pictures of Lucas in uniform. They murmured prayers with hands clasped. Poor son of mine, his mother wailed: Was he hungry? Was he fighting? Was he afraid? We waited. We were there when someone, at the very highest level of government, decided that none of it was worth anything. Not the lives of the hostages, not the lives of the *terrucos* or the rioting thieves, or any of it. The president came on the television to talk about his heavy heart, about the most difficult decision he'd ever had to make. All the hostages were young, he said, and would die for their country. If there were innocents, the president said, it was too late for them now. The moment called for action. There would be no future. And this is how it ended. This is how Lucas died: the helicopters buzzed overhead and the tanks pulled into position. They weren't going to take the University back. They were going to set it on fire. They began the cataclysm. Renán didn't turn away. The walls crumbled to ash and the tanks fired cannon shots. There was singing. The bombs fell and we felt the dry mountains shake. ●

Explorations of the Text

1. Why does Alarcón juxtapose the flood with the narrator's and Lucas's story and the story of the boys, the gangs? Discuss the significance of the flood.

2. How does the setting develop the meaning of the story? Interpret the following symbolic statement about the lagoon: "Like everything beautiful around here, no one had ever seen it."

3. How do the political, economic, and social conditions contribute to the boys' fates (for example, the war against terrorism, the flood, poverty, gang warfare)?

4. Discuss Lucas's character. Why do Renán and the narrator admire him?

5. In what ways is this work a coming-of-age story? What do the narrator and Renán learn? How are they changed as a result of their imprisonment? As a result of the riots at the prison?

6. Compare and contrast the protagonists' rites of passage in this work with Georgeann's in "Rose-Johnny."

The Reading/Writing Connection

1. Respond in a freewrite to the following sentence: "Our city was built for dying."

2. Choose five words or phrases from this work and create a poem. Then suggest how your poem reveals themes of the work.

3. Discuss images of anarchy and/or violence in this work. What do they signify?

Ideas for Writing

1. Create a character analysis of one of the protagonists in the work. Consider his appearance, attitudes, actions, inner thoughts, and gestures as well as the environment that he lives in.

2. This story takes place in Lima, Peru. How does that world compare to that of an urban area in the United States? What contemporary events and issues does the story represent?

3. **Write an Argument:** Create an argument presenting the causes and hypothetical effects of the riots. In order to discuss the impact of the riots, you will need to create a short sequel to the story. Then use that sequel as the basis of your argument.

4. **Write an Argument:** Edward P. Jones suggests that Daniel Alarcón "pre[sents] worlds we have only imagined or heard about in less truthful and poetic ways." Do you agree with his evaluation of Alarcón's work?

Raymond Carver *(1938–1989)*

Cathedral *1984*

This blind man, an old friend of my wife's, he was on his way to spend the night. His wife had died. So he was visiting the dead wife's relatives in Connecticut. He called my wife from his in-laws'. Arrangements were made. He would come by train, a five-hour trip, and my wife would meet him at the station. She hadn't seen him since she worked for him one summer in Seattle ten years ago. But she and the blind man had kept in touch. They made tapes and mailed them back and forth. I wasn't enthusiastic about his visit. He was no one I knew. And his being blind bothered me. My idea of blindness came from the movies. In the movies, the blind moved slowly and never laughed. Sometimes they were led by seeing-eye dogs. A blind man in my house was not something I looked forward to.

That summer in Seattle she had needed a job. She didn't have any money. The man she was going to marry at the end of the summer was in officers' training school. He didn't have any money, either. But she was in love with the guy, and he was in love with her, etc. She'd seen something in the paper: HELP WANTED—*Reading to Blind Man*, and a telephone number. She phoned and went over, was hired on the spot. She'd worked with this blind man all summer. She read stuff to him, case studies, reports, that sort of thing. She helped him organize his little office in the county social-service department. They'd become good friends, my wife and the blind man. How do I know these things? She told me. And she told me something else. On her last day in the office, the blind man asked if he could touch her face. She agreed to this. She told me he touched his fingers to every part of her face, her nose—even her neck! She never forgot it. She even tried to write a poem about it. She was always trying to write a poem. She wrote a poem or two every year, usually after something really important had happened to her.

When we first started going out together, she showed me the poem. In the poem, she recalled his fingers and the way they had moved around over her face. In the poem, she talked about what she had felt at the time, about what went through her mind when the blind man touched her nose and lips. I can remember I didn't think much of the poem. Of course, I didn't tell her that. Maybe I just don't understand poetry. I admit it's not the first thing I reach for when I pick up something to read.

Anyway, this man who'd first enjoyed her favors, the officer-to-be, he'd been her child-hood sweetheart. So okay. I'm saying that at the end of the summer she let the blind man run his hands over her face, said goodbye to him, married her childhood etc., who was now a commissioned officer, and she moved away from Seattle. But they'd kept in touch, she and the blind man. She made the first contact after a year or so. She called him up one night from an Air Force base in Alabama. She wanted to talk. They talked.

He asked her to send him a tape and tell him about her life. She did this. She sent the tape. On the tape, she told the blind man about her husband and about their life together in the military. She told the blind man she loved her husband but she didn't like it where they lived and she didn't like it that he was a part of the military-industrial thing. She told the blind man she'd written a poem and he was in it. She told him that she was writing a poem about what it was like to be an Air Force officer's wife. The poem wasn't finished yet. She was still writing it. The blind man made a tape. He sent her the tape. She made a tape. This went on for years. My wife's officer was posted to one base and then another. She sent tapes from Moody AFB, McGuire, McConnell, and finally Travis, near Sacramento, where one night she got to feeling lonely and cut off from people she kept losing in that moving-around life. She got to feeling she couldn't go it another step. She went in and swallowed all the pills and capsules in the medicine chest and washed them down with a bottle of gin. Then she got into a hot bath and passed out.

But instead of dying, she got sick. She threw up. Her officer—why should he have 5
a name? he was the childhood sweetheart, and what more does he want?—came home from somewhere, found her, and called the ambulance. In time, she put it all on a tape and sent the tape to the blind man. Over the years, she put all kinds of stuff on tapes and sent the tapes off lickety-split. Next to writing a poem every year, I think it was her chief means of recreation. On one tape, she told the blind man she'd decided to live away from her officer for a time. On another tape, she told him about her divorce. She and I began going out, and of course she told her blind man about it. She told him everything, or so it seemed to me. Once she asked me if I'd like to hear the latest tape from the blind man. This was a year ago. I was on the tape, she said. So I said okay, I'd listen to it. I got us drinks and we settled down in the living room. We made ready to listen. First she inserted the tape into the player and adjusted a couple of dials. Then she pushed a lever. The tape squeaked and someone began to talk in this loud voice. She lowered the volume. After a few minutes of harmless chitchat, I heard my own name in the mouth of this stranger, this blind man I didn't even know! And then this: "From all you've said about him, I can only conclude—" But we were interrupted, a knock at the door, something, and we didn't ever get back to the tape. Maybe it was just as well. I'd heard all I wanted to.

Now this same blind man was coming to sleep in my house.

"Maybe I could take him bowling," I said to my wife. She was at the draining board doing scalloped potatoes. She put down the knife she was using and turned around.

"If you love me," she said, "you can do this for me. If you don't love me, okay. But if you had a friend, any friend, and the friend came to visit, I'd make him feel comfortable." She wiped her hands with the dish towel.

"I don't have any blind friends," I said.

"You don't have *any* friends," she said. "Period. Besides," she said, "goddamn it, his 10
wife's just died! Don't you understand that? The man's lost his wife!"

I didn't answer. She'd told me a little about the blind man's wife. Her name was Beulah. Beulah! That's a name for a colored woman.

"Was his wife a Negro?" I asked.

"Are you crazy?" my wife said. "Have you just flipped or something?" She picked up a potato. I saw it hit the floor, then roll under the stove. "What's wrong with you?" she said. "Are you drunk?"

"I'm just asking," I said.

Right then my wife filled me in with more detail than I cared to know. I made a 15
drink and sat at the kitchen table to listen. Pieces of the story began to fall into place.

Beulah had gone to work for the blind man the summer after my wife had stopped
working for him. Pretty soon Beulah and the blind man had themselves a church wedding. It was a little wedding—who'd want to go to such a wedding in the first place?—
just the two of them, plus the minister and the minister's wife. But it was a church
wedding just the same. It was what Beulah had wanted, he's said. But even then Beulah
must have been carrying the cancer in her glands. After they had been inseparable for
eight years—my wife's word, *inseparable*—Beulah's health went into a rapid decline.
She died in a Seattle hospital room, the blind man sitting beside the bed and holding
on to her hand. They'd married, lived and worked together, slept together—had sex,
sure—and then the blind man had to bury her. All this without his having ever seen
what the goddamned woman looked like. It was beyond my understanding. Hearing
this, I felt sorry for the blind man for a little bit. And then I found myself thinking what
a pitiful life this woman must have led. Imagine a woman who could never see herself
as she was seen in the eyes of her loved one. A woman who could go on day after day
and never receive the smallest compliment from her beloved. A woman whose husband
could never read the expression on her face, be it misery or something better. Someone
who could wear makeup or not—what difference to him? She could, if she wanted,
wear green eye-shadow around one eye, a straight pin in her nostril, yellow slacks and
purple shoes, no matter. And then to slip off into death, the blind man's hand on her
hand, his blind eyes streaming tears—I'm imagining now—her last thought maybe
this: that he never even knew what she looked like, and she on an express to the grave.
Robert was left with a small insurance policy and half of a twenty-peso Mexican coin.
The other half of the coin went into the box with her. Pathetic.

So when the time rolled around, my wife went to the depot to pick him up. With
nothing to do but wait—sure, I blamed him for that—I was having a drink and watching the TV when I heard the car pull into the drive. I got up from the sofa with my
drink and went to the window to have a look.

I saw my wife laughing as she parked the car. I saw her get out of the car and shut
the door. She was still wearing a smile. Just amazing. She went around to the other side
of the car to where the blind man was already starting to get out. This blind man, feature this, he was wearing a full beard! A beard on a blind man! Too much, I say. The
blind man reached into the back seat and dragged out a suitcase. My wife took his arm,
shut the car door, and, talking all the way, moved him down the drive and then up the
steps to the front porch. I turned off the TV. I finished my drink, rinsed the glass, dried
my hands. Then I went to the door.

My wife said, "I want you to meet Robert. Robert, this is my husband. I've told
you all about him." She was beaming. She had this blind man by his coat sleeve.

The blind man let go of his suitcase and up came his hand. 20

I took it. He squeezed hard, held my hand, and then he let it go.

"I feel like we've already met," he boomed.

"Likewise," I said. I didn't know what else to say. Then I said, "Welcome. I've heard
a lot about you." We began to move then, a little group, from the porch into the living
room, my wife guiding him by the arm. The blind man was carrying his suitcase in
his other hand. My wife said things like, "To your left here, Robert. That's right. Now
watch it, there's a chair. That's it. Sit down right here. This is the sofa. We just bought
this sofa two weeks ago."

I started to say something about the old sofa. I'd liked that old sofa. But I didn't say anything. Then I wanted to say something else, small-talk, about the scenic ride along the Hudson. How going *to* New York, you should sit on the right-hand side of the train, and coming *from* New York, the left-hand side.

"Did you have a good train ride?" I said. "Which side of the train did you sit on, by the way?"

"What a question, which side!" my wife said. "What's it matter which side?" she said.

"I just asked," I said.

"Right side," the blind man said. "I hadn't been on a train in nearly forty years. Not since I was a kid. With my folks. That's been a long time. I'd nearly forgotten the sensation. I have winter in my beard now," he said. "So I've been told, anyway. Do I look distinguished, my dear?" the blind man said to my wife.

"You look distinguished, Robert," she said. "Robert," she said. "Robert, it's just so good to see you."

My wife finally took her eyes off the blind man and looked at me. I had the feeling she didn't like what she saw. I shrugged.

I've never met, or personally known, anyone who was blind. This blind man was late forties, a heavy-set, balding man with stooped shoulders, as if he carried a great weight there. He wore brown slacks, brown shoes, a light-brown shirt, a tie, a sports coat. Spiffy. He also had this full beard. But he didn't use a cane and he didn't wear dark glasses. I'd always thought dark glasses were a must for the blind. Fact was, I wished he had a pair. At first glance, his eyes looked like anyone else's eyes. But if you looked close, there was something different about them. Too much white in the iris, for one thing, and the pupils seemed to move around in the sockets without his knowing it or being able to stop it. Creepy. As I stared at his face, I saw the left pupil turn in toward his nose while the other made an effort to keep in one place. But it was only an effort, for that eye was on the roam without his knowing it or wanting it to be.

I said, "Let me get you a drink. What's your pleasure? We have a little of everything. It's one of our pastimes."

"Bub, I'm a Scotch man myself," he said fast enough in this big voice.

"Right," I said. Bub! "Sure you are. I knew it."

He let his fingers touch his suitcase, which was sitting alongside the sofa. He was taking his bearings. I didn't blame him for that.

"I'll move that up to your room," my wife said.

"No, that's fine," the blind man said loudly. "It can go up when I go up."

"A little water with the Scotch?" I said.

"Very little," he said.

"I knew it," I said.

He said, "Just a tad. The Irish actor, Barry Fitzgerald? I'm like that fellow. When I drink water, Fitzgerald said, I drink water. When I drink whiskey, I drink whiskey." My wife laughed. The blind man brought his hand up under his beard. He lifted his beard slowly and let it drop.

I did the drinks, three big glasses of Scotch with a splash of water in each. Then we made ourselves comfortable and talked about Robert's travels. First the long flight from the West Coast to Connecticut, we covered that. Then from Connecticut up here by train. We had another drink concerning that leg of the trip.

I remembered having read somewhere that the blind didn't smoke because, as speculation had it, they couldn't see the smoke they exhaled. I thought I knew that much and that much only about blind people. But this blind man smoked his cigarette down to the nubbin and then lit another one. This blind man filled his ashtray and my wife emptied it.

When we sat down at the table for dinner, we had another drink. My wife heaped Robert's plate with cube steak, scalloped potatoes, green beans. I buttered him up two slices of bread. I said, "Here's bread and butter for you." I swallowed some of my drink. "Now let us pray," I said, and the blind man lowered his head. My wife looked at me, her mouth agape. "Pray the phone won't ring and the food doesn't get cold," I said.

We dug in. We ate everything there was to eat on the table. We ate like there was 45
no tomorrow. We didn't talk. We ate. We scarfed. We grazed that table. We were into serious eating. The blind man had right away located his foods, he knew just where everything was on his plate. I watched with admiration as he used his knife and fork on the meat. He'd cut two pieces of meat, fork the meat into his mouth, and then go all out for the scalloped potatoes, the beans next, and then he'd tear off a hunk of buttered bread and eat that. He'd follow this up with a big drink of milk. It didn't seem to bother him to use his fingers once in a while, either.

We finished everything, including half a strawberry pie. For a few moments, we sat as if stunned. Sweat beaded on our faces. Finally, we got up from the table and left the dirty plates. We didn't look back. We took ourselves into the living room and sank into our places again. Robert and my wife sat on the sofa. I took the big chair. We had us two or three more drinks while they talked about the major things that had come to pass for them in the past ten years. For the most part, I just listened. Now and then I joined in. I didn't want him to think I'd left the room, and I didn't want her to think I was feeling left out. They talked of things that had happened to them—to them!— these past ten years. I waited in vain to hear my name on my wife's sweet lips: "And then my dear husband came into my life"—something like that. But I heard nothing of the sort. More talk of Robert. Robert had done a little of everything, it seemed, a regular blind jack-of-all-trades. But most recently he and his wife had had an Amway distributorship, from which, I gathered, they'd earned their living, such as it was. The blind man was also a ham radio operator. He talked in his loud voice about conversations he'd had with fellow operators in Guam, in the Philippines, in Alaska, and even in Tahiti. He said he'd have a lot of friends there if he ever wanted to go visit those places. From time to time, he'd turn his blind face toward me, put his hand under his beard, ask me something. How long had I been in my present position? (Three years.) Did I like my work? (I didn't.) Was I going to stay with it? (What were the options?) Finally, when I thought he was beginning to run down, I got up and turned on the TV.

My wife looked at me with irritation. She was heading toward a boil. Then she looked at the blind man and said, "Robert, do you have a TV?"

The blind man said, "My dear, I have two TVs. I have a color set and a black-and-white thing, an old relic. It's funny, but if I turn the TV on, and I'm always turning it on, I turn on the color set. It's funny, don't you think?"

I didn't know what to say to that. I had absolutely nothing to say to that. No opinion. So I watched the news program and tried to listen to what the announcer was saying.

"This is a color TV," the blind man said. "Don't ask me how, but I can tell." 50

"We traded up a while ago," I said.

The blind man had another taste of his drink. He lifted his beard, sniffed it, and let it fall. He leaned forward on the sofa. He positioned his ashtray on the coffee table, then put the lighter to his cigarette. He leaned back on the sofa and crossed his legs at the ankles.

My wife covered her mouth, and then she yawned. She stretched. She said, "I think I'll go upstairs and put on my robe. I think I'll change into something else. Robert, you make yourself comfortable," she said.

"I'm comfortable," the blind man said.

"I want you to feel comfortable in this house," she said.   55

"I am comfortable," the blind man said.

After she'd left the room, he and I listened to the weather report and then to the sports roundup. By that time, she'd been gone so long I didn't know if she was going to come back. I thought she might have gone to bed. I wished she'd come back downstairs. I didn't want to be left alone with a blind man. I asked him if he wanted another drink, and he said sure. Then I asked if he wanted to smoke some dope with me. I said I'd just rolled a number. I hadn't, but I planned to do so in about two shakes.

"I'll try some with you," he said.

"Damn right," I said. "That's the stuff."

I got our drinks and sat down on the sofa with him. Then I rolled us two fat num-   60
bers. I lit one and passed it. I brought it to his fingers. He took it and inhaled.

"Hold it as long as you can," I said. I could tell he didn't know the first thing.

My wife came back downstairs wearing her pink robe and her pink slippers.

"What do I smell?" she said.

"We thought we'd have us some cannabis," I said.

My wife gave me a savage look. Then she looked at the blind man and said,   65
"Robert, I didn't know you smoked."

He said, "I do now, my dear. There's a first time for everything. But I don't feel anything yet."

"This stuff is pretty mellow," I said. "This stuff is mild. It's dope you can reason with," I said. "It doesn't mess you up."

"Not much it doesn't, bub," he said, and laughed.

My wife sat on the sofa between the blind man and me. I passed her the number. She took it and toked and then passed it back to me. "Which way is this going?" she said. Then she said, "I shouldn't be smoking this. I can hardly keep my eyes open as it is. That dinner did me in. I shouldn't have eaten so much."

"It was the strawberry pie," the blind man said. "That's what did it," he said, and   70
he laughed his big laugh. Then he shook his head.

"There's more strawberry pie," I said.

"Do you want some more, Robert?" my wife said.

"Maybe in a little while," he said.

We gave our attention to the TV. My wife yawned again. She said, "Your bed is made up when you feel like going to bed, Robert. I know you must have had a long day. When you're ready to go to bed, say so." She pulled his arm. "Robert?"

He came to and said, "I've had a real nice time. This beats tapes, doesn't it?"   75

I said, "Coming at you," and I put the number between his fingers. He inhaled, held the smoke, and then let it go. It was like he'd been doing it since he was nine years old.

"Thanks, bub," he said. "But I think this is all for me. I think I'm beginning to feel it," he said. He held the burning roach out for my wife.

"Same here," she said. "Ditto. Me, too." She took the roach and passed it to me. "I may just sit here for a while between you two guys with my eyes closed. But don't let me bother you, okay? Either one of you. If it bothers you, say so. Otherwise, I may just sit here with my eyes closed until you're ready to go to bed," she said. "Your bed's made up, Robert, when you're ready. It's right next to our room at the top of the stairs. We'll show you up when you're ready. You wake me up now, you guys, if I fall asleep." She said that and then she closed her eyes and went to sleep.

The news program ended. I got up and changed the channel. I sat back down on the sofa. I wished my wife hadn't pooped out. Her head lay across the back of the sofa, her mouth open. She'd turned so that her robe had slipped away from her legs, exposing a juicy thigh. I reached to draw her robe back over her, and it was then that I glanced at the blind man. What the hell! I flipped the robe open again.

"You say when you want some strawberry pie," I said.   80

"I will," he said.

I said, "Are you tired? Do you want me to take you up to your bed? Are you ready to hit the hay?"

"Not yet," he said. "No, I'll stay up with you, bub. If that's all right. I'll stay up until you're ready to turn in. We haven't had a chance to talk. Know what I mean? I feel like me and her monopolized the evening." He lifted his beard and he let it fall. He picked up his cigarettes and his lighter.

"That's all right," I said. Then I said, "I'm glad for the company."

And I guess I was. Every night I smoked dope and stayed up as long as I could be-   85
fore I fell asleep. My wife and I hardly ever went to bed at the same time. When I did go to sleep, I had these dreams. Sometimes I'd wake up from one of them, my heart going crazy.

Something about the church and the Middle Ages was on the TV. Not your run-of-the-mill TV fare. I wanted to watch something else. I turned to the other channels. But there was nothing on them, either. So I turned back to the first channel and apologized.

"Bub, it's all right," the blind man said. "It's fine with me. Whatever you want to watch is okay. I'm always learning something. Learning never ends. It won't hurt me to learn something tonight. I got ears," he said.

We didn't say anything for a time. He was leaning forward with his head turned at me, his right ear aimed in the direction of the set. Very disconcerting. Now and then his eyelids drooped and then they snapped open again. Now and then he put his fingers into his beard and tugged, like he was thinking about something he was hearing on the television.

On the screen, a group of men wearing cowls was being set upon and tormented by men dressed in skeleton costumes and men dressed as devils. The men dressed as devils wore devil masks, horns, and long tails. This pageant was part of a procession. The Englishman who was narrating the thing said it took place in Spain once a year. I tried to explain to the blind man what was happening.

"Skeletons," he said. "I know about skeletons," he said, and he nodded.   90

The TV showed this one cathedral. Then there was a long, slow look at another one. Finally, the picture switched to the famous one in Paris, with its flying buttresses and its spires reaching up to the clouds. The camera pulled away to show the whole of the cathedral rising above the skyline.

There were times when the Englishman who was telling the thing would shut up, would simply let the camera move around over the cathedrals. Or else the camera would tour the countryside, men in fields walking behind oxen. I waited as long as I could. Then I felt I had to say something. I said, "They're showing the outside of this cathedral now. Gargoyles. Little statues carved to look like monsters. Now I guess they're in Italy. Yeah, they're in Italy. There's paintings on the walls of this one church."

"Are those fresco paintings, bub?" he asked, and he sipped from his drink.

I reached for my glass. But it was empty. I tried to remember what I could remember. "You're asking me are those frescoes?" I said. "That's a good question. I don't know."

The camera moved to a cathedral outside Lisbon. The differences in the Portuguese 95
cathedral compared with the French and Italian were not that great. But they were there. Mostly the interior stuff. Then something occurred to me, and I said, "Something has occurred to me. Do you have any idea what a cathedral is? What they look like, that is? Do you follow me? If somebody says cathedral to you, do you have any notion what they're talking about? Do you know the difference between that and a Baptist church, say?"

He let the smoke dribble from his mouth. "I know they took hundreds of workers fifty or a hundred years to build," he said. "I just heard the man say that, of course. I know generations of the same families worked on a cathedral. I heard him say that, too. The men who began their life's work on them, they never lived to see the completion of their work. In that wise, bub, they're no different from the rest of us, right?" He laughed. Then his eyelids drooped again. His head nodded. He seemed to be snoozing. Maybe he was imagining himself in Portugal. The TV was showing another cathedral now. This one was in Germany. The Englishman's voice droned on. "Cathedrals," the blind man said. He sat up and rolled his head back and forth. "If you want the truth, bub, that's about all I know. What I just said. What I heard him say. But maybe you could describe one to me? I wish you'd do it. I'd like that. If you want to know, I really don't have a good idea."

I stared hard at the shot of the cathedral on the TV. How could I even begin to describe it? But say my life depended on it. Say my life was being threatened by an insane guy who said I had to do it or else.

I stared some more at the cathedral before the picture flipped off into the countryside. There was no use. I turned to the blind man and said, "To begin with, they're very tall." I was looking around the room for clues. "They reach way up. Up and up. Toward the sky. They're so big, some of them, they have to have these supports. To help hold them up, so to speak. These supports are called buttresses. They remind me of viaducts, for some reason. But maybe you don't know viaducts, either? Sometimes the cathedrals have devils and such carved into the front. Sometimes lords and ladies. Don't ask me why this is," I said.

He was nodding. The whole upper part of his body seemed to be moving back and forth.

"I'm not doing so good, am I?" I said. 100

He stopped nodding and leaned forward on the edge of the sofa. As he listened to me, he was running his fingers through his beard. I wasn't getting through to him,

I could see that. But he waited for me to go on just the same. He nodded, like he was trying to encourage me. I tried to think what else to say. "They're really big," I said. "They're massive. They're built of stone. Marble, too, sometimes. In those olden days, when they built cathedrals, men wanted to be close to God. In those olden days, God was an important part of everyone's life. You could tell this from their cathedral-building. I'm sorry," I said, "but it looks like that's the best I can do for you. I'm just no good at it."

"That's all right, bub," the blind man said. "Hey, listen. I hope you don't mind my asking you. Can I ask you something? Let me ask you a simple question, yes or no. I'm just curious and there's no offense. You're my host. But let me ask if you are in any way religious? You don't mind my asking?"

I shook my head. He couldn't see that, though. A wink is the same as a nod to a blind man. "I guess I don't believe in it. In anything. Sometimes it's hard. You know what I'm saying?"

"Sure, I do," he said.

"Right," I said.   105

The Englishman was still holding forth. My wife sighed in her sleep. She drew a long breath and went on with her sleeping.

"You'll have to forgive me," I said. "But I can't tell you what a cathedral looks like. It just isn't in me to do it. I can't do any more than I've done."

The blind man sat very still, his head down, as he listened to me.

I said, "The truth is, cathedrals don't mean anything special to me. Nothing. Cathedrals. They're something to look at on late-night TV. That's all they are."

It was then that the blind man cleared his throat. He brought something up. He   110
took a handkerchief from his back pocket. Then he said, "I get it, bub. It's okay. It happens. Don't worry about it," he said. "Hey, listen to me. Will you do me a favor? I got an idea. Why don't you find us some heavy paper? And a pen. We'll do something. We'll draw one together. Get us a pen and some heavy paper. Go on, bub, get the stuff," he said.

So I went upstairs. My legs felt like they didn't have any strength in them. They felt like they did after I'd done some running. In my wife's room, I looked around. I found some ballpoints in a little basket on her table. And then I tried to think where to look for the kind of paper he was talking about.

Downstairs, in the kitchen, I found a shopping bag with onion skins in the bottom of the bag. I emptied the bag and shook it. I brought it into the living room and sat down with it near his legs. I moved some things, smoothed the wrinkles from the bag, spread it out on the coffee table.

The blind man got down from the sofa and sat next to me on the carpet.

He ran his fingers over the paper. He went up and down the sides of the paper. The edges, even the edges. He fingered the corners.

"All right," he said. "All right, let's do her."   115

He found my hand, the hand with the pen. He closed his hand over my hand. "Go ahead, bub, draw," he said. "Draw. You'll see. I'll follow along with you. It'll be okay. Just begin now like I'm telling you. You'll see. Draw," the blind man said.

So I began. First I drew a box that looked like a house. It could have been the house I lived in. Then I put a roof on it. At either end of the roof, I drew spires. Crazy.

"Swell," he said. "Terrific. You're doing fine," he said. "Never thought anything like this could happen in your lifetime, did you, bub? Well, it's a strange life, we all know that. Go on now. Keep it up."

I put in windows with arches. I drew flying buttresses.[1] I hung great doors. I couldn't stop. The TV station went off the air. I put down the pen and closed and opened my fingers. The blind man felt around over the paper. He moved the tips of his fingers over the paper, all over what I had drawn, and he nodded.

"Doing fine," the blind man said.   120

I took up the pen again, and he found my hand. I kept at it. I'm no artist. But I kept drawing just the same.

My wife opened up her eyes and gazed at us. She sat up on the sofa, her robe hanging open. She said, "What are you doing? Tell me, I want to know."

I didn't answer her.

The blind man said, "We're drawing a cathedral. Me and him are working on it. Press hard," he said to me. "That's right. That's good," he said. "Sure. You got it, bub. I can tell. You didn't think you could. But you can, can't you? You're cooking with gas now. You know what I'm saying? We're going to really have us something here in a minute. How's the old arm?" he said. "Put some people in there now. What's a cathedral without people?"

My wife said, "What's going on? Robert, what are you doing? What's going on?"   125

"It's all right," he said to her. "Close your eyes now," the blind man said to me.

I did it. I closed them just like he said.

"Are they closed?" he said. "Don't fudge."

"They're closed," I said.

"Keep them that way," he said. He said, "Don't stop now. Draw."   130

So we kept on with it. His fingers rode my fingers as my hand went over the paper. It was like nothing else in my life up to now.

Then he said, "I think that's it. I think you got it," he said. "Take a look. What do you think?"

But I had my eyes closed. I thought I'd keep them that way for a little longer. I thought it was something I ought to do.

"Well?" he said. "Are you looking?"

My eyes were still closed. I was in my house. I knew that. But I didn't feel like I   135
was inside anything.

"It's really something," I said. •

Explorations of the Text

1. Examine the character of the speaker: his attitudes, values, actions, speech.
2. Why does only the blind man have a name? Describe his attitudes, his physical characteristics, and his capacity for friendship.
3. What is the nature of the relationship between the wife and Robert? Between the wife and the narrator?
4. Why does the woman leave Robert and the narrator together? Is her action deliberate?

---

[1] **flying buttresses:** A crucial part of the architecture of Gothic cathedrals; an external support arch that carries an outward and downward thrust to a solid buttress, thereby creating a vertical thrust against a masonry wall to help hold the structure.

5. Does the incident concerning the cathedral have religious meaning? What is the symbolism of the title? In what way does the narrator change at the end of the story?

The Reading/Writing Connection

1. "Think" Topic: What does the narrator mean when he says, "I didn't feel like I was inside anything"?

2. Journal Entry: Extend the narrative: write about possible changes in the narrator when the blind man leaves.

Ideas for Writing

1. Write a character analysis of the wife that takes into account her first marriage, her suicide attempt, her friendship with Robert, and her present life.

2. Explore the symbolism of the cathedral.

3. **Write an Argument:** Carver mentions television numerous times in the opening paragraphs of the story. Why? Use evidence from the story to support your thesis.

Fairy Tales/Fiction

Nadine Gordimer   *(1923–   )*

Once upon a Time   *1989*

Someone has written to ask me to contribute to an anthology of stories for children. I reply that I don't write children's stories; and he writes back that at a recent congress/book fair/seminar a certain novelist said every writer ought to write at least one story for children. I think of sending a postcard saying I don't accept that I "ought" to write anything.

And then last night I woke up—or rather was awakened without knowing what had roused me.

A voice in the echo-chamber of the subconscious?

A sound.

A creaking of the kind made by the weight carried by one foot after another along   5
a wooden floor. I listened. I felt the apertures of my ears distend with concentration. Again: the creaking. I was waiting for it; waiting to hear if it indicated that feet were moving from room to room, coming up the passage—to my door. I have no burglar bars, no gun under my pillow, but I have the same fears as people who do take these precautions, and my windowpanes are thin as rime, could shatter like a wineglass. A woman was murdered (how do they put it) in broad daylight in a house two blocks away, last year, and the fierce dogs who guarded an old widower and his collection of antique clocks were strangled before he was knifed by a casual laborer he had dismissed without pay.

I was staring at the door, making it out in my mind rather than seeing it, in the dark. I lay quite still—a victim already—but the arrhythmia of my heart was fleeing, knocking this way and that against its body-cage. How finely tuned the senses are, just out of rest, sleep! I could never listen intently as that in the distractions of the day; I was reading every faintest sound, identifying and classifying its possible threat.

But I learned that I was to be neither threatened nor spared. There was no human weight pressing on the boards, the creaking was a buckling, an epicenter of stress. I was in it. The house that surrounds me when I sleep is built on undermined ground; far beneath my bed, the floor, the house's foundations, the stopes and passages of gold mines have hollowed the rock, and when some face trembles, detaches and falls, three thousand feet below, the whole house shifts slightly, bringing uneasy strain to the balance and counterbalance of brick, cement, wood and glass that hold it as a structure around me. The misbeats of my heart tailed off like the last muffled flourishes on one of the wooden xylophones made by the Chopi and Tsonga[1] migrant miners who might have been down there, under me in the earth at that moment. The stope where the fall was could have been disused, dripping water from its ruptured veins; or men might now be interred there in the most profound of tombs.

I couldn't find a position in which my mind would let go of my body—release me to sleep again. So I began to tell myself a story; a bedtime story.

In a house, in a suburb, in a city, there were a man and his wife who loved each other very much and were living happily ever after. They had a little boy, and they loved him very much. They had a cat and a dog that the little boy loved very much. They had a car and a caravan trailer for holidays, and a swimming-pool which was fenced so that the little boy and his playmates would not fall in and drown. They had a housemaid who was absolutely trustworthy and an itinerant gardener who was highly recommended by the neighbors. For when they began to live happily ever after they were warned by that wise old witch, the husband's mother, not to take on anyone off the street. They were inscribed in a medical benefit society, their pet dog was licensed, they were insured against fire, flood damage and theft, and they subscribed to the local Neighborhood Watch, which supplied them with a plaque for their gates lettered YOU HAVE BEEN WARNED over the silhouette of a would-be intruder. He was masked; it could not be said if he was black or white, and therefore proved the owner was no racist.

It was not possible to insure the house, the swimming-pool or the car against riot 10 damage. There were riots, but these were outside the city, where people of another color were quartered. These people were not allowed into the suburb except as reliable housemaids and gardeners, so there was nothing to fear, the husband told the wife. Yet she was afraid that some day such people might come up the street and tear off the plaque YOU HAVE BEEN WARNED and open the gates and stream in . . . Nonsense, my dear, said the husband, there are police and soldiers and tear-gas and guns to keep them away. But to please her—for he loved her very much and buses were being burned, cars stoned, and schoolchildren shot by the police in those quarters out of sight and hearing of the suburb—he had electronically controlled gates fitted. Anyone who pulled off the sign YOU HAVE BEEN WARNED and tried to open the gates would have to announce his intentions by pressing a button and speaking into a receiver relayed to the

---

[1] **Chopi and Tsonga:** two peoples from Mozambique, northeast of South Africa.

house. The little boy was fascinated by the device and used it as a walkie-talkie in cops and robbers play with his small friends.

The riots were suppressed, but there were many burglaries in the suburb and somebody's trusted housemaid was tied up and shut in a cupboard by thieves while she was in charge of her employers' house. The trusted housemaid of the man and wife and little boy was so upset by this misfortune befalling a friend left, as she herself often was, with responsibility for the possessions of the man and his wife and the little boy that she implored her employers to have burglar bars attached to the doors and windows of the house, and an alarm system installed. The wife said, She is right, let us take heed of her advice. So from every window and door in the house where they were living happily ever after they now saw the trees and sky through bars, and when the little boy's pet cat tried to climb in by the fanlight to keep him company in his little bed at night, as it customarily had done, it set off the alarm keening through the house.

The alarm was often answered—it seemed—by other burglar alarms, in other houses, that had been triggered by pet cats or nibbling mice. The alarms called to one another across the gardens in shrills and bleats and wails that everyone soon became accustomed to, so that the din aroused the inhabitants of the suburb no more than the croak of frogs and musical grating of cicadas' legs. Under cover of the electronic harpies' discourse, intruders sawed the iron bars and broke into homes, taking away hi-fi equipment, television sets, cassette players, cameras and radios, jewelry and clothing, and sometimes were hungry enough to devour everything in the refrigerator or paused audaciously to drink the whisky in the cabinets or patio bars. Insurance companies paid no compensation for single malt,[2] a loss made keener by the property owner's knowledge that the thieves wouldn't even have been able to appreciate what it was they were drinking.

Then the time came when many of the people who were not trusted housemaids and gardeners hung about the suburb because they were unemployed. Some importuned for a job: weeding or painting a roof; anything, *baas*,[3] madam. But the man and his wife remembered the warning about taking on anyone off the street. Some drank liquor and fouled the street with discarded bottles. Some begged, waiting for the man and his wife to drive the car out of the electronically operated gates. They sat about with their feet in the gutters, under the jacaranda trees that made a green tunnel of the street—for it was a beautiful suburb, spoiled only by their presence—and sometimes they fell asleep lying right before the gates in the midday sun. The wife could never see anyone go hungry. She sent the trusted housemaid out with bread and tea, but the trusted housemaid said these were loafers and *tsotsis*,[4] who would come and tie her up and shut her up in a cupboard. The husband said, She's right. Take heed of her advice. You only encourage them with your bread and tea. They are looking for their chance . . . And he brought the little boy's tricycle from the garden into the house every night, because if the house was surely secure, once locked and with the alarm set, someone might still be able to climb over the wall or the electronically closed gates into the garden.

You are right, said the wife, then the wall should be higher. And the wise old witch, the husband's mother, paid for the extra bricks as her Christmas present to her son and his wife—the little boy got a Space Man outfit and a book of fairy tales.

---

[2]**single malt:** Expensive Scotch whisky.   [3]*baas:* Boss.   [4]*tsotsis:* Hooligans.

But every week there were more reports of intrusion: in broad daylight and the   15
dead of night, in the early hours of the morning, and even in the lovely summer twilight—a certain family was at dinner while the bedrooms were being ransacked upstairs. The man and his wife, talking of the latest armed robbery in the suburb, were
distracted by the sight of the little boy's pet cat effortlessly arriving over the seven-foot
wall, descending first with a rapid bracing of extended forepaws down on the sheer vertical surface, and then a graceful launch, landing with swishing tail within the property. The whitewashed wall was marked with the cat's comings and goings; and on the
street side of the wall there were larger red-earth smudges that could have been made
by the kind of broken running shoes, seen on the feet of unemployed loiterers, that had
no innocent destination.

When the man and wife and little boy took the pet dog for a walk round the
neighborhood streets, they no longer paused to admire this show of roses or that perfect lawn; these were hidden behind an array of different varieties of security fences,
walls, and devices. The man, wife, little boy and dog passed a remarkable choice: there
was the low-cost option of pieces of broken glass embedded in cement along the top of
walls, there were iron grilles ending in lance-points, there were attempts at reconciling
the aesthetics of prison architecture with the Spanish Villa style (spikes painted pink)
and with the plaster urns of neoclassical façades (twelve-inch pikes finned like zigzags
of lightning and painted pure white). Some walls had a small board affixed, giving the
name and telephone number of the firm responsible for the installation of the devices.
While the little boy and the pet dog raced ahead, the husband and wife found themselves comparing the possible effectiveness of each style against its appearance; and
after several weeks when they paused before this barricade or that without needing to
speak, both came out with the conclusion that only one was worth considering. It was
the ugliest but the most honest in its suggestion of the pure concentration-camp style,
no frills, all evident efficacy. Placed the length of walls, it consisted of a continuous coil
of stiff and shining metal serrated into jagged blades, so that there would be no way of
climbing over it and no way through its tunnel without getting entangled in its fangs.
There would be no way out, only a struggle getting bloodier and bloodier, a deeper and
sharper hooking and tearing of flesh. The wife shuddered to look at it. You're right,
said the husband, anyone would think twice. . . And they took heed of the advice on
the small board fixed to the wall: Consult DRAGON'S TEETH The People for Total
Security.

Next day a gang of workmen came and stretched the razor-bladed coils all round
the walls of the house where the husband and wife and little boy and pet dog and cat
were living happily ever after. The sunlight flashed and slashed off the serrations; the
cornice of razor thorns encircled the home, shining. The husband said, Never mind.
It will weather. The wife said, You're wrong. They guarantee it's rust-proof. And she
waited until the little boy had run off to play before she said, I hope the cat will take
heed . . . The husband said, Don't worry, my dear, cats always look before they leap.
And it was true that from that day on the cat slept in the little boy's bed and kept to the
garden, never risking a try at breaching security.

One evening, the mother read the little boy to sleep with a fairy story from the
book the wise old witch had given him at Christmas. Next day he pretended to be the
Prince who braves the terrible thicket of thorns to enter the palace and kiss the Sleeping Beauty back to life: he dragged a ladder to the wall, the shining coiled tunnel was
just wide enough for his body to creep in, and with the first fixing of its razor-teeth in

his knees and hands and head he screamed and struggled deeper into its tangle. The trusted housemaid and itinerant gardener, whose "day" it was, came running, the first to see and to scream with him, and the itinerant gardener tore his hands trying to get at the little boy. Then the man and his wife burst wildly into the garden and for some reason (the cat, probably) the alarm set up wailing against the screams while the bleeding mass of the little boy was hacked out of the security coil with saws, wire-cutters, choppers, and they carried it—the man, the wife, the hysterical trusted housemaid, and the weeping gardener—into the house. •

Angela Carter   *(1940–1992)*

The Company of Wolves   *1979*

One beast and only one howls in the woods by night.
The wolf is carnivore incarnate and he's as cunning as he is ferocious; once he's had a taste of flesh then nothing else will do.

At night, the eyes of wolves shine like candle flames, yellowish, reddish, but that is because the pupils of their eyes fatten on darkness and catch the light from your lantern to flash it back to you—red for danger; if a wolf's eyes reflect only moonlight, then they gleam a cold and unnatural green, a mineral, a piercing color. If the benighted traveller spies those luminous, terrible sequins stitched suddenly on the black thickets, then he knows he must run, if fear has not struck him stock-still.

But those eyes are all you will be able to glimpse of the forest assassins as they cluster invisibly round your smell of meat as you go through the wood unwisely late. They will be like shadows, they will be like wraiths, grey members of a congregation of nightmare; hark! his long, wavering howl . . . an aria of fear made audible.

The wolfsong is the sound of the rending you will suffer, in itself a murdering.   5

It is winter and cold weather. In this region of mountain and forest, there is now nothing for the wolves to eat. Goats and sheep are locked up in the byre, the deer departed for the remaining pasturage on the southern slopes—wolves grow lean and famished. There is so little flesh on them that you could count the starveling ribs through their pelts, if they gave you time before they pounced. Those slavering jaws; the lolling tongue; the rime of saliva on the grizzled chops—of all the teeming perils of the night and the forest, ghosts, hobgoblins, ogres that grill babies upon gridirons, witches that fatten their captives in cages for cannibal tables, the wolf is worst for he cannot listen to reason.

You are always in danger in the forest, where no people are. Step between the portals of the great pines where the shaggy branches tangle about you, trapping the unwary traveller in nets as if the vegetation itself were in a plot with the wolves who live there, as though the wicked trees go fishing on behalf of their friends—step between the gateposts of the forest with the greatest trepidation and infinite precautions, for if you stray from the path for one instant, the wolves will eat you. They are grey as famine, they are as unkind as plague.

The grave-eyed children of the sparse villages always carry knives with them when they go out to tend the little flocks of goats that provide the homesteads with acrid milk and rank, maggoty cheeses. Their knives are half as big as they are, the blades are sharpened daily.

But the wolves have ways of arriving at your own hearthside. We try and try but sometimes we cannot keep them out. There is no winter's night the cottager does not fear to see a lean, grey, famished snout questing under the door, and there was a woman once bitten in her own kitchen as she was straining the macaroni.

Fear and flee the wolf; for, worst of all, the wolf may be more than he seems. 10

There was a hunter once, near here, that trapped a wolf in a pit. This wolf had massacred the sheep and goats; eaten up a mad old man who used to live by himself in a hut halfway up the mountain and sing to Jesus all day; pounced on a girl looking after the sheep, but she made such a commotion that men came with rifles and scared him away and tried to track him into the forest but he was cunning and easily gave them the slip. So this hunter dug a pit and put a duck in it, for bait, all alive-oh; and he covered the pit with straw smeared with wolf dung. Quack, quack! went the duck and a wolf came slinking out of the forest, a big one, a heavy one, he weighed as much as a grown man and the straw gave way beneath him—into the pit he tumbled. The hunter jumped down after him, slit his throat, cut off all his paws for a trophy.

And then no wolf at all lay in front of the hunter but the bloody trunk of a man, headless, footless, dying, dead.

A witch from up the valley once turned an entire wedding party into wolves because the groom had settled on another girl. She used to order them to visit her, at night, from spite, and they would sit and howl around her cottage for her, serenading her with their misery.

Not so very long ago, a young woman in our village married a man who vanished clean away on her wedding night. The bed was made with new sheets and the bride lay down in it; the groom said, he was going out to relieve himself, insisted on it, for the sake of decency, and she drew the coverlet up to her chin and she lay there. And she waited and she waited and then she waited again—surely he's been gone a long time? Until she jumps up in bed and shrieks to hear a howling, coming on the wind from the forest.

That long-drawn, wavering howl has, for all its fearful resonance, some inherent 15 sadness in it, as if the beasts would love to be less beastly if only they knew how and never cease to mourn their own condition. There is a vast melancholy in the canticles of the wolves, melancholy infinite as the forest, endless as these long nights of winter and yet that ghastly sadness, that mourning for their own, irremediable appetites, can never move the heart for not one phrase in it hints at the possibility of redemption; grace could not come to the wolf from its own despair, only through some external mediator, so that, sometimes, the beast will look as if he half welcomes the knife that despatches him.

The young woman's brothers searched the outhouses and the haystacks but never found any remains so the sensible girl dried her eyes and found herself another husband not too shy to piss into a pot who spent the nights indoors. She gave him a pair of bonny babies and all went right as a trivet until, one freezing night, the night of the solstice, the hinge of the year when things do not fit together as well as they should, the longest night, her first good man came home again.

A great thump on the door announced him as she was stirring the soup for the father of her children and she knew him the moment she lifted the latch to him although it was years since she'd worn black for him and now he was in rags and his hair hung down his back and never saw a comb, alive with lice.

"Here I am again, missus," he said. "Get me my bowl of cabbage and be quick about it."

Then her second husband came in with wood for the fire and when the first one saw she'd slept with another man and, worse, clapped his red eyes on her little children who'd crept into the kitchen to see what all the din was about, he shouted: "I wish I were a wolf again, to teach this whore a lesson!" So a wolf he instantly became and tore off the eldest boy's left foot before he was chopped up with the hatchet they used for chopping logs. But when the wolf lay bleeding and gasping its last, the pelt peeled off again and he was just as he had been, years ago, when he ran away from his marriage bed, so that she wept and her second husband beat her.

They say there's an ointment the Devil gives you that turns you into a wolf the [20] minute you rub it on. Or, that he was born feet first and had a wolf for his father and his torso is a man's but his legs and genitals are a wolf's. And he has a wolf's heart.

Seven years is a werewolf's natural span but if you burn his human clothing you condemn him to wolfishness for the rest of his life, so old wives hereabouts think it some protection to throw a hat or an apron at the werewolf, as if clothes made the man. Yet by the eyes, those phosphorescent eyes, you know him in all his shapes; the eyes alone unchanged by metamorphosis.

Before he can become a wolf, the lycanthrope strips stark naked. If you spy a naked man among the pines, you must run as if the Devil were after you.

It is midwinter and the robin, the friend of man, sits on the handle of the gardener's spade and sings. It is the worst time in all the year for wolves but this strong-minded child insists she will go off through the wood. She is quite sure the wild beasts cannot harm her although, well-warned, she lays a carving knife in the basket her mother has packed with cheeses. There is a bottle of harsh liquor distilled from brambles; a batch of flat oatcakes baked on the hearthstone; a pot or two of jam. The flaxen-haired girl will take these delicious gifts to a reclusive grandmother so old the burden of her years is crushing her to death. Granny lives two hours' trudge through the winter woods; the child wraps herself up in her thick shawl, draws it over her head. She steps into her stout wooden shoes; she is dressed and ready and it is Christmas Eve. The malign door of the solstice still swings upon its hinges but she has been too much loved ever to feel scared.

Children do not stay young for long in this savage country. There are no toys for them to play with so they work hard and grow wise but this one, so pretty and the youngest of her family, a little late-comer, had been indulged by her mother and the grandmother who'd knitted her the red shawl that, today, has the ominous if brilliant look of blood on snow. Her breasts have just begun to swell; her hair is like lint, so fair it hardly makes a shadow on her pale forehead; her cheeks are an emblematic scarlet and white and she has just started her woman's bleeding, the clock inside her that will strike, henceforward, once a month.

She stands and moves within the invisible pentacle[1] of her own virginity. She is [25] an unbroken egg; she is a sealed vessel; she has inside her a magic space the entrance to which is shut tight with a plug of membrane; she is a closed system; she does not know how to shiver. She has her knife and she is afraid of nothing,

Her father might forbid her, if he were home, but he is away in the forest, gathering wood, and her mother cannot deny her.

The forest closed upon her like a pair of jaws.

---

[1]**pentacle:** A figure of a five-pointed star within a circle.

There is always something to look at in the forest, even in the middle of winter—the huddled mounds of birds, succumbed to the lethargy of the season, heaped on the creaking boughs and too forlorn to sing; the bright frills of the winter fungi on the blotched trunks of the trees; the cuneiform slots of rabbits and deer, the herringbone tracks of the birds, a hare as lean as a rasher of bacon streaking across the path where the thin sunlight dapples the russet brakes of last year's bracken.

When she heard the freezing howl of a distant wolf, her practised hand sprang to the handle of her knife, but she saw no sign of a wolf at all, nor of a naked man, neither, but then she heard a clattering among the brushwood and there sprang on to the path a fully clothed one, a very handsome young one, in the green coat and wide-awake hat of a hunter, laden with carcasses of game birds. She had her hand on her knife at the first rustle of twigs but he laughed with a flash of white teeth when he saw her and made her a comic yet flattering little bow; she'd never seen such a fine fellow before, not among the rustic clowns of her native village. So on they went together, through the thickening light of the afternoon.

Soon they were laughing and joking like old friends. When he offered to carry   30
her basket, she gave it to him although her knife was in it because he told her his rifle would protect them. As the day darkened, it began to snow again; she felt the first flakes settle on her eyelashes but now there was only half a mile to go and there would be a fire, and hot tea, and a welcome, a warm one, surely, for the dashing huntsman as well as for herself.

This young man had a remarkable object in his pocket. It was a compass. She looked at the little round glass face in the palm of his hand and watched the wavering needle with a vague wonder. He assured her this compass had taken him safely through the wood on his hunting trip because the needle always told him with perfect accuracy where the north was. She did not believe it; she knew she should never leave the path on the way through the wood or else she would be lost instantly. He laughed at her again; gleaming trails of spittle clung to his teeth. He said, if he plunged off the path into the forest that surrounded them, he could guarantee to arrive at her grandmother's house a good quarter of an hour before she did, plotting his way through the undergrowth with his compass, while she trudged the long way, along the winding path.

I don't believe you. Besides, aren't you afraid of the wolves?

He only tapped the gleaming butt of his rifle and grinned.

Is it a bet? he asked her. Shall we make a game of it? What will you give me if I get to your grandmother's house before you?

What would you like? she asked disingenuously.   35

A kiss.

Commonplaces of a rustic seduction; she lowered her eyes and blushed. He went through the undergrowth and took her basket with him but she forgot to be afraid of the beasts, although now the moon was rising, for she wanted to dawdle on her way to make sure the handsome gentleman would win his wager.

Grandmother's house stood by itself a little way out of the village. The freshly falling snow blew in eddies about the kitchen garden and the young man stepped delicately up the snowy path to the door as if he were reluctant to get his feet wet, swinging his bundle of game and the girl's basket and humming a little tune to himself.

There is a faint trace of blood on his chin; he has been snacking on his catch.

He rapped upon the panels with his knuckles.   40

Aged and frail, granny is three-quarters succumbed to the mortality the ache in her bones promises her and almost ready to give in entirely. A boy came out from the village to build up her hearth for the night an hour ago and the kitchen crackles with busy firelight. She has her Bible for company, she is a pious old woman. She is propped up on several pillows in the bed set into the wall peasant-fashion, wrapped up in the patchwork quilt she made before she was married, more years ago than she cares to remember. Two china spaniels with liver-coloured blotches on their coats and black noses sit on either side of the fireplace. There is a bright rug of woven rags on the pantiles. The grandfather clock ticks away her eroding time.

We keep the wolves outside by living well.

He rapped upon the panels with his hairy knuckles.

It is your granddaughter, he mimicked in a high soprano.

Lift up the latch and walk in, my darling.   45

You can tell them by their eyes, eyes of a beast of prey, nocturnal, devastating eyes as red as a wound; you can hurl your Bible at him and your apron after, granny, you thought that was a sure prophylactic against these infernal vermin . . . now call on Christ and his mother and all the angels in heaven to protect you but it won't do you any good.

His feral muzzle is sharp as a knife; he drops his golden burden of gnawed pheasant on the table and puts down your dear girl's basket, too. Oh, my God, what have you done with her?

Off with his disguise, that coat of forest-coloured cloth, the hat with the feather tucked into the ribbon; his matted hair streams down his white shirt and she can see the lice moving in it. The sticks in the hearth shift and hiss; night and the forest has come into the kitchen with darkness tangled in its hair.

He strips off his shirt. His skin is the colour and texture of vellum. A crisp stripe of hair runs down his belly, his nipples are ripe and dark as poison fruit but he's so thin you could count the ribs under his skin if only he gave you the time. He strips off his trousers and she can see how hairy his legs are. His genitals, huge. Ah! huge.

The last thing the old lady saw in all this world was a young man, eyes like cinders, 50 naked as a stone, approaching her bed.

The wolf is carnivore incarnate.

When he had finished with her, he licked his chops and quickly dressed himself again, until he was just as he had been when he came through her door. He burned the inedible hair in the fireplace and wrapped the bones, up in a napkin that he hid away under the bed in the wooden chest in which he found a clean pair of sheets. These he carefully put on the bed instead of the tell-tale stained ones he stowed away in the laundry basket. He plumped up the pillows and shook out the patchwork quilt, he picked up the Bible from the floor, closed it and laid it on the table. All was as it had been before except that grandmother was gone. The sticks twitched in the grate, the clock ticked and the young man sat patiently, deceitfully beside the bed in granny's nightcap.

Rat-a-tap-tap.

Who's there, he quavers in granny's antique falsetto.

Only your granddaughter.   55

So she came in, bringing with her a flurry of snow that melted in tears on the tiles, and perhaps she was a little disappointed to see only her grandmother sitting beside the fire. But then he flung off the blanket and sprang to the door, pressing his back against it so that she could not get out again.

The girl looked round the room and saw there was not even the indentation of a head on the smooth cheek of the pillow and how, for the first time she'd seen it so, the Bible lay closed on the table. The tick of the clock cracked like a whip. She wanted her knife from her basket but she did not dare reach for it because his eyes were fixed upon her—huge eyes that now seemed to shine with a unique, interior light, eyes the size of saucers, saucers full of Greek fire, diabolic phosphorescence.

What big eyes you have.

All the better to see you with.

No trace at all of the old woman except for a tuft of white hair that had caught in 60 the bark of an unburned log. When the girl saw that, she knew she was in danger of death.

Where is my grandmother?

There's nobody here but we two, my darling.

Now a great howling rose up all around them, near, very near, as close as the kitchen garden, the howling of a multitude of wolves; she knew the worst wolves are hairy on the inside and she shivered, in spite of the scarlet shawl she pulled more closely round herself as if it could protect her although it was as red as the blood she must spill.

Who has come to sing us carols, she said.

Those are the voices of my brothers, darling; I love the company of wolves. Look 65 out of the window and you'll see them.

Snow half-caked the lattice and she opened it to look into the garden. It was a white night of moon and snow; the blizzard whirled round the gaunt, grey beasts who squatted on their haunches among the rows of winter cabbage, pointing their sharp snouts to the moon and howling as if their hearts would break. Ten wolves; twenty wolves—so many wolves she could not count them, howling in concert as if demented or deranged. Their eyes reflected the light from the kitchen and shone like a hundred candles.

It is very cold, poor things, she said; no wonder they howl so.

She closed the window on the wolves' threnody[2] and took off her scarlet shawl, the colour of poppies, the colour of sacrifices, the colour of her menses, and, since her fear did her no good, she ceased to be afraid.

What shall I do with my shawl?

Throw it on the fire, dear one. You won't need it again. 70

She bundled up her shawl and threw it on the blaze, which instantly consumed it. Then she drew her blouse over her head; her small breasts gleamed as if the snow had invaded the room.

What shall I do with my blouse?

Into the fire with it, too, my pet.

The thin muslin went flaring up the chimney like a magic bird and now off came her skirt, her woollen stockings, her shoes, and on to the fire they went, too, and were gone for good. The firelight shone through the edges of her skin; now she was clothed only in her untouched integument of flesh. This dazzling, naked she combed out her hair with her fingers; her hair looked white as the snow outside. Then went directly to the man with red eyes in whose unkempt mane the lice moved; she stood up on tiptoe and unbuttoned the collar of his shirt.

What big arms you have. 75

---

[2] **threnody:** A lamentation song; a dirge.

All the better to hug you with.

Every wolf in the world now howled a prothalamion[3] outside the window as she freely gave the kiss she owed him.

What big teeth you have!

She saw how his jaw began to slaver and the room was full of the clamour of the forest's Liebestod[4] but the wise child never flinched, even when he answered:

All the better to eat you with.

The girl burst out laughing; she knew she was nobody's meat. She laughed at him full in the face, she ripped off his shirt for him and flung it into the fire, in the fiery wake of her own discarded clothing. The flames danced like dead souls on Walpurgisnacht[5] and the old bones under the bed set up a terrible clattering but she did not pay them any heed.

Carnivore incarnate, only immaculate flesh appeases him.

She will lay his fearful head on her lap and she will pick out the lice from his pelt and perhaps she will put the lice into her mouth and eat them, as he will bid her, as she would do in a savage marriage ceremony.

The blizzard will die down.

The blizzard died down, leaving the mountains as randomly covered with snow as if a blind woman had thrown a sheet over them, the upper branches of the forest pines limed, creaking, swollen with the fall.

Snowlight, moonlight, a confusion of paw-prints.

All silent, all still.

Midnight; and the clock strikes. It is Christmas Day, the werewolves' birthday, the door of the solstice stands wide open; let them all sink through.

See! sweet and sound she sleeps in granny's bed, between the paws of the tender wolf. ●

Explorations of the Text

1. What prompts Nadine Gordimer to write a children's story? Refer to Bruno Bettelheim's essay in this chapter. Consider his view that literature, including children's books, gives a reader "access to deeper meaning," to an "understanding of what the meaning of one's life may or ought to be." How does the introduction in the story relate to Bettelheim's views and frame the work? Develop thematic significance?

2. How does Angela Carter change the story of Little Red Riding Hood (i.e., the development of character, plot, and symbolism)? How does Carter's version differ from the original tale?

3. How do both Nadine Gordimer and Angela Carter incorporate and subvert fairy tale motifs, such as the haunted palace, children lost in the wilderness, the prince as savior, the wicked witch? What is the impact of these changes?

4. What happens to the "happily ever after" ending? What do the denouements of both works suggest about the state of the world?

---

[3]**prothalamion:** A song in celebration of a marriage.   [4]**Liebestod:** Literally, love-death.   [5]**Walpurgisnacht:** The eve of May Day, when, according to legend, witches rendezvous.

The Reading/Writing Connection

1. Write sequels to one of these stories. What happens to the main characters?
2. Begin a freewrite with "Once upon a time . . ."
3. Create your own modern version of a fairy tale. Consider how you will work with the original story and change it.

4. Write a monologue in the voice of Little Red Riding Hood or the Wolf in Carter's story.

Ideas for Writing

1. How do both stories represent the journey from innocence to experience or the tension between good and evil? You also may refer to other works in the fairy tale cluster.
2. Read another story from Angela Carter's *The Bloody Chamber*. Compare her version with the original tale. Or ana-lyze Anne Sexton's "Cinderella." How does Sexton change the tale?
3. What fairy tales, children's stories, or animated films were your favorites? Why were they important to you?
4. Debate Topic: Are parents powerless to protect their children? Present your views on this issue.

 On the Web: *Introduction to Fairy Tales*

Please visit http://www.academic.cengage.com/english/Schmidt/Legacies4e/ for links to the following online resources.

The Children's Literature Association:
"The Little Red Riding Hood Project"
"The Cinderella Project"
Aaron Goranson, "When the Aliens Came"

POETRY

Diane Wakoski   *(1937–   )*

Wind Secrets   *1966*

I like the wind
with its puffed cheeks and closed eyes.
Nice wind.
I like its gentle sounds
and fierce bites.　　　　　　　　　　　　　　　　　　　5
When I was little
I used to sit by the black, potbellied stove and stare
at a spot on the ceiling,
while the wind breathed and blew
outside.　　　　　　　　　　　　　　　　　　　　　10

"Nice wind,"
I murmured to myself.

I would ask mother when she kneeled to tie my shoes
what the wind said.

Mother knew.　　　　　　　　　　　　　　　　　　15

And the wind whistled and roared outside
while the coals opened their eyes in anger
at me.
I would hear mother crying under the wind.
"Nice wind," I said,　　　　　　　　　　　　　　　20
But my heart leapt like a darting fish.
I remember the wind better than any sound.
It was the first thing I heard
with blazing ears,
a sound that didn't murmur and coo,　　　　　　　　25
and the sounds wrapped round my head
and huffed open my eyes.
It was the first thing I heard
besides my father beating my mother.
The sounds slashed at my ears like scissors.　　　　30
Nice wind.

The wind blows
while the glowing coals from the stove look at me
with angry eyes.

Nice wind.
Nice wind.
Oh, close your eyes.   35
There was nothing I could do.

Explorations of the Text

1. Discuss the speaker's point of view. Is it a child's or an adult's voice? Explain.
2. What comparisons create the dramatic effects and momentum in the poem?

What do they suggest about the child's state of mind?

3. Explore the symbolism of the "eyes." Whose "eyes" are they?

The Reading/Writing Connection

1. Journal Entry: Create a moment from childhood in which you use nature imagery to suggest your state of mind

(You may create a poem or a drawing for this entry).

Ideas for Writing

1. Write a monologue in the voice of the mother.
2. Discuss the use of figurative language in this poem. How does the language develop the theme?

3. Compare this poem with "Incident." Focus on loss of innocence.

Countee Cullen *(1903–1946)*

Incident *1925*

Once riding in old Baltimore,
  Heart-filled, head-filled with glee,
I saw a Baltimorean
  Keep looking straight at me.

Now I was eight and very small,   5
  And he was no whit bigger,
And so I smiled, but he poked out
  His tongue and called me, "Nigger."

I saw the whole of Baltimore
  From May until December: 10
Of all the things that happened there
  That's all that I remember.

Explorations of the Text

1. What is the nature of the interaction between the two boys?
2. Why does the speaker remember nothing more than the incident, even though he stayed in Baltimore from "May until December"?
3. What aspects of this poem are similar to the story by Heker?

The Reading/Writing Connection

1. In a paragraph compare your experience of prejudice with the persona in the poem.
2. "Think" Topic: Compare the reactions of the persona with those in the works by Heker and Erdrich.

Ideas for Writing

1. What do its form and rhyme add to this poem?
2. What is the power of language? What are the effects of the use of the term *nigger?*

Walt Whitman   *(1819–1892)*

Out of the Cradle Endlessly Rocking   *1859*

Out of the cradle endlessly rocking,
Out of the mocking-bird's throat, the musical shuttle,
Out of the Ninth-month[1] midnight,
Over the sterile sands and the fields beyond, where the child leaving his bed
    wander'd alone, bareheaded, barefoot,
Down from the shower'd halo,   5
Up from the mystic play of shadows twining and twisting as if they were alive,
Out from the patches of briers and blackberries,
From the memories of the bird that chanted to me,
From your memories sad brother, from the fitful risings and fallings I heard,
From under that yellow half-moon late-risen and swollen as if with tears,   10
From those beginning notes of yearning and love there in the mist,
From the thousand responses of my heart never to cease,
From the myriad thence-arous'd words,
From the word stronger and more delicious than any,
For such as now they start the scene revisiting,   15
As a flock, twittering, rising, or overhead passing,
Borne hither, ere all eludes me, hurriedly,
A man, yet by these tears a little boy again,
Throwing myself on the sand, confronting the waves,
I, chanter of pains and joys, uniter of here and hereafter,   20
Taking all hints to use them, but swiftly leaping beyond them,
A reminiscence sing.

---

[1]**Ninth-month:** Quaker name for September.

Once Paumanok,
When the lilac-scent was in the air and Fifth-month grass was growing,
Up this seashore in some briers,   25
Two feather'd guests from Alabama, two together,
And their nest, and four light-green eggs spotted with brown,
And every day the he-bird to and fro near at hand,
And every day the she-bird crouch'd on her nest, silent, with bright eyes,
And every day I, a curious boy, never too close, never disturbing them,   30
Cautiously peering, absorbing, translating.

Shine! shine! shine!
Pour down your warmth, great sun!
While we bask, we two together.

Two together!   35
Winds blow south, or winds blow north,
Day come white, or night come black,
Home, or rivers and mountains from home,
Singing all time, minding no time,
While we two keep together.   40

Till of a sudden,
May-be kill'd, unknown to her mate,
One forenoon the she-bird crouch'd not on the nest,
Nor return'd that afternoon, nor the next,
Nor ever appear'd again.   45

And thenceforward all summer in the sound of the sea,
And at night under the full of the moon in calmer weather,
Over the hoarse surging of the sea,
Or flitting from brier to brier by day,
I saw, I heard at intervals the remaining one, the he-bird,   50
The solitary guest from Alabama.

Blow! blow! blow!
Blow up sea-winds along Paumanok's shore;
I wait and I wait till you blow my mate to me.

Yes, when the stars glisten'd,   55
All night long on the prong of a moss-scallop'd stake,
Down almost amid the slapping waves,
Sat the lone singer wonderful causing tears.
He call'd on his mate,
He pour'd forth the meanings which I of all men know.   60

Yes my brother I know,
The rest might not, but I have treasur'd every note,
For more than once dimly down to the beach gliding,

Silent, avoiding the moonbeams, blending myself with the shadows,
Recalling now the obscure shapes, the echoes, the sounds and sights after   65
   their sorts,
The white arms out in the breakers tirelessly tossing,
I, with bare feet, a child, the wind wafting my hair,
Listen'd long and long.

Listen'd to keep, to sing, now translating the notes,
Following you my brother.   70

Soothe! soothe! soothe!
Close on its wave soothes the wave behind,
And again another behind embracing and lapping, every one close,
But my love soothes not me, not me.

Low hangs the moon, it rose late,   75
It is lagging—O I think it is heavy with love, with love.

O madly the sea pushes upon the land,
With love, with love.

O night! do I not see my love fluttering out among the breakers?
What is that little black thing I see there in the white?   80

Loud! loud! loud!
Loud I call to you, my love!
High and clear I shoot my voice over the waves,
Surely you must know who is here, is here,
You must know who I am, my love.   85

Low-hanging moon!
What is that dusky spot in your brown yellow?
O it is the shape, the shape of my mate!
O moon do not keep her from me any longer.

Land! land! O land!   90
Whichever way I turn, O I think you could give me my mate back again if you
   only would,
For I am almost sure I see her dimly whichever way I look.

O rising stars!
Perhaps the one I want so much will rise, will rise with some of you.

O throat! O trembling throat!   95
Sound clearer through the atmosphere!
Pierce the woods, the earth,
Somewhere listening to catch you must be the one I want.

Shake out carols!
Solitary here, the night's carols!   100
Carols of lonesome love! death's carols!
Carols under that lagging, yellow, waning moon!
O under that moon where she droops down into the sea!
O reckless despairing carols.

But soft! sink low!   105
Soft! let me just murmur,
And do you wait a moment you husky-nois'd sea,
For somewhere I believe I heard my mate responding to me,
So faint, I must be still, be still to listen,
But not altogether still, for then she might not come immediately to me.   110

Hither my love!
Here I am! here!
With this just-sustain'd note I announce myself to you,
This gentle call is for you my love, for you.

Do not be decoy'd elsewhere,   115
That is the whistle of the wind, it is not my voice,
That is the fluttering, the fluttering of the spray,
Those are the shadows of leaves.

O darkness! O in vain!
O I am very sick and sorrowful.   120

O brown halo in the sky near the moon, drooping upon the sea!
O troubled reflection in the sea!

O throat! O throbbing heart!
And I singing uselessly, uselessly all the night.

O past! O happy life! O songs of joy!   125
In the air, in the woods, over fields,
Loved! loved! loved! loved! loved!
But my mate no more, no more with me!
We two together no more.

The aria[2] sinking,   130
All else continuing, the stars shining,
The winds blowing, the notes of the bird continuous echoing,
With angry moans the fierce old mother incessantly moaning,
On the sands of Paumanok's shore gray and rustling,
The yellow half-moon enlarged, sagging down, drooping, the face of the   135
    sea almost touching

---

[2] **aria:** A song performed by a single voice in opera.

The boy ecstatic, with his bare feet the waves, with his hair the atmosphere
    dallying,
The love in the heart long pent, now loose, now at last tumultuously bursting,
The aria's meaning, the ears, the soul, swiftly depositing,
The strange tears down the cheeks coursing,
The colloquy there, the trio, each uttering,   140
The undertone, the savage old mother incessantly crying,
To the boy's soul's questions sullenly timing, some drown'd secret hissing,
To the outsetting bard.[3]

Demon or bird! (said the boy's soul,)
Is it indeed toward your mate you sing? or is it really to me?   145
For I, that was a child, my tongue's use sleeping, now I have heard you,
Now in a moment I know what I am for, I awake,
And already a thousand singers, a thousand songs, clearer, louder and
    more sorrowful than yours,
A thousand warbling echoes have started to live within me, never to die.

O you singer solitary, singing by yourself, projecting me,   150
O solitary me listening, never more shall I cease perpetuating you,
Never more shall I escape, never more the reverberations,
Never more the cries of unsatisfied love be absent from me,
Never again leave me to be the peaceful child I was before what there in the
    night,
By the sea under the yellow and sagging moon,   155
The messenger there arous'd, the fire, the sweet hell within,
The unknown want, the destiny of me.

O give me the clew! (it lurks in the night here somewhere,)
O if I am to have so much, let me have more!

A word then, (for I will conquer it,)   160
The word final, superior to all,
Subtle, sent up—what is it?—I listen;
Are you whispering it, and have been all the time, you sea waves?
Is that it from your liquid rims and wet sands?

Whereto answering, the sea,   165
Delaying not, hurrying not,
Whisper'd me through the night, and very plainly before daybreak,
Lisp'd to me the low and delicious word death,
And again death, death, death, death,
Hissing melodious, neither like the bird nor like my arous'd child's heart,   170
But edging near as privately for me rustling at my feet,
Creeping thence steadily up to my ears and laving me softly all over,
Death, death, death, death, death.

---

[3]**bard:** A poet.

Which I do not forget,
But fuse the song of my dusky demon and brother,   175
That he sang to me in the moonlight on Paumanok's gray beach,
With the thousand responsive songs at random,
My own songs awaked from that hour,
And with them the key, the word up from the waves,
The word of the sweetest song and all songs,   180
The strong and delicious word which, creeping to my feet,
(Or like some old crone rocking the cradle, swathed in sweet garments,
    bending aside,)
The sea whisper'd me.

Explorations of the Text

1. About what does the speaker reminisce? What is the speaker's motivation for this "reminiscence" song?
2. What is the mood of the prologue?
3. What is the message of the he-bird's lament? Is the personification effective?
4. What does the boy learn of life through the "reminiscence" song? What does the adult speaker learn?
5. Explore the connections of birth, love, and death expressed in this poem.
6. Whitman is known for his organic free verse (poetry that has music, form, and rhythm, but not a standard metric or rhythmic pattern); see the Glossary and Chapter 11. How does Whitman's free verse work in this poem?

The Reading/Writing Connection

1. Choose one line from the poem, and in a journal entry respond to the line.
2. Study the he-bird's song. Create a free verse monologue spoken by a bird or other creature. In a concrete manner, convey an abstract idea, such as loss, betrayal, death, or love.

Ideas for Writing

1. Analyze the persona. (See lines 1–21 and 130–182.)
2. What do the repeated symbols of the star, bird, and sea suggest?

Gary Soto   *(1952–   )*

Oranges   *1985*

The first time I walked
With a girl, I was twelve,
Cold, and weighted down
With two oranges in my jacket.
December. Frost cracking   5
Beneath my steps, my breath
Before me, then gone,

As I walked toward
Her house, the one whose
Porch light burned yellow   10
Night and day, in any weather.
A dog barked at me, until
She came out pulling
At her gloves, face bright
With rouge. I smiled,   15
Touched her shoulder, and led
Her down the street, across
A used car lot and a line
Of newly planted trees,
Until we were breathing   20
Before a drugstore. We
Entered, the tiny bell
Bringing a saleslady
Down a narrow aisle of goods.
I turned to the candies   25
Tiered like bleachers,
And asked what she wanted—
Light in her eyes, a smile
Starting at the corners
Of her mouth. I fingered   30
A nickel in my pocket,
And when she lifted a chocolate
That cost a dime,
I didn't say anything.
I took the nickel from   35
My pocket, then an orange,
And set them quietly on
The counter. When I looked up,
The lady's eyes met mine,
And held them, knowing   40
Very well what it was all
About.
      Outside,
A few cars hissing past,
Fog hanging like old
Coats between the trees.   45
I took my girl's hand
In mine for two blocks,
Then released it to let
Her unwrap the chocolate.
I peeled my orange   50
That was so bright against
The gray of December
That, from some distance,
Someone might have thought
I was making a fire in my hands.   55

Explorations of the Text

1. Discuss the significance of the purchase at the drugstore.
2. Explore the symbolism of peeling the paper from the chocolate, peeling the orange, and the last line. What do these images suggest?

3. Examine the images associated with weather. How does the time of year enhance the mood of the poem?

The Reading/Writing Connection

1. In a journal entry, write about your first date.
2. Write a monologue in the voice of the young girl.

3. "Think" Topic: How does the outside world, the environment, influence the speaker's experience? Are there clues in the poem?

Ideas for Writing

1. **Write an Argument:** What do the last two lines of the poem mean? Do they present a satisfying conclusion?

2. Compare the state of mind of the speaker with that of Audre Lorde's adolescent girl in "Hanging Fire."

Audre Lorde *(1934–1992)*

Hanging Fire   *1978*

I am fourteen
and my skin has betrayed me
the boy I cannot live without
still sucks his thumb
in secret   5
how come my knees are
always so ashy
what if I die
before morning
and momma's in the bedroom   10
with the door closed.

I have to learn how to dance
in time for the next party
my room is too small for me
suppose I die before graduation   15
they will sing sad melodies
but finally
tell the truth about me
There is nothing I want to do
and too much   20
that has to be done

and momma's in the bedroom
with the door closed.

Nobody even stops to think
about my side of it   25
I should have been on Math Team
my marks were better than his
why do I have to be
the one
wearing braces   30
I have nothing to wear tomorrow
will I live long enough
to grow up
and momma's in the bedroom
with the door closed.   35

Explorations of the Text

1. Characterize the voice and the tone of the speaker. Discuss the speaker's conflict. What is her view of her body?
2. What is "momma's" role in her life?
3. Discuss the impact of the repetition in the poem.

4. What does the poem reveal about being "fourteen"? Explore the meaning of the title.

The Reading/Writing Connection

1. Freewrite about being an adolescent. Does the poem present a realistic portrait of early adolescence?

Ideas for Writing

1. Compare the vision of adolescence in this work with those in "Oranges," and "Adolescence I, II, III."

2. How can parents help adolescents negotiate this difficult stage of life? Write a letter to the mother in this poem.

Nikki Giovanni   *(1943–)*

Ego Tripping   *1973*

(there may be a reason why)

I was born in the congo
I walked to the fertile crescent and built
    the sphinx[1]

---

[1] **sphinx**: A mythical creature with the head of a human or animal, the body of a lion, and the wings of an eagle. One of the famous monuments in ancient Egypt, near the pyramids. In Greek mythology, the Sphinx proposed a riddle to Oedipus; and when he answered it, she killed herself.

I designed a pyramid so tough that a star
    that only glows every one hundred years falls
    into the center giving divine perfect light
I am bad

I sat on the throne
    drinking nectar with allah[2]
I got hot and sent an ice age to europe
    to cool my thirst
My oldest daughter is nefertiti[3]
    the tears from my birth pains
    created the nile[4]
I am a beautiful woman

I gazed on the forest and burned
    out the sahara desert
    with a packet of goat's meat
    and a change of clothes
I crossed it in two hours
I am a gazelle so swift
    so swift you can't catch me

    For a birthday present when he was three
I gave my son hannibal[5] an elephant
    He gave me rome for mother's day
My strength flows ever on
My son noah built new/ark and
I stood proudly at the helm
    as we sailed on a soft summer day
I turned myself into myself and was
    jesus
    men intone my loving name

    All praises All praises
I am the one who would save

I sowed diamonds in my back yard
My bowels deliver uranium
    the filings from my fingernails are
    semi-precious jewels
    On a trip north

Line numbers: 5, 10, 15, 20, 25, 30, 35

---

[2]**Allah:** In Islam, the name of God; Supreme Being.   [3]**Nefertiti:** An Egyptian queen (fourteenth century B.C.), known for her beauty.   [4]**the Nile:** Longest river in Africa, flowing north from Lake Victoria to the Mediterranean.   [5]**Hannibal:** A Carthaginian general who crossed the Mediterranean and the Alps and attacked Italy. Carthage—a country in North Africa.

I caught a cold and blew   40
My nose giving oil to the arab world
I am so hip even my errors are correct
I sailed west to reach east and had to round off
   the earth as I went
      The hair from my head thinned and gold was laid   45
   across three continents

I am so perfect so divine so ethereal so surreal
I cannot be comprehended
   except by my permission

I mean . . . I . . . can fly   50
   like a bird in the sky . . .

Nikki Giovanni   *(1943–)*

Quilts   *2007*

(For Sally Sellers)

Like a fading piece of cloth
I am a failure

No longer do I cover tables filled with food and laughter
My seams are frayed my hems fall-
ing my strength no longer able   5
To hold the hot and cold

I wish for those first days
When just woven I could keep water
From seeping through
Repelled stains with the tightness of my weave   10
Dazzled the sunlight with my
Reflection

I grow old though pleased with my memories
The tasks I can no longer complete
Are balanced by the love of the tasks gone past   15

I offer no apology only
This plea:

When I am frayed and stained and drizzled at the end
Please someone cut a square and put me in a quilt
That I might keep some child warm   20

And some old person with no one else to talk to
Will hear my whispers

And cuddle
Near

Explorations of the Text—"Ego Tripping"

1. What is the speaker's view of herself? What character traits does she attribute to herself?
2. How is the title a clue to the meaning of the poem? In what ways does the poem extend its themes beyond the ego?
3. How does the poet use such devices from oral tradition as exaggeration and **anaphora** (repetition) to create an impact?
4. How does humor contribute to the poem's effect?
5. Identify the historical and anthropological references in the poem. How do these allusions enrich this work?
6. Contrast the speaker's sense of self with the persona's identity in "Suicide Note."

The Reading/Writing Connection

1. Do a double-entry for a section of the poem as preparation for one of the assigned ideas for writing.
2. "Think" Topic: What are the advantages and disadvantages of **hyperbole** (exaggeration)? Use details from this poem to support your position.

Ideas for Writing

1. Analyze the voice and tone of the speaker.
2. Write a short essay that explicates one of the allusions in the poem.
3. Nikki Giovanni published "Ego Tripping" in 1979 and "Quilts" in 2007. She wrote "Ego Tripping" when she was young while "Quilts" depicts the struggles of an older woman. Compare and contrast the character of the speaker, the point of view and tone, and the imagery used to depict the self in this work with that of "Ego Tripping." What do you conclude?

Anne Sexton (1928–1974)

Cinderella 1971

You always read about it:
the plumber with twelve children
who wins the Irish Sweepstakes.
From toilets to riches.

That story.　　　　　　　　　　　　　　　　　　　5
Or the nursemaid,
some luscious sweet from Denmark
who captures the oldest son's heart.
From diapers to Dior.
That story.　　　　　　　　　　　　　　　　　　10

Or a milkman who serves the wealthy,
eggs, cream, butter, yogurt, milk,
the white truck like an ambulance
who goes into real estate
and makes a pile.　　　　　　　　　　　　　　　15
From homogenized to martinis at lunch.

Or the charwoman
who is on the bus when it cracks up
and collects enough from the insurance.
From mops to Bonwit Teller.[1]　　　　　　　　20
That story.

Once
the wife of a rich man was on her deathbed
and she said to her daughter Cinderella:
Be devout. Be good. Then I will smile　　　　　25
down from heaven in the seam of a cloud.
The man took another wife who had
two daughters, pretty enough
but with hearts like blackjacks.
Cinderella was their maid.　　　　　　　　　　30
She slept on the sooty hearth each night
and walked around looking like Al Jolson.
Her father brought presents home from town,
jewels and gowns for the other women
but the twig of a tree for Cinderella.　　　　　35
She planted that twig on her mother's grave
and it grew to a tree where a white dove sat.
Whenever she wished for anything the dove
would drop it like an egg upon the ground.
The bird is important, my dears, so heed him.　　40

Next came the ball, as you all know.
It was a marriage market.
The prince was looking for a wife.
All but Cinderella were preparing
and gussying up for the big event.　　　　　　45
Cinderella begged to go too.

---

[1]**Bonwit Teller:** An exclusive department store in New York City.

Her stepmother threw a dish of lentils
into the cinders and said: Pick them
up in an hour and you shall go.
The white dove brought all his friends;   50
all the warm wings of the fatherland came,
and picked up the lentils in a jiffy.
No, Cinderella, said the stepmother,
you have no clothes and cannot dance.
That's the way with stepmothers.   55

Cinderella went to the tree at the grave
and cried forth like a gospel singer:
Mama! Mama! My turtledove,
send me to the prince's ball!
The bird dropped down a golden dress   60
and delicate little gold slippers.
Rather a large package for a simple bird.
So she went. Which is no surprise.
Her stepmother and sisters didn't
recognize her without her cinder face   65
and the prince took her hand on the spot
and danced with no other the whole day.

As nightfall came she thought she'd better
get home. The prince walked her home
and she disappeared into the pigeon house   70
and although the prince took an axe and broke
it open she was gone. Back to her cinders.
These events repeated themselves for three days.
However on the third day the prince
covered the palace steps with cobbler's wax   75
and Cinderella's gold shoe stuck upon it.
Now he would find whom the shoe fit
and find his strange dancing girl for keeps.
He went to their house and the two sisters
were delighted because they had lovely feet.   80
The eldest went into a room to try the slipper on
but her big toe got in the way so she simply
sliced it off and put on the slipper.
The prince rode away with her until the white dove
told him to look at the blood pouring forth.   85
That is the way with amputations.
They don't just heal up like a wish.
The other sister cut off her heel
but the blood told as blood will.
The prince was getting tired.   90
He began to feel like a shoe salesman.
But he gave it one last try.

This time Cinderella fit into the shoe
like a love letter into its envelope.

At the wedding ceremony   95
the two sisters came to curry favor
and the white dove pecked their eyes out.
Two hollow spots were left
like soup spoons.

Cinderella and the prince   100
lived, they say, happily ever after,
like two dolls in a museum case
never bothered by diapers or dust,
never arguing over the timing of an egg,
never telling the same story twice,   105
never getting a middle-aged spread,
their darling smiles pasted on for eternity.
Regular Bobbsey Twins.[2]
That story.

Explorations of the Text

1. Characterize the speaker's point of view and tone. List the particular words that convey tone. What is their impact?
2. Why does Sexton introduce the Cinderella story with the "toilet to riches" stories in the first four stanzas? What purpose do they serve? Why does she repeat "that story"?

3. Research Perrault's "Cinderella." How does Sexton change the story through her use of figurative language and imagery? Contrast the original text with Sexton's imaginative rendering of the tale.
4. Analyze the closing stanza's commentary on the "rags to riches" theme. Discuss Sexton's use of irony.

The Reading/Writing Connection

1. Do a double-entry notebook for one section of the poem. What is the impact of the imagery, figurative language, form, and diction?
2. This poem is drawn from Sexton's poetry volume, *Transformations,* which contains her imaginative retellings of many other fairy tales. You may consult that volume as inspiration. Using Sexton's work as a model, create your own retelling of a fairy tale or a children's story with which you are familiar.

Ideas for Writing

1. How do the writers in the fairy tale cluster in this chapter depict the mythic battle between good and evil?
2. Compare Sexton's treatment of romance with a selected poem about love in Chapter 7.

---

[2] **Bobbsey Twins:** Twins in a series of children's books published in the 1950s.

Shirley Geok-Lin Lim (1944–)

Ah Mah 1998

Grandmother was smaller
than me at eight. Had she
been a child forever?

Helpless, hopeless, chin sharp
as a knuckle, fan face   5
hardly half-opened, not a scrap

of fat anywhere: she tottered
in black silk, leaning on
handmaids, on two tortured

fins. At sixty, his sons all   10
married, grandfather bought
her, Soochow flower song girl.

Every bone in her feet
had been broken, bound tighter
than any neighbor's sweet   15

daughter's. Ten toes and instep
curled inwards, yellow petals
of chrysanthemum, wrapped

in gold cloth. He bought the young
face, small knobby breasts   20
he swore he'd not dress in sarong

of maternity. Each night
he held her feet in his palms,
like lotus in the tight

hollows of celestial lakes.   25
In his calloused flesh, her
weightless soles, cool, and slack,

clenched in his stranger's fever.

Explorations of the Text

1. This autobiographical poem is about
the speaker's grandmother. Explore
the granddaughter's attitude toward
her grandmother. What do her questions in stanza 1, her description of her
grandmother's past, and her grandmother's bound feet reveal? Why are the
grandmother's feet described as "yellow
petals/of chrysanthemum" or "lotus"?
What does the flower imagery imply?

2. Why does the poet break up the narrative moments in separate stanzas? What is the significance of the final line: "clenched in his stranger's fever"?
3. Shirley Geok-Lin Lim alludes to the myth of the mermaid in her portrayal of her grandmother. According to the myth, when a mermaid ventures out of the water, she is unable to walk and slithers onto the land. How does this allusion enlarge the portrayal of her grandmother?
4. Compare and contrast Geok-Lin Lim's treatment of fairy tale motifs with Sexton's treatment in "Cinderella."

The Reading/Writing Connection

1. "Think" Topic: How does the speaker view her heritage? Compare her treatment of her lineage with Agha Shahid Ali's in "Snowmen" (Chapter 6).
2. Foot binding was a common practice among the upper classes in traditional Confucian Chinese society until the Communist Revolution in 1948–1949 when the practice was outlawed. Why do you think foot binding was practiced? What other rituals, practices, or social codes in other past or present cultures have constrained women (see "The Yellow Wallpaper" in Chapter 7)? What is the attitude toward foot binding portrayed in the poem?

Ideas for Writing

1. Often we have a complex relationship with our heritage—positive and negative attitudes toward our pasts. Compare and contrast several writers' views of their lineage, for example, Cathy Song's "Lost Sister," Nikki Giovanni's "Quilts," and Etheridge Knight's "The Idea of Ancestry" (Chapter 6).

2. **Write an Argument:** What have women throughout the ages done to themselves in order to become beautiful? For example, recently, some women in New York City had their toes broken in order to wear pointy shoes. Or think about such shows as *The Swan* or *Extreme Makover*. Discuss the significance of these cultural practices. Why would women subject themselves to such torture in order to achieve beauty? Or what do men do to enhance their masculinity (i.e., taking steroids)? Do you think the pain is worth it?

Neal Bowers *(1948–)*

Driving Lessons   *2003*

I learned to drive in a parking lot
on Sundays, when the stores were closed—
slow maneuvers out beyond the light-poles,
no destination, just the ritual of clutch and gas,
my father clenching with the grinding gears,
finally giving up and leaving my mother
to buck and plunge with me and say,
repeatedly, "Once more. Try just once more."

5

She walked out on him once
when I was six or seven, my father   10
driving beside her, slow as a beginner,
pleading, my baby brother and I
crying out the windows, "Mama, don't go!"
It was a scene to break your heart
or make you laugh—those wailing kids,   15
a woman walking briskly with a suitcase,
the slow car following like a faithful dog.

I don't know why she finally got in
and let us take her back
to whatever she had made up her mind to leave;   20
but the old world swallowed her up
as soon as she opened that door,
and the other life she might have lived
lay down forever in its dark infancy.

Sometimes, when I'm home, driving   25
through the old neighborhoods, stopping
in front of each little house we rented,
my stillborn other life gets in,
the boy I would have been if
my mother had kept on walking.   30
He wants to be just like her,
far away and gone forever, wants
me to press down on the gas;
but however fast I squeal away,
the shaggy past keeps loping behind,   35
sniffing every turn.

When I stop in the weedy parking lot,
the failed stores of the old mall
make a dark wall straight ahead;
and I'm alone again, until my parents get in,   40
unchanged after all these years,
my father, impatient, my mother
trying hard to smile, waiting for me
to steer my way across this emptiness.

Stephen Dunn   *(1939–)*

The Sacred   *1989*

After the teacher asked if anyone had
          a sacred place
and the students fidgeted and shrank

in their chairs, the most serious of them all
> said it was his car,   5
being in it alone, his tape deck playing

things he'd chosen, and others knew the truth
> had been spoken
and began speaking about their rooms,

their hiding places, but the car kept coming up,   10
> the car in motion,
music filling it, and sometimes one other person

who understood the bright altar of the dashboard
> and how far away
a car could take him from the need   15

to speak, or to answer, the key
> in having a key
and putting it in, and going.

Barbara Hamby   *(1952–   )*

Ode to My 1977 Toyota   *2003*

Engine like a Singer sewing machine, where have you
> not carried me—to dance class, grocery shopping,
into the heart of darkness and back again? O the fruit
> you've transported—cherries, peaches, blueberries,
watermelons, thousands of Fuji apples—books,   5
> and all my dark thoughts, the giddy ones, too,
like bottles of champagne popped at the wedding of two people
> who will pass each other on the street as strangers
in twenty years. Ronald Reagan was president when I walked
> into Big Chief Motors and saw you glimmering   10
on the lot like a slice of broiled mahi mahi or sushi
> without its topknot of tuna. Remember the months
I drove you to work singing "Some Enchanted Evening"?
> Those were scary times. All I thought about
was getting on I-10 with you and not stopping. Would you   15
> have made it to New Orleans? What would our life
have been like there? I'd forgotten about poetry. Thank God,
> I remembered her. She saved us both. We were young
together. Now we're not. College boys stop us at traffic lights
> and tell me how cool you are. Like an ice cube, I say,   20
though you've never had air conditioning. Who needed it?
> I would have missed so many smells without you—

confederate jasmine, magnolia blossoms, the briny sigh
   of the Gulf of Mexico, rotting 'possums scattered
along 319 between Sopchoppy and Panacea. How many holes   25
   are there in the ballet shoes in your back seat?
How did that pair of men's white loafers end up in your trunk?
   Why do I have so many questions, and why
are the answers like the animals that dart in front of your headlights
   as we drive home from the coast, the Milky Way   30
strung across the black velvet bowl of the sky like the tiara
   of some impossibly fat empress who rules the universe
but doesn't know if tomorrow is December or Tuesday or June first.

Explorations of the Text

1. In each of these poems, the car functions as a symbol. What does the car represent?

2. In Neal Bowers' "Driving Lessons," what do the driving lessons suggest about the relationship between his parents? Why does he create the image of "a faithful dog" to portray both the car "driven by his father" and the "shaggy past. . . ."?

3. Does the journey, the road trip, in each poem open up or close off possibility?

4. In Stephen Dunn's "The Sacred," why is the car "sacred"? What is the significance of "the key"?

5. How do cars suggest and evoke memories of a stage of one's life? Refer to Barbara Hamby's "Ode to My 1977 Toyota."

The Reading/Writing Connection

1. Describe your car. Is it important to you?

2. **Write an Argument:** Argue pro or con. My car is a "sacred place."

3. Write about a "first" associated with a car: your driving test, the first time that you drove alone, or a road trip that you took with your family or with your friends.

Ideas for Writing

1. **Write an Argument:** Do road trips offer an escape from everyday life or problems, or do they offer opportunities for personal growth? The Beat writers, for instance, saw road trips as a way to escape the confines of a conventional, humdrum existence and find self-fulfillment. Create a cause-effect argument about the impact of road trips.

2. Write a descriptive essay about a "sacred place" in your life.

Metamorphoses/Poetry

Cathy Song   *(1955–   )*

Lost Sister   *1983*

1

In China,
even the peasants
named their first daughters
Jade—
the stone that in the far fields   5
could moisten the dry season,
could make men move mountains
for the healing green of the inner hills
glistening like slices of winter melon.

And the daughters were grateful: 10
They never left home.
To move freely was a luxury
stolen from them at birth.
Instead, they gathered patience,
learning to walk in shoes   15
the size of teacups,
without breaking—
the arc of their movements
as dormant as the rooted willow,
as redundant as the farmyard hens.   20
But they traveled far
in surviving,
learning to stretch the family rice,
to quiet the demons,
the noisy stomachs.   25

2

There is a sister
across the ocean,
who relinquished her name,
diluting jade green
with the blue of the Pacific.   30
Rising with a tide of locusts,
she swarmed with others
to inundate another shore.

In America,
there are many roads
and women can stride along with men.

35

But in another wilderness,
the possibilities,
the loneliness,
can strangulate like jungle vines.
The meager provisions and sentiments
of once belonging—
fermented roots, Mah-Jong[1] tiles and firecrackers—set but
a flimsy household
in a forest of nightless cities.
A giant snake rattles above,
spewing black clouds into your kitchen.
Dough-faced landlords
slip in and out of your keyholes,
making claims you don't understand,
tapping into your communication systems
of laundry lines and restaurant chains.

40

45

50

You find you need China:
your one fragile identification,
a jade link
handcuffed to your wrist.
You remember your mother
who walked for centuries.
footless—
and like her,
you have left no footprints,
but only because
there is an ocean in between,
the unremitting space of your rebellion.

55

60

Naomi Shihab Nye   *(1952–   )*

Biography of an Armenian Schoolgirl   *1993*

I have lived in the room of stone
where voices become bones
buried under us long ago.
You could dig for years
uncovering the same sweet dust.

5

---

[1]**Mah-Jong:** Chinese game, similar to dominoes.

My hands dream crescent-shaped cakes,
trapped moons on a narrow veined earth.
All day I am studying my hands—giving them
    new things to hold.

Travel, I say. They become boats.   10
Go—the bird squirms to detach from the arm.
Across the courtyards, a radio rises up and explodes.

What is the history of Europe to us if we cannot
    choose our own husbands?
Yesterday my father met with the widower,   15
    the man with no hair.
How will I sleep with him, I who have never slept
    away from my mother?

Once I bought bread from the vendor with the
    humped back.   20
I carried it home singing,
the days had doors in them
that would swing open in front of me.

Now I copy the alphabets of three languages,
imagining the loops in my Arabic letters are eyes.   25
What you do when you are tired of what you see,

what happens to the gray body
when it is laid in the earth,
these are the subjects which concern me.
But they teach algebra.   30
They pull our hair back and examine our nails.

Every afternoon, predictable passage of sun
    across a wall.
I would fly out of here. Travel, I say.
I would go so far away my life would be   35
    a small thing behind me.

They teach physics, chemistry.
I throw my book out the window,
watch the pages scatter like wings.
I stitch the professor's[1] jacket   40
to the back of his chair.

---

[1] **professor:** A high school teacher.

There is something else we were born for.
I almost remember it. While I write,
a ghost writes on the same tablet,
achieves a different sum.   45

Louise Erdrich *(1954–)*

Indian Boarding School: The Runaways   *1984*

Home's the place we head for in our sleep.
Boxcars stumbling north in dreams
don't wait for us. We catch them on the run.
The rails, old lacerations that we love,
shoot parallel across the face and break   5
just under Turtle Mountains.[1] Riding scars
you can't get lost. Home is the place they cross.

The lame guard strikes a match and makes the dark
less tolerant. We watch through cracks in boards
as the land starts rolling, rolling till it hurts   10
to be here, cold in regulation clothes.
We know the sheriff's waiting at midrun
to take us back. His car is dumb and warm.
The highway doesn't rock, it only hums
like a wing of long insults. The worn-down welts   15
of ancient punishments lead back and forth.
All runaways wear dresses, long green ones,
the color you would think shame was. We scrub
the sidewalks down because it's shameful work.
Our brushes cut the stone in watered arcs   20
and in the soak frail outlines shiver clear
a moment, things us kids pressed on the dark
face before it hardened, place, remembering
delicate old injuries, the spines of names and leaves.

Janice Mirikitani *(1942–)*

Suicide Note   *1983*

> *. . . An Asian American college student was reported to have jumped to her
> death from her dormitory window. Her body was found two days later under a
> deep cover of snow. Her suicide note contained an apology to her parents for having
> received less than a perfect four point grade average . . .*

---

[1]**Turtle Mountains:** The location of a Chippewa Indian reservation in North Dakota.

How many notes written . . .
ink smeared like birdprints in snow.

not good enough   not pretty enough   not smart enough
dear mother and father.
I apologize   5
for disappointing you.
I've worked very hard,
        not good enough
harder, perhaps to please you.
If only I were a son, shoulders broad   10
as the sunset threading through pine,
I would see the light in my mother's
eyes, or the golden pride reflected
in my father's dream
of my wide, male hands worthy of work   15
and comfort.
I would swagger through life
muscled and bold and assured,
drawing praises to me
like currents in the bed of wind, virile   20
with confidence.
    not good enough   not strong enough   not good enough

I apologize.
Tasks do not come easily.
Each failure, a glacier.   25
Each disapproval, a bootprint.
Each disappointment,
ice above my river.
So I have worked hard.
        not good enough   30
My sacrifice I will drop
bone by bone, perched
on the ledge of my womanhood,
fragile as wings.
        not strong enough   35
It is snowing steadily
surely not good weather
for flying—this sparrow
sillied and dizzied by the wind
on the edge.   40
        not smart enough
I make this ledge my altar
to offer penance.
This air will not hold me,
The snow burdens my crippled wings,   45

my tears drop like bitter cloth
softly into the gutter below.
    not good enough   not strong enough   not smart enough
          Choices thin as shaved
          ice. Notes shredded   50
          drift like snow
on my broken body,
covers me like whispers
of sorries
sorries.   55
Perhaps when they find me
they will bury
my bird bones beneath
a sturdy pine
and scatter my feathers like   60
unspoken song
over this white and cold and silent
breast of earth.

Ha Jin *(1956–)*

The Past   *1996*

I have supposed my past is a part of myself.
As my shadow appears whenever I'm in the sun
the past cannot be thrown off and its weight
must be borne, or I will become another man.

But I saw someone wall his past into a garden   5
whose produce is always in fashion.
If you enter his property without permission
he will welcome you with a watchdog or a gun.

I saw someone set up his past as a harbor.
Wherever it sails, his boat is safe—   10
if a storm comes, he can always head for home.
His voyage is the adventure of a kite.

I saw someone drop his past like trash.
He buried it and shed it altogether.
He has shown me that without the past   15
one can also move ahead and get somewhere.

Like a shroud my past surrounds me,
but I will cut it and stitch it,
to make good shoes with it,
shoes that fit my feet.   20

General Ulysses S. Awesome

Who Places Things Exactly   *2005*

where they
don't belong

is he who knows
how hard

it is to find   5
things, gone

from where
he knows to look.

Explorations of the Text

1. What kinds of conflicts or changes do these speakers experience? Are these conflicts resolved? Do the changes prompt personal growth and identity development?

2. What metaphors in each poem suggest metamorphoses? Are the images positive or negative? What do they suggest about a process of change?

3. Explore the attitudes toward home expressed in the works.

4. What are the different speakers' dreams and desires? Do you think that they will be fulfilled?

The Reading/Writing Connection

1. Write a letter expressing who you are—where you come from, what your interests are, and/or what your goals are. Or pen a letter in the voice of one of the speakers from one of the poems in the cluster.

2. Explore a moment of change or transition in your own life. Some possibilities include a coming-of-age experience in high school, an awareness that you experienced about the state of the world, a first in your life, or the transition from high school to college.

Ideas for Writing

1. **Write an Argument:** How many ways can a person be "lost"? Discuss the ways in which the personae in the poems in this cluster are "lost." Will they find themselves? You also may refer to Gretel Ehrlich's "Looking for a Lost Dog," which also appears in this chapter.

DRAMA

Paula Vogel *(1951–)*

How I Learned to Drive   *1998*

A VOICE announces, as the house lights dim: Safety first—you and driver education.

Then the sound of a key turning the ignition of a car. Li'l Bit steps into a spotlight on the stage; "well-endowed," she is a softer-looking woman in the present time than she was at seventeen.

LI'L BIT. Sometimes to tell a secret, you first have to teach a lesson. We're going to start our lesson tonight on an early, warm summer evening.

In a parking lot overlooking the Beltsville Agricultural Farms in suburban Maryland.

Less than a mile away, the crumbling concrete of U.S. One wends its way past one room revival churches, the porno drive-in, and boarded up motels with For Sale signs tumbling down.

Like I said, it's a warm summer evening.

Here on the land the department of Agriculture owns, the smell of sleeping farm animal is thick on the air. The smells of clover and hay mix in with the smells of the leather dashboard. You can still imagine how Maryland used to be, before the malls took over. This countryside was once dotted with farmhouses—from their porches you could have witnessed the civil war raging in the front fields.

Oh yes. There's a moon over Maryland tonight, that spills into the car where I sit beside a man old enough to be—did I mention how still the night is? Damp soil and tranquil air. It's the kind of night that makes a middle-aged man with a mortgage feel like a country boy again.

It's 1969. And I am very old, very cynical of the world, and I know it all. In short, I am seventeen years old, parking off a dark lane with a married man on an early summer night.

(Lights up on two chairs facing front—or a Buick Riviera, if you will. Waiting patiently, with a smile on his face, Peck sits sniffing the night air. Li'l Bit climbs in beside him, seventeen years old and tense. Throughout the following, the two sit facing directly front. They do not touch. Their bodies remain passive. Only their facial expressions emote.)

PECK. Ummm. I love the smell of your hair.
LI'L BIT. Uh-huh.
PECK. Oh, Lord. Ummmm. *(Beat.)* A man could die happy like this.
LI'L BIT. Well, *don't.*
PECK. What shampoo is this?
LI'L BIT. Herbal Essence.

5

PECK. Herbal Essence. I'm gonna buy me some. Herbal Essence. And when I'm all alone in the house, I'm going to get into the bathtub, and uncap the bottle and—

LI'L BIT. —Be good.

PECK. What?

LI'L BIT. Stop being . . . bad.

PECK. What did you think I was going to say? What do you think I'm going to do with the shampoo?

LI'L BIT. I don't want to know. I don't want to hear it.

PECK. I'm going to wash my hair. That's all.

LI'L BIT. Oh.

PECK. What did you think I was going to do?

LI'L BIT. Nothing. . . . I don't know. Something . . . nasty.

PECK. With shampoo? Lord, gal—your mind!

LI'L BIT. And whose fault is it?

PECK. Not mine. I've got the mind of a boy scout.

LI'L BIT. Right. A horny boy scout.

PECK. Boy scouts are always horny. What do you think the first Merit Badge is for?

LI'L BIT. There. You're going to be nasty again.

PECK. Oh, no. I'm good. Very good.

LI'L BIT. It's getting late.

PECK. Don't change the subject. I was talking about how good I am. *(Beat.)* Are you ever gonna let me show you how good I am?

LI'L BIT. Don't go over the line now.

PECK. I won't. I'm not gonna do anything you don't want me to do.

LI'L BIT. That's right.

PECK. And I've been good all week.

LI'L BIT. You have?

PECK. Yes. All week. Not a single drink.

LI'L BIT. Good boy.

PECK. Do I get a reward? For not drinking?

LI'L BIT. A small one. It's getting late.

PECK. Just let me undo you. I'll do you back up.

LI'L BIT. All right. But be quick about it. *(Peck pantomimes undoing Li'l Bit's brassiere with one hand.)* You know, that's amazing. The way you can undo the hooks through my blouse with one hand.

PECK. Years of practice.

LI'L BIT. You would make an incredible brain surgeon with that dexterity.

PECK. I'll bet Clyde—what's the name of the boy taking you to the prom?

LI'L BIT. Claude Souders.

PECK. Claude Souders. I'll bet it takes him two hands, lights on, and you helping him on to get to first base.

LI'L BIT. Maybe. *(Beat.)*

PECK. Can I . . . kiss them? Please?

LI'L BIT. I don't know.

PECK. Don't make a grown man beg.

LI'L BIT. Just one kiss.

PECK. I'm going to lift your blouse.

LI'L BIT. It's a little cold. *(Peck laughs gently.)*

PECK. That's not why you're shivering. *(They sit, perfectly still, for a long moment of* 50 *silence. Peck makes gentle, concentric circles with his thumbs in the air in front of him.)* How does that feel? *(Li'l Bit closes her eyes, carefully keeps her voice calm.)*

LI'L BIT. It's . . . okay. *(Sacred music, organ music or boy's choir, swells beneath the following.)*

PECK. I tell you, you can keep all the cathedrals of Europe. Just give me a second with these—these celestial orbs—*(Peck bows his head as if praying. But he is kissing her nipple. Li'l Bit, eyes still closed, rears back her head on the leather Buick car seat.)*

LI'L BIT. Uncle Peck—we've got to go. I've got graduation rehearsal at school tomorrow morning. And you should get on home to Aunt Mary—

PECK. —All right, Li'l Bit.

LI'L BIT. —*Don't* call me that no more. *(Calmer.)* Any more. I'm a big girl now, Uncle 55 Peck. As you know. *(Li'l Bit pantomimes refastening her bra behind her back.)*

PECK. That you are. Going on eighteen. Kittens will turn into cats. *(Sighs.)*—I live all week long for these few minutes with you—you know that?

LI'L BIT. I'll drive.

VOICE. *(Cutting in.)* Idling in the neutral gear. *(Sound of car revving cuts off the sacred music; Li'l Bit, now an adult, rises out of the car and comes to us.)*

LI'L BIT. In most families, relatives get names like, "Junior," or "Brother," or "Bubba." In my family, if we call someone "Big Papa," it's not because he's tall. In my family, folks tend to get nicknamed for their genitalia. Uncle Peck, for example. My Mama's adage was "the titless wonder," and my cousin Bobby got branded for life as "B.B."—*(In unison with Greek Chorus.)*

LI'L BIT.	**GREEK CHORUS.**	60
"For blue balls."	"For blue balls."	

(Female Greek Chorus, as Mother, continues.)

FEMALE GREEK CHORUS. *(As Mother.)* And of course, we were so excited to have a baby girl—that when the nurse brought you in and said "It's a girl! It's a baby girl!" I just had to see for myself. So we whipped your diapers down and parted your chubby little legs—and right between your legs there was—*(Peck has come over during the above and chimes along.)*

PECK.	**GREEK CHORUS.**
"Just a little bit."	"Just a little bit."

FEMALE GREEK CHORUS. *(As Mother.)* And when you were born, you were so tiny that you fit in Uncle Peck's outstretched hand. *(Peck stretches his hand out.)*

PECK. Now that's a fact. I held you, one day old, right in this hand. *(A traffic signal is projected of a bicycle in a circle with a diagonal red slash.)*

LI'L BIT. Even with my family background, I was sixteen or so before I realized that 65 pedophilia did not mean people who loved to bicycle. . . .

VOICE. *(Intruding.)* Driving in first gear.

LI'L BIT. 1969. A typical family dinner.

FEMALE GREEK CHORUS. *(As Mother.)* Look, Grandma. Li'l Bit's getting to be as big in the bust as you are.

LI'L BIT. Mother! Could we please change the subject?

TEENAGE GREEK CHORUS. *(As Grandmother.)* Well, I hope you are buying her 70 some decent bras. I never had a decent bra, growing up in the Depression, and now my shoulders are just crippled—crippled from the weight hanging on my shoulders—the dents from my bra straps are big enough to put your finger in—here, let me show you—*(As Grandmother starts to open her blouse.)*

LI'L BIT. Grandma! Please don't undress at the dinner table.

PECK. I thought the entertainment came *after* the dinner.

LI'L BIT. *(To us.)* This is how it always starts. My grandfather, Big Papa will chime in next with—

MALE GREEK CHORUS. *(As Grandfather.)* Yup. If Li'l Bit gets any bigger, we're gonna haveta buy her a wheelbarrow to carry in front of her—

LI'L BIT. —Damn it—   75

PECK. —How about those Redskins on Sunday, Big Papa?

LI'L BIT. *(To us.)*—The only sport Big Papa followed was chasing Grandma around the house—

MALE GREEK CHORUS. *(As Grandfather.)*—Or we could write to Kate Smith. Ask her for somma her used brassieres she don't want anymore—she could maybe give to Li'l Bit here—

LI'L BIT. I can't stand it. I can't.

PECK. Now, honey, that's just their way—   80

FEMALE GREEK CHORUS. *(As Mother.)* I tell you, Grandma, Li'l Bit's at that age. She's so sensitive, you can't say boo—

LI'L BIT. I'd like some privacy, that's all. Okay? Some goddamn privacy—

PECK. Well, at least she didn't use the savior's name—

LI'L BIT. *(To us.)* And Big Papa wouldn't let a dead dog lie. No sirree:

MALE GREEK CHORUS. *(As Grandfather)* Well, she'd better stop being so sensitive.   85
'Cause five minutes before Li'l Bit turns the corner, her tits turn first—

LI'L BIT. *(Starting to rise from the table.)*—That's it. That's it.

PECK. Li'l Bit, you can't let him get to you. Then he wins.

LI'L BIT. I hate him. *Hate* him.

PECK. That's fine. But hate him and eat a good dinner at the same time. *(Li'l Bit calms down and sits with perfect dignity.)*

LI'L BIT. The gumbo is really good, Grandma.   90

MALE GREEK CHORUS. *(As Grandfather.)* A'course, Li'l Bit's got a big surprise coming for her when she goes to that fancy college this fall—

PECK. Big Papa—let it go.

MALE GREEK CHORUS. *(As Grandfather.)* What does she need a college degree for? She's got all the credentials she'll need on her chest—

LI'L BIT. —Maybe I want to learn things. Read. Rise above my cracker background—

PECK. —Whoa, now, Li'l Bit—   95

MALE GREEK CHORUS. *(As Grandfather.)* What kind of things do you want to read?

LI'L BIT. There's a whole semester course, for example, on Shakespeare—*(Greek Chorus, as Grandfather, laughs until he weeps.)*

MALE GREEK CHORUS. *(As Grandfather.)* Shakespeare. That's a good one. Shakespeare is really going to help you in life.

PECK. I think it's wonderful. And on scholarship!

MALE GREEK CHORUS. *(As Grandfather.)* How is Shakespeare going to help her   100
lie on her back in the dark? *(Li'l Bit is on her feet.)*

LI'L BIT. You're getting old, Big Papa. You are going to die—Very very soon. Maybe even *tonight.* And when you get to heaven, God's going to be a beautiful black woman in a long white robe. She's gonna look at your chart and say: uh-oh. Fornication. Doguly mean with blood-relatives. Oh. Uh-oh. Voted for George Wallace. Well, one last chance: if you can name the play, all will be forgiven—And then she'll quote:—"The quality of mercy is not strained—" Your answer?—oh, too bad—*Merchant of Venice:* Act IV, scene iii—and then she'll send your ass to fry in hell with all the other crackers. Excuse me, please. *(To us.)* And as I left the house, I would always hear Big Papa say:

MALE GREEK CHORUS. *(As Grandfather.)* Lucy, your daughter's got a mouth on her. Well, no sense in wasting good gumbo. Pass me her plate, Mama.

LI'L BIT. And Aunt Mary would come up to Uncle Peck:

FEMALE GREEK CHORUS. *(As Aunt Mary.)* Peck, go after her, will you? You're the only one she'll listen to when she gets like this.

PECK. She just needs to cool off.   105

FEMALE GREEK CHORUS. *(As Aunt Mary.)* Please, honey—Grandma's been on her feet cooking all day.

PECK. All right.

LI'L BIT. And as he left the room, Aunt Mary would say:

FEMALE GREEK CHORUS. *(As Aunt Mary.)* Peck's so good with them when they get to be this age. *(Li'l Bit has stormed to another part of the stage, her back turned, weeping with a teenage fury. Peck, cautiously, as if stalking a deer, comes to her. She turns away even more. He waits a bit.)*

PECK. I don't suppose you're talking to family. *(No response.)* Does it help that I'm   110
in-law?

LI'L BIT. Don't you dare make fun of this.

PECK. I'm not. There's nothing funny about this. *(Beat.)* Although I'll bet when Big Papa is about to meet his maker, he'll remember *The Merchant of Venice.*

LI'L BIT. I've got to get away from here.

PECK. You're going away. Soon. Here, take this. *(Peck hands her his folded handkerchief. Li'l Bit uses it, noisily. Hands it back. Without her seeing, he reverently puts it back.)*

LI'L BIT. I hate this family.   115

PECK. Your grandfather's ignorant. And you're right—he's going to die soon. But he's family. Family is . . . family.

LI'L BIT. Grown-ups are always saying that. Family.

PECK. Well, when you get a little older, you'll see what we're saying.

LI'L BIT. Uh-huh. So family is another acquired taste, like French kissing?

PECK. Come again?   120

LI'L BIT. You know, at first it really grosses you out, but in time you grow to like it?

PECK. Girl, you are . . . a handful.

LI'L BIT. Uncle Peck—you have the keys to your car?

PECK. Where do you want to go?

LI'L BIT. Just up the road.   125

PECK. I'll come with you.

LI'L BIT. No—please? I just need to—to drive for a little bit. Alone. *(Peck tosses her the keys.)*

PECK. When can I see you alone again?

LI'L BIT. Tonight. *(Li'l Bit crosses to C. while lights dim around her.)*

THE VOICE. *(Directs.)* Shifting forward from first to second gear.   130

LI'L BIT. There were a lot of rumors about why I got kicked out of that fancy school in 1970. Some say I got caught with a man in my room. Some say as a kid on scholarship I fooled around with a rich man's daughter. *(Li'l Bit smiles innocently at us.)*

I'm not talking.

But the real truth was I had a constant companion in my dorm room—who was less than discrete. Canadian V.O. A fifth a day.

1970. A Nixon recession. I slept on the floors of friends who were out of work themselves. Took factory work when I could find it. A string of dead-end day jobs that didn't last very long.

What I did, most nights, was cruise the Beltway and the back roads of Maryland, where there was still country, past the battlefields and farm houses. Racing in a 1965 mustang—and as long as I had gasoline for my car and whiskey for me, the nights would pass. Fully tanked, I would speed past the churches and the trees on the bend, thinking just one notch of the steering wheel would be all it would take, and yet some . . . reflex took over. My hands on the wheel in the nine and three o'clock position—I never so much got a ticket. He taught me well.

A VOICE. *(Announces.)* You and the reverse gear.

LI'L BIT. Back up. 1968. On the Eastern Shore. A celebration dinner. *(Li'l Bit joins Peck at a table in a restaurant.)*

PECK. Feeling better, Missy?

LI'L BIT. The bathroom's really amazing here, Uncle Peck! They have these little soaps—instead of borax or something—and they're in the shape of shells. 135

PECK. I'll have to take a trip to the gentleman's room just to see.

LI'L BIT. How did you know about this place?

PECK. This Inn is famous on the Eastern Shore—it's been open since the 17th century. And I know how you like history—*(Li'l Bit is shy and pleased.)*

LI'L BIT. It's great.

PECK. And you've just done your first, legal, long-distance drive. You must be hungry. 140

LI'L BIT. I'm starved.

PECK. I would suggest a dozen oysters to start, and the crab imperial—*(Li'l Bit is genuinely agog.)*—You might be interested to know the town history. When the British sailed up this very river in the dead of night—see outside where I'm pointing?—they were going to bombard the heck out of this town. But the town fathers were ready for them. They crept up all the trees with lanterns so that the British would think they saw the town lights and they aimed their cannons too high. And that's why the Inn is still here for business today.

LI'L BIT. That's a great story.

PECK. *(Casually.)* Would you like to start with a cocktail?

LI'L BIT. You're not—you're not going to start drinking, are you, Uncle Peck? 145

PECK. Not me. I told you, as long as you're with me, I'll never drink. I asked you if *you'd* like a cocktail before dinner. It's nice to have a little something with the oysters.

LI'L BIT. But—I'm not . . . legal. We could get arrested. Uncle Peck, they'll never believe I'm twenty-one!

PECK. So? Today we celebrate your driver's license—on the first try. This establishment reminds me a lot of places back home.

LI'L BIT. What does that mean?

PECK. In South Carolina, like here on the Eastern Shore, they're—*(Searches for the* 150 *right euphemism.)*—"European." Not so puritanical. And very understanding if gentlemen wish to escort very attractive young ladies who might want a before-dinner cocktail. If you want one, I'll order one.

LI'L BIT. Well—sure. Just . . . one. *(The Female Greek Chorus appears in a spot.)*

FEMALE GREEK CHORUS. *(As Mother.)* A mother's guide to social drinking:

A lady never gets sloppy—she may, however, get tipsy and a little gay.

Never drink on an empty stomach. Avail yourself of the bread basket and generous portions of butter. *Slather* the butter on your bread.

Sip your drink, slowly, let the beverage linger in your mouth—interspersed with interesting, fascinating conversation. Sip, never . . . slurp or gulp. Your glass should always be three-quarters full when his glass is empty.

Stay away from "ladies'" drinks: drinks like pink ladies, sloe gin fizzes, daiquiris, gold cadillacs, Long Island iced teas, margaritas, piña coladas, mai tais, planters punch, white Russians, black Russians, red Russians, melon balls, blue balls, blue Hawaiians, green Arkansans, hummingbirds, hemorrhages and hurricanes. In short, avoid anything with sugar, or anything with an umbrella. Get your vitamin C from *fruit.* Don't order anything with Voodoo or Vixen in the title or sexual positions in the name like Dead Man Screw or the Missionary. *(She sort of titters.)*

Believe me, they are lethal. . . . I think you were conceived after one of those.

Drink, instead, like a man: straight up or on the rocks, with plenty of water in between.

Oh, yes. And never mix your drinks. Stay with one all night long, like the man you came in with: bourbon, gin, or tequila 'til dawn, damn the torpedoes, full speed ahead! *(As the Female Greek Chorus retreats, the Male Greek Chorus approaches the table as a Waiter.)*

MALE GREEK CHORUS. *(As Waiter.)* I hope you all are having a pleasant evening. Is there something I can bring you, sir, before you order? *(Li'l Bit waits in anxious fear; carefully, Uncle Peck says with command.)*

PECK. I'll have a plain iced tea. The lady would like a drink, I believe. *(The Male Greek Chorus does a double-take; there is a moment when Uncle Peck and he are in silent communication.)*

MALE GREEK CHORUS. *(As Waiter.)* Very good. What would the . . . lady like? 155

LI'L BIT. *(A bit flushed.)* Is there—is there any sugar in a martini?

PECK. None that I know of.

LI'L BIT. That's what I'd like then—a dry martini. And could we maybe have some bread?

PECK. A drink fit for a woman of the world.—Please bring the lady a dry martini, be generous with the olives, straight up. *(The Male Greek Chorus anticipates a large tip.)*

MALE GREEK CHORUS. *(As Waiter.)* Right away. Very good, sir. *(The Male Greek* 160 *Chorus returns with an empty martini glass which he puts in front of Li'l Bit.)*

PECK. Your glass is empty. Another martini, madam?

LI'L BIT. Yes, thank you. *(Peck signals the Male Greek Chorus, who nods.)* So why did you leave South Carolina, Uncle Peck?

PECK. I was stationed in DC after the war, and decided to stay. Go North, Young
 Man, someone might have said.
LI'L BIT. What did you do in the service anyway?
PECK. *(Suddenly taciturn.)* I . . . I did just this and that. Nothing heroic or   165
 spectacular.
LI'L BIT. But did you see fighting? Or go to Europe?
PECK. I served in the Pacific Theater. It's really nothing interesting to talk about.
LI'L BIT. It is to me. *(The Waiter has brought another empty glass.)* Oh, goody. I love
 the color of the swizzle sticks. What were we talking about?
PECK. Swizzle sticks.
LI'L BIT. Do you ever think of going back?   170
PECK. To the Marines?
LI'L BIT. No—to South Carolina.
PECK. Well, we do go back. To visit.
LI'L BIT. No, I mean to live.
PECK. Not very likely. I think it's better if my mother doesn't have a daily reminder   175
 of her disappointment.
LI'L BIT. Are these floorboards slanted?
PECK. Yes, the floor is very slanted. I think this is the original floor.
LI'L BIT. Oh, good. *(The Female Greek Chorus as Mother enters swaying a little, a
 little past tipsy.)*
FEMALE GREEK CHORUS. *(As Mother.)* Don't leave your drink unattended when
 you visit the ladies' room. There is such a thing as white slavery; the modus
 operandi is to spike an unsuspecting young girl's drink with a "mickey" when
 she's left the room to powder her nose.
  But if you feel you have had more than your sufficiency in liquor, do
 go to the ladies room—often. Pop your head out of doors for a refreshing
 breath of the night air. If you must, wet your face and head with tap water.
 Don't be afraid to dunk your head if necessary. A wet woman is still less
 conspicuous than a drunk woman. *(The Female Greek Chorus stumbles a little;
 conspiratorially:)*
  When in the course of human events it becomes necessary, go to a corner
 stall and insert the index and middle finger down the throat almost to the
 epiglottis. Divulge your stomach contents by such persuasion, and then wait a
 few moments before rejoining your beau waiting for you at your table.
  Oh, no. Don't be shy or embarrassed. In the very best of establishments,
 there's always one or two debutantes crouched in the corner stalls, their beaded
 purses tossed willy-nilly, sounding like cats in heat, heaving up the contents of
 their stomachs. *(The Female Greek Chorus begins to wander off:)*
  I wonder what it is they do in the men's rooms . . .
LI'L BIT. So why is your mother disappointed in you, Uncle Peck?   180
PECK. Every mother in Horry County has Great Expectations.
LI'L BIT. —Could I have another mar-ti-ni, please?
PECK. I think this is your last one. *(Peck signals the Waiter. The Waiter looks at
 her, and shakes his head no. Peck raises his eyebrow, raises his finger to the
 number one, and rubs his fingers together. It looks like a secret code. The Waiter,
 sighs, shakes his head sadly, and brings over another empty martini glass. He glares
 at Peck.)*

LI'L BIT. The name of the county where you grew up is "Horry?" *(Li'l Bit, plastered, begins to laugh. Then she stops.)* I think your mother should be proud of you. *(Peck signals for the check.)*

PECK. Well, missy, she wanted me to do—to *be* everything my father was not. She   185
wanted me to amount to something.

LI'L BIT. But you have! You've amounted a lot. . . .

PECK. I'm just a very ordinary man. *(The Waiter has brought the check and waits. Peck draws out a large bill and hands it to the waiter. Li'l Bit is to the soppy stage.)*

LI'L BIT. I'll bet your mother loves you, Uncle Peck. *(Peck freezes a bit. To Male Greek Chorus as Waiter.)*

PECK. Thank you. The service was exceptional. Please keep the change.

MALE GREEK CHORUS. *(As Waiter, in a tone that could freeze.)* Thank you, sir.   190
Will you be needing any help?

PECK. I think we can manage, thank you. *(Just then, the Female Greek Chorus as Mother lurches on stage; the Male Greek Chorus as Waiter escorts her off as she delivers:)*

FEMALE GREEK CHORUS. *(As Mother.)* Thanks to judicious planning and several trips to the ladies loo, your mother once out-drank an entire regiment of British officers on a good-will visit to Washington! Every last man of them! Milque-toasts! How'd they ever kick Hitler's cahones, huh? No match for an American lady—I could drink every man in here under the table—*(She delivers one last crucial hint before she is gently "bounced:")*—As a last resort, when going out for an evening on the town, be sure to wear a skin-tight girdle, so tight that only a surgical knife or acetylene torch can get it off you—so that if you do pass out in the arms of your escort, he'll end up with rubber burns on his fingers before he can steal your virtue—

A VOICE. *(Puncturing the interlude.)* Vehicle failure. Even with careful maintenance and preventive operation of your automobile, it is all too common for us to experience an unexpected breakdown. If you are driving at any speed when a breakdown occurs, you must slow down and guide the automobile to the side of the road. *(Peck is slowly propping up Li'l Bit as they work their way to his car in the parking lot of the Inn.)*

PECK. How are you doing, missy?

LI'L BIT. It's so far to the car, Uncle Peck. Like the lanterns in the trees the British   195
fired on—*(Li'l Bit stumbles. Peck swoops her up in his arms.)*

PECK. Okay. I think we're going to take a more direct route—*(Li'l Bit closes her eyes.)* Dizzy? *(She nods her head.)* Don't look at the ground. Almost there—do you feel sick to your stomach? *(Li'l Bit nods. They reach the "car." Peck gently deposits her on the front seat.)* Just settle here a little while until things stop spinning. *(Li'l Bit opens her eyes.)*

LI'L BIT. What are we doing?

PECK. We're just going to sit here until your tummy settles down.

LI'L BIT. It's such nice upholst'ry—

PECK. Think you can go for a ride, now?   200

LI'L BIT. Where are you taking me?

PECK. Home.

LI'L BIT. You're not taking me—upstairs? There's no room at the Inn? *(Li'l Bit giggles.)*

PECK. Do you want to go upstairs? *(Li'l Bit doesn't answer.)* Or home?

LI'L BIT. —This isn't right, Uncle Peck.   205

PECK. What isn't right?

LI'L BIT. What we're doing. It's wrong. It's very wrong.

PECK. What are we doing? *(Li'l Bit does not answer.)* We're just going out to dinner.

LI'L BIT. You know. It's not nice to Aunt Mary.

PECK. You let me be the judge of what's nice and not nice to my wife. *(Beat.)*   210

LI'L BIT. Now you're mad.

PECK. I'm not mad. It's just that I thought you . . . understood me, Li'l Bit. I think you're the only one who does.

LI'L BIT. Someone will get hurt.

PECK. Have I forced you to do anything? *(There is a long pause as Li'l Bit tries to get sober enough to think this through.)*

LI'L BIT. . . . I guess not.   215

PECK. We are just enjoying each other's company. I've told you, nothing is going to happen between us until you want it to. Do you know that?

LI'L BIT. Yes.

PECK. Nothing is going to happen until you want it to. *(A second more, with Peck staring ahead at the river at the wheel of his car. Then, softly:)* Do you want something to happen? *(Peck reaches over and strokes her face, very gently. Li'l Bit softens, reaches for him, and buries her head in his neck. Then she kisses him. Then she moves away, dizzy again.)*

LI'L BIT. —I don't know. *(Peck smiles; this has been good news for him—it hasn't been a "no.")*

PECK. Then I'll wait. I'm a very patient man. I've been waiting for a long time. I don't mind waiting.   220

LI'L BIT. Someone is going to get hurt.

PECK. No one is going to get hurt. *(Li'l Bit closes her eyes.)* Are you feeling sick?

LI'L BIT. Sleepy. *(Carefully, Peck props Li'l Bit up on the seat.)*

PECK. Stay here a second.

LI'L BIT. Where're you going?   225

PECK. I'm getting something from the back seat.

LI'L BIT. *(Scared; too loud.)* What? What are you going to do? *(Peck reappears in the front seat with a lap rug.)*

PECK. Shhhh. *(Peck covers Li'l Bit. She calms down.)* There. Think you can sleep? *(Li'l Bit nods. She slides over to rest on his shoulder. With a look of happiness, Peck turns the ignition key. Beat. Peck leaves Li'l Bit sleeping in the car and strolls down to us. Wagner's "Flying Dutchman" comes up faintly.)*

VOICE. *(Interjecting.)* Idling in the neutral gear.

TEENAGE GREEK CHORUS. Uncle Peck teaches cousin Bobby how to fish: 230

PECK. I get back once or twice a year—supposedly to visit Mama and the family, but the real truth is to fish. I miss this the most of all. There's a smell in the Low Country—where the swamp and fresh inlet join the saltwater—a scent of sand and cypress—that I haven't found anywhere yet.

I don't say this very often up North because it will just play into the stereotype everyone has, but I will tell you: I didn't wear shoes in the summertime until I was sixteen. It's unnatural down here to pen up your feet in leather. Go ahead—take 'em off. Let yourself breathe—it really will make you feel better.

We're going to aim for some Pompano today—and I have to tell you, they're a very shy, mercurial fish. Takes patience, and psychology. You have to believe it doesn't matter if you catch one or not.

Sky's pretty spectacular. . . . There's some beer in the cooler next to the crab salad I packed, so help yourself if you get hungry. Are you hungry? Thirsty? Holler if you are.

Okay. You don't want to lean over the bridge like that—pompano feed in shallow water, and you don't want to get too close—

Okay, cast it in, like I showed you. That's great! I can taste that pompano now, sautéed with some pecans and butter, a little bourbon—now—let it lie on the bottom—now, reel, jerk, reel, jerk—Look—look at your line. There's something calling, all right. Okay, tip the rod up—not too sharp—and *hook* it—all right, now easy, reel and then rest—let it play. And reel—play it out, that's right—really good! I can't believe it! It's a pompano—Good work! Way to go! You are an official fisherman now. Pompano are hard to catch. We are going to have a delicious little—

What? Well, I don't know how much pain a fish feels—you can't think of that. Oh, no, don't cry, come on now, it's just a fish—the other guys are going to see you—No, no, you're just real sensitive, and I think that's wonderful at your age—look, do you want me to cut it free? You do?

Okay, hand me those pliers—look, I'm cutting the hook—okay? and we're just going to drop it in—no I'm not mad. It's just for fun, okay? There—*(Peck bends down, very earnest.)*

I don't want you to feel ashamed about crying. I'm not going to tell anyone, okay? I can keep secrets. You know, men cry all the time. They just don't tell anybody, and they don't let anybody catch them. There's nothing you could do that would make me feel ashamed of you. Do you know that? Okay. *(Peck straightens up, smiles.)*

Do you want to pack up and call it a day? I tell you what—I think I can still remember—there's a really neat tree house where I used to stay for days— I think it's still here—it was the last time I looked. But it's a secret place— you can't tell anybody we've gone there—least of all your mom or your sisters— this is something special just between you and me? Sound good? We'll climb up there and have a beer and some crab salad—okay, B.B.? Bobby? Robert. . . . *(Li'l Bit sits at a kitchen table with the two Female Greek Chorus members.)*

LI'L BIT. *(To us.)* Three women, three generations, sit at the kitchen table. On Men, Sex, and Women: Part I.

FEMALE GREEK CHORUS. *(As Mother.)* Men only want one thing.

LI'L BIT. *(Wide-eyed.)* But what? What is it they want?

FEMALE GREEK CHORUS. *(As Mother.)* And once they have it, they lose all interest. So Don't Give It to Them.

TEENAGE GREEK CHORUS. *(As Grandmother.)* I never had the luxury of the rhythm method. Your grandfather is just a big bull. A big bull. Every morning, every evening.

FEMALE GREEK CHORUS. *(As Mother, whispers to Li'l Bit.)* And he used to come home for lunch every day.

235

LI'L BIT. My god, Grandma!

TEENAGE GREEK CHORUS. *(As Grandmother.)* Your grandfather only cares that I do two things: have the table set and the bed turned down.

FEMALE GREEK CHORUS. *(As Mother.)* And in all that time, mother, you never have experienced—? 240

LI'L BIT. *(To us.)*—Now my grandmother believed in all the sacraments of the church, to the day she died. She believed in Santa Claus and the Easter Bunny until she was fifteen. But she didn't believe in—

TEENAGE GREEK CHORUS. *(As Grandmother)*—Orgasm! That's just something you and Mary have made up! I don't believe you.

FEMALE GREEK CHORUS. *(As Mother.)* Mother, it happens to women all the time—

TEENAGE GREEK CHORUS. *(As Grandmother.)*—Oh, now you're going to tell me about the G force!

LI'L BIT. No, Grandma, I think that's astronauts— 245

FEMALE GREEK CHORUS. *(As Mother.)* Well, Mama, after all, you were a child bride when Big Papa came and got you—you were a married woman and you still believed in Santa Claus.

TEENAGE GREEK CHORUS. *(As Grandmother.)*—It was legal, what Daddy and I did! I was fourteen and in those days, fourteen was a grown-up woman—*(Big Papa shuffles in the kitchen for a cookie.)*

MALE GREEK CHORUS. *(As Grandfather.)*—Oh, now we're off on Grandma and the Rape of the Sa-bean Women!

TEENAGE GREEK CHORUS. *(As Grandmother.)*—Well, you were the one in such a big hurry—

MALE GREEK CHORUS. *(As Grandfather to Li'l Bit.)* I picked your grandmother 250 out of that herd of sisters just like a lion chooses the gazelle—the plump, slow, flaky gazelle dawdling at the edge of the herd—your sisters were too smart and too fast and too scrawny—

LI'L BIT. *(To us.)*—The family story is that when Big Papa came for Grandma, my Aunt Lily was waiting for him with a broom—and she beat him over the head all the way down the stairs as he was carrying out Grandma's hope chest—

MALE GREEK CHORUS. *(As Grandfather.)*—And they were *mean.* 'Specially Lily.

FEMALE GREEK CHORUS. *(As Mother.)* Well, you were robbing the baby of the family!

TEENAGE GREEK CHORUS. *(As Grandmother.)* I still keep a broom handy in the kitchen! And I know how to use it! So get your hand out of the cookie jar and don't you spoil your appetite for dinner—out of the kitchen! *(Male Greek Chorus as Grandfather leaves chuckling with a cookie.)*

FEMALE GREEK CHORUS. *(As Mother.)* Just one thing a married woman needs 255 to know how to use—the rolling pin or the broom. I prefer a heavy, cast-iron fry pan—they're great on a man's head, no matter how thick the skull is.

TEENAGE GREEK CHORUS. *(As Grandmother.)* Yes, sir, your father is ruled by only two bosses! Mr. Gut and Mr. Peter! And sometimes, first thing in the morning, Mr. Sphincter Muscle!

FEMALE GREEK CHORUS. *(As Mother.)* It's true. Men are like children. Just like little boys.

TEENAGE GREEK CHORUS. *(As Grandmother.)* Men are bulls! Big bulls! *(The Greek Chorus is getting aroused.)*

FEMALE GREEK CHORUS. *(As Mother.)* They'd still be crouched on their haunches over a fire in a cave if we hadn't cleaned them up!

TEENAGE GREEK CHORUS. *(As Grandmother, flushed.)* Coming in smelling of 260
sweat—

FEMALE GREEK CHORUS. *(As Mother.)* Looking at those naughty pictures like boys in a dime store with a dollar in their pockets!

TEENAGE GREEK CHORUS. *(As Grandmother; raucous.)* No matter to them what they smell like! They've got to have it, right then, on the spot, right there! Nasty!—

FEMALE GREEK CHORUS. *(As Mother.)* Vulgar!

TEENAGE GREEK CHORUS. *(As Grandmother.)* Primitive!—

FEMALE GREEK CHORUS. *(As Mother.)*—Hot!— 265

LI'L BIT. And just about then, Big Papa would shuffle in with—

MALE GREEK CHORUS. *(As Grandfather.)* What are you all cackling about in here?

TEENAGE GREEK CHORUS. *(As Grandmother.)* Stay out of the kitchen! This is just for girls! *(As Grandfather leaves.)*

MALE GREEK CHORUS. *(As Grandfather.)* Lucy, you'd better not be filling Mama's head with sex! Every time you and Mary come over and start in about sex, when I ask a simple question like "what time is dinner going to be ready?," Mama snaps my head off!

TEENAGE GREEK CHORUS. *(As Grandmother.)* Dinner will be ready when I'm 270
good and ready! Stay out of this kitchen! *(Li'l Bit steps out.)*

VOICE. *(Directs:)* When making a left turn, you must downshift while going forward.

LI'L BIT. 1979. A long bus trip to upstate New York. I settled in to read, when a young man sat beside me.

MALE GREEK CHORUS. *(As Young Man; Voice cracking.)* "What are you reading?"

LI'L BIT. He asked. His voice broke into that miserable equivalent of vocal acne, not quite falsetto and not tenor, either. I glanced a side view. He was appealing in an odd way, huge ears at a defiant angle springing forward at 90 degrees. He must have been shaving, because his face, with a peach sheen, was speckled with nicks and styptic. "I have a class tomorrow." I told him.

MALE GREEK CHORUS. *(As Young Man.)* "You're taking a class?" 275

LI'L BIT. "I'm teaching a class." He concentrated on lowering his voice.

MALE GREEK CHORUS. *(As Young Man.)* "I'm a senior. Walt Whitman High."

LI'L BIT. The light was fading outside; so perhaps he was. With a very high voice.
I felt his "interest" quicken. Five steps ahead of the hopes in his head, I slowed down, waited, pretended surprise, acted at listening, all the while knowing we would get off the bus, he would just then seem to think to ask me to dinner, he would chivalrously insist on walking me home, he would continue to converse in the street until I would casually invite him up to my room— and—I was only into the second moment of conversation and I could see the whole evening before me.
And dramaturgically speaking, after the faltering and slightly comical "first act," there was the very briefest of intermissions, and an extremely capable and

forceful and *sustained* second act. And after the second act climax and a gentle denouement—before the post-play discussion—I lay on my back in the dark and I thought about you, Uncle Peck. Oh: oh—this is the allure. Being older. Being the first. Being the translator, the teacher, the epicure, the already jaded. This is how the giver gets taken. *(Li'l Bit changes her tone.)*

On Men, Sex, and Women: Part II *(Li'l Bit steps back into the scene as a fifteen-year-old, gawky and quiet as the gazelle at the edge of the herd.)*

TEENAGE GREEK CHORUS. *(As Grandmother; to Li'l Bit.)* You're being mighty quiet, Missy. Cat Got Your Tongue?

LI'L BIT. I'm just listening. Just thinking. 280

TEENAGE GREEK CHORUS. *(As Grandmother.)* Oh, yes, Little Miss Radar Ears? Soaking it all in? Little Miss Sponge? Penny for your thoughts? *(Li'l Bit hesitates to ask but she really wants to know.)*

LI'L BIT. Does it—when you do it—you know, theoretically when I do it and I haven't done it before—I mean—does it hurt?

FEMALE GREEK CHORUS. *(As Mother.)* Does what hurt, honey?

LI'L BIT. When a—when a girl does it for the first time—with a man—does it hurt?

TEENAGE GREEK CHORUS. *(Grandmother; horrified.)* That's what you're 285 thinking about?

FEMALE GREEK CHORUS. *(As Mother; calm.)* Well, just a little bit. Like a pinch. And there's a little blood.

TEENAGE GREEK CHORUS. *(As Grandmother.)* Don't tell her that! She's too young to be thinking those things!

FEMALE GREEK CHORUS. *(As Mother.)* Well, if she doesn't find out from me, where is she going to find out? In the street?

TEENAGE GREEK CHORUS. *(As Grandmother.)* Tell her it hurts! It's agony! You think you're going to die! Especially if you do it before marriage!

FEMALE GREEK CHORUS. *(As Mother.)* Mama! I'm going to tell her the truth! 290 Unlike you, you left me and Mary completely in the dark with fairy tales and told us to go to the Priest! What does an 80-year-old priest know about love-making with girls!

LI'L BIT. *(Getting upset.)* It's not fair!

FEMALE GREEK CHORUS. *(As Mother)* Now, see, she's getting upset—you're scaring her.

TEENAGE GREEK CHORUS. *(As Grandmother.)* Good! Let her be good and scared! It hurts! You bleed like a stuck pig! And you lay there and say, "Why, O Lord, have you forsaken me?!"

LI'L BIT. —It's not fair! Why does everything have to hurt for girls? Why is there always blood?

FEMALE GREEK CHORUS. *(As Mother.)* It's not a lot of blood—and it feels 295 wonderful after the pain subsides—

TEENAGE GREEK CHORUS. *(As Grandmother.)* You're encouraging her to just go out and find out with the first drugstore joe who buys her a milk shake!

FEMALE GREEK CHORUS. *(As Mother.)* Don't be scared. It won't hurt you—if the man you go to bed with really loves you. It's important that he loves you.

TEENAGE GREEK CHORUS. *(As Grandmother.)*—Why don't you just go out and rent a motel room for her, Lucy?

FEMALE GREEK CHORUS. *(As Mother.)* I believe in telling my daughter the truth! We have a very close relationship! I want her to be able to ask me anything—I'm not scaring her with stories about Eve's sin and snakes crawling on their bellies for eternity and women bearing children in mortal pain—

TEENAGE GREEK CHORUS. *(As Grandmother.)* If she stops and thinks before she 300 takes her knickers off, maybe someone in this family will finish high school! *(Li'l Bit knows what is about to happen and starts to retreat from the scene at this point.)*

FEMALE GREEK CHORUS. *(As Mother.)* Mother! If you and Daddy had helped me—I wouldn't have had to marry that—that no-good-son-of-a—

TEENAGE GREEK CHORUS. *(As Grandmother.)*—He was good enough for you on a full moon! I hold you responsible!

FEMALE GREEK CHORUS. *(As Mother.)*—You could have helped me! You could have told me something about the facts of life!

TEENAGE GREEK CHORUS. *(As Grandmother.)*—I told you what my mother told me! A girl with her skirt up can outrun a man with his pants down!—*(The Male Greek Chorus enters the fray; Li'l Bit edges further D.)*

FEMALE GREEK CHORUS. *(As Mother.)* And when I turned to you for a little 305 help, all I got afterwards was—

MALE GREEK CHORUS. *(As Grandfather.)*—You Made Your Bed; Now Lie on It! *(The Greek Chorus freeze, mouths open, argumentatively.)*

LI'L BIT. *(To us.)* Oh, please! I still can't bear to listen to it, after all these years—*(The Male Greek Chorus "unfreezes," but out of his open mouth, as if to his surprise, comes a base refrain from a Motown song.)*

MALE GREEK CHORUS. "Do-Bee-Do-Wah!": *(The Female Greek Chorus member is also surprised; but she, too, unfreezes.)*

FEMALE GREEK CHORUS. "Shoo-doo-be-doo-be-doo; shoo-doo-be-doo-be-doo": *(The Male and Female Greek choral members continue with their harmony, until the Teenage member of the Chorus starts in with Motown lyrics such as "Dedicated to the One I Love" or "In the Still of the Night," or "Hold Me"—any Sam Cooke will do. The three modulate down into three part harmony, softly, until they are submerged by the actual recording playing over the radio in the car in which Uncle Peck sits in the driver's seat, waiting. Li'l Bit sits in the passenger's seat.)*

LI'L BIT. Ahh. That's better. *(Uncle Peck reaches over and turns the volume down; to 310 Li'l Bit.)*

PECK. How can you hear yourself think? *(Li'l Bit does not answer.)*

A VOICE. *(Insinuating itself in the pause:)* Before you drive. Always check under your car for obstructions—broken bottles, fallen tree branches, and the bodies of small children. Each year hundreds of children are crushed beneath the wheels of unwary drivers in their own driveways. Children depend on *you* to watch them. *(Pause.)*

ANOTHER VOICE. You and the Reverse Gear. *(In the following section, it would be nice to have slides of erotic photographs of women and cars: women posed over the hood; women draped along the sideboards; women with water hoses spraying the car; and the actress playing Li'l Bit with a Bel Air or any 1950s car one can find as the finale.)*

LI'L BIT. 1967. In a parking lot of the Beltsville Agricultural Farms. The Initiation into a Boy's First Love.

PECK. *(With a soft look on his face.)* Of course, my favorite car will always be the '56   315
Bel Air Sports Coupe. Chevy sold more '55s, but the '56!—a V-8 with corvette
option, 225 horsepower; went from 0–60 miles per hour in 8.9 seconds.

LI'L BIT. *(To us.)* Long after a mother's tits, but before a woman's breasts:

PECK. Super-Turbo-Fire! What a Power Pack—mechanical lifters, twin four-barrel
carbs, lightweight valves; dual exhausts—

LI'L BIT. *(To us.)* After the milk but before the beer:

PECK. A specific intake manifold, higher-lift camshaft, and the tightest squeeze
Chevy had ever made—

LI'L BIT. *(To us.)* Long after he's squeezed down the birth canal but before he's   320
pushed his way back in: the boy falls in love with the thing that bears his
weight with speed:

PECK. I want you to know your automobile inside and out.—Are you there? Li'l Bit?
(Slides end here.)

LI'L BIT. —What?

PECK. You're drifting. I need you to concentrate.

LI'L BIT. Sorry.

PECK. Okay. Get into the driver's seat. *(Li'l Bit does.)* Okay. Now. Show me what   325
you're going to do before you start the car. *(Li'l Bit sits, with her hands in her
lap. She starts to giggle.)*

LI'L BIT. I don't know, Uncle Peck.

PECK. Now, come on. What's the first thing you're going to adjust?

LI'L BIT. My bra strap—?

PECK. Li'l Bit. What's the most important thing to have control of on the inside of
the car?

LI'L BIT. That's easy. The radio. I tune the radio from Mama's old fart tunes to: *(Li'l*   330
*Bit turns the radio up so we can hear a 1960s tune. With surprising firmness, Peck
commands.)*

PECK. Radio off. Right now. *(Li'l Bit turns the radio off.)* When you are driving your
car, with your license, you can fiddle with the stations all you want. But when
you are driving with a learner's permit in my car, I want all your attention to be
on the road.

LI'L BIT. Yes sir.

PECK. Okay. Now the seat—forward and up. *(Li'l Bit pushes it forward.)* Do you
want a cushion?

LI'L BIT. No—I'm good.

PECK. You should be able to reach all the switches and controls. Your feet should be   335
able to push the accelerator, brake and clutch all the way down. Can you do that?

LI'L BIT. Yes.

PECK. Okay, the side mirrors. You want to be able to see just a bit of the right side of
the car in the right mirror—can you?

LI'L BIT. Turn it out more—

PECK. Okay. How's that?

LI'L BIT. A little more. . . . Okay, that's good.   340

PECK. Now the left—again, you want to be able to see behind you but the left
lane—adjust it until you feel comfortable. *(Li'l Bit does so.)* Next. I want you to
check the rear view mirror. Angle it so you have a clear vision of the back. *(Li'l
Bit does so.)* Okay. Lock your door. Make sure all the doors are locked.

LI'L BIT. *(Making a joke of it.)* But then I'm locked in with you.

PECK. Don't fool.

LI'L BIT. All right. We're locked in.

PECK. We'll deal with the air vents and defroster later. I'm teaching you on a   345
    manual—once you learn manual, you can drive anything. I want you to be
    able to drive any car, any machine. Manual gives you *control*. In ice, if your
    brakes fail, if you need more power—okay? It's a little harder at first, but then it
    becomes like breathing. Now. Put your hands on the wheel. I never want to see
    you driving with one hand. Always two hands. *(Li'l Bit hesitates.)* What? What
    is it now?

LI'L BIT. If I put my hands on the wheel—how do I defend myself?

PECK. *(Softly.)* Now listen. Listen up close. We're not going to fool around with
    this. This is serious business. I will never touch you when you are driving a car.
    Understand?

LI'L BIT. Okay.

PECK. Hands on the nine o'clock and three o'clock position gives you maximum
    control and turn. *(Peck goes silent for a while. Li'l Bit waits for more
    instruction.)*

        Okay. Just relax and listen to me, Li'l Bit, okay? I want you to lift your
    hands for a second and look at them—*(Li'l Bit feels a bit silly, but does it.)*

        Those are your two hands. When you are driving, your life is in your own
    two hands. Understand? *(Li'l Bit nods.)*

        I don't have any sons. You're the nearest to a son I'll ever have—and I want
    to give you something. Something that really matters to me.

        There's something about driving—when you're in control of the car, just
    you and the machine and the road—that nobody can take from you. A power.
    I feel more myself in my car than anywhere else. And that's what I want to give
    to you.

        There's a lot of assholes out there. Crazy men, arrogant idiots, drunks,
    angry kids, geezers who are blind—and you have to be ready for them. I want
    to teach you to drive like a man.

LI'L BIT. What does that mean?   350

PECK. Men are taught to drive with confidence—with aggression. The road belongs
    to them. They drive defensively—always looking out for the other guy. Women
    tend to be polite—to hesitate. And that can be fatal.

        You're going to learn to think what the other guy is going to do before he
    does it. If there's an accident, and ten cars pile up, and people get killed, you're
    the one who's gonna steer through it, put your foot on the gas if you have to,
    and be the only one to walk away. I don't know how long you or I are going to
    live, but we're for damned sure not going to die in a car.

        So if you're going to drive with me, I want you to take this very seriously.

LI'L BIT. I will, Uncle Peck. I want you to teach me to drive.

PECK. Good. You're going to pass your test on the first try. Perfect score. Before the
    next four weeks are over, you're going to know this baby inside and out. Treat
    her with respect.

LI'L BIT. Why is it a "she"?

PECK. Good question. It doesn't have to be a "she"—but when you close your eyes   355
    and think of someone who responds to your touch—someone who performs

just for you and gives you what you ask for—I guess I always see a "she." You can call her what you like.

LI'L BIT. *(To us.)* I closed my eyes—and decided not to change the gender.

THE VOICE. *(Continues:)* Defensive driving involves defending yourself from hazardous and sudden changes in your automotive environment. By thinking ahead, the defensive driver can adjust to weather, road conditions and road kill. Good defensive driving involves mental and physical preparation. Are you prepared?

ANOTHER VOICE. *(Chiming in.)* You and the reverse gear.

LI'L BIT. 1966. The anthropology of the female body in Ninth Grade; Or A Walk Down Mammary Lane. *(Throughout the following, there is occasional rhythmic beeping, like a transmitter signalling. Li'l Bit is aware of it, but can't figure out where it is coming from. No one else seems to hear it.)*

MALE GREEK CHORUS. In the hallway of Francis Scott Key Middle School. *(A bell rings; the Greek Chorus is changing classes and meet in the hall, conspiratorially.)*   360

TEENAGE GREEK CHORUS. She's coming! *(Li'l Bit enters the scene; the Male Greek Chorus member has a sudden, violent sneezing and lethal allergy attack.)*

FEMALE GREEK CHORUS. Jerome? Jerome? Are you all right?

MALE GREEK CHORUS. I—don't—know. I can't breathe—get Li'l Bit—

TEENAGE GREEK CHORUS. He needs oxygen!

FEMALE GREEK CHORUS. —Can you help us here?   365

LI'L BIT. What's wrong? Do you want me to get the school nurse—*(The Male Greek Chorus member wheezes, grabs his throat, and sniffs at Li'l Bit's chest, which is beeping away.)*

MALE GREEK CHORUS. No—it's okay—I only get this way when I'm around an allergy trigger—

LI'L BIT. Golly. What are you allergic to?

MALE GREEK CHORUS. *(With a sudden grab of her breast.)* Foam rubber. *(The Greek Chorus members break up with hilarity; Jerome leaps away from Li'l Bit's kicking rage with agility; as he retreats:)*

LI'L BIT. Jerome! Creep! Cretin! Cro-Magnon!   370

TEENAGE GREEK CHORUS. Rage is not attractive in a girl.

FEMALE GREEK CHORUS. Really. Get a Sense of Humor.

THE VOICE. *(Echoes:)* Good defensive driving involves mental and physical preparation. Were you prepared?

FEMALE GREEK CHORUS. Gym Class: In the showers. *(The sudden sound of water; the Female Greek Chorus members and Li'l Bit, while fully clothed, drape towels across their fronts, miming nudity. They stand, hesitate, at an imaginary shower's edge.)*

LI'L BIT. Water looks hot.   375

FEMALE GREEK CHORUS. Yesss. . . . *(Female Greek Chorus members are not going to make the first move. One dips a tentative toe under the water, clutching the towel around her.)*

LI'L BIT. Well, I guess we'd better shower and get out of here.

FEMALE GREEK CHORUS. Yep. You go ahead. I'm still cooling off.

LI'L BIT. Okay.—Sally? Are you gonna shower?

TEENAGE GREEK CHORUS. After you—*(Li'l Bit takes a deep breath for courage,*   380
*drops the towel and plunges in: the two Female Greek Chorus members look at Li'l
Bit in the all together, laugh, gasp, and high-five each other.)* Oh my god! Can you
believe—

FEMALE GREEK CHORUS. Told you! It's not foam rubber! I win! Jerome owes
me fifty cents!

THE VOICE. *(Editorializes:)* Were you prepared? *(Li'l Bit tries to cover up; exposed, as
suddenly 1960s Motown fills the room and we segue into:)*

FEMALE GREEK CHORUS. The Sock Hop. *(Li'l Bit stands up against the wall
with her female classmates. Teenage Greek Chorus is mesmerized by the music and
just sways alone, lip-synching the lyrics.)*

LI'L BIT. I don't know. Maybe it's just me—but—do you ever feel like you're just a
walking Mary Jane joke?

FEMALE GREEK CHORUS. I don't know what you mean.   385

LI'L BIT. You haven't heard the Mary Jane jokes? *(Female Greek Chorus member
shakes her head no.)* Okay. "Little Mary Jane is walking through the woods,
when all of a sudden this man who was hiding behind a tree *jumps* out, *rips*
open Mary Jane's blouse, and *plunges* his hands on her breasts. And Little Mary
Jane just laughed and laughed because she knew her money was in her shoes."
(Li'l Bit laughs; the Female Greek Chorus does not.)

FEMALE GREEK CHORUS. You're weird. *(In another space, in a strange light,
Uncle Peck stands and stares at Li'l Bit's body. He is setting up a tripod, but he just
stands, appreciative, watching her.)*

LI'L BIT. Well, don't you ever feel . . . self-conscious? Like you're being looked at all
the time?

FEMALE GREEK CHORUS. That's not a problem for me.—Oh—look—Greg's
coming over to ask you to dance. *(Teenage Greek Chorus becomes attentive,
flustered. Male Greek Chorus member, as Greg, bends slightly as a very short young
man, whose head is at Li'l Bit's chest level. Ardent, sincere and socially inept, Greg
will become a successful gynecologist.)*

TEENAGE GREEK CHORUS. *(Softly.)* Hi, Greg. *(Greg does not hear. He is intent*   390
on only one thing.)

MALE GREEK CHORUS. *(As Greg, to Li'l Bit.)* Good Evening. Would you care to
dance?

LI'L BIT. *(Gently.)* Thank you very much, Greg—but I'm going to sit this one out.

MALE GREEK CHORUS. *(As Greg.)* Oh. Okay. I'll try my luck later. *(He
disappears.)*

TEENAGE GREEK CHORUS. Oohhh. *(Li'l Bit relaxes. Then she tenses, aware of
Peck's gaze.)*

FEMALE GREEK CHORUS. Take pity on him. Someone should.   395

LI'L BIT. But he's so short.

TEENAGE GREEK CHORUS. He can't help it.

LI'L BIT. But his head comes up to—*(Li'l Bit gestures.)*—Here. And I think he asks
me on the fast dances so he can watch me—you know—jiggle.

FEMALE GREEK CHORUS. I wish I had your problems. *(The tune changes; Greg is
across the room in a flash.)*

MALE GREEK CHORUS. *(As Greg.)* Evening again. May I ask you for the honor of   400
a spin on the floor?

LI'L BIT. I'm . . . very complimented, Greg. But I . . . I just don't do fast dances.

MALE GREEK CHORUS. *(As Greg.)* Oh. No problem. That's okay. *(He disappears. Teenage Greek Chorus watches him go.)*

TEENAGE GREEK CHORUS. That is just so—*sad. (Li'l Bit becomes aware of Peck waiting.)*

FEMALE GREEK CHORUS. You know, you should take it as a compliment that the guys want to watch you jiggle. They're guys. That's what they're supposed to do.

LI'L BIT. I guess you're right. But sometimes I feel like these alien life forces, these 405 two mounds of flesh have grafted themselves onto my chest, and they're using me until they can "propagate" and take over the world and they'll just keep growing, with a mind of their own until I collapse under their weight and they suck all the nourishment out of my body and I finally just waste away while they get bigger and bigger and—*(Li'l Bit's classmates are just staring at her in disbelief.)*

FEMALE GREEK CHORUS. You are the strangest girl I have ever met. *(Li'l Bit's trying to joke but feels on the verge of tears.)*

LI'L BIT. Or maybe someone's implanted radio transmitters in my chest at a frequency I can't hear, that girls can't detect, but they're sending out these signals to men who get mesmerized, like sirens, calling them to dash themselves on these "rocks": *(Just then, the music segues into a slow dance, perhaps a Beach Boys tune like "Little Surfer," but over the music there's a rhythmic, hypnotic beeping transmitted, that both Greg and Peck hear. Li'l Bit hears it too, and in horror she stares at her chest. She, too, is almost hypnotized: in a trance, Greg responds to the signals and is called to her side—actually, her front. Like a zombie, he stands in front of her, his eyes planted on her two orbs.)*

MALE GREEK CHORUS. *(As Greg.)* This one's a slow dance. I hope your dance card isn't . . . filled? *(Li'l Bit is aware of Peck; but the signals are calling her to him. The signals are no longer transmitters, but an electromagnetic force, pulling Li'l Bit to his side, where he again waits for her to join him. She must get away from the dance floor.)*

LI'L BIT. Greg—you really are a nice boy. But I don't like to dance.

MALE GREEK CHORUS. *(As Greg.)* That's okay. We don't have to move or 410 anything. I could just hold you and we could just *sway* a little—

LI'L BIT. No! I'm sorry—but I think I have to leave; I hear someone calling me—*(Li'l Bit starts across the dance floor, leaving Greg behind. The beeping stops. The lights change, although the music does not. As Li'l Bit talks to us, she continues to change and prepare for the coming session. She should be wearing a tight tank top or a sheer blouse and very tight pants. To us.)*

In every man's home some small room, some zone in his house is set aside. It might be the attic, or the study, or a den. And there's an invisible sign as if from the old treehouse: Girls Keep Out.

Here, away from female eyes, lace doilies and crochet, he keeps his manly toys: the Vargas pin-ups, the tackle. A scent of tobacco and WD-40. *(She inhales deeply.)*

A dash of his Bay Rum. Ahhh—*(Li'l Bit savors it for just a moment more.)*

Here he keeps his secrets: a violin or saxophone, drum set or dark room, and the stacks of Playboy. *(In a whisper.)*

Here, in my aunt's home, it was the basement. Uncle Peck's turf.

VOICE. *(Commands.)* You and the reverse gear.

LI'L BIT. 1965. The Photo-Shoot. *(Li'l Bit steps into the scene as a nervous but curious thirteen-year-old. Music, from the previous scene, continues to play, changing into something like Roy Orbison later—something seductive with a beat. Peck fiddles, all business, with his camera. As in the driving lesson, he is all competency and concentration. Li'l Bit stands awkwardly. He looks through the Leica camera on the tripod, adjusts the back lighting, etc.)*

PECK. Are you cold? The lights should heat up some in a few minutes—

LI'L BIT. —Aunt Mary is?   415

PECK. At the National Theatre matinee. With your mother. We have time.

LI'L BIT. But—what if—

PECK. —And so what if they return? I told them you and I were going to be working with my camera. They won't come down. *(Li'l Bit is quiet, apprehensive.)*—Look, are you sure you want to do this?

LI'L BIT. I said I'd do it. But—

PECK. —I know. You've drawn the lines.   420

LI'L BIT. *(Reassured.)* That's right. No frontal nudity.

PECK. Good heavens, girl, where did you pick that up?

LI'L BIT. *(Defensive.)* I read. *(Peck tries not to laugh.)*

PECK. And I read *Playboy* for the interviews. Okay. Let's try some different music. *(Peck goes to an expensive reel to reel and forwards. Something like "Sweet Dreams" begins to play.)*

LI'L BIT. I didn't know you listened to this.   425

PECK. I'm not dead, you know. I try to keep up. Do you like this song? *(Li'l Bit nods with pleasure.)* Good. Now listen—at professional photo shoots, they always play music for the models. Okay? I want you to just enjoy the music. Listen to it with your body, and just—respond.

LI'L BIT. Respond to the music with my . . . body?

PECK. Right. Almost like dancing. Here—let's get you on the stool, first. *(Peck comes over and helps her up.)*

LI'L BIT. But nothing showing—*(Peck firmly, with his large capable hands, brushes back her hair, angles her face. Li'l Bit turns to him like a plant to the sun.)*

PECK. Nothing showing. Just a peek. *(He holds her by the shoulder, looking at her*   430 *critically. Then he unbuttons her blouse to the mid-point, and runs his hands over the flesh of her exposed sternum, arranging the fabric, just touching her. Deliberately, calmly. Asexually. Li'l Bit quiets, sits perfectly still, and closes her eyes.)* Okay?

LI'L BIT. Yes. *(Peck goes back to his camera.)*

PECK. I'm going to keep talking to you. Listen without responding to what I'm saying; you want to *listen* to the music. Sway, move just your torso or your head—I've got to check the light meter:

LI'L BIT. But—you'll be watching.

PECK. No—I'm not here—just my voice. Pretend you're in your room all alone on a Friday night with your mirror—and the music feels good—just move for me, Li'l Bit—*(Li'l Bit closes her eyes. At first self-conscious, she gets more into the music and begins to sway: we hear the camera start to whir. Throughout the shoot, there can be a slide montage of actual shots of the actor playing Li'l Bit—interspersed with other models à la* Playboy, *Calvin Klein and Victoriana/Lewis Carroll's Alice Liddell.)*

That's it. That looks great. Okay. Just keep doing that. Lift your head up a bit more, good, good, just keep moving, that a girl—you're a very beautiful young woman. Do you know that? *(Li'l Bit looks up, blushes. Peck shoots the camera. We should see this shot on the screen.)*

LI'L BIT. No. I don't know that.   435

PECK. Listen to the music. *(Li'l Bit closes her eyes again.)* Well you are. For a thirteen-year-old, you have a body a twenty-year-old woman would die for.

LI'L BIT. The boys in school don't think so.

PECK. The boys in school are little Neanderthals in short pants. You're ten years ahead of them in maturity; it's gonna take a while for them to catch up. *(Peck clicks another shot; we see a faint smile on Li'l Bit on the screen.)* Girls turn into women long before boys turn into men.

LI'L BIT. Why is that?

PECK. I don't know, Li'l Bit. But it's a blessing for men. *(Li'l Bit turns silent.)* Keep   440
moving. Try arching your back on the stool, hands behind you, and throw your head back—*(The slide shows a* Playboy *model in this pose.)* Oohh, great. That one was great. Turn your head away, same position—*(Whir.)* Beautiful. *(Li'l Bit looks at him a bit defiantly.)*

LI'L BIT. I think Aunt Mary is beautiful. *(Peck stands still.)*

PECK. My wife is a very beautiful woman. Her beauty doesn't cancel yours out. *(More casually; he returns to the camera.)* All the women in your family are beautiful. In fact, I think all women are. You're not listening to the music. *(Peck shoots some more film in silence.)* All right, Turn your head to the left. Good. Now take the back of your right hand and put in on your right cheek—your elbow angled up— now slowly, slowly, stroke your cheek, draw back your hair with the back of your hand—*(Another classic* Playboy *or Vargas.)* Good. One hand above and behind your head; stretch your body; smile—*(Another pose.)* Li'l Bit. I want you to think of something that makes you laugh—

LI'L BIT. I can't think of anything.

PECK. Okay. Think of Big Papa chasing Grandma around the living room—*(Li'l Bit lifts her head and laughs. Click. We should see this shot.)* Good. Both hands behind your head. Great! Hold that—*(From behind his camera.)* You're doing great work. If we keep this up, in five years we'll have a really professional portfolio—*(Li'l Bit stops.)*

LI'L BIT. What do you mean in five years?   445

PECK. You can't submit work to *Playboy* until you're eighteen. *(Peck continues to shoot; he knows he's made a mistake.)*

LI'L BIT. —Wait a minute. You're joking, aren't you, Uncle Peck?

PECK. Heck, no. You can't get into *Playboy* unless you're the very best. And you are the very best.

LI'L BIT. I would never do that! *(Peck stops shooting. He turns off the music.)*

PECK. Why? There's nothing wrong with *Playboy*—it's a very classy maga—   450

LI'L BIT. *(More upset.)* But I thought you said I should go to college!

PECK. Wait—Li'l Bit—it's nothing like that. Very respectable women model for *Playboy*—actresses with major careers—women in college—there's an Ivy League issue every—

LI'L BIT. —I'm never doing anything like that! You'd show other people these—other *men*—these—what I'm doing—why would you do that?!

Any *boy* around here could just pick up, just go into The Stop & Go and *buy*—Why would you ever want to—to share—

PECK. Whoa, whoa. Just stop a second and listen to me. Li'l Bit. Listen. There's nothing wrong in what we're doing. I'm very proud of you. I think you have a wonderful body and an even more wonderful mind. And of course I want other people to *appreciate* it. It's not anything shameful.

LI'L BIT. *(Hurt.)* But this is something—that I'm only doing for you. This is   455
something—that you said was just between us.

PECK. It is. And if that's how you feel, five years from now, it will remain that way. Okay? I know you're not going to do anything you don't feel like doing. *(He walks back to the camera.)* Do you want to stop now? I've got just a few more shots on this roll—

LI'L BIT. I don't want anyone seeing this.

PECK. I swear to you. No one will. I'll treasure this—that you're doing this only for me. *(Li'l Bit, still shaken, sits on the stool. She closes her eyes.)* Li'l Bit? Open your eyes and look at me. *(Li'l Bit shakes her head no.)* Come on. Just open your eyes, honey.

LI'L BIT. If I look at you—if I look at the camera: you're gonna know what I'm thinking. You'll see right through me—

PECK. —No, I won't. I want you to look at me. All right, then. I just want you   460
to listen. Li'l Bit. *(She waits.)* I love you. *(Li'l Bit opens her eyes; startled. Peck captures the shot. On the screen we see right though her. Peck says softly:)* Do you know that? *(Li'l Bit nods her head yes.)* I have loved you every day since the day you were born.

LI'L BIT. Yes. *(Li'l Bit and Peck just look at each other. Beat. Beneath the shot of herself on the screen, Li'l Bit, still looking at her uncle, begins to unbutton her blouse.)*

A NEUTRAL VOICE. *(Cutting off the above scene.)* Implied consent. As an individual operating a motor vehicle in the state of Maryland, you must abide by 'Implied Consent.' If you do not consent to take the Blood Alcohol Content test, there may be severe penalties: a suspension of license, a fine, community service and a possible *jail* sentence. *(Shifting tone.)* Idling in the neutral gear:

MALE GREEK CHORUS. *(Announcing.)* Aunt Mary on behalf of her husband. *(Female Greek Chorus checks her appearance, and with dignity comes to the front of the stage and sits down to talk to us.)*

FEMALE GREEK CHORUS. *(As Aunt Mary.)* My husband was such a good man—is. Is such a good man. Every night, he does the dishes. The second he comes home, he's taking out the garbage, or doing yard work, lifting the heavy things I can't. Everyone in the neighborhood borrows Peck—it's true—women with husbands of their own, men who just don't have Peck's abilities—there's always a knock on our door for a jump start on cold mornings, when anyone needs a ride, or help shoveling the sidewalk—I look out, and there Peck is, without a coat, pitching in.

I know I'm lucky. The man works from dawn to dusk. And the overtime he does every year—my poor sister. She sits every Christmas when I come to dinner with a new stole, or diamonds, or with the tickets to Bermuda.

I know he has troubles. And we don't talk about them. I wonder, sometimes, what happened to him during the war. The men who fought World War II didn't have "rap sessions" to talk about their feelings. Men in his generation were expected to be quiet about it and get on with their lives. And sometimes I can feel him just fighting the trouble—whatever has burrowed deeper than the scar tissue—and we don't talk about it. I know he's having a bad spell because he comes looking for me in the house, and just hangs around me until it passes. And I keep my banter light—I discuss a new recipe, or sales, or gossip—because I think domesticity can be a balm for men when they're lost. We sit in the house and listen to the peace of the clock ticking in his well-ordered living room, until it passes. *(Sharply.)*

I'm not a fool. I know what's going on. I wish you could feel how hard Peck fights against it—he's swimming against the tide, and what he needs is to see me on the shore, believing in him, knowing he won't go under, he won't give up—

And I want to say this about my niece. She's a sly one, that one is. She knows exactly what she's doing; she's twisted Peck around her little finger and thinks it's all a big secret. Yet another one who's borrowing my husband until it doesn't suit her anymore.

Well. I'm counting the days until she goes away to school. And she manipulates someone else. And then he'll come back again, and sit in the kitchen while I bake, or beside me on the sofa when I sew in the evenings. I'm a very patient woman. But I'd like my husband back.

I am counting the days.

VOICE. *(Repeats.)* You and the reverse gear.

MALE GREEK CHORUS. Li'l Bit's 13th Christmas. Uncle Peck Does the Dishes. Christmas 1964. *(Peck stands in a dress shirt and tie, nice pants, with an apron. He is washing dishes. He's in a mood we haven't seen. Quiet, brooding. Li'l Bit watches him a moment before seeking him out.)*

LI'L BIT. Uncle Peck? *(He does not answer. He continues to work on the pots.)* I didn't know where you'd gone to. *(He nods. She takes this as a sign to come in.)* Don't you want to sit with us for a while?

PECK. No. I'd rather do the dishes. *(Pause. Li'l Bit watches him.)*

LI'L BIT. You're the only man I know who does dishes. *(Peck says nothing.)* I think it's really nice.

PECK. My wife has been on her feet all day. So's your grandmother and your mother.

LI'L BIT. I know. *(Beat.)* Do you want some help?

PECK. No. *(He softens a bit towards her.)* You can help by just talking to me.

LI'L BIT. Big Papa never does the dishes. I think it's nice.

PECK. I think men should be nice to women. Women are always working for us. There's nothing particularly manly in wolfing down food and then sitting around in a stupor while the women clean up.

LI'L BIT. That looks like a really neat camera that Aunt Mary got you.

PECK. It is. It's a very nice one. *(Pause, as Peck works on the dishes and some demon that Li'l Bit intuits.)*

LI'L BIT. Did Big Papa hurt your feelings?

PECK. *(Tired.)* What? Oh, no—it doesn't hurt me. Family is family. I'd rather have him picking on me than—I don't pay him any mind, Li'l Bit.

LI'L BIT. Are you angry with us?

PECK. No, Li'l Bit. I'm not angry. *(Another pause.)*

LI'L BIT. We missed you at Thanksgiving. . . . I did. I missed you.

PECK. Well, there were . . . "things" going on. I didn't want to spoil anyone's Thanksgiving.

LI'L BIT. Uncle Peck? *(Very carefully.)* Please don't drink anymore tonight.

PECK. I'm not . . . "over-doing" it.

LI'L BIT. I know. *(Beat.)* Why do you drink so much? *(Peck stops and thinks, carefully.)* 485

PECK. Well, Li'l Bit—let me explain it this way. There are some people who have a—a "fire" in the belly. I think they go to work on Wall Street or they run for office. And then there are people who have a "fire" in their heads—and they become writers or scientists or historians. *(He smiles a little at her.)* You. You've got a "fire" in the head. And then there are people like me.

LI'L BIT. Where do you have . . . a fire?

PECK. I have a fire in my heart. And sometimes the drinking helps.

LI'L BIT. There's got to be other things that can help.

PECK. I suppose there are. 490

LI'L BIT. Does it help—to talk to me?

PECK. Yes. It does. *(Quiet.)* I don't get to see you very much.

LI'L BIT. I know. *(Li'l Bit thinks.)* You could talk to me more.

PECK. Oh?

LI'L BIT. I could make a deal with you, Uncle Peck. 495

PECK. I'm listening.

LI'L BIT. We could meet and talk—once a week. You could just store up whatever's bothering you during the week—and then we could talk.

PECK. Would you like that?

LI'L BIT. As long as you don't drink. I'd meet you somewhere for lunch or for a walk—on the weekends—as long as you stop drinking. And we could talk about whatever you want.

PECK. You would do that for me? 500

LI'L BIT. I don't think I'd want Mom to know. Or Aunt Mary. I wouldn't want them to think—

PECK. —No. It would just be us talking.

LI'L BIT. I'll tell Mom I'm going to a girlfriend's. To study. Mom doesn't get home until six, so you can call me after school and tell me where to meet you.

PECK. You get home at four?

LI'L BIT. We can meet once a week. But only in public. You've got to let me—draw the line. And once it's drawn, you mustn't cross it. 505

PECK. Understood.

LI'L BIT. Would that help? *(Peck is very moved.)*

PECK. Yes. Very much.

LI'L BIT. —I'm going to join the others in the living room now. *(Li'l Bit turns to go.)*

PECK. Merry Christmas, Li'l Bit. *(Li'l Bit bestows a very warm smile on him.)* 510

LI'L BIT. Merry Christmas, Uncle Peck.

VOICE. *(Dictates.)* Shifting forward from second to third gear. *(The Male and Female Greek Chorus members come forward.)*

MALE GREEK CHORUS. 1969. Days and gifts: a Countdown:

FEMALE GREEK CHORUS. A note. "September 3, 1969. Li'l Bit: you've only been away two days and it feels like months. Hope your dorm room is cozy. I'm sending you this tape cassette—it's a new model—so you'll have some music in your room. Also that music you're reading about for class—Carmina Burana. Hope you enjoy. Only 90 days to go!—Peck."

MALE GREEK CHORUS. September 22. A bouquet of roses. A note: "Miss you 515 like crazy. 69 days . . ."

TEENAGE GREEK CHORUS. September 25. A box of chocolates. A card: "Don't worry about the weight gain. You still look great. Got a post office box—write to me there. 66 days—Love, your candy man."

MALE GREEK CHORUS. October 16. A note: "Am trying to get through the Jane Austin you're reading—*Emma*—here's a book in return: *Liaisons Dangereuse*. Hope you're saving time for me." Scrawled in the margin the number: "47"

FEMALE GREEK CHORUS. "November 16: sixteen days to go!—hope you like the perfume—having a hard time reaching you on the dorm phone. You must be in the library a lot. Won't you think about me getting you your own phone so we can talk?"

TEENAGE GREEK CHORUS. November 18: "Li'l Bit—got a package returned to the PO Box. Have you changed dorms? Call me at work or write to the PO. Am still on the wagon. Waiting to see you. Only two weeks more!"

MALE GREEK CHORUS. November 23: A letter: "Li'l Bit. So disappointed you 520 couldn't come home for the turkey. Sending you some money for a nice dinner out—nine days and counting!"

GREEK CHORUS. *(In unison.)* November 25th: a letter:

LI'L BIT. "Dear Uncle Peck: I am sending this to you at work. Don't come up next weekend for my birthday. I will not be here—"

VOICE. *(Directs.)* Shifting forward from third to fourth gear.

MALE GREEK CHORUS. December 10, 1969. A hotel room. Philadelphia. There is no moon tonight. *(Peck sits on the side of the bed while Li'l Bit paces. He can't believe she's in his room, but there's a desperate edge to his happiness. Li'l Bit is furious, edgy. There is a bottle of champagne in an ice bucket in a very nice hotel room.)*

PECK. Why don't you sit? 525

LI'L BIT. I don't want to.—What's the champagne for?

PECK. I thought we might toast your birthday—

LI'L BIT. —I am so pissed off at you, Uncle Peck.

PECK. —Why?

LI'L BIT. —I mean, are you crazy? 530

PECK. What did I do?

LI'L BIT. You scared the holy crap out of me—sending me that stuff in the mail—

PECK. —They were gifts! I just wanted to give you some little perks your first semester—

LI'L BIT. —Well, what the hell were those numbers all about! 44 days to go—only two more weeks—and then just numbers—69—68—67—like some serial killer!

PECK. Li'l Bit! Whoa! This is me you're talking to—I was just trying to pick up your 535 spirits, trying to celebrate your birthday—

LI'L BIT. My *eighteenth* birthday. I'm not a child, Uncle Peck. You were counting down to my eighteenth birthday.

PECK. So?

LI'L BIT. So? So statutory rape is not in effect when a young woman turns eighteen. And you and I both know it. *(Peck is walking on ice.)*

PECK. I think you misunderstand.

LI'L BIT. I think I understand all too well. I know what you want to do five steps 540
ahead of you doing it. Defensive driving 101.

PECK. Then why did you suggest we meet here instead of the restaurant?

LI'L BIT. I don't want to have this conversation in public.

PECK. Fine. Fine. We have a lot to talk about.

LI'L BIT. Yeah. We do. *(Li'l Bit doesn't want to do what she has to do.)* Could I—have some of that champagne?

PECK. Of course, madam! *(Peck makes a big show of it.)* 545
Let me do the honors. I wasn't sure which you might prefer—Taittingers or Veuve Cliquot—so I thought we'd start out with an old standard—Perrier Jouet. *(The bottle is popped.)*
Quick—Li'l Bit—your glass! *(Uncle Peck fills Li'l Bit's glass. He puts the bottle back in the ice and goes for a can of ginger ale.)*
Let me get some of this ginger ale—my bubbly—and toast you—*(He turns and sees that Li'l Bit has not waited for him.)*

LI'L BIT. Oh—sorry, Uncle Peck. Let me have another—*(Peck fills her glass and reaches for his ginger ale: she stops him.)* Uncle Peck—maybe you should join me in the champagne.

PECK. You want me to—drink?

LI'L BIT. It's not polite to let a lady drink alone.

PECK. Well, missy, if you insist—*(Peck hesitates.)*—Just one. It's been a while. *(Peck fills another flute for himself.)* There. I'd like to propose a toast to you and your birthday! *(Peck sips it tentatively.)* I'm not used to this anymore.

LI'L BIT. You don't have anywhere to go tonight, do you? *(Peck hopes this is a good* 550
sign.)

PECK. I'm all yours.—God, it's good to see you! I've gotten so used to . . . to . . . talking to you in my head. I'm used to seeing you every week—there's so much—I don't quite know where to begin. How's school, Li'l Bit?

LI'L BIT. I—it's hard. Uncle Peck. Harder than I thought it would be. I'm in the middle of exams and papers and—I don't know.

PECK. You'll pull through. You always do.

LI'L BIT. Maybe. I . . . might be flunking out.

PECK. You always think the worse, Li'l Bit, but when the going gets tough—*(Li'l Bit* 555
shrugs and pours herself another glass.) Hey, honey, go easy on that stuff, okay?

LI'L BIT. Is it very expensive?

PECK. Only the best for you. But the cost doesn't matter—champagne should be "sipped." *(Li'l Bit is quiet.)* Look—if you're in trouble in school—you can always come back home for a while.

LI'L BIT. *No—(Li'l Bit tries not to be so harsh.)* Thanks, Uncle Peck, but I'll figure some way out of this.

PECK. You're supposed to get in scrapes, your first year away from home.

LI'L BIT. Right. How's Aunt Mary? 560

PECK. She's fine. *(Pause.)* Well—how about the new car?

LI'L BIT. It's real nice. What is it, again?

PECK. It's a Cadillac El Dorado.

LI'L BIT. Oh. Well, I'm real happy for you, Uncle Peck.

PECK. I got it for you. 565

LI'L BIT. What?

PECK. I always wanted to get a Cadillac—but I thought, Peck, wait until Li'l Bit's old enough—and thought maybe you'd like to drive it, too.

LI'L BIT. *(Confused.)* Why would I want to drive your car?

PECK. Just because it's the best—I want you to have the best. *(They are running out of "gas": small talk.)*

LI'L BIT.	**PECK.**	570
(Simultaneously.)	*(Simultaneously.)*	
Listen, Uncle Peck, I don't	I have been thinking of how	
know how to begin this,	to say this in my head, over	
but—	and over—	

PECK. Sorry.

LI'L BIT. You first.

PECK. Well, your going away—has just made me realize how much I miss you. Talking to you and being alone with you. I've really come to depend on you, Li'l Bit. And it's been so hard to get in touch with you lately—the distance and—and you're never in when I call—I guess you've been living in the library—

LI'L BIT. No—the problem is, I haven't been in the library—

PECK. Well, it doesn't matter—I hope you've been missing me as much. 575

LI'L BIT. Uncle Peck—I've been thinking a lot about this—and I came here tonight to tell you that—I'm not doing very well. I'm getting very confused—I can't concentrate on my work—and now that I'm away—I've been going over and over it in my mind—and I don't want us to "see" each other anymore. Other than with the rest of the family.

PECK. *(Quiet.)* Are you seeing other men?

LI'L BIT. *(Getting agitated.)* I—no, that's not the reason—I—well, yes, I am seeing other—listen, it's not really anybody's business!

PECK. Are you in love with anyone else?

LI'L BIT. That's not what this is about. 580

PECK. Li'l Bit—you're scared. Your mother and your grandparents have filled your head with all kinds of nonsense about men—I hear them working on you all the time—and you're scared. It won't hurt you—if the man you go to bed with really loves you. *(Li'l Bit is scared. She starts to tremble.)* And I have loved you since the day I held you in my hand. And I think everyone's just gotten you frightened to death about something that is just like breathing—

LI'L BIT. Oh, my god—*(She takes a breath.)* I can't see you anymore, Uncle Peck. *(Peck downs the rest of his champagne.)*

PECK. Li'l Bit. Listen. Listen. Open your eyes and look at me. Come on. Just open your eyes, honey. *(Li'l Bit, eyes squeezed shut, refuses.)* All right then. I just want you to listen. Li'l Bit—I'm going to ask you just this once. Of your own free will. Just lie down on the bed with me—our clothes on—just lie down with me, a man and a woman—and let's—hold one another. Nothing else. Before you say anything else. I want the chance to—hold you. Because sometimes the body knows things that the mind isn't listening to . . . and after I've held you, then I want you to tell me what you feel.

LI'L BIT. You'll just . . . hold me?

PECK. Yes. And then you can tell me what you're feeling. *(Li'l Bit—half wanting to* 585 *run, half wanting to get it over with, half wanting to be held by him.)*

LI'L BIT. Yes. All right. Just hold. Nothing else. *(Peck lies down on the bed and holds his arms out to her. Li'l Bit lies beside him, putting her head on his chest. He looks as if he's trying to soak her into his pores by osmosis. He strokes her hair, and she lies very still. The Male Greek Chorus member and the Female Greek Chorus member as Aunt Mary come into the room.)*

MALE GREEK CHORUS. Recipe for a Southern Boy:

FEMALE GREEK CHORUS. *(As Aunt Mary.)* A drawl of molasses in the way he speaks.

MALE GREEK CHORUS. A gumbo of red and brown mixed in the cream of his skin. *(While Peck lies, his eyes closed, Li'l Bit rises in the bed and responds to her Aunt.)*

LI'L BIT. Warm brown eyes— 590

FEMALE GREEK CHORUS. *(As Aunt Mary.)*—Bedroom eyes—

MALE GREEK CHORUS. —A dash of Southern Baptist Fire and Brimstone—

LI'L BIT. A curl of Elvis on his forehead—

FEMALE GREEK CHORUS. *(As Aunt Mary.)* A splash of Bay Rum—

MALE GREEK CHORUS. A closely shaven beard that he razors just for you— 595

FEMALE GREEK CHORUS. *(As Aunt Mary.)* Large hands—rough hands—

LI'L BIT. —Warm hands—

MALE GREEK CHORUS. The steel of Marines in his walk—

LI'L BIT. The slouch of the fishing skiff in his walk—

MALE GREEK CHORUS. Neatly pressed khakis— 600

FEMALE GREEK CHORUS. *(As Aunt Mary.)* And under the wide leather of the belt—

LI'L BIT. Sweat of cypress and sand—

MALE GREEK CHORUS. Neatly pressed khakis—

LI'L BIT. His heart beating Dixie—

FEMALE GREEK CHORUS. *(As Aunt Mary.)* The whisper of the zipper—you 605 could reach out with your hand and—

LI'L BIT. His mouth—

FEMALE GREEK CHORUS. *(As Aunt Mary.)* You could just reach out and—

LI'L BIT. Hold him in your hand—

FEMALE GREEK CHORUS. *(As Aunt Mary.)* And his mouth—(*Li'l Bit rises above her uncle and looks at his mouth; starts to lower herself to kiss him—and wrenches herself free. She gets up from the bed.)*

LI'L BIT. —I've got to get back. 610

PECK. Wait—Li'l Bit. Did you . . . feel nothing?

LI'L BIT. *(Lying.)* No. Nothing.

PECK. Do you—do you think of me? *(The Greek Chorus whispers.)*

FEMALE GREEK CHORUS. Khakis—

MALE GREEK CHORUS. Bay Rum— 615

FEMALE GREEK CHORUS. The whisper of the—

LI'L BIT. —No. *(Peck, in a rush, trembling, gets something out of his pocket.)*

PECK. I'm forty-five. That's not old for a man. And I haven't been able to do anything else but think of you. I can't concentrate on my work—Li'l Bit. You've got to—I want you to think about what I am about to ask you.

LI'L BIT. I'm listening. *(Peck opens a small ring box.)*

PECK. I want you to be my wife.

LI'L BIT. This isn't happening.

PECK. I'll tell Mary I want a divorce. We're not blood-related. It would be legal—

LI'L BIT. —What have you been thinking! You are married to my aunt, Uncle Peck. She's my family. You have—you have gone way over the line. Family is family. *(Quickly, Li'l Bit flies through the room, gets her coat.)*

I'm leaving. Now. I am not seeing you. Again. *(Peck lies down on the bed for a moment, trying to absorb the terrible news. For a moment, he almost curls into a fetal position.)*

I'm not coming home for Christmas. You should go home to Aunt Mary. Go home now, Uncle Peck. *(Peck gets control, and sits, rigid.)*

Uncle Peck?—I'm sorry but I have to go. *(Pause.)*

Are you all right. *(With a discipline that comes from being told that boys don't cry, Peck stands upright.)*

PECK. I'm fine. I just think—I need a real drink. *(The Male Greek Chorus has become a Bartender—at a small counter, he is lining up shots for Peck. As Li'l Bit narrates, we see Peck sitting, carefully and calmly downing shot glasses.)*

LI'L BIT. *(To us.)* I never saw him again. I stayed away from Christmas and Thanksgiving for years after.

It took my uncle seven years to drink himself to death. First he lost his job, then his wife, and finally his driver's license. He retreated to his house, and had his bottles delivered. *(Peck stands, and puts his hands in front of him—almost like Superman flying.)*

One night he tried to go downstairs to the basement—and he flew down the steep basement stairs. My aunt came by weekly to put food on the porch—and she noticed the mail and the papers stacked up, uncollected.

They found him at the bottom of the stairs. Just steps away from his dark room.

Now that I'm old enough, there are some questions I would have liked to have asked him. Who did it to you, Uncle Peck? How old were you? Were you eleven? *(Peck moves to the driver's seat of a car and waits.)*

Sometimes I think of my uncle as a kind of Flying Dutchman. In the opera, the Dutchman is doomed to wander the sea; but every seven years he can come ashore—and if he finds a maiden who will love him of her own free will—he will be released.

And I see Uncle Peck in my mind, in his Chevy '56, a spirit driving up and down the back roads of Carolina—looking for a young girl who, of her own free will, will love him. Release him.

VOICE. *(States.)* You and the reverse gear.

LI'L BIT. The summer of 1962. On Men, Sex, and Women: Part III. *(Li'l Bit steps, as an eleven-year-old, into:)*

FEMALE GREEK CHORUS. It is out of the question. End of Discussion.

LI'L BIT. But why?

FEMALE GREEK CHORUS. Li'l Bit—we are not discussing this. I said no.

LI'L BIT. But I could spend an extra week at the beach! You're not telling me why!

FEMALE GREEK CHORUS. Your Uncle pays entirely too much attention to you.

LI'L BIT. He listens to me when I talk. And—and he talks to me. He teaches me about things. Mama—he knows an awful lot.

FEMALE GREEK CHORUS. He's a small town hick who's learned how to mix drinks from Hugh Hefner.

LI'L BIT. Who's Hugh Hefner? *(Beat.)*   635

FEMALE GREEK CHORUS. I am not letting an 11-year-old girl spend seven hours alone in the car with a man. . . . I don't like the way your uncle looks at you.

LI'L BIT. For God's sake, mother! Just because you've gone through a bad time with my father—you think every man is evil!

FEMALE GREEK CHORUS. Oh no, Li'l Bit—not all men. . . . We . . . we just haven't been very lucky with the men in our family.

LI'L BIT. Just because you lost your husband—I still deserve a chance at having a father! Someone! A man who will look out for me! Don't I get a chance?

FEMALE GREEK CHORUS. I will feel terrible if something happens.   640

LI'L BIT. Mother! It's in your head! Nothing will happen! I can take care of myself. And I can certainly handle Uncle Peck.

FEMALE GREEK CHORUS. All right. But I'm warning you—if anything happens, I hold you responsible. *(Li'l Bit moves out of this scene and towards the car.)*

LI'L BIT. 1962. On the back roads of Carolina: the First Driving Lesson. *(The Teenage Greek Chorus member stands apart on stage. She will speak all the lines. Li'l Bit sits beside Peck in the front seat. She looks at him closely, remembering.)*

PECK. Li'l Bit? Are you getting tired?

TEENAGE GREEK CHORUS. A little.   645

PECK. It's a long drive. But we're making really good time. We can take the back road from here and see . . . a little scenery. Say—I've got an idea—*(Peck checks his rear view mirror.)*

TEENAGE GREEK CHORUS. Are we stopping, Uncle Peck?

PECK. There's no traffic here. Do you want to drive?

TEENAGE GREEK CHORUS. I can't drive.

PECK. It's easy. I'll show you how. I started driving when I was your age. Don't you   650
want to?

TEENAGE GREEK CHORUS. —But it's against the law at my age!

PECK. And that's why you can't tell anyone I'm letting you do this—

TEENAGE GREEK CHORUS. But—I can't reach the pedals.

PECK. You can sit in my lap and steer. I'll push the pedals for you. Did your father ever let you drive his car?

TEENAGE GREEK CHORUS. No way.   655

PECK. Want to try?

TEENAGE GREEK CHORUS. Okay. *(Li'l Bit moves into Peck's lap. She leans against him, closing her eyes.)*

PECK. You're just a little thing, aren't you? Okay—now think of the wheel as a big clock—I want you to put your right hand on the clock where three o'clock would be; and your left hand on the nine—*(Li'l Bit puts one hand to Peck's face, to stroke him. Then, she takes the wheel.)*

TEENAGE GREEK CHORUS. Am I doing it right?

PECK. That's right. Now, whatever you do, don't let go of the wheel. You tell me   660
whether to go faster or slower—

TEENAGE GREEK CHORUS. Not so fast, Uncle Peck!

PECK. Li'l Bit—I need you to watch the road—*(Peck puts his hands on Li'l Bit's breasts. She relaxes against him, silent, accepting his touch.)*

TEENAGE GREEK CHORUS. Uncle Peck—what are you doing?
PECK. Keep driving. *(He slips his hands under her blouse.)*
TEENAGE GREEK CHORUS. Uncle Peck—please don't do this—
PECK. Just a moment longer—*(Peck tenses against Li'l Bit.)*
TEENAGE GREEK CHORUS. *(Trying not to cry.)* This isn't happening. *(Peck tenses more, sharply. He buries his face in Li'l Bit's neck, and moans softly. The Teenage Greek Chorus exits, and Li'l Bit steps out of the car. Peck, too, disappears.)*
VOICE. *(Reflects.)* Driving in today's world.
LI'L BIT. That day was the last day I lived in my body. I retreated above the neck, and I've lived inside the "fire" in my head ever since.

And now that seems like a long, long time ago. When we were both very young.

And before you know it, I'll be thirty-five. That's getting up there for a woman. And I find myself believing in things that a younger self vowed never to believe in. Things like family and forgiveness.

I know I'm lucky. Although I still have never known what it feels like to jog or dance. Any thing that . . . "jiggles." I do like to watch people on the dance floor, or out on the running paths, just jiggling away. And I say—good for them. *(Li'l Bit moves to the car with pleasure.)*

The nearest sensation I feel—of flight in the body—I guess I feel when I'm driving. On a day like today. It's five A.M. The radio says it's going to be clear and crisp. I've got five hundred miles of highway ahead of me—and some back roads too. I filled the tank last night, and had the oil checked. Checked the tires, too. You've got to treat her . . . with respect.

First thing I do is: check under the car. To see if any two-year-olds or household cats have crawled beneath—and strategically placed their skulls behind my back tires—*(Li'l Bit crouches.)*

Nope. Then I get in the car. *(Li'l Bit does so.)*

I lock the doors. And turn the key. Then I adjust the most important control on the dashboard—the radio—*(Li'l Bit turns the radio on: we hear all of the Greek Chorus overlapping, and static:)*
FEMALE GREEK CHORUS. *(Overlapping.)*—"You were so tiny you fit in his hand"—
MALE GREEK CHORUS. *(Overlapping.)*—"How is Shakespeare gonna help her lie on her back in the—"
TEENAGE GREEK CHORUS. *(Overlapping.)*—"Am I doing it right?" *(Li'l Bit fine-tunes the radio station. A song like "Dedicated to the One I Love" or Orbison's "Sweet Dreams" comes on, and cuts off the Greek Chorus.)*
LI'L BIT. Ahh . . . *(Beat.)* I fasten my seat belt. Adjust the seat. Then I check the right side mirror—check the left side. *(She does.)* Finally, I adjust the rear view mirror. *(As Li'l Bit adjusts the rear view mirror, a faint light strikes the spirit of Uncle Peck, who is sitting in the back seat of the car. She sees him in the mirror. She smiles at him, and he nods at her. They are happy to be going for a long drive together. Li'l Bit slips the car into first gear—to us:)* And then—I floor it. *(Sound of a car taking off. Blackout.)*

END OF PLAY

Explorations of the Text

1. How does Vogel humanize Uncle Peck? Does he have any positive qualities? Does she present causes of his pedophilia? Focus on Uncle Peck's experiences in the war and the fishing episode with Bobby. How does Aunt Mary treat her husband?

2. Why is Li'l Bit drawn to Uncle Peck? Why does she finally reject him when he visits her in college?

3. How do sexual and gender roles define the family members? Consider their names.

4. Characterize Li'l Bit at different stages in her life. In what ways is she an outsider in her family? How does she change? How does her relationship with Uncle Peck change? Explore her changing relationship with her female body. Discuss the impact of the abuse.

5. How does the Greek Chorus function in the play? Does it act as character foils? Does it comment on the action? Present cultural contexts? Why do you think Vogel used the technique of having one actor play several roles in the Chorus?

6. Why is the story told in reverse chronological order; that is, the story begins when the protagonist is thirty-five and ends when she is eleven. How do the stream-of-consciousness structure and retrospective perspective develop themes of the drama?

7. How does the car function as a symbol in the work? Consider Uncle Peck's statement: "There's something about driving—when you're in control of the car, just you and the machine and the road—that nobody can take from you. A power." In what ways is this statement ironic? Explore the significance of the motif of driving lessons and the driving instructions that preface each scene in the play.

8. What role does music play in the drama? How does the music create the world of the 1960s? Compare the use of music in this work with the symbolic role that it plays in Oates's "Where Are You Going, Where Have You Been?"

9. Does Li'l Bit come to terms with her past? Does she forgive her Uncle? Analyze the last scene in the play, "Driving in Today's World."

10. Compare and contrast Li'l Bit's coming of age journey with Nora's in *A Doll's House*, which also appears in this chapter.

The Reading/Writing Connection

1. "Think" Topic: In what ways is Li'l Bit a teenage rebel?

2. In order to understand Li'l Bit's psychological development, examine the scenes in chronological order, noting what you think is significant in her relationship with Uncle Peck, in her place in her family and the larger world, and in her sense of self. What do you conclude?

Ideas for Writing

1. Compare and contrast the symbolism of the car and/or driving lessons presented in this work and in the works in the poetry cluster entitled "Road Trips."

Henrik Ibsen *(1828–1906)*

A Doll's House   *1879*

Characters

Torvald Helmer, *a lawyer*
Nora, *his wife*
Dr. Rank
Mrs. Kristine Linde
Nils Krogstad
Anne Marie, *the nursemaid*
Helene, *the maid*
The Helmers' three children
A Porter

Scene

The action takes place in the Helmers' flat.

> Act I
>
> *A pleasant room, tastefully but not expensively furnished. On the back wall, one door on the right leads to the entrance hall, a second door on the left leads to Helmer's study. Between these two doors, a piano. In the middle of the left wall, a door; and downstage from it, a window. Near the window a round table with armchairs and a small sofa. In the right wall, upstage, a door; and on the same wall downstage, a porcelain stove with a couple of armchairs and a rocking chair. Between the stove and the door a small table. Etchings on the walls. A whatnot with china and other small objets d'art; a small bookcase with books in handsome bindings. Carpet on the floor; a fire burns in the stove. A winter's day.*
>
> *The front door-bell rings in the hall; a moment later, there is the sound of the front door being opened. Nora comes into the room, happily humming to herself. She is dressed in her outdoor things, and is carrying lots of parcels which she then puts down on the table, right. She leaves the door into the hall standing open; a Porter can be seen outside holding a Christmas tree and a basket; he hands them to the Maid who has opened the door for them.*

Nora: Hide the Christmas tree away carefully, Helene. The children mustn't see it till this evening when it's decorated. *(To the Porter, taking out her purse.)* How much?

Porter: Fifty öre.

Nora: There's a crown. Keep the change.

> *(The Porter thanks her and goes. Nora shuts the door. She continues to laugh quietly and happily to herself as she takes off her things. She takes a bag of macaroons out of her pocket and eats one or two; then she walks stealthily across and listens at her husband's door.)*

Nora: Yes, he's in.

> *(She begins humming again as she walks over to the table, right.)*

Helmer: *(In his study.)* Is that my little sky-lark chirruping out there?

5

Nora: *(Busy opening some of the parcels.)* Yes, it is.

Helmer: Is that my little squirrel frisking about?

Nora: Yes!

Helmer: When did my little squirrel get home?

Nora: Just this minute. *(She stuffs the bag of macaroons in her pocket and wipes her mouth.)* Come on out, Torvald, and see what I've bought. 10

Helmer: I don't want to be disturbed! *(A moment later, he opens the door and looks out, his pen in his hand.)* "Bought," did you say? All that? Has my little spendthrift been out squandering money again?

Nora: But, Torvald, surely this year we can spread ourselves just a little. This is the first Christmas we haven't had to go carefully.

Helmer: Ah, but that doesn't mean we can afford to be extravagant, you know.

Nora: Oh yes, Torvald, surely we can afford to be just a little bit extravagant now, can't we? Just a teeny-weeny bit. You are getting quite a good salary now, and you are going to earn lots and lots of money.

Helmer: Yes, after the New Year. But it's going to be three whole months before the 15 first pay check comes in.

Nora: Pooh! We can always borrow in the meantime.

Helmer: Nora! *(Crosses to her and takes her playfully by the ear.)* Here we go again, you and your frivolous ideas! Suppose I went and borrowed a thousand crowns today, and you went and spent it over Christmas, then on New Year's Eve a slate fell and hit me on the head and there I was. . . .

Nora: *(Putting her hand over his mouth.)* Sh! Don't say such horrid things.

Helmer: Yes, but supposing something like that did happen . . . what then?

Nora: If anything as awful as that did happen, I wouldn't care if I owed anybody 20 anything or not.

Helmer: Yes, but what about the people I'd borrowed from?

Nora: Them? Who cares about them! They are only strangers!

Helmer: Nora, Nora! Just like a woman! Seriously though, Nora, you know what I think about these things. No debts! Never borrow! There's always something inhibited, something unpleasant, about a home built on credit and borrowed money. We two have managed to stick it out so far, and that's the way we'll go on for the little time that remains.

Nora: *(Walks over to the store.)* Very well, just as you say, Torvald.

Helmer: *(Following her.)* There, there! My little singing bird mustn't go drooping her 25 wings, eh? Has it got the sulks, that little squirrel of mine? *(Takes out his wallet.)* Nora, what do you think I've got here?

Nora: *(Quickly turning around.)* Money!

Helmer: There! *(He hands her some notes.)* Good heavens, I know only too well how Christmas runs away with the housekeeping.

Nora: *(Counts.)* Ten, twenty, thirty, forty. Oh, thank you, thank you. Torvald! This will see me quite a long way.

Helmer: Yes, it'll have to.

Nora: Yes, yes, I'll see that it does. But come over here, I want to show you all the 30 things I've bought. And so cheap! Look, some new clothes for Ivar . . . and a little sword. There's a horse and a trumpet for Bob. And a doll and a doll's cot for Emmy. They are not very grand but she'll have them all broken before long anyway. And I've got some dress material and some handkerchiefs for the maids. Though, really, dear old Anne Marie should have had something better.

Helmer: And what's in this parcel here?

Nora: *(Shrieking.)* No, Torvald! You mustn't see that till tonight!

Helmer: All right. But tell me now, what did my little spendthrift fancy for herself?

Nora: For me? Pooh, I don't really want anything.

Helmer: Of course you do. Anything reasonable that you think you might like, just tell me.   35

Nora: Well, I don't really know. As a matter of fact, though, Torvald . . .

Helmer: Well?

Nora: *(Toying with his coat buttons, and without looking at him.)* If you did want to give me something, you could . . . you could always . . .

Helmer: Well, well, out with it!

Nora: *(Quickly.)* You could always give me money, Torvald. Only what you think you   40
could spare. And then I could buy myself something with it later on.

Helmer: But Nora . . .

Nora: Oh, please, Torvald dear! Please! I beg you. Then I'd wrap the money up in some pretty gilt paper and hang it on the Christmas tree. Wouldn't that be fun?

Helmer: What do we call my pretty little pet when it runs away with all the money?

Nora: I know, I know, we call it a spendthrift. But please let's do what I said, Torvald. Then I'll have a bit of time to think about what I need most. Isn't that awfully sensible, now, eh?

Helmer: *(Smiling.)* Yes, it is indeed—that is, if only you really could hold on to the   45
money I gave you, and really did buy something for yourself with it. But it just gets mixed up with the housekeeping and frittered away on all sorts of useless things, and then I have to dig into my pocket all over again.

Nora: Oh but, Torvald . . .

Helmer: You can't deny it, Nora dear. *(Puts his arm around her waist.)* My pretty little pet is very sweet, but it runs away with an awful lot of money. It's incredible how expensive it is for a man to keep such a pet.

Nora: For shame! How can you say such a thing? As a matter of fact I save everything I can.

Helmer: *(Laughs.)* Yes, you are right there. Everything you *can*. But you simply can't.

Nora: *(Hums and smiles quietly and happily.)* Ah, if you only knew how many   50
expenses the likes of us sky-larks and squirrels have, Torvald!

Helmer: What a funny little one you are! Just like your father. Always on the look-out for money, wherever you can lay your hands on it; but as soon as you've got it, it just seems to slip through your fingers. You never seem to know what you've done with it. Well, one must accept you as you are. It's in the blood. Oh yes, it is, Nora. That sort of thing is hereditary.

Nora: Oh, I only wish I'd inherited a few more of Daddy's qualities.

Helmer: And I wouldn't want my pretty little song-bird to be the least bit different from what she is now. But come to think of it, you look rather . . . rather . . . how shall I put it? . . . rather guilty today. . . .

Nora: Do I?

Helmer: Yes, you do indeed. Look me straight in the eye.   55

Nora: *(Looks at him.)* Well?

Helmer: *(Wagging his finger at her.)* My little sweet-tooth surely didn't forget herself in town today?

Nora: No, whatever makes you think that?

Helmer: She didn't just pop into the confectioner's for a moment?

Nora: No, I assure you, Torvald . . . ! 60

Helmer: Didn't try sampling the preserves?

Nora: No, really I didn't.

Helmer: Didn't go nibbling a macaroon or two?

Nora: No, Torvald, honestly, you must believe me . . . !

Helmer: All right then! It's really just my little joke. . . . 65

Nora: *(Crosses to the table.)* I would never dream of doing anything you didn't want me to.

Helmer: Of course not, I know that. And then you've given me your word. . . . *(Crosses to her.)* Well then, Nora dearest, you shall keep your little Christmas secrets. They'll all come out tonight, I dare say, when we light the tree.

Nora: Did you remember to invite Dr. Rank?

Helmer: No. But there's really no need. Of course he'll come and have dinner with us. Anyway, I can ask him when he looks in this morning. I've ordered some good wine. Nora, you can't imagine how I am looking forward to this evening.

Nora: So am I. And won't the children enjoy it, Torvald! 70

Helmer: Oh, what a glorious feeling it is, knowing you've got a nice, safe job, and a good fat income. Don't you agree? Isn't it wonderful, just thinking about it?

Nora: Oh, it's marvelous!

Helmer: Do you remember last Christmas? Three whole weeks beforehand you shut yourself up every evening till after midnight making flowers for the Christmas tree and all the other splendid things you wanted to surprise us with. Ugh, I never felt so bored in all my life.

Nora: I wasn't the least bit bored.

Helmer: *(Smiling.)* But it turned out a bit of an anticlimax, Nora. 75

Nora: Oh, you are not going to tease me about that again! How was I to know the cat would get in and pull everything to bits?

Helmer: No, of course you couldn't. Poor little Nora! All you wanted was for us to have a nice time—and it's the thought behind it that counts, after all. All the same, it's a good thing we've seen the back of those lean times.

Nora: Yes, really it's marvelous.

Helmer: Now there's no need for me to sit here all on my own, bored to tears. And you don't have to strain your dear little eyes, and work those dainty little fingers to the bone. . . .

Nora: *(Clapping her hands.)* No, Torvald, I don't do I? Not any more. Oh, how 80 marvelous it is to hear that! *(Takes his arm.)* Now I want to tell you how I've been thinking we might arrange things, Torvald. As soon as Christmas is over. . . . *(The door-bell rings in the hall.)* Oh, there's the bell. *(Tidies one or two things in the room.)* It's probably a visitor. What a nuisance!

Helmer: Remember I'm not at home to callers.

Maid: *(In the doorway.)* There's a lady to see you, ma'am.

Nora: Show her in, please.

Maid: *(To Helmer.)* And the doctor's just arrived, too, sir.

Helmer: Did he go straight into my room? 85

Maid: Yes, he did, sir.

> *(Helmer goes into his study. The Maid shows in Mrs. Linde, who is in traveling clothes, and closes the door after her.)*

Mrs. Linde: *(Subdued and rather hesitantly.)* How do you do, Nora?

Nora: *(Uncertainly.)* How do you do?

Mrs. Linde: I'm afraid you don't recognize me.

Nora: No, I don't think I . . . And yet I seem to. . . . *(Bursts out suddenly.)* Why! Kristine! Is it really you?   90

Mrs. Linde: Yes, it's me.

Nora: Fancy not recognizing you again! But how was I to, when . . . *(Gently.)* How you've changed, Kristine!

Mrs. Linde: I dare say I have. In nine . . . ten years. . . .

Nora: Is it so long since we last saw each other? Yes, it must be. Oh, believe me these last eight years have been such a happy time. And now you've come up to town, too? All that long journey in wintertime. That took courage.

Mrs. Linde: I just arrived this morning on the steamer.   95

Nora: To enjoy yourself over Christmas, of course. How lovely! Oh, we'll have such fun, you'll see. Do take off your things. You are not cold, are you? *(Helps her.)* There now! Now let's sit down here in comfort beside the stove. No, here, you take the armchair, I'll sit here on the rocking chair. *(Takes her hands.)* Ah, now you look a bit more like your old self again. It was just that when I first saw you. . . . But you are a little paler, Kristine . . . and perhaps even a bit thinner!

Mrs. Linde: And much, much older, Nora.

Nora: Yes, perhaps a little older . . . very, very little, not really very much. *(Stops suddenly and looks serious.)* Oh, what a thoughtless creature I am, sitting here chattering on like this! Dear, sweet Kristine, can you forgive me?

Mrs. Linde: What do you mean, Nora?

Nora: *(Gently.)* Poor Kristine, of course you're a widow now.   100

Mrs. Linde: Yes, my husband died three years ago.

Nora: Oh, I remember now. I read about it in the papers. Oh, Kristine, believe me I often thought at the time of writing to you. But I kept putting it off, something always seemed to crop up.

Mrs. Linde: My dear Nora, I understand so well.

Nora: No, it wasn't very nice of me, Kristine. Oh, you poor thing, what you must have gone through. And didn't he leave you anything?

Mrs. Linde: No.   105

Nora: And no children?

Mrs. Linde: No.

Nora: Absolutely nothing?

Mrs. Linde: Nothing at all . . . not even a broken heart to grieve over.

Nora: *(Looks at her incredulously.)* But, Kristine, is that possible?   110

Mrs. Linde: *(Smiles sadly and strokes Nora's hair.)* Oh, it sometimes happens, Nora.

Nora: So utterly alone. How terribly sad that must be for you. I have three lovely children. You can't see them for the moment, because they're out with their nanny. But now you must tell me all about yourself. . . .

Mrs. Linde: No, no, I want to hear about you.

Nora: No, you start. I won't be selfish today. I must think only about your affairs today. But there's just one thing I really must tell you. Have you heard about the great stroke of luck we've had in the last few days?

Mrs. Linde: No. What is it?   115

Nora: What do you think? My husband has just been made Bank Manager!

Mrs. Linde: Your husband? How splendid!

Nora: Isn't it tremendous! It's not a very steady way of making a living, you know, being a lawyer, especially if he refuses to take on anything that's the least bit shady—which of course is what Torvald does, and I think he's quite right. You can imagine how pleased we are! He starts at the bank straight after New Year, and he's getting a big salary and lots of commission. From now on we'll be able to live quite differently . . . we'll do just what we want. Oh, Kristine, I'm so happy and relieved. I must say it's lovely to have plenty of money and not have to worry. Isn't it?

Mrs. Linde: Yes. It must be nice to have enough, at any rate.

Nora: No, not just enough, but pots and pots of money.   120

Mrs. Linde: *(Smiles.)* Nora, Nora, haven't you learned any sense yet? At school you used to be an awful spendthrift.

Nora: Yes, Torvald still says I am. *(Wags her finger.)* But little Nora isn't as stupid as everybody thinks. Oh, we haven't really been in a position where I could afford to spend a lot of money. We've both had to work.

Mrs. Linde: You too?

Nora: Yes, odd jobs—sewing, crochet-work, embroidery and things like that. *(Casually.)* And one or two other things, besides. I suppose you know that Torvald left the Ministry when we got married. There weren't any prospects of promotion in his department, and of course he needed to earn more money than he had before. But the first year he wore himself out completely. He had to take on all kinds of extra jobs, you know, and he found himself working all hours of the day and night. But he couldn't go on like that, and he became seriously ill. The doctors said it was essential for him to go South.

Mrs. Linde: Yes, I believe you spent a whole year in Italy, didn't you?   125

Nora: That's right. It wasn't easy to get away, I can tell you. It was just after I'd had Ivar. But of course we had to go. Oh, it was an absolutely marvelous trip. And it saved Torvald's life. But it cost an awful lot of money, Kristine.

Mrs. Linde: That I can well imagine.

Nora: Twelve hundred dollars. Four thousand eight hundred crowns. That's a lot of money, Kristine.

Mrs. Linde: Yes, but in such circumstances, one is very lucky if one has it.

Nora: Well, we got it from Daddy, you see.   130

Mrs. Linde: Ah, that was it. It was just about then your father died, I believe, wasn't it?

Nora: Yes, Kristine, just about then. And do you know, I couldn't even go and look after him. Here was I expecting Ivar any day. And I also had poor Torvald, gravely ill, on my hands. Dear, kind Daddy! I never saw him again, Kristine. Oh, that's the saddest thing that has happened to me in all my married life.

Mrs. Linde: I know you were very fond of him. But after that you left for Italy?

Nora: Yes, we had the money then, and the doctors said it was urgent. We left a month later.

Mrs. Linde: And your husband came back completely cured?   135

Nora: Fit as a fiddle!

Mrs. Linde: But . . . what about the doctor?

Nora: How do you mean?

Mrs. Linde: I thought the maid said something about the gentleman who came at the same time as me being a doctor.

Nora: Yes, that was Dr. Rank. But this isn't a professional visit. He's our best friend and 140 he always looks in at least once a day. No, Torvald has never had a day's illness since. And the children are fit and healthy, and so am I. *(Jumps up and claps her hands.)* Oh God, oh God, isn't it marvelous to be alive, and to be happy, Kristine! . . . Oh but I ought to be ashamed of myself . . . Here I go on talking about nothing but myself. *(She sits on a low stool near Mrs. Linde and lays her arms on her lap.)* Oh, please, you mustn't be angry with me! Tell me, is it really true that you didn't love your husband? What made you marry him, then?

Mrs. Linde: My mother was still alive; she was bedridden and helpless. And then I had two young brothers to look after as well. I didn't think I would be justified in refusing him.

Nora: No, I dare say you are right. I suppose he was fairly wealthy then?

Mrs. Linde: He was quite well off, I believe. But the business was shaky. When he died, it went all to pieces, and there just wasn't anything left.

Nora: What then?

Mrs. Linde: Well, I had to fend for myself, opening a little shop, running a little 145 school, anything I could turn my hand to. These last three years have been one long relentless drudge. But now it's finished, Nora. My poor dear mother doesn't need me any more, she's passed away. Nor the boys either; they're at work now, they can look after themselves.

Nora: What a relief you must find it. . . .

Mrs. Linde: No, Nora! Just unutterably empty. Nobody to live for any more. *(Stands up restlessly.)* That's why I couldn't stand it any longer being cut off up there. Surely it must be a bit easier here to find something to occupy your mind. If only I could manage to find a steady job of some kind, in an office perhaps. . . .

Nora: But, Kristine, that's terribly exhausting; and you look so worn out even before you start. The best thing for you would be a little holiday at some quiet little resort.

Mrs. Linde: *(Crosses to the window.)* I haven't any father I can fall back on for the money, Nora.

Nora: *(Rises.)* Oh, please, you mustn't be angry with me! 150

Mrs. Linde: *(Goes to her.)* My dear Nora, you mustn't be angry with me either. That's the worst thing about people in my position, they become so bitter. One has nobody to work for, yet one has to be on the look-out all the time. Life has to go on, and one starts thinking only of oneself. Believe it or not, when you told me the good news about your step up, I was pleased not so much for your sake as for mine.

Nora: How do you mean? Ah, I see. You think Torvald might be able to do something for you.

Mrs. Linde: Yes, that's exactly what I thought.

Nora: And so he shall, Kristine. Just leave things to me. I'll bring it up so cleverly. . . . I'll think up something to put him in a good mood. Oh, I do so much want to help you.

Mrs. Linde: It is awfully kind of you, Nora, offering to do all this for me,   155
    particularly in your case, where you haven't known much trouble or hardship in
    your own life.

Nora: When I . . . ? I haven't known much . . . ?

Mrs. Linde: *(Smiling.)* Well, good heavens, a little bit of sewing to do and a few
    things like that. What a child you are, Nora!

Nora: *(Tosses her head and walks across the room.)* I wouldn't be too sure of that, if I
    were you.

Mrs. Linde: Oh?

Nora: You're just like the rest of them. You all think I'm useless when it comes to   160
    anything really serious. . . .

Mrs. Linde: Come, come. . . .

Nora: You think I've never had anything much to contend with in this hard world.

Mrs. Linde: Nora dear, you've only just been telling me all the things you've had to
    put up with.

Nora: Pooh! They were just trivialities! *(Softly.)* I haven't told you about the really big
    thing.

Mrs. Linde: What big thing? What do you mean?   165

Nora: I know you rather tend to look down on me, Kristine. But you shouldn't, you
    know. You are proud of having worked so hard and so long for your mother.

Mrs. Linde: I'm sure I don't look down on anybody. But it's true what you say: I am
    both proud and happy when I think of how I was able to make Mother's life a
    little easier towards the end.

Nora: And you are proud when you think of what you have done for your brothers,
    too.

Mrs. Linde: I think I have every right to be.

Nora: I think so too. But now I'm going to tell you something, Kristine. I too have   170
    something to be proud and happy about.

Mrs. Linde: I don't doubt that. But what is it you mean?

Nora: Not so loud. Imagine if Torvald were to hear! He must never on any
    account . . . nobody must know about it, Kristine, nobody but you.

Mrs. Linde: But what is it?

Nora: Come over here. *(She pulls her down on the sofa beside her.)* Yes, Kristine, I
    too have something to be proud and happy about. I was the one who saved
    Torvald's life.

Mrs. Linde: Saved . . . ? How . . . ?   175

Nora: I told you about our trip to Italy. Torvald would never have recovered but for
    that. . . .

Mrs. Linde: Well? Your father gave you what money was necessary.

Nora: *(Smiles.)* That's what Torvald thinks, and everybody else. But . . .

Mrs. Linde: But . . . ?

Nora: Daddy never gave us a penny. I was the one who raised the money.   180

Mrs. Linde: You? All that money?

Nora: Twelve hundred dollars. Four thousand eight hundred crowns. What do you
    say to that!

Mrs. Linde: But, Nora, how was it possible? Had you won a sweepstake or
    something?

Nora: *(Contemptuously.)* A sweepstake? Pooh! There would have been nothing to it then.

Mrs. Linde: Where did you get it from, then?   185
Nora: *(Hums and smiles secretively.)* H'm, tra-la-la!
Mrs. Linde: Because what you couldn't do was borrow it.
Nora: Oh? Why not?
Mrs. Linde: Well, a wife can't borrow without her husband's consent.
Nora: *(Tossing her head.)* Ah, but when it happens to be a wife with a bit of a sense for   190
     business . . . a wife who knows her way about things, then. . . .
Mrs. Linde: But, Nora, I just don't understand. . . .
Nora: You don't have to. I haven't said I did borrow the money. I might have got it
     some other way. *(Throws herself back on the sofa.)* I might even have got it from
     some admirer. Anyone as reasonably attractive as I am. . . .
Mrs. Linde: Don't be so silly!
Nora: Now you must be dying of curiosity, Kristine.
Mrs. Linde: Listen to me now, Nora dear—you haven't done anything rash, have   195
     you?
Nora: *(Sitting up again.)* Is it rash to save your husband's life?
Mrs. Linde: I think it was rash to do anything without telling him. . . .
Nora: But the whole point was that he mustn't know anything. Good heavens, can't
     you see! He wasn't even supposed to know how desperately ill he was. It was
     me the doctors came and told his life was in danger, that the only way to save
     him was to go South for a while. Do you think I didn't try talking him into
     it first? I began dropping hints about how nice it would be if I could be taken
     on a little trip abroad, like other young wives. I wept, I pleaded. I told him he
     ought to show some consideration for my condition, and let me have a bit of my
     own way. And then I suggested he might take out a loan. But at that he nearly
     lost his temper, Kristine. He said I was being frivolous, that it was his duty as a
     husband not to give in to all these whims and fancies of mine—as I do believe
     he called them. All right, I thought, somehow you've got to be saved. And it
     was then I found a way. . . .
Mrs. Linde: Did your husband never find out from your father that the money
     hadn't come from him?
Nora: No, never. It was just about the time Daddy died. I'd intended letting him into   200
     the secret and asking him not to give me away. But when he was so ill . . . I'm
     sorry to say it never became necessary.
Mrs. Linde: And you never confided in your husband?
Nora: Good heavens, how could you ever imagine such a thing! When he's so strict
     about such matters! Besides, Torvald is a man with a good deal of pride—it
     would be terribly embarrassing and humiliating for him if he thought he owed
     anything to me. It would spoil everything between us; this happy home of ours
     would never be the same again.
Mrs. Linde: Are you never going to tell him?
Nora: *(Reflectively, half-smiling.)* Oh yes, some day perhaps . . . in many years time,
     when I'm no longer as pretty as I am now. You mustn't laugh! What I mean
     of course is when Torvald isn't quite so much in love with me as he is now,
     when he's lost interest in watching me dance, or get dressed up, or recite. Then
     it might be a good thing to have something in reserve. . . . *(Breaks off.)* What
     nonsense! That day will never come. Well, what have you got to say to my
     big secret, Kristine? Still think I'm not much good for anything? One thing,

though, it's meant a lot of worry for me, I can tell you. It hasn't always been easy to meet my obligations when the time came. You know in business there is something called quarterly interest, and other things called installments, and these are always terribly difficult things to cope with. So what I've had to do is save a little here and there, you see, wherever I could. I couldn't really save anything out of the housekeeping, because Torvald has to live in decent style. I couldn't let the children go about badly dressed either—I felt any money I got for them had to go on them alone. Such sweet little things!

Mrs. Linde: Poor Nora! So it had to come out of your own allowance? 205

Nora: Of course. After all, I was the one it concerned most. Whenever Torvald gave me money for new clothes and such-like, I never spent more than half. And always I bought the simplest and cheapest things. It's a blessing most things look well on me, so Torvald never noticed anything. But sometimes I did feel it was a bit hard, Kristine, because it is nice to be well dressed, isn't it?

Mrs. Linde: Yes, I suppose it is.

Nora: I have had some other sources of income, of course. Last winter I was lucky enough to get quite a bit of copying to do. So I shut myself up every night and sat and wrote through to the small hours of the morning. Oh, sometimes I was so tired, so tired. But it was tremendous fun all the same, sitting there working and earning money like that. It was almost like being a man.

Mrs. Linde: And how much have you been able to pay off like this?

Nora: Well, I can't tell exactly. It's not easy to know where you are with transactions 210 of this kind, you understand. All I know is I've paid off just as much as I could scrape together. Many's the time I was at my wit's end. *(Smiles)* Then I used to sit here and pretend that some rich old gentleman had fallen in love with me. . . .

Mrs. Linde: What! What gentleman?

Nora: Oh, rubbish! . . . and that now he had died, and when they opened his will, there in big letters were the words: "My entire fortune is to be paid over, immediately and in cash, to charming Mrs. Nora Helmer."

Mrs. Linde: But my dear Nora—who is this man?

Nora: Good heavens, don't you understand? There never was any old gentleman; it was just something I used to sit here pretending, time and time again, when I didn't know where to turn next for money. But it doesn't make very much difference; as far as I'm concerned the old boy can do what he likes, I'm tired of him; I can't be bothered any more with him or his will. Because now all my worries are over. *(Jumping up.)* Oh God, what a glorious thought, Kristine! No more worries! Just think of being without a care in the world . . . being able to romp with the children, and making the house nice and attractive, and having things just as Torvald likes to have them? And then spring will soon be here, and blue skies. And maybe we can go away somewhere. I might even see something of the sea again. Oh yes! When you're happy, life is a wonderful thing!

(The door-bell is heard in the hall.)

Mrs. Linde: *(Gets up.)* There's the bell. Perhaps I'd better go. 215

Nora: No, do stay, please. I don't suppose it's for me; it's probably somebody for Torvald. . . .

Maid: *(In the doorway.)* Excuse me, ma'am, but there's a gentleman here wants to see Mr. Helmer, and I didn't quite know . . . because the Doctor is in there. . . .

Nora: Who is the gentleman?

Krogstad: *(In the doorway.)* It's me, Mrs. Helmer.

(Mrs. Linde starts, then turns away to the window.)

Nora: *(Tense, takes a step towards him and speaks in a low voice.)* You? What is it? 220
What do you want to talk to my husband about?

Krogstad: Bank matters . . . in a manner of speaking. I work at the bank, and I hear
your husband is to be the new manager. . . .

Nora: So it's . . .

Krogstad: Just routine business matters, Mrs. Helmer. Absolutely nothing else.

*(She nods impassively and shuts the hall door behind him; then she walks across and
sees to the stove.)*

Mrs. Linde: Nora . . . who was that man?

Nora: His name is Krogstad. 225

Mrs. Linde: So it really was him.

Nora: Do you know the man?

Mrs. Linde: I used to know him . . . a good many years ago. He was a solicitor's clerk
in our district for a while.

Nora: Yes, so he was.

Mrs. Linde: How he's changed! 230

Nora: His marriage wasn't a very happy one, I believe.

Mrs. Linde: He's a widower now, isn't he?

Nora: With a lot of children. There, it'll burn better now.

(She closes the stove door and moves the rocking chair a little to one side.)

Mrs. Linde: He does a certain amount of business on the side, they say?

Nora: Oh? Yes, it's always possible. I just don't know. . . . But let's not think about 235
business . . . it's all so dull.

(Dr. Rank comes in from Helmer's study.)

Dr. Rank: *(Still in the doorway.)* No, no, Torvald, I won't intrude. I'll just look in on
your wife for a moment. *(Shuts the door and notices Mrs. Linde.)* Oh, I beg your
pardon. I'm afraid I'm intruding here as well.

Nora: No, not at all! *(Introduces them.)* Dr. Rank . . . Mrs. Linde.

Rank: Ah! A name I've often heard mentioned in this house. I believe I came past
you on the stairs as I came in.

Mrs. Linde: I have to take things slowly going upstairs. I find it rather a trial.

Nora: Ah, some little disability somewhere, eh? 240

Mrs. Linde: Just a bit run down, I think, actually.

Rank: Is that all? Then I suppose you've come to town for a good rest—doing the
rounds of the parties?

Mrs. Linde: I have come to look for work.

Rank: Is that supposed to be some kind of sovereign remedy for being run down?

Mrs. Linde: One must live, Doctor. 245

Rank: Yes, it's generally thought to be necessary.

Nora: Come, come, Dr. Rank. You are quite as keen to live as anybody.

Rank: Quite keen, yes. Miserable as I am, I'm quite ready to let things drag on as
long as possible. All my patients are the same. Even those with a moral affliction
are no different. As a matter of fact, there's a bad case of that kind in talking
with Helmer at this very moment. . . .

Mrs. Linde: *(Softly.)* Ah!

Nora: Whom do you mean? 250

Rank: A person called Krogstad—nobody you would know. He's rotten to the core. But even he began talking about having to *live,* as though it were something terribly important.

Nora: Oh? And what did he want to talk to Torvald about?

Rank: I honestly don't know. All I heard was something about the Bank.

Nora: I didn't know that Krog . . . that this Mr. Krogstad had anything to do with the Bank.

Rank: Oh yes, he's got some kind of job down there. *(To Mrs. Linde.)* I wonder if 255 you've got people in your part of the country too who go rushing round sniffing out cases of moral corruption, and then installing the individuals concerned in nice, well-paid jobs where they can keep them under observation. Sound, decent people have to be content to stay out in the cold.

Mrs. Linde: Yet surely it's the sick who most need to be brought in.

Rank: *(Shrugs his shoulders.)* Well, there we have it. It's that attitude that's turning society into a clinic.

(Nora, lost in her own thoughts, breaks into smothered laughter and claps her hands.)

Rank: Why are you laughing at that? Do you know in fact what society is?

Nora: What do I care about your silly old society? I was laughing about something quite different . . . something frightfully funny. Tell me, Dr. Rank, are all the people who work at the bank dependent on Torvald now?

Rank: Is *that* what you find so frightfully funny? 260

Nora: *(Smiles and hums.)* Never you mind! Never you mind! *(Walks about the room.)* Yes, it really is terribly amusing to think that we . . . that Torvald now has power over so many people. *(She takes the bag out of her pocket.)* Dr. Rank, what about a little macaroon?

Rank: Look at this, eh? Macaroons. I thought they were forbidden here.

Nora: Yes, but these are some Kristine gave me.

Mrs. Linde: What? I . . . ?

Nora: Now, now, you needn't be alarmed. You weren't to know that Torvald had 265 forbidden them. He's worried in case they ruin my teeth, you know. Still . . . what's it matter once in a while! Don't you think so, Dr. Rank? Here! *(She pops a macaroon into his mouth.)* And you too, Kristine. And I shall have one as well; just a little one . . . or two at the most. *(She walks about the room again.)* Really I am so happy. There's just one little thing I'd love to do now.

Rank: What's that?

Nora: Something I'd love to say in front of Torvald.

Rank: Then why can't you?

Nora: No, I daren't. It's not very nice.

Mrs. Linde: Not very nice? 270

Rank: Well, in that case it might not be wise. But to us, I don't see why. . . . What is this you would love to say in front of Helmer?

Nora: I would simply love to say: "Damn."

Rank: Are you mad!

Mrs. Linde: Good gracious, Nora . . . !

Rank: Say it! Here he is! 275
Nora: *(Hiding the bag of macaroons.)* Sh! Sh!

(Helmer comes out of his room, his overcoat over his arm and his hat in his hand.)

Nora: *(Going over to him.)* Well, Torvald dear, did you get rid of him?
Helmer: Yes, he's just gone.
Nora: Let me introduce you. This is Kristine, who has just arrived in town. . . .
Helmer: Kristine . . . ? You must forgive me, but I don't think I know . . . 280
Nora: Mrs. Linde, Torvald dear. Kristine Linde.
Helmer: Ah, indeed. A school-friend of my wife's, presumably.
Mrs. Linde: Yes, we were girls together.
Nora: Fancy, Torvald, she's come all this long way just to have a word with you.
Helmer: How is that? 285
Mrs. Linde: Well, it wasn't really. . . .
Nora: The thing is, Kristine is terribly clever at office work, and she's frightfully keen on finding a job with some efficient man, so that she can learn even more. . . .
Helmer: Very sensible, Mrs. Linde.
Nora: And then when she read you'd been made Bank Manager—there was a bit in the paper about it—she set off at once. Torvald, please! You *will* try and do something for Kristine, won't you? For my sake?
Helmer: Well, that's not altogether impossible. You are a widow, I presume? 290
Mrs. Linde: Yes.
Helmer: And you've had some experience in business?
Mrs. Linde: A fair amount.
Helmer: Well, it's quite probable I can find you a job, I think. . . .
Nora: *(Clapping her hands.)* There, you see! 295
Helmer: You have come at a fortunate moment, Mrs. Linde. . . .
Mrs. Linde: Oh, how can I ever thank you . . . ?
Helmer: Not a bit. *(He puts on his overcoat.)* But for the present I must ask you to excuse me. . . .
Rank: Wait. I'm coming with you.

(He fetches his fur coat from the hall and warms it at the stove.)

Nora: Don't be long, Torvald dear. 300
Helmer: Not more than an hour, that's all.
Nora: Are you leaving too, Kristine?
Mrs. Linde: *(Putting on her things.)* Yes, I must go and see if I can't find myself a room.
Helmer: Perhaps we can all walk down the road together.
Nora: *(Helping her.)* What a nuisance we are so limited for space here. I'm afraid it 305 just isn't possible. . . .
Mrs. Linde: Oh, you mustn't dream of it! Goodbye, Nora dear, and thanks for everything.
Nora: Goodbye for the present. But . . . you'll be coming back this evening, of course. And you too, Dr. Rank? What's that? If you are up to it? Of course you'll be up to it. Just wrap yourself up well.

(They go out, talking, into the hall; Children's voices can be heard on the stairs.)

Nora: Here they are! Here they are! *(She runs to the front door and opens it. Anne Marie, the nursemaid, enters with the Children.)* Come in! Come in! *(She bends* *down and kisses them.)* Ah! my sweet little darlings. . . . You see them, Kristine? Aren't they lovely!

Rank: Don't stand here chattering in this draft!

Helmer: Come along, Mrs. Linde. The place now becomes unbearable for anybody except mothers. 310

> *(Dr. Rank, Helmer, and Mrs. Linde go down the stairs: the Nursemaid comes into the room with the Children, then Nora, shutting the door behind her.)*

Nora: How fresh and bright you look! My, what red cheeks you've got! Like apples and roses. *(During the following, the Children keep chattering away to her.)* Have you had a nice time? That's splendid. And you gave Emmy and Bob a ride on your sledge? Did you now! Both together! Fancy that! There's a clever boy, Ivar. Oh, let me take her a little while, Anne Marie. There's my sweet little baby-doll! *(She takes the youngest of the Children from the Nursemaid and dances with her.)* All right, Mummy will dance with Bobby too. What? You've been throwing snowballs? Oh, I wish I'd been there. No, don't bother, Anne Marie, I'll help them off with their things. No, please let me—I like doing it. You go on in, you look frozen. You'll find some hot coffee on the stove. *(The Nursemaid goes into the room, left. Nora takes off the Children's coats and hats and throws them down anywhere, while the Children all talk at once.)* Really! A great big dog came running after you? But he didn't bite. No, the doggies wouldn't bite my pretty little dollies. You mustn't touch the parcels, Ivar! What are they? Wouldn't you like to know! No, no, that's nasty. Now? Shall we play something? What shall we play? Hide and seek? Yes, let's play hide and seek. Bob can hide first. Me first? All right, let me hide first.

> *(She and the other Children play, laughing and shrieking, in this room and in the adjacent room on the right. Finally Nora hides under the table; the Children come rushing in to look for her but cannot find her; they hear her stifled laughter, rush to the table, lift up the tablecloth and find her. Tremendous shouts of delight. She creeps out and pretends to frighten them. More shouts. Meanwhile there has been a knock at the front door, which nobody has heard. The door half opens, and Krogstad can be seen. He waits a little; the game continues.)*

Krogstad: I beg your pardon, Mrs. Helmer. . . .

Nora: *(Turns with a stifled cry and half jumps up.)* Ah! What do you want?

Krogstad: Excuse me. The front door was standing open. Somebody must have forgotten to shut it. . . .

Nora: *(Standing up.)* My husband isn't at home, Mr. Krogstad. 315

Krogstad: I know.

Nora: Well . . . what are you doing here?

Krogstad: I want a word with you.

Nora: With . . . ? *(Quietly, to the Children.)* Go to Anne Marie. What? No, the strange man won't do anything to Mummy. When he's gone we'll have another game. *(She leads the Children into the room, left, and shuts the door after them; tense and uneasy.)* You want to speak to me?

Krogstad: Yes, I do. 320

Nora: Today? But it isn't the first of the month yet. . . .

Krogstad: No, it's Christmas Eve. It depends entirely on you what sort of Christmas you have.

Nora: What do you want? Today I can't possibly . . .

Krogstad: Let's not talk about that for the moment. It's something else. You've got a moment to spare?

Nora: Yes, I suppose so, though . . . 325

Krogstad: Good. I was sitting in Olsen's cafe, and I saw your husband go down the road . . .

Nora: Did you?

Krogstad: . . . with a lady.

Nora: Well?

Krogstad: May I be so bold as to ask whether that lady was Mrs. Linde? 330

Nora: Yes.

Krogstad: Just arrived in town?

Nora: Yes, today.

Krogstad: And she's a good friend of yours?

Nora: Yes, she is. But I can't see . . . 335

Krogstad: I also knew her once.

Nora: I know.

Krogstad: Oh? So you know all about it. I thought as much. Well, I want to ask you straight: is Mrs. Linde getting a job in the Bank?

Nora: How dare you cross-examine me like this, Mr. Krogstad? You, one of my husband's subordinates? But since you've asked me, I'll tell you. Yes, Mrs. Linde *has* got a job. And I'm the one who got it for her, Mr. Krogstad. Now you know.

Krogstad: So my guess was right. 340

Nora: (*Walking up and down.*) Oh, I think I can say that some of us have a little influence now and again. Just because one happens to be a woman, that doesn't mean. . . . People in subordinate positions ought to take care they don't offend anybody . . . who . . . hm . . .

Krogstad: . . . has influence?

Nora: Exactly.

Krogstad: (*Changing his tone.*) Mrs. Helmer, will you have the goodness to use your influence on my behalf?

Nora: What? What do you mean? 345

Krogstad: Will you be so good as to see that I keep my modest little job at the Bank?

Nora: What do you mean? Who wants to take it away from you?

Krogstad: Oh, you needn't try and pretend to me you don't know. I can quite see that this friend of yours isn't particularly anxious to bump up against me. And I can also see now whom I can thank for being given the sack.

Nora: But I assure you. . . .

Krogstad: All right, all right. But to come to the point: there's still time. And I 350 advise you to use your influence to stop it.

Nora: But, Mr. Krogstad, I *have* no influence.

Krogstad: Haven't you? I thought just now you said yourself . . .

Nora: I didn't mean it that way, of course. Me? What makes you think I've got any influence of that kind over my husband?

Krogstad: I know your husband from our student days. I don't suppose he is any more steadfast than other married men.

Nora: You speak disrespectfully of my husband like that and I'll show you the door. 355

Krogstad: So the lady's got courage.

Nora: I'm not frightened of you any more. After New Year I'll soon be finished with the whole business.

Krogstad: *(Controlling himself.)* Listen to me, Mrs. Helmer. If necessary I shall fight for my little job in the bank as if I were fighting for my life.

Nora: So it seems.

Krogstad: It's not just for the money, that's the last thing I care about. There's 360 something else . . . well, I might as well out with it. You see it's like this. You know as well as anybody that some years ago I got myself mixed up in a bit of trouble.

Nora: I believe I've heard something of the sort.

Krogstad: It never got as far as the courts; but immediately it was as if all paths were barred to me. So I started going in for the sort of business you know about. I had to do something, and I think I can say I haven't been one of the worst. But now I have to get out of it. My sons are growing up; for their sake I must try and win back what respectability I can. That job in the bank was like the first step on the ladder for me. And now your husband wants to kick me off the ladder again, back into the mud.

Nora: But in God's name, Mr. Krogstad, it's quite beyond my power to help you.

Krogstad: That's because you haven't the will to help me. But I have ways of making you.

Nora: You wouldn't go and tell my husband I owe you money? 365

Krogstad: Suppose I did tell him?

Nora: It would be a rotten shame. *(Half choking with tears.)* That secret is all my pride and joy—why should he have to hear about it in this nasty, horrid way . . . hear about it from *you*. You would make things horribly unpleasant for me. . . .

Krogstad: Merely unpleasant?

Nora: *(Vehemently.)* Go on, do it then! It'll be all the worse for you. Because then my husband will see for himself what a bad man you are, and then you certainly won't be able to keep your job.

Krogstad: I asked whether it was only a bit of domestic unpleasantness you were 370 afraid of?

Nora: If my husband gets to know about it, he'll pay off what's owing at once. And then we'd have nothing more to do with you.

Krogstad: *(Taking a pace towards her.)* Listen, Mrs. Helmer, either you haven't a very good memory, or else you don't understand much about business. I'd better make the position a little bit clearer for you.

Nora: How do you mean?

Krogstad: When your husband was ill, you came to me for the loan of twelve hundred dollars.

Nora: I didn't know of anybody else. 375

Krogstad: I promised to find you the money. . . .

Nora: And you did find it.

Krogstad: I promised to find you the money on certain conditions. At the time you were so concerned about your husband's illness, and so anxious to get the money for going away with, that I don't think you paid very much attention to all the incidentals. So there is perhaps some point in reminding you of them. Well, I promised to find you the money against an IOU which I drew up for you.

Nora: Yes, and which I signed.

Krogstad: Very good. But below that I added a few lines, by which your father was   380
to stand security. This your father was to sign.

Nora: Was to . . . ? He did sign it.

Krogstad: I had left the date blank. The idea was that your father was to add the date
himself when he signed it. Remember?

Nora: Yes, I think. . . .

Krogstad: I then gave you the IOU to post to your father. Wasn't that so?

Nora: Yes.   385

Krogstad: Which of course you did at once. Because only about five or six days later
you brought it back to me with your father's signature. I then paid out the
money.

Nora: Well? Haven't I paid the installments regularly?

Krogstad: Yes, fairly. But . . . coming back to what we were talking about . . . that
was a pretty bad period you were going through then, Mrs. Helmer.

Nora: Yes, it was.

Krogstad: Your father was seriously ill, I believe.   390

Nora: He was very near the end.

Krogstad: And died shortly afterwards?

Nora: Yes.

Krogstad: Tell me, Mrs. Helmer, do you happen to remember which day your father
died? The exact date, I mean.

Nora: Daddy died on 29 September.   395

Krogstad: Quite correct. I made some inquiries. Which brings up a rather curious
point *(Takes out a paper.)* which I simply cannot explain.

Nora: Curious . . . ? I don't know . . .

Krogstad: The curious thing is, Mrs. Helmer, that your father signed this document
three days after his death.

Nora: What? I don't understand. . . .

Krogstad: Your father died on 29 September. But look here. Your father has dated   400
his signature 2 October. Isn't that rather curious, Mrs. Helmer? *(Nora remains
silent.)* It's also remarkable that the words "2 October" and the year are not in
your father's handwriting, but in a handwriting I rather think I recognize. Well,
perhaps that could be explained. Your father might have forgotten to date his
signature, and then somebody else might have made a guess at the date later,
before the fact of your father's death was known. There is nothing wrong in
that. What really matters is the signature. And *that* is of course genuine, Mrs.
Helmer? It really was your father who wrote his name here?

Nora: *(After a moment's silence, throws her head back and looks at him defiantly.)* No, it
wasn't. It was me who signed father's name.

Krogstad: Listen to me. I suppose you realize that that is a very dangerous
confession?

Nora: Why? You'll soon have all your money back.

Krogstad: Let me ask you a question: why didn't you send that document to your
father?

Nora: It was impossible. Daddy was ill. If I'd asked him for his signature, I'd have   405
had to tell him what the money was for. Don't you see, when he was as ill as
that I couldn't go and tell him that my husband's life was in danger. It was
simply impossible.

Krogstad: It would have been better for you if you had abandoned the whole trip.

Nora: No, that was impossible. This was the thing that was to save my husband's life. I couldn't give it up.

Krogstad: But did it never strike you that this was fraudulent . . . ?

Nora: That wouldn't have meant anything to me. Why should I worry about you? I couldn't stand you, not when you insisted on going through with all those cold-blooded formalities, knowing all the time what a critical state my husband was in.

Krogstad: Mrs. Helmer, it's quite clear you still haven't the faintest idea what it is   410
you've committed. But let me tell you, my own offense was no more and no worse than that, and it ruined my entire reputation.

Nora: You? Are you trying to tell me that you once risked everything to save your wife's life?

Krogstad: The law takes no account of motives.

Nora: Then they must be very bad laws.

Krogstad: Bad or not, if I produce this document in court, you'll be condemned according to them.

Nora: I don't believe it. Isn't a daughter entitled to try and save her father from worry   415
and anxiety on his deathbed? Isn't a wife entitled to save her husband's life? I might not know very much about the law, but I feel sure of one thing: it must say somewhere that things like this are allowed. You mean to say you don't know that—you, when it's your job? You must have been a rotten lawyer, Mr. Krogstad.

Krogstad: That may be. But when it comes to business transactions—like the sort between us two—perhaps you'll admit I know something about them? Good. Now you must please yourself. But I tell you this: if I'm pitched out a second time, you are going to keep me company.

(He bows and goes out through the hall.)

Nora: *(Stands thoughtfully for a moment, then tosses her head.)* Rubbish! He's just trying to scare me. I'm not such a fool as all that. *(Begins gathering up the Children's clothes; after a moment she stops.)* Yet . . . ? No, it's impossible! I did it for love, didn't I?

The Children: *(In the doorway, left.)* Mummy, the gentleman's just gone out of the gate.

Nora: Yes, I know. But you mustn't say anything to anybody about that gentleman. You hear? Not even to Daddy!

The Children: All right, Mummy. Are you going to play again?   420

Nora: No, not just now.

The Children: But Mummy, you promised!

Nora: Yes, but I can't just now. Off you go now, I have a lot to do. Off you go, my darlings.

(She herds them carefully into the other room and shuts the door behind them. She sits down on the sofa, picks up her embroidery and works a few stitches, but soon stops.) No! *(She flings her work down, stands up, goes to the hall door and calls out.)* Helene! Fetch the tree in for me, please. *(She walks across to the table, left, and opens the drawer; again pauses.)* No, really, it's quite impossible!

Maid: *(With the Christmas tree.)* Where shall I put it, ma'am?

Nora: On the floor there, in the middle.   425

Maid: Anything else you want me to bring?

Nora: No, thank you. I've got what I want.

(The Maid has put the tree down and goes out.)

Nora: *(Busy decorating the tree.)* Candles here . . . and flowers here.—Revolting man! It's all nonsense! There's nothing to worry about. We'll have a lovely Christmas tree. And I'll do anything you want me to, Torvald; I'll sing for you, dance for you. . . .

(Helmer, with a bundle of documents under his arm, comes in by the hall door.)

Nora: Ah, back again already?

Helmer: Yes. Anybody been?   430

Nora: Here? No.

Helmer: That's funny. I just saw Krogstad leave the house.

Nora: Oh? O yes, that's right. Krogstad was here a minute.

Helmer: Nora, I can tell by your face he's been asking you to put a good word in for him.

Nora: Yes.   435

Helmer: And you were to pretend it was your own idea? You were to keep quiet about his having been here. He asked you to do that as well, didn't he?

Nora: Yes, Torvald. But . . .

Helmer: Nora, Nora, what possessed you to do a thing like that? Talking to a person like him, making him promises? And then on top of everything, to tell me a lie!

Nora: A lie . . . ?

Helmer: Didn't you say that nobody had been here? *(Wagging his finger at her.)* Never   440 again must my little song-bird do a thing like that! Little song-birds must keep their pretty little beaks out of mischief; no chirruping out of tune! *(Puts his arm around her waist.)* Isn't that the way we want things to be? Yes, of course it is. *(Lets her go.)* So let's say no more about it. *(Sits down by the stove.)* Ah, nice and cozy here!

(He glances through his papers.)

Nora: *(Busy with the Christmas tree, after a short pause.)* Torvald!

Helmer: Yes.

Nora: I'm terribly looking forward to that fancy dress ball at the Stenborgs' on Boxing Day.[1]

Helmer: And I'm terribly curious to see what sort of surprise you've got for me.   445

Nora: Oh, it's too silly.

Helmer: Oh?

Nora: I just can't think of anything suitable. Everything seems so absurd, so pointless.

Helmer: Has my little Nora come to *that* conclusion?

Nora: *(Behind his chair, her arms on the chairback.)* Are you very busy, Torvald?   450

Helmer: Oh . . .

Nora: What are all those papers?

Helmer: Bank matters.

Nora: Already?

Helmer: I have persuaded the retiring manager to give me authority to make any changes in organization or personnel I think necessary. I have to work on it over the Christmas week. I want everything straight by the New Year.

---

[1] **Boxing Day:** The first weekday after Christmas.

Nora: So that was why that poor Krogstad. . . . 455

Helmer: Hm!

Nora: *(Still leaning against the back of the chair, running her fingers through his hair.)* If you hadn't been so busy, Torvald, I'd have asked you to do me an awfully big favor.

Helmer: Let me hear it. What's it to be?

Nora: Nobody's got such good taste as you. And the thing is I do so want to look my best at the fancy dress ball. Torvald, couldn't you give me some advice and tell me what you think I ought to go as, and how I should arrange my costume?

Helmer: Aha! So my impulsive little woman is asking for somebody to come to her 460 rescue, eh?

Nora: Please Torvald, I never get anywhere without your help.

Helmer: Very well, I'll think about it. We'll find something.

Nora: That's sweet of you. *(She goes across to the tree again; pause.)* How pretty these red flowers look.—Tell me, was it really something terribly wrong this man Krogstad did?

Helmer: Forgery. Have you any idea what that means?

Nora: Perhaps circumstances left him no choice? 465

Helmer: Maybe. Or perhaps, like so many others, he just didn't think. I am not so heartless that I would necessarily want to condemn a man for a single mistake like that.

Nora: Oh no, Torvald, of course not!

Helmer: Many a man might be able to redeem himself, if he honestly confessed his guilt and took his punishment.

Nora: Punishment?

Helmer: But that wasn't the way Krogstad chose. He dodged what was due to him by 470 a cunning trick. And that's what has been the cause of his corruption.

Nora: Do you think it would . . . ?

Helmer: Just think how a man with a thing like that on his conscience will always be having to lie and cheat and dissemble; he can never drop the mask, not even with his own wife and children. And the children—*that's* the most terrible part of it, Nora.

Nora: Why?

Helmer: A fog of lies like that in a household, and it spreads disease and infection to every part of it. Every breath the children take in that kind of house is reeking with evil germs.

Nora: *(Closer to him.)* Are you sure of that? 475

Helmer: My dear Nora, as a lawyer I know what I'm talking about. Practically all juvenile delinquents come from homes where the mother is dishonest.

Nora: Why mothers particularly?

Helmer: It's generally traceable to the mothers, but of course fathers can have the same influence. Every lawyer knows that only too well. And yet there's Krogstad been poisoning his own children for years with lies and deceit. That's the reason I call him morally depraved. *(Holds out his hands to her.)* That's why my sweet little Nora must promise me not to try putting in any more good words for him. Shake hands on it. Well? What's this? Give me your hand. There now! That's settled. I assure you I would have found it impossible to work with him. I quite literally feel physically sick in the presence of such people.

Nora: *(Draws her hand away and walks over to the other side of the Christmas tree.)* How hot it is in here! And I still have such a lot to do.

Helmer: *(Stands up and collects his papers together.)* Yes, I'd better think of getting some of this read before dinner. I must also think about your costume. And I might even be able to lay my hands on something to wrap in gold paper and hang on the Christmas tree. *(He lays his hand on her head.)* My precious little singing bird. 480

(He goes into his study and shuts the door behind him.)

Nora: *(Quietly, after a pause.)* Nonsense! It can't be. It's impossible. It *must* be impossible.

Maid: *(In the doorway, left.)* The children keep asking so nicely if they can come in and see Mummy.

Nora: No, no, don't let them in! You stay with them, Anne Marie.

Maid: Very well, ma'am.

(She shuts the door.)

Nora: *(Pale with terror.)* Corrupt my children . . . ! Poison my home? *(Short pause; she throws back her head.)* It's not true! It could never, never be true! 485

Act II

The same room. In the corner beside the piano stands the Christmas tree, stripped, bedraggled and with its candles burnt out. Nora's outdoor things lie on the sofa. Nora, alone there, walks about restlessly; at last she stops by the sofa and picks up her coat.

Nora: *(Putting her coat down again.)* Somebody's coming! *(Crosses to the door, listens.)* No, it's nobody. Nobody will come today, of course, Christmas Day—nor tomorrow, either. But perhaps. . . . *(She opens the door and looks out.)* No, nothing in the letter box; quite empty. *(Comes forward.)* Oh, nonsense! He didn't mean it seriously. Things like that *can't* happen. It's impossible! Why, I have three small children.

(The Nursemaid comes from the room, left, carrying a big cardboard box.)

Nursemaid: I finally found it, the box with the fancy dress costumes.

Nora: Thank you. Put it on the table, please.

Nursemaid: *(Does this.)* But I'm afraid they are in an awful mess.

Nora: Oh, if only I could rip them up into a thousand pieces! 5

Nursemaid: Good heavens, they can be mended all right, with a bit of patience.

Nora: Yes, I'll go over and get Mrs. Linde to help me.

Nursemaid: Out again? In this terrible weather? You'll catch your death of cold, Ma'am.

Nora: Oh, worse things might happen.—How are the children?

Nursemaid: Playing with their Christmas presents, poor little things, but . . . 10

Nora: Do they keep asking for me?

Nursemaid: They are so used to being with their Mummy.

Nora: Yes, Anne Marie, from now on I can't be with them as often as I was before.

Nursemaid: Ah well, children get used to anything in time.

Nora: Do you think so? Do you think they would forget their Mummy if she went away for good? 15

Nursemaid: Good gracious—for good?

Nora: Tell me, Anne Marie—I've often wondered—how on earth could you bear to hand your children over to strangers?

Nursemaid: Well, there was nothing else for it when I had to come and nurse my little Nora.

Nora: Yes but . . . how could you *bring* yourself to do it?

Nursemaid: When I had the chance of such a good place? When a poor girl's been in 20 trouble she must make the best of things. Because *he* didn't help, the rotter.

Nora: But your daughter will have forgotten you.

Nursemaid: Oh no, she hasn't. She wrote to me when she got confirmed, and again when she got married.

Nora: *(Putting her arms around her neck.)* Dear old Anne Marie, you were a good mother to me when I was little.

Nursemaid: My poor little Nora never had any other mother but me. 25

Nora: And if my little ones only had you, I know you would . . . Oh, what am I talking about! *(She opens the box.)* Go in to them. I must . . . Tomorrow I'll let you see how pretty I am going to look.

(She goes into the room, left.)

Nora: *(Begins unpacking the box, but soon throws it down.)* Oh, if only I dare go out. If only I could be sure nobody would come. And that nothing would happen in the meantime here at home. Rubbish—nobody's going to come. I mustn't think about it. Brush this muff. Pretty gloves, pretty gloves! I'll put it right out of my mind. One, two, three, four, five, six. . . . *(Screams.)* Ah, they are coming. . . . *(She starts towards the door, but stops irresolute. Mrs. Linde comes from the hall, where she has taken off her things.)* Oh, it's you, Kristine. There's nobody else out there, is there? I'm so glad you've come.

Mrs. Linde: I heard you'd been over looking for me.

Nora: Yes, I was just passing. There's something you must help me with. Come and sit beside me on the sofa here. You see, the Stenborgs are having a fancy dress party upstairs tomorrow evening, and now Torvald wants me to go as a Neapolitan fisher lass and dance the tarantella. I learned it in Capri, you know.

Mrs. Linde: Well, well! So you are going to do a party piece?

Nora: Torvald says I should. Look, here's the costume, Torvald had it made for me 30 down there. But it's got all torn and I simply don't know. . . .

Mrs. Linde: We'll soon have that put right. It's only the trimming come away here and there. Got a needle and thread? Ah, here's what we are after.

Nora: It's awfully kind of you.

Mrs. Linde: So you are going to be all dressed up tomorrow, Nora? Tell you what— I'll pop over for a minute to see you in all your finery. But I'm quite forgetting to thank you for the pleasant time we had last night.

Nora: *(Gets up and walks across the room.)* Somehow I didn't think yesterday was as nice as things generally are.—You should have come to town a little earlier, Kristine.—Yes, Torvald certainly knows how to make things pleasant about the place.

Mrs. Linde: You too, I should say. You are not your father's daughter for nothing. 35 But tell me, is Dr. Rank always as depressed as he was last night?

Nora: No, last night it was rather obvious. He's got something seriously wrong with him, you know. Tuberculosis of the spine, poor fellow. His father was a horrible man, who used to have mistresses and things like that. That's why the son was always ailing, right from being a child.

Mrs. Linde: *(Lowering her sewing.)* But my dear Nora, how do you come to know about things like that?

Nora: *(Walking about the room.)* Huh! When you've got three children, you get these visits from . . . women who have had a certain amount of medical training. And you hear all sorts of things from them.

Mrs. Linde: *(Begins sewing again; short silence.)* Does Dr. Rank call in every day?

Nora: Every single day. He was Torvald's best friend as a boy, and he's a good friend   40
of *mine*, too. Dr. Rank is almost like one of the family.

Mrs. Linde: But tell me—is he really genuine? What I mean is: doesn't he sometimes rather turn on the charm?

Nora: No, on the contrary. What makes you think that?

Mrs. Linde: When you introduced me yesterday, he claimed he'd often heard my name in this house. Afterwards I noticed your husband hadn't the faintest idea who I was. Then how is it that Dr. Rank should. . . .

Nora: Oh yes, it was quite right what he said, Kristine. You see Torvald is so terribly in love with me that he says he wants me all to himself. When we were first married, it even used to make him sort of jealous if I only as much as mentioned any of my old friends from back home. So of course I stopped doing it. But I often talk to Dr. Rank about such things. He likes hearing about them.

Mrs. Linde: Listen, Nora! In lots of ways you are still a child. Now, I'm a good deal   45
older than you, and a bit more experienced. I'll tell you something: I think you ought to give up all this business with Dr. Rank.

Nora: Give up what business?

Mrs. Linde: The whole thing, I should say. Weren't you saying yesterday something about a rich admirer who was to provide you with money. . . .

Nora: One who's never existed, I regret to say. But what of it?

Mrs. Linde: Has Dr. Rank money?

Nora: Yes, he has.   50

Mrs. Linde: And no dependents?

Nora: No, nobody. But . . . ?

Mrs. Linde: And he comes to the house every day?

Nora: Yes, I told you.

Mrs. Linde: But how can a man of his position want to pester you like this?   55

Nora: I simply don't understand.

Mrs. Linde: Don't pretend, Nora. Do you think I don't see now who you borrowed the twelve hundred from?

Nora: Are you out of your mind? Do you really think that? A friend of ours who comes here every day? The whole situation would have been absolutely intolerable.

Mrs. Linde: It *really* isn't him?

Nora: No, I give you my word. It would never have occurred to me for one   60
moment. . . . Anyway, he didn't have the money to lend then. He didn't inherit it till later.

Mrs. Linde: Just as well for you, I'd say, my dear Nora.

Nora: No, it would never have occurred to me to ask Dr. Rank. . . . All the same I'm pretty certain if I were to ask him . . .

Mrs. Linde: But of course you won't.

Nora: No, of course not. I can't ever imagine it being necessary. But I'm quite certain if ever I were to mention it to Dr. Rank . . .

Mrs. Linde: Behind your husband's back? 65

Nora: I have to get myself out of that other business. That's also behind his back. I *must* get myself out of that.

Mrs. Linde: Yes, that's what I said yesterday. But . . .

Nora: (*Walking up and down.*) A man's better at coping with these things than a woman. . . .

Mrs. Linde: Your own husband, yes.

Nora: Nonsense! (*Stops.*) When you've paid everything you owe, you do get your 70 IOU back again, don't you?

Mrs. Linde: Of course.

Nora: And you can tear it up into a thousand pieces and burn it—the nasty, filthy thing!

Mrs. Linde: (*Looking fixedly at her, puts down her sewing and slowly rises.*) Nora, you are hiding something from me.

Nora: Is it so obvious?

Mrs. Linde: Something has happened to you since yesterday morning. Nora, what is it? 75

Nora: (*Going towards her.*) Kristine! (*Listens.*) Hush! There's Torvald back. Look, you go and sit in there beside the children for the time being. Torvald can't stand the sight of mending lying about. Get Anne Marie to help you.

Mrs. Linde: (*Gathering a lot of things together.*) All right, but I'm not leaving until we have thrashed this thing out.

(*She goes into the room, left; at the same time Helmer comes in from the hall.*)

Nora: (*Goes to meet him.*) I've been longing for you to be back, Torvald, dear.

Helmer: Was that the dressmaker . . . ?

Nora: No, it was Kristine; she's helping me with my costume. I think it's going to 80 look very nice. . . .

Helmer: Wasn't that a good idea of mine, now?

Nora: Wonderful! But wasn't it also nice of me to let you have your way?

Helmer: (*Taking her under the chin.*) Nice of you—because you let your husband have his way? All right, you little rogue, I know you didn't mean it that way. But I don't want to disturb you. You'll be wanting to try the costume on, I suppose.

Nora: And I dare say you've got work to do? 85

Helmer: Yes. (*Shows her a bundle of papers.*) Look at this. I've been down at the Bank. . . .

(*He turns to go into his study.*)

Nora: Torvald!

Helmer: (*Stopping.*) Yes.

Nora: If a little squirrel were to ask ever so nicely . . . ?

Helmer: Well? 90

Nora: Would you do something for it?

Helmer: Naturally I would first have to know what it is.

Nora: Please, if only you would let it have its way, and do what it wants, it'd scamper about and do all sorts of marvelous tricks.

Helmer: What is it?

Nora: And the pretty little sky-lark would sing all day long. . . .

Helmer: Huh! It does that anyway.   95

Nora: I'd pretend I was an elfin child and dance a moonlight dance for you, Torvald.

Helmer: Nora—I hope it's not that business you started on this morning?

Nora: *(Coming closer.)* Yes, it is, Torvald. I implore you!

Helmer: You have the nerve to bring that up again?

Nora: Yes, yes, you *must* listen to me. You must let Krogstad keep his job at the Bank.   100

Helmer: My dear Nora, I'm giving his job to Mrs. Linde.

Nora: Yes, it's awfully sweet of you. But couldn't you get rid of somebody else in the office instead of Krogstad?

Helmer: This really is the most incredible obstinacy! Just because you go and make some thoughtless promise to put in a good word for him, you expect me . . .

Nora: It's not that, Torvald. It's for your own sake. That man writes in all the nastiest papers, you told me that yourself. He can do you no end of harm. He terrifies me to death. . . .

Helmer: Aha, now I see. It's your memories of what happened before that are   105
frightening you.

Nora: What do you mean?

Helmer: It's your father you are thinking of.

Nora: Yes . . . yes, that's right. You remember all the nasty insinuations those wicked people put in the papers about Daddy? I honestly think they would have had him dismissed if the Ministry hadn't sent you down to investigate, and you hadn't been so kind and helpful.

Helmer: My dear little Nora, there is a considerable difference between your father and me. Your father's professional conduct was not entirely above suspicion. Mine is. And I hope it's going to stay that way as long as I hold this position.

Nora: But nobody knows what some of these evil people are capable of. Things could   110
be so nice and pleasant for us here, in the peace and quiet of our home—you and me and the children, Torvald! That's why I implore you. . . .

Helmer: The more you plead for him, the more impossible you make it for me to keep him on. It's already known down at the bank that I am going to give Krogstad his notice. If it ever got around that the new manager had been talked over by his wife. . . .

Nora: What of it?

Helmer: Oh, nothing! As long as the little woman gets her own stubborn way . . . ! Do you want me to make myself a laughing stock in the office? . . . Give the people the idea that I am susceptible to any kind of outside pressure? You can imagine how soon I'd feel the consequences of that! Anyway, there's one other consideration that makes it impossible to have Krogstad in the bank as long as I am manager.

Nora: What's that?

Helmer: At a pinch I might have overlooked his past lapses. . . .   115

Nora: Of course you could, Torvald!

Helmer: And I'm told he's not bad at his job, either. But we knew each other rather well when we were younger. It was one of those rather rash friendships that prove embarrassing in later life. There's no reason why you shouldn't know we were once on terms of some familiarity. And he, in his tactless way, makes no attempt to hide the fact, particularly when other people are present. On the contrary, he thinks he has every right to treat me as an equal, with his "Torvald this" and "Torvald that" every time he opens his mouth. I find it extremely irritating, I can tell you. He would make my position at the bank absolutely intolerable.

Nora: Torvald, surely you aren't serious?

Helmer: Oh? Why not?

Nora: Well, it's all so petty. 120

Helmer: What's that you say? Petty? Do you think I'm petty?

Nora: No, not at all, Torvald dear! And that's why . . .

Helmer: Doesn't make any difference! . . . You call my motives petty; so I must be petty too. Petty! Indeed! Well, we'll put a stop to that, once and for all. *(He opens the hall door and calls.)* Helene!

Nora: What are you going to do?

Helmer: *(Searching among his papers.)* Settle things. *(The Maid comes in.)* See this 125 letter? I want you to take it down at once. Get hold of a messenger and get him to deliver it. Quickly. The address is on the outside. There's the money.

Maid: Very good, sir. *(She goes with the letter.)*

Helmer: *(Putting his papers together.)* There now, my stubborn little miss.

Nora: *(Breathless.)* Torvald . . . what was that letter?

Helmer: Krogstad's notice.

Nora: Get it back, Torvald! There's still time! Oh, Torvald, get it back! Please for my 130 sake, for your sake, for the sake of the children! Listen, Torvald, please! You don't realize what it can do to us.

Helmer: Too late.

Nora: Yes, too late.

Helmer: My dear Nora, I forgive you this anxiety of yours, although it is actually a bit of an insult. Oh, but it is, I tell you! It's hardly flattering to suppose that anything this miserable pen-pusher wrote could frighten *me!* But I forgive you all the same, because it is rather a sweet way of showing how much you love me. *(He takes her in his arms.)* This is how things must be, my own darling Nora. When it comes to the point, I've enough strength and enough courage, believe me, for whatever happens. You'll find I'm man enough to take everything on myself.

Nora: *(Terrified.)* What do you mean?

Helmer: Everything, I said. . . . 135

Nora: *(In command of herself.)* That is something you shall never, never do.

Helmer: All right, then we'll share it, Nora—as man and wife. That's what we'll do. *(Caressing her.)* Does that make you happy now? There, there, don't look at me with those eyes, like a little frightened dove. The whole thing is sheer imagination.—Why don't you run through the tarantella and try out the tambourine? I'll go into my study and shut both the doors, then I won't hear anything. You can make all the noise you want. *(Turns in the doorway.)* And when Rank comes, tell him where he can find me.

(He nods to her, goes with his papers into his room, and shuts the door behind him.)

Nora: *(Wild-eyed with terror, stands as though transfixed.)* He's quite capable of doing it! He would do it! No matter what, he'd do it.—No, never in this world!

Anything but that! Help? Some way out . . . ? *(The door-bell rings in the hall.)* Dr. Rank . . . ! Anything but that, *anything!* (She brushes her hands over her face, pulls herself together and opens the door into the hall. Dr. Rank is standing outside hanging up his fur coat. During what follows it begins to grow dark.)* Hello, Dr. Rank. I recognized your ring. Do you mind not going in to Torvald just yet, I think he's busy.

Rank: And you?

(Dr. Rank comes into the room and she closes the door behind him.)

Nora: Oh, you know very well I've always got time for you.   140

Rank: Thank you. A privilege I shall take advantage of as long as I am able.

Nora: What do you mean—as long as you are able?

Rank: Does that frighten you?

Nora: Well, its just that it sounds so strange. Is anything likely to happen?

Rank: Only what I have long expected. But I didn't think it would come quite so   145
soon.

Nora: *(Catching at his arm.)* What have you found out? Dr. Rank, you must tell me!

Rank: I'm slowly sinking. There's nothing to be done about it.

Nora: *(With a sigh of relief.)* Oh, it's *you* you're . . . ?

Rank: Who else? No point in deceiving oneself. I am the most wretched of all my patients, Mrs. Helmer. These last few days I've made a careful analysis of my internal economy. Bankrupt! Within a month I shall probably be lying rotting up there in the churchyard.

Nora: Come now, what a ghastly thing to say!   150

Rank: The whole damned thing is ghastly. But the worst thing is all the ghastliness that has to be gone through first. I only have one more test to make; and when that's done I'll know pretty well when the final disintegration will start. There's something I want to ask you. Helmer is a sensitive soul; he loathes anything that's ugly. I don't want him visiting me. . . .

Nora: But Dr. Rank. . . .

Rank: On no account must he. I won't have it. I'll lock the door on him.—As soon as I'm absolutely certain of the worst, I'll send you my visiting card with a black cross on it. You'll know then the final horrible disintegration has begun.

Nora: Really, you are being quite absurd today. And here I was hoping you would be in a thoroughly good mood.

Rank: With death staring me in the face? Why should I suffer for another man's sins?   155
What justice is there in that? Somewhere, somehow, every single family must be suffering some such cruel retribution. . . .

Nora: *(Stopping up her ears.)* Rubbish! Do cheer up!

Rank: Yes, really the whole thing's nothing but a huge joke. My poor innocent spine must do penance for my father's gay subaltern life.

Nora: *(By the table, left.)* Wasn't he rather partial to asparagus and *pâté de foie gras?*

Rank: Yes, he was. And truffles.

Nora: Truffles, yes. And oysters, too, I believe?   160

Rank: Yes, oysters, oysters, of course.

Nora: And all the port and champagne that goes with them. It does seem a pity all these delicious things should attack the spine.

Rank: Especially when they attack a poor spine that never had any fun out of them.

Nora: Yes, that is an awful pity.

Rank: *(Looks at her sharply.)* Hm . . .   165

Nora: *(After a pause.)* Why did you smile?

Rank: No, it was you who laughed.

Nora: No, it was you who smiled, Dr. Rank!

Rank: *(Getting up.)* You are a bigger rascal than I thought you were.

Nora: I feel full of mischief today.   170

Rank: So it seems.

Nora: *(Putting her hands on his shoulders.)* Dear, dear Dr. Rank, you mustn't go and die on Torvald and me.

Rank: You wouldn't miss me for long. When you are gone, you are soon forgotten.

Nora: *(Looking at him anxiously.)* Do you think so?

Rank: People make new contacts, then . . .   175

Nora: Who makes new contacts?

Rank: Both you and Helmer will, when I'm gone. You yourself are already well on the way, it seems to me. What was this Mrs. Linde doing here last night?

Nora: Surely you aren't jealous of poor Kristine?

Rank: Yes, I am. She'll be my successor in this house. When I'm done for, I can see this woman . . .

Nora: Hush! Don't talk so loud, she's in there.   180

Rank: Today as well? There you are, you see!

Nora: Just to do some sewing on my dress. Good Lord, how absurd you are! *(She sits down on the sofa.)* Now Dr. Rank, cheer up. You'll see tomorrow how nicely I can dance. And you can pretend I'm doing it just for you—and for Torvald as well, of course. *(She takes various things out of the box.)* Come here, Dr. Rank. I want to show you something.

Rank: *(Sits.)* What is it?

Nora: Look!

Rank: Silk stockings.   185

Nora: Flesh-colored! Aren't they lovely! Of course, it's dark here now, but tomorrow. . . . No, no, no, you can only look at the feet. Oh well, you might as well see a bit higher up, too.

Rank: Hm . . .

Nora: Why are you looking so critical? Don't you think they'll fit?

Rank: I couldn't possibly offer any informed opinion about that.

Nora: *(Looks at him for a moment.)* Shame on you. *(Hits him lightly across the ear with*   190
the stockings.) Take that! *(Folds them up again.)*

Rank: And what other delights am I to be allowed to see?

Nora: Not another thing. You are too naughty. *(She hums a little and searches among her things.)*

Rank: *(After a short pause.)* Sitting here so intimately like this with you, I can't imagine . . . I simply cannot conceive what would have become of me if I had never come to this house.

Nora: *(Smiles.)* Yes, I rather think you do enjoy coming here.

Rank: *(In a low voice, looking fixedly ahead.)* And the thought of having to leave it   195
all . . .

Nora: Nonsense. You aren't leaving.

Rank: *(In the same tone.)* . . . without being able to leave behind even the slightest
token of gratitude, hardly a fleeting regret even . . . nothing but an empty place
to be filled by the first person that comes along.
Nora: Supposing I were to ask you to . . . ? No . . .
Rank: What?
Nora: . . . to show me the extent of your friendship . . .   200
Rank: Yes?
Nora: I mean . . . to do me a tremendous favor. . . .
Rank: Would you really, for once, give me that pleasure?
Nora: You have no idea what it is.
Rank: All right, tell me.   205
Nora: No, really I can't, Dr. Rank. It's altogether too much to ask . . . because I need
your advice and help as well. . . .
Rank: The more the better. I cannot imagine what you have in mind. But tell me
anyway. You do trust me, don't you?
Nora: Yes, I trust you more than anybody I know. You are my best and my most
faithful friend. I know that. So I will tell you. Well then, Dr. Rank, there
is something you must help me to prevent. You know how deeply, how
passionately Torvald is in love with me. He would never hesitate for a moment
to sacrifice his life for my sake.
Rank: *(Bending towards her.)* Nora . . . do you think he's the only one who . . . ?
Nora: *(Stiffening slightly.)* Who . . . ?   210
Rank: Who wouldn't gladly give his life for your sake.
Nora: *(Sadly.)* Oh!
Rank: I swore to myself you would know before I went. I'll never have a better
opportunity. Well, Nora! Now you know. And now you know too that you can
confide in me as in nobody else.
Nora: *(Rises and speaks evenly and calmly.)* Let me past.
Rank: *(Makes way for her, but remains seated.)* Nora . . .   215
Nora: *(In the hall doorway.)* Helene, bring the lamp in, please. *(Walks over to the
stove.)* Oh, my dear Dr. Rank, that really was rather horrid of you.
Rank: *(Getting up.)* That I have loved you every bit as much as anybody? Is *that*
horrid?
Nora: No, but that you had to go and tell me. When it was all so unnecessary. . . .
Rank: What do you mean? Did you know . . . ?

(The Maid comes in with the lamp, puts in on the table, and goes out again.)

Rank: Nora . . . Mrs. Helmer . . . I'm asking you if you knew?   220
Nora: How can I tell whether I did or didn't. I simply can't tell you. . . . Oh, how
could you be so clumsy, Dr. Rank! When everything was so nice.
Rank: Anyway, you know now that I'm at your service, body and soul. So you can
speak out.
Nora: *(Looking at him.)* After this?
Rank: I beg you to tell me what it is.
Nora: I can tell you nothing now.   225
Rank: You must. You can't torment me like this. Give me a chance—I'll do anything
that's humanly possible.

Nora: You can do nothing for me now. Actually, I don't really need any help. It's all just my imagination, really it is. Of course! *(She sits down in the rocking chair, looks at him and smiles.)* I must say, you are a nice one, Dr. Rank! Don't you feel ashamed of yourself, now the lamp's been brought in?

Rank: No, not exactly. But perhaps I ought to go—for good?

Nora: No, you mustn't do that. You must keep coming just as you've always done. You know very well Torvald would miss you terribly.

Rank: And *you?* 230

Nora: I always think it's tremendous fun having you.

Rank: That's exactly what gave me the wrong ideas. I just can't puzzle you out. I often used to feel you'd just as soon be with me as with Helmer.

Nora: Well, you see, there are those people you love and those people you'd almost rather *be* with.

Rank: Yes, there's something in that.

Nora: When I was a girl at home, I loved Daddy best, of course. But I also thought 235 it great fun if I could slip into the maids' room. For one thing they never preached at me. And they always talked about such exciting things.

Rank: Aha! So it's their role I've taken over!

Nora: *(Jumps up and crosses to him.)* Oh, my dear, kind Dr. Rank, I didn't mean that at all. But you can see how it's a bit with Torvald as it was with Daddy. . . .

(The Maid comes in from the hall.)

Maid: Please, ma'am . . . !

(She whispers and hands her a card.)

Nora: *(Glances at the card.)* Ah!

(She puts it in her pocket.)

Rank: Anything wrong? 240

Nora: No, no, not at all. It's just . . . it's my new costume. . . .

Rank: How is that? There's your costume in there.

Nora: That one, yes. But this is another one. I've ordered it. Torvald mustn't hear about it. . . .

Rank: Ah, so that's the big secret, is it!

Nora: Yes, that's right. Just go in and see him, will you? He's in the study. Keep him 245 occupied for the time being. . . .

Rank: Don't worry. He shan't escape me.

(He goes into Helmer's study.)

Nora: *(To the Maid.)* Is he waiting in the kitchen?

Maid: Yes, he came up the back stairs. . . .

Nora: But didn't you tell him somebody was here?

Maid: Yes, but it was no good. 250

Nora: Won't he go?

Maid: No, he won't till he's seen you.

Nora: Let him in, then. But quietly. Helene, you mustn't tell anybody about this. It's a surprise for my husband.

Maid: I understand, ma'am. . . .

(She goes out.)

Nora: Here it comes! What I've been dreading! No, no, it can't happen, it *can't*   255
happen.

(*She walks over and bolts Helmer's door. The Maid opens the hall door for Krogstad
and shuts it again behind him. He is wearing a fur coat, overshoes, and a fur cap.*)

Nora: (*Goes towards him.*) Keep your voice down, my husband is at home.
Krogstad: What if he is?
Nora: What do you want with me?
Krogstad: To find out something.
Nora: Hurry, then. What is it?   260
Krogstad: You know I've been given notice.
Nora: I couldn't prevent it, Mr. Krogstad. I did my utmost for you, but it was no use.
Krogstad: Has your husband so little affection for you? He knows what I can do to
you, yet he dares. . . .
Nora: You don't imagine he knows about it!
Krogstad: No, I didn't imagine he did. It didn't seem a bit like my good friend   265
Torvald Helmer to show that much courage. . . .
Nora: Mr. Krogstad, I must ask you to show some respect for my husband.
Krogstad: Oh, sure! All due respect! But since you are so anxious to keep this
business quiet, Mrs. Helmer, I take it you now have a rather clearer idea of just
what it is you've done, than you had yesterday.
Nora: Clearer than *you* could ever have given me.
Krogstad: Yes, being as I am such a rotten lawyer. . . .
Nora: What do you want with me?   270
Krogstad: I just wanted to see how things stood, Mrs. Helmer. I've been thinking
about you all day. Even a mere money-lender, a hack journalist, a—well, even
somebody like me has a bit of what you might call feeling.
Nora: Show it then. Think of my little children.
Krogstad: Did you or your husband think of mine? But what does it matter now?
There was just one thing I wanted to say: you needn't take this business too
seriously. I shan't start any proceedings, for the present.
Nora: Ah, I knew you wouldn't.
Krogstad: The whole thing can be arranged quite amicably. Nobody need know. Just   275
the three of us.
Nora: My husband must never know.
Krogstad: How can you prevent it? Can you pay off the balance?
Nora: No, not immediately.
Krogstad: Perhaps you've some way of getting hold of the money in the next few
days.
Nora: None I want to make use of.   280
Krogstad: Well, it wouldn't have been very much help to you if you had. Even if you
stood there with the cash in your hand and to spare, you still wouldn't get your
IOU back from me now.
Nora: What are you going to do with it?
Krogstad: Just keep it—have it in my possession. Nobody who isn't implicated need
know about it. So if you are thinking of trying any desperate remedies . . .
Nora: Which I am. . . .
Krogstad: . . . if you happen to be thinking of running away . . .   285

Nora: Which I am!

Krogstad: . . . or anything worse . . .

Nora: How did you know?

Krogstad: . . . forget it!

Nora: How did you know I was thinking of *that?* 290

Krogstad: Most of us think of *that,* to begin with. I did, too; but I didn't have the courage. . . .

Nora: *(Tonelessly.)* I haven't either.

Krogstad: *(Relieved.)* So you haven't the courage either, eh?

Nora: No, I haven't! I haven't!

Krogstad: It would also be very stupid. There'd only be the first domestic storm to 295
get over. . . . I've got a letter to your husband in my pocket here. . . .

Nora: And it's all in there?

Krogstad: In as tactful a way as possible.

Nora: *(Quickly.)* He must never read that letter. Tear it up. I'll find the money somehow.

Krogstad: Excuse me, Mrs. Helmer, but I've just told you. . . .

Nora: I'm not talking about the money I owe you. I want to know how much you are 300
demanding from my husband, and I'll get the money.

Krogstad: I want no money from your husband.

Nora: What do you want?

Krogstad: I'll tell you. I want to get on my feet again, Mrs. Helmer; I want to get to
the top. And your husband is going to help me. For the last eighteen months
I've gone straight; all that time it's been hard going; I was content to work my
way up, step by step. Now I'm being kicked out, and I won't stand for being
taken back again as an act of charity. I'm going to get to the top, I tell you. I'm
going back into that bank—with a better job. Your husband is going to create a
new vacancy, just for me. . . .

Nora: He'll never do that!

Krogstad: He will do it. I know him. He'll do it without so much as a whimper. And 305
once I'm in there with him, you'll see what's what. In less than a year I'll be his
right-hand man. It'll be Nils Krogstad, not Torvald Helmer, who'll be running
that bank.

Nora: You'll never live to see that day!

Krogstad: You mean you . . . ?

Nora: Now I have the courage.

Krogstad: You can't frighten me! A precious pampered little thing like you. . . .

Nora: I'll show you! I'll show you! 310

Krogstad: Under the ice, maybe? Down in the cold, black water? Then being washed
up in the spring, bloated, hairless, unrecognizable. . . .

Nora: You can't frighten me.

Krogstad: You can't frighten me, either. People don't do that sort of thing,
Mrs. Helmer. There wouldn't be any point to it, anyway, I'd still have him in
my pocket.

Nora: Afterwards? When I'm no longer . . .

Krogstad: Aren't you forgetting that your reputation would then be entirely in my 315
hands? *(Nora stands looking at him, speechless.)* Well, I've warned you. Don't
do anything silly. When Helmer gets my letter, I expect to hear from him.

And don't forget: it's him who is forcing me off the straight and narrow again, your own husband! That's something I'll never forgive him for. Goodbye, Mrs. Helmer.

(He goes out through the hall. Nora crosses to the door, opens it slightly, and listens.)

Nora: He's going. He hasn't left the letter. No, no, that would be impossible! *(Opens the door further and further.)* What's he doing? He's stopped outside. He's not going down the stairs. Has he changed his mind? Is he . . . ? *(A letter falls into the letter-box. Then Krogstad's footsteps are heard receding as he walks downstairs. Nora gives a stifled cry, runs across the room to the sofa table; pause.)* In the letter-box! *(She creeps stealthily across to the hall door.)* There it is! Torvald, Torvald! It's hopeless now!

Mrs. Linde: *(Comes into the room, left, carrying the costume.)* There, I think that's everything. Shall we try it on?

Nora: *(In a low, hoarse voice.)* Kristine, come here.

Mrs. Linde: *(Throws the dress down on the sofa.)* What's wrong with you? You look upset.

Nora: Come here. Do you see that letter? *There,* look! Through the glass in the letter-box.   320

Mrs. Linde: Yes, yes, I can see it.

Nora: It's a letter from Krogstad.

Mrs. Linde: Nora! It was Krogstad who lent you the money!

Nora: Yes. And now Torvald will get to know everything.

Mrs. Linde: Believe me, Nora, it's best for you both.   325

Nora: But there's more to it than that. I forged a signature. . . .

Mrs. Linde: Heavens above!

Nora: Listen, I want to tell you something, Kristine, so you can be my witness.

Mrs. Linde: What do you mean "witness"? What do you want me to . . . ?

Nora: If I should go mad . . . which might easily happen . . .   330

Mrs. Linde: Nora!

Nora: Or if anything happened to me . . . which meant I couldn't be here. . . .

Mrs. Linde: Nora, Nora! Are you out of your mind?

Nora: And if somebody else wanted to take it all upon himself, the whole blame, you understand. . . .

Mrs. Linde: Yes, yes. But what makes you think . . . ?   335

Nora: Then you must testify that it isn't true, Kristine. I'm not out of my mind; I'm quite sane now. And I tell you this: nobody else knew anything, I alone was responsible for the whole thing. Remember that!

Mrs. Linde: I will. But I don't understand a word of it.

Nora: Why should you? You see something miraculous is going to happen.

Mrs. Linde: Something miraculous?

Nora: Yes, a miracle. But something so terrible as well, Kristine—oh, it must *never*   340 happen, not for anything.

Mrs. Linde: I'm going straight over to talk to Krogstad.

Nora: Don't go. He'll only do you harm.

Mrs. Linde: There was a time when he would have done anything for me.

Nora: Him!

Mrs. Linde: Where does he live?   345

Nora: How do I know . . . ? Wait a minute. *(She feels in her pocket.)* Here's his card. But the letter, the letter . . . !

Helmer: *(From his study, knocking on the door.)* Nora!

Nora: *(Cries out in terror.)* What's that? What do you want?

Helmer: Don't be frightened. We're not coming in. You've locked the door. Are you trying on?

Nora: Yes, yes, I'm trying on. It looks so nice on me, Torvald.   350

Mrs. Linde: *(Who has read the card.)* He lives just round the corner.

Nora: It's no use. It's hopeless. The letter is there in the box.

Mrs. Linde: Your husband keeps the key?

Nora: Always.

Mrs. Linde: Krogstad must ask for his letter back unread, he must find some sort of   355
excuse. . . .

Nora: But this is just the time that Torvald generally . . .

Mrs. Linde: Put him off! Go in and keep him busy. I'll be back as soon as I can.

(She goes out hastily by the hall door. Nora walks over to Helmer's door, opens it, and peeps in.)

Nora: Torvald!

Helmer: *(In the study.)* Well, can a man get into his own living room again now? Come along, Rank, now we'll see . . . *(In the doorway.)* But what's this?

Nora: What, Torvald dear?   360

Helmer: Rank led me to expect some kind of marvelous transformation.

Rank: *(In the doorway.)* That's what I thought too, but I must have been mistaken.

Nora: I'm not showing myself off to anybody before tomorrow.

Helmer: Nora dear, you look tired. You haven't been practicing too hard?

Nora: No, I haven't practiced at all yet.   365

Helmer: You'll have to, though.

Nora: Yes, I certainly must, Torvald. But I just can't get anywhere without your help: I've completely forgotten it.

Helmer: We'll soon polish it up.

Nora: Yes, do help me, Torvald. Promise? I'm so nervous. All those people. . . . You must devote yourself exclusively to me this evening. Pens away! Forget all about the office! Promise me, Torvald dear!

Helmer: I promise. This evening I am wholly and entirely at your service . . . helpless   370
little thing that you are. Oh, but while I remember, I'll just look first . . .

(He goes towards the hall door.)

Nora: What do you want out there?

Helmer: Just want to see if there are any letters.

Nora: No, don't, Torvald!

Helmer: Why not?

Nora: Torvald, *please!* There aren't any.   375

Helmer: Just let me see.

(He starts to go. Nora, at the piano, plays the opening bars of the tarantella.)

Helmer: *(At the door, stops.)* Aha!

Nora: I shan't be able to dance tomorrow if I don't rehearse it with you.

Helmer: *(Walks to her.)* Are you really so nervous, Nora dear?

Nora: Terribly nervous. Let me run through it now. There's still time before supper. 380
Come and sit here and play for me, Torvald dear. Tell me what to do, keep me
right—as you always do.

Helmer: Certainly, with pleasure, if that's what you want.

*(He sits at the piano. Nora snatches the tambourine out of the box, and also a long
gaily-colored shawl which she drapes around herself, then with a bound she leaps
forward.)*

Nora: *(Shouts.)* Now play for me! Now I'll dance!

*(Helmer plays and Nora dances; Dr. Rank stands at the piano behind Helmer and
looks on.)*

Helmer: *(Playing.)* Not so fast! Not so fast!

Nora: I can't help it.

Helmer: Not so wild, Nora! 385

Nora: This is how it has to be.

Helmer: *(Stops.)* No, no, that won't do at all.

Nora: *(Laughs and swings the tambourine.)* Didn't I tell you?

Rank: Let me play for her.

Helmer: *(Gets up.)* Yes, do. Then I'll be better able to tell her what to do. 390

*(Rank sits down at the piano and plays. Nora dances more and more wildly.
Helmer stands by the stove giving her repeated directions as she dances; she does not
seem to hear them. Her hair comes undone and falls about her shoulders; she pays no
attention and goes on dancing. Mrs. Linde enters.)*

Mrs. Linde: *(Standing as though spellbound in the doorway.)* Ah . . . !

Nora: *(Dancing.)* See what fun we are having, Kristine.

Helmer: But my dear darling Nora, you are dancing as though your life depended
on it.

Nora: It does.

Helmer: Stop, Rank! This is sheer madness. Stop, I say. 395

(Rank stops playing and Nora comes to a sudden halt.)

Helmer: *(Crosses to her.)* I would never have believed it. You have forgotten
everything I ever taught you.

Nora: *(Throwing away the tambourine.)* There you are, you see.

Helmer: Well, some more instruction is certainly needed there.

Nora: Yes, you see how necessary it is. You must go on coaching me right up to the
last minute. Promise me, Torvald?

Helmer: You can rely on me. 400

Nora: You mustn't think about anything else but me until after tomorrow . . .
mustn't open any letters . . . mustn't touch the letter-box.

Helmer: Ah, you are still frightened of what that man might . . .

Nora: Yes, yes, I am.

Helmer: I can see from your face there's already a letter there from him.

Nora: I don't know. I think so. But you mustn't read anything like that now. We 405
don't want anything horrid coming between us until all this is over.

Rank: *(Softly to Helmer.)* I shouldn't cross her.

Helmer: *(Puts his arm around her.)* The child must have her way. But tomorrow night, when your dance is done. . . .

Nora: Then you are free.

Maid: *(In the doorway, right.)* Dinner is served, madam.

Nora: We'll have champagne, Helene.   410

Maid: Very good, madam.

    (She goes.)

Helmer: Aha! It's to be quite a banquet, eh?

Nora: With champagne flowing until dawn. *(Shouts.)* And some macaroons, Helene . . . lots of them, for once in a while.

Helmer: *(Seizing her hands.)* Now, now, not so wild and excitable! Let me see you being my own little singing bird again.

Nora: Oh yes, I will. And if you'll just go in . . . you, too, Dr. Rank. Kristine, you   415
must help me to do my hair.

Rank: *(Softly, as they leave.)* There isn't anything . . . anything as it were, impending, is there?

Helmer: No, not at all, my dear fellow. It's nothing but these childish fears I was telling you about.

    (They go out to the right.)

Nora: Well?

Mrs. Linde: He's left town.

Nora: I saw it in your face.   420

Mrs. Linde: He's coming back tomorrow evening. I left a note for him.

Nora: You shouldn't have done that. You must let things take their course. Because really it's a case for rejoicing, waiting like this for the miracle.

Mrs. Linde: What is it you are waiting for?

Nora: Oh, you wouldn't understand. Go and join the other two. I'll be there in a minute.

    (Mrs. Linde goes into the dining-room. Nora stands for a moment as though to collect herself, then looks at her watch.)

Nora: Five. Seven hours to midnight. Then twenty-four hours till the next midnight.   425
Then the tarantella will be over. Twenty-four and seven? Thirty-one hours to live.

Helmer: *(In the doorway, right.)* What's happened to our little sky-lark?

Nora: *(Running towards him with open arms.)* Here she is!

Act III

The same room. The round table has been moved to the center of the room, and the chairs placed round it. A lamp is burning on the table. The door to the hall stands open. Dance music can be heard coming from the floor above. Mrs. Linde is sitting by the table, idly turning over the pages of a book; she tries to read, but does not seem able to concentrate. Once or twice she listens, tensely, for a sound at the front door.

Mrs. Linde: *(Looking at her watch.)* Still not here. There isn't much time left. I only hope he hasn't . . . *(She listens again.)* Ah, there he is. *(She goes out into the hall, and cautiously opens the front door. Soft footsteps can be heard on the stairs. She whispers.)* Come in. There's nobody here.

Krogstad: *(In the doorway.)* I found a note from you at home. What does it all mean?

Mrs. Linde: I *had* to talk to you.

Krogstad: Oh? And did it have to be here, in this house?

Mrs. Linde: It wasn't possible over at my place, it hasn't a separate entrance. Come   5
in. We are quite alone. The maid's asleep and the Helmers are at a party
upstairs.

Krogstad: *(Comes into the room.)* Well, well! So the Helmers are out dancing tonight!
Really?

Mrs. Linde: Yes, why not?

Krogstad: Why not indeed!

Mrs. Linde: Well then, Nils. Let's talk.

Krogstad: Have we two anything more to talk about?   10

Mrs. Linde: We have a great deal to talk about.

Krogstad: I shouldn't have thought so.

Mrs. Linde: That's because you never really understood me.

Krogstad: What else was there to understand, apart from the old, old story? A
heartless woman throws a man over the moment something more profitable
offers itself.

Mrs. Linde: Do you really think I'm so heartless? Do you think I found it easy to   15
break it off?

Krogstad: Didn't you?

Mrs. Linde: You didn't really believe that?

Krogstad: If that wasn't the case, why did you write to me as you did?

Mrs. Linde: There was nothing else I could do. If I had to make the break, I felt in
duty bound to destroy any feeling that you had for me.

Krogstad: *(Clenching his hands.)* So that's how it was. And all that . . . was for money!   20

Mrs. Linde: You mustn't forget I had a helpless mother and two young brothers. We
couldn't wait for you, Nils. At that time you hadn't much immediate prospect
of anything.

Krogstad: That may be. But you had no right to throw me over for somebody else.

Mrs. Linde: Well, I don't know. Many's the time I've asked myself whether I was
justified.

Krogstad: *(More quietly.)* When I lost you, it was just as if the ground had slipped
away from under my feet. Look at me now: a broken man clinging to the wreck
of his life.

Mrs. Linde: Help might be near.   25

Krogstad: It *was* near. Then you came along and got in the way.

Mrs. Linde: Quite without knowing, Nils. I only heard today it's you I'm supposed
to be replacing at the bank.

Krogstad: If you say so, I believe you. But now you do know, aren't you going to
withdraw?

Mrs. Linde: No, that wouldn't benefit you in the slightest.

Krogstad: Benefit, benefit . . . ! I would do it just the same.   30

Mrs. Linde: I have learned to go carefully. Life and hard, bitter necessity have taught
me that.

Krogstad: And life has taught me not to believe in pretty speeches.

Mrs. Linde: Then life has taught you a very sensible thing. But deeds are something
you surely must believe in?

Krogstad: How do you mean?

Mrs. Linde: You said you were like a broken man clinging to the wreck of his life.   35

Krogstad: And I said it with good reason.

Mrs. Linde: And I am like a broken woman clinging to the wreck of her life. Nobody to care about, and nobody to care for.

Krogstad: It was your own choice.

Mrs. Linde: At the time there was no other choice.

Krogstad: Well, what of it?   40

Mrs. Linde: Nils, what about us two castaways joining forces?

Krogstad: What's that you say?

Mrs. Linde: Two of us on *one* wreck surely stand a better chance than each on his own.

Krogstad: Kristine!

Mrs. Linde: Why do you suppose I came to town?   45

Krogstad: You mean, you thought of me?

Mrs. Linde: Without work I couldn't live. All my life I have worked, for as long as I can remember; that has always been my one great joy. But now I'm completely alone in the world, and feeling horribly empty and forlorn. There's no pleasure in working only for yourself. Nils, give me somebody and something to work for.

Krogstad: I don't believe all this. It's only a woman's hysteria, wanting to be all magnanimous and self-sacrificing.

Mrs. Linde: Have you ever known me hysterical before?

Krogstad: Would you really do this? Tell me—do you know all about my past?   50

Mrs. Linde: Yes.

Krogstad: And you know what people think about me?

Mrs. Linde: Just now you hinted you thought you might have been a different person with me.

Krogstad: I'm convinced I would.

Mrs. Linde: Couldn't it still happen?   55

Krogstad: Kristine! You know what you are saying, don't you? Yes, you do. I can see you do. Have you really the courage . . . ?

Mrs. Linde: I need someone to mother, and your children need a mother. We two need each other. Nils, I have faith in what, deep down, you are. With you I can face anything.

Krogstad: *(Seizing her hands.)* Thank you, thank you, Kristine. And I'll soon have everybody looking up to me, or I'll know the reason why. Ah, but I was forgetting. . . .

Mrs. Linde: Hush! The tarantella! You must go!

Krogstad: Why? What is it?   60

Mrs. Linde: You hear that dance upstairs? When it's finished they'll be coming.

Krogstad: Yes, I'll go. It's too late to do anything. Of course, you know nothing about what steps I've taken against the Helmers.

Mrs. Linde: Yes, Nils, I do know.

Krogstad: Yet you still want to go on. . . .

Mrs. Linde: I know how far a man like you can be driven by despair.   65

Krogstad: Oh, if only I could undo what I've done!

Mrs. Linde: You still can. Your letter is still there in the box.

Krogstad: Are you sure?

Mrs. Linde: Quite sure. But . . .

Krogstad: *(Regards her searching.)* Is that how things are? You want to save your   70
friend at any price? Tell me straight. Is that it?

Mrs. Linde: When you've sold yourself *once* for other people's sake, you don't do it
again.

Krogstad: I shall demand my letter back.

Mrs. Linde: No, no.

Krogstad: Of course I will, I'll wait here till Helmer comes. I'll tell him he has to
give me my letter back . . . that it's only about my notice . . . that he mustn't
read it. . . .

Mrs. Linde: No, Nils, don't ask for it back.   75

Krogstad: But wasn't that the very reason you got me here?

Mrs. Linde: Yes, that was my first terrified reaction. But that was yesterday, and it's
quite incredible the things I've witnessed in this house in the last twenty-four
hours. Helmer must know everything. This unhappy secret must come out.
Those two must have the whole thing out between them. All this secrecy and
deception, it just can't go on.

Krogstad: Well, if you want to risk it. . . . But one thing I can do, and I'll do it at
once. . . .

Mrs. Linde: *(Listening.)* Hurry! Go, go! The dance has stopped. We aren't safe a
moment longer.

Krogstad: I'll wait for you downstairs.   80

Mrs. Linde: Yes, do. You must see me home.

Krogstad: I've never been so incredibly happy before.

(He goes out by the front door. The door out into the hall remains standing open.)

Mrs. Linde: *(Tidies the room a little and gets her hat and coat ready.)* How things
change! How things change! Somebody to work for . . . to live for. A home to
bring happiness into. Just let me get down to it. . . . I wish they'd come. . . .
(Listens.) Ah, there they are. . . . Get my things.

*(She takes her coat and hat. The voices of Helmer and Nora are heard outside. A key
is turned and Helmer pushes Nora almost forcibly into the hall. She is dressed in the
Italian costume, with a big black shawl over it. He is in evening dress, and over it a
black cloak, open.)*

Nora: *(Still in the doorway, reluctantly.)* No, no, not in here! I want to go back up
again. I don't want to leave so early.

Helmer: But my dearest Nora . . .   85

Nora: Oh, please, Torvald, I beg you. . . . *Please,* just for another hour.

Helmer: Not another minute, Nora my sweet. You remember what we agreed. There
now, come along in. You'll catch cold standing there.

(He leads her, in spite of her resistance, gently but firmly into the room.)

Mrs. Linde: Good evening.

Nora: Kristine!

Helmer: Why, Mrs. Linde. You here so late?   90

Mrs. Linde: Yes. You must forgive me but I did so want to see Nora all dressed up.

Nora: Have you been sitting here waiting for me?

Mrs. Linde: Yes, I'm afraid I wasn't in time to catch you before you went upstairs. And I felt I couldn't leave again without seeing you.

Helmer: *(Removing Nora's shawl.)* Well, take a good look at her. I think I can say she's worth looking at. Isn't she lovely, Mrs. Linde?

Mrs. Linde: Yes, I must say. . . . 95

Helmer: Isn't she quite extraordinarily lovely? That's what everybody at the party thought, too. But she's dreadfully stubborn . . . the sweet little thing! And what shall we do about that? Would you believe it, I nearly had to use force to get her away.

Nora: Oh Torvald, you'll be sorry you didn't let me stay, even for half an hour.

Helmer: You hear that, Mrs. Linde? She dances her tarantella, there's wild applause—which was well deserved, although the performance was perhaps rather realistic . . . I mean, rather more so than was strictly necessary from the artistic point of view. But anyway! The main thing is she was a success, a tremendous success. Was I supposed to let her stay after that? Spoil the effect? No, thank you! I took my lovely little Capri girl—my capricious little Capri girl, I might say—by the arm, whisked her once round the room, a curtsey all round, and then—as they say in novels—the beautiful vision vanished. An exit should always be effective, Mrs. Linde. But I just can't get Nora to see that. Phew! It's warm in here. *(He throws his cloak over a chair and opens the door to his study.)* What? It's dark. Oh yes, of course. Excuse me. . . .

(He goes in and lights a few candles.)

Nora: *(Quickly, in a breathless whisper.)* Well?

Mrs. Linde: *(Softly.)* I've spoken to him. 100

Nora: And . . . ?

Mrs. Linde: Nora . . . you must tell your husband everything.

Nora: *(Tonelessly.)* I knew it.

Mrs. Linde: You've got nothing to fear from Krogstad. But you must speak.

Nora: I won't. 105

Mrs. Linde: Then the letter will.

Nora: Thank you, Kristine. Now I know what's to be done. Hush . . . !

Helmer: *(Comes in again.)* Well, Mrs. Linde, have you finished admiring her?

Mrs. Linde: Yes. And now I must say good night.

Helmer: Oh, already? Is this yours, this knitting? 110

Mrs. Linde: *(Takes it.)* Yes, thank you. I nearly forgot it.

Helmer: So you knit, eh?

Mrs. Linde: Yes.

Helmer: You should embroider instead, you know.

Mrs. Linde: Oh? Why? 115

Helmer: So much prettier. Watch! You hold the embroidery like this in the left hand, and then you take the needle in the right hand, like this, and you describe a long, graceful curve. Isn't that right?

Mrs. Linde: Yes, I suppose so. . . .

Helmer: Whereas knitting, on the other hand, just can't help being ugly. Look! Arms pressed into the sides, the knitting needles going up and down—there's something Chinese about it. . . . Ah, that was marvelous champagne they served tonight.

Mrs. Linde: Well, good night, Nora! And stop being so stubborn.

Helmer: Well said, Mrs. Linde! 120

Mrs. Linde: Good night, Mr. Helmer.

Helmer: *(Accompanying her to the door.)* Good night, good night! You'll get home all right, I hope? I'd be only too pleased to . . . But you haven't far to walk. Good night, good night! *(She goes; he shuts the door behind her and comes in again.)* There we are, got rid of her at last. She's a frightful bore, that woman.

Nora: Are you very tired, Torvald?

Helmer: Not in the least.

Nora: Not sleepy? 125

Helmer: Not at all. On the contrary, I feel extremely lively. What about you? Yes, you look quite tired and sleepy.

Nora: Yes, I'm very tired. I just want to fall straight off to sleep.

Helmer: There you are, you see! Wasn't I right in thinking we shouldn't stay any longer.

Nora: Oh, everything you do is right.

Helmer: *(Kissing her forehead.)* There's my little sky-lark talking common sense. Did 130 you notice how gay Rank was this evening?

Nora: Oh, was he? I didn't get a chance to talk to him.

Helmer: I hardly did either. But it's a long time since I saw him in such a good mood. *(Looks at Nora for a moment or two, then comes nearer her.)* Ah, it's wonderful to be back in our own home again, and quite alone with you. How irresistibly lovely you are, Nora!

Nora: Don't look at me like that, Torvald!

Helmer: Can't I look at my most treasured possession? At all this loveliness that's mine and mine alone, completely and utterly mine.

Nora: *(Walks round to the other side of the table.)* You mustn't talk to me like that 135 tonight.

Helmer: *(Following her.)* You still have the tarantella in your blood, I see. And that makes you even more desirable. Listen! The guests are beginning to leave now. *(Softly.)* Nora . . . soon the whole house will be silent.

Nora: I should hope so.

Helmer: Of course you do, don't you, Nora my darling? You know, whenever I'm out at a party with you . . . do you know why I never talk to you very much, why I always stand away from you and only steal a quick glance at you now and then . . . do you know why I do that? It's because I'm pretending we are secretly in love, secretly engaged and nobody suspects there is anything between us.

Nora: Yes, yes. I know your thoughts are always with me, of course.

Helmer: And when it's time to go, and I lay your shawl round those shapely, young 140 shoulders, round the exquisite curve of your neck . . . I pretend that you are my young bride, that we are just leaving our wedding, that I am taking you to our new home for the first time . . . to be alone with you for the first time . . . quite alone with your young and trembling loveliness! All evening I've been longing for you, and nothing else. And as I watched you darting and swaying in the tarantella, my blood was on fire . . . I couldn't bear it any longer . . . and that's why I brought you down here with me so early. . . .

Nora: Go away, Torvald! Please leave me alone. I won't have it.

Helmer: What's this? It's just your little game isn't it, my little Nora. Won't Won't! Am I not your husband . . . ?

(There is a knock on the front door.)

Nora: *(Startled.)* Listen . . . !

Helmer: *(Going towards the hall.)* Who's there?

Rank: *(Outside.)* It's me. Can I come in for a minute? 145

Helmer: *(In a low voice, annoyed.)* Oh, what does he want now? *(Aloud.)* Wait a moment. *(He walks across and opens the door.)* How nice of you to look in on your way out.

Rank: I fancied I heard your voice and I thought I would just look in. *(He takes a quick glance round.)* Ah yes, this dear, familiar old place! How cozy and comfortable you've got things here, you two.

Helmer: You seemed to be having a pretty good time upstairs yourself.

Rank: Capital! Why shouldn't I? Why not make the most of things in this world? At least as much as one can, and for as long as one can. The wine was excellent. . . .

Helmer: Especially the champagne. 150

Rank: You noticed that too, did you? It's incredible the amount I was able to put away.

Nora: Torvald also drank a lot of champagne this evening.

Rank: Oh?

Nora: Yes, and that always makes him quite merry.

Rank: Well, why shouldn't a man allow himself a jolly evening after a day well spent? 155

Helmer: Well spent? I'm afraid I can't exactly claim that.

Rank: *(Clapping him on the shoulder.)* But I can, you see!

Nora: Dr. Rank, am I right in thinking you carried out a certain laboratory test today?

Rank: Exactly.

Helmer: Look at our little Nora talking about laboratory tests! 160

Nora: And may I congratulate you on the result?

Rank: You may indeed.

Nora: So it was good?

Rank: The best possible, for both doctor and patient—certainty!

Nora: *(Quickly and searchingly.)* Certainty? 165

Rank: Absolute certainty. So why shouldn't I allow myself a jolly evening after that?

Nora: Quite right, Dr. Rank.

Helmer: I quite agree. As long as you don't suffer for it in the morning.

Rank: Well, you never get anything for nothing in this life.

Nora: Dr. Rank . . . you are very fond of masquerades, aren't you? 170

Rank: Yes, when there are plenty of amusing disguises. . . .

Nora: Tell me, what shall we two go as next time?

Helmer: There's frivolity for you . . . thinking about the next time already!

Rank: We two? I'll tell you. You must go as Lady Luck. . . .

Helmer: Yes, but how do you find a costume to suggest *that?* 175

Rank: Your wife could simply go in her everyday clothes. . . .

Helmer: That was nicely said. But don't you know what you would be?

Rank: Yes, my dear friend, I know exactly what I shall be.

Helmer: Well?

Rank: At the next masquerade, I shall be invisible.   180

Helmer: That's a funny idea!

Rank: There's a big black cloak . . . haven't you heard of the cloak of invisibility? That comes right down over you, and then nobody can see you.

Helmer: *(Suppressing a smile.)* Of course, that's right.

Rank: But I'm clean forgetting what I came for. Helmer, give me a cigar, one of the dark Havanas.

Helmer: With the greatest of pleasure.   185

(He offers his case.)

Rank: *(Takes one and cuts the end off.)* Thanks.

Nora: *(Strikes a match.)* Let me give you a light.

Rank: Thank you. *(She holds out the match and he lights his cigar.)* And now, goodbye!

Helmer: Goodbye, goodbye, my dear fellow!

Nora: Sleep well, Dr. Rank.   190

Rank: Thank you for that wish.

Nora: Wish me the same.

Rank: You? All right, if you want me to. . . . Sleep well. And thanks for the light.

(He nods to them both, and goes.)

Helmer: *(Subdued.)* He's had a lot to drink.

Nora: *(Absently.)* Very likely.   195

(Helmer takes a bunch of keys out of his pocket and goes out into the hall.)

Nora: Torvald . . . what do you want there?

Helmer: I must empty the letter-box, it's quite full. There'll be no room for the papers in the morning. . . .

Nora: Are you going to work tonight?

Helmer: You know very well I'm not. Hello, what's this? Somebody's been at the lock.

Nora: At the lock?   200

Helmer: Yes, I'm sure of it. Why should that be? I'd hardly have thought the maids . . . ? Here's a broken hair-pin. Nora, it's one of yours. . . .

Nora: *(Quickly.)* It must have been the children. . . .

Helmer: Then you'd better tell them not to. Ah . . . there . . . I've managed to get it open. *(He takes the things out and shouts into the kitchen.)* Helene! . . . Helene, put the light out in the hall. *(He comes into the room again with the letters in his hand and shuts the hall door.)* Look how it all mounts up. *(Runs through them.)* What's this?

Nora: The letter! Oh no, Torvald, no!

Helmer: Two visiting cards . . . from Dr. Rank.   205

Nora: From Dr. Rank?

Helmer: *(Looking at them.)* Dr. Rank, Medical Practitioner. They were on top. He must have put them in as he left.

Nora: Is there anything on them?

Helmer: There's a black cross above his name. Look. What an uncanny idea. It's just as if he were announcing his own death.

Nora: He is.   210

Helmer: What? What do you know about it? Has he said anything to you?

Nora: Yes. He said when these cards came, he would have taken his last leave of us. He was going to shut himself up and die.

Helmer: Poor fellow! Of course I knew we couldn't keep him with us very long. But so soon. . . . And hiding himself away like a wounded animal.

Nora: When it has to happen, it's best that it should happen without words. Don't you think so, Torvald?

Helmer: *(Walking up and down.)* He had grown so close to us. I don't think I can imagine him gone. His suffering and his loneliness seemed almost to provide a background of dark cloud to the sunshine of our lives. Well, perhaps it's all for the best. For him at any rate. *(Pauses.)* And maybe for us as well, Nora. Now there's just the two of us. *(Puts his arms around her.)* Oh, my darling wife, I can't hold you close enough. You know, Nora . . . many's the time I wish you were threatened by some terrible danger so I could risk everything, body and soul, for your sake.

Nora: *(Tears herself free and says firmly and decisively.)* Now you must read your letters, Torvald.

Helmer: No, no, not tonight. I want to be with you, my darling wife.

Nora: Knowing all the time your friend is dying . . . ?

Helmer: You are right. It's been a shock to both of us. This ugly thing has come between us . . . thoughts of death and decay. We must try to free ourselves from it. Until then . . . we shall go our separate ways.

Nora: *(Her arms round his neck.)* Torvald . . . good night! Good night!

Helmer: *(Kisses her forehead.)* Goodnight, my little singing bird. Sleep well, Nora, I'll just read through my letters.

(He takes the letters into his room and shuts the door behind him.)

Nora: *(Gropes around her, wild-eyed, seizes Helmer's cloak, wraps it round herself, and whispers quickly, hoarsely, spasmodically.)* Never see him again. Never, never, never. *(Throws her shawl over her head.)* And never see the children again either. Never, never. Oh, that black icy water. Oh, that bottomless . . . ! If only it were all over! He's got it now. Now he's reading it. Oh no, no! Not yet! Torvald, goodbye . . . and my children. . . .

(She rushes out in the direction of the hall; at the same moment Helmer flings open his door and stands there with an open letter in his hand.)

Helmer: Nora!

Nora: *(Shrieks.)* Ah!

Helmer: What is this? Do you know what is in this letter?

Nora: Yes, I know. Let me go! Let me out!

Helmer: *(Holds her back.)* Where are you going?

Nora: *(Trying to tear herself free.)* You mustn't try to save me, Torvald!

Helmer: *(Reels back.)* True! Is it true what he writes? How dreadful! No, no, it can't possibly be true.

Nora: It *is* true. I loved you more than anything else in the world.

Helmer: Don't come to me with a lot of paltry excuses!

Nora: *(Taking a step towards him.)* Torvald . . . !

Helmer: Miserable woman . . . what is this you have done?

Nora: Let me go. I won't have you taking the blame for me. You mustn't take it on yourself.

215

220

225

230

Helmer: Stop play-acting! *(Locks the front door.)* You are staying here to give an   235
account of yourself. Do you understand what you have done? Answer me! Do
you understand?

Nora: *(Looking fixedly at him, her face hardening.)* Yes, now I'm really beginning to
understand.

Helmer: *(Walking up and down.)* Oh, what a terrible awakening this is. All these
eight years . . . this woman who was my pride and joy . . . a hypocrite, a liar,
worse than that, a criminal! Oh, how utterly squalid it all is! Ugh! Ugh! *(Nora
remains silent and looks fixedly at him.)* I should have realized something like
this would happen. I should have seen it coming. All your father's irresponsible
ways . . . Quiet! All your father's irresponsible ways are coming out in you. No
religion, no morals, no sense of duty . . . Oh, this is my punishment for turning
a blind eye to him. It was for your sake I did it, and this is what I get for it.

Nora: Yes, this.

Helmer: Now you have ruined my entire happiness, jeopardized my whole future.
It's terrible to think of. Here I am, at the mercy of a thoroughly unscrupulous
person; he can do whatever he likes with me, demand anything he wants, order
me about just as he chooses . . . and I daren't even whimper. I'm done for, a
miserable failure, and it's all the fault of a feather-brained woman!

Nora: When I've left this world behind, you will be free.   240

Helmer: Oh, stop pretending! Your father was just the same, always ready with fine
phrases. What good would it do me if you left this world behind, as you put it?
Not the slightest bit of good. He can still let it all come out, if he likes; and if
he does, people might even suspect me of being an accomplice in these criminal
acts of yours; they might even think I was the one behind it all, that it was I
who pushed you into it! And it's you I have to thank for this . . . and when I've
taken such good care of you, all our married life. Now do you understand what
you have done to me?

Nora: *(Coldly and calmly.)* Yes.

Helmer: I just can't understand it, it's so incredible. But we must see about putting
things right. Take that shawl off. Take it off, I tell you! I must see if I can't find
some way or other of appeasing him. The thing must be hushed up at all costs.
And as far as you and I are concerned, things must appear to go on exactly as
before. But only in the eyes of the world, of course. In other words you'll go
on living here; that's understood. But you will not be allowed to bring up the
children; I can't trust you with them. . . . Oh, that I should have to say this to
the woman I loved so dearly, the woman I still . . . Well, that must be all over
and done with. From now on, there can be no question of happiness. All we
can do is save the bits and pieces from the wreck, preserve appearances . . . *(The
front door-bell rings. Helmer gives a start.)* What's that? So late? How terrible,
supposing . . . If he should . . . ? Hide, Nora! Say you are not well.

(Nora stands motionless. Helmer walks across and opens the door into the hall.)

Maid: *(Half dressed, in the hall.)* It's a note for Mrs. Helmer.

Helmer: Give it to me. *(He snatches the note and shuts the door.)* Yes, it's from him.   245
You can't have it. I want to read it myself.

Nora: You read it then.

Helmer: *(By the lamp.)* I hardly dare. Perhaps this is the end, for both of us. Well,
I *must* know. *(He opens the note hurriedly, reads a few lines, looks at another*

enclosed sheet, and gives a cry of joy.) Nora! *(Nora looks at him inquiringly.)* Nora! I must read it again. Yes, yes, it's true! I am saved! Nora, I am saved!

Nora: And me?

Helmer: You too, of course, we are both saved, you as well as me. Look, he's sent your IOU back. He sends his regrets and apologies for what he has done. . . . His luck has changed. . . . Oh, what does it matter what he says. We are saved, Nora! Nobody can do anything to you now. Oh, Nora, Nora . . . but let's get rid of this disgusting thing first. Let me see. . . . *(He glances at the IOU.)* No, I don't want to see it. I don't want it to be anything but a dream. *(He tears up the IOU and both letters, throws all the pieces into the stove and watches them burn.)* Well, that's the end of that. He said in his note you'd known since Christmas Eve. . . . You must have had three terrible days of it, Nora.

Nora: These three days haven't been easy. 250

Helmer: The agonies you must have gone through! When the only way out seemed to be. . . . No, let's forget the whole ghastly thing. We can rejoice and say: It's all over! It's all over! Listen to me, Nora! You don't seem to understand: it's all over! Why this grim look on your face? Oh, poor little Nora, of course I understand. You can't bring yourself to believe I've forgiven you. But I have. Nora, I swear it. I forgive you everything. I know you did what you did because you loved me.

Nora: That's true.

Helmer: You loved me as a wife should love her husband. It was simply that you didn't have the experience to judge what was the best way of going about things. But do you think I love you any the less for that; just because you don't know how to act on your own responsibility? No, no, you just lean on me. I shall give you all the advice and guidance you need. I wouldn't be a proper man if I didn't find a woman doubly attractive for being so obviously helpless. You mustn't dwell on the harsh things I said in the first moment of horror, when I thought everything was going to come crashing down about my ears. I have forgiven you, Nora, I swear it! I have forgiven you!

Nora: Thank you for your forgiveness.

(She goes out through the door, right.)

Helmer: No, don't go! *(He looks through the doorway.)* What are you doing in the spare room? 255

Nora: Taking off this fancy dress.

Helmer: *(Standing at the open door.)* Yes, do. You try and get some rest, and set your mind at peace again, my frightened little song-bird. Have a good long sleep; you know you are safe and sound under my wing. *(Walks up and down near the door.)* What a nice, cozy little home we have here, Nora! Here you can find refuge. Here I shall hold you like a hunted dove I have rescued unscathed from the cruel talons of the hawk, and calm your poor beating heart. And that will come, gradually, Nora, believe me. Tomorrow you'll see everything quite differently. Soon everything will be just as it was before. You won't need me to keep on telling you I've forgiven you: you'll feel convinced of it in your own heart. You don't really imagine me ever thinking of turning you out, or even of reproaching you? Oh, a real man isn't made that way, you know, Nora. For a man, there's something indescribably moving and very satisfying in knowing that he has forgiven his wife—forgiven her, completely and genuinely, from the depths of his heart. It's as though it made her his property in a double sense: he has, as it were, given her a new life, and she becomes in a way both his wife and at the same time his child. That is how you will seem to me after today, helpless, perplexed little thing that you are. Don't you worry your pretty little head about anything, Nora. Just you be frank with me, and I'll make all the decisions for you. . . . What's this? Not in bed? You've changed your things?

Nora: *(In her everyday dress.)* Yes, Torvald, I've changed.

Helmer: What for? It's late.

Nora: I shan't sleep tonight.

Helmer: But my dear Nora. . . .   260

Nora: *(Looks at her watch.)* It's not so terribly late. Sit down, Torvald. We two have a lot to talk about.

    (She sits down at one side of the table.)

Helmer: Nora, what is all this? Why so grim?

Nora: Sit down. It'll take some time. I have a lot to say to you.

Helmer: *(Sits down at the table opposite her.)* You frighten me, Nora. I don't   265
understand you.

Nora: Exactly. You don't understand me. And I have never understood you, either—until tonight. No, don't interrupt. I just want you to listen to what I have to say. We are going to have things out, Torvald.

Helmer: What do you mean?

Nora: Isn't there anything that strikes you about the way we two are sitting here?

Helmer: What's that?

Nora: We have now been married eight years. Hasn't it struck you this is the first   270
time you and I, man and wife, have had a serious talk together?

Helmer: Depends what you mean by "serious."

Nora: Eight whole years—no, more, ever since we first knew each other—and never have we exchanged one serious word about serious things.

Helmer: What did you want me to do? Get you involved in worries that you couldn't possibly help me to bear?

Nora: I'm not talking about worries. I say we've never once sat down together and seriously tried to get to the bottom of anything.

Helmer: But, my dear Nora, would that have been a thing for you?   275

Nora: That's just it. You have never understood me . . . I've been greatly wronged, Torvald. First by my father, and then by you.

Helmer: What! Us two! The two people who loved you more than anybody?

Nora: *(Shakes her head.)* You two never loved me. You only thought how nice it was to be in love with me.

Helmer: But, Nora, what's this you are saying?

Nora: It's right, you know, Torvald. At home, Daddy used to tell me what he   280
thought, then I thought the same. And if I thought differently, I kept quiet about it, because he wouldn't have liked it. He used to call me his baby doll, and he played with me as I used to play with my dolls. Then I came to live in your house. . . .

Helmer: What way is that to talk about our marriage?

Nora: *(Imperturbably.)* What I mean is: I passed out of Daddy's hands into yours. You arranged everything to your tastes, and I acquired the same tastes. Or pretended to . . . I don't really know . . . I think it was a bit of both, sometimes one thing and sometimes the other. When I looked back, it seems to me I have been living here like a beggar, from hand to mouth. I lived by doing tricks for you, Torvald. But that's the way you wanted it. You and Daddy did me a great wrong. It's your fault that I've never made anything of my life.

Helmer: Nora, how unreasonable . . . how ungrateful you are! Haven't you been happy here?

Nora: No, never. I thought I was, but I wasn't really.

Helmer: Not . . . not happy! 285

Nora: No, just gay. And you've always been so kind to me. But our house has never been anything but a play-room. I have been your doll wife, just as at home I was Daddy's doll child. And the children in turn have been my dolls. I thought it was fun when you came and played with me, just as they thought it was fun when I went and played with them. That's been our marriage, Torvald.

Helmer: There is some truth in what you say, exaggerated and hysterical though it is. But from now on it will be different. Play-time is over; now comes the time for lessons.

Nora: Whose lessons? Mine or the children?

Helmer: Both yours and the children's, my dear Nora.

Nora: Ah, Torvald, you are not the man to teach me to be a good wife for you. 290

Helmer: How can you say that?

Nora: And what sort of qualifications have I to teach the children?

Helmer: Nora!

Nora: Didn't you say yourself, a minute or two ago, that you couldn't trust me with that job.

Helmer: In the heat of the moment! You shouldn't pay any attention to that. 295

Nora: On the contrary, you were quite right. I'm not up to it. There's another problem needs solving first. I must take steps to educate myself. You are not the man to help me there. That's something I must do on my own. That's why I'm leaving you.

Helmer: *(Jumps up.)* What did you say?

Nora: If I'm ever to reach any understanding of myself and the things around me, I must learn to stand alone. That's why I can't stay here with you any longer.

Helmer: Nora! Nora!

Nora: I'm leaving here at once. I dare say Kristine will put me up for tonight. . . . 300

Helmer: You are out of your mind! I won't let you! I forbid you!

Nora: It's no use forbidding me anything now. I'm taking with me my own personal belongings. I don't want anything of yours, either now or later.

Helmer: This is madness!

Nora: Tomorrow I'm going home—to what used to be my home, I mean. It will be easier for me to find something to do there.

Helmer: Oh, you blind, inexperienced . . . 305

Nora: I must set about *getting* experience, Torvald.

Helmer: And leave your home, your husband and your children? Don't you care what people will say?

Nora: That's no concern of mine. All I know is that this is necessary for *me*.

Helmer: This is outrageous! You are betraying your most sacred duty.

Nora: And what do you consider to be my most sacred duty? 310

Helmer: Does it take me to tell you that? Isn't it your duty to your husband and your children?

Nora: I have another duty equally sacred.

Helmer: You have not. What duty might *that* be?

Nora: My duty to myself.

Helmer: First and foremost, you are a wife and mother. 315

Nora: That I don't believe any more. I believe that first and foremost I am an individual, just as much as you are—or at least I'm going to try to be. I know most people agree with you, Torvald, and that's also what it says in books. But I'm not content any more with what most people say, or with what it says in books. I have to think things out for myself, and get things clear.

Helmer: Surely you are clear about your position in your own home? Haven't you an infallible guide in questions like these? Haven't you your religion?

Nora: Oh, Torvald, I don't really know what religion is.

Helmer: What do you say?

Nora: All I know is what Pastor Hansen said when I was confirmed. He said religion 320 was this, that and the other. When I'm away from all this and on my own, I'll go into that, too. I want to find out whether what Pastor Hansen told me was right—or at least whether it's right for *me*.

Helmer: This is incredible talk from a young woman! But if religion cannot keep you on the right path, let me at least stir your conscience. I suppose you do have some moral sense? Or tell me—perhaps you don't?

Nora: Well, Torvald, that's not easy to say. I simply don't know. I'm really confused about such things. All I know is my ideas about such things are very different from yours. I've also learned that the law is different from what I thought; but I simply can't get it into my head that that particular law is right. Apparently a woman has no right to spare her old father on his death-bed, or to save her husband's life, even. I just don't believe it.

Helmer: You are talking like a child. You understand nothing about the society you live in.

Nora: No, I don't. But I shall go into that too. I must try to discover who is right, society or me.

Helmer: You are ill, Nora. You are delirious. I'm half inclined to think you are out of 325 your mind.

Nora: Never have I felt so calm and collected as I do tonight.

Helmer: Calm and collected enough to leave your husband and children?

Nora: Yes.

Helmer: Then only one explanation is possible.

Nora: And that is? 330

Helmer: You don't love me any more.

Nora: Exactly.

Helmer: Nora! Can you say that!

Nora: I'm desperately sorry, Torvald. Because you have always been so kind to me. But I can't help it. I don't love you any more.

Helmer: *(Struggling to keep his composure.)* Is that also a "calm and collected" decision 335 you've made?

Nora: Yes, absolutely calm and collected. That's why I don't want to stay here.

Helmer: And can you also account for how I forfeited your love?

Nora: Yes, very easily. It was tonight, when the miracle didn't happen. It was then I realized you weren't the man I thought you were.

Helmer: Explain yourself more clearly. I don't understand.

Nora: For eight years I have been patiently waiting. Because, heavens, I knew   340
miracles didn't happen every day. Then this devastating business started, and I became absolutely convinced the miracle *would* happen. All the time Krogstad's letter lay there, it never so much as crossed my mind that you would ever submit to that man's conditions. I was absolutely convinced you would say to him: Tell the whole wide world if you like. And when that was done . . .

Helmer: Yes, then what? After I had exposed my wife to dishonor and shame . . . !

Nora: When that was done, I was absolutely convinced you would come forward and take everything on yourself, and say: I am the guilty one.

Helmer: Nora!

Nora: You mean I'd never let you make such a sacrifice for my sake? Of course not. But what would my story have counted for against yours?—That was the miracle I went in hope and dread of. It was to prevent it that I was ready to end my life.

Helmer: I would gladly toil day and night for you, Nora, enduring all manner of   345
sorrow and distress. But nobody sacrifices his *honor* for the one he loves.

Nora: Hundreds and thousands of women have.

Helmer: Oh, you think and talk like a stupid child.

Nora: All right. But you neither think nor talk like the man I would want to share my life with. When you had got over your fright—and you weren't concerned about me but only about what might happen to you—and when all danger was past, you acted as though nothing had happened. I was your little sky-lark again, your little doll, exactly as before; except you would have to protect it twice as carefully as before, now that it had shown itself to be so weak and fragile. *(Rises.)* Torvald, that was the moment I realized that for eight years I'd been living with a stranger, and had borne him three children. . . . Oh, I can't bear to think about it! I could tear myself to shreds.

Helmer: *(Sadly.)* I see. I see. There is a tremendous gulf dividing us. But, Nora, is there no way we might bridge it?

Nora: As I am now, I am no wife for you.   350

Helmer: I still have it in me to change.

Nora: Perhaps . . . if you have your doll taken away.

Helmer: And be separated from you! No, no, Nora, the very thought of it is inconceivable.

Nora: *(Goes into the room, right.)* All the more reason why it must be done.

(She comes back with her outdoor things and a small traveling bag which she puts on the chair beside the table.)

Helmer: Nora, Nora, not now! Wait till the morning.   355

Nora: *(Putting on her coat.)* I can't spend the night in a strange man's room.

Helmer: Couldn't we go on living here like brother and sister . . . ?

Nora: *(Tying on her hat.)* You know very well that wouldn't last. *(She draws the shawl round her.)* Goodbye, Torvald. I don't want to see the children. I know they are in better hands than mine. As I am now, I can never be anything to them.

Helmer: But some day, Nora, some day . . . ?

Nora: How should I know? I've no idea what I might turn out to be.   360

Helmer: But you are my wife, whatever you are.

Nora: Listen, Torvald, from what I've heard, when a wife leaves her husband's house
    as I am doing now, he is absolved by law of all responsibility for her. I can,
    at any rate, free you from all responsibility. You must not feel in any way
    bound, any more than I shall. There must be full freedom on both sides. Look,
    here's your ring back. Give me mine.

Helmer: That too?

Nora: That too.

Helmer: There it is.   365

Nora: Well, that's the end of that. I'll put the keys down here. The maids know where
    everything is in the house—better than I do, in fact. Kristine will come in the
    morning after I've left to pack up the few things I brought with me from home.
    I want them sent on.

Helmer: The end! Nora, will you never think of me?

Nora: I dare say I'll often think about you and the children and this house.

Helmer: May I write to you, Nora?

Nora: No, never. I won't let you.   370

Helmer: But surely I can send you . . .

Nora: Nothing, nothing.

Helmer: Can't I help you if ever you need it?

Nora: I said "no." I don't accept things from strangers.

Helmer: Nora, can I never be anything more to you than a stranger?   375

Nora: *(Takes her bag.)* Ah, Torvald, only by a miracle of miracles. . . .

Helmer: Name it, this miracle of miracles!

Nora: Both you and I would have to change to the point where . . . Oh, Torvald, I
    don't believe in miracles any more.

Helmer: But I *will* believe. Name it! Change to the point where . . . ?

Nora: Where we could make a real marriage of our lives together. Goodbye!   380

    (She goes out through the hall door.)

Helmer: *(Sinks down on a chair near the door, and covers his face with his hands.)* Nora!
    Nora! *(He rises and looks round.)* Empty! She's gone! *(With sudden hope.)* The
    miracle of miracles . . . ?

    (The heavy sound of a door being slammed is heard from below.)

    THE CURTAIN FALLS.

Explorations of the Text

1. What are your first impressions of Nora's and Torvald's personalities? Of their relationship? Why does Torvald call Nora "my pretty little pet" or "my little squirrel"? What do these nicknames suggest about his attitude toward her?

2. Do you think that Nora was justified in taking out the loan, breaking the law and forging her father's signature? Consider Krogstad's statement: "The law takes no account of motives." Should she have revealed her "secret" to Torvald right away?

3. Discuss Nora's relationship with her children in Act I. What is significant about her actions?

4. How does the conflict between Nora and Torvald escalate in Act II? What motivates each character's behavior? Examine their interaction in the dance scene at the end of Act II. What is the significance of the tarantella?

5. List the other conflicts in the drama. How do they evolve in Acts II and III? How do Mrs. Linde, Krogstad, and Dr. Rank serve as character foils? What roles do they play in determining Nora's fate?

6. The conflict between Nora and Torvald reaches its climax in Act III. Examine Torvald's and Nora's differing moral positions. Is Torvald justified in condemning her? With whom are you more sympathetic?

7. How does Nora change from the beginning to the end of the play?

8. Why does Nora leave? Do you think that Nora should have left her children?

9. Compare and contrast Nora with the narrator in "The Yellow Wallpaper" (Chapter 7).

The Reading/Writing Connection

1. "Think" Topic: What is the meaning of the title?

2. Freewrite: What do you think is the basis for a successful marriage?

3. What do you think happens to Nora after the end of the play?

Ideas for Writing

1. Write a character analysis of Nora or of Torvald.

2. **Write an Argument:** Should Nora have left Torvald and her children? Compose an argumentative essay that presents your position on this question. Use specific evidence from the text to support your views.

3. Both Li'l Bit and Nora are trapped by their pasts. In what ways?

NONFICTION

Lynn Smith

Betwixt and Bewildered: Scholars Are Intrigued by the Angst of "Emerging Adults" *2001*

When she was 18, the mother of a 21-year-old son recalled, she hardly could wait to go away to school and move out of her parents' house. Most of her friends felt the same way. Nobody knew who they went out with, where they went, what they did or when they got in.

But her son lives at home and likes it. A junior in the California State University system, he doesn't have to pay rent or buy groceries. "He has a TV, a computer and a double bed. What more could a guy want?"

"The one thing that's been weird has been having his girlfriend spend the night," said the single mother, who also has a boyfriend. "How can I say, 'I can, but you can't'?" she asked. "When do you say he's an adult?"

It's a common question, and one that a growing number of parents and researchers are trying to answer. Social and economic realities have suspended the traditional markers of adulthood—moving out, finishing school, starting a job, getting married and having children. Old expectations for independence have been joined by new ones for career success and happiness.

Indeed, scholars say the path to adulthood, never particularly smooth, is not only 5 longer, but also more circuitous, complex, expensive and vaguely defined than ever before. Rather than settling down with a spouse and children as their grandparents did, most high school seniors go on to college or pursue advanced degrees. They move about and hop from job to job. They live with various friends or significant others. An ever-increasing number move back home with their parents at some point after they move out.

Some specialists in human development believe the years between 18 and 25 are more than an extended adolescence, that they compose a distinct life stage that is neither adolescent nor adult, a heretofore nameless world of angst and hope. Jeffrey Arnett, an independent scholar based at the University of Maryland, calls it "emerging adulthood." Terri Apter, a research psychologist in Cambridge, England, and author of "The Myth of Maturity," calls those young adults "thresholders."

The members of this group, Arnett said, are living in a state marked by more risk and exploration than adolescence itself. Emerging adults, he said, are "freer now than they have ever been in American history. It used to be just for the elite. Now it's for the majority."

Even as they document this new stage of life, scholars disagree about whether these changes should be a cause for celebration or concern. A boom-and-bust marketplace, overly involved parents and mixed expectations are creating new pressures for young adults who fear they might never make it on their own. Others say the longer transition offers an unparalleled opportunity. Especially for those from disadvantaged or dysfunctional families, they say, this make-or-break phase can be a chance to invent or reinvent a life.

"We're going through a real sea change in how we define what adulthood is, what maturity is, what dependence is, what a steady job is," said Stephanie Coontz, a family historian at Evergreen State College in Olympia, Wash. Although the young aren't the only ones trying to sort out their life paths, they are the most obvious, she said. "They have to make decisions right now—when to get married, when to move out."

Bill Fitzsimmons, Harvard University dean of admissions and financial aid, said he has seen a consistent growth in anxiety levels among college students over the last two decades. The cause, he believes, is too little freedom, rather than too much. Overscheduled and controlled throughout childhood by their parents, many students are burned out and unable to be introspective about their own futures, he said. Some college students are so frenzied, they have to schedule a 20-minute meeting at 7 a.m. just to catch up with a friend, he said. Others might fail classes, consciously or unconsciously, as a way to deal with parents who have imposed inappropriate majors on them. 10

University officials have found students mature remarkably in just a year if they can take time off from school, Fitzsimmons said. But Jeylan Mortimer, a life-course specialist at the University of Michigan, said most students don't have the resources to take time off, travel or spend time mulling over their possibilities. "They're struggling to find their way, moving in and out of school and work, running into financial problems. They struggle with the whole process."

Increasingly young people are unable to leave home permanently the first time they move out. "It's like stopping smoking. You have to keep trying a couple of times," said Frances Goldscheider, professor of sociology at Brown University. "In the 1930s, only 25 percent of those who left home returned. By the mid-'80s, it was up to 40 percent." Now, although she doesn't have current numbers, she estimates that the figures are higher.

Apter believes too many parents feel they shouldn't be helping their thresholder children. "We're used to thinking about the dangers of keeping our children connected to us. These are real concerns in some cases, but what's happened is our awareness of the dangers of being too close has made us devalue normal healthy closeness and connection," she said.

One problem with studying the transition to adulthood is that researchers usually have limited funds and turn most often to students as subjects. Another is that there has been little information about how people experience that phase of life.

Among the first to describe how it feels to navigate this extended transition are Alexandra Robbins and Abby Wilner, authors of "Quarterlife Crisis." They say young adults like themselves face nearly unlimited options and are jolted by "overwhelming helplessness and cluelessness, indecision and apprehension." 15

The authors, in their twenties, have said many people mistakenly think the twenties are easy and carefree. In fact, they said, many young adults are emotionally paralyzed and turn to antidepressants to deal with the angst of growing up. One chapter of their book is titled, "What if I'm Scared to Stop Being a Kid?"

Arnett noted that many students do not finish college, or at least not in four consecutive years. Only one-third of the college population obtains a bachelor's degree in their twenties, he said. "They're talking about the most fortunate segment of the most affluent generation of the most affluent society in human history. And all they can talk about is how tough they have it? It's like a rich guy complaining about the problems he's having with his Mercedes."

Many emerging adults have legitimate problems stemming from educational loans and credit card debt, he said.

At the same time, a "lottery-based society" has created pressures unrelated to one's finances, background or parents, said family historian Coontz. "It doesn't matter how stable you grew up; the person next to you, just by luck, got out of the stock market at just the right time and is now wandering around a millionaire while someone else, just by luck, lost out. It creates a 'why me?' mindset interspersed with grandiose, narcissistic dreams of really making it."

Despite their problems, most of the 200 young people Arnett interviewed over the 20 last seven years, he said, were much happier than they had been as adolescents.

They get along with parents and regret that they were rude, he said. Most are full of hope and ambition, even if their backgrounds were difficult.

Some scholars said emerging adulthood is a luxury of the educated middle and upper classes, experienced only by those who stay in school and remain childless.

Nevertheless, Arnett said, it is an especially important opportunity for people whose parents were poor or dysfunctional in some way. "Emerging adulthood represents a chance to remake your life," he said.

For the poor, it might be now or never. "Children and adolescents are really at the mercy of families, for better or worse. The chances to turn your life around are not in childhood and adolescence. And in a way, there won't be any once you take on new long-term commitments, especially children," he said.

Barbara Schneider, professor of sociology at the University of Chicago, said it is 25 imperative to understand that young adults, although they might be grouped in a single generation, are not all alike, one way or another. In her studies of 1,221 adolescents whom she followed into adulthood, Schneider found they fell into three groups: those who had a clear idea about what they wanted to do in the future, a transitional group whose members are trying to find themselves, and a "diffuse" group of young adults who had no idea what they wanted to do.

The diffuse group tended most to founder, changing colleges and taking longer to get a degree. Transitional students also have a difficult time if they don't establish a path for themselves by their junior year, she said. "This is the group that at the end of college is more likely to feel they have not lived up to their expectations. Mom says, 'We spent all this money and you want to be a what?'" ●

Explorations of the Text

1. What is the major claim (the main position) of the article?

2. Smith presents a cause-effect argument. Outline the essay. What are the causes of this state of "extended adolescence" or "emerging adulthood"? the effects on this generation? What forms of proof does she use to support her points?

3. Of the characters in the selected fictional works in this chapter, who do you think fits the category of "thresholder": Sammy in John Updike's "A & P"; Janice Mirikitani's speaker in "Suicide Note"; or the unnamed narrator in Raymond Carver's "Cathedral"?

4. Compare Smith's state of "extended adolescence" with Joan Didion's description of her life in New York in "Goodbye to All That." Was Didion a "threshholder"?

The Reading/Writing Connection

1. **Write an Argument:** Based on your observations and experiences, do you think adolescents today experience more "anxiety" than "college students over the last two decades," as Bill Fitzsimmons theorizes? Why or why not?

2. Ask several of your peers to read this article. Then have a group discussion about its major points. What do you learn? Write up your conclusions.

Ideas for Writing

1. **Write an Argument:** This article presents the term, "thresholder," to define this generation of eighteen- to twenty-five-year-olds. Do you think that this is an accurate depiction of your generation? Argue pro or con.

2. Create your own definition for the experiences of your generation of adolescents and college students. Using this essay as a model, examine causes and effects of this phenomenon.

Gretel Ehrlich   (1946–)

Looking for a Lost Dog   1995

The most valuable thoughts which I entertain are anything but what I thought. Nature abhors a vacuum, and if I can only walk with sufficient carelessness I am sure to be filled.

—Henry David Thoreau

I started off this morning looking for my lost dog. He's a red heeler, blotched brown and white, and I tell people he looks like a big saddle shoe. Born at Christmas on a thirty-below-zero night, he's tough, though his right front leg is crooked where it froze to the ground.

It's the old needle-in-the-haystack routine: small dog, huge landscape, and rugged terrain. While moving cows once, he fell in a hole and disappeared. We heard him whining but couldn't see him. When we put our ears to the ground, we could hear the hole that had swallowed him.

It's no wonder human beings are so narcissistic. The way our ears are constructed, we can only hear what's right next to us or else the internal monologue inside. I've taken to cupping my hands behind my ears—mule-like—and pricking them all the way forward or back to hear what's happened or what's ahead.

"Life is polyphonic," a Hungarian friend in her eighties said. She was a child prodigy from Budapest who had soloed on the violin in Paris and Berlin by the time she was twelve. "Childishly, I once thought hearing had mostly to do with music," she said.

"Now that I'm too old to play the fiddle, I know it has to do with the great suspiration of life everywhere."

But back to the dog. I'm walking and looking and listening for him, though there is no trail, no clue, no direction to the search. Whimsically, I head north toward the falls. They're set in a deep gorge where Precambrian rock piles up to ten thousand feet on either side. A raven creaks overhead, flies into the cleft, glides toward a panel of white water splashing over a ledge, and comes out cawing.

To find what is lost is an art in some cultures. The Navajos employ "hand tremblers," usually women, who go into a trance and "see" where the lost article or person is located. When I asked one such diviner what it was like when she was in trance, she said, "Lots of noise, but noise that's hard to hear."

Near the falls the ground flattens into a high-altitude valley before the mountains rise vertically. The falls roar, but they're overgrown with spruce, pine, willow, and wild rose, and the closer I get, the harder it is to see the water. Perhaps that is how it will be in my search for the dog.

We're worried about Frenchy because last summer he was bitten three times by rattlesnakes. After the first bite he walked toward me, reeled dramatically, and collapsed. I could see the two holes in his nose where the fangs went in, and I felt sure he was dying. I drove him twenty miles to the vet; by the time we arrived, Frenchy resembled a monster. His nose and neck had swollen as though a football had been sewn under the skin.

I walk and walk. Past the falls, through a pass, toward a larger, rowdier creek. The sky goes black. In the distance snow on the Owl Creek Mountains glares. A blue ocean seems to stretch between, and the black sky hangs over like a frown. A string of cottonwoods whose new, tender leaves are the color of limes pulls me downstream. I come into the meadow with the abandoned apple orchard. The trees have leaves but have lost most of their blossoms. I feel as if I had caught strangers undressed.

The sun comes back, and the wind. It brings no dog, but ducks slide overhead. An Eskimo from Barrow, Alaska, told me the reason spring has such fierce winds is so birds coming north will have something to fly on.

To find what's lost; to lose what's found. Several times I've thought I might be "losing my mind." Of course, minds aren't literally misplaced—on the contrary, we live too much under them. As with viewing the falls, we can lose sight of what is too close. It is between the distant and close-up views that the struggle between impulse and reason, logic and passion takes place.

The feet move; the mind wanders. In his journals Thoreau wrote: "The saunterer, in the good sense, is no more vagrant than the meandering river, which is all the while sedulously seeking the shortest course to the sea."

Today I'm filled with longings—for what I'm not, for what is impossible, for people I love who can't be in my life. Passions of all sorts struggle soundlessly, or else, like the falls, they are all noise but can't be seen. My hybrid anguish spends itself as recklessly and purposefully as water.

Now I'm following a game trail up a sidehill. It's a mosaic of tracks—elk, deer, rabbit, and bird. If city dwellers could leave imprints in cement, it would look this way: tracks would overlap, go backward and forward like the peregrine saunterings of the mind.

I see a dog's track, or is it a coyote's? I get down on my hands and knees to sniff out a scent. What am I doing? I entertain expectations of myself as preposterous as when I landed in Toyko—I felt so at home there that I thought I would break into fluent

Japanese. Now I sniff the ground and smell only dirt. If I spent ten years sniffing, would I learn scents?

The tracks veer off the trail and disappear. Descending into a dry wash whose elegant, tortured junipers and tumbled boulders resemble a Japanese garden, I trip on a sagebrush root. I look. Deep in the center of the plant there is a bird's nest, but instead of eggs, a locust stares up at me.

Some days I think this one place isn't enough. That's when nothing is enough, when I want to live multiple lives and be allowed to love without limits. Those days, like today, I walk with a purpose but no destination. Only then do I see, at least momentarily, that everything is here. To my left a towering cottonwood is lunatic with birdsong. Under it I'm a listening post while its great gray trunk—like a baton or the source of something—heaves its green symphony into the air.

I walk and walk: from the falls, over Grouse Hill, to the dry wash. Today it is enough to make a shadow. ●

Explorations of the Text

1. How does the Henry David Thoreau quotation establish the direction of the essay? What did you predict the essay would be about?

2. Is the essay about "looking for a lost dog"? What is Ehrlich's subject matter? What is the narrator's internal conflict?

3. What is "lost"? Isolate several passages that provide clues.

4. Explain the significance of the following statements: "My hybrid anguish spends itself as recklessly and purposefully as water," and "I walk with a purpose but no destination."

5. What is the final revelation in the essay? Examine the last two paragraphs.

The Reading/Writing Connection

1. Freewrite: Discuss Ehrlich's inner conflict. What does she mean by "today it is enough to make a shadow." What does the "shadow" signify?

2. Select a significant passage in the essay, and use it as the starting point for a freewrite.

3. "Think" Topic: Ehrlich uses allusions and quotations to enlarge the scope of her argument. Choose one allusion or quotation, and discuss how it develops her point. Is this technique effective?

4. Make a list of the sense details in this work. What is the impact of the sensory language? How does it contribute to the development of Ehrlich's message?

Ideas for Writing

1. Write about a journey that you have taken—a hike, a car trip, or travel abroad or at home. Create a short synopsis of the event, and then write as descriptively as possible. Finally, jot down any discoveries about the event that have emerged through writing. Use this writing as the basis of a descriptive essay.

2. Compare the journey in Ehrlich's work with that in Cathy Song's poem.

Bruno Bettelheim   *(1903–1990)*

Introduction: The Struggle for Meaning   1975
From *The Uses of Enchantment*

If we hope to live not just from moment to moment, but in true consciousness of our existence, then our greatest need and most difficult achievement is to find meaning in our lives. It is well known how many have lost the will to live, and have stopped trying, because such meaning has evaded them. An understanding of the meaning of one's life is not suddenly acquired at a particular age, not even when one has reached chronological maturity. On the contrary, gaining a secure understanding of what the meaning of one's life may or ought to be—this is what constitutes having attained psychological maturity. And this achievement is the end result of a long development: at each age we seek, and must be able to find, some modicum of meaning congruent with how our minds and understanding have already developed.

Contrary to the ancient myth, wisdom does not burst forth fully developed like Athena out of Zeus's head; it is built up, small step by small step, from most irrational beginnings. Only in adulthood can an intelligent understanding of the meaning of one's existence in this world be gained from one's experiences in it. Unfortunately, too many parents want their children's minds to function as their own do—as if mature understanding of ourselves and the world, and our ideas about the meaning of life, did not have to develop as slowly as our bodies and minds.

Today, as in times past, the most important and also the most difficult task in raising a child is helping him to find meaning in life. Many growth experiences are needed to achieve this. The child, as he develops, must learn step by step to understand himself better; with this he becomes more able to understand others, and eventually can relate to them in ways which are mutually satisfying and meaningful.

To find deeper meaning, one must become able to transcend the narrow confines of a self-centered existence and believe that one will make a significant contribution to life—if not right now, then at some future time. This feeling is necessary if a person is to be satisfied with himself and with what he is doing. In order not to be at the mercy of the vagaries of life, one must develop one's inner resources, so that one's emotions, imagination, and intellect mutually support and enrich one another. Our positive feelings give us the strength to develop our rationality; only hope for the future can sustain us in the adversities we unavoidably encounter.

As an educator and therapist of severely disturbed children, my main task was to restore meaning to their lives. This work made it obvious to me that if children were reared so that life was meaningful to them, they would not need special help. I was confronted with the problem of deducing what experiences in a child's life are most suited to promote his ability to find meaning in his life; to endow life in general with more meaning. Regarding this task, nothing is more important than the impact of parents and others who take care of the child; second in importance is our cultural heritage, when transmitted to the child in the right manner. When children are young, it is literature that carries such information best.

Given this fact, I became deeply dissatisfied with much of the literature intended to develop the child's mind and personality, because it fails to stimulate and nurture those resources he needs most in order to cope with his difficult inner problems. The preprimers and primers from which he is taught to read in school are designed to teach the necessary skills, irrespective of meaning. The overwhelming bulk of the rest of so-called "children's literature" attempts to entertain or to inform, or both. But most of these books are so shallow in substance that little of significance can be gained from them. The acquisition of skills, including the ability to read, becomes devalued when what one has learned to read adds nothing of importance to one's life.

We all tend to assess the future merits of an activity on the basis of what it offers now. But this is especially true for the child, who, much more than the adult, lives in the present and, although he has anxieties about his future, has only the vaguest notions of what it may require or be like. The idea that learning to read may enable one later to enrich one's life is experienced as an empty promise when the stories the child listens to, or is reading at the moment, are vacuous. The worst feature of these children's books is that they cheat the child of what he ought to gain from the experience of literature: access to deeper meaning, and that which is meaningful to him at his stage of development.

For a story truly to hold the child's attention, it must entertain him and arouse his curiosity. But to enrich his life, it must stimulate his imagination; help him to develop his intellect and to clarify his emotions; be attuned to his anxieties and aspirations; give full recognition to his difficulties, while at the same time suggesting solutions to the problems which perturb him. In short, it must at one and the same time relate to all aspects of his personality—and this without ever belittling but, on the contrary, giving full credence to the seriousness of the child's predicaments, while simultaneously promoting confidence in himself and in his future.

In all these and many other respects, of the entire "children's literature"—with rare exceptions—nothing can be as enriching and satisfying to child and adult alike as the folk fairy tale. True, on an overt level fairy tales teach little about the specific conditions of life in modern mass society; these tales were created long before it came into being. But more can be learned from them about the inner problems of human beings, and of the right solutions to their predicaments in any society, than from any other type of story within a child's comprehension. Since the child at every moment of his life is exposed to the society in which he lives, he will certainly learn to cope with its conditions, provided his inner resources permit him to do so.

Just because his life is often bewildering to him, the child needs even more to be given the chance to understand himself in this complex world with which he must learn to cope. To be able to do so, the child must be helped to make some coherent sense out of the turmoil of his feelings. He needs ideas on how to bring his inner house into order, and on that basis be able to create order in his life. He needs—and this hardly requires emphasis at this moment in our history—a moral education which subtly, and by implication only, conveys to him the advantages of moral behavior, not through abstract ethical concepts but through that which seems tangibly right and therefore meaningful to him.

The child finds this kind of meaning through fairy tales. Like many other modern psychological insights, this was anticipated long ago by poets. The German poet Schiller wrote: "Deeper meaning resides in the fairy tales told to me in my childhood than in the truth that is taught by life." (*The Piccolomini,* III, 4.)

Through the centuries (if not millennia) during which, in their retelling, fairy tales became ever more refined, they came to convey at the same time overt and covert meanings—came to speak simultaneously to all levels of the human personality, communicating in a manner which reaches the uneducated mind of the child as well as that

of the sophisticated adult. Applying the psychoanalytic model of the human personality, fairy tales carry important messages to the conscious, the preconscious, and the
unconscious mind, on whatever level each is functioning at the time. By dealing with
universal human problems, particularly those which preoccupy the child's mind, these
stories speak to his budding ego and encourage its development, while at the same time
relieving preconscious and unconscious pressures. As the stories unfold, they give conscious credence and body to id pressures and show ways to satisfy these that are in line
with ego and superego requirements.

But my interest in fairy tales is not the result of such a technical analysis of their
merits. It is, on the contrary, the consequence of asking myself why, in my experience,
children—normal and abnormal alike, and at all levels of intelligence—find folk fairy
tales more satisfying than all other children's stories.

The more I tried to understand why these stories are so successful at enriching
the inner life of the child, the more I realized that these tales, in a touch deeper sense
than any other reading material, start where the child really is in his psychological and
emotional being. They speak about his severe inner pressures in a way that the child
unconsciously understands, and—without belittling the most serious inner struggles
which growing up entails—offer examples of both temporary and permanent solutions
to pressing difficulties.

When a grant from the Spencer Foundation provided the leisure to study what   15
contributions psychoanalysis can make to the education of children—and since reading and being read to are essential means of education—it seemed appropriate to use
this opportunity to explore in greater detail and depth why folk fairy tales are so valuable in the upbringing of children. My hope is that a proper understanding of the
unique merits of fairy tales will induce parents and teachers to assign them once again
to that central role in the life of the child they held for centuries.

Fairy Tales and the Existential Predicament

In order to master the psychological problems of growing up—overcoming narcissistic disappointments, oedipal dilemmas, sibling rivalries; becoming able to relinquish
childhood dependencies; gaining a feeling of selfhood and of self-worth, and a sense of
moral obligation—a child needs to understand what is going on within his conscious
self so that he can also cope with that which goes on in his unconscious. He can achieve
this understanding, and with it the ability to cope, not through rational comprehension of the nature and content of his unconscious, but by becoming familiar with
it through spinning out daydreams—ruminating, rearranging, and fantasizing about
suitable story elements in response to unconscious pressures. By doing this, the child
fits unconscious content into conscious fantasies, which then enable him to deal with
that content. It is here that fairy tales have unequaled value, because they offer new dimensions to the child's imagination which would be impossible for him to discover as
truly on his own. Even more important, the form and structure of fairy tales suggest
images to the child by which he can structure his daydreams and with them give better direction to his life.

In child or adult, the unconscious is a powerful determinant of behavior. When the
unconscious is repressed and its content denied entrance into awareness, then eventually
the person's conscious mind will be partially overwhelmed by derivatives of these unconscious elements, or else he is forced to keep such rigid, compulsive control over them that

his personality may become severely crippled. But when unconscious material *is* to some degree permitted to come to awareness and worked through in imagination, its potential for causing harm—to ourselves or others—is much reduced; some of its forces can then be made to serve positive purposes. However, the prevalent parental belief is that a child must be diverted from what troubles him most: his formless, nameless anxieties, and his chaotic, angry, and even violent fantasies. Many parents believe that only conscious reality or pleasant and wish-fulfilling images should be presented to the child—that he should be exposed only to the sunny side of things. But such one-sided fare nourishes the mind only in a onesided way, and real life is not all sunny.

There is a widespread refusal to let children know that the source of much that goes wrong in life is due to our very own natures—the propensity of all men for acting aggressively, asocially, selfishly, out of anger and anxiety. Instead, we want our children to believe that, inherently, all men are good. But children know that *they* are not always good; and often, even when they are, they would prefer not to be. This contradicts what they are told by their parents, and therefore makes the child a monster in his own eyes.

The dominant culture wishes to pretend, particularly where children are concerned, that the dark side of man does not exist, and professes a belief in an optimistic meliorism. Psychoanalysis itself is viewed as having the purpose of making life easy—but this is not what its founder intended. Psychoanalysis was created to enable man to accept the problematic nature of life without being defeated by it, or giving in to escapism. Freud's prescription is that only by struggling courageously against what seem like overwhelming odds can man succeed in wringing meaning out of his existence.

This is exactly the message that fairy tales get across to the child in manifold form: 20 that a struggle against severe difficulties in life is unavoidable, is an intrinsic part of human existence—but that if one does not shy away, but steadfastly meets unexpected and often unjust hardships, one masters all obstacles and at the end emerges victorious.

Modern stories written for young children mainly avoid these existential problems, although they are crucial issues for all of us. The child needs most particularly to be given suggestions in symbolic form about how he may deal with these issues and grow safely into maturity. "Safe" stories mention neither death nor aging, the limits to our existence, nor the wish for eternal life. The fairy tale, by contrast, confronts the child squarely with the basic human predicaments.

For example, many fairy stories begin with the death of a mother or father; in these tales the death of the parent creates the most agonizing problems, as it (or the fear of it) does in real life. Other stories tell about an aging parent who decides that the time has come to let the new generation take over. But before this can happen, the successor has to prove himself capable and worthy. The Brothers Grimm's story "The Three Feathers" begins: "There was once upon a time a king who had three sons. . . . When the king had become old and weak, and was thinking of his end, he did not know which of his sons should inherit the kingdom after him." In order to decide, the king sets all his sons a difficult task; the son who meets it best "shall be king after my death."

It is characteristic of fairy tales to state an existential dilemma briefly and pointedly. This permits the child to come to grips with the problem in its most essential form, where a more complex plot would confuse matters for him. The fairy tale simplifies all situations. Its figures are clearly drawn; and details, unless very important, are eliminated. All characters are typical rather than unique.

Contrary to what takes place in many modern children's stories, in fairy tales evil is as omnipresent as virtue. In practically every fairy tale good and evil are given body in the form of some figures and their actions, as good and evil are omnipresent in life and the propensities for both are present in every man. It is this duality which poses the moral problem, and requires the struggle to solve it.

Evil is not without its attractions—symbolized by the mighty giant or dragon, the 25 power of the witch, the cunning queen in "Snow White"—and often it is temporarily in the ascendancy. In many fairy tales a usurper succeeds for a time in seizing the place which rightfully belongs to the hero—as the wicked sisters do in "Cinderella." It is not that the evildoer is punished at the story's end which makes immersing oneself in fairy stories an experience in moral education, although this is part of it. In fairy tales, as in life, punishment or fear of it is only a limited deterrent to crime. The conviction that crime does not pay is a much more effective deterrent, and that is why in fairy tales the bad person always loses out. It is not the fact that virtue wins out at the end which promotes morality, but that the hero is most attractive to the child, who identifies with the hero in all his struggles. Because of this identification the child imagines that he suffers with the hero his trials and tribulations, and triumphs with him as virtue is victorious. The child makes such identifications all on his own, and the inner and outer struggles of the hero imprint morality on him.

The figures in fairy tales are not ambivalent—not good and bad at the same time, as we all are in reality. But since polarization dominates the child's mind, it also dominates fairy tales. A person is either good or bad, nothing in between. One brother is stupid, the other is clever. One sister is virtuous and industrious, the others are vile and lazy. One is beautiful, the others are ugly. One parent is all good, the other evil. The juxtaposition of opposite characters is not for the purpose of stressing right behavior, as would be true for cautionary tales. (There are some amoral fairy tales where goodness or badness, beauty or ugliness play no role at all.) Presenting the polarities of character permits the child to comprehend easily the difference between the two, which he could not do as readily were the figures drawn more true to life, with all the complexities that characterize real people. Ambiguities must wait until a relatively firm personality has been established on the basis of positive identifications. Then the child has a basis for understanding that there are great differences between people, and that therefore one has to make choices about who one wants to be. This basic decision, on which all later personality development will build, is facilitated by the polarizations of the fairy tale.

Furthermore, a child's choices are based, not so much on right versus wrong, as on who arouses his sympathy and who his antipathy. The more simple and straightforward a good character, the easier it is for a child to identify with it and to reject the bad other. The child identifies with the good hero not because of his goodness, but because the hero's condition makes a deep positive appeal to him. The question for the child is not "Do I want to be good?" but "Who do I want to be like?" The child decides this on the basis of projecting himself wholeheartedly into one character. If this fairy-tale figure is a very good person, then the child decides that he wants to be good, too.

Amoral fairy tales show no polarization or juxtaposition of good and bad persons; that is because these amoral stories serve an entirely different purpose. Such tales or type figures as "Puss in Boots," who arranges for the hero's success through trickery, and Jack, who steals the giant's treasure, build character not by promoting choices between good and bad, but by giving the child the hope that even the meekest can succeed in life. After all, what's the use of choosing to become a good person when one feels so insignificant that he fears he will never amount to anything? Morality is not the issue in these tales, but rather, assurance that one can succeed. Whether one meets life with a belief in the possibility of mastering its difficulties or with the expectation of defeat is also a very important existential problem.

The deep inner conflicts originating in our primitive drives and our violent emotions are all denied in much of modern children's literature, and so the child is not helped in coping with them. But the child is subject to desperate feelings of loneliness and isolation, and he often experiences mortal anxiety. More often than not, he is unable to express these feelings in words, or he can do so only by indirection: fear of the dark, of some animal, anxiety about his body. Since it creates discomfort in a parent to recognize these emotions in his child, the parent tends to overlook them, or he belittles these spoken fears out of his own anxiety, believing this will cover over the child's fears.

The fairy tale, by contrast, takes these existential anxieties and dilemmas very seri- 30 ously and addresses itself directly to them: the need to be loved and the fear that one is thought worthless; the love of life, and the fear of death. Further, the fairy tale offers solutions in ways that the child can grasp on his level of understanding. For example, fairy tales pose the dilemma of wishing to live eternally by occasionally concluding: "If they have not died, they are still alive." The other ending—"And they lived happily ever after"—does not for a moment fool the child that eternal life is possible. But it does indicate that which alone can take the sting out of the narrow limits of our time on this earth: forming a truly satisfying bond to another. The tales teach that when one has done this, one has reached the ultimate in emotional security of existence and permanence of relation available to man; and this alone can dissipate the fear of death. If one has found true adult love, the fairy story also tells, one doesn't need to wish for eternal life. This is suggested by another ending found in fairy tales: "They lived for a long time afterward, happy and in pleasure."

An uninformed view of the fairy tale sees in this type of ending an unrealistic wish-fulfillment, missing completely the important message it conveys to the child. These tales tell him that by forming a true interpersonal relation, one escapes the separation anxiety which haunts him (and which sets the stage for many fairy tales, but is always resolved at the story's ending). Furthermore, the story tells, this ending is not made possible, as the child wishes and believes, by holding on to his mother eternally. If we try to escape separation anxiety and death anxiety by desperately keeping our grasp on our parents, we will only be cruelly forced out, like Hansel and Gretel.

Only by going out into the world can the fairy-tale hero (child) find himself there; and as he does, he will also find the other with whom he will be able to live happily ever after; that is, without ever again having to experience separation anxiety. The fairy tale is future-oriented and guides the child—in terms he can understand in both his conscious and his unconscious mind—to relinquish his infantile dependency wishes and achieve a more satisfying independent existence.

Today children no longer grow up within the security of an extended family, or of a well-integrated community. Therefore, even more than at the times fairy tales were invented, it is important to provide the modern child with images of heroes who have to go out into the world all by themselves and who, although originally ignorant of the ultimate things, find secure places in the world by following their right way with deep inner confidence.

The fairy-tale hero proceeds for a time in isolation, as the modern child often feels isolated. The hero is helped by being in touch with primitive things—a tree, an animal, nature—as the child feels more in touch with those things than most adults do. The fate of these heroes convinces the child that, like them, he may feel outcast and abandoned in the world, groping in the dark, but, like them, in the course of his life he will be guided step by step, and given help when it is needed. Today, even more than in past times, the child needs the reassurance offered by the image of the isolated man who nevertheless is capable of achieving meaningful and rewarding relations with the world around him. ●

Explorations of the Text

1. According to Bettelheim, what is the main reason to read fairy tales? What is the difference for children between reading these tales and other forms of children's literature?
2. What are the differences between the ways in which children and adults gain meaning from experience? According to Bettelheim, what is "the most difficult task in raising a child"?
3. How do children benefit from reading fairy tales? Do you agree with Bettelheim's conclusions?
4. What does Bettelheim mean by the "existential predicament"?
5. Do you agree with Bettelheim's contention that reading fairy tales provides a way for children to deal with "deep inner conflicts"?
6. How do Gordimer and Carter portray what Bettelheim labels as "the existential predicament"?

The Reading/Writing Connection

1. Bettelheim's essay is in the form of an argument. Gloss and annotate the text, pinpointing the main claim, reasons, and evidence. Do you think that the work is persuasive?
2. Select one statement about the function of fairy tales, and relate it to your own experience of reading a fairy tale or seeing an animated version of a tale as a child. What do you learn?

Ideas for Writing

1. Web Research: Find one fairy tale to consider. Some popular ones include "Rapunzel," "Snow White," "Hansel and Gretel," and "Jack and the Beanstalk." Then apply Bettelheim's theory of reading to the work. What do you conclude?
2. View the movie *Shrek, Shrek 2,* or *Shrek 3*. How does the movie allude to and subvert fairy tale motifs? Write a short essay.

3. **Write an Argument:** Agree or disagree with one of the following of Bettelheim's contentions in a short argument essay.

"Much of the literature intended to develop the child's mind and personality . . . fails to stimulate and nurture those resources he needs most in order to cope with his difficult inner problems. The preprimer and primers from which he is taught to read in school are designed to teach the necessary skills irrespective of meaning."

OR

"Today, even more than in past times, the child needs the reassurance offered [in fairy tales of] the image of the isolated man who nevertheless is capable of achieving meaningful and rewarding relations with the world around him."

Bettelheim wrote *The Uses of Enchantment* in the mid-1970s. Are these arguments still relevant today? Refer to your own experience of schooling or of reading children's literature.

4. Bettelheim suggests that it is important for people to find "meaning" in their lives. Relate this idea to the character development in the following works: the grandmother in O'Connor's "A Good Man Is Hard to Find" (Chapter 9), the unnamed narrator in Carver's "Cathedral," or Nora in *A Doll's House.*

5. Bettelheim points out a predominant motif in fairy tales: heroines who are saved by men. Compare and contrast the fates of female characters in such works as Oates's "Where Are You Going, Where Have You Been?"; Kingsolver's "Rose-Johnny"; or the animated films *Shrek* or *Mulan.*

Azar Nafisi *(1950–)*

from *Reading* Lolita *in Tehran*   *2003*

In the fall of 1995, after resigning from my last academic post, I decided to indulge myself and fulfill a dream. I chose seven of my best and most committed students and invited them to come to my home every Thursday morning to discuss literature. They were all women—to teach a mixed class in the privacy of my home was too risky, even if we were discussing harmless works of fiction.

For nearly two years, almost every Thursday morning, rain or shine, they came to my house, and almost every time, I could not get over the shock of seeing them shed their mandatory veils and robes and burst into color. When my students came into that room, they took off more than their scarves and robes. Gradually, each one gained an outline and a shape, becoming her own inimitable self. Our world in that living room with its window framing my beloved Elburz Mountains became our sanctuary, our self-contained universe, mocking the reality of black-scarved, timid faces in the city that sprawled below.

The theme of the class was the relationship between fiction and reality. We would read Persian classical literature, such as the tales of our own lady of fiction, Scheherazade, from *A Thousand and One Nights,* along with Western classics—*Pride and Prejudice, Madame Bovary, Daisy Miller, The Dean's December,* and *Lolita,* the work of fiction that perhaps most resonated with our lives in the Islamic Republic of Iran. For the first time in many years, I felt a sense of anticipation that was not marred by tension: I would not need to go through the tortuous rituals that had marked my days when I taught at the university—rituals governing what I was forced to wear, how I was expected to act, the gestures I had to remember to control.

Life in the Islamic Republic was as capricious as the month of April, when short periods of sunshine would suddenly give way to showers and storms. It was unpredictable: The regime would go through cycles of some tolerance, followed by a crackdown. Now, in the mid-1990s, after a period of relative calm and so-called liberalization, we had again entered a time of hardships. Universities had once more become the targets of attack by the cultural purists, who were busy imposing stricter sets of laws, going so far as to segregate men and women in classes and punishing disobedient professors.

The University of Allameh Tabatabai, where I had been teaching since 1987, had been singled out as the most liberal university in Iran. It was rumored that someone   5 in the Ministry of Higher Education had asked, rhetorically, if the faculty at Allameh thought they lived in Switzerland. Switzerland had somehow become a byword for Western laxity. Any program or action that was deemed un-Islamic was reproached with a mocking reminder that Iran was by no means Switzerland.

The pressure was hardest on the students. I felt helpless as I listened to their endless tales of woe. Female students were being penalized for running up the stairs when they were late for classes, for laughing in the hallways, for talking to members of the opposite sex. One day Sanaz had barged into class near the end of the session, crying. In between bursts of tears, she explained that she was late because the female guards at the door, finding a blush in her bag, had tried to send her home with a reprimand.

Why did I stop teaching so suddenly? I had asked myself this question many times. Was it the declining quality of the university? The ever-increasing indifference among the remaining faculty members and students? The daily struggle against arbitrary rules and restrictions?

I often went over in my mind the reaction of the university officials to my letter of resignation. They had harassed and limited me in all manner of ways, monitoring my visitors, controlling my actions, refusing my long-overdue tenure; and when I resigned, they infuriated me by suddenly commiserating and by refusing to accept my resignation. The students had threatened to boycott classes, and it was of some satisfaction to me to find out later that despite threats of reprisals, they in fact did boycott my replacement. Everyone thought I would break down and eventually return. It took two more years before they finally accepted my resignation.

Teaching in the Islamic Republic, like any other vocation, was subservient to politics and subject to arbitrary rules. Always, the joy of teaching was marred by diversions and considerations forced on us by the regime—how well could one teach when the main concern of university officials was not the quality of one's work but the color of one's lips, the subversive potential of a single strand of hair? Could one really concentrate on one's job when what preoccupied the faculty was how to excise the word "wine" from a Hemingway story, when they decided not to teach Bronte because she appeared to condone adultery?

In selecting students for study in my home, I did not take into consideration their 10 ideological or religious backgrounds. Later, I would count it as the class's great achievement that such a mixed group, with different and at times conflicting backgrounds, personal as well as religious and social, remained so loyal to its goals and ideals. One reason for my choice of these particular girls was the peculiar mixture of fragility and courage I sensed in them. They were what you would call loners, who did not belong to any particular group or sect. I admired their ability to survive not despite but in some ways because of their solitary lives.

One of the first books we read was Nabokov's *Invitation to a Beheading*. Nabokov creates for us in this novel not the actual physical pain and torture of a totalitarian regime but the nightmarish quality of living in an atmosphere of perpetual dread. Cincinnatus C. is frail, he is passive, he is a hero without knowing or acknowledging it: He fights with his instincts, and his acts of writing are his means of escape. He is a hero because he refuses to become like all the rest.

We formed a special bond with Nabokov despite the difficulty of his prose. This went deeper than our identification with his themes. His novels are shaped around invisible trapdoors, sudden gaps that constantly pull the carpet from under the reader's feet. They are filled with mistrust of what we call everyday reality, an acute sense of that reality's fickleness and frailty. There was something, both in his fiction and in his life, that we instinctively related to and grasped, the possibility of a boundless freedom when all options are taken away.

Nabokov used the term "fragile unreality" to explain his own state of exile; it also describes our existence in the Islamic Republic of Iran. We lived in a culture that denied any merit to literary works, considering them important only when they were handmaidens to something seemingly more urgent—namely, ideology. This was a country where all gestures, even the most private, were interpreted in political terms. The colors of my head scarf or my father's tie were symbols of Western decadence and imperialist tendencies. Not wearing a beard, shaking hands with members of the opposite sex, clapping or whistling in public meetings, were likewise considered Western and therefore decadent, part of the plot by imperialists to bring down our culture.

Our class was shaped within this context. There, in that living room, we rediscovered that we were also living, breathing human beings; and no matter how repressive the state became, no matter how intimidated and frightened we were, like Lolita we tried to escape and to create our own little pockets of freedom. And, like Lolita, we took every opportunity to flaunt our insubordination: by showing a little hair from under our scarves, insinuating a little color into the drab uniformity of our appearances, growing our nails, falling in love, and listening to forbidden music.

How can I create this other world outside the room? I have no choice but to appeal to your imagination. Let's imagine one of the girls, say Sanaz, leaving my house, and let us follow her from there to her final destination. She says her goodbyes and puts on her black robe and scarf over her orange shirt and jeans, coiling her scarf around her neck to cover her huge gold earrings. She directs wayward strands of hair under the scarf, puts her notes into her large bag, straps it on over her shoulder, and walks out into the hall. She pauses for a moment on top of the stairs to put on thin, lacy, black gloves to hide her nail polish. 15

We follow Sanaz down the stairs, out the door, and into the street. You might notice that her gait and her gestures have changed. It is in her best interest not to be seen, not to be heard or noticed. She doesn't walk upright, but bends her head toward the ground and doesn't look at passers-by. She walks quickly and with a sense of determination. The streets of Tehran and other Iranian cities are patrolled by militia, who ride in white Toyota patrols—four gun-carrying men and women, sometimes followed by a minibus. They are called the Blood of God. They patrol the streets to make sure that women like Sanaz wear their veils properly, do not wear makeup, do not walk in public with men who are not their fathers, brothers, or husbands. If she gets on a bus, the seating is segregated. She must enter through the rear door and sit in the back seats, allocated to women.

You might well ask, What is Sanaz thinking as she walks the streets of Tehran? How much does this experience affect her? Most probably, she tries to distance her mind as much as possible from her surroundings. Perhaps she is thinking of her distant boyfriend and the time when she will meet him in Turkey. Does she compare her own situation with her mother's when she was the same age? Is she angry that women of her mother's generation could walk the streets freely, enjoy the company of the opposite sex, join the police force, become pilots, live under laws that were among the most progressive in the world regarding women? Does she feel humiliated by the new laws, by the fact that after the revolution, the age of marriage was lowered from eighteen to nine, that stoning became once more the punishment for adultery and prostitution?

In the course of nearly two decades, the streets have been turned into a war zone, where young women who disobey the rules are hurled into patrol cars, taken to jail, flogged, fined, forced to wash the toilets and humiliated—and, as soon as they leave, they go back and do the same thing. Is she aware, Sanaz, of her own power? Does she realize how dangerous she can be when her every stray gesture is a disturbance to public safety? Does she think how vulnerable are the Revolutionary Guards, who for over eighteen years have patrolled the streets of Tehran and have had to endure young women like herself, and those of other generations, walking, talking, showing a strand of hair just to remind them that they have not converted?

These girls had both a real history and a fabricated one. Although they came from very different backgrounds, the regime that ruled them had tried to make their personal identities and histories irrelevant. They were never free of the regime's definition of them as Muslim women.

Take the youngest in our class, Yassi. There she is, in a photograph I have of the 20 students, with a wistful look on her face. She is bending her head to one side, unsure of what expression to choose. She is wearing a thin white-and-gray scarf, loosely tied at the throat—a perfunctory homage to her family's strict religious background. Yassi was a freshman who audited my graduate courses in my last year of teaching. She felt intimidated by the older students, who, she thought, by virtue of their seniority, were blessed not only with greater knowledge and a better command of English but also with more wisdom. Although she understood the most difficult texts better than many of the graduate students, and although she read the texts more dutifully and with more pleasure than most, she felt secure only in her terrible sense of insecurity.

About a month after I had decided privately to leave Allameh Tabatabai, Yassi and I were standing in front of the green gate at the entrance of the university. What I remember most distinctly about the university now is that green gate. I owe my memory of that gate to Yassi: She mentioned it in one of her poems. The poem is called "How Small Are the Things That I Like." In it, she describes her favorite objects—an orange backpack, a colorful coat, a bicycle just like her cousin's—and she also describes how much she likes to enter the university through the green gate. The gate appears in this poem, and in some of her other writings, as a magical entrance into the forbidden world of all the ordinary things she had been denied in life.

Yet that green gate was closed to her, and to all my girls. Next to the gate there was a small opening with a curtain hanging from it. Through this opening all the female students went into a small, dark room to be inspected. Yassi would describe later what was done to her in this room: "I would first be checked to see if I have the right clothes: the color of my coat, the length of my uniform, the thickness of my scarf, the form of my shoes, the objects in my bag, the visible traces of even the mildest makeup, the size of my rings and their level of attractiveness, all would be checked before I could enter the campus of the university, the same university in which men also study. And to them the main door, with its immense portals and emblems and flags, is generously open."

In the sunny intimacy of our encounter that day, I asked Yassi to have an ice cream with me. We went to a small shop, where, sitting opposite each other with two tall *cafés glacés* between us, our mood changed. We became, if not somber, quite serious. Yassi came from an enlightened religious family that had been badly hurt by the revolution.

They felt the Islamic Republic was a betrayal of Islam rather than its assertion. At the start of the revolution, Yassi's mother and older aunt joined a progressive Muslim women's group that, when the new government started to crack down on its former supporters, was forced to go underground. Yassi's mother and aunt went into hiding for a long time. This aunt had four daughters, all older than Yassi, all of whom in one way or another supported an opposition group that was popular with young religious Iranians. They were all but one arrested, tortured, and jailed. When they were released, every one of them married within a year. They married almost haphazardly, as if to negate their former rebellious selves. Yassi felt that they had survived the jail but could not escape the bonds of traditional marriage.

To me, Yassi was the real rebel. She did not join any political group or organization. As a teenager she had defied family traditions and, in the face of strong opposition, had taken up music. Listening to any form of nonreligious music, even on the radio, was forbidden in her family, but Yassi forced her will. Her rebellion did not stop there: She did not marry the right suitor at the right time and instead insisted on leaving her hometown, Shiraz, to go to college in Tehran. Now she lived partly with her older sister and husband and partly in the home of an uncle with fanatical religious leanings. The university, with its low academic standards, its shabby morality, and its ideological limitations, had been a disappointment to her.

What could she do? She did not believe in politics and did not want to marry, but [25] she was curious about love. That day, she explained why all the normal acts of life had become small acts of rebellion and political insubordination to her and to other young people like her. All her life she was shielded. She was never let out of sight; she never had a private corner in which to think, to feel, to dream, to write. She was not allowed to meet any young men on her own. Her family not only instructed her on how to behave around men, but seemed to think they could tell her how she should feel about them as well. What seems natural to someone like you, she said, is so strange and unfamiliar to me.

Again she repeated that she would never get married. She said that for her a man always existed in books, that she would spend the rest of her life with Mr. Darcy—even in the books, there were few men for her. What was wrong with that? She wanted to go to America, like her uncles, like me. Her mother and her aunts had not been allowed to go, but her uncles were given the chance. Could she ever overcome all the obstacles and go to America? Should she go to America? She wanted me to advise her; they all wanted that. But what could I offer her, she who wanted so much more from life than she had been given?

There was nothing in reality that I could give her, so I told her instead about Nabokov's "other world." I asked her if she had noticed how in most of Nabokov's novels, there was always the shadow of another world, one that was attainable only through fiction. It is this world that prevents his heroes and heroines from utter despair, that becomes their refuge in a life that is consistently brutal.

Take *Lolita*. This was the story of a twelve-year-old girl who had nowhere to go. Humbert had tried to turn her into his fantasy, into his dead love, and he had destroyed her. The desperate truth of Lolita's story is not the rape of a twelve-year-old by a dirty old man but the confiscation of one individual's life by another. We don't know what Lolita would have become if Humbert had not engulfed her. Yet the novel, the finished work, is hopeful, beautiful even, a defense not just of beauty but of life, ordinary everyday life, all the normal pleasures that Lolita, like Yassi, was deprived of.

Warming up and suddenly inspired, I added that, in fact, Nabokov had taken revenge against our own solipsizers; he had taken revenge on the Ayatollah Khomeini and those like him. They had tried to shape others according to their own dreams and desires, but Nabokov, through his portrayal of Humbert, had exposed all solipsists who take over other people's lives. She, Yassi, had much potential; she could be whatever she wanted to be—a good wife or a teacher and poet. What mattered was for her to know what she wanted.

I want to emphasize that we were not Lolita, the Ayatollah was not Humbert, 30 and this republic was not what Humbert called his princedom by the sea. *Lolita* was not a critique of the Islamic Republic, but it went against the grain of all totalitarian perspectives.

At some point, the truth of Iran's past became as immaterial to those who had appropriated it as the truth of Lolita's is to Humbert. It became immaterial in the same way that Lolita's truth, her desires and life, must lose color before Humbert's one obsession, his desire to turn a twelve-year-old unruly child into his mistress.

This is how I read Lolita. Again and again as we discussed Lolita in that class, our discussions were colored by my students' hidden personal sorrows and joys. Like tear stains on a letter, these forays into the hidden and the personal shaded all our discussions of Nabokov.

Humbert never possesses his victim; she always eludes him, just as objects of fantasy are always simultaneously within reach and inaccessible. No matter how they may be broken, the victims will not be forced into submission.

This was on my mind one Thursday evening after class, as I was looking at the diaries my girls had left behind, with their new essays and poems. At the start of our class, I had asked them to describe their image of themselves. They were not ready then to face that question, but every once in a while I returned to it and asked them again. Now, as I sat curled up on the love seat, I looked at dozens of pages of their recent responses.

I have one of these responses in front of me. It belongs to Sanaz, who handed it in 35 shortly after a recent experience in jail, on trumped-up morality charges. It is a simple drawing in black and white, of a naked girl, the white of her body caught in a black bubble. She is crouched in an almost fetal position, hugging one bent knee. Her other leg is stretched out behind her. Her long, straight hair follows the same curved line as the contour of her back, but her face is hidden. The bubble is lifted in the air by a giant bird with long black talons. What interests me is a small detail: the girl's hand reaches out of the bubble and holds on to the talon. Her subservient nakedness is dependent on that talon, and she reaches out to it.

The drawing immediately brought to my mind Nabokov's statement in his famous afterword to *Lolita*, about how the "first little throb of Lolita" went through him in 1939 or early 1940, when he was ill with a severe attack of intercostal neuralgia. He recalls that "the initial shiver of inspiration was somehow prompted by a newspaper story about an ape in the Jardin des Plantes, who, after months of coaxing by a scientist, produced the first drawing ever charcoaled by an animal: this sketch showed the bars of the poor creature's cage."

The two images, one from the novel and the other from reality, reveal a terrible truth. Its terribleness goes beyond the fact that in each case an act of violence has been committed. It goes beyond the bars, revealing the victim's proximity and intimacy with its jailer. Our focus in each is on the delicate spot where the prisoner touches the bar, on the invisible contact between flesh and cold metal.

Most of the other students expressed themselves in words. Manna saw herself as fog, moving over concrete objects, taking on their form but never becoming concrete herself. Yassi described herself as a figment. Nassrin, in one response, gave me the *Oxford English Dictionary*'s definition of the word "paradox." Implicit in almost all of their descriptions was the way they saw themselves in the context of an outside reality that prevented them from defining themselves clearly and separately.

Manna had once written about a pair of pink socks for which she was reprimanded by the Muslim Students' Association. When she complained to a favorite professor, he started teasing her about how she had already ensnared and trapped her man, Nima, and did not need the pink socks to entrap him further.

These students, like the rest of their generation, were different from my genera- 40 tion in one fundamental aspect. My generation complained of a loss, the void in our lives that was created when our past was stolen from us, making us exiles in our own country. Yet we had a past to compare with the present; we had memories and images of what had been taken away. But my girls spoke constantly of stolen kisses, films they had never seen, and the wind they had never felt on their skin. This generation had no past. Their memory was of a half-articulated desire, something they never had. It was this lack, their sense of longing for the ordinary, taken-for-granted aspects of life, that gave their words a certain luminous quality akin to poetry.

I had asked my students if they remembered the dance scene in *Invitation to a Beheading*: The jailer invites Cincinnatus to a dance. They begin a waltz and move out into the hall. In a corner they run into a guard: "They described a circle near him and glided back into the cell, and now Cincinnatus regretted that the swoon's friendly embrace had been so brief." This movement in circles is the main movement of the novel. As long as he accepts the sham world the jailers impose upon him, Cincinnatus will remain their prisoner and will move within the circles of their creation. The worst crime committed by totalitarian mind-sets is that they force their citizens, including their victims, to become complicit in their crimes. Dancing with your jailer, participating in your own execution, that is an act of utmost brutality. My students witnessed it in show trials on television and enacted it every time they went out into the streets dressed as they were told to dress. They had not become part of the crowd who watched the executions, but they did not have the power to protest them, either.

The only way to leave the circle, to stop dancing with the jailer, is to find a way to preserve one's individuality, that unique quality which evades description but differentiates one human being from the other. That is why, in their world, rituals—empty rituals—become so central.

There was not much difference between our jailers and Cincinnatus's executioners. They invaded all private spaces and tried to shape every gesture, to force us to become one of them, and that in itself is another form of execution.

In the end, when Cincinnatus is led to the scaffold, and as he lays his head on the block, in preparation for his execution, he repeats the magic mantra: "by myself." This constant reminder of his uniqueness, and his attempts to write, to articulate and create a language different from the one imposed upon him by his jailers, saves him at the last moment, when he takes his head in his hands and walks away toward voices that beckon him from that other world, while the scaffold and all the sham world around him, along with his executioner, disintegrate.

Explorations of the Text

1. *Reading* Lolita *in Tehran* describes the two years from 1995 to 1997 that Nafisi spent conducting a clandestine reading group with seven of her most talented and committed women students after she resigned from the liberal university in Iran where she taught literature. In another passage in the memoir, she describes their meetings in her living room as "our sanctuary," "our self-contained universe." What does Nafisi mean by "sanctuary"? What two worlds do she and the women inhabit? How does the Revolution control the women's private and public lives? What role does reading and literature play in the lives? How are Nafisi's and her students' interpretation of Nabokov's *Lolita* shaped by their experiences in the Islamic Republic?

2. Why is Nafisi's generation different from the generation that came of age during the Revolution? What does Nafisi mean when she states "this generation has no past"?

3. What do the images that the women create to describe themselves reveal about their identities?

4. Explore the significance of the following: "The worst crime committed by totalitarian mind-sets is that they force their citizens, including their victims, to become complicit in their crimes." The victims had to "[dance] with [their] jailer." What does she mean by these statements?

5. What is the role of language and imagination in a totalitarian regime? Consider both the excerpts from *Persepolis* and this section of Nafisi's memoir.

The Reading/Writing Connection

1. "Think" Topic: Compare the private and public worlds in this work, in "Flood," and in "Rose-Johnny." How does the public world (political, social, and cultural forces) thwart the development of identity? How do the protagonists resist and preserve their senses of self?

2. Create a visual image or metaphor that represents your state of selfhood. What does it signify?

Ideas for Writing

1. Examine the portrayal of women's roles in these excerpts from *Reading* Lolita *in Tehran* and *Persepolis*. You may want to read more of both books.

2. **Write an Argument:** Do you think that "acts of writing are . . . [a] means of escape" from an oppressive reality? Can they free an individual?

3. **Write an Argument:** Even in our democratic society, there are social and cultural forces that insidiously shape our thinking, attitudes, and values. Argue pro or con.

Pilgrimages . . . Escape or Enlightenment?/ Nonfiction

Jonathan Lethem   *(1964–)*

13, 1977, 21   *1995*

1. In the summer of 1977 I saw *Star Wars*—the original, which is all I want to discuss here—twenty-one times. Better to blurt this at the start so I'm less tempted to retreat from what still seems to me a sort of raw, howling confession, one I've long hidden in shame. Again, to pin myself like a Nabokovian butterfly (no highlit reference is going to bail me out here, I know) to my page in geek history: I watched *Star Wars* twenty-one times in the space of four months. I was that kid alone in the ticket line, slipping past ushers who'd begun to recognize me, muttering in impatience at a urinal before finding my favorite seat. That was me, occult as a porn customer, yes, though I've sometimes denied it. Now, a quarter of a century later, I'm ready for my close-up. Sort of.

2. That year I was thirteen, and likely as ideal an audience member as any mogul could have drooled for. Say every kid in the United States with even the passingest fondness for comic books or adventure fiction, *any kid with a television, even,* had bought a ticket for the same film in a single summer: blah, blah, right, that's what happened. So figure that for every hundred kids who traveled an ordinary path (*Cool movie. Wouldn't mind seeing it again with my friends*) there might be one who'd make himself ill returning to the cookie jar five or six times (*It's really still good the fourth time, I swear!*) before copping to a tummy ache. Next figure that for each *five* hundred, one or two would slip into some brain-warped identificatory obsession (*I am Star Wars. Star Wars am me, goo goo ga joob*) and return to the primal site often enough to push into the realm of trance and memorization. That's me, with my gaudy *twenty-one,* like DiMaggio's *fifty-six.* But what actually occurred within the secret brackets of that experience? What emotions lurk within that ludicrous temple of hours? *What the fuck was I thinking?*

3. Every one of those twenty-one viewings took place at the Loew's Astor Plaza on Forty-fourth Street, just off Times Square. I'd never seen a movie there before (and unless you count *The Empire Strikes Back,* I didn't again until 1999—*The Matrix*). And I've still never seen *Star Wars* anywhere else. The Astor Plaza was a low, deep-stretched hall with a massive screen and state-of-the-art sound, and newly enough renovated to be free of too much soda-rotted carpet, a plague among New York theaters those days. Though architecturally undistinguished, it was a superior place to see anything. I suppose. But for me it was a shrine meant for just one purpose—I took it as weirdly significant that "Astor: could be rearranged into "astro"—and in a very *New Yorker*-coverish way I believed it to be the only real and right place to see *Star Wars,* the very ground zero of the phenomenon. I felt a definite but not at all urgent pity for any benighted fools stuck watching it elsewhere. I think I associated the Astor Plaza with the Death Star, in a way. Getting in always felt like an accomplishment, both elevating and slightly dangerous.

4. Along those lines I should say it was vaguely unnerving to be a white kid in spectacles routinely visiting Times Square by subway in the middle of the 1970s. Nobody ever said anything clearly about what was wrong or fascinating about that part of the

city we lived in—the information was absorbed in hints and mutterings from a polyphony of sources. In fact, though I was conscious of a certain seamy energy in those acres of sex shows and drug dealers and their furtive sidewalk customers, I was never once hassled (and this was a time when my home neighborhood, in Brooklyn, was a minefield for me personally). But the zone's reputation ensured I'd always plan my visits to fall wholly within summer's long daylight hours.

5. Problem: it doesn't seem at all likely that I went to the movie alone the first time, but I can't remember who I was with. I've polled a few of my likeliest friends from that period, but they're unable to help. In truth I can't recall a "first time" in any real sense, though I do retain a flash memory of the moment the prologue first began to crawl in tilted perspective up the screen, an Alice-in-Wonderland doorway to dream. I'd been so primed, so attuned and ready to love it (I remember mocking my friend Evan for his thinking that the title meant it was going to be some kind of all-star cavalcade of a comedy, like *It's a Mad Mad Mad Mad World* or *Smokey and the Bandit*) that my first time was gulped impatiently, then covered quickly in the memory of return visits. From the first I was "seeing it again." I think this memory glitch is significant. I associate it with my practice of bluffing familiarity with various drug experiences, later (not much later). My refusal to recall or admit to a first time was an assertion of maturity: I was *always already* a *Star Wars* fanatic.

6. I didn't buy twenty-one tickets. My count was amassed by seeing the movie twice in a day over and over again. And one famous day (famous to myself) I sat through it three times. That practice of seeing a film twice through originated earlier. Somebody—my mother?—had floated the idea that it wasn't important to be on time for a movie, or even, to check the screening times before going. Instead, moviegoing in Brooklyn Heights or on Fulton Street with my brother or with friends, we'd pop in at any point in the story, watch to the end, then sit through the break and watch the beginning. Which led naturally, if the film was any good, to staying past the original point of entry to see the end twice. Which itself led to routinely twice-watching a movie we liked, even if we hadn't been late. This was encouraged, partly according to a general *Steal This Book*-ish anticapitalist imperative for taking freebies in my parents' circle in the seventies. Of course somebody—my mother?—had also figured out a convenient way to get the kids out of the house for long stretches.

7. I hate arriving late for movies now and would never watch one in this broken fashion. (It seems to me, though, that I probably learned something about the construction of narratives from the practice.) The life-long moviegoing habit which does originate for me with *Star Wars* is that of sitting in movie theaters alone. I probably only had company in the Loew's Astor Plaza four or five times. The rest of my visits were solitary, which is certainly central to any guesses I'd make about the emotional meaning of the ritual viewings.

8. I still go to the movies alone, all the time. In the absenting of self which results—so different from the quality of solitude at my writing desk—this seems to me as near as I come in my life to any reverent or worshipful or meditational practice. That's not to say it isn't also indulgent, with a frisson of guilt, of stolen privilege, every time. I'm acutely conscious of this joyous guilt in the fact that when as a solitary moviegoer I take a break to go to the bathroom *I can return to another part of the theater and watch from a different seat.* I first discovered this thrill during my *Star Wars* summer, and it's one which never diminishes. The rupture of the spectator's contract with perspective feels as transgressive as wife-swapping.

9. The function or dysfunction of my *Star Wars* obsession was paradoxical. I was using the movie as a place to hide, sure. That's obvious. At the same time, this activity of hiding inside the Loew's Astor Plaza, and inside my private, *deeper-than-yours, deeper-than-anyone's* communion with the film itself, was something I boasted widely about. By building my lamebrain World Record for screenings (fat chance, I learned later) I was teaching myself to package my own craving for solitude, and my own obsessive tendencies, as something to be admired. *You can't join me inside this box where I hide,* I was saying, *but you sure can praise the box. You're permitted to marvel at me for going inside.*

10. What I was hiding from is easy, though. My parents had separated a couple of years earlier. Then my mother had begun having seizures, been diagnosed with a brain tumor, and had had the first of two surgeries. The summer of *Star Wars* she was five or six months from the second, unsuccessful surgery, and a year from dying.

11. I took my brother, and he stayed through it twice. We may have done that together more than once—neither of us clearly remembers. I took a girl, on a quasidate: Alissa, the sister of my best friend, Joel. I took my mother. I tried to take my grandmother.

12. That same summer I once followed Alissa to a ballet class at Carnegie Hall and hung around the studio, expressing a polite curiosity which was cover for another, less polite curiosity. The instructor was misled or chose to misunderstand—a thirteen-year-old boy willing to set foot inside a ballet studio was a commodity, a raw material. I was offered free classes, and the teacher called my house and strong-armed my parents. I remember vividly my mother's pleasure in refusing on my behalf—I was too much of a coward—and how strongly she fastened on the fact that my visit had had nothing to do with any interest in ballet. For years this seemed to me an inexplicable cruelty in my mother toward the ballet teacher. Later I understood that in those first years of adolescence I was giving off a lot of signals to my parents that I might be gay. I was a delicate, obedient, and bookish kid, a constant teacher's pet. Earlier that year my father had questioned me regarding a series of distended cartoon noses I'd drawn in ballpoint on my loose-leaf binder—they had come out looking a lot like penises. And my proclaimed favorite *Star Wars* character was the tweaking English robot, C-3PO.

13. I did and do find C-3PO sexy. It's as if a strand of DNA from Fritz Lang's fetishized girl robot in *Metropolis* has carried forward to the bland world of *Star Wars.* Also, whereas Carrie Fisher's robes went to her ankles, C-3PO is obviously naked, and ashamed of it.

14. Alissa thought the movie was okay (my overstated claims generally cued a compensating shrug in others) and that was our last date, if it was a date. We're friends now.

15. 1 don't know how much of an effort it was for my mother to travel by subway to a movie theater in Manhattan by the summer of '77, but I do know it was unusual, and that she was certainly doing it to oblige me. It might have been one of our last ventures out together, before it was impossible for her. I remember fussing over rituals inside the theater, showing her my favorite seat, and straining not to watch her watch it throughout, not to hang on her every reaction. Afterward she too found the movie just okay. It wasn't her kind of thing, but she could understand why I liked it so much. Those were pretty close to her exact words. Maybe with her characteristic Queens hardboiled tone: *I see why you like it, kiddo.* Then, in a turn I find painful to relate, she left me there to watch it a second time, and took the subway home alone. What a heartbreaking rehearsal! I was saying, in effect: *Come and see my future, post-mom self. Enact with me your parting from it. Here's the world of cinema and stories and obsessive iden-*

tification I'm using to survive your going—now go. How generous of her to play in this masquerade, if she knew.

16. I spent a certain amount of time that year trying hopelessly to distract my grandmother from the coming loss of her only child—it would mostly wreck her—by pushing my new enthusiasms at her. For instance she and I had a recurrent argument about rock and roll, one which it now strikes me was probably a faint echo, for her, of struggles over my mother's dropping out of Queens College in favor of a Greenwich Village beatnik-folk lifestyle. I worked to find a hit song she couldn't quibble with, and thought I'd found one in Wings' "Mull of Kintyre," which is really just a strummy faux-Irish folk song. I played it for her at top volume and she grimaced, her displeasure not at the music but at the apparent trump card I'd played. Then, on the fade, Paul McCartney gave out a kind of *whoop-whoop* holler and my grandmother seized on this, with relish: "You hear that? He had to go and scream. It wasn't good enough just to sing, he had to scream like an animal!" Her will was too much for me. So when she re-sisted being dragged to *Star Wars* I probably didn't mind, being uninterested in having her trample on my secret sand castle. She and I were ultimately in a kind of argument about whether or not our family was a site of tragedy, and I probably sensed I was on the losing end of that one.

17. My father lived in a commune for part of that summer, though my mother's ill-ness sometimes drew him back into the house. There was a man in the commune—call him George Lucas—whose married life, which included two young children, was com-ing apart. George Lucas was the person I knew who'd seen *Star Wars* the most times, apart from me, and we had a ritualized bond over it. He'd ask me how many times I'd seen the film and I'd report, like an emissary with good news from the front. George Lucas had a copy of the soundtrack and we'd sit in the commune's living room and play it on the stereo, which I seem to remember being somewhat unpopular with the commune's larger membership. George Lucas, who played piano and had some clas-sical training, would always proclaim that the score was *really pretty good symphonic composition*—he'd also play me Gustav Holst's *Planets Suite* as a kind of primer, and to show me how the Death Star theme came from Holst's Jupiter—I would dutifully par-rot this for my friends, with great severity: John Williams's score was *really pretty good symphonic composition.*

18. The movie itself, right: of course, I must have enjoyed it immensely the first few times. That's what I least recall. Instead I recall now how as I memorized, scenes I fought my impatience, and yet fought not to know I was fighting impatience—all that mattered were the winnowed satisfactions of crucial moments occurring once again, like stations of the cross: "Help me, Obi-Wan Kenobi, you're my only hope," "These aren't the droids you're looking for," "If you strike me down, I'll become more power-ful than you can possibly imagine," and the dunk shot of Luke's missiles entering the Death Star's duct. I hated, absolutely, the scene in the Death Star's sewers. I hated Han Solo and Princess Leia's flirtation, after a while, feeling I was being manipulated, that it was too mannered and rote: of course they're grumbling now, that's how it *always* goes. I hated the triumphalist ceremony at the end, though the spiffing-up of the robots was a consolation, a necessary relief. I think I came to hate a lot of the film, but I couldn't permit myself to know it. I even came, within a year or so, to hate the fact that I'd seen the movie twenty-one times.

19. Why that number? Probably I thought it was safely ridiculous and extreme to get my record into the twenties, yet stopping at only twenty seemed too mechanically

round. Adding one more felt plausibly arbitrary, more *realistic.* That was likely all I could stand. Perhaps at twenty-one I'd also attained the symbolic number of adulthood, of maturity. By bringing together *thirteen* and *twenty-one* I'd made *Star Wars* my Bar Mitzvah, a ritual I didn't have and probably could have used that year. Now I was a man.

20. By the time I was fifteen, not only had I long since quit boasting about my love of *Star Wars* but it had become privately crucial to have another favorite movie inscribed in its place. I decided Kubrick's *2001: A Space Odyssey* was a suitably noble and alienated choice, but that in order to make it official I'd have to see it more times than *Star Wars.* An exhausting proposition, but I went right at it. One day at the Thalia on West Ninety-fifth Street I sat alone through *2001* three times in a row in a nearly empty theater, a commitment of some nine hours. That day I brought along a tape recorder in order to whisper notes on this immersion experience to my friend Eliot—I also taped *Also sprach Zarathustra* all six times. If *Star Wars* was my Bar Mitzvah then *2001* was getting laid, an experience requiring a more persuasive maturity, and one which I more honestly enjoyed, especially fifteen or twenty showings in. Oddly enough, though, I never did completely overwrite *Star Wars* with *2001.* Instead I stuck at precisely twenty-one viewings of the second movie as well, leaving the two in a dead heat. Even that number was only attained years later, at the University Theater in Berkeley, California, two days after the 1989 Loma Prieta earthquake. There was a mild aftershock which rumbled the old theater during the Star Gate sequence, a nice touch.

21. I'll never see another film so many times, though I still count. I've seen *The Searchers* twelve times—a cheat, since it was partly research. Otherwise, I usually peak out at six or seven viewings, as with *Bringing Up Baby* and *Three Women* and *Love Streams* and *Vertigo,* all films I believe I love more than either *Star Wars* or *2001.* But that kid who still can't decide which of the two futuristic epics to let win the struggle for his mortal soul, the kid who left the question hanging, the kid who partly invented himself in the vacuum collision of *Star Wars*—and real loss—that kid is me. ◉

Joan Didion   *(1934–)*

Goodbye to All That   *1968*

> *How many miles to Babylon?*
> *Three score miles and ten—*
> *Can I get there by candlelight?*
> *Yes, and back again—*
> *If your feet are nimble and light*
> *You can get there by candlelight.*

It is easy to see the beginnings of things, and harder to see the ends. I can remember now, with a clarity that makes the nerves in the back of my neck constrict, when New York began for me, but I cannot lay my finger upon the moment it ended, can never cut through the ambiguities and second starts and broken resolves to the exact place on the page where the heroine is no longer as optimistic as she once was. When I first saw New York I was twenty, and it was summertime, and I got off a DC-7 at the old Idlewild temporary terminal in a new dress which had seemed very smart in Sacramento but seemed less smart already, even in the old Idlewild temporary terminal, and the warm air smelled of mildew and some instinct, programmed by all the movies I had ever seen and all the songs I had ever heard sung and all the stories I had ever read about New York, informed me that it would never be quite the same again. In fact it never was. Some time later there was a song on all the jukeboxes on the upper East Side that went "but where is the schoolgirl who used to be me," and if it was late enough at night I used to wonder that. I know now that almost everyone wonders something like that, sooner or later and no matter what he or she is doing, but one of the mixed blessings of being twenty and twenty-one and even twenty-three is the conviction that nothing like this, all evidence to the contrary notwithstanding, has ever happened to anyone before.

Of course it might have been some other city, had circumstances been different and the time been different and had I been different, might have been Paris or Chicago or even San Francisco, but because I am talking about myself I am talking here about New York. That first night I opened my window on the bus into town and watched for the skyline, but all I could see were the wastes of Queens and the big signs that said MIDTOWN TUNNEL THIS LANE and then a flood of summer rain (even that seemed remarkable and exotic, for I had come out of the West where there was no summer rain), and for the next three days I sat wrapped in blankets in a hotel room air-conditioned to 35° and tried to get over a bad cold and a high fever. It did not occur to me to call a doctor, because I knew none, and although it did occur to me to call the desk and ask that the air conditioner be turned off, I never called, because I did not know how much to tip whoever might come—was anyone ever so young? I am here to tell you that someone was. All I could do during those three days was talk long-distance to the boy I already knew I would never marry in the spring. I would stay in New York, I told him, just six months, and I could see the Brooklyn Bridge from my window. As it turned out the bridge was the Triborough, and I stayed eight years.

In retrospect it seems to me that those days before I knew the names of all the bridges were happier than the ones that came later, but perhaps you will see that as we go along. Part of what I want to tell you is what it is like to be young in New York, how six months can become eight years with the deceptive ease of a film dissolve, for that is how those years appear to me now, in a long sequence of sentimental dissolves and old-fashioned trick shots—the Seagram Building fountains dissolve into snowflakes, I enter a revolving door at twenty and come out a good deal older, and on a different street. But most particularly I want to explain to you, and in the process perhaps to myself, why I no longer live in New York. It is often said that New York is a city for only the very rich and the very poor. It is less often said that New York is also, at least for those of us who came there from somewhere else, a city for only the very young.

I remember once, one cold bright December evening in New York, suggesting to a friend who complained of having been around too long that he come with me to a party where there would be, I assured him with the bright resourcefulness of twenty-three, "new faces." He laughed literally until he choked, and I had to roll down the taxi window and hit him on the back. "New faces," he said finally, "don't tell me about *new faces.*" It seemed that the last time he had gone to a party where he had been promised "new faces," there had been fifteen people in the room, and he had already slept with five of the women and owed money to all but two of the men. I laughed with him, but the first snow had just begun to fall and the big Christmas trees glittered yellow and white as far as I could see up Park Avenue and I had a new dress and it would be a long while before I would come to understand the particular moral of the story.

It would be a long while because, quite simply, I was in love with New York. I do not mean "love" in any colloquial way, I mean that I was in love with the city, the way you love the first person who ever touches you and never love anyone quite that way again. I remember walking across Sixty-second Street one twilight that first spring, or the second spring, they were all alike for a while. I was late to meet someone but I stopped at Lexington Avenue and bought a peach and stood on the corner eating it and knew that I had come out of the West and reached the mirage. I could taste the peach and feel the soft air blowing from a subway grating on my legs and I could smell lilac and garbage and expensive perfume and I knew that it would cost something sooner or later—because I did not belong there, did not come from there—but when you are twenty-two or twenty-three, you figure that later you will have a high emotional balance, and be able to pay whatever it costs. I still believed in possibilities then, still had the sense, so peculiar to New York, that something extraordinary would happen any minute, any day, any month. I was making only $65 or $70 a week then ("Put yourself in Hattie Carnegie's hands," I was advised without the slightest trace of irony by an editor of the magazine for which I worked), so little money that some weeks I had to charge food at Bloomingdale's gourmet shop in order to eat, a fact which went unmentioned in the letters I wrote to California. I never told my father that I needed money because then he would have sent it, and I would never know if I could do it by myself. At that time making a living seemed a game to me, with arbitrary but quite inflexible rules. And except on a certain kind of winter evening—six-thirty in the Seventies, say, already dark and bitter with a wind off the river, when I would be walking very fast toward a bus and would look in the bright windows of brownstones and see cooks working in clean kitchens and imagine women lighting candles on the floor above and beautiful children being bathed on the floor above that—except on nights like those, I never felt poor; I had the feeling that if I needed money I could always get it. I could write a syndicated column for teenagers under the name "Debbi Lynn" or I could smuggle gold into India or I could become a $100 call girl, and none of it would matter.

Nothing was irrevocable; everything was within reach. Just around every corner lay something curious and interesting, something I had never before seen or done or known about. I could go to a party and meet someone who called himself Mr. Emotional Appeal and ran The Emotional Appeal Institute or Tina Onassis Blandford or a Florida cracker who was then a regular on what he called "the Big C," the Southampton-El Morocco circuit ("I'm well-connected on the Big C, honey," he would tell me over collard greens on his vast borrowed terrace), or the widow of the celery king of the Harlem market or a piano salesman from Bonne Terre, Missouri, or someone who had already made and lost two fortunes in Midland, Texas. I could make promises to myself and to other people and there would be all the time in the world to keep them. I could stay up all night and make mistakes, and none of it would count.

You see I was in a curious position in New York: it never occurred to me that I was living a real life there. In my imagination I was always there for just another few months, just until Christmas or Easter or the first warm day in May. For that reason I was most comfortable in the company of Southerners. They seemed to be in New York as I was, on some indefinitely extended leave from wherever they belonged, disinclined to consider the future, temporary exiles who always knew when the flights left for New Orleans or Memphis or Richmond or, in my case, California. Someone who lives always with a plane schedule in the drawer lives on a slightly different calendar. Christmas, for example, was a difficult season. Other people could take it in stride, going to Stowe or going abroad or going for the day to their mothers' places in Connecticut; those of us who believed that we lived somewhere else would spend it making and canceling airline reservations, waiting for weatherbound flights as if for the last plane out of Lisbon in 1940, and finally comforting one another, those of us who were left, with the oranges and mementos and smoked-oyster stuffings of childhood, gathering close, colonials in a far country.

Which is precisely what we were. I am not sure that it is possible for anyone brought up in the East to appreciate entirely what New York, the idea of New York, means to those of us who came out of the West and the South. To an Eastern child, particularly a child who has always had an uncle on Wall Street and who has spent several hundred Saturdays first at F. A. O. Schwarz and being fitted for shoes at Best's and then waiting under the Biltmore clock and dancing to Lester Lanin, New York is just a city, albeit *the* city, a plausible place for people to live. But to those of us who came from places where no one had heard of Lester Lanin and Grand Central Station was a Saturday radio program, where Wall Street and Fifth Avenue and Madison Avenue were not places at all but abstractions ("Money," and "High Fashion," and "The Hucksters"), New York was no mere city. It was instead an infinitely romantic notion, the mysterious nexus of all love and money and power, the shining and perishable dream itself. To think of "living" there was to reduce the miraculous to the mundane; one does not "live" at Xanadu.

In fact it was difficult in the extreme for me to understand those young women for whom New York was not simply an ephemeral Estoril but a real place, girls who bought toasters and installed new cabinets in their apartments and committed themselves to some reasonable future. I never bought any furniture in New York. For a year or so I lived in other people's apartments; after that I lived in the Nineties in an apartment furnished entirely with things taken from storage by a friend whose wife had moved away. And when I left the apartment in the Nineties (that was when I was leaving everything, when it was all breaking up) I left everything in it, even my winter clothes and the map of Sacramento County I had hung on the bedroom wall to remind me who I was, and I moved into a monastic four-room floor-through on Seventy-fifth Street. "Monastic" is perhaps misleading here, implying some chic severity; until after I was married and my husband moved some furniture in, there was nothing at all in those four rooms except a cheap double mattress and box springs, ordered by telephone the day I decided to move, and two French garden chairs lent me by a friend who imported them. (It strikes me now that the people I knew in New York all had curious and self-defeating sidelines. They imported garden chairs which did not sell very well at Ham-macher Schlemmer or they tried to market hair straighteners in Harlem or they ghosted exposés of Murder Incorporated for Sunday supplements. I think that perhaps none of us was very serious, *engagé* only about our most private lives.)

All I ever did to that apartment was hang fifty yards of yellow theatrical silk across 10 the bedroom windows, because I had some idea that the gold light would make me feel better, but I did not bother to weight the curtains correctly and all that summer the long panels of transparent golden silk would blow out the windows and get tangled and drenched in the afternoon thunderstorms. That was the year, my twenty-eighth, when I was discovering that not all of the promises would be kept, that some things are in fact irrevocable and that it had counted after all, every evasion and every procrastination, every mistake, every word, all of it.

That is what it was all about, wasn't it? Promises? Now when New York comes back to me it comes in hallucinatory flashes, so clinically detailed that I sometimes wish that memory would effect the distortion with which it is commonly credited. For a lot of the time I was in New York I used a perfume called *Fleurs de Rocaille,* and then *L'Air du Temps,* and now the slightest trace of either can short-circuit my connections for the rest of the day. Nor can I smell Henri Bendel jasmine soap without falling back into the past, or the particular mixture of spices used for boiling crabs. There were barrels of crab boil in a Czech place in the Eighties where I once shopped. Smells, of course, are notorious memory stimuli, but there are other things which affect me the same way. Blue-and-white striped sheets. Vermouth cassis. Some faded nightgowns which were new in 1959 or 1960, and some chiffon scarves I bought about the same time.

I suppose that a lot of us who have been young in New York have the same scenes on our home screens. I remember sitting in a lot of apartments with a slight headache about five o'clock in the morning. I had a friend who could not sleep, and he knew a few other people who had the same trouble, and we would watch the sky lighten and have a last drink with no ice and then go home in the early morning light, when the streets were clean and wet (had it rained in the night? we never knew) and the few cruising taxis still had their headlights on and the only color was the red and green of traffic signals. The White Rose bars opened very early in the morning; I recall waiting in one of them to watch an astronaut go into space, waiting so long that at the moment it actually happened I had my eyes not on the television screen but on a cockroach on the tile floor. I liked the bleak branches above Washington Square at dawn, and the monochromatic flatness of Second Avenue, the fire escapes and the grilled storefronts peculiar and empty in their perspective.

It is relatively hard to fight at six-thirty or seven in the morning without any sleep, which was perhaps one reason we stayed up all night, and it seemed to me a pleasant time of day. The windows were shuttered in that apartment in the Nineties and I could sleep a few hours and then go to work. I could work then on two or three hours' sleep and a container of coffee from Chock Full O' Nuts. I liked going to work, liked the soothing and satisfactory rhythm of getting out a magazine, liked the orderly progression of four-color closings and two-color closings and black-and-white closings and then The Product, no abstraction but something which looked effortlessly glossy and could be picked up on a newsstand and weighed in the hand. I liked all the minutiae of proofs and layouts, liked working late on the nights the magazine went to press, sitting and reading *Variety* and waiting for the copy desk to call. From my office I could look across town to the weather signal on the Mutual of New York Building and the lights that alternately spelled out TIME and LIFE above Rockefeller Plaza; that pleased me obscurely, and so did walking uptown in the mauve eight o'clocks of early summer evenings and looking at things, Lowestoft tureens in Fifty-seventh Street windows, people in evening clothes trying to get taxis, the trees just coming into full leaf, the lambent air, all the sweet promises of money and summer.

Some years passed, but I still did not lose that sense of wonder about New York. I began to cherish the loneliness of it, the sense that at any given time no one need know where I was or what I was doing. I liked walking, from the East River over to the Hudson and back on brisk days, down around the Village on warm days. A friend would leave me the key to her apartment in the West Village when she was out of town, and sometimes I would just move down there, because by that time the telephone was beginning to bother me (the canker, you see, was already in the rose) and not many people had that number. I remember one day when someone who did have the West Village number came to pick me up for lunch there, and we both had hangovers, and I cut my finger opening him a beer and burst into tears, and we walked to a Spanish restaurant and drank Bloody Marys and *gazpacho* until we felt better. I was not then guilt-ridden about spending afternoons that way, because I still had all the afternoons in the world.

And even that late in the game I still liked going to parties, all parties, bad parties, 15 Saturday-afternoon parties given by recently married couples who lived in Stuyvesant Town, West Side parties given by unpublished or failed writers who served cheap red wine and talked about going to Guadalajara, Village parties where all the guests worked for advertising agencies and voted for Reform Democrats, press parties at Sardi's, the worst kinds of parties. You will have perceived by now that I was not one to profit by the experience of others, that it was a very long time indeed before I stopped believing in new faces and began to understand the lesson in that story, which was that it is distinctly possible to stay too long at the Fair.

I could not tell you when I began to understand that. All I know is that it was very bad when I was twenty-eight. Everything that was said to me I seemed to have heard before, and I could no longer listen. I could no longer sit in little bars near Grand Central and listen to someone complaining of his wife's inability to cope with the help while he missed another train to Connecticut. I no longer had any interest in hearing about the advances other people had received from their publishers, about plays which were having second-act trouble in Philadelphia, or about people I would like very much if only I would come out and meet them. I had already met them, always. There were certain parts of the city which I had to avoid. I could not bear upper Madison Avenue on weekday mornings (this was a particularly inconvenient aversion, since I then lived just fifty or sixty feet east of Madison), because I would see women walking Yorkshire terriers and shopping at Gristede's, and some Veblenesque gorge would rise in my throat. I could not go to Times Square in the afternoon, or to the New York Public Library for any reason whatsoever. One day I could not go into a Schrafft's; the next day it would be Bonwit Teller.

I hurt the people I cared about, and insulted those I did not. I cut myself off from the one person who was closer to me than any other. I cried until I was not even aware when I was crying and when I was not, cried in elevators and in taxis and in Chinese laundries, and when I went to the doctor he said only that I seemed to be depressed, and should see a "specialist." He wrote down a psychiatrist's name and address for me, but I did not go.

Instead I got married, which as it turned out was a very good thing to do but badly timed, since I still could not walk on upper Madison Avenue in the mornings and still could not talk to people and still cried in Chinese laundries. I had never before understood what "despair" meant, and I am not sure that I understand now, but I understood that year. Of course I could not work. I could not even get dinner with any degree of certainty, and I would sit in the apartment on Seventy-fifth Street paralyzed until my husband would call from his office and say gently that I did not have to get dinner, that I could meet him at Michael's Pub or at Toots Shor's or at Sardi's East. And then one morning in April (we had been married in January) he called and told me that he wanted to get out of New York for a while, that he would take a six-month leave of absence, that we would go somewhere.

It was three years ago that he told me that, and we have lived in Los Angeles since. Many of the people we knew in New York think this a curious aberration, and in fact tell us so. There is no possible, no adequate answer to that, and so we give certain stock answers, the answers everyone gives. I talk about how difficult it would be for us to "afford" to live in New York right now, about how much "space" we need. All I mean is that I was very young in New York, and that at some point the golden rhythm was broken, and I am not that young any more. The last time I was in New York was in a cold January, and everyone was ill and tired. Many of the people I used to know there had moved to Dallas or had gone on Antabuse or had bought a farm in New Hampshire. We stayed ten days, and then we took an afternoon flight back to Los Angeles, and on the way home from the airport that night I could see the moon on the Pacific and smell jasmine all around and we both knew that there was no longer any point in keeping the apartment we still kept in New York. There were years when I called Los Angeles "the Coast," but they seem a long time ago. ●

Explorations of the Text

1. What does the "idea" of New York mean for Didion? Characterize her state of mind when she first comes to New York at twenty. How do her views about the city change? As she says at the beginning of par. 2, could her experiences have taken place in "some other city"? Why does Didion decide to leave New York City at twenty-eight?

2. Look at Didion's sensuous language and choice of words. Why does she use the phrase, "reached the mirage" (par. 5), for example? How do the sensory details and imagery create the atmosphere of New York at the time?

3. Why does Lethem view *Star Wars* twenty-one times during a space of four months in 1977? What are the reasons for his obsession? What does he learn about himself (see pars. 9 and 18, for example)?

4. Discuss the significance of the following: "By being together between thirteen and twenty-one I'd made *Star Wars* my Bar Mitzvah, a ritual I didn't have and probably could have used that year. Now I was a man" (par. 19).

5. How does the retrospective point of view contribute to the mood and themes of the two works?

The Reading/Writing Connection

1. Use one of the lines in "Goodbye to All That" as the beginning of a freewrite or a poem: Suggested lines: "The golden rhythm was broken. . . ."; "It is easy to see the beginnings of things, and harder to see the ends."; "I still believed in possibilities. . . ."

2. **Write an Argument:** Do you agree: "New York is a city of only the very rich and the very poor" as well as "the very young"?

3. "Think" Topic: Lethem uses *Stars War* and *2001: A Space Odyssey* as symbolic motifs in his essay. Suggest how these works illuminate his inner conflicts and stages of growth. Why doesn't he include more facts about the movies? OR What movies were central to your coming of age?

Ideas for Writing

1. Based on your own experiences, your reading of the essays in this cluster, and the works in the thematic cluster, "Road Trips," what purposes do you think pilgrimages have?

2. **Write an Argument:** Pilgrimage involves similar experiences as the heroic journey: a departure from home, a test of the self, the opportunity to experience freedom, the risks and challenges incurred by facing physical and emotional obstacles to growth, and the possibility for self-discovery and maturation. Consider these elements of pilgrimage in relation to the works in this cluster.

www **On the Web:** *Pilgrimages/Road Trips*

Please visit http://www.academic.cengage.com/english/Schmidt/Legacies4e/ for links to the following online resources.

Sarah Dickerson, "Hometown"
Deanne Stillman, "The Winding Road to Joshua Tree"

GRAPHIC LITERATURE

Marjane Satrapi *(1969–)*

The Veil *2003*
from *Persepolis: The Story of a Childhood*

AND ALSO BECAUSE THE YEAR BEFORE, IN 1979, WE WERE IN A FRENCH NON-RELIGIOUS SCHOOL.

WHERE BOYS AND GIRLS WERE TOGETHER.

AND THEN SUDDENLY IN 1980...

ALL BILINGUAL SCHOOLS MUST BE CLOSED DOWN.

THEY ARE SYMBOLS OF CAPITALISM.

BRAVO!

WHAT WISDOM!

OF DECADENCE.

THIS IS CALLED A "CULTURAL REVOLUTION."

WE FOUND OURSELVES VEILED AND SEPARATED FROM OUR FRIENDS.

AND THAT WAS THAT...

EVERYWHERE IN THE STREETS THERE WERE DEMONSTRATIONS FOR AND AGAINST THE VEIL.

AT ONE OF THE DEMONSTRATIONS, A GERMAN JOURNALIST TOOK A PHOTO OF MY MOTHER.

I WAS REALLY PROUD OF HER. HER PHOTO WAS PUBLISHED IN ALL THE EUROPEAN NEWSPAPERS.

AND EVEN IN ONE MAGAZINE IN IRAN. MY MOTHER WAS REALLY SCARED.

SHE DYED HER HAIR,

AND WORE DARK GLASSES FOR A LONG TIME.

Black Market Tapes

FOR A YEAR NOW, THE FOOD SHORTAGE HAD BEEN RESOLVED BY THE GROWTH OF THE BLACK MARKET. HOWEVER, FINDING TAPES WAS A LITTLE MORE COMPLICATED. ON GANDHI AVENUE YOU COULD FIND THEM SOMETIMES.

ESTEVIE VONDER

ABBA, BEE GEES

YAZOO

JULIO IGLESIAS,

PINK FLOYD

JIKAEL MACKSON

VIDEOS, MUSIC, CARDS, LIPSTICK, NAIL POLISH, CHESS SET, PANTYHOSE, CHOCOLATE, ...,....

I BOUGHT TWO TAPES: KIM WILDE AND CAMEL.

HOW MUCH?

110 TUMANS.

♪WE'RE THE KIDS IN AMERICA ♪WHOA...

YOU! STOP!

THEY WERE GUARDIANS OF THE REVOLUTION, THE WOMEN'S BRANCH. THIS GROUP HAD BEEN ADDED IN 1982, TO ARREST WOMEN WHO WERE IMPROPERLY VEILED. (LIKE ME, FOR EXAMPLE.)

THEIR JOB WAS TO PUT US BACK ON THE STRAIGHT AND NARROW BY EXPLAINING THE DUTIES OF MUSLIM WOMEN.

WHY ARE YOU WEARING THOSE "PUNK" SHOES?

WHAT PUNK SHOES?

THOSE!

BUT THESE ARE SNEAKERS!

SHUT UP! THEY'RE PUNK.

IT WAS OBVIOUS THAT SHE HAD NO IDEA WHAT PUNK WAS.

THERE WAS NO ALTERNATIVE. I HAD TO LIE.

I WEAR THESE BECAUSE I PLAY BASKETBALL.

I'M ON MY SCHOOL'S TEAM.

OH SURE. I CAN TELL BY YOUR HEIGHT!

AND YOU WEAR THIS JACKET FOR BASKETBALL TOO??

WHAT DO I SEE HERE? MICHAEL JACKSON! THAT SYMBOL OF DECADENCE?

NO, IT'S MALCOLM X, THE LEADER OF BLACK MUSLIMS IN AMERICA.

DON'T GIVE ME THAT! IT'S MICHAEL JACKSON!

WHO? I DON'T KNOW HIM.

BACK THEN, MICHAEL JACKSON WAS STILL BLACK.

LOWER YOUR SCARF, YOU LITTLE WHORE!

AREN'T YOU ASHAMED TO WEAR TIGHT JEANS LIKE THESE??

THEY SHRANK!!

GO ON, GET IN THE CAR. WE'RE TAKING YOU DOWN TO THE COMMITTEE.

THE COMMITTEE WAS THE HQ OF THE GUARDIANS OF THE REVOLUTION.

AT THE COMMITTEE, THEY DIDN'T HAVE TO INFORM MY PARENTS. THEY COULD DETAIN ME FOR HOURS, OR FOR DAYS. I COULD BE WHIPPED. IN SHORT, ANYTHING COULD HAPPEN TO ME. IT WAS TIME FOR ACTION.

I'M SORRY MA'AM! I'LL NEVER DO IT AGAIN...

GET IN THE CAR!

MA'AM, MY MOTHER'S DEAD. MY STEPMOTHER IS REALLY CRUEL AND IF I DON'T GO HOME RIGHT AWAY, SHE'LL KILL ME...

SHE'LL BURN ME WITH THE CLOTHES IRON!

SHE'LL MAKE MY FATHER PUT ME IN AN ORPHANAGE

MAYBE SHE BELIEVED ME, MAYBE SHE JUST PRETENDED TO. BUT, MIRACULOUSLY, SHE LET ME GO.

BACK HOME...

MARJI! WHAT HAPPENED? HAVE YOU BEEN CRYING?

NO MOM. I'M JUST TIRED. I'M GOING TO MY ROOM.

THERE WAS NO WAY I COULD TELL THE TRUTH. SHE NEVER WOULD HAVE LET ME GO OUT ALONE AGAIN.

I GOT OFF PRETTY EASY, CONSIDERING. THE GUARDIANS OF THE REVOLUTION DIDN'T FIND MY TAPES.

♫ WE'RE THE KIDS IN AMERICA WHOAO ♫

TO EACH HIS OWN WAY OF CALMING DOWN.

Explorations of the Text

1. What is the first person autobiographical persona's attitude toward "the Islamic Revolution"? Discuss her point of view. How does she respond to wearing the veil? How does she view her mother's protest?
2. How does Marjane respond when the guardians of the revolution stop her because she is not properly veiled?
3. What does wearing the veil suggest about the treatment of women in the Islamic Republic after 1980? Compare this portrayal of women with that in the excerpt from Azar Nafisi's *Reading Lolita in Tehran.*
4. Look at a frame of the graphic memoir. How do the black and white images suggest Marjane's state of mind?

The Reading/Writing Connection

1. Freewrite: What does clothing suggest about who we are? How would you feel if you were told that you had to wear specific garb that covered your hair or body?
2. After the Islamic Revolution, Azar Nafisi, a writer and academic who enjoyed the freedoms that a secular Iran afforded to women, found that she had to conform to the strict Islamic code for the behavior of women. She explains in her memoir that "she . . . [became] someone who was a stranger to herself." Are there hints of this phenomenon in "The Veil"?

Ideas for Writing

1. What are some of the freedoms that you take for granted?

WRITING ASSIGNMENTS

1. a. Contrast views of cultural identity in this chapter.
   b. Compare your view of cultural pride and identity with the views in two of the following poems: "Ego Tripping," "Indian Boarding School: The Runaways," "Lost Sister," and "Suicide Note."
2. a. Compare the view of gaining sexual awareness and identity for men and for women in any of the works in this chapter.
   b. Interview several people about their experiences in gaining sexual awareness.
   c. Based on the works in this chapter and/or your interviews, write an essay that classifies ways in which adolescents acquire sexual knowledge.
3. Argue pro or con: Control of the body leads to control of the mind and imagination. You may define control in terms of social, political, or cultural forces.
4. One of the themes of this chapter is the way that the body can be marked and constrained by social, cultural, and political forces and the consequences for the development of identity. And, conversely, are there ways that people take control of their bodies, use their bodies to define their identities, through tattooing, piercing, or taking diet pills or steroids, for example? Explore the treatment of the body in several works in this chapter. (Suggestions: "Rose-Johnny," "Cathedral," and "The Veil.")
5. Rites of passage may be characterized as those that involve loss, those that entail facing death, those that include isolation, and those that involve gaining new

knowledge. Analyze two or three of the works in the chapter according to one of these categories.

6. Coming of age and initiation experiences prompt adolescents either to accept or to reject adult responsibilities. Analyze the conflicts of a character in one of the works in this chapter in light of this idea.

7. Consider one of David Espey's statements about travel:

   "Travel, which often begins in a need to escape the confines of home, may end with a new appreciation and understanding of home and its meaning to the traveler." OR "Travel can be an intensely individual pursuit, often an escape from the constrictions of a traveler's own society or community."

   What views toward travel do you see represented in works in the Pilgrimage cluster?

8. Visit the World.Hum.com website and select a "road-trip" narrative. Compare one of the pilgrimage essays in this chapter with your selected work. Consider treatment of such features as point of view, nature of the journey, state of awareness, or change.
   a. Write about a memorable road trip that you took. What impact did the places visited have on you? The mode of travel? The people you met? What did you learn? How did you change?
   b. Compare your journey with one of the pilgrimages or road trips presented in works in this chapter.

9. Argument: You can go on a pilgrimage without leaving home. Argue pro or con. Refer to several works in this chapter to prove your points.

10. a. Freewrite on a coming-of-age ritual you have experienced.
    b. Read about coming-of-age rituals in a particular culture. Take notes. Examine the origins, the evolution, and the current practice of the ritual (for example, bar mitzvah in Jewish culture). Write an outline, draft, revision, and final version of a research paper concerning one such ritual.

11. Here are stages of an assignment that focuses on your Facebook or MySpace page:
    a. Examine your own Facebook or MySpace page. What does the page reveal about your identity, attitudes, or values?
    b. Create a Facebook or MySpace page for one of the characters in one of the stories. What does it reveal about the protagonist's character?
    c. In a formal essay, compare and contrast your MySpace profile with that of the character's. Compare and contrast the visions of identity presented on the pages.

12. a. List the ways in which you have conformed and the ways in which you have rebelled.
    b. Write about a single event that symbolizes the conflict between conformity and rebellion.

13. Discuss how a scene or vignette from a story or play functions in the development of a particular character.

14. As a reader you gain multiple perspectives about a work through rereading, discussing the work in collaboration with others, and applying different critical lens through which to examine the work. Multiple readings can lead you to an expansive vision of a text. For this assignment, begin with a freewrite that focuses on one dimension of a work. Next study the work again from another

perspective. Finally, compose an essay that presents an interpretation of the multiple layers of a text. For example, you might compose a freewrite that focuses on Li'l Bit's response to her molestation in *How I Learned to Drive.* Then applying a feminist critical lens, you might study the portrayal of gender roles: the worlds of men and women in 1960s, rural Maryland. This thematic thread would lead you to consider how gender roles influenced the characters' development of identity. Your essay then would place Li'l Bit's experiences within a larger cultural context.

15. Many of the works in this chapter depend on *irony.* Choose two or three selections, and discuss the function and effects of irony. (Suggestions: "Flood," "The Stolen Party," "Cinderella," "Rose-Johnny," and "Once upon a Time.")

16. a. Write a journal entry on your search for selfhood.
    b. Compare your process of individuation with the struggles of a character in a work in this chapter.
    c. Discuss the themes concerning the search for self.

17. a. Interview your parents or other adults about conflicts between parents and children in adolescence.
    b. Interview several teenagers about their perspectives concerning conflicts between parents and adolescents.
    c. Write a summary of these responses.
    d. Write an essay that compares these perspectives.

18. Choose a quotation or a song that illuminates a theme or main impression of character for one of the selected texts in the chapter. Create an argument demonstrating how your quotation applies to the work.

19. Choose several stories in this chapter and discuss whether those stories' portrayal of adolescence is still relevant today.

20. Explore your personal responses to one of the works in this chapter. You may frame your response as a letter to the writer. (See Staci Ferris's essay, "Response to Greg Delanty's 'Leavetaking.'")

21. Fairy tales often end with the promise of a "happily ever after" life. Do the stories in this chapter conclude in this manner? Compare the endings of several works in this chapter. Are the conclusions unexpected, or are they the predictable outcomes of characters' plights?

22. Much of what goes wrong in life is caused by our own natures. Relate this idea to such works as "Rose-Johnny," *A Doll's House,* and/or other works from this chapter.

23. According to an article in *The Chronicle of Higher Education* (1/12/07), researchers have discovered that "the adolescent brain seems to be hard-wired to seek out exciting and potentially dangerous situations." Do you see evidence of this behavior pattern in works in this chapter?

24. According to Bettelheim it is important for people to find meaning in their lives.
    a. Write about a time in your life that challenged you, that pushed you beyond your own comfort level and prompted you to find new meanings in life.
    b. Focus on this same struggle for protagonists in such works as "Cathedral," *A Doll's House,* or *How I Learned to Drive.*
    c. Compare and contrast you own search for meaning with that of one or several of the protagonists in the above works.

25. Bettelheim discusses the "images of heroes who have to go out into the world all by themselves," like the narrator in "Flood" or Georgeann in "Rose-Johnny."

Discuss how or why these characters achieve or fail to achieve meaningful relations with the world around them.

26. "Treasures" and "Loss": Both of these words characterize our relationships with our pasts.
    a. Use each word as the basis of a freewrite. What were the treasures and the losses of your childhood and adolescence?
    b. Compare your complex relationship with your own past with that of several characters from works in this chapter. (Suggestions: "The Attic," "Biography of an Armenian Schoolgirl," and "Ah Mah.")

27. Create a character analysis in creative or analytic form of one of the protagonists in one of the works in this chapter. See Patrick Lindo's "Where Wolf."

STUDENT ESSAYS
Personal Response Essay

Greg Delanty   *(1958–)*

Leavetaking   *1992*

After you board the train, you sit & wait,
   to begin your first real journey alone.
You read to avoid the window's awkwardness,
   knowing he's anxious to catch your eye,
     loitering out in never-ending rain,   5
to wave, a bit shy, another final goodbye;
you are afraid of having to wave too soon.

And for the moment you think it's the train
   next to you has begun, but it is yours,
and your face, pressed to the windowpane,   10
   is distorted & numbed by the icy glass,
     pinning your eyes upon your father,
as he cranes to defy your disappearing train.
Both of you waving, eternally, to each other.

Staci Anna Marie Ferris

Response to Greg Delanty's "Leavetaking"

Dear Greg,

   Your poem "Leavetaking" brought memories flowing back into my mind. Memories of the day that I left my home and family in Switzerland and headed to college on a train. Memories of many tears and yet memories of excitement. Reading your poem was like having someone read my mind and put the memories of that day on paper. I am amazed at how much alike our feelings and experiences were about leaving home.

The first thing about the poem that struck me as a coincidence was the train. I also left home a little more than two months ago on a train. When you talk about "sit[ting] and wait[ing]/to begin your first real journey alone," as I read, memories of the day of leavetaking began to flow back into my mind as vividly as the day I left. I remember stepping on the train and taking my seat next to the window. On the other side of the window was my family. I felt as if I were already over the ocean, and they still were at home in Switzerland. I felt the window's "awkwardness." The window of the train was like a barrier between home and the future, my future. I could not look at them out the window for fear that I would break out into tears.

But yet at the same time I wanted to look at them, to capture the memory of every line of my family's faces, hair, the clothes that they were wearing, and, most importantly, the look in their eyes. Everyone had looks of sadness on their faces and tears in their eyes, except my little cousins who were too young to understand what was happening—that I was going to be away for a long time. My cousins were all standing there with ice cream in their hands, smiling and waving. All I could think was how I wished that I was that little again and wasn't on the train about to leave. I only looked at them at short glances thinking what would happen if I just jumped off the train and decided to stay home. But I continued to sit on the train for what seemed an eternity.

Another line that struck me was "you are afraid of having to wave too soon." I remember that I was too afraid to wave because I thought that once I began to wave the train would move, and I would be slowly moving down the track away from my family and home. I kept thinking—my "face pressed to the windowpane"—that if I didn't wave, then the train wouldn't move; I could just sit there forever taking short glances at my family. However, finally the train began to move, and I got a funny feeling in the pit of my stomach, a sick feeling perhaps. I began to wave out the window at my family, and they waved back. They were crying and waving, and I was doing the same. All of us waving, "eternally, to each other," hoping that I wasn't really leaving and that they could still see me. As the miles passed and the mountains became practically invisible, I realized that I had left home and my family to start this new journey, new beginning, a new chapter of my life: a chapter filled with new people and places, but still containing my family and my home. However, I would be living at a distance from them and not seeing them as much.

Greg, your poem took me back to a very important and vivid day in my life. Thank you for reminding me of that day and the moment that the train started to move on the tracks.

Yours truly,
Staci Ferris

Creative Response to Literature Essay

Patrick Lindo

Where Wolf

I was with my family when they came to visit my uncle in the country for Christmas. I had not been to this part of the country since I was a little boy, and that was during the summer. While eating breakfast by the fire in my uncle's cottage, we heard the howl of wolves; I thought it was a beautiful sound. It sounded like the wolves were singing joyously to each other. My aunt was frightened by it and said that during the winter, when there was no food, the wolves would attack people. I knew this to be false, as there had never been a documented case of a wolf attacking a human unless the wolf was sick or injured. I was amused by her ignorance. My aunt warned me to be careful and not to get lost or leave the trails as wolves might be waiting for me. She said, "If you come across a naked man in the forest, run away, because he is a werewolf." She told stories about how some farmer trapped and killed a wolf, and that the dead body was that of a man, and another story about a witch, who turned men into wolves. The way she told these tales, she undoubtedly believed them to be true. I found her stories funny and ridiculous, but I listened without commenting on her foolishness. I knew the villagers had some odd beliefs, but I thought they were mainly superstitious about the weather or issues relating to their farms and crops. She was probably worried about me being a city boy in the country, and this was her way of telling me to be careful. The people in this area are so uneducated.

I became bored by her stories and decided to go out hunting for some game birds to add to our Christmas feast. My father and I hunted every season in the countryside near the city where we lived. I was generally comfortable outside of the city, but my uncle lived far from civilization, and I felt isolated. I was sixteen years old, and now old enough to hunt alone. I looked forward to getting out in the bush, as hunting was one of the few pleasures the country afforded; however, the locals mostly hunted out of the necessity for food. This endless pursuit of sustenance was not how I envisioned my life. I was thinking about what college to attend.

I dressed in my hunting gear, grabbed my compass, rifle, and game sack, and headed out to the countryside. The temperature was not too cold and the snow was not so deep as to hinder my trekking. Soon I was far from the cottage and into the wild. The fresh air was wonderful. It was quiet and peaceful. Being alone in the woods with my gun gave me feelings of adventure and contentment. For the first time, I felt in control of my life. Nobody from my neighborhood or school was here. I wasn't worried about doing or saying something that would result in my embarrassment or harassment. The insecurity I felt in city was absent. During the first hour, I was mainly surveying the landscape for good places to find my quarry. I noticed that the most of the village farms looked dark and gloomy. It was as if there was a bad aura hanging over the place. This feeling of doom vanished once I began to see the signs of pheasant and grouse. My first shot was a kill, and I was feeling good. After I bagged a few more birds, I heard the faint cry of a wolf in the distance. I thought about what my aunt had said and then realized how ridiculous it was to worry. I had a rifle and the knowledge that wolves are actually afraid of men. I thought, how could a person actually believe in werewolves? Does everyone in this area think werewolves exist? The hicks probably do.

I worked my way through some underbrush and found my way onto a trail. There happened to be a girl on the path, and I startled her. She looked scared, so I jokingly bowed to her as if she were royalty. She seemed amused and it eased her fear. Pretty soon we were talking together, down the path, laughing and fooling around. Normally I would feel anxiety while talking to a girl, but somehow I didn't. She was younger than me and cute, and my flirting with her seemed to come naturally. If I had acted this way toward any of the girls in the city, they would have told everyone I liked them and the teasing would be endless. I already got picked on enough. Trying to be a gentleman, I asked if I could carry her basket, and she handed it to me. This girl in the red shawl was unlike the city girls I knew; she was attentive and genuinely interested in what I was saying. I felt a confidence in myself that I had never before experienced, and I didn't want it to end. I was just walking with her, feeling exuberant and forgetting all about the hunt. A gentle snowfall had begun, and being unfamiliar with the terrain, I took out my compass to get a bearing on where I was, as sundown was approaching. She was surprised that I had a compass. She had walked this trail many times before; therefore, she knew exactly where she was and had no need for a compass. I felt foolish, so I boasted that with the compass, I could find my way through the woods, to any destination. She asked, "aren't you afraid of the wolves"? I tapped my rifle and smiled. She said she would not leave the trail to her grandmother's home. So I bet her that I could get there faster than her. She asked what I would want if I won the bet. I didn't know what to say so I blurted out, "a kiss." I couldn't believe I said it, but she didn't make fun of me. She said, "okay it's a bet." I slid into the underbrush, cool and collected, knowing I was not going to let her beat me to granny's.

Once I knew she could not hear me rustling in the woods, I raced to her grandmother's house. While running through the dense bushes I scratched my face, and my chin was bleeding a little. Some pine needles and small twigs had worked there way under my shirt. My clothes were completely soaked from snow and sweat. I arrived at the cottage before the girl. I knocked on the door and when asked who it was, I was so out of breath that I gasped out in a high pitch, "your granddaughter's friend," as I tried to regain my voice in mid sentence. Granny said, "Come in." I opened the door, went inside, and placed my birds and the basket on the table. I removed my cloak, and hung it by the fire to dry. I opened the top button on my shirt to pick out some of the needles and twigs stuck to my skin, and that was when granny saw me. She must not have heard me say I was a friend as she had a look of terror in her eyes. Granny screamed in a frail voice, "What have you done with my granddaughter?" and, "You're a werewolf come to eat me!" I tried to calm her and tell her I was not going to harm her, but the shock of my unexpected presence was too much for her weak heart. She fell silent and was motionless. I tried to revive her. I shook her, but she was not responding. I put my coat back on, and I lifted her out of the bed, thinking I would try to bring her to help, but we were in the country and it was now dark, snowing pretty hard, and I didn't know where to go. How could this stupid werewolf superstition actually lead to someone's death? Country people are so dumb. I was frantic. What was going to happen to me? I thought I should hide the body and act as if granny was not home when I arrived. Hurriedly, I pushed her body under the bed. I made up the bedroom as if nobody was there. The room was neat and tidy. I placed granny's bible on the nightstand, like it was waiting to be opened for the night's reading.

I knew this plan would not work, but before I could think of what else to do, there was a knock on the door. Choking back tears, I stupidly asked, "Who's there?" She replied, "It's your Granddaughter," and entered the cottage. Before she could see what had happened, I jumped in front of the door to stop her from running away in fear. I wanted to explain what had happened. I was hoping she would understand, but I must have looked like a maniac with my bloodshot, bulging eyes and sweating, scratched-up face. She commented, "What big eyes you have!" and I said, "The better to see you with." Even with the trauma I was about to inflict on her I wished we were back in the first moments of our meeting, when everything between us seemed magical. I noticed a small lock of granny's hair near the fire and as I did her eyes also fell upon it. I sensed her fear growing. She asked me where her grandmother was and I lied and told her we were alone. Just as the lie exited my lips there began a howling outside.

It sounded as if hundreds of wolves were at the door, wanting an invitation inside. The sound no longer seemed beautiful and was now haunting me. It sounded painful. She looked panicked, so I said, "Don't be afraid, the wolves will not harm you; they are my friends." I couldn't believe what I had said, considering all the werewolf lore. I was still trying to salvage some hope of her understanding what really happened. I wanted her to like me. I noticed she kept glancing toward her basket on the table but I had no idea why. Maybe she just didn't want to look me in the eyes, because I didn't want her to either.

She went over to the window and opened it. The howling wolves were all over the yard baying in what seemed to me to be a unified yearning. Their intense hunger was expressed in every note. Somehow, she now appeared totally calm as she closed the window, mentioning that she felt sorry for them out in the cold. I was trying to think of a way to tell her about what happened, without having her hate me. I sensed that she already knew and, for some reason, forgave me. There was new connection developing between us, something deeper than the childish flirting. It was a mature feeling, something I couldn't explain, but it felt completely natural. My anxiety was dissipating.

She removed her shawl, rolled it up, and tossed it on the fire. I didn't think anything of it as I was mesmerized by her movements. She was no longer the cute girl, but a beautiful young woman. She pulled her blouse over her head, revealing her breasts. She removed her skirt, stockings, and shoes. She was standing there completely nude, running her fingers sensually through her hair. I felt like I was dreaming. She tiptoed over to me, unbuttoned my shirt and picked the pine needles and twigs off me. I was shivering with anticipation. She slowly ran her fingers up and down the muscles of my arms and said, "What big arms you have!" and I replied, "The better to hold you with." The wolves howled a little louder. Then she kissed me, the one she owed me from the bet, and it was wonderful. I stared into her eyes and smiled. She said, "What big teeth you have!" and my reply was, "The better to eat you up with." My response sounded corny, but I was enraptured. There was still a leg of this journey not finished. She laughed, tore off the rest of my clothes and threw them in the fire. The passion overwhelmed us; our only thoughts were carnal. The wolves, the blizzard, and granny's dead body under the bed were out of mind. Nothing in my life was ever so perfect as that embrace. I wished the experience would last forever.

Watching her as she slept in my arms, an epiphany came to me. I realized that flirting, wanting her to like me and the lies I told her were to keep the momentum of building her trust in me and forging a perceived bond between us. It was all a subconscious attempt by me to bring us to the moment of sexual gratification. I gained an insight that would change my interactions with girls forever. I recollected an essay that I had read in school, titled, "Where Are You Going, Where Have You Been?," by Joyce Carol Oates. The story was about how a young girl can be manipulated by a person who knows her vulnerabilities. If I could find and then exploit the insecurities of young girls, I might be able to get them to willingly give in to my desires.

The wolves were in full serenade, and it was as though they were reading my thoughts. Their howls were acknowledging an ancient rite of passage that I triumphed over. I was being initiated into the brotherhood of wolves, and whether I am in the country or the city, the hunt is on.

Works Cited

Carter, Angela. "The Company of Wolves." <u>Legacies: Fiction, Poetry, Drama, Nonfiction</u>, Fourth Edition. Eds. Jan Zlotnik Schmidt, Lynne Crockett, and Carley Rees Bogarad. Boston: Cengage Learning Wadsworth, 2008. 129-135.

Oates, Joyce Carol. "Where Are You Going, Where Have You Been?" <u>Legacies: Fiction, Poetry, Drama, Nonfiction</u>, Fourth Edition. Eds. Jan Zlotnik Schmidt, Lynne Crockett, and Carley Rees Bogarad. Boston: Cengage Learning Wadsworth, 2008. 51-61.

6

The Self and Beyond

Introduction

We live our lives like chips in a kaleidoscope, always
part of patterns that are larger than ourselves and somehow
more than the sum of their parts.

Salvadore Minuchin, Family Kaleidoscope

We live as part of a kaleidoscope that is "larger than ourselves." The "chips" of the pattern are variegated, beautiful, and complex. The fundamental pieces of the pattern upon which the others depend are family members. They provide the initial forms of bonding: the crucial experiences of security and insecurity, of love and hate. These early relationships of intimacy, connection, and conflict with parents and siblings influence our responses to the world.

Perhaps one of the enduring facts of family life is that family members exist in separate worlds. Each person in the kaleidoscope harbors secret thoughts, wishes, dreams—an inner life of which others have no knowledge. Another is that we often are haunted by the ghosts of the past: personal, familial, historical, and cultural traumatic events. Family dynamics, the relationships between parents and children, inevitably are complicated. Literature is replete, for example, with images of the father as the authority figure, as the protector, and as the provider. What happens when fathers fail to fulfill these obligations? A number of works in this chapter explore the question. Of course, relationships with fathers not only are destructive but also life-giving and nurturing. Literature also represents fathers who demonstrate their values and teach their children to live in the world as several works in Chapter 6 illustrate. Like the bonds of fathers with their children, the relationships of mothers with their sons and daughters not only are fraught with anxiety, but also are life-giving, and nurturing.

The works in this chapter concerning parents and children, then, are stories of love and nurture as well as of loss and recognition of loss. As some stories demonstrate complex and positive relationships between parents and children, some demonstrate the failings of parents, and they record the anger of children who perceive that their parents have failed them—failed them because of their own limits, failed them because of desire for their children to be perfect, to be like them, and to compensate for their deficiencies.

We not only are members of a nuclear family but also of an extended family, of a tribe, and of a community. We are the products of personal, familial, and cultural histories, often expressed in the rituals of daily life—the foods we eat, the ceremonies we take part in. The same kaleidoscope of relationships that characterize parents and children exists among siblings and friends. Several poems and essays affirm kinship ties, those bonds with others that become sources of strength. As Etheridge Knight's persona reveals: "I am all of them,/they are all of me, I am me, they are they, and I have no children/to float in the space between."

Crossing the Genres
Family Secrets

Mary Gaitskill   *(1954–)*

Tiny, Smiling Daddy   *1988*

The phone rang five times before he got up to answer it. It was his friend Norm. They greeted each other and then Norm, his voice strangely weighted, said, "I saw the issue of *Self* with Kitty in it."

He waited for an explanation. None came so he said, "What? Issue of *Self?* What's *Self?*"

"Good grief, Stew, I thought for sure you'd of seen it. Now I feel awkward."

"So do I. Do you want to tell me what this is about?"

"My daughter's got a subscription to this magazine, *Self.* And they printed an ar-   5 ticle that Kitty wrote about fathers and daughters talking to each other, and she well, she wrote about you. Laurel showed it to me."

"My God."

"It's ridiculous that I'm the one to tell you. I just thought—"

"It was bad?"

"No. No, she didn't say anything bad. I just didn't understand the whole idea of it. And I wondered what you thought."

He got off the phone and walked back into the living room, shocked. His daughter   10 Kitty was living in South Carolina working in a record store and making pots, vases, and statuettes which she sold on commission. She had never written anything that he knew of, yet she'd apparently published an article in a national magazine about him without telling him. He lifted his arms and put them on the window sill; the air from the open window cooled his underarms. Outside, the Starlings' tiny dog marched officiously up and down the pavement, looking for someone to bark at. Maybe she had written an article about how wonderful he was, and she was too shy to show him right away. This was doubtful. Kitty was quiet but she wasn't shy. She was untactful and she could be aggressive. Uncertainty only made her doubly aggressive.

He turned the edge of one nostril over with his thumb and nervously stroked his nose-hairs with one finger. He knew it was a nasty habit but it soothed him. When Kitty was a little girl he would do it to make her laugh: "Well," he'd say, "do you think it's time we played with the hairs in our nose?" And she would giggle, holding her hands against her face, eyes sparkling over her knuckles.

Then she was fourteen, and as scornful and rejecting as any girl he had ever thrown a spitball at when he was that age. They didn't get along so well any more. Once, they were sitting in the rec room watching TV, he on the couch, she on the footstool. There was a Charlie Chan[1] movie on TV, but he was mostly watching her back and her long, thick brown hair, which she had just washed and was brushing. She dropped her head

---

[1] **Charlie Chan**: A Chinese-American detective featured in movies from the 1930s and 1940s.

forward from the neck to let the hair fall between her spread legs, and began slowly stroking it with a pink nylon brush.

"Say, don't you think it's time we played with the hairs in our nose?"

No reaction from bent back and hair.

"Who wants to play with the hairs in their nose?" Nothing.

"Hairs in the nose, hairs in the nose," he sang.

She bolted violently up from the stool. "You are so gross you disgust me!" She stormed from the room, shoulders in a tailored jacket of indignation.

Sometimes he said it just to see her exasperation, to feel the adorable, futile outrage of her violated girl delicacy.

He wished that his wife would come home with the car so that he could drive to the store and buy a copy of *Self*. His car was being repaired and he could not walk to the little cluster of stores and parking lots that constituted "town" in this heat. It would take a good twenty minutes and he would be completely worn out when he got there. He would find the magazine and stand there in the drugstore and read it and if it was something bad, he might not have the strength to walk back.

He went into the kitchen, opened a beer and brought it into the living room. His wife had been gone for over an hour, and God knows how much longer she would be. She could spend literally all day driving around the county doing nothing but buying a jar of honey or a bag of apples. Of course, he could call Kitty, but he'd probably just get her answering machine, and besides, he didn't want to talk to her before he understood the situation. He felt helplessness move through his body like a swimmer feels a large sea creature pass beneath him. How could she have done this to him? She knew how he dreaded exposure of any kind, she knew the way he guarded himself against strangers, the way he carefully drew all the curtains when twilight approached so that no one could see them walking through the house. She knew how ashamed he had been when, at sixteen, she had announced that she was lesbian.

The Starling dog was now across the street, yapping at the heels of a bow-legged old lady in a blue dress who was trying to walk down the street. "Dammit," he said. He left the window and got the afternoon opera station on the radio. They were in the final act of *La Bohème*.

He did not remember precisely when it had happened, but Kitty, his beautiful, happy little girl, turned into a glum, weird teenager that other kids picked on. She got skinny and ugly. Her blue eyes, which had been so sensitive and bright, turned filmy, as if the real Kitty had retreated so far from the surface that her eyes existed to shield rather than reflect her. It was as if she deliberately held her beauty away from them, only showing glimpses of it during unavoidable lapses, like the time she sat before the TV, daydreaming and lazily brushing her hair. At moments like this, her dormant charm broke his heart. It also annoyed him. What did she have to retreat from? They had both loved her. When she was little, and she couldn't sleep at night, Marsha would sit with her in bed for hours. She praised her stories and her drawings as if she were a genius. When Kitty was seven, she and her mother had special times, during which they went off together and talked about whatever Kitty wanted to talk about.

He tried to compare the sullen, morbid Kitty of sixteen with the slender, self-possessed twenty-eight-year-old lesbian who wrote articles for *Self*. He pictured himself in court, waving a copy of *Self* before a shocked jury. The case would be taken up by the press. He saw the headlines: Dad Sues Mag—Dyke Daughter Reveals . . . reveals what? What had Kitty found to say about him that was of interest to the entire country that she didn't want him to know about?

Anger overrode his helplessness. Kitty could be vicious. He hadn't seen her vicious side in years, but he knew it was there. He remembered the time he'd stood behind the half-open front door when fifteen-year-old Kitty sat hunched on the front steps with one of her few friends, a homely blond who wore white lipstick and a white leather jacket. He had come to the door to view the weather and say something to the girls, but they were muttering so intently that curiosity got the better of him, and he hung back a moment to listen. "Well, at least your mom's smart," said Kitty. "My mom's not only a bitch, she's stupid."

This after the lullabies and special times! It wasn't just an isolated incident either; every time he'd come home from work, his wife had something bad to say about Kitty. She hadn't set the table until she had been asked four times. She'd gone to Lois's house instead of coming straight home like she'd been told to do. She'd worn a dress to school that was short enough to show the tops of her panty hose.

By the time Kitty came to dinner, looking as if she'd been doing slave labor all day, he would be mad at her. He couldn't help it. Here was his wife doing her damnedest to raise a family and cook dinner and here was this awful kid looking ugly, acting mean and not setting the table. It seemed unreasonable that she should turn out so badly after taking up so much time. Her afflicted expression made him angry too. What had anybody ever done to her?

He sat forward and gently gnawed the insides of his mouth as he listened to the dying girl in *La Bohème*. He saw his wife's car pull into the driveway. He walked to the back door, almost wringing his hands, and waited for her to come through the door. When she did, he snatched the grocery bag from her arms and said, "Give me the keys." She stood open-mouthed in the stair-well, looking at him with idiotic consternation. "Give me the keys!"

"What is it, Stew? What's happened?"

"I'll tell you when I get back."

He got in the car and became part of it, this panting, mobile case propelling him through the incredibly complex and fast-moving world of other people, their houses, their children, their dogs, their lives. He wasn't usually so aware of this unpleasant sense of disconnection between him and everyone else, but he had the feeling that it had been there all along, underneath what he thought of most of the time. It was ironic that it should rear up so visibly at a time when there was in fact a mundane yet invasive and horribly real connection between him and everyone else in Wayne County: the hundreds of copies of *Self* magazine sitting in countless drugstores, bookstores, groceries, and libraries. It was as if there was a tentacle plugged into the side of the car, linking him with the random humans who picked up the magazine, possibly his very neighbors. He stopped at a crowded intersection, feeling like an ant in an enemy swarm.

Kitty had projected herself out of the house and into this swarm very early, ostensibly because life with him and Marsha had been so awful. Well, it had been awful, but because of Kitty, not them. As if it wasn't enough to be sullen and dull, she turned into a lesbian. Kids followed her down the street jeering at her. Somebody dropped her books in a toilet. She got into a fistfight. Their neighbors gave them looks. This reaction seemed only to steel Kitty's grip on her new identity; it made her romanticize herself like the kid she was. She wrote poems about heroic women warriors, she brought home strange books and magazines which, among other things, seemed to glorify prostitutes. Marsha looked for them and threw them away. Kitty screamed at her, the tendons leaping out on her slender neck. He hit Kitty, Marsha tried to stop him and he yelled at her. Kitty leapt between them, as if to defend her mother. He grabbed her and shook her but he could not shake the conviction off her face.

Most of the time though, they continued as always, eating dinner together, watching TV, making jokes. That was the worst thing; he would look at Kitty and see his daughter, now familiar in her withdrawn sullenness, and feel comfort and affection. Then he would remember that she was a lesbian and a morass of complication and wrongness would come down between them, making it impossible for him to see her. Then she would be just Kitty again. He hated it.

She ran away at sixteen and the police found her in the apartment of an eighteen-year-old body builder named Dolores who had a naked woman tattooed on her sinister bicep. Marsha made them put her in a mental hospital so psychiatrists could observe her, but he hated the psychiatrists—mean, supercilious sons of bitches who delighted in the trick question—so he took her back out. She finished school and they told her if she wanted to leave it was all right with them. She didn't waste any time getting out of the house.

She moved into an apartment near Detroit with a girl named George and took a job at a home for retarded kids. She would appear for visits with a huge bag of laundry every few weeks. She was thin and neurotically muscular, her body having the look of a fighting dog on a leash. She wore her hair like a boy's and wore black sunglasses, black leather half-gloves and leather belts. The only remnant of her beauty was her erect martial carriage and her efficient movements; she walked through a room like the commander of a guerrilla force. She would sit at the dining room table with Marsha, drinking tea and having a laconic verbal conversation, her body speaking its precise martial language while the washing machine droned from the utility room and he wandered in and out trying to make sense of what she said. Sometimes she would stay into the evening to eat dinner and watch *All in the Family*. Then Marsha would send her home with a jar of homemade tapioca pudding or a bag of apples and oranges.

One day instead of a visit they got a letter postmarked San Francisco. She had left George, she said. She listed strange details about her current environment and was vague about how she was supporting herself. He had nightmares about Kitty, with her brave, proudly muscular little body, lost among big fleshy women who danced naked in go-go bars and took drugs with needles, terrible women who his confused romantic daughter invested with oppressed heroism and intensely female glamour. He got up at night and stumbled into the bathroom for stomach medicine, the familiar darkness of the house heavy with menacing images that pressed about him, images that he saw reflected in his own expression when he turned on the bathroom light over the mirror.

Then one year she came home for Christmas. She came into the house with her luggage and a shopping bag of gifts for them and he saw that she was beautiful again. It was a beauty that both offended and titillated his senses. Her short spiky hair was streaked with purple, her dainty mouth was lipsticked, her nose and ears were pierced with amethyst and dangling silver. Her face had opened in thousands of petals. Her eyes shone with quick perception as she put down her bag and he knew that she had seen him see her beauty. She moved towards him with fluid hips, she embraced him

35

for the first time in years. He felt her live, lithe body against him and his heart pulsed a message of blood and love. "Merry Christmas, Daddy," she said.

Her voice was husky and coarse, it reeked of knowledge and confidence. Her T-shirt said "Chicks With Balls." She was twenty-two years old.

She stayed for a week, discharging her strange jangling beauty into the house and changing the molecules of its air. She talked about the girls she shared an apartment with, her job at a coffee shop, how Californians were different from Michiganders. She talked about her friends: Lorraine, who was so pretty men fell off their bicycles as they twisted their bodies for a better look at her; Judy, a martial arts expert; and Meredith, who was raising a child with her husband, Angela. She talked of poetry readings, ceramics classes, celebrations of spring.

He realized, as he watched her, that she was now doing things that were as bad as or worse than the things that had made him angry at her five years before, yet they didn't quarrel. It seemed that a large white space existed between him and her, and that it was impossible to enter this space or to argue across it. Besides, she might never come back if he yelled at her.

Instead, he watched her, puzzling at the metamorphosis she had undergone. First she had been a beautiful, happy child turned homely, snotty, miserable adolescent. From there she had become a martinet girl with the eyes of a stifled pervert. Now she was a vibrant imp living, it seemed, in a world constructed of topsy-turvy junk pasted with rhinestones. Where had these three different people come from? Not even Marsha, who had spent so much time with her as a child, could trace the genesis of the new Kitty from the old one. Sometimes he bitterly reflected that he and Marsha weren't even real parents anymore, but bereft old people rattling around in a house, connected not to a real child who was going to college, or who at least had some kind of understandable life, but a changeling who was the product of only their most obscure quirks, a being who came from recesses that neither of them suspected they'd had.

There were only a few cars in the parking lot. He wheeled through it with pointless deliberation before parking near the drugstore. He spent irritating seconds searching for *Self* until he realized that its airbrushed cover girl was grinning right at him. He stormed the table of contents, then headed for the back of the magazine. "Speak Easy" was written sideways across the top of the appointed page in round turquoise letters. At the bottom was his daughter's name in a little box. "Kitty Thorne is a ceramic artist living in South Carolina." His hands were trembling.

It was hard for him to rationally ingest the beginning paragraphs which seemed, incredibly, to be about a phone conversation they'd had some time ago about the emptiness and selfishness of people who have sex but don't get married and have children. A few phrases that stood out clearly: ". . . my father may love me but he doesn't love the way I live." ". . . even more complicated because I'm gay." "Because it still hurts me."

For reasons he didn't understand, he felt a nervous smile tremble under his skin. He suppressed it.

"This hurt has its roots deep in our relationship, starting, I think, when I was a teenager."

He had a horrible sensation of being in public so he paid for the thing and took it out to the car with him. He slowly drove to another spot in the lot, as far away from the drugstore as possible, picked up the magazine, and began again. She described "the terrible difficulties" between him and her. She recounted, briefly and with hieroglyphic politeness, the fighting, the running away, the return, the tacit reconciliation.

"There is an emotional distance that we have both accepted and chosen to work around, hoping the occasional contact—love, anger, something—will get through."

He put the magazine down and looked out the window. It was near dusk; most of the stores in the little mall were closed. There were only two other cars in the parking lot, and a big, slow, frowning woman with two grocery bags was getting ready to drive one away. He was parked before a weedy piece of land at the edge of the parking lot. In it were rough, picky weeds spread out like big green tarantulas, young yellow dandelions, frail old dandelions, and bunches of tough blue chickweed. Even in his distress he vaguely appreciated the beauty of the blue weeds against the cool white and grey sky. For a moment the sound of insects comforted him. Images of Kitty passed through his memory with terrible speed: her nine-year-old forehead bent over her dish of ice cream, her tiny nightgowned form ran up the stairs, her ringed hand brushed her face, the keys on her belt jiggled as she walked her slow blue-jeaned walk away from the house. Gone, all gone.

The article went on to describe how Kitty hung up the phone feeling frustrated and then listed all the things she could've said to him to let him know how hurt she was, paving the way for "real communication," all in ghastly talk-show language. He was unable to put these words together with the Kitty he had last seen lounging around the house. She was twenty-eight now and she no longer dyed her hair or wore jewels in her nose. Her demeanor was serious, bookish, almost old-maidish. Once he'd overheard her talking to Marsha and heard her say, "So then this Italian girl gives me the once-over and says to Joanne, 'You 'ang around with too many Wasp.' And I said, 'I'm not a Wasp, I'm white trash.'"

"Speak for yourself," he'd said.

"If the worst occurred and my father was unable to respond to me in kind, I still 50 would have done a good thing. I would have acknowledged my own needs and created the possibility to connect with what therapists call 'the good parent' in myself."

Well, if that was the kind of thing she was going to say to him, he was relieved she hadn't said it. But if she hadn't said it to him, why was she saying it to the rest of the country?

He turned on the radio. It sang: "Try to remember, and if you remember, then follow, follow." He turned it off. He closed his eyes. When he was nine or ten an uncle of his had told him, "Everybody makes his own world. You see what you want to see and hear what you want to hear. You can do it right now. If you blink ten times and then close your eyes real tight, you can see anything you want to see in front of you." He'd tried it rather half-heartedly and hadn't seen anything but the vague suggestion of a yellowish-white ball moving creepily through the dark. At the time, he'd thought it was perhaps because he hadn't tried hard enough.

He had told Kitty to do the same thing, or something like it, when she was eight or nine. They were on the back porch sitting in striped lawn chairs, holding hands and watching the fire-flies turn off and on.

She closed her eyes for a long time. Then very seriously, she said, "I see big balls of color, like shaggy flowers. They're pink and red and turquoise. I see an island with palm trees and pink rocks. There's dolphins and mermaids swimming in the water around it." He'd been almost awed by her belief in this impossible vision. Then he was sad because she would never see what she wanted to see.

His memory floated back to his boyhood; he was walking down the middle of the 55 street at dusk, sweating lightly after a basketball game. There were crickets and the muted barks of dogs and the low, affirming mumble of people on their front porches. He felt securely held by the warm light and its sounds, he felt an exquisite blend of happiness and sorrow that life could contain this perfect moment, and sadness that he would soon arrive home, walk into bright light and be on his way into the next day, with its loud noise and alarming possibility. He resolved to hold this evening walk in his mind forever, to imprint all the sensations that occurred to him as he walked by the Oatlander's house in a permanent place, so that he could always take it out and look at it. He dimly recalled feeling that if he could successfully do that, he could stop time and hold it.

He knew he had to go home soon. He didn't want to talk about the article with Marsha, but the idea of sitting in the house with her and not talking about it was hard to bear. He imagined the conversation grinding into being, a future conversation with Kitty gestating within it. The conversation was a vast, complex machine like those that occasionally appeared in his dreams; if he could only pull the switch everything would be all right, but he felt too stupefied by the weight and complexity of the thing to do so. Besides, in this case, everything might not be all right. He put the magazine under his seat and started the car.

Marsha was in her armchair reading. She looked up and the expression on her face seemed like the result of internal conflict as complicated and strong as his own, but cross-pulled in different directions, uncomprehending of him and what he knew. In his mind he withdrew from her so quickly that for a moment the familiar room was fraught with the inexplicable horror of a banal nightmare. Then the ordinariness of the scene threw the extraordinary event of the day into relief and he felt so angry and bewildered he could've howled.

"Everything all right, Stew?" asked Marsha.

"No, nothing is all right. I'm a tired old man in a shitty world I don't want to be in. I go out there, it's like walking on knives. Everything is an attack, the ugliness, the cheapness, the rudeness, everything." He sensed her withdrawing from him into her own world of disgruntlement, her lips drawn together in that look of exasperated perseverance she'd gotten from her mother. Like Kitty, like everyone, she was leaving him. "I don't have a real daughter and I don't have a real wife who's here with me because she's too busy running around on some—"

"We've been through this before. We agreed I could—"

"That was different! That was when we had two cars!" His voice tore through his throat in a jagged whiplash and came out a cracked half-scream. "I don't have a car, remember? That means I'm stranded, all alone for hours and Norm Pisarro can just call me up and casually tell me that my lesbian daughter has just betrayed me in a national magazine and what do I think about that?" He wanted to punch the wall until his hand was bloody. He wanted Kitty to see the blood. Marsha's expression broke into soft open-mouthed consternation. The helplessness of it made his anger seem huge and terrible, then impotent and helpless itself. He sat down on the couch and instead of anger felt pain.

"What did Kitty do? What happened? What does Norm have—"

"She wrote an article in *Self* magazine about being a lesbian and her problems and something to do with me. I don't know, I could barely read the crap."

Marsha looked down at her nails.

He looked at her and saw the aged beauty of her ivory skin, sagging under the weight of her years and her cock-eyed bifocals, the emotional receptivity of her face, the dark down on her upper lip, the childish pearl buttons of her sweater, only the top button done.

"I'm surprised at Norm, that he would call you like that."

"Oh, who the hell knows what he thought." His heart was soothed and slowed by her words, even if they didn't address its real unhappiness.

"Here," she said, "let me rub your shoulders."

He allowed her to approach him and they sat sideways on the couch, his weight balanced on the edge by his awkwardly planted legs, she sitting primly on one hip with her legs tightly crossed. The discomfort of the position negated the practical value of the massage, but he welcomed her touch. Marsha had strong, intelligent hands that spoke to his muscles of deep safety and love and delight of physical life. In her effort, she leaned close and her sweatered breast touched him, releasing his tension almost against his will. Through half-closed eyes he observed her sneakers on the floor—he could not quite get over this phenomenon of adult women wearing what had been boys' shoes—in the dim light, one toe atop the other as though cuddling, their laces in pretty disorganization.

Poor Kitty. It hadn't really been so bad that she hadn't set the table on time. He 70 couldn't remember why he and Marsha had been so angry over the table. Unless it was Kitty's coldness, her always turning away, her sarcastic voice. But she was a teenager and that's what teenagers did. Well, it was too bad, but it couldn't be helped now.

He thought of his father. That was too bad too, and nobody was writing articles about that. There had been a distance between them too, so great and so absolute that the word "distance" seemed inadequate to describe it. But that was probably because he had only known his father when he was a very young child; if his father had lived longer, perhaps they would've become closer. He could recall his father's face clearly only at the breakfast table, where it appeared silent and still except for lip and jaw motions, comforting in its constancy. His father ate his oatmeal with one hand working the spoon, one elbow on the table, eyes down, sometimes his other hand holding a cold rag to his head, which always hurt with what seemed to be a noble pain, willingly taken on with his duties as a husband and father. He had loved to stare at the big face with its deep lines and long earlobes, its thin lips and loose, loopily chewing jaws. Its almost godlike stillness and expressionlessness filled him with admiration and reassurance, until one day, his father slowly looked up from his cereal, met his eyes and said, "Stop staring at me, you little shit."

In the other memories, his father was a large, heavy body with a vague oblong face. He saw him sleeping in the armchair in the living room, his large, hairy-knuckled hands grazing the floor. He saw him walking up the front walk with the quick, clipped steps that he always used coming home from work, the straight-backed choppy gait that gave the big body an awesome mechanicalness. His shirt was wet under the arms, his head down, the eyes abstracted but alert, as though keeping careful watch on the outside world in case something nasty came at him, while he attended to the more important business inside.

"The good parent in yourself."

What did the well-meaning idiots who thought of these phrases mean by them? When a father dies, he is gone, there is no tiny, smiling daddy who appears, waving happily, in a secret pocket in your chest. Some kinds of loss are absolute. And no amount of self-realization or self-expression will change that.

As if she heard him, Marsha urgently pressed her weight into her hands and ap- 75
plied all her strength to relaxing his muscles. Her sweat and scented deodorant filtered
through her sweater, which added its muted woolliness to her smell. "All righty!" She
rubbed his shoulders and briskly patted him. He reached back and touched her hand
in thanks.

Across from where they sat had once been a red chair, and in it had once sat Kitty,
gripping her face in her hand, her expression mottled by tears. "And if you ever try to
come back here I'm going to spit in your face. I don't care if I'm on my deathbed, I'll
still have the energy to spit in your face," he had said.

Marsha's hands lingered on him for a moment. Then she moved and sat away from
him on the couch. ●

Edwidge Danticat *(1969–)*

Night Talkers *2004*

He thought that the mountain would kill him, that he would never see the other
side. He had been walking for two hours when suddenly he felt a sharp pain in his
side. He tried some breathing exercises he remembered from medical shows on television, but it was hard to concentrate. All he could think of, besides the pain, was his
roommate, Michel, who'd had an emergency appendectomy a few weeks before in New
York. What if he was suddenly stricken with appendicitis, here on top of a mountain,
deep in the Haitian countryside, where the closest village seemed like a grain of sand
in the valley below?

Hugging his midsection, he left the narrow trail and took cover from the scorch-
ing midday sun under a tall, arched, wind-deformed tree. Avoiding a row of anthills,
he slid down onto his back over a patch of grainy pebbled soil and closed his eyes,
shutting out, along with the sapphire sky, the craggy hills that made up the rest of his
journey.

He was on his way to visit his aunt Estina, his father's older sister, whom he'd not
seen since he moved to New York ten years before. He had lost his parents to the dictatorship twenty-five years before that, when he was a boy, and his aunt Estina had
raised him in the capital. After he moved to New York, she returned to her home in
the mountains where she'd always taken him during school holidays. This was the first
time he was going to her village, as he'd come to think of it, without her. If she had
been with him, she would have made him start his journey earlier in the day. They
would have boarded a camion[1] at the bus depot in Port-au-Prince[2] before dawn and
started climbing the mountain at sunrise to avoid sunstroke at high noon. If she had
known he was coming, she would have hired him a mule and sent a child to meet
him halfway, a child who would know all the shortcuts to her village. She also would
have advised him to wear a sun hat and bring more than the two bottles of water he'd
consumed hours ago.

---

[1]**camion**: A bus.   [2]**Port-au-Prince**: Capital of Haiti.

But no, he'd wanted to surprise her; however, the only person he was surprising was himself, by getting lost and nearly passing out and possibly lying there long enough to draw a few mountain vultures to come pick his skeleton clean.

When he finally opened his eyes, the sun was beating down on his face in pretty, symmetrical designs. Filtered through the long, upturned branches of what he now recognized as a giant saguaro cactus, the sun rays had patterned themselves into hearts, starfishes, and circles looped around one another.

He reached over and touched the cactus's thick trunk, which felt like a needle-filled pincushion or a field of dry grass. The roots were close to the soil, a design that his aunt Estina had once told him would allow the plant to collect as much rainwater as possible. Further up along the spine, on the stem, was a tiny cobalt flower. He wanted to pluck it and carry it with him the rest of the way, but his aunt would scold him. Most cactus flowers bloomed only for a few short days, then withered and died. He should let the cactus enjoy its flower for this brief time, his aunt would say.

The pain in his midsection had subsided, so he decided to get up and continue walking. There were many paths to his aunt's house, and seeing the lone saguaro[3] had convinced him that he was on one of them.

He soon found himself entering a village, where a girl was pounding a pestle in a mortar, forming a small crater in the ground beneath the mortar as a group of younger children watched.

The girl stopped her pounding as soon as she saw him, causing the other children to turn their almost identical brown faces toward him.

"Bonjou, cousins," he said, remembering the childhood greeting his aunt had taught him. When he was a boy, in spite of the loss of his parents, he had thought himself part of a massive family, every child his cousin and every adult his aunt or uncle.

"Bonjou," the children replied.

"Ki jan w ye?" the oldest girl added, distinguishing herself. How are you?

"Could I have some water, please?" he said to her, determining that she was indeed the one in charge.

The girl turned her pestle over to the next-oldest child and ran into the limestone house as he dropped his backpack on the ground and collapsed on the front gallery. The ground felt chilly against his bare legs, as though he'd stumbled into a cold stream with his shorts and T-shirt on.

As one of the younger boys ran off behind the house, the other children settled down on the ground next to him, some of them reaching over and stroking his backpack.

The oldest girl came back with a glass in one hand and an earthen jar in the other. He watched as she poured the water, wondering if it, like her, was a mirage fabricated by his intense thirst. When she handed him the water, he drank it faster than it took her to pour him another glass, then another and another, until the earthen jar was clearly empty.

She asked if he wanted more.

"Non," he replied. "Mèsi." Thank you.

The girl went back into the house to put the earthen jar and glass away. The children were staring up at him, too coy to question him and too curious not to stare.

---

[3]**saguaro**: tall cactus.

When the girl returned, she went back to her spot behind the mortar and pestle and just stood there as though she no longer knew what to do.

An old man carrying a machete and a sisal[4] knapsack walked up to the bamboo gate that separated the road from the house. The young boy who had run off earlier was at his side.

"How are you, konpè?" the old man asked.

"Uncle," he said, "I was dying of thirst until your granddaughter here gave me some water to drink."

"My granddaughter?" The old man laughed. "She's my daughter. Do you think I look that old?"

Toothless, he did look old, with a grizzly white beard and a face full of folds and creases that seemed to map out every road he had traveled in his life.

The old man reached over and grabbed one of three wooden poles that held up the front of the house. He stood there for a while, saying nothing, catching his breath. After the children had brought him a calabash[5] filled with water—the glass and earthen jar were obviously reserved for strangers—and two chairs for him and the stranger, he lit his pipe, exhaled a fragrant cloud of fresh tobacco, and asked, "Where are you going, my son?"

"I'm going to see my aunt, Estina Estème," he replied. "She lives in Beau Jour."

The old man removed the pipe from his mouth and reached up to scratch his beard.

"Estina Estème? The same Estina Estème from Beau Jour?"

"The same," he said, growing hopeful that he was not too far from his aunt's house.

"You say she is your aunt?"

"She is," he replied. "You know her?"

"Know her?" the old man retorted. "There are no strangers in these mountains. My grandfather Nozial and her grandfather Dormēus were cousins. Who was your father?"

"My father was Maxo Jean Dorméus," he said.

"The one killed with his wife in that fire?" the old man asked. "They only had the one boy. Estina nearly died in that fire too. Only the boy came out whole."

"I am the boy," he said, an egg-sized lump growing in his throat. He hadn't expected to be talking about these things so soon. He had prepared himself for only one conversation about his parents' death, the one he would inevitably have with his aunt.

The children moved a few inches closer to him, their eyes beaming as though they were being treated to a frightening folktale in the middle of the day.

"Even after all these years," the old man said, "I'm still so sad for you. So you are that young man who used to come here with Estina, the one who went to New York some years back?"

The old man looked him up and down, as if searching for burn marks on his body, then ordered the children to retreat.

"Shoo," he commanded. "This is no talk for young ears."

---

[4]**sisal**: A fiber from the sisal hemp plant.   [5]**calabash**: gourd hollowed out to use as a container.

The children quickly vanished, the oldest girl resuming her work with the mortar   40
and pestle.

Rising from his chair, the old man said, "Come, I'll take you to Estina Estème."

Estina Estème lived in a valley between two lime-green mountains and a giant waterfall, which sprayed a fine mist over the banana grove that surrounded her one-room
house and the teal ten-place mausoleum that harbored the bones of many of her forebears. Her nephew recognized the house as soon as he saw it. It had not changed much,
the sloped tin roof and the wooden frame intact. His aunt's banana grove seemed to
have flourished, it was greener and denser than he remembered. Her garden was packed
with orange and avocado trees—a miracle, given the barren mountain range he'd just
traveled through.

When he entered his aunt's yard, he was greeted by a flock of hens and roosters that
scattered quickly, seeking shelter on top of the family mausoleum.

He rushed to the front porch, where an old faded skirt and blouse were drying on
the wooden railing. The door was open, so he ran into the house, leaving behind the
old man and a group of neighbors whom the old man had enticed into following them
by announcing as he passed their houses that he had with him Estina Estème's only
nephew.

In the small room was his aunt's cot, covered with a pale blue sheet. Nearby was a   45
calabash filled with water, within easy reach so she could drink from it at night without
leaving her bed. Under the cot was her porcelain chamber pot and baskets filled with a
few Sunday dresses, hats, and shoes.

The old man peeked in to ask, "She's not here?"

"No," he replied, "she's not."

He was growing annoyed with the old man, even though he would never have
found his aunt's house so quickly without his help.

When he walked out of the house, he found himself facing a dozen or so more
people gathered in his aunt's yard. He scanned the faces and recognized one or two, but
couldn't recall the names. Many in the group were nudging one another, whispering
while pointing at him. Others called out, "Dany, don't you know me anymore?"

He walked over and kissed the women, shook hands with the men, and patted the   50
children's heads.

"Please, where's my aunt?" he asked of the entire crowd.

"She'll soon be here," a woman replied. "We sent for her."

Once he knew his aunt was on her way, he did his best to appear interested in
catching up. Many in the crowd complained that once he got to New York, he forgot
about them, never sending the watch or necklace or radio he'd promised. Surprised
that they'd taken his youthful pledges so seriously, he offered some feeble excuses. "It's
not so easy to earn money in New York. . . . I thought you'd moved to the capital. . . .
I didn't know your address."

"Where would we have gone?" one of the men rebutted. "We were not so lucky as
you."

He was glad when he heard his aunt's voice, calling his name. The crowd parted   55
and she appeared, pudgy yet graceful in a drop-waist dress. Her face was round and
full, her skin silken and very black, her few wrinkles, in his estimation, more like
beauty marks than signs of old age. Two people were guiding her by the elbows. As they

were leading her to him, she pulled herself away and raised her hands in front of her, searching for him in the breeze. He had almost forgotten that she was blind, had been since the day of the fire that had taken his parents' lives.

The crowd moved back a few feet as he ran into her arms. She held him tightly, angling her head to kiss the side of his face.

"Dany, is it you?" She patted his back and shoulders to make sure.

"I brought him here for you," the old man said.

"Old Zo, why is it that you're always mixed up in everything?" she asked, joking.

"True to my name," the old man replied, "I'm a bone that fits every stew."   60

The crowd laughed.

"Let's go in the house," his aunt told him. "It's hot out here."

As they started for her front door, he took her hand and tried to guide her, but found himself an obstacle in her path and let go. Once they were inside, she felt her way to her cot and sat down on the edge.

"Sit with me, Da," she said. "You have made your old aunt a young woman again."

"How are you?" He sat down next to her. "Truly?"   65

"*Truly* fine," she said. "Did Popo tell you different?"

For years now, he'd been paying a boyhood friend in Port-au-Prince, Popo, to come and check on her once a month. He would send Popo money to buy her whatever she needed and Popo would in turn call him in New York to brief him on how she was doing.

"No," he said. "Popo didn't tell me anything."

"Then why did you come?" she asked. "I'm not unhappy to see you, but you just dropped out of the sky. There must be a reason." She felt for his face, found it, and kissed it for what seemed like the hundredth time. "Were you sent back?" she asked. "We have a few boys here in the village who have been sent back. Many don't even speak Creole anymore. They come here because this is the only place they have any family. There's one boy not far from here. I'll take you to visit him. You can speak to him, one American to another."

"You still go on your visits?" he asked.   70

"When they came to fetch me, I was with a girl in labor," she said.

"Still midwifing?"

"Helping the midwife," she replied. "You know I know every corner of these mountains. If a new tree grows, I learn where it is. Same with children. A baby's still born the same way it was when I had sight."

"I meant to come sooner," he said, watching her join and separate her fingers like tree branches brushing against each other. Both her hands had been burned during the fire that had followed the explosion at his parents' house, but over the years the burn marks had smoothed into her skin and were now barely visible.

"I knew that once the time was right you'd come back," she said. "But why didn't   75 you send word that you were on your way?"

"You're right," he said. "I didn't just drop out of the sky. I came because I want to tell you something."

"What is it, Da?" she asked, weaving and unweaving her fingers. "Are you finally getting married?"

"No," he said. "That's not it. I found him. I found him in New York, the man who killed Papa and Manman and took your sight."

Why the old man chose that exact moment to come through the door he would never know. Perhaps it was chance, serendipity, or maybe simply because the old man was a nosy pain in the ass. But just then Old Zo came in, pushing the mortar-and-pestle girl ahead of him. She was carrying a covered plate of food.

"We brought you something to refresh you," he told Dany.   80

His aunt seemed neither distressed nor irritated by the interruption. She could have sent Old Zo and the girl away, but she didn't. Instead she told them to put their offering on an old table in the corner. The girl quietly put the plate down and backed out of the room, avoiding Dany's eyes.

"I hope you're both hungry," the old man said, not moving from his spot. "Everyone is going to bring you something."

Clusters of food-bearing people streamed in and out of the house all afternoon. He and his aunt would sample each plate, then share the rest with the next visitor until everyone in the valley had tasted at least one of their neighbors' dishes.

By the time all the visitors had left and he and his aunt were alone together, it was dark and his aunt showed no interest in hearing what he had to say. Instead she offered him her cot, but he talked her into letting him have the sisal mat she'd spread out on the floor for herself.

She fell asleep much more quickly than he did. Middream, she laughed, paid com-   85
pliments, made promises, or gave warnings. "Listen, don't go too far. Come back soon. What a strong baby! I'll make you a dress. I'll make you coffee." Then she sat up in her cot to scold herself, "Estina, you are waking the boy," before drifting once again into the images in her head.

In the dark, listening to his aunt conduct entire conversations in her sleep, he realized that aside from blood, she and he shared nocturnal habits. They were both palannits, night talkers, people who wet their beds, not with urine but with words. He too spoke his dreams aloud in the night, to the point of sometimes jolting himself awake with the sound of his own voice. Usually he could remember only the very last words he spoke, but remained with a lingering sensation that he had been talking, laughing, and at times crying all night long.

His aunt was already awake by the time he got up the next morning. With help from Old Zo's daughter, who seemed to have been rented out to his aunt for the duration of his visit, she had already set up breakfast on the small table brought out to the front gallery from inside the house. His aunt seemed restless, almost anxious, as if she'd been waiting for him to rise for hours.

"Go wash yourself, Da," she said, handing him a towel. "I'll be waiting for you here."

Low shrubs covered in dew brushed against his ankles as he made his way down a trail toward the stream at the bottom of the fall. The water was freezing cold when he slipped in, but he welcomed the sensation of having almost every muscle in his body contract, as if to salute the dawn.

Had his father ever bathed in this stream? Had his parents soaked here together, in   90
this same spot, when they'd come to stay with his aunt? He had so little information and so few memories to draw on that every once in a while he would substitute moments from his own life in trying to re-create theirs. But lately what was taking up the most space in his mind was not the way his parents had lived but the way they had died.

A group of women were coming down the path toward the river with calabashes and plastic jugs balancing on top of their heads. They would bathe, then fill their containers further up, closer to the fall. He remembered spending hours as a boy watching the women bathe topless, their breasts flapping against their chests as they soaped and scrubbed themselves with mint and parsley sprigs, as if to eradicate every speck of night dust from their skin.

When he got back to his aunt's house, he had a visitor, a short, muscular boy with a restrained smile and an overly firm handshake. The boy's brawny arms were covered with tattoos from his elbows down to his wrists, his skin a canvas of Chinese characters, plus kings and queens from a card deck. One-Eyed Jack, Hector, Lancelot, Judith, Rachel, Argine, and Palas, they were all there in miniature, carved into his nut-brown skin in navy blue and red ink.

"I sent for Claude," his aunt announced. "He's the one I was telling you about, one of the boys who was sent back."

Claude was sitting next to his aunt, on the top step in front of the house, dipping his bread in the coffee Old Zo's daughter had just made.

"Claude understands Creole and is learning to speak bit by bit," his aunt said, "but he has no one to speak English to. I would like you to talk with him." 95

Claude was probably in his late teens, too young, it seemed, to have been expatriated twice, from both his native country and his adopted land. Dany sat down on the step next to Claude, and Old Zo's daughter handed him a cup of coffee and a piece of bread.

"How long have you been here?" he asked Claude.

"Too long, man," Claude replied, "but I guess it could be worse. I could be down in the city, in Port, eating crap and sleeping on the street. Everyone here's been really cool to me, especially your aunt. She's really taken me under her wing."

Claude flapped his heavily tattooed arms, as if to illustrate the word "wing."

"When I first got here," he continued, "I thought I'd get stoned. I mean, I thought 100 people would throw rocks at me, man. Not the other kind of stoned. I mean, coming out of New York, then being in prison in Port for three months because I had no place to go, then finally my moms, who didn't speak to me for the whole time I was locked up, came to Port and hooked me up with some family up here."

His aunt was leaning forward with both hands holding up her face, her white hair braided like a crown of gardenias around her head. She was listening to them speak, like someone trying to capture the indefinable essence of a great piece of music. Watching her face, the pleasure she was taking in the unfamiliar words made him want to talk even more, find something drawn-out to say, tell a story of some kind, even recite some poetry, if only he knew any.

"So you're getting by all right?" he asked Claude.

"It took a lot of getting used to, but I'm settling in," Claude replied. "I got a roof over my head and it's quiet as hell here. No trouble worth a damn to get into. It's cool that you've come back to see your aunt, man. Some of the folks around here told me she had someone back in New York. I had a feeling when she'd ask me to speak English for her."

Claude reached down and picked up a couple of pebbles from the ground. It seemed to Dany that he could easily crush them if he wanted to, pulverize them with his fingertips. But instead he took turns throwing them up in the air and catching them, like a one-handed juggler. "It's real big that you didn't forget her, that you didn't forget your folks," he went on. "I wish I'd stayed in touch more with my people, you know, then it wouldn't be so weird showing up here like I did. These people don't even know me, man. They've never seen my face before, not even in pictures. They still took me in, after everything I did, because my moms told them I was their blood. I look at them and I see nothing of me, man, blank, nada, but they look at me and they say he has so-and-so's nose and his grandmother's forehead, or some shit like that." One of Claude's pebbles fell on the ground, missing his hand. He did not bend down to pick it up, but threw the others after it. "It's like a puzzle, a weird-ass kind of puzzle, man," he said. "I'm the puzzle and these people are putting me back together, telling me things about myself and my family that I never knew or gave a fuck about. Man, if I'd run into these people back in Brooklyn, I'd have laughed my ass off at them. I would've called them backward-ass peasants. But here I am."

His aunt was engrossed, enthralled by Claude's speech, smiling at times while the   105
morning rays danced across her eyes, never penetrating her pupils. He was starting to think of his aunt's eyes as a strange kind of prism, one that consumed light rather than reflected it.

"I can't honestly say I love it here," Claude seemed to be wrapping up, "but it's worked out good for me. It saved my life. I'm at peace here, and my family seems to have made peace with me. I came around; I can honestly say I was reformed in prison. I would've been a better citizen than most if they hadn't deported me."

"You still have a chance," Dany said, not believing it himself. "You can do something with your life. Maybe you're back here for a reason, to make things better."

He was growing tired of Claude, tired of what he considered his lame excuses and an apparent lack of remorse for whatever it was he'd done.

"How long will you be staying?" Claude asked.

"A while," Dany said.   110

"Is there anything you want to do?" Claude asked. "I know the area pretty well now. I take lots of walks to clear my head. I could show you around."

"I know where things are," Dany said. "And if I don't remember, my aunt can—"

"It's just with her not being able to see—"

"She can see, in her own way."

"Cool, man. I was just trying to be helpful."   115

Even with the brusque way their conversation ended, Claude seemed happy as he left. He had gotten his chance to speak English and tell his entire life story in the process.

After Claude's departure, Old Zo's daughter came up and took the empty coffee cup from Dany's hand. She lingered in front of him for a minute, her palm accidentally brushing against his fingertips. At times, she seemed older than she looked. Maybe she was twenty, twenty-five, but she looked twelve. He wondered what her story was. Were those children he had seen in Old Zo's yard hers? Did she have a husband? Was he in the city? Dead?

She hesitated before stepping away, as though she gave too much thought to every move she made. When she finally walked away, Dany's aunt asked him, "Do you know why Claude was in prison?"

"He didn't say."

"Do you know what his people say?"   120

"What do his people say?"

"They say he killed his father."

That night, Dany dreamed that he was having the conversation he'd come to have with his aunt. They were sitting on the step where he and Claude had spoken. He began the conversation by recalling with his aunt the day his parents died.

He was six years old and his father was working as a gardener in Port-au-Prince. The night of the explosion, he had been at home with his parents and his aunt, who was visiting from Beau Jour, when they heard a loud crash outside. His father went out first, followed by his mother. Dany was about to go after them when he heard the shots. His aunt grabbed him and pinned him to the ground, but somehow he managed to wiggle out of her grasp.

Outside, most of the wooden porch was already on fire. The smoke was so dense he 125 could barely see his parents, his mother slumped over his father on the ground.

Behind him the front door was covered in flames. He ran out to the yard and called out for his aunt at the top of his lungs.

"Shut up now or I'll shoot you too!" someone was shouting from the street.

It was a large man with a face like a soccer ball and a widow's peak dipping into the middle of his forehead. The man was waving a gun at him as he opened his car door, and he only lowered the gun to drive away. His aunt then crawled out of the house and away from the porch, coughing the smoke out of her lungs. She was unable to see.

He dreamed his aunt saying, "Yes, this is how it happened, Da," then urging him to elaborate on what he'd begun to tell her before Old Zo and his daughter had walked into her house. "You said you saw that same man in New York, Da? Are you sure it was him?"

The man who had killed his parents was now a barber in New York. He had a wife 130 and a grown daughter, who visited often. Some guys from work had told him that a barber was renting a room in the basement of his house. When he went to the barbershop to ask about the room, he recognized the barber as the man who had waved the gun at him outside his parents' house.

"It's been so many years," the dream aunt said. "Are you sure he's the one?"

He took the empty room in the barber's basement. He couldn't sleep for months, spending his weekends in nightclubs to pass the time. He visited the barbershop regularly for haircuts, arriving early in the morning soon after he opened. He would sit and watch the barber, now a much thinner man, turn on his radio, then sweep the entire shop before lining up his tools and calling him to the chair. His heart would race as the barber draped a black cape over his chest, then sheared paths through his hair until barely a stubble was left on top of his head. All the while he would study the pictures on the walls, campaign posters for local elections, hairstyle samples that he never chose from, asking the barber only to "cut as much as you can."

The barber never made conversation, never said, "How do you like the basement?" He only asked in a soft voice that sounded nothing like the hoarse and angry voice that had threatened him so many years ago, "Would you like a shave?"

He never turned down the shaves, for he thought it would give the barber a chance to have a closer look at his face, to remember him. He always expected the barber's large hands to tremble, but it was his own body that quivered instead, his forehead and neck that became covered with sweat, melting the shaving cream on his chin, forcing the barber to offer him extra napkins and towels and warn him to stay still to avoid nicks and cuts.

Finally, two nights ago, when the barber's wife was away at a religious retreat— 135 he looked for such opportunities all the time and hadn't found one until then—he climbed the splintered steps to the first floor, then made his way with a flashlight to the barber's bedroom.

"What did you do?" the dream aunt asked.

He stood there and listened to the barber breathing. The barber was snoring, each round of snores beginning with a grunt and ending in a high-pitched moan. He lowered his face toward the barber's widow's peak, hoping he would wake him up and startle him to death. When he was a boy, he'd heard about political prisoners being choked in their sleep, their faces swelling, their eyes bulging out of their heads. He wanted to do the same thing now to the barber. Or maybe press a pillow down on his face. Or simply wake him up to ask him "Why?"

Looking down at the barber's face, which had shrunk so much over the years, he lost the desire to kill. It wasn't that he was afraid, for he was momentarily feeling bold, fearless. It wasn't pity, either. He was too angry to feel pity. It was something else, something less measurable. It was the dread of being wrong, of harming the wrong man, of making the wrong woman a widow and the wrong child an orphan. It was the realization that he would never know why—why one single person had been given the power to destroy his entire life.

He was trembling again. His whole body, it seemed, was soaked with sweat as he tiptoed out of the barber's room. Even when he was back in the basement calling about flights to Port-au-Prince, he couldn't shake the feeling that after all these years the barber might finally make good on his promise to shoot him, just as he had his parents.

Dany woke himself with the sound of his own voice reciting his story. His aunt was 140 awake too, he could make out her outline in the dark. It looked as though she was sitting up in her cot, pushing the chamber pot beneath her, to relieve herself.

"Da, were you dreaming about your parents?" She leaned over and replaced the chamber pot back under the bed. "You were calling their names."

"Was I?" He would have thought he was calling the barber.

"You were calling your parents," she said, "just this instant."

He was still back there, on the burning porch, hoping that his mother and father would rise and put out the fire. He was in the yard, watching the barber's car speed away and his aunt crawling off the porch, on her belly, like a blind snake. He was in that room in Brooklyn, with the barber, watching him sleep. Now his aunt's voice was just an echo of things he could no longer enjoy—his mother's voice, his father's laugh.

"I'm sorry I woke you," he said, wiping the sweat off his forehead with the backs 145 of his hands.

"I should have let you continue telling me what you came here to say." His aunt's voice seemed to be floating toward him in the dark. "It's like walking up these mountains and losing something precious halfway. For you, it would be no problem walking back to find it because you're still young and strong, but for me it would take a lot more time and effort."

He heard the cot squeak as she lay back down.

"Tante Estina," he said, lying back on the small sisal mat himself.

"Wi, Da," she replied.

"Were my parents in politics?" 150

"Oh, Da," she said, as if protesting the question.

"Please," he said.

"No more than any of us," she said.

"What do you mean?" he asked.

"They didn't do anything bad, Da," she said, "or anything at all. I didn't know all 155 my brother's secrets, but I think he was taken for somebody else."

"Who?" he asked.

"M pa konnen," she said.

He thought maybe she'd said a name, Lubin or Firmin.

"Who were they mistaken for?" he asked her again.

"M pa konnen," she repeated. "I don't know, Da. Maybe they were mistaken for 160
all of us. There's a belief that if you kill people, you can take their knowledge, become
everything they were. Maybe they wanted to take all that knowledge for themselves. I
don't know, Da. All I know is I'm very tired now. Let me sleep."

He decided to let her rest. They should have a chance to talk again. She went back
to sleep, whispering something he could not hear under her breath, then growing silent.
When he woke up the next morning, she was dead.

It was Old Zo's daughter who let out the first cry, announcing the death to the entire
valley. Sitting near the body, on the edge of his aunt's cot, Dany was doubled over with
an intense bellyache. Old Zo's daughter took over immediately, brewing him some tea
while waiting for their neighbors to arrive.

The tea did nothing for him. He wasn't expecting it to. Part of him was grateful for
the pain, for the physically agonizing diversion it provided him.

Soon after Old Zo's daughter's cry, a few of the village women started to arrive. It
was only then that he learned Old Zo's daughter's name, at least her nickname, Ti Fanm,
Little Woman, which the others kept shouting as they badgered her with questions.

"What happened, Ti Fanm?" 165

"Ti Fanm, did she die in her sleep?"

"Did she fall, Ti Fanm?"

"Ti Fanm, did she suffer?"

"Ti Fanm, she wasn't even sick."

"She was old," Ti Fanm said in a firm and mature voice. "It can happen like that." 170

They didn't bother asking him anything. He wouldn't have known how to answer
anyway. After he and his aunt had spoken in the middle of the night, he thought she
had fallen asleep. When he woke up in the morning, even later than he had the day before, she was still lying there, her eyes shut, her hands resting on her belly, her fingers
intertwined. He tried to find her pulse, but she had none. He lowered his face to her
nose and felt no breath; then he walked out of the house and found Ti Fanm, sitting on
the steps, waiting to cook their breakfast. The pain was already starting in his stomach.
Ti Fanm came in and performed her own investigation on his aunt, then let out that
cry, a cry as loud as any siren he had heard on the streets of New York.

His aunt's house was filled with people now, each of them taking turns examining
his aunt's body for signs of life, and when finding none immediately assigning themselves, and one another, tasks related to her burial. One group ran off to get purple
curtains, to hang shroudlike over the front door to show that this was a household in
mourning. Another group went off to fetch an unused washbasin to bathe the corpse.
Others were searching through the baskets beneath his aunt's cot for an appropriate
dress to change her into after her bath. Another went looking for a carpenter to build
her coffin.

The men assigned themselves to him and his pain.

"He's in shock," they said.

"Can't you see he's not able to speak?" 175

"He's not even looking at her. He's looking at the floor."

"He has a stomachache," Ti Fanm intercepted.

She brought him some salted coffee, which he drank in one gulp.

"He should lie down," one of the men said.

"But where?" another rebutted. "Not next to her." 180

"He must have known she was going to die." He heard Old Zo's voice rising above the others. "He came just in time. Blood calls blood. She made him come so he could see her before she died. It would have been sad if she'd died behind his back, especially given the way he lost his parents."

They were speaking about him as though he couldn't understand, as if he were solely an English speaker, like Claude. He wished that his stomach would stop hurting, that he could rise from the edge of the cot and take control of the situation, or at least participate in the preparations, but all he wanted to do was lie down next to his aunt, rest his head on her chest, and wrap his arms around her waist, the way he had done when he was a boy. He wanted to close his eyes until he could wake up from this unusual dream where everyone was able to speak except the two of them.

By midday, he felt well enough to join Old Zo and some of the men who were opening an empty slot in the family mausoleum. He was in less pain now, but was still uncomfortable and moved slower than the others.

Old Zo announced that a Protestant minister would be coming by the next morning to say a prayer during the burial. Old Zo had wanted to transport the body to a church in the next village for a full service, but Dany was sure that his aunt wouldn't have wanted to travel so far, only to return to her own yard to be buried.

"I've been told that the coffin's almost ready," Old Zo said. "She'll be able to rest 185 in it during the wake."

Ti Fanm and the other women were inside the house, bathing his aunt's body and changing her into a blue dress he'd sent her last Christmas through Popo. He had seen the dress in a store window on Nostrand Avenue and had chosen it for her, remembering that blue was her favorite color. The wrapping was still intact; she had never worn it.

Before he left the room he watched as Ti Fanm handed a pair of rusty scissors along with the dress to one of the oldest women, who proceeded to clip three small pieces from the inner lining. As the old woman "marked" the dress, the others moaned, some whispering and some shouting, "Estina, this is your final dress. Don't let anyone take it from you. Even if among the other dead there are some who are naked, this is your dress and yours alone. Don't give it away."

He'd heard his aunt talk about this ritual, this branding of the final clothes, but had never seen it done before. His parents' clothes had not been marked because they had been secretly and hastily buried. Now in his pocket he had three tiny pieces of cloth that had been removed from the lining of his aunt's last dress, and he would carry them with him forever, like some people carry locks of hair or fingernails.

He had always been perplexed by the mixture of jubilation and sorrow that was part of Beau Jour's wakes, by the fact that some of the participants played cards and dominoes while others served tea and wept. But what he most enjoyed was the time carved out for the mourners to tell stories about the deceased, singular tales of first or last encounters, which could make one either chuckle or weep.

The people of his aunt's village were telling such stories about her now. They told 190 of how she had once tried to make coffee and filtered dirt through her coffee pouch, how she had once delivered the village's only triplets, saving all three babies and the mother.

"In the city that kind of birthing might have required a serious operation," Old Zo said, "but we didn't need the city doctors. Estina knew what to do."

"Here's one she brought into the world," a man said, pushing a boy forward.

"Here's another," someone else said.

"She birthed me," a young man said. "Since my mother died, she's been like a mother to me, because she was the only other person present at my birth."

They told of how as a young woman his aunt had embroidered a trousseau that she carried everywhere with her, thinking it would attract a husband. They spoke of her ambition, of her wanting to be a baby seamstress, so she could make clothes for the very same children she was ushering into the world. If he could have managed it, he would have told her neighbors how she had treated her burns herself after the fire, with poultices and herbs. He'd have spoken of her sacrifices, of the fact that she had spent most of her life trying to keep him safe. He would have told of how he hadn't wanted to leave her, to go to New York, but she'd insisted that he go so he would be as far away as possible from the people who'd murdered his parents.

Claude arrived at the wake just as it was winding down, at a time when everyone was too tired to do anything but sit, stare, and moan, when through sleepy eyes the reason for the all-night gathering had become all too clear, when the purple shroud blowing from the doorway into the night breeze could no longer be ignored.

"I'm sorry, man," Claude said. "Your aunt was such good people. One of a kind. I'm truly sorry."

Claude moved forward, as if to hug Dany, his broad shoulders towering over Dany's head. Dany stepped back, cringing. Maybe it was what his aunt had told him, about Claude having killed his father, but he didn't want Claude to touch him.

Claude got the message and walked away, drifting toward a group of men who were nodding off at a table near the porch railing.

When he walked back inside the house, Dany found a few women sitting near the plain pine coffin, keeping watch over his aunt. He was still unable to look at her in the coffin for too long. He envied these women the ten years they'd spent with her while he was gone. He dragged his sisal mat, the one he'd been sleeping on these last two nights, to a corner, one as far away from the coffin as possible.

It could happen like that, Ti Fanm had said. A person his aunt's age could fall asleep talking and wake up dead. He wouldn't have believed it if he hadn't seen it for himself. Death was supposed to be either quick and furious or drawn out and dull, after a long illness. Maybe Old Zo was right. Blood calls blood. Perhaps she had summoned him here so he could at last witness a peaceful death and see how it was meant to be mourned. Perhaps the barber was not his parents' murderer after all, but just a phantom who'd shown up to escort him back here.

He could not fall asleep, not with the women keeping watch over his aunt's body being so close by. Not with Ti Fanm coming over every hour with a cup of tea, which was supposed to cure his bellyaches forever.

He didn't like her nickname, was uncomfortable using it. It felt too generic to him, as though she were one of many from a single mold, with no distinctive traits of her own.

"What's your name?" he asked when she brought him her latest brew.

She seemed baffled, as though she were thinking he might need a stronger infu- 205
sion, something to calm his nerves and a memory aid too.

"Ti Fanm," she replied.

"Non," he said. "Your true name, your full name."

"Denise Auguste," she said.

The women who were keeping watch over his aunt were listening to their conversation, cocking their heads ever so slightly in their direction.

"How old are you?" he asked. 210

"Twenty," she said.

"Thank you," he said.

"You're deserving," she said, using an old-fashioned way of acknowledging his
gratitude.

She was no longer avoiding his eyes, as though his grief and stomach ailment and
the fact that he'd asked her real name had rendered them equals.

He got up and walked outside, where many of his aunt's neighbors were sleeping on 215
mats on the porch. There was a full moon overhead and a calm in the air that he was
not expecting. In the distance, he could hear the waterfall, a sound that, once you got
used to it, you never paid much attention to. He walked over to the mausoleum, removed his shirt, and began to wipe it, starting at the base and working his way toward the flat top surface and the cross. It was clean already. The men had done a good
job removing the leaves, pebbles, and dust that had accumulated on it while they were
opening his aunt's slot, but he wanted to make sure it was spotless, that every piece of
debris that had fallen on it since was gone.

"Need help?" Claude asked from a few feet away.

He'd been sitting on the porch with some of the men.

Dany threw his dusty shirt on the ground, climbed on top of the mausoleum, and
sat down. His aunt's body would be placed in one of the higher slots, one of two not
yet taken.

"Excuse me," Dany said, "for earlier."

"I understand," Claude said. "I'd be a real asshole if I got pissed off at you for any- 220
thing you did or said to me at a time like this. You're in pain, man. I get that."

"I don't know if I'd call it pain," Dany said. "There's no word yet for it. No one has
thought of a word yet."

"I know, man," Claude said. "It's a real bitch."

In spite of his huge muscles and oversized tattoos, Claude seemed oddly defenseless, like a refugee lost at sea, or a child looking for his parents in a supermarket aisle.
Or maybe that's just how Dany wanted to see him, to make him seem more normal,
less frightening.

"I hear you killed your father," Dany said.

The words sounded less severe coming out of his mouth than they did rolling 225
around in his head. Claude pushed both his hands into his pants pockets and looked
off into the distance toward the banana groves.

"Can I sit?" he asked, turning his face back toward the mausoleum platform, where
Dany was sitting.

"I didn't mean to say it like that," Dany said. "It's not my business."

"Yes, I killed my old man," Claude said in the same abrupt tone that he used for everything else. "Everyone here knows that by now. I wish I could say it was an accident. I

wish I could say he was a bastard who beat the crap out of me and forced me to defend myself. I wish I could tell you I hated him, never loved him, didn't give a fuck about him at all. I was fourteen and strung out on shit. He came into my room and took the shit. It wasn't just my shit. It was shit I was hustling for someone else. I was really fucked up and wanted the shit back. I had a gun I was using to protect myself out on the street. I threatened him with it. He wouldn't give my shit back, so I shot him."

There was even less sorrow in Claude's voice than Dany had expected. Perhaps Claude too had never learned how to grieve or help others grieve. Maybe the death of a parent early in life, either by one's own hand or by others, eliminated that instinct in a person.

"I'm sorry," Dany said, feeling that someone should also think of a better word for their particular type of sorrow. 230

"Sorry?" Claude wiped a shadow of a tear from his face with a quick swipe of the back of his hand. "I'm the luckiest fucker alive. I've done something really bad that makes me want to live my life like a fucking angel now. If I hadn't been a minor, I'd have been locked up for the rest of my life. They might have even given me the chair. And if the prisons in Port had had more room, or if the police down there were worth a damn, I'd be in a small cell with a thousand people right now, not sitting here talking to you."

Claude threw his hands up in the air and, raising his voice, as if to call out to the stars slowly evaporating from the sky, shouted, "Even with everything I've done, with everything that's happened to me, I'm the luckiest fucker on this goddamned planet. Someone somewhere must be looking out for my ass."

It would be an hour or so now before Dany's aunt's burial at dawn. The moon was already fading, slipping away, on its way to someplace else. The only thing Dany could think to do for his aunt now was to keep Claude speaking, which wouldn't be so hard, since Claude was already one of them, a member of their tribe. Claude was a palannit, a night talker, one of those who spoke their nightmares out loud to themselves. Except Claude was even luckier than he realized, for he was able to speak his nightmares to himself as well as to others, in the nighttime as well as in the hours past dawn, when the moon had completely vanished from the sky. ●

Robyn Joy Leff *(1964–   )*

Burn Your Maps *2003*

Six days after Halloween my nine-year-old, Wes, is still dressing in the furry, puffed-out uniform of a Mongolian nomad. He goes to school in the bushy fake fez he ordered off the Internet, tromps across the light Portland snow in his bloated felt boots. What seemed impossibly clever at the end of October has by November grown a bit disconcerting. We threw the gap-toothed pumpkin out two days ago, and Wes merely yawned. But just try to touch his hat—say, to wash his hair—and he turns all claws and parental condemnations.

Wes's father, Connor, is more annoyed than troubled by this unexpected detour into Ulan Bator. Connor, who sells next-generation CAT- and PET-scan equipment to major medical centers, survives on his ability to make up other people's minds, to blunt dissent with reason.

At dinner he shouts at our son, one word at a time: "Who are you?"

"I'm a yak herder, sir."

"Who are you really, though?" 5

Wes considers the question carefully. "For now," he says, "you can call me Baltnai."

Connor refuses to call his son Baltnai. On the seventh day, at breakfast, we all sit in silence and glare: I at Connor, Connor at Wes, Wes at no one in particular. When Wes is in the bathroom, Connor seriously suggests that we stage a midnight raid, rip off the kid's costume while he's asleep, and toss it in the trash compactor. End of Mongolian story.

"A fledgling imagination is at stake here," I say. "We can't just crush it."

"I've got this weird stomach thing again," Connor says, tossing away his pumpernickel bagel. "Every morning."

"Connor, he's only nine. The developing brain is wacky." 10

"Wes is not going to be wacky."

I touch my hand to his shoulder. "What I'm saying is, he has a lot of good reasons."

Wes comes out of the bathroom dragging a huge ball of toilet paper, at least three quarters of the roll, wrapped into an amorphous blob and hitched to his wrist with mint-flavored floss.

"What in the world are you doing?" Connor asks.

"Now I have a flock," Wes says. "A little lamb." 15

"What about Ethel?" I worry all the time about my son's fading allegiance to our elderly dachshund, about his breaking her very fine heart.

"She's a dog. This is a lamb."

"You're not dragging that pile of crap to school," Connor says with a snort.

"It's not a pile of crap," Wes states, entirely cool. "And Dad, even in Mongolia sheep don't go to school."

In our usual routine, Connor drops Wes in front of Hawkins Elementary and me at the 20
equally dour-looking community center. Wes gets a kiss, but I don't.

"Why don't you ask one of your freaky child-psych friends," he says when I'm already halfway out of the car.

"Connor, you're making too big a deal. Do you know my brother swore he was Spider-Man for a month? One day he started up our garage and he actually thought his hands would stick. The fricking moron broke his leg, pissed off my dad, and ended the superhero summer."

"Lovely. Your brother. Alise, let me ask you something." Connor doesn't even turn off NPR. "You ever had any Mongolian students?"

"Probably. We cover the globe here in the Pacific Northwest."

"You think that has anything to do with it?" 25

"It's going to be my fault now—is that the concept?" I zip my jacket high over my throat.

"It's just a question," Connor says. "A line of inquiry."

"It was a National Geographic special, Con. That's what Wes says. Ask himself, Mr. Inquiry."

"That damned Discovery Channel," Connor says. "They act as if all information is equal."

"I think it's TBS," I say. 30

"He watches too much TV as it is," Connor says.

"Con, it's not like we let him watch *Wild Police Videos.*"

"Let's review this later," he says.

"Have a nice day," I say.

I teach English as a Second Language. My students come from Mongolia or Turkey or Laos, yet I rarely know it. They are the tired, the huddled, the oddly uniform masses who yearn for Oprah and Wolfgang Puck and Intel. They all wear Gap-ish clothing, even if it's secondhand or Kmart. They bring lunches that have nothing to do with where they come from—the Polish woman eats supermarket sushi, the Japanese teenager downs a burger, the Somali carries in boxes of Chinese takeout and snakes cold spicy noodles into his mouth with his equally serpentine fingers.

I used to love all this, used to get off on the very odor of the classroom—a volatile magic of knockoff perfumes, ethnic spices, and cheap wet leather. I could smell the hunger to fit in, to regenerate into fatter, tanner, more legend-worthy versions of themselves, and it aroused me intellectually. I wanted to feed that hunger, wanted to snake American customs and social niceties and the correct use of adjectives into their heads like so many cold spicy noodles. But that was before burnout set in, before I saw too many of my students get nowhere or get terminally frustrated or get deported, their well-taught English turned to spite.

This year, for the first time in a long while, I have a favorite. I actually find myself bouncing to class, pleased to sit authoritatively behind my desk waiting for Ismail to walk in, always with that loose neon-blue backpack bumping toward his high ass, always with the slightest, smoothest shift of the eyes, always catching my eyes with the very corner of his.

He is a Pakistani in his forties, short, and lean. He was an engineer in his former life—something to do with mines, I believe, though I fantasize that he is a bridge builder. Earlier in the quarter I asked my students to write a short essay titled "My Advice to New Immigrants Coming to the USA." I got a lot of funny answers—"There are many bad drivers." "Bring earplugs." "You must have some lucky." "Eat ketchup, yum."—but Ismail's actually stopped me in my tracks. He wrote,

> Throw out all maps. Rip them from your books. Rip them from your heart. Or they will break it. I guarantee. Toss all globes from the roof until you have plastic pieces. Burn any atlas. You can't understand them anyway. They are offensive, like fairy tales from another tribe. The lines make no sense and no longer make mountains. You have come to the land where no one looks back. Remember, don't look back. Don't look out the window. Don't dare turn your head. You could grow dizzy. You could fall down. Throw out all your maps. Burn them.

I asked him to stay after class the day I returned the papers. I underlined the A on his essay twice.

"Your essay was so poetic and so sad," I said. "Your written English is quite excellent."

"Yes, it is for crying," he said. "I am this year forty-five, but I am learning like an American boy. Every day I see MTV. Now I rap better than talk. You enjoy Snoop Doggy Dogg, teacher?"

I snorted. He wasn't the gloomy or downtrodden sort I'd expected. "I don't know, we're more into 'NSync at my house. Tell me, Ismail, what are you hoping to do here in America? Return to engineering?"

"No, not one chance. I want to have a coffee shop. Coffee makes all the world happy."

"Not me, actually. Burns my stomach."

He frowned. "For you, for you then, teacher, we have something very special. We have sweet milk, or mint tea, or a drink of almonds. No worries. We make you happy. We will. No doubts."

For some reason in that moment I believed him, and we became friends after that, talking after class about the vagaries of Portland's traffic laws, about the cultural accuracy of *The Godfather,* sometimes even about Connor and Wes. Ismail never talked about his own family, and I didn't push in that area. After all, he was a man who advocated throwing away all maps—and what were families if not sharp demarcations in the flesh?

But on this day, when all the others have shuffled from the room with their admittedly cushy assignment to write a New Year's party menu, I sit on the floor next to Ismail's folding chair and say, "I've never asked, but do you have children?"

"What do you mean with 'have'?" He smiles slyly. It is impossible to know if he is teasing, playing the coy student.

"Are you a father?"

"Of course," he answers. "But my children, they are not with me in my home. So I think I do not 'have' them, as you say."

"Oh," I say. "I'm sorry, then."

"That's no problem," he says. "But you. I think you look very bad. Unhappy."

"No sleep. My son is acting a little weird, and my husband is angry."

"Anger is for husbands," Ismail says with a shrug. "That is the way."

"I know, but this is different. We disagree about Wes. About how best to raise him. You understand?"

Ismail, perched above me in his chair, lowers a hand, seemingly toward my hair, and then lets it slide away. "In this country," he says, "I cannot imagine to be a father. Your problems, they are so—" I think he's going to say "ridiculous"—"decadent."

"Well, Wes wants to be a Mongolian."

"What do you mean by this?" Ismail is no less confused than I.

"He wears a little tunic and pretends he's from Inner Asia. I don't know why—something he saw on TV or read on the Internet. It struck him as, I don't know, a kind of home."

"Mongolia? Like, as in, Mongolia?"

"Yeah, Mongolia."

"Shitty Mongolia?" Ismail shouts. "Dirty, ugly, poor Mongolia?"

We both start to laugh, the kind of musical laughter that feeds on itself, until Ismail puts a long finger to his stilled top lip and settles himself deep into the impossibly flimsy-looking chair beneath him.

It always ends this way. No matter how Ismail and I begin our conversations, they always complete themselves just like this. We both shut up and just sit together. We don't look in each other's eyes. We don't touch. We just slump, staring into space, breathing lightly, together. At first I found it quite odd, disturbing, indefinite; but now I'm beginning to wonder if it isn't some previously undiscovered form of love.

Wes leads his toilet-paper sheep to the dinner table on night number seven. Connor makes strange faces at me, curling and crushing his lips.

"I met a neurosurgeon from the Ukraine today," he begins, spinning yet another tale of MD heroics for Wes's future benefit. "He was all of five-foot-one, ugly little guy, but they say he has magical hands. He can make precise movements of a millimeter or less. You know how big that is?"

"Has he been to Mongolia?" Wes asks.

"Didn't ask. He uses something called a gamma knife. To blast right through tumors. Is that cool or what?"

"Mongolia isn't that far from the Ukraine," Wes points out.

"How was it in Mongolia today?" I ask.

Connor clicks his tongue at me.

"It was cold," Wes says, "but then, it always is. It was windy, too. It's almost time for *dzud*."

"What's *dzud*?"

"It means the slow white death," Wes says.

"Jesus," Connor says. "Are you okay with this?" He is pointing his fork at me, a piece of spinach waving limply.

"Wes," I say, ignoring Connor, "what is it you like so much about being Mongolian?"

He squints at me. "Can I sleep on the stairs tonight?"

"Why, Wes?"

"Baltnai," he corrects. "Because that's where the Mongolians live. On the steps."

"That's s-t-e-p-p-e, you know. It means a plateau, like a high, flat piece of land."

"I know what it is, Mom," he says, in the fierce way of smart boys. "But since I'm here, I got to do what I can to be there."

"Name me one reason," Connor says before bed.

I could name him three, not the least of which is that we are on the verge of separation. On the verge, we say, as if it were a bungee-jumping platform, as if we could just step backward at any point and laugh at what we almost did. But I don't want to start that talk tonight, so I say, "Grandpa Firth."

"Absurd," Connor says. He is lying on top of the covers in his briefs, fingertips jammed just under the band, which incongruously screams JOE BOXER. He doesn't look as if he could sell firewood to an Eskimo. He looks like a little boy himself. He turns to the right and hugs the bottom of his naked ribs. I toss his half of the blanket over him. He shrinks to a lump beneath it.

"Slow white death," I say. "You think that's a coincidence?"

"Alise," he says.

Two months ago Connor's father died in our television room, surrounded by hospital equipment and cases of Ensure. Before that we saw Grandpa Firth maybe once every other year, guilted into occasional holidays. Wes barely knew him. Hell, I barely knew him. Connor used to say he didn't want him spreading his lies to Wes. I knew only that Connor was like a nine-year-old himself in the old man's presence.

"You don't see the connection?"

"Between my old man and Mongolia? You're just pushing any button you can find."

"No—I mean, maybe there's something there. About the incredible transience of human contact. Or something. I mean, I don't know what I mean."

"No shit, Sherlock."

He shuffles and moves in closer, his skin sharp with cold, igniting that lingering instinct to warm what's next to you. It's almost as though we could drop this whole pretense of so many years, wiggle into one another, make sweat-happy teenage love. Instead I slide the sole of a foot onto his icy calf.

"I think Grandpa Firth told Wes that he used to be a CIA agent in Singapore."

"I'd say it was the chemo talking, but that was him. In translation, he meant he once had too many drinks in a bar in Singapore."

"I'm just saying that Wes liked his stories. He's got that storytelling thing now. It's like an addiction." 95

"My dad was real good with addictions."

"It kills you that anyone could like Will Firth, doesn't it?"

Connor wriggles a little. "You're so wrong it's hilarious, Alise. That's the only thing around here I'm happy about. Wes was the only one who ever made my dad—" He clears his throat as if he's going to cry, but of course he doesn't. "But you know," he goes on, "maybe it's you, and the way you give him so much freedom. He lacks a sense of that one thing Will Firth gave me—boundaries."

I snort, but then suddenly I'm the one who's crying. Lightly, but still crying.

Boundaries. Borders. Maps. I retreat fully from Connor's body, drop my foot off 100 his warming leg, tuck into full fetal position. It could be worse, I suppose. I have a friend, a child psychologist as it happens, who keeps separate bedrooms with her artist husband. He has sleep issues, Krista tells me, and he can't fall asleep if someone else is in the room. So once every two weeks or so they come to each other to make love, but she tells me it's like visiting a stranger's bed: they are awkward and silly, and when they're done, they wipe up and return to their separate islands.

Separate islands, my brain sings near sleep. Then, before I drop off, I begin to wonder just how many young nomad boys in the heart of Inner Mongolia—*most?* *50 percent?*—are lying in their yurts right now humming to the Backstreet Boys on some Walkman a tourist left behind, fully engaged in the reverse of Wes's fantasy, certain they were meant to be born American.

I'm sure I have plenty of culpability. Unlike Connor, I don't consider myself that free a parent. Wes may watch some TV shows but not others. A 9:00 P.M. bed curfew is enforced. I've spanked him several times, but never with premeditation. My worst sin may be that I have spent so many nights on Wes's bedcovers, my favorite globe spinning under my fingers. Ismail's nightmare, our little game.

"It's all so close together," Wes said, giggling, in September, because that's what happens when all you do is trace your finger from one land to another: the very shape of distance falls away, becomes an impossible geometry.

"That's just an illusion," I said.

It was a huge error. People of my generation feel we have good excuses for our lone- 105 liness. But what about Wes? He flicks through dozens of search-engine hits for Mongolia, and learns that the world's millions are within his reach. So how can he know it's still okay to feel that no one on Earth can understand him, that no one can comfort him if he sits in his room, a micro-lump in the middle of Oregon in the middle of America in the middle of the world, losing it?

■ ■ ■

Connor doesn't speak at breakfast. He just clutches his slight paunch. "Are you going to call the doctor?" I ask.

"About Wes?"

"About your bellyache, Con. You see a million doctors every day."

"They're head guys. I need a GI man."

"Like GI Joe," Wes says.   110

"'GI' means 'gastrointestinal' in medical talk. Like guts."

"Ew, that's gross," Wes says. He rubs his nubby wool hat violently.

"Bet your hair really itches," Connor teases.

"When it does, I meditate. It's like praying, only you do it to Buddha"—Wes says *Butt-ah*—"instead of God."

"Where do you get this stuff?" Connor asks.   115

"I don't know. Encarta and stuff."

"You know, nomads don't really have the Internet or CD-ROMs."

"Duh, Dad. They don't need it, anyway."

"Why not?"

"Everything they need is right there. They don't have to order stuff from UPS." He   120
is unflinching, standing up to his father. Connor must secretly be proud.

"And where is everything you need, Wes?"

Wes shrugs and squints, making his features so small and pointed that I want to put him back to my breast, grow him all over again. "I don't know," he says. "Where?"

So much purpling blood pours into Connor's face that I am certain he is going to scream. But instead he shuffles quickly toward the bathroom, where he remains until we are all going to be late.

Thank God it is Friday. I'm not exactly looking forward to the weekend, with everything building to a head over Mongolia, but Friday is my student-conference day, when I meet with anyone who makes an appointment to see me. Ismail always makes an appointment.

My Friday slots are almost always filled. Most of my students come desperately   125
seeking help—but not with their English. Today a tall, balding Sri Lankan inquires whether I know any performing-arts agents. His son has an Asian-techno hip-hop band, and if the kid can just snag a record contract, they'll be able to afford a bigger apartment. I tell him to try a book at the library, which makes him belly laugh for a good long minute. At least I'm useful for something.

Sometimes I think I am a fraud, because I myself can barely speak a second language. I can squeak by with some Spanish and a tad of Farsi, and I have painstakingly memorized certain Chinese characters, but I lack that magical ability some annoying linguists have to slide simply between two tongues, easing back and forth between one way of speaking and another. I admit that I am attached to the shapes my tongue makes, to the comforting way my throat opens and closes day after day.

I didn't mean to do this kind of teaching. First I wanted to be a ballet dancer, but my hips bloomed round; then I wanted to be in the Peace Corps, but I met Con; then I fantasized about becoming one of those brilliant private school matrons who mold little geniuses into men and women of the world, only that was just silly. Of course, it was the same for Connor, who wanted to be a brain surgeon but kept failing chemistry. Nothing quite turns out in our lives. But that's what gets me: there might still be a very few remote places in the world—deepest Mongolia, maybe—where a person comes to live exactly the life expected, exactly as offered. I didn't. None of my students has. Wes, child of his times already, doesn't even have a shot at it. And yet somehow it thrills me—and maybe Wes as well—to know that such a thing remains imaginable.

By 3:00 P.M. Ismail should have arrived, but he is late. In his absence I draw thin, malformed yaks on my doodle pad and think about Connor's stomach. Mostly I imagine it's a problem of emptiness. He has lost twenty pounds in the past six months, has started taking a kickboxing class on the weekends, has stopped buying ice cream. I wonder if this has affected Wes at all—his father's slipping away, disappearing, reducing himself. I wonder also if Connor is doing it for me. Is that possible? Is it wicked to hope that his ill health is rooted in thwarted passion?

When Ismail arrives, he is breathless, agitated. He walks right across my office to the window, which looks on a parking lot overgrown with peeling, rusted Subarus.

"You think *you* have some trouble," he says. 130

"Is something wrong?"

"Lahore has called. A son may be arrested."

I think of going to him, but I know that's not what he wants. His skin—what I can see of it—seems to sag, pulled toward the window and away from me.

"Why?"

"It is not known. Maybe some drugs, maybe some politics, maybe, I don't know 135 how to say, crazy, crazy, crazy."

"Will you go there?"

At last he turns around, and I can see his face, which looks no different—as soft and yielding around the lips and jawline as ever, eyes still shifted to the side.

"I cannot, you see."

"Can I do anything? To help?"

He saunters back to my desk, forcing a slow grin. 140

"Let us discuss the *Austin Powers,*" he says. "I do not get this one."

"Ismail," I say, "I can't talk about *Austin Powers* right now."

"Why so?"

"You've upset me. You're upset. It's outrageous."

He sits on top of my desk, the way a boy with a crush would. "Everything is what 145 you say: outrageous," he says.

He's so damn glib it infuriates me. I scrunch up my doodle page, yaks and all, and throw it at him. Hard.

He glares at me, finally revealing a glint of hurt. Then he grabs a slim paperback off a shelf and hurls it at my shoulder.

I return fire with a catapulted rubber band. Ismail takes up chalk from my board and strafes my side of the desk with several pieces. One hits me square in the cheek, smarting immediately. I rise and move toward the bookshelves. A paper clip ricochets off my breast. Blindly I grab at a stapler. He takes my wrist. I take his waist.

We crumple into each other, almost hugging. But not. Our arms fall to our sides, the stapler falls to the floor, and we tremble. But we say nothing. We do not touch. We do not look in each other's eyes. We do nothing but stand there.

Finally he steps back and says, "Thank you. You are a good teacher." 150

"Ismail," I say.

"Shush—we cross no line," he says.

We cross no line, he says. Or at least we pretend not to. You choose your home and you burn all your maps, but that doesn't mean you might not find yourself lost and speechless where the lines fall away and the mountains blur and the silence feels better than years and years of conversation.

Ismail and I walk casually to the parking lot, talking of *Austin Powers*. "Okay," he says. "But why is this funny?"

"Analysis kills humor," I tell him. 155

"Why does joy break so easy? This is one shitty substance."

I see Connor in the Toyota, biting his nails. I imagine him winking at me. "Try *Groundhog Day*," I say. "And please, your son, if there's anything—"

He laughs, just like the Sri Lankan—the most frequent response to offers of assistance these days.

In the car Connor says, "That your Mongolian?"

"Oh, Lord. He's Pakistani, Con. He was wondering why *Austin Powers* is funny." 160

"Wrong person to ask."

"What does that mean?"

"Alise. Let's not. Hey, I talked to a doctor today."

"About your stomach?"

"About Wes. A neuropsychologist, top gun, Harvard, the whole schmeer. He says 165 we're in trouble. We have to nip it in the bud."

"Nip what? What about your stomach?"

"He says that obsessions can literally reshape the landscape of the brain. Neurons get stuck in little pathways, draw new maps. It can be permanent."

"Does he have kids?"

"What?"

"Does he have a nine-year-old son on whom he experiments?" 170

"I don't know, Alise. The point is he knows the brain."

"The brain is just a bit."

"The most important bit," Connor says.

I exhale into my fist. "So what does he say we should do?"

"Take the costume." 175

"Take the costume," I repeat.

"Throw it away, bury it, burn it. Free Wes of the compulsion."

"Oh, Connor, that seems needlessly cruel."

"Are you saying I'm cruel?"

"Not you, Con. The idea of it." 180

"Just like that, you know more than the experts, huh?"

"I know my son," I say.

"I know my son too," he says.

The Toyota pulls hard to a halt in front of the library, where Wes waits inside, no doubt reading up on Mongolia. I find myself unable to undo my seat belt. Connor doesn't take his off either. We just sit there a moment, strapped in, he tapping on the dashboard, I fiddling in the cavern of my handbag for something I cannot name.

Saturday afternoon, day nine, Wes walks Ethel the dachshund up and down my back. 185 This is a ritual we began about a year ago, when I started getting fierce cramps in my trapezius. Wes told me he'd read that Gypsies used to walk pet bears up and down people's backs for money. He has always been that kind of kid—digging up weird facts and anecdotes wherever he could find them. Nondiscriminatory about information, I guess, all of it worth paying out.

The truth is that a lot of his info is crap. But with Ethel he hit gold. She loves being the masseuse, and I can tell by the way her sweeping tail draws broad smiles up and down my torso. I, in turn, love the feeling of the paws pressing into my sinews, their animal motion so much more random and unflinching than a human rubdown. Just a walk on the back. Pure, motiveless attention.

I am grateful, as usual, after the mini-hound massage, so I brew Wes a pot of tea, since that is what he says Mongolians drink. Tea and lots of vodka, he says pointedly, but I roll my eyes, so we have Celestial Seasonings Cranberry Cove instead.

Connor is at his kickboxing class, which means that Wes and I can talk about his idea of building a *ger* in the back yard.

"It's like a tent, but it's round," he tells me. "I just need sticks and animal skins."

"Your father will have a cow," I say. 190

"A cow skin would be good," he says. I wish his smile would last longer.

"Wes," I say. "Are you mad at us?"

"At who?"

"At me. Or your father."

"Not really." He wrinkles his perfectly smooth face. "Not exactly." 195

"Are you still sad about Grandpa Firth?"

"It's okay, you know. I think he'll be reincarnated. Maybe as a Javanese rhino, but he'll be born in a zoo, because they're almost extinct."

"Wes," I say, "you've got to tell me the truth. Do you hate your life?"

"You're freaking, Mom."

"Really. You can tell me. Do you hate your life with us, with me and your dad, 200 here in America?"

He takes a sloppy sip of tea and then smiles sympathetically at me, as if I'm a hundred moves behind him. "Silly worrywart," he says. "You guys always think it's 'cause of you. But sometimes that's not true. Sometimes a person just wants to be a Mongolian, okay?"

"Okay," I say. "If that's what you feel like."

But it's not okay, because when Connor comes home from his kickboxing class, his forehead is taut and shiny, his cheeks are fat and ruddy, and he stands in the foyer huffing.

"Are you all right?" I ask.

"Stop it with the stomach." 205

"You seem a little off is all."

"I'm good. I had a great workout." He smells salty and smoky, like winter air.

"Good," I say. "Tougher and stronger every day."

"Are you mocking me?"

"Jesus," I say. "Can't I say something nice?" But I am thinking, *Mocking, the bane* 210 *of our times,* and *Why don't I ever feel the instinct for niceness first anymore?*

"Let's go to the movies," he says. "It's icy as hell out there, so it won't be crowded. We'll get hot cocoa and popcorn, be a real fam."

"Okay," I say. "Let's be a real fam."

He stands there for a second. "Where's Wes?"

"In his room. On the computer, I think."

"Wes," Connor calls. 215

"I think he's going to be okay," I say suddenly. I don't know why.

"Wes," Connor calls in a louder voice.

"He's really such a smart kid."

He appears in front of us, a smart kid in a tunic, felt boots, and a wool fez, dragging crumpled toilet paper.

"Do you want to go to the movies?" Connor asks. "That thing with Keanu 220 Reeves?"

"Really?"

"It's not R?" I interrupt.

"Really," Connor says.

"That's so radical, Dad. It's all CGI—computer animation, you know."

"Great. Why don't you put on your jeans and a sweater, and we'll go get the 225 tickets."

"What do you mean?" Wes asks.

"Connor, please," I say.

"I mean, just go change into something normal, and we'll go."

"I'm a nomad, Dad. Take it or leave it."

"I'll leave it," Connor says. The edge has taken over his entire voice, lopped off the 230 soft bits. "You can wear the hat, but the rest is history. That's my final deal."

"I'm going upstairs," Wes says, and shrugs. "I'll be on the modem. 'Night, Mommy."

"No computer," Connor says.

"What?"

"No computer until you take that stuff off."

"Mom?" Wes looks at me urgently. 235

"Con, let's just rent a video and have a nice night," I plead. I feel like an envoy to the Middle East, my centrist position as dangerous as any.

"I want to see a movie," Connor says.

"Well, I want to see a video," I say.

"Well, I want to have a loving wife and a sane son, but you can't always get what you want."

"Take that back." Wes jumps in his father's face now, looking fierce and ancient in 240 his little nomad uniform. If he had a scimitar, somebody would get hurt.

"Listen, Wes—" Connor says.

"No," Wes says. "I won't. Not till you take it back."

"Take what back?"

"You know what. Take it back."

Connor bends slightly at the waist, and his knees seem to make small circles. I can 245 see how badly he wants to take it back, how the very pull is shredding his innards. But he can't. He can't take it back because he has no more room to stash anything.

"Take it back, Dad," Wes says again in a hoarse whisper.

But his father, my husband, is paralyzed where he stands, in the foyer, at the base of the stairs. Wes pushes past us and races out the front door, whipping it shut on the beat of a sharp sniffle.

I want to say something to Connor, something he won't ever forget, but he looks so bereft that I can't imagine doing further damage. So I button my shirt to the neck and head out into air that has the essence of conscious razor blades, cutting you just for having the gall to breathe it in.

What I find first, on the Swenson's lawn, is a fur cap laced with strands of greasy hair. Then I see the tunic on a tree stump across Ashford Avenue, and the sash and the fat yellow boots near the bus stop. They have been violently strewn, ripped away. Bits of thread are everywhere in the snow, like shrapnel. I follow the line of them, contemplating just how cold it really is, just how long it would take a naked nine-year-old boy to develop hypothermia.

It's amazing how fast he can run in the snow, as if he was born to it. My lungs are 250 like meat in a freezer, all elasticity gone. I am forced to crawl at the bus-stop corner, because the sidewalks are far too icy to get traction with my sneakers.

I almost lose him, but near the school I find a footprint rarely seen in the snow—light as a snow angel, with individual little ellipses of toe shapes. They lead me to an anemic bush inside whose silver arms Wes is huddled, snorting snot into his trembling hands. His body is bright red, but it looks strong. As I get closer, I see that what I thought were white blisters on his belly are actually frail bubbles of water. He looks more inviolate than I ever imagined he could be.

I grab at him anyway, search his limbs for wounds, feel his baby-thin skin for aberrations. Then I catch his eyes, the whites expanding like the universe, and I see him searching for something in mine, for some reason or explanation or even just a nano-glimmer of hope that will set this all back to bearable. He begins to laugh.

"It's not funny," I protest. "You could die out here like this."

"I'm naked in the snow," he giggles. "I'm a naked Mongolian. My butt has ice on it."

This part is true. He is in shockingly dirty blue Gap briefs, which are soaked with snow and sagging off him. I start to laugh too. 255

We both look up and see Connor approaching, lurching and sliding and completely off-kilter. When he reaches us, his chest heaves; his breath steams out his mouth.

"What in the hell are you two—" he starts, but then he stops.

That's what gets me. He stops.

"Oh, Christ, you both must be freezing," he says. "Come here."

I scoop Wes in my arms, his wet bottom drenching my shirt. Connor has had the 260 presence of mind to take a wool coat on his way out, and now he wraps it around all three of us, making a kind of mobile cave. For the first time I realize that I am freezing, that my fingers, nipples, and nose are buzzing near numb. Inside the coat Wes and I cling to each other and to Connor's almost fiery warmth. We start walking home, three bodies moving through the night under one cloak, picking up pieces of Mongolia the whole way.

It's very quiet out. The night is so cold and so amply hushed that I can hear the constellations hum like halogen lamps. We say nothing to one another. When we get to the house, before we separate and rush for the door, for a single moment I almost speak. I almost say, "We're home."

But I cannot tell a lie. I don't know that we're home, because it's as if we don't belong anyplace on this Earth, in any country, or any house, or anywhere, really, but in this ragged circle of wool. ●

Robert Hayden *(1913–1980)*

Those Winter Sundays   *1962*

Sundays too my father got up early
and put his clothes on in the blueblack cold,
then with cracked hands that ached
from labor in the weekday weather made
banked fires blaze. No one ever thanked him.   5

I'd wake and hear the cold splintering, breaking.
When the rooms were warm, he'd call,

and slowly I would rise and dress,
fearing the chronic angers of that house,

Speaking indifferently to him,   10
who had driven out the cold
and polished my good shoes as well.
What did I know, what did I know
of love's austere and lonely offices?

bell hooks *(1955–)*

bone black   *1996*
Chapters 49, 50, and 51

49

They have never heard their mama and daddy fussing or fighting. They have heard
him be harsh, complain that the house should be cleaner, that he should not have
to come home from work to a house that is not cleaned just right. They know he gets
mad. When he gets mad about the house he begins to clean it himself to show that he
can do better. Although he never cooks he knows how. He would not be able to judge
her cooking if he did not cook himself. They are afraid of him when he is mad. They
go upstairs to get out of his way. He does not come upstairs. Taking care of children is
not a man's work. It does not concern him. He is not even interested—that is, unless
something goes wrong. Then he can show her that she is not very good at parenting.
They know they have a good mama, the best. Even though they fear him they are not
moved by his opinions. She tries to remember a time when she felt loved by him. She
remembers it as being the time when she was a baby girl, a small girl. She remembers
him taking her places, taking her to the world inhabited by black men, the barbershop,
the pool hall. He took his affections away from her abruptly. She never understood
why, only that they went and did not come back. She remembered trying to do whatever she could to bring them back, only they never came. Growing up she stopped trying. He mainly ignored her. She mainly tried to stay out of his way. In her own way she
grew to hate wanting his love and not being able to get it. She hated that part of herself
that kept wanting his love or even just his approval long after she could see that he was
never, never going to give it.

Out of nowhere he comes home from work angry. He reaches the porch yelling
and screaming at the woman inside—yelling that she is his wife, he can do with her
what he wants. They do not understand what is happening. He is pushing, hitting, telling her to shut up. She is pleading—crying. He does not want to hear, to listen. They
catch his angry words in their hands like lightning bugs—store them in a jar to sort
them out later. Words about other men, about phone calls, about how he had told
her. They do not know what he has told her. They have never heard them talk in an
angry way.

She thinks of all the nights she lies awake in her bed hearing the woman's voice,
her mother's voice, hearing his voice. She wonders if it is then that he is telling her

everything—warning her. Yelling, screaming, hitting: they stare at the red blood that trickles through the crying mouth. They cannot believe this pleading, crying woman, this woman who does not fight back, is the same person they know. The person they know is strong, gets things done, is a woman of ways and means, a woman of action. They do not know her still, paralyzed, waiting for the next blow, pleading. They do not know their mama afraid. Even if she does not hit back they want her to run, to run and to not stop running. She wants her to hit him with the table light, the ashtray, the one near her hand. She does not want to see her like this, not fighting back. He notices them, long enough to tell them to get out, go upstairs. She refuses to move. She cannot move. She cannot leave her mama alone. When he says What are you staring at, do you want some, too? she is afraid enough to move. She will not take her orders from him. She asks the woman if it is right to leave her alone. The woman—her mother—nods her head yes. She still stands still. It is his movement in her direction that sends her up the stairs. She cannot believe all her sisters and her brother are not taking a stand, that they go to sleep. She cannot bear their betrayal. When the father is not looking she creeps down the steps. She wants the woman to know that she is not alone. She wants to bear witness.

They say she is near death, that we must go and see her because it may be the last time. I will not go. I have my own ideas about death. I see her all the time. I see her as she moves about the house doing things, cooking, cleaning, fussing. I refuse to go. I cannot tell them why, that I do not want to have the last sight of her be there in the white hospital bed, surrounded by strangers and the smell of death. She does not die. She comes home angry, not wanting to see the uncaring daughter, the one who would not even come to say good-bye. She is in control. She is not yet ready to love. She does not understand. Upstairs in my hiding place I cry. They tell her she is upstairs crying and will not stop. She sends me orders to stop crying right this minute, that I have nothing to cry about, that she should be crying to have such a terrible daughter. When I go to her, sitting on the bed, with my longing and my tears she knows that she breaks my heart a little. She thinks I break her heart a little. She cannot know the joy we feel that she is home, alive.

50

All that she does not understand about marriage, about men and women, is explained ₅ to her one night. In her dark place on the stairs she is seeing over and over again the still body of the woman pleading, crying, the moving body of the man angry, yelling. She sees that the man has a gun. She hears him tell the woman that he will kill her. She sits in her place on the stair and demands to know of herself is she able to come to the rescue, is she willing to fight, is she ready to die. Her body shakes with the answers. She is fighting back the tears. When he leaves the room she comes to ask the woman if she is all right, if there is anything she can do. The woman's voice is full of tenderness and hurt. She is in her role as mother. She tells her daughter to go upstairs and go to sleep, that everything will be all right. The daughter does not believe her. Her eyes are pleading. She does not want to be told to go. She hovers in the shadows. When he returns he tells her that he has told her to get her ass upstairs. She does not look at him. He turns to the woman, tells her to leave, tells her to take the daughter with her.

The woman does not protest. She moves like a robot, hurriedly throwing things into suitcases, boxes. She says nothing to the man. He is still screaming, muttering.

When she tries to say to him he is wrong, so wrong, he is more angry, threatening. All the neat drawers are emptied out on the bed, all the precious belongings that can be carried, stuffed, are to be taken. There is sorrow in every gesture, sorrow and pain— like a dust collecting on everything, so thick she can gather it in her hands. She is seeing that the man owns everything, that the woman has only her clothes, her shoes, and other personal belongings. She is seeing that the woman can be told to go, can be sent away in the silent, long hours of the night. She is hearing in her head the man's threats to kill. She can feel the cool metal as if it is resting against her cheek. She can hear the click, the blast. She can see the woman's body falling. No, it is not her body, it is the body of love. She witnesses the death of love. If love were alive she believes it would stop everything. It would steady the man's voice, calm his rage. Love would take the woman's hand, caress her cheek and with a clean handkerchief wipe her eyes. The gun is pointed at love. He lays it on the table. He wants his wife to finish her packing, to go.

She is again in her role as mother. She tells the daughter that she does not have to flee in the middle of the night, that it is not her fight. The daughter is silent, staring into the woman's eyes. She is looking for the bright lights, the care and adoration she has shown the man. The eyes are dark with grief, swollen. She feels that a fire inside the woman is dying out, that she is cold. She is sure the woman will freeze to death if she goes out into the night alone. She takes her hand, ready to go with her. Yet she hopes there will be no going. She hopes when the mother's brother comes he will be strong enough to take love's body and give it, mouth-to-mouth, the life it has lost. She hopes he will talk to the man, guide him. When he finally comes, her mother's favorite brother, she cannot believe the calm way he lifts suitcase, box, sack, carries them to the car without question. She cannot bear his silent agreement that the man is right, that he has done what men are able to do. She cannot take the bits and pieces of her mother's heart and put them together again.

51

I am always fighting with mama. Everything has come between us. She no longer stands between me and all that would hurt me. She is hurting me. This is my dream of her—that she will stand between me and all that hurts me, that she will protect me at all cost. It is only a dream. In some way I understand that it has to do with marriage, that to be the wife to the husband she must be willing to sacrifice even her daughters for his good. For the mother it is not simple. She is always torn. She works hard to fulfill his needs, our needs. When they are not the same she must maneuver, manipulate, choose. She has chosen. She has decided in his favor. She is a religious woman. She has been told that a man should obey god, that a woman should obey man, that children should obey their fathers and mothers, particularly their mothers. I will not obey.

She says that she punishes me for my own good. I do not know what it is I have done this time. I know that she is ready with her switches, that I am to stand still while she lashes out again and again. In my mind there is the memory of a woman sitting still while she is being hit, punished. In my mind I am remembering how much I want that woman to fight back. Before I can think clearly my hands reach out, grab the switches, are raised as if to hit her back. For a moment she is stunned, unbelieving. She is shocked. She tells me that I must never *ever* as long as I live raise my hand against my mother. I tell her I do not have a mother. She is even more shocked. Enraged, she lashes out again. This time I am still. This time I cry. I see the hurt in her eyes when I say I do not have a mother. I am ready to be punished. My desire was to stop the pain, not to hurt. I am ashamed and torn. I do not want to stand still and be punished but I never want to hurt mama. It is better to hurt than to cause her pain. She warns me that she will tell daddy when he comes home, that I will be punished again. I cannot understand her acts of betrayal. I cannot understand that she must be against me to be for him. He and I are strangers. Deep in the night we parted from one another, knowing that nothing would ever be the same. He did not say good-bye. I did not look him in the face. Now we avoid one another. He speaks to me through her.

Although they act as if everything between them is the same, that life is as it was. 10 It is only a game. They pretend. There is no pain in the pretense. Everything is hidden. Secrets find a way out in sleep. My sisters say to mama She cries in her sleep, calls out. In her sleep is the place of remembering. It is the place where there is no pretense. She is dreaming always the same dream. A movie is showing. It is a tragic story of jealousy and lost love. It is called *Crime of Passion*. In the movie a man has killed his wife and daughter. He has killed his wife because he believes she has lovers. He killed the daughter because she witnesses the death of the wife. When they go to trial all the remaining family come to speak on behalf of the man. At his job he is calm and quiet, a hardworking man, a family man. Neighbors come to testify that the dead woman was young and restless, that the daughter was wild and rebellious. Everyone sympathizes with the man. His story is so sad that they begin to weep. All their handkerchiefs are clean and white. Like flags waving, they are a signal of peace, of surrender. They are a gesture to the man that he can go on with life. ●

Explorations of the Text

1. Examine the relationships between parents and children. What are the children's roles in the families?

2. Discuss the failure to communicate—what Leff in "Burn Your Maps" describes as the "transience of human contact"—portrayed in these works. Analyze the silences in family life.

3. What are the secrets of the main characters? How do the protagonists live on "separate islands" (as suggested in Leff's "Burn Your Maps")? What do the protagonists yearn for? What losses do they experience? Do the children absorb the anxieties, insecurities, suppressed emotions, dreams, and desires of their parents? Do family secrets damage the children?

4. How would each work in this cluster change if the point of view were different? (Example: What if the third person narrative in hooks's work were changed to first person?)

5. Explore the theme of the dysfunctional family in these works. How do these works redefine "home"?

6. How does setting in these works serve as a symbol of family life?

7. How do parental power and control shape the destinies of children?

The Reading/Writing Connection

1. Freewrite: Respond to this line from "Burn Your Maps": "Throw out all maps. Rip them out from your books. Rip them from your heart." Does this statement convey truths about the dynamics of family relationships, of other intimate relationships (e.g., friendship or love relationships)? Argue pro or con.

2. Have your parents disappointed you? When did you realize that your parents were not perfect human beings? Answer either or both questions in a journal entry.

3. Write a letter to one of your parents expressing your feelings concerning an issue or an experience about which you have kept silent, or say something (positive or negative) that you always have wanted to express to them.

4. Create a monologue or a journal entry for one of the characters that reveals the character's inner life.

5. Create a new title for one of the works, and then justify your choice. As an alternative, create an artwork or collage that represents your response to the work, and then explain what it signifies about the work.

Ideas for Writing

1. How do the secrets or obsessions of parents have consequences for their children? How do the secrets shape the children's destinies? Once the secrets are revealed, what are the consequences? Analyze this thematic motif in works in this cluster.

2. In the excerpt from *bone black*, hooks observes that "the silent agreement that the man is right" is operative in the marriage of her parents. How are the dynamics of the marital relationships portrayed in the works in this cluster governed by social conditioning? Create a feminist critique of one of the marital relationships. As an alternative, based on your observations and experience, do you believe the roles in marriage have changed? Present your views on this issue.

3. **Write an Argument:** Just as parents have power over children, children have the ability to hurt their parents. In "Tiny, Smiling Daddy," Kitty publishes an article about her relationship with her father, knowing that "he dreaded exposure of any kind." In "bone black," the protagonist refuses to take an order from her father. In "Night Talkers," Claude kills his father. Consider the power in the relationships between parents and children portrayed in this cluster of works and create an argument stating one of the following:

   a) Children have more power over their parents than is generally recognized.

   b) Parental control of and power over children is stronger than children's over parents.

   c) There is a dynamic relationship within families in which children and parents negotiate for power.

4. Interpret this quotation from Paul Simon's song "The Sound of Silence": "Silence like a cancer grows." Connect it with the conflicts of several protagonists in these works.

FICTION

Tillie Olsen *(1913–2007)*

I Stand Here Ironing *1953*

I stand here ironing, and what you asked me moves tormented back and forth with the iron.

"I wish you would manage the time to come and talk with me about your daughter. I'm sure you can help me understand her. She's a youngster who needs help and whom I'm deeply interested in helping."

"Who needs help." . . . Even if I came, what good would it do? You think because I am her mother I have a key, or that in some way you could use me as a key? She has lived for nineteen years. There is all that life that has happened outside of me, beyond me.

And when is there time to remember, to sift, to weigh, to estimate, to total? I will start and there will be an interruption and I will have to gather it all together again. Or I will become engulfed with all I did or did not do, with what should have been and what cannot be helped.

She was a beautiful baby. The first and only one of our five that was beautiful at birth. You do not guess how new and uneasy her tenancy in her now-loveliness. You did not know her all those years she was thought homely, or see her poring over her baby pictures, making me tell her over and over how beautiful she had been—and would be, I would tell her—and was now, to the seeing eye. But the seeing eyes were few or nonexistent. Including mine.

I nursed her. They feel that's important nowadays. I nursed all the children, but with her, with all the fierce rigidity of first motherhood, I did like the books then said. Though her cries battered me to trembling and my breasts ached with swollenness, I waited till the clock decreed.

Why do I put that first? I do not even know if it matters, or if it explains anything.

She was a beautiful baby. She blew shining bubbles of sound. She loved motion, loved light, loved color and music and textures. She would lie on the floor in her blue overalls patting the surface so hard in ecstasy her hands and feet would blur. She was a miracle to me, but when she was eight months old I had to leave her daytimes with the woman downstairs to whom she was no miracle at all, for I worked or looked for work and for Emily's father, who "could no longer endure" (he wrote in his good-bye note) "sharing want with us."

I was nineteen. It was the pre-relief, pre-WPA[1] world of the Depression. I would start running as soon as I got off the streetcar, running up the stairs, the place smelling sour, and awake or asleep to startle awake, when she saw me she would break into a clogged weeping that could not be comforted, a weeping I can hear yet.

---

[1] **WPA**: Works Progress Administration: a federal agency that administered public works to relieve unemployment from 1935 to 1943.

After a while I found a job hashing at night so I could be with her days, and it was 10 better. But it came to where I had to bring her to his family and leave her.

It took a long time to raise the money for her fare back. Then she got chicken pox and I had to wait longer. When she finally came, I hardly knew her, walking quick and nervous like her father, looking like her father, thin, and dressed in a shoddy red that yellowed her skin and glared at the pockmarks. All the baby loveliness gone.

She was two. Old enough for nursery school they said, and I did not know then what I know now—the fatigue of the long day, and the lacerations of group life in the kinds of nurseries that are only parking places for children.

Except that it would have made no difference if I had known. It was the only place there was. It was the only way we could be together, the only way I could hold a job.

And even without knowing, I knew. I knew the teacher that was evil because all these years it has curdled into my memory, the little boy hunched in the corner, her rasp, "why aren't you outside, because Alvin hits you? that's no reason, go out, scaredy." I knew Emily hated it even if she did not clutch and implore "don't go Mommy" like the other children, mornings.

She always had a reason why we should stay home. Momma, you look sick. Momma, 15 I feel sick. Momma, the teachers aren't there today, they're sick. Momma, we can't go, there was a fire there last night. Momma, it's a holiday today, no school, they told me.

But never a direct protest, never rebellion. I think of our others in their three-, four-year-oldness—the explosions, the tempers, the denunciations, the demands—and I feel suddenly ill. I put the iron down. What in me demanded that goodness in her? And what was the cost, the cost to her of such goodness?

The old man living in the back once said in his gentle way: "You should smile at Emily more when you look at her." What *was* in my face when I looked at her? I loved her. There were all the acts of love.

It was only with the others I remembered what he said, and it was the face of joy, and not of care or tightness or worry I turned to them—too late for Emily. She does not smile easily, let alone almost always as her brothers and sisters do. Her face is closed and sombre, but when she wants, how fluid. You must have seen it in her pantomimes, you spoke of her rare gift for comedy on the stage that rouses a laughter out of the audience so dear they applaud and applaud and do not want to let her go.

Where does it come from, that comedy? There was none of it in her when she came back to me that second time, after I had had to send her away again. She had a new daddy now to learn to love, and I think perhaps it was a better time.

Except when we left her alone nights, telling ourselves she was old enough. 20

"Can't you go some other time, Mommy, like tomorrow?" she would ask. "Will it be just a little while you'll be gone? Do you promise?"

The time we came back, the front door open, the clock on the floor in the hall. She rigid awake. "It wasn't just a little while. I didn't cry. Three times I called you, just three times, and then I ran downstairs to open the door so you could come faster. The clock talked loud. I threw it away, it scared me what it talked."

She said the clock talked loud again that night I went to the hospital to have Susan. She was delirious with the fever that comes before red measles, but she was fully conscious all the week I was gone and the week after we were home when she could not come near the new baby or me.

She did not get well. She stayed skeleton thin, not wanting to eat, and night after night she had nightmares. She would call for me, and I would rouse from exhaustion to sleepily call back: "You're all right, darling, go to sleep, it's just a dream," and if she still called, in a sterner voice, "now go to sleep, Emily, there's nothing to hurt you." Twice, only twice, when I had to get up for Susan anyhow, I went in to sit with her.

Now when it is too late (as if she would let me hold and comfort her like I do the others) I get up and go to her at once at her moan or restless stirring. "Are you awake, Emily? Can I get you something?" And the answer is always the same: "No, I'm all right, go back to sleep, Mother." 25

They persuaded me at the clinic to send her away to a convalescent home in the country where "she can have the kind of food and care you can't manage for her, and you'll be free to concentrate on the new baby." They still send children to that place. I see pictures on the society page of sleek young women planning affairs to raise money for it, or dancing at the affairs, or decorating Easter eggs or filling Christmas stockings for the children.

They never have a picture of the children so I do not know if the girls still wear those gigantic red bows and the ravaged looks on the every other Sunday when parents can come to visit "unless otherwise notified"—as we were notified the first six weeks.

Oh it is a handsome place, green lawns and tall trees and fluted flower beds. High up on the balconies of each cottage the children stand, the girls in their red bows and white dresses, the boys in white suits and giant red ties. The parents stand below shrieking up to be heard, and the children shriek down to be heard, and between them the invisible wall "Not to Be Contaminated by Parental Germs or Physical Affection."

There was a tiny girl who always stood hand in hand with Emily. Her parents never came. One visit she was gone. "They moved her to Rose Cottage," Emily shouted in explanation. "They don't like you to love anybody here."

She wrote once a week, the labored writing of a seven-year-old. "I am fine. How is the baby. If I write my leter nicly I will have a star. Love" There never was a star. We wrote every other day, letters she could never hold or keep but only hear read—once. "We simply do not have room for children to keep any personal possessions," they patiently explained when we pieced one Sunday's shrieking together to plead how much it would mean to Emily, who loved so to keep things, to be allowed to keep her letters and cards. 30

Each visit she looked frailer. "She isn't eating," they told us.

(They had runny eggs for breakfast or mush with lumps, Emily said later, I'd hold it in my mouth and not swallow. Nothing ever tasted good, just when they had chicken.)

It took us eight months to get her released home, and only the fact that she gained back so little of her seven lost pounds convinced the social worker.

I used to try to hold and love her after she came back, but her body would stay stiff, and after a while she'd push away. She ate little. Food sickened her, and I think much of life too. Oh she had physical lightness and brightness, twinkling by on skates, bouncing like a ball up and down up and down over the jump rope, skimming over the hill; but these were momentary.

She fretted about her appearance, thin and dark and foreign-looking at a time when every little girl was supposed to look or thought she should look a chubby blonde replica of Shirley Temple. The doorbell sometimes rang for her, but no one seemed to come and play in the house or be a best friend. Maybe because we moved so much. 35

There was a boy she loved painfully through two school semesters. Months later she told me how she had taken pennies from my purse to buy him candy. "Licorice was his favorite and I brought him some every day, but he still liked Jennifer better'n me. Why, Mommy?" The kind of question for which there is no answer.

School was a worry to her. She was not glib or quick in a world where glibness and quickness were easily confused with ability to learn. To her overworked and exasperated teachers she was an overconscientious "slow learner" who kept trying to catch up and was absent entirely too often.

I let her be absent, though sometimes the illness was imaginary. How different from my now-strictness about attendance with the others. I wasn't working. We had a new baby, I was home anyhow. Sometimes, after Susan grew old enough, I would keep her home from school, too, to have them all together.

Mostly Emily had asthma, and her breathing, harsh and labored, would fill the house with a curiously tranquil sound. I would bring the two old dresser mirrors and her boxes of collections to her bed. She would select beads and single earrings, bottle tops and shells, dried flowers and pebbles, old postcards and scraps, all sorts of oddments; then she and Susan would play Kingdom, setting up landscapes and furniture, peopling them with action.

Those were the only times of peaceful companionship between her and Susan. I   40 have edged away from it, that poisonous feeling between them, that terrible balancing of hurts and needs I had to do between the two, and did so badly, those earlier years.

Oh there are conflicts between the others too, each one human, needing, demanding, hurting, taking—but only between Emily and Susan, no, Emily toward Susan that corroding resentment. It seems so obvious on the surface, yet it is not obvious. Susan, the second child, Susan, golden- and curly-haired and chubby, quick and articulate and assured, everything in appearance and manner Emily was not; Susan, not able to resist Emily's precious things, losing or sometimes clumsily breaking them; Susan telling jokes and riddles to company for applause while Emily sat silent (to say to me later: that was *my* riddle, Mother, I told it to Susan); Susan, who for all the five years' difference in age was just a year behind Emily in developing physically.

I am glad for that slow physical development that widened the difference between her and her contemporaries, though she suffered over it. She was too vulnerable for that terrible world of youthful competition, of preening and parading, of constant measuring of yourself against every other, of envy, "If I had that copper hair," "If I had that skin. . . ." She tormented herself enough about not looking like the others, there was enough of the unsureness, the having to be conscious of words before you speak, the constant caring—what are they thinking of me? without having it all magnified by the merciless physical drives.

Ronnie is calling. He is wet and I change him. It is rare there is such a cry now. That time of motherhood is almost behind me when the ear is not one's own but must always be racked and listening for the child cry, the child call. We sit for a while and I hold him, looking out over the city spread in charcoal with its soft aisles of light. *"Shoogily,"* he breathes and curls closer. I carry him back to bed, asleep. *Shoogily.* A funny word, a family word, inherited from Emily, invented by her to say: *comfort.*

In this and other ways she leaves her seal, I say aloud. And startle at my saying it. What do I mean? What did I start to gather together, to try and make coherent? I was at the terrible, growing years. War years. I do not remember them well. I was working, there were four smaller ones now, there was not time for her. She had to help be a mother, and housekeeper, and shopper. She had to set her seal. Mornings of crisis and near hysteria trying to get lunches packed, hair combed, coats and shoes found, everyone to school or Child Care on time, the baby ready for transportation. And always the paper scribbled on by a smaller one, the book looked at by Susan then mislaid, the homework not done. Running out to that huge school where she was one, she was lost, she was a drop; suffering over the unpreparedness, stammering and unsure in her classes.

There was so little time left at night after the kids were bedded down. She would struggle over books, always eating (it was in those years she developed her enormous appetite that is legendary in our family) and I would be ironing, or preparing food for the next day, or writing V-mail to Bill, or tending the baby. Sometimes, to make me laugh, or out of her despair, she would imitate happenings or types at school.

I think I said once: "Why don't you do something like this in the school amateur show?" One morning she phoned me at work, hardly understandable through the weeping: "Mother, I did it. I won, I won; they gave me first prize; they clapped and clapped and wouldn't let me go."

Now suddenly she was Somebody, and as imprisoned in her difference as she had been in anonymity.

She began to be asked to perform at other high schools, even in colleges, then at city and statewide affairs. The first one we went to, I only recognized her that first moment when thin, shy, she almost drowned herself into the curtains. Then: Was this Emily? The control, the command, the convulsing and deadly clowning, the spell, then the roaring, stamping audience, unwilling to let this rare and precious laughter out of their lives.

Afterwards: You ought to do something about her with a gift like that—but without money or knowing how, what does one do? We have left it all to her, and the gift has as often eddied inside, clogged and clotted, as been used and growing.

She is coming. She runs up the stairs two at a time with her light graceful step, and I know she is happy tonight. Whatever it was that occasioned your call did not happen today.

"Aren't you ever going to finish the ironing, Mother? Whistler[2] painted his mother in a rocker. I'd have to paint mine standing over an ironing board." This is one of her communicative nights and she tells me everything and nothing as she fixes herself a plate of food out of the icebox.

She is so lovely. Why did you want me to come in at all? Why were you concerned? She will find her way.

She starts up the stairs to bed. "Don't get me up with the rest in the morning." "But I thought you were having midterms." "Oh, those," she comes back in, kisses me, and says quite lightly, "in a couple of years when we'll all be atom-dead they won't matter a bit."

She has said it before. She *believes* it. But because I have been dredging the past, and all that compounds a human being is so heavy and meaningful in me, I cannot endure it tonight.

I will never total it all. I will never come in to say: She was a child seldom smiled at. Her father left me before she was a year old. I had to work her first six years when there was work, or I sent her home and to his relatives. There were years she had care she hated. She was dark and thin and foreign-looking in a world where the prestige went to blondeness and curly hair and dimples, she was slow where glibness was prized.

---

[2]**Whistler**: James (Abbott) McNeill Whistler (1834–1903), United States painter and etcher.

She was a child of anxious, not proud, love. We were poor and could not afford for her the soil of easy growth. I was a young mother, I was a distracted mother. There were other children pushing up, demanding. Her younger sister seemed all that she was not. There were years she did not want me to touch her. She kept too much in herself, her life was such she had to keep too much in herself. My wisdom came too late. She has much to her and probably little will come of it. She is a child of her age, of depression, of war, of fear.

Let her be. So all that is in her will not bloom—but in how many does it? There is still enough left to live by. Only help her to know—help make it so there is cause for her to know—that she is more than this dress on the ironing board, helpless before the iron. •

Explorations of the Text

1. How does the mother view her daughter Emily as a baby?
2. How do economic and social circumstances affect the mother's ability to take care of Emily?
3. Characterize Emily as a baby and at different stages in her life. According to the narrator, what needs, yearnings, and conflicts shape the daughter's view of herself?
4. Analyze the images describing Emily's body. How do societal conceptions of beauty figure in Emily's development?
5. How does the mother feel about herself as a parent? Is she a "good mother"? Is she to blame for what has happened to Emily?
6. Explore the significance of the title and the symbol of ironing. Discuss Tillie Olsen's critique of woman's position in society.
7. How does the opening, the interchange between the unnamed social worker and the mother, develop the story?

The Reading/Writing Connection

1. "Think" Topic: What effect does the first-person point of view have on the story? Rewrite several passages in third person. How does the perspective change?
2. Write a monologue in the voice of Emily, and present her version of her upbringing. Or write a letter from Emily to her mother.

Ideas for Writing

1. Compare this story with "Scar" and/or "Burn Your Maps."
2. Some psychologists suggest that "wounds" in childhood may later become sources of creativity. Is there support for this theory in the story?
3. Continue the story. What is going to happen to Emily?

Dean Bakopoulos *(1975–)*

Some Memories of My Father *2005*

I missed my father's cheese sandwiches, the way most nights around nine o'clock he'd go to the fridge, take out two slices of Wonder bread and two pieces of individually wrapped American cheese, and make a sandwich. The process by which he did this was nearly surgical and it yielded a perfect sandwich, square and neat, nothing falling out from the sides. He never left a crumb on the counter. He simply put the perfect sandwich on a clean plate, set a pickle down beside it, and returned to the television, where he was watching, no doubt, PBS or the evening news. Such methodical operations my father sometimes had, and I missed them. I missed the smell of his breakfast in the morning (one poached egg, dark rye toast, Nescafé). I missed the way he folded his newspaper, leaving it, finally, at day's end, open to the crossword puzzle (which he always seemed able to finish, every slot, using a green felttip pen). I missed the slippers at his bedside, the smell of cigarette smoke hanging in the bathroom, the cracking of his knuckles, the precise way he folded towels.

Yes, it's true that I missed my father, but in a larger sense, I missed all the fathers. I'd drive into other neighborhoods, neighborhoods with names like Quail Ridge and Oak Hills where people could not even imagine the mass exodus we had experienced, and I'd watch the fathers washing cars or practicing golf swings. In these neighborhoods, fathers could be seen strolling up and down driveways, monitoring the progress of the landscapers and deck-builders and sprinkler-system-installers. Neighborhoods like this could have been a million miles away from us.

What I missed most was the collective drone of our fathers' lives, their big and clumsy presence. I even missed their cussing and their labored breathing from too many cigarettes. I missed the roar of the sick engines inside the hoods of the hobby cars that would never run quite right. I missed their beer and coffee breath, missed their cheap aftershave that stunk up the church on Sunday mornings. I missed the cranking of their power tools on Saturday afternoons, and the roar of their voices while watching the Lions play on television. I even missed the yelling, the arguments gone over the edge, the occasional sound of a fist going through the door.

Still, in truth, I could remember very little about my father. Already, in a matter of less than a year, his image had grown vague and hazy. I listed the few memories I had in a notebook, afraid they might leave me:

I am three years old, my father is smoking and sweating, swearing at some sort of 5 machine, while I sit on a concrete floor, banging an old coffee can with a screwdriver.

I am four. My father and I are stacking firewood at the side of the house. A hornet swirls around my head and lands on the small log that I am holding. My father says nothing, puts his hand out. I give him the log. The hornet doesn't budge. My father takes his pocketknife, flips it open with one hand, and sticks the blade into the hornet, pinning it to the wood. I hear an anemic buzz and the hornet falls to the grass in two pieces.

Five years old. We are at a wedding. It is late. Ambulances have arrived. Somebody has had a heart attack. Some adult, a mustached man with floppy gray hair, pours beers on my head. I start to cry. My father grabs the beer-pourer by his necktie and throws him to the floor.

When I am six, my father lives in the basement for a week. He sleeps on the couch, does not shave, never goes to work. Sometimes my mother and I hear him vomiting in the bathroom down there. My mother says he is sick. We sometimes hear him crying, loud sobs. I am not allowed to go downstairs. He stays there for another week, a third week. My mother goes downstairs only after I am in bed, and they yell at each other so that I can't sleep. One night there is the crash of a broken mirror and the sound of a hole being kicked into the wood paneling. In the morning, my father joins us for breakfast and, clean-shaven, returns to work.

When I am seven, my father disappears for a weekend. Eventually, my mother calls the police, who find him hitchhiking on I-75. My mother asks: Where were you going? My father says: Maybe Florida?

When I am eight, my father announces that he is breaking the Good Friday fast, and that he doesn't want any goddamn fish, what he wants is kielbasa and ham. He rips into our Easter meats and sits at the table, drinking beer and eating pork. My mother yells at him; she tries to call the priest on the telephone but he doesn't answer. My father inhales the smoky smell of kielbasa and offers me a piece. I take it, eat it, then eat several more. My mother yells for me to stop. My mother begs me, but my father laughs and so I laugh with him. Later, my father leaves the house, and it's me and my mother in the kitchen. She is trying to salvage what's left of the meat for basket blessing the next afternoon. She says I've done a horrible, sinful thing. In my room that night, I stay up as late as I can, crying and saying the Rosary, begging the Virgin Mary to ask Jesus to forgive me, although, because it is Good Friday, I am not sure if Jesus is available.

When I am nine, my father announces that we are moving to Arizona, and he and my mother stay up all night fighting. My mother says, "What do you hope is different for us in goddamn Tucson, Roman?" And my father says, "Everything." But by morning, my father no longer mentions Arizona, and we never move or discuss it again.

When I am ten, my father kisses a woman at an office party. He confesses this to my mother, moves out for a week, and then comes back home, bearing two large pizzas and a jug of root beer.

When I am eleven, my father gets a ticket for drunk driving. My mother threatens to leave him.

When I am twelve, my father grows a beard and mustache and begins to work in the garden, bird-watch, and listen to opera. He quits drinking for six months and buys a family pass to the Detroit Symphony Orchestra.

When I am thirteen, while we're eating cheeseburgers at a White Castle, my father tells me that I should prepare myself for disappointment. "This is the way our lives turn out, Mikey," he says. "Disappointing."

When I am fourteen, my father and I drive to Florida after his uncle Five dies. We think we are set to inherit nearly half a million, but instead, we find that Uncle Five has spent all his money on his widow, a thirty-one-year-old waitress who won't let us in the house. On the way home, my father says, "This is what I mean by disappointment."

These were my fragments of my father. I could remember only his many phases, his fleeting obsessions, and his periodic bouts with depression. I'm not saying there was no happiness in my childhood. No, I remember my father as a loving, bighearted man capable of hitting low points that lasted for weeks. I remember him often looking confused and broken, as if he'd just woken up from a long sleep plagued by sad dreams. Still, although I tried and I tried, I couldn't retrieve a single extended memory: there was no camping trip that we took alone, no long talk in which he offered me advice, no fishing from a metal rowboat, just us guys, our lines in the water and the sun barely starting to rise. And this is one of the things that I was afraid of that my father was gone for good and that my memories of him weren't clear and lasting. Perhaps my memory was just bad. My memories of my childhood were pleasant ones, mostly. But they were dim, and my father was a shadow in them all.

Now only one thing remains:

When I was sixteen, my father went to the moon. •

Explorations of the Text

1. Upon reading the first paragraph of the story, how would you characterize the protagonist's father? Finish the story. Was your characterization correct?

2. Why might the men in the protagonist's neighborhood have gone "to the moon," fled their homes, when men in other neighborhoods remained with their families? The narrator says that in "neighborhoods with names like Quail Ridge and Oak Hills" the fathers had remained with their families. Within this context, what might the road names symbolize?

3. The narrator, Mikey, is afraid he will forget his father, and much of the story consists of a series of fragments, or memories, that he has pasted together. What images or themes are consistent throughout the memories? Do the fragments lead to a picture of the narrator's father? The narrator's mother? The narrator?

The Reading/Writing Connection

1. Journal entry: Write down some memories you have of your father or mother. Is there a unifying theme that connects the memories? Do you think that another member of your family would remember the same events similarly? Why or why not?

Ideas for Writing

1. **Write an Argument:** The narrator's father tells his son that life is "disappointing." Do you agree with the father? Create an argument that supports or disproves this statement.

2. **Write an Argument:** Bakopoulos's story portrays a family that has been deserted by the father. Statistically more fathers leave their families than do mothers. Considering the context of this story and "bone black," what pressures might lead fathers to desert families? Create a cause-and-effect argument that examines why fathers may seek a new life away from their families.

James Baldwin *(1924–1987)*

Sonny's Blues *1957*

I read about it in the paper, in the subway, on my way to work. I read it, and I couldn't believe it, and I read it again. Then perhaps I just stared at it, at the newsprint spelling out his name, spelling out the story. I stared at it in the swinging lights of the subway car, and in the faces and bodies of the people, and in my own face, trapped in the darkness which roared outside.

It was not to be believed and I kept telling myself that, as I walked from the subway station to the high school. And at the same time I couldn't doubt it. I was scared, scared for Sonny. He became real to me again. A great block of ice got settled in my belly and kept melting there slowly all day long, while I taught my classes algebra. It was a special kind of ice. It kept melting, sending trickles of ice water all up and down my veins, but it never got less. Sometimes it hardened and seemed to expand until I felt my guts were going to come spilling out or that I was going to choke or scream. This would always be at a moment when I was remembering some specific thing Sonny had once said or done.

When he was about as old as the boys in my classes his face had been bright and open, there was a lot of copper in it; and he'd had wonderfully direct brown eyes, and great gentleness and privacy. I wondered what he looked like now. He had been picked up, the evening before, in a raid on an apartment downtown, for peddling and using heroin.

I couldn't believe it: but what I mean by that is that I couldn't find any room for it anywhere inside me. I had kept it outside me for a long time. I hadn't wanted to know. I had had suspicions, but I didn't name them, I kept putting them away. I told myself that Sonny was wild, but he wasn't crazy. And he'd always been a good boy, he hadn't ever turned hard or evil or disrespectful, the way kids can, so quick, so quick, especially in Harlem. I didn't want to believe that I'd ever see my brother going down, coming to nothing, all that light in his face gone out, in the condition I'd already seen so many others. Yet it had happened and here I was, talking about algebra to a lot of boys who might, every one of them for all I knew, be popping off needles every time they went to the head. Maybe it did more for them than algebra could.

I was sure that the first time Sonny had ever had horse, he couldn't have been much older than these boys were now. These boys, now, were living as we'd been living then, they were growing up with a rush and their heads bumped abruptly against the low ceiling of their actual possibilities. They were filled with rage. All they really knew were two darknesses, the darkness of their lives, which was now closing in on them, and the darkness of the movies, which had blinded them to that other darkness, and in which they now, vindictively, dreamed, at once more together than they were at any other time, and more alone.

When the last bell rang, the last class ended, I let out my breath. It seemed I'd been holding it for all that time. My clothes were wet—I may have looked as though I'd been sitting in a steam bath, all dressed up, all afternoon. I sat alone in the classroom a long time. I listened to the boys outside, downstairs, shouting and cursing and laughing. Their laughter struck me for perhaps the first time. It was not the joyous laughter which—God knows why—one associates with children. It was mocking and insular, its intent was to denigrate. It was disenchanted, and in this, also, lay the authority of their curses. Perhaps I was listening to them because I was thinking about my brother and in them I heard my brother. And myself.

One boy was whistling a tune, at once very complicated and very simple, it seemed to be pouring out of him as though he were a bird, and it sounded very cool and moving through all that harsh, bright air, only just holding its own through all those other sounds.

I stood up and walked over to the window and looked down into the courtyard. It was the beginning of the spring and the sap was rising in the boys. A teacher passed through them every now and again, quickly, as though he or she couldn't wait to get out of that courtyard, to get those boys out of their sight and off their minds. I started collecting my stuff. I thought I'd better get home and talk to Isabel.

The courtyard was almost deserted by the time I got downstairs. I saw this boy standing in the shadow of a doorway, looking just like Sonny. I almost called his name. Then I saw that it wasn't Sonny, but somebody we used to know, a boy from around our block. He'd been Sonny's friend. He'd never been mine, having been too young for me, and, anyway, I'd never liked him. And now, even though he was a grown-up man, he still hung around that block, still spent hours on the street corners, was always high and raggy. I used to run into him from time to time and he'd often work around to asking me for a quarter or fifty cents. He always had some real good excuse, too, and I always gave it to him, I don't know why.

But now, abruptly, I hated him. I couldn't stand the way he looked at me, partly 10 like a dog, partly like a cunning child. I wanted to ask him what the hell he was doing in the school courtyard.

He sort of shuffled over to me, and he said, "I see you got the papers. So you already know about it."

"You mean about Sonny? Yes, I already know about it. How come they didn't get you?"

He grinned. It made him repulsive and it also brought to mind what he'd looked like as a kid. "I wasn't there. I stay away from them people."

"Good for you." I offered him a cigarette and I watched him through the smoke. "You come all the way down here just to tell me about Sonny?"

"That's right." He was sort of shaking his head and his eyes looked strange, as 15 though they were about to cross. The bright sun deadened his damp dark brown skin and it made his eyes look yellow and showed up the dirt in his kinked hair. He smelled funky. I moved a little away from him and I said, "Well, thanks. But I already know about it and I got to get home."

"I'll walk you a little ways," he said. We started walking. There were a couple of kids still loitering in the courtyard and one of them said goodnight to me and looked strangely at the boy beside me.

"What're you going to do?" he asked me. "I mean, about Sonny?"

"Look. I haven't seen Sonny for over a year, I'm not sure I'm going to do anything. Anyway, what the hell *can* I do?"

"That's right," he said quickly, "ain't nothing you can do. Can't much help old Sonny no more, I guess."

It was what I was thinking and so it seemed to me he had no right to say it. 20

"I'm surprised at Sonny, though," he went on—he had a funny way of talking, he looked straight ahead as though he were talking to himself—"I thought Sonny was a smart boy, I thought he was too smart to get hung."

"I guess he thought so too," I said sharply, "and that's how he got hung. And now about you? You're pretty goddamn smart, I bet."

Then he looked directly at me, just for a minute. "I ain't smart," he said. "If I was smart, I'd have reached for a pistol a long time ago."

"Look. Don't tell *me* your sad story, if it was up to me, I'd give you one." Then I felt guilty—guilty, probably, for never having supposed that the poor bastard *had* a story of his own, much less a sad one, and I asked, quickly, "What's going to happen to him now?"

He didn't answer this. He was off by himself some place. "Funny thing," he said, and from his tone we might have been discussing the quickest way to get to Brooklyn, "when I saw the papers this morning, the first thing I asked myself was if I had anything to do with it. I felt sort of responsible." 25

I began to listen more carefully. The subway station was on the corner, just before us, and I stopped. He stopped, too. We were in front of a bar and he ducked slightly, peering in, but whoever he was looking for didn't seem to be there. The juke box was blasting away with something black and bouncy and I half watched the barmaid as she danced her way from the juke box to her place behind the bar. And I watched her face as she laughingly responded to something someone said to her, still keeping time to the music. When she smiled one saw the little girl, one sensed the doomed, still-struggling woman beneath the battered face of the semi-whore.

"I never give Sonny nothing," the boy said finally, "but a long time ago I come to school high and Sonny asked me how it felt." He paused, I couldn't bear to watch him, I watched the barmaid, and I listened to the music which seemed to be causing the pavement to shake. "I told him it felt great." The music stopped, the barmaid paused and watched the juke box until the music began again. "It did."

All this way carrying me some place I didn't want to go. I certainly didn't want to know how it felt. It filled everything, the people, the houses, the music, the dark, quick-silver barmaid, with menace: and this menace was their reality.

"What's going to happen to him now?" I asked again.

"They'll send him away some place and they'll try to cure him." He shook his head. "Maybe he'll even think he's kicked the habit. Then they'll let him loose"—he gestured, throwing his cigarette into the gutter. "That's all." 30

"What do you mean, that's *all?*"

But I knew what he meant.

"I mean, that's *all*." He turned his head and looked at me, pulling down the corners of his mouth. "Don't you know what I mean?" he asked, softly.

"How the hell would I know what you mean?" I almost whispered it. I don't know why.

"That's right," he said to the air, "how would he know what I mean?" He turned toward me again, patient and calm, and yet I somehow felt him shaking, shaking as though he were going to fall apart. I felt that ice in my guts again, the dread I'd felt all afternoon; and again I watched the barmaid, moving about the bar, washing glasses, and singing. "Listen. They'll let him out and then it'll just start all over again. That's what I mean." 35

"You mean—they'll let him out. And then he'll just start working his way back in again. You mean he'll never kick the habit. Is that what you mean?"

"That's right," he said, cheerfully. "You see what I mean."

"Tell me," I said at last, "why does he want to die? He must want to die, he's killing himself, why does he want to die?"

He looked at me in surprise. He licked his lips. "He don't want to die. He wants to live. Don't nobody want to die, ever."

Then I wanted to ask him—too many things. He could not have answered, or if he had, I could not have borne the answers. I started walking. "Well, I guess it's none of my business." 40

"It's going to be rough on old Sonny," he said. We reached the subway station. "This is your station?" he asked. I nodded. I took one step down. "Damn!" he said, suddenly. I looked up at him. He grinned again. "Damn it if I didn't leave all my money home. You ain't got a dollar on you, have you? Just for a couple of days, is all."

All at once something inside gave and threatened to come pouring out of me. I didn't hate him any more, I felt that in another moment I'd start crying like a child.

"Sure," I said. "Don't swear." I looked in my wallet and didn't have a dollar, I only had a five. "Here," I said. "That hold you?"

He didn't look at it—he didn't want to look at it. A terrible, closed look came over his face, as though he were keeping the number on the bill a secret from him and me. "Thanks," he said, and now he was dying to see me go. "Don't worry about Sonny. Maybe I'll write him or something."

"Sure," I said. "You do that. So long." 45

"Be seeing you," he said. I went down the steps.

And I didn't write Sonny or send him anything for a long time. When I finally did, it was just after my little girl died, he wrote me back a letter which made me feel like a bastard.

Here's what he said:

Dear Brother,

You don't know how much I needed to hear from you. I wanted to write you many a time but I dug how much I must have hurt you and so I didn't write. But now I feel like a man who's been trying to climb up out of some deep, real deep and funky hole and just saw the sun up there, outside. I got to get outside.

I can't tell you much about how I got here. I mean I don't know how to tell you. I guess I was afraid of something or I was trying to escape from something and you know I have never been very strong in the head (smile). I'm glad Mama and Daddy are dead and can't see what's happened to their son and I swear if I'd known what I was doing I would never have hurt you so, you and a lot of other fine people who were nice to me and who believed in me.

I don't want you to think it had anything to do with me being a musician. It's more than that. Or maybe less than that. I can't get anything straight in my head down here and I try not to think about what's going to happen to me when I get outside again. Sometime I think I'm going to flip and never get outside and sometime I think I'll come straight back, I tell you one thing, though. I'd rather blow my brains out than go through this again. But that's what they all say, so they tell me. If I tell you when I'm coming to New York and if you could meet me, I sure would appreciate it. Give my love to Isabel and the kids and I was sure sorry to hear about little Gracie. I wish I could be like Mama and say the Lord's will be done, but I don't know it seems to me that trouble is the one thing that never does get stopped and I don't know what good it does to blame it on the Lord. But maybe it does some good if you believe it.

Your brother,
Sonny

Then I kept in constant touch with him and I sent him whatever I could and I went to meet him when he came back to New York. When I saw him many things I thought I had forgotten came flooding back to me. This was because I had begun, finally, to wonder about Sonny, about the life that Sonny lived inside. This life, whatever it was, had made him older and thinner and it had deepened the distant stillness in which he had always moved. He looked very unlike my baby brother. Yet, when he smiled, when we shook hands, the baby brother I'd never known looked out from the depths of his private life, like an animal waiting to be coaxed into the light.

"How you been keeping?" he asked me. 50

"All right. And you?"

"Just fine." He was smiling all over his face. "It's good to see you again."

"It's good to see you."

The seven years' difference in our ages lay between us like a chasm: I wondered if these years would ever operate between us as a bridge. I was remembering, and it made it hard to catch my breath, that I had been there when he was born; and I had heard the first words he had ever spoken. When he started to walk, he walked from our mother straight to me. I caught him just before he fell when he took the first steps he ever took in this world.

"How's Isabel?" 55

"Just fine. She's dying to see you."

"And the boys?"

"They're fine, too. They're anxious to see their uncle."

"Oh, come on. You know they don't remember me."

"Are you kidding? Of course they remember you." 60

He grinned again. We got into a taxi. We had a lot to say to each other, far too much to know how to begin.

As the taxi began to move, I asked, "You still want to go to India?"

He laughed. "You still remember that. Hell, no. This place is Indian enough for me."

"It used to belong to them," I said.

And he laughed again. "They damn sure knew what they were doing when they 65 got rid of it."

Years ago, when he was around fourteen, he'd been all hipped on the idea of going to India. He read books about people sitting on rocks, naked, in all kinds of weather, but mostly bad, naturally, and walking barefoot through hot coals and arriving at wisdom. I used to say that it sounded to me as though they were getting away from wisdom as fast as they could. I think he sort of looked down on me for that.

"Do you mind," he asked, "if we have the driver drive alongside the park? On the west side—I haven't seen the city in so long."

"Of course not," I said. I was afraid that I might sound as though I were humoring him, but I hoped he wouldn't take it that way.

So we drove along, between the green of the park and the stony, lifeless elegance of hotels and apartment buildings, toward the vivid, killing streets of our childhood. These streets hadn't changed, though housing projects jutted up out of them now like rocks in the middle of a boiling sea. Most of the houses in which we had grown up had vanished, as had the stores from which we had stolen, the basements in which we had first tried sex, the rooftops from which we had hurled tin cans and bricks. But houses exactly like the houses of our past yet dominated the landscape, boys exactly like the boys we once had been found themselves smothering in these houses, came down into the streets for light and air and found themselves encircled by disaster. Some escaped the trap, most didn't. Those who got out always left something of themselves behind, as some animals amputate a leg and leave it in the trap. It might be said, perhaps, that I had escaped, after all, I was a school teacher; or that Sonny had, he hadn't lived in Harlem for years. Yet, as the cab moved uptown through streets which seemed, with a rush, to darken with dark people, and as I covertly studied Sonny's face, it came to me that what we both were seeking through our separate cab windows was that part of ourselves which had been left behind. It's always at the hour of trouble and confrontation that the missing member aches.

We hit 110th Street and started rolling up Lenox Avenue. And I'd known this av- 70
enue all my life, but it seemed to me again, as it had seemed on the day I'd first heard about Sonny's trouble, filled with a hidden menace which was its very breath of life.

"We almost there," said Sonny.

"Almost." We were both too nervous to say anything more.

We live in a housing project. It hasn't been up long. A few days after it was up it seemed uninhabitably new, now, of course, it's already rundown. It looks like a parody of the good, clean, faceless life—God knows the people who live in it do their best to make it a parody. The beat-looking grass lying around isn't enough to make their lives green, the hedges will never hold out the streets, and they know it. The big windows fool no one, they aren't big enough to make space out of no space. They don't bother with the windows, they watch the TV screen instead. The playground is most popular with the children who don't play at jacks, or skip rope, or roller skate, or swing, and they can be found in it after dark. We moved in partly because it's not too far from where I teach, and partly for the kids; but it's really just like the houses in which Sonny and I grew up. The same things happen, they'll have the same things to remember. The moment Sonny and I started into the house I had the feeling that I was simply bringing him back into the danger he had almost died trying to escape.

Sonny has never been talkative. So I don't know why I was sure he'd be dying to talk to me when supper was over the first night. Everything went fine, the oldest boy remembered him, and the youngest boy liked him, and Sonny had remembered to bring something for each of them; and Isabel, who is really much nicer than I am, more open and giving, had gone to a lot of trouble about dinner and was genuinely glad to see him. And she's always been able to tease Sonny in a way that I haven't. It was nice to see her face so vivid again and to hear her laugh and watch her make Sonny laugh. She wasn't, or, anyway, she didn't seem to be, at all uneasy or embarrassed. She chatted as though there were no subject which had to be avoided and she got Sonny past his first, faint stiffness. And thank God she was there, for I was filled with that icy dread again. Everything I did seemed awkward to me, and everything I said sounded freighted with hidden meaning. I was trying to remember everything I'd heard about dope addiction and I couldn't help watching Sonny for signs. I wasn't doing it out of malice. I was trying to find out something about my brother. I was dying to hear him tell he was safe.

"Safe!" my father grunted, whenever Mama suggested trying to move to a neigh- 75
borhood which might be safer for children. "Safe, hell! Ain't no place safe for kids, nor nobody."

He always went on like this, but he wasn't, ever, really as bad as he sounded, not even on weekends, when he got drunk. As a matter of fact, he was always on the lookout for "something a little better," but he died before he found it. He died suddenly, during a drunken weekend in the middle of the war, when Sonny was fifteen. He and Sonny hadn't ever got on too well. And this was partly because Sonny was the apple of his father's eye. It was because he loved Sonny so much and was frightened for him, that he was always fighting with him. It doesn't do any good to fight with Sonny. Sonny just moves back, inside himself, where he can't be reached. But the principal reason that they never hit it off is that they were so much alike. Daddy was big and rough and loud-talking, just the opposite of Sonny, but they both had—that same privacy.

Mama tried to tell me something about this, just after Daddy died. I was home on leave from the army.

This was the last time I ever saw my mother alive. Just the same, this picture gets all mixed up in my mind with pictures I had of her when she was younger. The way I always see her is the way she used to be on a Sunday afternoon, say, when the old folks were talking after the big Sunday dinner. I always see her wearing pale blue. She'd be sitting on the sofa. And my father would be sitting in the easy chair, not far from her. And the living room would be full of church folks and relatives. There they sit, in chairs all around the living room, and the night is creeping up outside, but nobody knows it yet. You can see the darkness growing against the windowpanes and you hear the street noises every now and again, or maybe the jangling beat of a tambourine from one of the churches close by, but it's real quiet in the room. For a moment nobody's talking, but every face looks darkening, like the sky outside. And my mother rocks a little from the waist, and my father's eyes are closed. Everyone is looking at something a child can't see. For a minute they've forgotten the children. Maybe a kid is lying on the rug, half asleep. Maybe somebody's got a kid in his lap and is absent-mindedly stroking the kid's head. Maybe there's a kid, quiet and big-eyed, curled up on a big chair in the corner. The silence, the darkness coming, and the darkness in the faces frightens the child obscurely. He hopes that the hand which strokes his forehead will never stop—will never die. He hopes that there will never come a time when the old folks won't be sitting around the living room, talking about where they've come from, and what they've seen, and what's happened to them and their kinfolk.

But something deep and watchful in the child knows that this is bound to end, is already ending. In a moment someone will get up and turn on the light. Then the old folks will remember the children and they won't talk any more that day. And when light fills the room, the child is filled with darkness. He knows that every time this happens he's moved just a little closer to that darkness outside. The darkness outside is what the old folks have been talking about. It's what they've come from. It's what they endure. The child knows that they won't talk any more because if he knows too much about what's happened to *them,* he'll know too much too soon, about what's going to happen to *him.*

The last time I talked to my mother, I remember I was restless. I wanted to get out and see Isabel. We weren't married then and we had a lot to straighten out between us. 80

There Mama sat, in black, by the window. She was humming an old church song, *Lord, you brought me from a long ways off.* Sonny was out somewhere. Mama kept watching the streets.

"I don't know," she said, "if I'll ever see you again, after you go off from here. But I hope you'll remember the things I tried to teach you."

"Don't talk like that," I said, and smiled. "You'll be here a long time yet."

She smiled, too, but she said nothing. She was quiet for a long time. And I said, "Mama, don't you worry about nothing. I'll be writing all the time, and you be getting the checks. . . ."

"I want to talk to you about your brother," she said, suddenly. "If anything happens to me he ain't going to have nobody to look out for him." 85

"Mama," I said, "ain't nothing going to happen to you *or* Sonny. Sonny's all right. He's a good boy and he's got good sense."

"It ain't a question of his being a good boy," Mama said, "nor of his having good sense. It ain't only the bad ones, nor yet the dumb ones that gets sucked under." She stopped, looking at me. "Your Daddy once had a brother," she said, and she smiled in a way that made me feel she was in pain. "You didn't never know that, did you?"

"No," I said, "I never knew that," and I watched her face.

"Oh, yes," she said, "your Daddy had a brother." She looked out of the window again. "I know you never saw your Daddy cry. But *I* did—many a time, through all these years."

I asked her, "What happened to his brother? How come nobody's ever talked about him?" ⁹⁰

This was the first time I ever saw my mother look old.

"His brother got killed," she said, "when he was just a little younger than you are now. I knew him. He was a fine boy. He was maybe a little full of the devil, but he didn't mean nobody no harm."

Then she stopped and the room was silent, exactly as it had sometimes been on those Sunday afternoons. Mama kept looking out into the streets.

"He used to have a job in the mill," she said, "and, like all young folks, he just liked to perform on Saturday nights. Saturday nights, him and your father would drift around to different places, go to dances and things like that, or just sit around with people they knew, and your father's brother would sing, he had a fine voice, and play along with himself on his guitar. Well, this particular Saturday night, him and your father was coming home from some place, and they were both a little drunk and there was a moon that night, it was bright like day. Your father's brother was feeling kind of good, and he was whistling to himself, and he had his guitar slung over this shoulder. They was coming down a hill and beneath them was a road that turned off from the highway. Well, your father's brother, being always kind of frisky, decided to run down this hill, and he did, with that guitar banging and clanging behind him, and he ran across the road, and he was making water behind a tree. And your father was sort of amused at him and he was still coming down the hill, kind of slow. Then he heard a car motor and that same minute his brother stepped from behind the tree, into the road, in the moonlight. And he started to cross the road. And your father started to run down the hill, he says he don't know why. This car was full of white men. They was all drunk, and when they seen your father's brother they let out a great whoop and holler and they aimed the car straight at him. They was having fun, they just wanted to scare him, the way they do sometimes, you know. But they was drunk. And I guess the boy, being drunk, too, and scared, kind of lost his head. By the time he jumped it was too late. Your father says he heard his brother scream when the car rolled over him, and he heard the wood of that guitar when it give, and he heard them strings go flying, and he heard them white men shouting, and the car kept on a-going and it ain't stopped till this day. And, time your father got down the hill, his brother weren't nothing but blood and pulp."

Tears were gleaming on my mother's face. There wasn't anything I could say. ⁹⁵

"He never mentioned it," she said, "because I never let him mention it before you children. Your Daddy was like a crazy man that night and for many a night thereafter. He says he never in his life seen anything as dark as that road after the lights of that car had gone away. Weren't nothing, weren't nobody on that road, just your Daddy and his brother and that busted guitar. Oh, yes. Your Daddy never did really get right again. Till the day he died he weren't sure but that every white man he saw was the man that killed his brother."

She stopped and took out her handkerchief and dried her eyes and looked at me.

"I ain't telling you all this," she said, "to make you scared or bitter or to make you hate nobody. I'm telling you this because you got a brother. And the world ain't changed."

I guess I didn't want to believe this. I guess she saw this in my face. She turned away from me, toward the window again, searching those streets.

"But I praise my Redeemer," she said at last, "that He called your Daddy home be- 100 fore me. I ain't saying it to throw no flowers at myself, but, I declare, it keeps me from feeling too cast down to know I helped your father get safely through this world. Your father always acted like he was the roughest, strongest man on earth. And everybody took him to be like that. But if he hadn't had *me* there—to see his tears!"

She was crying again. Still, I couldn't move. I said, "Lord, Lord, Mama, I didn't know it was like that."

"Oh, honey," she said, "there's a lot that you don't know. But you are going to find it out." She stood up from the window and came over to me. "You got to hold on to your brother," she said, "and don't let him fall, no matter what it looks like is happening to him and no matter how evil you gets with him. You going to be evil with him many a time. But don't you forget what I told you, you hear?"

"I won't forget," I said. "Don't you worry, I won't forget. I won't let nothing happen to Sonny."

My mother smiled as though she were amused at something she saw in my face. Then, "You may not be able to stop nothing from happening. But you got to let him know you's *there*."

Two days later I was married, and then I was gone. And I had a lot of things on my 105 mind and I pretty well forgot my promise to Mama until I got shipped home on a special furlough for her funeral.

And after the funeral, with just Sonny and me alone in the empty kitchen, I tried to find out something about him.

"What do you want to do?" I asked him.

"I'm going to be a musician," he said.

For he had graduated, in the time I had been away, from dancing to the juke box to finding out who was playing what, and what they were doing with it, and he had bought himself a set of drums.

"You mean, you want to be a drummer?" I somehow had the feeling that being a 110 drummer might be all right for other people but not for my brother Sonny.

"I don't think," he said, looking at me very gravely, "that I'll ever be a good drummer. But I think I can play a piano."

I frowned. I'd never played the role of the older brother quite so seriously before, had scarcely ever, in fact, *asked* Sonny a damn thing. I sensed myself in the presence of something I didn't really know how to handle, didn't understand. So I made my frown a little deeper as I asked: "What kind of musician do you want to be?"

He grinned, "How many kinds do you think there are?"

"Be *serious*," I said.

He laughed, throwing his head back, and then looked at me. "I *am* serious." 115

"Well, then, for Christ's sake, stop kidding around and answer a serious question. I mean, do you want to be a concert pianist, you want to play classical music and all that, or—or what?" Long before I finished he was laughing again. "For Christ's *sake*, Sonny!"

He sobered, but with difficulty. "I'm sorry, But you sound so—*scared!*" and he was off again.

"Well, you may think it's funny now, baby, but it's not going to be so funny when you have to make your living at it, let me tell you *that*." I was furious because I knew he was laughing at me and I didn't know why.

"No," he said, very sober now, and afraid, perhaps, that he'd hurt me. "I don't want to be a classical pianist. That isn't what interests me. I mean"—he paused, looking hard at me, as though his eyes would help me to understand, and then gestured helplessly, as though perhaps his hand would help—"I mean, I'll have a lot of studying to do, and I'll have to study *everything*, but, I mean, I want to play *with*—jazz musicians." He stopped, "I want to play jazz," he said.

Well, the word had never before sounded as heavy, as real, as it sounded that after- 120
noon in Sonny's mouth. I just looked at him and I was probably frowning a real frown by this time. I simply couldn't see why on earth he'd want to spend his time hanging around nightclubs, clowning around on bandstands, while people pushed each other around a dance floor. It seemed—beneath him, somehow. I had never thought about it before, had never been forced to, but I suppose I had always put jazz musicians in a class with what Daddy called "good-time people."

"Are you *serious*?"

"Hell, *yes*, I'm serious."

He looked more helpless than ever, and annoyed, and deeply hurt.

I suggested, helpfully: "You mean—like Louis Armstrong?"[1]

His face closed as though I'd struck him. "No. I'm not talking about none of that 125
old-time, down home crap."

"Well, look, Sonny, I'm sorry, don't get mad. I just don't altogether get it, that's all. Name somebody—you know, a jazz musician you admire."

"Bird."

"Who?"

"Bird! Charlie Parker![2] Don't they teach you nothing in the goddamn army?"

I lit a cigarette. I was surprised and then a little amused to discover that I was trem- 130
bling. "I've been out of touch," I said. "You'll have to be patient with me. Now. Who's this Parker character?"

"He's just one of the greatest jazz musicians alive," said Sonny, sullenly, his hands in his pockets, his back to me. "Maybe *the* greatest," he added, bitterly, "that's probably why *you* never heard of him."

"All right," I said, "I'm ignorant. I'm sorry. I'll go out and buy all the cat's records right away, all right?"

"It don't," said Sonny, with dignity, "make any difference to me. I don't care what you listen to. Don't do me no favors."

I was beginning to realize that I'd never seen him so upset before. With another part of my mind I was thinking that this would probably turn out to be one of those things kids go through and that I shouldn't make it seem important by pushing it too hard. Still, I didn't think it would do any harm to ask: "Doesn't all this take a lot of time? Can you make a living at it?"

He turned back to me and half leaned, half sat, on the kitchen table. "Everything 135
takes time," he said, "and—well, yes, sure, I can make a living at it. But what I don't seem to be able to make you understand is that it's the only thing I want to do."

---

[1]**Louis Armstrong**: Famous jazz trumpet player.   [2]**Charlie Parker**: Famous jazz musician, nick-named Bird.

"Well, Sonny," I said, gently, "you know people can't always do exactly what they *want* to do—"

"*No,* I don't know that," said Sonny, surprising me. "I think people *ought* to do what they want to do, what else are they alive for?"

"You getting to be a big boy," I said desperately, "it's time you started thinking about your future."

"I'm thinking about my future," said Sonny, grimly. "I think about it all the time."

I gave up. I decided, if he didn't change his mind, that we could always talk about it later. "In the meantime," I said, "you got to finish school." We had already decided that he'd have to move in with Isabel and her folks. I knew this wasn't the ideal arrangement because Isabel's folks are inclined to be dicty[3] and they hadn't especially wanted Isabel to marry me. But I didn't know what else to do. "And we have to get you fixed up at Isabel's."

There was a long silence. He moved from the kitchen table to the window. "That's a terrible idea. You know it yourself."

"Do you have a *better* idea?"

He just walked up and down the kitchen for a minute. He was as tall as I was. He had started to shave. I suddenly had the feeling that I didn't know him at all.

He stopped at the kitchen table and picked up my cigarettes. Looking at me with a kind of mocking, amused defiance, he put one between his lips. "You mind?"

"You smoking already?"

He lit the cigarette and nodded, watching me through the smoke. "I just wanted to see if I'd have the courage to smoke in front of you." He grinned and blew a great cloud of smoke to the ceiling. "It was easy." He looked at my face. "Come on, now. I bet you was smoking at my age, tell the truth."

I didn't say anything but the truth was on my face, and he laughed. But now there was something very strained in his laugh. "Sure. And I bet that ain't all you was doing."

He was frightening me a little. "Cut the crap," I said. "We already decided that you was going to go and live at Isabel's. Now what's got into you all of a sudden?"

"*You* decided it," he pointed out. "*I* didn't decide nothing." He stopped in front of me, leaning against the stove, arms loosely folded. "Look, brother. I don't want to stay in Harlem no more, I really don't." He was very earnest. He looked at me, then over toward the kitchen window. There was something in his eyes I'd never seen before, some thoughtfulness, some worry all his own. He rubbed the muscle of one arm. "It's time I was getting out of here."

"Where do you want to *go,* Sonny?"

"I want to join the army. Or the navy, I don't care. If I say I'm old enough, they'll believe me."

Then I got mad. It was because I was so scared. "You must be crazy. You goddamn fool, what the hell do you want to go and join the *army* for?"

"I just told you. To get out of Harlem."

"Sonny, you haven't even finished *school.* And if you really want to be a musician, how do you expect to study if you're in the *army?*"

He looked at me, trapped, and in anguish. "There's ways. I might be able to work out some kind of deal. Anyway, I'll have the G.I. Bill when I come out."

---

[3] **dicty**: Putting on fine airs.

"*If* you come out." We stared at each other. "Sonny, please. Be reasonable. I know the setup is far from perfect. But we got to do the best we can."

"I ain't learning nothing in school," he said. "Even when I go." He turned away from me and opened the window and threw his cigarette out into the narrow alley. I watched his back. "At least, I ain't learning nothing you'd want me to learn." He slammed the window so hard I thought the glass would fly out, and turned back to me. "And I'm sick of the stink of these garbage cans!"

"Sonny," I said, "I know how you feel. But if you don't finish school now, you're going to be sorry later that you didn't." I grabbed him by the shoulders. "And you only got another year. It ain't so bad. And I'll come back and I swear I'll help you do *whatever* you want to do. Just try to put up with it till I come back. Will you please do that? For me?"

He didn't answer and he wouldn't look at me.

"Sonny. You hear me?"

He pulled away. "I hear you. But you never hear anything *I* say." 160

I didn't know what to say to that. He looked out of the window and then back at me. "OK," he said, and sighed. "I'll try."

Then I said, trying to cheer him up a little, "They got a piano at Isabel's. You can practice on it."

And as a matter of fact, it did cheer him up for a minute. "That's right," he said to himself. "I forgot that." His face relaxed a little. But the worry, the thoughtfulness, played on it still, the way shadows play on a face which is staring into the fire.

But I thought I'd never hear the end of that piano. At first, Isabel, would write me, 165 saying how nice it was that Sonny was so serious about his music and how, as soon as he came in from school, or wherever he had been when he was supposed to be at school, he went straight to that piano and stayed there until suppertime. And, after supper, he went back to that piano and stayed there until everybody went to bed. He was at the piano all day Saturday and all day Sunday. Then he bought a record player and started playing records. He'd play one record over and over again, all day long sometimes, and he'd improvise along with it on the piano. Or he'd play one section of the record, one chord, one change, one progression, then he'd do it on the piano. Then back to the record. Then back to the piano.

Well, I really don't know how they stood it. Isabel finally confessed that it wasn't like living with a person at all, it was like living with sound. And the sound didn't make any sense to her, didn't make any sense to any of them—naturally. They began, in a way, to be afflicted by this presence that was living in their home. It was as though Sonny were some sort of god, or monster. He moved in an atmosphere which wasn't like theirs at all. They fed him and he ate, he washed himself, he walked in and out of their door; he certainly wasn't nasty or unpleasant or rude, Sonny isn't any of those things; but it was as though he were all wrapped up in some cloud, some fire, some vision all his own; and there wasn't any way to reach him.

At the same time, he wasn't really a man yet, he was still a child, and they had to watch out for him in all kinds of ways. They certainly couldn't throw him out. Neither did they dare to make a great scene about that piano because even they dimly sensed, as I sensed, from so many thousands of miles away, that Sonny was at that piano playing for his life.

But he hadn't been going to school. One day a letter came from the school board and Isabel's mother got it—there had, apparently, been other letters but Sonny had torn them up. This day, when Sonny came in, Isabel's mother showed him the letter and asked where he'd been spending his time. And she finally got it out of him that he'd been down in Greenwich Village, with musicians and other characters, in a white girl's apartment. And this scared her and she started to scream at him and what came up, once she began—though she denies it to this day—was what sacrifices they were making to give Sonny a decent home and how little he appreciated it.

Sonny didn't play the piano that day. By evening, Isabel's mother had calmed down but then there was the old man to deal with, and Isabel herself. Isabel says she did her best to be calm but she broke down and started crying. She says she just watched Sonny's face. She could tell, by watching him, what was happening with him. And what was happening was that they penetrated his cloud, they had reached him. Even if their fingers had been a thousand times more gentle than human fingers ever are, he could hardly help feeling that they had stripped him naked and were spitting on that nakedness. For he also had to see that his presence, that music, which was life or death to him, had been torture for them and that they had endured it, not at all for his sake, but only for mine. And Sonny couldn't take that. He can take it a little better today than he could then but he's still not very good at it and, frankly, I don't know anybody who is.

The silence of the next few days must have been louder than the sound of all the music ever played since time began. One morning, before she went to work, Isabel was in his room for something and she suddenly realized that all of his records were gone. And she knew for certain that he was gone. And he was. He went as far as the navy would carry him. He finally sent me a postcard from some place in Greece and that was the first I knew that Sonny was still alive. I didn't see him any more until we were both back in New York and the war had long been over.

He was a man by then, of course, but I wasn't willing to see it. He came by the house from time to time, but we fought almost every time we met. I didn't like the way he carried himself, loose and dreamlike all the time, and I didn't like his friends, and his music seemed to be merely an excuse for the life he led. It sounded just that weird and disordered.

Then we had a fight, a pretty awful fight, and I didn't see him for months. By and by I looked him up, where he was living, in a furnished room in the Village, and I tried to make it up. But there were lots of other people in the room and Sonny just lay on his bed, and he wouldn't come downstairs with me, and he treated these other people as though they were his family and I weren't. So I got mad and then he got mad, and then I told him that he might just as well be dead as live the way he was living. Then he stood up and he told me not to worry about him any more in life, that he *was* dead as far as I was concerned. Then he pushed me to the door and the other people looked on as though nothing were happening, and he slammed the door behind me. I stood in the hallway, staring at the door. I heard somebody laugh in the room and then the tears came to my eyes. I started down the steps, whistling to keep from crying. I kept whistling to myself, *You going to need me, baby, one of these cold, rainy days.*

I read about Sonny's trouble in the spring. Little Grace died in the fall. She was a beautiful little girl. But she only lived a little over two years. She died of polio and she suffered. She had a slight fever for a couple of days, but it didn't seem like anything and we just kept her in bed. And we would certainly have called the doctor, but the fever dropped, and she seemed to be all right. So we thought it had just been a cold. Then, one day, she was up, playing, Isabel was in the kitchen fixing lunch for the two boys when they'd come in from school, and she heard Grace fall down in the living room. When you have a lot of children you don't always start running when one of them falls, unless they start screaming or something. And, this time, Grace was quiet. Yet, Isabel says that when she heard that *thump* and then that silence, something happened in her to make her afraid. And she ran to the living room and there was little Grace on the floor, all twisted up, and the reason she hadn't screamed was that she couldn't get her breath. And when she did scream, it was the worst sound, Isabel says, that she'd ever heard in all her life, and she still hears it sometimes in her dreams. Isabel will sometimes wake me up with a low, moaning, strangled sound and I have to be quick to awaken her and hold her to me and where Isabel is weeping against me seems a mortal wound.

I think I may have written Sonny the very day that little Grace was buried. I was sitting in the living room in the dark, by myself, and I suddenly thought of Sonny. My trouble made his real.

One Saturday afternoon, when Sonny had been living with us, or, anyway, been in 175
our house, for nearly two weeks, I found myself wandering aimlessly about the living room, drinking from a can of beer, and trying to work up the courage to search Sonny's room. He was out, he was usually out whenever I was home, and Isabel had taken the children to see their grandparents. Suddenly I was standing still in front of the living room window, watching Seventh Avenue. The idea of searching Sonny's room made me still. I scarcely dared to admit to myself what I'd be searching for. I didn't know what I'd do if I found it. Or if I didn't.

On the sidewalk across from me, near the entrance to a barbecue joint, some people were holding an old-fashioned revival meeting. The barbecue cook, wearing a dirty white apron, his conked hair reddish and metallic in the pale sun, and a cigarette between his lips, stood in the doorway, watching them. Kids and older people paused in their errands and stood there, along with some older men and a couple of very tough-looking women who watched everything that happened on the avenue, as though they owned it, or were maybe owned by it. Well, they were watching this, too. The revival was being carried on by three sisters in black, and a brother. All they had were their voices and their Bibles and a tambourine. The brother was testifying and while he testified two of the sisters stood together, seeming to say, amen, and the third sister walked around with the tambourine outstretched and a couple of people dropped coins into it. Then the brother's testimony ended and the sister who had been taking up the collection dumped the coins into her palm and transferred them to the pocket of her long black robe. Then she raised both hands, striking the tambourine against the air, and then against one hand, and she started to sing. And the two other sisters and the brother joined in.

It was strange, suddenly, to watch, though I had been seeing these street meetings all my life. So, of course, had everybody else down there. Yet, they paused and watched and listened and I stood still at the window. *"Tis the old ship of Zion,"* they sang, and the sister with the tambourine kept a steady, jangling beat, *"it has rescued many a thousand!"* Not a soul under the sound of their voices was hearing this song for the first time, not one of them had been rescued. Nor had they seen much in the way of rescue work being done around them. Neither did they especially believe in the holiness of the three sisters and the brother, they knew too much about them, knew where they lived, and how. The woman with the tambourine, whose voice dominated the air, whose face was bright with joy, was divided by very little from the woman who stood watching her, a cigarette between her heavy, chapped lips, her hair a cuckoo's nest, her face scarred and swollen from many beatings, and her black eyes glittering like coal. Perhaps they both knew this, which was why, when, as rarely, they addressed each other, they addressed each other as Sister. As the singing filled the air the watching, listening faces underwent a change, and eyes focusing on something within; the music seemed to soothe a poison out of them; and time seemed, nearly, to fall away from the sullen, belligerent, battered faces, as though they were fleeing back to their first condition, while dreaming of their last. The barbecue cook half shook his head and smiled, and dropped his cigarette and disappeared into his joint. A man fumbled in his pockets for change and stood holding it in his hand impatiently, as though he had just remembered a pressing appointment further up the avenue. He looked furious. Then I saw Sonny, standing on the edge of the crowd. He was carrying a wide, flat notebook with a green cover, and it made him look, from where I was standing, almost like a schoolboy. The coppery sun brought out the copper in his skin, he was very faintly smiling, standing very still. Then the singing stopped, the tambourine turned into a collection plate again. The furious man dropped in his coins and vanished, so did a couple of the women, and Sonny dropped some change in the plate, looking directly at the woman with a little smile. He started across the avenue, toward the house. He has a slow, loping walk, something like the way Harlem hipsters walk, only he's imposed on this his own half-beat. I had never really noticed it before.

I stayed at the window, both relieved and apprehensive. As Sonny disappeared from my sight, they began singing again. And they were still singing when his key turned in the lock.

"Hey," he said.

"Hey, yourself. You want some beer?" 180

"No. Well, maybe." But he came up to the window and stood beside me, looking out. "What a warm voice," he said.

They were singing *If I could only hear my mother pray again!*

"Yes," I said, "and she can sure beat that tambourine."

"But what a terrible song," he said, and laughed. He dropped his notebook on the sofa and disappeared into the kitchen. "Where's Isabel and the kids?"

"I think they went to see their grandparents. You hungry?" 185

"No." He came back into the living room with his can of beer. "You want to come some place with me tonight?"

I sensed, I don't know how, that I couldn't possibly say no. "Sure. Where?"

He sat down on the sofa and picked up his notebook and started leafing through it. "I'm going to sit in with some fellows in a joint in the Village."

"You mean, you're going to play, tonight?"

"That's right." He took a swallow of his beer and moved back to the window. He 190 gave me a sidelong look. "If you can stand it."

"I'll try," I said.

He smiled to himself and we both watched as the meeting across the way broke up. The three sisters and the brother, heads bowed, were singing *God be with you till we meet again.* The faces around them were very quiet. Then the song ended. The small crowd dispersed. We watched the three women and the lone man walk slowly up the avenue.

"When she was singing before," said Sonny, abruptly, "her voice reminded me for a minute of what heroin feels like sometimes—when it's in your veins. It makes you feel sort of warm and cool at the same time. And distant. And—and sure." He sipped his beer, very deliberately not looking at me. I watched his face. "It makes you feel—in control. Sometimes you've got to have that feeling."

"Do you?" I sat down slowly in the easy chair.

"Sometimes." He went to the sofa and picked up his notebook again. "Some 195 people do."

"In order," I asked, "to play?" And my voice was very ugly, full of contempt and anger.

"Well"—he looked at me with great, troubled eyes, as though, in fact, he hoped his eyes would tell me things he could never otherwise say—"they *think* so. And *if* they think so—!"

"And what do *you* think?" I asked.

He sat on the sofa and put his can of beer on the floor. "I don't know," he said, and I couldn't be sure if he were answering my question or pursuing his thoughts. He face didn't tell me. "It's not so much to *play*. It's to *stand* it, to be able to make it at all. On any level." He frowned and smiled: "In order to keep from shaking to pieces."

"But these friends of yours," I said, "they seem to shake themselves to pieces pretty 200 goddamn fast."

"Maybe." He played with the notebook. And something told me that I should curb my tongue, that Sonny was doing his best to talk, that I should listen. "But of course you only know the ones that've gone to pieces. Some don't—or at least they haven't *yet* and that's just about all *any* of us can say." He paused. "And then there are some who just live, really, in hell, and they know it and they see what's happening and they go right on. I don't know." He sighed, dropped the notebook, folded his arms. "Some guys, you can tell from the way they play, they on something *all* the time. And you can see that, well, it makes something real for them. But of course," he picked up his beer from the floor and sipped it and put the can down again, "they *want* to, too, you've got to see that. Even some of them that say they don't—*some,* not all.

"And what about you?" I asked—I couldn't help it. "What about you? Do *you* want to?"

He stood up and walked to the window and remained silent for a long time. Then he sighed. "Me," he said. Then: "While I was downstairs before, on my way here, listening to that woman sing, it struck me all of a sudden how much suffering she must have had to go through—to sing like that. It's *repulsive* to think you have to suffer that much."

I said: "But there's no way not to suffer—is there, Sonny?"

"I believe not," he said and smiled, "but that's never stopped anyone from try- 205 ing." He looked at me. "Has it?" I realized, with this mocking look, that there stood between us, forever, beyond the power of time or forgiveness, the fact that I had held silence—so long!—when he had needed human speech to help him. He turned back to the window. "No, there's no way not to suffer. But you try all kinds of ways to keep from drowning in it, to keep on top of it, and to make it seem—well, like *you*. Like you did something, all right, and now you're suffering for it. You know?" I said nothing. "Well you know," he said, impatiently, "why *do* people suffer? Maybe it's better to do something to give it a reason, *any* reason."

"But we just agreed," I said, "that there's no way not to suffer. Isn't it better, then, just to—take it?"

"But nobody just takes it," Sonny cried, "that's what I'm telling you! *Everybody* tries not to. You're just hung up on the *way* some people try—it's not *your* way!"

The hair on my face began to itch, my face felt wet. "That's not true," I said, "that's not true. I don't give a damn what other people do, I don't even care how they suffer. I just care how *you* suffer." And he looked at me. "Please believe me," I said, "I don't want to see you—die—trying not to suffer."

"I won't," he said, flatly, "die trying not to suffer. At least, not any faster than anybody else."

"But there's no need," I said, trying to laugh, "is there? in killing yourself."   210

I wanted to say more, but I couldn't. I wanted to talk about will power and how life could be—well, beautiful. I wanted to say that it was all within; but was it? or, rather, wasn't that exactly the trouble? And I wanted to promise that I would never fail him again. But it would all have sounded—empty words and lies.

So I made the promise to myself and prayed that I would keep it.

"It's terrible sometimes, inside," he said, "that's what's the trouble. You walk these streets, black and funky and cold, and there's not really a living ass to talk to, and there's nothing shaking, and there's no way of getting it out—that storm inside. You can't talk it and you can't make love with it, and when you finally try to get with it and play it, you realize *nobody's* listening. So *you've* got to listen. You got to find a way to listen."

And then he walked away from the window and sat on the sofa again, as though all the wind had suddenly been knocked out of him. "Sometimes you'll do *anything* to play, even cut your mother's throat." He laughed and looked at me. "Or your brother's." Then he sobered. "Or your own." Then: "Don't worry. I'm all right now and I think I'll *be* all right. But I can't forget—where I've been. I don't mean just the physical place I've been, I mean where I've *been*. And *what* I've been."

"What have you been, Sonny?" I asked.   215

He smiled—but sat sideways on the sofa, his elbow resting on the back, his fingers playing with his mouth and chin, not looking at me. "I've been something I didn't recognize, didn't know I could be. Didn't know anybody could be." He stopped, looking inward, looking helplessly young, looking old. "I'm not talking about it now because I feel *guilty* or anything like that—maybe it would be better if I did, I don't know. Anyway, I can't really talk about it. Not to you, not to anybody," and now he turned and faced me. "Sometimes, you know, and it was actually when I was most *out* of the world, I felt that I was in it, that I was *with* it, really, and I could play or I didn't really have to *play*, it just came out of me, it was there. And I don't know how I played, thinking about it now, but I know I did awful things, those times, sometimes, to people. Or it wasn't that I *did* anything to them—it was that they weren't real." He picked up the beer can; it was empty; he rolled it between his palms: "And other times—well, I needed a fix, I needed to find a place to lean, I needed to clear a space to *listen*—and I couldn't find it, and I—went crazy, I did terrible things to *me*, I was terrible *for* me." He began pressing the beer can between his hands, I watched the metal begin to give. It glittered, as he played with it, like a knife, and I was afraid he would cut himself, but I said nothing. "Oh well, I can never tell you. I was all by myself at the bottom of something, stinking and sweating and crying and shaking, and I smelled it, you know? *my* stink, and I thought I'd die if I couldn't get away from it and yet, all the same, I knew that everything I was doing was just locking me in with it. And I didn't know," he paused, still flattening the beer can, "I didn't know, I still *don't* know, something kept telling me that maybe it was good to smell your own stink, but I didn't think that *that* was what I'd been trying to do—and—who can stand it?" and he abruptly dropped the ruined beer can, looking at me with a small, still smile, and then rose, walking to the window as though it were the lodestone rock. I watched his face, he watched the avenue. "I couldn't tell you when Mama died—but the reason I wanted to leave Harlem so bad was to get away from drugs. And then, when I ran away, that's what I was running from—really. When I came back, nothing had changed, *I* hadn't changed, I was just—older." And he stopped, drumming with his fingers on the windowpane. The sun had vanished, soon darkness would fall. I watched his face. "It can come again," he said, almost as though speaking to himself. Then he turned to me. "It can come again," he repeated. "I just want you to know that."

"All right," I said, at last. "So it can come again, All right."

He smiled, but the smile was sorrowful. "I had to try to tell you," he said.

"Yes," I said. "I understand that."

"You're my brother," he said, looking straight at me, and not smiling at all.   220

"Yes," I repeated, "yes. I understand that."

He turned back to the window, looking out. "All that hatred down there," he said, "all that hatred and misery and love. It's a wonder it doesn't blow the avenue apart."

We went to the only nightclub on a short, dark street, downtown. We squeezed through the narrow, chattering, jampacked bar to the entrance of the big room, where the bandstand was. And we stood there for a moment, for the lights were very dim in this room and we couldn't see. Then, "Hello, boy," said a voice and an enormous black man, much older than Sonny or myself, erupted out of all that atmospheric lighting and put an arm around Sonny's shoulder. "I been sitting right here," he said, "waiting for you."

He had a big voice, too, and heads in the darkness turned toward us.

Sonny grinned and pulled a little away, and said, "Creole, this is my brother. I told   225 you about him."

Creole shook my hand. "I'm glad to meet you, son," he said, and it was clear that he was glad to meet me *there,* for Sonny's sake. And he smiled, "You got a real musician in *your* family," and he took his arm from Sonny's shoulder and slapped him, lightly, affectionately, with the back of his hand.

"Well. Now I've heard it all," said a voice behind us. This was another musician, and a friend of Sonny's, a coal-black, cheerful-looking man, built close to the ground. He immediately began confiding to me, at the top of his lungs, the most terrible things about Sonny, his teeth gleaming like a lighthouse and his laugh coming up out of him like the beginning of an earthquake. And it turned out that everyone at the bar knew Sonny, or almost everyone; some were musicians, working there, or nearby, or not working, some were simply hangers-on, and some were there to hear Sonny play. I was introduced to all of them and they were all very polite to me. Yet it was clear that, for them, I was only Sonny's brother. Here, I was in Sonny's world. Or, rather: his kingdom. Here, it was not even a question that his veins bore royal blood.

They were going to play soon and Creole installed me, by myself, at a table in a dark corner. Then I watched them, Creole, and the little black man, and Sonny, and the others, while they horsed around, standing just below the bandstand. The light from the bandstand spilled just a little short of them and, watching them laughing and gesturing and moving about, I had the feeling that they, nevertheless, were being most careful not to step into that circle of light too suddenly: that if they moved into the light too suddenly, without thinking, they would perish in flame. Then, while I watched, one of them, the small, black man, moved into the light and crossed the bandstand and started fooling around with his drums. Then—being funny and being, also, extremely ceremonious—Creole took Sonny by the arm and led him to the piano. A woman's voice called Sonny's name and a few hands started clapping. And Sonny, also being funny and being ceremonious, and so touched, I think, that he could have cried, but neither hiding it nor showing it, riding it like a man, grinned, and put both hands to his heart and bowed from the waist.

Creole then went to the bass fiddle and a lean, very bright-skinned brown man jumped up on the bandstand and picked up his horn. So there they were, and the atmosphere on the bandstand and in the room began to change and tighten. Someone stepped up to the microphone and announced them. Then there were all kinds of murmurs. Some people at the bar shushed others. The waitress ran around, frantically getting in the last orders, guys and chicks got closer to each other, and the lights on the bandstand, on the quartet, turned to a kind of indigo. Then they all looked different there. Creole looked about him for the last time, as though he were making certain that all his chickens were in the coop, and then he—jumped and struck the fiddle. And there they were.

All I know about music is that not many people ever really hear it. And even then, on the rare occasions when something opens within, and the music enters, what we mainly hear, or hear corroborated, are personal, private, vanishing evocations. But the man who creates the music is hearing something else, is dealing with the roar rising from the void and imposing order on it as it hits the air. What is evoked in him, then, is of another order, more terrible because it has no words, and triumphant, too, for that same reason. And his triumph, when he triumphs, is ours. I just watched Sonny's face. His face was troubled, he was working hard, but he wasn't with it. And I had the feeling that, in a way, everyone on the bandstand was waiting for him, both waiting for him and pushing him along. But as I began to watch Creole, I realized that it was Creole who held them all back. He had them on a short rein. Up there, keeping the beat with his whole body, wailing on the fiddle, with his eyes half closed, he was listening to everything, but he was listening to Sonny. He was having a dialogue with Sonny. He wanted Sonny to leave the shoreline and strike out for the deep water. He was Sonny's witness that deep water and drowning were not the same thing—he had been there, and he knew. And he wanted Sonny to know. He was waiting for Sonny to do the things on the keys which would let Creole know that Sonny was in the water.

And, while Creole listened, Sonny moved, deep within, exactly like someone in torment. I had never before thought of how awful the relationship must be between the musician and his instrument. He has to fill it, this instrument, with the breath of life, his own. He has to make it do what he wants it to do. And a piano is just a piano. It's made out of so much wood and wires and little hammers and big ones, and ivory. While there's only so much you can do with it, the only way to find this out is to try; to try and make it do everything.

And Sonny hadn't been near a piano for over a year. And he wasn't on much better terms with his life, not the life that stretched before him now. He and the piano stammered, started one way, got scared, stopped; started another way, panicked, marked time, started again; then seemed to have found a direction, panicked again, got stuck. And the face I saw on Sonny I'd never seen before. Everything had been burned out of

230

it, and, at the same time, things usually hidden were being burned in, by the fire and fury of the battle which was occurring in him up there.

Yet, watching Creole's face as they neared the end of the first set, I had the feeling that something had happened, something I hadn't heard. Then they finished, there was scattered applause, and then, without an instant's warning, Creole started into something else, it was almost sardonic, it was *Am I Blue*. And, as though he commanded, Sonny began to play. Something began to happen. And Creole let out the reins. The dry, low, black man said something awful on the drums, Creole answered, and the drums talked back. Then the horn insisted, sweet and high, slightly detached perhaps, and Creole listened, commenting now and then, dry, and driving, beautiful and calm and old. Then they all came together again, and Sonny was part of the family again. I could tell this from his face. He seemed to have found, right there beneath his fingers, a damn brand-new piano. It seemed that he couldn't get over it. Then, for awhile, just being happy with Sonny, they seemed to be agreeing with him that brand-new pianos certainly were a gas.

Then Creole stepped forward to remind them that what they were playing was the blues. He hit something in all of them, he hit something in me, myself, and the music tightened and deepened, apprehension began to beat the air. Creole began to tell us what the blues were all about. They were not about anything very new. He and his boys up there were keeping it new, at the risk of ruin, destruction, madness, and death, in order to find new ways to make us listen. For, while the tale of how we suffer, and how we are delighted, and how we may triumph is never new, it always must be heard. There isn't any other tale to tell, it's the only light we've got in all this darkness.

And this tale, according to that face, that body, those strong hands on those strings, has another aspect in every country, and a new depth in every generation. Listen, Creole seemed to be saying, listen. Now these are Sonny's blues. He made the little black man on the drums know it, and the bright, brown man on the horn. Creole wasn't trying any longer to get Sonny in the water. He was wishing him Godspeed. Then he stepped back, very slowly, filling the air with the immense suggestion that Sonny speak for himself. 235

Then they all gathered around Sonny and Sonny played. Every now and again one of them seemed to say, amen. Sonny's fingers filled the air with life, his life. But that life contained so many others. And Sonny went all the way back, he really began with the spare, flat statement of the opening phrase of the song. Then he began to make it his. It was very beautiful because it wasn't hurried and it was no longer a lament. I seemed to hear with what burning he had made it his, with what burning we had yet to make it ours, how we could cease lamenting. Freedom lurked around us and I understood, at last, that he could help us to be free if we would listen, that he would never be free until we did. Yet, there was no battle in his face now. I heard what he had gone through, and would continue to go through until he came to rest in earth. He had made it his: that long line, of which we knew only Mama and Daddy. And he was giving it back, as everything must be given back, so that, passing through death, it can live forever. I saw my mother's face again, and felt, for the first time, how the stones of the road she had walked on must have bruised her feet. I saw the moonlit road where my father's brother died. And it brought something else back to me, and carried me past it, I saw my little girl again and felt Isabel's tears again, and I felt my own tears begin to rise. And I was yet aware that this was only a moment, that the world waited outside, as hungry as a tiger, and that trouble stretched above us, longer than the sky.

Then it was over. Creole and Sonny let out their breath, both soaking wet, and grinning. There was a lot of applause and some of it was real. In the dark, the girl came by and I asked her to take drinks to the bandstand. There was a long pause, while they talked up there in the indigo light and after awhile I saw a girl put a Scotch and milk on top of the piano for Sonny. He didn't seem to notice it, but just before they started playing again, he sipped from it and looked toward me, and nodded. Then he put it back on top of the piano. For me, then, as they began to play again, it glowed and shook above my brother's head like the very cup of trembling.[4] ●

Explorations of the Text

1. After reading the first paragraph, what do you predict about the **narrator** and about the **plot** of the story? Why is the narrator's face "trapped in the darkness which roared outside"? What does the "darkness . . . outside" signify to the children? To the adult narrator? To us as readers?

2. Explore the metaphor of "the block of ice." What does the metaphor reveal about the narrator's feelings for Sonny?

3. Characterize the narrator. What is revealed about his personality in his constant position as an onlooker (at the window in the schoolroom, at the window in his apartment, at the jazz club)?

4. Compare and contrast the narrator and Sonny. Why have they grown up differently?

5. Why does Sonny turn to the life of the streets? drugs? What importance does music play in his life? Will Sonny be saved by music?

6. Why does the relationship between the narrator and Sonny change? What are the narrator's feelings for his brother at the end of the story?

7. What is the meaning of the scene in the club at the end? What does the narrator realize? What does the scotch and milk cocktail that the narrator sends up to Sonny symbolize?

8. The story is told through a series of **flashbacks**. What would the story lose if it were structured chronologically?

The Reading/Writing Connection

1. Baldwin published this story in 1957 about life in Harlem. Does this vision of life still seem real? What might Baldwin write about today?

2. Freewrite and respond to a nonverbal art form (a photograph, a painting, a piece of music) so that someone unfamiliar with the work can share your feelings.

Ideas for Writing

1. Is violence part of the life of the nuclear family? Explore this **theme** in the works of Hayden, Danticat, and/or hooks.

2. Imagine Sonny's future. What are the causes of Sonny's problems? Propose possible solutions.

---

[4]**cup of trembling**: An allusion to the Bible, Isaiah 51:22; "I have taken out of thine hand the cup of trembling . . . thou shalt no more drink it again. . . . "

Alice Walker *(1944–)*

Everyday Use *1973*

For your grandmama

I will wait for her in the yard that Maggie and I made so clean and wavy yesterday afternoon. A yard like this is more comfortable than most people know. It is not just a yard. It is like an extended living room. When the hard clay is swept clean as a floor and the fine sand around the edges lined with tiny, irregular grooves, anyone can come and sit and look up into the elm tree and wait for the breezes that never come inside the house.

Maggie will be nervous until after her sister goes: she will stand hopelessly in corners homely and ashamed of the burn scars down her arms and legs, eyeing her sister with a mixture of envy and awe. She thinks her sister had held life always in the palm of one hand, that "no" is a word the world never learned to say to her.

You've no doubt seen those TV shows where the child who has "made it" is confronted, as a surprise, by her own mother and father, tottering in weakly from backstage. (A pleasant surprise, of course: What would they do if parent and child came on the show only to curse out and insult each other?) On TV mother and child embrace and smile into each other's faces. Sometimes the mother and father weep, the child wraps them in her arms and leans across the table to tell how she would not have made it without their help. I have seen these programs.

Sometimes I dream a dream in which Dee and I are suddenly brought together on a TV program of this sort. Out of a dark and soft-seated limousine I am ushered into a bright room filled with many people. There I meet a smiling, gray, sporty man like Johnny Carson who shakes my hand and tells me what a fine girl I have. Then we are on the stage and Dee is embracing me with tears in her eyes. She pins on my dress a large orchid, even though she has told me once that she thinks orchids are tacky flowers.

In real life I am a large, big-boned woman with rough, man-working hands. In 5 the winter I wear flannel nightgowns to bed and overalls during the day. I can kill and clean a hog as mercilessly as a man. My fat keeps me hot in zero weather. I can work outside all day, breaking ice to get water for washing. I can eat pork liver cooked over the open fire minutes after it comes steaming from the hog. One winter I knocked a bull calf straight in the brain between the eyes with a sledge hammer and had the meat hung up to chill before nightfall. But of course all this does not show on television. I am the way my daughter would want me to be: a hundred pounds lighter, my skin like an uncooked barley pancake. My hair glistens in the hot bright lights. Johnny Carson has much to do to keep up with my quick and witty tongue.

But that is a mistake. I know even before I wake up. Who ever knew a Johnson with a quick tongue? Who can even imagine me looking a strange white man in the eye? It seems to me I have talked to them always with one foot raised in flight, with my head turned in whichever way is farthest from them. Dee, though. She would always look anyone in the eye. Hesitation was no part of her nature.

"How do I look, Mama?" Maggie says, showing just enough of her thin body enveloped in pink skirt and red blouse for me to know she's there, almost hidden by the door.

"Come out into the yard," I say.

Have you ever seen a lame animal, perhaps a dog run over by some careless person rich enough to own a car, sidle up to someone who is ignorant enough to be kind to him? That is the way my Maggie walks. She has been like this, chin on chest, eyes on ground, feet in shuffle, ever since the fire that burned the other house to the ground.

Dee is lighter than Maggie, with nicer hair and a fuller figure. She's a woman now, though sometimes I forget. How long ago was it that the other house burned? Ten, twelve years? Sometimes I can still hear the flames and feel Maggie's arms sticking to me, her hair smoking and her dress falling off her in little black papery flakes. Her eyes seemed stretched open, blazed open by the flames reflected in them. And Dee. I see her standing off under the sweet gum tree she used to dig gum out of; a look of concentration on her face as she watched the last dingy gray board of the house fall in toward the red-hot brick chimney. Why don't you do a dance around the ashes? I'd wanted to ask her. She had hated the house that much.

I used to think she hated Maggie, too. But that was before we raised the money, the church and me, to send her to Augusta to school. She used to read to us without pity; forcing words, lies, other folks' habits, whole lives upon us two, sitting trapped and ignorant underneath her voice. She washed us in a river of make-believe, burned us with a lot of knowledge we didn't necessarily need to know. Pressed us to her with the serious way she read, to shove us away at just the moment, like dimwits, we seemed about to understand.

Dee wanted nice things. A yellow organdy dress to wear to her graduation from high school; black pumps to match a green suit she'd made from an old suit somebody gave me. She was determined to stare down any disaster in her efforts. Her eyelids would not flicker for minutes at a time. Often I fought off the temptation to shake her. At sixteen she had a style of her own: and knew what style was.

I never had an education myself. After second grade the school was closed down. Don't ask me why: in 1927 colored asked fewer questions than they do now. Sometimes Maggie reads to me. She stumbles along goodnaturedly but can't see well. She knows she is not bright. Like good looks and money, quickness passed her by. She will marry John Thomas (who has mossy teeth in an earnest face) and then I'll be free to sit here and I guess just sing church songs to myself. Although I never was a good singer. Never could carry a tune. I was always better at a man's job. I used to love to milk till I was hoofed in the side in '49. Cows are soothing and slow and don't bother you, unless you try to milk them the wrong way.

I have deliberately turned my back on the house. It is three rooms, just like the one that burned, except the roof is tin; they don't make shingle roofs any more. There are no real windows, just some holes cut in the sides, like the portholes in a ship, but not round and not square, with rawhide holding the shutters up on the outside. This house is in a pasture, too, like the other one. No doubt when Dee sees it she will want to tear it down. She wrote me once that no matter where we "choose" to live, she will manage to come see us. But she will never bring her friends. Maggie and I thought about this and Maggie asked me, "Mama, when did Dee ever *have* any friends?"

She had a few. Furtive boys in pink shirts hanging about on washday after school. Nervous girls who never laughed. Impressed with her they worshiped the well-turned phrase, the cute shape, the scalding humor that erupted like bubbles in lye. She read to them.

When she was courting Jimmy T she didn't have much time to pay to us, but turned all her faultfinding power on him. He *flew* to marry a cheap gal from a family of ignorant flashy people. She hardly had time to recompose herself.

When she comes I will meet—but there they are!

Maggie attempts to make a dash for the house, in her shuffling way, but I stay her with my hand. "Come back here," I say. And she stops and tries to dig a well in the sand with her toe.

It is hard to see them clearly through the strong sun. But even the first glimpse of leg out of the car tells me it is Dee. Her feet were always neat-looking, as if God himself had shaped them with a certain style. From the other side of the car comes a short, stocky man. Hair is all over his head a foot long and hanging from his chin like a kinky mule tail. I hear Maggie suck in her breath. "Uhnnnh," is what it sounds like. Like when you see the wriggling end of a snake just in front of your foot on the road. "Uhnnnh."

Dee next. A dress down to the ground, in this hot weather. A dress so loud it hurts   20
my eyes. There are yellows and oranges enough to throw back the light of the sun. I feel my whole face warming from the heat waves it throws out. Earrings, too, gold and hanging down to her shoulders. Bracelets dangling and making noises when she moves her arm up to shake the folds of the dress out of her armpits. The dress is loose and flows, and as she walks closer, I like it. I hear Maggie go "Uhnnnh" again. It is her sister's hair. It stands straight up like the wool on a sheep. It is black as night and around the edges are two long pigtails that rope about like small lizards disappearing behind her ears.

"Wa-su-zo-Tean-o!" she says, coming on in that gliding way the dress makes her move. The short stocky fellow with the hair to his navel is all grinning and he follows up with "Asalamalakim, my mother and sister!" He moves to hug Maggie but she falls back, right up against the back of my chair. I feel her trembling there and when I look up I see the perspiration falling off her chin.

"Don't get up," says Dee. Since I am stout it takes something of a push. You can see me trying to move a second or two before I make it. She turns, showing white heels through her sandals, and goes back to the car. Out she peeks next with a Polaroid. She stoops down quickly and lines up picture after picture of me sitting there in front of the house with Maggie cowering behind me. She never takes a shot without making sure the house is included. When a cow comes nibbling around the edge of the yard she snaps it and me and Maggie *and* the house. Then she puts the Polaroid in the back seat of the car, and comes up and kisses me on the forehead.

Meanwhile Asalamalakim is going through the motions with Maggie's hand. Maggie's hand is as limp as a fish, and probably as cold, despite the sweat, and she keeps trying to pull it back. It looks like Asalamalakim wants to shake hands but wants to do it fancy. Or maybe he don't know how people shake hands. Anyhow, he soon gives up on Maggie.

"Well," I say, "Dee."

"No, Mama," she says. "Not 'Dee,' Wangero Leewanika Kemanjo!"   25

"What happened to 'Dee'?" I wanted to know.

"She's dead," Wangero said. "I couldn't bear it any longer being named after the people who oppress me."

"You know as well as me you was named after your aunt Dicie," I said. Dicie is my sister. She named Dee. We called her "Big Dee" after Dee was born.

"But who was *she* named after?" asked Wangero.

"I guess after Grandma Dee," I said.   30

"And who was she named after?" asked Wangero.

"Her mother," I said, and saw Wangero was getting tired. "That's about as far back as I can trace it," I said. Though, in fact, I probably could have carried it back beyond the Civil War through the branches.

"Well," said Asalamalakim, "there you are."

"Uhnnnh," I heard Maggie say.

"There I was not," I said, "before 'Dicie' cropped up in our family, so why should   35
I try to trace it that far back?"

He just stood there grinning, looking down on me like somebody inspecting a Model A car. Every once in a while he and Wangero sent eye signals over my head.

"How do you pronounce this name?" I asked.

"You don't have to call me by it if you don't want to," said Wangero.

"Why shouldn't I?" I asked. "If that's what you want us to call you, we'll call you."

"I know it might sound awkward at first," said Wangero.   40

"I'll get used to it," I said. "Ream it out again."

Well, soon we got the name out of the way. Asalamalakim had a name twice as long and three times as hard. After I tripped over it two or three times he told me to just call him Hakim-a-barber. I wanted to ask him was he a barber, but I didn't really think he was, so I didn't ask.

"You must belong to those beef-cattle peoples down the road," I said. They said "Asalamalakim" when they met you, too, but they didn't shake hands. Always too busy: feeding the cattle, fixing the fences, putting up saltlick shelters, throwing down hay. When the white folks poisoned some of the herd the men stayed up all night with rifles in their hands. I walked a mile and a half just to see the sight.

Hakim-a-barber said, "I accept some of their doctrines, but farming and raising cattle is not my style." (They didn't tell me, and I didn't ask, whether Wangero [Dee] had really gone and married him.)

We sat down to eat and right away he said he didn't eat collards and pork was un-   45
clean. Wangero, though, went on through the chitlins and corn bread, the greens and everything else. She talked a blue streak over the sweet potatoes. Everything delighted her. Even the fact that we still used the benches her daddy made for the table when we couldn't afford to buy chairs.

"Oh, Mama!" she cried. Then turned to Hakim-a-barber. "I never knew how lovely these benches are. You can feel the rump prints," she said, running her hands underneath her and along the bench. Then she gave a sigh and her hand closed over Grandma Dee's butter dish. "That's it!" she said. "I knew there was something I wanted to ask you if I could have." She jumped up from the table and went over in the corner where the churn stood, the milk in it clabber by now. She looked at the churn and looked at it.

"This churn top is what I need," she said. "Didn't Uncle Buddy whittle it out of a tree you all used to have?"

"Yes," I said.

"Uh huh," she said happily. "And I want the dasher, too."

"Uncle Buddy whittle that, too?" asked the barber.   50

Dee (Wangero) looked up at me.

"Aunt Dee's first husband whittled the dash," said Maggie so low you almost couldn't hear her. "His name was Henry, but they called him Stash."

"Maggie's brain is like an elephant's," Wangero said, laughing. "I can use the churn top as a centerpiece for the alcove table," she said, sliding a plate over the churn, "and I'll think of something artistic to do with the dasher."

When she finished wrapping the clasher the handle stuck out. I took it for a moment in my hands. You didn't even have to look close to see where hands pushing the dasher up and down to make butter had left a kind of sink in the wood. In fact, there were a lot of small sinks; you could see where thumbs and fingers had sunk into the wood. It was beautiful light yellow wood, from a tree that grew in the yard where Big Dee and Stash had lived.

After dinner Dee (Wangero) went to the trunk at the foot of my bed and started 55 rifling through it. Maggie hung back in the kitchen over the dishpan. Out came Wangero with two quilts. They had been pieced by Grandma Dee and then Big Dee and me had hung them on the quilt frames on the front porch and quilted them. One was in the Lone Star pattern. The other was Walk Around the Mountain. In both of them were scraps of dresses Grandma Dee had worn fifty and more years ago. Bits and pieces of Grandpa Jarrell's paisley shirts. And one teeny faded blue piece, about the size of a penny matchbox, that was from Great Grandpa Ezra's uniform that he wore in the Civil War.

"Mama," Wangero said sweet as a bird. "Can I have these old quilts?"

I heard something fall in the kitchen, and a minute later the kitchen door slammed.

"Why don't you take one or two of the others?" I asked. "These old things was just done by me and Big Dee from some tops your grandma pieced before she died."

"No," said Wangero. "I don't want those. They are stitched around the borders by machine."

"That's make them last better," I said. 60

"That's not the point," said Wangero. "These are all pieces of dresses Grandma used to wear. She did all this stitching by hand. Imagine!" She held the quilts securely in her arms, stroking them.

"Some of the pieces, like those lavender ones, come from old clothes her mother handed down to her," I said, moving up to touch the quilts. Dee (Wangero) moved back just enough so that I couldn't reach the quilts. They already belonged to her.

"Imagine!" she breathed again, clutching them closely to her bosom.

"The truth is," I said, "I promised to give them quilts to Maggie, for when she marries John Thomas."

She gasped like a bee had stung her. 65

"Maggie can't appreciate these quilts!" she said. "She'd probably be backward enough to put them to everyday use."

"I reckon she would," I said. "God knows I been saving 'em for long enough with nobody using 'em. I hope she will!" I didn't want to bring up how I had offered Dee (Wangero) a quilt when she went away to college. Then she had told me they were old-fashioned, out of style.

"But they're *priceless!*" she was saying now, furiously; for she has a temper. "Maggie would put them on the bed and in five years they'd be in rags. Less than that!"

"She can always make some more," I said. "Maggie knows how to quilt."

Dee (Wangero) looked at me with hatred. "You just will not understand. The point 70 is these quilts, *these* quilts!"

"Well," I said, stumped. "What would *you* do with them?"

"Hang them," she said. As if that was the only thing you *could* do with quilts.

Maggie by now was standing in the door. I could almost hear the sound her feet made as they scraped over each other.

"She can have them, Mama," she said, like somebody used to never winning anything, or having anything reserved for her. "I can 'member Grandma Dee without the quilts."

I looked at her hard. She had filled her bottom lip with checkerberry snuff and it gave her face a kind of dopey, hangdog look. It was Grandma Dee and Big Dee who taught her how to quilt herself. She stood there with her scarred hands hidden in the folds of her skirt. She looked at her sister with something like fear but she wasn't mad at her. This was Maggie's portion. This was the way she knew God to work.

When I looked at her like that something hit me in the top of my head and ran down to the soles of my feet. Just like when I'm in church and the spirit of God touches me and I get happy and shout. I did something I never had done before: hugged Maggie to me, then dragged her on into the room, snatched the quilts out of Miss Wangero's hands and dumped them into Maggie's lap. Maggie just sat there on my bed with her mouth open.

"Take one or two of the others," I said to Dee.

But she turned without a word and went out to Hakim-a-barber.

"You just don't understand," she said, as Maggie and I came out to the car.

"What don't I understand?" I wanted to know.

"Your heritage," she said. And then she turned to Maggie, kissed her, and said, "You ought to try to make something of yourself, too, Maggie. It's really a new day for us. But from the way you and Mama still live you'd never know it."

She put on some sunglasses that hid everything above the tip of her nose and her chin.

Maggie smiled; maybe at the sunglasses. But a real smile, not scared. After we watched the car dust settle I asked Maggie to bring me a dip of snuff. And then the two of us sat there just enjoying, until it was time to go in the house and go to bed. ●

Explorations of the Text

1. Explain the title of the story. Why is it significant?
2. Why does Wangero, who was once embarrassed by her family's poverty, now embrace it?
3. Explain the symbolism of the quilts. Why does Maggie's mother insist that she, and not Wangero, keep them?
4. Wangero accuses her mother and Maggie of not understanding their heritage. What does "heritage" mean to Wangero? To Maggie and her mother?
5. Geeta Kothari and Chang-rae Lee write about the foods that remind them of home. What memories of home might Maggie bring to her new home with her husband? How are these memories of food or beloved possessions related to heritage?

The Reading/Writing Connection

1. In the third paragraph of the story, Walker inserts a line in parentheses, "What would they do if parent and child came on the [TV] show only to curse out and insult each other?" Walker's story was written in 1973 when

Jerry Springer and others did not encourage people to publicly confront one another. Create a skit in which Wangero and her mother are on the Jerry Springer show. What would they say to one another?

2. Write about objects from your home that remind you of your own heritage.

Explain the symbolic importance of each object.

3. Find some quilting images online (search for Gee's Bend Quilts). Design a quilt that would best represent your family.

Ideas for Writing

1. **Write an Argument:** Write an argument in which you take Wangero's perspective that the old family quilts need to be protected against "everyday use." Or argue from the other side.

2. In embracing her heritage, is Wangero actually distancing herself from it?

Write an essay in which you explain the complex themes of heritage that exist in this story.

3. Write a feminist analysis of Walker's story using Nikki Giovanni's poem "Quilts" (Chapter 5) as a critical lens.

Amy Tan *(1952–)*

Scar *1989*
From *The Joy Luck Club*

When I was a young girl in China, my grandmother told me my mother was a ghost. This did not mean my mother was dead. In those days, a ghost was anything we were forbidden to talk about. So I knew Popo wanted me to forget my mother on purpose, and this is how I came to remember nothing of her. The life that I knew began in the large house in Ningpo with the cold hallways and tall stairs. This was my uncle and auntie's family house, where I lived with Popo and my little brother.

But I often heard stories of a ghost who tried to take children away, especially strong-willed little girls who were disobedient. Many times Popo said aloud to all who could hear that my brother and I had fallen out of the bowels of a stupid goose, two eggs that nobody wanted, not even good enough to crack over rice porridge. She said this so that the ghosts would not steal us away. So you see, to Popo we were also very precious.

All my life, Popo scared me. I became even more scared when she grew sick. This was in 1923, when I was nine years old. Popo had swollen up like an overripe squash, so full her flesh had gone soft and rotten with a bad smell. She would call me into her room with the terrible stink and tell me stories. "An-mei," she said, calling me by my school name. "Listen carefully." She told me stories I could not understand.

One was about a greedy girl whose belly grew fatter and fatter. This girl poisoned herself after refusing to say whose child she carried. When the monks cut open her body, they found inside a large white winter melon.

"If you are greedy, what is inside you is what makes you always hungry," said 5
Popo.

Another time, Popo told me about a girl who refused to listen to her elders. One day this bad girl shook her head so vigorously to refuse her auntie's simple request that a little white ball fell from her ear and out poured all her brains, as clear as chicken broth.

"Your own thoughts are so busy swimming inside that everything else gets pushed out," Popo told me.

Right before Popo became so sick she could no longer speak, she pulled me close and talked to me about my mother. "Never say her name," she warned. "To say her name is to spit on your father's grave."

The only father I knew was a big painting that hung in the main hall. He was a large, unsmiling man, unhappy to be so still on the wall. His restless eyes followed me around the house. Even from my room at the end of the hall, I could see my father's watching eyes. Popo said he watched me for any signs of disrespect. So sometimes, when I had thrown pebbles at other children at school, or had lost a book through carelessness, I would quickly walk by my father with a know-nothing look and hide in a corner of my room where he could not see my face.

I felt our house was so unhappy, but my little brother did not seem to think   10 so. He rode his bicycle through the courtyard, chasing chickens and other children, laughing over which ones shrieked the loudest. Inside the quiet house, he jumped up and down on Uncle and Auntie's best feather sofas when they were away visiting village friends.

But even my brother's happiness went away. One hot summer day when Popo was already very sick, we stood outside watching a village funeral procession marching by our courtyard. Just as it passed our gate, the heavy framed picture of the dead man toppled from its stand and fell to the dusty ground. An old lady screamed and fainted. My brother laughed and Auntie slapped him.

My auntie, who had a very bad temper with children, told him he had no *shou*, no respect for ancestors or family, just like our mother. Auntie had a tongue like hungry scissors eating silk cloth. So when my brother gave her a sour look, Auntie said our mother was so thoughtless she had fled north in a big hurry, without taking the dowry furniture from her marriage to my father, without bringing her ten pairs of silver chopsticks, without paying respect to my father's grave and those of our ancestors. When my brother accused Auntie of frightening our mother away, Auntie shouted that our mother had married a man named Wu Tsing who already had a wife, two concubines, and other bad children.

And when my brother shouted that Auntie was a talking chicken without a head, she pushed my brother against the gate and spat on his face.

"You throw strong words at me, but you are nothing," Auntie said. "You are the son of a mother who has so little respect she has become *ni*, a traitor to our ancestors. She is so beneath others that even the devil must look down to see her."

That is when I began to understand the stories Popo taught me, the lessons I   15 had to learn for my mother. "When you lose your face, An-mei," Popo often said, "it is like dropping your necklace down a well. The only way you can get it back is to fall in after it."

Now I could imagine my mother, a thoughtless woman who laughed and shook her head, who dipped her chopsticks many times to eat another piece of sweet fruit, happy to be free of Popo, her unhappy husband on the wall, and her two disobedient children. I felt unlucky that she was my mother and unlucky that she had left us. These were the thoughts I had while hiding in the corner of my room where my father could not watch me.

I was sitting at the top of the stairs when she arrived. I knew it was my mother even though I had not seen her in all my memory. She stood just inside the doorway so that her face became a dark shadow. She was much taller than my auntie, almost as tall as my uncle. She looked strange, too, like the missionary ladies at our school who were insolent and bossy in their too-tall shoes, foreign clothes, and short hair.

My auntie quickly looked away and did not call her by name or offer her tea. An old servant hurried away with a displeased look. I tried to keep very still, but my heart felt like crickets scratching to get out of a cage. My mother must have heard, because she looked up. And when she did, I saw my own face looking back at me. Eyes that stayed wide open and saw too much.

In Popo's room my auntie protested, "Too late, too late," as my mother approached the bed. But this did not stop my mother.

"Come back, stay here," murmured my mother to Popo. "*Nuyer* is here. Your ⟨20⟩ daughter is back." Popo's eyes were open, but now her mind ran in many different directions, not staying long enough to see anything. If Popo's mind had been clear she would have raised her two arms and flung my mother out of the room.

I watched my mother, seeing her for the first time, this pretty woman with her white skin and oval face, not too round like Auntie's or sharp like Popo's. I saw that she had a long white neck, just like the goose that had laid me. That she seemed to float back and forth like a ghost, dipping cool cloths to lay on Popo's bloated face. As she peered into Popo's eyes, she clucked soft worried sounds. I watched her carefully, yet it was her voice that confused me, a familiar sound from a forgotten dream.

When I returned to my room later that afternoon, she was there, standing tall. And because I remember Popo told me not to speak her name, I stood there, mute. She took my hand and led me to the settee. And then she also sat down as though we had done this every day.

My mother began to loosen my braids and brush my hair with long sweeping strokes.

"An-mei, you have been a good daughter?" she asked, smiling a secret look.

I looked at her with my know-nothing face, but inside I was trembling. I was the ⟨25⟩ girl whose belly held a colorless winter melon.

"An-mei, you know who I am," she said with a small scold in her voice. This time I did not look for fear my head would burst and my brains would dribble out of my ears.

She stopped brushing. And then I could feel her long smooth fingers rubbing and searching under my chin, finding the spot that was my smooth-neck scar. As she rubbed this spot, I became very still. It was as though she were rubbing the memory back into my skin. And then her hand dropped and she began to cry, wrapping her hands around her own neck. She cried with a wailing voice that was so sad. And then I remembered the dream with my mother's voice.

I was four years old. My chin was just above the dinner table, and I could see my baby brother sitting on Popo's lap, crying with an angry face. I could hear voices praising a steaming dark soup brought to the table, voices murmuring politely, *"Ching! Ching!"*—Please, eat!

And then the talking stopped. My uncle rose from his chair. Everyone turned to look at the door, where a tall woman stood. I was the only one who spoke.

"Ma," I had cried, rushing off my chair, but my auntie slapped my face and pushed me back down. Now everyone was standing up and shouting, and I heard my mother's voice crying, "An-mei! An-mei!" Above this noise, Popo's shrill voice spoke. 30

"Who is this ghost? Not an honored widow. Just a number-three concubine. If you take your daughter, she will become like you. No face. Never able to lift up her head."

Still my mother shouted for me to come. I remember her voice so clearly now. An-mei! An-mei! I could see my mother's face across the table. Between us stood the soup pot on its heavy chimney-pot stand—rocking slowly, back and forth. And then with one shout this dark boiling soup spilled forward and fell all over my neck. It was as though everyone's anger were pouring all over me.

This was the kind of pain so terrible that a little child should never remember it. But it is still in my skin's memory. I cried out loud only a little, because soon my flesh began to burst inside and out and cut off my breathing air.

I could not speak because of this terrible choking feeling. I could not see because of all the tears that poured out to wash away the pain. But I could hear my mother's crying voice. Popo and Auntie were shouting. And then my mother's voice went away.

Later that night Popo's voice came to me. 35

"An-mei, listen carefully." Her voice had the same scolding tone she used when I ran up and down the hallway. "An-mei, we have made your dying clothes and shoes for you. They are all white cotton."

I listened, scared.

"An-mei," she murmured, now more gently. "Your dying clothes are very plain. They are not fancy, because you are still a child. If you die, you will have a short life and you will still owe your family a debt. Your funeral will be very small. Our mourning time for you will be very short."

And then Popo said something that was worse than the burning on my neck.

"Even your mother has used up her tears and left. If you do not get well soon, she will forget you." 40

Popo was very smart. I came hurrying back from the other world to find my mother.

Every night I cried so that both my eyes and my neck burned. Next to my bed sat Popo. She would pour cool water over my neck from the hollowed cup of a large grape-fruit. She would pour and pour until my breathing became soft and I could fall asleep. In the morning, Popo would use her sharp fingernails like tweezers and peel off the dead membranes.

In two years' time, my scar became pale and shiny and I had no memory of my mother. That is the way it is with a wound. The wound begins to close in on itself, to protect what is hurting so much. And once it is closed, you no longer see what is underneath, what started the pain.

I worshipped this mother from my dream. But the woman standing by Popo's bed was not the mother of my memory. Yet I came to love this mother as well. Not because she came to me and begged me to forgive her. She did not. She did not need to explain that Popo chased her out of the house when I was dying. This I knew. She did not need to tell me she married Wu Tsing to exchange one unhappiness for another. I knew this as well.

Here is how I came to love my mother. How I saw in her my own true nature. What was beneath my skin. Inside my bones. 45

It was late at night when I went to Popo's room. My auntie said it was Popo's dying time and I must show respect. I put on a clean dress and stood between my auntie and uncle at the foot of Popo's bed. I cried a little, not too loud.

I saw my mother on the other side of the room. Quiet and sad. She was cooking a soup, pouring herbs and medicines into the steaming pot. And then I saw her pull up her sleeve and pull out a sharp knife. She put this knife on the softest part of her arm. I tried to close my eyes, but could not.

And then my mother cut a piece of meat from her arm. Tears poured from her face and blood spilled to the floor.

My mother took her flesh and put it in the soup. She cooked magic in the ancient tradition to try to cure her mother this one last time. She opened Popo's mouth, already too tight from trying to keep her spirit in. She fed her this soup, but that night Popo flew away with her illness.

Even though I was young, I could see the pain of the flesh and the worth of the 50 pain.

This is how a daughter honors her mother. It is *shou* so deep it is in your bones. The pain of the flesh is nothing. The pain you must forget. Because sometimes that is the only way to remember what is in your bones. You must peel off your skin, and that of your mother, and her mother before her. Until there is nothing. No scar, no skin, no flesh. ●

Explorations of the Text

1. Why is An-Mei Hsu's mother considered a "ghost" by the family? Why is she a "ghost" to the little girl?
2. Why does Popo tell the child scary stories?
3. What are An-Mei's feelings about her father? Explain the symbolism of the portrait.
4. What motivates Auntie's behavior? What effect do her actions have on An-Mei and on her brother?
5. Does An-Mei feel that her mother loves her when her mother returns?
6. What are the symbolic implications of the scenes in which An-Mei becomes sick because the soup spilled and in which An-Mei's mother cuts her own flesh and puts it into the soup for her mother, Popo?

The Reading/Writing Connection

1. "Think" Topic: What is the importance of the scar? Discuss the meaning of this passage: "In two years' time, my scar became pale and shiny and I had no memory of my mother. That is the way it is with a wound. The wound begins to close in on itself, to protect what is hurting so much. And once it is closed, you no longer see what is underneath, what started the pain."
2. What does the closing paragraph reveal? What is meant by "You must peel off your skin, and that of your mother, and her mother before her. Until there is nothing. No scar, no skin, no flesh"? Create a double-entry for the ending of the work.

Ideas for Writing

1. What does "Scar" imply about the relationships between parents and children in Chinese society? How are children supposed to behave? What values are important?

2. Explore the theme of intense connectedness between mothers and their daughters in "Girl," "Scar," and/or "Beginning Dialogues."

3. Explore the theme of loss between parents and children in "Scar," "Persimmons," "Daddy," "Night Talkers," and/or "Some Memories of My Father."

Louise Erdrich *(1954–   )*

The Shawl 2001

Among the Anishinaabeg on the road where I live, it is told how a woman loved a man other than her husband and went off into the bush and bore his child. Her name was Aanakwad, which means cloud, and like a cloud she was changeable. She was moody and sullen one moment, her lower lip jutting and her eyes flashing, filled with storms. The next, she would shake her hair over her face and blow it straight out in front of her to make her children scream with laughter. For she also had two children by her husband, one a yearning boy of five years and the other a capable daughter of nine.

When Aanakwad brought the new baby out of the trees that autumn, the older girl was like a second mother, even waking in the night to clean the baby and nudge it to her mother's breast. Aanakwad slept through its cries, hardly woke. It wasn't that she didn't love her baby; no, it was the opposite—she loved it too much, the way she loved its father, and not her husband. This passion ate away at her, and her feelings were unbearable. If she could have thrown off that wronghearted love, she would have, but the thought of the other man, who lived across the lake, was with her always. She became a gray sky, stared monotonously at the walls, sometimes wept into her hands for hours at a time. Soon, she couldn't rise to cook or keep the cabin neat, and it was too much for the girl, who curled up each night exhausted in her red-and-brown plaid shawl, and slept and slept, until the husband had to wake her to awaken her mother, for he was afraid of his wife's bad temper, and it was he who roused Aanakwad into anger by the sheer fact that he was himself and not the other.

At last, even though he loved Aanakwad, the husband had to admit that their life together was no good anymore. And it was he who sent for the other man's uncle. In those days, our people lived widely scattered, along the shores and in the islands, even out on the plains. There were no roads then, just trails, though we had horses and wagons and, for the winter, sleds. When the uncle came around to fetch Aanakwad, in his wagon fitted out with sled runners, it was very hard, for she and her husband had argued right up to the last about the children, argued fiercely until the husband had finally given in. He turned his face to the wall, and did not move to see the daughter, whom he treasured, sit down beside her mother, wrapped in her plaid robe in the wagon bed. They left right away, with their bundles and sacks, not bothering to heat up the stones to warm their feet. The father had stopped his ears, so he did not hear his son cry out when he suddenly understood that he would be left behind.

As the uncle slapped the reins and the horse lurched forward, the boy tried to jump into the wagon, but his mother pried his hands off the boards, crying, *Gego.gego,* and he fell down hard. But there was something in him that would not let her leave. He jumped up and, although he was wearing only light clothing, he ran behind the wagon over the packed drifts. The horses picked up speed. His chest was scorched with pain, and yet he pushed himself on. He'd never run so fast, so hard and furiously, but he was determined, and he refused to believe that the increasing distance between him and the wagon was real. He kept going until his throat closed, he saw red, and in the ice of the air his lungs shut. Then, as he fell onto the board-hard snow, he raised his head. He watched the back of the wagon and the tiny figures of his mother and sister disappear, and something failed in him. Something broke. At that moment he truly did not care if he was alive or dead. So when he saw the gray shapes, the shadows, bounding lightly from the trees to either side of the trail, far ahead, he was not afraid.

The next the boy knew, his father had him wrapped on a blanket and was carrying him home. His father's chest was broad and, although he already spat the tubercular blood that would write the end of his story, he was still a strong man. It would take him many years to die. In those years, the father would tell the boy, who had forgotten this part entirely, that at first when he talked about the shadows the father thought he'd been visited by *manidoog*. But then, as the boy described the shapes, his father had understood that they were not spirits. Uneasy, he had decided to take his gun back along the trail. He had built up the fire in the cabin, and settled his boy near it, and gone back out into the snow. Perhaps the story spread through our settlements because the father had to tell what he saw, again and again, in order to get rid of it. Perhaps as with all frightful dreams, *amaniso,* he had to talk about it to destroy its power—though in this case nothing could stop the dream from being real.

The shadows' tracks were the tracks of wolves, and in those days, when our guns had taken all their food for furs and hides to sell, the wolves were bold and had abandoned the old agreement between them and the first humans. For a time, until we understood and let the game increase, the wolves hunted us. The father bounded forward when he saw the tracks. He could see where the pack, desperate, had tried to slash the tendons of the horses' legs. Next, where they'd leaped for the back of the wagon. He hurried on to where the trail gave out at the broad empty ice of the lake. There, he saw what he saw, scattered, and the ravens, attending to the bitter small leavings of the wolves.

For a time, the boy had no understanding of what had happened. His father kept what he knew to himself, at least that first year, and when his son asked about his sister's torn plaid shawl, and why it was kept in the house, his father said nothing. But he wept when the boy asked if his sister was cold. It was only after his father had been weakened by the disease that he began to tell the story, far too often and always the same way: he told how when the wolves closed in Aanakwad had thrown her daughter to them.

When his father said those words, the boy went still. What had his sister felt? What had thrust through her heart? Had something broken inside her, too, as it had in him? Even then, he knew that this broken place inside him would not be mended, except by some terrible means. For he kept seeing his mother put the baby down and grip his sister around the waist. He saw Aanakwad swing the girl lightly out over the side of the wagon. He saw the brown shawl with its red lines flying open. He saw the shadows, the wolves, rush together, quick and avid, as the wagon with sled runners disappeared into the distance—forever, for neither he nor his father saw Aanakwad again.

When I was little, my own father terrified us with his drinking. This was after we lost our mother, because before that the only time I was aware that he touched the *ishkode waaboo* was on an occasional weekend when they got home late, or sometimes during berry-picking gatherings when we went out to the bush and camped with others. Not until she died did he start the heavy sort of drinking, the continuous drinking, where we were left alone in the house for days. The kind where, when he came home, we'd jump out the window and hide in the woods while he barged around, shouting for us. We'd go back only after he had fallen dead asleep.

There were three of us: me, the oldest at ten, and my little sister and brother, twins, and only six years old. I was surprisingly good at taking care of them, I think, and because we learned to survive together during those drinking years we have always been close. Their names are Doris and Raymond, and they married a brother and sister. When we get together, which is often, for we live on the same road, there come times in the talking and card-playing, and maybe even in the light beer now and then, when we will bring up those days. Most people understand how it was. Our story isn't uncommon. But for us it helps to compare our points of view.

How else would I know, for instance, that Raymond saw me the first time I hid my father's belt? I pulled it from around his waist while he was passed out, and then I buried it in the woods. I kept doing it after that. Our father couldn't understand why his belt was always stolen when he went to town drinking. He even accused his *shkwebii* buddies of the theft. But I had good reasons. Not only was he embarrassed, afterward, to go out with his pants held up by rope, but he couldn't snake his belt out in anger and snap the hooked buckle end in the air. He couldn't hit us with it. Of course, being resourceful, he used other things. There was a board. A willow wand. And there was himself—his hands and fists and boots—and things he could throw. But eventually it became easy to evade him, and after a while we rarely suffered a bruise or a scratch. We had our own place in the woods, even a little campfire for the cold nights. And we'd take money from him every chance we got, slip it from his shoe, where he thought it well hidden. He became, for us, a thing to be avoided, outsmarted, and exploited. We survived off him as if he were a capricious and dangerous line of work. I suppose we stopped thinking of him as a human being, certainly as a father.

I got my growth earlier than some boys, and, one night when I was thirteen and Doris and Raymond and I were sitting around wishing for something besides the oatmeal and commodity canned milk I'd stashed so he couldn't sell them, I heard him coming down the road. He was shouting and making noise all the way to the house, and Doris and Raymond looked at me and headed for the back window. When they saw that I wasn't coming, they stopped. C'mon, *ondaas,* get with it—they tried to pull me along. I shook them off and told them to get out quickly—I was staying. I think I can take him now is what I said.

He was big; he hadn't yet wasted away from the alcohol. His nose had been pushed to one side in a fight, then slammed back to the other side, so now it was straight. His teeth were half gone, and he smelled the way he had to smell, being five days drunk. When he came in the door, he paused for a moment, his eyes red and swollen, tiny slits. Then he saw that I was waiting for him, and he smiled in a bad way. My first punch surprised him. I had been practicing on a hay-stuffed bag, then on a padded board, toughening my fists, and I'd got so quick I flickered like fire. I still wasn't as strong as he was, and he had a good twenty pounds on me. Yet I'd do some damage, I was sure of it. I'd teach him not to mess with me. What I didn't foresee was how the fight itself would get right into me.

There is something terrible about fighting your father. It came on suddenly, with the second blow—a frightful kind of joy. A power surged up from the center of me, and I danced at him, light and giddy, full of a heady rightness. Here is the thing: I wanted to waste him, waste him good. I wanted to smack the living shit out of him. Kill him, if I must. A punch for Doris, a kick for Raymond. And all the while I was silent, then screaming, then silent again, in this rage of happiness that filled me with a simultaneous despair so that, I guess you could say, I stood apart from myself.

He came at me, crashed over a chair that was already broken, then threw the pieces. I grabbed one of the legs and whacked him on the ear so that his head spun and turned back to me, bloody, I watched myself striking him again and again. I knew what I was doing, but not really, not in the ordinary sense. It was as if I were standing calm, against the wall with my arms folded, pitying us both. I saw the boy, the chair leg, the man fold and fall, his hands held up in begging fashion. Then I also saw that, for a while now, the bigger man had not even bothered to fight back.

Suddenly, he was my father again. And when I knelt down next to him, I was his son. I reached for the closest rag, and picked up this piece of blanket that my father always kept with him for some reason. And as I picked it up and wiped the blood off his face, I said to him. Your nose is crooked again. He looked at me, steady and quizzical, as though he had never had a drink in his life, and I wiped his face again with that frayed piece of blanket. Well, it was a shawl, really, a kind of old-fashioned woman's blanket-shawl. Once, maybe, it had been plaid. You could still see lines, some red, the background a faded brown. He watched intently as my hand brought the rag to his face. I was pretty sure, then, that I'd clocked him too hard, that he'd really lost it now. Gently, though, he clasped one hand around my wrist. With the other hand he took the shawl. He crumpled it and held it to the middle of his forehead. It was as if he were praying, as if he were having thoughts he wanted to collect in that piece of cloth. For a while he lay like that, and I, crouched over, let him be, hardly breathing. Something told me to sit there, still. And then at last he said to me, in the sober new voice I would hear from then on, *Did you know I had a sister once?*

There was a time when the government moved everybody off the farthest reaches of the reservation, onto roads, into towns, into housing. It looked good at first, and then it all went sour. Shortly afterward, it seemed that anyone who was someone was either drunk, killed, near suicide, or had just dusted himself. None of the old sort were left, it seemed—the old kind of people, the Geteanishinaabeg, who are kind beyond kindness and would do anything for others. It was during that time that my mother died and my father hurt us, as I have said.

Now, gradually, that term of despair has lifted somewhat and yielded up its survivors. But we still have sorrows that are passed to us from early generations, sorrows to handle in addition to our own, and cruelties lodged where we cannot forget them. We have the need to forget. We are always walking on oblivion's edge.

Some get away, like my brother and sister, married now and living quietly down the road. And me, to some degree, though I prefer to live alone. And even my father, who recently found a woman. Once, when he brought up the old days, and we went over the story again, I told him at last the two things I had been thinking.

First, I told him that keeping his sister's shawl was wrong, because we never keep the clothing of the dead. Now's the time to burn it, I said. Send it off to cloak her spirit. And he agreed.

The other thing I said to him was in the form of a question. Have you ever considered, I asked him, given how tenderhearted your sister was, and how brave, that she looked at the whole situation? She saw that the wolves were only hungry. She knew that their need was only need. She knew that you were back there, alone in the snow. She understood that the baby she loved would not live without a mother, and that only the uncle knew the way. She saw clearly that one person on the wagon had to be offered up, or they all would die. And in that moment of knowledge, don't you think, being who she was, of the old sort of Anishinaabeg, who thinks of the good of the people first, she jumped, my father, *n'dede,* brother to that little girl? Don't you think she lifted her shawl and flew? ●

Explorations of the Text

1. Why does Erdrich begin the story with the Anishinaabeg tale? How does the tale relate to the narrator's life story? Discuss the symbolism of the wolves.
2. Analyze the narrator's role in the family. How does he differ from his brother and his sister? Characterize the children's relationship with their father.
3. How does the power dynamic, the relationship between father and son, shift in the climactic scene of the narrator's confrontation with his father? What do the descriptive details of the fight suggest about their relationship?
4. What does the father reveal about his past life? Interpret the symbolism of the shawl.
5. Consider the theme of generational legacies in the story. How does the narrator retell both the Anishinaabeg tale and his father's story? How does it continue the life of the tribe?
6. Explore the concept of bearing witness in this work and in hooks's autobiographical narrative.

The Reading/Writing Connection

1. Freewrite about a treasured object from your childhood. What does it signify in your life?
2. "Think" Topic: Compare the symbolism of wolves in this work with Carter's "The Company of Wolves" (Chapter 5).
3. Journal entry: Write about a family story that has been handed down from one generation to the next, or write about an incident from the past. Ask several family members to relate the same event. How do their versions differ? What do you conclude?

Ideas for Writing

1. In an essay entitled, "Language and Literature from a Pueblo Indian Perspective," Leslie Silko suggests that storytelling is vital to the survival of a community. How does this vision of talk-story apply to Erdrich's "The Shawl"? To Silko's "Yellow Woman" (Chapter 7)? To Kingston's "No Name Woman" (Chapter 7)?
2. Compare and contrast the symbolism of the shawl in this work with that of Ozick's "The Shawl" (Chapter 8).

The Family Gothic/Fiction

Nathaniel Hawthorne *(1804–1864)*

Rappaccini's Daughter *1846*

A young man, named Giovanni Guasconti, came, very long ago, from the more southern region of Italy, to pursue his studies at the University of Padua. Giovanni, who had but a scanty supply of gold ducats[1] in his pocket, took lodgings in a high gloomy chamber of an old edifice which looked not unworthy to have been the palace of a Paduan noble, and which, in fact, exhibited over its entrance the armorial bearings of a family long since extinct. The young stranger, who was not unstudied in the great poem of his country, recollected that one of the ancestors of this family, and perhaps an occupant of this very mansion, had been pictured by Dante as a partaker of the immortal agonies of his Inferno.[2] These reminiscences and associations, together with the tendency to heartbreak natural to a young man for the first time out of his native sphere, caused Giovanni to sigh heavily as he looked around the desolate and ill-furnished apartment.

"Holy Virgin, signor!" cried old Dame Lisabetta, who, won by the youth's remarkable beauty of person was kindly endeavoring to give the chamber a habitable air, "what a sigh was that to come out of a young man's heart! Do you find this old mansion gloomy? For the love of Heaven, then, put your head out of the window, and you will see as bright sunshine as you have left in Naples."

Guasconti mechanically did as the old woman advised, but could not quite agree with her that the Paduan sunshine was as cheerful as that of southern Italy. Such as it was, however, it fell upon a garden beneath the window and expended its fostering influences on a variety of plants, which seemed to have been cultivated with exceeding care.

"Does this garden belong to the house?" asked Giovanni.

"Heaven forbid, signor, unless it were fruitful of better pot herbs than any that grow there now," answered old Lisabetta. "No; that garden is cultivated by the own hands of Signor Giacomo Rappaccini, the famous doctor, who, I warrant him, has been heard of as far as Naples. It is said that he distils these plants into medicines that are as potent as a charm. Oftentimes you may see the signor doctor at work, and perchance the signora, his daughter, too, gathering the strange flowers that grow in the garden."

The old woman had now done what she could for the aspect of the chamber; and, commending the young man to the protection of the saints, took her departure.

Giovanni still found no better occupation than to look down into the garden beneath his window. From its appearance, he judged it to be one of those botanic gardens which were of earlier date in Padua than elsewhere in Italy or in the world. Or, not improbably, it might once have been the pleasure-place of an opulent family; for there

---

[1]**gold ducats**: Gold coins.   [2]**Inferno:**In *Inferno* 18:71, Dante mentions an unnamed Paduan nobleman among those who have committed crimes against Nature.

was the ruin of a marble fountain in the centre, sculptured with rare art, but so wofully shattered that it was impossible to trace the original design from the chaos of remaining fragments. The water, however, continued to gush and sparkle into the sunbeams as cheerfully as ever. A little gurgling sound ascended to the young man's window and made him feel as if the fountain were an immortal spirit that sung its song unceasingly and without heeding the vicissitudes around it, while one century imbodied it in marble and another scattered the perishable garniture on the soil. All about the pool into which the water subsided grew various plants, that seemed to require a plentiful supply of moisture for the nourishment of gigantic leaves, and, in some instances, flowers gorgeously magnificent. There was one shrub in particular, set in a marble vase in the midst of the pool, that bore a profusion of purple blossoms, each of which had the lustre and richness of a gem; and the whole together made a show so resplendent that it seemed enough to illuminate the garden, even had there been no sunshine. Every portion of the soil was peopled with plants and herbs, which, if less beautiful, still bore tokens of assiduous care, as if all had their individual virtues, known to the scientific mind that fostered them. Some were placed in urns, rich with old carving, and others in common garden pots; some crept serpent-like along the ground or climbed on high, using whatever means of ascent was offered them. One plant had wreathed itself round a statue of Vertumnus,[3] which was thus quite veiled and shrouded in a drapery of hanging foliage, so happily arranged that it might have served a sculptor for a study.

While Giovanni stood at the window he heard a rustling behind a screen of leaves, and became aware that a person was at work in the garden. His figure soon emerged into view, and showed itself to be that of no common laborer, but a tall, emaciated, sallow, and sickly-looking man, dressed in a scholar's garb of black. He was beyond the middle term of life, with gray hair, a thin, gray beard, and a face singularly marked with intellect and cultivation, but which could never, even in his more youthful days, have expressed much warmth of heart.

Nothing could exceed the intentness with which this scientific gardener examined every shrub which grew in his path: it seemed as if he was looking into their inmost nature, making observations in regard to their creative essence, and discovering why one leaf grew in this shape and another in that, and wherefore such and such flowers differed among themselves in hue and perfume. Nevertheless, in spite of this deep intelligence on his part, there was no approach to intimacy between himself and these vegetable existences. On the contrary, he avoided their actual touch or the direct inhaling of their odors with a caution that impressed Giovanni most disagreeably; for the man's demeanor was that of one walking among malignant influences, such as savage beasts, or deadly snakes, or evil spirit, which, should he allow them one moment of license, would wreak upon him some terrible fatality. It was strangely frightful to the young man's imagination to see this air of insecurity in a person cultivating a garden, that most simple and innocent of human toils, and which has been alike the joy and labor of the unfallen parents of the race. Was this garden, then, the Eden of the present world? And this man, with such a perception of harm in what his own hands caused to grow,—was he the Adam?

The distrustful gardener, while plucking away the dead leaves or pruning the too luxuriant growth of the shrubs, defended his hands with a pair of thick gloves. Nor were these his only armor. When, in his walk through the garden, he came to the mag-

10

---

[3]**Vertumnus**: The Roman god of the seasons.

nificent plant that hung its purple gems beside the marble fountain, he placed a kind of mask over his mouth and nostrils, as if all this beauty did but conceal a deadlier malice; but, finding his task still too dangerous, he drew back, removed the mask, and called loudly, but in the infirm voice of a person affected with inward disease,—

"Beatrice! Beatrice!"

"Here am I, my father. What would you?" cried a rich and youthful voice from the window of the opposite house—a voice as rich as a tropical sunset, and which made Giovanni, though he knew not why, think of deep hues of purple or crimson and of perfumes heavily delectable. "Are you in the garden?"

"Yes, Beatrice," answered the gardener; "and I need your help."

Soon there emerged from under a sculptured portal the figure of a young girl, arrayed with as much richness of taste as the most splendid of the flowers, beautiful as the day, and with a bloom so deep and vivid that one shade more would have been too much. She looked redundant with life, health, and energy; all of which attributes were bound down and compressed, as it were, and girdled tensely, in their luxuriance, by her virgin zone.[4] Yet Giovanni's fancy must have grown morbid while he looked down into the garden; for the impression which the fair stranger made upon him was as if here were another flower, the human sister of those vegetable ones, as beautiful as they, more beautiful than the richest of them, but still to be touched only with a glove, nor to be approached without a mask. As Beatrice came down the garden path, it was observable that she handled and inhaled the odor of several of the plants which her father had most sedulously avoided.

"Here, Beatrice," said the latter, "see how many needful offices require to be done 15 to our chief treasure. Yet, shattered as I am, my life might pay the penalty of approaching it so closely as circumstances demand. Henceforth, I fear, this plant must be consigned to your sole charge."

"And gladly will I undertake it," cried again the rich tones of the young lady, as she bent towards the magnificent plant and opened her arms as if to embrace it. "Yes, my sister, my splendor, it shall be Beatrice's task to nurse and serve thee; and thou shalt reward her with thy kisses and perfumed breath, which to her is as the breath of life."

Then, with all the tenderness in her manner that was so strikingly expressed in her words, she busied herself with such attentions as the plant seemed to require; and Giovanni, at his lofty window, rubbed his eyes, and almost doubted whether it were a girl tending her favorite flower, or one sister performing the duties of affection to another. The scene soon terminated. Whether Dr. Rappaccini had finished his labors in the garden, or that his watchful eye had caught the stranger's face, he now took his daughter's arm and retired. Night was already closing in; oppressive exhalations seemed to proceed from the plants and steal upward past the open window; and Giovanni, closing the lattice, went to this couch and dreamed of a rich flower and beautiful girl. Flower and maiden were different, and yet the same, and fraught with some strange peril in either shape.

But there is an influence in the light of morning that tends to rectify whatever errors of fancy, or even of judgment, we may have incurred during the sun's decline, or among the shadows of the night, or in the less wholesome glow of moonshine. Giovanni's first movement, on starting from sleep, was to throw open the window and gaze down into the garden which his dreams had made so fertile of mysteries. He was sur-

---

[4]**virgin zone**: Her belt, "virgin" because Beatrice appears to be an unmarried girl.

prised, and a little ashamed, to find how real and matter-of-fact an affair it proved to be, in the first rays of the sun which gilded the dewdrops that hung upon leaf and blossom, and while giving a brighter beauty to each rare flower, brought every thing within the limits of ordinary experience. The young man rejoiced that, in the heart of the barren city, he had the privilege of overlooking this spot of lovely and luxuriant vegetation. It would serve, he said to himself, as a symbolic language to keep him in communion with Nature. Neither the sickly and thoughtworn Dr. Giacomo Rappaccini, it is true, nor his brilliant daughter, were now visible; so that Giovanni could not determine how much of the singularity which he attributed to both was due to their own qualities and how much to his wonder-working fancy; but he was inclined to take a most rational view of the whole matter.

In the course of the day he paid his respects to Signor Pietro Baglioni, professor of medicine in the university, a physician of eminent repute, to whom Giovanni had brought a letter of introduction. The professor was an elderly personage, apparently of genial nature and habits that might almost be called jovial. He kept the young man to dinner, and made himself very agreeable by the freedom and liveliness of his conversation, especially when warmed by a flask or two of Tuscan wine. Giovanni, conceiving that men of science, inhabitants of the same city, must needs be on familiar terms with one another, took an opportunity to mention the name of Dr. Rappaccini. But the professor did not respond with so much cordiality as he had anticipated.

"Ill would it become a teacher of the divine art of medicine," said Professor Pietro Baglioni, in answer to a question of Giovanni, "to withhold due and well-considered praise of a physician so eminently skilled as Rappaccini; but, on the other hand, I should answer it but scantily to my conscience were I to permit a worthy like yourself, Signor Giovanni, the son of an ancient friend, to imbibe erroneous ideas respecting a man who might hereafter chance to hold your life and death in his hands. The truth is, our worshipful Dr. Rappaccini has as much science as any member of the faculty—with perhaps one single exception—in Padua, or all Italy; but there are certain grave objections to his professional character." [20]

"And what are they?" asked the young man.

"Has my friend Giovanni any disease of body or heart, that he is so inquisitive about physicians?" said the professor, with a smile. "But as for Rappaccini, it is said of him—and I, who know the man well, can answer for its truth—that he cares infinitely more for science than for mankind. His patients are interesting to him only as subjects for some new experiment. He would sacrifice human life, his own among the rest, or whatever else was dearest to him, for the sake of adding so much as a grain of mustard seed to the great heap of his accumulated knowledge."

"Methinks he is an awful[5] man indeed," remarked Guasconti, mentally recalling the cold and purely intellectual aspect of Rappaccini. "And yet, worshipful professor, is it not a noble spirit? Are there many men capable of so spiritual a love or science?"

"God forbid," answered the professor, somewhat testily; "at least, unless they take sounder views of the healing art than those adopted by Rappaccini. It is his theory that all medicinal virtues are comprised within those substances which we term vegetable poisons. These he cultivates with his own hands, and is said even to have produced new varieties of poison, more horribly deleterious than Nature, without the assistance of this learned person, would ever have plagued the world withal. That the signor doctor

---

[5] **awful**: Frightful, inspiring fear; dreadful.

does less mischief than might be expected with such dangerous substances, is undeniable. Now and then, it must be owned, he has effected, or seemed to effect, a marvellous cure; but, to tell you my private mind, Signor Giovanni, he should receive little credit for such instances of success,—they being probably the work of chance,—but should be held strictly accountable for his failures, which may justly be considered his own work."

The youth might have taken Baglioni's opinions with many grains of allowance 25
had he known that there was a professional warfare of long continuance between him and Dr. Rappaccini, in which the latter was generally thought to have gained the advantage. If the reader be inclined to judge for himself, we refer him to certain blackletter tracts on both sides, preserved in the medical department of the University of Padua.

"I know not, most learned professor," returned Giovanni, after musing on what had been said of Rappaccini's exclusive zeal for science,—"I know not how dearly this physician may love his art; but surely there is one object more dear to him. He has a daughter."

"Aha!" cried the professor, with a laugh. "So now our friend Giovanni's secret is out. You have heard of this daughter, whom all the young men in Padua are wild about, though not half a dozen have ever had the good hap to see her face. I know little of the Signora Beatrice save that Rappaccini is said to have instructed her deeply in his science, and that, young and beautiful as fame reports her, she is already qualified to fill a professor's chair. Perchance her father destines her for mine! Other absurd rumors there be, not worth talking about or listening to. So now, Signor Giovanni, drink off your glass of lachryma."[6]

Guasconti returned to his lodgings somewhat heated with the wine he had quaffed, and which caused his brain to swim with strange fantasies in reference to Dr. Rappaccini and the beautiful Beatrice. On his way, happening to pass by a florist's, he bought a fresh bouquet of flowers.

Ascending to his chamber, he seated himself near the window, but within the shadow thrown by the depth of the wall, so that he could look down into the garden with little risk of being discovered. All beneath his eye was a solitude. The strange plants were basking in the sunshine, and now and then nodding gently to one another, as if in acknowledgment of sympathy and kindred. In the midst, by the shattered fountain, grew the magnificent shrub, with its purple gems clustering all over it; they glowed in the air, and gleamed back again out of the depths of the pool, which thus seemed to overflow with colored radiance from the rich reflection that was steeped in it. At first, as we have said, the garden was a solitude. Soon, however,—as Giovanni had half hoped, half feared, would be the case,—a figure appeared beneath the antique sculptured portal, and came down between the rows of plants, inhaling their various perfumes as if she were one of those beings of old classic fable that lived upon sweet odors. On again beholding Beatrice, the young man was even startled to perceive how much her beauty exceeded his recollection of it; so brilliant, so vivid, was its character, that she glowed amid the sunlight, and, as Giovanni whispered to himself, positively illuminated the more shadowy intervals of the garden path. Her face being now more revealed than on the former occasion, he was struck by its expression of simplicity and sweetness—qualities that had not entered into his idea of her character, and which

---

[6]**lachryma**: Italian wine, grown near Mount Vesuvius; lachrymal also pertains to tears.

made him ask anew what manner of mortal she might be. Nor did he fail again to observe, or imagine, an analogy between the beautiful girl and the gorgeous shrub that hung its gemlike flowers over the fountain—a resemblance which Beatrice seemed to have indulged a fantastic humor in heightening, both by the arrangement of her dress and the selection of its hues.

Approaching the shrub, she threw open her arms, as with a passionate ardor, and drew its branches into an intimate embrace—so intimate that her features were hidden in its leafy bosom and her glistening ringlets all intermingled with the flowers. 30

"Give me thy breath, my sister," exclaimed Beatrice; "for I am faint with common air. And give me this flower of thine, which I separate with gentlest fingers from the stem and place it close beside my heart."

With these words the beautiful daughter of Rappaccini plucked one of the richest blossoms of the shrub, and was about to fasten it in her bosom. But now, unless Giovanni's draughts of wine had bewildered his senses, a singular incident occurred. A small orange-colored reptile, of the lizard or chameleon species, chanced to be creeping along the path, just at the feet of Beatrice. It appeared to Giovanni,—but, at the distance from which he gazed, he could scarcely have seen any thing so minute,—it appeared to him, however, that a drop or two of moisture from the broken stem of the flower descended upon the lizard's head. For an instant the reptile contorted itself violently, and then lay motionless in the sunshine. Beatrice observed this remarkable phenomenon, and crossed herself, sadly, but without surprise; nor did she therefore hesitate to arrange the fatal flower in her bosom. There it blushed, and almost glimmered with the dazzling effect of a precious stone, adding to her dress and aspect the one appropriate charm which nothing else in the world could have supplied. But Giovanni, out of the shadow of his window, bent forward and shrank bank, and murmured and trembled.

"Am I awake? Have I my senses?" said he to himself. "What is this being? Beautiful shall I call her, or inexpressibly terrible?"

Beatrice now strayed carelessly through the garden, approaching closer beneath Giovanni's window, so that he was compelled to thrust his head quite out of its concealment in order to gratify the intense and painful curiosity which she excited. At this moment there came a beautiful insect over the garden wall: it had, perhaps, wandered through the city, and found no flowers or verdure among those antique haunts of men until the heavy perfumes of Dr. Rappaccini's shrubs had lured it from afar. Without alighting on the flowers, this winged brightness seemed to be attracted by Beatrice, and lingered in the air and fluttered about her head. Now, here it could not be but that Giovanni Guasconti's eyes deceived him. Be that as it might, he fancied that, while Beatrice was gazing at the insect with childish delight, it grew faint and fell at her feet; its bright wings shivered; it was dead—from no cause that he could discern, unless it were the atmosphere of her breath. Again Beatrice crossed herself and sighed heavily as she bent over the dead insect.

An impulsive movement of Giovanni drew her eyes to the window. There she beheld the beautiful head of the young man—rather a Grecian than an Italian head, with fair, regular features, and a glistening of gold among his ringlets—gazing down upon her like a being that hovered in mid air. Scarcely knowing what he did, Giovanni threw down the bouquet which he had hitherto held in his hand. 35

"Signora," said he, "there are pure and healthful flowers. Wear them for the sake of Giovanni Guasconti."

"Thanks, signor," replied Beatrice, with her rich voice, that came forth as it were like a gush of music, and with a mirthful expression half childish and half womanlike. "I accept your gift, and would fain recompense it with this precious purple flower; but, if I toss it into the air, it will not reach you. So Signor Guasconti must even content himself with my thanks."

She lifted the bouquet from the ground, and then, as if inwardly ashamed at having stepped aside from her maidenly reserve to respond to a stranger's greeting, passed swiftly homeward through the garden. But, few as the moments were, it seemed to Giovanni, when she was on the point of vanishing beneath the sculptured portal, that his beautiful bouquet was already beginning to wither in her grasp. It was an idle thought; there could be no possibility of distinguishing a faded flower from a fresh one at so great a distance.

For many days after this incident the young man avoided the window that looked into Dr. Rappaccini's garden, as if something ugly and monstrous would have blasted his eyesight had he been betrayed into a glance. He felt conscious of having put himself, to a certain extent, within the influence of an unintelligible power by the communication which he had opened with Beatrice. The wisest course would have been, if his heart were in any real danger, to quit his lodging and Padua itself at once; the next wiser, to have accustomed himself, as far as possible, to the familiar and daylight view of Beatrice—thus bringing her rigidly and systematically within the limits of ordinary experience. Least of all, while avoiding her sight, ought Giovanni to have remained so near this extraordinary being that the proximity and possibility even of intercourse should give a kind of substance and reality to the wild vagaries which his imagination ran riot continually in producing. Guasconti had not a deep heart—or, at all events, its depths were not sounded now; but he had a quick fancy, and an ardent southern temperament, which rose every instant to a higher fever pitch. Whether or not Beatrice possessed those terrible attributes, that fatal breath, the affinity with those so beautiful and deadly flowers which were indicated by what Giovanni had witnessed, she had at least instilled a fierce and subtle poison in his system. It was not love, although her rich beauty was a madness to him; nor horror, even while he fancied her spirit to be imbued with the same baneful essence that seemed to pervade her physical frame; but a wild offspring of both love and horror that had each parent in it, and burned like one and shivered like the other. Giovanni knew not what to dread; still less did he know what to hope; yet hope and dread kept a continual warfare in his breast, alternately vanquishing one another and starting up afresh to renew the contest. Blessed are all simple emotions, be they dark or bright! It is the lurid intermixture of the two that produces the illuminating blaze of the infernal regions.

Sometimes he endeavored to assuage the fever of his spirit by a rapid walk through ₄₀ the streets of Padua or beyond its gates: his footsteps kept time with the throbbings of his brain, so that the walk was apt to accelerate itself to a race. One day he found himself arrested; his arm was seized by a portly personage, who had turned back on recognizing the young man and expended much breath in overtaking him.

"Signor Giovanni! Stay, my young friend!" cried he. "Have you forgotten me? That might well be the case if I were as much altered as yourself."

It was Baglioni, whom Giovanni had avoided ever since their first meeting, from a doubt that the professor's sagacity would look too deeply into his secrets. Endeavoring to recover himself, he stared forth wildly from his inner world into the outer one and spoke like a man in a dream.

"Yes; I am Giovanni Guasconti. You are Professor Pietro Baglioni. Now let me pass!"

"Not yet, not yet, Signor Giovanni Guasconti," said the professor, smiling, but at the same time scrutinizing the youth with an earnest glance. "What! did I grow up side by side with your father? and shall his son pass me like a stranger in these old streets of Padua? Stand still, Signor Giovanni; for we must have a word or two before we part."

"Speedily, then, most worshipful professor, speedily," said Giovanni, with feverish impatience. "Does not your worship see that I am in haste?"

Now, while he was speaking there came a man in black along the street, stooping and moving feebly like a person in inferior health. His face was all overspread with a most sickly and sallow hue, but yet so pervaded with an expression of piercing and active intellect that an observer might easily have overlooked the merely physical attributes and have seen only this wonderful energy. As he passed, this person exchanged a cold and distant salutation with Baglioni, but fixed his eyes upon Giovanni with an intentness that seemed to bring out whatever was within him worthy of notice. Nevertheless, there was a peculiar quietness in the look, as if taking merely a speculative, not a human, interest in the young man.

"It is Dr. Rappaccini!" whispered the professor when the stranger had passed. "Has he ever seen your face before?"

"Not that I know," answered Giovanni, starting at the name.

He *has* seen you! he must have seen you!" said Baglioni, hastily. "For some purpose or other, this man of science is making a study of you. I know that look of his! It is the same that coldly illuminates his face as he bends over a bird, a mouse, or a butterfly; which, in pursuance of some experiment, he has killed by the perfume of a flower; a look as deep as Nature itself, but without Nature's warmth of love. Signor Giovanni, I will stake my life upon it, you are the subject of one of Rappaccini's experiments!"

"Will you make a fool of me?" cried Giovanni, passionately. "*That,* signor professor, were an untoward experiment."

"Patience! patience!" replied the imperturbable professor. "I tell thee, my poor Giovanni, that Rappaccini has a scientific interest in thee. Thou hast fallen into fearful hands! And the Signora Beatrice,—what part does she act in this mystery?"

But Guasconti, finding Baglioni's pertinacity intolerable, here broke away, and was gone before the professor could again seize his arm. He looked after the young man intently and shook his head.

"This must not be," said Baglioni to himself. "The youth is the son of my old friend, and shall not come to any harm from which the arcana[7] of medical science can preserve him. Besides, it is too insufferable an impertinence in Rappaccini thus to snatch the lad out of my own hands, as I may say, and make use of him for his infernal experiments. This daughter of his! It shall be looked to. Perchance, most learned Rappaccini, I may foil you where you little dream of it!"

Meanwhile Giovanni had pursued a circuitous route, and at length found himself at the door of his lodgings. As he crossed the threshold he was met by old Lisabetta, who smirked and smiled, and was evidently desirous to attract his attention; vainly, however, as the ebullition of his feelings had momentarily subsided into a cold and dull vacuity. He turned his eyes full upon the withered face that was puckering itself into

---

[7]**arcana:** Secrets.

a smile, but seemed to behold it not. The old dame, therefore, laid her grasp upon his cloak.

"Signor! signor!" whispered she, still with a smile over the whole breadth of her vis- 55 age, so that it looked not unlike a grotesque carving in wood, darkened by centuries. "Listen, signor! There is a private entrance into the garden!"

"What do you say?" exclaimed Giovanni, turning quickly about, as if an inanimate thing should start into feverish life. "A private entrance into Dr. Rappaccini's garden?"

"Hush, hush! not so loud!" whispered Lisabetta, putting her hand over his mouth. "Yes; into the worshipful doctor's garden, where you may see all his fine shrubbery. Many a young man in Padua would give gold to be admitted among those flowers."

Giovanni put a piece of gold into her hand.

"Show me the way," said he.

A surmise, probably excited by his conversation with Baglioni, crossed his mind, 60 that this interposition of old Lisabetta might perchance be connected with the intrigue, whatever were its nature, in which the professor seemed to suppose that Dr. Rappaccini was involving him. But such a suspicion, though it disturbed Giovanni, was inadequate to restrain him. The instant that he was aware of the possibility of approaching Beatrice, it seemed an absolute necessity of his existence to do so. It mattered not whether she were angel or demon; he was irrevocably within her sphere, and must obey the law that whirled him onward, in ever-lessening circles, towards a result which he did not attempt to foreshadow; and yet, strange to say, there came across him a sudden doubt whether this intense interest on his part were not delusory; whether it were really of so deep and positive a nature as to justify him in now thrusting himself into an incalculable position; whether it were not merely the fantasy of a young man's brain, only slightly or not at all connected with his heart.

He paused, hesitated, turned half about, but again went on. His withered guide led him along several obscure passages, and finally undid a door, through which, as it was opened, there came the sight and sound of rustling leaves, with the broken sunshine glimmering among them. Giovanni stepped forth, and, forcing himself through the entanglement of a shrub that wreathed its tendrils over the hidden entrance, stood beneath his own window in the open area of Dr. Rappaccini's garden.

How often is it the case that, when impossibilities have come to pass and dreams have condensed their misty substance into tangible realities, we find ourselves calm, and even coldly self-possessed, amid circumstances which it would have been a delirium of joy or agony to anticipate! Fate delights to thwart us thus. Passion will choose his own time to rush upon the scene, and lingers sluggishly behind when an appropriate adjustment of events would seem to summon his appearance. So was it now with Giovanni. Day after day his pulses had throbbed with feverish blood at the improbably idea of an interview with Beatrice, and of standing with her, face to face, in this very garden, basking in the Oriental sunshine of her beauty, and snatching from her full gaze the mystery which he deemed the riddle of his own existence. But now there was a singular and untimely equanimity within this breast. He threw a glance around the garden to discover if Beatrice or her father were present, and, perceiving that he was alone, began a critical observation of the plants.

The aspect of one and all of them dissatisfied him; their gorgeousness seemed fierce, passionate, and even unnatural. There was hardly an individual shrub which a wanderer, straying by himself through a forest, would not have been startled to find growing wild, as if an unearthly face had glared at him out of the thicket. Several also would have shocked a delicate instinct by an appearance of artificialness indicating that there had been such commixture, and, as it were, adultery of various vegetable species, that the production was not longer of God's making, but the monstrous offspring of man's depraved fancy, glowing with only an evil mockery of beauty. They were probably the result of experiment, which in one or two cases had succeeded in mingling plants individually lovely into a compound possessing the questionable and ominous character that distinguished the whole growth of the garden. In fine, Giovanni recognized but two or three plants in the collection, and those of a kind that he well knew to be poisonous. While busy with these contemplations he heard the rustling of a silken garment, and, turning, beheld Beatrice emerging from beneath the sculptured portal.

Giovanni had not considered with himself what should be his deportment; whether he should apologize for his intrusion into the garden, or assume that he was there with the privity at least, if not by the desire, of Dr. Rappaccini or his daughter; but Beatrice's manner placed him at his ease, though leaving him still in doubt by what agency he had gained admittance. She came lightly along the path and met him near the broken fountain. There was surprise in her face, but brightened by a simple and kind expression of pleasure.

"You are a connoisseur in flowers, signor," said Beatrice, with a smile, alluding to 65 the bouquet which he had flung her from the window. "It is no marvel, therefore, if the sight of my father's rare collection has tempted you to take a nearer view. If he were here, he could tell you many strange and interesting facts as to the nature and habits of these shrubs; for he has spent a lifetime in such studies, and this garden is his world."

"And yourself, lady," observed Giovanni, "if fame says true,—you likewise are deeply skilled in the virtues indicated by these rich blossoms and these spicy perfumes. Would you deign to be my instructress, I should prove an apter scholar than if taught by Signor Rappaccini himself."

"Are there such idle rumors?" asked Beatrice, with the music of a pleasant laugh. "Do people say that I am skilled in my father's science of plants? What a jest is there! No; though I have grown up among these flowers, I know no more of them than their hues and perfume; and sometimes methinks I would fain rid myself of even that small knowledge. There are many flowers here, and those not the least brilliant, that shock and offend me when they meet my eye. But pray, signor, do not believe these stories about my science. Believe nothing of me save what you see with your own eyes."

"And must I believe all that I have seen with my own eyes?" asked Giovanni, pointedly, while the recollection of former scenes made him shrink. "No, signora; you demand too little of me. Bid me believe nothing save what comes from your own lips."

It would appear that Beatrice understood him. There came a deep flush to her cheek; but she looked full into Giovanni's eyes, and responded to his gaze of uneasy suspicion with a queenlike haughtiness.

"I do so bid you, signor," she replied. "Forget whatever you may have fancied in 70 regard to me. If true to the outward senses, still it may be false in its essence; but the words of Beatrice Rappaccini's lips are true from the depths of the heart outward. Those you may believe."

A fervor glowed in her whole aspect and beamed upon Giovanni's consciousness like the light of truth itself; but while she spoke there was a fragrance in the atmosphere around her, rich and delightful, though evanescent, yet which the young man, from an indefinable reluctance, scarcely dared to draw into his lungs. It might be the odor of the flowers. Could it be Beatrice's breath which thus embalmed her words with a strange richness, as if by steeping them in her heart? A faintness passed like a shadow over Giovanni and flitted away; he seemed to gaze through the beautiful girl's eyes into her transparent soul, and felt no more doubt or fear.

The tinge of passion that had colored Beatrice's manner vanished; she became gay, and appeared to derive a pure delight from her communion with the youth not unlike what the maiden of a lonely island might have felt conversing with a voyager from the civilized world. Evidently her experience of life had been confined within the limits of that garden. She talked now about matters as simple as the daylight or summer clouds, and now asked questions in reference to the city, or Giovanni's distant home, his friends, his mother, and his sisters—questions indicating such seclusion, and such lack of familiarity with modes and forms, that Giovanni responded as if to an infant. Her spirit gushed out before him like a fresh rill that was just catching its first glimpse of the sunlight and wondering at the reflections of earth and sky which were flung into its bosom. There came thoughts, too, from a deep source, and fantasies of a gemlike brilliancy, as if diamonds and rubies sparkled upward among the bubbles of the fountain. Ever and anon there gleamed across the young man's mind a sense of wonder that he should be walking side by side with the being who had so wrought upon his imagination, whom he had idealized in such hues of terror, in whom he had positively witnessed such manifestations of dreadful attributes—that he should be conversing with Beatrice like a brother, and should find her so human and so maidenlike. But such reflections were only momentary; the effect of her character was too real not to make itself familiar at once.

In this free intercourse they had strayed through the garden, and now, after many turns among its avenues, were come to the shattered fountain, beside which grew the magnificent shrub, with its treasury of flowing blossoms. A fragrance was diffused from it which Giovanni recognized as identical with that which he had attributed to Beatrice's breath, but incomparably more powerful. As her eyes fell upon it, Giovanni beheld her press her hand to her bosom as if her heart were throbbing suddenly and painfully.

"For the first time in my life," murmured she, addressing the shrub, "I had forgotten thee."

"I remember, signora," said Giovanni, "that you once promised to reward me with ₇₅ one of these living gems for the bouquet which I had the happy boldness to fling to your feet. Permit me now to pluck it as a memorial of this interview."

He made a step towards the shrub with extended hand; but Beatrice darted forward, uttering a shriek that went through his heart like a dagger. She caught his hand and drew it back with the whole force of her slender figure. Giovanni felt her touch thrilling through his fibres.

"Touch it not!" exclaimed she, in a voice of agony. "Not for thy life! It is fatal!"

Then, hiding her face, she fled from him and vanished beneath the sculptured portal. As Giovanni followed her with his eyes, he beheld the emaciated figure and pale intelligence of Dr. Rappaccini, who had been watching the scene, he knew not how long, within the shadow of the entrance.

No sooner was Guasconti alone in his chamber than the image of Beatrice came back to his passionate musings, invested with all the witchery that had been gathering around it ever since his first glimpse of her, and now likewise imbued with a tender warmth of girlish womanhood. She was human; her nature was endowed with all gentle and feminine qualities; she was worthiest to be worshipped; she was capable, surely, on her part, of the height and heroism of love. Those tokens which he had hitherto considered as proofs of a frightful peculiarity in her physical and moral system were now either forgotten or by the subtle sophistry of passion transmitted into a golden crown of enchantment, rendering Beatrice the more admirable by so much as she was the more unique. Whatever had looked ugly was not beautiful; or, if incapable of such a change, it stole away and hid itself among those shapeless half ideas which throng the dim region beyond the daylight of our perfect consciousness. Thus did he spend the night, nor fell asleep until the dawn had begun to awake the slumbering flowers in Dr. Rappaccini's garden, whither Giovanni's dreams doubtless led him. Up rose the sun in his due season, and, flinging his beams upon the young man's eyelids, awoke him to a sense of pain. When thoroughly aroused, he became sensible of a burning and tingling agony in his hand—in his right hand—the very hand which Beatrice had grasped in her own when he was on the point of plucking one of the gemlike flowers. On the back of that hand there was now a purple print like that of four small fingers, and the likeness of a slender thumb upon his wrist.

O, how stubbornly does love,—or even that cunning semblance of love which 80 flourishes in the imagination, but strikes no depth of root into the heart,—how stubbornly does it hold its faith until the moment comes when it is doomed to vanish into thin mist! Giovanni wrapped a handkerchief about his hand and wondered what evil thing had stung him, and soon forgot his pain in a revery of Beatrice.

After the first interview, a second was in the inevitable course of what we call fate. A third; a fourth; and a meeting with Beatrice in the garden was no longer an incident in Giovanni's daily life, but the whole space in which he might be said to live; for the anticipation and memory of that ecstatic hour made up the remainder. Nor was it otherwise with the daughter of Rappaccini. She watched for the youth's appearance and flew to his side with confidence as unreserved as if they had been playmates from early infancy—as if they were such playmates still. If, by any unwonted chance, he failed to come at the appointed moment, she stood beneath the window and sent up the rich sweetness of her tones to float around him in his chamber and echo and reverberate throughout his heart—"Giovanni! Giovanni! Why tarriest thou? Come down!" And down he hastened into that Eden of poisonous flowers.

But, with all this intimate familiarity, there was still a reserve in Beatrice's demeanor, so rigidly and invariably sustained that the idea of infringing it scarcely occurred to his imagination. By all appreciable signs, they loved; they had looked love with eyes that conveyed the holy secret from the depths of one soul into the depths of the other, as if it were too sacred to be whispered by the way; they had even spoken love in those gushes of passion when their spirits darted forth in articulated breath like tongues of long hidden flame; and yet there had been no seal of lips, no clasp of hands, nor any slightest caress such as love claims and hallows. He had never touched one of the gleaming ringlets of her hair; her garment—so marked was the physical barrier between them—had never been waved against him by a breeze. On the few occasions when Giovanni had seemed tempted to overstep the limit, Beatrice grew so sad, so stern, and withal wore such a look of desolate separation, shuddering at itself, that not a spoken word was requisite to repel him. At such times he was startled at the horrible suspicions that rose, monster-like, out of the caverns of his heart and stared him in the face; his love grew thin and faint as the morning mist; his doubts alone had substance. But, when Beatrice's face brightened again after the momentary shadow, she was transformed at once from the mysterious, questionable being whom he had watched with so much awe and horror; she was now the beautiful and unsophisticated girl whom he felt that his spirit knew with a certainty beyond all other knowledge.

A considerable time had now passed since Giovanni's last meeting with Baglioni. One morning, however, he was disagreeably surprised by a visit from the professor, whom he had scarcely thought of for whole weeks, and would willingly have forgotten still longer. Given up as he had long been to a pervading excitement, he could tolerate no companions except upon condition of their perfect sympathy with his present state of feeling. Such sympathy was not to be expected from Professor Baglioni.

The visitor chatted carelessly for a few moments about the gossip of the city and the university, and then took up another topic.

"I have been reading an old classic author lately," said he, "and met with a story   85 that strangely interested me. Possibly you may remember it. It is of an Indian prince, who sent a beautiful woman as a present to Alexander the Great. She was as lovely as the dawn and gorgeous as the sunset; but what especially distinguished her was a certain rich perfume in her breath—richer than a garden of Persian roses. Alexander, as was natural to a youthful conqueror, fell in love at first sight with this magnificent stranger; but a certain sage physician, happening to be present, discovered a terrible secret in regard to her."

"And what was that?" asked Giovanni, turning his eyes downward to avoid those of the professor.

"That this lovely woman," continued Baglioni, with emphasis, "had been nourished with poisons from her birth upward, until her whole nature was so imbued with them that she herself had become the deadliest poison in existence. Poison was her element of life. With that rich perfume of her breath she blasted the very air. Her love would have been poison—her embrace death. Is not this a marvellous tale?"

"A childish fable," answered Giovanni, nervously starting from his chair. "I marvel how your worship finds time to read such nonsense among your graver studies."

"By the by," said the professor, looking uneasily about him, "what singular fragrance is this in your apartment? Is it the perfume of your gloves? It is faint, but delicious; and yet, after all, by no means agreeable. Were I to breathe it long, methinks it would make me ill. It is like the breath of a flower; but I see no flowers in the chamber."

"Nor are there any," replied Giovanni, who had turned pale as the professor spoke;   90 "nor, I think, is there any fragrance except in your worship's imagination. Odors, being a sort of element combined of the sensual and the spiritual, are apt to deceive us in this matter. The recollection of a perfume, the bare idea of it, may easily be mistaken for a present reality."

"Ay; but my sober imagination does not often play such tricks," said Baglioni; "and, were I to fancy any kind of odor, it would be that of some vile apothecary drug, wherewith my fingers are likely enough to be imbued. Our worshipful friend Rappaccini, as I have heard, tinctures his medicaments with odors richer than those of Araby.[8] Doubtless, likewise, the fair and learned Signora Beatrice would minister to her patients with draughts as sweet as a maiden's breath; but woe to him that sips them!"

Giovanni's face evinced many contending emotions. The tone in which the professor alluded to the pure and lovely daughter of Rappaccini was a torture to his soul; and

---

[8]**Araby:** Arabia.

yet the intimation of a view of her character, opposite to his own, gave instantaneous distinctness to a thousand dim suspicions, which now grinned at him like so many demons. But he strove hard to quell them and to respond to Baglioni with a true lover's perfect faith.

"Signor professor," said he, "you were my father's friend; perchance, too, it is your purpose to act a friendly part towards his son. I would fain feel nothing towards you save respect and deference; but I pray you to observe, signor, that there is one subject on which we must not speak. You know not the Signora Beatrice. You cannot, therefore, estimate the wrong—the blasphemy, I may even say—that is offered to her character by a light or injurious word."

"Giovanni! my poor Giovanni!" answered the professor, with a calm expression of pity. "I know this wretched girl far better than yourself. You shall hear the truth in respect to the poisoner Rappaccini and his poisonous daughter; yes, poisonous as she is beautiful. Listen; for, even should you do violence to my gray hairs, it shall not silence me. That old fable of the Indian woman has become a truth by the deep and deadly science of Rappaccini and in the person of the lovely Beatrice."

Giovanni groaned and hid his face.   95

"Her father," continued Baglioni, "was not restrained by natural affection from offering up his child in this horrible manner as the victim of his insane zeal for science; for, let us do him justice, he is as true a man of science as ever distilled his own heart in an alembic. What, then, will be your fate? Beyond a doubt you are selected as the material of some new experiment. Perhaps the result is to be death; perhaps a fate more awful still. Rappaccini, with what he calls the interest of science before his eyes, will hesitate at nothing."

"It is a dream," muttered Giovanni to himself; "surely it is a dream."

"But," resumed the professor, "be of good cheer, son of my friend. It is not yet too late for the rescue. Possibly we may even succeed in bringing back this miserable child within the limits of ordinary nature, from which her father's madness has estranged her. Behold this little silver vase! It was wrought by the hands of the renowned Benvenuto Cellini,[9] and is well worthy to be a love gift to the fairest dame in Italy. But its contents are invaluable. One little sip of this antidote would have rendered the most virulent poisons of the Borgias[10] innocuous. Doubt not that it will be as efficacious against those of Rappaccini. Bestow the vase, and the precious liquid within it, on your Beatrice, and hopefully await the result."

Baglioni laid a small, exquisitely wrought silver vial on the table and withdrew, leaving what he had said to produce its effect upon the young man's mind.

"We will thwart Rappaccini yet," thought he, chuckling to himself, as he descended   100
the stairs; "but, let us confess the truth of him, he is a wonderful man—a wonderful man indeed; a vile empiric,[11] however, in his practice, and therefore not to be tolerated by those who respect the good old rules of the medical profession."

Throughout Giovanni's whole acquaintance with Beatrice, he had occasionally, as we have said, been haunted by dark surmises as to her character; yet so thoroughly had she made herself felt by him as a simple, natural, most affectionate, and guileless creature, that the image now held up by Professor Baglioni looked as strange and incredible as if it were not in accordance with his own original conception. True, there

---

[9]**Benvenuto Cellini**: (1500–71), an Italian sculptor.   [10]**Borgias**: Notorious, powerful Italian Renaissance family, noted for cruelty and political intrigues.   [11]**vile empiric**: Charlatan.

were ugly recollections connected with his first glimpses of the beautiful girl; he could not quite forget the bouquet that withered in her grasp, and the insect that perished amid the sunny air, by no ostensible agency save the fragrance of her breath. These incidents, however, dissolving in the pure light of her character, had no longer the efficacy of facts, but were acknowledged as mistaken fantasies, by whatever testimony of the senses they might appear to be substantiated. There is something truer and more real than what we can see with the eyes and touch with the finger. On such better evidence had Giovanni founded his confidence in Beatrice, though rather by the necessary force of her high attributes than by any deep and generous faith on his part. But now his spirit was incapable of sustaining itself at the height to which the early enthusiasm of passion had exalted it; he fell down, grovelling among earthly doubts, and defiled therewith the pure whiteness of Beatrice's image. Not that he gave her up; he did but distrust. He resolved to institute some decisive test that should satisfy him, once for all, whether there were those dreadful peculiarities in her physical nature which could not be supposed to exist without some corresponding monstrosity of soul. His eyes, gazing down afar, might have deceived him as to the lizard, the insect, and the flowers; but if he could witness, at the distance of a few paces, the sudden blight of one fresh and healthful flower in Beatrice's hand, there would be room for no further question. With this idea he hastened to the florist's and purchased a bouquet that was still gemmed with the morning dewdrops.

It was now the customary hour of his daily interview with Beatrice. Before descending into the garden, Giovanni failed not to look at his figure in the mirror—a vanity to be expected in a beautiful young man, yet, as displaying itself at that troubled and feverish moment, the token of a certain shallowness of feeling and insincerity of character. He did gaze, however, and said to himself that his features had never before possessed so rich a grace, nor his eyes such vivacity, nor his cheeks so warm a hue of superabundant life.

"At least," thought he, "her poison has not yet insinuated itself into my system. I am no flower to perish in her grasp."

With that thought he turned his eyes on the bouquet, which he had never once laid aside from his hand. A thrill of indefinable horror shot through his frame on perceiving that those dewy flowers were already beginning to droop; they wore the aspect of things that had been fresh and lovely yesterday. Giovanni grew white as marble, and stood motionless before the mirror, staring at his own reflection there as at the likeness of something frightful. He remembered Baglioni's remark about the fragrance that seemed to pervade the chamber. It must have been the poison in his breath! Then he shuddered—shuddered at himself. Recovering from his stupor, he began to watch with curious eye a spider that was busily at work hanging its web from the antique cornice of the apartment, crossing and recrossing the artful system of interwoven lines—as vigorous and active a spider as ever dangled from an old ceiling. Giovanni bent towards the insect, and emitted a deep, long breath. The spider suddenly ceased its toil; the web vibrated with a tremor originating in the body of the small artisan. Again Giovanni sent forth a breath, deeper, longer, and imbued with a venomous feeling out of his heart: he knew not whether he were wicked, or only desperate. The spider made a convulsive gripe with his limbs and hung dead across the window.

"Accursed! accursed!" muttered Giovanni, addressing himself. "Hast thou grown so poisonous that this deadly insect perishes by thy breath?" 105

At that moment a rich, sweet voice came floating up from the garden.

"Giovanni! Giovanni! It is past the hour! Why tarriest thou? Come down!"

"Yes," muttered Giovanni again. "she is the only being whom my breath may not slay! Would that it might!"

He rushed down, and in an instant was standing before the bright and loving eyes of Beatrice. A moment ago his wrath and despair had been so fierce that he could have desired nothing so much as to wither her by a glance; but with her actual presence there came influences which had too real an existence to be at once shaken off; recollections of the delicate and benign power of her feminine nature, which had so often enveloped him in a religious calm; recollections of many a holy and passionate outgush of her heart, when the pure fountain had been unsealed from its depths and made visible in its transparency to his mental eye; recollections which, had Giovanni known how to estimate them, would have assured him that all this ugly mystery was but an earthly illusion, and that, whatever mist of evil might seem to have gathered over her, the real Beatrice was a heavenly angel. Incapable as he was of such high faith, still her presence had not utterly lost its magic. Giovanni's rage was quelled into an aspect of sullen insensibility. Beatrice, with a quick spiritual sense, immediately felt that there was a gulf of blackness between them which neither he nor she could pass. They walked on together, sad and silent, and came thus to the marble fountain and to its pool of water on the ground, in the midst of which grew the shrub that bore gemlike blossoms. Giovanni was affrighted at the eager enjoyment—the appetite, as it were—with which he found himself inhaling the fragrance of the flowers.

"Beatrice," asked he, abruptly, "whence came this shrub?" 110

"My father created it," answered she, with simplicity.

"Created it! created it!" repeated Giovanni. "What mean you, Beatrice?"

"He is a man fearfully acquainted with the secrets of Nature," replied Beatrice; "and, at the hour when I first drew breath, this plant sprang from the soil, the offspring of his science, of his intellect, while I was but his earthly child. Approach it not!" continued she, observing with terror that Giovanni was drawing nearer to the shrub. "It has qualities that you little dream of. But I, dearest Giovanni,—I grew up and blossomed with the plant and was nourished with its breath. It was my sister, and I loved it with a human affection; for, alas!—hast thou not suspected it?—there was an awful doom."

Here Giovanni frowned so darkly upon her that Beatrice paused and trembled. But her faith in his tenderness reassured her, and made her blush that she had doubted for an instant.

"There was an awful doom," she continued, "The effect of my father's fatal love 115 of science, which estranged me from all society of my kind. Until Heaven sent thee, dearest Giovanni, O, how lonely was thy poor Beatrice!"

"Was it a hard doom?" asked Giovanni, fixing his eyes upon her.

"Only of late have I known how hard it was," answered she, tenderly. "O, yes; but my heart was torpid, and therefore quiet."

Giovanni's rage broke forth from his sullen gloom like a lightning flash out of a dark cloud.

"Accursed one!" cried he, with venomous scorn and anger. "And, finding thy solitude wearisome, thou hast severed me likewise from all the warmth of life and enticed me into thy region of unspeakable horror!"

"Giovanni!" exclaimed Beatrice, turning her large bright eyes upon his face. The 120 force of his words had not found it way into her mind; she was merely thunderstruck.

"Yes, poisonous thing!" repeated Giovanni, beside himself with passion. "Thou hast done it! Thou hast blasted me! Thou hast filled my veins with poison! Thou hast made me as hateful, as ugly, as loathsome and deadly a creature as thyself—a world's wonder of hideous monstrosity! Now, if our breath be happily as fatal to ourselves as to all other, let us join our lips in one kiss of unutterable hatred, and so die!"

"What has befallen me?" murmured Beatrice, with a low moan out of her heart. "Holy Virgin, pity me, a poor heart-broken child!"

"Thou,—dost thou pray?" cried Giovanni, still with the same fiendish scorn. "Thy very prayers, as they come from thy lips, taint the atmosphere with death. Yes, yes; let us pray! Let us to church and dip our fingers in the holy water at the portal! They that come after us will perish as by a pestilence! Let us sign crosses in the air! It will be scattering curses abroad in the likeness of holy symbols!"

"Giovanni," said Beatrice, calmly, for her grief was beyond passion, "why dost thou join thyself with me thus in those terrible words? I, it is true, am the horrible thing thou namest me. But thou,—what hast thou to do, save with one other shudder at my hideous misery to go forth out of the garden and mingle with thy race, and forget that there ever crawled on earth such a monster as poor Beatrice?"

"Dost thou pretend ignorance?" asked Giovanni, scowling upon her. "Behold! this 125 power have I gained from the pure daughter of Rappaccini."

There was a swarm of summer insects flitting through the air in search of the food promised by the flower odors of the fatal garden. They circled round Giovanni's head, and were evidently attracted towards him by the same influence which had drawn them for an instant within the sphere of several of the shrubs. He sent forth a breath among them, and smiled bitterly at Beatrice as at least a score of the insects fell dead upon the ground.

"I see it! I see it!" shrieked Beatrice. "It is my father's fatal science! No, no, Giovanni; it was not I! Never! never! I dreamed only to love thee and be with thee a little time, and so to let thee pass away, leaving but thine image in mine heart; for, Giovanni, believe it, though my body be nourished with poison, my spirit is God's creature, and craves love as its daily food. But my father,—he has united us in this fearful sympathy. Yes; spurn me, tread upon me, kill me! O, what is death after such words as thine? But it was not I. Not for a world of bliss would I have done it."

Giovanni's passion had exhausted itself in its outburst from his lips. There now came across him a sense, mournful, and not without tenderness, of the intimate and peculiar relationship between Beatrice and himself. They stood, as it were, in an utter solitude, which would be made none the less solitary by the densest throng of human life. Ought not, then, the desert of humanity around them to press this insulated pair closer together? If they should be cruel to one another, who was there to be kind to them? Besides, thought Giovanni, might there not still be a hope of his returning within the limits of ordinary nature, and leading Beatrice, the redeemed Beatrice, by the hand? O, weak, and selfish, and unworthy spirit, that could dream of an earthly union and earthly happiness as possible, after such deep love had been so bitterly wronged as was Beatrice's love by Giovanni's blighting words! No, no; there could be no such hope. She must pass heavily, with that broken heart, across the borders of Time—she must bathe her hurts in some fount of paradise, and forget her grief in the light of immortality, and *there* be well.

But Giovanni did not know it.

"Dear Beatrice," said he, approaching her, while she shrank away as always at his approach, but now with a different impulse, "dearest Beatrice, our fate is not yet so desperate. Behold! there is a medicine, potent, as a wise physician has assured me, and almost divine in its efficacy. It is composed of ingredients the most opposite to those by which thy awful father has brought this calamity upon thee and me. It is distilled of blessed herbs. Shall we not quaff it together, and thus be purified from evil?"

"Give it me!" said Beatrice, extending her hand to receive the little silver vial which Giovanni took from his bosom. She added, with a peculiar emphasis, "I will drink; but do thou await the result."

She put Baglioni's antidote to her lips; and, at the same moment, the figure of Rappaccini emerged from the portal and came slowly towards the marble fountain. As he drew near, the pale man of science seemed to gaze with a triumphant expression at the beautiful youth and maiden, as might an artist who should spend his life in achieving a picture or a group of statuary and finally be satisfied with his success. He paused; his bent form grew erect with conscious power; he spread out his hands over them in the attitude of a father imploring a blessing upon his children; but those were the same hands that had thrown poison into the stream of their lives. Giovanni trembled. Beatrice shuddered nervously, and pressed her hand upon her heart.

"My daughter," said Rappaccini, "thou art no longer lonely in the world. Pluck one of those precious gems from thy sister shrub and bid thy bridegroom wear it in his bosom. It will not harm him now. My science and the sympathy between thee and him have so wrought within his system that he now stands apart from common men, as thou dost, daughter of my pride and triumph, from ordinary women. Pass on, then, through the world, most dear to one another and dreadful to all besides!"

"My father," said Beatrice, feebly—and still as she spoke she kept her hand upon her heart,—"wherefore didst thou inflict this miserable doom upon thy child?"

"Miserable!" exclaimed Rappaccini. "What mean you, foolish girl. Dost thou deem it misery to be endowed with marvellous gifts against which no power nor strength could avail an enemy—misery, to be able to quell the mightiest with a breath—misery, to be as terrible as thou art beautiful? Wouldst thou, then, have preferred the condition of a weak woman, exposed to all evil and capable of none?"

"I would fain have been loved, not feared," murmured Beatrice, sinking down upon the ground. "But now it matters not. I am going, father, where the evil which thou hast striven to mingle with my being will pass away like a dream—like the fragrance of these poisonous flowers, which will no longer taint my breath among the flowers of Eden. Farewell, Giovanni! Thy words of hatred are like lead within my heart; but they, too, will fall away as I ascend. O, was there not, from the first, more poison in thy nature than in mine?"

To Beatrice,—so radically had her earthly part been wrought upon by Rappaccini's skill,—as poison had been life, so the powerful antidote was death; and thus the poor victim of man's ingenuity and of thwarted nature, and of the fatality that attends all such efforts of perverted wisdom, perished there, at the feet of her father and Giovanni. Just at that moment Professor Pietro Baglioni looked forth from the window, and called loudly, in a tone of triumph mixed with horror, to the thunderstricken man of science,—

"Rappaccini! Rappaccini! and is *this* the upshot of your experiment?"

William Faulkner *(1897–1962)*

A Rose for Emily   *1931*

I

When Miss Emily Grierson died, our whole town went to her funeral: the men through a sort of respectful affection for a fallen monument, the women mostly out of curiosity to see the inside of her house, which no one save an old manservant—a combined gardener and cook—had seen in at least ten years.

It was a big, squarish frame house that had once been white, decorated with cupolas and spires and scrolled balconies in the heavily lightsome style of the seventies, set on what had once been our most select street. But garages and cotton gins had encroached and obliterated even the august names of that neighborhood; only Miss Emily's house was left, lifting its stubborn and coquettish decay above the cotton wagons and the gasoline pumps—an eyesore among eyesores. And now Miss Emily had gone to join the representatives of those august names where they lay in the cedar-bemused cemetery among the ranked and anonymous graves of Union and Confederate soldiers who fell at the battle of Jefferson.

Alive, Miss Emily had been a tradition, a duty, and a care; a sort of hereditary obligation upon the town, dating from that day in 1894 when Colonel Sartoris, the mayor—he who fathered the edict that no Negro woman should appear on the streets without an apron—remitted her taxes, the dispensation dating from the death of her father on into perpetuity. Not that Miss Emily would have accepted charity. Colonel Sartoris invented an involved tale to the effect that Miss Emily's father had loaned money to the town, which the town, as a matter of business, preferred this way of repaying. Only a man of Colonel Sartoris' generation and thought could have invented it, and only a woman could have believed it.

When the next generation, with its more modern ideas, became mayors and aldermen, this arrangement created some little dissatisfaction. On the first of the year they mailed her a tax notice. February came, and there was no reply. They wrote her a formal letter, asking her to call at the sheriff's office at her convenience. A week later the mayor wrote her himself, offering to call or to send his car for her, and received in reply a note on paper of an archaic shape, in a thin, flowing calligraphy in faded ink, to the effect that she no longer went out at all. The tax notice was also enclosed, without comment.

They called a special meeting of the Board of Aldermen. A deputation waited upon her, knocked at the door through which no visitor had passed since she ceased giving chinapainting lessons eight or ten years earlier. They were admitted by the old Negro into a dim hall from which a stairway mounted into still more shadow. It smelled of dust and disuse—a close, dank smell. The Negro led them into the parlor. It was furnished in heavy, leather-covered furniture. When the Negro opened the blinds of one window, they could see that the leather was cracked; and when they sat down, a faint dust rose sluggishly about their thighs, spinning with slow motes in the single sun-ray. On a tarnished gilt easel before the fireplace stood a crayon portrait of Miss Emily's father.

They rose when she entered—a small, fat woman in black, with a thin gold chain descending to her waist and vanishing into her belt, leaning on an ebony cane with a tarnished gold head. Her skeleton was small and spare; perhaps that was why what would have been merely plumpness in another was obesity in her. She looked bloated, like a body long submerged in motionless water, and of that pallid hue. Her eyes, lost in the fatty ridges of her face, looked like two small pieces of coal pressed into a lump of dough as they moved from one face to another while the visitors stated their errand.

She did not ask them to sit. She just stood in the door and listened quietly until the spokesman came to a stumbling halt. Then they could hear the invisible watch ticking at the end of the gold chain.

Her voice was dry and cold. "I have no taxes in Jefferson. Colonel Sartoris explained it to me. Perhaps one of you can gain access to the city records and satisfy yourselves."

"But we have. We are the city authorities, Miss Emily. Didn't you get a notice from the sheriff, signed by him?"

"I received a paper, yes," Miss Emily said. "Perhaps he considers himself the 10 sheriff. . . . I have no taxes in Jefferson."

"But there is nothing on the books to show that, you see. We must go by the—"

"See Colonel Sartoris. I have no taxes in Jefferson."

"But, Miss Emily—"

"See Colonel Sartoris." (Colonel Sartoris had been dead almost ten years.) "I have no taxes in Jefferson. Tobe!" The Negro appeared. "Show these gentlemen out."

II

So she vanquished them, horse and foot, just as she had vanquished their fathers thirty 15 years before about the smell. That was two years after her father's death and a short time after her sweetheart—the one we believed would marry her—had deserted her. After her father's death she went out very little; after her sweetheart went away, people hardly saw her at all. A few of the ladies had the temerity to call, but were not received, and the only sign of life about the place was the Negro man—a young man then—going in and out with a market basket.

"Just as if a man—any man—could keep a kitchen properly," the ladies said; so they were not surprised when the smell developed. It was another link between the gross, teeming world and the high and mighty Griersons.

A neighbor, a woman, complained to the mayor, Judge Stevens, eighty years old.

"But what will you have me do about it, madam?" he said.

"Why, send her word to stop it," the woman said. "Isn't there a law?"

"I'm sure that won't be necessary," Judge Stevens said. "It's probably just a snake or 20 a rat that nigger of hers killed in the yard. I'll speak to him about it."

The next day he received two more complaints, one from a man who came in diffident deprecation. "We really must do something about it, Judge. I'd be the last one in the world to bother Miss Emily, but we've got to do something." That night the Board of Aldermen met—three graybeards and one younger man, a member of the rising generation.

"It's simple enough," he said. "Send her word to have her place cleaned up. Give her a certain time to do it in, and if she don't. . . . "

"Dammit, sir," Judge Stevens said, "will you accuse a lady to her face of smelling bad?"

So the next night, after midnight, four men crossed Miss Emily's lawn and slunk about the house like burglars, sniffing along the base of the brickwork and at the cellar openings while one of them performed a regular sowing motion with his hand out of a sack slung from his shoulder. They broke open the cellar door and sprinkled lime there, and in all the outbuildings. As they recrossed the lawn, a window that had been dark was lighted and Miss Emily sat in it, the light behind her, and her upright torso motionless as that of an idol. They crept quietly across the lawn and into the shadow of the locusts that lined the street. After a week or two the smell went away.

That was when people had begun to feel really sorry for her. People in our town,   25 remembering how old lady Wyatt, her great-aunt, had gone completely crazy at last, believed that the Griersons held themselves a little too high for what they really were. None of the young men were quite good enough for Miss Emily and such. We had long thought of them as a tableau, Miss Emily a slender figure in white in the background, her father a spraddled silhouette in the foreground, his back to her and clutching a horsewhip, the two of them framed by the backflung front door. So when she got to be thirty and was still single, we were not pleased exactly, but vindicated; even with insanity in the family she wouldn't have turned down all of her chances if they had really materialized.

When her father died, it got about that the house was all that was left to her; and in a way, people were glad. At last they could pity Miss Emily. Being left alone, and a pauper, she had become humanized. Now she too would know the old thrill and the old despair of a penny more or less.

The day after his death all the ladies prepared to call at the house and offer condolence and aid, as is our custom. Miss Emily met them at the door, dressed as usual and with no trace of grief on her face. She told them that her father was not dead. She did that for three days, with the ministers calling on her, and the doctors, trying to persuade her to let them dispose of the body. Just as they were about to resort to law and force, she broke down, and they buried her father quickly.

We did not say she was crazy then. We believed she had to do that. We remembered all the young men her father had driven away, and we knew that with nothing left, she would have to cling to that which had robbed her, as people will.

III

She was sick for a long time. When we saw her again, her hair was cut short, making her look like a girl, with a vague resemblance to those angels in colored church windows—sort of tragic and serene.

The town had just let the contracts for paving the sidewalks, and in the summer   30 after her father's death they began the work. The construction company came with niggers and mules and machinery, and a foreman named Homer Barron, a Yankee—a big, dark, ready man, with a big voice and eyes lighter than his face. The little boys would follow in groups to hear him cuss the niggers, and the niggers singing in time to the rise and fall of picks. Pretty soon he knew everybody in town. Whenever you heard a lot of laughing anywhere about the square, Homer Barron would be in the center of the group. Presently, we began to see him and Miss Emily on Sunday afternoons driving in the yellow-wheeled buggy and the matched team of bays from the livery stable.

At first we were glad that Miss Emily would have an interest, because the ladies all said, "Of course a Grierson would not think seriously of a Northerner, a day laborer." But there were still others, older people, who said that even grief could not cause a real lady to forget *noblesse oblige*—without calling it *noblesse oblige*. They just said, "Poor Emily. Her kinsfolk should come to her." She had some kin in Alabama; but years ago her father had fallen out with them over the estate of old lady Wyatt, the crazy woman, and there was no communication between the two families. They had not even been represented at the funeral.

And as soon as the old people said, "Poor Emily," the whispering began. "Do you suppose it's really so?" they said to one another. "Of course it is. What else could. . . . " This behind their hands; rustling of craned silk and satin behind jalousies closed upon the sun of Sunday afternoon as the thin, swift clop-clop-clop of the matched team passed: "Poor Emily."

She carried her head high enough—even when we believed that she was fallen. It was as if she demanded more than ever the recognition of her dignity as the last Grierson; as if it had wanted that touch of earthiness to reaffirm her imperviousness. Like when she bought the rat poison, the arsenic. That was over a year after they had begun to say "Poor Emily," and while the two female cousins were visiting her.

"I want some poison," she said to the druggist. She was over thirty then, still a slight woman, though thinner than usual, with cold, haughty black eyes in a face the flesh of which was strained across the temples and about the eye-sockets as you imagine a lighthouse-keeper's face ought to look. "I want some poison," she said.

"Yes, Miss Emily. What kind? For rats and such? I'd recom—"   35

"I want the best you have. I don't care what kind."

The druggist named several. "They'll kill anything up to an elephant. But what you want is—"

"Arsenic," Miss Emily said. "Is that a good one?"

"Is . . . arsenic? Yes, ma'am. But what you want—"

"I want arsenic."   40

The druggist looked down at her. She looked back at him, erect, her face like a strained flag. "Why, of course," the druggist said. "If that's what you want. But the law requires you to tell what you are going to use it for."

Miss Emily just stared at him, her head tilted back in order to look him eye for eye, until he looked away and went and got the arsenic and wrapped it up. The Negro delivery boy brought her the package; the druggist didn't come back. When she opened the package at home there was written on the box, under the skull and bones: "For rats."

IV

So the next day we all said, "She will kill herself"; and we said it would be the best thing. When she had first begun to be seen with Homer Barron, we had said, "She will marry him." Then we said, "She will persuade him yet," because Homer himself had remarked—he liked men, and it was known that he drank with the younger men in the Elks' Club—that he was not a marrying man. Later we said, "Poor Emily" behind the jalousies as they passed on Sunday afternoon in the glittering buggy, Miss Emily with her head high and Homer Barron with his hat cocked and a cigar in his teeth, reins and whip in a yellow glove.

Then some of the ladies began to say that it was a disgrace to the town and a bad example to the young people. The men did not want to interfere, but at last the ladies forced the Baptist minister—Miss Emily's people were Episcopal—to call upon her. He would never divulge what happened during that interview, but he refused to go back again. The next Sunday they again drove about the streets, and the following day the minister's wife wrote to Miss Emily's relations in Alabama.

So she had blood-kin under her roof again and we sat back to watch developments. 45
At first nothing happened. Then we were sure that they were to be married. We learned
that Miss Emily had been to the jeweler's and ordered a man's toilet set in silver, with
the letters H.B. on each piece. Two days later we learned that she had bought a complete outfit of men's clothing, including a nightshirt, and we said, "They are married."
We were really glad. We were glad because the two female cousins were even more
Grierson than Miss Emily had ever been.

So we were not surprised when Homer Barron—the streets had been finished
some time since—was gone. We were a little disappointed that there was not a public
blowing-off, but we believed that he had gone on to prepare for Miss Emily's coming,
or to give her a chance to get rid of the cousins. (By that time it was a cabal, and we
were all Miss Emily's allies to help circumvent the cousins.) Sure enough, after another week they departed. And, as we had expected all along, within three days Homer
Barron was back in town. A neighbor saw the Negro man admit him at the kitchen
door at dusk one evening.

And that was the last we saw of Homer Barron. And of Miss Emily for some time.
The Negro man went in and out with the market basket, but the front door remained
closed. Now and then we would see her at the window for a moment, as the men did
that night when they sprinkled the lime, but for almost six months she did not appear
on the streets. Then we knew that this was to be expected too; as if that quality of her
father which had thwarted her woman's life so many times had been too virulent and
too furious to die.

When we next saw Miss Emily, she had grown fat and her hair was turning
gray. During the next few years it grew grayer and grayer until it attained an even
pepper-and-salt iron-gray when it ceased turning. Up to the day of her death at seventy-
four it was still that vigorous iron-gray, like the hair of an active man.

From that time on her front door remained closed, save during a period of six or
seven years, when she was about forty, during which she gave lessons in china-painting.
She fitted up a studio in one of the downstairs rooms, where the daughters and grand-
daughters of Colonel Sartoris' contemporaries were sent to her with the same regularity
and in the same spirit that they were sent to church on Sundays with a twenty-five-cent
piece for the collection plate. Meanwhile her taxes had been remitted.

Then the newer generation became the backbone and the spirit of the town, and 50
the painting pupils grew up and fell away and did not send their children to her with
boxes of color and tedious brushes and pictures cut from the ladies' magazines. The
front door closed upon the last one and remained closed for good. When the town got
free postal delivery, Miss Emily alone refused to let them fasten the metal numbers
above her door and attach a mailbox to it. She would not listen to them.

Daily, monthly, yearly we watched the Negro grow grayer and more stooped, going in and out with the market basket. Each December we sent her a tax notice, which
would be returned by the post office a week later, unclaimed. Now and then we would
see her in one of the downstairs windows—she had evidently shut up the top floor of
the house—like the carven torso of an idol in a niche, looking or not looking at us, we
could never tell which. Thus she passed from generation to generation—dear, inescapable, impervious, tranquil, and perverse.

And so she died. Fell ill in the house filled with dust and shadows, with only a
doddering Negro man to wait on her. We did not even know she was sick; we had long

since given up trying to get any information from the Negro. He talked to no one, probably not even to her, for his voice had grown harsh and rusty, as if from disuse.

She died in one of the downstairs rooms, in a heavy walnut bed with a curtain, her gray head propped on a pillow yellow and moldy with age and lack of sunlight.

V

The Negro met the first of the ladies at the front door and let them in, with their hushed, sibilant voices and their quick, curious glances, and then he disappeared. He walked right through the house and out the back and was not seen again.

The two female cousins came at once. They held the funeral on the second day, 55 with the town coming to look at Miss Emily beneath a mass of bought flowers, with the crayon face of her father musing profoundly above the bier and the ladies sibilant and macabre; and the very old men—some in their brushed Confederate uniforms—on the porch and the lawn, talking of Miss Emily as if she had been a contemporary of theirs, believing that they had danced with her and courted her perhaps, confusing time with its mathematical progression, as the old do, to whom all the past is not a diminishing road but, instead, a huge meadow which no winter ever quite touches, divided from them now by the narrow bottleneck of the most recent decade of years.

Already we knew that there was one room in that region above stairs which no one had seen in forty years, and which would have to be forced. They waited until Miss Emily was decently in the ground before they opened it.

The violence of breaking down the door seemed to fill this room with pervading dust. A thin, acrid pall as of the tomb seemed to lie everywhere upon this room decked and furnished as for a bridal: upon the valance curtains of faded rose color, upon the rose-shaded lights, upon the dressing table, upon the delicate array of crystal and the man's toilet things backed with tarnished silver, silver so tarnished that the monogram was obscured. Among them lay a collar and tie, as if they had just been removed, which, lifted, left upon the surface a pale crescent in the dust. Upon a chair hung the suit, carefully folded; beneath it the two mute shoes and the discarded socks.

The man himself lay in the bed.

For a long while we just stood there, looking down at the profound and fleshless grin. The body had apparently once lain in the attitude of an embrace, but now the long sleep that outlasts love, that conquers even the grimace of love, had cuckolded him. What was left of him, rotted beneath what was left of the nightshirt, had become inextricable from the bed in which he lay; and upon him and upon the pillow beside him lay that even coating of the patient and biding dust.

Then we noticed that in the second pillow was the indentation of a head. One of 60 us lifted something from it, and leaning forward, that faint and invisible dust dry and acrid in the nostrils, we saw a long strand of iron-gray hair.

Mary Gordon *(1949–)*

City Life *2006*

Peter had always been more than thoughtful in not pressing her about her past, and Beatrice was sure it was a reason for her choice of him. Most men, coming of age in a time that extolled openness and disclosure, would have thought themselves remiss in questioning her so little. Perhaps because he was a New Englander—one of four sons in a family that had been stable for generations—perhaps because he was a mathematician, perhaps because both the sight of her and her way of living had pleased him from the first and continued to please him, he had been satisfied with what she was willing to tell. "My parents are dead. We lived in western New York State, near Rochester. I am an only child. I have no family left."

She preferred saying "I have no family left"—creating with her words an absence, a darkness, rather than to say what had been there, what she had ruthlessly left, with a ruthlessness that would have shocked anyone who knew her later. She had left them so thoroughly that she really didn't know if they were still living. When she tried to locate them, with her marriage and her children and the warm weight of her domestic safety at her back, there was no trace of them. It had shocked and frightened her how completely they had failed to leave a trace. This was the sort of thing most people didn't think of: how possible it was for people like her parents to impress themselves so little on the surface, the many surfaces of the world, that they would leave it or inhabit it with the same lack of a mark.

They were horrors, her parents, the sort people wanted to avert their eyes from, that people felt it was healthful to avert their eyes from. They had let their lives slip very far, further than anyone Beatrice now knew could even begin to imagine. But it had always been like that: a slippage so continuous that there was simultaneously a sense of slippage and of already having slipped.

It was terribly clear to her. She was brought up in filth. Most people, Beatrice knew, believed that filth was temporary, one of those things, unlike disease or insanity or social hatred—that didn't root itself in but was an affair of surfaces, therefore dislodgeable by effort, will, and the meagerest brand of intelligence. That was, Beatrice knew, because people didn't understand filth. They mistook its historical ordinariness for simplicity. They didn't understand the way it could invade and settle, take over, dominate, and for good, until it became, inevitably, the only true thing about a place and the only lives that could be lived there. Dust, grime, the grease of foods, the residues of bodies, the smells that lived in the air, palpable, malign, unidentifiable, impossible to differentiate: an ugly population of refugees from an unknowable location, permanent, stubborn, knife-faced settlers who had right of occupancy—the place was theirs now—and would never leave.

Beatrice's parents had money for food, and the rent must have been paid to some-   5
one. They had always lived in the one house: her mother, her father, and herself. Who could have owned it? Who would have put money down for such a place? One-story, nearly windowless, the outside walls made of soft shingle in the semblance of pinkish gray brick. It must have been built from the first entirely without love, with the most cynical understanding, Beatrice had always thought, of the human need for shelter

and the dollar value that it could bring. Everything was cheap and thin, done with the minimum of expense and of attention. No thought was given to ornament or amplitude, or even to the long, practical run: what wouldn't age horribly or crumble, splinter, quickly fade.

As she grew older, she believed the house had been built to hide some sort of criminality. It was in the middle of the woods, down a dirt road half a mile down Highway 117, which led nowhere she knew, or maybe south, she somehow thought, to Pennsylvania. Her parents said it had once been a hunting lodge, but she didn't believe it. When she was old enough to have learned about bootlegging, and knew that whiskey had been smuggled in from Canada, she was convinced that the house had had something to do with that. She could always imagine petty gangsters, local thugs in mean felt hats and thin-soled shoes trading liquor for money, throwing their cigarette butts down on the hard, infertile ground, then driving away from the house, not giving it a thought until it was time for their next deal.

Sometimes she thought it was the long periods of uninhabitedness that gave the house its closed, and vengeful, character. But when she began to think like that, it wasn't long before she understood that kind of thought to be fantastical. It wasn't the house, houses had no will or nature. Her parents had natures, and it was their lives and the way they lived that made their dwelling a monstrosity.

She had awakened each day in dread, afraid to open her eyes, knowing the first thing they fell on would be ugly. She didn't even know where she could get something for herself that might be beautiful. The word couldn't have formed itself in her mind in any way that could attach to an object that was familiar to her, or that she could even imagine having access to. She heard, as if from a great distance, people using the word "beautiful" in relation to things like trees or sunsets, but her faculty for understanding things like this had been so crippled that the attempt to comprehend what people were saying when they spoke like this filled her with a kind of panic. She couldn't call up even the first step that would allow her, even in the far future, to come close to what they meant. They were talking about things out of doors when they talked about trees and sunsets. And what was the good of that? You could go out of doors. The blueness of the sky, the brightness of the sun, the freshness of a tree would greet you, but in the end you would only have to go back somewhere to sleep. And that would not be beautiful; it would be where you lived. So beauty seemed a dangerous, foreign, and irrelevant idea. She turned for solace, not to it, but to the nature of enclosure. Everything in her life strained toward the ideal of separations: how to keep the horror of her parents' life from everything that could be called her life.

She learned what it was she wanted from watching her grade school teachers cutting simple shapes—squares, triangles—and writing numbers in straight columns on the blackboard or on paper with crisp, straight blue lines. The whiteness of pages, the unmuddled black of print, struck her as desirable; the dry rasping of the scissors, the click of a stapler, the riffling of a rubber band around a set of children's tests. She understood all these things as prosperity, and knew that her family was not prosperous; they were poor. But she knew as well that their real affliction wasn't poverty but something different—you might, perhaps, say worse—but not connected to money. If she could have pointed to that—a simple lack of money—it would have been more hopeful for her. But she knew it wasn't poverty that was the problem. It was the way her parents were. It was what they did.

They drank. That was what they did. It was, properly speaking, the only thing they did. But no, she always told herself when she began to think that way, it wasn't the only thing. Her father, after all, had gone out to work. He was a gravedigger in a Catholic cemetery. Each morning he woke in the dark house. Massive, nearly toothless, and still in his underwear, he drank black coffee with a shot in it for breakfast, and then put on his dark olive work pants and shirts, his heavy boots—in winter a fleece-lined coat and cap—and started the reluctant car driving down the dirt road. He came home at night, with a clutch of bottles in a paper bag, to begin drinking. He wasn't violent or abusive; he was interested only in the stupor he could enter and inhabit. This, Beatrice knew early on, was his true home.

Her mother woke late, her hair in pin curls wrapped in a kerchief, which she rarely bothered to undo. She was skeletally thin; her skin was always in a state of dull eruptions; red spidery veins on her legs always seemed to Beatrice to be the tracks of a slow disease. Just out of bed, she poured herself a drink, not bothering to hide it in coffee, and drank it from a glass that had held cheese spread mixed with pimentos, which her parents ate on crackers when they drank, and which was often Beatrice's supper. Beatrice's mother would sit for a while on the plaid couch, watch television, then go back to bed. The house was nearly always silent; there were as few words in the house as there were ornaments. It was another reason Peter liked her. She had a gift, he said, for silence, a gift he respected, that he said too few people had. She wondered if he would have prized this treasure if he'd known its provenance.

Beatrice saw everything her parents did because she slept in the large room. When she was born, her parents had put a crib for her in the corner of the room nearest their bedroom, opposite the wall where the sink, the stove, and the refrigerator were. It didn't occur to them that she might want privacy; when she grew taller, they replaced her crib with a bed, but they never imagined she had any more rights or desires than an infant. The torpor, the disorder of their lives, spread into her quarters. For years, it anguished her to see their slippers, their half-read newspapers, broken bobby pins, half-empty glasses, butt-filled ashtrays traveling like bacilli into the area she thought of as hers. When she was ten, she bought some clothesline and some tacks. She bought an Indian bedspread from a hippie store in town; rose-colored, with a print of tigers; the only vivid thing in the place. She made a barrier between herself and them. Her father said something unkind about it, but she took no notice.

For the six years after that, she came home as little as she could, staying in the school library until it closed, walking home miles in the darkness. She sat on her bed, did what was left of her homework, and, as early as possible, lay down to sleep. At sunrise, she would leave the house, walking the roads till something opened in the town—the library, the five-and-ten, the luncheonette—then walking for more hours till sunset. She didn't love the woods; she didn't think of them as nature, with all the implications she had read about. But they were someplace she could be until she had no choice but to be *there* again, but not quite *there,* not in the place that was *theirs,* but her place, behind her curtain, where she needn't see the way they lived.

She moved out of her parents' house two days after she graduated from high school. She packed her few things and moved to Buffalo, where she got a job in a tool and die factory, took night courses at the community college. She did this for five years, then took all her savings and enrolled in the elementary education program at the University of Buffalo full-time. She'd planned it all out carefully, in her tiny room, living on yogurt she made from powdered milk, allowing it to ferment in a series of thermoses she'd bought at garage sales, eating the good parts of half-rotten fruit and vegetables she'd bought for pennies, the fresh middle parts of loaves of day-old bread. Never, in those years, did she buy a new blouse or skirt or pair of jeans. She got her clothes from the Salvation Army; it was only later, after she married, that she learned to sew.

In her second semester, she met Peter in a very large class: European History 1789– 1945. He said he'd fallen in love with several things about her almost at once: the look of her notebooks, the brilliant white of the collar of her shirt as it peeked over the top of her pastel blue Shetland sweater, the sheer pink curves of her fingernails. He said he'd been particularly taken by her thumb. Most women's thumbs were ugly and betrayed the incompleteness of their femininity, the essential coarseness of it. The fineness of her thumb, the way the nail curved and was placed within the flesh, showed there wasn't a trace of coarseness in her: everything connected with her was, and would always be, fine. He didn't find out until they'd dated a few times that she was older, more than three years older than he was. He accepted that she'd had to work those years because her parents had—tragically—died.

Beatrice knew what Peter saw when he looked at her: clarity and simplicity and thrift, an almost holy sign of order, a plain creature without hidden parts or edges, who would sail through life before him making a path through murky seas, leaving to him plain sailing: nothing in the world to obstruct him or the free play of his mind. She knew that he didn't realize that he had picked her in part for the emptiness of her past, imagining a beautiful blankness, blameless, unpopulated, clear. His pity for her increased her value for him: she was an exile in the ordinary world he was born into, lacking the encumbrances that could make for problems in his life. He believed that life could be simple, that he would leave from a cloudless day and drop into the teeming fog of mathematics, which for him was peopled, creatured, a tumultuous society he had to colonize and civilize and rule.

She knew he felt he could leave all the rest to her, turning to her at night with the anomaly of his ardor, another equation she could elegantly solve. His curiosity about the shape of her desire was as tenderly blunted as his curiosity about her past, and she was as glad of the one as of the other. Making love to him, an occurrence she found surprisingly frequent, she could pretend she was sitting through a violent and fascinating storm that certainly would pass. Having got through it, she could be covered over in grateful tenderness for the life that he made possible: a life of clean linen and bright rooms, of matched dishes and a variety of specialized kitchen items: each unique, for one use only, and not, as everything in her mother's house was, interchangeable.

So the children came, three boys, and then the farmhouse, bought as a wreck, transformed by Beatrice Talbot into a treasure, something acquaintances came to see as much (more, she thought, if they were honest) as they did the family itself. Then Peter's tenure, and additions on the house: a sewing room, a greenhouse, then uncovering the old woodwork, searching out antique stores, auctions, flea markets for the right furniture—all this researched in the university library and in the local library—and the children growing and needing care so that by the time Peter came home with the news that was the first breakup of the smooth plane that had been their life together, the children had become, somehow, twelve, ten, and eight.

He had won a really spectacular fellowship at Columbia, three years being paid twice what he made at Cornell and no teaching, and a chance to work beside the man who was tops in his field. Peter asked Beatrice what she thought, but only formally. They both knew. They would be going to New York.

Nights in the house ten miles above Ithaca—it was summer and in her panic she could hear the crickets and, toward dawn, smell the freshness of the wet grass—she lay awake in terror of the packing job ahead of her. Everything, each thing she owned, would have to be wrapped and collected. She lived in dread of losing something, breaking something, for each carefully selected, carefully tended object that she owned was a proof of faith against the dark clutching power of the past. She typed on an index card a brief but wholly accurate description of the house, and the housing office presented her with a couple from Berlin—particle physicists, the both of them, and without children, she was grateful to hear. They seemed clean and thorough; they wanted to live in the country, they were the type who would know enough to act in time if a problem was occurring, who wouldn't let things get too far.

Peter and Beatrice were assured by everyone they talked to in New York that their apartment was a jewel. Sally Rodier, the wife of Peter's collaborator, who also helped Beatrice place the children in private schools, kept telling her how incredibly lucky they were, to have been given an apartment in one of the buildings on Riverside Drive. The view could be better, but they had a glimpse of the river. Really, they were almost disgustingly lucky, she said, laughing. Did they know what people would do to get what they had?

But Beatrice's heart sank at the grayness of the grout between the small octagonal bathroom floor tiles, the uneven job of polyurethaning on the living room floor, the small hole in the floor by the radiator base, the stiff door on one of the kitchen cabinets, the frosted glass on the window near the shower that she couldn't, whatever she did, make look clean.

For nearly a month she worked, making the small repairs herself, unheard-of behavior, Sally Rodier said, in a Columbia tenant. She poured a lake of bleach on the bathroom floor, left it for six hours, then, sopping it up, found she had created a field of dazzling whiteness. She made curtains; she scraped the edges of the window frames. Then she began to venture out. She had been so few places, had done so little, that the city streets, although they frightened her, began to seem a place of quite exciting possibilities. Because she did her errands, for the first time in her life, on foot, she could have human contact with no fear of revelation. She could be among her kind without fear every second that they would find out about her: where and what she'd come from, who she really was. Each day the super left mail on her threshold; they would exchange a pleasant word or two. He was a compact and competent man who had left his family in Peru. She could imagine that he and the Bangladeshi doormen, and the people on the streets, all possessed a dark and complicated past, things they'd prefer to have hidden as she did. In Buffalo, in Ithaca, people had seemed to be expressing everything they were. Even their reserve seemed legible and therefore relatively simple. But, riding on the bus and walking out on Broadway, she felt for the first time part of the web of concealment, of lives constructed like a house with rooms that gave access only to each other, rooms far from the initial entrance, with no source of natural light.

By Thanksgiving, she was able to tell Peter, who feared that she would suffer separation from her beloved house, that she was enjoying herself very much. The boys, whose lives, apart from their aspects of animal survival, never seemed to have much to do with her, were absorbed in the thick worlds of their schools—activities till five or six most nights, homework, and supper and more homework. Weekends, she could leave them to Peter, who was happy to take them to the park for football, or to the university pool, or the indoor track. She would often go to the Metropolitan Museum, to look at the collection of American furniture or, accompanied by a guidebook, on an architectural tour.

One Thursday night, Peter was working in the library and the boys were playing basketball in the room the two younger ones shared, throwing a ball made of foam through the hoop Peter had nailed against the door. Beatrice was surprised to hear the bell ring; people rarely came without telephoning first. She opened the door to a stranger, but catching a glimpse of her neighbor across the hall, a history professor, opening her door, she didn't feel afraid.

The man at the doorway was unlike anyone she had spoken to in New York, anyone she'd spoken to since she'd left home. But in an instant she recognized him. She thought he was there to tell her the story of her life, and to tell Peter and everyone she knew. She'd never met him, as himself, before. But he could have lived in the house she'd been born in. He had an unrushed look, as if he had all the time in the world. He took a moment to meet her eyes, but when he did, finally, she understood the scope of everything he knew.

She kept the door mostly closed, leaving only enough space for her body. She would allow him to hurt her, if that was what he came for, but she wouldn't let him in the house.

"I'm your downstairs neighbor," he said.

She opened the door wider. He was wearing a greasy-looking ski jacket which had once been royal blue; a shiny layer of black grime covered the surface like soot on old snow. The laces on his black sneakers had no tips. His pants were olive green; his hands were in his pockets. It was impossible to guess how old he was. He was missing several top teeth, which made him look not young, but his hair fell over his eyes in a way that bestowed youth. She stepped back a pace further into the hall.

"What can I do for you?"

"You've got kids?"

For a moment, she thought he meant to take the children. She could hear them in the back of the apartment, running, laughing, innocent of what she was sure would befall them. A sense of heavy torpor took her up. She felt that whatever this man wanted, she would have to let him take. A half-enjoyable lassitude came over her. She knew she couldn't move.

He was waiting for her answer. "I have three boys," she said.

"Well, what you can do for me is to tell them to stop their racket. All day, all night, night and day, bouncing the ball. The plaster is coming down off the ceiling. It's hitting me in my bed. That's not too much to ask, is it? You can see that's not too much to ask."

"No, of course not. No," she said. "I'll see to it right away."

She closed the door very quickly. Walking to the back part of the apartment, she had to dig her nails into the palms of her hands so that she wouldn't scream the words to her children. "They didn't know, they didn't know," she kept saying to herself. It wasn't their fault. They weren't used to living in an apartment. It wasn't anybody's fault. But she was longing to scream at them, for having made this happen. For doing something so she would have to see that man, would have to think about him. An immense distaste for her children came over her. They seemed loud and gross and spoiled and careless. They knew nothing of the world. They were passing the ball back and forth to one another, their blond hair gleaming in the light that shone down from the fixture overhead.

She forced herself to speak calmly. "I'm afraid you can't play basketball here," she said. "The man downstairs complained."

"What'd you say to him?" asked Jeff, the oldest.

"I said I'd make you stop."

"What'd you say that for? We have just as much right as he does."   40

She looked at her son coldly. "I'm afraid you don't."

The three of them looked back at her, as if they'd never seen her.

"I'll make supper now," she said. "But I have a terrible headache. After I put dinner on the table, I'm going to lie down."

While she was cooking, the phone rang. It was her neighbor across the hall. "Terribly sorry to intrude," she said. "I hope I'm not being a busybody, but I couldn't help over-hear the rather unpleasant exchange you had with our neighbor. I just thought you should understand a few things."

I understand everything, Beatrice wanted to say. There's nothing I don't   45 understand.

"He's a pathetic case. Used to be a big shot in the chemistry department. Boy genius. Then he blew it. Just stopped going to classes, stopped showing up in the de-partment. But some bigwigs in the administration were on his side, and he's been on disability and allowed to keep the apartment. We're all stuck with him. If he ever opens the door and you're near, you get a whiff of the place. Unbelievable. It's unbelievable how people live. What I'm trying to tell you is, don't let him get you bent out of shape. Occasionally he crawls out of his cave and growls something, but he's quite harmless."

"Thank you," said Beatrice. "Thank you for calling. Thank you very much."

She put down the phone, walked into her bedroom, turned out all the lights, and lay down on her bed.

Lying in the dark, she knew it was impossible that he was underneath her. If his room was below the children's, it was near the other side of the apartment, far from where she was.

But she imagined she could hear his breathing. It matched her own: in-out-in-out.   50 Just like hers.

She breathed with him. In and out, and in and out. Frightened, afraid to leave the bed, she lay under a quilt she'd made herself. She forced herself to think of the silver scissors, her gold thimble, the spools and spools of pale thread. Tried and tried to call them back, a pastel shimmering cloud, a thickness glowing softly in this darkness. It would come, then fade, swallowed up in darkness. Soon the darkness was all there was. It was everything. It was everything she wanted and her only terror was that she would have to leave it and go back. Outside the closed door, she could hear the voices of her husband and her sons. She put her fingers in her ears so she couldn't hear them. She prayed, she didn't know to whom, to someone who inhabited the same darkness. This was the only thing about the one she prayed to that she knew. She prayed that her fam-ily would forget about her, leave her. She dreaded the door's cracking, the intrusion of the light. If she could just be here, in darkness, breathing in and out, with him as he breathed in and out. Then she didn't know. But it would be something that she feared.

"How about you tone it down and let your mother sleep?"

She closed her eyes as tightly as a child in nightmare. Then she knew that she had been, in fact, asleep because when Peter came in, sank his weight onto the bed, she understood she had to start pretending to be sleeping.

After that night, she began staying in bed all day long. She had so rarely been sick, had met the occasional cold or bout of flu with so much stoicism that Peter couldn't help but believe her when she complained of a debilitating headache. And it would have been impossible for him to connect her behavior with the man downstairs. He hadn't even seen him. No one had seen him except her and the woman across the hall who told her what she didn't need to know, what she already knew, what she couldn't help knowing.

She wondered how long it would be before Peter suggested calling a doctor. That 55 was what worried her as she lay in the darkness: what would happen, what would be the thing she wouldn't be able to resist, the thing that would force her to get up.

She cut herself off fully from the life of the family. She had no idea what kind of life was going on outside her door. Peter was coping very well, without a question or murmur of complaint. Cynically, she thought it was easier for him not to question: he might learn something he didn't want to know. He had joined up with her so they could create a world free from disturbance, from disturbances. Now the disturbance rumbled beneath them, and it only stood to reason that he wouldn't know of it and wouldn't want to know.

Each morning, she heard the door close as Peter left with the children for school. Then she got up, bathed, fixed herself a breakfast, and, exhausted, fell back into a heavy sleep. She would sleep through the afternoon. In the evening, Peter brought her supper on a tray. The weak light from the lamp on the bed table hurt her eyes; the taste and textures of the food hurt her palate, grown fragile from so much silence, so much sleep.

She didn't ask what the children were doing and they didn't come in to see her. Peter assumed she was in excruciating pain. She said nothing to give him that idea, and nothing to relieve him of it.

After her fourth day in the dark, she heard the doorbell ring. It was early evening, the beginning of December. Night had completely fallen and the radiators hissed and cooed. She tried not to hear what was going on outside, so at first she heard only isolated words that Peter was shouting. "Children." "Natural." "Ordinary." "Play." "Rights." "No right."

Alarm, a spot of electric blue spreading beneath one of her ribs, made her under- 60 stand that Peter was shouting at the man downstairs. She jumped out of bed and stood at the door of the bedroom. She could see Peter's back, tensed as she had, in fourteen years of marriage, never seen it. His fists were clenched at his sides.

"You come here, bothering my wife, disturbing my family. I don't know where the hell . . . what makes you think . . . but you've got the wrong number, mister. My sons are going to play ball occasionally at a reasonable hour. It's five-ten in the afternoon. Don't tell me you're trying to sleep."

"All right, buddy. All right. We'll just see about sleeping. Some night come midnight when everyone in your house is fast asleep, you want to hear about disturbing. Believe me, buddy, I know how to make a disturbance."

Peter shut the door in the man's face. He turned around, pale, his fists not yet unclenched.

"Why didn't you tell me about that guy?" he said, standing so close to her that his voice hurt her ears, which had heard very little in the last four days.

"I wasn't feeling well," she said.   65

He nodded. She knew he hadn't heard her.

"Better get back into bed."

The doorbell rang again. Peter ran to it, his fists clenched once again. But it wasn't the man downstairs, it was the woman across the hall. Beatrice could hear her telling Peter the same story she'd told her, but with more details. "The apartment is full of broken machines, he takes them apart for some experiment he says he's doing. He says he's going to be able to create enough energy to power the whole world. He brags that he can live on five dollars a week."

"Low overhead," said Peter, and the two of them laughed.

She was back in the darkness. Her heart was a swollen muscle; she spread her hands   70
over her chest to slow it down. She heard Peter calling Al Rodier.

"Do you believe it . . . university building . . . speak to someone in real estate first thing . . . right to the top if necessary . . . will not put up with it . . . hard to evict, but not impossible. Despoiling the environment . . . polluting the air we breathe."

The word "pollution" spun in her brain like one of those headlines in old movies: one word finally comprehensible after the turning blur: Strike. War.

Pollution. It suggested a defilement so complete, so permanent, that nothing could reverse it. Clear streams turned black and tarlike, verdant forests transformed to soot-covered stumps, the air full of black flakes that settled on the skin and couldn't be washed off.

Was that what the man downstairs was doing? He was living the way he wanted to, perhaps the only way he could. Before this incident, he hadn't disturbed them. They were the first to disturb him. People had a right not to hear thumping over their heads. Suppose he was trying to read, listening to music, working out a scientific formula. Suppose, when the children were making that noise, he was on the phone making an important call, the call that could change his life.

It wasn't likely. What was more likely was that he was lying in the dark, as   75
she was. But not as she was. He wasn't lying in an empty bed. He bedded down in garbage. And the sound of thumping over his head was the sound of all his fear: that he would be named the names that he knew fit him, but could bear if they weren't said. "Disreputable." "Illegitimate."

They would send him out into the world. If only he could be left alone. If only he could be left to himself. And her children with their loud feet, the shouts of their un-knowingness told him what he most feared, what he was right to fear, but what he only wanted to forget. At any minute they would tell him he was nothing, he was worse than nothing. Everything was theirs and they could take it rightfully, at any moment. Not because they were unjust or cruel. They were not unjust. Justice was entirely on their side. He couldn't possibly, in justice, speak a word in his own defense. Stone-faced, empty-handed, he would have to follow them into the open air.

She heard Peter on the phone calling the people they knew in the building who'd invited them for coffee or for brunch. She kept hearing him say his name—Peter

Talbot—and his department—Mathematics, and the number of their apartment—4A. He was urging them to band together in his living room, the next night, to come up with a plan of action before, he kept saying, over and over, "things get more out of hand. And when you think," he kept saying, "of the qualified people who'd give their eyeteeth for what he's got, what he's destroying for everyone who comes after him. I'll bet every one of you knows someone who deserves that apartment more than him."

She saw them filing into her house, their crisp short hair, their well-tended shoes, the smiles cutting across their faces like a rifle shot. They would march in, certain of their right to be there, their duty to keep order. Not questioning the essential rightness of clearing out the swamp, the place where disease bred, and necessarily, of course, removing the breeders and the spreaders who, if left to themselves, would contaminate the world.

And Beatrice knew that they were right, that was the terrible thing about them, their unquestionable rightness. Right to clear out, break in, burn, tear, demolish, so that the health of the world might be preserved.

She sank down deeper. She was there with those who wallowed, burrowed, 80 hoarded, their weak eyes half-closed, their sour voices, not really sour but hopeless at the prospect of trying to raise some objection, of offering some resistance. They knew there could be no negotiation, since they had no rights. So their petition turned into a growl, a growl that only stiffened the righteousness of their purpose. "Leave me alone" is all the ones who hid were saying. They would have liked to beseech but they were afraid to. Also full of hate. "Leave me alone."

Of course they wouldn't be left alone. They couldn't be. Beatrice understood that.

The skin around her eyes felt flayed, her limbs were heavy, her spine too weak to hold her up. "Leave me alone." The sweetness of the warm darkness, like a poultice, was all that could protect her from the brutality of open air on her raw skin.

She and the man downstairs breathed. In and out. She heard their joined breath and, underneath that sound, the opening of doors, the rush of violent armies, of flame, of tidal wave, lightning cleaving a moss-covered tree in two. And then something else below that: "Cannot. Cannot. Leave me alone." Unheeded.

She turned the light on in the bedroom. She put on a pair of turquoise sweatpants and a matching sweatshirt. On her feet she wore immaculate white socks and the white sneakers she'd varnished to brilliance with a product called Sneaker White she'd bought especially. She put on earrings, perfume, but no lipstick and no blush. She walked out of the apartment. She knew that Peter, in the back with the children, wouldn't hear the door close.

She walked down the dank, faintly ill-smelling stairs to the apartment situated exactly 85 as hers was—3A—and rang the bell.

He opened the door a crack. The stench of rotting food and unwashed clothes ought to have made her sick, but she knew she was beyond that sort of thing.

She looked him in the eye. "I need to talk to you," she said.

He shrugged, then smiled. Most of his top teeth were gone and the ones that were left were yellowed and streaked. He pushed the lock of his blondish hair that fell into his forehead back, away from his eyes. Then he took a comb out of his pocket and pulled it through his hair.

"Make yourself at home," he said, laughing morosely.

There was hardly a place to stand. The floor space was taken up by broken radios, 90 blenders, ancient portable TVs revealing blown tubes, disconnected wires, a double-size mattress. Beside the mattress were paper plates with hardened sandwiches, glimpses of pink ham, tomatoes turned to felt between stone-colored slices of bread, magazines with wrinkled pages, unopened envelopes (yellow, white, mustard-colored), sloping hills of clean underwear mixed up with balled socks, and opened cans of Coke. There were no sheets on the mattress; sheets, she could tell, had been given up long ago. Loosely spread over the blue ticking was a pinkish blanket, its trim a trap, a bracelet for the foot to catch itself in during the uneasy night.

A few feet from the mattress was a Barcalounger[1] whose upholstery must once have been mustard-colored. The headrest was a darker shade, almost brown; she understood that the discoloration was from the grease of his hair when he leaned back. She moved some copies of *Popular Mechanics* and some Styrofoam containers, hamburger-sized, to make room for herself to sit. She tried to imagine what she looked like, in her turquoise sweatsuit, sitting in this chair.

"I came to warn you," she said. "They're having a meeting. Right now in my apartment. They want to have you evicted."

He laughed, and she could see that his top teeth looked striated, lines of brownish yellow striping the enamel in a way she didn't remember seeing on anyone else.

"Relax," he said. "It'll never happen. They keep trying, but it'll never happen. This is New York. I'm a disabled person. I'm on disability. You understand what that means? Nobody like me gets evicted in New York. Don't worry about it. I'll be here forever."

She looked at her neighbor and gave him a smile so radiant that it seemed to par- 95 take of prayer. And then a torpor that was not somnolent, but full of joy, took hold of her. Her eyes were closing themselves with happiness. She needed rest. Why hadn't she ever known before that rest was the one thing she had always needed?

She saw her white bathroom floor, gleaming from the lake of bleach she had poured on it. Just thinking of it hurt her eyes. Here, there was nothing that would hurt her. She wanted to tell him it was beautiful here, it was wonderful, it was just like home. But she was too tired to speak. And that was fine, she knew he understood. Here, where they both were, there was no need to say a word.

But he was saying something. She could hear it through her sleep, and she had to swim up to get it, like a fish surfacing for crumbs. She couldn't seem, quite, to open her eyes and she fell back down to the dark water. Then she felt him shaking her by the shoulders.

"What are you doing? What are you doing? You can't do that here."

She looked at his eyes. They weren't looking at her kindly. She had thought he would be kind. She blinked several times, then closed her eyes again. When she opened them, he was still standing above her, his hands on her shoulders, shaking them, his eyes unkind.

"You can't do that here. You can't just come down here and go to sleep like that. 100 This is my place. Now get out."

He was telling her she had to leave. She supposed she understood that. She couldn't stay here if he didn't want her. She had thought he'd understand that what she needed

---

[1]**Barcalounger**: An arm chair.

was a place to rest, just that, she wouldn't be taking anything from him. But he was treating her like a thief. He was making her leave as if she were a criminal. There was no choice now but to leave, shamefully, like a criminal.

He closed the door behind her. Although her back was to the door, she felt he was closing it in her face and she felt the force of it exactly on her face as if his hand had struck it. She stood completely still, her back nearly touching the brown door.

She couldn't move. She couldn't move because she could think of no direction that seemed sensible. But the shame of his having thrown her out propelled her toward the stairs. She wondered if she could simply walk out of the building as she was. With no coat, no money, nothing to identify her. But she knew that wasn't possible. It was winter, and it was New York.

She walked up the stairs. She stood on the straw mat in front of her own door. She'd have to ring the bell; she hadn't brought her keys. Peter would wonder where she had gone. She didn't know what she'd tell him. There was nothing to say.

She didn't know what would happen now. She knew only that she must ring the bell and see her husband's face and then walk into the apartment. It was the place she lived and she had nowhere else to go. ● 105

Explorations of the Text

1. Gothic literature is characterized by several features: ruins or decay; secrets; a sense of mystery; and the presence or the possibility of death. The gothic tends to be a world of disorder, of chaos. In this cluster, how is the sense of mystery enhanced by any of the above elements? Does "City Life," written more recently than the other stories, employ gothic techniques differently?

2. Each of the stories in this cluster is a mystery, each mystery revolves around a family secret, and in each the characters' perception of reality helps to shape the secret and sense of mystery. What unusual or unique characteristics do the protagonists of these stories possess that make them perfect gothic heroes?

3. Compare the family secrets in these stories to those held by the characters in "Night Talkers."

The Reading/Writing Connection

1. List some of the themes represented in the stories of this cluster. What theme of family life is represented in two of these stories? How do the gothic elements reinforce these themes?

Ideas for Writing

1. **Write an Argument:** How do the secrets or obsessions of the characters have consequences for other people, either members of their communities or families? Argue that secrets are necessary or harmful to the characters in Hawthorne's, Faulkner's, or Gordon's stories.

2. Create a gothic mystery that involves secrets from your family. You may exaggerate real secrets or make them up. As you write, consider the setting, imagery, and tone that you want to create for your audience.

On the Web: *Visions of Hauntings*

Please visit http://www.academic.cengage.com/english/Schmidt/Legacies4e/ for links to the following online resources.

- Short Stories by Edgar Allan Poe
  "The Fall of the House of Usher"
  "The Tell-Tale Heart"
- Robert Harris, "Introduction to the Gothic"

POETRY

Amiri Baraka *(1934–)*

Preface to a Twenty Volume Suicide Note   *1961*

For Kellie Jones, born 16 May 1959

Lately, I've become accustomed to the way
The ground opens up and envelops me
Each time I go out to walk the dog.
Or the broad-edged silly music the wind
Makes when I run for a bus . . .   5

Things have come to that.

And now, each night I count the stars,
And each night I get the same number.
And when they will not come to be counted,
I count the holes they leave.   10

Nobody sings anymore.

And then last night, I tiptoed up
To my daughter's room and heard her
Talking to someone, and when I opened
The door, there was no one there . . .   15
Only she on her knees, peeking into

Her own clasped hands.

Explorations of the Text

1. What is the mood of the speaker in the opening lines? What images suggest his feelings?
2. What is the significance of the daughter's gesture of peeking into "her own clasped hands"?
3. What does the title mean? How does it explain the closing line?
4. Why does Baraka have three short lines, separated as stanzas? How do they convey the message of the poem?
5. Why does Baraka begin stanzas with "Lately," "And now," and "And then"? What do these transition words accomplish?
6. How does the speaker feel about his daughter? What does she represent to him?

The Reading/Writing Connection

1. "Think" Topic: Do you think that the experience of parenting differs for mothers and for fathers? Refer to two works that you have read.

Ideas for Writing

1. How does Baraka use figurative language in this poem? Is the figurative language effective?
2. What do children represent and give to their parents in two of the following poems: "Preface to a Twenty Volume Suicide Note," "Making the Jam Without You," "My Little Girl, My Stringbean, My Lovely Woman"?

Grace Paley *(1922–2007)*

Fathers *2003*

Fathers are
more fathering
these days they have
accomplished this by
being more mothering   5

what luck for them that
women's lib happened then
the dream of new fathering
began to shine in the eyes
for free women and was irresistible   10

on the New York subways
and the mass transits
of other cities one may
see fatherings of many colors
with their round babies on   15
their laps this may also
happen in the countryside

these scenes were brand-new
exciting for an old woman who
had watched the old fathers   20
gathering once again in
familiar Army camps and comfortable
war rooms to consider
the necessary eradication of
the new fathering fathers   25
(who are their sons) as well
as the women and children who
will surely be in the way.

Explorations of the Text

1. Consider Paley's use of the word "fathering," especially in the third stanza when she describes "fatherings of many colors." What might she mean by "fathering," and why might she use the plural "fatherings" rather than "fathers"? What is the effect of this word?

2. Why might Paley have shifted the poem's focus in the last stanza from that of fathering to war? How does this stanza change the vision of men from that offered in the first three stanzas?

3. In the first three lines of the poem Paley explains that "Fathers are/ more fathering/ these days . . ." Paley's poem was written in 2003. Contrast her image of fathering with that presented in Plath's 1962 poem, "Daddy." In what ways do the authors' visions of fathers differ?

The Reading/Writing Connection

1. "Think" topic: Research gender roles of the 1950s and 1960s; then consider Paley's poem in relation to the roles of men in the past.

2. Write a journal entry about your father. Compare your experience of fathering with that in Paley's poem. How is it similar? Different?

3. Write a prose poem or short story about future fathers. How might parenting differ in 2107 from now?

Ideas for Writing

1. **Write an Argument:** Fathers now are able to spend more time nurturing their children because the feminist movement has liberated them from restrictive roles. Argue pro or con.

2. In the last stanza, Paley refers to "old fathers" planning in "war rooms" for the "necessary eradication of/the new fathering fathers." Create an analysis essay, using this stanza as a lens through which to read the rest of the poem.

Sylvia Plath *(1932–1963)*

Daddy *1962*

You do not do, you do not do
Any more, black shoe
In which I have lived like a foot
For thirty years, poor and white,
Barely daring to breathe or Achoo.   5

Daddy, I have had to kill you.
You died before I had time—
Marble-heavy, a bag full of God,
Ghastly statue[1] with one grey toe
Big as a Frisco seal   10

---

[1]**Ghastly statue**: The Colossus at Rhodes, a gigantic statue of Apollo protecting the harbor at Rhodes; the Colossus was known as one of the seven wonders of the world.

And a head in the freakish Atlantic
Where it pours bean green over blue
In the waters off beautiful Nauset.[2]
I used to pray to recover you.
Ach, du.[3]   15

In the German tongue, in the Polish town
Scraped flat by the roller
Of wars, wars, wars.
But the name of the town is common.
My Polack friend   20

Says there are a dozen or two.
So I never could tell where you
Put your foot, your root,
I never could talk to you.
The tongue stuck in my jaw.   25

It stuck in a barb wire snare.
Ich, ich, ich, ich,[4]
I could hardly speak.
I thought every German was you.
And the language obscene   30

An engine, an engine
Chuffing me off like a Jew.
A Jew to Dachau, Auschwitz, Belsen.[5]
I began to talk like a Jew.
I think I may well be a Jew.   35

The snows of the Tyrol,[6] the clear beer of Vienna
Are not very pure or true.
With my gypsy ancestress and my weird luck
And my Taroc pack and my Taroc pack
I may be a bit of a Jew.   40

I have always been scared of *you,*
With your Luftwaffe,[7] your gobbledygoo.
And your neat moustache
And your Aryan[8] eye, bright blue.
Panzer-man,[9] panzer-man, O You—   45

---

[2]**Nauset**: place on the shore on Cape Cod in Massachusetts.   [3]**Ach, du**: "Oh, you" (translation from German).   [4]**Ich, ich, ich, ich**: "I, I, I, I" (translation from German).   [5]**Dachau, Auschwitz, Belsen**: Locations of concentration camps.   [6]**Tyrol**: Region of the Alps in West Austria and Northern Italy.   [7]**Luftwaffe**: The German air force.   [8]**Aryan**: Of or pertaining to a presumed ethnic type descended from early speakers of Indo-European languages; a term used by the Nazi party in World War II to denote racial purity.   [9]**Panzer-man**: A *panzer* is a "tank" (translation from German).

Not God but a swastika
So black no sky could squeak through.
Every woman adores a Fascist,
The boot in the face, the brute
Brute heart of a brute like you. 50

You stand at the blackboard, daddy,
In the picture I have of you,
A cleft in your chin instead of your foot
But no less a devil for that, no not
Any less the black man who 55

Bit my pretty red heart in two.
I was ten when they buried you.
At twenty I tried to die
And get back, back, back to you.
I thought even the bones would do. 60

But they pulled me out of the sack,
And they stuck me together with glue.
And then I knew what to do.
I made a model of you,
A man in black with a Meinkampf[10] look 65

And a love of the rack and the screw.[11]
And I said I do, I do.
So daddy, I'm finally through.
The black telephone's off at the root,
The voices just can't worm through. 70

If I've killed one man, I've killed two—
The vampire who said he was you
And drank my blood for a year,
Seven years, if you want to know.
Daddy, you can lie back now. 75

There's a stake in your fat black heart
And the villagers never liked you.
They are dancing and stamping on you.
They always *knew* it was you.
Daddy, daddy, you bastard, I'm through. 80

---

[10]**Meinkampf**: Book written by Hitler; *My Struggle* (translation from German). [11]**the rack and the screw**: Instruments of torture.

Explorations of the Text

1. What is the significance of the "black shoe"?
2. To what nursery rhyme does the poet allude? How does the allusion dictate the rhyme scheme? What is the emotional effect of the dominant sounds of the rhyme scheme?
3. How does the speaker first present her father? Why does she envision him as "Marble-heavy, a bag full of God"?
4. Why does she compare her father to a German? a Nazi? Why does she compare herself to a Jew?
5. Why does she compare her father to a "devil"?
6. Why does the speaker try to kill herself at twenty?
7. Why does the speaker state: "If I've killed one man, I've killed two"?
8. To what does the movie imagery in the last stanza refer? What is the effect of Plath's use of black humor?
9. Compare Plath's vision with the characterization of the father in "Rappaccini's Daughter."

The Reading/Writing Connection

1. "Think" Topic: Plath described the persona as a girl with an Electra complex. What is an Electra complex? Is this an adequate explanation for the behavior of the persona in the poem?

Ideas for Writing

1. How does Plath use sound and rhyme in "Daddy"? How do these techniques develop themes of the poem?
2. Why is the persona so angry at "Daddy"? Is the conflict resolved? Is she "through"?
3. Compare the point of view and tone of the speaker in this poem with that of one speaker in another poem in this chapter.

Simon Ortiz *(1941–)*

My Father's Song *1976*

Wanting to say things,
I miss my father tonight.
His voice, the slight catch,
the depth from his thin chest,
the tremble of emotion   5
in something he has just said
to his son, his song:

We planted corn one Spring at Acu—
we planted several times
but this one particular time   10
I remember the soft damp sand
in my hand.

My father had stopped at one point
to show me an overturned furrow;
the plowshare had unearthed   15
the burrow nest of a mouse
in the soft moist sand.

Very gently, he scooped tiny pink animals
into the palm of his hand
and told me to touch them.   20
We took them to the edge
of the field and put them in the shade
of a sand moist clod.

I remember the very softness
of cool and warm sand and tiny alive mice   25
and my father saying things.

Explorations of the Text

1. Who is the speaker in the first stanza
of the poem? Who is the speaker in the
last four stanzas?
2. What picture emerges of the father in
the first stanza? What images give you
clues?
3. What does "his song" suggest about the
speaker, his father, and his grandfather?

4. What is the significance of the central
images of "cool and warm sand" and
"tiny alive mice"? What do the furrows
and the ploughing suggest?
5. What inheritance does the grandfather
want to give to his son? What does the
father want to leave to the speaker?

The Reading/Writing Connection

1. Freewrite: Respond to the philosophy of
life presented in the poem.

2. Contrast the inability to communicate
in "Daddy" with the memory of voice
in "My Father's Song."

Ideas for Writing

1. Explicate and evaluate this poem. (See
Chapter 11.)

2. What is the relation of human beings to
the earth in "My Father's Song"?

Li-Young Lee   *(1957–   )*

Persimmons   *1986*

In sixth grade Mrs. Walker
slapped the back of my head
and made me stand in the corner
for not knowing the difference
between *persimmon* and *precision*.   5
How to choose

persimmons. This is precision.
Ripe ones are soft and brown-spotted.
Sniff the bottoms. The sweet one
will be fragrant. How to eat: 10
put the knife away, lay down newspaper.
Peel the skin tenderly, not to tear the meat.
Chew the skin, suck it,
and swallow. Now, eat
the meat of the fruit,   15
so sweet,
all of it, to the heart.

Donna undresses, her stomach is white.
In the yard, dewy and shivering
with crickets, we lie naked,   20
face-up, face-down.
I teach her Chinese.
Crickets: *chiu chiu.* Dew: I've forgotten.
Naked: I've forgotten.
Ni, wo: you and me.   25
I part her legs,
remember to tell her
she is beautiful as the moon.
Other words
that got me into trouble were   30
fight and *fright, wren* and *yarn.*
Fight was what I did when I was frightened,
fright was what I felt when I was fighting.
Wrens are small, plain birds,
yarn is what one knits with.   35
Wrens are soft as yarn.
My mother made birds out of yarn.
I loved to watch her tie the stuff;
a bird, a rabbit, a wee man.

Mrs. Walker brought a persimmon to class   40
and cut it up
so everyone could taste

a *Chinese apple.* Knowing
it wasn't ripe or sweet, I didn't eat
but watched the other faces.   45

My mother said every persimmon has a sun
inside, something golden, glowing,
warm as my face.

Once, in the cellar, I found two wrapped in newspaper,
forgotten and not yet ripe.   50
I took them and set both on my bedroom windowsill,
where each morning a cardinal
sang, *The sun, the sun.*

Finally understanding
he was going blind,   55
my father sat up all one night
waiting for a song, a ghost.
I gave him the persimmons,
swelled, heavy as sadness,
and sweet as love.   60

This year, in the muddy lighting
of my parent's cellar, I rummage, looking
for something I lost.
My father sits on the tired, wooden stairs,
black cane between his knees,   65
hand over hand, gripping the handle.

He's so happy that I've come home.
I ask how his eyes are, a stupid question.
All gone, he answers.

Under some blankets, I find a box.   70
Inside the box I find three scrolls.
I sit beside him and untie
three paintings by my father:
Hibiscus leaf and a white flower.
Two cats preening.   75
Two persimmons, so full they want to drop from the cloth.

He raises both hands to touch the cloth,
asks, *Which is this?*

This is persimmons, Father.

Oh, the feel of the wolftail on the silk,   80
the strength, the tense

precision in the wrist.
I painted them hundreds of times
eyes closed. These I painted blind.
Some things never leave a person: 85
scent of the hair of one you love,
the texture of persimmons,
in your palm, the ripe weight.

Explorations of the Text

1. Characterize the voice and the tone of the speaker.
2. What does the symbolism of persimmons suggest about the speaker's background? Attitude toward his heritage? Relationship with his father?
3. Why does the poet insert the love scene in stanza 2?
4. List the words that the speaker confuses and then discuss their significance.
5. Explore the meaning of the dialogue between father and son in the last six stanzas. What does the son learn about their relationship? Analyze the play on words of "sun" and "son."

The Reading/Writing Connection

1. Write a monologue in the voice of the father.
2. Journal entry: Imagine other incidents between father and son. Create a series of scenes and narrative moments.

Ideas for Writing

1. "Think" Topic: Are the fathers in "Persimmons" and in "Those Winter Sundays" good fathers? Do they nurture their sons? Are the speakers good sons? Do they relate to and know their fathers?
2. In a journal entry discuss how cultural expectations have shaped the father's and son's lives in "Persimmons."

Seamus Heaney *(1939–)*

Digging *1966*

Between my finger and my thumb
The squat pen rests; snug as a gun.

Under my window, a clean rasping sound
When the spade sinks into gravelly ground:
My father, digging. I look down 5

Till his straining rump among the flowerbeds
Bends low, comes up twenty years away

Stooping in rhythm through potato drills
Where he was digging.

The coarse boot nestled on the lug, the shaft   10
Against the inside knee was levered firmly.
He rooted out tall tops, buried the bright edge deep
To scatter new potatoes that we picked
Loving their cool hardness in our hands.

By God, the old man could handle a spade.   15
Just like his old man.

My grandfather cut more turf in a day
Than any other man on Toner's bog.
Once I carried him milk in a bottle
Corked sloppily with paper. He straightened up   20

To drink it, then fell to right away
Nicking and slicing neatly, heaving sods
Over his shoulder, going down and down
For the good turf. Digging.

The cold smell of potato mould, the squelch and slap   25
Of soggy peat, the curt cuts of an edge
Through living roots awaken in my head.
But I've no spade to follow men like them.

Between my finger and my thumb
The squat pen rests.   30
I'll dig with it.

Explorations of the Text

1. Contrast the speaker's sense of vocation with his representation of his father's and grandfather's work. Explicate the line: "The squat pen rests." Why does he use the word "squat"?

2. How does the poet describe the father's and grandfather's "digging"? What met-aphors are used to describe their labors? Explore the multiple meanings of the title, "Digging."

3. What does the speaker realize about his ancestry?

The Reading/Writing Connection

1. Journal entry: Contrast a physical act or gesture that you associate with a grand-parent or with a parent and one of your own. What do you learn about your connection with your past?

2. "Think" Topic: What views of labor and of artistry are expressed in this work?

Ideas for Writing

1. Create a dialogue among three fathers presented in three poems in this chapter.

2. Explicate this poem: Focus on point of view, tone, imagery, structure, and word choice.

Jamaica Kincaid *(1949–)*

Girl *1977*

Wash the white clothes on Monday and put them on the stone heap; wash the color clothes on Tuesday and put them on the clothesline to dry; don't walk barehead in the hot sun; cook pumpkin fritters in very hot sweet oil; soak your little cloths right after you take them off; when buying cotton to make yourself a nice blouse, be sure that it doesn't have gum on it, because that way it won't hold up well after a wash; soak   5
salt fish overnight before you cook it; is it true that you sing benna[1] in Sunday school?; always eat your food in such a way that it won't turn someone else's stomach; on Sundays try to walk like a lady and not like the slut you are so bent on becoming; don't sing benna in Sunday school; you mustn't speak to wharf-rat boys, not even to give directions; don't eat fruits on the street—flies will follow you; *but I don't sing benna on*   10
Sundays at all and never in Sunday school; this is how to sew on a button; this is how to make a button-hole for the button you have just sewed on; this is how to hem a dress when you see the hem coming down and so to prevent yourself from looking like the slut I know you are so bent on becoming; this is how you iron your father's khaki shirt so that it doesn't have a crease; this is how you iron your father's khaki pants so that   15
they don't have a crease, this is how you grow okra—far from the house, because okra tree harbors red ants: when you are growing dasheen,[2] make sure it gets plenty of water or else it makes your throat itch when you are eating it; this is how you sweep a corner; this is how you sweep a whole house; this is how you sweep a yard; this is how you smile to someone you don't like too much; this is how you smile to someone you don't like   20
at all; this is how you smile to someone you like completely; this is how you set a table for tea; this is how you set a table for dinner; this is how you set a table for dinner with an important guest; this is how you set a table for lunch; this is how you set a table for breakfast; this is how to behave in the presence of men who don't know you very well, and this way they won't recognize immediately the slut I have warned you against be-   25
coming; be sure to wash every day, even if it is with your own spit; don't squat down to play marbles—you are not a boy, you know; don't pick people's flowers—you might catch something; don't throw stones at blackbirds, because it might not be a blackbird at all; this is how to make a bread pudding; this is how to make doukona,[3] this is how to make pepper pot;[4] this is how to make a good medicine for a cold; this is how to   30
make a good medicine to throw away a child before it even becomes a child; this is how to catch a fish; this is how to throw back a fish you don't like, and that way something bad won't fall on you; this is how to bully a man; this is how a man bullies you; this is

---

[1]**benna**: Calypso music.   [2]**dasheen**: A kind of potato.   [3]**doukona**: A spicy pudding made of plantains.   [4]**pepper pot**: A kind of stew.

how to love a man, and if this doesn't work there are other ways, and if they don't work don't feel too bad about giving up; this is how to spit up in the air if you feel like it, and ₃₅ this is how to move quick so that it doesn't fall on you; this is how to make ends meet; always squeeze bread to make sure it's fresh; *but what if the baker won't let me feel the bread?;* you mean to say that after all you are really going to be the kind of woman who the baker won't let near the bread?

Explorations of the Text

1. Who speaks which lines in the poem?
2. The speech is a single sentence filled with commands. What do they suggest about the main speaker's intentions? Characterize the speaker.
3. What is the main speaker's tone? What is the significance of the variations of the phrase, "not like the slut you are so bent on becoming"?
4. What do the girl's lines reveal about her character? about her relationship with the speaker?

5. Why does the speaker say, "You mean to say that after all you are really going to be the kind of woman who the baker won't let near the bread?"
6. What vision of female roles emerges in this piece?
7. What is the impact of the repeated phrasing, of the parallel structure, and of its form as a single sentence?

The Reading/Writing Connection

1. Create an imitation of this speech as a mother/father giving advice to a child in North America. You may create the voice of your parent talking to you.

2. Become a representative figure and give advice (e.g., a teenager giving advice about how to be a "teen" in North America to a foreign student; a senior giving advice to a college freshman).

Ideas for Writing

1. What motivates the mother's speech? Is her approach effective? Why? Why not?

Pauline Powers Uchmanowicz   *(1957–)*

Knee Deep in Mud My Mother | *2004*

Would you be so terrifying
uncoffined, dried earth caked on your calves,
disintegrating in a field among weeds
like an animal whose death
makes a place large and strange?   5

Or, they could wait, they could
place us in one box,
carry us someplace pleasant
we have never visited and then
waking beside you in a strange city   10
I would be home.

Billy Collins   *(1941–   )*

The Lanyard   *2005*

The other day as I was ricocheting slowly
off the pale blue walls of this room,
bouncing from typewriter to piano,
from bookshelf to an envelope lying on the floor,
I found myself in the L section of the dictionary   5
where my eyes fell upon the word lanyard.

No cookie nibbled by a French novelist
could send one more suddenly into the past—
a past where I sat at a workbench at a camp
by a deep Adirondack lake   10
learning how to braid thin plastic strips
into a lanyard, a gift for my mother.

I had never seen anyone use a lanyard
or wear one, if that's what you did with them,
but that did not keep me from crossing   15
strand over strand again and again
until I had made a boxy
red and white lanyard for my mother.

She gave me life and milk from her breasts,
and I gave her a lanyard.   20
She nursed me in many a sickroom,
lifted teaspoons of medicine to my lips,
set cold face-cloths on my forehead,
and then led me out into the airy light

and taught me to walk and swim,   25
and I, in turn, presented her with a lanyard.
Here are thousands of meals, she said,
and here is clothing and a good education.
And here is your lanyard, I replied,
which I made with a little help from a counselor.   30

Here is a breathing body and a beating heart,
strong legs, bones and teeth,
and two clear eyes to read the world, she whispered,
and here, I said, is the lanyard I made at camp.
And here, I wish to say to her now,   35
is a smaller gift—not the archaic truth

that you can never repay your mother,
but the rueful admission that when she took
the two-tone lanyard from my hands,
I was as sure as a boy could be   40
that this useless, worthless thing I wove
out of boredom would be enough to make us even.

Explorations of the Text

1. Both Collins and Uchmanowicz use images of body and earth to describe their connections to their mothers. List the words, phrases, and lines that denote these ideas and discuss their significance within the poems.
2. Collins uses humor and irony to convey a deeper message of love and gratitude. Does it work? Explain why or why not.
3. Several of the works in this chapter address the power of "home," including "Coming Home Again" and "Common Scents." Choose one of these works and compare that author's image of home with Uchmanowicz's. What does she mean in the last line, "I would be home"?
4. Is the point of view of the narrator in Collins' poem that of a child or a man? In Uchmanowicz's poem, is the point of view from a child or a woman? Explain.

The Reading/Writing Connection

1. Uchmanowicz shows the close connection between a mother and a child through the images of earth and death. Create a list of images, symbols, or metaphors to illustrate the relationship between you and one of your parents, then write a poem or prose poem (like "Girl") using one or more items from your list.

Ideas for Writing

1. **Write an Argument:** Are parents "terrifying" to children, as Uchmanowicz states in the first line of her poem? Argue pro or con.

2. **Write an Argument:** It is not possible to return to your parents all that they have done for you. Argue pro or con.

Etheridge Knight *(1931–1991)*

The Idea of Ancestry *1968*

1

Taped to the wall of my cell are 47 pictures: 47 black
faces: my father, mother, grandmothers (1 dead), grandfathers (both dead), brothers, sisters, uncles, aunts,
cousins (1st & 2nd), nieces, and nephews. They stare
across the space at me sprawling on my bunk. I know   5
their dark eyes, they know mine. I know their style,
they know mine. I am all of them, they are all of me;
they are farmers, I am a thief, I am me, they are thee.

I have at one time or other been in love with my mother,
1 grandmother, 2 sisters, 2 aunts (1 went to the asylum),   10
and 5 cousins. I am now in love with a 7 yr old niece
(she sends me letters written in large block print, and
her picture is the only one that smiles at me).

I have the same name as 1 grandfather, 3 cousins, 3 nephews,
and 1 uncle. The uncle disappeared when he was 15, just took   15
off and caught a freight (they say). He's discussed each year
when the family has a reunion, he causes uneasiness in
the clan, he is an empty space. My father's mother, who is 93
and who keeps the Family Bible with everybody's birth dates
(and death dates) in it, always mentions him. There is no   20
place in her Bible for "whereabouts unknown."

Each fall the graves of my grandfathers call me, the brown
hills and red gullies of mississippi send out their electric
messages, galvanizing my genes. Last yr / like a salmon quitting
the cold ocean-leaping and bucking up his birthstream / I   25
hitchhiked my way from L.A. with 16 caps¹ in my pocket and a
monkey on my back.² And I almost kicked it with the kinfolks.
I walked barefooted in my grandmother's backyard / I smelled the old
land and the woods / I sipped cornwhiskey from fruit jars with the men /
I flirted with the women / I had a ball till the caps ran out   30
and my habit came down. That night I looked at my grandmother
and split / my guts were screaming for junk³ / but I was almost
contented / I had almost caught up with me.
(The next day in Memphis I cracked a croaker's crib for a fix.)

This yr there is a gray stone wall damming my stream, and when   35
the falling leaves stir my genes, I pace my cell or flop on my bunk

---

¹**caps**: Capsules or vials of drugs.   ²**monkey on my back**: Being high; having a drug
habit.   ³**junk**: Heroin.

and stare at 47 black faces across the space. I am all of them,
they are all of me, I am me, they are thee, and I have no children
to float in the space between.

Agha Shahid Ali   *(1949–   )*

Snowmen   *1987*

My ancestor, a man
of Himalayan snow,
came to Kashmir from Samarkand,
carrying a bag
of whale bones: 5
heirlooms from sea funerals.
His skeleton
carved from glaciers, his breath
arctic,
he froze women in his embrace.   10
His wife thawed into stony water,
her old age a clear
evaporation.

This heirloom,
his skeleton under my skin, passed   15
from son to grandson,
generations of snowmen on my back.
They tap every year on my window,
their voices hushed to ice.

No, they won't let me out of winter,   20
and I've promised myself,
even if I'm the last snowman,
that I'll ride into spring
on their melting shoulders.

Explorations of the Text

1. What is the importance of the setting in the two poems?
2. In "The Idea of Ancestry," what does the refrain "I am all of them, they are all of me" suggest?
3. Discuss the concept of the extended family in each poem. What is the progression, stanza by stanza?
4. What is the meaning of the line, "I cracked a croaker's crib for a fix" in Knight's poem?
5. How do the speakers' ancestors help them to survive? Do the closing lines of the poems offer clues?
6. How do the levels of style (e.g., slang, Biblical language) add to the effect of the poems?
7. Find lines that state a thesis of the poems.

The Reading/Writing Connection

1. "Think" Topic: What is one "Idea of Ancestry" in these poems?
2. Assume that you are confined in a room or in a space for a prolonged period.

How would you choose to decorate the walls? Or select one character from this chapter and create a room for him or her. Respond in a journal entry.

Ideas for Writing

1. What consequences of incarceration are expressed in Knight's poem?
2. Write about the African American concept of extended family and of

community. Use this poem and other works in this chapter to support your analysis.

Marilyn Chin *(1957–)*

Turtle Soup *1994*

for Ben Huang

You go home one evening tired from work,
and your mother boils you turtle soup.
Twelve hours hunched over the hearth
(who knows what else is in that cauldron).

You say, "Ma, you've poached the symbol of long life;   5
that turtle lived four thousand years, swam
the Wei, up the Yellow, over the Yangtze.[1]
Witnessed the Bronze Age, the High Tang,
grazed on splendid sericulture."
(So, she boils the life out of him.)   10

"All our ancestors have been fools.
Remember Uncle Wu who rode ten thousand miles
to kill a famous Manchu and ended up
with his head on a pole? Eat, child,
its liver will make you strong."   15

"Sometimes you're the life, sometimes the sacrifice."
Her sobbing is inconsolable.
So, you spread that gentle napkin
over your lap in decorous Pasadena.

---

[1]**Wei . . . Yellow . . . Yangtze**: Rivers in China.

Baby, some high priestess has got it wrong.   20
The golden decal on the green underbelly
says "Made in Hong Kong."

Is there nothing left but the shell
and humanity's strange inscriptions,
the songs, the rites, the oracles?   25

Explorations of the Text

1. Notice the author's choice of the word "cauldron" in line 4. What images or connections does this word evoke? Why might the author have chosen "cauldron" rather than "pot"?

2. Chin refers to "the Wei," "the Yellow," and "the Yangtze." Why does she reference these rivers in China? Why not include the Nile, the Amazon, or the Mississippi?

3. What is the tone of this poem?

4. "Turtle Soup" describes a meal made by a mother for her child. List similar themes of food and family in "Persimmons," "Coca-cola and Coco Frío," "Coming Home Again," and "You Are What You Eat." Why is food so often connected to family? How do the mother/child/food connections in this poem differ or seem similar to those in one of the other works?

The Reading/Writing Connection

1. "Think" topic: In the second stanza, the narrator reproaches the mother for having "poached the symbol of long life." Why is the mother's action significant, especially in relation to the final stanza?

2. Explain the lines from the fifth stanza, "The golden decal on the [turtle's] green underbelly/says 'Made in Hong Kong.'" You can write your explanation as a journal entry, as a letter to the turtle or to the narrator, or as a poem.

Ideas for Writing

1. "'Sometimes you're the life, sometimes the sacrifice.'" Write about this quote within the context of an immigrant family. What might a family gain or lose by moving to a new land?

2. **Write an Argument:** Is it necessary for immigrants to have "nothing left but the shell"? Argue pro or con. (You may want to refer to Marjorie Agosin's poem, "The Foreigner," in Chapter 9).

Loss and Family/Poetry

Frances Ellen Watkins Harper *(1825–1911)*

The Slave Mother *1854*

Heard you that shriek? It rose
    So wildly on the air.
It seemed as if a burden'd heart
    Was breaking in despair.

Saw you those hands so sadly clasped—   5
    The bowed the feeble head—
The shuddering of that fragile form—
    That look of grief and dread?

Saw you the sad, imploring eye?
    Its every glance was pain,   10
As if a storm of agony
    Were sweeping through the brain.

She is a mother, pale with fear,
    Her boy clings to her side,
And in her kirtle[1] vainly tries   15
    His trembling form to hide.

He is not hers, although she bore
    For him a mother's pains;
He is not hers, although her blood
    Is coursing through his veins!   20

He is not hers, for cruel hands
    May rudely tear apart
The only wreath of household love
    That binds her breaking heart.

His love has been a joyous light   25
    That o'er her pathway smiled,
A fountain gushing ever new,
    Amid life's desert wild.

His lightest word has been a tone
    Of music round her heart,   30

---

[1]**kirtle**: Loose-fitting gown.

Their lives a streamlet blent in one—
    Oh, Father! must they part?

They tear him from her circling arms,
    Her last and fond embrace.
Oh! never more may her sad eyes   35
    Gaze on his mournful face.

No marvel, then, these bitter shrieks
    Disturb the listening air:
She is a mother, and her heart
    Is breaking in despair.   40

D. H. Lawrence   *(1885–1930)*

Piano   *1918*

Softly, in the dusk, a woman is singing to me;
Taking me back down the vista of years, till I see
A child sitting under the piano, in the boom of the tingling strings
And pressing the small, poised feet of a mother who smiles as she sings.

In spite of myself, the insidious mastery of song   5
Betrays me back, till the heart of me weeps to belong
To the old Sunday evenings at home, with winter outside
And hymns in the cozy parlour, the tinkling piano our guide.

So now it is vain for the singer to burst into clamour
With the great black piano appassionato. The glamour   10
Of childish days is upon me, my manhood is cast
Down in the flood of remembrance, I weep like a child for the past.

Harold A. Zlotnik   *(1914–)*

Odyssey   *1948*

(For My Daughter)

Take this, my child, O World, and
    give her strength
As durable as grass that hugs the
    earth
In its vicissitudes; insure the length   5
Of summer days, uncradling from
    birth
A sky of living with that pine ter-
    rain

Of solitude; and let forgiveness,
    grow   10
Pervasive as the democratic rain
In hostile moments. Just as others
    know
Compassion past their grief, let her   15
    receive
That night-wind as the balm for
    desert heat
Her cool, diurnal hope, and soon
    perceive   20
The beacon stars in crisis or retreat,
And mix her blood divinely with the
    sun
For faith to burn in glory and be
    won.   25

Martín Espada *(1957–)*

Coca-Cola and Coco Frío *1993*

On his first visit to Puerto Rico,
island of family folklore,
the fat boy wandered
from table to table
with his mouth open.   5
At every table, some great-aunt
would steer him with cool spotted hands
to a glass of Coca-Cola.
One even sang to him, in all the English
she could remember, a Coca-Cola jingle   10
from the forties. He drank obediently, though
he was bored with this potion, familiar
from soda fountains in Brooklyn.

Then, at a roadside stand off the beach, the fat boy
opened his mouth to coco frío, a coconut   15
chilled, then scalped by a machete
so that a straw could inhale the clear milk.
The boy tilted the green shell overhead
and drooled coconut milk down his chin;
suddenly, Puerto Rico was not Coca-Cola   20
or Brooklyn, and neither was he.

For years afterward, the boy marveled at an island
where the people drank Coca-Cola
and sang jingles from World War II
in a language they did not speak,   25

while so many coconuts in the trees
sagged heavy with milk, swollen
and unsuckled.

Dwight Okita   *(1958–)*

The Nice Thing about Counting Stars   *1992*

for my parents Fred and Patsy Okita

In 1942, over 100,000 Americans of Japanese descent were evacuated from their homes by the American government and forced to relocate in internment camps. They wound up staying for three years. My mother, Patsy Takeyo Okita, was one of them. This poem includes excerpts from her memoirs.

"In the hot summers of the 30's, we would
sit on the steps and sing for hours. We
even counted the stars in the sky and it
was always beautiful."
So my mother begins   5
writing her life down, Jackie Onassis
thinking in the car behind dark glasses.
She recalls the luxury
of growing up—she and her sisters
buying jelly bismarcks on Sundays   10
and eating them in the back seat
of their father's Packard
parked on the drive.
Pretending they were going
somewhere, and they were.   15
Not knowing years later they would
be headed for just such an exotic place.
Somewhere far from Fresno, their white stone house
on F Street, the blackboard in the kitchen
where they learned math,   20
          long division, remainders,
    what is left
    after you divide something.

"When Executive Order 9066 came telling
all Japanese-Americans to leave their   25
houses, we cleared out of Fresno real
fast. They gave us three days. I remember
carrying a washboard to the camp. I don't
know how it got in my hands. Someone must
have told me—Here, take this."   30

They were given three days to move
what had taken them years to acquire—
sewing machines, refrigerators, pianos, expensive fishing

rods from Italy. A war was on—Japs
had bombed Pearl Harbor.   35
Burma Shave billboards littered the highways:

SLAP
                    THE JAP

"Take only what you can carry."
My mother's family left the Packard   40
and with it left Sundays in the back seat.
Others walked away from acres of land,
drugstores, photo albums.

I think of turtles.
How they carry their whole lives   45
on their backs. My neighbor Jimmy
told me one night how they
make turtle soup down south.
A huge sea turtle—take a sledge hammer
to the massive shell, wedge it open   50
with one simple, solid blow
till the turtle can feel
no home above him, till everything
is taken away
and there is nothing   55
he will carry away from this moment.

My parents had three days
to relocate.
"Take only what you can carry."
One simple, solid blow—   60
They felt no home above them.

    Dear Sirs:
    Of course I'll come. I've packed my galoshes
    and three packets of tomato seeds. Janet calls them
    "love apples." My father says where we're going   65
    they won't grow.

    I am a fourteen-year-old girl with bad spelling
    and a messy room. If it helps any, I will tell you
    I have always felt funny using chopsticks
    and my favorite food is hot dogs.   70
    My best friend is a white girl named Denise—
    we look at boys together. She sat in front of me
    all through grade school because of our names:
    O'Connor, Ozawa. I know the back of Denise's head very well.
    I tell her she's going bald. She tells me I copy on tests. 75
    We are best friends.

I saw Denise today in Geography class,
She was sitting on the other side of the room.
"You're trying to start a war," she said, "giving secrets away
to the Enemy, Why can't you keep your big mouth shut?"   80
I didn't know what to say.
I gave her a packet of tomato seeds
and asked her to plant them for me, told her
when the first tomato ripens
to miss me.   85

    "We were sent to Jerome, Arkansas.
    Arriving there, I wondered how long
    we would be fenced in."

The nice thing about counting stars is
you can do it just about anywhere.   90
Even in a relocation camp
miles from home, even in Jerome, Arkansas
where a barbed wire fence crisscrosses itself
making stars of its own—but nothing
worth counting, nothing worth singing to.   95

My father remembers only two things:

    washing dishes in the mess hall each morning
    beside George Kaminishi and

    listening to Bing Crosby sing "White Christmas"
    on the radio in the barracks late at night.   100

One morning, George looked up from a greasy skillet
at my dad and said Yosh, you're a happy-go-lucky guy.
What do you want to do with your life?
It was the first time he realized he had a life
to do things with. He was fifteen. He didn't know.   105
It was only later that Dad found out George
had colon cancer and had no life to do things with.
And when Bing sang late at night that song
Dad could only think, He's not singing to me he's
singing to white people.   110

    "I'm dreaming of a white Christmas,
    just like the ones I used to know."

My mother meanwhile was in a different camp
and hadn't met my father. At night, she'd lie
in bed and think about the old family car   115
back in the driveway—were the windows smashed
and broken into, the thing driven away by thieves?

Or was the grass a foot tall now, erasing the
Goodyear tires that were so shiny and new?
There was a hole in the week where Sunday   120
used to be, and she *wanted* jelly bismarcks
more than ever.

    "Somehow we adjusted. There were weekly
    dances for the young. Dad sent away
    for a huge rice paper umbrella of vivid colors,   125
    and Peg and I hugged it during the stormy
    days."

Tonight, almost half a century later,
my father celebrates his 60th birthday.
He sits marking papers in the orange chair   130
in the living room, my mother enters grades
in the gradebook. In one corner
a brass gooseneck umbrella stand has been turned
into a planter—an ivy climbing its way
out. The oscillating fan shakes its head.   135

He remembers high school, Mrs. Barnett in Latin class,
himself at the head of it. A few days
before relocation, she took him aside.
So you'll be leaving us? she asked.
My father nodded.   140
She looked out the window at a maple tree
giving its leaves back to the earth,
at the chalky swirls of dust
on the blackboard for some good word
at the end of it all: 145

    Look on it as an adventure, she said.

Julia Alvarez   *(1950–   )*

Homecoming   *1984*

When my cousin Carmen married, the guards
at her father's *finca*[1] took the guests' bracelets
and wedding rings and put them in an armored truck
for safekeeping while wealthy, dark-skinned men,
their plump, white women and spoiled children   5
bathed in a river whose bottom had been cleaned
for the occasion. She was Uncle's only daughter,

---

[1] *finca*: Plantation; farm.

and he wanted to show her husband's family,
a bewildered group of sunburnt Minnesotans,
that she was valued. He sat me at their table   10
to show off my English, and when he danced with me,
fondling my shoulder blades beneath my bridesmaid's gown
as if they were breasts, he found me skinny
but pretty at seventeen, and clever.
Come back from that cold place, Vermont, he said,   15
all this is yours! Over his shoulder
a dozen workmen hauled in blocks of ice
to keep the champagne lukewarm and stole
glances at the wedding cake, a dollhouse duplicate
of the family *rancho,* the shutters marzipan,   20
the cobbles almonds. A maiden aunt housekept,
touching up whipped cream roses with a syringe
of eggwhites, rescuing the groom when the heat
melted his chocolate shoes into the frosting.
On too much rum Uncle led me across the dance floor,   25
dusted with talcum for easy gliding, a smell
of babies underfoot. He twirled me often,
excited by my pleas of dizziness, teasing me,
saying that my merengue had lost its Caribbean.
Above us, Chinese lanterns strung between posts   30
came on and one snapped off and rose
into a purple postcard sky.
A grandmother cried: *The children all grow up too fast.*
The Minnesotans finally broke loose and danced a Charleston
and were pronounced good gringos with latino hearts.   35
The little sister, freckled with a week of beach,
her hair as blonde as movie stars, was asked
by maids if they could touch her hair or skin,
and she backed off, until it was explained to her,
they meant no harm. *This is all yours,*   40
Uncle whispered, pressing himself into my dress.
The workmen costumed in their workclothes danced
a workman's jig. The maids went by with trays
of wedding bells and matchbooks monogrammed
with Dick's and Carmen's names. It would be years   45
before I took the courses that would change my mind
in schools paid for by sugar from the fields around us,
years before I could begin to comprehend
how one does not see the maids when they pass by. . . .
—It was too late, or early, to be wise—   50
The sun was coming up beyond the amber waves
of cane, the roosters crowed, the band struck up
Las Mañanitas, a morning serenade. I had a vision
that I blamed on the champagne:
the fields around us were burning. At last   55

a yawning bride and groom got up and cut
the wedding cake, but everyone was full
of drink and eggs, roast pig, and rice and beans.
Except the maids and workmen,
sitting on stoops behind the sugar house,   60
ate with their fingers from their open palms
windows, shutters, walls, pillars, doors,
made from the cane they had cut in the fields.

Sharon Olds   *(1942–)*

I Go Back to May 1937   *1997*

I see them standing at the formal gates of their colleges,
I see my father strolling out
under the ochre sandstone arch, the
red tiles glinting like bent
plates of blood behind his head, I   5
see my mother with a few light books at her hip
standing at the pillar made of tiny bricks with the
wrought-iron gate still open behind her, its
sword-tips black in the May air,
they are about to graduate, they are about to get married,   10
they are kids, they are dumb, all they know is they are
innocent, they would never hurt anybody.
I want to go up to them and say Stop,
don't do it—she's the wrong woman,
he's the wrong man, you are going to do things   15
you cannot imagine you would ever do,
you are going to do bad things to children,
you are going to suffer in ways you never heard of,
you are going to want to die. I want to go
up to them there in the late May sunlight and say it,   20
her hungry pretty blank face turning to me,
her pitiful beautiful untouched body,
his arrogant handsome blind face turning to me,
his pitiful beautiful untouched body,
but I don't do it. I want to live. I   25
take them up like the male and female
paper dolls and bang them together
at the hips like chips of flint as if to
strike sparks from them, I say
Do what you are going to do, and I will tell about it.   30

Explorations of the Text

1. The poems in this cluster describe different types of losses. List the losses experienced in three of the poems and categorize them. In what ways are they similar? Different?
2. The poem "Odyssey" was written by a father for his daughter. Why might it be included in a cluster entitled Loss and Family? What gifts does the father offer to his daughter?
3. "Coca-Cola and Coco Frío," "The Nice Thing About Counting Stars," and "Homecoming" all depict a loss of culture. Explain the relationship between culture and family. Why might a loss of heritage be as painful or destructive as a more physical loss?
4. In several of the poems—"Coca-Cola and Coco Frío," "I Go Back to May 1937," "The Nice Thing about Counting Stars," "Homecoming," "Piano," and "Odyssey"—loss is closely connected with time and memory. Since memory is a recollection of the past, is it possible to remember something without a sense of loss? Consider this question in relation to other works in this chapter (Danticat, Bakopoulos, Gordon, and Derricotte, for example) that rely on memory to convey ideas.

The Reading/Writing Connection

1. Journal entry: Write about a loss that you or your family experienced. You can write this as a poem or as a prose entry. Try to capture the emotion of the loss through the use of imagery, symbolism, or metaphor.
2. In "Piano," the piano itself, played by a woman, reminds the narrator of his mother. Freewrite about something that reminds you of one of your parents.

Ideas for Writing

1. **Write an Argument:** Losses in families, including the loss of family members to death, desertion, or divorce; the loss of culture or heritage; or loss due to change in attitude toward one's family or culture, have long lasting consequences that can affect future generations. Argue pro or con.

DRAMA

August Wilson *(1945–2005)*

The Piano Lesson *1990*

> Gin my cotton
> Sell my seed
> Buy my baby
> Everything she need
>
> —Skip James

DOAKER

BOY WILLIE

LYMON

BERNIECE

MARETHA

AVERY

WINING BOY

GRACE

The Setting

The action of the play takes place in the kitchen and parlor of the house where Doaker Charles lives with his niece, Berniece, and her eleven-year-old daughter, Maretha. The house is sparsely furnished, and although there is evidence of a woman's touch, there is a lack of warmth and vigor. Berniece and Maretha occupy the upstairs rooms. Doaker's room is prominent and opens onto the kitchen. Dominating the parlor is an old upright piano. On the legs of the piano, carved in the manner of African sculpture, are mask-like figures resembling totems. The carvings are rendered with a grace and power of invention that lifts them out of the realm of craftsmanship and into the realm of art. At left is a staircase leading to the upstairs.

Act 1
Scene 1
(The lights come up on the Charles household. It is five o'clock in the morning. The dawn is beginning to announce itself, but there is something in the air that belongs to the night. A stillness that is a portent, a gathering, a coming together of something akin to a storm. There is a loud knock at the door.)

BOY WILLIE: *(Offstage, calling.)* Hey, Doaker . . . Doaker!

(He knocks again and calls.)

Hey, Doaker! Hey, Berniece! Berniece!

(DOAKER *enters from his room. He is a tall, thin man of forty-seven, with severe features, who has for all intents and purposes retired from the world though he works full-time as a railroad cook.*)

DOAKER: Who is it?

BOY WILLIE: Open the door, nigger! It's me . . . Boy Willie!

DOAKER: Who?

BOY WILLIE: Boy Willie! Open the door!   5

(DOAKER *opens the door and* BOY WILLIE *and* LYMON *enter.* BOY WILLIE *is thirty years old. He has an infectious grin and a boyishness that is apt for his name. He is brash and impulsive, talkative and somewhat crude in speech and manner.* LYMON *is twenty-nine.* BOY WILLIE'*s partner, he talks little, and then with a straightforwardness that is often disarming.*)

DOAKER: What you doing up here?

BOY WILLIE: I told you, Lymon. Lymon talking about you might be sleep. This is Lymon. You remember Lymon Jackson from down home? This my Uncle Doaker.

DOAKER: What you doing up here? I couldn't figure out who that was. I thought you was still down in Mississippi.

BOY WILLIE: Me and Lymon selling watermelons. We got a truck out there. Got a whole truckload of watermelons. We brought them up here to sell. Where's Berniece?

(Calls.)

Hey, Berniece!

DOAKER: Berniece up there sleep.   10

BOY WILLIE: Well, let her get up.

(Calls.)

Hey, Berniece!

DOAKER: She got to go to work in the morning.

BOY WILLIE: Well she can get up and say hi. It's been three years since I seen her.

(Calls.)

Hey, Berniece! It's me . . . Boy Willie.

DOAKER: Berniece don't like all that hollering now. She got to work in the morning.

BOY WILLIE: She can go on back to bed. Me and Lymon been riding two days in   15
that truck . . . the least she can do is get up and say hi.

DOAKER: *(Looking out the window.)* Where you all get that truck from?

BOY WILLIE: It's Lymon's. I told him let's get a load of watermelons and bring them up here.

LYMON: Boy Willie say he going back, but I'm gonna stay. See what it's like up here.

BOY WILLIE: You gonna carry me down there first.

LYMON: I told you I ain't going back down there and take a chance on that truck   20
breaking down again. You can take the train. Hey, tell him Doaker, he can take the train back. After we sell them watermelons he have enough money he can buy him a whole railroad car.

DOAKER: You got all them watermelons stacked up there no wonder the truck broke down. I'm surprised you made it this far with a load like that. Where you break down at?

BOY WILLIE: We broke down three times! It took us two and a half days to get here. It's a good thing we picked them watermelons fresh.

LYMON: We broke down twice in West Virginia. The first time was just as soon as we got out of Sunflower. About forty miles out she broke down. We got it going and got all the way to West Virginia before she broke down again.

BOY WILLIE: We had to walk about five miles for some water.

LYMON: It got a hole in the radiator but it runs pretty good. You have to pump the   25
brakes sometime before they catch. Boy Willie have his door open and be ready to jump when that happens.

BOY WILLIE: Lymon think that's funny. I told the nigger I give him ten dollars to get the brakes fixed. But he thinks that funny.

LYMON: They don't need fixing. All you got to do is pump them till they catch.

(BERNIECE *enters on the stairs. Thirty-five years old, with an eleven-year-old daughter, she is still in mourning for her husband after three years.*)

BERNIECE: What you doing all that hollering for?

BOY WILLIE: Hey, Berniece. Doaker said you was sleep. I said at least you could get up and say hi.

BERNIECE: It's five o'clock in the morning and you come in here with all this noise.   30
You can't come like normal folks. You got to bring all that noise with you.

BOY WILLIE: Hell, I ain't done nothing but come in and say hi. I ain't got in the house good.

BERNIECE: That's what I'm talking about. You start all that hollering and carry on as soon as you hit the door.

BOY WILLIE: Aw hell, woman, I was glad to see Doaker. You ain't had to come down if you didn't want to. I come eighteen hundred miles to see my sister I figure she might want to get up and say hi. Other than that you can go back upstairs. What you got, Doaker? Where your bottle? Me and Lymon want a drink.

(*To* BERNIECE.)

This is Lymon. You remember Lymon Jackson from down home.

LYMON: How you doing, Berniece. You look just like I thought you looked.

BERNIECE: Why you all got to come in hollering and carrying on? Waking the   35
neighbors with all that noise.

BOY WILLIE: They can come over and join the party. We fixing to have a party. Doaker, where your bottle? Me and Lymon celebrating. The Ghosts of the Yellow Dog got Sutter.

BERNIECE: Say what?

BOY WILLIE: Ask Lymon, they found him the next morning. Say he drowned in his well.

DOAKER: When this happen, Boy Willie?

BOY WILLIE: About three weeks ago. Me and Lymon was over in Stoner County   40
when we heard about it. We laughed. We thought it was funny. A great big old three-hundred-and-forty-pound man gonna fall down his well.

LYMON: It remind me of Humpty Dumpty.

BOY WILLIE: Everybody say the Ghosts of the Yellow Dog pushed him.

BERNIECE: I don't want to hear that nonsense. Somebody down there pushing them people in their wells.

DOAKER: What was you and Lymon doing over in Stoner County?

BOY WILLIE: We was down there working. Lymon got some people down there.   45

LYMON: My cousin got some land down there. We was helping him.

BOY WILLIE: Got near about a hundred acres. He got it set up real nice. Me and Lymon was down there chopping down trees. We was using Lymon's truck to haul the wood. Me and Lymon used to haul wood all around them parts.

(*To* BERNIECE.)

Me and Lymon got a truckload of watermelons out there.

(BERNIECE *crosses to the window to the parlor.*)

Doaker, where your bottle? I know you got a bottle stuck up in your room. Come on, me and Lymon want a drink.

(DOAKER *exits into his room.*)

BERNIECE: Where you all get that truck from?

BOY WILLIE: I told you it's Lymon's.

BERNIECE: Where you get the truck from, Lymon?   50

LYMON: I bought it.

BERNIECE: Where he get that truck from, Boy Willie?

BOY WILLIE: He told you he bought it. Bought it for a hundred and twenty dollars. I can't say where he got that hundred and twenty dollars from . . . but he bought that old piece of truck from Henry Porter. (*To* LYMON.) Where you get that hundred and twenty dollars from, nigger?

LYMON: I got it like you get yours. I know how to take care of money.

(DOAKER *brings a bottle and sets it on the table.*)

BOY WILLIE: Aw hell, Doaker got some of that good whiskey. Don't give Lymon   55
none of that. He ain't used to good whiskey. He liable to get sick.

LYMON: I done had good whiskey before.

BOY WILLIE: Lymon bought that truck so he have him a place to sleep. He down there wasn't doing no work or nothing. Sheriff looking for him. He bought that truck to keep away from the sheriff. Got Stovall looking for him too. He down there sleeping in that truck ducking and dodging both of them. I told him come on let's go up and see my sister.

BERNIECE: What the sheriff looking for you for, Lymon?

BOY WILLIE: The man don't want you to know all his business. He's my company. He ain't asking you no questions.

LYMON: It wasn't nothing. It was just a misunderstanding.   60

BERNIECE: He in my house. You say the sheriff looking for him, I wanna know what he looking for him for. Otherwise you all can go back out there and be where nobody don't have to ask you nothing.

LYMON: It was just a misunderstanding. Sometimes me and the sheriff we don't think alike. So we just got crossed on each other.

BERNIECE: Might be looking for him about that truck. He might have stole that truck.

BOY WILLIE: We ain't stole no truck, woman. I told you Lymon bought it.

DOAKER: Boy Willie and Lymon got more sense than to ride all the way up here   65
in a stolen truck with a load of watermelons. Now they might have stole them
watermelons, but I don't believe they stole that truck.

BOY WILLIE: You don't even know the man good and you calling him a thief. And
we ain't stole them watermelons either. Them old man Pitterford's watermelons.
He give me and Lymon all we could load for ten dollars.

DOAKER: No wonder you got them stacked up out there. You must have five
hundred watermelons stacked up out there.

BERNIECE: Boy Willie, when you and Lymon planning on going back?

BOY WILLIE: Lymon say he staying. As soon as we sell them watermelons I'm going
on back.

BERNIECE: *(Starts to exit up the stairs.)* That's what you need to do. And you need   70
to do it quick. Come in here disrupting the house. I don't want all that loud
carrying on around here. I'm surprised you ain't woke Maretha up.

BOY WILLIE: I was fixing to get her now.

(Calls.)

Hey, Maretha!

DOAKER: Berniece don't like all that hollering now.

BERNIECE: Don't you wake that child up!

BOY WILLIE: You going up there . . . wake her up and tell her her uncle's here. I
ain't seen her in three years. Wake her up and send her down here. She can go
back to bed.

BERNIECE: I ain't waking that child up . . . and don't you be making all that noise.   75
You and Lymon need to sell them watermelons and go on back.

(BERNIECE exits up the stairs.)

BOY WILLIE: I see Berniece still try to be stuck up.

DOAKER: Berniece alright. She don't want you making all that noise. Maretha up
there sleep. Let her sleep until she get up. She can see you then.

BOY WILLIE: I ain't thinking about Berniece. You hear from Wining Boy? You
know Cleotha died?

DOAKER: Yeah, I heard that. He come by here about a year ago. Had a whole sack
of money. He stayed here about two weeks. Ain't offered nothing. Berniece
asked him for three dollars to buy some food and he got mad and left.

LYMON: Who's Wining Boy?   80

BOY WILLIE: That's my uncle. That's Doaker's brother. You heard me talk about
Wining Boy. He play piano. He done made some records and everything. He
still doing that, Doaker?

DOAKER: He made one or two records a long time ago. That's the only ones I ever
known him to make. If you let him tell it he a big recording star.

BOY WILLIE: He stopped down home about two years ago. That's what I hear. I
don't know. Me and Lymon was up on Parchman Farm doing them three years.

DOAKER: He don't never stay in one place. Now, he been here about eight months
ago. Back in the winter. Now, you subject not to see him for another two years.
It's liable to be that long before he stop by.

BOY WILLIE: If he had a whole sack of money you liable never to see him. You ain't   85
gonna see him until he get broke. Just as soon as that sack of money is gone you
look up and he be on your doorstep.

LYMON: *(Noticing the piano.)* Is that the piano?

BOY WILLIE: Yeah . . . look here, Lymon. See how it got all cash money. He don't know I found out the most Stovall how it's carved up real nice and polished and everything? You never find you another piano like that.

LYMON: Yeah, that look real nice.

BOY WILLIE: I told you. See how it's polished? My mama used to polish it every day. See all them pictures carved on it? That's what I was talking about. You can get a nice price for that piano.

LYMON: That's all Boy Willie talked about the whole trip up here. I got tired of hearing him talk about the piano. 90

BOY WILLIE: All you want to talk about is women. You ought to hear this nigger, Doaker. Talking about all the women he gonna get when he get up here. He ain't had none down there but he gonna get a hundred when he get up here.

DOAKER: How your people doing down there, Lymon?

LYMON: They alright. They still there. I come up here to see what it's like up here. Boy Willie trying to get me to go back and farm with him.

BOY WILLIE: Sutter's brother selling the land. He say he gonna sell it to me. That's why I come up here. I got one part of it. Sell them watermelons and get me another part. Get Berniece to sell that piano and I'll have the third part.

DOAKER: Berniece ain't gonna sell that piano. 95

BOY WILLIE: I'm gonna talk to her. When she see I got a chance to get Sutter's land she'll come around.

DOAKER: You can put that thought out your mind. Berniece ain't gonna sell that piano.

BOY WILLIE: I'm gonna talk to her. She been playing on it?

DOAKER: You know she won't touch that piano. I ain't never known her to touch it since Mama Ola died. That's over seven years now. She say it got blood on it. She got Maretha playing on it though. Say Maretha can go on and do everything she can't do. Got her in an extra school down at the Irene Kaufman Settlement House. She want Maretha to grow up and be a schoolteacher. Say she good enough she can teach on the piano.

BOY WILLIE: Maretha don't need to be playing on no piano. She can play on the guitar. 100

DOAKER: How much land Sutter got left?

BOY WILLIE: Got a hundred acres. Good land. He done sold it piece by piece, he kept the good part for himself. Now he got to give that up. His brother come down from Chicago for the funeral . . . he up there in Chicago got some kind of business with soda fountain equipment. He anxious to sell the land, Doaker. He don't want to be bothered with it. He called me to him and said cause of how long our families done known each other and how we been good friends and all, say he wanted to sell the land to me. Say he'd rather see me with it than Jim Stovall. Told me he'd let me have it for two thousand dollars cash money. He don't know I found out the most Stovall would give him for it was fifteen hundred dollars. He trying to get that extra five hundred out of me telling me he doing me a favor. I thanked him just as nice. Told him what a good man Sutter was and how he had my sympathy and all. Told him to give me two weeks. He said he'd wait on me. That's why I come up here. Sell them watermelons. Get Berniece to sell that piano. Put them two parts with the part

I done saved. Walk in there. Tip my hat. Lay my money down on the table. Get my deed and walk on out. This time I get to keep all the cotton. Hire me some men to work it for me. Gin my cotton. Get my seed. And I'll see you again next year. Might even plant some tobacco or some oats.

DOAKER: You gonna have a hard time trying to get Berniece to sell that piano. You know Avery Brown from down there don't you? He up here now. He followed Berniece up here trying to get her to marry him after Crawley got killed. He been up here about two years. He call himself a preacher now.

BOY WILLIE: I know Avery. I know him from when he used to work on the Willshaw place. Lymon know him too.

DOAKER: He after Berniece to marry him. She keep telling him no but he won't give up. He keep pressing her on it.   105

BOY WILLIE: Avery think all white men is bigshots. He don't know there some white men ain't got as much as he got.

DOAKER: He supposed to come past here this morning. Berniece going down to the bank with him to see if he can get a loan to start his church. That's why I know Berniece ain't gonna sell that piano. He tried to get her to sell it to help him start his church. Sent the man around and everything.

BOY WILLIE: What man?

DOAKER: Some white fellow was going around to all the colored people's houses looking to buy up musical instruments. He'd buy anything. Drums. Guitars. Harmonicas. Pianos. Avery sent him past here. He looked at the piano and got excited. Offered her a nice price. She turned him down and got on Avery for sending him past. The man kept on her about two weeks. He seen where she wasn't gonna sell it, he gave her his number and told her if she ever wanted to sell it to call him first. Say he'd go one better than what anybody else would give her for it.

BOY WILLIE: How much he offer her for it?   110

DOAKER: Now you know me. She didn't say and I didn't ask. I just know it was a nice price.

LYMON: All you got to do is find out who he is and tell him somebody else wanna buy it from you. Tell him you can't make up your mind who to sell it to, and if he like Doaker say, he'll give you anything you want for it.

BOY WILLIE: That's what I'm gonna do. I'm gonna find out who he is from Avery.

DOAKER: It ain't gonna do you no good. Berniece ain't gonna sell that piano.

BOY WILLIE: She ain't got to sell it. I'm gonna sell it. I own just as much of it as she   115
does.

BERNIECE: (*Offstage, hollers.*) Doaker! Go on get away. Doaker!

DOAKER: (*Calling.*) Berniece?

(DOAKER and BOY WILLIE *rush to the stairs,* BOY WILLIE *runs up the stairs, passing* BERNIECE *as she enters, running.*)

DOAKER: Berniece, what's the matter? You alright? What's the matter?

(BERNIECE *tries to catch her breath. She is unable to speak.*)

DOAKER: That's alright. Take your time. You alright. What's the matter?

(*He calls.*)

Hey, Boy Willie?

BOY WILLIE: *(Offstage.)* Ain't nobody up here. 120

BERNIECE: Sutter . . . Sutter's standing at the top of the steps.

DOAKER: *(Calls.)* Boy Willie!

(LYMON *crosses to the stairs and looks up.* BOY WILLIE *enters from the stairs.)*

BOY WILLIE: Hey Doaker, what's wrong with her? Berniece, what's wrong? Who was you talking to?

DOAKER: She say she seen Sutter's ghost standing at the top of the stairs.

BOY WILLIE: Seen what? Sutter? She ain't seen no Sutter. 125

BERNIECE: He was standing right up there.

BOY WILLIE: *(Entering on the stairs.)* That's all in Berniece's head. Ain't nobody up there. Go on up there, Doaker.

DOAKER: I'll take your word for it. Berniece talking about what she seen. She say Sutter's ghost standing at the top of the steps. She ain't just make all that up.

BOY WILLIE: She up there dreaming. She ain't seen no ghost.

LYMON: You want a glass of water, Berniece? Get her a glass of water, Boy Willie. 130

BOY WILLIE: She don't need no water. She ain't seen nothing. Go on up there and look. Ain't nobody up there but Maretha.

DOAKER: Let Berniece tell it.

BOY WILLIE: I ain't stopping her from telling it.

DOAKER: What happened, Berniece?

BERNIECE: I come out my room to come back down here and Sutter was standing 135 there in the hall.

BOY WILLIE: What he look like?

BERNIECE: He look like Sutter. He look like he always look.

BOY WILLIE: Sutter couldn't find his way from Big Sandy to Little Sandy. How he gonna find his way all the way up here to Pittsburgh? Sutter ain't never even heard of Pittsburgh.

DOAKER: Go on, Berniece.

BERNIECE: Just standing there with the blue suit on. 140

BOY WILLIE: The man ain't never left Marlin County when he was living . . . and he's gonna come all the way up here now that he's dead?

DOAKER: Let her finish. I want to hear what she got to say.

BOY WILLIE: I'll tell you this. If Berniece had seen him like she think she seen him she'd still be running.

DOAKER: Go on, Berniece. Don't pay Boy Willie no mind.

BERNIECE: He was standing there . . . had his hand on top of his head. Look like 145 he might have thought if he took his hand down his head might have fallen off.

LYMON: Did he have on a hat?

BERNIECE: Just had on that blue suit . . . I told him to go away and he just stood there looking at me . . . calling Boy Willie's name.

BOY WILLIE: What he calling my name for?

BERNIECE: I believe you pushed him in the well.

BOY WILLIE: Now what kind of sense that make? You telling me I'm gonna go out 150 there and hide in the weeds with all them dogs and things he got around there . . . I'm gonna hide and wait till I catch him looking down his well just right . . . then I'm gonna run over and push him in. A great big old three-hundred-and-forty-pound man.

BERNIECE: Well, what he calling your name for?

BOY WILLIE: He bending over looking down his well, woman . . . how he know who pushed him? It could have been anybody. Where was you when Sutter fell in his well? Where was Doaker? Me and Lymon was over in Stoner County. Tell her, Lymon. The Ghosts of the Yellow Dog got Sutter. That's what happened. to him.

BERNIECE: You can talk all that Ghosts of the Yellow Dog stuff if you want. I know better.

LYMON: The Ghosts of the Yellow Dog pushed him. That's what the people say. They found him in his well and all the people say it must be the Ghosts of the Yellow Dog. Just like all them other men.

BOY WILLIE: Come talking about he looking for me. What he come all the way   155
up here for? If he looking for me all he got to do is wait. He could have saved himself a trip if he looking for me. That ain't nothing but in Berniece's head. Ain't no telling what she liable to come up with next.

BERNIECE: Boy Willie, I want you and Lymon to go ahead and leave my house. Just go on somewhere. You don't do nothing but bring trouble with you everywhere you go. If it wasn't for you Crawley would still be alive.

BOY WILLIE: Crawley what? I ain't had nothing to do with Crawley getting killed. Crawley three time seven. He had his own mind.

BERNIECE: Just go on and leave. Let Sutter go somewhere else looking for you.

BOY WILLIE: I'm leaving. Soon as we sell them watermelons. Other than that I ain't going nowhere. Hell, I just got here. Talking about Sutter looking for me. Sutter was looking for that piano. That's what he was looking for. He had to die to find out where that piano was at . . . If I was you I'd get rid of it. That's the way to get rid of Sutter's ghost. Get rid of that piano.

BERNIECE: I want you and Lymon to go on and take all this confusion out of my   160
house!

BOY WILLIE: Hey, tell her, Doaker. What kind of sense that make? I told you, Lymon, as soon as Berniece see me she was gonna start something. Didn't I tell you that? Now she done made up that story about Sutter just so she could tell me to leave her house. Well, hell, I ain't going nowhere till I sell them watermelons.

BERNIECE: Well why don't you go out there and sell them! Sell them and go on back!

BOY WILLIE: We waiting till the people get up.

LYMON: Boy Willie say if you get out there too early and wake the people up they get mad at you and won't buy nothing from you.

DOAKER: You won't be waiting long. You done let the sun catch up with you. This   165
the time everybody be getting up around here.

BERNIECE: Come on, Doaker, walk up here with me. Let me get Maretha up and get her started. I got to get ready myself. Boy Willie, just go on out there and sell them watermelons and you and Lymon leave my house.

(BERNIECE and DOAKER *exit up the stairs.*)

BOY WILLIE: *(Calling after them.)* If you see Sutter up there . . . tell him I'm down here waiting on him.

LYMON: What if she see him again?

BOY WILLIE: That's all in her head. There ain't no ghost up there.

(*Calls.*)

Hey, Doaker . . . I told you ain't nothing up there.

LYMON: I'm glad he didn't say he was looking for me.   170

BOY WILLIE: I wish I would see Sutter's ghost. Give me a chance to put a whupping on him.

LYMON: You ought to stay up here with me. You be down there working his land . . . he might come looking for you all the time.

BOY WILLIE: I ain't thinking about Sutter. And I ain't thinking about staying up here. You stay up here. I'm going back and get Sutter's land. You think you ain't got to work up here. You think this the land of milk and honey. But I ain't scared of work. I'm going back and farm every acre of that land.

(DOAKER *enters from the stairs.*)

I told you there ain't nothing up there, Doaker. Berniece dreaming all that.

DOAKER: I believe Berniece seen something. Berniece levelheaded. She ain't just made all that up. She say Sutter had on a suit. I don't believe she ever seen Sutter in a suit. I believe that's what he was buried in, and that's what Berniece saw.

BOY WILLIE: Well, let her keep on seeing him then. As long as he don't mess   175
with me.

(DOAKER *starts to cook his breakfast.*)

I heard about you, Doaker. They say you got all the women looking out for you down home. They be looking to see you coming. Say you got a different one every two weeks. Say they be fighting one another for you to stay with them.

(*To* LYMON.)

Look at him, Lymon. He know it's true.

DOAKER: I ain't thinking about no women. They never get me tied up with them. After Coreen I ain't got no use for them. I stay up on Jack Slattery's place when I be down there. All them women want is somebody with a steady payday.

BOY WILLIE: That ain't what I hear. I hear every two weeks the women all put on their dresses and line up at the railroad station.

DOAKER: I don't get down there but once a month. I used to go down there every two weeks but they keep switching me around. They keep switching all the fellows around.

BOY WILLIE: Doaker can't turn that railroad loose. He was working the railroad when I was walking around crying for sugartit. My mama used to brag on him.

DOAKER: I'm cooking now, but I used to line track. I pieced together the Yellow   180
Dog stitch by stitch. Rail by rail. Line track all up around there. I lined track all up around Sunflower and Clarksdale. Wining Boy worked with me. He helped put in some of that track. He'd work it for six months and quit. Go back to playing piano and gambling.

BOY WILLIE: How long you been with the railroad now?

DOAKER: Twenty-seven years. Now, I'll tell you something about the railroad. What I done learned after twenty-seven years. See, you got North. You got West. You look over here you got South. Over there you got East. Now, you can start from anywhere. Don't care where you at. You got to go one of them four ways. And whichever way you decide to go they got a railroad that will take you there. Now, that's something simple. You think anybody would be able to understand that. But you'd be surprised how many people trying to go North get on a train going West. They think the train's supposed to go where they going rather than where it's going.

Now, why people going? Their sister's sick. They leaving before they kill somebody . . . and they sitting across from somebody who's leaving to keep from getting killed. They leaving cause they can't get satisfied. They going to meet someone. I wish I had a dollar for every time that someone wasn't at the station to meet them. I done seen that a lot. In between the time they sent the telegram and the time the person get there . . . they done forgot all about them.

They got so many trains out there they have a hard time keeping them from running into each other. Got trains going every whichaway. Got people on all of them. Somebody going where somebody just left. If everybody stay in one place I believe this would be a better world. Now what I done learned after twenty-seven years of railroading is this . . . if the train stays on the track . . . it's going to get where it's going. It might not be where you going. If it ain't, then all you got to do is sit and wait cause the train's coming back to get you. The train don't never stop. It'll come back every time. Now I'll tell you another thing . . .

BOY WILLIE: What you cooking over there, Doaker? Me and Lymon's hungry.

DOAKER: Go on down there to Wylie and Kirkpatrick to Eddie's restaurant. Coffee cost a nickel and you can get two eggs, sausage, and grits for fifteen cents. He even give you a biscuit with it.

BOY WILLIE: That look good what you got. Give me a little piece of that grilled bread.   185

DOAKER: Here . . . go on take the whole piece.

BOY WILLIE: Here you go, Lymon . . . you want a piece?

(He gives LYMON a piece of toast. MARETHA enters from the stairs.)

BOY WILLIE: Hey, sugar. Come here and give me a hug. Come on give Uncle Boy Willie a hug. Don't be shy. Look at her, Doaker. She done got bigger. Ain't she got big?

DOAKER: Yeah, she getting up there.

BOY WILLIE: How you doing, sugar?   190

MARETHA: Fine.

BOY WILLIE: You was just a little old thing last time I seen you. You remember me, don't you? This your Uncle Boy Willie from down South. That there's Lymon. He my friend. We come up here to sell watermelons. You like watermelons?

(MARETHA nods.)

We got a whole truckload out front. You can have as many as you want. What you been doing?

MARETHA: Nothing.

BOY WILLIE: Don't be shy now. Look at you getting all big. How old is you?

MARETHA: Eleven. I'm gonna be twelve soon.   195

BOY WILLIE: You like it up here? You like the North?

MARETHA: It's alright.

BOY WILLIE: That there's Lymon. Did you say hi to Lymon?

MARETHA: Hi.

LYMON: How you doing? You look just like your mama. I remember you when you   200
was wearing diapers.

BOY WILLIE: You gonna come down South and see me? Uncle Boy Willie gonna
get him a farm. Gonna get a great big old farm. Come down there and I'll teach
you how to ride a mule. Teach you how to kill a chicken, too.

MARETHA: I seen my mama do that.

BOY WILLIE: Ain't nothing to it. You just grab him by his neck and twist it. Get
you a real good grip and then you just wring his neck and throw him in the
pot. Cook him up. Then you got some good eating. What you like to eat? What
kind of food you like?

MARETHA: I like everything . . . except I don't like no black-eyed peas.

BOY WILLIE: Uncle Doaker tell me your mama got you playing that piano. Come   205
on play something for me.

(BOY WILLIE *crosses over to the piano followed by* MARETHA.)

Show me what you can do. Come on now. Here . . . Uncle Boy Willie give you
a dime . . . show me what you can do. Don't be bashful now. That dime say you
can't be bashful.

(MARETHA *plays. It is something any beginner first learns.*)

Here, let me show you something.

(BOY WILLIE *sits and plays a simple boogie-woogie.*)

See that? See what I'm doing? That's what you call the boogie-woogie. See
now . . . you can get up and dance to that. That's how good it sound. It sound
like you wanna dance. You can dance to that. It'll hold you up. Whatever kind
of dance you wanna do you can dance to that right there. See that? See how it
go? Ain't nothing to it. Go on you do it.

MARETHA: I got to read it on the paper.

BOY WILLIE: You don't need no paper. Go on. Do just like that there.

BERNIECE: Maretha! You get up here and get ready to go so you be on time. Ain't
no need you trying to take advantage of company.

MARETHA: I got to go.

BOY WILLIE: Uncle Boy Willie gonna get you a guitar. Let Uncle Doaker teach   210
you how to play that. You don't need to read no paper to play the guitar. Your
mama told you about that piano? You know how them pictures got on there?

MARETHA: She say it just always been like that since she got it.

BOY WILLIE: You hear that, Doaker? And you sitting up here in the house with
Berniece.

DOAKER: I ain't got nothing to do with that. I don't get in the way of Berniece's
raising her.

BOY WILLIE: You tell your mama to tell you about that piano. You ask her how
them pictures got on there. If she don't tell you I'll tell you.

BERNIECE: Maretha!   215

MARETHA: I got to get ready to go.

BOY WILLIE: She getting big, Doaker. You remember her, Lymon?

LYMON: She used to be real little.

(There is a knock on the door. DOAKER goes to answer it. AVERY enters. Thirty-eight years old, honest and ambitious, he has taken to the city like a fish to water, finding in it opportunities for growth and advancement that did not exist for him in the rural South. He is dressed in a suit and tie with a gold cross around his neck. He carries a small Bible.)

DOAKER: Hey, Avery, come on in. Berniece upstairs.

BOY WILLIE: Look at him . . . look at him . . . he don't know what to say. He `220`
wasn't expecting to see me.

AVERY: Hey, Boy Willie. What you doing up here?

BOY WILLIE: Look at him, Lymon.

AVERY: Is that Lymon? Lymon Jackson?

BOY WILLIE: Yeah, you know Lymon.

DOAKER: Berniece be ready in a minute, Avery. `225`

BOY WILLIE: Doaker say you a preacher now. What . . . we supposed to call you
Reverend? You used to be plain old Avery. When you get to be a preacher,
nigger?

LYMON: Avery say he gonna be a preacher so he don't have to work.

BOY WILLIE: I remember when you was down there on the Willshaw place
planting cotton. You wasn't thinking about no Reverend then.

AVERY: That must be your truck out there. I saw that truck with them watermelons,
I was trying to figure out what it was doing in front of the house.

BOY WILLIE: Yeah, me and Lymon selling watermelons. That's Lymon's truck. `230`

DOAKER: Berniece say you all going down to the bank.

AVERY: Yeah, they give me a half day off work. I got an appointment to talk to the
bank about getting a loan to start my church.

BOY WILLIE: Lymon say preachers don't have to work. Where you working at,
nigger?

DOAKER: Avery got him one of them good jobs. He working at one of them
skyscrapers downtown.

AVERY: I'm working down there at the Gulf Building running an elevator. Got a `235`
pension and everything. They even give you a turkey on Thanksgiving.

LYMON: How you know the rope ain't gonna break? Ain't you scared the rope's
gonna break?

AVERY: That's steel. They got steel cables hold it up. It take a whole lot of breaking
to break that steel. Naw, I ain't worried about nothing like that. It ain't nothing
but a little old elevator. Now, I wouldn't get in none of them airplanes. You
couldn't pay me to do nothing like that.

LYMON: That be fun. I'd rather do that than ride in one of them elevators.

BOY WILLIE: How many of them watermelons you wanna buy?

AVERY: I thought you was gonna give me one seeing as how you got a whole truck `240`
full.

BOY WILLIE: You can get one, get two. I'll give you two for a dollar.

AVERY: I can't eat but one. How much are they?

BOY WILLIE: Aw, nigger, you know I'll give you a watermelon. Go on, take as
many as you want. Just leave some for me and Lymon to sell.

AVERY: I don't want but one.

BOY WILLIE: How you get to be a preacher, Avery? I might want to be a preacher `245`
one day. Have everybody call me Reverend Boy Willie.

AVERY: It come to me in a dream. God called me and told me he wanted me to be a shepherd for his flock. That's what I'm gonna call my church . . . The Good Shepherd Church of God in Christ.

DOAKER: Tell him what you told me. Tell him about the three hobos.

AVERY: Boy Willie don't want to hear all that.

LYMON: I do. Lots a people say your dreams can come true.   250

AVERY: Naw. You don't want to hear all that.

DOAKER: Go on. I told him you was a preacher. He didn't want to believe me. Tell him about the three hobos.

AVERY: Well, it come to me in a dream. See . . . I was sitting out in this railroad yard watching the trains go by. The train stopped and these three hobos got off. They told me they had come from Nazareth and was on their way to Jerusalem. They had three candles. They gave me one and told me to light it . . . but to be careful that it didn't go out. Next thing I knew I was standing in front of this house. Something told me to go knock on the door. This old woman opened the door and said they had been waiting on me. Then she led me into this room. It was a big room and it was full of all kinds of different people. They looked like anybody else except they all had sheep heads and was making noise like sheep make. I heard somebody call my name. I looked around and there was these same three hobos. They told me to take off my clothes and they give me a blue robe with gold thread. They washed my feet and combed my hair. Then they showed me these three doors and told me to pick one.

    I went through one of them doors and that flame leapt off that candle and it seemed like my whole head caught fire. I looked around and there was four or five other men standing there with these same blue robes on. Then we heard a voice tell us to look out across this valley. We looked out and saw the valley was full of wolves. The voice told us that these sheep people that I had seen in the other room had to go over to the other side of this valley and somebody had to take them. Then I heard another voice say, "Who shall I send?" Next thing I knew I said, "Here I am. Send me." That's when I met Jesus. He say, "If you go, I'll go with you." Something told me to say, "Come on. Let's go." That's when I woke up. My head still felt like it was on fire . . . but I had a peace about myself that was hard to explain. I knew right then that I had been filled with the Holy Ghost and called to be a servant of the Lord. It took me a while before I could accept that. But then a lot of little ways God showed me that it was true. So I became a preacher.

LYMON: I see why you gonna call it the Good Shepherd Church. You dreaming about them sheep people. I can see that easy.

BOY WILLIE: Doaker say you sent some white man past the house to look at that piano. Say he was going around to all the colored people's houses looking to buy up musical instruments.

AVERY: Yeah, but Berniece didn't want to sell that piano. After she told me about   255
it . . . I could see why she didn't want to sell it.

BOY WILLIE: What's this man's name?

AVERY: Oh, that's a while back now. I done forgot his name. He give Berniece a card with his name and telephone number on it, but I believe she threwed it away.

    (BERNIECE *and* MARETHA *enter from the stairs.*)

BERNIECE: Maretha, run back upstairs and get my pocket-book. And wipe that hair grease off your forehead. Go ahead, hurry up.

(MARETHA exits up the stairs.)

How you doing, Avery? You done got all dressed up. You look nice. Boy Willie, I thought you and Lymon was going to sell them watermelons.

BOY WILLIE: Lymon done got sleepy. We liable to get some sleep first.

LYMON: I ain't sleepy.   260

DOAKER: As many watermelons as you got stacked up on that truck out there, you ought to have been gone.

BOY WILLIE: We gonna go in a minute. We going.

BERNIECE: Doaker. I'm gonna stop down there on Logan Street. You want anything?

DOAKER: You can pick up some ham hocks if you going down there. See if you can get the smoked ones. If they ain't got that get the fresh ones. Don't get the ones that got all that fat under the skin. Look for the long ones. They nice and lean.

(He gives her a dollar.)

Don't get the short ones lessen they smoked. If you got to get the fresh ones make sure that they the long ones. If they ain't got them smoked then go ahead and get the short ones.

(Pause.)

You may as well get some turnip greens while you down there. I got some buttermilk . . . if you pick up some cornmeal I'll make me some cornbread and cook up them turnip greens.

(MARETHA enters from the stairs.)

MARETHA: We gonna take the streetcar?   265

BERNIECE: Me and Avery gonna drop you off at the settlement house. You mind them people down there. Don't be going down there showing your color. Boy Willie, I done told you what to do. I'll see you later, Doaker.

AVERY: I'll be seeing you again, Boy Willie.

BOY WILLIE: Hey, Berniece . . . what's the name of that man Avery sent past say he want to buy the piano?

BERNIECE: I knew it. I knew it when I first seen you. I knew you was up to something.

BOY WILLIE: Sutter's brother say he selling the land to me. He waiting on me now.   270
Told me he'd give me two weeks. I got one part. Sell them watermelons get me another part. Then we can sell that piano and I'll have the third part.

BERNIECE: I ain't selling that piano, Boy Willie. If that's why you come up here you can just forget about it.

(To DOAKER.)

Doaker, I'll see you later. Boy Willie ain't nothing but a whole lot of mouth. I ain't paying him no mind. If he come up here thinking he gonna sell that piano then he done come up here for nothing.

(BERNIECE, AVERY, and MARETHA exit the front door.)

BOY WILLIE: Hey, Lymon! You ready to go sell these watermelons.

(BOY WILLIE and LYMON start to exit. At the door BOY WILLIE turns to DOAKER.)

Hey, Doaker . . . if Berniece don't want sell that piano . . . I'm gonna cut it in half and go on and sell my half.

(BOY WILLIE and LYMON exit.)

(The lights go down on the scene.)

Scene 2

(The lights come up on the kitchen. It is three days later. WINING BOY sits at the kitchen table. There is a half-empty pint bottle on the table. DOAKER busies himself washing pots. WINING BOY is fifty-six years old. DOAKER's older brother, he tries to present the image of a successful musician and gambler, but his music, his clothes, and even his manner of presentation are old. He is a man who looking back over his life continues to live it with an odd mixture of zest and sorrow.)

WINING BOY: So the Ghosts of the Yellow Dog got Sutter. That just go to show you I believe I always lived right. They say every dog gonna have his day and time it go around it sure come back to you. I done seen that a thousand times. I know the truth of that. But I'll tell you outright . . . . if I see Sutter's ghost I'll be on the first thing I find that got wheels on it.

(DOAKER enters from his room.)

DOAKER: Wining Boy!

WINING BOY: And I'll tell you another thing . . . Berniece ain't gonna sell that piano.

DOAKER: That's what she told him. He say he gonna cut it in half and go on and sell his half. They been around here three days trying to sell them watermelons. They trying to get out to where the white folks live but the truck keep breaking down. They go a block or two and it break down again. They trying to get out to Squirrel Hill and can't get around the corner. He say soon as he can get that truck empty to where he can set the piano up in there he gonna take it out of here and go sell it.

WINING BOY: What about them boys Sutter got? How come they ain't farming that land?

DOAKER: One of them going to school. He left down there and come North to school. The other one ain't got as much sense as that frying pan over yonder. That is the dumbest white man I ever seen. He'd stand in the river and watch it rise till it drown him.

WINING BOY: Other than seeing Sutter's ghost how's Berniece doing?

DOAKER: She doing alright. She still got Crawley on her mind. He been dead three years but she still holding on to him. She need to go out here and let one of these fellows grab a whole handful of whatever she got. She act like it done got precious.

WINING BOY: They always told me any fish will bite if you got good bait.

DOAKER: She stuck up on it. She think it's better than she is. I believe she messing around with Avery. They got something going. He a preacher now. If you let him tell it the Holy Ghost sat on his head and heaven opened up with thunder and lightning and God was calling his name. Told him to go out and preach and tend to his flock. That's what he gonna call his church. The Good Shepherd Church.

WINING BOY: They had that joker down in Spear walking around talking about he Jesus Christ. He gonna live the life of Christ. Went through the Last Supper and everything. Rented him a mule on Palm Sunday and rode through the town. Did everything . . . talking about he Christ. He did everything until they got up to that crucifixion part. Got up to that part and told everybody to go home and quit pretending. He got up to the crucifixion part and changed his mind. Had a whole bunch of folks come down there to see him get nailed to the cross. I don't know who's the worse fool. Him or them. Had all them folks come down there . . . even carried the cross up this little hill. People standing around waiting to see him get nailed to the cross and he stop everything and preach a little sermon and told everybody to go home. Had enough nerve to tell them to come to church on Easter Sunday to celebrate his resurrection.

DOAKER: I'm surprised Avery ain't thought about that. He trying every little thing to get him a congregation together. They meeting over at his house till he get him a church.

WINING BOY: Ain't nothing wrong with being a preacher. You got the preacher on one hand and the gambler on the other. Sometimes there ain't too much difference in them.

DOAKER: How long you been in Kansas City?

WINING BOY: Since I left here. I got tied up with some old gal down there.   15

(Pause.)

You know Cleotha died.

DOAKER: Yeah, I heard that last time I was down there. I was sorry to hear that.

WINING BOY: One of her friends wrote and told me. I got the letter right here.

(He takes the letter out of his pocket.)

I was down in Kansas City and she wrote and told me Cleotha had died. Name of Willa Bryant. She say she know cousin Rupert.

(He opens the letter and reads.)

Dear Wining Boy: I am writing this letter to let you know Miss Cleotha Holman passed on Saturday the first of May she departed this world in the loving arms of her sister Miss Alberta Samuels. I know you would want to know this and am writing as a friend of Cleotha. There have been many hardships since last you seen her but she survived them all and to the end was a good woman whom I hope have God's grace and is in His Paradise. Your cousin Rupert Bates is my friend also and he give me your address and I pray this reaches you about Cleotha. Miss Willa Bryant. A friend.

(He folds the letter and returns it to his pocket.)

They was nailing her coffin shut by the time I heard about it. I never knew she was sick. I believe it was that yellow jaundice. That's what killed her mama.

DOAKER: Cleotha wasn't but forty-some.

WINING BOY: She was forty-six. I got ten years on her. I met her when she was sixteen. You remember I used to run around there. Couldn't nothing keep me still. Much as I loved Cleotha I loved to ramble. Couldn't nothing keep me still. We got married and we used to fight about it all the time. Then one day she asked me to leave. Told me she loved me before I left. Told me, Wining Boy, you got a home as long as I got mine.

And I believe in my heart I always felt that and that kept me safe.

DOAKER: Cleotha always did have a nice way about her.

WINING BOY: Man that woman was something. I used to thank the Lord. Many a night I sat up and looked out over my life. Said, well, I had Cleotha. When it didn't look like there was nothing else for me, I said, thank God, at least I had that. If ever I go anywhere in this life I done known a good woman. And that used to hold me till the next morning.

(Pause.)

What you got? Give me a little nip. I know you got something stuck up in your room.

DOAKER: I ain't seen you walk in here and put nothing on the table. You done sat there and drank up your whiskey. Now you talking about what you got.

WINING BOY: I got plenty money. Give me a little nip.

(DOAKER carries a glass into his room and returns with it half-filled. He sets it on the table in front of WINING BOY.)

WINING BOY: You hear from Coreen?

DOAKER: She up in New York. I let her go from my mind.

WINING BOY: She was something back then. She wasn't too pretty but she had a way of looking at you made you know there was a whole lot of woman there. You got married and snatched her out from under us and we all got mad at you.

DOAKER: She up in New York City. That's what I hear.

(The door opens and BOY WILLIE and LYMON enter.)

BOY WILLIE: Aw hell . . . look here! We was just talking about you. Doaker say you left out of here with a whole sack of money. I told him we wasn't going see you till you got broke.

WINING BOY: What you mean broke? I got a whole pocketful of money.

DOAKER: Did you all get that truck fixed?

BOY WILLIE: We got it running and got halfway out there on Centre and it broke down again. Lymon went out there and messed it up some more. Fellow told us we got to wait till tomorrow to get it fixed. Say he have it running like new. Lymon going back down there and sleep in the truck so the people don't take the watermelons.

LYMON: Lymon nothing. You go down there and sleep in it.

BOY WILLIE: You was sleeping in it down home, nigger! I don't know nothing about sleeping in no truck.

LYMON: I ain't sleeping in no truck.

BOY WILLIE: They can take all the watermelons. I don't care. Wining Boy, where you coming from? Where you been?

WINING BOY: I been down in Kansas City.

BOY WILLIE: You remember Lymon? Lymon Jackson.

WINING BOY: Yeah, I used to know his daddy.

BOY WILLIE: Doaker say you don't never leave no address with nobody. Say he got to depend on your whim. See when it strike you to pay a visit.

WINING BOY: I got four or five addresses.

BOY WILLIE: Doaker say Berniece asked you for three dollars and you got mad and left.

WINING BOY: Berniece try and rule over you too much for me. That's why I left. It wasn't about no three dollars.

BOY WILLIE: Where you getting all these sacks of money from? I need to be with you. Doaker say you had a whole sack of money . . . turn some of it loose.

WINING BOY: I was just fixing to ask you for five dollars.

BOY WILLIE: I ain't got no money. I'm trying to get some. Doaker tell you about Sutter? The Ghosts of the Yellow Dog got him about three weeks ago. Berniece done seen his ghost and everything. He right upstairs.

(Calls.)

Hey Sutter! Wining Boy's here. Come on, get a drink!

WINING BOY: How many that make the Ghosts of the Yellow Dog done got?

BOY WILLIE: Must be about nine or ten, eleven or twelve. I don't know.

DOAKER: You got Ed Saunders. Howard Peterson. Charlie Webb.

WINING BOY: Robert Smith. That fellow that shot Becky's boy . . . say he was stealing peaches . . .

DOAKER: You talking about Bob Mallory.

BOY WILLIE: Berniece say she don't believe all that about the Ghosts of the Yellow Dog.

WINING BOY: She ain't got to believe. You go ask them white folks in Sunflower County if they believe. You go ask Sutter if he believe. I don't care if Berniece believe or not. I done been to where the Southern cross the Yellow Dog and called out their names. They talk back to you, too.

LYMON: What they sound like? The wind or something?

BOY WILLIE: You done been there for real, Wining Boy?

WINING BOY: Nineteen thirty. July of nineteen thirty I stood right there on that spot. It didn't look like nothing was going right in my life. I said everything can't go wrong all the time . . . let me go down there and call on the Ghosts of the Yellow Dog, see if they can help me. I went down there and right there where them two railroads cross each other . . . I stood right there on that spot and called out their names. They talk back to you, too.

LYMON: People say you can ask them questions. They talk to you like that?

WINING BOY: A lot of things you got to find out on your own. I can't say how they talked to nobody else. But to me it just filled me up in a strange sort of way to be standing there on that spot. I didn't want to leave. It felt like the longer I stood there the bigger I got. I seen the train coming and it seem like I was bigger than the train. I started not to move. But something told me to go ahead and get on out the way. The train passed and I started to go back up there and stand some more. But something told me not to do it. I walked away from there feeling like a king. Went on and had a stroke of luck that run on for three years. So I don't care if Berniece believe or not. Berniece ain't got to believe. I know cause I been there. Now Doaker'll tell you about the Ghosts of the Yellow Dog.

DOAKER: I don't try and talk that stuff with Berniece. Avery got her all tied up in that church. She just think it's a whole lot of nonsense.

BOY WILLIE: Berniece don't believe in nothing. She just think she believe. She believe in anything if it's convenient for her to believe. But when that convenience run out then she ain't got nothing to stand on.

WINING BOY: Let's not get on Berniece now. Doaker tell me you talking about   60
selling that piano.

BOY WILLIE: Yeah . . . hey, Doaker, I got the name of that man Avery was talking
about. The man what's fixing the truck gave me his name. Everybody know
him. Say he buy up anything you can make music with. I got his name and his
telephone number. Hey, Wining Boy, Sutter's brother say he selling the land to
me. I got one part. Sell them watermelons get me the second part. Then
. . . soon as I get them watermelons out that truck I'm gonna take and sell
that piano and get the third part.

DOAKER: That land ain't worth nothing no more. The smart white man's up here in
these cities. He cut the land loose and step back and watch you and the dumb
white man argue over it.

WINING BOY: How you know Sutter's brother ain't sold it already? You talking
about selling the piano and the man's liable to sold the land two or three
times.

BOY WILLIE: He say he waiting on me. He say he give me two weeks. That's
two weeks from Friday. Say if I ain't back by then he might gonna sell it to
somebody else. He say he wanna see me with it.

WINING BOY: You know as well as I know the man gonna sell the land to the first   65
one walk up and hand him the money.

BOY WILLIE: That's just who I'm gonna be. Look, you ain't gotta know he
waiting on me. I know. Okay. I know what the man told me. Stoval already
done tried to buy the land from him and he told him no. The man say he
waiting on me . . . he waiting on me. Hey, Doaker . . . give me a drink. I see
Wining Boy got his glass.

(DOAKER *exits into his room.*)

Wining Boy, what you doing in Kansas City? What they got down there?

LYMON: I hear they got some nice-looking women in Kansas City. I sure like to go
down there and find out.

WINING BOY: Man, the women down there is something else.

(DOAKER *enters with a bottle of whiskey. He sets it on the table with some glasses.*)

DOAKER: You wanna sit up here and drink up my whiskey, leave a dollar on the
table when you get up.

BOY WILLIE: You ain't doing nothing but showing your hospitality. I know we   70
ain't got to pay for your hospitality.

WINING BOY: Doaker say they had you and Lymon down on the Parchman Farm.
Had you on my old stomping grounds.

BOY WILLIE: Me and Lymon was down there hauling wood for Jim Miller and
keeping us a little bit to sell. Some white fellows tried to run us off of it. That's
when Crawley got killed. They put me and Lymon in the penitentiary.

LYMON: They ambushed us right there where that road dip down and around that
bend in the creek. Crawley tried to fight them. Me and Boy Willie got away but
the sheriff got us. Say we was stealing wood. They shot me in my stomach.

BOY WILLIE: They looking for Lymon down there now. They rounded him up and
put him in jail for not working.

LYMON: Fined me a hundred dollars. Mr. Stovall come and paid my hundred   75
dollars and the judge say I got to work for him to pay him back his hundred

dollars. I told them I'd rather take my thirty days but they wouldn't let me do that.

BOY WILLIE: As soon as Stovall turned his back, Lymon was gone. He down there living in that truck dodging the sheriff and Stovall. He got both of them looking for him. So I brought him up here.

LYMON: I told Boy Willie I'm gonna stay up here. I ain't going back with him.

BOY WILLIE: Ain't nobody twisting your arm to make you go back. You can do what you want to do.

WINING BOY: I'll go back with you. I'm on my way down there. You gonna take the train? I'm gonna take the train.

LYMON: They treat you better up here.   80

BOY WILLIE: I ain't worried about nobody mistreating me. They treat you like you let them treat you. They mistreat me I mistreat them right back. Ain't no difference in me and the white man.

WINING BOY: Ain't no difference as far as how somebody supposed to treat you. I agree with that. But I'll tell you the difference between the colored man and the white man. Alright. Now you take and eat some berries. They taste real good to you. So you say I'm gonna go out and get me a whole pot of these berries and cook them up to make a pie or whatever. But you ain't looked to see them berries is sitting in the white fellow's yard. Ain't got no fence around them. You figure anybody want something they'd fence it in. Alright. Now the white man come along and say that's my land. Therefore everything that grow on it belong to me. He tell the sheriff, "I want you to put this nigger in jail as a warning to all the other niggers. Otherwise first thing you know these niggers have everything that belong to us."

BOY WILLIE: I'd come back at night and haul off his whole patch while he was sleep.

WINING BOY: Alright. Now Mr. So and So, he sell the land to you. And he come to you and say, "John, you own the land. It's all yours now. But them is my berries. And come time to pick them I'm gonna send my boys over. You got the land . . . but them berries, I'm gonna keep them. They mine." And he go and fix it with the law that them is his berries. Now that's the difference between the colored man and the white man. The colored man can't fix nothing with the law.

BOY WILLIE: I don't go by what the law say. The law's liable to say anything. I go   85
by if it's right or not. It don't matter to me what the law say. I take and look at it for myself.

LYMON: That's why you gonna end up back down there on the Parchman Farm.

BOY WILLIE: I ain't thinking about no Parchman Farm. You liable to go back before me.

LYMON: They work you too hard down there. All that weeding and hoeing and chopping down trees. I didn't like all that.

WINING BOY: You ain't got to like your job on Parchman. Hey, tell him, Doaker, the only one got to like his job is the waterboy.

DOAKER: If he don't like his job he need to set that bucket down.   90

BOY WILLIE: That's what they told Lymon. They had Lymon on water and everybody got mad at him cause he was lazy.

LYMON: That water was heavy.

BOY WILLIE: They had Lymon down there singing:

(Sings.)

O Lord Berta Berta O Lord gal oh-ah
O Lord Berta Berta O Lord gal well

(LYMON and WINING BOY join in.)

Go 'head marry don't you wait on me oh-ah
Go 'head marry don't you wait on me well
Might not want you when I go free oh-ah
Might not want you when I go free well

BOY WILLIE: Come on, Doaker. Doaker know this one.

(As DOAKER joins in the men stamp and clap to keep time. They sing in harmony with great fervor and style.)

BOY WILLIE: I don't want to see them either. Hey, Wining Boy, come on play some 95 piano. You a piano player, play some piano. Lymon wanna hear you.

WINING BOY: I give that piano up. That was the best thing that ever happened to me, getting rid of that piano. That piano got so big and I'm carrying it around on my back. I don't wish that on nobody. See, you think it's all fun being a recording star. Got to carrying that piano around and man did I get slow. Got just like molasses. The world just slipping by me and I'm walking around with that piano. Alright. Now, there ain't but so many places you can go. Only so many road wide enough for you and that piano. And that piano get heavier and heavier. Go to a place and they find out you play piano, the first thing they want to do is give you a drink, find you a piano, and sit you right down. And that's where you gonna be for the next eight hours. They ain't gonna let you get up! Now, the first three or four years of that is fun. You can't get enough whiskey and you can't get enough women and you don't never get tired of playing that piano. But that only last so long. You look up one day and you hate the whiskey, and you hate the women, and you hate the piano. But that's all you got. You can't do nothing else. All you know how to do is play that piano. Now, who am I? Am I me? Or am I the piano player? Sometime it seem like the only thing to do is shoot the piano player cause he the cause of all the trouble I'm having.

DOAKER: What you gonna do when your troubles get like mine?

LYMON: If I knew how to play it, I'd play it. That's a nice piano.

BOY WILLIE: Whoever playing better play quick. Sutter's brother say he waiting on me. I sell them watermelons.

O Lord Berta Berta O Lord gal oh-ah
O Lord Berta Berta O Lord gal well

Raise them up higher, let them drop on down oh-ah
Raise them up higher, let them drop on down well

Don't know the difference when the sun go down oh-ah
Don't know the difference when the sun go down well

Berta in Meridan and she living at ease oh-ah
Berta in Meridan and she living at ease well
I'm on old Parchman, got to work or leave oh-ah
I'm on old Parchman, got to work or leave well

O Alberta, Berta, O Lord gal oh-ah
O Alberta, Berta, O Lord gal well

When you marry, don't marry no farming man oh-ah
When you marry, don't marry no farming man well
Everyday Monday, hoe handle in your hand oh-ah
Everyday Monday, hoe handle in your hand well

When you marry, marry a railroad man, oh-ah
When you marry, marry a railroad man, well
Everyday Sunday, dollar in your hand oh-ah
Everyday Sunday, dollar in your hand well

O Alberta, Berta, O Lord gal oh-ah
O Alberta, Berta, O Lord gal well

BOY WILLIE: Doaker like that part. He like that railroad part.   100
LYMON: Doaker sound like Tangleye. He can't sing a lick.
BOY WILLIE: Hey, Doaker, they still talk about you down on Parchman. They ask
   me, "You Doaker Boy's nephew?" I say, "Yeah, me and him is family." They
   treated me alright soon as I told them that. Say, "Yeah, he my uncle."
DOAKER: I don't never want to see none of them niggers no more.
   Get Berniece to sell that piano. Put them two parts with the part I done saved . . .
WINING BOY: Berniece ain't gonna sell that piano. I don't see why you don't know
   that.
BOY WILLIE: What she gonna do with it? She ain't doing nothing but letting it sit   105
   up there and rot. That piano ain't doing nobody no good.
LYMON: That's a nice piano. If I had it I'd sell it. Unless I knew how to play like
   Wining Boy. You can get a nice price for that piano.
DOAKER: Now I'm gonna tell you something, Lymon don't know this . . . but
   I'm gonna tell you why me and Wining Boy say Berniece ain't gonna sell that
   piano.
BOY WILLIE: She ain't got to sell it! I'm gonna sell it! Berniece ain't got no more
   rights to that piano than I do.
DOAKER: I'm talking to the man . . . let me talk to the man. See, now . . . to
   understand why we say that . . . to understand about that piano . . . you got to
   go back to slavery time. See, our family was owned by a fellow named Robert
   Sutter. That was Sutter's grandfather. Alright. The piano was owned by a fellow
   named Joel Nolander. He was one of the Nolander brothers from down in

Georgia. It was coming up on Sutter's wedding anniversary and he was looking to buy his wife . . . Miss Ophelia was her name . . . he was looking to buy her an anniversary present. Only thing with him . . . he ain't had no money. But he had some niggers. So he asked Mr. Nolander to see if maybe he could trade off some of his niggers for that piano. Told him he would give him one and a half niggers for it. That's the way he told him. Say he could have one full grown and one half grown. Mr. Nolander agreed only he say he had to pick them. He didn't want Sutter to give him just any old nigger. He say he wanted to have the pick of the litter. So Sutter lined up his niggers and Mr. Nolander looked them over and out of the whole bunch he picked my grandmother . . . her name was Berniece . . . sample like Berniece . . . and he picked my daddy when he wasn't nothing but a little boy nine years old. They made the trade off and Miss Ophelia was so happy with that piano that it got to be just about all she would do was play on that piano.

WINING BOY: Just get up in the morning, get all dressed up and sit down and play on that piano. 110

DOAKER: Alright. Time go along. Time go along. Miss Ophelia got to missing my grandmother . . . the way she would cook and clean the house and talk to her and what not. And she missed having my daddy around the house to fetch things for her. So she asked to see if maybe she could trade back that piano and get her niggers back. Mr. Nolander said no. Said a deal was a deal. Him and Sutter had a big falling out about it and Miss Ophelia took sick to the bed. Wouldn't get out of the bed in the morning. She just lay there. The doctor said she was wasting away.

WINING BOY: That's when Sutter called our granddaddy up to the house.

DOAKER: Now, our granddaddy's name was Boy Willie. That's who Boy Willie's named after . . . only they called him Willie Boy. Now, he was a worker of wood. He could make you anything you wanted out of wood. He'd make you a desk. A table. A lamp. Anything you wanted. Them white fellows around there used to come up to Mr. Sutter and get him to make all kinds of things for them. Then they'd pay Mr. Sutter a nice price. See, everything my granddaddy made Mr. Sutter owned cause he owned him. That's why when Mr. Nolander offered to buy him to keep the family together Mr. Sutter wouldn't sell him. Told Mr. Nolander he didn't have enough money to buy him. Now . . . am I telling it right, Wining Boy?

WINING BOY: You telling it.

DOAKER: Sutter called him up to the house and told him to carve my grandmother and my daddy's picture on the piano for Miss Ophelia. And he took and carved this . . . 115

(DOAKER *crosses over to the piano.*)

See that right there? That's my grandmother Berniece. She looked just like that. And he put a picture of my daddy when he wasn't nothing but a little boy the way he remembered him. He made them up out of his memory. Only thing . . . he didn't stop there. He carved all this. He got a picture of his mama . . . Mama Esther . . . and his daddy, Boy Charles.

WINING BOY: That was the first Boy Charles.

DOAKER: Then he put on the side here all kinds of things. See that? That's when him and Mama Berniece got married. They called it jumping the broom. That's how you got married in them days. Then he got here when my daddy was born . . . and here he got Mama Esther's funeral . . . and down here he got Mr. Nolander taking Mama Berniece and my daddy away down to his place in Georgia. He got all kinds of things what happened with our family. When Mr. Sutter seen the piano with all them carvings on it he got mad. He didn't ask for all that. But see . . . there wasn't nothing he could do about it. When Miss Ophelia seen it . . . she got excited. Now she had her piano and her niggers too. She took back to playing it and played on it right up till the day she died. Alright . . . now see, our brother Boy Charles . . . that's Berniece and Boy Willie's daddy . . . he was the oldest of us three boys. He's dead now. But he would have been fifty-seven if he had lived. He died in 1911 when he was thirty-one years old. Boy Charles used to talk about that piano all the time. He never could get it off his mind. Two or three months go by and the be talking about it again. He be talking about taking it out of Sutter's house. Say it was the story of our whole family and as long as Sutter had it . . . he had us. Say we was still in slavery. Me and Wining Boy tried to talk him out of it but it wouldn't do any good. Soon as he quiet down about it he'd start up again. We seen where he wasn't gonna get it off his mind . . . so, on the Fourth of July, 1911 . . . when Sutter was at the picnic what the county give every year . . . me and Wining Boy went on down there with him and took that piano out of Sutter's house. We put it on a wagon and me and Wining Boy carried it over into the next county with Mama Ola's people. Boy Charles decided to stay around there and wait until Sutter got home to make it look like business as usual.

    Now, I don't know what happened when Sutter came home and found that piano gone. But somebody went up to Boy Charles's house and set it on fire. But he wasn't in there. He must have seen them coming cause he went down and caught the 3:57 Yellow Dog. He didn't know they was gonna come down and stop the train. Stopped the train and found Boy Charles in the boxcar with four of them hobos. Must have got mad when they couldn't find the piano cause they set the boxcar afire and killed everybody. Now, nobody know who done that. Some people say it was Sutter cause it was his piano. Some people say it was Sheriff Carter. Some people say it was Robert Smith and Ed Saunders. But don't nobody know for sure. It was about two months after that that Ed Saunders fell down his well. Just upped and fell down his well for no reason. People say it was the ghost of them men who burned up in the boxcar that pushed him in his well. They started calling them the Ghosts of the Yellow Dog. Now, that's how all that got started and that why we say Berniece ain't gonna sell that piano. Cause her daddy died over it.

BOY WILLIE: All that's in the past. If my daddy had seen where he could have traded that piano in for some land of his own, it wouldn't be sitting up here now. He spent his whole life farming on somebody else's land. I ain't gonna do that. See, he couldn't do no better. When he come along he ain't had nothing he could build on. His daddy ain't had nothing to give him. The only thing my daddy had to give me was that piano. And he died over giving me that. I ain't gonna let it sit up there and rot without trying to do something with it. If

Berniece can't see that, then I'm gonna go ahead and sell my half. And you and Wining Boy know I'm right.

DOAKER: Ain't nobody said nothing about who's right and who's wrong. I was just telling the man about the piano. I was telling him why we say Berniece ain't gonna sell it.

LYMON: Yeah, I can see why you say that now. I told Boy Willie he ought to stay up 120 here with me.

BOY WILLIE: You stay! I'm going back! That's what I'm gonna do with my life! Why I got to come up here and learn to do something I don't know how to do when I already know how to farm? You stay up here and make your own way if that's what you want to do. I'm going back and live my life the way I want to live it.

(WINING BOY *gets up and crosses to the piano.*)

WINING BOY: Let's see what we got here. I ain't played on this thing for a while.

DOAKER: You can stop telling that. You was playing on it the last time you was through here. We couldn't get you off of it. Go on and play something.

(WINING BOY *sits down at the piand and plays and sings. The song is one which has put many dimes and quarters in his pocket, long ago, in dimly remembered towns and way stations. He plays badly, without hesitation, and sings in a forceful voice.*)

WINING BOY: (*Singing.*)

> I am a rambling gambling man
> I gambled in many towns
> I rambled this wide world over
> I rambled this world around
> I had my ups and downs in life
> And bitter times I saw
> But I never knew what misery was
> Till I lit on old Arkansas.
>
> I started out one morning
> to meet that early train
> He said, "You better work for me
> I have some land to drain.
> I'll give you fifty cents a day,
> Your washing, board and all
> And you shall be a different man
> In the state of Arkansas."
>
> I worked six months for the rascal
> Joe Herrin was his name
> He fed me old corn dodgers
> They was hard as any rock
> My tooth is all got loosened
> And my knees begin to knock
> That was the kind of hash I got
> In the state of Arkansas.

Traveling man
I've traveled all around this world
Traveling man
I've traveled from land to land
Traveling man
I've traveled all around this world
Well it ain't no use
writing no news
I'm a traveling man.

(The door opens and BERNIECE *enters with* MARETHA.*)*

BERNIECE: Is that . . . Lord, I know that ain't Wining Boy sitting there.   125
WINING BOY: Hey, Berniece.
BERNIECE: You all had this planned. You and Boy Willie had this planned.
WINING BOY: I didn't know he was gonna be here. I'm on my way down home. I
   stopped by to see you and Doaker first.
DOAKER: I told the nigger he left out of here with that sack of money, we thought
   we might never see him again. Boy Willie say he wasn't gonna see him till he
   got broke. I looked up and seen him sitting on the doorstep asking for two
   dollars. Look at him laughing. He know it's the truth.
BERNIECE: Boy Willie, I didn't see that truck out there. I thought you was out   130
   selling watermelons.
BOY WILLIE: We done sold them all. Sold the truck too.
BERNIECE: I don't want to go through none of your stuff. I done told you to go
   back where you belong.
BOY WILLIE: I was just teasing you, woman. You can't take no teasing?
BERNIECE: Wining Boy, when you get here?
WINING BOY: A little while ago. I took the train from Kansas City.   135
BERNIECE: Let me go upstairs and change and then I'll cook you something to eat.
BOY WILLIE: You ain't cooked me nothing when I come.
BERNIECE: Boy Willie, go on and leave me alone. Come on, Maretha, get up here
   and change your clothes before you get them dirty.

*(*BERNIECE *exits up the stairs, followed by* MARETHA.*)*

WINING BOY: Maretha sure getting big, ain't she, Doaker. And just as pretty as she
   want to be. I didn't know Crawley had it in him.

*(*BOY WILLIE *crosses to the piano.)*

BOY WILLIE: Hey, Lymon . . . get up on the other side of this piano and let me see   140
   something.
WINING BOY: Boy Willie, what is you doing?
BOY WILLIE: I'm seeing how heavy this piano is. Get up over there, Lymon.
WINING BOY: Go on and leave that piano alone. You ain't taking that piano out of
   here and selling it.
BOY WILLIE: Just as soon as I get them watermelons out that truck.
WINING BOY: Well, I got something to say about that.   145
BOY WILLIE: This my daddy's piano.
WINING BOY: He ain't took it by himself. Me and Doaker helped him.

BOY WILLIE: He died by himself. Where was you and Doaker at then? Don't come telling me nothing about this piano. This is me and Berniece's piano. Am I right, Doaker?

DOAKER: Yeah, you right.

BOY WILLIE: Let's see if we can lift it up, Lymon. Get a good grip on it and pick it 150
up on your end. Ready? Lift!

(As they start to move the piano, the sound of SUTTER's GHOST *is heard.* DOAKER *is the only one to hear it. With difficulty they move the piano a little bit so it is out of place.)*

BOY WILLIE: What you think?

LYMON: It's heavy . . . but you can move it. Only it ain't gonna be easy.

BOY WILLIE: It wasn't that heavy to me. Okay, let's put it back.

(The sound of SUTTER's GHOST *is heard again. They all hear it as* BERNIECE *enters on the stairs.)*

BERNIECE: Boy Willie . . . you gonna play around with me one too many times. And then God's gonna bless you and West is gonna dress you. Now set that piano back over there. I done told you a hundred times I ain't selling that piano.

BOY WILLIE: I'm trying to get me some land, woman. I need that piano to get me 155
some money so I can buy Sutter's land.

BERNIECE: Money can't buy what that piano cost. You can't sell your soul for money. It won't go with the buyer. It'll shrivel and shrink to know that you ain't taken on to it. But it won't go with the buyer.

BOY WILLIE: I ain't talking about all that, woman. I ain't talking about selling my soul. I'm talking about trading that piece of wood for some land. Get something under your feet. Land the only thing God ain't making no more of. You can always get you another piano. I'm talking about some land. What you get something out the ground from. That's what I'm talking about. You can't do nothing with that piano but sit up there and look at it.

BERNIECE: That's just what I'm gonna do. Wining Boy, you want me to fry you some pork chops?

BOY WILLIE: Now, I'm gonna tell you the way I see it. The only thing that make that piano worth something is them carvings Papa Willie Boy put on there. That's what make it worth something. That was my great-grandaddy. Papa Boy Charles brought that piano into the house. Now, I'm supposed to build on what they left me. You can't do nothing with that piano sitting up here in the house. That's just like if I let them watermelons sit out there and rot. I'd be a fool. Alright now, if you say to me, Boy Willie, I'm using that piano. I give out lessons on it and that help me make my rent or whatever. Then that be something else. I'd have to go on and say, well, Berniece using that piano. She building on it. Let her go on and use it. I got to find another way to get Sutter's land. But Doaker say you ain't touched that piano the whole time it's been up here. So why you wanna stand in my way? See, you just looking at the sentimental value. See, that's good. That's alright. I take my hat off whenever somebody say my daddy's name. But I ain't gonna be no fool about no sentimental value. You can sit up here and look at the piano for the next hundred years and it's just gonna be a piano. You can't make more than that. Now I want to get Sutter's land with that piano. I get Sutter's land and I can go down and cash in the crop and get my seed. As long as I got the land and the seed then I'm alright. I can always get me a little something else. Cause that land give back to you. I can make me another crop and cash that in. I still got the land and the seed. But that piano don't put out nothing else. You ain't got nothing working for you. Now, the kind of man my daddy was he would have understood that. I'm sorry you can't see it that way. But that's why I'm gonna take that piano out of here and sell it.

BERNIECE: You ain't taking that piano out of my house.   160

(She crosses to the piano.)

Look at this piano. Look at it. Mama Ola polished this piano with her tears for seventeen years. For seventeen years she rubbed on it till her hands bled. Then she rubbed the blood in . . . mixed it up with the rest of the blood on it. Every day that God breathed life into her body she rubbed and cleaned and polished and prayed over it. "Play something for me, Berniece. Play something for me, Berniece." Every day. "I cleaned it up for you, play something for me, Berniece." You always talking about your daddy but you ain't never stopped to look at what his foolishness cost your mama. Seventeen years' worth of cold nights and an empty bed. For what? For a piano? For a piece of wood? To get even with somebody? I look at you and you're all the same. You, Papa Boy Charles, Wining Boy, Doaker, Crawley . . . you're all alike. All this thieving and killing and thieving and killing. And what it ever lead to? More killing and more thieving. I ain't never seen it come to nothing. People getting burned up. People getting shot. People falling down their wells. It don't never stop.

DOAKER: Come on now, Berniece, ain't no need in getting upset.

BOY WILLIE: I done a little bit of stealing here and there, but I ain't never killed nobody. I can't be speaking for nobody else. You all got to speak for yourself, but I ain't never killed nobody.

BERNIECE: You killed Crawley just as sure as if you pulled the trigger.

BOY WILLIE: See, that's ignorant. That's downright foolish for you to say something like that. You ain't doing nothing but showing your ignorance. If the nigger was here I'd whup his ass for getting me and Lymon shot at.

BERNIECE: Crawley ain't knew about the wood.   165

BOY WILLIE: We told the man about the wood. Ask Lymon. He knew all about the wood. He seen we was sneaking it. Why else we gonna be out there at night? Don't come telling me Crawley ain't knew about the wood. Them fellows come up on us and Crawley tried to bully them. Me and Lymon seen the sheriff with them and give in. Wasn't no sense in getting killed over fifty dollars' worth of wood.

BERNIECE: Crawley ain't knew you stole that wood.

BOY WILLIE: We ain't stole no wood. Me and Lymon was hauling wood for Jim Miller and keeping us a little bit on the side. We dumped our little bit down there by the creek till we had enough to make a load. Some fellows seen us and we figured we better get it before they did. We come up there and got Crawley to help us load it. Figured we'd cut him in. Crawley trying to keep the wolf from his door . . . we was trying to help him.

LYMON: Me and Boy Willie told him about the wood. We told him some fellows might be trying to beat us to it. He say let me go back and get my thirty-eight. That's what caused all the trouble.

BOY WILLIE: If Crawley ain't had the gun he'd be alive today.   170

LYMON: We had it about half loaded when they come up on us. We seen the sheriff with them and we tried to get away. We ducked around near the bend in the creek . . . but they was down there too. Boy Willie say let's give in. But Crawley pulled out his gun and started shooting. That's when they started shooting back.

BERNIECE: All I know is Crawley would be alive if you hadn't come up there and got him.

BOY WILLIE: I ain't had nothing to do with Crawley getting killed. That was his own fault.

BERNIECE: Crawley's dead and in the ground and you still walking around here eating. That's all I know. He went off to load some wood with you and ain't never come back.

BOY WILLIE: I told you, woman . . . I ain't had nothing to do with . . .   175

BERNIECE: He ain't here, is he? He ain't here!

(BERNIECE hits BOY WILLIE.)

I said he ain't here. Is he?

(BERNIECE continues to hit BOY WILLIE, who doesn't move to defend himself, other than back up and turning his head so that most of the blows fall on his chest and arms.)

DOAKER: *(Grabbing BERNIECE.)* Come on, Berniece . . . let it go, it ain't his fault.

BERNIECE: He ain't here, is he? Is he?

BOY WILLIE: I told you I ain't responsible for Crawley.

BERNIECE: He ain't here.   180

BOY WILLIE: Come on now, Berniece . . . don't do this now. Doaker get her. I ain't had nothing to do with Crawley . . .

BERNIECE: You come up there and got him!

BOY WILLIE: I done told you now. Doaker, get her. I ain't playing.

DOAKER: Come on. Berniece.

(MARETHA is heard screaming upstairs. It is a scream of stark terror.)

MARETHA: Mama! . . . Mama!   185

(The lights go down to black. End of Act One.)

Act 2

Scene 1

(The lights come up on the kitchen. It is the following morning. DOAKER is ironing the pants to his uniform. He has a pot cooking on the stove at the same time. He is singing a song. The song provides him with the rhythm for his work and he moves about the kitchen with the ease born of many years as a railroad cook.)

DOAKER:

Gonna leave Jackson Mississippi
and go to Memphis
and double back to Jackson
Come on down to Hattiesburg
Change cars on the Y. D.

coming through the territory to
Meridian
and Meridian to Greenville
and Greenville to Memphis
I'm on my way and I know where

Change cars on the Katy
Leaving Jackson
and going through Clarksdale
Hello Winona!
Courtland!
Bateville!
Como!
Senitobia!
Lewisberg!
Sunflower!
Glendora!
Sharkey!
And double back to Jackson
Hello Greenwood
I'm on my way Memphis
Clarksdale
Moorhead
Indianola
Can a highball pass through?
Highball on through sir
Grand Carson!
Thirty First Street Depot
Fourth Street Depot
Memphis!

(**WINING BOY** *enters carrying a suit of clothes.*)

DOAKER: I thought you took that suit to the pawnshop?

WINING BOY: I went down there and the man tell me the suit is too old. Look at this suit. This is one hundred percent silk! How a silk suit gonna get too old? I know what it was he just didn't want to give me five dollars for it. Best he wanna give me is three dollars. I figure a silk suit is worth five dollars all over the world. I wasn't gonna part with it for no three dollars so I brought it back.

DOAKER: They got another pawnshop up on Wylie.

WINING BOY: I carried it up there. He say he don't take no clothes. Only thing he 5 take is guns and radios. Maybe a guitar or two. Where's Berniece?

DOAKER: Berniece still at work. Boy Willie went down there to meet Lymon this morning. I guess they got that truck fixed, they been out there all day and ain't come back yet. Maretha scared to sleep up there now. Berniece don't know, but I seen Sutter before she did.

WINING BOY: Say what?

DOAKER: About three weeks ago. I had just come back from down there. Sutter couldn't have been dead more than three days. He was sitting over there at the piano. I come out to go to work . . . and he was sitting right there. Had his hand on top of his head just like Berniece said. I believe he broke his neck when he fell in the well. I kept quiet about it. I didn't see no reason to upset Berniece.

WINING BOY: Did he say anything? Did he say he was looking for Boy Willie?

DOAKER: He was just sitting there. He ain't said nothing. I went on out the door and left him sitting there. I figure as long as he was on the other side of the room everything be alright. I don't know what I would have done if he had started walking toward me. 10

WINING BOY: Berniece say he was calling Boy Willie's name.

DOAKER: I ain't heard him say nothing. He was just sitting there when I seen him. But I don't believe Boy Willie pushed him in the well. Sutter here cause of that piano. I heard him playing on it one time. I thought it was Berniece but then she don't play that kind of music. I come out here and ain't seen nobody, but them piano keys was moving a mile a minute. Berniece need to go on and get rid of it. It ain't done nothing but cause trouble.

WINING BOY: I agree with Berniece. Boy Charles ain't took it to give it back. He took it cause he figure he had more right to it than Sutter did. If Sutter can't understand that . . . then that's just the way that go. Sutter dead and in the ground . . . don't care where his ghost is. He can hover around and play on the piano all he want. I want to see him carry it out the house. That's what I want to see. What time Berniece get home? I don't see how I let her get away from me this morning.

DOAKER: You up there sleep. Berniece leave out of here early in the morning. She out there in Squirrel Hill cleaning house for some bigshot down there at the steel mill. They don't like you to come late. You come late they won't give you your carfare. What kind of business you got with Berniece?

WINING BOY: My business. I ain't asked you what kind of business you got. 15

DOAKER: Berniece ain't got no money. If that's why you was trying to catch her. She having a hard enough time trying to get by as it is. If she go ahead and marry Avery . . . he working every day . . . she go ahead and marry him they could do alright for themselves. But as it stands she ain't got no money.

WINING BOY: Well, let me have five dollars.

DOAKER: I just give you a dollar before you left out of here. You ain't gonna take my five dollars out there and gamble and drink it up.

WINING BOY: Aw, nigger, give me five dollars. I'll give it back to you.

DOAKER: You wasn't looking to give me five dollars when you had that sack of money. You wasn't looking to throw nothing my way. Now you wanna come in here and borrow five dollars. If you going back with Boy Willie you need to be trying to figure out how you gonna get train fare. 20

WINING BOY: That's why I need the five dollars. If I had five dollars I could get me some money.

(DOAKER *goes into his pocket.*)

Make it seven.

DOAKER: You take this five dollars . . . and you bring my money back here too.

(BOY WILLIE and LYMON enter. They are happy and excited. They have money in all of their pockets and are anxious to count it.)

DOAKER: How'd you do out there?

BOY WILLIE: They was lining up for them.

LYMON: Me and Boy Willie couldn't sell them fast enough. Time we got one sold   25
we'd sell another.

BOY WILLIE: I seen what was happening and told Lymon to up the price on them.

LYMON: Boy Willie say charge them a quarter more. They didn't care. A couple of
people give me a dollar and told me to keep the change.

BOY WILLIE: One fellow bought five. I say now what he gonna do with five
watermelons? He can't eat them all. I sold him the five and asked him did he
want to buy five more.

LYMON: I ain't never seen nobody snatch a dollar fast as Boy Willie.

BOY WILLIE: One lady asked me say, "Is they sweet?" I told her say, "Lady,   30
where we grow these watermelons we put sugar in the ground." You know,
she believed me. Talking about she had never heard of that before. Lymon
was laughing his head off. I told her, "Oh, yeah, we put the sugar right in the
ground with the seed." She say, "Well, give me another one." Them white folks
is something else . . . ain't they, Lymon?

LYMON: Soon as you holler watermelons they come right out their door. Then they
go and get their neighbors. Look like they having a contest to see who can buy
the most.

WINING BOY: I got something for Lymon.

(WINING BOY goes to get his suit. BOY WILLIE and LYMON continue to count their money.)

BOY WILLIE: I know you got more than that. You ain't sold all them watermelons
for that little bit of money.

LYMON: I'm still looking. That ain't all you got either. Where's all them quarters?

BOY WILLIE: You let me worry about the quarters. Just put the money on the table.   35

WINING BOY: *(Entering with his suit.)* Look here, Lymon . . . see this? Look at his
eyes getting big. He ain't never seen a suit like this. This is one hundred percent
silk. Go ahead . . . put it on. See if it fit you.

(LYMON tries the suit coat on.)

Look at that. Feel it. That's one hundred percent genuine silk. I got that in
Chicago. You can't get clothes like that nowhere but New York and Chicago.
You can't get clothes like that in Pittsburgh. These folks in Pittsburgh ain't
never seen clothes like that.

LYMON: This is nice, feel real nice and smooth.

WINING BOY: That's a fifty-five-dollar suit. That's the kind of suit the bigshots
wear. You need a pistol and a pocketful of money to wear that suit. I'll let you
have it for three dollars. The women will fall out their windows they see you in
a suit like that. Give me three dollars and go on and wear it down the street and
get you a woman.

BOY WILLIE: That looks nice, Lymon. Put the pants on. Let me see it with the
pants.

(LYMON begins to try on the pants.)

WINING BOY: Look at that . . . see how it fits you? Give me three dollars and go on 40
and take it. Look at that, Doaker . . . don't he look nice?

DOAKER: Yeah . . . that's a nice suit.

WINING BOY: Got a shirt to go with it. Cost you an extra dollar. Four dollars you
got the whole deal.

LYMON: How this look, Boy Willie?

BOY WILLIE: That look nice . . . if you like that kind of thing. I don't like them
dress-up kind of clothes. If you like it, look real nice.

WINING BOY: That's the kind of suit you need for up here in the North. 45

LYMON: Four dollars for everything? The suit and the shirt?

WINING BOY: That's cheap. I should be charging you twenty dollars. I give you a
break cause you a homeboy. That's the only way I let you have it for four dollars.

LYMON: *(Going into his pocket.)* Okay . . . here go the four dollars.

WINING BOY: You got some shoes? What size you wear?

LYMON: Size nine. 50

WINING BOY: That's what size I got! Size nine. I let you have them for three
dollars.

LYMON: Where they at? Let me see them.

WINING BOY: They real nice shoes, too. Got a nice tip to them. Got pointy toe just
like you want.

(WINING BOY *goes to get his shoes.*)

LYMON: Come on, Boy Willie, let's go out tonight. I wanna see what it looks like up
here. Maybe we go to a picture show. Hey, Doaker, they got picture shows up
here?

DOAKER: The Rhumba Theater. Right down there on Fullerton Street. Can't miss 55
it. Got the speakers outside on the sidewalk. You can hear it a block away. Boy
Willie know where it's at.

(DOAKER *exits into his room.*)

LYMON: Let's go to the picture show, Boy Willie. Let's go find some women.

BOY WILLIE: Hey, Lymon, how many of them watermelons would you say we got
left? We got just under a half a load . . . right?

LYMON: About that much. Maybe a little more.

BOY WILLIE: You think that piano will fit up in there?

LYMON: If we stack them watermelons you can sit it up in the front there. 60

BOY WILLIE: I'm gonna call that man tomorrow.

WINING BOY: *(Returns with his shoes.)* Here you go . . . size nine. Put them on.
Cost you three dollars. That's a Florsheim shoe. That's the kind Staggerlee wore.

LYMON: *(Trying on the shoes.)* You sure these size nine?

WINING BOY: You can look at my feet and see we wear the same size. Man, you
put on that suit and them shoes and you got something there. You ready for
whatever's out there. But is they ready for you? With them shoes on you be the
King of the Walk. Have everybody stop to look at your shoes. Wishing they
had a pair. I'll give you a break. Go on and take them for two dollars.

(LYMON *pays* WINING BOY *two dollars.*)

LYMON: Come on, Boy Willie . . . let's go find some women. I'm gonna go upstairs 65
and get ready. I'll be ready to go in a minute. Ain't you gonna get dressed?

BOY WILLIE: I'm gonna wear what I got on. I ain't dressing up for these city niggers.

(LYMON *exits up the stairs.)*

That's all Lymon think about is women.

WINING BOY: His daddy was the same way. I used to run around with him. I know his mama too. Two strokes back and I would have been his daddy! His daddy's dead now . . . but I got the nigger out of jail one time. They was fixing to name him Daniel and walk him through the Lion's Den. He got in a tussle with one of them white fellows and the sheriff lit on him like white on rice. That's how the whole thing come about between me and Lymon's mama. She knew me and his daddy used to run together and he got in jail and she went down there and took the sheriff a hundred dollars. Don't get me to lying about where she got it from. I don't know. The sheriff *looked at that hundred dollars and turned his nose up* Told her, say, "That ain't gonna do him no good. You got to put another hundred on top of that." She come up *there and got me where I was playing at this saloon* . . . said she had all but fifty dollars and asked me if I could help. Now the way I figured it . . . without that fifty dollars the sheriff was gonna turn him over to Parchman. The sheriff turn him over to Parchman it be three years before anybody see him again. Now I'm gonna say it right . . . I will give anybody fifty dollars to keep them out of jail for three years. I give her the fifty dollars and she told me to come over to the house. I ain't asked her. I figure if she was nice enough to invite me I ought to go. I ain't had to say a word. She invited me over just as nice. Say, "Why don't you come over to the house?" She ain't had to say nothing else. Them words rolled off her tongue just as nice. I went on down there and sat about three hours. Started to leave and changed my mind. She grabbed hold to me and say, "Baby, it's all night long." That was one of the shortest nights I have ever spent on this earth! I could have used another eight hours. Lymon's daddy didn't even say nothing to me when he got out. He just looked at me funny. He had a good notion something had happened between me an' her. L. D. Jackson. That was one bad-luck nigger. Got killed at some dance. Fellow walked in and shot him thinking he was somebody else.

(DOAKER *enters from his room.)*

Hey, Doaker, you remember L. D. Jackson?

DOAKER: That's Lymon's daddy. That was one bad-luck nigger.

BOY WILLIE: Look like you ready to railroad some.

DOAKER: Yeah, I got to make that run.

70

(LYMON *enters from the stairs. He is dressed in his new suit and shoes, to which he has added a cheap straw hat.)*

LYMON: How I look?

WINING BOY: You look like a million dollars. Don't he look good, Doaker? Come on, let's play some cards. You wanna play some cards?

BOY WILLIE: We ain't gonna play no cards with you. Me and Lymon gonna find some women. Hey, Lymon, don't play no cards with Wining Boy. He'll take all your money.

WINING BOY: *(To* LYMON.*)* You got a magic suit there. You can get you a woman easy with that suit . . . but you got to know the magic words. You know the magic words to get you a woman?

LYMON: I just talk to them to see if I like them and they like me. 75

WINING BOY: You just walk right up to them and say, "If you got the harbor I got the ship." If that don't work ask them if you can put them in your pocket. The first thing they gonna say is, "It's too small." That's when you look them dead in the eye and say, "Baby, ain't nothing small about me." If that don't work then you move on to another one. Am I telling him right, Doaker?

DOAKER: That man don't need you to tell him nothing about no women. These women these days ain't gonna fall for that kind of stuff. You got to buy them a present. That's what they looking for these days.

BOY WILLIE: Come on, I'm ready. You ready, Lymon? Come on, let's go find some women.

WINING BOY: Here, let me walk out with you, I wanna see the women fall out their window when they see Lymon.
(They all exit and the lights go down on the scene.)

Scene 2
(The lights come up on the kitchen. It is late evening of the same day. BERNIECE *has set a tub for her bath in the kitchen. She is heating up water on the stove. There is a knock at the door.)*

BERNIECE: Who is it?

AVERY: It's me, Avery.

(BERNIECE opens the door and lets him in.)

BERNIECE: Avery, come on in. I was just fixing to take my bath.

AVERY: Where Boy Willie? I see that truck out there almost empty. They done sold almost all them watermelons.

BERNIECE: They was gone when I come home. I don't know where they went off 5 to. Boy Willie around here about to drive me crazy.

AVERY: They sell them watermelons . . . he'll be gone soon.

BERNIECE: What Mr. Cohen say about letting you have the place?

AVERY: He say he'll let me have it for thirty dollars a month. I talked him out of thirty-five and he say he'll let me have it for thirty.

BERNIECE: That's a nice spot next to Benny Diamond's store.

AVERY: Berniece . . . I be at home and I get to thinking you up here an' I'm down 10 there. I get to thinking how that look to have a preacher that ain't married. It makes for a better congregation if the preacher was settled down and married.

BERNIECE: Avery . . . not now. I was fixing to take my bath.

AVERY: You know how I feel about you, Berniece. Now . . . I done got the place from Mr. Cohen. I get the money from the bank and I can fix it up real nice. They give me a ten cents a hour raise down there on the job . . . now Berniece, I ain't got much in the way of comforts. I got a hole in my pockets near about as far as money is concerned. I ain't never found no way through life to a woman I care about like I care about you. I need that. I need somebody on my bond side. I need a woman that fits in my hand.

BERNIECE: Avery, I ain't ready to get married now.

AVERY: You too young a woman to close up, Berniece.

BERNIECE: I ain't said nothing about closing up. I got a lot of woman left in me. 15

AVERY: Where's it at? When's the last time you looked at it?

BERNIECE: *(Stunned by his remark.)* That's a nasty thing to say. And you call yourself a preacher.

AVERY: Anytime I get anywhere near you . . . you push me away.

BERNIECE: I got enough on my hands with Maretha. I got enough people to love and take care of.

AVERY: Who you got to love you? Can't nobody get close enough to you. Doaker   20
can't half say nothing to you. You jump all over Boy Willie. Who you got to love you, Berniece?

BERNIECE: You trying to tell me a woman can't be nothing without a man. But you alright, huh? You can just walk out of here without me—without a woman—and still be a man. That's alright. Ain't nobody gonna ask you, "Avery, who you got to love you?" That's alright for you. But everybody gonna be worried about Berniece. "How Berniece gonna take care of herself? How she gonna raise that child without a man? Wonder what she do with herself. How she gonna live like that?" Everybody got all kinds of questions for Berniece. Everybody telling me I can't be a woman unless I got a man. Well, you tell me, Avery—you know—how much woman am I?

AVERY: It wasn't me, Berniece. You can't blame me for nobody else. I'll own up to my own shortcomings. But you can't blame me for Crawley or nobody else.

BERNIECE: I ain't blaming nobody for nothing. I'm just stating the facts.

AVERY: How long you gonna carry Crawley with you, Berniece? It's been over three years. At some point you got to let go and go on. Life's got all kinds of twists and turns. That don't mean you stop living. That don't mean you cut yourself off from life. You can't go through life carrying Crawley's ghost with you. Crawley's been dead three years. Three years, Berniece.

BERNIECE: I know how long Crawley's been dead. You ain't got to tell me that. I   25
just ain't ready to get married right now.

AVERY: What is you ready for, Berniece? You just gonna drift along from day to day. Life is more than making it from one day to another. You gonna look up one day and it's all gonna be past you. Life's gonna be gone out of your hands—there won't be enough to make nothing with. I'm standing here now, Berniece—but I don't know how much longer I'm gonna be standing here waiting on you.

BERNIECE: Avery, I told you . . . when you get your church we'll sit down and talk about this. I got too many other things to deal with right now. Boy Willie and the piano . . . and Sutter's ghost. I thought I might have been seeing things, but Maretha done seen Sutter's ghost, too.

AVERY: When this happen, Berniece?

BERNIECE: Right after I came home yesterday. Me and Boy Willie was arguing about the piano and Sutter's ghost was standing at the top of the stairs. Maretha scared to sleep up there now. Maybe if you bless the house he'll go away.

AVERY: I don't know, Berniece. I don't know if I should fool around with something   30
like that.

BERNIECE: I can't have Maretha scared to go to sleep up there. Seem like if you bless the house he would go away.

AVERY: You might have to be a special kind of preacher to do something like that.

BERNIECE: I keep telling myself when Boy Willie leave he'll go on and leave with him. I believe Boy Willie pushed him in the well.

AVERY: That's been going on down there a long time. The Ghosts of the Yellow Dog been pushing people in their wells long before Boy Willie got grown.

BERNIECE: Somebody down there pushing them people in their wells. They ain't just upped and fell. Ain't no wind pushed nobody in their well. 35

AVERY: Oh, I don't know. God works in mysterious ways.

BERNIECE: He ain't pushed nobody in their wells.

AVERY: He caused it to happen. God is the Great Causer. He can do anything. He parted the Red-Sea. He say I will smite my enemies. Reverend Thompson used to preach on the Ghosts of the Yellow Dog as the hand of God.

BERNIECE: I don't care who preached what. Somebody down there pushing them people in their wells. Somebody like Boy Willie. I can see him doing something like that. You ain't gonna tell me that Sutter just upped and fell in his well. I believe Boy Willie pushed him so he could get his land.

AVERY: What Doaker say about Boy Willie selling the piano? 40

BERNIECE: Doaker don't want no part of that piano. He ain't never wanted no part of it. He blames himself for not staying behind with Papa Boy Charles. He washed his hands of that piano a long time ago. He didn't want me to bring it up here—but I wasn't gonna leave it down there.

AVERY: Well, it seems to me somebody ought to be able to talk to Boy Willie.

BERNIECE: You can't talk to Boy Willie. He been that way all his life. Mama Ola had her hands full trying to talk to him. He don't listen to nobody. He just like my daddy. He get his mind fixed on something and can't nobody turn him from it.

AVERY: You ought to start a choir at the church. Maybe if he seen you was doing something with it—if you told him you was gonna put it in my church—maybe he'd see it different. You ought to put it down in the church and start a choir. The Bible say "Make a joyful noise unto the Lord." Maybe if Boy Willie see you was doing something with it he'd see it different.

BERNIECE: I done told you I don't play on that piano. Ain't no need in you to keep 45 talking this choir stuff. When my mama died I shut the top on that piano and I ain't never opened it since. I was only playing it for her. When my daddy died seem like all her life went into that piano. She used to have me playing on it . . . had Miss Eula come in and teach me . . . say when I played it she could hear my daddy talking to her. I used to think them pictures came alive and walked through the house. Sometime late at night I could hear my mama talking to them. I said that wasn't gonna happen to me. I don't play that piano cause I don't want to wake them spirits. They never be walking around in this house.

AVERY: You got to put all that behind you, Berniece.

BERNIECE: I got Maretha playing on it. She don't know nothing about it. Let her go on and be a schoolteacher or something. She don't have to carry all of that with her. She got a chance I didn't have. I ain't gonna burden her with that piano.

AVERY: You got to put all of that behind you, Berniece. That's the same thing like Crawley. Everybody got stones in their passway. You got to step over them or walk around them. You picking them up and carrying them with you. All you got to do is set them down by the side of the road. You ain't got to carry them with you. You can walk over there right now and play that piano. You can walk over there right now and God will walk over there with you. Right now you can set that sack of stones down by the side of the road and walk away from it. You don't have to carry it with you. You can do it right now.

(AVERY crosses over to the piano and raises the lid.)

Come on, Berniece . . . set it down and walk away from it. Come on, play "Old Ship of Zion." Walk over here and claim it as an instrument of the Lord. You can walk over here right now and make it into a celebration.

(BERNIECE moves toward the piano.)

BERNIECE: Avery . . . I done told you I don't want to play that piano. Now or no other time.

AVERY: The Bible say, "The Lord is my refuge . . . and my strength!" With the strength of God you can put the past behind you, Berniece. With the strength of God you can do anything! God got a bright tomorrow. God don't ask what you done . . . God ask what you gonna do. The strength of God can move mountains! God's got a bright tomorrow for you . . . all you got to do is walk over here and claim it. 50

BERNIECE: Avery, just go on and let me finish my bath. I'll see you tomorrow.

AVERY: Okay, Berniece. I'm gonna go home. I'm gonna go home and read up on my Bible. And tomorrow . . . if the good Lord give me strength tomorrow . . . I'm gonna come by and bless the house . . . and show you the power of the Lord.

(AVERY crosses to the door.)

It's gonna be alright, Berniece. God say he will soothe the troubled waters. I'll come by tomorrow and bless the house.

(The lights go down to black.)

Scene 3
(Several hours later. The house is dark. BERNIECE has retired for the night. BOY WILLIE enters the darkened house with GRACE.)

BOY WILLIE: Come on in. This my sister's house. My sister live here. Come on, I ain't gonna bite you.

GRACE: Put some light on. I can't see.

BOY WILLIE: You don't need to see nothing, baby. This here is all you need to see. All you need to do is see me. If you can't see me you can feel me in the dark. How's that, sugar?

(He attempts to kiss her.)

GRACE: Go on now . . . wait!

BOY WILLIE: Just give me one little old kiss. 5

GRACE: *(Pushing him away.)* Come on, now. Where I'm gonna sleep at?

BOY WILLIE: We got to sleep out here on the couch. Come on, my sister don't mind. Lymon come back he just got to sleep on the floor. He run off with Dolly somewhere he better stay there. Come on, sugar.

GRACE: Wait now . . . you ain't told me nothing about no couch. I thought you had a bed. Both of us can't sleep on that little old couch.

BOY WILLIE: It don't make no difference. We can sleep on the floor. Let Lymon sleep on the couch.

GRACE: You ain't told me nothing about no couch.

BOY WILLIE: What difference it make? You just wanna be with me.

GRACE: I don't want to be with you on no couch. Ain't you got no bed?

BOY WILLIE: You don't need no bed, woman. My granddaddy used to take women on the backs of horses. What you need a bed for? You just want to be with me.

GRACE: You sure is country. I didn't know you was this country.

BOY WILLIE: There's a lot of things you don't know about me. Come on, let me show you what this country boy can do.

GRACE: Let's go to my place. I got a room with a bed if Leroy don't come back there.

BOY WILLIE: Who's Leroy? You ain't said nothing about no Leroy.

GRACE: He used to be my man. He ain't coming back. He gone off with some other gal.

BOY WILLIE: You let him have your key?

GRACE: He ain't coming back.

BOY WILLIE: Did you let him have your key?

GRACE: He got a key but he ain't coming back. He took off with some other gal.

BOY WILLIE: I don't wanna go nowhere he might come. Let's stay here. Come on, sugar.

(He pulls her over to the couch.)

Let me heist your hood and check your oil. See if your battery needs charged.

(He pulls her to him. They kiss and tug at each other's clothing. In their anxiety they knock over a lamp.)

BERNIECE: Who's that . . . Wining Boy?

BOY WILLIE: It's me . . . Boy Willie. Go on back to sleep. Everything's alright.

(To GRACE.)

That's my sister. Everything's alright, Berniece. Go on back to sleep.

BERNIECE: What you doing down there? What you done knocked over?

BOY WILLIE: It wasn't nothing. Everything's alright. Go on back to sleep.

(To GRACE.)

That's my sister. We alright. She gone back to sleep.

(They begin to kiss. BERNIECE enters from the stairs dressed in a nightgown. She cuts on the light.)

BERNIECE: Boy Willie, what you doing down here?

BOY WILLIE: It was just that there lamp. It ain't broke. It's okay. Everything's alright. Go on back to bed.

BERNIECE: Boy Willie, I don't allow that in my house. You gonna have to take your company someplace else.

BOY WILLIE: It's alright. We ain't doing nothing. We just sitting here talking. This here is Grace. That's my sister Berniece.

BERNIECE: You know I don't allow that kind of stuff in my house.

BOY WILLIE: Allow what? We just sitting here talking.

BERNIECE: Well, your company gonna have to leave. Come back and talk in the morning.

BOY WILLIE: Go on back upstairs now.

BERNIECE: I got an eleven-year-old girl upstairs. I can't allow that around here.

BOY WILLIE: Ain't nobody said nothing about that. I told you we just talking.

GRACE: Come on . . . let's go to my place. Ain't nobody got to tell me to leave but once.

BOY WILLIE: You ain't got to be like that, Berniece.

BERNIECE: I'm sorry, Miss. But he know I don't allow that in here.   40

GRACE: You ain't got to tell me but once. I don't stay nowhere I ain't wanted.

BOY WILLIE: I don't know why you want to embarrass me in front of my company.

GRACE: Come on, take me home.

BERNIECE: Go on, Boy Willie. Just go on with your company.

> (BOY WILLIE *and* GRACE *exit.* BERNIECE *puts the light on in the kitchen and puts on the teakettle. Presently there is a knock at the door.* BERNIECE *goes to answer it.* BERNIECE *opens the door.* LYMON *enters.)*

LYMON: How you doing, Berniece? I thought you'd be asleep. Boy Willie been back   45
here?

BERNIECE: He just left out of here a minute ago.

LYMON: I went out to see a picture show and never got there. We always end up doing something else. I was with this woman she just wanted to drink up all my money. So I left her there and came back looking for Boy Willie.

BERNIECE: You just missed him. He just left out of here.

LYMON: They got some nice-looking women in this city. I'm gonna like it up here real good. I like seeing them with their dresses on. Got them high heels. I like that. Make them look like they real precious. Boy Willie met a real nice one today. I wish I had met her before he did.

BERNIECE: He come by here with some woman a little while ago. I told him to go   50
on and take all that out of my house.

LYMON: What she look like, the woman he was with? Was she a brown-skinned woman about this high? Nice and healthy? Got nice hips on her?

BERNIECE: She had on a red dress.

LYMON: That's her! That's Grace. She real nice. Laugh a lot. Lot of fun to be with. She don't be trying to put on. Some of these woman act like they the Queen of Sheba. I don't like them kind. Grace ain't like that. She real nice with herself.

BERNIECE: I don't know what she was like. He come in here all drunk knocking over the lamp, and making all kind of noise. I told them to take that somewhere else. I can't really say what she was like.

LYMON: She real nice. I seen her before he did. I was trying not to act like I seen   55
her. I wanted to look at her a while before I said something. She seen me when I come into the saloon. I tried to act like I didn't see her. Time I looked around Boy Willie was talking to her. She was talking to him kept looking at me. That's when her friend Dolly came. I asked her if she wanted to go to the picture show. She told me to buy her a drink while she thought about it. Next thing I knew she done had three drinks talking about she too tired to go. I bought her another drink, then I left. Boy Willie was gone and I thought he might have come back here. Doaker gone, huh? He say he had to make a trip.

BERNIECE: Yeah, he gone on his trip. This is when I can usually get me some peace and quiet, Maretha asleep.

LYMON: She look just like you. Got them big eyes. I remember her when she was in diapers.

BERNIECE: Time just keep on. It go on with or without you. She going on twelve.

LYMON: She sure is pretty. I like kids.

BERNIECE: Boy Willie say you staying . . . what you gonna do up here in this big 60
city? You thought about that?

LYMON: They never get me back down there. The sheriff looking for me. All
because they gonna try and make me work for somebody when I don't want to.
They gonna try and make me work for Stovall when he don't pay nothing. It
ain't like that up here. Up here you more or less do what you want to. I figure I
find me a job and try to get set up and then see what the year brings. I tried to
do that two or three times down there . . . but it never would work out. I was
always in the wrong place.

BERNIECE: This ain't a bad city once you get to know your way around.

LYMON: Up here is different. I'm gonna get me a job unloading boxcars or
something. One fellow told me say he know a place. I'm gonna go over there
with him next week. Me and Boy Willie finish selling them watermelons I'll
have enough money to hold me for a while. But I'm gonna go over there and see
what kind of jobs they have.

BERNIECE: You shouldn't have too much trouble finding a job. It's all in how you
present yourself. See now, Boy Willie couldn't get no job up here. Somebody
hire him they got a pack of trouble on their hands. Soon as they find that out
they fire him. He don't want to do nothing unless he do it his way.

LYMON: I know. I told him let's go to the picture show first and see if there was any 65
women down there. They might get tired of sitting at home and walk down to
the picture show. He say he wanna look around first. We never did get down
there. We tried a couple of places and then we went to this saloon where he met
Grace. I tried to meet her before he did but he beat me to her. We left Wining
Boy sitting down there running his mouth. He told me if I wear this suit I'd
find me a woman. He was almost right.

BERNIECE: You don't need to be out there in them saloons. Ain't no telling what
you liable to run into out there. This one liable to cut you as quick as that one
shoot you. You don't need to be out there. You start out that fast life you can't
keep it up. It makes you old quick. I don't know what them women out there be
thinking about.

LYMON: Mostly they be lonely and looking for somebody to spend the night with
them. Sometimes it matters who it is and sometimes it don't. I used to be the
same way. Now it got to matter. That's why I'm here now. Dolly liable not to
even recognize me if she sees me again. I don't like women like that. I like
my women to be with me in a nice and easy way. That way we can both enjoy
ourselves. The way I see it we the only two people like us in the world. We
got to see how we fit together. A woman that don't want to take the time to
do that I don't bother with. Used to. Used to bother with all of them. Then I
woke up one time with this woman and I didn't know who she was. She was
the prettiest woman I had ever seen in my life. I spent the whole night with her
and didn't even know it. I had never taken the time to look at her. I guess she
kinda knew I ain't never really looked at her. She must have known that cause
she ain't wanted to see me no more. If she had wanted to see me I believe we
might have got married. How come you ain't married? It seem like to me you
would be married. I remember Avery from down home. I used to call him plain

old Avery. Now he Reverend Avery. That's kinda funny about him becoming a preacher. I like when he told about how that come to him in a dream about them sheep people and them hobos. Nothing ever come to me in a dream like that. I just dream about women. Can't never seem to find the right one.

BERNIECE: She out there somewhere. You just got to get yourself ready to meet her. That's what I'm trying to do. Avery's alright. I ain't really got nobody in mind.

LYMON: I get me a job and a little place and get set up to where I can make a woman comfortable I might get married. Avery's nice. You ought to go ahead and get married. You be a preacher's wife you won't have to work. I hate living by myself. I didn't want to be no strain on my mama so I left home when I was about sixteen. Everything I tried seem like it just didn't work out. Now I'm trying this.

BERNIECE: You keep trying it'll work out for you.   70

LYMON: You ever go down there to the picture show?

BERNIECE: I don't go in for all that.

LYMON: Ain't nothing wrong with it. It ain't like gambling and sinning. I went to one down in Jackson once. It was fun.

BERNIECE: I just stay home most of the time. Take care of Maretha.

LYMON: It's getting kind of late. I don't know where Boy Willie went off to. He's   75
liable not to come back. I'm gonna take off these shoes. My feet hurt. Was you in bed? I don't mean to be keeping you up.

BERNIECE: You ain't keeping me up. I couldn't sleep after that Boy Willie woke me up.

LYMON: You got on that nightgown. I likes women when they wear them fancy nightclothes and all. It makes their skin look real pretty.

BERNIECE: I got this at the five-and-ten-cents store. It ain't so fancy.

LYMON: I don't too often get to see a woman dressed like that.

(There is a long pause. LYMON takes off his suit coat.)

Well, I'm gonna sleep here on the couch. I'm supposed to sleep on the floor but I don't reckon Boy Willie's coming back tonight. Wining Boy sold me this suit. Told me it was a magic suit. I'm gonna put it on again tomorrow. Maybe it bring me a woman like he say.

(He goes into his coat pocket and takes out a small bottle of perfume.)

I almost forgot I had this. Some man sold me this for a dollar. Say it come from Paris. This is the same kind of perfume the Queen of France wear. That's what he told me. I don't know if it's true or not. I smelled it. It smelled good to me. Here . . . smell it see if you like it. I was gonna give it to Dolly. But I didn't like her too much.

BERNIECE: *(Takes the bottle.)* It smells nice.   80

LYMON: I was gonna give it to Dolly if she had went to the picture with me. Go on, you take it.

BERNIECE: I can't take it. Here . . . go on you keep it. You'll find somebody to give it to.

LYMON: I wanna give it to you. Make you smell nice.

(He takes the bottle and puts perfume behind BERNIECE's ear.)

They tell me you supposed to put it right here behind your ear. Say if you put it there you smell nice all day.

(BERNIECE *stiffens at his touch.* LYMON *bends down to smell her.*)

There . . . you smell real good now.

(He kisses her neck.)

You smell real good for Lymon.

(He kisses her again. BERNIECE *returns the kiss, then breaks the embrace and crosses to the stairs. She turns and they look silently at each other.* LYMON *hands her the bottle of perfume.* BERNIECE *exits up the stairs.* LYMON *picks up his suit coat and strokes it lovingly with the full knowledge that it is indeed a magic suit. The lights go down on the scene.)*

Scene 4

(It is late the next morning. The lights come up on the parlor. LYMON *is asleep on the sofa.* BOY WILLIE *enters the front door.)*

BOY WILLIE: Hey, Lymon! Lymon, come on get up.

LYMON: Leave me alone.

BOY WILLIE: Come on, get up, nigger! Wake up, Lymon.

LYMON: What you want?

BOY WILLIE: Come on, let's go. I done called the man about the piano.   5

LYMON: What piano?

BOY WILLIE: *(Dumps* LYMON *on the floor.)* Come on, get up!

LYMON: Why you leave, I looked around and you was gone.

BOY WILLIE: I come back here with Grace, then I went looking for you. I figured you'd be with Dolly.

LYMON: She just want to drink and spend up your money. I come on back here   10
looking for you to see if you wanted to go to the picture show.

BOY WILLIE: I been up at Grace's house. Some nigger named Leroy come by but I had a chair up against the door. He got mad when he couldn't get in. He went off somewhere and I got out of there before he could come back. Berniece got mad when we came here.

LYMON: She say you was knocking over the lamp busting up the place.

BOY WILLIE: That was Grace doing all that.

LYMON: Wining Boy seen Sutter's ghost last night.

BOY WILLIE: Wining Boy's liable to see anything. I'm surprised he found the right   15
house. Come on, I done called the man about the piano.

LYMON: What he say?

BOY WILLIE: He say to bring it on out. I told him I was calling for my sister, Miss Berniece Charles. I told him some man wanted to buy it for eleven hundred dollars and asked him if he would go any better. He said yeah, he would give me eleven hundred and fifty dollars for it if it was the same piano. I described it to him again and he told me to bring it out.

LYMON: Why didn't you tell him to come and pick it up?

BOY WILLIE: I didn't want to have no problem with Berniece.

This way we just take it on out there and it be out the way. He want to charge twenty-five dollars to pick it up.

LYMON: You should have told him the man was gonna give you twelve hundred   20
for it.

BOY WILLIE: I figure I was taking a chance with that eleven hundred. If I had told him twelve hundred he might have run off. Now I wish I had told him twelve-fifty. It's hard to figure out white folks sometimes.

LYMON: You might have been able to tell him anything. White folks got a lot of money.

BOY WILLIE: Come on, let's get it loaded before Berniece come back. Get that end over there. All you got to do is pick it up on that side. Don't worry about this side. You wanna stretch you' back for a minute?

LYMON: I'm ready.

BOY WILLIE: Get a real good grip on it now.   25

(The sound of SUTTER's GHOST *is heard. They do not hear it.)*

LYMON: I got this end. You get that end.

BOY WILLIE: Wait till I say ready now. Alright. You got it good? You got a grip on it?

LYMON: Yeah, I got it. You lift up on that end.

BOY WILLIE: Ready? Lift!

(The piano will not budge.)

LYMON: Man, this piano is heavy! It's gonna take more than me and you to move   30
this piano.

BOY WILLIE: We can do it. Come on—we did it before.

LYMON: Nigger—you crazy! That piano weighs five hundred pounds!

BOY WILLIE: I got three hundred pounds of it! I know you can carry two hundred pounds! You be lifting them cotton sacks! Come on lift this piano!

(They try to move the piano again without success.)

LYMON: It's stuck. Something holding it.

BOY WILLIE: How the piano gonna be stuck? We just moved it. Slide you' end out.   35

LYMON: Naw—we gonna need two or three more people. How this big old piano get in the house?

BOY WILLIE: I don't know how it got in the house. I know how it's going out though! You get on this end. I'll carry three hundred and fifty pounds of it. All you got to do is slide your end out. Ready?

(They switch sides and try again without success. DOAKER *enters from his room as they try to push and shove it.)*

LYMON: Hey, Doaker . . . how this piano get in the house?

DOAKER: Boy Willie, what you doing?

BOY WILLIE: I'm carrying this piano out the house. What it look like I'm doing?   40
Come on, Lymon, let's try again.

DOAKER: Go on let the piano sit there till Berniece come home.

BOY WILLIE: You ain't got nothing to do with this, Doaker. This my business.

DOAKER: This is my house, nigger! I ain't gonna let you or nobody else carry nothing out of it. You ain't gonna carry nothing out of here without my permission!

BOY WILLIE: This is my piano. I don't need your permission to carry my belongings out of your house. This is mine. This ain't got nothing to do with you.

DOAKER: I say leave it over there till Berniece come home. She got part of it too. 45 Leave it set there till you see what she say.

BOY WILLIE: I don't care what Berniece say. Come on, Lymon. I got this side.

DOAKER: Go on and cut it half in two if you want to. Just leave Berniece's half sitting over there. I can't tell you what to do with your piano. But I can't let you take her half out of here.

BOY WILLIE: Go on, Doaker. You ain't got nothing to do with this. I don't want you starting nothing now. Just go on and leave me alone. Come on, Lymon. I got this end.

(DOAKER *goes into his room.* BOY WILLIE *and* LYMON *prepare to move the piano.*)

LYMON: How we gonna get it in the truck?

BOY WILLIE: Don't worry about how we gonna get it on the truck. You got to get 50 it out the house first.

LYMON: It's gonna take more than me and you to move this piano.

BOY WILLIE: Just lift up on that end, nigger!

(DOAKER *comes to the doorway of his room and stands.*)

DOAKER: (*Quietly with authority.*) Leave that piano set over there till Berniece come back. I don't care what you do with it then. But you gonna leave it sit over there right now.

BOY WILLIE: Alright . . . I'm gonna tell you this, Doaker. I'm going out of here . . . I'm gonna get me some rope . . . find me a plank and some wheels . . . and I'm coming back. Then I'm gonna carry that piano out of here . . . sell it and give Berniece half the money. See . . . now that's what I'm gonna do. And you . . . or nobody else is gonna stop me. Come on, Lymon . . . let's go get some rope and stuff. I'll be back, Doaker.

(BOY WILLIE *and* LYMON *exit. The lights go down on the scene.*)

Scene 5
(*The lights come up.* BOY WILLIE *sits on the sofa, screwing casters on a wooden plank.* MARETHA *is sitting on the piano stool.* DOAKER *sits at the table playing solitaire.*)

BOY WILLIE: (*To* MARETHA.) Then after that them white folks down around there started falling their wells. You ever seen a well? A well got a wall around it. It's hard to fall down a well. You got to be leaning way over. Couldn't nobody figure out too much what was making these fellows fall down their well . . . so everybody says the Ghosts of the Yellow Dog must have pushed them. That's what everybody called them four men what got burned up in the boxcar.

MARETHA: Why they call them that?

BOY WILLIE: Cause the Yazoo Delta railroad got yellow boxcars. Sometime the way the whistle blow sound like an old dog howling so the people call it the Yellow Dog.

MARETHA: Anybody ever see the Ghosts?

BOY WILLIE: I told you they like the wind. Can you see the wind? 5
MARETHA: No.
BOY WILLIE: They like the wind you can't see them. But sometimes you be
in trouble they might be around to help you. They say if you go where the
Southern cross the Yellow Dog . . . you go to where them two railroads cross
each other . . . and call out their names . . . they say they talk back to you. I
don't know, I ain't never done that. But Uncle Wining Boy he say he been down
there and talked to them. You have to ask him about that part.

(BERNIECE *has entered from the front door.*)

BERNIECE: Maretha, you go on and get ready for me to do your hair.

(MARETHA *crosses to the steps.*)

Boy Willie, I done told you to leave my house.

(*To* MARETHA.)

Go on, Maretha.

(MARETHA *is hesitant about going up the stairs.*)

BOY WILLIE: Don't be scared. Here, I'll go up there with you. If we see Sutter's
ghost I'll put a whupping on him. Come on, Uncle Boy Willie going with you.

(BOY WILLIE *and* MARETHA *exit up the stairs.*)

BERNIECE: Doaker—what is going on here? 10
DOAKER: I come home and him and Lymon was moving the piano. I told them to
leave it over there till you got home. He went out and got that board and them
wheels. He say he gonna take that piano out of here and ain't nobody gonna
stop him.
BERNIECE: I ain't playing with Boy Willie. I got Crawley's gun upstairs. He don't
know but I'm through with it. Where Lymon go?
DOAKER: Boy Willie sent him for some rope just before you come in.
BERNIECE: I ain't studying Boy Willie or Lymon—or the rope. Boy Willie ain't
taking that piano out this house. That's all there is to it.

(BOY WILLIE *and* MARETHA *enter on the stairs.* MARETHA *carries a hot
comb and a can of hair grease.* BOY WILLIE *crosses over and continues to screw
the wheels on the board.*)

MARETHA: Mama, all the hair grease is gone. There ain't but this little bit left. 15
BERNIECE: (*Gives her a dollar.*) Here . . . run across the street and get another can.
You come straight back, too. Don't you be playing around out there. And watch
the cars. Be careful when you cross the street.

(MARETHA *exits out the front door.*)

Boy Willie, I done told you to leave my house.
BOY WILLIE: I ain't in you' house. I'm in Doaker's house. If he ask me to leave then
I'll go on and leave. But consider me done left your part.
BERNIECE: Doaker, tell him to leave. Tell him to go on.
DOAKER: Boy Willie ain't done nothing for me to put him out of the house. I told
you if you can't get along just go on and don't have nothing to do with each
other.
BOY WILLIE: I ain't thinking about Berniece. 20

(He gets up and draws a line across the floor with his foot.)

There! Now I'm out of your part of the house. Consider me done left your part. Soon as Lymon come back with that rope. I'm gonna take that piano out of here and sell it.

BERNIECE: You ain't gonna touch that piano.

BOY WILLIE: Carry it out of here just as big and bold. Do like my daddy would have done come time to get Sutter's land.

BERNIECE: I got something to make you leave it over there.

BOY WILLIE: It's got to come better than this thirty-two-twenty.

DOAKER: Why don't you stop all that! Boy Willie, go on and leave her alone. You know how Berniece get. Why you wanna sit there and pick with her?

BOY WILLIE: I ain't picking with her. I told her the truth. She the one talking about what she got. I just told her what she better have.

BERNIECE: That's alright, Doaker. Leave him alone.

BOY WILLIE: She trying to scare me. Hell, I ain't scared of dying. I look around and see people dying every day. You got to die to make room for somebody else. I had a dog that died. Wasn't nothing but a puppy. I picked it up and put it in a bag and carried it up there to Reverend C. L. Thompson's church. I carried it up there and prayed and asked Jesus to make it live like he did the man in the Bible. I prayed real hard. Knelt down and everything. Say ask in Jesus' name. Well, I must have called Jesus' name two hundred times. I called his name till my mouth got sore. I got up and looked in the bag and the dog still dead. It ain't moved a muscle! I say, "Well, ain't nothing precious." And then I went out and killed me a cat. That's when I discovered the power of death. See, a nigger that ain't afraid to die is the worse kind of nigger for the white man. He can't hold that power over you. That's what I learned when I killed that cat. I got the power of death too. I can command him. I can call him up. The white man don't like to see that. He don't like for you to stand up and look him square in the eye and say, "I got it too." Then he got to deal with you square up.

BERNIECE: That's why I don't talk to him, Doaker. You try and talk to him and that's the only kind of stuff that comes out his mouth.

DOAKER: You say Avery went home to get his Bible?

BOY WILLIE: What Avery gonna do? Avery can't do nothing with me. I wish Avery would say something to me about this piano.

DOAKER: Berniece ain't said about that. Avery went home to get his Bible. He coming by to bless the house see if he can get rid of Sutter's ghost.

BOY WILLIE: Ain't nothing but a house full of ghosts down there at the church. What Avery look like chasing away somebody's ghost?

(MARETHA enters the front door.)

BERNIECE: Light that stove and set that comb over there to get hot. Get something to put around your shoulders.

BOY WILLIE: The Bible say an eye for an eye, a tooth for a tooth, and a life for a life. Tit for tat. But you and Avery don't want to believe that. You gonna pass up that part and pretend it ain't in there. Everything else you gonna agree with. But if you gonna agree with part of it you got to agree with all of it. You can't do nothing halfway. You gonna go at the Bible halfway. You gonna act like that part ain't in there. But you pull out the Bible and open it and see what it say.

Ask Avery. He a preacher. He'll tell you it's in there. He the Good Shepherd. Unless he gonna shepherd you to heaven with half the Bible.

BERNIECE: Maretha, bring me that comb. Make sure it's hot.

(MARETHA *brings the comb.* BERNIECE *begins to do her hair.*)

BOY WILLIE: I will say this for Avery. He done figured out a path to go through life. I don't agree with it. But he done fixed it so he can go right through it real smooth. Hell, he liable to end up with a million dollars that he done got from selling bread and wine.

MARETHA: OWWWWWWW!

BERNIECE: Be still, Maretha. If you was a boy I wouldn't be going through this.

BOY WILLIE: Don't you tell that girl that. Why you wanna tell her that?   40

BERNIECE: You ain't got nothing to do with this child.

BOY WILLIE: Telling her you wished she was a boy. How's that gonna make her feel?

BERNIECE: Boy Willie, go on and leave me alone.

DOAKER: Why don't you leave her alone? What you got to pick with her for? Why don't you go on out and see what's out there in the streets? Have something to tell the fellows down home.

BOY WILLIE: I'm waiting on Lymon to get back with that truck. Why don't you go   45 on out and see what's out there in the streets? You ain't got to work tomorrow. Talking about me . . . why don't you go out there? It's Friday night.

DOAKER: I got to stay around here and keep you all from killing one another.

BOY WILLIE: You ain't got to worry about me. I'm gonna be here just as long as it takes Lymon to get back here with that truck. You ought to be talking to Berniece. Sitting up there telling Maretha she wished she was a boy. What kind of thing is that to tell a child? If you want to tell her something tell her about that piano. You ain't even told her about that piano. Like that's something to be ashamed of. Like she supposed to go off and hide somewhere about that piano. You ought to mark down on the calendar the day that Papa Boy Charles brought that piano into the house. You ought to mark that day down and draw a circle around it . . . and every year when it come up throw a party. Have a celebration. If you did that she wouldn't have no problem in life. She could walk around here with her head held high. I'm talking about a big party!

Invite everybody! Mark that day down with a special meaning. That way she know where she at in the world. You got her going out here thinking she wrong in the world. Like there ain't no part of it belong to her.

BERNIECE: Let me take care of my child. When you get one of your own then you can teach it what you want to teach it.

(DOAKER *exits into his room.*)

BOY WILLIE: What I want to bring a child into this world for? Why I wanna bring somebody else into all this for? I'll tell you this . . . If I was Rockefeller I'd have forty or fifty. I'd make one every day. Cause they gonna start out in life with all the advantages. I ain't got no advantages to offer nobody. Many is the time I looked at my daddy and seen him staring off at his hands. I got a little older I know what he was thinking. He sitting there saying, "I got these big old hands but what I'm gonna do with them? Best I can do is make a fifty-acre crop for

Mr. Stovall. Got these big old hands capable of doing anything. I can take and build something with these hands. But where's the tools? All I got is these hands. Unless I go out here and kill me somebody and take what they got . . . it's a long row to hoe for me to get something of my own. So what I'm gonna do with these big old hands? What would you do?"

See now . . . if he had his own land he wouldn't have felt that way. If he had something under his feet that belonged to him he could stand up taller. That's what I'm talking about. Hell, the land is there for everybody. All you got to do is figure out how to get you a piece. Ain't no mystery to life. You just got to go out and meet it square on. If you got a piece of land you'll find everything else fall right into place. You can stand right up next to the white man and talk about the price of cotton . . . the weather, and anything else you want to talk about. If you teach that girl that she living at the bottom of life, she's gonna grow up and hate you.

BERNIECE: I'm gonna teach her the truth. That's just where she living. Only she 50
ain't got to stay there.

(To MARETHA.)

Turn you' head over to the other side.

BOY WILLIE: This might be your bottom but it ain't mine. I'm living at the top of life. I ain't gonna just take my life and throw it away at the bottom. I'm in the world like everybody else. The way I see it everybody else got to come up a little taste to be where I am.

BERNIECE: You right at the bottom with the rest of us.

BOY WILLIE: I'll tell you this . . . and ain't a living soul can put a come back on it. If you believe that's where you at then you gonna act that way. If you act that way then that's where you gonna be. It's as simple as that. Ain't no mystery to life. I don't know how you come to believe that stuff. Crawley didn't think like that. He wasn't living at the bottom of life. Papa Boy Charles and Mama Ola wasn't living at the bottom of life. You ain't never heard them say nothing like that. They would have taken a strap to you if they heard you say something like that.

(DOAKER enters from his room.)

Hey, Doaker . . . Berniece say the colored folks is living at the bottom of life. I tried to tell her if she think that . . . that's where she gonna be. You think you living at the bottom of life? Is that how you see yourself?

DOAKER: I'm just living the best way I know how. I ain't thinking about no top or no bottom.

BOY WILLIE: That's what I tried to tell Berniece. I don't know where she got that 55
from. That sound like something Avery would say. Avery think cause the white man give him a turkey for Thanksgiving that makes him better than everybody else. That's gonna raise him out of the bottom of life. I don't need nobody to give me a turkey. I can get my own turkey. All you have to do is get out my way. I'll get me two or three turkeys.

BERNIECE: You can't even get a chicken let alone two or three turkeys. Talking about get out your way. Ain't nobody in your way.

(To MARETHA.)

Straighten your head, Maretha! Don't be bending down like that. Hold your head up!

(To BOY WILLIE.*)*

All you got going for you is talk. You' whole life that's all you ever had going for you.

BOY WILLIE: See now . . . I'll tell you something about me. I done strung along and strung along. Going this way and that. Whatever way would lead me to a moment of peace. That's all I want. To be as easy with everything. But I wasn't born to that. I was born to a time of fire.

The world ain't wanted no part of me. I could see that since I was about seven. The world say it's better off without me. See, Berniece accept that. She trying to come up to where she can prove something to the world. Hell, the world a better place cause of me. I don't see it like Berniece. I got a heart that beats here and it beats just as loud as the next fellow's. Don't care if he black or white. Sometime it beats louder. When it beats louder, then everybody can hear it. Some people get scared of that. Like Berniece. Some people get scared to hear a nigger's heart beating. They think you ought to lay low with that heart. Make it beat quiet and go along with everything the way it is. But my mama ain't birthed me for nothing. So what I got to do? I got to mark my passing on the road. Just like you write on a tree, "Boy Willie was here."

That's all I'm trying to do with that piano. Trying to put my mark on the road. Like my daddy done. My heart say for me to sell that piano and get me some land so I can make a life for myself to live in my own way. Other than that I ain't thinking about nothing Berniece got to say.

(There is a knock at the door. BOY WILLIE *crosses to it and yanks it open thinking it is* LYMON. AVERY *enters. He carries a Bible.)*

BOY WILLIE: Where you been, nigger? Aw . . . I thought you was Lymon. Hey, Berniece, look who's here.

BERNIECE: Come on in, Avery. Don't you pay Boy Willie no mind.

BOY WILLIE: Hey . . . Hey, Avery . . . tell me this . . . can you get to heaven with half the Bible? 60

BERNIECE: Boy Willie . . . I done told you to leave me alone.

BOY WILLIE: I just ask the man a question. He can answer. He don't need you to speak for him. Avery . . . if you only believe on half the Bible and don't want to accept the other half . . . you think God let you in heaven? Or do you got to have the whole Bible? Tell Berniece . . . if you only believe in part of it . . . when you see God he gonna ask you why you ain't believed in the other part . . . then he gonna send you straight to Hell.

AVERY: You got to be born again. Jesus say unless a man be born again he cannot come unto the Father and who so ever heareth my words and believeth them not shall be cast into a fiery pit.

BOY WILLIE: That's what I was trying to tell Berniece. You got to believe in it all. You can't go at nothing halfway. She think she going to heaven with half the Bible.

(To BERNIECE.*)*

You hear that . . . Jesus say you got to believe in it all.

BERNIECE: You keep messing with me.

BOY WILLIE: I ain't thinking about you.

DOAKER: Come on in, Avery, and have a seat. Don't pay neither one of them no mind. They been arguing all day.

BERNIECE: Come on in, Avery.

AVERY: How's everybody in here?

BERNIECE: Here, set this comb back over there on that stove.

(To AVERY.*)*

Don't pay Boy Willie no mind. He been around here bothering me since I come home from work.

BOY WILLIE: Boy Willie ain't bothering you. Boy Willie ain't bothering nobody. I'm just waiting on Lymon to get back. I ain't thinking about you. You heard the man say I was right and you still don't want to believe it. You just wanna go and make up anythin'. Well there's Avery . . . there's the preacher . . . go on and ask him.

AVERY: Berniece believe in the Bible. She been baptized.

BOY WILLIE: What about that part that say an eye for an eye a tooth for a tooth and a life for a life? Ain't that in there?

DOAKER: What they say down there at the bank, Avery?

AVERY: Oh, they talked to me real nice. I told Berniece . . . they say maybe they let me borrow the money. They done talked to my boss down at work and everything.

DOAKER: That's what I told Berniece. You working every day you ought to be able to borrow some money.

AVERY: I'm getting more people in my congregation every day. Berniece says she gonna be the Deaconess. I get me my church I can get married and settled down. That's what I told Berniece.

DOAKER: That be nice. You all ought to go ahead and get married. Berniece don't need to be by herself. I tell her that all the time.

BERNIECE: I ain't said nothing about getting married. I said I was thinking about it.

DOAKER: Avery get him his church you all can make it nice.

(To AVERY.*)*

Berniece said you was coming by to bless the house.

AVERY: Yeah, I done read up on my Bible. She asked me to come by and see if I can get rid of Sutter's ghost.

BOY WILLIE: Ain't no ghost in this house. That's all in Berniece's head. Go on up there and see if you see him. I'll give you a hundred dollars if you see him. That's all in her imagination.

DOAKER: Well, let her find that out then. If Avery blessing the house is gonna make her feel better . . . what you got to do with it?

AVERY: Berniece say Maretha seen him too. I don't know, but I found a part in the Bible to bless the house. If he is here then that ought to make him go.

BOY WILLIE: You worse than Berniece believing all that stuff. Talking about . . . if he here. Go on up there and find out. I been up there I ain't seen him. If you reading from that Bible gonna make him leave out of Berniece imagination, well, you might be right. But if you talking about . . .

DOAKER: Boy Willie, why don't you just be quiet? Getting all up in the man's business. This ain't got nothing to do with you. Let him go ahead and do what he gonna do.

BOY WILLIE: I ain't stopping him. Avery ain't got no power to do nothing.

AVERY: Oh, I ain't got no power. God got the power! God got power over everything in His creation. God can do anything. God say, "As I commandeth so it shall be." God said, "Let there be light," and there was light. He made the world in six days and rested on the seventh. God's got a wonderful power. He got power over life and death. Jesus raised Lazareth from the dead. They was getting ready to bury him and Jesus told him say, "Rise up and walk." He got up and walked and the people made great rejoicing at the power of God. I ain't worried about him chasing away a little old ghost!

(There is a knock at the door. BOY WILLIE *goes to answer it.* LYMON *enters carrying a coil of rope.)*

BOY WILLIE: Where you been? I been waiting on you and you run off somewhere.

LYMON: I ran into Grace. I stopped and bought her drink. She say she gonna go to the picture show with me. 90

BOY WILLIE: I ain't thinking about no Grace nothing.

LYMON: Hi, Berniece.

BOY WILLIE: Give me that rope and get up on this side of the piano.

DOAKER: Boy Willie, don't start nothing now. Leave the piano alone.

BOY WILLIE: Get that board there, Lymon. Stay out of this, Doaker. 95

*(*BERNIECE *exits up the stairs.)*

DOAKER: You just can't take the piano. How you gonna take the piano? Berniece ain't said nothing about selling that piano.

BOY WILLIE: She ain't got to say nothing. Come on, Lymon. We got to lift one end at a time up on the board. You got to watch so that the board don't slide up under there.

LYMON: What we gonna do with the rope?

BOY WILLIE: Let me worry about the rope. You just get up on this side over here with me.

*(*BERNIECE *enters from the stairs. She has her hand in her pocket where she has Crawley's gun.)*

AVERY: Boy Willie . . . Berniece . . . why don't you all sit down and talk this out now? 100

BERNIECE: Ain't nothing to talk out.

BOY WILLIE: I'm through talking to Berniece. You can talk to Berniece till you get blue in the face, and it don't make no difference. Get up on that side, Lymon. Throw that rope around there and tie it to the leg.

LYMON: Wait a minute . . . wait a minute, Boy Willie. Berniece got to say. Hey, Berniece . . . did you tell Boy Willie he could take this piano?

BERNIECE: Boy Willie ain't taking nothing out of my house but himself. Now you let him go ahead and try.

BOY WILLIE: Come on, Lymon, get up on this side with me. 105

*(*LYMON *stands undecided.)*

Come on, nigger! What you standing there for?

LYMON: Maybe Berniece is right, Boy Willie. Maybe you shouldn't sell it.

AVERY: You all ought to sit down and talk it out. See if you can come to an agreement.

DOAKER: That's what I been trying to tell them. Seem like one of them ought to respect the other one's wishes.

BERNIECE: I wish Boy Willie would go on and leave my house. That's what I wish. Now, he can respect that. Cause he's leaving here one way or another.

BOY WILLIE: What you mean one way or another? What's that supposed to mean? 110
I ain't scared of no gun.

DOAKER: Come on, Berniece, leave him alone with that.

BOY WILLIE: I don't care what Berniece say. I'm selling my half. I can't help it if her half got to go along with it. It ain't like I'm trying to cheat her out of her half. Come on, Lymon.

LYMON: Berniece . . . I got to do this . . . Boy Willie say he gonna give you half of the money . . . say he want to get Sutter's land.

BERNIECE: Go on, Lymon. Just go on . . . I done told Boy Willie what to do.

BOY WILLIE: Here, Lymon . . . put that rope up over there. 115

LYMON: Boy Willie, you sure you want to do this? The way I figure it . . . I might be wrong . . . but I figure she gonna shoot you first.

BOY WILLIE: She just gonna have to shoot me.

BERNIECE: Maretha, get on out the way. Get her out the way, Doaker.

DOAKER: Go on, do what your mama told you.

BERNIECE: Put her in your room. 120

(MARETHA *exits to Doaker's room.* BOY WILLIE *and* LYMON *try to lift the piano. The door opens and* WINING BOY *enters. He has been drinking.*)

WINING BOY: Man, these niggers around here! I stopped down there at Seefus. . . . These folks standing around talking about Patchneck Red's coming. They jumping back and getting off the sidewalk talking about Patchneck Red this and Patchneck Red that. Come to find out . . . you know who they was talking about? Old John D. from up around Tyler! Used to run around with Otis Smith. He got everybody scared of him. Calling him Patchneck Red. They don't know I whupped the nigger's head in one time.

BOY WILLIE: Just make sure that board don't slide, Lymon.

LYMON: I got this side. You watch that side.

WINING BOY: Hey, Boy Willie, what you got? I know you got a pint stuck up in your coat.

BOY WILLIE: Wining Boy, get out the way! 125

WINING BOY: Hey, Doaker. What you got? Gimme a drink. I want a drink.

DOAKER: It look like you had enough of whatever it was. Come talking about "What you got?" You ought to be trying to find somewhere to lay down.

WINING BOY: I ain't worried about no place to lay down. I can always find me a place to lay down in Berniece's house. Ain't that right, Berniece?

BERNIECE: Wining Boy, sit down somewhere. You been out there drinking all day. Come in here smelling like an old polecat. Sit on down there, you don't need nothing to drink.

DOAKER: You know Berniece don't like all that drinking. 130

WINING BOY: I ain't disrespecting Berniece. Berniece, am I disrespecting you? I'm just trying to be nice. I been with strangers all day and they treated me like family. I come in here to family and you treat me like a stranger. I don't need your whiskey. I can buy my own. I wanted your company, not your whiskey.

DOAKER: Nigger, why don't you go upstairs and lay down? You don't need nothing to drink.

WINING BOY: I ain't thinking about no laying down. Me and Boy Willie fixing to party. Ain't that right, Boy Willie? Tell him. I'm fixing to play me some piano. Watch this.

(WINING BOY sits down at the piano.)

BOY WILLIE: Come on, Wining Boy! Me and Lymon fixing to move the piano.

WINING BOY: Wait a minute . . . wait a minute. This a song I wrote for Cleotha. I   135
wrote this song in memory of Cleotha.

(He begins to play and sing.)

Hey little woman what's the matter with you now
Had a storm last night and blowed the line all down

Tell me how long
Is I got to wait
Can I get it now
Or must I hesitate

It takes a hesitating stocking in her hesitating shoe
It takes a hesitating woman wanna sing the blues

Tell me how long
Is I got to wait
Can I kiss you now
Or must I hesitate.

BOY WILLIE: Come on, Wining Boy, get up! Get up, Wining Boy! Me and
Lymon's fixing to move the piano.

WINING BOY: Naw . . . Naw . . . you ain't gonna move this piano!

BOY WILLIE: Get out the way, Wining Boy.

(WINING BOY, his back to the piano, spreads his arms out over the piano.)

WINING BOY: You ain't taking this piano out the house. You got to take me with it!

BOY WILLIE: Get on out the way, Wining Boy! Doaker get him!   140

(There is a knock on the door.)

BERNIECE: I got him, Doaker. Come on, Wining Boy. I done told Boy Willie he
ain't taking the piano.

(BERNIECE tries to take WINING BOY away from the piano.)

WINING BOY: He got to take me with it!

(DOAKER goes to answer the door. GRACE enters.)

GRACE: Is Lymon here?

DOAKER: Lymon.   145

WINING BOY: He ain't taking that piano.

BERNIECE: I ain't gonna let him take it.

GRACE: I thought you was coming back. I ain't gonna sit in that truck all day.

LYMON: I told you I was coming back.

GRACE: *(Sees* BOY WILLIE.*)* Oh, hi, Boy Willie. Lymon told me you was gone back down South.

LYMON: I said he was going back. I didn't say he had left already.   150

GRACE: That's what you told me.

BERNIECE: Lymon, you got to take your company some-place else.

LYMON: Berniece, this is Grace. That there is Berniece. That's Boy Willie's sister.

GRACE: Nice to meet you.

> *(To* LYMON.*)*

> I ain't gonna sit out in that truck all day. You told me you was gonna take me to the movie.

LYMON: I told you I had something to do first. You supposed to wait on me.   155

BERNIECE: Lymon, just go on and leave. Take Grace or whoever with you. Just go on get out my house.

BOY WILLIE: You gonna help me move this piano first, nigger!

LYMON: *(To* GRACE.*)* I got to help Boy Willie move the piano first.

> *(Everybody but* GRACE *suddenly senses* SUTTER's *presence.)*

GRACE: I ain't waiting on you. Told me you was coming right back. Now you got to move a piano. You just like all the other men.

> *(*GRACE *now senses something.)*

> Something ain't right here. I knew I shouldn't have come back up in this house.

> *(*GRACE *exits.)*

LYMON: Hey, Grace! I'll be right back, Boy Willie.   160

BOY WILLIE: Where you going, nigger?

LYMON: I'll be back. I got to take Grace home.

BOY WILLIE: Come on, let's move the piano first!

LYMON: I got to take Grace home. I told you I'll be back.

> *(*LYMON *exits.* BOY WILLIE *exits and calls after him.)*

BOY WILLIE: Come on, Lymon! Hey . . . Lymon! Lymon . . . come on!   165

> *(Again, the presence of* SUTTER *is felt.)*

WINING BOY: Hey, Doaker, did you feel that? Hey, Berniece . . . did you get cold? Hey, Doaker . . .

DOAKER: What you calling me for?

WINING BOY: I believe that's Sutter.

DOAKER: Well, let him stay up there. As long as he don't mess with me.

BERNIECE: Avery, go on and bless the house.   170

DOAKER: You need to bless that piano. That's what you need to bless. It ain't done nothing but cause trouble. If you gonna bless anything go on and bless that.

WINING BOY: Hey, Doaker, if he gonna bless something let him bless everything. The kitchen . . . the upstairs. Go on and bless it all.

BOY WILLIE: Ain't no ghost in this house. He need to bless Berniece's head. That's what he need to bless.

AVERY: Seem like that piano's causing all the trouble. I can bless that. Berniece, put me some water in that bottle.

(AVERY takes a small bottle from his pocket and hands it to BERNIECE, who goes into the kitchen to get water. AVERY takes a candle from his pocket and lights it. He gives it to BERNIECE as she gives him the water.)

Hold this candle. Whatever you do make sure it don't go out.

O Holy Father we gather here this evening in the Holy Name to cast out the spirit of one James Sutter. May this vial of water be empowered with thy spirit. May each drop of it be a weapon and a shield against the presence of all evil and may it be a cleansing and blessing of this humble abode.

Just as Our Father taught us how to pray so He say, "I will prepare a table for you in the midst of mine enemies," and in His hands we place ourselves to come unto his presence. Where there is Good so shall it cause Evil to scatter to the Four Winds.

(He throws water at the piano at each commandment.)

AVERY: Get thee behind me, Satan! Get thee behind the face of Righteousness as we   175
Glorify His Holy Name! Get thee behind the Hammer of Truth that breaketh down the Wall of Falsehood! Father. Father. Praise. Praise. We ask in Jesus' name and call forth the power of the Holy Spirit as it is written. . . .

(He opens the Bible and reads from it.)

I will sprinkle clean water upon thee and ye shall be clean.

BOY WILLIE: All this old preaching stuff. Hell, just tell him to leave.

(AVERY continues reading throughout BOY WILLIE's outburst.)

AVERY: I will sprinkle clean water upon you and you shall be clean: from all your uncleanliness, and from all your idols, will I cleanse you. A new heart also will I give you, and a new spirit will I put within you: and I will take out of your flesh the heart of stone, and I will give you a heart of flesh. And I will put my spirit within you, and cause you to walk in my statutes, and ye shall keep my judgments, and do them.

(BOY WILLIE grabs a pot of water from the stove and begins to fling it around the room.)

BOY WILLIE: Hey Sutter! Sutter! Get your ass out this house! Sutter! Come on and get some of this water! You done drowned in the well, come on and get some more of this water!

(BOY WILLIE is working himself into a frenzy as he runs around the room throwing water and calling SUTTER's name. AVERY continues reading.)

BOY WILLIE: Come on, Sutter!

(He starts up the stairs.)

Come on, get some water! Come on, Sutter!

(The sound of SUTTER's GHOST is heard. As BOY WILLIE approaches the steps he is suddenly thrown back by the unseen force, which is choking him. As he struggles he frees himself, then dashes up the stairs.)

BOY WILLIE: Come on, Sutter!   180

AVERY: *(Continuing.)* A new heart also will I give you and a new spirit will I put within you: and I will take out of your flesh the heart of stone, and I will give you a heart of flesh. And I will put my spirit within you, and cause you to walk in my statutes, and ye shall keep my judgments, and do them.

(There are loud sounds heard from upstairs as BOY WILLIE begins to wrestle with SUTTER's GHOST. It is a life-and-death struggle fraught with perils and faultless terror. BOY WILLIE is thrown down the stairs. AVERY is stunned into silence. BOY WILLIE picks himself up and dashes back upstairs.)

AVERY: Berniece, I can't do it.

(There are more sounds heard from upstairs. DOAKER and WINING BOY stare at one another in stunned disbelief. It is in this moment, from somewhere old, that BERNIECE realizes what she must do. She crosses to the piano. She begins to play. The song is found piece by piece. It is an old urge to song that is both a commandment and a plea. With each repetition it gains in strength. It is intended as an exorcism and a dressing for battle. A rustle of wind blowing across two continents.)

BERNIECE: *(Singing.)*
I want you to help me
I want you to help me
I want you to help me
I want you to help me
I want you to help me
I want you to help me
Mama Berniece
I want you to help me
Mama Esther
I want you to help me
Papa Boy Charles
I want you to help me
Mama Ola
I want you to help me

I want you to help me
I want you to help me
I want you to help me
I want you to help me
I want you to help me
I want you to help me
I want you to help me
I want you to help me

(The sound of a train approaching is heard. The noise upstairs subsides.)

BOY WILLIE: Come on, Sutter! Come back, Sutter!

(BERNIECE begins to chant:)

BERNIECE:
Thank you.

Thank you.
Thank you.

(A calm comes over the house. MARETHA enters from DOAKER's room. BOY WILLIE enters on the stairs. He pauses a moment to watch BERNIECE at the piano.)

BERNIECE:
Thank you.
Thank you.

BOY WILLIE: Wining Boy, you ready to go back down home?
Hey, Doaker, what time the train leave?

DOAKER: You still got time to make it.

(MARETHA crosses and embraces BOY WILLIE.)

BOY WILLIE: Hey Berniece . . . if you and Maretha don't keep playing on that piano . . . ain't no telling . . . me and Sutter both liable to be back.

(He exits.)

BERNIECE: Thank you.   190
(The lights go down to black.)

Explorations of the Text

1. The piano not only is a family treasure, but it also plays a symbolic role in the play. What does the piano symbolize to the family? How might this symbol relate to American society as a whole?

2. Boy Willie wants to sell the piano to buy land for a farm. Discuss the relationship of the piano to the land; does Boy Willie's dream of his own farm also play a symbolic role in the play? In American society as a whole?

3. Discuss the characters of Berniece and Boy Willie as individuals and as family members. How are they different from each other? Analyze the conflict between them. How does it build throughout the play? What is the apex of the drama?

4. Consider the play's title. Why is it *The Piano Lesson,* not *The Piano?*

5. Is the ending of the play effective?

The Reading/Writing Connection

1. Write a monologue in the voice of Berniece describing the piano and what it means to her. Then write a monologue in the voice of Boy Willie, explaining his feelings about the piano. Finally, write a dialogue, using excerpts of your monologues, blending the brother and sister's voices. Or, write a third monologue in the voice of the piano. What do you discover?

2. "Think" Topic: In "Everyday Use," Wangero and Maggie both want the family quilt but for different reasons. Compare/contrast these sisters to Berniece and Boy Willie in *The Piano Lesson.*

Ideas for Writing

1. **Write an Argument:** August Wilson presents the female protagonist, Berniece, as a steady and responsible character whose values are less materialistic than those of her less stable brother, Boy Willie. Compare these characters to the brothers in "Sonny's Blues." Do you think that Wilson is providing a social critique or stereotyping young black males? Something else?

2. Analyze the theme of family legacies in the play, both the tangible and intangible.

NONFICTION

Toi Derricotte *(1941–)*

Beginning Dialogues   *1996*

On the way, he said, "When you visit the cemetery, you do it for yourself. They don't know you're there." But maybe some part of me believes she will know, that she's brought many good things to me after her death, that she's taking care. Maybe I visit her grave because she would have visited the grave of her mother, because she taught me to send thank-you notes and be a good girl. Maybe I'm going to find signs of whether she's still there; maybe she hasn't blown open the ground, and we'll find an angel lounging on her gravestone, saying, "She's not here. Go and find her elsewhere."

I don't seem to suffer the pains of anguish that many women whose mothers have died feel. Last night, a group about my age, all in that midlife past midlife, late fifties or early sixties, ate dinner and talked about our mothers' deaths. It's not a new conversation; women whose mothers have died always talk about it. They did even when I was in my twenties. Yet here no one is hearing these stories with expectancy; everyone has faced that which at one time was unthinkable. It's as if we're all in the same club, as if we have all finally arrived, as if we could all look back at those women on the other side and know we are totally new.

One woman talked about that inconsolable stabbing in the heart when she realized she wouldn't buy a Christmas present for her mother again this year. I've wondered about it, about perhaps having grieved the separation between my mother and me in my early childhood, for, in a way, I truly do not miss her like that, do not feel that irreversible moment of no return, as I did when she would go into the bathroom and shut the door, the ache that breaks the heart and has no answer. I felt the goneness of her then, as if the center of me was gone, and I tried to bring it back by peering through the crack at the bottom of the door, trying to see anything, even her feet.

I said this to the women who talked last night about their mothers. One woman, who said that her mother had died a few days after she was born, had always struck me before as cold, contained, and now, as she spoke, I noticed she was squeezing the fleshy part of her cheek, near her mouth, making a little fat bubble of flesh between her ring and baby fingers. I have seen that before, a kind of clumsy, unconscious pinching of the self, and it makes me feel great pity. Her fingers seemed squat, doing an act whose purpose I couldn't imagine—perhaps a partial holding to signify that she could not hold the whole of what she needed held. Now, clumsily, here was her body (was it her clumsy body that had killed her mother, ungracefully slipping out?)—her liveliness covered by a dreary cape, her hair dreary, her face unmade, as if who would care?—speaking about her mother's death (we had never heard of this, though we had known her for years!) without tears, just those two fingers clenching and opening, pinching a clump of cheek, letting go and clenching again, moving slightly, as if she couldn't find the right spot, and since the cheek is larger than what those two fingers can grasp, and since the two fingers form a small vise and take in only a slot of flesh, it seemed she was stopping the flesh from moving, clamping it in place. It seemed inadequate, incomplete, and ill chosen; in literature, the small thing signifies the whole of something we can imagine from the reference to the small thing, but here, the small reference did not convey. It was a clumsy effort, as a child might pinch the breast. Or perhaps it was an effort to make another mouth, to pucker the face, as the lips of the child might pucker for its mother's breast.

At my mother's grave, I tried to imagine what I should do. My partner had taken my picture at the grave and a picture of the inscription. He was sitting in the car. How long should I stay? My mind didn't know what to settle on. No particular feeling or idea carried me. I became lost in nothing. Just me, stuttering over an immensity that I couldn't absorb, the way I used to feel guilty for not feeling enough happiness at Christmas, after my mother's great efforts. I guess I felt that I was incompetent, too broken to hold. I sang her favorite song: "This little light of mine, I'm gonna let it shine." I wanted to give her a promise; I wanted to change my life because of her, just the way I did before.

I am struck by my own inability to feel grief. It feels like a refusal to face an end. I know I have great trouble facing boundaries, my own and others'. So, instead, perhaps there is this magical thinking built on my own inadequacy to face the truth: I say I get messages from my mother, that she is still in my life, and now, perhaps even more, she is reaching me, since her destruction is out of my way.

Once, when I called a friend to say I couldn't go on teaching at the prestigious workshop I was visiting because I could not stand the torturing voices in my head, twenty-four hours a day, saying I was no good, stupid, not as smart as the others, not as respected or loved, that I had no value, that I was there only because I was black, that I had done or said the wrong thing, that I was not really a poet, my friend said, "Why not ask the torturing voices from where they get their information?" I did, and without hesitation they answered, "From your mother."

Things had changed by then, so I flipped back, "You haven't got the latest information!"

Just a few months before she died, my mother turned the universe of an unloved daughter around with one sentence. Instead of screaming at me when I asked her not to come to one of my readings because I might read things that would make her uncomfortable, she said, "Oh, dear, would you be uncomfortable? I don't want you to be uncomfortable, so I won't come."

I've written a lot about messages from her—I won't repeat them here—just to say my conversation with my mother isn't over, and I think it isn't over for her, either.

In the manuscript of my mother's book, I read about the women in her childhood—her mother, aunts, and grandmother—who helped each other beyond the bounds of the imaginable. Because of their hard labor, our family succeeded. I read this manuscript, which she put into my hands to publish only two days before her death, and I think that, although my mother began writing after I did, after I was published, she was a writer before she began writing. Though she is dead, our stories are in dialogue: my writing has been against her writing, as if there was a war between us. It is more than our writing that is in dialogue; it is our lives.

When I was seven, she told me how, when she left the house of the rich white people her mother worked for, the white kids were waiting to beat her up on her way to school, and as soon as she crossed the line to the black part of town, the black kids were there to beat her up too. Why would she tell me that story? Why would a mother tell a seven-year-old such a sad story, such a defeating one? I thought it was her way of saying, "Trust no one but your mother," a way of binding me to her by making me fear.

It's a question—what she said and did that I didn't understand, what she did to hurt me. It is not over; it is still a riddle being solved. I do not need to be held, and so, therefore, isn't my mother free too? Is that why she told me those stories? Was I to be the mother who freed her?

My partner and I have just spent a delightful weekend together, a sunny, windy fall weekend with the trees half shredded, the bright blue sky both miraculous and unavoidable through the nude branches and their silence. On the drive home, my mind comes to how my life has changed since my mother's death: slowly, I have been loosed from those heavy, nearly inconsolable fears like Houdini's chains, lock by lock, as if some magician part of me occasionally appears, from some unseen and undetectable room, with one more chain gone. Finally, I am gloriously undrowned.

Everyone says that I changed for the better, as if, when my mother's slight body, 15 not even one hundred pounds, slipped into the earth, the whole world suddenly belonged to me. The first year I stopped jogging. People said it was grief, but whatever grief felt like—except for the first few days after her death, especially the burial day, heavy lodestar—it was too indistinct for me to grab on to. Two years later, I bought a house and found a man in my life, like a spectacular hat pin in just the right hat. The simple explanation would have been my mother's narcissism—the way she pushed me toward independence, screaming, "You're weighing me down," and yet, when I was sixteen and came in late one night, slamming the door, she was behind it in the shadows, like a burglar, and her hand went around my neck while she screamed, "I'll kill you!" Who hasn't wanted to kill the one she loved?

But there was so much unaccounted for, so much in my mother's past that I couldn't fix, not ever, or make up for. Maybe my mother never had such a weekend of happiness with a man as I have just had, though a former lover of hers once told me, when I asked about the affair, how much she had loved to make love to him. Perhaps he told me because he loved me and thought I should know that aspect of my mother, because knowing might help me put a necessary piece in the puzzle. Perhaps he had sympathy for me—in spite of the fact he had loved my mother—and didn't feel the need to protect her. Perhaps he thought it was better to give a daughter that important piece than to keep still about a dead woman. And perhaps he was bragging a bit when he said it.

My mother had slept alone, in another room, in another bed, for eighteen years of her marriage, until my parents divorced. I never saw her kiss my father, and the only touch was the time I heard him smash her against the table. My mother always gave abundantly with one hand and pushed you away with the other. The mystery of a beautiful woman. Perhaps in some reciprocal way, my unhappy, angry, guilt-producing mother had also been a planter, had been planting the seeds of my happiness with an invisible hand, the hand I didn't see. She left me enough money to buy a house. She told me all my life she loved me, as if she completely forgot the hundred slights, humiliations, threats, and insinuations. Of course she loved me; why would I think otherwise? She loved me more than anything. Sometimes she'd scream, as if my doubts were another evil, another proof of my unworthiness. How exasperating my complaints must have been when, all along, she was planting seeds with that invisible hand.

The women of that generation, my mother and aunts, counted their blessings: Chinese food and beer on Friday nights after work, and fried chicken breasts, twice-baked potatoes, and broccoli for early Sunday afternoon dinners. And there were parties with bounteous tables; polished glasses and silver, a chandelier, every bauble ammonia-shiny; and heat's seven coolnesses, the little cups of rice turned over and decorated, each small, white breast with a nipple of parsley. Polished floors, shopping trips, lunch at Hudson's—these were the good things, the punctuation marks that held back despondency, that danced away despair. No hardship was unredeemable to women who had one endless belief: bread on the water always comes home. It wasn't until I was in my sixties that I realized it did, but not necessarily to the ones who cast it. I am eating bread from hands that are no longer there. I cannot reach back to touch their actual bodies. It is good that they are gone.

My mother helps me. She sends me signs: her African violet bloomed for the first time on my windowsill three years after her death, on the first day of her death month. She says, "Remember me. My miracles are still there for you, still becoming apparent as you have eyes to see." I love my mother now in ways I could not have loved her when she was alive, fierce, terrifying, unpredictable, mad, shame-inducing, self-involved, relentless, and determined by any means necessary. When she was a child, to get what she wanted from her mother, she would hold her breath until she was blue and pass out. Even if she had to inflict the greatest pain—making me see her suffer, making me fear her death and that I had caused it—she would do it without thinking, without hesitation. That worst threat was always between us—that she could take herself away, that she could hurt herself in my eyes—and it was out of my control to stop it. She was the hostage of an insane government, her own body. And so I revoked my love: I took away, as much as I could, the only real currency between us. I would not count on her to save me from her death. And therefore I saved myself by cutting the part of my heart that was in her heart; I cut it off as if snipping a pigtail. It is only now, when I am at a safe distance, that my heart begins to grow again, as if a surgeon has inserted a little gray balloon to open it up to blood. There begins to be an invisible cell, a chamber, a thumping like the thump inside the embryo shell, tissues paper thin, of hardly any substance, except that, somewhere in it, it still knows what it is, what it will grow up to be used for. ◉

Explorations of the Text

1. Derricotte uses a series of memories to illustrate the power of her mother to shape her own identity and self-worth, and she likens the death of her mother to a loosening of chains that bound her. How is the image of being bound by her mother reflected in her feelings about her mother's death? Explain the ambiguity of Derricotte's feelings through the examination of this imagery.

2. Discuss the expectations that Derricotte's mother has for her daughter. How do these differ from Derricotte's expectations of her mother? Herself?

3. Derricotte wonders if her mother was unhappy because she did not experience the love of another the way that Derricotte herself has. Considering the stories in this chapter about broken relationships, do you believe that Derricotte may be right? Discuss the effect on children brought up in a family of parents who have a loveless relationship.

4. The title of Derricotte's essay is "Beginning Dialogues." Why are the dialogues "beginning"? Explain using references to the text to support your suppositions.

5. In her essay, Derricotte is writing of the loss of her mother through a series of memories of their lives together. How are her memories similar to or different from those of other women writing about their mothers? Refer to bell hooks, Amy Tan, and/or Pauline Uchmanowicz. Are there similar themes or feelings in these pieces?

The Reading/Writing Connection

1. Journal entry: Compare the voice of Derricotte's mother in her head with that of the narrator's mother in Kincaid's poem, "Girl." Write about a parental voice that you hear in your head: Whose voice is it? What does it say? How do you answer?

Ideas for Writing

1. **Write an Argument:** Derricotte is "struck by [her] own inability to feel grief." When reading her essay, do you find evidence that she is grieving the death of her mother? Write an argument that either claims she does feel grief, or one that proves what she states, that she does not feel grief. Use evidence from the text to support your feelings.

David Sedaris *(1957–)*

The Girl Next Door *2003*

"**W**ell that little experiment is over," my mother said. "You tried it, it didn't work out, so what do you say we just move on." She was dressed in her roll-up-the-shirtsleeves outfit: the faded turquoise skirt, a cotton head scarf, and one of the sporty blouses my father had bought in the hope she might take up golf. "We'll start with the kitchen," she said. "That's always the best way, isn't it?"

I was moving again. This time because of the neighbors.

"Oh, no," my mother said. "They're not to blame. Let's be honest now." She liked to take my problems back to the source, which was usually me. Like, for instance, when I got food poisoning it wasn't the chef's fault. "*You're* the one who wanted to go Oriental. *You're* the one who ordered the lomain."

"Lo mein. It's two words."

"Oh, he speaks Chinese now! Tell me, Charlie Chan,[1] what's the word for six straight hours of vomiting and diarrhea?"

What she meant was that I'd tried to save money. The cheap Chinese restaurant, the seventy-five-dollar-a-month apartment: "Cut corners and it'll always come back to bite you in the ass." That was one of her sayings. But if you didn't *have* money how could you *not* cut corners?

"And whose fault is it that you don't have any money? I'm not the one who turned up his nose at a full-time job. I'm not the one who spends his entire paycheck down at the hobby shop."

"I understand that."

---

[1] **Charlie Chan**: A Chinese-American detective featured in movies from the 1930s and 40s.

"Well good," she said, and then we began to wrap the breakables.

In my version of the story, the problem began with the child next door, a third grader 10
who, according to my mother, was bad news right from the start. "Put it together,"
she'd said when I first called to tell her about it. "Take a step back. Think."

But what was there to think about? She was a nine-year-old girl.

"Oh, they're the worst," my mother said. "What's her name?" I made something
up. "Brandi? Well that's cheap, isn't it."

"I'm sorry," I said. "But aren't I talking to someone who named her daughter *Tiffany?*"

"My hands were tied!" she shouted. "The damned Greeks had me against the wall
and you know it."

"Whatever you say." 15

"So this girl," my mother continued—and I knew what she would ask before she
even said it. "What does her father do?"

I told her there wasn't a father, at least not one that I knew about, and then I waited
as she lit a fresh cigarette. "Let's see," she said. "Nine-year-old girl named after an alcoholic beverage. Single mother in a neighborhood the police won't even go to. What else
have you got for me?" She spoke as if I'd formed these people out of clay, as if it were
my fault that the girl was nine years old and her mother couldn't keep a husband. "I
don't suppose this woman has a job, does she?"

"She's a bartender."

"Oh, that's splendid," my mother said. "Go on."

The woman worked nights and left her daughter alone from four in the afternoon 20
until two or three in the morning. Both were blond, their hair almost white, with invisible eyebrows and lashes. The mother darkened hers with pencil, but the girl appeared
to have none at all. Her face was like the weather in one of those places with no dis-
cernible seasons. Every now and then, the circles under her eyes would shade to purple.
She might show up with a fat lip or a scratch on her neck but her features betrayed
nothing.

You had to feel sorry for a girl like that. No father, no eyebrows, and that mother.
Our apartments shared a common wall, and every night I'd hear the woman stomping
home from work. Most often she was with someone, but whether alone or with company she'd find some excuse to bully her daughter out of bed. Brandi had left a dough-
nut on the TV or Brandi had forgotten to drain her bathwater. Those are important
lessons to learn, but there's something to be said for leading by example. I never went
into their apartment, but what I saw from the door was pretty rough, not simply messy
or chaotic but hopeless, the lair of a depressed person.

Given her home life, it wasn't surprising that Brandi latched onto me. A normal
mother might have wondered what was up—her nine-year-old daughter spending time
with a twenty-six-year-old man—but this one didn't seem to care. I was just free stuff to
her: a free babysitter, a free cigarette machine, the whole store. I'd hear her through the
wall sometimes. "Hey, go ask your friend for a roll of toilet paper." "Go ask your friend
to make you a sandwich." If company was coming and she wanted to be alone, she'd kick
the girl out. "Why don't you go next door and see what your little playmate is up to?"

Before I moved in, Brandi's mother had used the couple downstairs, but you could
tell that the relationship had soured. Next to the grocery carts chained to their porch
was a store-bought sign, the "No Trespassing" followed by a hand-written "This meens
you, Brandi!!!!"

There was a porch on the second floor as well, with one door leading to Brandi's bedroom and another door leading to mine. Technically, the two apartments were supposed to share it, but the entire thing was taken up with their junk and so I rarely used it.

"I can't wait until you get out of your little slumming phase," my mother had said 25 on first seeing the building. She spoke as if she'd been raised in splendor, but in fact her childhood home had been much worse. The suits she wore, the delicate bridges holding her teeth in place—it was all an invention. "You live in bad neighborhoods so you can feel superior," she'd say, the introduction, always, to a fight. "The point is to move up in the world. Even sideways will do in a pinch, but what's the point in moving down?"

As a relative newcomer to the middle class, she worried that her children might slip back into the world of public assistance and bad teeth. The finer things were not yet in our blood, or at least that was the way she saw it. My thrift-shop clothing drove her wild, as did the secondhand mattress lying without benefit of box springs upon my hardwood floor. "It's not *ironic*," she'd say. "It's not *ethnic*. It's filthy."

Bedroom suites were fine for people like my parents, but as an artist I preferred to rough it. Poverty lent my little dabblings a much needed veneer of authenticity, and I imagined myself repaying the debt by gently lifting the lives of those around me, not en masse but one by one, the old-fashioned way. It was, I thought, the least I could do.

I told my mother that I had allowed Brandi into my apartment, and she sighed deeply into the telephone. "And I bet you gave her the grand tour, didn't you? Mr. Showoff. Mr. Big Shot." We had a huge fight over that one. I didn't call her for two days. Then the phone rang. "Brother," she said, "you have no idea what you're getting yourself into."

A neglected girl comes to your door and what are you supposed to do, turn her away?

"Exactly," my mother said. "Throw her the hell out." 30

But I couldn't. What my mother defined as boasting I considered a standard show-and-tell. "This is my stereo system," I'd said to Brandi. "This is the electric skillet I received last Christmas, and here's a little something I picked up in Greece last summer." I thought I was exposing her to the things a regular person might own and appreciate, but all she heard was the possessive. "This is my honorable-mention ribbon" meant "It belongs to *me*. It's not yours." Every now and then, I'd give her a little something, convinced that she'd treasure it forever. A postcard of the Acropolis, prestamped envelopes, packaged towelettes bearing the insignia of Olympic Airways. "Really?" she'd say. "For me?"

The only thing she owned, the only thing special, was a foot-tall doll in a clear-plastic carrying case. It was a dimestore version of one of those Dolls from Many Countries, this one Spanish with a beet-red dress and a droopy mantilla on her head. Behind her, printed on cardboard, was the place where she lived: a piñata-lined street snaking up a hill to a dusty bullring. The doll had been given to Brandi by her grandmother, who was forty years old and lived in a trailer beside an Army base.

"What is this?" my mother asked. "A skit from 'Hee Haw'? Who the hell *are* these people?"

"These people," I said, "are my neighbors, and I'd appreciate it if you wouldn't make fun of them. The grandmother doesn't need it, I don't need it, and I'm pretty sure a nine-year-old-girl doesn't need it either." I didn't tell her that the grandmother was nicknamed Rascal or that, in the photograph Brandi showed me, the woman was wearing cutoff shorts and an ankle bracelet.

"We don't talk to her anymore," Brandi had said when I handed back the picture. 35
"She's out of our life, and we're glad of it." Her voice was dull and robotic, and I got
the impression that the line had been fed to her by her mother. She used a similar tone
when introducing her doll: "She's not for playing with. She's for display."

Whoever imposed this rule had obviously backed it up with a threat. Brandi would
trace her finger along the outside of the box, tempting herself, but never once did I
see her lift the lid. It was as if the doll would explode if removed from her natural
environment. Her world was the box, and a strange world it was.

"See," Brandi said one day. "She's on her way home to cook up those clams."

She was talking about the castanets dangling from the doll's wrist. It was a funny
thought, childish, and I probably should have let it go rather than playing the know-
it-all. "If she were an American doll those might be clams," I said. "But instead she's
from Spain, and those are called castanets." I wrote the word on a piece of paper.
"'Castanets,' look it up."

"She's not from Spain, she's from Fort Bragg."

"Well, maybe she was *bought* there," I said. "But she's supposed to be Spanish." 40

"And what's *that* supposed to mean?" It was hard to tell without the eyebrows, but
I think she was mad at me.

"It's not *supposed* to mean anything," I said. "It's just true."

"You're full of it. There's no such place."

"Sure there is," I said. "It's right next to France."

"Yeah, right. What's that, a store?" 45

I couldn't believe I was having this conversation. How could you not know that
Spain was a country? Even if you were nine years old, it seems you would have picked it
up on TV or something. "Oh, Brandi," I said. "We've got to find you a map."

Because I couldn't do it any other way, we fell into a tight routine. I had a part-time
construction job and would return home at exactly five-thirty. Five minutes later,
Brandi would knock on my door, and stand there blinking until I let her in. I was going
through a little wood-carving phase at the time, whittling figures whose heads resembled the various tools I worked with during the day: a hammer, a hatchet, a wire brush.
Before beginning, I'd arrange some paper and colored pencils on my desk. "Draw your
doll," I'd say. "Copy the bullring in her private environment. Express yourself!" I encouraged her to broaden her horizons, but she usually quit after the first few minutes,
claiming it was too much work.

Mainly she observed, her eyes shifting between my knife and the Spanish doll
parked before her on the desktop. She'd talk about how stupid her teachers were, and
then she'd ask what I would do if I had a million dollars. If I'd had a million dollars
at that time in my life I probably would have spent every last penny of it on drugs, but
I didn't admit it, because I wanted to set a good example. "Let's see," I'd say. "If I had
that kind of money, I'd probably give it away."

"Yeah, right. You'd what, just hand it out to people on the street?"

"No, I'd set up a foundation and try to make a difference in people's lives." At this 50
one even the doll was gagging.

When asked what she'd do with a million dollars Brandi described cars and gowns
and heavy bracelets encrusted with gems.

"But what about others? Don't you want to make them happy?"

"No. I want to make them jealous."

"You don't mean that," I'd say.

"Try me."   55

"Oh, Brandi." I'd make her a glass of chocolate milk and she'd elaborate on her list until six-fifty-five, when friendship period was officially over. If work had gone slowly and there weren't many shavings to sweep up, I might let her stay an extra two minutes, but never longer.

"Why do I have to go right this second?" she asked one evening. "Are you going to work or something?"

"Well no, not exactly."

"Then what's your hurry?"

I never should have told her. The good part about being an obsessive-compulsive is   60
that you're always on time for work. The bad part is that you're on time for everything. Rinsing your coffee cup, taking a bath, walking your clothes to the laundromat: there's no mystery to your comings and goings, no room for spontaneity. During that time of my life, I went to the IHOP every evening, heading over on my bike at exactly seven and returning at exactly nine. I never ate there, just drank coffee, facing the exact same direction in the exact same booth and reading library books for exactly an hour. After this, I would ride to the grocery store. Even if I didn't need anything I'd go, because that's what that time was allotted for. If the lines were short, I'd bike home the long way or circle the block a few times, unable to return early, as those five or ten minutes weren't scheduled for apartment time.

"What would happen if you were ten minutes late?" Brandi asked. My mother often asked the same question—everyone did. "You think the world will fall apart if you walk through that door at nine-o-four?"

They said it jokingly, but the answer was yes, that's exactly what I thought would happen. The world would fall apart. On the nights when another customer occupied my regular IHOP booth, I was shattered. "Is there a problem?" the waitress would ask, and I'd find that I couldn't even speak.

Brandi had been incorporated into my schedule for a little over a month when I started noticing certain things missing—things like pencil erasers and these little receipt books I'd picked up in Greece. In searching through my drawers and cabinets, I discovered that other things were missing as well: a box of tacks, a key ring in the form of a peanut.

"I see where this is going," my mother said. "The little sneak unlatched your porch door and wandered over while you were off at the pancake house. That's what happened, isn't it?"

I hated that she'd figured it out so quickly.   65

When I confronted Brandi, she broke down immediately. It was as if she'd been dying to confess, had rehearsed it even. The stammered apology, the plea for mercy. She hugged me around the waist, and when she finally pulled away I felt my shirt front, expecting to find it wet with tears. It wasn't. I don't know why I did what I did next, or, rather, I guess I do. It was all part of my ridiculous plan to set a good example. "You know what we have to do now, don't you?" I sounded firm and fair until I considered the consequences, at which point I faltered. "We've got to go . . . and tell your mother what you just *did*."

I half hoped that Brandi might talk me out of it, but instead she just shrugged.

"I bet she did," my mother said. "I mean, come on, you might as well have reported her to the cat. What did you expect that mother to do, needlepoint a sampler with the Ten Commandments? Wake up, Dopey, the woman's a whore."

Of course she was right. Brandi's mother listened with her arms crossed, a good sign until I realized that her anger was directed toward me rather than her daughter. In the far corner of the room a long-haired man cleaned beneath his fingernails with a pair of scissors. He looked my way for a moment, and then turned his attention back to the television.

"So she took a pencil eraser," Brandi's mother said. "What do you want me to do, dial 911?" She made it sound unbelievably petty. 70

"I just thought you should know what happened," I said.

"Well lucky me. Now I know."

I returned to my apartment and pressed my ear against the bedroom wall. "Who was that?" the guy asked.

"Oh, just some asshole," Brandi's mother said.

Things cooled down after that. I could forgive Brandi for breaking into my apart- 75 ment, but I could not forgive her mother. *Just some asshole.* I wanted to go to the place where she worked and burn it down. In relating the story, I found myself employing lines I'd probably heard on public radio. "Children *want* boundaries," I said. "They *need* them." It sounded sketchy to me, but everyone seemed to agree, especially my mother, who suggested that, in this particular case, a five-by-eleven cell might work. She wasn't yet placing the entire blame on me, so it was still enjoyable to tell her things, to warm myself against the comforting glow of her outrage.

The next time Brandi knocked, I pretended to be out—a ploy that fooled no one. She called my name, figured out where this was headed, and then went home to watch TV. I didn't plan to stay mad forever. A few weeks of the silent treatment and then I figured we'd pick up where we left off. In the meantime, I occasionally passed her in the front yard, just standing there as if she were waiting for someone normal to pick her up. I'd say, "Hello, how's it going?" and she'd give me this tight little smile, the sort you'd offer if someone you hated was walking around with chocolate stains on the back of his pants.

Back when our neighborhood was prosperous, the building we lived in was a single-family home, and sometimes I liked to imagine it as it once was: with proud rooms and chandeliers, a stately working household serviced by maids and coachmen. I was carrying out the trash one afternoon and came upon what used to be the coal cellar, a grim crawl space now littered with shingles and mildewed cardboard boxes. There were worn-out fuses and balls of electrical wire, and there, in the back, a pile of objects I recognized as my own, things I hadn't noticed missing—photographs, for instance, and slides of my bad art work. Moisture had fouled the casings, and when I backed out of the cellar and held them to the sun I saw that the film had been scratched, not by accident but intentionally, with a pin or a razor. "Yur a ashole," one of them read. "Suk my dick why dont you." The spelling was all over the place, the writing tiny and furious, bleeding into the mind-bending designs spewed by mental patients who don't know when to stop. It was the exact effect I'd been striving for in mybland, imitation folk art, so not only did I feel violated, I felt jealous. I mean, this girl was the real thing.

There were pages of slides, all of them etched with ugly messages. Photographs, too, were ruined. Here was me as a toddler with the word "Shity" scratched into my forehead. Here was my newly-wed mother netting crabs with her eyes clawed out. Included in the pile were all of the little presents accepted with such false gratitude, the envelopes and postcards, even the towelettes, everything systematically destroyed.

I gathered it all up and went straight to Brandi's mother. It was two o'clock in the afternoon and she was dressed in one of those thigh-length robes people wear when practicing karate. This was morning for her, and she stood drinking cola from a tall glass mug. "Fuck," she said. "Haven't we been through this?"

"Well, actually, no." My voice was higher than normal, and unstable. "Actually, we *haven't* been through this."

I'd considered myself an outsider in this neighborhood, something like a missionary among the savages, but standing there panting, my hair netted with cob-webs, I got the horrible feeling that I fit right in.

Brandi's mother glanced down at the filthy stack in my hand, frowning, as if these were things I was trying to sell door to door. "You know what?" she said. "I don't need this right now. No, you know what? I don't need it, period. Do you think having a baby was easy for me? I don't have nobody helping me out, a husband or day care or whatever, I'm all alone here, understand?"

I tried putting the conversation back on track, but as far as Brandi's mother was concerned there was no other track. It was all about her. "I work my own hours *and* cover shifts for Kathy fucking Cornelius and on my one day off I've got some faggot hassling me about some shit I don't even *know* about? I don't think so. Not today I don't, so why don't you go find somebody else to dump on."

She slammed the door in my face and I stood in the hallway wondering, *Who is Kathy Cornelius? What just happened?*

In the coming days, I ran the conversation over and over in my mind, thinking of all the fierce and sensible things I should have said, things like "Hey, *I'm* not the one who decided to have children," and "It's not *my* problem that you have to cover shifts for Kathy fucking Cornelius."

"It wouldn't have made any difference," my mother said. "A woman like that, the way she sees it she's a victim. Everyone's against her, no matter what."

I was so angry and shaken that I left the apartment and went to stay with my parents, on the other side of town. My mom drove me to the IHOP and back, right on schedule, but it wasn't the same. On my bike I was left to my own thoughts, but now I had her lecturing me, both coming and going. "What did you hope to gain by letting that girl into your apartment? And don't tell me you wanted to make a difference in her life, please, I just ate." I got it that night and then again the following morning. "Do you want me to give you a ride back to your little shantytown?" she asked, but I was mad at her, and so I took the bus.

I thought things couldn't get much worse and then, that evening, they did. I was just returning from the IHOP and was on the landing outside Brandi's door when I heard her whisper, "Faggot." She had her mouth to the keyhole and her voice was puny and melodic. It was the way I'd always imagined a moth might sound. "Faggot. What's the matter, faggot? What's wrong, huh?"

She laughed as I scrambled into my apartment, and then she ran to the porch and began to broadcast through my bedroom door. "Little faggot, little tattle-tale. You think you're so smart but you don't know shit."

"That's it," my mother said. "We've got to get you out of there." There was no talk of going to the police or social services, just "Pack up your things. She won."

"But can't I . . ."

"Ho ho no," my mother said. "You've got her mad now and there's no turning back. All she has to do is go to the authorities, saying you molested her. Is that what you want? One little phone call and your life is ruined."

"But I didn't do *anything*. I'm gay, remember?"

"That's not going to save you," she said. "Push comes to shove and who do you think they're going to believe, a nine-year-old girl or a full-grown man who gets his jollies carving little creatures out of balsa wood?"

"They're *not* little creatures!" I yelled. "They're tool people!" 95

"What the hell difference does it make? In the eyes of the law you're just some nut with a knife who sits in the pancake house staring at a goddam stop-watch. You dress that girl in something other than a tube top and prop her up on the witness stand—crying her eyes out—and what do you think is going to happen? Get that mother in on the act and you've got both a criminal trial *and* a civil suit on your hands."

"You watch too much TV."

"Not as much as they do," she said. "I can guaran-goddam-tee you that. You think these people can't smell money?"

"But I haven't got any."

"It's not your money they'll be after," she said. "It's mine." 100

"You mean Dad's." I was smarting over the "little creatures" comment and wanted to hurt her, but it didn't work.

"I mean *our* money," she said. "You think I don't know how these things work? I wasn't just born some middle-aged woman with a nice purse and a decent pair of shoes. My God, the things you don't know. My *God*."

My new apartment was eight blocks away, facing our city's first Episcopal church. My mother paid the deposit and the first month's rent and came with her station wagon to help me pack and move my things. Carrying a box of my featherweight balsa-wood sculptures out onto the landing, her hair gathered beneath a gingham scarf, how, I wondered, did she appear to Brandi, who was certainly watching through the keyhole. What did she represent to her? The word "mother" wouldn't do, as I don't really think she understood what it meant. A person who shepherds you along the way and helps you out when you're in trouble—what would she call that thing? A queen? A crutch? A teacher?

I heard a noise from behind the door, and then the little moth voice. "Bitch," Brandi whispered.

I fled back into the apartment, but my mother didn't even pause. "Sister," she said, 105 "you don't know the half of it." ●

Explorations of the Text

1. This essay is written not only from Sedaris's point of view but also as a dialogue between him and his mother. What do we learn about the situation from the two perspectives that we might not have learned from either Sedaris or his mother alone?

2. What constitutes a good mother or parent? List your criteria for a good parent and discuss the ways in which the two mothers in this essay do or do not meet your criteria.

3. Why does Sedaris let Brandi into his apartment and tell her so much about himself? Do you agree with his mother that the entire situation is his fault?

4. Sedaris's mother understands Brandi and her mother because as a child, she herself was poor. Considering this essay and "City Life," note the similarities between Sedaris's mother and Beatrice. How does their worldview differ from that of Sedaris?

The Reading/Writing Connection

1. Create a dialogue between Brandi and her therapist, twenty years later. What memories might Brandi have of her mother? Or, write a dialogue between David Sedaris and his therapist.

2. Freewrite about a time when a parent or another supportive adult helped you to deal with a difficult situation the way that Sedaris's mother helps him to move away from Brandi.

Ideas for Writing

1. **Write an Argument:** Hillary Clinton has famously said that it takes a village to raise a child, an idea shared by Barbara Kingsolver in "Stone Soup." Does it take a village to raise a child? Or, whose responsibility is it to care for children like Brandi, who are unwanted and neglected?

2. Write a short story featuring Brandi as a woman in her twenties or thirties. Is she a mother? If yes, how might her parenting differ from that of her own mother? If no, why does she decide not to have children?

Chang-rae Lee (1965–)

Coming Home Again   1996

When my mother began using the electronic pump that fed her liquids and medication, we moved her to the family room. The bedroom she shared with my father was upstairs, and it was impossible to carry the machine up and down all day and night. The pump itself was attached to a metal stand on casters, and she pulled it along wherever she went. From anywhere in the house, you could hear the sound of the wheels clicking out a steady time over the grout lines of the slate-tiled foyer, her main thoroughfare to the bathroom and the kitchen. Sometimes you would hear her halt after only a few steps, to catch her breath or steady her balance, and whatever you were doing was instantly suspended by a pall of silence.

I was usually in the kitchen, preparing lunch or dinner, poised over the butcher block with her favorite chef's knife in my hand and her old yellow apron slung around my neck. I'd be breathless in the sudden quiet, and, having ceased my mincing and chopping, would stare blankly at the brushed sheen of the blade. Eventually, she would clear her throat or call out to say she was fine, then begin to move again, starting her rhythmic *ka-jug;* and only then could I go on with my cooking, the world of our house turning once more, wheeling through the black.

I wasn't cooking for my mother but for the rest of us. When she first moved downstairs she was still eating, though scantily, more just to taste what we were having than from any genuine desire for food. The point was simply to sit together at the kitchen table and array ourselves like a family again. My mother would gently set herself down in her customary chair near the stove. I sat across from her, my father and sister to my left and right, and crammed in the center was all the food I had made—a spicy codfish stew, say, or a casserole of gingery beef, dishes that in my youth she had prepared for us a hundred times.

It had been ten years since we'd all lived together in the house, which at fifteen I had left to attend boarding school in New Hampshire. My mother would sometimes point this out, by speaking of our present time as being "just like before Exeter," which surprised me, given how proud she always was that I was a graduate of the school.

My going to such a place was part of my mother's not so secret plan to change my 5 character, which she worried was becoming too much like hers. I was clever and able enough, but without outside pressure I was readily given to sloth and vanity. The famous school—which none of us knew the first thing about—would prove my mettle. She was right, of course, and while I was there I would falter more than a few times, academically and otherwise. But I never thought that my leaving home then would ever be a problem for her, a private quarrel she would have even as her life waned.

Now her house was full again. My sister had just resigned from her job in New York City, and my father, who typically saw his psychiatric patients until eight or nine in the evening, was appearing in the driveway at four-thirty. I had been living at home for nearly a year and was in the final push of work on what would prove a dismal failure of a novel. When I wasn't struggling over my prose, I kept occupied with the things she usually did—the daily errands, the grocery shopping, the vacuuming and the cleaning, and, of course, all the cooking.

When I was six or seven years old, I used to watch my mother as she prepared our favorite meals. It was one of my daily pleasures. She shooed me away in the beginning, telling me that the kitchen wasn't my place, and adding, in her half-proud, half-deprecating way, that her kind of work would only serve to weaken me. "Go out and play with your friends," she'd snap in Korean, "or better yet, do your reading and homework." She knew that I had already done both, and that as the evening approached there was no place to go save her small and tidy kitchen, from which the clatter of her mixing bowls and pans would ring through the house.

I would enter the kitchen quietly and stand beside her, my chin lodging upon the point of her hip. Peering through the crook of her arm, I beheld the movements of her hands. For *kalbi,* she would take up a butchered short rib in her narrow hand, the flinty bone shaped like a section of an airplane wing and deeply embedded in gristle and flesh, and with the point of her knife cut so that the bone fell away, though not completely, leaving it connected to the meat by the barest opaque layer of tendon. Then she methodically butterflied the flesh, cutting and unfolding, repeating the action until the meat lay out on her board, glistening and ready for seasoning. She scored it diagonally, then sifted sugar into the crevices with her pinched fingers, gently rubbing in the crystals. The sugar would tenderize as well as sweeten the meat. She did this with each rib, and then set them all aside in a large shallow bowl. She minced a half-dozen cloves of garlic, a stub of ginger-root, sliced up a few scallions, and spread it all over the meat. She wiped her hands and took out a bottle of sesame oil, and, after pausing for a moment, streamed the dark oil in two swift circles around the bowl. After adding a few splashes of soy sauce, she thrust her hands in and kneaded the flesh, careful not to dislodge the bones. I asked her why it mattered that they remain connected, "The meat needs the bone nearby," she said, "to borrow its richness." She wiped her hands clean of the marinade, except for her little finger, which she would flick with her tongue from time to time, because she knew that the flavor of a good dish developed not at once but in stages.

Whenever I cook, I find myself working just as she would, readying the ingredients—a mash of garlic, a julienne of red peppers, fantails of shrimp—and piling them in little mounds about the cutting surface. My mother never left me any recipes, but this is how I learned to make her food, each dish coming not from a list or a card but from the aromatic spread of a board.

I've always thought it was particularly cruel that the cancer was in her stomach, 10 and that for a long time at the end she couldn't eat. The last meal I made for her was on New Year's Eve, 1990. My sister suggested that instead of a rib roast or a bird, or the usual overflow of Korean food, we make all sorts of finger dishes that our mother might fancy and pick at.

We set the meal out on the glass coffee table in the family room. I prepared a tray of smoked-salmon canapés, fried some Korean bean cakes, and made a few other dishes I thought she might enjoy. My sister supervised me, arranging the platters, and then with some pomp carried each dish in to our parents. Finally, I brought out a bottle of champagne in a bucket of ice. My mother had moved to the sofa and was sitting up, surveying the low table. "It looks pretty nice," she said. "I think I'm feeling hungry."

This made us all feel good, especially me, for I couldn't remember the last time she had felt any hunger or had eaten something I cooked. We began to eat. My mother picked up a piece of salmon toast and took a tiny corner in her mouth. She rolled it around for a moment and then pushed it out with the tip of her tongue, letting it fall back onto her plate. She swallowed hard, as if to quell a gag, then glanced up to see if we had noticed. Of course we all had. She attempted a bean cake, some cheese, and then a slice of fruit, but nothing was any use.

She nodded at me anyway, and said, "Oh, it's very good." But I was already feeling lost and I put down my plate abruptly, nearly shattering it on the thick glass. There was an ugly pause before my father asked me in a weary, gentle voice if anything was wrong, and I answered that it was nothing, it was the last night of a long year, and we were together, and I was simply relieved. At midnight, I poured out glasses of champagne, even one for my mother, who took a deep sip. Her manner grew playful and light, and I helped her shuffle to her mattress, and she lay down in the place where in a brief week she was dead.

My mother could whip up most anything, but during our first years of living in this country we ate only Korean foods. At my harangue-like behest, my mother set herself to learning how to cook exotic American dishes. Luckily, a kind neighbor, Mrs. Churchill, a tall, florid young woman with flaxen hair, taught my mother her most trusted recipes. Mrs. Churchill's two young sons, palish, weepy boys with identical crew cuts, always accompanied her, and though I liked them well enough, I would slip away from them after a few minutes, for I knew that the real action would be in the kitchen, where their mother was playing guide. Mrs. Churchill hailed from the state of Maine, where the finest Swedish meatballs and tuna casserole and angel food cake in America are made. She readily demonstrated certain techniques—how to layer wet sheets of pasta for a lasagna or whisk up a simple roux, for example. She often brought gift shoeboxes containing curious ingredients like dried oregano, instant yeast, and cream of mushroom soup. The two women, though at ease and jolly with each other, had difficulty communicating, and this was made worse by the often confusing terminology of Western cuisine ("corned beef," "deviled eggs"). Although I was just learning the language myself, I'd gladly play the interlocutor, jumping back and forth between their places at the counter, dipping my fingers into whatever sauce lay about.

I was an insistent child, and, being my mother's firstborn, much too prized. My 15 mother could say no to me, and did often enough, but anyone who knew us—particularly my father and sisters—could tell how much the denying pained her. And if I was overconscious of her indulgence even then, and suffered the rushing pangs of guilt that she could inflict upon me with the slightest wounded turn of her lip, I was too happily obtuse and venal to let her cease. She reminded me daily that I was her sole son, her reason for living, and that if she were to lose me, in either body or spirit, she wished that God would mercifully smite her, strike her down like a weak branch.

In the traditional fashion, she was the house accountant, the maid, the launderer, the disciplinarian, the driver, the secretary, and, of course, the cook. She was also my first basketball coach. In South Korea, where girls' high school basketball is a popular spectator sport, she had been a star, the point guard for the national high school team that once won the all-Asia championships. I learned this one Saturday during the summer, when I asked my father if he would go down to the schoolyard and shoot some baskets with me. I had just finished the fifth grade, and wanted desperately to make the middle school team the coming fall. He called for my mother and sister to come along. When we arrived, my sister immediately ran off to the swings, and I recall being annoyed that my mother wasn't following her. I dribbled clumsily around the key, on the verge of losing control of the ball, and flung a flat shot that caromed wildly off the rim. The ball bounced to my father, who took a few not so graceful dribbles and made an easy layup. He dribbled out and then drove to the hoop for a layup on the other side. He rebounded his shot and passed the ball to my mother, who had been watching us from the foul line. She turned from the basket and began heading the other way.

"*Um-mah,*" I cried at her, my exasperation already bubbling over, "the basket's over *here!*"

After a few steps she turned around, and from where the professional three-point line must be now, she effortlessly flipped the ball up in a two-handed set shot, its flight truer and higher than I'd witnessed from any boy or man. The ball arced cleanly into the hoop, stiffly popping the chain-link net. All afternoon, she rained in shot after shot, as my father and I scrambled after her.

When we got home from the playground, my mother showed me the photograph album of her team's championship run. For years I kept it in my room, on the same shelf that housed the scrapbooks I made of basketball stars, with magazine clippings of slick players like Bubbles Hawkins and Pistol Pete and George (the Iceman) Gervin.

It puzzled me how much she considered her own history to be immaterial, and if she never patently diminished herself, she was able to finesse a kind of self-removal by speaking of my father whenever she could. She zealously recounted his excellence as a student in medical school and reminded me, each night before I started my homework, of how hard he drove himself in his work to make a life for us. She said that because of his Asian face and imperfect English, he was "working two times the American doctors." I knew that she was building him up, buttressing him with both genuine admiration and her own brand of anxious braggadocio, and that her overarching concern was that I might fail to see him as she wished me to—in the most dawning light, his pose steadfast and solitary.

In the year before I left for Exeter, I became weary of her oft-repeated accounts of my father's success. I was a teenager, and so ever inclined to be dismissive and bitter toward anything that had to do with family and home. Often enough, my mother was the object of my derision. Suddenly, her life seemed so small to me. She was there, and sometimes, I thought, *always* there, as if she were confined to the four walls of our house. I would even complain about her cooking. Mostly, though, I was getting more and more impatient with the difficulty she encountered in doing everyday things. I was afraid for her. One day, we got into a terrible argument when she asked me to call the bank, to question a discrepancy she had discovered in the monthly statement. I asked her why she couldn't call herself. I was stupid and brutal, and I knew exactly how to wound her.

"Whom do I talk to?" she said. She would mostly speak to me in Korean, and I would answer in English.

"The bank manager, who else?"

"What do I say?"

"Whatever you want to say." 25

"Don't speak to me like that!" she cried.

"It's just that you should be able to do it yourself," I said.

"You know how I feel about this!"

"Well, maybe then you should consider it *practice*," I answered lightly, using the Korean word to make sure she understood.

Her face blanched, and her neck suddenly became rigid, as if I were throttling 30 her. She nearly struck me right then, but instead she bit her lip and ran upstairs. I followed her, pleading for forgiveness at her door. But it was the one time in our life that I couldn't convince her, melt her resolve with the blandishments of a spoiled son.

When my mother was feeling strong enough, or was in particularly good spirits, she would roll her machine into the kitchen and sit at the table and watch me work. She wore pajamas day and night, mostly old pairs of mine.

She said, "I can't tell, what are you making?"

"Mahn-doo filling."

"You didn't salt the cabbage and squash."

"Was I supposed to?" 35

"Of course. Look, it's too wet. Now the skins will get soggy before you can fry them."

"What should I do?"

"It's too late. Maybe it'll be OK if you work quickly. Why didn't you ask me?"

"You were finally sleeping."

"You should have woken me." 40

"No way."

She sighed, as deeply as her weary lungs would allow.

"I don't know how you were going to make it without me."

"I don't know, either. I'll remember the salt next time."

"You better. And not too much." 45

We often talked like this, our tone decidedly matter-of-fact, chin up, just this side of being able to bear it. Once, while inspecting a potato fritter batter I was making, she asked me if she had ever done anything that I wished she hadn't done. I thought for a moment, and told her no. In the next breath, she wondered aloud if it was right of her to have let me go to Exeter, to live away from the house while I was so young. She tested the batter's thickness with her finger and called for more flour. Then she asked if, given a choice, I would go to Exeter again.

I wasn't sure what she was getting at, and I told her that I couldn't be certain, but probably yes, I would. She snorted at this and said it was my leaving home that had once so troubled our relationship. "Remember how I had so much difficulty talking to you? Remember?"

She believed back then that I had found her more and more ignorant each time I came home. She said she never blamed me, for this was the way she knew it would be with my wonderful new education. Nothing I could say seemed to quell the notion. But I knew that the problem wasn't simply the *education;* the first time I saw her again after starting school, barely six weeks later, when she and my father visited me on Parents Day, she had already grown nervous and distant. After the usual campus events, we had gone to the motel where they were staying in a nearby town and sat on the beds in our room. She seemed to sneak looks at me, as though I might discover a horrible new truth if our eyes should meet.

My own secret feeling was that I had missed my parents greatly, my mother especially, and much more than I had anticipated. I couldn't tell them that these first weeks were a mere blur to me, that I felt completely overwhelmed by all the studies and my much brighter friends and the thousand irritating details of living alone, and that I had really learned nothing, save perhaps how to put on a necktie while sprinting to class. I felt as if I had plunged too deep into the world, which, to my great horror, was much larger than I had ever imagined.

I welcomed the lull of the motel room. My father and I had nearly dozed off when 50 my mother jumped up excitedly, murmured how stupid she was, and hurried to the closet by the door. She pulled out our old metal cooler and dragged it between the beds. She lifted the top and began unpacking plastic containers, and I thought she would never stop. One after the other they came out, each with a dish that traveled well—a salted stewed meat, rolls of Korean-style sushi. I opened a container of radish kimchi and suddenly the room bloomed with its odor, and I reveled in the very peculiar sensation (which perhaps only true kimchi lovers know) of simultaneously drooling and gagging as I breathed it all in. For the next few minutes, they watched me eat. I'm not certain that I was even hungry. But after weeks of pork parmigiana and chicken patties and wax beans, I suddenly realized that I had lost all the savor in my life. And it seemed I couldn't get enough of it back. I ate and I ate, so much and so fast that I actually went to the bathroom and vomited. I came out dizzy and sated with the phantom warmth of my binge.

And beneath the face of her worry, I thought, my mother was smiling.

From that day, my mother prepared a certain meal to welcome me home. It was always the same. Even as I rode the school's shuttle bus from Exeter to Logan airport, I could already see the exact arrangement of my mother's table.

I knew that we would eat in the kitchen, the table brimming with plates. There was the *kalbi,* of course, broiled or grilled depending on the season. Leaf lettuce, to wrap the meat with. Bowls of garlicky clam broth with miso and tofu and fresh spinach. Shavings of cod dusted in flour and then dipped in egg wash and fried. Glass noodles with onions and shiitake. Scallion-and-hot-pepper pancakes. Chilled steamed shrimp. Seasoned salads of bean sprouts, spinach, and white radish. Crispy squares of seaweed. Steamed rice with barley and red beans. Homemade kimchi. It was all there—the old flavors I knew, the beautiful salt, the sweet, the excellent taste.

After the meal, my father and I talked about school, but I could never say enough for it to make any sense. My father would often recall his high school principal, who had gone to England to study the methods and traditions of the public schools, and regaled students with stories of the great Eton man. My mother sat with us, paring fruit, not saying a word but taking everything in. When it was time to go to bed, my father said good night first. I usually watched television until the early morning. My mother would sit with me for an hour or two, perhaps until she was accustomed to me again, and only then would she kiss me and head upstairs to sleep.

During the following days, it was always the cooking that started our conversa- 55
tions. She'd hold an inquest over the cold leftovers we ate at lunch, discussing each dish in terms of its balance of flavors or what might have been prepared differently. But mostly I begged her to leave the dishes alone. I wish I had paid more attention. After her death, when my father and I were the only ones left in the house, drifting through the rooms like ghosts, I sometimes tried to make that meal for him. Though it was too much for two, I made each dish anyway, taking as much care as I could. But nothing turned out quite right—not the color, not the smell. At the table, neither of us said much of anything. And we had to eat the food for days.

I remember washing rice in the kitchen one day and my mother's saying in English, from her usual seat, "I made a big mistake."

"About Exeter?"

"Yes. I made a big mistake. You should be with us for that time. I should never let you go there."

"So why did you?" I said.

"Because I didn't know I was going to die." 60

I let her words pass. For the first time in her life, she was letting herself speak her full mind, so what else could I do?

"But you know what?" she spoke up. "It was better for you. If you stayed home, you would not like me so much now."

I suggested that maybe I would like her even more.

She shook her head. "Impossible."

Sometimes I still think about what she said, about having made a mistake. I 65
would have left home for college, that was never in doubt, but those years I was away at boarding school grew more precious to her as her illness progressed. After many months of exhaustion and pain and the haze of the drugs, I thought that her mind was beginning to fade, for more and more it seemed that she was seeing me again as her fifteen-year-old boy, the one she had dropped off in New Hampshire on a cloudy September afternoon.

I remember the first person I met, another new student, named Zack, who walked to the welcome picnic with me. I had planned to eat with my parents—my mother had brought a coolerful of food even that first day—but I learned of the cookout and told her that I should probably go. I wanted to go, of course. I was excited, and no doubt fearful and nervous, and I must have thought I was only thinking ahead. She agreed wholeheartedly, saying I certainly should. I walked them to the car, and perhaps I hugged them, before saying goodbye. One day, after she died, my father told me what happened on the long drive home to Syracuse.

He was driving the car, looking straight ahead. Traffic was light on the Massachusetts Turnpike, and the sky was nearly dark. They had driven for more than two hours and had not yet spoken a word. He then heard a strange sound from her, a kind of muffled chewing noise, as if something inside her were grinding its way out.

"So, what's the matter?" he said, trying to keep an edge to his voice.

She looked at him with her ashen face and she burst into tears. He began to cry himself, and pulled the car over onto the narrow shoulder of the turnpike, where they stayed for the next half hour or so, the blank-faced cars droning by them in the cold, onrushing; night.

Every once in a while, when I think of her, I'm driving alone somewhere on the highway. In the twilight, I see their car off to the side, a blue Olds coupe with a landau top, and as I pass them by I look back in the mirror and I see them again, the two figures huddling together in the front seat. Are they sleeping? Or kissing? Are they all right? ●

Explorations of the Text

1. How does Lee define his relationship with his mother through the cooking anecdotes? In what ways are the mother and son similar? Different?
2. Discuss Lee's mother's place in North American society. How is she hampered as a nonnative speaker of English? How is she caught between worlds? How do her language difficulties and ethnic background create a gulf between mother and son?
3. Explore the significance of the last scene (the last five paragraphs in the essay).

4. Why does Lee entitle the essay "Coming Home Again"? In tending to her in her final illness, in coping with her death, what does the narrator learn to appreciate about his mother? What does he discover through acts of autobiographical writing and reminiscing? Compare Lee's process of discovery with Kothari's. Do both writers come to terms with their pasts?

The Reading/Writing Connection

1. Journal entry: Write about your first few weeks in college or in high school.
2. Have your attitudes toward one of your parents changed over the years? Freewrite about this subject.

3. "Think" Topic: How does the symbolism of food function in the essay? What are the multiple ways that Lee uses this symbol?

Ideas for Writing

1. Create a character analysis of Lee's mother. Focus on her background, actions, attitudes, values, gestures, relationships with others, and speech.
2. Lee's work is an example of creative nonfiction. Analyze his style and approach. Consider such elements of creative nonfiction as point of view, use of descriptive detail, and figurative language. (Refer to Chapter 13 for ideas.)

Geeta Kothari *(1963–)*

If You Are What You Eat, Then What Am I? *2000*

To belong is to understand the tacit codes of the people you live with.

—Michael Ignatieff, *Blood and Belonging*

I

The first time my mother and I open a can of tuna, I am nine years old. We stand in the doorway of the kitchen, in semidarkness, the can tilted toward daylight. I want to eat what the kids at school eat: bologna, hot dogs, salami—foods my parents find repugnant because they contain pork and meat byproducts, crushed bone and hair glued together by chemicals and fat. Although she has never been able to tolerate the smell of fish, my mother buys the tuna, hoping to satisfy my longing for American food.

Indians, of course, do not eat such things.

The tuna smells fishy, which surprises me because I can't remember anyone's tuna sandwich actually smelling like fish. And the tuna in those sandwiches doesn't look like this, pink and shiny, like an internal organ. In fact, this looks similar to the bad foods my mother doesn't want me to eat. She is silent, holding her face away from the can while peering into it like a half-blind bird.

"What's wrong with it?" I ask.

She has no idea. My mother does not know that the tuna everyone else's mothers 5 made for them was tuna *salad*.

"Do you think it's botulism?"[1]

I have never seen botulism, but 1 have read about it, just as I have read about but never eaten steak and kidney pie.

There is so much my parents don't know. They are not like other parents, and they disappoint me and my sister. They are supposed to help us negotiate the world outside, teach us the signs, the clues to proper behavior: what to eat and how to eat it.

We have expectations, and my parents fail to meet them, especially my mother, who works full-time. I don't understand what it means, to have a mother who works outside and inside the home; I notice only the ways in which she disappoints me. She doesn't show up for school plays. She doesn't make chocolate-frosted cupcakes for my class. At night, if I want her attention, I have to sit in the kitchen and talk to her while she cooks the evening meal, attentive to every third or fourth word I say.

We throw the tuna away. This time my mother is disappointed. I go to school with 10 tuna eaters. I see their sandwiches, yet cannot explain the discrepancy between them and the stinking, oily fish in my mother's hand. We do not understand so many things, my mother and I.

II

On weekends, we eat fried chicken from Woolworth's on the back steps of my father's first-floor office in Murray Hill. The back steps face a small patch of garden—hedges, a couple of skinny trees, and gravel instead of grass. We can see the back window of

---

[1] **botulism**: A potentially fatal form of food poisoning.

the apartment my parents and I lived in until my sister was born. There, the doorman watched my mother, several months pregnant and wearing a sari, slip on the ice in front of the building.

My sister and I pretend we are in the country, where our American friends all have houses. We eat glazed doughnuts, also from Woolworth's, and french fries with ketchup.

III

My mother takes a catering class and learns that Miracle Whip and mustard are healthier than mayonnaise. She learns to make egg salad with chopped celery, deviled eggs dusted with paprika, a cream cheese spread with bits of fresh ginger and watercress, chicken liver pâté, and little brown-and-white checkerboard sand-wiches that we have only once. She makes chicken à la king in puff pastry shells and eggplant Parmesan. She acquires smooth wooden paddles, whose purpose is never clear, two different egg slicers, several wooden spoons, icing tubes, cookie cutters, and an electric mixer.

IV

I learn to make tuna salad by watching a friend. My sister never acquires a taste for it. Instead, she craves

    bologna
    hot dogs
    bacon
    sausages

and a range of unidentifiable meat products forbidden by my parents. Their restrictions are not about sacred cows, as everyone around us assumes; in a pinch, we are allowed hamburgers, though lamb burgers are preferable. A "pinch" means choosing not to draw attention to ourselves as outsiders, impolite visitors who won't eat what their host serves. But bologna is still taboo.

V

Things my sister refuses to eat: butter, veal, anything with jeera. The baby-sitter tries to   15
feed her butter sandwiches, threatens her with them, makes her cry in fear and disgust. My mother does not disappoint her; she does not believe in forcing us to eat, in using food as a weapon. In addition to pbj, my sister likes pasta and marinara sauce, bologna and Wonder Bread (when she can get it), and fried egg sandwiches with turkey, cheese, and horseradish. Her tastes, once established, are predictable.

VI

When we visit our relatives in India, food prepared outside the house is carefully monitored. In the hot, sticky monsoon months in New Delhi and Bombay, we cannot eat ice cream, salad, cold food, or any fruit that can't be peeled. Definitely no meat. People die from amoebic dysentery,[2] unexplained fevers, strange boils on their bodies. We drink boiled water only, no ice. No sweets except for jalebi, thin fried twists of dough

---

[2]**dysentery**: Intestinal disease.

in dripping hot sugar syrup. If we're caught outside with nothing to drink, Fanta, Limca, Thums Up (after Coca-Cola is thrown out by Mrs. Gandhi)[3] will do. Hot tea sweetened with sugar, served with thick creamy buffalo milk, is preferable. It should be boiled, to kill the germs on the cup.

My mother talks about "back home" as a safe place, a silk cocoon frozen in time where we are sheltered by family and friends. Back home, my sister and I do not argue about food with my parents. Home is where they know all the rules. We trust them to guide us safely through the maze of city streets for which they have no map, and we trust them to feed and take care of us, the way parents should.

Finally, though, one of us will get sick, hungry for the food we see our cousins and friends eating, too thirsty to ask for a straw, too polite to insist on properly boiled water.

At my uncle's diner in New Delhi, someone hands me a plate of aloo tikki, fried potato patties filled with mashed channa dal and served with a sweet and a sour chutney. The channa, mixed with hot chilies and spices, burns my tongue and throat. I reach for my Fanta, discard the paper straw, and gulp the sweet orange soda down, huge drafts that sting rather than soothe.

When I throw up later that day (or is it the next morning, when a stomachache [20] wakes me from deep sleep?), I cry over the frustration of being singled out, not from the pain my mother assumes I'm feeling as she holds my hair back from my face. The taste of orange lingers in my mouth, and I remember my lips touching the cold glass of the Fanta bottle.

At that moment, more than anything, I want to be like my cousins.

VII

In New York, at the first Indian restaurant in our neighborhood, my father orders with confidence, and my sister and I play with the silverware until the steaming plates of lamb biryani arrive.

What is Indian food? my friends ask, their noses crinkling up.

Later, this restaurant is run out of business by the new Indo-Pak-Bangladeshi combinations up and down the street, which serve similar food. They use plastic cutlery and Styrofoam cups. They do not distinguish between North and South Indian cooking, or between Indian, Pakistani, and Bangladeshi cooking, and their customers do not care. The food is fast, cheap, and tasty. Dosa, a rice flour crepe stuffed with masala potato, appears on the same trays as chicken makhani.

Now my friends want to know, Do you eat curry at home? [25]

One time my mother makes lamb vindaloo for guests. Like dosa, this is a South Indian dish, one that my Punjabi mother has to learn from a cookbook. For us, she cooks everyday food—yellow dal, rice, chapati, bhaji. Lentils, rice, bread, and vegetables. She has never referred to anything on our table as "curry" or "curried," but I know she has made chicken curry for guests. Vindaloo, she explains, is a curry too. I understand then that curry is a dish created for guests, outsiders, a food for people who eat in restaurants.

---

[3]**Mrs. Gandhi**: Indira Gandhi was Prime Minister of India from 1966 to 1977 and again from 1980 until her assassination in 1984. In 1977 Coca-Cola chose to leave India rather than relinquish sixty percent of its equity to the Indians who were attempting to bolster their economy.

VIII

I have inherited brown eyes, black hair, a long nose with a crooked bridge, and soft teeth with thin enamel. I am in my twenties, moving to a city far from my parents, before it occurs to me that jeera, the spice my sister avoids, must have an English name. I have to learn that haldi = turmeric, methi = fenugreek. What to make with fenugreek, I do not know. My grandmother used to make methi roti for our breakfast, cornbread with fresh fenugreek leaves served with a lump of homemade butter. No one makes it now that she's gone, though once in a while my mother will get a craving for it and produce a facsimile ("The cornmeal here is wrong") that only highlights what she's really missing: the smells and tastes of her mother's house.

I will never make my grandmother's methi roti or even my mother's unsatisfactory imitation of it. I attempt chapati; it takes six hours, three phone calls home, and leaves me with an aching back. I have to write translations down: jeera = cumin. My memory is unreliable. But I have always known garam = hot.

IX

My mother learns how to make brownies and apple pie. My father makes only Indian food, except for loaves of heavy, sweet brown bread that I eat with thin slices of American cheese and lettuce. The recipe is a secret, passed on to him by a woman at work. Years later, when he finally gives it to me, when I finally ask for it, I end up with three bricks of gluten that even the birds and my husband won't eat.

X

My parents send me to boarding school, outside of London. They imagine that I will overcome my shyness and find a place for myself in this all-girls' school. They have never lived in England, but as former subjects of the British Empire, they find London familiar, comfortable in a way New York—my mother's home for over twenty years by now—is not. Americans still don't know what to call us; their Indians live on reservations, not in Manhattan. Because they understand the English, my parents believe the English understand us.

I poke at my first school lunch—thin, overworked pastry in a puddle of lumpy gravy. The lumps are chewy mushrooms, maybe, or overcooked shrimp.

"What is this?" I don't want to ask, but I can't go on eating without knowing.

"Steak and kidney pie."

The girl next to me, red-haired, freckled, watches me take a bite from my plate. She has been put in charge of me, the new girl, and I follow her around all day, a foreigner at the mercy of a reluctant and angry tour guide. She is not used to explaining what is perfectly and utterly natural.

"What, you've never had steak and kidney pie? Bloody hell."

My classmates scoff, then marvel, then laugh at my ignorance. After a year, I understand what is on my plate: sausage rolls, blood pudding, Spam, roast beef in a thin, greasy gravy, all the bacon and sausage I could possibly want. My parents do not expect me to starve.

The girls at school expect conformity; it has been bred into them, through years of uniforms and strict rules about proper behavior. I am thirteen and contrary, even as I yearn for acceptance. I declare myself a vegetarian and doom myself to a diet of cauliflower, cheese, and baked beans on toast. The administration does not question my decision; they assume it's for vague, undefined religious reasons, although my father, the doctor, tells them it's for my health. My reasons, from this distance of many years, remain murky to me.

Perhaps I am my parents' daughter after all.

XI

When she is three, sitting on my cousin's lap in Bombay, my sister reaches for his plate and puts a chili in her mouth. She wants to be like the grownups, who dip green chilies in coarse salt and eat them like any other vegetable. She howls inconsolable animal pain for what must be hours. She doesn't have the vocabulary for the oily heat that stings her mouth and tongue, burns a trail through her small tender body. Only hot, sticky tears on my father's shoulder.

As an adult, she eats red chili paste, mango pickle, kimchee, foods that make my   40
eyes water and my stomach gurgle. My tastes are milder. I order raita at Indian restaurants and ask for food that won't sear the roof of my mouth and scar the insides of my cheeks. The waiters nod, and their eyes shift—a slight once-over that indicates they don't believe me. I am Indian, aren't I? My father seems to agree with them. He tells me I'm asking for the impossible, as if he believes the recipes are immutable, written in stone during the passage from India to America.

XII

I look around my boyfriend's freezer one day and find meat: pork chops, ground beef, chicken pieces, Italian sausage. Ham in the refrigerator, next to the homemade bolognese sauce. Tupperware filled with chili made from ground beef and pork.

He smells different from me. Foreign. Strange.

I marry him anyway.

He has inherited blue eyes that turn gray in bad weather, light brown hair, a sharp pointy nose, and excellent teeth. He learns to make chili with ground turkey and tofu, tomato sauce with red wine and portobello mushrooms, roast chicken with rosemary and slivers of garlic under the skin.

He eats steak when we are in separate cities, roast beef at his mother's house, ham-   45
burgers at work. Sometimes I smell them on his skin. I hope he doesn't notice me turning my face, a cheek instead of my lips, my nose wrinkled at the unfamiliar, musky smell.

XIII

And then I realize I don't want to be a person who can find Indian food only in restaurants. One day my parents will be gone and I will long for the foods of my childhood, the way they long for theirs. I prepare for this day the way people on TV prepare for the end of the world. They gather canned goods they will never eat while I stockpile recipes I cannot replicate. I am frantic, disorganized, grabbing what I can, filing scribbled notes haphazardly. I regret the tastes I've forgotten, the meals I have inhaled without a thought. I worry that I've come to this realization too late.

XIV

Who told my mother about Brie? One day we were eating Velveeta, the next day Brie, Gouda, Camembert, Port Salut, Havarti with caraway, Danish fontina, string cheese made with sheep's milk. Who opened the door to these foreigners that sit on the refrigerator shelf next to last night's dal?

Back home, there is one cheese only, which comes in a tin, looks like Bakelite, and tastes best when melted.

And how do we go from Chef Boyardee to fresh pasta and homemade sauce, made with Redpack tomatoes, crushed garlic, and dried oregano? Macaroni and cheese, made with fresh cheddar and whole milk, sprinkled with bread crumbs and paprika. Fresh eggplant and ricotta ravioli, baked with marinara sauce and fresh mozzarella.

My mother will never cook beef or pork in her kitchen, and the foods she knew in her childhood are unavailable. Because the only alternative to the supermarket, with its TV dinners and canned foods, is the gourmet Italian deli across the street, by default our meals become socially acceptable.

XV

If I really want to make myself sick, I worry that my husband will one day leave me for a meat-eater, for someone familiar who doesn't sniff him suspiciously for signs of alimentary infidelity.

XVI

Indians eat lentils. I understand this as absolute, a decree from an unidentifiable authority that watches and judges me.

So what does it mean that I cannot replicate my mother's dal? She and my father show me repeatedly, in their kitchen, in my kitchen. They coach me over the phone, buy me the best cookbooks, and finally write down their secrets. Things I'm supposed to know but don't. Recipes that should be, by now, engraved on my heart.

Living far from the comfort of people who require no explanation for what I do and who I am, I crave the foods we have shared. My mother convinces me that moong is the easiest dal to prepare, and yet it fails me every time: bland, watery, a sickly greenish yellow mush. These imperfect imitations remind me only of what I'm missing.

But I have never been fond of moong dal. At my mother's table it is the last thing I reach for. Now I worry that this antipathy toward dal signals something deeper, that somehow I am not my parents' daughter, not Indian, and because I cannot bear the touch and smell of raw meat, though I can eat it cooked (charred, dry, and overdone), I am not American either.

I worry about a lifetime purgatory in Indian restaurants where I will complain that all the food looks and tastes the same because they've used the same masala.

XVII

About the tuna and her attempts to feed us, my mother laughs. She says, "You were never fussy. You ate everything I made and never complained."

My mother is at the stove, wearing only her blouse and petticoat, her sari carefully folded and hung in the closet. She does not believe a girl's place is in the kitchen, but she expects me to know that too much hing can ruin a meal, to know without being told, without having to ask or write it down. Hing = asafetida.

She remembers the catering class. "Oh, that class. You know, I had to give it up when we got to lobster. I just couldn't stand the way it looked."

She says this apologetically, as if she has deprived us, as if she suspects that having a mother who could feed us lobster would have changed the course of our lives.

Intellectually, she understands that only certain people regularly eat lobster, people with money or those who live in Maine, or both. In her catering class there were people without jobs for whom preparing lobster was a part of their professional training as caterers. Like us, they wouldn't be eating lobster at home. For my mother, however, lobster was just another American food, like tuna—different, strange, not natural yet somehow essential to belonging.

I learned how to prepare and eat lobster from the same girl who taught me tuna salad. I ate bacon at her house too. And one day this girl, with her houses in the country and Martha's Vineyard, asked me how my uncle was going to pick me up from the airport in Bombay. In 1973, she was surprised to hear that he used a car, not an elephant. At home, my parents and I laughed, and though I never knew for sure if she was making fun of me, I still wanted her friendship.

My parents were afraid my sister and I would learn to despise the foods they loved, replace them with bologna and bacon and lose our taste for masala. For my mother, giving up her disgust of lobster, with its hard exterior and foreign smell, would mean renouncing some essential difference. It would mean becoming, decidedly, definitely, American—unafraid of meat in all its forms, able to consume large quantities of protein at any given meal. My willingness to toss a living being into boiling water and then get past its ugly appearance to the rich meat inside must mean to my mother that I am somehow someone she is not.

But I haven't eaten lobster in years. In my kitchen cupboards, there is a thirteen-pound bag of basmati rice, jars of lime pickle, mango pickle, and ghee, cans of tuna and anchovies, canned soups, coconut milk, and tomatoes, rice noodles, several kinds of pasta, dried mushrooms, and unlabeled bottles of spices: haldi, jeera, hing. When my husband tries to help me cook, he cannot identify all the spices. He gets confused when I forget their English names and remarks that my expectations of him are unreasonable.

I am my parents' daughter. Like them, I expect knowledge to pass from me to my husband without one word of explanation or translation. I want him to know what I know, see what I see, without having to tell him exactly what it is. I want to believe that recipes never change. ● 65

Explorations of the Text

1. Kothari uses food imagery as a way to illustrate her family's acclimation to the culture of the United States. Some of her paragraphs consist of lists of food eaten and enjoyed (or not) by her and her sister. How effective is this presentation of cultural differences? List what you have learned of Indian food, family life, and culture from reading this essay.

2. Throughout the essay, Kothari notes what people inherit from their families in terms of genetics and cultural tastes. At the end of the essay, what has Kothari kept of her family inheritance? What has changed from her parents' to her generation? Is this change characterized as a loss of culture? Or as an adap-

tation, a creation of a new life that can be considered a blending of two rather than a loss of one?

3. In "Common Scents," Lynda Barry describes the different smells she notices in people's homes. Kothari, too, notes that her husband "smells different from [her]. Foreign. Strange." What do the smells signify about cultural identity?

4. In Chang-rae Lee's "Coming Home Again," he, like Kothari, connects home and memories of childhood to food. Discuss the ways in which Lee and Kothari describe the process of learning how to cook as a means of connecting to and maintaining the memories of childhood.

The Reading/Writing Connection

1. Write about foods of your childhood. What do they represent?
2. Consider your impressions of other people based on what they eat or do not eat. Create a character sketch for a vegetarian (a person who will not eat meat) or a vegan (a person who eats no animal products, including milk, eggs,

or cheese), a person who only wants to eat hamburgers and French fries, and a person who is uncomfortable eating foods that are not culturally familiar (for instance, an American of German descent who would refuse to try sushi). In what ways do we stereotype people based on their diets? Are these stereotypes accurate?

Ideas for Writing

1. **Write an Argument:** Consider the title of the essay. Are you what you eat? Argue for or against this question, using evidence from Kothari's essay and from your own experience to support your argument.

Katherine Waugh *(1946–)*

Bucket of Blood   *2006*

Picture a family of five, sometime in the early nineteen fifties, nearing the end of dinner. They have sopped up the last pools of gravy; the bones are sucked clean. The father, a professor, has talked about a brilliant student he is encouraging to go on to Yale in Early American History. The older boy, nine years old, has educated the others, in almost New Yorkerish detail, on the habits of the box turtle. The younger son, a second grader, has spoken of his stamp collection and his ambition to be governor of Tasmania.[1] The five year old girl, who attends Catholic school, has held forth at some length on St. Francis of Assisi. Civilization has been upheld for one more day.

The mother, unusually silent, has so far added no tales of the day's doings, no amusing stories of victories over surly shopkeepers, no charming policemen out of issuing speeding tickets, no treasures found by the side of the road. Forks scrape plates, milk glasses are drained; the children calculate how soon they may ask to be excused from the table.

"I had an interesting experience today," the mother began with a pleased, faraway look. "I left home to go to the A&P Market, and there, on the corner by the Methodist Church, stood an old Negro man."

This was hardly unusual. Life in a Southern town at that time involved a certain amount of public standing about on the part of both black and white men.

"He had a bucket of blood at his feet." Her gaze swept the table. All thoughts of 5 being excused fled. One paused, napkin halfway to mouth. Another set his milk glass down gently. Other mothers would have fainted at the sight of a bucket of blood; the bravest might have shuddered and passed by, but not this one! She had driven through a forest fire, gone boating in a hurricane, swum across riptides.

---

[1] **Tasmania:** An island state of Australia.

She resumed her tale.

"I said, 'Well, Sir, what do you have there?' and he answered 'Swamp rat, ma'am.'"

At this point, any other mother we knew would have moved on, but not this one. Instead, she stood there in her dress, her stockings, her hat and white gloves, swinging her market basket and continued the conversation.

"I asked him what was swamp rat, and he told me some folks called it marsh rat. Then of course I realized it was muskrat."

Imagine three children, torn between pride in their mother and the horrified real-   10 ization of where this story of hers was inevitably headed.

"Leave now," they are thinking. "Depart from the corner of the Methodist Church. Say goodbye to the amiable Negro man. Ask no more questions. Go to the A&P Market to buy your family a pot roast, a chicken, some hamburger meat." But their Greek cho-rus was mute, not to mention after the fact, and their mother, oblivious as any Greek hero, moved toward the climax.

"So naturally I asked him how he fixed it, and he said he rolled it in some cornmeal and fried it right up. And," she smiled at her family, "I told him I'd take two!"

The children looked down at their plates, the little piles of bones, the small rib cages, the delicate vertebrae.

"May we please be excused from the table?"

"Yes, of course. Run along." ●   15

Explorations of the Text

1. From whose point of view is the moth-er's story told; who is the narrator?

2. What is your impression of the family pictured in the introduction? In what ways does this picture change by the time you read the conclusion?

3. Discuss the character of the mother. What role does she appear to play in the family? Why do the children know "where this story" is "headed"?

4. Is the ending satisfactory?

The Reading/Writing Connection

1. Journal entry: Write about a time when you ate something that many people might consider to be unusual. Why did you do it?

2. Re-write the ending to this essay. Or, continue the essay, focusing on the thoughts and conversations of the chil-dren once they leave the table.

3. Write a letter from the mother in this essay to Geeta Kothari, (author of "If You Are What You Eat, Then What Am I?") or vice versa.

Ideas for Writing

1. Argue pro or con: Meat is meat; it shouldn't matter if you eat cow, pig, deer, muskrat, or dog.

www   **On the Web:** *Food and Family*

Please visit http://www.academic.cengage.com/english/Schmidt/Legacies4e/ for links to the following online resources.

Ira Sukrungruang, "Chop Suey"

The Nuclear Family Redefined/Nonfiction

Barbara Kingsolver   (1955–   )

Stone Soup   1995

In the catalog of family values, where do we rank an occasion like this? A curly-haired boy who wanted to run before he walked, age seven now, a soccer player scoring a winning goal. He turns to the bleachers with his fists in the air and a smile wide as a gap-toothed galaxy. His own cheering section of grown-ups and kids all leap to their feet and hug each other, delirious with love for this boy. He's Andy, my best friend's son. The cheering section includes his mother and her friends, his brother, his father and stepmother, a stepbrother and stepsister, and a grandparent. Lucky is the child with this many relatives on hand to hail a proud accomplishment. I'm there too, witnessing a family fortune. But in spite of myself, defensive words take shape in my head. I am thinking: I dare *anybody* to call this a broken home.

Families change, and remain the same. Why are our names for home so slow to catch up the truth of where we live?

When I was a child, I had two parents who loved me without cease. One of them attended every excuse for attention I ever contrived, and the other made it to the ones with higher production values, like piano recitals and appendicitis. So I was a lucky child too. I played with a set of paper dolls called "The Family of Dolls," four in number, who came with the factory-assigned names of Dad, Mom, Sis, and Junior. I think you know what they looked like, at least before I loved them to death and their heads fell off.

Now I've replaced the dolls with a life. I knit my days around my daughter's survival and happiness, and am proud to say her head is still on. But we aren't the Family of Dolls. Maybe you're not, either. And if not. even though you are statistically no oddity, it's probably been suggested to you in a hundred ways that yours isn't exactly a real family, but an impostor family, a harbinger of cultural ruin, a slapdash substitute—something like counterfeit money. Here at the tail end of our century, most of us are up to our ears in the noisy business of trying to support and love a thing called family. But there's a current in the air with ferocious moral force that finds its way even into political campaigns, claiming there is only one right way to do it, the Way It Has Always Been.

In the face of a thriving, particolored world, this narrow view is so pickled and 5 absurd I'm astonished that it gets airplay. And I'm astonished that it still stings.

Every parent has endured the arrogance of a child-unfriendly grump sitting in judgment, explaining what those kids of ours really need (for example, "a good licking"). If we're polite, we move our crew to another bench in the park. If we're forthright (as I am in my mind, only, for the rest of the day), we fix them with a sweet imperious stare and say, "Come back and let's talk about it after you've changed a thousand diapers."

But it's harder somehow to shrug off the Family-of-Dolls Family Values crew when they judge (from their safe distance) that divorced people, blended families, gay families, and single parents are failures. That our children are at risk, and the whole arrangement is messy and embarrassing. A marriage that ends is not called "finished," it's called *failed*. The children of this family may have been born to a happy union, but now they are called *the children of divorce.*

I had no idea how thoroughly these assumptions overlaid my culture until I went through divorce myself. I wrote to a friend: "This might be worse than being widowed. Overnight I've suffered the same losses—companionship, financial and practical support, my identity as a wife and partner, the future I'd taken for granted. I am lonely, grieving, and hard-pressed to take care of my household alone. But instead of bringing casseroles, people are acting like I had a fit and broke up the family china."

Once upon a time I held these beliefs about divorce: that everyone who does it could have chosen not to do it. That it's a lazy way out of marital problems. That it selfishly puts personal happiness ahead of family integrity. Now I tremble for my ignorance. It's easy, in fortunate times, to forget about the ambush that could leave your head reeling: serious mental or physical illness, death in the family, abandonment, financial calamity, humiliation, violence, despair.

I started out like any child, intent on being the Family of Dolls. I set upon young 10 womanhood believing in most of the doctrines of my generation: I wore my skirts four inches above the knee. I had that Barbie with her zebra-striped swimsuit and a figure unlike anything found in nature. And I understood the Prince Charming Theory of Marriage, a quest for Mr. Right that ends smack dab where you find him. I did not completely understand that another whole story *begins* there, and no fairy tale prepared me for the combination of bad luck and persistent hope that would interrupt my dream and lead me to other arrangements. Like a cancer diagnosis, a dying marriage is a thing to fight, to deny, and finally, when there's no choice left, to dig in and survive. Casseroles would help. Likewise, I imagine it must be a painful reckoning in adolescence (or later on) to realize one's own true love will never look like the soft-focus fragrance ads because Prince Charming (surprise!) is a princess. Or vice versa. Or has skin the color your parents didn't want you messing with, except in the Crayola box.

It's awfully easy to hold in contempt the straw broken home, and that mythical category of persons who toss away nuclear family for the sheer fun of it. Even the legal terms we use have a suggestion of caprice. I resent the phrase "irreconcilable differences," which suggests a stubborn refusal to accept a spouse's little quirks. This is specious. Every happily married couple I know has loads of irreconcilable differences. Negotiating where to set the thermostat is not the point. A nonfunctioning marriage is a slow asphyxiation. It is waking up despised each morning, listening to the pulse of your own loneliness before the radio begins to blare its raucous gospel that you're nothing if you aren't loved. It is sharing your airless house with the threat of suicide or other kinds of violence, while the ghost that whispers, "Leave here and destroy your children," has passed over every door and nailed it shut. Disassembling a marriage in these circumstances is as much *fun* as amputating your own gangrenous leg. You do it, if you can, to save a life—or two, or more.

I know of no one who really went looking to hoe the harder row, especially the daunting one of single parenthood. Yet it seems to be the most American of customs to blame the burdened for their destiny. We'd like so desperately to believe in freedom and justice for all, we can hardly name that rogue bad luck, even when he's a close enough snake to bite us. In the wake of my divorce, some friends (even a few close ones) chose to vanish, rather than linger within striking distance of misfortune.

But most stuck around, bless their hearts, and if I'm any the wiser for my trials, it's from having learned the worth of steadfast friendship. And also, what not to say. The least helpful question is: "Did you want the divorce, or didn't you?" Did I want to keep that gangrenous leg, or not? How to explain, in a culture that venerates choice: two terrifying options are much worse than none at all. Give me any day the quick hand of cruel fate that will leave me scarred but blameless. As it was, I kept thinking of that wicked third-grade joke in which some boy comes up behind you and grabs your ear, starts in with a prolonged tug, and asks, "Do you want this ear any longer?"

Still, the friend who holds your hand and says the wrong thing is made of dearer stuff than the one who stays away. And generally, through all of it, you live. My favorite fictional character, Kate Vaiden (in the novel by Reynolds Price), advises: "Strength just comes in one brand—you stand up at sunrise and meet what they send you and keep your hair combed."

Once you've weathered the straits, you get to cross the tricky juncture from ca- 15 sualty to survivor. If you're on your feet at the end of a year or two, and have begun putting together a happy new existence, those friends who were kind enough to feel sorry for you when you needed it must now accept you back to the ranks of the living. If you're truly blessed, they will dance at your second wedding. Everybody else, for heavens sake, should stop throwing stones.

Arguing about whether nontraditional families deserve pity or tolerance is a little like the medieval debate about left-handedness as a mark of the devil. Divorce, remarriage, single parenthood, gay parents, and blended families simply are. They're facts of our time. Some of the reasons listed by sociologists for these family reconstructions are: the idea of marriage as a romantic partnership rather than a pragmatic one; a shift in women's expectations, from servility to self-respect and independence; and longevity (prior to antibiotics no marriage was expected to last many decades—in Colonial days the average couple lived to be married less than twelve years). Add to all this, our growing sense of entitlement to happiness and safety from abuse. Most would agree these are all good things. Yet their result—a culture in which serial monogamy and the consequent reshaping of families are the norm—gets diagnosed as "failing."

For many of us, once we have put ourselves Humpty-Dumpty—wise back together again, the main problem with our reorganized family is that other people think we have a problem. My daughter tells me the only time she's uncomfortable about being the child of divorced parents is when her friends say they feel sorry for her. It's a bizarre sympathy, given that half the kids in her school and nation are in the same boat, pursuing childish happiness with the same energy as their married-parent peers. When anyone asks how she feels about it, she spontaneously lists the benefits: our house is in the country and we have a dog, but she can go to her dad's neighborhood for the urban thrills of a pool and sidewalks for roller-skating. What's more, she has three sets of grandparents!

Why is it surprising that a child would revel in a widened family and the right to feel at home in more than one house? Isn't it the opposite that should worry us—a child with no home at all, or too few resources to feel safe? The child at risk is the one whose parents are too immature themselves to guide wisely; too diminished by poverty to nurture; too far from opportunity to offer hope. The number of children in the U.S. living in poverty at this moment is almost unfathomably large: twenty percent. There are families among us that need help all right, and by no means are they new on the landscape. The rate at which teenage girls had babies in 1957 (ninety-six per thousand) was twice what it is now. That remarkable statistic is ignored by the religious right—probably because the teen birth rate was cut in half mainly by legalized abortion. In fact, the policy gatekeepers who coined the phrase "family values" have steadfastly ignored the desperation of too-small families, and since 1979 have steadily reduced the amount of financial support available to a single parent. But, this camp's most outspoken attacks seem aimed at the notion of families getting too complex, with add-ons and extras such as a gay parent's partner, or a remarried mother's new husband and his children.

To judge a family's value by its tidy symmetry is to purchase a book for its cover. There's no moral authority there. The famous family comprised by Dad, Mom, Sis, and Junior living as an isolated economic unit is not built on historical bedrock. In *The Way We Never Were,* Stephanie Coontz writes. "Whenever people propose that we go back to the traditional family, I always suggest that they pick a ballpark date for the family they have in mind." Colonial families were tidily disciplined, but their members (meaning everyone but infants) labored incessantly and died young. Then the Victorian family adopted a new division of labor, in which women's role was domestic and children were allowed time for study and play, but this was an upper-class construct supported by myriad slaves. Coontz writes, "For every nineteenth-century middle-class family that protected its wife and child within the family circle, there was an Irish or German girl scrubbing floors . . . A Welsh boy mining coal to keep the homebaked goodies warm, a black girl doing the family laundry, a black mother and child picking cotton to be made into clothes for the family, and a Jewish or an Italian daughter in a sweatshop making 'ladies' dresses or artificial flowers for the family to purchase."

The abolition of slavery brought slightly more democratic arrangements, in which   20
extended families were harnessed together in cottage industries; at the turn of the century came a steep rise in child labor in mines and sweat-shops. Twenty percent of American children lived in orphanages at the time; their parents were not necessarily dead, but couldn't afford to keep them.

During the Depression and up to the end of World War II, many millions of U.S. households were more multigenerational than nuclear. Women my grandmother's age were likely to live with a fluid assortment of elderly relatives, inlaws, siblings, and children. In many cases they spent virtually every waking hour working in the company of other women—a companionable scenario in which it would be easier, I imagine, to tolerate an estranged or difficult spouse. I'm reluctant to idealize a life of so much hard work and so little spousal intimacy, but its advantage may have been resilience. A family so large and varied would not easily be brought down by a single blow: it could absorb a death, long-illness, an abandonment here or there, and any number of irreconcilable differences.

The Family of Dolls came along midcentury as a great American experiment. A booming economy required a mobile labor force and demanded that women surrender jobs to returning soldiers. Families came to be defined by a single breadwinner. They struck out for single-family homes at an earlier age than ever before, and in unprecedented numbers they raised children in suburban isolation. The nuclear family was launched to sink or swim.

More than a few sank. Social historians corroborate that the suburban family of the postwar economic boom, which we have recently selected as our definition of "traditional," was no panacea. Twenty-five percent of Americans were poor in the mid-1950s, and as yet there were no food stamps. Sixty percent of the elderly lived on less than $1,000 a year, and most had no medical insurance. In the sequestered suburbs, alcoholism and sexual abuse of children were far more widespread than anyone imagined.

Expectations soared, and the economy sagged. It's hard to depend on one other adult for everything, come what may. In the last three decades, that amorphous, adaptable structure we call "family" has been reshaped once more by economic tides. Compared with fifties families, mothers are far more likely now to be employed. We are statistically more likely to divorce, and to live in blended families or other extranuclear arrangements. We are also more likely to plan and space our children, and to rate our marriages as "happy." We are less likely to suffer abuse without recourse, or to stare out at our lives through a glaze of prescription tranquilizers. Our aged parents are less likely to be destitute, and we're half as likely to have a teenage daughter turn up a mother herself. All in all, I would say that if "intact" in modern family-values jargon means living quietly desperate in the bell jar, then hip-hip-hooray for "broken." A neat family model constructed to service the Baby Boom economy seems to be returning gradually to a grand, lumpy shape that human families apparently have tended toward since they first took root in the Olduvai Gorge.[1] We're social animals, deeply fond of companionship, and children love best to run in packs. If there is a *normal* for humans, at all, I expect it looks like two or three Families of Dolls, connected variously by kinship and passion, shuffled like cards and strewn over several shoeboxes.

The sooner we can let go the fairy tale of families functioning perfectly in isola- 25 tion, the better we might embrace the relief of community. Even the admirable parents who've stayed married through thick and thin are very likely, at present, to incorporate other adults into their families—household help and baby-sitters if they can afford them or neighbors and grandparents if they can't. For single parents, this support is the rock-bottom definition of family. And most parents who have split apart, however painfully, still manage to maintain family continuity for their children, creating in many cases a boisterous phenomenon that Constance Ahrons in her book *The Good Divorce* calls the "binuclear family." Call it what you will—when ex-spouses beat swords into plowshares and jump up and down at a soccer game together, it makes for happy kids.

Cinderella, look, who needs her? All those evil stepsisters? That story always seemed like too much cotton-picking fuss over clothes. A childhood tale that fascinated me more was the one called "Stone Soup," and the gist of it is this: Once upon a time, a pair of beleaguered soldiers straggled home to a village empty-handed, in a land ruined by war. They were famished, but the villagers had so little they shouted evil words and slammed their doors. So the soldiers dragged out a big kettle, filled it with water, and put it on a fire to boil. They rolled a clean round stone into the pot, while the villagers peered through their curtains in amazement.

"What kind of soup is that?" they hooted.

"Stone soup," the soldiers replied. "Everybody can have some when it's done."

"Well, thanks," one matron grumbled, coming out with a shriveled carrot. "But it'd be better if you threw this in."

And so on, of course, a vegetable at a time, until the whole suspicious village man- 30 aged to feed itself grandly.

Any family is a big empty pot, save for what gets thrown in. Each stew turns out different. Generosity, a resolve to turn bad luck into good, and respect for variety— these things will nourish a nation of children. Name-calling and suspicion will not. My soup contains a rock or two of hard times, and maybe yours does too. I expect it's a heck of a bouillabaisse. ●

---

[1] **Olduvai Gorge:** A gorge in Tanzania made famous by the discovery of ancient human fossils.

Judith Wallerstein, Julia Lewis, and Sandra Blakeslee

Growing Up Is Harder *2000*
from *The Unexpected Legacy of Divorce*

One of the many myths of our divorce culture is that divorce automatically rescues children from an unhappy marriage. Indeed, many parents cling to this belief as a way of making themselves feel less guilty. No one wants to hurt his or her child, and thinking that divorce is a solution to everyone's pain genuinely helps. Moreover, it's true that divorce delivers a child from a violent or cruel marriage. . . . However, when one looks at the thousands of children that my colleagues and I have interviewed at our center since 1980, most of whom were from moderately unhappy marriages that ended in divorce, one message is clear: the children do not say they are happier. Rather, they say flatly, "The day my parents divorced is the day my childhood ended."

What do they mean? Typically parent and child relationships change radically after divorce—temporarily or, as in Karen's family, permanently. Ten years after the breakup only one-half of the mothers and one-quarter of the fathers in our study were able to provide the kind of nurturant care that had distinguished their parenting before the divorce. To go back to what Gary said about his parents being "offstage" while he grew up, after a divorce one or both parents often move onto center stage and refuse to budge. The child becomes the backstage prop manager making sure the show goes on.

What most parents don't realize is that their children can be reasonably content despite the failing marriage. Kids are not necessarily overwhelmed with distress because Mommy and Daddy are arguing. In fact, children and adults can cope pretty well in protecting one another during the stress of a failing marriage or unhappy intact marriage. Mothers and fathers often make every effort to shield their marital troubles from their children. It's only after one or both have decided to divorce that they fight in full view. Children who sense tension at home turn their attention outside, spending more time with friends and participating in school activities. (Gary, whose parents' marriage was often unhappy, did exactly the same thing.) Children learn at an early age to turn a deaf ear to their parents' quarrels. The notion that all or even most parents who divorce are locked into screaming conflict that their children witness is plainly wrong. In many unhappy marriages, one or both people suffer for many years in total silence—feeling lonely, sexually deprived, and profoundly disappointed. Most of the children of divorce say that they had no idea their parents' marriage was teetering on the brink. Although some had secretly thought about divorce or discussed it with their siblings, they had no inkling that their parents were planning to break up. Nor did they understand the reality of what divorce would entail for them.

For children, divorce is a watershed that permanently alters their lives. The world is newly perceived as a far less reliable, more dangerous place because the closest relationships in their lives can no longer be expected to hold firm. More than anything else, this new anxiety represents the end of childhood.

Karen confirmed this change in several of our follow-up interviews. Ten years after her parents' divorce, I learned that she was attending the University of California at Santa Cruz so that she could run home on weekends and be available for crises. And there were plenty of those, mostly involving both her younger brother and sister. When she was twenty, she told me angrily, "Since their divorce I've been responsible for both my parents. My dad became a pathetically needy man who always wants a woman to 5 take care of him. I'm the backup when his girlfriends leave him. My mom is still a mess, always involved with the wrong kind of men. I've had to take care of them as well as my brother and sister."

Many Losses

When most people hear the word "divorce," they think it means one failed marriage. The child of divorce is thought to experience one huge loss of the intact family after which stability and a second, happier marriage comes along. But this is not what happens to most children of divorce. They experience not one, not two, but many more losses as their parents go in search of new lovers or partners. Each of these "transitions" (as demographers call them) throws the child's life into turmoil and brings back painful reminders of the first loss. National studies show that the more transitions there are, the more the child is harmed because the impact of repeated loss is cumulative. The prevalence of this instability in the lives of these children hasn't been properly weighed or even recognized by most people. While we do have legal records of second, third, and fourth remarriages and divorces, we have no reliable count of how many live-in or long-term lovers a child of divorce will typically encounter. Children observe each of their parents' courtships with a mixture of excitement and anxiety. For adolescents, the erotic stimulation of seeing their parents with changing partners can be difficult to contain. Several young teenage girls in the study began their own sexual activity when they observed a parent's involvement in a passionate affair. Children and adolescents watch their parents' lovers, with everything from love to resentment, hoping for some clue about the future. They participate actively as helper, critic, and audience and are not afraid to intervene. One mother returning home from a date found her school-age children asleep in her bed. Since they'd told her earlier that they didn't like her boyfriend, she took the hint. Many new lovers are attentive to the children, regularly bringing little gifts. But even the most charming lovers can disappear overnight. Second marriages with children are much more likely to end in divorce than first marriage. Thus the child's typical experience is not one marriage followed by the one divorce, but several or sometimes many relationships for both their mother and father followed by loss or by eventual stability.

Karen's experience is typical of many that I have seen. Her father's second wife, who was nice to the children, left without warning three years into the marriage. After she was gone, her father had four more girlfriends who caused him a great deal of suffering when they also left. Karen's mother had three unhappy love affairs prior to her remarriage, which ended after five years. Obviously Karen and her siblings experienced more than "one divorce." Their childhoods were filled with a history of new attachments followed by losses and consequent distress for both parents. Karen's brother, at age thirty, told me: "What is marriage? Only a piece of paper and a piece of metal. If you love someone, it breaks your heart."

In this study, only 7 of the original 131 children experienced stable second marriages in which they had good relationships with a stepparent and stepsiblings on both sides of the divorced family. Two-thirds of the children grew up in families where they experienced multiple divorces and remarriages of one or both of their parents. Such figures don't capture the many cohabitations and brief love affairs that never become legal relationships. Given this experience, can we be surprised that so many children of divorce conclude that love is fleeting?

Ghosts of Childhood

When I turned to the notes of my interview with Karen fifteen years after her parents' divorce, the image of a young woman crying inconsolably entered my mind. Karen was sitting on the sofa in my old office, with her chin in her hands and elbows on her knees, telling me about her live-in relationship with her boyfriend Nick.

"I've made a terrible mistake," she said, twisting a damp tissue into the shape of a rope. "I can't believe I've gotten myself into this. I never should have done it. It's like my worst nightmare come to life. It's what I grew up dreading most and look what happened." Karen gripped her fingers tightly until her knuckles shone like moons.

"What's wrong?" I asked, as gently as I could.

"Everything," she moaned. "He drinks beer. He has no ambition, no life goals, no education, no regular job. He's going nowhere. When I come home after work, he's just sitting there in front of the TV and that's where he's been all day." Then Karen's voice dropped. "But he loves me," she said in anguish. "He would be devastated if I ever left him." Even in her great distress and anger she was intensely cognizant of her boyfriend's suffering. I thought to myself, this epitomizes Karen—she's always aware of other people's hurts and suffering.

"But then why did you move in with him?"

"I'm not sure. I knew I didn't love him. But I was scared of marriage. I was scared of divorce, and I'm terrified of being alone. Look, you can hope for love but you can't expect it! When Nick asked me to live with him, I was afraid that I'd get older and that I wouldn't have another chance. I kept thinking that I'd end up lonely like my dad. And Mom."

I looked at this beautiful young woman and shook my head in disbelief. Could she really think that shacking up with a man she didn't love was all she could hope for? Karen must have read my mind because she quickly said, "I know. People have been telling me how pretty I am since I was a child. But I don't believe it. And I don't care. Looks were always important to my mother. She wears tons of makeup and dresses like a model. I thought she was silly and still do. I don't want to look like her or live my life that way."

"How did you meet Nick?"

She sighed as she answered, "Well, we hardly knew each other in high school. We were never lovers or even friends. I think that he had a crush on me from afar. Then in my junior year I broke my ankle and during the six weeks that I was hobbling around, he was very kind to me, carrying my stuff and visiting me. He was the only one who took any care of me. He also comes from a divorced family with lots of troubles. When he dropped out of school, I felt very sorry for him."

"Then how did he come back into your life?"

"I was having a real bad time. My brother was getting into serious trouble with the law and my dad wouldn't do anything to help. I pleaded with him but he was totally indifferent. I was frantic and beginning to realize that all my efforts to hold my family together were wasted. So when Nick asked me to move in with him, I said yes. Anything to get away, even though I knew from the outset he had no plans for the future, no training, no formal education. After the first day, I said to myself, 'Oh, my God, what did I do?' But at least I know he won't betray me. At least I'm safe from that."

"Karen, this fear of betrayal is pretty central to you. You keep mentioning it."

"It's been central to my life," she agreed. "Both my parents played around. I saw it all around me. They felt that if you are not getting what you want, you just look elsewhere." (I've never heard anyone put the alternative morality of our divorce culture so succinctly.)

Karen took her hands away from her face and silently ripped the tissue in half. "There's another reason I moved in with him," she, whispered. "It will probably distress you." Karen spoke hesitantly, clasped her hands in her lap, and elaborated slowly, as if every word were painful and she had to extract them one by one. "I figured that this is one man who will never leave me." Silence. "Because he has no ambitions, he will always have fewer choices than me. So if I stay with him and even marry him someday, I won't ever have to worry about his walking out."

Karen was right about my being distressed. Her statement was chilling. How utterly tragic that this lovely woman would begin her adult journey so burdened down with fears. What kind of life could she build on such fragile foundations?

Like a good caregiver child, Karen reinstalled her troubled relationships with her mother and father into her early relationships with men. As rescuers, most young women like Karen are used to giving priority to the needs of others. Indeed, they are usually not aware of their own needs or desires. Karen confessed that she had never in her life thought about what would make her happy. "That would be like asking for the moon," she said. "I was always too worried about my family to ask for me." As a result, these young women are often trapped into rescuing a troubled man. How can they reject a pitiful man who clings to them? The guilt would be unbearable. Others find troubled men more exciting. One young woman who had frequent contact with both parents during her growing up years explained: "I think I subconsciously pick men who are not going to work out. Men who are nice and considerate bore me. My latest is irresponsible. I don't trust him. I'm sure he cheats. But he's the one I want."

What prompts so many children of divorce to rush into a cohabitation or early marriage with as much forethought as buying a new pair of shoes? Answers lie in the ghosts that rise to haunt them as they enter adulthood. Men and women from divorced families live in fear that they will repeat their parents' history, hardly daring to hope that they can do better. These fears, which were present but less commanding during adolescence, become overpowering in young adulthood, more so if one or both of their parents failed to achieve a lasting relationship after a first or second divorce. Dating and courtship raise their hopes of being loved sky-high—but also their fears of being hurt and rejected. Being alone raises memories of lonely years in the postdivorce family and feels like the abandonment they dread. They're trapped between the wish for love and the fear of loss.

This amalgam of fear and loneliness can lead to multiple affairs, hasty marriages, early divorce, and—if no take-home lessons are gleaned from it all—a second and third round of the same. Or they can stay trapped in bad relationships for many years. Here's how it works: at the threshold of young adulthood, relationships move center stage. But for many that stage is barren of good memories for how an adult man and woman can live together in a loving relationship. This is the central impediment blocking the developmental journey for children of divorce. The psychological scaffolding that they need to construct a happy marriage has been badly damaged by the two people they depended on while growing up.

Let's look closely at the process of growing up. Children learn all kinds of lessons at their parents' knees, from the time they are born to the time they leave home. There is no landscape more fascinating to the baby than the mother's face. There is no more exciting image to the child than the frame that includes Mom and Dad kissing, fighting, conferring, frowning, crying, yelling, or hugging in the adjoining room. These thousand and one images are internalized and they form the template for the child's view of how men and women treat each other, how parents and children communicate, how brothers and sisters get along. From day one, children watch their parents and absorb the minutiae of human interaction. They observe their parents as private persons (when the adult thinks no one is paying attention) and as public persons onstage outside the home. They listen carefully to what the parents say (although they often pretend not to hear) and they ponder what the parents fail to say. No scientist ever looked through a microscope more intently than the average child who observes her family day in and night out. And they make judgments from early on. Children as young as four years old tell me, "I want to be a daddy like my dad" or "I won't be a mommy like my mommy." They have powerful feelings of love, hate, envy, admiration, pity, respect, and disdain. This is the theater of our lives—our first and most important school for learning about ourselves and all others. From this we extrapolate the interactions of human society. The images of each family are imprinted on each child's heart and mind, becoming the inner theater that shapes expectations, hopes, and fears.

But over and beyond the child's view of mother and father as individuals is the child's view of the relationship between them—the nature of the relationship *as a couple*. Our scholarly literature is full of mother—child and, more recently, father–child experiments, but as every child could tell the professors, the child sees her parents as a twosome. She is intensely and passionately aware of their interaction. What could be more important or more enthralling? These complex images of parental interaction are central to the family theater and are of lasting importance to children of divorce and to children from intact families.

All the young people in the intact families described the relationship between their parents as if they had followed them around day and night. They described their parents' laughter, their teasing, how they knew how to push each other's buttons and how they comforted one another. They even speculated in detail about their parents' sex life. They told me whether Dad kissed Mom when he returned home or whether he pinched her bottom or whether the parents were reserved. Others wondered what their parents had in common or why they stayed married. Along with these observations, they made moral judgments and they reached conclusions that had direct implications for their future lives.

How is the inner template of the child of divorce different from that of the young 30 adult in the intact family—especially if the child of divorce, in accord with the current advice of mediators and court personnel, has access to both parents and the parents refrain from fighting during the postdivorce years?

As every child of divorce told me, no matter how often they see their parents, the image of them together as a loving couple is forever lost. A father in one home and a mother in another home does not represent a marriage, however well they communicate. Separate may be equal but it is not together. As children grow up and choose partners of their own, they lack this central image of the intact marriage. In its place they confront a void that threatens to swallow them whole. Unlike children from intact families, children of divorce in our study spoke very little about their parents' interaction. They hardly ever referred to their parents' behavior at the breakup. By and large their central complaint is that no one had explained the divorce to them and that the reasons were shrouded in mystery. When reasons were offered, they sounded to them like platitudes designed to avoid telling what really happened. Their parents said, we were different people, we had nothing in common. Children of divorce hardly mentioned their parents together except to express their disdain when the parents continued to fight or behave badly with each other at the birthdays of grandchildren and the like. Indeed, the parents' interaction was a black hole—as if the couple had vanished from memory and the children's conscious inner life.

This need for a good internal image of the parents as a couple is important to the child's development throughout her growing up years, but at adolescence, the significance of this internal template of manwoman relationships rises. Memories and images from past and present come together and crescendo in a mighty chorus of voices at entry into young adulthood when the young person confronts for real the issues of choice in love and commitment. In the old Yiddish folk song, the marriage broker asks the maiden, "Whom will you marry?" and her first words echo the contemporary theme of Karen and her millions of sisters and brothers. She replies, "Who will be true to me? Will he take care of me? Will he leave at the crack of dawn when we have our first fight? Will he love me?"

But children of divorce have one more strike against them. Unlike children who lose a parent due to illness, accident, or war, children of divorce lose the template they need because of their parents' *failure*. Parents who divorce may think of their decision to end the marriage as wise, courageous, and the best remedy for their unhappiness— indeed, it may be so—but for the child the divorce carries one meaning: the parents have failed at one of the central tasks of adulthood. Together and separately, they failed to maintain the marriage. Even if the young person decides as an adult that the divorce was necessary, that in fact the parents had little in common to begin with, the divorce still represents failure—failture to keep the man or the woman, failure to maintain the relationship, failure to be faithful, or failure to stick around. This failure in turn shapes the child's inner template of self and family. If they failed, I can fail, too. And if, as happens so frequently, the child observes more failed relationships in the years after divorce, the conclusion is simple. *I have never seen a man and a woman together on the same beam. Failure is inevitable.*

Courtship is always fraught with excitement, yearning, and anxiety. Every adult is aware that this is the most important decision of one's life. Fear of making the wrong choice and of being rejected and betrayed is certainly not confined to children of divorce. But the differences between the children of divorce and those from intact marriages were striking beyond my expectations. The young men and women from intact families, along with their fears, brought a confidence that they had seen it work, that they had some very clear ideas about how to do it. They said so in very convincing terms.

No single adult in the divorced group spoke this way. Their memories and internal images were by contrast impoverished or frightening because they lacked guidelines to use in muting their fears. Indeed, they were helpless in the face of their fears.

Gina, a forty-year-old successful executive in an international company, told me, "I grew up feeling that men are unreliable, just flaky, that like my dad they only really want to play with toys. I know that I've gone out with men who seemed reliable and wonderful, but still, putting all my eggs in one basket with one man is totally frightening. I'm better off relying on me."

Growing Up Takes Longer

When Karen came to see me in 1994 on the eve of her marriage, she was bursting to tell me everything that had happened since our last visit. I remembered her crying her eyes out, complaining about Nick, and here she was, glowing with happiness and optimism. What happened to her between the ages of twenty-five and thirty-four?

First, she described her decision to leave Nick, a journey that took her to a new life in Washington, D.C., where she stayed with a close friend from college and examined her options. "I realized that I wanted to help children but that to make a difference I'd need a degree, I'd need some expertise," she said. Working her contacts, Karen soon heard about a masters of public health program at Johns Hopkins that would allow her to combine her interest in child welfare and community organization. Drawing on student loans and what remained from her grandmother's inheritance, she applied and was accepted into the three-year program, moved to Baltimore, and worked part-time in a pediatric outreach program while attending school. Karen, at last following her own desires, was an outstanding student who soon caught the attention of senior professors who mentored her as she negotiated career opportunities. "I have the best job," Karen informed me. "I work with severely handicapped children in five southern states where I run a rural outreach program. We're based in Chapel Hill. I love my work, Judy. I make it my business to spend a lot of time out in the community working with the children. People ask how I can stand it but I don't find it depressing because I get a lot of gifts from the children. They open up and share things with me, their hopes, their dreams, the things they want to do, and the many things they fear. I realize from being with them how precious life is and how you only have this day."

"Karen, you've been helping other people ever since I met you, when you were ten years old. But now it looks like you decided to take a chance on what you want. Maybe the dice will fall your way."

"That's right. I decided to take a chance and I discovered what I want. And I finally figured out what I don't want. I don't want another edition of my relationships with my mom or dad. I don't want a man who is dependent on me." 40

"And you do want?"

"I want a lover and a husband. I'm no longer frantic to find just anybody because if I have to, I can live alone. I can stand on my own two feet. I'm no longer afraid." And then the sadness around her eyes returned. "But it's not really all behind me. Like I told you, part of me is always waiting for disaster to strike. I keep reminding myself that I'm doing this to myself, but the truth is that I live in dread that something bad will happen to me. Some terrible loss that will change my life. It gets worse as things get better for me. Maybe that's the permanent result of their divorce." She leaned forward so that she was almost doubled at the waist, as if holding herself in one piece. "Gavin teases me all the time about being afraid of change. But I think I've learned how to contain it. I no longer wake up in terror when I go to sleep happy." She paused to think about what she meant. "But it never really goes away, never."

On hearing her story, I realized that Karen's journey into full adulthood required several more steps. Leaving her first serious relationship was only an overture. The Karen who graduated in public health and who had helped establish a successful regional program to help crippled children was a different person altogether. She had acquired a new identity as a competent and proud young woman who could if necessary manage by herself. Over and beyond her professional achievements, Karen was finally able to relinquish her role as the person responsible for her parents and siblings. This was a slow and painful process. The turning point was her realization that her brother and sister were adults who were exploiting her generosity. "I had to move on," she said. "I'd done enough." With that she closed the door, a free woman. Having achieved intellectual and emotional growth, she was ready to be the partner of an adult man who wanted a lover and a wife, not a caregiver. In loving a man who loved her and treated her as an equal, she felt safe for the first time in her life and was able to vanquish her fears. Although residues of her early fears did not disappear, they faded into the background. Within this relationship, Karen completed her struggle to reach adulthood.

In hearing story after story like Karen's about how difficult life was during their twenties, I realized that compared to children from intact families, children of divorce follow a different trajectory for growing up. *It takes them longer.* Their adolescence is protracted and their entry into adulthood is delayed.

Children of divorce need more time to grow up because they have to accomplish 45 more: they must simultaneously let go of the past and create mental models for where they are headed, carving their own way. Those who succeed deserve gold medals for integrity and perseverance. Having rejected their parents as role models, they have to invent who they want to be and what they want to achieve in adult life. This is far and beyond what most adolescents are expected to achieve. Given the normal challenges of growing up—which they had to accomplish on their own—it's no surprise that children of divorce get waylaid by ill-fated love affairs and similar derailments. Most are well into their late twenties and thirties before they graduate into adulthood.

My analysis may not seem to match the pseudomaturity exhibited by many children of divorce who often appear on a fast track to adulthood. Compared with youngsters from more protected families, they get into the trappings of adolescent culture at an earlier age. Sex, drugs, and alcohol are rites of passage into being accepted by an older crowd. At the same time, they're independent and justifiably proud of their ability to make their own decisions and to advise their parents.

But let's not be fooled by the swagger. The developmental path from adolescence into adulthood is thrown out of sync after divorce. Many children of divorce can't get past adolescence because they cannot bring closure to the normal process of separating from their parents. In the normal course of adolescence, children spend several years in a kind of push and pull pas de deux with their parents, slowly weaning themselves from home. But Karen hardly experienced this separation process. By the time she left for college at age eighteen, she was still tied to her parents by her needs and theirs.

And she was not alone. By late adolescence most children of divorce are more tied to their parents and paradoxically more eager to let go than their peers in intact families. Like the folk story of Brer Rabbit and the Tar Baby, the divorce is as sticky as the tar that held the rabbit. The young people want out but can't move on because of unfinished business at home.

Children of divorce are held back from adulthood because the vision of it is so frightening. From the outset, they are more anxious and uncomfortable with the opposite sex and it's harder for them to build a relationship and gradually give it time to develop. Feeling vulnerable, bewildered, and terribly alone, and driven by biology and social pressures, these young men and women throw themselves into a shadow play of the real thing involving sex without love, passion without commitment, togetherness without a future. . . .

The fact that Karen and others were able to turn their lives around is very good 50 news for all of us who have been worried about the longterm effects of divorce on children. It sometimes took many years and several failed relationships, but close to half of the women and over a third of the men in our study were finally able to create a new template with themselves in starring roles. They did it the hard way—by learning from their own experience. They got hurt, kept going, and tried again. Some had relatives, especially grandparents, who loved them and provided close-up role models for what was possible. Some had childhood memories from before the divorce that gave them hope and self confidence when they felt like giving up. Only a few had mentors, but when they came along they were greatly appreciated. One young man told me, "My boss has been like a father to me, the father that I always wanted and never had." Men and women alike were especially grateful to lovers who stood by them and insisted that they stick around for the long haul. Karen's husband undoubtedly played a major part in her recovery. Finally, a third of the men and women in our study sought professional help from therapists and found, in individual sessions, that they could establish a trusting relationship with another person and use it to get at the roots of their difficulties. It helped that they were young because it meant they had the energy and determination to really change their lives. Clearly people enter adulthood "unfinished," which means the decade of the twenties lends itself to personal development and change. ●

Explorations of the Text

1. Both Kingsolver and Wallerstein, Lewis, and Blakeslee structure their essays as arguments. Which argument do you find most effective? Discuss purpose and audience.

2. Do you think that families and the definition of what a "normal" family consists of is changing in our society? Discuss.

3. From reading these two essays, do you think that the expectations of society for families with children are too lenient? Perfectly reasonable? Too strict? Explain.

4. Wallerstein, Lewis, and Blakeslee describe the instability suffered by children of divorce. Considering this essay and Bakopoulos's "Some Memories of My Father," argue whether these works support or dispute their position.

The Reading/Writing Connection

1. Using a double-entry journal, write key passages from the essays in the left column and your impressions of them in the right column. What important points do the authors make? What, if anything, do you feel is left out of the essays?

2. Wallerstein, Lewis, and Blakeslee describe the fear of loneliness and abandonment suffered by children of divorce. Kingsolver provides an example of a family in which the children have more support and interaction than one normally finds in a family that is not divorced. Write a journal entry expressing your feelings about these two visions. In your experience, which seems most realistic? Or do you have a different perspective?

3. Writing in the style of "Girl," offer advice to someone who lives in a blended family.

4. In "I Go Back to May 1937," Sharon Olds writes of her parents, young and hopeful, entering into a doomed marriage. Do you think it is possible for people to avoid relationships that will end in divorce? Plan a high school course that will help people to choose suitable mates.

Ideas for Writing

1. **Write an Argument:** Kingsolver talks about the way that divorced parents are often abandoned by friends after their divorce. In our society, where half of all marriages end in divorce, do you think we have a double standard in which we all know people who are divorced yet we refuse to acknowledge that divorce is common and, in fact, normal? Argue in favor of a more open, supportive attitude toward divorce. Or, argue that we need to continue to consider divorce a failure so that people will try to make marriages work.

2. **Write an Argument:** Wallerstein, Lewis, and Blakeslee claim that the changes that occur in a family after divorce hurt a child's development. Create an argument in which you agree that parents should remain together for the child's welfare. Or, create an argument that agrees with Kingsolver that growing up in a hostile, loveless family is destructive to a child's healthy development. In your conclusion, propose a solution to either (or both) of the problems.

GRAPHIC LITERATURE

Lynda Barry *(1956–)*

Common Scents *2002*
From *One! Hundred! Demons!*

BUT THERE WERE BAD MYS-
TERIES TOO, LIKE THE MYSTERY
OF THE BLEACH PEOPLE WHOSE
HOUSE GAVE OFF FUMES YOU
COULD SMELL FROM THE STREET.
WE KEPT WAITING FOR THAT
HOUSE TO EXPLODE. THE BUGS
DIDN'T EVEN GO IN THEIR YARD.

ALSO GIVING OFF BLEACH FUMES

HEYA, JANINA.

HEYA.

'N I ASK YOU A PERSONAL THING?

POSSIBLY.

HOW COME YOUR HOUSE SMELLS LIKE THAT?

SMELLS LIKE WHAT?

SOME SMELLS WERE MYS-
TERIOUSLY WONDERFUL LIKE
AT THE PALINKI'S WHERE IT WAS
A COMBINATION OF MINT, TAN-
GERINES, AND LIBRARY BOOKS.
BUT HOW? I NEVER SAW ANY
OF THOSE THINGS THERE.

WHAT'S YOUR KIND OF AIR FRESHENER, BECAUSE THAT'S THE KIND I WANT MY MOM TO GET.

I DON'T USE AIR FRESHENER, DEAR.

WELL, THAT'S WEIRD BECAUSE YOUR HOUSE SMELLS PERFECT.

SHE HAD THOSE CAR FRESHENER CHRISTMAS TREE THINGS HANGING EVERYWHERE. EVEN THE MARSHMALLOW TREATS SHE MADE HAD A FRESH PINE-SPRAY FLAVOR. SHE WAS FREE WITH HER OBSERVATIONS ABOUT THE SMELL OF OTHERS.

YOUR ORIENTALS HAVE AN ARRAY, WITH YOUR CHINESE SMELLING STRONGER THAN YOUR JAPANESE AND YOUR KOREANS FALLING SOMEWHERES IN THE MIDDLE AND DON'T GET ME STARTED ON YOUR FILIPINOS.

SHE DETAILED THE SMELLS OF BLACKS, MEXICANS, ITAL-IANS, SOME PEOPLE I NEVER HEARD OF CALLED "BO-HUNKS" AND THE DIFFERENCE IT MADE IF THEY WERE WET OR DRY, FAT OR SKINNY. NATURALLY I BROUGHT THIS INFORMATION HOME.

AIE N'AKO! WHITE LADIES SMELL BAD TOO, NAMAN! SHE NEVER WASH HER POOKIE! HER KILI-KILI ALWAYS SWEAT-SWEATING! THE OLD ONES SMELL LIKE E-HEE! THAT LADY IS TUNG-AH!

[1] **duran fruits**: The durian is an Asian fruit that gives off a disagreeable odor but has a creamy, tasty flesh.

Explorations of the Text

1. What do we learn about Barry's family from her description of smells? The dialogue? The pictures? Describe the way that each detail works closely with the next to create a whole image.

2. Discuss Barry's use of humor to convey ideas. Would this piece work if it were written as a serious essay?

3. Air fresheners play an important role in Barry's piece. Why does Barry imply that Americans use air fresheners so frequently? Why are air fresheners funny? What does Americans' obsession with air fresheners imply about our cultural attitudes toward the body?

4. From the food, animal, cigarette, cleaning fluids, and other smells, what picture does Barry present of American life? Why does each person think that her own house doesn't smell? What underlying message might Barry be presenting of our attitudes toward other cultures?

5. In "Everyday Use," Maggie and her mother are comfortable with their lives, whereas Wangero is not. Compare Walker's story to Lynda Barry's "Common Scents." Describe the families that seem to be comfortable with their lives and those who are not. How does Barry achieve this insight through a seemingly simple comic?

6. How do Barry's drawings add to the comic effect?

The Reading/Writing Connection

1. Create an illustrated story about your family either as a comic or in prose with an accompanying drawing. What details do you choose to keep objective? Which do you exaggerate? Think about your artistic choices with both the words and the drawing.

2. Think Topic: Barry's comic both embraces and critiques American culture. Write about the power of consumerism and its creation of dissatisfaction within Barry's work.

Ideas for Writing

1. **Write an Argument:** Considering Geeta Kothari's "You Are What You Eat," write an argument entitled, "You Are What You Smell." Argue in favor of or against the truth of this title, using evidence from Kothari and Barry to support your points.

2. Barry's philosophical grandmother has answers to all of Barry's questions. Write a character analysis of the grandmother as a unifying presence within the piece. How does Barry's grandmother help Barry to accept her own and other families' limitations?

WRITING ASSIGNMENTS

1. a. Based on the selections in this chapter, freewrite about what you learned regarding the experience of parenting or of childhood that was revelatory to you.

   b. Write a journal entry comparing one example of the parent/child relationship presented in the works in this chapter with your own experience.

   c. Make a list of questions that emerge from these explorations of parent/child relationships. Write an answer to one of these questions. Refer to three works in this chapter.

2. a. Diagram a family tree for the central relationships in your life. Include extended family and friends. Draw straight lines for the relationships that represent solidity and broken lines (————) for those that seem fragile or negative.

   b. Write your conclusions in your journal.

   c. Compare the positive and negative aspects of family dynamics in your life with one work in this chapter.

3. a. Think of a moment from your past—a moment of conflict or of closeness. Write a point-of-view piece, a monologue, for each family member.

   b. After you write these pieces, construct several freewrites about characters' conflicts within family settings presented in three works in this chapter. Then create monologues for these characters.

   c. Write an essay about sources of closeness or of conflict between parents and their children. Choose three works from this chapter. Include specific evidence from the texts.

4. Analyze the impact of mothers or fathers on their children. What are major issues in parent/child relationships evident in works in this chapter? Choose several works for discussion.

5. a. Define a good parent. (You may do this as either a freewrite or a journal entry.)

   b. Watch several situation comedies about families. What images of parents appear?

   c. Do any television programs present a realistic view of family life? Your analysis may become an argumentative essay.

   d. Compare a comedy from the fifties or sixties with one that is contemporary.

6. a. Interview several people with backgrounds different from your own. Concentrate on family life, particularly on the roles and responsibilities of parents and of children. What do you conclude?

   b. Based on your interviews and the selections in this chapter, compare the roles of parents or children in two different cultures. Do parents' roles differ? Are there different cultural expectations for children?

   c. Write an analysis of cultural roles for parents and/or children in such works as Tan's "Scar," Baldwin's "Sonny's Blues," or Ortiz's "My Father's Song." (Choose two.)

7. Explore the use of allusions to myth, fable, and fairy tale as a literary technique in "My Little Girl, My Stringbean, My Lovely Woman," and/or "Sonny's Blues."

8. Explore the idea of kinship, of extended family, and of community as these ideas are depicted in several works in this chapter.

9. Is the idea of the nuclear family in North America being redefined? Defend your position. You may use evidence from the works you have read or do research on this topic to support your argument.

10. Explicate one of the poems in this chapter. Concentrate on point of view, tone, imagery, figurative language, and form. How do these aspects of the work develop theme?

11. Several of the essays in this chapter are autobiographical. Reread these works and determine what creates effective autobiographical writing. (Refer to Chapter 13 for directions for analysis.)

12. a. Interview one of your family members. What knowledge, attitudes, and values have been passed down from generation to generation?

    b. Compare your family legacies with that of a protagonist in one of the works in the "Generational Legacies" cluster.

13. Using examples from the works in this chapter, discuss how as a culture we might better help families to cope with difficult times.

14. Write the recipe for a favorite family dish; then describe one or more memories of preparing and/or eating it.

15. Both intimacy and distance—closeness and separation—exist in family life. Explore this theme in several works in this chapter.

16. Parents inscribe traditional gender roles on their children. Consider this theme in relation to such works as Tan's "The Scar," Kincaid's "Girl," and Heaney's "Digging."

17. How do the expectations of parents shape their children's lives? You may consider Mirikitani's "Suicide Note," and Hawthorne's "Rappaccini's Daughter."

18. In the excerpt from *bone black,* the autobiographical persona reveals: "She hated that part of herself that kept wanting . . . love or even his [her father's] approval long after she could see that he was never, never going to give it." How is the child's desire for approval portrayed in works in this chapter?

19. Many of these stories in this chapter end ambivalently. Write sequels to several of the stories. What happens to the characters? (Suggestions: Danticat's "Night Talkers," Baldwin's "Sonny's Blues," and Gordon's "City Life.") Compare and contrast your endings. What do they reveal about characters and theme of the works?

20. In Baldwin's "Sonny's Blues," the narrator's mother tells her son about the white men who killed his father's brother. This death, witnessed by the father, haunted him throughout his life. Similarly, in Erdrich's "The Shawl," the father is haunted by witnessing the death of his daughter. The loss of family deeply affects characters in works in this chapter (e.g., Plath's "Daddy," Danticat's "Night Talkers," Lee's "Coming Home Again," and in Chapter 8, Busch's "Ralph the Duck," Ozick's "The Shawl," and Sophocles's *Antigone*).

    a. Compare and contrast one character from each work. How are the lives of these characters changed by the death of a family member?

    b. Choose a work in which the family remains intact, in which no one dies. Compare and contrast it with a depiction of a family that has lost someone to death. How does the death of one person alter the family dynamic and affect every person within?

21. In the excerpt from *bone black,* bell hooks reveals that "she wants to bear witness." How do characters in the works in this chapter "bear witness" to the tragedies of family life? What larger social issues are revealed?

22. Gloria Steinem suggests that "happy or unhappy, families are all mysterious." How do these "mysteries" manifest themselves in familial interactions? What is it we do not know about family members? What are the superficial ways in which we behave within family? What are the deeper, often unspoken connections?

a. With these questions in mind, examine the family dynamics in several works in this chapter (Suggestions: Baldwin's "Sonny Blues," Lee's "Persimmons," Lee's "Coming Home Again," and Leff's "Burn Your Maps.")

b. Compare the family dynamics in one of these works to those in your family.

STUDENT ESSAYS

Comparison/Contrast Essay

Katherine Beatty

Compare/Contrast and Character Analysis

Family, a crucial part of most people's lives, can be considered a primary cause for human behavior. Families reinforce cultural values, uphold certain traditions, and ask of their members to perform certain established social roles. In most nuclear families, moreover, oftentimes one or two people exist as the dominant members; they may affect the rest of the family in such a way as to make others fear them. In such cases, the other members are left feeling uneasy and anxious, keeping to themselves and never confronting their feelings. The family becomes a fragile unit. It is inevitable that with these strict standards come emotional problems, making weaker members vulnerable to their authority figures. If certain rules are enforced with extremity and pressured upon those within the family, then conflicts between those who are inflicting the pain and those who are receiving it are bound to occur.

In "Eveline," by James Joyce, the authoritative power is clearly exhibited by Eveline's father, who both physically and verbally abuses his children, causing them grief and anxiety. With no other parent in the household, Eveline's father assumes all control and ultimately belittles anyone who stands in his way. His forceful nature causes Eveline stress and leaves her emotionally trapped, functioning only in ways that her father allows. He threatens Eveline, saying "what he would do to her [is] only for her dead mother's sake" and physically abuses his sons "with his [big] blackthorn stick" (Joyce 708, 707). He sarcastically disparages Eveline, "[asking] if she [has] any intention of buying Sunday's dinner" (Joyce 708). Eveline's father also makes her give "her entire wages—seven shillings [to him] . . . for he [is] usually fairly bad of a Saturday night" (Joyce 708). Her father is undoubtedly cruel and controlling, abusing his power as the only authority figure in the house. Without the option or strength to argue against him, Eveline is left to live a burdened life with "nobody to protect her" (Joyce 708). She assumes most of the responsibility in the household, and, despite the fact that she is nineteen years old, her father still insists that she follow his rules of the family, walking, talking and breathing to his very own liking (Joyce 707). He even comes between her and her lover, "[forbidding] her to have anything to say to him" (Joyce 708). All of his negative attitudes toward Eveline cause her to feel bound to this lifestyle. She "feels herself in danger of her father's violence," yet remains in the situation of vulnerable entrapment (Joyce 708).

"Scar" by Amy Tan, also displays the issue of family in a clear-cut manner. An-Mei grows up psychologically pressured to function as the perfect Chinese daughter, to respect elders and to ultimately honor the "shou" (Tan 459). Her fierce grandmother, the authority figure here, sets the rules of the household and inflicts her own power upon An-Mei. Her means of making sure An-Mei follows the rules of the family is by disparaging An-Mei's mother and terrifying An-Mei with the consequences that could arise should she fail to follow these rules. Throughout the story, Popo refers to An-Mei's mother as a ghost: "a ghost [is] anything [the family] is forbidden to talk about" (Tan 458). An-Mei must learn to accept the fact that her mother is a "ni, a traitor to [all] the ancestors" (Tan 459). Popo refers to An-Mei's mother as being "'so beneath others that even the devil must look down to see her'" (Tan 459). And all these thoughts circle inside An-Mei's head, causing her grief and leaving her to "imagine [her] mother [as] a thoughtless woman" as An-Mei "hides in the corner of [her] room" (Tan 459). The stories of consequence that her grandmother tells her are of punishment and discipline that An-Mei will suffer should she go against the accepted behavior of the household. Her grandmother's stories consist of disobedience, mainly refusal to listen to elders. In one story a girl's brains fall out and in another "a ghost . . . tried to take children away . . ." (Tan 459, 458). Story after story, An-Mei is repeatedly reminded by her grandmother of how to act and function in order to remain a part of this family, and An-Mei never underestimates her grandmother's power.

Our duties and obligations to our families play a key role in how we should work in order to please those who we reside with. It is evident in James Joyce's "Eveline" that Eveline's duty is to remain loyal to the family and act as a mother and wife toward her father and her siblings. "Rush[ing] out as quickly as she could to do her marketing" and "[giving] her entire wages," all with having "nobody to protect her," are only some of the day-to-day tasks that she needs to carry out (Joyce 708). But more wearisome is the heavy burden of her obligation to her mother: "to keep the home together as long as she could" (Joyce 709). As a nineteen-year-old girl, Eveline is to "see that the two young children who had been left to her charge [go] to school regularly and get their meals regularly" (Joyce 708). Sealing this responsibility is like sealing a deal with confinement. Her duty, in hindsight, is to look after her own siblings and essentially to provide for the family, all under the watchful eye of her violent father. In fact, he only makes Eveline more fearful of the consequences if she does not do as she is told. If she forgets about a single task, her father knows how to handle it. Her obligation is apparent. It isn't a concern that her father "threatens her" (Joyce 708). It is specifically up to her to carry out her task and fulfill the responsibility. "She [has] to work hard both in the house and at business . . . elbow[ing] her way through the crowds and returning home late under her load of provisions" (Joyce 707, 708). Eveline must carry out her promise to her mother and fulfill her responsibilities in order to please her father and to keep him and the rest of the family satisfied.

Similarly, in "Scar," the understandable duty is respect, better know as "shou" (Tan 459). Her grandmother enforces that An-Mei carry out her obligation to her family, frightening her with the thought that her father's watchful eyes in the painting study her for any "signs of disrespect" (Tan 459). Taught by her grandmother, through harsh words and her father's painting, An-Mei became cognizant of her duty, "when [she] was [just] a young girl in China" (Tan 458). An-Mei's grandmother makes sure she doesn't underestimate what these duties in life are and uses her father as a tool for scaring An-Mei. "He was a large, unsmiling man, unhappy to be so still on the wall. His restless eyes followed [An-Mei] around the house" (Tan 459). If An-Mei "[threw] pebbles at other children at school, or . . . lost a book through carelessness, [she] would quickly walk by [her] father . . . and hide in a corner of [her] room where he could not see [her] face" (Tan 459). In traditional Chinese families, "both urban and rural adolescents continue to [express] a strong sense of obligation to support, assist, and respect the authority of their families" (Fuligini 1). An-Mei's duty is to carry out her grandmother's wise words and teachings, even if she does not necessarily agree with them. An-Mei, afraid of the consequences, hopes never to disrespect her family, and more importantly, her grandmother.

The authority figures in Eveline's and An-Mei's lives dominate them, causing them stress and making them concerned with going against the set of rules of the family. It is these rules and the overall obligations that bind Eveline and An-Mei to the lifestyles that their cultures insist upon. It is easy to say that everyone is affected by society, peers, school, media and so forth, but family plays a much larger part in our behavioral patterns. The components of a family determine whether it is functional or dysfunctional, and though both Chinese and Irish families are discussed, a dysfunctional family can occur in any race, any culture, and any religion. In today's society, abuse, divorce rates, and obligations are all rising steadily. Every family has its own issues, and sometimes no one will ever know for sure what happens behind closed doors. However, family members either can choose to maintain the family situation or walk away from it. Eveline and An-Mei are, indeed, trapped in their own family circumstances; and as readers we don't know whether they will continue to be oppressed or to escape the pain and break free. Sometimes in literature, the authors give the reader a chance to imagine and determine the fates of characters.

Works Cited

Fuligini, A.J. and W. Zhang. "Attitudes Toward Family Obligation Among Adolescents In Contemporary Urban and Rural China." Adolescent Attitudes Regarding Family Obligations in Mainland China. 75(2004). 20 October 2006. http://www.srcd.org/journals/cdev/1-1/Fuligini.pdf

Joyce, James. "Eveline." Legacies: Fiction, Poetry, Drama, Nonfiction, Fourth Edition. Eds. Jan Zlotnik Schmidt, Lynne Crockett, and Carley Rees Bogarad. Boston: Cengage Learning Wadsworth, 2008. 658–661.

Tan, Amy. "Scar." Legacies: Fiction, Poetry, Drama, Nonfiction, Fourth Edition. Eds. Jan Zlotnik Schmidt, Lynne Crockett, and Carley Rees Bogarad. Boston: Cengage Learning Wadsworth, 2008. 376–380.

7

Gender and Sexuality

Introduction

"Ah, love, let us be true
To one another . . ."

"Dover Beach," Matthew Arnold

From the words of Matthew Arnold, from the love songs of Sappho, from Kalidosa's *Shakuntala,* from "The Song of Solomon," from William Shakespeare's sonnets to Anna Akhmatova's poetry, works have expressed the longing for love. This yearning represents a need deeper than sexual attraction or survival of the species; it represents the desire for connection that emerges as strongly as the urge for food or drink.

Intimacy takes on many forms: friendship, platonic love, passion, regret over lost or diminished love. Inevitably, lovers face challenges and obstacles in relationships, but they also discover the pleasures and the fulfillment that love offers. People fall in and out of love, remain in long and enduring relationships, and along the way, they discern more about themselves and continue a process of growth borne out of bonds with others.

The works in Crossing the Genres/The Elusive Sexual Self, present the struggles inherent in gender and sexual identity formation and the conflicts apparent in same-sex relationships and the intimacy that prevails in such unions. Other questions about love are posed in many of the works. What is romantic love? What constitutes romantic fantasy? Passion? Young love? Some works ask why love fails and portray the obstacles in relationships and the distance between lovers. Other works explore the risks of sexual encounters. The desire for union may turn into an obsessive and dangerous quest for the other.

Experiencing passion, of course, need not always lead to danger. Many of the works in this chapter celebrate the joys of passion. Desire—of the young and old, of the married and unmarried—remains central to the experience of loving.

Other dimensions of love are the expectations, shaped by social mores, that men and women have of roles and behaviors in relationships. Are men and women doomed to reach out and yet misunderstand each other? Are gender roles for men and women socially constructed? How has the lack of equality affected women's and men's existences? Indeed, the questions of what it means to have an identity as a woman or as a man still seem as relevant today as they did for Virginia Woolf seventy-five years ago. Ultimately, although the experience of love on some level remains mysterious, throughout the centuries, philosophers and writers have tried to explain and to analyze the human need to bond with another.

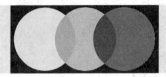

Crossing the Genres
The Elusive Sexual Self

ZZ Packer   *(1973–   )*

Drinking Coffee Elsewhere   *2003*

Orientation games began the day I arrived at Yale from Baltimore. In my group we played heady, frustrating games for smart people. One game appeared to be charades reinterpreted by existentialists; another involved listening to rocks. Then a freshman counsellor made everyone play Trust. The idea was that if you had the faith to fall backward and wait for four scrawny former high-school geniuses to catch you, just before your head cracked on the slate sidewalk, then you might learn to trust your fellow-students. Russian roulette sounded like a better game.

"No way," I said. The white boys were waiting for me to fall, holding their arms out for me, sincerely, gallantly. "No fucking way."

"It's all cool, it's all cool," the counsellor said. Her hair was a shade of blond I'd seen only on *Playboy* covers, and she raised her hands as though backing away from a growling dog. "Sister," she said, in an I'm-down-with-the-struggle voice, "you don't have to play this game. As a person of color, you shouldn't have to fit into any white, patriarchal system."

I said, "It's a bit too late for that."

In the next game, all I had to do was wait in a circle until it was my turn to say   5 what inanimate object I wanted to be. One guy said he'd like to be a gadfly, like Socrates. "Stop me if I wax Platonic," he said. The girl next to him was eating a rice cake. She wanted to be the Earth, she said. Earth with a capital "E."

There was one other black person in the circle. He wore an Exeter T-shirt and his overly elastic expressions resembled a series of facial exercises. At the end of each person's turn, he smiled and bobbed his head with unfettered enthusiasm. "Oh, that was good," he said, as if the game were an experiment he'd set up and the results were turning out better than he'd expected. "Good, good good!"

When it was my turn I said, "My name is Dina, and if I had to be any object, I guess I'd be a revolver." The sunlight dulled as if on cue. Clouds passed rapidly overhead, presaging rain. I don't know why I said it. Until that moment I'd been good in all the ways that were meant to matter. I was an honor-roll student—though I'd learned long ago not to mention it in the part of Baltimore where I lived. Suddenly I was hard-bitten and recalcitrant, the kind of kid who took pleasure in sticking pins into cats; the kind who chased down smart kids to spray them with mace.

"A revolver," a counsellor said, stroking his chin, as if it had grown a rabbinical beard. "Could you please elaborate?"

The black guy cocked his head and frowned, as if the beakers and Erlenmeyer flasks of his experiment had grown legs and scurried off.

"You were just kidding," the dean said, "about wiping out all of mankind. That, I sup-   10 pose, was a joke." She squinted at me. One of her hands curved atop the other to form a pink, freckled molehill on her desk.

"Well," I said, "maybe I meant it at the time." I quickly saw that was not the answer she wanted. "I don't know. I think it's the architecture."

Through the dimming light of the dean's-office window, I could see the fortress of the old campus. On my ride from the bus station to the campus, I'd barely glimpsed New Haven—a flash of crumpled building here, a trio of straggly kids there. A lot like Baltimore. But everything had changed when we reached those streets hooded by the Gothic buildings. I imagined how the college must have looked when it was founded, when most of the students owned slaves. I pictured men wearing tights and knickers, smoking pipes.

"The architecture," the dean repeated. She bit her lip and seemed to be making a calculation of some sort. I noticed that she blinked less often than most people. I sat there, waiting to see how long it would be before she blinked again.

My revolver comment won me a year's worth of psychiatric counselling, weekly meetings with Dean Guest, and—since the parents of the roommate I'd never met weren't too hip on the idea of their Amy sharing a bunk bed with a budding homicidal loony— my very own room.

Shortly after getting my first D, I also received the first knock on my door. The female counsellors never knocked. The dean had spoken to them; I was a priority. Every other day, right before dinnertime, they'd look in on me, unannounced. "Just checking up," a counsellor would say. It was the voice of a suburban mother in training. By the second week, I had made a point of sitting in a chair in front of the door, just when I expected a counsellor to pop her head around. This was intended to startle them. I also made a point of being naked. The unannounced visits ended.

The knocking persisted. Through the peephole I saw a white face, distorted and balloonish.

"Let me in." The person looked like a boy but sounded like a girl. "Let me in," the voice repeated.

"Not a chance," I said.

Then the person began to sob, and I heard a back slump against the door. If I hadn't known the person was white from the peephole, I'd have known it from a display like this. Black people didn't knock on strangers' doors, crying. Not that I understood the black people at Yale. There was something pitiful in how cool they were. Occasionally one would reach out to me with missionary zeal, but I'd rebuff that person with haughty silence.

"I don't have anyone to talk to!" the person on the other side of the door cried.

"That is correct."

"When I was a child," the person said, "I played by myself in a corner of the schoolyard all alone. I hated dolls and I hated games, animals were not friendly and birds flew away. If anyone was looking for me I hid behind a tree and cried out 'I am an orphan—'"

I opened the door. It was a she.

"Plagiarist!" I yelled. She had just recited a Frank O'Hara poem[1] as though she'd thought it up herself. I knew the poem because it was one of the few things I'd been forced to read that I wished I'd written myself.

The girl turned to face me, smiling weakly, as though her triumph were not in getting me to open the door but in the fact that she was able to smile at all when she was

---

[1] **Frank O'Hara** (1926–1966): Part of the New York School of poets in the 1950s.

so accustomed to crying. She was large but not obese, and crying had turned her face the color of raw chicken. She blew her nose into the waist end of her T-shirt, revealing a pale belly.

"How do you know that poem?"

She sniffed. "I'm in your Contemporary Poetry class."

She was Canadian and her name was Heidi, although she said she wanted people to call her Henrik. "That's a guy's name," I said. "What do you want? A sex change?"

She looked at me with so little surprise that I suspected she hadn't discounted this as an option. Then her story came out in teary, hiccup-like bursts. She had sucked some "cute guy's dick" and he'd told everybody and now people thought she was "a slut."

"Why'd you suck his dick? Aren't you a lesbian?"   30

She fit the bill. Short hair, hard, roach-stomping shoes. Dressed like an aspiring plumber. The lesbians I'd seen on TV were wiry, thin strips of muscle, but Heidi was round and soft and had a moonlike face. Drab mud-colored hair. And lesbians had cats. "Do you have a cat?" I asked.

Her eyes turned glossy with new tears. "No," she said, her voice wavering, "and I'm not a lesbian. Are you?"

"Do I look like one?" I said.

She didn't answer.

"O.K.," I said. "I could suck a guy's dick, too, if I wanted. But I don't. The hu- 35
man penis is one of the most germ-ridden objects there is." Heidi looked at me, unconvinced. "What I meant to say," I began again, "is that I don't like anybody. Period.
Guys or girls. I'm a misanthrope."

"I am, too."

"No," I said, guiding her back through my door and out into the hallway. "You're not."

"Have you had dinner?" she asked. "Let's go to Commons."

I pointed to a pyramid of ramen noodle packages on my windowsill. "See that? That means I never have to go to Commons. Aside from class, I have contact with no one."

"I hate it here, too," she said. "I should have gone to McGill, eh."   40

"The way to feel better," I said, "is to get some ramen and lock yourself in your room. Everyone will forget about you and that guy's dick and you won't have to see anyone ever again. If anyone looks for you—"

"I'll hide behind a tree."

"A revolver?" Dr. Raeburn said, flipping through a manila folder. He looked up at me as if to ask another question, but he didn't.

Dr. Raeburn was the psychiatrist. He had the gray hair and whiskers of a Civil War general. He was also a chain smoker with beige teeth and a navy wool jacket smeared with ash. He asked about the revolver at the beginning of my first visit. When I was unable to explain myself he smiled, as if this were perfectly respectable.

"Tell me about your parents."   45

I wondered what he already had on file. The folder was thick, though I hadn't said a thing of significance since Day One.

"My father was a dick and my mother seemed to like him."

He patted his pockets for his cigarettes. "That's some heavy stuff," he said. "How do you feel about Dad?" The man couldn't say the word "father." "Is Dad someone you see often?"

"I hate my father almost as much as I hate the word 'Dad.'"

He started tapping his cigarette.

"You can't smoke in here."

"That's right," he said, and slipped the cigarette back into the packet. He smiled, widening his eyes brightly. "Don't ever start."

I thought that that first encounter would be the last of Heidi, but then her head appeared in a window of Linsly-Chit during my Chaucer class. Next, she swooped down a flight of stairs in Harkness. She hailed me from across Elm Street and found me in the Sterling Library stacks. After one of my meetings with Dr. Raeburn, she was waiting for me outside Health Services, legs crossed, cleaning her fingernails.

"You know," she said, as we walked through Old Campus, "you've got to stop eating ramen. Not only does it lack a single nutrient but it's full of MSG."

"I like eating chemicals," I said. "It keeps the skin radiant."

"There's also hepatitis." She already knew how to get my attention—mention a disease.

"You get hepatitis from unwashed lettuce," I said. "If there's anything safe from the perils of the food chain, it's ramen."

"But you refrigerate what you don't eat. Each time you reheat it, you're killing good bacteria, which then can't keep the bad bacteria in check. A guy got sick from reheating Chinese noodles, and his son died from it. I read it in the *Times*." With this, she put a jovial arm around my neck. I continued walking, a little stunned. Then, just as quickly, she dropped her arm and stopped walking. I stopped, too.

"Did you notice that I put my arm around you?"

"Yes," I said. "Next time, I'll have to chop it off."

"I don't want you to get sick," she said. "Let's eat at Commons."

In the cold air, her arm had felt good.

The problem with Commons was that it was too big; its ceiling was as high as a cathedral's, but below it there were no awestruck worshippers, only eighteen-year-olds at heavy wooden tables, chatting over veal patties and Jell-O.

We got our food, tacos stuffed with meat substitute, and made our way through the maze of tables. The Koreans had a table. Each singing group had a table. The crew team sat at a long table of its own. We passed the black table. The sheer quantity of Heidi's flesh accentuated just how white she was.

"How you doing, sista?" a guy asked, his voice full of accusation, eyeballing me as though I were clad in a Klansman's sheet and hood. "I guess we won't see you till graduation."

"If," I said, "you graduate."

The remark was not well received. As I walked past, I heard protests, angry and loud, as if they'd discovered a cheat at their poker game. Heidi and I found an unoccupied table along the periphery, which was isolated and dark. We sat down. Heidi prayed over her tacos.

"I thought you didn't believe in God," I said.

"Not in the God depicted in the Judeo-Christian Bible, but I do believe that nature's essence is a spirit that—"

"All right," I said. I had begun to eat, and cubes of diced tomato fell from my mouth when I spoke. "Stop right there. Tacos and spirits don't mix."

"You've always got to be so flip," she said. "I'm going to apply for another friend."

"There's always Mr. Dick," I said. "Slurp, slurp."

"You are so lame. So unbelievably lame. I'm going out with Mr. Dick. Thursday night at Atticus. His name is Keith."

Heidi hadn't mentioned Mr. Dick since the day I'd met her. That was more than a month ago and we'd spent a lot of that time together. I checked for signs that she was lying, her habit of smiling too much, her eyes bright and cheeks full, so that she looked like a chipmunk. But she looked normal. Pleased, even, to see me so flustered.

"You're insane! What are you going to do this time?" I asked. "Sleep with him? 75 Then when he makes fun of you, what? Come pound your head on my door reciting the 'Collected Poems of Sylvia Plath'?"

"He's going to apologize for before. And don't call me insane. You're the one going to the psychiatrist."

"Well, I'm not going to suck his dick, that's for sure."

She put her arm around me in mock comfort, but I pushed it off, and ignored her. She touched my shoulder again, and I turned, annoyed, but it wasn't Heidi after all; a sepia-toned boy dressed in khakis and a crisp plaid shirt was standing behind me. He handed me a hot-pink square of paper without a word, then briskly made his way toward the other end of Commons, where the crowds blossomed. Heidi leaned over and read it: "Wear Black Leather—the Less, the Better."

"It's a gay party," I said, crumpling the card. "He thinks we're fucking gay."

Heidi and I signed on to work at the Saybrook Dining Hall as dishwashers. The job 80 consisted of dumping food from plates and trays into a vat of rustling water. It seemed straightforward, but then I learned better. You wouldn't believe what people could do with food until you worked in a dish room. Lettuce and crackers and soup would be bullied into a pulp in the bowl of some bored anorexic; ziti would be mixed with honey and granola; trays would appear heaped with mashed-potato snow women with melted chocolate ice cream for hair. Frat boys arrived at the dish-room window, en masse. They liked to fill glasses with food, then seal them, airtight, onto their trays. If you tried to prize them off, milk, Worcestershire sauce, peas, chunks of bread vomited onto your dish-room uniform.

When this happened one day in the middle of the lunch rush, for what seemed like the hundredth time, I tipped the tray toward one of the frat boys, popping the glasses off so that the mess spurted onto his Shetland sweater.

He looked down at his sweater. "Lesbo bitch!"

"No," I said, "that would be your mother."

Heidi, next to me, clenched my arm in support, but I remained motionless, waiting to see what the frat boy would do. He glared at me for a minute, then walked away.

"Let's take a smoke break," Heidi said. 85

I didn't smoke, but Heidi had begun to, because she thought it would help her lose weight. As I hefted a stack of glasses through the steamer, she lit up.

"Soft packs remind me of you," she said. "Just when you've smoked them all and you think there's none left, there's always one more, hiding in that little crushed corner." Before I could respond she said, "Oh, God. Not another mouse. You know whose job that is."

By the end of the rush, the floor mats got full and slippery with food. This was when mice tended to appear, scurrying over our shoes; more often than not, a mouse got caught in the grating that covered the drains in the floor. Sometimes the mouse was already dead by the time we noticed it. This one was alive.

"No way," I said. "This time you're going to help. Get some gloves and a trash bag."

"That's all I'm getting. I'm not getting that mouse out of there." 90

"Put on the gloves," I ordered. She winced, but put them on. "Reach down," I said. "At an angle, so you get at its middle. Otherwise, if you try to get it by its tail, the tail will break off."

"This is filthy, eh."

"That's why we're here," I said. "To clean up filth. Eh."

She reached down, but would not touch the mouse. I put my hand around her arm and pushed it till her hand made contact. The cries from the mouse were soft, songlike. "Oh, my God," she said. "Oh, my God, ohmigod." She wrestled it out of the grating and turned her head away.

"Don't you let it go," I said. 95

"Where's the food bag? It'll smother itself if I drop it in the food bag. Quick," she said, her head still turned away, her eyes closed. "Lead me to it."

"No. We are not going to smother this mouse. We've got to break its neck."

"You're one heartless bitch."

I wondered how to explain that if death is unavoidable it should be quick and painless. My mother had died slowly. At the hospital, they'd said it was kidney failure, but I knew that, in the end, it was my father. He made her scared to live in her own home, until she was finally driven away from it in an ambulance.

"Breaking its neck will save it the pain of smothering," I said. "Breaking its neck 100 is more humane. Take the trash bag and cover it so you won't get any blood on you, then crush."

The loud jets of the steamer had shut off automatically and the dish room grew quiet. Heidi breathed in deeply, then crushed the mouse. She shuddered, disgusted. "Now what?"

"What do you mean, 'Now what?' Throw the little bastard in the trash."

At our third session, I told Dr. Raeburn I didn't mind if he smoked. He sat on the sill of his open window, smoking behind a jungle screen of office plants.

We spent the first ten minutes discussing the Iliad, and whether or not the text actually states that Achilles had been dipped in the River Styx. He said it did, and I said it didn't. After we'd finished with the Iliad, and with my new job in what he called "the scullery," he asked more questions about my parents. I told him nothing. It was none of his business. Instead, I talked about Heidi. I told him about that day in Commons, Heidi's plan to go on a date with Mr. Dick, and the invitation we'd been given to the gay party.

"You seem preoccupied by this soirée." He arched his eyebrows at the word 105 "soirée."

"Wouldn't you be?"

"Dina," he said slowly, in a way that made my name seem like a song title, "have you ever had a romantic interest?"

"You want to know if I've ever had a boyfriend?" I said. "Just go ahead and ask if I've ever fucked anybody."

This appeared to surprise him. "I think that you are having a crisis of identity," he said.

"Oh, is that what this is?" 110

His profession had taught him not to roll his eyes. Instead, his exasperation revealed itself with a tiny pursing of his lips, as though he'd just tasted something awful and were trying very hard not to offend the cook.

"It doesn't have to be, as you say, someone you've fucked, it doesn't have to be a boyfriend," he said.

"Well, what are you trying to say? If it's not a boy, then you're saying it's a girl—"

"Calm down. It could be a crush, Dina." He lit one cigarette off another. "A crush on a male teacher, a crush on a dog, for heaven's sake. An interest. Not necessarily a relationship."

It was sacrifice time. If I could spend the next half hour talking about some boy, 115 then I'd have given him what he wanted.

So I told him about the boy with the nice shoes.

I was sixteen and had spent the last few coins in my pocket on bus fare to buy groceries. I didn't like going to the Super Fresh two blocks away from my house, plunking government food stamps into the hands of the cashiers.

"There she go reading," one of them once said, even though I was only carrying a book. "Don't your eyes get tired?"

On Greenmount Avenue you could read schoolbooks—that was understandable. The government and your teachers forced you to read them. But anything else was antisocial. It meant you'd rather submit to the words of some white dude than shoot the breeze with your neighbors.

I hated those cashiers, and I hated them seeing me with food stamps, so I took the bus 120 and shopped elsewhere. That day, I got off the bus at Govans, and though the neighborhood was black like my own—hair salon after hair salon of airbrushed signs promising arabesque hair styles and inch-long fingernails—the houses were neat and orderly, nothing at all like Greenmount, where every other house had at least one shattered window. The store was well swept, and people quietly checked long grocery lists—no screaming kids, no loud cashier-customer altercations. I got the groceries and left the store.

I decided to walk back. It was a fall day, and I walked for blocks. Then I sensed someone following me. I walked more quickly, my arms around the sack, the leafy lettuce tickling my nose. I didn't want to hold the sack so close that it would break the eggs or squash the hamburger buns, but it was slipping, and as I looked behind a boy my age, maybe older, rushed toward me.

"Let me help you," he said.

"That's all right." I set the bag on the sidewalk. Maybe I saw his face, maybe it was handsome enough, but what I noticed first, splayed on either side of the bag, were his shoes. They were nice shoes, real leather, a stitched design like a widow's peak on each one, or like birds' wings, and for the first time in my life I understood what people meant when they said "wing-tip shoes."

"I watched you carry them groceries out that store, then you look around, like you're lost, but like you liked being lost, then you walk down the sidewalk for blocks and blocks. Rearranging that bag, it almost gone to slip, then hefting it back up again."

"Huh, huh," I said. 125

"And then I passed my own house and was still following you. And then your bag really look like it was gone crash and everything. So I just thought I'd help." He sucked in his bottom lip, as if to keep it from making a smile. "What's your name?" When I told him, he said, "Dina, my name is Cecil." Then he said, "'D' comes right after 'C.'"

"Yes," I said, "it does, doesn't it."

Then, half question, half statement, he said, "I could carry your groceries for you? And walk you home?"

I stopped the story there. Dr. Raeburn kept looking at me. "Then what happened?"

I couldn't tell him the rest: that I had not wanted the boy to walk me home, that I   130 didn't want someone with such nice shoes to see where I lived.

Dr. Raeburn would only have pitied me if I'd told him that I ran down the sidewalk after I told the boy no, that I fell, the bag slipped, and the eggs cracked, their yolks running all over the lettuce. Clear amniotic fluid coated the can of cinnamon rolls. I left the bag there on the sidewalk, the groceries spilled out randomly like cards loosed from a deck. When I returned home, I told my mother that I'd lost the food stamps.

"Lost?" she said. I'd expected her to get angry, I'd wanted her to get angry, but she hadn't. "Lost?" she repeated. Why had I been so clumsy and nervous around a harmless boy? I could have brought the groceries home and washed off the egg yolk, but, instead, I'd just left them there. "Come on," Mama said, snuffing her tears, pulling my arm, trying to get me to join her and start yanking cushions off the couch. "We'll find enough change here. We got to get something for dinner before your father gets back."

We'd already searched the couch for money the previous week, and I knew there'd be nothing now, but I began to push my fingers into the couch's boniest corners, pretending that it was only a matter of time before I'd find some change or a lost watch or an earring. Something pawnable, perhaps.

"What happened next?" Dr. Raeburn asked again. "Did you let the boy walk you home?"

"My house was far, so we went to his house instead." Though I was sure Dr. Rae-   135 burn knew that I was making this part up, I continued. "We made out on his sofa. He kissed me."

Dr. Raeburn lit his next cigarette like a detective. Cool, suspicious. "How did it feel?"

"You know," I said. "Like a kiss feels. It felt nice. The kiss felt very, very nice."

Raeburn smiled gently, though he seemed unconvinced. When he called time on our session his cigarette had become one long pole of ash. I left his office, walking quickly down the corridor, afraid to look back. It would be like him to trot after me, his navy blazer flapping, just to eke the truth out of me. *You never kissed anyone.* The words slid from my brain, and knotted in my stomach.

When I reached my dorm, I found an old record player blocking my door and a Charles Mingus[2] LP propped beside it. I carried them inside and then, lying on the floor, I played the Mingus over and over again until I fell asleep. I slept feeling as though Dr. Raeburn had attached electrodes to my head, willing into my mind a dream about my mother. I saw the lemon meringue of her skin, the long bone of her arm as she reached down to clip her toenails. I'd come home from a school trip to an aquarium, and I was explaining the differences between baleen and sperm whales according to the size of their heads, the range of their habitats, their feeding patterns.

I awoke remembering the expression on her face after I'd finished my dizzying   140 whale lecture. She looked like a tourist who'd asked for directions to a place she thought was simple enough to get to only to hear a series of hypothetical turns, alleys, one-way

---

[2]**Charles Mingus** (1922–1979): Bassist, jazz musician, and composer.

streets. Her response was to nod politely at the perilous elaborateness of it all; to nod in the knowledge that she would never be able to get where she wanted to go.

The dishwashers always closed down the dining hall. One night, after everyone else had punched out, Heidi and I took a break, and though I wasn't a smoker, we set two milk crates upside down on the floor and smoked cigarettes.

The dishwashing machines were off, but steam still rose from them like a jungle mist. Outside in the winter air, students were singing carols in their groomed and tailored singing-group voices. The Whiffenpoofs were back in New Haven after a tour around the world, and I guess their return was a huge deal. Heidi and I craned our necks to watch the year's first snow through an open window.

"What are you going to do when you're finished?" Heidi asked. Sexy question marks of smoke drifted up to the windows before vanishing.

"Take a bath."

She swatted me with her free hand. "No, silly. Three years from now. When you leave Yale." 145

"I don't know. Open up a library. Somewhere where no one comes in for books. A library in a desert."

She looked at me as though she'd expected this sort of answer and didn't know why she'd asked in the first place.

"What are you going to do?" I asked her.

"Open up a psych clinic. In a desert. And my only patient will be some wacko who runs a library."

"Ha," I said. "Whatever you do, don't work in a dish room ever again. You're no good." I got up from the crate. "C'mon. Let's hose the place down." 150

We put out our cigarettes on the floor, since it was our job to clean it, anyway. We held squirt guns in one hand and used the other to douse the floors with the standard-issue, eye-burning cleaning solution. We hosed the dish room, the kitchen, the serving line, sending the water and crud and suds into the drains. Then we hosed them again so the solution wouldn't eat holes in our shoes as we left. Then I had an idea. I unbuckled my belt.

"What the hell are you doing?" Heidi said.

"Listen, it's too cold to go outside with our uniforms all wet. We could just take a shower right here. There's nobody but us."

"What the fuck, eh?"

I let my pants drop, then took off my shirt and panties. I didn't wear a bra, since I 155 didn't have much to fill one. I took off my shoes and hung my clothes on the stepladder.

"You've flipped," Heidi said. "I mean, really, psych-ward flipped."

I soaped up with the liquid hand soap until I felt as glazed as a ham. "Stand back and spray me."

"Oh, my God," she said. I didn't know whether she was confused or delighted, but she picked up the squirt gun and sprayed me. She was laughing. Then she got too close and the water started to sting.

"God damn it!" I said. "That hurt!"

"I was wondering what it would take to make you say that." 160

When all the soap had been rinsed off, I put on my regular clothes and said, "O.K. You're up next."

"No way," she said.

"Yes way."

She started to take off her uniform shirt, then stopped.

"What?" 165

"I'm too fat."

"You goddam right." She always said she was fat. One time, I'd told her that she should shut up about it, that large black women wore their fat like mink coats. "You're big as a house," I said now. "Frozen yogurt may be low in calories but not if you eat five tubs of it. Take your clothes off. I want to get out of here."

She began taking off her uniform, then stood there, hands cupped over her breasts, crouching at the pubic bone.

"Open up," I said, "or we'll never get done."

Her hands remained where they were. I threw the bottle of liquid soap at her, and 170 she had to catch it, revealing herself as she did.

I turned on the squirt gun, and she stood there, stiff, arms at her sides, eyes closed, as though awaiting mummification. I began with the water on low, and she turned around in a full circle, hesitantly, letting the droplets from the spray fall on her as if she were submitting to a death by stoning.

When I increased the water pressure, she slipped and fell on the sudsy floor. She stood up and then slipped again. This time she laughed and remained on the floor, rolling around on it as I sprayed.

I think I began to love Heidi that night in the dish room, but who is to say that I hadn't begun to love her the first time I met her? I sprayed her and sprayed her, and she turned over and over like a large beautiful dolphin, lolling about in the sun.

Heidi started sleeping at my place. Sometimes she slept on the floor; sometimes we slept sardinelike, my feet at her head, until she complained that my feet were "taunt-ing" her. When we finally slept head to head, she said, "Much better." She was so close I could smell her toothpaste. "I like your hair," she told me, touching it through the darkness. "You should wear it out more often."

"White people always say that about black people's hair. The worse it looks, the 175 more they say they like it."

I'd expected her to disagree, but she kept touching my hair, her hands passing through it till my scalp tingled. When she began to touch the hair around the edge of my face, I felt myself quake. Her fingertips stopped for a moment, as if checking my pulse, then resumed.

"I like how it feels right here. See, mine just starts with the same old texture as the rest of my hair." She found my hand under the blanket and brought it to her hairline. "See," she said.

It was dark. As I touched her hair, it seemed as though I could smell it, too. Not a shampoo smell. Something richer, murkier. A bit dead, but sweet, like the decaying wood of a ship. She guided my hand.

"I see," I said. The record she'd given me was playing in my mind, and I kept trying to shut it off. I could also hear my mother saying that this is what happens when you've been around white people: things get weird. So weird I could hear the stylus etching its way into the flat vinyl of the record. "Listen," I said finally, when the bass and saxes started up. I heard Heidi breathe deeply, but she said nothing.

We spent the winter and some of the spring in my room—never hers—missing tests, 180
listening to music, looking out my window to comment on people who wouldn't have
given us a second thought. We read books related to none of our classes. I got riled up
by "The Autobiography of Malcolm X" and "The Chomsky Reader";[3] Heidi read aloud
passages from "The Anxiety of Influence."[4] We guiltily read mysteries and "Clan of the
Cave Bear,"[5] then immediately threw them away. Once, we looked up from our books
at exactly the same moment, as though trapped at a dinner table with nothing to say.
A pleasant trap of silence.

Then one weekend I went back to Baltimore. When I returned, to a sleepy, tree-
scented spring, a group of students were holding what was called "Coming Out Day."
I watched it from my room.

The m.c. was the sepia boy who'd invited us to that party months back. His speech
was strident but still smooth, and peppered with jokes. There was a speech about AIDS,
with lots of statistics: nothing that seemed to make "coming out" worth it. Then the
women spoke. One girl pronounced herself "out" as casually as if she'd announced the
time. Another said nothing at all: she appeared at the microphone accompanied by a
woman who began cutting off her waist-length, bleached-blond hair. The woman doing the cutting tossed the shorn hair in every direction as she cut. People were clapping
and cheering and catching the locks of hair.

And then there was Heidi. She was proud that she liked girls, she said when she
reached the microphone. She loved them, wanted to sleep with them. She was a dyke,
she said repeatedly, stabbing her finger to her chest in case anyone was unsure to whom
she was referring. She could not have seen me. I was across the street, three stories up.
And yet, when everyone clapped for her, she seemed to be looking straight at me.

Heidi knocked. "Let me in."

It was like the first time I met her. The tears, the raw pink of her face. 185

We hadn't spoken in weeks. Outside, pink-and-white blossoms hung from the Old
Campus trees. Students played hackeysack in T-shirts and shorts. Though I was the one
who'd broken away after she went up to that podium, I still half expected her to poke
her head out a window in Linsly-Chit, or tap on my back in Harkness, or even join me
in the Commons dining hall, where I'd asked for my dish-room shift to be transferred.
She did none of these.

"Well," I said, "what is it?"

She looked at me. "My mother," she said.

She continued to cry, but it seemed to have grown so silent in my room I wondered
if I could hear the numbers change on my digital clock.

"When my parents were getting divorced," she said, "my mother bought a car. A 190
used one. An El Dorado. It was filthy. It looked like a huge crushed can coming up the
street. She kept trying to clean it out. I mean—"

I nodded and tried to think what to say in the pause she left behind. Finally I said,
"We had one of those," though I was sure ours was an Impala.

---

[3]**Noam Chomsky** (1928–): Professor of Linguistics at Massachusetts Institute of Technology and author of works on linguistics, intellectual history, international affairs, and U.S. foreign
policy. [4]*The Anxiety of Influence:* Work of literary criticism by Harold Bloom, published in
1973. [5]*Clan of the Cave Bear:* The first in Jean Auel's series of novels about prehistoric humans,
published in 1980.

She looked at me, eyes steely from trying not to cry. "Anyway she'd drive me around in it and although she didn't like me to eat in it, I always did. One day, I was eating cantaloupe slices, spitting the seeds on the floor. Maybe a month later, I saw this little sprout, growing right up from the car floor. I just started laughing and she kept saying what, what? I was laughing and then I saw she was so—"

She didn't finish. So what? So sad? So awful? Heidi looked a me with what seemed to be a renewed vigor. "We could have gotten a better car, eh?"

"It's all right. It's not a big deal," I said.

Of course, that was the wrong thing to say. And I really didn't mean it to sound 195 the way it had come out.

I told Dr. Raeburn about Heidi's mother having cancer and how I'd said it wasn't a big deal, though I'd wanted to say exactly the opposite. I meant that I knew what it was like to have a parent die. My mother had died. I knew how eventually one accustoms oneself to the physical world's lack of sympathy: the buses that still run on time, the kids who still play in the street, the clocks that won't stop ticking for the person who's gone.

"You're pretending," Dr. Raeburn said, not sage or professional but a little shocked by the discovery, as if I'd been trying to hide a pack of his cigarettes behind my back.

"I'm pretending?" I shook my head. "All those years of psych grad," I said. "And to tell me *that?*"

"You construct stories about yourself and dish them out—one for you, one for you—" Here he reenacted the process, showing me handing out lies as if they were apples.

"Pretending. I believe the professional name for it might be denial," I said. "Are 200 you calling me gay?"

He pursed his lips noncommittally. "No, Dina. I don't think you're gay."

I checked his eyes. I couldn't read them.

"No. Not at all," he said, sounding as if he were telling a subtle joke. "But maybe you'll finally understand."

"Understand what?"

"That constantly saying what one doesn't mean accustoms the mouth to meaning- 205 less phrases." His eyes narrowed. "Maybe you'll understand that when you need to express something truly significant, your mouth will revert to the insignificant nonsense it knows so well." He looked at me, his hands sputtering in the air in a gesture of defeat. "Who knows?" he asked, with a glib, psychiatric smile I'd never seen before. "Maybe its your survival mechanism. Black living in a white world."

I heard him, but only vaguely. I'd hooked on to that one word, pretending. What Dr. Raeburn would never understand was that pretending was what had got me this far. I remembered the morning of my mother's funeral. I'd been given milk to settle my stomach; I'd pretended it was coffee. I imagined I was drinking coffee elsewhere. Some Arabic-speaking country where the thick coffee served in little cups was so strong it could keep you awake for days. Some Arabic country where I'd sit in a tented café and be more than happy to don a veil.

Heidi wanted me to go with her to the funeral. She'd sent this message through the dean. "We'll pay for your ticket to Vancouver," the dean said.

"What about my ticket back?" I asked. "Maybe the shrink will pay for that."

The dean looked at me as though I were an insect she'd like to squash. "We'll pay for the whole thing. We might even pay for some lessons in manners."

So I packed my suitcase and walked from my suicide-single dorm to Heidi's room. 210 A thin wispy girl in ragged cutoffs and a shirt that read "LSBN!" answered the door. A group of short-haired girls in thick black leather jackets, bundled up despite the summer heat, encircled Heidi in a protective fairy ring. They looked at me critically, clearly wondering if Heidi was too fragile for my company.

"You've got our numbers," one said, holding onto Heidi's shoulder. "And Vancouver's got a great gay community."

"Oh God," I said. "She's going to a funeral, not a 'save the Dykes' rally."

One of the girls stepped in front of me.

"It's O.K., Cynthia," Heidi said. Then she ushered me into her bedroom and closed the door. A suitcase was on her bed, half packed. She folded a polka-dotted T-shirt that was wrong for any occasion. "Why haven't you talked to me?" she said. "Why haven't you talked to me in two months?"

"I don't know," I said. 215

"You don't know," she said, each syllable seeped in sarcasm. "You don't know. Well, I know. You thought I was going to try to sleep with you."

"Try to? We slept together all winter!"

"Smelling your feet is not 'sleeping together.' You've got a lot to learn." She seemed thinner and meaner.

"So tell me," I said. "What can you show me that I need to learn?" But as soon as I said it I somehow knew that she still hadn't slept with anyone.

"Am I supposed to come over there and sweep your enraged self into my arms?" 220 I said. "Like in the movies? Is this the part where we're both so mad we kiss each other?"

She shook her head and smiled weakly. "You don't get it," she said. "My mother is dead." She closed her suitcase, clicking shut the old-fashioned locks. "My mother is dead," she said again, this time reminding herself. She set the suitcase upright on the floor and sat on it. She looked like someone waiting for a train.

"Fine," I said. "And she's going to be dead for a long time." Though it sounded stupid, I felt good saying it. As though I had my own locks to click shut.

Heidi went to Vancouver for her mother's funeral. I didn't go. Instead, I went back to Baltimore and moved in with an aunt I barely knew. Every day was the same: I read and smoked outside my aunt's apartment, studying the row of hair salons across the street, where girls in denim cut-offs and tank tops would troop in and come out hours later, a flash of neon nails, coifs the color and sheen of patent leather. And every day I imagined visiting Heidi in Vancouver. Her house would not be large, but it would be clean. Flowery shrubs would line the walks. The Canadian wind would whip us about like pennants. I'd be visiting her at some vague time in the future, deliberately vague, for people like me, who realign past events to suit themselves. In that future time, you always have a chance to catch the groceries before they fall, your words can always be rewound and erased, rewritten and revised.

But once I imagined Heidi visiting me. There would be no psychiatrists or deans. No boys with nice shoes or flip cashiers. Just me in my single room. She would knock on the door and say, "Open up." ●

Andrew Lam (1964–   )

Grandma's Tales *1996*

The day after Mama and Papa took off to Las Vegas, Grandma died. Nancy and I, we didn't know what to do, Vietnamese traditional funerals with incense sticks and chanting Buddhist monks not being our thing. We have a big freezer, Nancy said. Why don't we freeze her. Really. Why bother Mama and Papa. What's another day or two for Grandma now anyway?

Nancy's older than me, and since I didn't have any better idea, we iced her.

Grandma was 94 years, 8 months, and 6 days old when she died. She lived through three wars, two famines, and a full hard life. America, besides, was not all that good for her. She had been confined to the second floor of our big Victorian home, as her health was failing, and she did not speak English, only a little French, like *Oui monsieur, c'est evidemment un petit monstre,* and, *Non, Madame, vous n'êtes pas du tout enceinte, je vous assure.* She was a head nurse in the maternity ward of the Hanoi hospital during the French colonial time. I used to love her stories about delivering all these strange two-headed babies and Siamese triplets connected at the hip whom she named Happy, Liberation, and Day.

Grandma's death came when she was eating spring rolls with me and Nancy. Nancy was wearing a nice black miniskirt and her lips were painted red, and Grandma said you look like a high-class whore. Nancy made a face and said she was preparing to go to one of her famous San Francisco artsy cocktail parties where waiters were better dressed than most upper-class Vietnamese men back home, and there were silver trays of duck paté and salmon mousse, and ice sculptures with wings and live musicians playing Vivaldi.

So get off my case, Grandma, because I'm no whore.   5

It was a compliment, Grandma said, winking at me, but I guess it's wasted on you, child. Then she laughed, as Nancy prepared to leave. Child, do the cha-cha-cha for me. I didn't get to do it when I was young, with my clubbed foot and the wars and everything else.

Sure, Grandma, Nancy said, and rolled her pretty eyes.

Then Grandma dropped her chopsticks on the hardwood floor—clack, clack, clatter, clack, clack—closed her eyes, and stopped breathing. Just like that.

So we iced her. She was small, the freezer was large. We wrapped her body in plastic wrap first, then sent a message to Circus-Circus, where Mama and Papa were staying.

Meanwhile Nancy had a party to go to, and I had to meet Eric for a movie.   10

I didn't care about the movie, but cared about Eric. He's got eyes so blue you can swim in them, and a warm laugh, and is really beautiful, a year older than me, a senior. Eric liked Grandma. Neither one knew the other's language, but there was this thing between them, mutual respect, like one cool old chic to one cool young dude. (Sometimes I would translate but not always 'cause my English is not all that good and my Vietnamese sucks.) What was so cool about Grandma was she was the only one who knew I'm bisexual. Even though she was Confucian bound and trained and a Buddhist and all, she was really cool about it.

One night, we were sitting in the living room watching a John Wayne movie together, *The Green Berets,* and Eric was there with me and Grandma. (Mama and Papa had just gone to bed and Nancy was at some weird black and white ball or something like that.) And Eric leaned over and kissed me on the lips and Grandma said, That's real nice, and I translated and we all laughed and John Wayne shot dead five guys. Just like that. But Grandma didn't mind, really. She's seen Americans like John Wayne shooting her people in the movies before. She always thought of him as a bad guy, uglier than a water buffalo's ass. And she'd seen us more passionate than a kiss on the lips and didn't mind. She used to tell us to be careful and not make any babies—obviously a joke—'cause she'd done delivering them. So you see, we liked Grandma a lot.

Anyway, after Nancy and I packed Grandma down into the 12 degree Fahrenheit, I went out to meet Eric, and later we came back to the house. We made out on the couch. After a while I said, Eric, I have to tell you something. Grandma's dead. You're kidding me, he whispered, with his beautiful smile. I kid you not, I said. She's dead, and Nancy and me, we iced her. Shit! He said. Why? 'Cause otherwise she would start to smell, duh, and we have to wait for my parents to perform a traditional Vietnamese funeral. We fell silent. Then Eric said, can I take a peek at Grandma? Sure, I said, sure you can, she was as much yours as she was mine, and we went to the freezer and looked in.

The weird thing was the freezer was on defrost and Grandma was nowhere in sight. There was a trail of water and plastic wrap leading from the freezer to her bedroom. We followed it. On the bed, all wet, sat Grandma, counting her Buddhist rosary and chanting her diamond sutra. What's weirder is that she looked real young. I mean around 54 now, not 94, the high cheeks, the rosy lips. When she saw us she smiled and said: "What do you say we all go to one of those famous cocktail parties that Nancy's gone to, the three of us?" I wasn't scared because she said it in English, I mean accentless, Californian English.

Wow, Grandma, Eric said, your English is excellent.   15

"I know," Grandma said, "that's just a side benefit of being reborn. But enough with compliments, we got to party."

Cool, said Eric. Cool, I said, though I was a little jealous 'cause I had to go through junior high and high school and all those damn ESL classes and everything to learn the same language while Grandma just got it down cold because she was reborn. Grandma put on this nice brocaded red blouse and black silk pants and sequined velvet shoes and fixed her hair real nice and we drove off downtown.

Boy, you should've seen Nancy's face when we arrived at her cocktail party. She nearly tripped over herself. She laid her face against the wing of an ice sculpture to calm herself. Then she walked straight up to us, haughty, and said, It's invitation only, how'd ya'll get in?

"Calm yourself, child," said Grandma, "I told them that I was a board member of the Cancer Society and flashed my jade bracelet and diamond ring and gave the man a forty dollar tip."

Nancy had the same reaction Eric and I had: Grandma, your English is flawless!   20
Grandma was oblivious to compliments. She went straight to the punch bowl for some spirits. Since her clubbed foot was cured she had an elegant grace about her. Her hair floated like gray-black clouds behind her. Everyone stared, mesmerized.

Needless to say Grandma was the big hit of the party. She had so many interesting stories to tell. The feminists, it seemed, loved her the most. They crowded around her as she told them how she'd been married early and had eight children while being the matriarch of a middle-class family during the Viet Minh uprising. She told them about my grandfather, a brilliant man who was well versed in Moliére and Shakespeare and who was an accomplished violinist but who drank himself to death because he was helpless against the colonial powers of the French. She told everyone how single-handedly she had raised her children after his death and they all became doctors and lawyers and pilots and famous composers. Then she started telling them how the twenty-four-year-old civil war divided her family up and brothers fought brothers over ideological notions that proved bloody pointless. Then she told them about our journey across the Pacific Ocean in a crowded fishing boat where thirst and starvation nearly did us all in until it was her idea to eat some of the dead and drink their blood so that the rest of us could survive to catch glimpses of this beautiful America and become Americans.

She started telling them, too, about the fate of Vietnamese women who had to marry and see their husbands and sons go to war and never come back. Then she recited poems and told fairy tales with sad endings, fairy tales she herself had learned as a child, the kind she used to tell me and my cousins when we were young. There was this princess, you see, who fell in love with a fisherman and he didn't know about her 'cause she only heard his beautiful voice singing from a distance, so when he drifted away downriver one day she died, her heart turning into this ruby with the image of his boat imprinted on it. (In Grandma's stories, the husbands and fishermen always come home, but they come home always too late and there was nothing they could do but mourn and grieve.)

Grandma's voice was sad and seductive and words came pouring out of her like rain and the whole place turned quiet and Nancy sobbed because she understood and Eric stood close to me and I cried a little, too. "I lost four of my children," Grandma said, "twelve of my grandchildren, and countless relatives and friends to wars and famines and I lost everything I owned when I left my beautiful country behind. Mine is a story of suffering and sorrow, suffering and sorrow being the way of Vietnamese life. But now I have a second chance and I am not who I was, and yet I have all the memories, so wherever I go I will keep telling my stories and songs."

Applause broke out, then a rich-looking man with gray hair came up to Grandma and they talked quietly for a while. When they were done Grandma came to me and Nancy and Eric and said goodbye. She said she was not going to wait for my parents to come home for a traditional funeral. She had a lot of living still to do since Buddha had given her the gift to live twice in one life and this man, some famous novelist from Colombia, was going to take her places. He might even help her write her book. So she was going to the *mediteranée* to get a tan and to Venice to see the festivals and ride the gondolas and maybe afterward she'd go by Hanoi and see what they'd done to her childhood home and visit some long-forgotten ancestral graves and relatives and then who knows where she'd go. She'd send postcards though and don't you wait up. Then before we knew it Grandma was already out of the door with the famous novelist and the music started up again. Eric and I ran out after her but outside there was only this city under a velvety night sky, its highrises shining like glass cages, with little diamonds and gold coins kept locked inside them.

Mama and Papa came home two days later. They brought incense sticks and ox- 25
hide drums and wooden fish and copper gongs and jasmine wreaths and Oolong tea and paper offerings, all the things that we were supposed to have for a traditional funeral. A monk had even sent a fax of his chanting rate and schedule because he was real busy, and the relatives started pouring in.

It was hard to explain then what had happened, what we had always expected as the tragic ending of things, human frailty the point of mourning and grief. And wasn't epic loss what made us tell our stories? It was difficult for me to mourn now, though. Difficult 'cause while the incense smoke drifted all over the mansion and the crying and wailing resounded like cicadas humming on the tamarind tree in the summer back in Vietnam, Grandma wasn't around. ●

Alma Luz Villanueva *(1944–)*

Crazy Courage *1996*

To Michael B.

Why do I think of Michael . . .
He came to my fiction class
as a man (dressed in men's
clothes); then he came

to my poetry class   5
as a woman (dressed in women's
clothes; but he was still
a man under the clothes).

Was I moved in the face of
such courage (man/woman   10
woman/man) . . .
Was I moved by the gentleness

of his masculinity; the strength
of his femininity . . .
His presence at the class poetry   15
reading, dressed in a miniskirt,

high boots, bright purple tights,
a scooped-neck blouse, carrying
a single, living, red rose, in a
vase, to the podium (the visitors,   20

not from the class, shocked—
the young, seen-it-all MTV crowd—
into silence as he's introduced,
"Michael . . .") And what it was, I think,

was his perfect dignity, the offering   25
of his living, red rose to the perceptive,
to the blind, to the amused, to the impressed,
to those who would kill him, and

to those who would love him.
And of course I remember the surprise   30
of his foamy breasts as we hugged
goodbye, his face blossomed
open, set apart, the pain of it,
the joy of it (the crazy courage
to be whole, as a rose is   35
whole, as a child is

whole before they're
punished for including
everything in their
innocence).   40

Mark Doty   *(1953–)*

Tiara   *1990*

Peter died in a paper tiara
cut from a book of princess paper dolls;
he loved royalty, sashes

and jewels. *I don't know,*
he said, when he woke in the hospice,   5
I was watching the Bette Davis[1] *film festival*

on Channel 57 and then—
At the wake, the tension broke
when someone guessed

the casket closed because   10
he was *in there in a big wig*
and heels, and someone said,

You know he's always late,
he probably isn't here yet—
he's still fixing his makeup.   15

And someone said he asked for it.
Asked for it—
when all he did was go down

into the salt tide
of wanting as much as he wanted,   20
giving himself over so drunk

---

[1]**Bette Davis:** An American movie actress (1908–1989).

or stoned it almost didn't matter who,
though they were beautiful,
stampeding into him in the simple,

ravishing music of their hurry.   25
I think heaven is perfect stasis
poised over the realms of desire,

where dreaming and waking men lie
on the grass while wet horses
roam among them, huge fragments   30

of the music we die into
in the body's paradise.
Sometimes we wake not knowing

how we came to lie here,
or who has crowned us with these temporary,   35
precious stones. And given

the world's perfectly turned shoulders,
the deep hollows blued by longing,
given the irreplaceable silk

of horses rippling in orchards,   40
fruit thundering and chiming down,
given the ordinary marvels of form

and gravity, what could he do,
what could any of us ever do
but ask for it.   45

David Henry Hwang *(1957–   )*

M Butterfly *1986*

The Characters

Rene Gallimard
Song Liling
Marc/Man No. 2/Consul Sharpless
Renee/Woman at Party/Pinup Girl
Comrade Chin/Suzuki/Shu-Fang
Helga
Toulon/Man No. 1/Judge
Dancers

Time and Place

> *The action of the play takes place in a Paris prison in the present, and, in recall, during the decade 1960–1970 in Beijing, and from 1966 to the present in Paris.*

Playwright's Notes

> *A former French diplomat and a Chinese opera singer have been sentenced to six years in jail for spying for China after a two-day trial that traced a story of clandestine love and mistaken sexual identity. . . .*
>
> > *Mr. Boursicot was accused of passing information to China after he fell in love with Mr. Shi, whom he believed for twenty years to be a woman.*
>
> <div align="right">—New York Times, <i>May 11, 1986</i></div>

> *This play was suggested by international newspaper accounts of a recent espionage trial. For purposes of dramatization, names have been changed, characters created, and incidents devised or altered, and this play does not purport to be a factual record of real events or real people.*

I could escape this feeling
With my China girl . . .
—*David Bowie & Iggy Pop*

Act 1

Scene 1

M. Gallimard's prison cell. Paris. 1988.

> *Lights fade up to reveal Rene Gallimard, sixty-five, in a prison cell. He wears a comfortable bathrobe and looks old and tired. The sparsely furnished cell contains a wooden crate, upon which sits a hot plate with a kettle and a portable tape recorder. Gallimard sits on the crate staring at the recorder, a sad smile on his face.*
>
> *Upstage Song, who appears as a beautiful woman in traditional Chinese garb, dances a traditional piece from the Peking Opera, surrounded by the percussive clatter of Chinese music.*
>
> *Then, slowly, lights and sound cross-fade; the Chinese opera music dissolves into a Western opera, the "Love Duet" from Puccini's* Madame Butterfly. *Song continues dancing, now to the Western accompaniment. Though her movements are the same, the difference in music now gives them a balletic quality.*
>
> *Gallimard rises, and turns upstage towards the figure of Song, who dances without acknowledging him.*

Gallimard: Butterfly, Butterfly . . .

(He forces himself to turn away, as the image of Song fades out, and talks to us.)

Gallimard: The limits of my cell are as such: four-and-a-half meters by five. There's one window against the far wall; a door, very strong, to protect me from autograph hounds. I'm responsible for the tape recorder, the hot plate, and this charming coffee table.

When I want to eat, I'm marched off to the dining room—hot, steaming slop appears on my plate. When I want to sleep, the light bulb turns itself off—the work of fairies. It's an enchanted space I occupy. The French—we know how to run a prison.

But, to be honest, I'm not treated like an ordinary prisoner. Why? Because I'm a celebrity. You see, I make people laugh.

I never dreamed this day would arrive. I've never been considered witty or clever. In fact, as a young boy, in an informal poll among my grammar school classmates, I was voted "least likely to be invited to a party." It's a title I managed to hold on to for many years. Despite some stiff competition.

But now, how the tables turn! Look at me: the life of every social function in Paris. Paris? Why be modest: My fame has spread to Amsterdam, London, New York. Listen to them! In the world's smartest parlors. I'm the one who lifts their spirits!

(With a flourish, Gallimard directs our attention to another part of the stage.)

Scene 2
A party, 1988.
    Lights go up on a chic-looking parlor, where a well-dressed trio, two men and one woman, make conversation. Gallimard also remains lit; he observes them from his cell.

Woman: And what of Gallimard?

Man 1: Gallimard?

Man 2: Gallimard!

Gallimard *(To us.)*: You see? They're all determined to say my name, as if it were some new dance.

Woman: He still claims not to believe the truth.   5

Man 1: What? Still? Even since the trial?

Woman: Yes. Isn't it mad?

Man 2 *(Laughing.)*: He says . . . it was dark . . . and she was very modest!

(The trio break into laughter.)

Man 1: So—what? He never touched her with his hands?

Man 2: Perhaps he did, and simply misidentified the equipment. A compelling case   10 for sex education in the schools.

Woman: To protect the National Security—the Church can't argue with that.

Man 1: That's impossible! How could he not know?

Man 2: Simple ignorance.

Man 1: For twenty years?

Man 2: Time flies when you're being stupid.   15

Woman: Well, I thought the French were ladies' men.

Man 2: It seems Monsieur Gallimard was overly anxious to live up to his national reputation.

Woman: Well, he's not very good-looking.

Man 1: No, he's not.

Man 2: Certainly not.   20

Woman: Actually, I feel sorry for him.

Man 2: A toast! To Monsieur Gallimard!

Woman: Yes! To Gallimard!

Man 1: To Gallimard!

Man 2: *Vive la différence!*   25

(They toast, laughing. Lights down on them.)

Scene 3
M. Gallimard's cell.

Gallimard *(Smiling.)* You see? They toast me. I've become a patron saint of the socially inept. Can they really be so foolish? Men like that—they should be scratching at my door, begging to learn my secrets! For I, Rene Gallimard, you see, I have known, and been loved by . . . the Perfect Woman.

Alone in this cell, I sit night after night, watching our story play through my head, always searching for a new ending, one which redeems my honor, where she returns at last to my arms. And I imagine you—my ideal audience—who come to understand and even, perhaps just a little, to envy me.

(He turns on his tape recorder. Over the house speakers, we hear the opening phrases of Madame Butterfly.)

Gallimard: In order for you to understand what I did and why, I must introduce you to my favorite opera: *Madame Butterfly.* By Giacomo Puccini. First produced at La Scala, Milan, in 1904, it is now beloved throughout the Western world.

(As Gallimard describes the opera, the tape segues in and out to sections he may be describing.)

Gallimard: And why not? Its heroine, Cio-Cio-San, also known as Butterfly, is a feminine ideal, beautiful and brave. And its hero, the man for whom she gives up everything, is—*(He pulls out a naval officer's cap from under his crate, pops it on his head, and struts about.)*—not very good-looking, not too bright, and pretty much a wimp: Benjamin Franklin Pinkerton of the U.S. Navy. As the curtain rises, he's just closed on two great bargains: one on a house, the other on a woman—call it a package deal.

Pinkerton purchased the rights to Butterfly for one hundred yen—in modern currency, equivalent to about . . . sixty-six cents. So, he's feeling pretty pleased with himself as Sharpless, the American consul, arrives to witness the marriage.

(Marc, wearing an official cap to designate Sharpless, enters and plays the character.)

Sharpless/Marc: Pinkerton!

Pinkerton/Gallimard: Sharpless! How's it hangin'? It's a great day, just great. Between my house, my wife, and the rickshaw ride in from town, I've saved nineteen cents just this morning.

Sharpless: Wonderful. I can see the inscription on your tombstone already: "I saved a dollar, here I lie." *(He looks around.)* Nice house.

Pinkerton: It's artistic. Artistic, don't you think? Like the way the shoji screens slide open to reveal the wet bar and disco mirror ball? Classy, huh? Great for impressing the chicks.

Sharpless: "Chicks"? Pinkerton, you're going to be a married man!

Pinkerton: Well, sort of.

Sharpless: What do you mean?

Pinkerton: This country—Sharpless, it is okay. You got all these geisha girls running around—

Sharpless: I know! I live here!

Pinkerton: Then, you know the marriage laws, right? I split for one month, it's annulled!

Sharpless: Leave it to you to read the fine print. Who's the lucky girl?

Pinkerton: Cio-Cio-San. Her friends call her Butterfly. Sharpless, she eats out of my hand!

Sharpless: She's probably very hungry.

Pinkerton: Not like American girls. It's true what they say about Oriental girls. They want to be treated bad! 15

Sharpless: Oh, please!

Pinkerton: It's true!

Sharpless: Are you serious about this girl?

Pinkerton: I'm marrying her, aren't I?

Sharpless: Yes—with generous trade-in terms. 20

Pinkerton: When I leave, she'll know what it's like to have loved a real man. And I'll even buy her a few nylons.

Sharpless: You aren't planning to take her with you?

Pinkerton: Huh? Where?

Sharpless: Home!

Pinkerton: You mean, America? Are you crazy? Can you see her trying to buy rice in St. Louis? 25

Sharpless: So, you're not serious.

(Pause.)

Pinkerton/Gallimard *(As Pinkerton.)*: Consul, I am a sailor in port. *(As Gallimard.)* They then proceed to sing the famous duet, "The Whole World Over."

(The duet plays on the speakers. Gallimard, as Pinkerton, lip-syncs his lines from the opera.)

Gallimard: To give a rough translation: "The whole world over, the Yankee travels, casting his anchor wherever he wants. Life's not worth living unless he can win the hearts of the fairest maidens, then hotfoot it off the premises ASAP." *(He turns towards Marc.)* In the preceding scene, I played Pinkerton, the womanizing cad, and my friend Marc from school . . . *(Marc bows grandly for our benefit.)* played Sharpless, the sensitive soul of reason. In life, however, our positions were usually—no, always—reversed.

Scene 4
École Nationale.[1] *Aix-en-Provence. 1947.*

Gallimard: No, Marc, I think I'd rather stay home.

Marc: Are you crazy?! We are going to Dad's condo in Marseilles! You know what happened last time?

Gallimard: Of course I do.

Marc: Of course you don't! You never know. . . . They stripped, Rene!

Gallimard: Who stripped?

Marc: The girls! 5

Gallimard: Girls? Who said anything about girls?

Marc: Rene, we're a buncha university guys goin' up to the woods. What are we gonna do—talk philosophy?

Gallimard: What girls? Where do you get them?

---

[1]**École Nationale:** National School.

Marc: Who cares? The point is, they come. On trucks. Packed in like sardines. The back flips open, babes hop out, we're ready to roll. 10

Gallimard: You mean, they just—?

Marc: Before you know it, every last one of them—they're stripped and splashing around my pool. There's no moon out, they can't see what's going on, their boobs are flapping, right? You close your eyes, reach out—it's grab bag, get it? Doesn't matter whose ass is between whose legs, whose teeth are sinking into who. You're just in there, going at it, eyes closed, on and on for as long as you can stand. *(Pause.)* Some fun, huh?

Gallimard: What happens in the morning?

Marc: In the morning, you're ready to talk some philosophy. *(Beat.)* So how 'bout it?

Gallimard: Marc, I can't . . . I'm afraid they'll say no—the girls. So I never ask. 15

Marc: You don't have to ask! That's the beauty—don't you see? They don't have to say yes. It's perfect for a guy like you, really.

Gallimard: You go ahead . . . I may come later.

Marc: Hey, Rene—it doesn't matter that you're clumsy and got zits—they're not looking!

Gallimard: Thank you very much.

Marc: Wimp. 20

(Marc walks over to the other side of the stage, and starts waving and smiling at women in the audience.)

Gallimard *(To us.)*: We now return to my version of *Madame Butterfly* and the events leading to my recent conviction for treason.

(Gallimard notices Marc making lewd gestures.)

Gallimard: Marc, what are you doing?

Marc: Huh? *(Sotto voce.)* Rene, there're a lotta great babes out there. They're probably lookin' at me and thinking, "What a dangerous guy."

Gallimard: Yes—how could they help but be impressed by your cool sophistication?

(Gallimard pops the Sharpless cap on Marc's head, and points him offstage. Marc exits, leering.)

Scene 5
M. Gallimard's cell.

Gallimard: Next, Butterfly makes her entrance. We learn her age—fifteen . . . but very mature for her years.

(Lights come up on the area where we saw Song dancing at the top of the play. She appears there again, now dressed as Madame Butterfly, moving to the "Love Duet." Gallimard turns upstage slightly to watch, transfixed.)

Gallimard: But as she glides past him, beautiful, laughing softly behind her fan, don't we who are men sigh with hope? We, who are not handsome, nor brave, nor powerful, yet somehow believe, like Pinkerton, that we deserve a Butterfly. She arrives with all her possessions in the folds of her sleeves, lays them all out, for her man to do with as he pleases. Even her life itself—she bows her head as she whispers that she's not even worth the hundred yen he paid for her. He's already given too much, when we know he's really had to give nothing at all.

(Music and lights on Song out. Gallimard sits at his crate.)

Gallimard: In real life, women who put their total worth at less than sixty-six cents are quite hard to find. The closest we come is in the pages of these magazines. *(He reaches into his crate, pulls out a stack of girlie magazines, and begins flipping through them.)* Quite a necessity in prison. For three or four dollars, you get seven or eight women.

　　I first discovered these magazines at my uncle's house. One day, as a boy of twelve. The first time I saw them in his closet . . . all lined up—my body shook. Not with lust—no, with power. Here were women—a shelfful—who would do exactly as I wanted.

(The "Love Duet" creeps in over the speakers. Special comes up, revealing, not Song this time, but a pinup girl in a sexy negligee, her back to us. Gallimard turns upstage and looks at her.)

Girl: I know you're watching me.

Gallimard: My throat . . . it's dry.

Girl: I leave my blinds open every night before I go to bed.

Gallimard: I can't move.

Girl: I leave my blinds open and the lights on. 5

Gallimard: I'm shaking. My skin is hot, but my penis is soft. Why?

Girl: I stand in front of the window.

Gallimard: What is she going to do?

Girl: I toss my hair, and I let my lips part . . . barely. 10

Gallimard: I shouldn't be seeing this. It's so dirty. I'm so bad.

Girl: Then, slowly, I lift off my nightdress.

Gallimard: Oh, god. I can't believe it. I can't—

Girl: I toss it to the ground.

Gallimard: Now, she's going to walk away. She's going to— 15

Girl: I stand there, in the light, displaying myself.

Gallimard: No. She's—why is she naked?

Girl: To you.

Gallimard: In front of a window? This is wrong. No—

Girl: Without shame. 20

Gallimard: No, she must . . . like it.

Girl: I like it.

Gallimard: She . . . she wants me to see.

Girl: I want you to see.

Gallimard: I can't believe it! She's getting excited! 25

Girl: I can't see you. You can do whatever you want.

Gallimard: I can't do a thing. Why?

Girl: What would you like me to do . . . next?

(Lights go down on her. Music off. Silence, as Gallimard puts away his magazines. Then he resumes talking to us.)

Gallimard: Act Two begins with Butterfly staring at the ocean. Pinkerton's been called back to the U.S., and he's given his wife a detailed schedule of his plans. In the column marked "return date," he's written "when the robins nest." This failed to ignite her suspicions. Now, three years have passed without a peep from him. Which brings a response from her faithful servant, Suzuki.

(Comrade Chin enters, playing Suzuki.)

Suzuki: Girl, he's a loser. What'd he ever give you? Nineteen cents and those ugly   30
Day-Glo stockings? Look, it's finished! Kaput! Done! And you should be glad! I
mean, the guy was a woofer! He tried before, you know—before he met you, he
went down to geisha central and plunked down his spare change in front of the
usual candidates—everyone else gagged! These are hungry prostitutes, and they
were not interested, get the picture? Now, stop slathering when an American
ship sails in, and let's make some bucks—I mean, yen! We are broke!

    Now, what about Yamadori? Hey, hey—don't look away—the man is a
prince—figuratively, and, what's even better, literally. He's rich, he's handsome,
he says he'll die if you don't marry him—and he's even willing to overlook the
little fact that you've been deflowered all over the place by a foreign devil. What
do you mean, "But he's Japanese"? What do you think you are? You think
you've been touched by the whitey god? He was a sailor with dirty hands!

(Suzuki stalks offstage.)

Gallimard: She's also visited by Consul Sharpless, sent by Pinkerton on a minor
errand.

(Marc enters, as Sharpless.)

Sharpless: I hate this job.

Gallimard: This Pinkerton—he doesn't show up personally to tell his wife he's
abandoning her. No, he sends a government diplomat . . . at taxpayers' expense.

Sharpless: Butterfly? Butterfly? I have some bad—I'm going to be ill. Butterfly, I
came to tell you—

Gallimard: Butterfly says she knows he'll return and if he doesn't she'll kill herself   35
rather than go back to her own people. *(Beat.)* This causes a lull in the
conversation.

Sharpless: Let's put it this way . . .

Gallimard: Butterfly runs into the next room, and returns holding—

(Sound cue: a baby crying. Sharpless, "seeing" this, backs away.)

Sharpless: Well, good. Happy to see things going so well. I suppose I'll be going
now. Ta ta. Ciao. *(He turns away. Sound cue out.)* I hate this job. *(He exits.)*

Gallimard: At that moment, Butterfly spots in the harbor an American ship—the
Abramo Lincoln!

*(Music cue: "The Flower Duet." Song, still dressed as Butterfly, changes into a
wedding kimono, moving to the music.)*

Gallimard: This is the moment that redeems her years of waiting. With Suzuki's
help, they cover the room with flowers—

(Chin, as Suzuki, trudges onstage and drops a lone flower without much enthusiasm.)

Gallimard: —and she changes into her wedding dress to prepare for Pinkerton's
arrival.

*(Suzuki helps Butterfly change. Helga enters, and helps Gallimard change into a
tuxedo.)*

Gallimard: I married a woman older than myself—Helga.

Helga: My father was ambassador to Australia. I grew up among criminals and   40
kangaroos.

Gallimard: Hearing that brought me to the altar—

(Helga exits.)

Gallimard: —where I took a vow renouncing love. No fantasy woman would ever want me, so, yes, I would settle for a quick leap up the career ladder. Passion, I banish, and in its place—practicality!

But my vows had long since lost their charm by the time we arrived in China. The sad truth is that all men want a beautiful woman, and the uglier the man, the greater the want.

(Suzuki makes final adjustments of Butterfly's costume, as does Gallimard of his tuxedo.)

Gallimard: I married late, at age thirty-one. I was faithful to my marriage for eight years. Until the day when, as a junior-level diplomat in puritanical Peking, in a parlor at the German ambassador's house, during the "Reign of a Hundred Flowers,"[2] I first saw her . . . singing the death scene from *Madame Butterfly*.

(Suzuki runs offstage.)

Scene 6

German ambassador's house. Beijing, 1960.

The upstage special area now becomes a stage. Several chairs face upstage, representing seating for some twenty guests in the parlor. A few "diplomats"—Renee, Marc, Toulon—in formal dress enter and take seats.

Gallimard also sits down, but turns towards us and continues to talk. Orchestral accompaniment on the tape is now replaced by a simple piano. Song picks up the death scene from the point where Butterfly uncovers the hara-kiri knife.

Gallimard: The ending is pitiful. Pinkerton, in an act of great courage, stays home and sends his American wife to pick up Butterfly's child. The truth, long deferred, has come up to her door.

(Song, playing Butterfly, sings the lines from the opera in her own voice—which, though not classical, should be decent.)

Song: "Con onor muore / chi non puo serbar / vita con onore."
Gallimard *(Simultaneously.)*: "Death with honor / Is better than life / Life with dishonor."

(The stage is illuminated; we are now completely within an elegant diplomat's residence. Song proceeds to play out an abbreviated death scene. Everyone in the room applauds. Song, shyly, takes her bows. Others in the room rush to congratulate her. Gallimard remains with us.)

Gallimard: They say in opera the voice is everything. That's probably why I'd never before enjoyed opera. Here . . . here was a Butterfly with little or no voice—but she had the grace, the delicacy . . . I believed this girl. I believed her suffering. I wanted to take her in my arms—so delicate, even I could protect her, take her home, pamper her until she smiled.

(Over the course of the preceding speech, Song has broken from the upstage crowd and moved directly upstage of Gallimard.)

---

[2]**Reign of a Hundred Flowers:** A time in 1957 when there was freedom of expression in China.

Song: Excuse me. Monsieur . . . ?

(*Gallimard turns upstage, shocked.*)

Gallimard: Oh! Gallimard. Mademoiselle . . . ? A beautiful. . . .

Song: Song Liling.

Gallimard: A beautiful performance.

Song: Oh, please.

Gallimard: I usually—

Song: You make me blush. I'm no opera singer at all.

Gallimard: I usually don't like *Butterfly*.

Song: I can't blame you in the least.

Gallimard: I mean, the story—

Song: Ridiculous.

Gallimard: I like the story, but . . . what?

Song: Oh, you like it?

Gallimard: I . . . what I mean is, I've always seen it played by huge women in so much bad makeup.

Song: Bad makeup is not unique to the West.

Gallimard: But, who can believe them?

Song: And you believe me?

Gallimard: Absolutely. You were utterly convincing. It's the first time—

Song: Convincing? As a Japanese woman? The Japanese used hundreds of our people for medical experiments during the war, you know. But I gather such an irony is lost on you.

Gallimard: No! I was about to say, it's the first time I've seen the beauty of the story.

Song: Really?

Gallimard: Of her death. It's a . . . a pure sacrifice. He's unworthy, but what can she do? She loves him . . . so much. It's a very beautiful story.

Song: Well, yes, to a Westerner.

Gallimard: Excuse me?

Song: It's one of your favorite fantasies, isn't it? The submissive Oriental woman and the cruel white man.

Gallimard: Well, I didn't quite mean . . .

Song: Consider it this way: what would you say if a blonde homecoming queen fell in love with a short Japanese businessman? He treats her cruelly, then goes home for three years, during which time she prays to his picture and turns down marriage from a young Kennedy. Then, when she learns he has remarried, she kills herself. Now, I believe you would consider this girl to be a deranged idiot, correct? But because it's an Oriental who kills herself for a Westerner—ah!— you find it beautiful.

(*Silence.*)

Gallimard: Yes . . . well . . . I see your point . . .

Song: I will never do Butterfly again, Monsieur Gallimard. If you wish to see some real theater, come to the Peking Opera sometime. Expand your mind.

(*Song walks offstage. Other guests exit with her.*)

Gallimard (*To us.*): So much for protecting her in my big Western arms.

Scene 7
M. Gallimard's apartment. Beijing. 1960.
Gallimard changes from his tux into a casual suit. Helga enters.

Gallimard: The Chinese are an incredibly arrogant people.

Helga: They warned us about that in Paris, remember?

Gallimard: Even Parisians consider them arrogant. That's a switch.

Helga: What is it that Madame Su says? "We are a very old civilization." I never
know if she's talking about her country or herself.

Gallimard: I walk around here, all I hear every day, everywhere is how *old* this   5
culture is. The fact that "old" may be synonymous with "senile" doesn't occur to
them.

Helga: You're not going to change them. "East is east, west is west, and . . ." whatever
that guy said.

Gallimard: It's just that—silly. I met . . . at Ambassador Koening's tonight—you
should've been there.

Helga: Koening? Oh god, no. Did he enchant you all again with the history of
Bavaria?

Gallimard: No. I met, I suppose, the Chinese equivalent of a diva. She's a singer in
the Chinese opera.

Helga: They have an opera, too? Do they sing in Chinese? Or maybe—in Italian?   10

Gallimard: Tonight, she did sing in Italian.

Helga: How'd she manage that?

Gallimard: She must've been educated in the West before the Revolution. Her
French is very good also. Anyway, she sang the death scene from *Madame
Butterfly.*

Helga: *Madame Butterfly!* Then I should have come. *(She begins humming, floating
around the room as if dragging long kimono sleeves.)* Did she have a nice costume?
I think it's a classic piece of music.

Gallimard: That's what *I* thought, too. Don't let her hear you say that.   15

Helga: What's wrong?

Gallimard: Evidently the Chinese hate it.

Helga: She hated it, but she performed it anyway? Is she perverse?

Gallimard: They hate it because the white man gets the girl. Sour grapes if you ask me.

Helga: Politics again? Why can't they just hear it as a piece of beautiful music? So,   20
what's in their opera?

Gallimard: I don't know. But, whatever it is, I'm sure it must be *old.*

(Helga exits.)

Scene 8
Chinese opera house and the streets of Beijing. 1960.
The sound of gongs clanging fills the stage.

Gallimard: My wife's innocent question kept ringing in my ears. I asked around,
but no one knew anything about the Chinese opera. It took four weeks, but
my curiosity overcame my cowardice. This Chinese diva—this unwilling
Butterfly—what did she do to make her so proud?

    The room was hot, and full of smoke. Wrinkled faces, old women, teeth
missing—a man with a growth on his neck, like a human toad. All smiling,

pipes falling from their mouths, cracking nuts between their teeth, a live chicken pecking at my foot—all looking, screaming, gawking . . . at her.

(The upstage area is suddenly hit with a harsh white light. It has become the stage for the Chinese opera performance. Two dancers enter, along with Song. Gallimard stands apart, watching. Song glides gracefully amidst the two dancers. Drums suddenly slam to a halt. Song strikes a pose, looking straight at Gallimard. Dancers exit. Light change. Pause, then Song walks right off the stage and straight up to Gallimard.)

Song: Yes. You. White man. I'm looking straight at you.

Gallimard: Me?

Song: You see any other white men? It was too easy to spot you. How often does a man in my audience come in a tie?

(Song starts to remove her costume. Underneath, she wears simple baggy clothes. They are now backstage. The show is over.)

Song: So, you are an adventurous imperialist?

Gallimard: I . . . thought it would further my education.

Song: It took you four weeks. Why?

Gallimard: I've been busy.

Song: Well, education has always been undervalued in the West, hasn't it?

Gallimard *(Laughing.)*: I don't think that's true.

Song: No, you wouldn't. You're a Westerner. How can you objectively judge your own values?

Gallimard: I think it's possible to achieve some distance.

Song: Do you? *(Pause.)* It stinks in here. Let's go.

Gallimard: These are the smells of your loyal fans.

Song: I love them for being my fans, I hate the smell they leave behind. I too can distance myself from my people. *(She looks around, then whispers in his ear.)* "Art for the masses" is a shitty excuse to keep artists poor. *(She pops a cigarette in her mouth.)* Be a gentleman, will you? And light my cigarette.

(Gallimard fumbles for a match.)

Gallimard: I don't . . . smoke.

Song *(Lighting her own.)*: Your loss. Had you lit my cigarette, I might have blown a puff of smoke right between your eyes. Come.

(They start to walk about the stage. It is a summer night on the Beijing streets. Sounds of the city play on the house speakers.)

Song: How I wish there were even a tiny café to sit in. With cappuccinos, and men in tuxedos and bad expatriate jazz.

Gallimard: If my history serves me correctly, you weren't even allowed into the clubs in Shanghai before the Revolution.

Song: Your history serves you poorly, Monsieur Gallimard. True, there were signs reading "No dogs and Chinamen." But a woman, especially a delicate Oriental woman—we always go where we please. Could you imagine it otherwise? Clubs in China filled with pasty, big-thighed white women, while thousands of slender lotus blossoms wait just outside the door? Never. The clubs would be empty. *(Beat.)* We have always held a certain fascination for you Caucasian men, have we not?

Gallimard: But . . . that fascination is imperialist, or so you tell me. 20

Song: Do you believe everything I tell you? Yes. It is always imperialist. But sometimes . . . sometimes, it is also mutual. Oh—this is my flat.

Gallimard: I didn't even—

Song: Thank you. Come another time and we will further expand your mind.

(Song exits. Gallimard continues roaming the streets as he speaks to us.)

Gallimard: What was that? What did she mean, "Sometimes . . . it is mutual"? Women do not flirt with me. And I normally can't talk to them. But tonight, I held up my end of the conversation.

Scene 9
Gallimard's bedroom. Beijing. 1960.
Helga enters.

Helga: You didn't tell me you'd be home late.

Gallimard: I didn't intend to. Something came up.

Helga: Oh? Like what?

Gallimard: I went to the . . . to the Dutch ambassador's home.

Helga: Again? 5

Gallimard: There was a reception for a visiting scholar. He's writing a six-volume treatise on the Chinese revolution. We all gathered that meant he'd have to live here long enough to actually write six volumes, and we all expressed our deepest sympathies.

Helga: Well, I had a good night too. I went with the ladies to a martial arts demonstration. Some of those men—when they break those thick boards—*(She mimes fanning herself.)* whoo-whoo!

(Helga exits. Lights dim.)

Gallimard: I lied to my wife. Why? I've never had any reason to lie before. But what reason did I have tonight? I didn't do anything wrong. That night, I had a dream. Other people, I've been told, have dreams when angels appear. Or dragons, or Sophia Loren in a towel. In my dream, Marc from school appeared.

(Marc enters, in a nightshirt and cap.)

Marc: Rene! You met a girl!

(Gallimard and Marc stumble down the Beijing streets. Night sounds over the speakers.)

Gallimard: It's not that amazing, thank you. 10

Marc: No! It's so monumental, I heard about it halfway around the world in my sleep!

Gallimard: I've met girls before, you know.

Marc: Name one. I've come across time and space to congratulate you. *(He hands (Gallimard a bottle of wine.)*

Gallimard: Marc, this is expensive.

Marc: On those rare occasions when you become a formless spirit, why not steal the best? 15

(Marc pops open the bottle, begins to share it with Gallimard.)

Gallimard: You embarrass me. She . . . there's no reason to think she likes me.

Marc: "Sometimes, it is mutual"?

Gallimard: Oh.

Marc: "Mutual"? "Mutual"? What does that mean?

Gallimard: You heard?   20

Marc: It means the money is in the bank, you only have to write the check!

Gallimard: I am a married man!

Marc: And an excellent one too. I cheated after . . . six months. Then again and again, until now—three hundred girls in twelve years.

Gallimard: I don't think we should hold that up as a model.

Marc: Of course not! My life—it is disgusting! Phooey! Phooey! But, you—you are   25 the model husband.

Gallimard: Anyway, it's impossible. I'm a foreigner.

Marc: Ah, yes. She cannot love you, it is taboo, but something deep inside her heart . . . she cannot help herself . . . she must surrender to you. It is her destiny.

Gallimard: How do you imagine all this?

Marc: The same way you do. It's an old story. It's in our blood. They fear us, Rene. Their women fear us. And their men—their men hate us. And, you know something? They are all correct.

(They spot a light in a window.)

Marc: There! There, Rene!   30

Gallimard: It's her window.

Marc: Late at night—it burns. The light—it burns for you.

Gallimard: I won't look. It's not respectful.

Marc: We don't have to be respectful. We're foreign devils.

(Enter Song, in a sheer robe, her face completely swathed in black cloth. The "One Fine Day" aria creeps in over the speakers. With her back to us, Song mimes attending to her toilette. Her robe comes loose, revealing her white shoulders.)

Marc: All your life you've waited for a beautiful girl who would lay down for you. All   35 your life you've smiled like a saint when it's happened to every other man you know. And you see them in magazines and you see them in movies. And you wonder, what's wrong with me? Will anyone beautiful ever want me? As the years pass, your hair thins and you struggle to hold on to even your hopes. Stop struggling, Rene. The wait is over. *(He exits.)*

Gallimard: Marc? Marc?

(At that moment, Song, her back still towards us, drops her robe. A second of her naked back, then a sound cue: a phone ringing, very loud. Blackout, followed in the next beat by a special up on the bedroom area, where a phone now sits. Gallimard stumbles across the stage and picks up the phone. Sound cue out. Over the course of his conversation, area lights fill in the vicinity of his bed. It is the following morning.)

Gallimard: Yes? Hello?

Song *(Offstage.)*: Is it very early?

Gallimard: Why, yes.

Song *(Offstage.)*: How early?

Gallimard: It's . . . it's 5:30. Why are you—?   40

Song *(Offstage.)*: But it's light outside. Already.

Gallimard: It is. The sun must be in confusion today.

(Over the course of Song's next speech, her upstage special comes up again. She sits in a chair, legs crossed, in a robe, telephone to her ear.)

Song: I waited until I saw the sun. That was as much discipline as I could manage for one night. Do you forgive me?

Gallimard: Of course . . . for what?   45

Song: Then I'll ask you quickly. Are you really interested in the opera?

Gallimard: Why, yes. Yes I am.

Song: Then come again next Thursday. I am playing *The Drunken Beauty*. May I count on you?

Gallimard: Yes. You may.

Song: Perfect. Well, I must be getting to bed. I'm exhausted. It's been a very long   50
night for me.

(Song hangs up; special on her goes off. Gallimard begins to dress for work.)

Scene 10
Song Liling's apartment. Beijing. 1960.

Gallimard: I returned to the opera that next week, and the week after that . . . she keeps our meetings so short—perhaps fifteen, twenty minutes at most. So I am left each week with a thirst which is intensified. In this way, fifteen weeks have gone by. I am starting to doubt the words of my friend Marc. But no, not really. In my heart, I know she has . . . an interest in me. I suspect this is her way. She is outwardly bold and outspoken, yet her heart is shy and afraid. It is the Oriental in her at war with her Western education.

Song *(Offstage.):* I will be out in an instant. Ask the servant for anything you want.

Gallimard: Tonight, I have finally been invited to enter her apartment. Though the idea is almost beyond belief, I believe she is afraid of me.

(Gallimard looks around the room. He picks up a picture in a frame, studies it. Without his noticing, Song enters, dressed elegantly in a black gown from the twenties. She stands in the doorway looking like Anna May Wong.[3])   5

Song: That is my father.

Gallimard *(Surprised.):* Mademoiselle Song . . .

(She glides up to him, snatches away the picture.)

Song: It is very good that he did not live to see the Revolution. They would, no doubt, have made him kneel on broken glass. Not that he didn't deserve such a punishment. But he is my father. I would've hated to see it happen.

Gallimard: I'm very honored that you've allowed me to visit your home.

(Song curtseys.)

Song: Thank you. Oh! Haven't you been poured any tea?   10

Gallimard: I'm really not—

Song *(To her offstage servant.):* Shu-Fang! Cha! Kwai-lah! *(To Gallimard.)* I'm sorry. You want everything to be perfect—

Gallimard: Please.

---

[3]**Anna May Wong** (1905–1961): First actress of Chinese descent to become famous in Hollywood.

Song: —and before the evening even begins—
Gallimard: I'm really not thirsty.
Song: —it's ruined.
Gallimard *(Sharply.)*: Mademoiselle Song!

> *(Song sits down.)*

Song: I'm sorry.
Gallimard: What are you apologizing for now?

> *(Pause; Song starts to giggle.)*

Song: I don't know!

> *(Gallimard laughs.)*

Gallimard: Exactly my point.
Song: Oh, I am silly. Light-headed. I promise not to apologize for anything else tonight, do you hear me?
Gallimard: That's a good girl.

> *(Shu-Fang, a servant girl, comes out with a tea tray and starts to pour.)*

Song *(To Shu-Fang.)*: No! I'll pour myself for the gentleman!

> *(Shu-Fang, staring at Gallimard, exits.)*

Gallimard: You have a beautiful home.
Song: No, I . . . I don't even know why I invited you up.
Gallimard: Well, I'm glad you did.

> *(Song looks around the room.)*

Song: There is an element of danger to your presence.
Gallimard: Oh?
Song: You must know.
Gallimard: It doesn't concern me. We both know why I'm here.
Song: It doesn't concern me either. No . . . well perhaps . . .
Gallimard: What?
Song: Perhaps I am slightly afraid of scandal.
Gallimard: What are we doing?
Song: I'm entertaining you. In my parlor.
Gallimard: In France, that would hardly—
Song: France. France is a country living in the modern era. Perhaps even ahead of it. China is a nation whose soul is firmly rooted two thousand years in the past. What I do, even pouring the tea for you now . . . it has . . . implications. The walls and windows say so. Even my own heart, strapped inside this Western dress . . . even it says things—things I don't care to hear.

> *(Song hands Gallimard a cup of tea. Gallimard puts his hand over both the teacup and Song's hand.)*

Gallimard: This is a beautiful dress.
Song: Don't.
Gallimard: What?
Song: I don't even know if it looks right on me.
Gallimard: Believe me—
Song: You are from France. You see so many beautiful women.

Gallimard: France? Since when are the European women—?
Song: Oh! What am I trying to do, anyway?!

(Song runs to the door, composes herself, then turns towards Gallimard.)

Song: Monsieur Gallimard, perhaps you should go.
Gallimard: But . . . why?
Song: There's something wrong about this.
Gallimard: I don't see what.
Song: I feel . . . I am not myself.
Gallimard: No. You're nervous.
Song: Please. Hard as I try to be modern, to speak like a man, to hold a Western woman's strong face up to my own . . . in the end, I fail. A small, frightened heart beats too quickly and gives me away. Monsieur Gallimard, I'm a Chinese girl. I've never . . . never invited a man up to my flat before. The forwardness of my actions makes my skin burn.
Gallimard: What are you afraid of? Certainly not me, I hope.
Song: I'm a modest girl.
Gallimard: I know. And very beautiful. *(He touches her hair.)*
Song: Please—go now. The next time you see me, I shall again be myself.
Gallimard: I like you the way you are right now.
Song: You are a cad.
Gallimard: What do you expect? I'm a foreign devil.

(Gallimard walks downstage. Song exits.)

Gallimard *(to us)*: Did you hear the way she talked about Western women? Much differently than the first night. She does—she feels inferior to them—and to me.

Scene 11
The French embassy. Beijing. 1960.
Gallimard moves towards a desk.

Gallimard: I determined to try an experiment. In *Madame Butterfly*, Cio-Cio-San fears that the Western man who catches a butterfly will pierce its heart with a needle, then leave it to perish. I began to wonder: had I, too, caught a butterfly who would writhe on a needle?

(Marc enters, dressed as a bureaucrat, holding a stack of papers. As Gallimard speaks, Marc hands papers to him. He peruses, then signs, stamps, or rejects them.)

Gallimard: Over the next five weeks, I worked like a dynamo. I stopped going to the opera, I didn't phone or write her. I knew this little flower was waiting for me to call, and, as I wickedly refused to do so, I felt for the first time that rush of power—the absolute power of a man.

(Mark continues acting as the bureaucrat, but he now speaks as himself.)

Mark: Rene! It's me.
Gallimard: Marc—I hear your voice everywhere now. Even in the midst of work.
Marc: That's because I'm watching you—all the time.
Gallimard: You were always the most popular guy in school.
Marc: Well, there's no guarantee of failure in life like happiness in high school. Somehow I knew I'd end up in the suburbs working for Renault and you'd

be in the Orient picking exotic women off the trees. And they say there's no justice.

Gallimard: That's why you were my friend?

Marc: I gave you a little of my life, so that now you can give me some of yours. *(Pause.)* Remember Isabelle?

Gallimard: Of course I remember! She was my first experience.

Marc: We all wanted to ball her. But she only wanted me.

Gallimard: I had her.

Marc: Right. You balled her.

Gallimard: You were the only one who ever believed me.

Marc: Well, there's a good reason for that. *(Beat.)* C'mon. You must've guessed.

Gallimard: You told me to wait in the bushes by the cafeteria that night. The next thing I knew, she was on me. Dress up in the air.

Marc: She never wore underwear.

Gallimard: My arms were pinned to the dirt.

Marc: She loved the superior position. A girl ahead of her time.

Gallimard: I looked up, and there was this woman . . . bouncing up and down on my loins.

Marc: Screaming, right?

Gallimard: Screaming, and breaking off the branches all around me, and pounding my butt up and down into the dirt.

Marc: Huffing and puffing like a locomotive.

Gallimard: And in the middle of all this, the leaves were getting into my mouth, my legs were losing circulation, I thought, "God. So this is *it?*"

Marc: You thought that?

Gallimard: Well, I was worried about my legs falling off.

Marc: You didn't have a good time?

Gallimard: No, that's not what I—I had a great time!

Marc: You're sure?

Gallimard: Yeah. Really.

Marc: 'Cuz I wanted you to have a good time.

Gallimard: I did.

(Pause.)

Marc: Shit. *(Pause.)* When all is said and done, she was kind of a lousy lay, wasn't she? I mean, there was a lot of energy there, but you never knew what she was doing with it. Like when she yelled "I'm coming!"—hell, it was so loud, you wanted to go, "Look, it's not that big a deal."

Gallimard: I got scared. I thought she meant someone was actually coming. *(Pause.)* But, Marc?

Marc: What?

Gallimard: Thanks.

Marc: Oh, don't mention it.

Gallimard: It was my first experience.

Marc: Yeah. You got her.

Gallimard: I got her.

Marc: Wait! Look at that letter again!

(Gallimard picks up one of the papers he's been stamping, and rereads it.)

Gallimard *(To us.)*: After six weeks, they began to arrive. The letters.

(Upstage special on Song, as Madame Butterfly. The scene is underscored by the "Love Duet.")

Song: Did we fight? I do not know. Is the opera no longer of interest to you? Please come—my audiences miss the white devil in their midst.

(Gallimard looks up from the letter, towards us.)

Gallimard *(To us.)*: A concession, but much too dignified. *(Beat; he discards the letter.)* I skipped the opera again that week to complete a position paper on trade.

(The bureaucrat hands him another letter.)

Song: Six weeks have passed since last we met. Is this your practice—to leave friends in the lurch? Sometimes I hate you, sometimes I hate myself, but always I miss you.

Gallimard *(To us.)*: Better, but I don't like the way she calls me "friend." When a   45
woman calls a man her "friend," she's calling him a eunuch or a homosexual. *(Beat; he discards the letter.)* I was absent from the opera for the seventh week, feeling a sudden urge to clean out my files.

(Bureaucrat hands him another letter.)

Song: Your rudeness is beyond belief. I don't deserve this cruelty. Don't bother to call. I'll have you turned away at the door.

Gallimard *(To us.)*: I didn't. *(He discards the letter; bureaucrat hands him another.)* And then finally, the letter that concluded my experiment.

Song: I am out of words. I can hide behind dignity no longer. What do you want? I have already given you my shame.

(Gallimard gives the letter back to Marc, slowly. Special on Song fades out.)

Gallimard *(To us.)*: Reading it, I became suddenly ashamed. Yes, my experiment had been a success. She was turning on my needle. But the victory seemed hollow.

Marc: Hollow?! Are you crazy?   50

Gallimard: Nothing, Marc. Please go away.

Marc *(Exiting, with papers.)*: Haven't I taught you anything?

Gallimard: "I have already given you my shame." I had to attend a reception that evening. On the way, I felt sick. If there is a God, surely he would punish me now. I had finally gained power over a beautiful woman, only to abuse it cruelly. There must be justice in the world. I had the strange feeling that the ax would fall this very evening.

Scene 12

Ambassador Toulon's residence. Beijing. 1960.

Sound cue: party noises. Light change. We are now in a spacious residence. Toulon, the French ambassador, enters and taps Gallimard on the shoulder.

Toulon: Gallimard? Can I have a word? Over here.

Gallimard *(To us.)*: Manuel Toulon. French ambassador to China. He likes to think of us all as his children. Rather like God.

Toulon: Look, Gallimard, there's not much to say. I've liked you. From the day you walked in. You were no leader, but you were tidy and efficient.

Gallimard: Thank you, sir.

Toulon: Don't jump the gun. Okay, our needs in China are changing. It's embarrassing 5
that we lost Indochina. Someone just wasn't on the ball there. I don't mean you
personally, of course.

Gallimard: Thank you, sir.

Toulon: We're going to be doing a lot more information-gathering in the future. The
nature of our work here is changing. Some people are just going to have to go.
It's nothing personal.

Gallimard: Oh.

Toulon: Want to know a secret? Vice-Consul LeBon is being transferred.

Gallimard *(To us.)*: My immediate superior! 10

Toulon: And most of his department.

Gallimard *(To us.)*: Just as I feared! God has seen my evil heart—

Toulon: But not you.

Gallimard *(To us.)*: —and he's taking her away just as . . . *(To Toulon.)* Excuse me, sir?

Toulon: Scare you? I think I did. Cheer up, Gallimard. I want you to replace LeBon 15
as vice-consul.

Gallimard: You—? Yes, well, thank you, sir.

Toulon: Anytime.

Gallimard: I . . . accept with great humility.

Toulon: Humility won't be part of the job. You're going to coordinate the revamped
intelligence division. Want to know a secret? A year ago, you would've been out.
But the past few months, I don't know how it happened, you've become this
new aggressive confident . . . thing. And they also tell me you get along with
the Chinese. So I think you're a lucky man, Gallimard. Congratulations.

*(They shake hands. Toulon exits. Party noises out. Gallimard stumbles across a
darkened stage.)*

Gallimard: Vice-consul? Impossible! As I stumbled out of the party, I saw it written 20
across the sky: There is no God. Or, no—say that there is a God. But that
God . . . understands. Of course! God who creates Eve to serve Adam, who
blesses Solomon with his harem but ties Jezebel to a burning bed—that God
is a man. And he understands! At age thirty-nine, I was suddenly initiated into
the way of the world.

Scene 13
Song Liling's apartment. Beijing. 1960.
Song enters, in a sheer dressing gown.

Song: Are you crazy?

Gallimard: Mademoiselle Song—

Song: To come here—at this hour? After . . . after eight weeks?

Gallimard: It's the most amazing—

Song: You bang on my door? Scare my servants, scandalize the neighbors? 5

Gallimard: I've been promoted. To vice-consul.

(Pause.)

Song: And what is that supposed to mean to me?

Gallimard: Are you my Butterfly?

Song: What are you saying?

Gallimard: I've come tonight for an answer: are you my Butterfly?   10
Song: Don't you know already?
Gallimard: I want you to say it.
Song: I don't want to say it.
Gallimard: So, that is your answer?
Song: You know how I feel about—   15
Gallimard: I do remember one thing.
Song: What?
Gallimard: In the letter I received today.
Song: Don't.
Gallimard: "I have already given you my shame."   20
Song: It's enough that I even wrote it.
Gallimard: Well, then—
Song: I shouldn't have it splashed across my face.
Gallimard:—if that's all true—
Song: Stop!   25
Gallimard: Then what is one more short answer?
Song: I don't want to!
Gallimard: Are you my Butterfly? *(Silence; he crosses the room and begins to touch her hair.)* I want from you honesty. There should be nothing false between us. No false pride.

> *(Pause.)*

Song: Yes, I am. I am your Butterfly.
Gallimard: Then let me be honest with you. It is because of you that I was promoted   30
tonight. You have changed my life forever. My little Butterfly, there should be
no more secrets: I love you.

> *(He starts to kiss her roughly. She resists slightly.)*

Song: No . . . no . . . gently . . . please, I've never . . .
Gallimard: No?
Song: I've tried to appear experienced, but . . . the truth is . . . no.
Gallimard: Are you cold?
Song: Yes. Cold.   35
Gallimard: Then we will go very, very slowly.

> *(He starts to caress her; her gown begins to open.)*

Song: No . . . let me . . . keep my clothes . . .
Gallimard: But . . .
Song: Please . . . it all frightens me. I'm a modest Chinese girl.
Gallimard: My poor little treasure.   40
Song: I am your treasure. Though inexperienced, I am not . . . ignorant. They teach
us things, our mothers, about pleasing a man.
Gallimard: Yes?
Song: I'll do my best to make you happy. Turn off the lights.

> *(Gallimard gets up and heads for a lamp. Song, propped up on one elbow, tosses her hair back and smiles.)*

Song: Monsieur Gallimard?
Gallimard: Yes, Butterfly?   45

Song: *"Vieni, vieni!"*
Gallimard: "Come, darling."
Song: *"Ah! Dolce notte!"*
Gallimard: "Beautiful night."
Song: *"Tutto estatico d'amor ride il ciel!"* 50
Gallimard: "All ecstatic with love, the heavens are filled with laughter."

(He turns off the lamp. Blackout.)

Act 2
Scene 1
M. Gallimard's cell. Paris. 1988.
Lights up on Gallimard. He sits in his cell, reading from a leaflet.

Gallimard: This, from a contemporary critic's commentary on *Madame Butterfly*: "Pinkerton suffers from . . . being an obnoxious bounder whom every man in the audience itches to kick." Bully for us men in the audience! Then, in the same note: "Butterfly is the most irresistibly appealing of Puccini's 'Little Women.' Watching the succession of her humiliations is like watching a child under torture." *(He tosses the pamphlet over his shoulder.)* I suggest that, while we men may all want to kick Pinkerton, very few of us would pass up the opportunity to *be* Pinkerton.

(Gallimard moves out of his cell.)

Scene 2
Gallimard and Butterfly's flat. Beijing. 1960.
We are in a simple but well-decorated parlor. Gallimard moves to sit on a sofa, while Song, dressed in a cheongsam,[1] enters and curls up at his feet.

Gallimard *(To us.)*: We secured a flat on the outskirts of Peking. Butterfly, as I was calling her now, decorated our "home" with Western furniture and Chinese antiques. And there, on a few stolen afternoons or evenings each week, Butterfly commenced her education.
Song: The Chinese men—they keep us down.
Gallimard: Even in the "New Society"?
Song: In the "New Society," we are all kept ignorant equally. That's one of the exciting things about loving a Western man. I know you are not threatened by a woman's education.
Gallimard: I'm no saint, Butterfly. 5
Song: But you come from a progressive society.
Gallimard: We're not always reminding each other how "old" we are, if that's what you mean.
Song: Exactly. We Chinese—once, I suppose, it is true, we ruled the world. But so what? How much more exciting to be part of the society ruling the world today. Tell me—what's happening in Vietnam?
Gallimard: Oh, Butterfly—you want me to bring my work home?

---

[1]**cheongsam:** A dress with a slit skirt and mandarin collar.

Song: I want to know what you know. To be impressed by my man. It's not the particulars so much as the fact that you're making decisions which change the shape of the world.   10

Gallimard: Not the world. At best, a small corner.

(Toulon enters, and sits at a desk upstage.)

Scene 3
French embassy. Beijing. 1961.
Gallimard moves downstage, to Toulon's desk. Song remains upstage, watching.

Toulon: And a more troublesome corner is hard to imagine.

Gallimard: So, the Americans plan to begin bombing?

Toulon: This is very secret, Gallimard: yes. The Americans don't have an embassy here. They're asking us to be their eyes and ears. Say Jack Kennedy signed an order to bomb North Vietnam, Laos. How would the Chinese react?

Gallimard: I think the Chinese will squawk—

Toulon: Uh-huh   5

Gallimard: —but, in their hearts, they don't even like Ho Chi Minh.[2]

(Pause.)

Toulon: What a bunch of jerks. Vietnam was our colony. Not only didn't the Americans help us fight to keep them, but now, seven years later, they've come back to grab the territory for themselves. It's very irritating,

Gallimard: With all due respect, sir, why should the Americans have won our war for us back in fifty-four if we didn't have the will to win it ourselves?

Toulon: You're kidding, aren't you?

(Pause.)

Gallimard: The Orientals simply want to be associated with whoever shows the most strength and power. You live with the Chinese, sir. Do you think they like Communism?   10

Toulon: I live in China. Not with the Chinese.

Gallimard: Well, I—

Toulon: *You* live with the Chinese.

Gallimard: Excuse me?

Toulon: I can't keep a secret.   15

Gallimard: What are you saying?

Toulon: Only that I'm not immune to gossip. So, you're keeping a native mistress? Don't answer. It's none of my business. *(Pause.)* I'm sure she must be gorgeous.

Gallimard: Well . . .

Toulon: I'm impressed. You had the stamina to go out into the streets and hunt one down. Some of us have to be content with the wives of the expatriate community.

Gallimard: I do feel . . . fortunate.   20

Toulon: So, Gallimard, you've got the inside knowledge—what *do* the Chinese think?

Gallimard: Deep down, they miss the old days. You know, cappuccinos, men in tuxedos—

---

[2]**Ho Chi Minh** (1890–1969): First president of North Vietnam (1945–1969).

Toulon: So what do we tell the Americans about Vietnam?

Gallimard: Tell them there's a natural affinity between the West and the Orient.

Toulon: And that you speak from experience?

Gallimard: The Orientals are people too. They want the good things we can give them. If the Americans demonstrate the will to win, the Vietnamese will welcome them into a mutually beneficial union.

Toulon: I don't see how the Vietnamese can stand up to American firepower.

Gallimard: Orientals will always submit to a greater force.

Toulon: I'll note your opinions in my report. The Americans always love to hear how "welcome" they'll be. *(He starts to exit.)*

Gallimard: Sir?

Toulon: Mmmm?

Gallimard: This . . . rumor you've heard.

Toulon: Uh-huh?

Gallimard: How . . . widespread do you think it is?

Toulon: It's only widespread within this embassy. Where nobody talks because everybody is guilty. We were worried about you, Gallimard. We thought you were the only one here without a secret. Now you go and find a lotus blossom . . . and top us all. *(He exits.)*

Gallimard *(To us.)* Toulon knows! And he approves! I was learning the benefits of being a man. We form our own clubs, sit behind thick doors, smoke—and celebrate the fact that we're still boys. *(He starts to move downstage, towards Song.)* So, over the—

(Suddenly Comrade Chin enters. Gallimard backs away.)

Gallimard *(To Song.)* No! Why does she have to come in?

Song: Rene, be sensible. How can they understand the story without her? Now, don't embarrass yourself.

(Gallimard moves down center.)

Gallimard *(To us.)* Now, you will see why my story is so amusing to so many people. Why they snicker at parties in disbelief. Please—try to understand it from my point of view. We are all prisoners of our time and place. *(He exits.)*

Scene 4
Gallimard and Butterfly's flat. Beijing. 1961

Song *(To us.)* 1961. The flat Monsieur Gallimard rented for us. An evening after he has gone.

Chin: Okay, see if you can find out when the Americans plan to start bombing Vietnam. If you can find out what cities, even better.

Song: I'll do my best, but I don't want to arouse his suspicions.

Chin: Yeah, sure, of course. So, what else?

Song: The Americans will increase troops in Vietnam to 170,000 soldiers with 120,000 militia and 11,000 American advisors.

Chin *(Writing.)* Wait, wait, 120,000 militia and—

Song: —11,000 American—

Chin: —American advisors. *(Beat.)* How do you remember so much?

Song: I'm an actor.

Chin: Yeah. *(Beat.)* Is that how come you dress like that?   10
Song: Like what, Miss Chin?
Chin: Like that dress! You're wearing a dress. And every time I come here, you're wearing a dress. Is that because you're an actor? Or what?
Song: It's a . . . disguise, Miss Chin.
Chin: Actors, I think they're all weirdos. My mother tells me actors are like gamblers or prostitutes or—
Song: It helps me in my assignment.   15

(Pause.)

Chin: You're not gathering information in any way that violates Communist Party principles, are you?
Song: Why would I do that?
Chin: Just checking. Remember; when working for the Great Proletarian State, you represent our Chairman Mao in every position you take.
Song: I'll try to imagine the Chairman taking my positions.
Chin: We all think of him this way. Good-bye, comrade. *(She starts to exit.)* Comrade?   20
Song: Yes?
Chin: Don't forget: there is no homosexuality in China!
Song: Yes, I've heard.
Chin: Just checking. *(She exits.)*
Song *(To us.)*: What passes for a woman in modern China.   25

(Gallimard sticks his head out from the wings.)

Gallimard: Is she gone?
Song: Yes, Rene. Please continue in your own fashion.

Scene 5
Beijing. 1961–1963.
Gallimard moves to the couch where Song still sits. He lies down in her lap, and she strokes his forehead.

Gallimard *(To us.)*: And so, over the years 1961, '62, '63, we settled into our routine, Butterfly and I. She would always have prepared a light snack and then, ever so delicately, and only if I agreed, she would start to pleasure me. With her hands, her mouth . . . too many ways to explain, and too sad, given my present situation. But mostly we would talk. About my life. Perhaps there is nothing more rare than to find a woman who passionately listens.

(Song remains upstage, listening, as Helga enters and plays a scene downstage with Gallimard.)

Helga: Rene, I visited Dr. Bolleart this morning.
Gallimard: Why? Are you ill?
Helga: No, no. You see, I wanted to ask him . . . that question we've been discussing.
Gallimard: And I told you, it's only a matter of time. Why did you bring a doctor into this? We just have to keep trying—like a crapshoot, actually.   5
Helga: I went, I'm sorry. But listen: he says there's nothing wrong with me.
Gallimard: You see? Now, will you stop—?
Helga: Rene, he says he'd like you to go in and take some tests.
Gallimard: Why? So he can find there's nothing wrong with both of us?

Helga: Rene, I don't ask for much. One trip! One visit! And then, whatever you want 10
to do about it—you decide.

Gallimard: You're assuming he'll find something defective!

Helga: No! Of course not! Whatever he finds—if he finds nothing, we decide what to
do about nothing! But go!

Gallimard: If he finds nothing, we keep trying. Just like we do now.

Helga: But at least we'll know! *(Pause.)* I'm sorry. *(She starts to exit.)*

Gallimard: Do you really want me to see Dr. Bolleart? 15

Helga: Only if you want a child, Rene. We have to face the fact that time is running
out. Only if you want a child. *(She exits.)*

Gallimard *(To Song.)*: I'm a modern man, Butterfly. And yet, I don't want to go. It's
the same old voodoo. I feel like God himself is laughing at me if I can't produce
a child.

Song: You men of the West—you're obsessed by your odd desire for equality. Your
wife can't give you a child, and *you're* going to the doctor?

Gallimard: Well, you see, she's already gone.

Song: And because this incompetent can't find the defect, you now have to subject 20
yourself to him? It's unnatural.

Gallimard: Well, what is the "natural" solution?

Song: In Imperial China, when a man found that one wife was inadequate, he turned
to another—to give him his son.

Gallimard: What do you—? I can't . . . marry you, yet.

Song: Please. I'm not asking you to be my husband. But I am already your wife.

Gallimard: Do you want to . . . have my child? 25

Song: I thought you'd never ask.

Gallimard: But, your career . . . your—

Song: Phooey on my career! That's your Western mind, twisting itself into strange
shapes again. Of course I love my career. But what would I love most of all? To
feel something inside me—day and night—something I know is yours. *(Pause.)*
Promise me . . . you won't go to this doctor. Who is this Western quack to set
himself as judge over the man I love? I know who is a man, and who is not. *(She
exits.)*

Gallimard *(To us.)*: Dr. Bolleart? Of course I didn't go. What man would?

Scene 6
Beijing. 1963.
Party noises over the house speakers. Renee enters, wearing a revealing gown.

Gallimard: 1963. A party at the Austrian embassy. None of us could remember the
Austrian ambassador's name, which seemed somehow appropriate. *(To Renee.)*
So, I tell the Americans, Diem[3] must go. The U.S. wants to be respected by
the Vietnamese, and yet they're propping up this nobody seminarian as her
president. A man whose claim to fame is his sister-in-law imposing fanatic
"moral order" campaigns? Oriental women—when they're good, they're very
good, but when they're bad, they're Christians.

---

[3]**Diem:** Ngo Dinh Diem (1901–1963), Vietnamese political leader and president of South Vietnam
(1955–1963), assassinated in a coup d'état orchestrated by Vietnamese generals and supported by
the United States.

Renee: Yeah.

Gallimard: And what do you do?

Renee: I'm a student. My father exports a lot of useless stuff to the Third World.

Gallimard: How useless? 5

Renee: You know. Squirt guns, confectioner's sugar, Hula Hoops . . .

Gallimard: I'm sure they appreciate the sugar.

Renee: I'm here for two years to study Chinese.

Gallimard: Two years!

Renee: That's what everybody says. 10

Gallimard: When did you arrive?

Renee: Three weeks ago.

Gallimard: And?

Renee: I like it. Its primitive, but . . . well, this is the place to learn Chinese, so here I am.

Gallimard: Why Chinese? 15

Renee: I think it'll be important someday.

Gallimard: You do?

Renee: Don't ask me when, but . . . that's what I think.

Gallimard: Well, I agree with you. One hundred percent. That's very farsighted.

Renee: Yeah. Well of course, my father thinks I'm a complete weirdo. 20

Gallimard: He'll thank you someday.

Renee: Like when the Chinese start buying Hula Hoops?

Gallimard: There're a billion bellies out there.

Renee: And if they end up taking over the world—well, then I'll be lucky to know Chinese too, right?

(Pause.)

Gallimard: At this point, I don't see how the Chinese can possibly take— 25

Renee: You know what I *don't* like about China?

Gallimard: Excuse me? No—what?

Renee: Nothing to do at night.

Gallimard: You come to parties at embassies like everyone else.

Renee: Yeah, but they get out at ten. And then what? 30

Gallimard: I'm afraid the Chinese idea of a dance hall is a dirt floor and a man with a flute.

Renee: Are you married?

Gallimard: Yes. Why?

Renee: You wanna . . . fool around?

(Pause.)

Gallimard: Sure. 35

Renee: I'll wait for you outside. What's your name?

Gallimard: Gallimard. Rene.

Renee: Weird. I'm Renee too. *(She exits.)*

Gallimard *(To us.)*: And so, I embarked on my first extra-extramarital affair. Renee was picture perfect. With a body like those girls in the magazines. If I put a tissue paper over my eyes, I wouldn't have been able to tell the difference. And it was exciting to be with someone who wasn't afraid to be seen completely naked.

But is it possible for a woman to be *too* uninhibited, *too* willing, so as to seem almost too . . . masculine?

(*Chuck Berry*[4] *blares from the house speakers, then comes down in volume as Renee enters, toweling her hair.*)

Renee: You have a nice weenie.

Gallimard: What?

Renee: Penis. You have a nice penis.

Gallimard: Oh. Well, thank you. That's very . . .

Renee : What—can't take a compliment?

Gallimard: No, it's very . . . reassuring.

Renee: But most girls don't come out and say it, huh?

Gallimard: And also . . . what did you call it?

Renee: Oh. Most girls don't call it a "weenie," huh?

Gallimard: It sounds very—

Renee: Small, I know.

Gallimard: I was going to say, "young."

Renee: Yeah. Young, small, same thing. Most guys are pretty, uh, sensitive about that. Like, you know, I had a boyfriend back home in Denmark. I got mad at him once and called him a little weeniehead. He got so mad! He said at least I should call him a great big weeniehead.

Gallimard: I suppose I just say "penis."

Renee: Yeah. That's pretty clinical. There's "cock," but that sounds like a chicken. And "prick" is painful, and "dick" is like you're talking about someone who's not in the room.

Gallimard: Yes. It's a . . . bigger problem than I imagined.

Renee: I—I think maybe it's because I really don't know what to do with them— that's why I call them "weenies."

Gallimard: Well, you did quite well with . . . mine.

Renee: Thanks, but I mean, really *do* with them. Like, okay, have you ever looked at one? I mean, really?

Gallimard: No, I suppose when it's part of you, you sort of take it for granted.

Renee: I guess. But, like, it just hangs there. This little . . . flap of flesh. And there's so much fuss that we make about it. Like, I think the reason we fight wars is because we wear clothes. Because no one knows—between the men, I mean— who has the biggest . . . weenie. So, if I'm a guy with a small one, I'm going to build a really big building or take over a really big piece of land or write a really long book so the other men don't know, right? But, see, it never really works, that's the problem. I mean, you conquer the country, or whatever, but you're still wearing clothes, so there's no way to prove absolutely whose is bigger or smaller. And that's what we call a civilized society. The whole world run by a bunch of men with pricks the size of pins. (*She exits.*)

Gallimard (*To us.*): This was simply not acceptable.

(*A high-pitched chime rings through the air. Song, dressed as Butterfly, appears in the upstage special. She is obviously distressed. Her body swoons as she attempts to clip the stems of flowers she's arranging in a vase.*)

---

[4]**Chuck Berry** (b. 1926): American rock 'n' roll musician.

Gallimard: But I kept up our affair, wildly, for several months. Why? I believe because of Butterfly. She knew the secret I was trying to hide. But, unlike a Western woman, she didn't confront me, threaten, even pout. I remembered the words of Puccini's *Butterfly:*

Song: *"Noi siamo gente avvezza / alle piccole cose / umili e silenziose."*

Gallimard: "I come from a people / Who are accustomed to little / Humble and silent." I saw Pinkerton and Butterfly, and what she would say if he were unfaithful . . . nothing. She would cry, alone, into those wildly soft sleeves, once full of possessions, now empty to collect her tears. It was her tears and her silence that excited me, every time I visited Renee.

Toulon *(Offstage.)*: Gallimard!   65

(Toulon enters. Gallimard turns towards him. During the next section, Song, up center, begins to dance with the flowers. It is a drunken, reckless dance, where she breaks small pieces off the stems.)

Toulon: They're killing him.

Gallimard: Who? I'm sorry? What?

Toulon: Bother you to come over at this late hour?

Gallimard: No . . . of course not.

Toulon: Not after you hear my secret. Champagne?   70

Gallimard: Um . . . thank you.

Toulon: You're surprised. There's something that you've wanted, Gallimard. No, not a promotion. Next time. Something in the world. You're not aware of this, but there's an informal gossip circle among intelligence agents. And some of ours heard from some of the Americans—

Gallimard: Yes?

Toulon: That the U.S. will allow the Vietnamese generals to stage a coup . . . and assassinate President Diem.

(The chime rings again. Toulon freezes. Gallimard turns upstage and looks at Butterfly, who slowly and deliberately clips a flower off its stem. Gallimard turns back towards Toulon.)

Gallimard: I think . . . that's a very wise move!   75

(Toulon unfreezes.)

Toulon: It's what you've been advocating. A toast?

Gallimard: Sure. I consider this a vindication.

Toulon: Not exactly. "To the test. Let's hope you pass."

(They drink. The chime rings again. Toulon freezes. Gallimard turns upstage, and Song clips another flower.)

Gallimard *(To Toulon.)*: The test?

Toulon *(Unfreezing.)*: It's a test of everything you've been saying. I personally think   80
the generals probably will stop the Communists. And you'll be a hero. But if anything goes wrong, then your opinions won't be worth a pig's ear. I'm sure that won't happen. But sometimes it's easier when they don't listen to you.

Gallimard: They're your opinions too, aren't they?

Toulon: Personally, yes.

Gallimard: So we agree.

Toulon: But my opinions aren't on that report. Yours are. Cheers.

(Toulon turns away from Gallimard and raises his glass. At that instant Song picks up the vase and hurls it to the ground. It shatters. Song sinks down amidst the shards of the vase, in a calm, childlike trance. She sings softly, as if reciting a child's nursery rhyme.)

Song *(Repeat as necessary.)*: "The whole world over, the white man travels, setting   85
    anchor, wherever he likes. Life's not worth living, unless he finds, the finest
    maidens, of every land . . ."

(Gallimard turns downstage towards us. Song continues singing.)

Gallimard: I shook as I left his house. That coward! That worm! To put the burden
    for his decisions on my shoulders!
        I started for Renee's. But no, that was all I needed. A schoolgirl who would
    question the role of the penis in modern society. What I wanted was revenge. A
    vessel to contain my humiliation. Though I hadn't seen her in several weeks, I
    headed for Butterfly's.

(Gallimard enters Song's apartment.)

Song: Oh! Rene . . . I was dreaming!

Gallimard: You've been drinking?

Song: If I can't sleep, then yes, I drink. But then, it gives me these dreams which—
    Rene, it's been almost three weeks since you visited me last.

Gallimard: I know. There's been a lot going on in the world.   90

Song: Fortunately I am drunk. So I can speak freely. It's not the world, it's you and
    me. And an old problem. Even the softest skin becomes like leather to a man
    who's touched it too often. I confess I don't know how to stop it. I don't know
    how to become another woman.

Gallimard: I have a request.

Song: Is this a solution? Or are you ready to give up the flat?

Gallimard: It may be a solution. But I'm sure you won't like it.

Song: Oh well, that's very important. "Like it?" Do you think I "like" lying here   95
    alone, waiting, always waiting for your return? Please—don't worry about what
    I may not "like."

Gallimard: I want to see you . . . naked.

(Silence.)

Song: I thought you understood my modesty. So you want me to—what—strip? Like
    a big cowboy girl? Shiny pasties on my breasts? Shall I fling my kimono over my
    head and yell "ya-hoo" in the process? I thought you respected my shame!

Gallimard: I believe you gave me your shame many years ago.

Song: Yes—and it is just like a white devil to use it against me. I can't believe it. I
    thought myself so repulsed by the passive Oriental and the cruel white man.
    Now I see—we are always most revolted by the things hidden within us.

Gallimard: I just mean—   100

Song: Yes?

Gallimard: —that it will remove the only barrier left between us.

Song: No, Rene. Don't couch your request in sweet words. Be yourself—a cad—and
    know that my love is enough, that I submit—submit to the worst you can give
    me. *(Pause.)* Well, come. Strip me. Whatever happens, know that you have
    willed it. Our love, in your hands. I'm helpless before my man,

(Gallimard starts to cross the room.)

Gallimard: Did I not undress her because I knew, somewhere deep down, what I would find? Perhaps. Happiness is so rare that our mind can turn somersaults to protect it.

At the time, I only knew that I was seeing Pinkerton stalking towards his Butterfly, ready to reward her love with his lecherous hands. The image sickened me, pulled me to my knees, so I was crawling towards her like a worm. By the time I reached her, Pinkerton . . . had vanished from my heart. To be replaced by something new, something unnatural, that flew in the face of all I'd learned in the world—something very close to love.

(He grabs her around the waist; she strokes his hair.)

Gallimard: Butterfly, forgive me. 105

Song: Rene . . .

Gallimard: For everything. From the start.

Song: I'm . . .

Gallimard: I want to—

Song: I'm pregnant. *(Beat.)* I'm pregnant. *(Beat.)* I'm pregnant. 110

(Beat.)

Gallimard: I want to marry you!

Scene 7

Gallimard and Butterfly's flat. Beijing. 1963.

Downstage, Song paces as Comrade Chin reads from her notepad. Upstage, Gallimard is still kneeling. He remains on his knees throughout the scene, watching it.

Song: I need a baby.

Chin *(From pad.)*: He's been spotted going to a dorm.

Song: I need a baby.

Chin: At the Foreign Language Institute.

Song: I need a baby. 5

Chin: The room of a Danish girl. . . . What do you mean, you need a baby?!

Song: Tell Comrade Kang—last night, the entire mission, it could've ended.

Chin: What do you mean?

Song: Tell Kang—he told me to strip.

Chin: Strip?! 10

Song: Write!

Chin: I tell you, I don't understand nothing about this case anymore. Nothing.

Song: He told me to strip, and I took a chance. Oh, we Chinese, we know how to gamble.

Chin *(Writing.)*: ". . . told him to strip."

Song: My palms were wet, I had to make a split-second decision. 15

Chin: Hey! Can you slow down?!

(Pause.)

Song: You write faster, I'm the artist here. Suddenly, it hit me—"All he wants is for her to submit. Once a woman submits, a man is always ready to become 'generous.'"

Chin: You're just gonna end up with rough notes.

Song: And it worked! He gave in! Now, if I can just present him with a baby. A Chinese baby with blond hair—he'll be mine for life!

Chin: Kang will never agree! The trading of babies has to be a counterrevolutionary act! 20
Song: Sometimes, a counterrevolutionary act is necessary to counter a counterrevolutionary act.

(Pause.)

Chin: Wait.
Song: I need one . . . in seven months. Make sure it's a boy.
Chin: This doesn't sound like something the Chairman would do. Maybe you'd better talk to Comrade Kang yourself.
Song: Good. I will. 25

(Chin gets up to leave.)

Song: Miss Chin? Why, in the Peking Opera, are women's roles played by men?
Chin: I don't know. Maybe, a reactionary remnant of male—
Song: No. *(Beat.)* Because only a man knows how a woman is supposed to act.

(Chin exits. Song, turns upstage, towards Gallimard.)

Gallimard *(Calling after Chin.)*: Good riddance! *(To Song.)* I could forget all that betrayal in an instant, you know. If you'd just come back and become Butterfly again.
Song: Fat chance. You're here in prison, rotting in a cell. And I'm on a plane, winging 30 my way back to China. Your President pardoned me of our treason, you know.
Gallimard: Yes, I read about that.
Song: Must make you feel . . . lower than shit.
Gallimard: But don't you, even a litle bit, wish you were here with me?
Song: I'm an artist, Rene. You were my greatest . . . acting challenge. *(She laughs.)* It doesn't matter how rotten I answer, does it? You still adore me. That's why I love you, Rene. *(She points to us.)* So—you were telling your audience about the night I announced I was pregnant.

(Gallimard puts his arms around Song's waist. He and Song are in the positions they were in at the end of Scene 6.)

Scene 8
Same.

Gallimard: I'll divorce my wife. We'll live together here, and then later in France.
Song: I feel so . . . ashamed.
Gallimard: Why?
Song: I had begun to lose faith. And now, you shame me with your generosity.
Gallimard: Generosity? No, I'm proposing for very selfish reasons. 5
Song: Your apologies only make me feel more ashamed. My outburst a moment ago!
Gallimard: Your outburst? What about my request?!
Song: You've been very patient dealing with my . . . eccentricities. A Western man, used to women freer with their bodies—
Gallimard: It was sick! Don't make excuses for me.
Song: I have to. You don't seem willing to make them for yourself. 10

(Pause.)

Gallimard: You're crazy.
Song: I'm happy. Which often looks like crazy.
Gallimard: Then make me crazy. Marry me.

(Pause.)

Song: No.

Gallimard: What?

Song: Do I sound silly, a slave, if I say I'm not worthy?

Gallimard: Yes. In fact you do. No one has loved me like you.

Song: Thank you. And no one ever will. I'll see to that.

Gallimard: So what is the problem?

Song: Rene, we Chinese are realists. We understand rice, gold, and guns. You are a diplomat. Your career is skyrocketing. Now, what would happen if you divorced your wife to marry a Communist Chinese actress?

Gallimard: That's not being realistic. That's defeating yourself before you begin.

Song: We conserve our strength for the battles we can win.

Gallimard: That sounds like a fortune cookie!

Song: Where do you think fortune cookies come from!

Gallimard: I don't care.

Song: You do. So do I. And we should. That is why I say I'm not worthy. I'm worthy to love and even to be loved by you. But I am not worthy to end the career of one of the West's most promising diplomats.

Gallimard: It's not that great a career! I made it sound like more than it is!

Song: Modesty will get you nowhere. Flatter yourself, and you flatter me. I'm flattered to decline your offer. *(She exits.)*

Gallimard *(To us.)*: Butterfly and I argued all night. And, in the end, I left, knowing I would never be her husband. She went away for several months—to the countryside, like a small animal. Until one night I received her call.

(A baby's cry from offstage. Song enters, carrying a child.)

Song: He looks like you.

Gallimard: Oh! *(Beat; he approaches the baby.)* Well, babies are never very attractive at birth.

Song: Stop!

Gallimard: I'm sure he'll grow more beautiful with age. More like his mother.

Song: *"Chi vide mai / a bimbo del Giappon . . ."*

Gallimard: "What baby, I wonder, was ever born in Japan"—or China, for that matter—

Song: *". . . occhi azzurrini?"*

Gallimard: "With azure eyes"—they're actually sort of brown, wouldn't you say?

Song: *"E il labbro."*

Gallimard: "And such lips!" *(He kisses Song.)* And such lips.

Song: *"E i ricciolini d'oro schietto?"*

Gallimard: "And such a head of golden"—if slightly patchy—"curls?"

Song: I'm going to call him "Peepee."

Gallimard: Darling, could you repeat that because I'm sure a rickshaw just flew by overhead.

Song: You heard me.

Gallimard: "Song Peepee"? May I suggest Michael, or Stephan, or Adolph?

Song: You may, but I won't listen.

Gallimard: You can't be serious. Can you imagine the time this child will have in school?

Song: In the West, yes.

Gallimard: It's worse than naming him Ping Pong or Long Dong or—

Song: But he's never going to live in the West, is he?   50

(*Pause.*)

Gallimard: That wasn't my choice.

Song: It is mine. And this is my promise to you: I will raise him, he will be our child, but he will never burden you outside of China.

Gallimard: Why do you make these promises? I want to be burdened! I want a scandal to cover the papers!

Song (*To us.*): Prophetic.

Gallimard: I'm serious.   55

Song: So am I. His name is as I registered it. And he will never live in the West.

(*Song exits with the child.*)

Gallimard (*To us.*): Is it possible that her stubbornness only made me want her more? That drawing back at the moment of my capitulation was the most brilliant strategy she could have chosen? It is possible. But it is also possible that by this point she could have said, could have done . . . anything, and I would have adored her still.

Scene 9
Beijing. 1966.
> *A driving rhythm of Chinese percussion fills the stage.*

Gallimard: And then, China began to change. Mao became very old, and his cult became very strong. And, like many old men, he entered his second childhood. So he handed over the reins of state to those with minds like his own. And children ruled the Middle Kingdom[5] with complete caprice. The doctrine of the Cultural Revolution[6] implied continuous anarchy. Contact between Chinese and foreigners became impossible. Our flat was confiscated. Her fame and my money now counted against us.

(*Two dancers in Mao suits and red-starred caps enter, and begin crudely mimicking revolutionary violence, in an agitprop fashion.*)

Gallimard: And somehow the American war went wrong, too. Four hundred thousand dollars were being spent for every Viet Cong[7] killed; so General Westmoreland's[8] remark that the Oriental does not value life the way Americans do was oddly accurate. Why weren't the Vietnamese people giving in? Why were they content instead to die and die and die again?

(*Toulon enters. Percussion and dancers continue upstage.*)

---

[5]**Middle Kingdom:** The Middle Empire (581–960).   [6]**Cultural Revolution:** Mao's reform campaign of 1965–1967 to purge counterrevolutionary thought and rekindle revolutionary fervor in China. He did so with the help of the Red Guards, young followers who operated on the provincial level to purge China of capitalist elements.   [7]**Viet Cong:** Member of the National Liberation Front of South Vietnam, against which U.S. forces were fighting.   [8]**General Westmoreland** (b. 1914): Commanded American troops in Vietnam from 1964 to 1968.

Toulon: Congratulations, Gallimard.

Gallimard: Excuse me, sir?

Toulon: Not a promotion. That was last time. You're going home.   5

Gallimard: What?

Toulon: Don't say I didn't warn you.

Gallimard: I'm being transferred . . . because I was wrong about the American war?

Toulon: Of course not. We don't care about the Americans. We care about your
mind. The quality of your analysis. In general, everything you've predicted here
in the Orient . . . just hasn't happened.

Gallimard: I think that's premature.   10

Toulon: Don't force me to be blunt. Okay, you said China was ready to open to
Western trade. The only thing they're trading out there are Western heads. And,
yes, you said the Americans would succeed in Indochina. You were kidding,
right?

Gallimard: I think the end is in sight.

Toulon: Don't be pathetic. And don't take this personally. You were wrong. It's not
your fault.

Gallimard: But I'm going home.

Toulon: Right. Could I have the number of your mistress? *(Beat.)* Joke! Joke! Eat a   15
croissant for me.

*(Toulon exits. Song, wearing a Mao suit, is dragged in from the wings as part of the
upstage dance. They "beat" her, then lampoon the acrobatics of the Chinese opera, as
she is made to kneel onstage.)*

Gallimard *(Simultaneously.)*: I don't care to recall how Butterfly and I said our
hurried farewell. Perhaps it was better to end our affair before it killed her.

*(Gallimard exits. Percussion rises in volume. The lampooning becomes faster, more
frenetic. At its height, Comrade Chin walks across the stage with a banner reading:
"The Actor Renounces His Decadent Profession!" She reaches the kneeling Song. At
the moment Chin touches Song's chin, percussion stops with a thud. Dancers strike
poses.)*

Chin: Actor-oppressor, for years you have lived above the common people and looked
down on their labor. While the farmer ate millet—

Song: I ate pastries from France and sweetmeats from silver trays.

Chin: And how did you come to live in such an exalted position?

Song: I was a plaything for the imperialists!   20

Chin: What did you do?

Song: I shamed China by allowing myself to be corrupted by a foreigner . . .

Chin: What does this mean? The People demand a full confession!

Song: I engaged in the lowest perversions with China's enemies!

Chin: What perversions? Be more clear!   25

Song: I let him put it up my ass!

(Dancers look over, disgusted.)

Chin: Aaaa-ya! How can you use such sickening language?!

Song: My language . . . is only as foul as the crimes I committed . . .

Chin: Yeah. That's better. So—what do you want to do . . . now?

Song: I want to serve the people!   30

(Percussion starts up, with Chinese strings.)

Chin: What?
Song: I want to serve the people!

(Dancers regain their revolutionary smiles, and begin a dance of victory.)

Chin: What?!
Song: I want to serve the people!!

(Dancers unveil a banner: "The Actor Is Re-Habilitated!" Song remains kneeling before Chin, as the dancers bounce around them, then exit. Music out.)

Scene 10
A commune. Hunan Province. 1970.

Chin: How you planning to do that?
Song: I've already worked four years in the fields of Hunan, Comrade Chin.
Chin: So? Farmers work all their lives. Let me see your hands.

(Song holds them out for her inspection.)

Chin: Goddamn! Still so smooth! How long does it take to turn you actors into good anythings? Hunh. You've just spent too many years in luxury to be any good to the Revolution.
Song: I served the Revolution.   5
Chin: Serve the Revolution? Bullshit! You wore dresses! Don't tell me—I was there. I saw you! You and your white vice-consul! Stuck up there in your flat, living off the People's Treasury! Yeah, I knew what was going on! You two . . . homos! Homos! Homos! *(Pause; she composes herself.)* Ah! Well . . . you will serve the people, all right. But not with the Revolution's money. This time, you use your own money.
Song: I have no money.
Chin: Shut up! And you won't stink up China anymore with your pervert stuff. You'll pollute the place where pollution begins—the West.
Song: What do you mean?
Chin: Shut up! You're going to France. Without a cent in your pocket. You find your   10
consul's house, you make him pay your expenses—
Song: No.
Chin: And you give us weekly reports! Useful information!
Song: That's crazy. It's been four years.
Chin: Either that, or back to rehabilitation center!
Song: Comrade Chin, he's not going to support me! Not in France! He's a white   15
man! I was just his plaything—
Chin: Oh yuck! Again with the sickening language? Where's my stick?
Song: You don't understand the mind of a man.

(Pause.)

Chin: Oh no? No I don't? Then how come I'm married, huh? How come I got a man? Five, six years ago, you always tell me those kind of things, I felt very bad. But not now! Because what does the Chairman say? He tells us *I'm* now the smart one, you're now the nincompoop! *You're* the blockhead, the harebrain, the nitwit! You think you're so smart? You understand "The Mind of a Man"? Good! Then *you* go to France and be a pervert for Chairman Mao!

(Chin and Song exit in opposite directions.)

Scene 11
Paris. 1968–1970.
Gallimard enters.

Gallimard: And what was waiting for me back in Paris? Well, better Chinese food than I'd eaten in China. Friends and relatives. A little accounting, regular schedule, keeping track of traffic violations in the suburbs. . . . And the indignity of students shouting the slogans of Chairman Mao at me—in French.

Helga: Rene? Rene? *(She enters, soaking wet.)* I've had a . . . problem.

(She sneezes.)

Gallimard: You're wet.

Helga: Yes, I . . . coming back from the grocer's. A group of students, waving red flags, they—

(Gallimard fetches a towel.)

Helga: —they ran by, I was caught up along with them. Before I knew what was happening—

(Gallimard gives her the towel.)

Helga: Thank you. The police started firing water cannons at us. I tried to shout, to tell them I was the wife of a diplomat, but—you know how it is . . . *(Pause.)* Needless to say, I lost the groceries. Rene, what's happening to France?

Gallimard: What's—? Well, nothing, really. 5

Helga: Nothing?! The storefronts are in flames, there's glass in the streets, buildings are toppling—and I'm wet!

Gallimard: Nothing! . . . that I care to think about.

Helga: And is that why you stay in this room?

Gallimard: Yes, in fact.

Helga: With the incense burning? You know something? I hate incense. It smells so 10 sickly sweet.

Gallimard: Well, I hate the French. Who just smell—period!

Helga: And the Chinese were better?

Gallimard: Please—don't start.

Helga: When we left, this exact same thing, the riots—

Gallimard: No, no . . . 15

Helga: Students screaming slogans, smashing down doors—

Gallimard: Helga—

Helga: It was all going on in China, too. Don't you remember?!

Gallimard: Helga! Please! *(Pause.)* You have never understood China, have you? You walk in here with these ridiculous ideas, that the West is falling apart, that China was spitting in our faces. You come in, dripping of the streets, and you leave water all over my floor. *(He grabs Helga's towel, begins mopping up the floor.)*

Helga: But it's the truth! 20

Gallimard: Helga, I want a divorce.

(Pause; Gallimard continues mopping the floor.)

Helga: I take it back. China is . . . beautiful. Incense, I like incense.

Gallimard: I've had a mistress.

Helga: So?

Gallimard: For eight years.

Helga: I knew you would. I knew you would the day I married you. And now what? You want to marry her?

Gallimard: I can't. She's in China.

Helga: I see. You know that no one else is ever going to marry me, right?

Gallimard: I'm sorry.

Helga: And you want to leave. For someone who's not here, is that right?

Gallimard: That's right.

Helga: You can't live with her, but still you don't want to live with me.

Gallimard: That's right.

(*Pause.*)

Helga: Shit. How terrible that I can figure that out. (*Pause.*) I never thought I'd say it. But, in China, I was happy. I knew, in my own way, I knew that you were not everything you pretended to be. But the pretense—going on your arm to the embassy ball, visiting your office and the guards saying, "Good morning, good morning, Madame Gallimard"—the pretense . . . was very good indeed. (*Pause.*) I hope everyone is mean to you for the rest of your life. (*She exits.*)

Gallimard (*To us.*): Prophetic.

(*Marc enters with two drinks.*)

Gallimard (*To Marc.*): In China, I was different from all other men.

Marc: Sure. You were white. Here's your drink.

Gallimard: I felt . . . touched.

Marc: In the head? Rene, I don't want to hear about the Oriental love goddess. Okay? One night—can we just drink and throw up without a lot of conversation?

Gallimard: You still don't believe me, do you?

Marc: Sure I do. She was the most beautiful, et cetera, et cetera, blasé, blasé.

(*Pause.*)

Gallimard: My life in the West has been such a disappointment.

Marc: Life in the West is like that. You'll get used to it. Look, you're driving me away. I'm leaving. Happy, now? (*He exits, then returns.*) Look, I have a date tomorrow night. You wanna come? I can fix you up with—

Gallimard: Of course. I would love to come.

(*Pause.*)

Marc: Uh—on second thought, no. You'd better get ahold of yourself first.

(*He exits; Gallimard nurses his drink.*)

Gallimard (*To us.*): This is the ultimate cruelty, isn't it? That I can talk and talk and to anyone listening, it's only air—too rich a diet to be swallowed by a mundane world. Why can't anyone understand? That in China, I once loved, and was loved by, very simply, the Perfect Woman.

(*Song enters, dressed as Butterfly in wedding dress.*)

Gallimard (*To Song.*): Not again. My imagination is hell. Am I asleep this time? Or did I drink too much?

Song: Rene!

Gallimard: God, it's too painful! That you speak?

Song: What are you talking about? Rene—touch me. 50

Gallimard: Why?

Song: I'm real. Take my hand.

Gallimard: Why? So you can disappear again and leave me clutching at the air? For the entertainment of my neighbors who—?

(Song touches Gallimard.)

Song: Rene?

(Gallimard takes Song's hand. Silence.)

Gallimard: Butterfly? I never doubted you'd return. 55

Song: You hadn't . . . forgotten—?

Gallimard: Yes, actually, I've forgotten everything. My mind, you see—there wasn't enough room in this hard head—not for the world and for you. No, there was only room for one. *(Beat.)* Come, look. See? Your bed has been waiting, with the Klimt[9] poster you like, and—see? The *xiang lu*[10] you gave me?

Song: I . . . I don't know what to say.

Gallimard: There's nothing to say. Not at the end of a long trip. Can I make you some tea?

Song: But where's your wife? 60

Gallimard: She's by my side. She's by my side at last.

(Gallimard reaches to embrace Song. Song sidesteps, dodging him.)

Gallimard: Why?!

Song *(To us.)*: So I did return to Rene in Paris. Where I found—

Gallimard: Why do you run away? Can't we show them how we embraced that evening?

Song: Please. I'm talking. 65

Gallimard: You have to do what I say! I'm conjuring you up in *my* mind!

Song: Rene, I've never done what you've said. Why should it be any different in your mind? Now split—the story moves on, and I must change.

Gallimard: I welcomed you into my home! I didn't have to, you know! I could've left you penniless on the streets of Paris! But I took you in!

Song: Thank you.

Gallimard: So . . . please . . . don't change. 70

Song: You know I have to. You know I will. And anyway, what difference does it make? No matter what your eyes tell you, you can't ignore the truth. You already know too much.

(Gallimard exits. Song turns to us.)

Song: The change I'm going to make requires about five minutes. So I thought you might want to take this opportunity to stretch your legs, enjoy a drink, or listen to the musicians. I'll be here, when you return, right where you left me.

(Song goes to a mirror in front of which is a wash basin of water. She starts to remove her makeup as stagelights go to half and houselights come up.)

---

[9]**Klimt:** Gustav Klimt (1863–1918), Austrian painter.   [10]**xiang lu:** Incense burner.

Act 3
Scene 1
A courthouse in Paris. 1986.

As he promised, Song has completed the bulk of his transformation onstage by the time the houselights go down and the stagelights come up full. As he speaks to us, he removes his wig and kimono, leaving them on the floor. Underneath, he wears a well-cut suit.

Song: So I'd done my job better than I had a right to expect. Well, give him some credit, too. He's right—I was in a fix when I arrived in Paris. I walked from the airport into town, then I located, by blind groping, the Chinatown district. Let me make one thing clear: whatever else may be said about the Chinese, they are stingy! I slept in doorways three days until I could find a tailor who would make me this kimono on credit. As it turns out, maybe I didn't even need it. Maybe he would've been happy to see me in a simple shift and mascara. But . . . better safe than sorry.

That was 1970, when I arrived in Paris. For the next fifteen years, yes, I lived a very comfy life. Some relief, believe me, after four years on a fucking commune in Nowheresville, China. Rene supported the boy and me, and I did some demonstrations around the country as part of my "cultural exchange" cover. And then there was the spying.

(Song moves upstage, to a chair. Toulon enters as a judge, wearing the appropriate wig and robes. He sits near Song. It's 1986, and Song is testifying in a courtroom.)

Song: Not much at first. Rene had lost all his high-level contacts. Comrade Chin wasn't very interested in parking-ticket statistics. But finally, at my urging, Rene got a job as a courier, handling sensitive documents. He'd photograph them for me, and I'd pass them on to the Chinese embassy.
Judge: Did he understand the extent of his activity?
Song: He didn't ask. He knew that I needed those documents, and that was enough.
Judge: But he must've known he was passing classified information.
Song: I can't say.   5
Judge: He never asked what you were going to do with them?
Song: Nope.

(Pause.)

Judge: There is one thing that the court—indeed, that all of France—would like to know.
Song: Fire away.
Judge: Did Monsieur Gallimard know you were a man?   10
Song: Well, he never saw me completely naked. Ever.
Judge: But surely, he must've . . . how can I put this?
Song: Put it however you like. I'm not shy. He must've felt around?
Judge: Mmmmm.
Song: Not really. I did all the work. He just laid back. Of course we did enjoy more . . . 15
complete union, and I suppose he *might* have wondered why I was always on my stomach, but. . . . But what you're thinking is, "Of course a wrist must've brushed . . . a hand hit . . . over twenty years!" Yeah. Well, Your Honor, it was my job to make him think I was a woman. And chew on this: it wasn't all that hard.

See, my mother was a prostitute along the Bundt before the Revolution. And, uh, I think it's fair to say she learned a few things about Western men. So I borrowed her knowledge. In service to my country.

Judge: Would you care to enlighten the court with this secret knowledge? I'm sure we're all very curious.

Song: I'm sure you are. *(Pause.)* Okay, Rule One is: Men always believe what they want to hear. So a girl can tell the most obnoxious lies and the guys will believe them every time—"This is my first time"—"That's the biggest I've ever seen"—or *both,* which, if you really think about it, is not possible in a single lifetime. You've maybe heard those phrases a few times in your own life, yes, Your Honor?

Judge: It's not my life, Monsieur Song, which is on trial today.

Song: Okay, okay, just trying to lighten up the proceedings. Tough room.

Judge: Go on.   20

Song: Rule Two: As soon as a Western man comes into contact with the East—he's already confused. The West has sort of an international rape mentality towards the East. Do you know rape mentality?

Judge: Give us your definition, please.

Song: Basically, "Her mouth says no, but her eyes say yes."

> The West thinks of itself as masculine—big guns, big industry, big money—so the East is feminine—weak, delicate, poor . . . but good at art, and full of inscrutable wisdom—the feminine mystique.

> Her mouth says no, but her eyes say yes. The West believes the East, deep down, *wants* to be dominated—because a woman can't think for herself.

Judge: What does this have to do with my question?

Song: You expect Oriental countries to submit to your guns, and you expect Oriental   25
women to be submissive to your men. That's why you say they make the best wives.

Judge: But why would that make it possible for you to fool Monsieur Gallimard? Please—get to the point.

Song: One, because when he finally met his fantasy woman, he wanted more than anything to believe that she was, in fact, a woman. And second, I am an Oriental. And being an Oriental, I could never be completely a man.

> *(Pause.)*

Judge: Your armchair political theory is tenuous, Monsieur Song.

Song: You think so? That's why you'll lose in all your dealings with the East.

Judge: Just answer my question: did he know you were a man?   30

> *(Pause.)*

Song: You know, Your Honor, I never asked.

Scene 2
Same.
> *Music from the "Death Scene" from Butterfly blares over the house speakers. It is the loudest thing we've heard in this play.*
> *Gallimard enters, crawling towards Song's wig and kimono.*

Gallimard: Butterfly? Butterfly?

> *(Song remains a man, in the witness box, delivering a testimony we do not hear.)*

Gallimard (*To us.*): In my moment of greatest shame, here, in this courtroom—with that . . . person up there, telling the world. . . . What strikes me especially is how shallow he is, how glib and obsequious . . . completely . . . without substance! The type that prowls around discos with a gold medallion stinking of garlic. So little like my Butterfly.

　　Yet even in this moment my mind remains agile, flip-flopping like a man on a trampoline. Even now, my picture dissolves, and I see that . . . witness . . . talking to me.

　　(*Song suddenly stands straight up in his witness box, and looks at Gallimard.*)

Song: Yes. You. White man.

　　(*Song steps out of the witness box, and moves downstage towards Gallimard. Light change.*)

Gallimard (*To Song.*): Who? Me?

Song: Do you see any other white men?

Gallimard: Yes. There're white men all around. This is a French courtroom.　　5

Song: So you are an adventurous imperialist. Tell me, why did it take you so long? To come back to this place?

Gallimard: What place?

Song: This theater in China. Where we met many years ago. . . .

Gallimard (*To us.*): And once again, against my will, I am transported.

　　(*Chinese opera music comes up on the speakers. Song begins to do opera moves, as he did the night they met.*)

Song: Do you remember? The night you gave your heart?　　10

Gallimard: It was a long time ago.

Song: Not long enough. A night that turned your world upside down.

Gallimard: Perhaps.

Song: Oh, be honest with me. What's another bit of flattery when you've already given me twenty years' worth? It's a wonder my head hasn't swollen to the size of China.

Gallimard: Who's to say it hasn't?　　15

Song: Who's to say? And what's the shame? In pride? You think I could've pulled this off if I wasn't already full of pride when we met? No, not just pride. Arrogance. It takes arrogance, really—to believe you can will, with your eyes and your lips, the destiny of another. (*He dances.*) C'mon. Admit it. You still want me. Even in slacks and a button-down collar.

Gallimard: I don't see what the point of—

Song: You don't? Well maybe, Rene, just maybe—I want you.

Gallimard: You do?

Song: Then again, maybe I'm just playing with you. How can you tell? (*Reprising his feminine character, he sidles up to Gallimard.*) "How I wish there were even a small café to sit in. With men in tuxedos, and cappuccinos, and bad expatriate jazz." Now you want to kiss me, don't you?　　20

Gallimard (*Pulling away.*): What makes you—?

Song: —so sure? See? I take the words from your mouth. Then I wait for you to come and retrieve them. (*He reclines on the floor.*)

Gallimard: Why?! Why do you treat me so cruelly?

Song: Perhaps I was treating you cruelly. But now—I'm being nice. Come here, my little one.

Gallimard: I'm not your little one!   25
Song: My mistake. It's I who am *your* little one, right?
Gallimard: Yes, I—
Song: So come get your little one. If you like, I may even let you strip me.
Gallimard: I mean, you were! Before . . . but not like this!
Song: I was? Then perhaps I still am. If you look hard enough. *(He starts to remove his*   30
  clothes.)
Gallimard: What—what are you doing?
Song: Helping you to see through my act.
Gallimard: Stop that! I don't want to! I don't—
Song: Oh, but you asked me to strip, remember?
Gallimard: What? That was years ago! And I took it back!   35
Song: No. You postponed it. Postponed the inevitable. Today, the inevitable has
  come calling.

  (From the speakers, cacophony: Butterfly mixed in with Chinese gongs.)

Gallimard: No! Stop! I don't want to see!
Song: Then look away.
Gallimard: You're only in my mind! All this is in my mind! I order you! To stop!
Song: To what? To strip? That's just what I'm—   40
Gallimard: No! Stop! I want you—!
Song: You want me?
Gallimard: To stop!
Song: You know something, Rene? Your mouth says no, but your eyes say yes. Turn
  them away. I dare you.
Gallimard: I don't have to! Every night, you say you're going to strip, but then I beg   45
  you and you stop!
Song: I guess tonight is different.
Gallimard: Why? Why should that be?
Song: Maybe I've become frustrated. Maybe I'm saying "Look at me, you fool!" Or
  maybe I'm just feeling . . . sexy. *(He is down to his briefs.)*
Gallimard: Please. This is unnecessary. I know what you are.
Song: You do? What am I?   50
Gallimard: A—a man.
Song: You don't really believe that.
Gallimard: Yes I do! I knew all the time somewhere that my happiness was
  temporary, my love a deception. But my mind kept the knowledge at bay. To
  make the wait bearable.
Song: Monsieur Gallimard—the wait is over.

  (Song drops his briefs. He is naked. Sound cue out. Slowly, we and Song came to
  the realization that what we had thought to be Gallimard's sobbing is actually his
  laughter.)

Gallimard: Oh god! What an idiot! Of course!   55
Song: Rene—what?
Gallimard: Look at you! You're a man! *(He bursts into laughter again.)*
Song: I fail to see what's so funny!
Gallimard: "You fail to see—!" I mean, you never did have much of a sense of humor,
  did you? I just think it's ridiculously funny that I've wasted so much time on just
  a man!

Song: Wait. I'm not "just a man." 60
Gallimard: No? Isn't that what you've been trying to convince me of?
Song: Yes, but what I mean—
Gallimard: And now, I finally believe you, and you tell me it's not true? I think you must have some kind of identity problem.
Song: Will you listen to me?
Gallimard: Why?! I've been listening to you for twenty years. Don't I deserve a 65 vacation?
Song: I'm not just any man!
Gallimard: Then, what exactly are you?
Song: Rene, how can you ask—? Okay, what about this?

(He picks up Butterfly's robes, starts to dance around. No music.)

Gallimard: Yes, that's very nice. I have to admit.

(Song holds out his arm to Gallimard.)

Song: It's the same skin you've worshipped for years. Touch it. 70
Gallimard: Yes, it does feel the same.
Song: Now—close your eyes.

(Song covers Gallimard's eyes with one hand. With the other, Song draws Gallimard's hand up to his face. Gallimard, like a blind man, lets his hands run over Song's face.)

Gallimard: This skin, I remember. The curve of her face, the softness of her cheek, her hair against the back of my hand . . .
Song: I'm your Butterfly. Under the robes, beneath everything, it was always me. Now, open your eyes and admit it—you adore me. *(He removes his hand from Gallimard's eyes.)*
Gallimard: You, who knew every inch of my desires—how could you, of all people, 75 have made such a mistake?
Song: What?
Gallimard: You showed me your true self. When all I loved was the lie. A perfect lie, which you let fall to the ground—and now, it's old and soiled.
Song: So—you never really loved me? Only when I was playing a part?
Gallimard: I'm a man who loved a woman created by a man. Everything else—simply falls short.

(Pause.)

Song: What am I supposed to do now? 80
Gallimard: You were a fine spy, Monsieur Song, with an even finer accomplice. But now I believe you should go. Get out of my life!
Song: Go where? Rene, you can't live without me. Not after twenty years.
Gallimard: I certainly can't live with you—not after twenty years of betrayal.
Song: Don't be stubborn! Where will you go?
Gallimard: I have a date . . . with my Butterfly. 85
Song: So, throw away your pride. And come . . .
Gallimard: Get away from me! Tonight, I've finally learned to tell fantasy from reality. And, knowing the difference, I choose fantasy.
Song: *I'm* your fantasy!
Gallimard: You? You're as real as hamburger. Now get out! I have a date with my Butterfly and I don't want your body polluting the room! *(He tosses Song's suit at him.)* Look at these—you dress like a pimp.

Song: Hey! These are Armani slacks and—! *(He puts on his briefs and slacks.)* Let's just   90
say . . . I'm disappointed in you, Rene. In the crush of your adoration, I thought
you'd become something more. More like . . . a woman.

But no. Men. You're like the rest of them. It's all in the way we dress,
and make up our faces, and bat our eyelashes. You really have so little
imagination!

Gallimard: You, Monsieur Song? Accuse me of too little imagination? You, if
anyone, should know—I am pure imagination. And in imagination I will
remain. Now get out!

(Gallimard bodily removes Song from the stage, taking his kimono.)

Song: Rene! I'll never put on those robes again! You'll be sorry!

Gallimard *(To Song.)*: I'm already sorry! *(Looking at the kimono in his hands.)* Exactly
as sorry . . . as a Butterfly.

Scene 3
M. Gallimard's prison cell. Paris. 1988.

Gallimard: I've played out the events of my life night after night, always searching
for a new ending to my story, one where I leave this cell and return forever to
my Butterfly's arms.

Tonight I realize my search is over. That I've looked all along in the wrong
place. And now, to you, I will prove that my love was not in vain—by returning
to the world of fantasy where I first met her.

(He picks up the kimono; dancers enter.)

Gallimard: There is a vision of the Orient that I have. Of slender women in
cheongsams and kimonos who die for the love of unworthy foreign devils. Who
are born and raised to be the perfect women. Who take whatever punishment
we give them, and bounce back, strengthened by love, unconditionally. It is a
vision that has become my life.

(Dancers bring the washbasin to him and help him make up his face.)

Gallimard: In public, I have continued to deny that Song Liling is a man. This
brings me headlines, and is a source of great embarrassment to my French
colleagues, who can now be sent into a coughing fit by the mere mention of
Chinese food. But alone, in my cell, I have long since faced the truth.

And the truth demands a sacrifice. For mistakes made over the course of a
lifetime. My mistakes were simple and absolute—the man I loved was a cad, a
bounder. He deserved nothing but a kick in the behind, and instead I gave
him . . . all my love.

Yes—love. Why not admit it all? That was my undoing, wasn't it? Love
warped my judgment, blinded my eyes, rearranged the very lines on my face . . .
until I could look in the mirror and see nothing but . . . a woman.

(Dancers help him put on the Butterfly wig.)

Gallimard: I have a vision. Of the Orient. That, deep within its almond eyes, there
are still women. Women willing to sacrifice themselves for the love of a man.
Even a man whose love is completely without worth.

(Dancers assist Gallimard in donning the kimono. They hand him a knife.)

Gallimard: Death with honor is better than life . . . life with dishonor. *(He sets himself center stage, in a seppuku position.)* The love of a Butterfly can withstand many things—unfaithfulness, loss, even abandonment. But how can it face the one sin that implies all others? The devastating knowledge that, underneath it all, the object of her love was nothing more, nothing less than . . . a man. *(He sets the tip of the knife against his body.)* It is 1988. And I have found her at last. In a prison on the outskirts of Paris. My name is Rene Gallimard—also known as Madame Butterfly.

> *(Gallimard turns upstage and plunges the knife into his body, as music from the "Love Duet" blares over the speakers. He collapses into the arms of the dancers, who lay him reverently on the floor. The image holds for several beats. Then a tight special up on Song, who stands as a man, staring at the dead Gallimard. He smokes a cigarette; the smoke filters up through the lights. Two words leave his lips.)*

Song: Butterfly? Butterfly?

> *(Smoke rises as lights fade slowly to black.)*

Bernard Cooper *(1951–)*

Burl's   *1996*

I

I loved the restaurant's name, a compact curve of a word. Its sign, five big letters rimmed in neon, hovered above the roof. I almost never saw the sign with its neon lit; my parents took me there for early summer dinners, and even by the time we left—father cleaning his teeth with a toothpick, mother carrying steak bones in a doggie bag—the sky was still bright. Heat rippled off the cars parked along Hollywood Boulevard, the asphalt gummy from hours of sun.

With its sleek architecture, chrome appliances, and arctic temperature, Burl's offered a refuge from the street. We usually sat at one of the booths in front of the plate-glass windows. During our dinner, people came to a halt before the news-vending machine on the corner and burrowed in their pockets and purses for change.

The waitresses at Burl's wore brown uniforms edged in checked gingham. From their breast pockets frothed white lace handkerchiefs. In between reconnaissance missions to the table, they busied themselves behind the counter and shouted "Tuna to travel" or "Scorch that patty" to a harried short-order cook who manned the grill. Miniature pitchers of cream and individual pats of butter were extracted from an industrial refrigerator. Coca-Cola shot from a glinting spigot. Waitresses dodged and bumped one another, frantic as atoms.

My parents usually lingered after the meal, nursing cups of coffee while I played with the beads of condensation on my glass of ice water, tasted Tabasco sauce, or twisted pieces of my paper napkin into mangled animals. One evening, annoyed with my restlessness, my father gave me a dime and asked me to buy him a *Herald Examiner* from the vending machine in front of the restaurant.

Shouldering open the heavy glass door, I was seared by a sudden gust of heat. Traffic 5 roared past me and stirred the air. Walking toward the newspaper machine, I held the dime so tightly it seemed to melt in my palm. Duty made me feel large and important.

I inserted the dime and opened the box, yanking a *Herald* from the spring contraption that held it as tight as a mousetrap. When I turned around, paper in hand, I saw two women walking toward me.

Their high heels clicked on the sun-baked pavement. They were tall, broad-shouldered women who moved with a mixture of haste and defiance. They'd teased their hair into nearly identical black beehives. Dangling earrings flashed in the sun, brilliant as prisms. Each of them wore the kind of clinging, strapless outfit my mother referred to as a cocktail dress. The silky fabric—one dress was purple, the other pink—accentuated their breasts and hips and rippled with insolent highlights. The dresses exposed their bare arms, the slope of their shoulders, and the smooth, powdered plane of flesh where their cleavage began.

I owned at the time a book called *Things for Boys and Girls to Do.* There were pages to color, intricate mazes, and connect-the-dots. But another type of puzzle came to mind as I watched those women walking toward me: What's Wrong With This Picture? Say the drawing of a dining room looked normal at first glance; on closer inspection, a chair was missing its leg and the man who sat atop it wore half a pair of glasses.

The women had Adam's apples.

The closer they came, the shallower my breathing was. I blocked the sidewalk, an incredulous child stalled in their path. When they saw me staring, they shifted their purses and linked their arms. There was something sisterly and conspiratorial about their sudden closeness. Though their mouths didn't move, I thought they might have been communicating without moving their lips, so telepathic did they seem as they joined arms and pressed together, synchronizing their heavy steps. The pages of the *Herald* fluttered in the wind. I felt them against my arm, light as batted lashes.

The woman in pink shot me a haughty glance and yet she seemed pleased that I'd taken notice, hungry to be admired by a man, or even an awestruck eight-year-old boy. She tried to stifle a grin, her red lipstick more voluptuous than the lips it painted. Rouge deepened her cheekbones. Eye shadow dusted her lids, a clumsy abundance of blue. Her face was like a page in *Things for Boys and Girls to Do,* colored by a kid who went outside the lines. 10

At close range, I saw that her wig was slightly askew. I was certain it was a wig because my mother owned several; three Styrofoam heads lined a shelf in my mother's closet; upon them were perched a Page-Boy, an Empress, and a Baby-Doll, all in shades of auburn. The woman in the pink dress wore her wig like a crown of glory.

But it was the woman in the purple dress who passed nearest me, and I saw that her jaw was heavily powdered, a half-successful attempt to disguise the telltale shadow of a beard. Just as I noticed this, her heel caught on a crack in the pavement and she reeled on her stilettos. It was then that I witnessed a rift in her composure, a window through which I could glimpse the shades of maleness that her dress and wig and makeup obscured. She shifted her shoulders and threw out her hands like a surfer riding a curl. The instant she regained her balance, she smoothed her dress, patted her hair, and sauntered onward.

Any woman might be a man. The fact of it clanged through the chambers of my brain. In broad day, in the midst of traffic, with my parents drinking coffee a few feet away, I felt as if everything I understood, everything I had taken for granted up to that moment—the curve of the earth, the heat of the sun, the reliability of my own eyes—had been squeezed out of me. Who were those men? Did they help each other get inside those dresses? How many other people and things were not what they seemed? From the back, the impostors looked like women once again, slinky and curvaceous, purple and pink. I watched them disappear into the distance, their disguises so convincing that other people on the street seemed to take no notice, and for a moment I wondered if I had imagined the whole encounter, a visitation by two unlikely muses.

Frozen in the middle of the sidewalk, I caught my reflection in the window of Burl's, a silhouette floating between his parents. They faced one another across a table. Once the solid embodiments of woman and man, pedestrians and traffic appeared to pass through them.

II

There were some mornings, seconds before my eyes opened and my senses gathered into consciousness, that the child I was seemed to hover above the bed, and I couldn't tell what form my waking would take—the body of a boy or the body of a girl. Finally stirring, I'd blink against the early light and greet each incarnation as a male with mild surprise. My sex, in other words, didn't seem to be an absolute fact so much as a pleasant, recurring accident.

By the age of eight, I'd experienced this groggy phenomenon several times. Those ethereal moments above my bed made waking up in the tangled blankets, a boy steeped in body heat, all the more astonishing. That this might be an unusual experience never occurred to me; it was one among a flood of sensations I could neither name nor ignore.

And so, shocked as I was when those transvestites passed me in front of Burl's, they confirmed something about which I already had an inkling: the hazy border between the sexes. My father, after all, raised his pinky when he drank from a teacup, and my mother looked as faded and plain as my father until she fixed her hair and painted her face.

Like most children, I once thought it possible to divide the world into male and female columns. Blue/Pink. Rooster/Hens. Trousers/Skirts. Such divisions were easy, not to mention comforting, for they simplified matter into compatible pairs. But there also existed a vast range of things that didn't fit neatly into either camp: clocks, milk, telephones, grass. There were nights I fell into a fitful sleep while trying to sex the world correctly.

Nothing typified the realms of male and female as clearly as my parents' walk-in closets. Home alone for any length of time, I always found my way inside them. I could stare at my parents' clothes for hours, grateful for the stillness and silence, haunting the very heart of their privacy.

The overhead light in my father's closet was a bare bulb. Whenever I groped for the chain in the dark, it wagged back and forth and resisted my grasp. Once the light clicked on, I saw dozens of ties hanging like stalactites. A monogrammed silk bathrobe sagged from a hook, a gift my father had received on a long-ago birthday and, thinking it fussy, rarely wore. Shirts were cramped together along the length of an aluminum pole, their starched sleeves sticking out as if in a halfhearted gesture of greeting. The medicinal odor of mothballs permeated the boxer shorts that were folded and stacked in a built-in drawer. Immaculate underwear was proof of a tenderness my mother couldn't otherwise express; she may not have touched my father often, but she laundered his boxers with infinite care. Even back then, I suspected that a sense of duty was the final erotic link between them.

Sitting in a neat row on the closet floor were my father's boots and slippers and dress shoes. I'd try on his wingtips and clomp around, slipping out of them with every step.

My wary, unnatural stride made me all the more desperate to effect some authority. I'd whisper orders to imagined lackeys and take my invisible wife in my arms. But no matter how much I wanted them to fit, those shoes were as cold and hard as marble.

My mother's shoes were just as uncomfortable, but a lot more fun. From a brightly colored array of pumps and slingbacks, I'd pick a pair with the glee and deliberation of someone choosing a chocolate. Whatever embarrassment I felt was overwhelmed by the exhilaration of being taller in a pair of high heels. Things will look like this some-day, I said to myself, gazing out from my new and improved vantage point as if from a crow's nest. Calves elongated, arms akimbo, I gauged each step so that I didn't fall over and moved with what might have passed for grace had someone seen me, a possibility I scrupulously avoided by locking the door.

Back and forth I went. The longer I wore a pair of heels, the better my balance. In the periphery of my vision, the shelf of wigs looked like a throng of kindly bystanders. Light streamed down from a high window, causing crystal bottles to glitter, the air ripe with perfume. A makeup mirror above the dressing table invited my self-absorption. Sound was muffled. Time slowed. It seemed as if nothing bad could happen as long as I stayed within those walls.

Though I'd never been discovered in my mother's closet, my parents knew that I was drawn toward girlish things—dolls and jump rope and jewelry—as well as to the games and preoccupations that were expected of a boy. I'm not sure now if it was my ef-feminacy itself that bothered them as much as my ability to slide back and forth, with-out the slightest warning, between male and female mannerisms. After I'd finished building the model of an F-17 bomber, say, I'd sit back to examine my handiwork, pursing my lips in concentration and crossing my legs at the knee.

III

One day my mother caught me standing in the middle of my bedroom doing an imita- 25 tion of Mary Injijikian, a dark, overeager Armenian girl with whom I believed myself to be in love, not only because she was pretty but because I wanted to be like her. Col-lector of effortless A's, Mary seemed to know all the answers in class. Before the teacher had even finished asking a question, Mary would let out a little grunt and practically levitate out of her seat, as if her hand were filled with helium. "Could we please hear from someone else today besides Miss Injijikian," the teacher would say. *Miss Injijikian.* Those were the words I was repeating over and over to myself when my mother caught me. To utter them was rhythmic, delicious, and under their spell I raised my hand and wiggled like Mary. I heard a cough and spun around. My mother froze in the doorway. She clutched the folded sheets to her stomach and turned without saying a word. My sudden flush of shame confused me. Weren't boys supposed to swoon over girls? Hadn't I seen babbling, heartsick men in a dozen movies?

Shortly after the Injijikian incident, my parents decided to send me to gymnastics class at the Los Angeles Athletic Club, a brick relic of a building on Olive Street. One of the oldest establishments of its kind in Los Angeles, the club prohibited women from the premises. My parents didn't have to say it aloud: they hoped a fraternal atmosphere would toughen me up and tilt me toward the male side of my nature.

My father drove me downtown so I could sign up for the class, meet the instruc-tor, and get a tour of the place. On the way there, he reminisced about sports. Since he'd grown up in a rough Philadelphia neighborhood, sports consisted of kick-the-can or rolling a hoop down the street with a stick. The more he talked about his physical prowess, the more convinced I became that my daydreams and shyness were a disappointment to him.

The hushed lobby of the athletic club was paneled in dark wood. A few solitary figures were hidden in wing chairs. My father and I introduced ourselves to a man at the front desk who seemed unimpressed by our presence. His aloofness unnerved me, which wasn't hard considering that no matter how my parents put it, I knew their sending me here was a form of disapproval, a way of banishing the part of me they didn't care to know.

A call went out over the intercom for someone to show us around. While we waited, I noticed that the sand in the standing ashtrays had been raked into perfect furrows. The glossy leaves of the potted plants looked as if they'd been polished by hand. The place seemed more like a well-tended hotel than an atheletic club. Finally, a stoop-shouldered old man hobbled toward us, his head shrouded in a cloud of white hair. He wore a T-shirt that said "Instructor"; his arms were so wrinkled and anemic, I thought I might have misread it. While we followed him to the elevator, I readjusted my expectations, which had involved fantasies of a hulking drill sergeant barking orders at a flock of scrawny boys.

The instructor, mumbling to himself and never turning around to see if we were   30
behind him, showed us where the gymnastics class took place. I'm certain the building was big, but the size of the room must be exaggerated by a trick of memory, because when I envision it, I picture a vast and windowless warehouse. Mats covered the wooden floor. Here and there, in remote and lonely pools of light, stood a pommel horse, a balance beam, and parallel bars. Tiers of bleachers rose into darkness. Unlike the cloistered air of a closet, the room seemed incomplete without a crowd.

Next we visited the dressing room, empty except for a naked middle-aged man. He sat on a narrow bench and clipped his formidable toenails. Moles dotted his back. He glistened like a fish.

We continued to follow the instructor down an aisle lined with numbered lockers. At the far end, steam billowed from the doorway that led to the showers. Fresh towels stacked on a nearby table made me think of my mother; I knew she liked to have me at home with her—I was often her only companion—and I resented her complicity in the plan to send me here.

The tour ended when the instructor gave me a sign-up sheet. Only a few names preceded mine. They were signatures, or so I imagined, of other soft and wayward sons.

IV

When the day of the first gymnastics class arrived, my mother gave me money and a gym bag and sent me to the corner of Hollywood and Western to wait for a bus. The sun was bright, the traffic heavy. While I sat there, an argument raged inside my head, the familiar, battering debate between the wish to be like other boys and the wish to be like myself. Why shouldn't I simply get up and go back home, where I'd be left alone to read and think? On the other hand, wouldn't life be easier if I liked athletics, or learned to like them?

No sooner did I steel my resolve to get on the bus than I thought of something bet-   35
ter: I could spend the morning wandering through Woolworth's, then tell my parents I'd gone to the class. But would my lie stand up to scrutiny? As I practiced describing

phantom gymnastics, I became aware of a car circling the block. It was a large car in whose shaded interior I could barely make out the driver, but I thought it might be the man who owned the local pet store. I'd often gone there on the pretext of looking at the cocker spaniel puppies huddled together in their pen, but I really went to gawk at the owner, whose tan chest, in the V of his shirt, was the place I most wanted to rest my head. Every time the man moved, counting stock or writing a receipt, his shirt parted, my mouth went dry, and I smelled the musk of sawdust and dogs.

I found myself hoping that the driver was the man who ran the pet store. I was thrilled by the unlikely possibility that the sight of me, slumped on a bus bench in my T-shirt and shorts, had caused such a man to circle the block. Up to that point in my life, lovemaking hovered somewhere in the future, an impulse a boy might aspire to but didn't indulge. And there I was, sitting on a bus bench in the middle of the city, dreaming I could seduce an adult. I showered the owner of the pet store with kisses and, as aquariums bubbled, birds sang, and mice raced in a wire wheel, slipped my hand beneath his shirt. The roar of traffic brought me to my senses. I breathed deeply and blinked against the sun. I crossed my legs at the knee in order to hide an erection. My fantasy left me both drained and changed. The continent of sex had drifted closer.

The car made another round. This time the driver leaned across the passenger seat and peered at me through the window. He was a complete stranger, whose gaze filled me with fear. It wasn't the surprise of not recognizing him that frightened me, it was what I did recognize—the unmistakable shame in his expression, and the weary temptation that drove him in circles. Before the car behind him honked, he mouthed "hello" and cocked his head. What now, he seemed to be asking. A bold, unbearable question.

I bolted to my feet, slung the gym bag over my shoulder, and hurried toward home. Now and then I turned around to make sure he wasn't trailing me, both relieved and disappointed when I didn't see his car. Even after I became convinced that he wasn't at my back—my sudden flight had scared him off—I kept turning around to see what was making me so nervous, as if I might spot the source of my discomfort somewhere on the street. I walked faster and faster, trying to outrace myself. Eventually, the bus I was supposed to have taken roared past. Turning the corner, I watched it bob eastward.

Closing the kitchen door behind me, I vowed never to leave home again. I was resolute in this decision without fully understanding why, or what it was I hoped to avoid; I was only aware of the need to hide and a vague notion, fading fast, that my trouble had something to do with sex. Already the mechanism of self-deception was at work. By the time my mother rushed into the kitchen to see why I'd returned so early, the thrill I'd felt while waiting for the bus had given way to indignation.

I poured out the story of the man circling the block and protested, with perhaps 40 too great a passion, my own innocence. "I was just sitting there," I said again and again. I was so determined to deflect suspicion away from myself, and to justify my missing the class, that I portrayed the man as a grizzled pervert who drunkenly veered from lane to lane as he followed me halfway home.

My mother cinched her housecoat. She seemed moved and shocked by what I told her, if a bit incredulous, which prompted me to be more dramatic. "It wouldn't be safe," I insisted, "for me to wait at the bus stop again."

No matter how overwrought my story, I knew my mother wouldn't question it, wouldn't bring the subject up again; sex of any kind, especially sex between a man and a boy, was simply not discussed in our house. The gymnastics class, my parents agreed, was something I could do another time.

And so I spent the remainder of that summer at home with my mother, stirring cake batter, holding the dustpan, helping her fold the sheets. For a while I was proud of myself for engineering a reprieve from the athletic club. But as the days wore on, I began to see that my mother had wanted me with her all along, and forcing that to happen wasn't such a feat. Soon a sense of compromise set in; by expressing disgust for the man in the car, I'd expressed disgust for an aspect of myself. Now I had all the time in the world to sit around and contemplate my desire for men. The days grew long and stifling and hot, an endless sentence of self-examination.

Only trips to the pet store offered any respite. Every time I went there, I was too electrified with longing to think about longing in the abstract. The bell tinkled above the door, animals stirred within their cages, and the handsome owner glanced up from his work.

V

I handed my father the *Herald*. He opened the paper and disappeared behind it. My mother stirred her coffee and sighed. She gazed at the sweltering passersby and probably thought herself lucky. I slid into the vinyl booth and took my place beside my parents.

For a moment, I considered asking them about what had happened on the street, but they would have reacted with censure and alarm, and I sensed there was more to the story than they'd ever be willing to tell me. Men in dresses were only the tip of the iceberg. Who knew what other wonders existed—a boy, for example, who wanted to kiss a man—exceptions the world did its best to keep hidden.

It would be years before I heard the word "transvestite," so I struggled to find a word for what I'd seen. "He-she" came to mind, as lilting as "Injijikian." "Burl's" would have been perfect, like "boys" and "girls" spliced together, but I can't claim to have thought of this back then.

I must have looked stricken as I tried to figure it all out, because my mother put down her coffee cup and asked if I was O.K. She stopped just short of feeling my forehead. I assured her I was fine, but something within me had shifted, had given way to a heady doubt. When the waitress came and slapped down our check—"Thank You," it read, "Dine out more often"—I wondered if her lofty hairdo or the breasts on which her nametag quaked were real. Wax carnations bloomed at every table. Phony wood paneled the walls. Plastic food sat in a display case: fried eggs, a hamburger sandwich, a sundae topped with a garish cherry. ●

Explorations of the Text

1. How do societal and familial expectations concerning gender roles shape the identities and actions of the protagonists in these sections?

2. How are the struggles of the protagonists with their sexual identities similar or different? Which characters seem to be most comfortable with their sexual orientation? With their sexual selves?

3. In "Burl's" Cooper's eight-year-old persona perceives the "hazy border between the sexes," stating that "sex . . . didn't seem to be an absolute fact so much as a pleasant, recurring accident." In what ways does *M Butterfly* portray this "hazy border"? How do other works in this cluster depict the fluidity of sexual identity?

4. Several of the works present the idea of pretense and role playing as a predominant force in relationships. What roles do characters adopt? What roles do the characters reject?

5. How do longing and desire exert their hold on the protagonists?

6. In "Drinking Coffee Elsewhere," in "Grandma's Tales," and in *M Butterfly*, character foils exist: Heidi in "Drinking Coffee Elsewhere," Nancy in "Grandma's Tales," and Song Liling in *M Butterfly*. What are their roles in these works? What do they reveal about the personalities, attitude, and internal struggles of the main characters?

7. In "Drinking Coffee Elsewhere," the main character, Dina, retreats to a world of her own—her words—"always rewound and erased, rewritten and revised." How do other characters in the works in this cluster live in fantasy worlds? What purpose do these constructed worlds serve in their lives? How do the fantasy worlds collide with reality?

8. How do class and race figure in the internal conflicts of the protagonists?

9. In "Arts of the Contact Zone," Mary Louise Pratt defines a "contact zone" as a "social space where cultures meet, clash, and grapple with each other, often in contexts of highly asymmetrical relations of power, such as colonialism, slavery, or their aftermaths as they are lived out in many parts of the world today." In such a space, patterns of domination and submission exist. Explore this motif in several works in this cluster.

The Reading/Writing Connection

1. "Think" Topic: Explore the theme of the outsider as presented in several works in this cluster.

2. "Think" Topic: Examine the ways in which protagonists in these works adopt different roles and identities. How do they behave differently based on their new roles? How do you change your behavior in different social situations or with different people? Does your sense of yourself change? In what ways?

3. Develop a character sketch of an elderly figure in your life whom you have been influenced by. Focus on his/her appearance, past history, actions, interactions with others, values and attitudes, and impact on your development.

4. Freewrite: What are the different ways that people can be reborn?

Ideas for Writing

1. Explore the tension between reality and illusion as presented in several works in this cluster.

2. **Write an Argument:** In "Grandma's Tales," Grandma talks about the three wars that she lived through, and, consequently, the three very different stages of her life and of her development of selfhood. She talks about having "a second chance." Based on your observations and experiences, do you think people get "second chance[s]" in their lives? Argue pro or con.

3. Respond to this question from "Grandma's Tales": "And wasn't epic loss what made us tell our stories?" Do you think storytelling arises from a sense of "loss"? What are other reasons for creating and telling stories?

FICTION

Anton Chekhov   *(1860–1904)*   Translated by David Magarshack

Lady with Lapdog   *1899*

I

The appearance on the front of a new arrival—a lady with a lapdog—became the topic of general conversation. Dmitry Dmitrich Gurov, who had been a fortnight in Yalta[1] and got used to its ways, was also interested in new arrivals. One day, sitting on the terrace of Vernet's restaurant, he saw a young woman walking along the promenade; she was fair, not very tall, and wore a toque;[2] behind her trotted a white pomeranian.

Later he came across her in the park and in the square several times a day. She was always alone, always wearing the same toque, followed by the white pomeranian. No one knew who she was, and she became known simply as the lady with the lapdog.

"If she's here without her husband and without any friends," thought Gurov, "it wouldn't be a bad idea to strike up an acquaintance with her."

He was not yet forty, but he had a twelve-year-old daughter and two schoolboy sons. He had been married off when he was still in his second year at the university, and his wife seemed to him now to be almost twice his age. She was a tall, black-browed woman, erect, dignified, austere, and, as she liked to describe herself, a "thinking person." She was a great reader, preferred the new "advanced" spelling, called her husband by the more formal "Dimitry" and not the familiar "Dmitry"; and though he secretly considered her not particularly intelligent, narrow-minded, and inelegant, he was afraid of her and disliked being at home. He had been unfaithful to her for a long time, he was often unfaithful to her, and that was why, perhaps, he almost always spoke ill of women, and when men discussed women in his presence, he described them as *the lower breed*.

He could not help feeling that he had had enough bitter experience to have the right to call them as he pleased, but all the same without *the lower breed* he could not have existed a couple of days. He was bored and ill at ease among men, with whom he was reticent and cold, but when he was among women he felt at ease, he knew what to talk about with them and how to behave, even when he was silent in their company he experienced no feeling of constraint. There was something attractive, something elusive in his appearance, in his character and his whole person that women found interesting and irresistible; he was aware of it, and was himself drawn to them by some irresistible force.

Long and indeed bitter experience had taught him that every new affair, which at first relieved the monotony of life so pleasantly and appeared to be such a charming and light adventure, among decent people and especially among Muscovites, who are so irresolute and so hard to rouse, inevitably developed into an extremely complicated problem and finally the whole situation became rather cumbersome. But at every new

---

[1]**Yalta:** A seaport in the Ukraine on the Black Sea.   [2]**toque:** A kind of hat.

meeting with an attractive woman he forgot all about this experience, he wanted to enjoy life so badly and it all seemed so simple and amusing.

And so one afternoon, while he was having dinner at a restaurant in the park, the woman in the toque walked in unhurriedly and took a seat at the table next to him. The way she looked, walked and dressed, wore her hair, told him that she was of good social standing, that she was married, that she was in Yalta for the first time, that she was alone and bored. . . . There was a great deal of exaggeration in the stories about the laxity of morals among the Yalta visitors, and he dismissed them with contempt, for he knew that such stories were mostly made up by people who would gladly have sinned themselves if they had had any idea how to go about it; but when the woman sat down at the table three yards away from him he remembered these stories of easy conquests and excursions to the mountains and the tempting thought of a quiet and fleeting affair, an affair with a strange woman whose very name he did not know, suddenly took possession of him.

He tried to attract the attention of the dog by calling softly to it, and when the pomeranian came up to him he shook a finger at it. The pomeranian growled. Gurov again shook a finger at it.

The woman looked up at him and immediately lowered her eyes.

"He doesn't bite," she said and blushed.   10

"May I give him a bone?" he asked, and when she nodded, he said amiably: "Have you been long in Yalta?"

"About five days."

"And I am just finishing my second week here."

They said nothing for the next few minutes.

"Time flies," she said without looking at him, "and yet it's so boring here."   15

"That's what one usually hears people saying here. A man may be living in Belev and Zhizdra or some other God-forsaken hole and he isn't bored, but the moment he comes here all you hear from him is 'Oh, it's so boring! Oh, the dust!' You'd think he'd come from Granada!"

She laughed. Then both went on eating in silence, like complete strangers; but after dinner they strolled off together, and they embarked on the light playful conversation of free and contented people who do not care where they go or what they talk about. They walked, and talked about the strange light that fell on the sea: the water was of such a soft and warm lilac, and the moon threw a shaft of gold across it. They talked about how close it was after a hot day. Gurov told her that he lived in Moscow, that he was a graduate in philology but worked in a bank, that he had at one time thought of singing in a private opera company but had given up the idea, that he owned two houses in Moscow. . . . From her he learnt that she had grown up in Petersburg, but had got married in the town of S _____ , where she had been living for the past two years, that she would stay another month in Yalta, and that her husband, who also needed a rest, might join her. She was quite unable to tell him what her husband's job was, whether he served in the offices of the provincial governor or the rural council, and she found this rather amusing herself. Gurov also found out that her name and patronymic were Anna Sergeyevna.

Later, in his hotel room, he thought about her and felt sure that he would meet her again the next day. It had to be. As he went to bed he remembered that she had only recently left her boarding school, that she had been a schoolgirl like his own daughter; he recalled how much diffidence and angularity there was in her laughter and her conversation with a stranger—it was probably the first time in her life she had found herself alone, in a situation when men followed her, looked at her, and spoke to her with only one secret intention, an intention she could hardly fail to guess. He remembered her slender, weak neck, her beautiful grey eyes.

"There's something pathetic about her, all the same," he thought as he fell asleep.

II

A week had passed since their first meeting. It was a holiday. It was close indoors, while in the streets a strong wind raised clouds of dust and tore off people's hats. All day long one felt thirsty, and Gurov kept going to the terrace of the restaurant, offering Anna Sergeyevna fruit drinks and ices. There was nowhere to go.

In the evening, when the wind had dropped a little, they went to the pier to watch the arrival of the steamer. There were a great many people taking a walk on the landing pier; some were meeting friends, they had bunches of flowers in their hands. It was there that two peculiarities of the Yalta smart set at once arrested attention: the middle-aged women dressed as if they were still young girls and there was a great number of generals.

Because of the rough sea the steamer arrived late, after the sun had set, and she had to swing backwards and forwards several times before getting alongside the pier. Anna Sergeyevna looked at the steamer and the passengers through her lorgnette, as though trying to make out some friends, and when she turned to Gurov her eyes were sparkling. She talked a lot, asked many abrupt questions, and immediately forgot what it was she had wanted to know; then she lost her lorgnette in the crowd of people.

The smartly dressed crowd dispersed; soon they were all gone, the wind had dropped completely, but Gurov and Anna were still standing there as though waiting to see if someone else would come off the boat. Anna Sergeyevna was no longer talking. She was smelling her flowers without looking at Gurov.

"It's a nice evening," he said. "Where shall we go now? Shall we go for a drive?"

She made no answer.

Then he looked keenly at her and suddenly put his arms round her and kissed her on the mouth. He felt the fragrance and dampness of the flowers and immediately looked around him fearfully; had anyone seen them?

"Let's go to your room," he said softly.

And both walked off quickly.

It was very close in her hotel room, which was full of the smell of the scents she had bought in a Japanese shop. Looking at her now, Gurov thought: "Life is full of strange encounters!" From his past he preserved the memory of carefree, good-natured women, whom love had made gay and who were grateful to him for the happiness he gave them, however short-lived; and of women like his wife, who made love without sincerity, with unnecessary talk, affectedly, hysterically, with such an expression, as though it were not love or passion, but something much more significant; and of two or three very beautiful, frigid women, whose faces suddenly lit up with a predatory expression, an obstinate desire to take, to snatch from life more than it could give; these were women no longer in their first youth, capricious, unreasoning, despotic, unintelligent women, and when Gurov lost interest in them, their beauty merely aroused hatred in him and the lace trimmings on their négligés looked to him then like the scales of a snake.

But here there was still the same diffidence and angularity of inexperienced youth— ³⁰ an awkward feeling; and there was also the impression of embarrassment, as if someone had just knocked at the door. Anna Sergeyevna, this lady with the lapdog, apparently regarded what had happened in a peculiar sort of way, very seriously, as though she had become a fallen woman—so it seemed to him, and he found it odd and disconcerting. Her features lengthened and drooped, and her long hair hung mournfully on either side of her face; she sank into thought in a despondent pose, like a woman taken in adultery in an old painting.

"It's wrong," she said. "You'll be the first not to respect me now."

There was a water-melon on the table. Gurov cut himself a slice and began to eat it slowly. At least half an hour passed in silence.

Anna Sergeyevna was very touching; there was an air of pure, decent, naïve woman about her, a woman who had very little experience of life; the solitary candle burning on the table scarcely lighted up her face, but it was obvious that she was unhappy.

"But, darling, why should I stop respecting you?" Gurov asked. "You don't know yourself what you're saying."

"May God forgive me," she said, and her eyes filled with tears. "It's terrible." ³⁵

"You seem to wish to justify yourself."

"How can I justify myself? I am a bad, despicable creature. I despise myself and have no thought of justifying myself. I haven't deceived my husband, I've deceived myself. And not only now. I've been deceiving myself for a long time. My husband is, I'm sure, a good and honest man, but, you see, he is a flunkey. I don't know what he does at his office, all I know is that he is a flunkey. I was only twenty when I married him, I was eaten up by curiosity, I wanted something better. There surely must be a different kind of life, I said to myself. I wanted to live. To live, to live! I was burning with curiosity. I don't think you know what I am talking about, but I swear I could no longer control myself, something was happening to me. I could not be held back. I told my husband I was ill, and I came here. . . . Here too I was going about as though in a daze, as though I was mad, and now I've become a vulgar worthless woman whom everyone has a right to despise."

Gurov could not help feeling bored as he listened to her; he was irritated by her naïve tone of voice and her repentance, which was so unexpected and so out of place; but for the tears in her eyes, he might have thought that she was joking or play-acting.

"I don't understand," he said gently, "what it is you want."

She buried her face on his chest and clung close to him. ⁴⁰

"Please, please believe me," she said. "I love a pure, honest life. I hate immorality. I don't know myself what I am doing. The common people say 'the devil led her astray,' I too can now say about myself that the devil has led me astray."

"There, there . . ." he murmured.

He gazed into her staring, frightened eyes, kissed her, spoke gently and affectionately to her, and gradually she calmed down and her cheerfulness returned; both of them were soon laughing.

Later, when they went out, there was not a soul on the promenade, the town with its cypresses looked quite dead, but the sea was still roaring and dashing itself against the shore; a single launch tossed on the waves, its lamp flickering sleepily.

They hailed a cab and drove to Oreanda. ⁴⁵

"I've just found out your surname, downstairs in the lobby," said Gurov. "Von Diederitz. Is your husband a German?"

"No. I believe his grandfather was German. He is of the Orthodox faith himself."

In Oreanda they sat on a bench not far from the church, looked down on the sea, and were silent. Yalta could scarcely be seen through the morning mist. White clouds lay motionless on the mountain tops. Not a leaf stirred on the trees, the cicadas chirped, and the monotonous, hollow roar of the sea, coming up from below, spoke of rest, of eternal sleep awaiting us all. The sea had roared like that down below when there was no Yalta or Oreanda, it was roaring now, and it would go on roaring as indifferently and hollowly when we were here no more. And in this constancy, in this complete indifference to life and death of each one of us, there is perhaps hidden the guarantee of our eternal salvation, the never-ceasing movement of life on earth, the never-ceasing movement towards perfection. Sitting beside a young woman who looked so beautiful at the break of day, soothed and enchanted by the sight of all that fairy-land scenery—the sea, the mountains, the clouds, the wide sky—Gurov reflected that, when you came to think of it, everything in the world was really really beautiful, everything but our own thoughts and actions when we lose sight of the higher aims of existence and our dignity as human beings.

Someone walked up to them, a watchman probably, looked at them, and went away. And there seemed to be something mysterious and also beautiful in this fact, too. They could see the Theodosia boat coming towards the pier, lit up by the sunrise, and with no lights.

"There's dew on the grass," said Anna Sergeyevna, breaking the silence.   50

"Yes. Time to go home."

They went back to town.

After that they met on the front every day at twelve o'clock, had lunch and dinner together, went for walks, admired the sea. She complained of sleeping badly and of her heart beating uneasily, asked the same questions, alternately worried by feelings of jealousy and by fear that he did not respect her sufficiently. And again and again in the park or in the square, when there was no one in sight, he would draw her to him and kiss her passionately. The complete idleness, these kisses in broad daylight, always having to look round for fear of someone watching them, the heat, the smell of the sea, and the constant looming into sight of idle, well-dressed, and well-fed people seemed to have made a new man of him; he told Anna Sergeyevna that she was beautiful, that she was desirable, made passionate love to her, never left her side, while she was often lost in thought and kept asking him to admit that he did not really respect her, that he was not in the least in love with her and only saw in her a vulgar woman. Almost every night they drove out of town, to Oreanda or to the waterfall; the excursion was always a success, and every time their impressions were invariably grand and beautiful.

They kept expecting her husband to arrive. But a letter came from him in which he wrote that he was having trouble with his eyes and implored his wife to return home as soon as possible. Anna Sergeyevna lost no time in getting ready for her journey home.

"It's a good thing I'm going," she said to Gurov. "It's fate."   55

She took a carriage to the railway station, and he saw her off. The drive took a whole day. When she got into the express train, after the second bell, she said:

"Let me have another look at you. . . . One last look. So."

She did not cry, but looked sad, just as if she were ill, and her face quivered.

"I'll be thinking of you, remembering you," she said. "Good-bye. You're staying, aren't you? Don't think badly of me. We are parting for ever. Yes, it must be so, for we should never have met. Well, good-bye. . . ."

The train moved rapidly out of the station; its lights soon disappeared, and a min- 60
ute later it could not even be heard, just as though everything had conspired to put a
quick end to this sweet trance, this madness. And standing alone on the platform gazing into the dark distance, Gurov listened to the chirping of the grasshoppers and the
humming of the telegraph wires with a feeling as though he had just woken up. He
told himself that this had been just one more affair in his life, just one more adventure,
and that it too was over, leaving nothing but a memory. He was moved and sad, and
felt a little penitent that the young woman, whom he would never see again, had not
been happy with him; he had been amiable and affectionate with her, but all the same
in his behavior to her, in the tone of his voice and in his caresses, there was a suspicion
of light irony, the somewhat coarse arrogance of the successful male, who was, moreover, almost twice her age. All the time she called him good, wonderful, high-minded;
evidently she must have taken him to be quite different from what he really was, which
meant that he had involuntarily deceived her.

At the railway station there was already a whiff of autumn in the air; the evening
was chilly.

"Time I went north, too," thought Gurov, as he walked off the platform. "High
time!"

III

At home in Moscow everything was already like winter: the stoves were heated, and it
was still dark in the morning when the children were getting ready to go to school and
having breakfast, so that the nurse had to light the lamp for a short time. The frosts
had set in. When the first snow falls and the first day one goes out for a ride in a sleigh,
one is glad to see the white ground, the white roofs, the air is so soft and wonderful to
breathe, and one remembers the days of one's youth. The old lime trees and birches,
white with rime, have such a benignant look, they are nearer to one's heart than cypresses and palms, and beside them one no longer wants to think of mountains and
the sea.

Gurov had been born and bred in Moscow, and he returned to Moscow on a fine
frosty day; and when he put on his fur coat and warm gloves and took a walk down
Petrovka Street, and when on Saturday evening he heard the church bells ringing, his
recent holiday trip and the places he had visited lost their charm for him. Gradually
he became immersed in Moscow life, eagerly reading three newspapers a day and declaring that he never read Moscow papers on principle. Once more, he could not resist
the attraction of restaurants, clubs, banquets, and anniversary celebrations, and once
more he felt flattered that well-known lawyers and actors came to see him and that in
the Medical Club he played cards with a professor as his partner. Once again he was
capable of eating a whole portion of the Moscow speciality of sour cabbage and meat
served in a frying-pan. . . .

Another month and, he thought, nothing but a memory would remain of Anna 65
Sergeyevna; he would remember her as through a haze and only occasionally dream of
her with a wistful smile, as he did of the others before her. But over a month passed,
winter was at its height, and he remembered her as clearly as though he had only parted
from her the day before. His memories haunted him more and more persistently. Every
time the voices of his children doing their homework reached him in his study in the
stillness of the evening, every time he heard a popular song or some music in a restau-

rant, every time the wind howled in the chimney—it all came back to him: their walks on the pier, early morning with the mist on the mountains, the Theodosia boat, and the kisses. He kept pacing the room for hours remembering it all and smiling, and then his memories turned into daydreams and the past mingled in his imagination with what was going to happen. He did not dream of Anna Sergeyevna, she accompanied him everywhere like his shadow and followed him wherever he went. Closing his eyes, he saw her as clearly as if she were before him, and she seemed to him lovelier, younger, and tenderer than she had been; and he thought that he too was much better than he had been in Yalta. In the evenings she gazed at him from the bookcase, from the fireplace, from the corner—he heard her breathing, the sweet rustle of her dress. In the street he followed women with his eyes, looking for anyone who resembled her. . . .

He was beginning to be overcome by an overwhelming desire to share his memories with someone. But at home it was impossible to talk of his love, and outside his home there was no one he could talk to. Not the tenants who lived in his house, and certainly not his colleagues in the bank. And what was he to tell them? Had he been in love then? Had there been anything beautiful, poetic, edifying, or even anything interesting about his relations with Anna Sergeyevna? So he had to talk in general terms about love and women, and no one guessed what he was driving at, and his wife merely raised her black eyebrows and said:

"Really, Dimitry, the role of a coxcomb doesn't suit you at all!"

One evening, as he left the Medical Club with his partner, a civil servant, he could not restrain himself, and said:

"If you knew what a fascinating woman I met in Yalta!"

The civil servant got into his sleigh and was about to be driven off, but suddenly he turned round and called out:

"I say!"

"Yes?"

"You were quite right; the sturgeon *was* a bit off."

These words, so ordinary in themselves, for some reason hurt Gurov's feelings: they seemed to him humiliating and indecent. What savage manners! What faces! What stupid nights! What uninteresting, wasted days! Crazy gambling at cards, gluttony, drunkenness, endless talk about one and the same thing. Business that was of no use to anyone and talk about one and the same thing absorbed the greater part of one's time and energy, and what was left in the end was a sort of dock-tailed, barren life, a sort of nonsensical existence, and it was impossible to escape from it, just as though you were in a lunatic asylum or a convict chaingang!

Gurov lay awake all night, fretting and fuming, and had a splitting headache the whole of the next day. The following nights too he slept badly, sitting up in bed thinking, or walking up and down his room. He was tired of his children, tired of the bank, he did not feel like going out anywhere or talking about anything.

In December, during the Christmas holidays, he packed his things, told his wife that he was going to Petersburg to get a job for a young man he knew, and set off for the town of S _____ . Why? He had no very clear idea himself. He wanted to see Anna Sergeyevna, to talk to her, to arrange a meeting, if possible.

He arrived in S _____ in the morning and took the best room in a hotel, with a fitted carpet of military grey cloth and an inkstand grey with dust on the table, surmounted by a horseman with raised hand and no head. The hall porter supplied him with all the necessary information: Von Diederitz lived in a house of his own in Old

Potter's Street, not far from the hotel. He lived well, was rich, kept his own carriage horses, the whole town knew him. The hall porter pronounced the name: Dridiritz.

Gurov took a leisurely walk down Old Potter's Street and found the house. In front of it was a long grey fence studded with upturned nails.

"A fence like that would make anyone wish to run away," thought Gurov, scanning the windows and the fence.

As it was a holiday, he thought, her husband was probably at home. It did not matter either way, though, for he could not very well embarrass her by calling at the house. If he were to send in a note it might fall into the hands of the husband and ruin everything. The best thing was to rely on chance. And he kept walking up and down the street and along the fence, waiting for his chance. He watched a beggar enter the gate and the dogs attack him; then, an hour later, he heard the faint indistinct sounds of a piano. That must have been Anna Sergeyevna playing. Suddenly the front door opened and an old woman came out, followed by the familiar white pomeranian. Gurov was about to call to the dog, but his heart began to beat violently and in his excitement he could not remember its name.

He went on walking up and down the street, hating the grey fence more and more, and he was already saying to himself that Anna Sergeyevna had forgotten him and had perhaps been having a good time with someone else, which was indeed quite natural for a young woman who had to look at that damned fence from morning till night. He went back to his hotel room and sat on the sofa for a long time, not knowing what to do, then he had dinner and after dinner a long sleep.

"How stupid and disturbing it all is," he thought, waking up and staring at the dark windows: it was already evening. "Well, I've had a good sleep, so what now? What am I going to do tonight?"

He sat on a bed covered by a cheap grey blanket looking exactly like a hospital blanket, and taunted himself in vexation:

"A *lady* with a lapdog! Some adventure, I must say! Serves you right!"

At the railway station that morning he had noticed a poster announcing in huge letters the first performance of *The Geisha Girl* at the local theatre. He recalled it now, and decided to go to the theatre.

"Quite possibly she goes to first nights," he thought.

The theatre was full. As in all provincial theatres, there was a mist over the chandeliers and the people in the gallery kept up a noisy and excited conversation; in the first row of the stalls stood the local dandies with their hands crossed behind their backs; here, too, in the front seat of the Governor's box, sat the Governor's daughter, wearing a feather boa, while the Governor himself hid modestly behind the portière so that only his hands were visible; the curtain stirred, the orchestra took a long time tuning up. Gurov scanned the audience eagerly as they filed in and occupied their seats.

Anna Sergeyevna came in too. She took her seat in the third row, and when Gurov glanced at her his heart missed a beat and he realized clearly that there was no one in the world nearer and dearer or more important to him than that little woman with the stupid lorgnette in her hand, who was in no way remarkable. That woman lost in a provincial crowd now filled his whole life, was his misfortune, his joy, and the only happiness that he wished for himself. Listening to the bad orchestra and the wretched violins played by second-rate musicians, he thought how beautiful she was. He thought and dreamed.

A very tall, round-shouldered young man with small whiskers had come in with Anna Sergeyevna and sat down beside her; he nodded at every step he took and seemed to be continually bowing to someone. This was probably her husband, whom in a fit of bitterness at Yalta she had called a flunkey. And indeed there was something of a lackey's obsequiousness in his lank figure, his whiskers, and the little bald spot on the top of his head. He smiled sweetly, and the gleaming insignia of some scientific society which he wore in his buttonhole looked like the number on a waiter's coat.

In the first interval the husband went out to smoke and she was left in her seat. 90 Gurov, who also had a seat in the stalls, went up to her and said in a trembling voice and with a forced smile:

"Good evening!"

She looked up at him and turned pale, then looked at him again in panic, unable to believe her eyes, clenching her fan and lorgnette in her hand and apparently trying hard not to fall into a dead faint. Both were silent. She sat and he stood, frightened by her embarrassment and not daring to sit down beside her. The violinists and the flautist began tuning their instruments, and they suddenly felt terrified, as though they were being watched from all the boxes. But a moment later she got up and walked rapidly towards one of the exits; he followed her, and both of them walked aimlessly along corridors and up and down stairs. Figures in all sorts of uniforms—lawyers, teachers, civil servants, all wearing badges—flashed by them: ladies, fur coats hanging on pegs, the cold draught bringing with it the odour of cigarette-ends. Gurov, whose heart was beating violently, thought:

"Oh, Lord, what are all these people, that orchestra, doing here?"

At that moment, he suddenly remembered how after seeing Anna Sergeyevna off he had told himself that evening at the station that all was over and that they would never meet again. But how far they still were from the end!

She stopped on a dark, narrow staircase with a notice over it: "To the Upper 95 Circle."

"How you frightened me!" she said, breathing heavily, still looking pale and stunned. "Oh, dear, how you frightened me! I'm scarcely alive. Why did you come? Why?"

"But, please, try to understand, Anna," he murmured hurriedly. "I beg you, please, try to understand. . . ."

She looked at him with fear, entreaty, love, looked at him intently, so as to fix his features firmly in her mind.

"I've suffered so much," she went on, without listening to him. "I've been thinking of you all the time. The thought of you kept me alive. And yet I tried so hard to forget you—why, oh, why did you come?"

On the landing above two schoolboys were smoking and looking down, but Gurov 100 did not care. He drew Anna Sergeyevna towards him and began kissing her face, her lips, her hands.

"What are you doing? What are you doing?" she said in horror, pushing him away. "We've both gone mad. You must go back tonight, this minute. I implore you, by all that's sacred . . . Somebody's coming!"

Somebody was coming up the stairs.

"You must go back," continued Anna Sergeyevna in a whisper. "Do you hear? I'll come to you in Moscow. I've never been happy, I'm unhappy now, and I shall never be happy, never! So please don't make me suffer still more. I swear I'll come to you in Moscow. But now we must part. Oh, my sweet, my darling, we must part!"

She pressed his hand and went quickly down the stairs, looking back at him all the time, and he could see from the expression in her eyes that she really was unhappy.

Gurov stood listening for a short time, and when all was quiet he went to look for his coat and left the theatre.

IV

Anna Sergeyevna began going to Moscow to see him. Every two or three months she   105
left the town of S _____ , telling her husband that she was going to consult a Moscow gynaecologist, and her husband believed and did not believe her. In Moscow she stayed at the Slav Bazaar and immediately sent a porter in a red cap to inform Gurov of her arrival. Gurov went to her hotel, and no one in Moscow knew about it.

One winter morning he went to her hotel as usual (the porter had called with his message at his house the evening before, but he had not been in). He had his daughter with him, and he was glad of the opportunity of taking her to school, which was on the way to the hotel. Snow was falling in thick wet flakes.

"It's three degrees above zero," Gurov was saying to his daughter, "and yet it's snowing. But then, you see, it's only warm on the earth's surface, in the upper layers of the atmosphere the temperature's quite different."

"Why isn't there any thunder in winter, Daddy?"

He explained that, too. As he was speaking, he kept thinking that he was going to meet his mistress and not a living soul knew about it. He led a double life: one for all who were interested to see, full of conventional truth and conventional deception, exactly like the lives of his friends and acquaintances; and another which went on in secret. And by a kind of strange concatenation of circumstances, possibly quite by accident, everything that was important, interesting, essential, everything about which he was sincere and did not deceive himself, everything that made up the quintessence of his life, went on in secret, while everything that was a lie, everything that was merely the husk in which he hid himself to conceal the truth, like his work at the bank, for instance, his discussions at the club, his ideas of the lower breed, his going to anniversary functions with his wife—all that happened in the sight of all. He judged others by himself, did not believe what he saw, and was always of the opinion that every man's real and most interesting life went on in secret, under cover of night. The personal, private life of an individual was kept a secret, and perhaps that was partly the reason why civilized man was so anxious that his personal secrets should be respected.

Having seen his daughter off to her school, Gurov went to the Slav Bazaar. He took   110
off his fur coat in the cloakroom, went upstairs, and knocked softly on the door. Anna Sergeyevna, wearing the grey dress he liked most, tired out by her journey and by the suspense of waiting for him, had been expecting him since the evening before; she was pale, looked at him without smiling, but was in his arms the moment he went into the room. Their kiss was long and lingering, as if they had not seen each other for two years.

"Well," he asked, "how are you getting on there? Anything new?"

"Wait, I'll tell you in a moment. . . . I can't . . ."

She could not speak because she was crying. She turned away from him and pressed her handkerchief to her eyes.

"Well, let her have her cry," he thought, sitting down in an armchair. "I'll wait."

Then he rang the bell and ordered tea; while he was having his tea, she was still   115
standing there with her face to the window. She wept because she could not control her emotions, because she was bitterly conscious of the fact that their life was so sad: they could only meet in secret, they had to hide from people, like thieves! Was not their life ruined?

"Please stop crying!" he said.

It was quite clear to him that their love would not come to an end for a long time, if ever. Anna Sergeyevna was getting attached to him more and more strongly, she worshipped him, and it would have been absurd to tell her that all this would have to come to an end one day. She would not have believed it, anyway.

He went up to her and took her by the shoulders, wishing to be nice to her, to make her smile; and at that moment he caught sight of himself in the looking glass.

His hair was already beginning to turn grey. It struck him as strange that he should have aged so much, that he should have lost his good looks in the last few years. The shoulders on which his hands lay were warm and quivering. He felt so sorry for this life, still so warm and beautiful, but probably soon to fade and wilt like his own. Why did she love him so? To women he always seemed different from what he was, and they loved in him not himself, but the man their imagination conjured up and whom they had eagerly been looking for all their lives; and when they discovered their mistake they still loved him. And not one of them had ever been happy with him. Time had passed, he had met women, made love to them, parted from them, but not once had he been in love; there had been everything between them, but no love.

It was only now, when his hair was beginning to turn grey, that he had fallen in love properly, in good earnest for the first time in his life.

He and Anna Sergeyevna loved each other as people do who are very dear and near, as man and wife or close friends love each other; they could not help feeling that fate itself had intended them for one another, and they were unable to understand why he should have a wife and she a husband; they were like two migrating birds, male and female, who had been caught and forced to live in separate cages. They had forgiven each other what they had been ashamed of in the past, and forgave each other everything in their present, and felt that this love of theirs had changed them both.

Before, when he felt depressed, he had comforted himself by all sorts of arguments that happened to occur to him on the spur of the moment, but now he had more serious things to think of, he felt profound compassion, he longed to be sincere, tender. . . .

"Don't cry, my sweet," he said. "That'll do, you've had your cry. . . . Let's talk now, let's think of something."

Then they had a long talk. They tried to think how they could get rid of the necessity of hiding, telling lies, living in different towns, not seeing one another for so long. How were they to free themselves from their intolerable chains?

"How? How?" he asked himself, clutching at his head. "How?"

And it seemed to them that in only a few more minutes a solution would be found and a new, beautiful life would begin; but both of them knew very well that the end was still a long, long way away and that the most complicated and difficult part was only just beginning. ●

Explorations of the Text

1. Analyze Dmitry Gurov's attitude toward women in Part I. Why has he been "unfaithful" to his wife? Why does he describe women as the "lower breed"?

2. Discuss Anna Sergeyevna's character. Why does she have an affair with Gurov?

3. After lovemaking, why does Anna consider herself "a bad, despicable creature"? Is Gurov sympathetic to her?

4. Explain the symbolism of the landscape of Oreanda.

5. After they return to their homes and spouses, do the feelings of Anna and

Gurov for each other change? Do they have a deep commitment to each other? Are they deluded?

6. What critique of Russian society and culture is apparent in the story?

The Reading/Writing Connection

1. "Think" Topic: With which character do you most sympathize? Why?

2. In a journal entry, explore a love relationship that changed your life or that changed you.

Ideas for Writing

1. Chekhov said about his fictional method that he was not a judge of human character; he simply presented problems. Does this story support his view of his fictional strategy?

2. Chekhov is considered a master of the short story. What are his strengths as a fiction writer? (See the evaluation checklist in Chapter 10.)

Ernest Hemingway *(1899–1961)*

Hills Like White Elephants *1927*

The hills across the valley of the Ebro[1] were long and white. On this side there was no shade and no trees and the station was between two lines of rails in the sun. Close against the side of the station there was the warm shadow of the building and a curtain, made of strings of bamboo beads, hung across the open door into the bar, to keep out flies. The American and the girl with him sat at a table in the shade, outside the building. It was very hot and the express from Barcelona would come in forty minutes. It stopped at this junction for two minutes and went on to Madrid.

"What should we drink?" the girl asked. She had taken off her hat and put it on the table.

"It's pretty hot," the man said.

"Let's drink beer."

"Dos cervezas,"[2] the man said into the curtain.

"Big ones?" a woman asked from the doorway.

"Yes. Two big ones."

The woman brought two glasses of beer and two felt pads. She put the felt pads and the beer glasses on the table and looked at the man and the girl. The girl was looking off at the line of hills. They were white in the sun and the country was brown and dry.

"They look like white elephants," she said.

"I've never seen one," the man drank his beer.

"No, you wouldn't have."

"I might have," the man said. "Just because you say I wouldn't have doesn't prove anything."

5

10

---

[1] **Ebro:** River in Spain.   [2] **Dos cervezas:** Two beers.

The girl looked at the bead curtain. "They've painted something on it," she said. "What does it say?"

"Anis del Toro. It's a drink."

"Could we try it?"   15

The man called "Listen" through the curtain. The woman came out from the bar. "Four reales."

"We want two Anis del Toro."

"With water?"

"Do you want it with water?"   20

"I don't know," the girl said. "Is it good with water?"

"It's all right."

"You want them with water?" asked the woman.

"Yes, with water."

"It tastes like licorice," the girl said and put the glass down.   25

"That's the way with everything."

"Yes," said the girl. "Everything tastes of licorice. Especially all the things you've waited so long for, like absinthe."

"Oh, cut it out."

"You started it," the girl said. "I was being amused. I was having a fine time."

"Well, let's try and have a fine time."   30

"All right. I was trying. I said the mountains looked like white elephants. Wasn't that bright?"

"That was bright."

"I wanted to try this new drink. That's all we do, isn't it—look at things and try new drinks?"

"I guess so."

The girl looked across the hills.   35

"They're lovely hills," she said. "They don't really look like white elephants. I just meant the coloring of their skin through the trees."

"Should we have another drink?"

"All right."

The warm wind blew the bead curtain against the table.

"The beer's nice and cool," the man said.   40

"It's lovely," the girl said.

"It's really an awfully simple operation, Jig," the man said. "It's not really an operation at all."

The girl looked at the ground the table legs rested on.

"I know you wouldn't mind it, Jig. It's really not anything. It's just to let the air in."

The girl did not say anything.   45

"I'll go with you and I'll stay with you all the time. They just let the air in and then it's all perfectly natural."

"Then what will we do afterward?"

"We'll be fine afterward. Just like we were before."

"What makes you think so?"

"That's the only thing that bothers us. It's the only thing that's made us   50
unhappy."

The girl looked at the bead curtain, put her hand out and took hold of two of the strings of beads.

"And you think then we'll be all right and be happy."

"I know we will. You don't have to be afraid. I've known lots of people that have done it."

"So have I," said the girl. "And afterward they were all happy."

"Well," the man said, "if you don't want to you don't have to. I wouldn't have you do it if you didn't want to. But I know it's perfectly simple." 55

"And you really want to?"

"I think it's the best thing to do. But I don't want you to do it if you don't really want to."

"And if I do it you'll be happy and things will be like they were and you'll love me?"

"I love you now. You know I love you."

"I know. But if I do it, then it will be nice again if I say things are like white elephants, and you'll like it?" 60

"I'll love it. I love it now but I just can't think about it. You know how I get when I worry."

"If I do it you won't ever worry?"

"I won't worry about that because it's perfectly simple."

"Then I'll do it. Because I don't care about me."

"What do you mean?" 65

"I don't care about me."

"Well, I care about you."

"Oh, yes. But I don't care about me. And I'll do it and then everything will be fine."

The girl stood up and walked to the end of the station. Across, on the other side, were fields of grain and trees along the banks of the Ebro. Far away, beyond the river, were mountains. The shadow of a cloud moved across the field of grain and she saw the river through the trees.

"And we could have all this," she said. "And we could have everything and every day we make it more impossible." 70

"What did you say?"

"I said we could have everything."

"We can have everything."

"No, we can't."

"We can have the whole world." 75

"No, we can't."

"We can go everywhere."

"No, we can't. It isn't ours any more."

"It's ours."

"No, it isn't. And once they take it away, you never get it back." 80

"But they haven't taken it away."

"We'll wait and see."

"Come on back in the shade," he said. "You mustn't feel that way."

"I don't feel any way," the girl said. "I just know things."

"I don't want you to do anything that you don't want to do—" 85

"Nor that isn't good for me," she said. "I know. Could we have another beer?"

"All right. But you've got to realize—"

"I realize," the girl said. "Can't we maybe stop talking?"

They sat down at the table and the girl looked across at the hills on the dry side of the valley and the man looked at her and at the table.

"You've got to realize," he said, "that I don't want you to do it if you don't want to. I'm perfectly willing to go through with it if it means anything to you."

"Doesn't it mean anything to you? We could get along."

"Of course it does. But I don't want anybody but you. I don't want any one else. And I know it's perfectly simple."

"Yes, you know it's perfectly simple."

"It's all right for you to say that, but I do know it."

"Would you do something for me now?"

"I'd do anything for you."

"Would you please please please please please please please stop talking?"

He did not say anything but looked at the bags against the wall of the station. There were labels on them from all the hotels where they had spent nights.

"But I don't want you to," he said, "I don't care anything about it."

"I'll scream," the girl said.

The woman came out through the curtains with two glasses of beer and put them down on the damp felt pads. "The train comes in five minutes," she said.

"What did she say?" asked the girl.

"That the train is coming in five minutes."

The girl smiled brightly at the woman, to thank her.

"I'd better take the bags over to the other side of the station," the man said. She smiled at him.

"All right. Then come back and we'll finish the beer."

He picked up the two heavy bags and carried them around the station to the other tracks. He looked up the tracks but could not see the train. Coming back, he walked through the barroom, where people waiting for the train were drinking. He drank an Anis at the bar and looked at the people. They were all waiting reasonably for the train. He went out through the bead curtain. She was sitting at the table and smiled at him.

"Do you feel better?" he asked.

"I feel fine," she said. "There's nothing wrong with me. I feel fine." ●

Explorations of the Text

1. What mood is created at the beginning of the story?

2. Examine Jig's and the man's dialogue before the discussion of the operation. What can you infer about the woman's and the man's characters?

3. What is "it"? "the operation"? How does the symbol of the "white elephant" relate to the operation?

4. What is the source of the conflict between Jig and the man?

5. Discuss Jig's state of mind. What are her concerns? Isolate statements that reveal her feelings.

6. What are the man's reasons for wanting her to have "the operation"? Discuss his attitudes toward the woman and their relationship.

7. Why does she want him to "please . . . please stop talking"?

8. Explain the irony of Jig's last statement: "I feel fine. . . . There's nothing wrong with me. I feel fine."

9. Analyze the symbolism of the setting. How does setting develop themes of the story?

The Reading/Writing Connection

1. In a journal entry, write about what you would say to them if you were a marriage counselor.
2. Does Hemingway sympathize with either character? How can you tell?
3. Create a **monologue** in the voice of Jig or of the man several months or years later.

Ideas for Writing

1. Compare Hemingway's view of relationships with Braverman's in "Pagan Night."
2. Why does Hemingway choose to present the story almost totally in **dialogue**? Evaluate this technique.

James Joyce *(1882–1941)*

Eveline *1914*

She sat at the window watching the evening invade the avenue. Her head was leaned against the window curtains and in her nostrils was the odour of dusty cretonne.[1] She was tired.

Few people passed. The man out of the last house passed on his way home; she heard his footsteps clacking along the concrete pavement and afterwards crunching on the cinder path before the new red houses. One time there used to be a field there in which they used to play every evening with other people's children. Then a man from Belfast[2] bought the field and built houses in it—not like their little brown houses but bright brick houses with shining roofs. The children of the avenue used to play together in that field—the Devines, the Waters, the Dunns, little Keogh the cripple, she and her brothers and sisters. Ernest, however, never played: he was too grown up. Her father used often to hunt them in out of the field with his blackthorn stick; but usually little Keogh used to keep *nix*[3] and call out when he saw her father coming. Still they seemed to have been rather happy then. Her father was not so bad then; and besides, her mother was alive. That was a long time ago; she and her brothers and sisters were all grown up; her mother was dead. Tizzie Dunn was dead, too, and the Waters had gone back to England. Everything changes. Now she was going to go away like the others, to leave her home.

Home! She looked round the room, reviewing all its familiar objects which she had dusted once a week for so many years, wondering where on earth all the dust came from. Perhaps she would never see again those familiar objects from which she had never dreamed of being divided. And yet during all those years she had never found out the name of the priest whose yellowing photograph hung on the wall above the broken harmonium beside the coloured print of the promises made to Blessed Margaret Mary

---

[1]**cretonne:** A heavy cotton material used for draperies and slipcovers.   [2]**Belfast:** Capital of present-day Northern Ireland; a city in Ireland before the partition.   [3]*nix:* Keep watch (slang expression).

Alacoque. He had been a school friend of her father. Whenever he showed the photograph to a visitor her father used to pass it with a casual word:

"He is in Melbourne now."

She had consented to go away, to leave her home. Was that wise? She tried to weigh each side of the question. In her home anyway she had shelter and food; she had those whom she had known all her life about her. Of course she had to work hard both in the house and at business. What would they say of her in the Stores when they found out that she had run away with a fellow? Say she was a fool, perhaps; and her place would be filled up by advertisement. Miss Gavan would be glad. She had always had an edge on her, especially whenever there were people listening.

"Miss Hill, don't you see these ladies are waiting?"

"Look lively, Miss Hill, please."

She would not cry many tears at leaving the Stores.

But in her new home, in a distant unknown country, it would not be like that. Then she would be married—she, Eveline. People would treat her with respect then. She would not be treated as her mother had been. Even now, though she was over nineteen, she sometimes felt herself in danger of her father's violence. She knew it was that that had given her the palpitations. When they were growing up he had never gone for her, like he used to go for Harry and Ernest, because she was a girl; but latterly he had begun to threaten her and say what he would do to her only for her dead mother's sake. And now she had nobody to protect her. Ernest was dead and Harry, who was in the church decorating business, was nearly always down somewhere in the country. Besides, the invariable squabble for money on Saturday nights had begun to weary her unspeakably. She always gave her entire wages—seven shillings—and Harry always sent up what he could but the trouble was to get any money from her father. He said she used to squander the money, that she had no head, that he wasn't going to give her his hard-earned money to throw about the streets, and much more, for he was usually fairly bad of a Saturday night. In the end he would give her the money and ask her had she any intention of buying Sunday's dinner. Then she had to rush out as quickly as she could and do her marketing, holding her black leather purse tightly in her hand as she elbowed her way through the crowds and returning home late under her load of provisions. She had hard work to keep the house together and to see that the two young children who had been left to her charge went to school regularly and got their meals regularly. It was hard work—a hard life—but now that she was about to leave it she did not find it a wholly undesirable life.

She was about to explore another life with Frank. Frank was very kind, manly, open-hearted. She was to go away with him by the night-boat to be his wife and to live with him in Buenos Ayres where he had a home waiting for her. How well she remembered the first time she had seen him; he was lodging in a house on the main road where she used to visit. It seemed a few weeks ago. He was standing at the gate, his peaked cap pushed back on his head and his hair tumbled forward over a face of bronze. Then they had come to know each other. He used to meet her outside the Stores every evening and see her home. He took her to see *The Bohemian Girl* and she felt elated as she sat in an unaccustomed part of the theatre with him. He was awfully fond of music and sang a little. People knew that they were courting and, when he sang about the lass that loves a sailor, she always felt pleasantly confused. He used to call her Poppens out of fun. First of all it had been an excitement for her to have a fellow and then she had begun to like him. He had tales of distant countries. He had started as a deck boy at a pound a month on a ship of the Allan Line going out to Canada. He told her the names of the ships he had been on and the names of the different services. He had sailed through the Straits of Magellan[4] and he told her stories of the terrible Patagonians.[5] He had fallen on his feet in Buenos Ayres, he said, and had come over to the old country just for a holiday. Of course, her father had found out the affair and had forbidden her to have anything to say to him.

"I know these sailor chaps," he said.

One day he had quarrelled with Frank and after that she had to meet her lover secretly.

The evening deepened in the avenue. The white of two letters in her lap grew indistinct. One was to Harry; the other was to her father. Ernest had been her favourite but she liked Harry too. Her father was becoming old lately, she noticed; he would miss her. Sometimes he could be very nice. Not long before, when she had been laid up for a day, he had read her out a ghost story and made toast for her at the fire. Another day, when their mother was alive, they had all gone for a picnic to the Hill of Howth. She remembered her father putting on her mother's bonnet to make the children laugh.

Her time was running out but she continued to sit by the window, leaning her head against the window curtain, inhaling the odour of dusty cretonne. Down far in the avenue she could hear a street organ playing. She knew the air. Strange that it should come that very night to remind her of the promise to her mother, her promise to keep the home together as long as she could. She remembered the last night of her mother's illness; she was again in the close dark room at the other side of the hall and outside she heard a melancholy air of Italy. The organ-player had been ordered to go away and given sixpence. She remembered her father strutting back into the sickroom saying:

"Damned Italians! coming over here!"   15

As she mused the pitiful vision of her mother's life laid its spell on the very quick of her being—that life of commonplace sacrifices closing in final craziness. She trembled as she heard again her mother's voice saying constantly with foolish insistence:

"Derevaun Seraun! Derevaun Seraun!"[6]

She stood up in a sudden impulse of terror. Escape! She must escape! Frank would save her. He would give her life, perhaps love, too. But she wanted to live. Why should she be unhappy? She had a right to happiness. Frank would take her in his arms, fold her in his arms. He would save her.

She stood among the swaying crowd in the station at the North Wall. He held her hand and she knew that he was speaking to her, saying something about the passage over and over again. The station was full of soldiers with brown baggages. Through the wide doors of the sheds she caught a glimpse of the black mass of the boat, lying in beside the quay[7] wall, with illumined portholes. She answered nothing. She felt her cheek pale and cold and, out of a maze of distress, she prayed to God to direct her, to show her what was her duty. The boat blew a long mournful whistle into the mist.

---

[4]**Straits of Magellan:** Channel linking the Atlantic and Pacific oceans at the tip of South America.   [5]**Patagonians:** People inhabiting the region of Patagonia in southern Argentina and Chile.   [6]**Derevaun Seraun!:** This exclamation, according to scholars, has never been completely understood; it is assumed to be gibberish spoken by the mother in her delirium.   [7]**quay:** A landing place beside a body of water; a wharf.

If she went, tomorrow she would be on the sea with Frank, steaming toward Buenos Ayres. Their passage had been booked. Could she still draw back after all he had done for her? Her distress awoke a nausea in her body and she kept moving her lips in silent fervent prayer.

A bell clanged upon her heart. She felt him seize her hand: 20
"Come!"

All the seas of the world tumbled about her heart. He was drawing her into them: he would drown her. She gripped with both hands at the iron railing.

"Come!"

No! no! No! It was impossible. Her hands clutched the iron in frenzy. Amid the seas she sent a cry of anguish!

"Eveline! Evvy!" 25

He rushed beyond the barrier and called to her to follow. He was shouted at to go on but he still called to her. She set her white face to him, passive, like a helpless animal. Her eyes gave him no sign of love or farewell or recognition. ●

Explorations of the Text

1. How do the first two paragraphs create the setting and mood of the story? What details are most significant? What do the details suggest about Eveline's situation?

2. Why is Eveline drawn to Frank? Discuss Eveline's inner conflict.

3. Analyze the symbol of the cretonne curtain and the window.

4. Discuss the conclusion of the story. What is Eveline's epiphany? Do you think that she leaves with Frank?

The Reading/Writing Connection

1. "Think" Topic: Does Eveline leave with Frank? Create a debate in class based on this question. As preparation for the debate, list pros and cons.

2. Journal Entry: Write about leaving home. Consult Greg Delanty's poem, "Leavetaking," and Staci Ferris's Personal Response Essay in Chapter 5. What are the challenges? Rewards?

3. Continue the narrative. Write a monologue in Frank's or Eveline's voice.

Ideas for Writing

1. Write an essay on risk taking. Use your own experiences and that of two other protagonists in works from this chapter. (Consider, for example, Norma Jean in "Shiloh.")

2. Joyce is considered a master of the modern short story. How do the elements of the story (consult the checklist for fiction in Chapter 10) develop themes of the work?

3. Using criteria that you create for a successful short story, evaluate this work.

4. **Write an Argument:** Present your position about Eveline's leaving home. Use the "Think" topic as prewriting material.

Junot Díaz *(1968–)*

How to Date a Browngirl, Blackgirl, Whitegirl, or Halfie   *1996*

Wait for your brother and your mother to leave the apartment. You've already told them that you're feeling too sick to go to Union City to visit that tía who likes to squeeze your nuts. (He's gotten big, she'll say.) And even though your moms knows you ain't sick you stuck to your story until finally she said, Go ahead and stay, malcriado.

Clear the government cheese from the refrigerator. If the girl's from the Terrace stack the boxes behind the milk. If she's from the Park or Society Hill hide the cheese in the cabinet above the oven, way up where she'll never see. Leave yourself a reminder to get it out before morning or your moms will kick your ass. Take down any embarrassing photos of your family in the campo, especially the one with the half-naked kids dragging a goat on a rope leash. The kids are your cousins and by now they're old enough to understand why you're doing what you're doing. Hide the pictures of yourself with an Afro. Make sure the bathroom is presentable. Put the basket with all the crapped-on toilet paper under the sink. Spray the bucket with Lysol, then close the cabinet.

Shower, comb, dress. Sit on the couch and watch TV. If she's an outsider her father will be bringing her, maybe her mother. Neither of them want her seeing any boys from the Terrace—people get stabbed in the Terrace—but she's strong-headed and this time will get her way. If she's a whitegirl you know you'll at least get a hand job.

The directions were in your best handwriting, so her parents won't think you're an idiot. Get up from the couch and check the parking lot. Nothing. If the girl's local, don't sweat it. She'll flow over when she's good and ready. Sometimes she'll run into her other friends and a whole crowd will show up at your apartment and even though that means you ain't getting shit it will be fun anyway and you'll wish these people would come over more often. Sometimes the girl won't flow over at all and the next day in school she'll say sorry, smile and you'll be stupid enough to believe her and ask her out again.

Wait and after an hour go out to your corner. The neighborhood is full of traffic. 5 Give one of your boys a shout and when he says, Are you still waiting on that bitch? say, Hell yeah.

Get back inside. Call her house and when her father picks up ask if she's there. He'll ask, Who is this? Hang up. He sounds like a principal or a police chief, the sort of dude with a big neck, who never has to watch his back. Sit and wait. By the time your stomach's ready to give out on you, a Honda or maybe a Jeep pulls in and out she comes.

Hey, you'll say.

Look, she'll say. My mom wants to meet you. She's got herself all worried about nothing.

Don't panic. Say, Hey, no problem. Run a hand through your hair like the whiteboys do even though the only thing that runs easily through your hair is Africa. She will look good. The white ones are the ones you want the most, aren't they, but usually the out-of-towners are black, blackgirls who grew up with ballet and Girl Scouts, who have three cars in their driveways. If she's a halfie don't be surprised that her mother is white. Say, Hi. Her moms will say hi and you'll see that you don't scare her, not really. She will say that she needs easier directions to get out and even though she has the best directions in her lap give her new ones. Make her happy.

You have choices. If the girl's from around the way, take her to El Cibao for din- 10 ner. Order everything in your busted-up Spanish. Let her correct you if she's Latina and amaze her if she's black. If she's not from around the way, Wendy's will do. As you walk to the restaurant talk about school. A local girl won't need stories about the neighborhood but the other ones might. Supply the story about the loco who'd been storing canisters of tear gas in his basement for years, how one day the canisters cracked and the whole neighborhood got a dose of the military strength stuff. Don't tell her that your moms knew right away what it was, that she recognized its smell from the year the United States invaded your island.

Hope that you don't run into your nemesis, Howie, the Puerto Rican kid with the two killer mutts. He walks them all over the neighborhood and every now and then the mutts corner themselves a cat and tear it to shreds, Howie laughing as the cat flips up in the air, its neck twisted around like an owl, red meat showing through the soft fur. If his dogs haven't cornered a cat, he will walk behind you and ask, Hey, Yunior, is that your new fuckbuddy?

Let him talk. Howie weighs about two hundred pounds and could eat you if he wanted. At the field he will turn away. He has new sneakers, and doesn't want them muddy. If the girl's an outsider she will hiss now and say, What a fucking asshole. A homegirl would have been yelling back at him the whole time, unless she was shy. Either way don't feel bad that you didn't do anything. Never lose a fight on a first date or that will be the end of it.

Dinner will be tense. You are not good at talking to people you don't know. A halfie will tell you that her parents met in the Movement, will say, Back then people thought it a radical thing to do. It will sound like something her parents made her memorize. Your brother once heard that one and said, Man, that sounds like a whole lot of Uncle Tomming to me. Don't repeat this.

Put down your hamburger and say, It must have been hard.

She will appreciate your interest. She will tell you more. Black people, she will say, 15 treat me real bad. That's why I don't like them. You'll wonder how she feels about Dominicans. Don't ask. Let her speak on it and when you're both finished eating walk back into the neighborhood. The skies will be magnificent. Pollutants have made Jersey sunsets one of the wonders of the world. Point it out. Touch her shoulder and say, That's nice, right?

Get serious. Watch TV but stay alert. Sip some of the Bermúdez your father left in the cabinet, which nobody touches. A local girl may have hips and a thick ass but she won't be quick about letting you touch. She has to live in the same neighborhood you do, has to deal with you being all up in her business. She might just chill with you and then go home. She might kiss you and then go, or she might, if she's reckless, give it up, but that's rare. Kissing will suffice. A whitegirl might just give it up right then. Don't stop her. She'll take her gum out of her mouth, stick it to the plastic sofa covers and then will move close to you. You have nice eyes, she might say.

Tell her that you love her hair, that you love her skin, her lips, because, in truth, you love them more than you love your own.

She'll say, I like Spanish guys, and even though you've never been to Spain, say, I like you. You'll sound smooth.

You'll be with her until about eight-thirty and then she will want to wash up. In the bathroom she will hum a song from the radio and her waist will keep the beat against the lip of the sink. Imagine her old lady coming to get her, what she would say if she knew her daughter had just lain under you and blown your name, pronounced with her eighth-grade Spanish, into your ear. While she's in the bathroom call one of your boys and say, Lo hice, loco. Or just sit back on the couch and smile.

But usually it won't work this way. Be prepared. She will not want to kiss you. Just cool it, she'll say. The halfie might lean back, breaking away from you. She will cross her arms, say, I hate my tits. Stroke her hair but she will pull away. I don't like anybody touching my hair, she will say. She will act like somebody you don't know. In school she is known for her attention-grabbing laugh, as high and far-ranging as a gull, but here she will worry you. You will not know what to say. 20

You're the only kind of guy who asks me out, she will say. Your neighbors will start their hyena calls, now that the alcohol is in them. You and the blackboys.

Say nothing. Let her button her shirt, let her comb her hair, the sound of it stretching like a sheet of fire between you. When her father pulls in and beeps, let her go without too much of a good-bye. She won't want it. During the next hour the phone will ring. You will be tempted to pick it up. Don't. Watch the shows you want to watch, without a family around to debate you. Don't go downstairs. Don't fall asleep. It won't help. Put the government cheese back in its place before your moms kills you. ●

Explorations of the Text

1. This work presents a dramatic monologue. Analyze the speaker's point of view and tone. Is he a reliable narrator? Characterize the speaker. What do you imagine he looks like? What is he wearing? What are his interests? What is his attitude toward women? Dating?

2. Analyze his instructions for dating. For each "girl," note the specifics: his actions and the girl's behavior. What do you conclude? What do their actions reveal about class and ethnic identities?

3. How does the narrator use sex? What is implied about his view of sexuality? Masculinity? Femininity? Relationships?

4. Analyze the style of the work. Is the use of the vernacular and of commands effective?

5. Compare and contrast the main character in this work with Dalton in "Pagan Night." What are both characters searching for?

The Reading/Writing Connection

1. Create a list of instructions, a "how to" manual for dating. You may be serious, humorous, satiric, or ironic. Choose details that suggest a larger, more universal message about relationships, dating, social codes, or cultural values.

2. Create a monologue for one of the young women whom the speaker has dated.

Ideas for Writing

1. Imagine this protagonist has a session with a school counselor. What would he say?

2. **Write an Argument:** Do you think that this is a realistic portrait of the dating game? Why or why not?

Lara Vapnyar   *(1971–)*

Broccoli   *2004*

Here's another one, seduced and abandoned," Nina's husband often said, pulling a bunch of wilted, yellowed broccoli from the refrigerator shelf. He held it, pinched between two fingers, his handsome face contorted in disgust, as though it smelled.

Nina, blushing, took the broccoli away from him and threw it in the garbage. She told him she was sorry; she had been busy all week and never had time to cook. Nina worked in Manhattan. By the time she got home to Brooklyn, it was already seven-thirty, sometimes eight, and the most she could do was make her husband and herself sandwiches, or boil some meat dumplings from a Russian supermarket.

"I know," her husband said. "But why buy all these vegetables if you know you won't have time to cook them?"

Nina shrugged. She liked shopping for vegetables.

She couldn't say exactly when she'd first felt the urge—possibly two years earlier,   5
on her second day in America, when she and her husband had left her sister's Brooklyn apartment for the first time to explore the nearest shopping street. Nina's sister, who'd lived in America for fourteen years and called herself an American, assumed that Nina would be impatient to see it. "Go, go," she said. "But don't buy anything. There are two rules you have to remember in order to survive in America. First: Never buy anything in expensive stores unless they're having a fifty-per-cent-off sale. Second: Never buy anything in cheap stores."

On the unimaginatively named Avenue M, Nina and her husband browsed through stores that all looked alike to them, no matter what was being sold: food, electronics, clothes, or hardware. They seemed to be walking in and out of the same store over and over, simply to hear the doorbell chime.

It was a pale, cold February morning, and Nina was hiding her reddened nose in the fur collar of her Russian coat. She clutched her husband's elbow, stepping carefully over piles of garbage, reluctant to look up at the ashen sky or sideways at the motley signs of the shops. She was feeling dizzy and a little nauseated from the flight and the all-night talk with her sister that had followed. Only one store attracted her attention—a small Chinese grocery, with fruit and vegetables set outside on plywood stands. Colorful piles of oranges, tomatoes, cucumbers—everything was sparklingly clean and bright. Nina read the side of the box of tomatoes: "Sunripe." She was still learning English, and every new expression seemed to her exciting and rich with meaning. "Sunripe" brought to mind a vegetable patch on a summer afternoon, the smell of dark soil heated by the sun, pale-green stems bent and bursting under the weight of juicy tomatoes. She wanted to touch the tomatoes in the box to see if their skin was still warm from the sun that shone on them as they ripened. She was just reaching out her hand when her husband pulled her away to another store.

Now Nina shopped for vegetables alone every Saturday morning—her husband loved to sleep late on weekends. She drove to Eighty-sixth Street and shopped in the Chinese and Russian stores between Bay Parkway and Twenty-third Avenue. The stores all offered pretty much the same selection of produce, but Nina liked to explore them all, in search of something surprising: the occasional white asparagus, plastic baskets of gooseberries, tiny, nutlike new potatoes. On the days when there was nothing new, it was still interesting to compare the stores. In one, the onions might be large and firm but the heads of lettuce wilted and colorless. Another might have the freshest greens and onions that were soft and gray, hiding timidly in string bags.

Nina felt a thrill as soon she got out of the car and placed her feet on the sidewalk, littered with torn lettuce leaves, onion peels, and overripe tomatoes. In the stores, she walked up and down the aisles, running her fingers over tomatoes as smooth and glossy as polished furniture. She cupped avocados, feeling their lumpy peel with her palms. Sometimes she dug a fingernail into the rind of an orange until it spat out a little of its pungent juice. She avoided touching the hairy, egg-shaped kiwis and the worm-like string beans, but she liked to stroke the feathery bunches of dill and parsley and squeeze the artichokes, which felt like soft pine cones. She patted cantaloupes and she tapped watermelons with her index finger, listening to the hollow sound they made. But, most of all, Nina loved broccoli. It smelled of young spring grass, and it looked like a tree, with its hard solid stem and its luxuriant crown of tight, grainy florets.

Nina bought a bunch of broccoli every week, along with various other vegetables. [10] She carried big brown bags to her car, firmly believing that this weekend she would find time to cook. There was still Saturday afternoon ahead, and then all of Sunday. She would wash the vegetables as soon as she got home and then cook something with them—spinach gnocchi, maybe, or grilled zucchini parcels, or three-cheese broccoli gratin.

But as soon as she got home Nina found herself in a whirl of things to do. She had to shower, curl her hair, brush it out if it started to go frizzy, try on and reject several sweaters and pairs of pants, put on makeup, find her husband's missing sock, iron his shirt, check that the gas was off, and lock the door. It seemed only minutes before she found herself in the car again, on the way to a party, glancing back and forth between her husband in the driver's seat and her own reflection in the mirror on the sun visor. Her husband was deep in his thoughts, which was natural, Nina told herself, since he was driving. And her reflection was unsatisfying—despite her efforts, her hair was still frizzy, her soft-featured, round face was poorly made up, and her blue angora sweater was too tight around the armpits. Clothes bought at fifty-percent-off sales were always either the wrong size or the wrong style.

In the car, Nina rarely thought about her vegetables. They lay abandoned on the cramped refrigerator shelves: tomatoes buried under zucchinis, lettuce leaves caught in the edge of the vegetable drawer, a bunch of broccoli that wouldn't fit in the drawer sitting by itself on the third shelf.

The parties were thrown by Pavlik, a friend of Nina's husband from work, whose wife had divorced him a few years earlier. Pavlik was a heavy man with an uneven ginger-colored beard. He wore ill-fitting trousers and shirts that never seemed clean. He loved to laugh heartily and smack his friends on the back. "Don't mind the mess!" he yelled as his guests wandered through the dusty labyrinth of his house, stumbling over secondhand furniture, broken electronic equipment, and heavy volumes of Russian literature. It seemed to Nina that Pavlik's functions as a host were limited to calling out that phrase. He didn't feed or entertain his guests. People arrived with their own food and wine, their own plastic dinnerware, their own guitars, and sometimes their own poems, written on scraps of notebook paper.

None of Pavlik's guests were professional poets or musicians. Most of them worked as computer programmers, an occupation that they had taken up in America, where they found it easier and more profitable than trying to prove the value of their Russian degrees in science or the arts. Some of them, Nina's husband included, adopted a condescending attitude toward their new profession: it was boring; it was beneath them. "Computer programming, like everyone else," they answered reluctantly when asked their occupation, "but that's not what I did in my previous life." They preferred to talk about art or music or such exciting hobbies as alpinism, rafting, and photographing Alaskan sunsets.

Nina was a computer programmer, too, but she had always been a computer programmer. She didn't know much about poetry or music, and she didn't have any exciting talents or hobbies.

"My wife is a vegetable lover," Nina's husband would say, introducing her to Pavlik's circle.

Nina didn't like Pavlik's guests. The men were untidy and unattractive. They loaded their paper plates with cold cuts and smoked too much. They said the same things over and over, and it seemed to Nina that there was always a piece of ham or salami hanging out of their mouths when they talked.

The women, with one or two exceptions, were attractive, but in an unpleasant way. They were thin and sophisticated; they had straight hair; they had strong hands with long, powerful fingers, toughened by playing piano or guitar; they had soulful eyes, saddened by all the poetry they'd read; they had mysterious expressions of eternal fatigue. They had everything that Nina lacked.

Nina usually spent the evening in one corner of Pavlik's stiff sofa, away from her husband and the other guests, who sat on the floor by the cold fireplace. The sound of their laughter, their singing, and their reading floated around the room, but didn't seem to reach Nina. The food and wine, arranged on a rickety folding table by the window, were more accessible. She made frequent trips to that table, where the cold cuts were spread out on paper plates, loaves of bread sat on cutting boards, and pickles swam in glass jars. There were usually a few unopened bottles of vodka and a five-litre box of Burgundy or Chablis. The wine dripped from a little plastic faucet onto the beige carpet, forming intricate patterns, so that by the end of the party Pavlik's modest floor covering looked like a fancy Turkish rug.

When Nina and her husband first started coming to Pavlik's parties, she had joined the others by the fireplace. She'd loved to sit across from her husband and watch his face as he played the guitar. His head tilted forward, and the bangs of his dark hair fell to his half-closed eyes. From time to time, he glanced at her, and his eyes flickered through the forest of his hair like two fireflies. At those moments, Nina felt that he was playing for her alone, and the music touched her, making her skin prickle and her throat hurt.

With time, though, Nina noticed that she wasn't the only person watching her husband as he played. Other women watched, too, and in exactly the same way. Nina saw how their faces lit up under his fleeting gaze, just as hers did. Those women probably felt that he was playing for them, too, and sometimes Nina thought that they had more right to be played for by her husband than she did. When they looked over at Nina, she felt as if she were expanding, bloating, metamorphosing into an oversized exhibit of a dull, talentless woman with the wrong clothes and the wrong makeup. She knew that they were all asking themselves why this interesting, talented man had married her. Her sister didn't ask. "You were his ticket to America," she reminded Nina frequently. "Can you disprove that?"

Nina couldn't. It was true that her husband had always wanted to emigrate but, without close relatives in the United States, hadn't been able to obtain a visa. It was true that, having married Nina, he had got his visa. It was true that Nina hadn't wanted to emigrate but had yielded to her husband's wishes. It wasn't true, though, that he had married Nina for those reasons alone, and it wasn't true that he didn't love her. Nina's sister didn't know what Nina knew. She didn't know that when Nina had been in the hospital with appendicitis her husband hadn't left her room for even a minute. She had begged him to go and get some coffee or a breath of fresh air, but he had stayed with her. He'd held Nina's hand and squeezed it involuntarily every time she moaned. Nina's sister also didn't know how he'd sometimes hug Nina from behind and bury his face in her hair and whisper, "There is nothing like this. Nothing in the world." She could feel his sharp nose and his hot breath on the nape of her neck, and her eyes filled with tears. Nina's sister didn't know that he often said the same words when they were making love.

It was a relief to come home after the parties and find herself in bed with a book, next to her husband. Nina's nightstand was piled with cookbooks, bought at a fifty-per-cent discount at Barnes & Noble. She read lying on her back, resting the book on her stomach. The thick, glossy pages rustled against her satin nightgowns, bought at a fifty-per-cent-off sale at Victoria's Secret. She loved that sound as much as she loved the prickly sensation on the soles of her feet when they brushed up against her husband's hairy legs. And she loved the euphoric feeling she got when she looked at lustrous photographs of okra-and-tomato stew in rustic clay bowls, baskets of fresh vegetables shot against a background of meadows or olive groves. In her favorite book, "Italian Cuisine: The Taste of the Sun," there were also images of the cooking process. In those photographs, smooth, light-skinned female hands with evenly trimmed fingernails performed magical actions on vegetables. The hands looked like Nina's hands, and Nina fantasized that they were her hands. That it was she who had made those perfectly curled carrot strips. It was she who had pushed the stubborn stuffing inside the bell peppers. It was she who had rinsed the grit off the greens and chopped the broccoli, scattering tiny green seeds all over the table. Nina's lips moved to form the almost passionate words of the cooking instructions. "Brush with olive oil," "Bring to a boil and simmer gently," "Scoop out the pulp," "Peel," "Chop," "Slice," "Crush." When she put the book away and stretched out against her husband's back, her lips continued moving for some time.

Nina's husband left her at the end of the summer, just as the tomatoes and the peaches were performing their yearly invasion of the fruit-and-vegetable stores on Eighty-sixth Street. Nina's refrigerator was full of them when her sister opened it.

"The fifth week is the worst," Nina's sister was saying. "The first four weeks it hasn't 25 sunk in yet—you feel the shock, but you don't feel the pain. It's like you're numb. But the fifth week . . . Brace yourself for the fifth week." She crouched by the refrigerator, unloading the food she had brought over. She had come to console Nina with four large bags from a Russian supermarket. Nina felt tired. She sat at the table, staring at her sister's broad back. She was thinking that if you banged on it with a hammer it would produce a loud, reverberating sound, as if it were made of hard wood. The refrigerator shelves filled quickly: cartons of currant juice ("Currant juice saved my life—I basically lived on it when Volodya left me"), cream cheese, farmer's cheese, soft cheese, Swiss cheese, bread, pickles, a jar of cherry compote.

"Nina!" her sister shrieked. "What is that?" She had pulled out the vegetable drawer. Inside, there was a pile of old tomatoes, with white beards of mold growing in the places where their skins had split; there were peaches covered with brown spots;

there were dark and slimy bunches of collard greens. "You've got a whole vegetable graveyard in here," Nina's sister grumbled, emptying the drawer into the garbage. The vegetables made squelching sounds as they landed.

A faint rotten smell stayed in the kitchen for a long time after Nina's sister had left. It wasn't unpleasant. It was the simple, cozy smell of a kitchen, the smell of vegetable soup simmering on the stove, the kind that her mother used to make.

Contrary to her sister's prediction, the fifth week didn't bring Nina any extreme pain. It only added to the fatigue. She felt as if she were recovering from a long, exhausting illness. She tried to do as few household chores as possible. She didn't shop for vegetables anymore. She still read her cookbooks after work, but she was too tired to do much more than scan the index. She ran her finger over the smooth pages and neat columns of tiny letters. The austere phrases were logical and easy to read. "Broccoli: gratin—17; macaroni with—72; penne and—78." She had no desire to look up the recipes. She just went on to the next entry. "Eggplant: braised chicken with onions and—137; and tomato, baked—162." "Zucchini: and mushrooms, sauteed—34; shredded, jasmine rice with—201; soup—41; stuffed—57."

Pavlik's booming voice on the answering machine broke into the elegant sequence of artichoke recipes. Nina had turned off the ringer on her phone weeks before, and now she listened to the messages as they came through her old scratchy answering machine. Most of them were from her sister, calling to ask if she was eating well and to tell her the latest news: that Nina's husband had been spotted on Brighton Beach with some "dried herring," that he was moving to Boston, that he had already moved. Nina's sister's voice seemed to her distant and somewhat unnatural. Pavlik's voice made her jump. "Hey! Nina! Are you home?" he shouted. On impulse, Nina looked at the front door. It was hard to believe that the roaring was coming from the modest plastic box on the wall. Then Pavlik's voice dropped too low, and it was hard to make out his words. "Don't disappear," he said, if Nina heard him correctly.

Pavlik's place looked different. Nina realized it as soon as she stepped into the living   30 room, but she couldn't quite figure out how it was different. The rickety table still stood on the stained rug, the fireplace was stacked with old magazines, Pavlik's big frame was shaking with laughter, the vacant sofa was waiting for Nina. Everything was there, everything was in place, and yet something had undeniably changed. "The size—it's become bigger," Nina decided, taking her seat in the corner of the sofa. Pavlik's house had more space and more air than it had had before.

A thin, delicate woman with a guitar was singing something about a little path in the woods that meandered through the trees. Nina liked the song. When it ended, the singer put the guitar down and walked to the food table. She was wearing a long blue cardigan with drooping pockets. There was nothing mysterious about her. A man with receding hair and a closely trimmed gray beard took over the guitar. Nina's eyes travelled from the man's moving, outstretched elbow, protruding through his shabby corduroy sleeve, to his hunched shoulders and the greasy line of his hair. She suddenly understood that his untidiness wasn't a kind of snobbish fashion statement but a sign of loneliness, of neglect. She saw that the women sitting in a circle were watching the man, just as they had watched her husband. They were tired, lonely women, just like her. There was nothing mysterious about them, either. Nina also noticed that she wasn't the only one sitting outside the circle. In fact, there were only a few people in it. Others were scattered all around Pavlik's house. She could see lonely figures here and there, sitting quietly on a chair, an old box, a windowsill, or wandering through the house. From time to time, the paths of the lonely figures intersected and then conversations were struck up. Awkward yet hopeful conversations, just like the one that Nina was having now.

"You're a vegetable lover, aren't you?" asked a man who had seated himself in the opposite corner of Nina's sofa. Nina nodded. "I thought I heard that from somebody. Do you like to cook vegetables?" Nina nodded again. "You know, I love vegetables, myself. My wife hates it when I cook, though." The man rolled his eyes, making Nina smile. He was short, with thin rusty-red hair and a very pale complexion. He had a tiny piece of toilet paper with a spot of dried blood stuck to his cheek.

"Are you a computer programmer like everyone else?" Nina asked. The man nodded with a smile. "And in your previous life?"

"A high-school physics teacher. But I can't say that I miss it. I used to be terrified of my students."

Nina laughed. He was easy to talk to. She looked at his smiling eyes, then down at his 35
hands—white fingers, short fingernails, red hair on the knuckles. She tried to imagine what it would be like if one of these hands were to accidentally brush against her breast.

Nina wiped the little beads of sweat off her nose. He was a strange, married, not particularly attractive man.

"So what's your favorite vegetable?" she asked.

"Probably fennel. Fennel has an incredible flavor, reminds me of a wild apple and, oddly enough, freshly sawed wood. Do you like fennel?"

Nina nodded. She liked fennel: it had a funny, slightly ribbed surface, it was heavy, it had weird green shoots that seemed to grow out of nowhere. Nina had never tasted fennel. "I like broccoli," she said.

"Oh, broccoli! I love how they cook it in Chinese places. How do you cook it?" The 40
man with the piece of tissue stuck to his cheek looked safe enough to confide in.

"I've never cooked broccoli, or any other vegetable," Nina said.

Nina spent the better part of the following Saturday shopping for cooking utensils. "Let's have a cooking date," the man from the party had suggested. A cooking date. Nina was sure that, at some point in the past, she had been as excited as she was now, but she couldn't remember when. She went to Macy's and, breaking the fifty-per-cent-discount rule for the first time, bought two drastically overpriced skillets, a set of shiny stainless-steel saucepans, a steamer, and a pretty wooden spoon with a carved handle. "Do you want wedding gift wrap?" the cashier asked.

Halfway home, Nina realized that she hadn't bought nearly enough. Knives! She needed knives, and a cutting board, and a colander, and God knew what else. She swerved her car in the direction of Avenue M, where, breaking the rule about never buying anything in the cheap stores, she bought a set of knives, two cutting boards— one wooden and one plastic—a colander, a curved grapefruit knife, because it looked so cute, a vegetable peeler, a set of stainless-steel bowls, and two aprons with pictures of wild mushrooms on yellow backgrounds. In a grocery store next door, Nina bought olive oil, black pepper, chili pepper, and a jar of dry dark-green stuff with Chinese characters on the label.

By two-thirty—half an hour before the man was due to arrive—Nina had everything ready. The sparkling sauce-pans and the skillet stood proudly on the stove, and the bowls, the colander, the cutting boards, and the knives were arranged on the kitchen counter in careful disarray around the centerpiece: "Italian Cuisine: The Taste of the Sun." Nina observed her kitchen, trying to shake off her embarrassing excess of excitement.

The man came on time, early even. At five to three, he stood in Nina's hallway, removing his bulky leather jacket and cap, sprinkled with raindrops. He smelled of wet leather. He handed Nina a bottle of wine and a baguette in a sodden paper bag.

"In the movies, when a man hands a woman a baguette and a bottle of wine, it always seems chic, doesn't it?" he asked.

Nina nodded. He was more homely than she remembered. Her memory had somehow managed to erase the red spots on his pasty cheeks, to color his brows and eyelashes, to make him slimmer and add an inch or two to his height. It was strange to see him in her house, especially in her tiny hallway, where every object was familiar, its position carefully chosen. He clashed with the surroundings like a mismatched piece of furniture. Nina quickly led him into the kitchen.

"So, are we cooking broccoli today?" the man asked, leafing through "Italian Cuisine: The Taste of the Sun," his freshly washed hands still smelling of Nina's soap.

"Broccoli, yes," Nina mumbled, suddenly struck by a dreadful suspicion, which she confirmed on opening the refrigerator. She had forgotten to buy the vegetables.

She jerked out the vegetable drawer, hoping for a miracle. It was empty and clean, wiped down with a kitchen towel dipped in Clorox by Nina's sister's firm hand. There was only a tiny strip of onion skin stuck between the edge of the drawer and the shelf above. Nina turned to the man, motioning to the empty drawer; she found it hard to speak, as if someone were squeezing her throat. Everything seemed hopeless and ridiculous. The counter crammed with its gleaming kitchenware. The barren vegetable drawer. This perfect stranger, who had come to cook in her kitchen. Nina herself, her energy drained away, standing now with her forehead pressed to the cold rubber lining of the refrigerator door.

"Do you want me to go to the supermarket?" the man asked. Nina shook her head. Now that everything had been exposed to her in all its absurdity, she knew that it would never work.

A bunch of broccoli was stuck between the third shelf and the back of the refrigerator. It hung upside down, the florets nearly touching the shelf below. The man saw it first and pointed it out to Nina. The broccoli wasn't yellow or covered with slime. During the weeks that it had hung between the shelves, it had become darker and dryer. In a few more weeks it would have become a broccoli mummy. It smelled all right—or, rather, it didn't smell of anything.

"I'm sure we can still cook it," the man said.

Nina ran cold water over the florets, then shook the bunch fiercely, letting out a shower of green drops. She chopped off the stem, then cut off the base of each floret, watching with fascination as each piece split into tiny new bunches of broccoli. She peeled the stem and cut it into even, star-shaped slices. Some things turned out to be different from her cooking fantasies, others exactly the same. Some were disappointing, others better than she had ever imagined. Then, when the broccoli was in the pot on the stove, boiling water sputtering under the saucepan's shiny lid, the man suggested that Nina move one of her kitchen chairs closer to the stove and stand on it. "Climb up and inhale," the man said. "The hot air travels up. The strongest aroma should be right under the ceiling."

Nina stood on the chair, her hair almost touching the ceiling, her eyes closed, her 55 face pointed upward, her nostrils dilated. The warm smell of broccoli rose, caressing her face, enveloping her whole. ●

Explorations of the Text

1. Why does Nina shop for vegetables? (See par. 7, for example.) Why does she read cookbooks? What do the vegetables symbolize about her state of mind? About her relationship with her husband? How do the meanings of this symbolism change as the story progresses?

2. Why does her husband marry Nina? Does he love her? How is he different from Nina?

3. What role do Pavlik's parties play in the lives of the émigrés who attend?

4. Analyze the conclusion of the story. What do cooking the broccoli and smelling its "aroma" suggest? What is going to happen to Nina? Compare the ending of this work with that of "Shiloh" or with "Lady with Lapdog." Do you think that the relationships will endure?

The Reading/Writing Connection

1. What do you think is Nina's definition of love? Create a monologue in her voice.

2. Discuss themes of isolation and loneliness portrayed in the work.

3. Create a poem or a short prose poem in which food suggests the state of love or desire. Then explicate your work.

Ideas for Writing

1. **Write an Argument:** Compare and contrast the vision of immigration in this work with that in Jhumpa Lahiri's "The Third and Final Continent" (Chapter 9). How do the protagonists adjust to life in the United States? What are the obstacles that they face? Do you think that they find their new lives fulfilling? Do you think that this is a positive or negative vision of immigrants' lives?

2. Explore the various ways that Vapnyar uses vegetables to symbolize Nina's state of mind, her marriage, and her response to life in the United States.

Charlotte Perkins Gilman   *(1860–1935)*

The Yellow Wallpaper   *1892*

It is very seldom that mere ordinary people like John and myself secure ancestral halls for the summer.

A colonial mansion, a hereditary estate, I would say a haunted house and reach the height of romantic felicity—but that would be asking too much of fate!

Still I will proudly declare that there is something queer about it.

Else, why should it be let so cheaply? And why have stood so long untenanted?

John laughs at me, of course, but one expects that.   5

John is practical in the extreme. He has no patience with faith, an intense horror of superstition, and he scoffs openly at any talk of things not to be felt and seen and put down in figures.

John is a physician, and *perhaps*—(I would not say it to a living soul, of course, but this is dead paper and a great relief to my mind)—*perhaps* that is one reason I do not get well faster.

You see he does not believe I am sick! And what can one do?

If a physician of high standing, and one's own husband, assures friends and relatives that there is really nothing the matter with one but temporary nervous depression—a slight hysterical tendency[1]—what is one to do?

My brother is also a physician, and also of high standing, and he says the same   10
thing.

So I take phosphates[2] or phosphites—whichever it is—and tonics, and air and exercise, and journeys, and am absolutely forbidden to "work" until I am well again.

Personally, I disagree with their ideas.

Personally, I believe that congenial work, with excitement and change, would do me good.

But what is one to do?

I did write for a while in spite of them; but it *does* exhaust me a good deal—having   15
to be so sly about it, or else meet with heavy opposition.

I sometimes fancy that in my condition, if I had less opposition and more society and stimulus—but John says the very worst thing I can do is to think about my condition, and I confess it always makes me feel bad.

So I will let it alone and talk about the house.

The most beautiful place! It is quite alone, standing well back from the road, quite three miles from the village. It makes me think of English places that you read about, for there are hedges and walls and gates that lock, and lots of separate little houses for the gardeners and people.

There is a *delicious* garden! I never saw such a garden—large and shady, full of box-bordered paths, and lined with long grape-covered arbors with seats under them.

There were greenhouses, but they are all broken now.   20

There was some legal trouble, I believe, something about the heirs and co-heirs; anyhow, the place has been empty for years.

That spoils my ghostliness, I am afraid, but I don't care—there is something strange about the house—I can feel it.

I even said so to John one moonlight evening, but he said what I felt was a draught, and shut the window.

I get unreasonably angry with John sometimes. I'm sure I never used to be so sensitive. I think it is due to this nervous condition.

But John says if I feel so I shall neglect proper self-control; so I take pains to con-   25
trol myself—before him, at least, and that makes me very tired.

---

[1]**hysterical tendency:** Hysteria was a general nervous condition, often diagnosed in women in the late nineteenth century. Symptoms included tension, anxiety, nervousness, and depression.   [2]**phosphates:** A carbonated beverage made of water, fruit syrup, and phosphoric acid, used for medicinal purposes.

I don't like our room a bit. I wanted one downstairs that opened onto the piazza and had roses all over the window, and such pretty old-fashioned chintz hangings! But John would not hear of it.

He said there was only one window and not room for two beds, and no near room for him if he took another.

He is very careful and loving, and hardly lets me stir without special direction.

I have a schedule prescription for each hour in the day; he takes all care from me, and so I feel basely ungrateful not to value it more.

He said we came here solely on my account, that I was to have perfect rest and all 30 the air I could get. "Your exercise depends on your strength, my dear," said he, "and your food somewhat on your appetite; but air you can absorb all the time." So we took the nursery at the top of the house.

It is a big, airy room, the whole floor nearly, with windows that look all ways, and air and sunshine galore. It was nursery first, and then playroom and gymnasium, I should judge, for the windows are barred for little children, and there are rings and things in the walls.

The paint and paper look as if a boys' school had used it. It is stripped off—the paper—in great patches all around the head of my bed, about as far as I can reach, and in a great place on the other side of the room low down. I never saw a worse paper in my life. One of those sprawling, flamboyant patterns committing every artistic sin.

It is dull enough to confuse the eye in following, pronounced enough to constantly irritate and provoke study, and when you follow the lame uncertain curves for a little distance they suddenly commit suicide—plunge off at outrageous angles, destroy themselves in unheard-of contradictions.

The color is repellent, almost revolting: a smouldering unclean yellow, strangely faded by the slow-turning sunlight. It is a dull yet lurid orange in some places, a sickly sulphur tint in others.

No wonder the children hated it! I should hate it myself if I had to live in this room 35 long.

There comes John, and I must put this away—he hates to have me write a word.

We have been here two weeks, and I haven't felt like writing before, since that first day.

I am sitting by the window now, up in this atrocious nursery, and there is nothing to hinder my writing as much as I please, save lack of strength.

John is away all day, and even some nights when his cases are serious.

I am glad my case is not serious! 40

But these nervous troubles are dreadfully depressing.

John does not know how much I really suffer. He knows there is no reason to suffer, and that satisfies him.

Of course it is only nervousness. It does weigh on me so not to do my duty in any way!

I meant to be such a help to John, such a real rest and comfort, and here I am a comparative burden already!

Nobody would believe what an effort it is to do what little I am able—to dress and 45 entertain, and order things.

It is fortunate Mary is so good with the baby. Such a dear baby!

And yet I *cannot* be with him, it makes me so nervous.

I suppose John never was nervous in his life. He laughs at me so about this wallpaper!

At first he meant to repaper the room, but afterward he said that I was letting it get the better of me, and that nothing was worse for a nervous patient than to give way to such fancies.

He said that after the wallpaper was changed it would be the heavy bedstead, and then the barred windows, and then that gate at the head of the stairs, and so on.

"You know the place is doing you good," he said, "and really, dear, I don't care to renovate the house just for a three months' rental."

"Then do let us go downstairs," I said. "There are such pretty rooms there."

Then he took me in his arms and called me a blessed little goose, and said he would go down to the cellar, if I wished, and have it whitewashed into the bargain.

But he is right enough about the beds and windows and things.

It is as airy and comfortable room as anyone need wish, and, of course, I would not be so silly as to make him uncomfortable just for a whim.

I'm really getting quite fond of the big room, all but that horrid paper.

Out of one window I can see the garden—those mysterious deep-shaded arbors, the riotous old-fashioned flowers, and bushes and gnarly trees.

Out of another I get a lovely view of the bay and a little private wharf belonging to the estate. There is a beautiful shaded lane that runs down there from the house. I always fancy I see people walking in these numerous paths and arbors, but John has cautioned me not to give way to fancy in the least. He says that with my imaginative power and habit of story-making, a nervous weakness like mine is sure to lead to all manner of excited fancies, and that I ought to use my will and good sense to check the tendency. So I try.

I think sometimes that if I were only well enough to write a little it would relieve the press of ideas and rest me.

But I find I get pretty tired when I try.

It is so discouraging not to have any advice and companionship about my work. When I get really well, John says we will ask Cousin Henry and Julia down for a long visit; but he says he would as soon put fireworks in my pillow-case as to let me have those stimulating people about now.

I wish I could get well faster.

But I must not think about that. This paper looks to me as if it *knew* what a vicious influence it had!

There is a recurrent spot where the pattern lolls like a broken neck and two bulbous eyes stare at you upside down.

I get positively angry with the impertinence of it and the everlastingness. Up and down and sideways they crawl, and those absurd unblinking eyes are everywhere. There is one place where two breadths didn't match, and the eyes go all up and down the line, one a little higher than the other.

I never saw so much expression in an inanimate thing before, and we all know how much expression they have! I used to lie awake as a child and get more entertainment and terror out of blank walls and plain furniture than most children could find in a toy-store.

I remember what a kindly wink the knobs of our big old bureau used to have, and there was one chair that always seemed like a strong friend.

I used to feel that if any of the other things looked too fierce I could always hop into that chair and be safe.

The furniture in this room is no worse than inharmonious, however, for we had to bring it all from downstairs. I suppose when this was used as a playroom they had to take the nursery things out, and no wonder! I never saw such ravages as the children have made here.

The wallpaper, as I said before, is torn off in spots, and it sticketh closer than a brother—they must have had perseverance as well as hatred. 70

Then the floor is scratched and gouged and splintered, the plaster itself is dug out here and there, and this great heavy bed, which is all we found in the room, looks as if it had been through the wars.

But I don't mind it a bit—only the paper.

There comes John's sister. Such a dear girl as she is, and so careful of me! I must not let her find me writing.

She is a perfect and enthusiastic housekeeper, and hopes for no better profession. I verily believe she thinks it is the writing which made me sick!

But I can write when she is out, and see her a long way off from these windows. 75

There is one that commands the road, a lovely shaded winding road, and one that just looks off over the country. A lovely country, too, full of great elms and velvet meadows.

This wallpaper has a kind of sub-pattern in a different shade, a particularly irritating one, for you can only see it in certain lights, and not clearly then.

But in the places where it isn't faded and where the sun is just so—I can see a strange, provoking, formless sort of figure that seems to skulk about behind that silly and conspicuous front design.

There's sister on the stairs!

Well, the Fourth of July is over! The people are all gone, and I am tired out. John 80 thought it might do me good to see a little company, so we just had mother and Nellie and the children down for a week.

Of course I didn't do a thing. Jennie sees to everything now.

But it tired me all the same.

John says if I don't pick up faster he shall send me to Weir Mitchell[3] in the fall.

But I don't want to go there at all. I had a friend who was in his hands once, and she says he is just like John and my brother, only more so!

Besides, it is such an undertaking to go so far. 85

I don't feel as if it was worthwhile to turn my hand over for anything, and I'm getting dreadfully fretful and querulous.

I cry at nothing, and cry most of the time.

Of course I don't when John is here, or anybody else, but when I am alone.

And I am alone a good deal just now. John is kept in town very often by serious cases, and Jennie is good and lets me alone when I want her to.

So I walk a little in the garden or down that lovely lane, sit on the porch under the 90 roses, and lie down up here a good deal.

I'm getting really fond of the room in spite of the wallpaper. Perhaps *because* of the wallpaper.

It dwells in my mind so!

---

[3] **Weir Mitchell:** American neurologist who invented the "rest cure" for hysteria and who treated Gilman herself.

I lie here on this great immovable bed—it is nailed down, I believe—and follow that pattern about by the hour. It is as good as gymnastics, I assure you. I start, we'll say, at the bottom, down in the corner over there where it has not been touched, and I determine for the thousandth time that I *will* follow that pointless pattern to some sort of a conclusion.

I know a little of the principle of design, and I know this thing was not arranged on any laws of radiation, or alternation, or repetition, or symmetry, or anything else that I ever heard of.

It is repeated, of course, by the breadths, but not otherwise.

Looked at in one way, each breadth stands alone; the bloated curves and flourishes—a kind of "debased Romanesque"[4] with *delirium tremens*[5]—go waddling up and down in isolated columns of fatuity.

But, on the other hand, they connect diagonally, and the sprawling outlines run off in great slanting waves of optic horror, like a lot of wallowing sea-weeds in full chase.

The whole thing goes horizontally, too, at least it seems so, and I exhaust myself in trying to distinguish the order of its going in that direction.

They have used a horizontal breadth for a frieze,[6] and that adds wonderfully to the confusion.

There is one end of the room where it is almost intact, and there, when the crosslights fade and the low sun shines directly upon it, I can almost fancy radiation after all—the interminable grotesque seems to form around a common center and rush off in headlong plunges of equal distraction.

It makes me tired to follow it. I will take a nap, I guess.

I don't know why I should write this.

I don't want to.

I don't feel able.

And I know John would think it absurd. But I *must* say what I feel and think in some way—it is such a relief!

But the effort is getting to be greater than the relief.

Half the time now I am awfully lazy, and lie down ever so much. John says I mustn't lose my strength, and has me take cod liver oil and lots of tonics and things, to say nothing of ale and wine and rare meat.

Dear John! He loves me very dearly, and hates to have me sick. I tried to have a real earnest reasonable talk with him the other day, and tell him how I wish he would let me go and make a visit to Cousin Henry and Julia.

But he said I wasn't able to go, nor able to stand it after I got there; and I did not make out a very good case for myself, for I was crying before I had finished.

It is getting to be a great effort for me to think straight. Just this nervous weakness, I suppose.

And dear John gathered me up in his arms, and just carried me upstairs and laid me on the bed, and sat by me and read to me till it tired my head.

---

[4]**Romanesque:** Style of architecture prevalent from the ninth to twelfth centuries in Europe, characterized by rounded arches and heavy masonry and design. [5]*delirium tremens*: Condition caused by excessive use of alcohol and characterized by physical trembling and hallucinations. [6]**frieze:** A decorative band with lettering or sculpture.

He said I was his darling and his comfort and all he had, and that I must take care of myself for his sake, and keep well.

He says no one but myself can help me out of it, that I must use my will and self-control and not let any silly fancies run away with me.

There's one comfort—the baby is well and happy, and does not have to occupy this nursery with the horrid wallpaper.

If we had not used it, that blessed child would have! What a fortunate escape! 115 Why, I wouldn't have a child of mine, an impressionable little thing, live in such a room for worlds.

I never thought of it before, but it is lucky that John kept me here after all; I can stand it so much easier than a baby, you see.

Of course I never mention it to them any more—I am too wise—but I keep watch for it all the same.

There are things in that wallpaper that nobody knows about but me, or ever will.

Behind that outside pattern the dim shapes get clearer every day.

It is always the same shape, only very numerous. 120

And it is like a woman stooping down and creeping about behind that pattern. I don't like it a bit. I wonder—I begin to think—I wish John would take me away from here!

It is so hard to talk with John about my case, because he is so wise, and because he loves me so.

But I tried it last night.

It was moonlight. The moon shines in all around just as the sun does.

I hate to see it sometimes, it creeps so slowly, and always comes in by one window 125 or another.

John was asleep and I hated to waken him, so I kept still and watched the moonlight on that undulating wallpaper till I felt creepy.

The faint figure behind seemed to shake the pattern, just as if she wanted to get out.

I got up softly and went to feel and see if the paper *did* move, and when I came back John was awake.

"What is it, little girl?" he said. "Don't go walking about like that—you'll get cold."

I thought it was a good time to talk, so I told him that I really was not gaining 130 here, and that I wished he would take me away.

"Why, darling!" said he. "Our lease will be up in three weeks, and I can't see how to leave before.

"The repairs are not done at home, and I cannot possibly leave town just now. Of course, if you were in any danger, I could and would, but you really are better, dear, whether you can see it or not. I am a doctor, dear, and I know. You are gaining flesh and color, your appetite is better, I feel really much easier about you."

"I don't weigh a bit more," said I, "nor as much; and my appetite may be better in the evening when you are here but it is worse in the morning when you are away!"

"Bless her little heart!" said he with a big hug. "She shall be as sick as she pleases! But now let's improve the shining hours by going to sleep, and talk about it in the morning!"

"And you won't go away?" I asked gloomily. 135

"Why, how can I, dear? It is only three weeks more and then we will take a nice little trip of a few days while Jennie is getting the house ready. Really, dear, you are better!"

"Better in body perhaps—" I began, and stopped short, for he sat up straight and looked at me with such a stern, reproachful look that I could not say another word.

"My darling," said he, "I beg of you, for my sake and for our child's sake, as well as for your own, that you will never for one instant let that idea enter your mind! There is nothing so dangerous, so fascinating, to a temperament like yours. It is a false and foolish fancy. Can you not trust me as a physician when I tell you so?"

So of course I said no more on that score, and we went to sleep before long. He thought I was asleep first, but I wasn't, and lay there for hours trying to decide whether that front pattern and the back pattern really did move together or separately.

On a pattern like this, by daylight, there is a lack of sequence, a defiance of law, that is a constant irritant to a normal mind. 140

The color is hideous enough, and unreliable enough, and infuriating enough, but the pattern is torturing.

You think you have mastered it, but just as you get well under way in following, it turns a back-somersault and there you are. It slaps you in the face, knocks you down, and tramples upon you. It is like a bad dream.

The outside pattern is a florid arabesque, reminding one of a fungus. If you can imagine a toadstool in joints, an interminable string of toadstools, budding and sprouting in endless convolutions—why, that is something like it.

That is, sometimes!

There is one marked peculiarity about this paper, a thing nobody seems to notice 145 but myself, and that is that it changes as the light changes.

When the sun shoots in through the east window—I always watch for that first long, straight ray—it changes so quickly that I never can quite believe it.

That is why I watch it always.

By moonlight—the moon shines in all night when there is a moon—I wouldn't know it was the same paper.

At night in any kind of light, in twilight, candlelight, lamplight, and worst of all by moonlight, it becomes bars! The outside pattern, I mean, and the woman behind it is as plain as can be.

I didn't realize for a long time what the thing was that showed behind, that dim 150 subpattern, but now I am quite sure it is a woman.

By daylight she is subdued, quiet. I fancy it is the pattern that keeps her so still. It is so puzzling. It keeps me quiet by the hour.

I lie down ever so much now. John says it is good for me, and to sleep all I can.

Indeed he started the habit by making me lie down for an hour after each meal.

It is a very bad habit, I am convinced, for you see, I don't sleep.

And that cultivates deceit, for I don't tell them I'm awake—oh, no! 155

The fact is I am getting a little afraid of John.

He seems very queer sometimes, and even Jennie has an inexplicable look.

It strikes me occasionally, just as a scientific hypothesis, that perhaps it is the paper!

I have watched John when he did not know I was looking, and come into the room suddenly on the most innocent excuses, and I've caught him several times *looking at the paper!* And Jennie too. I caught Jennie with her hand on it once.

She didn't know I was in the room, and when I asked her in a quiet, a very quiet 160 voice, with the most restrained manner possible, what she was doing with the paper, she turned around as if she had been caught stealing, and looked quite angry—asked me why I should frighten her so!

Then she said that the paper stained everything it touched, that she had found yellow smooches on all my clothes and John's, and she wished we would be more careful!

Did not that sound innocent? But I know she was studying that pattern and I am determined that nobody shall find it out but myself!

Life is very much more exciting now than it used to be. You see, I have something more to expect, to look forward to, to watch. I really do eat better, and am more quiet than I was.

John is so pleased to see me improve! He laughed a little the other day, and said I seemed to be flourishing in spite of my wallpaper.

I turned it off with a laugh. I had no intention of telling him it was *because* of the 165 wallpaper—he would make fun of me. He might even want to take me away.

I don't want to leave now until I have found it out. There is a week more, and I think that will be enough.

I'm feeling so much better!

I don't sleep much at night, for it is so interesting to watch developments; but I sleep a good deal during the daytime.

In the daytime it is tiresome and perplexing.

There are always new shoots on the fungus, and new shades of yellow all over it. I 170 cannot keep count of them, though I have tried conscientiously. It is the strangest yellow, that wallpaper! It makes me think of all the yellow things I ever saw—not beautiful ones like buttercups, but old, foul, bad yellow things.

But there is something else about that paper—the smell! I noticed it the moment we came into the room, but with so much air and sun it was not bad. Now we have had a week of fog and rain, and whether the windows are open or not, the smell is here.

It creeps all over the house.

I find it hovering in the dining-room, skulking in the parlor, hiding in the hall, lying in wait for me on the stairs.

It gets into my hair.

Even when I go to ride, if I turn my head suddenly and surprise it—there is that 175 smell!

Such a peculiar odor, too! I have spent hours in trying to analyze it, to find what it smelled like.

It is not bad—at first—and very gentle, but quite the subtlest, most enduring odor I ever met.

In this damp weather it is awful. I wake up in the night and find it hanging over me.

It used to disturb me at first. I thought seriously of burning the house—to reach the smell.

But now I am used to it. The only thing I can think of that it is like is the *color* of 180 the paper! A yellow smell.

There is a very funny mark on this wall, low down, near the mopboard. A streak that runs round the room. It goes behind every piece of furniture, except the bed, a long, straight, even *smooch,* as if it had been rubbed over and over.

I wonder how it was done and who did it, and what they did it for. Round and round and round—round and round and round—it makes me dizzy!

I really have discovered something at last.

Through watching so much at night, when it changes so, I have finally found out.

The front pattern *does* move—and no wonder! The woman behind shakes it! 185

Sometimes I think there are a great many women behind, and sometimes only one, and she crawls around fast, and her crawling shakes it all over.

Then in the very bright spots she keeps still, and in the very shady spots she just takes hold of the bars and shakes them hard.

And she is all the time trying to climb through. But nobody could climb through that pattern—it strangles so; I think that is why it has so many heads.

They get through, and then the pattern strangles them off and turns them upside down, and makes their eyes white!

If those heads were covered or taken off it would not be half so bad.   190

I think that woman gets out in the daytime!

And I'll tell you why—privately—I've seen her!

I can see her out of every one of my windows!

It is the same woman, I know, for she is always creeping, and most women do not creep by daylight.

I see her in that long shaded lane, creeping up and down. I see her in those dark   195
grape arbors, creeping all around the garden.

I see her on that long road under the trees, creeping along, and when a carriage comes she hides under the blackberry vines.

I don't blame her a bit. It must be very humiliating to be caught creeping by daylight!

I always lock the door when I creep by daylight. I can't do it at night, for I know John would suspect something at once.

And John is so queer now that I don't want to irritate him. I wish he would take another room! Besides, I don't want anybody to get that woman out at night but myself.

I often wonder if I could see her out of all the windows at once.   200

But, turn as fast as I can, I can only see out of one at one time.

And though I always see her, she *may* be able to creep faster than I can turn! I have watched her sometimes away off in the open country, creeping as fast as a cloud shadow in a wind.

If only that top pattern could be gotten off from the under one! I mean to try it, little by little.

I have found out another funny thing, but I shan't tell it this time! It does not do to trust people too much.

There are only two more days to get this paper off, and I believe John is beginning   205
to notice. I don't like the look in his eyes.

And I heard him ask Jennie a lot of professional questions about me. She had a very good report to give.

She said I slept a good deal in the daytime.

John knows I don't sleep very well at night, for all I'm so quiet!

He asked me all sorts of questions, too, and pretended to be very loving and kind.

As if I couldn't see through him!   210

Still, I don't wonder he acts so, sleeping under this paper for three months.

It only interests me, but I feel sure John and Jennie are secretly affected by it. Hurrah! This is the last day, but it is enough. John to stay in town over night, and won't be out until this evening.

Jennie wanted to sleep with me—the sly thing; but I told her I should undoubtedly rest better for a night all alone.

That was clever, for really I wasn't alone a bit! As soon as it was moonlight and that poor thing began to crawl and shake the pattern, I got up and ran to help her.

I pulled and she shook. I shook and she pulled, and before morning we had peeled 215 off yards of that paper.

A strip about as high as my head and half around the room.

And then when the sun came and that awful pattern began to laugh at me, I declared I would finish it today!

We go away tomorrow, and they are moving all my furniture down again to leave things as they were before.

Jennie looked at the wall in amazement, but I told her merrily that I did it out of pure spite at the vicious thing.

She laughed and said she wouldn't mind doing it herself, but I must not get tired. 220

How she betrayed herself that time!

But I am here, and no person touches this paper but Me—not *alive!*

She tried to get me out of the room—it was too patent! But I said it was so quiet and empty and clean now that I believed I would lie down again and sleep all I could, and not to wake me even for dinner—I would call when I woke.

So now she is gone, and the servants are gone, and the things are gone, and there is nothing left but that great bedstead nailed down, with the canvas mattress we found on it.

We shall sleep downstairs tonight, and take the boat home tomorrow. 225

I quite enjoy the room, now it is bare again.

How those children did tear about here!

This bedstead is fairly gnawed!

But I must get to work.

I have locked the door and thrown the key down into the front path. 230

I don't want to go out, and I don't want to have anybody come in, till John comes.

I want to astonish him.

I've got a rope up here that even Jennie did not find. If that woman does get out, and tries to get away, I can tie her!

But I forgot I could not reach far without anything to stand on!

This bed will *not* move! 235

I tried to lift and push it until I was lame, and then I got so angry I bit off a little piece at one corner—but it hurt my teeth.

Then I peeled off all the paper I could reach standing on the floor. It sticks horribly and the pattern just enjoys it! All those strangled heads and bulbous eyes and waddling fungus growths just shriek with derision!

I am getting angry enough to do something desperate. To jump out of the window would be admirable exercise, but the bars are too strong even to try.

Besides I wouldn't do it. Of course not. I know well enough that a step like that is improper and might be misconstrued.

I don't like to *look* out of the windows even—there are so many of those creeping 240 women, and they creep so fast.

I wonder if they all come out of that wallpaper as I did?

But I am securely fastened now by my well-hidden rope—you don't get *me* out in the road there!

I suppose I shall have to get back behind the pattern when it comes night, and that is hard!

It is so pleasant to be out in this great room and creep around as I please!

I don't want to go outside. I won't, even if Jennie asks me to. 245

For outside you have to creep on the ground, and everything is green instead of yellow.

But here I can creep smoothly on the floor, and my shoulder just fits in that long smooch around the wall, so I cannot lose my way.

Why, there's John at the door!

It is no use, young man, you can't open it!

How he does call and pound! 250

Now he's crying to Jennie for an axe.

It would be a shame to break down that beautiful door!

"John dear!" said I in the gentlest voice. "The key is down by the front steps, under a plantain leaf!"

That silenced him for a few moments.

Then he said, very quietly indeed. "Open the door, my darling!" 255

"I can't," said I. "The key is down by the front door under a plantain leaf!" And then I said it again, several times, very gently and slowly, and said it so often that he had to go and see, and he got it of course, and came in. He stopped short by the door.

"What is the matter?" he cried. "For God's sake, what are you doing!"

I kept on creeping just the same, but I looked at him over my shoulder.

"I've got out at last," said I, "in spite of you and Jane. And I've pulled off most of the paper, so you can't put me back!"

Now why should that man have fainted? But he did, and right across my path by 260
the wall, so that I had to creep over him every time! ●

Explorations of the Text

1. What attitudes characterize John's treatment of his wife? Do his attitudes contribute to the narrator's situation? Look carefully at terms of endearment.

2. Is the narrator correct in her suspicions about her husband? about her brother? How do her attitudes change in the story?

3. What is the significance of the fact that the narrator's room was originally a nursery?

4. Why does John not want her to write? Why does she want to write?

5. What are the stages in the narrator's psychological breakdown? How are these stages reflected in her obsession with the wallpaper?

6. Who is the "woman" in the wallpaper? Discuss the symbolism of the figure. What does the yellow wallpaper finally symbolize?

7. What does the ending mean? What happens to the narrator? What is the husband's reaction?

8. Explore the point of view and the imagery in this story. How do they contribute to the story's emotional impact?

The Reading/Writing Connection

1. Create a character sketch of the narrator or John. Incorporate specifics from the story.

2. Charlotte Perkins Gilman's doctor, treating her for nervous depression, once told her "never to touch pen, brush or pencil again." Imagine a situation in which you were asked to give up a creative process. How would you feel?

Ideas for Writing

> 1. **Write an Argument:** "The Yellow Wallpaper" was anthologized as a horror or ghost story for many years. Write a defense of "The Yellow Wallpaper" either as a horror story or as more serious fiction.

Leslie Marmon Silko *(1948–   )*

Yellow Woman *1992*

I

My thigh clung to his with dampness, and I watched the sun rising up through the tamaracks and willows. The small brown water birds came to the river and hopped across the mud, leaving brown scratches in the alkali-white crust. They bathed in the river silently. I could hear the water, almost at our feet where the narrow fast channel bubbled and washed green ragged moss and fern leaves. I looked at him beside me, rolled in the red blanket on the white river sand. I cleaned the sand out of the cracks between my toes, squinting because the sun was above the willow trees. I looked at him for the last time, sleeping on the white river sand.

I felt hungry and followed the river south the way we had come the afternoon before, following our footprints that were already blurred by lizard tracks and bug trails. The horses were still lying down, and the black one whinnied when he saw me but he did not get up—maybe it was because the corral was made out of thick cedar branches and the horses had not yet felt the sun like I had. I tried to look beyond the pale red mesas to the pueblo. I knew it was there, even if I could not see it, on the sandrock hill above the river, the same river that moved past me now and had reflected the moon last night.

The horse felt warm underneath me. He shook his head and pawed the sand. The bay whinnied and leaned against the gate trying to follow, and I remembered him asleep in the red blanket beside the river. I slid off the horse and tied him close to the other horse. I walked north with the river again, and the white sand broke loose in footprints over footprints.

"Wake up."

He moved in the blanket and turned his face to me with his eyes still closed. I knelt 5
down to touch him.

"I'm leaving."

He smiled now, eyes still closed. "You are coming with me, remember?" He sat up now with his bare dark chest and belly in the sun.

"Where?"

"To my place."

"And will I come back?" 10

He pulled his pants on. I walked away from him, feeling him behind me and smelling the willows.

"Yellow Woman," he said.

I turned to face him. "Who are you?" I asked.

He laughed and knelt on the low, sandy bank, washing his face in the river. "Last night you guessed my name, and you knew why I had come."

I stared past him at the shallow moving water and tried to remember the night, but I could only see the moon in the water and remember his warmth around me.

"But I only said that you were him and that I was Yellow Woman—I'm not really her—I have my own name and I come from the pueblo on the other side of the mesa. Your name is Silva and you are a stranger I met by the river yesterday afternoon."

He laughed softly. "What happened yesterday has nothing to do with what you will do today, Yellow Woman."

"I know—that's what I'm saying—the old stories about the ka'tsina spirit and Yellow Woman can't mean us."

My old grandpa liked to tell those stories best. There is one about Badger and Coyote who went hunting and were gone all day, and when the sun was going down they found a house. There was a girl living there alone, and she had light hair and eyes and she told them that they could sleep with her. Coyote wanted to be with her all night so he sent Badger into a prairie-dog hole, telling him he thought he saw something in it. As soon as Badger crawled in, Coyote blocked up the entrance with rocks and hurried back to Yellow Woman.

"Come here," he said gently.

He touched my neck and I moved close to him to feel his breathing and to hear his heart. I was wondering if Yellow Woman had known who she was—if she knew that she would become part of the stories. Maybe she'd had another name that her husband and relatives called her so that only the ka'tsina from the north and the storytellers would know her as Yellow Woman. But I didn't go on; I felt him all around me, pushing me down into the white river sand.

"Yellow Woman went away with the spirit from the north and lived with him and his relatives. She was gone for a long time, but then one day she came back and she brought twin boys.

"Do you know the story?"

"What story?" He smiled and pulled me close to him as he said this. I was afraid lying there on the red blanket. All I could know was the way he felt, warm, damp, his body beside me. This is the way it happens in the stories. I was thinking, with no thought beyond the moment she meets the ka'tsina spirit and they go.

"I don't have to go. What they tell in stories was real only then, back in time immemorial, like they say."

He stood up and pointed at my clothes tangled in the blanket. "Let's go," he said.

I walked beside him, breathing hard because he walked fast, his hand around my wrist. I had stopped trying to pull away from him, because his hand felt cool and the sun was high, drying the river bed into alkali. I will see someone, eventually I will see someone, and then I will be certain that he is only a man—some man from nearby— and I will be sure that I am not Yellow Woman. Because she is from out of time past and I live now and I've been to school and there are highways and pickup trucks that Yellow Woman never saw.

It was an easy ride north on horseback. I watched the change from the cottonwood trees along the river to the junipers that brushed past us in the foothills, and finally there were only piñons, and when I looked up at the rim of the mountain plateau I could see pine trees growing on the edge. Once I stopped to look down, but the pale sandstone had disappeared and the river was gone and the dark lava hills were all around. He touched my hand, not speaking, but always singing softly a mountain song and looking into my eyes.

I felt hungry and wondered what they were doing at home now—my mother, my grandmother, my husband, and the baby. Cooking breakfast, saying, "Where did she go?—maybe kidnapped," and Al going to the tribal police with the details: "She went walking along the river."

The house was made with black lava rock and red mud. It was high above the spreading miles of arroyos and long mesas. I smelled a mountain smell of pitch and buck brush. I stood there beside the black horse, looking down on the small, dim country we had passed, and I shivered.

"Yellow Woman, come inside where it's warm."

II

He lit a fire in the stove. It was an old stove with a round belly and an enamel coffee-pot on top. There was only the stove, some faded Navajo blankets, and a bedroll and cardboard box. The floor was made of smooth adobe plaster, and there was one small window facing east. He pointed at the box.

"There's some potatoes and the frying pan." He sat on the floor with his arms around his knees pulling them close to his chest and he watched me fry the potatoes. I didn't mind him watching me because he was always watching me—he had been watching me since I came upon him sitting on the river bank trimming leaves from a willow twig with his knife. We ate from the pan and he wiped the grease from his fingers on his Levis.

"Have you brought women here before?" He smiled and kept chewing, so I said, "Do you always use the same tricks?"

"What tricks?" He looked at me like he didn't understand.

"The story about being a ka'tsina from the mountains. The story about Yellow Woman."

Silva was silent, his face was calm.

"I don't believe it. Those stories couldn't happen now," I said.

He shook his head and said softly, "But someday they will talk about us, and they will say, 'Those two lived long ago when things like that happened.'"

He stood up and went out. I ate the rest of the potatoes and thought about things—about the noise the stove was making and the sound of the mountain wind outside. I remembered yesterday and the day before, and then I went outside.

I walked past the corral to the edge where the narrow trail cut through the black rim rock. I was standing in the sky with nothing around me but the wind that came down from the mountain peak behind me. I could see faint mountain images in the distance miles across the vast spread of mesa and valleys and plains. I wondered who was over there to feel the mountain wind on those sheer blue edges—who walks on the pine needles in those blue mountains.

"Can you see the pueblo?" Silva was standing behind me.

I shook my head. "We're too far away."

"From here I can see the world." He stepped out on the edge. "The Navajo reservation begins over there." He pointed to the east. "The Pueblo boundaries are over here." He looked below us to the south, where the narrow trail seemed to come from. "The Texans have their ranches over there, starting with that valley, the Concho Valley. The Mexicans run some cattle over there too."

"Do you ever work for them?"

"I steal from them," Silva answered. The sun was dropping behind us and shadows were filling the land below. I turned away from the edge that dropped forever into the valleys below.

"I'm cold," I said; "I'm going inside." I started wondering about this man who could speak the Pueblo language so well but who lived on a mountain and rustled cattle. I decided that this man Silva must be Navajo, because Pueblo men didn't do things like that.

"You must be a Navajo."

Silva shook his head gently. "Little Yellow Woman," he said, "you never give up, do you? I have told you who I am. The Navajo people know me, too." He knelt down and unrolled the bedroll and spread the extra blankets out on a piece of canvas. The sun was down, and the only light in the house came from outside—the dim orange light from sundown.

I stood there and waited for him to crawl under the blankets. 50

"What are you waiting for?" he said, and I lay down beside him. He undressed me slowly like the night before beside the river—kissing my face gently and running his hands up and down my belly and legs. He took off my pants and then he laughed.

"Why are you laughing?"

"You are breathing so hard."

I pulled away from him and turned my back to him.

He pulled me around and pinned me down with his arms and chest. "You don't 55 understand, do you, little Yellow Woman? You will do what I want."

And again he was all around me with his skin slippery against mine, and I was afraid because I understood that his strength could hurt me. I lay beneath him and I knew that he could destroy me. But later, while he slept beside me, I touched his face and had a feeling—the kind of feeling for him that overcame me that morning along the river. I kissed him on the forehead and he reached out for me.

When I woke up in the morning he was gone. It gave me a strange feeling because for a long time I sat there on the blankets and looked around the little house for some object of his—some proof that he had been there or maybe that he was coming back. Only the blanket and the cardboard box remained. The .30-30 that had been leaning in the corner was gone, and so was the knife I had used the night before. He was gone, and I had my chance to go now. But first I had to eat, because I knew it would be a long walk home.

I found some dried apricots in the cardboard box, and I sat down on a rock at the edge of the plateau rim. There was no wind and the sun warmed me. I was surrounded by silence. I drowsed with apricots in my mouth, and I didn't believe that there were highways or railroads or cattle to steal.

When I woke up, I stared down at my feet in the black mountain dirt. Little black ants were swarming over the pine needles around my foot. They must have smelled the apricots. I thought about my family far below me. They would be wondering about me, because this had never happened to me before. The tribal police would file a report. But if old Grandpa weren't dead he would tell them what happened—he would laugh and say, "Stolen by a ka'tsina, a mountain spirit. She'll come home—they usually do." There are enough of them to handle things. My mother and grandmother will raise the baby like they raised me. Al will find someone else, and they will go on like before, except that there will be a story about the day I disappeared while I was walking along the river. Silva had come for me; he said he had. I did not decide to go. I just went. Moonflowers blossom in the sand hills before dawn just as I followed him. That's what I was thinking as I wandered along the trail through the pine trees.

It was noon when I got back. When I saw the stone house I remembered that I had to go home. But that didn't seem important any more, maybe because there were little blue flowers growing in the meadow behind the stone house and the gray squirrels were playing in the pines next to the house. The horses were standing in the corral, and there was a beef carcass hanging on the shady side of a big pine in front of the house. Flies buzzed around the clotted blood that hung from the carcass. Silva was washing his hands in a bucket full of water. He must have heard me coming because he spoke to me without turning to face me. 60

"I've been waiting for you."

"I went walking in the big pine trees."

I looked into the bucket full of bloody water with brown-and-white animal hairs floating in it. Silva stood there letting his hand drip, examining me intently.

"Are you coming with me?"

"Where?" I asked him. 65

"To sell the meat in Marquez."

"If you're sure it's O.K."

"I wouldn't ask you if it wasn't," he answered.

He sloshed the water around in the bucket before he dumped it out and set the bucket upside down near the door. I followed him to the corral and watched him saddle the horses. Even beside the horses he looked tall, and I asked him again if he wasn't Navajo. He didn't say anything; he just shook his head and kept cinching up the saddle.

"But Navajos are tall." 70

"Get on the horse," he said, "and let's go."

The last thing he did before we started down the steep trail was to grab the .30-30 from the corner. He slid the rifle into the scabbard that hung from his saddle.

"Do they ever try to catch you?" I asked.

"They don't know who I am."

"Then why did you bring the rifle?" 75

"Because we are going to Marquez where the Mexicans live."

///

The trail leveled out on a narrow ridge that was steep on both sides like an animal spine. On one side I could see where the trail went around the rocky gray hills and disappeared into the southeast where the pale sandrock mesas stood in the distance near my home. On the other side was a trail that went west, and as I looked far into the distance I thought I saw the little town. But Silva said no, that I was looking in the wrong place, that I just thought I saw houses. After that I quit looking off into the distance; it was hot and the wildflowers were closing up their deep-yellow petals. Only the waxy cactus flowers bloomed in the bright sun, and I saw every color that a cactus blossom can be: the white ones and the red ones were still buds, but the purple and the yellow were blossoms, open full and the most beautiful of all.

Silva saw him before I did. The white man was riding a big gray horse, coming up the trail toward us. He was traveling fast and the gray horse's feet sent rocks rolling off the trail into the dry tumbleweeds. Silva motioned for me to stop and we watched the white man. He didn't see us right away, but finally his horse whinnied at our horses and he stopped. He looked at us briefly before he loped the gray horse across the three hundred yards that separated us. He stopped his horse in front of Silva, and his young fat face was shadowed by the brim of his hat. He didn't look mad, but his small, pale eyes moved from the blood-soaked gunny sacks hanging from my saddle to Silva's face and then back to my face.

"Where did you get the fresh meat?" the white man asked.

"I've been hunting," Silva said, and when he shifted his weight in the saddle the 80 leather creaked.

"The hell you have, Indian. You've been rustling cattle. We've been looking for the thief for a long time."

The rancher was fat, and sweat began to soak through his white cowboy shirt and the wet cloth stuck to the thick rolls of belly fat. He almost seemed to be panting from the exertion of talking, and he smelled rancid, maybe because Silva scared him.

Silva turned to me and smiled. "Go back up the mountain, Yellow Woman."

The white man got angry when he heard Silva speak in a language he couldn't understand. "Don't try anything, Indian. Just keep riding to Marquez. We'll call the state police from there."

The rancher must have been unarmed because he was very frightened and if he 85 had a gun he would have pulled it out then. I turned my horse around and the rancher yelled, "Stop!" I looked at Silva for an instant and there was something ancient and dark—something I could feel in my stomach—in his eyes, and when I glanced at his hand I saw his finger on the trigger of the .30-30 that was still in the saddle scabbard. I slapped my horse across the flank and the sacks of raw meat swung against my knees as the horse leaped up the trail. It was hard to keep my balance, and once I thought I felt the saddle slipping backward; it was because of this that I could not look back.

I didn't stop until I reached the ridge where the trail forked. The horse was breathing deep gasps and there was a dark film of sweat on its neck. I looked down in the direction I had come from, but I couldn't see the place. I waited. The wind came up and pushed warm air past me. I looked up at the sky, pale blue and full of thin clouds and fading vapor trails left by jets.

I think four shots were fired—I remember hearing four hollow explosions that reminded me of deer hunting. There could have been more shots after that, but I couldn't have heard them because my horse was running again and the loose rocks were making too much noise as they scattered around his feet.

Horses have a hard time running downhill, but I went that way instead of uphill to the mountain because I thought it was safer. I felt better with the horse running southeast past the round gray hills that were covered with cedar trees and black lava rock. When I got to the plain in the distance I could see the dark green patches of tamaracks that grew along the river; and beyond the river I could see the beginning of the pale sandrock mesas. I stopped the horse and looked back to see if anyone was coming; then I got off the horse and turned the horse around, wondering if it would go back to its corral under the pines on the mountain. It looked back at me for a moment and then plucked a mouthful of green tumbleweeds before it trotted back up the trail with its ears pointed forward, carrying its head daintily to one side to avoid stepping on the dragging reins. When the horse disappeared over the last hill, the gunny sacks full of meat were still swinging and bouncing.

IV

I walked toward the river on a wood-hauler's road that I knew would eventually lead to the paved road. I was thinking about waiting beside the road for someone to drive by, but by the time I got to the pavement I had decided it wasn't very far to walk if I followed the river back the way Silva and I had come.

The river water tasted good, and I sat in the shade under a cluster of silvery willows. 90 I thought about Silva, and I felt sad at leaving him; still, there was something strange about him, and I tried to figure it out all the way back home.

I came back to the place on the river bank where he had been sitting the first time I saw him. The green willow leaves that he had trimmed from the branch were still lying there, wilted in the sand. I saw the leaves and I wanted to go back to him—to kiss him and to touch him—but the mountains were too far away now. And I told myself, because I believe it, he will come back sometime and be waiting again by the river.

■ ■ ■

I followed the path up from the river into the village. The sun was getting low, and I could smell supper cooking when I got to the screen door of my house. I could hear their voices inside—my mother was telling my grandmother how to fix the Jell-o and my husband, Al, was playing with the baby. I decided to tell them that some Navajo had kidnapped me, but I was sorry that old Grandpa wasn't alive to hear my story because it was the Yellow Woman stories he liked to tell best. ●

Explorations of the Text

1. How does the story of Yellow Woman and the ka'tsina function in this work?
2. Describe the relationship between the speaker and Silva. How does it change in each section?
3. How do details about the setting and about the horses emphasize the mythic elements of the story? How do the same details emphasize the sexual fascination between the two characters?
4. Discuss Silva's character. Why does he live a solitary life? Why does he steal horses? Why does he have a gun?
5. Why does Yellow Woman agree to help Silva sell the meat? What does the symbolism of the dead animal and of the blood signify?
6. Analyze the encounter between Silva and the rancher. Why does the narrator ride down the mountain? Does she make conscious choices?
7. Is the ending optimistic or pessimistic?
8. Discuss the depiction of sexual roles in the story. Compare with Maxine Hong Kingston's "No Name Woman."

The Reading/Writing Connection

1. Extend the story to part five. Imitate Silko's style.
2. Freewrite about Silva.
3. "Think" Topic: Does the narrator return to her husband? Argue pro or con.

Ideas for Writing

1. Analyze the love relationship in this story. Are the male and female roles stereotypical?

Bobbie Ann Mason *(1940–   )*

Shiloh   *1982*

Leroy Moffitt's wife, Norma Jean, is working on her pectorals. She lifts three-pound dumbbells to warm up, then progresses to a twenty-pound barbell. Standing with her legs apart, she reminds Leroy of Wonder Woman.

"I'd give anything if I could just get these muscles to where they're real hard," says Norma Jean. "Feel this arm. It's not as hard as the other one."

"That's 'cause you're right-handed," says Leroy, dodging as she swings the barbell in an arc.

"Do you think so?"

"Sure."

Leroy is a truckdriver. He injured his leg in a highway accident four months ago, and his physical therapy, which involves weights and a pulley, prompted Norma Jean to try building herself up. Now she is attending a body-building class. Leroy has been collecting temporary disability since his tractor-trailer jackknifed in Missouri, badly twisting his left leg in its socket. He has a steel pin in his hip. He will probably not be able to drive his rig again. It sits in the backyard, like a gigantic bird that has flown home to roost. Leroy has been home in Kentucky for three months, and his leg is almost healed, but the accident frightened him and he does not want to drive any more long hauls. He is not sure what to do next. In the meantime, he makes things from craft kits. He started by building a miniature log cabin from notched Popsicle sticks. He varnished it and placed it on the TV set, where it remains. It reminds him of a rustic Nativity scene. Then he tried string art (sailing ships on black velvet), a macramé owl kit, a snap-together B-17 Flying Fortress,[1] and a lamp made out of a model truck, with a light fixture screwed in the top of the cab. At first the kits were diversions, something to kill time, but now he is thinking about building a full-scale log house from a kit. It would be considerably cheaper than building a regular house, and besides, Leroy has grown to appreciate how things are put together. He has begun to realize that in all the years he was on the road he never took time to examine anything. He was always flying past scenery.

"They won't let you build a log cabin in any of the new subdivisions," Norma Jean tells him.

"They will if I tell them it's for you," he says, teasing her. Ever since they were married, he has promised Norma Jean he would build her a new home one day. They have always rented, and the house they live in is small and nondescript. It does not even feel like a home, Leroy realizes now.

5

---

[1] **B-17 Flying Fortress:** A model of a heavy bomber used by the U.S. Army in World War II.

Norma Jean works at the Rexall drugstore, and she has acquired an amazing amount of information about cosmetics. When she explains to Leroy the three stages of complexion care, involving creams, toners, and moisturizers, he thinks happily of other petroleum products—axle grease, diesel fuel. This is a connection between him and Norma Jean. Since he has been home, he has felt unusually tender about his wife and guilty over his long absences. But he can't tell what she feels about him. Norma Jean has never complained about his traveling; she has never made hurtful remarks, like calling his truck a "widow-maker." He is reasonably certain she has been faithful to him, but he wishes she would celebrate his permanent home-coming more happily. Norma Jean is often startled to find Leroy at home, and he thinks she seems a little disappointed about it. Perhaps he reminds her too much of the early days of their marriage, before he went on the road. They had a child who died as an infant, years ago. They never speak about their memories of Randy, which have almost faded, but now that Leroy is home all the time, they sometimes feel awkward around each other, and Leroy wonders if one of them should mention the child. He has the feeling that they are waking up out of a dream together—that they must create a new marriage, start afresh. They are lucky they are still married. Leroy has read that for most people losing a child destroys the marriage—or else he heard this on *Donahue*.[2] He can't always remember where he learns things anymore.

At Christmas, Leroy bought an electric organ for Norma Jean. She used to play   10
the piano when she was in high school. "It don't leave you," she told him once. "It's like riding a bicycle."

The new instrument had so many keys and buttons that she was bewildered by it at first. She touched the keys tentatively, pushed some buttons, then pecked out "Chopsticks." It came out in an amplified fox-trot rhythm, with marimba sounds.

"It's an orchestra!" she cried.

The organ had a pecan-look finish and eighteen preset chords, with optional flute, violin, trumpet, clarinet, and banjo accompaniments. Norma Jean mastered the organ almost immediately. At first she played Christmas songs. Then she bought *The Sixties Songbook* and learned every tune in it, adding variations to each with the rows of brightly colored buttons.

"I didn't like these old songs back then," she said. "But I have this crazy feeling I missed something."

"You didn't miss a thing," said Leroy.   15

Leroy likes to lie on the couch and smoke a joint and listen to Norma Jean play "Can't Take My Eyes Off You" and "I'll Be Back." He is back again. After fifteen years on the road, he is finally settling down with the woman he loves. She is still pretty. Her skin is flawless. Her frosted curls resemble pencil trimmings.

Now that Leroy has come home to stay, he notices how much the town has changed. Subdivisions are spreading across western Kentucky like an oil slick. The sign at the edge of town says "Pop: 11,500"—only seven hundred more than it said twenty years before. Leroy can't figure out who is living in all the new houses. The farmers who used to gather around the courthouse square on Saturday afternoons to play checkers and spit tobacco juice have gone. It has been years since Leroy has thought about the farmers, and they have disappeared without his noticing.

---

[2] ***Donahue:*** Popular television talk show hosted by Phil Donahue.

Leroy meets a kid named Stevie Hamilton in the parking lot at the new shopping center. While they pretend to be strangers meeting over a stalled car, Stevie tosses an ounce of marijuana under the front seat of Leroy's car. Stevie is wearing orange jogging shoes and a T-shirt that says CHATTAHOOCHEE SUPER-RAT. His father is a prominent doctor who lives in one of the expensive subdivisions in a new white-columned brick house that looks like a funeral parlor. In the phone book under his name there is a separate number, with the listing "Teenagers."

"Where do you get this stuff?" asks Leroy. "From your pappy?"

"That's for me to know and you to find out," Stevie says. He is slit-eyed and skinny. 20

"What else you got?"

"What you interested in?"

"Nothing special. Just wondered."

Leroy used to take speed on the road. Now he has to go slowly. He needs to be mellow. He leans back against the car and stays, "I'm aiming to build me a log house, soon as I get time. My wife, though, I don't think she likes the idea."

"Well, let me know when you want me again," Stevie says. He has a cigarette in his 25 cupped palm, as though sheltering it from the wind. He takes a long drag, then stomps it on the asphalt and slouches away.

Stevie's father was two years ahead of Leroy in high school. Leroy is thirty-four. He married Norma Jean when they were both eighteen, and their child Randy was born a few months later, but he died at the age of four months and three days. He would be about Stevie's age now. Norma Jean and Leroy were at the drive-in, watching a double feature (*Dr. Strangelove* and *Lover Come Back*), and the baby was sleeping in the back seat. When the first movie ended, the baby was dead. It was the sudden infant death syndrome. Leroy remembers handing Randy to a nurse at the emergency room, as though he were offering her a large doll as a present. A dead baby feels like a sack of flour. "It just happens sometimes," said the doctor, in what Leroy always recalls as a nonchalant tone. Leroy can hardly remember the child anymore, but he still sees vividly a scene from *Dr. Strangelove* in which the President of the United States was talking in a folksy voice on the hot line to the Soviet premier about the bomber accidentally headed toward Russia. He was in the War Room, and the world map was lit up. Leroy remembers Norma Jean standing catatonically beside him in the hospital and himself thinking: Who is this strange girl? He had forgotten who she was. Now scientists are saying that crib death is caused by a virus. Nobody knows anything, Leroy thinks. The answers are always changing.

When Leroy gets home from the shopping center, Norma Jean's mother, Mabel Beasley, is there. Until this year, Leroy has not realized how much time she spends with Norma Jean. When she visits, she inspects the closets and then the plants, informing Norma Jean when a plant is droopy or yellow. Mabel calls the plants "flowers," although there are never any blooms. She also notices if Norma Jean's laundry is piling up. Mabel is a short, overweight woman whose tight, brown-dyed curls look more like a wig than the actual wig she sometimes wears. Today she has brought Norma Jean an off-white dust ruffle she made for the bed; Mabel works in a custom-upholstery shop.

"This is the tenth one I made this year," Mabel says. "I got started and couldn't stop."

"It's real pretty," says Norma Jean.

"Now we can hide things under the bed," says Leroy, who gets along with his 30 mother-in-law primarily by joking with her. Mabel has never really forgiven him for disgracing her by getting Norma Jean pregnant. When the baby died, she said that fate was mocking her.

"What's that thing?" Mabel says to Leroy in a loud voice, pointing to a tangle of yarn on a piece of canvas.

Leroy holds it up for Mabel to see. "It's my needlepoint," he explains. "This is a *Star Trek* pillow cover."

"That's what a woman would do," says Mabel. "Great day in the morning!"

"All the big football players on TV do it," he says.

"Why, Leroy, you're always trying to fool me. I don't believe you for one minute. You don't know what to do with yourself—that's the whole trouble. Sewing!"

"I'm aiming to build us a log house," says Leroy. "Soon as my plans come."

"Like *heck* you are," says Norma Jean. She takes Leroy's needlepoint and shoves it into a drawer. "You have to find a job first. Nobody can afford to build now anyway."

Mabel straightens her girdle and says, "I still think before you get tied down y'all ought to take a little run to Shiloh."

"One of these days, Mama," Norma Jean says impatiently.

Mabel is talking about Shiloh, Tennessee. For the past few years, she has been urging Leroy and Norma Jean to visit the Civil War battleground there. Mabel went there on her honeymoon—the only real trip she ever took. Her husband died of a perforated ulcer when Norma Jean was ten, but Mabel, who was accepted into the United Daughters of the Confederacy in 1975, is still preoccupied with going back to Shiloh.

"I've been to kingdom come and back in that truck out yonder," Leroy says to Mabel, "but we never yet set foot in that battleground. Ain't that something? How did I miss it?"

"It's not even that far," Mabel says.

After Mabel leaves, Norma Jean reads to Leroy from a list she has made. "Things you could do," she announces. "You could get a job as a guard at Union Carbide, where they'd let you set on a stool. You could get on at the lumberyard. You could do a little carpenter work, if you want to build so bad. You could—"

"I can't do something where I'd have to stand up all day."

"You ought to try standing up all day behind a cosmetics counter. It's amazing that I have strong feet, coming from two parents that never had strong feet at all." At the moment Norma Jean is holding on to the kitchen counter, raising her knees one at a time as she talks. She is wearing two-pound ankle weights.

"Don't worry," says Leroy. "I'll do something."

"You could truck calves to slaughter for somebody. You wouldn't have to drive any big old truck for that."

"I'm going to build you this house," says Leroy. "I want to make you a real home."

"I don't want to live in any log cabin."

"It's not a cabin. It's a house."

"I don't care. It looks like a cabin."

"You and me together could lift those logs. It's just like lifting weights."

Norma Jean doesn't answer. Under her breath, she is counting. Now she is marching through the kitchen. She is doing goose steps.

Before his accident, when Leroy came home he used to stay in the house with Norma Jean, watching TV in bed and playing cards. She would cook fried chicken, picnic ham, chocolate pie—all his favorites. Now he is home alone much of the time. In the mornings, Norma Jean disappears, leaving a cooling place in the bed. She eats a cereal called Body Buddies, and she leaves the bowl on the table, with the soggy tan balls floating in a milk puddle. He sees things about Norma Jean that he never realized before. When she chops onions, she stares off into a corner, as if she can't bear to look. She puts on her house slippers almost precisely at nine o'clock every evening and nudges her jogging shoes under the couch. She saves bread heels for the birds. Leroy watches the birds at the feeder. He notices the peculiar way goldfinches fly past the window. They close their wings, then fall, then spread their wings to catch and lift themselves. He wonders if they close their eyes when they fall. Norma Jean closes her eyes when they are in bed. She wants the lights turned out. Even then, he is sure she closes her eyes.

He goes for long drives around town. He tends to drive a car rather carelessly. 55 Power steering and an automatic shift make a car feel so small and inconsequential that his body is hardly involved in the driving process. His injured leg stretches out comfortably. Once or twice he has almost hit something, but even the prospect of an accident seems minor in a car. He cruises the new subdivisions, feeling like a criminal rehearsing for a robbery. Norma Jean is probably right about a log house being inappropriate here in the new subdivision. All the houses look grand and complicated. They depress him.

One day when Leroy comes home from a drive he finds Norma Jean in tears. She is in the kitchen making a potato and mushroom-soup casserole, with grated cheese topping. She is crying because her mother caught her smoking.

"I didn't hear her coming. I was standing here puffing away pretty as you please," Norma Jean says, wiping her eyes.

"I knew it would happen sooner or later," says Leroy, putting his arm around her.

"She don't know the meaning of the word 'knock,'" says Norma Jean. "It's a wonder she hadn't caught me years ago."

"Think of it this way," Leroy says. "What if she caught me with a joint?" 60

"You better not let her!" Norma Jean shrieks. "I'm warning you, Leroy Moffitt!"

"I'm just kidding. Here, play me a tune. That'll help you relax."

Norma Jean puts the casserole in the oven and sets the timer. Then she plays a ragtime tune, with horns and banjo, as Leroy lights up a joint and lies on the couch, laughing to himself about Mabel's catching him at it. He thinks of Stevie Hamilton—a doctor's son pushing grass. Everything is funny. The whole town seems crazy and small. He is reminded of Virgil Mathis, a boastful policeman Leroy used to shoot pool with. Virgil recently led a drug bust in a back room at a bowling alley, where he seized ten thousand dollars' worth of marijuana. The newspaper had a picture of him holding up the bags of grass and grinning widely. Right now, Leroy can imagine Virgil breaking down the door and arresting him with a lungful of smoke. Virgil would probably have been alerted to the scene because of all the racket Norma Jean is making. Now she sounds like a hard-rock band. Norma Jean is terrific. When she switches to a Latin-rhythm version of "Sunshine Superman," Leroy hums along. Norma Jean's foot goes up and down, up and down.

"Well, what do you think?" Leroy says, when Norma Jean pauses to search through her music.

"What do I think about what?"

His mind has gone blank. Then he says, "I'll sell my rig and build us a house." That 65 wasn't what he wanted to say. He wanted to know what she thought—what she *really* thought—about them.

"Don't start in on that again," says Norma Jean. She begins playing "Who'll Be the Next in Line?"

Leroy used to tell hitchhikers his whole life story—about his travels, his hometown, the baby. He would end with a question: "Well, what do you think?" It was just a rhetorical question. In time, he had the feeling that he'd been telling the same story over and over to the same hitchhikers. He quit talking to hitchhikers when he realized how his voice sounded—whining and self-pitying, like some teenage-tragedy song. Now Leroy has the sudden impulse to tell Norma Jean about himself, as if he had just met her. They have known each other so long they have forgotten a lot about each other. They could become reacquainted. But when the oven timer goes off and she runs to the kitchen, he forgets why he wants to do this.

The next day, Mabel drops by. It is Saturday and Norma Jean is cleaning. Leroy is studying the plans of his log house, which have finally come in the mail. He has them spread out on the table—big sheets of stiff blue paper, with diagrams and numbers printed in white. While Norma Jean runs the vacuum, Mabel drinks coffee. She sets her coffee cup on a blueprint.

"I'm just waiting for time to pass," she says to Leroy, drumming her fingers on the table. 70

As soon as Norma Jean switches off the vacuum, Mabel says in a loud voice, "Did you hear about the datsun dog that killed the baby?"

Norma Jeans says, "The word is 'dachshund.'"

"They put the dog on trial. It chewed the baby's legs off. The mother was in the next room all the time." She raises her voice. "They thought it was neglect."

Norma Jean is holding her ears. Leroy manages to open the refrigerator and get some Diet Pepsi to offer Mabel. Mabel still has some coffee and she waves away the Pepsi.

"Datsuns are like that," Mabel says. "They're jealous dogs. They'll tear a place to 75 pieces if you don't keep an eye on them."

"You better watch out what you're saying, Mabel," says Leroy.

"Well, facts is facts."

Leroy looks out the window at his rig. It is like a huge piece of furniture gathering dust in the backyard. Pretty soon it will be an antique. He hears the vacuum cleaner. Norma Jean seems to be cleaning the living room rug again.

Later, she says to Leroy, "She just said that about the baby because she caught me smoking. She's trying to pay me back."

"What are you talking about?" Leroy says, nervously shuffling blueprints. 80

"You know good and well," Norma Jean says. She is sitting in a kitchen chair with her feet up and her arms wrapped around her knees. She looks small and helpless. She says, "The very idea, her bringing up a subject like that! Saying it was neglect."

"She didn't mean that," Leroy says.

"She might not have *thought* she meant it. She always says things like that. You don't know how she goes on."

"But she didn't really mean it. She was just talking."

Leroy opens a king-sized bottle of beer and pours it into two glasses, dividing it 85 carefully. He hands a glass to Norma Jean and she takes it from him mechanically. For a long time, they sit by the kitchen window watching the birds at the feeder.

Something is happening. Norma Jean is going to night school. She has graduated from her six-week body-building course and now she is taking an adult-education course in composition at Paducah Community College. She spends her evenings outlining paragraphs.

"First, you have a topic sentence," she explains to Leroy. "Then you divide it up. Your secondary topic has to be connected to your primary topic."

To Leroy, this sounds intimidating. "I never was any good in English," he says.

"It makes a lot of sense."

"What are you doing this for, anyhow?"   90

She shrugs. "It's something to do." She stands up and lifts her dumbbells a few times.

"Driving a rig, nobody cared about my English."

"I'm not criticizing your English."

Norma Jean used to say, "If I lose ten minutes' sleep, I just drag all day." Now she stays up late, writing compositions. She got a B on her first paper—a how-to theme on soup-based casseroles. Recently Norma Jean has been cooking unusual foods—tacos, lasagna, Bombay chicken. She doesn't play the organ anymore, though her second paper was called "Why Music Is Important to Me." She sits at the kitchen table, concentrating on her outlines, while Leroy plays with his log house plans, practicing with a set of Lincoln logs. The thought of getting a truckload of notched, numbered logs scares him, and he wants to be prepared. As he and Norma Jean work together at the kitchen table, Leroy has the hopeful thought that they are sharing something, but he knows he is a fool to think this. Norma Jean is miles away. He knows he is going to lose her. Like Mabel, he is just waiting for time to pass.

One day, Mabel is there before Norma Jean gets home from work, and Leroy finds   95
himself confiding in her. Mabel, he realizes, must know Norma Jean better than he does.

"I don't know what's got into that girl," Mabel says. "She used to go to bed with the chickens. Now you say she's up all hours. Plus her a-smoking. I like to died."

"I want to make her this beautiful house," Leroy says, indicating the Lincoln Logs. "I don't think she even wants it. Maybe she was happier with me gone."

"She don't know what to make of you, coming home like this."

"Is that it?"

Mabel takes the roof off his Lincoln Log cabin. "You couldn't get *me* in a log   100
cabin," she says. "I was raised in one. It's no picnic, let me tell you."

"They're different now," says Leroy.

"I tell you what," Mabel says, smiling oddly at Leroy.

"What?"

"Take her on down to Shiloh. Y'all need to get out together, stir a little. Her brain's all balled up over them books."

Leroy can see traces of Norma Jean's features in her mother's face. Mabel's worn   105
face has the texture of crinkled cotton, but suddenly she looks pretty. It occurs to Leroy that Mabel has been hinting all along that she wants them to take her with them to Shiloh.

"Let's all go to Shiloh," he says. "You and me and her. Come Sunday."

Mabel throws up her hand in protest. "Oh, no, not me. Young folks want to be by theirselves."

When Norma Jean comes in with groceries, Leroy says excitedly, "Your mama here's been dying to go to Shiloh for thirty-five years. It's about time we went, don't you think?"

"I'm not going to butt in on anybody's second honeymoon," Mabel says.

"Who's going on a honeymoon, for Christ's sake?" Norma Jean says loudly. 110

"I never raised no daughter of mine to talk that-a-way," Mabel says.

"You ain't seen nothing yet," says Norma Jean. She starts putting away boxes and cans, slamming cabinet doors.

"There's a log cabin at Shiloh," Mabel says. "It was there during the battle. There's bullet holes in it."

"When are you going to *shut up* about Shiloh, Mama?" asks Norma Jean.

"I always thought Shiloh was the prettiest place, so full of history," Mabel goes on. 115
"I just hoped y'all could see it once before I die, so you could tell me about it." Later, she whispers to Leroy, "You do what I said. A little change is what she needs."

"Your name means 'the king,'" Norma Jean says to Leroy that evening. He is trying to get her to go to Shiloh, and she is reading a book about another century.

"Well, I reckon I ought to be right proud."

"I guess so."

"Am I still king around here?"

Norma Jean flexes her biceps and feels them for hardness. "I'm not fooling around 120
with anybody, if that's what you mean," she says.

"Would you tell me if you were?"

"I don't know."

"What does your name mean?"

"It was Marilyn Monroe's real name."

"No kidding!" 125

"Norma comes from the Normans. They were invaders," she says. She closes her book and looks hard at Leroy. "I'll go to Shiloh with you if you'll stop staring at me."

On Sunday, Norma Jean packs a picnic and they go to Shiloh.[3] To Leroy's relief Mabel says she does not want to come with them. Norma Jean drives, and Leroy, sitting beside her, feels like some boring hitchhiker she has picked up. He tries some conversation, but she answers him in monosyllables. At Shiloh, she drives aimlessly through the park, past bluffs and trails and steep ravines. Shiloh is an immense place, and Leroy cannot see it as a battleground. It is not what he expected. He thought it would look like a golf course. Monuments are everywhere, showing through the thick clusters of trees. Norma Jean passes the log cabin Mabel mentioned. It is surrounded by tourists looking for bullet holes.

"That's not the kind of log house I've got in mind," says Leroy apologetically.

"I know *that*."

"This is a pretty place. Your mama was right." 130

"It's O.K.," says Norma Jean. "Well, we've seen it. I hope she's satisfied."

They burst out laughing together.

At the park museum, a movie on Shiloh is shown every half hour, but they decide that they don't want to see it. They buy a souvenir Confederate flag for Mabel, and then they find a picnic spot near the cemetery. Norma Jean has brought a picnic cooler, with pimento sandwiches, soft drinks, and Yodels. Leroy eats a sandwich and then smokes a

---

[3]**Shiloh:** Site of a famous Civil War battle fought in southwestern Tennessee, April 6–7, 1862. The battle resulted in a victory for the North, but there were large numbers of casualties on both sides.

joint, hiding it behind the picnic cooler. Norma Jean has quit smoking altogether. She is picking cake crumbs from the cellophane wrapper, like a fussy bird.

Leroy says, "So the boys in gray ended up in Corinth. The Union soldiers zapped 'em finally. April 7, 1862."

They both know that he doesn't know any history. He is just talking about some 135 of the historical plaques they have read. He feels awkward, like a boy on a date with an older girl. They are still just making conversation.

"Corinth is where Mama eloped to," says Norma Jean.

They sit in silence and stare at the cemetery for the Union dead and, beyond, at a tall cluster of trees. Campers are parked nearby, bumper to bumper, and small children in bright clothing are cavorting and squealing. Norma Jean wads up the cake wrapper and squeezes it tightly in her hand. Without looking at Leroy, she says, "I want to leave you."

Leroy takes a bottle of Coke out of the cooler and flips off the cap. He holds the bottle poised near his mouth but cannot remember to take a drink. Finally he says, "No, you don't."

"Yes, I do."

"I won't let you."   140

"You can't stop me."

"Don't do me that way."

Leroy knows Norma Jean will have her own way. "Didn't I promise to be home from now on?" he says.

"In some ways, a woman prefers a man who wanders," says Norma Jean. "That sounds crazy, I know."

"You're not crazy."   145

Leroy remembers to drink from his Coke. Then he says, "Yes, you *are* crazy. You and me could start all over again. Right back at the beginning."

"We *have* started all over again," says Norma Jean. "And this is how it turned out."

"What did I do wrong?"

"Nothing."

"Is this one of those women's lib things?" Leroy asks.   150

"Don't be funny."

The cemetery, a green slope dotted with white markers, looks like a subdivision site. Leroy is trying to comprehend that his marriage is breaking up, but for some reason he is wondering about white slabs in a graveyard.

"Everything was fine till Mama caught me smoking," says Norma Jean, standing up. "That set something off."

"What are you talking about?"

"She won't leave me alone—*you* won't leave me alone." Norma Jean seems to be 155 crying, but she is looking away from him. "I feel eighteen again. I can't face that all over again." She starts walking away. "No, it *wasn't* fine. I don't know what I'm saying. Forget it."

Leroy takes a lungful of smoke and closes his eyes as Norma Jean's words sink in. He tries to focus on the fact that thirty-five hundred soldiers died on the grounds around him. He can only think of that war as a board game with plastic soldiers. Leroy almost smiles, as he compares the Confederates' daring attack on the Union camps and Virgil Mathis's raid on the bowling alley. General Grant, drunk and furious, shoved the Southerners back to Corinth,[4] where Mabel and Jet Beasley were married years later, when Mabel was still thin and good-looking. The next day, Mabel and Jet visited the battleground, and then Norma Jean was born, and then she married Leroy and they had a baby, which they lost, and now Leroy and Norma Jean are here at the same battleground. Leroy knows he is leaving out a lot. He is leaving out the insides of history. History was always just names and dates to him. It occurs to him that building a house of logs is similarly empty—too simple. And the real inner workings of a marriage, like most of history, have escaped him. Now he sees that building a log house is the dumbest idea he could have had. It was clumsy of him to think Norma Jean would want a log house. It was a crazy idea. He'll have to think of something else, quickly. He will wad the blueprints into tight balls and fling them into the lake. Then he'll get moving again. He opens his eyes. Norma Jean has moved away and is walking through the cemetery, following a serpentine[5] brick path.

Leroy gets up to follow his wife, but his good leg is asleep and his bad leg still hurts him. Norma Jean is far away, walking rapidly toward the bluff by the river, and he tries to hobble toward her. Some children run past him, screaming noisily. Norma Jean has reached the bluff, and she is looking out over the Tennessee River. Now she turns toward Leroy and waves her arms. Is she beckoning to him? She seems to be doing an exercise for her chest muscles. The sky is unusually pale—the color of the dust ruffle Mabel made for their bed. ●

Explorations of the Text

1. What does the opening scene with the barbells reveal about Leroy's and Norma Jean's characters?
2. Why is Leroy building the log house? How has Leroy changed since his accident? How has Norma Jean changed since Leroy first married her?
3. What is Mabel's role in the story?
4. Discuss the significance of the trip to Shiloh. Closely examine the last two paragraphs. Relate the following quotation to themes of the story: "History was always just names and dates to him. . . . And the real inner workings of a marriage, like most of history, have escaped him."
5. Compare the endings of this story and "Eveline."

The Reading/Writing Connection

1. Journal Entry: Continue the story. What happens to Norma Jean and to Leroy?
2. Create an exchange of letters between Norma Jean and another character in this chapter. Here is one possible scenario: Have Norma Jean ask this character for advice about her relationship with Leroy.
3. Imagine that you are a marriage counselor. What advice would you give Leroy and Norma Jean?

---

[4]**Corinth:** Corinth, Mississippi.   [5]**serpentine:** A winding path.

Ideas for Writing

1. **Write an Argument:** Who is responsible for the disintegration of the marriage: Leroy or Norma Jean? Write an argumentative essay defending your position.

2. Bobbie Ann Mason's work is noted for its minimalist style. The story seems straightforward and simply written, yet if one probes, one realizes that every detail builds the symbolic subtext of the work and the themes of the story. Choose one symbolic detail and explore its significance in building theme (e.g., the dust ruffle or the battle of Shiloh).

Margaret Atwood   *(1939–   )*

Happy Endings   *1983*

John and Mary meet.
What happens next?
If you want a happy ending, try A.

A

John and Mary fall in love and get married. They both have worthwhile and remunerative jobs which they find stimulating and challenging. They buy a charming house. Real estate values go up. Eventually, when they can afford live-in help, they have two children, to whom they are devoted. The children turn out well. John and Mary have a stimulating and challenging sex life and worthwhile friends. They go on fun vacations together. They retire. They both have hobbies which they find stimulating and challenging. Eventually they die. This is the end of the story.

B

Mary falls in love with John but John doesn't fall in love with Mary. He merely uses her body for selfish pleasure and ego gratification of a tepid kind. He comes to her apartment twice a week and she cooks him dinner, you'll notice that he doesn't even consider her worth the price of a dinner out, and after he's eaten the dinner he fucks her and after that he falls asleep, while she does the dishes so he won't think she's untidy, having all those dirty dishes lying around, and puts on fresh lipstick so she'll look good when he wakes up, but when he wakes up he doesn't even notice, he puts on his socks and his shorts and his pants and his shirt and his tie and his shoes, the reverse order from the one in which he took them off. He doesn't take off Mary's clothes, she takes them off herself, she acts as if she's dying for it every time, not because she likes sex exactly, she doesn't, but she wants John to think she does because if they do it often enough surely he'll get used to her, he'll come to depend on her and they will get married, but John goes out the door with hardly so much as a good-night and three days later he turns up at six o'clock and they do the whole thing over again.

Mary gets run-down. Crying is bad for your face, everyone knows that and so does Mary but she can't stop. People at work notice. Her friends tell her John is a rat, a pig, a dog, he isn't good enough for her, but she can't believe it. Inside John, she thinks, is another John, who is much nicer. This other John will emerge like a butterfly from a cocoon, a Jack from a box, a pit from a prune, if the first John is only squeezed enough.

One evening John complains about the food. He has never complained about the food before. Mary is hurt.

Her friends tell her they've seen him in a restaurant with another woman, whose name is Madge. It's not even Madge that finally gets to Mary: it's the restaurant. John has never taken Mary to a restaurant. Mary collects all the sleeping pills and aspirins she can find, and takes them and a half a bottle of sherry. You can see what kind of a woman she is by the fact that it's not even whiskey. She leaves a note for John. She hopes he'll discover her and get her to the hospital in time and repent and then they can get married, but this fails to happen and she dies.

John marries Madge and everything continues as in A.

C

John, who is an older man, falls in love with Mary, and Mary, who is only twenty-two, 10 feels sorry for him because he's worried about his hair falling out. She sleeps with him even though she's not in love with him. She met him at work. She's in love with someone called James, who is twenty-two also and not yet ready to settle down.

John on the contrary settled down long ago: this is what is bothering him. John has a steady, respectable job and is getting ahead in his field, but Mary isn't impressed by him, she's impressed by James, who has a motorcycle and a fabulous record collection. But James is often away on his motorcycle, being free. Freedom isn't the same for girls, so in the meantime Mary spends Thursday evenings with John. Thursdays are the only days John can get away.

John is married to a woman called Madge and they have two children, a charming house which they bought just before the real estate values went up, and hobbies which they find stimulating and challenging, when they have the time. John tells Mary how important she is to him, but of course he can't leave his wife because a commitment is a commitment. He goes on about this more than is necessary and Mary finds it boring, but older men can keep it up longer so on the whole she has a fairly good time.

One day James breezes in on his motorcycle with some top-grade California hybrid and James and Mary get higher than you'd believe possible and they climb into bed. Everything becomes very underwater, but along comes John, who has a key to Mary's apartment. He finds them stoned and entwined. He's hardly in any position to be jealous, considering Madge, but nevertheless he's overcome with despair. Finally he's middle-aged, in two years he'll be bald as an egg and he can't stand it. He purchases a handgun, saying he needs it for target practice—this is the thin part of the plot, but it can be dealt with later—and shoots the two of them and himself.

Madge, after a suitable period of mourning, marries an understanding man called Fred and everything continues as in A, but under different names.

D

Fred and Madge have no problems. They get along exceptionally well and are good at 15 working out any little difficulties that may arise. But their charming house is by the seashore and one day a giant tidal wave approaches. Real estate values go down. The rest of the story is about what caused the tidal wave and how they escape from it. They do, though thousands drown, but Fred and Madge are virtuous and lucky. Finally on high ground they clasp each other, wet and dripping and grateful, and continue as in A.

E

Yes, but Fred has a bad heart. The rest of the story is about how kind and understanding they both are until Fred dies. Then Madge devotes herself to charity work until the end of A. If you like, it can be "Madge," "cancer," "guilty and confused," and "bird watching."

F

If you think this is all too bourgeois, make John a revolutionary and Mary a counter-espionage agent and see how far that gets you. Remember, this is Canada. You'll still end up with A, though in between you may get a lustful brawling saga of passionate involvement, a chronicle of our times, sort of.

You'll have to face it, the endings are the same however you slice it. Don't be deluded by any other endings, they're all fake, either deliberately fake, with malicious intent to deceive, or just motivated by excessive optimism if not by downright sentimentality.

The only authentic ending is the one provided here:
John and Mary die. John and Mary die. John and Mary die.   20

So much for endings. Beginnings are always more fun. True connoisseurs, however, are known to favor the stretch in between, since it's the hardest to do anything with.

That's about all that can be said for plots, which anyway are just one thing after another, a what and a what and a what.

Now try How and Why. ●

Explorations of the Text

1. Compare and contrast the versions of John and Mary's love story. What do they suggest about love and marriage?

2. Explore the significance of the last four paragraphs. Analyze and interpret the following: "The only authentic ending is the one provided here. John and Mary die. John and Mary die. John and Mary die." Why does Atwood repeat the sentence three times? Why are "beginnings . . . more fun"? What does "the stretch in between . . ." suggest?

3. Is this a story about love, about writing fiction, or both?

4. Discuss the critique of relationships and women's roles presented in the work. Discuss the criticism of bourgeois culture.

5. How does the humor convey Atwood's theme?

The Reading/Writing Connection

1. Write several different versions of a relationship in which you have been involved. What do you learn?

2. Atwood's work is an example of metafiction (see Glossary). How does Atwood handle this genre?

Ideas for Writing

1. Compare and contrast the feminist critique of relationships in this work and in Gilman's "The Yellow Wallpaper."

Sandra Cisneros *(1954–)*

Barbie-Q *1991*

for Licha

Yours is the one with mean eyes and a ponytail. Striped swimsuit, stilettos, sunglasses, and gold hoop earrings. Mine is the one with bubble hair. Red swimsuit, stilettos, pearl earrings, and a wire stand. But that's all we can afford, besides one extra outfit apiece. Yours, "Red Flair," sophisticated A-line coatdress with a Jackie Kennedy pillbox hat, white gloves, handbag, and heels included. Mine, "Solo in the Spotlight," evening elegance in black glitter strapless gown with a puffy skirt at the bottom like a mermaid tail, formal-length gloves, pink chiffon scarf, and mike included. From so much dressing and undressing, the black glitter wears off where her titties stick out. This and a dress invented from an old sock when we cut holes here and here and here, the cuff rolled over for the glamorous, fancy-free, off-the-shoulder look.

Every time the same story. Your Barbie is roommates with my Barbie, and my Barbie's boyfriend comes over and your Barbie steals him, okay? Kiss kiss kiss. Then the two Barbies fight. You dumbbell! He's mine. Oh no he's not, you stinky! Only Ken's invisible, right? Because we don't have money for a stupid-looking boy doll when we'd both rather ask for a new Barbie outfit next Christmas. We have to make do with your mean-eyed Barbie and my bubblehead Barbie and our one outfit apiece not including the sock dress.

Until next Sunday when we are walking through the flea market on Maxwell Street and *there!* Lying on the street next to some tool bits, and platform shoes with the heels all squashed, and a fluorescent green wicker wastebasket, and aluminum foil, and hubcaps, and a pink shag rug, and windshield wiper blades, and dusty mason jars, and a coffee can full of rusty nails. *There!* Where? Two Mattel boxes. One with the "Career Gal" ensemble, snappy black-and-white business suit, three-quarter-length sleeve jacket with kick-pleat skirt, red sleeveless shell, gloves, pumps, and matching hat included. The other, "Sweet Dreams," dreamy pink-and-white plaid nightgown and matching robe, lace-trimmed slippers, hair-brush and hand mirror included. How much? Please, please, please, please, please, please, please, until they say okay.

On the outside you and me skipping and humming but inside we are doing loopity-loops and pirouetting. Until at the next vendor's stand, next to boxed pies, and bright orange toilet brushes, and rubber gloves, and wrench sets, and bouquets of feather flowers, and glass towel racks, and steel wool, and Alvin and the Chipmunks records, *there!* And *there!* And *there!* And *there!* and *there!* and *there!* and *there!* Bendable Legs Barbie with her new page-boy hairdo. Midge, Barbie's best friend. Ken, Barbie's boyfriend. Skipper, Barbie's little sister. Tutti and Todd, Barbie and Skipper's tiny twin sister and brother. Skipper's friends, Scooter and Ricky. Alan, Ken's buddy. And Francie, Barbie's MOD'ern cousin.

Everybody today selling toys, all of them damaged with water and smelling of smoke. Because a big toy warehouse on Halsted Street burned down yesterday—see there?—the smoke still rising and drifting across the Dan Ryan expressway. And now there is a big fire sale at Maxwell Street, today only.

So what if we didn't get our new Bendable Legs Barbie and Midge and Ken and Skipper and Tutti and Todd and Scooter and Ricky and Alan and Francie in nice clean boxes and had to buy them on Maxwell Street, all water-soaked and sooty. So what if our Barbies smell like smoke when you hold them up to your nose even after you wash and wash and wash them. And if the prettiest doll, Barbie's MOD'ern cousin Francie with real eyelashes, eyelash brush included, has a left foot that's melted a little—so? If you dress her in her new "Prom Pinks" outfit, satin splendor with matching coat, gold belt, clutch, and hair bow included, so long as you don't lift her dress, right?—who's to know. ●

Explorations of the Text

1. What do the Barbie dolls represent to the narrator and to her friend? What do the clothes and the games that the girls play suggest about their identities?
2. Explore the play on words in the title. Explore the symbolism of the "water-soaked and sooty" Barbies that "smell like smoke when you hold them up to your nose even after you wash and wash and wash them." What is implied about the protagonist's class and social status?
3. Compare and contrast the portrait of Barbies in this work with that of Marge Piercy's "Barbie Doll." What visions of the female body and of gender roles do the works depict?

The Reading/Writing Connection

1. Write about a toy that you played with in childhood (for example, Teenage Mutant Ninja Turtles, American Girl dolls, Legos, or Transformers) and what it suggests about socially indoctrinated roles for girls or for boys and, in addition, societal values.

2. **Write an Argument:** Both "Barbie-Q" and "Barbie Doll" present arguments in literary form. Summarize the argument presented in one of the works and analyze the forms of appeal. Then agree or disagree with the position presented in the work.

Ideas for Writing

1. **Write an Argument:** In a *New Yorker* article (Dec. 4, 2006), "Little Hotties," Margaret Talbot reports that Barbie dolls are receiving competition from dolls called Bratz. "Bratz dolls have large heads and skinny bodies, . . . almond-shaped eyes . . . tilted upward at the edges and adorned with thick crescents of eye-shadow, and . . . lips . . . lush and pillowy, glossed to a candy-apple sheen." Although Talbot suggests these dolls do have a positive dimension because they evoke a multiracial and multi-ethnic identity and

appearance, she believes the company that manufactures the doll is intent on "making dolls that look like celebrity hotties." While Barbie caters to three- to six-year olds, Talbot reports that Bratz dolls are designed by the manufacturer for the "six-to-twelve year old market." Talbot theorizes: "Bratz dolls are both contributing to and feeding on . . . a culture in which girls play at being 'sassy'—the toy industry's favored euphemism for sexy—and discard traditional toys at a younger age. (Girls seem to be growing out of toys earlier than boys are, industry analysts say.) Toy marketers now invoke a phenomenon called K.G.O.Y.—Kids Getting Older Younger and talk about it as though it were a fact of modern life over which they have no control, rather than one which they have largely created." Do you think that girls are emerging from childhood earlier and growing up too quickly? Do you see evidence of this "tween" trend? Is there an equivalent pattern of experience for young boys? Do you think the industries that market products to this age group are responsible for creating this phenomenon? What other social forces are at work? Consider one or several of these questions and frame a response in the form of an argumentative essay.

Modern Love/Fiction

T. C. Boyle *(1948–)*

Modern Love *1987*

There was no exchange of body fluids on the first date, and that suited both of us just fine. I picked her up at seven, took her to Mee Grop, where she meticulously separated each sliver of meat from her Phat Thai, watched her down four bottles of Singha at three dollars per, and then gently stroked her balsam-smelling hair while she snoozed through *The Terminator* at the Circle Shopping Center theater. We had a late-night drink at Rigoletto's Pizza Bar (and two slices, plain cheese), and I dropped her off. The moment we pulled up in front of her apartment she had the door open. She turned to me with the long, elegant, mournful face of her Puritan ancestors and held out her hand.

"It's been fun," she said.

"Yes," I said, taking her hand.

She was wearing gloves.

"I'll call you," she said,

"Good," I said, giving her my richest smile. "And I'll call you."   5

On the second date we got acquainted.

"I can't tell you what a strain it was for me the other night," she said, staring down into her chocolate-mocha-fudge sundae. It was early afternoon, we were in Helmut's Olde Tyme Ice Cream Parlor in Mamaroneck, and the sun streamed through the thick frosted windows and lit the place like a convalescent home. The fixtures glowed behind the counter, the brass rail was buffed to a reflective sheen, and everything smelled of disinfectant. We were the only people in the place.

"What do you mean?" I said, my mouth glutinous with melted marshmallow and caramel.

"I mean Thai food, the seats in the movie theater, the *ladies' room* in that place for   10 god's sake . . ."

"Thai food?" I wasn't following her. I recalled the maneuver with the strips of pork and the fastidious dissection of the glass noodles. "You're a vegetarian?"

She looked away in exasperation, and then gave me the full, wide-eyed shock of her ice-blue eyes. "Have you seen the Health Department statistics on sanitary conditions in ethnic restaurants?"

I hadn't.

Her eyebrows leapt up. She was earnest. She was lecturing. "These people are refugees. They have—well, different standards. They haven't even been inoculated." I watched her dig the tiny spoon into the recesses of the dish and part her lips for a neat, foursquare morsel of ice cream and fudge.

"The illegals, anyway. And that's half of them." She swallowed with an almost imperceptible movement, a shudder, her throat dipping and rising like a gazelle's. "I got   15 drunk from fear," she said. "Blind panic. I couldn't help thinking I'd wind up with hepatitis or dysentery or dengue fever or something."

"Dengue fever?"

"I usually bring a disposable sanitary sheet for public theaters—just think of who might have been in that seat before you, and how many times, and what sort of nasty festering little cultures of this and that there must be in all those ancient dribbles of taffy and Coke and extra-butter popcorn—but I didn't want you to think I was too extreme or anything on the first date, so I didn't. And then the *ladies' room* . . . You don't think I'm overreacting, do you?"

As a matter of fact, I did. Of course I did. I liked Thai food—and sushi and ginger crab and greasy souvlaki at the corner stand too. There was the look of the mad saint in her eye, the obsessive, the mortifier of the flesh, but I didn't care. She was lovely, wilting, clear-eyed, and pure, as cool and matchless as if she'd stepped out of a Pre-Raphaelite painting, and I was in love. Besides, I tended a little that way myself. Hypochondria. Anal retentiveness. The ordered environment and alphabetized books. I was a thirty-three-year-old bachelor, I carried some scars and I read the newspapers—herpes, AIDS, the Asian clap that foiled every antibiotic in the book. I was willing to take it slow. "No," I said, "I don't think you're overreacting at all."

I paused to draw in a breath so deep it might have been a sigh. "I'm sorry," I whispered, giving her a doglike look of contrition. "I didn't know."

She reached out then and touched my hand—touched it, skin to skin—and mur-   20 mured that it was all right, she'd been through worse. "If you want to know," she breathed, "I like places like this."

I glanced around. The place was still empty, but for Helmut, in a blinding white jumpsuit and toque, studiously polishing the tile walls. "I know what you mean," I said.

We dated for a month—museums, drives in the country, French and German restaurants, ice-cream emporia, fern bars—before we kissed. And when we kissed, after a showing of *David and Lisa* at a revival house all the way up in Rhinebeck and on a night so cold no run-of-the-mill bacterium or commonplace virus could have survived it, it was the merest brushing of the lips. She was wearing a big-shouldered coat of synthetic fur and a knit hat pulled down over her brow and she hugged my arm as we stepped out of the theater and into the blast of the night. "God," she said, "did you see him when he screamed 'You touched me!'? Wasn't that priceless?" Her eyes were big and she seemed weirdly excited. "Sure," I said, "yeah, it was great," and then she pulled me close and kissed me. I felt the soft flicker of her lips against mine. "I love you," she said, "I think."

A month of dating and one dry fluttering kiss. At this point you might begin to wonder about me, but really, I didn't mind. As I say, I was willing to wait—I had the patience of Sisyphus—and it was enough just to be with her. Why rush things? I thought. This is good, this is charming, like the slow sweet unfolding of the romance in a Frank Capra movie, where sweetness and light always prevail. Sure, she had her idio-syncrasies, but who didn't? Frankly, I'd never been comfortable with the three-drinks-dinner-and-bed sort of thing, the girls who come on like they've been in prison for six years and just got out in time to put on their makeup and jump into the passenger seat of your car. Breda—that was her name, Breda Drumhill, and the very sound and syl-labification of it made me melt—was different.

Finally, two weeks after the trek to Rhinebeck, she invited me to her apartment. Cock-tails, she said. Dinner. A quiet evening in front of the tube.

She lived in Croton, on the ground floor of a restored Victorian, half a mile from the Harmon station, where she caught the train each morning for Manhattan and her job as an editor of *Anthropology Today*. She'd held the job since graduating from Barnard six years earlier (with a double major in Rhetoric and Alien Cultures), and it suited her temperament perfectly. Field anthropologists living among the River Dyak of Borneo or the Kurds of Kurdistan would send her rough and grammatically tor-tured accounts of their observations and she would whip them into shape for popular consumption. Naturally, filth and exotic disease, as well as outlandish customs and re-volting habits, played a leading role in her rewrites. Every other day or so she'd call me from work and in a voice that could barely contain its joy give me the details of some new and horrific disease she'd discovered.

She met me at the door in a silk kimono that featured a plunging neckline and a pair of dragons with intertwined tails. Her hair was pinned up as if she'd just stepped out of the bath and she smelled of Noxzema and pHisoHex. She pecked my cheek, took the bottle of Vouvray I held out in offering, and led me into the front room. "Chagas' disease," she said, grinning wide to show off her perfect, outsized teeth.

"Chagas' disease?" I echoed, not quite knowing what to do with myself. The room was as spare as a monk's cell. Two chairs, a loveseat, and a coffee table, in glass, chrome, and hard black plastic. No plants ("God knows what sort of insects might live on them—and the dirt, the dirt has got to be crawling with bacteria, not to mention spi-ders and worms and things") and no rug ("A breeding ground for fleas and ticks and chiggers").

Still grinning, she steered me to the hard black plastic loveseat and sat down beside me, the Vouvray cradled in her lap. "South America," she whispered, her eyes leaping with excitement. "In the jungle. These bugs—assassin bugs, they're called—isn't that wild? These bugs bite you and then, after they've sucked on you a while, they go potty next to the wound. When you scratch, it gets into your bloodstream, and anywhere from one to twenty years later you get a disease that's like a cross between malaria and AIDS."

"And then you die," I said.   30

"And then you die."

Her voice had turned somber. She wasn't grinning any longer. What could I say? I patted her hand and flashed a smile. "Yum," I said, mugging for her. "What's for dinner?"

She served a cold cream-of-tofu-carrot soup and little lentil-paste sandwiches for an appetizer and a garlic soufflé with biologically controlled vegetables for the entrée. Then it was snifters of cognac, the big-screen TV, and a movie called *The Boy in the Bubble,* about a kid raised in a totally antiseptic environment because he was born without an immune system. No one could touch him. Even the slightest sneeze would have killed him. Breda sniffled through the first half-hour, then pressed my hand and sobbed openly as the boy finally crawled out of the bubble, caught about thirty-seven different diseases, and died before the commercial break. "I've seen this movie six times now," she said, fighting to control her voice, "and it gets to me every time. What a life," she said, waving her snifter at the screen, "what a perfect life. Don't you envy him?"

I didn't envy him. I envied the jade pendant that dangled between her breasts and I told her so.

She might have giggled or gasped or lowered her eyes, but she didn't. She gave me a long slow look, as if she were deciding something, and then she allowed herself to blush, the color suffusing her throat in a delicious mottle of pink and white. "Give me a minute," she said mysteriously, and disappeared into the bathroom.

I was electrified. This was it. Finally. After all the avowals, the pressed hands, the   35 little jokes and routines, after all the miles driven, meals consumed, museums paced, and movies watched, we were finally, naturally, gracefully going to come together in the ultimate act of intimacy and love.

I felt hot. There were beads of sweat on my forehead. I didn't know whether to stand or sit. And then the lights dimmed, and there she was at the rheostat.

She was still in her kimono, but her hair was pinned up more severely, wound in a tight coil to the crown of her head, as if she'd girded herself for battle. And she held something in her hand—a slim package, wrapped in plastic. It rustled as she crossed the room.

"When you're in love, you make love," she said, easing down beside me on the rocklike settee, "—it's only natural." She handed me the package. "I don't want to give you the wrong impression," she said, her voice throaty and raw, "just because I'm careful and modest and because there's so much, well, filth in the world, but I have my passionate side too. I do. And I love you, I think."

"Yes," I said, groping for her, the package all but forgotten.

We kissed. I rubbed the back of her neck, felt something strange, an odd sag and   40 ripple, as if her skin had suddenly turned to Saran Wrap, and then she had her hand on my chest. "Wait," she breathed, "the, the thing."

I sat up. "Thing?"

The light was dim but I could see the blush invade her face now. She was sweet. Oh, she was sweet, my Little Em'ly, my Victorian princess. "It's Swedish," she said.

I looked down at the package in my lap. It was a clear, skin-like sheet of plastic, folded up in its transparent package like a heavy-duty garbage bag. I held it up to her huge, trembling eyes. A crazy idea darted in and out of my head. No, I thought.

"It's the newest thing," she said, the words coming in a rush, "the safest . . . I mean, nothing could possibly—"

My face was hot. "No," I said.

"It's a condom," she said, tears starting up in her eyes, "my doctor got them for me they're . . . they're Swedish." Her face wrinkled up and she began to cry. "It's a condom," she sobbed, crying so hard the kimono fell open and I could see the outline of the thing against the swell of her nipples, "a full-body condom."

I was offended. I admit it. It wasn't so much her obsession with germs and contagion, but that she didn't trust me after all that time. I was clean. Quintessentially clean. I was a man of moderate habits and good health, I changed my underwear and socks daily— sometimes twice a day—and I worked in an office, with clean, crisp, unequivocal numbers, managing my late father's chain of shoe stores (and he died cleanly himself, of a myocardial infarction, at seventy-five). "But Breda," I said, reaching out to console her and brushing her soft, plastic-clad breast in the process, "don't you trust me? Don't you believe in me? Don't you, don't you love me?" I took her by the shoulders, lifted her head, forced her to look me in the eye. "I'm clean," I said. "Trust me."

She looked away. "Do it for me," she said in her smallest voice, "if you really love me."

In the end, I did it. I looked at her, crying, crying for me, and I looked at the thin sheet of plastic clinging to her, and I did it. She helped me into the thing, poked two holes for my nostrils, zipped the plastic zipper up the back, and pulled it tight over my head. It fit like a wetsuit. And the whole thing—the stroking and the tenderness and the gentle yielding—was everything I'd hoped it would be.

Almost.

She called me from work the next day. I was playing with sales figures and thinking of her. "Hello," I said, practically cooing into the receiver.

"You've got to hear this." Her voice was giddy with excitement.

"Hey," I said, cutting her off in a passionate whisper, "last night was really special."

"Oh, yes," she said, "yes, last night. It was. And I love you, I do . . ." She paused to draw in her breath. "But listen to this: I just got a piece from a man and his wife living among the Tuareg of Nigeria—these are the people who follow cattle around, picking up the dung for their cooking fires?"

I made a small noise of awareness.

"Well, they make their huts of dung too—isn't that wild? And guess what—when times are hard, when the crops fail and the cattle can barely stand up, you know what they eat?"

"Let me guess," I said. "Dung?"

She let out a whoop. "Yes! Yes! Isn't it too much? They *eat* dung!"

I'd been saving one for her, a disease a doctor friend had told me about. "Onchocerciasis," I said. "You know it?"

There was a thrill in her voice. "Tell me."

"South America and Africa both. A fly bites you and lays its eggs in your bloodstream and when the eggs hatch, the larvae—these little white worms—migrate to your eyeballs, right underneath the membrane there, so you can see them wriggling around."

There was a silence on the other end of the line.

"Breda?"

"That's sick," she said. "That's really sick."

But I thought—? I trailed off. "Sorry," I said.

"Listen," and the edge came back into her voice, "the reason I called is because I love you, I think I love you, and I want you to meet somebody."

"Sure," I said.

"I want you to meet Michael. Michael Maloney."

"Sure. Who's he?"

She hesitated, paused just a beat, as if she knew she was going too far. "My doctor," she said.

You have to work at love. You have to bend, make subtle adjustments, sacrifices—love is nothing without sacrifice. I went to Dr. Maloney. Why not? I'd eaten tofu, bantered about leprosy and bilharziasis as if I were immune, and made love in a bag. If it made Breda happy—if it eased the nagging fears that ate at her day and night—then it was worth it.

The doctor's office was in Scarsdale, in his home, a two-tone mock Tudor with a winding drive and oaks as old as my grandfather's Chrysler. He was a young man—late thirties, I guessed—with a red beard, shaved head, and a pair of oversized spectacles in clear plastic frames. He took me right away—the very day I called—and met me at the door himself. "Breda's told me about you," he said, leading me into the floodlit vault of his office. He looked at me appraisingly a moment, murmuring "Yes, yes" into his beard, and then, with the aid of his nurses, Miss Archibald and Miss Slivovitz, put me through a battery of tests that would have embarrassed an astronaut.

First, there were the measurements, including digital joints, maxilla, cranium, penis, and earlobe. Next, the rectal exam, the EEG and urine sample. And then the tests. Stress tests, patch tests, reflex tests, lung-capacity tests (I blew up yellow balloons till they popped, then breathed into a machine the size of a Hammond organ), the X-rays, sperm count, and a closely printed, twenty-four-page questionnaire that included sections on dream analysis, genealogy, and logic and reasoning. He drew blood too, of course—to test vital-organ function and exposure to disease. "We're testing for antibodies to over fifty diseases," he said, eyes dodging behind the walls of his lenses. "You'd be surprised how many people have been infected without even knowing it." I couldn't tell if he was joking or not. On the way out he took my arm and told me he'd have the results in a week.

That week was the happiest of my life. I was with Breda every night, and over the weekend we drove up to Vermont to stay at a hygiene center her cousin had told her about. We dined by candlelight—on real food—and afterward we donned the Saran Wrap suits and made joyous, sanitary love. I wanted more, of course—the touch of skin on skin—but I was fulfilled and I was happy. Go slow, I told myself. All things in time. One night, as we lay entwined in the big white fortress of her bed, I stripped back the hood of the plastic suit and asked her if she'd ever trust me enough to make love in the way of the centuries, raw and unprotected. She twisted free of her own wrapping and looked away, giving me that matchless patrician profile. "Yes," she said, her voice pitched low, "yes, of course. Once the results are in."

"Results?"   75

She turned to me, her eyes searching mine. "Don't tell me you've forgotten?"

I had. Carried away, intense, passionate, brimming with love, I'd forgotten.

"Silly you," she murmured, tracing the line of my lips with a slim, plastic-clad finger, "Does the name Michael Maloney ring a bell?"

And then the roof fell in.

I called and there was no answer. I tried her at work and her secretary said she was   80
out. I left messages. She never called back. It was as if we'd never known one another, as if I were a stranger, a door-to-door salesman, a beggar on the street.

I took up a vigil in front of her house. For a solid week I sat in my parked car and watched the door with all the fanatic devotion of a pilgrim at a shrine. Nothing. She neither came nor went. I rang the phone off the hook, interrogated her friends, haunted the elevator, the hallway, and the reception room at her office. She'd disappeared.

Finally, in desperation, I called her cousin in Larchmont. I'd met her once—she was a homely, droopy-sweatered, baleful-looking girl who represented everything gone wrong in the genes that had come to such glorious fruition in Breda—and barely knew what to say to her. I'd made up a speech, something about how my mother was dying in Phoenix, the business was on the rocks, I was drinking too much and dwelling on thoughts of suicide, destruction, and final judgment, and I had to talk to Breda just one more time before the end, and did she by any chance know where she was? As it turned out, I didn't need the speech. Breda answered the phone.

"Breda, it's me," I choked. "I've been going crazy looking for you."

Silence.

"Breda, what's wrong? Didn't you get my messages?"   85

Her voice was halting, distant. "I can't see you anymore," she said.

"Can't see me?" I was stunned, hurt, angry. "What do you mean?"

"All those feet," she said.

"Feet?" It took me a minute to realize she was talking about the shoe business. "But I don't deal with anybody's feet—I work in an office. Like you. With air-conditioning and sealed windows. I haven't touched a foot since I was sixteen."

"Athlete's foot," she said. "Psoriasis. Eczema. Jungle rot."   90

"What is it? The physical?" My voice cracked with outrage. "Did I flunk the damn physical? Is that it?"

She wouldn't answer me.

A chill went through me. "What did he say? What did the son of a bitch say?"

There was a distant ticking over the line, the pulse of time and space, the gentle sway of Bell Telephone's hundred million miles of wire.

"Listen," I pleaded, "see me one more time, just once—that's all I ask. We'll talk   95
it over. We could go on a picnic. In the park. We could spread a blanket and, and we could sit on opposite corners—"

"Lyme disease," she said.

"Lyme disease?"

"Spread by tick bite. They're seething in the grass. You get Bell's palsy, meningitis, the lining of your brain swells up like dough."

"Rockefeller Center then," I said. "By the fountain."

Her voice was dead. "Pigeons," she said. "They're like flying rats."   100

"Helmut's. We can meet at Helmut's. Please. I love you."

"I'm sorry."

"Breda, please listen to me. We were so close—"

"Yes," she said, "we were close," and I thought of that first night in her apartment, the boy in the bubble and the Saran Wrap suit, thought of the whole dizzy spectacle of our romance till her voice came down like a hammer on the refrain, "but not that close." ●

Kate Braverman *(1950–   )*

Pagan Night   *1995*

Sometimes they called him Forest or Sky. Sometimes they called him River or Wind. Once, during a week of storms when she could not leave the van at all, not for seven consecutive days, they called him Gray. The baby with the floating name and how she carries him and he keeps crying, has one rash after another, coughs, seems to shudder and choke. It is a baby of spasms, of a twisted face turning colors. You wouldn't want to put his picture on the baby-food jar. You wouldn't want to carry his picture in your wallet, even if you had his photograph and she doesn't.

Of course, Dalton never wanted this baby. Neither did she. The baby was just something that happened and there didn't seem to be the time to make it not happen. They were on tour, two months of one-nighters between San Diego and Seattle and when it was over the band broke up. When it was over, they got drunk and sold the keyboards and video cameras for heroin. Then they were in San Francisco and she still had the apartment. Later, they had Dalton's van.

Then they had to leave San Francisco. Something about the equipment, the amplifiers Dalton insisted were his, that they had accrued to him by a process of decision and sacrifice. Then they had to wind through California with her belly already showing and all they had left were their black leather jackets and the silver-and-turquoise jewelry they had somehow acquired in Gallup or Flagstaff. Dalton kept talking about the drummer's kit, which he claimed was actually his, and they sold it in Reno and lived on the fortieth floor of an old hotel with a view of the mountains. They had room service for three weeks and by then she had stopped throwing up. After that there was more of Nevada and the van broke again on the other side of the state. There was the slow entry into Idaho, after mountains and desert and Utah and the snow had melted and then the baby they had almost forgotten about was born.

Dalton can't stand the baby crying. That's why she leaves the van, walks three miles into town along the river. When she has a dollar-fifty, she buys an espresso in the café where the waitress has heard of her band.

Sunny stays away from the van as long as she can. Sometimes someone will offer   5 her a ride to the park or the zoo or the shopping mall and she takes it. She's let her hair grow out, the purple and magenta streaks are nearly gone, seem an accident that could have happened to anyone, a mislabeled bottle, perhaps. Dalton says it's better to blend in. He's cut his hair, too, and wears a San Diego Padres baseball cap. He says it makes him feel closer to God.

Willow. Cottonwood. Creek. Eagle. She could call the baby Willow. But Dalton refuses to give it a name. He resists the gender, refers to the baby as it, not he. Just it, the creature that makes the noise. But it doesn't cost any money. She still feeds it from her body and the rashes come and go. It's because she doesn't have enough diapers. Sunny puts suntan lotion on the baby's sores, massage oil, whatever is left in her suitcase from the other life. Once she covered the baby's rash with layers of fluorescent orange lipstick, the last of her stage makeup.

Sunny has begun to realize that if she can't keep the baby quiet, Dalton will leave her. It won't always be summer here. There will come a season when she can't just walk all day, or sit in the mall or the lobby of the granite city hall, pretending to read a newspaper. She won't be able to spend the entire winter in the basement of the museum where they have built a replica of the town as it was in the beginning, with its penny-candy store and nickel barber shop and baths for a quarter. She won't be able to spend five or six months attempting to transport herself through time telepathically. She could work in the saloon, find an Indian to watch the baby. Later she could marry the sheriff.

Today, walking by the river, it occurred to Sunny that this landscape was different from any other she had known. It wasn't the punched-awake, intoxicated glow of the tropics, seductive and inflamed. It didn't tease you and make you want to die for it. That's what she thought of Hawaii. And it wasn't the rancid gleam like spoiled lemons that coated everything in a sort of bad childhood waxy veneer flashback. That's what she thought of Los Angeles where they had lived for two years. In Los Angeles, afternoon smelled of ash and some enormous August you could not placate or forget. Los Angeles air reminded her of what happened to children in foster homes at dusk when they took their clothes off, things that were done in stucco added-on garages with ropes and pieces of metal and the freeway rushing in the background like a cheap sound track. It was in sync, but it had no meaning.

This Idaho was an entirely separate area of the spectrum. There was something unstable about it, as if it had risen from a core of some vast, failed caution. It was the end of restlessness. It was what happened when you stopped looking over your shoulder. It was what happened when you dared to catch your breath, when you thought you were safe.

Sunny feels there is some mean streak to this still raw, still frontier, place. This 10 land knows it gets cold, winter stays too long, crops rot, you starve. This land knows about wind, how after storms the clouds continue to assemble every afternoon over the plain, gather and recombine and rain again and this can go on for weeks. Her shoes are always damp. Her feet are encased in white blisters. Always, the thunderheads are congregating and mating and their spawn is a cold rain.

Somedays the clouds are in remission, ringing the plain but staying low. On such afternoons, the three of them go down to the Snake River. They follow a dirt road to another dirt road and they've been instructed where to turn, near the hit-by-lightning willow. They park on a rise above the channel. Dalton leaves his guitar in the van and padlocks it, walks ahead of her and the baby with the fishing pole over his shoulder. They walk beneath black branches, find the path of smooth rocks down to the bank leading to a railroad bridge. It's a trestle over the Snake made from railroad ties with gaps between them and the tracks running down the center. This is how they cross the Snake, reach the other bank where the fishing is supposed to be good. There are tiny grassy islands Dalton can roll up his black jeans and wade out to. Dalton traded some-body in town for a fly-fishing rod. He probably traded drugs for the rod, though she realizes she hasn't seen her black leather jacket for more than a week.

On Sundays yellow with orioles and tiger monarchs and a sun that turns the grasses soft, Dalton takes them fishing on the far bank of the river. One late afternoon he caught four trout. Sunny could see their rainbows when the sun struck their skin. They looked sewed with red sequins. They were supposed to be sixteen inches. That was the rule for the South Fork of the Snake. Their trout were smaller, seven and eight inches, but they kept them anyway, cooked them on a stick over a fire they made near the van. Dalton said the eyes were the best part and he gave her one and it was white as a pried-open moon and she ate it.

Now she is walking into a yellow that makes her feel both restless and invigorated. A yellow of simultaneity and symbols and some arcane celebration she can vaguely sense. When she ate the trout eyes, they were like crisp white stones. She thought of rituals, primitive people, the fundamental meaning of blood. If one mastered these ele-ments, it might be possible to see better in the dark. She shakes her head as if to clear it, but nothing changes. Her entire life is a network of intuitions, the beginning of words, like neon and dome, pine, topaz, shadow, but then the baby starts crying.

Sunny knows it's all a matter of practice, even silence and erasure and absence. What it isn't is also a matter of practice. In the same way you can take piano or voice and train yourself to recognize and exploit your range, you can also teach yourself not to speak, not to remember. That's why when Dalton asks what's she thinking, she says, "Nothing." It's a kind of discipline. What she's really thinking about is what will hap-pen when summer is over. What will happen if she can't make the baby stop crying?

Sometimes when she is frightened, it calms her to think about Marilyn Monroe. 15 Sunny knows all about Marilyn's childhood, the foster homes, the uncles who fondled her breasts, kissed her seven-year-old nipples, and they got hard. Then Marilyn knew she was a bad girl. She would always be a bad girl. It was like being at a carnival, a pri-vate carnival, just for her. There were balloons and streamers, party hats and birthday cakes with chocolate frosting and her name written in a neon pink. And no one could tell her no. She had liked to think about Marilyn Monroe when they were driving in the van between gigs. The band was in its final incarnation then. Sunny was already pregnant and it was called Pagan Night.

When Dalton asks her what she's thinking and she says, "Nothing," she is really imagining winter and how she is certain there won't be enough to eat. Dalton says he'll shoot a cow. There are cows grazing outside of town, off half the dirt roads and along the banks of the river. Or he'll shoot a deer, an elk, he'll trap rabbits. He's been talk-ing to people in town, at the Rio Bar. He's traded something for the fly-fishing rig, but he still has both guns and the rifle. He'll never trade the weapons, not even for heroin, even if they could find any here.

Today, on this cool morning, Sunny has walked from the river to the zoo. Admis-sion is one dollar, but the woman in the booth knows her and has started to simply wave her in.

Sunny passes through a gate near a willow and she would like to name the baby Willow. It would be an omen and it would survive winter. Then she is entering the zoo, holding her baby without a name. She sits with her baby near the swan pond un-til someone gives her a quarter, a sandwich, a freshly purchased bag of popcorn. They simply hand it to her.

She has memorized each animal, bird, and fish in this miniature zoo. The birds stand by mossy waterfalls of the sort she imagines adorn the swimming pools of movie stars. She sits nursing her baby that she is pretending is named Willow. If anyone asks, and she knows no one will, she is prepared to say, His name is Willow.

Later, she stands in a patch of sun by an exhibit featuring a glassed-in bluish pool   20
that should contain a penguin or a seal, but is empty. It smells derelict, harsh and sour with something like the residue of trapped wind and the final thoughts of small mammals as they chew off their feet and bleed to death. You can walk down a flight of stairs and look through the glass, but nothing is swimming. She knows. She has climbed down twice.

Sunny likes to look at what isn't there, in the caged water whipped by sun. This is actually the grotto that is most full, with its battered streams of light like hieroglyphics, a language in flux, lost in shifting ripples.

She pauses in front of the golden eagle. It will not look at her, even when she whistles. The information stenciled to the cage says the golden eagle can live thirty years, longer than many movie stars, longer than Hendrix and Janis and Jim Morrison and James Dean. This particular bird will probably outlive her.

Sunny is thinking about how hungry she is, when someone offers her half a peanut butter and jelly sandwich. Actually, the woman has her child do this, reach out a baby arm to her as if she is now some declawed beast you could let your kid near.

Her own baby is wrapped in a shawl, the same shawl she had once laid across the sofa in the living room of her apartment in San Francisco. She had gone there to study modern dancing, tap, and ballet. Her father had wanted her to go to nursing school. If she went to nursing school, her father could believe she had finally forgotten. He could conclude that she was well and whole, and he could sleep without pills. His ulcer would disappear. He could take communion again.

Sunny took singing lessons and began to meet men with rock 'n' roll bands. Nurs-   25
ing school became white and distant. It became a sort of moon you could put between your teeth and swallow. She stopped envisioning herself in a starched cotton uniform with a stethoscope around her neck. What she wanted now was to smoke grass and hash and opium and stare out the window at Alcatraz. What she wanted to do was sniff powder drawn in lines across a wide square of mirror she kept on the side of the sofa, like a sort of magic screen where you could watch your face change forever.

Now, at the zoo, she stands on the wood slats surrounding the fish pond filled with keepers, twenty- and twenty-five- and thirty-inch rainbow trout. This is what keepers look like. On yellow Sundays, she and Dalton and the baby walk across the railroad trestle over the Snake River. But Dalton will never catch a fish this big.

She was afraid the first time they crossed the bridge. Dalton had to grab her hand. He hadn't touched her body since the baby was born. He had to pull her along. The bridge was higher than she had thought. The river was rushing underneath like a sequence of waves, but faster and sharper, without breath or cycles, and she was holding the baby. That day she was secretly calling the baby Sunday. And she was cradling Sunday with one arm and Dalton was holding her other hand, pulling her through the yellow. He was also holding the fishing rod he'd somehow procured at the Rio Bar, traded somebody something for, she is beginning to think it was her black leather jacket with the studs on the cuffs, the special studs sewed on by a woman who claimed she was a gypsy in Portland.

Dalton must think she won't need her leather jacket in winter. He isn't considering what she'll need in winter. Maybe they won't still be in Idaho. Maybe they won't still be together. And the bridge was wider than she had at first imagined. It was like a pier with its set of two railroad tracks down the center, one thinner, the other fatter, one unused set covered with rust. The bridge was made from railroad ties and there were gaps between them where a foot could get caught, something small could fall through. Dalton said, "Make a pattern. Step every other one. Don't look down." That's what she did, stepped every other one, didn't look down, but still she could hear the river in a kind of anguish beneath her and she was shaking.

"It's an abandoned bridge, isn't it?" she asked Dalton.

The first few times he said yes, but when they had crossed the fourth time, he said no. She stopped, found herself staring into sun. "What do you mean?" she demanded. 30

"Look at the rails. The larger set are clean. Trains do this." He pointed at the tracks. "Or they'd be covered with rust."

"What if the train came now? As we were crossing?" she finally asked.

"There are beams every twenty feet." Dalton pointed to a kind of metal girder. "We'd hang on the side until it passed."

She tries to imagine herself standing on the girder, holding the baby which in her mind is named Sunday in one of her arms. She cannot conceive of this. Instead she remembers, suddenly, a story Dalton once told her years ago, before they had gone on the road, when they first recited their secret information to each other, their collection of shame, where they were truly from, what had happened, what was irrevocable.

Dalton told her about a night in high school when he had been drinking beer with his friends. Perhaps it was spring. They had been drinking since dawn and now it was after midnight. It was Ohio. That's where Dalton was from. His friends had wandered down to the train station. His best friend had tried to hop a train. Johnny Mohawk. That's what they called him, Mohawk, because he said he was part Indian. Johnny Mohawk tried to hop a train and fell. It ran over him, amputating both legs, his right arm, and half of his left. 35

"He was so drunk, that's what saved him," Dalton explained. It must have been later. They were riding in a tour bus. They had an album out and the company had given them a roadie, a driver, and a bus. Outside was neon and wind and houses you didn't want to live in. "He was so drunk, he didn't feel it," Dalton was saying. "If he'd been more awake, the shock would have killed him."

Dalton glanced out the window, at some in-between stretch of California where there were waist-high grasses and wild flowers and a sense of too much sun, even in the darkness. She asked him what happened. She tried to imagine Johnny Mohawk, but she could not. Her mind refused to accommodate the brutal lack of symmetry, would produce only words like tunnel and agony, suffocate and scream. Even if she had gone to nursing school, even if she went right now, enrolled in the morning, she could do nothing about Johnny Mohawk. It would always be too late.

"It was the best thing ever happened to him," Dalton said. "He was on his way to becoming a professional drunk. Like his father, like his uncles and inbred cousins. After the accident, he got a scholarship to State. They gave him a tutor and a special car. Now he's an engineer for an oil company."

Sunny thinks about Johnny Mohawk as she stands in the zoo, in front of a grotto with grassy sides and a sleeping male and female lion. Their cage seems too small to contain them if they wanted to do anything other than sleep in the damp green grass. She wonders what would happen if she fell in, over the low metal bar.

Near her, a pregnant woman with three blond daughters, each with a different colored ribbon in their long yellow hair, tells her two-year-old, "Don't you climb up on that bar now. You fall in, there'd be no way to get you out. That hungry old lion would eat you right up."

Sunny feels the baby in her arms, how heavy it is, how it could so easily slide from her, through the bar, into the grassy grotto. She could never retrieve it. No one would expect her to.

Then she is walking past the one zebra. When Dalton asks her if she wants to talk about anything, she shakes her head, no. She is considering how filled each no is, glittering and yellow. Each no is a miniature carnival, with curled smiles and balloons on strings and a profusion of names for babies. And in this no are syllables like willow and cottonwood and shadow and Johnny Mohawk. And in this no is the railroad trestle above one hundred thousand rainbow trout.

Sunny's favorite exhibit is the snow leopard. It is strange that a zoo in a tiny town should have such an animal. They are so rare. She reads what the snow leopard eats, mammals and birds. Its social life is solitary. How long does it live? Twenty-five years. Not quite long enough to see its first record go platinum. And it isn't really asleep on the green slope behind its grid of bars as much as it is simply turned away. Perhaps it is thinking about the past, and on its lip is something that isn't quite a smile. Or perhaps he is simply listening to birds.

There are always birds when they cross the railroad trestle on Sunday, the Snake below them, the bald eagles and blue herons and swallows and robins, orioles and magpies, in the air near their shoulders. And there is no schedule for the train. She's called Union Pacific five times, waited for the man in charge to come back from vacation, to come back from the flu, to be at his desk, and there is no way to predict when the train runs over this particular trestle. It's a local. It gets put together at the last moment, no one knows when.

When they cross the bridge on Sunday, she is obsessively listening for trains. And there are so many birds, fat robins, unbelievably red, and orioles, the yellow of chalk from fourth grade when she got an A and her teacher let her write the entire spelling list for the week on the blackboard. And ducks and Canadian geese and loons, all of them stringing their syllables across the afternoon, hanging them near her face like a kind of party streamer. The baby is named Sunday or Sometimes and she feels how heavy it is, how it could just drop from her arms.

It's become obvious that these fishing Sundays are not about catching trout. It's a practice for something else entirely, for leaving, for erasure, silence, and absence. She understands now. It's the end of July. She won't be able to feed the baby from her body indefinitely or walk through town all day, looking for trash cans where she can deposit the diapers she has used over and over again.

Now it is time to rehearse. They are involved in a new show with an agenda they don't mention. It's a rehearsal for abandoning the baby. She practices leaving it on the bank, walking fifty steps away, smoking a cigarette. Then she rushes back to retrieve it, to press it against her. If she simply took a slightly longer path from the bank, permitted herself to smoke a joint, a third or fourth cigarette, she might not remember exactly where she placed the baby, not with all the foliage, the vines and brush, bushes and trees, the whole bank an ache of greenery. Something could have interceded, a sudden aberration in the river current or perhaps a hawk. She wouldn't be blamed.

In the children's petting zoo, a gray rabbit mounts a white one. Another white rabbit eats from a bowl. They eat and mate, eat and mate. In the winter, Dalton says he'll shoot a deer. He's made a deal with somebody at the Rio Bar, something about sharing and storing. There are always cattle, fish, rabbits, beavers, and otters that can be trapped.

During the day, Dalton says he's working on songs. He still has both guitars. He can only write music when the baby isn't crying or coughing. She wants to name the baby Music or Tears. Once she tells Dalton she wants to name the baby Bay. She remembers the apartment they had with the view of the bridge, the way at midnight the wind felt like a scalded blue. It was when everything seemed simultaneously anesthetized and hot. It was a moment she remembers as happy.

"It's not time to name it," Dalton said. He was strumming his twelve-string. He   50
said many African tribes didn't name a baby until it had survived a year. Dalton looked at her and smiled. His lips reminded her of Marilyn Monroe.

That's when she realized each day would have to be distinct and etched. She licks the baby's face. She sits on a bench in the sun at the zoo by a pond with a mossy waterfall in the center. There are swans in this pond. She closes her eyes and smells the baby and decides to name him Swan. She kisses his cheek and whispers in his ear, "Your name is Swan. Your name is Moss. Your name is Bye-Bye."

"What are you thinking?" Dalton asks. It was during the storm two weeks ago. He was drinking tequila. Rain struck the van and she thought of rocks and bullets and time travel.

"Nothing," she replied.

Wind. Hidden networks. The agenda that sparks. You know how night feels without candles, without light bulbs, maps, schedules. This is what we do not speak of Bye-bye-bye, baby. Bye-bye-bye.

Everyday, Dalton says he's going to write songs while she is gone. He has a joint in   55
his mouth, curled on his side in the back of the van on a ridge above the Snake River where they now live. He has a bottle of vodka tucked into his belt. The vodka is gone when she comes back. Sunny has to knock again and again on the side of the van, has to kick it with her foot, has to shout his name, until he wakes up.

Each day must be separate, an entity, like a species, a snow leopard, a zebra, or a rainbow trout. Each one with a distinct evolution and morphology, niches, complex accidents. Last Sunday, she smoked a joint and drank tequila. Then they crossed the river on the railroad ties. She has a pattern, left foot, skip one with the right, left foot, skip one with the right, don't look down.

She knows it will happen on a Sunday, perhaps next Sunday. Dalton will say, "Come over, look at this."

"I can't. I'm feeding the baby," she will answer.

"Put it down a second," he'll say. "You've got to see this."

She'll place the baby in the center of soft weeds. She'll follow the sound of his   60
voice, find Dalton on the bank with a great trout, twenty inches, thirty inches long. It will be their keeper and she will bend down, help him pull it in. Her feet will get wet. She will use her hat for a net, her red hat that says Wyoming Centennial 1990. The seconds will elongate, the minutes will spread into an afternoon, with no one counting or keeping track. When they've pulled the trout in, when they've finished the tequila,

it will be dark. They will begin searching for the baby, but there will be only shadow. No one could say they were at fault. No one could say anything. No one knows about them or the baby, and the van has got at least five thousand miles left in it. They could be in New York or Florida in two days.

Perhaps it will be a Sunday when they are crossing the bridge. She'll be holding the baby named Sometimes or Swan or Willow, and they'll have to leap onto the steel girders as the train rushes by. The baby will drop from her arms into the Snake and it will be taken on the current like Moses.

They will never mention the falling. They will not speak of it, not once. It will just be something caught in the edge of their smile, like a private carnival that went through town and maybe you saw it once and too briefly and then it was gone.

She knows Dalton believes they are purer, more muscle and bone, closer to an archetypal winter beyond artifice. That was part of why they called the band Pagan Night. They are animals, barbarians, heathens. They are savage and recognize this, its possibilities and what it costs. In China and India, girl children are often drowned at birth. There are fashions of surviving famines engraved on the nerves.

Maybe this Sunday they will be crossing the bridge when the train erupts from a spoil of foliage and shadow, willows and heron and orioles. Dalton will have left his guitar in the van, padlocked with his paperback myths of primitive people. Perhaps it will be a Sunday after Dalton returned from the Rio Bar with heroin. They will have cooked it up and had it that night, all night, and the next day, all day, until it was finished and there was nothing left, not even in the cotton in the spoon.

When she stands on the Sunday railroad trestle, she will think about ineluctable trajectories. There is a destiny to the direction and journey of all objects, stars and birds, babies and stones and rivers. Who can explain how or why that snow leopard came from Asia to reside in an obsolete grotto in a marginal farming town among barley and potato fields in southern Idaho? What shaped such a voyage, what miscalculations, what shift of wind or currents, what failure of which deity? 65

Sunny knows exactly what she will be thinking when it happens. There are always acres of sun and their fading. It is all a sequence of erasures and absences. Who is to say flesh into water or flesh into rock is not a form of perfection? What of Moses on the river with an ineluctable destiny to be plucked from reeds by a princess? Perhaps on some fishing Sunday when the baby is named Swallow or Tiger and falls from her arms, someone on a distant bank will look up and say they saw the sudden ascension of a god. ●

Explorations of the Text

1. In "Modern Love," does the narrator fall in love with Breda?

2. Characterize the narrator and Breda. How do they differ from each other?

3. Analyze Sunny's and Dalton's characters in "Pagan Night." How do their expectations for the relationship differ? How have they been shaped by their pasts? Discuss their differing attitudes toward the baby.

4. In both stories intimacy and risk-taking are central issues in their relationships. How do these issues affect the characters differently?

5. Both authors use symbolism to convey themes. T. C. Boyle's story is a humorous and satiric presentation of "modern love" in the nineties. What do the imagery of cleanliness and disease and the symbol of the full body condom sug-

gest about issues in relationships? "Pagan Night," in contrast, presents a disturbing and serious portrait of a young couple struggling with the experience of having a baby. What do the nature images (the descriptions of the Snake River), the baby's suggested names (i.e., "Willow, "Forest or Sky," or "River or Wind"), the visits to the zoo, the snow leopard, Moses, and the bridge at the end of the work suggest?

6. Consider Plato's definition of love in the excerpt from the *Symposium*. Are these couples searching for the missing part of themselves?

7. Compare and contrast Dalton and Sunny in "Pagan Night" with the couple in Ernest Hemingway's "Hills like White Elephants."

The Reading/Writing Connection

1. Write a monologue for one of the characters about the nature of love or of relationships. Or write a dialogue between the two characters about a conflict in their relationship. What do you conclude about the conflicts in their relationship?

2. Debate topic: Do you think that Sunny in "Pagan Night" will abandon her baby? Argue pro or con.

3. Freewrite: In both these stories the couples seem unable to connect. What are the components of a successful love relationship?

Ideas for Writing

1. In what ways do "Modern Love," "Pagan Night," or "Shiloh" illustrate developmental issues for adolescent girls and boys that often extend into adulthood as described by Mary Pipher and Williams Pollack in their essays in this chapter?

2. **Write an Argument:** Do these stories present realistic visions of "modern love"? Do they present the issues, conflicts, and/or obstacles that couples face in a relationship? Argue pro or con. You may refer to other works in this chapter.

 On the Web: *Essays: Love and Loss*

Please visit http://www.academic.cengage.com/english/Schmidt/Legacies4e/ for links to the following online resources.

Sheryl St. Germain, "What We're Good At"

Heather Eliot, "Sandbags in the Archipelago"

POETRY

William Shakespeare *(1564–1616)*

Let Me Not to the Marriage of True Minds *1609*

Let me not to the marriage of true minds
Admit impediments. Love is not love
Which alters when it alteration finds,
Or bends with the remover to remove.
O no, it is an ever-fixèd mark   5
That look on tempests and is never shaken;
It is the star to every wand'ring bark,[1]
Whose worth's unknown, although his height[2] be taken.
Love's not Time's fool,[3] though rosy lips and cheeks
Within his bending sickle's compass come;   10
Love alters not with his brief hours and weeks,
But bears it out[4] even to the edge of doom.[5]
If this be error and upon me proved,
I never writ, nor no man every loved.

Explorations of the Text

1. Why does the persona speak of a "marriage of true minds"?
2. Paraphrase the first two lines. What does the first statement mean?
3. Why does love not "[alter]" or "[bend]"? Why is it "an ever-fixèd mark"?
4. What do the navigational images mean?
5. Look at personification in this sonnet. What is personified? Why? What is the relationship of love and time? Why is love not "Time's fool"?
6. Discuss the final **couplet**. Solve the **paradox**.
7. Consider the view of love in this sonnet. Is the persona convincing in his contention that true love lasts "even to the edge of doom"?

The Reading/Writing Connection

1. Define love or another abstract idea by stating what it is not. Begin with: Love is not. . . .
2. "Think" Topic: Do you agree with the persona's view of true love?

Ideas for Writing

1. Some critics consider this poem to be Shakespeare's greatest sonnet. Evaluate "Let Me Not to the Marriage of True Minds." (See checklist in Chapter 11.)

---

[1]**bark:** Small ship.   [2]**height:** Altitude.   [3]**fool:** Slave.   [4]**bears it out:** Endures.   [5]**edge of doom:** The Last Judgment.

William Shakespeare *(1564–1616)*

Shall I Compare Thee to a Summer's Day? 1609

Shall I compare thee to a summer's day?
Thou art more lovely and more temperate.
Rough winds do shake the darling buds of May,
And summer's lease hath all too short a date.
Sometimes too hot the eye of heaven shines, 5
And often is his gold complexion dimmed;
And every fair from fair sometime declines,
By chance, or nature's changing course, untrimmed.
But thy eternal summer shall not fade,
Nor lose possession of that fair thou ow'st;[1] 10
Nor shall death brag thou wand'rest in his shade,
When in eternal lines to time thou grow'st.
So long as men can breathe or eyes can see,
So long lives this, and this gives life to thee.

Explorations of the Text

1. Why does the speaker consider his loved one more lovely than "a summer's day"? What are the positive qualities of the loved one?
2. List ways in which nature and time change beauty. Interpret lines 3–8.
3. Explain the shift in tone and in subject in line 9. Why does the speaker assure the lover that "eternal summer shall not fade"?
4. What is the relation of art and love? Look carefully at the **couplet** at the end. To what does "this" refer?
5. Identify **metaphors** and **similes** in the sonnet. How do they relate to theme?

The Reading/Writing Connection

1. Write about the timelessness of art and the fragility of beauty in this sonnet. What do you conclude?
2. Freewrite and create a portrait of a loved one through the use of figurative language (e.g., similes and metaphors).

Ideas for Writing

1. Explicate this sonnet. (Focus on imagery, figurative language, formal elements.)

---

[1]**ow'st:** Ownest.

John Donne *(1571–1631)*

A Valediction Forbidding Mourning   *1633*

As virtuous men pass mildly away,
    And whisper to their souls to go,
Whilst some of their sad friends do say
    The breath goes now, and some say, no:

So let us melt, and make no noise,   5
    No tear-floods, nor sigh-tempests move;
'Twere profanation[1] of our joys
    To tell the laity our love.

Moving of th' earth[2] brings harms and fears;
    Men reckon what it did and meant;   10
But trepidation of the spheres,[3]
    Though greater far, is innocent.

Dull sublunary lovers' love
    (Whose soul is sense)[4] cannot admit
Absence, because it doth remove   15
    Those things which elemented it.

But we, by a love so much refined
    That ourselves know not what it is,
Inter-assured of the mind,
    Care less, eyes, lips, and hands to miss.   20

Our two souls, therefore, which are one,
    Though I must go, endure not yet
A breach, but an expansion,[5]
    Like gold to airy thinness beat.

If they be two, they are two so   25
    As stiff twin compasses are two:[6]
Thy soul, the fixed foot, makes no show
    To move, but doth, if th' other do.

---

[1]**profanation:** The lovers are like priests, and their love is a mystery.   [2]**Moving of th' earth:** Earthquakes.   [3]**trepidation of the spheres:** Prior to Newton's explanation of the equinoxes, people assumed that stars and planets had circular positions. The observation of irregularities (the result of the wobbling of the earth's axis) was explained by the theory of trepidation, a trembling that occurred in outer spheres around the earth.   [4]**(Whose soul is sense):** A completely physical attraction.   [5]**expansion:** Gold is quite malleable.   [6]**twin compasses are two:** Compasses used for drawing circles.

> And though it in the center sit,
>   Yet when the other far doth roam,   30
> It leans and harkens after it,
>   And grows erect as that comes home.
>
> Such wilt thou be to me, who must,
>   Like th' other foot, obliquely run;
> Thy firmness makes my circle just,[7]   35
>   And makes me end where I begun.

Explorations of the Text

1. To what event does the speaker compare his separation from his beloved in the first stanza?
2. What does he mean by the "trepidation of the spheres"?
3. Why can "dull" lovers not part easily? Why can they not tolerate "absence"?
4. What does the "refined" love of the speaker require? (See stanza 5.)
5. How does the gold imagery in lines 21–24 expand the vision of the lovers' communion?
6. Examine the metaphysical conceit comparing the lovers to "twin compasses." Is this extended figure effective?
7. Is the speaker's argument against "mourning" persuasive?

The Reading/Writing Connection

1. "Think" Topic: Write a letter to the speaker of the poem, responding to his view of love.

Ideas for Writing

1. Both Shakespeare and Donne refer to "the marriage of true minds," a love more refined than ordinary relationship. Take a position on ideal love or on grand passion.
2. Compare Plato's concept of union with Donne's ideas.

Heather McHugh *(1948–)*

Earthmoving Malediction   *1988*

> Bulldoze the bed where we made love,
> bulldoze the goddamn room.
> Let rubble be our evidence
> and wreck our home.

---

[7] **... makes my circle just:** Round.

I can't give touching up
by inches, can't give beating up
by heart. So set the comforter
on fire, and turn the dirt

to some advantage—palaces of pigweed,
treasuries of turd. The fist
will vindicate the hand,
and tooth and nail

refuse to burn, and I
must not look back, as Mrs. Lot
was named for such a little—
something in a cemetery,

or a man. Bulldoze the coupled
ploys away, the cute exclusives
in the social mall. We dwell

on earth, where beds
are brown, where swoops
are fell. Bulldoze

the pearly gates:
if paradise comes down
there is no hell.

5

10

15

20

25

Explorations of the Text

1. Discuss the speaker's point of view and tone and attitude toward her lover. What do you imagine is the source of her anger?

2. What does the imagery of the bulldozer and "the rubble" suggest about her feelings?

3. How does the stanzaic form reinforce meaning? How does hyperbole add to the meaning of the work?

4. In what ways does John Donne's "Valediction: Forbidding Mourning" serve as the context for the poem?

The Reading/Writing Connection

1. Create a portrait of the speaker. What does she look like? How old is she? What is she wearing? Why is she angry? What do you conclude about her character?

2. Create a short dramatic scene based on the poem. Create a conflict situation and the dialogue between the lover and the speaker about this conflict. Or create a monologue for her lover.

Ideas for Writing

1. Look up the definitions of "malediction," "benediction," and "valediction." How do they play off of each other in this work?

2. Examine the theme of betrayal in this work and a work in the "Love and Betrayal" cluster.

Andrew Marvell *(1621–78)*

To His Coy Mistress *1681*

Had we but world enough and time,
This coyness, lady, were no crime.
We would sit down and think which way
To walk, and pass our long love's day.
Thou by the Indian Ganges'[1] side 5
Should'st rubies find; I by the tide
Of Humber[2] would complain.[3] I would
Love you ten years before the flood,
And you should, if you please, refuse
Till the conversion of the Jews. 10
My vegetable love should grow[4]
Vaster than empires, and more slow.
An hundred years should go to praise
Thine eyes, and on thy forehead gaze,
Two hundred to adore each breast, 15
But thirty thousand to the rest.
An age at least to every part,
And the last age should show your heart.
For, lady, you deserve this state,
Nor would I love at lower rate. 20
    But at my back I always hear
Time's wingèd chariot hurrying near,
And yonder all before us lie
Deserts of vast eternity.
Thy beauty shall no more be found, 25
Nor, in thy marble vault, shall sound
My echoing song; then worms shall try
That long-preserved virginity,
And your quaint honor turn to dust,
And into ashes all my lust. 30

---

[1]**Ganges':** River in India, sacred to Hindus.   [2]**Humber:** Small river that flows through Marvell's hometown of Hull.   [3]**would complain:** Compose love songs.   [4]**. . . should grow:** Slow, unconscious development.

The grave's a fine and private place,
But none, I think, do there embrace.
   Now therefore, while the youthful hue
Sits on thy skin like morning dew[5]
And while thy willing soul transpires[6]   35
At every pore with instant fires,
Now let us sport us while we may;
And now, like amorous birds of prey,
Rather at once our time devour
Than languish in his slow-chapped[7] power.   40
Let us roll all our strength and all
Our sweetness up into one ball
And tear our pleasures with rough strife
Thorough the iron gates of life.
Thus, though we cannot make our sun   45
Stand still, yet we will make him run.

Explorations of the Text

1. In what ways does the speaker suggest the lovers might pass their "long love's day" if only they had time?
2. Why is the lady "coy"?
3. Trace the steps in the argument that begin on lines 1, 21, and 33.
4. What concepts of time and of death does the speaker present? What are the consequences to the beloved?
5. Why does he suggest that "worms" will "try" her "virginity" and her "quaint honor"?
6. In the conclusion, how does his description of proposed acts of love function? How will the lovers make the sun "run"?
7. How does hyperbole add to the humorous and whimsical tone? Contrast the tone of this poem with "The Dover Bitch," and "The Flea."

The Reading/Writing Connection

1. In a mini-essay, write a feminist critique of this poem.
2. In a monologue, persuade someone to change his or her attitude or behavior about a love relationship. Use **hyperbole** in an effort to be persuasive.

Ideas for Writing

1. Outline and critique the argument in "To His Coy Mistress."
2. Write a paper on virginity. Consider such questions as abstinence, social and cultural values, peer pressure, and marriage.

---

[5]**Sits on thy skin:** Glow.   [6]**transpires:** Breathes.   [7]**slow-chapped:** Slow-jawed.

Matthew Arnold   *(1822–1888)*

Dover Beach   *1851*

The sea is calm tonight,
The tide is full, the moon lies fair
Upon the straits; on the French coast the light
Gleams and is gone; the cliffs of England stand,
Glimmering and vast, out in the tranquil bay.   5
Come to the window, sweet is the night-air!
Only, from the long line of spray

Where the sea meets the moon-blanched land,
Listen! you hear the grating roar
Of pebbles which the waves draw back, and fling,   10
At their return, up the high strand,
Begin, and cease, and then again begin,
With tremulous cadence slow, and bring
The eternal note of sadness in.[1]

Sophocles long ago   15
Heard it on the Aegean, and it brought
Into his mind the turbid ebb and flow
Of human misery; we
Find also in the sound a thought,
Hearing it by this distant northern sea.   20

The Sea of Faith
Was once, too, at the full, and round earth's shore
Lay like the folds of a bright girdle[2] furled.
But now I only hear
Its melancholy, long, withdrawing roar,   25
Retreating, to the breath
Of the night-wind, down the vast edges drear
And naked shingles[3] of the world.

Ah, love, let us be true
To one another! for the world, which seems   30
To lie before us like a land of dreams,
So various, so beautiful, so new,
Hath really neither joy, nor love, nor light,

---

[1] **sadness in:** A reference to *Antigone* where Sophocles alludes to the tragedies that plague the House of Oedipus as a "mourning tide."   [2] **bright girdle:** Belt or cord.   [3] **naked shingles:** Beaches covered with small stones or pebbles.

Nor certitude, nor peace, nor help for pain;
And we are here as on a darkling plain   35
Swept with confused alarms of struggle and flight,
Where ignorant armies clash by night.

Explorations of the Text

1. Compare the initial description with the closing lines (33–37). What is the difference? Are both effective?
2. To whom is the poem addressed? Why?
3. What is "the eternal note of sadness"? What creates the motion and sound of the sea?
4. What is the significance of the "withdrawing roar" of the "Sea of Faith"?
5. What can the lovers do to avoid despair? What can anyone do? Is the speaker hopeful?
6. Discuss the title and the setting. Is the sadness a modern attitude, or has it always been central to the human condition?

The Reading/Writing Connection

1. In a paragraph, describe the setting and its effect on the persona and on the themes.
2. "Think" Topic: Choose the best lines in the poem, and discuss the word choice, sound, and imagery that make them effective.

Ideas for Writing

1. M. H. Abrams has called a poem that uses landscape as a prelude to meditation "the greater romantic lyric." The first part creates the setting; the second section presents the meditation; the third transforms the landscape according to the persona's insights. Analyze "Dover Beach" as a lyric in this mode.
2. Write a meditation in lyric or prose form.

Anthony Hecht *(1923–2004)*

The Dover Bitch   *1968*
A Criticism of Life

for Andrews Wanning

So there stood Matthew Arnold and this girl
With the cliffs of England crumbling away behind them,
And he said to her, "Try to be true to me,
And I'll do the same for you, for things are bad
All over, etc., etc."   5

Well now, I knew this girl. It's true she had read
Sophocles in a fairly good translation
And caught that bitter allusion to the sea,
But all the time he was talking she had in mind
The notion of what his whiskers would feel like   10
On the back of her neck. She told me later on
That after a while she got to looking out
At the lights across the channel, and really felt sad,
Thinking of all the wine and enormous beds
And blandishments in French and the perfumes.   15
And then she got really angry. To have been brought
All the way down from London, and then be addressed
As a sort of mournful cosmic last resort—
Is really tough on a girl, and she was pretty.
Anyway, she watched him pace the room   20
And finger his watch-chain and seem to sweat a bit,
And then she said one or two unprintable things.
But you mustn't judge her by that. What I mean to say is,
She's really all right. I still see her once in a while
And she always treats me right. We have a drink   25
And I give her a good time, and perhaps it's a year
Before I see her again, but there she is,
Running to fat, but dependable as they come.
And sometimes I bring her a bottle of *Nuit d'Amour.*

Explorations of the Text

1. How does "The Dover Bitch" comment on "Dover Beach"? Consider the change in point of view, tone, setting, plot, and the characterization of the speaker and the loved one.

2. What views of love does "The Dover Bitch" present?

3. Why do you think that Hecht chose the title? Point to specific images and themes of the work to justify your interpretation.

The Reading/Writing Connection

1. Characterize the speaker or his paramour.

2. Write a poem in response to a work in this chapter.

Ideas for Writing

1. Compare "Dover Beach" and "The Dover Bitch."

Pablo Neruda *(1904–1973)*   Translated from the Spanish by Alastair Reid

Sweetness, always   *1958*

Why such harsh machinery?
Why, to write down the stuff
and people of every day,
must poems be dressed up in gold,
in old and fearful stone?   5

I want verses of felt or feather
which scarcely weigh, mild verses
with the intimacy of beds
where people have loved and dreamed.
I want poems stained   10
by hands and everydayness.

Verses of pastry which melt
into milk and sugar in the mouth,
air and water to drink,
the bites and kisses of love.   15
I long for eatable sonnets,
poems of honey and flour.

Vanity keeps prodding us
to lift ourselves skyward
or to make deep and useless   20
tunnels underground.
So we forget the joyous
love-needs of our bodies.
We forget about pastries.
We are not feeding the world.   25

In Madras[1] a long time since,
I saw a sugary pyramid,
a tower of confectionery—
one level after another,
and in the construction, rubies,   30
and other blushing delights,
medieval and yellow.

Someone dirtied his hands
to cook up so much sweetness.
Brother poets from here   35
and there, from earth and sky,

---

[1] **Madras:** Industrial city in India.

from Medellin,[2] from Veracruz,[3]
Abyssinia,[4] Antofagasta,[5]
do you know the recipe for honeycombs?
Let's forget about all that stone.   40

Let your poetry fill up
the equinoctial pastry shop
our mouths long to devour—
all the children's mouths
and the poor adults' also.   45
Don't go on without seeing,
relishing, understanding
all these hearts of sugar.
Don't be afraid of sweetness.

With us or without us,   50
sweetness will go on living
and is infinitely alive,
forever being revived,
for it's in a man's mouth,
whether he's eating or singing,   55
that sweetness has its place.

Explorations of the Text

1. Whom does the speaker address in the first stanza? Why does he believe that "the stuff/and people of every day" need not be written in "gold" or in "stone"?

2. What kind of poetry does the persona want? Why?

3. Discuss the extended metaphor of "sweetness." What is the connection between love and sweetness?

4. What are the barriers to the poetry of sweetness, to the "eatable sonnets"? What does the speaker mean when he declares, "We are not feeding the world"?

5. Why does he tell about the incident in Madras? Why does he emphasize the cook's dirty hands?

6. The speaker contends that sweetness "is infinitely alive," that "it's in a man's mouth." What does he mean?

7. Contrast Neruda's "sweetness" and Arnold's "sadness." What views of life are implied?

The Reading/Writing Connection

1. **Write an Argument:** In a mini-essay, agree or disagree with the speaker's position.

2. Write a short piece in which images of confections represent love. Do not be sentimental; control your material.

---

[2]**Medellin:** City in Colombia. [3]**Veracruz:** Mexican seaport. [4]**Abyssinia:** Ethiopia. [5]**Antofagasta:** Coastal city in Chile.

Ideas for Writing

1. **Write an Argument:** Answer Neruda's "Sweetness, always." Argue that poetry does not avoid "sweetness" and that poets are not afraid of it.

2. Why does the persona speak only to male poets? Analyze the attitude toward gender presented in the work.

3. Contrast Arnold's vision of "sadness" and Neruda's view of "sweetness." What philosophical stances are suggested?

Pablo Neruda   *(1904–1973)*   Translated by W. S. Merwin, 1969

Tonight I Can Write . . .   *1924*

Tonight I can write the saddest lines.

Write, for example, "The night is shattered
and the blue stars shiver in the distance."

The night wind revolves in the sky and sings.

Tonight I can write the saddest lines.   5
I loved her, and sometimes she loved me too.

Through nights like this one I held her in my arms.
I kissed her again and again under the endless sky.

She loved me, sometimes I loved her too.
How could one not have loved her great still eyes.   10

Tonight I can write the saddest lines.
To think that I do not have her. To feel that I have lost her.

To hear the immense night, still more immense without her.
And the verse falls to the soul like dew to the pasture.

What does it matter that my love could not keep her.   15
The night is shattered and she is not with me.

This is all. In the distance someone is singing. In the distance.
My soul is not satisfied that it has lost her.

My sight searches for her as though to go to her.
My heart looks for her, and she is not with me.   20

The same night whitening the same trees.
We, of that time, are no longer the same.

I no longer love her, that's certain, but how I loved her.
My voice tried to find the wind to touch her hearing.

Another's. She will be another's. Like my kisses before.   25
Her voice. Her bright body. Her infinite eyes.

I no longer love her, that's certain, but maybe I love her.
Love is so short, forgetting is so long.

Because through nights like this one I held her in my arms
my soul is not satisfied that it has lost her.   30

Though this be the last pain that she makes me suffer
and these the last verses that I write for her.

Explorations of the Text

1. Describe the voice and point of view of the persona.
2. Discuss images of night, darkness, and loss in the poem.

3. How do the two-line stanzas deepen mood and heighten themes of the work?
4. Discuss the meaning of this line, "Love is so short, forgetting is so long."

The Reading/Writing Connection

1. What makes this work a powerful love poem? Respond in a freewrite.

2. In a mini-essay, compare the view of love expressed in this poem with your own feelings and experiences.

Ideas for Writing

1. Contrast the view of love in "Sweetness, Always" with the vision of love in this poem.

Liz Rosenberg   *(1955–)*

In The End, We Are All Light   1986

I love how old men carry purses for their wives,
those stiff light beige or navy wedge-shaped bags
that match the women's pumps,
with small gold clasps that click open and shut.
The men drowse off in medical center waiting rooms,   5
with bags perched in their laps like big tame birds
too worn to flap away. Within, the wives slowly undress,
put on the thin white robes, consult, come out
and wake the husbands dreaming openmouthed.

And when they both rise up   10
to take their constitutional,
walk up and down the block, her arms are free as air,
his right hand dangles down.

So I, desiring to shed this skin
for some light silken one,   15
will tell my husband, "Here, hold this,"
and watch him amble off into the mall among the shining
cans of motor oil, my leather bag
slung over his massive shoulder bone,
so prettily slender-waisted, so forgiving of the ways   20
we hold each other down, that watching him
I see how men love women, and women men,
and how the burden of the other comes to be
light as a feather blown, more quickly vanishing.

Explorations of the Text

1. Discuss the characters of the "old men" and "their wives." Focus on the simile of the "big tame birds" and on the images of hands.
2. What does the husbands' carrying of their wives' "purses" suggest about their relationships?
3. What is unexpected in this portrayal of marriage and love?
4. Characterize the tone of the poem. Does it shift? Look carefully at the images of "light." What word play is evident in the use of "light"?
5. Discuss the speaker's revelation at "how the burden of the other comes to be/ light as a feather blown, more quickly vanishing."
6. What do you learn about long-lasting marriages? about the state of older people in love?
7. Contrast this marriage with that of the couples in *M Butterfly* and in *Trifles*.

The Reading/Writing Connection

1. Journal Entry: Go to a public place. Observe several couples in love. What does their body language reveal about their relationships?
2. Imagine a young couple whom you know. Describe their lives after fifty years of marriage. Write a scene with them in it.

Ideas for Writing

1. Use your first journal entry as the basis of portraits of several couples in love. As Rosenberg does, isolate particular details that evoke visions of the people's characters and relationships.
2. Compare the "old men" and Prufrock in Eliot's Poem, "The Love Song of J. Alfred Prufrock," which appears later in this chapter.

Virginia Hamilton Adair *(1913–2004)*

Peeling an Orange 1996

Between you and a bowl of oranges I lie nude
Reading *The World's Illusion* through my tears.
You reach across me hungry for global fruit,
Your bare arm hard, furry and warm on my belly.
Your fingers pry the skin of a navel orange   5
Releasing tiny explosions of spicy oil.
You place peeled disks of gold in a bizarre pattern
On my white body. Rearranging, you bend and bite
The disks to release further their eager scent.
I say "Stop, you're tickling," my eyes still on the page.   10
Aromas of groves arise. Through green leaves
Glow the lofty snows. Through red lips
Your white teeth close on a translucent segment.
Your face over my face eclipses *The World's Illusion*.
Pulp and juice pass into my mouth from your mouth.   15
We laugh against each other's lips. I hold my book
Behind your head, still reading, still weeping a little.
You say "Read on, I'm just an illusion," rolling
Over upon me soothingly, gently moving,
Smiling greenly through long lashes. And soon   20
I say "Don't stop. Don't disillusion me."
Snows melt. The mountain silvers into many a stream.
The oranges are golden worlds in a dark dream.

Explorations of the Text

1. Characterize the speaker's voice and persona.
2. Discuss the use of the imagery of "peeling an orange." What is the significance of the statement: "You reach across me hungry for global fruit."
3. Analyze the juxtaposition of illusion and reality in the work. How does the imagery develop this theme? Why does the speaker state: " 'Don't disillusion me.' " What is the irony?
4. Explore the sensuality of the imagery. What is the impact of the word choice?

The Reading/Writing Connection

1. "Think" Topic: Compare and contrast the treatment of passion in this work with that of Neruda's "Sweetness, Always" or with Robert Browning's "Porphyria's Lover."
2. Neruda's "Sweetness, Always" and this poem use food metaphors to suggest passion. Which poem do you think is most effective? Write a paragraph presenting your evaluation of this technique in one work.
3. Compose a journal entry or a monologue for the beloved in this poem. Use Hecht's "The Dover Bitch" as a model.

Ideas for Writing

1. Write your own poem about passion
   using food or fruit as a symbolic motif,
   and then explicate your work. (See Gary
   Soto's "Oranges" in Chapter 5.)

Marge Piercy (1936–)

Barbie doll *1973*

This girlchild was born as usual
and presented dolls that did pee-pee
and miniature GE stoves and irons
and wee lipsticks the color of cherry candy.
Then in the magic of puberty, a classmate said: 5
You have a great big nose and fat legs.

She was healthy, tested intelligent,
possessed strong arms and back,
abundant sexual drive and manual dexterity.
She went to and fro apologizing.   10
Everyone saw a fat nose on thick legs.

She was advised to play coy,
exhorted to come on hearty,
exercise, diet, smile and wheedle.
Her good nature wore out   15
like a fan belt.
So she cut off her nose and legs
and offered them up.

In the casket displayed on satin she lay
with the undertaker's cosmetics painted on,   20
a turned-up putty nose,
dressed in a pink and white nightie.
Doesn't she look pretty? everyone said.
Consummation at last.
To every woman a happy ending.   25

Explorations of the Text

1. Analyze the point of view and the persona in the poem. Who do you imagine
   the speaker to be?
2. What does the symbolism of the Barbie doll suggest about girl's socialization? List all the images that relate to
   the "girlchild['s]" adolescent body. How
   does the girl conform to gender stereotypes? How does she not fit the stereotypes? What do you conclude?

3. What advice does the girl receive? Discuss its significance.
4. Analyze and interpret the ironies at the conclusion of the poem. What is the "consummation"?

5. Compare the feminist critique in this work with that of Atwood's "Happy Endings" and Cisneros's "Barbie-Q."

The Reading/Writing Connection

1. Write a poem for a G.I. Joe doll. What gender stereotypes prevail for adolescent boys?

2. Write a letter to your body in the voice of your adolescent or adult persona.

Ideas for Writing

1. **Write an Argument:** Young girls today are less likely to be taken in by media images of the perfect body.

2. Compare and contrast the images of the female body in this work, in Woolf's "Professions for Women," and/or in

Kingston's "No Name Woman." How do the female protagonists in Oates's "Where Are You Going, Where Have You Been?" (Chapter 5) and Kingsolver's "Rose-Johnny" (Chapter 5) relate to their female bodies?

Anna Akhmatova *(1889–1966)*   Translated from the Russian by D. M. Thomas

Lot's Wife   *1922–24*

And the just man trailed God's messenger,
His huge, light shape devoured the black hill.
But uneasiness shadowed his wife and spoke to her:
"It's not too late, you can look back still[1]

At the red towers of Sodom,[2] the place that bore you,   5
The square in which you sang, the spinning-shed,
At the empty windows of that upper storey
Where children blessed your happy marriage-bed."

Her eyes that were still turning when a bolt
Of pain shot through them, were instantly blind;   10
Her body turned into transparent salt,
And her swift legs were rooted to the ground.

---

[1]**you can look back still:** Lot was the nephew of Abraham. His wife was transformed into a pillar of salt for looking back during their flight from Sodom (Genesis 13–19). [2]**Sodom:** An ancient city destroyed by God because of its wickedness (Genesis 18–19).

Who mourns one woman in a holocaust?
Surely her death has no significance?
Yet in my heart she never will be lost,   15
She who gave up her life to steal one glance.

Explorations of the Text

1. Review the story of Sodom and Go-
morrah in Genesis 19. Who is the "just
man"? "God's messenger"?
2. Explore the significance of the line,
"His huge, light shape devoured the
black hill." Whose "shape" is it?
3. In Akhmatova's poem, why does Lot's
wife look back? What does her glance
reveal about women's values and
concerns?
4. Why is "uneasiness" personified? What
does it signify?

5. What is the significance of the speaker's questions in the last stanza? Why
will Lot's wife "never . . . be lost" in the
speaker's "heart"?
6. In what ways has Akhmatova changed
the story? Why?
7. Why have women always been pillars of
salt? What does the salt symbolize?
8. Why is Lot's wife never named? What
does this detail suggest about the view
of woman's position?

The Reading/Writing Connection

1. Defend the choices of Lot and of his
wife. You may write in monologue form.

Ideas for Writing

1. In *Slaughterhouse Five,* Kurt Vonnegut
reflects that it is both necessary and terrifying to look back. Examine the poem

in the context of this assertion by Vonnegut. Why is it necessary to look back?
Why is it so terrifying?

T. S. Eliot   *(1888–1965)*

The Love Song of J. Alfred Prufrock   *1910–11*

S'io credessi che mia risposta fosse
A persona che mai tornasse al mondo,
Questa fiamma staria senza piu scosse.
Ma perciocche giammai di questo fondo
Non torno vivo alcun, s'i'odo il vero,
Senza tema d'infamia ti rispondo.[1]

---

[1] **The epigraph from Dante's *Inferno*:** Spoken by Guido da Montefeltro, "If I thought that my reply were to someone who could ever return to the world, this flame would shake no more. But since
no one has ever returned alive from this place, if what I hear is true, without fear of infamy I answer
you," suggests Prufrock's "damnation" and psychological torment.

Let us go then, you and I,
When the evening is spread out against the sky
Like a patient etherized upon a table;
Let us go, through certain half-deserted streets,
The muttering retreats   5
Of restless nights in one-night cheap hotels
And sawdust restaurants with oyster-shells:
Streets that follow like a tedious argument
Of insidious intent
To lead you to an overwhelming question . . .   10
Oh, do not ask, "What is it?"
Let us go and make our visit.

    In the room the women come and go
Talking of Michelangelo.

    The yellow fog that rubs its back upon the window-panes,   15
The yellow smoke that rubs its muzzle on the window-panes
Licked its tongue into the corners of the evening,
Lingered upon the pools that stand in drains,
Let fall upon its back the soot that falls from chimneys,
Slipped by the terrace, made a sudden leap,   20
And seeing that it was a soft October night,
Curled once about the house, and fell asleep.

    And indeed there will be time
For the yellow smoke that slides along the street,
Rubbing its back upon the window-panes;   25
There will be time, there will be time
To prepare a face to meet the faces that you meet;
There will be time to murder and create,
And time for all the works and days[2] of hands
That lift and drop a question on your plate;   30
Time for you and time for me,
And time yet for a hundred indecisions,
And for a hundred visions and revisions,
Before the taking of a toast and tea.

    In the room the women come and go   35
Talking of Michelangelo.

    And indeed there will be time
To wonder, "Do I dare?" and, "Do I dare?"
Time to turn back and descend the stair,
With a bald spot in the middle of my hair—   40
(They will say: "How his hair is growing thin!")

---

[2]**works and days:** Reference to a poem by Hesiod, an eighth-century Greek writer.

My morning coat, my collar mounting firmly to the chin,
My necktie rich and modest, but asserted by a simple pin—
(They will say: "But how his arms and legs are thin!")
Do I dare   45
Disturb the universe?
In a minute there is time
For decisions and revisions which a minute will reverse.

    For I have known them all already, known them all:
Have known the evenings, mornings, afternoons,   50
I have measured out my life with coffee spoons;
I know the voices dying with a dying fall[3]
Beneath the music from a farther room.
    So how should I presume?

    And I have known the eyes already, known them all—   55
The eyes that fix you in a formulated phrase,
And when I am formulated, sprawling on a pin,
When I am pinned and wriggling on the wall,
Then how should I begin
To spit out all the butt-ends of my days and ways?   60
    And how should I presume?

    And I have known the arms already, known them all—
Arms that are braceleted and white and bare
(But in the lamplight, downed with light brown hair!)
Is it perfume from a dress   65
That makes me so digress?
Arms that lie along a table, or wrap about a shawl.
    And should I then presume?
    And how should I begin? . . .

■ ■ ■

Shall I say, I have gone at dusk through narrow streets   70
And watched the smoke that rises from the pipes
Of lonely men in shirt-sleeves, leaning out of windows? . . .
    I should have been a pair of ragged claws
Scuttling across the floors of silent seas.

■ ■ ■

And the afternoon, the evening, sleeps so peacefully!   75
Smoothed by long fingers,
Asleep . . . tired . . . or it malingers,
Stretched on the floor, here beside you and me.

---

[3]**dying fall:** Allusion to Orsino's speech in Shakespeare's *Twelfth Night* (I, i), "That strain again! It had a dying fall."

Should I, after tea and cakes and ices,
Have the strength to force the moment to its crisis? 80
But though I have wept and fasted, wept and prayed,
Though I have seen my head (grown slightly bald) brought in upon a platter,[4]
I am no prophet—and here's no great matter;
I have seen the moment of my greatness flicker,
And I have seen the eternal Footman[5] hold my coat, and snicker, 85
And in short, I was afraid.

    And would it have been worth it, after all,
After the cups, the marmalade, the tea,
Among the porcelain, among some talk of you and me,
Would it have been worth while, 90
To have bitten off the matter with a smile,
To have squeezed the universe into a ball
To roll it toward some overwhelming question,
To say: "I am Lazarus,[6] come from the dead,
Come back to tell you all, I shall tell you all"— 95
If one, settling a pillow by her head,
    Should say: "That is not what I meant at all.
    That is not it, at all."

    And would it have been worth while, after all
Would it have been worth while, 100
After the sunsets and the dooryards and the sprinkled streets,
After the novels, after the teacups, after the skirts that trail along the floor—
And this, and so much more?—
It is impossible to say just what I mean!
But as if a magic lantern threw the nerves in patterns on a screen: 105
Would it have been worth while
If one, settling a pillow or throwing off a shawl,
And turning toward the window, should say:
    "That is not it at all,
    That is not what I meant, at all." 110

■ ■ ■

No! I am not Prince Hamlet, nor was meant to be;
Am an attendant lord, one that will do
To swell a progress,[7] start a scene or two,
Advise the prince; no doubt, an easy tool,
Deferential, glad to be of use, 115
Politic, cautious, and meticulous;

---

[4] **I have seen my head . . . platter:** Reference to John the Baptist, who was beheaded by King Herod (Matthew 14:3–11). [5] **eternal Footman:** Figure of death or fate. [6] **Lazarus:** Lazarus was raised from the dead by Jesus (John 11:1–44). [7] **progress:** A royal journey (Elizabethan English).

Full of high sentence,[8] but a bit obtuse;
At times, indeed, almost ridiculous—
Almost, at times, the Fool.[9]

I grow old . . . I grow old . . .   120
I shall wear the bottoms of my trousers rolled.

Shall I part my hair behind? Do I dare to eat a peach?
I shall wear white flannel trousers, and walk upon the beach.
I have heard the mermaids singing, each to each.

I do not think that they will sing to me.   125

I have seen them riding seaward on the waves
Combing the white hair of the waves blown back
When the wind blows the water white and black.

We have lingered in the chambers of the sea
By sea-girls wreathed with seaweed red and brown   130
Till human voices wake us, and we drown.

Explorations of the Text

1. Identify the "you" and "I." What are the possibilities?
2. What atmosphere do the opening simile of the evening and the personification of "the yellow smoke" and "yellow fog" create?
3. What is the state of mind of the persona, the "I" of the poem, in the first six stanzas? Why is he so concerned with "time"?
4. Why does he ask, "Do I dare/Disturb the universe?" Which details about his appearance (stanza 6) reveal his view of himself?
5. What is the significance of the refrain, "In the room the women come and go / Talking of Michelangelo"?
6. How do the concerns change in the next five stanzas? Whom and what has he "known"? Explore his state of mind.
7. What is his "crisis" in the last nine stanzas? How do the allusions to John the Baptist, Lazarus, and Hamlet enlarge the scope of his conflict?
8. In the last stanza, what is the significance of the sea imagery and of the mermaids?
9. Explore Eliot's use of figurative language (personification, simile, metaphor) and irony. What is the impact of these techniques?
10. Examine Eliot's use of repetition and parallelism. What impact do these devices have?
11. Compare Prufrock and Minnie Wright (*Trifles*).

---

[8]**high sentence:** Ideals, sentiments.   [9]**Fool:** Reference to the stock figure of a Fool, appearing in many dramas (e.g., Shakespeare's *King Lear*).

The Reading/Writing Connection

1. "Think" Topic: Isolate a simile or metaphor and explain its role in developing a portrait of Prufrock.
2. Write a monologue for Prufrock five years after this "love song." What is his future?

3. Use one line from this work as a beginning for your own poem.

Ideas for Writing

1. Create a character analysis of Prufrock. Focus on his appearance, his questions, and his actions.
2. **Write an Argument:** Will Prufrock ever find love? Construct an argumentative response to this question.
3. Do the literary allusions add to or detract from this poem? Do they confuse and intimidate a reader, or do they add depth to Eliot's vision?
4. Is this a "love song"? Why? Why not?
5. Prufrock is considered a modern anti-hero. Analyze his character in this context.

Marie Howe *(1950–)*

The Boy *1998*

My older brother is walking down the sidewalk into the suburban
     summer night:
white T-shirt, blue jeans—to the field at the end of the street.

Hangers Hideout the boys called it, an undeveloped plot, a pit
     overgrown
with weeds, some old furniture thrown down there,

and some metal hangers clinking in the trees like wind chimes.   5
He's running away from home because our father wants to cut his hair.

And in two more days our father will convince me to go to him—you know
where he is—and talk to him: No reprisals. He promised. A small parade
     of kids

in feet pajamas will accompany me, their voices like the first peepers
     in spring.
And my brother will walk ahead of us home, and my father   10

will shave his head bald, and my brother will not speak to anyone the next
month, not a word, not *pass the milk,* nothing.

What happened in our house taught my brothers how to leave, how to walk
down a sidewalk without looking back.

I was the girl. What happened taught me to follow him, whoever he was,   15
calling and calling his name.

William Carlos Williams   *(1883–1963)*

Danse Russe   *1923*

If when my wife is sleeping
and the baby and Kathleen
are sleeping
and the sun is a flame-white disc
in silken mists   5
above shining trees,—
if I in my north room
dance naked, grotesquely
before my mirror
waving my shirt round my head   10
and singing softly to myself:
"I am lonely, lonely.
I was born to be lonely,
I am best so!"
If I admire my arms, my face,   15
my shoulders, flanks, buttocks
against the yellow drawn shades,—

Who shall say I am not
the happy genius of my household?

Thom Gunn   *(1929–2004)*

The Missing   *(1987; 1992)*

Now as I watch the progress of the plague[1]
The friends surrounding me fall sick, grow thin,
And drop away. Bared, is my shape less vague
—Sharply exposed and with a sculpted skin?

I do not like the statue's chill contour,   5
Not nowadays. The warmth investing me
Let outward through mind, limb, feeling, and more
In an involved increasing family.

Contact of friend led to another friend,
Supple entwinement through the living mass   10
Which for all that I knew might have no end,
Image of an unlimited embrace.

---

[1] **plague:** The AIDS epidemic.

I did not just feel ease, though comfortable:
Aggressive as in some ideal of sport,
With ceaseless movement thrilling through the whole,   15
Their push kept me as firm as their support.

But death—Their deaths have left me less defined:
It was their pulsing presence made me clear.
I borrowed from it, I was unconfined,
Who tonight balance unsupported here,   20

Eyes glaring from raw marble, in a pose
Languorously part-buried in the block,
Shins perfect and no calves, as if I froze
Between potential and a finished work.

—Abandoned incomplete, shape of a shape,   25
In which exact detail shows the more strange,
Trapped in unwholeness, I find no escape
Back to the play of constant give and change.

Explorations of the Text

1. How do the poems present the boy's or man's relationship to his body? What do the images of the body suggest about the speakers' states of mind?
2. Are the speakers happy or unhappy? Isolated? Alone? What are their positions in their families? In their communities?
3. What do the works suggest about man's ability to reach out, to develop intimate relationships? In William Pollack's terms in "Inside the World of Boys," do the personae adopt "mask[s] of masculinity"?
4. Compare and contrast the depiction of masculine gender roles in these works with that of "Pagan Night" or "Hills Like White Elephants."

The Reading/Writing Connection

1. Use the closing question in "Danse Russe" as the basis of a freewrite.
2. "Think" Topic: Compare and contrast the portrayal of the fathers in "Danse Russe" and "The Boy."
3. Have you ever wanted to run away from home? Why? Respond in a freewrite.

Ideas for Writing

1. Discuss the state of psychic "incomplete[ness]" presented in these three poems. What are the different reasons for the speakers' "unwholeness"? How are they shaped by this reality?

2. **Write an Argument:** Is aloneness an inevitable aspect of human existence even in fulfilling love relationships? Respond in a persuasive essay.

Love and Betrayal/Poetry

John Donne *(1572–1631)*

The Flea *1633*

Mark[1] but this flea, and mark in this,
How little that which thou deniest me is;
It sucked me first, and now sucks thee,
And in this flea our two bloods mingled be;
Thou know'st that this cannot be said[2]   5
A sin, nor shame, nor loss of maidenhead,
    Yet this enjoys before it woo,[3]
    And pampered swells with one blood made of two,
    And this, alas, is more than we would do.

Oh stay, three lives in one flea spare,   10
Where we almost, yea more than married, are.
This flea is you and I, and this
Our marriage bed and marriage temple is;
Though parents grudge, and you, we are met,
And cloistered in these living walls of jet.   15
    Though use[4] make you apt to kill me
    Let not to that, self-murder added be,
    And sacrilege, three sins in killing three.

Cruel and sudden, hast thou since
Purpled thy nail, in blood of innocence?   20
Wherein could this flea guilty be,
Except in that drop which it sucked from thee?
Yet thou triumph'st and say'st that thou
Find'st not thy self nor me the weaker now;
    'Tis true, then learn how false fears be;   25
    Just so much honor, when thou yield'st to me,
    Will waste, as this flea's death took life from thee.

---

[1]**Mark:** Note, look at. [2]**said:** Called. [3]**woo:** Marry. [4]**use:** Custom.

John Keats *(1795–1821)*

La Belle Dame Sans Merci[1] *1819*

O what can ail thee, knight-at-arms,
  Alone and palely loitering?
The sedge[2] has withered from the lake,
  And no birds sing.

O what can ail thee, knight-at-arms,   5
  So haggard and so woe-begone?
The squirrel's granary is full,
  And the harvest's done.

I see a lily on thy brow,
  With anguish moist and fever dew,   10
And on thy cheeks a fading rose
  Fast withereth too.

I met a lady in the meads,[3]
  Full beautiful—a faery's child,
Her hair was long, her foot was light,   15
  And her eyes were wild.

I made a garland for her head,
  And bracelets too, and fragrant zone;[4]
She looked at me as she did love,
  And made sweet moan.   20

I set her on my pacing steed,
  And nothing else saw all day long,
For sidelong would she bend, and sing
  A faery's song.

She found me roots of relish sweet,   25
  And honey wild, and manna dew,
And sure in language strange she said,
  "I love thee true."

---

[1]**La Belle . . . :** The title taken from a medieval poem means "The Beautiful Lady Without Mercy."   [2]**sedge:** Grasslike or marshlike vegetation growing in wet places.   [3]**meads:** Meadows.   [4]**zone:** Belt.

She took me to her elfin grot,
    And there she wept, and sighed full sore,
And there I shut her wild wild eyes   30
    With kisses four.

And there she lullèd me asleep,
    And there I dreamed—Ah! woe betide!
The latest[5] dream I ever dreamed   35
    On the cold hill side.

I saw pale kings and princes too,
    Pale warriors, death-pale were they all;
They cried—"La Belle Dame sans Merci
    "Hath thee in thrall!"   40

I saw their starved lips in the gloam,[6]
    With horrid warning gapèd wide,
And I awoke and found me here,
    On the cold hill's side.

And this is why I soujourn here,   45
    Alone and palely loitering,
Though the sedge has withered from the lake,
    And no birds sing.

Robert Browning   *(1812–1889)*

Porphyria's Lover   1834

The rain set early in tonight,
    The sullen wind was soon awake,
It tore the elm-tops down for spite,
    and did its worst to vex the lake:
    I listened with heart fit to break.   5
When glided in Porphyria; straight
    She shut the cold out and the storm,
And kneeled and made the cheerless grate
    Blaze up, and all the cottage warm;
    Which done, she rose, and from her form   10
Withdrew the dripping cloak and shawl,
    And laid her soiled gloves by, untied
Her hat and let the damp hair fall,
    And, last, she sat down by my side
    And called me. When no voice replied,   15

---

[5]**latest:** Last.   [6]**gloam:** Twilight.

She put my arm about her waist,
  And made her smooth white shoulder bare,
And all her yellow hair displaced,
  And, stooping, made my cheek lie there,
  And spread, o'er all, her yellow hair,   20
Murmuring how she loved me—she
  Too weak, for all her heart's endeavor,
To set its struggling passion free
  From pride, and vainer ties dissever,
  And give herself to me forever.   25
But passion sometimes would prevail,
  Nor could tonight's gay feast restrain
A sudden thought of one so pale
  For love of her, and all in vain:
  So, she was come through wind and rain.   30
Be sure I looked up at her eyes
  Happy and proud; at last I knew
Porphyria worshiped me: surprise
  Made my heart swell, and still it grew
  While I debated what to do.   35
That moment she was mine, mine, fair,
  Perfectly pure and good: I found
A thing to do, and all her hair
  In one long yellow string I wound
  Three times her little throat around,   40
And strangled her. No pain felt she;
  I am quite sure she felt no pain.
As a shut bud that holds a bee,
  I warily oped her lids: again
  Laughed the blue eyes without a stain.   45
And I untightened next the tress
  About her neck; her cheek once more
Blushed bright beneath my burning kiss:
  I propped her head up as before
  Only, this time my shoulder bore   50
Her head, which droops upon it still:
  The smiling rosy little head,
So glad it has its utmost will,
  That all it scorned at once is fled,
  And I, its love, am gained instead!   55
Porphyria's love: she guessed not how
  Her darling one wish would be heard.
And thus we sit together now,
  And all night long we have not stirred,
  And yet God has not said a word!   60

Christina Rossetti *(1830–1894)*

Goblin Market *(1859, 1862)*

Morning and evening
Maids heard the goblins cry:
'Come buy our orchard fruits,
Come buy, come buy:
Apples and quinces, 5
Lemons and oranges,
Plump unpecked cherries,
Melons and raspberries,
Bloom-down-cheeked peaches,
Swart-headed mulberries, 10
Wild free-born cranberries,
Crab-apples, dewberries,
Pine-apples, blackberries,
Apricots, strawberries;—
All ripe together 15
In summer weather,—
Morns that pass by,
Fair eves that fly;
Come buy, come buy:
Our grapes fresh from the vine, 20
Pomegranates full and fine,
Dates and sharp bullaces,[1]
Rare pears and greengages,
Damsons and bilberries,
Taste them and try: 25
Currants and gooseberries,
Bright-fire-like barberries,
Figs to fill your mouth,
Citrons from the South,
Sweet to tongue and sound to eye; 30
Come buy, come buy.'

Evening by evening
Among the brookside rushes,
Laura bowed her head to hear,
Lizzie veiled her blushes: 35
Crouching close together
In the cooling weather,
With clasping arms and cautioning lips,
With tingling cheeks and finger tips.
'Lie close,' Laura said, 40
Pricking up her golden head:

---

[1] **bullaces:** European plum.

'We must not look at goblin men,
We must not buy their fruits:
Who knows upon what soil they fed
Their hungry thirsty roots?'   45
'Come buy,' call the goblins
Hobbling down the glen.
'Oh,' cried Lizzie, 'Laura, Laura,
You should not peep at goblin men.'
Lizzie covered up her eyes,   50
Covered close lest they should look;
Laura reared her glossy head,
And whispered like the restless brook:
'Look, Lizzie, look, Lizzie,
Down the glen tramp little men.   55
One hauls a basket,
One bears a plate,
One lugs a golden dish
Of many pounds weight.
How fair the vine must grow   60
Whose grapes are so luscious;
How warm the wind must blow
Thro' those fruit bushes.'
'No,' said Lizzie: 'No, no, no;
Their offers should not charm us,   65
Their evil gifts would harm us.'
She thrust a dimpled finger
In each ear, shut eyes and ran:
Curious Laura chose to linger
Wondering at each merchant man.   70
One had a cat's face,
One whisked a tail,
One tramped at a rat's pace,
One crawled like a snail,
One like a wombat prowled obtuse and furry,   75
One like a ratel[2] tumbled hurry skurry.
She heard a voice like voice of doves
Cooing all together:
They sounded kind and full of loves
In the pleasant weather.   80

Laura stretched her gleaming neck
Like a rush-imbedded swan,
Like a lily from the beck,
Like a moonlit poplar branch,
Like a vessel at the launch   85
When its last restraint is gone.

---

[2]**ratel:** An African or Asian carnivorous mammal resembling the badger.

Backwards up the mossy glen
Turned and trooped the goblin men,
With their shrill repeated cry,
'Come buy, come buy.'   90
When they reached where Laura was
They stood stock still upon the moss,
Leering at each other,
Brother with queer brother;
Signalling each other,   95
Brother with sly brother.
One set his basket down,
One reared his plate;
One began to weave a crown
Of tendrils, leaves and rough nuts brown   100
(Men sell not such in any town);
One heaved the golden weight
Of dish and fruit to offer her;
'Come buy, come buy,' was still their cry.

Laura stared but did not stir,   105
Longed but had no money:
The whisk-tailed merchant bade her taste
In tones as smooth as honey,
The cat-faced purr'd,
The rat-paced spoke a word   110
Of welcome, and the snail-paced even was heard;
One parrot-voiced and jolly
Cried 'Pretty Goblin' still for 'Pretty Polly;'—
One whistled like a bird.

But sweet-tooth Laura spoke in haste;   115
'Good folk, I have no coin;
To take were to purloin:
I have no copper in my purse,
I have no silver either,
And all my gold is on the furze   120
That shakes in windy weather
Above the rusty heather.'
'You have much gold upon your head,'
They answered all together:
'Buy from us with a golden curl.'   125
She clipped a precious golden lock,
She dropped a tear more rare than pearl,
Then sucked their fruit globes fair or red:
Sweeter than honey from the rock,
Stronger than man-rejoicing wine,   130
Clearer than water flowed that juice;
She never tasted such before,

How should it cloy with length of use?
She sucked and sucked and sucked the more
Fruits which that unknown orchard bore;   135
She sucked until her lips were sore;
Then flung the emptied rinds away
But gathered up one kernel-stone,
And knew not was it night or day
As she turned home alone.   140

Lizzie met her at the gate
Full of wise upbraidings:
'Dear, you should not stay so late,
Twilight is not good for maidens;
Should not loiter in the glen   145
In the haunts of goblin men.
Do you not remember Jeanie,
How she met them in the moonlight,
Took their gifts both choice and many,
Ate their fruits and wore their flowers   150
Plucked from bowers
Where summer ripens at all hours?
But ever in the noonlight
She pined and pined away;
Sought them by night and day,   155
Found them no more but dwindled and grew grey;
Then fell with the first snow,
While to this day no grass will grow
Where she lies low:
I planted daisies there a year ago   160
That never blow.
You should not loiter so.'
'Nay, hush,' said Laura:
'Nay, hush, my sister:
I ate and ate my fill,   165
Yet my mouth waters still;
Tomorrow night I will
Buy more:' and kissed her:
'Have done with sorrow;
I'll bring you plums tomorrow   170
Fresh on their mother twigs,
Cherries worth getting;
You cannot think what figs
My teeth have met in,
What melons icy-cold.   175
Piled on a dish of gold
Too huge for me to hold,
What peaches with a velvet nap,
Pellucid grapes without one seed:

Odorous indeed must be the mead   180
Whereon they grow, and pure the wave they drink
With lilies at the brink,
And sugar-sweet their sap.'

Golden head by golden head,
Like two pigeons in one nest   185
Folded in each other's wings,
They lay down in their curtained bed:
Like two blossoms on one stem,
Like two flakes of new-fall'n snow,
Like two wands of ivory   190
Tipped with gold for awful kings.
Moon and stars gazed in at them,
Wind sang to them lullaby,
Lumbering owls forbore to fly,
Not a bat flapped to and fro   195
Round their rest:
Cheek to cheek and breast to breast
Locked together in one nest.

Early in the morning
When the first cock crowed his warning,   200
Neat like bees, as sweet and busy,
Laura rose with Lizzie:
Fetched in honey, milked the cows,
Aired and set to rights the house,
Kneaded cakes of whitest wheat,   205
Cakes for dainty mouths to eat,
Next churned butter, whipped up cream,
Fed their poultry, sat and sewed;
Talked as modest maidens should:
Lizzie with an open heart,   210
Laura in an absent dream,
One content, one sick in part;
One warbling for the mere bright day's delight,
One longing for the night.
At length slow evening came: 215
They went with pitchers to the reedy brook;
Lizzie most placid in her look,
Laura most like a leaping flame.
They drew the gurgling water from its deep;
Lizzie plucked purple and rich golden flags,[3]   220
Then turning homewards said: 'The sunset flushes
Those furthest loftiest crags;

---

[3]**flags:** Lilies.

Come, Laura, not another maiden lags,
No wilful squirrel wags,
The beasts and birds are fast asleep.'   225
But Laura loitered still among the rushes
And said the bank was steep.

And said the hour was early still,
The dew not fall'n, the wind not chill:
Listening ever, but not catching   230
The customary cry,
'Come buy, come buy,'
With its iterated jingle
Of sugar-baited words:
Not for all her watching   235
Once discerning even one goblin
Racing, whisking, tumbling, hobbling;
Let alone the herds
That used to tramp along the glen,
In groups or single,   240
Of brisk fruit-merchant men.
Till Lizzie urged, 'O Laura, come;
I hear the fruit-call but I dare not look:
You should not loiter longer at this brook:
Come with me home.   245
The stars rise, the moon bends her arc,
Each glowworm winks her spark,
Let us get home before the night grows dark:
For clouds may gather
Tho' this is summer weather,   250
Put out the lights and drench us thro';
Then if we lost our way what should we do?'

Laura turned cold as stone
To find her sister heard that cry alone,
That goblin cry,   255
'Come buy our fruits, come buy.'
Must she then buy no more such dainty fruit?
Must she no more such succous pasture find,
Gone deaf and blind?
Her tree of life drooped from the root: 260
She said not one word in her heart's sore ache;
But peering thro' the dimness, nought discerning,
Trudged home, her pitcher dripping all the way;
So crept to bed, and lay
Silent till Lizzie slept;   265
Then sat up in a passionate yearning,
And gnashed her teeth for baulked desire, and wept
As if her heart would break.

Day after day, night after night,
Laura kept watch in vain   270
In sullen silence of exceeding pain.
She never caught again the goblin cry:
'Come buy, come buy;'—
She never spied the goblin men
Hawking their fruits along the glen: 275
But when the noon waxed bright
Her hair grew thin and gray;
She dwindled, as the fair full moon doth turn
To swift decay and burn
Her fire away.   280

One day remembering her kernel-stone
She set it by a wall that faced the south;
Dewed it with tears, hoped for a root,
Watched for a waxing shoot,
But there came none;   285
It never saw the sun,
It never felt the trickling moisture run:
While with sunk eyes and faded mouth
She dreamed of melons, as a traveller sees
False waves in desert drouth   290
With shade of leaf-crowned trees,
And burns the thirstier in the sandful breeze.

She no more swept the house,
Tended the fowls or cows,
Fetched honey, kneaded cakes of wheat,   295
Brought water from the brook:
But sat down listless in the chimney-nook
And would not eat.

Tender Lizzie could not bear
To watch her sister's cankerous care   300
Yet not to share.
She night and morning
Caught the goblins' cry:
'Come buy our orchard fruits,
Come buy, come buy:'—   305
Beside the brook, along the glen,
She heard the tramp of goblin men,
The voice and stir
Poor Laura could not hear;
Longed to buy fruit to comfort her,   310
But feared to pay too dear.
She thought of Jeanie in her grave,
Who should have been a bride;

But who for joys brides hope to have
Fell sick and died   315
In her gay prime,
In earliest Winter time,
With the first glazing rime,
With the first snow-fall of crisp Winter time.

Till Laura dwindling   320
Seemed knocking at Death's door:
Then Lizzie weighed no more
Better and worse;
But put a silver penny in her purse,
Kissed Laura, crossed the heath with clumps of furze   325
At twilight, halted by the brook:
And for the first time in her life
Began to listen and look.

Laughed every goblin
When they spied her peeping: 330
Came towards her hobbling,
Flying, running, leaping,
Puffing and blowing,
Chuckling, clapping, crowing,
Clucking and gobbling,   335
Mopping and mowing,
Full of airs and graces,
Pulling wry faces,
Demure grimaces,
Cat-like and rat-like,   340
Ratel- and wombat-like,
Snail-paced in a hurry,
Parrot-voiced and whistler,
Helter skelter, hurry skurry,
Chattering like magpies,   345
Fluttering like pigeons,
Gliding like fishes,—
Hugged her and kissed her,
Squeezed and caressed her:
Stretched up their dishes,   350
Panniers, and plates:
'Look at our apples
Russet and dun,
Bob at our cherries,
Bite at our peaches,   355
Citrons and dates,
Grapes for the asking,
Pears red with basking
Out in the sun,

Plums on their twigs;   360
Pluck them and suck them,
Pomegranates, figs.'—

'Good folk,' said Lizzie,
Mindful of Jeanie:
'Give me much and many:'—   365
Held out her apron,
Tossed them her penny.
'Nay, take a seat with us,
Honour and eat with us,'
They answered grinning: 370
'Our feast is but beginning.
Night yet is early,
Warm and dew-pearly,
Wakeful and starry:
Such fruits as these   375
No man can carry;
Half their bloom would fly,
Half their dew would dry,
Half their flavour would pass by.
Sit down and feast with us,   380
Be welcome guest with us,
Cheer you and rest with us.'—
'Thank you,' said Lizzie: 'But one waits
At home alone for me:
So without further parleying,   385
If you will not sell me any
Of your fruits tho' much and many,
Give me back my silver penny
I tossed you for a fee.'—
They began to scratch their pates,   390
No longer wagging, purring,
But visibly demurring,
Grunting and snarling.
One called her proud,
Cross-grained, uncivil;   395
Their tones waxed loud,
Their looks were evil.
Lashing their tails
They trod and hustled her,
Elbowed and jostled her,   400
Clawed with their nails,
Barking, mewing, hissing, mocking,
Tore her gown and soiled her stocking,
Twitched her hair out by the roots,
Stamped upon her tender feet,   405
Held her hands and squeezed their fruits

Against her mouth to make her eat.
White and golden Lizzie stood,
Like a lily in a flood,—
Like a rock of blue-veined stone   410
Lashed by tides obstreperously,—
Like a beacon left alone
In a hoary roaring sea,
Sending up a golden fire,—
Like a fruit-crowned orange-tree   415
White with blossoms honey-sweet
Sore beset by wasp and bee,—
Like a royal virgin town
Topped with gilded dome and spire
Close beleaguered by a fleet   420
Mad to tug her standard down.

One may lead a horse to water,
Twenty cannot make him drink.
Tho' the goblins cuffed and caught her,
Coaxed and fought her,   425
Bullied and besought her,
Scratched her, pinched her black as ink,
Kicked and knocked her,
Mauled and mocked her,
Lizzie uttered not a word;   430
Would not open lip from lip
Lest they should cram a mouthful in:
But laughed in heart to feel the drip
Of juice that syrupped all her face,
And lodged in dimples of her chin,   435
And streaked her neck which quaked like curd.
At last the evil people
Worn out by her resistance
Flung back her penny, kicked their fruit
Along whichever road they took,   440
Not leaving root or stone or shoot;
Some writhed into the ground,
Some dived into the brook
With ring and ripple,
Some scudded on the gale without a sound,   445
Some vanished in the distance.

In a smart, ache, tingle,
Lizzie went her way;
Knew not was it night or day;
Sprang up the bank, tore thro' the furze,   450
Threaded copse and dingle,
And heard her penny jingle

Bouncing in her purse,
Its bounce was music to her ear.
She ran and ran   455
As if she feared some goblin man
Dogged her with gibe or curse
Or something worse:
But not one goblin skurried after,
Nor was she pricked by fear;   460
The kind heart made her windy-paced
That urged her home quite out of breath with haste
And inward laughter.

She cried 'Laura,' up the garden,
'Did you miss me?   465
Come and kiss me.
Never mind my bruises,
Hug me, kiss me, suck my juices
Squeezed from goblin fruits for you,
Goblin pulp and goblin dew.   470
Eat me, drink me, love me;
Laura, make much of me:
For your sake I have braved the glen
And had to do with goblin merchant men.'

Laura started from her chair,   475
Flung her arms up in the air,
Clutched her hair:
'Lizzie, Lizzie, have you tasted
For my sake the fruit forbidden?
Must your light like mine be hidden,   480
Your young life like mine be wasted,
Undone in mine undoing
And ruined in my ruin,
Thirsty, cankered, goblin-ridden?'—
She clung about her sister,   485
Kissed and kissed and kissed her:
Tears once again
Refreshed her shrunken eyes,
Dropping like rain
After long sultry drouth;   490
Shaking with aguish fear, and pain,
She kissed and kissed her with a hungry mouth.

Her lips began to scorch,[4]
That juice was wormwood to her tongue,

---

[4] **scorch:** A European plant that has a bitter oil, used in absinthe; something bitter.

She loathed the feast: 495
Writhing as one possessed she leaped and sung,
Rent all her robe, and wrung
Her hands in lamentable haste,
And beat her breast.
Her locks streamed like the torch   500
Borne by a racer at full speed,
Or like the mane of horses in their flight,
Or like an eagle when she stems the light
Straight toward the sun,
Or like a caged thing freed,   505
Or like a flying flag when armies run.

Swift fire spread thro' her veins, knocked at her heart,
Met the fire smouldering there
And overbore its lesser flame;
She gorged on bitterness without a name: 510
Ah! fool, to choose such part
Of soul-consuming care!
Sense failed in the mortal strife:
Like the watch-tower of a town
Which an earthquake shatters down,   515
Like a lightning-stricken mast,
Like a wind-uprooted tree
Spun about,
Like a foam-topped waterspout
Cast down headlong in the sea,   520
She fell at last;
Pleasure past and anguish past,
Is it death or is it life?

Life out of death.
That night long Lizzie watched by her,   525
Counted her pulse's flagging stir,
Felt for her breath,
Held water to her lips, and cooled her face
With tears and fanning leaves:
But when the first birds chirped about their eaves,   530
And early reapers plodded to the place
Of golden sheaves,
And dew-wet grass
Bowed in the morning winds so brisk to pass,
And new buds with new day   535
Opened of cup-like lilies on the stream,
Laura awoke as from a dream,
Laughed in the innocent old way,
Hugged Lizzie but not twice or thrice;
Her gleaming locks showed not one thread of grey,   540

Her breath was sweet as May
And light danced in her eyes.

Days, weeks, months, years
Afterwards, when both were wives
With children of their own;   545
Their mother-hearts beset with fears,
Their lives bound up in tender lives;
Laura would call the little ones
And tell them of her early prime,
Those pleasant days long gone   550
Of not-returning time:
Would talk about the haunted glen,
The wicked, quaint fruit-merchant men,
Their fruits like honey to the throat
But poison in the blood;   555
(Men sell not such in any town:)
Would tell them how her sister stood
In deadly peril to do her good,
And win the fiery antidote:
Then joining hands to little hands   560
Would bid them cling together,
'For there is no friend like a sister
In calm or stormy weather;
To cheer one on the tedious way,
To fetch one if one goes astray,   565
To lift one if one totters down,
To strengthen whilst one stands.'

Gabriela Mistral *(1889–1957)*

Dusk *1922*

I feel my heart melting
in the mildness like candles:
my veins are slow oil
and not wine,
and I feel my life fleeing   5
hushed and gentle like the gazelle.

Carley Rees Bogarad *(1936–1995)*

Kudzu *1995*

vines cover the land
in Opelika, Alabama,
        twining

and
    twining   5
over
   poles
   and
   trees,
They grow a foot a day,   10
inundating the South;
cotton plants in the fields
open their small hands,
white in supplication. In Japan
kudzu is used   15
   for hay
   for soil erosion;
they can make anything
useful. Here the leaves choke
and choke, leaving nothing alive.   20
   In
   a
   dream
I watch you roll hot
against someone else's skin.   25

Bart Edelman   *(1951–)*

Bed and Brimstone   *2005*

The tussle of love
Knuckles between us,
Red sheets askew
Before blue fire
Burns the bed black.   5
By next morning
Only powdered ash remains
And white heat that hovers
Above our prickly pink skin.
Now we know how easily   10
Desire consumes souls
We were saving for God,
Long before it became time
To find an acre of Paradise
In the only garden named Eden.   15
Here is where we return
To learn apocryphal lessons
Lust has in mind for us
When it slithers through the grass
On its empty belly.   20

Yet, for the moment,
Our only worry is simply
The replacement of this bed
And the sheer cost involved
To clean up residue,   25
Ridding the room of smoke
And the smell of brimstone
We are unable to escape.

Explorations of the Text

1. Categorize the forms of betrayal.
2. What images do writers use to describe the inner landscape of love? How do they project their inner turmoil on external symbols?
3. Describe the way that the authors use images of the body to capture the abstract nature or emotion of love.
4. John Donne's "The Flea" uses an extended metaphysical conceit (see Glossary). Create a conceit of your own state of love.
5. Discuss the ideas of revenge or jealousy in the poems and in *Othello*.

The Reading/Writing Connection

1. "Think" Topic: Examine patterns of domination and submission in these poems. Why do relationships have these dynamics? Are there other models?
2. Journal entry: Does the one who loves the least have the most power? Is there ever equality in love?

Ideas for Writing

1. Analyze the nature imagery in two or more of the poems. Why are natural images so often connected to love?

2. **Write an Argument:** In "Bed and Brimstone," Bart Edelman writes: "[The Garden of Eden] is where we return/ To learn apocryphal lessons/ Lust has in mind for us/ as it slithers through the grass/ on its empty belly." Is love a kind of paradise? Or is it the garden of evil? Argue pro or con.

3. **Write an Argument:** Does passion prompt us to take leave of our senses? Consider the poems in the cluster and the last encounter between Othello and Desdemona (Act 5, Scene 3).

 On the Web: *Cultural Contexts/Gender*

Please visit http://www.academic.cengage.com/english/Schmidt/Legacies4e/ for links to the following online resources.

The Victorian Web: Literature, History, and Culture in the Age of Victoria
Gender Matters
Robert Browning: Gender Matters
Keunjung Cho, "Female Silence and Male Self-Consciousness in Browning's Poetry"

DRAMA

Susan Glaspell (1882–1948)

Trifles 1916

Characters

County Attorney   Hale
Mrs. Peters   Mrs. Hale
Sheriff

> (Scene: The kitchen in the now abandoned farmhouse of John Wright, a gloomy kitchen, and left without having been put in order—unwashed pans under the sink, a loaf of bread outside the bread-box, a dish-towel on the table—other signs of incompleted work. At the rear the outer door opens and the Sheriff comes in followed by the County Attorney and Hale. The Sheriff and Hale are men in middle life, the County Attorney is a young man; all are much bundled up and go at once to the stove. They are followed by two women—the Sheriff's wife first; she is a slight wiry woman, a thin nervous face. Mrs. Hale is larger and would ordinarily be called more comfortable looking, but she is disturbed now and looks fearfully about as she enters. The women have come in slowly, and stand close together near the door.)

County Attorney: (*Rubbing his hands.*) This feels good. Come up to the fire, ladies.

Mrs. Peters: (*After taking a step forward.*) I'm not—cold.

Sheriff: (*Unbuttoning his overcoat and stepping away from the stove as if to mark the beginning of official business.*) Now, Mr. Hale, before we move things about, you explain to Mr. Henderson just what you saw when you came here yesterday morning.

County Attorney: By the way, has anything been moved? Are things just as you left them yesterday?

Sheriff: (*Looking about.*) It's just the same. When it dropped below zero last night I thought I'd better send Frank out this morning to make a fire for us—no use getting pneumonia with a big case on, but I told him not to touch anything except the stove—and you know Frank.

County Attorney: Somebody should have been left here yesterday.

Sheriff: Oh—yesterday. When I had to send Frank to Morris Center for that man who went crazy—I want you to know I had my hands full yesterday. I knew you could get back from Omaha by today and as long as I went over everything here myself—

County Attorney: Well, Mr. Hale, tell just what happened when you came here yesterday morning.

Hale: Harry and I had started to town with a load of potatoes. We came along the road from my place and as I got here I said, "I'm going to see if I can't get John Wright to go in with me on a party telephone." I spoke to Wright about it once before and he put me off, saying folks talked too much anyway, and all he asked

5

was peace and quiet—I guess you know about how much he talked himself;
but I thought maybe if I went to the house and talked about it before his wife,
though I said to Harry that I didn't know as what his wife wanted made much
difference to John—

County Attorney: Let's talk about that later, Mr. Hale. I do want to talk about that,   10
but tell now just what happened when you got to the house.

Hale: I didn't hear or see anything; I knocked at the door, and still it was all quiet
inside. I knew they must be up, it was past eight o'clock. So I knocked again,
and I thought I heard somebody say, "Come in." I wasn't sure, I'm not sure
yet, but I opened the door—this door *(Indicating the door by which the two
women are still standing.)* and there in that rocker—*(Pointing to it.)* sat
Mrs. Wright.

(They all look at the rocker.)

County Attorney: What—was she doing?

Hale: She was rockin' back and forth. She had her apron in her hand and was kind
of—pleating it.

County Attorney: And how did she—look?

Hale: Well, she looked queer.   15

County Attorney: How do you mean—queer?

Hale: Well, as if she didn't know what she was going to do next. And kind of done up.

County Attorney: How did she seem to feel about your coming?

Hale: Why, I don't think she minded—one way or other. She didn't pay much
attention. I said, "How do, Mrs. Wright, it's cold, ain't it?" And she said, "Is
it?"—and went on kind of pleating at her apron. Well, I was surprised; she
didn't ask me to come up to the stove, or to set down, but just sat there, not
even looking at me, so I said, "I want to see John." And then she—laughed. I
guess you would call it a laugh. I thought of Harry and the team outside, so I
said a little sharp: "Can't I see John?" "No," she says, kind o' dull like. "Ain't
he home?" says I. "Yes," says she, "he's home." "Then why can't I see him?" I
asked her, out of patience. "'Cause he's dead," says she. *"Dead?"* says I. She just
nodded her head, not getting a bit excited, but rockin' back and forth. "Why—
where is he?" says I, not knowing what to say. She just pointed upstairs—like
that *(Himself pointing to the room above.)*. I got up, with the idea of going up
there. I walked from there to here—then I says, "Why, what did he die of?"
"He died of a rope round his neck," says she, and just went on pleatin' at her
apron. Well, I went out and called Harry. I thought I might—need help. We
went upstairs and there he was lying—

County Attorney: I think I'd rather have you go into that upstairs, where you can   20
point it all out. Just go on now with the rest of the story.

Hale: Well, my first thought was to get that rope off. It looked . . . *(Stops, his face
twitches.)* . . . but Harry, he went up to him, and he said, No, he's dead all right,
and we'd better not touch anything. So we went back down stairs. She was still
sitting that same way. "Has anybody been notified?" I asked. "No," says she,
unconcerned. "Who did this, Mrs. Wright?" said Harry. He said it business-
like—and she stopped pleatin' of her apron. "I don't know," she says. "You
don't *know?*" says Harry. "No," says she. "Weren't you sleepin' in the bed with
him?" says Harry. "Yes," says she, "but I was on the inside." "Somebody slipped

a rope round his neck and strangled him and you didn't wake up?" says Harry. "I didn't wake up," she said after him. We must 'a looked as if we didn't see how that could be, for after a minute she said, "I sleep sound." Harry was going to ask her more questions but I said maybe we ought to let her tell her story first to the coroner, or the sheriff, so Harry went fast as he could to Rivers' place, where there's a telephone.

County Attorney: And what did Mrs. Wright do when she knew that you had gone for the coroner?

Hale: She moved from that chair to this one over here *(Pointing to a small chair in the corner.)* and just sat there with her hands held together and looking down. I got a feeling that I ought to make some conversation, so I said I had come in to see if John wanted to put in a telephone, and at that she started to laugh, and then she stopped and looked at me—scared. *(The County Attorney, who has had his notebook out, makes a note.)* I dunno, maybe it wasn't scared. I wouldn't like to say it was. Soon Harry got back, and then Dr. Lloyd came, and you, Mr. Peters, and so I guess that's all I know that you don't.

County Attorney: *(Looking around.)* I guess we'll go upstairs first—and then out to the barn and around there. *(To the Sheriff.)* You're convinced that there was nothing important here—nothing that would point to any motive.

Sheriff: Nothing here but kitchen things. 25

(The County Attorney, after again looking around the kitchen, opens the door of a cupboard closet. He gets up on a chair and looks on a shelf. Pulls his hand away, sticky.)

County Attorney: Here's a nice mess.

(The women draw nearer.)

Mrs. Peters: *(To the other woman.)* Oh, her fruit; it did freeze. *(To the County Attorney.)* She worried about that when it turned so cold. She said the fire'd go out and her jars would break.

Sheriff: Well, can you beat the women! Held for murder and worryin' about her preserves.

County Attorney: I guess before we're through she may have something more serious than preserves to worry about.

Hale: Well, women are used to worrying over trifles. 30

(The two women move a little closer together.)

County Attorney: *(With the gallantry of a young politician.)* And yet, for all their worries, what would we do without the ladies? *(The women do not unbend. He goes to the sink, takes a dipperful of water from the pail and pouring it into a basin, washes his hands. Starts to wipe them on the roller-towel, turns it for a cleaner place.)* Dirty towels! *(Kicks his foot against the pans under the sink.)* Not much of a housekeeper, would you say, ladies?

Mrs. Hale: *(Stiffly.)* There's a great deal of work to be done on a farm.

County Attorney: To be sure. And yet *(With a little bow to her.)* I know there are some Dickson county farmhouses which do not have such roller towels.

(He gives it a pull to expose its full length again.)

Mrs. Hale: Those towels get dirty awful quick. Men's hands aren't always as clean as they might be.

County Attorney: Ah, loyal to your sex, I see. But you and Mrs. Wright were   35
   neighbors. I suppose you were friends, too.

Mrs. Hale: *(Shaking her head.)* I've not seen much of her of late years. I've not been in
   this house—it's more than a year.

County Attorney: And why was that? You didn't like her?

Mrs. Hale: I liked her all well enough. Farmers' wives have their hands full,
   Mr. Henderson. And then—

County Attorney: Yes—?

Mrs. Hale: *(Looking about.)* It never seemed a very cheerful place.   40

County Attorney: No—it's not cheerful. I shouldn't say she had the homemaking
   instinct.

Mrs. Hale: Well, I don't know as Wright had, either.

County Attorney: You mean that they didn't get on very well?

Mrs. Hale: No, I don't mean anything. But I don't think a place'd be any cheerfuller
   for John Wright's being in it.

County Attorney: I'd like to talk more of that a little later. I want to get the lay of   45
   things upstairs now.

(He goes to the left, where three steps lead to a stair door.)

Sheriff: I suppose anything Mrs. Peters does'll be all right. She was to take in some
   clothes for her, you know, and a few little things. We left in such a hurry
   yesterday.

County Attorney: Yes, but I would like to see what you take, Mrs. Peters, and keep
   an eye out for anything that might be of use to us.

Mrs. Peters: Yes, Mr. Henderson.

(The women listen to the men's steps on the stairs, then look about the kitchen.)

Mrs. Hale: I'd hate to have men coming into my kitchen, snooping around and
   criticising.

*(She arranges the pans under sink which the County Attorney had shoved out of
place.)*

Mrs. Peters: Of course it's no more than their duty.   50

Mrs. Hale: Duty's all right, but I guess that deputy sheriff that came out to make
   the fire might have got a little of this on. *(Gives the roller towel a pull.)* Wish
   I'd thought of that sooner. Seems mean to talk about her for not having things
   slicked up when she had to come away in such a hurry.

Mrs. Peters: *(Who has gone to a small table in the left rear corner of the room, and lifted
one end of a towel that covers a pan.)* She had bread set.

(Stands still.)

Mrs. Hale: *(Eyes fixed on a loaf of bread beside the breadbox, which is on a low shelf at
the other side of the room. Moves slowly toward it.)* She was going to put this in
there. *(Picks up loaf, then abruptly drops it. In a manner of returning to familiar
things.)* It's a shame about her fruit. I wonder if it's all gone. *(Gets up on the chair
and looks.)* I think there's some here that's all right, Mrs. Peters. Yes—here;
(Holding it toward the window.) this is cherries, too. *(Looking again.)* I declare
I believe that's the only one. *(Gets down, bottle in her hand. Goes to the sink and
wipes it off on the outside.)* She'll feel awful bad after all her hard work in the hot
weather. I remember the afternoon I put up my cherries last summer.

(She puts the bottle on the big kitchen table, center of the room. With a sigh, is about to sit down in the rocking-chair. Before she is seated realizes what chair it is; with a slow look at it, steps back. The chair, which she has touched, rocks back and forth.)

Mrs. Peters: Well, I must get those things from the front room closet. *(She goes to the door at the right, but after looking into the other room, steps back.)* You coming with me, Mrs. Hale? You could help me carry them.

(They go in the other room; reappear, Mrs. Peters carrying a dress and skirt, Mrs. Hale following with a pair of shoes.)

Mrs. Peters: My, it's cold in there. 55

(She puts the clothes on the big table, and hurries to the stove.)

Mrs. Hale: *(Examining her skirt.)* Wright was close. I think maybe that's why she kept so much to herself. She didn't even belong to the Ladies Aid. I suppose she felt she couldn't do her part, and then you don't enjoy things when you feel shabby. She used to wear pretty clothes and be lively, when she was Minnie Foster, one of the town girls singing in the choir. But that—oh, that was thirty years ago. This all you was to take in?

Mrs. Peters: She said she wanted an apron. Funny thing to want, for there isn't much to get you dirty in jail, goodness knows. But I suppose just to make her feel more natural. She said they was in the top drawer in this cupboard. Yes, here. And then her little shawl that always hung behind the door. *(Opens stair door and looks.)* Yes, here it is.

(Quickly shuts door leading upstairs.)

Mrs. Hale: *(Abruptly moving toward her.)* Mrs. Peters?

Mrs. Peters: Yes, Mrs. Hale?

Mrs. Hale: Do you think she did it? 60

Mrs. Peters: *(In a frightened voice.)* Oh, I don't know.

Mrs. Hale: Well, I don't think she did. Asking for an apron and her little shawl. Worrying about her fruit.

Mrs. Peters: *(Starts to speak, glances up, where footsteps are heard in the room above. In a low voice.)* Mr. Peters says it looks bad for her. Mr. Henderson is awful sarcastic in a speech and he'll make fun of her sayin' she didn't wake up.

Mrs. Hale: Well, I guess John Wright didn't wake when they was slipping that rope under his neck.

Mrs. Peters: No, it's strange. It must have been done awful crafty and still. They say 65 it was such a—funny way to kill a man, rigging it all up like that.

Mrs. Hale: That's just what Mr. Hale said. There was a gun in the house. He says that's what he can't understand.

Mrs. Peters: Mr. Henderson said coming out that what was needed for the case was a motive; something to show anger, or—sudden feeling.

Mrs. Hale: *(Who is standing by the table.)* Well, I don't see any signs of anger around here. *(She puts her hand on the dish towel which lies on the table, stands looking down at table, one half of which is clean, the other half messy.)* It's wiped to here. *(Makes a move as if to finish work, then turns and looks at loaf of bread outside the breadbox. Drops towel. In that voice of coming back to familiar things.)* Wonder how they are finding things upstairs. I hope she had it a little more red-up up there. You know, it seems kind of *sneaking*. Locking her up in town and then coming out here and trying to get her own house to turn against her!

Mrs. Peters: But Mrs. Hale, the law is the law.

Mrs. Hale: I s'pose 'tis. (*Unbuttoning her coat.*) Better loosen up your things,   70
Mrs. Peters. You won't feel them when you go out.

(*Mrs. Peters takes off her fur tippet, goes to hang it on hook at back of room, stands looking at the under part of the small corner table.*)

Mrs. Peters: She was piecing a quilt.

(*She brings the large sewing basket and they look at the bright pieces.*)

Mrs. Hale: It's log cabin pattern. Pretty, isn't it? I wonder if she was goin' to quilt it or just knot it?

(*Footsteps have been heard coming down the stairs. The Sheriff enters followed by Hale and the County Attorney.*)

Sheriff: They wonder if she was going to quilt it or just knot it!

(*The men laugh; the women look abashed.*)

County Attorney: (*Rubbing his hands over the stove.*) Frank's fire didn't do much up there, did it? Well, let's go out to the barn and get that cleared up.

(*The men go outside.*)

Mrs. Hale: (*Resentfully.*) I don't know as there's anything so strange, our takin' up   75
our time with little things while we're waiting for them to get the evidence. (*She sits down at the big table smoothing out a block with decision.*) I don't see as it's anything to laugh about.

Mrs. Peters: (*Apologetically.*) Of course they've got awful important things on their minds.

(*Pulls up a chair and joins Mrs. Hale at the table.*)

Mrs. Hale: (*Examining another block.*) Mrs. Peters, look at this one. Here, this is the one she was working on, and look at the sewing! All the rest of it has been so nice and even. And look at this! It's all over the place! Why, it looks as if she didn't know what she was about!

(*After she has said this they look at each other, then start to glance back at the door. After an instant Mrs. Hale has pulled at a knot and ripped the sewing.*)

Mrs. Peters: Oh, what are you doing, Mrs. Hale?

Mrs. Hale: (*Mildly.*) Just pulling out a stitch or two that's not sewed very good. (*Threading a needle.*) Bad sewing always made me fidgety.

Mrs. Peters: (*Nervously.*) I don't think we ought to touch things.   80

Mrs. Hale: I'll just finish up this end. (*Suddenly stopping and leaning forward.*) Mrs. Peters?

Mrs. Peters: Yes, Mrs. Hale?

Mrs. Hale: What do you suppose she was so nervous about?

Mrs. Peters: Oh—I don't know. I don't know as she was nervous. I sometimes sew awful queer when I'm just tired. (*Mrs. Hale starts to say something, looks at Mrs. Peters, then goes on sewing.*) Well, I must get these things wrapped up. They may be through sooner than we think. (*Putting apron and other things together.*) I wonder where I can find a piece of paper, and string.

Mrs. Hale: In that cupboard, maybe. 85

Mrs. Peters: *(Looking in cupboard.)* Why, here's a bird-cage. *(Holds it up.)* Did she have a bird, Mrs. Hale?

Mrs. Hale: Why, I don't know whether she did or not—I've not been here for so long. There was a man around last year selling canaries cheap, but I don't know as she took one; maybe she did. She used to sing real pretty herself.

Mrs. Peters: *(Glancing around.)* Seems funny to think of a bird here. But she must have had one, or why would she have a cage? I wonder what happened to it.

Mrs. Hale: I s'pose maybe the cat got it.

Mrs. Peters: No, she didn't have a cat. She's got that feeling some people have about 90
cats—being afraid of them. My cat got in her room and she both real upset and asked me to take it out.

Mrs. Hale: My sister Bessie was like that. Queer, ain't it?

Mrs. Peters: *(Examining the cage.)* Why, look at this door. It's broke. One hinge is pulled apart.

Mrs. Hale: *(Looking too.)* Looks as if someone must have been rough with it.

Mrs. Peters: Why, yes.

(She brings the cage forward and puts it on the table.)

Mrs. Hale: I wish if they're going to find any evidence they'd be about it. I don't like 95
this place.

Mrs. Peters: But I'm awful glad you came with me, Mrs. Hale. It would be lonesome for me sitting here alone.

Mrs. Hale: It would, wouldn't it? *(Dropping her sewing.)* But I tell you what I do wish, Mrs. Peters. I wish I had come over sometimes when she was here. I—*(Looking around the room.)*—wish I had.

Mrs. Peters: But of course you were awful busy, Mrs. Hale—your house and your children.

Mrs. Hale: I could've come. I stayed away because it weren't cheerful—and that's why I ought to have come. I—I've never liked this place. Maybe because it's down in a hollow and you don't see the road. I dunno what it is but it's a lonesome place and always was. I wish I had come over to see Minnie Foster sometimes. I can see now—

(Shakes her head.)

Mrs. Peters: Well, you mustn't reproach yourself, Mrs. Hale. Somehow we just don't 100
see how it is with other folks until—something comes up.

Mrs. Hale: Not having children makes less work—but it makes a quiet house, and Wright out to work all day, and no company when he did come in. Did you know John Wright, Mrs. Peters?

Mrs. Peters: Not to know him; I've seen him in town. They say he was a good man.

Mrs. Hale: Yes—good; he didn't drink, and kept his word as well as most, I guess, and paid his debts. But he was a hard man, Mrs. Peters. Just to pass the time of day with him—*(Shivers.)* Like a raw wind that gets to the bone. *(Pauses, her eye falling on the cage.)* I should think she would 'a wanted a bird. But what do you suppose went with it?

Mrs. Peters: I don't know, unless it got sick and died.

(She reaches over and swings the broken door, swings it again. Both women watch it.)

Mrs. Hale: You weren't raised round here, were you? *(Mrs. Peters shakes her head.)*   105
You didn't know—her?

Mrs. Peters: Not till they brought her yesterday.

Mrs. Hale: She—come to think of it, she was kind of like a bird herself—real
sweet and pretty, but kind of timid and—fluttery. How—she—did—change.
*(Silence; then as if struck by a happy thought and relieved to get back to everyday
things.)* Tell you what, Mrs. Peters, why don't you take the quilt in with you? It
might take up her mind.

Mrs. Peters: Why, I think that's a real nice idea, Mrs. Hale. There couldn't possibly
be any objection to it, could there? Now, just what would I take? I wonder if her
patches are in here—and her things.

(They look in the sewing basket.)

Mrs. Hale: Here's some red. I expect this has got sewing things in it. *(Brings out a
fancy box.)* What a pretty box. Looks like something somebody would give you.
Maybe her scissors are in here. *(Opens box. Suddenly puts her hand to her nose.)*
Why—*(Mrs. Peters bends nearer, then turns her face away.)* There's something
wrapped up in this piece of silk.

Mrs. Peters: Why, this isn't her scissors.   110

Mrs. Hale: *(Lifting the silk.)* Oh, Mrs. Peters—it's—

(Mrs. Peters bends closer.)

Mrs. Peters: It's the bird.

Mrs. Hale: *(Jumping up.)* But, Mrs. Peters—look at it! Its neck! Look at its neck! It's
all—other side to.

Mrs. Peters: Somebody—wrung—its—neck.

*(Their eyes meet. A look of growing comprehension, of horror. Steps are heard
outside. Mrs. Hale slips box under quilt pieces, and sinks into her chair. Enter
Sheriff and County Attorney. Mrs. Peters rises.)*

County Attorney: *(As one turning from serious things to little pleasantries.)* Well, ladies,   115
have you decided whether she was going to quilt it or knot it?

Mrs. Peters: We think she was going to—knot it.

County Attorney: Well, that's interesting, I'm sure. *(Seeing the bird-cage.)* Has the
bird flown?

Mrs. Hale: *(Putting more quilt pieces over the box.)* We think the—cat got it.

County Attorney: *(Preoccupied.)* Is there a cat?

(Mrs. Hale glances in a quick covert way at Mrs. Peters.)

Mrs. Peters: Well, not now. They're superstitious, you know. They leave.   120

County Attorney: *(To Sheriff Peters, continuing an interrupted conversation.)* No sign
at all of anyone having come from the outside. Their own rope. Now let's go up
again and go over it piece by piece. *(They start upstairs.)* It would have to have
been someone who knew just the—

*(Mrs. Peters sits down. The two women sit there not looking at one another, but as if
peering into something and at the same time holding back. When they talk now it is
in the manner of feeling their way over strange ground, as if afraid of what they are
saying, but as if they can not help saying it.)*

Mrs. Hale: She liked the bird. She was going to bury it in that pretty box.

Mrs. Peters: *(In a whisper.)* When I was a girl—my kitten—there was a boy took a hatchet, and before my eyes—and before I could get there—*(Covers her face an instant.)* If they hadn't held me back I would have—*(Catches herself, looks upstairs where steps are heard, falters weakly.)*—hurt him.

Mrs. Hale: *(With a slow look around her.)* I wonder how it would seem never to have had any children around. *(Pause.)* No, Wright wouldn't like the bird—a thing that sang. She used to sing. He killed that, too.

Mrs. Peters: *(Moving uneasily.)* We don't know who killed the bird.   125

Mrs. Hale: I knew John Wright.

Mrs. Peters: It was an awful thing was done in this house that night, Mrs. Hale. Killing a man while he slept, slipping a rope around his neck that choked the life out of him.

Mrs. Hale: His neck. Choked the life out of him.

(Her hand goes out and rests on the bird-cage.)

Mrs. Peters: *(With rising voice.)* We don't know who killed him. We don't know.

Mrs. Hale: *(Her own feeling not interrupted.)* If there'd been years and years of   130 nothing, then a bird to sing to you, it would be awful—still, after the bird was still.

Mrs. Peters: *(Something within her speaking.)* I know what stillness is. When we homesteaded in Dakota, and my first baby died—after he was two years old, and me with no other then—

Mrs. Hale: *(Moving.)* How soon do you suppose they'll be through, looking for the evidence?

Mrs. Peters: I know what stillness is. *(Pulling herself back.)* The law has got to punish crime, Mrs. Hale.

Mrs. Hale: *(Not as if answering that.)* I wish you'd seen Minnie Foster when she wore a white dress with blue ribbons and stood up there in the choir and sang. *(A look around the room.)* Oh, I wish I'd come over here once in a while! That was a crime! That was a crime! Who's going to punish that?

Mrs. Peters: *(Looking upstairs.)* We mustn't—take on.   135

Mrs. Hale: I might have known she needed help! I know how things can be—for women. I tell you, it's queer, Mrs. Peters. We live close together and we live far apart. We all go through the same things—it's all just a different kind of the same thing. *(Brushes her eyes, noticing the bottle of fruit, reaches out for it.)* If I was you I wouldn't tell her her fruit was gone. Tell her it *ain't*. Tell her it's all right. Take this in to prove it to her. She—she may never know whether it was broke or not.

Mrs. Peters: *(Takes the bottle, looks about for something to wrap it in; takes petticoat from the clothes brought from the other room, very nervously begins winding this around the bottle. In a false voice.)* My, it's a good thing the men couldn't hear us. Wouldn't they just laugh! Getting all stirred up over a little thing like a— dead canary. As if that could have anything to do with—with—wouldn't they laugh!

(The men are heard coming down stairs.)

Mrs. Hale: *(Under her breath.)* Maybe they would—maybe they wouldn't.

County Attorney: No, Peters, it's all perfectly clear except a reason for doing it. But you know juries when it comes to women. If there was some definite thing.

Something to show—something to make a story about—a thing that would connect up with this strange way of doing it—

(The women's eyes meet for an instant. Enter Hale from outer door.)

Hale: Well, I've got the team around. Pretty cold out there. 140

County Attorney: I'm going to stay here a while by myself. *(To the Sheriff.)* You can send Frank out for me, can't you? I want to go over everything. I'm not satisfied that we can't do better.

Sheriff: Do you want to see what Mrs. Peters is going to take in?

(The County Attorney goes to the table, picks up the apron, laughs.)

County Attorney: Oh, I guess they're not very dangerous things the ladies have picked out. *(Moves a few things about, disturbing the quilt pieces which cover the box. Steps back.)* No, Mrs. Peters doesn't need supervising. For that matter, a sheriff's wife is married to the law. Ever think of it that way, Mrs. Peters?

Mrs. Peters: Not—just that way.

Sheriff: *(Chuckling.)* Married to the law. *(Moves toward the other room.)* I just want 145 you to come in here a minute, George. We ought to take a look at these windows.

County Attorney: *(Scoffingly.)* Oh, windows!

Sheriff: We'll be right out, Mr. Hale.

(Hale goes outside. The Sheriff follows the County Attorney into the other room. Then Mrs. Hale rises, hands tight together, looking intensely at Mrs. Peters, whose eyes make a slow turn, finally meeting Mrs. Hale's. A moment Mrs. Hale holds her, then her own eyes point the way to where the box is concealed. Suddenly Mrs. Peters throws back quilt pieces and tries to put the box in the bag she is wearing. It is too big. She opens box, starts to take bird out, cannot touch it, goes to pieces, stands there helpless. Sound of a knob turning in the other room. Mrs. Hale snatches the box and puts it in the pocket of her big coat. Enter County Attorney and Sheriff.)

County Attorney: *(Facetiously.)* Well, Henry, at least we found out that she was not going to quilt it. She was going to—what is it you call it, ladies?

Mrs. Hale: *(Her hand against her pocket.)* We call it—knot it, Mr. Henderson.

(Curtain.)

Explorations of the Text

1. Characterize Mrs. Hale and Mrs. Peters at the beginning of the play. How do they differ?

2. What clues lead the women to conclude that Minnie Wright killed her husband?

3. How do the men differ from the women? from each other?

4. What do the men discover? Why do they conclude "Nothing here but kitchen things"? What do the women discover?

5. Why do the men and women find different clues about the murder? What does Glaspell imply about the ways in which men and women were conditioned to view the world?

6. Do Mrs. Hale and Mrs. Peters change? Why? How? What makes them sympathize with Minnie Wright? Discuss the symbolism of the broken cage and the dead canary.

7. Characterize Minnie Wright and her husband. Describe their relationship.

Why is Minnie Wright absent from the play?

8. Interpret the ending and the title. With what "crime" should Minnie Wright be charged?

9. Compare the marriage of the Wrights with those in other works in this chapter.

10. Compare Glaspell's critique of gender roles and of women's place in society with treatments of these issues by Gilman and Chopin.

The Reading/Writing Connection

1. Write a journal entry in Minnie Wright's voice.

2. Are Mrs. Hale and Mrs. Peters justified in withholding evidence concerning John Wright's murder?

Ideas for Writing

1. Susan Glaspell claimed that the idea for the play came from a story that she covered as a reporter. Construct your version of her article.

2. What are the strengths and weaknesses of *Trifles?* Consider conflict, characters, setting, theme, symbol, irony, emotion, and/or general effect.

3. After the play was produced, Glaspell wrote a short story, "A Jury of Her Peers," about this subject. Read the story, and decide which version is better. Defend your choice.

4. **Write an Argument:** Should Minnie Wright be found guilty for her actions? Defend your position in an essay.

David Ives   *(1950–)*

Sure Thing   *1995*

Characters

Bill, in his late twenties
Betty, in her late twenties

Setting

A café table, with a couple of chairs.

Scene

Betty, reading at the table. An empty chair opposite her. Bill enters.

Bill: Excuse me. Is this chair taken?
Betty: Excuse me?
Bill: Is this taken?
Betty: Yes, it is.
Bill: Oh. Sorry.
Betty: Sure thing.

(A bell rings softly.)

Bill: Excuse me. Is this chair taken?
Betty: Excuse me?
Bill: Is this taken?
Betty: No, but I'm expecting somebody in a minute.   10
Bill: Oh. Thanks anyway.
Betty: Sure thing.

(A bell rings softly.)

Bill: Excuse me. Is this chair taken?
Betty: No, but I'm expecting somebody very shortly.
Bill: Would you mind if I sit here till he or she or it comes?   15
Betty: *(Glances at her watch.)* They seem to be pretty late . . .
Bill: You never know who you might be turning down.
Betty: Sorry. Nice try, though.
Bill: Sure thing.

(Bell.)

Bill: Is this seat taken?   20
Betty: No, it's not.
Bill: Would you mind if I sit here?
Betty: Yes, I would.
Bill: Oh.

(Bell.)

Bill: Is this chair taken?   25
Betty: No, it's not.
Bill: Would you mind if I sit here?
Betty: No. Go ahead.
Bill: Thanks. *(He sits. She continues reading.)* Every place else seems to be taken.
Betty: Mm-hm.   30
Bill: Great place.
Betty: Mm-hm.
Bill: What's the book?
Betty: I just wanted to read in quiet, if you don't mind.
Bill: No. Sure thing.   35

(Bell.)

Bill: Everyplace else seems to be taken.
Betty: Mm-hm.
Bill: Great place for reading.
Betty: Yes, I like it.
Bill: What's the book?   40
Betty: "The Sound and the Fury."
Bill: Oh. Hemingway.[1]

(Bell.)

Bill: What's the book?

---

[1]**Ernest Hemingway (1899–1961):** U.S. novelist, short story writer.

Betty: "The Sound and the Fury."
Bill: Oh. Faulkner.[2]
Betty: Have you read it?
Bill: Not . . . actually. I've read *about* it, though. It's supposed to be great.
Betty: It is great.
Bill: I hear it's great. *(Small pause.)* Waiter?

   (Bell.)

Bill: What's the book?
Betty: "The Sound and the Fury."
Bill: Oh. Faulkner.
Betty: Have you read it?
Bill: I'm a Mets fan, myself.

   (Bell.)

Betty: Have you read it?
Bill: Yeah, I read it in college.
Betty: Where was college?
Bill: I went to Oral Roberts University.

   (Bell.)

Betty: Where was college?
Bill: I was lying. I never really went to college. I just like to party.

   (Bell.)

Betty: Where was college?
Bill: Harvard.
Betty: Did you like Faulkner?
Bill: I love Faulkner. I spent a whole winter reading him once.
Betty: I've just started.
Bill: I was so excited after ten pages that I went out and bought everything else
    he wrote. One of the greatest reading experiences of my life. I mean, all that
    incredible psychological understanding. Page after page of gorgeous prose. His
    profound grasp of the mystery of time and human existence. The smells of the
    earth . . . What do you think?
Betty: I think it's pretty boring.

   (Bell.)

Bill: What's the book?
Betty: "The Sound and the Fury."
Bill: Oh! Faulkner!
Betty: Do you like Faulkner?
Bill: I love Faulkner.
Betty: He's incredible.
Bill: I spent a whole winter reading him once.
Betty: I was so excited after ten pages that I went out and bought everything else he
    wrote.
Bill: All that incredible psychological understanding.

---

[2]**William Faulkner (1897–1962):** U.S. novelist, short story writer.

Betty: And the prose is so gorgeous.

Bill: And the way he's grasped the mystery of time—

Betty: —and human existence. I can't believe I've waited this long to read him.

Bill: You never know. You might not have liked him before.   80

Betty: That's true.

Bill: You might not have been ready for him. You have to hit these things at the right moment or it's no good.

Betty: That's happened to me.

Bill: It's all in the timing. *(Small pause.)* My name's Bill, by the way.

Betty: I'm Betty.   85

Bill: Hi.

Betty: Hi.

> *(Small pause.)*

Bill: Yes, I thought reading Faulkner was . . . a great experience.

Betty: Yes.

> *(Small pause.)*

Bill: "The Sound and the Fury" . . .   90

> *(Another small pause.)*

Betty: Well. Onwards and upwards. *(She goes back to her book.)*

Bill: Waiter—?

> *(Bell.)*

Bill: You have to hit these things at the right moment or it's no good.

Betty: That's happened to me.

Bill: It's all in the timing. My name's Bill, by the way.   95

Betty: I'm Betty.

Bill: Hi.

Betty: Hi.

Bill: Do you come in here a lot?

Betty: Actually I'm just in town for two days from Pakistan.   100

Bill: Oh. Pakistan.

> *(Bell.)*

Bill: My name's Bill, by the way.

Betty: I'm Betty.

Bill: Hi.

Betty: Hi.   105

Bill: Do you come in here a lot?

Betty: Every once in a while. Do you?

Bill: No much anymore. Not as much as I used to. Before my nervous breakdown.

> *(Bell.)*

Bill: Do you come in here a lot?

Betty: Why are you asking?   110

Bill: Just interested.

Betty: Are you really interested, or do you just want to pick me up?

Bill: No, I'm really interested.

Betty: Why would you be interested in whether I come in here a lot?

Bill: Just . . . getting acquainted. 115

Betty: Maybe you're only interested for the sake of making small talk long enough to ask me back to your place to listen to some music, or because you've just rented some great tape for your VCR, or because you've got some terrific unknown Django Reinhardt[3] record, only all you'll really want to do is fuck—which you won't do very well—after which you'll go into the bathroom and pee very loudly, then pad into the kitchen and get yourself a beer from the refrigerator without asking me whether I'd like anything, and then you'll proceed to lie back down beside me and confess that you've got a girlfriend named Stephanie who's away at medical school in Belgium for a year, and that you've been involved with her—*off and on*—in what you'll call a very intricate relationship, for about *seven YEARS*. None of which *interests* me, mister!

Bill: Okay.

(Bell.)

Bill: Do you come in here a lot?

Betty: Every other day, I think.

Bill: I come in here quite a lot and I don't remember seeing you. 120

Betty: I guess we must be on different schedules.

Bill: Missed connections.

Betty: Yes. Different time zones.

Bill: Amazing how you can live right next door to somebody in this town and never even know it.

Betty: I know. 125

Bill: City life.

Betty: It's crazy.

Bill: We probably pass each other in the street every day. Right in front of this place, probably.

Betty: Yep.

Bill: *(Looks around.)* Well, the waiters here sure seem to be in some different time 130 zone. I don't see one anywhere . . . Waiter! *(He looks back.)* So what do you . . . *(He sees that she's gone back to her book.)*

Betty: I beg pardon?

Bill: Nothing. Sorry.

(Bell.)

Betty: I guess we must be on different schedules.

Bill: Missed connections.

Betty: Yes. Different time zones. 135

Bill: Amazing how you can live right next door to somebody in this town and never even know it.

Betty: I know.

Bill: City life.

Betty: It's crazy.

Bill: You weren't waiting for somebody when I came in, were you? 140

Betty: Actually I was.

---

[3] **Django Reinhardt:** Famous jazz guitarist, originally named Jean-Baptiste Reinhardt (1910–1943), of Gypsy origin. One of the originals of European jazz, he performed with the Duke Ellington orchestra in 1946.

Bill: Oh. Boyfriend?
Betty: Sort of.
Bill: What's a sort-of boyfriend?
Betty: My husband.   145
Bill: Ah-ha.

> *(Bell.)*

Bill: You weren't waiting for somebody when I came in, were you?
Betty: Actually I was.
Bill: Oh. Boyfriend?
Betty: Sort of.   150
Bill: What's a sort-of boyfriend?
Betty: We were meeting here to break up.
Bill: Mm-hm . . .

> *(Bell.)*

Bill: What's a sort-of boyfriend?
Betty: My lover. Here she comes right now!   155

> *(Bell.)*

Bill: You weren't waiting for somebody when I came in, were you?
Betty: No, just reading.
Bill: Sort of a sad occupation for a Friday night, isn't it? Reading here, all by yourself?
Betty: Do you think so?
Bill: Well sure. I mean, what's a good-looking woman like you doing out alone on a   160
  Friday night?
Betty: Trying to keep away from lines like that.
Bill: No, listen—

> *(Bell.)*

Bill: You weren't waiting for somebody when I came in, were you?
Betty: No, just reading.
Bill: Sort of a sad occupation for a Friday night, isn't it? Reading here all by yourself?   165
Betty: I guess it is, in a way.
Bill: What's a good-looking woman like you doing out alone on a Friday night? No
  offense, but . . .
Betty: I'm out alone on a Friday night for the first time in a very long time.
Bill: Oh.
Betty: You see, I just recently ended a relationship.   170
Bill: Oh.
Betty: Of rather long standing.
Bill: I'm sorry—Well listen, since reading by yourself is such a sad occupation for a
  Friday night, would you like to go elsewhere?
Betty: No . . .
Bill: Do something else?   175
Betty: No thanks.
Bill: I was headed out to the movies in a while anyway.
Betty: I don't think so.
Bill: Big chance to let Faulkner catch his breath. All those long sentences get him
  pretty tired.

Betty: Thanks anyway. 180
Bill: Okay.
Betty: I appreciate the invitation.
Bill: Sure thing.

(*Bell.*)

Bill: You weren't waiting for somebody when I came in, were you?
Betty: No, just reading. 185
Bill: Sort of a sad occupation for a Friday night, isn't it? Reading here all by yourself?
Betty: I guess I was trying to think of it as existentially romantic. You know—capuccino, great literature, rainy night . . .
Bill: That only works in Paris. We *could* hop the late plane to Paris. Get on a Concorde. Find a café . . .
Betty: I'm a little short on plane fare tonight.
Bill: Darn it, so am I. 190
Betty: To tell you the truth, I was headed to the movies after I finished this section. Would you like to come along? Since you can't locate a waiter?
Bill: That's a very nice offer, but—I can't.
Betty: Uh-huh. Girlfriend?
Bill: Two of them, actually. One of them's pregnant, and Stephanie—

(*Bell.*)

Betty: Girlfriend? 195
Bill: No, I don't have a girlfriend. Not if you mean the castrating bitch I dumped last night.

(*Bell.*)

Betty: Girlfriend?
Bill: Sort of. Sort of . . .
Betty: What's a sort-of girlfriend?
Bill: My mother. 200

(*Bell.*)

Bill: I just ended a relationship, actually.
Betty: Oh.
Bill: Of rather long standing.
Betty: I'm sorry to hear it.
Bill: This is my first night out alone in a long time. I feel a little bit at sea, to tell you 205 the truth.
Betty: So you didn't stop to talk because you're a Moonie,[4] or you have some weird political affiliation—?
Bill: Nope. Straight-down-the-ticket Republican.

(*Bell.*)

Straight-down-the-ticket Democrat.

(*Bell.*)

Can I tell you something about politics?

(*Bell.*)

---

[4]**Moonie:** Member of a religious cult.

I consider myself a citizen of the universe.

(Bell.)

I'm unaffiliated.

Betty: That's a relief. So am I.

Bill: I vote my beliefs.

Betty: Labels are not important.   210

Bill: Labels are not important, exactly. Like me, for example. I mean, what does it matter if I had a two-point—

(Bell.)

—three-point—

(Bell.)

—four-point at college, or if I did come from Pittsburgh—

(Bell.)

—Cleveland—

(Bell.)

—Westchester County?

Betty: Sure.

Bill: I believe that a man is what he is.

(Bell.)

A person is what he is.

(Bell.)

A person is what they are.

Betty: I think so, too.

Bill: So what if I admire Trotsky?[5]   215

(Bell.)

So what if I once had a total body liposuction?

(Bell.)

So what if I don't have a penis?

(Bell.)

So what if I spent a year in the Peace Corps? I was acting on my convictions.

Betty: Convictions are important.

Bill: You just can't hang a sign on a person.

Betty: Absolutely. I'll bet you're a Scorpio.

(Many bells ring.)

Betty: Listen, I was headed to the movies after I finished this section. Would you like to come along?

Bill: That sounds like fun. What's playing?   220

Betty: A couple of the really early Woody Allen movies.

Bill: Oh.

Betty: Don't you like Woody Allen?

---

[5]**Leon Trotsky (1879–1940):** Russian revolutionary and writer.

Bill: Sure. I like Woody Allen.
Betty: But you're not crazy about Woody Allen. 225
Bill: Those early ones kind of get on my nerves.
Betty: Uh-huh.

> *(Bell.)*

Bill:	*(Simultaneously.)*	**Betty:**
	Y'know, I was headed	I was thinking about . . .
	to the . . .	

Bill: I'm sorry.
Betty: No, go ahead. 230
Bill: I was just going to say that I was headed to the movies in a little while, and . . .
Betty: So was I.
Bill: The Woody Allen festival?
Betty: Just up the street.
Bill: Do you like the early ones? 235
Betty: I think anybody who doesn't ought to be run off the planet.
Bill: How many times have you seen "Bananas"?[6]
Betty: Eight times.
Bill: Twelve. So are you still interested?
Betty: Do you like Entenmann's crumb cake? 240
Bill: I went out at two o'clock this morning to buy one. Did you have an Etch-a-Sketch as a child?
Betty: Yes! Do you like brussel sprouts?
Bill: I think they're gross.
Betty: They *are* gross!
Bill: Do you still believe in marriage in spite of current sentiments against it? 245
Betty: Yes.
Bill: And children?
Betty: Three of them.
Bill: Two girls and a boy.
Betty: Harvard, Vassar, and Brown. 250
Bill: And will you love me?
Betty: Yes.
Bill: And cherish me forever?
Betty: Yes.
Bill: Do you still want to go to the movies? 255
Betty: Sure thing.
Bill and Betty: *(Together.)* Waiter!

> *(Blackout.)*

Explorations of the Text

1. Why does Ives choose the names Betty and Bill for his protagonists?

2. What is the significance of the setting—the café? What does the bell signify?

---

[6]**"Bananas":** A movie produced and directed by Woody Allen.

3. Discuss the irony of the repeated line, "Sure thing."

4. How do the interactions between the two characters in each scene differ from one another? How do the scenes build upon one another? Discuss the climactic last interchange.

5. What views of dating and relationships does the play suggest? Are they believable?

6. Discuss the impact of the humor in the play.

The Reading/Writing Connection

1. Using this work as a model, create a dramatic scene or dialogue that conveys a satiric view of relationships. Then in a short paragraph analyze the themes of your work.

Ideas for Writing

1. Analyze this work as an example of the theater of the absurd (refer to Chapter 12).

2. **Write an Argument:** Do you relate to the play's vision of the dating game? Create an argumentative mini-essay presenting your response to this question.

William Shakespeare   *(1564–1616)*

Othello, the Moor of Venice   *(1622)*

Characters

Duke of Venice
Brabantio, *a Senator*
Other Senators
Gratiano, *Brabantio's brother*
Lodovico, *Brabantio's kinsman*
Othello, *a noble Moor in the service of the Venetian state*
Cassio, *his lieutenant*
Iago, *his ensign*
Montano, *Othello's predecessor in the government of Cyprus*
Roderigo, *a Venetian gentleman*
Clown, *Othello's servant*
Desdemona, *Brabantio's daughter and Othello's wife*
Emilia, *Iago's wife*
Bianca, *Cassio's mistress*
Sailor, MESSENGER, HERALD, OFFICERS, GENTLEMEN, MUSICIANS, *and* ATTENDANTS

Scene

Venice, and a seaport in Cyprus.

ACT 1
Scene 1.
Venice. A street.

(Enter RODERIGO *and* IAGO.*)*

Roderigo. Tush, never tell me! I take it much unkindly
    That thou, Iago, who hast had my purse
    As if the strings were thine, shouldst know of this.
Iago. 'Sblood, but you will not hear me.
    If ever I did dream of such a matter,   5
    Abhor me.
Roderigo. Thou told'st me thou didst hold him in thy hate.
Iago. Despise me if I do not. Three great ones of the city,
    In personal suit to make me his Lieutenant,
    Off-capped to him. And, by the faith of man,   10
    I know my price, I am worth no worse a place.
    But he, as loving his own pride and purposes,
    Evades them, with a bombast circumstance
    Horribly stuffed with epithets of war.
    And, in conclusion,   15
    Nonsuits° my mediators, for, "Certes," says he,
    "I have already chose my officer,"
    And what was he?
    Forsooth, a great arithmetician,°
    One Michael Cassio, a Florentine,   20
    A fellow almost damned in a fair wife,°
    That never set a squadron in the field,
    Nor the division of a battle knows
    More than a spinster, unless the bookish theoric,
    Wherein the toged Consuls can propose   25
    As masterly as he—mere prattle without practice
    Is all his soldiership. But he, sir, had the election.
    And I, of whom his eyes had seen the proof
    At Rhodes, at Cyprus, and on other grounds
    Christian and heathen, must be beleed° and calmed   30
    By debitor and creditor. This countercaster,°
    He, in good time,° must his Lieutenant be,
    And I—God bless the mark!—his Moorship's Ancient.°
Roderigo. By Heaven, I rather would have been his hangman.

---

16. **Nonsuits:** Rejects the petition of   19. **arithmetician:** Contemporary books on military tactics are full of elaborate diagrams and numerals to explain military formations. Cassio is a student of such books.   21. **almost . . . wife:** A much-disputed phrase. There is an Italian proverb, "You have married a fair wife? You are damned." If Iago has this in mind, he means by *almost* that Cassio is about to marry.   30. **beleed:** placed on the lee (or unfavorable) side   31. **countercaster:** calculator (repeating the idea of arithmetician). Counters were used in making calculations.   32. **in good time:** a phrase expressing indignation   33. **Ancient:** Ensign, the third officer in the company of which Othello is Captain and Cassio Lieutenant

Iago. Why, there's no remedy. 'Tis the curse of service,   35
    Preferment goes by letter and affection,
    And not by old gradation,° where each second
    Stood heir to the first. Now, sir, be judge yourself
    Whether I in any just term am affined°
    To love the Moor.
Roderigo.   I would not follow him, then.   40
Iago. Oh, sir, content you,
    I follow him to serve my turn upon him.
    We cannot all be masters, nor all masters
    Cannot be truly followed. You shall mark
    Many a duteous and knee-crooking knave   45
    That doting on his own obsequious bondage
    Wears out his time, much like his master's ass,
    For naught but provender, and when he's old, cashiered.
    Whip me such honest knaves. Others there are
    Who, trimmed in forms and visages of duty,   50
    Keep yet their hearts attending on themselves,
    And throwing but shows of service on their lords
    Do well thrive by them, and when they have lined their coats
    Do themselves homage. These fellows have some soul,
    And such a one do I profess myself. For, sir,   55
    It is as sure as you are Roderigo,
    Were I the Moor, I would not be Iago.
    In following him, I follow but myself.
    Heaven is my judge, not I for love and duty,
    But seeming so, for my peculiar end.   60
    For when my outward action doth demonstrate
    The native act and figure of my heart
    In compliment extern, 'tis not long after
    But I will wear my heart upon my sleeve
    For daws to peck at. I am not what I am.   65
Roderigo. What a full fortune does the thick-lips owe°
    If he can carry 't thus!°
Iago.   Call up her father,
    Rouse him. Make after him, poison his delight,
    Proclaim him in the streets. Incense her kinsmen,
    And though he in a fertile climate dwell,   70
    Plague him with flies. Though that his joy be joy,
    Yet throw such changes of vexation on 't
    As it may lose some color.
Roderigo. Here is her father's house, I'll call aloud.

36–37. **Preferment . . . gradation:** Promotion comes through private recommendation and favoritism and not by order of seniority. 39. **affined:** tied by affection 66. **owe:** own 67. **carry 't thus:** i.e., bring off this marriage

Iago. Do, with like timorous° accent and dire yell   75
     As when, by night and negligence, the fire
     Is spied in populous cities.
Roderigo. What ho, Brabantio! Signior Brabantio, ho!
Iago. Awake! What ho, Brabantio! Thieves! Thieves! Thieves!
     Look to your house, your daughter and your bags!°   80
     Thieves! Thieves! (BRABANTIO *appears above, at a window.*)
Brabantio. What is the reason of this terrible summons?
     What is the matter there?
Roderigo. Signior, is all your family within?
Iago. Are your doors locked?
Brabantio.   Why, wherefore ask you this?   85
Iago. 'Zounds, sir, you're robbed. For shame, put on your gown,
     Your heart is burst, you have lost half your soul.
     Even now, now, very now, an old black ram
     Is tupping your white ewe. Arise, arise,
     Awake the snorting° citizens with the bell,   90
     Or else the Devil° will make a grandsire of you.
     Arise, I say.
Brabantio.   What, have you lost your wits?
Roderigo. Most reverend signior, do you know my voice?
Brabantio. Not I. What are you?
Roderigo. My name is Roderigo.
Brabantio.   The worser welcome.   95
     I have charged thee not to haunt about my doors.
     In honest plainness thou hast heard me say
     My daughter is not for thee, and now, in madness,
     Being full of supper and distempering draughts,
     Upon malicious bravery° dost thou come   100
     To start° my quiet.
Roderigo. Sir, sir, sir—
Brabantio.   But thou must needs be sure
     My spirit and my place have in them power
     To make this bitter to thee.
Roderigo.   Patience, good sir.
Brabantio. What tell'st thou me of robbing? This is Venice,   105
     My house is not a grange.°
Roderigo.   Most grave Brabantio,
     In simple and pure soul I come to you.
Iago. 'Zounds, sir, you are one of those that will not serve God if the Devil bid you.
     Because we come to do you service and you think we are ruffians, you'll have
     your daughter covered with a Barbary° horse, you'll have your nephews° neigh
     to you, you'll have coursers for cousins,° and jennets° for germans.°   112

---

75. **timorous:** terrifying   80. **bags:** moneybags   90. **snorting:** snoring   91. **Devil:** The Devil in old pictures and woodcuts was represented as black.   100. **bravery:** defiance   101. **start:** startle 106. **grange:** lonely farm   110. **Barbary:** Moorish   111. **nephews:** grandsons   112. **cousins:** near relations   **jennets:** Moorish ponies   **germans:** kinsmen

Brabantio. What profane wretch art thou?

Iago. I am one, sir, that comes to tell you your daughter and the Moor are now
    making the beast with two backs.

Brabantio. Thou art a villain.

Iago.   You are—a Senator.

Brabantio. This thou shalt answer. I know thee, Roderigo.

Roderigo. Sir, I will answer anything. But I beseech you
    If 't be your pleasure and most wise consent,
    As partly I find it is, that your fair daughter,   120
    At this odd-even° and dull watch o' the night,
    Transported with no worse nor better guard
    But with a knave of common hire, a gondolier,
    To the gross clasps of a lascivious Moor—
    If this be known to you, and your allowance,°   125
    We then have done you bold and saucy wrongs.
    But if you know not this, my manners tell me
    We have your wrong rebuke. Do not believe
    That, from the sense of all civility,
    I thus would play and trifle with your reverence.   130
    Your daughter, if you have not given her leave,
    I say again, hath made a gross revolt,
    Tying her duty, beauty, wit, and fortunes
    In an extravagant° and wheeling° stranger
    Of here and everywhere. Straight satisfy yourself.   135
    If she be in her chamber or your house,
    Let loose on me the justice of the state
    For thus deluding you.

Brabantio. Strike on the tinder,° ho!
    Give me a taper!° Call up all my people!
    This accident is not unlike my dream.   140
    Belief of it oppresses me already.
    Light, I say! Light! *(Exit above.)*

Iago.   Farewell, for I must leave you.
    It seems not meet, nor wholesome to my place,°
    To be produced—as if I stay I shall—
    Against the Moor. For I do know the state,   145
    However this may gall him with some check,
    Cannot with safety cast° him. For he's embarked
    With such loud reason to the Cyprus wars,
    Which even now stand in act, that, for their souls,
    Another of his fathom they have none   150
    To lead their business. In which regard,
    Though I do hate him as I do Hell pains,

---

121. **odd-even:** about midnight   125. **your allowance:** by your permission   134. **extravagant:**
vagabond   **wheeling:** wandering   138. **tinder:** the primitive method of making fire, used before
the invention of matches   139. **taper:** candle   143. **place:** i.e., as Othello's officer   147. **cast:** dismiss from service

Yet for necessity of present life
I must show out a flag and sign of love,
Which is indeed but sign. That you shall surely find him,   155
Lead to the Sagittary the raisèd search,
And there will I be with him. So farewell.

(Exit IAGO. *Enter, below,* BRABANTIO, *in his nightgown, and* SERVANTS *with torches.)*

Brabantio. It is too true an evil. Gone she is,
And what's to come of my despisèd time
Is naught but bitterness. Now, Roderigo,   160
Where didst thou see her? Oh, unhappy girl!
With the Moor, say'st thou? Who would be a father!
How didst thou know 'twas she? Oh, she deceives me
Past thought! What said she to you? Get more tapers.
Raise all my kindred. Are they married, think you?   165
Roderigo. Truly, I think they are.
Brabantio. Oh Heaven! How got she out? Oh, treason of the blood!
Fathers, from hence trust not your daughters' minds
By what you see them act. Are there not charms°
By which the property° of youth and maidhood   170
May be abused?° Have you not read, Roderigo,
Of some such thing?
Roderigo.   Yes, sir, I have indeed.
Brabantio. Call up my brother.—Oh, would you had had her!—
Some one way, some another.—Do you know
Where we may apprehend her and the Moor?   175
Roderigo. I think I can discover him, if you please
To get good guard and go along with me.
Brabantio. Pray you, lead on. At every house I'll call,
I may command° at most. Get weapons, ho!
And raise some special officers of night.   180
On, good Roderigo, I'll deserve your pains.° *(Exeunt.)*

Scene 2.
Another street.

(Enter OTHELLO, IAGO, *and* ATTENDANTS *with torches.)*

Iago. Though in the trade of war I have slain men,
Yet do I hold it very stuff o' the conscience
To do no contrivèd murder. I lack iniquity
Sometimes to do me service. Nine or ten times
I had thought to have yerked him here under the ribs.   5
Othello. 'Tis better as it is.
Iago.   Nay, but he prated
And spoke such scurvy and provoking terms

---

169. **charms:** magic spells   170. **property:** nature   171. **abused:** deceived   179. **command:** find supporters   181. **deserve your pains:** reward your labor

Against your honor
That, with the little godliness I have,
I did full hard forbear him. But I pray you, sir, 10
Are you fast married? Be assured of this,
That the Magnifico is much beloved,
And hath in his effect a voice potential
As double as° the Duke's. He will divorce you,
Or put upon you what restraint and grievance 15
The law, with all his might to enforce it on,
Will give him cable.

Othello. Let him do his spite.
My services which I have done the signiory°
Shall out-tongue his complaints. 'Tis yet to know— 20
Which, when I know that boasting is an honor,
I shall promulgate—I fetch my life and being
From men of royal siege, and my demerits°
May speak unbonneted to as proud a fortune
As this that I have reached. For know, Iago, 25
But that I love the gentle Desdemona,
I would not my unhousèd° free condition
Put into circumscription and confine
For the sea's worth. But look! What lights come yond?

Iago. Those are the raisèd father and his friends.
You were best go in.

Othello. Not I, I must be found. 30
My parts, my title, and my perfect soul
Shall manifest me rightly. Is it they?

Iago. By Janus, I think no.

(*Enter* CASSIO, *and certain* OFFICERS *with torches.*)

Othello. The servants of the Duke, and my Lieutenant.
The goodness of the night upon you, friends! 35
What is the news?

Cassio. The Duke does greet you, General,
And he requires your haste-posthaste appearance,
Even on the instant.

Othello. What is the matter, think you?

Cassio. Something from Cyprus, as I may divine.
It is a business of some heat. The galleys 40
Have sent a dozen sequent messengers
This very night at one another's heels,
And many of the consuls, raised and met,
Are at the Duke's already. You have been hotly called for
When, being not at your lodging to be found, 45
The Senate hath sent about three several° quests
To search you out.

13–14. **potential . . . as:** twice as powerful as   18. **signiory:** state of Venice   22. **demerits:**
deserts   26. **unhousèd:** unmarried   46. **several:** separate

Othello.   'Tis well I am found by you.
    I will but spend a word here in the house
    And go with you. *(Exit.)*
Cassio.   Ancient, what makes he here?
Iago. Faith, he tonight hath boarded a land carrack.°   50
    If it prove lawful prize, he's made forever.
Cassio. I do not understand.
Iago. He's married.
Cassio. To who? *(Re-enter* OTHELLO.*)*
Iago. Marry, to—Come, Captain, will you go?
Othello. Have with you.
Cassio. Here comes another troop to seek for you.
Iago. It is Brabantio. General, be advised,   55
    He comes to bad intent.

    (Enter BRABANTIO, RODERIGO, *and* OFFICERS *with torches and weapons.)*

Othello.   Holloa! Stand there!
Roderigo. Signior, it is the Moor.
Brabantio.   Down with him, thief!

    (They draw on both sides.)

Iago. You, Roderigo! Come, sir, I am for you.
Othello. Keep up° your bright swords, for the dew will rust them.
    Good signior, you shall more command with years   60
    Than with your weapons.
Brabantio. O thou foul thief, where hast thou stowed my daughter?
    Damned as thou art, thou hast enchanted her.
    For I'll refer me to all things of sense
    If she in chains of magic were not bound,   65
    Whether a maid so tender, fair, and happy,
    So opposite to marriage that she shunned
    The wealthy curlèd darlings of our nation,
    Would ever have, to incur a general mock,
    Run from her guardage° to the sooty bosom   70
    Of such a thing as thou, to fear, not to delight.
    Judge me the world if 'tis not gross in sense
    That thou hast practiced on her with foul charms,
    Abused her delicate youth with drugs or minerals
    That weaken motion.° I'll have 't disputed on,   75
    'Tis probable, and palpable to thinking.
    I therefore apprehend and do attach° thee
    For an abuser of the world, a practicer
    Of arts inhibited and out of warrant.
    Lay hold upon him. If he do resist,   80
    Subdue him at his peril.

---

50. **carrack:** large merchant ship   59. **Keep up:** Sheathe   70. **guardage:** guardianship
75. **motion:** sense   77. **attach:** arrest

Othello.   Hold your hands,
  Both you of my inclining and the rest.
  Were it my cue to fight, I should have known it
  Without a prompter. Where will you that I go
  To answer this your charge?
Brabantio.   To prison, till fit time   85
  Of law and course of direct session
  Call thee to answer.
Othello.   What if I do obey?
  How may the Duke be therewith satisfied,
  Whose messengers are here about my side
  Upon some present business of the state   90
  To bring me to him?
First Officer.   'Tis true, most worthy signior.
  The Duke's in council, and your noble self
  I am sure is sent for.
Brabantio.   How? The Duke in council?
  In this time of the night? Bring him away.
  Mine's not an idle cause. The Duke himself,   95
  Or any of my brothers of the state,
  Cannot but feel this wrong as 'twere their own.
  For if such actions may have passage free,
  Bondslaves and pagans shall our statesmen be. *(Exeunt.)*

  Scene 3.
  A council chamber.

(The DUKE *and* SENATORS *sitting at a table,* OFFICERS *attending.)*

Duke. There is no composition° in these news°
  That gives them credit.
First Senator.   Indeed they are disproportioned.
  My letters say a hundred and seven galleys.
Duke. And mine, a hundred and forty.
Second Senator.   And mine, two hundred.
  But though they jump not on a just account°—   5
  As in these cases, where the aim reports,°
  'Tis oft with difference—yet do they all confirm
  A Turkish fleet, and bearing up to Cyprus.
Duke. Nay, it is possible enough to judgment.
  I do not so secure me in the error,°   10
  But the main article° I do approve
  In fearful° sense.
Sailor *(Within.)*   What ho! What ho! What ho!

---

1. **composition:** agreement   **news:** reports   5. **jump . . . account:** do not agree with an exact estimate   6. **aim reports:** i.e., intelligence reports of an enemy's intention often differ in the details   10. **I . . . error:** I do not consider myself free from danger, because the reports may not all be accurate.   11. **main article:** general report   12. **fearful:** to he feared

First Officer. A messenger from the galleys. *(Enter* SAILOR.*)*

Duke.   Now, what's the business?

Sailor. The Turkish preparation makes for Rhodes.

So was I bid report here to the state   15

By Signior Angelo.

Duke. How say you by this charge?

First Senator.   This cannot be,

By no assay of reason. 'Tis a pageant

To keep us in false gaze. When we consider

The importancy of Cyprus to the Turk,   20

And let ourselves again but understand

That as it more concerns the Turk than Rhodes,

So may he with more facile question bear it,°

For that it stands not in such warlike brace

But altogether lacks the abilities   25

That Rhodes is dressed in—if we make thought of this,

We must not think the Turk is so unskillful

To leave that latest which concerns him first,

Neglecting an attempt of ease and gain

To wake and wage a danger profitless.   30

Duke. Nay, in all confidence, he's not for Rhodes.

First Officer. Here is more news. *(Enter a* MESSENGER.*)*

Messenger. The Ottomites,° Reverend and Gracious,

Steering with due course toward the isle of Rhodes,

Have there injointed° them with an after-fleet.°   35

First Senator. Aye, so I thought. How many, as you guess?

Messenger. Of thirty sail. And now they do restem°

Their backward course, bearing with frank appearance

Their purposes toward Cyprus. Signior Montano,

Your trusty and most valiant servitor,   40

With his free duty recommends you thus,

And prays you to believe him.

Duke. 'Tis certain then for Cyprus.

Marcus Luccicos, is not he in town?

First Senator. He's now in Florence.   45

Duke. Write from us to him, post-posthaste dispatch.

First Senator. Here comes Brabantio and the valiant Moor. *(Enter* BRABANTIO,

OTHELLO, IAGO, RODERIGO, *and* OFFICERS.*)*

Duke. Valiant Othello, we must straight employ you

Against the general enemy Ottoman.

(To BRABANTIO.*)* I did not see you. Welcome, gentle signior,   50

We lacked your counsel and your help tonight.

Brabantio. So did I yours. Good your Grace, pardon me,

Neither my place nor aught I heard of business

Hath raised me from my bed, nor doth the general care

---

23. **with . . . it:** take it more easily   33. **Ottomites:** Turks   35. **injointed:** joined   **after-fleet:**
second fleet   37. **restem:** steer again

Take hold on me. For my particular° grief 55
Is of so floodgate and o'erbearing nature
That it engluts and swallows other sorrows,
And it is still itself.

Duke.   Why, what's the matter?

Brabantio. My daughter! Oh, my daughter!

All.   Dead?

Brabantio.   Aye, to me.
She is abused, stol'n from me and corrupted 60
By spells and medicines bought of mountebanks.
For nature so preposterously to err,
Being not deficient, blind, or lame of sense,
Sans° witchcraft could not.

Duke. Whoe'er he be that in this foul proceeding 65
Hath thus beguiled your daughter of herself
And you of her, the bloody book of law
You shall yourself read in the bitter letter
After your own sense—yea, though our proper° son
Stood in your action.

Brabantio.   Humbly I thank your Grace. 70
Here is the man, this Moor, whom now, it seems,
Your special mandate for the state affairs
Hath hither brought.

All.   We are very sorry for't.

Duke (*To* OTHELLO.) What in your own part can you say to this?

Brabantio. Nothing but this is so. 75

Othello. Most potent, grave, and reverend signiors,
My very noble and approved good masters,
That I have ta'en away this old man's daughter,
It is most true—true, I have married her.
The very head and front of my offending 80
Hath this extent, no more. Rude am I in my speech,
And little blest with the soft phrase of peace,
For since these arms of mine had seven years' pith
Till now some nine moons wasted, they have used
Their dearest action in the tented field; 85
And little of this great world can I speak,
More than pertains to feats of broil and battle,
And therefore little shall I grace my cause
In speaking for myself. Yet, by your gracious patience,
I will a round unvarnished tale° deliver 90
Of my whole course of love—what drugs, what charms,
What conjuration and what mighty magic—
For such proceeding I am charged withal—
I won his daughter.

---

55. **particular:** personal   64. **Sans:** Without   69. **proper:** own   90. **round . . . tale:** direct, unadorned account

Brabantio.   A maiden never bold,
Of spirit so still and quiet that her motion   95
Blushed at herself, and she—in spite of nature,
Of years, of country, credit,° everything—
To fall in love with what she feared to look on!
It is a judgment maimed and most imperfect
That will confess perfection so could err   100
Against all rules of nature, and must be driven
To find out practices of cunning Hell
Why this should be. I therefore vouch again
That with some mixtures powerful o'er the blood,
Or with some dram conjured to this effect,   105
He wrought upon her.
Duke.   To vouch this is no proo
Without more certain and more overt test
Than these thin habits and poor likelihoods
Of modern seeming do prefer against him.
First Senator. But, Othello, speak.   110
Did you by indirect and forcèd courses
Subdue and poison this young maid's affections?
Or came it by request, and such fair question
As soul to soul affordeth?
Othello.   I do beseech you
Send for the lady to the Sagittary,   115
And let her speak of me before her father.
If you do find me foul in her report,
The trust, the office I do hold of you,
Not only take away, but let your sentence
Even fall upon my life.
Duke.   Fetch Desdemona hither.   120
Othello. Ancient, conduct them, you best know the place.

(*Exeunt* IAGO *and* ATTENDANTS.)

And till she come, as truly as to Heaven
I do confess the vices of my blood,
So justly to your grave ears I'll present
How I did thrive in this fair lady's love   125
And she in mine.
Duke.   Say it, Othello.
Othello. Her father loved me, oft invited me,
Still° questioned me the story of my life
From year to year, the battles, sieges, fortunes,
That I have passed.   130
I ran it through, even from my boyish days
To the very moment that he bade me tell it.
Wherein I spake of most disastrous chances,

---

97. **credit:** reputation   128. **Still:** Always

Of moving accidents by flood and field,
Of hairbreadth 'scapes i' the imminent deadly breach,   135
Of being taken by the insolent foe
And sold to slavery, of my redemption thence,
And portance in my travels' history.
Wherein of antres° vast and deserts idle,
Rough quarries, rocks, and hills whose heads touch heaven,   140
It was my hint to speak—such was the process.
And of the cannibals that each other eat,
The anthropophagi,° and men whose heads
Do grow beneath their shoulders. This to hear
Would Desdemona seriously incline.   145
But still the house affairs would draw her thence,
Which ever as she could with haste dispatch,
She'd come again, and with a greedy ear
Devour up my discourse. Which I observing,
Took once a pliant hour and found good means   150
To draw from her a prayer of earnest heart
That I would all my pilgrimage dilate,
Whereof by parcels she had something heard,
But not intentively. I did consent,
And often did beguile her of her tears   155
When I did speak of some distressful stroke
That my youth suffered. My story being done,
She gave me for my pains a world of sighs.
She swore, in faith, 'twas strange, 'twas passing strange,
'Twas pitiful, 'twas wondrous pitiful.   160
She wished she had not heard it, yet she wished
That Heaven had made her such a man. She thanked me,
And bade me, if I had a friend that loved her,
I should but teach him how to tell my story
And that would woo her. Upon this hint I spake.   165
She loved me for the dangers I had passed,
And I loved her that she did pity them.
This only is the witchcraft I have used.
Here comes the lady, let her witness it.

(*Enter* DESDEMONA, IAGO, *and* ATTENDANTS.)

Duke. I think this tale would win my daughter too.   170
Good Brabantio,
Take up this mangled matter at the best.°
Men do their broken weapons rather use
Than their bare hands.

Brabantio.   I pray you hear her speak.
If she confess that she was half the wooer,   175

---

139. **antres:** caves   143. **anthropophagi:** cannibals   172. **Take . . . best:** Make the best settlement you can of this confused business.

Destruction on my head if my bad blame
Light on the man! Come hither, gentle mistress.
Do you perceive in all this noble company
Where most you owe obedience?

Desdemona.   My noble father,
    I do perceive here a divided duty.   180
    To you I am bound for life and education,
    My life and education both do learn me
    How to respect you; you are the lord of duty,
    I am hitherto your daughter. But here's my husband,
    And so much duty as my mother showed   185
    To you, preferring you before her father,
    So much I challenge that I may profess
    Due to the Moor my lord.

Brabantio.   God be with you! I have done.
    Please it your Grace, on to the state affairs.
    I had rather to adopt a child than get° it.   190
    Come hither, Moor.
    I here do give thee that with all my heart
    Which, but thou hast already, with all my heart
    I would keep from thee. For your sake, jewel,
    I am glad at soul I have no other child,   195
    For thy escape would teach me tyranny,
    To hang clogs on them. I have done, my lord.

Duke. Let me speak like yourself, and lay a sentence°
    Which, as a grise° or step, may help these lovers
    Into your favor.   200
    When remedies are past, the griefs are ended
    By seeing the worst, which late on hopes depended.
    To mourn a mischief that is past and gone
    Is the next way to draw new mischief on.
    What cannot be preserved when fortune takes,   205
    Patience her injury a mockery makes.
    The robbed that smiles steals something from the thief.
    He robs himself that spends a bootless grief.

Brabantio. So let the Turk of Cyprus us beguile,
    We lose it not so long as we can smile.   210
    He bears the sentence well that nothing bears
    But the free comfort which from thence he hears.
    But he bears both the sentence and the sorrow
    That, to pay grief, must of poor patience borrow.
    These sentences, to sugar or to gall,   215
    Being strong on both sides, are equivocal.
    But words are words. I never yet did hear
    That the bruisèd heart was piercèd through the ear.
    I humbly beseech you, proceed to the affairs of state.

---

190. **get:** beget   198. **sentence:** proverbial saying   199. **grise:** degree

Duke. The Turk with a most mightly preparation makes for Cyprus.
Othello, the fortitude of the place is best known to you, and though we have
there a substitute° of most allowed sufficiency, yet opinion, a sovereign mistress
of effects, throws a more safer voice on you. You must therefore be content to
slubber° the gloss of your new fortunes with this more stubborn and boisterous
expedition. 225

Othello. The tyrant custom, most grave Senators,
Hath made the flinty and steel couch of war
My thrice-driven bed of down. I do agnize°
A natural and prompt alacrity
I find in hardness,° and do undertake 230
These present wars against the Ottomites.
Most humbly therefore bending to your state,
I crave fit disposition for my wife,
Due reference of place and exhibition,°
With such accommodation and besort° 235
As levels with her breeding.

Duke.   If you please,
Be 't at her father's.

Brabantio.   I'll not have it so.

Othello. Nor I.

Desdemona.   Nor I. I would not there reside,
To put my father in impatient thoughts
By being in his eye. Most gracious Duke, 240
To my unfolding lend your prosperous° ear,
And let me find a charter in your voice
To assist my simpleness.

Duke. What would you, Desdemona?

Desdemona. That I did love the Moor to live with him, 245
My downright violence and storm of fortunes
May trumpet to the world. My heart's subdued
Even to the very quality° of my lord.
I saw Othello's visage in his mind,
And to his honors and his valiant parts° 250
Did I my soul and fortunes consecrate.
So that, dear lords, if I be left behind,
A moth of peace, and he go to the war,
The rites for which I love him are bereft me,
And I a heavy interim shall support 255
By his dear absence. Let me go with him.

Othello. Let her have your voices.
Vouch with me, Heaven, I therefore beg it not
To please the palate of my appetite,

---

222. **substitute:** deputy commander   224. **slubber:** tarnish   228. **agnize:** confess   230. **hardness:** hardship   234. **exhibition:** allowance   235. **besort:** attendants   241. **prosperous:** favorable   248. **quality:** profession   250. **parts:** qualities

Nor to comply with heat—the young affects   260
In me defunct°—and proper satisfaction,
But to be free and bounteous to her mind.°
And Heaven defend your good souls, that you think
I will your serious and great business scant
For she is with me. No, when light-winged toys   265
Of feathered Cupid seel° with wanton dullness
My speculative and officed instruments,°
That my disports° corrupt and taint my business,
Let housewives make a skillet of my helm,
And all indign° and base adversities   270
Make head against my estimation!°

Duke. Be it as you shall privately determine,
Either for her stay or going. The affair cries haste,
And speed must answer 't. You must hence tonight.

Desdemona. Tonight, my lord?

Duke.   This night.

Othello.   With all my heart.   275

Duke. At nine i' the morning here we'll meet again.
Othello, leave some officer behind,
And he shall our commission bring to you,
With such things else of quality and respect
As doth import you.

Othello.   So please your Grace, my Ancient,   280
A man he is of honesty and trust.
To his conveyance I assign my wife,
With what else needful your good Grace shall think
To be sent after me.

Duke.   Let it be so.
Good night to everyone. *(To* BRABANTIO.*)* And, noble signior,   285
If virtue no delighted beauty lack,
Your son-in-law is far more fair than black.°

First Senator. Adieu, brave Moor. Use Desdemona well.

Brabantio. Look to her, Moor, if thou hast eyes to see.
She has deceived her father, and may thee.   290

(Exeunt DUKE, SENATORS, OFFICERS, *etc.)*

Othello. My life upon her faith! Honest Iago,
My Desdemona must I leave to thee.
I prithee, let thy wife attend on her,
And bring them after in the best advantage.
Come, Desdemona, I have but an hour   295

260–61. **young . . . defunct:** In me the passion of youth is dead.   262. **to . . . mind:** Othello repeats
Desdemona's claim that this is a marriage of minds.   266. **seel:** close up   267. **speculative
. . . instruments:** powers of sight and action; i.e., my efficiency as your general   268. **disports:**
amusements   270. **indign:** unworthy   271. **estimation:** reputation   286–87. **If . . . black:** If worthiness is a beautiful thing in itself, your son-in-law, though black, has beauty.

Of love, of worldly matters and direction,
To spend with thee. We must obey the time.

(Exeunt OTHELLO *and* DESDEMONA.*)*

Roderigo. Iago!

Iago. What sayest thou, noble heart?

Roderigo. What will I do, thinkest thou?   300

Iago. Why, go to bed and sleep.

Roderigo. I will incontinently° drown myself.

Iago. If thou dost, I shall never love thee after. Why, thou silly gentleman!

Roderigo. It is silliness to live when to live is torment, and then have we a
    prescription to die when death is our physician.   306

Iago. Oh, villainous! I have looked upon the world for four times seven years, and
    since I could distinguish betwixt a benefit and an injury I never found man that
    knew how to love himself. Ere I would say I would drown myself for the love of
    a guinea hen, I would change my humanity with a baboon.   311

Roderigo. What should I do? I confess it is my shame to be so fond, but it is not in
    my virtue to amend it.

Iago. Virtue! A fig! 'Tis in ourselves that we are thus or thus. Our bodies are gardens,
    to the which our wills are gardeners. So that if we will plant nettles or sow
    lettuce, set hyssop and weed up thyme, supply it with one gender of herbs or
    distract it with many, either to have it sterile with idleness or manured with
    industry—why, the power and corrigible° authority of this lies in our wills.
    If the balance of our lives had not one scale of reason to poise another of
    sensuality, the blood and baseness of our natures would conduct us to most
    preposterous conclusions. But we have reason to cool our raging motions, our
    carnal stings, our unbitted lusts, whereof I take this that you call love to be a
    sect or scion.°

Roderigo. It cannot be.   325

Iago. It is merely a lust of the blood and a permission of the will. Come, be a man!
    Drown thyself? Drown cats and blind puppies! I have professed me thy friend,
    and I confess me knit to thy deserving with cables of perdurable toughness. I
    could never better stead thee than now. Put money in thy purse, follow thou the
    wars, defeat thy favor with an usurped beard°—I say put money in thy purse.
    It cannot be that Desdemona should long continue her love to the Moor—put
    money in thy purse—nor he his to her. It was a violent commencement, and
    thou shalt see an answerable sequestration°—put but money in thy purse.
    These Moors are changeable in their wills.—Fill thy purse with money. The
    food that to him now is as luscious as locusts shall be to him shortly as bitter as
    coloquintida. She must change for youth. When she is sated with his body, she
    will find the error of her choice. She must have change, she must—therefore put
    money in thy purse. If thou wilt needs damn thyself, do it a more delicate way

---

302. **incontinently:** immediately   319. **corrigible:** correcting, directing   324. **sect or scion:** Both
words mean a slip taken from a tree and planted to produce a new growth.   330–31. **defeat
. . . beard:** disguise your face by growing a beard   334–35. **answerable sequestration:** corresponding separation; i.e., reaction

than drowning. Make all the money thou canst°. If sanctimony and a frail vow betwixt an erring° barbarian and a supersubtle Venetian be not too hard for my wits and all the tribe of Hell, thou shalt enjoy her—therefore make money. A pox of drowning thyself! It is clean out of the way. Seek thou rather to be hanged in compassing thy joy than to be drowned and go without her.   347

Roderigo. Wilt thou be fast to my hopes if I depend on the issue?

Iago. Thou art sure of me. Go, make money. I have told thee often, and I retell thee again and again, I hate the Moor. My cause is hearted,° thine hath no less reason. Let us be conjunctive in our revenge against him. If thou canst cuckold him thou dost thyself a pleasure, me a sport. There are many events in the womb of time which will be delivered. Traverse, go, provide thy money. We will have more of this tomorrow. Adieu.   355

Roderigo. Where shall we meet i' the morning?

Iago. At my lodging.

Roderigo. I'll be with thee betimes.

Iago. Go to, farewell. Do you hear, Roderigo?

Roderigo. What say you?   360

Iago. No more of drowning, do you hear?

Roderigo. I am changed. I'll go sell all my land. *(Exit.)*

Iago. Thus do I ever make my fool my purse,
For I mine own gained knowledge should profane
If I would time expend with such a snipe   365
But for my sport and profit. I hate the Moor,
And it is thought abroad that 'twixt my sheets
He's done my office. I know not if 't be true,
But I for mere suspicion in that kind
Will do as if for surety. He holds me well,   370
The better shall my purpose work on him.
Cassio's a proper° man. Let me see now,
To get his place, and to plume up° my will
In double knavery—How, how?—Let's see.—
After some time, to abuse Othello's ear   375
That he is too familiar with his wife.
He hath a person and a smooth dispose
To be suspected,° framed to make women false.
The Moor is of a free and open nature
That thinks men honest that but seem to be so,   380
And will as tenderly be led by the nose
As asses are.
I have't. It is engendered. Hell and night
Must bring this monstrous birth to the world's light. *(Exit.)*

---

342. **Make . . . canst:** Turn all you can into ready cash.   343. **erring:** vagabond   351. **hearted:** heartfelt   372. **proper:** handsome   373. **plume up:** glorify   377–78. **He . . . suspected:** He has an easy way about him that is naturally suspected.

ACT 2

Scene 1.

A seaport in Cyprus. An open place near the wharf.

(Enter MONTANO *and two* GENTLEMEN.*)*

Montano. What from the cape can you discern at sea?
First Gentleman. Nothing at all. It is a high-wrought flood.
 I cannot 'twixt the heaven and the main
 Descry a sail.
Montano. Methinks the wind hath spoke aloud at land,   5
 A fuller blast ne'er shook our battlements.
 If it hath ruffianed so upon the sea,
 What ribs of oak, when mountains melt on them,
 Can hold the mortise? What shall we hear of this?
Second Gentleman. A segregation° of the Turkish fleet.   10
 For do but stand upon the foaming shore,
 The chidden billow seems to pelt the clouds,
 The wind-shaked surge, with high and monstrous mane,
 Seems to cast water on the burning Bear,
 And quench the guards of the ever-fixèd Pole.   15
 I never did like molestation view
 On the enchafèd flood.
Montano.   If that the Turkish fleet
 Be not ensheltered and embayed, they are drowned.
 It is impossible to bear it out. *(Enter a* THIRD GENTLEMAN.*)*
Third Gentleman. News, lads! Our wars are done.   20
 The desperate tempest hath so banged the Turks
 That their designment halts. A noble ship of Venice
 Hath seen a grievous wreck and sufferance°
 On most part of their fleet.
Montano. How! Is this true?
Third Gentleman.   The ship is here put in,   25
A Veronesa. Michael Cassio,
 Lieutenant to the warlike Moor Othello,
 Is come on shore, the Moor himself at sea,
 And is in full commission here for Cyprus.
Montano. I am glad on't. 'Tis a worthy governor.   30
Third Gentleman. But this same Cassio, though he speak of comfort
 Touching the Turkish loss, yet he looks sadly
 And prays the Moor be safe, for they were parted
 With foul and violent tempest.
Montano.   Pray Heavens he be,
 For I have served him, and the man commands   35
 Like a full soldier. Let's to the seaside, ho!
 As well to see the vessel that's come in
 As to throw out our eyes for brave Othello,

---

10. **segregation:** separation   23. **sufferance:** damage

Even till we make the main and the aerial blue
An indistinct regard.

Third Gentleman.   Come, let's do so.   40
For every minute is expectancy
Of more arrivance. *(Enter* CASSIO.*)*

Cassio. Thanks, you the valiant of this warlike isle
That so approve the Moor! Oh, let the heavens
Give him defense against the elements,   45
For I have lost him on a dangerous sea.

Montano. Is he well shipped?

Cassio. His bark is stoutly timbered, and his pilot
Of very expert and approved allowance.
Therefore my hopes, not surfeited to death,   50
Stand in bold cure.

   (A cry within: "A sail, a sail, a sail!" *Enter a* FOURTH GENTLEMAN.*)*

   What noise?

Fourth Gentleman. The town is empty. On the brow o' the sea
Stand ranks of people and they cry "A sail!"

Cassio. My hopes do shape him for the governor. *(Guns heard.)*   55

Second Gentleman. They do discharge their shot of courtesy.
Our friends, at least.

Cassio.   I pray you, sir, go forth,
And give us truth who 'tis that is arrived.

Second Gentleman. I shall. *(Exit.)*

Montano. But, good Lieutenant, is your General wived?   60

Cassio. Most fortunately. He hath achieved a maid
That paragons description and wild fame,
One that excels the quirks of blazoning pens
And in the essential vesture of creation
Does tire the ingener.° *(Re-enter* SECOND GENTLEMAN.*)*
       How now! Who has put in?   65

Second Gentleman. 'Tis one Iago, Ancient to the General.

Cassio. He has had most favorable and happy speed.
Tempests themselves, high seas, and howling winds,
The guttered rocks, and congregated sands,
Traitors ensteeped to clog the guiltless keel,   70
As having sense of beauty, do omit
Their mortal° natures, letting go safely by
The divine Desdemona.

Montano.   What is she?

Cassio. She that I spake of, our great Captain's captain,
Left in the conduct of the bold Iago,   75
Whose footing here anticipates our thoughts

63–65. **One . . . ingener:** One that is too good for the fancy phrases *(quirks)* of painting pens
(i.e., poets) and in her absolute perfection wearies the artist (i.e., the painter)   **ingener:** inventor
72. **mortal:** deadly

A sennight's° speed. Great Jove, Othello guard,
And swell his sail with thine own powerful breath,
That he may bless this bay with his tall ship,
Make love's quick pants in Desdemona's arms,   80
Give renewed fire to our extincted spirits,
And bring all Cyprus comfort.

(Enter DESDEMONA, EMILIA, IAGO, RODERIGO, *and* ATTENDANTS.*)*

                Oh, behold,
The riches of the ship is come on shore!
Ye men of Cyprus, let her have your knees.
Hail to thee, lady! And the grace of Heaven,   85
Before, behind thee, and on every hand,
Enwheel thee round!

Desdemona.   I thank you, valiant Cassio.
What tidings can you tell me of my lord?

Cassio. He is not yet arrived, nor know I aught
But that he's well and will be shortly here.   90

Desdemona. Oh, but I fear—How lost you company?

Cassio. The great contention of the sea and skies
Parted our fellowship.—But hark! A sail.

(A cry within: "A sail, a sail!" *Guns heard.)*

Second Gentleman. They give their greeting to the citadel.
This likewise is a friend.

Cassio.   See for the news. *(Exit* GENTLEMAN.*)*   95
Good Ancient, you are welcome. *(To* EMILIA.*)* Welcome, mistress.
Let it not gall your patience, good Iago,
That I extend my manners. 'Tis my breeding
That gives me this bold show of courtesy. *(Kissing her.)*

Iago. Sir, would she give you so much of her lips
As of her tongue she oft bestows on me,   100
You'd have enough.

Desdemona.   Alas, she has no speech.

Iago. In faith, too much,
I find it still when I have list° to sleep.
Marry, before your ladyship, I grant,   105
She puts her tongue a little in her heart
And chides with thinking.

Emilia. You have little cause to say so.

Iago. Come on, come on. You are pictures° out of doors,
Bells° in your parlors, wildcats in your kitchens,   110
Saints in your injuries,° devils being offended,
Players in your housewifery, and housewives in your beds.

Desdemona. Oh, fie upon thee, slanderer!

---

77. **sennight's:** week's   104. **list:** desire   109. **pictures:** i.e., painted and dumb   110. **Bells:** i.e.,
ever clacking   111. **Saints . . . injuries:** Saints when you hurt anyone else

Iago. Nay, it is true, or else I am a Turk.
　　You rise to play, and go to bed to work.　　　　　　　　　　115
Emilia. You shall not write my praise.
Iago.　　　　　　　　　　　　　No, let me not.
Desdemona. What wouldst thou write of me if thou shouldst praise me?
Iago. O gentle lady, do not put me to 't,
　　For I am nothing if not critical.
Desdemona. Come on, assay.°—There's one gone to the harbor?　　　120
Iago. Aye, madam.
Desdemona *(Aside.)* I am not merry, but I do beguile
　　The thing I am by seeming otherwise.—
　　Come, how wouldst thou praise me?
Iago. I am about it, but indeed my invention　　　　　　　　125
　　Comes from my pate as birdlime does from frieze°—
　　It plucks out brains and all. But my Muse labors,
　　And thus she is delivered:
　　If she be fair and wise, fairness and wit,
　　The one's for use, the other useth it.　　　　　　　　　　130
Desdemona. Well praised! How if she be black and witty?
Iago. If she be black, and thereto have a wit,
　　She'll find a white° that shall her blackness fit.
Desdemona. Worse and worse.
Emilia. How if fair and foolish?　　　　　　　　　　　135
Iago. She never yet was foolish that was fair,
　　For even her folly helped her to an heir.
Desdemona. These are old fond paradoxes to make fools laugh i' the alehouse. What
　　miserable praise hast thou for her that's foul and foolish?　　140
Iago. There's none so foul, and foolish thereunto,
　　But does foul pranks which fair and wise ones do.
Desdemona. Oh, heavy ignorance! Thou praisest the worst best. But what praise
　　couldst thou bestow on a deserving woman indeed, one that in the authority of
　　her merit did justly put on the vouch of very malice itself?°　　146
Iago. She that was ever fair and never proud,
　　Had tongue at will° and yet was never loud,
　　Never lacked gold and yet went never gay,
　　Fled from her wish and yet said "Now I may";　　　　　　150
　　She that, being angered, her revenge being nigh,
　　Bade her wrong stay and her displeasure fly;
　　She that in wisdom never was so frail
　　To change the cod's head for the salmon's tail;°
　　She that could think and ne'er disclose her mind,　　　　　155

---

120. **assay:** try　125–26. **my . . . frieze:** my literary effort *(invention)* is as hard to pull out of
my head as frieze (cloth with a nap)　133. **white:** with a pun on *wight* (line 156), man, person
144–46. **one . . . itself:** one so deserving that even malice would declare her good　148. **tongue . . .
will:** a ready flow of words　154. **To . . . tail:** To prefer the tail end of a good thing to the head of a
poor thing

See suitors following and not look behind;
She was a wight, if ever such wight were—
Desdemona. To do what?
Iago. To suckle fools and chronicle small beer.
Desdemona. Oh, most lame and impotent conclusion! Do not learn of him, Emilia,
    though he be thy husband. How say you, Cassio? Is he not a most profane and
    liberal° counselor?   162
Cassio. He speaks home, madam. You may relish him more in the soldier than in the
    scholar.
Iago *(Aside.)* He takes her by the palm. Aye, well said, whisper. With as little a web
    as this will I ensnare as great a fly as Cassio. Aye, smile upon her, do, I will gyve
    thee in thine own courtship. You say true, 'tis so indeed. If such tricks as these
    strip you out of your Lieutenantry, it had been better you had not kissed your
    three fingers° so oft, which now again you are most apt to play the sir° in. Very
    good, well kissed! An excellent courtesy! 'Tis so indeed. Yet again your fingers
    to your lips? Would they were clyster pipes° for your sake! *(Trumpet within.)* The
    Moor! I know his trumpet.   173
Cassio. 'Tis truly so.
Desdemona. Let's meet him and receive him.   175
Cassio. Lo where he comes! *(Enter* OTHELLO *and* ATTENDANTS.*)*
Othello. O my fair warrior!°
Desdemona.   My dear Othello!
Othello. It gives me wonder great as my content
    To see you here before me. O my soul's joy!
    If after every tempest come such calms,   180
    May the winds blow till they have wakened death!
    And let the laboring bark climb hills of seas
    Olympus-high, and duck again as low
    As Hell's from Heaven! If it were now to die,
    'Twere now to be most happy, for I fear   185
    My soul hath her content so absolute
    That not another comfort like to this
    Succeeds in unknown fate.
Desdemona.   The Heavens forbid
    But that our loves and comforts should increase,
    Even as our days do grow!
Othello.   Amen to that, sweet powers!   190
    I cannot speak enough of this content.
    It stops me here,° it is too much of joy.
    And this, and this, the greatest discords be *(Kissing her.)*
    That e'er our hearts shall make!
Iago *(Aside.)*   Oh, you are well tuned now,
    But I'll set down the pegs° that make this music,   195
    As honest as I am.

---

162. **liberal:** gross   169. **kissed . . . fingers:** a gesture of gallantry   170. **play the sir:** act the fine
gentleman   172. **clyster pipes:** an enema syringe   177. **warrior:** because she is a soldier's wife
192. **here:** i.e., in the heart   195. **set . . . pegs:** i.e., make you sing out of tune. A stringed instrument was tuned by the pegs.

Othello.   Come, let us to the castle.
   News, friends! Our wars are done, the Turks are drowned.
   How does my old acquaintance of this isle?
   Honey, you shall be well desired in Cyprus,
   I have found great love amongst them. O my sweet,   200
   I prattle out of fashion, and I dote
   In mine own comforts. I prithee, good Iago,
   Go to the bay and disembark my coffers.°
   Bring thou the master° to the citadel.
   He is a good one, and his worthiness   205
   Does challenge much respect. Come, Desdemona,
   Once more well met at Cyprus. *(Exeunt all but* IAGO *and* RODERIGO.*)*

Iago. Do thou meet me presently at the harbor. Come hither. If thou beest valiant—
   as they say base men being in love have then a nobility in their natures more
   than is native to them—list me. The Lieutenant tonight watches on the court of
   guard. First, I must tell thee this. Desdemona is directly in love with him.   212

Roderigo. With him! Why, 'tis not possible.

Iago. Lay thy finger thus,° and let thy soul be instructed. Mark me with what
   violence she first loved the Moor, but for bragging and telling her fantastical
   lies. And will she love him still for prating? Let not thy discreet heart think
   it. Her eye must be fed, and what delight shall she have to look on the Devil?
   When the blood is made dull with the act of sport, there should be, again to
   inflame it and to give satiety a fresh appetite, loveliness in favor,° sympathy
   in years, manners, and beauties, all which the Moor is defective in. Now, for
   want of these required conveniences, her delicate tenderness will find itself
   abused, begin to heave the gorge, disrelish and abhor the Moor. Very nature
   will instruct her in it and compel her to some second choice. Now, sir, this
   granted—as it is a most pregnant and unforced position°—who stands so
   eminently in the degree of this fortune as Cassio does? A knave very voluble,
   no further conscionable° than in putting on the mere form of civil and humane
   seeming° for the better compassing of his salt° and most hidden loose affection?
   Why, none, why, none. A slipper° and subtle knave, a finder-out of occasions,
   that has an eye can stamp and counterfeit advantages,° though true advantage
   never present itself. A devilish knave! Besides, the knave is handsome, young,
   and hath all those requisites in him that folly and green minds look after. A
   pestilent complete knave, and the woman hath found him already.   235

Roderigo. I cannot believe that in her. She's full of most blest condition.°

Iago. Blest fig's-end! The wine she drinks is made of grapes. If she had been blest, she
   would never have loved the Moor. Blest pudding! Didst thou not see her paddle
   with the palm of his hand? Didst not mark that?   241

Roderigo. Yes, that I did, but that was but courtesy.

---

203. **coffers:** trunks   204. **master:** captain of the ship   214. **thus:** i.e., on the lips   220. **favor:**
face   225–26. **pregnant . . . position:** very significant and probable argument   227. **no . . .**
conscionable: who has no more conscience   228. **humane seeming:** courteous appearance
229. **salt:** lecherous   230. **slipper:** slippery   231. **stamp . . . advantages:** forge false opportunities   237. **condition:** disposition

Iago. Lechery, by his hand, an index and obscure prologue to the history of lust and foul thoughts. They met so near with their lips that their breaths embraced together. Villainous thoughts, Roderigo! When these mutualities so marshal the way, hard at hand comes the master and main exercise, the incorporate° conclusion. Pish! But, sir, be you ruled by me. I have brought you from Venice. Watch you tonight. For the command, I'll lay 't upon you. Cassio knows you not. I'll not be far from you. Do you find some occasion to anger Cassio, either by speaking too loud, or tainting° his discipline, or from what other course you please which the time shall more favorably minister.

Roderigo. Well.   253

Iago. Sir, he is rash and very sudden in choler,° and haply may strike at you. Provoke him, that he may, for even out of that will I cause these of Cyprus to mutiny, whose qualification shall come into no true taste again but by the displanting of Cassio. So shall you have a shorter journey to your desires by the means I shall then have to prefer° them, and the impediment most profitably removed without the which there were no expectation of our prosperity.   260

Roderigo. I will do this, if I can bring it to any opportunity.

Iago. I warrant thee. Meet me by and by at the citadel. I must fetch his necessaries ashore. Farewell.

Roderigo. Adieu. *(Exit.)*

Iago. That Cassio loves her, I do well believe it.   265
    That she loves him, 'tis apt and of great credit.°
    The Moor, howbeit that I endure him not,
    Is of a constant, loving, noble nature,
    And I dare think he'll prove to Desdemona
    A most dear husband. Now, I do love her too,   270
    Not out of absolute lust, though peradventure
    I stand accountant for as great a sin,
    But partly led to diet° my revenge
    For that I do suspect the lusty Moor
    Hath leaped into my seat. The thought whereof   275
    Doth like a poisonous mineral gnaw my inwards,
    And nothing can or shall content my soul
    Till I am evened with him, wife for wife.
    Or failing so, yet that I put the Moor
    At least into a jealousy so strong   280
    That judgment cannot cure. Which thing to do,
    If this poor trash of Venice, whom I trash
    For his quick hunting, stand the putting-on,
    I'll have our Michael Cassio on the hip,
    Abuse him to the Moor in the rank garb°—   285
    For I fear Cassio with my nightcap too—
    Make the Moor thank me, love me, and reward me
    For making him egregiously an ass

---

247. **incorporate:** bodily   251. **tainting:** disparaging   254. **choler:** anger   259. **prefer:** promote   266. **apt . . . credit:** likely and very creditable   273. **diet:** feed   285. **rank garb:** gross manner; i.e., by accusing him of being Desdemona's lover

And practicing upon his peace and quiet
Even to madness. 'Tis here, but yet confused. 290
Knavery's plain face is never seen till used. *(Exit.)*

Scene 2.
A street.

(Enter a HERALD *with a proclamation,* PEOPLE *following.)*

Herald. It is Othello's pleasure, our noble and valiant General, that upon certain
tidings now arrived, importing the mere perdition° of the Turkish fleet, every
man put himself into triumph°—some to dance, some to make bonfires,
each man to what sport and revels his addiction leads him. For, besides these
beneficial news, it is the celebration of his nuptial. So much was his pleasure
should be proclaimed. All offices° are open, and there is full liberty of feasting
from this present hour of five till the bell have told eleven. Heaven bless the isle
of Cyprus and our noble General Othello! *(Exeunt.)*

Scene 3.
A hall in the castle.

(Enter OTHELLO, DESDEMONA, CASSIO, *and* ATTENDANTS.*)*

Othello. Good Michael, look you to the guard tonight.
Let's teach ourselves that honorable stop,
Not to outsport discretion.°
Cassio. Iago hath directions what to do,
But notwithstanding with my personal eye 5
Will I look to 't.
Othello.   Iago is most honest.
Michael, good night. Tomorrow with your earliest
Let me have speech with you. *(To* DESDEMONA.*)* Come, my dear love,
The purchase made, the fruits are to ensue—
That profit's yet to come 'tween me and you. 10
Good night. *(Exeunt all but* CASSIO. *Enter* IAGO.*)*
Cassio. Welcome, Iago. We must to the watch.
Iago. Not this hour, Lieutenant, 'tis not yet ten o'clock. Our General cast° us thus
early for the love of his Desdemona, who let us not therefore blame. He hath
not yet made wanton the night with her, and she is sport for Jove. 16
Casio. She's a most exquisite lady.
Iago. And, I'll warrant her, full of game.
Cassio. Indeed she's a most fresh and delicate creature.
Iago. What an eye she has! Methinks it sounds a parley to provocation. 20
Cassio. An inviting eye, and yet methinks right modest.
Iago. And when she speaks, is it not an alarum to love?
Cassio. She is indeed perfection.

---

2. **mere perdition:** absolute destruction   3. **put . . . triumph:** celebrate   7. **offices:** the kitchen
and buttery—i.e., free food and drink for all   3. **outsport discretion:** let the fun go too far.
14. **cast:** dismissed

Iago. Well, happiness to their sheets! Come, Lieutenant, I have a stoup of wine, and there without are a brace of Cyprus gallants that would fain have a measure to the health of black Othello. 27

Cassio. Not tonight, good Iago. I have very poor and unhappy brains for drinking. I could well wish courtesy would invent some other custom of entertainment. 30

Iago. Oh, they are our friends. But one cup—I'll drink for you.

Cassio. I have drunk but one cup tonight, and that was craftily qualified too, and behold what innovation it makes here. I am unfortunate in the infirmity, and dare not task my weakness with any more.

Iago. What, man! 'Tis a night of revels. The gallants desire it. 35

Cassio. Where are they?

Iago. Here at the door. I pray you call them in.

Cassio. I'll do 't, but it dislikes me. *(Exit.)*

Iago. If I can fasten but one cup upon him,
    With that which he hath drunk tonight already, 40
    He'll be as full of quarrel and offense
    As my young mistress' dog. Now my sick fool Roderigo,
    Whom love hath turned almost the wrong side out,
    To Desdemona hath tonight caroused
    Potations pottle-deep, and he's to watch. 45
    Three lads of Cyprus, noble swelling spirits
    That hold their honors in a wary distance,
    The very elements° of this warlike isle,
    Have I tonight flustered with flowing cups,
    And they watch too. Now, 'mongst this flock of drunkards, 50
    Am I to put our Cassio in some action
    That may offend the isle. But here they come.
    If consequence do but approve my dream,
    My boat sails freely, both with wind and stream.

(Re-enter CASSIO, *with him* MONTANO *and* GENTLEMEN, SERVANTS *following with wine.)*

Cassio. 'Fore God, they have given me a rouse already. 55

Montano. Good faith, a little one—not past a pint, as I am a soldier.

Iago. Some wine, ho! *(Sings.)*
        "And let me the cannikin clink, clink
        And let me the cannikin clink.
          A soldier's a man, 60
          A life's but a span.°
        Why, then let a soldier drink."
    Some wine, boys!

Cassio. 'Fore God, an excellent song.

Iago. I learned it in England, where indeed they are most potent in potting.° Your Dane, your German, and your swag-bellied Hollander—Drink, ho!—are nothing to your English. 67

---

48. **very elements:** typical specimens   61. **span:** lit., the measure between the thumb and little finger of the outstretched hand; about 9 inches   65–66. **potting:** drinking

Cassio. Is your Englishman so expert in his drinking?

Iago. Why, he drinks you with facility your Dane dead drunk, he sweats not to
overthrow your Almain,° he gives your Hollander a vomit° ere the next pottle
can be filled. 71

Cassio. To the health of our General!

Montano. I am for it, Lieutenant, and I'll do you justice.

Iago. O sweet England! *(Sings.)*

> "King Stephen was a worthy peer, 75
>   His breeches cost him but a crown.
> He held them sixpence all too dear,
>   With that he called the tailor lown.°
>
> "He was a wight of high renown,
>   And thou art but of low degree. 80
> 'Tis pride that pulls the country down.
>   Then take thine auld cloak about thee."

Some wine, ho!

Cassio. Why, this is a more exquisite song than the other.

Iago. Will you hear 't again? 85

Cassio. No, for I hold him to be unworthy of his place that does those things. Well,
God's above all, and there be souls must be saved and there be souls must not
be saved.

Iago. It's true, good Lieutenant.

Cassio. For mine own part—no offense to the General, nor any man of quality—I
hope to be saved. 91

Iago. And so do I too, Lieutenant.

Cassio. Aye, but, by your leave, not before me. The Lieutenant is to be saved before
the Ancient. Let's have no more of this, let's to our affairs. God forgive us our
sins! Gentlemen, let's look to our business. Do not think, gentlemen, I am
drunk. This is my Ancient, this is my right hand and this is my left. I am not
drunk now, I can stand well enough and speak well enough. 98

All. Excellent well.

Cassio. Why, very well, then, you must not think then that I am drunk. *(Exit.)*

Montano. To the platform, masters. Come, let's set the watch. 101

Iago. You see this fellow that is gone before.
He is a soldier fit to stand by Caesar
And give direction. And do but see his vice.
'Tis to his virtue a just equinox, 105
The one as long as the other. 'Tis pity of him.
I fear the trust Othello puts him in
On some odd time of his infirmity
Will shake this island.

Montano.   But is he often thus?

Iago. 'Tis evermore the prologue to his sleep. 110
He'll watch the horologe a double set,°
If drink rock not his cradle.

---

70. **Almain:** German   **gives . . . vomit:** drinks as much as will make a Dutchman throw up
78. **lown:** lout   111. **watch . . . set:** stay awake the clock twice round

Montano.   It were well
    The General were put in mind of it.
    Perhaps he sees it not, or his good nature
    Prizes the virtue that appears in Cassio   115
    And looks not on his evils. Is not this true? *(Enter* RODERIGO.*)*
Iago *(Aside to him.)* How now, Roderigo! I pray you, after the Lieutenant. Go.
    (Exit RODERIGO.*)*
Montano. And 'tis great pity that the noble Moor
    Should hazard such a place as his own second   120
    With one of an ingraft infirmity.
    It were an honest action to say
    So to the Moor.
Iago.   Not I, for this fair island.
    I do love Cassio well, and would do much
    To cure him of this evil—But hark! What noise?   125

    (A cry within: "Help! Help!" *Re-enter* CASSIO, *driving in* RODERIGO.*)*

Cassio. 'Zounds! You rogue! You rascal!
Montano. What's the matter, Lieutenant?
Cassio. A knave teach me my duty! But I'll beat the knave into a wicker bottle.
Roderigo. Beat me!   130
Cassio. Does thou prate, rogue? *(Striking* RODERIGO.*)*
Montano. Nay, good Lieutenant, *(Staying him.)*
          I pray you sir, hold your hand.
Cassio. Let me go, sir, or I'll knock you o'er the mazzard.°
Montano. Come, come, you're drunk.
Cassio. Drunk! *(They fight.)*   135
Iago *(Aside to* RODERIGO.*)* Away, I say. Go out and cry a mutiny.

    (Exit RODERIGO.*)*

    Nay, good Lieutenant! God's will, gentlemen!
    Help, ho!—Lieutenant—sir—Montano—sir—
    Help, masters!—Here's a goodly watch indeed! *(A bell rings.)*
    Who's that that rings the bell?—Diablo, ho!   140
    The town will rise. God's will, Lieutenant, hold—
    You will be ashamed forever. *(Re-enter* OTHELLO *and* ATTENDANTS.*)*
Othello. What is the matter here?
Montano. 'Zounds, I bleed still, I am hurt to death. *(Faints.)*
Othello. Hold, for your lives!
Iago. Hold, ho! Lieutenant—sir—Montano—gentlemen—   145
    Have you forgot all sense of place and duty?
    Hold! The General speaks to you. Hold, hold, for shame!
Othello. Why, how now, ho! From whence ariseth this?
    Are we turned Turks, and to ourselves do that
    Which Heaven hath forbid the Ottomites?   150
    For Christian shame, put by this barbarous brawl.
    He that stirs next to carve for his own rage

---

133. **mazzard:** head

Holds his soul light, he dies upon his motion.
Silence that dreadful bell. It frights the isle
From her propriety. What is the matter, masters? 155
Honest Iago, that look'st dead with grieving,
Speak, who began this? On thy love, I charge thee.
Iago. I do not know. Friends all but now, even now,
In quarter and in terms like bride and groom
Devesting them for bed. And then, but now, 160
As if some planet had unwitted men,
Swords out, and tilting one at other's breast
In opposition bloody. I cannot speak
Any beginning to this peevish odds,
And would in action glorious I had lost 165
Those legs that brought me to a part of it!
Othello. How comes it, Michael, you are thus forgot?°
Cassio. I pray you, pardon me, I cannot speak.
Othello. Worthy Montano, you were wont be civil.
The gravity and stillness of your youth 170
The world hath noted, and your name is great
In mouths of wisest censure.° What's the matter
That you unlace your reputation thus
And spend your rich opinion for the name
Of a night brawler? Give me answer to it. 175
Montano. Worthy Othello, I am hurt to danger.
Your officer, Iago, can inform you—
While I spare speech, which something now offends me—
Of all that I do know. Nor know I aught
By me that's said or done amiss this night, 180
Unless self-charity° be sometimes a vice,
And to defend ourselves it be a sin
When violence assails us.
Othello.   Now, by Heaven,
My blood begins my safer guides to rule,
And passion, having my best judgment collied,° 185
Assays to lead the way. If I once stir,
Or do but lift this arm, the best of you
Shall sink in my rebuke. Give me to know
How this foul rout began, who set it on,
And he that is approved° in this offense, 190
Though he had twinned with me, both at a birth,
Shall lose me. What! In a town of war,
Yet wild, the people's hearts brimful of fear,
To manage private and domestic quarrel,
In night, and on the court and guard of safety! 195
'Tis monstrous. Iago, who began 't?

---

167. **are thus forgot:** have so forgotten yourself   172. **censure:** judgment   181. **self-charity:** love for oneself   185. **collied:** darkened   190. **approved:** proved guilty

Montano. If partially affined or leagued in office,
    Thou dost deliver more or less than truth,
    Thou art no soldier.
Iago.   Touch me not so near.
    I had rather have this tongue cut from my mouth   200
    Than it should do offense to Michael Cassio.
    Yet I persuade myself to speak the truth
    Shall nothing wrong him. Thus it is, General.
    Montano and myself being in speech,
    There comes a fellow crying out for help,   205
    And Cassio following him with determined sword
    To execute upon him. Sir, this gentleman
    Steps in to Cassio and entreats his pause.
    Myself the crying fellow did pursue
    Lest by his clamor—as it so fell out—   210
    The town might fall in fright. He, swift of foot,
    Outran my purpose, and I returned the rather
    For that I heard the clink and fall of swords,
    And Cassio high in oath, which till tonight
    I ne'er might say before. When I came back—   215
    For this was brief—I found them close together,
    At blow and thrust, even as again they were
    When you yourself did part them.
    More of this matter cannot I report.
    But men are men, the best sometimes forget.   220
    Though Cassio did some little wrong to him,
    As men in rage strike those that wish them best,
    Yet surely Cassio, I believe, received
    From him that fled some strange indignity,
    Which patience could not pass.
Othello.   I know, Iago,   225
    Thy honesty and love doth mince this matter,
    Making it light to Cassio. Cassio, I love thee,
    But never more be officer of mine. *(Re-enter* DESDEMONA, *attended.)*
    Look, if my gentle love be not raised up!
    I'll make thee an example.
Desdemona.   What's the matter?   230
Othello. All's well now, sweeting. Come away to bed.

    (To MONTANO, *who is led off.)*

    Sir, for your hurts, myself will be your surgeon.
    Lead him off.
    Iago, look with care about the town,
    And silence those whom this vile brawl distracted.   235
    Come, Desdemona. 'Tis the soldier's life
    To have their balmy slumbers waked with strife.

    (Exeunt all but IAGO *and* CASSIO.)*

Iago. What, are you hurt, Lieutenant?

Cassio. Aye, past all surgery.

Iago. Marry, Heaven forbid!   240

Cassio. Reputation, reputation, reputation! Oh, I have lost my reputation! I have lost the immortal part of myself, and what remains is bestial. My reputation, Iago, my reputation!

Iago. As I am an honest man, I thought you had received some bodily wound. There is more sense in that than in reputation. Reputation is an idle and most false imposition, oft got without merit and lost without deserving. You have lost no reputation at all unless you repute yourself such a loser. What, man! There are ways to recover the General again. You are but now cast in his mood,° a punishment more in policy° than in malice—even so as one would beat his offenseless dog to affright an imperious lion.° Sue to him again and he's yours.   252

Cassio. I will rather sue to be despised than to deceive so good a commander with so slight, so drunken, and so indiscreet an officer. Drunk? And speak parrot°? And squabble? Swagger? Swear? And discourse fustian° with one's own shadow? O thou invisible spirit of wine, if thou hast no name to be known by, let us call thee devil!   258

Iago. What was he that you followed with your sword? What had he done to you?   260

Cassio. I know not.

Iago. Is 't possible?

Cassio. I remember a mass of things, but nothing distinctly—a quarrel, but nothing wherefore. Oh God, that men should put an enemy in their mouths to steal away their brains! That we should, with joy, pleasance, revel, and applause, transform ourselves into beasts!   266

Iago. Why, but you are now well enough. How came you thus recovered?

Cassio. It hath pleased the devil drunkenness to give place to the devil wrath. One unperfectness shows me another, to make me frankly despise myself.   271

Iago. Come, you are too severe a moraler. As the time, the place, and the condition of this country stands, I could heartily wish this had not befallen. But since it is as it is, mend it for your own good.   274

Cassio. I will ask him for my place again, he shall tell me I am a drunkard! Had I as many mouths as Hydra, such an answer would stop them all. To be now a sensible man, by and by a fool, and presently a beast! Oh, strange! Every inordinate cup is unblest, and the ingredient is a devil.

Iago. Come, come, good wine is a good familiar creature, if it be well used. Exclaim no more against it. And, good Lieutenant, I think you think I love you.   282

Cassio. I have well approved it, sir. I drunk!

Iago. You or any man living may be drunk at some time, man. I'll tell you what you shall do. Our General's wife is now the General. I may say so in this respect, for that he hath devoted and given up himself to the contemplation, mark, and denotement of her parts and graces. Confess yourself freely to her, importune

---

249. **cast . . . mood:** dismissed because he is in a bad mood   250. **in policy:** i.e., because he must appear to be angry before the Cypriots   250–51. **even . . . lion:** a proverb meaning that when the lion sees the dog beaten, he will know what is coming to him   255. **speak parrot:** babble 256. **fustian:** nonsense

her help to put you in your place again. She is of so free, so kind, so apt, so blessed a disposition, she holds it a vice in her goodness not to do more than she is requested. This broken joint between you and her husband entreat her to splinter° and, my fortunes against any lay° worth naming, this crack of your love shall grow stronger than it was before.   293

Cassio. You advise me well.

Iago. I protest, in the sincerity of love and honest kindness.

Cassio. I think it freely, and betimes in the morning I will beseech the virtuous Desdemona to undertake for me. I am desperate of my fortunes if they check me here.

Iago. You are in the right. Good night, Lieutenant, I must to the watch.

Cassio. Good night, honest Iago. *(Exit.)*   300

Iago. And what's he then that says I play the villain?
When this advice is free I give and honest,
Probal° to thinking, and indeed the course
To win the Moor again? For 'tis most easy
The inclining Desdemona to subdue   305
In any honest suit. She's framed as fruitful
As the free elements. And then for her
To win the Moor, were't to renounce his baptism,
All seals and symbols of redeemèd sin,
His soul is so enfettered to her love   310
That she may make, unmake, do what she list,
Even as her appetite shall play the god
With his weak function. How am I then a villain
To counsel Cassio to this parallel course,
Directly to his good? Divinity of Hell!   315
When devils will the blackest sins put on,
They do suggest at first with heavenly shows,
As I do now. For whiles this honest fool
Plies Desdemona to repair his fortunes,
And she for him pleads strongly to the Moor,   320
I'll pour this pestilence into his ear,
That she repeals° him for her body's lust,
And by how much she strives to do him good,
She shall undo her credit with the Moor.
So will I turn her virtue into pitch,   325
And out of her own goodness make the net
That shall enmesh them all. *(Enter* RODERIGO.*)*
                    How now, Roderigo!

Roderigo. I do follow here in the chase, not like a hound that hunts but one that fills up the cry. My money is almost spent, I have been tonight exceedingly well cudgeled, and I think the issue will be I shall have so much experience from my pains and so, with no money at all and a little more wit, return again to Venice.   332

Iago. How poor are they that have not patience!
What wound did ever heal but by degrees?

---

292. **splinter:** put in splints   **lay:** bet   303. **Probal:** Probable   322. **repeals:** calls back

Thou know'st we work by wit and not by witchcraft, 335
And wit depends on dilatory Time.
Does 't not go well? Cassio hath beaten thee,
And thou by that small hurt hast cashiered Cassio.
Though other things grow fair against the sun,
Yet fruits that blossom first will first be ripe. 340
Content thyself awhile. By the mass, 'tis morning.
Pleasure and action make the hours seem short.
Retire thee, go where thou art billeted.
Away, I say. Thou shalt know more hereafter.
Nay, get thee gone. *(Exit* RODERIGO.*)*
               Two things are to be done: 345
My wife must move for Cassio to her mistress,
I'll set her on,
Myself the while to draw the Moor apart
And bring him jump° when he may Cassio find
Soliciting his wife. Aye, that's the way. 350
Dull not device by coldness and delay. *(Exit.)*

ACT 3
Scene 1.
Before the castle.

(Enter CASSIO *and some* MUSICIANS.*)*

Cassio. Masters, play here, I will content your pains°—
    Something that's brief, and bid "Good morrow, General."°

(Music. Enter CLOWN.*)*

Clown. Why, masters, have your instruments been in Naples, that they speak i' the
    nose thus?
First Musician. How, sir, how? 5
Clown. Are these, I pray you, wind instruments?
First Musician. Aye, marry are they, sir.
Clown. Oh, thereby hangs a tail.
First Musician. Whereby hangs a tale, sir?
Clown. Marry, sir, by many a wind instrument that I know. But, masters, here's
    money for you. And the General so likes your music that he desires you, for
    love's sake, to make no more noise with it. 12
First Musician. Well, sir, we will not.
Clown. If you have any music that may not be heard, to 't again. But, as they say, to
    hear music the General does not greatly care. 15
First Musician. We have none such, sir.
Clown. Then put up your pipes in your bag, for I'll away. Go, vanish into air, away!
    (Exeunt MUSICIANS.*)*
Cassio. Dost thou hear, my honest friend?

---

349. **jump:** at the moment   1. **content your pains:** reward your labor   2. **bid . . . General.":** It
was a common custom to play or sing a song beneath the bedroom window of a distinguished guest
or of a newly wedded couple on the morning after their wedding night.

Clown. No, I hear not your honest friend, I hear you. 20

Cassio. Prithee keep up thy quillets.° There's a poor piece of gold for thee. If the
gentlewoman that attends the General's wife be stirring, tell her there's one
Cassio entreats her a little favor of speech. Wilt thou do this?

Clown. She is stirring, sir. If she will stir hither, I shall seem to notify unto her. 26

Cassio. Do, good my friend. *(Exit* CLOWN. *Enter* IAGO.*)*
                                In happy time, Iago.

Iago. You have not been abed, then?

Cassio. Why, no, the day had broke
      Before we parted. I have made bold, Iago, 30
      To send in to your wife. My suit to her
      Is that she will to virtuous Desdemona
      Procure me some access.

Iago.   I'll send her to you presently,
      And I'll devise a mean to draw the Moor
      Out of the way, that your convérse and business 35
      May be more free.

Cassio. I humbly thank you for 't. *(Exit* IAGO.*)*
                                I never knew
      A Florentine more kind and honest. *(Enter* EMILIA.*)*

Emilia. Good morrow, good Lieutenant. I am sorry
      For your displeasure, but all will sure be well. 40
      The General and his wife are talking of it,
      And she speaks for you stoutly. The Moor replies
      That he you hurt is of great fame in Cyprus
      And great affinity,° and that in wholesome wisdom
      He might not but refuse you. But he protests he loves you, 45
      And needs no other suitor but his likings
      To take the safest occasion by the front
      To bring you in again.

Cassio.   Yet I beseech you
      If you think fit, or that it may be done,
      Give me advantage of some brief discourse 50
      With Desdemona alone.

Emilia.   Pray you, come in.
      I will bestow you where you shall have time
      To speak your bosom freely.

Cassio.   I am much bound to you. *(Exeunt.)*

        Scene 2.
        A room in the castle.

(Enter OTHELLO, IAGO, *and* GENTLEMEN.*)*

Othello. These letters give, Iago, to the pilot,
      And by him do my duties to the Senate.
      That done, I will be walking on the works.°
      Repair there to me.

---

21. **keep . . . quillets:** put away your wisecracks   44. **affinity:** kindred   3. **works:** fortifications

Iago.   Well, my good lord, I'll do 't.
Othello. This fortification, gentlemen, shall we see 't?   5
Gentlemen. We'll wait upon your lordship. *(Exeunt.)*

Scene 3.
The garden of the castle.

(Enter DESDEMONA, CASSIO, *and* EMILIA.*)*

Desdemona. Be thou assured, good Cassio, I will do
   All my abilities in thy behalf.
Emilia. Good madam, do. I warrant it grieves my husband
   As if the case were his.
Desdemona. Oh, that's an honest fellow. Do not doubt, Cassio,   5
   But I will have my lord and you again
   As friendly as you were.
Cassio.   Bounteous madam,
   Whatever shall become of Michael Cassio,
   He's never anything but your true servant.
Desdemona. I know 't. I thank you. You do love my lord.   10
   You have known him long, and be you well assured
   He shall in strangeness stand no farther off
   Than in a politic distance.°
Cassio.   Aye, but lady,
   That policy may either last so long,
   Or feed upon such nice and waterish diet,   15
   Or breed itself so out of circumstance,
   That, I being absent and my place supplied,
   My General will forget my love and service.
Desdemona. Do not doubt° that. Before Emilia here
   I give thee warrant of thy place. Assure thee,   20
   If I do vow a friendship, I'll perform it
   To the last article. My lord shall never rest.
   I'll watch him tame and talk him out of patience,
   His bed shall seem a school, his board a shrift.
   I'll intermingle every thing he does   25
   With Cassio's suit. Therefore be merry, Cassio,
   For thy solicitor shall rather die
   Than give thy cause away. *(Enter* OTHELLO *and* IAGO, *at a distance.)*
Emilia. Madam, here comes my lord.
Cassio. Madam, I'll take my leave.   30
Desdemona. Nay, stay and hear me speak.
Cassio. Madam, not now. I am very ill at ease,
   Unfit for mine own purposes.
Desdemona. Well, do your discretion. *(Exit* CASSIO.*)*
Iago. Ha! I like not that.   35

12–13: **He . . . distance:** i.e., his apparent coldness to you shall only be so much as his official position demands for reasons of policy.   19. **doubt:** fear

Othello. What dost thou say?

Iago. Nothing, my lord. Or if—I know not what.

Othello. Was not that Cassio parted from my wife?

Iago. Cassio, my lord! No, sure, I cannot think it,

    That he would steal away so guilty-like, 40

    Seeing you coming.

Othello.   I do believe 'twas he.

Desdemona. How now, my lord!

    I have been talking with a suitor here,

    A man that languishes in your displeasure.

Othello. Who is 't you mean? 45

Desdemona. Why, your Lieutenant, Cassio. Good my lord,

    If I have any grace or power to move you,

    His present reconciliation take.°

    For if he be not one that truly loves you,

    That errs in ignorance and not in cunning, 50

    I have no judgment in an honest face.

    I prithee call him back.

Othello.   Went he hence now?

Desdemona. Aye, sooth, so humbled

    That he hath left part of his grief with me,

    To suffer with him. Good love, call him back. 55

Othello. Not now, sweet Desdemona, some other time.

Desdemona. But shall 't be shortly?

Othello.   The sooner, sweet, for you.

Desdemona. Shall 't be tonight at supper?

Othello.   No, not tonight.

Desdemona. Tomorrow dinner then?

Othello.   I shall not dine at home.

    I meet the captains at the citadel. 60

Desdemona. Why, then tomorrow night or Tuesday morn,

    On Tuesday noon, or night, on Wednesday morn.

    I prithee name the time, but let it not

    Exceed three days. In faith, he's penitent,

    And yet his trespass, in our common reason— 65

    Save that, they say, the wars must make examples

    Out of their best—is not almost° a fault

    To incur a private check.° When shall he come?

    Tell me, Othello. I wonder in my soul

    What you would ask me that I should deny, 70

    Or stand so mammering° on. What! Michael Cassio,

    That came a-wooing with you, and so many a time

    When I have spoke of you dispraisingly

    Hath ta'en your part—to have So much to do

    To bring him in! Trust me, I could do much— 75

---

48. **His . . . take:** Accept his immediate apology and forgive him.   67. **not almost:** hardly
68. **check:** rebuke   71. **mammering:** hesitating

Othello. Prithee, no more. Let him come when he will.
    I will deny thee nothing.
Desdemona.   Why, this is not a boon.
    'Tis as I should entreat you wear your gloves,
    Or feed on nourishing dishes, or keep you warm,
    Or sue to you to do a peculiar profit   80
    To your own person. Nay, when I have a suit
    Wherein I mean to touch your love indeed,
    It shall be full of poise and difficult weight,
    And fearful to be granted.
Othello.   I will deny thee nothing.
    Whereon I do beseech thee grant me this,   85
    To leave me but a little to myself.
Desdemona. Shall I deny you? No. Farewell, my lord.
Othello. Farewell, my Desdemona. I'll come to thee straight.
Desdemona. Emilia, come. Be as your fancies teach you.
    Whate'er you be, I am obedient.   90

(Exeunt DESDEMONA *and* EMILIA.*)*

Othello. Excellent wretch! Perdition catch my soul
    But I do love thee! And when I love thee not,
    Chaos is come again.
Iago. My noble lord—
Othello.   What dost thou say, Iago?
Iago. Did Michael Cassio, when you wooed my lady,   95
    Know of your love?
Othello. He did, from first to last. Why dost thou ask?
Iago. But for a satisfaction of my thought,
    No further harm.
Othello.   Why of thy thought, Iago?
Iago. I did not think he had been acquainted with her.   100
Othello. Oh yes, and went between us very oft.
Iago. Indeed!
Othello. Indeed! Aye, indeed. Discern'st thou aught in that?
    Is he not honest?
Iago.   Honest, my lord!
Othello.   Honest! Aye, honest.
Iago. My lord, for aught I know.
Othello.   What dost thou think?   105
Iago. Think, my lord!
Othello. Think, my lord! By Heaven, he echoes me
    As if there were some monster in his thought
    Too hideous to be shown. Thou dost mean something.
    I heard thee say even now that thou likedst not that   110
    When Cassio left my wife. What didst not like?
    And when I told thee he was of my counsel
    In my whole course of wooing, thou criedst "Indeed!"
    And didst contract and purse thy brow together

As if thou then hadst shut up in thy brain 115
Some horrible conceit. If thou dost love me,
Show me thy thought.

Iago. My lord, you know I love you.

Othello.   I think thou dost,
And for I know thou'rt full of love and honesty
And weigh'st thy words before thou givest them breath, 120
Therefore these stops of thine fright me the more.
For such things in a false disloyal knave
Are tricks of custom, but in a man that's just
They're close delations,° working from the heart,
That passion cannot rule.

Iago.   For Michael Cassio, 125
I dare be sworn I think that he is honest.

Othello. I think so too.

Iago.   Men should be what they seem,
Or those that be not, would they might seem none!°

Othello. Certain, men should be what they seem.

Iago. Why, then I think Cassio's an honest man. 130

Othello. Nay, yet there's more in this.
I prithee speak to me as to thy thinkings,
As thou dost ruminate, and give thy worst of thoughts
The worst of words.

Iago.   Good my lord, pardon me.
Though I am bound to every act of duty, 135
I am not bound to that all slaves are free to.
Utter my thoughts? Why, say they are vile and false,
As where's that palace whereinto foul things
Sometimes intrude not? Who has a breast so pure
But some uncleanly apprehensions 140
Keep leets° and law days, and in session sit
With meditations lawful?

Othello. Thou dost conspire against thy friend, Iago,
If thou but think'st him wronged and makest his ear
A stranger to thy thoughts.

Iago.   I do beseech you— 145
Though I perchance am vicious in my guess,
As, I confess, it is my nature's plague
To spy into abuses, and oft my jealousy°
Shapes faults that are not—that your wisdom yet,
From one that so imperfectly conceits,° 150
Would take no notice, nor build yourself a trouble
Out of his scattering and unsure observance.°
It were not for your quiet nor your good,

---

124. **close delations:** concealed accusations   128. **seem none:** i.e., not seem to be honest men
141. **leets:** courts   148. **jealousy:** suspicion   150. **conceits:** conceives   152. **observance:**
observation

Nor for my manhood, honesty, or wisdom,
To let you know my thoughts.

Othello.   What dost thou mean?   155

Iago. Good name in man and woman, dear my lord,
Is the immediate jewel of their souls.
Who steals my purse steals trash—'tis something, nothing,
'Twas mine, 'tis his, and has been slave to thousands—
But he that filches from me my good name   160
Robs me of that which not enriches him
And makes me poor indeed.

Othello. By Heaven, I'll know thy thoughts.

Iago. You cannot, if my heart were in your hand,
Nor shall not, whilst 'tis in my custody.   165

Othello. Ha!

Iago.   Oh, beware, my lord, of jealousy.
It is the green-eyed monster which doth mock
The meat it feeds on. That cuckold lives in bliss
Who, certain of his fate, loves not his wronger.°
But, oh, what damned minutes tells he o'er   170
Who dotes, yet doubts, suspects, yet strongly loves!

Othello. Oh misery!

Iago. Poor and content is rich, and rich enough,
But riches fineless° is as poor as winter
To him that ever fears he shall be poor.   175
Good God, the souls of all my tribe defend
From jealousy!

Othello.   Why, why is this?
Think'st thou I'd make a life of jealousy,
To follow still the changes of the moon
With fresh suspicions? No, to be once in doubt   180
Is once to be resolved.° Exchange me for a goat
When I shall turn the business of my soul
To such exsufflicate° and blown surmises,
Matching thy inference.° 'Tis not to make me jealous
To say my wife is fair, feeds well, loves company,   185
Is free of speech, sings, plays, and dances well.
Where virtue is, these are more virtuous.
Nor from mine own weak merits will I draw
The smallest fear or doubt of her revolt,
For she had eyes, and chose me. No, Iago,   190
I'll see before I doubt, when I doubt, prove,

168–69. **That . . . wronger:** i.e., the cuckold who hates his wife and knows her falseness is not tormented by suspicious jealousy.   174. **fineless:** limitless   180–81. **to . . . resolved:** whenever I find myself in doubt I at once seek out the truth.   182–84. **When . . . inference:** When I shall allow that which concerns me most dearly to be influenced by such trifling suggestions as yours **exsufflicate:** blown up like a bubble

And on the proof, there is no more but this—
Away at once with love or jealousy!

Iago. I am glad of it, for now I shall have reason
    To show the love and duty that I bear you 195
    With franker spirit. Therefore, as I am bound,
    Receive it from me. I speak not yet of proof.
    Look to your wife. Observe her well with Cassio.
    Wear your eye thus, not jealous nor secure.°
    I would not have your free and noble nature 200
    Out of self-bounty° be abused. Look to 't.
    I know our country disposition well.
    In Venice° they do let Heaven see the pranks
    They dare not show their husbands. Their best conscience
    Is not to leave 't undone, but keep 't unknown. 205

Othello. Dost thou say so?

Iago. She did deceive her father, marrying you,
    And when she seemed to shake and fear your looks,
    She loved them most.

Othello.   And so she did.

Iago.   Why, go to, then.
    She that so young could give out such a seeming 210
    To seel° her father's eyes up close as oak—
    He thought 'twas witchcraft—but I am much to blame.
    I humbly do beseech you of your pardon
    For too much loving you.

Othello.   I am bound to thee forever.

Iago. I see this hath a little dashed your spirits. 215

Othello. Not a jot, not a jot.

Iago.   I' faith, I fear it has.
    I hope you will consider what is spoke
    Comes from my love. But I do see you're moved.
    I am to pray you not to strain my speech
    To grosser issues nor to larger reach
    Than to suspicion. 220

Othello. I will not.

Iago.   Should you do so, my lord,
    My speech should fall into such vile success
    As my thoughts aim not at. Cassio's my worthy friend.—
    My lord, I see you're moved.

Othello.   No, not so much moved. 225
    I do not think but Desdemona's honest.°

Iago. Long live she so! And long live you to think so!

Othello. And yet, how nature erring from itself—

---

199. **secure:** overconfident   201. **self-bounty:** natural goodness   203. **In Venice:** Venice was notorious for its loose women; the Venetian courtesans were among the sights of Europe and were much commented upon by travelers.   211. **seel:** blind   226. **honest:** When applied to Desdemona, "honest" means "chaste," but applied to Iago it has the modern meaning of "open and sincere."

Iago. Aye, there's the point. As—to be bold with you—
  Not to affect° many proposèd matches   230
  Of her own clime, complexion, and degree,
  Whereto we see in all things nature tends°—
  Foh! One may smell in such a will most rank,°
  Foul disproportion, thoughts unnatural.
  But pardon me. I do not in position   235
  Distinctly speak of her, though I may fear
  Her will, recoiling to her better judgment,
  May fall to match° you with her country forms,°
  And happily° repent.
Othello.   Farewell, farewell.
  If more thou dost perceive, let me know more.   240
  Set on thy wife to observe. Leave me, Iago.
Iago *(Going.)* My lord, I take my leave.
Othello. Why did I marry? This honest creature doubtless
  Sees and knows more, much more, than he unfolds.
Iago *(Returning.)* My lord, I would I might entreat your honor   245
  To scan this thing no further. Leave it to time.
  Though it be fit that Cassio have his place,
  For sure he fills it up with great ability,
  Yet if you please to hold him off awhile,
  You shall by that perceive him and his means.   250
  Note if your lady strain his entertainment°
  With any strong or vehement importunity—
  Much will be seen in that. In the meantime,
  Let me be thought too busy in my fears—
  As worthy cause I have to fear I am—   255
  And hold her free, I do beseech your Honor.
Othello. Fear not my government.°
Iago. I once more take my leave. *(Exit.)*
Othello. This fellow's of exceeding honesty,
  And knows all qualities, with a learned spirit,   260
  Of human dealings. If I do prove her haggard,°
  Though that her jesses° were my dear heartstrings,
  I'd whistle her off and let her down the wind
  To prey at fortune.° Haply, for I am black
  And have not those soft parts of conversation   265
  That chamberers° have, or for I am declined

---

230. **affect:** be inclined to   232. **in . . . tends:** i.e., a woman naturally marries a man of her own
country, color, and rank.   233. **will . . . rank:** desire most lustful   238. **match:** compare
country forms: the appearance of her countrymen, i.e., white men   239. **happily:** haply, by
chance   251. **strain his entertainment:** urge you to receive him   257. **government:** self-
control   261. **haggard:** a wild hawk   261–64. **If . . . fortune:** Othello keeps up the imagery of
falconry throughout. He means: If I find that she is wild, I'll whistle her off the game and let her go
where she will, for she's not worth keeping.   262. **jesses:** the straps attached to a hawk's legs
266. **chamberers:** playboys

Into the vale of years—yet that's not much—
She's gone, I am abused, and my relief
Must be to loathe her. Oh, curse of marriage,
That we can call these delicate creatures ours, 270
And not their appetites! I had rather be a toad
And live upon the vapor of a dungeon
Than keep a corner in the thing I love
For others' uses. Yet, 'tis the plague of great ones,
Prerogatived are they less than the base. 275
'Tis destiny unshunnable, like death.
Even then this forkèd plague° is fated to us
When we do quicken.° Desdemona comes.
(Re-enter DESDEMONA *and* EMILIA.*)*
If she be false, oh, then Heaven mocks itself!
I'll not believe 't.

Desdemona.   How now, my dear Othello! 280
Your dinner, and the generous° islanders
By you invited, do attend your presence.

Othello. I am to blame.

Desdemona.   Why do you speak so faintly?
Are you not well?

Othello. I have a pain upon my forehead here. 285

Desdemona. Faith, that's with watching,° 'twill away again.
Let me but bind it hard, within this hour
It will be well.

Othello.   Your napkin° is too little,
(He puts the handkerchief from him, and it drops.)
Let it alone. Come, I'll go in with you.

Desdemona. I am very sorry that you are not well. 290
(Exeunt OTHELLO *and* DESDEMONA.*)*

Emilia. I am glad I have found this napkin.
This was her first remembrance from the Moor.
My wayward° husband hath a hundred times
Wooed me to steal it, but she so loves the token,
For he conjured° her she should ever keep it, 295
That she reserves it evermore about her
To kiss and talk to. I'll have the work ta'en out,°
And give 't to Iago. What he will do with it
Heaven knows, not I.
I nothing know, but for his fantasy.° *(Re-enter* IAGO.*)* 300

Iago. How now! What do you here alone?

Emilia. Do not you chide, I have a thing for you.

Iago. A thing for me? It is a common thing—

---

277. **forkèd plague:** i.e., to be a cuckold 278. **quicken:** stir in our mother's womb 281. **generous:** noble 286. **watching:** lack of sleep 288. **napkin:** handkerchief 293. **wayward:** unac-
countable 295. **conjured:** begged with an oath 297. **work . . . out:** pattern copied
300. **fantasy:** whim

Emilia. Ha!

Iago. To have a foolish wife. 305

Emilia. Oh, is that all? What will you give me now
    For that same handkerchief?

Iago.   What handkerchief?

Emilia. What handkerchief!
    Why, that the Moor first gave to Desdemona,
    That which so often you did bid me steal. 310

Iago. Hast stol'n it from her?

Emilia. No, faith, she let it drop by negligence,
    And, to the advantage, I being here took 't up.
    Look, here it is.

Iago.   A good wench. Give it me.

Emilia. What will you do with 't, that you have been so earnest 315
    To have me filch it?

Iago *(Snatching it.)*   Why, what's that to you?

Emilia. If 't be not for some purpose of import,
    Give 't me again. Poor lady, she'll run mad
    When she shall lack it.

Iago. Be not acknown on 't,° I have use for it. 320
    Go, leave me. *(Exit* EMILIA.*)*
    I will in Cassio's lodging lose this napkin,
    And let him find it. Trifles light as air
    Are to the jealous confirmations strong
    As proofs of Holy Writ. This may do something. 325
    The Moor already changes with my poison.
    Dangerous conceits are in their natures poisons,
    Which at the first are scarce found to distaste,
    But, with a little, act upon the blood,
    Burn like the mines of sulphur. I did say so.° 330
    Look where he comes! *(Re-enter* OTHELLO.*)*
                 Not poppy,° nor mandragora,°
    Nor all the drowsy syrups of the world,
    Shall ever medicine thee to that sweet sleep
    Which thou owedst° yesterday,

Othello.   Ha! Ha! False to me?

Iago. Why, how now, General! No more of that. 335

Othello. Avaunt! Be gone! Thou hast set me on the rack.
    I swear 'tis better to be much abused
    Than but to know 't a little.

Iago.   How now, my lord!

Othello. What sense had I of her stol'n hours of lust?
    I saw 't not, thought it not, it harmed not me. 340
    I slept the next night well, was free and merry.
    I found not Cassio's kisses on her lips.

---

320. **Be . . . 't:** Know nothing about it   330. **I . . . so:** As Iago says this, Othello is seen approaching, with all the signs of his agitation out-wardly visible.   331. **poppy:** opium   **mandragora:** called also mandrake—a root used as a drug to bring sleep   334. **owedst:** owned

He that is robbed, not wanting° what is stol'n,
Let him not know 't and he's not robbed at all.

Iago. I am sorry to hear this.

Othello. I had been happy if the general camp,
Pioners° and all, had tasted her sweet body,
So I had nothing known. Oh, now forever
Farewell the tranquil mind! Farewell content!
Farewell the plumèd troop and the big wars
That make ambition virtue! Oh farewell,
Farewell the neighing steed and the shrill trump,
The spirit-stirring drum, the ear-piercing fife,
The royal banner, and all quality,
Pride, pomp, and circumstance of glorious war!
And, O you mortal engines,° whose rude throats
The immortal Jove's dread clamors counterfeit,
Farewell! Othello's occupation's gone!

Iago. Is 't possible, my lord?

Othello. Villain, be sure thou prove my love a whore,
Be sure of it, give me the ocular proof.
Or by the worth of man's eternal soul,
Thou hadst been better have been born a dog
Than answer my waked wrath!

Iago.   Is 't come to this?

Othello. Make me to see 't, or at the least so prove it
That the probation° bear no hinge nor loop
To hang a doubt on, or woe upon thy life!

Iago. My noble lord—

Othello. If thou dost slander her and torture me,
Never pray more, abandon all remorse.°
On horror's head horrors accumulate,
Do deeds to make Heaven weep, all earth amazed,
For nothing canst thou to damnation add
Greater than that.

Iago.   Oh, grace! Oh, Heaven defend me!
Are you a man? Have you a soul or sense?
God be wi' you, take mine office. O wretched fool,
That livest to make thine honesty a vice!
O monstrous world! Take note, take note, O world,
To be direct and honest is not safe.
I thank you for this profit, and from hence
I'll love no friend, sith° love breeds such offense.

Othello. Nay, stay. Thou shouldst be honest.

Iago. I should be wise, for honesty's a fool,
And loses that it works for.

345
350
355
360
365
370
375
380

---

343. **wanting:** missing   347. **Pioners:** Pioneers, the lowest type of soldier   356. **mortal engines:**
deadly cannon   366. **probation:** proof   370. **remorse:** pity   381. **sith:** since

Othello.   By the world,
I think my wife be honest, and think she is not.   385
I think that thou are just, and think thou art not.
I'll have some proof. Her name, that was as fresh
As Dian's° visage, is now begrimed and black
As mine own face. If there be cords, or knives,
Poison, or fire, or suffocating streams,   390
I'll not endure it. Would I were satisfied!
Iago. I see, sir, you are eaten up with passion.
I do repent me that I put it to you.
You would be satisfied?

Othello.   Would! Nay, I will.
Iago. And may, but how? How satisfied, my lord?   395
Would you, the supervisor,° grossly gape on?
Behold her topped?

Othello.   Death and damnation! Oh!
Iago. It were a tedious difficulty, I think,
To bring them to that prospect. Damn them then,
If ever mortal eyes do see them bolster°   400
More than their own! What then? How then?
What shall I say? Where's satisfaction?
It is impossible you should see this,
Were they as prime° as goats, as hot as monkeys,
As salt° as wolves in pride,° and fools as gross   405
As ignorance made drunk. But yet I say
If imputation° and strong circumstances,
Which lead directly to the door of truth,
Will give you satisfaction, you may have 't.

Othello. Give me a living reason she's disloyal.   410
Iago. I do not like the office.
But sith I am entered in this cause so far,
Pricked to 't by foolish honesty and love,
I will go on. I lay with Cassio lately,
And being troubled with a raging tooth,   415
I could not sleep.
There are a kind of men so loose of soul
That in their sleeps will mutter their affairs.
One of this kind is Cassio.
In sleep I heard him say "Sweet Desdemona,   420
Let us be wary, let us hide our loves."
And then, sir, would he gripe° and wring my hand,
Cry "O sweet creature!" and then kiss me hard,
As if he plucked up kisses by the roots
That grew upon my lips. Then laid his leg   425

---

388. **Dian:** Diana, goddess of chastity   396. **supervisor:** looker-on   400. **bolster:** sleep together   404. **prime:** lustful   405. **salt:** eager   **pride:** in heat   407. **imputation:** probability   422. **gripe:** grip

Over my thigh, and sighed and kissed, and then
Cried "Cursed fate that gave thee to the Moor!"

Othello. Oh, monstrous! Monstrous!

Iago.   Nay, this was but his dream.

Othello. But this denoted a foregone conclusion.
'Tis a shrewd doubt,° though it be but a dream.   430

Iago. And this may help to thicken other proofs
That do demonstrate thinly.

Othello.   I'll tear her all to pieces.

Iago. Nay, but be wise. Yet we see nothing done.
She may be honest yet. Tell me this:
Have you not sometimes seen a handkerchief   435
Spotted with strawberries in your wife's hand?

Othello. I gave her such a one, 'twas my first gift.

Iago. I know not that. But such a handkerchief—
I am sure it was your wife's—did I today
See Cassio wipe his beard with.

Othello.   If it be that—   440

Iago. If it be that, or any that was hers,
It speaks against her with the other proofs.

Othello. Oh, that the slave had forty thousand lives!
One is too poor, too weak, for my revenge.
Now do I see 'tis true. Look here, Iago,   445
All my fond love thus do I blow to Heaven—
'Tis gone.
Arise, black Vengeance, from thy hollow cell!
Yield up, O Love, thy crown and hearted throne
To tyrannous hate! Swell, bosom, with thy fraught,°   450
For 'tis of aspics'° tongues!

Iago.   Yet be content.

Othello. Oh, blood, blood, blood!

Iago. Patience, I say. Your mind perhaps may change.

Othello. Never, Iago. Like to the Pontic Sea,
Whose icy current and compulsive course   455
Ne'er feels retiring ebb but keeps due on
To the Propontic and the Hellespont;
Even so my bloody thoughts, with violent pace,
Shall ne'er look back, ne'er ebb to humble love,
Till that a capable° and wide revenge   460
Swallow them up. Now, by yond marble Heaven,
In the due reverence of a sacred vow *(Kneels.)*
I here engage my words.

Iago.   Do not rise yet. *(Kneels.)*
Witness, you ever burning lights above,
You elements that clip° us round about,   465

---

430. **shrewd doubt:** bitter suspicion   450. **fraught:** freight   451. **aspics':** asps'   460. **capable:** comprehensive   465. **clip:** embrace

Witness that here Iago doth give up
The execution of his wit, hands, heart,
To wronged Othello's service! Let him command,
And to obey shall be in me remorse,°
What bloody business ever. *(They rise.)*

Othello.   I greet thy love,   470
Not with vain thanks, but with acceptance bounteous,
And will upon the instant put thee to 't.
Within these three days let me hear thee say
That Cassio's not alive.

Iago. My friend is dead. 'Tis done at your request.   475
But let her live.

Othello. Damn her, lewd minx! Oh, damn her!
Come, go with me apart. I will withdraw,
To furnish me with some swift means of death
For the fair devil. Now art thou my Lieutenant.   480

Iago. I am your own forever. *(Exeunt.)*

Scene 4
Before the castle.

(Enter DESDEMONA, EMILIA, *and* CLOWN.*)*

Desdemona. Do you know, sirrah, where Lieutenant Cassio lies?
Clown. I dare not say he lies anywhere.
Desdemona. Why, man?
Clown. He's a soldier, and for one to say a soldier lies is stabbing.
Desdemona. Go to. Where lodges he?   5
Clown. To tell you where he lodges is to tell you where I lie.
Desdemona. Can anything be made of this?
Clown. I know not where he lodges, and for me to devise a lodging, and say he lies here or he lies there, were to lie in mine own throat.
Desdemona. Can you inquire him out and be edified by report?°   10
Clown. I will catechize the world for him; that is, make questions and by them answer.
Desdemona. Seek him, bid him come hither. Tell him I have moved my lord on his behalf and hope all will be well.
Clown. To do this is within the compass of man's wit, and therefore I will attempt the doing it. *(Exit.)*   16
Desdemona. Where should I lose that handkerchief, Emilia?
Emilia. I know not, madam.
Desdemona. Believe me, I had rather have lost my purse
Full of crusados. And, but my noble Moor   20
Is true of mind and made of no such baseness
As jealous creatures are, it were enough
To put him to ill thinking.

---

469. **remorse:** solemn oblication   10. **edified by report:** enlightened by the information. Desdemona speaks with mock pomposity.

Emilia.   Is he not jealous?

Desdemona. Who, he? I think the sun where he was born Drew all such humors
    from him.

Emilia.   Look where he comes.   25

Desdemona. I will not leave him now till Cassio
    Be called to him. *(Enter* OTHELLO.*)*
          How is 't with you, my lord?

Othello. Well, my good lady. *(Aside.)* Oh, hardness to dissemble!
    How do you, Desdemona?

Desdemona.   Well, my good lord.

Othello. Give me your hand. This hand is moist,° my lady.   30

Desdemona. It yet has felt no age nor known no sorrow.

Othello. This argues fruitfulness and liberal heart.
    Hot, hot, and moist—this hand of yours requires
    A sequester from liberty, fasting and prayer,
    Much castigation, exercise devout.   35
    For here's a young and sweating devil here,
    That commonly rebels. 'Tis a good hand,
    A frank one.

Desdemona. You may indeed say so,
    For 'twas that hand that gave away my heart.

Othello. A liberal° hand. The hearts of old gave hands,   40
    But our new heraldry is hands, not hearts.°

Desdemona. I cannot speak of this. Come now, your promise.

Othello. What promise, chuck?°

Desdemona. I have sent to bid Cassio come speak with you.

Othello. I have a salt and sorry rheum offends me.   45
    Lend me thy handkerchief.

Desdemona.   Here, my lord.

Othello. That which I gave you.

Desdemona.   I have it not about me.

Othello. Not?

Desdemona. No indeed, my lord.

Othello. That's a fault. That handkerchief
    Did an Egyptian to my mother give.   50
    She was a charmer, and could almost read
    The thoughts of people. She told her while she kept it
    'Twould make her amiable and subdue my father
    Entirely to her love, but if she lost it
    Or made a gift of it, my father's eye   55
    Should hold her loathèd and his spirits should hunt
    After new fancies. She dying gave it me,
    And bid me, when my fate would have me wive,

---

30. **moist:** A hot moist palm was believed to show desire.   40. **liberal:** overgenerous   40–41. **The
. . . hearts:** Once love and deeds went together, but now it is all deeds (i.e., faithlessness) and no
love.   43. **chuck:** A term of affection, but not the kind of word with which a person of Othello's dignity would normally address his wife. He is beginning to treat her with contemptuous familiarity.

To give it her. I did so. And take heed on 't,
Make it a darling like your precious eye.   60
To lose 't or give 't away were such perdition
As nothing else could match.
Desdemona.   Is 't possible?
Othello. 'Tis true. There's magic in the web of it.
A sibyl that had numbered in the world
The sun to course two hundred compasses   65
In her prophetic fury sewed the work.
The worms were hallowed that did breed the silk,
And it was dyed in mummy which the skillful
Conserved° of maiden's hearts.
Desdemona.   Indeed! Is 't true?
Othello. Most veritable, therefore look to 't well.   70
Desdemona. Then would God that I had never seen 't.
Othello. Ha! Wherefore?
Desdemona. Why do you speak so startingly and rash?
Othello. Is 't lost? Is 't gone? Speak, is it out o' the way?
Desdemona. Heaven bless us!   75
Othello. Say you?
Desdemona. It is not lost, but what an if it were?
Othello. How!
Desdemona. I say it is not lost.
Othello.   Fetch 't, let me see it.
Desdemona. Why, so I can, sir, but I will not now.   80
This is a trick to put me from my suit.
Pray you let Cassio be received again.
Othello. Fetch me the handkerchief. My mind misgives.
Desdemona. Come, come,
You'll never meet a more sufficient man.   85
Othello. The handkerchief!
Desdemona.   I pray talk me of Cassio.
Othello. The handkerchief!
Desdemona.   A man that all this time
Hath founded his good fortunes on your love,
Shared dangers with you—
Othello. The handkerchief!   90
Desdemona. In sooth, you are to blame.
Othello. Away! *(Exit.)*
Emilia. Is not this man jealous?
Desdemona. I ne'er saw this before.
Sure there's some wonder in this handkerchief.   95
I am most unhappy in the loss of it.
Emilia. 'Tis not a year or two shows us a man.°
They are all but stomachs and we all but food.

---

69. **Conserved:** Prepared   97. **'Tis . . . man:** It does not take a couple of years to discover the
nature of a man; i.e., he soon shows his real nature.

They eat us hungerly, and when they are full
They belch us. Look you, Cassio and my husband.   100

(Enter CASSIO *and* IAGO.)

Iago. There is no other way, 'tis she must do 't.
And, lo, the happiness!° Go and impórtune her.
Desdemona. How now, good Cassio! What's the news with you?
Cassio. Madam, my former suit. I do beseech you
That by your virtuous means I may again   105
Exist, and be a member of his love
Whom I with all the office of my heart
Entirely honor. I would not be delayed.
If my offense be of such mortal kind
That nor my service past nor present sorrows   110
Nor purposed merit in futurity
Can ransom me into his love again,
But to know so must be my benefit.
So shall I clothe me in a forced content
And shut myself up in some other course   115
To Fortune's alms.
Desdemona.   Alas, thrice-gentle Cassio!
My advocation° is not now in tune.
My lord is not my lord, nor should I know him
Were he in favor as in humor altered.
So help me every spirit sanctified,   120
As I have spoken for you all my best
And stood within the blank° of his displeasure
For my free speech! You must awhile be patient.
What I can do I will, and more I will
Than for myself I dare. Let that suffice you.   125
Iago. Is my lord angry?
Emilia.   He went hence but now,
And certainly in strange unquietness.
Iago. Can he be angry? I have seen the cannon
When it hath blown his ranks into the air,
And, like the Devil, from his very arm   130
Puffed his own brother, and can he be angry?
Something of moment then. I will go meet him.
There's matter in 't indeed if he be angry.
Desdemona. I prithee do so. *(Exit* IAGO.)
                        Something sure of state,
Either from Venice, or some unhatched practice   135
Made demonstrable° here in Cyprus to him,
Hath puddled his clear spirit. And in such cases
Men's natures wrangle with inferior things,

---

102. **And . . . happiness!:** What good luck, here she is!   117. **advocation:** advocacy   122. **blank:**
aim   135–36. **unhatched . . . demonstrable:** some plot, not yet matured, which has been revealed

Though great ones are their object. 'Tis even so,
For let our finger ache and it indues 140
Our other healthful members even to that sense
Of pain. Nay, we must think men are not gods,
Nor of them look for such observancy
As fits the bridal.° Beshrew me much, Emilia,
I was, unhandsome warrior° as I am, 145
Arraigning his unkindness with my soul,
But now I find I had suborned the witness,
And he's indicted falsely.

Emilia. Pray Heaven it be state matters, as you think,
And no conception nor no jealous toy° 150
Concerning you.

Desdemona. Alas the day, I never gave him cause!

Emilia. But jealous souls will not be answered so.
They are not ever jealous for the cause,
But jealous for they are jealous. 'Tis a monster 155
Begot upon itself, born on itself.

Desdemona. Heaven keep that monster from Othello's mind!

Emilia. Lady, amen.

Desdemona. I will go seek him. Cassio, walk hereabout.
If I do find him fit, I'll move your suit, 160
And seek to effect it to my uttermost.

Cassio. I humbly thank your ladyship.

(Exeunt DESDEMONA *and* EMILIA. *Enter* BIANCA.*)*

Bianca. Save you, friend Cassio!

Cassio.   What make you from home?
How is it with you, my most fair Bianca?
I' faith, sweet love, I was coming to your house. 165

Bianca. And I was going to your lodging, Cassio.
What, keep a week away? Seven days and nights?
Eightscore eight hours? And lovers' absent hours,
More tedious than the dial eightscore times?
Oh, weary reckoning!

Cassio.   Pardon me, Bianca. 170
I have this while with leaden thoughts been pressed,
But I shall in a more continuate time
Strike off this score of absence. Sweet Bianca,

(Giving her DESDEMONA'S *handkerchief.)*

Take me this work out.

Bianca.   O Cassio, whence came this?
This is some token from a newer friend. 175
To the felt absence now I feel a cause.
Is 't come to this? Well, well.

---

144. **bridal:** honeymoon   145. **unhandsome warrior:** clumsy soldier. Desdemona continually
thinks of herself as Othello's companion in arms. Cf. 1.3.248 ff.   150. **jealous toy:** silly suspicion

Cassio.   Go to, woman!
Throw your vile guesses in the Devil's teeth,
From whence you have them. You are jealous now
That this is from some mistress, some remembrance.   180
No, by my faith, Bianca.
Bianca.   Why, whose is it?
Cassio. I know not, sweet. I found it in my chamber.
I like the work well. Ere it be demanded—
As like enough it will—I'd have it copied.
Take it, and do 't, and leave me for this time.   185
Bianca. Leave you! Wherefore?
Cassio. I do attend here on the General,
And think it no addition,° nor my wish
To have him see me womaned.°
Bianca.   Why, I pray you?
Cassio. Not that I love you not.
Bianca.   But that you do not love me.   190
I pray you bring me on the way a little,
And say if I shall see you soon at night.
Cassio. 'Tis but a little way that I can bring you,
For I attend here. But I'll see you soon.
Bianca. 'Tis very good, I must be circumstanced.° *(Exeunt.)*   195

ACT 4
Scene 1.
Cyprus. Before the castle.

(Enter OTHELLO *and* IAGO.*)*

Iago. Will you think so?
Othello.   Think so, Iago!
Iago.   What,
To kiss in private?
Othello.   An unauthorized kiss.
Iago. Or to be naked with her friend in bed
An hour or more, not meaning any harm?
Othello. Naked in bed, Iago, and not mean harm!   5
It is hypocrisy against the Devil.
They that mean virtuously and yet do so,
The Devil their virtue tempts and they tempt Heaven.
Iago. So they do nothing, 'tis a venial° slip.
But if I give my wife a handkerchief—   10
Othello. What then?
Iago. Why, then, 'tis hers, my lord, and being hers,
She may, I think, bestow 't on any man.

---

188. **addition:** honor   189. **womaned:** with a woman   195. **circumstanced:** put off
9. **venial:** pardonable

Othello. She is protectress of her honor too.
 May she give that?   15
Iago. Her honor is an essence that's not seen.
 They have it very oft that have it not.
 But for the handkerchief—
Othello. By Heaven, I would most gladly have forgot it.
 Thou said'st—oh, it comes o'er my memory,   20
 As doth the raven o'er the infected house
 Boding to all—he had my handkerchief.
Iago. Aye, what of that?
Othello.   That's not so good now.
Iago.   What
 If I had said I had seen him do you wrong?
 Or heard him say—as knaves be such abroad,   25
 Who having, by their own importunate suit,
 Or voluntary dotage of some mistress,
 Convincèd or supplied° them, cannot choose
 But they must blab—
Othello.   Hath he said anything?
Iago. He hath, my lord, but be you well assured,   30
 No more than he'll unswear.
Othello.   What hath he said?
Iago. Faith, that he did—I know not what he did.
Othello. What? What?
Iago. Lie—
Othello. With her?
Iago.   With her, on her, what you will.   34
Othello. Lie° with her! Lie on her!—We say lie on her when they belie her.—Lie with
 her. 'Zounds, that's fulsome!° Handkerchief— confessions—handkerchief!—
 To confess, and be hanged for his labor. First to be hanged, and then to confess.
 I tremble at it. Nature would not invest herself in such shadowing passion
 without some instruction.° It is not words that shake me thus. Pish! Noses, ears,
 and lips. Is 't possible?—Confess?—Handkerchief?—Oh, devil!

 (Falls in a trance.)   41

Iago. Work on,
 My medicine, work! Thus credulous fools are caught,
 And many worthy and chaste dames even thus,
 All guiltless, meet reproach. What ho! My lord!   45
 My lord, I say! Othello! *(Enter* CASSIO.*)*
        How now, Cassio!
Cassio. What's the matter?
Iago. My lord is fall'n into an epilepsy.
 This is his second fit, he had one yesterday.

---

28. **Convincèd or supplied:** Overcome or satisfied their desires   35–41. **Lie . . . devil:** Othello
breaks into incoherent muttering before he falls down in a fit.   36. **fulsome:** disgusting
38–40. **Nature . . . instruction:** Nature would not fill me with such overwhelming emotion unless
there was some cause.

Cassio. Rub him about the temples.

Iago.   No, forbear,   50
    The lethargy° must have his quiet course.
    If not, he foams at mouth and by and by
    Breaks out to savage madness. Look, he stirs.
    Do you withdraw yourself a little while,
    He will recover straight. When he is gone,   55
    I would on great occasion speak with you. *(Exit* CASSIO.*)*
    How is it, General? Have you not hurt your head?°

Othello. Dost thou mock me?

Iago.   I mock you! No, by Heaven.
    Would you would bear your fortune like a man!

Othello. A hornèd man's a monster and a beast.   60

Iago. There's many a beast, then, in a populous city,
    And many a civil monster.

Othello. Did he confess it?

Iago.   Good sir, be a man.
    Think every bearded fellow that's but yoked°
    May draw with you.° There's millions now alive   65
    That nightly lie in those unproper beds
    Which they dare swear peculiar.° Your case is better.
    Oh, 'tis the spite of Hell, the Fiend's arch-mock,
    To lip° a wanton in a secure couch°
    And to suppose her chaste! No, let me know,   70
    And knowing what I am, I know what she shall be.

Othello. Oh, thou art wise, 'tis certain.

Iago.   Stand you awhile apart,
    Confine yourself but in a patient list.°
    Whilst you were here o'erwhelmèd with your grief—
    A passion most unsuiting such a man—   75
    Cassio came hither. I shifted him away,
    And laid good 'scuse upon your ecstasy,°
    Bade him anon return and here speak with me,
    The which he promised. Do but encave yourself,
    And mark the fleers, the gibes, and notable scorns,   80
    That dwell in every region of his face.
    For I will make him tell the tale anew,
    Where, how, how oft, how long ago, and when
    He hath and is again to cope° your wife.
    I say but mark his gesture. Marry, patience,   85

---

51. **lethargy:** epileptic fit   57. **Have . . . head?:** With brutal cynicism Iago asks whether Othello is suffering from cuckold's headache.   64. **yoked:** married   65. **draw with you:** be your yoke fellow   66–67. **That . . . peculiar:** That lie nightly in beds which they believe are their own but which others have shared   69. **lip:** kiss   **secure couch:** lit., a carefree bed; i.e., a bed which has been used by the wife's lover, but secretly   73. **patient list:** confines of patience   77. **ecstasy:** fit   84. **cope:** encounter

Or I shall say you are all in all in spleen,
And nothing of a man.

Othello.   Dost thou hear, Iago?
I will be found most cunning in my patience,
But—dost thou hear?—most bloody.

Iago.   That's not amiss.
But yet keep time in all. Will you withdraw? *(OTHELLO retires.)*   90
Now will I question Cassio of Bianca,
A housewife° that by selling her desires
Buys herself bread and clothes. It is a creature
That dotes on Cassio, as 'tis the strumpet's plague
To beguile many and be beguiled by one.   95
He, when he hears of her, cannot refrain
From the excess of laughter. Here he comes. *(Re-enter* CASSIO.)
As he shall smile, Othello shall go mad,
And his unbookish° jealousy must construe
Poor Cassio's smiles, gestures, and light behavior   100
Quite in the wrong. How do you now, Lieutenant?

Cassio. The worser that you give me the addition°
Whose want even kills me.

Iago. Ply Desdemona well, and you are sure on't.
Now, if this suit lay in Bianca's power,   105
How quickly should you speed!

Cassio.   Alas, poor caitiff!°

Othello. Look how he laughs already!

Iago. I never knew a woman love man so.

Cassio. Alas, poor rogue! I think i' faith, she loves me.

Othello. Now he denies it faintly and laughs it out.   110

Iago. Do you hear, Cassio?

Othello.   Now he impórtunes him
To tell it o'er. Go to. Well said, well said.

Iago. She gives it out that you shall marry her.
Do you intend to?

Cassio. Ha, ha, ha!   115

Othello. Do you triumph, Roman?° Do you triumph?

Cassio. I marry her! What, a customer!° I prithee bear some charity to my wit. Do
not think it so unwholesome. Ha, ha, ha!

Othello. So, so, so, so. They laugh that win.

Iago. Faith, the cry goes that you shall marry her.   120

Cassio. Prithee say true.

Iago. I am a very villain else.

Othello. Have you scored° me? Well.

---

92. **housewife:** hussy   99. **unbookish:** unlearned   102. **addition:** title (Lieutenant) which he has
lost   106. **caitiff:** wretch   116. **triumph, Roman:** The word "triumph" suggests "Roman" because
the Romans celebrated their victories with triumphs, elaborate shows, and processions.   117. **customer:** harlot   123. **scored:** marked, as with a blow from a whip

Cassio. This is the monkey's own giving out. She is persuaded I will marry her out of her own love and flattery, not out of my promise. 126

Othello. Iago beckons me, now he begins the story.

Cassio. She was here even now. She haunts me in every place. I was the other day talking on the sea bank with certain Venetians, and thither comes the bauble, and, by this hand, she falls me thus about my neck— 131

Othello. Crying "O dear Cassio!" as it were. His gesture imports it.

Cassio. So hangs and lolls and weeps upon me, so hales and pulls me. Ha, ha, ha!

Othello. Now he tells how she plucked him to my chamber. Oh, I see that nose of yours, but not that dog I shall throw it to. 136

Cassio. Well, I must leave her company.

Iago. Before me!° Look where she comes.

Classio. 'Tis such another fitchew!° Marry, a perfumed one.

(Enter BIANCA.*)*

What do you mean by this haunting of me? 140

Bianca. Let the Devil and his dam haunt you! What did you mean by that same handkerchief you gave me even now? I was a fine fool to take it. I must take out the work? A likely piece of work, that you should find it in your chamber and not know who left it there! This is some minx's token, and I must take out the work? There, give it your hobby-horse. Wheresoever you had it, I'll take out no work on't. 146

Cassio. How now, my sweet Bianca! How now! How now!

Othello. By Heaven, that should be my handkerchief!

Bianca. An° you'll come to supper tonight, you may. An you will not, come when you are next prepared for. *(Exit.)* 150

Iago. After her, after her.

Cassio. Faith, I must, she'll rail i' the street else.

Iago. Will you sup there?

Cassio. Faith, I intend so.

Iago. Well, I may chance to see you, for I would very fain speak with you. 156

Cassio. Prithee, come, will you?

Iago. Go to. Say no more. *(Exit* CASSIO.*)*

Othello *(Advancing.)* How shall I murder him, Iago?

Iago. Did you perceive how he laughed at his vice? 160

Othello. Oh, Iago!

Iago. And did you see the handkerchief?

Othello. Was that mine?

Iago. Yours, by this hand. And to see how he prizes the foolish woman your wife? She gave it him, and he hath given it his whore. 165

Othello. I would have him nine years a-killing. A fine woman! A fair woman! A sweet woman!

Iago. Nay, you must forget that.

Othello. Aye, let her rot, and perish, and be damned tonight, for she shall not live. No, my heart is turned to stone, I strike it and it hurts my hand. Oh, the world hath not a sweeter creature. She might lie by an emperor's side, and command him tasks. 172

---

138. **Before me!:** By my soul!   139. **fitchew:** polecat   149. **An:** If

Iago. Nay, that's not your way.°

Othello. Hang her! I do but say what she is, so delicate with her needle, an admirable
musician—oh, she will sing the savageness out of a bear—of so high and
plenteous wit and invention— 176

Iago. She's the worse for all this.

Othello. Oh, a thousand times. And then, of so gentle a condition!

Iago. Aye, too gentle.

Othello. Nay, that's certain. But yet the pity of it, Iago! O Iago, the pity of it, Iago! 181

Iago. If you are so fond over her iniquity, give her patent to offend, for if it touch not
you, it comes near nobody.

Othello. I will chop her into messes. Cuckold me!

Iago. Oh, 'tis foul in her. 185

Othello. With mine officer!

Iago. That's fouler.

Othello. Get me some poison, Iago, this night. I'll not expostulate with her, lest her
body and beauty unprovide my mind again. This night, Iago. 190

Iago. Do it not with poison, strangle her in her bed, even the bed she hath
contaminated.

Othello. Good, good. The justice of it pleases. Very good.

Iago. And for Cassio, let me be his undertaker.°
You shall hear more by midnight. 195

Othello. Excellent good. *(A trumpet within.)* What trumpet is that same?

Iago. Something from Venice, sure. 'Tis Lodovico
Come from the Duke. And see, your wife is with him.

(Enter LODOVICO, DESDEMONA, *and* ATTENDANTS.*)*

Lodovico. God save the worthy General! 200

Othello. With all my heart, sir.

Lodovico. The Duke and Senators of Venice greet you. *(Gives him a letter.)*

Othello. I kiss the instrument of their pleasures.

(Opens the letter, and reads.)

Desdemona. And what's the news, good Cousin Lodovico?

Iago. I am very glad to see you, signior. 205
Welcome to Cyprus.

Lodovico. I thank you. How does Lieutenant Cassio?

Iago. Lives, sir.

Desdemona. Cousin, there's fall'n between him and my lord An unkind breach, but
you shall make all well. 210

Othello. Are you sure of that?

Desdemona. My lord?

Othello *(Reads.)* "This fail you not to do, as you will—"

Lodovico. He did not call, he's busy in the paper.
Is there division 'twixt my lord and Cassio? 215

Desdemona. A most unhappy one. I would do much
To atone° them, for the love I bear to Cassio.

---

173. **Nay . . . way:** i.e., don't get soft thoughts about her   194. **be his undertaker:** undertake
to manage his business. In Shakespeare's plays the word does *not* mean "mortician."
217. **atone:** reconcile

Othello. Fire and brimstone!

Desdemona. My lord?

Othello. Are you wise?°

Desdemona. What, is he angry?

Lodovico. Maybe the letter moved him,
    For, as I think, they do command him home,   220
    Deputing Cassio in his government.

Desdemona. By my troth, I am glad on 't.

Othello. Indeed!

Desdemona. My lord?

Othello. I am glad to see you mad.

Desdemona. Why, sweet Othello?

Othello. Devil! *(Striking her.)*

Desdemona. I have not deserved this.   225

Lodovieo. My lord, this would not be believed in Venice
    Though I should swear I saw 't. 'Tis very much.
    Make her amends, she weeps.

Othello. O devil, devil!
    If that the earth could teeth with a woman's tears,
    Each drop she falls would prove a crocodile.°   230
    Out of my sight!

Desdemona. I will not stay to offend you. *(Going.)*

Lodovico. Truly, an obedient lady.
    I do beseech your lordship, call her back.

Othello. Mistress!

Desdemona. My lord?   235

Othello. What would you with her, sir?

Lodovico. Who, I, my lord?

Othello. Aye, you did wish that I would make her turn.
    Sir, she can turn and turn, and yet go on
    And turn again. And she can weep, sir, weep.
    And she's obedient, as you say, obedient,   240
    Very obedient.—Proceed you in your tears—
    Concerning this, sir—oh, well-painted passion!—
    I am commanded home.—Get you away.
    I'll send for you anon.—Sir, I obey the mandate,
    And will return to Venice.—Hence, avaunt! *(Exit* DESDEMONA.*)*
    Cassio shall have my place. And, sir, tonight,   246
    I do entreat that we may sup together.
    You are welcome, sir, to Cyprus.—Goats and monkeys! *(Exit.)*

Lodovico. Is this the noble Moor whom our full Senate
    Call all-in-all sufficient? This the nature   250
    Whom passion could not shake? Whose solid virtue

---

218. **Are you wise?:** i.e., in saying you bear love to Cassio   229–30. **If . . . crocodile:** If the earth could breed from woman's tears, each tear that she lets tall would become a crocodile. It was believed that the crocodile would cry and sob to attract the sympathetic passer-by, who was then snapped up.

The shot of accident nor dart of chance
Could neither graze nor pierce?
Iago.   He is much changed.
Lodovico. Are his wits safe? Is he not light of brain?
Iago. He's that he is. I may not breathe my censure   255
What he might be. If what he might he is not,
I would to Heaven he were!
Lodovico.   What, strike his wife!
Iago. Faith, that was not so well, yet would I knew
That stroke would prove the worst!
Lodovico.   Is it his use?
Or did the letters work upon his blood,   260
And new-create this fault?
Iago.   Alas, alas!
It is not honesty in me to speak
What I have seen and known. You shall observe him,
And his own courses will denote him so
That I may save my speech. Do but go after,   265
And mark how he continues.
Lodovico. I am sorry that I am deceived in him. *(Exeunt.)*

Scene 2.
A room in the castle.

(Enter OTHELLO *and* EMILIA.*)*

Othello. You have seen nothing, then?
Emilia. Nor ever heard, nor ever did suspect.
Othello. Yes, you have seen Cassio and she together.
Emilia. But then I saw no harm, and then I heard
Each syllable that breath made up between them.   5
Othello. What, did they never whisper?
Emilia.   Never, my lord.
Othello. Nor send you out o'the way?
Emilia. Never.
Othello. To fetch her fan, her gloves, her mask, nor nothing?
Emilia. Never, my lord.   10
Othello. That's strange.
Emilia. I durst, my lord, to wager she is honest,
Lay down my soul at stake. If you think other,
Remove your thought, it doth abuse your bosom.
If any wretch have put this in your head,   15
Let Heaven requite it with the serpent's curse!
For if she be not honest, chaste, and true,
There's no man happy, the purest of their wives
Is foul as slander.
Othello.   Bid her come hither. Go. *(Exit* EMILIA.*)*
She says enough. Yet she's a simple bawd   20
That cannot say as much. This is a subtle whore,

A closet lock and key of villainous secrets.
And yet she'll kneel and pray, I have seen her do 't.

(Enter DESDEMONA *with* EMILIA.*)*

Desdemona. My lord, what is your will?
Othello.   Pray, chuck, come hither.
Desdemona. What is your pleasure?
Othello.   Let me see your eyes.   25
　　Look in my face.
Desdemona.   What horrible fancy's this?
Othello *(To* EMILIA.*)* Some of your function,° mistress.
　　Leave procreants alone and shut the door,
　　Cough, or cry hem, if anybody come.
　　Your mystery,° your mystery. Nay, dispatch. *(Exit* EMILIA.*)*   30
Desdemona. Upon my knees, what doth your speech import?
　　I understand a fury in your words,
　　But not the words.
Othello.   Why, what art thou?
Desdemona. Your wife, my lord, your true and loyal wife.
Othello. Come, swear it, damn thyself,   35
　　Lest, being like one of Heaven,° the devils themselves
　　Should fear to seize thee. Therefore be double-damned.
　　Swear thou art honest.
Desdemona.   Heaven doth truly know it.
Othello. Heaven truly knows that thou art false as Hell.
Desdemona. To whom, my lord? With whom? How am I false?   40
Othello. O Desdemona! Away! Away! Away!
Desdemona. Alas the heavy day! Why do you weep!
　　Am I the motive of these tears, my lord?
　　If haply you my father do suspect
　　An instrument of this your calling-back,   45
　　Lay not your blame on me. If you have lost him,
　　Why, I have lost him too.
Othello.   Had it pleased Heaven
　　To try me with affliction, had they rained
　　All kinds of sores and shames on my bare head,
　　Steeped me in poverty to the very lips,   50
　　Given to captivity me and my utmost hopes,
　　I should have found in some place of my soul
　　A drop of patience. But, alas, to make me
　　A fixèd figure for the time of scorn
　　To point his slow unmoving finger at!   55
　　Yet could I bear that too, well, very well.
　　But there where I have garnered up my heart,

---

27. **Some . . . function:** Get about your business, i.e., prostitution. Othello pretends that Emilia is keeper of a brothel and Desdemona one of the women.   30. **mystery:** profession   36. **being . . . Heaven:** because you look like an angel

Where either I must live or bear no life,
The fountain from the which my current runs
Or else dries up—to be discarded thence!   60
Or keep it as a cistern for foul toads
To knot and gender in! Turn thy complexion there,
Patience, thou young and rose-lipped cherubin—
Aye, there, look grim as Hell!
Desdemona. I hope my noble lord esteems me honest.   65
Othello. Oh, aye, as summer flies are in the shambles,°
That quicken even with blowing.° O thou weed,
Who art so lovely fair and smell'st so sweet
That the sense aches at thee, would thou hadst ne'er been born!
Desdemona. Alas, what ignorant sin have I committed?   70
Othello. Was this fair paper,° this most goodly book,
Made to write "whore" upon? What committed!
Committed! O thou public commoner!°
I should make very forges of my cheeks
That would to cinders burn up modesty   75
Did I but speak thy deeds. What committed!
Heaven stops the nose at it, and the moon winks.
The bawdy wind, that kisses all it meets,
Is hushed within the hollow mine of earth
And will not hear it. What committed!   80
Impudent strumpet!
Desdemona.   By Heaven, you do me wrong.
Othello. Are not you a strumpet?
Desdemona.   No, as I am a Christian.
If to preserve this vessel for my lord
From any other foul unlawful touch
Be not to be a strumpet, I am none.   85
Othello. What, not a whore?
Desdemona.   No, as I shall be saved.
Othello. Is 't possible?
Desdemona. Oh, Heaven forgive us!
Othello.   I cry you mercy, then.
I took you for that cunning whore of Venice
That married with Othello. *(Raising his voice.)* You mistress,   90
That have the office opposite to Saint Peter,
And keep the gate of Hell! *(Re-enter* EMILIA.*)*
                           You, you, aye, you!
We have done our course, there's money for your pains.
I pray you turn the key, and keep our counsel. *(Exit.)*
Emilia. Alas, what does this gentleman conceive?   95
How do you, madam? How do you, my good lady?

---

66. **shambles:** slaughterhouse   67. **quicken . . . blowing:** come to life as soon as the eggs are
laid   71. **fair paper:** i.e., her white body   73. **public commoner:** one who offers herself to all
comers

Desdemona. Faith, half-asleep.

Emilia. Good madam, what's the matter with my lord?

Desdemona. With who?

Emilia. Why, with my lord, madam. 100

Desdemona. Who is thy lord?

Emilia.   He that is yours, sweet lady.

Desdemona. I have none. Do not talk to me, Emilia.
    I cannot weep, nor answer have I none
    But what should go by water.° Prithee tonight
    Lay on my bed my wedding sheets. Remember, 105
    And call thy husband hither.

Emilia.   Here's a change indeed! *(Exit.)*

Desdemona. 'Tis meet I should be used so, very meet.
    How have I been behaved that he might stick
    The small'st opinion on my least misuse?°

(Re-enter EMILIA *with* IAGO.*)*

Iago. What is your pleasure, madam? How is 't with you? 110

Desdemona. I cannot tell. Those that do teach young babes
    Do it with gentle means and easy tasks.
    He might have chid me so, for, in good faith,
    I am a child to chiding.

Iago.   What's the matter, lady?

Emilia. Alas, Iago, my lord hath so bewhored her, 115
    Thrown such despite and heavy terms upon her,
    As true hearts cannot bear.

Desdemona. Am I that name, Iago?

Iago.   What name, fair lady?

Desdemona. Such as she says my lord did say I was.

Emilia. He called her whore. A beggar in his drink 120
    Could not have laid such terms upon his callet.

Iago. Why did he so?

Desdemona. I do not know. I am sure I am none such.

Iago. Do not weep, do not weep. Alas the day!

Emilia. Hath she forsook so many noble matches, 125
    Her father and her country and her friends,
    To be called whore? Would it not make one weep?

Desdemona. It is my wretched fortune.

Iago.   Beshrew him for 't!
    How comes this trick upon him?

Desdemona.   Nay, Heaven doth know.

Emilia. I will be hanged if some eternal villain, 130
    Some busy and insinuating rogue,
    Some cogging, cozening slave, to get some office,
    Have not devised this slander. I'll be hanged else.

Iago. Fie, there is no such man, it is impossible.

---

104. go by water: be expressed in tears   **109. misuse:** mistake

Desdemona. If any such there be, heaven pardon him!   135
Emilia. A halter pardon him! And Hell gnaw his bones!
    Why should he call her whore? Who keeps her company?
    What place? What time? What form? What likelihood?
    The Moor's abused by some most villainous knave,
    Some base notorious knave, some scurvy fellow.   140
    O Heaven, that such companions° Thou'dst unfold,°
    And put in every honest hand a whip
    To lash the rascals naked through the world
    Even from the east to the west!
Iago.   Speak withindoor.°
Emilia. Oh, fie upon them! Some such squire he was   145
    That turned your wit the seamy side without,
    And made you to suspect me with the Moor.
Iago. You are a foot. Go to.°
Desdemona.   O good Iago,
    What shall I do to win my lord again?
    Good friend, go to him, for, by this light of Heaven,   150
    I know not how I lost him. Here I kneel.
    If e'er my will did trespass 'gainst his love
    Either in discourse of thought or actual deed,
    Or that mine eyes, mine ears, or any sense
    Delighted them in any other form,   155
    Or that I do not yet, and ever did,
    And ever will, though he do shake me off
    To beggarly divorcement, love him dearly,
    Comfort forswear me! Unkindness may do much,
    And his unkindness may defeat my life,   160
    But never taint my love. I cannot say "whore,"
    It doth abhor me now I speak the word.
    To do the act that might the addition° earn
    Not the world's mass of vanity° could make me.
Iago. I pray you be content, 'tis but his humor.   165
    The business of the state does him offense,
    And he does chide with you.
Desdemona.   If 'twere no other—
Iago. 'Tis but so, I warrant. *(Trumpets within.)*
    Hark how these instruments summon to supper!
    The messengers of Venice stay the meat.°   170
    Go in, and weep not, all things shall be well.

    (Exeunt DESDEMONA *and* EMILIA. *Enter* RODERIGO.*)*

    How now, Roderigo!
Roderigo. I do not find that thou dealest justly with me.

---

141. **companions:** low creatures   **unfold:** bring to light   144. **Speak withindoor:** Don't shout so
loud that all the street will hear you.   148. **Go to:** an expression of derision   163. **addition:** title
164. **vanity:** i.e., riches   170. **meat:** serving of supper

Iago. What in the contrary?

Roderigo. Every day thou daffest me with some device, Iago, and rather, as it seems to me now, keepest from me all conveniency than suppliest me with the least advantage of hope. I will indeed no longer endure it, nor am I yet persuaded to put up in peace what already I have foolishly suffered.   179

Iago. Will you hear me, Roderigo?

Roderigo. Faith, I have heard too much, for your words and performances are no kin together.

Iago. You charge me most unjustly.

Roderigo. With naught but truth. I have wasted myself out of my means. The jewels you have had from me to deliver to Desdemona would half have corrupted a votarist.° You have told me she hath received them, and returned me expectations and comforts of sudden respect and acquaintance, but I find none.   188

Iago. Well, go to, very well.

Roderigo. Very well! Go to! I cannot go to, man, nor'tis not very well. By this hand, I say 'tis very scurvy, and begin to find myself fopped in it.   192

Iago. Very well.

Roderigo. I tell you 'tis not very well. I will make myself known to Desdemona. If she will return me my jewels, I will give over my suit and repent my unlawful solicitation. If not, assure yourself I will seek satisfaction of you.   197

Iago. You have said now.°

Roderigo. Aye, and said nothing but what I protest intendment of doing.

Iago. Why, now I see there's mettle in thee, and even from this instant do build on thee a better opinion than ever before. Give me thy hand, Roderigo. Thou hast taken against me a most just exception, but yet I protest I have dealt most directly in thy affair.   204

Roderigo. It hath not appeared.

Iago. I grant indeed it hath not appeared, and your suspicion is not without wit and judgment. But, Roderigo, if thou hast that in thee indeed which I have greater reason to believe now than ever—I mean purpose, courage, and valor—this night show it. If thou the next night following enjoy not Desdemona, take me from this world with treachery and devise engines° for my life.   211

Roderigo. Well, what is it? Is it within reason and compass?

Iago. Sir, there is especial commission come from Venice to depute Cassio in Othello's place.

Roderigo. Is that true? Why, then Othello and Desdemona return again to Venice.   216

Iago. Oh, no. He goes into Mauritania, and takes away with him the fair Desdemona, unless his abode be lingered here by some accident, wherein none can be so determinate as the removing of Cassio.

Roderigo. How do you mean, "removing of" him?   220

Iago. Why, by making him uncapable of Othello's place, knocking out his brains.

Roderigo. And that you would have me to do?

Iago. Aye, if you dare do yourself a profit and a right. He sups tonight with a harlotry,° and thither will I go to him. He knows not yet of his honorable fortune. If you will watch his going thence, which I will fashion to fall out

---

186. **votarist:** nun   198. **You . . . now:** or in modern slang, "Oh yeah."   211. **engines:** instruments of torture   225. **harlotry:** harlot

between twelve and one, you may take him at your pleasure. I will be near to second your attempt, and he shall fall between us. Come, stand not amazed at it, but go along with me. I will show you such a necessity in his death that you shall think yourself bound to put it on him. It is now high suppertime and the night grows to waste. About it.

232

Roderigo. I will hear further reason for this.

Iago. And you shall be satisfied. *(Exeunt.)*

Scene 3.
Another room in the castle.

(Enter OTHELLO, LODOVICO, DESDEMONA, EMILIA, *and* ATTENDANTS.*)*

Lodovico. I do beseech you, sir, trouble yourself no further.

Othello. Oh, pardon me, 'twill do me good to walk.

Lodovico. Madam, good night. I humbly thank your ladyship.

Desdemona. Your Honor is most welcome.

Othello.   Will you walk, sir?

Oh—Desdemona—   5

Desdemona. My lord?

Othello. Get you to bed on the instant, I will be returned forthwith.

Dismiss your attendant there. Look it be done.

Desdemona. I will, my lord.

(Exeunt OTHELLO, LODOVICO, *and* ATTENDANTS.*)*

Emilia. How goes it now? He looks gentler than he did.   10

Desdemona. He says he will return incontinent.°

He hath commanded me to go to bed,

And bade me to dismiss you.

Emilia.   Dismiss me!

Desdemona. It was his bidding, therefore, good Emilia,

Give me my nightly wearing, and adieu.   15

We must not now displease him.

Emilia. I would you had never seen him!

Desdemona. So would not I. My love doth so approve him

That even his stubbornness, his checks, his frowns—

Prithee, unpin me—have grace and favor in them.   20

Emilia. I have laid those sheets you bade me on the bed.

Desdemona. All's one. Good faith, how foolish are our minds!

If I do die before thee, prithee shroud me

In one of those same sheets.

Emilia.   Come, come, you talk.

Desdemona. My mother had a maid called Barbary.   25

She was in love, and he she loved proved mad

And did forsake her. She had a song of "willow"°—

An old thing 'twas, but it expressed her fortune,

And she died singing it. That song tonight

---

11. **incontinent:** immediately   27. **willow:** the emblem of the forlorn lover

Will not go from my mind. I have much to do 30
But to go hang my head all at one side
And sing it like poor Barbary. Prithee, dispatch.
Emilia. Shall I go fetch your nightgown?
Desdemona.   No, unpin me here.
This Lodovico is a proper man.
Emilia. A very handsome man. 35
Desdemona. He speaks well.
Emilia. I know a lady in Venice would have walked barefoot to Palestine for a touch
of his nether lip.
Desdemona *(Singing.)*
   "The poor soul sat sighing by a sycamore tree,
      Sing all a green willow. 40
   Her hand on her bosom, her head on her knee,
      Sing willow, willow, willow.
   The fresh streams ran by her, and murmured her moans,
      Sing willow, willow, willow.
   Her salt tears fell from her, and softened the stones—" 45
Lay by these—*(Singing.)*
   "Sing willow, willow, willow,"
Prithee, hie thee, he'll come anon.—*(Singing.)*
   "Sing all a green willow must be my garland.
   Let nobody blame him, his scorn I approve—" 50
Nay, that's not next. Hark! Who is 't that knocks?
Emilia. It's the wind.
Desdemona *(Singing.)*
      "I called my love false love, but what said he then?
         Sing willow, willow, willow.
      If I court moe° women, you'll couch with moe men." 55
So get thee gone, good night. Mine eyes do itch.
Doth that bode weeping?
Emilia.   'Tis neither here nor there.
Desdemona. I have heard it said so. Oh, these men, these men!
Dost thou in conscience think—tell me, Emilia—
That there be women do abuse their husbands 60
In such gross kind?
Emilia.   There be some such, no question.
Desdemona. Wouldst thou do such a deed for all the world?
Emilia. Why, would not you?
Desdemona.   No, by this heavenly light!
Emilia. Nor I neither by this heavenly light.
I might do 't as well i' the dark. 65
Desdemona. Would thou do such a deed for all the world?
Emilia. The world's a huge thing. It is a great price
For a small vice.
Desdemona.   In troth, I think thou wouldst not.

---

55. **moe:** more

Emilia. In troth, I think I should, and undo 't when I had done. Marry, I would
not do such a thing for a joint ring,° nor for measures of lawn, nor for gowns,
petticoats, nor caps, nor any petty exhibition;° but for the whole world—why,
who would not make her husband a cuckold to make him a monarch? I should
venture Purgatory for 't. 73

Desdemona. Beshrew me if I would do such a wrong for the whole world.

Emilia. Why, the wrong is but a wrong i' the world, and having the world for your
labor, 'tis a wrong in your own world and you might quickly make it right. 78

Desdemona. I do not think there is any such woman.

Emilia. Yes, a dozen, and as many to the vantage as would store the world they
played for.
But I do think it is their husbands' faults
If wives do fall. Say that they slack their duties
And pour our treasures into foreign laps,
Or else break out in peevish jealousies, 85
Throwing restraint upon us, or say they strike us,
Or scant our former having in despite,°
Why, we have galls,° and though we have some grace,
Yet have we some revenge. Let husbands know
Their wives have sense like them. They see and smell 90
And have their palates both for sweet and sour,
As husbands have. What is it that they do
When they change us for others? Is it sport?
I think it is. And doth affection breed it?
I think it doth. Is 't frailty that thus errs? 95
It is so too. And have not we affections,
Desires for sport, and frailty, as men have?
Then let them use us well. Else let them know
The ills we do, their ills instruct us so.

Desdemona. Good night, good night. Heaven me such uses send, 100
Not to pick bad from bad, but by bad mend! *(Exeunt.)*

ACT 5
Scene 1.
Cyprus. A street.

(Enter IAGO *and* RODERIGO.*)*

Iago. Here, stand behind this bulk, straight will he come.
Wear thy good rapier bare, and put it home.
Quick, quick, fear nothing. I'll be at thy elbow.
It makes us, or it mars us. Think on that,
And fix most firm thy resolution. 5

Roderigo. Be near at hand. I may miscarry in 't.

Iago. Here, at thy hand. Be bold, and take thy stand. *(Retires.)*

---

70. **joint ring:** ring made in two pieces, a lover's gift   71. **petty exhibition:** small allowance of
money   87. **scant . . . despite:** for spite cut down our allowance   88. **galls:** bile, the cause of
bitterness

Roderigo. I have no great devotion to the deed,
  And yet he hath given me satisfying reasons.
  'Tis but a man gone. Forth, my sword. He dies.   10
Iago. I have rubbed this young quat° almost to the sense,°
  And he grows angry. Now, whether he kill Cassio,
  Or Cassio him, or each do kill the other,
  Every way makes my gain. Live Roderigo,
  He calls me to a restitution large   15
  Of gold and jewels that I bobbed from him
  As gifts to Desdemona.
  It must not be. If Cassio do remain,
  He hath a daily beauty in his life
  That makes me ugly,° and besides, the Moor   20
  May unfold me to him. There stand I in much peril.
  No, he must die. Be 't so. I hear him coming. (*Enter* CASSIO.)
Roderigo. I know his gait, 'tis he. Villain, thou diest!

  (*Makes a pass at* CASSIO.)

Cassio. That thrust had been mine enemy indeed
  But that my coat is better than thou know'st.   25
  I will make proof of thine. (*Draws, and wounds* RODERIGO.)
Roderigo.   Oh, I am slain!

  (IAGO *from behind wounds* CASSIO *in the leg, and exits.*)

Cassio. I am maimed for ever. Help, ho! Murder! Murder!

  (*Falls. Enter* OTHELLO.)

Othello. The voice of Cassio. Iago keeps his word.
Roderigo. Oh, villain that I am!
Othello.   It is even so.
Cassio. Oh, help, ho! Light! A surgeon!   30
Othello. 'Tis he. O brave Iago, honest and just,
  That hast such noble sense of thy friend's wrong!
  Thou teachest me. Minion,° your dear friend lies dead,
  And your unblest fate hies. Strumpet, I come!
  Forth of my heart those charms, thine eyes, are blotted.   35
  Thy bed lust-stained shall with lust's blood be spotted.

  (*Exit. Enter* LODOVICO *and* GRATIANO.)

Cassio. What ho! No watch?° No passage?° Murder! Murder!
Gratiano. 'Tis some mischance, the cry is very direful.
Cassio. Oh, help!
Lodovico. Hark!   40
Roderigo. Oh, wretched villain!

---

11. **quat:** pimple   **sense:** quick   19–20. **He . . . ugly:** By comparison with him I am a poor thing.
Iago is conscious of his lack of social graces.   33. **Minion:** Darling, in a bad sense   37. **watch:** police   **No passage?:** Nobody passing?

Lodovico. Two or three groan. It is a heavy° night.
> These may be counterfeits. Let's think 't unsafe
> To come in to the cry without more help.

Roderigo. Nobody come? Then I shall bleed to death.   45

Lodovico. Hark! *(Re-enter* IAGO, *with a light.)*

Gratiano. Here's one comes in his shirt, with light and weapons.

Iago. Who's there? Whose noise is this that cries on murder?

Lodovico. We do not know.

Iago.   Did not you hear a cry?

Cassio. Here, here! For Heaven's sake, help me!

Iago.   What's the matter?   50

Gratiano. This is Othello's Ancient, as I take it.

Lodovico. The same indeed, a very valiant fellow.

Iago. What are you here that cry so grievously?

Cassio. Iago? Oh, I am spoiled, undone by villains! Give me some help.   55

Iago. Oh me, Lieutenant! What villains have done this?

Cassio. I think that one of them is hereabout,
> And cannot make away.

Iago.   Oh, treacherous villains!
> *(To* LODOVICO *and* GRATIANO.*)* What are you there?
> Come in and give some help.

Roderigo.   Oh, help me here!   60

Cassio. That's one of them.

Iago.   Oh, murderous slave! Oh, villain!

(Stabs RODERIGO.*)*

Roderigo. Oh, damned Iago! Oh, inhuman dog!

Iago. Kill men i' the dark! Where be these bloody thieves?
> How silent is this town! Ho! Murder! Murder!
> What may you be? Are you of good or evil?   65

Lodovico. As you shall prove us, praise us.

Iago. Signior Lodovico?

Lodovico. He, sir.

Iago. I cry your mercy. Here's Cassio hurt by villains.

Gratiano. Cassio!   70

Iago. How is 't, brother?

Cassio. My leg is cut in two.

Iago.   Marry, Heaven forbid!
> Light, gentlemen. I'll bind it with my shirt. *(Enter* BIANCA.*)*

Bianca. What is the matter, ho? Who is 't that cried?

Iago. Who is 't that cried!   75

Bianca. Oh, my dear Cassio! My sweet Cassio!
> Oh, Cassio, Cassio, Cassio!

Iago. Oh, notable strumpet! Cassio, may you suspect
> Who they should be that have thus mangled you?

Cassio. No.   80

---

42. **heavy:** thick

Gratiano. I am sorry to find you thus. I have been to seek you.

Iago. Lend me a garter. Oh, for a chair,
    To bear him easily hence!

Bianca. Alas, he faints! Oh, Cassio, Cassio, Cassio!

Iago. Gentlemen all, I do suspect this trash   85
    To be a party in this injury.
    Patience awhile, good Cassio. Come, come
    Lend me a light. Know we this face or no?
    Alas, my friend and my dear countryman
    Roderigo? No—yes, sure. Oh Heaven! Roderigo.   90

Gratiano. What, of Venice?

Iago. Even he, sir. Did you know him?

Gratiano.   Know him! Aye.

Iago. Signior Gratiano? I cry you gentle pardon.
    These bloody accidents must excuse my manners,
    That so neglected you.

Gratiano.   I am glad to see you.   95

Iago. How do you, Cassio? Oh, a chair, a chair!

Gratiano. Roderigo!

Iago. He, he, 'tis he. *(A chair brought in.)* Oh, that's well said, the chair.
    Some good man bear him carefully from hence.
    I'll fetch the General's surgeon. *(To* BIANCA.*)* For you, mistress,   100
    Save you your labor. He that lies slain here, Cassio,
    Was my dear friend. What malice between you?

Cassio. None in the world, nor do I know the man.

Iago *(To* BIANCA.*)* What, look you pale? Oh, bear him out o' the air.

*(*CASSIO *and* RODERIGO *are borne off.)*

    Stay you, good gentlemen. Look you pale, mistress?   105
    Do you perceive the gastness of her eye?
    Nay, if you stare, we shall hear more anon.
    Behold her well, I pray you look upon her.
    Do you see, gentlemen? Nay, guiltiness will speak,
    Though tongues were out of use. *(Enter* EMILIA.*)*   110

Emilia. 'Las, what's the matter? What's the matter, husband?

Iago. Cassio hath here been set on in the dark
    By Roderigo and fellows that are 'scaped.
    He's almost slain, and Roderigo dead.

Emilia. Alas, good gentleman! Alas, good Cassio!   115

Iago. This is the fruit of whoring. Prithee, Emilia,
    Go know of Cassio where he supped tonight.
    What, do you shake at that?

Bianca. He supped at my house, but I therefore shake not.

Iago. Oh, did he so? I charge you, go with me.   120

Emilia. Fie, fie upon thee, strumpet!

Bianca. I am no strumpet, but of life as honest
    As you that thus abuse me.

Emilia.   As I! Foh! Fie upon thee!

Iago. Kind gentlemen, let's go see poor Cassio dressed.°
    Come, mistress, you must tell's another tale. 125
    Emilia, run you to the citadel,
    And tell my lord and lady what hath happened!
    Will you go on afore? I pray. *(Aside.)* This is the night
    That either makes me or fordoes me quite. *(Exeunt.)*

Scene 2.

A bedchamber in the castle. DESDEMONA *in bed asleep, a light burning.*

(Enter OTHELLO.*)*

Othello. It is the cause,° it is the cause, my soul.
    Let me not name it to you, you chaste stars!
    It is the cause. Yet I'll not shed her blood,
    Nor scar that whiter skin of hers than snow
    And smooth as monumental alabaster. 5
    Yet she must die, else she'll betray more men.
    Put out the light, and then put out the light.
    If I quench thee, thou flaming minister,°
    I can again thy former light restore,
    Should I repent me. But once put out thy light, 10
    Thou cunning'st° pattern of excelling nature,
    I know not where is that Promethean heat
    That can thy light relume. When I have plucked the rose,
    I cannot give it vital growth again,
    It needs must wither. I'll smell it on the tree. *(Kissing her.)* 15
    Ah, balmy breath, that dost almost persuade
    Justice to break her sword! One more, one more.
    Be thus when thou art dead, and I will kill thee,
    And love thee after. One more, and this the last.
    So sweet was ne'er so fatal. I must weep, 20
    But they are cruel tears. This sorrow's heavenly,
    It strikes where it doth love. She wakes.
Desdemona. Who's there? Othello?
Othello.   Aye, Desdemona.
Desdemona. Will you come to bed, my lord?
Othello. Have you prayed tonight, Desdemona?
Desdemona.   Aye, my lord. 25
Othello. If you bethink yourself of any crime
    Unreconciled as yet to Heaven and grace,
    Solicit for it straight.
Desdemona. Alas, my lord, what may you mean by that?

---

124. **dressed:** i.e., his wound dressed   1. **It . . . cause:** The meaning of the opening lines of this speech has been much discussed. The *cause* is Desdemona's supposed faithless ness; Othello, at this moment, sees himself as embodied justice, the avenger of man betrayed by woman.   8. **minister:** servant   11. **cunning'st:** most skillfully made

Othello. Well, do it, and be brief. I will walk by.   30
    I would not kill thy unpreparèd spirit.
    No, Heaven forfend! I would not kill thy soul.
Desdemona. Talk you of killing?
Othello.   Aye, I do.
Desdemona.   Then Heaven
    Have mercy on me!
Othello.   Amen, with all my heart!
Desdemona. If you say so, I hope you will not kill me.   35
Othello. Hum!
Desdemona. And yet I fear you, for you are fatal then
    When your eyes roll so. Why I should fear I know not,
    Since guiltiness I know not, but yet I feel I fear.
Othello. Think on thy sins.
Desdemona.   They are loves I bear to you.   40
Othello. Aye, and for that thou diest.
Desdemona. That death's unnatural that kills for loving.
    Alas, why gnaw you so your nether lip?
    Some bloody passion shakes your very frame.
    These are portents, but yet I hope, I hope,   45
    They do not point on me.
Othello.   Peace, and be still!
Desdemona. I will so. What's the matter?
Othello. That handkerchief which I so loved and gave thee
    Thou gavest to Cassio.
Desdemona.   No, by my life and soul!
    Send for the man, and ask him.
Othello.   Sweet soul, take heed,   50
    Take heed of perjury, thou art on thy deathbed.
Desdemona. Aye, but not yet to die.
Othello.   Yes, presently.°
    Therefore confess thee freely of thy sin,
    For to deny each article with oath
    Cannot remove nor choke the strong conception   55
    That I do groan withal. Thou art to die.
Desdemona. Then Lord have mercy on me!
Othello.   I say amen.
Desdemona. And have you mercy too! I never did
    Offend you in my life, never loved Cassio
    But with such general warranty of Heaven   60
    As I might love. I never gave him token.
Othello. By Heaven, I saw my handkerchief in 's hand.
    O perjured woman! Thou dost stone° my heart,
    And makest me call what I intend to do
    A murder, which I thought a sacrifice.   65
    I saw the handkerchief.

---

52. **presently:** at once   63. **stone:** turn to stone

Desdemona.   He found it, then,
    I never gave it him. Send for him hither.
    Let him confess a truth.
Othello.   He hath confessed.
Desdemona. What, my lord?
Othello. That he hath used thee.
Desdemona.   How? Unlawfully?
Othello.   Aye.   70
Desdemona. He will not say so.
Othello.   No, his mouth is stopped.
    Honest Iago hath ta'en order for 't.
Desdemona. Oh, my fear interprets! What, is he dead?
Othello. Had all his hairs been lives, my great revenge
    Had stomach for them all.   75
Desdemona. Alas, he is betrayed, and I undone!
Othello. Out, strumpet! Weep'st thou for him to my face?
Desdemona. Oh, banish me, my lord, but kill me not!
Othello. Down, strumpet!
Desdemona. Kill me tomorrow, let me live tonight!   80
Othello. Nay, if you strive—
Desdemona. But half an hour!
Othello.   Being done, there is no pause.
Desdemona. But while I say one prayer!
Othello.   It is too late. *(He stifles her.)*
Emilia *(Within.)* My lord, my lord! What ho! My lord, my lord!
Othello. What noise is this? Not dead? Not yet quite dead?   85
    I that am cruel am yet merciful,
    I would not have thee linger in thy pain.
    So, so.
Emilia *(Within.)* What ho! My lord, my lord!
Othello.   Who's there?
Emilia *(Within.)* Oh, good my lord, I would speak a word with you!
Othello. Yes, 'tis Emilia. By and by. She's dead.   90
    'Tis like she comes to speak of Cassio's death.
    The noise was here. Ha! No more moving?
    Still as the grave. Shall she come in? Were 't good?
    I think she stirs again. No. What's best to do?
    If she come in, she'll sure speak to my wife.   95
    My wife! My wife! What wife? I have no wife.
    Oh, insupportable! Oh, heavy hour!
    Methinks it should be now a huge eclipse
    Of sun and moon, and that the affrighted globe
    Should yawn at alteration.
Emilia *(Within.)*   I do beseech you   100
    That I may speak with you, O good my lord!
Othello. I had forgot thee. Oh, come in, Emilia.
    Soft, by and by. Let me the curtains° draw.

---

103. **curtains:** i.e., of the bed

What art thou? *(Unlocks the door. Enter* EMILIA.*)*
                   What's the matter with thee now?
Emilia. Oh, my good lord, yonder's foul murders done!   105
Othello. What, now?
Emilia. But now, my lord.
Othello. It is the very error of the moon.
    She comes more nearer earth than she was wont
    And makes men mad.   110
Emilia. Cassio, my lord, hath killed a young Venetian
    Called Roderigo.
Othello.   Roderigo killed!
    And Cassio killed!
Emilia.   No, Cassio is not killed.
Othello. Not Cassio killed! Then murder's out of tune,
    And sweet revenge grows harsh.   115
Desdemona. Oh, falsely, falsely murdered!
Emilia.   Alas, what cry is that?
Othello. That! What?
Emilia. Out and alas! That was my lady's voice.
    Help! Help, ho! Help! O lady, speak again!
    Sweet Desdemona! O sweet mistress, speak!   120
Desdemona. A guiltless death I die.
Emilia. Oh, who hath done this deed?
Desdemona. Nobody, I myself. Farewell.
    Commend me to my kind lord. Oh, farewell! *(Dies.)*
Othello. Why, how should she be murdered?
Emilia.   Alas, who knows?   125
Othello. You heard her say herself it was not I.
Emilia. She said so. I must needs report the truth.
Othello. She's like a liar gone to burning Hell.
    'Twas I that killed her.
Emilia.   Oh, the more angel she,
    And you the blacker devil!   130
Othello. She turned to folly, and she was a whore.
Emilia. Thou dost belie her, and thou art a devil.
Othello. She was false as water.
Emilia.   Thou art rash as fire to say
    That she was false. Oh, she was heavenly true!
Othello. Cassio did top her, ask thy husband else.   135
    Oh, I were damned beneath all depth in Hell
    But that I did proceed upon just grounds
    To this extremity. Thy husband knew it all.
Emilia. My husband!
Othello. Thy husband.   140
Emilia. That she was false to wedlock?
Othello. Aye, with Cassio. Nay, had she been true,
    If Heaven would make me such another world
    Of one entire and perfect chrysolite,
    I'd not have sold her for it.

Emilia.   My husband!   145
Othello. Aye, 'twas he that told me first.
    An honest man he is, and hates the slime
    That sticks on filthy deeds.
Emilia.   My husband!
Othello. What needs this iteration, woman? I say thy husband.
Emilia. Oh, mistress, villainy hath made mocks with love!   150
    My husband say that she was false!
Othello.   He, woman.
    I say thy husband. Dost understand the word?
    My friend, thy husband, honest, honest Iago.
Emilia. If he say so, may his pernicious soul
    Rot half a grain a day! He lies to the heart.   155
    She was too fond of her most filthy bargain.
Othello. Ha!
Emilia. Do thy worst.
    This deed of thine is no more worthy Heaven
    Than thou wast worthy her.
Othello.   Peace, you were best.   160
Emilia. Thou hast not half that power to do me harm
    As I have to be hurt. O gull! O dolt!
    As ignorant as dirt! Thou hast done a deed—
    I care not for thy sword, I'll make thee known,
    Though I lost twenty lives. Help! Help! ho! Help!   165
    The Moor hath killed my mistress! Murder! Murder!
    (Enter MONTANO, GRATIANO, IAGO, *and others.)*
Montano. What is the matter? How now, General!
Emilia. Oh, are you come, Iago? You have done well,
    That men must lay their murders on your neck.
Gratiano. What is the matter?   170
Emilia. Disprove this villain, if thou be'st a man.
    He says thou told'st him that his wife was false.
    I know thou didst not, thou'rt not such a villain.
    Speak, for my heart is full.
Iago. I told him what I thought, and told no more   175
    Than what he found himself was apt and true.
Emilia. But did you ever tell him she was false?
Iago. I did.
Emilia. You told a lie, an odious, damnèd lie,
    Upon my soul, a lie, a wicked lie!   180
    She false with Cassio! Did you say with Cassio?
Iago. With Cassio, mistress. Go to, charm your tongue.°
Emilia. I will not charm my tongue, I am bound to speak.
    My mistress here lies murdered in her bed.
All. Oh, Heavens forfend!   185
Emilia. And your reports have set the murder on.

---

182. **charm your tongue:** be silent

Othello. Nay, stare not, masters. It is true indeed.

Gratiano. 'Tis a strange truth.

Montano. Oh, monstrous act!

Emilia.   Villainy, villainy, villainy!
    I think upon 't. I think I smell 't. Oh, villainy!   190
    I thought so then. I'll kill myself for grief.
    Oh, villainy, villainy!

Iago. What, are you mad? I charge you, get you home.

Emilia. Good gentlemen, let me have leave to speak.
    'Tis proper I obey him, but not now.   195
    Perchance, Iago, I will ne'er go home.

Othello. Oh! Oh! Oh! *(Falling on the bed.)*

Emilia.   Nay, lay thee down and roar,
    For thou has killed the sweetest innocent
    That e'er did lift up eye.

Othello *(Rising.)*   Oh, she was foul!
    I scarce did know you, Uncle. There lies your niece,   200
    Whose breath indeed these hands have newly stopped.
    I know this act shows horrible and grim.

Gratiano. Poor Desdemona! I am glad thy father's dead.
    Thy match was mortal to him, and pure grief
    Shore his old thread in twain. Did he live now,   205
    This sight would make him do a desperate turn—
    Yea, curse his better angel from his side,
    And fall to reprobation.°

Othello. 'Tis pitiful, but yet Iago knows
    That she with Cassio hath the act of shame   210
    A thousand times committed. Cassio confessed it.
    And she did gratify his amorous works
    With that recognizance and pledge of love
    Which I first gave her, I saw it in his hand.
    It was a handkerchief, an antique token   215
    My father gave my mother.

Emilia. Oh, Heaven! Oh, heavenly powers!

Iago. 'Zounds! Hold your peace.

Emilia.   'Twill out, 'twill out. I peace!
    No, I will speak as liberal as the north.°
    Let Heaven and men and devils, let them all,
    All, all, cry shame against me, yet I'll speak.   220

Iago. Be wise, and get you home.

Emilia.   I will not.

    (IAGO *offers to stab* EMILIA.)

Gratiano.   Fie!
    Your sword upon a woman!

---

208. **reprobation:** damnation; i.e., by self-murder   219. **liberal . . . north:** as freely as the north wind, which is loud and bitter

Emilia. O thou dull Moor! That handkerchief thou speak'st of
    I found by fortune and did give my husband,   225
    For often with a solemn earnestness,
    More than indeed belonged to such a trifle,
    He begged of me to steal it.
Iago.   Villainous whore!
Emilia. She give it Cassio! No, alas, I found it,
    And I did give 't my husband.
Iago.   Filth, thou liest!   230
Emilia. By Heaven, I do not, I do not, gentlemen.
    Oh, murderous coxcomb! What should such a fool
    Do with so good a wife!
Othello.   Are there no stones° in Heaven
    But what serve for the thunder? Precious villain!

(He runs at IAGO. IAGO, *from behind, stabs* EMILIA, *and exits.)*

Gratiano. The woman falls. Sure, he hath killed his wife.   235
Emilia. Aye. Aye. Oh, lay me by my mistress' side.
Gratiano. He's gone, but his wife's killed.
Montano. 'Tis a notorious villain. Take you this weapon,
    Which I have here recovered from the Moor.
    Come, guard the door without, let him not pass,   240
    But kill him rather. I'll after that same villain,
    For 'tis a damnèd slave. *(Exeunt all but* OTHELLO *and* EMILIA.*)*
Othello.   I am not valiant neither,
    But every puny whipster gets my sword.
    But why should honor outlive honesty?
    Let it go all.
Emilia.   What did thy song bode, lady?   245
    Hark, canst thou hear me? I will play the swan,
    And die in music. *(Singing.)*
               "Willow, willow, willow."
    Moor, she was chaste. She loved thee, cruel Moor,
    So come my soul to bliss as I speak true.
    So speaking as I think, I die, I die. *(Dies.)*   250
Othello. I have another weapon in this chamber.
    It is a sword of Spain, the ice brook's temper.—
    Oh, here it is. Uncle, I must come forth.
Gratiano *(within.)* If thou attempt it, it will cost thee dear.
    Thou hast no weapon, and perforce must suffer.   255
Othello. Look in upon me then, and speak with me, Or, naked° as I am, I will
    assault thee. *(Re-enter* GRATIANO.*)*
Gratiano. What is the matter?
Othello.   Behold, I have a weapon,
    A better never did itself sustain
    Upon a soldier's thigh. I have seen the day   260
    That with this little arm and this good sword

---

233. **stones:** thunderbolts

I have made my way through more impediments
Than twenty times your stop. But, oh, vain boast!
Who can control his fate? 'Tis not so now.
Be not afraid, though you do see me weaponed.   265
Here is my journey's end, here is my butt°
And very sea mark of my utmost sail.
Do you go back dismayed? 'Tis a lost fear.
Man but a rush° against Othello's breast,
And he retires. Where should Othello go?   270
Now, how dost thou look now? O ill-starred wench!
Pale as thy smock! When we shall meet at compt,°
This look of thine will hurl my soul from Heaven
And fiends will snatch at it. Cold, cold, my girl!
Even like thy chastity. Oh, cursed slave!   275
Whip me, ye devils,
From the possession of this heavenly sight!
Blow me about in winds! Roast me in sulphur!
Wash me in steep-down gulfs of liquid fire!
O Desdemona! Desdemona! Dead!   280
Oh! Oh! Oh!

(*Enter* LODOVICO, MONTANO, CASSIO *carried in a chair, and* OFFICERS *with* IAGO, *prisoner.*)

Lodovico. Where is this rash and most unfortunate man?
Othello. That's he that was Othello. Here I am.
Lodovico. Where is the viper? Bring the villain forth.
Othello. I look down toward his feet,° but that's a fable.   285
    If that thou be'st a devil, I cannot kill thee. (*Wounds* IAGO.)
Lodovico. Wrench his sword from him.
Iago.   I bleed, sir, but not killed.
Othello. I am not sorry neither. I'd have thee live,
    For, in my sense, 'tis happiness to die.
Lodovico. O thou Othello, that wert once so good,   290
    Fall'n in the practice° of a damnèd slave,
    What shall be said to thee?
Othello.   Why, anything.
    An honorable murderer, if you will,
    For naught did I in hate, but all in honor.
Lodovico. This wretch hath part confessed his villainy.   295
    Did you and he consent in Cassio's death?
Othello. Aye.
Cassio. Dear General, I never gave you cause.
Othello. I do believe it, and I ask your pardon.
    Will you, I pray, demand that demi-devil   300
    Why he hath thus ensnared my soul and body?

---

257. **naked:** unarmed   266. **butt:** aim   269. **Man . . . rush:** Attack with only a reed
272. **compt:** account; i.e., the Day of Judgment   285. **toward his feet:** i.e., to see if he has the
cloven hoot of a devil   291. **Fall'n . . . practice:** Destroyed by the plotting

Iago. Demand me nothing. What you know, you know.
　　From this time forth I never will speak word.

Lodovico. What, not to pray?

Gratiano. 　　　　　　Torments will ope your lips.

Othello. Well, thou dost best. 305

Lodovico. Sir, you shall understand what hath befall'n,
　　Which, as I think, you know not. Here is a letter
　　Found in the pocket of the slain Roderigo,
　　And here another. The one of them imports
　　The death of Cassio to be undertook 310
　　By Roderigo.

Othello. Oh, villain!

Cassio. 　　　　　Most heathenish and most gross!

Lodovico. Now here's another discontented paper,
　　Found in his pocket too. And this, it seems,
　　Roderigo meant to have sent this damnèd villain 315
　　But that, belike, Iago in the interim
　　Came in and satisfied him.

Othello. 　　　　　　　　Oh, the pernicious caitiff!
　　How come you, Cassio, by that handkerchief
　　That was my wife's?

Cassio. 　　　　　I found it in my chamber.
　　And he himself confessed but even now 320
　　That there he dropped it for a special purpose
　　Which wrought to his desire.

Othello. 　　　　　　　　O fool! Fool! Fool!

Cassio. There is besides in Roderigo's letter
　　How he upbraids Iago, that he made him
　　Brave° me upon the watch, whereon it came 325
　　That I was cast.° And even but now he spake
　　After long seeming dead, Iago hurt him,
　　Iago set him on.

Lodovico. You must forsake this room, and go with us.
　　Your power and your command is taken off, 330
　　And Cassio rules in Cyprus. For this slave,
　　If there be any cunning cruelty
　　That can torment him much and hold him long,°
　　It shall be his. You shall close prisoner rest
　　Till that the nature of your fault be known 335
　　To the Venetian state. Come, bring away.

Othello. Soft you, a word or two before you go.
　　I have done the state some service, and they know 't.
　　No more of that. I pray you, in your letters,
　　When you shall these unlucky deeds relate, 340
　　Speak of me as I am, nothing extenuate,
　　Nor set down aught in malice. Then must you speak
　　Of one that loved not wisely but too well;

---

325. **Brave:** Insult　326. **cast:** dismissed　333. **long:** i.e., in dying

Of one not easily jealous, but, being wrought,
Perplexed in the extreme; of one whose hand, 345
Like the base Indian, threw a pearl away
Richer than all his tribe; of one whose subdued eyes,
Albeit unusèd to the melting mood,
Drop tears as fast as the Arabian trees
Their medicinable gum. Set you down this, 350
And say besides that in Aleppo once,
Where a malignant and a turbaned Turk
Beat a Venetian and traduced the state,
I took by the throat the circumcisèd dog
And smote him, thus. *(Stabs himself.)* 355
Lodovico. Oh, bloody period!
Gratiano.   All that's spoke is marred.
Othello. I kissed thee ere I killed thee. No way but this,
   Killing myself, to die upon a kiss. *(Falls on the bed, and dies.)*
Cassio. This did I fear, but thought he had no weapon,
   For he was great of heart.
Lodovico *(To* IAGO.*)*   O Spartan° dog, 360
   More fell° than anguish, hunger, or the sea!
   Look on the tragic loading of this bed:
   This is thy work. The object poisons sight,
   Let it be hid.° Gratiano, keep the house,
   And seize upon the fortunes of the Moor, 365
   For they succeed on you. To you, Lord Governor,
   Remains the censure of this hellish villain,
   The time, the place, the torture.
   Oh, enforce it!
   Myself will straight aboard, and to the state 370
   This heavy act with heavy heart relate. *(Exeunt.)*

Explorations of the Text

Act I

1. As the play opens, we meet Iago before we are introduced to the title character Othello. Does it seem significant to you that we know a lot about Iago before we directly encounter Othello himself in scene ii? How would you describe their first interaction?

2. Look closely at the speech that Othello gives before the Duke of Venice in Act I, iii, lines 127–69. What does he reveal about his relationship with his new wife, Desdemona? In what ways does his background, as it is revealed here, contribute to our sense of who he is as a character?

3. Now look at Desdemona's speeches in lines 179–297 in the same scene. Clearly, this is a moment of great emotional intensity for her as she is forced to choose between her father and her new husband. What do we learn about her character and her motives in this section?

4. In reference to Iago's final speech in Act I, the English Romantic poet and

---

360. **Spartan:** i.e., hardhearted   361. **fell:** cruel   364. **Let . . . hid:** At these words the curtains are closed across the inner stage (or chamber, if this scene was acted aloft), concealing all three bodies.

critic Samuel Taylor Coleridge famously identified Iago as a villain driven by "the motive-hunting of motive-less malignity." What does this phrase mean? Do you agree with Coleridge's assessment of Iago's soliloquy? (A soliloquy is a speech delivered when no one else is on stage, usually intended to allow the viewer or reader to "see" the mental or emotional state of the character delivering the lines.)

5. What would you identify as the main conflict or conflicts in the play as we reach the end of Act I?

Act II

1. Consider Act II, scene i. What more do we learn about the interactions between Iago and the other characters from this scene? Pay particular attention to his two asides and final soliloquy. (An *aside* is a dramatic convention in which a character speaks to him- or herself or directly to the audience, while other characters on stage do not hear what is said.)

2. How does Iago make alcohol his accomplice in Act II, scene iii? What aspect of his character emerges in this scene?

3. "Reputation, reputation, reputation! Oh, I have lost my reputation!" cries Cassio in Act II, scene iii, lines 241–42. What does good "reputation" mean to Cassio, Iago, Othello, and Desdemona in the first two acts of this play?

4. The word *honest* is used by several characters throughout this act. What qualities or values does the word carry in Act II?

5. Many parts of the plot of *Othello* are in place by the end of Act II. Who controls most of the action in this play? Why do you say so?

Act III

1. Consider questions 3 and 4 from Act II. How do the concepts of honesty and reputation continue to be important in Act III?

2. What role does the serving woman Emilia appear to play when she takes up the "napkin" (i.e., handkerchief) and hands it over to Iago? (See Act III, scene iii, lines 291–331.)

3. In Act III, scene iv, lines 27–100 we learn a good deal more about the handkerchief introduced in the previous scene. What is important about this new information?

4. Why is Cassio in particular the object of Iago's deceit and guile?

5. Consider the long third scene of this act. How does Iago use psychological manipulation to provoke and fuel Othello's jealousy? Focus on two or three specific examples and explain how Iago's mind operates.

6. Focus on Othello's closing speech in Act III. In particular, what can be said about his words to Iago: "thou art my Lieutenant"? (See scene iii, line 480.)

Act IV

1. Before you begin to read Act IV, consider the story of *Othello* so far: what is the main conflict at this point in the play? What expectations do we have and what concerns as readers should be feeling?

2. Why do think Shakespeare makes Othello faint (or fall into an epileptic fit) in scene i?

3. What do we learn from the emotionally charged encounter between Othello and Desdemona in scene ii? In the overall structure of this play, why is this scene so important?

4. Emilia is certainly right that "The Moor's abused by some most villainous knave" (Act IV, scene ii, line 139). What is significant or ironic about her comment?

5. How would you advise the actress playing Desdemona to sing her "Willow Song" in Act IV, scene iii, lines 39–57? What emotional state does her song seem to suggest?

Act V

1. How important is the character Emilia at the end of the play? Give particular attention to her interaction with Othello in Act V, scene ii, but feel free to refer back to events or speeches in Acts III and IV.
2. Why is the handkerchief finally such an important stage prop (and symbol) in this play?
3. A classic question concerning the play *Othello* has to do with the extent to which Othello is the protagonist of this play and the extent to which Iago is. What do you think?
4. Are the circumstances of Othello's murder of Desdemona in any way symbolic of the jealous passions that motivate him?
5. In his long epitaph to himself in Act V, scene ii, lines 337–55, Othello characterizes himself as "one who loved not wisely but too well." Is he?

The Reading/Writing Connection

1. Select a single line, phrase, image, or very short selection of lines from the play that have particular meaning for you. Then write a poem, a rap, or song lyrics based on these words. Think about who is speaking: is it the same character as the one who speaks the words in *Othello*? Someone else?
2. Imagine that the characters in *Othello* live in your own age, with all the advantages of modern electronic communication. Select two important characters from the play: what would an instant-message or text-message exchange between them look like? Then write a short essay in which you explain the personal traits or motives of the two characters that are revealed in this exchange.
3. As in question 2, imagine that the characters of *Othello* live in the modern age, with all the benefits of advanced digital technology. Describe what the Facebook, Myspace, Tagworld, or personal Web site information for one of these characters would look like: Othello, Iago, Desdemona, Cassio, or Roderigo. Then explain your reasoning in a short essay.
4. You are given the opportunity to direct a production of *Othello*. Now it's the first meeting with the cast and you are going to start by working on Act I, scene i. What directions do you give to the actors playing Iago, Roderigo, and Brabantio to help them conceptualize this intense (and sexually suggestive) scene and to help set up the dynamics of the play as a whole? Write out your vision of how the scene should be played is if you were delivering it as a speech or "pep-talk" to these actors.
5. For the same production of *Othello,* you are asked to write a 300-word introduction to the play that will be included in the theater program all patrons receive as they enter the theater. Write this introduction for the program, then write a separate essay in which you explain to your instructor why you included the points you included and how you targeted the readers you targeted.

Ideas for Writing

1. Discuss one key relationship between characters in *Othello*. Some especially good pairings might include Iago and Roderigo, Desdemona and Emilia, Iago and Emilia, Othello and Cassio, or Othello, Othello and Desdemona, Iago and Roderigo, Desdemona and Emilia, Iago and Emilia, Othello and Cassio, or

Cassio and Iago. What does the relationship you chose tell us about the play as a whole?

2. After reading the play, choose two different film versions of *Othello* and watch them carefully for their different portrayals of one major character. (See the list of film versions below.) What does your comparison tell you about the depths and dramatic possibilities of the character you chose?

3. **Write an Argument:** Are Othello's jealousy and suspicions ever made to seem justified in this play? Why or why not? Write an argument essay in which you present evidence for either view.

4. Do research on the various actors who have played the role of Othello in the nineteenth and twentieth centuries. What conclusions do you draw concerning the issue of racial identity in the performance history of *Othello*?

5. How important is race in this play? Consider all five acts when answering this question.

6. *Othello* is an unusual Shakespearean tragedy in that the action remains almost entirely within a domestic realm. Very few, if any, political or civic consequences seem implied by the tragic events of Act V. Compare this play's tragic ending to the ending of another tragedy by Shakespeare. Some good choices would be *Titus Andronicus, Romeo and Juliet, Hamlet, King Lear,* or *Macbeth.*

Othello *on Film*

Othello has been filmed many times, and in several languages.

Othello (1952). Directed by Orson Welles. Stars Orson Welles, Robert Coote, Michael MacLiammour, and Suzanne Cloutier.

Othello (1965). Directed by Stuart Burge. Stars Laurence Olivier, Maggie Smith, Frank Findlay, Derek Jacobi.

Othello (1995). Directed by Oliver Parker. Stars Kenneth Branagh, Laurence Fishburn, Irene Jacob, Michael Maloney, and Nathaniel Parker.

Othello (2001). A modern adaptation directed by Geoffrey Sax. Stars Eammon Walker, Keeley Hawes, Christopher Eccleston, and Del Synnott.

O (2001). A modern retelling, set in the United States, directed by Tim Blake Nelson. Stars Mekhi Phifer, Julia Stiles, Martin Sheen, and Josh Hartnett.

 On the Web: *Othello*

Please visit http://www.academic.cengage.com/english/Schmidt/Legacies4e/ for links to the following online resources.

"Mr. William Shakespeare and the Internet"
"The Shakespeare Resource Center"
"The Globe Theatre"
Images of the first printing of *Othello*, The British Library Quarto copy (1622)
Second printing of *Othello*, 1623 First Folio

NONFICTION

Plato *(428–347 B.C.)* — Translated by Walter Hamilton

The Sexes *c. 387–367 B.C.*
From *The Symposium*

Well, Eryximachus," began Aristophanes,[1] "it is quite true that I intend to take a different line from you and Pausanias. Men seem to me to be utterly insensible of the power of Love; otherwise he would have had the largest temples and altars and the largest sacrifices. As it is, he has none of these things, though he deserves them most of all. For of all the gods he is the most friendly to man, and his helper and physician in those diseases whose cure constitutes the greatest happiness of the human race. I shall therefore try to initiate you into the secret of his power, and you in turn shall teach others.

"First of all, you must learn the constitution of man and the modifications which it has undergone, for originally it was different from what it is now. In the first place there were three sexes, not, as with us, two, male and female; the third partook of the nature of both the others and has vanished, though its name survives. The hermaphrodite was a distinct sex in form as well as in name, with the characteristics of both male and female, but now the name alone remains, and that solely as a term of abuse. Secondly, each human being was a rounded whole, with double back and flanks forming a complete circle; it has four hands and an equal number of legs, and two identically similar faces upon a circular neck, with one head common to both the faces, which were turned in opposite directions. It had four ears and two organs of generation and everything else to correspond. These people could walk upright like us in either direction, backwards or forwards, but when they wanted to run quickly they used all their eight limbs, and turned rapidly over and over in a circle, like tumblers who perform a cart-wheel and return to an upright position. The reason for the existence of three sexes and for their being of such a nature is that originally the male sprang from the sun and the female from the earth, while the sex which was both male and female came from the moon, which partakes of the nature of both sun and earth. Their circular shape and their hoop-like method of progression were both due to the fact that they were like their parents. Their strength and vigour made them very formidable, and their pride was overweening; they attacked the gods, and Homer's story of Ephialtes and Otus attempting to climb up to heaven and set upon the gods is related also of these beings.[2]

"So Zeus and the other gods debated what was to be done with them. For a long time they were at a loss, unable to bring themselves either to kill them by lightning, as they had the giants, and extinguish the race—thus depriving themselves for ever of

---

[1]**Aristophanes (448?–385? B.C.):** Athenian comic playwright. Eryximachus, Pausanias (following), and Agathon and Socrates (later) are other participants at the banquet, where love is the topic of discussions.   [2]**attempting . . . these beings:** Giants Ephialtes and Otus tried to climb to heaven by piling mountain upon mountain.

the honours and sacrifice due from humanity—or to let them go on in their insolence. At last, after much painful thought, Zeus had an idea. "I think," he said, "that I have found a way by which we can allow the human race to continue to exist and also put an end to their wickedness by making them weaker. I will cut each of them in two; in this way they will be weaker, and at the same time more profitable to us by being more numerous. They shall walk upright upon two legs. If there is any sign of wantonness in them after that, and they will not keep quiet, I will bisect them again, and they shall hop on one leg." With these words he cut the members of the human race in half, just like fruit which is to be dried and preserved, or like eggs which are cut with a hair. As he bisected each, he bade Apollo turn round the face and the half-neck attached to it towards the cut side, so that the victim, having the evidence of bisection before his eyes, might behave better in the future. He also bade him heal the wounds. So Apollo turned round the faces, and gathering together the skin, like a purse with drawstrings, on to what is now called the belly, he tied it tightly in the middle of the belly round a single aperture which men call the navel. He smoothed out the other wrinkles, which were numerous, and moulded the chest with a tool like those which cobblers use to smooth wrinkles in the leather on their last. But he left a few on the belly itself round the navel, to remind man of the state from which he had fallen.

"Man's original body having been thus cut in two, each half yearned for the half from which it had been severed. When they met they threw their arms round one another and embraced, in their longing to grow together again, and they perished of hunger and general neglect of their concerns, because they would not do anything apart. When one member of a pair died and the other was left, the latter sought after and embraced another partner, which might be the half either of a female whole (what is now called a woman) or a male. So they went on perishing till Zeus took pity on them, and hit upon a second plan. He moved their reproductive organs to the front: hitherto they had been placed on the outer side of their bodies, and the processes of begetting and birth had been carried on not by the physical union of the sexes, but by emission on to the ground, as is the case with grasshoppers. By moving their genitals to the front, as they are now, Zeus made it possible for reproduction to take place by the intercourse of the male with the female. His object in making this change was twofold; if male coupled with female, children might be begotten and the race thus continued, but if male coupled with male, at any rate the desire for intercourse would be satisfied, and men set free from it to turn to other activities and to attend to the rest of the business of life. It is from this distant epoch, then, that we may date the innate love which human beings feel for one another, the love which restores us to our ancient state by attempting to weld two beings into one and to heal the wounds which humanity suffered.

"Each of us then is the mere broken tally of a man, the result of a bisection which has reduced us to a condition like that of flat fish, and each of us is perpetually in search of his corresponding tally. Those men who are halves of a being of the common sex, which was called, as I told you, hermaphrodite, are lovers of women, and most adulterers come from this class, as also do women who are mad about men and sexually promiscuous. Women who are halves of a female whole direct their affections towards women and pay little attention to men; Lesbians belong to this category. But those who are halves of a male whole pursue males, and being slices, so to speak, of the male, love men throughout their boyhood, and take pleasure in physical contact with men. Such boys and lads are the best of their generation, because they are the most manly. Some people say that they are shameless, but they are wrong. It is not shamelessness which inspires their behaviour, but high spirit and manliness and virility, which lead them to welcome the society of their own kind. A striking proof of this is that such boys alone, when they reach maturity, engage in public life. When they grow to be men, they become lovers of boys, and it requires the compulsion of convention to overcome their natural disinclination to marriage and procreation; they are quite content to live with one another unwed. In a word, such persons are devoted to lovers in boyhood and themselves lovers of boys in manhood, because they always cleave to what is akin to themselves.

"Whenever the lover of boys—or any other person for that matter—has the good fortune to encounter his own actual other half, affection and kinship and love combined inspire in him an emotion which is quite overwhelming, and such a pair practically refuse ever to be separated even for a moment. It is people like these who form lifelong partnerships, although they would find it difficult to say what they hope to gain from one another's society. No one can suppose that it is mere physical enjoyment which causes the one to take such intense delight in the company of the other. It is clear that the soul of each has some other longing which it cannot express, but can only surmise and obscurely hint at. Suppose Hephaestus with his tools were to visit them as they lie together, and stand over them and ask: "What is it, mortals, that you hope to gain from one another?" Suppose too that when they could not answer he repeated his question in these terms: "Is the object of your desire to be always together as much as possible, and never to be separated from one another day or night? If that is what you want, I am ready to melt and weld you together, so that, instead of two, you shall be one flesh; as long as you live you shall live a common life, and when you die, you shall suffer a common death, and be still one, not two, even in the next world. Would such a fate as this content you, and satisfy your longings?" We know what their answer would be; no one would refuse the offer; it would be plain that this is what everybody wants, and everybody would regard it as the precise expression of the desire which he had long felt but had been unable to formulate, that he should melt into his beloved, and that henceforth they should be one being instead of two. The reason is that this was our primitive condition when we were wholes, and love is simply the name of the desire and pursuit of the whole. Originally, as I say, we were whole beings, before our wickedness caused us to be split by Zeus, as the Arcadians have been split apart by the Spartans.[3] We have reason to fear that if we do not behave ourselves in the sight of heaven, we may be split in two again, like dice which are bisected for tallies, and go about like the people represented in profile on tombstones, sawn in two vertically down the line of our noses. That is why we ought to exhort everyone to conduct himself reverently towards the gods; we shall thus escape a worse fate, and even win the blessing which Love has in his power to bestow, if we take him for our guide and captain. Let no man set himself in opposition to Love—which is the same thing as incurring the hatred of the gods—for if we are his friends and make our peace with him, we shall succeed, as few at present succeed, in finding the person to love who in the strictest sense belongs to us. I know that Eryximachus is anxious to make fun of my speech, but he is not to suppose that in saying this I am pointing at Pausanias and Agathon. They may, no doubt, belong to this class, for they are both unquestionably halves of male wholes, but I am speaking of men and women in general when I say that the way to happiness for

---

[3] **Arcadians have been split apart by the Spartans:** The conquering Spartans forced the residents of the Arcadian city of Mantinea to live in four separate villages.

our race lies in fulfilling the behests of Love, and in each finding for himself the mate who properly belongs to him; in a word, in returning to our original condition. If that condition was the best, it follows that it is best for us to come as near to it as our present circumstances allow; and the way to do that is to find a sympathetic and congenial object for our affections.

"If we are to praise the god who confers this benefit upon us, it is to Love that our praises should be addressed. It is Love who is the author of our well-being in this present life, by leading us towards what is akin to us, and it is Love who gives us a sure hope that, if we conduct ourselves well in the sight of heaven, he will hereafter make us blessed and happy by restoring us to our former state and healing our wounds.

"There is my speech about Love, Eryximachus, and you will see that it is of quite a different type from yours. Remember my request, and don't make fun of it, but let us hear what each of the others has to say. I should have said 'each of the other two,' for only Agathon and Socrates are left." ●

Explorations of the Text

1. Explore the descriptions of the "three sexes," particularly of the "third" sex. How do you react to this description?
2. Describe this myth of the "fall." Compare it to the Biblical creation story and to the fall of Adam and Eve.
3. What is the concept of the "bisection"? How does Aristophanes explain homosexuality and heterosexuality?
4. How does the myth account for love?
5. What will happen if human beings set themselves "in opposition to Love"?
6. According to Aristophanes, what is "the way to happiness" for the race? Why?
7. What are Aristophanes's point of view and tone? Find key words and phrases that reveal his perspective.

The Reading/Writing Connection

1. Create a myth or a fable that provides an explanation for one of the following: a) Why people fall in love; b) The nature of love or relationships; c) The nature of gender roles.
2. "Think" Topic: Take issue with one point in this treatise. Construct a counterargument.

Ideas for Writing

1. **Write an Argument:** Agree or disagree with Aristophanes that happiness lies in "fulfilling the behests of love" and in finding the proper mate.
2. Are we only "half" selves, yearning for completion through our mates or through our love relationships?
3. Compare Aristophanes's views of love with the view in one of the love poems in this chapter. OR Respond in the persona of a character in one of the works in this chapter.

Maxine Hong Kingston (1940–)

No Name Woman *1976*

Y ou must not tell anyone," my mother said, "what I am about to tell you. In China your father had a sister who killed herself. She jumped into the family well. We say that your father has all brothers because it is as if she had never been born.

"In 1924 just a few days after our village celebrated seventeen hurry-up weddings— to make sure that every young man who went 'out on the road' would responsibly come home—your father and his brothers and your grandfather and his brothers and your aunt's new husband sailed for America, the Gold Mountain. It was your grandfather's last trip. Those lucky enough to get contracts waved good-bye from the decks. They fed and guarded the stowaways and helped them off in Cuba, New York, Bali, Hawaii. "We'll meet in California next year," they said. All of them sent money home.

"I remember looking at your aunt one day when she and I were dressing; I had not noticed before that she had such a protruding melon of a stomach. But I did not think, 'She's pregnant,' until she began to look like other pregnant women, her shirt pulling and the white tops of her black pants showing. She could not have been pregnant, you see, because her husband had been gone for years. No one said anything. We did not discuss it. In early summer she was ready to have the child, long after the time when it could have been possible.

"The village had also been counting. On the night the baby was to be born the villagers raided our house. Some were crying. Like a great saw, teeth strung with lights, files of people walked zigzag across our land, tearing the rice. Their lanterns doubled in the disturbed black water, which drained away through the broken bunds. As the villagers closed in, we could see that some of them, probably men and women we knew well, wore white masks. The people with long hair hung it over their faces. Women with short hair made it stand up on end. Some had tied white bands around their foreheads, arms, and legs.

"At first they threw mud and rocks at the house. Then they threw eggs and began slaughtering our stock. We could hear the animals scream their deaths—the roosters, the pigs, a last great roar from the ox. Familiar wild heads flared in our night windows; the villagers encircled us. Some of the faces stopped to peer at us, their eyes rushing like searchlights. The hands flattened against the panes, framed heads, and left red prints.

"The villagers broke in the front and the back doors at the same time, even though we had not locked the doors against them. Their knives dripped with the blood of our animals. They smeared blood on the doors and walls. One woman swung a chicken, whose throat she had slit, splattering blood in red arcs about her. We stood together in the middle of our house, in the family hall with the pictures and tables of the ancestors around us, and looked straight ahead.

"At that time the house had only two wings. When the men came back, we would build two more to enclose our courtyard and a third one to begin a second courtyard. The villagers pushed through both wings, even your grandparents' rooms, to find your aunt's, which was also mine until the men returned. From this room a new wing for one of the younger families would grow. They ripped up her clothes and shoes and broke her combs, grinding them underfoot. They tore her work from the loom. They scattered the cooking fire and rolled the new weaving in it. We could hear them in the kitchen breaking our bowls and banging the pots. They overturned the great waist-high earthenware jugs; duck eggs, pickled fruits, vegetables burst out and mixed in acrid torrents. The old woman from the next field swept a broom through the air and loosed the spirits-of-the-broom over our heads. 'Pig.' 'Ghost.' 'Pig,' they sobbed and scolded while they ruined our house.

"When they left, they took sugar and oranges to bless themselves. They cut pieces from the dead animals. Some of them took bowls that were not broken and clothes that were not torn. Afterward we swept up the rice and sewed it back up into sacks. But the smells from the spilled preserves lasted. Your aunt gave birth in the pigsty that night. The next morning when I went for the water, I found her and the baby plugging up the family well.

"Don't let your father know that I told you. He denies her. Now that you have started to menstruate, what happened to her could happen to you. Don't humiliate us. You wouldn't like to be forgotten as if you had never been born. The villagers are watchful."

Whenever she had to warn us about life, my mother told stories that ran like this 10 one, a story to grow up on. She tested our strength to establish realities. Those in the emigrant generations who could not reassert brute survival died young and far from home. Those of us in the first American generations have had to figure out how the invisible world the emigrants built around our childhoods fit in solid America.

The emigrants confused the gods by diverting their curses, misleading them with crooked streets and false names. They must try to confuse their offspring as well, who, I suppose, threaten them in similar ways—always trying to get things straight, always trying to name the unspeakable. The Chinese I know hide their names; sojourners take new names when their lives change and guard their real names with silence.

Chinese-Americans, when you try to understand what things in you are Chinese, how do you separate what is peculiar to childhood, to poverty, insanities, one family, your mother who marked your growing with stories, from what is Chinese? What is Chinese tradition and what is the movies?

If I want to learn what clothes my aunt wore, whether flashy or ordinary, I would have to begin, "Remember Father's drowned-in-the-well sister?" I cannot ask that. My mother has told me once and for all the useful parts. She will add nothing unless powered by Necessity, a riverbank that guides her life. She plants vegetable gardens rather than lawns; she carries the odd-shaped tomatoes home from the fields and eats food left for the gods.

Whenever we did frivolous things, we used up energy; we flew high kites. We children came up off the ground over the melting cones our parents brought home from work and the American movie on New Year's Day—*Oh, You Beautiful Doll* with Betty Grable one year, and *She Wore a Yellow Ribbon* with John Wayne another year. After the one carnival ride each, we paid in guilt; our tired father counted his change on the dark walk home.

Adultery is extravagance. Could people who hatch their own chicks and eat the em- 15 bryos and the heads for delicacies and boil the feet in vinegar for party food, leaving only the gravel, eating even the gizzard lining—could such people engender a prodigal aunt? To be a woman, to have a daughter in starvation time was a waste enough. My aunt could not have been the lone romantic who gave up everything for sex. Women in the old China did not choose. Some man had commanded her to lie with him and be his secret evil. I wonder whether he masked himself when he joined the raid on her family.

Perhaps she encountered him in the fields or on the mountain where the daughters-in-law collected fuel. Or perhaps he first noticed her in the marketplace. He was not a stranger because the village housed no strangers. She had to have dealings with him other than sex. Perhaps he worked an adjoining field, or he sold her the cloth for the dress she sewed and wore. His demand must have surprised, then terrified her. She obeyed him; she always did as she was told.

When the family found a young man in the next village to be her husband, she stood tractably beside the best rooster, his proxy, and promised before they met that she would be his forever. She was lucky that he was her age and she would be the first wife, an advantage secure now. The night she first saw him, he had sex with her. Then he left for America. She had almost forgotten what he looked like. When she tried to envision him, she only saw the black and white face in the group photograph the men had had taken before leaving.

The other man was not, after all, much different from her husband. They both gave orders: she followed. "If you tell your family, I'll beat you. I'll kill you. Be here again next week." No one talked sex, ever. And she might have separated the rapes from the rest of living if only she did not have to buy her oil from him or gather wood in the same forest. I want her fear to have lasted just as long as rape lasted so that the fear could have been contained. No drawn-out fear. But women at sex hazarded birth and hence lifetimes. The fear did not stop but permeated everywhere. She told the man, "I think I'm pregnant." He organized the raid against her.

On nights when my mother and father talked about their life back home, sometimes they mentioned an "outcast table" whose business they still seemed to be settling, their voices tight. In a commensal tradition,[1] where food is precious, the powerful older people made wrongdoers eat alone. Instead of letting them start separate new lives like the Japanese, who could become samurais and geishas, the Chinese family, faces averted but eyes glowering sideways, hung on to the offenders and fed them leftovers. My aunt must have lived in the same house as my parents and eaten at an outcast table. My mother spoke about the raid as if she had seen it, when she and my aunt, a daughter-in-law to a different household, should not have been living together at all. Daughters-in-law lived with their husbands' parents, not their own; a synonym for marriage in Chinese is "taking a daughter-in-law." Her husband's parents could have sold her, mortgaged her, stoned her. But they had sent her back to her own mother and father, a mysterious act hinting at disgraces not told me. Perhaps they had thrown her out to deflect the avengers.

She was the only daughter; her four brothers went with her father, husband, and uncles "out on the road" and for some years became western men. When the goods were divided among the family, three of the brothers took land, and the youngest, my father, chose an education. After my grandparents gave their daughter away to her husband's family, they had dispensed all the adventure and all the property. They expected her alone to keep the traditional ways, which her brothers, now among the barbarians, could fumble without detection. The heavy, deep-rooted women were to maintain the past against the flood, safe for returning. But the rare urge west had fixed upon our family, and so my aunt crossed boundaries not delineated in space.

The work of preservation demands that the feelings playing about in one's guts not be turned into action. Just watch their passing like cherry blossoms. But perhaps

20

---

[1]**commensal tradition:** A tradition that values communal meals—people's sharing of meals.

my aunt, my forerunner, caught in a slow life, let dreams grow and fade and after some months or years went toward what persisted. Fear at the enormities of the forbidden kept her desires delicate, wire and bone. She looked at a man because she liked the way the hair was tucked behind his ears, or she liked the question-mark line of a long torso curving at the shoulder and straight at the hip. For warm eyes or a soft voice or a slow walk—that's all—a few hairs, a line, a brightness, a sound, a pace, she gave up family. She offered us up for a charm that vanished with tiredness, a pigtail that didn't toss when the wind died. Why, the wrong lighting could erase the dearest thing about him.

It could very well have been, however, that my aunt did not take subtle enjoyment of her friend, but, a wild woman, kept rollicking company. Imagining her free with sex doesn't fit, though. I don't know any women like that, or men either. Unless I see her life branching into mine, she gives me no ancestral help.

To sustain her being in love, she often worked at herself in the mirror, guessing at the colors and shapes that would interest him, changing them frequently in order to hit on the right combination. She wanted him to look back.

On a farm near the sea, a woman who tended her appearance reaped a reputation for eccentricity. All the married women blunt-cut their hair in flaps about their ears or pulled it back in tight buns. No nonsense. Neither style blew easily into heart-catching tangles. And at their weddings they displayed themselves in their long hair for the last time. "It brushed the backs of my knees," my mother tells me. "It was braided, and even so, it brushed the backs of my knees."

At the mirror my aunt combed individuality into her bob. A bun could have been contrived to escape into black streamers blowing in the wind or in quiet wisps about her face, but only the older women in our picture album wear buns. She brushed her hair back from her forehead, tucking the flaps behind her ears. She looped a piece of thread, knotted into a circle between her index fingers and thumbs, and ran the double strand across her forehead. When she closed her fingers as if she were making a pair of shadow geese bite, the string twisted together catching the little hairs. Then she pulled the thread away from her skin, ripping the hairs out neatly, her eyes watering from the needles of pain. Opening her fingers, she cleaned the thread, then rolled it along her hairline and the tops of her eyebrows. My mother did the same to me and my sisters and herself. I used to believe that the expression "caught by the short hairs" meant a captive held with a depilatory string. It especially hurt at the temples, but my mother said we were lucky we didn't have to have our feet bound when we were seven. Sisters used to sit on their beds and cry together, she said, as their mothers or their slaves removed the bandages for a few minutes each night and let the blood gush back into their veins. I hope that the man my aunt loved appreciated a smooth brow, that he wasn't just a tits-and-ass man.

Once my aunt found a freckle on her chin, at a spot that the almanac said predestined her for unhappiness. She dug it out with a hot needle and washed the wound with peroxide.

More attention to her looks than these pullings of hairs and pickings at spots would have caused gossip among the villagers. They owned work clothes and good clothes, and they wore good clothes for feasting the new seasons. But since a woman combing her hair hexes beginnings, my aunt rarely found an occasion to look her best. Women looked like great sea snails—the corded wood, babies, and laundry they carried were the whorls on their backs. The Chinese did not admire a bent back: goddesses and warriors stood straight. Still there must have been a marvelous freeing of beauty when a worker laid down her burden and stretched and arched.

Such commonplace loveliness, however, was not enough for my aunt. She dreamed of a lover for the fifteen days of New Year's, the time for families to exchange visits, money, and food. She plied her secret comb. And sure enough she cursed the year, the family, the village, and herself.

Even as her hair lured her imminent lover, many other men looked at her. Uncles, cousins, nephews, brothers would have looked, too, had they been home between journeys. Perhaps they had already been restraining their curiosity, and they left, fearful that their glances, like a field of nesting birds, might be startled and caught. Poverty hurt, and that was their first reason for leaving. But another, final reason for leaving the crowded house was the never-said.

She may have been unusually beloved, the precious only daughter, spoiled and mirror gazing because of the affection the family lavished on her. When her husband left, they welcomed the chance to take her back from the in-laws; she could live like the little daughter for just a while longer. There are stories that my grandfather was different from other people, "crazy ever since the little Jap bayoneted him in the head." He used to put his naked penis on the dinner table, laughing. And one day he brought home a baby girl, wrapped up inside his brown western-style greatcoat. He had traded one of his sons, probably my father, the youngest, for her. My grandmother made him trade back. When he finally got a daughter of his own, he doted on her. They must have all loved her, except perhaps my father, the only brother who never went back to China, having once been traded for a girl.

Brothers and sisters, newly men and women, had to efface their sexual color and present plain miens.[2] Disturbing hair and eyes, a smile like no other threatened the ideal of five generations living under one roof. To focus blurs, people shouted face to face and yelled from room to room. The immigrants I know have loud voices, unmodulated to American tones even after years away from the village where they called their friendships out across the fields. I have not been able to stop my mother's screams in public libraries or over telephones. Walking erect (knees straight, toes pointed forward, not pigeon-toed, which is Chinese-feminine) and speaking in an inaudible voice, I have tried to turn myself American-feminine. Chinese communication was loud, public. Only sick people had to whisper. But at the dinner table, where the family members came nearest one another, no one could talk, not the outcasts nor any eaters. Every word that falls from the mouth is a coin lost. Silently they gave and accepted food with both hands. A preoccupied child who took his bowl with one hand got a sideways glare. A complete moment of total attention is due everyone alike. Children and lovers have no singularity here, but my aunt used a secret voice, a separate attentiveness.

She kept the man's name to herself throughout her labor and dying; she did not accuse him that he be punished with her. To save her inseminator's name she gave silent birth.

He may have been somebody in her own household, but intercourse with a man outside the family would have been no less abhorrent. All the village were kinsmen, and the titles shouted in loud country voices never let kinship be forgotten. Any man within visiting distance would have been neutralized as a lover—"brother," "younger brother," "older brother"—one hundred and fifteen relationship titles. Parents researched birth charts probably not so much to assure good fortune as to circumvent incest in a popu-

30

---

[2]**miens:** Looks.

lation that has but one hundred surnames. Everybody has eight million relatives. How useless then sexual mannerisms, how dangerous.

As if it came from an atavism[3] deeper than fear, I used to add "brother" silently to boys' names. It hexed the boys, who would or would not ask me to dance, and made them less scary and as familiar and deserving of benevolence as girls.

But, of course, I hexed myself also—no dates. I should have stood up, both arms waving, and shouted out across libraries, "Hey, you! Love me back." I had no idea, though, how to make attraction selective, how to control its direction and magnitude. If I made myself American-pretty so that the five or six Chinese boys in the class fell in love with me, everyone else—the Caucasian, Negro, and Japanese boys—would too. Sisterliness, dignified and honorable, made much more sense.

Attraction eludes control so stubbornly that whole societies designed to organize relationships among people cannot keep order, not even when they bind people to one another from childhood and raise them together. Among the very poor and the wealthy, brothers married their adopted sisters, like doves. Our family allowed some romance, paying adult brides' prices and providing dowries so that their sons and daughters could marry strangers. Marriage promises to turn strangers into friendly relatives—a nation of siblings.

In the village structure, spirits shimmered among the live creatures, balanced and held in equilibrium by time and land. But one human being flaring up into violence could open up a black hole, a maelstrom that pulled in the sky. The frightened villagers, who depended on one another to maintain the real, went to my aunt to show her a personal, physical representation of the break she had made in the "roundness." Misallying couples snapped off the future, which was to be embodied in true offspring. The villagers punished her for acting as if she could have a private life, secret and apart from them.

If my aunt had betrayed the family at a time of large grain yields and peace, when many boys were born, and wings were being built on many houses, perhaps she might have escaped such severe punishment. But the men—hungry, greedy, tired of planting in dry soil, cuckolded—had had to leave the village in order to send food-money home. There were ghost plagues, bandit plagues, wars with the Japanese, floods. My Chinese brother and sister had died of an unknown sickness. Adultery, perhaps only a mistake during good times, became a crime when the village needed food.

The round moon cakes and round doorways, the round tables of graduated size that fit one roundness inside another, round windows and rice bowls—these talismen had lost their power to warn this family of the law: a family must be whole, faithfully keeping the descent line by having sons to feed the old and the dead, who in turn look after the family. The villagers came to show my aunt and her lover-in-hiding a broken house. The villagers were speeding up the circling of events because she was too short-sighted to see that her infidelity had already harmed the village, that waves of consequences would return unpredictably, sometimes in disguise, as now, to hurt her. This roundness had to be made coin-sized so that she would see its circumference: punish her at the birth of her baby. Awaken her to the inexorable. People who refused fatalism because they could invent small resources insisted on culpability. Deny accidents and wrest fault from the stars.

After the villagers left, their lanterns now scattering in various directions toward home, the family broke their silence and cursed her. "Aiaa, we're going to die. Death is

---

[3]**atavism:** Reversion to a primitive or an earlier type (or ancestral form).

coming. Death is coming. Look what you've done. You've killed us. Ghost! Dead ghost! You've never been born." She ran out into the fields, far enough from the house so that she could no longer hear their voices, and pressed herself against the earth, her own land no more. When she felt the birth coming, she thought that she had been hurt. Her body seized together. "They've hurt me too much," she thought. "This is gall, and it will kill me." Her forehead and knees against the earth, her body convulsed and then released her onto her back. The black well of sky and stars went out and out and out forever; her body and her complexity seemed to disappear. She was one of the stars, a bright dot in blackness, without home, without a companion, in eternal cold and silence. An agoraphobia rose in her, speeding higher and higher, bigger and bigger; she would not be able to contain it; there would be no end to fear.

Flayed, unprotected against space, she felt pain return, focusing her body. This pain chilled her—a cold, steady kind of surface pain. Inside, spasmodically, the other pain, the pain of the child, heated her. For hours she lay on the ground, alternately body and space. Sometimes a vision of normal comfort obliterated reality: she saw the family in the evening gambling at the dinner table, the young people massaging their elders' backs. She saw them congratulating one another, high joy on the mornings the rice shoots came up. When these pictures burst, the stars drew yet further apart. Black space opened.

She got to her feet to fight better and remembered that old-fashioned women gave birth in their pigsties to fool the jealous, pain-dealing gods, who do not snatch piglets. Before the next spasms could stop her, she ran to the pigsty, each step a rushing out into emptiness. She climbed over the fence and knelt in the dirt. It was good to have a fence enclosing her, a tribal person alone.

Laboring, this woman who had carried her child as a foreign growth that sickened her every day, expelled it at last. She reached down to touch the hot, wet, moving mass, surely smaller than anything human, and could feel that it was human after all—fingers, toes, nails, nose. She pulled it up on to her belly, and it lay curled there, butt in the air, feet precisely tucked one under the other. She opened her loose shirt and buttoned the child inside. After resting, it squirmed and thrashed and she pushed it up to her breast. It turned its head this way and that until it found her nipple. There, it made little snuffling noises. She clenched her teeth at its preciousness, lovely as a young calf, a piglet, a little dog.

She may have gone to the pigsty as a last act of responsibility: she would protect this child as she had protected its father. It would look after her soul, leaving supplies on her grave. But how would this tiny child without family find her grave when there would be no marker for her anywhere, neither in the earth nor the family hall? No one would give her a family hall name. She had taken the child with her into the wastes. At its birth the two of them had felt the same raw pain of separation, a wound that only the family pressing tight could close. A child with no descent line would not soften her life but only trail after her, ghostlike, begging her to give it purpose. At dawn the villagers on their way to the fields would stand around the fence and look.

Full of milk, the little ghost slept. When it awoke, she hardened her breasts against the milk that crying loosens. Toward morning she picked up the baby and walked to the well. 45

Carrying the baby to the well shows loving. Otherwise abandon it. Turn its face into the mud. Mothers who love their children take them along. It was probably a girl; there is some hope of forgiveness for boys.

■　■　■

"Don't tell anyone you had an aunt. Your father does not want to hear her name. She has never been born." I have believed that sex was unspeakable and words so strong and fathers so frail that "aunt" would do my father mysterious harm. I have thought that my family, having settled among immigrants who had also been their neighbors in the ancestral land, needed to clean their name, and a wrong word would incite the kinspeople even here. But there is more to this silence: they want me to participate in her punishment. And I have.

In the twenty years since I heard this story I have not asked for details nor said my aunt's name; I do not know it. People who can comfort the dead can also chase after them to hurt them further—a reverse ancestor worship. The real punishment was not the raid swiftly inflicted by the villagers, but the family's deliberately forgetting her. Her betrayal so maddened them, they saw to it that she would suffer forever, even after death. Always hungry, always needing, she would have to beg food from other ghosts, snatch and steal it from those whose living descendants give them gifts. She would have to fight the ghosts massed at crossroads for the buns a few thoughtful citizens leave to decoy her away from village and home so that the ancestral spirits could feast unharassed. At peace, they could act like gods, not ghosts, their descent lines providing them with paper suits and dresses, spirit money, paper houses, paper automobiles, chicken, meat, and rice into eternity—essences delivered up in smoke and flames, steam and incense rising from each rice bowl. In an attempt to make the Chinese care for people outside the family, Chairman Mao[4] encourages us now to give our paper replicas to the spirits of outstanding soldiers and workers, no matter whose ancestors they may be. My aunt remains forever hungry. Goods are not distributed evenly among the dead.

My aunt haunts me—her ghost drawn to me because now, after fifty years of neglect, I alone devote pages of paper to her, though not origamied[5] into houses and clothes. I do not think she always means me well. I am telling on her, and she was a spite suicide, drowning herself in the drinking water. The Chinese are always very frightened of the drowned one, whose weeping ghost, wet hair hanging and skin bloated, waits silently by the water to pull down a substitute. ●

Explorations of the Text

1. Why does the mother tell her story about the narrator's aunt? Why is the aunt considered to have "never been born"?

2. What are the conditions—social, cultural, economic, and personal—that drive the aunt to another man?

3. Why do the villagers storm and raid the house? What do the actions in the scene suggest about the villagers and their values?

4. What is the purpose of storytelling for these first-generation Chinese American women? What additional motives for the mother's narrative emerge?

5. Why do Chinese "guard their real names with silence"? Why do they want to confuse the gods?

6. Explain: "Adultery is extravagance." Relate the statement to Chinese values and philosophy of life.

---

[4]**Chairman Mao:** Chinese Communist leader (1893–1976).   [5]**Origami:** The Japanese art of decorative paper folding.

7. How does the daughter reinterpret the story of her aunt? Is it an initiation story?

8. How does the daughter view her aunt as her precursor? Look at details of hair and appearance.

9. Why is the aunt's pregnancy so threatening to the society?

10. Why does the aunt give birth in a pigsty? Why does she drown herself and her baby in the well?

11. What are the attitudes toward sexuality, love, marriage, and women's roles in China at the time of this story?

The Reading/Writing Connection

1. Gloss and annotate the text and explore the theme of silence in "No Name Woman."

2. Explain the imagery of the ghost and of the "No Name Woman." Why does she have no name?

Ideas for Writing

1. Consider the title. What are views of language and of identity in this work? What do words mean to the daughter?

2. Write a short scene for a play in which the aunt and Minnie Wright talk with each other. Write monologues and/or dialogue for each character.

Virginia Woolf *(1882–1941)*

Professions for Women *1942*

When your secretary invited me to come here, she told me that your Society is concerned with the employment of women and she suggested that I might tell you something about my own professional experiences. It is true I am a woman; it is true I am employed; but what professional experiences have I had? it is difficult to say. My profession is literature; and in that profession there are fewer experiences for women than in any other, with the exception of the stage—fewer, I mean, that are peculiar to women. For the road was cut many years ago—by Fanny Burney, by Aphra Behn, by Harriet Martineau, by Jane Austen, by George Eliot[1]—many famous women, and many more unknown and forgotten, have been before me, making the path smooth, and regulating my steps. Thus, when I came to write, there were very few material obstacles in my way. Writing was a reputable and harmless occupation. The family peace was not broken by the scratching of a pen. No demand was made upon the family purse. For ten and sixpence one can buy paper enough to write all the plays of Shakespeare—if one has a mind that way. Pianos and models, Paris, Vienna and Berlin, masters and mistresses, are not needed by a writer. The cheapness of writing paper is, of course, the reason why women have succeeded as writers before they have succeeded in the other professions.

---

[1] **Fanny Burney . . . George Eliot:** Famous women writers: Fanny Burney (1752–1840), English novelist and diarist; Aphra Behn (1640–89), English dramatist and novelist; Harriet Martineau (1802–76), English novelist; Jane Austen (1775–1817), English novelist; and George Eliot (1819–80), pen name of Mary Ann Evans, English novelist.

But to tell you my story—it is a simple one. You have only got to figure to yourselves a girl in a bedroom with a pen in her hand. She had only to move that pen from left to right—from ten o'clock to one. Then it occurred to her to do what is simple and cheap enough after all—to slip a few of those pages into an envelope, fix a penny stamp in the corner, and drop the envelope into the red box at the corner. It was thus that I became a journalist; and my effort was rewarded on the first day of the following month—a very glorious day it was for me—by a letter from an editor containing a cheque for one pound ten shillings and sixpence. But to show you how little I deserve to be called a professional woman, how little I know of the struggles and difficulties of such lives, I have to admit that instead of spending that sum upon bread and butter, rent, shoes and stockings, or butcher's bills, I went out and bought a cat—a beautiful cat, a Persian cat, which very soon involved me in bitter disputes with my neighbours.

What could be easier than to write articles and to buy Persian cats with the profits? But wait a moment. Articles have to be about something. Mine, I seem to remember, was about a novel by a famous man. And while I was writing this review, I discovered that if I were going to review books I should need to do battle with a certain phantom. And the phantom was a woman, and when I came to know her better I called her after the heroine of a famous poem, The Angel in the House.[2] It was she who used to come between me and my paper when I was writing reviews. It was she who bothered me and wasted my time and so tormented me that as last I killed her. You who come of a younger and happier generation may not have heard of her—you may not know what I mean by the Angel in the House. I will describe her as shortly as I can. She was intensely sympathetic. She was immensely charming. She was utterly unselfish. She excelled in the difficult arts of family life. She sacrificed herself daily. If there was chicken, she took the leg; if there was a draught she sat in it—in short she was so constituted that she never had a mind or a wish of her own, but preferred to sympathize always with the minds and wishes of others. Above all—I need not say it—she was pure. Her purity was supposed to be her chief beauty—her blushes, her great grace. In those days—the last of Queen Victoria—every house had its Angel. And when I came to write I encountered her with the very first words. The shadow of her wings fell on my page; I heard the rustling of her skirts in the room. Directly, that is to say, I took my pen in hand to review that novel by a famous man, she slipped behind me and whispered: "My dear, you are a young woman. You are writing about a book that has been written by a man. Be sympathetic; be tender; flatter; deceive; use all the arts and wiles of our sex. Never let anybody guess that you have a mind of your own. Above all, be pure." And she made as if to guide my pen. I now record the one act for which I take some credit to myself, though the credit rightly belongs to some excellent ancestors of mine who left me a certain sum of money—shall we say five hundred pounds a year?—so that it was not necessary for me to depend solely on charm for my living. I turned upon her and caught her by the throat. I did my best to kill her. My excuse, if I were to be had up in a court of law, would be that I acted in self-defence. Had I not killed her she would have killed me. She would have plucked the heart out of my writing. For, as I found, directly I put pen to paper, you cannot review even a novel without having a mind of your own, without expressing what you think to be the truth about human relations, morality,

---

[2] **The Angel in the House:** Woolf took the term from a poem by Coventry Patmore, an English poet and essayist (1823–96).

sex. And all these questions, according to the Angel in the House, cannot be dealt with freely and openly by women; they must charm, they must conciliate, they must—to put it bluntly—tell lies if they are to succeed. Thus, whenever I felt the shadow of her wing or the radiance of her halo upon my page, I took up the inkpot and flung it at her. She died hard. Her fictitious nature was of great assistance to her. It is far harder to kill a phantom than a reality. She was always creeping back when I thought I had despatched her. Though I flatter myself that I killed her in the end, the struggle was severe; it took much time that had better have been spent upon learning Greek grammar; or in roaming the world in search of adventures. But it was a real experience; it was an experience that was bound to befall all women writers at that time. Killing the Angel in the House was part of the occupation of a woman writer.

But to continue my story. The Angel was dead; what then remained? You may say that what remained was a simple and common object—a young woman in a bedroom with an inkpot. In other words, now that she had rid herself of falsehood, that young woman had only to be herself. Ah, but what is "herself"? I mean, what is a woman? I assure you, I do not know. I do not believe that you know. I do not believe that anybody can know until she has expressed herself in all the arts and professions open to human skill. That indeed is one of the reasons why I have come here—out of respect for you, who are in process of showing us by your experiments what a woman is, who are in process of providing us, by your failures and successes, with that extremely important piece of information.

But to continue the story of my professional experiences. I made one pound ten   5
and six by my first review; and I bought a Persian cat with the proceeds. Then I grew ambitious. A Persian cat is all very well, I said; but a Persian cat is not enough. I must have a motor car. And it was thus that I became a novelist—for it is a very strange thing that people will give you a motor car if you will tell them a story. It is a still stranger thing that there is nothing so delightful in the world as telling stories. It is far pleasanter than writing reviews of famous novels. And yet, if I am to obey your secretary and tell you my professional experiences as a novelist, I must tell you about a very strange experience that befell me as a novelist. And to understand it you must try first to imagine a novelist's state of mind. I hope I am not giving away professional secrets if I say that a novelist's chief desire is to be as unconscious as possible. He has to induce in himself a state of perpetual lethargy. He wants life to proceed with the utmost quiet and regularity. He wants to see the same faces, to read the same books, to do the same things day after day, month after month, while he is writing, so that nothing may break the illusion in which he is living—so that nothing may disturb or disquiet the mysterious nosings about, feelings round, darts, dashes and sudden discoveries of that very shy and illusive spirit, the imagination. I suspect that this state is the same both for men and women. Be that as it may, I want you to imagine me writing a novel in a state of trance. I want you to figure to yourselves a girl sitting with a pen in her hand, which for minutes, and indeed for hours, she never dips into the inkpot. The image that comes to my mind when I think of this girl is the image of a fisherman lying sunk in dreams on the verge of a deep lake with a rod held out over the water. She was letting her imagination sweep unchecked round every rock and cranny of the world that lies submerged in the depths of our unconscious being. Now came the experience, the experience that I believe to be far commoner with women writers than with men. The line raced through the girl's fingers. Her imagination had rushed away. It had sought

the pools, and depths, the dark places where the largest fish slumber. And then there was a smash. There was an explosion. There was foam and confusion. The imagination had dashed itself against something hard. The girl was roused from her dream. She was indeed in a state of the most acute and difficult distress. To speak without figure she had thought of something, something about the body, about the passions which it was unfitting for her as a woman to say. Men, her reason told her, would be shocked. The consciousness of what men will say of a woman who speaks the truth about her passions had roused her from her artist's state of unconsciousness. She could write no more. The trance was over. Her imagination could work no longer. This I believe to be a very common experience with women writers—they are impeded by the extreme conventionality of the other sex. For though men sensibly allow themselves great freedom in these respects, I doubt that they realize or can control the extreme severity with which they condemn such freedom in women.

These then were two very genuine experiences of my own. These were two of the adventures of my professional life. The first—killing the Angel in the House—I think I solved. She died. But the second, telling the truth about my own experiences as a body, I do not think I solved. I doubt that any woman has solved it yet. The obstacles against her are still immensely powerful—and yet they are very difficult to define. Outwardly, what is simpler than to write books? Outwardly, what obstacles are there for a woman rather than for a man? Inwardly, I think, the case is very different; she has still many ghosts to fight, many prejudices to overcome. Indeed it will be a long time still, I think, before a woman can sit down to write a book without finding a phantom to be slain, a rock to be dashed against. And if this is so in literature, the freest of all professions for women, how is it in the new professions which you are now for the first time entering?

Those are the questions that I should like, had I time, to ask you. And indeed, if I have laid stress upon these professional experiences of mine, it is because I believe that they are, though in different forms, yours also. Even when the path is nominally open—when there is nothing to prevent a woman from being a doctor, a lawyer, a civil servant—there are many phantoms and obstacles, as I believe, looming in her way. To discuss and define them is I think of great value and importance; for thus only can the labour be shared, the difficulties be solved. But besides this, it is necessary also to discuss the ends and the aims for which we are fighting, for which we are doing battle with these formidable obstacles. Those aims cannot be taken for granted; they must be perpetually questioned and examined. The whole position, as I see it—here in this hall surrounded by women practising for the first time in history I know not how many different professions—is one of extraordinary interest and importance. You have won rooms of your own in the house hitherto exclusively owned by men. You are able, though not without great labour and effort, to pay the rent. You are earning your five hundred pounds a year. But this freedom is only a beginning; the room is your own, but it is still bare. It has to be furnished; it has to be decorated; it has to be shared. How are you going to furnish it, how are you going to decorate it? With whom are you going to share it, and upon what terms? These, I think are questions of the utmost importance and interest. For the first time in history you are able to ask them; for the first time you are able to decide for yourselves what the answers should be. Willingly would I stay and discuss those questions and answers—but not tonight. My time is up; and I must cease. ●

Explorations of the Text

1. How does Woolf view the professions of journalist and writer?
2. Explore the image of the "Angel in the House." What is Woolf's attitude toward this "phantom"? How does the "Angel" affect Woolf's writing career?
3. Discuss Woolf's process of creating a novel. Contrast this process with her work as a journalist.
4. Analyze the "image of a fisherman" and "the girl" extending her line. What is the challenge Woolf faces as a woman writer?
5. Compare Woolf's vision of "telling the truth about [her] own experiences as a body" with the experiences of one or several of the female figures in the thematic cluster, "Love and Betrayal."

The Reading/Writing Connection

1. What does Woolf mean by her "own experiences as a body"? Freewrite in response to this quotation.
2. "Think" Topic: Woolf wrote this essay in 1931. Do you think that women artists today face these same "obstacles"?
3. Write a mini-essay in response to one of the statements or questions in the last paragraph of the essay. Probe the statement or question; relate it to your own observations, experiences, and reading; analyze it; and come to conclusions.

Ideas for Writing

1. Explicate the image of a "room of [one's] own." How are women today exercising their "freedom"? "furnish[ing]" "room[s]"?
2. Debate Topic: Do men need to create similar places?
3. Choose a character from this chapter and imagine the kind of "room" this character would create. Create diary entries in the voice of this character.
4. Create a drawing of this room; furnish and decorate it. Or create a poem for a character from this chapter who is now living in a "room of [her] own."

Simone de Beauvoir   *(1908–1986)*

Woman as Other   *1949*

What is a woman?

To state the question is, to me, to suggest, at once, a preliminary answer. The fact that I ask it is in itself significant. A man would never get the notion of writing a book on the peculiar situation of the human male. But if I wish to define myself, I must first of all say: "I am a woman"; on this truth must be based all further discussion. A man never begins by presenting himself as an individual of a certain sex; it goes without saying that he is a man. The terms *masculine* and *feminine* are used symmetrically only as a matter of form, as on legal papers. In actuality the relation of the two sexes is not quite like that of two electrical poles, for man represents both the positive and the neutral, as is indicated by the common use of *man* to designate human beings in general; whereas woman represents only the negative, defined by limiting criteria, without reciprocity. In the midst of an abstract discussion it is vexing to hear a man say: "You think thus and so because you are a woman"; but I know that my only defense is to reply: "I think thus and so because it is true," thereby removing my subjective self from the argument. It would be out of the question to reply: "And you think the contrary because you are a man," for it is understood that the fact of being a man is no peculiarity. A man is in the right in being a man; it is the woman who is in the wrong. It amounts to this: just as for the ancients there was an absolute vertical with reference to which the oblique was defined, so there is an absolute human type, the masculine. Woman has ovaries, a uterus; these peculiarities imprison her in her subjectivity, circumscribe her within the limits of her own nature. It is often said that she thinks with her glands. Man superbly ignores the fact that his anatomy also includes glands, such as the testicles, and that they secrete hormones. He thinks of his body as a direct and normal connection with the world, which he believes he apprehends objectively, whereas he regards the body of woman as a hindrance, a prison, weighed down by everything peculiar to it. "The female is a female by virtue of a certain *lack* of qualities," said Aristotle;[1] "we should regard the female nature as afflicted with a natural defectiveness." And St. Thomas[2] for his part pronounced women to be an "imperfect man," an "incidental" being. This is symbolized in Genesis where Eve is depicted as made from what Bossuet[3] called "a supernumerary bone" of Adam.

Thus humanity is male and man defines woman not in herself but as relative to him; she is not regarded as an autonomous being. Michelet[4] writes: "Woman, the relative being. . . ." And Benda[5] is most positive in his *Rapport d'Uriel:* "The body of man makes sense in itself quite apart from that of woman, whereas the latter seems wanting in significance by itself. . . . Man can think of himself without woman. She cannot think of herself without man." And she is simply what man decrees; thus she is called "the sex," by which is meant that she appears essentially to the male as a sexual being. For him she is sex— absolute sex, no less. She is defined and differentiated with reference to man and not he with reference to her; she is the incidental, the inessential as opposed to the essential. He is the Subject, he is the Absolute—she is the Other.

The category of the *Other* is as primordial as consciousness itself. In the most primitive societies, in the most ancient mythologies, one finds the expression of a duality—that of the Self and the Other. This duality was not originally attached to the division of the sexes; it was not dependent upon any empirical facts. It is revealed in such works as that of Granet[6] on Chinese thought and those of Dumézil[7] on the East Indies and Rome. The feminine element was at first no more involved in such pairs as Varuna-Mitra, Uranus-Zeus, Sun-Moon, and Day-Night[8] than it was in the contrasts

---

[1]**Aristotle:** Greek philosopher (384–322 B.C.).   [2]**Saint Thomas Aquinas:** ecclesiastical writer and philosopher (1224?-1225–1274).   [3]**Jacques Bossuet:** French bishop, defended the rights of the French church against papal authority. His literary works include *Funeral Panegyrics* and *Four Great Personages* (1627–1704).   [4]**Michelet:** French historian (1798–1874).   [5]**Julian Benda:** French novelist and philosopher (1867–1956).   [6]**Francois Marius Granet:** French painter and watercolorist (1775–1849).   [7]**Dumézil:** Expert on mythology.   [8]**Varuna-Mitra . . . Day-Night:** Varuna—Vedic god of skies and sea; Mitra—Vedic god of moon; Uranus—god/father of the Titans in Greek mythology; Zeus—king of the gods in Greek mythology; oppositions.

between Good and Evil, lucky and unlucky auspices, right and left, God and Lucifer. Otherness is a fundamental category of human thought.

Thus it is that no group ever sets itself up as the One without at once setting up the 5 Other over against itself. If three travelers chance to occupy the same compartment, that is enough to make vaguely hostile "others" out of all the rest of the passengers on the train. In small-town eyes all persons not belonging to the village are "strangers" and suspect; to the native of a country all who inhabit other countries are "foreigners"; Jews are "different" for the anti-Semite, Negroes are "inferior" for American racists, aborigines are "natives" for colonists, proletarians are the "lower class" for the privileged.

Lévi-Strauss,[9] at the end of a profound work on the various forms of primitive societies, reaches the following conclusion: "Passage from the state of Nature to the state of Culture is marked by man's ability to view biological relations as a series of contrasts; duality, alternation, opposition, and symmetry, whether under definite or vague forms, constitute not so much phenomena to be explained as fundamental and immediately given data of social reality." These phenomena would be incomprehensible if in fact human society were simply a *Mitsein* or fellowship based on solidarity and friendliness. Things become clear, on the contrary, if, following Hegel,[10] we find in consciousness itself a fundamental hostility toward every other consciousness; the subject can be posed only in being opposed—he sets himself up as the essential, as opposed to the other, the inessential, the object.

But the other consciousness, the other ego, sets up a reciprocal claim. The native traveling abroad is shocked to find himself in turn regarded as a "stranger" by the natives of neighboring countries. As a matter of fact, wars, festivals, trading, treaties, and contests among tribes, nations, and classes tend to deprive the concept *Other* of its absolute sense and to make manifest its relativity; willy-nilly, individuals and groups are forced to realize the reciprocity of their relations. How is it, then, that this reciprocity has not been recognized between the sexes, that one of the contrasting terms is set up as the sole essential, denying any relativity in regard to its correlative and defining the latter as pure otherness? Why is it that women do not dispute male sovereignty? No subject will readily volunteer to become the object, the inessential; it is not the Other who, in defining himself as the Other, establishes the One. The Other is posed as such by the One in defining himself as the One. But if the Other is not to regain the status of being the One, he must be submissive enough to accept this alien point of view. Whence comes this submission in the case of woman?

There are, to be sure, other cases in which a certain category has been able to dominate another completely for a time. Very often this privilege depends upon inequality of numbers—the majority imposes its rule upon the minority or persecutes it. But women are not a minority, like the American Negroes or the Jews; there are as many women as men on earth. Again, the two groups concerned have often been originally independent; they may have been formerly unaware of each other's existence, or perhaps they recognized each other's autonomy. But a historical event has resulted in the subjugation of the weaker by the stronger. The scattering of the Jews, the introduction of slavery into America, the conquests of imperialism are examples in point. In these

---

[9]**Claude Lévi-Strauss:** French anthropologist (1908–). [10]**Georg Wilhelm Friedrich Hegel:** German philosopher who developed the theory of dialectic (1770–1831).

cases the oppressed retained at least the memory of former days; they possessed in common a past, a tradition, sometimes a religion or a culture.

The parallel drawn by Bebel[11] between women and the proletariat is valid in that neither ever formed a minority or a separate collective unit of mankind. And instead of a single historical event it is in both cases a historical development that explains their status as a class and accounts for the membership of *particular individuals* in that class. But proletarians have not always existed, whereas there have always been women. They are women in virtue of their anatomy and physiology. Throughout history they have always been subordinated to men, and hence their dependency is not the result of a historical event or a social change—it was not something that *occurred*. The reason why otherness in this case seems to be an absolute is in part that it lacks the contingent or incidental nature of historical facts. A condition brought about at a certain time can be abolished at some other time, as the Negroes of Haiti[12] and others have proved; but it might seem that a natural condition is beyond the possibility of change. In truth, however, the nature of things is no more immutably given, once for all, than is historical reality. If woman seems to be the inessential which never becomes the essential, it is because she herself fails to bring about this change. Proletarians say "We"; Negroes also. Regarding themselves as subjects, they transform the bourgeois, the whites, into "others." But women do not say "We," except at some congress of feminists or similar formal demonstration; men say "women," and women use the same word in referring to themselves. They do not authentically assume a subjective attitude. The proletarians have accomplished the revolution in Russia, the Negroes in Haiti, the Indochinese are battling for it in Indochina;[13] but the women's effort has never been anything more than a symbolic agitation. They have gained only what men have been willing to grant; they have taken nothing, they have only received.

The reason for this is that women lack concrete means for organizing themselves into a unit which can stand face to face with the correlative unit. They have no past, no history, no religion of their own; and they have no such solidarity of work and interest as that of the proletariat. They are not even promiscuously herded together in the way that creates community feeling among the American Negroes, the ghetto Jews, the workers of Saint-Denis,[14] or the factory hands of Renault.[15] They live dispersed among the males, attached through residence, housework, economic condition, and social standing to certain men—fathers or husbands—more firmly than they are to other women. If they belong to the bourgeoisie, they feel solidarity with men of that class, not with proletarian women; if they are white, their allegiance is to white men, not to Negro women. The proletariat can propose to massacre the ruling class, and a sufficiently fanatical Jew or Negro might dream of getting sole possession of the atomic bomb and making humanity wholly Jewish or black; but woman cannot even dream of exterminating the males. The bond that unites her to her oppressors is not comparable to any other. The division of the sexes is a biological fact, not an event in human

10

---

[11] **August Bebel:** German Social Democrat leader and writer (1840–1913).   [12] **Haiti:** Country of the West Indies.   [13] **Indochina:** Peninsula of Southeast Asia composed of Vietnam, Laos, Cambodia, Thailand, Burma, and the Malay Peninsula; name given to group of former French colonies.   [14] **Saint-Denis:** City in north central France, near Paris.   [15] **Renault:** French car manufacturer.

history. Male and female stand opposed within a primordial *Mitsein,* and woman has not broken it. The couple is a fundamental unity with its two halves riveted together, and the cleavage of society along the line of sex is impossible. Here is to be found the basic trait of woman: she is the Other in a totality of which the two components are necessary to one another.

One could suppose that this reciprocity might have facilitated the liberation of woman. When Hercules sat at the feet of Omphale[16] and helped with her spinning, his desire for her held him captive; but why did she fail to gain a lasting power? To revenge herself on Jason, Medea[17] killed their children: and this grim legend would seem to suggest that she might have obtained a formidable influence over him through his love for his offspring. In *Lysistrata* Aristophanes[18] gaily depicts a band of women who joined forces to gain social ends through the sexual needs of their men; but this is only a play. In the legend of the Sabine women,[19] the latter soon abandoned their plan of remaining sterile to punish their ravishers. In truth woman has not been socially emancipated through man's need—sexual desire and the desire for offspring—which makes the male dependent for satisfaction upon the female.

Master and slave, also, are united by a reciprocal need, in this case economic, which does not liberate the slave. In the relation of master to slave the master does not make a point of the need that he has for the other; he has in his grasp the power of satisfying this need through his own action; whereas the slave, in his dependent condition, his hope and fear, is quite conscious of the need he has for his master. Even if the need is at bottom equally urgent for both, it always works in favor of the oppressor and against the oppressed. That is why the liberation of the working class, for example, has been slow.

Now, woman has always been man's dependent, if not his slave; the two sexes have never shared the world in equality. And even today woman is heavily handicapped, though her situation is beginning to change. Almost nowhere is her legal status the same as man's, and frequently it is much to her disadvantage. Even when her rights are legally recognized in the abstract, long-standing custom prevents their full expression in the mores. In the economic sphere men and women can almost be said to make up two castes; other things being equal, the former hold the better jobs, get higher wages, and have more opportunity for success than their new competitors. In industry and politics men have a great many more positions and they monopolize the most important posts. In addition to all this, they enjoy a traditional prestige that the education of children tends in every way to support, for the present enshrines the past—and in the past all history has been made by men. At the present time, when women are beginning to take part in the affairs of the world, it is still a world that belongs to men—they have no doubt of it

---

[16]**Hercules . . . Omphale:** Hercules—hero of Greek mythology, known for his strength; as punishment, Zeus condemned Hercules to serve as a slave to Queen Omphale, who required him to dress as a woman and to do women's chores.   [17]**Jason, Medea:** Jason—Thessalian hero who journeyed with the Argonauts in search of the Golden Fleece. Medea—a magician or sorceress who aided Jason and later murdered their two children when he betrayed her.   [18]**Aristophanes:** Athenian dramatist (448–380? B.C.). *Lysistrata,* a comedy by Aristophanes, features a rebellion by women who protest war by denying their husbands sexual favors.   [19]**Sabine women:** Allusion to the abduction of the Sabine women by the Romans (c. 290 B.C.).

at all and women have scarcely any. To decline to be the Other, to refuse to be a party to the deal—this would be for women to renounce all the advantages conferred upon them by their alliance with the superior caste. Man-the-sovereign will provide woman-the-liege with material protection and will undertake the moral justification of her existence; thus she can evade at once both economic risk and the metaphysical risk of a liberty in which ends and aims must be contrived without assistance. Indeed, along with the ethical urge of each individual to affirm his subjective existence, there is also the temptation to forgo liberty and become a thing. This is an inauspicious road, for he who takes it—passive, lost, ruined—becomes henceforth the creature of another's will, frustrated in his transcendence and deprived of every value. But it is an easy road; on it one avoids the strain involved in undertaking an authentic existence. When man makes of woman the *Other,* he may, then, expect her to manifest deep-seated tendencies toward complicity. Thus, woman may fail to lay claim to the status of subject because she lacks definite resources, because she feels the necessary bond that ties her to man regardless of reciprocity, and because she is often very well pleased with her role as the *Other.* ●

Explorations of the Text

1. Why does de Beauvoir begin with a question? with the need for definition?
2. Do you agree with her assessment that "man represents both the positive and the neutral . . . whereas woman represents only the negative"?
3. What does de Beauvoir mean when she states that woman is "imprison[ed] in her subjectivity" and that "she thinks with her glands"?
4. State in your own words her concept of "the Other." Agree or disagree with her position.
5. Why does de Beauvoir include references to the ideas of "reciprocity" and of "duality"? to master-slave relations?
6. How has woman's sexuality led historically to her position as "Other"? Why have women failed to break out of this position?
7. Outline de Beauvoir's argument. Does she argue through definition, causal analysis, or comparison? Does she argue inductively or deductively? Who is her audience?
8. Why does she include references to Haiti and Indochina, to Jews and African Americans? Why does she include references to Hercules, Jason and Medea, *Lysistrata,* and the Sabine Women? Are the allusions effective?
9. De Beauvoir wrote *The Second Sex* in 1949. Do her ideas still apply to contemporary society? What aspects of women's status have changed?

The Reading/Writing Connection

1. **Write an Argument:** Define the "Other." Do you agree with de Beauvoir's characterization of woman as "Other"?
2. What do you see as a current issue for men and women in North American society? Is de Beauvoir's critique still relevant? Evaluate her arguments. Write a journal response to one of these questions.

Ideas for Writing

1. Compare de Beauvoir's view of the woman as "Other" with the roles of several women in works in this chapter.

2. Conceive of an alternative relationship for men and women. What do you see as ideal?

The 3rd WWWave

The 3rd WWWave: Who We Are, and Why We Need to Speak *1997*

For the Second Wave: We Are Not You (And That's Not a Bad Thing)

The spiral goes on. A new generation of women is emerging into the adult world, the first generation who knew about the ERA and "Women's Lib" from early childhood. Many of our mothers went back to school to get higher degrees that were postponed when they had children; many worked outside the home; many were divorced or separated. We grew up hearing "you can be anything you want to be," and yet we knew also that the world didn't welcome high-achieving girls as it did boys. We knew women had the right to have any job that a man could have, and yet we saw few female auto mechanics, engineers, and athletes. We heard about valuing everyone for their contributions—including stay-at-home dads as well as career women—but nonetheless we observed men going to work, pooh-poohing the concept of raising kids, and women either staying at home exclusively or holding a job *and* doing all the housework on top of that.

Clearly feminism is not "finished" now that women have moved into the workplace and everyone knows to say "chairperson" instead of "chairman."

And yet even though a majority of women support the *goals* of feminism, a majority of those will not call themselves "feminist." Feminism has a problem. It has come to be associated with the academic feminists of the university Women's Studies departments. It has come to represent a rigid "agenda" and a fixed set of beliefs which more and more women are not comfortable adhering to. Feminism used to have so many faces, but now only one is considered "legitimate."

What about women who want to get married and have children even though they believe strongly in equal opportunity for men and women? Have they bowed down to the patriarchy? Can they really claim to be feminists?

What about women who want to make money? Who work hard for that promo- 5 tion, manage their money in the stock market, and use their financial power to get things they want? Have they bowed down to the evil capitalist empire? Can they really claim to be feminists?

What about women who like to shoot guns, who write pornographic short stories, who use the Internet instead of sending out hand-written flyers? Do they "qualify" as feminists?

Yes. If they want to.

We proudly call ourselves feminists, and we are! It seems that young women these days are getting a lot of criticism from old-guard feminists who call their efforts puny and invalid. Our main crime seems to be that we are not replicas of the 60s activists who started the second wave. Some of feminism's image problem is being *created* by second-wave feminists themselves! It is a shame to disown people from your own movement just because they don't conform to your exact model. Times have changed; we need new strategies. We are happy to learn from what you did, but we also need to move on to new efforts that fit the way women live *today*.

Maybe you just need the question asked in a different way: Do you think the suffragists of the first wave would have enthusiastically supported the 1960s counterculture and the sexual revolution as a logical extension of their feminist efforts? No? So why do you want us to be just like you?

The third wave is gearing up. We know it's unfair that women work just as hard   10
as men outside the home (indeed, *harder* than men just to be considered competent), then come home to do 75% of the housework. We sense that our very value system still rewards men's achievements simply because they are done by men, and that women will never "measure up" on the male yardstick. There's plenty more to do in the name of feminism. We of the third wave are more hard-boiled than the second, lacking the idealism of the 1960s. But we are just as angry, and in a better financial position. Don't underestimate our drive and clout.

Now don't get me wrong. I for one am very grateful to the second wave for helping me get to this point. I have opportunities my mother never did. I am protected by laws that it took sweat, blood, and tears to pass 30 years ago. I will never suffer through some of the humiliating and painful experiences that members of the second wave endured to bring women the rights and priviledges they have now. I am not taking you for granted. But I *am* champing at the bit to fly off in my own direction with these wings you helped me gain! Don't tell me where to fly!

And don't lament the loss of your "Movement"! It's not dead; it's been reborn in a new form appropriate for the 90s. It is moving off in new directions that you couldn't have anticipated 30 years ago. We are not you, and that's not a bad thing. (Are you just like *your* mother?) The third wave has arrived.

For The Women: "But Isn't Feminism a Thing of the Past?"

I hear this all the time from career women. These are smart women, with college degrees or beyond, often in the midst of a tricky balancing act between job, children, and personal pursuits. They landed a decent job, got a promotion in a couple years, had a family. They "have it all," just like the magazines promised they would. Who needs feminism? Aren't feminists just a bunch of angry man-haters who see sexism in everything and want to add new pronouns like "hir" to the English language?

Sigh. No.

Did you ever ask yourself, why do I get up at 5:30 am so I can get the kids dressed   15
and pack their lunches and send them off to school, then rush off to my job from 8 to 6, then rush home to cook dinner, do a couple hours of cleaning, catch up on reading for work, then collapse in bed? Is this "having it all," or is it merely "doing it all"?

We don't deny that you have much more than your mother did. A better education, a higher-paying job, more laws protecting your rights—all these things are crucial advances that we have made because of second wave feminism. But it's a very different thing to say that feminism is over, that it's finished, that nothing more needs to be done, or that everything will "work itself out" now that the first bricks have been laid.

There are questions you can ask yourself. Why do women who hold outside jobs still do 75% of the housework? Didn't feminism enlighten all the men to regard sharing a home as genuine *sharing?* Why do most high school kids still learn that history is a series of wars, kings, pacts, and economic movements? Didn't feminism enlighten educators to the existence of important women and their impact on culture? Where are the female athletes, scientists, auto mechanics, and construction workers that feminism was supposed to create by showing that "girls were as good as boys"? Where are the househusbands who no longer tie their egos to supporting a family, but find joy instead in raising children while their wives work? Where is the *respect* for women or men who choose stereotypically female pursuits?

The last question is the key. Feminism has not broken the gender stereotypes that imprison men and women in fundamentally unequal roles. It has allowed very specific women to gain respect because they follow certain rules. Let me say loudly and clearly that I am **not** criticizing these women—heck, I'm one of them!—and that I firmly believe our recently gained economic freedom from men is the best advance we've made.

But the stereotypes *persist.* Part of the problem is that the Reagan years reentrenched these gender roles like a tick diving back down under flesh. When it comes right down to it, men do pretty much the same things that they ever did: get an education, get a job, have a family, earn money. The difference now is that women have broken into the job arena. But we still do the lion's share of housework, emotional upkeep in relationships, raising children, caring for elderly family members, and supporting men psychologically.

This was not the goal of the second wave, nor is it especially good for women. Do 20 you really like spending all that money on daycare, rushing around to ten places at once—all so your boss can pay you less overtime, decide that you aren't as "committed" to your career as a man, and subtley decrease your earnings compared to men over the long haul? Do you really think that the male lifestyle of sacrificing personal development and relation-ships for a career is the *only* lifestyle worthy of rewards and respect? Do you get the feeling America has no concept of "healthy balance"?

Some people are starting to decide that feminists are to blame for this situation. Women say, "I'm not a feminist," by which they mean, "Don't worry—I won't be out there waving a sign that might hurt my position in the company. And by the way, I have to leave at 4 to pick up Bobby from daycare." Translation: feminists are troublemakers and who has time for that anyway when I'm booked 20 hours out of 24? Men say, "Feminism failed. My wife is miserable with all the stress from her job and then having to take care of the kids on top of that." Translation: why can't you women just stay home like you're supposed to? ('Share' the childcare? What does that mean?)

If you're unhappy with the way work and family balance (or fail to balance) for women, that's a clue that feminism is not "a thing of the past." The working world has grudgingly allowed us to enter, but we haven't had a say in the rules! Why can't we have more flexible work schedules, more on-site child care, more telecommuting? Why can't we respect men who want to stay home? Why can't we respect women who want to stay home? People are shifting around in the worlds of work and family, but somehow, the old edifice remains in place. The old values, the old structures. Feminism of the 90s—or at least part of it—is about making new structures that fit the way women live now, not the way men lived in the 1950s.

It will mean that men have to change too. We address that in other parts of this site. The point is, feminism isn't a "thing of the past." It's here now, from the present into the future, in a new form than you remember it. And it can help answer all those nagging questions we asked above. The third wave has arrived.

For the Men: How Does Third-wave Feminism Relate to You?

Too many men get 100% of their emotional support from women. Sure, you've got your buddies and your coworkers and your online friends. But when you are nervous about an upcoming job interview, unhappy with your boss, or concerned about your mother's health, you turn *exclusively* to your wife or girlfriend. When was the last emotional, vulnerable, heart-to-heart talk you had with another man?

You get *all* your support from us, and almost none from other men. This is an in-   25
credible burden to place on another human, and it isn't fair. We have our own emotions to manage, and it is downright tiring to manage yours too. Everyone needs support from their friends and relatives, and of course we care about you as lovers and friends, but please don't ask us to be the only person in your life who fulfills that role. So many men are absolutely *cut adrift* when their relationships break up. Suddenly you have no one you can talk to because you *only* talked to your girlfriend!

I believe this is why men are so often compared to children. You are emotionally needy. I think it is also why so many murders are committed by men who have just broken up with their girlfriends or wives. Losing that special person makes you absolutely despondent and isolated because you have no other close connections. It is unhealthy to structure your life that way.

Many years ago, women were totally dependent on men financially, which in some sense "balanced" the total dependence of men on women emotionally. (Obviously, it was an unstable equilibrium.) Now we are learning to support ourselves money-wise. We can't count on a lifelong income from our husbands— and we can't even count on alimony or child support. We have jobs. We work to live, just like you. (And I happen to think this is a good thing!)

Now you must do your share. Learn not to depend on us for 100% of your emotional support. We just can't do that for you anymore. It's too exhausting when we are trying to deal with our own jobs and lives at the same time.

The third wave of feminism is about helping women learn to use their freedom, power, money, and influence wisely and for the common good. We have no desire to leave our brothers, boyfriends, husbands, and male friends behind because we care about our relationships with you. But we will not do your work for you. We cannot be your surrogate Mom now that you are all grown up. Run alongside us! And please start helping *each other*. ●

Explorations of the Text

1. How does the author distinguish between the second and third wave of feminism? According to The 3rd WWWave, what characterizes the first "generation of women . . . emerging into the adult world . . . [who] knew about the ERA and Women's Liberation"?

2. What is the third wave's critique of second wave feminism? What are the goals of third wave feminists?

3. Summarize the feminist positions presented in Simone de Beauvoir's "Woman as Other"; Virginia Woolf's "Professions for Women"; and "The 3rd

WWWave . . ." How does each author tackle the political and social inequalities endemic to her age? How does each woman confront a different set of problems for women? How are their views similar?

The Reading/Writing Connection

1. "Think" Topic: Do you think that the feminist revolution is over? Respond in a freewrite.
2. Argument: Isolate one of the controversial statements in "The 3rd WWWave."

4. According to the essay, what more needs to be done in the struggle for gender equity?

(For example, "Too many men get 100% of their emotional support from women.") Do you agree with her?

Ideas for Writing

1. **Write an Argument:** "Is feminism "a thing of the past"? Would you consider yourself a feminist? What do you consider to be the goals of feminism? Write an essay exploring your views in response to one of these questions.

2. **Write an Argument:** Do you agree with the author's assertion that one of the goals of third wave feminism is to address the issue of women "having it all" yet "doing it all"? She suggests that the feminist movement has not changed the assumptions about women's and men's work and/or stereotypical gender roles in regard to domestic responsibilities and childcare. In addition, a recent report issued by the American Association of University Women Educational Foundation states that the salary gap between men and women starts immediately after college and continues to widen throughout their careers.

Masculinities/Femininities—Conditioned or Constructed/Nonfiction

Mary Pipher *(1947–)*

Saplings in the Storm   *1994*
from *Reviving Ophelia: Saving the Selves of Adolescent Girls*

When my cousin Polly was a girl, she was energy in motion. She danced, did cartwheels and splits, played football, basketball and baseball with the neighborhood boys, wrestled with my brothers, biked, climbed trees and rode horses. She was as lithe and as resilient as a willow branch and as unrestrained as a lion cub. Polly talked as much as she moved. She yelled out orders and advice, shrieked for joy when she won a bet or heard a good joke, laughed with her mouth wide open, argued with kids and grown-ups and insulted her foes in the language of a construction worker.

We formed the Marauders, a secret club that met over her garage. Polly was the Tom Sawyer of the club. She planned the initiations, led the spying expeditions and hikes to haunted houses. She showed us the rituals to become blood "brothers" and taught us card tricks and how to smoke.

Then Polly had her first period and started junior high. She tried to keep up her old ways, but she was called a tomboy and chided for not acting more ladylike. She was excluded by her boy pals and by the girls, who were moving into makeup and romances.

This left Polly confused and shaky. She had temper tantrums and withdrew from both the boys' and girls' groups. Later she quieted down and reentered as Becky Thatcher. She wore stylish clothes and watched from the sidelines as the boys acted and spoke. Once again she was accepted and popular. She glided smoothly through our small society. No one spoke of the changes or mourned the loss of our town's most dynamic citizen. I was the only one who felt that a tragedy had transpired.

Girls in what Freud called the latency period, roughly age six or seven through puberty, are anything but latent. I think of my daughter Sara during those years—performing chemistry experiments and magic tricks, playing her violin, starring in her own plays, rescuing wild animals and biking all over town. I think of her friend Tamara, who wrote a 300-page novel the summer of her sixth-grade year. I remember myself, reading every children's book in the library of my town. One week I planned to be a great doctor like Albert Schweitzer. The next week I wanted to write like Louisa May Alcott or dance in Paris like Isadora Duncan. I have never since had as much confidence or ambition. 5

Most preadolescent girls are marvelous company because they are interested in everything—sports, nature, people, music and books. Almost all the heroines of girls' literature come from this age group—Anne of Green Gables, Heidi, Pippi Longstocking and Caddie Woodlawn. Girls this age bake pies, solve mysteries and go on quests. They can take care of themselves and are not yet burdened with caring for others. They have a brief respite from the female role and can be tomboys, a word that conveys courage, competency and irreverence.

They can be androgynous, having the ability to act adaptively in any situation regardless of gender role constraints. An androgynous person can comfort a baby or change a tire, cook a meal or chair a meeting. Research has shown that, since they are free to act without worrying if their behavior is feminine or masculine, androgynous adults are the most well adjusted.

Girls between seven and eleven rarely come to therapy. They don't need it. I can count on my fingers the girls this age whom I have seen: Coreen, who was physically abused; Anna, whose parents were divorcing; and Brenda, whose father killed himself. These girls were courageous and resilient. Brenda said, "If my father didn't want to stick around, that's his loss." Coreen and Anna were angry, not at themselves, but rather at the grown-ups, who they felt were making mistakes. It's amazing how little help these girls needed from me to heal and move on.

A horticulturist told me a revealing story. She led a tour of junior-high girls who were attending a math and science fair on her campus. She showed them side oats grama, bluestem, Indian grass and trees—redbud, maple, walnut and willow. The younger girls interrupted each other with their questions and tumbled forward to see, touch and smell everything. The older girls, the ninth-graders, were different. They hung back. They didn't touch plants or shout out questions. They stood primly to the side, looking bored and even a little disgusted by the enthusiasm of their younger classmates.

My friend asked herself, What's happened to these girls? What's gone wrong? She told me, "I wanted to shake them, to say, 'Wake up, come back. Is anybody home at your house?'"

Recently I sat sunning on a bench outside my favorite ice-cream store. A mother 10 and her teenage daughter stopped in front of me and waited for the light to change. I heard the mother say, "You have got to stop blackmailing your father and me. Every time you don't get what you want, you tell us that you want to run away from home or kill yourself. What's happened to you? You used to be able to handle not getting your way."

The daughter stared straight ahead, barely acknowledging her mother's words. The light changed. I licked my ice-cream cone. Another mother approached the same light with her preadolescent daughter in tow. They were holding hands. The daughter said to her mother, "This is fun. Let's do this all afternoon."

Something dramatic happens to girls in early adolescence. Just as planes and ships disappear mysteriously into the Bermuda Triangle, so do the selves of girls go down in droves. They crash and burn in a social and developmental Bermuda Triangle. In early adolescence, studies show that girls' IQ scores drop and their math and science scores plummet. They lose their resiliency and optimism and become less curious and inclined to take risks. They lose their assertive, energetic and "tomboyish" personalities and become more deferential, self-critical and depressed. They report great unhappiness with their own bodies.

Psychology documents but does not explain the crashes. Girls who rushed to drink in experiences in enormous gulps sit quietly in the corner. Writers such as Sylvia Plath, Margaret Atwood and Olive Schreiner have described the wreckage. Diderot, in writing to his young friend Sophie Volland, described his observations harshly: "You all die at 15."

Fairy tales capture the essence of this phenomenon. Young women eat poisoned apples or prick their fingers with poisoned needles and fall asleep for a hundred years. They wander away from home, encounter great dangers, are rescued by princes and are transformed into passive and docile creatures.

The story of Ophelia, from Shakespeare's *Hamlet,* shows the destructive forces that 15 affect young women. As a girl, Ophelia is happy and free, but with adolescence she loses herself. When she falls in love with Hamlet, she lives only for his approval. She has no inner direction; rather she struggles to meet the demands of Hamlet and her father. Her value is determined utterly by their approval. Ophelia is torn apart by her efforts to please. When Hamlet spurns her because she is an obedient daughter, she goes mad with grief. Dressed in elegant clothes that weigh her down, she drowns in a stream filled with flowers.

Girls know they are losing themselves. One girl said, "Everything good in me died in junior high." Wholeness is shattered by the chaos of adolescence. Girls become fragmented, their selves split into mysterious contradictions. They are sensitive and tenderhearted, mean and competitive, superficial and idealistic. They are confident in the morning and overwhelmed with anxiety by nightfall. They rush through their days with wild energy and then collapse into lethargy. They try on new roles every week—this week the good student, next week the delinquent and the next, the artist. And they expect their families to keep up with these changes.

My clients in early adolescence are elusive and slow to trust adults. They are easily offended by a glance, a clearing of the throat, a silence, a lack of sufficient enthusiasm or a sentence that doesn't meet their immediate needs. Their voices have gone underground—their speech is more tentative and less articulate. Their moods swing widely. One week they love their world and their families, the next they are critical of everyone. Much of their behavior is unreadable. Their problems are complicated and metaphorical—eating disorders, school phobias and self-inflicted injuries. I need to ask again and again in a dozen different ways, "What are you trying to tell me?"

Michelle, for example, was a beautiful, intelligent seventeen-year-old. Her mother brought her in after she became pregnant for the third time in three years. I tried to talk about why this was happening. She smiled a Mona Lisa smile to all my questions. "No, I don't care all that much for sex." "No, I didn't plan this. It just happened." When Michelle left a session, I felt like I'd been talking in the wrong language to someone far away.

Holly was another mystery. She was shy, soft-spoken and slow-moving, pretty under all her makeup and teased red hair. She was a Prince fan and wore only purple. Her father brought her in after a suicide attempt. She wouldn't study, do chores, join any school activities or find a job. Holly answered questions in patient, polite monosyllables. She really talked only when the topic was Prince. For several weeks we talked about him. She played me his tapes. Prince somehow spoke for her and to her.

Gail burned and cut herself when she was unhappy. Dressed in black, thin as a straw, she sat silently before me, her hair a mess, her ears, lips and nose all pierced with rings. She spoke about Bosnia and the hole in the ozone layer and asked me if I liked rave music. When I asked about her life, she fingered her earrings and sat silently.   20

My clients are not different from girls who are not seen in therapy. I teach at a small liberal arts college and the young women in my classes have essentially the same experiences as my therapy clients. One student worried about her best friend who'd been sexually assaulted. Another student missed class after being beaten by her boyfriend. Another asked what she should do about crank calls from a man threatening to rape her. When stressed, another student stabbed her hand with paper clips until she drew blood. Many students have wanted advice on eating disorders.

After I speak at high schools, girls approach me to say that they have been raped, or they want to run away from home, or that they have a friend who is anorexic or alcoholic. At first all this trauma surprised me. Now I expect it.

Psychology has a long history of ignoring girls this age. Until recently adolescent girls haven't been studied by academics, and they have long baffled therapists. Because they are secretive with adults and full of contradictions, they are difficult to study. So much is happening internally that's not communicated on the surface.

Simone de Beauvoir believed adolescence is when girls realize that men have the power and that their only power comes from consenting to become submissive adored objects. They do not suffer from the penis envy Freud postulated, but from power envy.

She described the Bermuda Triangle this way: Girls who were the subjects of their   25 own lives become the objects of others' lives. "Young girls slowly bury their childhood, put away their independent and imperious selves and submissively enter adult existence." Adolescent girls experience a conflict between their autonomous selves and their need to be feminine, between their status as human beings and their vocation as females. De Beauvoir says, "Girls stop being and start seeming."

Girls become "female impersonators" who fit their whole selves into small, crowded spaces. Vibrant, confident girls become shy, doubting young women. Girls stop thinking, "Who am I? What do I want?" and start thinking, "What must I do to please others?"

This gap between girls' true selves and cultural prescriptions for what is properly female creates enormous problems. To paraphrase a Stevie Smith poem about swimming in the sea, "they are not waving, they are drowning." And just when they most need help, they are unable to take their parents' hands.

Olive Schreiner wrote of her experiences as a young girl in *The Story of an African Farm.* "The world tells us what we are to be and shapes us by the ends it sets before us. To men it says, work. To us, it says, seem. The less a woman has in her head the lighter she is for carrying." She described the finishing school that she attended in this way: "It was a machine for condensing the soul into the smallest possible area. I have seen some souls so compressed that they would have filled a small thimble."

Margaret Mead believed that the ideal culture is one in which there is a place for every human gift. By her standards, our Western culture is far from ideal for women. So many gifts are unused and unappreciated. So many voices are stilled. Stendhal wrote: "All geniuses born women are lost to the public good."

Alice Miller wrote of the pressures on some young children to deny their true selves 30 and assume false selves to please their parents. *Reviving Ophelia* suggests that adolescent girls experience a similar pressure to split into true and false selves, but this time the pressure comes not from parents but from the culture. Adolescence is when girls experience social pressure to put aside their authentic selves and to display only a small portion of their gifts.

This pressure disorients and depresses most girls. They sense the pressure to be someone they are not. They fight back, but they are fighting a "problem with no name." One girl put it this way: "I'm a perfectly good carrot that everyone is trying to turn into a rose. As a carrot, I have good color and a nice leafy top. When I'm carved into a rose, I turn brown and wither."

Adolescent girls are saplings in a hurricane. They are young and vulnerable trees that the winds blow with gale strength. Three factors make young women vulnerable to the hurricane. One is their developmental level. Everything is changing—body shape, hormones, skin and hair. Calmness is replaced by anxiety. Their way of thinking is changing. Far below the surface they are struggling with the most basic of human questions: What is my place in the universe, what is my meaning?

Second, American culture has always smacked girls on the head in early adolescence. This is when they move into a broader culture that is rife with girl-hurting "isms," such as sexism, capitalism and lookism, which is the evaluation of a person solely on the basis of appearance.

Third, American girls are expected to distance from parents just at the time when they most need their support. As they struggle with countless new pressures, they must relinquish the protection and closeness they've felt with their families in childhood. They turn to their none-too-constant peers for support.

Parents know only too well that something is happening to their daughters. Calm, 35 considerate daughters grow moody, demanding and distant. Girls who loved to talk are sullen and secretive. Girls who liked to hug now bristle when touched. Mothers complain that they can do nothing right in the eyes of their daughters. Involved fathers bemoan their sudden banishment from their daughters' lives. But few parents realize how universal their experiences are. Their daughters are entering a new land, a dangerous place that parents can scarcely comprehend. Just when they most need a home base, they cut themselves loose without radio communications.

Most parents of adolescent girls have the goal of keeping their daughters safe while they grow up and explore the world. The parents' job is to protect. The daughters' job is to explore. Always these different tasks have created tension in parent-daughter relationships, but now it's even harder. Generally parents are more protective of their daughters than is corporate America. Parents aren't trying to make money off their daughters by selling them designer jeans or cigarettes, they just want them to be well adjusted. They don't see their daughters as sex objects or consumers but as real people with talents and interests. But daughters turn away from their parents as they enter the new land. They befriend their peers, who are their fellow inhabitants of the strange country and who share a common language and set of customs. They often embrace the junk values of mass culture.

This turning away from parents is partly for developmental reasons. Early adolescence is a time of physical and psychological change, self-absorption, preoccupation with peer approval and identity formation. It's a time when girls focus inward on their own fascinating changes.

It's partly for cultural reasons. In America we define adulthood as a moving away from families into broader culture. Adolescence is the time for cutting bonds and breaking free. Adolescents may claim great independence from parents, but they are aware and ashamed of their parents' smallest deviation from the norm. They don't like to be seen with them and find their imperfections upsetting. A mother's haircut or a father's joke can ruin their day. Teenagers are furious at parents who say the wrong things or do not respond with perfect answers. Adolescents claim not to hear their parents, but with their friends they discuss endlessly all parental attitudes. With amazing acuity, they sense nuances, doubt, shades of ambiguity, discrepancy and hypocrisy.

Adolescents still have some of the magical thinking of childhood and believe that parents have the power to keep them safe and happy. They blame their parents for their misery, yet they make a point of not telling their parents how they think and feel; they have secrets, so things can get crazy. For example, girls who are raped may not tell their parents. Instead, they become hostile and rebellious. Parents bring girls in because of their anger and out-of-control behavior. When I hear about this unexplainable anger, I ask about rape. Ironically, girls are often angrier at their parents than at the rapists. They feel their parents should have known about the danger and been more protective; afterward, they should have sensed the pain and helped.

Most parents feel like failures during this time. They feel shut out, impotent and misunderstood. They often attribute the difficulties of this time to their daughters and their own failings. They don't understand that these problems go with the developmental stage, the culture and the times. 40

Parents experience an enormous sense of loss when their girls enter this new land. They miss the daughters who sang in the kitchen, who read them school papers, who accompanied them on fishing trips and to ball games. They miss the daughters who liked to bake cookies, play Pictionary and be kissed goodnight. In place of their lively, affectionate daughters they have changelings—new girls who are sadder, angrier and more complicated. Everyone is grieving.

Fortunately adolescence is time-limited. By late high school most girls are stronger and the winds are dying down. Some of the worst problems—cliques, a total focus on looks and struggles with parents—are on the wane. But the way girls handle the problems of adolescence can have implications for their adult lives. Without some help, the loss of wholeness, self-confidence and self-direction can last well into adulthood. Many adult clients struggle with the same issues that overwhelmed them as adolescent girls. Thirty-year-old accountants and realtors, forty-year-old homemakers and doctors, and thirty-five-year-old nurses and schoolteachers ask the same questions and struggle with the same problems as their teenage daughters.

Even sadder are the women who are not struggling, who have forgotten that they have selves worth defending. They have repressed the pain of their adolescence, the betrayals of self in order to be pleasing. These women come to therapy with the goal of becoming even more pleasing to others. They come to lose weight, to save their marriages or to rescue their children. When I ask them about their own needs, they are confused by the question.

Most women struggled alone with the trauma of adolescence and have led decades of adult life with their adolescent experiences unexamined. The lessons learned in adolescence are forgotten and their memories of pain are minimized. They come into therapy because their marriage is in trouble, or they hate their job, or their own daughter is giving them fits. Maybe their daughter's pain awakens their own pain. Some are depressed or chemically addicted or have stress-related illnesses—ulcers, colitis, migraines or psoriasis. Many have tried to be perfect women and failed. Even though they followed the rules and did as they were told, the world has not rewarded them. They feel angry and betrayed. They feel miserable and taken for granted, used rather than loved.

Women often know how everyone in their family thinks and feels except them- 45 selves. They are great at balancing the needs of their coworkers, husbands, children and friends, but they forget to put themselves into the equation. They struggle with adolescent questions still unresolved: How important are looks and popularity? How do I care for myself and not be selfish? How can I be honest and still be loved? How can I achieve and not threaten others? How can I be sexual and not a sex object? How can I be responsive but not responsible for everyone?

As we talk, the years fall away. We are back in junior high with the cliques, the shame, the embarrassment about bodies, the desire to be accepted and the doubts about ability. So many adult women think they are stupid and ugly. Many feel guilty if they take time for themselves. They do not express anger or ask for help.

We talk about childhood—what the woman was like at ten and at fifteen. We piece together a picture of childhood lost. We review her own particular story, her own time in the hurricane. Memories flood in. Often there are tears, angry outbursts, sadness for what has been lost. So much time has been wasted pretending to be who others wanted. But also, there's a new energy that comes from making connections, from choosing awareness over denial and from the telling of secrets.

We work now, twenty years behind schedule. We reestablish each woman as the subject of her life, not as the object of others' lives. We answer Freud's patronizing question "What do women want?" Each woman wants something different and particular and yet each woman wants the same thing—to be who she truly is, to become who she can become.

Many women regain their preadolescent authenticity with menopause. Because they are no longer beautiful objects occupied primarily with caring for others, they are free once again to become the subjects of their own lives. They become more confident, self-directed and energetic. Margaret Mead noticed this phenomenon in cultures all over the world and called it "pmz," postmenopausal zest. She noted that some cultures revere these older women. Others burn them at the stake.

■ ■ ■

Before I studied psychology, I studied cultural anthropology. I have always been in- 50 terested in that place where culture and individual psychology intersect, in why cultures create certain personalities and not others, in how they pull for certain strengths in their members, in how certain talents are utilized while others atrophy from lack of attention. I'm interested in the role cultures play in the development of individual pathology.

For a student of culture and personality, adolescence is fascinating. It's an extraordinary time when individual, developmental and cultural factors combine in ways that shape adulthood. It's a time of marked internal development and massive cultural indoctrination.

I want to try . . . to connect each girl's story with larger cultural issues—to examine the intersection of the personal and the political. It's a murky place; the personal and political are intertwined in all of our lives. Our minds, which are shaped by the society in which we live, can oppress us. And yet our minds can also analyze and work to change our culture. ●

William Pollack

Inside the World of Boys: Behind the Mask of Masculinity
from *Real Boys' Voices*   2001

> *"I get a little down," Adam confessed, "but I'm very good at hiding it. It's like I wear a mask. Even when the kids call me names or taunt me, I never show them how much it crushes me inside. I keep it all in."*

The Boy Code: "Everything's Just Fine"

Adam is a fourteen-year-old boy whose mother sought me out after a workshop I was leading on the subject of boys and families. Adam, she told me, had been performing very well in school, but now she felt something was wrong.

Adam had shown such promise that he had been selected to join a special program for talented students, and the program was available only at a different—and more academically prestigious—school than the one Adam had attended. The new school was located in a well-to-do section of town, more affluent than Adam's own neighborhood. Adam's mother had been pleased when her son had qualified for the program and even more delighted that he would be given a scholarship to pay for it. And so Adam had set off on this new life.

At the time we talked, Mrs. Harrison's delight had turned to worry. Adam was not doing well at the new school. His grades were mediocre, and at midterm he had been given a warning that he might fail algebra. Yet Adam continued to insist, "I'm fine. Everything's just fine." He said this both at home and at school. Adam's mother was perplexed, as was the guidance counselor at his new school. "Adam seems cheerful and has no complaints," the counselor told her. "But something must be wrong." His mother tried to talk to Adam, hoping to find out what was troubling him and causing him to do so poorly in school. "But the more I questioned him about what was going on," she said, "the more he continued to deny any problems."

Adam was a quiet and rather shy boy, small for his age. In his bright blue eyes I detected an inner pain, a malaise whose cause I could not easily fathom. I had seen a similar look on the faces of a number of boys of different ages, including many boys in the "Listening to Boys' Voices" study. Adam looked wary, hurt, closed-in, self-protective. Most of all, he looked alone.

One day, his mother continued, Adam came home with a black eye. She asked   5
him what had happened. "Just an accident," Adam had mumbled. He'd kept his eyes cast down, she remembered, as if he felt guilty or ashamed. His mother probed more deeply. She told him that she knew something was wrong, something upsetting was going on, and that—whatever it was—they could deal with it, they could face it together. Suddenly, Adam erupted in tears, and the story he had been holding inside came pouring out.

Adam was being picked on at school, heckled on the bus, goaded into fights in the schoolyard. "Hey, White Trash!" the other boys shouted at him. "You don't belong here with *us!*" taunted a twelfth-grade bully. "Why don't you go back to your own side of town!" The taunts often led to physical attacks, and Adam found himself having to fight back in order to defend himself. "But I never throw the first punch," Adam explained to his mother. "I don't show them they can hurt me. I don't want to embarrass myself in front of everybody."

I turned to Adam. "How do you feel about all this?" I asked. "How do you handle your feelings of anger and frustration?" His answer was, I'm sad to say, a refrain I hear often when I am able to connect to the inner lives of boys.

"I get a little down," Adam confessed, "but I'm very good at hiding it. It's like I wear a mask. Even when the kids call me names or taunt me, I never show them how much it crushes me inside. I keep it all in."

"What do you do with the sadness?" I asked.

"I tend to let it boil inside until I can't hold it any longer, and then it explodes. It's   10
like I have a breakdown, screaming and yelling. But I only do it inside my own room at home, where nobody can hear. Where nobody will know about it." He paused a moment. "I think I got this from my dad, unfortunately."

Adam was doing what I find so many boys do: he was hiding behind a mask, and using it to hide his deepest thoughts and feelings—his real self—from everyone, even the people closest to him. This mask of masculinity enabled Adam to make a bold (if inaccurate) statement to the world: "I can handle it. Everything's fine. I am invincible."

Adam, like other boys, wore this mask as an invisible shield, a persona to show the outside world a feigned self-confidence and bravado, and to hide the shame he felt at his feelings of vulnerability, powerlessness, and isolation. He couldn't handle the school situation alone—very few boys or girls of fourteen could—and he didn't know how to ask for help, even from people he knew loved him. As a result, Adam was unhappy and was falling behind in his academic performance.

Many of the boys I see today are like Adam, living behind a mask of masculine bravado that hides the genuine self to conform to our society's expectations; they feel it is necessary to cut themselves off from any feelings that society teaches them are unacceptable for men and boys—fear, uncertainty, feelings of loneliness and need.

Many boys, like Adam, also think it's necessary that they handle their problems alone. A boy is not expected to reach out—to his family, his friends, his counselors, or coaches—for help, comfort, understanding, and support. And so he is simply not as close as he could be to the people who love him and yearn to give him the human connections of love, caring, and affection every person needs.

The problem for those of us who want to help is that, on the outside, the boy who is ₁₅ having problems may seem cheerful and resilient while keeping inside the feelings that don't fit the male model—being troubled, lonely, afraid, desperate. Boys learn to wear the mask so skillfully—in fact, they don't even know they're doing it—that it can be difficult to detect what is really going on when they are suffering at school, when their friendships are not working out, when they are being bullied, becoming depressed, even dangerously so, to the point of feeling suicidal. The problems below the surface become obvious only when boys go "over the edge" and get into trouble at school, start to fight with friends, take drugs or abuse alcohol, are diagnosed with clinical depression or attention deficit disorder, erupt into physical violence, or come home with a black eye, as Adam did. Adam's mother, for example, did not know from her son that anything was wrong until Adam came home with an eye swollen shut; all she knew was that he had those perplexingly poor grades.

The Gender Straitjacket

Many years ago, when I began my research into boys, I had assumed that since America was revising its ideas about girls and women, it must have also been reevaluating its traditional ideas about boys, men, and masculinity. But over the years my research findings have shown that as far as boys today are concerned, the old Boy Code—the outdated and constricting assumptions, models, and rules about boys that our society has used since the nineteenth century—is still operating in force. I have been surprised to find that even in the most progressive schools and the most politically correct communities in every part of the country and in families of all types, the Boy Code continues to affect the behavior of all of us—the boys themselves, their parents, their teachers, and society as a whole. None of us is immune—it is so ingrained. I have caught myself behaving in accordance with the code, despite my awareness of its falseness—denying sometimes that I'm emotionally in pain when in fact I am; insisting that everything is all right, when it is not.

The Boy Code puts boys and men into a gender straitjacket that constrains not only them but everyone else, reducing us all as human beings, and eventually making us strangers to ourselves and to one another—or, at least, not as strongly connected to one another as we long to be.

Ophelia's Brothers

In Shakespeare's *Hamlet,* Ophelia is lover to the young prince of Denmark. Despondent over the death of his father, Hamlet turns away from Ophelia. She, in turn, is devastated and she eventually commits suicide. In recent years, Mary Pipher's book on adolescent girls, *Reviving Ophelia,* has made Ophelia a symbolic figure for troubled, voiceless adolescent girls. But what of Hamlet? What of Ophelia's brothers?

For Hamlet fared little better than Ophelia. Alienated from himself, as well as from his mother and father, he was plagued by doubt and erupted in uncontrolled outbursts. He grew increasingly isolated, desolate, and alone, and those who loved him were never able to get through to him. In the end, he died a tragic and unnecessary death.

The boys we care for, much like the girls we cherish, often seem to feel they must ₂₀ live semi-inauthentic lives, lives that conceal much of their true selves and feelings, and studies show they do so in order to fit in and be loved. The boys I see—in the

"Listening to Boys' Voices" study, in schools, and in private practice—often are hiding not only a wide range of their feelings but also some of their creativity and originality, showing in effect only a handful of primary colors rather than a broad spectrum of colors and hues of the self.

The Boy Code is so strong, yet so subtle, in its influence that boys may not even know they are living their lives in accordance with it. In fact, they may not realize there is such a thing until they violate the code in some way or try to ignore it. When they do, however, society tends to let them know—swiftly and forcefully—in the form of a taunt by a sibling, a rebuke by a parent or a teacher, or ostracism by classmates.

But, it doesn't have to be this way. I know that Adam could have been saved a great deal of pain if his parents and the well-meaning school authorities had known how to help him, how to make him feel safe to express his real feelings, beginning with the entirely natural anxiety about starting at a new school. This could have eased the transition from one school to a new one, rather than leaving Adam to tough it out by himself—even though Adam would have said, "Everything's all right."

How to Get Behind the Mask

As we'll discuss . . . there are many ways that we can learn how to understand a boy's deepest feelings and experience, to come to know who he *really* is, and to help him love and feel comfortable with his genuine self. The starting place for parents—as well as for teachers and other mentors of our boys—is to become sensitive to the early signs of the masking of feelings. These signs include everything from bad grades to rowdy behavior, from "seeming quiet" to manifesting symptoms of depression, from using drugs or alcohol to becoming a perpetrator or victim of violence; and sometimes, as in the case of Adam, the mask may accompany the mantra that "everything is fine."

The second step to getting behind the mask is learning a new way to talk to boys so that they don't feel afraid or ashamed to share their true feelings. For example, when a boy like Adam comes home with a black eye, rather than saying "Oh my God! Just *what* is happening to you at school?" or "What the heck happened to you?" less intimidating language can be used, such as "What is going on—can you tell me?" or "I've noticed things seem a little different for you lately—now I can see something's wrong. Let's talk about it."

The third step is to learn how to accept a boy's own *emotional schedule*. As we'll 25 discuss more in this book, boys who do share their feelings often take longer to do so than girls do. Whereas a girl might share her feelings as soon as she's asked what's going wrong, a boy will often refuse (or ignore us) the first time he's approached. We have to learn how to give the boy the time he needs and how to recognize in his words and actions the signals that he is ready to talk.

A boy's need to be silent—and then his subsequent readiness to share what he is feeling—is what we will call the *timed silence syndrome*. It's the boy who usually needs to set the clock himself—to determine how much time he needs to remain silent before opening up to share his feelings. If we learn to become sensitive to each boy's unique timing, we become better at respecting how he copes with emotions and make it more possible for him to be honest about the feelings behind the mask.

The fourth step involves what I call *connection through action*. This means that rather than nudging a boy to sit down and share his feelings with us, we begin by simply joining him in an activity that he enjoys. Often by simply *doing* something with the boy—playing a game with him, joining him for a duet on the piano, taking him to an amusement park—we forge a connection that then enables him to open up. In the middle of the game, the duet, or the Ferris wheel ride, a boy may often feel close and safe enough to share the feelings he'd otherwise keep hidden.

Finally, we can often help boys take off their masks by telling them stories about our own experiences. We can tell them "war stories" about when we were young and had to deal with life's ups and downs, or we can share recent experiences that challenged us. Even if our boy groans or rolls his eyes when we begin to share our story, he almost always benefits from the empathy that telling the story inevitably conveys. By discovering that, yes, we too have felt scared, embarrassed, or disappointed, the boy begins to feel less ashamed of his own vulnerable feelings. He feels our empathy and discovers that we understand, love, and respect the real boy in him.

For schools, getting behind the mask to help a boy like Adam requires several specific additional steps. First, as we'll learn throughout this book, teachers, school administrators, guidance counselors, and others all need to learn about how the Boy Code operates. They need to be actually trained to understand how this code restricts boys from being their true selves and how it pushes them to put on the mask. Second, I often suggest that schools assign to each boy an adult mentor who is sensitive and empathic to that boy's unique personality and interests. For example, the mentor for a boy who loves sports might be one of the gym teachers, whereas the mentor for the boy who loves poetry might be the English teacher. By assigning a mentor whose interests mirror those of the boy, the boy gains an adult friend with whom he can talk, somebody with whom he might feel comfortable sharing his deepest feelings and thoughts. Third, schools need to monitor closely those areas where the Boy Code operates most intensely. These include bus rides (where boys are often completely unsupervised), gym class, recess, and extracurricular sports. In such situations, teachers and other supervisors need to be especially vigilant about making sure that each boy is doing all right. Fourth, when teachers or others do intervene to help a boy who seems to be hurting behind the mask, it's important that they use the kind of nonshaming approach I discussed above. For example, when a boy seems to be the victim of a lot of teasing, rather than intervening suddenly by saying "Hey, what's going on here? Cut that out!" the adult supervisor might take aside the boys involved, individually and at separate times, and investigate what's happening in the particular situation. Finally, as I'll discuss more in this book, schools need to give boys a "report card" that covers not only their academic progress and classroom conduct but also their social life. By keeping an eye on a boy's social adjustment, schools are much better able to stay in touch with a boy's genuine emotional experience.

Preparing a Boy for Change

In addition to learning how to get to know the real boy, it's important for us as adults to anticipate situations such as important life changes—a move, a divorce, the birth of a new sibling—that are likely to bring up the kinds of painful feelings that force many boys to retreat behind the mask. For example, a new school, knowing that a boy like Adam was coming there from a less advantaged neighborhood, might have anticipated difficulties, assigned a buddy or mentor to Adam, an older boy who could teach him the ropes, introduce him to other boys, help him to become an insider rather than remain an outsider, and be a friend to ease him through the first weeks of school. The school counselors might have been in contact with Adam's mother from the first sign of an academic dip. Adam's teachers, too, might have been encouraged to help him get acquainted. Adam's parents might have spent more time with Adam during the first few weeks, and also prepared him in advance for his new experience, talking with him about what to expect, meeting with other parents and boys who had been involved in the same program, looking for another parent with a boy in the new school who might befriend Adam or talk with that parent about the school, visiting the school with Adam before his first day, and exploring the new neighborhood so he could adjust to the scene. Once he began to experience academic difficulties, which was the first indication to them that something was amiss, his parents might have tried to create safe spaces or activities to do together in which Adam might have felt able to open up and share his feelings; they might also have talked about their own memories of going away to college or feeling alone in a new experience.

A Mother's Instincts

One of the things I especially noticed in Adam's story is a hallmark of other boys' stories too—the mother's instincts were accurate; she *knew* in her heart that something was wrong. But she distrusted her own knowledge, and went along with the Boy Code and with Adam's saying, "Every thing is all right." In her denial of what she in fact knew, and in her acceptance of society's code for boys, she disconnected from her own instincts, not realizing she knew better; she didn't feel empowered to listen to her own intuitions about her son or take action that might have been outside the code but could have helped Adam before the situation came to a crisis. With the very best of intentions, everyone involved—the parents and authorities at both schools—had pushed Adam away from help and connection, from the full range of expressing himself. Everyone believed that the special school program represented a great opportunity for him, as indeed it did; but they failed to realize that it also represented a change in his social setting that needed to be handled for and with the boy.

Adam tried to tough it out on his own, the way boys do. It's part of the code.

Behind the Mask of Masculinity: Shame and the Trauma of Separation

Just as Adam and his parents unwittingly adhered to the Boy Code, most parents and schools do the same. It has been ingrained in our society for so long, we're unaware of it. One educational expert recently suggested that the way to achieve equality in schooling would be by "teaching girls to raise their voices and boys to develop their ears." Of course boys should learn to listen. They should also speak clearly, in their own personal voices. I believe, however, that it's not boys who cannot hear us—it is we who are unable to hear them.

Researchers have found that at birth, and for several months afterward, *male infants are actually more emotionally expressive than female babies.* But by the time boys reach elementary school much of their emotional expressiveness has been lost or has gone underground. Boys at five or six become less likely than girls to express hurt or distress, either to their teachers or to their own parents. Many parents have asked me what triggers this remarkable transformation, this squelching of a boy's natural emotional expressiveness. What makes a boy who was open and exuberant unwilling to show the whole range of his emotions?

Recent research points to two primary causes for this change, and both of them 35 grow out of assumptions about and attitudes toward boys that are deeply ingrained in the codes of our society.

The first reason is the use of shame in the toughening-up process by which it's assumed boys need to be raised. Little boys are made to feel ashamed of their feelings, guilty especially about feelings of weakness, vulnerability, fear, and despair.

The second reason is the separation process as it applies to boys, the emphasis society places on a boy's separating emotionally from his mother at an unnecessarily early age, usually by the time the boys are six years old and then again in adolescence.

The use of shame to "control" boys is pervasive; it is so corrosive I will devote a whole chapter to it in this book. Boys are made to feel shame over and over, in the midst of growing up, through what I call society's shame-hardening process. The idea is that a boy needs to be disciplined, toughened up, made to act like a "real man," be independent, keep the emotions in check. A boy is told that "big boys don't cry," that he shouldn't be "a mama's boy." If these things aren't said directly, these messages dominate in subtle ways in how boys are treated—and therefore how boys come to think of themselves. Shame is at the heart of how others behave toward boys on our playing fields, in schoolrooms, summer camps, and in our homes. A number of other societal factors contribute to this old-fashioned process of shame-hardening boys, and I'll have more to say about shame in the next chapter.

The second reason we lose sight of the real boy behind a mask of masculinity, and ultimately lose the boy himself, is the premature separation of a boy from his mother and all things maternal at the beginning of school. Mothers are encouraged to separate from their sons, and the act of forced separation is so common that it is generally considered to be "normal." But I have come to understand that this forcing of early separation is so acutely hurtful to boys that it can only be called a trauma—an emotional blow of damaging proportions. I also believe that it is an unnecessary trauma. Boys, like girls, will separate very naturally from their mothers, if allowed to do so at their own pace.

As if the trauma of separation at age six were not wrenching enough, boys often suffer a second separation trauma when they reach sexual maturity. As a boy enters adolescence, our society becomes concerned and confused about the mother-son relationship. We feel unsure about how intimate a mother should be with her sexually mature son. We worry that an intense and loving relationship between the two will somehow get in the way of the boy's ability to form friendships with girls his own age. As a result, parents—encouraged by the society around them—may once again push the boy away from the family and, in particular, the nurturing female realm. Our society tells us this is "good" for the boy, that he needs to be pushed out of the nest or he will never fly. But I believe that the opposite is true—that a boy will make the leap when he is ready, and he will do it better if he feels that there is someone there to catch him if he falls.

This double trauma of boyhood contributes to the creation in boys of a deep wellspring of grief and sadness that may last throughout their lives.

Mixed Messages: Society's New Expectations for Boys

But there is another problem too: society's new expectations for boys today are in direct conflict with the teachings of the Boy Code—and we have done little to resolve the contradiction. We now say that we want boys to share their vulnerable feelings, but at the same time we expect them to cover their need for dependency and *hide* their natural feelings of love and caring behind the mask of masculine autonomy and strength. It's an impossible assignment for any boy, or, for that matter, any human being.

The Silence of Lost Boys

Often, the result of all this conflation of signals is that the boys decide to be silent. They learn to suffer quietly, in retreat behind the mask of masculinity. They cannot speak, and we cannot hear. It's this silence that is often confusing to those of us concerned about the well-being of boys because it fools us into thinking that all is well, when much may be awry—that a boy doesn't need us, when in fact he needs us very much.

The good news is that we now know of many ways that we can help boys, and they are based on various patterns we now understand about typical boy behavior. Under-standing these patterns, these ways of a real boy's life, will, I believe, help us raise boys of all ages in more successful and authentic ways. For the truth is that once we help boys shed the straitjacket of gender—once we hear and understand what a real boy says, feels, and sees—the silence is broken and replaced by a lively roar of communica-tion. The disconnection quickly becomes reconnection. And once we reconnect with one boy, it can lead to stronger bonds with all the males in our lives—our brothers and fathers and husbands and sons. It can also help boys to connect again with their deep-est feelings, their true selves.

Living with Half a Self—the "Heroic" Half

Until now, many boys have been able to live out and express only *half* of their emo-tional lives—they feel free to show their "heroic," tough, action-oriented side, their physical prowess, as well as their anger and rage. What the Boy Code dictates is that they should suppress all other emotions and cover up the more gentle, caring, vulner-able sides of themselves. In the "Listening to Boys' Voices" study, many boys told me that they feel frightened and yearn to make a connection but can't. "At school, and even most times with my parents," one boy explained, "you can't act like you're a weakling. If you start acting scared or freaking out like a crybaby, my parents get mad, other kids punch you out or just tell you to shut up and cut it out." One mother told me what she expected of her nine-year-old son. "I don't mind it when Tony complains a little bit," she said, "but if he starts getting really teary-eyed and whiny I tell him to just put a lid on it. It's for his own good because if the other boys in the area hear him crying, they'll make it tough for him. Plus, his father really hates that kind of thing!" 45

Boys suppress feelings of rejection and loss also. One sixteen-year-old boy was told by his first girlfriend, after months of going together, that she didn't love him anymore. "You feel sick," confessed Cam. "But you just keep it inside. You don't tell anybody about it. And, then, maybe after a while, it just sort of goes away."

"It must feel like such a terrible burden, though, being so alone with it," I remarked.

"Yep," Cam sighed, fighting off tears. "But that's what a guy has to do, isn't it?"

Jason, age fifteen, recently wrote the following in an essay about expressing feelings:

> If something happens to you, you have to say: "Yeah, no big deal," even when you're really hurting. . . . When it's a tragedy—like my friend's father died—you can go up to a guy and give him a hug. But if it's anything less . . . you have to punch things and brush it off. I've punched so many lockers in my life, it's not even funny. When I get home, I'll cry about it.

I believe, and my studies indicate, that many boys are eager to be heard and that 50 we, as parents and professionals, must use all our resources to reach out and help them. As adults, we have both the power and perspective to see through the boys' false front of machismo, especially when we know enough to expect it and to understand it for what it is—a way to look in-charge and cool.

A four-year-old boy shrugs and tries to smile after he is hit in the eye with a baseball, while blinking back tears of pain. A ten-year-old boy whose parents have just divorced behaves so boisterously and entertainingly in class he's branded the "class clown," but underneath that bravado is a lot of suffering; he longs for the days when his parents were together and he didn't need that kind of attention. A fourteen-year-old flips listlessly through a sports magazine while his school counselor discusses the boy's poor conduct. When the counselor warns the boy that his behavior may well lead to failure and suspension from school—trying to discipline through shame, through a threat of rejection—the boy retorts, "So what?"

Unfortunately, at times we all believe the mask because it fits so well and is worn so often it becomes more than just a barrier to genuine communication or intimacy. The tragedy is that the mask can actually become impossible to remove, leaving boys emotionally hollowed out and vulnerable to failure at school, depression, substance abuse, violence, even suicide.

Boys Today are Falling Behind

While it may seem as if we live in a "man's world," at least in relation to power and wealth in adult society we do not live in a "boy's world." Boys on the whole are not faring well in our schools, especially in our public schools. It is in the classroom that we see some of the most destructive effects of society's misunderstanding of boys. Thrust into competition with their peers, some boys invest so much energy into keeping up their emotional guard and disguising their deepest and most vulnerable feelings, they often have little or no energy left to apply themselves to their schoolwork. No doubt boys still show up as small minorities at the top of a few academic lists, playing starring roles as some teachers' best students. But, most often, boys form the majority of the bottom of the class. Over the last decade we've been forced to confront some staggering statistics. From elementary grades through high school, boys receive lower grades than girls. Eighth-grade boys are held back 50 percent more often than girls. By high school, boys account for two thirds of the students in special education classes. Fewer boys than girls now attend and graduate from college. Fifty-nine percent of all master's degree candidates are now women, and the percentage of men in graduate-level professional education is shrinking each year.

So, there is a gender gap in academic performance, and boys are falling to the bottom of the heap. The problem stems as much from boys' lack of confidence in their ability to perform at school as from their actual inability to perform.

When eighth-grade students are asked about their futures, girls are now twice as 55 likely as boys to say they want to pursue a career in management, the professions, or business. Boys experience more difficulty adjusting to school, are up to ten times more likely to suffer from "hyper-activity" than girls, and account for 71 percent of all school suspensions. In recent years, girls have been making great strides in math and science. In the same period, boys have been severely lagging behind in reading and writing.

Boys' Self-Esteem—and Bragging

The fact is that *boys' self-esteem as learners is far more fragile than that of most girls*. A recent North Carolina study of students in grades six to eight concluded that "Boys have a much lower image of themselves as students than girls do." Conducted by Dr. William Purkey, this study contradicts the myth that adolescent boys are more likely than girls to see themselves as smart enough to succeed in society. Boys tend to brag, according to Purkey, as a "shield to hide deep-seated lack of confidence." It is the mask at work once again, a facade of confidence and bravado that boys erect to hide what they perceive as a shameful sense of vulnerability. Girls, on the other hand, brag less and do better in school. It is probably no surprise that a recent U.S. Department of Education study found that among high school seniors fewer boys than girls expect to pursue graduate studies, work toward a law degree, or go to medical school.

What we really need for boys is the same upswing in self-esteem as learners that we have begun to achieve for girls—to recognize the specialized academic needs of boys and girls in order to turn us into a more gender-savvy society.

Overwhelmingly, recent research indicates that girls not only outperform boys academically but also feel far more confident and capable. Indeed the boys in my study reported, over and over again, how it was not "cool" to be too smart in class, for it could lead to being labeled a nerd, dork, wimp, or fag. As one boy put it, "I'm not stupid enough to sit in the front row and act like some sort of teacher's pet. If I did, I'd end up with a head full of spitballs and then get my butt kicked in." Just as girls in coeducational environments have been forced to suppress their voices of certainty and truth, boys feel pressured to hide their yearnings for genuine relationships and their thirst for knowledge. To garner acceptance among their peers and protect themselves from being shamed, boys often focus on maintaining their masks and on doing whatever they can to avoid seeming interested in things creative or intellectual. To distance themselves from the things that the stereotype identifies as "feminine," many boys sit through classes without contributing and tease other boys who speak up and participate. Others pull pranks during class, start fights, skip classes, or even drop out of school entirely.

Schools and the Need for Gender Understanding

Regrettably, instead of working with boys to convince them it is desirable and even "cool" to perform well at school, teachers, too, are often fooled by the mask and believe the stereotype; and this helps to make the lack of achievement self-fulfilling. If a teacher believes that boys who are not doing well are simply uninterested, incapable, or delinquent, and signals this, it helps to make it so. Indeed when boys feel pain at school, they sometimes put on the mask and then "act out." Teachers, rather than exploring the emotional reasons behind a boy's misconduct, may instead apply behavioral control techniques that are intended somehow to better "civilize" boys.

Sal, a third-grader, arrived home with a note from his teacher. "Sal had to be disci- 60 plined today for his disruptive behavior," the teacher had written. "Usually he is a very cooperative student, and I hope this behavior does not repeat itself."

Sal's mother, Audrey, asked her son what he had done.

"I was talking out of turn in class," he said.

"That's it?" she asked. "And how did your teacher discipline you?"

"She made me stay in during recess. She made me write an essay about why talking in class is disruptive and inconsiderate." Sal hung his head.

"I was appalled," recalls Audrey. "If the teacher had spent one minute with my 65 child, trying to figure out why he was behaving badly, this whole thing could have been avoided." The teacher had known Sal to be "a very cooperative student." It seems that, the night before, Sal had learned that a favorite uncle had been killed in a car crash. "I told my son that I understood that he was having a really hard day because of his uncle, but that, even so, it's wrong to disrupt class. He was very relieved that I wasn't mad," Audrey said. "The episode made me think about how boys get treated in school. I think the teacher assumed that Sal was just 'being a boy.' And so, although what he really needed was a little understanding and extra attention instead she humiliated him. It reminded me to think about how Sal must be feeling when something like this happens, because he often won't talk about what's bothering him unless we prompt him to."

As a frequent guest in schools across the country, I have observed a practice I consider to be inappropriate, even dangerous—and based on a misunderstanding of boys. Elementary school teachers will offer the boys in their class a special "reward"—such as a better grade, an early recess, or an extra star on their good-behavior tally sheet—if the boys will *not* raise their hand more than once per class period. They find that some boys are so eager to talk and so boisterous in clamoring to be called on that their behavior disrupts the order of the classroom.

High school teachers sometimes adopt the same practice with their adolescent boy students, particularly those who act up or talk out of turn in class. The teachers will let the boys leave early or take a short break from class if they demonstrate that they can keep quiet and "behave." In other words, instead of trying to look behind the behavior to the real boy, to what is going on inside him, teachers assume a negative, and ask these boys to make themselves even *more* invisible and to suppress their genuine selves further. Ironically, they're asking boys to act more like the old stereotype of the passive, "feminine" girl. The teachers may get what they want—a quiet classroom—but at what cost? Such approaches silence boys' voices of resistance and struggle and individuality, and serve to perpetuate boys' attention-seeking acts of irreverence.

We need to develop a new code for real boys, gender-informed schools, and a more gender-savvy society where both boys and girls are drawn out to be themselves.

If we want boys to become more empathic, we must be more empathic toward them.

The Potency of Connection—a New Code for Boys and Girls

Growing up as a boy brings its own special difficulties, but the good news is that boys 70 can and do overcome them when and if they feel connected to their families, friends, and communities. My research demonstrates that despite society's traumatizing pressure on boys to disconnect from their vulnerable inner selves, many, if not most, boys maintain an inner well-spring of emotional connectedness, a resilience, that helps to sustain them. Sometimes these affective ties are formed with special male friends—boys' "chumships." Boys may also forge empathic and meaningful friendships with girls and young women, relationships that are often platonic.

The fact is that boys experience deep subliminal yearnings for connection—a *hidden yearning for relationship*—that makes them long to be close to parents, teachers, coaches, friends, and family. Boys are full of love and empathy for others and long to stay "attached" to their parents and closest mentors. These yearnings, in turn, can empower parents and professionals to become more deeply connected to the boys in their lives, much as Professor Carol Gilligan at Harvard and researchers at the Stone Center Group at Wellesley College have so eloquently advocated we do for girls. This intense power to connect of parents and others is part of the "potency of connection" that needs to be at the heart of a revised real-boy code. Through the potency of connection a boy can be helped to become himself, to grow into manhood in his own individual way—to be fully the "real boy" we know he is. ●

Explorations of the Text

1. Both Mary Pipher and William Pollack analyze and portray the inner lives of adolescents. What does Pipher envision as the major developmental changes and issues for young girls as they move from childhood to adolescence, from elementary school to junior high? What characterizes the "latency period" for preadolescent girls? According to Pipher, how and why do they "[lose] themselves"? To what does Pipher attribute this change? If adolescent girls do not attend to their psychological needs and listen to their inner voices, what does Pipher think will transpire? How does Pollack portray boy's inner life? According to Pollack, what causes boys to adopt a "mask of masculinity"? What is the result of this behavior? According to Pollack, what is the way out for boys from this "gender straitjacket"?

2. Both authors examine the complex interplay between the individual and society. Pipher states: "For a student of culture and personality, adolescence is fascinating. It's an extraordinary time when individual, developmental and cultural factors combine in ways that shape adulthood. It's a time of marked internal developmental and massive cultural indoctrination." How do their case studies illustrate their findings? Can you think of examples drawn from your life that confirm or dispute their theories? Do you find their arguments convincing? Do the authors present alternatives to cultural indoctrination?

3. Using Pipher's and/or Pollack's developmental theories as a framework for analysis, examine the characters of Sunny and Dalton in "Pagan Night," Norma Jean and LeRoy in "Shiloh," or protagonists in another story in this chapter. You also may go back to one of the stories in Chapters 5 or 6 such as Kingsolver's "Rose-Johnny," Liliana Heker's "The Stolen Party" (Chapter 5), or James Baldwin's "Sonny's Blues" (Chapter 6).

The Reading/Writing Connection

1. **Write an Argument:** Do you find Pipher's and Pollack's visions of adolescence credible? Do they present patterns of behavior that you recognize in yourself or in your peers? Consider your own psychological growth, your home and school life, and your relationships throughout the years with your peers.

2. At the end of Pollack's essay, he suggests that "we need to develop a new code for real boys, gender-informed schools, and a more-gender savvy society where both boys and girls are drawn out to be themselves." Imagine you are an educator. Create such a code for a school.

Ideas for Writing

1. **Write an Argument:** Both Pipher and Pollack focus on social conditioning as the primary force shaping gender roles for young men and women. Do you agree or disagree? What about biological/genetic factors influencing development? What about a person's individual capacity for decision-making? How much of psychological growth is influenced by family or by peers? What do you think are the forces influencing gender development? You may want to do research on this issue. For example, some recent articles suggest that certain aspects of behavior seem to be biologically based and different for men and women.

2. **Write an Argument:** After many years of scholarly attention to girls' development, at the present time, a number of scholars suggest that there is a "gender gap"; that is, boys are experiencing more developmental issues and more difficulties in school than young women. They are lagging behind women in levels of achievement in school and in attendance at college. Based on your own observations and experiences, do you think that these findings are valid?

3. **Write an Argument:** Do you think that our society is fulfilling its obligations in preparing young people for adulthood, in helping adolescents become responsible, confident adults who possess healthy senses of self and gender identities? Present your views in response to this question.

On the Web: *Masulinities and Femininities*

Please visit http://www.academic.cengage.com/english/Schmidt/Legacies4e/ for links to the following online resources.

Meghan O'Rourke, "Theories of the Erotic"

On the Web: *Selections from "Modern Love," the* New York Times

Please visit http://www.academic.cengage.com/english/Schmidt/Legacies4e/ for links to the following online resources.

Sophia Raday, "Diary of a Soldier's Wife: Tie-Dye and Camo Don't Mix" (June 18, 2006)
Alison Luterman, "Married, but Certainly Not to Tradition" (July 16, 2006)
Victoria Loustalot, "Fatherly Memories Scattered to the Wind" (November 19, 2006)

GRAPHIC LITERATURE

Alison Bechdel *(1960–)*

Old Father, Old Artificer *2006*
from *Fun Home*

CHAPTER 1

LIKE MANY FATHERS, MINE COULD OCCASIONALLY BE PREVAILED ON FOR A SPOT OF "AIRPLANE."

AS HE LAUNCHED ME, MY FULL WEIGHT WOULD FALL ON THE PIVOT POINT BETWEEN HIS FEET AND MY STOMACH.

OOF!

IT WAS A DISCOMFORT WELL WORTH THE RARE PHYSICAL CONTACT, AND CERTAINLY WORTH THE MOMENT OF PERFECT BALANCE WHEN I SOARED ABOVE HIM.

IN THE CIRCUS, ACROBATICS WHERE ONE PERSON LIES ON THE FLOOR BALANCING ANOTHER ARE CALLED "ICARIAN GAMES."

CONSIDERING THE FATE OF ICARUS AFTER HE FLOUTED HIS FATHER'S ADVICE AND FLEW SO CLOSE TO THE SUN HIS WINGS MELTED, PERHAPS SOME DARK HUMOR IS INTENDED.

BUT BEFORE HE DID SO, HE MANAGED TO GET QUITE A LOT DONE.

HIS GREATEST ACHIEVEMENT, ARGUABLY, WAS HIS MONOMANIACAL RESTORATION OF OUR OLD HOUSE.

WHEN OTHER CHILDREN CALLED OUR HOUSE A MANSION, I WOULD DEMUR. I RESENTED THE IMPLICATION THAT MY FAMILY WAS RICH, OR UNUSUAL IN ANY WAY.

IN FACT, WE WERE UNUSUAL, THOUGH I WOULDN'T APPRECIATE EXACTLY HOW UNUSUAL UNTIL MUCH LATER. BUT WE WERE NOT RICH.

THE GILT CORNICES, THE MARBLE FIREPLACE, THE CRYSTAL CHANDELIERS, THE SHELVES OF CALF-BOUND BOOKS--THESE WERE NOT SO MUCH BOUGHT AS PRODUCED FROM THIN AIR BY MY FATHER'S REMARKABLE LEGERDEMAIN.

MY FATHER COULD SPIN GARBAGE...

...INTO GOLD.

HE COULD TRANSFIGURE A ROOM WITH THE SMALLEST OFFHAND FLOURISH.

HE COULD CONJURE AN ENTIRE, FINISHED PERIOD INTERIOR FROM A PAINT CHIP.

THIS SHOULD GO AT AN ANGLE.

AMAZING.

HIS SISTER

MY ARM'S FALLING OFF.

HE WAS AN ALCHEMIST OF APPEARANCE, A SAVANT OF SURFACE, A DAEDALUS OF DECOR.

SLIGHTLY PERFECT.

FOR IF MY FATHER WAS ICARUS, HE WAS ALSO DAEDALUS—THAT SKILLFUL ARTIFICER, THAT MAD SCIENTIST WHO BUILT THE WINGS FOR HIS SON AND DESIGNED THE FAMOUS LABYRINTH...

THIS IS THE WALLPAPER FOR MY ROOM?

...AND WHO ANSWERED NOT TO THE LAWS OF SOCIETY, BUT TO THOSE OF HIS CRAFT.

BUT I **HATE** PINK! I **HATE** FLOWERS!

TOUGH TITTY.

HISTORICAL RESTORATION WASN'T HIS JOB.

(TWELFTH-GRADE ENGLISH)

ARCHI-TECTURAL DIGEST

IT WAS HIS PASSION. AND I MEAN PASSION IN EVERY SENSE OF THE WORD.

LIBIDINAL. MANIC. MARTYRED.

OUR GOTHIC REVIVAL HOUSE HAD BEEN BUILT DURING THE SMALL PENNSYLVANIA TOWN'S ONE BRIEF MOMENT OF WEALTH, FROM THE LUMBER INDUSTRY, IN 1867.

BUT LOCAL FORTUNES HAD DECLINED STEADILY FROM THAT POINT, AND WHEN MY PARENTS BOUGHT THE PLACE IN 1962, IT WAS A SHELL OF ITS FORMER SELF.

THE SHUTTERS AND SCROLLWORK WERE GONE. THE CLAPBOARDS HAD BEEN SHEATHED WITH SCABROUS SHINGLES.

THE BARE LIGHTBULBS REVEALED DINGY WARTIME WALLPAPER AND WOODWORK PAINTED PASTEL GREEN.

ALL THAT WAS LEFT OF THE HOUSE'S LUMBER-ERA GLORY WERE THE EXUBERANT FRONT PORCH SUPPORTS.

BUT OVER THE NEXT EIGHTEEN YEARS, MY FATHER WOULD RESTORE THE HOUSE TO ITS ORIGINAL CONDITION, AND THEN SOME.

JESUS! THIS MUST BE THE PATTERN FOR THE ORIGINAL BARGEBOARD!

HE WOULD PERFORM, AS DAEDALUS DID, DAZZLING DISPLAYS OF ARTFULNESS.

HE WOULD CULTIVATE THE BARREN YARD...

...INTO A LUSH, FLOWERING LANDSCAPE.

HE WOULD MANIPULATE FLAGSTONES THAT WEIGHED HALF A TON...

...AND THE THINNEST, QUIVERING LAYERS OF GOLD LEAF.

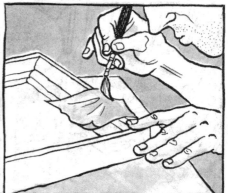

IT COULD HAVE BEEN A ROMANTIC STORY, LIKE IN *IT'S A WONDERFUL LIFE*, WHEN JIMMY STEWART AND DONNA REED FIX UP THAT BIG OLD HOUSE AND RAISE THEIR FAMILY THERE.

BUT IN THE MOVIE WHEN JIMMY STEWART COMES HOME ONE NIGHT AND STARTS YELLING AT EVERYONE...

...IT'S OUT OF THE ORDINARY.

DAEDALUS, TOO, WAS INDIFFERENT TO THE HUMAN COST OF HIS PROJECTS.

HE BLITHELY BETRAYED THE KING, FOR EXAMPLE, WHEN THE QUEEN ASKED HIM TO BUILD HER A COW DISGUISE SO SHE COULD SEDUCE THE WHITE BULL.

INDEED, THE RESULT OF THAT SCHEME--A HALF-BULL, HALF-MAN MONSTER--INSPIRED DAEDALUS'S GREATEST CREATION YET.

HE HID THE MINOTAUR IN THE LABYRINTH-- A MAZE OF PASSAGES AND ROOMS OPENING ENDLESSLY INTO ONE ANOTHER...

...AND FROM WHICH, AS STRAY YOUTHS AND MAIDENS DISCOVERED TO THEIR PERIL...

...ESCAPE WAS IMPOSSIBLE.

THEN THERE ARE THOSE FAMOUS WINGS. WAS DAEDALUS REALLY STRICKEN WITH GRIEF WHEN ICARUS FELL INTO THE SEA?

OR JUST DISAPPOINTED BY THE DESIGN FAILURE?

SOMETIMES, WHEN THINGS WERE GOING WELL, I THINK MY FATHER ACTUALLY ENJOYED HAVING A FAMILY.

OR AT LEAST, THE AIR OF AUTHENTICITY WE LENT TO HIS EXHIBIT. A SORT OF STILL LIFE WITH CHILDREN.

AND OF COURSE, MY BROTHERS AND I WERE FREE LABOR. DAD CONSIDERED US EXTENSIONS OF HIS OWN BODY, LIKE PRECISION ROBOT ARMS.

PUT HOT, SOAPY WATER IN THE SINK AND GET SOME CLEAN RAGS.

IN THIS REGARD, IT WAS LIKE BEING RAISED NOT BY JIMMY BUT BY MARTHA STEWART.

IN THEORY, HIS ARRANGEMENT WITH MY MOTHER WAS MORE COOPERATIVE.

WHAT DO YOU THINK OF THIS GAS CHANDELIER?

BORDELLO.

AUCTION CATALOG

IN PRACTICE, IT WAS NOT.

WE EACH RESISTED IN OUR OWN WAYS, BUT IN THE END WE WERE EQUALLY POWERLESS BEFORE MY FATHER'S CURATORIAL ONSLAUGHT.

MY BROTHERS AND I COULDN'T COMPETE WITH THE ASTRAL LAMPS AND GIRANDOLES AND HEPPLEWHITE SUITE CHAIRS. THEY WERE PERFECT.

I GREW TO RESENT THE WAY MY FATHER TREATED HIS FURNITURE LIKE CHILDREN, AND HIS CHILDREN LIKE FURNITURE.

MY OWN DECIDED PREFERENCE FOR THE UNADORNED AND PURELY FUNCTIONAL EMERGED EARLY.

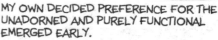

I WAS SPARTAN TO MY FATHER'S ATHENIAN.

MODERN TO HIS VICTORIAN.

BUTCH TO HIS NELLY.

UTILITARIAN TO HIS AESTHETE.

I DEVELOPED A CONTEMPT FOR USE-LESS ORNAMENT. WHAT FUNCTION WAS SERVED BY THE SCROLLS, TASSELS, AND BRIC-A-BRAC THAT INFESTED OUR HOUSE?

IF ANYTHING, THEY OBSCURED FUNCTION. THEY WERE EMBELLISHMENTS IN THE WORST SENSE.

MY FATHER BEGAN TO SEEM MORALLY SUSPECT TO ME LONG BEFORE I KNEW THAT HE ACTUALLY HAD A DARK SECRET.

HE USED HIS SKILLFUL ARTIFICE NOT TO MAKE THINGS, BUT TO MAKE THINGS APPEAR TO BE WHAT THEY WERE NOT.

HE APPEARED TO BE AN IDEAL HUSBAND AND FATHER, FOR EXAMPLE.

BUT WOULD AN IDEAL HUSBAND AND FATHER HAVE SEX WITH TEENAGE BOYS?

IT'S TEMPTING TO SUGGEST, IN RETRO-SPECT, THAT OUR FAMILY WAS A SHAM.

THAT OUR HOUSE WAS NOT A REAL HOME AT ALL BUT THE SIMULACRUM OF ONE, A MUSEUM.

YET WE REALLY WERE A FAMILY, AND WE REALLY DID LIVE IN THOSE PERIOD ROOMS.

I CAN'T FIND THE SCISSORS!

LOOK IN THE CHIPPEN-DALE.

STILL, SOMETHING VITAL WAS MISSING.

WELL?

ME, AGE 4

MY BROTHER CHRISTIAN, AGE 3

AN ELASTICITY, A MARGIN FOR ERROR.

HOW DID THIS VASE GET SO CLOSE TO THE EDGE OF THE TABLE?

BUT I DIDN'T DO ANYTHING!

MOST PEOPLE, I IMAGINE, LEARN TO ACCEPT THAT THEY'RE NOT PERFECT.

BUT AN IDLE REMARK ABOUT MY FATHER'S TIE OVER BREAKFAST COULD SEND HIM INTO A TAILSPIN.

PEACE, MAN.

DON'T CHANGE IT! WE'RE LATE!

ALSO AN ENGLISH TEACHER

MY MOTHER ESTABLISHED A RULE.

NO COMMENTS ON HIS APPEARANCE. IS THAT UNDERSTOOD?

WHAT IF IT'S SOMETHING GOOD?

GOOD, BAD, IT DOESN'T MATTER.

IF WE COULDN'T CRITICIZE MY FATHER, SHOWING AFFECTION FOR HIM WAS AN EVEN DICIER VENTURE.

WE WERE NOT A PHYSICALLY EXPRESSIVE FAMILY, TO SAY THE LEAST. BUT ONCE I WAS UNACCOUNTABLY MOVED TO KISS MY FATHER GOOD NIGHT.

HAVING LITTLE PRACTICE WITH THE GESTURE, ALL I MANAGED WAS TO GRAB HIS HAND AND BUSS THE KNUCKLES LIGHTLY...

...AS IF HE WERE A BISHOP OR AN ELEGANT LADY, BEFORE RUSHING FROM THE ROOM IN EMBARRASSMENT.

THIS EMBARRASSMENT ON MY PART WAS A TINY SCALE MODEL OF MY FATHER'S MORE FULLY DEVELOPED SELF-LOATHING.

HIS SHAME INHABITED OUR HOUSE AS PERVASIVELY AND INVISIBLY AS THE AROMATIC MUSK OF AGING MAHOGANY.

IN FACT, THE METICULOUS, PERIOD INTERIORS WERE EXPRESSLY DESIGNED TO CONCEAL IT.

MIRRORS, DISTRACTING BRONZES, MULTIPLE DOORWAYS. VISITORS OFTEN GOT LOST UPSTAIRS.

GRACIOUS, I ALMOST WALKED RIGHT INTO THIS!

MY MOTHER, MY BROTHERS, AND I KNEW OUR WAY AROUND WELL ENOUGH, BUT IT WAS IMPOSSIBLE TO TELL IF THE MINOTAUR LAY BEYOND THE NEXT CORNER.

AND THE CONSTANT TENSION WAS HEIGHT-ENED BY THE FACT THAT SOME ENCOUNTERS COULD BE QUITE PLEASANT.

HIS BURSTS OF KINDNESS WERE AS INCANDESCENT AS HIS TANTRUMS WERE DARK.

ALTHOUGH I'M GOOD AT ENUMERATING MY FATHER'S FLAWS, IT'S HARD FOR ME TO SUSTAIN MUCH ANGER AT HIM.

STOP SPLASHING!

I EXPECT THIS IS PARTLY BECAUSE HE'S DEAD, AND PARTLY BECAUSE THE BAR IS LOWER FOR FATHERS THAN FOR MOTHERS.

IN MY EYES!

HOLD STILL, DAMMIT!

MY MOTHER MUST HAVE BATHED ME HUNDREDS OF TIMES. BUT IT'S MY FATHER RINSING ME OFF WITH THE PURPLE METAL CUP THAT I REMEMBER MOST CLEARLY.

THE SUFFUSION OF WARMTH AS THE HOT WATER SLUICED OVER ME...

...THE SUDDEN, UNBEARABLE COLD OF ITS ABSENCE.

AGAIN!

WAS HE A GOOD FATHER? I WANT TO SAY, "AT LEAST HE STUCK AROUND." BUT OF COURSE, HE DIDN'T.

IT'S TRUE THAT HE DIDN'T KILL HIMSELF UNTIL I WAS NEARLY TWENTY.

BUT HIS ABSENCE RESONATED RETRO-ACTIVELY, ECHOING BACK THROUGH ALL THE TIME I KNEW HIM.

MAYBE IT WAS THE CONVERSE OF THE WAY AMPUTEES FEEL PAIN IN A MISSING LIMB.

HE REALLY WAS THERE ALL THOSE YEARS, A FLESH-AND-BLOOD PRESENCE STEAMING OFF THE WALLPAPER, DIGGING UP THE DOGWOODS, POLISHING THE FINIALS...

...SMELLING OF SAWDUST AND SWEAT AND DESIGNER COLOGNE.

BUT I ACHED AS IF HE WERE ALREADY GONE.

Explorations of the Text

1. Why does the autobiographical persona call her father an "old artificer"? Why does she include the myth of Daedalus, Icarus, and the Minotaur? What motivates her father to fix the house?
2. Characterize her father's relationships with his wife and children.
3. How does her father's hidden life, his secrets, influence his behavior toward his children?
4. In what ways does Alison's father "wear a mask"? What concepts of masculinity and femininity emerge in the work? Consider Pipher's and Pollack's essays.
5. First read the words. Then look at the images. Analyze them separately, and then consider how they work together. How does the narrative voice develop character, conflict, and theme? How do the images enhance the vision of characters?

The Reading/Writing Connection

1. Create a graphic representation of a moment in the life of your family. What does it suggest about your family dynamics?
2. Explore the role of "home" in your own life. What does home mean to you?

Ideas for Writing

1. Analyze the tension between appearance and reality in the work. Do the images reinforce this tension? What do they suggest?
2. Discuss the significance of the mythic allusions to Daedalus.

WRITING ASSIGNMENTS

1. a. What is platonic or ideal love? Write a definition.
   b. Define your ideal lover.
   c. Discuss platonic or ideal love in Donne, in Shakespeare's "Let Me Not to the Marriage of True Minds," in Arnold, and/or in Rosenberg.
2. a. What is romantic love? Why do people fall in love? Respond in a journal entry.
   b. Explore the vision of romantic love in several works in this chapter.
   c. Compare three views of romantic love and marriage in this chapter.
3. a. What are the major problems in love relationships? Write a journal entry.
   b. Analyze the essay by Woolf. What obstacles does she enumerate?
   c. Write an essay on obstacles in love relationships. Use three works in this chapter to support your points. Refer to Woolf and to your journal entry.
4. a. In a journal entry, explore your conceptions of young love, married love, and love in old age.
   b. Categorize kinds of love. Refer to works that represent different states of love.

5. Have any of these works changed your attitude about love? Which ones? Why? Why not?

6. Write about the end of love, the acceptance of loss. Refer to Mason, Akhmatova, Hemingway, Braverman, and/or Joyce.

7. a. Trace the phases of a relationship you have experienced or observed.

   b. Trace the phases of the love relationship in one of the texts in this chapter.

   c. Compare your relationship with the view of love in one of the works in the text.

8. a. Interview three people from the same cultural background. Ask about gender roles, socialization, and responsibilities.

   b. Write an essay on roles of men and women in that culture. Have gender roles changed in that culture in the twentieth century?

   c. Write an analysis of gender roles in three works in this chapter. You may choose works in other chapters if you wish.

9. a. Interview men about women; women about men. Ask about conceptions of the opposite sex, relationships, and social roles. Summarize your interviews.

   b. Analyze the results of the interviews. What misconceptions do men have about women? Women about men?

   c. "Men and women are doomed never to understand one another." Develop an argument in response to this quotation.

10. a. Freewrite about ways in which men and women might perceive conflict differently.

    b. Choose one experience, and write a monologue for each person involved in the incident.

    c. Based on a work in this chapter, write an essay about how a man and a woman develop different views of a conflict. How does the conflict resolve itself?

11. a. Have you ever felt like an "Other"? Write about this experience in your journal.

    b. In your own words, define "Other." Use your journal entry as a basis for your definition.

    c. Analyze the experience of the woman as "Other" in three works in this chapter.

    d. What separates people; what binds them together?

12. Examine the conflicts and characters in *Trifles* and in *M Butterfly*. How does symbolism help to create character and theme?

13. a. Interview another person who has read one of the works in this chapter. Ask questions about speaker, conflict, theme, language, and other literary elements. Summarize your interview.

    b. Write an essay about your interview.

14. a. Have gender roles in marriage changed during the last twenty years? Interview several people in long-term marriages. How do they see their defined roles? Do they perceive that roles for men and women have changed over the years?

    b. Compare their views of roles in marriage with your observations about your generation's conceptions of roles for men and for women.

    c. Examine the treatment of marital relationships on television programs. You may view such situation comedies as *I Love Lucy* from the 1950s, *The Brady Bunch* from the 1970s, *The Simpsons* from the 1990s, or *Everybody Loves Raymond* and *Desperate Housewives* from the 2000s.

15. Focus on the theme of disappointment with love.
    a. Write about your own disappointments—a failed love relationship.
    b. Compare your sense of loss with that of a character in one of the stories in this chapter, such as Joyce's "Eveline," Chekhov's "Lady with Lapdog," Braverman's "Pagan Night," and Mason's "Shiloh."

16. Find a copy of the old English poem "The Demon Lover." Analyze the symbolism of the figure of the lover, and then explore this psychosexual, symbolic motif in several of the following works: Oates's "Where Are You Going, Where Have You Been?" (Chapter 5), Hwang's *M Butterfly,* Faulkner's "A Rose for Emily" (Chapter 6), and Rossetti's "Goblin Market."

17. What does it mean to be a man or a woman in contemporary society? What images of the male and female body are promoted in the media? What are North American society's overt and covert attitudes toward young men and women? How does the society claim to treat young men and women? How does it really treat them? Examine these questions through scrutinizing advertisements, particularly women's or men's magazines, television programs, or films such as *Kids* or *Thirteen.* What do they reveal? What images of men and women are portrayed? After doing this research, write an argumentative essay presenting your position on this issue.

18. a. Focus on a favorite love song. What vision of love is presented?
    b. Connect the song with a particular work in the chapter.

19. Examine the patterns of socially proscribed gender roles presented in works in this chapter. Are there characters who break out of their socially defined roles? Are there ways out of the "gender straitjacket" (William Pollack's term)?

20. Using Pipher and Pollack's case studies in their essays as models, create a case study of your own that illustrates a developmental conflict for an adolescent boy or girl; then interpret and analyze your study.

21. In their book, *Madame Bovarie's Ovaries,* David and Nanelle Barrash provide a Darwinian reading of literature. For instance, in Chapter 2, "Othello and Other Angry Fellows," they determine that Othello was jealous because he is a man: "The truly important thing about Othello wasn't the color of his skin, his age, or his war record. Rather, Othello was all about sperm; Desdemona, eggs." According to this reading, human males have evolved to spread their sperm widely and create as many offspring as possible. In the process they recognize that other males are attempting to do the same. This recognition creates suspicion of other males. Jealousy occurs more easily in males because of this biological determined behavior. Choose two or more texts from this chapter and write an analysis essay using a Darwinian reading of the works. To help with this assignment, you may want to research evolutionary psychology in your library or on the Internet.

STUDENT ESSAY
Thematic Analysis Essay and Movie Review
Kimberley Thomas

The Concept of Love in *The English Patient*

There are several types of love, ranging from romantic love to platonic love to parental love, all of which are expressed in Michael Ondaatje's novel, The English Patient.
Oxford's Mini-Reference Dictionary and Thesaurus states that love is "warm liking or
affection" between people. Yet, love is a difficult concept to understand. Emma Goldman, Russian-born writer of the nineteenth and twentieth centuries, once labeled an
iconoclast, writes in her essay "Marriage and Love":

> Love, the strongest and deepest element in all life, the harbinger of hope, of
> joy, of ecstasy; love, the defier of all laws, of all conventions; love, the freest,
> the most powerful molder of human destiny. (242)

Love is unpredictable. Love is security. "Love needs no protection; it is its own protection" (Goldman 243). Love is perplexing. Love should be, but is not, permanent. Love
hurts. "Love has the magic power to make a beggar a king" (Goldman 242). Love has
the ability to conquer all people, regardless of age or race.

Where does the concept of love come from? From where does love arise? Greek
philosopher Aristophanes explains this strange and unknown concept in Plato's Symposium: "I shall therefore try to initiate you in the secret of [the] power" of love (Plato
870). He explains to his audience about the three sexes of the world: males, females,
and hermaphrodites. These hermaphrodites, both male and female, were "formidable,
and their pride was overweening; they attacked the gods" (Plato 870). As punishment
for their sin, the god Zeus decided to split them up. This is the reason why people love
others: "Each of us is perpetually in search of his corresponding tally" (Plato 871).
Aristophanes explains, "Love . . . restores us to our ancient state by attempting to
weld two beings into one" (Plato 871).

Romantic love is the kind of love that exists between the characters Hana and
Kip and Almasy and Katharine; however, their affection for one another is not established immediately. Kip, the Indian sapper, stumbles into Hana's life as she is playing
the piano in the Villa San Girolamo, "an old nunnery, taken over by the Germans, then
converted into a hospital" (Ondaatje 28). Upon hearing the music, the sapper rushes
towards the villa, fearing that there is a destructive mine implanted in the piano, a tactic that the Germans tended to use. Kip resides in a tent in the garden of the villa and,
over time, Hana begins to realize she is attracted to Kip. Several times, she "suddenly
[realizes that] she is watching him" (Ondaatje 73). She watches while he works, noticing insignificant things, such as "the darker brown skin of his wrist" (Ondaatje 74);
things most people would not pay much attention to. Hana has a "crush" on Kip, reminding the reader of her child-like ways.

The relationship between Almasy and Katharine Clifton begins when Katherine
arrives in the desert with her new husband, Geoffrey Clifton, in 1936. The film version of The English Patient depicts Almasy as standoffish upon the arrival of the new-
lyweds. The reason for his behavior is left untold, but one can speculate that it is one

of two things: 1) the fact that she is the only woman among a group of desert explorers; or 2) because Almasy wants to disguise his attraction to her. It is as she recites a poem that he "[falls] in love with a voice" (Ondaatje 144). Almasy states: "This is a story of how I fell in love with a woman . . . I heard the words she spoke across the fire" (Ondaatje 233). For Almasy this is appropriate. He is a man of languages, a man of words. He explains this at one point to Caravaggio: "Words, Caravaggio. They have a power" (Ondaatje 234).

Love is unpredictable, because a person cannot help with whom he or she falls in love. Love is blind, overlooking all things such as age, race, or status. Both Katharine and Hana fall in love with "international bastards" (Ondaatje 176). Writer Gloria Anzaldúa expresses ideas similar to this in her poem "To live in the Borderlands means you": "To survive in the Borderlands/you must live sin fronteras/be a crossroads."

How could Hana know that she would fall in love with an Indian sapper? How could Katharine know that she would love someone fifteen years her senior? How could Almasy know that he would love a married woman? Such things are irrelevant when it comes down to loving someone. Some things cannot be resisted. Different in more ways than one in the light, the lovers were "equal in darkness" (Ondaatje 225).

Although romantic love exists between the couples, it seems as though Kip and Hana are more affectionate while Almasy and Katharine are more passionate. In the novel, Hana and Kip are usually depicted as holding each other: "There is the one month when Hana and Kip sleep beside each other. A formal celibacy between them" (Ondaatje 225). Kip also mentions several times that he simply wants to touch Hana:

> He wanted Hana's shoulder, wanted to place his palm over it as he had done in the sunlight when she slept and he had lain there as if in someone's rifle sights, awkward with her. (Ondaatje 114).

On the other hand, Almasy and Katharine have a more physical relationship. In the film, they are constantly keeping their romantic affair to themselves, sneaking around to share their love for one another. Katharine says to Almasy, "I want you to ravish me" (Ondaatje 236).

There is another type of love that exists in <u>The English Patient</u> between Hana and Kip and Almasy and Katharine. It is physical love, not sexual intercourse, but a love of the physical body. While observing Kip, Hana is described by the narrator: "She loves most the wet colours of his neck when he bathes . . . and his chest with its sweat" (Ondaatje 127). In return, Kip "loves most her face's smart look . . . he loves her voice . . . and the way she crawls in against his body like a saint" (Ondaatje 128). Another time, Hana comments to Kip, "It's your mouth that I'm most purely in love with" (Ondaatje 128). Almasy and Katharine have the same type of physical love: "This is my shoulder, he thinks, not her husband's, this is my shoulder. As lovers they have offered parts of their bodies to each other, like this" (Ondaatje 156). Almasy loves Katharine's vaccination scar, the "pale aureole on her arm" (Ondaatje 158). He also loves the hollow at the base of a woman's neck that he likes to call the "Bosphorus" and which he later discovers is called the "vascular sizood" (Ondaatje 241).

Is marriage the next step after falling in love? Author Stanley N. Bernard writes "[l]ove, lust, and marriage go hand in hand" (in "Love, Lust, and Marriage"), while feminist author Emma Goldman disagrees, stating in her essay that "marriage and love have nothing in common" (233). She discusses the concept of free love, which is love without church and state, the type of love shared between Almasy and Katharine and Hana and Kip. They were free to love one another without the burden of marriage. Although Goldman was married, divorced, and then remarried, she still believes that "it is utterly false that love results in marriage" (233).

A major question to ask is: are the couples in The English Patient truly in love? 10 Hana, after the loss of her child, the father of the child, and her own father is seeking love and comfort. She is searching for her "half," her "corresponding tally" (Plato 871). Plato's Symposium discusses this idea. He suggests that we yearn for our other half and experience love as a result of this "weld[ing] of two beings into one . . ." (Plato 871). The relationship between Almasy and Katharine is slightly more complicated. Katharine is married to Geoffrey during the affair. Geoffry loves her, but the novel does not describe Katharine's feelings for him in return. Is it possible to be in love with two people at once? In an article found on Jet Online ("Which Urge Is Stronger—Sex or Love?"), psychologist Dr. Grace Cornish discusses the age-old belief that "women give sex just to feel love and men will say 'I love you' just to have the sex." Almasy has a burning desire for Katharine, which might be mistaken for lust since "love endears while lust desires" (Bernard); however, the reader is encouraged to believe that Almasy is truly in love with Katharine.

"The strongest human desire for most people is to be loved" ("Which Urge"), and when that love is gone, the lovers's world comes crashing down. As singer Mariah Carey once sang: "Love takes time to heal when you're hurting so much . . . I can't escape the pain inside, 'cause love takes time'." Katharine breaks off the short-lived love affair, because she is "too proud to be a lover, a secret" (Ondaatje 171). Almasy is distraught but remains calm, stating "I don't miss you yet" (Ondaatje 171). Knowing that absence makes the heart grow fonder, Katharine simply replies, "You will" (Ondaatje 158). Unknown by the lovers, however, Geoffrey Clifton has discovered the truth about their relationship and plans a murder-suicide. He deliberately attempts to crash the plane carrying himself and Katharine into Almasy, killing them all.

The tragedy leaves Clifton dead, Katharine severely injured with broken ribs and a broken wrist, and Almasy unharmed. Almasy and Katharine are separated for several months, and during this time Almasy "ha[s] grown bitter" (Ondaatje 172). He believes that Katharine has found another lover and "did not trust her last endearments to him anymore" (Ondaatje 172), but he still loves her enough to take care of her after the accident. Placing her in the Cave of Swimmers, he vows to get help and return for her. He does keep his promise to her, but is unable to return for three years. When he arrives at the cave, he finds his love dead. Almasy, as well as Kip, proves that love is security. He does all that he can to bring aid to the woman he loves, possibly the only woman whom he has ever loved (this fact is not mentioned in the novel).

Kip's actions also suggest that love means security. One day, he discovers a mine hidden in the garden of the villa. Hana comes along, sees what he is doing and offers her help. Kip responds, "You must leave" (Ondaatje 101). He is trying to protect her, but Hana, with her stubborn nature, stays by his side, holding the wire that he must cut in her left hand. Later, Kip is somewhat angry with her for not leaving and going to safety. If Almasy and Kip did not truly love their women, Katharine and Hana, then they might not have tried to protect them. "Love is your head and heart" ("Which Urge"), and this is what the men seem to believe when their lovers are in danger.

Though the lovers are unable to remain together, due to the unfortunate death of Katharine and the unexpected flight of Kip, they are never forgotten. Almasy, as an amnesiac burn patient, frequently slips into the past, telling his story to those who are around him. At the end of the film, which centers on his memory of the romantic affair between him and Katharine, he requests an overdose of morphine, allowing him to die peacefully and to be reunited with his greatest love. The end of the novel reveals that Kip returns to India after he leaves the villa, marries, and has a family of his own. He still reminisces about the young, Canadian girl, child-like in nature, whom he loved. Both situations imply that love can be found and lost, but never forgotten.

In his poem "September 1, 1939," W.H. Auden observes: 15

> For the error bred in the bone
> Of each woman and each man
> Craves what it cannot have,
> Not universal love
> But to be loved alone.

Aristophanes from Plato's Symposium believed this concept, too. Men and women simply want their other half:

> The way to happiness for our race lies in fulfilling the behests of Love, and in each finding for himself [herself] the mate who properly belongs to him [her]; in a word, in returning to our original condition. (Plato 872-873)

Love should never be repelled or taken advantage of. Remember, as another writer once taught, "The greatest thing you'll ever learn is just to love and be loved in return."

Works Cited

Anzaldúa, Gloria. "To live in the Borderlands means you." Legacies: Fiction, Poetry, Drama, Nonfiction, Fourth Edition. Eds. Jan Zlotnik Schmidt, Lynne Crockett, and Carley Bogarad. Boston: Cengage Learning Wadsworth, 2008. 1275-1276.

Auden, W. H. "September 1, 1939." 3 April 2002. http://www.auden.com.

Bernard, Stanley N. "Love, Lust, and Marriage." Humanist. November 2000. http://www.findarticles.com.

Goldman, Emma. Anarchism and Other Essays. Third Revised Edition. New York: Mother Earth Publishing Association, 1917.

Ondaatje, Michael. The English Patient. New York: Vintage International, 1992.

Plato. "The Sexes" from The Symposium. Legacies: Fiction, Poetry, Drama, Nonfiction, Fourth Edition. Eds. Jan Zlotnik Schmidt, Lynne Crockett, and Carley Bogarad. Boston: Cengage Learning Wadsworth, 2008. 870-873.

"Which Urge is Stronger—Sex or Love?" Jet Online. 3 April 2000. http://www.findarticles.com.

Sites of Conflict

Introduction

There is a cyclone fence between
ourselves and the slaughter and behind it
we hover in a calm, protected world like
netted fish, exactly like netted fish.
It is either the beginning or the end
of the world, and the choice is ourselves
or nothing.

Carolyn Forché, "Ourselves or Nothing"

Whereas once people felt that they perhaps could "hover in a calm, protected world," after 9/11 it seems impossible to escape the presence of the "slaughter." People live with a heightened sense of fear and vulnerability because of the threat of terrorist acts, because of the knowledge of sites of conflict worldwide. No longer may people assume that they will remain untouched by acts of violence. The writers in this chapter explore both the new ideas of threat and those sites of conflict (from the physical to the verbal) that exist within and independent of terrorism.

The works in Crossing the Genres/Terror and Terrorism explore the impact of terrorism on characters in very different parts of the world. In the additional thematic cluster, "Visions of the Holocaust," another version of the "end" is portrayed: the Nazi genocide during World War II. The Holocaust marked a time in history when concepts of good and evil, moral responsibility, and the idea of civilization itself were challenged.

The poems in the 9/11 cluster attest to the need to commemorate the dead through acts of remembrance and writing.

Another site of conflict explored in this chapter is a way to oppose the "slaughter": the awareness of and fight against forms of racial oppression. Despite advances, forms of racism and oppression still persist; people are still treated as "nobodies" both in North American society and in the global world. However, the dream of an ideal—of freedom and of a true America—persists. The works in the additional thematic cluster, American Dreams Lost and Found, present the tension between the ideal and the real in American life. In these texts, images of destruction and renewal are intertwined.

War represents the ultimate form of destruction. Diverse works attest to the physical and the emotional burdens that soldiers and those caught in the crossfire bear. Acts of violence, however, do not always occur through acts of terror, oppression, or war;

they also can manifest themselves when the will of the majority defeats the will of the individual.

Opportunities for moments of resistance, for social transformation, however, still exist. Indeed, the works in this chapter attest to the power of art to incite questioning, awareness, and, hopefully, social change. As Forché reminds us, "all things human take time."

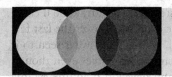

Crossing the Genres
Terror and Terrorism

Luisa Valenzuela *(1938–1976)*

The Verb to Kill 1976

He kills—he killed—he will kill—he has killed—he had killed—he will have killed—he would have killed—he is killing—he was killing—he has been killing—he would have been killing—he will have been killing—he will be killing—he would be killing—he may kill.

We decided that none of these tenses or moods suited him. Did he kill, will he kill, will he have killed? We think he *is* killing, with every step, with every breath, with every . . . We don't like him to get close to us but we come across him when we go clam-digging on the beach. We walk from north to south, and he comes from south to north, closer to the dunes, as if looking for pebbles. He looks at us and we look at him—did he kill, will he kill, would he have killed, is he killing? We put down the sack with the clams and hold each other's hand till he passes. He doesn't throw so much as one little pebble at us, he doesn't even look at us, but afterward we're too weak in the knees to go on digging clams.

The other day he walked by us and right afterward we found an injured sea gull on the beach. We took the poor thing home and on the way we told it that we were good, not like him, that it didn't have to be afraid of us, and we even covered it up with my jacket so the cold wind wouldn't hurt its broken wing. Later we ate it in a stew. A little tough, but tasty.

The next day we went back to run on the beach. We didn't see him and we didn't find a single injured sea gull. He may be bad, but he's got something that attracts animals. For example, when we were fishing: hours without a bite until he suddenly showed up and then we caught a splendid sea bass. He didn't look at our catch or smile, and it's good he didn't because he looked more like a murderer than ever with his long bushy hair and gleaming eyes. He just went on gathering his pebbles as though nothing were wrong, thinking about the girls that he has killed, will kill, kills.

When he passes by we're petrified—will it be our turn someday? In school we con- 5 jugate the verb *to kill* and the shiver that goes up our spine isn't the same as when we see him passing on the beach, all puffed up with pride and gathering his pebbles. The shiver on the beach is lower down in our bodies and more stimulating, like sea air. He gathers all those pebbles to cover up the graves of his victims—very small, transparent pebbles that he holds up to the sun and looks through from time to time so as to make certain that the sun exists. Mama says that if he spends all day looking for pebbles, it's because he *eats* them. Mama can't think about anything but food, but I'm sure he eats something else. The last breath of his victims, for example. There's nothing more nourishing than the last sigh, the one that brings with it everything that a person has gathered over the years. He must have some secret for trapping this essence that escapes his victims, and that's why he doesn't need vitamins. My sister and I are afraid he'll catch us some night and kill us to absorb everything that we've been eating over the last few years. We're terribly afraid because we're well nourished, Mama has always seen to it that we eat balanced meals and we've never lacked for fruit or vegetables even though they're very expensive in this part of the country. And clams have lots of iodine, Mama says, and fish are the healthiest food there is even though the taste of it bores us but why should he be bored because while he kills his victims (always girls, of course) he must do those terrible things to them that my sister and I keep imagining, just for fun. We spend hours talking about the things that he does to his victims before killing them just for fun. The papers often talk about degenerates like him but he's one of the worst because that's all he eats. The other day we spied on him while he was talking to the lettuce he has growing in his garden (he's crazy as well as degenerate). He was saying affectionate things to it and we were certain it was poisoned lettuce. For our part we don't say anything to lettuce, we have to eat it with oil and lemon even though it's disgusting, all because Mama says it has lots of vitamins. And now we have to swallow vitamins for him, what a bother, because the better fed we are the happier we'll make him and the more he'll like doing those terrible things the papers talk about and we imagine, just before killing us so as to gulp down our last breath full of vitamins in one big mouthful. He's going to do a whole bunch of things so repulsive we'll be ashamed to tell anybody, and we only say them in a whisper when we're on the beach and there's nobody within miles. He's going to take our last breath and then he'll be as strong as a bull to go kill other little girls like us. I hope he catches Pocha. But I hope he doesn't do any of those repulsive things to her before killing her because she might like it, the dirty thing. I hope he kills her straightaway by plunging a knife in her belly. But he'll have his fun with us for a long time because we're pretty and he'll like our bodies and our voices when we scream. And we will scream and scream but nobody will hear us because he's going to take us to a place very far away and then he will put in our mouths that terrible thing we know he has. Pocha already told us about it—he must have an enormous thing that he uses to kill his victims.

An enormous one, even though we've never seen it. To show how brave we are, we tried to watch him while he made peepee, but he saw us and chased us away. I wonder why he didn't want to show it to us. Maybe it's because he wants to surprise us on our last day here and catch us while we're pure so's to get more pleasure. That must be it. He's saving himself for our last day and that's why he doesn't try to get close to us.

Not anymore.

Papa finally lent us the rifle after we asked and asked for it to hunt rabbits. He told us we were big girls now, that we can go out alone with the rifle if we want to, but to be careful, and he said it was a reward for doing so well in school. It's true we're doing well in school. It isn't hard at all to learn to conjugate verbs:

He will be killed—he is killed—he has been killed. ●

Uwem Akpan

My Parents' Bedroom [1] *2006*

I'm nine years and seven months old. I'm at home playing peekaboo in my room with my little brother, Jean. It's Saturday evening and the sun has fallen behind the hills. There's silence outside our bungalow, but from time to time the evening wind carries a shout to us. Our parents have kept us indoors since yesterday.

Maman comes into the room and turns off the light before we see her. Jean cries in the darkness, but once she starts kissing him he begins to giggle. He reaches up to be held, but she's in a hurry.

"Don't turn on any lights tonight," she whispers to me.

I nod. "*Yego,* Maman."

"Come with your brother." I carry Jean and follow her. "And don't open the door 5 for anybody. Your papa is not home, I'm not home, nobody is home. Do you hear me, Monique, huh?"

"*Yego,* Maman."

"Swallow all your questions now, bright daughter. When your papa and uncle return, they'll explain things to you."

Maman leads us through the corridor and into her room, where she lights a candle that she has taken from our family altar, in the parlor. She starts to undress, tossing her clothes on the floor. She tells us that she's going out for the night and that she's already late. She's panting, as if she'd been running; her body is shining with sweat. She slips into the beautiful black evening dress that Papa likes and combs out her soft hair. I help her with the zipper at the back of her dress. She paints her lips a deep red and presses them together. The sequins on her dress glitter in the candlelight as if her heart were on fire.

My mother is a very beautiful Tutsi woman. She has high cheekbones, a narrow nose, a sweet mouth, slim fingers, big eyes, and a lean frame. Her skin is so light that you can see the blue veins on the back of her hands, as you can on the hands of Le Père Mertens, our parish priest, who's from Belgium. I look like Maman, and when I grow up I'll be as tall as she is. This is why Papa and all his Hutu people call me Shenge, which means "my little one" in Kinyarwanda.

Papa looks like most Hutus, very black. He has a round face, a wide nose, and 10 brown eyes. His lips are as full as a banana. He is a jolly, jolly man who can make you laugh till you cry. Jean looks like him.

---

[1] ***My Parents' Bedroom:*** During the Rwandan genocide of 1994, 500,000 people, mostly Tutsi, were massacred in three months—100 days—between April and June, mostly by Hutus. The immediate cause of the genocide was the killing of the Hutu President, Juvenal Habyarimana, whose plane was shot down on April 6, 1994. Immediately following this incident, a reign of terror spread from the capital, Kigali, to the rest of the country during which Hutus murdered members of the minority Tutsi population. Ethnic tensions between the majority Hutus and minority Tutsi had been present during the country's history and were deepened during colonial rule by the Belgian government's favoritism of the minority Tutsi population, particularly in giving them educational and economic opportunities. After the country gained independence, the Hutus gained control of the government. The genocide ended when the Rwandan Patriotic Front (the rebels) captured the capital in July of 1994.

"But, Maman, you told me that only bad women go out at night."

"Monique, no questions tonight, I told you."

She stops and stares at me. As I'm about to open my mouth, she shouts, "Quiet! Go, sit with your brother!"

Maman never shouts at me. She's strange today. Tears shine in her eyes. I pick up a bottle of Amour Bruxelles, the perfume Papa gives her because he loves her. Everybody in the neighborhood knows her by its sweet smell. When I put the bottle in her hands, she shivers, as if her mind has just returned to her. Instead of spraying it on herself, she puts it on Jean. He's excited, sniffing his hands and clothes. I beg Maman to put some on me, but she refuses.

"When they ask you," she says sternly, without looking at me, "say you're one of 15 them, O.K.?"

"Who?"

"Anybody. You have to learn to take care of Jean, Monique. You just have to, huh?"

"I will, Maman."

"Promise?"

"Promise." 20

Maman heads for the parlor, and Jean trails after. He's whimpering to be held. I carry the candle. We sit down on our big sofa, and Maman blows the candle out. Our parlor is never totally dark, because of the crucifix in the corner, which glows yellow-green. All-translucent, as Papa likes to say. Jean toddles to the altar, as usual. He places his hands on the crucifix, as if playing with a toy. The glow enters into his fingers, making them green, and he turns to us and laughs. In quick strides, I bring him back. I don't want him to pull down the crucifix, which leans against the wall, or the vase of bougainvillea beside it. It's part of my duty to tend to the altar. I love the crucifix; all my relatives do. Except Tonton Nzeyimana—the Wizard.

The Wizard is Papa's father's brother. He is a pagan and he is very powerful. If he doesn't like you, unless you're a strong Catholic, he can put his spell on you, until you become useless. The color of his skin is milk with a little coffee. He never married because he says he hates his skin and doesn't want to pass it on. Sometimes he paints himself with charcoal until the rain comes to wash away his blackness. I don't know where he got his color from. My parents say it's a complicated story about intermarriage. He's so old that he walks with a stick. His lips are long and droopy, because he uses them to blow bad luck and disease into people. He likes to frighten children with his ugly face. Whenever I see the Wizard, I run away. Papa, his own nephew, doesn't want him in our house, but Maman tolerates the Wizard. "No matter, he's our relative," she says. Tonton André, Papa's only brother, hates him even more. They don't even greet each on the road.

Though I'm a girl, Papa says that the crucifix will be mine when he dies, because I'm the firstborn of the family. I will carry it till I give it to my child. Some people laugh at Papa for saying that it'll come to me, a girl. Others shrug and agree with Papa, because he went to university and works in a government ministry. Sometimes when Tonton André and his wife, Tantine Annette, visit us, they praise Papa for this decision. Tantine Annette is pregnant, and I know that they would do the same if God gave them a girl first.

Without his I.D., you'd never know that Tonton André is Papa's brother. He's a cross between Papa and Maman—as tall as Maman but not quite as dark as Papa. He's got a tiny beard. Tantine Annette is Maman's best friend. Though she's Tutsi like Maman, she's as dark as Papa. Sometimes on the road, the police ask for her I.D., to be sure of her roots. These days, my parents tease her that she'll give birth to six babies, because her pregnant stomach is very big. Each time she becomes pregnant, she miscarries, and everybody knows that it's the Wizard's spell. But the couple have been strong in their faith. Sometimes they kiss in public, like Belgians do on TV, and our people don't like this very much. But they don't care. Tonton André takes her to a good hospital in Kigali for checkups, and Papa and our other relatives contribute money to help them, because both of them are only poor primary-school teachers. The Wizard offered to give his money, too, but we don't allow him to. If he gave even one franc, his bad money would swallow all the good contributions, like the sickly, hungry cows in Pharaoh's dream.

Maman stands up suddenly. "Monique, remember to lock the door behind me! Your papa will soon be back." I hear her going into the kitchen. She opens the back door and stops for a moment. Then the door slams. She's gone.

I light the candle again and go into the kitchen and lock the door. We eat rice and fish and return to our room. I dress Jean in his flannel pajamas and sing him to sleep. I change into my nightie, and lie down beside him.

In a dream, I hear Tonton Andre's voice. He sounds as anxious as he did yesterday afternoon, when he came to call Papa away. "Shenge, Shenge, you must open the door for me!" Tonton André shouts.

"Wait, I'm coming," I try to tell him, but in my dream I have no voice, and my legs have melted like butter in the sun. There's a lot of commotion, and gunshots that sound like bombs.

"Come to the front door, quick!" he shouts again.

I wake up. Tonton André is actually yelling outside our house.

I go into the parlor and turn on the fluorescent lights. My eyes hurt. People are banging on our front door. I see the blades of machetes and axes stabbing through the door, making holes in the plywood. Two windows are smashed, and rifle butts and *udufuni* are poking in. I don't know what's going on. The attackers can't get in through the windows with their guns and small hoes, because they're covered with metal bars. Afraid, I squat on the floor, with my hands covering my head, till the people outside stop and pull back.

I hear Tonton André's voice again, but this time it's calm and deep, as usual, and everything in quiet outside.

"Poor, sweet thing, don't be afraid," he says, now laughing confidently like Jean. "They're gone. Your papa is here with me."

I pick my way through the broken glass and open the door. But Tonton André comes in with a group. Men and women, all armed.

"Where's Maman?" he asks me.

"Maman went out."

He looks like a madman. His hair is rough, as if he had not combed it for a year. His green shirt is unbuttoned and he's without shoes.

"*Yagiye hehe?*" someone from the mob asks, disappointed. "Where's she gone?"

"She didn't say," I answer.

"Have you seen your papa this evening?" Tonton André asks.

"*Oya.*"

"No? I'll kill you," he says, his face swollen with seriousness.

I scan the mob. "You told me Papa was with you. . . . Papa! Papa!"

"The coward has escaped," someone in the crowd says.

"Nta butungane burimo!" others shout. "Unfair!" 45

They look victorious, like football champions. I know some of them. Our church usher, Monsieur Paschal, is humming and chanting and wears a bandanna. Mademoiselle Angeline, my teacher's daughter, is dancing to the chants, as if to reggae beats. She gives a thumbs-up to Monsieur Francois, who is the preacher at the nearby Adventist church.

Some of them brandish their I.D.s, as if they were conducting a census. Others are now searching our home. Sniffing around like dogs, they've traced Maman's Amour Bruxelles to Jean and are bothering him so he begins to cry. I run to our room and carry him back to the parlor. I can hear them all over the place, overturning beds and breaking down Closets.

Suddenly, I see the Wizard by the altar. He turns and winks at me. Then he swings his stick at the crucifix, once, twice, and Christ's body breaks from the cross, crashing to the floor. Limbless, it rolls to my feet. Only bits of its hands and legs are still hanging on the cross, hollow and jagged. The cross has fallen off the altar too. The Wizard smiles at me, enjoying my frustration. When he's distracted for a moment, I grab Jesus' broken body and hide it under Jean's pajama top. I sit down on the sofa and put Jean in my lap. The Wizard now searches excitedly for the body of Jesus. He is like an overgrown kid looking for his toy.

He turns to me. "Shenge, do you have it?"

I look away. "No." 50

"Look at me, girl."

"I don't have it."

I hold on tighter to Jean.

The Wizard switches off the lights. Jean bursts into laughter, because now his stomach glows like Jesus. The Wizard turns the lights on again and comes toward us, smiling a bad smile. Jean is not afraid of the old man. When the Wizard reaches for Jesus, Jean fights him off, bending almost double to protect his treasure. The Wizard is laughing, but Jean bites the man's fingers with his eight teeth. I wish he had iron teeth and could bite off the Wizard's whole hand, because it's not funny. But the old man teases us, dangling his tongue and making stupid faces. When he laughs, you can see his gums and all the pits left by his fallen teeth. Now wheezing from too much laughter, he snatches Christ's body from Jean and puts it in his pagan pocket.

Tonton André is bitter and restless. Since I told him that my parents have gone out, 55 he hasn't spoken to me. I'm angry at him, too, because he lied to get in and now the Wizard has destroyed my crucifix and stolen Christ's body.

When I hear noises in my parents' room, I run in there with Jean, because my parents never allow visitors in their bedroom. There are two men rummaging through their closet. One man is bald and wearing stained yellow trousers, the bottoms rolled up—no shirt, no shoes. He has a few strands of hair on his chest, and his belly is huge and firm. The other man is young, secondary-school age. His hair and beard are very neat, as if he were coming from the barber. He's bug-eyed and tall and is wearing jean overalls, a T-shirt, and dirty blue tennis shoes.

The big-bellied man looks at the younger man mischievously and asks me to hug him. Before I can say anything, he wriggles out of his yellow trousers and reaches for me. But I avoid his hands and slip under the bed with Jean. He pulls me out by my ankles. Pressing me down on the floor, the naked man grabs my two wrists with his left hand. He pushes up my nightie with the right and tears my underpants. I shout at the top of my voice. I call out to Tonton André, who is pacing in the corridor. He doesn't come. I keep screaming. I'm twisting and holding my knees together. Then I snap at the naked man with my teeth. He hits my face, this way and that, until my saliva is salted with blood. I spit in his face. Twice. He bangs my head on the floor, pinning my neck down, punching my left thigh.

"*Oya!* No! Shenge is one of us!" the Wizard tells him, rushing into the room.

"Ah . . . leave this little thing . . . to me," the naked man says slowly. His short pee is pouring on my thighs and my nightie, warm and thick like baby food. I can't breathe, because he has collapsed on me with his whole weight, like a dead man. When he finally gets up, hiding his nakedness with his trousers, the Wizard bends down, peering at me, and breathes a sigh of relief.

"Shenge, can you hear me?" the Wizard says.   60

"Ummh."

"I say, you're all right!"

"All right."

"Bad days, girl, bad days. Be strong." He turns to my attacker and growls, "You're lucky you didn't open her womb. I would've strangled you myself!"

"Jean," I whisper. "Where's my brother?"   65

The overalls man finds him under the bed, curled up like a python, and drags him out. Jean lays his big head on my chest. An ache beats in my head as if the man were still banging it on the floor. My eyes show me many men in yellow trousers and overalls, many Wizards. The floor is rising and falling. I try to keep my eyes open but can't. Jean keeps feeling my busted mouth.

Someone lifts me and Jean up and takes us back to the parlor. Tonton André is sitting between two men, who are consoling him. He's got his head in his hands, and the Wizard is standing behind him, patting his shoulder gently.

As soon as Tonton André sees us, he springs to his feet. But they pull him down and scold him and tell him to get ahold of himself. He's not listening, though.

"My bastard brother and his wife are not home?" he says very slowly, as if he were   70
coming out of a deep sleep. "He owes me this one. And I'm killing these children if I don't see him."

"My nephew," the Wizard says, thudding his stick once on the floor. "Don't worry. He must pay, too. Nobody can escape our wrath this time. Nobody."

"*Koko, ni impamo tuzabigira,*" people start murmuring in agreement.

I don't know what Papa could owe his younger brother. Papa is richer than he is. Whatever it is, I'm sure that he'll repay him tomorrow.

The crowd calms down. People stand is groups and carry out their conversations, like women at the market. I get the impression that there are more people outside. Only Monsieur François is impatient, telling the others to hurry up so that they can go elsewhere, that the government didn't buy them machetes and guns to be idle.

After a while, the Wizard leaves Tonton André and comes over to us. "Young girl," he says, "you say you don't know where your parents are?"

"I don't know," I say.   75

"When they return, tell them all the roads are blocked. No escape. And you, clever girl," the old man says, tapping me on the chest, "if you want to live, don't leave this house for anything. Ghosts are all over our land. Bad ghosts." He whisks his cane and tosses his head as if he were commanding the ghosts into existence. And then he goes out, in the flow of the crowd.

I lock up as soon as everyone has left. The flowers are crushed, the altar cloth trampled upon. Pieces of glass are everywhere. The drawers from the writing desk are hanging out, and the bookshelf has fallen over. The TV is now facing the wall, and a cold wind ruffles the window blinds. I find the cross, and put it back on the altar.

I want to sleep, but fear follows me into my room. My fingers are shivering. My head feels heavy and swollen. There's a pebble in my left thigh where the naked man hit me. My mouth is still bleeding, staining the front of my nightie. I shouldn't have tricked the Wizard. What are the ghosts he summoned going to do to us? He has put his spell on Tonton André, too. Jean is covered in goose bumps. I'm too afraid to tidy up our room. We huddle in one corner, on the mattress, which has been tossed onto the floor. I start to pray.

I wake to the sound of my parents and other people arguing in the parlor. There's a lot of noise. It's not yet dawn, and my whole body is sore. One side of my upper lip is swollen as if I had a toffee between it and my gum. I don't see Jean.   80

I limp into the parlor but see only my parents and Jean. Maybe I was dreaming the other voices. My parents stop talking as soon as they see me. Maman is seated on the sofa like a statue of Marie Mére des Douleurs, looking down. Papa stands near the altar, holding Jean and scooping hot spoonfuls of oatmeal into his mouth. Jean's eyes are dull and watery, as if he hadn't slept for days. Shaking his head, he shrieks and pushes the food away. "Eat up, kid, eat up," Papa says impatiently. "You'll need the energy."

My family isn't preparing for Mass this Sunday morning. The parlor lights are off, the furniture still scattered from last nights. The doors and windows are closed, as they have been since Friday, and the dinner table is now pushed up against the front door. Our home feels haunted, as if the ghosts from the Wizard's stick were still inside.

I hurry toward my father. "Good morning, Papa!"

"Sh-h-h . . . yeah, good morning,"he whispers. He puts Jean down on the floor and squats and holds my two hands. "No noise. Don't be afraid. I won't let anyone touch you again, O.K.?"

"*Yego,* Papa."   85

I want to hug him, but he blocks me with his hands. "Don't turn on any rights, and don't bother Maman now."

"The Wizard said that ghosts are—"

"No ghosts here. . . . Listen, no Mass today. Le Père Mertens went on home leave last week." He's not looking at me but peering out through the window.

I hear a sneeze from the kitchen, stifled like a sick cat's. I search my parents' faces, but they're blank. A sudden fear enters my body. Maybe I'm still dreaming, maybe not. I push closer to Papa and ask him, "Tonton Andrél is now friends with the Wizard?"

"Don't mention André in my house anymore."   90

"He brought a man to tear my underpants."

"I say leave me alone!"

He goes to the window and holds on to the iron bars so that his hands are steady, but his body is trembling. His eyes are blinking fast and his face is tightened. When Papa gets quiet like this, he's ready to pounce on anyone. I go to the sofa and sit down silently. When I slide over to Maman, she pushes me away with one hand. I resist, bending like a tree in the wind, then returning to my position. Nothing interests

Maman today, not even Jean, her favorite child. She doesn't say any sweet thing to him or even touch him today. She acts dumb, bewitched, like a goat that the neighborhood children have fed sorghum beer.

From the window, Papa turns and looks at me as if I'm no longer his sweet Shenge. When he sees Jean sleeping on the carpet by Maman's feet, he puts the blame on me: "Stubborn girl, have you no eyes to see that your brother needs a bed? Put him in the bedroom and stop disturbing my life."

But I circle the parlor, like an ant whose hole has been blocked. I am scared to go to my room, because of the ghosts. Papa grabs my wrist and drags me into my room. He turns on the light. Our toys litter the floor. He puts the mattress back on the bed and rearranges the room. But it's still messy. Papa is cursing the toys, destroying the special treats that he and Maman bought for us when they visited America. He kicks the Teddy bear against the wall and stamps on Tweety and Mickey Mouse. Papa's hands are very dirty, the gutters around his nails swollen with black mud. When he sees me looking at him, he says, "What are you staring at?"

"I'm sorry, Papa."   95

"I told you not to turn on the lights. Who turned on this light?" I turn off the light. "Go get your stupid brother and put him to bed. You must love him."

"*Yego,* Papa."

I go to the parlor and hope that Maman will intervene. She doesn't, so I bring Jean back to the bed.

"And stay here, girl," Papa says. He goes back to the parlor, slamming the door.

When I was younger, I used to ride into the hills on Papa's wide shoulders. We were   100
always visiting Maman's family's place, in the next valley. Papa told me that when he first met Maman she was my age, and they played together in these hills. They went to the same primary school and university.

In the hills, you can see the clouds moving away, like incense smoke in a church. Our country is full of winds, and in the hills they below at your eyes until tears stain your cheeks. They suck through the valleys, like hungry cows. The birds rise and tumble and swing, their voices mixing with the winds. When Papa laughs his jolly-jolly laugh, the winds carry his voice, too. From the top of the hills, you can see that the earth is red. You can see stands of banana and plantain trees, their middle leaves rolled up, like yellow-green swords slicing the wind. You can see fields of coffee, with farmers wading through them, piggybacking their baskets. When you climb the hills in the dry season, your feet are powdered with dust. When it rains, the red earth runs like blood under a green skin. There are tendrils everywhere, and insects come out of the soil.

I walk tall and proud in our neighborhood. The bullies all know that Papa would attack anyone who messes with me. Even when he is drunk on banana beer, my tears sober him. Sometimes he even goes after Maman, for making his girl sad. He scolds his relatives when they say that it's risky that I look so much like Maman. Papa likes to tell me that he wanted to go against his people and wed Maman in our church when I was born, even though she hadn't given him a son yet. Maman wouldn't hear of it, he says. She wanted to give him a male child before they had the sacrament of matrimony. Papa tells me everything.

Maman's love for me is different. Sometimes she looks at me and becomes sad. She never likes going out in public with me, as she does with Jean. She is always tense, as if a lion will leap out and eat us.

"Maman, I'll always be beautiful!" I told her one day, as Papa was driving us back from a lakeside picnic. Maman was in the passenger's seat, Jean on her lap. I was behind.

"You could be beautiful in other ways, Monique," she said.   105

"Leave the poor girl alone," Papa told her.

"I don't understand," I said.

"You will when you grow up," she said.

This time when I wake up, rays of yellow morning are leaking in through the holes in the door and the torn blinds. They riddle the gloom, and I can see dust particles dancing within them. Our neighborhood is quiet. When I go into the parlor, Papa is moving from window to window to insure that the blinds leave no space for outsiders to peep in. Maman is standing at the table, straining her eyes as she examines two framed photographs.

One is from my parents' traditional wedding. It's ten years old. I was in Maman's 110 belly then. All the women are elegantly dressed, the *imyitero* draping over them like Le Père Mertens's short vestment. Married women who have given birth to sons wear *urugoli* crowns. Maman got hers only last year, when Jean was born. There are some cows tethered in the background. They were part of the dowry Papa offered for Maman. But no matter what I try to focus on, my eyes go to Tonton André's smiley face. I cover it with my hand, but Maman pushes my fingers off. I look at the other picture instead, which was taken last year, after my parents' church wedding. Papa, Maman, and I are in front. I'm the flower girl, my hands gloved and a flower basket hanging down from my neck with white ribbons. Maman holds baby Jean close to her heart, like a wedding bouquet.

"Maman, Jean is lonely in the bedroom," I say.

"I hope he sleeps the whole day," she says, without looking at me.

"Won't ghosts steal him?"

"He'll get used to them. Go get yourself some food, Monique."

"*Oya,* Maman, I don't want to eat."   115

"Then go and shower."

"Alone? I don't want to shower."

She touches my nightie. "You need to shower."

"Maman, when wizards pee . . ."

"Don't tell me now." She looks at Papa. "She needs a shower."   120

Hearing this, I raise my nightie to show Maman my swollen thigh, but she slaps it down, saying, "You'll get a new pair of underpants. Your face will be beautiful again."

I return my attention to the pictures. I scratch at Tonton André's face with my nails to erase him from our family. But the glass saves him.

Maman isn't looking at the photos anymore; her eyes are closed, as if in prayer. I pick up a brass letter opener and begin to scratch the glass over my Tonton's face. The sound distracts Papa from the window and he gives me a bad look. I stop.

"Why did you come down—come *back?*" he says to Maman, searching my face to see whether I've understood the question.

I haven't.   125

He turns back to Maman. "Woman, why? Return to where you were last night. Please. Leave."

"Whatever you do," she says, "do not let my daughter know."

"She should!" he says, then recoils from the force in his own voice.

My parents are hiding something from me. Maman is very stubborn about it. Their sentences enter my ears as randomly as a toss of the dice on our Ludo board. Papa looks guilty, like a child who can't keep a secret.

"I can't bear it," he says. "I can't." 130

"If Monique knew where I was last night," Maman argues, "your family would've forced it out of her and shed blood."

As they talk, invisible people are breathing everywhere—at least twenty ghosts are in the air around us. When Maman speaks, the ghosts let out groans of agreement, but my parents don't seem to hear them.

Papa shakes his head. "I mean, you should never have come back. I could have convinced them . . ."

"We needed to be with the children."

I don't understand why Maman is saying she wants to be with me when she won't 135 even look my way. I see dirty water dripping down the white wall beside me. It is coming from the ceiling. At first, it comes down in two thin lines. Then the lines widen and swell into one. Then two more lines come down, in spurts, like little spiders gliding down on threads from a branch of the mango tree in our yard. I touch the liquid with the tip of my finger. Blood.

"Ghost! Ghost!" I scream, diving toward Papa.

"It's not blood," he says.

"You are lying! It's blood! It's blood!"

Papa tries to get between me and the wall, but I get in front of him and hug him. I cling to his body, climbing upward until my hands are around his neck and my legs wrapped around his waist. He tries to muffle my shouts with his hands, but I wriggle and twist till he bows under my weight, and we nearly topple over. He staggers and regains his balance, then he releases his breath, and his stiff body softens. He puts his arms around me and carries me to the sofa. He holds my face to his heart, hiding me from the blood. I stop shouting. Maman is grinding her teeth, and there is a stubborn look on her face—maybe the Wizard has fixed her, too.

My body continues to tremble, no matter how hard Papa holds me. I tell him 140 about last night, and he consoles me, telling me not to cry. Tears fill his eyes, too, then pour down onto me, warm and fast. I've never seen him cry before. Now he can't stop, like me. He's telling me he will always love me, putting my head on his shoulder, stroking my braided hair. Once again, I'm Papa's Shenge.

"They're good ghosts," he sobs, kissing my forehead. "Good people who died."

"Papa, I tricked the Wizard."

"Don't think of last night."

He gives me a piggyback ride to the bathroom. He takes off my nightie and tosses it into the dustbin, then turns on the taps to run the bath. In the walls, the pipes whistle and sigh, but today it feels as if I were hearing the blood flowing through the strange veins of ghosts. The heat of the bath sends mist through the room, and Papa moves within it, still sobbing and wiping his tears with the sleeve of his shirt.

When he cleans my face, his hands smell like raw eggs. I reach out and switch on 145 the light; his dirty hands seem to shock him. He washes them in the sink. We're sweating in the heat and the steam. But when I try to pull back the window blinds, he stops me. In the mirror, my mouth looks as if I'd been dropped on it. I can't brush my teeth. With warm water and iodine from the closet, he cleanses my lip.

He leaves me to wash myself, tells me that I should not be afraid; he'll be right outside the door. After the bath, he goes with me to my room, and I dress in a pair of jeans and a pink T-shirt.

Back in the parlor, we sit together, away from the blood wall, my head on his shoulder. I'm hungry. He offers to make me food, but I say no, because I can't move my mouth to eat.

"Look, we cannot run away from this," Maman says.

Papa shrugs. "But I cannot do it. How do I do it?"

They're talking about secret things again.

"You can," she says. "Yesterday you did it to Annette." 150

"I should never have gone to André's place yesterday. Big mistake."

"We owe André our coöperation. He's a madman now."

Papa goes to the window, and looks out. "I think we should run to those U.N. soldiers by the street corner."

"*Ndabyanze!* No way! If your brother doesn't get what he wants when he returns, 155 he will hurt all of us."

"The soldiers are our only hope."

"They? Hopeless."

"No."

"My husband, whatever you decide, let our children live, O.K.?"

"Maman, are we going to die?" I ask. 160

"No, no, my dear," Maman says. "You're not going to die. *Uzabaho.* You will live."

Outside, the mid-morning sun is now very bright, and, though the blinds are still drawn, I can see my parents' clothes clearly now. Papa's light-brown jeans are covered with dark stains. Maman is very dirty, her dress covered with dust and dirt, as if she'd been wrestling on the ground all night. She smells of sweat. I knew that it was a bad idea for her to go out last night; she never goes out at night. She tells me that there are many bad women who do, because Rwanda is getting poorer and poorer.

"Maman, Maman!" Jean shrieks suddenly. He must be having a nightmare. She shakes her head guiltily but doesn't go to him, as if she'd lost her right to be our mother. I go with Papa into our bedroom, and Jean climbs all over him, but wails for Maman. A muffled sneeze breaks the silence again. A ghost is gasping for air, as if it were being stifled. We hold on to Papa, who has brought holy water into the bedroom with him.

"It's O.K., it's O.K.," Papa says, looking around and sprinkling the holy water, as if he has come to console the ghosts, not us. Together we listen to the ghost's raspy breathing. The breaths come further and further apart. They stop. Papa and the other ghosts start to sigh, as if the ailing one had died a second death. There are tears in Papa's eyes, and his mouth is moving without words. He is commanding ghosts, like the Wizard, but without a stick.

Someone begins to pound on our front door. Papa quickly hands Jean to me. 165 "Don't open the door!" he hisses to Maman in the parlor, then turns to me. "And don't take your brother out there!" He stays with us, but his mind is in the parlor, where we can hear Maman pushing aside the table, opening the front door, and whispering to people. We hear chairs and tables being moved. Then there's a grating sound. On the roof, I can hear big birds flapping their wings for takeoff. Then quiet. The people must have left, and Maman is alone again in the parlor.

Somebody wails in a house down the road. Jean begins to cry. I pat him on the back and sing for him in a whisper. He's licking his lips, because he wants food. Papa takes us into the parlor and offers Jean the remains of the oatmeal. He chews the cold chunks hungrily. 'Young man, I told you to eat the whole thing in the morning," Papa says. "You children are a burden to us!" He gives me bread slices and milk from the fridge. I soak the slices and swallow them without chewing.

A mob is chanting in the distance; it sounds like it's making its way toward our house. Papa goes to the window. Another voice begins to wail. A third voice, a fourth, a fifth, a child's—it sounds like my friend Hélène. Before I can say anything, Papa says, "Shenge, forget about that Twa girl."

Hélène and I sit next to each other at school. She's the brightest in our class, and during recreation we jump rope together in the schoolyard. She's petite and hairy, with a flat forehead like a monkey. Most of the Twa people are like that. They're few in our country. My parents say that they're peaceful and that when the world talks about our country they're never mentioned.

Hélène is an orphan, because the Wizard fixed her parents last year. Mademoiselle Angeline said that he cursed them with AIDS by throwing his grisgris over their roof. Now Papa is paying Hélène's school fees. We're also in the same catechism class and Papa has promised to throw a joint party for our first Holy Communion. Last year, Hélène took the first prize in community service in our class—organized by Le Père Mertens. I came in second. We fetched the most buckets of water for old people in the neighborhood. He said if you're Hutu you should fetch for the Tutsis or the Twa. If you're Tutsi, you do it for the Hutus or the Twa. If you're Twa, you serve the other two. Being both Tutsi and Hutu, I fetched for everybody with my small bucket.

"We can't take her in," Papa says, and shrugs. "And how does this crisis concern 170 the Twa?"

Suddenly, Maman yanks the table away from the door again and unlocks it. But she doesn't open the door, just leans on it. More choked cries crack the day like a whip. There are gunshots in the distance. Papa approaches Maman, his hands shaking. He locks the door and takes her back to her seat. He pushes the table back against the door.

Maman stands up suddenly and pulls out the biggest roll of money I've ever seen from inside her dress. The notes are squeezed and damp, as if she had been holding on to them all night. "This should help for a while," she says, offering the roll to Papa. "I hope the banks will reopen soon." He doesn't touch the money. "For our children, then," she says, placing the money on the table.

I tell Papa, "We must give the money to Tonton André to pay him back."

"Ego imana y'Urwanda!" Maman swears, cutting me off. "My daughter, shut up. Do you want to die?"

Her lips quake as if she has malaria. Papa pulls his I.D. from his back pocket and 175 considers the details with disgust. He gets Maman's card out of his pocket, too. Joining the two together, he tears them into large pieces, then into tiny pieces, like confetti. He puts the scraps on the table and goes back to his security post at the window. Then he comes back and gathers them up, but he can't repair the damage. He puts the pieces into his pocket.

Evening is falling. Maman walks stiffly across the room and kneels by the altar. Papa speaks to her, but she doesn't reply. He touches her and she begins to sob.

"By this, your Shenge's crucifix," Maman says, getting up, "promise me you won't betray the people who've run to us for safety."

He nods. "I promise . . . *ndakwijeje.*"

Slowly, Maman removes the gold ring from her finger and holds it out for Papa.

"Sell this and take care of yourself and the children." 180

Papa backs away, his eyes closed. When he opens them, they're clouded, like a rainy day. Maman comes over to me and places the money on my palms and puts the ring on top of it.

"Don't go away, Maman. Papa loves you."

"I know, Monique, I know."

"Is it because you went out last night?"

"No, no, I did not go out last night!" she says. I leave everything on the altar, kneel 185 in front of Papa, and beg him with all my love to forgive her though she's lying. He turns away. I go back to the sofa. "Your papa is a good man," Maman says, hugging me.

I push Jean against her, but she avoids his eyes. I think of Le Père Mertens. I plead with Maman to wait for him to return from Belgium to reconcile them. "If you confess to Le Père Mertens," I say, "Jesus shall forgive you."

There's a light knock on the door. Maman sits up, pushing Jean off like a scorpion. Someone is crying softly outside our door. Maman walks past Papa to push aside the table and open the door. It's Hélène. She's sprawled on our doorstep. Maman quickly carries her inside, and Papa locks the door.

Hélène is soaked in blood and has been crawling through the dust. Her right foot is dangling on strings, like a shoe tied to the clothesline by its lace. Papa binds her foot with a towel, but the blood soaks through. I hold her hand, which is cold and sticky.

"You'll be O.K., Hélène," I tell her. She faints.

"No, St. Jude Thadée, no!" Maman exclaims, gathering Hélène's limp body in a 190 hug. "Monique, your friend will be fine."

I can hear a mob coming, but my parents are more interested in Hélène. Papa climbs onto a chair, then onto the table. He opens the hatch of the parlor ceiling and asks Maman to relay Hélène to him.

"Remember, we've too many up there," Maman says. "When I came down, you had five in there . . . and I put two more in just hours ago. The ceiling will collapse."

They take Hélène into our room, and Maman pulls open the hatch. A cloud of fine dust explodes into the room from the ceiling. They shove Hélène's body in.

Now I understand—they are hiding people in our ceiling. Maman was in the ceiling last night. She tricked me. Nobody is telling me the truth today. Tomorrow I must remind them that lying is a sin.

As the mob closes in on the house, chanting, the ceiling people begin to pray. I recog- 195 nize their voices as those of our Tutsi neighbors and fellow-parishioners. They're silent as Papa opens the front door to the crowd, which is bigger than last night and pushes into our home like floodwater. These people look tired, yet they sing on like drunks. Their weapons and hands and shoes and clothes are covered with blood, their palms slimy. Our house smells suddenly like an abattoir. I see the man who attacked me; his yellow trousers are now reddish brown. He stares at me; I hold on to Papa, who is hanging his head.

Maman runs into her bedroom. Four men are restraining Tonton André, who still wants to kill us all. I run to Maman and sit with her on the bed. Soon, the mob enters the room, too, bringing Papa. They give Papa a big machete. He begins to tremble, his eyes blinking. A man tears me away from Maman and pushes me toward Jean, who's in the corner. Papa is standing before Maman, his fingers on the knife's handle.

"My people," he mumbles, "let another do it. Please."

"No, you do it, traitor!" Tonton André shouts, struggling with those holding him. "You were with us when I killed Annette yesterday. My pregnant wife. You can't keep yours. Where did you disappear to when we came last night? You love your family more than I loved mine? Yes?"

"If we kill your wife for you," the Wizard says, "we must kill you. And your children, too." He thuds his stick. "Otherwise, after cleansing our land of Tutsi nuisance, your children will come after us. We must remain one. Nothing shall dilute our blood. Not God. Not marriage."

Tonton André shouts, "Shenge, how many Tutsis has Papa hidden—" 200

"My husband, be a man," Maman interrupts, looking down.

"Shenge, answer!" someone yells. The crowd of Hutus murmur and become impatient. *Wowe, subiza.*

"My husband, you promised me."

Papa lands the machete on Maman's head. Her voice chokes and she falls off the bed and onto her back on the wooden floor. It's like a dream. The knife tumbles out of Papa's hand. His eyes are closed, his face calm, though he's shaking.

Maman straightens out on the floor as if she were yawning. Her feet kick, and her 205 chest rises and locks as if she were holding her breath. There's blood everywhere—on everybody around her. It flows into Maman's eyes. She looks at us through the blood. She sees Papa become a wizard, sees his people telling him bad things. The blood overflows her eyelids, and Maman is weeping red tears. My bladder softens and pee flows down my legs toward the blood. The blood overpowers it, bathing my feet. Papa opens his eyes slowly. His breaths are long and slow. He bends down and closes Maman's eyes with shaky hands.

"If you let any Tutsi live," they tell him, "you're dead." And then they begin to leave, some patting him on the back. Tonton André is calm now, stroking his goatee. He tugs at Papa's sleeve. Papa covers Maman with a white bedspread and then goes off with the mob, without looking at me or Jean. Maman's ring and money disappear with them.

I cry with the ceiling people until my voice cracks and my tongue dries up. No one can ever call me Shenge again. I want to sit with Maman forever, and I want to run away at the same time. Sometimes I think she's sleeping and hugging Hélène under the bedspread and the blood is Hélène's. I don't want to wake them up. My mind is no longer mine; it's doing things on its own. It begins to run backward, and I see the blood flowing back into Maman. I see her rising suddenly, as suddenly as she fell. I see Papa's knife lifting from her hair. She's saying, "Me promised you."

"Yes, Maman," I say. "You promised me!"

Jean is startled by my shout. He stamps around in the blood, as if he were playing in mud.

I begin to think of Maman as one of the people in the ceiling. It's not safe for 210 her to come down yet. She's lying up there quietly, holding on to the rafters, just as she must have been last night when the man in the yellow trousers attacked me. She's waiting for the right time to cry with me. I think that Tonton André is hiding Tantine Annette in his ceiling and fooling everyone into believing that he killed her. I see her lying, face up, on a wooden beam, with her mountain belly, the way I lie on the lowest branch of our mango tree and try to count the fruit. Soon, Tonton André will bring her down gently. She'll give birth, and my uncle will cover her mouth with Belgian kisses.

Jean yanks the cloth off Maman and tries to wake her. He straightens her finger, but it bends back slowly, as if she were teasing him. He sticks his fingers into Maman's hair and kneads it, the blood thick like red shampoo. As the ceiling people weep, he wipes his hands on her clothes and walks outside, giggling.

I wander from room to room, listening for her voice among the ceiling voices. When there's silence, her presence fills my heart.

"Forgive us, Monique," Madame Thérèse says from the parlor ceiling.

"We'll always support you and Jean," her husband stammers from above my room. "Your parents are good people, Monique. We'll pay your school fees. You're ours now."

"Get this dead body off me," Grandmaman de Martin groans from the corridor. 215 "It's dead, it's dead!"

"Just be patient," someone close to her says. "We'll send the dead down carefully before they fall through."

Some praise God for the way my parents' marriage has saved them. Grandmaman de Martin becomes hysterical, forcing everyone else to rearrange themselves in the ceiling in the hallway. I identify each voice, but Maman's voice isn't there. Why hasn't she said something to me? Why doesn't she order me to go and shower?

All the things that Maman used to tell me come at me at once, and yet separately—in play, in anger, in fear. There is a command, a lullaby, the sound of her kiss on my cheek. Perhaps she is still trying to protect me from what is to come. She's capable of doing that, I know, just as she stopped Papa from telling me that he was going to smash her head.

"I'm waiting for Maman," I tell the ceiling people.

"She's gone, Monique." 220

"No, no, I know now. She's up there."

"*Yagiye hehe?* Where?"

"Stop lying! Tell my mother to talk to me."

The parlor ceiling is now creaking and sagging in the middle, and Madame Thérèse starts to laugh like a drunk. "You're right, Monique. We're just kidding. Smart girl, yes, your maman is here but she will come down only if you go outside to get Jean. She's had a long day."

"*Yego,* Madame," I say, "wake her up." 225

"She's hearing you," Monsieur Pierre Nsabimana says suddenly from the kitchen. He hasn't said anything all this while. His voice calms me, and I move toward it, my eyes fixed on the ceiling. Someone begins the Catena in a harsh, rapid whisper. It's not Maman. She always takes her time to say her prayer.

"Do you want your maman to fall with the ceiling on you?" Monsieur Pierre says.

"No."

"Then, girl, leave the house, and don't come back!"

The ceiling above the altar begins to tear apart from the wall and people scurry away 230 from that end, like giant lizards. I pick up the broken crucifix and hurry outside.

There are corpses everywhere. Their clothes are dancing in the wind. Where blood has soaked the earth, the grass doesn't move. Vultures are poking the dead with their long beaks; Jean is driving them away, stamping his feet and swirling his arms. His hands are stained, because he's been trying to raise the dead. He's not laughing anymore. His eyes are wide open, and there's a frown on his babyish forehead.

Then he wanders toward the U.N. soldiers at the corner, their rifles shiny in the twilight. They're walking away from him, as if they were a mirage. The vultures are following Jean. I scream at them, but they continue to taunt him, like stubborn mosquitoes. Jean doesn't hear. He sits on the ground, kicking his legs and crying because the soldiers won't wait for him. I squat before my brother, begging him to climb on my back. He does and keeps quiet.

We limp on into the chilly night, ascending the stony road into the hills. The blood has dried into our clothes like starch. There's a smaller mob coming toward us. Monsieur Henri is among them. He's carrying a huge torch, and the flame is eating the night in large, windy gulps. These are our people on Maman's side, and they're all in military clothes. Like another football fan club, they're chanting about how they're going to kill Papa's people. Some of them have guns. If Papa couldn't spare Maman's life, would my mother's relatives spare mine? Or my brother's?

I slip into the bush, with Jean on my back, one hand holding the crucifix, the other shielding my eyes from the tall grass and the branches, my feet cold and bracing for thorns. Jean presses hard against me, his face digging into my back. "Maman says do not be afraid," I tell him. Then we lie down on the crucifix to hide its brightness. We want to live; we don't want to die. I must be strong.

After the mob runs past us, I return to the road and look back. They drag Maman 235 out by the legs and set fire to the house. By the time their fellow-Tutsis in the ceiling begin to shout, the fire is unstoppable. They run on. They run after Papa's people. We walk forward. Everywhere is dark, and the wind spreads black clouds like blankets across the sky. My brother is toying with the glow of the crucifix, babbling like mad. ●

Senadin Musabegović *(1970–)*   Translated from the Bosnian by Ulvija Tanović

The Oath   *2007*

On my ninth birthday, in 1979, after my party, my father took the kitchen knife that my mother used to cut the cake and marked my height on the wardrobe in my room. On the knife, white and blue lines of icing that had covered the chocolate cake reminded me of an old man frowning, dissatisfied by my excitement, because for a moment I imagined that in my parents' eyes 5 I was the center of the world. As Father dragged the glittering blade above my head the icing stuck to strands of my hair. On the wooden wardrobe, where stickers of soccer players smiled, Mother marked my height in red pencil beside their greatness: one meter, thirty-four.

On my tenth birthday, in 1980, my height was marked on the wardrobe with 10 a white pencil: one meter, forty-two. During the party I was sad, because I thought I would never reach the height of Tito's picture, which smiled its icy smile at me from the corner of the room.

In 1981—in red Adidas trainers with three blue stripes, a white Lacoste shirt
with the alligator logo that twisted its head around giving my body new   15
strength, and Levi's that didn't bend at the knees, my height was marked
with a blue pencil: one meter, fifty-six. Everyone in the family was excited
about my growth.

On the wardrobe stood three colors of the Yugoslav flag illustrating my growth.

In 1989, as we made our oath to the army. I was standing in the front row   20
next to the Yugoslav flag due to my height. Nobody noticed that at the peak
of the ceremony, as we pledged our life-long allegiance to our homeland, the
bayonet fell from the top of my musket and bounced off the cold asphalt
three times.

In 1993, I measured one meter, ninety-one centimeters. I was standing   25
next to a window two meters high, watching a corpse that had been hit
by a sniper and was now spread across four flag-stones on the sidewalk. Its
fingers touched the asphalt, the sun reflected off its golden bracelet three
times. I could not count the droplets of steam that were gathering on the
windowpane.   30
The seconds followed in a row:
one,
two,
three,
four . . .   35
In a fraction of a second I felt on my head the ruler with which my father's
hand measured the border between me and the world.

Jessica Hagedorn *(1949–   )*

The Song of Bullets *1993*

Formalized
by middle age
we avoid crowds
but still
love music.   5

Day after day
with less surprise
we sit
in apartments
and count   10
the dead.

Awake,
my daughter croons
her sudden cries

and growls   15
my new language.
While she sleeps
we memorize
a list of casualties:

The photographer's brother   20
the doctor is missing.
Or I could say:
"Victor's brother Oscar
has been gone for two years . . .
It's easier for the family   25
to think of him dead."

Victor sends
a Christmas card
from El Salvador:
"Things still the same."   30

And there are others
who don't play
by the rules—
someone else's brother
perhaps mine   35
languishes in a hospital;
everyone's grown tired
of his nightmares
and pretends
he's not there.   40

Someone else's father
perhaps mine
will be executed
when the time comes.
Someone else's mother   45
perhaps mine
telephones incessantly
her husband is absent
her son has gone mad
her lover has committed suicide   50
she's a survivor
who can't appreciate
herself.

The sight
of my daughter's
pink and luscious flesh   55
undoes me.
I fight

my weakening rage
I must remember   60
to commit
those names to memory
and stay angry.

Friends send postcards:
"Alternating between hectic   65
social Manila life & rural wonders
of Sagata[1] . . . on to Hongkong and Bangkok—
Love . . ."

Assassins cruise the streets
in obtrusive limousines   70
sunbathers idle
on the beach

War is predicted
in five years
ten years   75
any day now
I always thought
it was already happening

snipers and poets locked
in a secret embrace   80
the country
my child may never see

a heritage
of women in heat
and men   85
skilled at betrayal

dancing
to the song
of bullets.

Carolyn Forché *(1950–)*

The Colonel   *1981*

What you have heard is true. I was in his house. His wife carried a tray of
coffee and sugar. His daughter filed her nails, his son went out for the night.
There were daily papers, pet dogs, a pistol on the cushion beside him. The

---

[1]**Sagata:** Area with caves in the Philippines.

moon swung bare on its black cord over the house. On the television was
a cop show. It was in English. Broken bottles were embedded in the walls 5
around the house to scoop the kneecaps from a man's legs or cut his hands to
lace. On the windows there were gratings like those in liquor stores. We had
dinner, rack of lamb, good wine, a gold bell was on the table for calling the
maid. The maid brought green mangoes, salt, a type of bread. I was asked
how I enjoyed the country. There was a brief commercial in Spanish. His 10
wife took everything away. There was some talk then of how difficult it had
become to govern. The parrot said hello on the terrace. The colonel told it to
shut up, and pushed himself from the table. My friend said to me with his
eyes: say nothing. The colonel returned with a sack used to bring groceries
home. He spilled many human ears on the table. They were like dried peach 15
halves. There is no other way to say this. He took one of them in his hands,
shook it in our faces, dropped it into a water glass. It came alive there. I am
tired of fooling around he said. As for the rights of anyone, tell your people
they can go fuck themselves. He swept the ears to the floor with his arm and
held the last of his wine in the air. Something for your poetry, no? he said. 20
Some of the ears on the floor caught this scrap of his voice. Some of the ears
on the floor were pressed to the ground.

Robert Waugh *(1944–)*

The Bodies of This Century

The bodies are swinging, the bodies
are falling, holes in their heads,
in the parlor, the bodies choke on gas, *en masse*
a stench steeps in the piles of bodies heaped
on lawns, on porches, in guacamole kitchens, 5
bodies in tallow, in jars upon the pantry
shelves, tallow on telephone lines, tallow
upon the tongue, tallow of tallow, bodies sawn
in half, bodies bulldozed into pits
in the back of our national forests (one night I looked 10
into ten eyeless heads
on a backroad in Indiana), bodies raked up, bodies
hoes chop up into furrows for your harvest,
bodies and pumpkins, bodies and straw-berry-
red wet cheeks, bodies against the wall 15
rat-a-tat-tat, bodies of fertilizer
scattered across the fields, bone crush of bone,
bodies that sit behind you in the drive-in
watching you making out, reaching up, bodies that sit
in church to watch you pray and pour the blood 20
into the chalice, bodies
spattered in boulevards, bodies on barbed
wire, bodies on street corners waiting for the light,
bodies in towers, bodies.

Naomi Shihab Nye *(1952–)*

All Things Not Considered *2002*

You cannot stitch the breath
back into this boy.

A brother and sister were playing with toys
when their room exploded.

In what language   5
is this holy?

The Jewish boys killed in the cave
were skipping school, having an adventure.

Asel Asleh, Palestinian, age 17, believed in the field
beyond right and wrong where people   10
   come together

to talk. He kneeled to help someone else
stand up before he was shot.

If this is holy,
could we have some new religions please?   15

Mohammed al-Durra huddled against his father
in the street, terrified. The whole world saw him die.

An Arab father on crutches burying his 4 month girl
   weeps,
"I spit in the face of this ugly world."   20

   *

Most of us would take our children over land.
We would walk the fields forever homeless
with our children,
huddle under cliffs, eat crumbs and berries,
to keep our children.   25
This is what we say from a distance
because we can say whatever we want.

   *

No one was right.
Everyone was wrong.

What if they'd get together   30
and say that?
At a certain point
the flawed narrator wins.

People made mistakes for decades.
Everyone hurt in similar ways   35
at different times.
Some picked up guns because guns were given.

If they were holy it was okay to use guns.
Some picked up stones because they had them.
They had millions of them.   40
They might have picked up turnip roots
or olive pits.
Picking up things to throw and shoot:
at the same time people were studying history,
going to school.   45

*

The curl of a baby's graceful ear.

The calm of a bucket
waiting for water.

Orchards of the old Arab men
who knew each tree.   50

Jewish and Arab women
standing silently together.

Generations of black.

Are people the only holy land?

Laura Blumenfeld *(1964–)*

The Apology: Letters from a Terrorist *2002*

The gunman was not at home. "Come in," his mother said. "Would you like some orange soda?" My knocking must have shaken her out of a nap; she was wearing slippers and a pink embroidered bathrobe. Inside, the living room was full of family members, young and old.

"That's him," the woman said, pointing over her grandchildren's heads to the gunman's photograph. "He tried to kill someone," she said in an easy voice.

"Who?" I asked.

"Some Jew," said a boy, who appeared to be about twelve years old. He smiled crookedly, and added, "I don't know who—a Mossad[1] agent.

"I'm not sure he was a Mossad agent," a man who introduced himself as Saed, the gunman's older brother, said. "He was a person from the outside—a leader from New York. We heard he was doing something against Palestinians. Why else would they choose him to be shot?"

"Why did he fire only once?" I asked.

"It was in the marketplace," Saed said.

"After the shooting, he threw the gun in the air, and it fell to the ground," his mother said. She began to chuckle and the others joined in.

The attack had taken place in the early spring of 1986. It had been a quiet time in Jerusalem: people could walk through the Old City without fear. In March, all that changed when Palestinian terrorists began gunning down foreign tourists—Americans, British, Germans. Their first target was an American man; he had been shot as he strolled through the Arab market shortly after sundown. The gunman had aimed a little too high, and the bullet had grazed his scalp.

Twelve years later, I arrived in Israel for an extended honeymoon with my husband. While he did part-time legal work, I took a leave of absence from my job at the *Washington Post* to do research for a book about the culture of vengeance—the thirst for settling scores which has created so much turmoil in the Middle East and throughout the world. My research took me to Albania, Sicily, Iran, and other countries; between trips I looked for the gunman who had shot the American in the market. From records in the Jerusalem District Attorney's office, I learned that several Palestinians in a pro-Syria breakaway faction of the Palestine Liberation Organization had been convicted in 1986 for the shooting of foreigners. The man who had shot the American was named Omar Khatib. He had been tried and convicted in an Israeli court, and was now serving a sentence of twenty-five years in Shikma Prison, in Ashkelon.

The Khatibs lived in the West Bank, in the last house on a narrow, rutted lane, which ended at a limestone quarry. Trash and rusty appliances spilled over the precipice. Their house, which was behind a red gate, was really a number of buildings joined together—cement improvisations with raw concrete steps and half-stacked cinder blocks. In rudimentary Arabic, I introduced myself as an American journalist.

"Why did he do it?" I asked the gunman's father, a tall, bony man in a gray robe.

The father's response was terse. "He did his duty," he said. "Every Palestinian must do it. Then there will be justice."

Another brother of the gunman came into the room. He introduced himself as Imad. His mustache and goatee were dyed burnt orange, and he was wearing a silly red-and-black shirt. He told me that he had been a member of the Popular Front for the Liberation of Palestine, a radical faction of the P.L.O., and that he had returned to Palestine, after twenty-five years of exile in Jordan, in 1994, the summer after the Israelis and the Palestinians signed the Oslo peace accords. "Anybody would do what my brother did under those circumstances," he said. "If you pretend to be a Palestinian for five minutes, you'll feel what we feel."

"And what about the man he tried to kill?" I asked.

---

[1] **Mossad:** Intelligence agency in Israel.

"It wasn't a personal vendetta," Imad replied. "It was public relations. It was like telling the media to pay attention to us."

"Won't someone from the victim's family kill one of your people?" I asked.

"My brother never met the man," Imad said. "Nothing personal, so no revenge."

For me, however, the shooting was personal. The man whom Imad's brother had tried to kill was my father.

■ ■ ■

In March of 1986, when I was an undergraduate at Harvard, my father, in his capacity as executive director of the New York Holocaust Memorial Commission, went to Israel to look at the country's various Holocaust museums. One evening, after a visit to the Western Wall,[2] in Jerusalem, one of the Holy Land's most sacred sites, he was walking back to his hotel when he was shot by an unseen assailant. He was treated for the head wound in an Israeli hospital, and the story of the shooting made front-page news.

"Did you ever wonder who the gunman was or what he looked like?" I later asked my father. "I never thought about it," he replied. But, for me, putting the incident out of my mind wasn't so easy. I understood that people who commit acts of terrorism are less concerned with what happens to their victims than with advancing their cause, but I had resolved to find a way to make my father human in the gunman's eyes. And I wanted him to see that what he had done was horrible. I thought about introducing myself as the daughter of his victim but discarded the idea, because I did not want him to regard me as "a Jew" or as an adversary. Given the Palestinians' eagerness to get their views out to the world, I reasoned that the best way to gain access to him would be to identify myself to him and his family simply as an American journalist who was interested in hearing his story.

Several weeks after I met Omar's family, I went back to their house to return some clippings about the shooting which they had given me to photocopy. I was greeted by Omar's mother and his brother Imad, and led to an upstairs bedroom. We sat down on the couch where Omar had slept before his imprisonment.

"His head was here, his feet were here," his mother said, brushing the upholstery with her fingers. She brought out a black attaché case and opened it. Inside was a karate manual, a picture of Omar in martial-arts dress, executing a kick, and a black-belt certificate that he had won in 1979. The picture showed a slim young man with an angry expression on his face. There was also a copy of the Koran, a book entitled "Theories About Revolution and National Liberation," and a copy of "Measure for Measure."[3]

"He was at Bethlehem University, studying English," Imad pointed out.

"And business, too," his mother said. "He got a ninety-five in public relations." 25

I was shown Omar's report cards, his birth certificate from a hospital on the Mount of Olives, and a high-school certificate of graduation that read, "The school administration certifies that Mr. Omar Kamel Said Al Khatib was a student in 1980–81. His

---

[2]**Western Wall:** The most sacred and holy place in the Jewish religion, the Western Wall in the Old City of Jerusalem is the remaining section of the Temple Mount, which has remained intact since 70 C.E., the destruction of the Second Jerusalem Temple.   [3]**Koran . . . :** The sacred writing of Islam revealed by God to the prophet Muhannad; *Measure for Measure,* a Shakespeare play.

conduct was very good." Before saying goodbye, Imad offered to take a letter from me to his brother in prison. Only immediate relatives were allowed contact with such prisoners, but Imad agreed to deliver whatever I wanted to write.

■ ■ ■

In my first letter to Omar, I explained that I was an American journalist who was writing a book about the region, and that I was curious about his life in an Israeli prison. I asked him about his hobbies and his plans for the future. At the end of the letter, I wrote, "And finally, I would like to hear about the events that led to your arrest. What happened? When you think back on it, what were your feelings then? How do you feel about it today?"

Six weeks later, Omar wrote back, in an intricate light-blue scrawl, on eight sheets of tissue paper:

> *Dear Laura,*
>
> *I would like first to extend my appreciation and regard for your message, which I have read with interest and care. This is not a dream, but a real fact we are seeking to incarnate on land through the long march of our revolution and in accordance with rules of justice and equality and the right of people to liberate their lands, this sacred right which was secured by international law. We, as sons to this people, and part of its past and present, have on our shoulders the burden of holding the difficulty of the liberation road; it's our mission to let the rifles live.*
>
> *I would like you to know that our choice in the military struggle is a legitimate choice on a historical basis that takes into account the fact that the enemy we are facing is one who stands on a Zionist ideology that is racist in its basis and fascist in its aims and means. It is an enemy with a huge military destructive machine higher in its ability than any other superpower state. It's an enemy that can be faced and defeated only by force. . . .*
>
> *There is a huge difference, my dear, between "terror" and the right of self-determination, between a criminal and a revolutionary. . . . It is hard for us, as prisoners, to accept a peace process which does not answer all the questions that the Israeli/Palestinian conflict has raised. We continue in our efforts to affect what is going on outside the walls of our prisons.*
>
> *Sincerely,*
> *Omar Kamel Al Khatib*

The letter read more like a manifesto than like an exchange between two people. I wanted to know Omar as he really was, beneath the layers of ideology, and the next day I wrote to him again and inquired about what he was currently reading, what he could tell me about his family's history, and what, in particular, had inflamed his feelings against Israel.

A month later, he replied: 30

> *I love English literature, and have been reading it from the first years of my imprisonment; lately I have dedicated my time to the reading of theoretical and philosophical books. . . . I have read the works of Tolstoy and Dostoevsky. I do suggest that you read Dostoevsky's "Memoirs from the House of the Dead"; it will help you in the work you are conducting.*

My chances of being released now are big because of my deteriorating health conditions. I suffer from asthma, an illness which puts me very near death. I'm living in unhealthy conditions, with ten of my friends in a small, cold cell very full of humidity. They smoke, cook, and do all their daily activities, which brings me a hard time. You can't imagine how it feels when you find yourself being chased even by the breath you breathe.

I don't know if the Israelis consider me as "having blood on my hands," but I do know that there is no meaning in keeping me in prison after more than 13 years. The term "blood on their hands" is a bad term I do not like to hear. It is a racist term used to fulfill some political purpose aimed to distort our identity as freedom fighters.

He went on to say that he had been "chosen" to join the rebel Abu Musa faction of the Palestine Liberation Organization in 1985, with orders to "create a state of unrest," whose objective was to put an end to Israel's occupation of Palestine.

I was young at that time, but since then I have discovered that violence is not in my personality. Maybe this is the answer to your question of why I shot just one shot at that man, despite the fact that my pistol was very full of bullets.

When Israel became a state, in 1948, Omar said, his mother's family had been forced to leave their home in Jaffa and migrate to Lebanon. Omar's father was born in the West Bank, but after his marriage to Omar's mother he had gone to live in Jerusalem, where the couple had brought up their children.

He continued:

This city has shaped my identity; she planted in my mind unforgettable memories. I witnessed the Israeli aggression of the Six-Day War. I was four years old then, but enough aware to understand what was going on. I remember when my mother used to hide us with the rest of our neighbors who came to have shelter in our small room. We were so frightened by the darkness and the sound of guns. Six days, and the history entered into a new stage, the stage of the occupation.

The resistance movement began, and at the end of the '60s my brother was arrested and sent to prison. . . . I saw the painful time that my family went through, searching to know the fate of my brother. I remember visiting him with my mother once or twice, but after that he was expelled to Jordan. . . . There he was sent to prison for no reason but under the pretext of crossing the borders illegally.

We were such a poor family at the time, we didn't have enough money to eat. . . . I will never forget the exhaustion and pain of the journey when I accompanied my mother to visit my brother. . . . Do you know when I saw [my brother] next?! It was 25 years later. This time I was the prisoner, and he was the visitor. After the signing of the Oslo agreement he got the chance to return to his home land. He came to visit me at Ashkelon prison. It was a very sad meeting, we both couldn't stop crying. I had no words to say, I had forgotten everything, but felt the need of touching him, and kissing him.

For all its self-justifying tone, the letter was more candid on a personal level, and in my reply I asked Omar to describe how he had felt when he shot the man in the marketplace. I also asked him what he would say to the man if the two of them were to meet again. In his next two letters, he dwelled on the hardships of prison life and the satisfaction he felt in taking a college correspondence course. He said that he had learned French and Hebrew, and that he had written a book of grammar for his fellow-prisoners entitled "The Practical Use of English Structure." He said that he had six more courses to complete before earning his B.A.

In my next letter, I again asked Omar why he had shot the American tourist. Omar   35
wrote back:

> With regard to David Blumenfeld—I hope he can understand the reasons behind my act. If I were him I would. I have thought a lot about meeting him one day. We have been in a state of war, and now we are passing through a new stage of historical reconciliation where there is no place for hatred and detestation. In this new era and atmosphere, he is welcome to be my guest in Jerusalem.

The letter hinted that Omar was capable of remorse, though an earlier reference to my father as a "chosen military site" had made me wince. And Omar's lofty talk about "historical reconciliation" made me wonder whether we were both involved in an elaborate game of manipulation, each for a different purpose. To give him a better sense of David Blumenfeld, I replied that I had contacted David, and discovered that his grandparents had been killed in the Holocaust, and that he had come to Israel to gather material for building a Holocaust museum in New York. I told him that David was not hostile to the Palestinian cause but that he was concerned about whether Omar would ever again resort to violence against anyone, innocent or not. Omar began his next letter with an account of an examination that he had undergone for his asthma, in the hope of winning a release from prison on medical grounds:

> When the van stopped in front of Ramallah hospital, it was as if I were an alien from another world. Each of the guards took his place around my vehicle. Guns were ready for use. The door was opened, and all around me I saw people looking at me strangely. I touched the ground with slow steps because my hands and legs were tied. I took a deep breath and looked at the sky, feeling the need to fly. . . . And all the people looked at me with pity and wonder because of my weak appearance.

> They led me to an elevator to the main section of the testing area. We waited till a very beautiful Moroccan girl came to lead us to the examination room. I introduced myself to her and spoke with her a little about the prison while she conducted the test three times. She was shocked to see the bad test results.

In his next letter, he wrote:

> Back to David, I do admire his talking to you and I appreciate his understanding, his support for my people. If these feelings are really from the depth of his heart, this may contribute a lot to our friendship. Of course, my answer to his question [about committing an act of violence again] is NO.

∎ ∎ ∎

A few weeks later, I learned that the parole board had rejected Omar's petition for release. Two months later, his petition came up again, on appeal to a higher court. I asked Imad if I could attend the hearing, and he agreed.

The courtroom was packed with defendants and their families—Israelis and Palestinians together on the benches. Omar's mother and his brother Imad were there, along with nine other relatives. I took a seat directly in front of them. Three judges filed into the room, and finally Omar arrived. Although he was in ankle chains, his entrance was triumphant. He greeted the other prisoners effusively, shaking their hands and clapping them on the back. And yet the effects of his incarceration were visible: the skin on his face was so taut that his cheekbones cast a skeletal shadow under his eyes; there was a noticeable swelling around his mouth. His mother rushed over to him and kissed him. Imad ruffled his hair. Then Imad pointed to me. "Laura is here," he said.

"Laura!" Omar said, smiling. "I hoped to meet you one day, but not in this set- 40 ting." I couldn't keep my hands from shaking as I smiled back.

"I need to know if you're sorry," I said.

"I will write David a long letter," he said.

"No, I need to know now," I said. For a moment our eyes met, and then a court officer led him away.

Several hours passed before Omar's lawyer, an energetic Israeli woman, presented the case to the judges. They listened to the details of Omar's asthma, and then gave orders for the petition to be sent back to the medical-parole committee for further review. As Omar and his family got up to leave, I realized that this was my last chance to confront him. I stood up and said, "I am David Blumenfeld's daughter, Laura Blumenfeld." For a moment, Omar and his family stared at me. Then Omar's mother, Imad, and several other relatives began to weep. I tried to explain why I had concealed my identity for so long. "I did it for one reason," I said. "This conflict is between human beings, and not between disembodied Arabs and Jews. And we're people. Not military targets. We're people with families." I turned to Omar. He looked stunned. "You promised me you would never hurt anyone again," I said. He looked at me and said nothing. As he was led away, his family rushed over to embrace me.

A few weeks later, I received another letter from Omar: 45

> *A week has passed since the day of the hearing, and all that is in my mind and imagination is the picture of you standing in front of the court, and the echo of your voice.*
>
> *You made me feel so stupid that once I was the cause of your and your kind mother's pain. Sorry and please understand.*
>
> *Of course I was shocked to learn that you are David's daughter. I didn't sleep for almost two days. I reread all your precious letters trying to rearrange the whole puzzle again.*

■ ■ ■

My stay in Israel was nearly over. Before leaving for America, I visited Omar's family one last time. The house was full of people, and in honor of my departure Omar's mother had laid out plates of vegetables, bread, and cheese. Arabic music was coming from a tape player, and several of the women and children invited me to dance with them. Imad presented me with gifts from Omar—two gold necklaces, one for me and one for my father, with Omar's name inscribed on it. I felt unsure of this display of warmth: only a short while ago, these same people had condoned the attempted killing of my father, as they might condone other attacks on innocent bystanders in their struggle with Israel, if the fragile peace process broke down.

A few weeks after I had returned to America, my father received a letter from Omar that I have read many times since, in the hope that its sentiments are genuine:

Dear David,

Thirteen years have passed. Yes, it's so late to come and ask you about your injuries, but I would like you to know that I've prayed a lot for you. I hope you are well today.

I admit to having some good feeling toward you from the beginning, a feeling that made me hope to meet you one day. It seems to me that this good feeling is coming to be a reality. . . . I would like first to express to you my deep pain and sorrow for what I caused you. I've learned many things about you. You are supposed to be a very close friend to my people. I hope you believe that we both were victims of this long historical conflict. . . . Laura was the mirror that made me see your face as a human person deserving to be admired and respected. I apologize for not understanding her message from the beginning.

If God helps and I get to be released, I hope you accept my invitation to be my guest in the holy city of peace, Jerusalem. ●

Sara Corbett *(1970–)*

The Lost Boys[1] *2001*

One evening in late January, Peter Dut, twenty-one, leads his two teenage brothers through the brightly lit corridors of the Minneapolis airport, trying to mask his confusion. Two days earlier, the brothers, refugees from Africa, encountered their first light switch and their first set of stairs. An aid worker in Nairobi demonstrated the flush toilet to them—also the seat belt, the shoelace, the fork. And now they find themselves alone in Minneapolis, three bone-thin African boys confronted by a swirling river of white faces and rolling suitcases.

Finally, a traveling businessman recognizes their uncertainty. "Where are you flying to?" he asks kindly, and the eldest brother tells him in halting, bookish English. A few days earlier, they left a small mud hut in a blistering hot Kenyan refugee camp, where they had lived as orphans for nine years after walking for hundreds of miles across Sudan. They are now headed to a new home in the U.S.A. "Where?" the man asks in disbelief when Peter Dut says the city's name. "Fargo? North Dakota? You gotta be kidding me. It's too cold there. You'll never survive it!"

And then he laughs. Peter Dut has no idea why.

---

[1] *The Lost Boys:* In the second phase of the Sudanese Civil War (since 1983) between Northern Islamic government forces and Southern black African rebel tribes, the government has killed one out of five of the southern Sudanese populations and four million have been forced to flee. In the latest humanitarian crisis in the war, in the western Darfur region, Arab Sudanese militias (Janjaweed), backed by the government, retaliating for a rebel uprising, have attacked and pillaged Sudanese villages, taken women and children into slavery, and killed and tortured hundreds of thousands. The violence in Darfur since 2003 has taken two hundred thousand lives and two million have fled their homes, many to refugee camps in Chad. The civil war not only is fueled by ethnic divisions but also by a struggle for arable land and resources.

In the meantime, the temperature in Fargo has dropped to 15 below. The boys tell me that until now, all they have ever known about cold is what they felt grasping a bottle of frozen water. An aid worker handed it to them one day during a "cultural orientation" session at the Kakuma Refugee Camp, a place where the temperature hovers around 100 degrees.

Peter Dut and his two brothers belong to an unusual group of refugees referred to by aid organizations as the Lost Boys of Sudan, a group of roughly 10,000 boys who arrived in Kenya in 1992 seeking refuge from their country's fractious civil war. The fighting pits a northern Islamic government against rebels in the south who practice Christianity and tribal religions.

The Lost Boys were named after Peter Pan's posse of orphans. According to U.S. State Department estimates, some 17,000 boys were separated from their families and fled southern Sudan in an exodus of biblical proportions after fighting intensified in 1987. They arrived in throngs, homeless and parentless, having trekked about 1000 miles, from Sudan to Ethiopia, back to Sudan, and finally to Kenya. The majority of the boys belonged to the Dinka and Nuer tribes, and most were then between the ages of eight and eighteen. (Most of the boys don't know for sure how old they are; aid workers assigned them approximate ages after they arrived in 1992.)

Along the way, the boys endured attacks from the northern army and marauding bandits as well as lions, who preyed on the slowest and weakest among them. Many died from starvation or thirst. Others drowned or were eaten by crocodiles as they tried to cross a swollen Ethiopian river. By the time the Lost Boys reached the Kakuma Refugee Camp, their numbers had been cut nearly in half.

Now, after nine years of subsisting on rationed corn mush and lentils and living largely ungoverned by adults, the Lost Boys of Sudan are coming to America. In 1999, the United Nations High Commissioner for Refugees, which handles refugee cases around the world, and the U.S. government agreed to send 3600 of the boys to the United States—since going back to Sudan was out of the question. About 500 of the Lost Boys still under the age of eighteen will be living in apartments or foster homes across the United States by the end of this year. The boys will start school at a grade level normal for their age, thanks to a tough English-language program at their refugee camp. The remaining 3100 Lost Boys will be resettled as adults. After five years, each boy will be eligible for citizenship, provided he has turned twenty-one.

Nighttime in America?

On the night that I stand waiting for Peter Dut and his brothers to land in Fargo, tendrils of snow are snaking across the tarmac. The three boys file through the gate without money or coats or luggage beyond their small backpacks. The younger brothers, Maduk, seventeen, and Riak, fifteen, appear petrified. As a social worker passes out coats, Peter Dut studies the black night through the airport window. "Excuse me," he says worriedly. "Can you tell me, please, is it now night or day?"

This is a stove burner. This is a can opener. This is a brush for your teeth. The new things come in a tumble. The brothers' home is a sparsely furnished two-bedroom apartment in a complex on Fargo's south side. Rent is $445 a month. It has been stocked with donations from area churches and businesses: toothpaste, bread, beans, bananas.

A caseworker empties a garbage bag full of donated clothing, which looks to have come straight from the closet of an elderly man. I know how lucky the boys are: the

State Department estimates that war, famine, and disease in southern Sudan have killed more than 2 million people and displaced another 4 million. Still I cringe to think of the boys showing up for school in these clothes.

The next day, when I return to the apartment at noon, the boys have been up since five and are terribly hungry. "What about your food?" I ask, gesturing to the bread and bananas and the box of cereal sitting on the counter.

Peter grins sheepishly. I suddenly realize that the boys, in a lifetime of cooking maize and beans over a fire pit, have never opened a box. I am placed in the role of teacher. And so begins an opening spree. We open potato chips. We open a can of beans. We untwist the tie on the bagged loaf of bread. Soon the boys are seated and eating a hot meal.

Living on Leaves and Berries

The three brothers have come a long way since they fled their village in Sudan with their parents and three sisters, all of whom were later killed by Sudanese army soldiers. The Lost Boys first survived a six- to ten-week walk to Ethiopia, often subsisting on leaves and berries and the occasional boon of a warthog carcass. Some boys staved off dehydration by drinking their own urine. Many fell behind; some were devoured by lions or trampled by buffalo.

The Lost Boys lived for three years in Ethiopia, in UN-supported camps, before   15
they were forced back into Sudan by a new Ethiopian government no longer sympathetic to their plight. Somehow, more than 10,000 of the boys miraculously trailed into Kenya's UN camps in the summer of 1992—as Sudanese government planes bombed the rear of their procession.

For the Lost Boys, then, a new life in America might easily seem to be the answer to every dream. But the real world has been more complicated than that. Within weeks of arriving, Riak is placed in a local junior high; Maduk starts high school classes; and Peter begins adult education classes.

Refugee Blues

Five weeks later, Riak listens quietly through a lesson on Elizabethan history at school, all but ignored by white students around him.

Nearby, at Fargo South High School, Maduk is frequently alone as well, copying passages from his geography textbook, trying not to look at the short skirts worn by many of the girls.

Peter Dut worries about money. The three brothers say they receive just $107 in food stamps each month and spend most of their $510 monthly cash assistance on rent and utilities.

Resettlement workers say the brothers are just undergoing the normal transition.   20
Scott Burtsfield, who coordinates resettlement efforts in Fargo through Lutheran Social Services, says, "The first three months are always the toughest. It really does get better."

The Lost Boys can only hope so; they have few other options. A return to southern Sudan could be fatal. "There is nothing left for the Lost Boys to go home to—it's a war zone," says Mary Anne Fitzgerald, a Nairobi-based relief consultant.

Some Sudanese elders have criticized sending boys to the United States. They worry that their children will lose their African identity. One afternoon an eighteen-year-old Lost Boy translated a part of a tape an elder had sent along with many boys: "He is saying, 'Don't drink. Don't smoke. Don't kill. Go to school every day, and remember, America is not your home.'"

But if adjustment is hard, the boys also experience consoling moments. One of these came on a quiet Friday night last winter. As the boys make a dinner of rice and lentils, Peter changes into an African outfit, a finely woven green tunic with a skullcap to match, bought with precious food rations at Kakuma.

Just then the doorbell rings unexpectedly. And out of the cold tumble four Sudanese boys—all of whom have resettled as refugees over the past several years. I watch one, an eighteen-year-old named Sunday, wrap his arms encouragingly around Peter Dut. "It's a hard life here," Sunday whispers to the older boy, "but it's a free life, too." ●

Explorations of the Text

1. In his "Brief History of Terrorism," Martin Walker states that "well into the twentieth century, terror usually meant state-sponsored terror," evoking images of Nazi Germany and the Soviet secret police. After World War II, however, terror tactics began to be used by such revolutionary groups as the National Liberation Front of Algeria and the Irish Republican army in Northern Ireland to promote their causes. He then contends that suicide bombers represent a third kind of terrorist group, "implacable new fanatics . . . who simply want to blow up the peace table along with everything else." After reading the works in this thematic cluster and considering Walker's categorization of terrorists, create your definition of terrorism. Use evidence from the works to support your points.

2. Explore the mindset of the terrorist or the fanatic as presented in selected works in this cluster. What are the similarities or the differences in these various states of mind?

3. How does terror differ from terrorism? Discuss the aftermath of terror as envisioned by several authors in this cluster. How are the main characters, for example, in Uwem Akpan's "My Parents' Bedroom," affected by terrorist acts?

4. After 9/11, we in the United States certainly live with a heightened sense of fear and vulnerability. How do several writers in this cluster portray the intrusions of terror into everyday life?

5. What do Luisa Valenzuela, Laura Blumenfeld, and Carolyn Forché envision as antidotes to fanaticism?

6. Do any of the authors conceive of a possible resolution of tribal conflicts? Ethnic tensions? What does Blumenfeld propose as alternatives to demonizing the enemy?

7. When we witness disaster, we often are left speechless. In many ways acts of terror or terrorism are unimaginable. What techniques do several of the writers in this cluster use to portray inconceivable horror (e.g., use of descriptive detail, irony, imagery, etc.)? You also may examine the poems in the 9/11 cluster or the works dealing with the Holocaust.

The Reading/Writing Connection

1. Choose a passage or symbol from one of the readings that you find particularly meaningful. In a freewrite, respond to that passage. Suggestions: the conjugation of the verb "to kill" in "The Verb to Kill"; or the broken crucifix in "My Parents' Bedroom."

2. Imagine a dialogue between the children in Ukem's and Corbett's works about the aftermath of horror. You also may write letters or journal entries for the characters or narrators.

3. Write a poem in response to one of the works in this cluster.

Ideas for Writing

1. For Europeans who survived World War II, the destruction and carnage resulting from war became "natural law," according to Milosz in "American Ignorance of War." We have entered a new era in which the fact of terrorism has reshaped our visions of our world. How do several of the authors envision what has become "natural" in a society threatened by terrorism? What are the human costs of terrorist actions? See Robert Waugh's "The Bodies."

2. How do several of the writers treat the incomprehensibility of the terrorist act?

3. What do Naomi Shihab Nye and Laura Blumenfeld propose as forces that could combat fanaticism? Do you agree with their positions?

4. In the aftermath of 9/11, acts of witnessing—acts of commemoration— have abounded. What do you learn about aesthetic techniques of witnessing from analyzing several works in this

4. Create a memorial for someone you've lost or for those lost on 9/11 or in the Iraq War—or in another historical event, such as the explosion of the *Challenger* or the tsunami. Describe the design of your memorial and the reasons for your design.

cluster? Explore the role of the writer as witness.

5. In "In the Ruins of the Future: Reflections on Terror, Loss and Time in the Shadow of September, 11," which appeared in *Harper's* in November 2001, Don DeLillo theorizes: "Terror's response is a narrative that has been developing over years, only now becoming inescapable. It is our lives and minds that are occupied now. This catastrophic event changes the way we think and act, moment to moment, week to week, for unknown weeks and months to come, and steely years. . . ."

Although DeLillo is reflecting on Americans' response to 9/11, does this reaction describe the protagonists' response to terror in the works in this cluster? You also may refer to Larry Carr's play, "Scrabble and Tabouli" (Chapter 9).

FICTION

Chimamanda Ngozi Adichie   *(1977–)*

Half of a Yellow Sun[1]   *2002*
From *Zoetrope: All-Story*

The Igbo say that a mature eagle feather will always remain spotless.

It was the kind of day in the middle of the rainy season when the sun felt like an orange flame placed close to my skin, yet it was raining, and I remembered when I was a child, when I would run around on days like this and sing songs about the dueling sun and rain, urging the sun to win. The lukewarm raindrops mixed with my sweat and ran down my face as I walked back to my hostel after the rally in Nsukka. I was still holding the placard that read REMEMBER THE MASSACRES, still marveling at my new—at our new—identity. It was late May, Ojukwu had just announced the secession, and we were no longer Nigerians. We were Biafrans.

When we gathered in Freedom Square for the rally, thousands of us students shouted Igbo songs and swayed, riverlike. Somebody said that in the market outside our campus, the women were dancing, giving away groundnuts and mangoes. Nnamdi and I stood next to each other and our shoulders touched as we waved green dogonyaro branches and cardboard placards. Nnamdi's placard read SECESSION NOW. Even though he was one of the student leaders, he chose to be with me in the crowd. The other leaders were in front carrying a coffin with NIGERIA written on it in white chalk. When they dug a shallow hole and buried the coffin, a cheer rose and snaked around the crowd, uniting us, elevating us, until it was one cheer, until we all became one.

I cheered loudly, although the coffin reminded me of Aunty Ifeka, Mama's half sister, the woman whose breast I sucked because Mama's dried up after I was born. Aunty Ifeka was killed during the massacres in the north. So was Arize, her pregnant daughter. They must have cut open Arize's stomach and beheaded the baby first—it was what they did to the pregnant women. I didn't tell Nnamdi that I was thinking of Aunty Ifeka and Arize again. Not because I had lost only two relatives while he had lost three uncles and six cousins. But because he would caress my face and say, "I've told you, don't dwell on the massacres. Isn't it why we seceded? Biafra is born! Dwell on that instead. We will turn our pain into a mighty nation, we will turn our pain into the pride of Africa."

Nnamdi was like that; sometimes I looked at him and saw what he would have been two hundred years before: an Igbo warrior leading his hamlet in battle (but only a fair battle), shouting and charging with his fire-warmed machete, returning with the most heads lolling on sticks.   5

---

[1] **Half of a Yellow Sun:** Nigeria became an independent nation in 1960. Later, civil unrest broke out between the Hausa and Igbo peoples, and the Igbos fled to the east, where they formed the independent nation of Biafra and seceded from Nigeria. The war lasted from 1967 to 1970, when the Biafrans surrendered. During the last phase of the war, Nigeria created a blockade that stopped food and supplies from entering Biafra. There was widespread illness, famine, and starvation.

I was in front of my hostel when the rain stopped; the sun had won the fight. Inside the lounge, crowds of girls were singing. Girls I had seen struggle at the water pump and hit each other with plastic buckets, girls who had cut holes in each other's bras as they hung out to dry, now held hands and sang. Instead of "Nigeria, we hail thee," they sang, "Biafra, we hail thee." I joined them, singing, clapping, talking. We did not mention the massacres, the way Igbos had been hunted house to house, pulled from where they crouched in trees, by bright-eyed people screaming *Jihad,* screaming *Nyamiri, nyamiri.* Instead, we talked about Ojukwu, how his speeches brought tears to our eyes and goose bumps to our skin, how easily his charisma would make him stand out among other leaders—Nkurumah would look like a plastic doll next to him. "*Imakwa,* Biafra has more doctors and lawyers than all of Black Africa!" somebody said. "Ah, Biafra will save Africa!" another said. We laughed, deliriously proud of people we would never even know.

We laughed more in the following weeks—we laughed when our expatriate lecturers went back to Britain and India and America, because even if war came, it would take us only one week to crush Nigeria. We laughed at the Nigerian navy ships blocking our ports, because the blockade could not possibly last. We laughed as we gathered under the gmelina trees to discuss Biafra's future foreign policy, as we took down the UNIVERSITY OF NIGERIA, NSUKKA sign and replaced it with UNIVERSITY OF BIAFRA, NSUKKA. Nnamdi hammered in the first nail. He was first, too, to join the Biafran Army, before the rest of his friends followed. I went with him to the army enlistment office, which still smelled of fresh paint, to collect his uniform. He looked so broad-shouldered in it, so capable, and later I did not let him take it all off; I held on to the grainy khaki shirt as he moved inside me.

My life—our lives—had taken on a sheen. A sheen like patent leather. We all felt as if liquid steel, instead of blood, flowed through our veins, as if we could stand bare-foot over red-hot embers.

I heard the guns from my hostel room. They sounded close, like thunder funneling up from the lounge. Somebody was shouting outside with a loudspeaker. Evacuate now! Evacuate now! There was the sound of feet, frenzied feet, in the hallway. I threw things into a suitcase, nearly forgetting my underwear in the drawer. As I left the hostel, I saw a girl's stylish sandal left lying on the stairs.

The Igbo say who knows how water entered the stalk of a pumpkin?   10

The air in Enugu smelled of rain and fresh grass and hope and new anthills. I watched as market traders and grandmothers and little boys hugged Nnamdi, caressed his army uniform. Justifiable heroism, Obi called it. Obi was thirteen, my bespectacled brother who read a book a day and went to the Advanced School for Gifted Children and was researching the African origin of Greek civilization. He didn't just touch Nnamdi's uniform, he wanted to try it on, wanted to know exactly what the guns sounded like. Mama invited Nnamdi over and made him a mango pie. "Your uniform is so *debonair,* darling," she said, and hung around him as if he were her son, as if she had not muttered that I was too young, that his family was not quite "suitable," when we got engaged a year ago.

Papa suggested Nnamdi and I get married right away, so that Nnamdi could wear his uniform at the wedding and our first son could be named Biafrus. Papa was joking, of course, but perhaps because something had weighed on my chest since Nnamdi entered the army, I imagined having a child now. A child with skin the color of a polished mahogany desk, like his. When I told Nnamdi about this, about the distant longing somewhere inside me, he pricked his thumb, pricked mine, and, although he was not usually superstitious, we smeared our blood together. Then we laughed because we were not even sure what the hell that meant exactly.

The Igbo say that the maker of the lion does not let the lion eat grass.

I watched Nnamdi go, watched until the red dust had covered his boot prints, and felt the moistness of pride on my skin, in my eyes. Pride at his smart olive uniform with the image of the sun rising halfway on the sleeve. It was the same symbol, half of a yellow sun, that was tacked onto the garish cotton tie Papa now wore to his new job at the War Research Directorate every day. Papa ignored all his other ties, the silk ones, the symbol-free ones. And Mama, elegant Mama with the manicured nails, sold some of her London-bought dresses and organized a women's group at St. Paul's to sew for the soldiers. I joined the group; we sewed singlets and sang Igbo songs. Afterward, Mama and I walked home (we didn't drive, to save petrol), and when Papa came home in the evenings, during those slow months, we would sit on the veranda and eat fresh anara with groundnut paste and listen to Radio Biafra, the kerosene lamp casting amber shadows all around. Radio Biafra brought stories of victories, of Nigerian corpses lining the roads. And from the War Research Directorate, Papa brought stories of our people's genius: we made brake fluid from coconut oil, we created car engines from scrap metal, we refined crude oil in cooking pots, we had perfected a homegrown mine. The blockade would not deter us. Often we ended those evenings by telling each other, "We have a just cause," as if we did not already know. Necessary affirmation, Obi called it.

It was on one of those evenings that a friend dropped by to say that Nnamdi's battalion had conquered Benin, that Nnamdi was fine. We toasted Nnamdi with palm wine. "To our future son-in-law," Papa said, raising his mug toward me. Papa let Obi drink as much as he wanted. Papa was a cognac man, but he couldn't find Rémy Martin even on the black market, because of the blockade. After a few mugs Papa said, with his upper lip coated in white foam, that he preferred palm wine now: at least he didn't have to drink it in snifters. And we all laughed too loudly.

The Igbo say the walking ground squirrel sometimes breaks into a trot, in case the need to run arises.

Enugu fell on the kind of day in the middle of the harmattan when the wind blew hard, carrying dust and bits of paper and dried leaves, covering hair and clothes with a fine brown film. Mama and I were cooking pepper soup—I cut up the tripe while Mama ground the peppers—when we heard the guns. At first I thought it was thunder, the rumbling thunder that preceded harmattan storms. It couldn't be the Federal guns because Radio Biafra said the Federals were far away, being driven back. But Papa dashed into the kitchen moments later, his cotton tie skewed. "Get in the car now!" he said. "Now! Our directorate is evacuating."

We didn't know what to take. Mama took her manicure kit, her small radio, clothes, the pot of half-cooked pepper soup wrapped in a dish towel. I snatched a packet of crackers. Obi grabbed the books on the dining table. As we drove away in Papa's Peugeot, Mama said we would be back soon anyway, our troops would recover Enugu. So it didn't matter that all her lovely china was left behind, our radiogram, her new wig imported from Paris in that case of such an unusual lavender color. "My leather-bound books," Obi added. I was grateful that nobody brought up the Biafran soldiers we saw

15

dashing past, on the retreat. I didn't want to imagine Nnamdi like that, running like a chicken drenched by heavy rain. Papa stopped the car often to wipe the dust off the windscreen, and he drove at a crawl, because of the crowds. Women with babies tied to their backs, pulling at toddlers, carrying pots on their heads. Men pulling goats and bicycles, carrying wood boxes and yams. Children, so many children. The dust swirled all around like a translucent brown blanket. An exodus clothed in dusty hope. It took a while before it struck me that, like these people, we were now refugees.

The Igbo say that the place from where one wakes up is his home.

Papa's old friend Akubueze was a man with a sad smile whose greeting was "God 20 bless Biafra." He had lost all his children in the massacres. As he showed us the smoke-blackened kitchen and pit latrine and room with the stained walls, I wanted to cry. Not because of the room we would rent from Akubueze, but because of Akubueze. Because of the apology in his eyes. I placed our raffia sleeping mats at the corners of the room, next to our bags and food. But the radio stayed in the center of the room, and we walked around it every day, listened to it, cleaned it. We sang along when the soldiers' marching songs were broadcast. *We are Biafrans, fighting for survival, in the name of Jesus, we shall conquer, hip hop, one two.* Sometimes the people in the yard joined us, our new neighbors. Singing meant that we did not have to wonder aloud about our old house with the marble staircase and airy verandas. Singing meant we did not have to acknowledge aloud that Enugu remained fallen and that the War Research Directorate was no longer paying salaries and what Papa got now was an "allowance." Papa gave every note, even the white slip with his name and ID number printed in smudgy ink, to Mama. I would look at the money and think how much prettier than Nigerian pounds Biafran pounds were, the elegant writing, the bold faces. But they could buy so little at the market.

The market was a cluster of dusty, sparse tables. There were more flies than food, the flies buzzing thickly over the graying pieces of meat, the black-spotted bananas. The flies looked healthier, fresher, than the meats and fruits. I looked over everything, I insisted, as if it were the peacetime market and I still had the leisure that came with choice. In the end, I bought cassava, always, because it was the most filling and economical. Sickly tubers, the ones with grisly pink skin. We had never eaten those before. I told Mama, half teasing, that they could be poisonous. And Mama laughed and said, "People are eating the peels now, honey. It used to be goat food."

The months crawled past and I noted them when my periods came, scant, more mud-colored than red now. I worried about Nnamdi, that he would not find us, that something would happen to him and nobody would know where to find me. I followed the news on Radio Biafra carefully, although Radio Nigeria intercepted the signal so often now. Deliberate jamming, Obi called it. Radio Biafra described the thousands of Federal bodies floating on the Niger. Radio Nigeria listed the thousands of dead and defecting Biafran soldiers. I listened to both with equal attention, and afterward, I created my own truths and inhabited them, believed them.

The Igbo say that unless a snake shows its venom, little children will use it for tying firewood.

Nnamdi appeared at our door on a dry-aired morning, with a scar above his eye and the skin of his face stretched too thin and his worn trousers barely staying on his waist. Mama dashed out to the market and bought three chicken necks and two wings, and fried them in a little palm oil. "Especially for Nnamdi," she said gaily. Mama, who used to make coq au vin without a cookbook.

I took Nnamdi to the nearby farm that had been harvested too early. All the farms 25 looked that way now, raided at night, raided of corn ears so tender they had not yet formed kernels and yams so young they were barely the size of my fist. Harvest of desperation, Obi called it. Nnamdi pulled me down to the ground, under an ukpaka tree. I could feel his bones through his skin. He scratched my back, bit my sweaty neck, held me down so hard I felt the sand pierce my skin. And he stayed inside me so long, so tightly, that I felt our hearts were pumping blood at the same rhythm. I wished in a twisted way that the war would never end so that it would always have this quality, like nutmeg, tart and lasting. Afterward, Nnamdi started to cry. I had never even considered that he could cry. He said the British were giving more arms to Nigeria, Nigeria had Russian planes and Egyptian pilots, the Americans didn't want to help us, we were still blockaded, his battalion was down to two men using one gun, some battalions had resorted to machetes and cutlasses. "Didn't they kill babies in the north for being born Igbo, eh?" he asked.

I pressed my face to his, but he wouldn't stop crying. "Is there a God?" he asked me. "Is there a God?" So I held him close and listened to him cry, and listened to the shrilling of the crickets. He said goodbye two days later, holding me too long. Mama gave him a small bag of boiled rice.

I hoarded that memory, and every other memory of Nnamdi, used each sparingly. I used them most during the air raids, when the screeching *ka-ka-ka* of the antiaircraft guns disrupted a hot afternoon and everybody in the yard dashed to the bunker—the room-size hole in the ground covered with logs—and slid into the moist earth underneath. Exhilarating, Obi called it, even though he got scratches and cuts. I would smell the organic walls and floor, like a freshly tilled farm, and watch the children crawl around looking for crickets and earthworms, until the bombing stopped. I would rub the soil between my fingers and savor thoughts of Nnamdi's teeth, tongue, voice.

The Igbo say let us salute the deaf, for if the heavens don't hear, then the earth will hear.

So many things became transient, and more valuable. I savored a plate of cornmeal that tasted like cloth, because I might have to leave it and run into the bunker, because when I came out a neighbor might have eaten it or given it to one of the children.

Obi suggested that we teach classes for those children, so many of them running 30 around the yard chasing lizards. "They think bombings are normal," Obi said, shaking his head. He picked a cool spot under the kolanut tree for our classroom. I placed planks across cement blocks for benches, a wooden sheet against the tree for a blackboard. I taught English, Obi taught mathematics and history, and the children did not whisper and giggle in his classes as they did in mine. He seemed to hold them somehow, as he talked and gestured and scrawled on the board with charcoal (when he ran his hands over his sweaty face, they left black patterns like a design).

Perhaps it was that he mixed learning and playing—once he asked the children to role-play the Berlin Conference. They became Europeans partitioning Africa, giving hills and rivers to each other although they didn't know where the hills and rivers were. Obi played Bismarck. "My contribution to the young Biafrans, our leaders of tomorrow," he said, glowing with mischief.

I laughed, because he seemed to forget that he too was a future Biafran leader. Sometimes even I forgot how young he was. "Do you remember when I used to half-chew your beef and then put it in your mouth so it would be easier for you to chew?" I teased. And Obi made a face and said he did not remember.

The classes were in the morning, before the afternoon sun turned fierce. After the classes, Obi and I joined the local militia—a mix of young people and married women and injured men—and went combing, to root out Federal soldiers or Biafran saboteurs hiding in the bush, although all we found were dried fruits and groundnuts. We talked about dead Nigerians, we talked about the braveness of the French and Tanzanians in supporting Biafra, the evil of the British. We did not talk about dead Biafrans. We talked about anti-kwash too, how it really worked, how many children in the early stages of kwashiorkor had been cured. I knew that anti-kwash was absolute nonsense, that those leaves were from a tree nobody used to eat; they filled the children's bellies but gave no nourishment, definitely no protein. But we *needed* to believe stories like that. When you were stripped down to sickly cassava, you used everything else fiercely and selfishly—especially the discretion to choose what to believe and what not to believe.

I enjoyed those stories we told, the lull of our voices, until one day; we were at an abandoned farm wading through tall grass when we stumbled upon something. A body. I smelled it before I saw it, an odor that gagged me, suffocated me, left me lightheaded. "Hei! He's a Nigerian!" a woman said. The flies rose from the bloated body of the Nigerian soldier as we gathered around. His skin was ashy, his eyes were open, his tribal marks were thick, eerie lines running across his swollen face. "I wish we had seen him alive," a young boy said. "*Nkakwu*, ugly rat," somebody else said. A young girl spat at the body. Vultures landed a few feet away. A woman vomited. Nobody suggested burying him. I stood there, dizzy from the smell and the buzzing flies and the heat, and wondered how he had died, what his life had been like. I wondered about his family. A wife who would be looking outside, her eyes on the road, for news of her husband. Little children who would be told, "Papa will be home soon." A mother who had cried when he left. Brothers and sisters and cousins. I imagined the things he left behind—clothes, a prayer mat, a wooden cup used to drink kunu.

I started to cry.

Obi held me and looked at me with a calm disgust. "It was people like him who killed Aunty Ifeka," Obi said. "It was people like him who beheaded unborn babies." I brushed Obi away and kept crying.

The Igbo say that a fish that does not swallow other fish does not grow fat.

There was no news of Nnamdi. When neighbors heard from their sons or husbands on the front, I hung around their rooms for days, willing their good fortunes to myself. "Nnamdi is fine," Obi said in a tone so normal I wanted to believe him. He said it often during those months of boiled cassava, months of moldy yams, months when we shared our dreams of vegetable oil and fish and salt.

Because of the neighbors, I hid what little food we had, wrapped in a mat and stuck behind the door. The neighbors hid their own food, too. In the evenings, we all unwrapped our food and clustered in the kitchen, cooking and talking about salt. There was salt in Nigeria; salt was the reason our people were crossing the border to the other side, salt was the reason a woman down the road was said to have run out of her kitchen and torn her clothes off and rolled in the dirt, wailing. I sat on the kitchen floor and listened to the chatter and tried to remember what salt tasted like. It seemed surreal now, that we had a crystal saltshaker back home. That I had even wasted salt, rinsing

35

away the clumpy bottom before refilling the shaker. Fresh salt. I interspersed thoughts of Nnamdi with thoughts of salty food.

And when Akubueze told us that our old pastor, Father Damian, was working in a refugee camp in Amandugba, two towns away, I thought about salt. Akubueze was not sure; stories drifted around about so many people being in so many places. Still, I suggested to Mama that we go and see Father Damian. Mama said yes, we would go to see if he was well, it had been two long years since we saw him. I humored her and said it had been long—as if we still paid social calls. We did not say anything about the food Caritas Internationalis sent to priests by secret night flights, the food the priests gave away, the corned beef and glucose and dried milk. And salt. 40

Father Damian was thinner, with hollows and shadows on his face. But he looked healthy next to the children in the refugee camp. Stick-thin children whose bones stuck out, so unnaturally, so sharply. Children with rust-colored hair and stomachs like balloons. Children whose eyes were swallowed deep in their faces. Father Damian introduced Mama and me to the other priests, Irish missionaries of the Holy Ghost, white men with sun-reddened skin and smiles so brave I wanted to tug at their faces and see if they were real. Father Damian talked a lot about his work, about the dying children, but Mama kept changing the subject. It was so unlike her, something she would call "unmannered" if somebody else did it. Father Damian finally stopped talking about the children, about kwashiorkor, and he looked almost disappointed as he watched us leave, Mama holding the bag of salt and corned beef and fish powder he had given us.

"Why was Father Damian telling us about those children?" Mama shouted as we walked home. "What can we do for them?" I calmed her down, told her he probably just needed to talk to someone about his work and did she remember how he used to sing those silly, off-tune songs at church bazaars to make the children laugh?

But Mama kept shouting. And I too began shouting, the words tumbling out of my mouth. Why the hell did Father Damian tell us about those dying children, anyway? Did we need to know? Didn't we have enough to deal with?

Shouting. A man walked up the street, beating a metal gong, asking us to pray for the good white people who were flying food in for the relief center, the new one they set up in St. Johns. Not all white people were killers, *gong, gong, gong,* not all were arming the Nigerians, *gong, gong, gong.*

At the relief center, I fought hard, kicking through the crowds, risking the flogging militia. I lied, cajoled, begged. I spoke British-accented English to show how educated I was, to distinguish myself from the common villagers, and afterward I felt tears building up, as if I only had to blink and they would flow down. But I didn't blink as I walked home, I kept my eyes roundly open, my hands tightly wrapped around whatever food I got. When I got food. Dried egg yolk. Dried milk. Dried fish. Cornmeal. 45

Shell-shocked soldiers in filthy shirts roamed around the relief center, muttering gibberish, children running away from them. They followed me, first begging, then trying to snatch my food. I shoved at them and cursed them and spat in their direction. Once I shoved so hard one of the men fell down, and I didn't turn to see if he got up all right. I didn't want to imagine, either, that they had once been proud Biafran soldiers, like Nnamdi.

Perhaps it was the food from the relief center that made Obi sick, or all the other things we ate, the things we brushed blue mold from, or picked ants out of. He threw up, and when he was emptied, he still retched and clutched at his belly. Mama brought in an old bucket for him, helped him use it, took it out afterward. I'm a chamber-pot man, Obi joked. He still taught his classes but he talked less about Biafra and more about the past, like did I remember how Mama used to give herself facials with a paste of honey and milk? And did I remember the soursop tree in our backyard, how the yellow bees formed columns on it? Mama went to Albatross Hospital and dropped the names of all the famous doctors she had known in Enugu, so that the doctor would see her before the hundreds of women thronging the corridors. It worked, and he gave her diarrhea tablets. He could spare only five and told her to break each in two so they would last long enough to control Obi's diarrhea. Mama said she doubted that the "doctor" had even reached his fourth year in medical school, but this was Biafra two years into the war, and medical students had to play doctors because the real doctors were cutting off arms and legs to keep people alive. Then Mama said that part of the roof of Albatross Hospital had been blown off during an air raid. I didn't know what was funny about that, but Obi laughed, and Mama joined in, and finally I did too.

Obi was still sick, still in bed, when Ihuoma came running into our room. Her daughter was lying in the yard, inhaling a foul concoction of spices and urine that somebody said cured asthma. "The soldiers are coming," Ihuoma said. She was a simple woman, a market trader, the kind of woman who would have had nothing in common with Mama before Biafra. But now she and Mama plaited each other's hair every week. "Hurry," she said. "Bring Obi to the outer room—he can hide in the ceiling!" It took me a moment to understand, although Mama was already helping Obi up, rushing him out of the room. We had heard that the Biafran soldiers were conscripting young men, children really, and taking them to the front, that it had happened in the yard down our street a week ago, although Obi said he doubted they had really taken a twelve-year-old. We heard too that the mother of the boy was from Abakaliki, where people cut their hair when their children died, and after she watched them take her son, she took a razor and shaved all her hair off.

The soldiers came shortly after Obi and two other boys climbed into a hole in the ceiling, a hole that had appeared when the wood gave way after a bombing. Four soldiers with bony bodies and tired eyes. I asked if they knew Nnamdi, if they'd heard of him, even though I knew they hadn't. The soldiers looked inside the latrine, asked Mama if she was sure she was not hiding anybody, because that would make her a saboteur and saboteurs were worse than Nigerians. Mama smiled at them, then used her old voice, the voice of when she hosted three-course dinners for Papa's friends, and offered them some water before they left. Afterward, Obi said he would enlist when he felt better. He owed it to Biafra, and besides, fifteen-year-olds had fought in the Persian War. Before Mama left the room, she walked up to Obi and slapped his face so hard I saw the immediate slender welts on his cheek.

The Igbo say that the chicken frowns at the cooking pot, and yet ignores the knife. 50

Mama and I were close to the bunker when we heard the antiaircraft guns. "Good timing," Mama joked, and although I tried, I could not smile. My lips were too sore; the harmattan winds had dried them to a bloody crisp during our walk to the relief center, and besides, we had not been lucky: we got no food.

Inside the bunker, people were shouting *Lord, Jesus, God Almighty, Jehovah.* A woman was crumpled next to me, holding her toddler in her arms. The bunker was dim, but I could see the crusty ringworm marks all over the toddler's body. Mama was looking around. "Where is Obi?" she asked, clutching my arm. "What is wrong with that boy, didn't he hear the guns?" Mama got up, saying she had to find Obi, saying the bombing was far away. But it wasn't, it was really close, loud, and I tried to hold Mama, to keep her still, but I was weak from the walk and hunger and Mama pushed past me and climbed out.

The explosion that followed shook something inside my ear loose, and I felt that if I bent my head sideways, something hardsoft, like cartilage, would fall out. I heard things breaking and falling above, cement walls and glass louvers and trees. I closed my eyes and thought of Nnamdi's voice, just his voice, until the bombing stopped and I scrambled out of the bunker. The bodies strewn about the street, some painfully close to the bunker entrance, were still quivering, writhing. They reminded me of the chickens our steward used to kill in Enugu, how they flapped around in the dust after their throats had been slit, over and over, before finally lying quiet. Dignity dance, Obi called it. I was bawling as I stared at the bodies, all people I knew, trying to identify Mama and Obi. But they were not there. They were in the yard, Mama helping to wash the wounded, Obi writing in the dust with his finger. Mama did not scold Obi for his earlier carelessness, and I did not rebuke Mama for dashing out like that either. I went into the kitchen to soak some dried cassava for dinner.

Obi died that night. Or maybe he died in the morning. I don't know. I simply know that when Papa tugged at him in the morning and then when Mama threw herself on him, he did not stir. I went over and shook him, shook him, shook him. He was cold.

"*Nwa m anwugo,*" Papa said, as if he had to say it aloud to believe it. Mama brought out her manicure kit and started to clip Obi's nails. "What are you doing?" Papa asked. He was crying. Not the kind of manly crying that is silence accompanied by tears. He was wailing, sobbing. I watched him, he seemed to swell before my eyes, the room was unsteady. Something was on my chest, something heavy like a jerry can full of water. I started to roll on the floor to ease the weight. Outside, I heard shouting. Or was it inside? Was it Papa? Was it Papa saying *Nwa m anwugo, nwa m anwugo?* Obi was dead. I grasped around, frantic, trying to remember Obi, to remember the concrete things about him. And I could not. My baby brother who made wisecracks, and yet I could not remember any of them. I could not even remember anything he said the night before. I had felt I would have Obi for a long, long time and that I didn't need to notice him, really notice him. He was there, I believed he would always be there. With Obi, I never had the fear I had with Nnamdi, the fear that I might mourn someday. And so I did not know how to mourn Obi, if I could mourn Obi. My hair was itching and I started to tear at it, to feel the warm blood on my scalp. I tore some more and then more. With my hair littering our floor, I wrapped my arms around myself and watched as Mama calmly filed Obi's nails.

There was something feverish about the days after Obi's death, something malarial, something so numbingly fast it left me free not to feel. Even Obi's burial in the backyard was fast, although Papa spent hours fashioning a cross from old wood. After the neighbors and Father Damian and the crying children dispersed, Mama called the cross shabby and kicked it, broke it, flung the wood away.

Papa stopped going to the War Research Directorate and dropped his patriotic tie into the pit latrine, and day after day, week after week, we sat in front of our room—Papa, Mama, and me—staring at the yard. The morning a woman from down the street dashed into our yard I did not look up, until I heard her shouting. She was waving a green branch. Such a brilliant, wet-looking green. I wondered where she got it;

55

the plants and trees around us were scorched by January's harmattan sun, blown bare by the dusty winds. The earth was sallow.

The war is lost, Papa said. He didn't need to say it though; we already knew. We knew when Obi died. The neighbors were packing in a hurry, to go into the smaller villages because we had heard the Federal soldiers were coming with truckloads of whips. We got up to pack. It struck me how little we had, as we packed, and how we had stopped noticing how little we had.

The Igbo say that when a man falls, it is his god who has pushed him down.

Nnamdi clutched my hand too tightly at our wedding. He did everything with extra effort now, as if he were compensating for his amputated left arm, as if he were shielding his shame. Papa took photos, telling me to smile wider, telling Nnamdi not to slouch. But Papa slouched himself, he had slouched since the war ended, since the bank gave him fifty Nigerian pounds for all the money he had in Biafra. And he had lost his house—our house, with the marble staircase—because it was declared abandoned property and now a civil servant lived there, a woman who had threatened Mama with a fierce dog when Mama defied Papa and went to see her beloved house. All she wanted was our china and our radiogram, she told the woman. But the woman whistled for the dog. 60

"Wait," Mama said to Papa, and came over to fix my hat. She had made my wedding dress and sewn sequins onto a secondhand hat. After the wedding we had pastries in a café, and as we ate, Papa told me about the wedding cake he used to dream about for me, a pink multilayered cake, so tall it would shield my face and Nnamdi's face and the cake-cutting photo would capture only the groomsman's face, only Obi's face.

I envied Papa, that he could talk about Obi like that. It was the year Obi would have turned seventeen, the year Nigeria changed from driving on the left-hand side of the road to the right. We were Nigerians again. ●

Explorations of the Text

1. What attitudes toward the Biafran War for independence do the main characters exhibit? How do their views of Biafra and the war change as the struggle progresses? What is the impact of the civil war on the family? The community?

2. How does the story treat the realities of war? Discuss the contrast between the facts of everyday life and the realities of civil war. Point to specific examples in the text. What is the difference in the

family's position and status before, during, and after the war?

3. Why do the Igbo sayings preface each section of the story? How do they introduce themes of each section?

4. How is the narrator's relationship with Nnamdi changed by the war?

5. Discuss the significance of the title.

6. Discuss the differences between the rhetoric and the reality of war in this work, in Jose Rivera's "Gas," and in the soldiers' blogs.

The Reading/Writing Connection

1. Create a double-entry notebook for one section of the story. What do you learn?

2. Take one of the Igbo sayings and create your own narrative; include an experience evoked by the saying.

3. Create a dialogue about the state of war between the narrator in this work and the one in Tim O'Brien's "How to Tell a True War Story."

Ideas for Writing

1. In "American Ignorance of War," Milosz suggests that in a post-war world the "natural order" shifts. How does this work portray the idea that a war produces a new kind of "natural order," that what is conceived of as normal radically changes?

2. Discuss the contrasts of love and war revealed in this work.

Cynthia Ozick *(1928–)*

The Shawl   *1980*

Stella, cold, cold, the coldness of hell. How they walked on the roads together, Rosa with Magda curled up between sore breasts, Magda wound up in the shawl. Sometimes Stella carried Magda. But she was jealous of Magda. A thin girl of fourteen, too small, with thin breasts of her own, Stella wanted to be wrapped in a shawl, hidden away, asleep, rocked by the march, a baby, a round infant in arms. Magda took Rosa's nipple, and Rosa never stopped walking, a walking cradle. There was not enough milk; sometimes Magda sucked air; then she screamed. Stella was ravenous. Her knees were tumors on sticks, her elbows chicken bones.

Rosa did not feel hunger; she felt light, not like someone walking but like someone in a faint, in trance, arrested in a fit, someone who is already a floating angel, alert and seeing everything, but in the air, not there, not touching the road. As if teetering on the tips of her fingernails. She looked into Magda's face through a gap in the shawl: a squirrel in a nest, safe, no one could reach her inside the little house of the shawl's windings. The face, very round, a pocket mirror of a face: but it was not Rosa's bleak complexion, dark like cholera, it was another kind of face altogether, eyes blue as air, smooth feathers of hair nearly as yellow as the Star sewn into Rosa's coat. You could think she was one of *their* babies.

Rosa, floating, dreamed of giving Magda away in one of the villages. She could leave the line for a minute and push Magda into the hands of any woman on the side of the road. But if she moved out of line they might shoot. And even if she fled the line for half a second and pushed the shawl-bundle at a stranger, would the woman take it? She might be surprised, or afraid; she might drop the shawl, and Magda would fall out and strike her head and die. The little round head. Such a good child, she gave up screaming, and sucked now only for the taste of the drying nipple itself. The neat grip of the tiny gums. One mite of a tooth tip sticking up in the bottom gum, how shining, an elfin tombstone of white marble, gleaming there. Without complaining, Magda relinquished Rosa's teats, first the left, then the right; both were cracked, not a sniff of milk. The duct crevice extinct, a dead volcano, blind eye, chill hole, so Magda took the corner of the shawl and milked it instead. She sucked and sucked, flooding the threads with wetness. The shawl's good flavor, milk of linen.

It was a magic shawl, it could nourish an infant for three days and three nights. Magda did not die, she stayed alive, although very quiet. A peculiar smell, of cinnamon and almonds, lifted out of her mouth. She held her eyes open every moment, forgetting how to blink or nap, and Rosa and sometimes Stella studied their blueness. On the road they raised one burden of a leg after another and studied Magda's face. "Aryan," Stella said, in a voice grown as thin as a string; and Rosa thought how Stella gazed at Magda like a young cannibal. And the time that Stella said "Aryan," it sounded to Rosa as if Stella had really said, "Let us devour her."

But Magda lived to walk. She lived that long, but she did not walk very well, partly 5
because she was only fifteen months old, and partly because the spindles of her legs could not hold up her fat belly. It was fat with air, full and round. Rosa gave almost all her food to Magda, Stella gave nothing; Stella was ravenous, a growing child herself, but not growing much. Stella did not menstruate. Rosa did not menstruate. Rosa was ravenous, but also not; she learned from Magda how to drink the taste of a finger in one's mouth. They were in a place without pity, all pity was annihilated in Rosa, she looked at Stella's bones without pity. She was sure that Stella was waiting for Magda to die so she could put her teeth into the little thighs.

Rosa knew Magda was going to die very soon; she should have been dead already, but she had been buried away deep inside the magic shawl, mistaken there for the shivering mound of Rosa's breasts; Rosa clung to the shawl as if it covered only herself. No one took it away from her. Magda was mute. She never cried. Rosa hid her in the barracks, under the shawl, but she knew that one day someone would inform; or one day someone, not even Stella, would steal Magda to eat her. When Magda began to walk Rosa knew that Magda was going to die very soon, something would happen. She was afraid to fall asleep; she slept with the weight of her thigh on Magda's body; she was afraid she would smother Magda under her thigh. The weight of Rosa was becoming less and less, Rosa and Stella were slowly turning into air.

Magda was quiet, but her eyes were horribly alive, like blue tigers. She watched. Sometimes she laughed—it seemed a laugh, but how could it be? Magda had never seen anyone laugh. Still, Magda laughed at her shawl when the wind blew its corners, the bad wind with pieces of black in it, that made Stella's and Rosa's eyes tear. Magda's eyes were always clear and tearless. She watched like a tiger. She guarded her shawl. No one could touch it; only Rosa could touch it. Stella was not allowed. The shawl was Magda's own baby, her pet, her little sister. She tangled herself up in it and sucked on one of the corners when she wanted to be very still.

Then Stella took the shawl away and made Magda die.

Afterward Stella said: "I was cold."

And afterward she was always cold, always. The cold went into her heart: Rosa 10
saw that Stella's heart was cold. Magda flopped onward with her little pencil legs scribbling this way and that, in search of the shawl; the pencils faltered at the barracks opening, where the light began. Rosa saw and pursued. But already Magda was in the square outside the barracks, in the jolly light. It was the roll-call arena. Every morning Rosa had to conceal Magda under the shawl against a wall of the barracks and go out and stand in the arena with Stella and hundreds of others, sometimes for hours, and Magda, deserted, was quiet under the shawl, sucking on her corner. Every day Magda was silent, and so she did not die. Rosa saw that today Magda was going to die, and at the same time a fearful joy ran in Rosa's two palms, her fingers were on fire, she was astonished, febrile: Magda, in the sunlight, swaying on her pencil legs, was howling. Ever since the drying up of Rosa's nipples, ever since Magda's last scream on the road, Magda had been devoid of any syllable; Magda was a mute. Rosa believed that some-

thing had gone wrong with her vocal cords, with her windpipe, with the cave of her larynx; Magda was defective, without a voice; perhaps she was deaf; there might be something amiss with her intelligence; Magda was dumb. Even the laugh that came when the ash-stippled wind made a clown out of Magda's shawl was only the air-blown showing of her teeth. Even when the lice, head lice and body lice, crazed her so that she became as wild as one of the big rats that plundered the barracks at daybreak looking for carrion, she rubbed and scratched and kicked and bit and rolled without a whimper. But now Magda's mouth was spilling a long viscous rope of clamor.

"Maaaa—"

It was the first noise Magda had ever sent out from her throat since the drying up of Rosa's nipples.

"Maaaa . . . aaa!"

Again! Magda was wavering in the perilous sunlight of the arena, scribbling on such pitiful little bent shins. Rosa saw. She saw that Magda was grieving the loss of her shawl, she saw that Magda was going to die. A tide of commands hammered in Rosa's nipples: Fetch, get, bring! But she did not know which to go after first, Magda or the shawl. If she jumped out into the arena to snatch Magda up, the howling would not stop, because Magda would still not have the shawl; but if she ran back into the barracks to find the shawl, and if she found it, and if she came after Magda holding it and shaking it, then she would get Magda back, Magda would put the shawl in her mouth and turn dumb again.

Rosa entered the dark. It was easy to discover the shawl. Stella was heaped under it, asleep in her thin bones. Rosa tore the shawl free and flew—she could fly, she was only air—into the arena. The sunheat murmured of another life, of butterflies in summer. The light was placid, mellow. On the other side of the steel fence, far away, there were green meadows speckled with dandelions and deep-colored violets; beyond them, even farther, innocent tiger lilies, tall, lifting their orange bonnets. In the barracks they spoke of "flowers," of "rain": excrement, thick turd-braids, and the slow stinking maroon waterfall that slunk down from the upper bunks, the stink mixed with a bitter fatty floating smoke that greased Rosa's skin. She stood for an instant at the margin of the arena. Sometimes the electricity inside the fence would seem to hum; even Stella said it was only an imagining, but Rosa heard real sounds in the wire: grainy sad voices. The farther she was from the fence, the more clearly the voices crowded at her. The lamenting voices strummed so convincingly, so passionately, it was impossible to suspect them of being phantoms. The voices told her to hold up the shawl, high; the voices told her to shake it, to whip with it, to unfurl it like a flag. Rosa lifted, shook, whipped, unfurled. Far off, very far, Magda leaned across her air-fed belly, reaching out with the rods of her arms. She was high up, elevated, riding someone's shoulder. But the shoulder that carried Magda was not coming toward Rosa and the shawl, it was drifting away, the speck of Magda was moving more and more into the smoky distance. Above the shoulder a helmet glinted. A light tapped the helmet and sparkled it into a goblet. Below the helmet a black body like a domino and a pair of black boots hurled themselves in the direction of the electrified fence. The electric voices began to chatter wildly. "Maamaa, maaamaaa," they all hummed together. How far Magda was from Rosa now, across the whole square, past a dozen barracks, all the way on the other side! She was no bigger than a moth.

All at once Magda was swimming through the air. The whole of Magda traveled through loftiness. She looked like a butterfly touching a silver vine. And the moment

Magda's feathered round head and her pencil legs and balloonish belly and zigzag arms splashed against the fence, the steel voices went mad in their growling, urging Rosa to run and run to the spot where Magda had fallen from her flight against the electrified fence; but of course Rosa did not obey them. She only stood, because if she ran they would shoot, and if she tried to pick up the sticks of Magda's body they would shoot, and if she let the wolf's screech ascending now through the ladder of her skeleton break out, they would shoot; so she took Magda's shawl and filled her own mouth with it, stuffed it in and stuffed it in, until she was swallowing up the wolf's screech and tasting the cinnamon and almond depth of Magda's saliva; and Rosa drank Magda's shawl until it dried. ●

Explorations of the Text

1. Describe the agony of Rosa, Stella, and Magda as they walk to the camp. What is the attitude of each toward the shawl?

2. Why does Magda's existence remain secret?

3. Explore Stella's relationships with Rosa and with Magda.

4. Examine the agony of Magda's first cry. Consider the language that describes Magda's death. What are the major images?

5. Explain the ending: "Rosa drank Magda's shawl until it dried." Has Ozick chosen the right response for Rosa? Why? Why not?

6. Why does the speaker begin her description of Magda's death only to interrupt it with a fantasy of saving her?

7. How does Stella "make" Magda die? Why is Stella's heart "cold"?

8. Compare the fates of the central characters in works by O'Brien, Endō, Adichie, and Valenzuela.

The Reading/Writing Connection

1. In a paragraph discuss the symbolism of the shawl.

2. **Write an Argument:** Is Stella to be blamed for Magda's death? Argue pro or con.

Ideas for Writing

1. Evaluate the descriptive language in this story. Does it enhance and create meaning?

2. Discuss "The Shawl's" portrayal of the inhumanity and cruelty of the concentration camps during the Holocaust. Is it powerful?

3. Analyze Rosa's or Stella's character.

Sara Nomberg-Przytyk (1915–)

Natasha's Triumph   1985

Every day deathly undernourished women and hundreds of mortally sick people came through the doors of the infirmary to which was attached a little cottage that housed the personnel who worked in the infirmary. Actually, it was not really a cottage but a little shack without windows. The total area of the shack was about two by six meters. Inside there were two three-decker beds and a small table. We thought that it was the most wonderful habitation in the world. It was our corner, different from the terrible barracks.

One sunny day we received a notice that hit us like a clap of thunder. It was a summer evening in 1944 when Orli brought us the news that we would have to move out of our little shack because Mengele had decided to create a ward for mentally disturbed women. At night we removed our meager possessions. The next morning we waited for the patients. The whole affair looked very suspicious to me. It was difficult to understand why Mengele would create a ward for the mentally sick in the infirmary. Until now there had been no such ward. We had a feeling that Mengele must have a new trick up his sleeve.

First thing in the morning they brought the first patient. Her name was Natasha. The *blokowa* brought her in.

"She has to stay here with you in the infirmary," the *blokowa* said and left.

Before me stood a young girl, straight as a tree, with a gloomy, rebellious face. She 5
was nineteen years old and from Leningrad. She would not tell us anything else. Our Jewish doctors were not invited to examine her, since their findings were set at no value. Natasha immediately took an upper bunk. She lay there quietly, saying nothing, but when we brought her some soup she came to life, and a big smile brightened up her face. She ate while she continued to lie there without saying a word.

The same afternoon, five new patients were brought in, including two German, one Dutch, and two French women. They were all very young and very sad. At first we were afraid of them. We imagined that they would cause trouble, maybe have fits. Perhaps we would have to use physical force to subdue them. We had no experience in handling such cases. But the new patients lay quietly in their beds, or else they sat bent over on the edge of the bed.

I remember that I made several attempts to talk to them, but my words did not reach them. That same day, just before roll call, a few more women were brought in. By this time a few of the beds were being shared by two women. A couple of mornings later we prepared the infirmary to receive a visit from Dr. Mengele.[1] We knew that he would come to examine the new "ward." That morning, as we were admitting the sick to the hospital, we did not accept the very sick ones. We sent them back to the blocks. We knew that if he started looking at them he would certainly send them to the ovens. It was with heavy hearts that we sent those women away to do heavy labor, women who were barely alive, with swollen legs and terrible sores all over their bodies. But we well knew the monster in the white coat who had the face of a Romeo. He would assign them to the gas and then would say to us, "You see yourselves that these women are not strong enough to live. Why should they suffer? I am sending them to the gas for their own good."

Mengele arrived about twelve o'clock.

"Achtung," shouted Marusia.

The selection of the sick and the signing of the cards started. Everything was go- 10
ing smoothly, without a hitch. All of a sudden, from the next room, we heard a loud, happy voice calling,

---

[1] **Dr. Mengele:** The Nazi doctor at Auschwitz who determined who lived and died—who was to be sent to the gas chambers—and who performed medical experiments on inmates. He was called the Angel of Death.

"Hey, you! Doctor! Maybe you can come in and see us."

It was Natasha calling to Mengele; she was speaking to him in beautiful German, her voice radiant with happiness.

"What are you afraid of, coward, you who can murder women and children? Come here. We will discuss your Hitler's crimes. Maybe you want to discuss Stalingrad, where you are dying like mad dogs."

We turned to stone. Every one of us pretended to be very busy. We were afraid to look in his direction. We knew that in a minute something terrible would happen. Natasha's ringing, violent voice floated in from the other room.

"You will all die in Russia, the way Napoleon did. You are afraid to come to me. 15 You don't want to listen to the truth, you specialist of the gas chambers."

Suddenly we saw Mengele get up and go into the other room. I waited for a shot and automatically covered my ears with my fists.

"Come, sit next to us. We will have a chat."

Mengele did not say a thing. Only the voice of Natasha could be heard.

"Hitler, that human garbage, destroyed Germany. All the nations will hate you through the ages. You will see. Even if you live through the war, you will have to hide from human revenge like a worm."

We stood there completely motionless, as though hypnotized. Natasha started to 20 sing. What a wonderful voice she had.

She finished the interview with an abrupt, "Get out of here. I can't stand to look at your shiny mug any more."

Mengele got up and left without a word. Only after he had crossed the threshold of the infirmary and had looked at our pale faces did he shout out the order to dress all the sick, because the orderly would come to pick them up after lunch.

"The Russian is to stay here," he added in closing.

We knew what that meant. The orderly would give them an injection of phenol, and in the evening the *leichenauto* would take them to the gas chambers. Natasha had to remain here. Why? Maybe he was preparing a more agonizing death for her.

The next day they brought a new batch of women. They, too, were sad and silent. 25 About lunch time Mengele came in again.

"Come here, hero of the gas chambers," Natasha called again. "We will discuss your death. If you wish, I will tell you how you're going to die."

With wonder we watched him approach Natasha. For an hour she carried on a tirade against Hitler. She sang Russia's praises. Mengele sat on the chair with his head hung low on his chest.

I remember looking at him and not believing my own eyes. What was going on here? What was drawing that predator to his prey? To this very day I cannot understand what secret was lurking behind his behavior. Maybe it was just one more aberration. Perhaps the flagellation he received from Natasha's tongue gave him some sort of satisfaction.

Every day the sanitation worker took the sick for the szpryce (injection). That was their term for murder by phenol in Auschwitz. Every day Mengele came to listen to Natasha's speeches. One evening I decided to have a talk with Natasha. I told her everything about myself, waiting for her to get up enough confidence so that she would be willing to tell me about her life. I was not mistaken.

Natasha had been a student. Her parents had been professors of German. It was 30 from them that she had learned such elegant German. After that conversation I was certain that Natasha was not mentally ill and that she was feigning mental illness in order to be able to get away with telling the Germans exactly how she felt about them.

"But dear Natasha," I screamed with anguish, "do you know what they do to mentally ill people? They don't heal but kill."

"I know," said Natasha. "But I don't want to live in this rotten world."

The next day Dr. Koenig came for the inspection instead of Mengele. We closed the door to the little room. Maybe we could hide the sick from him.

"Hey, you, Doctor of death," Natasha shouted in a loud voice. "Come here, we will discuss your Hitler."

Koenig shuddered. He pushed open the door and went into the little room. The room was almost completely dark. On the beds sat the huddled figures.   35

"What, you're afraid to come in, you Hitler's coward?"

Then there was a shot. All the sick screamed at the same time, with a terrible, hollow voice.

When we reached Natasha she was already dead. ●

Explorations of the Text

1. Describe the position of the narrator. Who do you imagine her to be?
2. Why does the narrator admire Natasha?
3. Why does Natasha confront Mengele? Why is it important that she speaks to him in "beautiful German"? What does her confrontation symbolize?

The Reading/Writing Connection

1. Discuss the theme of silence and speech in this work. What is the power of language?
2. Debate Topic: Is Natasha insane?
3. Freewrite in response to this question: What is "Natasha's Triumph"?

Ideas for Writing

1. How does Natasha turn victimization into heroism? Why does she inspire others?

Shusaku Endō *(1923–1996)*

The War Generation   *1979*

Outside it was raining, and the restaurant was crowded. A steaming pot on a white charcoal brazier in front of them, office workers and various other customers blew on their onions and *kiritanpo*[1] before eating them. A young woman dressed in a dark blue kimono with white splashes went from table to table setting down bottles of *sake*.[2]

---

[1]**kiritanpo:** A kind of stew, pounded into a mortar and served with chicken.   [2]**sake:** A kind of alcoholic beverage, made from rice and served warm.

"Are these seats taken?" a businessman with a young woman in tow asked Konishi.

"No." With his *sake* cup still at his lips, Konishi shook his head sourly. In truth he had wanted this table all to himself.

"Shall we have the fish broth?"

"Anything. I'm starving." 5

She took a cigarette from her brown handbag and began to smoke. Looking at her, Konishi thought of his wife and daughters waiting for him at home. This woman would be about the same age as his oldest girl, but she brought the cigarette to her lips like a habitual smoker. It was a distressing sight.

"Don't you think they're charging a little too much for the year-end party this time?"

"What can we do? We have to go."

Listening without interest to the whispered conversation between these two, Konishi concluded that they must work in the same section at some company. Their talk shifted from the cost of the year-end party to backbiting against their co-workers.

He consumed a good deal of time slowly drinking down his second bottle of *sake*. 10 At home, his wife and daughters had probably already started dinner. He often stopped off for a few drinks on his way home from work, so his family would wait until seven o'clock and then go ahead and eat without him. Konishi felt more comfortable having them do that than making them wait for him.

As intoxication began to settle in, Konishi thought about the funeral of one of his fellow workers that he had attended the previous day. Mimura had been Personnel Director at the company, and was the same age as Konishi—fifty-two. He had heard that Mimura's blood pressure was a little high, but when the two of them had been tested together a year before in the company examination room, Konishi's blood pressure had been 150, Mimura's around 160. They had talked about how, by taking medicine, the pressure could be held below 200, and so there was nothing to worry about. But Mimura had died suddenly of a heart attack.

A photograph of Mimura, smiling and wearing a golfing hat, had been placed above the Buddhist memorial tablet surrounded by chrysanthemums. To one side sat the drooping figures of Mimura's wife, dressed in mourning kimono, and his son, wearing his high-school uniform. As he pressed his hands together reverently and gazed at Mimura's photograph, Konishi thought that this would be happening to him too before very long. Death, which had until now seemed still some distance away, had suddenly closed in on him with a whirr. In fact, two other funerals he had attended this year were for men in their fifties; he had to be on his guard.

"On my guard . . . ?" he muttered to himself. The woman who was sharing his table was putting fish and onions from the broth into a bowl for her date. The man, puffing on a cigarette, watched her as though he expected such treatment. Doubtless they had already slept together.

I must be on my guard. . . . But what was he supposed to do at this point? He was by no means satisfied with his job, but he had no intention of leaving. Eventually he would become an executive. Thereby he would avoid mandatory retirement. These days he had to feel very grateful for the position he was in. In his youth he had never imagined that his declining years would take their present shape. When he entered the Department of Law, he had planned to become a government official. Those plans had been aborted when he was taken out of school and sent off to war.

But Konishi had not been the only one that had happened to. All around him in those days were people who had had to change the direction of their lives because of the war. It was a matter of course for Konishi's generation.

He finished off his second bottle, and while he was debating whether to order a third, the glass door of the restaurant opened with a clatter. In the artificial light the rain looked like needles. A tall, thin woman in a black raincoat, around fifty or so, came into the restaurant.

Her nose was as pronounced as a foreigner's. Flecks of silver streaked her hair, like a foreigner's. Droplets of rain glimmered on her black raincoat. She asked the kimono-clad hostess a brief question and disappeared into a room at the back.

Still holding the empty *sake* bottle in his hand, Konishi let out an unintentional gasp. The man at the next table gave him a peculiar look.

None of the other customers in the restaurant knew who the woman was. But Konishi recognized the middle-aged woman as the violinist Ono Mari.

There was not a single clear sky over Tokyo in the days just before Konishi went into the army. Each day was leadenly overcast.

Though he knew it couldn't be the case, he wondered if the ashen skies over Tokyo had something to do with the city being as dark as his own feelings at the time. He had been at the university, and his boarding-house was located at Shinano-machi. Even the main road from there to Shinjuku was always deserted, every store had its glass doors tightly shut and displayed signs reading "Closed." Outside the shops, sandbags, buckets and fire blankets had been stacked in preparation for air raids. But there were no signs of human life.

Every day the sky looked as though it had been stuffed full of tattered cotton swabs. He could remember hearing sounds like faint explosions echoing constantly from the sky.

There was no longer anything resembling classes at the university. Instead, students like Konishi were sent to the F. Heavy Industries factory in Kawasaki, where they assembled airplane parts.

On the wintry mornings, factory workers and students dressed in work clothes and gaiters and carrying knapsacks over their shoulders lined up in single file on the square in front of Kawasaki Station. Buffeted by the cold wind, they waited and waited for their bus to come. Inside Konishi's knapsack he had some soya beans wrapped in paper, the only food that would help in some small way to stave off his hunger throughout the entire day.

Towards the end of 1944, the factory suffered a shortage of raw materials, and many machines ground to a halt. Even so, Konishi and the other grease-covered students had to stand in front of their drill presses all day long. Supervisors continued to make their rounds, marking down the names of any students whose work was slack. Those whose names were logged were not given any of the watery porridge that was brought around each day at three o'clock. Diluted as it was, the ravenous students coveted the porridge.

They were starved for more than just food. They likewise craved books. They yearned for heated rooms. They were hungry for human conversation, and for love. And so during the noon break, as they lined up in groups of five or six with their backs to the sunlit concrete wall, they discussed food and books. Then with sighs of longing they talked about certain members of the women's volunteer corps, who worked in a separate building. Dressed in their work pantaloons and wearing headbands, these women sorted the various machine parts. Throughout the factory hung posters that read: "Advance to Attu Island!"[3]

As that year drew to a close, however, one after another of the young men who basked in that noonday sun received their draft notices printed on red paper. Each morning at the factory it was easy to tell from the looks on people's faces just who had received their orders. They would try to force a smile, but the dark, heavy circles under their eyes betrayed them.

"It's come," the latest recipient would announce to everyone in a low voice, as though he were confessing some dark secret.

"When do you leave?"

"In two weeks." 30

Of course, no one mouthed empty phrases like "Congratulations" or "Give it your best!" Sooner or later the same piece of paper would be coming their way. They all stared at the tall factory chimney. Again today the smoke from the chimney swirled straight up into the sombre sky. The scene was unchanged from yesterday or the day before. It seemed as though it would stay that way for eternity.

"When is this war going to end?" No one knew. They felt as though it would linger on and on for ever.

Whenever a new recruit left Tokyo, everyone assembled at Shinjuku or Tokyo Station to see him off. The students formed a circle on the crowded platform and sang their school song in an angry roar. They howled and leaped about, less interested in seeing off their friend than in masking the anxiety and fear that lurked in their own hearts. As the train carrying their comrade vanished from sight, looks of bleak emptiness appeared on the faces of those who had been so boisterous just a few moments before.

1945 came, and still Konishi had not received his induction notice. Around that time the enemy air raids gradually intensified. The previous November the Nakashima Aircraft Plant in Musashino had been bombed, and enemy planes appeared fifteen times the following month. Strangely, F. Factory in Kawasaki was untouched. Often the trains packed with exhausted workers at the end of the day would come to a stop with a groan. Sometimes there appeared to be an attack over the downtown area; from the train windows they could see the sky in that direction glowing a dark red. The train service was often suspended, and Konishi would have to crouch for a long while on a connecting platform at Tokyo Station, staring at the reddened sky, realizing with a start that death was all that lay before them.

On 28 February his good friend Inami received his draft notice, and the feeling 35 that his own turn was coming soon struck Konishi with greater force than ever before. The night Inami's orders came, four or five of them gathered in his room for a farewell party. They drank rationed liquor and some watered-down medicinal alcohol they had stolen from the factory. Later that night, the landlord and the owner of an electrical shop who represented the local veterans' association came in and clumsily began to chant some Chinese poetry. "Do your best! Work for your country." They spouted callous words of encouragement. Inami, his face sallow, sat up straight in the student uniform he had not put on for some time.

That night he and Konishi slept in his room under the same blanket. Inami turned over, and Konishi could hear him weeping softly. He listened in silence for a while, then whispered, "I'll be getting drafted too, before long."

---

[3] **Attu Island:** Island southwest of Alaska, the most western of the Aleutians.

"Uh-huh," Inami nodded. He turned so that Konishi could see the profile of his face. "If you want anything of mine, you can have it."

"I don't want any books. My red slip will be coming before I could finish reading any of them."

"Probably. In that case, would you go to a concert in my place? I had to fight to get the ticket. I wanted to go to just one concert before the army got me." He slipped out of bed in his worn-out underwear and rifled through his desk drawer until he found a brown-coloured ticket. Inami was engrossed in music: he had his own record collection, and even had a phonograph in his room.

"Whose concert?"

"Ono Mari on the violin. You've heard of her, haven't you—Ono Mari? They say she's a young genius."

"I've heard the name a lot."

In the dim light from the lamp swathed in a black cloth, Konishi looked at the brown ticket. On the coarse paper had been printed the words: "Ono Mari Solo Violin Concert, March 10." It hardly seemed possible that a concert could be held in Tokyo now that death was everywhere.

"Are you sure I can have this?"

"Please go. In my place."

Inami set out from Shinjuku Station the following morning. The usual clusters of students had gathered in circles on the platform to sing. Inami seemed thinner and shorter than the other students who were boarding the trains. He blinked his eyes behind glasses that kept sliding down his nose, and bowed his head repeatedly to his friends.

On the night of 9 March, a large formation of B-29s attacked Tokyo. The hour was approximately 12 a.m.

There was a strong northerly wind that night. A heavy snow had fallen in Tokyo two or three days earlier, and a thick layer of black ice still remained along the sides of the streets. Around six o'clock, Mari finished rehearsing for the following day's performance at the home of her accompanist, a White Russian named Sapholo, who lived nearby. She returned home, but because of the wind that had stirred up around noon, the long hair that was her trademark kept blowing across her face, and she had to stop many times along the way.

At the age of fourteen, she had left all the older violinists in the dust and taken first place in a music competition sponsored by the Mainichi Newspaper Corporation. Thereafter she attracted many fans. As a young child she had been in poor health, and the rowdy children at elementary school had made fun of her. Unable to endure the atmosphere, she had pleaded with her parents not to make her continue in school; they had agreed to let her pursue her violin and other essential studies at home. Perhaps that was why she was fawned upon there.

That evening, as she warmed her legs under the *kotatsu*[4] and ate the potato pie and unsweetened black tea her mother had prepared for her, she discussed with her parents the possibility of going to Manchuria.[5] The Musicians' Patriotic Society had proposed

---

[4]**kotatsu:** Heated charcoal, wrapped in cloth or blankets to preserve warmth and often covered with a box. Used only in winter, the *kotatsu* can be placed in a central location at dinner so that everyone seated for the meal can enjoy the comfort of the heat. [5]**Manchuria:** A region in Northeast China, including Heilongjiang, Tilin, and Liaoning provinces and part of Inner Mongolia.

a series of concerts in Manchuria, and if possible she wanted her mother to go with her. Her father, wearing a frayed dressing-gown, agreed that they should go for about half a year, treating it as a kind of evacuation; there would be no air raids in Manchuria, and they would probably not have to contend with food shortages.

"This war should be over within half a year anyway." Her artist father, who had studied in France as a young man, hated the military. He took an active part in air-raid drills and went to pay his respects to departing soldiers, but at the dinner table he often shared his grim outlook on the war situation with his wife and daughter.

Mari eventually grew tired and put her hand to her mouth to yawn. The radio had been playing a song called "Look, a Parachute!," but suddenly it was interrupted by a shrill buzzer, and the announcer began to read a report from the Eastern Military Command.

"Enemy planes have been sighted over the ocean south of the city. They are approaching the mainland." The announcer repeated the words three times.

"It's all right," Mari's mother said. "They're probably just reconnaissance planes."

"Why don't we just go to bed instead of putting out the lights," her father replied,　55 extinguishing the coals in the *kotatsu*. "I'm not about to do everything the army wants us to do."

Mari fell asleep in her upstairs room. She had placed her violin case, air-raid hood and knapsack by her pillow, ready for an emergency, and had then dropped off to sleep as swiftly as a shower of falling pebbles. Soon in her dreams the orchestra members began to tune their instruments. The reverberations from the instruments were jumbled and confused, and somehow refused to modulate together as they usually did. Someone was beating on the kettledrum.

"Wake up! Mari, wake up!"

Someone was shouting at her bedside. She opened her eyes and dimly saw her father standing there wearing a metal helmet. Her ears still rang with the discordant strains of the orchestra.

"We've got to get away. It's an air raid! The flames are coming closer to us!"

For some reason her father's voice seemed to come from far away. She felt no sense　60 of urgency at the words "air raid." Like a marionette she did as she was instructed and stumbled out of bed. It was then that she realized the noises in her ears were not those of an orchestra tuning up, but the crackling of fires somewhere nearby.

They joined her mother at the foot of the stairs and started for the air-raid shelter in the garden. As they hurried along, they looked up and saw that the sky over Honjo and Fukagawa was a flaming red. There was a popping sound like roasting beans, and they could hear the shouting, clamouring voices of many people. When they reached the shelter, their noses were stung by the smells of straw and damp earth.

"We can't stay here. We've got to run!" her father shouted. To her mother, who was carrying a rucksack and her purse, he called, "Leave that. You don't need it." Carrying just one rucksack on his back, he hurried the two women out through the gate. From the neighbouring Yoshimura house came clattering noises of others preparing to flee; on a road nearby a child cried, "Ma-a-ama!"

The main street was already a maelstrom of people. The sky behind them was a sombre red. In the torrent were a man pulling his belongings along in a bicycle trailer, a young man carrying bedding in a hand-cart and a woman with a blanket wrapped around her body. All of them streamed towards the west, as though drawn by some phantom power. Time and again Mari's father shouted, "Stay together!" Mari realized that the only thing she was carrying was her violin case. Another explosion shook the sky. The white bodies of the B-29s, their arms outstretched, appeared in the searchlights. The anti-aircraft guns opened fire, but the B-29s continued to soar calmly overhead. The wind still blew fiercely. From the distance echoed a succession of thunderous noises, as though a pile-driver were pounding the ground.

At his Shinano-machi boarding-house, Konishi was unable to get to sleep until about 2 a.m., thanks to the searchlights that glanced off his window and the explosion of anti-aircraft guns in the distance. The next morning he learned from the Imperial Headquarters bulletin that part of the city had been indiscriminately bombed by a hundred and thirty B-29s. The information bureau of the Headquarters and the newspapers reported without comment that fifty of the enemy planes had been damaged and fifteen shot down. But that day as he set out for the factory on the sporadically paralysed train line, Konishi saw that nearly all of the downtown sector had been consumed by fire in the previous night's raid. At the plant, workers gathered in small groups here and there, talking in subdued voices. Many of the labourers they were used to seeing had not shown up for work. From the student workforce, Taguchi, Ueno and Fujimoto were absent. A supervisor appeared and roared at the group, "Get back to work!"

The ticket he had received from Inami was still carefully tucked into his train pass holder, but as he worked, Konishi began to have doubts that the concert would be held under the present circumstances. Besides, even if he tried to go to the concert, and there was another air raid like the one the night before, he would not be able to get back to his boarding-house. He decided it would be better not to go. When he reached that conclusion, though, he could hear Inami's plaintive voice echoing in his ears: "I had to fight to get the ticket. Please go in my place." He began to feel that wasting the brown ticket would be akin to betraying his friend. Without even asking, Konishi knew full well what sort of trials Inami was now enduring in the army.

At five o'clock the long, heavy siren announcing the end of the working day blared out. Still uncertain whether or not to go to the concert, Konishi crowded into the bus for Kawasaki Station with the other workers, then transferred to the equally packed train. Those who had found seats and those who dangled from the straps all had their eyes closed, and their faces looked as if they belonged to overworked beasts of burden.

It was pitch black at the deserted Yūraku-chō Station when Konishi got off the train and started walking towards Hibiya Public Hall. Along the way he took some of the paper-wrapped soya beans from his knapsack and chewed them. At the end of the day's labours his legs felt heavy and his stomach empty. When the dark hall at last came into view, he had to sit down on a rock in the park and rest for a while. Then he stood up and walked to the steps of the hall, where about fifty people had gathered by the entrance. Each of them wore gaiters and work pants and carried a knapsack on his shoulders.

As it was nearly six o'clock and the doors still hadn't been opened, someone asked his neighbour in the queue, "Is there going to be a concert or not?" Word of mouth had it that the fires caused by the previous night's air raid had driven both Mari and her accompanist Sapholo from their homes; their whereabouts were unknown, and the hall was presently attempting to contact them. Still no one made a move to leave; they all stood patiently at the entrance.

Two men with stern faces, dressed in patriotic uniforms, appeared and bellowed, "Hmph, what are you doing listening to enemy music in times like these? Go home, all of you!" The group lowered their eyes and said nothing. The men shrugged their shoulders and disappeared.

Before long a timid, middle-aged employee came out of the hall and announced apologetically, "We have not been able to make contact. The concert is cancelled. I'm very sorry." 70

No one protested. With shadows of resignation flickering on their backs, they silently began to disperse. Feeling somehow relieved, Konishi started to follow them out of the park. Just then a man at the front of the procession called, "She's here!"

Everyone stopped walking. A weary, long-haired girl dressed in men's trousers and carrying a violin case was walking towards the hall with a look of pain on her face. It was Ono Mari.

"There's going to be a concert!" The shout passed from one person to the next like the baton in a relay race. The music enthusiasts turned on their heels like a flock of ducks and went back to the hall.

It was a peculiar concert, the sort not likely to have been seen before or since. The audience filled only half of Hibiya Public Hall, so the patrons dressed in their working clothes picked out seats to their liking and waited eagerly for Ono Mari to make her appearance.

Soon Mari came out onto the dusty stage, clutching her violin and bow in one hand. She had not had time to adjust her make-up, and the pained expression lingered as she stood in the centre of the stage. Exhaustion was etched into her face, and the renowned long hair and the wide, almost European eyes seemed agonizingly incongruous with the tattered men's trousers she was wearing. But no one laughed. 75

"We were burned out of our house," she apologized, the violin and bow dangling from her hands. "The trains couldn't go any further than Yotsuya . . . I walked here from Yotsuya. I had to come . . . knowing this might be my last concert."

She bit her lip, and the audience knew she was choking down her emotions. There was not even a suggestion of applause. Everyone remained silent, pondering what she had just said.

At that moment, Konishi thought, "This just might be the last concert I'll ever hear."

Mari shook her head vigorously to get the hair out of her face, tucked the violin under her chin, leaned forward, bent her slender wrist sharply, and adjusted her bow.

From beneath that wrist the strains of Fauré's Elegy[6] began to pour out. Not a single cough came from the audience. The tired, begrimed patrons closed their eyes and listened to the music, absorbed in their own private thoughts and individual griefs. The dark, low melody pierced the hearts of each one. As he followed the music, Konishi thought about the dying city of Tokyo. He thought of the scorched, reddish sky he had seen from the station platform. He thought of the drafted workers and students waiting in the chill winter wind for a bus to pick them up at Kawasaki Station. He remembered the thin face of Inami, the tear-stained face he had buried in his bedcovers the night before his induction. Perhaps the air-raid sirens would whine again tonight, and many more people would die. Tomorrow morning Konishi, the other members of the audience and Ono Mari might be reduced to charred grey corpses. Even if he did not die 80

---

[6]**Fauré's Elegy:** François-Félix Fauré, French composer (1843–1924).

today, before long he would be carted off to the battlefield. When that happened, only the strains of this melody would remain to reach the ears of those who survived.

When she finished the Elegy, Mari played Fauré's Après un réve, then performed the Saint-Saëns "Rondo Capriccioso"[7] and Beethoven's "Romance." No one even considered the possibility that at any moment the alarms might sound, that the sky might be filled with a deafening roar, and that bombs might start to fall with a screeching howl.

Something sticky brushed against his head. A spider had woven its web in the yatsude plants in front of his house. Konishi clicked his tongue and opened the glass door.

From the parlour he could hear music playing on the television. As a man in his fifties, he could not begin to comprehend the electric guitar music that so delighted his daughters. It sounded to him like nothing more than someone banging noisily on metal buckets.

He was balancing himself with one hand on the shoe cabinet and removing his shoes when his wife came out of the parlour. "Welcome home," she said, and a moment later his second daughter, a high-school girl, appeared and begrudgingly repeated the greeting.

"Clean up the entranceway. How many times do I have to tell you?"   85

His wife and daughter said nothing. With a sour expression he washed his hands in the bathroom and then gargled, making a sound exactly like a duck. When he had changed his clothes he went into the parlour. The two daughters who had been watching television got abruptly to their feet, looked at him coldly, and muttering, "We've got homework to do," headed for their rooms. Konishi cast a disappointed glance after them.

Konishi's wife chattered as she filled his rice bowl, "Remember I told you that the owner of the Azusa-ya was complaining of stiff shoulders?" The Azusa-ya was a grocery store by the bus stop. "He's gone into hospital. His wife says he's got some kind of growth in his chest. It looks like cancer."

The shop-owner was not much older than Konishi. Once again he felt death closing in on him with a whirring sound. He remembered the funeral of Mimura, his co-worker who had died of a heart attack. No, death was not closing in on them. Since their schooldays, death had always lived alongside the members of his generation. That smouldering red sky he had seen from the platform at Tokyo Station. The buzz of enemy planes that constantly filled the clogged grey skies. Inami had died of an illness on the battlefield in Korea. Other friends had been killed in the South Seas or on islands in the Pacific. Somewhere within, he felt as though the postwar period was just an extension of life that he had been granted.

"Toshiko wants to go on a vacation to Guam with some of her friends." Glumly he continued to eat while his wife went on talking. Her face was fleshy around the eyelids and chin. It occurred to him that when he had seen Ono Mari in the restaurant tonight, her hair was streaked with flecks of silver.

"I saw Ono Mari today," he said, almost to himself.   90

"Who's she?" His wife smothered a yawn. ●

---

[7] **"Rondo Capriccioso":** Charles Camille Saint-Saëns, French composer (1835–1921).

Explorations of the Text

1. Describe the occasion and the setting. What do you learn about Konishi in the restaurant?
2. Why does Endō emphasize sky imagery?
3. Discuss Konishi's experience in the factory during the war. Why are the young men so unhappy when the red paper arrives?
4. Analyze the section on Ono Mari and her family. Why is this section in the narrative?
5. Why is Konishi so moved by Ono Mari's appearance in the restaurant many years later? What is the significance of her "hair streaked with flecks of silver"?
6. Examine Konishi's relationships at home. What accounts for his estrangement from his wife and daughters?
7. What are the ironies of the end of the story?
8. Compare the view of the brutality of war in this story with the treatment of the same theme in O'Brien's "How to Tell a True War Story" (below).

The Reading/Writing Connection

1. List your preconceptions of the Japanese during World War II. Does this story change your views in any way?

Ideas for Writing

1. Characterize Konishi. What does he fear? How does he represent and symbolize the "war generation"?
2. What does the story reveal about life in Japan during World War II? Use exercise 1 in The Reading/Writing Connection as a beginning.
3. What is Ono Mari's role in the story?
4. Discuss Endō's use of imagery, tone, and point of view.

Tim O'Brien *(1946–   )*

How to Tell a True War Story   *1990*

This is true.

I had a buddy in Vietnam. His name was Bob Kiley, but everybody called him Rat.

A friend of his gets killed, so about a week later Rat sits down and writes a letter to the guy's sister. Rat tells her what a great brother she had, how together the guy was, a number one pal and comrade. A real soldier's soldier, Rat says. Then he tells a few stories to make the point, how her brother would always volunteer for stuff nobody else would volunteer for in a million years, dangerous stuff, like doing recon or going out on these really badass night patrols. Stainless steel balls, Rat tells her. The guy was a little crazy, for sure, but crazy in a good way, a real daredevil, because he liked the challenge of it, he liked testing himself, just man against gook. A great, great guy, Rat says.

Anyway, it's a terrific letter, very personal and touching. Rat almost bawls writing it. He gets all teary telling about the good times they had together, how her brother made the war seem almost fun, always raising hell and lighting up villes and bringing smoke to bear every which way. A great sense of humor, too. Like the time at this river when he went fishing with a whole damn crate of hand grenades. Probably the funniest thing in world history, Rat says, all that gore, about twenty zillion dead gook fish. Her brother, he had the right attitude. He knew how to have a good time. On Halloween, this real hot spooky night, the dude paints up his body all different colors and puts on this weird mask and hikes over to a ville and goes trick-or-treating almost stark naked, just boots and balls and an M-16. A tremendous human being, Rat says. Pretty nutso sometimes, but you could trust him with your life.

And then the letter gets very sad and serious. Rat pours his heart out. He says he 5 loved the guy. He says the guy was his best friend in the world. They were like soul mates, he says, like twins or something, they had a whole lot in common. He tells the guy's sister he'll look her up when the war's over.

So what happens?

Rat mails the letter. He waits two months. The dumb cooze never writes back.

A true war story is never moral. It does not instruct, nor encourage virtue, nor suggest models of proper human behavior, nor restrain men from doing the things men have always done. If a story seems moral, do not believe it. If at the end of a war story you feel uplifted, or if you feel that some small bit of rectitude has been salvaged from the larger waste, then you have been made the victim of a very old and terrible lie. There is no rectitude whatsoever. There is no virtue. As a first rule of thumb, therefore, you can tell a true war story by its absolute and uncompromising allegiance to obscenity and evil. Listen to Rat Kiley. Cooze, he says. He does not say bitch. He certainly does not say woman, or girl. He says cooze. Then he spits and stares. He's nineteen years old —it's too much for him—so he looks at you with those big sad gentle killer eyes and says cooze, because his friend is dead, and because it's so incredibly sad and true: she never wrote back.

You can tell a true war story if it embarrasses you. If you don't care for obscenity, you don't care for the truth; if you don't care for the truth, watch how you vote. Send guys to war, they come home talking dirty.

Listen to Rat: "Jesus Christ, man, I write this beautiful fuckin' letter, I slave over 10 it, and what happens? The dumb cooze never writes back."

The dead guy's name was Curt Lemon. What happened was, we crossed a muddy river and marched west into the mountains, and on the third day we took a break along a trail junction in deep jungle. Right away, Lemon and Rat Kiley started goofing. They didn't understand about the spookiness. They were kids; they just didn't know. A nature hike, they thought, not even a war, so they went off into the shade of some giant trees—quadruple canopy, no sunlight at all—and they were giggling and calling each other yellow mother and playing a silly game they'd invented. The game involved smoke grenades, which were harmless unless you did stupid things, and what they did was pull out the pin and stand a few feet apart and play catch under the shade of those huge trees. Whoever chickened out was a yellow mother. And if nobody chickened out, the grenade would make a light popping sound and they'd be covered with smoke and they'd laugh and dance around and then do it again.

It's all exactly true.

It happened, to *me,* nearly twenty years ago, and I still remember that trail junction and those giant trees and a soft dripping sound somewhere beyond the trees. I remember the smell of moss. Up in the canopy there were tiny white blossoms, but no sunlight at all, and I remember the shadows spreading out under the trees where Curt Lemon and Rat Kiley were playing catch with smoke grenades. Mitchell Sanders sat flipping his yo-yo. Norman Bowker and Kiowa and Dave Jensen were dozing, or half dozing, and all around us were those ragged green mountains.

Except for the laughter things were quiet.

At one point, I remember, Mitchell Sanders turned and looked at me, not quite   15
nodding, as if to warn me about something, as if he already *knew,* then after a while he rolled up his yo-yo and moved away.

It's hard to tell you what happened next.

They were just goofing. There was a noise, I suppose, which must've been the detonator, so I glanced behind me and watched Lemon step from the shade into bright sunlight. His face was suddenly brown and shining. A handsome kid, really. Sharp gray eyes, lean and narrow-waisted, and when he died it was almost beautiful, the way the sunlight came around him and lifted him up and sucked him high into a tree full of moss and vines and white blossoms.

In any war story, but especially a true one, it's difficult to separate what happened from what seemed to happen. What seems to happen becomes its own happening and has to be told that way. The angles of vision are skewed. When a booby trap explodes, you close your eyes and duck and float outside yourself. When a guy dies, like Curt Lemon, you look away and then look back for a moment and then look away again. The pictures get jumbled; you tend to miss a lot. And then afterward, when you go to tell about it, there is always that surreal seemingness, which makes the story seem untrue, but which in fact represents the hard and exact truth as it *seemed.*

■ ■ ■

In many cases a true war story cannot be believed. If you believe it, be skeptical. It's a question of credibility. Often the crazy stuff is true and the normal stuff isn't, because the normal stuff is necessary to make you believe the truly incredible craziness.

In other cases you can't even tell a true war story. Sometimes it's just beyond   20
telling.

I heard this one, for example, from Mitchell Sanders. It was near dusk and we were sitting at my foxhole along a wide muddy river north of Quang Ngai. I remember how peaceful the twilight was. A deep pinkish red spilled out on the river, which moved without sound, and in the morning we would cross the river and march west into the mountains. The occasion was right for a good story.

"God's truth," Mitchell Sanders said. "A six-man patrol goes up into the mountains on a basic listening-post operation. The idea's to spend a week up there, just lie low and listen for enemy movement. They've got a radio along, so if they hear anything suspicious—anything—they're supposed to call in artillery or gunships, whatever it takes. Otherwise they keep strict field discipline. Absolute silence. They just listen."

Sanders glanced at me to make sure I had the scenario. He was playing with his yo-yo, dancing it with short, tight little strokes of the wrist.

His face was blank in the dusk.

"We're talking regulation, by-the-book LP. These six guys, they don't say boo for a 25 solid week. They don't got tongues. *All* ears."

"Right," I said.

"Understand me?"

"Invisible."

Sanders nodded.

"Affirm," he said. "Invisible. So what happens is, these guys get themselves deep 30 in the bush, all camouflaged up, and they lie down and wait and that's all they do, nothing else, they lie there for seven straight days and just listen. And man, I'll tell you—it's spooky. This is mountains. You don't *know* spooky till you been there. Jungle, sort of, except it's way up in the clouds and there's always this fog—like rain, except it's not raining—everything's all wet and swirly and tangled up and you can't see jack, you can't find your own pecker to piss with. Like you don't even have a body. Serious spooky. You just go with the vapors—the fog sort of takes you in . . . And the sounds, man. The sounds carry forever. You hear stuff nobody should *ever* hear."

Sanders was quiet for a second, just working the yo-yo, then he smiled at me.

"So after a couple days the guys start hearing this real soft, kind of wacked-out music. Weird echoes and stuff. Like a radio or something, but it's not a radio, it's this strange gook music that comes right out of the rocks. Faraway, sort of, but right up close, too. They try to ignore it. But it's a listening post, right? So they listen. And every night they keep hearing that crazyass gook concert. All kinds of chimes and xylophones. I mean, this is wilderness—no way, it can't be real—but there it is, like the mountains are tuned in to Radio fucking Hanoi. Naturally they get nervous. One guy sticks Juicy Fruit in his ears. Another guy almost flips. Thing is, though, they can't report music. They can't get on the horn and call back to base and say, 'Hey, listen, we need some firepower, we got to blow away this weirdo gook rock band.' They can't do that. It wouldn't go down. So they lie there in the fog and keep their mouths shut. And what makes it extra bad, see, is the poor dudes can't horse around like normal. Can't joke it away. Can't even talk to each other except maybe in whispers, all hush-hush, and that just revs up the willies. All they do is listen."

Again there was some silence as Mitchell Sanders looked out on the river. The dark was coming on hard now, and off to the west I could see the mountains rising in silhouette, all the mysteries and unknowns.

"This next part," Sanders said quietly, "you won't believe."

"Probably not," I said. 35

"You won't. And you know why?" He gave me a long, tired smile. "Because it happened. Because every word is absolutely dead-on true."

Sanders made a sound in his throat, like a sigh, as if to say he didn't care if I believed him or not. But he did care. He wanted me to feel the truth, to believe by the raw force of feeling. He seemed sad, in a way.

"These six guys," he said, "they're pretty fried out by now, and one night they start hearing voices. Like at a cocktail party. That's what it sounds like, this big swank gook cocktail party somewhere out there in the fog. Music and chitchat and stuff. It's crazy, I know, but they hear the champagne corks. They hear the actual martini glasses. Real hoity-toity, all very civilized, except this isn't civilization. This is Nam.

"Anyway, the guys try to be cool. They just lie there and groove, but after a while they start hearing—you won't believe this—they hear chamber music. They hear violins and cellos. They hear this terrific mama-san soprano. Then after a while they hear gook opera and a glee club and the Haiphong Boys Choir and a barbershop quartet and all kinds of weird chanting and Buddha-Buddha stuff. And the whole time, in the background, there's still that cocktail party going on. All these different voices. Not human voices, though. Because it's the mountains. Follow me? The rock—it's *talking*. And the fog, too, and the grass and the goddamn mongooses. Everything talks. The trees talk politics, the monkeys talk religion. The whole country. Vietnam. The place talks. It talks. Understand? Nam—it truly *talks*.

"The guys can't cope. They lose it. They get on the radio and report enemy movement—a whole army, they say—and they order up the firepower. They get arty and gunships. They call in air strikes. And I'll tell you, they fuckin' crash that cocktail party. All night long, they just smoke those mountains. They make jungle juice. They blow away trees and glee clubs and whatever else there is to blow away. Scorch time. They walk napalm up and down the ridges. They bring in the Cobras and F-4s[1], they use Willie Peter and HE and incendiaries. It's all fire. They make those mountains burn.

"Around dawn things finally get quiet. Like you never even *heard* quiet before. One of those real thick, real misty days—just clouds and fog, they're off in this special zone—and the mountains are absolutely dead-flat silent. Like Brigadoon—pure vapor, you know? Everything's all sucked up inside the fog. Not a single sound, except they still *hear* it.

"So they pack up and start humping. They head down the mountain, back to base camp, and when they get there they don't say diddly. They don't talk. Not a word, like they're deaf and dumb. Later on this fat bird colonel comes up and asks what the hell happened out there. What'd they hear? Why all the ordnance? The man's ragged out, he gets down tight on their case. I mean, they spent six trillion dollars on firepower, and this fatass colonel wants answers, he wants to know what the fuckin' story is.

"But the guys don't say zip. They just look at him for a while, sort of funny like, sort of amazed, and the whole war is right there in that stare. It says everything you can't ever say. It says, man, you got wax in your ears. It says, poor bastard, you'll never know—wrong frequency—you don't *even* want to hear this. Then they salute the fucker and walk away, because certain stories you don't ever tell."

You can tell a true war story by the way it never seems to end. Not then, not ever. Not when Mitchell Sanders stood up and moved off into the dark.

It all happened.

Even now, at this instant, I remember that yo-yo. In a way, I suppose, you had to be there, you had to hear it, but I could tell how desperately Sanders wanted me to believe him, his frustration at not quite getting the details right, not quite pinning down the final and definitive truth.

And I remember sitting at my foxhole that night, watching the shadows of Quang Ngai, thinking about the coming day and how we would cross the river and march west into the mountains, all the ways I might die, all the things I did not understand.

Late in the night Mitchell Sanders touched my shoulder.

"Just came to me," he whispered. "The moral, I mean. Nobody listens. Nobody hears nothin'. Like that fatass colonel. The politicians, all the civilian types. Your girlfriend. My girlfriend. Everybody's sweet little virgin girlfriend. What they need is to go out on LP. The vapors, man. Trees and rocks—you got to *listen* to your enemy."

---

[1] **F-4s:** Fighter jets.

■ ■ ■

And then again, in the morning, Sanders came up to me. The platoon was prepar- 50
ing to move out, checking weapons, going through all the little rituals that preceded
a day's march. Already the lead squad had crossed the river and was filing off toward
the west.

"I got a confession to make," Sanders said. "Last night, man, I had to make up a
few things."

"I know that."

"The glee club. There wasn't any glee club."

"Right."

"No opera." 55

"Forget it, I understand."

"Yeah, but listen, it's still true. Those six guys, they heard wicked sound out there.
They heard sound you just plain won't believe."

Sanders pulled on his rucksack, closed his eyes for a moment, then almost smiled
at me. I knew what was coming.

"All right," I said, "what's the moral?"

"Forget it." 60

"No, go ahead."

For a long while he was quiet, looking away, and the silence kept stretching out
until it was almost embarrassing. Then he shrugged and gave me a stare that lasted
all day.

"Hear that quiet, man?" he said. "That quiet—just listen. There's your moral."

In a true war story, if there's a moral at all, it's like the thread that makes the cloth. You
can't tease it out. You can't extract the meaning without unraveling the deeper meaning. And in the end, really, there's nothing much to say about a true war story, except
maybe "Oh."

True war stories do not generalize. They do not indulge in abstraction or analysis. 65

For example: War is hell. As a moral declaration the old truism seems perfectly
true, and yet because it abstracts, because it generalizes, I can't believe it with my
stomach. Nothing turns inside.

It comes down to gut instinct. A true war story, if truly told, makes the stomach
believe.

■ ■ ■

This one does it for me. I've told it before—many times, many versions—but here's
what actually happened.

We crossed that river and marched west into the mountains. On the third day,
Curt Lemon stepped on a booby-trapped 105 round. He was playing catch with Rat
Kiley, laughing, and then he was dead. The trees were thick; it took nearly an hour to
cut an LZ for the dustoff.

Later, higher in the mountains, we came across a baby VC water buffalo. What it 70
was doing there I don't know—no farms or paddies—but we chased it down and got a
rope around it and led it along to a deserted village where we set up for the night. After
supper Rat Kiley went over and stroked its nose.

He opened up a can of C rations, pork and beans, but the baby buffalo wasn't
interested.

Rat shrugged.

He stepped back and shot it through the right front knee. The animal did not make a sound. It went down hard, then got up again, and Rat took careful aim and shot off an ear. He shot it in the hindquarters and in the little hump at its back. He shot it twice in the flanks. It wasn't to kill; it was to hurt. He put the rifle muzzle up against the mouth and shot the mouth away. Nobody said much. The whole platoon stood there watching, feeling all kinds of things, but there wasn't a great deal of pity for the baby water buffalo. Curt Lemon was dead. Rat Kiley had lost his best friend in the world. Later in the week he would write a long personal letter to the guy's sister, who would not write back, but for now it was a question of pain. He shot off the tail. He shot away chunks of meat below the ribs. All around us there was the smell of smoke and filth and deep greenery, and the evening was humid and very hot. Rat went to automatic. He shot randomly, almost casually, quick little spurts in the belly and butt. Then he reloaded, squatted down, and shot it in the left front knee. Again the animal fell hard and tried to get up, but this time it couldn't quite make it. It wobbled and went down sideways. Rat shot it in the nose. He bent forward and whispered something, as if talking to a pet, then he shot it in the throat. All the while the baby buffalo was silent, or almost silent, just a light bubbling sound where the nose had been. It lay very still. Nothing moved except the eyes, which were enormous, the pupils shiny black and dumb.

Rat Kiley was crying. He tried to say something, but then cradled his rifle and went off by himself.

The rest of us stood in a ragged circle around the baby buffalo. For a time no one spoke. We had witnessed something essential, something brand-new and profound, a piece of the world so startling there was not yet a name for it. 75

Somebody kicked the baby buffalo.

It was still alive, though just barely, just in the eyes.

"Amazing," Dave Jensen said. "My whole life, I never seen anything like it."

"Never?"

"Not hardly. Not once," 80

Kiowa and Mitchell Sanders picked up the baby buffalo. They hauled it across the open square, hoisted it up, and dumped it in the village well.

Afterward, we sat waiting for Rat to get himself together.

"Amazing," Dave Jensen kept saying. "A new wrinkle. I never seen it before."

Mitchell Sanders took out his yo-yo. "Well, that's Nam," he said. "Garden of Evil. Over here, man, every sin's real fresh and original."

How do you generalize? 85

War is hell, but that's not the half of it, because war is also mystery and terror and adventure and courage and discovery and holiness and pity and despair and longing and love. War is nasty; war is fun. War is thrilling; war is drudgery. War makes you a man; war makes you dead.

The truths are contradictory. It can be argued, for instance, that war is grotesque. But in truth war is also beauty. For all its horror, you can't help but gape at the awful majesty of combat. You stare out at tracer rounds unwinding through the dark like brilliant red ribbons. You crouch in ambush as a cool, impassive moon rises over the nighttime paddies. You admire the fluid symmetries of troops on the move, the harmonies of sound and shape and proportion, the great sheets of metal-fire streaming down from a gunship, the illumination rounds, the white phosphorus, the purply orange glow of napalm, the rocket's red glare. It's not pretty, exactly. It's astonishing. It fills the eye. It commands you. You hate it, yes, but your eyes do not. Like a killer forest fire, like cancer under a microscope, any battle or bombing raid or artillery barrage has the aesthetic purity of absolute moral indifference—a powerful, implacable beauty—and a true war story will tell the truth about this, though the truth is ugly.

To generalize about war is like generalizing about peace. Almost everything is true. Almost nothing is true. At its core, perhaps, war is just another name for death, and yet any soldier will tell you, if he tells the truth, that proximity to death brings with it a corresponding proximity to life. After a firefight, there is always the immense pleasure of aliveness. The trees are alive. The grass, the soil—everything. All around you things are purely living, and you among them, and the aliveness makes you tremble. You feel an intense, out-of-the-skin awareness of your living self—your truest self, the human being you want to be and then become by the force of wanting it. In the midst of evil you want to be a good man. You want decency. You want justice and courtesy and human concord, things you never knew you wanted. There is a kind of largeness to it, a kind of godliness. Though it's odd, you're never more alive than when you're almost dead. You recognize what's valuable. Freshly, as if for the first time, you love what's best in yourself and in the world, all that might be lost. At the hour of dusk you sit at your foxhole and look out on a wide river turning pinkish red, and at the mountains beyond, and although in the morning you must cross the river and go into the mountains and do terrible things and maybe die, even so, you find yourself studying the fine colors on the river, you feel wonder and awe at the setting of the sun, and you are filled with a hard, aching love for how the world could be and always should be, but now is not.

Mitchell Sanders was right. For the common soldier, at least, war has the feel—the spiritual texture—of a great ghostly fog, thick and permanent. There is no clarity. Everything swirls. The old rules are no longer binding, the old truths no longer true. Right spills over into wrong. Order blends into chaos, love into hate, ugliness into beauty, law into anarchy, civility into savagery. The vapors suck you in. You can't tell where you are, or why you're there, and the only certainty is overwhelming ambiguity.

In war you lose your sense of the definite, hence your sense of truth itself, and 90 therefore it's safe to say that in a true war story nothing is ever absolutely true.

Often in a true war story there is not even a point, or else the point doesn't hit you until twenty years later, in your sleep, and you wake up and shake your wife and start telling the story to her, except when you get to the end you've forgotten the point again. And then for a long time you lie there watching the story happen in your head. You listen to your wife's breathing. The war's over. You close your eyes. You smile and think, Christ, what's the *point*?

This one wakes me up.

In the mountains that day, I watched Lemon turn sideways. He laughed and said something to Rat Kiley. Then he took a peculiar half step, moving from shade into bright sunlight, and the booby-trapped 105 round blew him into a tree. The parts were just hanging there, so Dave Jensen and I were ordered to shinny up and peel him off. I remember the white bone of an arm. I remember pieces of skin and something wet and yellow that must've been the intestines. The gore was horrible, and stays with me.

But what wakes me up twenty years later is Dave Jensen singing "Lemon Tree"[2] as we threw down the parts.

You can tell a true war story by the questions you ask. Somebody tells a story, let's say, and afterward you ask, "Is it true?" and if the answer matters, you've got your answer.

For example, we've all heard this one. Four guys go down a trail. A grenade sails 95
out. One guy jumps on it and takes the blast and saves his three buddies.

Is it true?

The answer matters.

You'd feel cheated if it never happened. Without the grounding reality, it's just a trite bit of puffery, pure Hollywood, untrue in the way all such stories are untrue. Yet even if it did happen—and maybe it did, anything's possible—even then you know it can't be true, because a true war story does not depend upon that kind of truth. Absolute occurrence is irrelevant. A thing may happen and be a total lie; another thing may not happen and be truer than the truth. For example: Four guys go down a trail. A grenade sails out. One guy jumps on it and takes the blast, but it's a killer grenade and everybody dies anyway. Before they die, though, one of the dead guys says, "The fuck you do *that* for?" and the jumper says, "Story of my life, man," and the other guy starts to smile but he's dead.

That's a true story that never happened.

Twenty years later, I can still see the sunlight on Lemon's face. I can see him turning, 100
looking back at Rat Kiley, then he laughed and took that curious half step from shade into sunlight, his face suddenly brown and shining, and when his foot touched down, in that instant, he must've thought it was the sunlight that was killing him. It was not the sunlight. It was a rigged 105 round. But if I could ever get the story right, how the sun seemed to gather around him and pick him up and lift him high into a tree, if I could somehow recreate the fatal whiteness of that light, the quick glare, the obvious cause and effect, then you would believe the last thing Curt Lemon believed, which for him must've been the final truth.

Now and then, when I tell this story, someone will come up to me afterward and say she liked it. It's always a woman. Usually it's an older woman of kindly temperament and humane politics. She'll explain that as a rule she hates war stories; she can't understand why people want to wallow in all the blood and gore. But this one she liked. The poor baby buffalo, it made her sad. Sometimes, even, there are little tears. What I should do, she'll say, is put it all behind me. Find new stories to tell.

I won't say it but I'll think it.

I'll picture Rat Kiley's face, his grief, and I'll think, You *dumb cooze.*

Because she wasn't listening.

It *wasn't* a war story. It was a *love* story. 105

But you can't say that. All you can do is tell it one more time, patiently, adding and subtracting, making up a few things to get at the real truth. No Mitchell Sanders, you tell her. No Lemon, no Rat Riley. No trail junction. No baby buffalo. No vines or moss or white blossoms. Beginning to end, you tell her, it's all made up. Every goddamn detail—the mountains and the river and especially that poor dumb baby buffalo. None of

---

[2] **"Lemon Tree":** A popular folk song.

it happened. *None* of it. And even if it did happen, it didn't happen in the mountains, it happened in this little village on the Batangan Peninsula[3] and it was raining like crazy, and one night a guy named Stink Harris woke up screaming with a leech on his tongue. You can tell a true war story if you just keep on telling it.

And in the end, of course, a true war story is never about war. It's about sunlight. It's about the special way that dawn spreads out on a river when you know you must cross the river and march into the mountains and do things you are afraid to do. It's about love and memory. It's about sorrow. It's about sisters who never write back and people who never listen. ●

Explorations of the Text

1. What could be the reason why Curt Lemon's sister didn't respond to Rat's letter? Evaluate Rat's reaction. Why did it affect him so deeply?

2. What is innovative about this story? Consider the metafictional elements and distinctive narrative voice.

3. The narrator states: "It's difficult to separate what happened from what seemed to happen." Discuss the relationship between memory and truth.

4. Discuss the moral of Mitchell Sanders' story. Is there one? If so, what is it?

5. What is the attitude toward "truth" in this story? What is the attitude about "generalizations"? What relationship do these abstract concepts share?

6. This story contains a multitude of horrifying images; however, it also offers many images of beauty, which lend a strong sense of hope to the story. Contemplate these images of beauty amid horror. Why are they so important to the narrator?

7. How does this story exemplify the statement, "True war stories do not generalize. They do not indulge in abstraction or analysis."

8. Respond to the following statement: "It wasn't a war story. It was a love story." Why does the narrator view it as such?

9. Contrast the process of depersonalization, of dehumanization, presented in this work with that in Hartley's "I, Jailor" or Zachary Scott-Singley's blog.

The Reading/Writing Connection

1. This story blurs the lines between fact and fiction. Why? What effect does it create? Respond to this question in a paragraph.

2. For some, the process of writing may be therapeutic. Consider O'Brien's involvement as a soldier in the Vietnam War. Write one page on how the author is trying to battle his past through the manner in which he tells a war story and the manner in which this fictional story closely parallels many of his lived experiences.

Ideas for Writing

1. Respond to the narrator's suggestion that fiction sometimes seems truer than the truth because some truths are too hard to believe. How may the narrator be reaching for an emotional truth rather than a factual one?

---

[3]**Batangan Peninsula:** Area in central Vietnam, a Viet Cong stronghold during the Vietnam War.

2. Write about a time when you fabricated a factual truth to tap into a greater emotional truth.

3. Although it seems contradictory, the narrator bends the truth to make it believable. Freewrite about a truth (e.g., personal, political, etc.) that is so horrifying that it appears to be fictional.

In (Visibility): Minorities vs. Majorities/Fiction

Frederick Busch *(1941–)*

Ralph the Duck *1989*

I woke at up 5:25 because the dog was vomiting. I carried seventy-five pounds of heaving golden retriever to the door and poured him onto the silver, moonlit snow. "Good boy," I said because he'd done his only trick. Outside he retched, and I went back up, passing the sofa on which Fanny lay. I tiptoed with enough weight on my toes to let her know how considerate I was while she was deserting me. She blinked her eyes. I swear I heard her blink her eyes. Whenever I tell her that I hear her blink her eyes, she tells me I'm lying; but I can hear the damp slap of lash after I have made her weep.

In bed and warm again, noting the red digital numbers (5:29) and certain that I wouldn't sleep, I didn't. I read a book about men who kill each other for pay or for their honor. I forget which, and so did they. It was 5:45, the alarm would buzz at 6:00, and I would make a pot of coffee and start the wood stove; I would call Fanny and pour her coffee into her mug; I would apologize because I always did, and then she would forgive me if I hadn't been too awful—I didn't think I'd been that bad—and we would stagger through the day, exhausted but pretty sure we were all right, and we'd sleep that night, probably after sex, and then we'd waken in the same bed to the alarm at 6:00, or the dog, if he'd returned to the frozen deer carcass he'd been eating in the forest on our land. He loved what made him sick. The alarm went off, I got into jeans and woolen socks and a sweatshirt, and I went downstairs to let the dog in. He'd be hungry, of course.

I was the oldest college student in America, I thought. But of course I wasn't. There were always ancient women with their parchment for skin who graduated at seventy-nine from places like Barnard and the University of Georgia. I was only forty-two, and I hardly qualified as a student. I patrolled the college at night in a Bronco with a leaky exhaust system, and I went from room to room in the classroom buildings, kicking out students who were studying or humping in chairs—they'd do it anywhere—and answering emergency calls with my little blue light winking on top of the truck. I didn't carry a gun or a billy, but I had a flashlight that took six batteries and I'd used it twice on some of my overprivileged northeastern-playboy part-time classmates. On Tuesdays and Thursdays I would awaken at 6:00 with my wife, and I'd do my homework, and work around the house, and go to school at 11:30 to sit there for an hour and a half while thirty-five stomachs growled with hunger and boredom, and this guy gave instruction about books. Because I was on the staff, the college let me take a course for nothing every term. I was getting educated, in a kind of slow-motion way—it would have taken me something like fifteen or sixteen years to graduate, and I would no doubt get an F in gym and have to repeat—and there were times when I respected myself for it. Fanny often did, and that was fair incentive.

I am not unintelligent. *You are not an unintelligent writer,* my professor wrote on my paper about Nathaniel Hawthorne.[1] We had to read short stories, I and the other students, and then we had to write little essays about them. I told how I saw Kafka[2] and Hawthorne in a similar light, and I was not unintelligent, he said. He ran into me at dusk one time, when I answered a call about a dead battery and found out it was him. I jumped his Buick from the Bronco's battery, and he was looking me over, I could tell, while I clamped onto the terminals and cranked it up. He was a tall, handsome guy who never wore a suit. He wore khakis and sweaters, loafers or sneakers, and he was always talking to the female students with the brightest hair and best builds. But he couldn't get a Buick going on an ice-cold night, and he didn't know enough to look for cells going bad. I told him he was going to need a new battery and he looked me over the way men sometimes do with other men who fix their cars for them.

"Vietnam?"   5

I said, "Too old."

"Not at the beginning. Not if you were an adviser. So-called. Or one of the Phoenix Project fellas?"

I was wearing a watch cap made of navy wool and an old Marine fatigue jacket. Slick characters like my professor like it if you're a killer or at least a onetime middle-weight fighter. I smiled like I knew something. "Take it easy," I said, and I went back to the truck to swing around the cemetery at the top of the campus. They'd been known to screw in down-filled sleeping bags on horizontal stones up there, and the dean of students didn't want anybody dying of frostbite while joined at the hip to a matriculating fellow resident of our northeastern camp for the overindulged.

He blinked his high beams at me as I went. "You are not an unintelligent driver," I said.

Fanny had left me a bowl of something made with sausage and sauerkraut and pota-   10
toes, and the dog hadn't eaten too much more than his fair share. He watched me eat his leftovers and then make myself a king-sized drink composed of sourmash whiskey and ice. In our back room, which is on the northern end of the house, and cold for sit-ting in that close to dawn, I sat and watched the texture of the sky change. It was going to snow, and I wanted to see the storm come up the valley. I woke up that way, sitting in the rocker with its loose right arm, holding a watery drink, and thinking right away of the girl I'd convinced to go back inside. She'd been standing outside her dormitory, looking up at a window that was dark in the midst of all those lighted panes—they never turned a light off, and often let the faucets run half the night—crying onto her bathrobe. She was barefoot in shoe-pacs, the brown ones so many of them wore un-laced, and for all I know she was naked under her robe. She was beautiful, I thought,

---

[1]**Nathaniel Hawthorne** (1804–64): U.S. novelist and short story writer.   [2]**Franz Kafka** (1883–1924): Austrian novelist and short story writer who wrote nightmarish and surreal fiction.

and she was somebody's red-headed daughter, standing in a quadrangle how many miles from home weeping.

"He doesn't love anyone," the kid told me. "He doesn't love his wife—I mean his ex-wife. And he doesn't love the ex-wife before that, or the one before that. And you know what? He doesn't love me. I don't know anyone who *does!*"

"It isn't your fault if he isn't smart enough to love you," I said, steering her toward the truck.

She stopped. She turned. "You know him?"

I couldn't help it. I hugged her hard, and she let me, and then she stepped back, and of course I let her go. "Don't you *touch me!* Is this sexual harassment? Do you know the rules? Isn't this sexual harassment?"

"I'm sorry," I said at the door to the truck. "But I think I have to be able to give you 15 a grade before it counts as harassment."

She got in. I told her we were driving to the dean of students' house. She smelled like marijuana and something very sweet, maybe one of those coffee-with-cream liqueurs you don't buy unless you hate to drink.

As the heat of the truck struck her, she started going kind of clay-gray-green, and I reached across her to open the window.

"You touched my breast!" she said.

"It's the smallest one I've touched all night, I'm afraid."

She leaned out the window and gave her rendition of my dog. 20

But in my rocker, waking up, at whatever time in the morning in my silent house, I thought of her as someone's child. Which made me think of ours, of course. I went for more ice, and I started on a wet breakfast. At the door of the dean of students' house, she'd turned her chalky face to me and asked, "What grade would you give me, then?"

It was a week composed of two teachers locked out of their offices late at night, a Toyota with a flat and no spare, an attempted rape on a senior girl walking home from the library, a major fight outside a fraternity house (broken wrist and significant concussion), and variations on breaking-and-entering. I was scolded by the director of nonacademic services for embracing a student who was drunk; I told him to keep his job, but he called me back because I was right to hug her, he said, and also wrong, but what the hell, and would I please stay. I thought of the fringe benefits—graduation in only sixteen years—so I went back to work.

My professor assigned a story called "A Rose for Emily,"[3] and I wrote him a paper about the mechanics of corpse fucking, and how, since she clearly couldn't screw her dead boyfriend, she was keeping his rotten body in bed because she truly loved him. I called the paper "True Love." He gave me a B and wrote *See me, pls.* In his office after class, his feet up on his deck, he trimmed a cigar with a giant folding knife he kept in his drawer.

"You got to clean the hole out," he said, "or they don't draw."

"I don't smoke," I said. 25

"Bad habit. Real *habit*, though. I started in smoking 'em in Georgia, in the service. My C.O. smoked 'em. We collaborated on a brothel inspection one time, and we ended

---

[3] **"A Rose for Emily"**: A story by William Faulkner.

up smoking these with a couple of women—" He waggled his eyebrows at me, now that his malehood was established.

"Were the women smoking them too?"

He snorted laughter through his nose while the greasy smoke came curling off his thin, dry lips. "They were pretty smoky, I'll tell ya!" Then he propped his feet—he was wearing cowboy boots that day—and he sat forward. "It's a little hard to explain. But—hell. You just don't say *fuck* when you write an essay for a college prof. Okay?" Like a scoutmaster with a kid he'd caught in the outhouse jerking off: "All right? You don't wanna do that."

"Did it shock you?"

"Fuck, no, it didn't shock me. I just told you. It violates certain proprieties."   30

"But if I'm writing it to you, like a letter—"

"You're writing it for posterity. For some mythical reader someplace, not just me. You're making a *statement*."

"Right. My statement said how hard it must be for a woman to fuck with a corpse."

"And a point worth making. I said so. Here."

"But you said I shouldn't say it."   35

"No. Listen. Just because you're talking about fucking, you don't have to say *fuck*. Does that make it any clearer?"

"No."

"I wish you'd lied to me just now," he said.

I nodded. I did too.

"Where'd you do your service?" he asked.   40

"Baltimore. Baltimore, Maryland.

"What's in Baltimore?"

"Railroads. I liaised on freight runs of army matériel. I killed a couple of bums on the road with my bare hands, though."

He snorted again, but I could see how disappointed he was. He'd been banking on my having been a murderer. Interesting guy in one of my classes, he must have told some terrific woman at an overpriced meal: I just *know* the guy was a rubout specialist in the Nam, he had to have said. I figured I should come to work wearing my fatigue jacket and a red bandanna tied around my head. Say "Man" to him a couple of times, hang a fist in the air for grief and solidarity, and look terribly worn, exhausted by experiences he was fairly certain that he envied me. His dungarees were ironed, I noticed.

On Saturday we went back to the campus because Fanny wanted to see a movie called   45
The Seven Samurai. I fell asleep, and I'm afraid I snored. She let me sleep until the auditorium was almost empty. Then she kissed me awake. "Who was screaming in my dream?" I asked her.

"Kurosawa," she said.

"Who?"

"Ask your professor friend."

I looked around, but he wasn't there. "Not an un-weird man," I said.

We went home and cleaned up after the dog and put him out. We drank a little   50
Spanish brandy and went upstairs and made love. I was fairly premature, you might say, but one way and another by the time we fell asleep we were glad to be there with

each other, and glad that it was Sunday coming up the valley toward us, and nobody with it. The dog was howling at another dog someplace, or at the moon, or maybe just his moon-thrown shadow on the snow. I did not strangle him when I opened the back door and he limped happily past me and stumbled up the stairs. I followed him into our bedroom and groaned for just being satisfied as I got into bed. You'll notice I didn't say fuck.

He stopped me in the hall after class on a Thursday, and asked me How's it going, just one of the kickers drinking sour beer and eating pickled eggs and watching the tube in a country bar. How's it goin. I nodded. I wanted a grade from the man, and I did want to learn about expressing myself. I nodded and made what I thought was a smile. He'd let his mustache grow out and his hair grow longer. He was starting to wear dark shirts with lighter ties. I thought he looked like someone in *The Godfather*. He still wore those light little loafers or his high-heeled cowboy boots. His corduroy pants looked baggy. I guess he wanted them to look that way. He motioned me to the wall of the hallway, and he looked and said, "How about the Baltimore stuff?"

I said, "Yeah?"

"Was that really true?" He was almost blinking, he wanted so much for me to be a damaged Vietnam vet just looking for a bell tower to climb into and start firing from. The college didn't have a bell tower you could get up into, though I'd once spent an ugly hour chasing a drunken ATO down from the roof of the observatory. "You were just clocking through boxcars in Baltimore?"

"I said, "Nah."

"I thought so!" He gave a kind of sigh.   55

"I killed people," I said.

"You know, I could have sworn you did," he said.

I nodded, and he nodded back. I'd made him so happy.

The assignment was to write something to influence somebody. He called it Rhetoric and Persuasion. We read an essay by George Orwell and "A Modest Proposal" by Jonathan Swift. I liked the Orwell better, but I wasn't comfortable with it. He talked about "niggers," and I felt him saying it two ways.

I wrote "Ralph the Duck."   60

Once upon a time, there was a duck named Ralph who didn't have any feathers on either wing. So when the cold wind blew, Ralph said, Brr, and shivered and shook.

What's the matter? Ralph's mommy asked.

I'm *cold*, Ralph said.

Oh, the mommy said. Here. I'll keep you warm.

So she spread her big, feathery wings, and hugged Ralph tight, and when the cold   65
wind blew, Ralph was warm and snuggly, and fell fast asleep.

■ ■ ■

The next Thursday, he was wearing canvas pants and hiking boots. He mentioned kind of casually to some of the girls in the class how whenever there was a storm he wore his Lake District walking outfit. He had a big, hairy sweater on. I kept waiting for him to make a noise like a mountain goat. But the girls seemed to like it. His boots made a creaky squeak on the linoleum of the hall when he caught up with me after class.

"As I told you," he said, "it isn't unappealing. It's just—not a college theme."

"Right," I said. "Okay. You want me to do it over?"

"No," he said. "Not at all. The D will remain your grade. But I'll read something else if you want to write it."

"This'll be fine," I said.

"Did you understand the assignment?"

"Write something to influence someone—Rhetoric and Persuasion."

We were at his office door and the redheaded kid who had gotten sick in my truck was waiting for him. She looked at me like one of us was in the wrong place, which struck me as accurate enough. He was interested in getting into his office with the redhead, but he remembered to turn around and flash me a grin he seemed to think he was known for.

Instead of going on shift a few hours after class, the way I'm supposed to, I told my supervisor I was sick, and I went home. Fanny was frightened when I came in, because I don't get sick and I don't miss work. She looked at my face and she grew sad. I kissed her hello and went upstairs to change. I always used to change my clothes when I was a kid, as soon as I came from school. I put on jeans and a flannel shirt and thick wool socks, and I made myself a dark drink of sourmash. Fanny poured herself some wine and came into the cold northern room a few minutes later. I was sitting in the rocker, looking over the valley. The wind was lining up a lot of rows of cloud so that the sky looked like a baked trout when you lift the skin off. "It'll snow," I said to her.

She sat on the old sofa and waited. After a while, she said, "I wonder why they always call it a mackerel sky?"

"Good eating, mackerel," I said.

Fanny said, "Shit! You're never that laconic unless you feel crazy. What's wrong? Who'd you punch out at the playground?"

"We had to write a composition," I said.

"Did he like it?"

"He gave me a D."

"Well, you're familiar enough with D's. I never saw you get this low over a grade."

"I wrote about Ralph the Duck."

She said, "You did?" She said, "Honey." She came over and stood beside the rocker and leaned into me and hugged my head and neck. "Honey," she said. "Honey."

It was the worst of the winter's storms, and one of the worst in years. That afternoon they closed the college, which they almost never do. But the roads were jammed with snow over ice, and now it was freezing rain on top of that, and the only people working at the school that night were the operator who took emergency calls and me. Everyone else had gone home except the students, and most of them were inside. The ones who weren't were drunk, and I kept on sending them in and telling them to act like grown-ups. A number of them said they were, and I really couldn't argue. I had the bright beams on, the defroster set high, the little blue light winking, and a thermos of sourmash and hot coffee that I sipped from every time I had to get out of the truck or every time I realized how cold all that wetness was out there.

About eight o'clock, as the rain was turning back to snow and the cold was worse, the roads impossible, just as I was done helping a county sander on the edge of the campus pull a panel truck out of a snowbank, I got the emergency call from the college operator. We had a student missing. The roommate thought the kid was headed for the quarry. This meant I had to get the Bronco up on a narrow road above the campus, above the old cemetery, into all kinds of woods and rough track that I figured would be chocked with ice and snow. Any kid up there would really have to want to be there, and I couldn't go in on foot, because you'd only want to be there on account of drugs, booze, or craziness, and either way I'd be needing blankets and heat, and then a fast ride down to the hospital in town. So I dropped into four-wheel drive to get me up the hill above the campus, bucking snow and sliding on ice, putting all the heater's warmth up onto the windshield because I couldn't see much more than swarming snow. My feet were still cold from the tow job, and it didn't seem to matter that I had on heavy socks and insulated boots I'd coated with waterproofing. I shivered, and I thought of Ralph the Duck.

I had to grind the rest of the way, from the cemetery, in four-wheel low, and in spite of the cold I was smoking my gearbox by the time I was close enough to the quarry—they really did take a lot of rocks for the campus buildings from there—to see I'd have to make my way on foot to where she was. It was a kind of scooped-out shape, maybe four or five stories high, where she stood—well, wobbled is more like it. She was as chalky as she'd been the last time, and her red hair didn't catch the light anymore. It just lay on her like something that had died on top of her head. She was in a white nightgown that was plastered to her body. She had her arms crossed as if she wanted to be warm. She swayed, kind of, in front of the big, dark, scooped-out rock face, where the trees and brush had been cleared for trucks and earthmovers. She looked tiny against all the darkness. From where I stood, I could see the snow driving down in front of the lights I'd left on, but I couldn't see it near her. All it looked like around her was dark. She was shaking with the cold, and she was crying.

I had a blanket with me, and I shoved it down the front of my coat to keep it dry for her, and because I was so cold. I waved. I stood in the lights and I waved. I don't know what she saw—a big shadow, maybe. I surely didn't reassure her, because when she saw me she backed up, until she was near the face of the quarry. She couldn't go any farther.

I called, "Hello! I brought a blanket. Are you cold? I thought you might want a blanket."

Her roommates had told the operator about pills, so I didn't bring her the coffee laced with mash. I figured I didn't have all that much time, anyway, to get her down and pumped out. The booze with whatever pills she'd taken would make her die that much faster.

I hated that word. Die. It made me furious with her. I heard myself seething when I breathed. I pulled my scarf and collar up above my mouth. I didn't want her to see how close I might come to wanting to kill her because she wanted to die. 90

I called, "Remember me?"

I was closer now. I could see the purple mottling of her skin. I didn't know if it was cold or dying. It probably didn't matter much to distinguish between them right now, I thought. That made me smile. I felt the smile, and I pulled the scarf down so she could look at it. She didn't seem awfully reassured.

"You're the sexual harassment guy," she said. She said it very slowly. Her lips were clumsy. It was like looking at a ventriloquist's dummy.

"I gave you an A," I said.

"When?"

"It's a joke," I said. "You don't want me making jokes. You want me to give you a nice warm blanket, though. And then you want me to take you home."

She leaned against the rock face when I approached. I pulled the blanket out, then zipped my jacket back up. The snow had stopped. I realized, and that wasn't really a very good sign. It felt like an arctic cold descending in its place. I held the blanket out to her, but she only looked at it.

"You'll just have to turn me in," I said. "I'm gonna hug you again."

She screamed, "No more! I don't want any more hugs!"

But she kept her arms on her chest, and I wrapped the blanket around her and stuffed a piece into each of her tight, small fists. I didn't know what to do for her feet. Finally, I got down on my haunches in front of her. She crouched down too, protecting herself.

"No," I said. "No. You're fine."

I took off the woolen mittens I'd been wearing. Mittens keep you warmer than gloves because they trap your hand's heat around the fingers and palms at once. Fanny had knitted them for me. I put a mitten as far onto each of her feet as I could. She let me. She was going to collapse, I thought.

"Now, let's go home," I said. "Let's get you better."

With her funny, stiff lips, she said. "I've been very self-indulgent and weird and I'm sorry. But I'd really like to die." She sounded so reasonable that I found myself nodding in agreement as she spoke.

"You can't just die," I said.

"Aren't I dying already? I took all of them, and then"—she giggled like a child, which of course is what she was—"I borrowed different ones from other people's rooms. See, this isn't some teenage cry for like *help*. Understand? I'm seriously interested in death and I have to like stay out here a little longer and fall asleep. All right?"

"You can't do that," I said. "You ever hear of Vietnam?"

"I saw that movie," she said. "With the opera in it? *Apocalypse?* Whatever."

"I was there!" I said. "I killed people! I helped to kill them! And when they die, you see their bones later on. You dream about their bones and blood on the ends of the splintered ones, and this kind of mucous stuff coming out of their eyes. You probably heard of guys having dreams like that, didn't you? Whacked-out Vietnam vets? That's me, see? So I'm telling you, I know about dead people and their eyeballs and everything falling out. And people keep dreaming about the dead people they knew, see? You can't make people dream about you like that! It isn't fair!"

"You dream about me?" She was ready to go. She was ready to fall down, and I was going to lift her up and get her to the truck.

"I will," I said. "If you die."

"I want you to," she said. Her lips were hardly moving now. Her eyes were closed. "I want you all to."

I dropped my shoulder and put it into her waist and picked her up and carried her down to the Bronco. She was talking, but not a lot, and her voice leaked down my back. I jammed her into the truck and wrapped the blanket around her better and then put another one down around her feet. I strapped her in with the seat belt. She was shaking, and her eyes were closed and her mouth open. She was breathing. I checked that twice, once when I strapped her in, and then again when I strapped myself in and backed up hard into a sapling and took it down. I got us into first gear, held the clutch in, leaned over to listen for breathing, heard it—heard it—shallow panting, like a kid asleep on your lap for a nap—and then I put the gear in and howled down the hillside on what I thought might be the road.

We passed the cemetery. I told her that was good sign. She didn't respond. I found myself panting too, as if we were breathing for each other. It made me dizzy, but I couldn't stop. We passed the highest dorm, and I dropped the truck into four-wheel high. The cab smelled like burnt oil and hot metal. We were past the chapel now, and the observatory, the president's house, then the bookstore. I had the blue light winking and the V-6 roaring, and I drove on the edge of out-of-control, sensing the skids just before I slid into them, and getting back out of them as I needed to. I took a little fender off once, and a bit of the corner of a classroom building, but I worked us back on course, and all I needed to do now was negotiate the sharp left turn around the Administration Building past the library, then floor it for the straight run to the town's main street and then the hospital.

I was panting into the mike, and the operator kept saying, "Say again?"   115

I made myself slow down some, and I said we'd need stomach pumping, and to get the names of the pills from her friends in the dorm, and I'd be there in less than five or we were crumpled up someplace and dead.

"Roger," the radio said. "Roger all that." My throat tightened and tears came into my eyes. They were helping us, they'd told me: Roger.

I said to the girl, whose head was slumped and whose face looked too blue all through its whiteness, "You know, I had girl once. My wife, Fanny. She and I had small girl one time."

I reached over and touched her cheek. It was cold. The truck swerved, and I got my hands on the wheel. I'd made the turn past the Ad Building using just my left. "I can do it in the dark," I sang to no tune I'd ever learned. "I can do it with one hand." I said to her, "We had a girl child, very small. Now, I do not want you dying."

I came to the campus gates doing fifty on the ice and snow, smoking the engine,   120
grinding the clutch, and I bounced off a wrought iron fence to give me the curve going left that I needed. On a pool table, it would have been a bank shot worth applause. The town cop picked me up and got out ahead of me and let the street have all the lights and noise it could want. We banged up to the emergency room entrance and I was out and at the other door before the cop on duty, Elmo St. John, could loosen his seat belt. I loosened hers, and they took her away from me. I tried to talk to them, but they made me sit down and do my shaking on a dirty sofa decorated with drawings of little spinning wheels. Somebody brought me hot coffee, I think it was Elmo, but I couldn't hold it.

"They won't," he kept saying to me. "They won't."

"What?"

"You just been sitting there for a minute and a half like St. Vitus dancing, telling me, 'Don't let her die. Don't let her die.' "

"Oh."

"You all *right?*"   125

"How about the kid?"

"They'll tell us soon."

"She better be all right."

"That's right."

"She—somebody's gonna have to tell me plenty if she isn't." 130

"That's right."

"She better not die this time," I guess I said.

Fanny came downstairs to look for me. I was at the northern windows, looking through the mullions down the valley to the faint red line along the mounds and little peaks of the ridge beyond the valley. The sun was going to come up, and I was looking for it.

Fanny stood behind me. I could hear her. I could smell her hair and the sleep on her. The crimson line widened, and I squinted at it. I heard the dog limp in behind her, catching up. He panted and I knew why his panting sounded familiar. She put her hands on my shoulders and arms. I made muscles to impress her with, and then I let them go, and let my head drop down until my chin was on my chest.

"I didn't think you'd be able to sleep after that," Fanny said. 135

"I brought enough adrenaline home to run a football team."

"But you hate being a hero, huh? You're hiding in here because somebody's going to call, or come over, and want to talk to you—her parents for shooting sure, sooner or later. Or is that supposed to be part of the service up at the playground! Saving their suicidal daughters. Almost dying to find them in the woods and driving too fast for any weather, much less what we had last night. Getting their babies home. The bastards." She was crying. I knew she would be, sooner or later. I could hear the soft sound of her lashes. She sniffed and I could feel her arm move as she felt for the tissues on the coffee table.

"I have them over here," I said. "On the windowsill."

"Yes." She blew her nose, and the dog thumped his tail. He seemed to think it one of Fanny's finer tricks, and he had wagged for her for thirteen years whenever she'd done it. "Well, you're going to have to talk to them."

"I will," I said. "I will." The sun was in our sky now, climbing. We had built the 140 room so we could watch it climb. "I think that jackass with the smile, my prof? She showed up a lot at his office, the last few weeks. He called her 'my advisee,' you know? The way those guys sound about what they're achieving by getting up and shaving and going to work and saying the same thing every day? Every year? Well, she was his advisee, I bet. He was shoving home the old advice."

"She'll be okay," Fanny said. "Her parents will take her home and love her up and get her some help." She began to cry again, then she stopped. She blew her nose, and the dog's tail thumped. She kept a hand between my shoulder and my neck. "So tell me what you'll tell a waiting world. How'd you talk her out?"

"Well, I didn't, really. I got up close and picked her up and carried her is all."

"You didn't say anything?"

"Sure I did. Kid's standing in the snow outside of a lot of pills, you're gonna say something.

"So what'd you say?" 145

"I told her stories," I said. "I did Rhetoric and Persuasion."

Fanny said, "Then you go in early on Thursday, you go in half an hour early, and you get that guy to jack up your grade." ●

Allegra Goodman (1967–)

The Local Production of Cinderella *1999*

You couldn't tell anymore that they had separate desks. For fifteen years, Roselva and Helen had worked together at H.D.H.S., the Hawaii Department of Human Services, and their two gray steel desks, pushed together in the Great Hall of the State Administration Building, were covered with layers of notes and client files and forms to be filled out. This was in 1978, and they worked on twin sea-foam-green I.B.M. Selectric typewriters.

Roselva was Chinese-Hawaiian-Portuguese. She was a religious woman and attended Calvary-by-the-Sea Church. Her skin was deeply tanned, her short hair smooth and black. Her features were soft, as were her brown eyes. She had a gentle face, and was always patient with her clients, whether they were runaways or battered wives, drug-addicted mothers or schizophrenic homeless people. She believed in her job; she believed in human services. Helen, on the other hand, had grown up on the mainland, in Maine, and was of German-Lutheran ancestry. Her skin was fair, her eyes dark. Her voice was weary. She talked all the time about how she wanted to leave social work and do something for herself—music or fine cooking or writing. The clients depressed her. She thought some people were just bad.

Of all the teams in the Great Hall, Roselva and Helen had been together the longest. They were true partners as they sifted the stacks of paperwork before them; effortlessly, they plucked forms from their shared mess. Often they took brown bags from their desk drawers and ate lunch together while they worked. On easy days, or after home visits, they ate outside, sitting on a dark-green bench in Tamarind Park. In the enormous shade of a monkey-pod tree, they would talk about Helen's daughters and Roselva's son, Thad, about their husbands, and about cleaning house.

On this day at the end of May, walking back to the office after lunch, they crossed South Beretania Street while they talked about Roselva's big night coming up. Thad's girlfriend, Clarysse, was a ballet major at Chaminade University of Honolulu, and that night she was going to dance the title role in "Cinderella." Everyone was going— Roselva's family, and Clarysse's. Helen and her husband, Sid, had tickets, too.

"I'm so nervous," Roselva confessed.   5

"Why?" asked Helen. "You don't have to get up and dance onstage."

"I'm nervous for Clarysse," Roselva said. "When she gets up there, I'm going to get butterflies for sure. She's my daughter, practically."

Helen sighed. For six years, Thad and Clarysse had been planning to get married. "Have they set a new date?" Helen asked.

"No," Roselva said. "I think her parents—"

"Yeah, they're pigs," Helen said. She often finished Roselva's sentences, although   10 not with the words Roselva would have chosen. "She's still holding out for the big wedding, huh? Or maybe she doesn't really want to marry Thad."

"Of course she does!"

All around them, lawyers in suits were streaming back to work. Men in aloha shirts and dress pants were walking up the steps to the state capitol building, with its open crater roof.

"Maybe they'll elope," Helen said.

Roselva was distracted. She was feeling guilty. That morning, she had read some of Helen's private writing. She had not done anything so clearly wrong since she was a child. She had come in to work a few minutes early, and put her purse in the file drawer, the way she always did. She began sorting through the papers in the "in" box, and there among them was a letter from Helen. It was written in black ink on the good heavy-weight bond paper. But it wasn't a letter to Roselva, or to anyone in particular. It was addressed, "Dear People of Hawaii." Roselva looked away. Then she glanced back. She hesitated just a moment. And then, in the empty Department of Human Services, she read the whole thing. Then she read it again. It made her queasy, but she couldn't stop. It was a cuckoo letter. Some kind of scary joke. This could not be Helen's writing, she thought. And yet it was her handwriting. This was not the Helen she knew. She wanted to hide the letter somewhere, stuff it away where she couldn't see it. But she put it back where she'd found it, among the pink, yellow, and white forms on the desk.

The letter still sat there when they returned from lunch. Maybe it was a warning 15 sign. Maybe it was a plea for help. In which case Roselva should speak up. That was what she always told her clients' families: first ask if anything is wrong.

As soon as Helen got up to go to the ladies' room, Roselva scooted forward in her swivel chair and slid the letter out once more.

Dear People of Hawaii:

The missionaries came to Hawaii in their Victorian dresses, whalebones and jet buttons. Imagine the black dresses soaking up the heat.

Missionaries planted roses—a buffet for gnats and slugs, caterpillars and aphids, not to mention black mold.

Now the universities plant their sick ideas. People of Hawaii, professors spread their ideology over you each day. They twist your history. Why do you sit silently in the valleys? Why do you sit patiently in the classrooms? Cut the white men down whether from New York or Michigan. Cut them down and plant them. Let them become succulent plants, night-blooming cereus blossoming under the moon. Heads of coral for the reef fish.

O People of Hawaii, I see your shopping malls and hotel luaus but then I see your revolution. A red tide, a taste of salt.

A new Queen rises in the fountain at the foot of Diamond Head. She wears a twelve-strand necklace of braided human hair, and a pendant of polished ivory. She outlaws ukuleles and slack-key guitars. But will the people rise up from their lei stands by the airport and romp across the asphalt back to the green valleys to reclaim their taro patches? Will you leave the front desks at the hotels and go back to plait pili grass and hold your ancient games? Stick throwing, javelin, smooth black rock bowling, and wrestling.

Without knowing it, Roselva had begun to read this letter aloud to herself. "The Queen will die," she whispered. "The dolphins will rise up and circle each island. The tide will come in up to the mountaintops. Hotels will dissolve like sand castles. In catamarans the children will sail from Pearl Harbor, gliding over sunken battleships. Honolulu will become a lost city, whales swishing through lobbies. Green sea turtles nosing empty rooms. The great white shark with pinpoint eyes will swim through sunken streets. There will be no humans left but bones and graves under the water."

What was this? What was this writing? It was like a love letter never sent. Or a speech Helen never gave. It was a crazy letter, some kind of crazy story. But Helen never acted crazy in real life. She was sarcastic in real life, always talking about her husband,

Sid, who taught at the university, and their three teen-age daughters. The professor and the princesses, she called them. Helen was cynical, maybe, but she'd never said a word about the old Hawaii. She talked about the old movies at the Honolulu Academy of Arts—Fred Astaire and Ginger Rogers. This letter wasn't Helen. And the place Helen described—the turtles and water? What was that place? Not Honolulu.

"Let me give you a piece of advice," Helen said.

Roselva practically jumped out of her chair. Helen was back from the ladies' room. 20 "Advice?" she asked.

"If you really want the kids to get married, offer to pay for the wedding."

Helen was talking about Thad and Clarysse, but Roselva's mind was still with the dolphins and the rising tide. That afternoon, she hung back a little until Helen left. She gathered up the letter along with the other papers on the desk and put the whole pile in her silk-screened orchid-pattern canvas tote bag.

Roselva's house was hot. She and her husband, Jimmy, lived in Niu Valley, and they had glassed in the lanai in the back. They had wanted a den, but they got a greenhouse effect. A ranch with three bedrooms and two plumeria trees in front, it was a tract house like every other one in the flat bottom of the valley. Roselva pulled up after work and parked her Dodge Omni in the carport. The car had a pyramidal sign on the roof, with "Student Driver" on one side and "Jimmy's Auto School" on the other. This was her husband's business, and his car, a green 1975 Pontiac, had a similar sign on its roof.

Indoors, Roselva opened the jalousies to cool down the living room and kitchen. Thad was already home. Jimmy would be next. The dance performance was that night, and her best friend was turning crazy on her. As if she didn't have enough to worry about. Of course, who told her to go around reading other people's private mail?

She stood at the counter, her brain zinging. She tried to cool down and watch 25 Thad eat. He was wearing gym shorts and an ancient T-shirt printed "13th Annual Haleiwa Surfing Classic." Long ago, Clarysse's parents, Edwin and Mitsuko, had announced that they were never going to pay for any wedding between Clarysse and Thad. Clarysse's parents tolerated Thad, but they did not approve of him. They thought their daughter should marry someone with a career like law or medicine, who could support a ballerina daughter. Clarysse's father owned a pool-cleaning-supplies store, and her mother taught the art of ikebana.

Thad bolted down his chicken and rice. He got up to look for a glass, then leaned over and drank from the kitchen tap as if it were a water fountain.

"Thad," Roselva said.

"Gotta go, Mom," he told her.

"It's still early yet," she said.

"Call is six o'clock!" he told her. He ran out to the driveway and started up Roselva's 30 car. He was taking Clarysse down to the Chaminade University theatre.

Any minute, Jimmy would come home. Roselva changed into a deep-green muumuu. She tried to read the newspaper. She opened the refrigerator and checked on the leis for Clarysse: a three-strand lei of pink Maui rosebuds and a matching haku lei of pink rosebuds, tiny orchids, and ferns, woven into a garland. The leis rested on damp paper towels in their clear plastic boxes.

The door slammed. It was Jimmy, in the living room. She heard him take his keys and wallet and smash them down onto the coffee table. She knew exactly what had happened. Jeannine Chung had failed her driving test. Patiently, painstakingly, Jimmy had been teaching this student, and had brought her along to a point where she was ready to take the exam. More than ready: prepared to ace that driving test. Jimmy had brought her to the D.M.V., let her take his driving-school car out on the test drive with the state examiner, gently pushed his student out of the nest—and the kid had flopped. Randall or Mike or one of the other examiners—Jimmy knew them all—had shuddered in the car and screamed at Jeannine, "*Never* do that. Never, *never* do that. Return to the testing station. Get out of the vehicle. Zero. You flunk!" Jimmy was Jeannine's instructor, and he was disgraced. Roselva knew how hard this hit him. He was the most careful teacher in the world. He never took a student to the D.M.V. until he or she was a perfect driver. But once in a while it all went wrong. Jimmy's flawless student driver would get to the test and fall apart. Panic while turning left into traffic. Fail to line up properly while parking. Block an intersection and turn into a snivelling mess.

Jimmy didn't say a word while they ate dinner. He didn't speak as they got into his car and drove to Chaminade. Roselva wanted to tell him what she'd done, and ask his advice. But she knew better than to open her mouth.

The car jerked ahead in the rushhour traffic. Tight-lipped, Jimmy accelerated to catch the tail end of a green light. They lurched forward. "Stop that!" Jimmy said to Roselva.

"Stop what?" she asked. Then she looked down at her feet. Without realizing it 35 she had been correcting Jimmy's driving with the car's specially added instructional passenger-side brake. Jimmy used the brake all the time to curb his wayward driving students, but he couldn't stand it when Roselva used the brake on him.

When they got to Chaminade, Jimmy let her out in front of the white, Spanish-style auditorium and drove off to park. Thad was waiting outside the auditorium door, and Roselva gave him the leis for Clarysse. Then she gave the usher her ticket and opened the door to the auditorium. The place was chilly, full of expectant talk. She went down the center aisle, past rows full of people. She was looking for Clarysse's parents, or for empty seats, but all she found were rows filled with strangers, and seats that were saved with programs folded over their backs. Then she heard someone calling her from down front.

"Roselva!" Helen was standing there, in the center of the third row. She had saved seats for her and Jimmy. Thad was there already, sitting next to her. Sid hadn't been able to come, Helen said.

"Thanks." Roselva squeezed in next to Helen. "Jimmy's parking. Oh, there he is." Her voice was breathy; she was so nervous. She should say something to Helen. She should speak up right now. The red velvet curtain loomed in front of her. The lights went down. She felt a sympathetic stagefright. When Jimmy took his seat she said a silent prayer. Lord Jesus, help us. Help Clarysse dance. And forgive me for what I did today. Show me the way.

Music started up from speakers in the wings. The curtains parted and the Chaminade dance majors appeared. Roselva had to put her glasses on in a hurry. The dancers jumped and pranced to the strains of Prokofiev, some more graceful and some less so, the women sometimes tall and willowy, in their tights and tutus, but sometimes short, with big thighs. Roselva's seat was excellent, almost too good. She could see the sweat trickling on the ballerinas' faces, glistening in their hair. When the dancers spun and turned, sweat flew off them as if they had been swimming and had just sprung out of the water.

Helen nudged Roselva. There was Clarysse. Her body was slender and her skin fair. 40 Her makeup made her look almost European. She had blushing pink cheeks and wide, blue-shadowed eyes. In her costume of gold lace, she descended the grand staircase at the ball. Her black hair was beautifully pinned up, her head suddenly small.

When Clarysse danced with her prince, she became more ordinary. The prince was a paid ringer from the Honolulu Opera Theatre, and he had a distant, professional manner. He looked less like an ardent lover than like a seasoned horse trainer as he led Clarysse this way and that. Her toe shoes clopped delicately on the wood floor of the stage as he took her through her paces. Oh, poor Thad, Roselva thought. What was he going to do with a dance major? How was he ever going to support her? But then, when Clarysse went into a solo, Roselva almost forgot her worries. When she sprang up in the air and beat he pointed feet, Roselva cheered silently against gravity. Even when Clarysse landed on the ground, she fell back lightly. She was on the verge of flying. Any second it was going to happen—Clarysse would become a princess and a bride, the fairy-tale star of her dream wedding.

All the way home, Roselva wished she had spoken to Helen. There Helen had been all evening, sitting and applauding with her. She had come to Clarysse's performance and sat at Roselva's side. And what had Roselva done? Only betrayed her colleague, her friend of fifteen years. In the car, Roselva couldn't stop thinking about Helen's words. The missionaries in their Victorian dresses. White men becoming succulent plants. What was that all about?

"Jimmy," she said. "You notice anything about Helen?"

"No," he said.

A red tide and a taste of salt, she thought. The white shark with pinpoint eyes.   45

At home in their bedroom, Roselva changed into her nightgown. Jimmy was lying in his underwear watching the news. His eyes were half closed.

"Helen wrote a letter," Roselva said. "I never should have read it, but—I'm worried she's sick. You think she's sick?" She tapped her head.

Jimmy didn't answer.

Roselva turned off the television. In a flash Jimmy opened his eyes. "I was watching that," he said.

"Can I show you this?" Roselva took Helen's letter from her bag. She handed Jimmy   50
his reading glasses and he read. He read the whole thing in silence, then handed it back.

"You sure that's Helen's?" he said.

"It's her handwriting," Roselva said.

"Maybe she copied it."

"Where would she copy something like that from?"

Jimmy shrugged.   55

"I just found it on the desk," Roselva said, "and now I can't figure out what to do."

"Put it back," Jimmy suggested.

"And what if it's some kind of call for help?"

"We just saw her," Jimmy said. He had turned on the news again. His eyes were starting to close.

Roselva bent her head down close to the words in the letter. Then she had an inspi-   60
ration. "Jimmy," she said. "This letter is a prophecy."

"Prophecy for what?"

"For the future," Roselva said. Her voice was hushed. "Look," she said. "The dolphins will rise up. The water will cover the city. There will be no humans left."

Jimmy opened his eyes. "What type prophecy is that?" he said.

"Armageddon type," Roselva replied. She lay down on the bed. For the first time that day, she felt some relief.

As soon as she came in on Monday morning, Roselva saw the newspaper clippings on the desk. Helen had clipped the review from her copy of the Sunday paper:

LOCAL PRODUCTION OF CINDERELLA TAKES WING

Chaminade University's spring offering, "Cinderella," sparkled with innovative choreography, energetic dancing, and dazzling costumes.

In the demanding title role, Clarysse Leong danced with verve and elegant extension. She was a lovely presence on the stage, and we hope to see much more of her in years to come.

"'Verve,'" Helen said to Roselva. "Not bad."   65

"Not too shabby," Roselva agreed.

"But you have to wonder what she's going to do with herself after graduation."

Roselva stared at Helen. "That's exactly what I was thinking at the performance."

"Poor Thad," Helen said.

"Poor Thad! That's just what I was thinking." Roselva shook her head.   70

But Helen was already at the steel file cabinet, gathering folders. They had a visit out on the North Shore. A homeless Tongan family camped out on the beach. Roselva felt sad whenever they drove out there. The family tent leaked. Mr. Tafesau was always trying to use the pay phone up the road to look for work trimming trees.

"Don't you start getting down already," Helen said, looking over at her.

"I can't believe it," Roselva whispered. "You've been reading my mind."

"Oh, Roselva, quit it." Helen took out her car keys.

"I mean, I read your letter." Roselva took it out of her bag and placed it on Helen's   75
desk. "I'm sorry," she said.

For just a second Helen was taken aback Then she shrugged. "My shrink says I should write. He says I have a lot of anger. I'm working on that."

"You're blessed," Roselva said.

"Yeah, I guess," Helen said. "I'm blessed with a lousy marriage, scum for clients, a daughter sleeping with her entire senior class."

"You're blessed with prophecy," Roselva said. "You see how it's all going to be."

"Oh, Roselva," Helen said. "I can't see two steps in front of me."   80

Roselva shook her head. "Look at this." She picked up Helen's letter. "No more selling leis. Whales in the lobby."

Helen took the letter, crumpled it up, and tossed it in the trash bin next to her desk.

Roselva blinked. She nearly went to fish the letter out again.

"That's just made up," Helen said. "None of that's going to happen."

"No, no," Roselva insisted. "You have the gift, you know the future."   85

"Fine. If you believe that kind of thing. It's like you believe in angels and Heaven and Hell."

"I do," Roselva said.

Helen shrugged. "O.K. I'm not going to argue with you."

"And what do you believe?"

"When you're dead, you're dead," Helen said. "That's the beauty of it. You just   90
stop."

"And then what?"

"Then nothing."

"I can't believe that's true."

"That's why they invented Heaven," Helen said.

"It's not," Roselva said.   95

"O.K., whatever you say," said Helen. "Listen, if you get up there, I'll go with you."

"But not too soon," Roselva said.

"It'll be like this," Helen said, and she leaned close. Roselva looked at her earnestly—just a little bit on guard, since Helen loved to make fun. And Helen said in her weary, half-serious voice, "We'll grow very old. And then we'll go to Heaven in clouds of smoke. Or to the shark palace. Wherever we go we'll kick off our shoes, and it'll all be the same. I'm still going to be working with you." ●

Explorations of the Text

1. What are your first impressions of the point of view of the narrators? Are they reliable narrators? Discuss voice and tone.

2. Summarize the main plot and subplots in both stories. How do they connect and reinforce each other? Why does Busch include the hints at the relationship between the professor and the red-headed girl? Is this subplot necessary to the development of the story?

3. Both works present stories within stories. Discuss the significance of the story of "Ralph the Duck." What does it mean to the narrator and to his wife? To the reader? In "The Local Production of Cinderella," examine the significance of Helen's letter and the Cinderella ballet as symbolic motifs. Discuss the levels of irony in both works.

4. Compare visions of friendship and community presented in both works.

The Reading/Writing Connection

1. "Think" Topic: In "Ralph the Duck" is the narrator a sympathetic character? Why or why not? Explain your choice.

2. **Write an Argument:** In "Ralph the Duck" do you think that the narrator actually went to war? Argue pro or con.

3. In "The Local Production of Cinderella," do you think that Helen is slightly mad? Argue pro or con.

4. In both stories how would the stories change if they were narrated from different points of view? For example, in "Ralph the Duck," how would the story change if it were narrated in third person from the wife's point of view? Write a portion of the story from this perspective and analyze the results. What is the impact of the change in point of view?

Ideas for Writing

1. Discuss war and Armageddon as central symbols in the two stories. How do these symbols connect the layers of the plot and suggest themes of the works?

2. The world of these stories can be described in terms of Mary Louise Pratt's vision of contact zones: "social spaces where cultures meet, clash, and grapple with each other, often in contexts of highly asymmetrical relations of power, such as colonialism, slavery, or their aftermaths as they are lived out in many parts of the world today." How do these social "spaces" affect the characters' attitudes, values, development?

POETRY

W. H. Auden *(1907–1973)*

Musée des Beaux Arts   *1940*

About suffering they were never wrong,
The Old Masters: how well they understood
Its human position; how it takes place
While someone else is eating or opening a window or just walking dully
    along
How, when the aged are reverently, passionately waiting   5
For the miraculous birth, there always must be
Children who did not specially want it to happen, skating
On a pond at the edge of the wood:
They never forgot
That even the dreadful martyrdom must run its course   10
Anyhow in a corner, some untidy spot
Where the dogs go on with their doggy life and the torturer's horse
Scratches its innocent behind on a tree.

In Brueghel's *Icarus,*[1] for instance: how everything turns away
Quite leisurely from the disaster; the ploughman may   15
Have heard the splash, the forsaken cry,
But for him it was not an important failure; the sun shone
As it had to on the white legs disappearing into the green
Water; and the expensive delicate ship that must have seen
Something amazing, a boy falling out of the sky,   20
Had somewhere to get to and sailed calmly on.

Explorations of the Text

1. About what were the "Old Masters" correct? What views did the "Old Masters" hold about suffering?

2. Characterize the persona. How does he view suffering? Contrast the speaker's vision with that of the "Old Masters."

3. Discuss the symbolism of Brueghel's painting. How does the symbolism develop themes of the poem?

4. What does the poem suggest about heroism, great deeds, and suffering?

5. How would the father in the story "War" respond to the poem?

---

[1] *Icarus:* Peter Brueghel, Flemish painter (ca. 1525–1569), whose painting, "Landscape with the Fall of Icarus," hangs in the Musees Royaux des Beaux-Arts in Brussels, Belgium. Icarus is a classical mythological figure who with his father, Daedalus, designed wings of wax and feathers, which they used to attempt to escape from Crete. Daedalus succeeded, but Icarus flew too close to the sun. The sun melted the boy's wings, and he plunged into the sea and drowned.

The Reading/Writing Connection

1. Respond to the speaker's view of suffering in this poem. Write a letter to the
   speaker.

Ideas for Writing

1. Compare the views presented in this
   poem with those in "American Ignorance of War" or in "Gas."

W. H. Auden   *(1907–1973)*

The Unknown Citizen   *1940*

(To JS/07/M/378
This Marble Monument
is Erected by the State)

He was found by the Bureau of Statistics to be
One against whom there was no official complaint,
And all the reports on his conduct agree
That, in the modern sense of an old-fashioned word, he was a saint,
For in everything he did he served the Greater Community.   5
Except for the War till the day he retired
He worked in a factory and never got fired,
But satisfied his employers, Fudge Motors Inc.
Yet he wasn't a scab or odd in his views,
For his Union reports that he paid his dues,   10
(Our report on his Union shows it was sound)
And our Social Psychology workers found
That he was popular with his mates and liked a drink.
The Press are convinced that he bought a paper every day
And that his reactions to advertisements were normal in every way.   15
Policies taken out in his name prove that he was fully insured,
And his Health-card shows he was once in hospital but left it cured.
Both Producers Research and High-Grade Living declare
He was fully sensible to the advantages of the Installment Plan
And had everything necessary to the Modern Man,   20
A phonograph, a radio, a car and a frigidaire.
Our researchers into Public Opinion are content
That he held the proper opinions for the time of year;
When there was peace, he was for peace; when there was war, he went.
He was married and added five children to the population,   25
Which our Eugenist[1] says was the right number for a parent of his generation,

---

[1]**Eugenist:** A scientist who studies ways to improve species, especially the human species, through careful selection of offspring by genetic means.

And our teachers report that he never interfered with their education.
Was he free? Was he happy? The question is absurd:
Had anything been wrong, we should certainly have heard.

Explorations of the Text

1. Identify the **allusion** in the title. Why is it ironic? What is the occasion?
2. Why is the citizen called a "saint" in "the modern sense" of this word? What is "the modern sense" of the word?
3. How does he serve "the Greater Community"? Describe his work and his relationship to his union.
4. In lines 18 to 21, "the unknown citizen" is depicted as a perfect consumer. How? Why?

5. What is the importance of the following line: "And our teachers report that he never interfered with their education"?
6. With all the sources of information on the citzen, "Was he free? Was he happy?" Does it matter? Why was he "unknown"?
7. What critique of modern culture does Auden offer? Is his analysis still relevant?

The Reading/Writing Connection

1. Make a list of ways in which you are a conformist or a nonconformist.

2. Discuss the **irony** in the closing.

Ideas for Writing

1. Characterize a contemporary unknown citizen.

2. Compare and contrast this poem with Ginsberg's "America."

Lao-tzu   *(6th century* B.C.)

Weapons at Best   *c. 500–200* B.C.

Weapons at best are tools of bad omen,
Loathed and avoided by those of the Way.

In the usage of men of good breeding,
Honor is had at the left;
Good omens belong on the left;   5
Bad omens belong on the right;
And warriors press to the right!
When the general stands at the right
His lieutenant is placed at the left.
So the usage of men of great power   10
Follows that of the funeral rite.

Weapons are tools of bad omen,
By gentlemen not to be used;
But when it cannot be avoided,

They use them with calm and restraint.   15
Even in victory's hour
These tools are unlovely to see;
For those who admire them truly
Are men who in murder delight.

As for those who delight to do murder,   20
It is certain they never can get
From the world what they sought when ambition
Urged them to power and rule.

A multitude slain!—and their death
Is a matter for grief and for tears;   25
The victory after a conflict
Is a theme for a funeral rite.

Explorations of the Text

1. What is the difference between "left" and "right" in stanza 2?
2. Why does Lao-tzu say that one may use arms "when it cannot be avoided?"

3. Why should the victor not rejoice? Why is taking pleasure in "a multitude slain" wrong, according to Lao-tzu?
4. Compare this poem with Owen's "Dulce et Decorum Est."

The Reading/Writing Connection

1. Respond to the following quotation from the *Tao-te-Ching*:
   "To quicken but not to own, to make but not to claim.

   To raise but not to rule, this is called profound virtue."
2. Explore themes of "Weapons at Best."

Ideas for Writing

1. Agree or disagree with the following statements: "Arms are unblest among tools and not the superior man's tools. Only when it is unavoidable he uses them."

2. Compare this work with "Arms and the Boy" by Owen (see Chapter 11).

Wilfred Owen   *(1893–1918)*

Dulce et Decorum Est   *1920*

Bent double, like old beggars under sacks,
Knock-kneed, coughing like hags, we cursed through sludge,
Till on the haunting flares we turned our backs

And towards our distant rest began to trudge.
Men marched asleep. Many had lost their boots   5
But limped on, blood-shod. All went lame; all blind;
Drunk with fatigue; deaf even to the hoots
Of tired, outstripped Five-Nines[1] that dropped behind.

Gas! Gas! Quick, boys!—An ecstasy of fumbling,
Fitting the clumsy helmets just in time;   10
But someone still was yelling out and stumbling
And flound'ring like a man in fire or lime . . .
Dim, through the misty panes and thick green light,
As under a green sea, I saw him drowning.

In all my dreams, before my helpless sight,   15
He plunges at me, guttering, choking, drowning.

If in some smothering dreams you too could pace
Behind the wagon that we flung him in,
And watch the white eyes writhing in his face,
His hanging face, like a devil's sick of sin;   20
If you could hear, at every jolt, the blood
Come gargling from the froth-corrupted lungs,
Obscene as cancer, bitter as the cud
Of vile, incurable sores on innocent tongues,—
My friend, you would not tell with such high zest   25
To children ardent for some desperate glory,
The old Lie: Dulce et decorum est
Pro patria mori.[2]

Explorations of the Text

1. Discuss the **similes** in lines 1 and 2. What images of the young soldiers does Owen present?

2. Find the words with negative **connotations** in stanza 1. Why are the men "lame," "blind," "drunk with fatigue," and "deaf"?

3. Why does Owen shift to the **first person** in the second verse? What effect does this highly personal testimony achieve?

4. Whom does the narrator address as "you" in stanza 4? What is his purpose? Who is the audience?

5. Give a synopsis of the narrative in this poem. What is the attitude of the speaker? Describe the tone.

6. Discuss figures of speech, rhyme scheme, and sound. How do they contribute to the effectiveness of this work?

7. Compare "Dulce et Decorum Est" to "How to Tell a True War Story."

---

[1] **Five-Nines:** Gas shells.   [2] **Dulce et decorum est:** "It is sweet and fitting to die for one's country" (Horace).

The Reading/Writing Connection

1. "Think" Topic: Gloss and annotate the text; identify and react to the similes in this poem.

Ideas for Writing

1. Write an essay that takes a position on Horace's quotation. Refer to works in the chapter to support your points.
2. Explicate this poem. Concentrate on point of view, tone, and imagery. (Look at the analysis of Owen's "Arms and the Boy" in Chapter 11 as a model.)

> **3. Write an Argument:** Does this poem persuade you that "war is Hell"? Why or why not?

Mary Jo Salter   (1954–   )

Welcome to Hiroshima   1985

is what you first see, stepping off the train:
a billboard brought to you in living English
by Toshiba Electric. While a channel
silent in the TV of the brain

projects those flickering re-runs of a cloud   5
that brims its risen columnful like beer
and, spilling over, hangs its foamy head,[1]
you feel a thirst for history: what year

it started to be safe to breathe the air,
and when to drink the blood and scum afloat   10
on the Ohta River.[2] But no, the water's clear,
they pour it for your morning cup of tea

in one of the countless sunny coffee shops
whose plastic dioramas advertise
mutations of cuisine behind the glass: 15
a pancake sandwich; a pizza someone tops

with a maraschino cherry. Passing by
the Peace Park's floral hypocenter[3] (where
how bravely, or with what mistaken cheer,
humanity erased its own erasure),   20

---

[1] **foamy head:** Reference to the telltale mushroom cloud of the atomic blast.   [2] **Ohta River:** River in Hiroshima.   [3] **Peace Park's floral hypocenter:** Epicenter of the blast.

you enter the memorial museum
and through more glass are served, as on a dish
of blistered grass, three mannequins. Like gloves
a mother clips to coatsleeves, strings of flesh

hang from their fingertips; or as if tied   25
to recall a duty for us, *Reverence*
the dead whose mourners too shall soon be dead,
but all commemoration's swallowed up

in questions of bad taste, how re-created
horror mocks the grim original,   30
and thinking at last *They should have left it all*
you stop. This is the wristwatch of a child.

Jammed on the moment's impact, resolute
to communicate some message, although mute,
it gestures with its hands at eight-fifteen   35
and eight-fifteen and eight-fifteen again

while tables of statistics on the wall
update the news by calling on a roll
of tape, death gummed on death, and in the case
adjacent, an exhibit under glass   40

is glass itself: a shard the bomb slammed in
a woman's arm at eight-fifteen, but some
three decades on—as if to make it plain
hope's only as renewable as pain,

and as if all the unsung   45
debasements of the past may one day come
rising to the surface once again—
worked its filthy way out like a tongue.

Explorations of the Text

1. Why does Salter use the "welcome" sign as the title and the first line of the poem? What impact does this wording have?

2. Discuss the persona's response to the exhibits at Hiroshima. How do the exhibits represent the nuclear holocaust? Focus particularly on stanza 5. What messages do these images convey? How does she use visceral, bodily images?

3. Why do the exhibits of the "wristwatch" and "shard of glass" capture the speaker's attention?

4. Explore the conception of witnessing enunciated in the last two stanzas.

5. How do the rhyme, rhythm, and stanzaic form further themes of the poem?

The Reading/Writing Connection

1. Freewrite and respond to the following line: "humanity erased its own erasure . . ." To what other historical events would this statement apply?
2. Gloss and annotate the poem. Explore the contrasting images of naïve hope versus understanding of pain; or present versus past realities.
3. "Think" Topic: What is the speaker's view of the exhibit? Connect her views with human beings' abilities to witness war.

Ideas for Writing

1. Compare the vision of witnessing war and genocide presented in this work with themes expressed in "American Ignorance of War" and "Song of Bullets."
2. Compare the views of war presented in this work with those suggested in "The War Generation."

Marilyn Chin *(1957–   )*

Love Poem from Nagasaki   *1987*

To say you are beautiful, to say
trees are, grass is, everything under
the weather—you are not really, no.

But the dark cloud exposing a rim of sun,
the river sedge dotted with strange new flowers,   5
ten thousand dragonflies spinning around the moon . . .

Suddenly, the earth emits a fragrance
deadlier than the teeming of flowers . . .
Tonight I am in love—
        from the squat houses of Nagaskai,   10

doves, bats, gnats
fly out
ecumenically.

Explorations of the Text

1. Contrast images of the "beautiful" with the aftereffects of the bombing of Nagasaki. According to the speaker, how has that world changed?
2. Discuss the juxtapositions of destruction and creation in the work.
3. Explain the closing lines of the poem. Why do "doves, bats, gnats/fly out/ecumenically"?
4. How does the poem move beyond Nagasaki to present a vision of a post–nuclear holocaust world?
5. Why does Chin entitle the work a "love poem"?

The Reading/Writing Connection

1. Create a love poem in which you juxtapose images of beauty and ugliness or growth and decay.
2. In a journal entry, compare and contrast the vision of Nagasaki in this work with Salter's portrayal of Hiroshima in "Welcome to Hiroshima." Focus on the depiction of setting, the aftermath of the bombing, and the speaker's stance as a witness.

Ideas for Writing

1. Create a portrait of the speaker: her appearance, attitudes, gestures, actions, and background. Imagine the setting that she is in. What do you learn from creating the world of the poem?

Yusef Komunyakaa   *(1947–   )*

Facing It   *1988*

My black face fades,
hiding inside the black granite.
I said I wouldn't,
dammit: No tears.
I'm stone. I'm flesh.   5
My clouded reflection eyes me
like a bird of prey, the profile of night
slanted against morning. I turn
this way—the stone lets me go.
I turn that way—I'm inside   10
the Vietnam Veterans Memorial
again, depending on the light
to make a difference.
I go down the 58,022 names,
half-expecting to find   15
my own in letters like smoke.
I touch the name Andrew Johnson;
I see the booby trap's white flash.
Names shimmer on a woman's blouse
but when she walks away   20
the names stay on the wall.
Brushstrokes flash, a red bird's
wings cutting across my stare.
The sky. A plane in the sky.
A white vet's image floats   25
closer to me, then his pale eyes
look through mine. I'm a widow.
He's lost his right arm
inside the stone. In the black mirror

a woman's trying to erase names;   30
No, she's brushing a boy's hair.

Yusef Komunyakaa *(1947–)*

Nude Interrogation   1988

Did you kill anyone over there? Angela shifts her gaze from the Janis
Joplin poster to the Jimi Hendrix, lifting the pale muslin blouse over her
head. The blacklight deepens the blues when the needle drops into the
first groove of "All Along the Watchtower." I don't want to look at the
floor. *Did you kill anyone? Did you dig a hole, crawl inside, and wait for*   5
your target? Her miniskirt drops into a rainbow at her feet. Sandalwood
incense hangs a slow comet of perfume over the room. I shake my head.
She unhooks her bra and flings it against a bookcase made of plywood
and cinderblocks. *Did you use an M-16, a handgrenade, a bayonet, or your*
own two strong hands, both thumbs pressed against that little bird in the   10
throat? She stands with her left thumb hooked into the elastic of her sky-
blue panties. When she flicks off the blacklight, snowy hills rush up to
the windows. *Did you kill anyone over there? Are you right-handed or left-*
handed? Did you drop your gun afterwards? Did you kneel beside the corpse
and turn it over? She's nude against the falling snow. Yes. The record spins   15
like a bull's-eye on the far wall of Xanadu. Yes, I say. *I was scared of the*
silence. The night was too big. *And afterwards, I couldn't stop looking up at*
the sky.

Explorations of the Text

1. How does the speaker respond to the
   Vietnam Wall in "Facing It"? List images that suggest his response.

2. Why does the poet use images of surface, depth, and reflection to depict
   the experience? What is the impact of
   portraying the speaker's face as "hiding
   inside the black granite"? Why is the
   speaker "inside/the Vietnam Veterans
   Memorial"?

3. What do the closing lines signify:
   ". . . In the black mirror/a woman's trying to erase names;/No she's brushing a
   boy's hair."

4. In "Nude Interrogation," analyze the
   speaker's character. Examine the conflict between the speaker and Angela.

5. In "Nude Interrogation," what does the
   italicized dialogue suggest?

6. Why does the poet include allusions to
   Janis Joplin, Jimi Hendrix, and Xanadu
   in "Nude Interrogation"?

7. Why does Komunyakaa use a love scene
   as the setting for a work about war? Is
   this a poem about love or war? Discuss
   the significance of the title.

8. Compare and contrast the motif
   of war stories in these works, in
   Rivera's "Gas," in Busch's "Ralph the
   Duck," and in O'Brien's "How to Tell
   a True War Story." What do the war
   stories reveal about the protagonists?
   What do they reveal about the state of
   war?

The Reading/Writing Connection

1. "Think" Topic: In O'Brien's "How to Tell a True War Story," the narrator suggests that war stories are, ultimately, "love" stories. How do these poems and Rivera's "Gas" prove or refute this point of view?

2. Choose one or two lines from one of these two poems about war or a line from another work about war in this chapter, and use it as the opening of your own poem about war.

3. In a journal entry, examine why you think that Komunyakaa wrote "Nude Interrogation" as a prose poem. Transform it into stanzaic form, and compare the two versions. What are the differences between the two? You also may examine Forché's "The Colonel," another example of the form.

Ideas for Writing

1. In "Making the Memorial," an autobiographical essay published in the *New York Review of Books,* Maya Lin suggests that memorials "should be . . . honest about the reality of war, about the loss of life in war." Do these poems project this sense of honesty? In what ways?

2. Lin also suggests in that essay that she saw "the wall as pure surface, an interface between light and dark," "an interface between the world of the living and the world of the dead." How does her vision of the memorial illuminate the poem?

Langston Hughes *(1902–1967)*

Let America be America Again   *1938*

Let America be America again.
Let it be the dream it used to be.
Let it be the pioneer on the plain
Seeking a home where he himself is free.

(America never was America to me.)   5

Let America be the dream the dreamers dreamed—
Let it be that great strong land of love
Where never kings connive nor tyrants scheme
That any man be crushed by one above.

(It never was America to me.)   10

O, let my land be a land where Liberty
Is crowned with no false patriotic wreath,
But opportunity is real, and life is free,
Equality is in the air we breathe.

(There's never been equality for me,   15
Nor freedom in this "homeland of the free.")

Say who are you that mumbles in the dark?
And who are you that draws your veil across the stars?

I am the poor white, fooled and pushed apart,
I am the red man driven from the land.   20
I am the refugee clutching the hope I seek—
But finding only the same old stupid plan

Of dog eat dog, of mighty crush the weak.
I am the Negro, "problem" to you all.
I am the people, humble, hungry, mean—   25
Hungry yet today despite the dream.
Beaten yet today—O, Pioneers!
I am the man who never got ahead,
The poorest worker bartered through the years.
Yet I'm the one who dreamt our basic dream   30
In that Old World while still a serf of kings,
Who dreamt a dream so strong, so brave, so true,
That even yet its mighty daring sings
In every brick and stone, in every furrow turned
That's made America the land it has become.   35
O, I'm the man who sailed those early seas
In search of what I meant to be my home—
For I'm the one who left dark Ireland's shore,
And Poland's plain, and England's grassy lea,
And torn from Black Africa's strand I came   40
To build a "homeland of the free."

The free?
Who said the free? Not me?
Surely not me? The millions on relief today?
The millions who have nothing for our pay   45
For all the dreams we've dreamed
And all the songs we've sung
And all the hopes we've held
And all the flags we've hung,
The millions who have nothing for our pay—   50
Except the dream we keep alive today.

O, let America be America again—
The land that never has been yet—
And yet must be—the land where every man is free.
The land that's mine—the poor man's, Indian's, Negro's, ME—   55
Who made America,
Whose sweat and blood, whose faith and pain,

Whose hand at the foundry, whose plow in the rain,
Must bring back our mighty dream again.

O, yes,
I say it plain,
America never was America to me,
And yet I swear this oath—
America will be!

60

Explorations of the Text

1. What does the title mean? Who is the speaker? For whom does he speak?
2. What dreams of America emerge in the first three stanzas? What is the meaning of America in the refrain?
3. Describe the transformation of the speaker which begins in line 19: "I am the poor white, fooled and pushed apart."
4. What criticisms of America does the speaker make? Compare them to Ginsberg's "America" and "Supermarket in California."

5. Analyze the **paradox:**
   "O let America be America again—
   The land that never has been yet—"
6. How does the speaker's attitude change in the last stanza?
7. Examine Hughes' use of **irony**. (See Chapter 12 for a discussion of irony.)
8. Consider the form of this poem—line length, repetition, stanza divisions—and compare this work with Whitman's "Out of the Cradle Endlessly Rocking" in Chapter 5.

The Reading/Writing Connection

1. "Think" Topic: Write about one of Hughes' two Americas.

2. Create a contemporary version of "Let America be America Again."

Ideas for Writing

1. **Write an Argument:** Agree or disagree with Hughes' analysis of America.
2. Explicate and evaluate this poem. Focus on point of view, imagery, paradox, tone, irony, and/or form.

3. Compare this poem with Ginsberg's "America," later in this chapter.

Langston Hughes *(1902–1967)*

Harlem   *1951*

What happens to a dream deferred?

Does it dry up
like a raisin in the sun?
Or fester like a sore—

And then run?   5
Does it stink like rotten meat?
Or crust and sugar over—
like a syrupy sweet?

Maybe it just sags
like a heavy load.   10

Or does it explode?

Explorations of the Text

1. What is the connection between the title and the opening question?
2. What possible consequences does the speaker suggest?
3. Why does Hughes create so many **similes**? Are they effective? Why does he use so many questions? Are they effective?
4. Why does the persona speak only one declarative sentence?

5. Why is the last question isolated and written in italics? What are the implications? What is the answer?
6. Examine the rhyme scheme and other formal elements in the poem. What makes "Harlem" work?
7. Compare themes in this poem to those in works by Auden, Ginsberg, and Angelou.

The Reading/Writing Connection

1. Gloss and annotate the poem, and write an end comment.
2. Journal Entry: Write about "a dream deferred" in your own life. Compare your experience with the lost hopes of the poem.

Ideas for Writing

1. Explicate formal elements—figures of speech, sound, rhyme, and rhythm—in "Harlem."
2. Consider each of the similes and paraphrase them. Write a cause-effect analysis of the "dream deferred."

Gwendolyn Brooks   *(1917–2000)*

The Chicago Defender Sends a Man to Little Rock   *1960*

In Little Rock[1] the people bear
Babes, and comb and part their hair
And watch the want ads, put repair

---

[1]**Little Rock, Arkansas:** scene of one test of the Supreme Court case *(Brown v. The Board of Education)* concerning desegregation of schools. Federal troops in 1957 had to be sent to enforce the Supreme Court decision and integrate Little Rock High School.

To roof and latch. While wheat toast burns
A woman waters multiferns. 5

Time upholds or overturns
The many, tight, and small concerns.

In Little Rock the people sing
Sunday hymns like anything,
Through Sunday pomp and polishing. 10

And after testament and tunes,
Some soften Sunday afternoons
With lemon tea and Lorna Doones.[2]

I forecast
And I believe 15
Come Christmas Little Rock will cleave
To Christmas tree and trifle, weave,
From laugh and tinsel, texture fast.

In Little Rock is baseball; Barcarolle.[3]
That hotness in July . . . the uniformed figures raw and implacable 20
And not intellectual,
Batting the hotness or clawing the suffering dust.
The Open Air Concert, on the special twilight green. . . .
When Beethoven[4] is brutal or whispers to lady-like air.
Blanket-sitters are solemn, as Johann[5] troubles to lean 25
To tell them what to mean. . . .

There is love, too, in Little Rock. Soft women softly
Opening themselves in kindness,
Or, pitying one's blindness,
Awaiting one's pleasure 30
In azure
Glory with anguished rose at the root. . . .
To wash away old semi-discomfitures.
They re-teach purple and unsullen blue.
The wispy soils go. And uncertain 35
Half-havings have they clarified to sures.

In Little Rock they know
Not answering the telephone is a way of rejecting life,

---

[2]**Lorna Doones:** Cookies.   [3]**Barcarolle:** Venetian boat song with a rowing rhythm or music imitating such songs.   [4]**Ludwig van Beethoven:** German composer (1770–1827).   [5]**Johann Sebastian Bach:** German composer (1685–1750).

That it is our business to be bothered, is our business
To cherish bores or boredom, be polite   40
To lies and love and many-faceted fuzziness.
I scratch my head, massage the hate-I-had.
I blink across my prim and pencilled pad.
The saga I was sent for is not down.
Because there is a puzzle in this town.   45
The biggest News I do not dare
Telegraph to the Editor's chair:
"They are like people everywhere."

The angry Editor would reply
In hundred harryings of Why.   50

And true, they are hurling spittle, rock,
Garbage and fruit in Little Rock.
And I saw coiling storm a-writhe
On bright madonnas. And a scythe
Of men harassing brownish girls.   55
(The bows and barrettes in the curls
And braids declined away from joy.)

I saw a bleeding brownish boy. . . .

The lariat lynch-wish I deplored.

The loveliest lynchee was our Lord.   60

Explorations of the Text

1. Examine the first four stanzas, and describe life in Little Rock.
2. Who is the narrator? Why is the narrator in Little Rock?
3. What is the nature of love in Little Rock? Describe the "soft women." Interpret this section carefully.
4. Why is the narrator so puzzled that the citizens of Little Rock "are like people everywhere"? What are the implications of this conclusion?
5. What has the man sent to Little Rock actually seen? What acts of harassment and violence happen there?
6. Why are the last three lines separated into stanzas? What is the effect?
7. What is traditional about the form of this poem?
8. Compare and contrast this poem with works by Hughes, Deavere Smith, and Ginsberg.

The Reading/Writing Connection

1. Freewrite. Respond to the idea that the people in Little Rock who opposed desegregation "are like people everywhere."
2. "Think" Topic: Is this poem still relevant, or is it an interesting and powerful description of a singular moment in history? Respond to this question in a paragraph.

Ideas for Writing

1. Write a brief research paper on the historical context of this poem.

2. What are the functions of setting in this poem?

Gwendolyn Brooks   *(1917–2000)*

The Boy Died in My Alley   *1981*

Without my having known.
Policeman said, next morning,
"Apparently died Alone."
"You heard a shot?" Policeman said.
Shots I hear and Shots I hear.   5
I never see the dead.

The Shot that killed him yes I heard
as I heard the Thousand shots before;
careening tinnily down the nights
across my years and arteries.   10

Policeman pounded on my door.
"Who is it?" "POLICE!" Policeman yelled.
"A Boy was dying in your alley.
Boy is dead, and in your alley.
And have you known this Boy before?"   15

I have known this Boy before.
I have known this Boy before, who
ornaments my alley.
I never saw his face at all.
I never saw his futurefall.   20
But I have known this Boy.

I have always heard him deal with death.
I have always heard the shout, the volley.
I have closed my heart-ears late and early.
And I have killed him ever.   25

I joined the Wild and killed him
with knowledgeable unknowing.
I saw where he was going.
I saw him Crossed. And seeing,
I did not take him down.   30

He cried not only "Father!"
but "Mother!
Sister!

Brother."
The cry climbed up the alley. 35
It went up to the wind.
It hung upon the heaven
for a long
stretch-strain of Moment.

The red floor of my alley 40
is a special speech to me.

Explorations of the Text

1. Examine the figure of the boy. Who do you imagine the boy to be? Why does the speaker state: "I have known the Boy before"?
2. Examine the extended imagery delineating the boy. Why are there a "Thousand shots . . ./careening tinnily down the nights"? Why has she "never [seen] his face" or "his futurefall"? Explore the paradox of the speaker's never seeing the boy but "know[ing]" his fate.

3. Explore the character and stance of the speaker. Why does the speaker reveal: "I have closed my heart-ears late and early/ And I have killed him ever"? How does the speaker's state of mind compare with the townspeople's in "Chicago Defender Sends a Man to Little Rock"?
4. Connect themes of this work with ideas in Goska's "Political Paralysis."

The Reading/Writing Connection

1. In a journal entry explore the religious symbolism in the poem.

Ideas for Writing

1. **Write an Argument:** Compare and contrast the speakers in Brooks's works with those in Ginsberg's two poems. In what ways are the speakers presenting arguments? Analyze the point of view, tone, and proofs in the works. Are you convinced as a reader by the visions in the works?

2. Connect Albert Einstein's statement: "The world is too dangerous to live in not because of the people who do evil, but because of the people who sit and let it happen" with themes of Brooks's two poems.

Allen Ginsberg *(1926–1997)*

America   *1956*

America I've given you all and now I'm nothing.
America two dollars and twentyseven cents January 17, 1956.
I can't stand my own mind.
America when will we end the human war?

Go fuck yourself with your atom bomb.   5
I don't feel good don't bother me.
I won't write my poem till I'm in my right mind.
America when will you be angelic?
When will you take off your clothes?
When will you look at yourself through the grave?   10
When will you be worthy of your million Trotskyites?[1]
America why are your libraries full of tears?
America when will you send your eggs to India?
I'm sick of your insane demands.
When can I go into the supermarket and buy what I need with my good   15
    looks?
America after all it is you and I who are perfect not the next world.
Your machinery is too much for me.
You made me want to be a saint.
There must be some other way to settle this argument.
Burroughs[2] is in Tangiers[3] I don't think he'll come back it's sinister.   20
Are you being sinister or is this some form of practical joke?
I'm trying to come to the point.
I refuse to give up my obsession.
America stop pushing I know what I'm doing.
America the plum blossoms are falling.   25
I haven't read the newspapers for months, everyday somebody goes on trial
    for murder.
America I feel sentimental about the Wobblies.[4]
America I used to be a communist when I was a kid I'm not sorry.
I smoke marijuana every chance I get.
I sit in my house for days on end and stare at the roses in the closet.   30
When I go to Chinatown I get drunk and never get laid.
My mind is made up there's going to be trouble.
You should have seen me reading Marx.[5]
My psychoanalyst thinks I'm perfectly right.
I won't say the Lord's Prayer.   35
I have mystical visions and cosmic vibrations.

America I still haven't told you what you did to Uncle Max after he came
    over from Russia.
I'm addressing you.
Are you going to let your emotional life be run by Time Magazine?
I'm obsessed by Time Magazine.   40

---

[1]**Trotskyites:** Those who believe in principles proposed by Leon Trotsky, especially the adoption of worldwide communism through revolution. [2]**William S. Burroughs:** American Beat novelist (1914–97). [3]**Tangiers:** Port on the Strait of Gibralter in North Morocco. [4]**Wobblies:** Members of the Industrial Workers of the World. [5]**Karl Marx:** German philosopher and Socialist (1818–83).

I read it every week.
Its cover stares at me every time I slink past the corner candystore.
I read it in the basement of the Berkeley Public Library.
It's always telling me about responsibility. Businessmen are serious.
       Movie producers are serious. Everybody's serious but me.
It occurs to me that I am America.   45
I am talking to myself again.

Asia is rising against me.
I haven't got a chinaman's chance.
I'd better consider my national resources.
My national resources consist of two joints of marijuana millions of genitals 50
    an unpublishable private literature that jetplanes 1400 miles
    an hour and twentyfive-thousand mental institutions.
I say nothing about my prisons nor the millions of underprivileged who
    live in my flowerpots under the light of five hundred suns.
I have abolished the whorehouses of France, Tangiers is the next to go.   55
My ambition is to be President despite the fact that I'm a Catholic.

America how can I write a holy litany in your silly mood?
I will continue like Henry Ford my strophes are as individual as his
    automobiles more so they're all different sexes.
America I will sell you strophes $2500 apiece $500 down on your old   60
    strophe
America free Tom Mooney[6]
America save the Spanish Loyalists[7]
America Sacco & Vanzetti must not die[8]
America I am the Scottsboro boys.[9]
America when I was seven momma took me to Communist Cell meetings 65
    they sold us garbanzos a handful per ticket a ticket costs a nickel
    and the speeches were free everybody was angelic and sentimental
    about the workers it was all so sincere you have no idea what a
    good thing the party was in 1835 Scott Nearing was a grand old
    man a real mensch Mother Bloor the Silk-strikers' Ewig-Weibliche[10] 70
    made me cry I once saw the Yiddish orator Israel Amter plain.[11]
    Everybody must have been a spy.
America you don't really want to go to war.
America it's them bad Russians.
Them Russians them Russians and them Chinamen. And them Russians. 75

---

[6]**Tom Mooney:** American Wobbly, convicted for murder in 1916 and pardoned more than twenty years latter. [7]**Spanish Loyalists:** Spaniards, Republicans, who opposed Franco's Nationalists during the Spanish Civil War (1936–39). [8]**Nicola Sacco (1891–1927):** and Bartolemeo Vanzetti (1888–1927), American anarchists who were executed. [9]**Scottsboro boys:** Nine African American youths convicted of raping two white women; a controversial case because of lack of evidence. [10]**Ewig-Weibliche:** "Eternal feminine" in German. [11]**Yiddish . . . plain:** Nearing, Bloor, and Amter; American leftists.

The Russia wants to eat us alive. The Russia's power mad. She wants to take
    our cars from out our garages.
Her wants to grab Chicago. Her needs a Red *Reader's Digest*. Her wants our
    auto plants in Siberia. Him big bureaucracy running our fillingstations.
That no good. Ugh. Him make Indians learn read. Him need big black niggers.
    Hah. Her make us all work sixteen hours a day. Help.
America this is quite serious.
America this is the impression I get from looking in the television set.   80
America is this correct?
I'd better get right down to the job.
It's true I don't want to join the Army or turn lathes in precision parts
    factories, I'm nearsighted and psychopathic anyway.
America I'm putting my queer shoulder to the wheel.

Explorations of the Text

1. Describe the speaker. Focus on his character traits, tone, values, and attitudes.
2. In addressing "America" as his audience, to whom does he speak? What are his criticisms of his culture?
3. Why does he state "It occurs to me that I am America./I am talking to myself again"?
4. Analyze the section beginning: "Asia is rising against me." From whose view is the persona speaking? Is this change of point of view effective?
5. How are the historical allusions—Spanish Loyalists, Sacco and Vanzetti, Communist cell meetings—important to the poem?
6. Why does he speak in baby talk, in "Indian" dialect? When does the voice shift?
7. What impact does the humor have? Does it develop themes of the work?
8. In the last line, does the speaker change his point of view and attitude? How?
9. Compare this poem to the poems by Brooks and Hughes.

The Reading/Writing Connection

1. Make a catalogue of the criticisms of America. Are they valid?
2. Write a humorous critique about some aspect of life in the United States. Begin with "America, I . . . ."

Ideas for Writing

1. Analyze the speaker in this poem. How does Ginsberg achieve this characterization? Discuss voice, tone, imagery, humor, word choice, and/or theme. Compose a diary entry in the speaker's voice.
2. Compare this poem with Whitman's "Out of the Cradle Endlessly Rocking" in Chapter 5.

Allen Ginsberg *(1926–1997)*

A Supermarket in California *1955*

What thoughts I have of you tonight, Walt Whitman, for I walked down the sidestreets under the trees with a headache self-conscious looking at the full moon.

In my hungry fatigue, and shopping for images, I went into the neon fruit supermarket, dreaming of your enumerations!

What peaches and what penumbras! Whole families shopping at night! Aisles full of husbands! Wives in the avocados, babies in the tomatoes!—and you, García Lorca, what were you doing down by the watermelons?

I saw you, Walt Whitman, childless, lonely old grubber, poking among the meats in the refrigerator and eyeing the grocery boys.

I heard you asking questions of each: Who killed the pork chops? What   5
price bananas? Are you my Angel?

I wandered in and out of the brilliant stacks of cans following you, and followed in my imagination by the store detective.

We strode down the open corridors together in our solitary fancy tasting artichokes, possessing every frozen delicacy, and never passing the cashier.

Where are we going, Walt Whitman? The doors close in an hour. Which way does your beard point tonight?

(I touch your book and dream of our odyssey in the supermarket and feel absurd.)

Will we walk all night through solitary streets? The trees add shade to   10
shade, lights out in the houses, we'll both be lonely.

Will we stroll dreaming of the lost America of love past blue automobiles in driveways, home to our silent cottage?

Ah, dear father, graybeard, lonely old courage-teacher, what America did you have when Charon quit poling his ferry and you got out on a smoking bank and stood watching the boat disappear on the black waters of Lethe?

Explorations of the Text

1. Why does Ginsberg compare himself to Walt Whitman? What does Whitman represent to him?

2. Discuss the critique of North American life presented through the images of the supermarket. How would Ginsberg respond today to the super-supermarkets like Super Stop 'n Shop or Wal-Mart? Is his critique still relevant?

3. How does the poem extend Ginsberg's vision presented in "America"?

4. Conceive of this work as a journey. What does the speaker learn?

The Reading/Writing Connection

1. **Write an Argument:** Take Ginsberg's stance. Become an outsider, experience from a distance some aspect of contemporary North American culture and then critique it. For example, you could write a cultural critique of tat-

> too parlors, Wal-Mart, malls, fast-food restaurants, reality television shows, *American Idol,* and so on. OR you could take on the persona of another liter-ary figure and then look at the world through his or her eyes as Ginsberg does in this poem.

Joy Harjo *(1951–)*

For Anna Mae Aquash Whose Spirit is Present Here and in the Dappled Stars   *1990*

For we remember the story and must tell it again so we may all live

Beneath a sky blurred with mist and wind,
                 I am amazed as I watch the violet
heads of crocuses erupt from the stiff earth
                    after dying for a season,
as I have watched my own dark head   5
                appear each morning after entering
the next world
           to come back to this one,
                  amazed.
It is the way in the natural world to understand the place   10
                the ghost dancers[1] named
after the heart breaking destruction.
               Anna Mae,
                everything and nothing changes
You are the shimmering young woman   15
               who found her voice
when you were warned to be silent, or have your body cut away
from you like an elegant weed.
            You are the one whose spirit is present in the dappled stars.
(They prance and lope like colored horses who stay with us   20
           through the streets of these steely cities. And I have seen them
         nuzzling the frozen bodies of tattered drunks
               on the corner.)
This morning when the last star is dimming
               and the buses grind toward   25
the middle of the city, I know it is ten years since they buried
you the second time in Lakota, a language that could
              free you.
I heard about it in Oklahoma, or New Mexico
           how the wind howled and pulled everything down   30
in a righteous anger.
(It was the women who told me) and we understood wordlessly

---

[1] **ghost dancers:** Dancers who performed the Ghost Dance, a group dance begun by late nineteenth-century Native Americans to promote the return of the dead and the restoration of the spiritual life of the tribe.

the ripe meaning of your murder.
  As I understand ten years later after the slow changing
        of the seasons   35
that we have just begun to touch
    the dazzling whirlwind of our anger,
we have just begun to perceive the amazed world the ghost
dancers entered
    crazily, beautifully.   40

Explorations of the Text

1. Describe the setting and season. What is the attitude of the speaker? Explain the following lines: "as I have watched my own dark head/appear each morning after entering/the next world/to come back to this one,/amazed." What is the place "the ghost dancers named"? How can it be understood?

2. How is Anna Mae invoked and described? Consider the star imagery and the extension of the **metaphor**.

3. What does the speaker mean when she says "I know it is ten years since they buried/you the second time in Lakota, a language that could/free you"?

4. Examine the last five lines. What is "the dazzling whirlwind" of anger? What is "the amazed world the ghost/dancers entered"?

5. Discuss the images of beauty and of destruction in this poem. How do they reveal theme?

6. Compare the political message of this poem to the ideas in Hughes's "Let America Be America Again" and Ginsberg's "America."

The Reading/Writing Connection

1. Imitate this poem, and write to someone who has died for a political cause.

2. Freewrite about the line: "everything and nothing changes."

Ideas for Writing

1. Characterize the speaker and Anna Mae.

2. Analyze the imagery in this poem.

Martín Espada *(1957–)*

Imagine the Angels of Bread *1996*

This is the year that squatters evict landlords,
gazing like admirals from the rail
of the roofdeck
or levitating hands in praise
of steam in the shower;   5
this is the year
that shawled refugees deport judges
who stare at the floor
and their swollen feet

as files are stamped   10
with their destination;
this is the year that police revolvers,
stove-hot, blister the fingers
of raging cops,
and nightsticks splinter   15
in their palms;
this is the year
that darkskinned men
lynched a century ago
return to sip coffee quietly   20
with the apologizing descendants
of their executioners.

This is the year that those
who swim the border's undertow
and shiver in boxcars   25
are greeted with trumpets and drums
at the first railroad crossing
on the other side;
this is the year that the hands
pulling tomatoes from the vine   30
uproot the deed to the earth that sprouts the vine,
the hands canning tomatoes
are named in the will
that owns the bedlam of the cannery;
this is the year that the eyes   35
stinging from the poison that purifies toilets
awaken at last to the sight
of a rooster-loud hillside,
pilgrimage of immigrant birth;
this is the year that cockroaches   40
become extinct, that no doctor
finds a roach embedded
in the ear of an infant;
this is the year that the food stamps
of adolescent mothers   45
are auctioned like gold doubloons,
and no coin is given to buy machetes
for the next bouquet of severed heads
in coffee plantation country.

If the abolition of slave-manacles   50
began as a vision of hands without manacles,
then this is the year;
if the shutdown of extermination camps
began as imagination of a land
without barbed wire or the crematorium,   55
then this is the year;

if every rebellion begins with the idea
that conquerors on horseback
are not many-legged gods, that they too drown
if plunged in the river, 60
then this is the year.

So may every humiliated mouth,
teeth like desecrated headstones,
fill with the angels of bread.

Explorations of the Text

1. Explicate the social and historical references in the poem. What social issues does the work treat?
2. Discuss the forms of resistance and rebellions presented in this work. Explore the reversals presented in the work. What forms of social transformation does Espada imagine?
3. Discuss the significance of the section of the poem beginning with "If the abolition of slave-manacles" and ending with "if plunged in the river,/then this is the year."
4. Explore the role of the imagination in inciting political change or transformation. For example, interpret these lines: "if the shutdown of extermination camps/began as imagination of a land/without barbed wire or the crematorium/then this is the year."
5. Analyze the concluding stanza. What does the image, "the angels of bread," signify?
6. Compare and contrast the ideas of political activism presented in this poem and in Veronica Goska's essay.

The Reading/Writing Connection

1. "Think" Topic: Find a copy of John Lennon's "Imagine." Compare and contrast the Utopian visions portrayed in Lennon's and Espada's works.
2. Choose one or two lines from the poem and respond in a freewrite.

Ideas for Writing

1. Create your own Utopian vision in prose or poetry. Then analyze your work, focusing on the themes presented.

2. **Write an Argument:** Do you think the kind of social change Espada imagines is possible? Why or why not? Present your position using examples from this poem, other works in the chapter, current events, and your own experiences and observations.

Maya Angelou *(1928–)*

Still I Rise *1978*

You may write me down in history
With your bitter, twisted lies,
You may trod me in the very dirt

But still, like dust, I'll rise.

Does my sassiness upset you?
Why are you beset with gloom?
'Cause I walk like I've got oil wells
Pumping in my living room.

Just like moons and like suns,
With the certainty of tides,
Just like hopes springing high,
Still I'll rise.

Did you want to see me broken?
Bowed head and lowered eyes?
Shoulders falling down like teardrops,
Weakened by my soulful cries.

Does my haughtiness offend you?
Don't you take it awful hard
'Cause I laugh like I've got gold mines
Diggin' in my own back yard.

You may shoot me with your words,
You may cut me with your eyes,
You may kill me with your hatefulness,
But still, like air, I'll rise.

Does my sexiness upset you?
Does it come as a surprise
That I dance like I've got diamonds
At the meeting of my thighs?

Out of the huts of history's shame
I rise
Up from a past that's rooted in pain
I rise
I'm a black ocean, leaping and wide,
Welling and swelling I bear in the tide.

Leaving behind nights of terror and fear
I rise
Into a daybreak that's wondrously clear
I rise
Bringing the gifts that my ancestors gave,
I am the dream and the hope of the slave.
I rise
I rise
I rise.

5

10

15

20

25

30

35

40

Explorations of the Text

1. Characterize the persona and point of view of the poem.
2. Why does Angelou include the images of "oil well," "gold mines," and "diamonds"?
3. How does the persona view her relationship with her past? To what historical events does she refer when she writes about "huts of history's shame," "broken/bowed head," and "nights of terror and fear"?
4. Will she triumph? Why?
5. Discuss the symbolism of "tides" and "ocean."
6. What effect does anaphora create? Does it add to or detract from the poem?

The Reading/Writing Connection

1. Write a poem or a voice piece in which you proclaim triumph or in which you brag about something that you accomplished.
2. Use one line as an opening to your own poem.

Ideas for Writing

1. **Write an Argument:** Compare the speaker in this poem with the one in "Ego Tripping" (See Chapter 5). How do both poets use allusions and historical references? Evaluate both poems. Which one do you think is more effective?

Lucille Clifton   *(1936–)*

Jasper Texas 1998[1]   *2000*

for j. byrd

i am a man's head hunched in the road.
i was chosen to speak by the members
of my body.   the arm as it pulled away
pointed toward me, the hand opened once
and was gone.   5

why and why and why
should i call a white man brother?
who is the human in this place,
the thing that is dragged or the dragger?
what does my daughter say?   10

---

[1]**Jasper, Texas:** In Jasper, Texas, on June 7, 1998, three white men, with ties to such hate groups as Aryan Nation, kidnapped James Bryd, Jr., an African-American man, beat him, dragged him behind a truck, and killed him. His head was severed from his body.

the sun is a blister overhead.
if i were alive i could not bear it.
the townsfolk sing we shall overcome
while hope bleeds slowly from my mouth
into the dirt that covers us all.   15
i am done with this dust.   i am done.

Explorations of the Text

1. Why does the speaker imagine herself as the "severed head"?
2. Why does the poet use bodily imagery and personification to portray racial violence? How do the imagery and figurative language develop themes of the work?
3. Discuss the confrontation between the "human" and the nonhuman in this work. Who is "human"—"the dragged" or "the dragger"?
4. Explicate the line: "The sun is a blister overhead."
5. Why does the poet use a small "i" instead of a capital?
6. Compare and contrast the persona in this work with that of the speaker in Angelou's "Still I Rise."

The Reading/Writing Connection

1. Etty Hillesum, a diarist and writer who lived in Amsterdam during the Holocaust chronicled her experiences during the war until her deportation to Auschwitz and described her own stance as a witness: "I want to be the thinking heart of the barracks." How does the poet convey the embodied response of a witness? How would the poem be different if Clifton omitted "i am. . ."
2. "Think" Topic: How does Clifton contrast the human and nonhuman? What themes emerge from this contrast?

Ideas for Writing

1. Compare and contrast the treatment of social injustice in this work with Anzaldua's "horse," Harjo's "For Anna Mae Aquash," and Angelou's "Still I Rise." Is there retribution? Resistance? Possibilities for social change?
2. Research the Orpheus myth. How does the myth enlarge the meaning of the work? What are the ironies in Clifton's use of the myth? See Rilke's "Sonnets to Orpheus" in Chapter 9.

Wole Soyinka   (1934–   )

Telephone Conversation   *1967*

The price seemed reasonable, location
Indifferent. The landlady swore she lived
Off premises. Nothing remained
But self-confession. "Madam," I warned,

"I hate a wasted journey—I am African."   5
Silence. Silenced transmission of
Pressurized good-breeding. Voice, when it came,
Lipstick coated, long gold-rolled
Cigarette-holder pipped. Caught I was, foully.

"HOW DARK?" . . . I had not misheard . . . "ARE YOU LIGHT   10
OR VERY DARK?" Button B. Button A. Stench
Of rancid breath of public hide-and-speak.
Red booth. Red pillar-box. Red double-tiered
Omnibus squelching tar. It was real! Shamed
By ill-mannered silence, surrender   15
Pushed dumbfoundment to beg simplification.
Considerate she was, varying the emphasis—

"ARE YOU DARK? OR VERY LIGHT?" Revelation came.
"You mean—like plain or milk chocolate?"
Her assent was clinical, crushing in its light   20
Impersonality. Rapidly, wave-length adjusted,
I chose. "West African sepia"—and as afterthought,
"Down in my passport." Silence for spectroscopic
Flight of fancy, till truthfulness clanged her accent
Hard on the mouthpiece. "WHAT'S THAT?" conceding   25
"DON'T KNOW WHAT THAT IS." "Like brunette."

"THAT'S DARK, ISN'T IT?" "Not altogether.
Facially, I am brunette, but madam, you should see
The rest of me. Palm of my hand, soles of my feet
Are a peroxide blonde. Friction, caused—   30
Foolishly madam—by sitting down, has turned
My bottom raven black—One moment madam!"—sensing
Her receiver rearing on the thunderclap
About my ears—"Madam," I pleaded, "wouldn't you rather
See for yourself?"   35

Explorations of the Text

1. In the opening lines, why is the tone reportial? What happens when the persona confesses that he is African?

2. Is the speaker surprised by the question? Where does this situation happen? Examine details in lines 11 to 14.

3. Characterize the persona. What does he intend when he describes his skin as "West African sepia"?

4. Characterize the landlady.

5. Examine the speaker's final description of his skin (beginning in line 28). What is the meaning of the narrator's last question?

6. What does Soyinka accomplish with humor? Compare this poem with the humor in the speech by Sojourner Truth.

The Reading/Writing Connection

1. Create a telephone conversation about renting a room or apartment. Like Soyinka, create a speaker who cannot succeed in his or her quest because of bigotry.

2. Respond in a journal entry to the closing lines of the poem.

Ideas for Writing

1. Discuss humor as a political response. Refer to this poem and to other works that you have read.

Emily Dickinson   *(1830–1886)*

I'm Nobody! Who are You?   *1929*

I'm Nobody! Who are you?
Are you—Nobody—Too?
Then there's a pair of us?
Don't tell! they'd advertise—you know!

How dreary—to be—Somebody!   5
How public—like a Frog—
To tell one's name—the livelong June—
To an admiring Bog!

Dagoberto Gilb   *(1950–)*

You Know Him By His Labors, But Not His Face   *2004*

The one who left wasn't the only one sleeping on a stained twin mattress under a carpet remnant in the room near the stench of sewage, wasn't the only one making shadows from a single light bulb dangling by a wire, who laughed at that old snoring dog, who liked to praise that dinner of beans and rice and chiles, not the only one who shared a torn love seat to watch a fuzzy TV with so many brothers drinking beer and soda and sisters getting married and having babies, that crowd of aunts, uncles, cousins, nephews and nieces, not the only one with unfaded scars and bad teeth, not the only one who complained about that so-loud radio always somewhere, not the only one who could pick out the best used retread tires.

He wasn't the only one loving a mother who wore that same housedress and apron, warming tortillas in the morning and early evening, who was still a beautiful woman.

He was the one who left and he will never stop loving her either. He had to leave behind a wife. The one who left had to leave behind his children. It was as though where he was going was a distant uncle's place, a man not blood, on his father's side, or it was the ex-husband of his godmother.

Somebody close to somebody else, somebody known but who is not in the family. That rich man has a successful construction business, or is a landowner, or he is just from "the States." He is the one many have seen drinking, laughing, talking loud in his language. He wouldn't live in even the nicest house in Mexico.

In "the States," there is work that pays and that is what the one who left needs and wants and he knows how to work, he is not afraid of any work, of earning. He is the one who left and he met good people, and bad people, and it was always dirty and mean, the same clothes no matter where or when or what. And that rich man does have lots of work. The one who left sweeps the sawdust and scrubs the cement and masonry tools and coils the hoses.

He stoops low for the cinder blocks and he lifts a beam that has to be set   5
high. He pushes the wheelbarrow and pounds spikes with a flattened waffle-face metal hammer and he pulls out pins with its claws. He hauls the trash scraps and he digs the plumbing trench.

He always says yes and he means yes. He is a cheap wage, and he is quiet because he is far from home, as paperless as birth, and he not only acts grateful, he is grateful, because there is always worse at home.

The one who left is nobody special, and he knows it him self.

There are so many others just like him, hungry, even hungrier once they've been paid. His only home is work and job. His only trust, his only confidence, is the work, the job.

The one who left lives near streets in the States that were the first and are now the last. He shops at markets where others who left go.

He does not go to banks, but of course he wants to. He does not have a   10
driver's license, but of course he wants one. He does not have a phone, but of course he wants one. He wants his family to be with him.

He learned early to live like a shadow watching a single light bulb and now he moves with almost a natural invisibility, carefully crossing into the light of night, not really seen when he's working in the sun.

He is someone who left his mother to get work.

He left his wife to find work.

He left his children to get work.

His citizenship is not in Mexico or in "the States" but is at a job.   15

He is not a part-time citizen, a temporary citizen.

He is loyal to work, and he is a patriot of its country.

He does not want to leave it in three years, or in six years. Like everyone else, he wants to become wealthy in his country.

Taslima Nasrin (1962–)

Translated from the Bengali by Carolyne Wright,
Mohammad Nurul Hada, and Taslima Nasrin

Things Cheaply Had   *1991*

In the market nothing can be had as cheap as women.
If they get a small bottle of *alta*[1] for their feet
        they spend three nights sleepless for sheer joy.
If they get a few bars of soap to scrub their skin
        and some scented oil for their hair   5
they become so submissive that they scoop out
        chunks of their flesh
to be sold in the flea market twice a week.
If they get a jewel for their nose
        they lick feet for seventy days or so,   10
a full three and a half months
        if it's a single striped sari.[2]

Even the mangy cur of the house barks now and then,
and over the mouths of women cheaply had
        there's a lock   15
a golden lock.

Explorations of the Text

1. Explore the contrast of the "nobody" and "somebody" presented in these three works.

2. Explore the significance of the repeated statement in Gilb's piece: "The one who left wasn't the only one sleeping . . ." Who is "the one who left"? Why does Gilb not name and describe the person more specifically?

3. Examine the actions associated with the ones "who left." What do you conclude?

4. Examine the imagery, figurative language, and form in each work. How do they develop meaning (for example, the use of questions, dashes and rhyme in Dickinson's work; the use of repetition in Gilb's work; and the body images in Nasrin's poem)?

5. Compare the symbolism of the "body" and "nobody" presented in these works with Robert Waugh's "Bodies" in the opening thematic cluster in this chapter.

The Reading/Writing Connection

1. Respond in a freewrite: Who are the "nobodies" in North American society or in another society with which you are familiar?

---

[1] **alta:** Lac-dye, a red liquid with which South Asian women decorate the borders of their feet on ceremonial occasions, such as weddings and dance performances. Alta is more in vogue among Hindus, but Bangladeshi women also use it, and it can be seen on the feet of Muslim heroines and harem women in Moghul miniature paintings. [Translator's note.]   [2] **sari:** A garment worn chiefly by women in India and Pakistan consisting of a long cloth wrapped around the body with one end draped over one shoulder or the head.

2. Create a poem using "somebody" or "nobody" as a title. Or start with one of the lines of the selected poems as a beginning. Then analyze your work. What themes are you presenting? What elements of your poem develop your message?

3. **Write an Argument:** Gilb builds his argument using specific examples and emotional appeals to an audience. Create a persuasive claim and support it through specific examples and emotional appeals.

Ideas for Writing

1. **Write an Argument:** Do you agree or disagree with Gilb's portrait of the illegal immigrant? Support your position with examples drawn from your observations, experiences, reading, and knowledge of current events.

2. Research the current immigration debate. Do you agree with President Bush's proposed guest worker plan? Do you think there should be a form of amnesty for illegal immigrants who have been in this country for more than a certain number of years? Do you think funneling money into more border patrols or a fence will stop the surge of immigrants into this country? Present your position on these issues.

3. Explore the process of dehumanization presented in these works. Select a quotation from Emma Goldman as a critical lens through which to explore the works. You also may include other selected works in this chapter or Szymborska's "Children of our Age" in Chapter 9.

4. Interview a recent immigrant to this country or someone in your family who has come here from another country. Ask them about their experiences of coming to the United States. Then write an essay based on your interview in which you explore the immigrant experience. You also may focus on your own experiences if you are an immigrant. An important collection of oral histories of immigrants is *Crossing the Boulevard.* You can access these oral histories via the Internet.

Anthony Hecht *(1923–)*

The Book of Yolek *(1990)*

Wir haben ein Gesetz,
Und nach dem Gesetz soll er sterben.[1]

The dowsed coals fume and hiss after your meal
Of grilled brook trout, and you saunter off for a walk
Down the fern trail, it doesn't matter where to,
Just so you're weeks and worlds away from home,

---

[1] **Wir haben . . . sterben:** "We have a law, and by the law he ought to die." From the German translation of John 19.7. The source of the poem is "Yanosz Korczak's Last Walk" by Hannah Mortkowitz-Olczakowa, which recounts events surrounding the Jewish Holocaust during World War II.

And among midsummer hills have set up camp 5
In the deep bronze glories of declining day.

You remember, peacefully, an earlier day
In childhood, remember a quite specific meal:
A corn roast and bonfire in summer camp.
That summer you got lost on a Nature Walk; 10
More than you dared admit, you thought of home;
No one else knows where the mind wanders to.

The fifth of August, 1942.
It was morning and very hot. It was the day
They came at dawn with rifles to The Home 15
For Jewish Children, cutting short the meal
Of bread and soup, lining them up to walk
In close formation off to a special camp.

How often you have thought about that camp,
As though in some strange way you were driven to, 20
And about the children, and how they were made to walk,
Yolek who had bad lungs, who wasn't a day
Over five years old, commanded to leave his meal
And shamble between armed guards to his long home.

We're approaching August again. It will drive home 25
The regulation torments of that camp
Yolek was sent to, his small, unfinished meal,
The electric fences, the numeral tattoo,
The quite extraordinary heat of the day
They all were forced to take that terrible walk. 30

Whether on a silent, solitary walk
Or among crowds, far off or safe at home,
You will remember, helplessly, that day,
And the smell of smoke, and the loudspeakers of the camp.
Wherever you are, Yolek will be there, too. 35
His unuttered name will interrupt your meal.

Prepare to receive him in your home some day.
Though they killed him in the camp they sent him to,
He will walk in as you're sitting down to a meal.

Explorations of the Text

1. Explore the stance of the speaker. How is he like one of Wiesel's witnesses?

2. Why does Hecht entitle the poem, "The Book of Yolek"? Is Yolek a representative figure?

3. Discuss contrasts of the ordinary and the horrific portrayed in the work. How do the specific, sensory details enlarge the vision of this tragic, historical moment?
4. Hecht uses Biblical imagery and religious symbolism (the Passover seder). How do these allusions develop meaning?
5. Discuss the work as an act of memorialization. Compare and contrast the works with the poems in the 9/11 cluster.

The Reading/Writing Connection

1. Whom do you imagine the speaker to be? Create a portrait of the speaker (age, appearance, gestures, attitudes, values, actions). Why is he creating "The Book of Yolek"?
2. "Think" Topic: Discuss the various meanings and associations ascribed to the word "home" in this work. What do you conclude?

Ideas for Writing

1. **Write an Argument:** Compare and contrast the treatment of the Holocaust in this work and in Paul Celan's "Death Fugue." Consider such formal features of a poem as point of view, tone, imagery, symbolism, formal elements, and theme. Or consider which poem affects you more. Why?

Poems for 9/11

Billy Collins *(1941–)*

The Names   2002

Yesterday, I lay awake in the palm of the night.
A fine rain stole in, unhelped by any breeze,
And when I saw the silver glaze on the windows,
I started with A, with Ackerman, as it happened,
Then Baxter and Calabro,   5
Davis and Eberling, names falling into place
As droplets fell through the dark.

Names printed on the ceiling of the night.
Names slipping around a watery bend.
Twenty-six willows on the banks of a stream.   10
In the morning, I walked out barefoot
Among thousands of flowers
Heavy with dew like the eyes of tears,

And each had a name—
Fiori inscribed on a yellow petal   15
Then Gonzalez and Han, Ishikawa and Jenkins.

Names written in the air
And stitched into the cloth of the day.
A name under a photograph taped to a mailbox.
Monogram on a torn shirt,   20
I see you spelled out on storefront windows
And on the bright unfurled awnings of this city.
I say the syllables as I turn a corner—
Kelly and Lee,
Medina, Nardella, and O'Connor.   25

When I peer into the woods,
I see a thick tangle where letters are hidden
As in a puzzle concocted for children.
Parker and Quigley in the twigs of an ash,
Rizzo, Schubert, Torres, and Upton,   30
Secrets in the boughs of an ancient maple.

Names written in the pale sky.
Names rising in the updraft amid buildings.
Names silent in stone
Or cried out behind a door.   35
Names blown over the earth and out to sea.

In the evening—weakening light, the last swallows.
A boy on a lake lifts his oars.
A woman by a window puts a match to a candle,
And the names are outlined on the rose clouds—   40
Vanacore and Wallace,
(let X stand, if it can, for the ones unfound)
Then Young and Ziminsky, the final jolt of Z.

Names etched on the head of a pin.
One name spanning a bridge, another undergoing a tunnel.   45
A blue name needled into the skin.
Names of citizens, workers, mothers and fathers,
The bright-eyed daughter, the quick son.
Alphabet of names in green rows in a field.
Names in the small tracks of birds.   50
Names lifted from a hat
Or balanced on the tip of the tongue.
Names wheeled into the dim warehouse of memory.
So many names, there is barely room on the walls of the heart.

Martín Espada *(1957–)*

Alabanza: In Praise of Local 100 *2002*

*for the 43 members of Hotel Employees and Restaurant Employees
Local 100, working at the Windows on the World restaurant,
who lost their lives in the attack on the World Trade Center*

Alabanza. Praise the cook with a shaven head
and a tattoo on his shoulder that said *Oye,*
a blue-eyed Puerto Rican with people from Fajardo,
the harbor of pirates centuries ago.
Praise the lighthouse in Fajardo, candle   5
glimmering white to worship the dark saint of the sea.
Alabanza. Praise the cook's yellow Pirates cap
worn in the name of Roberto Clemente, his plane
that flamed into the ocean loaded with cans for Nicaragua,
all the mouths chewing the ash of earthquakes.   10
Alabanza. Praise the kitchen radio, dial clicked
even before the dial on the oven, so that music and Spanish
rose before bread. Praise the bread. *Alabanza.*

Praise Manhattan from a hundred and seven flights up,
like Atlantis glimpsed through the windows of an ancient aquarium.   15
Praise the great windows where immigrants from the kitchen
could squint and almost see their world, hear the chant of nations:
Ecuador, Mexico, Republica Dominicana,
Haiti, Yemen, Ghana, Bangladesh.
Alabanza. Praise the kitchen in the morning,   20
where the gas burned blue on every stove
and exhaust fans fired their diminutive propellers,
hands cracked eggs with quick thumbs
or sliced open cartons to build an altar of cans.
Alabanza. Praise the busboy's music, the *chime-chime*   25
of his dishes and silverware in the tub.
Alabanza. Praise the dish-dog, the dishwasher
who worked that morning because another dishwasher
could not stop coughing, or because he needed overtime
to pile the sacks of rice and beans for a family   30
floating away on some Caribbean island plagued by frogs.
Alabanza. Praise the waitress who heard the radio in the kitchen
and sang to herself about a man gone. *Alabanza.*

After the thunder wilder than thunder,
after the shudder deep in the glass of the great windows,   35
after the radio stopped singing like a tree full of terrified frogs,
after night burst the dam of day and flooded the kitchen,
for a time the stoves glowed in darkness like the lighthouse in Fajardo,

like a cook's soul. Soul I say, even if the dead cannot tell us
about the bristles of God's beard because God has no face,   40
soul I say, to name the smoke-beings flung in constellations
across the night sky of this city and cities to come.
Alabanza I say, even if God has no face.

Alabanza. When the war began, from Manhattan and Kabul
two constellations of smoke rose and drifted to each other,   45
mingling in icy air, and one said with an Afghan tongue:
Teach me to dance. We have no music here.
And the other said with a Spanish tongue:
I will teach you. Music is all we have.

Adam Zagajewski   *(1945–)*   Translated, from the Polish, by Clare Cavanagh

Try to Praise the Mutilated World   *2001*

Try to praise the mutilated world.
Remember June's long days,
and wild strawberries, drops of wine, the dew.
The nettles that methodically overgrow
the abandoned homestead of exiles.   5
You must praise the mutilated world.
You watched the stylish yachts and ships;
one of them had a long trip ahead of it,
while salty oblivion awaited others.
You've seen the refugees heading nowhere,   10
you've heard the executioners sing joyfully.
You should praise the mutilated world.
Remember the moments when we were together
in a white room and the curtain fluttered.
Return in thought to the concert where music flared.   15
You gathered acorns in the park in autumn
and leaves eddied over the earth's scars.
Praise the mutilated world
and the gray feather a thrush lost,
and the gentle light that strays and vanishes   20
and returns.

Explorations of the Text

1. What impact does Collins's narrative method have—the names of people in alphabetical order?

2. How do the poets enlarge the scope of 9/11 and envision it as part of a "twen-

tieth century history of violent death"? Analyze the historical allusions.

3. How does the reader become a witness to disaster?

4. Although Zagajewski's "Try to Praise the Mutilated World" was not written

in response to 9/11 (Alice Quinn, the poetry editor of *The New Yorker,* chose it as the back page in the edition that came out directly after the date), how is the poem a comment on the tragedy?

5. The refrain in Zagajewski's "Try to Praise the Mutilated World" changes. What do these changes suggest about the perspective of the speaker?

6. Compare the speakers in Collins's "The Names," Zagajewski's "Try to Praise the Mutilated World," and Espada's "Alabanza . . ." How do they view the "mutilated world"? Who is more optimistic? More pessimistic? Do any of the speakers have hope for the future? Compare their stances with that of the speaker in Yeats's "The Second Coming" in Chapter 9.

The Reading/Writing Connection

1. Write your own 9/11 poem, autobiographical narrative, or short story. What do you remember about the day? What helped you to deal with the horror?

2. After 9/11, did you find comfort in any literary works, music, or art? If you had to add another work to this 9/11 cluster, what would it be? Explain your choice.

3. Begin a poem with "Try to . . ."

4. Analyze the use of repetition in the three works. What is the impact of this technique?

5. Write a letter to one of the poets, responding to the work and presenting your reactions to 9/11.

Ideas for Writing

1. Compare the attitudes of the speakers toward 9/11 and other historic calamities and tragedies. You may include your own 9/11 work. How do they treat the event? How do they envision the impact on people's daily lives? Do they see themselves living in a changed world? You also may refer to Milosz's "American Ignorance of War."

2. Using your response to question 2 in the Reading/Writing Connection as a starting point, compose an essay suggesting how a particular text helped you to cope with 9/11 or another tragic event. Focus on the specific elements of the work that proved to be comforting or instructive.

3. Often in eulolgizing a person, one wants to keep the person's memory alive through recounting special moments with the person or biographical facts. In this way, the person never dies. How does this work through its use of specifics become a song of praise, commemorating the lives of the workers?

4. Write a song of praise for someone whom you know who has died. Include the specifics that make the person come alive. You may write in poetic or prose form.

 On the Web: *Responses to 9/11—Wendell Berry*

Please visit http://www.academic.cengage.com/english/Schmidt/Legacies4e/ for links to the following online resources.

"Thoughts in the Presence of Fear"
Narratives about 9/11

The Ideal vs. the Real World/Poetry

William Blake *(1757–1827)*

London   *1794*

I wander through each chartered[1] street,
Near where the chartered Thames does flow,
And mark in every face I meet
Marks of weakness, marks of woe.

In every cry of every man,   5
In every Infant's cry of fear,
In every voice, in every ban,
The mind-forged manacles I hear.

How the Chimney-sweeper's cry
Every black'ning Church appalls;   10
And the hapless Soldier's sigh
Runs in blood down Palace walls.

But most through midnight streets I hear
How the youthful Harlot's curse
Blasts the new-born Infant's tear,   15
And blights with plagues the Marriage hearse.

Frances Ellen Watkins Harper   *(1825–1911)*

The Slave Auction   *1854*

The sale began—young girls were there,
    Defenceless in their wretchedness,
Whose stifled sobs of deep despair
    Revealed their anguish and distress.

And mothers stood with streaming eyes,   5
    And saw their dearest children sold;
Unheeded rose their bitter cries,
    While tyrants bartered them for gold.

And woman, with her love and truth—
    For these in sable[1] forms may dwell—   10

---

[1]**chartered:** Pre-empted by the State and leased by royal patent.   [1]**sable:** Black.

Gaz'd on the husband of her youth,
   With anguish none may paint or tell.

And men, whose sole crime was their hue,
   The impress of their Maker's hand,
And frail and shrinking children, too,   15
   Were gathered in that mournful band.

Ye who have laid your love to rest,
   And wept above their lifeless clay,
Know not the anguish of that breast,
   Whose lov'd are rudely torn away.   20

Ye may not know how desolate
   Are bosoms rudely forced to part,
And how a dull and heavy weight
   Will press the life-drops from the heart.

Paul Laurence Dunbar   *(1872–1906)*

Sympathy   *1893*

I know what the caged bird feels, alas!
   When the sun is bright on the upland slopes;
When the wind stirs soft through the springing grass,
And the river flows like a stream of glass;
   When the first bird sings and the first bud opens,   5
And the faint perfume from its chalice steals—
I know what the caged bird feels!

I know why the caged bird beats his wing
   Till its blood is red on the cruel bars;
For he must fly back to his perch and cling   10
When he fain would be on the bough a-swing;
   And a pain still throbs in the old, old scars
And they pulse again with a keener sting—
I know why he beats his wing!

I know why the caged bird sings, ah me,   15
   When his wing is bruised and his bosom sore,—
When he beats his bars and he would be free;
It is not a carol of joy or glee,
   But a prayer that he sends from his heart's deep core,
But a plea, that upward to Heaven he flings—   20
I know why the caged bird sings!

Gloria Anzaldúa *(1942–   )*

horse *1987*

(para la gente de Hargill, Texas)[1]

Great horse running in the fields
come thundering toward
the outstretched hands
nostrils flaring at the corn
only it was knives in the hidden hands   5
can a horse smell tempered steel?

Anoche[2] some kids cut up a horse
it was night and the *pueblo*[3] slept
the Mexicans mutter among themselves:
they hobbled the two front legs   10
the two hind legs, kids aged sixteen
but they're *gringos*[4]
and the sheriff won't do a thing
he'd just say boys will be boys
just following their instincts.   15

But it's the mind that kills
the animal the *mexicanos* murmur
killing it would have been a mercy
black horse running in the dark
came thundering toward   20
the outstretched hands
nostrils flaring at the smell
only it was knives in the hidden hands
did it pray all night for morning?

It was the owner came running   25
30–30 in his hand
put the *caballo*[5] out of its pain
the Chicanos shake their heads
turn away some rich father
fished out his wallet   30
held out the folds of green
as if green could staunch red

pools dripping from the ribbons
on the horse's flanks
could cast up testicles   35
grow back the ears on the horse's head
no ears of corn but sheaths
hiding blades of steel

---

[1]*para . . . Texas:* For the people of Hargill, Texas.   [2]*Anoche:* Last night.   [3]*pueblo:*
Village.   [4]*gringos:* Whites.   [5]*caballo:* Horse.

earth drinking blood sun rusting it
in that small Texas town   40
the *mexicanos* shuffle their feet
shut their faces stare at the ground.

Dead horse neighing in the night
come thundering toward the open faces
hooves iron-shod hurling lightning   45

only it is red red in the moonlight
in their sleep the *gringos* cry out
the *mexicanos* mumble if you're Mexican
you are born old.

Paul Celan *(1920–1970)*   Translated by Robert H. Waugh

Death Fugue   1952

Black milk of the morning we drink it at evening
we drink it at noon in the morning we drink it at night
we drink and we drink
we shovel a grave in the winds you don't lie there cramped
A man lives in the house he plays with snakes he writes   5
he writes when it darkens to Germany your gold hair Margaret
he writes and steps from the house the stars spark he whistles up hounds
he whistles his Jews out he has them shovel a grave in the earth
he commands us play for the dance

Black milk of the morning we drink you at night   10
we drink you morning and noon we drink you at evening
we drink and we drink
A man lives in the house he plays with the snakes he writes
he writes when it darkens to Germany your golden hair Margaret[1]
Your ashen hair Shulamite[2] we shovel a grave in the winds you don't lie there   15
cramped

He calls dig deeper into earth's kingdom you there you others sing and play
he grabs the iron in his belt he swings it his eyes are blue
dig deeper with your spades you there you others play on for the dance

Black milk of the morning we drink you at night
we drink you noon and morning we drink you at evening   20
we drink and we drink
a man lives in the house your golden hair Margaret
your ashen hair Shulamite he plays with the snakes

He calls play death more sweetly death is a German craftsman
he calls play the violins more darkly you will rise like smoke in the wind   25
you will have a grave in the clouds you won't lie there cramped

---

[1]**Margaret:** allusion to Gretchen in Goethe's *Faust*.   [2]**Shulamite:** the name of the beloved in *The Song of Songs*.

Black milk of the morning we drink you at night
we drink you at noon death is a German master
we drink you evenings mornings we drink and we drink
death is a German craftsman his eyes are blue   30
he hits you with a lead bullet he hits you now
a man lives in the house your golden hair Margaret
he sets his hounds on us he gives us a grave in the wind
he plays with the snakes and dreams death is a German master

your golden hair Margaret   35
your ashen hair Shulamite

Explorations of the Text

1. Compare and contrast the speaker's voice, point of view, and tone in these poems. Create a portrait of one of the speakers (age, appearance, gestures, attitudes, past experiences, values, likes and dislikes). What do you conclude? How is the character of the speaker important to the development of the poem?

2. What social issues and conflicts do the works represent? Discuss the historical and social contexts of the works.

3. What forms of oppression do the speakers experience? What are their responses to unjust treatment?

The Reading/Writing Connection

1. **Write an Argument:** Which poem do you think most forcefully presents its argument? Why? What techniques of argumentative writing does the poet use to convey his or her message (see Chapter 4)?

Ideas for Writing

1. Explore writing as a form of social protest. Examine the role of the poet in Allen Ginsberg's works and in works in this cluster.

2. Bertold Brecht's famous poem, "Motto," poses an important question and answer about art's response to atrocity and injustice:

"In the dark times, will there also be singing?
Yes, there will be singing
About the dark times."

Write an Argument: Do you think that it is possible to "[sing]" "about the dark times"? Is it possible to create beauty out of atrocity? Should we do so?

 On the Web: *Protest Songs*

Please visit http://www.academic.cengage.com/english/Schmidt/Legacies4e/ for links to the following online resources.

Woodie Guithrie, "The Dying Miners," "The Farmer Labor Train"
Abel Meeropol (pseudonym Lewis Allen), "Strange Fruit" as sung by Billie Holiday
Bob Dylan, "Blowing in the Wind"
John Lennon, "Imagine"
Green Day, "Holiday"
India Arie, "Video"
Jack Johnson, "In Times Like These"

DRAMA

Sophocles *(496–406 B.C.)* Translated by Dudley Fitts and Robert Fitzgerald

Antigone *(c. 441 B.C.)*

Characters

ANTIGONE
ISMENE } daughters of Oedipus
EURYDICE, *wife of Creon*
CREON, *King of Thebes*
HAIMON, *son of Creon*
TEIRESIAS, *a blind seer*
A SENTRY
A MESSENGER
CHORUS

> *Scene: Before the palace of* CREON, *King of Thebes. A central double door, and two lateral doors. A platform extends the length of the façade, and from this platform three steps lead down into the "orchestra" or chorus-ground.*
>
> *Time: dawn of the day after the repulse of the Argive army from the assault on Thebes.*

Prologue

(ANTIGONE *and* ISMENE *enter from the central door of the Palace.*)

Antigone: Ismene, dear sister,
    You would think that we had already suffered enough
    For the curse on Oedipus:[1]
    I cannot imagine any grief
    That you and I have not gone through. And now—   5
    Have they told you of the new decree of our King Creon?
Ismene: I have heard nothing: I know
    That two sisters lost two brothers, a double death
    In a single hour; and I know that the Argive army
    Fled in the night; but beyond this, nothing.   10
Antigone: I thought so. And that is why I wanted you
    To come out here with me. There is something we must do.
Ismene: Why do you speak so strangely?
Antigone: Listen, Ismene:

---

[1] **Oedipus:** Oedipus, father of Antigone, Ismene, Polyneices, and Eteocles, was King of Thebes. Unknowingly, he killed his father and married his mother. Upon learning what he had done, he put out his eyes and went into exile. Heirs to the throne, Polyneices and Eteocles eventually quarreled. Eteocles drove out Polyneices, but Polyneices returned to attack Thebes, and both brothers died in battle. Creon became king and ordered that Polyneices's body be left unburied.

Creon buried our brother Eteocles 15
With military honors, gave him a soldier's funeral,
And it was right that he should; but Polyneices,
Who fought as bravely and died as miserably,—
They say that Creon has sworn
No one shall bury him, no one mourn for him, 20
But his body must lie in the fields, a sweet treasure
For carrion birds to find as they search for food.
That is what they say, and our good Creon is coming here
To announce it publicly; and the penalty—
Stoning to death in the public square! 25
                There it is,
And now you can prove what you are:
A true sister, or a traitor to your family.
Ismene: Antigone, you are mad! What could I possibly do?
Antigone: You must decide whether you will help me or not. 30
Ismene: I do not understand you. Help you in what?
Antigone: Ismene, I am going to bury him. Will you come?
Ismene: Bury him! You have just said the new law forbids it.
Antigone: He is my brother. And he is your brother, too.
Ismene: But think of the danger! Think what Creon will do! 35
Antigone: Creon is not strong enough to stand in my way.
Ismene: Ah sister!
    Oedipus died, everyone hating him
For what his own search brought to light, his eyes
Ripped out by his own hand; and Iocaste died, 40
His mother and wife at once: she twisted the cords
That strangled her life; and our two brothers died,
Each killed by the other's sword. And we are left:
But oh, Antigone,
Think how much more terrible than these 45
Our own death would be if we should go against Creon
And do what he has forbidden! We are only women,
We cannot fight with men, Antigone!
The law is strong, we must give in to the law
In this thing, and in worse. I beg the Dead 50
To forgive me, but I am helpless: I must yield
To those in authority. And I think it is dangerous business
To be always meddling.
Antigone: If that is what you think,
I should not want you, even if you asked to come. 55
You have made your choice, you can be what you want to be
But I will bury him; and if I must die,
I say that this crime is holy: I shall lie down
With him in death, and I shall be as dear
To him as he to me. 60
              It is the dead,
Not the living, who make the longest demands:

We die for ever . . .

                    You may do as you like,

Since apparently the laws of the gods mean nothing to you.   65

Ismene: They mean a great deal to me; but I have no strength

   To break laws that were made for the public good.

Antigone: That must be your excuse, I suppose. But as for me,

   I will bury the brother I love.

Ismene: Antigone,   70

   I am so afraid for you!

Antigone: You need not be:

   You have yourself to consider, after all.

Ismene: But no one must hear of this, you must tell no one!

   I will keep it a secret, I promise!   75

Antigone: Oh tell it! Tell everyone!

   Think how they'll hate you when it all comes out

   If they learn that you knew about it all the time!

Ismene: So fiery! You should be cold, with fear.

Antigone: Perhaps. But I am doing only what I must.   80

Ismene: But can you do it? I say that you cannot.

Antigone: Very well: when my strength gives out, I shall do no more.

Ismene: Impossible things should not be tried at all.

Antigone: Go away, Ismene:

   I shall be hating you soon, and the dead will too,   85

   For your words are hateful. Leave me my foolish plan:

   I am not afraid of the danger; if it means death,

   It will not be the worst of deaths—death without

   honor.

Ismene: Go then, if you feel that you must.   90

   You are unwise,

   But a loyal friend indeed to those who love you.

(Exit into the Palace. ANTIGONE *goes off, left. Enter the* CHORUS.*)*

PARODOS[2] I • Strophe[3] 1

Chorus: Now the long blade of the sun, lying

   Level east to west, touches with glory

   Thebes of the Seven Gates. Open, unlidded

   Eye of golden day! O marching light

   Across the eddy and rush of Dirce's stream[4]   5

   Striking the white shields of the enemy

   Thrown headlong backward from the blaze of morning!

Choragos:[5] Polyneices their commander

   Roused them with windy phrases,

   He the wild eagle screaming   10

---

[2]**Parodos:** Sung by the Chorus upon entering.   [3]**Stophe:** Sung by the chorus as they move from stage right to stage left.   [4]**Dirce's stream:** Near Thebes.   [5]**Choragos:** Leader of the Chorus.

Insults above our land,
His wings their shields of snow,
His crest their marshalled helms.

Antistrophe[6] *1*

Chorus: Against our seven gates in a yawning ring
The famished spears came onward in the night;   15
But before his jaws were sated with our blood,
Or pinefire took the garland of our towers,
He was thrown back; and as he turned, great Thebes—
No tender victim for his noisy power—
Rose like a dragon behind him, shouting war.   20

Choragos: For God hates utterly
The bray of bragging tongues;
And when he beheld their smiling,
Their swagger of golden helms,
The frown of his thunder blasted   25
Their first man from our walls.

Strophe 2

Chorus: We heard his shout of triumph high in the air
Turn to a scream; far out in a flaming arc
He fell with his windy torch, and the earth struck him.
And others storming in fury no less than his   30
Found shock of death in the dusty joy of battle.

Choragos: Seven captains at seven gates
Yielded their clanging arms to the god
That bends the battle-line and breaks it.
These two only, brothers in blood,   35
Face to face in matchless rage,
Mirroring each the other's death,
Clashed in long combat.

Antistrophe 2

Chorus: But now in the beautiful morning of victory
Let Thebes of the many chariots sing for joy!   40
With hearts for dancing we'll take leave of war:
Our temples shall be sweet with hymns of praise,
And the long night shall echo with our chorus.

Scene 1

Choragos: But now at last our new King is coming:
Creon of Thebes, Menoikeus' son.
In this auspicious dawn of his reign
What are the new complexities

---

[6]**Antistrophe:** Sung by the chorus as they move from stage left to stage right.

That shifting Fate has woven for him? 5
What is his counsel? Why has he summoned
The old men to hear him?

(Enter CREON *from the Palace, center. He addresses the* CHORUS *from the top step.)*

Creon: Gentlemen: I have the honor to inform you that our Ship of State, which
recent storms have threatened to destroy, has come safely to harbor at last,
guided by the merciful wisdom of Heaven. I have summoned you here this 10
morning because I know that I can depend upon you: your devotion to
King Laios was absolute; you never hesitated in your duty to our late ruler
Oedipus; and when Oedipus died, your loyalty was transferred to his children.
Unfortunately, as you know, his two sons, the princes Eteocles and Polyneices,
have killed each other in battle; and I, as the next in blood, have succeeded to 15
the full power of the throne.

   I am aware, of course, that no Ruler can expect complete loyalty from his
subjects until he has been tested in office. Nevertheless, I say to you at the very
outset that I have nothing but contempt for the kind of Governor who is afraid,
for whatever reason, to follow the course that he knows is best for the State; and 20
as for the man who sets private friendship above the public welfare,—I have
no use for him, either. I call God to witness that if I saw my country headed
for ruin, I should not be afraid to speak out plainly; and I need hardly remind
you that I would never have any dealings with an enemy of the people. No one
values friendship more highly than I; but we must remember that friends made 25
at the risk of wrecking our Ship are not real friends at all.

   These are my principles, at any rate, and that is why I have made the
following decision concerning the sons of Oedipus: Eteocles, who died as a man
should die, fighting for his country, is to be buried with full military honors,
with all the ceremony that is usual when the greatest heroes die; but his brother 30
Polyneices, who broke his exile to come back with fire and sword against his
native city and the shrines of his fathers' gods, whose one idea was to spill the
blood of his blood and sell his own people into slavery—Polyneices, I say, is to
have no burial: no man is to touch him or say the least prayer for him; he shall
lie on the plain, unburied; and the birds and the scavenging dogs can do with 35
him whatever they like.

   This is my command, and you can see the wisdom behind it. As long as
I am King, no traitor is going to be honored with the loyal man. But whoever
shows by word and deed that he is on the side of the State,—he shall have my
respect while he is living, and my reverence when he is dead. 40

Choragos: If that is your will, Creon son of Menoikeus,
   You have the right to enforce it: we are yours.
Creon: That is my will. Take care that you do your part.
Choragos: We are old men: let the younger ones carry it out.
Creon: I do not mean that: the sentries have been appointed. 45
Choragos: Then what is it that you would have us do?
Creon: You will give no support to whoever breaks this law.
Choragos: Only a crazy man is in love with death!
Creon: And death it is; yet money talks, and the wisest
   Have sometimes been known to count a few coins too many. 50

   (Enter SENTRY *from left.)*

Sentry: I'll not say that I'm out of breath from running, King, because every time I
stopped to think about what I have to tell you, I felt like going back. And all
the time a voice kept saying, "You fool, don't you know you're walking straight
into trouble?"; and then another voice: "Yes, but if you let somebody else get
the news to Creon first, it will be even worse than that for you!" But good   55
sense won out, at least I hope it was good sense, and here I am with a story that
makes no sense at all; but I'll tell it anyhow, because, as they say, what's going
to happen's going to happen, and—

Creon: Come to the point. What have you to say?

Sentry: I did not do it. I did not see who did it. You must not punish me for what   60
someone else has done.

Creon: A comprehensive defense! More effective, perhaps,
If I knew its purpose. Come: what is it?

Sentry: A dreadful thing . . . I don't know how to put it—

Creon: Out with it!   65

Sentry: Well, then;
The dead man—
                Polyneices—
(*Pause. The* SENTRY *is overcome, fumbles for words.* CREON *waits impassively.*)
                out there—
                                someone,—   70
New dust on the slimy flesh!
(*Pause. No sign from* CREON.)
Someone has given it burial that way, and
Gone. . .
(*Long pause.* CREON *finally speaks with deadly control:*)

Creon: And the man who dared do this ?

Sentry: I swear I   75
Do not know! You must believe me!
                Listen:
The ground was dry, not a sign of digging, no,
Not a wheeltrack in the dust, no trace of anyone.
It was when they relieved us this morning: and one of them,   80
The corporal, pointed to it.
                There it was,
The strangest—
                Look:
The body, just mounded over with light dust: you see?   85
Not buried really, but as if they'd covered it
Just enough for the ghost's peace. And no sign
Of dogs or any wild animal that had been there.

And then what a scene there was! Every man of us
Accusing the other: we all proved the other man did it,   90
We all had proof that we could not have done it.
We were ready to take hot iron in our hands,
Walk through fire, swear by all the gods,
It was not I

> ***I do not know who it was, but it was not I!***   95
>
> (CREON's *rage has been mounting steadily, but the* SENTRY *is too intent upon his story to notice it.*)
>
> And then, when this came to nothing, someone said
> A thing that silenced us and made us stare
> Down at the ground: you had to be told the news,
> And one of us had to do it! We threw the dice,
> And the bad luck fell to me. So here I am,   100
> No happier to be here than you are to have me:
> Nobody likes the man who brings bad news.

Choragos: I have been wondering, King: can it be that the gods have done this?

Creon: *(Furiously.)* Stop!

> Must you doddering wrecks   105
> Go out of your heads entirely? "The gods!"
> Intolerable!
> The gods favor this corpse? Why? How had he served them?
> Tried to loot their temples, burn their images,
> Yes, and the whole State, and its laws with it!   110
> Is it your senile opinion that the gods love to honor bad men?
> A pious thought!—
>   No, from the very beginning
> There have been those who have whispered together,
> Stiff-necked anarchists, putting their heads together,   115
> Scheming against me in alleys. These are the men,
> And they have bribed my own guard to do this thing.
> *(Sententiously.)* Money!
> There's nothing in the world so demoralizing as money,
> Down go your cities,   120
> Homes gone, men gone, honest hearts corrupted,
> Crookedness of all kinds, and all for money!
> *(To* SENTRY.*)*   But you—!
> I swear by God and by the throne of God,
> The man who has done this thing shall pay for it!   125
> Find that man, bring him here to me, or your death
> Will be the least of your problems: I'll string you up
> Alive, and there will be certain ways to make you
> Discover your employer before you die;
> And the process may teach you a lesson you seem to have missed: 130
> The dearest profit is sometimes all too dear:
> That depends on the source. Do you understand me?
> A fortune won is often misfortune.

Sentry: King, may I speak?

Creon: Your very voice distresses me.   135

Sentry: Are you sure that it is my voice, and not your conscience?

Creon: By God, he wants to analyze me now!

Sentry: It is not what I say, but what has been done, that hurts you.

Creon: You talk too much.

Sentry: Maybe; but I've done nothing.   140

Creon: Sold your soul for some silver: that's all you've done.

Sentry: How dreadful it is when the right judge judges wrong!

Creon: Your figures of speech

May entertain you now; but unless you bring me the man,

You will get little profit from them in the end.   145

(Exit CREON *into the Palace.)*

Sentry: "Bring me the man"—!

I'd like nothing better than bringing him the man!

But bring him or not, you have seen the last of me here.

At any rate, I am safe!

(Exit SENTRY.*)*

    ODE I • Strophe 1

Chorus: Numberless are the world's wonders, but none

More wonderful than man; the stormgray sea

Yields to his prows, the huge crests bear him high;

Earth, holy and inexhaustible, is graven

With shining furrows where his plows have gone   5

Year after year, the timeless labor of stallions.

Antistrophe 1

The lightboned birds and beasts that cling to cover,

The lithe fish lighting their reaches of dim water,

All are taken, tamed in the net of his mind;

The lion on the hill, the wild horse windy-maned,   10

Resign to him; and his blunt yoke has broken

The sultry shoulders of the mountain bull.

Strophe 2

Words also, and thought as rapid as air,

He fashions to his good use; statecraft is his,

And his the skill that deflects the arrows of snow,   15

The spears of winter rain: from every wind

He has made himself secure—from all but one:

In the late wind of death he cannot stand.

Antistrophe 2

O clear intelligence, force beyond all measure!

O fate of man, working both good and evil!   20

When the laws are kept, how proudly his city stands!

When the laws are broken, what of his city then?

Never may the anarchic man find rest at my hearth,

Never be it said that my thoughts are his thoughts.

    Scene II

(Re-enter SENTRY *leading* ANTIGONE.*)*

Choragos: What does this mean? Surely this captive woman

Is the Princess, Antigone. Why should she be taken?

Sentry: Here is the one who did it! We caught her

In the very act of burying him.—Where is Creon?
Choragos: Just coming from the house.

(*Enter* CREON, *center.*)

Creon: What has happened?
Why have you come back so soon?
Sentry: (*Expansively.*)

                          O King,
A man should never be too sure of anything:
I would have sworn   10
That you'd not see me here again: your anger
Frightened me so, and the things you threatened me with;
But how could I tell then
That I'd be able to solve the case so soon?
No dice-throwing this time: I was only too glad to come!   15
Here is this woman. She is the guilty one:
We found her trying to bury him.
Take her, then; question her; judge her as you will.
I am through with the whole thing now, and glad of it.
Creon: But this is Antigone! Why have you brought her here?   20
Sentry: She was burying him, I tell you!
Creon: (*Severely.*)

                          Is this the truth?
Sentry: I saw her with my own eyes. Can I say more?
Creon: The details: come, tell me quickly!
Sentry: It was like this: 25
After those terrible threats of yours, King,
We went back and brushed the dust away from the body.
The flesh was soft by now, and stinking,
So we sat on a hill to windward and kept guard.
No napping this time! We kept each other awake.   30
But nothing happened until the white round sun
Whirled in the center of the round sky over us:
Then, suddenly,
A storm of dust roared up from the earth, and the sky
Went out, the plain vanished with all its trees   35
In the stinging dark. We closed our eyes and endured it.
The whirlwind lasted a long time, but it passed;
And then we looked, and there was Antigone!
I have seen
A mother bird come back to a stripped nest, heard   40
Her crying bitterly a broken note or two
For the young ones stolen. Just so, when this girl
Found the bare corpse, and all her love's work wasted,
She wept, and cried on heaven to damn the hands
That had done this thing.   45
                       And then she brought more dust
And sprinkled wine three times for her brother's ghost.

We ran and took her at once. She was not afraid,
Not even when we charged her with what she had done.
She denied nothing.   50
                         And this was a comfort to me,
And some uneasiness: for it is a good thing
To escape from death, but it is no great pleasure
To bring death to a friend.
                         Yet I always say   55
There is nothing so comfortable as your own safe skin!
Creon: *(Slowly, dangerously.)* And you, Antigone,
    You with your head hanging,—do you confess this thing?
Antigone: I do. I deny nothing.
Creon: *(To* SENTRY.*)* You may go.   60

                                                 (Exit SENTRY.*)*

    (To ANTIGONE.*)* Tell me, tell me briefly:
    Had you heard my proclamation touching this matter?
Antigone: It was public. Could I help hearing it?
Creon: And yet you dared defy the law.
Antigone: I dared.   65
    It was not God's proclamation. That final Justice
    That rules the world below makes no such laws.

    Your edict, King, was strong,
    But all your strength is weakness itself against
    The immortal unrecorded laws of God.   70
    They are not merely now: they were, and shall be,
    Operative for ever, beyond man utterly.

    I knew I must die, even without your decree:
    I am only mortal. And if I must die
    Now, before it is my time to die,   75
    Surely this is no hardship: can anyone
    Living, as I live, with evil all about me,
    Think Death less than a friend? This death of mine
    Is of no importance; but if I had left my brother
    Lying in death unburied, I should have suffered.   80
    Now I do not.
                         You smile at me. Ah Creon,
    Think me a fool, if you like; but it may well be
    That a fool convicts me of folly.
Choragos: Like father, like daughter: both headstrong, deaf to reason!   85
    She has never learned to yield.
Creon: She has much to learn.
    The inflexible heart breaks first, the toughest iron
    Cracks first, and the wildest horses bend their necks
    At the pull of the smallest curb.   90
                         Pride? In a slave?

This girl is guilty of a double insolence,
Breaking the given laws and boasting of it.
Who is the man here,
She or I, if this crime goes unpunished?   95
Sister's child, or more than sister's child,
Or closer yet in blood—she and her sister
Win bitter death for this!
(To SERVANTS.*)*   Go, some of you,
Arrest Ismene. I accuse her equally.   100
Bring her: you will find her sniffling in the house there.

Her mind's a traitor: crimes kept in the dark
Cry for light, and the guardian brain shudders;
But how much worse than this
Is brazen boasting of barefaced anarchy!   105
Antigone: Creon, what more do you want than my death?
Creon: Nothing.
   That gives me everything.
Antigone: Then I beg you: kill me.
   This talking is a great weariness: your words   110
   Are distasteful to me, and I am sure that mine
   Seem so to you. And yet they should not seem so:
   I should have praise and honor for what I have done.
   All these men here would praise me
   Were their lips not frozen shut with feat of you.   115
   (Bitterly.) Ah the good fortune of kings,
   Licensed to say and do whatever they please!
Creon: You are alone here in that opinion.
Antigone: No, they are with me. But they keep their tongues in leash.
Creon: Maybe. But you are guilty, and they are not.   120
Antigone: There is no guilt in reverence for the dead.
Creon: But Eteocles—was he not your brother too?
Antigone: My brother too.
Creon: And you insult his memory?
Antigone: *(Softly.)* The dead man would not say that I insult it.   125
Creon: He would: for you honor a traitor as much as him.
Antigone: His own brother; traitor or not, and equal in blood.
Creon: He made war on his country. Eteocles defended it.
Antigone: Nevertheless, there are honors due all the dead.
Creon: But not the same for the wicked as for the just.   130
Antigone: Ah Creon, Creon,
   Which of us can say what the gods hold wicked?
Creon: An enemy is an enemy, even dead.
Antigone: It is my nature to join in love, not hate.
Creon: *(Finally losing patience.)* Go join them, then; if you must have your love, 135
   Find it in hell!
Choragos: But see, Ismene comes:

(Enter ISMENE, *guarded.)*

Those tears are sisterly, the cloud
That shadows her eyes rains down gentle sorrow.

Creon: You too, Ismene,   140
    Snake in my ordered house, sucking my blood
    Stealthily—and all the time I never knew
    That these two sisters were aiming at my throne!

                                              Ismene,

    Do you confess your share in this crime, or deny it?   145
    Answer me.

Ismene: Yes, if she will let me say so. I am guilty.

Antigone: *(Coldly.)* No, Ismene. You have no right to say so.
    You would not help me, and I will not have you help me.

Ismene: But now I know what you meant; and I am here   150
    To join you, to take my share of punishment.

Antigone: The dead man and the gods who rule the dead
    Know whose act this was. Words are not friends.

Ismene: Do you refuse me, Antigone? I want to die with you:
    I too have a duty that I must discharge to the dead.   155

Antigone: You shall not lessen my death by sharing it.

Ismene: What do I care for life when you are dead?

Antigone: Ask Creon. You're always hanging on his opinions.

Ismene: You are laughing at me. Why, Antigone?

Antigone: It's a joyless laughter, Ismene.   160

Ismene: But can I do nothing?

Antigone: Yes. Save yourself. I shall not envy you.
    There are those who will praise you; I shall have honor, too.

Ismene: But we are equally guilty!

Antigone: No more, Ismene.   165
    You are alive, but I belong to Death.

Creon: *(To the* CHORUS.*)* Gentlemen, I beg you to observe these girls:
    One has just now lost her mind; the other,
    It seems, has never had a mind at all.

Ismene: Grief teaches the steadiest minds to waver, King.   170

Creon: Yours certainly did, when you assumed guilt with the guilty!

Ismene: But how could I go on living without her?

Creon: You are.
    She is already dead.

Ismene: But your own son's bride!   175

Creon: There are places enough for him to push his plow.
    I want no wicked women for my sons!

Ismene: O dearest Haimon, how your father wrongs you!

Creon: I've had enough of your childish talk of marriage!

Choragos: Do you really intend to steal this girl from your son?   180

Creon: No; Death will do that for me.

Choragos: Then she must die?

Creon: You dazzle me.

—But enough of this talk!
(To GUARDS.*)* You, there, take them away and guard them well: 185
For they are but women, and even brave men run
When they see Death coming.

(Exeunt ISMENE, ANTIGONE, *and* GUARDS.*)*

ODE II • Strophe 1

Chorus: Fortunate is the man who has never tasted God's vengeance!
Where once the anger of heaven has struck, that house is shaken
For ever: damnation rises behind each child
Like a wave cresting out of the black northeast,
When the long darkness under sea roars up   5
And bursts drumming death upon the windwhipped sand.

Antistrophe 1

I have seen this gathering sorrow from time long past
Loom upon Oedipus' children: generation from generation
Takes the compulsive rage of the enemy god.
So lately this last flower of Oedipus' line   10
Drank the sunlight! but now a passionate word
And a handful of dust have closed up all its beauty.

Strophe 2

  What mortal arrogance
  Transcends the wrath of Zeus?
Sleep cannot lull him, nor the effortless long months   15
Of the timeless gods: but he is young forever,
And his house is the shining day of high Olympos.
  All that is and shall be,
  And all the past, is his.
No pride on earth is free of the curse of heaven.   20

Antistrophe 2

  The straying dreams of men
  May bring them ghosts of joy:
But as they drowse, the waking embers bum them;
Or they walk with fixed eyes, as blind men walk.
But the ancient wisdom speaks for our own time: 25
  Fate works most for woe
  With Folly's fairest show.
Man's little pleasure is the spring of sorrow.

Scene III

Choragos: But here is Haimon, King, the last of all your sons.
Is it grief for Antigone that brings him here,
And bitterness at being robbed of his bride?

(Enter HAIMON.*)*

Creon: We shall soon see, and no need of diviners.

　　　　　　　　　　　　　　　　　　—Son, 5
You have heard my final judgment on that girl:
Have you come here hating me, or have you come
With deference and with love, whatever I do?
Haimon: I am your son, father. You are my guide.
You make things clear for me, and I obey you. 10
No marriage means more to me than your continuing wisdom.
Creon: Good. That is the way to behave: subordinate
Everything else, my son, to your father's will.
This is what a man prays for, that he may get
Sons attentive and dutiful in his house, 15
Each one hating his father's enemies,
Honoring his father's friends. But if his sons
Fail him, if they turn out unprofitably,
What has he fathered but trouble for himself
And amusement for the malicious? 20
　　　　　　　　　　　　　So you are right
Not to lose your head over this woman.
Your pleasure with her would soon grow cold, Haimon,
And then you'd have a hellcat in bed and elsewhere.
Let her find her husband in Hell! 25
Of all the people in this city, only she
Has had contempt for my law and broken it.

Do you want me to show myself weak before the people?
Or to break my sworn word? No, and I will not.
The woman dies. 30
I suppose she'll plead "family ties." Well, let her,
If I permit my own family to rebel,
How shall I earn the world's obedience?
Show me the man who keeps his house in hand,
He's fit for public authority. 35
　　　　　　　　　I'll have no dealings
With law-breakers, critics of the government:
Whoever is chosen to govern should be obeyed—
Must be obeyed, in all things, great and small,
Just and unjust! O Haimon, 40
The man who knows how to obey, and that man only,
Knows how to give commands when the time comes.
You can depend on him, no matter how fast
The spears come: he's a good soldier, he'll stick it out.
Anarchy, anarchy! Show me a greater evil! 45
This is why cities tumble and the great houses rain down,
This is what scatters armies!
No, no: good lives are made so by discipline.
We keep the laws then, and the lawmakers,
And no woman shall seduce us. If we must lose, 50
Let's lose to a man, at least! Is a woman stronger than we?

Choragos: Unless time has rusted my wits,
　　　What you say, King, is said with point and dignity.
Haimon: *(Boyishly earnest.)* Father:
　　　Reason is God's crowning gift to man, and you are right. 　　　　55
　　　To warn me against losing mine. I cannot say—
　　　I hope that I shall never want to say!—that you
　　　Have reasoned badly. Yet there are other men
　　　Who can reason, too; and their opinions might be helpful.
　　　You are not in a position to know everything 　　　　　　　60
　　　That people say or do, or what they feel:
　　　Your temper terrifies them—everyone
　　　Will tell you only what you like to hear.
　　　But I, at any rate, can listen; and I have heard them
　　　Muttering and whispering in the dark about this girl. 　　　65
　　　They say no woman has ever, so unreasonably,
　　　Died so shameful a death for a generous act:
　　　"She covered her brother's body. Is this indecent?
　　　She kept him from dogs and vultures. Is this a crime?
　　　Death?—She should have all the honor that we can give her!" 　70

　　　This is the way they talk out there in the city.

　　　You must believe me:
　　　Nothing is closer to me than your happiness.
　　　What could be closer? Must not any son
　　　Value his father's fortune as his father does his? 　　　　75
　　　I beg you, do not be unchangeable:
　　　Do not believe that you alone can be right.
　　　The man who thinks that,
　　　The man who maintains that only he has the power
　　　To reason correctly, the gift to speak, the soul— 　　　　80
　　　A man like that, when you know him, turns out empty.
　　　It is not reason never to yield to reason!

　　　In flood time you can see how some trees bend,
　　　And because they bend, even their twigs are safe,
　　　While stubborn trees are torn up, roots and all. 　　　　85
　　　And the same thing happens in sailing:
　　　Make your sheet fast, never slacken,—and over you go,
　　　Head over heels and under: and there's your voyage.
　　　Forget you are angry! Let yourself be moved!
　　　I know I am young; but please let me say this: 　　　　90
　　　The ideal condition
　　　Would be, I admit, that men should be right by instinct;
　　　But since we are all too likely to go astray,
　　　The reasonable thing is to learn from those who can teach.
Choragos: You will do well to listen to him. King, 　　　　95
　　　If what he says is sensible. And you, Haimon,

Must listen to your father. —Both speak well.

Creon: You consider it right for a man of my years and experience
to go to school to a boy?

Haimon: It is not right   100
If I am wrong. But if I am young, and right,
What does my age matter?

Creon: You think it right to stand up for an anarchist?

Haimon: Not at all. I pay no respect to criminals.

Creon: Then she is not a criminal?   105

Haimon: The City would deny it, to a man.

Creon: And the City proposes to teach me how to rule?

Haimon: Ah. Who is it that's talking like a boy now?

Creon: My voice is the one voice giving orders in this City!

Haimon: It is no City if it takes orders from one voice.   110

Creon: The State is the King!

Haimon: Yes, if the State is a desert.

    (Pause.)

Creon: This boy, it seems, has sold out to a woman.

Haimon: If you are a woman: my concern is only for you.

Creon: So? Your "concern"! In a public brawl with your father!   115

Haimon: How about you, in a public brawl with justice?

Creon: With justice, when all that I do is within my rights?

Haimon: You have no right to trample God's right.

Creon: *(Completely out of control.)* Fool, adolescent fool! Taken in by a woman!

Haimon: You'll never see me taken in by anything vile.   120

Creon: Every word you say is for her!

Haimon: *(Quietly, darkly.)*   And for you.
And for me. And for the gods under the earth.

Creon: You'll never marry her while she lives.

Haimon: Then she must die.—But her death will cause another.   125

Creon: Another?
Have you lost your senses? Is this an open threat?

Haimon: There is no threat in speaking to emptiness.

Creon: I swear you'll regret this superior tone of yours!
You are the empty one!   130

Haimon: If you were not my father,
I'd say you were perverse.

Creon: You girlstruck fool, don't play at words with me!

Haimon: I am sorry. You prefer silence.

Creon: Now, by God—!   135
I swear, by all the gods in heaven above us,
You'll watch it, I swear you shall!
(To the servants.*)*   Bring her out!
Bring the woman out! Let her die before his eyes!
Here, this instant, with her bridegroom beside her!   140

Haimon: Not here, no; she will not die here, King.
And you will never see my face again.

Go on raving as long as you've a friend to endure you.

(Exit HAIMON.*)*

Choragos: Gone, gone.
Creon, a young man in a rage is dangerous!   145
Creon: Let him do, or dream to do, more than a man can.
He shall not save these girls from death.
Choragos: These girls
You have sentenced them both?
Creon: No, you are right.   150
I will not kill the one whose hands are clean.
Choragos: But Antigone?
Creon: *(Somberly.)* I will carry her far away
Out there in the wilderness, and lock her
Living in a vault of stone. She shall have food,   155
As the custom is, to absolve the State of her death.
And there let her pray to the gods of hell:
They are her only gods:
Perhaps they will show her an escape from death,
Or she may learn,   160
                              though late,
That piety shown the dead is pity in vain.

(Exit CREON.*)*

ODE III • Strophe

Chorus: Love, unconquerable
Waster of rich men, keeper
Of warm lights and all-night vigil
In the soft face of a girl:
Sea-wanderer, forest-visitor!   5
Even the pure Immortals cannot escape you,
And mortal man, in his one day's dusk,
Trembles before your glory.

Antistrophe

Surely you swerve upon ruin
The just man's consenting heart,   10
As here you have made bright anger
Strike between father and son—
And none has conquered but Love!
A girl's glance working the will of heaven:
Pleasure to her alone who mocks us,   15
Merciless Aphrodite.

Scene IV

Choragos: *(As* ANTIGONE *enters guarded.)*
But I can no longer stand in awe of this,
Nor, seeing what I see, keep back my tears.
Here is Antigone, passing to that chamber

Where all find sleep at last.

Strophe 1

Antigone: Look upon me, friends, and pity me   5
Turning back at the night's edge to say
Good-by to the sun that shines for me no longer;
Now sleepy Death
Summons me down to Acheron, that cold shore:
There is no bridesong there, nor any music.   10

Chorus: Yet not unpraised, not without a kind of honor,
You walk at last into the underworld;
Untouched by sickness, broken by no sword.
What woman has ever found your way to death?

Antistrophe 1

Antigone: How often I have heard the story of Niobe,   15
Tantalos' wretched daughter, how the stone
Clung fast about her, ivy-close: and they say
The rain falls endlessly
And sifting soft snow; her tears are never done.
I feel the loneliness of her death in mine.   20

Chorus: But she was born of heaven, and you
Are woman, woman-born. If her death is yours,
A mortal woman's, is this not for you
Glory in our world and in the world beyond?

Strophe 2

Antigone: You laugh at me. Ah, friends, friends,   25
Can you not wait until I am dead? O Thebes,
O men many-charioted, in love with Fortune,
Dear springs of Dirce, sacred Theban grove,
Be witnesses for me, denied all pity,
Unjustly judged! and think a word of love   30
For her whose path turns
Under dark earth, where there are no more tears.

Chorus: You have passed beyond human daring and come at last
Into a place of stone where Justice sits.
I cannot tell   35
What shape of your father's guilt appears in this.

Antistrophe 2

Antigone: You have touched it at last: that bridal bed
Unspeakable, horror of son and mother mingling:
Their crime, infection of all our family!
O Oedipus, father and brother!   40
Your marriage strikes from the grave to murder mine.
I have been a stranger here in my own land:
All my life
The blasphemy of my birth has followed me.

Chorus: Reverence is a virtue, but strength   45

Lives in established law: that must prevail.
You have made your choice,
Your death is the doing of your conscious hand.

Epode

Antigone: Then let me go, since all your words are bitter,
And the very light of the sun is cold to me.   50
Lead me to my vigil, where I must have
Neither love nor lamentation; no song, but silence.

(CREON *interrupts impatiently.*)

Creon: If dirges and planned lamentations could put off death,
Men would be singing for ever.
(To the SERVANTS.*)*   Take her, go!   55
You know your orders: take her to the vault
And leave her alone there. And if she lives or dies,
That's her affair, not ours: our hands are clean.
Antigone: O tomb, vaulted bride-bed in eternal rock,
Soon I shall be with my own again   60
Where Persephone welcomes the thin ghosts underground:
And I shall see my father again, and you, mother,
And dearest Polyneices—

                          dearest indeed
To me, since it was my hand   65
That washed him clean and poured the ritual wine:
And my reward is death before my time!

And yet, as men's hearts know, I have done no wrong.
I have not sinned before God. Or if I have,
I shall know the truth in death. But if the guilt   70
Lies upon Creon who judged me, then, I pray,
May his punishment equal my own.
Choragos: O passionate heart,
Unyielding, tormented still by the same winds!
Creon: Her guards shall have good cause to regret their delaying.   75
Antigone: Ah! That voice is like the voice of death!
Creon: I can give you no reason to think you are mistaken.
Antigone: Thebes, and you my fathers' gods,
And rulers of Thebes, you see me now, the last
Unhappy daughter of a line of kings,   80
Your kings, led away to death. You will remember
What things I suffer, and at what men's hands,
Because I would not transgress the laws of heaven.
(To the GUARDS, *simply.*) Come: let us wait no longer.

(*Exit* ANTIGONE, *left, guarded.*)

ODE IV • Strophe 1

Chorus: All Danae's beauty was locked away
In a brazen cell where the sunlight could not come:

A small room, still as any grave, enclosed her.
Yet she was a princess too,
And Zeus in a rain of gold poured love upon her.   5
O child, child,
No power in wealth or war
Or tough sea-blackened ships
Can prevail against untiring Destiny!

Antistrophe 1

And Dryas' son[1] also, that furious king,   10
Bore the god's prisoning anger for his pride:
Sealed up by Dionysos in deaf stone,
His madness died among echoes.
So at the last he learned what dreadful power
His tongue had mocked: 15
For he had profaned the revels,
And fired the wrath of the nine
Implacable Sisters[2] that love the sound of the flute.

Strophe 2

And old men tell a half-remembered tale
Of horror done where a dark ledge splits the sea   20
And a double surf beats on the gray shores:
How a king's new woman,[3] sick
With hatred for the queen he had imprisoned,
Ripped out his two sons' eyes with her bloody hands
While grinning Ares watched the shuttle plunge   25
Four times: four blind wounds crying for revenge,

Antistrophe 2

Crying, tears and blood mingled.—Piteously born.
Those sons whose mother was of heavenly birth!
Her father was the god of the North Wind
And she was cradled by gales,   30
She raced with young colts on the glittering hills
And walked untrammeled in the open light:
But in her marriage deathless Fate found means
To build a tomb like yours for all her joy.

Scene V

(*Enter blind* TEIRESIAS, *led by a boy. The opening speeches of* TEIRESIAS *should be in singsong contrast to the realistic* CREON.)

Teiresias: This is the way the blind man comes, Princes, Princes,
    Lock-step, two heads lit by the eyes of one.
Creon: What new thing have you to tell us, Old Teiresias?

---

[1] **Dryas' son:** Lycurgus, King of Thrace. [2] **Implacable sisters:** The nine Muses. [3] **king's new woman:** Reference to Eidothea, wife of King Phineas.

Teiresias: I have much to tell you: listen to the prophet, Creon.
Creon: I am not aware that I have ever failed to listen. 5
Teiresias: Then you have done wisely, King, and ruled well.
Creon: I admit my debt to you. But what have you to say?
Teiresias: This, Creon: you stand once more on the edge of fate.
Creon: What do you mean? Your words are a kind of dread.
Teiresias: Listen, Creon: 10

> I was sitting in my chair of augury, at the place
> Where the birds gather about me. They were all a-chatter,
> As is their habit, when suddenly I heard
> A strange note in their jangling, a scream, a
> Whirring fury; I knew that they were fighting, 15
> Tearing each other, dying
> In a whirlwind of wings clashing. And I was afraid.
> I began the rites of burnt-offering at the altar,
> But Hephaistos failed me: instead of bright flame,
> There was only the sputtering slime of the fat thighflesh 20
> Melting: the entrails dissolved in gray smoke,
> The bare bone burst from the welter. And no blaze!
>
> This was a sign from heaven. My boy described it,
> Seeing for me as I see for others.
>
> I tell you, Creon, you yourself have brought 25
> This new calamity upon us. Our hearths and altars
> Are stained with the corruption of dogs and carrion birds
> That glut themselves on the corpse of Oedipus' son.
> The gods are deaf when we pray to them, their fire
> Recoils from our offering, their birds of omen 30
> Have no cry of comfort, for they are gorged
> With the thick blood of the dead.
>   O my son,
> These are no trifles! Think: all men make mistakes,
> But a good man yields when he knows his course is wrong, 35
> And repairs the evil. The only crime is pride.
>
> Give in to the dead man, then: do not fight with a corpse—
> What glory is it to kill a man who is dead?
> Think, I beg you:
> It is for your own good that I speak as I do. 40
> You should be able to yield for your own good.

Creon: It seems that prophets have made me their special province.

> All my life long
> I have been a kind of butt for the dull arrows
> Of doddering fortune-tellers! 45
>   No, Teiresias:
> If your birds—if the great eagles of God himself
> Should carry him stinking bit by bit to heaven,

I would not yield. I am not afraid of pollution:
No man can defile the gods.   50
                          Do what you will,
Go into business, make money, speculate
In India gold or that synthetic gold from Sardis,
Get rich otherwise than by my consent to bury him.
Teiresias, it is a sorry thing when a wise man   55
Sells his wisdom, lets out his words for hire!

Teiresias: Ah Creon! Is there no man left in the world—
Creon: To do what?—Come, let's have the aphorism!
Teiresias: No man who knows that wisdom outweighs any wealth?
Creon: As surely as bribes are baser than any baseness.   60
Teiresias: You are sick, Creon! You are deathly sick!
Creon: As you say: it is not my place to challenge a prophet.
Teiresias: Yet you have said my prophecy is for sale.
Creon: The generation of prophets has always loved gold.
Teiresias: The generation of kings has always loved brass.   65
Creon: You forget yourself! You are speaking to your King.
Teiresias: I know it. You are a king because of me.
Creon: You have a certain skill; but you have sold out.
Teiresias: King, you will drive me to words that—
Creon: Say them, say them!   70
Only remember: I will not pay you for them.
Teiresias: No, you will find them too costly.
Creon: No doubt. Speak:
Whatever you say, you will not change my will.
Teiresias: Then take this, and take it to heart!   75
The time is not far off when you shall pay back
Corpse for corpse, flesh of your own flesh.
You have thrust the child of this world into living night,
You have kept from the gods below the child that is theirs:
The one in a grave before her death, the other,   80
Dead, denied the grave. This is your crime:
And the Furies and the dark gods of Hell
Are swift with terrible punishment for you.

Do you want to buy me now, Creon?
                          Not many days,   85
And your house will be full of men and women weeping.
And curses will be hurled at you from far
Cities grieving for sons unburied, left to rot
Before the walls of Thebes.

These are my arrows, Creon: they are all for you.   90
(To BOY.*)* But come, child: lead me home.
Let him waste his fine anger upon younger men.
Maybe he will learn at last
To control a wiser tongue in a better head.

(Exit TEIRESIAS.*)*

Choragos: The old man has gone, King, but his words   95
  Remain to plague us. I am old, too,
  But I cannot remember that he was ever false.
Creon: That is true. . . . It troubles me.
  Oh it is hard to give in! but it is worse
  To risk everything for stubborn pride.   100
Choragos: Creon: take my advice.
Creon: What shall I do?
Choragos: Go quickly: free Antigone from her vault
  And build a tomb for the body of Polyneices.
Creon: You would have me do this?   105
Choragos: Creon, yes!
  And it must be done at once: God moves
  Swiftly to cancel the folly of stubborn men.
Creon: It is hard to deny the heart! But I
  Will do it: I will not fight with destiny.   110
Choragos: You must go yourself, you cannot leave it to others.
Creon: I will go.
  —Bring axes, servants:
  Come with me to the tomb. I buried her, I
  Will set her free.   115
                Oh quickly!
  My mind misgives—
  The laws of the gods are mighty, and a man must serve them
  To the last day of his life!

(Exit CREON.*)*

PAEAN • Strophe 1
Choragos: God of many names
Chorus: O Iacchos
                      son
  of Kadmeian Semele
                  O born of the Thunder!   5
  Guardian of the West
                  Regent
  of Eleusis' plain
                  O Prince of maenad Thebes
  and the Dragon Field by rippling Ismenos: 10
  Antistrophe 1

Choragos: God of many names
Chorus: the flame of torches
  flares on our hills
                      the nymphs of Iacchos
  dance at the spring of Castalia: 15
  From the vine-close mountain

come ah come in ivy:
Evohe evohe![1] sings through the streets of Thebes

Strophe 2

Choragos: God of many names

Chorus: Iacchos of Thebes   20
    heavenly Child
                    of Semele bride of the Thunderer!
The shadow of plague is upon us:
                            come
with clement feet   25
                    oh come from Parnasos
down the long slopes
                    across the lamenting water

Antistrophe 2

Choragos: Io Fire! Chorister of the throbbing stars!
    O purest among the voices of the night!   30
    Thou son of God, blaze for us!
Chorus: Come with choric rapture of circling Maenads
    Who cry *Io Iacche!*
                    God of many names!

EXODUS[1]

(Enter MESSENGER, *left.)*

Messenger: Men of the line of Kadmos, you who live
    Near Amphion's citadel[2]
                        I cannot say
Of any condition of human life "This is fixed,
This is clearly good, or bad". Fate raises up,   5
And Fate casts down the happy and unhappy alike:
No man can foretell his Fate.
                    Take the case of Creon:
Creon was happy once, as I count happiness:
Victorious in battle, sole governor of the land,   10
Fortunate father of children nobly born.
And now it has all gone from him! Who can say
That a man is still alive when his life's joy fails?
He is a walking dead man. Grant him rich,
Let him live like a king in his great house: 15
If his pleasure is gone, I would not give
So much as the shadow of smoke for all he owns.
Choragos: Your words hint at sorrow: what is your news for us?

---

[1] *Evohe evohe!:* "Come forth; come forth!"   [1] **Exodos:** Concluding scene.   [2] **Amphion's citadel:** Thebes.

Messenger: They are dead. The living are guilty of their death.
Choragos: Who is guilty? Who is dead? Speak!   20
Messenger: Haimon.
    Haimon is dead; and the hand that killed him
    Is his own hand.
Choragos: His father's? or his own?
Messenger: His own, driven mad by the murder his father had done.   25
Choragos: Teiresias, Teiresias, how clearly you saw it all!
Messenger: This is my news: you must draw what conclusions you can from it.
Choragos: But look: Eurydice, our Queen:
    Has she overheard us?

    (Enter EURYDICE from the Palace, center.)

Eurydice: I have heard something, friends: 30
    As I was unlocking the gate of Pallas' shrine,
    For I needed her help today, I heard a voice
    Telling of some new sorrow. And I fainted
    There at the temple with all my maidens about me.
    But speak again: whatever it is, I can bear it: 35
    Grief and I are no strangers.
Messenger: Dearest Lady,
    I will tell you plainly all that I have seen.
    I shall not try to comfort you: what is the use,
    Since comfort could lie only in what is not true?   40
    The truth is always best.
                                    I went with Creon
    To the outer plain where Polyneices was lying,
    No friend to pity him, his body shredded by dogs.
    We made our prayers in that place to Hecate   45
    And Pluto, that they would be merciful. And we bathed
    The corpse with holy water, and we brought
    Fresh-broken branches to burn what was left of it,
    And upon the urn we heaped up a towering barrow
    Of the earth of his own land.   50
                                    When we were done, we ran
    To the vault where Antigone lay on her couch of stone.
    One of the servants had gone ahead,
    And while he was yet far off he heard a voice
    Grieving within the chamber, and he came back   55
    And told Creon. And as the King went closer,
    The air was full of wailing, the words lost,
    And he begged us to make all haste. "Am I a prophet?"
    He said, weeping, "And must I walk this road,
    The saddest of all that I have gone before?   60
    My son's voice calls me on. Oh quickly, quickly!
    Look through the crevice there, and tell me
    If it is Haimon, or some deception of the gods!"

    We obeyed; and in the cavern's farthest comer

We saw her lying: 65
She had made a noose of her fine linen veil
And hanged herself. Haimon lay beside her,
His arms about her waist, lamenting her,
His love lost under ground, crying out
That his father had stolen her away from him.   70

When Creon saw him the tears rushed to his eyes
And he called to him: "What have you done, child?
    Speak to me.
What are you thinking that makes your eyes so strange?
O my son, my son, I come to you on my knees!"   75
But Haimon spat in his face. He said not a word,
Staring—
            And suddenly drew his sword
And lunged. Creon shrank back, the blade missed;
    and the boy,   80
Desperate against himself, drove it half its length
Into his own side, and fell. And as he died
He gathered Antigone close in his arms again,
Choking, his blood bright red on her white cheek.
And now he lies dead with the dead, and she is his   85
At last, his bride in the houses of the dead.

  (*Exit* EURYDICE *into the Palace.*)

Choragos: She has left us without a word. What can this mean?
Messenger: It troubles me, too; yet she knows what is best,
    Her grief is too great for public lamentation,
    And doubtless she has gone to her chamber to weep   90
    For her dead son, leading her maidens in his dirge.

  (*Pause.*)

Choragos: It may be so: but I fear this deep silence
Messenger: I will. see what she is doing. I will go in.

  (*Exit* MESSENGER *into the Palace. Enter* CREON *with attendants, bearing*
  HAIMON's *body.*)

Choragos: But here is the King himself: oh look at him,
    Bearing his own damnation in his arms.   95
Creon: Nothing you say can touch me any more.
    My own blind heart has brought me
    From darkness to final darkness. Here you see
    The father murdering, the murdered son—
    And all my civic wisdom!   100

Haimon my son, so young, so young to die,
I was the fool, not you; and you died for me.
Choragos: That is the truth; but you were late in learning it.
Creon: This truth is hard to bear. Surely a god

Has crushed me beneath the hugest weight of heaven, 105
And driven me headlong a barbaric way
To trample out the thing I held most dear.

The pains that men will take to come to pain!

(Enter MESSENGER *from the Palace.)*

Messenger: The burden you carry in your hands is heavy,
But it is not all: you will find more in your house. 110
Creon: What burden worse than this shall I find there?
Messenger: The Queen is dead.
Creon: O port of death, deaf world,
Is there no pity for me? And you, Angel of evil,
I was dead, and your words are death again. 115
Is it true, boy? Can it be true?
Is my wife dead? Has death bred death?
Messenger: You can see for yourself.

(The doors are opened, and the body of EURYDICE *is disclosed within.)*

Creon: Oh pity!
All true, all true, and more than I can bear! 120
O my wife, my son!
Messenger: She stood before the altar, and her heart
Welcomed the knife her own hand guided,
And a great cry burst from her lips for Megareus[3] dead,
And for Haimon dead, her sons; and her last breath 125
Was a curse for their father, the murderer of her sons.
And she fell, and the dark flowed in through her closing eyes.
Creon: O God, I am sick with fear.
Are there no swords here? Has no one a blow for me?
Messenger: Her curse is upon you for the deaths of both. 130
Creon: It is right that it should be. I alone am guilty.
I know it, and I say it. Lead me in,
Quickly, friends.
I have neither life nor substance. Lead me in.
Choragos: You are right, if there can be right in so much wrong. 135
The briefest way is best in a world of sorrow.
Creon: Let it come,
Let death come quickly, and be kind to me.
I would not ever see the sun again.
Choragos: All that will come when it will; but we, meanwhile, 140
Have much to do. Leave the future to itself.
Creon: All my heart was in that prayer!
Choragos: Then do not pray any more: the sky is deaf.
Creon: Lead me away. I have been rash and foolish.
I have killed my son and my wife. 145
I look for comfort; my comfort lies here dead.

---

[3]**Megareus:** Son of Creon, killed in the attack on Thebes.

Whatever my hands have touched has come to nothing.
Fate has brought all my pride to a thought of dust.

(As CREON *is being led into the house, the* CHORAGOS *advances and speaks directly to the audience.)*

Choragos: There is no happiness where there is no wisdom;
No wisdom but in submission to the gods. 150
Big words are always punished,
And proud men in old age learn to be wise.

Explorations of the Text

1. How did Eteocles and Polyneices die? Why is Eteocles buried with honor but Polyneices left to decompose in the open? Why does Antigone believe that they should both be buried? What is Ismene's position?

2. Who helps to convince Creon to free Antigone? Why might Sophocles have made Creon change his mind? What effect does this have on the play's message?

3. Why does Creon's son Haimon die? Give more than one answer—his death can be explained literally but also within the context of the play's deeper meaning. Who else dies?

4. What is the role of the chorus in this play? What is the role of Teiresias?

5. In Greek tragedy, a character often suffers for possessing a tragic flaw. One example of a tragic flaw is *hubris,* or excessive pride. In *Antigone,* who is tragically flawed, Creon or Antigone? Which is the tragic hero?

6. Do you admire Antigone? Why, or why not?

7. Compare/contrast Antigone's sense of moral responsibility with Natasha in "Natasha's Triumph."

The Reading/Writing Connection

1. Throughout history, there are times when people have chosen to break the law because it is the "right" thing to do. Write a journal entry explaining under what circumstances you think that following a law would be unethical. Use specific examples.

2. Write about a time that you refused to change your mind. List each of your reasons, and then write from the point of view of the chorus, convincing you to change.

Ideas for Writing

1. Teiresias tells Creon that "a good man yields when he knows his course is wrong." Referring to two other works in this chapter as evidence, argue either for or against this statement.

2. Write about a time when you felt that you were unjustly punished, and then revise it to become a short story. Use characters to fulfill the function of the chorus and the soothsayer.

3. Find Tim O'Brien's "On the Rainy River" in *The Things They Carried.* Compare the moral conflicts of the two main characters, and consider O'Brien's definition of cowardice.

Anna Deavere Smith (1950–)

"To Look Like Girls from Little" *1994*
from *Twilight: Los Angeles, 1992*

ELVIRA EVERS

General Worker and Cashier, Canteen Corporation
With a baby bottle in her hand. At her kitchen table. A black woman from Panama in her forties. Children can be heard offstage. A Panamanian accent. She had a gold front tooth.

So,
it was like a carnival out there
and I say
to my friend Frances,
"Frances, you see this?"   5
and she said, "Girl, you should see
that
is getting worse."
And I say, "Girl, let me take my butt
up there before something happen."   10
and um
when somebody throw a bottle
and I just,
then I felt,
like moist   15
and it was like a tingling sensation right?
And I dida like this *(Touching her stomach.)*
and it was like itchin',
and I say, "Frances, I'm *bleedin'*."
And she walk with me to her house   20
And she say, "Lift up your gown, let me see."
She say, "Elvira, iss a bullet!"
I say, "What?"
I say, "I didn't heard nothin'."
She say, "Yes, but iss a bullet."   25
She say, "Lay down there. Let me call St. Francis and tell them that
you been shot
and to send a ambulance."
and she say,
"Why you,   30
you don't mess with none of those people
Why they have to shoot you?"
So Frances say the ambulance be here in fifteen minutes
I say, "Frances,
I cannot wait that."   35
I say,

"I'm goin'!"
So I told my oldest son I say,
"Amant take care your brothers
I be right back."   40
Well by this time he was standing there he was crying.
All of them was crying.
What I did for them not to see the blood,
I took the gown and I cover it,
and I didn't cry   45
that way they didn't get nervous.
And I get in the car
I was goin' drive
Frances say, "What you doin'?"
I said, "I'm drivin'."   50
She say, "No, you're not!"
And we take all the back street,
and she was so supportive
because she say, "You alright?
You feel cold?   55
You feel dizzy?
The baby move?"
she say, "You nervous?"
I say, "No, I'm not nervous, I'm just worried about the baby."
I say, "I don't want to lose this baby."   60
She say, "Elvira everything will be alright." She say, "Just pray."
So there was a lot of cars we had to be blowing the horn
So finally we get to St. Francis *(Hospital.)*
and Frances told the front desk office she say,
"She been shot!"   65
and they say, "What she doin' walkin'?"
and I say, "I feel alright."
Everybody stop doin' what they was doin'
and they took me to the room
and put the monitor to see if the baby was fine   70
and they find the baby heart beat
and as long as I heard the baby heart beat I calmed down.
Long as I knew whoever it is boy or girl, it's alright,
and
matter of fact my doctor, Dr. Thomas, he was there   75
at
the emergency room
what a coincidence, right?
I was just lookin' for that familiar face
and soon as I saw him   80
I say, "Well I'm alright now."
Right?
So he bring me this other doctor and then told me:

"Elvira, we don't know how deep is the bullet
we don't know where it went. We gonna operate on
you.   85
But since that we gonna operate we gonna take the baby out
and you don't have to
go through all of that."
They say, "Do you understand
what we're saying?"   90
I say, "Yeah!"
and they say, "Okay sign here."
And I remember them preparing me
and I don't remember anything else   95
Nella! *(Calling to her child.)*
No.

(Turns to the side and admonishes the child, a girl about five years old.)

She likes company.
And in the background
I remember Dr. Thomas say, "You have a six-pound-twelve-ounces   100
little girl,"
he told me how much she weigh and her length
and he
say, "Um
she born   105
she had the bullet in her elbow,
but when we remove,
when we clean her up,
we find out that the bullet was still between two joints
so we did operate on her and your daughter is fine   110
and you are fine."

(Sound of a little child saying "Mommy.")

Nella!
She *wants to show the baby.*

(Listening to a question.)

Jessica. (Is her name.)
Bring the baby, Nella *(The baby is brought [imaginary]. She laughs.)*   115
Yes—*(Listening to a question.)*
yes
We don't like to keep the girls without earrings, we like the little girls
to look like girls from little.
I pierce hers   120
when I get out on Monday
by Wednesday I did it.
So by Monday she was five days
she was seven days,

and I
pierced her ears.
And the red band is just like for evil eyes   125
we really believe in Panama . . .
In English I can't explain too well.
And her doctor he told,   130
he explain to me,
that the bullet
destroyed the placenta
and
went through me   135
and she caught in her arm.

(Here you can hear the baby making noise, and a bell rings.)

If she didn't caught it in her arm,
Me, and her, would be dead.
See,
So it's like   140
open your eyes!
Watch what is goin' on!

Explorations of the Text

1. Examine the contrasts of life and death presented in this work and in José Rivera's "Gas."
2. What role does luck play in this work and in Szymborka's "Could Have"

(Chapter 9)? What vision of the human condition do these works present?

The Reading/Writing Connection

1. "Think" Topic: Danusha Goska's essay, "Political Paralysis" focuses on the individual's ability to make moral "choices" and to help others. Would this work dispute or confirm this view of human nature?

Ideas for Writing

1. **Write an Argument:** Based on your reading of these performance dramas, what are the qualities of an effective performance piece? Consider point of view, persona, content of monologue, figurative or descriptive language, and such dramatic elements as setting, dialogue, development of plot, and conflict.

2. How does a monologue or performance drama differ from a one-act play? See "Scrabble and Tabouli," for example, in Chapter 9 or "Trifles" in Chapter 7.

Suzan Lori-Parks *(1964–)*

Father Comes Home from the Wars (Part 1) *2006*
from *365 Days/365 Plays*

Father: Hi honey, Im home.
Mother: Yr home.
Father: Yes.
Mother: I wasnt expecting you. Ever.
Father: Should I go back out and come back in again? 5
Mother: Please.

> *(He goes back out and comes back in again.)*

Mother: Once more.
Father: Yr kidding.
Mother: Please.

> *(He goes back out and comes back in again.)*

Mother: Yr home. 10
Father: Yes.
Mother: Let me get a good look at you.
Father: I'll just turn around.
Mother: Please.

> *(He turns around once. Counterclockwise.)*

Mother: They should of sent a letter. A letter saying you were coming home. 15
Or at least a telephone call. That is the least they could do. Give a woman
and her family and her friends and neighbors a chance to get ready. A
chance to spruce things up. Put new ribbons in the hair of the dog. Get
the oil changed. Have everything running. Smoothly. And bake a cake of
course. Hang streamers. Tell the yard man to—tidy up his act. Oh God.
Long story. Oh God. Long story. I woulda invited the neighbors over. Had
everyone on the block jump out from their hiding places from behind the
brand-new furniture with the plastic still on it and say—WHAT? Say:
"Welcome Home" of course. And then after a few slices of cake and a few
drinks theyd all get the nerve to say what theyre really thinking. For now
itll stay unthought and unsaid. Well. You came home. All in one piece looks
like. We're lucky. I guess. We're lucky, right? Hhhhh.
Father: They sent a letter saying I was coming or at least they telephoned. Maybe you
didnt open the letter. I dont blame you. It could have been bad news. I see yr
unopened envelopes piled up. I dont blame you. I dont blame you at all. They
called several times. Maybe you were out. Maybe you were screwing the yard
man. If you had known I was coming you woulda put new ribbons in the hair
of the dog, got the oil changed, baked a cake and invited all the neighbors over
so they could jump out of their various hiding places behind the brand-new
furniture purchased with the blood of some people I used to know—and some
blood of some people I used to kill. Oh God. Long story. Oh God. Long story.
And theyd shout at me—WHAT? "Welcome Home" of course. And then after
a few slices of cake and a few drinks theyd get the nerve to tell me what they

really think: "Murderer, baby killer, racist, government pawn, ultimate patsy, stooge, fall guy, camp follower, dumbass, dope fiend, loser." Hhhhh.

Mother
Father

(*Rest.*)

Mother: I cant understand a word yr saying.
Father: I dont speak English anymore.   20
Mother: I dont blame you. SIT DOWN, I'LL FIX YOU SOMETHING.

> (*He sits. She takes a heavy frying pan and holds it over his head. Almost murder. She lowers the pan.*)

Mother
Father

(*Rest.*)

> (*He sits. Again she raises the frying pan and holds it over his head. Almost murder. She lowers the pan.*)

Father: Where are the children?
Mother: What children?   25

> (*Sound of the wind and the rain.*)

José Rivera   *(1955–   )*

Gas   1997

For Juan Carlos Rivera

Cast

Cheo

Time

Start of the ground offensive of the Persian Gulf War.

Place

A gas station

> (*A car at a gas station.* CHEO *stands next to the pump about to fill his car with gas. He is a working-class Latino. Before he pumps gas he speaks to the audience.*)

Cheo: His letters were coming once a week. I could feel his fear. It was in his handwriting. He sat in a tank. In the middle of the Saudi Arabian desert. Wrote six, seven, eight hours a day. These brilliant letters of fear. This big Puerto Rican guy! What the fuck's he doing out there? What the fucking hell sense that make? He's out there, in the Saudi sand, writing letters to me about how he's   5
gonna die from an Iraqi fucking missile. And he's got all this time on his hands to think about his own death. And there's nothing to do 'cause of these restrictions on him. No women, no magazines, 'cause the Saudis are afraid of the revolutionary effects of ads for women's lingerie on the population! Allah

would have a cow! There's nothing he's allowed to eat even remotely reminds [10]
him of home. Nothing but the fucking time to sit and think about what it's
gonna be like to have some fucking towel-head—as he calls them—run a
bayonet clean through his guts. He's sitting in the tank playing target practice
with the fucking camels. Shooting at the wind. The sand in all the food. Sand
in his dreaming. He and his buddies got a camel one day. They shaved that [15]
motherfucker clean! Completely shaved its ass! Then they spray-painted the
name of their company, in bright American spray-paint, on the side of the
camel, and sent it on its way! Scorpion fights in the tents! All those scenes from
fucking *Apocalypse Now* in his head. Fucking Marlon Brando decapitating that
guy and Martin Sheen going fucking nuts. That's what fills my brother's daily [20]
dreams as he sits out there in the desert contemplating his own death. The
Vietnam Syndrome those people are trying to eradicate. His early letters were
all about that. A chronicle. His way of laying it all down, saying it all for me, so
I would know what his last days, and months, and seconds were like. So when
he got offed by an Iraqi missile, I would at least know what it was like to be in [25]
his soul, if just for a little while. He couldn't write to save his life at first. Spelled
everything totally, unbelievably wrong. "Enough": e-n-u-f. "Thought": t-h-o-t.
"Any": e-n-y. But with time, he started to write beautifully. This angel started to
come out of the desert. This singing angel of words. Thoughts I honestly never
knew he had. Confessions. Ideas. We started to make plans. We start to be in [30]
sync for the first time since I stopped telling him I loved him. I used to kick his
fucking ass! It wasn't hard or nothing. That's not bragging, just me telling you a
simple truth. He was always sick. Always the first to cry. He played drums in a
parade back home. He couldn't even play the fucking instrument, he was so
uncoordinated. Spastic. But they let him march in the parade anyway— [35]
without drumsticks. He was the last guy in the parade, out of step, banging
make-believe drumsticks, phantom rhythms on this snare drum—playing air
drum for thousands of confused spectators! Then he got into uniforms and the
scouts. But I knew that bullshit was just a cover anyway. He didn't mean it.
Though after he joined the army and was in boot camp, he took particular [40]
delight in coming home and demonstrating the fifty neat new ways he learned
to kill a guy. One day he forgot he weighed twice my weight and nearly snapped
my spine like a fucking cucumber! I thought, in agony, "where's my bro?
Where's that peckerhead I used to kick around? The first one to cry when he
saw something beautiful. The first one to say 'I love that' or 'I love Mom' or 'I [45]
love you.'" He never got embarrassed by that, even after I got too old to deal
with my fucking little brother kissing me in front of other people. Even later, he
always, always, always ended every conversation with, "I love you bro," and I
couldn't say, "I love you" back, 'cause I was too hip to do that shit. But he got
deeper in it. The war thing. He wrote to say I'd never understand. He's fighting [50]
for my right to say whatever I want. To disagree. And I just fucking love how
they tell you on the news the fucking temperature in Riyadh, Saudi Arabia!
Like I fucking care! And a couple of times the son-of-a-bitch called me collect
from Saudi! *I said collect!* And I told him if Saddam Hussein didn't kill him, I
would! He told me about troubles with his wife back home. He'd just gotten [55]
married a month before shipping out. He didn't really know her and was
wondering if she still loved him. My brother always loved ugly women. It was a

thing with him. Low self-esteem or something. Like he couldn't love himself
and didn't understand a woman that would. So he sought out the absolute
losers of the planet: trucker whores with prison records who liked to tie him up   60
and whip him, stuff like that. I honestly have trouble contemplating my little
brother being whipped by some trucker whore in leather. Love! He didn't know
another way. Then he met a girl who on their first date confessed she hated
spiks—so my brother married her! This racist looked him in the eye,
disrespected his whole race to his face, and my brother says, "I do." Last night   65
somebody got on TV to say we shouldn't come down on rich people 'cause rich
people are a minority too, and coming down on them was a form of racism!
And I thought, they're fucking afraid of class warfare, and they should be! And
the news showed some little white punk putting up flags all over this dipshit
town in California and this little twirp's story absorbed twenty minutes of the   70
news—this little, blond Nazi kid with a smile full of teeth—and the protests
got shit. And this billboard went up in my town showing Stalin, Hitler, and
Hussein, saying we stopped him twice before we have to stop him again! This
billboard was put up by a local newspaper! The music, the computer graphics,
the generals coming out of retirement to become media stars, public hard ons.   75
And we gotta fight NAKED AGGRESSION—like his asshole president should
come to my *fucking neighborhood* if he wants to see naked aggression! I never
thought the ideas in the head of some politician would mean the death of my
brother and absolutely kill my mother. I'm telling you, that woman will not
survive the death of my brother no matter how much she believes in God, no   80
matter how much praying she does. But I keep that from him. I write back
about how it's not going to be another Vietnam. It's not going to be a whole
country that spits on you when you come back. That we don't forget the ones
we love and fight for us. Then his letters stopped. I combed the newspapers
trying to figure out what's going on over there, 'cause his letters said nothing   85
about where he was. He wasn't allowed to talk about locations, or troop size, or
movement, 'cause, like, I was going to personally transmit this information to
the Iraqi fucking Ministry of Defense! I thought about technology. The new
shit Iraq has that was made in the United States, shit that could penetrate a
tank's armour and literally travel through the guts of a tank, immolating every   90
living human soul inside, turning human Puerto Rican flesh into hot screaming
soup, the molecules of my brother's soul mixing with the metal molecules of the
iron coffin he loved so much. I couldn't sleep. My mother was suicidal. Why
wasn't he writing? The air war's continuing. They're bombing the shit out of
that motherfucking country! And I find myself ashamed. I think, "yeah, bomb   95
it more. Level it. Send it back to the Stone Age. Make it so every last elite
Republican Guard is dead. So my brother won't get killed." For the first time in
my life, I want a lot of people I don't hate to die 'cause I know one of them
could kill the man I love most in this fucked up world. If my brother is killed, I
will personally take a gun and blow out the brains of George Herbert Walker   100
Bush. And I'm sick. I'm sick of rooting for the bombs. Sick of loving every day
the air war continues. Sick of every air strike, every sortie. And being happy
another Iraqi tank got taken out and melted, another Iraqi bunker was bombed,
another bridge can't bring ammunition, can't deliver that one magic bullet that
will incapacitate my brother, bring him back a vegetable, bring him back dead   105

in his soul, or blinded, or butchered in some Iraqi concentration camp. That the Iraqi motherfucker that would torture him won't live now 'cause our smart bombs have killed that towelhead motherfucker in his sleep! They actually got me wanting this war to be bloody!

(Beat.)

Last night the ground war started. It started. The tanks are rolling. I find my gut empty now. I don't have thoughts. I don't have dreams. My mother is a shell. She has deserted herself and left behind a blathering cadaver, this pathetic creature with rosary beads in her hands looking up to Christ, and CNN, saying words like "Scud," "strategic interests," "collateral damage," "target rich environment"—words this woman from a little town in Puerto Rico has no right to know. So I fight my demons. I think of the cause. Blood for oil. I NEED MY CAR, DON'T I? I NEED MY CAR TO GET TO WORK SO I CAN PAY THE RENT AND NOT END UP A HOMELESS PERSON! DON'T I HAVE A RIGHT TO MY CAR AND MY GAS? AND WHAT ABOUT FREEING DEMOCRATIC KUWAIT?!

(Beat.)

So I wait for a sign, anything, a prayer, any sign. I'll take it. Just tell me he's okay. Tell me my brother's gonna kill well and make it through this alive. He's gonna come home and he's gonna come home the same person he left; the spastic one who couldn't spell . . . the one who couldn't play the drums.

(CHEO starts to pump gas. As he pumps the gas, he notices something horrifying. He pulls the nozzle out of the car. Blood comes out of the gas pump. CHEO stares and stares at the bloody trickle coming out of the gas pump.)

BLACKOUT

Explorations of the Text

1. Gloss and annotate the monologue. Concentrate on the narrator's perceptions of how his brother changed after he enlisted. What do the brother's letters reveal about the experience of being a solider?

2. What is the protagonist's attitude toward the Gulf War?

3. How has the brother's state affected the family?

4. How does the language of war—phrases such as "collateral damage" and "strategic interests"—contrast with the reality? What do they suggest, in general, about the ways in which politicians and the media portray the realities of war?

5. Explore the significance of the symbolism of the gas pump. Is it effective?

6. Compare and contrast the brother's experience of the Gulf War with that of Hartley's experience of the Iraq War in "I, Jailor" or Scott-Singley's war blog.

The Reading/Writing Connection

1. "Think" Topic: What do you think the speaker's attitude would be toward the Iraq War? Respond in a freewrite, or compose a series of letters between the brother in "Gas" and Hartley.

2. Create a dialogue among the speaker in "Gas," Jason Hartley, and the father in Parks's "Father Comes Home from the War."

Ideas for Writing

1. **Write an Argument:** Write an argumentative essay based on the following statement: "War Is Hell." As an alternative, agree or disagree with O'Brien that the experience of being a soldier in a war cannot be reduced to a single phrase. Use evidence from this play and from several other works.

NONFICTION

Sojourner Truth *(1797–1883)*

Ain't I a Woman?   *1851*

Well, children, where there is so much racket there must be something out of kilter. I think that 'twixt the negroes of the South and the women at the North, all talking about rights, the white men will be in a fix pretty soon. But what's all this here talking about?

That man over there says that women need to be helped into carriages, and lifted over ditches, and to have the best place everywhere. Nobody ever helps me into carriages, or over mud-puddles, or gives me any best place! And ain't I a woman? Look at me! Look at my arm! I have ploughed and planted, and gathered into barns, and no man could head me! And ain't I a woman? I could work as much and eat as much as a man—when I could get it—and bear the lash as well! And ain't I a woman? I have borne thirteen children, and seen them most all sold off to slavery, and when I cried out with my mother's grief, none but Jesus heard me! And ain't I a woman?

Then they talk about this thing in the head; what's this they call it? [Intellect, someone whispers.] That's it, honey. What's that got to do with women's rights or negro's rights? If my cup won't hold but a pint, and yours holds a quart, wouldn't you be mean not to let me have my little half-measure full?

Then that little man in black there, he says women can't have as much rights as men, 'cause Christ wasn't a woman! Where did your Christ come from? Where did your Christ come from? From God and a woman! Man had nothing to do with Him.

If the first woman God ever made was strong enough to turn the world upside   5 down all alone, these women together ought to be able to turn it back, and get it right side up again! And now they is asking to do it, the men better let them.

Obliged to you for hearing me, and now old Sojourner ain't got nothing more to say. ●

Explorations of the Text

1. What is the occasion? Why does Truth connect women's rights with racial issues in the first section of her speech? Characterize the voice of the speaker. Why was the speaker doubly vulnerable?

2. Examine the vision of woman presented in paragraph 2. What is the effect of the repetition of "ain't I a woman?"

3. What is the argument about intellect?

4. Why does she include religion in her speech? What does she accomplish

when she contends that "Man had nothing to do with [Jesus]"? How does she use humor?

5. Consider Truth's version of Eve, "the first woman." Is her argument logical or true?

6. What elements of persuasion does Truth use effectively? (See Chapters 4 and 13.)

The Reading/Writing Connection

1. In a journal entry, respond to the vision of "woman" presented in the speech.

Ideas for Writing

1. Analyze the rhetorical structure of Sojourner Truth's speech. See checklist for nonfiction in Chapter 13.

2. Compose a contemporary version of "Ain't I a Woman?"

Elie Wiesel *(1928–)*

Why I Write: Making No Become Yes   *1985*

Why do I write.

Perhaps in order not to go mad. Or, on the contrary, to touch the bottom of madness. Like Samuel Beckett,[1] the survivor expresses himself "en désepoir de cause"—out of desperation.

Speaking of the solitude of the survivor, the great Yiddish and Hebrew poet and thinker Aaron Zeitlin addresses those—his father, his brother, his friends—who have died and left him: "You have abandoned me," he says to them. "You are together, without me. I am here. Alone. And I make words."

So do I, just like him. I also say words, write words, reluctantly.

There are easier occupations, far more pleasant ones. But for the survivor, writing is 5 not a profession, but an occupation, a duty. Camus calls it "an honor." As he puts it: "I entered literature through worship." Other writers have said they did so through anger, through love. Speaking for myself, I would say—through silence.

It was by seeking, by probing silence that I began to discover the perils and power of the word. I never intended to be a philosopher, or a theologian. The only role I sought was that of witness. I believed that, having survived by chance, I was duty-bound to give meaning to my survival, to justify each moment of my life. I knew the story had to be told. Not to transmit an experience is to betray it. This is what Jewish tradition teaches us. But how to do this? "When Israel is in exile, so is the word," says the Zohar.[2] The word has deserted the meaning it was intended to convey—impossible to make them coincide. The displacement, the shift, is irrevocable.

This was never more true than right after the upheaval. We all knew that we could never, never say what had to be said, that we could never express in words, coherent, intelligible words, our experience of madness on an absolute scale. The walk through flaming night, the silence before and after the selection, the monotonous praying of the condemned, the Kaddish of the dying, the fear and hunger of the sick, the shame and suffering, the haunted eyes, the demented stares. I thought that I would never be able to speak of them. All words seemed inadequate, worn, foolish, lifeless, whereas I wanted them to be searing.

---

[1] **Samuel Beckett:** Irish playwright, essayist, poet, and novelist (1906–1989).   [2] **Zohar:** The source of the Kabbalah, Jewish mysticism.

Where was I to discover a fresh vocabulary, a primeval language? The language of night was not human, it was primitive, almost animal—hoarse shouting, screams, muffled moaning, savage howling, the sound of beating. A brute strikes out wildly, a body falls. An officer raises his arm and a whole community walks toward a common grave. A soldier shrugs his shoulders, and a thousand families are torn apart, to be reunited only by death. This was the concentration camp language. It negated all other language and took its place. Rather than a link, it became a wall. Could it be surmounted? Could the reader be brought to the other side? I knew the answer was negative, and yet knew that "no" had to become "yes." It was the last wish of the dead.

The fear of forgetting remains the main obsession of all those who have passed through the universe of the damned. The enemy counted on people's incredulity and forgetfulness. How could one foil this plot? And if memory grew hollow, empty of substance, what would happen to all we had accumulated along the way? Remember, said the father to his son, and the son to his friend. Gather the names, the faces, the tears. We had all taken an oath: "If, by some miracle, I emerge alive, I will devote my life to testifying on behalf of those whose shadow will fall on mine forever and ever."

That is why I write certain things rather than others—to remain faithful.   10

Of course, there are times of doubt for the survivor, times when one gives in to weakness, or longs for comfort. I hear a voice within me telling me to stop mourning the past. I too want to sing of love and of its magic. I too want to celebrate the sun, and the dawn that heralds the sun. I would like to shout, and shout loudly: "Listen, listen well! I too am capable of victory, do you hear? I too am open to laughter and joy! I want to stride, head high, my face unguarded, without having to point to the ashes over there on the horizon, without having to tamper with facts to hide their tragic ugliness. For a man born blind, God himself is blind, but look, I see, I am not blind." One feels like shouting this, but the shout changes to a murmur. One must make a choice; one must remain faithful. A big word, I know. Nevertheless, I use it, it suits me. Having written the things I have written, I feel I can afford no longer to play with words. If I say that the writer in me wants to remain loyal, it is because it is true. This sentiment moves all survivors; they owe nothing to anyone, but everything to the dead.

I owe them my roots and my memory. I am duty-bound to serve as their emissary, transmitting the history of their disappearance, even if it disturbs, even if it brings pain. Not to do so would be to betray them, and thus myself. And since I am incapable of communicating their cry by shouting, I simply look at them. I see them and I write.

While writing, I question them as I question myself. I believe I have said it before, elsewhere. I write to understand as much as to be understood. Will 1 succeed one day? Wherever one starts, one reaches darkness. God? He remains the God of darkness. Man? The source of darkness. The killers' derision, their victims' tears, the onlookers' indifference, their complicity and complacency—the divine role in all that I do not understand. A million children massacred—I shall never understand.

Jewish children—they haunt my writings. I see them again and again. I shall always see them. Hounded, humiliated, bent like the old men who surround them as though to protect them, unable to do so. They are thirsty, the children, and there is no one to give them water. They are hungry, but there is no one to give them a crust of bread. They are afraid, and there is no one to reassure them.

They walk in the middle of the road, like vagabonds. They are on the way to the   15
station, and they will never return. In sealed cars, without air or food, they travel toward another world. They guess where they are going, they know it, and they keep silent. Tense, thoughtful, they listen to the wind, the call of death in the distance.

All these children, these old people, I see them. I never stop seeing them. I belong to them.

But they, to whom do they belong?

People tend to think that a murderer weakens when facing a child. The child re-awakens the killer's lost humanity. The killer can no longer kill the child before him, the child inside him.

But with us it happened differently. Our Jewish children had no effect upon the killers. Nor upon the world. Nor upon God.

I think of them, I think of their childhood. Their childhood is a small Jewish town, and this town is no more. They frighten me; they reflect an image of myself, one that I pursue and run from at the same time—the image of a Jewish adolescent who knew no fear, except the fear of God, whose faith was whole, comforting, and not marked by anxiety. 20

No, I do not understand. And if I write, it is to warn the reader that he will not understand either. "You will not understand, you will never understand," were the words heard everywhere during the reign of night. I can only echo them. You, who never lived under a sky of blood, will never know what it was like. Even if you read all the books ever written, even if you listen to all the testimonies ever given, you will remain on this side of the wall, you will view the agony and death of a people from afar, through the screen of a memory that is not your own.

An admission of impotence and guilt? I do not know. All I know is that Treblinka and Auschwitz cannot be told. And yet I have tried. God knows I have tried.

Have I attempted too much or not enough? Among some twenty-five volumes, only three or four penetrate the phantasmagoric realm of the dead. In my other books, through my other books, I have tried to follow other roads. For it is danger-ous to linger among the dead, they hold on to you and you run the risk of speak-ing only to them. And so I have forced myself to turn away from them and study other periods, explore other destinies and teach other tales—the Bible and the Tal-mud, Hasidism[3] its fervor, the shtetl[4] and its songs, Jerusalem and its echoes, the Russian Jews and their anguish, their awakening, their courage. At times, it has seemed to me that I was speaking of other things with the sole purpose of keeping the essential—the personal experience—unspoken. At times I have wondered: And what if I was wrong? Perhaps I should not have heeded my own advice and stayed in my own world with the dead.

But then, I have not forgotten the dead. They have their rightful place even in the works about the Hasidic capitals Ruzhany and Korets, and Jerusalem. Even in my bib-lical and Midrashic tales[5] pursue their presence, mute and motionless. The presence of the dead then beckons in such tangible ways that it affects even the most removed char-acters. Thus they appear on Mount Moriah, where Abraham is about to sacrifice his son, a burnt offering to their common God. They appear on Mount Nebo, where Mo-ses enters solitude and death. They appear in Hasidic and Talmudic legends in which victims forever need defending against forces that would crush them. Technically, so to speak, they are of course elsewhere, in time and space, but on a deeper, truer plane, the dead are part of every story, of every scene.

---

[3]**Hasidism:** Popular Eastern European, Orthodox Jewish religious movement that developed in the 1700s. [4]**shtetl:** A village; usually refers to Jewish towns in Eastern Europe. [5]**Midrashic tales:** Readings and interpretations of biblical texts done by rabbis.

"But what is the connection?" you will ask. Believe me, there is one. After Ausch- 25
witz everything brings us back to Auschwitz. When I speak of Abraham, Isaac and
Jacob, when I invoke Rabbi Yohanan ben Zakkai and Rabbi Akiba,[6] it is the better to
understand them in the light of Auschwitz. As for the Maggid of Mezeritch[7] and his disciples, it is in order to encounter the followers of their followers that I reconstruct their
spellbound, spellbinding universe. I like to imagine them alive, exuberant, celebrating
life and hope. Their happiness is as necessary to me as it was once to themselves.

And yet—how did they manage to keep their faith intact? How did they manage
to sing as they went to meet the Angel of Death? I know Hasidim who never vacil-
lated—I respect their strength. I know others who chose rebellion, protest, rage—I respect their courage. For there comes a time when only those who do not believe in God
will not cry out to him in wrath and anguish.

Do not judge either group. Even the heroes perished as martyrs, even the martyrs
died as heroes. Who would dare oppose knives to prayers? The faith of some matters as
much as the strength of others. It is not ours to judge, it is only ours to tell the tale.

But where is one to begin? Whom is one to include? One meets a Hasid in all my
novels. And a child. And an old man. And a beggar. And a madman. They are all part
of my inner landscape. The reason why? Pursued and persecuted by the killers, I offer
them shelter. The enemy wanted to create a society purged of their presence, and I have
brought some of them back. The world denied them, repudiated them, so I let them live
at least within the feverish dreams of my characters.

It is for them that I write, and yet the survivor may experience remorse. He has
tried to bear witness; it was all in vain.

After the liberation, we had illusions. We were convinced that a new world would 30
be built upon the ruins of Europe. A new civilization would see the light. No more
wars, no more hate, no more intolerance, no fanaticism. And all this because the witnesses would speak. And speak they did, to no avail.

They will continue, for they cannot do otherwise. When man, in his grief, falls silent, Goethe[8] says, then God gives him the strength to sing his sorrows. From that moment on, he may no longer choose not to sing, whether his song is heard or not. What
matters is to struggle against silence with words, or through another form of silence.
What matters is to gather a smile here and there, a tear here and there, a word here and
there, and thus justify the faith placed in you, a long time ago, by so many victims.

Why do I write? To wrench those victims from oblivion. To help the dead vanquish death. ●

Explorations of the Text

1. As a survivor, why does Wiesel think that it is his "duty" to become a witness? What does he mean by witnessing? Give examples of his stance. What are the struggles that he endures as a witness?

---

[6]**Rabbi Yohanan . . . Rabbi Akiba:** Rabbi Yohanan ben Zakkai, disciple of Rabbi Hillel, responsible for continuation of Jewish scholarship after Jerusalem fell to Rome in 70 C.E.; Rabbi
Akiba (250–135 C.E.) became the first of Judaism's scholars.   [7]**Maggid of Mezeritch:** Hasidic
master.   [8]**Johann Wolfgang Goethe** (1749–1832): German playwright and poet.

2. Why does he state that he "write[s] certain things rather than others—to remain faithful" "to the dead"?

3. Wiesel's essay contains a series of paradoxes. Isolate the paradoxes, and analyze them. Why does Wiesel include so many paradoxical statements? What messages do they convey?

4. The tension between the impossibility of writing about the Holocaust and the necessity of doing so informs Wiesel's stance. Does he succeed in writing about the Holocaust—in making "no become yes"? Does this essay belie his contention that he is unable to probe the darkness?

5. Is Wiesel optimistic that acts of witnessing will create "a new civilization"? Is he optimistic about the future?

6. Do other writers in the Holocaust cluster effectively portray Holocaust worlds? Are they able to create what Wiesel calls "the language of night"? How do you think that they accomplish this impossible task?

The Reading/Writing Connection

1. Why do you write? Compare your reasons for writing with Wiesel's.

2. In a journal entry, explore the dangers of forgetting the past.

Ideas for Writing

1. Compare and contrast Wiesel's, and, in Chapter 9, Morrison's reasons for writing and your own.

2. In the essay, Wiesel states that he needed to "discover a fresh vocabulary, a primeval language . . . The language of night was not human, it was primitive, almost animal . . ." "This was the concentration camp language." What do you think he means? Are Pryztyk, Hecht, Spiegelman, Celan, or Ozick successful in creating this new language? Why, or why not?

3. Discuss the incomprehensibility of horror as it is portrayed by Wiesel, Pryztyk, and Ozick.

4. Compare Wiesel's use of paradox with Celan's in "Death Fugue."

Emma Goldman   *(1869–1940)*

Minorities vs. Majorities   *1910*

If I were to give a summary of the tendency of our times, I would say, Quantity. The multitude, the mass spirit, dominates everywhere, destroying quality. Our entire life—production, politics, and education—rests on quantity, on numbers. The worker who once took pride in the thoroughness and quality of his work, has been replaced by brainless, incompetent automatons, who turn out enormous quantities of things, valueless to themselves, and generally injurious to the rest of mankind. Thus quantity, instead of adding to life's comforts and peace, has merely increased man's burden.

In politics, naught but quantity counts. In proportion to its increase, however, principles, ideals, justice, and uprightness are completely swamped by the array of numbers. In the struggle for supremacy the various political parties outdo each other in trickery, deceit, cunning, and shady machinations, confident that the one who succeeds is sure to be hailed by the majority as the victor. That is the only god,—Success.

As to what expense, what terrible cost to character, is of no moment. We have not far to go in search of proof to verify this sad fact.

Never before did the corruption, the complete rottenness of our government stand so thoroughly exposed; never before were the American people brought face to face with the Judas nature of that political body, which has claimed for years to be absolutely beyond reproach, as the mainstay of our institutions, the true protector of the rights and liberties of the people.

Yet when the crimes of that party became so brazen that even the blind could see them, it needed but to muster up its minions, and its supremacy was assured. Thus the very victims, duped, betrayed, outraged a hundred times, decided, not against, but in favor of the victor. Bewildered, the few asked how could the majority betray the traditions of American liberty? Where was its judgment, its reasoning capacity? That is just it, the majority cannot reason; it has no judgment. Lacking utterly in originality and moral courage, the majority has always placed its destiny in the hands of others. Incapable of standing responsibilities, it has followed its leaders even unto destruction. Dr. Stockman[1] was right; "The most dangerous enemies of truth and justice in our midst are the compact majorities, the damned compact majority." Without ambition or initiative, the compact mass hates nothing so much as innovation. It has always opposed, condemned, and hounded the innovator, the pioneer of a new truth.

The oft repeated slogan of our time is, among all politicians, the Socialists, included, that ours is an era of individualism, of the minority. Only those who do not probe beneath the surface might be led to entertain this view. Have not the few accumulated the wealth of the world? Are they not the masters, the absolute kings of the situation? Their success, however, is due not to individualism, but to the inertia, the cravenness, the utter submission of the mass. The latter wants but to be dominated, to be led, to be coerced. As to individualism, at no time in human history did it have less chance of expression, less opportunity to assert itself in a normal, healthy manner.

■ ■ ■

Today, as then, public opinion is the omnipresent tyrant; today, as then, the majority represents a mass of cowards, willing to accept him who mirrors its own soul and mind poverty. That accounts for the unprecedented rise of a man like Roosevelt[2] He embodies the very worst element of mob psychology. A politician, he knows that the majority cares little for ideals or integrity. What it craves is display. It matters not whether that be a dog show, a prize fight, the lynching of a "nigger," the rounding up of some petty offender, the marriage exposition of an heiress, or the acrobatic stunts of an ex-president.[3] The more hideous the mental contortions, the greater the delight and bravos of the mass. Thus, poor in ideals and vulgar of soul, Roosevelt continues to be the man of the hour.

---

[1]**Dr. Stockman:** Medical officer of the Municipal Baths in Henrik Ibsen's play, *An Enemy of the People,* written in 1882. He is full of the spirit of innovation and enterprise and betrays the town by not telling them that the baths are built on a poisonous swamp and that the people using the baths to better their health will be infected with fever.   [2]**Theodore Roosevelt** (1858–1919): 26th President of U.S. (1901–1909). Called Rough Rider for his escapades and prosecution of the Spanish-American war.   [3]**It matters not . . . ex-president:** The dog show refers to a birthday party for Lady Astor's dog and the lynching refers to the lynching craze.

■ ■ ■

In the American struggle for liberty, the majority was no less of a stumbling block. Until this very day the ideas of Jefferson, of Patrick Henry, of Thomas Paine,[4] are denied and sold by their posterity. The mass wants none of them. The greatness and courage worshipped in Lincoln have been forgotten in the men who created the background for the panorama of that time. The true patron saints of the black men were represented in that handful of fighters in Boston, Lloyd Garrison, Wendell Phillips, Thoreau, Margaret Fuller,[5] and Theodore Parker, whose great courage and sturdiness culminated in that somber giant, John Brown.[6] Their untiring zeal, their eloquence and perseverance undermined the stronghold of the Southern lords. Lincoln and his minions followed only when abolition had become a practical issue, recognized as such by all.

About fifty years ago, a meteor-like idea made its appearance on the social horizon of the world, an idea so far-reaching, so revolutionary, so all-embracing as to spread terror in the hearts of tyrants everywhere. On the other hand, that idea was a harbinger of joy, of cheer, of hope to the millions. The pioneers knew the difficulties in their way, they knew the opposition, the persecution, the hardships that would meet them, but proud and unafraid they started on their march onward, ever onward. Now that idea has become a popular slogan. Almost everyone is a Socialist today: the rich man, as well as his poor victim; the upholders of law and authority, as well as their unfortunate culprits; the freethinker, as well as the perpetuator of religious falsehoods; the fashionable lady, as well as the shirtwaist girl. Why not? Now that the truth of fifty years ago has become a lie, now that it has been clipped of all its youthful imagination, and been robbed of its vigor, its strength, its revolutionary ideal—why not? Now that it is no longer a beautiful vision, but a "practical, workable scheme," resting on the will of the majority, why not? With the same political cunning and shrewdness the mass is petted, pampered, cheated daily. Its praise is being sung in many keys: the poor majority, the outraged, the abused, the giant majority, if only it would follow us.

Who has not heard this litany before? Who does not know this never-varying refrain of all politicians? That the mass bleeds, that it is being robbed and exploited, I know as well as our vote-baiters. But I insist that not the handful of parasites, but the mass itself is responsible for this horrible state of affairs. It clings to its masters, loves the whip, and is the first to cry Crucify! the moment a protesting voice is raised against the sacredness of capitalistic authority or any other decayed institution. Yet how long would authority and private property exist, if not for the willingness of the mass to become soldiers, policemen, jailers, and hangmen.

---

[4]**Thomas Jefferson** (1743–1826): one of the framers of the U.S. Constitution. **Patrick Henry** (1736–99): American revolutionary and statesman, whose oratorical skills made him famous. **Thomas Paine** (1737–1809): Revolutionary philosopher and writer. Born in England, he became a sailor. In 1774 he sailed for Philadelphia, where his pamphlet *Common Sense* (1776) argued for complete independence. [5]**Garrison** (1805–79): Abolitionist; **Phillips** (1811–84): U.S. orator and reformer; **Fuller** (1810–50): feminist and revolutionary, author of *Woman in the Nineteenth Century;* **Thoreau** (1817–62): essayist who wrote *Civil Disobedience*. [6]**John Brown:** An antislavery militant who led a raid on Harper's Ferry on October 16, 1859, in hopes of inciting a slave rebellion.

■ ■ ■

Yes, power, authority, coercion, and dependence rest on the mass, but never freedom, never the free unfoldment of the individual, never the birth of a free society.

Not because I do not feel with the oppressed, the disinherited of the earth; not because I do not know the shame, the horror, the indignity of the lives the people lead, do I repudiate the majority as a creative force for good. Oh, no, no! But because I know so well that as a compact mass it has never stood for justice or equality. It has suppressed the human voice, subdued the human spirit, chained the human body. As a mass its aim has always been to make life uniform, gray, and monotonous as the desert. As a mass it will always be the annihilator of individuality, of free initiative, of originality. I therefore believe with Emerson[7] that "the masses are crude, lame, pernicious in their demands and influence, and need not to be flattered, but to be schooled. I wish not to concede anything to them, but to drill, divide, and break them up, and draw individuals out of them. Masses! The calamity are the masses. I do not wish any mass at all, but honest men only, lovely, sweet, accomplished women only."

In other words, the living, vital truth of social and economic well-being will become a reality only through the zeal, courage, the non-compromising determination of intelligent minorities, and not through the mass. ●

Explorations of the Text

1. What does Goldman mean when she says the following: "Our entire life—production, politics and education—rests on quantity, on numbers"?

2. What does Goldman mean when she speaks about the "struggle for supremacy" of a political party, that "the one hailed by the majority is the victor"?

Do you see any comparisons between today's politics and those of 100 years ago?

3. Define Goldman's use of the following: "the mass," "the majority," and Socialism. What does she mean by "mob psychology"? Examine "mob psychology" in "My Parents' Bedroom."

The Reading/Writing Connection

1. How would you characterize the effect of the media on today's mass consciousness?

2. Characterize the meaning of success in Walker's story and in Goldman's essay. How do we define success today?

Ideas for Writing

1. **Write an Argument:** Take a statement from Goldman's essay, and write an argument essay either opposing or supporting it.

---

[7]**Ralph Waldo Emerson** (1803–82): Poet, essayist, born in Boston. He was a transcendentalist in philosophy, a rationalist in religion, and a bold advocate of spiritual individualism. Quote is from *The Conduct of Life.*

Czeslaw Milosz   *(1911–2004)*

American Ignorance of War   1953

Are Americans *really* stupid? I was asked in Warsaw. In the voice of the man who posed the question, there was despair, as well as the hope that I would contradict him. This question reveals the attitude of the average person in the people's democracies toward the West: It is despair mixed with a residue of hope.

During the last few years, the West has given these people a number of reasons to despair politically. In the case of the intellectual, other, more complicated reasons come into play. Before the countries of Central and Eastern Europe entered the sphere of the Imperium,[1] they lived through the Second World War. That war was much more devastating there than in the countries of Western Europe. It destroyed not only their economies but also a great many values which had seemed till then unshakable.

Man tends to regard the order he lives in as *natural*. The houses he passes on his way to work seem more like rocks rising out of the earth than like products of human hands. He considers the work he does in his office or factory as essential to the harmonious functioning of the world. The clothes he wears are exactly what they should be, and he laughs at the idea that he might equally well be wearing a Roman toga or medieval armor. He respects and envies a minister of state or a bank director, and regards the possession of a considerable amount of money as the main guarantee of peace and security. He cannot believe that one day a rider may appear on a street he knows well, where cats sleep and children play, and start catching passersby with his lasso. He is accustomed to satisfying those of his physiological needs which are considered private as discreetly as possible, without realizing that such a pattern of behavior is not common to all human societies. In a word, he behaves a little like Charlie Chaplin in *The Gold Rush,* bustling about in a shack poised precariously on the edge of a cliff.

His first stroll along a street littered with glass from bomb-shattered windows shakes his faith in the "naturalness" of his world. The wind scatters papers from hastily evacuated offices, papers labeled "Confidential" or "Top Secret" that evoke visions of safes, keys, conferences, couriers, and secretaries. Now the wind blows them through the street for anyone to read; yet no one does, for each man is more urgently concerned with finding a loaf of bread. Strangely enough, the world goes on even though the offices and secret files have lost all meaning. Farther down the street, he stops before a house split in half by a bomb, the privacy of people's homes—the family smells, the warmth of the beehive life, the furniture preserving the memory of loves and hatreds—cut open to public view. The house itself, no longer a rock, but a scaffolding of plaster, concrete, and brick; and on the third floor, a solitary white bathtub, rain-rinsed of all recollection of those who once bathed in it. Its formerly influential and respected owners, now destitute, walk the fields in search of stray potatoes. Thus overnight money loses its value and becomes a meaningless mass of printed paper. His walk takes him past a little boy poking a stick into a heap of smoking ruins and whistling a song about the great leader who will preserve the nation against all enemies. The song remains, but the leader of yesterday is already part of an extinct past.

He finds he acquires new habits quickly. Once, had he stumbled upon a corpse on the street, he would have called the police. A crowd would have gathered, and much talk

[1] **Imperium:** Empire; Sphere of dominance; Soviet Union.

and comment would have ensued. Now he knows he must avoid the dark body lying the gutter, and refrain from asking unnecessary questions. The man who fired the gun must have had his reasons; he might well have been executing an Underground sentence.

Nor is the average European accustomed to thinking of his native city as divided into segregated living areas, but a single decree can force him to this new pattern of life and thought. Quarter A may suddenly be designated for one race; B, for a second; C, for a third. As the resettlement deadline approaches, the streets become filled with long lines of wagons, carts, wheelbarrows, and people carrying bundles, beds, chests, caldrons, and bird cages. When all the moves are effected, 2,000 people may find themselves in a building that once housed 200, but each man is at last in the proper area. Then high walls are erected around Quarter C, and daily a given lot of men, women, and children are loaded into wagons that take them off to specially constructed factories where they are scientifically slaughtered and their bodies burned.

And even the rider with the lasso appears, in the form of a military van waiting at the corner of a street. A man passing that corner meets a leveled rifle, raises his hands, is pushed into the van, and from that moment is lost to his family and friends. He may be sent to a concentration camp, or he may face a firing squad, his lips sealed with plaster lest he cry out against the state; but, in any case, he serves as a warning to his fellow men. Perhaps one might escape such a fate by remaining at home. But the father of a family must go out in order to provide bread and soup for his wife and children; and every night they worry about whether or not he will return. Since these conditions last for years, everyone gradually comes to look upon the city as a jungle, and upon the fate of twentieth-century man as identical with that of a caveman living in the midst of powerful monsters.

It was once thought obvious that a man bears the same name and surname throughout his entire life; now it proves wiser for many reasons to change them and to memorize a new and fabricated biography. As a result, the records of the civilian state become completely confused. Everyone ceases to care about formalities, so that marriage, for example, comes to mean little more than living together.

Respectable citizens used to regard banditry as a crime. Today, bank robbers are heroes because the money they steal is destined for the Underground. Usually they are young boys, mothers' boys, but their appearance is deceiving. The killing of a man presents no great moral problem to them.

The nearness of death destroys shame. Men and women change as soon as they know that the date of their execution has been fixed by a fat little man with shiny boots and a riding crop. They copulate in public, on the small bit of ground surrounded by barbed wire—their last home on earth. Boys and girls in their teens, about to go off to the barricades to fight against tanks with pistols and bottles of gasoline, want to enjoy their youth and lose their respect for standards of decency.

Which world is "natural"? That which existed before, or the world of war? Both are natural, if both are within the realm of one's experience. All the concepts men live by are a product of the historic formation in which they find themselves. Fluidity and constant change are the characteristics of phenomena. And man is so plastic a being that one can even conceive of the day when a thoroughly self-respecting citizen will crawl on all fours, sporting a tail of brightly colored feathers as a sign of conformity to the order he lives in.

The man of the East cannot take Americans seriously because they have never undergone the experiences that teach men how relative their judgments and thinking habits are. Their resultant lack of imagination is appalling. Because they were born and raised in a given social order and in a given system of values, they believe that any other order must be "unnatural," and that it cannot last because it is incompatible with human nature. But even they may one day know fire, hunger, and the sword. In all probability this is what will occur; for it is hard to believe that when one half of the world is living through terrible disasters, the other half can continue a nineteenth-century mode of life, learning about the distress of its distant fellow men only from movies and newspapers. Recent examples teach us that this cannot be. An inhabitant of Warsaw or Budapest once looked at newsreels of bombed Spain or burning Shanghai, but in the end he learned how these and many other catastrophes appear in actuality. He read gloomy tales of the NKVD[2] until one day he himself had to deal with it. If *something exists in one place, it will exist everywhere.* This is the conclusion he draws from his observations, and so he has no particular faith in the momentary prosperity of America. He suspects that the years 1933–1945 in Europe[3] prefigure what will occur elsewhere. A hard school, where ignorance was punished not by bad marks but by death, has taught him to think sociologically and historically. But it has not freed him from irrational feelings. He is apt to believe in theories that foresee violent changes in the countries of the West, for he finds it unjust that they should escape the hardships he had to undergo. ●

Explorations of the Text

1. This essay appears in Milosz's first American volume, *The Captive Mind*, published shortly after World War II and after his defection from Poland in 1951 and thirty-five years before the birth of democracies in Eastern Europe and détente in Soviet Russia. Do you see evidence in the essay of the historical context of this work? To what historical events does the author refer?

2. Why does Milosz begin with the question: "Are Americans really stupid?" What is his perspective in the essay? How does the opening paragraph suggest his point of view, tone, and themes of the essay?

3. Consider Milosz's use of the term "nature." What is "natural" to man? Is he being ironic? Contrast the two views of human nature, modes of living, states of civilization presented in the essay.

4. What does he conclude about the world? Now fifty years after the publication of this essay, do you concur with his views expressed in paragraphs 11 and 12? Have Americans lost their innocence? Their sense of insularity from world events?

5. Compare the view of witnessing expressed in this essay with Creon's growth of awareness in *Antigone*.

The Reading/Writing Connection

1. "Think" Topic: Do Americans live in a state of willed "ignorance"? Freewrite in response to this question.

2. Choose a statement from this essay that you agree or disagree with. Create a dialogue with the author.

---

[2]**NKVD:** The Soviet secret police, 1935–43. [3]**1933–1945 in Europe:** The years of the rise, dominance, and demise of Nazism.

3. Do ordinary citizens bear the responsibility for the living and the dying? Respond in a journal entry.

Ideas for Writing

1. Evaluate Milosz's argument. How does Milosz build his argument? What forms of evidence does he use? Are his techniques effective?

2. Imagine that America has been invaded and occupied by another country. Create a short scene that demonstrates the consequences.

3. Debate Topics: Argue pro or con about one of these contentions.
   • Americans' "lack of imagination is appalling."
   • Americans have never experienced "fire, hunger, and the sword."
   • The state of war is "natural."

Jason Hartley   *(1974–   )*

I, Jailor   *2004*

This morning our battalion conducted several simultaneous pre-dawn raids. The first home my platoon hit went down in a fashion that's becoming the norm for us— moments before the ram is to hit the door for the dynamic entry that turgid grunts salivate over, the door is unlocked and opened from the inside by a man who is probably already on his second cup of Turkish coffee. People here wake up stupid early to get a jump on the long day of chicken herding or dirt farming or whatever. Some of the intel was of dubious credibility resulting in nothing but a lot of wide-eyed and confused detainees, as was the case with my platoon's target building, and some intel is rock solid. There were RPGs and belts of machine gun ammunition found at other target locations today, not a completely fruitless morning of raids.

I missed out on this morning's soiree pulling a twelve-hour shift of gate and jail guard instead. Our forward operations base's jail (detention center?) is right at the front gate, a messy configuration where detainees, local civilian contractors and politicians along with ICDC clowns, Iraqi police officers and all the other random visitors we get are being corralled through the same small area. Anyway, everyone was back by before 0800 at which point they dumped off all the men captured to our reluctant jailor. This "facility" is smaller than my apartment and with twenty-some-odd Ali Babba (the locals' term for evildoers) bound and blindfolded, it can be pretty cramped. One of the first detainees had on his person 3000 dinars (like 2 bucks), an ID card, and a slip of paper with what looked like some sort of apparent code handwritten on it. When the lieutenant in charge of performing ad-hoc in-processing saw this, he thought he might have struck gold by stumbling upon some sort of encrypted message. Looking at it, there were two lines of alpha-numeric text, each line five groups of five English alphabet characters separated by hyphens. Scrawled underneath was what looked like the word, "Word". The code looked incredibly familiar. Then it hit me. I kinda chuckled and told the Lieutenant that at best this implicated our detainee in the crime of software piracy. It was a couple of CD-keys, for Microsoft Word no doubt.

Once everyone had their restraints cut off and was farmed out evenly into the four cells, still blindfolded and seated facing the wall, an interpreter instructed each detainee that he would stay seated, not talk and not remove his blindfold. Each man was also informed that if he followed these rules and acted like a gentleman, he would be treated like a gentleman. Then began the Parade of Piss. "Mister, mister. Toilet, toilet." Once again, Jesus made manifest his displeasure with me for leaving his church. Had I stayed Mormon, gotten married ridiculously young, settled down, made a family, and took on the inevitable tour of duty of running the nursery at church while the other adults attended various meetings and Sunday classes, I would have been able to do my time in this life of taking rascals pee pee. In lieu of this duty I thought I had successfully dodged, I was now taking rascals pee pee that reeked of the body odor only a Middle-Eastern diet can create. So when are you being humane letting detainees urinate (the term this Lieutenant kept using was "titrate") as needed, and when are you just plain being taken advantage of by performing an endless round-robin of urinal runs? (There isn't actually any urinal, just a tube stuck in the dirt behind the jail.) Most of the soldiers I had with me had not worked with detainees yet and seemed to also be searching for a sense of what the right tone to set for a jail was. I felt myself walking a fine line between proper Geneva Convention–esque humane treatment of enemy combatants and being made a fool of by the same guys that have been making fools of us for the past few weeks by hitting our FOB almost nightly with mortars and RPGs who then always slip away into the night before we can catch them. It pretty much came down to the rule of thumb that if he did the pee pee dance for at least a half hour, he was probably legit and was allowed to go.

Once the initial shock and fear among the herd subsided, the chatter and blindfold fidgeting-with began. I'd say that most these guys were model detainees, but just like any Army platoon or company, there's always one or two problem children. First, two guys wouldn't stop whispering to each other. So I put them in separate cells. Then one kept pulling down his blindfold claiming allergy-beset eyes. We compromised and told him we'd loosen the blindfold if he faced the wall and shut up. He only partially complied. He was warned and re-warned by the Lieutenant and the interpreter. But like a child, he kept pushing the limit. The Lieutenant left as did the interpreter. More chatter, more blindfold-slippage. He started eyeballing me and some of the other soldiers. (If I were in East L.A., I'd be compelled to proclaim, "Why you mad doggin' me, yo?!") I yelled at him to shut up and pull the blind fold back up. He just smiled and gave me the thumbs up. I've said that the thumbs up in Iraq is a way of simultaneously telling someone both "okay" and "fuck you" at once, a trick this little bastard was now turning back on me deftly. Something I have to express here is that this childish way of pushing the limit and seeing what you can get away with is a pet peeve of mine. More last warnings, then I got fed up. I removed him from the cell, took his blindfold off and put on tightly a huge one made out of a first-aid cravat. I also flex-cuffed his hands, behind his back, also tight enough to be uncomfortable. A half hour later he had pulled the blindfold down with his teeth somehow. Last straw.

Everyone knows that duct tape can fix anything. In the Army, we have six-inch wide green duct tape that we call hundred mile-an-hour tape, a moniker apparently due to its ability to mend tears in the canvas wings of Wright Brothers–era planes, good up to one-hundred miles-an-hour. I put dickhead on his knees in the middle of his cell, removed the blindfold that he was now wearing as a dashing olive-drab scarf and wrapped the top half of his head with about ten layers of 100 MPH tape. Then one last piece across the bridge of his nose and around his head again to seal off the small gap that invariably is present at the bottom of one's field of vision when one is blindfolded. I tried to create as much drama as possible with the event. Our S-2 (intel) Master Sergeant happened to be present at the time, a mean-spirited quasi-sadist, the fulltime El Capitán of the jail, a job that he seems to relish, and was in the process of systematically interrogating the detainees. He kept saying, "Okay Sergeant, that's enough tape. Okay, that's enough. Okay, that's enough Sergeant." The distinct sound of duct tape being applied directly off the roll was loud and satisfying as it reverberated off the six cold concrete planes of wall, floor, and ceiling. I tried my best to seem stern and to disguise the fact that my heart was pounding. One layer or fifty layers, I figured it wouldn't make much difference as far as adhesive blindfolds go, I just wanted to give the impression of an excessive and final response to his juvenile game of tit for tat. I felt like my disciplinarian pious father (a relationship I'll never reconcile); I felt like I was on the wrong side of recurring anxiety dreams I've always had of being imprisoned; I felt stupid and petty and cowardly. I fucking loathe loathe loathe treating people like that. I'd rather be working with exceptional people, not dealing with troublesome people. Antagonistic relationships that have some constructive end or transparent layer of camaraderie, like the relationship a soldier has with a drill sergeant, I have no problem with. I actually endorse this sort of thing openly. But having to assert my assumed authority in front of my prisoners and my peers to make an example of this ne'er-do-well has no positive product as far as I'm concerned. There's a darkly intoxicating aspect to this kind of thing though. I'm over-armed with my rifle and grenade launcher and the veritable ammunition dump that is the vest over my body armor. Because of this my power over these men is near-absolute, especially if I were to consider spending life in Fort Leavenworth immaterial. I can see how the bully feels, how one could grow fond of this darkly amusing massive imbalance of power. I tried to keep in mind that even simple playful mockery of the detainees could easily be perceived as cold humor. I wanted to maintain order, I wanted to assert a measure of authority that was little to ask considering the situation, but most importantly I did not want to perpetrate something on others that I am deeply phobic of myself, to be imprisoned and tormented.

I let this guy sit and think about what he had done wrong. Isn't that how our parents used to put it? He finally broke his macho stoic silence after about forty-five minutes. "Mister. Mister. I'm sorry. I'm sorry." I was furious at this asshole. Not only was he apparently contrite now, but his English was getting better too. But mostly I was furious that he "made" me do this. I yelled some nonsense at him about how it was too late to be sorry, that he would continue to be sorry before I did anything for him. Not my words, just rhetorical crap I was regurgitating from a lifetime of being caught in a punishment-lecture-punishment-lecture cycle for serial rule-breaking. Working with me at the time was a medic, this forty-something-ish Hispanic specialist with an improbable number of vowels in his name and a thick salt-and-pepper moustache that seemed to exude an avuncular warmth. He had a pleasant and attentive demeanor and looked like he could be a dentist or a good-natured washing machine salesman at Sears. All day he had been eminently respectful to me, everything was a snappy Yes Sergeant, No Sergeant, something that always makes me uncomfortable when coming from someone so clearly my senior. He looked at me now like he had been suffering along with this guy the whole time, maybe empathetic because he's a medic or because he knew it would probably be his job to help separate tape from eyebrows in a few minutes. I assured him that I'd only let the guy stew for five more minutes tops, but after hemming and hawing for about five more seconds I finally just said Fuck it, let's just give this jerk his reprieve. From his knees again we unwrapped tapehead and I absurdly lectured him in an unavoidably paternal (patronizing?) way in a language I knew he couldn't understand but a tone that I knew he would. He looked up at me, his eyes red and watering (had he been crying or were his eyes actually irritated?) and he reverently uttered, "Thank you." After we locked the cell door (padlock on a grille-like door, not quite totally archetypical for a jail), all inside either sat or slept quietly, unmoving.

Hours later it was the problem child's turn to be interrogated and was escorted by several soldiers to an out-of-sight location by the Master Sergeant. I sat outside by the front gate, eating an MRE. My knife, a beloved Spyderco Delica with green handle and black blade, slayer of MRE packages, lay in front of me as I shoveled beef and mushroom into my mouth like the engineer fed coal into the furnace of his engine in the old Popeye cartoon. As they were walking, the Master Sergeant stopped for a moment to talk to someone. My favorite detainee now stood in front of me. He eyed my knife, then eyed me. I looked back at him and he didn't look away, or should I say he wouldn't look away. Honestly I couldn't tell if he was trying to read my eyes like I was trying to read his or if he was just trying to memorize my face, or maybe he just plain hated me and was indulging his fascination with the object of his hate, a thirst that you can never really slake.

Truth be told, I paid little attention to how he looked, not nearly as much attention as he seemed to pay to how I looked. If I saw him on the street right now, I probably wouldn't recognize him. Shame on me I guess. The first step is to remove the personness from your enemy. Once you remove his humanity in your mind, distance him from you, the human, it's easier to kill him if it comes down to that. He wore a green camouflage jacket making him stand out from the rest of the white and gray mandress wearers. In the back of the jacket on the bottom there was a buttoned flap. Ever since the advent of the man-dress (dish dash or pish posh or whatever they call them, I forget), when it came time to go into combat you'd reach between your legs, grab the back hem and pull it up into your belt in the front, creating a big man-diaper. My seminary teacher in junior high said this was called "girding up your loins." My guess is the flap on the back of this jacket was made for the same purpose, to turn the flowing man-dress of would-be fighters into MC Hammer pants. His hair was neat and short-cropped. I only know this really because I had to pull all that tape off his head. He was probably in his early twenties. I'd say if it came down to hand-to-hand, this guy, being most likely in the same weight-class as me, would give me a run for my money. But most non-farmer Iraqis are in absurdly bad shape, so I'd probably prevail. If not, I'd at least bite his nose off or something really dirty like that. So there he was, staring me down again, who knows what machinations going on in his head. ●

Zachary Scott-Singley *(1981–   )*

Military Blog   *2005*
from *A Soldier's Thoughts*

April 29, 2005—Memories of Death

There is good out there even though at times it all seems bleak. There is also death. How many have dealt in death? Some would call it murder. Well, I have a confession to make, my platoon and I have had over 192 confirmed kills during our first deployment here (during the war on our way to capture Baghdad). We targeted people and then they just disappeared. Why? They were going to kill me. I had my orders and they had theirs. We were mortal enemies because we were told that we were. There are some who would tell me to not think about what I had to do, or it will drive you insane.

For me, however, I can't help but think about it. They were men like me. Some of them were even conscripted into military service. What made them fight? Were they more scared of their leader than of us? What has become of their families? How could I forget or not think about all that I have done? Should I wash my hands of it all like Pontius Pilate? I think not. My choices have been made, my actions irreversible. So live I will, for we were the victors, right? The ones who survived. It is our victory, and our burden to carry, and I bear it with pride and with the greatest of remorse. Do you think that there is a special place in hell for people like me? Or will God judge me to have been a man of honor and duty?

When they told us how many we had killed my first thought was pride. Pride for such a high number. How does one feel pride for killing? Two years later and my thoughts are changed, transformed if you will. Those were just numbers so long ago when I first heard them. Now, however, I know that they were men with families like mine. It is crazy that we humans can be so destructive. There are people out there lining up to become martyrs, to kill themselves in order to kill others, and yet you still have people who fight tooth and nail to live for just one more minute longer. We are an oxymoron, humanity that is. What makes someone look down the sights of a rifle to take aim on a fellow human being? What does it take to pull the trigger? I have done those things. I have done them and would do it again if it meant returning to my wife and children again. Some of you may think that I am a beast and you are probably right. I am. I will kill, I will take aim and fire, I will call fire upon you from afar with rockets and bombs or anything I can get my hands on if it means that I will see my family one more time.

But, I will also choose to dwell on and live with my choices. I chose to enlist as a soldier. My time has been served and now it is becoming overtime, but I won't just run away. As much as I would love to just be done (and rightly so now that I have been involuntarily extended). One thing is all I ask of you. I ask that you not judge me. Let me be my own judge, for my judgment is harsher than any you could give me anyway. For I will always have those memories to remind me of what I have done and what I am. Please know that I pray for peace every day, that and to see my family again.

May 4, 2005—It Was Still Dark . . .

It was still dark. I got dressed in that darkness. When I was ready I grabbed an MRE s
(meal ready to eat) and got in the truck. I was going to go line the truck up in preparation for the raid we were about to go on. The targets were three houses where RPG attacks had come from a few days prior. Sitting there in that darkness listening to the briefing on how we were to execute the mission, I let my mind wander from the briefing and said a prayer. "Just one more day, God, let me live one more day and we will go from there . . ." It was the same prayer I said every day because every day I did the same thing. I left the base. With a small team I would go out each day on different missions. I was their translator.

There were different people to meet each day. There were some who would kill you if they could. They would look at you and you could see the hate in their eyes. I also met with people who would have given me everything they owned. People that were so thankful to us because we had rid them of Saddam. Well, this day was not really much different from all those other days so far. After the briefing we all got into our assigned seats and convoyed out to the raid site. I was to go in directly after the military police that would clear the building.

The raid began without a hitch. Inside one of the courtyards of one of the houses, talking to an Iraqi woman, checking to see if her story correlated with what the detained men had said, I heard gunfire. It was automatic gunfire. Ducking next to the stone wall I yelled at the woman to get inside her house, and when the gunfire stopped I peeked my head around the front gate. I saw a soldier amongst the others who was pulling rear security by our vehicles. This soldier I saw was still aiming his M249 (a fully automatic belt-fed machine gun) at a black truck off in the distance. His was the weapon I had heard.

I ran up near his position and overheard the captain in charge of the raid asking what had happened and why had this soldier opened fire. The soldier kept his weapon aimed and answered that he was sure he had seen a man holding an AK-47 in the back of the black truck. I was amongst the four (along with the soldier who had fired on the black truck) who had been selected to go and see what was up with that truck.

We were out of breath when we got to the gun truck nearest to the black civilian truck (a gun truck is a HUMMWV, sometimes called a Hummer by civilians, with a .50-caliber machine gun on its roof). There was a group of four Iraqis walking towards us from the black truck. They were carrying a body. When I saw this I ran forward and began to speak (in Arabic) to the man holding the body but I couldn't say a word.

There right in front of me in the arms of one of the men I saw a small boy (no more than three years old). His head was cocked back at the wrong angle and there was blood. So much blood. How could all that blood be from that small boy? I heard crying too. All of the Iraqi men standing there were crying and sobbing and asking me WHY? Someone behind me started screaming for a medic. It was the young soldier (around my age) who had fired his weapon. He screamed and screamed for a medic until his voice was hoarse and a medic came just to tell us what I already knew. The boy was dead. I was so numb.

I stood there looking at that little child, someone's child (just like mine), and seeing how red the clean white shirt of the man holding the boy was turning. It was then that I realized that I had been speaking to them, speaking in a voice that sounded so very far away. I heard my voice telling them (in Arabic) how sorry we were. My mouth was saying this but all my mind could focus on was the hole in the child's head. The white shirt covered in bright red blood. Every color was so bright. There were other colors too. The glistening white pieces of the child's skull still splattered on that so very white shirt. I couldn't stop looking at them even as I continued telling them how sorry we were.

I can still see it all to this very day. The raid was over, there were no weapons to be found, and we had accomplished nothing except killing a child of some unknowing mother. Not wanting to leave yet, I stayed as long as I could, talking to the man holding the child. I couldn't leave because I needed to know who they were. I wanted to remember. The man was the brother of the child's father. He was the boy's uncle, and he was watching him for his father who had gone to the market. They were carpenters

10

and the soldier who had fired upon the truck had seen someone holding a piece of wood and standing in the truck bed.

Before I left to go back to our base I saw the young soldier who had killed the boy. His eyes were unfocused and he was just standing there, staring off into the distance. My hand went to my canteen and I took a drink of water. That soldier looked so lost, so I offered him a drink from my canteen. In a hoarse voice he quietly thanked me and then gave me such a thankful look, like I had given him gold.

Later that day those of us who had been selected to go inspect the black truck were filling reports out about what we had witnessed for the investigation. The captain who had led the raid entered the room we were in and you could see that he was angry. He said, "Well this is just great! Now we have to go and give that family bags of money to shut them up." I wanted to kill him. I sat there trembling with my rage. Some family had just lost their beautiful baby boy and this man, this COMMISSIONED OFFICER in the United States Army is worried about trying to pay off the family's grief and sorrow. He must not have been a father, otherwise he would know that money doesn't even come close . . . I wanted to use my bare hands to kill him, but instead I just sat there and waited until the investigating officer called me into his office.

To this day I still think about that raid, that family, that boy. I wonder if they are making attacks on us now. I would be. If someone took the life of my son or my daughter nothing other than my own death would stop me from killing that person. I still cry too. I cry when the memory hits me. I cry when I think of how very far away I am from my family who needs me. I am not there just like the boy's father wasn't there. I pray every day for my family's safety and just that I was with them. I have served my time, I have my nightmares, I have enough blood on my hands. My contract with the Army has been involuntarily extended. I am not asking for medicine to help with the nightmares or for anything else, only that the Army would have held true to the contract I signed and let me be a father, a husband, a daddy again.

May 29, 2005—My Thoughts on Monsters

There is a place where the skies are blue, the water is clean, and life is good. This place cannot be found where I am at. Over here almost every single morning begins with violence, explosions, and people being killed. Over here the locals can't make enough money because it is so unsafe to be out and working. Over here things are different. Down is often up and up isn't down but sideways. In Iraq there are some who want only to see their children grow up, to grow old with their loved ones.

There are also monsters here. "Monsters?" you say. "Those can't be real." I tell you that they are. I have seen with my own eyes that they are. The worst part is that they look just like people. They aren't, though. They think that the way to do things is to violently end their lives. Most of the time they end up destroying and devastating those regular people who love their families. People who work honestly, those who have hearts. The monsters, however, are hard to spot because like I said, they look like regular people.

I have spoken with these monsters, seen their eyes. I wonder how you can fit so much hate in there. Maybe that is why they blow themselves up. They just can't contain all that hate . . .

Want to know what it is like to be one? I have come close before. Close, because I wanted to kill so badly, to destroy those same monsters, but I realized something. You are only a monster if you let yourself become one.

So now I dream not about monsters but about that place. It is so very far away that it doesn't seem like it is real anymore. That place is called home. I just hope that I make it back there.

June 17, 2005—Sticks and Stones but Words Can Never Hurt

I can't stop thinking about what a major said to me the other day. "The whole country of Iraq, every man, woman, and child . . . Kill every one of them and it still won't be worth one American's life."

Perhaps this is why we won't win here, because so many feel that the life of an Iraqi doesn't even register when compared to that of an American. This kind of mindset permeates the thoughts of many of the soldiers here in Iraq.

So often I hear, "I gotta go f—guard Hajji!" from the soldiers assigned the duty of watching over the Iraqi workers who are working on our base. Another thing I hear so very often is, "I'm gonna go shoot me some Hajji." The soldiers who say these things speak as if the Iraqi people were some kind of animal to be hunted. You might tell me that terrorists are nothing more than animals to be hunted but if you look at the statistics most of those killed are civilians not foreign fighters.

It is time to wake up and realize that there are more important things than the Michael Jackson trial. There are things like the value of a human life or the value of an *entire* nation that has been kicked so many times by tyrants that it may look downtrodden and useless but under it all there is the beauty of LIFE.

October 27, 2005—Our Walk Through Life

What is the human condition? Here in Iraq we fight terrorists and insurgents. We give them names (hajji, towelhead, raghead) to peel away their humanity. We focus only on the horrible things that have happened so that we can bring ourselves to kill, but in doing so we too become changed. No longer do we fit in when we get home. We become outsiders and misfits amongst our own families and distance ourselves as others too distance themselves from us.

Alone, it becomes easier with time to be that way. You can't let others know the things you have done because they would never understand and it would only serve to make us even more alone.

We must build as well; we become so proficient at building that we could be engineers. Walls are our specialty, so we build them thick and high around ourselves. These walls shut out all the pain and hurt we feel when others can't seem to understand why we are the way we are, or when they judge and condemn us as if they were God himself. The walls don't just keep those things out, but they serve to keep so much in as well. All of it, the guilt, the pain, and the fears we have can be kept deep inside where nobody will have to see them except ourselves.

That is OK though, because from there we can learn one last and important skill, that of the beast tamer. Like a monster everything we keep inside locked away can take on a mind of its own, creating even more pain. Some of us fall apart at this point, hitting the ground so hard that we decide we cannot get up. And so it ends.

The rest of us learn tricks to keep that beast inside so that nobody will ever have to see how much of a monster we have become. In doing so we can continue our walk through life. That is the soldier's cost of war, and it is ours to bear alone until the end. ●

Explorations of the Text

1. Czeslaw Milosz talks of the assumption by Americans that their way of seeing the world is "natural," normal. Do you notice this attitude in Hartley's "I, Jailor"? Explain.

2. Milosz asks, "Which world is 'natural'? That which existed before, or the world of war?" Answer this question, referring to Hartley's or Scott-Singley's description of Iraq.

3. The American soldiers call the Iraqis "Ali Babba," and the Iraqis use the thumbs-up signal to simultaneously convey "okay" and "fuck you." How might these uses of spoken and sign language indicate the birth of a new society?

4. Does Hartley seem to be "ignorant" by Milosz's standards? Why, or why not?

The Reading/Writing Connection

1. Why does Hartley duct-tape the detainee's eyes, even though he despises himself for doing so? Write about a time when you felt a similar sense of frustration. How did you act?

2. Zachary Scott-Singley was a sergeant in the 3rd Infantry Division, stationed in Tikrit, Iraq, when he composed this military blog, *A Soldier's Thoughts,* which is no longer active. Scott-Singley's blog depicts some of the impossible choices and decisions that soldiers make on a day-to-day basis. Choose one of his entries and analyze one of his experiences. How do you respond?

Ideas for Writing

1. Hartley explains that "the first step is to remove the person-ness from your enemy." Relate this to Milosz's concern that Americans are "ignorant" and to the attitude of the mob in "My Parents' Bedroom."

2. In Hartley's experience with the detainee, why might it be good for him not to consider the man as an equal, as human? Conversely, why might it be bad? What do you think might be the long-term result of having an occupying force treating people as subhumans? Write an argument in favor of or opposed to treating others as subhuman during a time of war.

3. Discuss the soldiers' choices, presented in these two blogs. As Scott-Singley states, "I . . . choose to dwell on and live with my choices." What do you learn about a soldier's thoughts, experiences, and psychological state? You also may refer to Tim O"Brien's "How to Tell a True War Story" or Jose Rivera's "Gas."

4. In "The Blogs of War," John Hockenberry discusses the phenomenon of military bloggers, or milbloggers as he labels them, who realistically portray the war in Iraq, whether they support or oppose the war. In the article, he quotes Danjel Bout, one of the bloggers, who states: "'The real value of milblogging may be that it brings to the United States the reality of what is becoming a long war,'" because "'Americans [who] are raised on a steady diet of action films and sound bites that slip from one supercharged scene to another'" have no idea of "'the confusing decisions and subtle details where most people actually spend their lives. . . . For people to really understand our day-to-day experience [in Iraq], they

need more than the highlight reel. They need to see the world through our eyes for a few minutes.'" Do you agree with Danjel Bout's conclusions? Do Hartley's and Scott-Singley's works illustrate this position?

Danusha Veronica Goska

Political Paralysis *2005*

It was September 1998, in Bloomington, Indiana. As part of the conference on Spirituality and Ecology: No Separation, a group of concerned citizens was gathered in the basement of St. Paul Catholic Center. They were thinking and talking about living their ideals. Some had planted trees in Africa. Some described ways that they honor the indigenous spirit of a place, and their own ancestors. Elderly nuns and young feminists recounted their part in women's struggle. One frustrated woman voiced the nagging worry of many. "I want to do something, but what can I do? I'm just one person, an average person. I can't have an impact. I live with the despair of my own powerlessness. I can't bring myself to do anything. The world is so screwed up, and I have so little power. I feel so *paralyzed*."

I practically exploded.

Years before I had been stricken by a debilitating illness. Perilymph fistula's symptoms are like those of multiple sclerosis. On some days I was functional. On others, and I could never predict when these days would strike, I was literally, not metaphorically, paralyzed. I couldn't leave the house; I could barely stand up. I had moved to Bloomington for grad school. I knew no one in town. I couldn't get health care because I hadn't enough money, and the Social Security administration, against the advice of its own physician and vocational advisors, denied my claim.

That's why I imitated Mount Vesuvius when the conference participant claimed that just one person, one average person, can't do anything significant to make the world a better place; that the only logical option was passivity, surrender, and despair.

I raised my hand and spoke. "I have an illness that causes intermittent bouts of 5 paralysis," I explained. "And that paralysis has taught me something. It has taught me that my protestations of my own powerlessness are bogus. Yes, some days I can't move or see. But you know what? Some days I can move. Some days I can see. And the difference between being able to walk across the room and not being able to walk across the room is epic.

"I commute to campus by foot along a railroad track. In spring, I come across turtles who have gotten stuck. The track is littered with the hollowing shells of turtles that couldn't escape the rails. So, I bend over, and I pick up the still living trapped turtles that I do find. I carry them to a wooded area and let them go. For those turtles, that much power that I have is enough.

"I'm just like those turtles. When I have been sick and housebound for days, I wish someone—anyone—would talk to me. To hear a human voice say my name; to be touched: that would mean the world to me.

"One day an attack hit me while I was walking home from campus. It was a snowy day. There was snow on the ground, and more snow was falling from the sky. I struggled with each step; wobbled and wove across the road. I must have looked like a drunk. One of my neighbors, whom I had never met, stopped and asked if I was okay. He drove me home.

"He didn't hand me the thousands of dollars I needed for surgery. He didn't take me in and empty my puke bucket. He just gave me one ride, one day. I am still grateful to him and touched by his gesture.

"I'd lived in the neighborhood for years, and so far he has been the only one to stop. The problem is not that we have so little power. The problem is that we don't use the power that we have."

■ ■ ■

Why do we deny that power? Why do we not honor what we can do?

Part of the reason is that "virtue" is often defined as the ultimate commodity, something exclusive, like a Porsche or a perfect figure, that only the rich and famous have access to. "Virtue" is defined as so outside of normal human experience or ability that you'd think, if you were doing it right, you'd know, because camera crews and an awards committee would appear on your lawn.

Thus the defining of virtue is surrendered to a Madison Avenue mentality. I remember when the Dalai Lama came to Bloomington in 1999. The words "virtue" and "celebrity" were confused until they became synonymous. The Dalai Lama's visit was the most glamorous event Bloomington had seen in years. Suddenly even our barbershop scuttlebutt featured more movie stars than an article from *People* magazine. "Did you see Steven Segal on Kirkwood Avenue? Richard Gere gets in tomorrow." Virtue becomes something farther and farther out of the reach of the common person.

I was once a Peace Corps volunteer. I also volunteered for the Sisters of Charity, the order begun by Mother Teresa. When people learn of these things, they sometimes act impressed. I am understood to be a virtuous person.

I did go far away, and I did wear a foreign costume. But I don't know that I was virtuous. I tried to be, but I was an immature, inadequately trained girl in foreign countries with obscenely unjust regimes and little to no avenues for progress. My impact was limited.

To put myself through college, I worked as a nurse's aid. I earned minimum wage. I wore a pink polyester uniform and I dealt with the elderly and the dying, ignored people who went years without seeing a loved one, who died alone. When I speak of this job, I never impress anyone. I am not understood to be a virtuous person. Rather, I am understood to be working class.

I loved this difficult, low-paid work not out of any masochistic sense of personal elevation through suffering. I loved it because I physically and emotionally touched people every day, all day long; I made them comfortable; I made them laugh; I challenged them; they rose to meet the challenges. In return, patients shared with me the most precious commodity in the universe: their humanity.

■ ■ ■

This essay is not a protest against selfishness, which, well done, can be a beautiful thing. There is nothing I envy, and appreciate, so much as a life led with genuinely unconscious, uncomplicated self-absorption. It's a sort of karmic performance art. Isn't that quality why some people so love observing cats? And I do not begrudge my fellow travelers' enthusiasm for glamour; there's nothing I like more. The right dress worn by the right starlet on Oscar night probably does as much to feed the soul as a perfect haiku.

Rather, I'm protesting the fallacy that to be virtuous, one must be on TV, one must be off to a meeting on how to be a better person, or one must have just come from a meeting on how to be a better person, but one can pass up every opportunity to actually *be* a better person.

It's sad how sometimes "virtue celebrities" intimidate us with their virtue résumés. We think, "Gee, I'll never travel to Malaysia and close a sweatshop; I'm not brave enough (or organized or articulate enough) to champion a cause. I have to go to work every day, and I just don't have the time or the gifts to be a virtuous person."

I go to a food bank every two weeks to get my food. I have no car. I can't carry two weeks worth of food the three miles back to my house. Every week, I get a ride home from other food bank patrons. These folks don't pause for a second to sigh, "Oh, problems are so big, I'm so powerless; will it really help anything if I give you this ride?" They don't look around to make sure some-one is watching. They just, invisibly, do the right thing. I get rides in old, old cars. In one car I could see the road beneath whiz past under broken-down flooring; in another, I shared space with a large, lapping dog. I once got a ride from a man who told me he'd just gotten out of jail. Another time, my chauffeur's tattoos ran up and down his naked chest and back. When I was sick, I went from agency to agency, begging people with glamorous titles and impressive virtue résumés for help. Most did nothing.

The *Lamed Vov Tzaddikim* are the thirty-six hidden saints of Jewish folklore. Unlettered and insignificant, they work at humble trades and pass unnoticed. Because of these anonymous saints, the world continues to exist. Without their insignificant, unnoticed virtue—Poof!—God loses divine patience, and the world goes up in smoke.

Sometimes we convince ourselves that the "unnoticed" gestures of "insignificant" people mean nothing. It's not enough to recycle our soda cans; we must Stop Global Warming Now. Since we can't Stop Global Warming Now, we may as well not recycle our soda cans. It's not enough to be our best selves; we have to be Gandhi. And yet when we study the biographies of our heroes, we learn that they spent years in preparation doing tiny, decent things before one historical moment propelled them to center stage.

Moments, as if animate, use the prepared to tilt empires. Ironically, saints we worship today, heroes we admire, were often ridiculed, tortured, or, most punishingly, ignored in their own lifetimes. St. John of the Cross gave the world the spiritual classic, *The Dark Night of the Soul.* It was inspired by his own experience of being imprisoned by the members of his own religious order. Before Solidarity, Lech Walesa, the Nobel Peace Prize winner who helped bring down communism, was a nonentity; a blue-collar worker in an oft-ridiculed Eastern European back-water. He was always active; one moment changed this small man's otherwise small-time, invisible activism into the kind of wedge that can topple a giant. Now, that moment past, Walesa has returned to relative obscurity.

■ ■ ■

Besides the pressure of virtue as an unattainable status reserved for the elect, there may be another reason why people don't live their own ideals. It may be that many who do not live what they believe have been stunted. They've been told many times: "What you feel does not matter; what you believe is ridiculous; what you envision is worthless; just sit back and obey the priest, the preacher, the teacher, the cop, the mob, the man in charge, or your own fear." When the still, small voice whispers to them that they ought to visit an elderly neighbor, or write a letter to the editor, or pull a few strings and let the indigent patient in to see the doctor, even though the red tape says they cannot, they tell the still, small voice "Stifle yourself!"

Such self-numbed people may see themselves as perpetual victims. "I have nothing!" they insist. "I have no power! I can't do anything! I have nothing to give! Everybody picks on me!" These are the folks who begrudge so much as a smile to their neighbors. Even as they live in houses, drive cars, enjoy health, they see themselves as naked, starving, homeless, penniless wretches waiting to be rescued by whomever is in charge. Their sense of victimization does not allow them to see that *they* are in charge—of their own choices.

While working or traveling in Africa, Asia, and Eastern Europe, I occasionally met people who really did have next to nothing, but who stunned me with their insistence on the abundance of their own humanity. One afternoon, as I trekked to my teaching post in the Himalayas, a monsoon storm turned day into night and a landslide wiped out my trail. I got terribly lost; coming to a strange village, exhausted, I sat on the porch of a peasant home. Inside, the family was eating roasted cow-corn kernels for dinner. Roasted cow-corn kernels were to be their entire dinner; there was nothing else on their menu.

A man inside saw that a human form was sitting on his porch. He couldn't have seen that I was American, or anything else, for that matter. It was dark night by then, in a village without electricity. In any case, I was wearing a sari. He whispered to his wife, "Someone is sitting on our porch. We have to cook rice." Rice is the highest status food in that economy. And, by "rice," they meant, for them, an elaborate meal consisting of rice, lentils, and vegetables.

This feeling of being seen, this conviction that every act one performs matters to a supremely consequential audience, can come from a belief in God. Psalm 139 articulates how thoroughly and consequentially *witnessed* the theist feels.

> O Lord, You have searched me
> and You know me.
> You know when I sit and when I rise;
> You perceive my thoughts from afar.
> . . . Before a word is on my tongue
> You know it completely, O Lord.
> Where can I go from Your Spirit?
> Where can I flee from Your presence?
> If I go up to the heavens, You are there;
> if I make my bed in the depths, You are there.

The very marrow of the believer's bones is impregnated with the conviction that everything he does is avidly witnessed by God, and that everything he does matters to God. Whether or not one's fellow incarnate beings see is secondary.

Non-theists, including atheists, can also have this feeling that one is witnessed, that everything one does matters. Not just a personalized God sees and tallies human action. Disembodied forces that can never be tampered with also weigh our deeds. For some, karma plays witness. You may be able to fool your fellow humans, but, ultimately, you can't cheat karma.

In many cultures, there is a disembodied force that demands that every action be ethical: honor. *"Bog, Honor, Ojczyzna,"* or "God, Honor, Country," is the Polish national motto. My stays in Poland introduced me to otherwise empty-handed activists who faced off against Nazis, Communists, and now, capitalism, with relentless personal power. "Burnout" and "apathy" were not in their vocabulary. Even when serving time in prisons that appeared on no map, they felt visible. Honor recorded their every deed, and ensured that it mattered.

■ ■ ■

I suspect that we all have our three-in-the-morning moments, when all of life seems one no-exit film noir, where any effort is pointless, where any hope seems to be born only to be dashed, like a fallen nestling on a summer sidewalk. When I have those moments, if I do nothing else, I remind myself: the ride in the snow; the volunteers at the food bank; the Nepali peasants who fed me. Activists like the Pole Wladyslaw Bartoszewski who, decades before he would earn any fame, got out of Auschwitz only to go on to even more resistance against the Nazis, and then the Soviets. Invisible, silent people who, day by day, choice by choice, unseen by me, unknown to me, force me to witness myself, invite me to keep making my own best choices, and keep me living my ideals. ●

Explorations of the Text

1. Outline Goska's essay. What is the main claim? Reasons? What patterns of argument and forms of proof does she incorporate to prove her points? Does she acknowledge opposing points of view? Describe her ethos.

2. According to Goska, what causes people to "deny . . . [their] power"? How can people regain their sense of "power"?

3. What does Goska mean by "honor"? What does she mean by feeling "visible"?

4. Which characters in stories in this chapter would agree with Goska's vision of making "choices"? Why?

The Reading/Writing Connection

1. Choose one of the controversial statements in this essay and freewrite in response to the statement.

2. "Think" Topic: Do you agree with Goska's vision of making "small choices" to help others? Is it possible to do so in today's world?

Ideas for Writing

1. Watch the movie *Babel* or *Pay It Forward*. Compare and contrast the vision of care and concern for others presented in one of the movies with Goska's views in her essay.

Andrew Sullivan *(1963–)*

What's So Bad About Hate? *2002*

I

I wonder what was going on in John William King's head two years ago when he tied James Byrd, Jr.'s feet to the back of a pickup truck and dragged him three miles down a road in rural Texas. King and two friends had picked up Byrd, who was black, when he was walking home, half drunk, from a party. As part of a bonding ritual in their fledgling white supremacist group, the three men took Byrd to a remote part of town, beat him, and chained his legs together before attaching them to the truck. Pathologists at King's trial testified that Byrd was probably alive and conscious until his body finally hit a culvert and split in two. When King was offered a chance to say something to Byrd's family at the trial, he smirked and uttered an obscenity.

We know all these details now, many months later. We know quite a large amount about what happened before and after. But I am still drawn, again and again, to the flash of ignition, the moment when fear and loathing became hate, the instant of transformation when King became hunter and Byrd became prey.

What was that? And what was it when Buford Furrow, Jr., longtime member of the Aryan Nations, calmly walked up to a Filipino-American mailman he happened to spot, asked him to mail a letter, and then shot him at point-blank range? Or when Russell Henderson beat Matthew Shepard, a young gay man, to a pulp, removed his shoes, and then, with the help of a friend, tied him to a post, like a dead coyote, to warn off others?

For all our documentation of these crimes and others, our political and moral disgust at them, our morbid fascination with them, our sensitivity to their social meaning, we seem at times to have no better idea now than we ever had of what exactly they were about. About what that moment means when, for some reason or other, one human being asserts absolute, immutable superiority over another. About not the violence, but what the violence expresses. About what—exactly—hate is. And what our own part in it may be.

I find myself wondering what hate actually is in part because we have created an 5 entirely new offense in American criminal law—a "hate crime"—to combat it. And barely a day goes by without someone somewhere declaring war against it. Last month President Clinton called for an expansion of hate-crime laws as "what America needs in our battle against hate." A couple of weeks later, Senator John McCain used a campaign speech to denounce the "hate" he said poisoned the land. New York's mayor, Rudolph Giuliani, recently tried to stop the Million Youth March in Harlem on the grounds that the event was organized by people "involved in hate marches and hate rhetoric."

The media concur in their emphasis. In 1985, there were eleven mentions of "hate crimes" in the national media database Nexis. By 1990, there were more than a thousand. In the first six months of 1999, there were seven thousand. "Sexy fun is one thing," wrote a *New York Times* reporter about sexual assaults in Woodstock '99's mosh pit. "But this was an orgy of lewdness tinged with hate." And when Benjamin Smith marked the Fourth of July this year by targeting blacks, Asians, and Jews for murder in Indiana and Illinois, the story wasn't merely about a twisted young man who had emerged on the scene. As the *Times* put it, "Hate arrived in the neighborhoods of Indiana University, in Bloomington, in the earlymorning darkness."

But what exactly was this thing that arrived in the early-morning darkness? For all our zeal to attack hate, we still have a remarkably vague idea of what it actually is. A single word, after all, tells us less, not more. For all its emotional punch, "hate" is far less nuanced an idea than prejudice, or bigotry, or bias, or anger, or even mere aversion to others. Is it to stand in for all these varieties of human experience—and everything in between? If so, then the war against it will be so vast as to be quixotic. Or is "hate" to stand for a very specific idea or belief, or set of beliefs, with a very specific object or group of objects? Then waging war against it is almost certainly unconstitutional. Perhaps these kinds of questions are of no concern to those waging war on hate. Perhaps it is enough for them that they share a sentiment that there is too much hate and never enough vigilance in combating it. But sentiment is a poor basis for law and a dangerous tool in politics. It is better to leave some unwinnable wars unfought.

II

Hate is everywhere. Human beings generalize all the time, ahead of time, about everyone and everything. A large part of it may even be hard-wired. At some point in our evolution, being able to know beforehand who was friend or foe was not merely a matter of philosophical reflection. It was a matter of survival. And even today it seems impossible to feel a loyalty without also feeling a disloyalty, a sense of belonging without an equal sense of unbelonging. We're social beings. We associate. Therefore we disassociate. And although it would be comforting to think that the one could happen without the other, we know in reality that it doesn't. How many patriots are there who have never felt a twinge of xenophobia?

Of course, by hate we mean something graver and darker than this kind of lazy prejudice. But the closer you look at this distinction, the fuzzier it gets. Much of the time, we harbor little or no malice toward people of other backgrounds or places or ethnicities or ways of life. But then a car cuts you off at an intersection and you find yourself noticing immediately that the driver is a woman, or black, or old, or fat, or white, or male. Or you are walking down a city street at night and hear footsteps quickening behind you. You look around and see that it is a white woman and not a black man, and you are instantly relieved. These impulses are so spontaneous they are almost involuntary. But where did they come from? The mindless need to be mad at someone—anyone—or the unconscious eruption of a darker prejudice festering within?

In 1993, in San Jose, California, two neighbors, one heterosexual, one homosexual, were engaged in a protracted squabble over grass clippings. (The full case is recounted in *Hate Crimes,* by James B. Jacobs and Kimberly Potter.) The gay man   10 regularly mowed his lawn without a grass catcher, which prompted his neighbor to complain on many occasions that grass clippings spilled over onto his driveway. Tensions grew until one day the gay man mowed his front yard, spilling clippings onto his neighbor's driveway, prompting the straight man to yell an obscene and common antigay insult. The wrangling escalated. At one point the gay man agreed to collect the clippings from his neighbor's driveway but then later found them dumped on his own porch. A fracas ensued, with the gay man spraying the straight man's son with a garden hose and the son hitting and kicking the gay man several times, yelling antigay slurs. The police were called, and the son was eventually convicted of a hate-motivated assault, a felony. But what was the nature of the hate, antigay bias or suburban property-owner madness?

Or take the Labor Day parade last year in Broad Channel, a small island in Jamaica Bay, Queens. Almost everyone there is white, and in recent years a group of local volunteer firefighters has taken to decorating a pickup truck for the parade in order to win the prize for "funniest float." Their themes have tended toward the outrageously provocative. Beginning in 1995, they won prizes for floats depicting "Hasidic Park," "Gooks of Hazzard," and "Happy Gays." Last year they called their float "Black to the Future, Broad Channel 2098." They imagined their community a century hence as a largely black enclave, with every stereotype imaginable: watermelons, basketballs, and so on. At one point during the parade, one of them mimicked the dragging death of James Byrd. It was caught on videotape, and before long the entire community was depicted as a caldron of hate.

It's an interesting case, because the float was indisputably in bad taste and the improvisation on the Byrd killing was grotesque. But was it hate? The men on the float were local heroes for their volunteer work; they had no record of bigoted activity and were not members of any racist organizations. In previous years they had made fun of many other groups, and they saw themselves more as provocateurs than bigots. When they were described as racists, it came as a shock to them. They apologized for poor taste but refused to confess to bigotry. "The people involved aren't horrible people," protested a local woman. "Was it a racist act? I don't know. Are they racists? I don't think so."

If hate is a self-conscious activity, she has a point. The men were primarily motivated by the desire to shock and to reflect what they thought was their community's culture. Their display was not aimed at any particular black people or at any blacks who lived in Broad Channel—almost none do. But if hate is primarily an unconscious activity, then the matter is obviously murkier. And by taking the horrific lynching of a black man as a spontaneous object of humor, the men were clearly advocating indifference to it. Was this an aberrant excess? Or the real truth about the men's feelings toward African-Americans? Hate or tastelessness? And how on earth is anyone, even perhaps the firefighters themselves, going to know for sure?

Or recall H. L. Mencken. He shared in the anti-Semitism of his time with more alacrity than most and was an indefatigable racist. "It is impossible," he wrote in his diary, "to talk anything resembling discretion or judgment into a colored woman. They are all essentially childlike, and even hard experience does not teach them anything." He wrote at another time of the "psychological stigmata" of the "Afro-American race." But it is also true that during much of his life, day to day, Mencken conducted himself with no regard to race and supported a politics that was clearly integrationist. As the editor of his diary has pointed out, Mencken published many black authors in his magazine, *The Mercury,* and lobbied on their behalf with his publisher, Alfred A. Knopf. The last thing Mencken ever wrote was a diatribe against racial segregation in Baltimore's public parks. He was good friends with leading black writers and journalists, including James Weldon Johnson, Walter White, and George S. Schuyler, and played an underappreciated role in promoting the Harlem Renaissance.

What would our modern view of hate do with Mencken? Probably ignore him, or   15 change the subject. But with regard to hate, I know lots of people like Mencken. He reminds me of conservative friends who oppose almost every measure for homosexual equality yet genuinely delight in the company of their gay friends. It would be easier for me to think of them as haters, and on paper, perhaps, there is a good case that they are. But in real life, I know they are not. Some of them clearly harbor no real malice toward me or other homosexuals whatsoever.

They are as hard to figure out as those liberal friends who support every gay rights measure they have ever heard of but do anything to avoid going into a gay bar with me. I have to ask myself in the same frustrating kind of way, are they liberal bigots or bigoted liberals? Or are they neither bigots nor liberals, but merely people?

III

Hate used to be easier to understand. When Sartre described anti-Semitism in his 1946 essay "Anti-Semite and Jew," he meant a very specific array of firmly held prejudices, with a history, an ideology, and even a pseudoscience to back them up. He meant a systematic attempt to demonize and eradicate an entire race. If you go to the Web site of the World Church of the Creator, the organization that inspired young Benjamin Smith to murder in Illinois earlier this year, you will find a similarly bizarre, pseudo-rational ideology. The kind of literature read by Buford Furrow before he rained terror on a Jewish kindergarten last month and then killed a mailman because of his color is full of the same paranoid loopiness. And when we talk about hate, we often mean this kind of phenomenon.

But this brand of hatred is mercifully rare in the United States. These professional maniacs are to hate what serial killers are to murder. They should certainly not be ignored, but they represent what Harold Meyerson, writing in *Salon,* called "niche haters": cold-blooded, somewhat deranged, often poorly socialized psychopaths. In a free society with relatively easy access to guns, they will always pose a menace.

But their menace is a limited one, and their hatred is hardly typical of anything very widespread. Take Buford Furrow. He famously issued a "wake-up call" to "kill Jews" in Los Angeles before he peppered a Jewish community center with gunfire. He did this in a state with two Jewish female senators, in a city with a large, prosperous Jewish population, in a country where out of several million Jewish Americans, a total of sixty-six were reported by the FBI as the targets of hate-crime assaults in 1997. However despicable Furrow's actions were, it would require a very large stretch to describe them as representative of anything but the deranged fringe of an American subculture.

Most hate is more common and more complicated, with as many varieties as there   20 are varieties of love. Just as there are possessive love and needy love, family love and friendship, romantic love and unrequited love, passion and respect, affection and obsession, so hatred has its shadings. There is hate that fears, and hate that merely feels contempt; there is hate that expresses power, and hate that comes from powerlessness;

there is revenge, and there is hate that comes from envy. There is hate that was love, and hate that is a curious expression of love. There is hate of the other, and hate of something that reminds us too much of ourselves. There is the oppressor's hate and the victim's hate. There is hate that burns slowly and hate that fades. And there is hate that explodes and hate that never catches fire.

The modern words that we have created to describe the varieties of hate—"sexism," "racism," "anti-Semitism," "homophobia"—tell us very little about any of this. They tell us merely the identities of the victims; they don't reveal the identities of the perpetrators, or what they think, or how they feel. They don't even tell us how the victims feel. And this simplicity is no accident. Coming from the theories of Marxist and post-Marxist academics, these isms are far better at alleging structures of power than at delineating the workings of the individual heart or mind. In fact, these isms can exist without mentioning individuals at all.

We speak of institutional racism, for example, as if an institution can feel anything. We talk of "hate" as an impersonal noun, with no hater specified. But when these abstractions are actually incarnated, when someone feels something as a result of them, when a hater actually interacts with a victim, the picture changes. We find that hates are often very different phenomena one from another, that they have very different psychological dynamics, that they might even be better understood by not seeing them as varieties of the same thing at all.

There is, for example, the now unfashionable distinction between reasonable hate and unreasonable hate. In recent years we have become accustomed to talking about hates as if they were all equally indefensible, as if it could never be the case that some hates might be legitimate, even necessary. But when some 800,000 Tutsis are murdered under the auspices of a Hutu regime in Rwanda, and when a few thousand Hutus are killed in revenge, the hates are not commensurate. Genocide is not an event like a hurricane, in which damage is random and universal; it is a planned and often merciless attack of one group upon another. The hate of the perpetrators is a monstrosity. The hate of the victims, and their survivors, is justified. What else, one wonders, were surviving Jews supposed to feel toward Germans after the Holocaust? Or, to a different degree, South African blacks after apartheid? If the victims overcome this hate, it is a supreme moral achievement. But if they don't, the victims are not as culpable as the perpetrators. So the hatred of Serbs for Kosovars today can never be equated with the hatred of Kosovars for Serbs.

Hate, like much of human feeling, is not rational, but it usually has its reasons. And it cannot be understood, let alone condemned, without knowing them. Similarly, the hate that comes from knowledge is always different from the hate that comes from ignorance. It is one of the most foolish clichés of our time that prejudice is always rooted in ignorance and can usually be overcome by familiarity with the objects of our loathing. The racism of many Southern whites under segregation was not appeased by familiarity with Southern blacks; the virulent loathing of Tutsis by many Hutus was not undermined by living next door to them for centuries. Theirs was a hatred that sprang, for whatever reasons, from experience. It cannot easily be compared with, for example, the resilience of anti-Semitism in Japan, or hostility to immigration in areas where immigrants are unknown, or fear of homosexuals by people who have never knowingly met one.

The same familiarity is an integral part of what has become known as "sexism." [25] Sexism isn't, properly speaking, a prejudice at all. Few men live without knowledge or constant awareness of women. Every single sexist man was born of a woman and is likely to be sexually attracted to women. His hostility is going to be very different from that of, say, a reclusive member of the Aryan Nations toward Jews he has never met.

In her book *The Anatomy of Prejudices,* the psychotherapist Elisabeth Young-Bruehl proposes a typology of three distinct kinds of hate: obsessive, hysterical, and narcissistic. It's not an exhaustive analysis, but it's a beginning in any serious attempt to understand hate rather than merely declaring war on it. The obsessives, for Young-Bruehl, are those, like the Nazis or Hutus, who fantasize a threat from a minority and obsessively try to rid themselves of it. For them, the very existence of the hated group is threatening. They often describe their loathing in almost physical terms: they experience what Patrick Buchanan, in reference to homosexuals, once described as a "visceral recoil" from the objects of their detestation. They often describe those they hate as diseased or sick, in need of a cure. Or they talk of "cleansing" them, as the Hutus talked of the Tutsis, or call them "cockroaches," as Yitzhak Shamir called the Palestinians. If you read material from the Family Research Council, it is clear that the group regards homosexuals as similar contaminants. A recent posting on its Web site about syphilis among gay men was headlined "Unclean."

Hysterical haters have a more complicated relationship with the objects of their aversion. In Young-Bruehl's words, hysterical prejudice is a prejudice that "a person uses unconsciously to appoint a group to act out in the world forbidden sexual and sexually aggressive desires that the person has repressed." Certain kinds of racists fit this pattern. White loathing of blacks is for some people at least partly about sexual and physical envy. A certain kind of white racist sees in black America all those impulses he wishes most to express himself but cannot. He idealizes in "blackness" a sexual freedom, a physical power, a Dionysian release that he detests but also longs for. His fantasy may not have any basis in reality, but it is powerful nonetheless. It is a form of love-hate, and it is impossible to understand the nuances of racism in, say, the American South, or in British imperial India, without it.

Unlike the obsessives, the hysterical haters do not want to eradicate the objects of their loathing; rather, they want to keep them in some kind of permanent and safe subjugation in order to indulge the attraction of their repulsion. A recent study, for example, found that the men most likely to be opposed to equal rights for homosexuals were those most likely to be aroused by homoerotic imagery. This makes little rational sense, but it has a certain psychological plausibility. If homosexuals were granted equality, then the hysterical gay-hater might panic that his repressed passions would run out of control, overwhelming him and the world he inhabits.

A narcissistic hate, according to Young-Bruehl's definition, is sexism. In its most common form, it is rooted in many men's inability even to imagine what it is to be a woman, a failing rarely challenged by men's control of our most powerful public social institutions. Women are not so much hated by most men as simply ignored in nonsexual contexts, or never conceived of as true equals. The implicit condescension is mixed, in many cases, with repressed and sublimated erotic desire. So the unawareness of women is sometimes commingled with a deep longing or contempt for them.

Each hate, of course, is more complicated than this, and in any one person hate can assume a uniquely configured combination of these types. So there are hysterical sexists who hate women because they need them so much, and narcissistic sexists who hardly notice that women exist, and sexists who oscillate between one of these positions and another. And there are gay-bashers who are threatened by masculine gay men and gay-haters who feel repulsed by effeminate ones. The soldier who beat his fellow sol-dier Barry Winchell to death with a baseball bat in July had earlier lost a fight to him. It was the image of a macho gay man—and the shame of being bested by him—that the vengeful soldier had to obliterate, even if he needed a gang of accomplices and a weapon to do so. But the murderers of Matthew Shepard seem to have had a differ-ent impulse: a visceral disgust at the thought of any sexual contact with an effeminate homosexual. Their anger was mixed with mockery, as the cruel spectacle at the side of the road suggested.

In the same way, the pathological anti-Semitism of Nazi Germany was obsessive, inasmuch as it tried to cleanse the world of Jews, but also, as Daniel Jonah Goldhagen shows in his book, *Hitler's Willing Executioners,* hysterical. The Germans were mysteri-ously compelled as well as repelled by Jews, devising elaborate ways, like death camps and death marches, to keep them alive even as they killed them. And the early Nazi phobia of interracial sex suggests as well a lingering erotic quality to the relationship, partaking of exactly the kind of sexual panic that persists among some homosexual-haters and antimiscegenation racists. So the concept of "homophobia," like that of "sexism" and "racism," is often a crude one. All three are essentially cookie-cutter for-mulas that try to understand human impulses merely through' the one-dimensional identity of the victims, rather than through the thoughts and feelings of the haters and hated.

This is deliberate. The theorists behind these isms want to ascribe all blame to one group in society—the "oppressors"—and render specific others—the "victims"—completely blameless. And they want to do this in order in part to side unequivocally with the underdog. But it doesn't take a genius to see how this approach too can gen-erate its own form of bias. It can justify blanket condemnations of whole groups of people—white straight males, for example—purely because of the color of their skin or the nature of their sexual orientation. And it can condescendingly ascribe innocence to whole groups of others. It does exactly what hate does: it hammers the uniqueness of each individual into the anvil of group identity. And it postures morally over the result.

In reality, human beings and human acts are far more complex, which is why these isms and the laws they have fomented are continually coming under strain and chal-lenge. Once again, hate wriggles free of its definers. It knows no monolithic groups of haters and hated. Like a river, it has many eddies, backwaters, and rapids. So there are anti-Semites who actually admire what they think of as Jewish power, and there are gay-haters who look up to homosexuals and some who want to sleep with them. And there are black racists, racist Jews, sexist women, and anti-Semitic homosexuals. Of course there are.

IV

Once you start thinking of these phenomena less as the isms of sexism, racism, and homophobia, once you think of them as independent psychological responses, it's also possible to see how they can work in a bewildering variety of ways in a bewildering number of people. To take one obvious and sad oddity: people who are demeaned and objectified in society may develop an aversion to their tormentors that is more hateful in its expression than the prejudice they have been subjected to. The FBI statistics on hate crimes throw up an interesting point. In America in the 1990s, blacks were up to three times as likely as whites to commit a hate crime, to express their hate by physically attacking their targets or their property. Just as sexual abusers have often been victims of sexual abuse and wife-beaters often grew up in violent households, so hate criminals may often be members of hated groups.

Even the Columbine murderers were in some sense victims of hate before they   35 were purveyors of it. Their classmates later admitted that Dylan Klebold and Eric Harris were regularly called "faggots" in the corridors and classrooms of Columbine High and that nothing was done to prevent or stop the harassment. This climate of hostility doesn't excuse the actions of Klebold and Harris, but it does provide a more plausible context. If they had been black, had routinely been called "nigger" in the school, and had then exploded into a shooting spree against white students, the response to the matter might well have been different. But the hate would have been the same. In other words, hate victims are often hate victimizers as well. This doesn't mean that all hates are equivalent, or that some are not more justified than others. It means merely that hate goes both ways; and if you try to regulate it among some, you will find yourself forced to regulate it among others.

It is no secret, for example, that some of the most vicious anti-Semites in America are black, and that some of the most virulent anti-Catholic bigots in America are gay. At what point, we are increasingly forced to ask, do these phenomena become as indefensible as white racism or religious toleration of antigay bigotry? That question becomes all the more difficult when we notice that it is often minorities who commit some of the most hate-filled offenses against what they see as their oppressors. It was the mainly gay AIDS activist group Act Up that perpetrated the hateful act of desecrating communion hosts at a mass at St. Patrick's Cathedral in New York. And here is the playwright Tony Kushner, who is gay, responding to the Matthew Shepard beating in *The Nation* magazine: "Pope John Paul II endorses murder. He, too, knows the price of discrimination, having declared anti-Semitism a sin. . . . He knows that discrimination kills. But when the Pope heard the news about Matthew Shepard, he, too, worried about spin. And so, on the subject of gay-bashing, the Pope and his cardinals and his bishops and priests maintain their cynical political silence. . . . To remain silent is to endorse murder." Kushner went on to describe the pope as a "homicidal liar."

Maybe the passion behind these words is justified. But it seems clear enough to me that Kushner is expressing, hate toward the institution of the Catholic Church and all those who perpetuate its doctrines. How else to interpret the way in which he accuses the pope of cynicism, lying, and murder? And how else either to understand the brutal parody of religious vocations expressed by the Sisters of Perpetual Indulgence, a group of gay men who dress in drag as nuns and engage in sexually explicit performances in public? Or T-shirts with the words "Recovering Catholic" on them, hot items among some gay and lesbian activists? The implication that someone's religious faith is a mental illness is clearly an expression of contempt. If that isn't covered under the definition of hate speech, what is?

Or take the following sentences: "The act male homosexuals commit is ugly and repugnant and afterwards they are disgusted with themselves. They drink and take drugs to palliate this, but they are disgusted with the act and they are always changing partners and cannot be really happy." The thoughts of Pat Robertson or Patrick Buchanan? Actually, that sentence was written by Gertrude Stein, one of the century's most notable lesbians. Or take the following, about how beating up "black boys like that made us feel *good* inside. . . . Every time I drove my foot into his [expletive], I felt better." It was written to describe the brutal assault on an innocent bystander for the sole reason of his race. By the end of the attack, the victim had blood gushing from his mouth as his attackers stomped on his genitals. Are we less appalled when we learn that the actual sentence was how beating up "white boys like that made us feel *good* inside. . . . Every time I drove my foot into his [expletive], I felt better"? It was written by Nathan McCall, an African-American who later in life became a successful journalist at the *Washington Post* and published his memoir of this "hate crime" to much acclaim.

In fact, one of the stranger aspects of hate is that the prejudice expressed by a group in power may often be milder in expression than the prejudice felt by the marginalized. After all, if you already enjoy privilege, you may not feel the anger that turns bias into hate. You may not need to. For this reason, most white racism may be more influential in society than most black racism—but also more calmly expressed.

So may other forms of minority loathing—especially hatred within minorities. 40 I'm sure that black conservatives like Clarence Thomas and Thomas Sowell have experienced their fair share of white racism. But I wonder whether it has ever reached the level of intensity of the hatred directed toward them by other blacks? In several years of being an openly gay writer and editor, I have experienced the gamut of responses to my sexual orientation. But I have only directly experienced articulated, passionate hate from other homosexuals. I have been accused over the years by other homosexuals of being a sellout, a hypocrite, a traitor, a sexist, a racist, a narcissist, a snob. I've been called selfish, callous, hateful, self-hating, and malevolent. At a reading, a group of lesbian activists portrayed my face on a poster within the crosshairs of a gun. Nothing from the religious right has come close to such vehemence.

I am not complaining. No harm has ever come to me or my property, and much of the criticism is rooted in the legitimate expression of political differences. But the visceral tone and style of the gay criticism can only be described as hateful. It is designed to wound personally, and it often does. But its intensity comes in part, one senses, from the pain of being excluded for so long, of anger long restrained bubbling up and directing itself more aggressively toward an alleged traitor than an alleged enemy. It is the hate of the hated. And it can be the most hateful hate of all. For this reason, hate-crime laws may themselves be an oddly biased category—biased against the victims of hate. Racism is everywhere, but the already victimized might be more desperate, more willing to express it violently. And so more prone to come under the suspicious eye of the law.

V

And why is hate for a group worse than hate for a person? In Laramie, Wyoming, the now-famous "epicenter of homophobia," where Matthew Shepard was brutally beaten to death, vicious murders are not unknown. In the previous twelve months, a fifteen-year-old pregnant girl was found east of the town with seventeen stab wounds. Her thirty-eight-year-old boyfriend was apparently angry that she had refused an abortion and left her in the Wyoming foothills to bleed to death. In the summer of 1998, an eight-year-old Laramie girl was abducted, raped, and murdered by a pedophile, who disposed of her young body in a garbage dump. Neither of these killings was deemed a hate crime, and neither would be designated as such under any existing hate-crime law. Perhaps because of this, one crime is an international legend; the other two are virtually unheard of.

But which crime was more filled with hate? Once you ask the question, you realize how difficult it is to answer. Is it more hateful to kill a stranger or a lover? Is it more hateful to kill a child than an, adult? Is it more hateful to kill your own child than another's? Under the law before the invention of hate crimes, these decisions didn't have to be taken. But under the law after hate crimes, a decision is essential. A decade ago, a murder was a murder. Now, in the era when group hate has emerged as our cardinal social sin, it all depends.

The supporters of laws against hate crimes argue that such crimes should be disproportionately punished because they victimize more than the victim. Such crimes, these advocates argue, spread fear, hatred, and panic among whole populations and therefore merit more concern. But of course all crimes victimize more than the victim and spread alarm in the society at large. Just think of the terrifying church shooting in Texas only two weeks ago. In fact, a purely random murder may be even more terrifying than a targeted one, since the entire community and not just a part of it feels threatened. High rates of murder, robbery, assault, and burglary victimize everyone, by spreading fear, suspicion, and distress everywhere. Which crime was more frightening to more people this summer: the mentally ill Buford Furrow's crazed attacks in Los Angeles, killing one, or Mark Barton's murder of his own family and several random day-traders in Atlanta, killing twelve? Almost certainly the latter. But only Furrow was guilty of "hate."

One response to this objection is that certain groups feel fear more intensely than others because of a history of persecution or intimidation. But doesn't this smack of a certain condescension toward minorities? Why, after all, should it be assumed that gay men or black women or Jews, for example, are as a group more easily intimidated than others? Surely in any of these communities there will be a vast range of responses, from panic to concern to complete indifference. The assumption otherwise is the kind of crude generalization the law is supposed to uproot in the first place. And among these groups, there are also likely to be vast differences. To equate a population once subjected to slavery with a population of Mexican immigrants or third-generation Holocaust survivors is to equate the unequatable. In fact, it is to set up a contest of vulnerability in which one group vies with another to establish its particular variety of suffering, a contest that can have no dignified solution.

Rape, for example, is not classified as a hate crime under most existing laws, pitting feminists against ethnic groups in a battle for recognition. If, as a solution to this problem, everyone except the white straight able-bodied male is regarded as a possible victim of a hate crime, then we have simply created a two-tier system of justice in which racial profiling is reversed, and white straight men are presumed guilty before being proved innocent, and members of minorities are free to hate them as gleefully as they like. But if we include the white straight male in the litany of potential victims, then we have effectively abolished the notion of a hate crime altogether, for if every crime is possibly a hate crime, then it is simply another name for crime. All we will have done is widened the search for possible bigotry, ratcheted up the sentences for everyone, and filled the jails up even further.

Hate-crime law advocates counter that extra penalties should be imposed on hate crimes because our society is experiencing an "epidemic" of such crimes. Mercifully, there is no hard evidence to support this notion. The federal government has only been recording the incidence of hate crimes in this decade, and the statistics tell a simple story. In 1992, there were 6,623 hate-crime incidents reported to the FBI by a total of 6,181 agencies, covering 51 percent of the population. In 1996, there were 8,734 incidents reported by 11,355 agencies, covering 84 percent of the population. That number dropped to 8,049 in 1997. These numbers are of course hazardous. They probably underreport the incidence of such crimes, but they are the only reliable figures we have. Yet even if they are faulty as an absolute number, they do not show an epidemic of hate crimes in the 1990s.

Is there evidence that the crimes themselves are becoming more vicious? None. More than 60 percent of recorded hate crimes in America involve no violent physical assault against another human being at all, and again, according to the FBI, that proportion has not budged much in the 1990s. These impersonal attacks are crimes against property or crimes of intimidation. Murder, which dominates media coverage of hate crimes, is a tiny proportion of the total. Of the 8,049 hate crimes reported to the FBI in 1997, a total of 8 were murders. Eight. The number of hate crimes that were aggravated assaults (generally involving a weapon) in 1997 is less than 15 percent of the total. That's 1,237 assaults too many, of course, but to put it in perspective, compare it with a reported 1,022,492 "equal opportunity" aggravated assaults in America in the same year. The number of hate crimes that were physical assaults is half the total. That's 4,000 assaults too many, of course, but to put it in perspective, it compares with around 3.8 million "equal opportunity" assaults in America annually.

The truth is, the distinction between a crime filled with personal hate and a crime filled with group hate is an essentially arbitrary one. It tells us nothing interesting about the psychological contours of the specific actor or his specific victim. It is a function primarily of politics, of special-interest groups carving out particular protections for themselves, rather than a serious response to a serious criminal concern. In such an endeavor, hate-crime law advocates cram an entire world of human motivations into an immutable, tiny box called hate and hope to have solved a problem. But nothing has been solved, and some harm may even have been done.

In an attempt to repudiate a past that treated people differently because of the color of their skin or their sex or religion or sexual orientation, we may merely create a future that permanently treats people differently because of the color of their skin or their sex, religion, or sexual orientation. This notion of a hate crime, and the concept of hate that lies behind it, takes a psychological mystery and turns it into a facile political artifact. Rather than compounding this error and extending it even further, we should seriously consider repealing the concept altogether.   50

To put it another way: violence can and should be stopped by the government. In a free society, hate can't and shouldn't be. The boundaries between hate and prejudice and between prejudice and opinion and between opinion and truth are so complicated and blurred that any attempt to construct legal and political fire walls is a doomed and illiberal venture. We know by now that hate will never disappear from human consciousness; in fact, it is probably, at some level, definitive of it. We know after decades of education measures that hate is not caused merely by ignorance and, after decades of legislation, that it isn't cured entirely by law.

To be sure, we have made much progress. Anyone who argues that America is as inhospitable to minorities and to women today as it has been in the past has not read much history. And we should of course be vigilant that our most powerful institutions, most notably the government, do not actively or formally propagate hatred, and insure that the violent expression of hate is curtailed by the same rules that punish all violent expression.

But after that, in an increasingly diverse culture, it is crazy to expect that hate, in all its variety, can be eradicated. A free country will always mean a hateful country. This may not be fair, or perfect, or admirable, but it is reality, and while we need not endorse it, we should not delude ourselves into thinking we can prevent it. That is surely the distinction between toleration and tolerance. Tolerance is the eradication of hate; toleration is coexistence despite it. We might do better as a culture and as a polity if we concentrated more on achieving the latter than the former. We would certainly be less frustrated.

And by aiming lower, we might actually reach higher. In some ways, some expression of prejudice serves a useful social purpose. It lets off steam; it allows natural tensions to express themselves incrementally; it can siphon off conflict through words rather than actions. Anyone who has lived in the ethnic shouting match that is New York City knows exactly what I mean. If New Yorkers disliked each other less, they wouldn't be able to get on so well. We may not all be able to pull off a Mencken—bigoted in words, egalitarian in action—but we might achieve a lesser form of virtue: a human acceptance of our need for differentiation without a total capitulation to it.

Do we not owe something more to the victims of hate? Perhaps we do. But it is also 55 true that there is nothing that government can do for the hated that the hated cannot better do for themselves. After all, most bigots are not foiled when they are punished specifically for their beliefs. In fact, many of the worst haters crave such attention and find vindication in such rebukes. Indeed, our media's obsession with "hate," our elevation of it above other social misdemeanors and crimes, may even play into the hands of the pathetic and the evil, may breathe air into the smoldering embers of their paranoid loathing. Sure, we can help create a climate in which such hate is disapproved of—and we should. But there is a danger that if we go too far, if we punish it too much, if we try to abolish it altogether, we may merely increase its mystique, and entrench the very categories of human difference that we are trying to erase.

For hate is only foiled not when the haters are punished but when the hated are immune to the bigot's power. A hater cannot psychologically wound if a victim cannot psychologically be wounded. And that immunity to hurt can never be given; it can merely be achieved. The racial epithet only strikes at someone's core if he lets it, if he allows the bigot's definition of him to be the final description of his life and his person—if somewhere in his heart of hearts, he believes the hateful slur to be true. The only final answer to this form of racism, then, is not majority persecution of it but minority indifference to it. The only permanent rebuke to homophobia is not the enforcement of tolerance but gay equanimity in the face of prejudice. The only effective answer to sexism is not a morass of legal proscriptions but the simple fact of female success. In this, as in so many other things, there is no solution to the problem. There is only a transcendence of it. For all our rhetoric, hate will never be destroyed. Hate, as our predecessors knew better, can merely be overcome. ●

Explorations of the text

1. What motivates Sullivan to compose this exploratory essay and argument? What does he "wonder" about? Why is he interested in what constitutes hate? (See part I, pars. 4 and 5.)

2. Sullivan presents a complex, multi-layered argument. Beginning in part II, gloss, annotate, and summarize each section of this essay. Isolate his major claims, reasons, and proof (use

of evidence). How does his argument progress? What does he conclude? Are his conclusions satisfying (See the last five paragraphs)?

3. Considering your own experiences and observations, do you find evidence of Young-Bruehl's kinds of hate?

4. Do you agree with Sullivan that "hate wriggles free of its definers"?

5. Why does Sullivan spend half of the essay attempting to figure out the origins and nature of hate before he tackles the issue of curbing hate crimes through legal means? Does he think that crimes can be eradicated through legal means?

6. Would Bernard and Marable agree with Sullivan's contention that "in a free society, hate can't and shouldn't be" "stopped"?

The Reading/Writing Connection

1. "Think" Topic: In a paragraph agree or disagree with one of Sullivan's controversial statements. For example: Hate "may even be hard-wired" into our biological makeup, that it may be part of a "survival instinct." OR "A free country will always mean a hateful country." OR "A hater cannot psychologically wound if a victim cannot psychologically be wounded."

Ideas for Writing

1. **Write an Argument:** Write a letter to the editor of the *New York Times Magazine* expressing your opinion about the work.

2. Create a talk show that focuses on the topic of hate or the excesses of shock radio. Choose several authors of nonfiction works or speakers from several poems to be the panelists. How would they respond to Sullivan's ideas? Create a dialogue among them. Possibilities include Laura Bluemenfeld, Elie Wiesel, Emily Bernard, Manning Marable, Maya Angelou's speaker in "Still I Rise," Countee Cullen's in "Incident," Joy Harjo's in "For Anna Mae Aquash" or Soyinka's in "Telephone Conversation."

The Prism of Race and Class/Nonfiction

Manning Marable *(1950–   )*

The Prism of Race   *1995*

The Prism of Race

Black and white. As long as I can remember, the fundamentally defining feature of my life, and the lives of my family, was the stark reality of race. Angular and unforgiving, race was so much more than the background for what occurred or the context for our relationships. It was the social gravity which set into motion our expectations and emotions, our language and dreams. Race seemed far more powerful than distinctions between people based on language, nationality, religion or income. Race seemed granite-like, fixed and permanent, as the center of the social universe. The reality of racial discrimination constantly fed the pessimism and doubts that we as black people felt about the apparent natural order of the world, the inherent unfairness of it all, as well as limiting our hopes for a better life somewhere in the distant future.

I am a child of Middle America. I was born in Dayton, Ohio, on 13 May 1950, at the height of McCarthyism[1] and on the eve of the Korean conflict.[2] One of the few rituals I remember about the anti-Communist hysteria sweeping the nation in the fifties were the obligatory exercises we performed in elementary school, "ducking and covering" ourselves beneath small wooden desks in our classroom to shield ourselves from the fallout and blast of a nuclear explosion. Most of what I now recall of growing up in south-central Ohio had little to do with nuclear war or communism, only the omnipresent reality of race.

In the 1950s, Dayton was a predominantly blue-collar, working-class town, situated on the banks of the Great Miami River. Neighborhoods were divided to some extent by class. Oakwood was the well-to-do, WASP-ish community, filled with the corporate executives and professionals who ran the city's enterprises. Dayton View on the northwest side was becoming increasingly Jewish. Kettering and Centerville were unpretentiously middle class, conservative and Republican. But beneath the divisions of income, religion and political affiliation seemed to be the broad polarization rooted in race. There appeared to be two parallel racial universes which cohabited the same city, each with its own set of religious institutions, cultural activities, social centers, clubs, political organizations and schools. African-Americans generally resided west of the Great Miami River. The central core of the ghetto was located along the corridors of West Third and West Fifth Street. With the great migration of southern blacks to Dayton immediately following World War II, the African-American population became much more dense, and began to spread west, out to the city's furthest boundaries.

---

[1]**McCarthyism:** The practice of making accusations of disloyalty, especially of pro-Communist sentiments, that often were unsupported or based on doubtful evidence.   [2]**Korean conflict:** The Korean War (1950–53); between North Korea (supported by Communist China) and South Korea (aided by the United States and other members of the United Nations.)

The black community existed largely in its own world, within the logic of institutions it had created to sustain itself. We were taught to be proud of our history and literature. Every day, on the way to Edison Elementary School, I would feel a surge of pride as we drove past the home of celebrated African American poet Paul Lawrence Dunbar. My parents, James and June Marable, were school teachers, a solidly middle-class profession by the standards of the status-conscious Negro elite. During the fifties, my father taught at predominantly black Dunbar and Roosevelt high schools during the day; after school was dismissed, he worked as a laborer in the second shift at Dayton tire factory. Although my father had a principal's certificate and a Master's degree, which qualified him to be appointed as a principal, he was constantly passed over by white administrators because of his fiercely independent spirit and self-initiative. Frustrated, my father eventually went into business for himself, borrowing the money to build a private nursery and daycare center for black children on the city's West Side.

Because of my parent's education and jobs, we were part of Dayton's Negro middle 5
class. Our family attorney, James McGee, was elected the city's first black mayor after the successes and reforms in the wake of the civilrights movement. Most of my parents' friends were physicians, dentists, lawyers, school teachers, entrepreneurs and professionals of various types. Despite their pretensions, most middle-class Negroes were barely two or three paychecks from poverty. Many of the businesses that sold consumer goods to blacks, which were located on West Third Street, were white-owned. Our own business sector consisted chiefly of funeral parlors, beauty salons, auto repair shops and small restaurants.

The college-educated Negro middle class had begun purchasing comfortable, spacious homes clustered high on the ridge which overlooked the West Side, not far from the mostly German farm families who lived in Jefferson Township. Poorer black families lived closer to the factories and foundries, near the dirt, smoke and industrial stench I vividly recall even today. Social class and income stratification were not unimportant. There seemed to be striking similarities between the houses and the manner in which working and poor people were dressed on "our" side of town and in "their" working-class neighborhoods. But color was the greatest denominator of all.

On Gettysburg Avenue there were a group of small rental properties and boarding houses which were within walking distance of the Veteran's Administration Hospital on the far West Side. In the front windows of most of these buildings were small cardboard signs, reading simply "No Colored." Blacks legally could not be denied entrance into the hotels or best restaurants downtown, but they were certainly not welcomed. White taxicab drivers often avoided picking up black passengers at the train station. Very few blacks were on the local police force. Black children weren't permitted to use the public swimming pool on Germantown Pike. In most aspects of public and private life, whites acted toward African-Americans as "superiors," and usually expected to be treated deferentially. There were exceptions, certainly. At my elementary school, there were white students who were friendly. There were white teachers who displayed kindness and sincerity towards their black students. But there was always an unbridgeable distance separating us. No white students with whom I attended school ever asked to come to my home. Although my parents taught in the Dayton Public School system, most white teachers and administrators maintained a strictly professional rather than personal relationship towards them. Whites were omnipresent in our lives, frequently as authority figures: politicians, police officers, bank-loan officers, school administrators, tax auditors, grocery-store managers. Race existed as a kind of prism through which we understood and saw the world, distorting and coloring everything before us.

Despite these experiences and numerous examples of discrimination, Dayton, Ohio was never the Deep South. Although the largest department stores downtown rarely employed Negroes, I recall that black customers were usually treated with courtesy. Whites were enrolled in every school I attended. Occasionally, whites attended our black church. Public institutions were largely desegregated. The color line was at its worse where it converged with the boundaries of class inequality. Blacks were treated most differently, for example, when it was also clear that they lacked money or material resources. Conversely, middle-class African-Americans certainly experienced prejudicial behavior by whites, but often encountered a less virulent form of hatred than their sisters and brothers who were poor. The recognition of class mobility and higher education gave a small number of blacks a buffer status from the worst forms of discrimination at a day-to-day level. But despite this relative privilege, we never forgot that we were black.

Every summer, we had the opportunity to encounter a far more racially charged society. At the end of the school year, my family packed our 1957 Chevrolet and traveled south, through Cincinnati and Nashville, along highways and narrow, two-lane country roads. Often at nights we were forced to sleep in the cramped confines of the automobile, because we could find no motel which permitted black people to stay overnight. We would stop along the highway to purchase gasoline, never knowing in advance whether we would be allowed to use the gas station's toilet facilities. If we were stopped for any reason by a highway patrol officer, we had to be prepared for some kind of verbal, racist abuse, and we had absolutely no recourse or appeal against his behavior or actions. Finally, we would arrive at my father's family home, Tuskegee, Alabama, where the sense of racial hostility and discrimination against African-Americans was the central theme of local life. I knew that Tuskegee then was in the midst of a major legal struggle initiated by blacks to outlaw the political gerrymandering of the city that had in effect disfranchised African-Americans.[3] We were taught that any open protest or violation of the norms of Jim Crow segregation was to court retaliation and retribution, personally and collectively. We learned that whites, with few exceptions, saw us as subhuman, without the rights to economic development, political expression and participation, and public accommodation which whites accepted and took for granted for themselves.

It was in Tuskegee, during my long visits to Alabama's Black Belt as a child, that 10 many of my basic impressions concerning the relative permanence and inflexibility of race were formed. Part of that consciousness was shaped by the experiences and stories of my father. James Marable was the grandson of slaves, and the second son of thirteen children. His father, Manning Marable, had owned and operated a small sawmill, cutting pulpwood for farm households. Along with other black rural families, they experienced the prism of race in hundreds of different ways, which formed the basic framework of their existence. From being denied the right to vote to being confined to unequal, segregated schools; from being harassed and intimidated by local white police

---

[3] **I knew . . . African Americans:** Seat of Macon County, east-central Alabama; home of the Tuskegee Institute, founded by Booker T. Washington in 1881. In 1957 the state legislature approved changes in the city's boundaries that resulted in the disenfranchisement of 400 black voters. In 1960 the U.S. Supreme Court declared that act to be unconstitutional.

officers to being forced to lower one's eyes when being directly addressed by a white man, "race" was ingrained in the smallest aspects of Southern daily life.

My father rarely talked at length about growing up black in the Deep South. But occasionally, and especially when we were visiting his large, extended family in Tuskegee, he would reflect about his own history, and recall the hostility and rudeness of whites toward himself, his family and his people. He was trying to prepare me for what I would surely experience. One of my father's stories I remember best occurred on a cold, early winter day in 1946. World War II had ended only months before, and millions of young people were going home. My father had served as a master sergeant in a segregated unit in the US Army Air Corps. Arriving in the Anniston, Alabama, bus station, he had to transfer to another local bus to make the final forty-mile trek to his family's home outside Wedowee, Alabama.

My father was wearing his army uniform, proudly displaying his medals. Quietly he purchased his ticket and stood patiently in line to enter the small bus. When my father finally reached the bus driver, the white man was staring intensely at him. With an ugly frown, the driver took a step. "Nigger," he spat at my father, "you look like you're going to give somebody some trouble. You had better wait here for the next bus." My father was immediately confused and angry. "As a soldier, you always felt sort of proud," my dad recalls. This white bus driver's remarks "hit me like a ton of bricks. Here I am, going home, and I'd been away from the South for four years. I wasn't being aggressive."

Dad turned around and saw that he was standing in front of three whites, who had purchased tickets after him. James Marable had forgotten, or had probably repressed, a central rule in the public etiquette of Jim Crow segregation.[4] Black people had to be constantly vigilant not to offend whites in any way. My father was supposed to have stepped out of line immediately, permitting the white patrons to move ahead of him. My father felt a burning sense of rage, which he could barely contain. "You get there some other way, nigger," the driver repeated with a laugh. The bus door shut in my father's face. The bus pulled away into the distance.

There was no other bus going to Wedowee that afternoon. My father wandered from the station into the street, feeling "really disgusted." Nothing he had accomplished in the previous four years, the sacrifices he had made for his country, seemed to matter. The rhetoric of democracy and freedom which had been popularized in the war against fascism rang hollow and empty. Although he eventually obtained a ride home by hitchhiking on the highway, my father never forgot the bitterness and hatred in the bus driver's words. Years later, he still felt his resentment and rage of that winter afternoon in Alabama. "When you go against the grain of racism," he warned me, "you pay for it, one way or another."

For both my father and myself, as well as for millions of black people for many generations, the living content of race was simultaneously and continuously created from within and imposed from without. That is, "race" is always an expression of how black people have defined themselves against the system of oppression, as well as a repressive structure of power and privilege which perpetuates an unequal status for African-Americans within a stratified social order. As an identity, race becomes a way of perceiving ourselves within a group. To be black in what seems to be a bipolar racial universe gives one in stantly a set of coordinates within space and time, a sense of

15

---

[4] **Jim Crow segregation:** Laws segregating, discriminating against Negroes.

geographical location along an endless boundary of color. Blackness as a function of the racial superstructure also gives meaning to collective memory; it allows us to place ourselves within a context of racial resistance, within the many struggles for human dignity, for our families and for material resources. This consciousness of racial pride and community awareness gave hope and strength to my grandfather and father; it was also the prime motivation for the Edward Wilmot Blydens, Marcus Garveys and Fannie Lou Hamers throughout black history.[5] In this way, the prism of race structures the community of the imagination, setting parameters for real activity and collective possibility.

But blackness in a racially stratified society is always simultaneously the "negation of whiteness." To be white is not a sign of culture, or a statement of biology or genetics: it is essentially a power relationship, a statement of authority, a social construct which is perpetuated by systems of privilege, the consolidation of property and status. There is no genius behind the idea of whiteness, only an empty husk filled with a mountain of lies about superiority and a series of crimes against "nonwhite" people. To be black in a white dominated social order, for instance, means that one's life chances are circumscribed and truncated in a thousand different ways. To be black means that when you go to the bank to borrow money, despite the fact that you have a credit profile identical to your white counterpart, you are nevertheless two or three times more likely to be denied the loan than the white. To be black means that when you are taken to the hospital for emergency health-care treatment, the quality of care you receive will be inadequate and substandard. To be black means that your children will not have the same academic experiences and access to higher learning resources as children in the white suburbs and exclusive urban enclaves. To be black means that your mere physical presence and the reality of your being can trigger surveillance cameras at shops, supermarkets, malls and fine stores everywhere. To be black, male, and to live in central Harlem in the 1990s, for example, means that you will have a life expectancy of forty-nine years of age—less than in Bangladesh. Race constantly represents itself to black people as an apparently unending series of moments of inequality, which constantly challenge us, sapping and draining our physical, mental and moral resources.

Perhaps this is what most white Americans have never fully comprehended about "race": the racism is not just social discrimination, political disfranchisement and acts of extra-legal violence and terror which proliferated under the Jim Crow segregation of my father's South. Nor is racism the socalled "silent discrimination" faced by my generation of African-Americans raised during the civil-rights era, who are still denied access to credit and capital by unfair banking practices, or who encounter the "glass ceiling" inside businesses which limits their job advancement. As its essential core, racism is most keenly felt in its smallest manifestations: the white merchant who drops change on the sales counter, rather than touch the hand of a black person; the white salesperson who follows you into the dressing room when you carry several items of clothing to try on, because he or she suspects that you are trying to steal; the white teacher who deliberately avoids the upraised hand of a Latino student in class, giving white pupils an unspoken yet under stood advantage; the white woman who wraps the strap of her purse several times tightly around her arm, just before walking past a black man; the white taxicab drivers who speed rapidly past African-Americans or Latinos, picking up

---

[5]**Blydens . . . Hamers:** Activists for equal rights for blacks. Marcus Garvey (1887–1940), for example, organized the first important American-based black nationalist movement (1919–1926).

whites on the next block. Each of these incidents, no matter how small, constructs the logic for the prism of race for the oppressed. We witness clear, unambiguous changes of behavior or language by whites toward us in public and private situations, and we code or interpret such changes as "racial." These minor actions reflect a structure of power, privilege and violence which most blacks can never forget.

The grandchildren of James Marable have never encountered Jim Crow segregation. They have never experienced signs reading "white" and "colored." They have never been refused service at lunch counters, access to hotel accommodation, restaurants or amusement parks, or admission to quality schools. They have never experienced the widespread unemployment, police brutality, substandard housing and the lack of educational opportunity which constitute the everyday lives of millions of African-American youth. For my children—eighteen-year-old Malaika, and sixteen-year old twins, Sojourner and Joshua—Martin Luther King, Jr., Medgar Evers, Fannie Lou Hamer and Ella Baker[6] are distant figures from the pages of black history books. Malcolm X is the charismatic image of Denzel Washington from Spike Lee's film, or perhaps the cinematic impression from several recent hip-hop music videos. "We shall Overcome" is an interesting but somewhat dated melody of the past, not a hopeful and militant anthem projecting an integrated America.

Yet, like my father before them, and like myself, my children are forced to view their world through the racial prism. They complain that their highschool textbooks don't have sufficient information about the activities and events related to African-Americans in the development of American society. In their classrooms, white students who claim to be their friends argue against affirmative action, insisting that the new "victims" of discrimination are overwhelmingly white and male. When Joshua goes to the shopping mall, he is followed and harassed by security guards. If he walks home alone through an affluent white neighborhood, he may be stopped by the police. White children have moved items away from the reach of my son because they have been taught the stereotype that "all blacks steal." Sojourner complains about her white teachers who have been hostile and unsympathetic toward her academic development, or who have given her lower grades for submitting virtually the identical level of work turned in by her white friends. As my daughter Malaika explains: "White people often misjudge you just by the way you look, without getting to know you. This makes me feel angry inside."

A new generation of African-Americans who never personally marched for civil   20 rights or Black Power, who never witnessed the crimes of segregation, feel the same rage expressed by my father half a century ago. When they watch the beating of Rodney King on television or the trial of O.J. Simpson, they instantly comprehend the racism of the Los Angeles police officers involved in each case, and the larger racial implications of both incidents. When they listen to members of Congress complain about "welfare dependency" and "crime," they recognize the racial stereotypes which are lurking just behind the code words. They have come to expect hypocritical behavior from the white "friends" who act cordially towards them at school but refuse to acknowledge or recognize them in another context. Race is a social force which still has real meaning to the generation of my children.

---

[6]**King, Jr. . . . Ella Baker:** Civil rights activists.

But the problem with the prism of race is that it simultaneously clarifies and distorts social reality. It both illuminates and obscures, creating false dichotomies and distinctions between people where none really exists. The constructive identity of race, the conceptual framework which the oppressed create to interpret their experiences of inequality and discrimination, often clouds the concrete reality of class, and blurs the actual structure of power and privilege. It creates tensions between oppressed groups which share common class interests, but which may have different physical appearances or colors. For example, on the recent debates concerning undocumented immigrants, a narrow racial perspective could convince African-Americans that they should be opposed to the civil rights and employment opportunities of Mexican Americans, Central Americans and other Latino people. We could see Latinos as potential competitors in the labor market rather than as allies in a struggle against corporate capital and conservatives within the political establishment. On affirmative action, a strict racist outlook might view the interest of lower-class and working-class whites as directly conflicting with programs which could increase opportunities for blacks and other people of color. The racial prism creates an illusion that "race" is permanent and finite; but, in reality, "race" is a complex expression of unequal relations which are dynamic and ever-changing. The dialectics of racial thinking pushes black people toward the logic and "us" versus "them," rather than a formulation which cuts across the perceived boundaries of color.

This observation is not a criticism of the world-views of my father, my children, or myself as I grew up in Dayton, Ohio. It is only common sense that most African-Americans perceive and interpret the basic struggle for equality and empowerment in distinctly racial terms. This perspective does speak to our experiences and social reality, but only to a portion of what that reality truly is. The parallel universes of race do not stand still. What was "black" and "white" in Booker T. Washington's Tuskegee of 1895 was not identical to categories of color and race in New Orleans a century ago; both are distinctly different from how we perceive and define race in the USA a generation after legal segregation. There is always a distance between our consciousness and the movement of social forces, between perception and historical reality. "Blackness" must inevitably be redefined in material terms ideologically, as millions of black and Hispanic people from the Caribbean, Africa and Latin America immigrate into the USA, assimilating within hundreds of urban centers and thousands of neighborhoods with other people of color. As languages, religions, cultural traditions and kinship networks among blacks in the USA become increasingly diverse and complex, our consciousness and our ideas of historical struggle against the leviathan of race also shift and move in new directions. This does not mean that "race" has declined in significance; it does mean that what we mean by "race" and how "race" is utilized as a means of dividing the oppressed are once again being transformed in many crucial respects.

At the beginning of the African presence in the Americas, an African-American culture, nationality and consciousness was constructed. Against great odds, inside the oppressive context of slavery and later racial segregation, the racial identity and perspective of resistance, a community empowered by imagination, was developed against the weight of institutional racism. That historic leap of collective self-definition and inner faith must once again occur, now inside the very different environment of mature capitalism. We must begin the process of redefining blackness in a manner which not only interprets but also transforms our world. ●

Emily Bernard *(1967–)*

Teaching the N-Word *2005*

> *Once riding in old Baltimore,*
> *Heart-filled, head-filled with glee,*
> *I saw a Baltimorean*
> *Keep looking straight at me.*
>
> *Now I was eight and very small,*
> *And he was no whit bigger,*
> *And so I smiled, but he poked out*
> *His tongue, and called me, "Nigger."*
>
> *I saw the whole of Baltimore*
> *From May until December;*
> *Of all the things that happened there*
> *That's all that I remember.*

—COUNTEE CULLEN, "Incident" (1925)

October 2004

Eric is crazy about queer theory. I think it is safe to say that Eve Sedgwick, Judith Butler, and Lee Edelman have changed his life. Every week, he comes to my office to report on the connections he is making between the works of these writers and the books he is reading for the class he is taking with me, African-American autobiography.

I like Eric. So tonight, even though it is well after six and I am eager to go home, I keep our conversation going. I ask him what he thinks about the word "queer," whether or not he believes, independent of the theorists he admires, that epithets can ever really be reclaimed and reinvented.

"'Queer' has important connotations for me," he says. "It's daring, political. I embrace it." He folds his arms across his chest, and then unfolds them.

I am suspicious.

"What about 'nigger'?" I ask. "If we're talking about the importance of transform- ⁵ ing hateful language, what about that word?" From my bookshelf I pull down Randall Kennedy's book *Nigger: The Strange Career of a Troublesome Word,* and turn it so its cover faces Eric. "Nigger," in stark white type against a black background, is staring at him, staring at anyone who happens to be walking past the open door behind him.

Over the next thirty minutes or so, Eric and I talk about "nigger." He is uncomfortable; every time he says "nigger," he drops his voice and does not meet my eyes. I know that he does not want to say the word; he is following my lead. He does not want to say it because he is white; he does not want to say it because I am black. I feel my power as his professor, the mentor he has so ardently adopted. I feel the power of Randall Kennedy's book in my hands, its title crude and unambiguous. *Say it,* we both instruct this white student. And he does.

It is late. No one moves through the hallway. I think about my colleagues, some of whom still sit at their own desks. At any minute, they might pass my office on their way out of the building. What would they make of this scene? Most of my colleagues are white. What would I think if I walked by an office and saw one of them holding up *Nigger* to a white student's face? A black student's face?

"I think I am going to add 'Who Can Say "Nigger"?' to our reading for next week," I say to Eric. "It's an article by Kennedy that covers some of the ideas in this book." I tap *Nigger* with my finger, and then put it down on my desk.

"I really wish there was a black student in our class," Eric says as he gathers his books to leave.

As usual, I have assigned way too much reading. Even though we begin class discus-   10
sion with references to three essays required for today, our conversation drifts quickly to "Who Can Say 'Nigger'?" and plants itself there. We talk about the word, who can say it, who won't say it, who wants to say it, and why. There are eleven students in the class. All of them are white.

Our discussion is lively and intense; everyone seems impatient to speak. We talk about language, history, and identity. Most students say "the n-word" instead of "nigger." Only one or two students actually use the word in their comments. When they do, they use the phrase "the word 'nigger,'" as if to cushion it. Sometimes they make quotation marks with their fingers. I notice Lauren looking around. Finally she raises her hand.

"I have a question; it's somewhat personal. I don't want to put you on the spot."

"Go ahead, Lauren," I say with relief.

"Okay, so how does it feel for you to hear us say that word?"

I have an answer ready.   15

"I don't enjoy hearing it. But I don't think that I feel more offended by it than you do. What I mean is, I don't think I have a special place of pain inside of me that the word touches because I am black." *We are both human beings,* I am trying to say. She nods her head, seemingly satisfied. Even inspired, I hope.

I am lying, of course.

I am grateful to Lauren for acknowledging my humanity in our discussion. But I do not want me—my feelings, my experiences, my humanity—to become the center of classroom discussion. Here at the University of Vermont, I routinely teach classrooms full of white students. I want to educate them, transform them. I want to teach them things about race they will never forget. To achieve this, I believe I must give of myself. I want to give to them—but I want to keep much of myself to myself. How much? I have a new answer to this question every week.

I always give my students a lecture at the beginning of every African-American studies course I teach. I tell them, in essence, not to confuse my body with the body of the text. I tell them that while it would be disingenuous for me to suggest that my own racial identity has nothing to do with my love for African-American literature, my race is only one of the many reasons why I stand before them. "I stand here," I say, "because I have a Ph.D., just like all your other professors." I make sure always to tell them that my Ph.D., like my B.A., comes from Yale.

"In order to get this Ph.D.," I continue, "I studied with some of this country's   20
foremost authorities on African-American literature, and a significant number of these people are white.

"I say this to suggest that if you fail to fully appreciate this material, it is a matter of your intellectual laziness, not your race. If you cannot grasp the significance of

Frederick Douglass's plight, for instance, you are not trying hard enough, and I will not accept that."

I have another part of this lecture. It goes: "Conversely, this material is not the exclusive property of students of color. This is literature. While these books will speak to us emotionally according to our different experiences, none of us is especially equipped to appreciate the intellectual and aesthetic complexities that characterize African-American literature. This is American literature, American experience, after all."

Sometimes I give this part of my lecture, but not always. Sometimes. I give it and then regret it later.

As soon as Lauren asks me how I feel, it is as if the walls of the room soften and collapse slightly, nudging us a little bit closer together. Suddenly, eleven pairs of eyes are beaming sweet messages at me. I want to laugh. I do. "Look at you all, leaning in," I say. "How close we have all become."

I sit at the end of a long narrow table. Lauren usually sits at the other end. The rest of the students flank us on either side. When I make my joke, a few students, all straight men, I notice, abruptly pull themselves back. They shift their eyes away from me, look instead at their notebooks, the table. I have made them ashamed to show that they care about me, I realize. They are following the cues I have been giving them since the beginning of the semester, cues that they should take this class seriously, that I will be offended if they do not. "African-American studies has had to struggle to exist at all," I have said. "You owe it your respect." *Don't be too familiar* is what I am really saying. *Don't be too familiar with me.*

Immediately, I regret having made a joke of their sincere attempt to offer me their care. They want to know me; they see this moment as an opportunity. But I can't stop. I make more jokes, mostly about them, and what they are saying and not saying. I can't seem to help myself.

Eric, who is sitting near me, does not recoil at my jokes; he does not respond to my not-so-subtle efforts to push him and everyone else back. He continues to lean in, his torso flat against the edge of the table. He looks at me. He raises his hand.

"Emily," he says, "would you tell them what you told me the other day in your office? You were talking about how you dress and what it means to you."

"Yes," I begin slowly. "I was telling Eric about how important it is to me that I come to class dressed up."

"And remember what you said about Todd? You said that Todd exercises his white privilege by dressing so casually for class."

Todd is one of my closest friends in the English department. His office is next door to mine. I don't remember talking about Todd's clothing habits with Eric, but I must have. I struggle to come up with a comfortably vague response to stop Eric's prodding. My face grows hot. Everyone is waiting.

"Well, I don't know if I put it exactly like that, but I do believe that Todd's style of dress reflects his ability to move in the world here—everywhere, really—less self-consciously than I do." As I sit here, I grow increasingly more alarmed at what I am revealing: my personal philosophies; my attitudes about my friend's style of dress; my insecurities; my feelings. I quietly will Eric to stop, even as I am impressed by his determination. I meet his eyes again.

"And you. You were saying that the way you dress, it means something too," Eric says. *On with this tug of war,* I think.

I relent, let go of the rope. "Listen, I will say this. I am aware that you guys, all of my students at UVM, have very few black professors. I am aware, in fact, that I may be the first black teacher many of you have ever had. And the way I dress for class reflects my awareness of that possibility." I look sharply at Eric. *That's it. No more.*

September 2004

On the first day of class, Nate asks me what I want to be called.

"Oh, I don't know," I say, fussing with equipment in the room. I know. But I feel embarrassed, as if I have been found out. "What do you think?" I ask them.

They shuffle around, equally embarrassed. We all know that I have to decide, and that whatever I decide will shape our classroom dynamic in very important ways.

"What does Gennari ask you to call him?" I have inherited several of these students from my husband, John Gennari, another professor of African-American studies. He is white.

"Oh, we call him John," Nate says with confidence. I am immediately envious of the easy warmth he seems to feel for John. I suspect it has to do with the name thing.

"Well, just call me Emily, then. This is an honors class, after all. And I do know several of you already. And then wouldn't it be strange to call the husband John and the wife Professor?" Okay, I have convinced myself.

Nate says, "Well, John and I play basketball in a pickup game on Wednesdays. So, you know, it would be weird for me to be checking him and calling him Professor Gennari."

We all laugh and move on to other topics. But my mind locks onto an image of my husband and Nate on the basketball court, two white men covered in sweat, body to body, heads down, focused on the ball.

October 2004

"It's not that I can't say it, it's that I don't want to. I will not say it," Sarah says. She wears her copper-red hair in a short, smart style that makes her look older than her years. When she smiles I remember how young she is. She is not smiling now. She looks indignant. She is indignant because I am insinuating that there is a problem with the fact that no one in the class will say "nigger." Her indignation pleases me.

Good.

"I'd just like to remind you all that just because a person refuses to say 'nigger,' that doesn't mean that person is not a racist," I say. They seem to consider this.

"And another thing," Sarah continues. "About dressing for class? I dislike it when my professors come to class in shorts, for instance. This is a profession. They should dress professionally."

Later, I tell my husband, John, about our class discussion. When I get to Sarah's comment about professors in shorts, he says, "Good for her."

I hold up *Nigger* and show its cover to the class. I hand it to the person on my left, gesture for him to pass the book around the room.

"Isn't it strange that when we refer to this book, we keep calling it 'the n-word'?"

Lauren comments on the affect of one student who actually said it. "Colin looked like he was being strangled." Of the effect on the other students, she says, "I saw us all collectively cringing."

"Would you be able to say it if I weren't here?" I blurt. A few students shake their heads. Tyler's hand shoots up. He always sits directly to my right.

"That's just bullshit," he says to the class, and I force myself not to raise an eyebrow at "bullshit." "If Emily weren't here, you all would be able to say that word."

I note that he himself has not said it, but I do not make this observation out loud.

"No." Sarah is firm. "I just don't want to be the kind of person who says that word, period."

"Even in this context?" I ask.   55

"Regardless of context," Sarah says.

"Even when it's the title of a book?"

I tell the students that I often work with a book called *Nigger Heaven,* written in 1926 by a white man, Carl Van Vechten.

"Look, I don't want to give you the impression that I am some-how longing for you guys to say 'nigger,'" I tell them, "but I do think that something is lost when you don't articulate it, especially if the context almost demands its articulation."

"What do you mean? What exactly is lost?" Sarah insists.   60

"I don't know," I say. I do know. But right here, in this moment, the last thing I want is to win an argument that winds up with Sarah saying "nigger" out loud.

Throughout our discussion, Nate is the only student who will say "nigger" out loud. He sports a shearling coat and a caesar haircut. He quotes Jay-Z. He makes a case for "nigga." He is that kind of white kid; he is down. "He is so down, he's almost up," Todd will say in December, when I show him the title page of Nate's final paper for this class. The page contains one word, "Nigger," in black type against a white background. It is an autobiographical essay. It is a very good paper.

October 1994

Nate reminds me of a student in the very first class I taught all on my own, a senior seminar called "Race and Representation." I was still in graduate school. It was 1994 and *Pulp Fiction* had just come out. I spent an entire three-hour class session arguing with my students over the way race was represented in the movie. One student in particular passionately resisted my attempts to analyze the way Tarantino used "nigger" in the movie.

"What is his investment in this word? What is he, as the white director, getting out of saying 'nigger' over and over again?" I asked.

After some protracted verbal arm wrestling, the student gave in.   65

"Okay, okay! I want to be the white guy who can say 'nigger' to black guys and get away with it. I want to be the cool white guy who can say 'nigger.'"

"Thank you! Thank you for admitting it!" I said, and everyone laughed.

He was tall. He wore tie-dyed T-shirts and had messy, curly brown hair. I don't remember his name.

After *Pulp Fiction* came out, I wrote my older brother an earnest, academic e-mail. I wanted to "initiate a dialogue" with him about the "cultural and political implications of the various usages of 'nigger' in popular culture."

His one-sentence reply went something like this: "Nigga, niggoo, niggu, negreaux,   70
negrette, niggrum."

"Do you guys ever read *The Source* magazine?" In 1994, my students knew about *The Source;* some of them had read James Bernard's column, "Doin' the Knowledge."

"He's my brother," I said, not bothering to mask my pride with anything like cool indifference. "He's coming to visit class in a couple of weeks, when we discuss hip-hop culture."

The eyes of the tie-dyed student glistened.

"Quentin Tarantino is a cool-ass white boy!" James said on the day he came to visit my class. "He is one cool white boy."

My students clapped and laughed.

"That's what I said," my tie-dyed student sighed.

James looked at me slyly. I narrowed my eyes at him. *Thanks a lot.*

September 2004

On the way to school in the morning, I park my car in the Allen House lot. Todd was the one who told me about the lot. He said, "Everyone thinks the lot at the library is closer, but the lot behind Allen House is so much better. Plus, there are always spaces, in part because everyone rushes for the library."

It is true that the library lot is nearly always full in the morning. It's also true that the Allen House lot is relatively empty, and much closer to my office. But if it were even just slightly possible for me to find a space in the library lot, I would probably try to park there, for one reason. To get to my office from Allen House, I have to cross a busy street. To get to my office from the library, I do not.

Several months ago, I was crossing the same busy street to get to my office after a class. It was late April, near the end of the semester, and it seemed as if everyone was outside. Parents were visiting, and students were yelling to each other, introducing family members from across the street. People smiled at me—wide, grinning smiles. I smiled back. We were all giddy with the promise of spring, which always comes so late in Vermont, if it comes at all.

Traffic was heavy, I noticed as I walked along the sidewalk, calculating the moment when I would attempt to cross. A car was stopped near me; I heard rough voices. Out of the corner of my eye, I looked into the car: all white. I looked away, but I could feel them surveying the small crowd that was carrying me along. As traffic picked up again, one of the male voices yelled out, "Queers! Fags!" There was laughter. Then the car roared off.

I was stunned. I stopped walking and let the words wash over me. *Queer. Fag.* Annihilating, surely. I remembered my role as a teacher, a mentor, in loco parentis, even though there were real parents everywhere. I looked around to check for the wounds caused by those hateful words. I peered down the street: too late for a license plate. All around me, students and parents marched to their destinations as if they hadn't heard. *Didn't you hear that?* I wanted to shout.

All the while I was thinking, *Not nigger. Not yet.*

October 2004

Nate jumps in.

"Don't you grant a word power by not saying it? Aren't we in some way amplifying its ugliness by avoiding it?" he asks.

"I am afraid of how I will be affected by saying it," Lauren says. "I just don't want that word in my mouth."

Tyler remembers a phrase attributed to Farai Chideya in Randall Kennedy's essay. He finds it and reads it to us. "She says that the n-word is the 'trump card, the nuclear bomb of racial epithets.'"

"Do you agree with that?" I ask.

Eleven heads nod vigorously.

"Nuclear bombs annihilate. What do you imagine will be destroyed if you guys   90 use the word in here?"

Shyly, they look at me, all of them, and I understand. Me. It is my annihilation they imagine.

November 2004

Some of My Best Friends, my anthology of essays about interracial friendship, came out in August, and the publicity department has arranged for various interviews and other promotional events. When I did an on-air interview on a New York radio show, one of the hosts, Janice, a black woman, told me that the reason she could not marry a white man was because she believed if things ever got heated between them, the white man would call her a nigger.

I nodded my head. I had heard this argument before. But strangely I had all but forgotten it. The fact that I had forgotten to fear "nigger" coming from the mouth of my white husband was more interesting to me than her fear, alive and ever-present.

"Are you biracial?"

"No."   95

"Are you married to a white man?"

"Yes."

These were among the first words exchanged between Janice, the radio host, and me. I could tell—by the way she looked at me, and didn't look at me; by the way she kept her body turned away from me; by her tone—that she had made up her mind about me before I entered the room. I could tell that she didn't like what she had decided about me, and that she had decided I was the wrong kind of black person. Maybe it was what I had written in *Some of My Best Friends.* Maybe it was the fact that I had decided to edit a collection about interracial friendships at all. When we met, she said, "I don't trust white people," as decisively and exactly as if she were handing me her business card. I knew she was telling me that I was foolish to trust them, to marry one. I was relieved to look inside myself and see that I was okay, I was still standing. A few years ago, her silent judgment—this silent judgment from any black person—would have crushed me.

When she said she could "tell" I was married to a white man, I asked her how. She said, "Because you are so friendly," and did a little dance with her shoulders. I laughed.

But Janice couldn't help it; she liked me in spite of herself. As the interview pro   100 gressed, she let the corners of her mouth turn up in a smile. She admitted that she had a few white friends, even if they sometimes drove her crazy. At a commercial break, she said, "Maybe I ought to try a white man." She was teasing me, of course. She hadn't changed her mind about white people, or dating a white man, but she had changed her mind about me. It mattered to me. I took what she was offering. But when the interview was over, I left it behind.

My husband thought my story about the interview was hilarious. When I got home, he listened to the tape they gave me at the station. He said he wanted to use the interview in one of his classes.

A few days later, I told him what Janice had said about dating a white man, that she won't because she is afraid he will call her a nigger. As I told him, I felt an unfamiliar shyness creep up on me.

"That's just so far out of . . . it's not in my head at all." He was having difficulty coming up with the words he wanted, I could tell. But that was okay. I knew what he meant. I looked at him sitting in his chair, the chair his mother gave us. I can usually find him in that chair when I come home. He is John, I told myself. And he is white. No more or less John and no more or less white than he was before the interview, and Janice's reminder of the fear that I had forgotten to feel.

I tell my students in the African-American autobiography class about Janice. I say, "You would not believe the indignities I have suffered in my humble attempts to 'move this product,' as they say in publishing." I say, "I have been surrounded by morons, and now I gratefully return to the land of the intellectually agile." They laugh.

I flatter them, in part because I feel guilty that I have missed so many classes in   105
order to do publicity for my book. But I cringe, thinking of how I have called Janice, another black woman, a "moron" in front of these white students. I do not tell my students she is black.

"Here is a story for your students," John tells me. We are in the car, on our way to Cambridge for the weekend. "The only time I ever heard 'nigger' in my home growing up was when my father's cousin was over for a visit. It was 1988, I remember. Jesse Jackson was running for president. My father's cousin was sitting in the kitchen, talking to my parents about the election. 'I'm going to vote for the nigger,' my father's cousin said. 'He's the only one who cares about the workingman.'"

John laughs. He often laughs when he hears something extraordinary, whether it's good or bad.

"That's fascinating," I say.

The next time class meets, I tell my students this story.

"So what do we care about in this sentence?" I say. "The fact that John's father's   110
cousin used a racial epithet, or the fact that his voting for Jackson conveys a kind of ultimate respect for him? Isn't his voting for Jackson more important for black progress than how his father's cousin *feels?*"

I don't remember what the students said. What I remember is that I tried to project for them a sense that I was untroubled by saying "nigger," by my husband's saying "nigger," by his father's cousin's having said "nigger," by his parents'—my in-laws'—tolerance of "nigger" in their home, years ago, long before I came along. What I remember is that I leaned on the word "feels" with a near sneer in my voice. *It's an intellectual issue,* I beamed at them, and then I directed it back at myself. *It has nothing to do with how it makes me feel.*

■ ■ ■

After my interview with Janice, I look at the white people around me differently, as if from a distance. I do this, from time to time, almost as an exercise. I even do it to my friends, particularly my friends. Which of them has "nigger" in the back of her throat?

I go out for drinks with David, my senior colleague. It is a ritual. We go on Thursdays after class, always to the same place. I know that he will order, in succession, two draft beers, and that he will ask the waitress to help him choose the second. "What do you have on draft that is interesting tonight?" he will say. I order red wine, and I, too, always ask the waitress's advice. Then we order a selection of cheeses, again soliciting assistance. We have our favorite waitresses. We like the ones who indulge us.

Tonight David orders a cosmopolitan.

We never say it, but I suspect we both like the waitresses who appreciate the odd   115
figure we cut. He is white, sixty-something, male. I am black, thirty-something, female. Not such an odd pairing elsewhere, perhaps, but uncommon in Burlington, insofar as black people are uncommon in Burlington.

Something you can't see is that we are both from the South. Different Souths, perhaps, thirty years apart, black and white. I am often surprised by how much I like his company. *All the way up here,* I sometimes think when I am with him, *and I am sitting with the South, the white South that, all of my childhood, I longed to escape.* I once had a white boyfriend from New Orleans. "A white southerner, Emily?" my mother asked, and sighed with worry. I understood. We broke up.

David and I catch up. We talk about the writing we have been doing. We talk each other out of bad feelings we are harboring against this and that person. (Like most southerners, like the South in general, David and I have long memories.) We talk about classes. I describe to him the conversation I have been having with my students about "nigger." He laughs at my anecdotes.

I am on my second glass of wine. I try to remember to keep my voice down. It's a very nice restaurant. *People in Burlington do not want to hear "nigger" while they are eating a nice dinner,* I say, chastising myself. I am tipsy.

As we leave, I accidentally knock my leg against a chair. *You are drunk,* I tell myself. *You are drunk and black in a restaurant in Burlington. What were you thinking?* I feel eyes on me as I walk out of the restaurant, eyes that may have been focused elsewhere, as far as I know, because I do not allow myself to look.

Later that evening, I am alone. I remember that David recently gave me a poem of his   120
to read, a poem about his racist grandmother, now dead, whom he remembers using the word "nigger" often and with relish. I lie in bed and reconstruct the scene of David and me in the restaurant, our conversation about "nigger." Was his grandmother at the table with us all along?

The next day, I see David in his office, which is next to mine, on the other side from Todd. I knock on the door. He invites me in. I sit in a chair, the chair I always sit in when I come to talk to him. He tells me how much he enjoyed our conversation the night before.

"Me too," I say. "But today it's as if I'm looking at you across from something," I say. "It has to do with race." I blame a book I am reading, a book for my African-American autobiography class, Toi Derricotte's *The Black Notebooks.*

"Have you read it?" David is a poet, like Derricotte.

"No, but I know Toi and enjoy her poetry. Everything I know about her and her work would lead me to believe that I would enjoy that book." He is leaning back in his chair, his arms folded behind his head.

"Well, it's making me think about things, remember the ways that you and I will always be different," I say abruptly. 125

David laughs. "I hope not." He looks puzzled.

"It's probably just temporary." I don't ask him my question about his grandmother, whether or not she is always somewhere with him, in him, in the back of his throat.

John is at an African-American studies conference in New York. Usually I am thrilled to have the house to myself for a few days. But this time I mope. I sit at the dining room table, write this essay, gaze out the window.

Today, when John calls, he describes the activity at the conference. He tells me delicious and predictable gossip about people we know, and the divas that we know of. The personalities, the infighting—greedily we sift over details on the phone.

"Did you enjoy your evening with David last night?" he asks. 130

"I did, very much," I say. "But give me more of the who-said-what." I know he's in a hurry. In fact, he's talking on a cell phone (my cell phone; he refuses to get one of his own) as he walks down a New York street.

"Oh, you know these Negroes." His voice jounces as he walks.

"Yeah," I say, laughing. I wonder who else can hear him.

Todd is married to Hilary, another of my close friends in the department. She is white. Like John, Todd is out of town this weekend. Since their two boys were born, our god-sons, John and I see them less frequently than we used to. But Hilary and I are determined to spend some time together this weekend, with our husbands away.

Burlington traffic keeps me from her and the boys for an hour, even though she lives only blocks away from me. When I get there, the boys are ready for their baths, one more feeding, and then bed. Finally they are down, and we settle into grown-up conversation. I tell her about my class, our discussions about "nigger," and my worries about David. 135

"That's the thing about the South," Hilary says. I agree, but then start to wonder about her grandmother. I decide I do not want to know, not tonight.

I do tell her, however, about the fear I have every day in Burlington, crossing that street to get back and forth from my office, what I do to guard myself against the fear.

"Did you grow up hearing that?" she asks. Even though we are close, and alone, she does not say the word.

I start to tell her a story I have never told anyone. It is a story about the only time I remember being called a nigger to my face.

"I was a teenager, maybe sixteen. I was standing on a sidewalk, trying to cross a busy street after school, to get to the mall and meet my friends. I happened to make eye contact with a white man in a car that was sort of stopped—traffic was heavy. Anyway, he just said it, kind of spit it up at me. 140

"Oh, that's why," I say, stunned, remembering the daily ritual I have just confessed to her. She looks at me, just as surprised.

December 2004

I am walking down a Burlington street with my friend Anh. My former quilting teacher, Anh is several years younger than I am. She has lived in Vermont her whole life. She is Vietnamese; her parents are white. Early in our friendship, she told me her father was a logger, as were most of the men in her family. *Generations of Vietnamese loggers in Vermont,* I mused. It wasn't until I started to describe her to someone else that I realized she must be adopted.

Anh and I talk about race, about being minorities in Burlington, but we usually do it indirectly. In quilting class, we would give each other looks sometimes that said, *You are not alone,* or *Oh, brother,* when the subject of race came up in our class, which was made up entirely of white women, aside from the two of us.

There was the time, for instance, when a student explained why black men found her so attractive. "I have a black girl's butt," she said. Anh and I looked at each other: *Oh, brother.* We bent our heads back over our sewing machines.

As we walk, I tell Anh about my African-American autobiography class, the dis- 145
cussions my students and I have been having about "nigger." She listens, and then de-
scribes to me the latest development in her on-again, off-again relationship with her fifty-year-old boyfriend, another native Vermonter, a blond scuba instructor.

"He says everything has changed," she tells me. "He's going to clean up the messes in his life." She laughs.

Once, Anh introduced me to the boyfriend she had before the scuba instructor when I ran into them at a restaurant. He is also white.

"I've heard a lot about you," I said, and put out my hand.

"I've never slept with a black woman," he said, and shook my hand. There was wonder in his voice. I excused myself and went back to my table. Later, when I looked over at them, they were sitting side by side, not speaking.

Even though Anh and I exchanged our usual glances that night, I doubted that we 150
would be able to recover our growing friendship.

Who could she be, dating someone like that? The next time I heard from her, months later, she had broken up with him.

I am rooting for the scuba instructor.

"He told me he's a new person," she says.

"Well, what did you say?" I ask her.

"In the immortal words of Jay-Z, I told him, 'Nigga, please.'" 155

I look at her and we laugh.

In lieu of a final class, my students come over for dinner. One by one, they file in. John takes coats while I pretend to look for things in the refrigerator. I can't stop smiling.

"The books of your life" is the topic for tonight. I have asked them to bring a book, a poem, a passage, some art that has affected them. Hazel has brought a children's book. Tyler talks about *Saved by the Bell.* Nate talks about Freud. Dave has a photo-graph. Eric reads "The Seacoast of Despair" from *Slouching Towards Bethlehem.*

I read from *Annie John* by Jamaica Kincaid. Later I will wonder why I did not read "Incident" by Countee Cullen, the poem that has been circulating in my head ever since we began our discussion about "nigger." *What held me back from bringing "Inci-dent" to class?* The question will stay with me for months.

The night of our dinner is an emotional one. I tell my students that they are the 160
kind of class a professor dreams about. They give me a gift certificate to the restaurant
that David and I frequent. I give them copies of *Some of My Best Friends* and inscribe
each one. Eric demands a hug, and then they all do; I happily comply. We talk about
meeting again as a class, maybe once or twice in the spring. The two students who will
be abroad promise to keep in touch through our listserv, which we all agree to keep
going until the end of the school year, at least. After they leave, the house is quiet and
empty.

Weeks later, I post "Incident" on our listserv and ask them to respond with their
reactions. Days go by, then weeks. Silence. After more prodding, finally Lauren posts
an analysis of the poem, and then her personal reactions to it. I thank her online and
ask for more responses. Silence.

I get e-mails and visits from these students about other matters, some of them race-
related. Eric still comes by my office regularly. Once he brings his mother to meet me,
a kind and engaging woman who gives me a redolent candle she purchased in France,
and tells me her son enjoyed the African-American autobiography class. Eric and I
smile at each other.

A few days later, I see Eric outside the campus bookstore.

"What did you think about 'Incident'?"

"I've been meaning to write you about it. I promise I will." 165

In the meantime, *Nigger* is back in its special place on my bookshelf. It is tucked
away so that only I can see the title on its spine, and then only with some effort. ●

Explorations of the Text

1. How does Bernard's essay, published
   in 2005, update and comment on "The
   Prism of Race," written and published
   in the 1990s, and on the double vulnerability expressed in Sojourner Truth's
   "'Ain't I A Woman,'" presented in 1851?

2. Bernard reflects on the use of the "N-
   word." How does the use of the word
   reveal her students', friends', colleagues',
   husband's, and the Vermont community's attitudes toward race? What does
   their behavior suggest? Are there unspoken assumptions that Bernard and the
   figures in her work won't reveal? Feel-

   ings that are taboo? In what ways are
   the subjects of this essay, including the
   author, products of a "long history"?

3. How do attitudes about race affect her
   stance as an African-American professor
   in a white community and university?
   Why do you think her students do not
   respond when she posts "Incident" on
   the class listserv?

4. Often creative nonfiction concludes
   with a discovery. What does Bernard
   realize as a result of writing about her
   experiences?

The Reading/Writing Connection

1. In a journal entry, examine the con-
   clusion of the essay and its relation to
   Countee Cullen's Poem, "Incident."
   Why is the poem significant to her?

2. In her essay, Bernard asks the students
   to think about what books are "the
   books of [their] lives. . . ." What is a
   "book, a poem, a passage, some art that
   has affected" your life?

3. **Write an Argument:** An African-American Studies scholar suggests that the use of the word "nigger" is important because the word carries with it the whole history of racism in this country from the time of slavery until the present, and, therefore, avoidance of the word perpetuates a denial of this history. Do you think that rejecting the N-word denies the history of slavery and oppression in this country? Or should the word be taboo because it evokes stereotypes and demeaning, negative images of African Americans?

Ideas for Writing

1. In "What's So Bad About Hate," Andrew Sullivan contends that "isms" (for instance, anti-Semitism, racism, sexism) designed to "describe the varieties of hate" do not represent the complexities of identity or "the workings of the individual heart or mind." Would Marable and Bernard agree with him? How do they portray the complexity of racial identity and racial politics?

2. **Write an Argument:** Do you concur with Sullivan's position? Use Bernard's and Marable's essays as well as other works from this chapter to support your argument.

3. How do you view your own racial, ethnic, or cultural identity and heritage? How has that heritage shaped your identity, actions, or values?

4. **Write an Argument:** Read Randall Kennedy's book, *Nigger: The Strange Career of a Troublesome Word*. Formulate an argument in response to one of the ideas in his work.

5. **Write an Argument:** After Don Imus was fired for disparaging the reputation and demeaning the members of the Rutgers women's basketball team, Bob Herbert in a column for *The New York Times* entitled "Signs of Infection" reflects that as a country "we have a problem. Not only is the society still permeated by racism and sexism and the stereotypes they spawn, but we have allowed a debased and profoundly immature culture to emerge in which the coarsest, most socially destructive images and language are an integral part of the everyday discourse." Write an essay in which you present your position on this issue. You may draw upon the essays in this cluster, rap music lyrics, shock radio, other forms of entertainment, other examples from popular culture or "everyday discourse."

 On the Web: *Civil Rights*

Please visit http://www.academic.cengage.com/english/Schmidt/Legacies4e/ for links to the following online resources.

Civil Rights Timeline
The Black Freedom Struggle Chronology (Civil Rights Timeline)

William E. B. Du Bois
The Souls of Black Folk, "Forethought" and Chapter 1
The Avalon Project at Yale Law School

Martin Luther King Speeches
The Martin Luther King Jr. Pages Project at Stanford University
Speeches (Text and Video)

GRAPHIC LITERATURE

Art Spiegelman *(1948–)*

Here My Troubles Began *1992*
from *MAUS II: A Survivor's Tale*[1]

---
[1] This excerpt is from *MAUS II: And Here My Trouble's Began,* the second volume of Art Spiegelman's autobiographical, graphic memoir. The memoir portrays his struggles as a second-generation

Holocaust child to come to terms with his relationship with his father and with his father's experiences during the war including his internment at Auschwitz. In this chapter, Spiegelman details the events following the publication of *MAUS I.*

Explorations of the Text

1. Discuss the contrasts between Spiegelman's present life with his own and his father's past. What do they reveal? Is he able to shed the burden of the past?

2. How does Spiegelman respond to the queries concerning his motivations for writing *MAUS*?

3. How do the visual elements, the portrayal of Jews as mice, the use of black and white, the lines, and the composition of the frame, develop meaning? (See, for example, frame 5 of the excerpt.)

The Reading/Writing Connection

1. "Think" Topic: Why does Spiegelman feel guilt? Does he think that others should feel guilt?

2. Create a narrative sequence in graphic form for a moment of conflict in your own life.

Ideas for Writing

1. **Write an Argument:** Elie Wiesel writes about the impossibility of finding words to represent the Shoah. Is Spiegelman's attempt to use images to represent the Holocaust successful and compelling? Why or why not? You may want to read *MAUS I* and *MAUS II* in order to explore this question.

WRITING ASSIGNMENTS

1. a. Discuss Marable's and Bernard's treatment of racism in the United States.
   b. Connect their views with two of the readings.
2. a. Write about law and justice. When is law just? When is it not? (Refer to Martin Luther King's speeches in the civil rights web cluster.)
   b. Is it ever right to disobey the law?
   c. Discuss the disobedience of Sojourner Truth.
3. a. Define cultural history.
   b. Write about your cultural history.
   c. Compare "Jasper Texas 1998," "horse," and "The Book of Yolek."
4. a. Gloss and annotate a political protest poem or song in this chapter. How effectively does the poet convey his/her political message?

    b. Analyze the poem that you have glossed and annotated. How does it achieve its impact? Focus, for example, on tone, imagery, symbolism, word choice, and/or form.

5. a. Write about the anger and dreams of retribution in the poems by Angelou, Anzaldúa, and Harjo.

    b. Is anger necessary for social change? Refer to three works in this chapter.

6. Write about the strength of the human spirit and the enduring dream of freedom and equality. Refer to works by Hughes, Angelou, Espada, and/or Ginsberg.

7. Write an essay on the statement that "Soldiers are dreamers." Refer to the works by O'Brien, Endō, Hartley and/or Adichie.

8. a. Make a list of political injustices presented in works in this chapter.

    b. Write on one writer's presentation of this issue.

    c. Support a point of view that counters the presentation of one of the works in this chapter.

9. Write a research paper on one of the following topics:

    a. Langston Hughes and the Harlem Renaissance.

    b. Tim O'Brien and the Vietnam War.

    c. A conflict between a minority group and the police (e.g., the Los Angeles riots, racial profiling).

    d. The use of chemical weapons in World War I or in another conflict.

    e. Ginsberg and the Beat generation.

    f. Human trafficking.

    g. Immigration.

    h. Some aspect of slavery in the United States, (e.g., the Underground Railroad).

    i. The Holocaust or another twentieth-century genocode (i.e., Rwanda).

    j. A contemporary site of conflict, civil war, or injustice (i.e., Darfur).

10. Analyze Sophocles's *Antigone* as a political tragedy. How does personal suffering become or cause public suffering?

11. Choose three works from this chapter and focus on their visions of the "natural order of the world." (See Milosz's "American Ignorance of War.")

12. Several different writers in this chapter envision their roles as witnesses to injustice.

    a. Referring to Wiesel's essay, define *witness*. Entertain these questions: Why witness injustice? How do you witness injustice? Why is forgetting injustice dangerous?

    b. Then explore three visions of witnessing (e.g., those of Brooks, Przytyk, Angelou, Espada, and/or Forché).

13. a. Gloss and annotate O'Brien's "How to Tell a True War Story," noting each definition of a "true war story."

    b. Apply one or several of O'Brien's definitions to other works in this chapter.

14. After reading the works in the cluster depicting terror and terrorism, create your own fictional version of "How to Tell a True Story about Terror." Use evidence from works in the chapter.

15. Examine the theme of "American Dreams: Lost and Found" in several works in the chapter. What dreams and ideals are represented? What is the underside of the American Dream? What dreams are lost? What hope exists?

16. Compare and contrast O'Brien's portrayal of being a soldier in Vietnam in "How to Tell a True War Story" with Rivera's experience of Desert Storm and with

Hartley's depiction of the Iraq war. How would the narrators respond to this passage from O'Brien's "How to Tell a True War Story": "For the common soldier, at least, war has the feel—the spiritual texture—of a great ghostly fog, thick and permanent. There is no clarity. The old rules are no longer binding, the old truths no longer true. Right spills into wrong"? You may create a dialogue among the characters.

17. In "How to Tell a True War Story," O'Brien states the following: "A true war story is never moral. . . ." What does he mean? Do you agree with him? Create a conversation among several characters or speakers in the texts on this subject.

18. Many of the characters in works in this chapter face moral dilemmas. What moral conflicts do they experience? How do they resolve these dilemmas? (Suggestions include *Antigone,* the narrator in "Ralph the Duck," and Jason Hartley.)

19. For the past two years, Nicholas Kristof, an award-winning *New York Times* journalist, has been sponsoring a contest in partnership with MySpace and with the *New York Times* in which a college student has the opportunity to travel with Kristof as a journalist and prepare blogs and video. The purpose of the trip, according to Kristof, is to give a student a global understanding of the world. Kristof states, for example, that the most college students are unaware of the fact that "a majority of the world's population lives on less than $2.00 a day." To participate in this contest, the student must write an essay explaining why he or she is qualified to take the trip and why he or she desires to go. Compose an essay for this contest. OR Present your opinion about whether you think that this contest is a good idea. Do you think that North American college students are unaware of issues in the larger world? OR Go to TimesSelect (which is now free for to all students or faculty who have an .edu address) and read Nicholas Kristof's columns about the crisis in the Darfur region of Sudan. Write short summaries of several of these articles; then synthesize the information and report what you have learned about the crisis. OR imagine you are a reporter covering the crisis in Darfur. Create a monologue.

20. **Write an Argument:** In its coverage of sites of conflict and the Iraq war, does the media perpetuate empty notions of heroism and victimization? Does it demonize the enemy? Argue pro or con. You may refer to other works in this chapter as well as information gained from research.

21. Explore the fates of children caught in a world of random violence or in the crossfire of ethnic violence, war, or civil strife. Suggestions: Corbett's "The Lost Boys of Sudan"; Brooks's "A Boy Died in My Alley"; Hecht's "The Book of Yolek"; Akpan's "My Parents' Bedroom," and Adichie's "Half a Yellow Sun."

22. Is it possible to change the world? To improve conditions in our society? In her essay, Goska maintains that we can escape "political paralysis." Do you agree or disagree?
    a) Freewrite in response to these questions and explore your own responses.
    b) Explore these questions in relation to several works in this chapter.
    c) Compose an argumentative essay, incorporating your own views and the visions of change presented in several works in the chapter.

23. Create a proposal for a memorial to commemorate a site of injustice. You may determine the site. Consider the appropriate place, design, ways that you want the public to experience the site, and symbolism. You may want to research the designs for the 9/11 memorial or another memorial with which you are familiar.

24. Find a copy of the "Declaration of Independence" and the "Declaration of Sentiments for Women" on the Internet. Create a new declaration for a particular group, for example, freshmen at a college.

25. a) Explore a film's portrayal of a social activist. What forces is the person rebelling or gainst? What form does his or her resistance take? How successful is the mode of resistance? Does the activism promote social change? Possible films include *Gandhi, The White Rose, Silkwood, Romero, Hotel Rwanda,* or *Malcolm X.*

    b) Explore a documentary's response to a social issue. Does the film present a persuasive argument? Use techniques of argumentation (see Chapter 4). Examples include *Bowling for Columbine* or *Supersize Me.*

STUDENT ESSAYS
Thematic Analysis and Research Essay

Melanie Chopko

A Mother's Survival

"I worry very much that this subject [the Holocaust] is corrupted by fiction and fiction in general corrupts history."

Cynthia Ozick

Though Cynthia Ozick worries that fiction can blur the essential facts that need to be taught to humanity, her writing does just the opposite. It is through her short story, "The Shawl," that those of us who did not experience the Holocaust are led into its horrors through the experiences of one mother, Rosa. In doing so, Ozick also explores the complex human experience of motherhood in the Holocaust and the incredible ritual of sacrifice. Through her exploration of motherhood, Ozick reveals the process of survival, showing us that temporary sustenance can be found through motherhood but true sustenance is found spiritually.

By placing the lyrical explorations of motherhood in juxtaposition to an unnamed death camp, Ozick emphasizes the very essence of motherhood: the continuity of life (survival) (Scrafford 11). As the story leads the reader on a journey defined by images of death (Rosa's breasts are cracked and dry while her niece's knees are swellings on sticks), the reader is made aware that the only life mentioned is in relation to Rosa and her baby, Magda. Motherhood is the only concept containing life that these marching prisoners are aware of, and it, therefore, defines their existence and offers a source of sustenance.

Ozick describes in great detail the hunger and physical sufferings of Rosa's niece, Stella, but her description of Rosa's presents a distinctly different response to the situation:

> Rosa did not feel hunger; she felt light, not like someone walking but like someone in a faint, in trance, arrested in a fit, someone who is already a floating angel, alert and seeing everything, but in the air, not there touching the ground. As if teetering on the tips of her fingernails. (3-4)

This description reveals that Rosa's existence is no longer defined by her physi- ⁵ cal presence; it has transcended her body. As her breasts dry from the lack of milk production and she ceases to menstruate, Rosa's body is unable to provide the life that her baby needs. In knowing that Magda's death is eminent, Rosa's existence becomes directed by instinct alone, her body a "walking cradle" (Scrafford 12). She transcends her physical need for survival to find sustenance in the emotional needs of her child.

With her existence defined by the maternal instinct to protect the life of her child, Rosa moves beyond normal human capabilities to provide for Magda. She does not eat but, rather, gives all of her food to her child. The warm shawl that Stella envies wraps the mother and child together like an umbilical cord, providing the wet nourishment Rosa's breasts cannot. Despite the knowledge that Magda will die in the near future from either starvation or discovery, Rosa protects her with this cloth extension of her body, both hiding her presence and vicariously nourishing her with the shawl (Scrafford 15).

The fictional Rosa's sacrifice opens a window to the real-life experiences of mothers who endured such suffering. While death defined nearly every part of existence in the Jewish ghettos and concentration camps, the sacrifices of mothers within these worlds testify that death was not the final victor. Portraits of women in both Lodz and Warsaw reveal that the sufferings of their families filled them with an incredible sense of purpose and strength. Their commitment sustained them as they worked eight to ten hours in factories and offices, as they provided food for their families (often through the dangerous act of smuggling), and as they returned home to fulfill their traditional roles (Ofer and Weitzman 10). Michael Unger's essay, "Women in the Lodz Ghetto," cites the diary entry of an anonymous young woman in response to her mother's sacrifice:

> March 11, 1942 . . . I ate all the honey. I am selfish. What will the family say?
> I'm not worthy of my mother, who works so hard . . . My mother looks awful,
> like a shadow. She works very hard. When I wake up at twelve or one o'clock
> at night she's sewing, and at six a.m. she's back on her feet. I have no heart,
> I have no pity. I eat anything that lands near me . . . I don't know what she
> lives on. She works the hardest and eats the least. (134)

Along with finding the strength to support their families through working, the women also were able to cope with hunger to a superhuman extent. In a desperate sacrifice for the lives of their children, mothers constantly deprived themselves of food and gave that sustenance to others despite the sickness it brought (Ofer and Weitzman 10).

Even through this deprivation, statistics show that these women had a higher ¹⁰ chance of survival than men. Their care of and responsibility for others protected against despair and violence, for their sacrifices were an extension of their prewar nurturing and responsibility to the family. Many accounts describe this act of extending care to be so essential for survival that it transcended the original ties of the family and led to the formation of surrogate families. The development of "camp sister" and "camp mother" relationships also instructed the men in survival, for the "lone wolf behavior" nearly always guaranteed death (Goldenburg 337).

Though caring for others could lead to survival, the instinct of a mother to live for her child most often began in hunger and ended in death. Mothers often were presented with the choice of a life alone as a worker or of death with their children. At Birkenau, in response to this choice, only two of about six hundred mothers of younger children presented themselves for work selection, while the others died, caring for their children until the end (Bondy 324). This commitment reveals that when faced with death, mothers continued the process of seeking sustenance and, in doing so, reached from emotion to find the spiritual nourishment that lasts for all time.

As shown in these accounts, the maternal instinct is so forceful that it battles the mother's own basic instinct for self-preservation. Because her mothering instinct is what drives her to survive, Rosa's thoughts are all directed toward Magda's life. Even Stella's bones are looked at without pity, only noticed because "[s]he [Rosa] was sure that Stella was waiting for Magda to die so that she could put her teeth into the little thighs" (Ozick 5). When Stella steals Magda's shawl selfishly for her own warmth, Magda is pushed out of the world of Rosa's protection and enters the roll-call arena of the death camp. Reduced to instinct alone, Magda's screams for her shawl are echoed in the buzzing voices of the electric fence around the arena, ordering Rosa, through her breasts, to run for the shawl in the hopes of saving her child.

It is only after Magda is thrown into the electric fence by a Nazi guard that Rosa is free to respond to her "instinct of self-preservation" (Scrafford 14). For the first time, she considers the consequences of following the command of her body to run to Magda's corpse and fights an internal battle to survive. Instead of following the instinct of motherhood, Rosa's scream in reaction to the death of her child is stifled by her pushing the scarf, which has become a symbol for Magda's life, into her mouth. This ingestion reveals the extent to which Rosa is controlled by this battle of instinct, for the action defines her existence as both a mother and an individual. By "swallowing" the shawl (Ozick 10), it becomes physically evident that Rosa has been reduced to a primitive creature (defined by instinct alone), behaving as a mother in the wild would, by consuming her young in a last attempt to save them from their predator (Scrafford 14).

With the emotional sustenance of motherhood unable to be claimed, Rosa is forced to acknowledge her physical needs. Just as the shawl provided nutrients for Magda in its wetness, Rosa now "drinks" the shawl both physically and spiritually (Ozick 10). By consuming that which defined Magda, Rosa makes her child a part of her own being, once again finding survival in motherhood. As "The Shawl" closes with Rosa swallowing the scarf, one is faced with the question of Rosa's survival. This question not only considers the mother's physical but also her emotional survival. Once a life is consumed by one purpose, the instinct of sacrifice over self-preservation, is it possible to meet all levels of need (physical, emotional, and spiritual) and, therefore, return to a balanced existence?

Just as the shawl provides nutrients to Magda, the symbol of the shawl provides more than physical sustenance to Rosa. It provides for her both emotionally and spiritually after the war. According to Lawrence S. Friedman, the shawl first preserves all levels of physical life by giving nourishment to Magda, warmth to Stella, and safety to Rosa. In doing so, the shawl unites the three characters into a symbol of the persecuted millions and alludes to another symbol of Jewish affiliation: the Jewish prayer shawl, the tallit (Friedman 115).

15

During the ritual of prayer, the believer covers his or her body with the tallit, a shawl with stripes on both ends that is large enough to enclose an entire frame. This action of being enclosed within the shawl represents the believer's communion with God (and with other believers) and His covenant with them. The lines on each end of the shawl are to encourage the wearer even more, for each stripe represents a swaying reed—bent but not broken by the winds of sorrow and suffering. In wrapping both Magda and Rosa's lives in the symbol of the tallit, Ozick assures her readers that even though Rosa, like the Jewish people, is bent nearly to the point of death, she is not broken. She will survive, for she is not alone. Because the use of the tallit was originally withheld from women due to fundamentalist beliefs of their uncleanness, the use of the shawl in Ozick's story has an even greater meaning, for it extends all of these covenantal promises to the gender that had for so long been excluded.

Despite its initial power, the shawl's reminder of the covenant loses its meaning to Rosa. Ozick's companion novella, "Rosa," reveals that Rosa's family was not pious but, rather, universal, denying their heritage as Jews and idolizing instead gentile culture. Rosa reduces the shawl from a Jewish emblem to a personal fetish. In idolizing this portion of her past, Rosa centers her life on idealizing it and creates a heritage separate from that which the Nazis destroyed (Friedman 116-118).

As a result, Rosa is unable to enter the present. She insists on honoring Magda's memory, but she also rejects her Jewishness. Rosa does not allow herself to claim the promises of the covenant promised by her heritage and is left without the ability to enter a postwar existence. The infliction of such inhuman suffering as Rosa experienced cannot be healed by human strength alone; it is only after Rosa moves to invite a character into her life who so blatantly represents the Jewish life she left behind that Ozick begins to speak about a rebirth of existence. As Rosa moves to invite her Jewish friend and all he symbolizes into her home, her emotional need for Magda finds a new source of fulfillment.

When Rosa finds rebirth in the acceptance of the spiritual symbols behind the shawl, Ozick reveals that the strength to survive is found not through the fulfillment of physical or emotional needs but, rather, through the eternal gift of spiritual sustenance. The maternal instinct can overcome the instinct for self-preservation of the body, but the fulfillment of both instincts is found in sustenance for the soul.

Works Consulted

Berger, Alan L. Crisis and Covenant: The Holocaust in American Jewish Fiction. Albany: State University of New York Press, 1985. 54.

Bondy, Ruth. "Women in Theresiensdat and the Family Camp in Birkenau." Women in the Holocaust. Eds. Dalia Ofer and Lenore J. Weitzman. New Haven: Yale University Press, 1998. 310-326.

Friedman, Lawrence S. Understanding Cynthia Ozick. Columbia: University of South Carolina Press, 1991.

Goldenberg, Myrna. "Memoirs of Auschwitz Survivors: The Burden of Gender." Women in the Holocaust. Eds. Dalia Ofer and Lenore J. Weitzman. New Haven: Yale University Press, 1998. 327-339.

Ofer, Dalia and Weitzman, Lenore J. "Introduction." Women in the Holocaust. Eds. Dalia Ofer and Lenore J. Weitzman. New Haven: Yale University Press, 1998. 1-18.

Ozick, Cynthia. The Shawl. New York: Alfred A. Knopf, 1989.

Scrafford, Barbara. "Nature's Silent Scream: A Commentary on Cynthia Ozick's 'The Shawl'." Critique 31.1 (1989):11-15.

Unger, Michael. "The Status and Plight of Women in the Lodz Ghetto." <u>Women in the Holocaust</u>. Eds. Dalia Ofer and Lenore J. Weitzman. New Haven: Yale University Press, 1998. 123–142.

Creative Response Essay

Gloria M. Winter

Rosa's Final Scream

New York City in springtime holds a certain charm. The air is filled with promises of new life and warmer days to come. People seem to be a little happier and more energetic. Children shed their long winter coats and mittens and play in the park while their mothers watch from the benches. The birds are busy, too, reconstructing their homes and preparing for new arrivals. During this time it is easy to forget about the past winter and the damage that it caused. Winter has a way of keeping people locked inside and out of the cold. For some, though, the past is tucked away and suppressed. Some memories are too painful to relive.

She doesn't exactly remember how she was rescued or when the troops arrived. At that time she was too weak to respond to the miracle at hand and collapsed from exhaustion. Rosa later woke up in a hospital with tubes in every part of her body. She was not afraid, nor was she excited. Rosa knew that Stella and Magda were gone and that she would be alone in this world. It was a bittersweet triumph because she survived and her daughters didn't. A part of Rosa did die, though. Her heart was heavy and her mind was numb. She could not speak about the horrors of the camp or the heinous murder of Magda. Poor Stella died of starvation only a few days before the troops came. Rosa felt that her survival was part of God's plan and that she needed to honor His wishes and carry on. She promised to start over but also to bury the past.

Rosa came to America after the war ended with the hopes of a new life and freedom. She did not let her conscious mind think about her past horrors but thanked God everyday for giving her the strength to live on. Rosa sailed to New York with other refugees and misplaced souls. They did not have much in tow or any idea where they were going to live. Some only had the clothes on their backs, but that did not matter. They were coming to the land of the free filled with opportunity. Milk and honey for everyone.

Rosa stayed in New York City, where she found a small apartment to live in and a job at the clothing factory. During her spare time she would take English lessons at the community center to learn to read and write. She did not want to work as a seamstress forever. Rosa wanted to take advantage of all this New World had to offer. It was a busy life for her, and some days she really felt at peace. But some days were very lonely. Rosa did not allow herself to think of Magda or Stella. The pain was too much to handle and too confusing to understand. Grieving was not a part of her life. She dreaded the nights when her unconscious mind dragged her back to the past and played a miserable dream of the Nazi soldiers. It was always the same dream about the soldiers taking away her tattered shawl and setting it on fire. They would laugh at her, while in silence she watched it burn. There was nothing she could do. Rosa would wake from this dream and pray for the morning. Somehow the daylight would make it go away.

Rosa also found solace at the art museum. Every Sunday she would take the bus to the Metropolitan Museum of Art. This was a special place for her. This was a place where she could learn about other cultures and see beautiful paintings. Most importantly, this was a place where she felt safe. The museum was always quiet and inviting. The only sounds that could be heard were the whispers of the art students, the occasional cough and sneeze or the clickety-click of high-heeled shoes on the wood floors. The Great Hall was always filled with grand flower arrangements and the most spectacular view of the balcony above. The ceilings seemed to reach Heaven. Rosa would spend all day walking through the galleries and special exhibits. She enjoyed looking at the paintings by Monet and Renoir. She observed how soft the colors were in Water Lilies and how happy the people looked in Le Moulin de la Galette. She thought that Chagall's paintings were amusing and that Van Gogh was an odd-looking fellow. The paintings were her friends, and she looked forward to visiting them each week. She never tired of the images, because each week she found something new to discover. Her love for art also furthered her English studies. Each week she would try to read the information at the museum library about the artists and their paintings. Rosa wanted to know everything. One day each week she felt special, intelligent, and complete. Her weekly ritual allowed her some temporary happiness. That is, until she saw the painting.

A new exhibit had opened the day before Rosa's usual Sunday visit. It was the Post-Impressionism exhibit. Rosa looked forward to making new friends with Cezanne, Seurat, and Gauguin. The museum was especially busy on this particular Sunday, and the gallery was filled with curious art connoisseurs. The exhibit contained paintings that were on loan from some of Europe's finest art museums. For some people, this would be their only chance to see these rare pieces of art. Rosa was amazed with all the excitement. She was also proud that she fumbled through that morning's New York Times article about the exhibit and had learned some interesting facts about the displayed artists. Rosa followed the crowd up the marble stairs and around the Great Hall balcony. She entered the new exhibit gallery and began her tour of the paintings. How wonderful everything looked! The Cezanne paintings hung on the wall with all their still-life glory. Rosa could almost taste the apples he painted. The next room contained her old friend Van Gogh and a new acquaintance named Toulouse-Lautrec. Vibrant colors and fantastic images were enfolded in these rooms. Rosa felt alive and radiant. She lost herself to the world of art, and for a moment in time, she became someone else. She was not a concentration camp survivor or the mother of forgotten children. She was Rosa, woman of the New World, art critic and a champion of life.

The tour was almost over, and there was one room left to view. She admired the Seurat and Picasso and blushed at Rousseau's painting, The Dream. The next artist was Munch. His paintings appeared intensely strange and horrifying. Rosa was not sure if she liked his work, and for the first time, she felt uncomfortable in the museum. The image of the Vampire frightened her, and Death in the Sickroom made her heart beat a little faster. Something uncontrollable was beginning to happen to Rosa, and she could not understand why. But there it was. The painting that brought it all back to her conscious mind. Rosa saw The Scream. The splashes of reddish-orange sky and bluish-purple water reminded her of the bloody ground and bruised bodies. The filth and stench and the swollen eyes and bellies. She then looked at the figure in the painting wearing black clothes and a frightened face. She suddenly imagined Stella was in the painting, too. Her poor skeleton body leaning on the figure and looking at Rosa from the canvas. She remembered it all. Once again Rosa saw her beautiful baby girl flying through the air. Her precious Magda had no idea that the fence would eat her body. It occurred to Rosa that she, herself, was the figure. This was her nightmare, her frightened face, and her scream. The sound that she muffled to remain alive by practically swallowing the shawl. Her mouth began to water, and she could taste the cinnamon and almond essence again. Rosa felt that scream in the depths of her soul, and this time she could not remain silent. Without a second thought, she opened her mouth and let herself cry in the middle of the room. She cried and wailed at the top of her lungs. Her scream filled the gallery and traveled through the museum. She screamed for her daughters. She screamed for her family and other camp victims. She screamed for humanity and prayed that this tragedy would never happen again. In an instant the madness was over, and Rosa fell to the ground. People rushed to help her, but it was too late.

Rosa died that afternoon in the museum. Nobody in the gallery could figure out why she screamed or what caused her heart to stop. To them, Rosa was just another visitor to the museum. They did not know about the other life she led or how she finally grieved for the loss of her daughters. Nor did they know how the soldiers stole her right to mourn for Magda when she was killed. How could they know unless they read the numbers on her wrist? Even then they would not truly understand that Rosa would be much happier in the afterlife. She cleansed her soul and lifted her burden by ultimately finding the courage and the voice to scream.

Online Forum and Discussion: Creative Responses to "horse"

In the assignment below, Rachel Rigolino, the instructor, asked her students to compose a creative response to the poem "horse" by Gloria Anzaldúa. The students were given a week and a half to compose their responses and also to critique one another's pieces.

Assignments(choose one):
1. Write a monologue in the voice of one of the boys.
2. Write a last stanza to the poem or a stanza that comes before the first stanza.
3. Write an official police report (or a poetic interpretation of an official police report) about the incident. Remembering the sheriff's attitude, what might actually appear in an "official" report?
4. Imagine that you are an elderly Mexican man or woman who is witness to what happens to the horse. Write a poetic monologue about your experience.

You can use my ideas as a starting point. Use your own creativity and choose another approach if you wish.

Forum: Quest. 5 "HORSE"
Date: 07-07-2004 22:34
Author: GREEN, KATHERINE ANNE
Subject: last stanza

> The blood has sunken deep within the soil
> And the evidence is hard to find
> But the guilty gringos have sown their seeds
> Which nature cannot ignore

New growth carries gross familiarity
And the gringos will someday harvest
Their tainted crops
Which will materialize beyond their wildest nightmares

Forum: Quest. 5 "HORSE"
Date: 07-14-2004 07:17
Author: DORRIAN, MARY F.
Subject: response last stanza

Hi Katie,

Wow! Great response!! Your response makes me think that even
though these "gringo boys" seem to have gotten away with killing
this horse and perhaps terrorizing these "Borderland People," retribution is not far behind. I do think that sooner or later we "reap
what we sow," and that is what your response made me think about.
Very creative, and I loved your choice of words. Your response had a
lot of strength, especially the lines "New growth carries gross famil-
iarity/and the gringos will someday harvest/Their tainted crops." I
think that these "boys" will perhaps be surprised at what the future
brings, and maybe this mighty horse will infiltrate their dreams
until they become nightmares. The violence these "boys" commit
against these people may very well "taint their crops." Clever way
to say that sooner or later their actions will catch up to them, and
it may just bleed into every part of their lives in a most uncomfortable fashion.

I have to say that your post is brilliant and extremely well-written.
You said a lot in a few lines, which made your response even more
powerful!

Great job, Katie!

Forum: Quest. 5 "HORSE"
Date: 07-09-2004 12:14
Author: TAMRAZ, LAUREN JOY
Subject: creative response:Witness

Rusting blood smell sours the wind
From the adobe porch I can see the caballo
No prayers can bring forgiveness to these boys
But they pray to a different god than I
They believe their god looks like them, thinks like them
I believe my god regrets creating them
Questions why they think they are another man's keeper
I almost pulled the children away,
Wanted to call them to the rio to help me with the washings

So they would not see the broken spirit of the village
Rusting in the sticky sun
But this will only become clearer as they grow,
What good to let them think otherwise?
I turn away from the scene
I string chilies for drying
The caballo and I,
The old lady,
rusting in the sun together.

Forum: Quest. 5 "HORSE"
Date: 07-16-2004 23:54
Author: HOEY, CHRISTOPHER ROBERT
Subject: Excellent job Lauren

Wow, excellent poem response, Lauren. I really enjoyed reading your piece. The lines you wrote "They believe their god looks like them, thinks like them/I believe my god regrets creating them" is really powerful and shows the deep racial tensions that Anzaldúa experienced growing up and expressed in her poem "horse." Your choice of words to end your response, "The caballo and I,/The old lady, rusting in the sun together," are very interesting. I wonder why you chose to have the old woman so accepting of the cruel actions against the horse and why she is so accepting of the horses and her fate? Maybe there has been just so much fighting that she just has no strength to fight back anymore, or perhaps she feels powerless in a land of such conflict? Good work on deciphering the meaning of the original poem and incorporating a very thoughtful response!

Forum: Quest. 5 "HORSE"
Date: 07-10-2004 20:36
Author: HERTZBERG, EMILY KATE
Subject: Emily's Last Stanza

memory like explosives in a feather pillow
hundreds of missing lines
horrible months torn from old
they melted the horse from their minds
like photographs taken by dead people with cameras without film
black out-of-tune notes playing a death dirge on a violin strung with barbwire
at a loss for a reason
surrounded by danger and uncertainty
hallucinating that the horse still rode in the night
breaking the mirror of silence
badly beaten by invisible things
water boiling underground
remember to remember
time to turn somebody in

it's now and never
never seen or heard from again

Forum: Quest. 5 "HORSE"
Date: 07-12-2004 16:50
Author: SORCI, REBECCA MARY
Subject: Re:creative police report

Incident 590890890028309890090
Type of Incident Wild Horse
Date- October 30th, 1987
Sheriff Racism of the Hargill Texas Police Dept.

On Monday October 30th, I was called to the town of Hargill, Texas at 1:30 am. Mr. Anzaldúa had called the police station claiming that two white boys killed his horse. When I got to the farm, Mr. Anzaldúa had the boys in his custody waiting for my arrival. The boys had told me that they were coming home from the creek, where they had been fishing all day. They were walking through Mr. Anzaldúa's land when they saw a beautiful black horse. They decided they wanted to take him for a quick ride. As they approached, the horse became wild and started to attack them, they did not know what to do. Tommy (a 16-year-old male) asked Bobby (a 16-year-old male) to hand them the knives they had used early to cut the fishing line. The horse continued to come at the two boys, out of protection the two boys sliced off the horse's legs. Anzaldúa told me he came out when heard noises coming from the barn, he saw the horse in much pain but still alive, he shot the horse to take it out of its misery. The father of the boys was called to the property and was told to take the two boys home. Mr. Anzaldúa was told to keep a better eye out for people on his property; he was also told that if he didn't keep his other animals tamed, he would receive a fine. Mr. Anzaldúa had trouble cooperating with my orders and questioned my authority by asking why the boys were not in trouble for trespassing and killing his horse. I told Mr. Anzaaluda to stop questioning my authority and told him, "boys will be boys, just following their instincts" (897). I then told Mr. Anzaldúa if he wanted to continue to talk back to me or question me, I could take him down to the station. I left the property at about 2:15 am.

Forum: Quest. 5 "HORSE"
Date: 07-12-2004 17:59
Author: LAROBARDIER, JOSEPHINE LOPANE
Subject: Re:Rebecca

Hi Rebecca,

Wow, I really like your response! You really capture the tone of the poem. The way you turn the situation around and put the blame on the poor rancher, Mr. Anzaldúa, was superb! I could see the whole event happening as I read your "police report," and I felt a bit ashamed that the poor man would be ignored by the authorities instead of being helped. Those boys really deserved to be punished, and it makes me sick that they got away scott-free. You made the whole thing very, very believable. Great Job!

JoAnn

Forum: Quest. 5 "HORSE"
Date: 07-12-2004 23:05
Author: REZMOVITS, DANIEL ADAM
Subject: Re: creative response as witness

I sit and watch over the field from my humble little hut
They say I am old, but I know I am young with a mind full of wisdom.
As I sit and watch the horses dance in the moonlight,
Out of the darkness comes a group of young gringos.
I know right away, nothing good will come of this,
With the children these days, nothing ever does.
They approach the beautiful animal at full speed,
As it screams in terror, bucking back and forth.
All I see is red, and it splashes down in bursts
The boys have done it again,
When will this killing stop?
The animal does nothing to deserve such a fate,
Yet all it can do now is wait for its end.
I sit and watch over the field from my humble little hut,
As I have for many years which have passed.
They say I am old, but I say I am young, with a mind full of wisdom,
The same way I have been, since the day I was born.

Borderlands

Introduction

> *"To survive the Borderlands*
> *you must live sin fronteras*
> *be a crossroads."*

Gloria Anzaldúa, "To Live in the Borderlands Means You"

The twenty-first century brings with it the dissolution of boundaries that once provided meaning and identity in a world of small communities. With widespread use of the Internet, satellite communication, and air travel, we are now aware of events that occur in countries all around the planet, and we recognize that these seemingly local happenings affect us all. International travel exposes people to different languages, cultures, and foods, leading to the creation of new, hybrid cultures. Travel is not restricted to humans; plants and nonhuman animals move across boundaries as pets, houseplants, or stowaways—sometimes wreaking havoc in their new environments. Both human and nonhuman animals have even traveled into outer space, a feat that was earlier imagined only in science-fiction stories. The works in this chapter explore the indeterminate areas that mark borderlands. Some of the boundaries these works explore include: the human/animal connection, the fluid and dissolving boundaries among countries, the transformation of wilderness into wasteland, the transition from life to death, and the inter-relationship of the material and the spiritual realm. The elimination of borders brings with it both anxiety and exhilaration. Gloria Anzaldúa challenges us to embrace our strange new world, to "be a crossroads," to live *"sin fronteras,"* without borders. If we are unable to accept her challenge, we may fulfill the prediction of science-fiction writers who foresee the world's future as filled with global conflict and eventual extinction.

Perhaps this place at the "crossroads"—a place envisioned by artists across four centuries—offers us the greatest challenge and the greatest possibilities for visions of community for the twenty-first century.

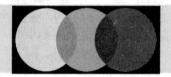

Crossing the Genres

The Human Animal

Lauren Slater *(1963–)*

Blue Beyond Blue *2005*

1

There once was a woman who had never had any children. This bothered her, and, as the years went by, the bother turned to grief. She lived alone, in a tidy house, while outside, in the fields, roses redder than crayons grew wild and thick. The woman liked to go for walks. She liked to pick flowers and see the pollen on her hands.

One day, while out walking, the woman came across a briar patch denser than any she had seen before, each enormous flower the size of a pink platter. These roses, strangely, had no thorns—their stalks were smooth and beaded with water—so the woman walked right into their thicket and there, lying on the ground in the shade, she saw a little egg.

"If I cannot have a child," the woman thought, "then perhaps I can at least have a small sparrow to keep me company." So she took the egg home with her, and put it on her windowsill, and then she waited for it to hatch.

Days passed and the egg, which started out as the size of a small speckled stone, did not hatch. Instead it just grew bigger, and by the end of the week it was as large as a melon, and strange scratching sounds were coming from inside it.

"This is obviously not a sparrow's egg," said the woman. "It must be an ostrich egg." 5

But after three weeks passed, and nothing had hatched, and the egg was as plump as a pumpkin, she thought, "Perhaps I have found some prehistoric creature, a dinosaur," and the woman grew scared.

The woman went to the town doctor. She explained her situation, and the doctor was so amazed that he rushed with her to her house.

Inside, the doctor looked for a long time at the giant egg. He took out his stethoscope and listened to its innards. He peered at its shell with his magnifying glass. He tapped at it with his little red rubber reflex hammer, all the while scratching his chin just like a learned man must.

At last he turned to the woman. His gaze was serious and direct. From his black bag he pulled a scalpel, but this was no ordinary scalpel. This had a blade as thin as hair, as sharp as Arctic wind, and its handle was made of carved bone. The doctor said, "I am giving you this scalpel as a gift, in light of what you have here. Wait until midnight, and then make a sideways slit in the shell, precisely four inches in length," he said, and with a marker he drew a line on the egg where she was to cut—at midnight.

The woman took the scalpel with its handle of bone. She felt scared. That evening, 10 darkness came fast and definite, snuffing out the contours of the land, swallowing sounds, making the roses bloom black in the fields. The woman trembled. Waiting until midnight, she could not help but think of all the sins she'd committed in her life, small sins but sins nonetheless, and she had the terrible sense that the egg contained these things, and that she would slit it open to see the darkest heart of herself.

Midnight came. An animal howled and a tiny red Mars blistered the sky like a sore. The woman now no longer wanted to cut open the egg, but a strange force called compulsion—and its kinder cousin, curiosity—both of those propelled her. She made the small slit, just as the doctor had instructed. At first, nothing happened, but then some liquid oozed from the incision, and then came a little white leg wearing, of all things, a flip-flop, and then came a second white leg, wearing, of all things, a flip-flop, and then a torso struggled out, the shell cracking, a girl, maybe three, maybe four, pulling her head free last, and in her hands she held a clean white envelope, which she offered immediately to the woman.

The woman, awestruck, took the envelope and opened it. There was a note, folded up. She unfolded the note. She saw:

$$==0^*))))$$
$$+++\%!\$no^\wedge$$

The woman squinted harder at the gibberish. It stayed just as it was, gibberish. Then she squinted at the little girl. "Who are you?" the woman said.

"I am your daughter," answered the girl.

Now, the woman could not believe this. It was just too good to be true. The darkness, it turned out, had augured not sin, but bounty, as darkness sometimes does. The woman just stood there and blinked and blinked. She said, "Show me your hands." 15

The little girl showed her her hands, which were, each one, five-fingered and perfect. The woman said, "Walk to the door and back," which the girl did, on two feet, wholly human, and then the woman said, "Pinch a piece of your skin, as hard as you can," which the girl did, until she cried out in pain, and the woman said, "Stop! Stop! I hear how you are human," and she took the girl to her, and tasted her tears.

2

Years went by. Mother and child were happy. They grew root vegetables and played harmonicas. They slept in two beds pushed side by side, and together they watched the moon move through the month, now plump as an egg, now a silver sliver, and, over time, the girl forgot where she was from, and believed she belonged wholly to her mother. And, over time, the mother, although she never forgot where the girl was from, believed the girl belonged wholly to her. Sometimes, when the girl slept, the mother anxiously, but oh so gently, checked the girl's toes and tongue, to make sure she was, well, a girl, and always her toes and tongue, plus everything else, looked normal.

The only thing that was not normal was the girl's voice, but in this instance abnormal was not bad, it was good. The girl had the most beautiful voice, like a piccolo was inside her, and when she sang all the birds stayed still in the trees and listened.

And so the years went by and mother and child slept side by side and kissed each other constantly and the woman had happiness at last. And then, during the summer of the girl's twelfth year, just as she should have begun to grow breasts, something very disconcerting happened.

The woman noticed, growing not from her front, but from her shoulder blades in 20 back, where the girl could not see, two tiny feathered mounds.

At first the mounds were so tiny they were more like downy patches, but day by day they sprouted and the woman was always trying to get a good look at them, and the daughter, who was twelve and becoming irritable, said, "Stop pressing on my back every other minute, would you?" and the woman said, "I am just trying to make sure your shirt is buttoned."

The daughter had no idea about the wings.

At night now, alone, the mother grieved. She recalled how, long ago, when she had slit open the strangest shell to find a tiny child whom she had come to think was of her, from her, she had known it was too good to be true. Her girl was not of this world. The mother cried. She got up one night, tiptoed across the creaking floorboards, and opened a locked box, where she had saved the scalpel and the mysterious letter. She unfolded the letter again, after all these years, and stared at its mysterious message.

$$==0*))))$$
$$+++\%!\$no^\wedge$$

and still she could make no sense out of it. She knew nothing of this written language, but what she did know was that if her daughter grew wings, as her body seemed to want so badly to do, then she would soon fly away from her, for one has wings only if one wishes to fly, and fly far, and then the woman would be all alone again, in a tidy house, with the wild roses growing in an abundant profusion.

The woman picked up the scalpel. Time had not blunted its blade, and the carved-bone handle had a pearly glisten. The daughter slept soundly. A white owl flew by the window, its wingspan massive, its eyes alarmed. The woman went toward her sleeping girl, drew back the covers like a nurse draws back a bandage to expose the flesh, and then there they were, the wings, two budding structures of piped bone and scaly feathers, not yet detected by their owner. The mother lowered the scalpel and then, in one swift swish, cut off the left wing, and then in one swift swish cut off the right wing, and the daughter did not awaken, but in her dreams she felt a searing pain, and saw birds falling from above.

The next morning, when the daughter awoke, she had a fever and her back badly 25 hurt. "What is wrong with my back, what is wrong with my back?" the child called out, and her tongue was swollen, her eyes gone glazed, and the mother, frantic, pressed cool washcloths to her forehead. Had she killed the girl? Would her daughter die?

For six days the child thrashed and moaned and then, on the seventh day, she was suddenly, remarkably, better. Glow crept back into her cheeks. She ate some sweet potatoes. She climbed out of bed and said, "Everything feels fine, except these spots on either side of my back," and she stood before the mirror and, twisting around, caught a glimpse of where the wounds were.

"What has happened to my back?" the daughter cried. Any wounds would be odd enough, but these wounds were odder still. Where the mother had cut were two slits, each one miraculously healing in a strip of shiny gold.

"Why do I have that funny color on my back?" the daughter said.

The mother searched in her head for an explanation. Of course she wasn't going to say, "Well, dear girl, while you were asleep I came at you with a scalpel because I didn't want you to leave me," so instead she did what many mothers do, she told a sort of half-truth, designed to protect both parties. She said, "You had a great fever and a golden rash for six days; you almost died, you almost left me, but now you are well, except for these minor markings, which do not matter. What matters is that we are together again, and will be together forever."

The girl, who was twelve and did not take anything about her body as minor, said, "I will never wear a bathing suit with these things on my back." She wept as though she'd been gored, which in a way she had. The mother rocked the girl and said, "Shhh, shhhh, it will be okay." The mother did not feel okay. Her heart was heavy. She loved her girl, but, until now, she had not known that love could be so sharp.

3

The girl grew up and grew beautiful and then, one day, fell in love with an acrobat. The mother said, "How will he support you, doing flips?" and the girl said, "We need very little," and, indeed, the mother knew this to be true, for she herself needed very little, except the love of this girl, who was leaving her now, for a man in a red stretch suit.

The girl and the acrobat planned their wedding for an April day. The acrobat was anxious to get through the ceremony, because every time he tried to undress his lover she said, "No no, wait until we are married," when in truth marriage was not the issue. She was embarrassed by her back, with its golden scars. On the actual wedding day, there were many feelings and fears experienced by many people. The girl felt frightened, for very soon she would have to take off her clothes and show her imperfect body, but she also felt excited, because she loved the acrobat. The acrobat felt anticipation. The girl's mother, who had helped plan the wedding, felt a deep melancholy, but also a sense of pride, for her daughter had grown to be beautiful and intelligent.

The wedding progressed with music and champagne, and then the bride and the bridegroom danced together, and then, as was the custom, everyone else had a dance with the bride. The officiator said, "It is now dusk. We have celebrated the union of this man and woman for a full joyous day, but we, as is our custom, cannot come to closure unless every man has danced with the bride. Is there any man here who has not had a chance to dance with the bride?"

And then, from out of the sky, a huge black bird appeared, circling slowly, dropping lower, calling, *Keeyaa keeyaa,* as though his heart were breaking. The wedding party hushed. The men stepped back instinctively, and the bird, black as obsidian, shiny as mica, revolved just over their heads. The girl, as though under a spell, walked into the center of the crowd, and she made gentle waving motions with her arms on the ground while the bird made gentle waving motions with his wings in the sky, and the girl opened her mouth and the most beautiful sounds came out, sounds of grief on this, her wedding day—the strangest song.

4

Most Things—but not all—change with time. The girl's grief was, in some sense, short-lived, because as soon as she was back in the arms of the acrobat, she felt an enveloping safety. On the other hand, the girl had a deeper grief, a grief that had been in her body ever since the night she'd lain asleep, scalpeled.

The girl and the acrobat went away to the acrobat's home at the outskirts of the village. The wedding party dispersed. The mother stood for a long time waving her handkerchief in farewell, and the mother thought, "Many years ago I tried to stop my child from flying away, but she has flown away anyway, because that is destiny, which cannot be cut."

The mother went home, back to her house. She was alone again. But she also knew her girl would come visit her, and so she was not wholly alone.

Even though years had passed since the night she had cut into her daughter, the mother had never been able to forgive herself for what she'd done. It was as though she had a stone in her stomach.

The girl, meanwhile, entered the acrobat's cottage, and the acrobat began, very gently, to peel off her clothes. The girl grew frightened. "No no," she cried, and the acrobat said, "Shush-sh, hush-sh," and he removed her clothes so gently and with such skill that she felt little twitches in her body, twitches that were part fear and part excitement.

And at last, when her clothes were fully removed, and she stood naked, and he walked around her, at last he saw the golden scars. "What are these?" he said.   40

"I don't know," the girl whispered. She hung her head. "I had some rash when I was little, they're ugly, I know," and she tried to hide herself by backing up against the wall.

"No no," said the acrobat. "They are beautiful," and he meant it. He turned her on her stomach on the bed and, standing over her, he kissed the scars with so much genuine passion that two fully formed wings burst upon her back, as though they'd just been waiting beneath the skin for a welcoming committee.

"What's that?" the girl cried, her face in the pillow. "What has come up upon my back?" and the acrobat, a man who loved adventure, who cherished the gaps between solid stones, who liked nothing better than to enter the air of utter possibility, said, "My love. You have wings! Those scars were hiding wings!" and there was delight in his voice.

The girl stood up and walked over to the mirror. "Oh my god," she said, for the wings were not diminutive. They were huge, white and gray, and she could make them flap. "What has happened to me?" she whispered.

"You are part angel," the acrobat said, and he came toward her and kissed her on   45
the mouth, and they made love and afterward he said, "You are more beautiful to me now than ever."

And, indeed, the girl felt, well, she felt for the first time, if not beautiful, then somehow *right*. She didn't understand why the wings felt so thoroughly comfortable. She didn't understand why she felt so strangely complete, so at peace. She realized that for a long, long time, there had been an ache in her body, a place of muffled pain, and now it was resolved, and her spirit felt light and yellow.

She sang and flew around the hut. The acrobat practiced flips and dips. They were an excellent couple.

The only thing was, the girl was too afraid to go home and visit her mother. "What will she think when she sees I have WINGS?" the girl wondered. "She will think it's the strangest thing, and I won't know how to explain it," but the girl missed her mother. A few times, she put on a big shirt sewn of sailcloth, her wings stuffed inside, and walked back to her mother's hut, but each time she got close, a dread filled her, and there was a terrific ache in her shoulder blades, the feeling of something slicing something off, and in her mind's eye, a drop of bright rich blood, and before she could help herself, she was whisked by her self straight up into the sky, and, flapping fast, went back to her second home.

5

Now, it just so happens that the mother, one day, was watching by the window and saw her daughter approach the house in a big white shirt, and then saw her daughter sail into the sky, the wings flapping fast and free. And the mother said, "She is afraid to come home to me. Her true body has triumphed and she doesn't want me to know." When the mother saw that the daughter's true body had triumphed, she did not feel dread or disappointment; she too felt a kind of yellow lightness, a certain lifting of the sodden spirit, because, well, for the mother, she saw how the wings were not only for leave-taking, but for return, and that pleased her. Even more importantly, the mother saw how the daughter's body was fluid in the sky, how she cartwheeled among clouds. She was a good mother with a great though imperfect love for her girl; in the end, it was love that won out, no question, it was love, as she watched the girl skim across the sky, and the mother's mouth opened into a joyful oh. Oh.

The mother went over to the locked box where, for all these years, she'd stored the scalpel and the mysterious note the girl had had with her in the egg. She put these things in a basket and set off to the acrobat's hut. On the way she found feathers scattered here and there across the ground, and she knew instinctively which feathers came from the body of her girl, which from the bodies of other birds. 50

When she got to the acrobat's hut, she knocked on the door and the girl opened it. "You don't have to hide from me," the mother said immediately. She touched her daughter's cheek. She remembered how she had waited, waited in the darkness for the egg to hatch, how she had seen the small white leg step over the cliff of cracks, how she had tasted her tears. "I know all about your wings," said the mother. She paused. "I have known about them for years."

"But I only just got them a few weeks ago," said the girl.

"May I come in?" asked the mother.

The girl stepped back to let her mother in. They sat together at the table. The mother, then, told her the entire story, how she had been born from an egg found in the woods, how, at twelve, she had started growing wings, how the mother, afraid of losing the girl to foreign lands, to the sky itself, had cut them off, and the mother cried in the telling, cried with a handkerchief wadded at her mouth, and the daughter cried too, and said, "Shhh, shhhh," and they kissed and tasted each other's tears.

"I did it because I loved you so much," said the mother, "and I did not understand how love can be so sharp." 55

"It is so strange," said the daughter, "because the very same hands that cut the wings from my body cradled the egg, birthed me, everything is always like that."

"Like what?" the mother said.

"Kindness and cutting, they're all mixed up together."

"Yes," said the mother.

"Yes," said the daughter, and then they ate some scones. 60

And then the mother gave to the daughter the scalpel she had long ago used to both birth her and hurt her, plus the mysterious folded note that she had had with her in the egg. "This scalpel," said the mother, "can bring life or break life; either way, it has great power. This note," said the mother, "may be gibberish or may be genius, I have no idea."

The daughter thanked the mother for the presents and put them away in the medicine chest, and life went on. She forgot about the presents, and she never read the note. She visited her mother three times a week and her mother grew a garden of eggplants and roses, and sea-green cucumbers that were so fat and healthy she sold them for an excellent price. Three years later, the girl got pregnant and there was great rejoicing all around. When it came time for delivery, the girl lay on her side and pushed and pushed, and the midwife said, "I see the head! I see the head!" and the acrobat wept, peering up into the tunnel that was his wife, and then out came the sphere of what they thought was the head but of course was really an egg.

Everyone was quiet. The egg lay there on the bed. The girl, panting, got up and went to the medicine chest, and now took out the note and the scalpel. She cut just as her mother had described to her, a four-inch slit on the surface of the egg, and she reached her hand in and pulled out a baby boy, who would, under the influence of time and testosterone, grow his own magnificent wings. Everybody understood that.

The girl, kneeling on the bed by bloody rags, her hair in a stream of sweat, opened the note from so long ago. It was written in the language of birds, which felt utterly familiar to her. The note said:

$$==0^*))))$$
$$+++\%!\$no^{\wedge}$$

Otherwise interpreted as (and she said it aloud):   65

I am yours
On loan from time
And the sky
So please give me back to
The blue beyond blue
As all good parents must do

And then the new baby boy let out a bellow, took his first breath, and began straightaway to grow up. ●

Charles Simic *(1938–)*

Summer Morning *1971*

I love to stay in bed
All morning,
Covers thrown off, naked,
Eyes closed, listening.

Outside they are opening   5
Their primers
In the little school
Of the corn field.

There's a smell of damp hay,
Of horses, laziness,   10
Summer sky and eternal life.

I know all the dark places
Where the sun hasn't reached yet,
Where the last cricket
Has just hushed; anthills   15
Where it sounds like it's raining;
Slumbering spiders spinning wedding dresses.

I pass over the farmhouses
Where the little mouths open to suck,
Barnyards where a man, naked to the waist,   20
Washes his face and shoulders with a hose,
Where the dishes begin to rattle in the kitchen.

The good tree with its voice
Of a mountain stream
Knows my steps.   25
It, too, hushes.

I stop and listen:
Somewhere close by
A stone cracks a knuckle,
Another rolls over in its sleep.   30

I hear a butterfly stirring
Inside a caterpillar,
I hear the dust talking
Of last night's storm.

Further ahead, someone   35
Even more silent
Passes over the grass
Without bending it.

And all of a sudden!
In the midst of that quiet,
It seems possible   40
To live simply on this earth.

Peter Singer *(1946–)*

Speciesism and the Equality of Animals *1977*

Speciesism—the word is not an attractive one, but I can think of no better term—is a prejudice or attitude of bias toward the interests of members of one's own species and against those of members of other species. It should be obvious that the fundamental objections to racism and sexism made by Thomas Jefferson and Sojourner Truth apply equally to speciesism. If possessing a higher degree of intelligence does not entitle one human to use another for his own ends, how can it entitle humans to exploit nonhumans for the same purpose?

Many philosophers and other writers have proposed the principle of equal consideration of interests, in some form or other, as a basic moral principle; but not many of them have recognized that this principle applies to members of other species as well as to our own. Jeremy Bentham was one of the few who did realize this. In a forward-looking passage written at a time when black slaves had been freed by the French but in the British dominions were still being treated in the way we now treat animals, Bentham wrote:

> The day *may* come when the rest of the animal creation may acquire those rights which never could have been withholden from them but by the hand of tyranny. The French have already discovered that the blackness of the skin is no reason why a human being should be abandoned without redress to the caprice of a tormentor. It may one day come to be recognized that the number of the legs, the villosity of the skin, or the termination of the *os sacrum* are reasons equally insufficient for abandoning a sensitive being to the same fate. What else is it that should trace the insuperable line? Is it the faculty of reason, or perhaps the faculty of discourse? But a full-grown horse or dog is beyond comparison a more rational, as well as a more conversable animal, than an infant of a day or a week or even a month, old. But suppose they were otherwise, what would it avail? The question is not, Can they *reason?* nor Can they *talk?* but, *Can they suffer?*

In this passage Bentham points to the capacity for suffering as the vital characteristic that gives a being the right to equal consideration. The capacity for suffering—or more strictly, for suffering and/or enjoyment or happiness—is not just another characteristic like the capacity for language or higher mathematics. Bentham is not saying that those who try to mark "the insuperable line" that determines whether the interests of a being should be considered happen to have chosen the wrong characteristic. By saying that we must consider the interests of all beings with the capacity for suffering or enjoyment Bentham does not arbitrarily exclude from consideration any interests at all—as those who draw the line with reference to the possession of reason or language do. The capacity for suffering and enjoyment is a *prerequisite for having interests at all,* a condition that must be satisfied before we can speak of interests in a meaningful way. It would be nonsense to say that it was not in the interests of a stone to be kicked along the road by a schoolboy. A stone does not have interests because it cannot suffer. Nothing that we can do to it could possibly make any difference to its welfare. A mouse, on the other hand, does have an interest in not being kicked along the road, because it will suffer if it is.

If a being suffers there can be no moral justification for refusing to take that suffering into consideration. No matter what the nature of the being, the principle of equality requires that its suffering be counted equally with the like suffering—insofar as rough comparisons can be made—of any other being. If a being is not capable of suffering, or of experiencing enjoyment or happiness, there is nothing to be taken into account. So the limit of sentience (using the term as a convenient if not strictly accurate shorthand for the capacity to suffer and/or experience enjoyment) is the only defensible boundary of concern for the interests of others. To mark this boundary by some other characteristic like intelligence or rationality would be to mark it in an arbitrary manner. Why not choose some other characteristic, like skin color?

The racist violates the principle of equality by giving greater weight to the interests of members of his own race when there is a clash between their interests and the interests of those of another race. The sexist violates the principle of equality by favoring the interests of his own sex. Similarly the speciesist allows the interests of his own species to override the greater interests of members of other species. The pattern is identical in each case.

Most human beings are speciesists. Ordinary human beings—not a few exceptionally cruel or heartless humans, but the overwhelming majority of humans—take an active part in, acquiesce in, and allow their taxes to pay for practices that require the sacrifice of the most important interests of members of other species in order to promote the most trivial interests of our own species. . . .

Speciesism In Practice

For the great majority of human beings, especially in urban, industrialized societies, the most direct form of contact with members of other species is at mealtimes: We eat them. In doing so we treat them purely as means to our ends. We regard their life and well-being as subordinate to our taste for a particular kind of dish. I say "taste" deliberately—this is purely a matter of pleasing our palate. There can be no defense of eating flesh in terms of satisfying nutritional needs, since it has been established beyond doubt that we could satisfy our need for protein and other essential nutrients far more efficiently with a diet that replaced animal flesh by soy beans, or products derived from soy beans, and other high protein vegetable products.

It is not merely the act of killing that indicates what we are ready to do to other species in order to gratify our tastes. The suffering we inflict on the animals while they are alive is perhaps an even clearer indication of our speciesism than the fact that we are prepared to kill them. In order to have meat on the table at a price that people can afford, our society tolerates methods of meat production that confine sentient animals in cramped, unsuitable conditions for the entire duration of their lives. Animals are treated like machines that convert fodder into flesh, and any innovation that results in a higher "conversion ratio" is liable to be adopted. As one authority on the subject has said, "cruelty is acknowledged only when profitability ceases." So hens are crowded four or five to a cage with a floor area of twenty inches by eighteen inches, or around the size of a single page of the *New York Times*. The cages have wire floors, since this reduces cleaning costs, though wire is unsuitable for the hens' feet; the floors slope, since this makes the eggs roll down for easy collection, although this makes it difficult for the hens to rest comfortably. In these conditions all the birds' natural instincts are thwarted: They cannot stretch their wings fully, walk freely, dust-bathe, scratch the ground, or build a nest. Although they have never known other conditions, observers have noticed that the birds vainly try to perform these actions. Frustrated at their inability to do so, they often develop what farmers call "vices," and peck each other to death. To prevent this, the beaks of young birds are often cut off.

This kind of treatment is not limited to poultry. Pigs are now also being reared in cages inside sheds. These animals are comparable to dogs in intelligence, and need a varied, stimulating environment if they are not to suffer from stress and boredom. Anyone who kept a dog in the way in which pigs are frequently kept would be liable to prosecution, in England at least, but because our interest in exploiting pigs is greater than our interest in exploiting dogs, we object to cruelty to dogs while consuming the produce of cruelty to pigs. Of the other animals, the condition of veal calves is perhaps worst of all, since these animals are so closely confined that they cannot even turn around or get up and lie down freely. In this way they do not develop unpalatable muscle. They are also made anaemic and kept short of roughage, to keep their flesh pale, since white veal fetches a higher price; as a result they develop a craving for iron and roughage, and have been observed to gnaw wood off the sides of their stalls, and lick greedily at any rusty hinge that is within reach.

Since, as I have said, none of these practices cater to anything more than our pleasures of taste, our practice of rearing and killing other animals in order to eat them is a clear instance of the sacrifice of the most important interests of other beings in order to satisfy trivial interests of our own. To avoid speciesism we must stop this practice, and each of us has a moral obligation to cease supporting the practice. Our custom is all the support that the meat industry needs. The decision to cease giving it that support may be difficult, but it is no more difficult than it would have been for a white Southerner to go against the traditions of his society and free his slaves; if we do not change our dietary habits, how can we censure those slaveholders who would not change their own way of living?

The same form of discrimination may be observed in the widespread practice of experimenting on other species in order to see if certain substances are safe for human beings, or to test some psychological theory about the effect of severe punishment on learning, or to try out various new compounds just in case something turns up. People sometimes think that all this experimentation is for vital medical purposes, and so will reduce suffering overall. This comfortable belief is very wide of the mark. Drug companies test new shampoos and cosmetics that they are intending to put on the market by dropping them into the eyes of rabbits, held open by metal clips, in order to observe what damage results. Food additives, like artificial colorings and preservatives, are tested by what is known as the "LD50"—a test designed to find the level of consumption at which 50 percent of a group of animals will die. In the process, nearly all of the animals are made very sick before some finally die, and others pull through. If the substance is relatively harmless, as it often is, huge doses have to be forcefed to the animals, until in some cases sheer volume or concentration of the substance causes death.

Much of this pointless cruelty goes on in the universities. In many areas of science, nonhuman animals are regarded as an item of laboratory equipment, to be used and expended as desired. In psychology laboratories experimenters devise endless variations and repetitions of experiments that were of little value in the first place. To quote just one example, from the experimenter's own account in a psychology journal: At the University of Pennsylvania, Perrin S. Cohen hung six dogs in hammocks with electrodes taped to their hind feet. Electric shock of varying intensity was then administered through the electrodes. If the dog learned to press its head against a panel on the left, the shock was turned off, but otherwise it remained on indefinitely. Three of the dogs, however, were required to wait periods varying from 2 to 7 seconds while being shocked before making the response that turned off the current. If they failed to wait, they received further shocks. Each dog was given from 26 to 46 "sessions" in the hammock, each session consisting of 80 "trials" or shocks, administered at intervals of one minute. The experimenter reported that the dogs, who were unable to move in the hammock, barked or bobbed their heads when the current was applied. The reported findings of the experiment were that there was a delay in the dogs' responses that increased proportionately to the time the dogs were required to endure the shock, but a gradual increase in the intensity of the shock had no systematic effect in the timing of the response. The experiment was funded by the National Institutes of Health, and the United States Public Health Service.

In this example, and countless cases like it, the possible benefits to mankind are either nonexistent or fantastically remote, while the certain losses to members of other species are very real. ●

Alice Walker *(1944–)*

Am I Blue? *1986*

"Ain't these tears in these eyes tellin' you?"

For about three years my companion and I rented a small house in the country that stood on the edge of a large meadow that appeared to run from the end of our deck straight into the mountains. The mountains, however, were quite far away, and between us and them there was, in fact, a town. It was one of the many pleasant aspects of the house that you never really were aware of this.

It was a house of many windows, low, wide, nearly floor to ceiling in the living room, which faced the meadow, and it was from one of these that I first saw our closest neighbor, a large white horse, cropping grass, flipping its mane, and ambling about—not over the entire meadow, which stretched well out of sight of the house, but over the five or so fenced-in acres that were next to the twenty-odd that we had rented. I soon learned that the horse, whose name was Blue, belonged to a man who lived in another town, but was boarded by our neighbors next door. Occasionally, one of the children, usually a stocky teen-ager, but sometimes a much younger girl or boy, could be seen riding Blue. They would appear in the meadow, climb up on his back, ride furiously for ten or fifteen minutes, then get off, slap Blue on the flanks, and not be seen again for a month or more.

There were many apple trees in our yard, and one by the fence Blue could almost reach. We were soon in the habit of feeding him apples, which he relished, especially because by the middle of summer the meadow grasses—so green and succulent since January—had dried out from lack of rain, and Blue stumbled about munching the dried stalks half-heartedly. Sometimes he would stand very still just by the apple tree, and when one of us came out he would whinny, snort loudly, or stamp the ground. This meant, of course: I want an apple.

It was quite wonderful to pick a few apples, or collect those that had fallen to the ground overnight, and patiently hold them, one by one, up to his large, toothy mouth. I remained as thrilled as a child by his flexible dark lips, huge, cubelike teeth that crunched the apples, core and all, with such finality, and his high, broad-breasted *enormity;* beside which, I felt small indeed. When I was a child, I used to ride horses, and was especially friendly with one named Nan until the day I was riding and my brother deliberately spooked her and I was thrown, head first, against the trunk of a tree. When I came to, I was in bed and my mother was bending worriedly over me; we silently agreed that perhaps horse-back riding was not the safest sport for me. Since then I have walked, and prefer walking to horse-back riding—but I had forgotten the depth of feeling one could see in horses' eyes.

I was therefore unprepared for the expression in Blue's. Blue was lonely. Blue was horribly lonely and bored. I was not shocked that this should be the case; five acres to tramp by yourself, endlessly, even in the most beautiful of meadows—and his was—cannot provide many interesting events, and once rainy season turned to dry that was about it. No, I was shocked that I had forgotten that human animals and nonhuman animals can communicate quite well; if we are brought up around animals as children we take this for granted. By the time we are adults we no longer remember. However, the animals have not changed. They are in fact *completed* creations (at least they seem to be, so much more than we) who are not likely to change; it is their nature to express themselves; What else are they going to express? And they do. And, generally speaking, they are ignored.

After giving Blue the apples, I would wander back to the house, aware that he was observing me. Were more apples not forthcoming then? Was that to be his sole entertainment for the day? My partner's small son had decided he wanted to learn how to piece a quilt; we worked in silence on our respective squares as I thought . . .

Well, about slavery: about white children, who were raised by black people, who knew their first all-accepting love from black women, and then, when they were twelve or so, were told they must "forget" the deep levels of communication between themselves and "mammy" that they knew. Later they would be able to relate quite calmly, "My old mammy was sold to another good family." "My old mammy was _____" Fill in the blank. Many more years later a white woman would say: "I can't understand these Negroes, these blacks. What do they want? They're so different from us."

And about the Indians, considered to be "like animals" by the "settlers" (a very benign euphemism for what they actually were), who did not understand their description as a compliment.

And about the thousands of American men who marry Japanese, Korean, Filipina, and other non–English-speaking women and of how happy they report they are, *"blissfully,"* until their brides learn to speak English, at which point the marriages tend to fall apart. What then did the men see, when they looked into the eyes of the women they married, before they could speak English? Apparently only their own reflections.

I thought of society's impatience with the young. "Why are they playing the music so loud?" Perhaps the children have listened to much of the music of oppressed people their parents danced to before they were born, with its passionate but soft cries for acceptance and love, and they have wondered why their parents failed to hear.

I do not know how long Blue had inhabited his five beautiful, boring acres before we moved into our house; a year after we had arrived—and had also traveled to other valleys, other cities, other worlds—he was still there.

But then, in our second year at the house, something happened in Blue's life. One morning, looking out the window at the fog that lay like a ribbon over the meadow, I saw another horse, a brown one, at the other end of Blue's field. Blue appeared to be afraid of it, and for several days made no attempt to go near. We went away for a week. When we returned, Blue had decided to make friends and the two horses ambled or galloped along together, and Blue did not come nearly as often to the fence underneath the apple tree.

When he did, bringing his new friend with him, there was a different look in his eyes. A look of independence, of self-possession, of inalienable *horseness*. His friend eventually became pregnant. For months and months there was, it seemed to me, a mutual feeling between me and the horses of justice, of peace. I fed apples to them both. The look in Blue's eyes was one of unabashed "this is *it*ness."

It did not, however, last forever. One day, after a visit to the city, I went out to give Blue some apples. He stood waiting, or so I thought, though not beneath the tree. When I shook the tree and jumped back from the shower of apples, he made no move. I carried some over to him. He managed to half-crunch one. The rest he let fall to the ground. I dreaded looking into his eyes—because I had of course noticed that Brown, his partner, had gone—but I did look. If I had been born into slavery, and my partner had been sold or killed, my eyes would have looked like that. The children next door explained that Blue's partner had been "put with him" (the same expression that old people used, I had noticed, when speaking of an ancestor during slavery who had been impregnated by her owner) so that they could mate and she conceive. Since that was accomplished, she had been taken back by her owner, who lived somewhere else.

Will she be back? I asked.

They didn't know.   15

Blue was like a crazed person. Blue *was*, to me, a crazed person. He galloped furiously, as if he were being ridden, around and around his five beautiful acres. He whinnied until he couldn't. He tore at the ground with his hooves. He butted himself against his single shade tree. He looked always and always toward the road down which his partner had gone. And then, occasionally, when he came up for apples, or I took apples to him, he looked at me. It was a look so piercing, so full of grief, a look so *human,* I almost laughed (I felt too sad to cry) to think there are people who do not know that animals suffer. People like me who have forgotten, and daily forget, all that animals try to tell us. "Everything you do to us will happen to you; we are your teachers, as you are ours. We are one lesson" is essentially it, I think. There are those who never once have even considered animals' rights: those who have been taught that animals actually want to be used and abused by us, as small children "love" to be frightened, or women "love" to be mutilated and raped. . . . They are the great-grandchildren of those who honestly thought, because someone taught them this: "Women can't think," and "niggers can't faint." But most disturbing of all, in Blue's large brown eyes was a new look, more painful than the look of despair: the look of disgust with human beings, with life; the look of hatred. And it was odd what the look of hatred did. It gave him, for the first time, the look of a beast. And what that meant was that he had put up a barrier within to protect himself from further violence; all the apples in the world wouldn't change that fact.

And so Blue remained, a beautiful part of our landscape, very peaceful to look at from the window, white against the grass. Once a friend came to visit and said, looking out on the soothing view: "And it *would* have to be a *white* horse; the very image of freedom." And I thought, yes, the animals are forced to become for us merely "images" of what they once so beautifully expressed. And we are used to drinking milk from containers showing "contented" cows, whose real lives we want to hear nothing about, eating eggs and drumsticks from "happy" hens, and munching hamburgers advertised by bulls of integrity who seem to command their fate.

As we talked of freedom and justice one day for all, we sat down to steaks. I am eating misery, I thought, as I took the first bite. And spit it out. •

Explorations of the Text

1. According to Terry Tempest Williams, "We are animals, in search of a home, in relationship to Other, an expanding community with a mosaic of habits, domestic and wild; there is nothing precious or nostalgic about it." Discuss this quote in relation to the works in this cluster. Why might she claim that we are "in search of a home"?

2. Charles Simic ends his poem, "Summer Morning," with the line: "It seems possible / To live simply on this earth." Gretel Ehrlich ends "Looking for a Lost Dog" (Chapter 5) with the line: "Today it is enough to make a shadow." What is the significance of these lines? Do you think that humans need nature, as some argue?

3. In "Blue Beyond Blue," the acrobat is described as "a man who loved adventure, who cherished the gaps between solid stones, who liked nothing better than to enter the air of utter possibility." Considering this description and his occupation, explain why the acrobat is or is not an appropriate mate for the girl.

4. Discuss the elements of fantasy in "Blue Beyond Blue." Do these fantastic features of the story help to create a message for the reader? If so, what is it?

5. Walker and Singer structure their essays as arguments. Summarize each argument; analyze the use of appeals; then determine which of the two is most effective.

The Reading/Writing Connection

1. Freewrite about a pet you have or have had in the past. What behaviors or habits did the pet have that you considered to be human? What behaviors of your own might you consider to be similar to those of nonhuman animals?

2. "Think" topic: Scientists claim that we are presently living through a period when more species are becoming extinct than during any time in the past history of the planet. Using your library or the Internet, research which species are becoming extinct and why. How will these extinctions affect humans?

Ideas for Writing

1. **Write an Argument:** Alice Walker and Peter Singer both compare the human treatment of nonhuman animals to slavery. Speciesism is, thus, comparable to racism. Argue pro or con this point of view.

2. **Write an Argument:** Create an argument as an analogy. Use Walker's essay as a model.

3. Although for more than a century scientists have recognized that humans belong to the animal kingdom, the boundary between human and nonhuman animals is as clearly drawn as ever. In an essay, analyze the concept of "human animal" in two or more of the works in this cluster. Consider the use of the word "animal" and its many meanings, from the most literal and scientific (a classification based on physiology), to its most metaphoric (the consideration of cruel behavior as "beastial").

FICTION

Kurt Vonnegut, Jr. *(1922–2007)*

Harrison Bergeron 1968

The year was 2081, and everybody was finally equal. They weren't only equal before God and the law. They were equal every which way. Nobody was smarter than anybody else. Nobody was better looking than anybody else. Nobody was stronger or quicker than anybody else. All this equality was due to the 211th, 212th, and 213th Amendments to the Constitution, and to the unceasing vigilance of agents of the United States Handicapper General.

Some things about living still weren't quite right, though. April, for instance, still drove people crazy by not being springtime. And it was in that clammy month that the H-G men took George and Hazel Bergeron's fourteen-year-old son, Harrison, away.

It was tragic, all right, but George and Hazel couldn't think about it very hard. Hazel had a perfectly average intelligence, which meant she couldn't think about anything except in short bursts. And George, while his intelligence was way above normal, had a little mental handicap radio in his ear. He was required by law to wear it at all times. It was tuned to a government transmitter. Every twenty seconds or so, the transmitter would send out some sharp noise to keep people like George from taking unfair advantage of their brains.

George and Hazel were watching television. There were tears on Hazel's cheeks, but she'd forgotten for the moment what they were about.

On the television screen were ballerinas.   5

A buzzer sounded in George's head. His thoughts fled in panic, like bandits from a burglar alarm.

"That was a real pretty dance, that dance they just did," said Hazel.

"Huh?" said George.

"That dance—it was nice," said Hazel.

"Yup," said George. He tried to think a little about the ballerinas. They weren't re-   10
ally very good—no better than anybody else would have been, anyway. They were burdened with sashweights and bags of birdshot, and their faces were masked, so that no one, seeing a free and graceful gesture or a pretty face, would feel like something the cat drug in. George was toying with the vague notion that maybe dancers shouldn't be handicapped. But he didn't get very far with it before another noise in his ear radio scattered his thoughts.

George winced. So did two out of the eight ballerinas.

Hazel saw him wince. Having no mental handicap herself, she had to ask George what the latest sound had been.

"Sounded like somebody hitting a milk bottle with a ball peen hammer," said George.

"I'd think it would be real interesting, hearing all the different sounds," said Hazel, a little envious. "All the things they think up."

"Um," said George.   15

"Only, if I was Handicapper General, you know what I would do?" said Hazel. Hazel, as a matter of fact, bore a strong resemblance to the Handicapper General, a woman named Diana Moon Glampers. "If I was Diana Moon Glampers," said Hazel, "I'd have chimes on Sunday—just chimes. Kind of in honor of religion."

"I could think, if it was just chimes," said George.

"Well—maybe make 'em real loud," said Hazel. "I think I'd make a good Handicapper General."

"Good as anybody else," said George.

"Who knows better'n I do what normal is?" said Hazel.   20

"Right," said George. He began to think glimmeringly about his abnormal son who was now in jail, about Harrison, but a twenty-one-gun salute in his head stopped that.

"Boy!" said Hazel, "that was a doozy, wasn't it?"

It was such a doozy that George was white and trembling, and tears stood on the rims of his red eyes. Two of the eight ballerinas had collapsed to the studio floor, were holding their temples.

"All of a sudden you look so tired," said Hazel. "Why don't you stretch out on the sofa, so's you can rest your handicap bag on the pillows, honeybunch." She was referring to the forty-seven pounds of birdshot in a canvas bag, which was padlocked around George's neck. "Go on and rest the bag for a little while," she said. "I don't care if you're not equal to me for a while."

George weighed the bag with his hands. "I don't mind it," he said. "I don't notice   25
it any more. It's just a part of me."

"You been so tired lately—kind of wore out," said Hazel. "If there was just some way we could make a little hole in the bottom of the bag, and just take out a few of them lead balls. Just a few."

"Two years in prison and two thousand dollars fine for every ball I took out," said George. "I don't call that a bargain."

"If you could just take a few out when you came home from work," said Hazel. "I mean—you don't compete with anybody around here. You just set around."

"If I tried to get away with it," said George, "then other people'd get away with it—and pretty soon we'd be right back to the dark ages again, with everybody competing against everybody else. You wouldn't like that, would you?"

"I'd hate it," said Hazel.   30

"There you are," said George. "The minute people start cheating on laws, what do you think happens to society?"

If Hazel hadn't been able to come up with an answer to this question, George couldn't have supplied one. A siren was going off in his head.

"Reckon it'd fall all apart," said Hazel.

"What would?" said George blankly.

"Society," said Hazel uncertainly. "Wasn't that what you just said?"   35

"Who knows?" said George.

The television program was suddenly interrupted for a news bulletin. It wasn't clear at first as to what the bulletin was about, since the announcer, like all announcers, had a serious speech impediment. For about half a minute, and in a state of high excitement, the announcer tried to say, "Ladies and gentlemen—"

He finally gave up, handed the bulletin to a ballerina to read.

"That's all right—" Hazel said of the announcer, "he tried. That's the big thing. He tried to do the best he could with what God gave him. He should get a nice raise for trying so hard."

"Ladies and gentlemen—" said the ballerina, reading the bulletin. She must have 40 been extraordinarily beautiful, because the mask she wore was hideous. And it was easy to see that she was the strongest and most graceful of all the dancers, for her handicap bags were as big as those worn by two-hundred-pound men.

And she had to apologize at once for her voice, which was a very unfair voice for a woman to use. Her voice was a warm, luminous, timeless melody. "Excuse me—" she said, and she began again, making her voice absolutely uncompetitive.

"Harrison Bergeron, age fourteen," she said in a grackle squawk, "has just escaped from jail, where he was held on suspicion of plotting to overthrow the government. He is a genius and an athlete, is under-handicapped, and should be regarded as extremely dangerous."

A police photograph of Harrison Bergeron was flashed on the screen upside down, then sideways, upside down again, then right side up. The picture showed the full length of Harrison against a background calibrated in feet and inches. He was exactly seven feet tall.

The rest of Harrison's appearance was Halloween and hardware. Nobody had ever borne heavier handicaps. He had outgrown hindrances faster than the H-G men could think them up. Instead of a little ear radio for a mental handicap, he wore a tremendous pair of earphones, and spectacles with thick wavy lenses. The spectacles were intended to make him not only half blind, but to give him whanging headaches besides.

Scrap metal was hung all over him. Ordinarily, there was a certain symmetry, a 45 military neatness to the handicaps issued to strong people, but Harrison looked like a walking junkyard. In the race of life, Harrison carried three hundred pounds.

And to offset his good looks, the H-G men required that he wear at all times a red rubber ball for a nose, keep his eyebrows shaved off, and cover his even white teeth with black caps at snaggle-tooth random.

"If you see this boy," said the ballerina, "do not—I repeat, do not—try to reason with him."

There was the shriek of a door being torn from its hinges.

Screams and barking cries of consternation came from the television set. The photograph of Harrison Bergeron on the screen jumped again and again, as though dancing to the tune of an earthquake.

George Bergeron correctly identified the earthquake, and well he might have—for 50 many was the time his own home had danced to the same crashing tune. "My God—" said George, "that must be Harrison!"

The realization was blasted from his mind instantly by the sound of an automobile collision in his head.

When George could open his eyes again, the photograph of Harrison was gone. A living, breathing Harrison filled the screen.

Clanking, clownish, and huge, Harrison stood in the center of the studio. The knob of the uprooted studio door was still in his hand. Ballerinas, technicians, musicians, and announcers cowered on their knees before him, expecting to die.

"I am the Emperor!" cried Harrison. "Do you hear? I am the Emperor! Everybody must do what I say at once!" He stamped his foot and the studio shook.

"Even as I stand here—" he bellowed, "crippled, hobbled, sickened—I am a greater 55 ruler than any man who ever lived! Now watch me become what I *can* become!"

Harrison tore the straps of his handicap harness like wet tissue paper, tore straps guaranteed to support five thousand pounds.

Harrison's scrap-iron handicaps crashed to the floor.

Harrison thrust his thumbs under the bar of the padlock that secured his head harness. The bar snapped like celery. Harrison smashed his headphones and spectacles against the wall.

He flung away his rubber-ball nose, revealed a man that would have awed Thor, the god of thunder.

"I shall now select my Empress!" he said, looking down on the cowering people. 60 "Let the first woman who dares rise to her feet claim her mate and her throne!"

A moment passed, and then a ballerina arose, swaying like a willow.

Harrison plucked the mental handicap from her ear, snapped off her physical handicaps with marvelous delicacy. Last of all, he removed her mask.

She was blindingly beautiful.

"Now—" said Harrison, taking her hand, "shall we show the people the meaning of the word dance? Music!" he commanded.

The musicians scrambled back into their chairs, and Harrison stripped them of 65 their handicaps, too. "Play your best," he told them, "and I'll make you barons and dukes and earls."

The music began. It was normal at first—cheap, silly, false. But Harrison snatched two musicians from their chairs, waved them like batons as he sang the music as he wanted it played. He slammed them back into their chairs.

The music began again and was much improved.

Harrison and his Empress merely listened to the music for a while—listened gravely, as though synchronizing their heartbeats with it.

They shifted their weights to their toes.

Harrison placed his big hands on the girl's tiny waist, letting her sense the weight- 70 lessness that would soon be hers.

And then, in an explosion of joy and grace, into the air they sprang!

Not only were the laws of the land abandoned, but the law of gravity and the laws of motion as well.

They reeled, whirled, swiveled, flounced, capered, gamboled, and spun.

They leaped like deer on the moon.

The studio ceiling was thirty feet high, but each leap brought the dancers nearer 75 to it.

It became their obvious intention to kiss the ceiling.

They kissed it.

And then, neutralizing gravity with love and pure will, they remained suspended in air inches below the ceiling, and they kissed each other for a long, long time.

It was then that Diana Moon Glampers, the Handicapper General, came into the studio with a double-barreled ten-gauge shotgun. She fired twice, and the Emperor and the Empress were dead before they hit the floor.

Diana Moon Glampers loaded the gun again. She aimed it at the musicians and 80 told them they had ten seconds to get their handicaps back on.

It was then that the Bergerons' television tube burned out.

Hazel turned to comment about the blackout to George. But George had gone out into the kitchen for a can of beer.

George came back in with the beer, paused while a handicap signal shook him up. And then he sat down again. "You been crying?" he said to Hazel.

"Yup," she said.

"What about?" he said.

"I forget," she said. "Something real sad on television."

"What was it?" he said.

"It's all kind of mixed up in my mind," said Hazel.

"Forget sad things," said George.

"I always do," said Hazel.

"That's my girl," said George. He winced. There was the sound of a rivetting gun in his head.

"Gee—I could tell that one was a doozy," said Hazel.

"You can say that again," said George.

"Gee—" said Hazel, "I could tell that one was a doozy." ●

Explorations of the Text

1. React to the first paragraph. What associations does the concept of "equality" evoke?

2. Analyze Harrison's appearance, character, behavior, and rebellion. Why is he depicted as a fourteen-year-old? Why is Harrison dangerous?

3. Explain the conclusion of the story. Is it **ironic?**

4. Evaluate the **satire** and humor in the story.

5. Why does Vonnegut create a series of short paragraphs to depict Harrison's and the ballerina's dance? What is the effect of this technique?

6. Discuss the world of 2081. What are its collective values? In what ways does Vonnegut criticize North American society and its values?

The Reading/Writing Connection

1. "Think" Topic: React to Vonnegut's vision of equality.

2. Begin a journal entry: "It was 2081 and. . . ." Freewrite. (Imagine that you are a character in a place.)

3. Write a monologue in Diana Moon Glampers's or in Harrison's voice.

4. **Write an Argument:** Which freedom would you most hate to lose: movement, speech, or imagination?

Ideas for Writing

1. What critique of North American society is presented?

2. Compare this story's view of individuality with the view of identity in "To live in the Borderlands means you."

Gabriel García Márquez *(1928–)*   Translated by Gregory Rabassa

The Handsomest Drowned Man In the World *1971*
A Tale for Children

The first children who saw the dark and slinky bulge approaching through the sea let themselves think it was an empty ship. Then they saw it had no flags or masts and they thought it was a whale. But when it washed up on the beach, they removed the clumps of seaweed, the jellyfish tentacles, and the remains of fish and flotsam, and only then did they see that it was a drowned man.

They had been playing with him all afternoon, burying him in the sand and digging him up again, when someone chanced to see them and spread the alarm in the village. The men who carried him to the nearest house noticed that he weighed more than any dead man they had ever known, almost as much as a horse, and they said to each other that maybe he'd been floating too long and the water had got into his bones. When they laid him on the floor they said he'd been taller than all other men because there was barely enough room for him in the house, but they thought that maybe the ability to keep on growing after death was part of the nature of certain drowned men. He had the smell of the sea about him and only his shape gave one to suppose that it was the corpse of a human being, because the skin was covered with a crust of mud and scales.

They did not even have to clean off his face to know that the dead man was a stranger. The village was made up of only twenty-odd wooden houses that had stone courtyards with no flowers and which were spread about on the end of a desertlike cape. There was so little land that mothers always went about with the fear that the wind would carry off their children and the few dead that the years had caused among them had to be thrown off the cliffs. But the sea was calm and bountiful and all the men fit into seven boats. So when they found the drowned man they simply had to look at one another to see that they were all there.

That night they did not go out to work at sea. While the men went to find out if anyone was missing in neighboring villages, the women stayed behind to care for the drowned man. They took the mud off with grass swabs, they removed the underwater stones entangled in his hair, and they scraped the crust off with tools used for scaling fish. As they were doing that they noticed that the vegetation on him came from faraway oceans and deep water and that his clothes were in tatters, as if he had sailed through labyrinths of coral. They noticed too that he bore his death with pride, for he did not have the lonely look of other drowned men who came out of the sea or that haggard, needy look of men who drowned in rivers. But only when they finished cleaning him off did they become aware of the kind of man he was and it left them breathless. Not only was he the tallest, strongest, most virile, and best built man they had ever seen, but even though they were looking at him there was no room for him in their imagination.

They could not find a bed in the village large enough to lay him on nor was there ⁵ a table solid enough to use for his wake. The tallest men's holiday pants would not fit him, nor the fattest ones' Sunday shirts, nor the shoes of the one with the biggest feet. Fascinated by his huge size and his beauty, the women then decided to make him some pants from a large piece of sail and a shirt from some bridal Brabant[1] linen so that he could continue through his death with dignity. As they sewed, sitting in a circle and gazing at the corpse between stitches, it seemed to them that the wind had never been so steady nor the sea so restless as on that night and they supposed that the change had something to do with the dead man. They thought that if that magnificent man had lived in the village, his house would have had the widest doors, and highest ceiling, and the strongest floor; his bedstead would have been made from a midship frame held together by iron bolts, and his wife would have been the happiest woman. They thought that he would have had so much authority that he could have drawn fish out of the sea simply by calling their names and that he would have put so much work into his

---

[1] **Brabant:** Former region of Western Europe including the current Brabant province of the Netherlands and Brabant and Antwerp regions of Belgium.

land that springs would have burst forth from among the rocks so that he would have been able to plant flowers on the cliffs. They secretly compared him to their own men, thinking that for all their lives theirs were incapable of doing what he could do in one night, and they ended up dismissing them deep in their hearts as the weakest, meanest, and most useless creatures on earth. They were wandering through that maze of fantasy when the oldest woman, who as the oldest had looked upon the drowned man with more compassion than passion, sighed:

"He has the face of someone called Esteban."

It was true. Most of them had only to take another look at him to see that he could not have any other name. The more stubborn among them, who were the youngest, still lived for a few hours with the illusion that when they put his clothes on and he lay among the flowers in patent leather shoes his name might be Lautaro. But it was a vain illusion. There had not been enough canvas, the poorly cut and worse sewn pants were too tight, and the hidden strength of his heart popped the buttons on his shirt. After midnight the whistling of the wind died down and the sea fell into its Wednesday drowsiness. The silence put an end to any last doubts: he was Esteban. The women who had dressed him, who had combed his hair, had cut his nails and shaved him were unable to hold back a shudder of pity when they had to resign themselves to his being dragged along the ground. It was then that they understood how unhappy he must have been with that huge body since it bothered him even after death. They could see him in life, condemned to going through doors sideways cracking his head on crossbeams, remaining on his feet during visits, not knowing what to do with his soft pink, sealion hands while the lady of the house looked for her most resistant chair and begged him, frightened to death, sit here, Esteban, please, and he, leaning against the wall, smiling, don't bother, ma'am, I'm fine where I am, his heels raw and his back roasted from having done the same thing so many times whenever he paid a visit, don't bother, ma'am, I'm fine where I am to avoid the embarrassment of breaking up the chair, and never knowing perhaps that the one who said don't go, Esteban, at least wait till the coffee's ready, were the ones who later on would whisper the big boob finally left, how nice, the handsome fool has gone. That was what the women were thinking beside the body a little before dawn. Later, when they covered his face with a handkerchief so that the light would not bother him, he looked so forever dead, so defenseless, so much like their men that the first furrows of tears opened in their hearts. It was one of the younger ones who began the weeping. The others, coming to, went from sighs to wails, and the more they sobbed the more they felt like weeping, because the drowned man was becoming all the more Esteban for them, and so they wept so much, for he was the most destitute, most peaceful, and most obliging man on earth, poor Esteban. So when the men returned with the news that the drowned man was not from the neighboring villages either, the women felt an opening of jubilation in the midst of their tears.

"Praise the Lord," they sighed, "he's ours!"

The men thought the fuss was only womanish frivolity. Fatigued because of the difficult nighttime inquiries, all they wanted was to get rid of the bother of the newcomer once and for all before the sun grew strong on that arid, windless day. They improvised a litter with the remains of foremasts and gaffs, tying it together with rigging so that it would bear the weight of the body until they reached the cliffs. They wanted to tie the anchor from a cargo ship to him so that he would sink easily into the deepest waves, where the fish are blind and divers die of nostalgia, and bad currents would not bring him back to shore, as had happened with other bodies. But the more they hurried, the more the women thought of ways to waste time. They walked about like startled hens, pecking with the sea charms on their breasts, some interfering on one side to put a scapular of the good wind on the drowned man, some on the other side to put a wrist compass on him, and after a great deal of *get away from there, woman, stay out of the way, look, you almost made me fall on top of the dead man,* the men began to feel mistrust in their livers and started grumbling about why so many main-altar decorations for a stranger, because no matter how many nails and holywater jars he had on him, the sharks would chew him all the same, but the women kept on piling on their junk relics, running back and forth, stumbling, while they released in sighs what they did not in tears, so that the men finally exploded with *since when has there ever been such a fuss over a drifting corpse, a drowned nobody, a piece of cold Wednesday meat.* One of the women, mortified by so much lack of care, then removed the handkerchief from the dead man's face and the men were left breathless too.

He was Esteban. It was not necessary to repeat it for them to recognize him. If they had been told Sir Walter Raleigh,[2] even they might have been impressed with his gringo accent, the macaw on his shoulder, his cannibal-killing blunderbuss, but there could be only one Esteban in the world and there he was, stretched out like a sperm whale, shoeless, wearing the pants of an undersized child, and with those stony nails that had to be cut with a knife. They had only to take the handkerchief off his face to see that he was ashamed, that it was not his fault that he was so big or so heavy or so handsome, and if he had known that this was going to happen, he would have looked for a more discreet place to drown in; seriously, I even would have tied the anchor off a galleon around my neck and staggered off a cliff like someone who doesn't like things in order not to be upsetting people now with this Wednesday dead body, as you people say, in order not to be bothering anyone with this filthy piece of cold meat that doesn't have anything to do with me. There was so much truth in his manner that even the most mistrustful men, the ones who felt the bitterness of endless nights at sea fearing that their women would tire of dreaming about them and begin to dream of drowned men, even they and others who were harder still shuddered in the marrow of their bones at Esteban's sincerity.

That was how they came to hold the most splendid funeral they could conceive of for an abandoned drowned man. Some women who had gone to get flowers in the neighboring villages returned with other women who could not believe what they had been told, and those women went back for more flowers when they saw the dead man, and they brought more and more until there were so many flowers and so many people that it was hard to walk about. At the final moment it pained them to return him to the waters as an orphan and they chose a father and mother from among the best people, and aunts and uncles and cousins, so that through him all the inhabitants of the village became kinsmen. Some sailors who heard the weeping from a distance went off course, and people heard of one who had himself tied to the mainmast, remembering ancient fables about sirens. While they fought for the privilege of carrying him on their shoulders along the steep escarpment by the cliffs, men and women became aware for the first time of the desolation of their streets, the dryness of their courtyards, the narrowness of their dreams as they faced the splendor and beauty of their drowned man. They let him go without an anchor so that he could come back if he wished and whenever he

---

[2]**Sir Walter Raleigh:** English navigator, courtier, and historian (1554–1618).

wished, and they all held their breath for the fraction of centuries the body took to fall into the abyss. They did not need to look to one another to realize that they were no longer all present, that they would never be. But they also knew that everything would be different from then on, that their houses would have wider doors, higher ceilings, and stronger floors so that Esteban's memory could go everywhere without bumping into beams and so that no one in the future would dare whisper the big boob finally died, too bad, the handsome fool has finally died, because they were going to paint their house fronts gay colors to make Esteban's memory eternal and they were going to break their backs digging for springs among the stones and planting flowers on the cliffs so that in future years at dawn the passengers on great liners would awaken, suffocated by the smell of gardens on the high seas, and the captain would have to come down from the bridge in his dress uniform, with his astrolabe,[3] his pole star, and his row of war medals and, pointing to the promontory of roses on the horizon, he would say in fourteen languages, look there, where the wind is so peaceful now that it's gone to sleep beneath the beds, over there, where the sun's so bright that the sunflowers don't know which way to turn, yes, over there, that's Esteban's village. ●

Explorations of the Text

1. Why does García Márquez subtitle the story "A Tale for Children"? What expectations does the subtitle create in the reader?
2. Why do the children play with the body? What is their attitude toward death?
3. What is the meaning of the symbolism of the vegetation and mud on the drowned man's body?
4. What are the consequences of the women's comparisons to their own men? What is the importance of identifying him as Esteban?
5. Examine the imaginary conversation about his size. How does he become "the big boob" and "the handsome fool"? Why do the villagers feel "jubilation" when Esteban becomes their drowned man?
6. Explore the men's attitudes, the funeral, and the behavior of the women. How does Esteban win the people with his sincerity?
7. Describe the ritual of the "most splendid funeral." How does the experience with the drowned man transform the people and the village?
8. Compare the transformation of the people in this story with the change in the narrator in Wright's "A Blessing."

The Reading/Writing Connection

1. Gloss and annotate the story. Consider the use of **hyperbole.**
2. React to the idea of Esteban as "the stranger" who is taken into the community. Write a short essay on this subject.

---

[3]**astrolabe:** An instrument used to observe and calculate the positions of stars and planets before the invention of the sextant.

Ideas for Writing

1. Analyze the transformation of the people and their village.
2. Discuss the symbolism of the drowned man.
3. How do the settings (village and sea) elucidate theme?
4. Look for elements of fairy tales in this story. How are they effective?

5. Compare the idea of community in García Márquez, Mukherjee, and Alexie.

6. **Write an Argument:** Without imagination, people live constricted, static lives. In an essay, argue pro or con.

Jhumpa Lahiri *(1967–)*

The Third and Final Continent   *1999*

I left India in 1964 with a certificate in commerce and the equivalent, in those days, of ten dollars to my name. For three weeks I sailed on the *SS Roma,* an Italian cargo vessel, in a cabin next to the ship's engine, across the Arabian Sea, the Red Sea, the Mediterranean, and finally to England. I lived in north London, in Finsbury Park, in a house occupied entirely by penniless Bengali bachelors like myself, at least a dozen and sometimes more, all struggling to educate and establish ourselves abroad.

I attended lectures at LSE[1] and worked at the university library to get by. We lived three or four to a room, shared a single, icy toilet, and took turns cooking pots of egg curry, which we ate with our hands on a table covered with newspapers. Apart from our jobs we had few responsibilities. On weekends we lounged barefoot in drawstring pajamas, drinking tea and smoking Rothmans, or set out to watch cricket at Lord's. Some weekends the house was crammed with still more Bengalis, to whom we had introduced ourselves at the greengrocer, or on the Tube, and we made yet more egg curry, and played Mukesh[2] on a Grundig reel-to-reel, and soaked our dirty dishes in the bathtub. Every now and then someone in the house moved out, to live with a woman whom his family back in Calcutta had determined he was to wed. In 1969, when I was thirty-six years old, my own marriage was arranged. Around the same time I was offered a full-time job in America, in the processing department of a library at MIT. The salary was generous enough to support a wife, and I was honored to be hired by a world-famous university, and so I obtained a sixth-preference green card, and prepared to travel farther still.

By now I had enough money to go by plane. I flew first to Calcutta, to attend my wedding, and a week later I flew to Boston, to begin my new job. During the flight I read *The Student Guide to North America,* a paperback volume that I'd bought before leaving London, for seven shillings six pence on Tottenham Court Road, for although I was no longer a student I was on a budget all the same. I learned that Americans drove on the right side of the road, not the left, and that they called a lift an elevator and an engaged phone busy. "The pace of life in North America is different from Britain as you will soon discover," the guidebook informed me. "Everybody feels he must get to the top. Don't

---

[1] **LSE:** London School of Economics.   [2] **Mukesh:** Popular playback singer of popular music and classical music in India.

expect an English cup of tea." As the plane began its descent over Boston Harbor, the pilot announced the weather and time, and that President Nixon had declared a national holiday: two American men had landed on the moon. Several passengers cheered. "God bless America!" one of them hollered. Across the aisle, I saw a woman praying.

I spent my first night at the YMCA in Central Square, Cambridge, an inexpensive accommodation recommended by my guidebook. It was walking distance from MIT, and steps from the post office and a supermarket called Purity Supreme. The room contained a cot, a desk, and a small wooden cross on one wall. A sign on the door said cooking was strictly forbidden. A bare window overlooked Massachusetts Avenue, a major thoroughfare with traffic in both directions. Car horns, shrill and prolonged, blared one after another. Flashing sirens heralded endless emergencies, and a fleet of buses rumbled past, their doors opening and closing with a powerful hiss, throughout the night. The noise was constantly distracting, at times suffocating. I felt it deep in my ribs, just as I had felt the furious drone of the engine on the *SS Roma*. But there was no ship's deck to escape to, no glittering ocean to thrill my soul, no breeze to cool my face, no one to talk to. I was too tired to pace the gloomy corridors of the YMCA in my drawstring pajamas. Instead I sat at the desk and stared out the window, at the city hall of Cambridge and a row of small shops. In the morning I reported to my job at the Dewey Library, a beige fortlike building by Memorial Drive. I also opened a bank account, rented a post office box, and bought a plastic bowl and a spoon at Woolworth's, a store whose name I recognized from London. I went to Purity Supreme, wandering up and down the aisles, converting ounces to grams and comparing prices to things in England. In the end I bought a small carton of milk and a box of cornflakes. This was my first meal in America. I ate it at my desk. I preferred it to hamburgers or hot dogs, the only alternative I could afford in the coffee shops on Massachusetts Avenue, and, besides, at the time I had yet to consume any beef. Even the simple chore of buying milk was new to me; in London we'd had bottles delivered each morning to our door.

In a week I had adjusted, more or less. I ate cornflakes and milk, morning and night, and bought some bananas for variety, slicing them into the bowl with the edge of my spoon. In addition I bought tea bags and a flask, which the salesman in Woolworth's referred to as a thermos (a flask, he informed me, was used to store whiskey, another thing I had never consumed). For the price of one cup of tea at a coffee shop, I filled the flask with boiling water on my way to work each morning, and brewed the four cups I drank in the course of a day. I bought a larger carton of milk, and learned to leave it on the shaded part of the windowsill, as I had seen another resident at the YMCA do. To pass the time in the evenings I read the *Boston Globe* downstairs, in a spacious room with stained-glass windows. I read every article and advertisement, so that I would grow familiar with things, and when my eyes grew tired I slept. Only I did not sleep well. Each night I had to keep the window wide open; it was the only source of air in the stifling room, and the noise was intolerable. I would lie on the cot with my fingers pressed into my ears, but when I drifted off to sleep my hands fell away, and the noise of the traffic would wake me up again. Pigeon feathers drifted onto the windowsill, and one evening, when I poured milk over my cornflakes, I saw that it had soured. Nevertheless I resolved to stay at the YMCA for six weeks, until my wife's passport and green card were ready. Once she arrived I would have to rent a proper apartment, and from time to time I studied the classified section of the newspaper, or stopped in at the housing office at MIT during my lunch break, to see what was available in my price range. It was in this manner that I discovered a room for immediate occupancy, in a house on a quiet street, the listing said, for eight dollars per week. I copied the number into my guidebook and dialed from a pay telephone, sorting through the coins with which I was still unfamiliar, smaller and lighter than shillings, heavier and brighter than *paisas*.

"Who is speaking?" a woman demanded. Her voice was bold and clamorous.

"Yes, good afternoon, madame. I am calling about the room for rent."

"Harvard or Tech?"

"I beg your pardon?"

"Are you from Harvard or Tech?"

Gathering that Tech referred to the Massachusetts Institute of Technology, I replied, "I work at Dewey Library," adding tentatively, "at Tech."

"I only rent rooms to boys from Harvard or Tech!"

"Yes, madame."

I was given an address and an appointment for seven o'clock that evening. Thirty minutes before the hour I set out, my guidebook in my pocket, my breath fresh with Listerine. I turned down a street shaded with trees, perpendicular to Massachusetts Avenue. Stray blades of grass poked between the cracks of the footpath. In spite of the heat I wore a coat and a tie, regarding the event as I would any other interview; I had never lived in the home of a person who was not Indian. The house, surrounded by a chain-link fence, was off-white with dark brown trim. Unlike the stucco row house I'd lived in in London, this house, fully detached, was covered with wooden shingles, with a tangle of forsythia bushes plastered against the front and sides. When I pressed the calling bell, the woman with whom I had spoken on the phone hollered from what seemed to be just the other side of the door, "One minute, please!"

Several minutes later the door was opened by a tiny, extremely old woman. A mass of snowy hair was arranged like a small sack on top of her head. As I stepped into the house she sat down on a wooden bench positioned at the bottom of a narrow carpeted staircase. Once she was settled on the bench, in a small pool of light, she peered up at me with undivided attention. She wore a long black skirt that spread like a stiff tent to the floor, and a starched white shirt edged with ruffles at the throat and cuffs. Her hands, folded together in her lap, had long pallid fingers, with swollen knuckles and tough yellow nails. Age had battered her features so that she almost resembled a man, with sharp, shrunken eyes and prominent creases on either side of her nose. Her lips, chapped and faded, had nearly disappeared, and her eyebrows were missing altogether. Nevertheless she looked fierce.

"Lock up!" she commanded. She shouted even though I stood only a few feet away. "Fasten the chain and firmly press that button on the knob! This is the first thing you shall do when you enter, is that clear?"

I locked the door as directed and examined the house. Next to the bench on which the woman sat was a small round table, its legs fully concealed, much like the woman's, by a skirt of lace. The table held a lamp, a transistor radio, a leather change purse with a silver clasp, and a telephone. A thick wooden cane coated with a layer of dust was propped against one side. There was a parlor to my right, lined with bookcases and filled with shabby claw-footed furniture. In the corner of the parlor I saw a grand piano with its top down, piled with papers. The piano's bench was missing; it seemed to be the one on which the woman was sitting. Somewhere in the house a clock chimed seven times.

"You're punctual!" the woman proclaimed. "I expect you shall be so with the rent!"

10

15

"I have a letter, madame." In my jacket pocket was a letter confirming my employment from MIT, which I had brought along to prove that I was indeed from Tech.

She stared at the letter, then handed it back to me carefully, gripping it with her fingers as if it were a dinner plate heaped with food instead of a sheet of paper. She did not wear glasses, and I wondered if she'd read a word of it. "The last boy was always late! Still owes me eight dollars! Harvard boys aren't what they used to be! Only Harvard and Tech in this house! How's Tech, boy?" 20

"It is very well."

"You checked the lock?"

"Yes, madame."

She slapped the space beside her on the bench with one hand, and told me to sit down. For a moment she was silent. Then she intoned as if she alone possessed this knowledge:

"There is an American flag on the moon!" 25

"Yes, madame." Until then I had not thought very much about the moon shot. It was in the newspaper, of course, article upon article. The astronauts had landed on the shores of the Sea of Tranquillity, I had read, traveling farther than anyone in the history of civilization. For a few hours they explored the moon's surface. They gathered rocks in their pockets, described their surroundings (a magnificent desolation, according to one astronaut), spoke by phone to the president, and planted a flag in lunar soil. The voyage was hailed as man's most awesome achievement. I had seen full-page photographs in the *Globe,* of the astronauts in their inflated costumes, and read about what certain people in Boston had been doing at the exact moment the astronauts landed, on a Sunday afternoon. A man said that he was operating a swan boat with a radio pressed to his ear; a woman had been baking rolls for her grandchildren.

The woman bellowed, "A flag on the moon, boy! I heard it on the radio! Isn't that splendid?"

"Yes, madame."

But she was not satisfied with my reply. Instead she commanded, "Say 'splendid'!"

I was both baffled and somewhat insulted by the request. It reminded me of the way I was taught multiplication tables as a child, repeating after the master, sitting cross-legged, without shoes or pencils, on the floor of my one-room Tollygunge school. It also reminded me of my wedding, when I had repeated endless Sanskrit verses after the priest, verses I barely understood, which joined me to my wife. I said nothing. 30

"Say 'splendid'!" the woman bellowed once again.

"Splendid," I murmured. I had to repeat the word a second time at the top of my lungs, so she could hear. I am soft-spoken by nature and was especially reluctant to raise my voice to an elderly woman whom I had met only moments ago, but she did not appear to be offended. If anything the reply pleased her because her next command was:

"Go see the room!"

I rose from the bench and mounted the narrow carpeted staircase. There were five doors, two on either side of an equally narrow hallway, and one at the opposite end. Only one door was partly open. The room contained a twin bed under a sloping ceiling, a brown oval rug, a basin with an exposed pipe, and a chest of drawers. One door, painted white, led to a closet, another to a toilet and a tub. The walls were covered with gray and ivory striped paper. The window was open; net curtains stirred in the breeze. I lifted them away and inspected the view: a small back yard, with a few fruit trees and an empty clothesline. I was satisfied. From the bottom of the stairs I heard the woman demand, "What is your decision?"

When I returned to the foyer and told her, she picked up the leather change purse 35 on the table, opened the clasp, fished about with her fingers, and produced a key on a thin wire hoop. She informed me that there was a kitchen at the back of the house, accessible through the parlor. I was welcome to use the stove as long as I left it as I found it. Sheets and towels were provided, but keeping them clean was my own responsibility. The rent was due Friday mornings on the ledge above the piano keys. "And no lady visitors!"

"I am a married man, madame." It was the first time I had announced this fact to anyone.

But she had not heard. "No lady visitors!" she insisted. She introduced herself as Mrs. Croft.

My wife's name was Mala. The marriage had been arranged by my older brother and his wife. I regarded the proposition with neither objection nor enthusiasm. It was a duty expected of me, as it was expected of every man. She was the daughter of a schoolteacher in Beleghata. I was told that she could cook, knit, embroider, sketch landscapes, and recite poems by Tagore, but these talents could not make up for the fact that she did not possess a fair complexion, and so a string of men had rejected her to her face. She was twenty-seven, an age when her parents had begun to fear that she would never marry, and so they were willing to ship their only child halfway across the world in order to save her from spinsterhood.

For five nights we shared a bed. Each of those nights, after applying cold cream and braiding her hair, which she tied up at the end with a black cotton string, she turned from me and wept; she missed her parents. Although I would be leaving the country in a few days, custom dictated that she was now a part of my household, and for the next six weeks she was to live with my brother and his wife, cooking, cleaning, serving tea and sweets to guests. I did nothing to console her. I lay on my own side of the bed, reading my guidebook by flashlight and anticipating my journey. At times I thought of the tiny room on the other side of the wall which had belonged to my mother. Now the room was practically empty; the wooden pallet on which she'd once slept was piled with trunks and old bedding. Nearly six years ago, before leaving for London, I had watched her die on that bed, had found her playing with her excrement in her final days. Before we cremated her I had cleaned each of her fingernails with a hairpin, and then, because my brother could not bear it, I had assumed the role of eldest son, and had touched the flame to her temple to release her tormented soul to heaven.

The next morning I moved into the room in Mrs. Croft's house. When I unlocked the 40 door I saw that she was sitting on the piano bench, on the same side as the previous evening. She wore the same black skirt, the same starched white blouse, and had her hands folded together the same way in her lap. She looked so much the same that I wondered if she'd spent the whole night on the bench. I put my suitcase upstairs, filled my flask with boiling water in the kitchen, and headed off to work. That evening when I came home from the university, she was still there.

"Sit down, boy!" She slapped the space beside her.

I perched beside her on the bench. I had a bag of groceries with me—more milk, more cornflakes, and more bananas, for my inspection of the kitchen earlier in the day had revealed no spare pots, pans, or cooking utensils. There were only two saucepans in the refrigerator, both containing some orange broth, and a copper kettle on the stove.

"Good evening, madame."

She asked me if I had checked the lock. I told her I had.

For a moment she was silent. Then suddenly she declared, with the equal measures of disbelief and delight as the night before, "There's an American flag on the moon, boy!"

"Yes, madame."

"A flag on the moon! Isn't that splendid?"

I nodded, dreading what I knew was coming. "Yes, madame."

"Say 'splendid'!"

This time I paused, looking to either side in case anyone were there to overhear me, though I knew perfectly well that the house was empty. I felt like an idiot. But it was a small enough thing to ask. "Splendid!" I cried out.

Within days it became our routine. In the mornings when I left for the library Mrs. Croft was either hidden away in her bedroom, on the other side of the staircase, or she was sitting on the bench, oblivious to my presence, listening to the news or classical music on the radio. But each evening when I returned the same thing happened: she slapped the bench, ordered me to sit down, declared that there was a flag on the moon, and declared that it was splendid. I said it was splendid, too, and then we sat in silence. As awkward as it was, and as endless as it felt to me then, the nightly encounter lasted only about ten minutes; inevitably she would drift off to sleep, her head falling abruptly toward her chest, leaving me free to retire to my room. By then, of course, there was no flag standing on the moon. The astronauts, I had read in the paper, had seen it fall before they flew back to Earth. But I did not have the heart to tell her.

Friday morning, when my first week's rent was due, I went to the piano in the parlor to place my money on the ledge. The piano keys were dull and discolored. When I pressed one, it made no sound at all. I had put eight one-dollar bills in an envelope and written Mrs. Croft's name on the front of it. I was not in the habit of leaving money unmarked and unattended. From where I stood I could see the profile of her tent-shaped skirt. She was sitting on the bench, listening to the radio. It seemed unnecessary to make her get up and walk all the way to the piano. I never saw her walking about, and assumed, from the cane always propped against the round table at her side, that she did so with difficulty. When I approached the bench she peered up at me and demanded:

"What is your business?"

"The rent, madame."

"On the ledge above the piano keys!"

"I have it here." I extended the envelope toward her, but her fingers, folded together in her lap, did not budge. I bowed slightly and lowered the envelope, so that it hovered just above her hands. After a moment she accepted, and nodded her head.

That night when I came home, she did not slap the bench, but out of habit I sat beside her as usual. She asked me if I had checked the lock, but she mentioned nothing about the flag on the moon. Instead she said:

"It was very kind of you!"

"I beg your pardon, madame?"

"Very kind of you!"

She was still holding the envelope in her hands.

■ ■ ■

On Sunday there was a knock on my door. An elderly woman introduced herself: she was Mrs. Croft's daughter, Helen. She walked into the room and looked at each of the walls as if for signs of change, glancing at the shirts that hung in the closet, the neckties draped over the doorknob, the box of cornflakes on the chest of drawers, the dirty bowl and spoon in the basin. She was short and thick-waisted, with cropped silver hair and bright pink lipstick. She wore a sleeveless summer dress, a row of white plastic beads, and spectacles on a chain that hung like a swing against her chest. The backs of her legs were mapped with dark blue veins, and her upper arms sagged like the flesh of a roasted eggplant. She told me she lived in Arlington, a town farther up Massachusetts Avenue. "I come once a week to bring Mother groceries. Has she sent you packing yet?"

"It is very well, madame."

"Some of the boys run screaming. But I think she likes you. You're the first boarder she's ever referred to as a gentleman."

"Not at all, madame." 65

She looked at me, noticing my bare feet (I still felt strange wearing shoes indoors, and always removed them before entering my room). "Are you new to Boston?"

"New to America, madame."

"From?" She raised her eyebrows.

"I am from Calcutta, India."

"Is that right? We had a Brazilian fellow, about a year ago. You'll find Cambridge 70 a very international city."

I nodded, and began to wonder how long our conversation would last. But at that moment we heard Mrs. Croft's electrifying voice rising up the stairs. When we stepped into the hallway we heard her hollering:

"You are to come downstairs immediately!"

"What is it?" Helen hollered back.

"Immediately!"

I put on my shoes at once. Helen sighed. 75

We walked down the staircase. It was too narrow for us to descend side by side, so I followed Helen, who seemed to be in no hurry, and complained at one point that she had a bad knee. "Have you been walking without your cane?" Helen called out. "You know you're not supposed to walk without that cane." She paused, resting her hand on the banister, and looked back at me. "She slips sometimes."

For the first time Mrs. Croft seemed vulnerable. I pictured her on the floor in front of the bench, flat on her back, staring at the ceiling, her feet pointing in opposite directions. But when we reached the bottom of the staircase she was sitting there as usual, her hands folded together in her lap. Two grocery bags were at her feet. When we stood before her she did not slap the bench, or ask us to sit down. She glared.

"What is it, Mother?"

"It's improper!"

"What's improper?" 80

"It is improper for a lady and gentleman who are not married to one another to hold a private conversation without a chaperone!"

Helen said she was sixty-eight years old, old enough to be my mother, but Mrs. Croft insisted that Helen and I speak to each other downstairs, in the parlor. She added that it was also improper for a lady of Helen's station to reveal her age, and to wear a dress so high above the ankle.

"For your information, Mother, it's 1969. What would you do if you actually left the house one day and saw a girl in a miniskirt?"

Mrs. Croft sniffed. "I'd have her arrested."

Helen shook her head and picked up one of the grocery bags. I picked up the other one, and followed her through the parlor and into the kitchen. The bags were filled with cans of soup, which Helen opened up one by one with a few cranks of a can opener. She tossed the old soup in the saucepans into the sink, rinsed the pans under the tap, filled them with soup from the newly opened cans, and put them back in the refrigerator. "A few years ago she could still open the cans herself," Helen said. "She hates that I do it for her now. But the piano killed her hands." She put on her spectacles, glanced at the cupboards, and spotted my tea bags. "Shall we have a cup?"

I filled the kettle on the stove. "I beg your pardon, madame. The piano?"

"She used to give lessons. For forty years. It was how she raised us after my father died." Helen put her hands on her hips, staring at the open refrigerator. She reached into the back, pulled out a wrapped stock of butter, frowned, and tossed it into the garbage. "That ought to do it," she said, and put the unopened cans of soup in the cupboard. I sat at the table and watched as Helen washed the dirty dishes, tied up the garbage bag, watered a spider plant over the sink, and poured boiling water into two cups. She handed one to me without milk, the string of the tea bag trailing over the side, and sat down at the table.

"Excuse me, madame, but is it enough?"

Helen took a sip of her tea. Her lipstick left a smiling pink stain on the inside rim of the cup. "Is what enough?"

"The soup in the pans. Is it enough food for Mrs. Croft?"

"She won't eat anything else. She stopped eating solids after she turned one hundred. That was, let's see, three years ago."

I was mortified. I had assumed Mrs. Croft was in her eighties, perhaps as old as ninety. I had never known a person who had lived for over a century. That this person was a widow who lived alone mortified me further still. It was widowhood that had driven my own mother insane. My father, who worked as a clerk at the General Post Office of Calcutta, died of encephalitis when I was sixteen. My mother refused to adjust to life without him; instead she sank deeper into a world of darkness from which neither I, nor my brother, nor concerned relatives, nor psychiatric clinics on Rash Behari Avenue could save her. What pained me most was to see her so unguarded, to hear her burp after meals or expel gas in front of company without the slightest embarrassment. After my father's death my brother abandoned his schooling and began to work in the jute mill he would eventually manage, in order to keep the household running. And so it was my job to sit by my mother's feet and study for my exams as she counted and recounted the bracelets on her arm as if they were the beads of an abacus. We tried to keep an eye on her. Once she had wandered half naked to the tram depot before we were able to bring her inside again.

"I am happy to warm Mrs. Croft's soup in the evenings," I suggested, removing the tea bag from my cup and squeezing out the liquor. "It is no trouble."

Helen looked at her watch, stood up, and poured the rest of her tea into the sink. "I wouldn't if I were you. That's the sort of thing that would kill her altogether."

■ ■ ■

That evening, when Helen had gone back to Arlington and Mrs. Croft and I were alone ₉₅ again, I began to worry. Now that I knew how very old she was, I worried that something would happen to her in the middle of the night, or when I was out during the day. As vigorous as her voice was, and imperious as she seemed, I knew that even a scratch or a cough could kill a person that old; each day she lived, I knew, was something of a miracle. Although Helen had seemed friendly enough, a small part of me worried that she might accuse me of negligence if anything were to happen. Helen didn't seem worried. She came and went, bringing soup for Mrs. Croft, one Sunday after the next.

In this manner the six weeks of that summer passed. I came home each evening, after my hours at the library, and spent a few minutes on the piano bench with Mrs. Croft. I gave her a bit of my company, and assured her that I had checked the lock, and told her that the flag on the moon was splendid. Some evenings I sat beside her long after she had drifted off to sleep, still in awe of how many years she had spent on this earth. At times I tried to picture the world she had been born into, in 1866—a world, I imagined, filled with women in long black skirts, and chaste conversations in the parlor. Now, when I looked at her hands, with their swollen knuckles folded together in her lap, I imagined them smooth and slim, striking the piano keys. At times I came downstairs before going to sleep, to make sure she was sitting upright on the bench, or was safe in her bedroom. On Fridays I made sure to put the rent in her hands. There was nothing I could do for her beyond these simple gestures. I was not her son, and apart from those eight dollars, I owed her nothing.

At the end of August, Mala's passport and green card were ready. I received a telegram with her flight information; my brother's house in Calcutta had no telephone. Around that time I also received a letter from her, written only a few days after we had parted. There was no salutation; addressing me by name would have assumed an intimacy we had not yet discovered. It contained only a few lines. "I write in English in preparation for the journey. Here I am very much lonely. Is it very cold there. Is there snow. Yours, Mala."

I was not touched by her words. We had spent only a handful of days in each other's company. And yet we were bound together; for six weeks she had worn an iron bangle on her wrist, and applied vermilion powder to the part in the hair, to signify to the world that she was a bride. In those six weeks I regarded her arrival as I would the arrival of a coming month, or season—something inevitable, but meaningless at the time. So little did I know her that, while details of her face sometimes rose to my memory, I could not conjure up the whole of it.

A few days after receiving the letter, as I was walking to work in the morning, I saw an Indian woman on the other side of Massachusetts Avenue, wearing a sari with its free end nearly dragging on the footpath, and pushing a child in a stroller. An American woman with a small black dog on a leash was walking to one side of her. Suddenly the dog began barking. From the other side of the street I watched as the Indian woman, startled, stopped in her path, at which point the dog leapt up and seized the end of the sari between its teeth. The American woman scolded the dog, appeared to apologize, and walked quickly away, leaving the Indian woman to fix her sari in the middle of the footpath, and quiet her crying child. She did not see me standing there, and eventually she continued on her way. Such a mishap, I realized that morning, would soon be my concern. It was my duty to take care of Mala, to welcome her and protect her. I would have to buy her her first pair of snow boots, her first winter coat. I would have to tell her which streets to avoid, which way the traffic came, tell her to wear her sari so that the free end did not drag on the footpath. A five-mile separation from her parents, I recalled with some irritation, had caused her to weep.

Unlike Mala, I was used to it all by then: used to cornflakes and milk, used to Helen's visits, used to sitting on the bench with Mrs. Croft. The only thing I was not used to was Mala. Nevertheless I did what I had to do. I went to the housing office at MIT and found a furnished apartment a few blocks away, with a double bed and a private kitchen and bath, for forty dollars a week. One last Friday I handed Mrs. Croft eight one-dollar bills in an envelope, brought my suitcase downstairs, and informed her that I was moving. She put my key into her change purse. The last thing she asked me to do was hand her the cane propped against the table, so that she could walk to the door and lock it behind me. "Good-bye, then," she said, and retreated back into the house. I did not expect any display of emotion, but I was disappointed all the same. I was only a boarder, a man who paid her a bit of money and passed in and out of her home for six weeks. Compared to a century, it was no time at all.

At the airport I recognized Mala immediately. The free end of her sari did not drag on the floor, but was draped in a sign of bridal modesty over her head, just as it had draped my mother until the day my father died. Her thin brown arms were stacked with gold bracelets, a small red circle was painted on her forehead, and the edges of her feet were tinted with a decorative red dye. I did not embrace her, or kiss her, or take her hand. Instead I asked her, speaking Bengali for the first time in America, if she was hungry.

She hesitated, then nodded yes.

I told her I had prepared some egg curry at home. "What did they give you to eat on the plane?"

"I didn't eat."

"All the way from Calcutta?"

"The menu said oxtail soup."

"But surely there were other items."

"The thought of eating an ox's tail made me lose my appetite."

When we arrived home, Mala opened up one of her suitcases, and presented me with two pullover sweaters, both made with bright blue wool, which she had knitted in the course of our separation, one with a V neck, the other covered with cables. I tried them on; both were tight under the arms. She had also brought me two new pairs of drawstring pajamas, a letter from my brother, and a packet of loose Darjeeling tea. I had no present for her apart from the egg curry. We sat at a bare table, each of us staring at our plates. We ate with our hands, another thing I had not yet done in America.

"The house is nice," she said. "Also the egg curry." With her left hand she held the end of her sari to her chest, so it would not slip off her head.

"I don't know many recipes."

She nodded, peeling the skin off each of her potatoes before eating them. At one point the sari slipped to her shoulders. She readjusted it at once.

"There is no need to cover your head," I said. "I don't mind. It doesn't matter here."

She kept it covered anyway.

I waited to get used to her, to her presence at my side, at my table and in my bed, but a week later we were still strangers. I still was not used to coming home to an apartment that smelled of steamed rice, and finding that the basin in the bathroom was always wiped clean, our two toothbrushes lying side by side, a cake of Pears soap from India resting in the soap dish. I was not used to the fragrance of the coconut oil she rubbed every other night into her scalp, or the delicate sound her bracelets made as she moved about the apartment. In the mornings she was always awake before I was. The first morning when I came into the kitchen she had heated up the leftovers and set a plate with a spoonful of salt on its edge on the table, assuming I would eat rice for breakfast, as most Bengali husbands did. I told her cereal would do, and the next morning when I came into the kitchen she had already poured the cornflakes into my bowl. One morning she walked with me down Massachusetts Avenue to MIT, where I gave her a short tour of the campus. On the way we stopped at a hardware store and I made a copy of the key, so that she could let herself into the apartment. The next morning before I left for work she asked me for a few dollars. I parted with them reluctantly, but I knew that this, too, was now normal. When I came home from work there was a potato peeler in the kitchen drawer, and a tablecloth on the table, and chicken curry made with fresh garlic and ginger on the stove. We did not have a television in those days. After dinner I read the newspaper, while Mala sat at the kitchen table, working on a cardigan for herself with more of the bright blue wool, or writing letters home.

At the end of our first week, on Friday, I suggested going out. Mala set down her knitting and disappeared into the bathroom. When she emerged I regretted the suggestion; she had put on a clean silk sari and extra bracelets, and coiled her hair with a flattering side part on top of her head. She was prepared as if for a party, or at the very least for the cinema, but I had no such destination in mind. The evening air was balmy. We walked several blocks down Massachusetts Avenue, looking into the windows of restaurants and shops. Then, without thinking, I led her down the quiet street where for so many nights I had walked alone.

"This is where I lived before you came," I said, stopping at Mrs. Croft's chain-link fence.

"In such a big house?"

"I had a small room upstairs. At the back."

"Who else lives there?" 120

"A very old woman."

"With her family?"

"Alone."

"But who takes care of her?"

I opened the gate. "For the most part she takes care of herself." 125

I wondered if Mrs. Croft would remember me; I wondered if she had a new boarder to sit with her on the bench each evening. When I pressed the bell I expected the same long wait as that day of our first meeting, when I did not have a key. But this time the door was opened almost immediately, by Helen. Mrs. Croft was not sitting on the bench. The bench was gone.

"Hello there," Helen said, smiling with her bright pink lips at Mala. "Mother's in the parlor. Will you be visiting awhile?"

"As you wish, madame."

"Then I think I'll run to the store, if you don't mind. She had a little accident. We can't leave her alone these days, not even for a minute."

I locked the door after Helen and walked into the parlor. Mrs. Croft was lying flat   130
on her back, her head on a peach-colored cushion, a thin white quilt spread over her
body. Her hands were folded together on top of her chest. When she saw me she pointed
at the sofa, and told me to sit down. I took my place as directed, but Mala wandered
over to the piano and sat on the bench, which was now positioned where it belonged.

"I broke my hip!" Mrs. Croft announced, as if no time had passed.

"Oh dear, madame."

"I fell off the bench!"

"I am so sorry, madame."

"It was the middle of the night! Do you know what I did, boy?"   135

I shook my head.

"I called the police!"

She stared up at the ceiling and grinned sedately, exposing a crowded row of long
gray teeth. Not one was missing. "What do you say to that, boy?"

As stunned as I was, I knew what I had to say. With no hesitation at all, I cried
out, "Splendid!"

Mala laughed then. Her voice was full of kindness, her eyes bright with amuse-   140
ment. I had never heard her laugh before, and it was loud enough so that Mrs. Croft
had heard, too. She turned to Mala and glared.

"Who is she, boy?"

"She is my wife, madame."

Mrs. Croft pressed her head at an angle against the cushion to get a better look.
"Can you play the piano?"

"No, madame," Mala replied.

"Then stand up!"   145

Mala rose to her feet, adjusting the end of her sari over her head and holding it to
her chest, and, for the first time since her arrival, I felt sympathy. I remembered my first
days in London, learning how to take the Tube to Russell Square, riding an escalator
for the first time, being unable to understand that when the man cried "piper" it meant
"paper," being unable to decipher, for a whole year, that the conductor said "mind the
gap" as the train pulled away from each station. Like me, Mala had traveled far from
home, not knowing where she was going, or what she would find, for no reason other
than to be my wife. As strange as it seemed, I knew in my heart that one day her death
would affect me, and stranger still, that mine would affect her. I wanted somehow to
explain this to Mrs. Croft, who was still scrutinizing Mala from top to toe with what
seemed to be placid disdain. I wondered if Mrs. Croft had ever seen a woman in a sari,
with a dot painted on her forehead and bracelets stacked on her wrists. I wondered
what she would object to. I wondered if she could see the red dye still vivid on Mala's
feet, all but obscured by the bottom edge of her sari. At last Mrs. Croft declared, with
the equal measures of disbelief and delight I knew well:

"She is a perfect lady!"

Now it was I who laughed. I did so quietly, and Mrs. Croft did not hear me. But
Mala had heard, and, for the first time, we looked at each other and smiled.

I like to think of that moment in Mrs. Croft's parlor as the moment when the distance
between Mala and me began to lessen. Although we were not yet fully in love, I like to

think of the months that followed as a honeymoon of sorts. Together we explored the city and met other Bengalis, some of whom are still friends today. We discovered that a man named Bill sold fresh fish on Prospect Street, and that a shop in Harvard Square called Cardullo's sold bay leaves and cloves. In the evenings we walked to the Charles River to watch sailboats drift across the water, or had ice cream cones in Harvard Yard. We bought an Instamatic camera with which to document our life together, and I took pictures of her posing in front of the Prudential building, so that she could send them to her parents. At night we kissed, shy at first but quickly bold, and discovered pleasure and solace in each other's arms. I told her about my voyage on the SS *Roma,* and about Finsbury Park and the YMCA, and my evenings on the bench with Mrs. Croft. When I told her stories about my mother, she wept. It was Mala who consoled me when, reading the *Globe* one evening, I came across Mrs. Croft's obituary. I had not thought of her in several months—by then those six weeks of the summer were already a remote interlude in my past—but when I learned of her death I was stricken, so much so that when Mala looked up from her knitting she found me staring at the wall, the newspaper neglected in my lap, unable to speak. Mrs. Croft's was the first death I mourned in America, for hers was the first life I had admired; she had left this world at last, ancient and alone, never to return.

As for me, I have not strayed much farther. Mala and I live in a town about twenty 150 miles from Boston, on a tree-lined street much like Mrs. Croft's, in a house we own, with a garden that saves us from buying tomatoes in summer, and room for guests. We are American citizens now, so that we can collect social security when it is time. Though we visit Calcutta every few years, and bring back more drawstring pajamas and Darjeeling tea, we have decided to grow old here. I work in a small college library. We have a son who attends Harvard University. Mala no longer drapes the end of her sari over her head, or weeps at night for her parents, but occasionally she weeps for our son. So we drive to Cambridge to visit him, or bring him home for a weekend, so that he can eat rice with us with his hands, and speak in Bengali, things we sometimes worry he will no longer do after we die.

Whenever we make that drive, I always make it a point to take Massachusetts Avenue, in spite of the traffic. I barely recognize the buildings now, but each time I am there I return instantly to those six weeks as if they were only the other day, and I slow down and point to Mrs. Croft's street, saying to my son, here was my first home in America, where I lived with a woman who was 103. "Remember?" Mala says, and smiles, amazed, as I am, that there was ever a time that we were strangers. My son always expresses his astonishment, not at Mrs. Croft's age, but at how little I paid in rent, a fact nearly as inconceivable to him as a flag on the moon was to a woman born in 1866. In my son's eyes I see the ambition that had first hurled me across the world. In a few years he will graduate and pave his way, alone and unprotected. But I remind myself that he has a father who is still living, a mother who is happy and strong. Whenever he is discouraged, I tell him that if I can survive on three continents, then there is no obstacle he cannot conquer. While the astronauts, heroes forever, spent mere hours on the moon, I have remained in this new world for nearly thirty years. I know that my achievement is quite ordinary. I am not the only man to seek his fortune far from home, and certainly I am not the first. Still, there are times I am bewildered by each mile I have traveled, each meal I have eaten, each person I have known, each room in which I have slept. As ordinary as it all appears, there are times when it is beyond my imagination. ●

Explorations of the Text

1. Describe the point of view of the narrator. What impact does this narrative perspective have?
2. Discuss the narrator's interactions with Mrs. Croft. In what ways are they both outsiders in North American society?
3. What does he learn from his experiences with Mrs. Croft? How does his relationship with her prepare him for his marriage? How does the narrator change as the story progresses?
4. What possible interpretations exist for the phrase, "the third and final continent"? What views do you gain of the immigrant experience in North America?
5. Explore the significance of the moon landing. How does the symbol develop themes of the story?

The Reading/Writing Connection

1. Do a freewrite on the topic of exile.

2. **Write an Argument:** Argue for or against arranged marriage.

Ideas for Writing

1. Explore the symbolism of the "third and final continent." How many different "third . . . continents" are there in this story? How do they intersect?

Bharati Mukherjee   *(1940–)*

Even Macau Girls Get the Blues   *1988*

I was born in a *hidalgo* with ochre walls and a red-tile roof in the leafy Fontainhas neighborhood of Panjim[1] when Goa[2] was still a Portuguese colony. *Hidalgo* was Mama's word for the dank, decrepit, verandah-wrapped house Father, Mama and I lived in. Though Mama was as cinnamon-brown as Father and I were, she claimed unadulterated Portuguese ancestry. She insisted that she was a direct descendant of the Portuguese viceroy who, over a hundred years ago, had founded Panjim. These days Panjim is known by its Indian name, Panaji; and Mama has made herself a fun life with a much younger husband in Belize.[3]

My late father, Jose Valladares, was the only one of the five watch-and-fine-jewelry-repairing Valladares brothers to stay on when India "liberated" us from Portugal. All my paternal uncles ran off to Australia or to Canada with their large families. Many of our Fontainhas neighbors, too, got out as fast as they could find jobs in other countries. Dr. Farias, the periodontist who'd owned the showy pink house across the street, fled to Perth.[4] Tristao Salgado, the bachelor actuary, vanished into the snows of Calgary.[5]

---

[1]**Panjim:** Capital of the Indian state of Goa.   [2]**Goa:** Indian state and former Portuguese colony on the Malabar coast.   [3]**Belize:** Independent state in Central America between Mexico and Guatamala.   [4]**Perth:** City in Western Australia.   [5]**Calgary:** City in Alberta, Canada.

My best friend, Seleena Pinto, was less lucky. She and all her brothers and sisters-in-law ended up in Maputo.[6] The three Misses Dyed-Hair De Souzas, school teachers who'd taught elocution and penmanship to both Mama and me, set up a "charm school" in Karachi.[7]

Father, Mama and I were the only ones to stay put in Fontainhas through the monsoon season of 1972. Then, early in September of that year, Father died of cholera, and Mama merry-widowed her way to Lisboa.[8]

The morning we buried Father, I shared with Mama my fantasy of learning the watch-repairing trade and keeping the Valladares reputation going. But Mama recommended that I take my half of whatever we got from the sale of the *hidalgo* and chase love and luck in a country where people still cared for fado.[9] She took her half and vanished within a month of the funeral. That Christmas, she sea-mailed me a photo of herself, looking pretty sleek in a white bathing suit. The photo changed my life. Philomena Valladares had been over-cautious or cowardly. I quit my nothing job as a shipping clerk, closed down my savings account, and bought myself a medium-quality forged Portuguese passport under a new name, Maria Pinto.

Maria Pinto looked for love and found heartbreak first in Penang,[10] then in Hong Kong. Then in the over-ripened month of August the following year, she took the ferry from Hong Kong and slipped into Macau.[11]

The cheap *hospedaria*[12] in Macau that I rented a room in was run by a Macanese widow named Mrs. Ribeiro. She looked to me to be about my mother's age, which is fifty-three. Mrs. Ribeiro had a motherly heart, a girlish waist, a love of poetry and a passion for gambling. Maybe it was the gambler in her that worked to my advantage. She not only didn't question the authenticity of my passport, but she introduced me to her high-rolling friends, many of whom turned out to be government officials and policemen.

My room at the *hospedaria* was a quarter the size of my room in Fontainhas. When I leaned out its only window, I smelled the sweet-and-sour tartness of garbage rotting in the alley below. All the same, Mrs. Ribeiro and I made a more convincing mother-daughter team than Mama and I ever had. She cooked me care packages of crab vindaloo, hot prawns and pork sorpatel. Some slow weekday afternoons, she took me on long strolls through the Camoes Gardens. On these afternoons, she declaimed epic lines from Luis de Camoes, the Portuguese poet after whom the Gardens were named. She found me temporary jobs by talking me up as a "data processor" to her business acquaintances. She taught me betting games with lilting names: *fan tan, dai siu, pai kao.* After a few weeks, she began dragging me—for luck, she claimed—into rooms reserved in casinos for the highest of high rollers. It was, of course, through Mrs. Ribeiro that I came to be courted by Orfeo Chang of the brokerage firm of Chang, Chang & Chang Associates.

I'd been a roomer at Mrs. Ribeiro's for over a year when she insisted that I tag along to a banquet at a Chinese highroller friend of hers. This man must have had a

---

[6]**Maputo:** Capital of Mozambique.   [7]**Karachi:** City in Pakistan.   [8]**Lisboa:** Capital of Portugal.   [9]**fado:** A form of Portuguese folk music similar to American blues.   [10]**Penang:** State in Malasia.   [11]**Macau:** Also known as Macao, a region of China formerly administered by Portugal and known for its casinos.   [12]***hospedaria:*** A small hotel or inn.

serious fortune to squander. Before that night, I'd not been in a mansion that huge and over-decorated, or to a party that boozy and deluxe. The upshot of this excess of hospitality was that both Mrs. Ribeiro and I had too many glasses of Mateus Rose. We flirted with the same handful of middle-aged playboys, and even let ourselves be groped so hard on a candle-lit balcony overlooking the ocean that wine sloshed on our matching silk blouses. Around dawn we ended up having to accept the favor of a ride home from a paunchy, bespectacled Chinese fellow guest.

For the next two days we coped with our worst-ever hangovers. By the third day, Mrs. Ribeiro felt recovered enough to hold forth on the good looks and the gallantry of that Chinese man. She recalled a boyish dimple on his left cheek. She went into rhapsodies about the elegant contours of his ears, the thinness of his lips, the subtle blue of his silk shirt, the deep blue of his sapphire cuff links. Even the pomade on his thick, black hair had smelled expensive. He had to be a man of means, she explained, as well as a genuine gentleman. After a couple of days, she moved on from the man's physical appearance to his personality. He was shy, she said. He was shy, but deeply romantic, because she now remembered him having ogled her from far all night. When his chance to introduce himself had finally come, he had seized it. That's what must have been behind his chauffeuring us back to the *hospedaria*. She'd heard from someone at the party that the man was our host's financial planner, so wasn't it plausible that he had planned the evening to end for her as it had? I had no reason to dispute Mrs. Ribeiro's memory that the rescuer had silently lusted after her.

For the next few days Mrs. Ribeiro kept vigil by her private phone. She sent him telepathic messages to call her. He went from being called "that kind man" to "my Chinese knight in shining armor" to "my beau." Pale-skinned and youthful to begin with, she grew paler, more girlish. When she became too paralyzed by lovesickness to do anything but pray for the phone to ring, I took over at the reception counter. The work wasn't taxing. A few tourists did come through every day, but after I'd shown them all available singles, doubles, and multiple-occupancies, they usually wandered away without renting. There were only three of us long-term roomers, the other two being ailing and elderly Macanese men who may have been Mrs. Ribeiro's relatives.

Sometimes, as I gave scruffy backpackers a tour, I saw the place that I'd made myself at home in through their eyes, and panicked. I didn't want to end up a sick, caustic, solitary roomer in a dead dump. Mrs. Ribeiro continued to sit by her phone, one sprightly hand on the receiver, and fantasize out loud about her first date with her stockbroker "beau."

The "beau" didn't call Mrs. Ribeiro. But he did send a sealed, business-size envelope by courier. The letter was addressed to Maria Pinto. Inside, on Chang, Chang & Chang Associates stationery was a single, word-processed line: YOU HAVE SET LOOSE LONGINGS I HAD CHAINED. ORFEO.

Mrs. Ribeiro was dozing in a wing chair, one hand resting on the phone. I could have broken her heart by waking her up and showing her the note. Or, I could treat the note as a hoax and tear it to shreds. My Fontainhas days as a shipping clerk and occasional watch-repairer hadn't prepared me for handling anonymous love calls. So why did I tuck the business-size envelope in my pocket book, and roam Macau's business district, tracking Orfeo?

The brokerage firm of Chang, Chang & Chang Associates turned out to be on the third floor of a tall, new office building. I checked out the names of the occupants on the board in the lobby: a few Changs and Lees, only one Young; many Singhs, Kumars, Swaminathans, Ranganathans, Mendozas, Da Silvas, Pintos, all operating gem businesses. Valladares wouldn't look at all out of place on that board. I felt part of a tribe of entrepreneurs who'd gambled on Macau to bring them better luck. On an impulse, I took the lift to the third floor.

A middle-aged Chinese man opened the glass-paneled front door to the offices of 15 Chang, Chang & Chang Associates. He had a paunch. He wore old-fashioned bifocals. Except that he was dressed in more formal clothes, he looked more or less like the courteous man who had driven Mrs. Ribeiro and me home. The man, however, didn't give away any sign that he had sent me the brief, passionate note. I could have been a client or a cleaning woman.

"Am I in the right place for leaving a message for Mr. Chang?" I mumbled. "A Mr. Orfeo Chang?"

The man bowed from his waist and gestured me to step inside. I took that as an admission that he was Orfeo Chang, but not necessarily the Orfeo of the roused passions.

"I don't know if I'm in the right place," I said. "I mean, I am not in need of financial planning; I don't have any money to invest, full stop."

The broker executed another bow. This time it was a slight dip and rise. The harsh office lights gave his balding head and his stooped, dress-shirted back a fluorescent halo. "Not to worry," he said. "After 5 p.m., I'm no longer a working stiff. I'm a poet." He closed the door behind me. Then he turned the lock. "You can't be too careful these days," he explained. "We've had burglaries. Two on this floor."

I didn't feel threatened. 20

Mrs. Ribeiro may have been wrong about her "beau" being a man of means. I took in the neat rows of metal desks and battered chairs; the outmoded computers, the clunky printer and the modest desktop copier. The drawers of the filing cabinets were so stuffed with folders that they stayed partly open. The offices of Mrs. Ribeiro's friends that I had temped in were definitely more upscale. A tall screen partitioned off a small, carpeted seating area, furnished with a pair of boxy, antique chairs and a set of nesting tables topped with an orchid blooming in an ornate, ceramic vase.

I thought it was in this screened-off area that Orfeo Chang and I would—over cups of tea from a thermos—separately intuit our next moves. But the broker escorted me to a neat, metal desk, and offering me his own cushioned, swivel-back chair on rollers, lowered himself into a smaller, sway-legged wooden chair.

"I am happy to receive you," he said. He absently touched the tops of three pens clipped to the pocket of his starched-crisp shirt. Each pen had the Mont Blanc white star on its cap. "Please to begin."

"I don't know what I was . . ."

He didn't help me out as I'd hoped. But by looking away from me, he didn't em- 25 barrass me either. That gave me hope. "I came to thank you," I gushed. "To thank you in person and to apologize."

"To apologize? Why?" He rocked his chair back and forth. The chair legs made soft, moaning noises under his weight.

I let missed cues sparkle like static in the stuffy air between us.

The broker started up again. "I commenced my first poem the night I made your acquaintance," he confessed. "I would like to recite a stanza to you. Oh, I don't mean from my own dilettante attempt. A verse from the world's greatest poet."

Then he launched into his recitation, eyes shut for concentration, paunch heaving with poetic feelings. The verse was in archaic Portuguese. I understood a phrase here and there, enough to guess that the poem was about a dark-skinned, beautiful woman who had stolen the perishable heart of the poet. But, mostly, I caught the mood of elegiac hopelessness that the words were meant to convey.

"Camoes," he said after he'd finished reciting. He opened his eyes.   30

In the broker's dark, dilated pupils I imagined I was detecting a lover's longings.

"Camoes visited your country. He became enamored of a slave there."

I said, "I should get going. Thank you very, very much for all your kindness."

"I did some checking up," he said.

The research was not on Camoes' travels in India.   35

"Philomena Vallardes," he said.

I'd almost forgotten the name I'd been christened.

Orfeo held out a courteous hand for me to shake. "Philomena Valladares, will I have the privilege of seeing you again?"

I had not guessed that being blackmailed felt so seductive.

The next morning I thumbed through the few books that Mrs. Ribeiro kept in a   40
locked glass cabinet beside her bed. Most of them were paperback mysteries. All the hardcover novels had the South China Seas as setting. The books with creased spines and faded gilt lettering were biographies of European adventurers and politicians I'd never heard of. There was also a fancily bound copy of Camoes' *Os Lusidas.* I was ready to give up when, jammed tight between two biographies, I found a skinny anthology of some of Camoes' short poems translated into Victorian English by a Viscount Strangford. I skimmed the anthology for the poem about the irresistible Goan slave. The Victorian viscount must not have approved of interracial, interclass romance. The only indirect acknowledgment he made of Camoes' love for a non-European woman was his explanation of the lines, *"I was caught in Folly's snare / And joined her giddy train / But found her soon the nurse of Care / And Punishment, and Pain."* "The nurse of Care and Punishment and Pain," Strangford speculated in his appendix to the anthology, was "a Negro girl" with whom Camoes committed "one of those little transgressions of which our Poet was often guilty."

I showed up at the Chang, Chang & Chang offices the next night, this time by prearrangement. Orfeo and I sat in the same chairs we had the evening before, this time side by side and touching hands instead of facing each other. He courted me by reading aloud his own sad, sweet English translation of the poem about the slave, the blackness of whose beauty and the luminosity of whose innocence makes the traveler-poet question all that he'd been taught about what's civilized and what's savage. All the time that Orfeo read, I couldn't take my eyes off his face. The skin on his forehead glowed with a passion that I had never expected abstractions such as "blackness" and "innocence" to generate.

Orfeo recited, then re-recited his translation.

I remembered how in Fontainhas, Mama slathered bleaching cream on her face every night. She'd tried the cream on me, too, but I'd broken out in rashes. She'd wept that I was doomed to a lifetime of cinnamon coloring. How could Mama claim for me as she did for herself a blood connection with the European adventurer who had founded Goa as a colony?

"Brownness," Orfeo improvised on the third recitation, "so mud-soft and smooth / That the whitest snow longs to be brown like you."

Suddenly, I was not shackled by Mama's anxieties for me. I was Maria Pinto of   45
Macau, a woman who had invented herself and her citizenship. I'd waged the battle
against Mama, but Orfeo and his beloved poet had speeded up my victory. He had
come to me not as a colonizer or missionary but as an accidental mentor. I felt potent,
and simultaneously, at peace with myself. In that mood, I leaned over the arms of my
office chair, seized Orfeo's shoulders with both hands and kissed him on the mouth. I
must have hurled myself at him with too much force. He pulled back instinctively. But
I was too intoxicated with Camoes' lawless love for the dark slave woman. I pressed my
sandaled feet hard against the floor for momentum, and lurched my chair with its cas-
tor wheels into Orfeo's stationary one. His feet kicked forward in self-defense. Was it
bewilderment that flushed his cologned and close-shaved face?

"Harlot!"

It was whispered. By a man who'd stumbled into a revelation. Paper cuts sting.
Flesh wounds leave permanent scars. In my grief, I ran to the front door.

An embarrassed Orfeo fished the key to the door out of his pants pocket. "Ever so
sorry," he kept mumbling. He could not let me go until I had allowed him to explain
himself, he insisted. He hadn't unburdened his love of poetry to me as a come-on. He
had found his Muse in me. That's what he had meant in the note. I had freed the poet
in him. He was eternally grateful to me. I had accomplished what no other woman in
his life had. If the note had misled me, it was because the wording had been the impre-
cise ones of a novice poet. For that he begged my forgiveness.

I made my bitter way to the *hospedaria* as fast as my high-heeled shoes and traffic
permitted. Mrs. Ribeiro was waiting up for me. She'd had shaming news from a friend.
The Chinese broker who had come on to her in the car under the pretext of seeing us
safely home was a married man with many scandals in his past. She invited me to join
her for a glass of port.

We had a glass, or two, maybe three. I rambled on and on about Mama's snobbish   50
family claims of being descended from a Portuguese nobleman. At dawn as pink fila-
ments of light marbled the sky over Macau, I asked Mrs. Ribeiro if the great Lusian
poet, Camoes, had found both luck and love in his lifetime.

The answer she provided was precise but not wholly satisfying. Camoes had
starved to death, probably in an alms house, but that all the same he had been a lucky
man, much luckier than me or her, because to the very end when he was penniless,
brokenhearted, abandoned by his patrons and avoided by all his friends, he had been
able to count on the love of one person, a Javanese slave named Antonio, whom he had
brought to Portugal from his Asian travels. Antonio had roamed the streets of Lisbon with a begging bowl and kept his master alive until the Good Lord had decided
otherwise.

The year is 1999, and the place still Macau. I own Mrs. Ribeiro's *hospedaria* now.
Mrs. Ribeiro sold me the place for next to nothing three years ago. She moved on to
Fall River, Massachusetts, saying she didn't want to be around when the Chinese took
over the colony. Some nights when I'm down, I mean really down, I think of making
my way to Fall River too, and legally changing my name to Maria Pinto. Who knows,
maybe love and good fortune are hiding out in Fall River. There's no listing for Orfeo
Chang in the phone book. He must have emigrated from Macau. I never, absolutely
never, read obits. ●

Explorations of the Text

1. Aside from their ages, Mrs. Ribeiro and the narrator are described as being similar in many ways, even down to their "matching silk blouses." In what ways are they similar? What purpose do the double characters serve within the work?

2. Why does the narrator change her name to Maria Pinto? If you were to change your name, what new name would you choose?

3. Consider Mr. Chang's infatuation with the narrator through the love poetry of Camoes about a dark-skinned slave girl. Why does Chang court her and then call her a "harlot" when she responds to his courtship? What role does her race, her brown skin, play in this interaction?

4. Explain the symbolic significance of the poet Camoes in the story.

5. Consider the last line of the story. Why might Mukherjee have chosen to end it as she did?

The Reading/Writing Connection

1. In your local library find a copy of Tom Robbins's novel, *Even Cowgirls Get the Blues.* Compare it with "Even Macau Girls Get the Blues." What similarities do you notice? Why might Mukherjee have chosen a similar title for her story?

2. Journal entry: Write about a time that the muse inspired you to create a poem, story, song, or other work of art. What form did the muse take? Or write about a poem, story, or song that inspired you.

Ideas for Writing

1. Do some research on Macau and then analyze the story's setting. Why might the narrator have ended up there rather than in Belize with her mother or in Massachusetts with Mrs. Ribeiro?

2. Read about Postcolonial Criticism (see Appendix B). In what ways are this story and Ben Okri's "A Prayer from the Living" postcolonial critiques?

3. Compare the visions of exile in this story with "The Third and Final Continent."

Flannery O'Connor   *(1925–1964)*

A Good Man Is Hard to Find   1955

The grandmother didn't want to go to Florida. She wanted to visit some of her connections in east Tennessee and she was seizing at every chance to change Bailey's mind. Bailey was the son she lived with, her only boy. He was sitting on the edge of his chair at the table, bent over the orange sports section of the *Journal.* "Now look here, Bailey," she said, "see here, read this," and she stood with one hand on her thin hip and the other rattling the newspaper at his bald head. "Here this fellow that calls himself The Misfit is aloose from the Federal Pen and headed toward Florida and you read here what it says he did to these people. Just you read it. I wouldn't take my children in any direction with a criminal like that aloose in it. I couldn't answer to my conscience if I did."

Bailey didn't look up from his reading so she wheeled around then and faced the children's mother, a young woman in slacks, whose face was as broad and innocent as a cabbage and was tied around with a green head-kerchief that had two points on the top like a rabbit's ears. She was sitting on the sofa, feeding the baby his apricots out of a jar. "The children have been to Florida before," the old lady said. "You all ought to take them somewhere else for a change so they would see different parts of the world and be broad. They never have been to east Tennessee."

The children's mother didn't seem to hear her but the eight-year-old boy, John Wesley, a stocky child with glasses, said, "If you don't want to go to Florida, why dontcha stay at home?" He and the little girl, June Star, were reading the funny papers on the floor.

"She wouldn't stay at home to be queen for a day," June Star said without raising her yellow head.

"Yes and what would you do if this fellow, The Misfit, caught you?" the grand-   5
mother asked.

"I'd smack his face," John Wesley said.

"She wouldn't stay at home for a million bucks," June Star said. "Afraid she'd miss something. She has to go everywhere we go."

"All right, Miss," the grandmother said. "Just remember that the next time you want me to curl your hair."

June Star said her hair was naturally curly.

The next morning the grandmother was the first one in the car, ready to go. She   10
had her big black valise that looked like the head of a hippopotamus in one corner, and underneath it she was hiding a basket with Pitty Sing, the cat, in it. She didn't intend for the cat to be left alone in the house for three days because he would miss her too much and she was afraid he might brush against one of the gas burners and accidentally asphyxiate himself. Her son, Bailey, didn't like to arrive at a motel with a cat.

She sat in the middle of the back seat with John Wesley and June Star on either side of her. Bailey and the children's mother and the baby sat in front and they left Atlanta at eight forty-five with the mileage on the car at 55890. The grandmother wrote this down because she thought it would be interesting to say how many miles they had been when they got back. It took them twenty minutes to reach the outskirts of the city.

The old lady settled herself comfortably, removing her white cotton gloves and putting them up with her purse on the shelf in front of the back window. The children's mother still had on slacks and still had her head tied up in a green kerchief, but the grandmother had on a navy blue straw sailor hat with a bunch of white violets on the brim and a navy blue dress with a small white dot in the print. Her collars and cuffs were white organdy trimmed with lace and at her neckline she had pinned a purple spray of cloth violets containing a sachet. In case of an accident, anyone seeing her dead on the highway would know at once that she was a lady.

She said she thought it was going to be a good day for driving, neither too hot nor too cold, and she cautioned Bailey that the speed limit was fifty-five miles an hour and that the patrolmen hid themselves behind billboards and small clumps of trees and sped out after you before you had a chance to slow down. She pointed out interesting details of the scenery: Stone Mountain; the blue granite that in some places came up to both sides of the highway; the brilliant red clay banks slightly streaked with purple; and the various crops that made rows of green lace-work on the ground. The trees were full of silver-white sunlight and the meanest of them sparkled. The children were reading comic magazines and their mother had gone back to sleep.

"Let's go through Georgia fast so we won't have to look at it much," John Wesley said.

"If I were a little boy," said the grandmother, "I wouldn't talk about my native state 15 that way. Tennessee has the mountains and Georgia has the hills."

"Tennessee is just a hillbilly dumping ground," John Wesley said, "and Georgia is a lousy state too."

"You said it," June Star said.

"In my time," said the grandmother, folding her thin veined fingers, "children were more respectful of their native states and their parents and everything else. People did right then. Oh look at the cute little pickaninny!" she said and pointed to a Negro child standing in the door of a shack. "Wouldn't that make a picture, now?" she asked and they all turned and looked at the little Negro out of the back window. He waved.

"He didn't have any britches on," June Star said.

"He probably didn't have any," the grandmother explained. "Little niggers in the 20 country don't have things like we do. If I could paint, I'd paint that picture," she said.

The children exchanged comic books.

The grandmother offered to hold the baby and the children's mother passed him over the front seat to her. She set him on her knee and bounced him and told him about the things they were passing. She rolled her eyes and screwed up her mouth and stuck her leathery thin face into his smooth bland one. Occasionally he gave her a faraway smile. They passed a large cotton field with five or six graves fenced in the middle of it, like a small island. "Look at the graveyard!" the grandmother said, pointing it out. "That was the old family burying ground. That belonged to the plantation."

"Where's the plantation?" John Wesley asked.

"Gone With the Wind," said the grandmother. "Ha. Ha."

When the children finished all the comic books they had brought, they opened the 25 lunch and ate it. The grandmother ate a peanut butter sandwich and an olive and would not let the children throw the box and the paper napkins out the window. When there was nothing else to do they played a game by choosing a cloud and making the other two guess what shape it suggested. John Wesley took one the shape of a cow and June Starr guessed a cow and John Wesley said, no, an automobile, and June Star said he didn't play fair, and they began to slap each other over the grandmother.

The grandmother said she would tell them a story if they would keep quiet. When she told a story, she rolled her eyes and waved her head and was very dramatic. She said once when she was a maiden lady she had been courted by a Mr. Edgar Atkins Teagarden from Jasper, Georgia. She said he was a very good-looking man and a gentleman and that he brought her a watermelon every Saturday afternoon with initials cut in it, E. A. T. Well, one Saturday, she said, Mr. Teagarden brought the watermelon and there was nobody at home and he left it on the front porch and returned in his buggy to Jasper, but she never got the watermelon, she said, because a nigger boy ate it when he saw the initials, E. A. T.! This story tickled John Wesley's funny bone and he giggled and giggled but June Star didn't think it was any good. She said she wouldn't marry a man that just brought her a watermelon on Saturday. The grandmother said she would have done well to marry Mr. Teagarden because he was a gentleman and had bought Coca-Cola stock when it first came out and that he had died only a few years ago, a very wealthy man.

They stopped at The Tower for barbecued sandwiches. The Tower was a part stucco and part wood filling station and dance hall set in a clearing outside of Timothy. A fat man named Red Sammy Butts ran it and there were signs stuck here and there on the building and for miles up and down the highway saying, TRY RED SAMMY'S

FAMOUS BARBECUE. NONE LIKE FAMOUS RED SAMMY'S! RED SAM! THE FAT BOY WITH THE HAPPY LAUGH! A VETERAN! RED SAMMY'S YOUR MAN!

Red Sammy was lying on the bare ground outside The Tower with his head under a truck while a gray monkey about a foot high, chained to a small chinaberry tree, chattered nearby. The monkey sprang back into the tree and got on the highest limb as soon as he saw the children jump out of the car and run toward him.

Inside, The Tower was a long dark room with a counter at one end and tables at the other and dancing space in the middle. They all sat down at a board table next to the nickelodeon and Red Sam's wife, a tall burnt-brown woman with hair and eyes lighter than her skin, came and took their order. The children's mother put a dime in the machine and played "The Tennessee Waltz," and the grandmother said that tune always made her want to dance. She asked Bailey if he would like to dance but he only glared at her. He didn't have a naturally sunny disposition like she did and trips made him nervous. The grandmother's brown eyes were very bright. She swayed her head from side to side and pretended she was dancing in her chair. June Star said play something she could tap to so the children's mother put in another dime and played a fast number and June Star stepped out onto the dance floor and did her tap routine.

"Ain't she cute?" Red Sam's wife said, leaning over the counter. "Would you like to come be my little girl?" 30

"No I certainly wouldn't," June Star said. "I wouldn't live in a broken-down place like this for a million bucks!" and she ran back to the table.

"Ain't she cute?" the woman repeated, stretching her mouth politely.

"Aren't you ashamed?" hissed the grandmother.

Red Sam came in and told his wife to quit lounging on the counter and hurry up with these people's order. His khaki trousers reached just to his hip bones and his stomach hung over them like a sack of meal swaying under his shirt. He came over and sat down at a table nearby and let out a combination sigh and yodel. "You can't win," he said. "You can't win," and he wiped his sweating red face off with a gray handkerchief. "These days you don't know who to trust," he said. "Ain't that the truth?"

"People are certainly not nice like they used to be," said the grandmother. 35

"Two fellers come in here last week," Red Sammy said, "driving a Chrysler. It was a old beat-up car but it was a good one and these boys looked all right to me. Said they worked at the mill and you know I let them fellers charge the gas they bought? Now why did I do that?"

"Because you're a good man!" the grandmother said at once.

"Yes'm, I suppose so," Red Sam said as if he were struck with this answer.

His wife brought the orders, carrying the five plates all at once without a tray, two in each hand and one balanced on her arm. "It isn't a soul in this green world of God's that you can trust," she said. "And I don't count nobody out of that, not nobody," she repeated, looking at Red Sammy.

"Did you read about the criminal, The Misfit, that's escaped?" asked the grand- 40 mother.

"I wouldn't be a bit surprised if he didn't attact this place right here," said the woman. "If he hears about it being here, I wouldn't be none surprised to see him. If he hears it's two cent in the cash register, I wouldn't be a tall surprised if he . . ."

"That'll do," Red Sam said. "Go bring these people their Co'-Colas," and the woman went off to get the rest of the order.

"A good man is hard to find," Red Sammy said. "Everything is getting terrible. I remember the day you could go off and leave your screen door unlatched. Not no more."

He and the grandmother discussed better times. The old lady said that in her opinion Europe was entirely to blame for the way things were now. She said the way Europe acted you would think we were made of money and Red Sam said it was no use talking about it, she was exactly right. The children ran outside into the white sunlight and looked at the monkey in the lacy chinaberry tree. He was busy catching fleas on himself and biting each one carefully between his teeth as if it were a delicacy.

They drove off again into the hot afternoon. The grandmother took cat naps and woke up every few minutes with her own snoring. Outside of Toombsboro she woke up and recalled an old plantation that she had visited in this neighborhood once when she was a young lady. She said the house had six white columns across the front and that there was an avenue of oaks leading up to it and two little wooden trellis arbors on either side in front where you sat down with your suitor after a stroll in the garden. She recalled exactly which road to turn off to get to it. She knew that Bailey would not be willing to lose any time looking at an old house, but the more she talked about it, the more she wanted to see it once again and find out if the little twin arbors were still standing. "There was a secret panel in this house," she said craftily, not telling the truth but wishing that she were, "and the story went that all the family silver was hidden in it when Sherman[1] came through but it was never found . . ."

"Hey!" John Wesley said. "Let's go see it! We'll find it! We'll poke all the woodwork and find it! Who lives there? Where do you turn off at? Hey Pop, can't we turn off there?"

"We never have seen a house with a secret panel!" June Star shrieked. "Let's go to the house with the secret panel! Hey Pop, can't we go see the house with the secret panel!"

"It's not far from here, I know," the grandmother said. "It wouldn't take over twenty minutes."

Bailey was looking straight ahead. His jaw was as rigid as a horseshoe. "No," he said.

The children began to yell and scream that they wanted to see the house with the secret panel. John Wesley kicked the back of the front seat and June Star hung over her mother's shoulder and whined desperately into her ear that they never had any fun even on their vacation, that they could never do what THEY wanted to do. The baby began to scream and John Wesley kicked the back of the seat so hard that his father could feel the blows in his kidney.

"All right!" he shouted and drew the car to a stop at the side of the road. "Will you all shut up? Will you just shut up for one second? If you don't shut up, we won't go anywhere."

"It would be very educational for them," the grandmother murmured.

"All right," Bailey said, "but get this: this is the only time we're going to stop for anything like this. This is the one and only time."

"The dirt road that you have to turn down is about a mile back," the grandmother directed. "I marked it when we passed."

"A dirt road," Bailey groaned.

After they had turned around and were headed toward the dirt road, the grandmother recalled other points about the house, the beautiful glass over the front

50

55

---

[1]**William Tecumseh Sherman** (1820–1891): Union general during the Civil War.

doorway and the candle-lamp in the hall. John Wesley said that the secret panel was probably in the fireplace.

"You can't go inside this house," Bailey said. "You don't know who lives there."

"While you all talk to the people in front, I'll run around behind and get in a window," John Wesley suggested.

"We'll all stay in the car," his mother said.

They turned onto the dirt road and the car raced roughly along in a swirl of pink 60 dust. The grandmother recalled the times when there were no paved roads and thirty miles was a day's journey. The dirt road was hilly and there were sudden washes in it and sharp curves on dangerous embankments. All at once they would be on a hill, looking down over the blue tops of trees for miles around, then the next minute, they would be in a red depression with the dust-coated trees looking down on them.

"This place had better turn up in a minute," Bailey said, "or I'm going to turn around."

The road looked as if no one had traveled on it in months.

"It's not much farther," the grandmother said and just as she said it, a horrible thought came to her. The thought was so embarrassing that she turned red in the face and her eyes dilated and her feet jumped up, upsetting her valise in the corner. The instant the valise moved, the newspaper top she had over the basket under it rose with a snarl and Pitty Sing, the cat, sprang onto Bailey's shoulder.

The children were thrown to the floor and their mother, clutching the baby, was thrown out the door onto the ground; the old lady was thrown into the front seat. The car turned over once and landed right-side-up in a gulch off the side of the road. Bailey remained in the driver's seat with the cat—gray-striped with a broad white face and an orange nose—clinging to his neck like a caterpillar.

As soon as the children saw they could move their arms and legs, they scram- 65 bled out of the car, shouting, "We've had an ACCIDENT!" The grandmother was curled up under the dashboard, hoping she was injured so that Bailey's wrath would not come down on her all at once. The horrible thought she had had before the accident was that the house she had remembered so vividly was not in Georgia but in Tennessee.

Bailey removed the cat from his neck with both hands and flung it out the window against the side of a pine tree. Then he got out of the car and started looking for the children's mother. She was sitting against the side of the red gutted ditch, holding the screaming baby, but she only had a cut down her face and a broken shoulder. "We've had an ACCIDENT!" the children screamed in a frenzy of delight.

"But nobody's killed," June Star said with disappointment as the grandmother limped out of the car, her hat still pinned to her head but the broken front brim standing up at a jaunty angle and the violet spray hanging off the side. They all sat down in the ditch, except the children, to recover from the shock. They were all shaking.

"Maybe a car will come along," said the children's mother hoarsely.

"I believe I have injured an organ," said the grandmother, pressing her side, but no one answered her. Bailey's teeth were clattering. He had on a yellow sport shirt with bright blue parrots designed in it and his face was as yellow as the shirt. The grandmother decided that she would not mention that the house was in Tennessee.

The road was about ten feet above and they could see only the tops of the trees on 70 the other side of it. Behind the ditch they were sitting in there were more woods, tall and dark and deep. In a few minutes they saw a car some distance away on top of a hill, coming slowly as if the occupants were watching them. The grandmother stood up and waved both arms dramatically to attract their attention. The car continued to come on slowly, disappeared around a bend and appeared again, moving even slower, on top of the hill they had gone over. It was a big black battered hearse-like automobile. There were three men in it.

It came to a stop just over them and for some minutes, the driver looked down with a steady expressionless gaze to where they were sitting, and didn't speak. Then he turned his head and muttered something to the other two and they got out. One was a fat boy in black trousers and a red sweat shirt with a silver stallion embossed on the front of it. He moved around on the right side of them and stood staring, his mouth partly open in a kind of loose grin. The other had on khaki pants and a blue striped coat and a gray hat pulled down very low, hiding most of his face. He came around slowly on the left side. Neither spoke.

The driver got out of the car and stood by the side of it, looking down at them. He was an older man than the other two. His hair was just beginning to gray and he wore silver-rimmed spectacles that gave him a scholarly look. He had a long creased face and didn't have on any shirt or undershirt. He had on blue jeans that were too tight for him and was holding a black hat and a gun. The two boys also had guns.

"We've had an ACCIDENT!" the children screamed.

The grandmother had the peculiar feeling that the bespectacled man was someone she knew. His face was as familiar to her as if she had known him all her life but she could not recall who he was. He moved away from the car and began to come down the embankment, placing his feet carefully so that he wouldn't slip. He had on tan and white shoes and no socks, and his ankles were red and thin. "Good afternoon," he said. "I see you all had you a little spill."

"We turned over twice!" said the grandmother.   75

"Oncet," he corrected. "We seen it happen. Try their car and see will it run, Hiram," he said quietly to the boy with the gray hat.

"What you got that gun for?" John Wesley asked. "Whatcha gonna do with that gun?"

"Lady," the man said to the children's mother, "would you mind calling them children to sit down by you? Children make me nervous. I want all you all to sit down right there together where you're at."

"What are you telling us what to do for?" June Star asked.

Behind them the line of woods gaped like a dark open mouth. "Come here," said   80
their mother.

"Look here now," Bailey began suddenly, "We're in a predicament! We're in . . ."

The grandmother shrieked. She scrambled to her feet and stood staring. "You're The Misfit!" she said. "I recognized you at once!"

"Yes'm," the man said, smiling slightly as if he were pleased in spite of himself to be known, "but it would have been better for all of you, lady, if you hadn't of recker-nized me."

Bailey turned his head sharply and said something to his mother that shocked even the children. The old lady began to cry and The Misfit reddened.

"Lady," he said, "don't you get upset. Sometimes a man says things he don't mean.   85
I don't reckon he meant to talk to you thataway."

"You wouldn't shoot a lady, would you?" the grandmother said and removed a clean handkerchief from her cuff and began to slap at her eyes with it.

The Misfit pointed the toe of his shoe into the ground and made a little hole and then covered it up again. "I would hate to have to," he said.

"Listen," the grandmother almost screamed, "I know you're a good man. You don't look a bit like you have common blood. I know you must come from nice people!"

"Yes main," he said, "finest people in the world." When he smiled he showed a row of strong white teeth. "God never made a finer woman than my mother and my daddy's heart was pure gold," he said. The boy with the red sweat shirt had come around behind them and was standing with his gun at his hip. The Misfit squatted down on the ground. "Watch them children, Bobby Lee," he said. "You know they make me nervous." He looked at the six of them huddled together in front of him and he seemed to be embarrassed as if he couldn't think of anything to say. "Ain't a cloud in the sky," he remarked, looking up at it. "Don't see no sun but don't see no cloud either."

"Yes, it's a beautiful day," said the grandmother. "Listen," she said, "you shouldn't call yourself The Misfit because I know you're a good man at heart. I can just look at you and tell." 90

"Hush!" Bailey yelled. "Hush! Everybody shut up and let me handle this!" He was squatting in the position of a runner about to sprint forward but he didn't move.

"I pre-chate that, lady," The Misfit said and drew a little circle in the ground with the butt of his gun.

"It'll take a half a hour to fix this here car," Hiram called, looking over the raised hood of it.

"Well, first you and Bobby Lee get him and that little boy to step over yonder with you," The Misfit said, pointing to Bailey and John Wesley. "The boys want to ast you something," he said to Bailey. "Would you mind stepping back in them woods there with them?"

"Listen," Bailey began, "we're in a terrible predicament! Nobody realizes what this is," and his voice cracked. His eyes were as blue and intense as the parrots in his shirt and he remained perfectly still. 95

The grandmother reached up to adjust her hat brim as if she were going to the woods with him but it came off in her hand. She stood staring at it and after a second she let it fall on the ground. Hiram pulled Bailey up by the arm as if he were assisting an old man. John Wesley caught hold of his father's hand and Bobby Lee followed. They went off toward the woods and just as they reached the dark edge, Bailey turned and supporting himself against a gray naked pine trunk, he shouted, "I'll be back in a minute, Mama, wait on me!"

"Come back this instant!" his mother shrilled but they all disappeared into the woods.

"Bailey Boy!" the grandmother called in a tragic voice but she found she was looking at The Misfit squatting on the ground in front of her. "I just know you're a good man," she said desperately. "You're not a bit common!"

"Nome, I ain't a good man," The Misfit said after a second as if he had considered her statement carefully, "but I ain't the worst in the world neither. My daddy said I was a different breed of dog from my brothers and sisters. 'You know,' Daddy said, 'it's some that can live their whole life out without asking about it and it's others has to know why it is, and this boy is one of the latters. He's going to be into everything!'" He put on his black hat and looked up suddenly and then away deep into the woods as if he were embarrassed again. "I'm sorry I don't have on a shirt before you ladies," he said, hunching his shoulders slightly "We buried our clothes that we had on when we escaped and we're just making do until we can get better. We borrowed these from some folks we met," he explained.

"That's perfectly all right," the grandmother said. "Maybe Bailey has an extra shirt in his suitcase." 100

"I'll look and see terrectly," The Misfit said.

"Where are they taking him?" the children's mother screamed.

"Daddy was a card himself," The Misfit said. "You couldn't put anything over on him. He never got in trouble with the Authorities though. Just had the knack of handling them."

"You could be honest too if you'd only try," said the grandmother. "Think how wonderful it would be to settle down and live a comfortable life and not have to think about somebody chasing you all the time."

The Misfit kept scratching in the ground with the butt of his gun as if he were thinking about it. "Yes'm, somebody is always after you," he murmured. 105

The grandmother noticed how thin his shoulder blades were just behind his hat because she was standing up looking down on him. "Do you ever pray?" she asked.

He shook his head. All she saw was the black hat wiggle between his shoulder blades.

"Nome," he said.

There was a pistol shot from the woods, followed closely by another. Then silence. The old lady's head jerked around. She could hear the wind move through the tree tops like a long satisfied insuck of breath. "Bailey Boy!" she called.

"I was a gospel singer for a while," The Misfit said. "I been most everything. Been in the arm service, both land and sea, at home and abroad, been twict married, been an under-taker, been with the railroads, plowed Mother Earth, been in a tornado, seen a man burnt alive oncet," and looked up at the children's mother and the little girl who were sitting close together, their faces white and their eyes glassy; "I even seen a woman flogged," he said.

"Pray, pray," the grandmother began, "pray, pray . . ." 110

"I never was a bad boy that I remember of," The Misfit said in an almost dreamy voice, "but somewheres along the line I done something wrong and got sent to the penitentiary. I was buried alive," and he looked up and held her attention to him by a steady stare.

"That's when you should have started to pray," she said. "What did you do to get sent to the penitentiary that first time?"

"Turn to the right, it was a wall," The Misfit said, looking up again at the cloudless sky. "Turn to the left, it was a wall. Look up it was a ceiling, look down it was a floor. I forget what I done, lady. I set there and set there, trying to remember what it was I done and I ain't recalled it to this day. Oncet in a while, I would think it was coming to me, but it never come."

"Maybe they put you in by mistake," the old lady said vaguely.

"Nome," he said. "It wasn't no mistake. They had the papers on me." 115

"You must have stolen something," she said.

The Misfit sneered slightly. "Nobody had nothing I wanted," he said. "It was a head-doctor at the penitentiary said what I had done was kill my daddy but I known that for a lie. My daddy died in nineteen ought nineteen of the epidemic flu and I never had a thing to do with it. He was buried in the Mount Hopewell Baptist churchyard and you can go there and see for yourself."

"If you would pray," the old lady said, "Jesus would help you."

"That's right," The Misfit said.

"Well then, why don't you pray?" she asked trembling with delight suddenly. 120

"I don't want no hep," he said. "I'm doing all right by myself."

Bobby Lee and Hiram came ambling back from the woods. Bobby Lee was dragging a yellow shirt with bright blue parrots in it.

"Thow me that shirt, Bobby Lee," The Misfit said. The shirt came flying at him and landed on his shoulder and he put it on. The grandmother couldn't name what the shirt reminded her of. "No, lady," The Misfit said while he was buttoning it up, "I found out the crime don't matter. You can do one thing or you can do another, kill a man or take a tire off his car, because sooner or later you're going to forget what it was you done and just be punished for it."

The children's mother had begun to make heaving noises as if she couldn't get her breath. "Lady," he asked, "would you and that little girl like to step off yonder with Bobby Lee and Hiram and join your husband?"

"Yes, thank you," the mother said faintly. Her left arm dangled helplessly and she   125
was holding the baby, who had gone to sleep, in the other. "Hep that lady up, Hiram," The Misfit said as she struggled to climb out of the ditch, "and Bobby Lee, you hold onto that little girl's hand."

"I don't want to hold hands with him," June Star said. "He reminds me of a pig."

The fat boy blushed and laughed and caught her by the arm and pulled her off into the woods after Hiram and her mother.

Alone with The Misfit, the grandmother found that she had lost her voice. There was not a cloud in the sky nor any sun. There was nothing around her but woods. She wanted to tell him that he must pray. She opened and closed her mouth several times before anything came out. Finally she found herself saying, "Jesus, Jesus," meaning, Jesus will help you, but the way she was saying it, it sounded as if she might be cursing.

"Yes'm," The Misfit said as if he agreed. "Jesus thown everything off balance. It was the same case with Him as with me except He hadn't committed any crime and they could prove I had committed one because they had the papers on me. Of course," he said, "they never shown me my papers. That's why I sign myself now. I said long ago, you get you a signature and sign everything you do and keep a copy of it. Then you'll know what you done and you can hold up the crime to the punishment and see do they match and in the end you'll have something to prove you ain't been treated right. I call myself The Misfit," he said, "because I can't make what all I done wrong fit what all I gone through in punishment."

There was a piercing scream from the woods, followed closely by a pistol report.   130
"Does it seem right to you, lady, that one is punished a heap and another ain't punished at all?"

"Jesus!" the old lady cried. "You've got good blood! I know you wouldn't shoot a lady! I know you come from nice people! Pray! Jesus, you ought not to shoot a lady. I'll give you all the money I've got!"

"Lady," The Misfit said, looking beyond her far into the woods, "there never was a body that give the undertaker a tip."

There were two more pistol reports and the grandmother raised her head like a parched old turkey hen crying for water and called, "Bailey Boy, Bailey Boy!" as if her heart would break.

"Jesus was the only One that ever raised the dead." The Misfit continued, "and He shouldn't have done it. He thrown everything off balance. If He did what He said, then it's nothing for you to do but throw away everything and follow Him, and if He didn't, then it's nothing for you to do but enjoy the few minutes you got left the best way you can—by killing somebody or burning down his house or doing some other meanness to him. No pleasure but meanness," he said and his voice had become almost a snarl.

"Maybe He didn't raise the dead," the old lady mumbled, not knowing what she   135
was saying and feeling so dizzy that she sank down in the ditch with her legs twisted under her.

"I wasn't there so I can't say He didn't," The Misfit said. "I wisht I had of been there," he said, hitting the ground with his fist. "It ain't right I wasn't there because if I had of been there I would of known. Listen lady," he said in a high voice, "if I had of been there I would of known and I wouldn't be like I am now." His voice seemed about to crack and the grandmother's head cleared for an instant. She saw the man's face twisted close to her own as if he were going to cry and she murmured, "Why you're one of my babies. You're one of my own children!" She reached out and touched him on the shoulder. The Misfit sprang back as if a snake had bitten him and shot her three times through the chest. Then he put his gun down on the ground and took off his glasses and began to clean them.

Hiram and Bobby Lee returned from the woods and stood over the ditch, looking down at the grandmother who half sat and half lay in a puddle of blood with her legs crossed under her like a child's and her face smiling up at the cloudless sky.

Without his glasses, The Misfit's eyes were red-rimmed and pale and defenseless-looking. "Take her off and throw her where you thrown the others," he said, picking up the cat that was rubbing itself against his leg.

"She was a talker, wasn't she?" Bobby Lee said, sliding down the ditch with a yodel.

"She would of been a good woman," The Misfit said, "if it had been somebody   140
there to shoot her every minute of her life."

"Some fun!" Bobby Lee said.

"Shut up, Bobby Lee," The Misfit said. "It's no real pleasure in life." ●

Explorations of the Text

1. Analyze the grandmother's character. Examine her relationship with her grandchildren, her son, and with her daughter-in-law. Discuss her concept of being a lady.
2. Discuss the episode in The Tower restaurant and the symbolism of the monkey.
3. What causes the accident?
4. What is your view of The Misfit? Is he a homicidal serial killer or a demented prophet?
5. Does the grandmother change? Does The Misfit change? Examine the grandmother's final confrontation with The Misfit.
6. Explore the significance of The Misfit's statement: "'She would of been a good woman,' . . . 'if it had been somebody there to shoot her every minute of her life.'"
7. Discuss the significance of the title.

The Reading/Writing Connection

1. List your questions about this story. Then answer one of them in a paragraph.
2. "Think" Topic: Is this a story about salvation or damnation?
3. Journal Entry: React to Red Sam's statement: "'These days you don't know who to trust.'"
4. **Write an Argument:** "The grandmother has become a good woman." Argue pro or con.

Ideas for Writing

1. Compare the treatment of violence in this story with "Where Are You Going, Where Have You Been?" (Chapter 5) or compare the endings of both stories.

2. Compare the grandmother's "coming of age" with the narrator's in "Cathedral" (Chapter 5).

3. Compare the spiritual vision in "What You Pawn I Will Redeem" with that of "A Good Man Is Hard to Find."

Sherman Alexie *(1966–)*

What You Pawn I Will Redeem   *2003*

Noon

One day you have a home and the next you don't, but I'm not going to tell you my particular reasons for being homeless, because it's my secret story, and Indians have to work hard to keep secrets from hungry white folks.

I'm a Spokane Indian boy, an Interior Salish,[1] and my people have lived within a one-hundred-mile radius of Spokane, Washington, for at least ten thousand years. I grew up in Spokane, moved to Seattle twenty-three years ago for college, flunked out within two semesters, worked various blue- and bluer-collar jobs for many years, married two or three times, fathered two or three kids, and then went crazy. Of course, "crazy" is not the official definition of my mental problem, but I don't think "asocial disorder" fits it, either, because that makes me sound like I'm a serial killer or something. I've never hurt another human being, or at least not physically. I've broken a few hearts in my time, but we've all done that, so I'm nothing special in that regard. I'm a boring heartbreaker, at that, because I've never abandoned one woman for another. I never dated or married more than one woman at a time. I didn't break hearts into pieces overnight. I broke them slowly and carefully. I didn't set any land-speed records running out the door. Piece by piece, I disappeared. And I've been disappearing ever since. But I'm not going to tell you any more about my brain or my soul.

I've been homeless for six years. If there's such a thing as being an effective homeless man, I suppose I'm effective. Being homeless is probably the only thing I've ever been good at. I know where to get the best free food. I've made friends with restaurant and convenience-store managers who let me use their bathrooms. I don't mean the public bathrooms, either. I mean the employees' bathrooms, the clean ones hidden in the back of the kitchen or the pantry or the cooler. I know it sounds strange to be proud of, but it means a lot to me, being truthworthy enough to piss in somebody else's clean bathroom. Maybe you don't understand the value of a clean bathroom, but I do.

Probably none of this interests you. I probably don't interest you much. Homeless Indians are everywhere in Seattle. We're common and boring, and you walk right on

---

[1] **Interior Salish:** A speaker of the Salishan languages, Native American languages of the Northwestern United States and British Columbia.

by us, with maybe a look of anger or disgust or even sadness at the terrible fate of the noble savage. But we have dreams and families. I'm friends with a homeless Plains Indian man whose son is the editor of a big-time newspaper back east. That's his story, but we Indians are great storytellers and liars and mythmakers, so maybe that Plains Indian hobo is a plain old everyday Indian. I'm kind of suspicious of him, because he describes himself only as Plains Indian, a generic term, and not by a specific tribe. When I asked him why he wouldn't tell me exactly what he is, he said, "Do any of us know exactly what we are?" Yeah, great, a philosophizing Indian. "Hey," I said, "you got to have a home to be that homely." He laughed and flipped me the eagle and walked away. But you probably want to know more about the story I'm really trying to tell you.

I wander the streets with a regular crew, my teammates, my defenders, and my posse. It's Rose of Sharon, Junior, and me. We matter to one another if we don't matter to anybody else. Rose of Sharon is a big woman, about seven feet tall if you're measuring overall effect, and about five feet tall if you're talking about the physical. She's a Yakama Indian of the Wishram variety. Junior is a Colville, but there are about 199 tribes that make up the Colville, so he could be anything. He's good-looking, though, like he just stepped out of some "Don't Litter the Earth" public-service advertisement. He's got those great big cheek-bones that are like planets, you know, with little moons orbiting around them. He gets me jealous, jealous, and jealous. If you put Junior and me next to each other, he's the Before Columbus Arrived Indian, and I'm the After Columbus Arrived Indian. I am living proof of the horrible damage that colonialism has done to us Skins. But I'm not going to let you know how scared I sometimes get of history and its ways. I'm a strong man, and I know that silence is the best way of dealing with white folks.

This whole story started at lunchtime, when Rose of Sharon, Junior, and I were panning the handle down at Pike Place Market. After about two hours of negotiating, we earned five dollars, good enough for a bottle of fortified courage from the most beautiful 7–Eleven in the world. So we headed over that way, feeling like warrior drunks, and we walked past this pawnshop I'd never noticed before. And that was strange, because we Indians have built-in pawnshop radar. But the strangest thing was the old powwow-dance regalia I saw hanging in the window.

"That's my grandmother's regalia," I said to Rose of Sharon and Junior.

"How do you know for sure?" Junior asked.

I didn't know for sure, because I hadn't seen that regalia in person ever. I'd seen only photographs of my grandmother dancing in it. And that was before somebody stole it from her fifty years ago. But it sure looked like my memory of it, and it had all the same colors of feathers and beads that my family always sewed into their powwow regalia.

"There's only one way to know for sure," I said.

So Rose of Sharon, Junior, and I walked into the pawnshop and greeted the old white man working behind the counter.

"How can I help you?" he asked.

"That's my grandmother's powwow regalia in your window," I said.

"Somebody stole it from her fifty years ago, and my family has been looking for it ever since."

The pawnbroker looked at me like I was a liar. I understood. Pawnshops are filled with liars.

"I'm not lying," I said. "Ask my friends here. They'll tell you."

"He's the most honest Indian I know," Rose of Sharon said.

"All right, honest Indian," the pawnbroker said. "I'll give you the benefit of the doubt. Can you prove it's your grandmother's regalia?"

Because they don't want to be perfect, because only God is perfect, Indian people sew flaws into their powwow regalia. My family always sewed one yellow bead somewhere on their regalia. But we always hid it where you had to search hard to find it.

"If it really is my grandmother's," I said, "there will be one yellow bead hidden somewhere on it." 20

"All right, then," the pawnbroker said. "Let's take a look."

He pulled the regalia out of the window, laid it down on his glass counter, and we searched for that yellow bead and found it hidden beneath the armpit.

"There it is," the pawnbroker said. He didn't sound surprised. "You were right. This is your grandmother's regalia."

"It's been missing for fifty years," Junior said.

"Hey, Junior," I said. "It's my family's story. Let me tell it." 25

"All right," he said. "I apologize. You go ahead."

"It's been missing for fifty years," I said.

"That's his family's sad story," Rose of Sharon said. "Are you going to give it back to him?"

"That would be the right thing to do," the pawnbroker said. "But I can't afford to do the right thing. I paid a thousand dollars for this. I can't give away a thousand dollars."

"We could go to the cops and tell them it was stolen," Rose of Sharon said. 30

"Hey," I said to her, "don't go threatening people."

The pawnbroker sighed. He was thinking hard about the possibilities.

"Well, I suppose you could go to the cops," he said. "But I don't think they'd believe a word you said."

He sounded sad about that. Like he was sorry for taking advantage of our disadvantages.

"What's your name?" the pawnbroker asked me. 35

"Jackson," I said.

"Is that first or last?" he asked.

"Both."

"Are you serious?"

"Yes, it's true. My mother and father named me Jackson Jackson. My family nickname is Jackson Squared. My family is funny." 40

"All right, Jackson Jackson," the pawnbroker said. "You wouldn't happen to have a thousand dollars, would you?"

"We've got five dollars total," I said.

"That's too bad," he said and thought hard about the possibilities. "I'd sell it to you for a thousand dollars if you had it. Heck, to make it fair, I'd sell it to you for nine hundred and ninety-nine dollars. I'd lose a dollar. It would be the moral thing to do in this case. To lose a dollar would be the right thing."

"We've got five dollars total," I said again.

"That's too bad," he said again and thought harder about the possibilities. "How about this? I'll give you twenty-four hours to come up with nine hundred and ninety-nine dollars. You come back here at lunchtime tomorrow with the money, and I'll sell it back to you. How does that sound?" 45

"It sounds good," I said.

"All right, then," he said. "We have a deal. And I'll get you started. Here's twenty bucks to get you started."

He opened up his wallet and pulled out a crisp twenty-dollar bill and gave it to me. Rose of Sharon, Junior, and I walked out into the daylight to search for nine hundred and seventy-four more dollars.

1:00 P.M.

Rose of Sharon, Junior, and I carried our twenty-dollar bill and our five dollars in loose change over to the 7–Eleven and spent it to buy three bottles of imagination. We needed to figure out how to raise all that money in one day. Thinking hard, we huddled in an alley beneath the Alaska Way Viaduct and finished off those bottles one, two, and three.

2:00 P.M.

Rose of Sharon was gone when I woke. I heard later she had hitchhiked back to   50
Toppenish and was living with her sister on the reservation.

Junior was passed out beside me, covered in his own vomit, or maybe somebody else's vomit, and my head hurt from thinking, so I left him alone and walked down to the water. I loved the smell of ocean water. Salt always smells like memory.

When I got to the wharf, I ran into three Aleut cousins who sat on a wooden bench and stared out at the bay and cried. Most of the homeless Indians in Seattle come from Alaska. One by one, each of them hopped a big working boat in Anchorage or Barrow or Juneau, fished his way south to Seattle, jumped off the boat with a pocketful of cash to party hard at one of the highly sacred and traditional Indian bars, went broke and broker, and has been trying to find his way back to the boat and the frozen north ever since.

These Aleuts smelled like salmon, I thought, and they told me they were going to sit on that wooden bench until their boat came back.

"How long has your boat been gone?" I asked.

"Eleven years," the elder Aleut said.   55

I cried with them for a while.

"Hey," I said. "Do you guys have any money I can borrow?"

They didn't.

3:00 P.M.

I walked back to Junior. He was still passed out. I put my face down near his mouth to make sure he was breathing. He was alive, so I dug around in his blue-jean pockets and found half a cigarette. I smoked it all the way down and thought about my grandmother.

Her name was Agnes, and she died of breast cancer when I was fourteen. My father   60
thought Agnes caught her tumors from the uranium mine on the reservation. But my mother said the disease started when Agnes was walking back from the powwow one night and got run over by a motorcycle. She broke three ribs, and my mother said those ribs never healed right, and tumors always take over when you don't heal right.

Sitting beside Junior, smelling the smoke and salt and vomit, I wondered if my grandmother's cancer had started when somebody stole her powwow regalia. Maybe the cancer started in her broken heart and then leaked out into her breasts. I know it's crazy, but I wondered if I could bring my grandmother back to life if I bought back her regalia.

I needed money, big money, so I left Junior and walked over to the Real Change office.

4:00 P.M.

"Real Change is a multifaceted organization that publishes a newspaper, supports cultural projects that empower the poor and homeless, and mobilizes the public around poverty issues. Real Change's mission is to organize, educate, and build alliances to create solutions to homelessness and poverty. They exist to provide a voice to poor people in our community."

I memorized Real Change's mission statement because I sometimes sell the newspaper on the streets. But you have to stay sober to sell it, and I'm not always good at staying sober. Anybody can sell the newspaper. You buy each copy for thirty cents and sell it for a dollar and keep the net profit.

"I need one thousand four hundred and thirty papers," I said to the Big Boss.　65

"That's a strange number," he said. "And that's a lot of papers."

"I need them."

The Big Boss pulled out the calculator and did the math. "It will cost you four hundred and twenty-nine dollars for that many," he said.

"If I had that kind of money, I wouldn't need to sell the papers."

"What's going on, Jackson-to-the-Second-Power?" he asked. He is the only one　70 who calls me that. He is a funny and kind man.

I told him about my grandmother's powwow regalia and how much money I needed to buy it back.

"We should call the police," he said.

"I don't want to do that," I said. "It's a quest now. I need to win it back by myself."

"I understand," he said. "And to be honest, I'd give you the papers to sell if I thought it would work. But the record for most papers sold in a day by one vendor is only three hundred and two."

"That would net me about two hundred bucks," I said.　75

The Big Boss used his calculator. "Two hundred and eleven dollars and forty cents," he said.

"That's not enough," I said.

"The most money anybody has made in one day is five hundred and twenty-five. And that's because somebody gave Old Blue five hundred-dollar bills for some dang reason. The average daily net is about thirty dollars."

"This isn't going to work."

"No."　80

"Can you lend me some money?"

"I can't do that," he said. "If I lend you money, I have to lend money to everybody."

"What can you do?"

"I'll give you fifty papers for free. But don't tell anybody I did it."

"Okay," I said.　85

He gathered up the newspapers and handed them to me. I held them to my chest. He hugged me. I carried the newspapers back toward the water.

5:00 P.M.

Back on the wharf, I stood near the Bainbridge Island Terminal and tried to sell papers to business commuters walking onto the ferry.

I sold five in one hour, dumped the other forty-five into a garbage can, and walked into the McDonald's, ordered four cheeseburgers for a dollar each, and slowly ate them.

After eating, I walked outside and vomited on the sidewalk. I hated to lose my food so soon after eating it. As an alcoholic Indian with a busted stomach, I always hope I can keep enough food in my stomach to stay alive.

6:00 P.M.

With one dollar in my pocket, I walked back to Junior. He was still passed out, so 90 I put my ear to his chest and listened for his heartbeat. He was alive, so I took off his shoes and socks and found one dollar in his left sock and fifty cents in his right sock. With two dollars and fifty cents in my hand, I sat beside Junior and thought about my grandmother and her stories.

When I was sixteen, my grandmother told me a story about World War II. She was a nurse at a military hospital in Sydney, Australia. Over the course of two years, she comforted and healed U.S. and Australian soldiers.

One day, she tended to a wounded Maori soldier. He was very darkskinned. His hair was black and curly, and his eyes were black and warm. His face with covered with bright tattoos.

"Are you Maori?" he asked my grandmother.

"No," she said. "I'm Spokane Indian. From the United States."

"Ah, yes," he said. "I have heard of your tribes. But you are the first American 95 Indian I have ever met."

"There's a lot of Indian soldiers fighting for the United States," she said. "I have a brother still fighting in Germany, and I lost another brother on Okinawa."

"I am sorry," he said. "I was on Okinawa as well. It was terrible."

He had lost his legs to an artillery attack.

"I am sorry about your legs," my grandmother said.

"It's funny, isn't it?" he asked. 100

"What's funny?"

"How we brown people are killing other brown people so white people will remain free."

"I hadn't thought of it that way."

"Well, sometimes I think of it that way. And other times, I think of it the way they want me to think of it. I get confused."

She fed him morphine. 105

"Do you believe in heaven?" he asked.

"Which heaven?" she asked.

"I'm talking about the heaven where my legs are waiting for me."

They laughed.

"Of course," he said, "my legs will probably run away from me when I get to 110 heaven. And how will I ever catch them?"

"You have to get your arms strong," my grandmother said. "So you can run on your hands."

They laughed again.

Sitting beside Junior, I laughed with the memory of my grandmother's story. I put my hand close to Junior's mouth to make sure he was still breathing. Yes, Junior was alive, so I took his two dollars and fifty cents and walked to the Korean grocery store over in Pioneer Square.

7:00 P.M.

In the Korean grocery store, I bought a fifty-cent cigar and two scratch lottery tickets for a dollar each. The maximum cash prize was five hundred dollars a ticket. If I won both, I would have enough money to buy back the regalia.

I loved Kay, the young Korean woman who worked the register. She was the daughter of the owners and sang all day.

"I love you," I said when I handed her the money.

"You always say you love me," she said.

"That's because I will always love you."

"You are a sentimental fool."

"I'm a romantic old man."

"Too old for me."

"I know I'm too old for you, but I can dream."

"Okay," she said. "I agree to be a part of your dreams, but I will only hold your hand in your dreams. No kissing and no sex. Not even in your dreams."

"Okay," I said. "No sex. Just romance."

"Good-bye, Jackson Jackson, my love, I will see you soon."

I left the store, walked over to Occidental Park, sat on a bench, and smoked my cigar all the way down.

Ten minutes after I finished the cigar, I scratched my first lottery ticket and won nothing. So I could win only five hundred dollars now, and that would be just half of what I needed.

Ten minutes later, I scratched my other lottery ticket and won a free ticket, a small consolation and one more chance to win money.

I walked back to Kay.

"Jackson Jackson," she said. "Have you come back to claim my heart?"

"I won a free ticket," I said.

"Just like a man," she said. "You love money and power more than you love me."

"It's true," I said. "And I'm sorry it's true."

She gave me another scratch ticket, and I carried it outside. I liked to scratch my tickets in private. Hopeful and sad, I scratched that third ticket and won real money. I carried it back inside to Kay.

"I won a hundred dollars," I said.

She examined the ticket and laughed. "That's a fortune," she said and counted out five twenties. Our fingertips touched as she handed me the money. I felt electric and constant.

"Thank you," I said and gave her one of the bills.

"I can't take that," she said. "It's your money."

"No, it's tribal. It's an Indian thing. When you win, you're supposed to share with your family."

"I'm not your family."

"Yes, you are."

She smiled. She kept the money. With eighty dollars in my pocket, I said good-bye to my dear Kay and walked out into the cold night air.

8:00 P.M.

I wanted to share the good news with Junior. I walked back to him, but he was gone. I later heard he had hitchhiked down to Portland, Oregon, and died of exposure in an alley behind the Hilton Hotel.

9:00 P.M.

Lonely for Indians, I carried my eighty dollars over to Big Heart's in South Downtown. Big Heart's is an all-Indian bar. Nobody knows how or why Indians migrate to one bar and turn it into an official Indian bar. But Big Heart's has been an Indian bar for twenty-three years. It used to be way up on Aurora Avenue, but a crazy Lummi Indian burned that one down, and the owners moved to the new location, a few blocks south of Safeco Field.

I walked inside Big Heart's and counted fifteen Indians, eight men and seven women. I didn't know any of them, but Indians like to belong, so we all pretended to be cousins.

"How much for whiskey shots?" I asked the bartender, a fat white guy.

"You want the bad stuff or the badder stuff?"

"As bad as you got."

"One dollar a shot."

I laid my eighty dollars on the bar top.

"All right," I said. "Me and all my cousins here are going to be drinking eighty shots. How many is that apiece?"

"Counting you," a woman shouted from behind me, "that's five shots for everybody."

I turned to look at her. She was a chubby and pale Indian sitting with a tall and skinny Indian man.

"All right, math genius," I said to her and then shouted for the whole bar to hear. "Five drinks for everybody!"

All of the other Indians rushed the bar, but I sat with the mathematician and her skinny friend. We took our time with our whiskey shots.

"What's your tribe?" I asked them.

"I'm Duwamish," she said. "And he's Crow."

"You're a long way from Montana," I said to him.

"I'm Crow," he said. "I flew here."

"What's your name?" I asked them.

"I'm Irene Muse," she said. "And this is Honey Boy."

She shook my hand hard, but he offered his hand like I was supposed to kiss it. So I kissed it. He giggled and blushed as well as a dark-skinned Crow can blush.

"You're one of them two-spirits, aren't you?" I asked him.

"I love women," he said. "And I love men."

"Sometimes both at the same time," Irene said.

We laughed.

"Man," I said to Honey Boy. "So you must have about eight or nine spirits going on inside of you, enit?"

"Sweetie," he said, "I'll be whatever you want me to be."

"Oh, no," Irene said. "Honey Boy is falling in love."

"It has nothing to do with love," he said.   170

We laughed.

"Wow," I said. "I'm flattered, Honey Boy, but I don't play on your team."

"Never say never," he said.

"You better be careful," Irene said. "Honey Boy knows all sorts of magic. He always makes straight boys fall for him."

"Honey Boy," I said, "you can try to seduce me. And Irene, you can try with him.   175
But my heart belongs to a woman named Kay."

"Is your Kay a virgin?" Honey Boy asked.

We laughed.

We drank our whiskey shots until they were gone. But the other Indians bought me more whiskey shots because I'd been so generous with my money. Honey Boy pulled out his credit card, and I drank and sailed on that plastic boat.

After a dozen shots, I asked Irene to dance. And she refused. But Honey Boy shuffled over to the jukebox, dropped in a quarter, and selected Willie Nelson's "Help Me Make It Through the Night." As Irene and I sat at the table and laughed and drank more whiskey, Honey Boy danced a slow circle around us and sang along with Willie.

"Are you serenading me?" I asked him.   180

He kept singing and dancing.

"Are you serenading me?" I asked him again.

"He's going to put a spell on you," Irene said.

I leaned over the table, spilling a few drinks, and kissed Irene hard. She kissed me back.

10:00 P.M.

Irene pushed me into the women's bathroom, into a stall, shut the door behind us,   185
and shoved her hand down my pants. She was short, so I had to lean over to kiss her. I grabbed and squeezed her everywhere I could reach, and she was wonderfully fat, and every part of her body felt like a large, warm, and soft breast.

Midnight

Nearly blind with alcohol, I stood alone at the bar and swore I'd been standing in the bathroom with Irene only a minute ago.

"One more shot!" I yelled at the bartender.

"You've got no more money!" he yelled.

"Somebody buy me a drink!" I shouted.

"They've got no more money!"   190

"Where's Irene and Honey Boy?"

"Long gone!"

2:00 A.M.

"Closing time!" the bartender shouted at the three or four Indians still drinking hard after a long hard day of drinking. Indian alcoholics are either sprinters or marathon runners.

"Where's Irene and Honey Bear?" I asked.

"They've been gone for hours," the bartender said.   195

"Where'd they go?"

"I told you a hundred times, I don't know."

"What am I supposed to do?"

"It's closing time. I don't care where you go, but you're not staying here."

"You are an ungrateful bastard. I've been good to you."   200

"You don't leave right now, I'm going to kick your ass."

"Come on, I know how to fight."

He came for me. I don't remember what happened after that.

4:00 A.M.

I emerged from the blackness and discovered myself walking behind a big ware-house. I didn't know where I was. My face hurt. I touched my nose and decided it might be broken. Exhausted and cold, I pulled a plastic tarp from a truck bed, wrapped it around me like a faithful lover, and fell asleep in the dirt.

6:00 A.M.

Somebody kicked me in the ribs. I opened my eyes and looked up at a white cop. 205

"Jackson," said the cop. "Is that you?"

"Officer Williams," I said. He was a good cop with a sweet tooth. He'd given me hundreds of candy bars over the years. I wonder if he knew I was diabetic.

"What the hell are you doing here?" he asked.

"I was cold and sleepy," I said. "So I laid down."

"You dumb-ass, you passed out on the railroad tracks."   210

I sat up and looked around. I was lying on the railroad tracks. Dockworkers stared at me. I should have been a railroad-track pizza, a double Indian pepperoni with extra cheese. Sick and scared, I leaned over and puked whiskey.

"What the hell's wrong with you?" Officer Williams asked. "You've never been this stupid."

"It's my grandmother," I said. "She died."

"I'm sorry, man. When did she die?"

"1972."   215

"And you're killing yourself now?"

"I've been killing myself ever since she died."

He shook his head. He was sad for me. Like I said, he was a good cop.

"And somebody beat the hell out of you," he said. "You remember who?"

"Mr. Grief and I went a few rounds."   220

"It looks like Mr. Grief knocked you out."

"Mr. Grief always wins."

"Come on," he said, "let's get you out of here."

He helped me stand and led me over to his squad car. He put me in the back. "You throw up in there," he said, "and you're cleaning it up."

"That's fair," I said.   225

He walked around the car and sat in the driver's seat. "I'm taking you over to detox," he said.

"No, man, that place is awful," I said. "It's full of drunk Indians."

We laughed. He drove away from the docks.

"I don't know how you guys do it," he said.

"What guys?" I asked.

"You Indians. How the hell do you laugh so much? I just picked your ass off the railroad tracks, and you're making jokes. Why the hell do you do that?"

"The two funniest tribes I've ever been around are Indians and Jews, so I guess that says something about the inherent humor of genocide."

We laughed.

"Listen to you, Jackson. You're so smart. Why the hell are you on the streets?"

"Give me a thousand dollars, and I'll tell you."

"You bet I'd give you a thousand dollars if I knew you'd straighten up your life."

He meant it. He was the second-best cop I'd ever known.

"You're a good cop," I said.

"Come on, Jackson," he said. "Don't blow smoke up my ass."

"No, really, you remind me of my grandfather."

"Yeah, that's what you Indians always tell me."

"No, man, my grandfather was a tribal cop. He was a good cop. He never arrested people. He took care of them. Just like you."

"I've arrested hundreds of scumbags, Jackson. And I've shot a couple in the ass."

"It don't matter. You're not a killer."

"I didn't kill them. I killed their asses. I'm an ass-killer."

We drove through downtown. The missions and shelters had already released their overnighters. Sleepy homeless men and women stood on corners and stared up at the gray sky. It was the morning after the night of the living dead.

"Did you ever get scared?" I asked Officer Williams.

"What do you mean?"

"I mean, being a cop, is it scary?"

He thought about that for a while. He contemplated it. I liked that about him.

"I guess I try not to think too much about being afraid," he said. "If you think about fear, then you'll be afraid. The job is boring most of the time. Just driving and looking into dark corners, you know, and seeing nothing. But then things get heavy. You're chasing somebody or fighting them or walking around a dark house and you just know some crazy guy is hiding around a corner, and hell yes, it's scary."

"My grandfather was killed in the line of duty," I said.

"I'm sorry. How'd it happen?"

I knew he'd listen closely to my story.

"He worked on the reservation. Everybody knew everybody. It was safe. We aren't like those crazy Sioux or Apache or any of those other warrior tribes. There's only been three murders on my reservation in the last hundred years."

"That is safe."

"Yeah, we Spokane, we're passive, you know? We're mean with words. And we'll cuss out anybody. But we don't shoot people. Or stab them. Not much, anyway."

"So what happened to your grandfather?"

"This man and his girlfriend were fighting down by Little Falls."

"Domestic dispute. Those are the worst."

"Yeah, but this guy was my grandfather's brother. My great-uncle."

"Oh, no."

"Yeah, it was awful. My grandfather just strolled into the house. He'd been there a thousand times. And his brother and his girlfriend were all drunk and beating on each other. And my grandfather stepped between them just like he'd done a hundred times before. And the girlfriend tripped or something. She fell down and hit her head and started crying. And my grandfather knelt down beside her to make sure she was all right. And for some reason, my great-uncle reached down, pulled my grandfather's pistol out of the holster, and shot him in the head."

"That's terrible. I'm sorry."

"Yeah, my great-uncle could never figure out why he did it. He went to prison for-ever, you know, and he always wrote these long letters. Like fifty pages of tiny little handwriting. And he was always trying to figure out why he did it. He'd write and write and write and try to figure it out. He never did. It's a great big mystery."

"Do you remember your grandfather?"

"A little bit. I remember the funeral. My grandmother wouldn't let them bury him. My father had to drag her away from the grave."

"I don't know what to say."

"I don't, either."

We stopped in front of the detox center.

"We're here," Officer Williams said.

"I can't go in there," I said.

"You have to."

"Please, no. They'll keep me for twenty-four hours. And then it will be too late."

"Too late for what?"

I told him about my grandmother's regalia and the deadline for buying it back.

"If it was stolen," he said, "then you need to file reports. I'll investigate it myself. If that thing is really your grandmother's, I'll get it back for you. Legally."

"No," I said. "That's not fair. The pawnbroker didn't know it was stolen. And be-sides, I'm on a mission here. I want to be a hero, you know? I want to win it back like a knight."

"That's romantic crap."

"It might be. But I care about it. It's been a long time since I really cared about something."

Officer Williams turned around in his seat and stared at me. He studied me.

"I'll give you some money," he said. "I don't have much. Only thirty bucks. I'm short until payday. And it's not enough to get back the regalia. But it's something."

"I'll take it," I said.

"I'm giving it to you because I believe in what you believe. I'm hoping, and I don't know why I'm hoping it, but I hope you can turn thirty bucks into a thousand somehow."

"I believe in magic."

"I believe you'll take my money and get drunk on it."

"Then why are you giving it to me?"

"There ain't no such thing as an atheist cop."

"Sure there is."

"Yeah, well, I'm not an atheist cop."

He let me out of the car, handed me two fives and a twenty, and shook my hand. "Take care of yourself, Jackson," he said. "Stay off the railroad tracks."

"I'll try," I said.

He drove away. Carrying my money, I headed back toward the water.

8:00 A.M.

On the wharf, those three Aleut men still waited on the wooden bench.

"Have you seen your ship?" I asked.

"Seen a lot of ships," the elder Aleut said. "But not our ship."

I sat on the bench with them. We sat in silence for a long time. I wondered whether we would fossilize if we sat there long enough.

I thought about my grandmother. I'd never seen her dance in her regalia. More than anything, I wished I'd seen her dance at a powwow.

"Do you guys know any songs?" I asked the Aleuts.

"I know all of Hank Williams," the elder Aleut said.

"How about Indian songs?"

"Hank Williams is Indian."

"How about sacred songs?"

"Hank Williams is sacred."

"I'm talking about ceremonial songs, you know, religious ones. The songs you sing back home when you're wishing and hoping."

"What are you wishing and hoping for?"

"I'm wishing my grandmother was still alive."

"Every song I know is about that."

"Well, sing me as many as you can."

The Aleuts sang their strange and beautiful songs. I listened. They sang about my grandmother and their grandmothers. They were lonely for the cold and snow. I was lonely for everybody.

10:00 A.M.

After the Aleuts finished their last song, we sat in silence. Indians are good at silence.

"Was that the last song?" I asked.

"We sang all the ones we could," the elder Aleut said. "All the others are just for our people."

I understood. We Indians have to keep our secrets. And these Aleuts were so secretive that they didn't refer to themselves as Indians.

"Are you guys hungry?" I asked.

They looked at one another and communicated without talking.

"We could eat," the elder Aleut said.

11:00 A.M.

The Aleuts and I walked over to Mother's Kitchen, a greasy diner in the International District. I knew they served homeless Indians who'd lucked in to money.

"Four for breakfast?" the waitress asked when we stepped inside.

"Yes, we're very hungry," the elder Aleut said.

She sat us in a booth near the kitchen. I could smell the food cooking. My stomach growled.

"You guys want separate checks?" the waitress asked.

"No, I'm paying for it," I said.

"Aren't you the generous one," she said.

"Don't do that," I said.

"Do what?" she asked.

"Don't ask me rhetorical questions. They scare me."

She looked puzzled, and then she laughed.

"Okay, Professor," she said. "I'll only ask you real questions from now on."

"Thank you."

"What do you guys want to eat?"

"That's the best question anybody can ask anybody," I said.

"How much money you got?" she asked.

"Another good question," I said. "I've got twenty-five dollars I can spend. Bring us all the breakfast you can, plus your tip."

She knew the math.

"All right, that's four specials and four coffees and fifteen percent for me."

The Aleuts and I waited in silence. Soon enough, the waitress returned and poured us four coffees, and we sipped at them until she returned again with four plates of food. Eggs, bacon, toast, hash-brown potatoes. It is amazing how much food you can buy for so little money.

Grateful, we feasted.

Noon

I said farewell to the Aleuts and walked toward the pawnshop. I later heard the Aleuts had waded into the saltwater near Dock 47 and disappeared. Some Indians said the Aleuts walked on the water and headed north. Other Indians saw the Aleuts drown. I don't know what happened to them.

I looked for the pawnshop and couldn't find it. I swear it wasn't located in the place where it had been before. I walked twenty or thirty blocks looking for the pawnshop, turned corners and bisected intersections, looked up its name in the phone books, and asked people walking past me if they'd ever heard of it. But that pawnshop seemed to have sailed away from me like a ghost ship. I wanted to cry. Right when I'd given up, when I turned one last corner and thought I might die if I didn't find that pawnshop, there it was, located in a space I swore it hadn't been filling up a few minutes before.

I walked inside and greeted the pawnbroker, who looked a little younger than he had before.

"It's you," he said.

"Yes, it's me," I said.

"Jackson Jackson."

"That is my name."

"Where are your friends?"

"They went traveling. But it's okay. Indians are everywhere."

"Do you have my money?"

"How much do you need again?" I asked and hoped the price had changed.

"Nine hundred and ninety-nine dollars."

It was still the same price. Of course it was the same price. Why would it change?

"I don't have that," I said.

"What do you have?"

"Five dollars."

I set the crumpled Lincoln on the countertop. The pawnbroker studied it.

"Is that the same five dollars from yesterday?"

"No, it's different."

He thought about the possibilities.

"Did you work hard for this money?" he asked.

"Yes," I said.   360

He closed his eyes and thought harder about the possibilities. Then he stepped into his back room and returned with my grandmother's regalia.

"Take it," he said and held it out to me.

"I don't have the money."

"I don't want your money."

"But I wanted to win it."   365

"You did win it. Now, take it before I change my mind."

Do you know how many good men live in this world? Too many to count!

I took my grandmother's regalia and walked outside. I knew that solitary yellow bead was part of me. I knew I was that yellow bead in part. Outside, I wrapped myself in my grandmother's regalia and breathed her in. I stepped off the sidewalk and into the intersection. Pedestrians stopped. Cars stopped. The city stopped. They all watched me dance with my grandmother. I was my grandmother, dancing. ●

Explorations of the Text

1. Explain the significance of the title.

2. Alexie's story opens with Jackson saying that "Indians have to work hard to keep secrets from hungry white folks." As the story continues, the theme of secrets and secrecy is returned to several times. Consider the significance of secrecy within the story.

3. Jackson says that the attempt to regain his grandmother's regalia is a "quest." When he gives the pawnbroker $5.00, he tells him that he wanted to "win," to be a "hero." What does Jackson mean? Why is this quest symbolic?

4. Why does the pawnbroker give the regalia to Jackson for $5.00? Does Jackson win?

5. In Alexie's story, many of the Native American characters that Jackson befriends are homeless, and all move on to new places. Why? Consider the meaning of their rootlessness.

6. Compare and contrast Jackson's quest with that of the narrator in "In Search of Epifano."

7. Is the symbolism of Jackson's regalia similar to that of the quilts in Alice Walker's "Everyday Use" (Chapter 6) or of the shawl in Cynthia Ozick's story (Chapter 8)? Explain.

8. Consider the themes of free will and determinism in Alexie's story and in Flannery O'Connor's "A Good Man is Hard to Find." Do the characters in these stories have control over their fates? Explain.

The Reading/Writing Connection

1. **Write an Argument:** Sherman Alexie's work is considered controversial because of his portrayal of Native Americans as poor, drunk, and dispirited. Go on the Internet and research the condition of Native Americans in the United States. Document your research in a writing journal. Then take a position in the Alexie controversy by agreeing with him that his portrayal of Native Americans is realistic or by opposing his portrayal as unnecessarily harsh.

2. Imagine that you are a judge and that Jackson's trial has come before you. Jackson claims that the regalia is his grandmother's, and he can prove it by the existence of the yellow bead. The pawnbroker insists that Jackson is lying. Using the evidence from Alexie's story, decide the case. Who would you decide for and why?

Ideas for Writing

1. In "Reflections on Exile," Edward Said wrote, "[Exile is] the unhealable rift forced between a human being and a native place, between the self and its true home: its essential sadness can never be surmounted. . . . The achievements of exile are permanently under-mined by the loss of something left behind forever." Analyze Alexie's story through Said's quotation. What images of exile are present in Alexie's story?

2. Consider the title of the story. What is redeemed?

Facing Death/Fiction

Ben Okri *(1959–)*

A Prayer from the Living   *1993*

We entered the town of the dying at sunset. We went from house to house. Everything was as expected, run-down, a desert, luminous with death and hidden life.

The gunrunners were everywhere. The world was now at the perfection of chaos. The little godfathers who controlled everything raided the food brought for us. They raided the airlifts and the relief aid and distributed most of the food among themselves and members of their clan.

We no longer cared. Food no longer mattered. I had done without for three weeks. Now I feed on the air and on the quest.

Every day, as I grow leaner, I see more things around us. I see the dead—all who had died of starvation. They are more joyful now; they are happier than we are; and they are everywhere, living their luminous lives as if nothing had happened, or as if they were more alive than we are.

The hungrier I became, the more I saw them—my old friends who had died before me, clutching onto flies. Now they feed on the light of the air. And they look at us—the living—with so much pity and compassion.

I suppose this is what the white ones cannot understand when they come with their TV cameras and their aid. They expect to see us weeping. Instead, they see us staring at them, without begging, and with a bulging placidity in our eyes. Maybe they are secretly horrified that we are not afraid of dying this way.

But after three weeks of hunger the mind no longer notices; you're more dead than alive; and it's the soul wanting to leave that suffers. It suffers because of the body's tenacity.

We should have come into the town at dawn. In the town everyone had died. The horses and cows were dying, too. I could say that the air stank of death, but that wouldn't be true. It smelled of rancid butter and poisoned heat and bad sewage. There was even the faint irony of flowers.

The only people who weren't dead were the dead. Singing golden songs in chorus, jubilant everywhere, they carried on their familiar lives. The only others who weren't dead were the soldiers. And they fought among themselves eternally. It didn't seem to matter to them how many died. All that mattered was how well they handled the grim mathematics of the wars, so that they could win the most important battle of all, which was for the leadership of the fabulous graveyard of this once beautiful and civilized land.

I was searching for my family and my lover. I wanted to know if they had died or not. If I didn't find out, I intended to hang on to life by its last tattered thread. If I knew that they, too, were dead and no longer needed me, I would die at peace.

All my information led me to this town. If my lover, my brothers, my family are anywhere, they are here. This is the last town in the world. Beyond its rusted gate lies the desert. The desert stretches all the way into the past; into history, to the Western world, and to the source of drought and famine—the mighty mountain of lovelessness. From its peaks, at night, the grim spirits of negation chant their awesome soul-shrinking songs. Their songs steal hope from us and make us yield to the air our energies. Their songs are cool and make us submit to the clarity of dying.

Behind us, in the past, before all this came to be, there were all the possibilities in the world. There were all the opportunities for starting from small things to create a sweet new history and future, if only we had seen them. But now, ahead, there lie only the songs of the mountain of death.

We search for our loved ones mechanically and with a dryness in our eyes. Our stomachs no longer exist. Nothing exists except the search. We turn the bodies over, looking for familiar faces. All the faces are familiar; death made them all my kin.

I search on, I come across an unfamiliar face; it is my brother. I nod. I pour dust on his flesh. Hours later, near a dry well, I come across the other members of my family. My mother holds on tightly to a bone so dry it wouldn't even nourish the flies. I nod twice. I pour dust on their bodies. I search on. There is one more face whose beautiful unfamiliarity will console me. When I have found the face, then I will submit myself to the mountain songs.

Sunset was approaching when, from an unfinished school building, I heard singing. It was the most magical sound I had ever heard and I thought only those who know how sweet life is can sing like that, can sing as if breathing were a prayer.

The singing was like the joyous beginning of all creation, the holy yes to the breath and light infusing all things, which makes the water shimmer, the plants sprout, the animals jump and play in the fields, and which makes the men and women look out into the first radiance of colors, the green of plants, the blue of sea, the gold of the air, the silver of the stars. It was the true end of my quest, the music to crown this treacherous life of mine, the end I couldn't have hoped for, or imagined.

It seemed to take an infinity of time to get to the school building. I had no strength left, and it was only the song's last echo, resounding through the vast spaces of my hunger, that sustained me. After maybe a century, when history had repeated itself and brought about exactly the same circumstances, because none of us ever learned our lesson, or loved enough to learn from our pain, I finally made it to the schoolroom door. But a cow, the only living thing left in the town, went in through the door before I did. It, too, must have been drawn by the singing. The cow went into the room, and I followed.

Inside, all the space was taken up with the dead. But here the air didn't have death in it. The air had prayer in it. The prayers stank more than the deaths. But all the dead here were differently dead from the corpses outside. The dead in the school were—forgive the paradox—*alive*. I have no other word to explain the serenity. I felt they had made the room holy because they had, in their last moments, thought not of themselves but of all people who suffer. I felt that to be the case because I felt myself doing the same thing. I crawled to a corner, sat against a wall, and felt myself praying for the whole human race.

I prayed—knowing full well that prayers are possibly an utter waste of time—but I prayed for everything that lived, for mountains and trees, for animals and streams, and for human beings, wherever they might be. I heard the great anguished cry of all mankind, its great haunting music as well. And I, too, without moving my mouth, for I had no energy, began to sing in silence. I sang all through the evening. And when I looked at the body next to me and found the luminous unfamiliarity of its face to be that of my lover's—I sang all through the recognition. I sang silently even when a good-hearted white man came into the school building with a television camera and, weeping, recorded the roomful of the dead for the world—and I hoped he recorded my singing, too.

And the dead were all about me, smiling, serene. They didn't urge me on; they were   20
just quietly and intensely joyful. They did not ask me to hurry to them, but left it to me. What could I choose? Human life—full of greed and bitterness, dim, low-oxygenated, judgmental and callous, gentle, too, and wonderful as well, but . . . human life had betrayed me. And besides, there was nothing left to save in me. Even my soul was dying of starvation.

I opened my eyes for the last time. I saw the cameras on us all. To them, we were the dead. As I passed through the agony of the light, I saw them as the dead, marooned in a world without pity or love.

As the cow wandered about in the apparent desolation of the room, it must have seemed odd to the people recording it all that I should have made myself so comfortable among the dead. I did. I stretched myself out and held the hand of my lover. With a painful breath and a gasp and a smile, I let myself go.

The smile must have puzzled the reporters. If they had understood my language, they would have known that it was my way of saying goodbye. ●

Rudolfo Anaya *(1937–)*

In Search of Epifano *2006*

She drove into the desert of Sonora in search of Epifano. For years, when summer came and she finished her classes, she had loaded her old Jeep with supplies and gone south into Mexico.

Now she was almost eighty, and she thought, ready for death, but not afraid of death. It was the pain of the bone-jarring journey which was her reality, not thoughts of death. But that did not diminish the urgency she felt as she drove south, across the desert. She was following the north rim of El Cañon de Cobre towards the land of the Tarahumaras.[1] In the Indian villages there was always a welcome and fresh water.

The battered Jeep kicked up a cloud of chalky dust which rose into the empty and searing sky of summer. Around her, nothing moved in the heat. Dry mirages rose and shimmered, without content, without form. Her bright, clear eyes remained fixed on the rocky, rutted road in front. Around her there was only the vast and empty space of the desert. The dry heat.

The Jeep wrenched sideways, the low gear groaning and complaining. It had broken down once, and had cost her many days' delay in Mexicali. The mechanic at

---

[1]**Tarahumaras:** Indigenous people of Northern Mexico.

the garage told her not to worry. In one day the parts would be in from Calexico and she would be on her way.

But she knew the way of the Mexican, so she rented a room in a hotel nearby. Yes, 5 she knew the Mexican. Part of her blood was Mexican, wasn't it? Her great-grandfather, Epifano, had come north to Chihuahua to ranch and mine. She knew the stories whispered about the man, how he had built the great ranch in the desert. His picture was preserved in the family album, at his side, his wife, a dark-haired woman. Around them, their sons.

The dry desert air burned her nostrils. A scent of the green ocotillo reached her, reminded her of other times, other years. She knew how to live in the sun, how to travel and how to survive, and she knew how to be alone under the stars. Night was her time in the desert. She liked to lie in her bedroll and look up at the swirling dance of the stars. In the cool of evening her pulse would quicken. The sure path of the stars was her map, drawing her south.

Sweat streaked her wrinkled skin. Sweat and dust, the scent commingling. She felt alive. "At least I'm not dry and dead," she said aloud. Sweat and pleasure, it came together.

The Jeep worried her now. A sound somewhere in the gear box was not right. "It has trouble," the mechanic had said, wiping his oily hands on a dirty rag. What he meant was that he did not trust his work. It was best to return home, he suggested with a shrug. He had seen her musing over the old and tattered map, and he was concerned about the old woman going south. Alone. It was no good.

"We all have trouble," she mumbled. We live too long and the bones get brittle and the blood dries up. Why can't I taste the desert in my mouth? Have I grown so old? Epifano? How does it feel to become a spirit of the desert?

Her back and arms ached from driving; she was covered with the dust of the des- 10 ert. Deep inside, in her liver or in her spleen, in one of those organs which the ancients called the seat of life, there was an ache, a dull, persistent pain. In her heart there was a tightness. Would she die and never reach the land of Epifano?

She slept while she waited for the Jeep to be repaired. Slept and dreamed under the shade of the laurel in the patio of the small hotel. Around her Mexican sounds and colors permeated her dream. What did she dream? That it was too late in her life to go once again into the desert? That she was an old woman and her life was lived, and the only evidence she would leave of her existence would be her sketches and paintings? Even now, as weariness filled her, the dreams came, and she slipped in and out of past and present. In her dreams she heard the voice of the old man, Epifano.

She saw his eyes, blue and bright like hers, piercing, but soft. The eyes of a kind man. He had died. Of course, he had died. He belonged to the past. But she had not forgotten him. In the family album, which she carried with her, his gaze was the one that looked out at her and drew her into the desert. She was the artist of the family. She had taken up painting. She heard voices. The voice of her great-grandfather. The rest of her family had forgotten the past, forgotten Mexico and the old man Epifano.

The groaning of the Jeep shattered the silence of the desert. She tasted dust in her mouth, she yearned for a drink of water. She smiled. A thirst to be satisfied. Always there was one more desire to be satisfied. Her paintings were like that, a desire from within to be satisfied, a call to do one more sketch of the desert in the molten light before night came. And always the voice of Epifano drawing her to the trek into the past.

The immense solitude of the desert swallowed her. She was only a moving shadow in the burning day. Overhead, vultures circled in the sky, the heat grew intense. She was alone on a dirt road she barely remembered, taking her bearings only by instinct, roughly following the north rim of the Cañon de Cobre, drawn by the thin line of the horizon, where the dull peaks of las montañas met the dull blue of the sky. Whirlwinds danced in her eyes, memories flooded at her soul.

She had married young. She thought she was in love; he was a man of ambition. It took her years to learn that he had little desire or passion. He could not, or would not, fulfill her. What was the fulfillment she sought? It had to do with something that lay even beneath the moments of love or children carried in the womb. Of that she was sure.

She turned to painting, she took classes, she traveled alone. She came to understand that she and the man were not meant for each other.

She remembered a strange thing had happened in the chapel where the family gathered to attend her marriage. An Indian had entered and stood at the back of the room. She had turned and looked at him. Then he was gone, and later she was not sure if the appearance was real or imagined.

But she did not forget. She had looked into his eyes. He had the features of a Tarahumara. Was he Epifano's messenger? Had he brought a warning? For a moment she hesitated, then she had turned and said yes to the preacher's question. Yes to the man who could never understand the depth of her passion. She did what was expected of her there in the land of ocean and sun. She bore him a daughter and a son. But in all those years, the man never understood the desire in her, he never explored her depth of passion. She turned to her dreams, and there she heard the voice of Epifano, a resonant voice imparting seductive images of the past.

Years later she left her husband, left everything, left the dream of southern California where there was no love in the arms of the man, no sweet juices in the nights of love pretended. She left the circle of pretend. She needed a meaning, she needed desperately to understand the voices which spoke in her soul. She drove south, alone, in search of Epifano. The desert dried her by day, but replenished her at night. She learned that the mystery of the stars, at night, was like the mystery in her soul.

She sketched, she painted, and each year in spring time she drove farther south. On her map she marked her goal, the place where once stood Epifano's hacienda.

In the desert the voices were clear. She followed the road into Tarahumara country, she dreamed of the old man, Epifano. She was his blood, the only one who remembered him.

At the end of day she stood at the side of a pool of water, a small, desert spring surrounded by desert trees. The smell in the air was cool, wet. At her feet, tracks of deer, a desert cat. Ocelot. She stooped to drink, like a cautious animal.

"Thank the gods for this water which quenches our thirst," she said, splashing the precious water on her face, knowing there is no life in the desert without the water which flows from deep within the earth. Around her, the first stars of dusk begin to appear.

She had come at last to the ranch of Epifano. There, below the spring where she stood, on the flat ground, was the hacienda. Now could be seen only the outlines of the foundation and the shape of the old corrals. From here his family had spread, northwest, up into Mexicali and finally into southern California. Seeds. Desert seeds seeking precious water. The water of desire. And only she had returned.

She sat and gazed at the desert, the peaceful quiet mauve of the setting sun. She felt a deep sadness within. An old woman, sitting alone in the wide desert, her dream done.

A noise causes her to turn. Perhaps an animal come to drink at the spring, the same spring where Epifano had once wet his lips. She waited, and in the shadows of the palo verde and the desert willows she saw the Indian appear. She smiled.

She was dressed in white, the color of desire not consummated. Shadows moved around her. She had come home, home to the arms of Epifano. The Indian was a tall, splendid man. Silent. He wore paint, as they did in the old days when they ran the game of the pelota up and down las montañas of the Cañon de Cobre.

"Epifano," she said, "I came in search of Epifano." He understood the name. Epifano. He held his hand to his chest. His eyes were bright and blue, not Tarahumara eyes, but the eyes of Epifano. He had known she would come. Around her other shadows moved, the women. Indian women of the desert. They moved silently around her, a circle of women, an old ceremony about to begin.

The sadness left her. She struggled to rise, and in the dying light of the sun a blinding flash filled her being. Like desire, or like an arrow from the bow of the Indian, the light filled her and she quivered.

The moan of love is like the moan of life. She was dressed in white. ●   30

Explorations of the Text

1. List common themes from the two stories and/or the web selection.
2. Characterize the portrayal of death in these works. What are the narrators' attitudes toward dying?
3. In "In Search of Epifano," the woman dies because she is old. Why are the people dying in "A Prayer from the Living"?
4. Consider the spiritual messages within the stories. What purpose do these messages serve?

5. In "A Prayer from the Living," the narrator cannot die until he or she finds the dead bodies of his or her family and lover and covers them with dust. In "In Search of Epifano," the narrator cannot die until her quest has ended. In Sophocles's *Antigone* (Chapter 8), Antigone's quest is to ensure the proper burial of her brother's body, and once she completes it, she is killed. Consider the symbolic relationship between the quest and death. Why does the quest so often end with death?

The Reading/Writing Connection

1. In "In Search of Epifano," the narrator dies in the desert with the stars overhead. In "A Prayer from the Living," the narrator dies in a church holding the hand of his or her lover. Write a poem or prose poem describing the place of your death.
2. Freewrite: If your life is a quest, for what are you searching?

Ideas for Writing

1. **Write an Argument:** Albert Camus wrote, "But in order to speak about all to all, one has to speak of what we know and the reality common to all. The sea, the rain, necessity, desire, and the struggle against death—these are the things that unite us all." Using evidence from the works in the cluster, agree or disagree with Camus's statement.

2. Analyze the themes and imagery of death in one of the works. Is death portrayed as a fearful or as a beautiful fate?

www **On the Web:** *Death in the Midst of Life*

Please visit http://www.academic.cengage.com/english/Schmidt/Legacies4e/ for a link to the following online resource.
Jeff Biggers, "Saying Goodbye in the Sierra Madre"

POETRY

William Butler Yeats   *(1865–1939)*

The Second Coming[1]   *1919*

Turning and turning in the widening gyre
The falcon cannot hear the falconer;
Things fall apart; the center cannot hold;
Mere anarchy is loosed upon the world,
The blood-dimmed tide is loosed, and everywhere   5
The ceremony of innocence is drowned;
The best lack all conviction, while the worst
Are full of passionate intensity.

Surely some revelation is at hand.
Surely the Second Coming is at hand.   10
The Second Coming! Hardly are those words out
When a vast image out of *Spiritus Mundi*[2]
Troubles my sight: somewhere in sands of the desert
A shape with lion body and the head of a man,[3]
A gaze blank and pitiless as the sun,   15
Is moving its slow thighs, while all about it
Reel shadows of the indignant desert birds.
The darkness drops again; but now I know
That twenty centuries[4] of stony sleep
Were vexed to nightmare[5] by a rocking cradle,   20
And what rough beast, its hour come round at last,
Slouches towards Bethlehem[6] to be born?

Explorations of the Text

1. What do the symbols of the "gyre," "the falcon," and "the falconer" suggest about the speaker's view of the state of the world?

2. Why do "Things fall apart"? Why is it that "the center cannot hold"?

3. Explore the significance of the images of the Egyptian sphinx, the "blank and pitiless" gaze, and the "shadows of the indignant desert birds."

---

[1] *The Second Coming*: Allusion to Jesus's prediction of his second coming. Written in 1919, the poem refers to the Black and Tan War in Ireland when British soldiers were sent to quell the republicans.   [2] *Spiritus Mundi*: The author's term for divine inspiration or for a place from which images are received, never invented.   [3] **A shape . . . man:** The Egyptian sphinx.   [4] **twenty centuries:** Reference to twenty centuries of Christianity.   [5] **vexed to nightmare:** Implication that Christianity created its opposite.   [6] **Bethlehem:** Birthplace of Jesus.

4. Why does Yeats choose the word "reel" in line 17? What is the effect of this word choice?

5. What is the speaker's view of the millennium? of the Apocalypse? What will be "born"?

6. Examine the rhyme scheme of the poem. Why do you think Yeats rhymes only certain lines?

7. Discuss the meaning and **irony** of the title and of the ending.

The Reading/Writing Connection

1. "Think" Topic: Do you agree with Yeats's view of the decline of civilization?

Ideas for Writing

1. Does Yeats's vision seem relevant today? What world events may be evoked by references in the poem?

2. Contrast Yeats's view of the future with the ideas in two other works in this chapter.

Rabindranath Tagore   *(1861–1941)*

Gitanjali: Songs I and II   *1910*

I

Thou hast made me endless, such is thy pleasure. This frail vessel
thou emptiest again and again, and fillest it ever with fresh life.
　　This little flute of a reed thou hast carried over hills and dales, and
has breathed through it melodies eternally new.
　　At the immortal touch of thy hands my little heart loses its limits   5
in joy, and gives birth to utterance ineffable.
　　Thy infinite gifts come to me only on these very small hands of
mine. Ages pass, and still thou pourest, and still there is room to fill.

II

When thou commandest me to sing, it seems that my heart would
break with pride; and I look to thy face, and tears come to my eyes.   10
　　All that is harsh and dissonant in my life melts into one sweet
harmony—and my adoration spreads wings like a glad bird on its
flight across the sea.
　　I know thou takest pleasure in my singing. I know that only as a
singer I come before thy presence.   15

Explorations of the Text

Song I

1. What does the speaker experience? Examine the images of the "vessel," the "flute," and the "heart."

2. What does the speaker mean when he describes "utterance ineffable"?

3. Interpret the last line. Explain the **paradox.**

Song II

1. What is the commandment "to sing"? Explain the bird **simile**.
2. Why does "all that is harsh and dissonant" melt? Describe the speaker's version of harmony, of joy.

3. Why can the speaker come into the presence of divinity only as a singer? What does the joy of "singing" suggest?
4. Compare Tagore's and Rilke's views of spirit and divinity.

The Reading/Writing Connection

1. Describe the voice in these lyrics.
2. Create your own version of a third song in this sequence. Consider speaker, tone, imagery, and theme.

Ideas for Writing

1. Characterize the speaker.
2. How does Tagore's poetry differ from other poets?

Rainer Maria Rilke   *(1875–1926)*

Sonnet 1   *1923*

There arose a tree. Oh, pure transcension!
Oh, Orpheus sings[1]! Oh, tall tree in the ear!
And all was still. But even in this suspension
new beginnings, signs, and changes were.

Animals from the silence, from the clear   5
now opened wood came forth from nest and den;
and it so came to pass that not from fear
or craftiness were they so quiet then,

but to be listening. Howling, cry, roar
seemed little to their hearts. Where scarce a   10

---

[1]**Orpheus sings:** According to Greek mythology, Orpheus was the son of Oeagrus, a river god, and one of the Muses (Polyhymnia, Clio, or Calliope). Born in Thrace, Orpheus may have been king of some Thracian tribes and was famous as a great singer, musician, and poet. In some legends, he supposedly invented the lyre. Because of the magic of his songs, all of nature responded to his music. Wild animals followed him, trees and plants leaned in his direction, and he tamed the souls of the wildest men.

The most famous exploit of Orpheus concerns his descent into the underworld to save his wife, Eurydice, who died when a serpent bit her. Inconsolable, he charmed monsters guarding the gates of hell and the gods of the dead in order to rescue her. For a brief moment, even the damned were relieved of pain by his music. The underworld deities, Hades and Persephone, agreed to allow Eurydice to return to earth with one stipulation: that Orpheus, followed by Eurydice, leave and that he not look back at her. When he could not resist temptation, he turned around, and she disappeared—lost to him forever.

humble
hut for such reception was before,

a hiding-place of the obscurest yearning,
with entrance shaft whose underpinnings tremble,
you made for the beasts temples in the hearing.   15

Rainer Maria Rilke *(1875–1926)*

Sonnet 29 *1923*

Still friend of many distances, feel yet
how your breathing is augmenting space.
From the beamwork of gloomy belfries let
yourself ring. What devours you will increase

more strongly from this food. Explore and win   5
knowledge of transformation through and
    through.
What experience was the worst for you?
Is drinking bitter, you must turn to wine.

Be the magic power of this immense   10
midnight at the crossroads of your senses,
be the purport of their strange meeting.
    Though

earth itself forgot your very name,
say unto the tranquil earth: I flow.   15
To the fleeting water speak: I am.

Explorations of the Text

1. In "Sonnet I," what is the "transcension" in the first quatrain? What does the tree symbolize? What is the "tall tree in the ear"?

2. In "Sonnet 29," who is the "friend"? How does the poet win "transformation"? What is the value of the "worst" "experience"?

3. In "Sonnet I," why do the animals come forth? Explicate: "Howling, cry, roar / seemed little to their hearts."

4. In "Sonnet 29," what does the speaker mean: "By the magic power of this immense / midnight at the crossroads of your senses"?

5. Interpret the last three lines of either poem. In "Sonnet I," who is "you"? In "Sonnet 29," what is the meaning of the declarations "I flow" and "I am"?

6. Compare the form of the two sonnets.

The Reading/Writing Connection

1. Gloss, annotate, and comment on one of the two sonnets.
2. "Think" Topic: Discuss transformation in Rilke's sonnets.

3. Write a poem in which you create a scene in which music or art transforms animals and/or people.

Ideas for Writing

1. Explicate and evaluate either sonnet. Use The Reading/Writing Connection 1 as a beginning, focusing on imagery and form (see Chapter 11).
2. Explore the theme of transformation in these poems, in "Diving into the Wreck," and in "My Name Is 'I am Living.'"

> 3. **Write an Argument:** Can the poet or his or her art change the world?

Adrienne Rich *(1929–)*

Diving into the Wreck *1972*

First having read the book of myths,
and loaded the camera,
and checked the edge of the knife-blade,
I put on
the body-armor of black rubber   5
the absurd flippers
the grave and awkward mask.
I am having to do this
not like Cousteau[1] with his
assiduous team   10
aboard the sun-flooded schooner
but here alone.

There is a ladder.
The ladder is always there
hanging innocently   15
close to the side of the schooner.
We know what it is for,
we who have used it.
Otherwise
it's a piece of maritime floss   20
some sundry equipment.

I go down.
Rung after rung and still

---

[1] **Cousteau:** French underwater explorer and filmmaker (1910–1997).

the oxygen immerses me
the blue light   25
the clear atoms
of our human air.
I go down.
My flippers cripple me,
I crawl like an insect down the ladder   30
and there is no one
to tell me when the ocean
will begin.

First the air is blue and then
it is bluer and then green and then   35
black I am blacking out and yet
my mask is powerful
it pumps my blood with power
the sea is another story
the sea is not a question of power   40
I have to learn alone
to turn my body without force
in the deep element.

And now: it is easy to forget
what I came for   45
among so many who have always
lived here
swaying their crenellated[2] fans
between the reefs
and besides   50
you breathe differently down here.

I came to explore the wreck.
The words are purposes.
The words are maps.
I came to see the damage that was done   55
and the treasures that prevail.
I stroke the beam of my lamp
slowly along the flank
of something more permanent
than fish or weed   60

the thing I came for:
the wreck and not the story of the wreck
the thing itself and not the myth
the drowned face always staring
toward the sun   65
the evidence of damage

---

[2]**crenellated:** Having notched or scalloped projections.

worn by salt and sway into this threadbare beauty
the ribs of the disaster
curving their assertion
among the tentative haunters.   70
This is the place.
And I am here, the mermaid whose dark hair
streams black, the merman in his armored body
We circle silently
about the wreck   75
we dive into the hold.
I am she: I am he

whose drowned face sleeps with open eyes
whose breasts still bear the stress
whose silver, copper, vermeil[3] cargo lies   80
obscurely inside barrels
half-wedged and left to rot
we are the half-destroyed instruments
that once held to a course
the water-eaten log   85
the fouled compass

We are, I am, you are
by cowardice or courage
the one who find our way
back to this scene   90
carrying a knife, a camera
a book of myths
in which
our names do not appear.

Derek Walcott   *(1930–)*

The Season of Phantasmal Peace   *1984*

Then all the nations of birds lifted together
the huge net of the shadows of this earth
in multitudinous dialects, twittering tongues,
stitching and crossing it. They lifted up
the shadows of long pines down trackless slopes,   5
the shadows of glass-faced towers down evening streets,
the shadow of a frail plant on a city sill—
the net rising soundless as night, the birds' cries soundless, until
there was no longer dusk, or season, decline, or weather,
only this passage of phantasmal light   10
that not the narrowest shadow dared to sever.

---

[3]**vermeil:** Metal that is gilded.

And men could not see, looking up, what the wild geese drew,
what the ospreys trailed behind them in silvery ropes
that flashed in the icy sunlight; they could not hear
battalions of starlings waging peaceful cries,   15
bearing the net higher, covering this world
like the vines of an orchard, or a mother drawing.
the trembling gauze over the trembling eyes
of a child fluttering to sleep;
                              it was the light   20
that you will see at evening on the side of a hill
in yellow October, and no one hearing knew
what change had brought into the raven's cawing,
the killdeer's screech, the ember-circling chough
such an immense, soundless, and high concern   25
for the fields and cities where the birds belong,
except it was their seasonal passing, Love,
made seasonless, or, from the high privilege of their birth,
something brighter than pity for the wingless ones
below them who shared dark holes in windows and in houses,   30
and higher they lifted the net with soundless voices
above all change, betrayals of falling suns,
and this season lasted one moment, like the pause
between dusk and darkness, between fury and peace,
but, for such as our earth is now, it lasted long.   35

Explorations of the Text

1. Walcott refers to the seasons in the title and in the poem itself. Discuss the significance of seasons within the poem.
2. Why is the "season of . . . peace" "phantasmal"?
3. What does "the huge net of the shadows of this earth" symbolize?
4. Walcott uses **personification** (see Glossary) when describing the birds. What effect does this have on the poem's meaning? List the reasons why he might have chosen to portray the birds in this manner. Why might he have used birds and not another creature or thing to lift the shadow?
5. Why can the men "not see" what the birds are doing?
6. Consider the portrayal of humans in this poem and in Alice Walker's "Am I Blue?" What might have influenced Walcott and Walker to describe humans as they do?

The Reading/Writing Connection

1. The poem begins with "Then . . . ," an indication that something must have come before. Write a stanza or two to precede "Then," explaining what led to the birds' action.
2. Compare visions of the future in this poem with that in Wislawa Szymborska's poems. Then, borrowing from their ideas, create your own vision of the future, either as a poem or as a short story or essay.

Ideas for Writing

1. Analyze the role of animals in Walcott's poem and two other works in this chapter. Consider the ways that the lives of nonhumans and humans are intertwined.

2. **Write an Argument:** Is peace "phantasmal"? Why?

Gloria Anzaldúa *(1942–2004)*

In this poem, the speaker begins by reflecting on being a "mulata"[1]—Hispanic, Indian, black, Spanish, and white.

To live in the Borderlands means you 1986

To live in the Borderlands means you
    are neither *hispana india negra española*[2]
    ni[3] *gabacha,*[4] *eres mestiza,*[5] *mulata,* half-breed
    caught in the crossfire between camps
    while carrying all five races on your back   5
    not knowing which side to turn to, run from;

To live in the Borderlands means knowing
    that the *india* in you, betrayed for 500 years,
    is no longer speaking to you,
    that *mexicanas* call you *rajetas,*[6]   10
    that denying the Anglo inside you
    is as bad as having denied the Indian or Black;

Cuando vives en la frontera[7]
    people walk through you, the wind steals your voice,
    you're a *burra,*[8] *buey,*[9] scapegoat,   15
    forerunner of a new race,
    half and half—both woman and man, neither—
    a new gender;

To live in the Borderlands means to
    put *chile* in the borscht,
    eat whole wheat *tortillas,*   20
    speak Tex-Mex with a Brooklyn accent;
    be stopped by *la migra* at the border checkpoints;

---

[1]**mulata:** A person of mixed racial ancestry. [2]**hispana india negra española:** Spanish, Indian, black, black Spanish woman. [3]**ni:** Neither (nor). [4]**gabacha:** A Chicano term for a white woman [Author's note]. [5]**eres mestiza:** You are of mixed blood. [6]**rajetas:** Literally, "Split," that is, having betrayed your word [Author's note]. [7]**Cuando vives en la frontera:** When you live in the borderlands. [8]**burra:** Donkey [Author's note]. [9]**buey:** Ox [Author's note].

Living in the Borderlands means you fight hard to
    resist the gold elixer beckoning from the bottle,   25
    the pull of the gun barrel,
    the rope crushing the hollow of your throat;

In the Borderlands
    you are the battleground
    where enemies are kin to each other;   30
    you are at home, a stranger,
    the border disputes have been settled
    the volley of shots have shattered the truce
    you are wounded, lost in action
    dead, fighting back;   35

To live in the Borderlands means
    the mill with the razor white teeth wants to shred off
    your olive-red skin, crush out the kernel, your heart
    pound you pinch you roll you out
    smelling like white bread but dead;   40

To survive the Borderlands
    you must live *sin fronteras*[10]
    be a crossroads.

Explorations of the Text

1. Who is "you"? How does the speaker characterize "you"?
2. In the Borderlands, "people walk through you, the wind steals your voice"—why?
3. How does the speaker extend her vision beyond the "mestiza"? Whom does her vision include? What are the other borders?
4. Analyze stanzas 5–8. To what specific historical contexts does Anzaldúa refer in stanzas 5 and 6?
5. Explain the symbolism of "the mill" in stanza 7. What is the central metaphor?
6. Examine the speaker's conclusion. What **paradox** is apparent?
7. Analyze the impact of the Spanish words. What do they add to the poem's effect?
8. Compare views of language, heritage, and naming in this poem with those in Rich's "Diving into the Wreck."

The Reading/Writing Connection

1. Freewrite. Respond to this poem. How do you react to the violent images?
2. "Think" Topic: Analyze the poem's structure as if it were an expository essay. What modes of development does Anzaldúa employ?

---

[10]**sin fronteras:** Without borders [Author's note].

Ideas for Writing

1. Compare processes of awakening and revelation in this poem and in "Diving into the Wreck."
2. How does Anzaldúa envision/re-envision North American ethnic identity? Do you agree?
3. Paraphrase and analyze the political argument of this poem.
4. Contrast Anzaldúa's view of "living in the borderlands" with Tagore's view of a limitless world.

Marjorie Agosin *(1955–)*

Far Away *2003*

My country is a slender pier
anchored inside me
curving between
my knees and skin
still damp from the sun.   5
My country is a tatter of stars like pockmarks
a rhapsody of useless voices
that come out to mourn the moon
through the ravished pelt
of plain daylight.   10

My country is a blue vial
hidden and radiant as the sea
or the shadow of your eyes
that never will be blue.

My country is a man   15
whom I loved
and when he kissed me
my legs turned to rain
to a grove
to a boundary of holy water.   20
My country is the color of smoke
and coal-heated irons
that drowsily envelop
the houses of adobe.

My country   25
is my house with the keys
hidden waiting for me,
on the beach.

Marjorie Agosin *(1955–)*

The Foreigner *2003*

You will search for another
landscape in which
to speak with
your dead.
No words   5
will respond to the voices of your love.
You will make up another gaze
and you will walk with your head bowed as if wounded
in borrowed cities.

You will know that there will be no return for you   10
and you will name those who made
of your memory
a language of orphanhood.
You will think of other breaths
because yours are distant and alone   15
because your language
carries the shadows of strangers.

Explorations of the Text

1. In "Far Away," metaphors define the speaker's relationship with her country. Explicate each one. What does each signify? How do the metaphors change? What do they suggest about her state of exile?

2. Explore the significance of the closing stanza.

3. In "The Foreigner," characterize the speaker's persona and voice.

4. In "The Foreigner," explore the significance of the "language of orphanhood." How does language separate her from others? How does it carry the memories of the past?

5. Who are "the strangers"? Discuss the significance of the closing two lines: "your language / carries the shadows of strangers."

6. A state of exile often is characterized by a sense of never feeling rooted, of being caught between worlds. Revisit Cervantes's "Refugee Ship" in Chapter 1 for a vision of this sense of rootlessness. How do these three poems portray this state?

The Reading/Writing Connection

1. "Think" Topic: How do these two poems use body imagery to suggest the speaker's state of being?

2. Create a poem of "return" OR, Create a sequel to "The Foreigner" in the voice of one of her forebears.

Ideas for Writing

1. Compare and contrast Agosin's "search" for roots with that of Eugene Gloria in "Assimilation."

Eugene Gloria

Assimilation 2001

On board the Victory Line Bus
boring down Kennon Road
from a weekend in Baguio[1]
is the bus driver's sideline:
a Coleman chest full of cold Cokes and Sprites,   5
a loaf sack of sandwiches
wrapped in pink napkin and cellophane.
My hunger sated by thin white
bread thick with mayonnaise,
diced pickles and slim slice of ham.   10
What's mere snack
for my gaunt Filipino seatmate,
was my American lunch, a habit
of eating, shaped by boyhood shame.
You see, there was a time when I believed   15
that a meal meant at least a plate of rice
with a sauced dish like *kare kare,*
or *pinakbet* pungent with *bagoong.*
But homeboys like us are marked
by experience of not being part of the whole   20
in a playground full of white kids lined
on red-painted benches in the fall chill of noon,
lunchpails bright with their favorite cartoons,
and a thermos of milk, or brown paper sacks
with Glad bags of chips, peeled Sunkist,   25
Mom's special sandwich with crisp leaf of lettuce,
and pressed turkey thick in between—
crumbed with the breakfast table bread.
I remember that first day of school, my mother
with the purest intention,   30
took two sheets of foil hollowed
with a cup of steamed rice
and a helping of last night's
caldereta: chunks of potatoes, sliced
red peppers, and a redder sauce with beef;   35
and I, with hunger, could not
bring myself to eat.
Ashamed to be more different
than what my face had already betrayed,
the rice, I hid from my schoolmates.   40

Next morning, my mother grasped
the appropriate combination: fruit,

---

[1]**Baguio:** A city in the Philippines.

sandwich cut into two triangles,
handful of chips, my best broken English.
And weeks passed while the scattered rice—   45
beneath the length of the red-painted bench—
blackened with the schoolyard's dirt.

Explorations of the Text

1. Consider the poem's title. Is "assimilation" something to be desired? What word might better describe an ideal situation for immigrants?

2. Discuss the food symbolism. Why did his Filipino lunch cause the speaker to feel ashamed? Why might Gloria have ended the poem with the image of "scattered rice / . . . blackened with the schoolyard's dirt"?

3. Why, when describing the American lunch prepared for him by his mother, does the poet include "my best broken English"? In what way does his "broken English" relate to the "handful of chips"?

4. In Marjorie Agosin's poems, "Far Away" and "The Foreigner," the theme of exile from one's native land is explored. Compare the concept of immigration in Agosin's work to Gloria's. What images are similar? In what ways do the writers present different visions?

5. In "The Case for Contamination," Kwame Anthony Appiah says that the "right approach" to globalization "starts by taking individuals—not nations, tribes, or 'peoples'—as the proper object of moral concern." Discuss this idea in relation to the speaker's situation in Gloria's poem.

The Reading/Writing Connection

1. Journal entry: Write about a time that you felt different, that you did not belong. What situation led to this feeling? What did you do to deal with it?

2. Double-entry journal: Using two columns, write words from the poem that describe the Filipino food, and words from the poem that describe the American food. Then, in another column, record your impressions about the foods and the cultures from which they come. What can we know about a culture by the preparation of its food?

Ideas for Writing

1. **Write an Argument:** The speaker's "shame" occurs when he is in school and wants to be the same as his schoolmates. Create a plan that schools can implement to welcome newcomers. Write this plan as an argument to present at a school board meeting.

Anna Lee Walters (1946–)

My Name Is "I Am Living" 1975

My name is "I am living."
My home is all directions and is everlasting.
Instructed and carried to you by the wind,
I have felt the feathers in pale clouds and bowed before the Sun
who watches me from a blanket of faded blue.   5

In a gentle whirlwind I was shaken,
made to see on earth in many ways,
And when in awe my mouth fell open,
I tasted a fine red clay.
Its flavor has remained after uncounted days.   10
This gave me cause to drink from a crystal stream
that only I have seen.
So I listened to all its flowing wisdom
and learned from it a Song—
This song the wind and I   15
have since sung together.
Unknowing, I was encircled by its water and cleansed.
Naked and damp, I was embraced and dried
by the warmth of your presence.
Dressed forever in the scent of dry cedar,   20
I am purified and free.
And I will not allow you to ignore me.
I have brought to you a gift.
It is all I have but it is yours.
You may reach out and enfold it.   25
It is only the strength in the caress of a gentle breeze,
But it will carry you to meet the eagle in the sky.
My name is "I am living." I am here.
My name is "I am living." I am here.

e. e. cummings *(1894–1962)*

the little horse is newlY   1950

the little horse is newlY

Born)he knows nothing,and feels
everything;all around whom is

perfectly a strange
ness Of sun   5
light and of fragrance and of

Singing)is ev
erywhere(a welcom
ing dream:is amazing)
a worlD.and in   10

this world lies:smoothbeautifuL
ly folded;a(brea
thing and a gro

Wing)silence,who;
is:somE   15

oNe.

Explorations of the Text

1. Who is the "I" in Walters's poem? Using words and images from Walters's and cummings's poems, define "I."

2. Note the structure of cummings's poem, his use of upper- and lower-case letters, line breaks, and punctuation. How does this structure create meaning? Compare it to the structure of Walters' poem.

3. Who is the narrator of "the little horse is newlY"? Who is the "somE / oNe" referred to in the last stanza?

4. At the end of "My Name is 'I Am Living,'" what is the "gift"? To whom is the gift given?

5. Consider the themes and images in "My Name is 'I Am Living'" and in Allen Ginsberg's "Sunflower Sutra." List the images in Ginsberg's poem that Walters's narrator might consider "gifts." Why are these gifts, and not other images in the poem?

The Reading/Writing Connection

1. Imagine that "My Name is 'I am Living'" is a song sung by the "little horse" during his first week of life. Write a narrative of the little horse as he discovers life, relating his experiences to some of the images in "My Name is 'I Am Living.'"

2. Using cummings's and Walters's poems, create an environmental philosophy of life.

Ideas for Writing

1. **Write an Argument:** In "The Ends of the World as We Know Them," Jared Diamond discusses the necessity for humans to respect the environment. Using the philosophy of life developed in question number 2 under "The Reading/Writing Connection," argue that this philosophy will help to avoid the collapse foreseen by Diamond if humans do not change their ways.

Mary Oliver   *(1935–)*

Spring   *2005*

Somewhere
   a black bear
      has just risen from sleep
        and is staring

down the mountain.   5
   All night
      in the brisk and shallow restlessness
        of early spring

I think of her,
   her four black fists   10
      flicking the gravel,
        her tongue

like a red fire
   touching the grass,
      the cold water.   15
         There is only one question:

how to love this world.
   I think of her
     rising
       like a black and leafy ledge   20

to sharpen her claws against
   the silence
     of the trees.
       Whatever else

my life is   25
   with its poems
     and its music
       and its glass cities,

it is also this dazzling darkness
   coming   30
     down the mountain,
       breathing and tasting;
   all day I think of her—
     her white teeth,
     her wordlessness,   35
       her perfect love.

Robert Frost *(1874–1963)*

The Bear *1928*

The bear puts both arms around the tree above her
And draws it down as if it were a lover
And its chokecherries lips to kiss good-by,
Then lets it snap back upright in the sky.
Her next step rocks a boulder on the wall   5
(She's making her cross-country in the fall).
Her great weight creaks the barbed wire in its staples
As she flings over and off down through the maples,
Leaving on one wire tooth a lock of hair.
Such is the uncaged progress of the bear.   10
The world has room to make a bear feel free;
The universe seems cramped to you and me.
Man acts more like the poor bear in a cage,
That all day fights a nervous inward rage,
His mood rejecting all his mind suggests.   15
He paces back and forth and never rests

The toenail click and shuffle of his feet,
The telescope at one end of his beat,
And at the other end the microscope,
Two instruments of nearly equal hope,   20
And in conjunction giving quite a spread.
Or if he rests from scientific tread,
'Tis only to sit back and sway his head
Through ninety-odd degrees of arc, it seems,
Between two metaphysical extremes.   25
He sits back on his fundamental butt
With lifted snout and eyes (if any) shut
(He almost looks religious but he's not),
And back and forth he sways from cheek to cheek,
At one extreme agreeing with one Greek,   30
At the other agreeing with another Greek,
Which may be thought, but only so to speak.
A baggy figure, equally pathetic
When sedentary and when peripatetic.

Explorations of the Text

1. Oliver's poem takes place in the spring, and Frost's is in the fall. How are the bears' activities different in the two seasons? What is the symbolic nature of these seasons in the poems?

2. Both Oliver and Frost characterize the bears in terms of love. Oliver ends the poem with the bear's "wordlessness, / her perfect love." Why might these writers use the words "love" and "lover" when writing of bears? In what context is a bear's love "perfect"?

3. Why do you think that Oliver and Frost chose the bear as the subject and not another animal? What might the bears symbolize?

4. Although the two poems focus on the bears, humanity is interjected, in Oliver's through the use of the word "I," and in Frost's through a meditation of humanity at the poem's end. Explain the connection in each poem between bears and humans.

5. Consider the picture of the world as portrayed in Walters's "My Name is 'I Am Living'" and Oliver's and Frost's poems. What message is being conveyed?

The Reading/Writing Connection

1. Write a poem or short story about an animal, using the animal as a symbol for humanity or as a way to convey a lesson about humanity. Then write a short explanation of why you chose the animal you did. You may refer to the excerpt from *Maus II* in Chapter 8 for ideas.

Ideas for Writing

1. **Write an Argument:** In Frost's poem, humans are portrayed as caged animals. Argue in favor of or in opposition to this image, using as examples evidence from this poem and two other works in this chapter.

2. Analyze one of the two poems using the other as a critical lens.
3. Both "Spring" and "The Bear" share spiritual visions of nature. Compare and contrast Oliver's and Frost's spiritual visions with that of Scott Russell Sanders in "The Force of Spirit."

Allen Ginsberg   *(1926–1997)*

Sunflower Sutra   *1955*

I walked on the banks of the tincan banana dock and
    sat down under the huge shade of a Southern
    Pacific locomotive to look at the sunset over the
    box house hills and cry.
Jack Kerouac sat beside me on a busted rusty iron   5
    pole, companion, we thought the same thoughts
    of the soul, bleak and blue and sad-eyed, surrounded
    by the gnarled steel roots of trees of machinery.
The oily water on the river mirrored the red sky, sun
    sank on top of final Frisco peaks, no fish in that   10
    stream, no hermit in those mounts, just ourselves
    rheumy-eyed and hungover like old bums on the
    riverbank, tired and wily.
Look at the Sunflower, he said, there was a dead gray
    shadow against the sky, big as a man, sitting dry on   15
    top of a pile of ancient sawdust—
—I rushed up enchanted—it was my first sunflower,
    memories of Blake—my visions—Harlem
and Hells of the Eastern rivers, bridges clanking Joes
    Greasy Sandwiches, dead baby carriages, black   20
    treadless tires forgotten and unretreaded, the poem
    of the riverbank, condoms & pots, steel knives,
    nothing stainless, only the dank muck and the
    razor-sharp artifacts passing into the past—
and the gray Sunflower poised against the sunset, crackly   25
    bleak and dusty with the smut and smog and smoke
    of olden locomotives in its eye—
corolla of bleary spikes pushed down and broken like a
    battered crown, seeds fallen out of its face, soon-to-be-
    toothless mouth of sunny air, sunrays obliterated on its   30
    hairy head like a dried wire spiderweb,
leaves stuck out like arms out of the stem, gestures from
    the sawdust root, broke pieces of plaster fallen out
    of the black twigs, a dead fly in its ear,
Unholy battered old thing you were, my sunflower O   35
    my soul, I loved you then!
The grime was no man's grime but death and human
    locomotives,
all that dress of dust, that veil of darkened railroad skin,

that smog of cheek, that eyelid of black mis'ry, that sooty   40
    hand or phallus or protuberance of artificial worse-than-
    dirt—industrial—modern—all that civilization spotting
    your crazy golden crown—
and those blear thoughts of death and dusty loveless
    eyes and ends and withered roots below, in the   45
    home-pile of sand and sawdust, rubber dollar bills,
    skin of machinery, the guts and innards of the
    weeping coughing car, the empty lonely tincans with
    their rusty tongues alack, what more could I name,
    the smoked ashes of some cock cigar, the cunts of   50
    wheelbarrows and the milky breasts of cars, wornout
    asses out of chairs & sphincters of dynamos—all these
entangled in your mummied roots—and you there standing
    before me in the sunset, all your glory in your form!
A perfect beauty of a sunflower! a perfect excellent lovely   55
    sunflower existence! a sweet natural eye to the new hip
    moon, woke up alive and excited grasping in the sunset
    shadow sunrise golden monthly breeze!
How many flies buzzed round you innocent of your grime,
    while you cursed the heavens of the railroad and your   60
    flower soul?
Poor dead flower? when did you forget you were a flower?
    when did you look at your skin and decide you were
    an impotent dirty old locomotive? the ghost of a
    locomotive? the specter and shade of a once powerful   65
    mad American locomotive?
You were never no locomotive, Sunflower, you were a
    sunflower!
And you Locomotive, you are a locomotive, forget me
    not!   70
So I grabbed up the skeleton thick sunflower and stuck it
    at my side like a scepter,
and deliver my sermon to my soul, and Jack's soul too, and
    anyone who'll listen,
—We're not our skin of grime, we're not our dread bleak   75
    dusty imageless locomotive, we're all beautiful golden
    sunflowers inside, we're blessed by our own seed &
    golden hairy naked accomplishment-bodies growing
    into mad black formal sunflowers in the sunset, spied
    on by our eyes under the shadow of the mad locomotive   80
    riverbank sunset Frisco hilly tincan evening sitdown vision.

Explorations of the Text

1. A "sutra" is a Buddhist scriptural narrative. What spiritual elements do you notice in the poem that characterize it as a sutra? Why might Ginsberg have written a sutra for the sunflower?

2. Allen Ginsberg and Jack Kerouac were members of the Beat movement (see Glossary), whose writing was characterized by its beatific, energetic, run-on sentences and contrasting images. List the elements of Beat writing that you find in Ginsberg's poem. How do these elements contribute to the poem's tone and meaning?

3. What does the locomotive symbolize in this poem? The sunflower? Explicate the poem's conclusion.

4. Allen Ginsberg claims to have been influenced by the poetry of Walt Whitman. Read "Out of the Cradle Endlessly Rocking" (Chapter 5), and compare the poetry of the two writers. What similarities do you notice between the style and structure of the writers' poems? Are the images, symbols, and meanings also similar? You may also want to read Ginsberg's poem "America" in Chapter 8.

The Reading/Writing Connection

1. "Think" topic: Ginsberg's poem was written in 1955. Do the images and attitudes in the poem seem as though they are consistent with what you know of 1950s America? Why or why not? Write a brief description of your perception of the time, and then contrast it to Ginsberg's portrayal.

2. Journal Entry: What memories does the sunflower unfold for Ginsberg? In a journal entry, describe your memories of the first time seeing a sunflower (or another flower). Write a short sutra for your flower memories.

Ideas for Writing

1. **Write an Argument:** The urban American landscape as described by Ginsberg in "Sunflower Sutra" has changed for the better since the poem was written in 1955. Argue pro or con.

2. Write a compare/contrast essay using images of the sunflower and images of the locomotive from Ginsberg's poem.

3. **Write an Argument:** Do the works of Ginsberg, Szymborska, and Walcott indicate hope for the future?

Wislawa Szymborska   *(1923–)*

The Century's Decline   *1986*

Our twentieth century was going to improve on the others.
It will never prove it now,
now that its years are numbered,
its gait is shaky,
its breath is short.   5

Too many things have happened
that weren't supposed to happen,
and what was supposed to come about
has not.

Happiness and spring, among other things,   10
were supposed to be getting closer.
Fear was expected to leave the mountains and the valleys.
Truth was supposed to hit home
before a lie.

A couple of problems weren't going   15
to come up anymore:
hunger, for example,
and war, and so forth.

There was going to be respect
for helpless people's helplessness,   20
trust, that kind of stuff.

Anyone who planned to enjoy the world
is now faced
with a hopeless task.

Stupidity isn't funny.   25
Wisdom isn't gay.
Hope
isn't that young girl anymore,
et cetera, alas.

God was finally going to believe   30
in a man both good and strong,
but good and strong
are still two different men.

"How should we live?" someone asked me in a letter.
I had meant to ask him   35
the same question.

Again, and as ever,
as may be seen above,
the most pressing questions
are naïve ones.   40

Wislawa Szymborska   *(1923–)*

Could Have   *1972*

It could have happened.
It had to happen.
It happened earlier. Later.
Nearer. Farther off.
It happened, but not to you.   5

You were saved because you were the first.
You were saved because you were the last.
Alone. With others.
On the right. The left.
Because it was raining. Because of the shade.   10
Because the day was sunny.

You were in luck—there was a forest.
You were in luck—there were no trees.
You were in luck—a rake, a hook, a beam, a brake,
a jamb, a turn, a quarter inch, an instant.   15
You were in luck—just then a straw went floating by.

As a result, because, although, despite.
What would have happened if a hand, a foot,
within an inch, a hairsbreadth from
an unfortunate coincidence.   20

So you're here? Still dizzy from another dodge, close shave,
    reprieve?
One hole in the net and you slipped through?
I couldn't be more shocked or speechless.
Listen,
how your heart pounds inside me.   25

Wislawa Szymborska   (1923–)

Hatred   *1993*

See how efficient it still is,
how it keeps itself in shape—
our century's hatred.
How easily it vaults the tallest obstacles.
How rapidly it pounces, tracks us down.   5

It's not like other feelings.
At once both older and younger.
It gives birth itself to the reasons
that give it life.
When it sleeps, it's never eternal rest.   10
And sleeplessness won't sap its strength; it feeds it.

One religion or another—
whatever gets it ready, in position.
One fatherland or another—
whatever helps it get a running start.   15
Justice also works well at the outset

until hate gets its own momentum going.
Hatred. Hatred.
Its face twisted in a grimace
of erotic ecstasy.   20

Oh these other feelings,
listless weaklings.
Since when does brotherhood
draw crowds?
Has compassion   25
ever finished first?
Does doubt ever really rouse the rabble?
Only hatred has just what it takes.
Gifted, diligent, hardworking.
Need we mention all the songs it has composed?   30
All the pages it has added to our history books?
All the human carpets it has spread
over countless city squares and football fields?

Let's face it:
it knows how to make beauty.   35
The splendid fire-glow in midnight skies.
Magnificent bursting bombs in rosy dawns.
You can't deny the inspiring pathos of ruins
and a certain bawdy humor to be found
in the sturdy column jutting from their midst.   40

Hatred is a master of contrast—
between explosions and dead quiet,
red blood and white snow.
Above all, it never tires
of its leitmotif—the impeccable executioner   45
towering over its soiled victim.

It's always ready for new challenges.
If it has to wait awhile, it will.
They say it's blind. Blind?
It has a sniper's keen sight   50
and gazes unflinchingly at the future
as only it can.

Wislawa Szymborska (1923–)

Children of Our Age   1986

We are children of our age,
it's a political age.

All day long, all through the night,
all affairs—yours, ours, theirs—
are political affairs. 5

Whether you like it or not,
your genes have a political past,
your skin, a political cast,
your eyes, a political slant.

Whatever you say reverberates, 10
whatever you don't say speaks for itself.
So either way you're talking politics.

Even when you take to the woods,
you're taking political steps
on political grounds. 15

Apolitical poems are also political,
and above us shines a moon
no longer purely lunar.
To be or not to be, that is the question.
And though it troubles the digestion 20
it's a question, as always, of politics.

To acquire a political meaning
you don't even have to be human.
Raw material will do,
or protein feed, or crude oil, 25

or a conference table whose shape
was quarreled over for months:
Should we arbitrate life and death
at a round table or a square one?

Meanwhile, people perished, 30
animals died,
houses burned,
and the fields ran wild
just as in times immemorial
and less political. 35

Explorations of the Text

1. In "Century's Decline," characterize the voice and tone of the speaker. Discuss the poet's use of irony.

2. Discuss the last two stanzas of "Century's Decline." What is the significance of the lines "the most pressing questions / are naive ones"? Does the poem answer the question "How should we live"?

3. In her poem "Children of Our Age," Wislawa Szymborska claims that we live in "a political age." Define "political."

4. In "Could Have," what "could have" happened? Who is the "you"? To whom is the persona speaking? Theorize the events to which the speaker is alluding. Are they necessarily specific? What does the poet accomplish by using abstract language?

5. In "Hatred," what poetic devices—forms of figurative language—does Szymborska use? Discuss the effect of this technique.

6. What view of fate is suggested in these poems?

7. What vision of the twentieth century is represented in the works?

8. Consider Szymborska's poetry through the lens of Dylan Thomas's "Do Not Go Gentle into That Good Night."

The Reading/Writing Connection

1. Journal Entry: Consider the idea of fate, of free will and determinism in Szymborska's poems. Create a double-entry journal of words and images that indicate our free will to change the future or deterministic elements that suggest the future is out of our control. Then analyze your journal entry and decide what position Syzmborska takes on this issue.

2. Write a poem in response to one of Szymborska's poems. You may choose to imitate her style.

Ideas for Writing

1. **Write an Argument:** Are Szymborksa's poems timeless, expressing truths about the past, present, and future, or are they firmly rooted in the events of the twentieth century?

2. Does "hatred" have the power the speaker ascribes to it? Compare and contrast Szymborska's vision of hatred with that of Andrew Sullivan (Chapter 8).

 On the Web: *Biographical and Critical Contexts, A Study of Wislawa Szymborska*

Please visit http://www.academic.cengage.com/english/Schmidt/Legacies4e/ for links to the following online resources.

Biography
Additional Poetry Selections
Banquet Speech
Critical Article: Malgorzata Anna Packalen, "A Domestication of Death: The Poetic Universe of Wislawa Szymborksa"
"Wislawa Szymborska Pages"

Linda Pastan *(1932–)*

Secrets *1981*

The secrets I keep
from myself
are the same secrets
the leaves keep

from the old trunk of the tree   5
even as they turn
color.

They are the garbled
secrets
of the waterfall   10
about to be stunned
on rock;
the sounds of the stream's
dry mouth
after weeks of drought.   15

Hush, says the nurse
to the new child howling
its one secret
into the world,
hush   20
as she buries
its mouth
in milk.

On the hearth the fire consumes
its own burning tongue,   25
I cannot read the ash.
By the gate
the trumpet flower sings
only silence
from its shapely   30
throat.

At night
I fall asleep
to the whippoorwill's
raucous lullabye,   35
old as the first garden:
never tell
never tell
never tell.

Robert Frost   *(1874–1963)*

Design   *1936*

I found a dimpled spider, fat and white,
On a white heal-all, holding up a moth
Like a white piece of rigid satin cloth—
Assorted characters of death and blight

Mixed ready to begin the morning right,   5
Like the ingredients of a witches' broth—
A snow-drop spider, a flower like a froth,
And dead wings carried like a paper kite.

What had that flower to do with being white,
The wayside blue and innocent heal-all?   10
What brought the kindred spider to that height,
Then steered the white moth thither in the night?
What but design of darkness to appall?—
If design govern in a thing so small.

Robert Frost *(1874–1963)*

After Apple-Picking   *1914*

My long two-pointed ladder's sticking through a tree
Toward heaven still,
And there's a barrel that I didn't fill
Beside it, and there may be two or three
Apples I didn't pick upon some bough.   5
But I am done with apple-picking now.
Essence of winter sleep is on the night,
The scent of apples: I am drowsing off.
I cannot rub the strangeness from my sight
I got from looking through a pane of glass   10
I skimmed this morning from the drinking trough
And held against the world of hoary grass.
It melted, and I let it fall and break.
But I was well
Upon my way to sleep before it fell,   15
And I could tell
What form my dreaming was about to take.
Magnified apples appear and disappear,
Stem end and blossom end,
And every fleck of russet showing clear.   20
My instep arch not only keeps the ache,
It keeps the pressure of a ladder-round.
I feel the ladder sway as the boughs bend.

And I keep hearing from the cellar bin
The rumbling sound   25
Of load on load of apples coming in.
For I have had too much
Of apple-picking: I am overtired
Of the great harvest I myself desired.

There were ten thousand thousand fruit to touch,   30
Cherish in hand, lift down, and not let fall.
For all
That struck the earth,
No matter if not bruised or spiked with stubble,
Went surely to the cider-apple heap   35
As of no worth.
One can see what will trouble
This sleep of mine, whatever sleep it is.
Were he not gone,
The woodchuck could say whether it's like his   40
Long sleep, as I describe its coming on,
Or just some human sleep.

Explorations of the Text

1. Linda Pastan notes that each living creature carries with it life's great secret. Why is "the new child howling" the only creature who tells the secret? Why is the secret a secret and not a message openly communicated to all?

2. In "After Apple-Picking," Frost refers to the importance of "cherish[ing]" each apple so as to avoid its being sent "to the cider-apple heap / As of no worth." Why might he have included these lines within a poem about seasonal change?

3. Why does Frost refer to the "design" of the spider's life "the design of darkness"? Why does "design . . . appall"?

4. List the themes and images that Pastan's and Frost's poems have in common. How is Pastan's secret present in "Design" and "After Apple-Picking"?

5. Discuss the relevance of seasons in Derek Walcott's "The Season of Phantasmal Peace," Frost's "After Apple-Picking," and at least one other poem in this chapter. Why are the seasons so frequently referred to in poetry?

The Reading/Writing Connection

1. Journal entry: Write a journal entry about a seasonal memory. Try to capture the sensual elements of the memory: the smells, sounds, and physical warmth or coldness of the time. How did the season influence your feelings at that time?

Ideas for Writing

1. Analyze these three poems, focusing on the design or pattern of life that lies behind each and is captured in the poems' images, themes, and ideas.

2. **Write an Argument:** Does Frost's poem "Design" indicate determinism? Does design necessarily conflict with free will?

Life in the Midst of Death/Poetry

Jorge Luis Borges   *(1899–1986)*   *Translated by Harold Morland*

Ars Poetica   1972

To gaze at the river made of time and water
And recall that time itself is another river,
To know we cease to be, just like the river,
And that our faces pass away, just like the water.

To feel that waking is another sleep   5
That dreams it does not sleep and that death,
Which our flesh dreads, is that very death
Of every night, which we call sleep.

To see in the day or in the year a symbol
Of mankind's days and of his years,   10
To transform the outrage of the years
Into a music, a rumor and a symbol,

To see in death a sleep, and in the sunset
A sad gold, of such is Poetry
Immortal and a pauper. For Poetry   15
Returns like the dawn and the sunset.

At times in the afternoons a face
Looks at us from the depths of a mirror;
Art must be like that mirror
That reveals to us this face of ours.   20

They tell how Ulysses,[1] glutted with wonders,
Wept with love to descry his Ithaca
Humble and green. Art is that Ithaca
Of green eternity, not of wonders.

It is also like an endless river   25
That passes and remains, a mirror for one same
Inconstant Heraclitus, who is the same
And another, like an endless river.

---

[1] **Ulysses:** Also known as Odysseus, hero of Homer's *Odyssey*. Ulysses was the son of Laertes, King of Ithaca, and participated in the Trojan War.

John Keats   *(1795–1821)*

Ode on a Grecian Urn   *1820*

I

Thou still unravished bride of quietness,
    Thou foster child of silence and slow time,
Sylvan[1] historian, who canst thus express
    A flowery tale more sweetly than our rhyme:
What leaf-fringed legend haunts about thy shape   5
    Of deities or mortals, or of both,
        In Tempe[2] or the dales of Arcady?[3]
    What men or gods are these? What maidens loath?
What mad pursuit? What struggle to escape?
        What pipes and timbrels? What wild ecstasy?   10

II

Heard melodies are sweet, but those unheard
    Are sweeter; therefore, ye soft pipes, play on;
Not to the sensual ear, but, more endeared,
    Pipe to the spirit ditties of no tone:
Fair youth, beneath the trees, thou canst not leave   15
    Thy song, nor ever can those trees be bare;
        Bold Lover, never, never canst thou kiss,
Though winning near the goal—yet, do not grieve;
        She cannot fade, though thou hast not thy bliss,
    Forever wilt thou love, and she be fair!   20

III

Ah, happy, happy boughs! that cannot shed
    Your leaves, nor ever bid the Spring adieu;
And, happy melodist, unweariéd,
    Forever piping songs forever new;
More happy love! more happy, happy love!   25
    Forever warm and still to be enjoyed,
        Forever panting, and forever young;
All breathing human passion far above,
    That leaves a heart high-sorrowful and cloyed,
        A burning forehead, and a parching tongue.   30

---

[1]**Sylvan:** Referring to woods or forest.   [2]**Tempe:** Valley in Greece.   [3]**Arcady:** Valleys of Arcadia, symbolic of pastoral life and beauty.

IV

Who are these coming to the sacrifice?
    To what green altar, O mysterious priest,
Lead'st thou that heifer lowing at the skies,
    And all her silken flanks with garlands dressed?
What little town by river or sea shore,   35
    Or mountain-built with peaceful citadel,
        Is emptied of this folk, this pious morn?
And, little town, thy streets forevermore
    Will silent be; and not a soul to tell
        Why thou art desolate, can e'er return.   40

V

O Attic[4] shape! Fair attitude! with brede[5]
    Of marble men and maidens overwrought,[6]
With forest branches and the trodden weed;
    Thou, silent form, dost tease us out of thought
As doth eternity: Cold Pastoral![7]   45
    When old age shall this generation waste,
        Thou shalt remain, in midst of other woe
    Than ours, a friend to man, to whom thou say'st,
"Beauty is truth, truth beauty,—that is all
    Ye know on earth, and all ye need to know."   50

Emily Dickinson   *(1830–1886)*

I heard a Fly buzz—when I died   *1862*

I heard a Fly buzz—when I died—
The Stillness in the Room
Was like the Stillness in the Air—
Between the Heaves of Storm—

The Eyes around—had wrung them dry—   5
And Breaths were gathering firm
For that last Onset—when the King
Be witnessed—in the Room—

I willed my Keepsakes—Signed away
What portion of me be   10
Assignable—and then it was

There interposed a Fly—

---

[4]**Attic:** Referring to Athens or Athenians.   [5]**brede:** Braid.   [6]**overwrought:** Elaborate; highly decorated.   [7]**Pastoral:** An idealized vision of country or rural life.

With Blue—uncertain stumbling Buzz—
Between the light—and me—
And then the Windows failed—and then   15
I could not see to see—

George Meredith   *(1828–1909)*

Dirge in Woods   *1870*

A wind sways the pines,
    And below
Not a breath of wild air—
Still as the mosses that glow
On the flooring and over the lines   5
Of the roots here and there.
The pine-tree drops its dead;
They are quiet, as under the sea.
Overhead, overhead
Rushes life in a race,   10
As the clouds the clouds chase;
    And we go,
And we drop like the fruits of the tree,
    Even we,
    Even so.   15

William Butler Yeats   *(1865–1939)*

Sailing to Byzantium[1]   *1926*

I

That is no country[2] for old men. The young
In one another's arms, birds in the trees
—Those dying generations—at their song,
The salmon-falls, the mackerel-crowded seas,
Fish, flesh, or fowl, commend all summer long   5
Whatever is begotten, born, and dies.
Caught in that sensual music all neglect
Monuments of unageing intellect.

---

[1]**Byzantium:** Capital of the Byzantine Empire; revered by Yeats as a place where artistry reached its apex. Now called Istanbul, "Byzantium was the center of European civilization and the source of its spiritual philosophy, so I symbolize the search for spiritual life by a journey to that city." (Yeats, BBC, 1931)   [2]**country:** Ireland.

II

An aged man is but a paltry thing,
A tattered coat upon a stick, unless   10
Soul clap its hands and sing, and louder sing
For every tatter in its mortal dress,
Nor is there singing school but studying
Monuments of its own magnificence;
And therefore I have sailed the seas and come   15
To the holy city of Byzantium.

III

O sages standing in God's holy fire
As in the gold mosaic of a wall,
Come from the holy fire, perne in a gyre[3]
And be the singing-masters of my soul.   20
Consume my heart away; sick with desire
And fastened to a dying animal
It knows not what it is; and gather me
Into the artifice of eternity.

IV

Once out of nature I shall never take   25
My bodily form from any natural thing,
But such a form as Grecian goldsmiths make
Of hammered gold and gold enamelling[4]
To keep a drowsy Emperor awake;
Or set upon a golden bough to sing   30
To lords and ladies of Byzantium
Of what is past, or passing, or to come.

Theodore Roethke *(1908–1963)*

The Waking *1953*

I wake to sleep, and take my waking slow.
I feel my fate in what I cannot fear.
I learn by going where I have to go.

---

[3]**gyre:** Whirl in spirals. The gyre or cone represented cycles of history and the fate of the individual. The speaker asks the sages in the mosaic to take him from the ordinary world and to the eternal world of art.   [4]**Of hammered . . . enamelling:** Yeats read that the emperor's palace contained a tree of gold and silver and artificial birds that could sing.

We think by feeling. What is there to know?
I hear my being dance from ear to ear. 5
I wake to sleep, and take my waking slow.

Of those so close beside me, which are you?
God bless the Ground! I shall walk softly there,
And learn by going where I have to go.

Light takes the Tree; but who can tell us how? 10
The lowly worm climbs up a winding stair;
I wake to sleep, and take my waking slow.

Great Nature has another thing to do
To you and me; so take the lively air,
And, lovely, learn by going where to go. 15

This shaking keeps me steady. I should know.
What falls away is always. And is near.
I wake to sleep, and take my waking slow.
I learn by going where I have to go.

Dylan Thomas   *(1914–1953)*

Do Not Go Gentle into That Good Night   *1951*

Do not go gentle into that good night,
Old age should burn and rave at close of day;
Rage, rage against the dying of the light.

Though wise men at their end know dark is right,
Because their words had forked no lightning they 5
Do not go gentle into that good night.

Good men, the last wave by, crying how bright
Their frail deeds might have danced in a green bay,
Rage, rage against the dying of the light.

Wild men who caught and sang the sun in flight, 10
And learn, too late, they grieved it on its way,
Do not go gentle into that good night.

Grave men, near death, who see with blinding sight
Blind eyes could blaze like meteors and be gay,
Rage, rage against the dying of the light. 15

And you, my father, there on the sad height,
Curse, bless, me now with your fierce tears, I pray.

Do not go gentle into that good night.
Rage, rage against the dying of the light.

James Wright *(1927–1980)*

A Blessing *1963*

Just off the highway to Rochester, Minnesota,
Twilight bounds softly forth on the grass.
And the eyes of those two Indian ponies
Darken with kindness.
They have come gladly out of the willows   5
To welcome my friend and me.
We step over the barbed wire into the pasture
Where they have been grazing all day, alone.
They ripple tensely, they can hardly contain their happiness
That we have come.   10
They bow shyly as wet swans. They love each other.
There is no loneliness like theirs.
At home once more,
They begin munching the young tufts of spring in the darkness.
I would like to hold the slenderer one in my arms.   15
For she has walked over to me
And nuzzled my left hand.
She is black and white,
Her mane falls wild on her forehead,
And the light breeze moves me to caress her long ear   20
That is delicate as the skin over a girl's wrist.
Suddenly I realize
That if I stepped out of my body I would break
Into blossom.

Jane Kenyon *(1947–1995)*

Otherwise *1996*

I got out of bed
on two strong legs.
It might have been
otherwise. I ate
cereal, sweet   5
milk, ripe, flawless
peach. It might
have been otherwise.
I took the dog uphill
to the birch wood.   10
All morning I did
the work I love.

At noon I lay down
with my mate. It might
have been otherwise.   15
We ate dinner together
at a table with silver
candlesticks. It might
have been otherwise.
I slept in a bed
in a room with paintings   20
on the walls, and
planned another day
just like this day.
But one day, I know,   25
it will be otherwise.

Ted Kooser *(1939–)*

Walking on Tiptoe   *2004*

Long ago we quit lifting our heels
like the others—horse, dog, and tiger—
though we thrill to their speed
as they flee. Even the mouse
bearing the great weight of a nugget   5
of dog food is enviably graceful.
There is little spring to our walk,
we are so burdened with responsibility,
all of the disciplinary actions
that have fallen to us, the punishments,   10
the killings, and all with our feet
bound stiff in the skins of the conquered.
But sometimes, in the early hours,
we can feel what it must have been like
to be one of them, up on our toes,   15
stealing past doors where others are sleeping,
and suddenly able to see in the dark.

Explorations of the Text

1. All of the poems in this cluster deal
with the concept of time or of timelessness. Characterize the time imagery in
three of the poems.

2. Describe the tone in three poems of
this cluster. Do the authors find the
approach of death to be a melancholy
prospect? One that is spiritually uplifting? Explain.

3. Several of the poets refer to the time-lessness of art, a timelessness that de-fies death. List the ways in which art is shown as timeless. Why or how might art supersede time? Refer to the poems in your answer.

4. Consider the idea of death as a return to a place of one's origins in one or more of the poems. To what place(s) do the dead return?

5. In Rudolfo Anaya's, "In Search of Epifano," the protagonist meets death at the end of her quest. Which one of the poems in this cluster best captures the idea of death as the reward at the end of a long quest?

The Reading/Writing Connection

1. The ideal world is characterized by Yeats as Byzantium. Write a poem or story in which you depict an ideal world.

2. Journal Entry: If you were to create a work of art that would survive long after your death, what would it be?

Ideas for Writing

1. Death is often thought of as a part of a cycle, the fulfillment of a pattern. Analyze two of the poems in this cluster or works in this chapter through the idea of life as a cycle.

DRAMA

Laurence Carr   *(1950–)*

Scrabble and Tabouli   *2005*

Characters

Mandy, 41, Phil's new friend
Phil, 37, Mandy's new friend

Setting

Mandy's eat-in kitchen in a mid-sized New Jersey town.
Time: Spring, 2004

> *(At rise: Mandy's kitchen. She's preparing a tabouli salad. Phil sits nearby. A small dining area is located just off the kitchen section.)*

Mandy: Red plates or blue plates?
Phil: Is this your blue plate special?

(Short pause.)

Mandy: Sort of . . .
Phil: Blue plates, then, I guess. Anyway- just to finish this up, I don't think the story worked. The story got lost.
Mandy: Where'd you see it?   5
Phil: Here.
Mandy: No, I mean- rental or big screen?
Phil: Rental.
Mandy: See, that's the point I was making. Some movies are for small screen, some are for big screen.
Phil: A story's a story.   10
Mandy: Yes- but- *(Short pause.)*
   There were movies we could just never rent- or rather I couldn't watch. Harley could watch anything. He was an addict. That and his crossword puzzles. I can't tell you the crappy movies he'd bring home.
Phil: If the story works-
Mandy: But it's about how it works. You can't watch Lawrence of Arabia on a small screen- you don't feel the heat. You can't watch Zhivago, you can't feel the cold.
Phil: A movie isn't a weather report.
Mandy: It's about feeling . . . something.   15
Phil: I totally get your point. *(Joking.)* I just don't have to agree with you.
Mandy: I'll bring you around.
Phil: I don't know. I think you met your match.
Mandy: *(Beat.)* Could you set the table? It's all on the counter.
Phil: Sure.   20
Mandy: Sorry I'm a little behind.

Phil: No problem- I think I was early.

Mandy: No, it's me. I couldn't get going on this.

Phil: Busy day.

Mandy: Same as yesterday.   25

> *(She watches him lay out the plates and flatware at two adjacent sides of the small dining table.)*

Oh, Phil- could you . . . let's sit across from each other. So we can talk.

Phil: Sure.

> *(He changes the settings. She continues preparing the food.)*

What are you making?

Mandy: Tabouli. From this Middle-Eastern cookbook. Cracked wheat, tomatoes, scallion, bed of lettuce.

Phil: Great. Fine.

Mandy: I should have asked you if this was okay.

Phil: Sounds a little healthy for me. Sounds good. *(Beat.)*   30

Mandy: Keep talking.

Phil: I'm thinking.

Mandy: Don't think. Talk.

Phil: I'm thinking about what to talk about.

Mandy: Just talk about what you were talking about last time. Stupid stuff.   35

Phil: I'm running out of stupid stuff.

Mandy: I mean unimportant. You know what I mean. I just want to hear about- your day.

Phil: Okay.

Mandy: Something mundane. Your day couldn't have been all that exciting.

Phil: I guess not.   40

Mandy: Or meaningful?

Phil: No.

Mandy: Good- So we're still at square one. Go on- please.

Phil: I got home about eight-thirty in the morning. I had a beer. I watched something stupid on the tube.

Mandy: Good. See- simple stuff. What was on?   45

Phil: I don't know.

Mandy: You were watching it?

Phil: But it wasn't registering. I don't know why I did that anyway. Turn on the tube. Reflex? You'd think after watching monitors in a hole in the ground for eight hours.

Mandy: What show?

Phil: I don't know. I used to watch the talk shows. Zone out. *Almost* sleep.   50
But they turn nasty. People yelling at each other. Threatening. Really angry- enraged with each other. Always- that far from throwing a punch.

Mandy: Phil . . .

Phil: I think that's where they want them to go. Talk is talk. But they want-

Mandy: Phil, where are we going?

Phil: The violence. You know it's going to show up- sooner or later.

Mandy: I never watch it anymore. I can't seem to-   55

Phil: Violence- same as cotton- the fabric of our lives. Somebody made that joke. Last night.

Mandy: It would all be blank anyway.

Phil: So- I switched to infomercials. They're- really interesting. It might be the only place in the world where there's no violence. It's a world without violence. I mean, they cut up a tomato with a knife you never have to sharpen, but . . . And after an hour or so of those soothing, caring voices and their demonstrations- that knife becomes that integral part of the universe, the missing link- the thing you can't live without. So, of course- I had to buy one. They have an 800 number tattooed on the screen. They use that knife to carve it right into you.

(Mandy breaks down. She drops the knife she's using and covers her face with her hands. She tries to pull back her emotions that are coming out.)

Phil: You okay?

Mandy: I'm sorry. I just have to play through this. You know . . .   60

Phil: Right. It's not belated whiplash or anything . . . ?

Mandy: I wish.

Phil: I'm sorry- Look, I should go- I don't want to make any more of a-

Mandy: No- just . . . I'm okay. Wouldn't that be great? Physical pain? Just plain old *physical* pain. I banged my head on the garage door yesterday- nothing. Didn't feel a thing. I burned my hand on the stove last month. Nothing. Still. Oh, I put my hand in the freezer- I went through all the motions. But- I'm going backwards-

Phil: Back to? – Oh, sorry- I'm prying.   65

Mandy: This is gray area. We're in gray area.

Phil: This is our third time. Meeting.

Mandy: Third date!?

Phil: Fourth if you count the first.

Mandy: You hit my car- that was not a date.   70

Phil: I backed into your car, by accident.

Mandy: You said you saw me get in.

Phil: Oh, right, and being a guy- my only thought was- there's a woman- if I back into her while she's pulling out- maybe we can start dating.

Mandy: Beats the Internet-

Phil: Sure, why use the Internet when I can play demolition derby in the Shop 'n Save   75 parking lot?

Mandy: It's more personal. More up close. I don't have to read about how you like long walks on the beach. And then look at the mug shot- not knowing if it's really you- and then hoping you don't find one who looks like-

(She shuts down. Beat.)

Phil: You only get to really know a person when they're pissed off.

Mandy: I wasn't pissed off. I was very- objective.

Phil: Saying "fuck" in *every* sentence is objective?

Mandy: It's a word to show that things are important. To keep your attention . . .   80
(Beat.) This is a mistake. We don't have to-

Phil: I can leave- this probably wasn't a good idea.

(He turns to leave.)

Mandy: I meant the tabouli. *(Beat.)* I mean- to say things I haven't said-

Phil: He died. I'm sorry. I don't need to know any more.

Mandy: No- about me.

Phil: Okay. *(Beat.)* 85

Mandy: Okay. *(Beat.)* I . . . was . . . a cutter. Am. Was. I'm saying *was*.

Phil: A cutter . . .

Mandy: Let's back up. This was before. When I was.

Phil: A cutter?

Mandy: We cut ourselves. 90

Phil: A bunch of you?

Mandy: No- just me- alone- I mean there are others. But- I mean- we don't do it together. It's not like some club or something.

Phil: Where?

Mandy: Most people ask "why"?

Phil: Do you tell most people? 95

Mandy: Why am I even telling you?

Phil: I don't know.

Mandy: You're not- most people. Maybe.

Phil: You're right- I'm not most people. So- why?

Mandy: You asked "where"? 100

Phil: Where?

Mandy: You need running water. To hide behind that sound. Flush the evidence. The blood. That's important. So you can walk away clean. And long sleeves help. We can look very proper. Prim. Some of us. Sorry. Where. In the kitchen. To get over the *little* attacks. Those are called "quickies." A fast in and out. In with the blade, out with the blood. It satisfies you enough to get through the rest of the day. Like quick sex. Not great sex, but sex that gets you over the hump.

(A small laugh comes from her joke.)

Then there's cutting you prep for. The ritual cut. We all have- had- our little rituals. Very intricate. Very personal. These are the ones in the bathroom- mostly. We- I- could always draw more there. Turn on the faucets. That running water. Very important. Soothing. You take a single razor. My weapon of choice. My friend. You've taped one side if it's double edged- because- hey- you don't want to cut yourself while you're cutting yourself . . . There's a favorite towel you sit or kneel on. Has to be that towel. Like your baby blanket. Usually two or three washcloths to clean up with. They rotate in a bucket of bleach. I could never get them really clean and it's just another thing to hide. All the same favorite color, though. I was into the green-blues. I used to love going through the catalogues looking at the names they made up for that color. Sea Foam. Spring Heather. Pond Slime. Bronchial Phlegm. I'd hold the catalogue page next to my arm to see if my blood would look good patted up by Sea Foam. Then I'd order a dozen. A little obsessive, but we're living in a world where you have to be prepared. The bomb could go off any time. Or- you might have to get away fast. Chemicals. Gas. WMDs, hidden in lunch boxes. Nestled in pink Barbie knapsacks. *(Beat.)* I never told Harley about my friend- when we were- "dating." It came out later, after we'd married. After it was too late. To stop or to leave. So we lived our lives together. The three of us.

(She ponders the knife she's been using.)

And now- Harley's dead. And my friend- seems to have left me, too. So- it's just me now.

Phil: So . . . arms?

Mandy: Forearms are good. But not around your wrist. You don't want to kill yourself for God's sake. But that means long sleeves. Legs. Calves. That means tights. Too hot in the summer. And you can always make up the excuse- "I cut myself shaving." You have to think of these things. Better to move it around. They get suspicious.

Phil: They?   105

Mandy: People. Like you. People who don't even know me. People that do. People.

Phil: And you feel better?

Mandy: Are you just curious or do you want to try it?

Phil: Sorry- I was just-

Mandy: No- sorry- it's me. I never really talked about it- you know- to a civilian. Just   110
my shrink and a couple women in that old club. You should have heard us- No, you shouldn't. But- it was funny. And sad. And painful. And- special. Now I'm in a new club. Very elite. A whole new addiction. Which is good- the old one was wearing thin. I was even losing my fear-

Phil: Your fear?

Mandy: The anxiety, the frustration-

Phil: Of what?

Mandy: You tell me.

Phil: Fear that-   115

Mandy: Yeah . . . go on. I spilled *my* can of beans.

Phil: That you're-

Mandy: It's your story now.

Phil: That I'm . . . that one can- slip away. Go from opaque to translucent to transparent- to invisible.

Mandy: To not being here.   120

Phil: But not dead. Just not part of anything.

Mandy: Hm.

Phil: There's this book. An anatomy book when I was on my pre-med track with these see-thru plastic pages. The first page shows a man- there's a woman further on-

Mandy: Good- I'd hate to think this was just a guy thing.

Phil: Naked- looking out at you. Standing there- in his skin. Turn the first plastic   125
page and his skin lifts off- like some medieval torture- showing everything under the skin- organs, skeleton, circulation-

Mandy: Blood-

Phil: Everything that makes him go. Now he's all about his organs. Turn the page. He's a Halloween skeleton. Turn the page. He's an outline of his blood flow. A maze of red and blue and purple lines. The journey of the heart.

Mandy: The last image of the woman- is there a single red stream flowing out of her arm dripping off the page?

Phil: I don't think so.

Mandy: Then the book was fiction.   130

Phil: No- it just wasn't about you.

Mandy: If it's not about me- then it's fiction.

Phil: Everything's fiction after it happens. Truth can't last for more than a second. Then it's over. It's a thing of the past. And it'll never be told the same way twice. And each time there'll be less and less truth to it.

Mandy: I think all we can do is to wait for the next thing to happen- and hope that it's different enough to start something new.

Phil: You're an optimist.   135

Mandy: Pessimistic optimist. It's all for shit, so what the hell- keep going.

Phil: So you're moving on?

Mandy: No. I haven't made it to the "let's move on" part. I'm still at the bottom looking for the dangling rope. It's everyone else who's pushing me.

Phil: People- like me?

Mandy: Oh, shut up- you're not them- I mean, my shrink, my sister, my new club.   140
"Now Mandy, it's coming up on one year. It's time to take a step- even if it's a baby step." They've been treating me like a baby for months. What- there's a fucking schedule I have to be on? Hey- It's three months- time to get back into those activities, six months, time to make new friends, ten months, time to start dating! It's the one year anniversary- time to go to the site, rip off my clothes and lay spread eagle in front of the construction workers. Here I am, boys! Just a little patriotic duty. A couple good fucks and I'll be back in the land of the living?

Phil: I'm not so sure about that-

Mandy: I don't know what's going on either. Maybe it's a hormone thing.

Phil: I could live with nothing for a while.
(He turns. Does she think he's leaving?)

Mandy: It's just supper A light supper. It's funny, the one thing that never changed was eating. Even on that day, a year ago. I was eating- like-

Phil: There was no tomorrow?   145

Mandy: But tomorrow came. And I had breakfast. Two scrambled eggs, whole wheat toast, and cantaloupe. I fixed it myself. Harley and I never had eggs at breakfast. But there I was making eggs and toast and cutting- cutting a cantaloupe. Did you know a ripe one has the same consistency as our skin? Tough.

Phil: I ate more junk food. More ordering out. More Mu-Shoo Pork. More cheezy tacos.

Mandy: Still?

Phil: Pretty much. Lots of greasy fast food at eight a.m. when I get off work. It's my reward.

Mandy: I was never good at cooking for one. I could always cook for six or more.   150
Family, college roommates, parties at work. Our freezer was always full. I started making food for church suppers. Churches I didn't even belong to. I'd just show up with a dish- and then leave. I was great at funerals. Wakes, rather. I was always first to show up with a casserole. My freezer's almost empty now. *(Beat.)* I'd love to cook again.

Phil: I'd just like to get some sleep.

Mandy: Sleep is good, too. One of our club girls calls it being "wrapped in the Arms of Morpheus."

Phil: Sounds like drugs.

Mandy: I think she's just horny all the time. Keeps saying she wants to be embedded. Goes with the territory.

Phil: Maybe she has a movie going on. Up here. *(He taps his head.)*   155

Mandy: Is yours running now?

Phil: *(Thinks.)* No.

Mandy: Sorry you can't sleep, but maybe you can get some rest. All I have up here is a blank white screen.

Phil: Lucky you.

Mandy: With nothing there. Before that day, I could always have something going on- drag up memories of- holidays, dinners, basketball games, bed . . . sex, long walks on the beach. But they all washed out. Now I just have my big blank screen. Not even a cartoon.

Phil: I'd kill for a blank screen.

Mandy: I'd kill for an old head movie. Even one about a little stream of blood finding its way.

Phil: You said you gave that up.

Mandy: Yeah, so? Never mind, you wouldn't understand.

Phil: You wouldn't understand my cutting either.

Mandy: You're a cutter?

Phil: Yeah. I'm a cutter.

Mandy: Men don't usually go in for-

Phil: Bloodsports? What d'ya mean- we invented them.

Mandy: Sure- men like to see others bleed. But they don't have the guts to open their own veins.

Phil: Suicide bombers.

Mandy: Fuck them. *(Beat.)* I hear they don't feel a thing either.

Phil: No- You're either a hero or you're the enemy. That's what both sides are making all of us into!

Mandy: Not Harley.

Phil: Harley, too. Everybody . . .

Mandy: Why?

Phil: To take away the frustration, hatred, the rage-

Mandy: I didn't cut myself because I hate this country, or to find God.

Phil: You had your own mini-war going on. Who was your enemy? You? Who was *your* terrorist? You?

Mandy: I was trying to find- some comfort. A safe place.

Phil: Same as everybody.

Mandy: What about you?

Phil: My safe place. It *was* two stories down in the ground. But- that's changed. There is no safe place! *(Beat.)*

Mandy: You should have one- somewhere.

Phil: I always used to be- up here. *(He touches his head.)* The only home I really had.

Mandy: Sounds safe.

Phil: My father was a machinist, military hardware, we moved around a lot, new towns, new schools. My mother tried to keep us together but the whole thing collapsed one winter. They terrorized each other into a divorce. We- my sister and I- she was four years older. She was all I had. I was always the kid brother. We ended up with an aunt and uncle in Northern California for most of high school. She joined the army the day after she graduated. Became an army nurse. That became her thing. She got stationed out here. I tagged along. That worked for a long time. But all I do now is lay on the couch, getting fat-

Mandy: You're not fat-

Phil: I'm on the junk food diet- in front of the tube. Watching people- go through the motions. Then to bed- sleep. Even better than sex. Sleep. I can't seem to get the hang of that. You lay there, you don't even know who to punch or scream at so you end up screaming at yourself. You end up . . .

Mandy: *(To herself.)* Cutting. *(Beat.)* Who did you lose? 190

Phil: My sister, Sarah, she was an army nurse. Over there. The hospital she was in was bombed.

Mandy: Suicide bomber?

Phil: Not that heroic.

Mandy: For who?

Phil: I don't know. For whoever makes heroes. Step right up- Win a medal, you're a 195 hero. I'm sorry-

Mandy: No- You're right. There are no heroes. Just people in the wrong place at the wrong time. *(Beat.)* How did Sarah die?

Phil: How was she killed? I love what they say. Friendly fire. Collateral damage. Ordinance gap. They said everything but- "We made a mistake, Someone screwed up and we dropped a bomb on your sister and her friends." It's all part of the show. We're all in on it. Like- like a dime I gave, in taxes, helped build the plane, another dime helped build the bomb, another dime trained the crew- hmm- they should have spent more dimes training the crew. So- I did my part- to help kill her. And it's all connected. Even further. Me- as a kid, in church, giving a dime every Sunday into a little wooden box. Dimes from us church kids to help feed some kid over there- or somewhere in the world- it was all a little hazy exactly where these dimes were going. But I remember saying in my kid voice, "What can you eat for ten cents- just candy!" And they'd say, "Oh, but thousands of children giving their dimes will feed the children of a whole village." OK, so we all bought that. We buy everything, don't we? So, I feed the village with my childhood dimes. And then later, my grownup dimes are building all kinds of weapons, too many for us, so we sell them to whoever wants them, until one day the Ten Cent Kid I helped feed has grown up strong and is handed a weapon that I helped build. And then the Ten Cent Kid becomes a man. He starts to think. About his place in the world. *His* world. Not our world. *His* world. *(Beat.)* So where's that leave us?

Mandy: I don't know. *(Beat.)* This is what I know. *(She fumbles in her pocket. Takes out a ring.)* I keep this ring in my pocket. This onyx ring. Harley's father gave it to him.

Phil: You don't wear it?

Mandy: I don't go there. 200

Phil: I have a Sarah ring, too. Was sent back to me. *(Fumbles it out of his pocket. It's the replica Super Bowl ring.)*

Mandy: *And* I keep the baseball he caught at a Yankee's game.

Phil: *And* her baby book our mom made. In happier times. That's in the Sarah box.

Mandy: I have the Harley trunk.

Phil: It's with the other stuff in the Sarah closet. 205

Mandy: See this? *(She fumbles in a hamper by the sink.)* This is Harley's favorite shirt. I sleep in it.

Phil: It doesn't keep you awake?

Mandy: It's a sleep shirt- not a stay up all night and terrorize myself shirt. You don't wear your sister's clothes?

Phil: And I don't go there.

Mandy: You might like it.

Phil: Yeah, right. Why's it out here? Am I keeping you from your nap?

Mandy: It was in the laundry hamper.

Phil: You wash it?

Mandy: Of course I wash it- just because I'm in mourning doesn't mean I have to smell like a gym.

Phil: Does it still . . . ?

Mandy: What? . . . What?

Phil: Smell like him?

Mandy: *(Beat.)* I don't think I could take that. But- a couple of drops of his after shave from the shelf- in the shrine- you know-

Phil: Yeah, I know.

Mandy: -does the trick. You have to trick yourself sometimes.

Phil: Or they start playing tricks on you. *(Beat.)* Do you remember the time- when we had answers for questions? Even simple questions?

Mandy: There was a time when I had all the answers.

Phil: Smarty-pants, huh?

Mandy: I knew what I knew and I knew I knew it.

Phil: Was another life.

Mandy: Now it's about wanting to stay invisible. But you know all about that.

Phil: Fading away.

Mandy: No- I always wanted to be- to be here- just not seen. They can't hurt what they can't see.

Phil: You still feel that way- after everything?

Mandy: That's a question.

Phil: Sorry. When I was a kid, I read *The Invisible Man* a dozen times. H. G. Wells.

Mandy: Isn't that an adolescent boy fantasy? Did you think you could sneak into houses and watch girls undress?

Phil: That's a question.

Mandy: It's a direct question- about *your* past. Are we still in the get-to-know-you part?

Phil: Like those horse fantasies young girls have? Did you have those?

Mandy: Maybe we should save this for next time.

Phil: Next time? *(Beat.)*

Mandy: Could you do the lettuce? It's washed.

Phil: Sure. *(He starts working with the lettuce.)* I miss West Coast produce.

Mandy: What do you mean? We get California produce all the time. All winter long.

Phil: Naw- it's not the same thing. They send all the second rate stuff out here. Then by the time it gets here- it's third rate.

Mandy: What are you, some kind of vegan? You're in the wrong house.

Phil: No. Just worked on some farms here and there. I spent a month cutting Iceberg lettuce.

Mandy: Was this in your hobo phase? Riding in box cars, eating beans from cans, a guitar slung on your back?

Phil: I actually tried that.

Mandy: You weren't, like, writing a book or something . . . ?

Phil: Never got that far. Lasted about three days. Sarah and Eric tracked me down. Was she ever pissed. Big sisters get mad at you like your mother never can. Eric just laughed. He'd actually done it for about a month. I guess I was trying to be like him- like both of them. I guess I was always tagging along. *(Beat.)* So- this Iceberg lettuce. You know they designed that shape so more could fit in a box.

Mandy: I love designer vegetables. Great for us who can't afford designer clothes.

Phil: Come on, I'm serious. Grew them to retain more water so they could travel long distances. Designed the flavor right out of them. Sarah and I used to pick lettuce and all sorts of stuff in our aunt's garden. Aunt Jean, the one we stayed with. Nothing tastes like that anymore.

Mandy: It's a different world now.   250

(Silence. He nods.)

Phil: Do you think it could happen to you? I mean, what are the odds?

Mandy: Then you play *their* game.

Phil: I didn't mean-

Mandy: I know what you meant. But it *is* a game. To the ones who report it. To the ones who can't get enough of it. They love the game. The Terror Game. The Hero Game. The Grief Game. The Retaliation Game. You should have heard the questions those reporters asked us- me- "So when did you first hear about <u>it</u>?" "Where were you?" "How did you <u>feel</u> when you heard?" I love that- "How did I feel?" You mean, what were the layers of emotions I was going through for the two minutes after I heard that Harley was blown up in that lobby? Into so many pieces they didn't know which ones were his? Gee, I don't know, I guess I felt pretty sad . . . But, I guess you only want footage of me being strong, being the hero, like you're making Harley and the others into . . . Fuckers. All of them.

Phil: Me, too?   255

Mandy: You were when you backed into my car.

Phil: Another random act of violence?

Mandy: There was a split second- when I thought- this is it. Just make it quick. Then I realized it was just some jerk who wasn't watching where he was going.

Phil: Do you know there are stats that say you're more likely to meet with an accident in a supermarket parking lot that any other public place?

Mandy: Terrorists have to eat, too. Do I think it can happen to me? Well, our little   260 meeting is living proof, isn't it? Yes, it can happen to me, to you, to anyone. Each of us is special, but no one is especially safe. Everybody's ground zero eventually.

Phil: Sure, but I'd like to be ground zero in my bed, asleep, dreaming of sipping an umbrella drink under a palm tree.

Mandy: Pussy.

Phil: But I don't have those dreams anymore.

Mandy: If these were the old days, I wouldn't be using this knife to just chop mint.

Phil: Cutting?   265

Mandy: Not in front of you. It's not a spectator sport. *(Short pause.)* You probably think I stopped when I became an adult. And put away childish things. No- it's always there. Not often. Once every nine . . . ten months or so- like visiting an old friend. A cup of tea, a plate of cookies, a trickle of blood. Then the day came. That divided my life. My life before the bomb. My life after the bomb.

Phil: You were there?

Mandy: No- I went there right after. There was still- blood. All over.

Phil: You saw it?

Mandy: No one wanted to talk about that part. They'd only use words like tragedy,   270
hero, honor, terrorist, patriot, innocent, heaven- no- they'd pull back on anything that sounded religious. They didn't want to offend anyone. But I kept asking, I wouldn't let them off the hook. Finally- we got down to it . . . Down to the bone. Words like piercing, sever, fragments, pieces . . . blood. It got to be too much. Not for me- for them. But I still had questions. The ones they didn't want to answer. So- I found a woman- like me- one of the club. And she knew a woman. An army . . . an army nurse. And she told me everything I needed to know. About exactly what a bombing does to a human body. Talked me through the whole thing. Like an anatomy class. Like a butcher shop. I never cried when she told me all that. I listened. I took it all in. We- I . . . We had a good marriage. Harley was a good husband. We were good together. A week after he died, I cut myself. And I saw what I was doing. I was doing just what the bomber wanted. What'd you call it- collateral damage. And then- when I got home from talking to her- the nurse- I cut. For the last time. It was my last gift to Harley. My goodbye. *(Beat.)* But it never ties up with a neat little bow- does it?

Phil: No.

Mandy: My old friend still comes by. Knocks on the door. I know it's her. I know her knock. But I haven't answered- I won't answer. Instead, I grab my jacket and I go downtown. To the clinic. The Red Cross Clinic. And I- give blood. Geez- they take a fucking pint! I never had that courage. But I do get orange juice and cookies after. For being a good girl. But you pay the price for being a good girl. Nothing's ever for free.

Phil: Oh, yeah . . .

Mandy: So what about your cutting?

Phil: We're back to that?   275

Mandy: I'm curious. So- you-

Phil: In my own way.

Mandy: Knife? Razor? No, you don't seem like a razor kind of guy. I'm sorry, it just doesn't seem like a guy thing to me-

Phil: Oh, there's no blood. Not that kind of cutting. I meant- cut up- class clown- go for the joke, that's was my weapon. Then I moved to cut out. Cut class, lots of detention- which I also cut. Lots of jobs I cut out on- lots of firings, lots of hirings. Six, eight months tops, then I'm out. Leave them with a joke. But leave. Invisible again. If you stay, they got you. Hostage. And that's where they have me now. Dark room. Watching the clock run out. Every night. Six screens. Can you believe it? I've had this job for ten months.

Mandy: You're due for a gold watch.   280

Phil: Long time, short time. There is no time when I'm down there.

Mandy: Where?

Phil: Sorry. The job? Night security guard. But I prefer the term- night watchman. Midnight to eight. No breaks. I check doors. Then I settle in watching the monitors. Six monitors. No channel surfing. Just six monitors with six images that never move. And nothing moves on them. Which is exactly what they want.

Mandy: *(Interrupts.)* You keep the place safe.

Phil: I took it to keep *me* safe. I thought it would. Seemed perfect. From twelve to eight, alone, two stories down, watching six monitors. Direct line next to me. All wired in so I can't fall asleep. And if I do, a buzzer sounds. But I never do. I just keep watching, until- my movies start up. Around two or three in the morning. A different one might start the ball rolling, but pretty soon, all six screens are going. Sarah, Eric, the Ten Cent Kid I fed at church.

Mandy: Sounds like-

Phil: Torture?

Mandy: No, I was going to say-

Phil: You were thinking torture.

Mandy: I wasn't thinking anything. I'm never thinking anything.

Phil: It must be good- not to have-

Mandy: Or it must be so good to have something going on inside you- even if it's-

Phil: Those pictures, the chatter-

Mandy: Blank space. Dead air.

Phil: Repeating. Night after night.

Mandy: Silence. No, it's a hum. A low hum. Like a computer on sleep.

Phil: Puzzle pieces. Linking together.

Mandy: Blank screen. Everything deleted.

Phil: Wired to me, each one like a-

Mandy: Razor?

Phil: I wasn't going to say razor.

Mandy: You were thinking razor.

Phil: Like a razor drawn across my skin.

Mandy: Yes.

Phil: Ride it out.

Mandy: Wait it out.

Phil: It can't go on forever.

Mandy: It has to stop sometime- something has to-

Phil: -Replace it. Has to-

Mandy: -Change sometime. Nothing-

Phil: -Lasts forever.

Mandy: No- not everything. "As long as you both shall live." We changed the vow, right before the wedding. To "As long as you both shall love." We thought- "Let's make it forever." Even after one of us is gone. The love won't end. The marriage can end- but not the love. Everything changes, everything ends- except the love. Do you believe that?

Phil: I don't know.

Mandy: I want to still believe that. I want to be with people who still believe that. With someone who still believes that.

Phil: Remarry?

Mandy: Oh, I don't know. This is what it is now.

Phil: Forever?

Mandy: I won't be here forever.

Phil: So- somewhere down the line, it might all change?

Mandy: Sure- at the end of the line.   320

Phil: But maybe you can change before you get to-

Mandy: -The end of the line?

Phil: Maybe.

Mandy: What about you?

Phil: What about me?   325

Mandy: Changing.

Phil: We're not talking about me.

Mandy: Oh, right- Mr. Big-Talk. As long as it's somebody else changing.

Phil: I think some people are able to change. I think others have to wait for it.

Mandy: Well, that covers all your bases, doesn't it?   330

Phil: If it comes-

Mandy: And if it doesn't?

Phil: Then you don't.

Mandy: Well, that sure sounds like Hell. Not being able to change. Who decides who's who?

Phil: What do you mean?   335

Mandy: I mean. Do I decide I change, do you decide for me, or does something- happen?

Phil: Something *did* happen- we know that one works.

Mandy: You got that right, Brother.

Phil: *(Slowly, feeling his way.)* I think we're both different people than we were- and I think- it's not an accident that we've come together.

Mandy: *(Pulling away.)* We've had three encounters.   340

Phil: We've been together three times.

Mandy: That sounds like dates.

Phil: One- when I ran into you.

Mandy: *That* was an accident! We talked while we were disengaging bumpers.

Phil: That still counts.   345

Mandy: Only if you're a man.

Phil: We met for me to give you a check after you got an estimate, an estimate, by the way that I think was too high.

Mandy: So sue me.

Phil: We had coffee.

Mandy: We went Dutch- I insisted. About that check. Was that to get out of calling   350
your insurance company?

Phil: I can't afford to have my insurance go up any more.

Mandy: DWI?

Phil: NO-

Mandy: Speeding tickets?

Phil: NO.   355

Mandy: Fender benders?

Phil: A couple.

Mandy: How many?

Phil: Four. Five.

Mandy: Is this how you pick up women?   360

Phil: Is this how you pick up men?

Mandy: I don't pick up men. I don't *do* anything! *(Beat.)*
Phil: The third time- we had a quick lunch at Zeno's. To make sure the car was all
   right.
Mandy: Sure.
Phil: To make sure you were all right.   365
Mandy: Was I?
Phil: No. And now this. I think you called it- a light supper. This is our fourth.

   (Long pause.)

Mandy: Do you think we'll have sex?
Phil: Tonight?
Mandy: No- not tonight- Geez! Sometime?   370
Phil: When sometime?
Mandy: I don't know- three months.
Phil: Why three months?
Mandy: That's when I think *you'll* be able to change!
Phil: How can you tell?   375
Mandy: I don't know! And you don't know anything about me. And I don't know
   anything about anything anymore. I just want to make this goddamn tabouli
   on a goddamn bed of lettuce. Have a glass of wine- talk about a boring movie
   or book- because that's about all I can handle. Still! And then say goodnight or
   goodbye. Or whatever- and just get back where it's safe. Me. Here. Alone.
Phil: I should leave- I'm sorry. We shouldn't be doing this-
Mandy: What? Having a bite together? Talking? Who else can we talk to? Have a
   carrot.
Phil: And I'll go back to my job. Into a basement to watch the monitors for seven
   hours. And then home by nine a.m. and then another try at sleep. A knockout
   with something the doctor's given me- sometimes. Then it's breakfast. Around
   five.
Mandy: Is this all wrong?   380
Phil: No- no- It's nice to have something different from my Egg McMuffin and a
   scotch. Then to work again. Back down into the mine. Like one of the seven
   dwarfs. Me and the six little screens. Then home again to my sleep of the not
   quite living. Then it starts all over again. Back down into the earth. To watch.
   Sarah in her last seconds. Eric in his last seconds. The Ten Cent Kid.
Mandy: You lost me.
Phil: The Ten Cent Kid! The kid we gave the dime to in church- for food. On the
   monitor, he's bought food for a nickel and saved the other nickel till he had
   enough to buy a gun. I see him in the background in the Sarah scenes, the Eric
   scenes.
Mandy: I got Sarah, I got the Ten Cent Kid- who's Eric?
Phil: A guy- a guy I knew. We knew. A friend of ours. Who was always there.   385
Mandy: What happened?
Phil: It's about what's happening. The six screens. In that basement- in that security
   room. When one screen gets to be too much I turn to another one-flashing-
   back and forth- till it's all one screen- one story- jumbled all together. I'd kill
   for your white blank screen and that no-noise noise you have. I'd die for it.
   (Short beat.) Do you ever think of suicide?

Mandy: *(Short beat.)* Why are you asking me that?

Phil: Because there's no one else to ask. I do. Think of it. Maybe that will be on one of the monitors tonight. But I don't think I could.

Mandy: Why?

Phil: Because I don't know if that would really end anything. What if it just went on? Forever.

Mandy: That would be Hell, wouldn't it?

Phil: So- do you?

Mandy: Every time I held the blade. Every time I cut a tomato.

Phil: Are you thinking of it now?

Mandy: *(Beat.)* No.

Phil: Then that's good.

Mandy: Is it? It would be *something* to think about.

Phil: I knew who you were. Not when I banged into you. After.

Mandy: Encounter number two.

Phil: When I saw you on TV. With the others- that group-

Mandy: The Bombed Widows Club- makes us sound like real party girls, doesn't it?

Phil: I saw that interview.

Mandy: Then you lied. You said you only watch-

Phil: I channel surf to get to QVC. All right?

Mandy: All right.

Phil: You and three others.

Mandy: Evie got cold feet. They needed a fourth- like Bridge.

Phil: The other three spoke.

Mandy: And I didn't. So what?

Phil: Why not?

Mandy: *(Defending and attacking.)* I'm shy goddammit!

Phil: Bullshit! Even when the mike was in your face.

Mandy: I hate those things.

Phil: Silence. When they came to you. Silence! On TV!!

Mandy: Yeah, so?

Phil: You don't get it. You were the only one saying anything.

Mandy: I froze.

Phil: The last thing I needed was more words.

Mandy: Well, you sure opened a can of- worms.

Phil: I wanted- I needed to see you again.

Mandy: Me, too, you owed me money.

Phil: That lunch.

Mandy: It was good. *(Beat.)* Did you want to talk then?

Phil: We did talk.

Mandy: No- I mean- talk about-

Phil: I don't know. I think I just wanted to listen.

Mandy: I don't know if I said anything.

Phil: No- you did.

Mandy: Small talk. All the small stuff you say when you can't talk about what you want to talk about.

Phil: It's what you said between the words.

390

395

400

405

410

415

420

425

430

Mandy: I like it when we talk. I like it when we don't. I like not having to talk. Just being- with- I haven't- been- with a man- since- Harley was killed. He was killed, you know.

Phil: Yes.

Mandy: He was in a bombing. Of the building he worked in. He was coming into the lobby through the glass doors. At 8:57 a.m. A van pulled up to the curb. The sign said- "No Parking- No Standing- 7 a.m. to 10 a.m." The driver must have missed that, the man who exploded the bomb. It's a real pet peeve of mine, you know, people who ignore parking signs. *(Beat.)* There were enough explosives in it to collapse the building. Eighteen stories. Harley was one of one-hundred and eleven people who were killed. My group- this crazy widow's club- told me to tell my story. As many times as I can. Work it out. All my stories. How we met. Dating. Marriage. They didn't say how graphic I should be about sex. The difficulty of having children. Jobs. Home improvements. Showing tax returns seems pretty boring though, doesn't it? They even said to talk about our differences. They never say "arguments." That would put a dent it "the story." Make us too much like real people. It's funny, when the media- shows up- they say they want real people, but they don't. They want the storybook. They like the tears, the heartbreak, the valiant baby steps toward a new life- but they don't want me. They don't want the blank page- feeling- nothing. They don't want to hear how I can't remember little details about him anymore. How every day, I remember one less thing. They want the others- the ones who can-sell it- hold the banner, speak to Congress, go on the talk show. Have Oprah understand their pain. Cry with Oprah. Hug Oprah. And they don't want to hear the joke Barbara made up. "So the Devil knocks on the door. Real Halloween type- red pantyhose, pitchfork, horns, pointy beard, and he says- "Hi, Barbara, you just won a million dollars! Here's your money! Oh, by the way, Jack's dead." A couple of us thought that was really funny. But that didn't make it on TV either. No one wants a flat, gray landscape- as far as you can see. That's not going to sell their deodorant and tacos.

(Beat. Phil gathers his forces to tell his story.)

Phil: Eric and I met in college. At the last of the two hundred colleges I went to. Sarah met him, too. They became good friends. Really tight. They never slept together. They liked each other too much. And I was always "the baby." That's who I was to her. Him too, I guess. But that was somebody else's life. Lives. Oh, hell, this doesn't make any sense.

Mandy: Yeah, it does, go on.

Phil: Right. Eric. The older brother I never had. Great mechanic, too. Used to fix Sarah's car all the time. He was always under the hood of that old Beemer. Loved trucks. Always working on a couple. Everybody wanted him but he dropped out, too. He went over there a couple months after Sarah. She volunteered. She didn't have to go, but- it's easier if I use the monitors- what I see every night. Monitor number one- Eric works on a big truck engine at a big truck plant. Monitor two- the company gets a big contract to repair military vehicles. Lots of smiling- lots of handshaking. Monitor three- Eric somewhere over there, an unknown location. Sun. Sand. He's waving at the camera. Monitor four- Eric in a small convoy. Going out to repair some supply vehicles.

435

Miles away. Monitor five- Firefight. Capture. Blindfolds. Chatter. Beating. Shouting. A tiny room. Demands. The waiting game. Monitor six- Eric kneeling in front of four men. Heads covered in black. He's denounced. We're denounced. A blade is unsheathed. The man with the knife comes to Eric. Raises the blade. Lowers the blade. A scream. Eric screaming for someone. Blood explodes. The four men behind Eric are spattered. Head and body separate. The bloody knife is held high. God is praised. The blood flows. Rewind. Play again. In sequence. Out of sequence. Random images repeat. Repeat. Monitor One- The blood hood comes off. The Ten Cent Kid is holding the knife. He hands it to Sarah. Monitor Two- Sarah- trying to save Eric. The Ten Cent Kid runs off. Laughing. Waving the knife. Whistle. Louder and louder. Sarah looking up in the sky. Watching it falling, coming right to her. Ground zero. Opens her arms like she's going to catch it. The bomb explodes. Silence- Rewind. Play again. All night long.

(The images surround him. They start to smother him.)

A dozen different ways- but they all end the same. That's *my* entertainment! My terrorist! My horror! My not understanding! My unknowing! My ignorance! My arrogance! My joy! My sorrow! My friend! My sister! My life! My past! My present! My what can never change! My what will never stop! My . . .

Mandy: *(Shouts.)* PHIL! . . . PHIL!! *(Beat.)* Do you like mint?
Phil: *(Beat. Recovers.)* I like mint.
Mandy: There used to be a lot of mint- out back- by the- where the water comes out- 440
Phil: -spigot-
Mandy: -and we- I- just let it go.
Phil: It is a problem, isn't it?
Mandy: Mint?
Phil: Pronouns. 445
Mandy: Most of the time, I'm just- "she." She sees the dishes. She walks past them. She makes toast. She eyeballs the paper. She goes to the grocery.
Phil: She meets him. In a parking lot accident.
Mandy: A random act of violence.
Phil: He offers to pay for the damages.
Mandy: She wishes all the damage could just be paid for and forgotten. 450
Phil: He calls her to find out how the car turned out.
Mandy: She says okay.
Phil: He asks if the check for the bill was enough.
Mandy: She says it cost an extra hundred for rustproofing.
Phil: He insists on paying the extra. 455
Mandy: She declines.
Phil: He really wants to.
Mandy: She declines again.
Phil: He asks if he can make up the difference over lunch.
Mandy: She hesitates. 460
Phil: He tries to sound non-threatening.
Mandy: She hasn't done this in so long.
Phil: He wants her to know- it's just lunch.
Mandy: She accepts. She orders the Niciose Salad.

Phil: He orders the turkey club. With a salad, not fries. 465

Mandy: She wonders- if it was his buddy- would he order the fries?

Phil: He fights not to order the fries.

Mandy: She orders the lemonade- no alcohol. God, a drink would sure calm her down.

Phil: He picks up the tab, but realizes the lunch doesn't add up to the hundred he owes her.

Mandy: She feels like she got a hundred dollars worth. It almost felt like a date. 470 When's the last time she dated? She knows the answer.

Phil: He doesn't want her to think he's cheap.

Mandy: She hears a voice that sounds like hers- "Come over for supper. On Friday. You can bring a bottle of wine."

Phil: He'll bring a good wine- he'll ask at the store what would be good. He should have learned more about how to do all of this. One bottle- no- one bottle looks cheap, and if it's expensive, it looks pretentious. Three bottles- no- that'll look like he wants to get her drunk- or that he's an alcoholic. Two bottles. One red, one white. Bases covered. He doesn't know what she's making. Does he know her well enough to ask?

Mandy: She'll make something fancy. No- She hasn't really cooked since- since that day. Geez- how many more neighbor's lasagnas can she eat! And did she still have her chops- her cooking chops? She keeps saying to herself- "It's not a date!"

Phil: He knows anything she makes will be good. And if it isn't, he'll pretend. They 475 can go out next time. Did he say that?

Mandy: Next time . . . Oh, God, is she- "seeing someone"? No- just payback for a collision.

Phil: A random act of violence?

Mandy: A random meeting. So strange- what brings people together.

Phil: Yes.

Mandy: I don't understand- anything. 480

Phil: I want to stop trying to.

Mandy: Tabouli. I could have made anything else. I should have. Nicoise Salad, turkey club. Food with no baggage.

Phil: You said we'd eat light.

Mandy: I need to do this. Make this. This was "the dish." "His" dish. "Our" dish. Awwwww- I hate pronouns!

Phil: It'll be okay- 485

Mandy: I have to make this. Today.

Phil: You could open a can of soup for all I care.

Mandy: I care!! But you have to stay and help when I can't do it and I throw the whole damn mess against the wall.

Phil: So if that happens- we'll order out.

Mandy: You'll stay even if I do that? 490

Phil: Yeah.

Mandy: Oh.

Phil: Is that the right answer?

Mandy: I don't have any answers to anything.

Phil: Okay, then- Supper. Do you serve red or white with tabouli? 495

Mandy: I don't know.

Phil: Me, either. So there's no wrong answer.

Mandy: And then- maybe- I can get through Thanksgiving with my sister, then maybe holiday baking and, oh God, spare me- shopping- and maybe through the end of the year- then a new year- and some more distance. I think I'm going for that long distance- like those marathon runners.

Phil: I'll hold a little cup of water when you run past.

Mandy: You'd do that? 500

Phil: Sure, why not?

Mandy: Look, if I can get through this- without doing any more damage to the food or us-

Phil: You're the one holding the knife.

Mandy: Oh, Geez- *(She puts it down.)*

Phil: No- Keep going- we'll get through this. 505

Mandy: If we- If we get through this- *(Beat.)* Will you come back- for Sunday brunch? Is that too early?

Phil: Sounds great.

Mandy: I'll buy the paper- another thing to get through. God, I've missed that Sunday paper. Would you-

Phil: What?

Mandy: I'm going to ask you to do something. 510

Phil: Amanda-

Mandy: No, Phil- I need you to do something with me.

Phil: Mandy- I haven't- been with anyone for a while. I can't focus enough to- you know- I don't know if I could-

Mandy: Play Scrabble with me. *(Beat.)* That's the next big hump. Help me get over that- and then maybe I can get to my sister's for Thanksgiving. Forget it- this is stupid.

Phil: No- *(Beat.)* Scrabble. Letters. Words on a grid. Yeah, I can do that. 515

Mandy: My sister makes Thanksgiving dinner at one o'clock. Always too early. I've always hated that. I can leave by six. I can be here by six thirty. What do you say?

Phil: About what?

Mandy: To make you a turkey club. It's same day turkey, it's not leftovers.

Phil: Do you drink red or white with turkey?

Mandy: How about a scotch? 520

Phil: I can do that.

Mandy: But no TV. No holiday acts of violence.

Phil: No Macy's balloons impaled on lamp posts.

Mandy: No TV.

Phil: The violence in football is highly organized. 525

Mandy: Is this going to be our first fight?

Phil: Why not?

Mandy: Taste this. *(She hands him a forkful of tabouli.)* Well?

Phil: Maybe a little wetter. And more garlic. More garlic.

Mandy: Then it won't be the same. 530

Phil: Then it'll be different.

(Phil hands her the knife. She takes it and continues preparing the meal. Lights fade to black.)

The End

Explorations of the Text

1. Think about the role of setting and props in this play. Why is it important that Mandy and Phil are setting a table and are about to eat dinner? What symbolic role does food play in the work?

2. Discuss the irony of Phil's statement: "A story's a story."; and Mandy's "Some movies are for small screen, some are for big screen." As you read further, consider the significance of this exchange.

3. Why does Mandy want to 'talk about' mundane things? Why does Phil concur with her desire?

4. Analyze the protagonists' inner conflicts and fears—their past histories and selves before they experience their great losses. For example, why does Mandy cut herself? Why does Phil "cut" out of jobs? Places? Why does Phil desire a "safe place"?

5. How are the characters affected by the "random violence" that changed their lives? How do loss and grief change them? What are the differences between "the old days" and the present ones—as Mandy says, "life before the bomb . . . life after the bomb"? List some of their behaviors. Discuss the symbolic significance of "ground zero," as the defining state of their lives.

6. What draws the protagonists together? Why are Mandy and Phil attracted to each other? What impact does telling their stories have on the two characters? Are they changed at the end of the drama? What do you imagine will occur in their lives?

7. Do you agree with Mandy's assessment of the media's and the public's reactions to what she calls the "Terror Game. The Hero Game. The Grief Game"? She critiques the media's voyeuristic response and the public's embrace of abstractions, of "words like tragedy, hero, honor, terrorist, patriot, innocent, heaven," to protect them from loss. She counters with the reality: "Finally, we [get] down to it . . . Down to the bone. Words like piercing, sever, fragments, pieces, blood." Compare this drama's portrayal of "random violence" with the ideas and images from Derek Walcott's vision of peace as "phantasmal."

The Reading/Writing Connection

1. Freewrite in response to one of the following statements: "'Violence—the same as cotton—the fabric of our lives.'" OR "'Everything's fiction after it happens. Truth can't last for more than a second. Then it's over. It's a thing of the past.'"

2. What is your "safe place"? Write a short, descriptive journal entry or a poem about the place.

3. **Write an Argument:** Do you think that the play realistically portrays a process of grieving and coming to terms with loss? Argue pro or con.

4. "Think" Topic: Phil states: "You're either a hero or you're the enemy. That's what both sides are making all of us into." Would Laura Blumenfeld, the author of "The Apology: Letters from a Terrorist" (Chapter 8), concur with Phil's world view? Why or why not?

Ideas for Writing

1. Write a character analysis of either Mandy or of Phil. Focus on their appearance, actions, behavior, gestures, dialogue, past histories, and interactions with others.

2. **Write an Argument:** Mandy asks: "'Do I decide to change, do you decide for me, or does something happen?'" Do you think people are capable of change? Or does change happen to them? Create an argument drawing upon your experiences and observations as well as the characters' lives portrayed in works in this chapter.

Lesli-Jo Morizono

Freakish Times *2002*

Characters

Young Woman, twenties.
Old Woman, fifties or older.

Times

Sometime in the future, after the apocalypse.

Setting

A graveyard.

> *Overcast sky hangs over a graveyard. Old Woman wanders through the yard with her nose in the air. She sniffs the air making loud hog-like sounds. She grows excited as she follows her nose, walking quickly with confident steps. She stops in front of an open grave and smiles. She leans over and reaches into the grave and holds up an arm and sniffs it. The body attached to the arm sits up. Old Woman recoils with surprise but recovers quickly.*

Young Woman: What year is it?

Old Woman: The — the twenty-fifth year after the plague. Were you napping, young girl, or have you come back from the dead?

Young Woman: I — I'm not quite sure. Is it night or day?

Old Woman: It is both.

(Old Woman smells Young Woman.)

Old Woman: Mmmm. You have no odor, you must be an undead. What a lucky day. ₅ How old might you be?

Young Woman: I don't remember.

Old Woman: Do you remember the plague?

Young Woman: What is this plague that you speak of?

(Old Woman smiles and opens her picnic basket. She removes a blanket and spreads it on the ground. She makes herself comfortable on it and takes out food and various jars.)

Old Woman: An evil time when the devil's blanket fell upon the earth and covered it whole. The year I was born the land became charred. We had no place to live except in the ocean. I grew up inside a whale's belly, and the year blood flowed between my legs the devil grew bored and took his blanket back. I walked on land for the first time. Babies became children before I learned how to use my legs properly, and when I was able to walk without fear the plague came.

Everywhere one saw only dead bodies. They say it was once called the black plague and came to a city called Euro hundreds of years ago, but we called it the red plague because the infected were covered with festering red sores that made the body hot as if a fire burned inside them. There was nothing we could do for them except listen to their screams. Eat this.

(She holds out a piece of bread.)

Young Woman: Thank you. I am glad I do not remember this red plague.　　10
Old Woman: What do you remember?
Young Woman: Well . . .
Old Woman: Do you remember a man named Trump?
Young Woman: Should I?
Old Woman: He was a formidable being, powerful enough to thwart the devil.　　15

(She pulls out of the basket a book and holds it up. It is a book by Donald Trump.)

Old Woman: When we walked on land we found hundreds, thousands of these books. His books and tins of Spam were the only things that the devil did not devour. Do you know of him? Perhaps he lived in your time.
Young Woman: I— I don't remember.

(Old Woman sprinkles salt on sticks of celery and gives it to Young Woman.)

Old Woman: Make sure you chew the root but not too fine.
Young Woman: I don't know you, yet you share your food. It is a good sign that perhaps this new life of mine will be blessed.
Old Woman: Wait until you see what we're having later. Give me your hands.　　20

(Old Woman holds up Young Woman's hands.)

Old Woman: Your flesh is ample yet firm. Death has preserved you well. What is this? One, two, three, four, five! You are missing two fingers. What happened to them?

(Old Woman holds up Young Woman's hands.)

Young Woman: I don't know what you mean. How many fingers do you have?
Old Woman: Seven, of course. Perhaps you were in an accident or your birth was cursed. What can you remember?

(Slight pause.)

Young Woman: I remember . . . Finding shade inside a mountain . . . a smile, yes, I remember a young buck's smile. Pain . . . a great deal of pain and blood. I remember being split into two . . . and an emptiness as if my insides had been scooped out . . . weariness, overwhelming weariness that's what I remember most.
Old Woman: Could this be a new plague or some unknown disease? Show me your　　25 teeth.

(Young Woman opens her mouth.)

Old Woman: You have all your teeth and they look young and strong. The dead always remember how they died, why can't you? Once I found a young man, so juicy and tender, who had walked into the ocean and realized he had forgotten how to swim. That's what walking on land will do. Another time I found a pack of young ones whose mother left them to hunt for food and didn't return. They were all bones and no meat. Most of the dead are victims of the plague. No one will touch them. Your body is ample and your skin is without marks or sores, so perhaps you did not die of disease.

Young Woman: I remember hearing a cry, a wail, high and shrill yet so sad and low. Even thinking of it now . . .

(She shivers as she covers her ears. Old Woman washes Young Woman's face and body, caressing her gently.)

Young Woman: You feed me and now you wash me. I am not used to such good fortune.

Old Woman: Your skin is soft and your meat lean, I will chew gently.

Young Woman: I remember . . . I remember a touch, yes, the way you're touching my body, I have felt this before. 30

Old Woman: Your belly is loose. I think I know how you died. You spawned a baby.

Young Woman: (*Surprised.*) But I have no memory of this. Surely one would never forget such a thing.

Old Woman: It is quite common to forget one's young. I never knew my mother. When you live in a whale's belly, it is easy to get separated and lost.

Young Woman: Do you have any memories of your mother?

Old Woman: The others say she died after giving birth to me. I like to think that she was a good female. Fair and kind who would have loved me no matter how different I am. I was told that my mother lived in the twenty-first century, after the great war and before the devil's blanket. The land was growing hotter and night became day. People roamed the land in search of shade and food until finally only the ocean was left. My mother must have been a wise female to convince a whale to share his belly. 35

Young Woman: Was it difficult to live inside a whale?

Old Woman: One can get used to anything, especially if one knows nothing else.

(Old Woman spreads grease on Young Woman's face and neck.)

Young Woman: What is that awful smell?

Old Woman: Your skin needs oil.

Young Woman: Why are you so kind to me? 40

Old Woman: You ask foolish questions.

Young Woman: No, you are proof that this life will be different. Perhaps I will even see the moon.

Old Woman: The moon exists only in stories, now hush before I change my mind. I curse this hunger in my belly. Living on land allows one to spawn many eggs. There is only so much spam to go around.

Young Woman: I have smelled this before. It is—fish oil!

Old Woman: Only the best for this feast. 45

Young Woman: Will I be going to your feast?

Old Woman: I will make you the guest of honor. Eat more bread. Color is coming back into your face. The others say that before the great war there was a celebration where people ate for days. It was a celebration to give thanks for all they had been given and they were given a lot although they did not think so. Berries and bread were eaten, but the main attraction was a bird, a large one that was roasted. They say it was an ugly-looking bird that walked on two legs.

I would have liked to have seen this bird. The others say he made a sound like this . . . *(Wails.)*

(Young Woman grows uneasy.)

Young Woman: Stop it!

Old Woman: Do not be cross, young one, it makes the intestines sour.

(Old Woman massages her again.)

Young Woman: What will be eaten at your feast? 50

Old Woman: Whatever one can find.

(Young Woman stands up almost losing her balance. She walks around testing her legs. Old Woman sniffs the air.)

Old Woman: What are you doing? Come back to me.

Young Woman: Your food has given me strength.

Old Woman: Sit down. You must not move too quickly. Bruised meat is tough.

Young Woman: The earth agrees with my feet. I must have walked on land before. 55
How long has it been since you first walked?

Old Woman: There are too many lines on my face to count. Now come to me.

Young Woman: Answer my question and then I will lie in your arms.

Old Woman: Soon after blood flowed from my legs we walked on land, now I am as
dry as the bread you greedily ate.

Young Woman: Perhaps I am not too late.

Old Woman: For what? 60

Young Woman: To find my young.

Old Woman: That is impossible. How can you look when you don't remember
anything?

Young Woman: I remember her cry.

Old Woman: You remember nothing.

Young Woman: The bird sounds you made remind me of my girl, yes, you see I 65
remember, I gave birth to a girl. She was the strangest-looking girl I had
ever seen. I gave birth to her at a time of great chaos. It was as if the earth had
turned upside down. Each day that passed more people died. Money
was useless, water and shade were the only things of value. People fought to
stand in the ocean and when that wasn't enough we had to go under water.
I swam with fishes and birds and when my contractions started, they helped me
find shelter in a cave that smelled of fish oil and that's where I gave birth.
Before I passed I saw her. I touched her face. I heard her wail. I want to
know if she survived.

Old Woman: That land is cool now but it is impossible for a young to survive alone,
especially if there were no others to teach her.

Young Woman: She was so unusual, perhaps she survived.

Old Woman: Impossible.

Young Woman: But you survived without your mother.

Old Woman: I had the others. Death has made you foolish. Now stop your chatter 70
and come to me. Let my hands soothe you.

Young Woman: It is too cruel to live your next life with the same bad memories of
before. I curse the gods who pulled me from the ground.

Old Woman: Let me help you ease your pain.

(Old Woman holds out her arms, but Young Woman remains still.)

Young Woman: Do you enjoy eating the dead?

Old Woman: The land produces only dead people.

Young Woman: How many will I feed?

Old Woman: My pack has ten. Your toes and fingers will be feed for the young.

Young Woman: How will I be cooked?

Old Woman: Wrapped in sheets of fish fat and seaweed and baked in the land for two days.

Young Woman: Will you be the one to cook me?

Old Woman: I will not leave your side. On the day you are served, the others will gather and sing and dance to our gods. Then we will laugh and talk as we feast pretending that our food is not of our dead but that of other creatures. We will drink sea water and say it is sweet and soothing. We will eat your flesh and remark how the meat falls from the bones enticing us to eat more. And when our bellies are full and the table is bare, the others will tell stories of life before the devil's blanket covered the land. A time when people had no need to eat their dead. Come to me.

(Old Woman holds out her hands.)

Young Woman: First you must make that bird sound again.

(Old Woman wails. Slowly Young Woman walks over to her, they embrace. Old Woman slowly rocks her in her arms.)

Young Woman: She is better off dead. One cannot live with a shadow over one's face.

Old Woman: What do you mean?

Young Woman: She was hideous-looking, a freak with no chance of surviving. Even if there were others to help she would have been an outcast. Death is the only kindness she could have known.

Old Woman: Hideous in what way?

Young Woman: One needs all the senses to survive.

Old Woman: You are the blind one now.

Young Woman: Where there should have been eyes was only skin. No eye sockets or anything remotely resembling eyes, only skin, smooth and blank. A nose, a mouth, and nothing else. It was as if the gods had suddenly lost interest and stopped work on her. She was a freak, no doubt about it. A freak for freakish times.

Old Woman: How do you know this? You died giving birth to her.

Young Woman: I saw her briefly before I passed. It was the sight of her that caused my heart to stop.

Old Woman: You speak of the impossible.

Young Woman: She is dead, and when I enter the other world perhaps this time your gods will favor me and allow me to meet her.

Old Woman: This is a cruel trick. I am old not stupid.

Young Woman: I am ready to be roasted. Take me, old woman, I am all yours. Only promise me that you will eat my heart. And when you chew, chew it well at least a hundred times or more. Although it is filled with pain, I give my heart to you.

(Young Woman holds out her hands to Old Woman who stares at her. Slight pause.)

Young Woman: What is wrong with you? Have you changed your mind about me? ⁹⁵
Perhaps I am too skinny for you. I assure you there is enough to feed your pack.
Look at my hips, see its width? The flesh on my chest and back will satisfy
the most hungry. Speak old woman. Do not tell me that you have lost your
appetite.

Old Woman: I hunger for you more than ever.

Young Woman: Then what is it?

*(Old Woman removes her veil and turns her face to the audience. She has no eyes. Young
Woman looks stunned. She looks at Old Woman with disbelief, then recognition, and
finally joy.)*

Young Woman: The gods have heard me.

(Blackout.)

Explorations of the Text

1. The play is set in the future. Characterize the events that have happened between now, our real time, and then, the futuristic time of the play's setting.

2. The young woman offers her heart to the old woman and asks her to chew it slowly, "at least one hundred times or more." Explain the symbolism of this gesture.

3. At the play's end, the characters recognize each other as mother and child. Will the child eat her mother even knowing who she is? Use evidence from the story to support your argument.

4. Discuss elements of magical realism (see Glossary) in Rudolfo Anaya's "In Search of Epifano" and Lesli-Jo Morizono's "Freakish Times." Are the authors' main ideas similar as well?

The Reading/Writing Connection

1. The old woman explains that after the plague all that remained were books by Donald Trump and cans of spam. Consider the symbolism of these items and then imagine what might remain if our world ended now. Write a satire of our present time by creating a futuristic story using items from the present as props.

Ideas for Writing

1. **Write an Argument:** Often futuristic literature is written as a warning so that people can alter their behavior and thus avert calamity. Argue whether Morizono's play is meant as a warning or something else.

2. Create a dialogue between Morizono and Szymborska about the state of the world.

NONFICTION

Toni Morrison (1931–)

The Nobel Prize Speech   1993

Members of the Swedish Academy, Ladies and Gentlemen: Narrative has never been merely entertainment for me. It is, I believe, one of the principal ways in which we absorb knowledge. I hope you will understand, then, why I begin these remarks with the opening phrase of what must be the oldest sentence in the world, and the earliest one we remember from childhood: "Once upon a time . . ."

"Once upon a time there was an old woman. Blind but wise." Or was it an old man? A guru, perhaps. Or a *griot*[1] soothing restless children. I have heard this story, or one exactly like it, in the lore of several cultures.

"Once upon a time there was an old woman. Blind. Wise."

In the version I know the woman is the daughter of slaves, black, American, and lives alone in a small house outside of town. Her reputation for wisdom is without peer and without question. Among her people she is both the law and its transgression. The honor she is paid and the awe in which she is held reach beyond her neighborhood to places far away; to the city where the intelligence of rural prophets is the source of much amusement.

One day the woman is visited by some young people who seem to be bent on disproving her clairvoyance and showing her up for the fraud they believe she is. Their plan is simple: they enter her house and ask the one question the answer to which rides solely on her difference from them, a difference they regard as a profound disability: her blindness. They stand before her, and one of them says,   5

"Old woman, I hold in my hand a bird. Tell me whether it is living or dead."

She does not answer, and the question is repeated. "Is the bird I am holding living or dead?"

Still she does not answer. She is blind and cannot see her visitors, let alone what is in their hands. She does not know their color, gender, or homeland. She knows only their motive.

The old woman's silence is so long, the young people have trouble holding their laughter.

Finally she speaks, and her voice is soft but stern. "I don't know," she says. "I don't   10 know whether the bird you are holding is dead or alive, but what I do know is that it is in your hands. It is in your hands."

Her answer can be taken to mean: if it is dead, you have either found it that way or you have killed it. If it is alive, you can still kill it. Whether it is to stay alive is your decision. Whatever the case, it is your responsibility.

For parading their power and her helplessness, the young visitors are reprimanded, told they are responsible not only for the act of mockery but also for the small bundle

---

[1] **griot:** A storyteller in western Africa.

of life sacrificed to achieve its aims. The blind woman shifts attention away from assertions of power to the instrument through which that power is exercised.

Speculation on what (other than its own frail body) that bird in the hand might signify has always been attractive to me, but especially so now, thinking as I have been about the work I do that has brought me to this company. So I choose to read the bird as language and the woman as a practiced writer.

She is worried about how the language she dreams in, given to her at birth, is handled, put into service, even withheld from her for certain nefarious purposes. Being a writer, she thinks of language partly as a system, partly as a living thing over which one has control, but mostly as agency—as an act with consequences. So the question the children put to her, "Is it living or dead?," is not unreal, because she thinks of language as susceptible to death, erasure; certainly imperiled and salvageable only by an effort of the will. She believes that if the bird in the hands of her visitors is dead, the custodians are responsible for the corpse. For her a dead language is not only one no longer spoken or written, it is unyielding language content to admire its own paralysis. Like statist language, censored and censoring. Ruthless in its policing duties, it has no desire or purpose other than to maintain the free range of its own narcotic narcissism, its own exclusivity and dominance. However moribund, it is not without effect, for it actively thwarts the intellect, stalls conscience, suppresses human potential. Unreceptive to interrogation, it cannot form or tolerate new ideas, shape other thoughts, tell another story, fill baffling silences. Official language smitheried to sanction ignorance and preserve privilege is a suit of armor, polished to shocking glitter, a husk from which the knight departed long ago. Yet there it is; dumb, predatory, sentimental. Exciting reverence in schoolchildren, providing shelter for despots, summoning false memories of stability, harmony among the public.

She is convinced that when language dies, out of carelessness, disuse, indifference, and absence of esteem, or killed by fiat, not only she herself but all users and makers are accountable for its demise. In her country children have bitten their tongues off and use bullets instead to iterate the void of speechlessness, of disabled and disabling language, of language adults have abandoned altogether as a device for grappling with meaning, providing guidance, or expressing love. But she knows tongue-suicide is not only the choice of children. It is common among the infantile heads of state and power merchants whose evacuated language leaves them with no access to what is left of their human instincts, for they speak only to those who obey, or in order to force obedience. 15

The systematic looting of language can be recognized by the tendency of its users to forgo its nuanced, complex, midwifery properties, replacing them with menace and subjugation. Oppressive language does more than represent violence; it is violence; does more than represent the limits of knowledge; it limits knowledge. Whether it is obscuring state language or the faux language of mindless media; whether it is the proud but calcified language of the academy or the commodity-driven language of science; whether it is the malign language of law-without-ethics, or language designed for the estrangement of minorities, hiding its racist plunder in its literary cheek—it must be rejected, altered, and exposed. It is the language that drinks blood, laps vulnerabilities, tucks its fascist boots under crinolines of respectability and patriotism as it moves relentlessly toward the bottom line and the bottomed-out mind. Sexist language, racist language, theistic language—all are typical of the policing languages of mastery, and cannot, do not, permit new knowledge or encourage the mutual exchange of ideas.

The old woman is keenly aware that no intellectual mercenary or insatiable dictator, no paid-for politician or demagogue, no counterfeit journalist would be persuaded by her thoughts. There is and will be rousing language to keep citizens armed and arming; slaughtered and slaughtering in the malls, courthouses, post offices, playgrounds, bedrooms, and boulevards; stirring, memorializing language to mask the pity and waste of needless death. There will be more diplomatic language to countenance rape, torture, assassination. There is and will be more seductive, mutant language designed to throttle women, to pack their throats like pâté-producing geese with their own unsayable, transgressive words; there will be more of the language of surveillance disguised as research; of politics and history calculated to render the suffering of millions mute; language glamorized to thrill the dissatisfied and bereft into assaulting their neighbors; arrogant pseudo-empirical language crafted to lock creative people into cages of inferiority and hopelessness.

Underneath the eloquence, the glamour, the scholarly associations, however stirring or seductive, the heart of such language is languishing, or perhaps not beating at all—if the bird is already dead.

She had thought about what could have been the intellectual history of any discipline if it had not insisted upon, or been forced into, the waste of time and life that rationalizations for and representations of dominance required—lethal discourses of exclusion blocking access to cognition for both the excluder and the excluded.

The conventional wisdom of the Tower of Babel story is that the collapse was a 20 misfortune. That it was the distraction or the weight of many languages that precipitated the tower's failed architecture. That one monolithic language would have expedited the building, and heaven would have been reached. Whose heaven, she wonders? And what kind? Perhaps the achievement of Paradise was premature, a little hasty if no one could take the time to understand other languages, other views, other narratives. Had they, the heaven they imagined might have been found at their feet. Complicated, demanding, yes, but a view of heaven as life; not heaven as post-life.

She would not want to leave her young visitors with the impression that language should be forced to stay alive merely to be. The vitality of language lies in its ability to limn the actual, imagined, and possible lives of its speakers, readers, writers. Although its poise is sometimes in displacing experience, it is not a substitute for it. It arcs toward the place where meaning may lie. When a president of the United States thought about the graveyard his country had become, and said, "The world will little note nor long remember what we say here. But it will never forget what they did here," his simple words were exhilarating in their life-sustaining properties because they refused to encapsulate the reality of 600,000 dead men in a cataclysmic race war. Refusing to monumentalize, disdaining the "final word," the precise "summing up," acknowledging their "poor power to add or detract," his words signal deference to the uncapturability of the life it mourns. It is deference that moves her, that recognition that language can never live up to life once and for all. Nor should it. Language can never "pin down" slavery, genocide, war. Nor should it yearn for the arrogance to be able to do so. Its force, its felicity, is in its reach toward the ineffable.

Be it grand or slender, burrowing, blasting or refusing to sanctify; whether it laughs out loud or is a cry without an alphabet, the choice word or the chosen silence, unmolested language surges toward knowledge, not its destruction. But who does not know of literature banned because it is interrogative; discredited because it is critical; erased because alternate? And how many are outraged by the thought of a self-ravaged tongue?

Word-work is sublime, she thinks, because it is generative; it makes meaning that secures our difference, our human difference—the way in which we are like no other life.

We die. That may be the meaning of life. But we do language. That may be the measure of our lives.

"Once upon a time . . ." Visitors ask an old woman a question. Who are they, these 25 children? What did they make of that encounter? What did they hear in those final words: "The bird is in your hands"? A sentence that gestures toward possibility, or one that drops a latch? Perhaps what the children heard was, "It's not my problem. I am old, female, black, blind. What wisdom I have now is in knowing I cannot help you. The future of language is yours."

They stand there. Suppose nothing was in their hands. Suppose the visit was only a ruse, a trick to get to be spoken to, taken seriously as they have not been before. A chance to interrupt, to violate the adult world, its miasma of discourse about them. Urgent questions are at stake, including the one they have asked: "Is the bird we are holding living or dead?" Perhaps the question meant: "Could someone tell us what is life? What is death?" No trick at all; no silliness. A straightforward question worthy of the attention of a wise one. An old one. And if the old and wise who have lived life and faced death cannot describe either, who can?

But she does not; she keeps her secret, her good opinion of herself, her gnomic pronouncements, her art without commitment. She keeps her distance, enforces it and retreats into the singularity of isolation, in sophisticated, privileged space.

Nothing, no word follows her declaration of transfer. That silence is deep, deeper than the meaning available in the words she has spoken. It shivers, this silence, and the children, annoyed, fill it with language invented on the spot.

"Is there no speech," they ask her, "no words you can give us that help us break through your dossier of failures" through the education you have just given us that is no education at all because we are paying close attention to what you have done as well as to what you have said? to the barrier you have erected between generosity and wisdom?

"We have no bird in our hands, living or dead. We have only you and our important 30 question. Is the nothing in our hands something you could not bear to contemplate, to even guess? Don't you remember being young, when language was magic without meaning? When what you could say, could not mean? When the invisible was what imagination strove to see? When questions and demands for answers burned so brightly you trembled with fury at not knowing?

"Do we have to begin consciousness with a battle heroes and heroines like you have already fought and lost, leaving us with nothing in our hands except what you imagined is there? Your answer is artful, but its artfulness embarrasses us and ought to embarrass you. Your answer is indecent in its self-congratulation. A made-for-television script that makes no sense if there is nothing in our hands.

"Why didn't you reach out, touch us with your soft fingers, delay the sound bite, the lesson, until you knew who we were? Did you so despise our trick, our modus operandi, that you could not see that we were baffled about how to get your attention? We are young. Unripe. We have heard all our short lives that we have to be responsible. What could that possibly mean in the catastrophe this world has become; where, as a poet said, 'nothing needs to be exposed since it is already barefaced'? Our inheritance is an affront. You want us to have your old, blank eyes and see only cruelty and mediocrity. Do you think we are stupid enough to perjure ourselves again and again with the fiction of nationhood? How dare you talk to us of duty when we stand waist deep in the toxin of our past?

"You trivialize us and trivialize the bird that is not in our hands. Is there no context for our lives? No song, no literature, no poem full of vitamins, no history connected to experience that you can pass along to help us start strong? You are an adult. The old one, the wise one. Stop thinking about saving your face. Think of our lives and tell us your particularized world. Make up a story. Narrative is radical, creating us at the very moment it is being created. We will not blame you if your reach exceeds your grasp; if love so ignites your words that they go down in flames and nothing is left but their scald. Or if, with the reticence of a surgeon's hands, your words suture only the places where blood might flow. We know you can never do it properly—once and for all. Passion is never enough; neither is skill. But try. For our sake and yours forget your name in the street; tell us what the world has been to you in the dark places and in the light. Don't tell us what to believe, what to fear. Show us belief's wide skirt and the stitch that unravels fear's caul. You, old woman, blessed with blindness, can speak the language that tells us what only language can: how to see without pictures. Language alone protects us from the scariness of things with no names. Language alone is meditation.

"Tell us what it is to be a woman so that we may know what it is to be a man. What moves at the margin. What it is to have no home in this place. To be set adrift from the one you knew. What it is to live at the edge of towns that cannot bear your company.

"Tell us about ships turned away from shorelines at Easter, placenta in a field. Tell us about a wagonload of slaves, how they sang so softly their breath was indistinguishable from the falling snow. How they knew from the hunch of the nearest shoulder that the next stop would be their last. How, with hands prayered in their sex, they thought of heat, then sun. Lifting their faces as though it was there for the taking. They stop at an inn. The driver and his mate go in with the lamp, leaving them humming in the dark. The horse's void steams into the snow beneath its hooves and the hiss and melt are the envoy of the freezing slaves. 35

"The inn door opens: a girl and a boy step away from its light. They climb into the wagon bed. The boy will have a gun in three years, but now he carries a lamp and a jug of warm cider. They pass it from mouth to mouth. The girl offers bread, pieces of meat, and something more: a glance into the eyes of the one she serves. One helping for each man, two for each woman. And a look. They look back. The next stop will be their last. But not this one. This one is warmed."

"It's quiet again when the children finish speaking, until the woman breaks into the silence.

"Finally," she says, "I trust you now. I trust you with the bird that is not in your hands because you have truly caught it. Look. How lovely it is, this thing we have done—together." •

Explorations of the Text

1. Consider an audience for this essay including and beyond: "Members of the Swedish Academy, Ladies and Gentlemen." To whom is this essay addressed?

2. At one point in the essay we read the following: "Narrative is radical, creating us at the very moment it is being created." Analyze and explain the complex

layers of narrative Morrison uses in this essay. What is the function, for example, of the story within a story?

3. Consider the various symbolic references to the bird. How does the symbolism of the bird change? What is the significance of the "bird in . . . [the] hand"?

4. As you interpret the references to the bird, consider the possibility of forms of narrative as a way into symbolic meaning. Is this a parable, a folk story, an allegory, or even a Socratic dialogue?

(Refer to Chapter 10 on forms of narrative; to the excerpt from *The Symposium* in Chapter 7; to "The Allegory of the Cave" in this chapter.)

5. Morrison makes numerous powerful, even provocative, statements about language in this essay. Examine and discuss at least three of these statements. Do you agree with her views of language?

6. What does the speech suggest about storytelling, language, and the power of words?

The Reading/Writing Connection

1. Gloss and annotate the text of the speech—concentrate on the symbolism of the bird—in preparation for class discussion of question 3 in Explorations of the Text.

2. After reading this speech, list several questions that you have about the work. Then answer one of your questions in the form of a paragraph.

Ideas for Writing

1. Choose one of Morrison's controversial statements about language. Agree or disagree with her. Your response may take the form of a letter to Morrison.

2. Is Morrison's speech effective? Convincing? Evaluate her work. Refer to the student portfolio in Chapter 13 for ideas.

Jared Diamond   *(1937–)*

The Ends of the World as We Know Them   *2005*

New Year's weekend traditionally is a time for us to reflect, and to make resolutions based on our reflections. In this fresh year, with the United States seemingly at the height of its power and at the start of a new presidential term, Americans are increasingly concerned and divided about where we are going. How long can America remain ascendant? Where will we stand ten years from now, or even next year?

Such questions seem especially appropriate this year. History warns us that when once-powerful societies collapse, they tend to do so quickly and unexpectedly. That shouldn't come as much of a surprise: peak power usually means peak population, peak needs, and hence peak vulnerability. What can be learned from history that could help us avoid joining the ranks of those who declined swiftly? We must expect the answers to be complex, because historical reality is complex: while some societies did indeed collapse spectacularly, others have managed to thrive for thousands of years without major reversal.

When it comes to historical collapses, five groups of interacting factors have been especially important: the damage that people have inflicted on their environment;

climate change; enemies; changes in friendly trading partners; and the society's political, economic and social responses to these shifts. That's not to say that all five causes play a role in every case. Instead, think of this as a useful checklist of factors that should be examined, but whose relative importance varies from case to case.

For instance, in the collapse of the Polynesian society on Easter Island[1] three centuries ago, environmental problems were dominant, and climate change, enemies and trade were insignificant; however, the latter three factors played big roles in the disappearance of the medieval Norse colonies on Greenland. Let's consider two examples of declines stemming from different mixes of causes: the falls of classic Maya civilization and of Polynesian settlements on the Pitcairn Islands.

Maya Native Americans of the Yucatan Peninsula and adjacent parts of Central   5
America developed the New World's most advanced civilization before Columbus. They were innovators in writing, astronomy, architecture and art. From local origins around 2,500 years ago, Maya societies rose especially after the year A.D. 250, reaching peaks of population and sophistication in the late eighth century.

Thereafter, societies in the most densely populated areas of the southern Yucatan underwent a steep political and cultural collapse: between 760 and 910, kings were overthrown, large areas were abandoned, and at least 90 percent of the population disappeared, leaving cities to become overgrown by jungle. The last known date recorded on a Maya monument by their so-called Long Count calendar corresponds to the year 909. What happened?

A major factor was environmental degradation by people: deforestation, soil erosion and water management problems, all of which resulted in less food. Those problems were exacerbated by droughts, which may have been partly caused by humans themselves through deforestation. Chronic warfare made matters worse, as more and more people fought over less and less land and resources.

Why weren't these problems obvious to the Maya kings, who could surely see their forests vanishing and their hills becoming eroded? Part of the reason was that the kings were able to insulate themselves from problems afflicting the rest of society. By extracting wealth from commoners, they could remain well fed while everyone else was slowly starving.

What's more, the kings were preoccupied with their own power struggles. They had to concentrate on fighting one another and keeping up their images through ostentatious displays of wealth. By insulating themselves in the short run from the problems of society, the elite merely bought themselves the privilege of being among the last to starve.

Whereas Maya societies were undone by problems of their own making, Polynesian   10
societies on Pitcairn and Henderson Islands in the tropical Pacific Ocean were undone largely by other people's mistakes. Pitcairn, the uninhabited island settled in 1790 by the *H.M.S. Bounty* mutineers, had actually been populated by Polynesians 800 years earlier. That society, which left behind temple platforms, stone and shell tools and huge garbage piles of fish and bird and turtle bones as evidence of its existence, survived for several centuries and then vanished. Why?

In many respects, Pitcairn and Henderson are tropical paradises, rich in some food sources and essential raw materials. Pitcairn is home to Southeast Polynesia's largest quarry of stone suited for making adzes, while Henderson has the region's largest breed-

---

[1]**Easter Island:** A remote South Pacific island known for giant Moai statues, which were toppled during a period of decline for the Rapa Nui people there.

ing seabird colony and its only nesting beach for sea turtles. Yet the islanders depended on imports from Mangareva Island, hundreds of miles away, for canoes, crops, livestock and oyster shells for making tools.

Unfortunately for the inhabitants of Pitcairn and Henderson, their Mangarevan trading partner collapsed for reasons similar to those underlying the Maya decline: deforestation, erosion and warfare. Deprived of essential imports in a Polynesian equivalent of the 1973 oil crisis, the Pitcairn and Henderson societies declined until everybody had died or fled.

The Maya and the Henderson and Pitcairn Islanders are not alone, of course. Over the centuries, many other societies have declined, collapsed or died out. Famous victims include the Anasazi in the American Southwest, who abandoned their cities in the twelfth century because of environmental problems and climate change, and the Greenland Norse, who disappeared in the fifteenth century because of all five interacting factors on the checklist. There were also the ancient Fertile Crescent societies, the Khmer at Angkor Wat, the Moche society of Peru—the list goes on.

But before we let ourselves get depressed, we should also remember that there is another long list of cultures that have managed to prosper for lengthy periods of time. Societies in Japan, Tonga, Tikopia, the New Guinea Highlands and Central and Northwest Europe, for example, have all found ways to sustain themselves. What separates the lost cultures from those that survived? Why did the Maya fail and the shogun succeed?

Half of the answer involves environmental differences: geography deals worse cards 15 to some societies than to others. Many of the societies that collapsed had the misfortune to occupy dry, cold or otherwise fragile environments, while many of the long-term survivors enjoyed more robust and fertile surroundings. But it's not the case that a congenial environment guarantees success: some societies (like the Maya) managed to ruin lush environments, while other societies—like the Incas, the Inuit, Icelanders and desert Australian Aborigines—have managed to carry on in some of the earth's most daunting environments.

The other half of the answer involves differences in a society's responses to problems. Ninth-century New Guinea Highland villagers, sixteenth-century German landowners, and the Tokugawa shoguns of seventeenth-century Japan all recognized the deforestation spreading around them and solved the problem, either by developing scientific reforestation (Japan and Germany) or by transplanting tree seedlings (New Guinea). Conversely, the Maya, Mangarevans and Easter Islanders failed to address their forestry problems and so collapsed.

Consider Japan. In the 1600s, the country faced its own crisis of deforestation, paradoxically brought on by the peace and prosperity following the Tokugawa shoguns' military triumph that ended 150 years of civil war. The subsequent explosion of Japan's population and economy set off rampant logging for construction of palaces and cities, and for fuel and fertilizer.

The shoguns responded with both negative and positive measures. They reduced wood consumption by turning to light-timbered construction, to fuel-efficient stoves and heaters, and to coal as a source of energy. At the same time, they increased wood production by developing and carefully managing plantation forests. Both the shoguns and the Japanese peasants took a long-term view: the former expected to pass on their power to their children, and the latter expected to pass on their land. In addition,

Japan's isolation at the time made it obvious that the country would have to depend on its own resources and couldn't meet its needs by pillaging other countries. Today, despite having the highest human population density of any large developed country, Japan is more than seventy percent forested.

There is a similar story from Iceland. When the island was first settled by the Norse around 870, its light volcanic soils presented colonists with unfamiliar challenges. They proceeded to cut down trees and stock sheep as if they were still in Norway, with its robust soils. Significant erosion ensued, carrying half of Iceland's topsoil into the ocean within a century or two. Icelanders became the poorest people in Europe. But they gradually learned from their mistakes, over time instituting stocking limits on sheep and other strict controls, and establishing an entire government department charged with landscape management. Today, Iceland boasts the sixth-highest per-capita income in the world.

What lessons can we draw from history? The most straightforward: take environ- 20 mental problems seriously. They destroyed societies in the past, and they are even more likely to do so now. If 6,000 Polynesians with stone tools were able to destroy Mangareva Island, consider what six billion people with metal tools and bulldozers are doing today. Moreover, while the Maya collapse affected just a few neighboring societies in Central America, globalization now means that any society's problems have the potential to affect anyone else. Just think how crises in Somalia, Afghanistan and Iraq have shaped the United States today.

Other lessons involve failures of group decision-making. There are many reasons why past societies made bad decisions, and thereby failed to solve or even to perceive the problems that would eventually destroy them. One reason involves conflicts of interest, whereby one group within a society (for instance, the pig farmers who caused the worst erosion in medieval Greenland and Iceland) can profit by engaging in practices that damage the rest of society. Another is the pursuit of short-term gains at the expense of long-term survival, as when fishermen overfish the stocks on which their livelihoods ultimately depend.

History also teaches us two deeper lessons about what separates successful societies from those heading toward failure. A society contains a built-in blueprint for failure if the elite insulates itself from the consequences of its actions. That's why Maya kings, Norse Greenlanders and Easter Island chiefs made choices that eventually undermined their societies. They themselves did not begin to feel deprived until they had irreversibly destroyed their landscape.

Could this happen in the United States? It's a thought that often occurs to me here in Los Angeles, when I drive by gated communities, guarded by private security patrols, and filled with people who drink bottled water, depend on private pensions, and send their children to private schools. By doing these things, they lose the motivation to support the police force, the municipal water supply, Social Security and public schools. If conditions deteriorate too much for poorer people, gates will not keep the rioters out. Rioters eventually burned the palaces of Maya kings and tore down the statues of Easter Island chiefs; they have also already threatened wealthy districts in Los Angeles twice in recent decades.

In contrast, the elite in seventeenth-century Japan, as in modern Scandinavia and the Netherlands, could not ignore or insulate themselves from broad societal problems. For instance, the Dutch upper class for hundreds of years has been unable to insulate itself from the Netherlands' water management problems for a simple reason: the rich live in the same drained lands below sea level as the poor. If the dikes and pumps keeping out the sea fail, the well-off Dutch know that they will drown along with everybody else, which is precisely what happened during the floods of 1953.

The other deep lesson involves a willingness to re-examine long-held core values, 25 when conditions change and those values no longer make sense. The medieval Greenland Norse lacked such a willingness: they continued to view themselves as transplanted Norwegian pastoralists, and to despise the Inuit as pagan hunters, even after Norway stopped sending trading ships and the climate had grown too cold for a pastoral existence. They died off as a result, leaving Greenland to the Inuit. On the other hand, the British in the 1950s faced up to the need for a painful reappraisal of their former status as rulers of a world empire set apart from Europe. They are now finding a different avenue to wealth and power, as part of a united Europe.

In this New Year, we Americans have our own painful reappraisals to face. Historically, we viewed the United States as a land of unlimited plenty, and so we practiced unrestrained consumerism, but that's no longer viable in a world of finite resources. We can't continue to deplete our own resources as well as those of much of the rest of the world.

Historically, oceans protected us from external threats; we stepped back from our isolationism only temporarily during the crises of two world wars. Now, technology and global interconnectedness have robbed us of our protection. In recent years, we have responded to foreign threats largely by seeking short-term military solutions at the last minute.

But how long can we keep this up? Though we are the richest nation on earth, there's simply no way we can afford (or muster the troops) to intervene in the dozens of countries where emerging threats lurk—particularly when each intervention these days can cost more than $100 billion and require more than 100,000 troops.

A genuine reappraisal would require us to recognize that it will be far less expensive and far more effective to address the underlying problems of public health, population and environment that ultimately cause threats to us to emerge in poor countries. In the past, we have regarded foreign aid as either charity or as buying support; now, it's an act of self-interest to preserve our own economy and protect American lives.

Do we have cause for hope? Many of my friends are pessimistic when they con- 30 template the world's growing population and human demands colliding with shrinking resources. But I draw hope from the knowledge that humanity's biggest problems today are ones entirely of our own making. Asteroids hurtling at us beyond our control don't figure high on our list of imminent dangers. To save ourselves, we don't need new technology: we just need the political will to face up to our problems of population and the environment.

I also draw hope from a unique advantage that we enjoy. Unlike any previous society in history, our global society today is the first with the opportunity to learn from the mistakes of societies remote from us in space and in time. When the Maya and Mangarevans were cutting down their trees, there were no historians or archaeologists, no newspapers or television, to warn them of the consequences of their actions. We, on the other hand, have a detailed chronicle of human successes and failures at our disposal. Will we choose to use it? ●

Explorations of the Text

1. Diamond's essay is structured as an argument. What is his position? Reasons? Who is his intended audience? What is his evidence? Is his argument effective?
2. Discuss the significance of the essay's title.
3. Why might Diamond refer to New Year's Eve twice in this essay? What symbolic purpose might this reference hold?
4. List the five factors that Diamond claims caused past societies to collapse.

Which one of these does Diamond find to be most significant for the United States?
5. What lessons does Diamond suggest that we learn from the past? Does he offer any hope for the future?
6. Compare Diamond's discussion of history and globalization with that of Kwame Anthony Appiah in "The Case for Contamination." How do their perspectives differ?

The Reading/Writing Connection

1. Write a poem, song, or short story using Diamond's title, "The Ends of the World as We Know Them."
2. Write a dialogue between two of the following authors from this chapter: Jared Diamond, Kwame Anthony Appiah, Peter Singer, or Alice Walker. In the dialogue, have the authors debate and perhaps offer possible solutions to

one of the world's great problems (environmental degradation, hunger, poverty, war, sexism, racism, etc.).
3. Journal Entry: Write a journal entry from yourself twenty-five years from today. In it, describe the environmental problems. Have they improved? Gotten worse? How do they affect your life?

Ideas for Writing

1. **Write an Argument:** In paragraph 20, Diamond tells us what we can learn from the collapse of past societies. In paragraph 23, he asks if the collapse he describes as having occurred in other societies can occur in the United States. And, in paragraph 30, he asks if we

"have cause for hope." Write an essay in which you use Diamond's points to argue that we can prevent environmental degradation from destroying our society. Or, conversely, write an essay in which you argue that it is too late and the United States is already in decline.

Albert Camus *(1913–1960)*

The Myth of Sisyphus   *1942*

The gods had condemned Sisyphus to ceaselessly rolling a rock to the top of a mountain, whence the stone would fall back of its own weight. They had thought with some reason that there is no more dreadful punishment than futile and hopeless labor.

If one believes Homer,[1] Sisyphus was the wisest and most prudent of mortals. According to another tradition, however, he was disposed to practice the profession of

---

[1]**Homer:** Greek epic poet (c. ninth to eighth centuries B.C.) who wrote about Sisyphus in *The Iliad*.

highwayman. I see no contradiction in this. Opinions differ as to the reasons why he became the futile laborer of the underworld. To begin with, he is accused of a certain levity in regard to the gods. He stole their secrets. Ægina,[2] the daughter of Æsopus, was carried off by Jupiter. The father was shocked by that disappearance and complained to Sisyphus. He, who knew of the abduction, offered to tell about it on condition that Æsopus would give water to the citadel of Corinth. To the celestial thunderbolts he preferred the benediction of water. He was punished for this in the underworld. Homer tells us also that Sisyphus had put Death in chains. Pluto[3] could not endure the sight of his deserted, silent empire. He dispatched the god of war, who liberated Death from the hands of her conqueror.

It is said also that Sisyphus, being near to death, rashly wanted to test his wife's love. He ordered her to cast his unburied body into the middle of the public square. Sisyphus woke up in the underworld. And there, annoyed by an obedience so contrary to human love, he obtained from Pluto permission to return to earth in order to chastise his wife. But when he had seen again the face of this world, enjoyed water and sun, warm stones and the sea, he no longer wanted to go back to the infernal darkness. Recalls, signs of anger, warnings were of no avail. Many years more he lived facing the curve of the gulf, the sparkling sea, and the smiles of earth. A decree of the gods was necessary. Mercury[4] came and seized the impudent man by the collar and, snatching him from his joys, led him forcibly back to the underworld, where his rock was ready for him.

You have already grasped that Sisyphus is the absurd hero. He is, as much through his passions as through his torture. His scorn of the gods, his hatred of death, and his passion for life won him that unspeakable penalty in which the whole being is exerted toward accomplishing nothing. This is the price that must be paid for the passions of this earth. Nothing is told us about Sisyphus in the underworld. Myths are made for the imagination to breathe life into them. As for this myth, one sees merely the whole effort of a body straining to raise the huge stone, to roll it and push it up a slope a hundred times over; one sees the face screwed up, the cheek tight against the stone, the shoulder bracing the clay-covered mass, the foot wedging it, the fresh start with arms outstretched, the wholly human security of two earth-clotted hands. At the very end of his long effort measured by skyless space and time without depth, the purpose is achieved. Then Sisyphus watches the stone rush down in a few moments toward that lower world whence he will have to push it up again toward the summit. He goes back down to the plain.

It is during that return, that pause, that Sisyphus interests me. A face that toils so close to stones is already stone itself! I see that man going back down with a heavy yet measured step toward the torment of which he will never know the end. That hour like a breathing space which returns as surely as his suffering, that is the hour of consciousness. At each of those moments when he leaves the heights and gradually sinks toward the lairs of the gods, he is superior to his fate. He is stronger than his rock.

If this myth is tragic, that is because its hero is conscious. Where would his torture be, indeed, if at every step the hope of succeeding upheld him? The workman of today

5

---

[2]**Ægina:** A story from Greek mythology.   [3]**Pluto:** Greek god of the underworld.   [4]**Mercury:** Roman god; messenger to the other gods.

works every day in his life at the same tasks, and this fate is no less absurd. But it is tragic only at the rare moments when it becomes conscious. Sisyphus, proletarian of the gods, powerless and rebellious, knows the whole extent of his wretched condition: it is what he thinks of during his descent. The lucidity that was to constitute his torture at the same time crowns his victory. There is no fate that cannot be surmounted by scorn.

If the descent is thus sometimes performed in sorrow, it can also take place in joy. This word is not too much. Again I fancy Sisyphus returning toward his rock, and the sorrow was in the beginning. When the images of earth cling too tightly to memory, when the call of happiness becomes too insistent, it happens that melancholy rises in man's heart: this is the rock's victory, this is the rock itself. The boundless grief is too heavy to bear. These are our nights of Gethsemane.[5] But crushing truths perish from being acknowledged. Thus, Oedipus at the outset obeys fate without knowing it. But from the moment he knows, his tragedy begins. Yet at the same moment, blind and desperate, he realizes that the only bond linking him to the world is the cool hand of a girl. Then a tremendous remark rings out: "Despite so many ordeals, my advanced age and the nobility of my soul make me conclude that all is well." Sophocles' Oedipus, like Dostoevsky's Kirilov,[6] thus gives the recipe for the absurd victory. Ancient wisdom confirms modern heroism.

One does not discover the absurd without being tempted to write a manual of happiness. "What! by such narrow ways—?" There is but one world, however. Happiness and the absurd are two sons of the same earth. They are inseparable. It would be a mistake to say that happiness necessarily springs from the absurd discovery. It happens as well that the feeling of the absurd springs from happiness. "I conclude that all is well," says Oedipus, and that remark is sacred. It echoes in the wild and limited universe of man. It teaches that all is not, has not been, exhausted. It drives out of this world a god who had come into it with dissatisfaction and a preference for futile sufferings. It makes a fate a human matter, which must be settled among men.

All Sisyphus' silent joy is contained therein. His fate belongs to him. His rock is his thing. Likewise, the absurd man, when he contemplates his torment, silences all the idols. In the universe suddenly restored to its silence, the myriad wondering little voices of the earth rise up. Unconscious, secret calls, invitations from all the faces, they are the necessary reverse and price of victory. There is no sun without shadow, and it is essential to know the night. The absurd man says yes and his effort will henceforth be unceasing. If there is a personal fate, there is no higher destiny, or at least there is but one which he concludes is inevitable and despicable. For the rest, he knows himself to be the master of his days. At that subtle moment when man glances backward over his life, Sisyphus returning toward his rock, in that slight pivoting he contemplates that series of unrelated actions which becomes his fate, created by him, combined under his memory's eye and soon sealed by his death. Thus, convinced of the wholly human origin of all that is human, a blind man eager to see who knows that the night has no end, he is still on the go. The rock is still rolling.

I leave Sisyphus at the foot of the mountain! One always finds one's burden again. But Sisyphus teaches the higher fidelity that negates the gods and raises rocks. He too 10

---

[5]**Gethsemane:** Garden outside Jerusalem. A reference to Jesus's discussion with his disciples the night before his crucifixion.   [6]**Kirilov:** Character who kills himself in Dostoevsky's novel, *The Possessed* (1871).

concludes that all is well. This universe henceforth without a master seems to him neither sterile nor futile. Each atom of that stone, each mineral flake of that night-filled mountain, in itself forms a world. The struggle itself toward the heights is enough to fill a man's heart. One must imagine Sisyphus happy. ●

Explorations of the Text

1. Why does Camus include two different versions of Sisyphus's fate? What common thread connects them? What does Sisyphus represent to Camus?

2. What does Camus mean by consciousness? Why does the "tragic" occur at the point of being "conscious"?

3. This excerpt is part of Camus's longer essay considered by critics to be a meditation on suicide. What arguments does Camus offer to oppose suicide?

4. Compare Camus's and Plato's views of enlightenment.

The Reading/Writing Connection

1. In a paragraph explore contemporary parallels for each aspect of the allegory (Sisyphus, his meaningless labor, his act of defiance, the gods).

2. "Think" Topic: Do you agree with Camus's view of the absurd universe? his vision of people's fates in such a world?

Ideas for Writing

1. Write an essay discussing Camus's concept of the absurd. Why is Sisyphus "the absurd hero"? What is the "absurd" man's fate?

2. Do you agree with Camus's statement: "The absurd man says yes, and his effort will henceforth be unceasing. If there is a personal fate, there is no higher destiny"?

Kwame Anthony Appiah   *(1954–)*

The Case for Contamination   *2006*

1.

I'm seated, with my mother, on a palace veranda, cooled by a breeze from the royal garden. Before us, on a dais, is an empty throne, its arms and legs embossed with polished brass, the back and seat covered in black-and-gold silk. In front of the steps to the dais, there are two columns of people, mostly men, facing one another, seated on carved wooden stools, the cloths they wear wrapped around their chests, leaving their shoulders bare. There is a quiet buzz of conversation. Outside in the garden, peacocks screech. At last, the blowing of a ram's horn announces the arrival of the king of Asante[1] its tones sounding his honorific, *kotokohene*, "porcupine chief." (Each quill of the porcupine, according to custom, signifies a warrior ready to kill and to die for the kingdom.) Everyone stands until the king has settled on the throne. Then, when we sit,

---

[1] **Asante:** Also known as Ashanti, an ethnic group in Ghana.

a chorus sings songs in praise of him, which are interspersed with the playing of a flute. It is a Wednesday festival day in Kumasi, the town in Ghana[2] where I grew up.

Unless you're one of a few million Ghanaians, this will probably seem a relatively unfamiliar world, perhaps even an exotic one. You might suppose that this Wednesday festival belongs quaintly to an African past. But before the king arrived, people were taking calls on cellphones, and among those passing the time in quiet conversation were a dozen men in suits, representatives of an insurance company. And the meetings in the office next to the veranda are about contemporary issues: H.I.V./AIDS, the educational needs of 21st-century children, the teaching of science and technology at the local university. When my turn comes to be formally presented, the king asks me about Princeton, where I teach. I ask him when he'll next be in the States. In a few weeks, he says cheerfully. He's got a meeting with the head of the World Bank.

Anywhere you travel in the world—today as always—you can find ceremonies like these, many of them rooted in centuries-old traditions. But you will also find everywhere—and this is something new—many intimate connections with places far away: Washington, Moscow, Mexico City, Beijing. Across the street from us, when we were growing up, there was a large house occupied by a number of families, among them a vast family of boys; one, about my age, was a good friend. He lives in London. His brother lives in Japan, where his wife is from. They have another brother who has been in Spain for a while and a couple more brothers who, last I heard, were in the United States. Some of them still live in Kumasi, one or two in Accra, Ghana's capital. Eddie, who lives in Japan, speaks his wife's language now. He has to. But he was never very comfortable in English, the language of our government and our schools. When he phones me from time to time, he prefers to speak Asante-Twi.

Over the years, the royal palace buildings in Kumasi have expanded. When I was a child, we used to visit the previous king, my great-uncle by marriage, in a small building that the British had allowed his predecessor to build when he returned from exile in the Seychelles[3] to a restored but diminished Asante kingship. That building is now a museum, dwarfed by the enormous house next door—built by his successor, my uncle by marriage—where the current king lives. Next to it is the suite of offices abutting the veranda where we were sitting, recently finished by the present king, my uncle's successor. The British, my mother's people, conquered Asante at the turn of the 20th century; now, at the turn of the 21st, the palace feels as it must have felt in the 19th century: a center of power. The president of Ghana comes from this world, too. He was born across the street from the palace to a member of the royal Oyoko clan. But he belongs to other worlds as well: he went to Oxford University; he's a member of one of the Inns of Court in London; he's a Catholic, with a picture of himself greeting the pope in his sitting room.

What are we to make of this? On Kumasi's Wednesday festival day, I've seen visitors from England and the United States wince at what they regard as the intrusion of modernity on timeless, traditional rituals—more evidence, they think, of a pressure in the modern world toward uniformity. They react like the assistant on the film set who's supposed to check that the extras in a sword-and-sandals movie aren't wearing wristwatches. And such purists are not alone. In the past couple of years, Unesco's[4] members

---

[2] **Ghana:** A country in West Africa.   [3] **Seychelles:** An island republic off the coast of East Africa north of Madagascar.   [4] **Unesco:** United Nations Educational, Scientific, and Cultural Organization.

have spent a great deal of time trying to hammer out a convention on the "protection and promotion" of cultural diversity. (It was finally approved at the Unesco General Conference in October 2005.) The drafters worried that "the processes of globalization . . . represent a challenge for cultural diversity, namely in view of risks of imbalances between rich and poor countries." The fear is that the values and images of Western mass culture, like some invasive weed, are threatening to choke out the world's native flora.

The contradictions in this argument aren't hard to find. This same Unesco document is careful to affirm the importance of the free flow of ideas, the freedom of thought and expression and human rights—values that, we know, will become universal only if we make them so. What's really important, then, cultures or people? In a world where Kumasi and New York—and Cairo and Leeds and Istanbul—are being drawn ever closer together, an ethics of globalization has proved elusive.

The right approach, I think, starts by taking individuals—not nations, tribes or "peoples"—as the proper object of moral concern. It doesn't much matter what we call such a creed, but in homage to Diogenes, the fourth-century Greek Cynic and the first philosopher to call himself a "citizen of the world," we could call it cosmopolitan. Cosmopolitans take cultural difference seriously, because they take the choices individual people make seriously. But because cultural difference is not the only thing that concerns them, they suspect that many of globalization's cultural critics are aiming at the wrong targets.

Yes, globalization can produce homogeneity. But globalization is also a threat to homogeneity. You can see this as clearly in Kumasi[5] as anywhere. One thing Kumasi isn't—simply because it's a city—is homogeneous. English, German, Chinese, Syrian, Lebanese, Burkinabe, Ivorian,[6] Nigerian, Indian: I can find you families of each description. I can find you Asante people, whose ancestors have lived in this town for centuries, but also Hausa[7] households that have been around for centuries, too. There are people there from every region of the country as well, speaking scores of languages. But if you travel just a little way outside Kumasi—20 miles, say, in the right direction—and if you drive off the main road down one of the many potholed side roads of red laterite, you won't have difficulty finding villages that are fairly monocultural. The people have mostly been to Kumasi and seen the big, polyglot, diverse world of the city. Where they live, though, there is one everyday language (aside from the English in the government schools) and an agrarian way of life based on some old crops, like yams, and some newer ones, like cocoa, which arrived in the late 19th century as a product for export. They may or may not have electricity. (This close to Kumasi, they probably do.) When people talk of the homogeneity produced by globalization, what they are talking about is this: Even here, the villagers will have radios (though the language will be local); you will be able to get a discussion going about Ronaldo, Mike Tyson or Tupac; and you will probably be able to find a bottle of Guinness or Coca-Cola (as well as of Star or Club, Ghana's own fine lagers). But has access to these things made the place more homogeneous or less? And what can you tell about people's souls from the fact that they drink Coca-Cola?

It's true that the enclaves of homogeneity you find these days—in Asante as in Pennsylvania—are less distinctive than they were a century ago, but mostly in good

---

[5]**Kumasi:** People from Burkinabe, a nation in West Africa.   [6]**Ivorian:** People from the Ivory Coast, a country in West Africa.   [7]**Hausa:** Also known as Haussa, an ethnic group primarily residing in North Nigeria and South Niger.

ways. More of them have access to effective medicines. More of them have access to clean drinking water, and more of them have schools. Where, as is still too common, they don't have these things, it's something not to celebrate but to deplore. And whatever loss of difference there has been, they are constantly inventing new forms of difference: new hairstyles, new slang, even, from time to time, new religions. No one could say that the world's villages are becoming anything like the same.

So why do people in these places sometimes feel that their identities are threat- 10 ened? Because the world, their world, is changing, and some of them don't like it. The pull of the global economy—witness those cocoa trees, whose chocolate is eaten all around the world—created some of the life they now live. If chocolate prices were to collapse again, as they did in the early 1990s, Asante farmers might have to find new crops or new forms of livelihood. That prospect is unsettling for some people (just as it is exciting for others). Missionaries came awhile ago, so many of these villagers will be Christian, even if they have also kept some of the rites from earlier days. But new Pentecostal messengers are challenging the churches they know and condemning the old rites as idolatrous. Again, some like it; some don't.

Above all, relationships are changing. When my father was young, a man in a village would farm some land that a chief had granted him, and his maternal clan (including his younger brothers) would work it with him. When a new house needed building, he would organize it. He would also make sure his dependents were fed and clothed, the children educated, marriages and funerals arranged and paid for. He could expect to pass the farm and the responsibilities along to the next generation.

Nowadays, everything is different. Cocoa prices have not kept pace with the cost of living. Gas prices have made the transportation of the crop more expensive. And there are new possibilities for the young in the towns, in other parts of the country and in other parts of the world. Once, perhaps, you could have commanded the young ones to stay. Now they have the right to leave—perhaps to seek work at one of the new data-processing centers down south in the nation's capital—and, anyway, you may not make enough to feed and clothe and educate them all. So the time of the successful farming family is passing, and those who were settled in that way of life are as sad to see it go as American family farmers are whose lands are accumulated by giant agribusinesses. We can sympathize with them. But we cannot force their children to stay in the name of protecting their authentic culture, and we cannot afford to subsidize indefinitely thousands of distinct islands of homogeneity that no longer make economic sense.

Nor should we want to. Human variety matters, cosmopolitans think, because people are entitled to options. What John Stuart Mill said more than a century ago in "On Liberty" about diversity within a society serves just as well as an argument for variety across the globe: "If it were only that people have diversities of taste, that is reason enough for not attempting to shape them all after one model. But different persons also require different conditions for their spiritual development; and can no more exist healthily in the same moral, than all the variety of plants can exist in the same physical, atmosphere and climate. The same things which are helps to one person towards the cultivation of his higher nature, are hindrances to another. . . . Unless there is a corresponding diversity in their modes of life, they neither obtain their fair share of happiness, nor grow up to the mental, moral, and aesthetic stature of which their nature is capable." If we want to preserve a wide range of human conditions because it allows free people the best chance to make their own lives, we can't enforce diversity by trapping people within differences they long to escape.

2.

Even if you grant that people shouldn't be compelled to sustain the older cultural practices, you might suppose that cosmopolitans should side with those who are busy around the world "preserving culture" and resisting "cultural imperialism." Yet behind these slogans you often find some curious assumptions. Take "preserving culture." It's one thing to help people sustain arts they want to sustain. I am all for festivals of Welsh bards in Llandudno[8] financed by the Welsh arts council. Long live the Ghana National Cultural Center in Kumasi, where you can go and learn traditional Akan dancing and drumming, especially since its classes are spirited and overflowing. Restore the deteriorating film stock of early Hollywood movies; continue the preservation of Old Norse and early Chinese and Ethiopian manuscripts; record, transcribe and analyze the oral narratives of Malay[9] and Masai[10] and Maori.[11] All these are undeniably valuable.

But preserving culture—in the sense of such cultural artifacts—is different from preserving cultures. And the cultural preservationists often pursue the latter, trying to ensure that the Huli of Papua New Guinea[12] (or even Sikhs in Toronto) maintain their "authentic" ways. What makes a cultural expression authentic, though? Are we to stop the importation of baseball caps into Vietnam so that the Zao will continue to wear their colorful red headdresses? Why not ask the Zao? Shouldn't the choice be theirs? 15

"They have no real choice," the cultural preservationists say. "We've dumped cheap Western clothes into their markets, and they can no longer afford the silk they used to wear. If they had what they really wanted, they'd still be dressed traditionally." But this is no longer an argument about authenticity. The claim is that they can't afford to do something that they'd really like to do, something that is expressive of an identity they care about and want to sustain. This is a genuine problem, one that afflicts people in many communities: they're too poor to live the life they want to lead. But if they do get richer, and they still run around in T-shirts, that's their choice. Talk of authenticity now just amounts to telling other people what they ought to value in their own traditions.

Not that this is likely to be a problem in the real world. People who can afford it mostly like to put on traditional garb—at least from time to time. I was best man once at a Scottish wedding at which the bridegroom wore a kilt and I wore kente cloth.[13] Andrew Oransay, the islander who piped us up the aisle, whispered in my ear at one point, "Here we all are then, in our tribal gear." In Kumasi, people who can afford them love to put on their kente cloths, especially the most "traditional" ones, woven in colorful silk strips in the town of Bonwire, as they have been for a couple of centuries. (The prices are high in part because demand outside Asante has risen. A fine kente for a man now costs more than the average Ghanaian earns in a year. Is that bad? Not for the people of Bonwire.)

---

[8]**Llandudno:** A town in Northwest Wales.   [9]**Malay:** People of the Malay Peninsula.   [10]**Masai:** People of East Africa, primarily Kenya and Tanzania.   [11]**Maori:** Indigenous people of New Zealand.   [12]**Huli of Papua New Guinea:** Indigenous people of Papua New Guinea, an island state in the South Pacific.   [13]**kente cloth:** Fabric made of interwoven strips of cloth; native to Ghana kente cloth.

Besides, trying to find some primordially authentic culture can be like peeling an onion. The textiles most people think of as traditional West African cloths are known as Java[14] prints; they arrived in the 19th century with the Javanese batiks sold, and often milled, by the Dutch. The traditional garb of Herero women in Namibia derives from the attire of 19th-century German missionaries, though it is still unmistakably Herero, not least because the fabrics used have a distinctly un-Lutheran range of colors. And so with our kente cloth: the silk was always imported, traded by Europeans, produced in Asia. This tradition was once an innovation. Should we reject it for that reason as untraditional? How far back must one go? Should we condemn the young men and women of the University of Science and Technology, a few miles outside Kumasi, who wear European-style gowns for graduation, lined with kente strips (as they do now at Howard and Morehouse, too)? Cultures are made of continuities and changes, and the identity of a society can survive through these changes. Societies without change aren't authentic; they're just dead.

3.

The preservationists often make their case by invoking the evil of "cultural imperialism." Their underlying picture, in broad strokes, is this: There is a world system of capitalism. It has a center and a periphery. At the center—in Europe and the United States—is a set of multinational corporations. Some of these are in the media business. The products they sell around the world promote the creation of desires that can be fulfilled only by the purchase and use of their products. They do this explicitly through advertising, but more insidiously, they also do so through the messages implicit in movies and in television drama. Herbert Schiller, a leading critic of "media-cultural imperialism," claimed that "it is the imagery and cultural perspectives of the ruling sector in the center that shape and structure consciousness throughout the system at large."

That's the theory, anyway. But the evidence doesn't bear it out. Researchers have [20] actually gone out into the world and explored the responses to the hit television series "Dallas" in Holland and among Israeli Arabs, Moroccan Jewish immigrants, kibbutzniks and new Russian immigrants to Israel. They have examined the actual content of the television media—whose penetration of everyday life far exceeds that of film—in Australia, Brazil, Canada, India and Mexico. They have looked at how American popular culture was taken up by the artists of Sophiatown, in South Africa. They have discussed "Days of Our Lives" and "The Bold and the Beautiful" with Zulu college students from traditional backgrounds.

And one thing they've found is that how people respond to these cultural imports depends on their existing cultural context. When the media scholar Larry Strelitz spoke to students from KwaZulu-Natal,[15] he found that they were anything but passive vessels. One of them, Sipho—a self-described "very, very strong Zulu man"—reported that he had drawn lessons from watching the American soap opera "Days of Our Lives," "especially relationship-wise." It fortified his view that "if a guy can tell a woman that he loves her, she should be able to do the same." What's more, after watching the show, Sipho "realized that I should be allowed to speak to my father. He should be my friend

---

[14]**Java:** An island near Indonesia.   [15]**KwaZulu-Natal:** A province of South Africa.

rather than just my father." It seems doubtful that that was the intended message of multinational capitalism's ruling sector.

But Sipho's response also confirmed that cultural consumers are not dupes. They can adapt products to suit their own needs, and they can decide for themselves what they do and do not approve of. Here's Sipho again:

"In terms of our culture, a girl is expected to enter into relationships when she is about 20. In the Western culture, a girl can be exposed to a relationship as early as 15 or 16. That one we shouldn't adopt in our culture. Another thing we shouldn't adopt from the Western culture has to do with the way they treat elderly people. I wouldn't like my family to be sent into an old-age home."

It wouldn't matter whether the "old-age homes" in American soap operas were safe places, full of kindly people. That wouldn't sell the idea to Sipho. Dutch viewers of "Dallas" saw not the pleasures of conspicuous consumption among the superrich—the message that theorists of "cultural imperialism" find in every episode—but a reminder that money and power don't protect you from tragedy. Israeli Arabs saw a program that confirmed that women abused by their husbands should return to their fathers. Mexican telenovelas remind Ghanaian women that, where sex is at issue, men are not to be trusted. If the telenovelas tried to tell them otherwise, they wouldn't believe it.

Talk of cultural imperialism "structuring the consciousnesses" of those in the periphery treats people like Sipho as blank slates on which global capitalism's moving finger writes its message, leaving behind another cultural automaton as it moves on. It is deeply condescending. And it isn't true. 25

In fact, one way that people sometimes respond to the onslaught of ideas from the West is to turn them against their originators. It's no accident that the West's fiercest adversaries among other societies tend to come from among the most Westernized of the group. Who in Ghana excoriated the British colonizers and built the movement for independence? Not the farmers and the peasants. Not the chiefs. It was the Western-educated bourgeoisie. And when Kwame Nkrumah—who went to college in Pennsylvania and lived in London—created a nationalist mass movement, at its core were soldiers who had returned from fighting a war in the British Army, urban market women who traded Dutch prints, unionists who worked in industries created by colonialism and the so-called veranda boys, who had been to colonial schools, learned English and studied history and geography in textbooks written in England. Who led the resistance to the British Raj? An Indian-born South African lawyer, trained in the British courts, whose name was Gandhi; an Indian named Nehru, who wore Savile Row suits and sent his daughter to an English boarding school; and Muhammad Ali Jinnah, founder of Pakistan, who joined Lincoln's Inn in London and became a barrister at the age of 19. The independence movements of the postwar world that led to the end of Europe's African and Asian empires were driven by the rhetoric that had guided the Allies' own struggle against Germany and Japan: democracy, freedom, equality. This wasn't a conflict between values. It was a conflict of interests couched in terms of the same values.

4.

Sometimes, though, people react to the incursions of the modern world not by appropriating the values espoused by the liberal democracies but by inverting them. One recent result has been a new worldwide fraternity that presents cosmopolitanism with something of a sinister mirror image. Indeed, you could think of its members as counter-cosmopolitans. They believe in human dignity across the nations, and they live their creed. They share these ideals with people in many countries, speaking many languages. As thoroughgoing globalists, they make full use of the World Wide Web. They resist the crass consumerism of modern Western society and deplore its influence in the rest of the world. But they also resist the temptations of the narrow nationalisms of the countries where they were born, along with the humble allegiances of kith and kin. They resist such humdrum loyalties because they get in the way of the one thing that matters: building a community of enlightened men and women across the world. That is one reason they reject traditional religious authorities (though they disapprove, too, of their obscurantism and temporizing). Sometimes they agonize in their discussions about whether they can reverse the world's evils or whether their struggle is hopeless. But mostly they soldier on in their efforts to make the world a better place.

These are not the heirs of Diogenes the Cynic. The community these comrades are building is not a polis; it's what they call the ummah, the global community of Muslims, and it is open to all who share their faith. They are young, global Muslim fundamentalists. The ummah's new globalists consider that they have returned to the fundamentals of Islam; much of what passes for Islam in the world, much of what has passed as Islam for centuries, they think a sham. As the French scholar Olivier Roy has observed, these religionists—his term for them is "neofundamentalists"—wish to cleanse Islam's pristine and universal message from the contingencies of mere history, of local cultures. For them, Roy notes, "globalization is a good opportunity to dissociate Islam from any given culture and to provide a model that could work beyond any culture." They have taken a set of doctrines that once came with a form of life, in other words, and thrown away that form of life.

Now, the vast majority of these fundamentalists are not going to blow anybody up. So they should not be confused with those other Muslims—the "radical neofundamentalists," Roy calls them—who want to turn jihad, interpreted as literal warfare against the West, into the sixth pillar of Islam. Whether to endorse the use of violence is a political decision, even if it is to be justified in religious terms. Nonetheless, the neofundamentalists present a classic challenge to cosmopolitanism, because they, too, offer a moral and, in its way, inclusive universalism.

Unlike cosmopolitanism, of course, it is universalist without being tolerant, and such intolerant universalism has often led to murder. It underlay the French Wars of Religion that bloodied the four decades before the Edict of Nantes of 1598, in which Henri IV of France finally granted to the Protestants in his realm the right to practice their faith. In the Thirty Years' War, which ravaged central Europe until 1648 and the Peace of Westphalia, Protestant and Catholic princes from Austria to Sweden struggled with one another, and hundreds of thousands of Germans died in battle. Millions starved or died of disease as roaming armies pillaged the countryside. The period of religious conflict in the British Isles, from the first Bishops' War of 1639 to the end of the English Civil War in 1651, which pitted Protestant armies against the forces of a Catholic king, resulted in the deaths of perhaps 10 percent of the population. All these conflicts involved issues beyond sectarian doctrine, of course. Still, many Enlightenment liberals drew the conclusion that enforcing one vision of universal truth could only lead the world back to the blood baths.

Yet tolerance by itself is not what distinguishes the cosmopolitan from the neofundamentalist. There are plenty of things that the heroes of radical Islam are happy to tolerate. They don't care if you eat kebabs or meatballs or kung pao chicken, as long as the meat is halal; your hijab can be silk or linen or viscose. At the same time, there are plenty of things that cosmopolitans will not tolerate. We will sometimes want to intervene in other places because what is going on there violates our principles so deeply. We, too, can see moral error. And when it is serious enough—genocide is the least-controversial case—we will not stop with conversation. Toleration has its limits.

Nor can you tell us apart by saying that the neofundamentalists believe in universal truth. Cosmopolitans believe in universal truth, too, though we are less certain that we already have all of it. It is not skepticism about the very idea of truth that guides us; it is realism about how hard the truth is to find. One tenet we hold to, however, is that every human being has obligations to every other. Everybody matters: that is our central idea. And again, it sharply limits the scope of our tolerance.

To say what, in principle, distinguishes the cosmopolitan from competing universalisms, we plainly need to go beyond talk of truth and tolerance. One distinctively cosmopolitan commitment is to pluralism. Cosmopolitans think that there are many values worth living by and that you cannot live by all of them. So we hope and expect that different people and different societies will embody different values. Another aspect of cosmopolitanism is what philosophers call fallibilism—the sense that our knowledge is imperfect, provisional, subject to revision in the face of new evidence.

The neofundamentalist conception of a global ummah, by contrast, admits of local variations—but only in matters that don't matter. These counter-cosmopolitans, like many Christian fundamentalists, do think that there is one right way for all human beings to live; that all the differences must be in the details. If what concerns you is global homogeneity, then this utopia, not the world that capitalism is producing, is the one you should worry about. Still, the universalisms in the name of religion are hardly the only ones that invert the cosmopolitan creed. In the name of universal humanity, you can be the kind of Marxist, like Mao or Pol Pot, who wants to eradicate all religion, just as easily as you can be the Grand Inquisitor supervising an auto-da-fé. All of these men want everyone on their side, so we can share with them the vision in their mirror. "Indeed, I'm a trustworthy adviser to you," Osama bin Laden said in a 2002 "message to the American people." "I invite you to the happiness of this world and the hereafter and to escape your dry, miserable, materialistic life that is without soul. I invite you to Islam, that calls to follow of the path of Allah alone Who has no partners, the path which calls for justice and forbids oppression and crimes." Join us, the counter-cosmopolitans say, and we will all be sisters and brothers. But each of them plans to trample on our differences—to trample us to death, if necessary—if we will not join them. Their motto might as well be the sardonic German saying Und willst du nicht mein Bruder sein, So schlag' ich Dir den Schädel ein. (If you don't want to be my brother, then I'll smash your skull in.)

That liberal pluralists are hostile to certain authoritarian ways of life—that they're intolerant of radical intolerance—is sometimes seen as kind of self-refutation. That's a mistake: you can care about individual freedom and still understand that the contours of that freedom will vary considerably from place to place. But we might as well admit that a concern for individual freedom isn't something that will appeal to every individual. In politics, including cultural politics, there are winners and losers—which is worth remembering when we think about international human rights treaties. When we seek to embody our concern for strangers in human rights law, and when we urge our government to enforce it, we are seeking to change the world of law in every nation on the planet. We have declared slavery a violation of international law. And, in so doing, we have committed ourselves, at a minimum, to the desirability of its eradication everywhere. This is no longer controversial in the capitals of the world. No one defends enslavement. But international treaties define slavery in ways that arguably include debt bondage, and debt bondage is a significant economic institution in parts of South Asia. I hold no brief for debt bondage. Still, we shouldn't be surprised if people whose incomes and style of life depend upon it are angry.

It's the same with the international movements to promote women's equality. We know that many Islamists are deeply disturbed by the way Western men and women behave. We permit women to swim almost naked with strange men, which is our business, but it is hard to keep the news of these acts of immodesty from Muslim women and children or to protect Muslim men from the temptations they inevitably create. As the Internet extends its reach, it will get even harder, and their children, especially their girls, will be tempted to ask for these freedoms, too. Worse, they say, we are now trying to force our conception of how women and men should behave upon them. We speak of women's rights. We make treaties enshrining these rights. And then we want their governments to enforce them.

Like many people in every nation, I support those treaties; I believe that women, like men, should have the vote, should be entitled to work outside their homes, should be protected from the physical abuse of men, including their fathers, brothers and husbands. But I also know that the changes these freedoms would bring will change the balance of power between men and women in everyday life. How do I know this? Because I have lived most of my adult life in the West as it has gone through just such a transition, and I know that the process is not yet complete.

So liberty and diversity may well be at odds, and the tensions between them aren't always easily resolved. But the rhetoric of cultural preservation isn't any help. Again, the contradictions are near to hand. Take another look at that Unesco Convention. It affirms the "principle of equal dignity of and respect for all cultures." (What, all cultures—including those of the K.K.K. and the Taliban?) It also affirms "the importance of culture for social cohesion in general, and in particular its potential for the enhancement of the status and role of women in society." (But doesn't "cohesion" argue for uniformity? And wouldn't enhancing the status and role of women involve changing, rather than preserving, cultures?) In Saudi Arabia, people can watch "Will and Grace" on satellite TV—officially proscribed, but available all the same—knowing that, under Saudi law, Will could be beheaded in a public square. In northern Nigeria, mullahs inveigh against polio vaccination while sentencing adulteresses to death by stoning. In India, thousands of wives are burned to death each year for failing to make their dowry payments. Vive la différence? Please.

5.

Living cultures do not, in any case, evolve from purity into contamination; change is more a gradual transformation from one mixture to a new mixture, a process that usually takes place at some distance from rules and rulers, in the conversations that occur across cultural boundaries. Such conversations are not so much about arguments and values as about the exchange of perspectives. I don't say that we can't change minds, but the reasons we offer in our conversation will seldom do much to persuade others who do not share our fundamental evaluative judgments already. When we make judgments, after all, it's rarely because we have applied well-thought-out principles to a set of facts and deduced an answer. Our efforts to justify what we have done—or what we plan to do—are typically made up after the event, rationalizations of what we have decided intuitively to do. And a good deal of what we intuitively take to be right, we take to be right just because it is what we are used to. That does not mean, however, that we cannot become accustomed to doing things differently.

Consider the practice of foot-binding in China, which persisted for a thousand years—and was largely eradicated within a generation. The antifoot-binding campaign, in the 1910's and 1920's, did circulate facts about the disadvantages of bound feet, but those couldn't have come as news to most people. Perhaps more effective was the campaign's emphasis that no other country went in for the practice; in the world at large, then, China was "losing face" because of it. (To China's cultural preservationists, of course, the fact that the practice was peculiar to the region was entirely a mark in its favor.) Natural-foot societies were formed, with members forswearing the practice and further pledging that their sons would not marry women with bound feet. As the movement took hold, scorn was heaped on older women with bound feet, and they were forced to endure the agonies of unbinding. What had been beautiful became ugly; ornamentation became disfigurement. The appeal to reason can explain neither the custom nor its abolition. 40

So, too, with other social trends. Just a couple of generations ago, most people in most of the industrialized world thought that middle-class women would ideally be housewives and mothers. If they had time on their hands, they could engage in charitable work or entertain one another; a few of them might engage in the arts, writing novels, painting, performing in music, theater and dance. But there was little place for them in the "learned professions"—as lawyers or doctors, priests or rabbis; and if they were to be academics, they would teach young women and probably remain unmarried. They were not likely to make their way in politics, except perhaps at the local level. And they were not made welcome in science.

How much of the shift away from these assumptions is a result of arguments? Isn't a significant part of it just the consequence of our getting used to new ways of doing things? The arguments that kept the old pattern in place were not—to put it mildly—terribly good. If the reasons for the old sexist way of doing things had been the problem, the women's movement could have been done in a couple of weeks.

Consider another example: In much of Europe and North America, in places where a generation ago homosexuals were social outcasts and homosexual acts were illegal, lesbian and gay couples are increasingly being recognized by their families, by society and by the law. This is true despite the continued opposition of major religious groups and a significant and persisting undercurrent of social disapproval. Both sides make arguments, some good, most bad. But if you ask the social scientists what has produced this change, they will rightly not start with a story about reasons. They will give you a historical account that concludes with a sort of perspectival shift. The increasing presence of "openly gay" people in social life and in the media has changed our habits. And over the last 30 years or so, instead of thinking about the private activity of gay sex, many Americans and Europeans started thinking about the public category of gay people.

One of the great savants of the postwar era, John von Neumann, liked to say, mischievously, that "in mathematics you don't understand things, you just get used to them." As in mathematical arguments, so in moral ones. Now, I don't deny that all the time, at every stage, people were talking, giving one another reasons to do things: accept their children, stop treating homosexuality as a medical disorder, disagree with their churches, come out. Still, the short version of the story is basically this: People got used to lesbians and gay men. I am urging that we should learn about people in other places, take an interest in their civilizations, their arguments, their errors, their achievements, not because that will bring us to agreement but because it will help us get used to one another—something we have a powerful need to do in this globalized era. If that is the aim, then the fact that we have all these opportunities for disagreement about values need not put us off. Understanding one another may be hard; it can certainly be interesting. But it doesn't require that we come to agreement.

6.

The ideals of purity and preservation have licensed a great deal of mischief in the past century, but they have never had much to do with lived culture. Ours may be an era of mass migration, but the global spread and hybridization of culture—through travel, trade or conquest—is hardly a recent development. Alexander's[16] empire molded both the states and the sculpture of Egypt and North India; the Mongols[17] and then the Mughals[18] shaped great swaths of Asia; the Bantu[19] migrations populated half the African continent. Islamic states stretch from Morocco to Indonesia; Christianity reached Africa, Europe and Asia within a few centuries of the death of Jesus of Nazareth; Buddhism long ago migrated from India into much of East and Southeast Asia. Jews and people whose ancestors came from many parts of China have long lived in vast diasporas. The traders of the Silk Road[20] changed the style of elite dress in Italy; someone buried Chinese pottery in 15th-century Swahili[21] graves. I have heard it said that the bagpipes started out in Egypt and came to Scotland with the Roman infantry. None of this is modern.

Our guide to what is going on here might as well be a former African slave named Publius Terentius Afer, whom we know as Terence.[22] Terence, born in Carthage,[23] was taken to Rome in the early second century B.C., and his plays—witty, elegant works that are, with Plautus's[24] earlier, less-cultivated works, essentially all we have of Roman comedy—were widely admired among the city's literary elite. Terence's own mode of writing—which involved freely incorporating any number of earlier Greek plays into a single Latin one—was known to Roman littérateurs as "contamination."

It's an evocative term. When people speak for an ideal of cultural purity, sustaining the authentic culture of the Asante or the American family farm, I find myself drawn to contamination as the name for a counterideal. Terence had a notably firm grasp on the range of human variety: "So many men, so many opinions" was a line of his. And it's in his comedy "The Self-Tormentor" that you'll find what may be the golden rule of cosmopolitanism—*Homo sum: humani nil a me alienum puto;* "I am human: nothing

---

[16]**Alexander the Great** (356–323 B.C.): The King of Macedon and conqueror of much of Asia. [17]**Mongols:** A group of people from Asia primarily living in China.   [18]**Mughals:** People from the Mughal Empire, which included Afghanistan, India, Pakistan, and Bangladesh.   [19]**Bantu:** People from Africa south of the Congo River.   [20]**Silk Road:** An ancient trade route from Eastern China to Central Asia and Europe.   [21]**Swahili:** Coastal inhabitants of Kenya, Tanzania, Somalia, Mozambique, Zanzibar, and Eastern Congo.   [22]**Terence** (c. 185 or 195–159 B.C.): Roman comedic writer.   [23]**Carthage:** An ancient city on the northern shore of Africa.   [24]**Plautus** (c. 254–184 B.C.): Roman comedic writer.

human is alien to me." The context is illuminating. A busybody farmer named Chremes is told by his neighbor to mind his own affairs; the homo sum credo is Chremes's breezy rejoinder. It isn't meant to be an ordinance from on high; it's just the case for gossip. Then again, gossip—the fascination people have for the small doings of other people—has been a powerful force for conversation among cultures.

The ideal of contamination has few exponents more eloquent than Salman Rushdie, who has insisted that the novel that occasioned his fatwa "celebrates hybridity, impurity, intermingling, the transformation that comes of new and unexpected combinations of human beings, cultures, ideas, politics, movies, songs. It rejoices in mongrelisation and fears the absolutism of the Pure. Mélange, hotch-potch, a bit of this and a bit of that is how newness enters the world." No doubt there can be an easy and spurious utopianism of "mixture," as there is of "purity" or "authenticity." And yet the larger human truth is on the side of contamination—that endless process of imitation and revision.

A tenable global ethics has to temper a respect for difference with a respect for the freedom of actual human beings to make their own choices. That's why cosmopolitans don't insist that everyone become cosmopolitan. They know they don't have all the answers. They're humble enough to think that they might learn from strangers; not too humble to think that strangers can't learn from them. Few remember what Chremes says after his "I am human" line, but it is equally suggestive: "If you're right, I'll do what you do. If you're wrong, I'll set you straight." ●

Explorations of the Text

1. Define "contamination" as used by Appiah in his essay. Is "contamination" desirable?

2. Appiah's essay is structured as an argument. What is his purpose in writing the essay? Who is Appiah's intended audience? What is his position? What evidence does he use to support his position?

3. Discuss Appiah's attitude toward globalization.

4. Would you say that the United States embraces cosmopolitanism? Explain why or why not.

5. **Write an Argument:** In her poem "Children of Our Age," Wislawa Szymborska claims that we live in "a political age." Using examples from her poem and Appiah's essay, argue that our age is or is not political.

The Reading/Writing Connection

1. Interview several older family members, and then write an essay describing the ways that your family's culture has changed over the past few generations. What is your family's attitude toward this change? What is your attitude?

Ideas for Writing

1. **Write an Argument:** Write an essay in which you argue in favor of "universalism" or "cosmopolitanism." Provide evidence from Appiah's essay to support your position.

2. Write an analysis of Sherman Alexie's "What You Pawn I Will Redeem" using the ideas within Kwame Anthony Appiah's "The Case for Contamination" as a critical lens.

3. **Write an Argument:** Should all cultures be valued equally? Argue pro or con.

Visions of the Spirit/Nonfiction

Plato *(428–347 B.C.)*   Translated by Benjamin Jowett

The Allegory of the Cave   *c. 387–367 B.C.*

The "Allegory of the Cave" appears in Plato's Republic.

And now, I[1] said, let me show in a figure how far our nature is enlightened or unenlightened:[2]—Behold! human beings housed in an underground cave, which has a long entrance open towards the light and as wide as the interior of the cave; here they have been from their childhood, and have their legs and necks chained, so that they cannot move and can only see before them, being prevented by the chains from turning round their heads. Above and behind them a fire is blazing at a distance, and between the fire and the prisoners there is a raised way; and you will see, if you look, a low wall built along the way, like the screen which marionette players have in front of them, over which they show the puppets.

I see.

And do you see, I said, men passing along the wall carrying all sorts of vessels, and statues and figures of animals made of wood and stone and various materials, which appear over the wall? While carrying their burdens, some of them, as you would expect, are talking, others silent.

You have shown me a strange image, and they are strange prisoners.

Like ourselves, I replied; for in the first place do you think they have seen anything   5
of themselves, and of one another, except the shadows which the fire throws on the opposite wall of the cave?

How could they do so, he asked, if throughout their lives they were never allowed to move their heads?

And of the objects which are being carried in like manner they would only see the shadows?

Yes, he said.

And if they were able to converse with one another, would they not suppose that the things they saw were the real things?

Very true.   10

And suppose further that the prison had an echo which came from the other side, would they not be sure to fancy when one of the passers-by spoke that the voice which they heard came from the passing shadow?

No question, he replied.

To them, I said, the truth would be literally nothing but the shadows of the images.

That is certain.

And now look again, and see in what manner they would be released from their   15
bonds, and cured of their error, whether the process would naturally be as follows. At

---

[1] **I:** From *The Republic,* Book 7. Socrates speaks to Glaucon.   [2] **unenlightened:** In the original Greek, the words for enlightened and unenlightened are *paideia* and *apaideusia.* The former, depending on context, also may be understood as "education," "culture," or "knowledge." [Translator's note.]

first, when any of them is liberated and compelled suddenly to stand up and turn his neck round and walk and look towards the light, he will suffer sharp pains; the glare will distress him, and he will be unable to see the realities of which in his former state he had seen the shadows; and then conceive someone saying to him that what he saw before was an illusion, but that now, when he is approaching nearer to being and his eye is turned towards more real existence, he has a clearer vision,—what will be his reply? And you may further imagine that his instructor is pointing to the objects as they pass and requiring him to name them,—will he not be perplexed? Will he not fancy that the shadows which he formerly saw are truer than the objects which are now shown to him?

Far truer.

And if he is compelled to look straight at the light, will he not have a pain in his eyes which will make him turn away to take refuge in the objects of vision which he can see, and which he will conceive to be in reality clearer than the things which are now being shown to him?

True, he said.

And suppose once more, that he is reluctantly dragged up that steep and rugged ascent, and held fast until he is forced into the presence of the sun himself, is he not likely to be pained and irritated? When he approaches the light his eyes will be dazzled, and he will not be able to see anything at all of what are now called realities.

Not all in a moment, he said. 20

He will require to grow accustomed to the sight of the upper world. And first he will see the shadows best, next the reflections of men and other objects in the water, and then the objects themselves; and, when he turned to the heavenly bodies and the heaven itself, he would find it easier to gaze upon the light of the moon and the stars at night than to see the sun or the light of the sun by day?

Certainly.

Last of all he will be able to see the sun, not turning aside to the illusory reflections of him in the water, but gazing directly at him in his own proper place, and contemplating him as he is.

Certainly.

He will then proceed to argue that this is he who gives the seasons and the years, 25 and is the guardian of all that is in the visible world, and in a certain way the cause of all things which he and his fellows have been accustomed to behold?

Clearly, he said, he would arrive at this conclusion after what he had seen.

And when he remembered his old habitation, and the wisdom of the cave and his fellow-prisoners, do you not suppose that he would felicitate himself on the change, and pity them?

Certainly, he would.

And if they were in the habit of conferring honours among themselves on those who were quickest to observe the passing shadows and to remark which of them went before and which followed after and which were together, and who were best able from these observations to divine the future do you think that he would be eager for such honours and glories, or envy those who attained honour and sovereignty among those men? Would he not say with Homer,[3]

"Better to be a serf, labouring for a landless master,"

---

[3]**Homer:** Greek epic poet (c. ninth–eighth centuries B.C.).

and to endure anything, rather than think as they do and live after their manner?

Yes, he said, I think that he would consent to suffer anything rather than live in this miserable manner.

Imagine once more, I said, such a one coming down suddenly out of the sunlight, and being replaced in his old seat; would he not be certain to have his eyes full of darkness?

To be sure, he said.

And if there were a contest, and he had to compete in measuring the shadows with the prisoners who had never moved out of the cave, while his sight was still weak, and before his eyes had become steady (and the time which would be needed to acquire this new habit of sight might be very considerable), would he not make himself ridiculous? Men would say of him that he had returned from the place above with his eyes ruined; and that it was better not even to think of ascending; and if anyone tried to loose another and lead him up to the light, let them only catch the offender, and they would put him to death.

No question, he said.

This entire allegory, I said, you may now append, dear Glaucon, to the previous argument; the prison-house is the world of sight, the light of the fire is the power of the sun, and you will not misapprehend me if you interpret the journey upwards to be the ascent of the soul into the intellectual world according to my surmise, which, at your desire, I have expressed—whether rightly or wrongly God knows. But, whether true or false, my opinion is that in the world of knowledge the Idea of good appears last of all, and is seen only with an effort; although, when seen, it is inferred to be the universal author of all things beautiful and right, parent of light and of the lord of light in the visible world, and the immediate and supreme source of reason and truth in the intellectual; and that this is the power upon which he who would act rationally either in public or private life must have his eye fixed.

I agree, he said, as far as I am able to understand you.

Moreover, I said, you must agree once more, and not wonder that those who attain to this vision are unwilling to take any part in human affairs; for their souls are ever hastening into the upper world where they desire to dwell; which desire of theirs is very natural, if our allegory may be trusted.

Yes, very natural.

Then, I said, the business of us who are the founders of the State will be to compel the best minds to attain that knowledge which we have already shown to be the greatest of all, namely, the vision of the good; they must make the ascent which we have described; but when they have ascended and seen enough we must now allow them to do as they do now.

What do you mean?

They are permitted to remain in the upper world, refusing to descend again among the prisoners in the cave, and partake of their labours and honours, whether they are worth having or not.

But is not this unjust? he said; ought we to give them a worse life, when they might have a better?

You have again forgotten, my friend, I said, the intention of our law, which does not aim at making any one class in the State happy above the rest; it seeks rather to spread happiness over the whole State, and to hold the citizens together by persuasion and necessity, making each share with others any benefit which he can confer upon the State; and the law aims at producing such citizens, not that they may be left to please themselves, but that they may serve in binding the State together.

True, he said, I had forgotten.

Observe, Glaucon, that we shall do no wrong to our philosophers but rather make a just demand, when we oblige them to have a care and providence of others; we shall explain to them that in other States, men of their class are not obliged to share in the toils of politics; and this is reasonable, for they grow up spontaneously, against the will of the governments in their several States; and things which grow up of themselves, and are indebted to no one for their nurture, cannot fairly be expected to pay dues for a culture which they have never received. But we have brought you into the world to be rulers of the hive, kings of yourselves and of the other citizens, and have educated you far better and more perfectly than they have been educated, and you are better able to share in the double duty. Wherefore each of you, when his turn comes, must go down to rejoin his companions, and acquire with them the habit of seeing things in the dark. As you acquire that habit, you will see ten thousand times better than the inhabitants of the cave, and you will know what the several images are and what they represent, because you have seen the beautiful and just and good in their truth. And thus our State, which is also yours, will be a reality and not a dream only, and will be administered in a spirit unlike that of other States, in which men fight with one another about shadows only and are distracted in the struggle for power, which in their eyes is a great good. Whereas the truth is that the State in which those who are to govern have least ambition to do so is always the best and most quietly governed, and the State in which they are most eager, the worst.

Quite true, he replied.

And will our pupils, when they hear this, refuse to take their turn at the toils of State, when they are allowed to spend the greater part of their time with one another in the heavenly light?

Impossible, he answered; for they are just men, and the commands which we impose upon them are just. But there can be no doubt that every one of them will take office as a stern necessity, contrary to the spirit of our present rulers of State.

Yes, my friend, I said; and there lies the point. You must contrive for your future rulers another and a better life than that of a ruler, and then you may have a well-ordered State; for only in the State which offers this, will they rule who are truly rich, not in gold, but in virtue and wisdom, which are the true blessings of life. Whereas if men who are destitute and starved of such personal goods go to the administration of public affairs, thinking to enrich themselves at the public expense, order there can never be; for they will be fighting about office, and the civil and domestic broils which thus arise will be the ruin of the rulers themselves and of the whole State.

Most true, he replied.

And the only life which looks down upon the life of political ambition is that of true philosophy. Do you know of any other?

Indeed, I do not, he said.

And those who govern should not "make love to their employment?" For, if they do there will be rival lovers, and they will fight.

No question.

Whom, then, will you compel to become guardians of the State? Surely those who excel in judgement of the means by which a State is administered, and who at the same time have other honours and another and a better life than that of politics?

None but these, he replied. ●

Scott Russell Sanders *(1945–)*

The Force of Spirit   *2001*

My wife's father is dying, and I can think of little else, because I love him and I love my wife. Once or twice a week, Ruth and I drive the forty miles of winding roads to visit him in the nursing home. Along the way we pass fields bursting with new corn, stands of trees heavy with fresh leaves, pastures deep in grass. In that long grass the lambs and calves and colts hunt for tender shoots to nibble and for the wet nipples of their mothers to suck. The meadows are thick with flowers, and butterflies waft over the blossoms like petals torn loose by wind. The spring this year was lavish, free of late frosts, well soaked with rain, and now in early June the Indiana countryside is all juiced up.

On our trip to the nursing home this morning, I drive while Ruth sits beside me, knitting. Strand by strand, a sweater grows under her hands. We don't talk much, because she must keep count of her stitches. To shape the silence, we play a tape of Mozart's *Requiem* from a recent concert in which Ruth sang, and I try to detect her clear soprano in the weave of voices. The car fills with the music of sorrow. The sound rouses aches in me from earlier losses, the way cold rouses pain from old bone breaks.

Yet when I look out through the windows at the blaze of sunlight and the blast of green, I forget for minutes at a time where we're going and what we're likely to see when we get there. Ruth must forget as well, because every now and again she glances up from her knitting to recall a story or a task or some odd discovery she's read about recently.

As we slow down for a hamlet named Cope—a cluster of frame houses gathered at a bend in the road—she describes a scientific article that she came across at the lab this past week. After puzzling over what distinguishes living organisms from dead matter, the author, a biologist, had concluded that the vital secret is the flow of electrons in association with oxygen.

I tell her that all sounds reasonable enough, but I wonder why oxygen goes hauling   5
electrons around in the first place.

"He hasn't figured that out yet," she replies.

"Wouldn't it be easier," I say, "for oxygen to sit still and leave matter alone? Why stir things up?"

"In other words, why life?"

"Yeah, why life?"

She laughs. "Ask me an easy one."   10

"All right," I say. "Why corn? Why shagbark hickories? Why moss and wolves? Why not just rock and dust?"

Used to my pestering her with questions, she normally answers with good humor and patience. But now she merely says, "You'll have to read the article."

A fly beats against the inside of the windshield. Suddenly the crazed, buzzing bit of stuff seems bizarre and precious. I lift one hand from the steering wheel, crank down a window, shoo the fly to freedom, then grip the wheel once more. Now my fingers seem utterly strange. How can they curl so exactly in the shape of my thoughts? The lurching of my heart surprises me, as if a desperate animal has crawled inside my chest. All at once my whole body feels like an implausible contraption, and my skin barely contains the storm of electrons.

What I feel is not exactly panic, because I'm spared for the moment the chill of knowing I will die. What I feel right now is amazement that anything lives, fly or hawk, virus or man. I stare at the radiant fields and woods flowing past our windows, and they seem far-fetched, outrageous. Why all those leaves waving? Why all those juicy stems thrusting at the sky? Why those silky black wings of crows slicing the air? And why am I set moving through this luminous world, only to feel such grief when some patch of woods falls before the saw, when a farm vanishes beneath the pavement of a shopping mall or a valley beneath a reservoir, when a man withers in a nursing home bed?

"What are you thinking?" I ask Ruth, just to make sure my voice works.   15

"I'm thinking I only need two more inches to finish the front of this sweater."

"About your dad, I mean."

She turns her brown eyes on me, reading my face, which has grown transparent to her gaze over thirty years of marriage. Her own heart-shaped face draws into a frown. "I'm wondering if he'll still know us."

"Surely he's not that far gone," I say.

"Maybe not yet," she agrees.   20

I turn my attention back to the music, and gradually Mozart restores my composure.

After a while Ruth sets down her knitting and takes up a stack of her father's insurance papers. She's been working on them for months, but the stack keeps growing thicker, each layer of papers recording another bout in the hospital, another round of tests. She circles numbers, places checkmarks beside dates, compares one statement with another, imposing order on this chronicle of illness. Congestive heart failure is the short name for what afflicts him. After coronary seizures, quadruple bypass surgery, the insertion of a pacemaker, and several strokes, and after seventy-eight years of faithfully pumping blood, Earl McClure's heart is simply wearing out.

Near a tiny settlement called Bud, we pass a white barn that bears a warning in letters six feet high: AT THE END THERE IS JUDGMENT! One side of the barn is painted with the silhouette of a man hanging on a cross, the figure entirely black except for two white rings marking the eyes, which glare out like searchlights. A caption explains, "He died for you."

Ruth and I have known since childhood who he is, this dangling man, for we both spent nearly all of our childhood Sundays in Methodist churches, singing hymns, memorizing Bible verses, listening to sermons, learning that Jesus saves. Although Ruth still sings regularly in a church choir and I sit in a pew on the occasional Sunday morning with a Bible in my lap, neither of us any longer feels confident that the man on the cross will preserve us from annihilation, nor that he will reunite us with our loved ones in heaven. The only meetings we count on are those we make in the flesh. The only time we're sure about is right now.

"Whenever we pass by here," Ruth says, "I wonder why anybody would paint such   25
a scary picture on a barn. Who'd want to look every day at those awful eyes?"

"They're meant to keep your mind on ultimate things as you milk the cows."

"They're creepy," she insists.

I agree, but I also understand the attraction of a faith that eases the sting of loss, including the loss of one's own precious life. Until I was twenty or so I embraced that faith, hoping for heaven; then I gradually surrendered it under the assault of science and in dismay over witnessing so much evil carried out in Christ's name. I no longer believe that Jesus can do our dying for us; we must do that for ourselves, one by one. Yet I've not given up believing in the power that was supposed to have sent him to redeem us, the Creator who laid the foundations of the world.

For the last few miles of our drive to the nursing home, I study the land. There's a shaping intelligence at work here, I feel sure of it. I sense a magnificent energy in the grasses bowing beneath the wind, in the butterflies flouncing from blossom to blossom, in the trees reaching skyward and the jays haranguing from the topmost branches and the clouds fluffing by. I sense in this rippling countryside a tremendous throb and surge, the same force that squeezes and relaxes my heart. Everything rides on one current. As I listen to the music of grief filling the car, as I go with my wife to visit her dying father, the world, for all its density and weight, seems made of breath.

Legend has it that Mozart died while composing the *Requiem,* a few measures into the   30
section beginning with the Latin word *Lacrimosa,* which means tearful or weeping. "On that day of weeping," the verse' proclaims,

> again from the ashes will arise
> guilty mankind, to be judged.

That much he orchestrated, but he never completed the remainder of the verse:

> Therefore, spare this one, O God,
> Merciful Lord Jesus,
> And grant them rest.

Officially, the one to be spared from God's wrath was the dearly departed wife of the count who had commissioned this mass for the dead, but the ailing Mozart must also have been mourning himself. Another scrap of legend claims that in those final days he said, "It is for myself that I am writing this." I suspect he was grieving as well for his own dearly departed, especially his mother, who had died some years earlier in Paris while he was there looking for work.

Ruth's mother died last October, not long before the chorus began rehearsing the *Requiem.* By the time of her death, Dessa McClure had been whittled away by Alzheimer's disease for half a dozen years, losing her memory, speech, balance, and strength, becoming again as a little child. This was not the sort of child she had aspired to become, for she meant to find her way to heaven by achieving a clear vision and a simple heart. Toward the end, her vision grew cloudy, and the world became a blur of strange rooms and unknown faces. And at the very end, while she was rising from a bath, her heart quit.

The nurse who'd been helping her at the time told us afterward, "She went limp all of a sudden and dropped right down and was gone."

Ruth's father, still able to get around fairly well back then, had just been to see Dessa in the special care unit, where patients suffering from various forms of dementia drifted about like husks blown by an idle breeze. She had seemed almost happy, he recalled. She even whistled a bit, and showed no signs of pain. And he was sure she'd recognized him by the way she squeezed his finger and smiled. He let that be his last glimpse of her, for he chose not to look at his wife's body after the nurses brought him news of her death.

But Ruth saw her laid out in the nursing home, still crumpled, as if, when breath departed, the body had collapsed like an empty sack. Ruth was so appalled by the image that she insisted on seeing her mother's body one more time before the cremation. And so, after we had finished our business in the funeral home, she and I slipped into a back room to gaze for a moment at the shell of her mother resting on a cart, all but the face hidden by a white sheet, the skin pale except for dark rings under the shut eyes. We knew this face, yet it seemed aloof and slack, for it had been peeled away from the person to whom it once belonged. Beneath the sheet, the body lay as motionless as a piece of furniture covered with drapery in a vacant house. I put my arm around Ruth, not so much to comfort her as to comfort me, to feel the warmth and weight of her. She tilted her head against my shoulder and stood there for a long while without speaking. Then she leaned forward, ran a hand over that forsaken face, and turned to go.

The heart is only a muscle. It's a meaty pump that shoves and sucks the blood that carries the oxygen that carries the electrons that keep us alive. It beats forty or a hundred and forty times a minute, hour after hour, day after day, until, between one contraction and the next, it falters and stops. When surgeons lay the heart open to repair valves and carve out damaged tissue, they find no spirit hiding there, no seat of the soul. Biologists can trace it back down the evolutionary path to the earliest twitchings of life in the sea. 35

Yet who can accept that we're merely meat? Who can shake the suspicion that we're more than two-legged heaps of dust accidentally sprung into motion? Whatever the doctors and biologists claim, we go on using the word "heart" as if it pointed to an emotional center, a core of integrity. We trust those who speak from the heart. We're wary of those who are heartless and hardhearted. Have a heart, we say, begging for kindness. Home is where the heart is, we say.

We're drawn irresistibly to our heartthrob, who knows how to pluck our heartstrings. We long to feel heart's-ease by fulfilling our heart's desire. In our earnest pronouncements, we appeal to hearts and minds, heart and soul. Swearing most solemnly, we cross our hearts and hope to die, if what we say should be a lie. Heartfelt and heartsick, heartland and heartache, heartwood and heartbreak: the word, like the muscle beating in our chest, is indispensable. The beliefs we truly live by, the ones we'll die for, are those we hold in our heart of hearts.

At the nursing home, we find Ruth's father drowsing on his bed, arms outstretched as if he has fallen there from a great height. He wears a white shirt, brown dress pants, low knit socks that leave his ankles bare, and lace-up leather shoes. His hair, still dark and full, is neatly combed. Except for his gauntness, he might be a man resting after a day at the office. Yet he's too frail even to stand up for more than a few minutes at a time. His wrists are sticks. His cheeks are hollow. Blue veins show through the translucent skin of his jaw.

I can see Ruth hesitate before waking him, because she wonders if he will recognize her. So long as he sleeps, she remains his daughter. At last she lightly touches one of those out-flung arms, and he startles awake. Behind thick spectacles, his eyes are milky and uncertain. He looks bewildered for a moment, and then he beams, reaching out to grasp Ruth's hand.

"Hey, there," he says. "I'd about given up on you." 40

"Don't you worry," she answers. "If I say I'm coming, I'm coming."

"Well, I was thinking—" he begins, then loses his way and falls silent with an embarrassed little shrug.

But he has said enough to assure Ruth that he knows her, that he's still there in his withered body. She asks how he's feeling, how he's eating, whether he's had any visitors, whether the nurses have been treating him well, and he answers each question in two or three words, staring up into her face and squeezing her hand.

To say that he is dying makes it sound as though he's doing something active, like singing or dancing, but really something's being done to him. Life is leaving him. From one visit to the next we can see it withdrawing, inch by inch, the way the tide retreating down a beach leaves behind dry sand. With each passing day he has more and more trouble completing sentences, as if words too were abandoning him.

I hang back, awkward before his terrible weakness. Eventually he notices me standing near the foot of his bed.

"Why, here's Scott," he says.

I step closer. "Came to see if you're behaving yourself."

"I am, pretty much," he says. "How was the drive over?"

"It was beautiful," I tell him, lifting my voice because I can see he's chosen not to wear his hearing aids. "Everything's blooming. The corn's shooting up. Some of the hay is cut and drying."

"Good, good," he murmurs. Then he asks if I've been watching the NBA tournament, which I haven't, and so he tells me, pausing for breath between sentences, how the Indiana Pacers lost to the New York Knicks. The Pacers had a lead going into the fourth quarter, but their legs gave out. "I understand tired legs," he says, and gives a rheumy laugh.

Ruth and I exchange looks, amazed that he's following basketball. He's also following our children, Eva and Jesse, for now he asks what they've been up to since our last visit. After we've told him, he repeats bits of what we've said, as if to pin memory down: "So Jesse's working in the restaurant. Is that right? And Eva's studying birds? She bought a new computer?" His voice is thin and soft, like a trickle of water over smooth stone.

Since we saw him last, Ruth and I have attended a college graduation in Ohio. He remembers this as well, and asks if we had a good time. We did, I answer. And then I tell him about watching the graduates troop across the stage as each name was called, most of them so young and spry they fairly danced in their black robes, while parents and friends and fellow students cheered. A few waddled heavily or limped stiffly. Two scooted across in electric chairs. Then, near the end of the ceremony, one slight woman who'd been waiting in line among those receiving degrees in nursing rose from a wheelchair, labored up the stairs, and slowly crossed the stage while holding on to the arm of a young man. When the president gave her the diploma and shook her hand, the audience broke out in the loudest applause of the afternoon. We clapped because many of us knew she was gravely ill with cancer, she'd not been expected to live until commencement, and yet she'd refused to give up. Now here she was, onstage for a moment, drawing our praise.

When I finish my story, which poured out of me before I thought how it might sound in the ears of a dying man, Ruth's father says, "She's got spunk."

"She does," I answer.

"I like that," he says. "You can never have too much spunk." He rouses a bit to report that he's going once a day to physical therapy. They wheel him down there in his chair, but then they make him stand up and push a walker across the room to build up his legs and make him lift dumbbells to build up his arms.

"Pumping iron, are you?" I say.

"I need to get my strength back." He raises an arm and the sleeve droops down, revealing the tender bruised skin of his wrist.

We learned from a doctor this week that his heart now pumps blood at 20 percent of the normal rate, and it will keep on dwindling. His eyes close, but he doesn't let go of Ruth's hand. She says we'd better let him get some rest. Does he need anything before we go? Yes, he answers, three things: his bathrobe, an extra pair of trousers, and his electric shaver.

I go to fetch them from his apartment on the floor below, a comfortable suite of rooms where he'll never be able to stay by himself again. Going there and coming back, I take the stairs two at a time. I rush down the halls past elderly residents who look at me as if I'm a lunatic. There's no reason to race, except that I still can, and so I do, savoring the bounce in my legs and the wild flutter in my chest.

I want a name for the force that keeps Earl McClure asking questions while the   60
tide of life withdraws from him. I want a name for the force that abandoned the body of Dessa McClure and left it like a piece of shrouded furniture on a cart in the funeral home. I want a name for the force that carried a woman dying of cancer through her studies and across a stage to claim her diploma. I want a name for the force that binds me to Ruth, to her parents, to my parents, to our children, to neighbors and friends, to the land and all its creatures.

This power is larger than life, although it contains life. It's tougher than love, although it contains love. It's akin to the power I sense in lambs nudging the teats of their dams to bring down milk, in the raucous tumult of crows high in trees, in the splendor of leaves gorging on sun. I recognize this force at work in children puzzling over a new fact, in grownups welcoming strangers, in our capacity, young and old, for laughter and kindness, for mercy and imagination.

No name is large enough to hold this power, but of all the inadequate names, the one that comes to me now is spirit. I know the risks of using such a churchy word. Believers may find me blasphemous for speaking of the wind that blows through all things without tracing the breath to God. Nonbelievers may find me superstitious for invoking any force beyond gravity, electromagnetism, and the binding energy of atoms. But I must run those risks, for I cannot understand the world, cannot understand my life, without appealing to the force of spirit. If what I feel for my wife or her father and mother is only a byproduct of hormones, then what I feel for swift rivers or slow turtles, for the shivering call of a screech owl or the green thrust of bloodroot breaking ground, is equally foolish. If we and the creatures who share the earth with us are only bundles of quarks in motion, however intricate or clever the shapes, then our affection for one another, our concern for other species, our devotion to wildness, our longing for union with the Creation are all mere delusions.

I can't prove it, but I believe we're more than accidental bundles of quarks, more than matter in motion. Our fellowship with other creatures is real, our union with the Creation is already achieved, because we all rise and fall on a single breath. You and I and the black-footed ferret, the earth, the sun, and the far-flung galaxies, are dust motes whirling in the same great wind. Whether we call that magnificent energy Spirit or Tao,[1] Creator or God, Allah or Atman,[2] or some other holy name, or no name at all, makes little difference, so long as we honor it. Wherever it flows—in person or place,

---

[1]**Tao:** A Chinese spiritual philosophy of life.   [2]**Atman:** Hindu principle of life.

in animal or plant or the whole of nature — we feel the pressure of the sacred, and that alone deserves our devotion.

A gusty breeze is pawing the grass and churning the ponds as Ruth and I drive back from the nursing home over the winding roads. Neither of us can bear to hear the *Requiem* again right now, so we talk. She remembers stories of her father from when he was strong—how he lifted her in and out of bed when she was down with rheumatic fever, how he laid fires in a charcoal grill when the family went camping, how he dug up the yard to plant roses. She recalls how, in their last house before the nursing home, her father and mother used to stand spellbound at the dining room window and watch birds at the feeders. And she recalls how, even in the final stark days, her mother shuffled to the birdcage in the special care unit and watched the fierce, tiny finches darting about, squabbling and courting. From inside the Alzheimer's daze, her mother would say nothing, but sometimes she whistled at the finches, and sometimes she laughed.

As if summoned by these memories of Dessa and Earl McClure, birds fill this blustery June afternoon here in southern Indiana. We see goldfinches dipping and rising as they graze among the waving seedheads of the tall grasses. We see red-winged blackbirds clinging to the tops of cattails that sway in the breeze. We see a kettle of hawks, a swirl of starlings, a fluster of crows. A great blue heron goes beating by, and six or eight geese plow the ruffled waters of a lake. Near the barn that's painted with the crucified man, more than a dozen turkey vultures spiral over a field, a lazy black funnel pointing down toward carrion. 65

There's an abundance in this teeming land that promises to make up for anything lost to vultures. The corn seems to have shot up higher since our drive over this morning. In the afternoon heat the woods bristle and the pastures heave and the fields are charged with light.

After a while Ruth takes up her knitting, clacks along for a few stitches, then puts it down again. Gazing out the window, she recalls in a soft voice how she thought of her mother at every rehearsal of the *Requiem,* and how moved she was at the performance itself when the conductor announced that the concert would be given in memory of Dessa McClure. Ruth had been forewarned of this gesture, but still she had to blink hard to read the opening measures.

We pass a hayfield where a tractor is rolling the cut grass into fat round bales, and I can't help thinking of the verse in Isaiah:

> All flesh is grass,
> and all its beauty is like the flower of the field.
> The grass withers, the flower fades,
> when the breath of the Lord blows upon it;
> surely the people is grass.

These days, I'm in no danger of forgetting how swiftly every living thing withers. But I also remember that grass, once cut, sprouts up again from the roots. Whatever Lord breathes upon this world of crickets and constellations blows beginnings as well as endings. The Latin word for breath is *spiritus,* which also means courage, air, and life. Our own word "spirit" carries all those overtones for me when I use it to speak of the current that lifts us into this life and bears us along and eventually lets us go.

We pass more fields scattered with round bales of hay like herds of slow, ungainly beasts. When we come up behind a truck on the road sagging under the weight of a single great bale, a stream of chaff comes blowing back at us, and loose bits float in through our open windows.

I reach over to brush some straw from Ruth's lap. She grabs my hand and 70 holds on.

"I hate to think of clearing out Daddy's things," she says. "We'll have to find who wants what, then get rid of the rest."

"Let's hope that won't be for a while yet," I say.

She doesn't answer. We drive on through the lush green countryside. I remember when we cleared out Dessa's things, how we found more than forty Bibles and hundreds of religious books, which she had long since lost the ability to read. In drawers and cupboards we found entry forms for sweepstakes, because she had decided, as her mind began to go, that winning some game of chance might set things right. And we found lists she had made of crucial events in her life—her marriage, her children's births, her surgeries, her husband's heart attack, the death of her parents, the moves from house to house—all the personal history that was slipping away from her. On page after page in a spiral notebook she wrote down in broken phrases what mattered to her, what defined her life, as if words on paper might preserve what the mind no longer could hold.

I make my own lists, in sentences and paragraphs rather than broken phrases, because language has not yet abandoned me. I am making such a list now, here in these pages. You've seen the long version. A short version of the story I've been telling you might say only:

Ruth, Earl, Dessa,
corn, crow, grass,
wind, dirt, sun. ⦿

Explorations of the Text

1. Scott Russell Sanders uses the word "spirit" instead of God, life, or love to describe the force that moves all creatures through life. Characterize the "spirit" within Plato's work. What force is at work within his tale?

2. In "The Allegory of the Cave," describe or draw the scene in the cave. Where are the "prisoners," "fire," and "screen"? What does the "light" signify? Why is it difficult for the prisoners to adjust to the "light"?

3. Plato's dialogue is meant to instruct. Does it? What might be the purpose of Sanders's essay?

4. Why does Sanders conclude his essay with a list? Is this an effective ending? Why?

5. Choose one poem from the "Life in the Midst of Death" cluster and characterize the spiritual elements within the poem. Is the poem most akin to Plato's or Sanders's vision of the spirit?

The Reading/Writing Connection

1. Does learning something or changing one's mind cause pain? Write about an incident or experience from your own life.

2. Like Plato, write an allegory or a fable to explain an abstraction (death, love, life). Like Sanders, try to come up with a word that most fits your sense of the abstraction.

Ideas for Writing

1. In Emily Dickinson's poem, "I heard a Fly buzz—when I died," the speaker is annoyed by a fly coming between her and the light. Analyze this poem using a Platonic interpretation of "light."

> 2. **Write an Argument:** Scott Russell Sanders writes: "There's a shaping intelligence at work here. I feel sure of it." Argue for Sanders's or Plato's vision of this "shaping intelligence." Or argue for another vision, using evidence from Sanders and Plato as counterarguments.

 On The Web: *Wilderness vs. Wasteland*

Please visit http://www.academic.cengage.com/english/Schmidt/Legacies4e/ for links to the following online resources.

Bill McKibben, "The Crunch"

The Nobel Peace Prize Speeches Including

Shirin Ebadi, Martin Luther King Jr., Aung San Suu Kyi, Wangari Maathai, Nelson Mandela, Desmond Tutu, Elie Wiesel, and Betty Williams

GRAPHIC LITERATURE

Gene Luen Yang

"The Myth of the Monkey King"

from American Born Chinese   *2006*

Explorations of the Text

1. In the beginning of the chapter, Flower-Fruit Mountain is described as a Garden of Eden. At the end, when the Monkey King returns, he notices the "thick smell of monkey fur," which he had "never noticed before." What has changed from the beginning to the end?

2. Look at the graphic depiction of the Monkey King and the other guests at the party. Why does the Monkey King expect to be admitted? Why do you think he is denied entry?

3. Compare the Monkey King's experience to that of the speaker in Gloria's poem, "Assimilation." What might the Monkey King do to assimilate, to fit in with the other guests at the party?

4. Compare ideas of home from scenes from Yang's graphic novel and from Agosin's poems.

The Reading/Writing Connection

1. Create a creation myth centered on an animal of your choice. You can illustrate it or write it as a graphic story, similar to Yang's.

2. Journal entry: Describe a time when you were made aware of something about yourself through the influence of others.

Ideas for Writing

1. **Write an Argument:** Argue that the Monkey King is a victim of speciesism, as defined by Peter Singer in his essay.

WRITING ASSIGNMENTS

1. Compare views of obedience and conformity suggested in Vonnegut's "Harrison Bergeron," in O'Connors's "A Good Man is Hard to Find," and Alexie's "What You Pawn I Will Redeem."

2. a. What does Anzaldúa mean by "borderland"?
   b. Describe a "borderland" in which you live.
   c. Compare your "borderland" with a work in this chapter that presents a "borderland."
   d. Compare Anzaldúa's view of "the borderland" with Agosin's conception of exile in her poetry.

3. a. Explain the concept of renewal in one work in this chapter.
   b. The possibility and impossibility of renewal and rebirth in a global world are recurring themes in this chapter. Compare and contrast three visions of renewal.
   c. Which works present the most convincing and/or believable visions?

4. Explicate "Diving into the Wreck" or one of Rilke's sonnets. Focus on point of view, imagery, figurative language, and form. (See Chapter 11.)

5. Compare the points of view of three speakers in three poems. How does point of view relate to tone, imagery, and theme?

6. a. What new myths of the future emerge in "Diving into the Wreck," "The Second Coming," and "The Season of Phantasmal Peace"?
   b. Create your own myth or allegory for a view of the future.

7. a. Ask several people to envision the world in 2102. What do they fear about the future, and what do they wish for the future?
   b. Analyze your results. What patterns do you perceive?
   c. Use one interview as the basis for an essay.
   d. Compare one of your interviewee's views of the future with a work in this chapter.

8. Create a science fiction short story. Develop a view of a utopian or dystopian society.

9. a. Evaluate your favorite work in this chapter. Argue for its inclusion in the next edition of this text. Write a letter to the authors.
   b. Evaluate your favorite work in this book. Assume that your audience is the publisher of this anthology.
   c. Select one work from *Legacies* that has changed your views. Explain your reaction to it. How did it change your perspective?

10. Write an argument, agreeing or disagreeing with Yeats's "The Second Coming." You may refer to other works in this chapter.

11. Discuss the ideal versus the reality of harmony among people of different races and/or cultures in the works in this chapter.

12. Compare the views of Plato, Camus, and Márquez on the cosmos and on human beings and their destinies. Compare the philosophies of life depicted in the works.

13. a. What is your view of the relationship between the individual and the community? The community may include nonhuman creatures.
    b. Discuss the sense of community represented in three works in this chapter.
    c. Which work exemplifies your view of the interrelationship between the individual and the community?

14. Many stories in this chapter, as in Chapter 8, portray humans as being violent toward one another. Meanwhile, most of us seek to live in a peaceful community. Do you consider this to be a basic human contradiction? Explain.

15. *Legacies* begins with an examination of identity in Chapter 5. Explain in an essay how one person can shape events, leading to the conflicts portrayed in Chapter 8 or to the bridging of barriers as seen in Chapter 9. Refer to three works as examples.

16. Mary Oliver, Robert Frost, and Scott Russell Sanders all perceive of organic life as fleeting, while the rocks and bones of the planet alone have lasting substance. Why might this perspective be significant when thinking of planetary history? Human history? Is this idea comforting or frightening?

17. In Keats's "Ode on a Grecian Urn," the speaker states, "Beauty is truth, truth beauty,—that is all / Ye know on earth, and all ye need to know," suggesting that the urge to conquer death through art is universal. Discuss this portrayal of this theme in Okri's "A Prayer from the Living," and Yeats's "Sailing to Byzantium."

18. Virginia Shabatay contends that "strangers in literature offer us images of individuals who live in some ways separate from the community." These stories lead us "to imagine an event from the side of another person, to grasp his

or her uniqueness." "The ability to appreciate otherness in individuals and communicate is a way of redeeming the stranger and of redeeming the world."

a. Write an essay explaining your personal and literary encounters with the stranger. What have they taught you?

b. Compare your state of "strangerhood" with that of a character in a work in this chapter. See Michael Mei's "Lost in Transition."

19. Write an Argument: Environmentalists are greatly concerned about the dangers of invasive species—insects, plants, or animals that enter a foreign environment and alter the environmental balance, sometimes wiping out native life. On the Internet, research invasive species, and write an argument relating the concept of invasive species to Appiah's discussion of contamination. Might environmental "contamination" create a new, diverse world by presenting opportunities for different species to arise, or is the world becoming a homogenous place in which much of life's diversity is destroyed?

20. Write an Argument: In "A Case for Contamination," Appiah writes of the breakdown of cultural borders as a positive and inevitable occurrence. Choosing one work from this chapter and one from another chapter in *Legacies* as evidence, argue in favor of or against Appiah's perspective.

STUDENT ESSAY

Cultural Analysis Essay

Michael Mei

Lost in Transition

Despite the subtle different transitional problems encountered by immigrants, the variables ultimately remain the same. They must assimilate themselves into a society with common, indelible goals inspired by the American dream or face the possibility of alienation. Jhumpa Lahiri's "The Third and Final Continent," from the short-story collection Interpreter of Maladies, reminds audiences that immigrants establish the diverse cultural society of the United States, but at a personal cost. Lahiri exposes the exploitation of the malleability and vulnerabilities of immigrants who are quick to conform for the purposes of adaptation and survival. Slowly but gradually, Lahiri's narrator epitomizes people who do not understand the intrinsic value of what they give up until it becomes irrevocably lost.

The title, "The Third and Final Continent," implies a long journey from one culture and society to the next—in this case, only to end up in America, a place where theoretically all identities cohesively weld. The narrator travels from the subcontinent of India (named because of its geographical placement and geological shape) to England, and then finally to the third and final continent, the United States. The narrator traverses three continents, representative of the three stages of the transition from his native Indian roots to a new American lifestyle. Just as a day is characterized by morning, afternoon, and night, the narrator's transition begins with light, hopes, and aspirations, but ends in the night, when he finds himself submerged by the darkness of a culture he has yet to understand or adapt to. The third and final continent represents two ideas: The narrator will finally stop moving from one impermanent situation to the next perceived destination and settle into a land where he can nurture his identity. On the pessimistic end of this spectrum, the narrator will settle into a melting-pot culture that will annihilate what remains of his ethnic roots from years of travel into and through three culturally different atmospheres.

Upon his arrival, the narrator (nameless by intention to represent all of the immigrants or former immigrants on U.S. soil who come knowing who they were but end up not knowing where they fit in because of their dual identities) willfully accepts the challenges and adversities of cultural adaptation. When he learns that "Americans [drive] on the right side of the road, not the left (India), and that they call a lift an elevator and an engaged phone busy (England)" (1244), he accepts and begins feeling comfortable with his new culture, expressions, and traditions. Prior to his Massachusetts Avenue apartment, he had "never lived in the home of a person who was not Indian" (1246), but now, he finds himself becoming familiarized with the infrastructure of developed North American society (i.e., post office and banks) in addition to the ubiquitous burgers and hotdogs on diner menus (1245). Having his cultural roots cultivated in India, his identity thus continues an aggravated process of decomposition since his arduous travels have considerably weakened his native Indian identity.

The protagonist learns quickly that American culture is characterized by the notion that "everybody feels he must get to the top" (1245), his first exposure to the American dream. Although an elusive ideal, many immigrants center their daily routines around the goal of seeing their version of the dream come to fruition. The actions of his landlady, Mrs. Croft, symbolize the habitual routines imposed on immigrant citizens. Each evening when the narrator returns home, he finds her sitting on the same bench inviting him to sit down and revel in the fact that an American man had landed and placed a United States flag on the moon (1247, 1249). Landing on the moon was without doubt one of humanity's greatest accomplishments but, on the consequential end, fueled the development of America's arrogance as a culture. Immigrants became seduced by a culture that yielded prosperity and a proud sense of nationalism.

Not only was there nationalism, there was also a growing sense of the affirmation in being nurtured in a capitalist economy. As a result, immigrants began considering themselves, in the context of this story, as American Indians rather than Indian Americans. Despite the subtle difference, and only in title, the distinction stands unequivocally. Upon realizing his uprooting, the narrator attempts to save his ethnic roots and cultural identity by complying with his arranged marriage to Mala. Despite resorting to an unorthodox method of preservation, the narrator persists in balancing his newly acquired American habits with his native Indian traditions.

Through the narrator's marriage, Lahiri explicitly reveals the innumerable cultural traditions that must continue, even if partially, to be practiced and/or implemented despite entering countries embedded with contrasting practices and/or traditions. The persistent notion of arranged marriages illuminates the often incomplete (accidental or engineered) cultural assimilation of immigrants. As a young Indian immigrant, he has been immersed into American society so much that his breakfast consists of cereal and milk, contrary to his traditional curry eggs and rice. Yet, when the discussion moves to marriage, a lifelong and life-altering event, he passively expresses his contentment with the arrangements already made for him by his brother and sister-in-law in India. "[He regards] the proposition with neither objection nor enthusiasm. It was a duty expected of [him], as it was expected of every man" (1248). Although merely acquiescing to tradition, the narrator expresses his contentment to preserve his heritage and background on a subconscious level of reality. For many Americans with backgrounds in foreign cultures, life becomes a matter of maintaining cultural values and traditions as a means of resisting cultural hegemony and preserving vestiges of their cultural identities. The narrator thus understands that the benefits of this arranged marriage far exceed any conceivable harm accompanying this institution. After arriving in the United States, Mala offers him a lifelong companion who shares similar cultural values and traditions from their native homeland. She also provides a character with whom the narrator can identify his immigrant struggles (1255). Her presence (even though the relationship between the two is not constructed on the foundations of love) offers the narrator a compassionate reminder that his roots are from India and that it is in his best interests to preserve such intrinsic aspects of his social life, even if it means having to conform to such a, by American standards, vehemently frowned upon institution. While the idea of an arranged marriage stands far from being a liberating experience, it is a comparatively small price to pay for the sake of cultural maintenance.

The narrator's relationship with Mrs Croft, though vicariously, presents him another opportunity (consciously or unconsciously) to preserve his ethnic roots. Helen (Mrs. Croft's daughter) visits only on a sporadic basis and leaves the elderly woman confined to her apartment. And even with her presence, the relationship between mother and daughter does not have deep intimacy, but the companionship that Helen fails to offer her mother, the protagonist succeeds in providing. He thinks back to how his mother died after years of widowhood-induced insanity and how he never had the chance to fulfill any notion of filial piety. This prompts him to acquiesce to each of Mrs. Croft's demands (1234). He checks the lock, accompanies her on her bench for conversations, professes the flag on the moon is "splendid," and always remembers to heat up her soup in the evenings (1231, 1232, 1234). "Although Helen had seemed friendly enough, a small part of [him] worried that she might accuse [him] of negligence if anything were to happen. Helen didn't seem worried" (1234). Helen, whose focus manifests itself in her self-interests demonstrated by her occasional and lack of perfunctory interest in such visits, typifies the American lifestyle that the narrator acknowledges he must resist. He does so by willingly acquiring the job that Helen fails to complete. Available to Mrs. Croft, he shows the respect with which a child should honor his or her parents, respect that he did not have the chance to pay his mother. However, his responsibility towards the landlady clearly illustrates that while he has acclimatized to physical elements of North American society like food, his cultural ethics and expectations have never been neglected.

However, the vast difficulties of transmitting and maintaining a native culture, especially in the successive generations, resurface when the narrator introduces his son. The United States continues to be a unique home to many immigrants who are able to survive only by the ethnic-American identities and social adjustments they are coerced into developing and making. Thus, for individuals like the narrator and his wife, as much as they are able to preserve parts of their cultural identities by implementing cultural practices and complying with traditional codes of conduct, the generations that they will watch grow up will retain even less of what they have accomplished. With every ensuing generation, immigrants experience a habitual decline in awareness of ethnic principles and practices of ancestral traditions. Typically, by the third or fourth generation, immigrant roots are so far removed that children like the narrator's son's children will begin to drop the title of Indian from Indian American altogether in pursuit of the American Dream and the rewards of a material culture. The narrator's son, if imbued with a sense of get-rich-now, will inevitably sacrifice his identity, discovering that to prosper in a racially and ethnically conscious country, he must become strictly American.

"The Third and Final Continent" reflects on the cultural transition from a native Indian culture based on subsistence to a culture of constant material acquisition. The narrator acknowledges in his final lines that

> [w]hile the astronauts, heroes forever, spent more hours on the moon, [he has] remained in this new world for nearly thirty years. [He] knows [his] achievement is quite ordinary. [He is] not the only man to seek his fortune far from home, and certainly not the first. Still, there are times [he is] bewildered by each mile [he has] traveled, each meal [he has] eaten, each person [he has] known and each room in which [he has] slept. As ordinary as it all appears, there are times when it is beyond [his] imagination. (1256)

The narrator humbly admits that his experiences cannot compare to the extraordinary first men and women who exchanged lives of familiarity in their native lands for lives isolated in unfamiliar territory and circumstances. He leads by example in pursuit of new dreams and aspirations in America, but he warns readers of the complementary but, potentially, overwhelming process of assimilation that, if continued at the current pace, threatens to dry out his cultural identity. People's infatuation with the prospects of financial stability and economic prosperity causes people to forget their need for native culture and identity. The American ethos inspires and reminds people of the foundation of motivation and persistence on which the original thirteen colonies rose, but today it has transpired into an oppressive hegemonic force that obliterates diverse cultures and ethnicities rather than encourage acceptance or tolerance for cultural multiplicity.

Lahiri's short stories remind me of just how much immigrants of one nation do, in actuality, face the same adversities and joys that immigrants of another country experience. Despite being born a citizen of the United States, I was raised in a sheltered, traditional Chinese household by Chinese immigrant parents. Until I reached the public school system of New York, I was utterly oblivious to the functions of American society. Thus, when I entered a classroom with students of all colors for the first time, I felt foreign in an atmosphere that required a considerable amount of time for me to become acclimated to. However, after tedious repetitions of daily routines that included making the Pledge of Allegiance to the United States each day at 10 A.M., like the narrator gets used to the fact that he needed to express how "splendid" a spectacle America's flag being stabbed on the moon was, I grew more and more accustomed to the American traditions that constituted the way of life in the United States. And like the narrator's preferences for food, I, too, went from eating traditional Chinese breakfasts to having cereal and milk in the mornings. Once I was exposed to the American lifestyles that I had been sheltered from as a child, I began to associate "an ends justifies the means" mentality in adapting to a new style of life. I found myself practicing less and less of the Chinese traditions, which included praying on every first and fifteenth of the Chinese Lunar Calendar. I even had the audacity to end my enrollment at Chinese school on the weekends in addition to neglecting to practice my calligraphy of Chinese characters altogether. The result? I am now an English major with Chinese roots that are so close to decimation that if I do not do something to revive these roots soon, the bridge that connects my children to my parents will be completely obliterated. However, for the sake of cultural maintenance, I will continue to practice Chinese traditions and cultural practices that remind me from time to time that I am a Chinese American and not that "Banana" everyone refers to me as.

Jhumpa Lahiri reminds us that whether we are immigrants or the children of immigrants, we must learn to weigh both the intrinsic and extrinsic benefits of assimilating into a new culture, especially one as pervasive as America's. There are always fringe benefits that possess the potential to be a curse in disguise. While she implicitly requests American citizens to be tolerant of foreign ethnic groups and cultures, she also asserts that immigrants like the protagonist must learn to resist the temptations of American hegemony.

Works Cited

Lahiri, Jhumpa. "The Third and Final Continent." <u>Legacies: Fiction, Poetry, Drama, Nonfiction</u>, Fourth Edition. Eds. Jan Zlotnik Schmidt, Lynne Crockett, and Carley Bogarad. Boston: Cengage Learning Wadsworth, 2008. 1216-1228.

3

[Reading and Writing about the Genres]

Fiction

Fiction is the imagined creation of character and action for the purpose of conveying a vision of life. Like forms of nonfictional narration (storytelling), fiction depends on a recording of a sequence of events (as in historical rendering) and on an organization of incident and action (as in reporting). Fiction also requires a colorful, vivid depiction of characters and action (as in oral storytelling).

Fundamental to short fiction is a concentration on characters and on the changes in characters brought about by events. Discussing the components of plot in *Aspects of the Novel,* E. M. Forster differentiates between an account of incidents and plot. He states that "The king died, and then the queen died" does not form a story line for fiction; however, the following presents the kernel of a tale, "The king died, and the queen died of grief." In the second version, the fiction emerges from the effect of the husband's death on the wife; a vision of mourning and loss is implied.

Forms of Narrative

The earliest forms of narrative stories are the **myths** that ancient people conceived to explain their worlds—natural phenomena, human behavior, beliefs, and values—and to satisfy their need for transcendent experiences and meanings. Creation myths appear in the Old Testament, in Norse legends, and in Native American tribal lore. Greek and Roman myths of gods and goddesses and the creation of the world are written in such works as Thesiod's *Theogeny* and Ovid's *Metamorphoses.* The *Vedas,* the sacred Sanskrit texts of the Hindus, explore the origins of the gods of India.

Many myths explain facts of life, death, and immortality. "Coyote and the Shadow People," a Nez Percé myth, for example, relates the story of Coyote, who longs for his wife's return from the dead. The Death Spirit permits Coyote's wife to live in the world as a shadow for a three-day trial, but, because Coyote touches his wife's shadow, he loses the opportunity to regain his wife permanently. In "Yellow Woman" (Chapter 7), Leslie Marmon Silko intertwines Native American myth and legend in the story of a young woman's journey of self-discovery.

Some stories, called **parables,** provide moral instruction or convey moral, religious, or spiritual truths. Consider the story of the prodigal son in the New Testament, a story in which the younger son squanders his share of his father's wealth in riotous living, while his older brother stays and works with the father. The prodigal son endures hard times and returns to his father to ask for mercy, and the father joyously welcomes him and celebrates his homecoming. When the elder son protests, the father replies, "Be glad: for this thy brother was dead and is alive again and was lost and is found." This tale teaches the need for charity, compassion, and forgiveness. Luisa Valenzuela's "The Verb to Kill"

(Chapter 8), a short story in parabolic form, suggests the impact of sites of conflict on young girls' developmental growth.

A **fable,** another kind of moralizing story, commonly features animals or inanimate objects endowed with human qualities. Their experiences and behavior teach a lesson, stated explicitly at the conclusion of the tale. Some of the oldest fables may be traced to Aesop, a sixth-century Roman. In his story, "The Tortoise and the Hare," for instance, the hare, conceited and overly confident, falls asleep during a race while the slower tortoise plods ahead and wins. The moral of the tale is "slow but steady wins the race." In "Blue Beyond Blue," the author uses fantasy to explore the nature of love and connection (Chapter 9).

Every culture also has its epics—stories of the exploits of heroes and mythical creatures—and folk tales that provide entertainment and present moral truths. Like myths, **epic poems** were passed from generation to generation as strictly oral entertainment before being written down and read as literature. *The Iliad* and *The Odyssey,* the oldest known Western epics, recount the exploits of the warriors of the Trojan War and the wanderings of the Greek hero Odysseus after the war. The *Mahabharata,* a monumental Hindu epic, depicts the strife of two Indian royal families and the spiritual development of the Indian hero, Krishna.

Each culture enjoys folk tales. The fairy tales we learned as children from Hans Christian Andersen or Disney were originally Danish and German stories. *Cinderella,* for example, has many incarnations as a French folk tale transcribed by Perrault; as a German story recorded by the Brothers Grimm; as Algonquin Indian and Chinese tales. Although each version transmits different cultural values, fairy tales around the world convey recurring and familiar motifs: they portray the struggle between parents and children, between innocence and corruption, between good and evil, and between life and death. Short story writers often draw on folk and fairy tales in the development of character, plot, and theme. Gabriel García Márquez deliberately titles "The Handsomest Drowned Man in the World" a "Tale for Children" to highlight its fairy tale elements (Chapter 9). In Chapter 5, the thematic cluster, "Fairy Tales," includes short fiction that incorporates fairy tale motifs.

Other forms of narrative emerged in the Middle Ages and the Renaissance. The epic, the tale of the hero, became transformed into romances in which knights fought battles for the love of their ladies. Sometimes the quest for romance also became a quest for spiritual salvation, as in many of the stories of King Arthur, his knights of the Round Table, and their search for the Holy Grail, as in the poem, *Sir Gawain and the Green Knight.*

The word **novella** came into existence to describe the short tales of Boccacio written in the fourteenth century. Now the term signifies a work of fiction longer than and more expansive than a short story but less complex than a novel. They were stories of love, designed as courtly entertainment. Boccacio's *The Decameron* is a collection of one hundred short stories told by ten residents of Florence who attempted to escape the plague.

Lady Murasaki of Japan wrote the first **novel,** *The Tale of Genji,* in 1022. The novel emerged as a form of fictional prose narrative in the seventeenth century in England with the advent of a middle class that had both the leisure and a level of literacy to read and to support magazines. The first English protonovels were Aphra Behn's *Oroonoko* (1688) and Daniel Defoe's *Robinson Crusoe* (1719), a tale of a man abandoned on an island. The reading public and the demand for novels grew in the eighteenth century.

The nineteenth century, however, became the great age of the British novel. The fullest representation of a story line, the novel captures a moment in time, a moment in a culture. This form incorporates the breadth and depth created by development of many characters, plots, subplots, and themes.

The invention of the modern **short story** is often attributed to Edgar Allan Poe. His most famous works include "The Masque of the Red Death," "The Pit and the Pendulum," and "The Telltale Heart." Poe suggested that a reader should be able complete a story in a single sitting. In the nineteenth century, the tradition of the American short story began with the publication of works by Poe, Nathaniel Hawthorne, Herman Melville, Mary Wilkins Freeman, Sarah Orne Jewett, and Kate Chopin. See, for example, Hawthorne's "Rappaccini's Daughter" (Chapter 6).

A single concentrated story line, a single plot that involves a conflict or crisis that leads to a climax and to a resolution, and a limited number of characters distinguish the short story. Another usual feature of the genre is that it, like poetry, is compressed so that all elements may develop character, plot, and theme.

The modern short story was influenced by James Joyce's conception that a central character should be involved in a conflict or momentary experience that leads to discovery or to an awakening—in Joyce's term—an epiphany. However, contemporary short stories portray characters caught in experiences that may not lead to a climax, resolution, or realization. The stories conclude without the characters undergoing any change or gaining any great insight. The characters—in stasis—remain in a cycle of sterility. According to its creators, this form of development mirrors the absurdity and lack of meaning in the modern world. Finally, many fiction writers today, aware of the history of the genre, mix narrative techniques and modes to create new forms of the short story. One new form is the metafiction in which the story itself reflects on the process of writing a story. Margaret Atwood's "Happy Endings" (Chapter 7) is an example of this form. Finally, another form of experimental fiction is graphic literature or the graphic novel. Graphic literature, which has its origins in the comic book, mixes visual and written text and has the same elements as a story: point of view, plot, a continuous narrative line (beginning, middle, and end), and complex characters. The visual and written elements work together to develop the impact of the work (see Appendix B for further discussion of graphic literature).

Elements of Fiction

Point of View

Many elements of fiction—**point of view, setting, plot, characters, conflict, symbolism,** and **theme**—combine to create a work. We use these elements when we create even a simple, informal narrative, as when we recount a tragedy reported in the news or describe the previous night's party. Read this ghost story:

> I woke up in the middle of the night because I thought someone was watching me.
> When I awakened, a girl, dressed in a white nightgown, stood at the foot of my bed.
> She had long, yellow hair and large, luminous eyes, staring at me. I was petrified.
> I freaked. I closed my eyes. She was still there. I pulled the pillow over my head. When
> I lifted the pillow, she had disappeared. Only later, much later, did I tell my husband

this story. He told me that he had shared the same experience. Later, much later, I learned that a little girl had died in our house in Kentucky, in the house where we experienced those nightmares.

Many elements of fiction are prevalent in this short tale, including a certain **point of view,** a narrative perspective. The choice of narrative perspective shapes the direction of the tale and is intertwined with plot, character, and theme. In this case, the story presents a first-person, singular point of view—"I." Writers create a sense of immediacy and personal involvement with first-person narrators.

An alternative to the first-person point of view is third-person narrative. To recognize the third-person point of view, look for the use of "he," "she," and "they." In third-person, the narrative perspective presents the characters and action and tells the tale from a certain distance. Recast the ghost story into third-person, using *she* and *her* in place of *I* and *me*. Such a change may result in a loss of intimacy, immediacy, and urgency.

There are several forms of third-person narration. An omniscient narrator assumes the vantage point of knowing everything in his or her characters' minds. Readers gain insights into the consciousness of all characters in the story. A narrator with limited knowledge discloses information about one or several, but not all, of the narrative points of view. In detached or dramatic narrative point of view, the speaker describes the characters and actions with no insight into characters' feelings. If the ghost story appeared in third-person, the narrator could develop his or her perspective, or possibly the husband's, or even the ghost's point of view. The story would progress differently. Consider this excerpt from Joyce Carol Oates' "Where Are You Going, Where Have You Been?" (Chapter 5):

> Her name was Connie. She was fifteen and she had a quick nervous giggling habit of craning her neck to glance into mirrors, or checking other people's faces to make sure her own was all right. Her mother, who noticed everything and knew everything and who hadn't much reason any longer to look at her own face, always scolded Connie about it. "Stop gawking at yourself, who are you? You think you're so pretty?" she would say. Connie would raise her eyebrows at these familiar complaints and look right through her mother, into a shadowy vision of herself as she was right at that moment: she knew she was pretty and that was everything. Her mother had been pretty once too, if you could believe those old snapshots in the album, but now her looks were gone and that was why she was always after Connie.

Oates creates a limited third-person narrative perspective to depict her main character's struggles in adolescence. The reader gains insight into Connie's feelings about her appearance and about her disdainful attitudes toward her mother, but does not learn anything about Connie from the mother's point of view.

We also may characterize a narrator as participant or as nonparticipant. A participant narrator is a presence within the story who creates and engages in the action. A nonparticipant narrator observes the action. In the ghost story, a participant first-person narrator tells her own tale. Imagine this first-person narrator as a nonparticipant in the action, a woman who recounts a tale she heard from her friend. The story would have a different dramatic impact.

A participant narrator also may be trustworthy or untrustworthy. We consider a narrator trustworthy when we accept his or her view of the situation, when we think it is credible or, perhaps, represents the position of the author. In a story with an untrustworthy narrator, we question the narrative's stance and ask if it is credible, biased, or even, perhaps, delusional or hysterical. We question the validity of the point of view and realize that a distinction exists between the narrative and authorial point of view. In the ghost story, the narrator is trustworthy because her responses seem skeptical and because she qualifies her discussion. We accept her version of the truth. Imagine an untrustworthy narrator, extremely overwrought, talking to the ghost—we would not believe her version.

Setting

Setting is the location, time, place, and/or environment in which the story takes place. In the ghost story, the location is the bedroom of a house, the time is night and the recent past; and the environment is a household in Kentucky. The setting creates a particular mood, sense of place, and context. The ghost story would have little impact if the event occurred in broad daylight, in a city, and in a less scientific and skeptical age.

Plot

A **plot** presents the sequence of events in a story. In a short story the sequence of events is concentrated and does not necessarily represent actual time. Events in daily life, perhaps having taken place over a period of time, or events that appear random or fragmentary are often shaped, developed, and given cohesive form. For example, routine trips to work on the bus may become the basis for a central episode in a story, or a chance encounter with an old friend may be transformed into the central action of a tale. In the case of the ghost story, the sighting may represent many nights of uneasy feelings or partial glimpses.

Since a short story is so compressed, usually the sequence of events narrows to a single moment, a series of moments, or action that reveals a larger truth of character and life. The sequence builds to a **climax,** a high point of action. In an adventure or horror short story, the climax may be an apex of suspense; in a short story focused on character, the climactic point may be a moment of discovery, awakening, or revelation. For example, in the ghost story, the most important event is not the appearance of the spirit, but the discovery that a child had died in the house, and, indeed, that the apparition could be a real ghost; in short, the narrator begins to recognize the possibility of supernatural occurrences.

Short story writers also manipulate the sequence of events in a story; they may not present the events in chronological (time) order. For example, the story may begin in the middle of the action or at the end of the sequence, and then the narrator may **flash back**—move back in time—to the beginning of the action. The ghost story, for instance, could have begun with the sighting of the ghost and then could have returned to the beginning of the night's sleep or even the girl's death. Flashback techniques add dramatic impact and meaning to the unfolding events since the reader already knows what will transpire; the technique also may shift the focus from the plot to character development because attention moves away from the rendering of the action. *Flash forward* is another method of manipulating time in which the narrator relates the beginning of the tale, then moves quickly to the ending, and then returns to the beginning of the story. This technique adds dramatic impact and irony (double meanings) to each stage of the action since the reader is aware of the contribution of each moment to the unfolding of the action. In a rendering of the ghost story, the narrator could have quickly moved to the sighting, then returned to see partial, mysterious glimpses of the face, hair, clothes, and eyes of a figure—these glimpses would have dramatic impact for a reader. Short stories also may unfold through associations and may move backward and forward in time.

Conflict

Conflict is the tension between two forces; the exposition of a problem; an internal battle between two forces, psychic or external. Major conflicts in fiction arise between people and nature, between people and their environments, among people, or within a person. In the ghost story, the conflict, an internal struggle, centers on whether the narrator believes that she has seen a ghost. The plot of the short story concentrates on and develops such a conflict until it is resolved after a moment of crisis. In conventional short stories, the climax prompts the resolution through a moment of reckoning, recognition, awakening, or discovery. However, many contemporary short stories do not present resolutions of conflict. Again in the ghost story, no answers exist to test the validity of the reported sighting of the apparition. The story leaves questions open. The story ends in an ambivalent, mysterious way.

Character

The short story primarily concentrates on the presentation of **characters:** the people in the story and their conflicts. In the ghost story, the characters are the first-person narrator, the apparition, and the husband. The conflict concerns the tension within the narrator between believing and negating the presence of the little girl. We learn about characters through action, dialogue, and physical appearance. Their personalities evolve through events and through interaction with others.

In fiction, E. M. Forster has distinguished between **round** and **flat** characters. Round characters are multidimensional, capable of growth and change. Flat characters, according to Forster, are one-dimensional and often stereotypical. The effective short story concentrates on presenting at least one round character in conflict with others. Because of the length and complicated texture of a short story, the writer of this genre cannot develop as many characters in depth as can writers of such longer forms as the novella or novel. In a further draft of the ghost story, the narrator could become the round character and the ghost of the little girl, the flat, one-dimensional character.

Language

The **language** in a short story is compressed. Each word is well chosen and contributes to the impact of the whole. Sharp, vivid sensory details involve the reader in the world of the narrator, in setting, in characters, in the unfolding drama of the plot. In addition, short story writers often choose elements of poetic diction: images, figurative language, symbolism, allusion, and irony to create their worlds (see Chapter 3).

Short story writers also work with the **denotations** (dictionary definitions) and **connotations** (associations) of words to create effect. Because the form is concentrated, each word must have impact and add to the presentation of theme (messages of the work). Think of the word "luminous" in the ghost story as it alludes to the physical presence of the ghost as transparent and also refers to the girl's wide-eyed stare. The connotations lead readers to form a picture of a ghost: mysterious, innocent, and yet scary.

Another element of language is the texture of the prose: the sounds and the rhythms of the language. Storytelling, originally oral entertainment, does exist as "music." Think of the tension between the liquid "l" sounds and the staccato "e" words, which reflects the narrator's state of mind. The repetition of the "s" and the "d" sounds evoke feelings of sharpness and of hardness, appropriate to a confrontation with the supernatural.

In addition, aspects of style that create the rhythm of language are repetition and parallelism (repeated and balanced wording). The short, simple sentences evoke the fear felt by the narrator.

For stories to be powerful, writers also avoid **clichés** (hackneyed or overused expressions and figures of speech). Clichés detract from impact because they belong to everyday conversational speech, not to the heightened language of fiction; and, therefore, they are jarring and destructive to the mood. They also do not add descriptive detail or image because they cannot evoke word pictures since their meanings are predictable and often taken for granted. In the ghost story, the narrator reverts to a level of colloquial language: "freaked." This shift is jarring. She could have used a stronger verb to convey both her fear and astonishment.

Tone

Tone, the sense of the narrator, emerges from the connotations, the inferences, of every word. Tone also conveys the attitude of the narrator toward his or her subject, for example, characters and events in the work. Apparent from the first word, tone colors every detail of the work—dialogue, imagery, symbol, and setting. In the ghost story, the tone shifts from fear to puzzlement to mystery as the narrator learns about the death of the child.

Symbolism

A **symbol** is a person, place, object, thing, name, title, aspect of setting that suggests something beyond itself and has a range of meanings. Since a short story, like poetry, is compressed, all aspects of the story—title, setting, characters' names, appearance, dialogue, and events of the plot—may contain symbolic meanings and create the theme. For example, even in the informal telling of the ghost story, the girl's yellow hair and white dress suggest her innocence; the head under the pillow, the denial of truth.

Theme

The **theme** of the short story is the message presented by the work. No story has a single central idea; there may be several themes. As he or she is crafting the story, the writer may be conscious of several themes of the work and may shape it with these ideas in mind. In addition, readers may discover other messages from careful analyses of the text. In the ghost story, one theme certainly is the mystery of supernatural occurrences.

Another theme concerns the omnipresence of death and the human drive to negate that reality.

All aspects of an effective short story may create themes: point of view, setting, plot, character, conflict, tone, and symbolism. In the narrator's story one theme centers on the impossibility of escaping death. The point of view—first person—gives the reader the thoughts of the woman facing the appearance of the ghost and the fact of death itself. The setting also develops this theme: it is the "middle of the night," a time of dream and unreality that contrasts with the stark presence of the apparition. The tension and conflict in the plot center on the narrator's vision of the ghost—is she real? The simple language builds the confrontation and mood of the work. The gesture of "[pulling] the pillow over [her] head" symbolically suggests the narrator's need for denial. This short story then becomes a tightly woven anecdote about facing the supernatural and the irrefutable fact of death.

The Reading/Writing Process: Fiction

In addition to critical reading responses, we recommend a process for understanding fiction. First, read the story. Involve yourself on the level of point of view and plot. Ask yourself who is telling the story, and explore your reactions to the narrative point of view. Is the narrator part of the story? Is the narrator objective about the events? Is the narrator trustworthy? As you read, remember the main events and follow the sequence of action. Who are the main characters? With whom do you sympathize? Locate the problems and conflicts. As you read, notice the shifts in conflict and the development of crisis. At the story's conclusion, ask yourself if the conflicts are resolved. Ask if any of the characters have changed. How have they developed? Ask if your sympathies and involvement with certain characters have shifted. What messages have you discovered in the text? Explore the emotional impact of the work. Ask how you felt after finishing the story. In a second or third reading, analyze the function of point of view, setting, tone, symbolism, word choice, detail, imagery, and figurative language used by the writer in building the story. Throughout your reading, explore your own reactions and associations with the story. Assess your reactions to the themes of the narrative.

Checklist for Reading and Writing about Short Fiction

1. What point of view is apparent? first person? third person? omniscient? limited? detached? What is the impact of this choice of narrative perspective? Is there a participant or nonparticipant narrative point of view?
2. What is the setting of the story? time? place? environment? What moods are created by the setting in the story? What social, cultural, historical contexts are established by setting?
3. What are the key events of the plot? Does the plot build to a climax? What are the conflicts in the story? Are the conflicts resolved? Is there a moment of awakening or discovery?

4. Who are the main characters? Are they round? flat? With whom do you relate? Sympathize? How are they related to each other? What is the role of minor characters?

5. What is the tone of the story? What can you tell about the tone from the opening? Why? From key descriptions and details?

6. Characterize word choice. Is there vivid detail? Figurative language? Irony?

7. What are the symbolic details (title, names, setting, gesture, objects, events)? How does symbolism help to develop the themes?

8. What are the themes of the work? Do all elements of the story contribute to the theme?

STUDENT PORTFOLIO

Response to Kate Chopin's "The Story of an Hour"

Kate Chopin   *(1850–1904)*

The Story of an Hour   *1894*

Knowing that Mrs. Mallard was afflicted with a heart trouble, great care was taken to break to her as gently as possible the news of her husband's death.

It was her sister Josephine who told her, in broken sentences; veiled hints that revealed in half concealing. Her husband's friend Richards was there, too, near her. It was he who had been in the newspaper office when intelligence of the railroad disaster was received, with Brently Mallard's name leading the list of "killed." He had only taken the time to assure himself of its truth by a second telegram, and had hastened to forestall any less careful, less tender friend in bearing the sad message.

She did not hear the story as many women have heard the same, with a paralyzed inability to accept its significance. She wept at once, with sudden, wild abandonment, in her sister's arms. When the storm of grief had spent itself she went away to her room alone. She would have no one follow her.

There stood, facing the open window, a comfortable, roomy armchair. Into this she sank, pressed down by a physical exhaustion that haunted her body and seemed to reach into her soul.

She could see in the open square before her house the tops of trees that were all   5 aquiver with the new spring life. The delicious breath of rain was in the air. In the street below a peddler was crying his wares. The notes of a distant song which some one was singing reached her faintly, and countless sparrows were twittering in the eaves.

There were patches of blue sky showing here and there through the clouds that had met and piled one above the other in the west facing her window.

She sat with her head thrown back upon the cushion of the chair, quite motionless, except when a sob came up into her throat and shook her, as a child who had cried itself to sleep continues to sob in its dreams.

She was young, with a fair, calm face, whose lines bespoke repression and even a certain strength. But now there was a dull stare in her eyes, whose gaze was fixed away off yonder on one of those patches of blue sky. It was not a glance of reflection, but rather indicated a suspension of intelligent thought.

There was something coming to her and she was waiting for it, fearfully. What was it? She did not know; it was too subtle and elusive to name. But she felt it, creeping out of the sky, reaching toward her through the sounds, the scents, the color that filled the air.

Now her bosom rose and fell tumultuously. She was beginning to recognize this thing that was approaching to possess her, and she was striving to beat it back with her will—as powerless as her two white slender hands would have been.

When she abandoned herself a little whispered word escaped her slightly parted lips. She said it over and over under her breath: "free, free, free!" The vacant stare and the look of terror that had followed it went from her eyes. They stayed keen and bright. Her pulses beat fast, and the cursing blood warmed and relaxed every inch of her body.

She did not stop to ask if it were or were not a monstrous joy that held her. A clear and exalted perception enabled her to dismiss the suggestion as trivial.

She knew that she would weep again when she saw the kind, tender hands folded in death; the face that had never looked save with love upon her, fixed and gray and dead. But she saw beyond that bitter moment a long procession of years to come that would belong to her absolutely. And she opened and spread her arms out to them in welcome.

There would be no one to live for her during those coming years; she would live for herself. There would be no powerful will bending hers in that blind persistence with which men and women believe they have a right to impose a private will upon a fellow-creature. A kind intention or a cruel intention made the act seem no less a crime as she looked upon it in that brief moment of illumination.

And yet she had loved him—sometimes. Often she had not. What did it matter! What could love, the unsolved mystery, count for in face of this possession of self-assertion which she suddenly recognized as the strongest impulse of her being!

"Free! Body and soul free!" she kept whispering.

Josephine was kneeling before the closed door with her lips to the keyhole, imploring for admission. "Louise, open the door! I beg; open the door—you will make yourself ill. What are you doing, Louise? For heaven's sake open the door."

"Go away. I am not making myself ill." No; she was drinking in a very elixir of life through that open window.

Her fancy was running riot along those days ahead of her. Spring days, and summer days, and all sorts of days that would be her own. She breathed a quick prayer that life might be long. It was only yesterday she had thought with a shudder that life might be long.

She arose at length and opened the door to her sister's importunities. There was a feverish triumph in her eyes, and she carried herself unwittingly like a goddess of Victory. She clasped her sister's waist, and together they descended the stairs. Richards stood waiting for them at the bottom.

Someone was opening the front door with a latchkey. It was Brently Mallard who entered, a little travel-stained, composedly carrying his grip-sack and umbrella. He had been far from the scene of the accident, and did not even know there had been one.

He stood amazed at Josephine's piercing cry; at Richards' quick motion to screen him from the view of his wife.

But Richards was too late.

When the doctors came they said she had died of heart disease—of joy that kills. ●

■ ■ ■

The following works present a student's reaction responses to Kate Chopin's "The Story of an Hour." To demonstrate the process of constructing a response essay to a work, we include Maria Taylor's initial journal entry and three drafts of her essay.

The thesis of the essay evolved from Taylor's freewrite (composed in her journal), designed to spur personal connections with the work. Students in the class were asked to write a monologue in the voice of Mrs. Mallard. After the completion of her assignment, Taylor discovered that she empathized with Mrs. Mallard and shared her feelings of imprisonment. Taylor's position is voiced in the lines: "I want to be free to be for me, only me." She begins with Mrs. Mallard's exclamations (" 'free, free, free. . . .' ") and moves to her own: "I never really felt free," and "It was the only house I knew as woman." She shifts from speaking in Mrs. Mallard's voice to voicing her own ideas and experiences. The discovery gained from the freewrite became the kernel of the first draft of the reaction essay. In this version, she expresses her yearning.

In her first draft, Taylor jumps from association to association: household duties, her relationship with her husband, the memories of his goodness and his abuse, her need for "balance," her panic, eating disorder, and fear. In her next two drafts, she more freely articulates her connections with Mrs. Mallard, organizes her thoughts, treats her responses in a systematic manner, and arranges them in stages that follow Mrs. Mallard's process of discovering her desire to be free. She also includes the quotations from the work that spark her insights.

Journal Entry

Freewrite: A Monologue Spoken by Mrs. Mallard
By Maria Taylor

I've said it over and over under my breath, "I want to be free, free, free." I want to be free to be for me, only me. To be no-one's mother, daughter, wife. I want to be free to come and go as I please, when I please, how I please. The words "free, free, free" speak to my longing soul.

I never really felt free. I went from Dad's household to my husband's control. The transition was easy for me; it was a role I always wanted. It was expected of me. It was the only role I knew as woman.

As a female, I was to be wife, mother, daughter, depending on "man" in all roles. I never realized then, in playing out my role I was always depending on a man for my well being. If I needed nurturing, I went to him. If I needed money, I went to him.

Note following reading of the story:

I could see so clearly the truth in the quotation "free." I see the dichotomy in her.

First Draft

I want to enjoy a relationship based on equality. Do I sound selfish? Well—it may be—but maybe it's my time, huh? I don't want to cook, clean, do laundry, shop, have to be home, say when I'll be home, where I'll be etc., be questioned about anything—anymore. I want to be free, and yet, I want to be connected. I suppose that would be with and to him. He is my husband, and he has been a good one. He is the father of my four incredible children, and he has been a good father. But there are the horrendous memories of his drinking and emotional and psychological abuse, all of which he denies to this day. He's demeaning of me and my role as woman, wife, person. I want out. I feel selfish and wrong and guilty, but I cannot continue to be a wife anymore. I want a balance in my life. No, this isn't even true. I want it all to be for me now. I know I cannot fulfill my roles anymore because my own health is beginning to fail. I have "panic attacks" regularly, and they are the most painful, terrorizing feelings I have ever experienced. I cannot control my food intake, anymore. Food has become my friend, lover, consoler, comforter. All things except what it truly is—I feel my own life has been fused to others for so long, and in that fusion, I've become lost. I am so frightened. I wonder how I can go on and on and what is left for me? Would I have been better off never knowing him or any man and just be for me?

Conclusion?

Is there ever a relationship between man and woman that is based on true equality and true freedom? Isn't love supposed to give these gifts? Will I, like Mrs. Mallard, have to die before I am truly free?

In the next draft, Taylor creates paragraphs to explore each topic.

Second Draft

It's almost too difficult to write, to express on paper, but I know this story. I have in many ways lived it.

I suppose you would have to be married for a while to understand Mrs. Mallard. I have been married for thirty-one years, so I understand her. (We can only really understand someone when we have walked in her shoes.)

I like Chopin's Mrs. Mallard's wish to be free. Free to be, for me—only me, no-one else. Free to sleep and eat, come and go—do, not do, whatever I want, when I want, for a while.

And yet am I afraid of this? Yes, for I have never lived for myself, lived by myself. I have never taken care of myself financially. I always took care of others and was taken care of financially by others.

I went from Dad's home living under his jurisdiction to my husband's home living under his jurisdiction. This sounds so cynical; doesn't it? But this is how I feel and how it was.

I never felt "free." Their control was always so subtle and elusive, but I knew it was there like Mr. Mallard and that I had to walk within the lines of their boundaries. If not, I would be abandoned, emotionally, physically and financially. Then how would I exist? I was programmed to believe I could not live without them.

And yet I love him. I believe I do anyway. But I so want to be free. I want to be like Mrs. Mallard looking out the window. I want to continue to love him, but I do not want to live within the confines of what he believes that love should be.

In the final draft, Taylor develops substantial responses and connection to the work.

Final Draft: "Free, Free, Free": Chopin's "The Story of an Hour"

Under her breath, Mrs. Mallard says, "free, free, free!" Over and over again. I have said the same words over and over again under my breath. I want to be free. Free to be for me, only me, to be no one's daughter, wife, or mother. I do not want to be caregiver, support, keeper. I want to live only for myself. I want to be free to come and go as I please, when I please, how I please.

The adjectives, "free, free, free," speak to my longing soul. And yet I am afraid. Yes, for I have never lived for myself, lived by myself. I have never taken care of myself financially. In many ways, I am like Mrs. Mallard's sobbing child. I always took care of others and was taken care of financially by others. I took care of both my parents when they were ill. Then I became a wife and mother. Emotionally, all of my energies were out there, caring for others all my life, leaving very little energy for nurturing myself. Consequently, I feel uncomfortable and I question whether or not I can be free. At fifty-one, this is a sorry commentary. Like Mrs. Mallard, I have never lived for myself.

I went from Dad's house, living under his jurisdiction, to my husband's home, living under his jurisdiction. Coming from a patriarchal home and environment, I thought that this simply was the way that it was for all women. I thought that the "powerful will bending [mine] in that blind persistence with which men and women believe they have a right to impose a private will upon a fellow-creature" was to be expected and the way it should be.

I never felt free. Their control was always so subtle and elusive, but I knew it was there and that I had to walk within the lines of their boundaries. If not, I would be abandoned, emotionally, physically and financially. Then how would I exist, survive? I was programmed to believe I could not live without them. As a result, I felt as if I danced around this big bear that lived in the center of the living room for most of my life. I do not want to dance anymore. Like Mrs. Mallard, who said "she would live for herself," I too wish for autonomy.

I want to continue a relationship with him, but I do not want to live within the confines of what he believes that love should be. I want to feel "spring days, and summer days . . . that would be [my] own."

My husband is a domineering man. He often treats me in a way that suffocates me. His constant questions, his lack of trust, his knee-jerk anger oppress and fatigue me. I understand his fear, that he will lose me, that he doesn't understand me any more, and I empathize with him. But I no longer can claim this shattering as my own. When I do, I become shattered myself. I love my husband, and yet I want to be free.

I want to enjoy a relationship based on equality and freedom. Can a relationship between a man and a woman be based on these things? Is it possible? Is it possible with my relationship with him? Has he snatched that away from me, too? Would I have been happier never knowing my love or any man and just be, for me? Will I, like Mrs. Mallard, have to die before I feel free, before I feel that "monstrous joy"—the "joy that kills?"

In the introduction to this last draft, Taylor states her thesis, the yearning "to be free" that she shares with Mrs. Mallard. In the middle paragraphs, she explains the origins of that desire, tracing her need for autonomy to her family background (paragraph 2), and to her marriage, an extension of that "patriarchal home and environment" (paragraph 3). She next presents (in paragraphs 5 and 6) her desire for autonomy; finally, she articulates her dilemma: the conflict between her love and loyalty to her husband and her need to find a "relationship based on equality and freedom." Her conclusion contains her pessimistic assessment: "Will I, like Mrs. Mallard, have to die before I feel free, before I feel that 'monstrous joy'—the 'joy that kills'?" She builds the essay to its dramatic conclusion.

Taylor also strives to include more quotations from the story so that the progression in her thinking mirrors, in some ways, the logic and progression of the plot of "The Story of An Hour." She begins by citing Mrs. Mallard's wish to be "free, free, free," which appears midway in Chopin's story. In the description of her relationship to her husband, she includes Mrs. Mallard's realization that after her husband's death, there will be no "powerful will bending [her]" into submission. By following the pattern of Mrs. Mallard's recognition, Taylor makes their situations analogous and strengthens the comparison of her situation with the character's plight. They both came to similar despairing assessments of the possibility of "true equality" in the relation of men and women. Chopin's character dies . . . death is her only release. Taylor despairs of the possibility of finding relationships based on a "true balance" between the sexes.

Taylor's connections with "The Story of an Hour" are made explicit: her understanding of Mrs. Mallard's imprisonment caused by her social role; Mrs. Mallard's inability to change her circumstances; the protagonist's inhibited desire for freedom and her ambivalent feelings toward her husband; her desire for release from a marriage that denies her autonomy.

[11]

Poetry

When asked to define poetry, a student responded, "Poems make words dance." This brief reply stimulates many provocative ideas and images concerning a difficult question. The excellent answer implies that poems are metaphorical, paradoxical, and dynamic. In poetry the images do not work if they do not inspire sudden connection and insight. The words must "dance," or they cannot create effective and astonishing meanings. This definition also suggests the necessity of rhythm, beat, and accent. If the work lacks these intrinsic qualities, it is not poetry.

What else does this definition signify? It indicates that poems create themes, character, and contexts through compressed language, through figures of speech, through economy of form, and through sound. If academic definitions always require appropriate language, then the student's answer insists upon such words. If academic definitions insist upon rhythm or meter, then the student's answer alludes to rhythm through the word "dance." If academic definitions require that poetry elicit feelings and imagination, the student's answer implies that poetry creates these responses in the reader or the listener.

The word "make," above all, connotes *art* and insists that words have the power of the visual to imitate, signify, please, mean, and construct new realities and truths. In ancient cultures, chants and religious rituals were poetry; epics and dramas were poetry. We appreciate the enduring value of the genre as an accessible source of wisdom and pleasure, a significant form of enrichment and of redemption, and an expression of the deepest experiences and truths of human existence.

Kinds of Poetry

In general, every poem falls into one of three broad categories: **narrative poetry** tells a story, **lyric poetry** gives a brief account of the person's feelings, ideas, or moods, and **dramatic poetry** presents monologues and soliloquies.

Narrative Poetry

Any poem that spins a tale may be defined as a *narrative work*. In Gwendolyn Brooks' "The Chicago Defender Sends a Man to Little Rock" (Chapter 8), the speaker catalogues the daily actions of citizens who bear children, celebrate holidays, play baseball, attend concerts, and love each other. The persona wants to report that "they are like people everywhere." Another story, however, exists in Little Rock; people are "hurling spittle, rocks, garbage, and fruit." The speaker must recount this conflict. Why? The Supreme Court had ordered desegregation of the schools in an historic decision in the case of *Brown* vs. *The Board of Education,* a case never directly mentioned in Brooks's narrative. Because of its political context, "The Chicago Defender Sends a Man to Little Rock" may be called a *protest poem.*

Other forms of narrative poetry include the epic and the ballad. **Epics,** written in many eras and in many cultures, derive from oral tradition and describe the adventures and accomplishments of great heroes. The story assumes grand proportions and often includes supernatural beings and their actions that create monumental consequences. The language of epics is formal and figurative, and almost all epics share similar conventions. *The Iliad* and *The Odyssey* by Homer (Greek), *The Epic of Gilgamesh* (Babylonian), *Sundiata* (Mali), and *Beowulf* (Anglo-Saxon) represent works in this tradition.

Ballads, another form of narrative poetry, also derive from oral tradition since originally they were songs. Literary ballads include most features of the oral form: repetition and refrain—phrases or lines reappearing at certain places in the poem. Ballads alternate lines of eight and six syllables, with rhymes in the second and fourth lines. Not every ballad must be written in the standard stanzaic pattern. Not every ballad contains a refrain. The Beatles, for example, wrote a humorous song about "Rocky Raccoon" that mimics "Frankie and Johnny"; both are ballads. More serious works tell stories of young women such as Thomas Hardy's "The Ruined Maid."

Lyric Poetry

Lyrics are short and subjective; in these poems, the speakers describe their thoughts or feelings. The original definition of the lyric meant a song accompanied by a lyre. This category includes the following forms:

1. An **elegy** mourns the death of a particular person, or sometimes, the inexorable fate of humans, their mortality. A variation of an elegy is Gwendolyn Brooks's "A Boy Died in My Alley" (Chapter 8).
2. A **meditation** centers on a particular object as a method for consideration of metaphysical ideas (see "Dover Beach" by Mathew Arnold in Chapter 7).
3. An **ode,** a song of praise, is long, serious, and formal in all of its aspects. It always has a complex stanzaic pattern. Keats's "Ode on a Grecian Urn" is an example of this form (Chapter 9).
4. A **pastoral** celebrates the idyllic nature of country life. James Wright's "A Blessing" represents a modern version of the pastoral (Chapter 9).

Matsuo Bashō, a Japanese poet who lived in the seventeenth century, wrote haiku, unrhymed three-line poems with seventeen syllables. Haiku also, may be considered lyrical in nature:

> Sleeping at noon
> the body of the blue heron
> poised in nobility
> (hiru neburu / aosagi no mi no / tōtosayo)
>
>   (translated by Earl Miner)

Notice that Bashō has compressed a strong image into three lines. The meaning depends on sudden insight and a connection between the heron's pose and a spiritual stance. At first glance, the poem seems to celebrate the serene immobility of the heron, "sleeping at noon." The closing line, however, implies a moment of spiritual awareness that transcends the physical.

Dramatic Poetry

In **dramatic poetry,** the speaker becomes an actor. In "Girl," for example, Jamaica Kincaid creates a **monologue** for a mother who is attempting to inculcate gender roles into her young daughter (Chapter 6).

Other forms of dramatic poems include epistolary monologues—letters written as poems. In the most familiar example of this kind of work, Ezra Pound's "The River Merchant's Wife: A Letter," loosely translated from a poem in Chinese written by Rihaku (also known as Li Po), the speaker has loved her husband deeply since childhood. The young Chinese wife waits patiently for his return and expresses her loneliness and longing in the letter. Admired as a model of dignity and of marital love, this eighth-century poem by Li Po presents great autobiographical detail in highly controlled and terse language.

Performance poetry, another kind of dramatic verse, has its roots in the oral tradition—in oral storytelling—particularly in its use of anaphora, in its conversational tone, and in its direct interaction with an audience. The form also developed out of the Dadaist artistic movement of the 1920s that advocated stream-of-consciousness writing, out of the works of the Beats of the 1950s who experimented with forms of spontaneous prose and poetry, and out of the improvisational structure of jazz. The form also was influenced by rap music and hip-hop—with their emphasis on word play, rhyme, street slang, and political messages. Performance poetry got its start at New York City's Nuyorican Café, founded by Miguel Algarin and Miguel Piñero, and was popularized by Russell Simmons's *Def Poetry Jam,* a dramatic enactment of a poetry slam that was featured on Broadway. Nikki Giovanni's "Ego Tripping" is an early example of the form (Chapter 5).

Although readers wish to designate strict categories for poems, some works defy such classification. Contemporary poetry often combines narrative and lyric modes; poets often extend the limits of traditional forms; and in their experiments, they create new language and images; they step into the borderland between narration and lyric, a place where new voices may sing and be heard.

Elements of Poetry

Voice

Poems, like fiction, present speakers who tell about events, experiences, emotions, or ideas. The poet remains separate from the persona or speaker, although in some works little distance exists between the two. In all cases, however, the reader should assume that poet and speaker have distinct identities. Often the poet creates a voice exceedingly different from him or herself. The speaker may even be anonymous.

One of the best methods of interpreting poetry is to define the voice, to discover as much as possible about its quality, mood, and concerns. In "Danaë," a voice poem based on Greek myth, the anonymous poet alludes to the imprisonment of the virgin, Danaë, by her father, a crime that he committed to circumvent the fulfillment of a prophecy that predicted the death of Acrisius at the hands of his grandson. Zeus, however, seduced Danaë in a shower of gold; and from this magical union, Perseus was born. Eventually the curse was fulfilled. Listen to the voice of Danaë. Consider the poem, and answer the following questions:

1. Who is the speaker?
2. What is the point of view?
3. What can you tell about the speaker? What is the situation of the speaker?
4. How is the story told? What story is being told?
5. What details and words characterize the speaker?
6. To whom does the speaker talk? Who is the audience?

Danaë

to be born to a curse
is all of history
that dark will
is all I knew
in the dark cavern   5
I lived
I saw just the
immediate edge of my body
the dark shadings and contours
of that shell   10
and you live in it
as if it were light
as if it gave you light
then one day
a rain came   15
a gold rain
a sheen of rain
a cool yellow breeze
a shimmer of gold
a sift of gold all over my skin   20
a wash of yellow light
and in this way
he came
my child
came as rain fell   25
came as silently
to life
came to me
a rinse of yellow gold
that boy child   30
my words
my history
my unsaid self
a blessing
too fragile   35
to be dreamt

The poet retells the story of Danaë with a first-person point of view and adds some new details to the ancient Greek myth. The persona expresses her sadness and loneliness as she considers her body as something to "live in." Subject to "the dark will," she exists in shadow "as if it were light." She seems concerned about the body, its history; and she feels resignation. She does not speak in anger, but she acknowledges indirectly that men and gods have power over her body. Yet the men are completely absent from the speaker's story.

The poet devotes half of the poem to the gold rain that impregnates Danaë and gives her a son. The repetition of "rain," "gold," "yellow," and "light" introduces a sense of quiet joy into the poem. These details about the conception of the child allow the speaker to claim herself, her history, and her child through words. In this connection between language and the body, the poet transforms Danaë into a contemporary woman.

Tone

The **tone** of a poem establishes the mood of the piece, the changing emotions of the speaker, or the attitude of the persona toward the subject. The poem may be sad, angry, shocking, nostalgic, or humorous. In "Daddy" by Sylvia Plath, the speaker begins with a mildly angry tone as she announces her rejection of her father, but the voice quickly becomes sad as she admits, "you died before I had time" (Chapter 6). In the monologue, the young woman, the persona, calls her father a god, a Nazi, and the devil. At the end, she attempts to exorcise him through a darkly humorous allusion to Dracula in vampire movies:

> There's a stake in your fat black heart
> And the villagers never liked you.
> They are dancing and stamping on you.
> They always knew it was you.
> Daddy, daddy, you bastard, I'm through.   5

Here the speaker refers to the only method that kills a vampire: a stake in the heart. She indicates that the villagers in Transylvania always knew that the vampire really was Count Dracula who lived in the eerie castle above the town. As a final shock, the speaker calls "Daddy" a "bastard" and declares wildly that she is "through." Some critics find the tone too exaggerated and do not believe that the ending convinces; others praise the poem for its devastating truth about the impact of the death of a parent and about the overwhelming anger of the betrayed and bereaved child.

Theme

Poems can explore any **theme,** any central idea. The poet can write about the terror of war, the ecstasy of love or religion, the mysteries or certainties of life or ideas. A poem may protest injustice, define itself, or mourn the death of a particular person. Many of these themes recur frequently. In every culture, poets write about time, death, love, and art. They celebrate achievements and laugh at and satirize human error and folly.

In order to determine the theme of a poem, look at images, voice, symbols, form, and sound. Combined, these aspects create the conceptions central to meaning. Because poetry is allusive and highly compressed, however, many interpretations become possible. Each reader may discover a different theme; but most of the time, a poem, rich in language and content, leads to certain agreements about thematic intent.

Chasing Fire Engines

The women in my family
always chase fire engines,
sirens wailing in their ears,
long funnels down and in,
a throb in their arms—   5
the urge to touch men,
the big hoses, eyes on the stream
arching toward smoke.
I was born with arson
in my heart, the desire   10
to light fires, to set
aflame every hand
that brushes my wrist,
to incinerate.

Now I dream of a stranger,   15
incendiary fingers on my breast.
I rise toward shadow,
light a match to identify
the face, to reach
the tender place;   20
and I smell ashes,
push the hand aside,
heat cooling

as I wake, women
in my family running   25
after fire engines, watching
men dowse flames,
water arching and arching:
the spray, the spray.

Then you turn to me in sleep,   30
move your leg over mine,
easy in your skin,
and I slide under you,
old luminations surround us,
the longing for arson   35
rising in my throat,

a moan subsides
as I chase the engines.
Fires, burning everywhere,
light the pillow where   40
your head circles mine.

In "Chasing Fire Engines," the persona speaks of natural curiosity and obsessions about sexuality; she feels the "heat cooling" and fantasizes about strangers; finally, she embraces her lover, familiar fires circling their heads on the pillow. Traditional themes about love and loss are deflated, but they remain relevant. The themes in this work center on the highly sexual nature of men and women, represented by the fire, the hoses, the spray. The heat cools in relationships, but most every person eventually discovers that familiarity and "old luminations" in love remain more important than initial and easy incendiary impulses.

Setting

Every poem presents a persona and a theme or themes; every poem takes place in a **setting**—the place, location, or atmosphere. Consider the various places in "Chasing Fire Engines." At first, the persona remembers the world of her childhood, a time when all of the men in the family served in the volunteer fire department and when the women and children hurried to watch the men in action. Of necessity, the town must have been small—perhaps, a village located in the South or Midwest. The setting also becomes a dream where a stranger touches the speaker, and the place seems shadowy and dark. As the third setting, the speaker alludes to a bed where she and her lover sleep; and, as they awaken, fire circles their heads on a pillow. Through an examination of setting, you can discover new aspects of meaning in every poem. By carefully describing locations in "Chasing Fire Engines," for example, you learn that the shifts in settings create important complications in the poem, complications that enrich its texture and significance.

Imagery

Everyone's first experience with reality begins with an **image**—a message from the world that comes to consciousness through the senses. It may enter through the eye as shape and shade; it may enter the nose as odor; it may enter the ear as sound; it may tingle the tongue as taste; it may caress the skin as touch. Every strong memory exists as an image or as a series or composite of images. Every dream emerges as vivid, often surreal, imagery. Scientists and poets confirm the inextricable relationship between ideas and images. Einstein arrived at his theory of relativity by picturing a man traveling on a wave of light. Goethe complained that he no sooner had an idea before "it [turned] into an image."

Certainly poetry cannot exist without **imagery.** Those things that appear as physical sensation are called **concrete images;** those that represent ideas may be **abstract images.** Consider this short poem by Margaret Atwood:

You Fit into Me

you fit into me
like a hook into an eye.

a fish hook
an open eye

The first two lines create the picture of the fitting together of the two parts of a familiar household fastener to connote a couple's embracing, caressing, or making love. The next two images twist the meaning—the hook becomes a fish hook penetrating a literal, not a metaphorical, eye—and they shock the reader with the deliberate announcement of pain. The relationship is an agonizing, not a loving, one.

Economy and brevity represent the advantages of images in poetry. They suggest; they enable readers to imagine experiences or sensations. They provide emotional connotations that color responses and evoke feelings in readers. William Carlos Williams's poem, "The Red Wheelbarrow," represents the compressed nature of poetry:

so much depends
upon

a red wheel
barrow

glazed with rain   5
water

beside the white
chickens.

What does the picture suggest? For a moment, the wet wheelbarrow beside the white chickens composes the world in a particular order, one that ascribes harmony and beauty to an ordinary scene. Through the first two lines Williams takes his representation of a bucolic scene and transforms it into a vision of the pleasures and purposes of perception. Williams suggests that the ability to perceive the relationship of images gives meaning to life. This poem exemplifies the tenets of the Imagist movement of the early twentieth century. Ezra Pound, who created such poetry, stated, "In a poem of this sort, one is trying to record the precise instant when a thing outward and objective transforms itself, or darts into a thing inward and subjective."

Poems often present highly complicated series of images that are woven through the entire work, strands that become a fabric of meaning. In this extension of imagery lies much of the pleasure of poetic form. In Walt Whitman's "When I Heard the Learn'd Astronomer," the speaker sits in a classroom and listens to a lecture. The first six lines of the poem introduce the astronomer and extend the images associated with him: "proofs," "figures," "charts and diagrams." The speaker, "sick" from the aridity of technical explanations, glides outside to enjoy the "mystical" experience of looking at the stars. The final lines emphasize and elaborate images of freedom in the natural world.

When I heard the learn'd astronomer,
When the proofs, the figures, were 'ranged in columns before me,

> When I was shown the charts and diagrams, to add, divide and measure
> them,
> When I sitting heard the astronomer where he lectured with much applause
> in the lecture-room,
> How soon unaccountable I became tired and sick   5
> Till rising and gliding out I wander'd off by myself,
> In the mystical moist night-air, and from time to time,
> Look'd up in perfect silence at the stars.

Note the passivity of the persona who listens, who "heard," and who "was shown," as the astronomer teaches in a "lecture-room." The speaker must perform calculations—"add, divide and measure"—in order to understand the "columns" placed before him. The proliferation and repetition ("when") of images denigrate the concrete, scientific atmosphere of the academy. The beautiful, abstract, active quality of the imagery that evokes the natural world, the world of "mystical moist night-air" and "stars," creates a "perfect" and silent contrast to the confinement of the lecture and the lecture-room. Whitman demonstrates the value of human experience and his view of the dangers of science by weaving images of a boring, sickening astronomy lecture and active perception of a starry night as threads through his work.

Figures of Speech

Figures of speech, expressions that suggest more than their literal meanings, present implied or direct comparisons that give readers the experience of an abstraction or of an emotion. Some figures are **metaphor, simile, personification, synecdoche, metonymy,** and **hyperbole.** In this famous section from Keats' "Endymion," the first line contains a metaphor:

> A thing of beauty is a joy for ever.
> Its loveliness increases; it will never
> Pass into nothingness; but still will keep
> A bower quiet for us, and a sleep
> Full of sweet dreams, and health, and quiet breathing.   5
> Therefore, on the morrow, are we wreathing
> A flowery band to bind us to the earth,
> Spite of despondence, of the inhuman death
> Of noble natures, of the gloomy days,
> Of all the unhealthy and o'er-darkened ways   10
> Made for our searching; yes, in spite of all,
> Some shape of beauty moves away the pall
> From our dark spirits.

Metaphor and Simile

The **metaphor** equates "A thing of beauty" with eternal joy and expresses Keats's belief that beauty transcends time, space, and matter, that beauty redeems the darkness in human life. A metaphor pictures a thing or an idea, "thing of beauty," and juxtaposes it with something different, "a joy forever," and implies an analogy between them. Look at the passage, and notice the additional comparisons that Keats creates. The "thing of beauty" becomes a "flowery band" and "some shape" that "moves away the pall." In fact, Keats extends the metaphor of beauty beyond the first line and elaborates the idea with numerous images. **Extended metaphors,** sometimes called conceits, often appear in poetry and serve to complicate its form and meaning, to create depth. In "The Love Song of J. Alfred Prufrock," T. S. Eliot describes the fog as a cat in stanzas two and three (Chapter 7). This extraordinary extended metaphor presents the fog in such a catlike manner that the comparison becomes obvious—even though Eliot never mentions the word *cat.*

Similes make a direct comparison of one thing to another; usually the words "like" or "as" serve to create connections. Keats, for example, could have written the first line of the passage from "Endymion" as a simile, "A thing of beauty is [like] a joy for ever." Think of William Wordsworth's "I Wandered Lonely as a Cloud." In this title, Wordsworth's speaker convinces the reader of his loneliness through a concrete object, a cloud. Its solitary movement in the sky suddenly illuminates the emotional state of the persona.

Personification, Synecdoche, Metonymy, and Hyperbole

These figures of speech appear frequently in poetry:

Personification is the attribution of human traits to objects, ideas, or creatures. In Keats's "Endymion" beauty possesses human powers to "keep" and to "move." Keats endows beautiful things with noble human qualities that can negate the dark nature of life.

Synecdoche, sometimes considered a special type of metonymy, is a figure of speech in which part of a thing is used to represent the whole. References to a monarch as the crown and to sailors as hands provide familiar samples of this technique.

Metonymy is a figure of speech in which a single name of a person, place, or thing stands for a more complex situation or experience with which the name is associated. Washington sometimes represents all branches of the government of the United States.

Hyperbole or **exaggeration** is overstatement of the situation, idea, person in order to shock, to create humor, to command attention. In Nikki Giovanni's "Ego Tripping," the entire poem becomes an exercise in hyperbole (Chapter 5). The speaker makes wild claims that she "gives oil to the Arab World," that her son is Hannibal, that she "cannot be comprehended."

Symbol, Myth, and Allusion

Symbol

A **symbol** is an object or event that represents something else or that has meaning beyond itself. Everyday objects become symbols when a red cross signifies an international relief organization, when ram's horns symbolize a football team, or when a swastika stands as a Nazi emblem.

In many cultures, poetic symbols have conventional meanings: cherry blossoms, jade, birds, and roses all have well-established significance in Japanese, Chinese, or English poetry. Many contemporary poets, however, create private symbols that readers may interpret from a close reading of the work. This development can make symbols more difficult to discover and to comprehend. Adrienne Rich's "Diving into the Wreck" presents a complex system of symbols that can be read simply as a dive to a sunken ship for treasure and as a personal search through the wreckage of a life (Chapter 9). In the end, however, the poet shifts from the first-person singular "I" to plural and multiple points of view:

> We are, I am, you are
> by cowardice or courage
> the one who finds our way
> back to this scene
> carrying a knife, a camera 5
> a book of myths
> in which our names do not appear

The "we" who dive into the wreck become an androgynous "one who finds our way/back" to a place where "a book of myths" denies existence through the absence of names. Rich seems to proclaim that none can have identity if the "book of myths" is not replaced by the recognition of personhood and autonomy for women as well as for men, for the oppressed as well as for the oppressors, by a merging, in fact, of these categories.

Myth

A **myth** is similar to a symbol, but it includes a story that stands for something else. In many cultures and traditions, myths explain the inexplicable and the mysterious; they preserve history, culture, customs; they describe the actions of supernatural beings. Some of these beings symbolize natural forces—fertility, harvest, the sea. Some of them represent abstract qualities—love, wisdom, cunning, evil. A **mythology,** a system or collection of myths, represents the beliefs of a culture or a particular group; these myths often originated in religious belief and ritual. Among the mythologies most commonly found in poetry are Greek, Roman, Germanic, Native American, and Egyptian.

Rilke's "Sonnets to Orpheus" (Chapter 9) incorporate the Orpheus myth; this myth provides the symbolic subtexts of the poems.

Allusion

An **allusion** refers to a well-known literary work, person, event, or place. Whether it is implicit or explicit, the allusion enlarges the world of the poem. In "Sailing to Byzantium," for example, Yeats refers to the city where the beauty and culture of the Byzantine empire reached its height in the fifth and sixth centuries (Chapter 9).

Structure

Stanzas

Historically poems originated as oral expression. Poets accompanied their songs with instruments, or they performed with choral or instrumental groups. The first aspect of the poem in any analysis of sound should be the visual picture of lines arranged on a page. The lines of a poem may be divided into separate groups or units called **stanzas** that function like paragraphs in fiction and in essays. Some questions to pose about stanzaic patterns include: How are the poetic groups or stanzas divided? Where do they begin and end? How does the punctuation provide cues for reading? The strong marks of punctuation—periods, semicolons, dashes, question marks, colons, exclamation points—require longer pauses than a comma. Examine Gwendolyn Brooks's poem:

We Real Cool *1960*
THE POOL PLAYERS
SEVEN AT THE GOLDEN SHOVEL

We real cool. We
Left school. We

Lurk late. We
Strike straight. We

Sing sin. We   5
Thin gin. We

Jazz June. We
Die soon.

The short sentences, each three words long, require a fast pace and regular beat. The two-line stanzas, called **couplets,** are open because each line and each couplet ends with "we." A line of poetry that ends without punctuation or pause is known as a run-on line, also as an **enjambment.** The internal periods command pauses, and the repetitions and positions of the pronoun "we" also demand emphasis. Read the poem as eight short sentences, and then read it according to stanzaic and line arrangements. What is the connection between sound and meaning?

Rhyme and Sound

Rhyme, the repetition of sounds usually at the ends of lines in regular patterns, represents a traditional technique that pleases the ear and enhances the effects of images and symbols. In Brooks's poem, each line rhymes because all except the last line end with the same word. In each couplet, Brooks has used internal rhyme: cool, school; late, straight; sin, gin; June, soon. If these rhymes were **end rhymes,** the **rhyme scheme**

would read aa, bb, cc, dd. To determine the scheme of any rhymed poem, simply assign letters of the alphabet to each new rhyming sound, and begin with *a*.

Another good example of rhyme is Shakespeare's "Shall I Compare Thee to a Summer's Day?" (Chapter 7). Its form, called a **Shakespearean** or **Elizabethan sonnet,** divides the traditional fourteen lines into three four-line verses or quatrains and a final couplet. The rhyme scheme reads abab, cdcd, efef, gg. Sonnets also may take **Petrarchan** form, named for the famous Italian poet, Petrarch. In this kind of sonnet, the poet writes two **quatrains,** called the **octave** (eight lines), and two **tercets,** three-line verses, called the **sestet** (six lines). The theme shifts radically at the ninth line in Petrarchan sonnets; this turn is known as the volta. The rhyme scheme in the octave usually reads abba abba. The sestet may rhyme in a number of ways: cdecde, cdccdc, cdedce. Another technique for rhyming in free verse or formal poetry includes slant or half rhyme, one in which words almost rhyme.

The sounds of the words contribute to the meaning of the poem. The repetition of the initial sounds of accented consonant syllables at close intervals, called **alliteration,** may create effects that enlarge, reinforce, or contradict the ideas and mood of the poem. In Brooks's work, for example, the alliteration begins with the identification of the speakers as *p*ool *p*layers, and she continues this pattern in *l*urk *l*ate, in *s*trike *s*traight, in *s*ing *s*in, in *j*azz *J*une. This frequent use of alliteration in such a short poem heightens the sense of jazz and music. Brooks also employs **assonance,** the repetition of vowel sounds of stressed syllables or important words at close intervals: c*oo*l sch*oo*l. Notice that this poem relies heavily on sound for meaning. Notice that the long, sighing vowel in die in the last line stands alone, a jarring conclusion.

Rhythm

One of the indispensable elements distinguishing poetry is **rhythm.** Like song or dance, no poem can exist without a beat that augments its meaning and beauty or contradicts and conflicts with its themes and images to create tension. Poets choose rhythms from four basic categories: *traditional meters, strong stress rhythms, syllabic counts,* and *free verse.*

Meter

Meter is a rhythmic pattern of stressed (/) and unstressed (˘) syllables in a poem. Each unit, called a *foot,* has either two or three syllables. The most common feet in poetry follow:

Foot	Designation	Example
iamb or iambic	(˘ /)	dĕlíght
trochee or trochaic	(/ ˘)	córăl
spondee or spondaic	(/ /)	hó húm
pyrrhus or pyrrhic	(˘ ˘)	advantăgĕ ŏf
anapest or anapestic	(˘ ˘ /)	iñ ă flásh
dactyl or dactylic	(/ ˘ ˘)	níght cŏmiñg

Line lengths can be measured in number of feet.

Line Length	Number of Feet
monometer	one foot
dimeter	two feet
trimeter	three feet
tetrameter	four feet
pentameter	five feet
hexameter	six feet
heptameter	seven feet
octometer	eight feet

Scansion

In order to discover the meter of a poem, each line is scanned for accented and unaccented syllables. This process, called **scansion,** enables you to examine the effects of rhythm in the work. Look at this scansion of Shakespeare's parody of the conceits in the sonnet tradition. Note that each syllable is marked to indicate stressed or unstressed pronunciations.

> My mistress' eyes, are nothing like the Sun;
> Coral is far more red, than her lips' red:
> If snow be white, why then her breasts are dun;
> If hairs be wires, black wires grow on her head.
> I have seen Roses damasked, red and white,   5
> But no such Roses see I in her cheeks;
> And in some perfumes is there more delight
> Than in the breath that from my Mistress reeks.
> I love to hear her speak, yet well I know
> That music hath a far more pleasing sound: 10
> I grant I never saw a goddess go,
> My Mistress, when she walks treads on the grounds.
> And yet, by heaven, I think my love as rare
> As any she belied with false compare.

With very little variation, this poem's meter is iambic pentameter (five iambic feet), the most frequent and natural rhythm in English. Line 2 contains a trochee (coral), as does line 6 (I in). Such variety prevents boredom, a sing-song quality, and commands attention. In this sonnet, Shakespeare makes little attempt to provide alternate rhythm. The boring regularity suits the purposes of his parody.

Strong Stress Meter

Early Anglo-Saxon and Germanic rhythms featured only strong stresses or **accents,** each line containing four stressed syllables. *Beowulf* and some Middle English poetry exemplify accentual meter. Strong stress rhythms still appear in such children's rhymes as "Hickory Dickory Dock." Gerard Manley Hopkins, an English poet, developed sprung rhythm, a variant of accentual meter, in the nineteenth century. In his poems, each line begins with a stressed syllable that may be followed by one, two, or three unaccented syllables or that may stand alone.

Syllabic Rhythm

Poetry also may receive its beat from patterns of **counted syllables,** a method that disregards accentual feet. In this mode, the poet chooses any combination of syllables and repeats the pattern. In Sylvia Plath's "Metaphors," she writes a riddle in nine lines, each containing nine syllables:

> 12 3 4 5 6   7 8 9
> I'm a riddle in nine syllables

> 1 2 3 4 5 6 7 8   9
> An elephant, a ponderous house

This clever poem catalogues metaphors about pregnancy. Japanese haiku also represents a form in which syllabic count is fixed and traditional: five syllables; seven; five syllables. Remember Bashō's lyric, "On New Year's Day."

Free Verse

More than eighty years ago, Ezra Pound theorized about composing "in the sequence of the metrical phrase, not in the sequence of a metronome. . . ." Pound noted that some poets had abandoned traditional meters and explored natural rhythms, and he advocated **free verse** as an exciting alternative to traditional meters. Pound was not the first poet to recognize the value of this approach, but his description certainly provides an apt definition.

Free verse has no strict meter or line length. Traditional feet appear but in natural order. Such rising feet as iambs and anapests may occur together; such falling feet as trochees and dactyls may occur together. One of the most famous examples of free verse is Walt Whitman's great poem of love and death, "Out of the Cradle Endlessly Rocking" (Chapter 5). Read the first few lines without any attempt at analysis; follow the surge of the sea.

> Out of the cradle endlessly rocking,
> Out of the mocking-bird's throat, the musical shuttle,
> Out of the Ninth-month midnight,

Over the sterile sands and the fields beyond, where the child
    leaving his bed wander'd alone, bareheaded, barefoot,
Down from the shower'd halo, ...   5

Anaphora—the repetition of phrases—in this case, adverbial phrases as "Out of" and biblical rhythm characterize this poem.

Needless to say, poets change and combine all of these categories. Every culture's poetic tradition recognizes rhythm as essential to the enjoyment and meaning of poetry because rhythm remains central to all natural movement: the beating of the heart, the rocking of the cradle, the swaying of the sea.

The Reading/Writing Process: Poetry

A poem requires more than one reading. Several examinations of the text may be necessary simply to understand the general idea of the piece. Any work of art worth attention—a Verdi opera, a Rembrandt painting, Lady Murasaki's *The Tale of Genji*—becomes more exciting and more valuable after careful examination.

The second task in understanding poetry should become the constant use of a dictionary. The multiple meanings of words in each poem result from the compression that characterizes this form. Any dictionary will suffice, but the *Oxford English Dictionary* presents the most comprehensive history of the meanings of words in English. A reader also should have access to other reference books on world mythology and to religious texts.

Listen to the sounds of poetry. Since poems originated in song and in oral tradition, the meaning resides in the sounds as well as in the words. Read poems aloud, and begin with your favorites. In your interpretation, be animated. Muriel Rukeyser once stated that fear of poetry is a fear of emotion. The feelings and meaning already exist in a poem; they will express themselves. In any attempt to render the work as an oral interpretation, find the patterns of rhythm, grammar, and punctuation. Try not to swallow the last lines or important words.

The central purpose of the poem becomes the next question. To comprehend the poem's purpose, characterize the voice of the speaker and paraphrase the action of the poem. Ask yourself: Who is speaking? What is happening in the poem? The speaker in "Daddy" feels angry and concludes: "Daddy, Daddy, you bastard, I'm through." Victimized like the Jews in Nazi concentration camps, she transforms her father from God into a devil and later into a vampire. The purpose of the poem appears to reside in the speaker's desire to resolve her feelings about her father's death.

Ask, then, about the achievement of purpose. How is it achieved? Find the answer by describing the organization of ideas in the poem. In Plath's soliloquy, she begins with fairy tale; then she describes Daddy as "a bag full of God." Her speaker relates his roots, his language, to German history; and she contends that every woman wants a brutal father and that her speaker marries a "man in black with a Meinkampf look" (like Hitler) in order to recover her father. Finally, both men are symbolically killed, and Daddy becomes the villain in a Dracuula movie. The purpose is achieved. Readers find the poem powerful; not everyone likes it or believes that the speaker has resolved her losses.

When reading a poem, give it what Shakespeare called "passionate attention." Consider voice, tone, theme, setting, imagery, figures of speech, symbols, sounds, and rhythm. These elements of poetry will reveal the richness of meaning and evoke responses and evaluation.

Checklist for Reading and Writing about Poetry

1. What is the category for the poem? Is it lyrical, narrative, or dramatic?
2. Who is the speaker? What is the point of view? What is the speaker's attitude toward the subject? What details, images, and uses of language give information about the persona?
3. What is the tone, and does it change? Why?
4. What is happening in the poem?
5. What are the significant figures of speech? How do they function?
6. Describe the setting.
7. Which senses do the images evoke? Does the poem have one image or a series of images? Are the images related? Is there a pattern? What concepts do the images represent? How do the images support the theme? How effective is the use of imagery?
8. What is the central symbol? Are the symbols universal or private? How does symbolism function in the poem?
9. Does the poem refer to mythological figures? Does the poet change the myth?
10. Are there any allusions? What are the specific historical events, names, and/or literary references in the poem? How do the allusions work? Are they effective?
11. What sounds are important? Does the poem contain alliteration or assonance? How does the poet arrange the lines?
12. What is the rhythm of the poem? How does rhythm function?
13. Does the poem have a conventional form? Is the poem a sonnet, villanelle, or sestina? Is the poem an open form?
14. Is the poem effective? What is best about this work? What are its flaws? What is the final evaluation of this work?

STUDENT PORTFOLIO

Response to Wilfred Owen's "Arms and the Boy"

Ursula Lebris's work presents a model of an explication of Wilfred Owen's "Arms and the Boy" and evolves from a gloss of the text, from notes, from freewriting, and from several drafts. An explication offers a careful analysis of a poem. The methodology requires an examination of the work to gain knowledge of each of its aspects and parts, and it attempts to determine the relation of all of the elements in the poem to the meaning of the whole. Note that the first draft of "Let the Boy Try" is articulate and structured but also seriously underdeveloped and lacking in precision. The final draft overcomes these deficiencies and demonstrates outstanding mastery of this poem.

*Title refers to weapons, but also to physical arms, protection.
Why?*

(imperative) **Lebris's Gloss of Wilfred Owen's**   *allusion?*
    Is the speaker cruel?   *"Arms and the Boy"*   <u>*Arms and the*</u>
                                                             <u>*Boy*</u>

Let the boy try along this bayonet-blade
How cold steel is, and keen with hunger of blood;   *alliteration*
Blue with all malice, like a madman's flash; ?   *(effect?)*
And thinly drawn with famishing for flesh.   *Tone serious*
                                                                         or ironic?

Why? (Again imperatives)

Lend him to stroke these blind, blunt bullet-heads
Which long to nuzzle in the hearts of lads,
Or give him cartridges of fine zinc teeth,
Sharp with the sharpness of grief and death.

                         repetition—good!

For his teeth seem for laughing round an apple.   *Why animal*
There lurk no claws behind his fingers supple;   *imagery?*
And God will grow no talons at his heels,
Nor antlers through the thickness of his curls.)   *Consonants*
                                                          used
        Can't or won't?   *throughout*
        Does speaker believe in God?   *poem.*
                                                               (effect?)

Notes

bayonet—a weapon attached to the muzzle of a rifle
keen—eager and sharp
malice—intention to injure others
thinly drawn—a sword is "drawn" in order to fight; the shape of the bayonet is like a
    thin line; also can mean drawn in (i.e., with hunger)
famishing—suffering extreme hunger
zinc—bluish white metallic element
talons—claws, esp. of a bird of prey
antlers—the horns of a stag or deer

Personification—the bayonet is starving to death ("famishing for flesh") and capable of
emotion ("blue with all malice."). The bullets "long to nuzzle" and the cartridges feel "grief
and death." The poem is divided into three quatrains; the first two discuss human weapons;
the third introduces "natural" (animal) weapons. I don't think the poem uses a particular
meter, but in the first two quatrains each line ends with a heavily stressed syllable. I really
hear this when I read the poem aloud. The emphasis (e.g., on "blade" and "blood") makes the
weapons seem more threatening.

    Alliteration—the hard "b" sounds are like explosions and the "sh" sounds are like the
hiss of bullets through the air.

    What about consonance (half-rhyme)? The words seem to rhyme at first but there is a
jarring effect. Is this significant?

    Simile—"like a madman's flash." This is weird. Is a flash a kind of fit? I suppose like a
flash of anger (malice). Why blue? Metal can look bluish. Ok. Also the blue flash of gunfire.

Metaphor—"blind, blunt bullet-heads." They are blunt but they are not literally blind. The bullets are made to seem vulnerable like newly born animals, but all they want to do is kill young "lads." They do not see their targets; they are not meant to see.

Freewrite

I remember years ago taking my father's gun out of its case, even though I was forbidden to touch it. I wanted to see what all the fuss was about. So I can understand why a young boy would want to test the sharpness of a blade or play with bullets and cartridges. But I don't understand why the speaker in the poem wants him to. I feel frustrated by the poem overall. I like the way the weapons are described as being alive because it makes them seem even more threatening. But allowing a kid to play with things which intend to kill him is pretty sadistic. I suppose it's the final verse which really throws me. Ok, the boy's teeth are innocent compared to the "grief and death" of the cartridge teeth, but why does the poet then go on to talk about claws and talons and antlers? Maybe the claw is meant to represent the trigger of a gun. "And God will grow no talons at his heels"—is it that God can protect the boy, but won't? Why "talons"? I suppose that unlike animals the boy has no natural defenses. So "give him cartridges of fine zinc teeth" so that he can protect himself. But I think the poet is implying that to fight is to go against God—human beings are not naturally equipped for battle ("Thou shalt not kill"). Anyway the poem is deliberately shocking because Owen wants to show how vulnerable the young boy is. Let him touch these weapons, and maybe he will realize how sick war is before it is too late.

First Draft: "Let the Boy Try"

At first "Arms and the Boy" may seem to be a cruel, even sadistic, poem, for in the first two stanzas a young boy is encouraged to play with potentially lethal weapons. However, in the final stanza the poet's compassion for the young lives lost in World War I is revealed. Although the poem is only twelve lines long, Owen makes the reader vividly aware of the vulnerability of youth by using several techniques to emphasize the horror of war.

The technique of personification is perhaps the most important. The bayonet is not only some starving animal "famishing for flesh." This simile likens the blue flash of gunfire to the indiscriminate malice of a madman. The bullets are also personified but in a different way. Far from being evil madmen, they are like the new-born young of some animal which "long to nuzzle in the hearts of lads." This perverse image is intended to shock: Owen wants the reader to realize how sick and unnatural war is.

The disturbing images of the first two quatrains are intensified through alliteration. The repetition of consonants in "blade," "blood," "blind," and "blunt" creates a hard, explosive effect like that of gunfire, while the "s," "f," and "sh" sounds suggest the hiss of blades or bullets through the air. These sounds, along with the strongly stressed syllables at the end of each line, give the poem a threatening tone, as though the speaker is talking through clenched teeth. The use of half-rhyme combines certain key images in the reader's mind while giving a jarring effect that adds to the tension in these first two quatrains.

The sinister effects created by personification, alliteration, and meter disappear in the final quatrain. The boy's youthful innocence is shown in the comparison between his laughing teeth and the "grief and death" of the cartridge teeth and by references to "his fingers supple" and "the thickness of his curls." These images emphasize how vulnerable he is. The boy has no natural defenses, and since "God will grow no talons at his heels" perhaps it is necessary to "give him cartridges of fine zinc teeth" so that he may survive. However, this is no answer because the weapons intended to protect him are bent on his destruction.

The figurative language and the several possible readings of the final quatrain make "Arms and the Boy" a somewhat difficult poem. But despite this the reader cannot help but share the poet's compassion for the young victims of armed conflict. And there is a more hopeful interpretation—perhaps if the boy experiences the 'grief and death' of the weapons now, he will decide against becoming part of the horror and insanity that is war.

Final Draft: "Let the Boy Try"

"Arms and the Boy" is a short lyric poem of great power, comprising three quatrains and employing the rhyme scheme AABB CCDD EEFF. The alliteration used throughout is an important feature, as it creates a tension appropriate to the subject matter. At first "Arms and the Boy" may seem to be a cruel, even sadistic, poem, for in the initial two stanzas, the speaker encourages another to give potentially lethal weapons to a young boy. The final stanza, however, reveals the deep compassion felt for the young lives lost on the battlefield. As an officer in the First World War, Wilfred Owen witnessed firsthand the atrocities inflicted by men upon other men. Although the poem is only twelve lines long, he succeeds in making the reader vividly aware of the vulnerability of youth and of the horror and perversity of war.

It is significant that the poem begins with an imperative statement: "Let the boy try along this bayonet-blade/ How cold steel is, and keen with hunger of blood." The note of challenge introduced here quickly becomes one of menace as the description of the bayonet shifts rapidly from the literal "cold steel" to the figurative "keen with hunger of blood." This personification of the weaponry is one of the most important devices used in the poem, as it transforms them from inanimate objects into evil personalities with conscious intentions. The bayonet, "keen" in the sense of both eager and sharp, is not only like a starving animal but also "Blue with all malice, like a madman's flash." This startling simile takes the blue flash of gunfire and likens it to the indiscriminate malice of a psychopath, a telling indication of how Owen himself had come to view military action. Note that "blue" also suggests the hue of cold steel and the pallor of death.

The second quatrain continues the menacing tone with another imperative statement: "Led him to stroke these blind, blunt bullet-heads/Which long to nuzzle in the hearts of lads." Again personification is used, but this time in a slightly different way. Far from being like evil madmen, the bullets are described as being like the new-born young of some animal. Paradoxically, it is they who seem vulnerable rather than the young boy who is being allowed to play with them. The use of the casual, inoffensive "lads" here is also significant; it strikes an even more chilling note into the metaphor. The sexual connotations of "stroke" and "nuzzle," in conjunction with the phallic symbolism of the bayonet and the bullets, create a very unsettling undercurrent in an already disturbing poem. That instruments of death should be described in sexual, hence creative, terms does, however, highlight the poem's main theme—that war is something perverse and unnatural.

The second quatrain concludes with the third imperative statement: "Or give him cartridges of fine zinc teeth,/Sharp with the sharpness of grief and death." There is an important progression here in the level of involvement implied: the boy was initially allowed to touch the bayonet, was then lent bullets, and is now given cartridges. Although it is never made clear whom the speaker in the poem is addressing, there is a note of accusation here which implicates a far wider group of people than just a few soldiers on sentry duty. That the boy should be encouraged to play with weapons which actively seek to harm him is the key paradox in the poem, and it is this action which gives the final quatrain its power.

The sinister mood of the first two quatrains is intensified through a variety of poetic devices. The alliteration in "blood," "blade," "blind," and "blunt" creates a hard, exploding effect like that of gunfire, while the softer "s," "f," and "sh" sounds suggest the hiss of blades or bullets through the air. These sounds, along with the strongly stressed syllables at the end of each line, further contribute to the threatening tone, as though the speaker is talking through clenched teeth. Although the poem does not employ any fixed metrical pattern, the groups of unstressed syllables followed by several stressed syllables ("Blue with all malice, like a madman's flash") seem to mimic the stabbing motion of a bayonet. Certain key images are combined in the reader's mind through consonance ("blade"/"blood"), while the jarring effect of the half-rhyme adds an appropriate air of tension to the first eight lines.

In the final quatrain, however, the tone changes, and the sinister effects created by personification, alliteration, and meter disappear. Consonance is still used, but weak rhyme replaces the strong, heavily stressed rhyme of the first two quatrains, giving the last four lines a much more gentle mood. The boy's youthful innocence is shown in the comparison between his teeth "laughing round an apple" and the "grief and death" of the cartridge teeth. It is at this point that the disturbing images of the first two quatrains are justified, and the apparent sadism of the speaker is now revealed as compassion. The poet emphasizes the boy's vulnerability through references to "his finger supple" and "the thickness of his curls," while his complete lack of aggression is expressed through a series of negative statements ("no claws," "no talons," "nor antlers"). The boy, unlike animals, has no natural defenses, and since "God will grow no talons at his heels," perhaps it is necessary to "give him cartridges of fine zinc teeth" so that he may survive. But the meaning of the poem cannot be quite as straightforward as this, because the implication is that for any human being to fight, whether boy or man, is to go against God. The poem's power comes from its tragic irony—that the weapons meant to protect the boy are intent only on his destruction.

The several possible readings of the final quatrain, along with the figurative language used throughout, make "Arms and the Boy" a somewhat difficult poem. It is also a shocking poem, and intentionally so, for Owen seems to have had in mind an audience of complacent armchair patriots. The poem's message is, of course, not limited to his contemporaries of the First World War but is, regrettably, still very relevant today. The knowledge that Owen himself was killed on the front lines at the age of twenty-five adds another dimension to the poem, but even without this fact, the reader cannot help but feel sadness and anger at the young lives which were, and still are, wasted on the battlefield. But there is a more hopeful interpretation—perhaps if the boy experiences the "grief and death" of weaponry secondhand, he will decide against becoming involved in the horror and insanity that is war.

The gloss and notes identify and explore the grammar, figurative language, sounds, and meaning of Owen's poem. The writer focuses on the formal elements of "Arms and the Boy" and on the connection between form and meaning. The journal entry describes a personal experience of touching a weapon and reveals the writer's attitudes toward violence, toward the poem, and toward war. In the journal the initial ideas for the essay are formulated.

The first draft contains an excellent introduction. The explication analyzes personification and alliteration in the first two stanzas or quatrains. The third paragraph discusses the meaning of the last verse, and the conclusion is excellent.

In the final version of "Let the Boy Try," the writer enlarges the vision of the poem and announces her view in the introduction that seems slightly cluttered with the rhyme scheme and with a comment concerning alliteration. Although the paper is well organized, the introduction fails to focus exclusively on the writer's plan. The beginning, however, engages the reader's interest and expresses the major ideas. The paragraphs on the three quatrains are brilliantly conceived and brilliantly illustrated. The careful reading of imagery, significant figures of speech, grammatical constructions (imperative statements), sounds, tone, speaker, and theme result in an exemplary performance. The introduction of biographi-cal details about Wilfred Owen emphasizes the dramatic conclusion about the "insanity that is war."

[12]

Drama

In *As You Like It,* Shakespeare claims that "all the world's a stage." His declaration captures the deep connection between dramatic literature and life; and, by extension, Shakespeare captures the human fascination with all of the imaginative arts. Every person views his or her experience as dramatic; each views the world as a setting for personal and public actions and ideas, for triumphs and crises, for the ordinary and the sublime. Plays and other forms of literature, therefore, are not simply imitations of life; they represent much more. They order, concentrate, and elevate acts of interpretation that may be crucial to daily life.

Theater existed in human cultures long before recorded history. Societies developed dramatic rituals with characters, costumes, makeup, masks, settings, and special effects to inspire, educate, entertain, initiate, worship the gods, and control the environment. Music became the universal accompaniment. In the rain dance of the Dieri in Australia, for instance, a lodge was constructed; and then, at the end of the ritual, it was destroyed by dancers who knocked it down with their heads. This ceremony signified the elimination of clouds so that rain could fall. In the drama of the Great Serpent held to celebrate the March moon, the Hopis burned fires in the kivas (ceremonial chambers) that they built; a prop person smothered the blazes to produce smoke curtains at certain intervals to facilitate changes in scenes and actors. They also devised sets with painted backdrops containing holes through which symbols of dancing serpents appeared. These performances exemplify the complexity of the drama before the practice of writing scripts. Some early comedies appeared as animal impersonations. For entertainment, one society in the Philippines created a comic play in which a searcher for honey experienced many outrageous indignations. Religious expression was central to many of these productions, but secular concerns also provided subject matter and impetus for public spectacles. Except for written scripts, the elements of modern drama—setting, character, action, plot—existed in prototype in these ceremonies.

The oldest evidences of scripts for drama are the fifty-five Pyramid Texts (3000 B.C.) of Egypt. Written on the walls of tombs and pyramids, they contain stage directions and lines for different characters. The major theme of these dramas was resurrection. Scholars estimate that more than four thousand texts once existed, developed, perhaps, from rituals celebrating the return of spring. The Egyptians also performed coronation festival plays that hailed the crowning of a new monarch.

Forms of Drama

Greek Drama

Much of the theater, as it exists today, originated in Greece. Performances to honor gods or to commemorate rites of spring developed into formal productions. The most famous ancient Greek playwrights, Aeschylus (525–426 B.C.), Sophocles (496–406 B.C.), and Euripedes (c. 480–406 B.C.) composed plays for the annual Dionysian festivals. Presented to a selection group and later evaluated by judges, the plays—three tragedies and one comedy by each playwright—were performed in a semicircular theater.

Differences Between Tragedy and Comedy

Tragedy is a form of drama about fortunes and misfortunes, about disaster. Broadly defined, tragedy refers to dramatic representations of serious and significant actions that result in disaster for the protagonist or main character. In classical plays, these disasters happened to human beings with high position and great power such as Oedipus, Agamemnon, and Antigone. These characters possessed noble qualities and high passion. In tragedy, these attributes could not, however, save them from self-destruction or from fate.

Aristotle's classic theory in the *Poetics* (fourth century B.C.) describes tragedy as "the imitation of an action that is serious and also, as having magnitude, complete in itself," written in dramatic form and in poetic language. The tragic drama features "incidents arousing pity and fear, wherewith to accomplish the catharsis of such emotion." This **catharsis,** or purging of emotion, implies that the play will leave the audience or reader with feelings of relief or even exaltation. According to Aristotle, the play focuses on a **tragic hero** who has higher than ordinary moral values. This hero suffers a change or reversal of fortune, caused by his or her **tragic flaw, hamartia,** an "error in judgment." One common expression of hamartia in Greek drama is **hubris** or excessive pride.

According to Aristotle, every successful drama must possess the three unities: action, time and place. By this, Aristotle means that a drama must be organic and continuous to be considered serious and believable. The action, therefore, must arise out of a clearly stated conflict, and the time and place must be logical and consistent to the action. Rarely is there a change of place or time in Greek drama because it would disturb the unity of the whole play. Elaborate set changes and special effects were not employed by the ancient Greek dramatists. Because the sets were simple and the power of the plays was largely psychological, violence in Greek tragedies occurs off stage.

To assure unity of action, time, and place, playwrights often employ the chorus to create a transition from one scene to another. The chorus serves as spectators and commentators who elaborate on events as they unfold within the drama. They also provide background information and note the passage of time. The choral odes frequently are divided into strophes, recited as the chorus moves across the stage in one direction, and antistrophes, recited while moving in the opposite direction. In the tragedies, comic relief can be provided by the chorus.

Greek **comedy** first appeared in fertility rites and in the worship of Dionysus. From the time of Aristophanes (c. 448–c. 380 B.C.), the greatest Greek comic playwright, the form has been associated primarily with drama. Aristophanes wrote a variety of comedies combining lyrics, dance, satire, social comment, fantasy, and buffoonery. He attempted to reveal truth by exposing political deceit and pretense in such plays as *Lysistrata, The Wasps,* and *The Peace.* His more philosophical works include *The Clouds, The Frogs,* and *The Birds.* Aristotle distinguished comedy from tragedy by suggesting that it features ordinary people in amusing, everyday situations. It derives from the word **komos** or revel.

While both tragedies and comedies deliver moral messages, tragedies do so by focusing on the downfall of the tragic hero, a superior individual, whereas comedies portray the actions of an ordinary person. The behavior of the tragic hero often leads not only to his own downfall but to the disintegration of his society, whereas the comic hero is responsible for the reinstitution of social order. In tragedies catharsis consists of pity and fear, whereas the emotions in comedies inspire the feelings of sympathy and ridicule.

Few of the early tragedies or comedies still exist, but those that have survived convey the beauty and wisdom, the bawdy humor, the awe and wonder of classical Greece. They establish without a doubt the incredible influence of the Greek theater on world drama during the past two thousand years.

Roman Drama

Fifteen years after the death of Aristophanes, scenic entertainments to appease the gods began in Rome (364 B.C.). Like Greek theater, Roman drama also originated in ritual ceremonies and secular entertainment. The most famous Roman dramatist was Seneca (3 B.C.–A.D. 65), although his tragedies may never have been performed in public.

During the Roman Empire, comedy employed two kinds of subjects: one derived from Greek dramas and the other concerned Roman materials. Seventy works from the Roman-based comedies are recorded, but the two best known Roman dramatists who wrote comedies depended on Greek plays. They are Maccius Plautus and Publius Terentius Afer, known as Terence. Plautus created the form known as **tragicomedy** by referring to the unconventional mixture of kings and servants in his play *Amphitrus,* as *tragico-comedia.* Choosing elements of both comedy and tragedy, the playwright attempted to balance a conflict of vision. The extant plays of both Plautus and Terence greatly influenced Elizabethan theater and, in turn, modern theater. Mime and pantomime, which developed as elaborate performances separate from dramas, also represent an original contribution of the Romans to the art.

English Drama

The theater did not die with the fall of Rome. Until the twelfth century, it survived in public entertainment and in religious performances, in particular, in cycles and in noncyclical plays. In England, Elizabethan drama developed from religious plays performed at medieval festivals during the twelfth and thirteenth centuries. These **mystery plays,** as they were called, presented Biblical stories—Noah and the ark, Jonah and the whale, the passion of Jesus—in town squares or in churches. As the dramas grew in popularity, platforms, called **pageants,** were wheeled from city to city; and the plays often expanded into a series that was enacted over a period of several days.

The **miracle play,** another dramatic genre related to the mystery play, presented saints' lives and miracles. It often centered on the divine acts of the Virgin Mary. A famous cycle of forty-two plays, the *Miracles de Notre Dame,* is extant in France. Other European examples are the German *Marienklage (The Complaint of Mary),* and the Dutch *Mariken Van Nieumaghen (Mary of Nieumaghen).* In England, where the cult of the Virgin Mary did not flourish, most miracle plays dramatized the lives of saints.

During the fourteenth and fifteenth centuries, **morality plays** allegorized Christian values. Characters symbolized Christian virtues and vices. The most famous play, *Everyman* (1500), presented positive and negative human qualities in a single representative figure whose conflicts mirrored all life processes.

In the sixteenth century, Greek and Roman drama began to influence English theater. Secular plays became popular as interest in religious dramatizations waned. At first the new plays, based on classic Greek models, focused on murder and revenge. Roman dramatists, Seneca and Menander, also influenced the writers of these plays. Professional actors performed plays in courtyards and later in theaters. Audiences were composed of both educated and illiterate spectators.

From the defeat of the Spanish Armada in 1588 until 1642 when all theaters were closed during the Civil War, the English theater reached its highest development through the genius of such playwrights as Christopher Marlowe, Ben Jonson, Thomas Kyd, Thomas Dekker, John Webster, and William Shakespeare. In *Tamburlaine* and *Dr. Faustus,* Marlowe (1564–93) invented blank verse, or unrhymed iambic pentameter, a rhythm that became the dominant meter of Elizabethan drama.

The greatest genius of the reigns of Queen Elizabeth I and James I was William Shakespeare. A writer of comedies, tragedies, and histories, Shakespeare was the best of many astonishingly fine dramatists. A member of the Lord Chamberlain's company (1594), he joined a group that constructed the Globe Theater (1599), a most successful structure, small enough to fit into the orchestra area of the Greek Theater of Dionysius. At most, the Globe could have accommodated two thousand people.

The stage was a platform that projected into the audience. In the rear was an area with a curtain for intimate scenes; above was a balcony. There was a trap door for such purposes as the gravedigger scene in *Hamlet,* and ghosts descended on ropes from a canopy. The theater had no painted sets, and props were minimal. As in Greek drama, all actors were male. Elizabethan theaters were designed like courtyards. Six hundred "groundlings" sat or stood in the open yards. More privileged spectators occupied tiers of covered balconies.

In *Hamlet,* the prince lectures the actors who perform the play-within-the-play and defines the purpose of drama: "to hold, as 'twere, the mirror up to nature." This blossoming of dramas in England focused on imitation of reality. At the same time, the performances of plays in the open theaters created a wonderful and wild public life—real entertainment.

The excitement of the Renaissance renewed interest in drama in Italy, France, and Germany; and audiences enjoyed many kinds of theater. No great dramatic literature emerged during the Renaissance in these countries. However, innovations in theater architecture influenced the development and form of modern drama: horseshoe seating, the **proscenium** arch (a frame enclosing the stage area behind which the front curtain hangs), painted sets, indoor lighting, and spectacular costumes.

In Spain, Lope de Vega and Calderón wrote spectacular plays, the most famous in Spanish literature. More than two thousand actors are listed in public records, and public playhouses in Spain developed in the same patterns as English theaters. They accommodated the same kind of enthusiastic audiences. Complete professionalization of theater and establishment of repertory groups represent significant accomplishments during this period.

In the seventeenth century, French theater was greatly influenced by Greek and Roman drama. During this time, the most significant drama was written by Molière, Racine, and Corneille. The actors developed revolutionary performing styles, and the first national European theater, the Comèdie Francaise, began.

During the Restoration in England (after 1688), the great achievement became the comedy of manners—hard, brilliant, accomplished. The major playwrights were George Etherege, William Wycherley, and William Congreve. In the eighteenth century in England, theater did not occupy a primary place. Oliver Goldsmith and Richard Brinsley Sheridan are notable exceptions. The art of acting, however, reached new heights; the best performer was the legendary David Garrick. This period also produced the **picture frame stage** and very large theaters.

On the European continent, Voltaire and Diderot in France and Goethe and Lessing in Germany wrote memorable and classic works. Dramatic theory and criticism received great attention. Many great actors emerged, and the number of theaters increased. Spectacular effects appeared in stage design. All of these developments received more attention in the nineteenth and twentieth centuries.

Nineteenth- and Twentieth-Century Drama

In Europe and in North America, three major movements in drama have developed in the last century: Realism, Theater of the Absurd, and Symbolist Drama.

Realism

At the end of the nineteenth century, writers began to create realistic dramas that presented accurate versions of the world and of human nature, of ordinary people leading ordinary lives. In dramatic literature, realism avoided all that was visionary and unbelievable. These dramatists chose serious, often tragic themes and well-developed characters who did not possess special status. They reacted against the spirit of Romanticism in England and in Europe, which emphasized the emotions and imagination above reason and intellect. They also reacted against melodrama, plays that depend on spectacle, action, and extravagant emotional appeal.

Realism, as it is defined and recognized today, is primarily the invention of Henrik Ibsen, a nineteenth century Norwegian playwright (see *A Doll's House* in Chapter 5). This dramatic movement corresponded to great cultural upheavals—the Napoleonic Wars, the Industrial Revolution, the rise of the middle class. People longed for critical analysis of social institutions.

In Russia, Anton Chekhov, Leo Tolstoy, and Maxim Gorki wrote realistic plays and fiction. In France, Émile Zola and Guy de Maupassant provided analysis of a movement that they called naturalism. The bases for this theory were Herbert Spencer's twist on Charles Darwin's idea of the survival of the fittest and Karl Marx's contention that economic conditions shape human life.

Ibsen influenced George Bernard Shaw, August Strindberg, and, subsequently, an entire generation of famous dramatists. Ibsen's work deeply affected Stanislavsky's teaching of method acting. Many North American playwrights—Eugene O'Neill,

Arthur Miller, and Tennessee Williams—adopted fundamental tenets of realism. August Wilson's *The Piano Lesson* (Chapter 6) is an example of realist drama.

Theater of the Absurd

The notion that life is absurd is not new, but it has acquired more specific meaning in the past century. Philosophers have defined the purposeless role of humans in a purposeless universe as absurd—mathematically, a *surd* is that which cannot be expressed in finite terms of ordinary numbers or quantities. It is in this mathematical sense that the philosophy of the absurd has been defined (see Camus' "The Myth of Sisyphus" in Chapter 9). The theatrical phrase was coined by Martin Esslin, who wrote *The Theatre of the Absurd* in 1961. Scholars trace the lineage of this form from Roman mime plays to the comic techniques of medieval and Renaissance drama, especially commedia dell'arte, comedy originating in the Italian Renaissance that featured improvisation, stock characters, and masks. Finally, Esslin cites the influence of August Strindberg and of Bertolt Brecht.

In the 1950s, this concept was expressed in a number of plays that focus on characters struggling with existential angst, anxiety, and anguish. The human condition is presented as essentially meaningless. The plays have no formal logic and lack conventional structure. The following dramatists and works represent this tradition: Samuel Beckett, *Waiting for Godot, Endgame;* Jean Genet, *Les Negres* (The Blacks), *Le Balcon* (The Balcony); Eugene Ionesco, *La Leçon* (The Lesson), *La Cantatrice Chauve* (The Bald Soprano), *Rhinoceros;* Harold Pinter, *The Birthday Party, The Homecoming;* Edward Albee, *The Zoo Story* and *The Sandbox.* David Ives's *Sure Thing* (Chapter 7) is a comic representation of Theater of the Absurd.

Symbolist Drama

With the advent of realism, twentieth-century theater relinquished many traditional sources of dramatic tension—poetic language, symbols, illusions, such as the ghost in *Hamlet.* Like symbols in poetry and fiction, the actions and characters in symbolist drama refer to eternal ideas, abstract concepts. In such a play, a woman might encounter an abandoned child. The situation would not be presented as criticism of a particular society. Instead, the event might indicate the woman's discovery of her real and autonomous self; it might mean that humans are always abandoned in life.

Most plays contain symbols, but most dramatists do not intend that all action be interpreted as symbolic. **Symbolist dramas,** however, may feature many traditional poetic symbols and allegorical names, and they employ dreamlike atmospheres. This mode traces its roots to Kabuki theater, to Nō plays, to morality plays, and to the folk dramas of William Butler Yeats and of John Millington Synge. Contemporary Chinese American playwright David Henry Hwang has written such symbolist dramas as *The Sound of a Voice* and *M. Butterfly* (Chapter 7).

Performance Drama

Performance drama has its roots in such diverse traditions as the oral narratives told by African griots and Native American seers; as the soliloquies of Shakespearean drama; as the surreal cabaret performances of the Dadaists and Surrealists of the 1920s (e.g.,

Andre Breton); as the monologues of stand-up comics; and as the performance art of the 1970s, which drew on forms of different media and often incorporated lighting, music, visuals, dance, and written text.

Performance drama combines elements of drama, poetry, and the short story as the genre also breaks down the boundaries between art forms. The central figure is a speaker, a solo artist who often creates an autobiographical persona or impersonates a collection of characters. The speaker presents interior monologues—a combination of inner thoughts, remembrance, and, often, social commentary. The approach is open and personal; the audience feels as if the persona is conversing in an intimate way with the public or letting the audience overhear his/her inner thoughts. The structure of the drama is open-ended and fluid. The script does not adhere to traditional forms of narrative or of dramatic structure, often following a stream-of-consciousness logic and using symbolism, dream, and anecdote to convey state of mind, character, and theme. The script, sometimes spontaneously improvised, also may draw on such poetic techniques as imagery, symbolism, and figurative language. One element of the form resembles the structure of the modern short story, created by James Joyce. The speaker often experiences a realization—an epiphany—by the end of the monologue, as does a protagonist in Joyce-ian short fiction. The performance also may include décor, costumes, settings, music, art, graphics, lighting, video—elements of other art forms. Finally, performance texts challenge orthodox notions of drama because they may be performed in such alternative spaces as cafes, coffeehouses, or art galleries instead of theaters, and therefore, attract public audiences who may not attend theatrical performances.

Like other forms of literature, the work also conveys a message—oftentimes a critique of everyday life or a vision of social protest. Some performance artists are noted for their comic, outrageous, or iconoclastic productions that challenge societal norms of appropriate behavior and North American cultural and social values. For example, in 1981, Laurie Anderson, combining elements of music, narrative, and visuals, created an eight-hour montage of song, story, and spectacle that critiqued the media culture of North America. In another performance scenario, "Constant State of Desire (1986)," Karen Finlay rebels quite vividly against the constraints of urban domesticity. Two important performance artists whose work expands the narrative and dramatic possibilities of the form are Spalding Gray, who in "Swimming to Cambodia" explores autobiographical landscapes of his life, and Eric Bogosian, who in several performance pieces critiques the character of men in America and what he views as an apathetic American society.

Anna Deavere Smith's *Twilight Los Angeles: 1992* portrays many characters who witnessed the Los Angeles riots. Her monologues, based on interviews, give readers multiple perspectives and visions of this moment in history (Chapter 8).

Film and Television

An important twentieth-century development that influences public interest in theater is the moving image—film. The advent of moving pictures and of television has changed the viewing habits of human beings forever.

Film

Film shares many characteristics with drama: setting, plot, character, conflict, dialogue, images, symbolism, and theme. The image adds new dimensions to language on screen; in drama, the work retains a more powerful position. Film, like drama, requires conventions. For example, movies generally have music in the background—a score that helps to determine tone or mood.

One advantage of film is the capacity to change settings and locations. Since movies are shot in small scenes and out of sequence, the screenwriter can defy all of the dramatic unities. A film can span centuries and continents. Now digital imaging and computer software can create virtual realities, computer-morphed images, and special effects.

Like fiction writers, screenwriters have enormous freedom with point of view. The camera lens can determine viewer response: a wide-angle lens gives a panoramic shot, a normal-angle lens what we can imagine as a realistic view, and a telephoto lens, a close-up, detailed image. A close-up can create the illusion of intimacy just as a first-person narrator in a novel may achieve the same effect. A wide angle provides distance, objectivity, and a sweeping view. A zoom can accomplish both purposes. Not only the camera lens but also the point of view from which the subject is filmed results in a change of perspective; you can manipulate point of view through camera angles. A high-angle shot has the scene viewed from above and from a distance, an eye-level angle from normal viewing distance, a low-angle shot from below, and a bird's eye view from above the subject. The camera also can film a shot from the perspective or gaze of a character in the film; this kind of shot creates a particular point of view. Films depend on cinematography, lighting, and music to create effects and to heighten the visual drama. For example, a wide-angle shot of helicopters in the air accompanied by Richard Wagner's "Ride of the Valkyries" playing in the background in Francis Ford Coppola's *Apocalypse Now* gives the viewer an idea of the idiocy of war and of the powerful exhilaration of battle before it subsides inescapably into horror. A close-up of Martin Sheen's face as he witnesses his friend's severed head renders the terror personal and human.

Checklist for Writing about Film

1. What is the function of the setting and props? Of the objects in the film?
2. Who are the main subjects? The main characters? Are they developed? What role do the minor characters play in the film?
3. How does the film handle plot? Are there flashbacks? Flash-forwards?
4. How does the director use composition (i.e., the placement of the image in the frame)?
5. How do the lens types, shots, and camera angles develop the story?
6. What is the impact of the cinematography?
7. Does the editing seem to be smooth?
8. What is the effect of the lighting? Is it dark? Is it soft?
9. What is the impact of the music? Does the music heighten the action? Develop character? Develop the theme?
10. How do all the elements of the film develop the theme?
11. Evaluate the film. Consider screenplay, acting, directing, editing, and cinematography.

Similarities and Differences Between Drama and Film

The elements that will be compared are those that are defined in terms of the "mise-en-scene" of a text, a term from drama that means those elements that the director manipulates to create a unified work. These elements include the following: scene, subjects, story, perspective, continuity, visuals, sound effects and music, symbolism, verbal or visual impact, and relationship with an audience. Understanding the similarities and differences between these two forms will help you to analyze and to write an essay about each genre or an essay comparing a dramatic and a filmed version of a text. For example, your instructor may ask you to compare two versions of *The Piano Lesson:* the original text and the film version.

The following chart provides you with some points of comparison and contrast between drama and film.

Drama	Film
Scene	
Similarities:	
Scene—physical location of a play	Settings where film occurs
Stage sets	Stage sets
Illusion of reality on stage	Illusion of reality
Symbolic role of scenes	Symbolic role of setting
Differences:	
Constructed sense of reality	On location sets
Illusion of reality on stage	Ability to have multiple settings and locations
	Visual impact of settings to create images, moods, and theme
	More expansive sense of setting
Subjects	
Similarities:	
Main characters	Main characters
Round or flat characters	Round or flat characters
Major and minor protagonists	Major or minor protagonists
Character foils	Character foils
Character revealed through appearance, gesture, action, dialogue, and relationships with others	Character revealed through appearance, gesture, action, dialogue, and relationships with others
Differences:	
Emphasis on character revelation through monologues and dialogue	More emphasis on physical presence on screen
Story	
Similarity:	
Script includes setting, characters, plot conflict, dialogue, and symbolism	Script includes setting, characters, plot, conflict, dialogue, and symbolism
Differences:	
Concentrated plot line	Multiple plot lines; ability to develop simultaneous stories through split-screen editing

Drama	**Film**
Stage directions may include instructions for character gestures, lighting, and music	Shooting script includes shots, camera placement, and angles

Perspective

Differences:

Limited ability to manipulate perspective	Perspective established by use of camera lens, shots, and by camera angles
Perspective dependant on use of parts of the stage (i.e., foreground and background); different sets; staging—movement of actors on the stage and in parts of the theater (i.e., actors speaking from balconies in the theater)	

Continuity

Similarity:

Continuity determined by sequence of plot and textual editing to create unity	Continuity determined by sequence of plot

Difference:

Plot devices, structural elements, and dialogue create unity	Editing of shots and film sequences to create unity; cuts to create transitions from one shot to the next

Visuals

Similarity:

Visuals include stage sets, costumes, props, and lighting	Visuals include settings, stage sets, props, costumes, and lighting

Difference:

Effects emanate from physical placement on stage and impact of lighting	Cinematography includes kind of film, texture of film, lighting, color, light and shadow

Sound Effects and Music

Similarity:

Use of sound effects and background music to create mood and theme	Use of sound effects and music to create mood and theme

Differences:

Limited use of sound effects	Heightened use of sound effects and music; more continuous use of sound effects and music
	Use of music as an underlying thread to develop themes and to unify work

Symbolism

Similarity:

Elements of setting, props, costumes, and lighting serve as symbols and develop the meanings of the work	Elements of setting, props, objects in film, characters' dress, and lighting serve as symbols and develop the meanings of the work

Difference:

Dialogue creates irony and symbolism	Cinematography and editing create symbolism

Drama	Film
Theme	
Similiarity:	
All elements develop the themes of the work	All elements develop the themes of the work
Verbal/Visual Medium	
Difference:	
Primarily a verbal medium; impact based on staged version of a text	Primarily a visual medium; impact arises from visual images, from cinematography
Impact on Audience	
Difference:	
Play's impact is from live performance and interaction with an audience	Audience is in a darkened theater, watching controlled moving images on a screen
Performances of a play may change based upon audience's reaction	The audience is passive
	The medium suggests larger-than-life images

Television

Television shares many techniques with film; the great difference, of course, is the size of the screen. Because the viewing area is confined, television employs more close-up shots. Programs are shaped by segments and by commercials, and series require twenty-six episodes each season. These constraints determine character, theme, conflict, and quality.

With the expansion of cable and pay per view television, specialty networks—news, music, science fiction, cartoons, movie, sports—make the possibilities endless. At the same time, Bruce Springsteen still sings that he has "fifty-seven channels and nothing to watch." Surely, more exciting productions will come from artists in the future as they explore the full potential of television.

Elements of Drama

Character

Imagined people stand at the center of almost all of the forms of literature. Anyone who appears in a work is called a **character,** a term chosen carefully for its meaning—those innate faculties that give a person identity and that distinguish him or her from others. Plays present a special framework for characters because the genre differs from fiction and from poetry since most dramas function without narration and narrators.

The *major* characters tend to be round, dynamic, and well-developed, whereas *minor* characters remain flat, static, and slightly developed. Often a character appears in order to illuminate, double, or contradict a main character—a foil. Because they are easily recognized types, some characters are known as **stereotypes** or **stock** characters.

In commedia dell'arte, for example, the harlequin always plays the same part—always acts in a predictable manner. All of the characters in this kind of drama are stereotypes by definition. This comfortable recognition allows the playwright to create characters easily.

The personae in most plays, however, grow and change; the development of the characters leads to important knowledge concerning the meaning of the drama. For example, at the end of *Antigone,* Creon recognizes his responsibility for the tragedy that has ruined both his life and the city of Thebes.

Soliloquy, Monologue, and Dialogue

A character's language reveals his or her feelings, values, situation, and/or beliefs. In a **soliloquy**—a long speech by one character, the speaker communicates special information to the audience. Think of Hamlet's famous words on suicide, "To be or not to be." Through this eloquent aside, the audience learns of Hamlet's pain as he contemplates his duty to exact revenge for his father's death, a pain that makes life unbearable. Hamlet resents his situation, his mother, his uncle; he feels increasingly angry, desperate, sad, and suicidal. Indeed, he cannot decide on an adequate response to the unreasonable demands of life. Unlike a soliloquy, a **monologue** may be addressed to other characters as well as to the audience. It serves the same function; it permits an extended discussion of information, attitudes, or ideas by one character.

Most words in a play, however, are spoken between two characters. This exchange, called **dialogue,** demonstrates agreements, conflicts, relationships, differing or similar beliefs and motives between personae. Dialogue becomes the main element in the play for the development of character, plot, and theme. Consider the following lines from Ibsen's *A Doll's House.* At the beginning of the play, the dialogue between Torvald Helmer and Nora Helmer and the language Helmer uses to describe his wife suggest his treatment of her as a child and his objectification of her, her acquiescence at that point in her role, and the dynamics of their relationship:

Helmer: . . . Is that my little sky-lark chirruping out there?
Nora: . . . Yes, it is.
Helmer: Is that my little squirrel frisking about?
Nora: Yes!
Helmer: When did my little squirrel get home?
Nora: Just this minute . . .

Action

Every character, played by an actor, not only speaks, but also acts and reacts to others and to events. A character may portray motivation through action. For example, in Act I of *A Doll's House* (Chapter 5), Nora's interaction with her children displays her concern for them and her attachment to them.

The audience also can learn about characters when they refuse to act according to normal expectations. In "Trifles," Mrs. Hale and Mrs. Peters do not reveal their knowledge about the Wright murder to the sheriff. They realize that Mrs. Wright was motivated to commit such violence by actions which the men would consider trifles (Chapter 7). In this play, Susan Glaspell artfully portrays character through *in*action.

Much of the interaction in drama becomes quite complicated. The tension in *A Doll's House* builds because of Krogstad's veiled threats to Nora and his speeches to Helmer, hinting at disaster. The subplot involving Krogstad's apparent desire to redeem himself also intensifies the conflict between Nora and Krogstad and Nora and her husband.

Plot

The **plot** in a dramatic or narrative work is the structure of its actions, ordered to achieve emotional and aesthetic effects. This definition becomes complicated by the relationship between plot and character. The actions, both verbal and physical, are performed by characters; they provide the vehicle through which characters reveal their moral and personal traits. Plot is more, much more, than the "story" of a play, which is a simple synopsis of the temporal events. Only when the story becomes related to discussions of relationships and organization of actions in order to produce meaning does it become part of the definition of plot.

Numerous patterns for plots exist; each depends on the mode of drama and its purposes. Is it tragedy? comedy? romance? satire? ritual? melodrama? Whatever the genre, all plots share certain elements in traditional forms of dramatic literature.

In any play, the interest centers on the protagonist—the hero or heroine. Usually this character struggles against an opponent or enemy, the character designated as the antagonist. The relationship between them becomes the conflict. Many, but not all, plays contain one or more conflicts. In *A Doll's House*, one central conflict is precipitated by the struggle between Nora, the protagonist, and Krogstad, the antagonist in the drama. It is from Krogstad that she has received the illegal loan that functions as the dark secret in the play. As the enemy, he propels the action of the play, blackmailing and pressuring Nora with the hope that she will prevail upon her husband to save Krogstad's position at the bank. The more important dynamic is the tension between Nora and Helmer that intensifies as the work progresses and takes over as the central conflict in the drama in Act III. This conflict centers on their relationship and Nora's realization of her need for independence and her desire to shed her traditional social role as a woman. Often the protagonist struggles in conflict with fate or circumstance; often the conflict resides within the main character. In *A Doll's House* several levels of conflict exist. Nora struggles with other characters and deals with the workings of fate and circumstance (that bring Krogstad to her doorstep) as well as her own inner, psychic turmoil.

Sometimes a character concocts a scheme that entraps another person, one who is naive, trusting, and vulnerable. This scheme is called intrigue. In *Othello*, although Othello is not naive, his vulnerability makes him susceptible to Iago's manipulations, and he becomes convinced of Desdemona's infidelity.

As the audience or reader begins to follow and to sympathize with characters, the plot builds **suspense** about its events and resolutions. If the action contradicts readers' expectations, the result becomes **surprise.** The relationship of suspense and surprise provides the essential dynamism in a play and must be predicated on the effectiveness of motive and of previous action.

A traditional plot has what Aristotle called **unity of action,** by which he meant that every part or event becomes necessary and integral to the whole and that the loss of any part destroys the whole. In *Antigone,* the recognition of Antigone as the guilty person sought by Creon, Creon's inflexibility, Haimon's betrothal to Antigone, and Creon's final change of heart, incident by incident, clue by clue, exemplifies this quality (Chapter 8).

Other plays include **double plots,** as in Elizabethan drama. Such plays involve a second story that becomes fascinating on its own merits and that enlarges understanding of the main plot. Such a **subplot** exists in *Othello* in the relationship between Othello and Desdemona (Chapter 7). Plays may have multiple subplots.

In the traditional definition of plot, a sequence of events provides a beginning that establishes the situation and introduces characters, a middle that complicates the actions and develops characters, and an end that completes the action. The apex of a play is the moment the conflict reaches its highest point of tension for the protagonist. In *Technique of the Drama* (1863), Gustav Freytag describes plot in a configuration known as Freytag's Pyramid. According to this schema, a plot begins with rising action; this rising action reaches a **climax** or **apex** for the hero. Then comes the crisis. Then the falling action leads to a catastrophe, as in the deaths of the main characters. This catastrophe may also be called the *denouement,* for not all plays end in tragic circumstances. Contemporary dramas often deliberately defy expectations of conventional plots, and some attempt to eliminate plot entirely. For example, in Laurence Carr's *Scrabble and Tabouli,* we do not know definitely what will come of the two main characters' relationship. Will they establish an intimate relationship? We are left only with their initial meeting and decision to have dinner again. The denouement is open ended.

A Doll's House has a plot configuration that would delight Freytag. In Act I the basic conflicts of the play are established. We learn that Nora borrowed money to take her husband on a trip to Italy that saved his life and that she never told her husband about the loan. We also learn that she forged her father's signature on the loan because women at the time could not take out loans in their own names and because she didn't want to bother her father when he was ill. Krogstad blackmails Nora and demands that Nora ask Helmer to save his job at the bank once Helmer becomes bank manager. The tension between Nora and Krogstad escalates in Act II, with Nora trying to persuade her husband to keep Krogstad at the bank. In Act III, at the **apex** of the drama, Nora confesses her transgressions to Helmer who rejects her and expresses his complete contempt for her behavior but then forgives her once he learns that Krogstad has ripped up the I.O.U. The crisis, the final confrontation between husband and wife during which Nora realizes that she has been a "doll wife," leads to the denouement, Nora's decision to leave home. The denouement is one of the most discussed endings in a drama.

Setting

In drama, **setting** differs greatly from other forms of literature because of the imperative for performance. In stage directions and in dialogue, the dramatist describes the place and time for the play. A designer creates stage sets that suggest the background for each scene. Shakespeare, for example, places Othello in Venice. The stage adds a dimension to drama that other forms of literature lack—visual and auditory images, live action, and spatial and temporal realities.

Props, scenery, costumes, and lights can change as the play progresses; but the setting on stage remains both limited and central to all productions. For instance, the set for *Trifles* should indicate the poverty of the modest cottage, a farmhouse in a barren, rural area. Unlike fiction writers and poets, the playwright does not describe place in great detail, and he or she leaves much more to the imagination or to the stage.

Symbolism

In dramatic literature, **symbols** often are not subtle. They appear on stage as visual reminders of their central place in the meaning of the play. In "Trifles," one of the symbols, the dead canary, suggests the husband's cruelty and Minnie Wright's caged and broken state of self.

Irony

Dramatic irony appears in a play or in fiction when a situation or action becomes apparent to the audience but remains unknown to a character or to characters. Consequently, the persona acts in ignorance and often inappropriately. The Greek tragedians, whose conflicts and stories were already known to their audiences, based their works on a constant use of this technique.

Other kinds of irony:

- **Verbal irony** is a statement in which the meaning is different from the message that is expressed. Jonathan Swift's "A Modest Proposal" for eating children as a solution to the problem caused by the potato famine in Ireland depends greatly on this device.
- **Structural irony** sustains double meaning throughout the work. In drama, this technique requires a naive protagonist; in fiction an unreliable narrator often serves this purpose.

Theme

The themes of a play are not its subjects, but rather its central idea or ideas. One theme of *Antigone* concerns the idea of individual moral responsibility versus obedience to authority. Should Antigone obey the dictates of conscience or submit to Creon's decree that her brother remain unburied? This question directs the action. The theme centers on the tension between an individual code of ethics and a socially sanctioned moral code.

The Reading/Writing Process: Drama

Interpreting drama begins with impressions about a play. Feelings often provide guidelines to intellectual analysis and responses. Reread the drama and examine its parts—character, plot, theme—to determine their relationship to the whole. Grasping the wholeness in a drama depends on looking carefully at all of its elements. Consider characters and their development; consider the conflicts and their complications and possible resolutions. Consider how themes emerge. Evaluate how well the play comes together.

Take notes, and be careful to pay close attention to stage directions, prologues, epilogues, and important quotations. Determine the play's meaning, and assess its ability to force a reader or audience to face matters of enduring value.

Checklist for Reading and Writing about Drama

1. Does the play have a **narrator?** How does this character function? Is he or she reliable?
2. Are the main characters fully developed? How do they change? What actions or words demonstrate such change? How do minor characters function in the play? What do you learn about characters from the dialogue of others? Is the character sympathetic? How would an audience react? What different interpretations of these characters are possible?
3. What is the central conflict? How is it resolved? Are there subplots? Which acts or scenes represent the **rising action?** Identify the **climax.** Is there suspense? Which acts or scenes represent the falling action? How are the **subplots** resolved?
4. How does the **dialogue** contribute to the **plot?** How do characters advance the plot or plots? How does **setting** function in relation to plot? Does offstage action contribute to the development of conflict? How?
5. Does the play contain **irony?** What kinds of irony are present? Is the irony effective?
6. Are there symbols that suggest the theme?
7. What information about production is included in the stage directions? What information does the play give about costume, set, lighting, sound effects?
8. What are central themes? What are other significant issues? How do characters and conflicts illuminate themes?
9. Discuss conflict, character, language, theme in relation to the total effect of the play. Does it work? What does it mean?
10. What is the best feature of the play? What is the weakest feature of the play? What is the final evaluation?

STUDENT PORTFOLIO

Character Analysis of Nora in
Henrik Ibsen's <u>A Doll's House</u>

Jenny Binnie, a student in Profesor Mary Fakler's class, was asked to write a character analysis essay about Nora in Henrik Ibsen's *A Doll's House.* What follows are the student's first draft with both her notations and changes and the teacher's comments; the teacher's feedback in the form of a letter to Jenny; and the final version of the paper. The first draft includes too much plot summary, does not have a clear argumentative thesis—a clear main impression of Nora's character—and is somewhat repetitive. The final draft shows vast improvement. The introduction and the thesis are clearer and more insightful. Having a stronger argumentative thesis made the paper easier to follow as a whole. In addition, precise details and quotes from the play were applied clearly to each of the main claims. With each example of textual evidence, Jenny further explained and supported her ideas. Her conclusion reinforces her claim.

Jenny Binnie

First Draft: Nora's Quest for Learning

In the beginning of Henrik Ibsen's play, *A Doll's House*, Nora Helmer seems like a wonderful mother. She plays with her three children, and she likes to spend time with them. ~~The children love their mother, and she dotes upon them.~~ At the end of the play, *though,* Nora leaves her *family.* ~~husband and consequently, the children.~~ She does not even say good-bye to the children, but tells Torvald, her husband, "I'll often think of you and the children. . . . " (Act 3, 1. 369). It sems *as if* ⟨like⟩ Nora simply decides to give up on motherhood and leave her children to be raised by their nurse, Anne. However, there is more to the story than this. Nora ~~has been~~ *is* in debt to a man named Nils Krogstad, but she ~~has hid~~ *hides* this debt from Torbald because she knows it will deeply upset him. *discovers this and the fact that* When Torvald ~~finds out that Nora has not only borrowed money, but that~~ she has also committed forgery, Torvald tells ~~Nora~~ *her* that she is not fit to be a mother. Although Nora's name is cleared, and she is no longer in danger, Nora realizes that she has been living with a veil over her eyes. Once she understands that she has never had a mind of her own, she decides to leave home. ⟨She agrees with Torvald that she is not fit to be a mother right now, because she herself knows nothing of life.⟩ She says [about her children], "I know they are in better hands than mine. As I am now, I can never be anything to them" (Act 3,1. 357-358). Thus, Nora does not abandon her children, but she leaves them to further her own education, in order to become a better person.

Thesis?

Possible Thesis?

You need paragraphs. OK? ¶ Nora could not abandon her children, because she loves them and is willing to sacrifice for them. The fact that Nora feels that love can demand sacrifices is clearly portrayed when Nora hopes for Torvald to take the blame for her forgery. She thinks that Torvald loves her, and so she expects him to want to sacrifice his honor to protect her. On a smaller scale, Nora's ideal love is portrayed through the way she treats her children. The play takes place, before, during, and after Christmas. Nora and Torvald are discussing the fact that they would have more money this Christmas than they had the year before, because Torvald was promoted at work. Torvald says about the year before, "Three weeks before hand you shut yourself up every evening till long after midnight, making flowers for the Christmas tree and all the other splendid things you wanted to surprise us with" (Act 1,1. 73). Because the Helmers did not have enough *New ¶ ?* money to buy their children nice things, Nora sacrificed her time, and spent it making nice things that her children could appreciate. She wanted them to have a special Christmas, even though they would not have nice gifts. [Besides loving them with an ideal love, Nora simply adores her children. She says to her friend Kristine: "I have three lovely children" (Act 1,1. 112). Nora is very proud of her children and the way that they look. A little bit later in the play, Torvald tells Nora that any child with a deceitful mother will end up doing bad things. Nora is horrified that she could corrupt her children. Talking to herself, she says, "Corrupt my children . . . Poison my home?" (Act 1. 1. 485). Nora is so worried that what has done will negatively affect her children; she does not want to harm them in any way, because she loves them.

Nora also could not have abandoned her children because she is not a selfish person. Throughout the beginning of the play, Nora proves that she is not a selfish person. For instance, Torvald and Nora are discussing money, and Nora asks Torvald for a little extra money. Torvald thinks Nora will spend the money on herself, but she says, "Pooh. I don't really want anything" (Act 1,1. 34). Nora is content to spend the money on her children and not to have nice things for herself. When Nora tells Kristine about her debt, she explains that she pays it off by doing odd jobs here and there. Concerning the money that Torvald gives her, she says, "I couldn't let the children go about badly dressed either—I felt any money I got for them had to go on them alone" (Act 1,1. 202-204). Nora could have used the money for herself, but she is not a selfish mother; she wants her children to have the best, so that they do not feel poor. She tells Kristine "Always I bought the simplest and cheapest things. . . . But sometimes I did feel it was a bit hard, Kristine—because it is nice to be well dressed, isn't it?" (Act 1,1. 205). Even though Nora would like to dress nicely, she makes sure that the money goes to her children. ~~Obviously, Nora loves her children very much, and she would do anything to make sure that they are comfortable and taken care of.~~ Because of this, she would not have willingly abandoned her children.

¶→ Nora leaves the "doll house" so that she can learn more about herself. Nora has lived a sheltered life with Torvald. He treats her like a doll; he plays with her, he admires her, he enjoys her charms, and he controls her. Torvald treats Nora as if she were a little girl; he does not realize that she is a full grown woman and is capable of having her own thoughts, feelings, and opinions. Because of this, Nora does not know who she is and what she is capable of. Before she leaves, she says to Torvald, "You arranged everything to your tastes, and I acquired the same tastes. Or pretended to. . . ." (Act 3, 1. 280). Nora only believe that Torvald says because he makes her feel that she has to. *Nora* ~~She~~ does not have her own opinions about life because she does not have to; Torvald dictates to her how she should feel and what she should think. Torvald says, "First and foremost, you are a wife and mother" (Act 3, l. 315). He would have Nora believe that she is not her own person, and that she lives solely to be his doll and the mother to his children. However, Nora responds by saying, "I believe that first and foremost I am an individual—or at least I'm going to try to be" (Act 3, l. 316). Nora understands now that she has never been her own person, ~~but now that the~~ *and she can try to change this.* ~~she knows this, she can try and change it~~. Thus, when Nora turns to leave the house, for the first time in her life, Nora is ~~making the decision to do something, and~~ *not basing her decision* ~~not basing it~~ on what anybody else wants or thinks. She says, "I must take steps to educate myself. . . . That's why I'm leaving you" (Act 3, l. 295).

　Nora also needs to leave her home in order to learn more about real life and real life responsibilities. While *Nora* ~~she~~ does love her children, she does not raise them by herself; she has a nurse that watches them while she cannot. Kristine even tells Nora that she "hasn't known much trouble or hardship in life" (Act 1, l. 155). Although Nora has worked small jobs to pay her loan, she still does not understand true hardship, because she has been sheltered by Torvald. Dr. Rank, a friend of Nora's, says to her: "Do you know in fact what society is?" Nora replies, "What do I care about your silly old society?" (Act 1, l. 257). Not only does Nora not understand society, but she does not want to understand it. She has lived a sheltered life, she knows it, and at first, she does not want to change it. However, at the end of the play, Nora says, "I'm not content any more with what most people say, or with what it says in books. I have to think things out for myself, and get things clear" (Act 3, l. 316).

Before this realization,
~~Previously,~~ Nora had simply believed whatever Torvald,
or anybody else had told her. She knew nothing ~~of reli-~~
outside of
~~gion, or law, except for~~ what she read in books. Now, she
wants to learn for herself and finally understand things
for what they are are. Evidently, Nora leaves her home
because she finally realizes that she has ~~been sheltered~~
her husband   *that*
~~to the point where she had~~ no real identity apart from
~~Torvald; and~~ ~~where~~ she knows absolutely nothing of the
world around her.

Nora does not intend to abandon her children,
but she knows that in order to be a better person,
she must leave them. There are many interpretations
of the ending of Ibsen's *A Doll's House*. Some think
that she leaves because she feels unloved. Some call
her selfish for deserting her children. However, Nora
simply realizes that she knows nothing about real life,
since she has been living under the protective and con-
not selfish when
trolling shadow of her husband. Nora is ~~actually self-~~
~~less when~~ she leaves her children, because she knows
that she cannot be a good mother unless she is a good
person first.

Works Cited

Ibsen, Henrik. <u>A Doll's House</u>. <u>Legacies: Fiction, Poetry, Drama, Nonfiction</u>. Fourth
Edition. Eds. Jan Zlotnik Schmidt, Lynne Crockett, and Carley Bogarad. Boston:
Cengage Learning Wadsworth, 2008. 199-249.

Profesor Fakler's Feedback
Letter to Jenny Binnie

Date: November 10, 2006
To: Jenny Binnie
From: Professor Fakler
Comments: "Nora's Quest for Learning"—Draft One

Jenny:

You have chosen a topic which is interesting and thought-provoking and has the
potential for a strong character analysis. Your response to Ibsen's play is well-thought-

out and articulated. You have made some good use of your sources and have competently used quotes from the play in support of your points.

Critique:

Your introduction is too abrupt. You have too much plot summary, and you jump into your discussion without signaling to the reader what the topic will be. You need to let the audience know that you will be discussing Ibsen's play, what your point will be about the play, and how you will support that point.

It is not clear what your thesis is. Every essay needs to have a clear purpose and a thesis. Remember the rhetorical situation: what is the subject, what is the purpose, who is the audience, what is the thesis? You need to clearly state, near the beginning of your essay, what your thesis will be. Remember it needs to be a main impression of Nora's character.

Your paragraphs are much too long. Separate out your ideas and break them into subtopics and paragraphs.

Some of the writing could be tightened. It is repetitive. For example, you tell us, at the very beginning, that Nora "plays with her three children, and she likes to spend time with them." Then you tell us that "she dotes upon them." This seems redundant.

And remember when a "because" subordinate clause comes at the end of the sentence, there is no comma before the "because."

This draft has a great deal of potential. I look forward to the next draft.

Jenny Binnie

Final Draft: Nora's Quest for Learning

"A thousand words will not leave so deep an impression as one deed" ("American Democracy Project"). This quote of Henrik Ibsen's applies very well to his play, *A Doll's House*. The dialogue of the entire play is eclipsed by the fact that the main character, Nora Helmer, leaves her family at the end. That one deed has led to much criticism and to many different interpretations of the ending. Some readers believe that Nora leaves her children because she is selfish or because she does not love them. In the beginning of the play, Nora seems like a wonderful mother: she likes to spend time with her three children, and she adores them. At the end of the play, though, Nora leaves without even saying good-bye to the children. It seems as if she gives up on motherhood because it is too difficult a task for her. In actuality, Nora has been living under the protective and controlling shadow of her husband, and she realizes that she has been sheltered her entire life. Therefore, Nora does not desert her children out of selfishness or lack of affection; instead, she leaves her family to learn more about herself and about life.

Although this seems like a horrible act for a mother to commit, Nora does not abandon her children out of selfishness because she is not a self-seeking person. For instance, when Nora asks her husband Torvald for a little extra money, Torvald thinks that she will spend it on herself. However, she says, "Pooh, I don't really want anything" (Act 1, 1.34). Nora is content to spend the money on her children, a sacrifice that will prevent her from having nice clothes. Although Nora works odd jobs to pay off a debt, the money Torvald gives her is not used as spending money for herself. Nora tells her friend, Kristine, that she "couldn't let the children go about badly dressed . . . any money I got for them had to go on them alone" (Act 1, 1. 204). Whatever money Torvald gives to Nora for her own clothes, she uses on her children because that is her obligation as a mother. She says "I bought the simplest and cheapest things . . . But sometimes I did feel it was a bit hard, Kristine because it is nice to be well dressed, isn't it" (Act 1, 1. 205 on). Even though Nora would like to dress nicely, she makes sure that the money is used for her children. She loves them and puts their needs over her own. These are certainly not the actions of a self-absorbed woman.

Nora loves her children too much for her departure to be seen as abandonment. The play takes place before, during, and after Christmas. Nora and Torvald discuss the fact that they will have more money this year than they had the year before since Torvald has been promoted at work. In reference to the previous year, Torvald says, "Three whole weeks beforehand you shut yourself up every evening . . . making flowers for the Christmas tree and all the other splendid things you wanted to surprise us with" (Act I, 1. 73). Because the Helmers did not have enough money to buy their children expensive gifts, Nora spent her time making nice things that her children could appreciate. She wanted them to have a special Christmas, even though they would not have new toys and clothes. Nora not only wants to provide for her children, but she simply adores them. She says to Kristine, "I have three lovely children" (Act I, 1.73). Nora is very proud of them; she brags about them the way loving mothers often do.

Nora does not leave "the doll house" because she is tired of motherhood—instead, she leaves in order to learn more about herself. Torvald treats Nora like a doll; he plays with, admires, and controls her. He treats Nora as if she were a little girl, not realizing that she is a woman, capable of her own thoughts and opinions. Consequently, Nora does not know who she is and what she is capable of. Before she leaves, she tells Torvald ". . . You arranged everything to your tastes, and I acquired the same tastes. Or pretended to. . . ." (Act 3, 1. 280). Nora lives her life in submission to Torvald and the ideas, thoughts, likes, and dislikes that he has. She has no personality of her own, and so she does not even know whether she really believes the way that Torvald does, or if she has just been pretending in order to please him.

In addition, Nora does not have her own tastes because she does not have to; Torvald dictates to her how she should be. He says: "First and foremost, you are a wife and a mother" (Act 3, 1. 315). He wants Nora to believe that she is not an individual, that she has no identity without him and their children. However, Nora responds by saying, "I believe that first and foremost I am an individual—or at least I'm going to try to be" (Act 3, 1. 316). Nora understands that she has never been her own person, but that it is not too late for her to change. For the first time in her life, Nora does not base a decision on what anybody else wants. She says, "I must take steps to educate myself. . . . That's why I'm leaving you" (Act 3, 1. 295). Nora must try to become a well-informed woman, and in order to do that, she has to live away from the person who restrained her for so long.

Nora also needs to leave home in order to learn more about life beyond "the doll house." At the beginning of the play, Kristine tells Nora that she (Nora) "hasn't known much trouble or hardship in life" (Act 1, 1. 155). Although Nora works to pay back her loan, she still does not understand true hardship. She does not even have to raise her own children; she has a nurse that watches them, and Nora only sees them when she wants to play with them. Dr. Rank, a friend of Nora, asks, "Do you know in fact what society is? Have you any notion what society really is?" Nora replies "What do I care about your silly old society?" (Act 1, 1. 257). Not only does Nora not understand society, but she also does not want to understand it. She lives a sheltered life, and, at first, she does not want to change her limited existence. However, by the end of the play, Nora understands that she "must take steps to educate [herself]" (Act 3, 1. 296). Nora will now be able to see society for what it really is, not from a sheltered viewpoint.

At the end of Henrik Ibsen's *A Doll's House*, Nora Helmer finally realizes that she has no identity separate from her role as a wife and a mother, and that she knows nothing of the world around her. Nora is really not selfish for leaving her children, nor is she apathetic towards them. Before she leaves, she says "I know [the children] are in better hands than mine. As I am now, I can never be anything to them" (Act 3, 1. 35). Nora must leave in order to avoid raising her children as sheltered and ignorant people. In leaving, she proves her selfless and affectionate nature; she understands that she cannot be an adequate and capable mother until she is a "reasonable human being."

Works Cited

"American Democracy Project: Quotes/Phrases." http://www.aascu.org/. 22 Nov. 2006. http://www. aascu.org/.

Ibsen, Henrik. A Doll's House. Legacies: Fiction, Poetry, Drama, Nonfiction. Fourth Edition. Eds. Jan Zlotnik Schmidt, Lynne Crockett, and Carley Bogarad. Boston: Cengage Learning Wadsworth, 2008. 199-249.

Nonfiction

When we think of nonfiction prose, we envision objective **expository** writing designed to convey information to an audience: newswriting, for example, or scientific and business communications. Nonfiction also may be creative, evocative essays replete with a sense of voice and power. Imaginative reaction, passionate commitment, and the urgency of personal perspective play a role in some kinds of nonfiction. Many forms have features of fiction, poetry, and drama: vivid, descriptive detail, narrative example, metaphoric language, and dialogue.

In nonfiction, we may be drawn into the world of the writing just as we are in fiction, in poetry, or in drama. However, we become involved in different ways. We read to absorb, to react, perhaps to be moved and enlightened by facts, arguments, issues, and ideas. As Susan Sontag suggests, "an essay could be as much an event, a transforming event, as a novel or a poem."

Forms of Nonfiction

Speech

As major civilizations and communal life flourished, public discourse evolved. The **speech,** oral communication designed to be delivered to an audience, became a popular form of public communication in Greek times, particularly during the fifth century B.C., the age of Pericles, at the height of Athenian democracy. In his treatise, *The Rhetoric,* Aristotle (384–322 B.C.), a Greek philosopher, categorized the three kinds of speeches prevalent in his society: orations delivered in the law courts, in the political arena, at ceremonial occasions. Many examples of these declamations, of course, did not survive because they were not transcribed. One famous speech is Pericles's funeral oration for the Athenian dead (430 B.C.), which appears in Thucydides's *History of the Peloponnesian Wars.* Among other arguments, Pericles praises the Athenian democratic "system of government" as a "model to others." Many famous Greek orators and teachers developed the form of the speech between the fifth and fourth centuries B.C., including Isocrates and Demosthenes whose political works are notable examples. Roman rhetoric was patterned after Greek models. Cicero (106–43 B.C.), a Roman statesman, politician, and rhetorician, excelled at oratory and published his own speeches, which still serve as exemplars of classical argument (see Chapter 4). Examples of speeches in *Legacies* include Sojourner Truth's "Ain't I a Woman?" (Chapter 8) and Martin Luther King's "Letter from Birmingham Jail" (Chapter 13).

Philosophical Treatise

Another human imperative has been to speculate on the state of the world and on human nature. One of the earliest forms of nonfiction has been the **philosophical treatise,** an extended formal meditation on a philosophical, religious, or political subject. Such treatises convey the central ideas, beliefs, and values of many Western and Eastern societies. Interestingly, at approximately the same time (c. 600 B.C.), Pythagoras wrote about mathematics in ancient Greece, Confucius was a teacher in China, and Hindu sages created the *Upanishads,* the central documents of Hindu thought in India.

Plato (428–347 B.C.), one of the foremost Greek philosophers, wrote tracts on such subjects as the nature of love, *The Symposium* (Chapter 7) and the ideal state, *The Republic* (Chapter 9). The wisdom of Confucius (551–479(?) B.C.), a Chinese scholar and teacher, instructed people to live a good life in harmony with others. Confucius suggests, for example, that a ruler must "govern by virtue. . . .": "Govern the people by virtue . . . and the people . . . will be reformed of themselves." Another Chinese philosopher, known as Lao-tzu (575–485(?) B.C.), assumes a different religious stance: withdrawal from the world, meditation, mysticism, and the cultivation of silence as the way of the spirit. Lao-tzu is considered responsible for the *Tao te Ching,* the opening line of which states, "The way that can be spoken of is not the way. . . ."

Examples of political, philosophical, and or religious treatises abound in world history. Think of the documents of the American or the French revolution; the Communist Manifesto; Chairman Mao's sayings; the sacred texts of world religions. The poem of Lao-tzu (Chapter 8) and the reflections of Albert Camus (Chapter 9) also exemplify this form of nonfiction.

Autobiography

One structured type of personal writing is **autobiography,** defined as writing about one's life. Autobiography became prevalent with the rise of Christianity as people had the urge to document their spiritual conversions. One of the earliest stories of such a conversion, St. Augustine's *Confessions,* written between A.D. 397 and 400, describes the author's childhood, his conversion to Christianity at thirty-two, and his transformation from sinner to Christian.

The desires to fashion a story of one's life, to create from memories—from inchoate reminiscences—an ordered vision of one's past, and to seek personal meaning from one's past are deep needs in human beings. The autobiographical impulse has taken hold of writers throughout the ages as diverse as Machiavelli, Helen Keller, and Maya Angelou. Autobiography becomes a particularly powerful means of expression for those groups who feel disenfranchised because this form of writing defines and asserts selfhood in response to the lack of recognition of ethnic identity. Alice Walker has written many autobiographical essays that explore her stance as an African American woman, for example, "Am I Blue?" (Chapter 9).

Memoir

As eras of conquest and travel progressed during the Middle Ages and the Renaissance, another autobiographical form emerged. **Memoir** presents the remembrances of a public figure and the events of an historical era. Perhaps, one of the earliest examples of such a document is Julius Caesar's record of his military campaigns in Gaul 102–44 B.C. Other examples of memoir include Marco Polo's travels in China and India (*The Travels of Marco Polo,* 1293), Leo Africanus's account of Africa written when he was taken captive and held as a slave by pirates (1526), and Babur's (Zahir Ud-Din Mohammed's) recounting of his battles in India (1526). Contemporary memoirists include Winston Churchill and Richard Nixon.

Journal

The **journal,** another form of personal writing, concerns the self exclusively, and the presumed audience is the author. Some of the earliest examples include the lists of Sei Shonogan—a form of a diary kept by a woman in the court of the emperor in tenth-century Japan. Titles from Shonogan's diary reveal "Things That Make One's Heart Beat Faster"; "Things That Arouse a Fond Memory of the Past"; "Hateful Things"; and "Depressing Things."

As journals developed, many types emerged: travel diaries, diaries of spiritual life, journals kept during the settlement of the frontier by the pioneers in North America, and diaries kept by women during the Civil War. Throughout literary history, numerous artists and writers were inveterate journal keepers: Leonardo da Vinci wrote and drew in sketchbooks; Henry David Thoreau composed more than 60,000 pages of journals; Anaïs Nin had at least sixteen volumes of journals.

Letter writing represents another form of personal expression; often in letter-writing, the assumption of a public as well as a private audience exists. Benjamin Franklin composed letters to his son; F. Scott Fitzgerald communicated by letter with his daughter, Scottie. Martin Luther King's "Letter from Birmingham Jail" presents a complex political argument that suggests the fusion of both the public and the private self and the impossibility of separating these selves in the response to political oppression (Chapter 13).

Essay

During the Renaissance, with its emphasis on individual will and consciousness, the **essay** developed, a form of prose that presented a person's reflections and ideas on a specific topic. The essay (derived from the French verb *assayer*—meaning to try, to attempt) presents a concise, prose discussion of a limited topic and of limited length, designed for a general audience. Although the origin of the essay can be traced to ancient Rome—to Seneca and to Plutarch who wrote works with such titles as "On Envy and Hate," "On the Control of Anger," and "On Having Many Friends,"—Francis Bacon, the English scientist and philosopher (1561–1628), often receives credit for inventing the modern form of the genre. He wrote volumes of essays on subjects as varied as the relation of parents and children, death, truth, adversity, anger, revenge, atheism, suspicion, and cunning. During the 1600s and 1700s, many writers experimented with this form, including Blaise Pascal, who produced his *Pensées* (Thoughts, 1670), a collection of his thoughts; Montaigne, who penned his *Essais* (1580), his meditations; and in England in the 1700s Joseph Addison and Richard Steele, who wrote essays for their literary journal, *The Spectator.* The essay flourished in the hands of such eighteenth-century British writers as Jonathan Swift, Samuel Johnson, and William

Hazlitt and such nineteenth-century North American writers as Henry David Thoreau and Ralph Waldo Emerson who wrote "Civil Disobedience" and "The American Scholar," respectively. Essay writing reached its apex in Britain and in North America in the eighteenth and nineteenth centuries.

Kinds of Essays

Exposition

Exposition, the main form of nonfiction, explains or conveys information to a particular audience. Exposition may have a range of approaches—objective, subjective, factual, or reflective. An expository essay may describe, explain, give examples, compare, define, analyze, or demonstrate cause and effect. Lynn Smith's "Betwixt and Bewildered: Scholars are Intrigued by the Angst of 'Emerging Adults'" (Chapter 5) explores the phenomenon of young people in their twenties who are between childhood and adulthood of our "hurried" lifestyle. Smith uses several rhetorical modes, including definition, exemplification, and cause and effect to develop her points.

Expository essays may fall into two classes: *formal* and *informal* writing. In a formal expository essay, the writing may be organized with an introduction, middle paragraphs, and conclusion. The essay is carefully and tightly developed: a thesis and subtopics exist; the writer orders ideas into supporting paragraphs with clear topic sentences and supporting evidence; a direct and logical progression of points moves toward the conclusion. The point of view and tone may be more objective and less personal. Singer's "Speciesism" (Chapter 9) represents a superb example of a tightly and formally organized essay. The informal essay may be organized by associations and may use techniques of fiction (personal, symbolic detail, dialogue, narrative excerpts) and of poetry (imagery, figurative language, repetition). Witness Maxine Hong Kingston's mix of description, reminiscence, narration, character sketch, and reflection in "No Name Woman" (Chapter 7).

Argumentation

In **argumentation,** one of the primary forms of nonfiction prose, the writer presents a personal opinion with the intention of convincing an audience about his or her point of view, constructs reasons for that position, and develops supporting evidence. Informal and formal modes of structuring argument exist. Informal argument may take the form of persuasive writing in which emotional appeals, detail, narrative and personal examples provide the proof designed to convince a reader. For instance, if a writer composed an essay for a local paper to convince the audience that eighteen-year-olds' drunken driving poses a serious threat to others, he or she refers to the experience of witnessing a violent and fatal accident caused by an eighteen-year-old. Or the writer may recount a tale about his or her child or another teenager in order to persuade readers. The intent is to convince an audience of the validity of the position or to persuade people to take some action.

In formal argument, the writer also will develop an argumentative thesis (a position) and reason with his or her audience in mind. However, the position and the thesis will be more objectively stated; the reasons supported with proofs, data, statistics, examples. One option is to shape an argument in classic, Aristotelian style (see

Chapter 4). Martin Luther King's "Letter from Birmingham Jail" (Chapter 13) is an excellent example of a formally structured, complex argumentative essay.

At the heart of argumentative writing remains a solid statement of thesis (position), development of reasons and supporting evidence, and sound, logical reasoning. Compare Toni Morrison's exploratory, allusive, lyrical, narrative political argument in "The Nobel Prize Speech" (Chapter 9) with Simone de Beauvoir's logically structured presentation of women's position as "object" in "Woman as Other" (Chapter 7).

For a full discussion of argument, see Chapter 4.

Forms of Creative Nonfiction

Creative nonfiction, once classified as the personal essay, is characterized by a strong sense of a personal voice and slant; an intimacy of tone—as if the writer is conversing with an imagined audience; experimental structure as opposed to academic essay form; and the use of literary devices. The literary techniques borrowed from fiction include shifts in point of view, setting, characterization, descriptive detail, and plot; from drama, character, conflict, and dialogue; and from poetry, imagery, figurative language, and symbolism. Creative nonfiction writers also balance the subjective and objective, showing and telling, narration and reflection. The essay embodies a process of discovery, moving from the personal to larger meanings and issues. As Janet Burroway suggests, "the essay begins in personal experiences but reaches out to a larger idea or area of thought about the human condition." Examples of this form includes Scott Russell Sanders's "The Force of Spirit" (Chapter 9).

Elements of Nonfiction

All forms of nonfiction share some similarities. A writer thinks of the audience, of the occasion for writing, of the reasons for the writing; he or she then shapes the writing with audience in mind. The writer becomes aware of purposes, intentions and overall goals and chooses relevant details, examples, facts, and reasons. Furthermore, he or she considers **point of view,** voice, the attitude and relationship to material and to audience, and thinks about the relationship between point of view and the persona in the work. This relationship provides readers with a sense of the writer as the character, the person behind the writing. Is the person honest? Does the voice sound real? truthful? distant? impassioned? angry? The persona and point of view of the writer influence the slant of the piece, the main idea, the thesis, the organization, the details, and the word choice. Rhetoricians label this consciousness of audience, occasion, purpose, goals, intent, and point of view the *rhetorical situation.*

Tone involves the feeling, mood, and **attitude** that readers infer from the content of the essay. In Alice Walker's "Am I Blue?" part of the tone emanates from a sense of righteous anger at the ways in which people treat animals (Chapter 9).

The crux of effective nonfiction prose, **detail** and **specific example,** makes the piece come alive. The power of nonfiction rests in the interplay of the general and of the specific, of the abstract and of the concrete. Return to the drunken driving example. Just saying eighteen-year-olds should not drive when they are drunk will not convince a reader. An example of a car accident or a statistic regarding the number of eighteen-year-olds involved in drunken-driving accidents and the consequence for others—death, injury of passengers—is much more persuasive.

A college freshman, Jody Levy, wrote the following paragraph. The **sensory details**, including "as a calm river, soon interrupted by rapids," intensify the description of a commonplace object.

Incense

I watched a stick of incense burn. It was a pale brown colored stick of musk incense, with a red hot tip that slowly smoldered downward. A stream of smoke rose from it, and moved with the wind. It was relaxing to watch the dreamy mist. It was calm and controlled, mesmerizing and hypnotic. The smoke ascended straight towards the ceiling, and, then broke its flow; it spurt, swirled, waved, and curled. It started as a calm river, soon interrupted by rapids. Ashes fell, and, crumbled on the tissue underneath, creating a pile of dirt. Dead and used. I let out a deep breath, and, the smoke scrambled. More ashes formed on the top as the red dot moved down. The ashes bent, and then broke, but they did not fall. They hung like a dead leaf on a tree. I followed the smoke with my eyes—thin, thick, straight, smooth, wavy, curly, spiral, fast, slow, short, long,—always moving and changing—floating lines and forms. A continuous flow of greyish, whitish, bluish smoke. Beautiful, like silk thread. . . . As the stick became shorter, the room smelled nicer; the smoke spiraled off with its musk scent. I liked the smell. The scent obscured the smell of my roommate's fat and odorous boyfriend. My roommate walked in; she hates the smell of incense. And the smoke rose in circles, like a horn shouting out scent. Two lines streamed from the stick, sometimes synchronized, cooperating to make forms. Other times, they crossed and waved in opposition, independently creating their own design, and then coming together again. The smoke formed a tunnel, and, then a spiral shell. . . . The incense neared its end, and spurted its last breaths of smoke that slowly floated away and disappeared; but they wafted somewhere in the air. For hours after the final stream of smoke was gone. The red glow faded and left the stick, solitary and lifeless, with a head of ashes. It died and left a lasting memory.

In this piece, the reader senses the persona of the observer: her awe as the stick of incense assumes a life of its own as a "river," as "dirt," as "a dead leaf," then as smoke "like silk thread." The details—color, shape, texture, and smell—of the concrete comparisons and figurative language give this vision of incense its "lasting" place in our minds.

The **organization** of an essay remains crucial. The introduction attracts readers and involves them in the world of the writing and the main idea (the thesis); the middle paragraphs compel through their treatment of evidence (the interplay of generalization and specifics, details and example); and the conclusion reinforces the thesis and leaves the reader with a view to contemplate, feeling enriched, enlivened, convinced, and intellectually aware.

Word choice and **style** are crucial in nonfiction. The writer selects words as carefully as a novelist, poet, or dramatist. He or she plays with words: ironic, witty, comic, lyrical; evocative wordplay and figurative language become crucial to nonfiction. Inexact or diffuse wording leads readers astray; and the work loses its impact. In "Incense" Jody Levy occasionally undermines vivid descriptions by the use of vague words and clichés. For example, after describing the "smoke" as "silk thread," Levy then depicts the room, which "smelled nicer." The "nicer" smell, vague, not at all suggestive of any odor, causes the piece to lose some of its power. The work also loses impact at the end because "lasting memory" is a cliché, a hackneyed means of stating the effect of a moment. Levy easily could have omitted the last sentence.

The total effect of a piece of nonfiction prose is its message: the total meaning of a work. As parts of a short story, drama, poem, build themes, so parts of a nonfiction essay build the message or thesis.

The Reading/Writing Process: Nonfiction

When you read nonfiction prose, a checklist of questions will help you analyze the text.

Checklist of Questions for Reading and Writing about Nonfiction Prose

1. What form of nonfiction prose am I reading: speech, treatise, autobiography, memoir, journal, essay, or creative nonfiction?
2. Is it exposition or argument?
3. What is the rhetorical situation (purpose, occasion, audience)?
4. What is the writer's point of view? Persona?
5. What is the writer's tone?
6. How do I, as a reader, respond to the point of view and tone?
7. What is the thesis? Supporting points?
8. What are significant details? Examples?
9. How is the essay organized? Formally? Informally? Experimentally?
10. What do I notice about style? Word choice?
11. What literary devices are used?
12. What have I learned from reading this work?

STUDENT PORTFOLIO
Response to King's "Letter from Birmingham Jail"[1]

The portfolio presents a model that demonstrates the stages in the process of writing an evaluation essay. Because King's work is so complex, Jack Ferguson created both a gloss and an outline of the essay to make sure that he grasped the structure of the argument. He next wrote a double-entry notebook. Finally, he composed first and final drafts of

---

[1]This response to a published statement by eight fellow clergymen from Alabama (Bishop C. C. J. Carpenter, Bishop Joseph A. Durick, Rabbi Hilton L. Grafman, Bishop Paul Hardin, Bishop Holan B. Harmon, the Reverend George M. Murray, the Reverend Edward V. Ramage and the Reverend Earl Stallings) was composed under somewhat constricting circumstances. Begun on the margins of the newspaper in which the statement appeared while I was in jail, the letter was continued on scraps of writing paper supplied by a friendly Negro trusty, and concluded on a pad my attorneys were eventually permitted to leave me. Although the text remains in substance unaltered, I have indulged in the author's prerogative of polishing it for publication. [King's note.]

his essay. In the final draft, the writer tightened the introduction, clarified King's use of appeals, and analyzed his style.

Ferguson's Gloss

My Dear Fellow Clergymen:

While confined here in the Birmingham city jail, I came across your recent statement calling my present activities "unwise and untimely." Seldom do I pause to answer criticism of my work and ideas. If I sought to answer all the criticisms that cross my desk, my secretaries would have little time for anything other than such correspondence in the course of the day, and I would have no time for constructive work. But since I feel that you are men of genuine good will and that your criticisms are sincerely set forth, I want to try to answer your statements in what I hope will be patient and reasonable terms.

King adopts a non-confrontational "Rogerian" stance.

Appeal to character— King wants to appear trustworthy.

I think I should indicate why I am here in Birmingham, since you have been influenced by the view which argues against "outsiders coming in." I have the honor of serving as president of the Southern Christian Leadership Conference, an organization operating in every southern state, with headquarters in Atlanta, Georgia. We have some eighty-five affiliated organizations across the South, and one of them is the Alabama Christian Movement for Human Rights. Frequently we share staff, educational and financial resources with our affiliates. Several months ago the affiliate here in Birmingham asked us to be on call to engage in a nonviolent direct-action program if such were deemed necessary. We readily consented, and when the hour came we lived up to our promise. So I, along with several members of my staff, am here because I was invited here. I am here because I have organizational ties here.

opposing argument #1 Refutation a)

Appeal to character— establishes credibility.

But more basically, I am in Birmingham because injustice is here. Just as the prophets of the eighth century B.C. left their villages and carried their "thus saith the

b)

Biblical allusions indicate his audience.

Lord" far beyond the boundaries of their home towns, and just as the Apostle Paul left his village of Tarsus and carried the gospel of Jesus Christ to the far corners of the Greco-Roman world, so am I (compelled) to carry the gospel of freedom beyond my own home town. Like Paul, I must constantly respond to the Macedonian call for aid.

Moreover, I am (cognizant) of the interrelatedness of all communities and states. I cannot sit idly by in Atlanta and not be concerned about what happens in Birmingham. Injustice anywhere is a threat to justice everywhere. We are caught in an inescapable network of mutuality, tied in a single garment of destiny. Whatever affects one directly, affects all indirectly. Never again can we afford to live with the narrow, provincial "outside agitator" idea. Anyone who lives inside the United States can never be considered an outsider anywhere within its bounds.

opposing argument #2

You deplore the demonstrations taking place in Birmingham. But your statement, I am sorry to say, fails to express a similar concern for the conditions that brought about the demonstrations. I am sure that none of you would want to rest content with the superficial kind of social analysis that deals merely with effects and does not grapple with underlying causes. It is unfortunate that demonstrations are taking place in Birmingham, but it is even more unfortunate that the city's white power structure left the Negro community with no alternative.

Rogerian approach to opponents.

Refutation

a)

In any nonviolent campaign there are four basic steps: collection of the facts to determine whether injustices exist; negotiation; self-purification; and direct action. We have gone through all these steps in Birmingham. There can be no (gainsaying) the fact that racial injustice engulfs this community. Birmingham is probably the most thoroughly segregated city in the United

Evidence—but maybe this could have been more specific.

States. Its ugly record of brutality is widely known. Negroes have experienced grossly unjust treatment in the courts. There have been more unsolved bombings of Negro homes and churches in Birmingham than in any other city in the nation. These are the hard, brutal facts of the case. On the basis of these conditions, Negro leaders sought to negotiate with the city fathers. But the latter consistently refused to engage in good-faith negotiation.

b)   Then, last September, came the opportunity to talk with leaders of Birmingham's economic community. In the course of the negotiations, certain promises were made by the merchants—for example, to remove the stores' humiliating racial signs. On the basis of these promises, the Reverend Fred Shuttlesworth and the leaders of the Alabama Christian Movement for Human Rights agreed to a moratorium on all demonstrations. As the weeks and months went by, we realized that we were the victims of a broken promise. A few signs, briefly removed, returned; the others remained.

c)   As in so many past experiences, our hopes had been blasted, and the shadow of deep disappointment settled upon us. We had no alternative except to prepare for direct action, whereby we would present our very bodies as a means of laying our case before the conscience of the local and the national community. Mindful of the difficulties involved, we decided to undertake a process of self-purification. We began a series of workshops on nonviolence, and we repeatedly asked ourselves : "Are you able to accept blows without retaliating?" "Are you able to endure the ordeal of jail?" We decided to schedule our direct-action program for the Easter season, realizing that except for Christmas, this is the main shopping period of the year. Knowing that a strong economic-withdrawal program would be the by-product of direct action, we felt that this would be the best time to bring pressure to bear on the merchants for the needed change.

Then it occurred to us that Birmingham's mayoral election was coming up in March, and we speedily decided to postpone action until after election day. When we discovered that the Commissioner of Public Safety, Eugene "Bull" Connor, had piled up enough votes to be in the run-off we decided again to postpone action until the day after the run-off so that the demonstrations could not be used to cloud the issues. Like many others, we wanted to see Mr. Connor defeated, and to this end we endured postponement after postponement. Having aided in this community need, we felt that our direct-action program could be delayed no longer.

Appeal to character.

d) You may well ask: "Why direct action? Why sit-ins, marches and so forth? Isn't negotiation a better path?" You are quite right in calling for negotiation. Indeed, this is the very purpose of direct action. Nonviolent direct action seeks to create such a crisis and foster such a tension that a community which has constantly refused to negotiate is forced to confront the issue. It seeks so to dramatize the issue that it can no longer be ignored. My citing the creation of tension as part of the work of the nonviolent-resister may sound rather shocking. But I must confess that I am not afraid of the word "tension." I have earnestly opposed violent tension, but there is a type of constructive, nonviolent tension which is necessary for growth. Just as Socrates felt that it was necessary to create a tension in the mind so that individuals could rise from the bondage of myths and half-truths to the unfettered realm of creative analysis and objective appraisal, we must we see the need for nonviolent gadflies to create the kind of tension in society that will help men rise from the dark depths of prejudice and racism to the majestic heights of understanding and brotherhood.

Appeal to reason.

Interesting!

King seeks to establish common ground.

The purpose of our direct-action program is to create a situation so crisis-packed that it will inevitably open the door to negotiation. <u>I therefore concur with you in your call for negotiation. Too long has our beloved Southland been bogged down in a tragic effort to live in monologue rather than dialogue.</u>

"Our" implies unity.

opposing argument #3

Refutation

One of the basic points in your statement is that the action that I and my associates have taken in Birmingham is untimely. Some have asked: "Why didn't you give the new city administration time to act?" The only answer that I can give to this query is that the new Birmingham administration must be prodded about as much as the outgoing one, before it will act. We are sadly mistaken if we feel that the election of Albert Boutwell as mayor will bring the millennium to Birmingham. While Mr. Boutwell is a much more gentle person than Mr. Connor, they are both segregationists, dedicated to maintenance of the status quo. I have hoped that Mr. Boutwell will be reasonable enough to see the futility of massive resistance to desegregation. But he will not see this without pressure from devotees of civil rights. My friends, I must say to you that we have not made a single gain in civil rights without determined legal and nonviolent pressure. <u>Lamentably, it is an historical fact that privileged groups seldom give up their privileges voluntarily. Individuals may see the moral light and voluntarily give up their unjust posture; but, as Reinhold Niebuhr has reminded us, groups tend to be more immoral than individuals.</u>

Appeal to reason.

Uses outside authority to support his argument.

We know through painful experience that freedom is never voluntarily given by the oppressor; it must be demanded by the oppressed. Frankly, I have yet to engage in a direct-action campaign that was "well timed" in the view of those who have not suffered unduly from the disease of segregation. For years now I have heard the word "Wait!" It rings in the ear of every Negro with piercing familiarity. This "Wait" has almost always meant "Never." We must come to see, with one of our distinguished jurists, that "justice too long delayed is justice denied." ✓

We have waited for more than 340 years for our constitutional and God-given rights. The nations of Asia and Africa are moving with jetlike speed toward gaining political independence, but we still creep at horse-and-buggy pace toward gaining a cup of coffee at a lunch counter. Perhaps it is easy for those who have never felt the stinging darts of segregation to say, "Wait." But when you have seen vicious mobs lynch your mothers and fathers at will and drown your sisters and brothers at whim; when you have seen hate-filled policemen curse, kick and even kill your black brothers and sisters; when you see the vast majority of your twenty million Negro brothers smothering in an airtight cage of poverty in the midst of an affluent society; when you suddenly find your tongue twisted and your speech stammering as you seek to explain to your six-year-old daughter why she can't go to the public amusement park that has just been advertised on television, and see tears welling up in her eyes when she is told that Funtown is closed to colored children, and see ominous clouds of inferiority beginning to form in her little mental sky, and see her beginning to distort her personality by developing an unconscious bitterness toward white people; when you have to concoct an answer for a five-year-old son who is asking: "Daddy, why do white people treat colored people so mean?"; when you take a cross-country drive and find it necessary to sleep night after night in the uncomfortable corners of your automobile because no motel will accept you; when you are humiliated day in and day out by nagging signs reading "white" and "col-

good contrast

Appeal to emotion.

parallelism and repetition

Personal examples— very persuasive

ored"; when your first name becomes "nigger," your middle name becomes "boy" (however old you are) and your last name becomes "John," and your wife and mother are never given the respected title "Mrs."; when you are harried by day and haunted by night by the fact that you are a Negro, living constantly at tiptoe stance, never quite knowing what to expect next, and are plagued with inner fears and outer resentments; when you are forever fighting a degenerating sense of "nobodiness"— then you will understand why we find it difficult to wait. There comes a time when the cup of endurance runs over, and men are no longer willing to be plunged into the abyss of despair. I hope, sirs, you can understand our legitimate and unavoidable impatience.

"Sirs" indicates respect— King does not want to alienate his audience.

You express a great deal of anxiety over our willingness to break laws. This is certainly a legitimate concern. Since we so diligently urge people to obey the Supreme Court's decision of 1954 outlawing segregation in the public schools, at first glance it may seem rather paradoxical for us consciously to break laws. One may well ask: "How can you advocate breaking some laws and obeying others?" The answer lies in the fact that there are two types of laws: just and unjust. I would be the first to advocate obeying just laws. One has not only a legal but a moral responsibility to obey just laws. Conversely, one has a moral responsibility to disobey unjust laws. I would agree with St. Augustine that "an unjust law is no law at all."

opposing argument #4

Refutation

Appeal to reason

Now, what is the difference between the two? How does one determine whether a law is just or unjust? A just law is a man-made code that squares with the moral law or the law of God. An unjust law is a code that is out of harmony with the moral law. To put it in the terms of St. Thomas Aquinas: An unjust law is a human law that is not rooted in eternal law and natural law.

Any law that uplifts human personality is just. Any law that degrades human personality is unjust. All segregation statutes are unjust because segregation distorts the soul and damages the personality. It gives the segregator a false sense of superiority and the segregated a false sense of inferiority. Segregation, to use the terminology of the Jewish philosopher Martin Buber, substitutes an "I-it" relationship for an "I-thou" relationship and ends up relegating persons to the status of things. Hence segregation is not only politically, economically and sociologically unsound, it is morally wrong and sinful. Paul Tillich has said that sin is separation. Is not segregation an existential expression of man's tragic separation, his awful estrangement, his terrible sinfulness? Thus it is that I can urge men to obey the 1954 decision of the Supreme Court, for it is morally right; and I can urge them to disobey segregation ordinances, for they are morally wrong.

Again King refers to a respected authority to support his argument.

Let us consider a more concrete example of just and unjust laws. An unjust law is a code that a numerical or power majority group compels a minority group to obey but does not make binding on itself. This is difference made legal. By the same token, a just law is a code that a majority compels a minority to follow and that it is willing to follow itself. This is sameness made legal.

Let me give another explanation. A law is unjust if it is inflicted on a minority that, as a result of being denied the right to vote, had no part in enacting or devising the law. Who can say that the legislature of Alabama which set up that state's segregation laws was democratically elected? Throughout Alabama all sorts of devious methods are used to prevent Negroes from becoming registered voters, and there are some counties in which, even though Negroes constitute a majority of the population, not a single Negro is registered. Can any law

Again I think his evidence could be more specific—what methods?

enacted under such circumstances be considered democratically structured?

Sometimes a law is just on its face and unjust in its application. For instance, I have been arrested on a charge of parading without a permit. Now, there is nothing wrong in having an ordinance which requires a permit for a parade. But such an ordinance becomes unjust when it is used to maintain segregation and to deny citizens the First-Amendment privilege of peaceful assembly and protest.

I hope you are able to see the distinction I am trying to point out. In no sense do I advocate evading or defying the law, as would the rabid segregationist. That would lead to anarchy. One who breaks an unjust law must do so openly, lovingly, and with a willingness to accept the penalty. I submit that an individual who breaks a law that conscience tells him is unjust and who willingly accepts the penalty of imprisonment in order to arouse the conscience of the community over its injustice, is in reality expressing the highest respect for law.

Of course, there is nothing new about this kind of civil disobedience. It was evidenced sublimely in the refusal of Shadrach, Meshach and Abednego to obey the laws of Nebuchadnezzar, on the ground that a higher moral law was at stake. It was practiced superbly by the early Christians, who were willing to face hungry lions and the excruciating pain of chopping blocks rather than submit to certain unjust laws of the Roman Empire. To a degree, academic freedom is a reality today because Socrates practiced civil disobedience. In our own nation, the Boston Tea Party represented a massive act of civil disobedience.

We should never forget that everything Adolf Hitler did in Germany was "legal" and everything the Hungar-

These biblica allusions create a common ground between King and his audience.

Wasn't Thoreau a big influence on M. L. King?

This is a pretty challenging parallel to draw.

ian fighters did in Hungary was "illegal." It was "illegal" to aid and comfort a Jew in Hitler's Germany. Even so, I am sure that, had I lived in Germany at the time, I would have aided and comforted my Jewish brothers. If today I lived in a Communist country where certain principles dear to the Christian faith are suppressed, I would openly advocate disobeying that country's anti-religious laws.

I must make two honest confessions to you, my Christian and Jewish brothers. First, I must confess that over the past few years I have been gravely disappointed with the white moderate. I have almost reached the regrettable conclusion that the Negro's great stumbling block in his stride toward freedom is not the White Citizen's Counciler or the Ku Klux Klanner, but the white moderate, who is more devoted to "order" than

parallelism

to justice; who prefers a negative peace which is the absence of tension to a positive peace which is the presence of justice; who constantly says, "I agree with you in the goal you seek, but I cannot agree with your methods of direct action"; who paternalistically believes he can set the timetable for another man's freedom; who lives by a mythical concept of time and who constantly advises the Negro to wait for a "more convenient season." Shallow understanding from people of good will is more frustrating than absolute misunderstanding from people of ill will. Lukewarm acceptance is much more bewildering than outright rejection.

I had hoped that the white moderate would understand that law and order exist for the purpose of establishing justice and that when they fail in this purpose they become the dangerously structured dams that

strong metaphor

block the flow of social progress. I had hoped that the white moderate would understand that the present tension in the South is a necessary phase of the transition from an obnoxious negative peace, in which the Negro passively accepted his unjust plight, to a substantive and positive peace, in which all men will respect the dignity and worth of human personality. Actually, we who engage in nonviolent direct action are not the creators of tension. <u>We merely bring to the surface the hidden tension that is already alive. We bring it out in the open, where it can be seen and dealt with. Like a boil that can never be cured so long as it is covered up but must be opened with all its ugliness to the natural medicines of air and light, injustice must be exposed, with all the tension its exposure creates, to the light of human conscience and the air of national opinion, before it can be cured.</u>

This is a great analogy— racism is something that festers beneath the surface.

opposing argument #5

In your statement you assert that our actions, even though peaceful, must be condemned because they precipitate violence. But is this a logical assertion? Isn't this like condemning a robbed man because his possession of money precipitated the evil act of robbery? Isn't this like condemning Socrates because his unswerving commitment to truth and his philosophical inquiries precipitated the act by the misguided populace in which they made him drink hemlock? Isn't this like condemning Jesus because his unique God consciousness and never-ceasing devotion to God's will precipitated the evil act of crucifixion? We must come to see that, as the federal courts have consistently affirmed, it is wrong to urge an individual to cease his efforts to gain his basic constitutional rights because the quest may precipitate violence. Society must protect the robbed and punish the robber.

False analogy maybe?

Isn't this a little weak? He uses rhetorical questions instead of specific evidence.

I had also hoped that the white moderate would reject the myth concerning time in relation to the struggle for freedom. I have just received a letter from a white brother in Texas. He writes: "All Christians know that the colored people will receive equal rights eventually, but it is possible that you are in too great a religious hurry. It has taken Christianity almost two thousand years to accomplish what it has. The teachings of Christ take time to come to earth." Such an attitude stems from a tragic misconception of time, from the strangely irrational notion that there is something in the very flow of time that will inevitably cure all ills. <u>Actually, time itself is neutral; it can be used either destructively or constructively.</u> ✓ More and more I feel that the people of ill will have used time much more effectively than have the people of good will. <u>We will have to repent in this generation not merely for the hateful words and actions of the bad people, but for the appalling silence of the good people.</u> Human progress never rolls in on wheels of inevitability; it comes through the tireless efforts of men willing to be co-workers with God, and without this hard work, time itself becomes an ally of the forces of social stagnation. We must use time creatively, in the knowledge that the time is always ripe to do right. Now is the time to make real the promise of democracy and transform our pending national elegy into a creative psalm of brotherhood. Now is the time to lift our national policy from the quicksand of racial injustice to the solid rock of human dignity.

opposing argument #6

refutation

You speak of our activity in Birmingham as extreme. At first I was rather disappointed that fellow clergymen would see my nonviolent efforts as those of an extremist. I began thinking about the fact that stand in the middle of two opposing forces in the Negro community. One is a force of complacency, made up in part of Negroes who, as a result of long years of oppression, are so drained of self-respect and a sense of "somebodiness" that they have adjusted to segregation; and in part of a few middle-class Negroes who, because of a degree of academic and economic security and because in some ways they profit by segregation, have become insensitive to the problems of the masses. The other force is one of bitterness and hatred, and it comes perilously close to advocating violence. It is expressed in the various black nationalist groups that are springing up across the nation, the largest and best-known being Elijah Muhammad's Muslim movement. Nourished by the Negro's frustration over the continued existence of racial discrimination, this movement is made up of people who have lost faith in America, who have absolutely repudiated Christianity, and who have concluded that the white man is an incorrigible "devil."

I have tried to stand between these two forces, saying that we need emulate neither the "do-nothingism" of the complacent nor the hatred and despair of the black nationalist. For there is the more excellent way of love and nonviolent protest. I am grateful to God that, through the influence of the Negro church, the way of nonviolence became an integral part of our struggle.

He constantly reminds his audience of this.

If this philosophy had not emerged, by now many streets of the South would, I am convinced, be flowing with blood. And I am further convinced that if our white brothers dismiss as "rabble-rousers" and "outside agitators" those of us who employ nonviolent direct action, and if they refuse to support our nonviolent efforts, millions of Negroes will, out of frustration and despair, seek solace and security in black-nationalist ideologies—a development that would inevitably lead to a frightening racial nightmare.

Oppressed people cannot remain oppressed forever. The yearning for freedom eventually manifests itself, and that is what has happened to the American Negro. Something within has reminded him of his birthright of freedom, and something without has reminded him that it can be gained. Consciously or unconsciously, he has been caught up by the Zeitgeist, and with his black brothers of Africa and his brown and yellow brothers of Asia, South America, and the Caribbean, the United States Negro is moving with a sense of great urgency toward the promised land of racial justice. If one recognizes this vital urge that has engulfed the Negro community, one should readily understand why public demonstrations are taking place. The Negro has many pent-up resentments and (latent) frustrations, and he must release them. So let him march; let him make prayer pilgrimages to the city hall; let him go on freedom rides—and try to understand why he must do so. If his repressed emotions are not released in nonviolent ways, they will seek expression through violence; this is not a threat but a fact of history. So I have not said to my people, "Get rid of your discontent." Rather, I have tried to say that this normal and healthy discontent can be channeled into the creative outlet of nonviolent direct action. And now this approach is being termed extremist.

Rhetorical qeustions create strong tone.

But though I was initially disappointed at being categorized as an extremist, as I continued to think about the matter I gradually gained a measure of satisfaction from the label. Was not Jesus an extremist for love: "Love your enemies, bless them that curse you, do good to them that hate you, and pray for them which despite-

Again parallism is used for emotional emphasis.

fully use you, and persecute you." Was not Amos an extremist for justice: "Let justice roll down like waters and righteousness like an everflowing stream." Was not Paul an extremist for the Christian gospel: "I bear in my body the marks of the Lord Jesus." Was not Martin Luther an extremist: "Here I stand; I cannot do otherwise, so help me God." And John Bunyan: "I will stay in jail

King wants to connect Christian tradition with American history.

to the end of my days before I make a butchery of my conscience." And Abraham Lincoln: "This nation cannot survive half slave and half free." And Thomas Jefferson: "We hold these truths to be self-evident, that all men are created equal. . . ." So the question is not whether we will be extremists, but what kind of extremists we will be. Will we be extremists for hate or for love? Will we be extremists for the preservation of injustice or for the extension of justice? In that dramatic scene on Calvary's hill three men were crucified. We must never forget that all three were crucified for the same crime— the crime of extremism. Two were extremists for immorality, and thus fell below their environment. The other, Jeans Christ, was an extremist for love, truth, and goodness, and thereby rose above his environment. <u>Perhaps the South, the nation, and the world are in dire need of creative extremists.</u>

I had hoped that the white moderate would see this need. Perhaps I was too optimistic; perhaps I expected too much. I suppose I should have realized that few members of the oppressor race can understand the <u>deep groans</u> and <u>passionate yearnings</u> of the oppressed race, and still fewer have the vision to see that injustice must be rooted out by strong, persistent, and determined action. I am thankful, however, that some of our white brothers in the South have grasped the meaning of this social revolution and committed themselves to it. They are still too few in quantity, but they are big in quality. Some—such as Ralph McGill, Lillian Smith, Harry Golden, James McBride Dabbs, Ann Braden, and Sarah Patton Boyle—have written about our struggle in eloquent and prophetic terms. Others have marched with us down nameless streets of the South. They have languished in filthy, roach-infested jails, suffering the abuse and brutality of policemen who view them as "dirty nigger-lovers." Unlike so many of their moderate brothers and sisters, they have recognized the urgency of the moment and sensed the need for powerful "action" antidotes to combat the disease of segregation.

Let me take note of my other major disappointment. I have been so greatly disappointed with the white church and its leadership. Of course, there are some notable exceptions. I am not unmindful of the fact that each of you has taken some significant stands on this issue. I commend you, Reverend Stallings, for your Christian stand on this past Sunday, in welcoming Negroes to your worship service on a nonsegregational basis. I commend the Catholic leaders of this state for integrating Spring Hill College several years ago.

But despite these notable exceptions, I must honestly (reiterate) that I have been disappointed with the church. I do not say this as one of those negative critics who can always find something wrong with the church. I say this as a minister of the gospel, who loves the church; who was nurtured in its bosom; who has been sustained by its spiritual blessings and who will remain true to it as long as the cord of life shall lengthen.

When I was suddenly catapulted into the leadership of the bus protest in Montgomery, Alabama, a few years ago, I felt we would be supported by the white church felt that the white ministers, priests, and rabbis of the South would be among our strongest allies. Instead, some have been outright opponents, refusing to understand the freedom movement and misrepresenting its leaders; all too many others have been more cautious than courageous and have remained silent behind the anesthetizing security of stained-glass windows.

In spite of my shattered dreams, I came to Birmingham with the hope that the white religious leadership of this community would see the justice of our cause and, with deep moral concern, would serve as the channel through which our just grievances could reach the power structure. I had hoped that each of you would understand. But again I have been disappointed.

I have heard numerous southern religious leaders admonish their worshipers to comply with a desegregation decision because it is the law, but I have longed to hear white ministers declare: "Follow this decree because integration is morally right and because the Negro is your brother." In the midst of blatant injustices inflicted upon the Negro, I have watched white churchmen stand on the sideline and mouth pious irrelevancies and sanctimonious trivialities. In the midst of a mighty struggle to rid our nation of racial and economic injustice, I have heard many ministers say: "Those are social issues, with which the gospel has no real concern." And I have watched many churches commit themselves to a completely otherworldly religion which makes a strange, un-Biblical distinction between body and soul, between the sacred and the secular.

I have traveled the length and breadth of Alabama, Mississippi and all the other southern states. On sweltering summer days and crisp autumn mornings I have looked at the South's beautiful churches with their lofty spires pointing heavenward. I have beheld the impressive outlines of her massive religious-education buildings. Over and over I have found myself asking: "What kind of people worship here? Who is their God? Where were their voices when the lips of Governor Barnett dripped with words of interposition and nullification? Where were they when Governor Wallace gave a clarion call for defiance and hatred? Where were their voices of support when bruised and weary Negro men and women decided to rise from the dark dungeons of complacency to the bright hills of creative protest?"

Yes, these questions are still in my mind. In deep disappointment I have wept over the laxity of the church. But be assured that my tears have been tears of love. There can be no deep disappointment where there is

Again, series of questions creates strong tone.

opposition

not deep love. Yes, I love the church. How could I do otherwise? I am in the rather unique position of being the son, the grandson and the great-grandson of preachers. Yes, I see the church as the body of Christ. But, oh! How we have blemished and scarred that body through social neglect and through fear of being nonconformists.

Note use of "we" here— King wants to create an impression of unity, rather than one of alienation.

There was a time when the church was very powerful—in the time when the early Christians rejoiced at being deemed worthy to suffer for what they believed. In those days the church was not merely a thermometer that recorded the ideas and principles of popular opinion; it was a thermostat that transformed the mores of society. Whenever the early Christians entered a town, the people in power became disturbed and immediately sought to convict the Christians for being "disturbers of the peace" and "outside agitators." But the Christians pressed on, in the conviction that they were "a colony of heaven," called to obey God rather than man. Small in number, they were big in commitment. They were too God intoxicated to be "astronomically intimidated." By their effort and example they brought an end to such ancient evils as infanticide. and gladiatorial contests.

Things are different now. So often the contemporary church is a weak, ineffectual voice with an uncertain sound. So often it is an archdefender of the status quo. Far from being disturbed by the presence of the church, the power structure of the average community is consoled by the church's silent—and often even vocal—sanction of things as they are.

But the judgment of God is upon the church as never before. If today's church does not recapture the sacrificial spirit of the early church, it will lose its authenticity, forfeit the loyalty of millions, and be dismissed as an irrelevant social club with no meaning for the twentieth century. Every day I meet young people whose disappointment with the church has turned into outright disgust.

Perhaps I have once again been too optimistic. Is organized religion too inextricably bound to the status quo to save our nation and the world? Perhaps I must turn my faith to the inner spiritual church, the church within the church, as the true ekklesia and the hope of the world. But again I am thankful to God that some noble souls from the ranks of organized religion have broken loose from the paralyzing chains of conformity and joined us as active partners in the struggle for freedom. They have left their secure congregations and walked the streets of Albany, Georgia, with us. They have gone down the highways of the South on tortuous rides for freedom. Yes, they have gone to jail with us. Some have been dismissed from their churches, have lost the support of their bishops and fellow ministers. But they have acted in the faith that right defeated is stronger than evil triumphant. Their witness has been the spiritual salt that has preserved the true meaning of the gospel in these troubled times. They have carved a tunnel of hope through the dark mountain of disappointment.

I hope the church as a whole will meet the challenge of this decisive hour. But even if the church does not come to the aid of justice, I have no despair about the future. I have no fear about the outcome of our struggle in Birmingham, even if our motives are at present misunderstood. We will reach the goal of freedom in Birmingham and all over the nation, because the goal of America is freedom. Abused and scorned though we may be, our destiny is tied up with America's destiny. Before the pilgrims landed at Plymouth, we were here. Before the pen of Jefferson etched the majestic words of the Declaration of Independence across the pages of history, we were here. For more than two centuries our forebears

This is an important aspect of his argument—the fate of the black Americans is linked with the fate of the nation as a whole.

labored in this country without wages; they made cotton king; they built the homes of their masters while suffering gross injustice and shameful humiliation—and yet out of a bottomless vitality they continued to thrive and develop. If the inexpressible cruelties of slavery could not stop us, the opposition we now face will surely fail. We will win our freedom because the sacred heritage of our nation and the eternal will of God are (embodied) in our echoing demands.

Before closing I feel impelled to mention one other point in your statement that has troubled me profoundly. You warmly commended the Birmingham police force for keeping "order" and "preventing violence." I doubt that you would have so warmly commended the police force if you had seen its dogs sinking their teeth into unarmed, nonviolent Negroes. I doubt that you would so quickly commend the policemen if you were to observe their ugly and inhumane treatment of Negroes here in the city jail; if you were to watch them push and curse old Negro women and young Negro girls; if you were to see them slap and kick old Negro men and young boys; if you were to observe them, as they did on two occasions, refuse to give us food because we wanted to sing our grace together. I cannot join you in your praise of the Birmingham police department.

more parallelisim

emotional language

It is true that the police have exercised a degree of discipline in handing the demonstrators. In this sense they have conducted themselves rather "nonviolently" in pubic. But for what purpose? To preserve the evil system of segregation. Over the past few years I have consistently preached that nonviolence demands that the means we use must be as pure as the ends we seek. I have tried to make clear that it is wrong to use immoral means to attain moral ends. But now I must affirm that it is just as wrong, or perhaps even more so,

Concedes opposing point of view but immediately modifies it.

to use moral means to preserve immoral ends. Perhaps Mr. Connor and his policemen have been rather nonviolent in public, as was Chief Pritchett in Albany, Georgia, but they have used the moral means of nonviolence to maintain the immoral end of racial injustice. As T. S. Eliot has said: "The last temptation is the greatest treason: To do the right deed for the wrong reason."

I wish you had commended the Negro sit-inners and demonstrators of Birmingham for their sublime courage, their willingness to suffer and their amazing discipline in the midst of great provocation. One day the South will recognize its real heroes. They will be the James Merediths, with the noble sense of purpose that enables them to face jeering, and hostile mobs, and with the agonizing loneliness that characterizes the life of the pioneer. They will be old, oppressed, battered Negro women, symbolized in a seventy-two-year-old woman in Montgomery, Alabama, who rose up with a sense of dignity and with her people decided not to ride segregated buses, and who responded with ungrammatical profundity to one who inquired about her weariness: "My feets is tired, but my soul is at rest." They will be the young high school and college students, the young ministers of the gospel and a host of their elders, courageously and nonviolently sitting in at lunch counters and willingly going to jail for conscience' sake. One day the South will know that when these disinherited children of God sat down at lunch counters, they were in reality standing up for what is best in the American dream and for the most sacred values in our Judaeo-Christian heritage, thereby bringing our nation back to those great wells of democracy which were dug deep by the founding fathers in their formulation of the Constitution and the Declaration of Independence.

Never before have I written so long a letter. I'm afraid it is much too long to take your precious time.

appeal to emotion

I can assure you that it would have been much shorter if I had been writing from a comfortable desk, but what else can one do when he is alone in a narrow jail cell, other than write long letters, think long thoughts, and pray long prayers?

appeal to character

If I have said anything in this letter that overstates the truth and indicates an unreasonable impatience, I beg you to forgive me. If I have said anything that understates the truth and indicates my having a patience that allows me to settle for anything less than brotherhood, I beg God to forgive me.

Figurative language here—to stir his readers' imaginations by reminding his audience of their common national identity

I hope this letter finds you strong in the faith. I also hope that circumstances will soon make it possible for me to meet each of you, not as an integrationist or a civil-rights leader but as a fellow clergyman and a Christian brother. Let us all hope that <u>the dark clouds of racial prejudice</u> will soon pass away and the <u>deep fog of misunderstanding will be lifted</u> from our <u>fear-drenched communities,</u> and in some not too distant tomorrow the <u>radiant stars</u> of love and brotherhood will shine over our great nation with all their scintillating beauty.

King addresses his audience directly to establish personal tone.

Yours for the cause of Peace and Brotherhood,

Martin Luther King, Jr.

This letter was written by King as a direct answer to the criticisms made by eight clergymen that his involvement in the Birmingham demonstrations was "unwise and untimely." For the most part, the essay consists of a point-by-point refutation of his opponents' arguments.

POINT 1: *As an "outsider," King has no right to be in Birmingham.*
Refutation:
(a) *As president of the Southern Christian Leadership Conference, King was invited by the Birmingham affiliate to take part in the demonstrations.*
(b) *As a Christian, King cannot ignore injustice, but must respond to any "call for aid" no matter where it comes from.*
(c) *The term "outside agitator" is dated and narrow-minded. "Injustice anywhere is a threat to justice everywhere."*

POINT 2: *The demonstrations in Birmingham were deplorable and cannot be justified.*
Refutation:
(a) *The Negro community had no choice. Birmingham is one of the most segregated cities in the country.*

(b) *Previous attempts at negotiation had failed.*

(c) *Self-purification workshops were held to ensure that the demonstrations were peaceful.*

(d) *Direct action is the only way to force a complacent system to face the issue.*

POINT 3: *The new Boutwell administration should have been given time to act.*

Refutation:

The new administration is also segregationist and will not act without direct pressure from the Negro community.

POINT 4: *The civil rights movement is hypocritical in its willingness to break certain laws while upholding others.*

Refutation:

Only just laws should be obeyed.

POINT 5: *Direct action leads to violence.*

Refutation:

It is illogical to condemn peaceful protestors for precipitating violence. The fault lies with those who seek to disrupt the demonstrations. Those seeking their constitutional rights should be protected from violence by law.

POINT 6: *King's activity in Birmingham has been extreme.*

Refutation:

King does, in fact, occupy a moderate position between the two extremes of violence and passivity. Without this moderate position, the streets of the South would be "flowing with blood."

King then expresses his disappointment with both the white moderates and the white church. He criticizes the church in particular for its lack of moral initiative, its lack of strong leadership, and its failure to support the civil rights movement.

King's last main point is that it is the demonstrators who should be commended for their self-control, not the police. He calls for the recognition of the "real heroes" of the civil rights movement, such as the "James Merediths."

The essay concludes on a uplifting note as King expresses his hope that "the dark clouds of racial prejudice will soon pass away . . . . and in some not too distant tomorrow the radiant stars of love and brotherhood will shine over our great nation with all their scintillating beauty."

Excerpt from Ferguson's Double-Entry Notebook

Quotes and Summaries

"I doubt you would have so warmly commended the police force if you had seen its dogs sinking their teeth into unarmed, nonviolent Negroes."

Reactions

King really knows how to use language to involve the reader emotionally. His reasonable tone allows him to do this without losing his reader's trust. So rather than just saying 'dogs attacking Negroes' he says "dogs sinking their teeth into unarmed, nonviolent Negroes." He's making an appeal to emotion here and uses parallelism to increase the effect ("if you were to watch," "if you were to see" etc.). His use of the word "Negro" makes me kind of uncomfortable. It seems so dated now. At first it makes it seem as though a lot has changed since King wrote this essay. But how much is different, really? We hardly live in an equitable society. Maybe that's why "Negro" bothers me so much. We've made the terminology "politically correct" but the injustices remain.

King concedes that the police officers may have appeared restrained in public, but argued that their behavior is still indefensible. No actions can be considered moral if they are used for immoral purposes.

King doesn't want to antagonize his audience, so he sometimes concedes the opposing point of view. Here he quickly turns the point around so that his own argument doesn't lose any ground. Nonviolent law enforcement cannot be commended if it is used to enforce unjust laws. It's important that King addresses this point because otherwise he might seem to be avoiding the issue. I mean, ignoring evidence in favor of the police would make him look biased. Instead, he makes this possible weakness into one of his strengths.

As T. S. Eliot has said, "The last temptation is the greatest treason: To do the right deed for the wrong reason."

King does this a lot—brings in some respected individual to support his argument. It shows that he is writing for a literate audience, and also that King himself is well educated (appeal to character again).

King suggests that his fellow clergymen commend the demonstrators for their self-control, not the police.

I admire King for his forthright criticisms of the white church. He's not afraid to say what he really thinks, despite his non-confrontational approach. I wonder how these clergymen reacted to the letter. I imagine it made them pretty uncomfortable. I hope so.

"One day the South will recognize its real heroes."

I've come to realize through studying this this essay that there is a reason for everything King does. Here I think he is deliberately bringing the focus back to ordinary people after a lot of fairly abstract discussion. The "My feets is tired but my soul is at rest" quote suddenly makes it all real. You can feel the struggle and frustration. Again King uses parallelism for emphasis.

One day the South will know that when these disinherited children of God sat down at lunch counters, they were in reality standing up for what is best in the American dream and for the most sacred values in our Judaeo Christian heritage, thereby bringing our nation back to those great wells of democracy which were dug deep by the founding fathers in their formulations of the Constitution and the Declaration of Independence.

I've quoted this whole passage because I think it's one of the most important in the whole essay. It gives the civil rights movement an historical context— this is not just about one town in the South; it's about American and Christian traditions. This prevents people from seeing the protest movement as "outside agitation." In referring to the Constitu tion, etc. King is playing on his audience's patriotic feelings and trying to stir their emotions. I think this is a legitimate tactic. He's not distorting anything—the American dream is meant to be about freedom and equality for all. But he is being quite clever here—these patriotic references ensure that no one can accuse him of being "un-American." I like the opposition between "sat down" and "standing up."

"Let us all hope that the dark clouds of racial prejudice will soon pass away and the deep fog of

King really likes long sentences. The repetition of "hope" is important—King wants to lift the tone of the essay and end on a positive note. He wants to involve the

misunderstanding will be lifted from our fear-drenched communities, and in some not too distant tomorrow the radiant stars of love and brotherhood will shine over our great nation with all their scintillating beauty."

reader emotionally so he uses a lot of figurative language. The "dark clouds" and "deep fog" are contrasted with the "radiant stars." (Religious imagery here? Dark vs light etc.) The reference to "our great nation" reminds the audience again of common national identity. These final sentences are uplifting and inspiring, but they rather depress me, too. We are still waiting for those "radiant stars of love and brother-hood" to shine. Has King's "not too distant tomorrow" come much closer in the past forty years, or not?

Ferguson's First Draft: An Analysis of "Letter from Birmingham Jail"

"Letter from Birmingham Jail" is a powerful, persuasive essay which argues for the necessity of direct, nonviolent action to end racial segregation in the city of Birmingham in 1963. King wrote it while in solitary confinement, in response to the published criticisms of eight white clergymen, but its scope goes far beyond that of a personal letter. In the course of the essay's pages, King demonstrates the most important aspects of argument, such as the use of appeals to character, emotion, and reason, logical structure and development, and the effective refutation of the opposition. Through reading "Letter from Birmingham Jail" I have a greater appreciation of persuasive writing and also of Martin Luther King himself.

King begins by establishing his own credibility—as the president of the Southern Christian Leadership Conference, he has a great deal of experience in the civil rights movement. This is part of the appeal to character which King maintains all the way through the essay. Aware that his audience is not sympathetic to his position, King also seeks to establish common ground between them by emphasizing their mutual involvement in the church. Himself a preacher, King draws attention to his thoroughly respectable background, "I am in the rather unique position of being the son, the grandson, and the great-grandson of preachers." By making a great many Biblical allusions, King hopes to win the trust of his opponents and so lead them towards his way of thinking. For the same reason, he presents their point of view in a calm and reasonable manner, "It is true that the police have exercised a degree of discipline in handling the demonstrators. In this sense, they have conducted themselves nonviolently in public. But for what purpose? To preserve the vile system of segregation." By fairly presenting the opposing point of view, which King does through the essay, he shows that he is unbiased and objective and, therefore, trustworthy.

The reasonable tone and the strong appeal to character allow King to manipulate his audience emotionally without losing his own credibility. He does this through the skillful use of such devices as vivid detail, metaphorical language, parallelism, and repetition. For instance, in response to the criticism that the campaign was "untimely," King creates a sharp metaphorical contrast to emphasize the natural impatience of the African American community, "We have waited more than 340 years for our constitutional and God-given rights. The nations of Africa and Asia are moving with jetlike speed toward gaining political independence, but we still creep at horse-and-buggy pace toward gaining a cup of coffee at a lunch counter." King builds on this point by using a great deal of vivid detail, as in "when you have seen hate-filled policemen curse, kick, and even kill your Negro brothers and sisters; when you see the vast majority of your Negro brothers smothering in an airtight cage of poverty in the midst of an affluent society . . .

This appeal to emotion is further strengthened through parallelism and repetition as King lists examples of his own personal humiliations. The reader cannot help but feel shocked and disgusted by these many injustices and must agree with King's final comment, "I hope, sirs, you can understand our legitimate and unavoidable impatience."

King also makes constant appeals to reason when refuting the opposing point of view, most notably when answering the criticism that the movement was too ready to break the law. While King agrees that this is "certainly a legitimate concern," he points out that "there are two types of law—just and unjust." In an extended appeal to reason, King argues that "An unjust law is a code that a numerical or power majority group compels a minority group to obey but does not make binding on itself." He then illustrates this by referring to the segregation laws of Alabama and further supports his argument by bringing in the opinions of respected individuals such as Paul Tillich and Martin Buber. King deliberately and methodically makes the distinction between just and unjust laws, and again draws on the Bible to remind his audience of the common ground between them.

In his powerful and moving conclusion, King expresses his hope that "the dark clouds of racial prejudice will soon pass away." A great deal may have changed in the forty years since King wrote "Letter from Birmingham Jail," but we are still waiting for "the radiant stars of love and brotherhood" to shine over "our great nation." Racism is still a "hidden tension" in our society, and we desperately need "creative extremists" such as Martin Luther King to bring it to the surface and cure it. The value of this essay is not just that it demonstrates the most important features of persuasive writing, but that it reminds us that racism is something that affects us all in our common identity as American citizens. As King said of himself and his followers, "our destiny is tied up with America's destiny."

Ferguson's Final Draft: An Analysis of "Letter from Birmingham Jail"

"Letter from Birmingham Jail" was written by Martin Luther King in 1963 while he was being held in solitary confinement for daring to lead a protest march against the city's segregationist policies. It is a direct response to the statement published by eight white clergymen criticizing King's direct action campaign, but its scope goes far beyond that of a personal letter. Rather than being simply a justification of his own actions, King's carefully constructed and eloquently worded argument is a justification of the civil rights movement itself. In his lengthy essay, King systematically addresses each of his opponents' points, refutes them in turn, and concludes with a series of his own criticisms of white moderates and church leaders. "Letter from Birmingham Jail" is a remarkable piece of persuasive writing which demonstrates both the principal features of argument and those individual aspects of King's style which made him such a powerful preacher and political activist.

Perhaps, the essay's greatest strength is King's non-confrontational or Rogerian approach to the argument. To avoid antagonizing an unsympathetic audience, King must appear to be a reasonable, well-informed individual whose views on this sensitive issue can be trusted. This is done very effectively in a number of ways. For instance, at the start of the essay he establishes his own credibility by describing his involvement in the Southern Christian Leadership Conference. As the president of this respected organization, it can be assumed that he has a great deal of experience in the civil rights movement. Furthermore, King constantly emphasizes his own involvement in the Church, pointing out that he is "the son, the grandson, and the great-grandson of preachers." He also compares himself with famous Christian figures, "Like Paul, I must constantly respond to the Macedonian call for aid." These somewhat obscure Biblical allusions not only show that King is thoroughly familiar with the Scriptures, but also establish a common ground between two adversaries who have little else in common but the Church. To further lessen any sense of conflict King refers to his fellow clergymen as "my friends" and "my Christian and Jewish brothers" and calls them "men of genuine good faith." Finally, King presents the opposing point of view in a calm and reasonable manner, often conceding its validity before presenting his own case: "It is true that the police have exercised a degree of discipline in handling the demonstrators. In this sense they have conducted themselves "nonviolently" in public. But for what purpose? To preserve the vile system of segregation." By fairly addressing the opposition, King shows that he is unbiased and capable of viewing the situation objectively. Therefore, when he attacks the white church for its lack of leadership and moral initiative, his criticisms carry real weight.

This strong appeal to character is maintained throughout and allows King to play on his audience's emotions without losing his own credibility. He proceeds through the constant use of metaphorical language, vivid detail, parallelism, and repetition, all of which combine to create his own unique style. For instance, in response to the criticism that the direct action campaign was "untimely" King stresses the natural impatience of his people:

> We have waited more than 340 years for our constitutional and God-given rights. The nations of Africa and Asia are moving with jetlike speed toward gaining political independence, but we still creep at horse-and-buggy pace toward gaining a cup of coffee at a lunch counter.

The contrast of these metaphors causes the reader to feel the frustration and humiliation of segregation. King builds on this by combining further metaphor with vivid detail, as in "when you have seen hate-filled policemen curse, kick, and even kill your Negro brothers and sisters; when you see the vast majority of your Negro brothers smothering in an airtight cage of poverty in the midst of an affluent society. . . ." This appeal to emotion is given even more impact through the skillful parallelism and repetition of "when you have seen . . . when you see . . . when you suddenly find . . . when you have to concoct . . ." The effect on the reader of this catalog of social injustice is one of shock and disgust, so that even the most conservative individual would have to concur with King's final comment, "I hope, sirs, you can understand our legitimate and unavoidable impatience." It is noteworthy that, despite the emotional intensity of this long passage, King never loses his self-control. With the simple insertion of "sirs" he maintains the modest and respectful tone which characterizes the whole essay.

While the appeals to character and emotion are arguably the most memorable aspects of the essay, King also makes constant appeals to reason in his defense of the direct action campaign in Birmingham. One of the best examples of his use of logic is his refutation of one of the most damaging criticisms of the movement—its "willingness to break laws." King concedes that this is "certainly a legitimate concern," but points out that "there are two types of law: just and unjust." In an extended appeal to reason, King argues that "An unjust law is a code that a numerical or power majority group compels a minority group to obey but does not make binding on itself." He then illustrates this general statement with a specific example:

> Who can say that the legislature of Alabama which set up that state's seg-
> regation laws was democratically elected? Throughout Alabama all sorts of
> devious methods are used to prevent Negroes from becoming registered vot-
> ers, and there are even some counties in which, even though Negroes consti-
> tute a majority of the population, not a single Negro is registered.

Perhaps King could have given more detailed evidence here, by describing the "devious methods" used and identifying the counties in question. He does, however, refer repeatedly to respected intellectuals such as Paul Tillich and Martin Buber to support his points, and it must be remembered that his essay was composed in a jail cell where there were no reference books.

In his powerful and moving conclusion, King expresses his hope that "the dark clouds of racial prejudice will soon pass away." The highly figurative language in this final paragraph creates another strong appeal to emotion, but this time the effect is one of promise and elation rather than shock and disgust. Throughout the letter, King has made references to the American Dream, the Constitution, and symbolic figures such as Thomas Jefferson and Abraham Lincoln, and this is continued in "our great nation." These references not only stir positive, patriotic feelings in his audience but also create a feeling of a shared national identity. For me, the value of this essay is not just in its tone, its skillful use of appeals, or its powerful language, but in its reminder that racism is something which affects us all in our common cultural identity. As King said of himself and of his followers, "our destiny is tied up with America's destiny." This is something none of us should forget. A great deal may have changed in the forty years since King wrote "Letter from Birmingham Jail," but we are still waiting for "the radiant stars of love and brotherhood" to shine. Racism is still a "hidden tension" in our society, and more than ever we need "creative extremists" such as Martin Luther King to bring it to the surface and to cure it.

In the final draft, the writer moves from a diffuse focus on imagery to a concentration on the three forms of appeal and the stylistic devices that create the appeals and that make them persuasive.

[Appendixes]

The Research Process and MLA Documentation

The reason for doing research is to attain information that will enlarge your understanding and analysis of a subject or topic. In your research, you may conceive of yourself as a detective, posing problems, deciphering the mysteries in the text or texts that need to be solved. You begin with clues, the words on a page; the clues reveal patterns. You discard false leads, red herrings, and develop a vision of a work or topic—your interpretation—expanded by information that you have gained from reading sources other than the work itself (if your subject concerns one particular text). The technical term in the research process for the work itself is the primary source. Other primary or original sources include autobiography, letters, journals, documents, and manuscripts. After you examine primary documents, then you study secondary sources that give you commentary about the topic. These materials may be biographical, historical, or critical.

An instructor may assign a specific subject for the research paper, for example, the vision of the tragic hero in *Antigone* (Chapter 8). Other instructors may offer you the opportunity to determine the topic. If no particular assignment is given, you may want to concentrate on one of these areas:

- The biography of the author.
- The relationship between the writer's life and works.
- The artistic influences upon the writer.
- Analysis of the process of the writer through examination of drafts.
- Features of a particular work, characteristics of the genre, such as point of view and symbolism in a short story, imagery and tone in a poem, character and conflict in a play.
- The social, historical, and political contexts of a work.
- A particular critical approach, such as a formalist analysis of Keats's "Ode on a Grecian Urn"; a feminist reading of "The Yellow Wallpaper."

These key topic areas may be posed as beginning questions for research:

- What biographical facts do I need to know about the writer that will help me understand the topic?
- What are the connections between the life and works?
- How did the writer develop his or her work? What can I learn by examining successive drafts of a work or by reading about the writer's artistic techniques?

- What features of the genre do I want to explore? Refer to the check-lists for the evaluation of short fiction, poetry, drama, and nonfiction in Chapters 10 through 13.
- What themes seem most important?
- How did the historical, social, political, and cultural realities of the time influence the writer?
- How are the intellectual movements of the writer's time evident in his or her work?
- How does the work represent social, political, and cultural realities?
- How will my reading of criticism enlarge my vision of the topic?
- What aspects of the subject do I find most puzzling?
- What interpretations of the topic do I find most debatable?
- What schools of thought will enlarge my understanding and provide new intellectual contexts and directions for further analysis?

Any one of these questions may provide a starting point.

The Research Process

For the sake of discussion, assume that you have chosen a particular work that interests or intrigues you. Before you begin your research project, you need to develop an understanding of the work. Perhaps you have discussed it in class. Perhaps you have talked about the reading in collaborative learning groups or with friends. Perhaps you have determined your own topic and have selected and studied a work not assigned or discussed in the course. After you analyze the text, you are ready to begin your research. Some suggested stages of the process follow. As you become more comfortable with the process, you may adapt or modify these stages to fit your needs.

Begin with a full exploration of the work. Engage in forms of reader response: annotate the text, brainstorm, freewrite, compose a double-entry notebook, and write several journal entries. Determine your interpretation, analyze your interpretation, and identify questions that remain. Discover the most puzzling areas concerning the topic. Then formulate a list of research questions. Check the most interesting queries. Have potential directions for research before you go to the library.

Next, explore other primary and secondary sources that will provide you with further information about the work. In the reference section of the library, you may want to consult a general encyclopedia for information on the writer and his or her work. Often the encyclopedia will have a signed entry by an expert and additional bibliographic sources. You may assume that the author of the encyclopedia entry is a reliable expert on the topic as are the other writers of cited secondary references. You now have a beginning point for research. After you complete this overview of a writer's life and works, you may choose a specialized biographical source, including the *Dictionary of National Biography*, *Dictionary of American Biography*, *Contemporary Authors*, *Twentieth-Century Authors*, *The Oxford Companion to American Literature*, and *The Oxford Companion to English Literature*. The Oxford Companion series also includes guides to other areas of literary study besides British and American literature (e.g., *The Oxford Companion to African American Literature*, *to American Theater*, etc.). Cambridge University Press also publishes literary reference guides. One title, for example, is *The Cam-*

bridge Guide to Asian Theatre (1993). Other valuable resources for background information include the following: *The Bloomsbury Guide to Women's Literature, The Feminist Companion to Literature in English: Women Writers from the Middle Ages to the Present,* and *The Penguin Companion to World Literature.* These reference books will give you a more comprehensive view of the writer and his or her work and additional sources for research.

After you gather information about a writer's life and works, you may narrow your focus to a single research area. At this point, you also will consult the computerized cataloglor computer indices of information to discover and gain additional secondary sources concerning biography and criticism. Other specialized indices in print form for research in journals and periodicals include the *Arts and Humanities Citation Index, Biography Index, Book Review Index,* and *Essay and General Literature Index.* Electronic databases include ProQuest, Wilson, JSTOR, Expanded Academic Index, Lexis-Nexis (abstracts and full texts from newspapers and journals), Info-Trac-One File, and Opposing Viewpoints. A very productive source of information for the study of literary texts is the Gale Literature Resource Center. The "Center" includes biographical, critical, and scholarly sources. Online indices include the Academic Index and Expanded Humanities Index. Note: First Search, a commercial database service to which many schools subscribe, allows you to find information on a broad range of subject areas. In many cases, collections of essays on the author and substantial critical treatments of the writer's life and works exist. You then survey and skim your materials with a slant or idea in mind. Before writing, in order to determine a focus, review biographical and critical materials so that you do not take too many preliminary notes.

As you consult sources, you write bibliographic entries. Each source may appear on a separate card, or you may devise some other system. The entry should contain the following information for a book: Author, Title, Publication Information (Place Published, Publisher, Date), and Library of Congress reference number so that you can find the book again without searching for it in the catalog. A bibliographic entry for a journal should contain the following: Author, Title of the Article, Journal, Publication Source, Volume, Year, Date, and Page. Include a brief evaluation of the source.

Book

Bundtzen, Lynda K.	PS 3566
Plath's Incarnations: A Woman and the Creative Process	.L27 Z588
Ann Arbor: University of Michigan Press, 1983	1983
Good evidence and analysis of theme of transcendence.	

Journal

Pollitt, Katha   PMLA Bibliography

"A Note of Triumph"
Nation.

16 January 1982: 52–55.

Excellent review of *Collected Poems* by Plath

Both biographical and critical treatments of the author and collections of essays may provide additional reference materials. You also may want to consult such general indices as the *Reader's Guide to Periodical Literature* (for information on current writers), the *New York Times Index,* and the *Book Review Digest* as well as computerized general subject indices for information in periodicals, magazines, journals, and newspapers and for reviews of current authors. The reference room also contains specialized bibliographies. For example, there are several bibliographies of women's studies materials (e.g., see *American Women Writers: A Critical Reference Guide from Colonial Times to the Present*). A standard bibliography for information on literature is the *Modern Language Association International Bibliography of Books and Articles on Modern Language and Literature.* This bibliography indexes the major scholarship in the discipline and lists entries for authors according to field of literature, nationality, and time period. For example, Ernest Hemingway's name would appear in the Twentieth Century American Literature section. Other specialized bibliographies include American Literary Scholarship, *American Literature and Language: A Guide to Information Sources, The New Cambridge Bibliography of English Literature,* and *The Oxford History of English Literature.* Also particularly helpful reference sources are the *Literary Criticism Index, Contemporary Literary Criticism, Contemporary Authors,* and *Gale Literary Criticism Series.*

After you have decided on a research question and after you have narrowed your focus and established a preliminary direction for research, isolate the materials that you plan to study. At this point, you have an initial list of "works consulted" and a working bibliography of those books and articles from which you genuinely intend to gather information. Your instructor may want to check your bibliography and to offer further directions for research. As you shape your bibliography, examine your sources of information. You want to be aware of the publication date of your secondary sources so that you do not rely on outdated materials or interpretations of works.

Now, the notetaking phase of the research process begins. Before you start taking notes, however, keep your research questions and possible subtopics or subheadings for analysis on a separate sheet of paper so that they are foremost in your mind. You also may draft a potential thesis and determine a tentative purpose and audience for your essay. The purposes of research essays about literature are informative, argumentative, or evaluative; that is, the writer explains an interpretation, argues a point of view, or evaluates the effectiveness of a work or a writer's use of a particular technique. You may assume that your audience is your instructor and a community of knowledgeable peers. Having a beginning idea of questions, of topics, of thesis, of purpose, and of audience will direct your thinking and notetaking and will help you to assess the information from your sources. As you take notes, be aware that you may change your approach, thesis, topics, purpose, and audience.

Read and review your secondary sources carefully. Some people prefer to take notes on index cards; others use sheets of paper; others take minimal notes on cards or paper and create a system of notes that refers to photocopied information. You may put notes in the margins of duplicated information. In addition, you may wish to enter data into a computer. Whatever method you use, as you take notes, you engage in a combination of summarizing, paraphrasing, and quoting. When you summarize, you compress the central idea and main points in a work. When you paraphrase, you "translate" a passage from a work into your own words. Paraphrasing keeps the length, spirit, tone, logic, and ideas of the original passage, but the wording is different. When you quote, you are recording the author's statement exactly. Be certain not to include any words from the original work within your summary or paraphrase without using quotation marks. Any material from a source in the words of the author must be quoted. For this reason, take notes meticulously. Summarize, paraphrase, and quote accurately on the front of a note card or page. Then write your reaction and comments on the back of the card or paper or photocopy so that you have carefully documented and differentiated between your words and the language in the source, between your view and the critic's interpretations.

Each note also should contain an abbreviated annotation for source and page and a heading so that you may arrange your notes into categories of discussion and reshuffle them as your thesis and topics evolve.

The Research Process Online

The stages of researching online are similar to traditional research methods: gain an overview of your topic by using an online encyclopedia (e.g., *Encyclopedia Britannica* on CD-ROM); develop a search strategy—narrow your topic; define and then refine your search terms and key words; and then limit your search and isolate appropriate online resources (CD-ROM; databases; indices; works online; other World Wide Web resources—public posting, home pages, etc.).

Consider carefully the search engine. Some search engines index general information according to subject areas (e.g., Google, Yahoo!) and compile information from other search engines, while others are more appropriate for literary research (Google Scholar or Academic Search Elite [EBSCO]). What follows are some important procedures for doing research online once you have chosen a search engine:

- Define the terms of your search (author, title, work, phrase).
- Identify a phrase or subject area by using parentheses or quotation marks.
- Limit your search by combining key words with Boolean operators. Remember that "and" narrows your search, "or" widens the search, and "not" excludes information.

- Check each search engine for appropriate field indicators and for directions as to how to search.
- Once you find sources, bookmark them.
- Create a list or folder of viable sources. You may create a hyperlinked bibliography.
- Print out the most important information.

It is especially important when you are doing research on the web that you evaluate your sources carefully and that you verify your information by using print sources. To assess web sources, consider these important questions about a website:

- Who is the author? Is he or she an expert in the field? What is the intended audience? Do you detect bias on the part of the authors?
- In what format is the site? a personal home page? newsgroup? article online? (Be aware that information from online dialogues and online forums may not be useful. The people are not likely to be authorities on a subject, so the information may be inaccurate.)
- What organization is sponsoring the website? Is the site a reputable one? an academic site? These abbreviations commonly indicate the kind of group sponsoring the site: .com = commercial site; .org = organization; .edu = educational institution; .gov = government site. (Be careful to distinguish between a personal home page and authorized sites for authors or for organizations.)
- Is the information accurate? current? verifiable?
- Is the treatment of the subject comprehensive? balanced?
- What is the date of the entry?

As you download material, be selective. Note the date that you accessed the material as well as the URL and information about the site.

Here is a list of selected search engines and helpful websites for literary research:

- Yahoo!—http://www.yahoo.com (a subject guide to the web with links to other sites and search engines).
- Google—http://www.google.com (a comprehensive search engine with links to more than a billion web pages).
- Ask Jeeves—http://www.ask.com (a resource for general information).
- Galaxy—http://www.galaxy.com (a resource for humanities and literature research).
- AltaVista—http://www.altavista.com (a search engine for humanities and literature topics).
- Lycos—http://www.lycos.com (another useful search engine).
- The Argus Clearinghouse—http://www.clearinghouse.net (a directory of subject guides, helpful to scholars).
- MLA on the web—http://www.mla.org (the site of the Modern Language Association with a link to guidelines for documenting sources in MLA format).
- The Voice of the Shuttle: web Pages for Humanities Research—http://www.vos.ucsb.edu/ (guide to websites on literary studies).
- The EServer (University of Washington)—http://eserver.org.

Principles of Documentation

You need to follow principles of documentation in your research process. Documentation indicates the sources of your information to a reader and demonstrates that you have absorbed and synthesized the materials from your secondary sources. Information that you should document in the text of your research paper includes the following:

- Facts that are not common knowledge (that could not be verified in several sources).
- Paraphrased information from a source (information from a source that you have put into your own words).
- Quoted material.
- Other people's views—even when they are paraphrased, not quoted— interviews, and other sources of information.

All of the above forms of information must be documented. If you do not document thoroughly or if you inadequately paraphrase the source, you will be plagiarizing. **Plagiarism** is the taking of someone else's ideas or words and representing them as your own. This act, which constitutes academic "theft," is a serious matter.

Once you have refined your research question, decided upon a focus for your research, a preliminary approach, thesis, and subtopics, and conducted research, you are ready to revise your thesis, to create an outline, and to draft your essay. The final stage in the research process is actually composing the essay. During this phase, you may repeat the acts of the writing process although you already have done considerable prewriting and planning: brainstorming, shaping, drafting, revising, and writing several versions of your paper. In this research-writing process, however, you must document carefully from all your sources.

For students, another issue in the research process becomes the value of their own opinions and thinking. During the drafting of a research essay, you focus on an original thesis and idea. Your thesis emerges from your thinking, reading, and research. The exploration, evaluation, and synthesis of evidence from sources also emanate from your own thinking. When you piece together your opinions, analysis, and information from primary and secondary sources, you may discover that you experience the satisfaction of exploring and validating your thesis and of sharing your findings with others.

Form of MLA Documentation— Citation Within the Text

All sources must be cited; that is, you must give the reader information about the material to which you refer. The accepted method of documenting information in research is MLA citation form that requires three steps: (1) use parenthetical references within your research essay; (2) include a "Works Cited" page that contains an alphabetized list of all of the primary and secondary sources that you have used in the development of your essay; and (3) include explanatory endnotes, if necessary.

The parenthetical reference involves two parts: an indication of author and of page. If the author's name is mentioned in the discussion, then you only need to indicate page number. If the author has written two books and if the title of the book is not given, then you should include an abbreviated title in the citation.

The common forms of parenthetical citation for papers about literature appear in the following examples. Examine these manuscript and punctuation forms—the conventions for citations:

1. Discussion (author and page)
   (Alexander 200).
2. Discussion—author already mentioned
   (79).
3. Two Works by Same Author whose name is mentioned
   ("Hope" 265) (*Ariel* 54).
4. Paraphrased and Summarized Material—author not mentioned
   (Alexander 302).
5. Direct Quotation—author mentioned
   Kroll states that "it is uncertain how seriously the speaker will entertain the theme of purity, and its related theme of transcendence" (178).
   Note: Citation appears after quotation mark and before final punctuation.
6. Indented quotation—more than two lines of poetry and four lines of prose:
   This poem is about two kinds of fire—
   the fires of hell, which merely
   agonize, and the fires of hell which
   purify. During the poem, the first
   suffers into the second. (Newman 62)

If you interpret only one literary work, you may indicate the paragraphs or pages of a short story, the lines of a poem, or the acts and scenes of a drama in a citation rather than the author and title since they previously have appeared in the introduction to the essay.

"Works Cited" Page

The "Works Cited" page also has a specific format, a particular pattern for each form of reference, dictated by the conventions of the MLA documentation system. The following are the most common bibliographic forms for the "Works Cited" page. Consult the handbook used in your school's freshman composition program for further information.

Common Forms of Bibliographic Entries for the "Works Cited" Page

For a Book

Gilligan, Carol. <u>In a Different Voice: Psychological Theory and Women's Development</u>. Cambridge: Harvard University Press, 1982.

Kincaid, Jamaica. <u>Annie John</u>. New York: Farrar, Straus, Giroux, 1985.

Morrison, Toni. <u>Beloved</u>. New York: Knopf, 1987.

The citation is double-spaced, the author's name is placed at the margin, and the second line indented (five spaces). There are periods between parts of the entry. The citation includes author's name, the title of the work and publication information—place published, publisher, and date.

For a Book with Two Authors

Flynn, Elizabeth A. and Patrocino Schweickart, eds. <u>Gender and Reading: Essays on Readers, Texts and Contexts</u>. Baltimore: Johns Hopkins Press, 1986.

When there are two authors, the second author's name is presented first name and then last name.

For an Author with Two Works

Rich, Adrienne. <u>An Atlas of a Difficult World: Poems 1988–1991</u>. New York: W. W. Norton, 1991.

—. <u>On Lies, Secrets and Silence: Selected Prose 1966–1978</u>. New York: W. W. Norton, 1979.

Note the alphabetical order of books for the author and a long (em) dash or three hyphens with a period to indicate the repeated name.

For Three or More Authors

Belenky, Mary Field, et al. <u>Women's Ways of Knowing: The Development of Self, Voice, and Mind</u>. New York: Basic Books, 1986.

Notice the use of "et al." to indicate the additional authors.

Translation

Wolf, Christa. <u>The Quest for Christa T</u>. Trans. Christopher Middletown. New York: Farrar, Straus, and Giroux, 1970.

Note that the translator's name appears after title and before publication information.

A Work Within an Anthology of Works

Mukherjee, Bharati. "Courtly Vision." <u>Sudden Fiction International: Sixty Short-Short Stories</u>. Eds. Robert Shapard and James Thomas. New York: W. W. Norton, 1989. 215–219.

The author's name and work appear before the title of the anthology. The names of the authors of the anthology are acknowledged, with the abbreviation indicating that they are the editors. Finally, the publication information is given.

Additional Entries for Works in an Anthology

Schmidt, Jan Zlotnik, Lynne Crockett, and Carley Bogarad, eds. <u>Legacies</u>. Boston: Cengage Learning Wadsworth, 2008.

Shakespeare, William. <u>Hamlet</u>. Schmidt, Bogarad, and Crockett, eds. 174–261.

Keats, John. "Ode on a Grecian Urn." Schmidt, Bogarad, and Crockett, eds. 1094–1095.

If you cite more than one selection from the same anthology, list the anthology as a separate entry with all publication information. If you use more than one work from the same anthology, also list each selection. Give the author's name and title of the selection, but mention only the name(s) of the editor(s) of the anthology and the page numbers.

Other Examples of a Short Story, Poem, or Play in an Edited Anthology

Borowski, Tadeusz. "Silence." <u>Literature: Reading, Reacting, Writing</u>. Eds. Laurie G. Kirzner and Stephen R. Mandell. Fort Worth: Harcourt Brace, 1993. 315–316.

Note the indication of page numbers.

Kumin, Maxine. "The Envelope." <u>Tangled Vines: A Collection of Mother and Daughter Poems</u>. Ed. Lyn Lifshin. New York: Harcourt, Brace, Jovanovich, 1992. 143.

Childress, Alice. <u>Wedding Band. 9 Plays by Black Women</u>. Ed. Margaret B. Wilkerson. New York: New American Library, 1986. 69–133.

Note that titles of short stories, poems, and essays require quotation marks and that titles of plays are underlined or italicized. As a general rule, complete works are underlined, and shorter works appear in quotation marks.

Work in Several Volumes

Eagleton, T. Allston. <u>A History of the New York Stage</u>. 3 vols. New York: Prentice Hall, 1987.

Note the indication of volumes.

One Work in a Several Volume Work

Eagleton, T. Allston. <u>A History of the New York Stage</u>. New York: Prentice Hall, 1987. Vol. 2.

Note the indication of the particular volume cited in the essay at the end of the note.

An Edited Anthology Cited as a Whole Work, Not as a Single Citation of a Particular Selection

Halpern, Daniel, ed. <u>The American Poetry Anthology</u>. New York: Avon, 1975.

Note the indication that Halpern is the editor.

An Article in a Critical Anthology

Volpe, Edmond L. "The Wasteland of Nathanael West." Nathanael West: A Collection of Critical Essays. Ed. Jay Martin. Englewood Cliffs, NJ: Prentice Hall, 1971. 91–101.

An Article or Selection in a Weekly Magazine for General Audiences, Paginated Anew in Each Issue

Barthelme, Frederick. "Law of Averages." The New Yorker, 5 October 1987: 36–39.

Notice the format for presentation of articles: Author, Title of Work, Name of Magazine, Date, a colon, and then pages.

An Article in an Academic Journal Paginated Continuously Throughout the Volume Year

Wilentz, Gay. "Toward a Diaspora Literature: Black Women Writers from Africa, the Caribbean and the United States." College English 54 (1992): 385–445.

Note the addition of volume number after the title of the journal and the placement of year within parentheses.

An Article in a Journal That Comes Out Once a Month, That Is Paginated Anew Each Month, and That Has a Volume and Issue Number

Muscatine, Charles. "Faculty Responsibility for the Curriculum." Academe 71.5 (1985): 18–21.

Notice that 71 is the volume number and that 5 is the issue number.

An Encyclopedia

Blotner, Joseph L. "James Joyce." The Webster Family Encyclopedia, 1984 ed.

You do not need to include publication information for well-known reference sources.

An Article in a Newspaper

Sontag, Deborah. "Making 'Refugee Experience' Less Daunting." New York Times 27 September 1992: Sec.1:1,35.

A Film or Book Review

Rafferty, Terrence. "Closing Time." Rev. of Leaving Las Vegas, dir. Mike Figgis with Nicholas Cage and Elizabeth Shue. The New Yorker. 6 Nov. 1995: 176–178.

Note: The reviewer's name and the title of the review precede the film or publication information.

A Film, Videotape, or DVD

The Manchurian Candidate. Screenplay by George Axelrod. Dir. John Frankenheimer. Prod. George Axelrod. Perf. Frank Sinatra, Laurence Harvey, Janet Leigh, and Angela Lansbury. MGM. 1962.

Artwork

Matisse, Henri. Goldfish. Museum of Modern Art. 1914–1915.

Interview

Dove, Rita. "An Interview with Helen Vendler." The National Humanities Center, January 16, 1989.

Bogarad, Carley. "Sylvia Plath's and Ted Hughes' Poetry." Talk given at State University of New York College at New Paltz. New Paltz, October 24, 1990.

Principles of Online Documentation

When you document online sources, follow these general guidelines. Begin with the author's name, title of the work, and publication information as you would for a print source. Next list the electronic publication date and then the date you accessed the information. Finally, include the URL (uniform resource locator). If the URL takes more than one line of text, split the citation following a slash. Do not break the URL with a hyphen.

What follows is a list of online resources for teaching Sherman Alexie's "This Is What It Means to Say Phoenix, Arizona" that Vika Shock, an ESL instructor at the State University of New York at New Paltz, compiled as background material for teaching the story.

Common Forms of Bibliographic Entries for Internet Sources on the "Works Cited" Page

Online Newspaper

"Sherman Alexie, Indian Country's Favorite Writer." Oklahoma Indian Times Online: The Native American Resources. 5 July 2000. <http://www.okit .com/news/2000/September/Best/shermanalexie.htm>

Online Not-for-Profit Organization

Soneda, Brian. "Sherman and the Heavy Hitters." ALKI: The Washington Library Association Journal. December 1998. WLA Online. 5 July 2000. <http://www.wla.org/alki/dec98/soneda.html>

Online Article from an Education Source

Luscher, Robert M. Anthology of Modern American Poetry. Book. *Modern American Poetry: Sherman Alexie (1966–)*. Multimedia Companion Online. University of Illinois at Urbana-Champaign. 1999. <http://www.english .uiuc.edu/maps/poets/a-f/alexie/alexie.htm>

Home Page

Rani. "The Official Sherman Alexie Site." Home page. January 1999. 5 July 2000. <http://www.fallsapart.com/>

Online Interview

West, Dennis and Joan M. West. Interview. "Sending Cinematic Smoke Signals: An Interview with Sherman Alexie." Cineaste v23, n4 (Fall, 1998): 28 (5 pages) 5 July 2000. <http://www.lib.berkeley.edu/MRC/alexie.html>

Online Encyclopedia

"Sherman Alexie." Britannica Online. 2004 Encylopedia Britannica. 5 July 2006. http://www.britannica.com

Article from Gale Literature Resource Center

"Sherman (Joseph Jr.) Alexie." Contemporary Authors Online. Thomson Gale. 2005 Sojourner Truth Library. SUNY New Paltz. New Paltz, New York. 5 July 2006. http://www.galenet.com/serlet/

Article from the Gale Literature Resource Center

McFarland, Ron. "Another Kind of Violence: Sherman Alexie's Poems." American Indian Quarterly 21,2 (Spring 1997): 252. Gale Literature Resource Center. Sojourner Truth Library. SUNY New Paltz. New Paltz, New York. 5 July 2006. http://galenet.galegroup.com/serlet/LitRc?vrsn

Full-Text Article Found in a Database (Academic Search Premier, EBSCO, JSTOR)

Ase Nygren. "A World of Story-Smoke: A Conversation with Sherman Alexie." Melus, 30,4 (Winter 2006): 159–169. Academic Search Premier. EBSCO. Sojourner Truth Library. SUNY New Paltz. New Paltz, New York. 5 July 2006. http://search.ebscohost.com/login.aspx?direct=true&db+aph&AN =195858.

Endnotes

When you use parenthetical citation form, you may create endnotes to include explanatory information that is not necessary to the text. This information may be additional sources, added biographical data, or an opposing critical view. Endnotes are numbered, follow in numerical order in the essay, and are indicated by a number in superscript above the line: [1]. The "Endnote" page, labeled "Notes," is doubled-spaced, appears after the last page of your paper, and is your last numbered page. The "Works Cited" page is the last page of your research essay.

Here is an example of an endnote designed to provide additional bibliographic information:

Text of Essay

In recent years, there have been many attempts to define women's separate ways of knowing and developing moral consciousness.[1]

Notes

[1] See, for example, Belenky et al. and Gilligan.

Here is an endnote designed to provide a differing critical view:

Text of Essay

The House on Mango Street is considered by many critics to be Cisneros's best work. This first, autobiographical work brought her critical acclaim.[1]

Notes

[1]Although *The House on Mango Street* brought Cisneros acclaim, I would contend that *Woman Hollering Creek* is a more complex and subtle work.

An Example of the Research Essay— MLA Documentation

Historical and Cultural Analysis and Argument

Eric Schoonebeek wrote his research paper in Composition II discussing literature as history and the representation of the Holocaust in Cynthia Ozick's "The Shawl."

Erik Schoonebeek

Literature as History

In the barracks they spoke of 'flowers,' of 'rain': excrement, thick turd-braids, and the slow stinking maroon waterfall that sunk from the upper bunks, the stink mixed with bitter fatty floating smoke that greased Rosa's skin (Ozick 8-9)

epigraph designed to provoke interest

What kind of wicked hell is this? What is this place where a steel fence is the division between a stinking, floating, greasy death and "green meadows speckled with dandelions and deep-colored violets . . . innocent tiger lilies lifting their orange bonnets" (Ozick 8)? This is the arena of dehumanization and the trivialization of life: the Nazi concentration camps of World War II, through the words of Cynthia Ozick.

Ozick's *The Shawl* is a historical narrative, surrounded by massive amounts of Holocaust documentation that historians have cemented in human chronology forever. But, how can one human fathom 6 million deaths? It is as much beyond the grasp of all imagination as the mind-set of the monster that ordered this mass murder. Without any personal experience in something that was so personal to so many people, we can only attempt to relate the Holocaust to our own consciousness through what is left behind. With the number of Holocaust survivors dwindling, eventually all that will be left behind are documents and Holocaust literature.

background information to establish context

"The Shawl" falls in the category of Holocaust literature and attempts to call to mind the humanity (or lack there of) of the Holocaust through the use of fiction. With Holocaust literature holding so much importance to the future understanding of history, Cynthia Ozick's piece becomes controversial, because it is fictional. One must ask if fiction, in the case of the Holocaust, is credible as a tool for understanding and preventing atrocity or if it merely portrays the imagination of the author, becoming a sort of folk tale, over time perverting the truth of documentation and first-hand accounts. To fully understand the role that "The Shawl" takes in relation to Holocaust history we must first define what it is not.

argumentative focus

excellent transition

"The Shawl" is not a memoir of Cynthia Ozick (she was not a victim of the Holocaust), nor is it a memoir of Rosa, the main character. Ozick chooses an omniscient narrator to stay at a distance to factual history throughout the story. She distances "The Shawl" from being tied to history to the point of refraining from using the terms "Holocaust," "Nazi," or even "concentration camp." Much of the documented history of WWII Germany is based around these terms, so frequently repeated that they begin to lose their meaning and the gravity of their associations.

counter-argument

Hayden White observes that such terms begin to be "associated with metaphysical concepts, religious beliefs or story forms" (398) and in becoming so, ironically, start to lose their true identity as we attempt to identify

use of authority as support

with them. To further this disassociation with history, it can also be observed that with the changing value of these terms history can take on an exotic quality simply due to the distance in time from our modern era. By these means we begin to associate documented history with cultures, people, and places that seem very different from our own. We overestimate the difference in the state of human consciousness from age to ago, and documented Holocaust history (even in its greatest detail) becomes quite foreign as the reader makes assumptions and associations in the context of his own era.

Extensively detailed histories can be seen to contain some qualities not usually associated with such strict observation. Many classic histories contain a sort of filler that is based on hypothesis as logical progression. This can happen when documentation of an era is lacking, and a history of this era can only be presumed by its context. Thus, detailed history (accepted as nonfiction) can take on a touch of the fictional. In *Fables of Identity*, Northrup Frye states that "when a historian's scheme gets to a certain point of comprehensiveness it becomes mythical in shape, and so approaches the poetic in structure" (as quoted in White 396). To say that the Holocaust documented history has become "mythical in shape" would come as quite a stretch to most. However, a minority has been swayed by the mythical capability of history in this case. "The number of books published that seek to deny the existence of the Nazi death camps now exceeds one hundred," states Czeslaw Milosz in his 1980 Nobel Peace Prize speech (as quoted in Hampl 632). This fact draws attention to one of the most basic, but most important, differences between documented history and narrative history.

History is constructive on two levels. First, as stated before, history can construct a public view that is either accurate or false, depending on who holds the power and the pen. Second, the historian is constructing history itself, from a sea of nothing but fact. There is no preconception to work from. Historians construct the concept. In contrast, narrative history works from the foundation laid down by historians. Narrative history can construct a public view, but it is not the goal. Much of narrative history appeals to the human aspects of history, making them tangible to the senses and, in effect, giving documentation a new solidity in the human consciousness. Hayden White aptly describes this relationship which is especially apparent in "The Shawl": ". . . the historical narrative does not reproduce the events it describes; it

argumentative thesis

tells us in what direction to think about the events and charges our thought about events with different emotional valences" (White 402). To see whether "The Shawl" truly does justice to the Holocaust in respect to White's comment, one must examine the images, modes of characterization, and symbols Ozick chooses.

The most widely used and important device in "The Shawl" is imagery. Ozick attempts to call to mind the feelings of loathing, shock, and desperation through the use of imagination, abstraction, and embellishment. Ozick assaults the senses to create a sense of tangibility and truth. Thirty-five years after the Holocaust, in "Rosa," Ozick describes Miami: "The streets were a furnace, the sun an executioner" (Ozick 14). "They [the citizens] were all scarecrows, blown about under the murdering sunball with empty rib cages" (Ozick 16). With this imagery, Miami takes on the likeness of a barren valley of decay, or a desert, suggesting that Rosa (now described as a "madwoman" and a "scavenger") is not free of her past in the death camp, but that it follows her like a black cloud. Ozick also plays with our senses in the description of the barracks and the beauty that lies outside (see epigraph). Again, in "Rosa," Rosa walks on a beach at night: "In the dark . . . hotel roofs held up their merciless teeth. Across the water the sky breathed a starless black; behind her, where the hotels bit down on the city, a dusty glow of brownish red lowered. Mud clouds. The sand was littered with bodies. Photograph of Pompeii: prone in the volcanic ash" (Ozick 47). All senses are involved in these bold and effectively graphic descriptions. Ozick also uses specific imagery and aptly unique descriptions in her construction of characters.

quotes from primary sources combined with paraphrase

Ozick embellishes some physical traits of Rosa, Magda, and Stella in "The Shawl" to create vital, weighty characters in a work that is only seven pages in length. Rosa's characterization in "The Shawl" is close to that of nonexistence. "Rosa did not feel hunger; she felt light . . . like someone in a faint, in trance . . . a floating angel, alert and seeing everything, but in the air, not there, not touching the road. As if teetering on the tips of her fingernails" (Ozick 4-5). Rosa becomes ethereal and ghostlike in quality with the embellishment of her emaciated state. Later, in "Rosa," Rosa takes on more human qualities as she interacts with people but is still described as a "scavenger" amongst death and decay as the sheets on her bed are described as "an umbilical cord. A shipwreck" (Ozick 30). Rosa tugs her dress out of the sheets "like a coarse colored worm . . ." (Ozick 33). Magda, Rosa's

topic sentence— character

paraphrase and summary

infant daughter, is also characterized by images, coupled with animal personification. Magda is surrounded by and compared to everything from a squirrel in a nest to having the eyes of a tiger and, most often, a butterfly. Ozick gives Magda "pencil legs," "zigzag arms," and a "balloonish belly" (10) as she flies through the air like a butterfly but as far away as a moth toward the electric fence. Stella has "knees like tumors on sticks, her elbows chicken bones" (Ozick 3). Some of this imagery is unclear if taken literally, but "historical narrative does not image the things it indicates; it calls to mind images of the things it indicates, in the same way metaphor does" (Ozick 402). Ozick's images conjure up different associations between the Holocaust and each reader's own life, and the work becomes personal. However, "The Shawl" not only is personal but also contains some key symbols that are universal in quality and of historical and traditional Jewish origin.

The entirety of "The Shawl" is inspired by one line from William Shirer's massive *The Rise and Fall of the Third Reich:* "that spoke about babies being thrown against the electrified fences" (Friedman 113). Ozick's short story stands upon a fifteen-hundred page foundation, which Shirer built, from 485 tons of documented fact. Ozick also uses symbols from Jewish mysticism. Magda's breath smelled of cinnamon and almonds, even though she hadn't been near anything of the sort. This smell calls to mind that of the Jewish besamin (spice box), which is sniffed at the havadalah ceremony, ending the Sabbath. To smell the scent of this box is to sustain one from any tribulations they may cross during the ordinary days of the week (Friedman 115). Rosa is sustained by Magda's meager survival, as if only her breath will guard her from evil.

summary of background information

The most important symbol in "The Shawl" is, of course, the shawl of the title. The shawl represents the one image of life in a sea of excrement and death. Magda "milks" the shawl, as it can suffice as a magical source of nourishment. Later, in "Rosa," Stella sends Rosa the shawl as it again brings about life, this time in Rosa's disillusionment as Magda fills the room "like a butterfly in this corner and that" upon the arrival of the shawl (Ozick 64). It converts to a dead baby to a "Queen of Bloom and Blossom" and Stella into the "Angel of Death" (Ozick 66). The shawl is not only a universal symbol of life but also affiliated with Judaism. The Jewish prayer shawl, or tallit, is worn at times of prayer when Jews are closer with their God and become a community (Friedman 115). When Magda is on her way to certain death, voices tell Rosa to "hold up the shawl, high . . . . to shake it, to whip with it, to unfurl it like a flag" (Ozick 9). Rosa does so, in a declaration of surrender, desperation, and a Jewish prayer for life. Following Magda's death, the shawl saves Rosa's own life as she stuffs her mouth with it, "swallowing the wolf's screech" so she would not be shot (Ozick 10).

Remaining consistent with Jewish symbolism, the "grainy sad voices" that Rosa hears emanating from the electric fence are most likely those of Jewish history (Ozick 8), telling Rosa to wave the shawl and attempt to save her baby (Lowin 109). The voices begin to take on the howling of Magda as she reaches the fence; "Maamaa, maaamaaa, they all hummed together" (Ozick 9). The symbols of the tallit, the besamin, and the electric fence are solid because they are rooted in history and tradition, giving "The Shawl" a strong basis for validity as an important historical narrative, with both its personal and historical qualities.

Cynthia Ozick is best represented in her writing philosophy: "History is the ground of our being, and together with imagination, that is what makes writing" By her own philosophy, "The Shawl" is great writing. Ozick doesn' t use imagination so much as she uses the Jewish tradition of memory, although the relationship between the two are very close: " . . memory impulsively reaches out its arms and embraces imagination. That is the resort to invention. It isn't a lie, but an act of necessity, as the innate urge to locate personal truth always is" (Hampl 631). Documented history focuses on the awareness of the masses, and historical narrative sets its sights on the necessity of a created version of the past on a more personal level as to be easily identifiable. And, in the most basic function of imagination and memory, "we can only know the actual by contrasting it with the imaginable" (White 406), as to create our own valid consciousness. Historical narratives serve this purpose.

conclusions

Tim O'Brien and Elie Wiesel, authors of *The Things They Carried* and *Night*, respectively, wrote their historical narratives in the form of autobiographical fiction and memoir, differing from Ozick. Even though each work consists primarily of the author's own personal experience, both authors see imagination as a necessity because both use fiction to make their work more accessible and malleable to the mind of the reader for means of more personal understanding while remaining in the realm of truth.

Two testimonials by Holocaust survivors, Brandla Small and Victor Frankl, are historical narratives that also aim for personal understanding by the reader. Both are completely nonfictional. But both do tug at the heart because they are very personal, with Frankl giving light to the invincibility of spirituality and Small to the importance of family as an undying source of healing. Both authors incorporate their stories into universal themes to make them familiar while providing vital information about the atrocity that was the Holocaust.

"The Shawl" is just as successful as memoir and the nonfictional testimonials of Holocaust survivors due to its historical foundation and, most importantly, its appeal to the human senses and heart through imagery. "The Shawl," with its conformity to the leader becomes more truthful than the hard fact of 6 million Holocaust victims. Ozick's writing can be swelled, tasted, seen, heard, and felt. As horrible as it may be, 6 million victims is simply unimaginable. Cynthia Ozick shows us a small piece as to better understand the whole.

Works Cited

Bolick, Katie. "The Many Faces of Cynthia Ozick," <u>The Atlantic Online</u> 15 May 1997. 15 April 2003. <u>http://www.theatlantic.com/unbound/factfict/ozick.html</u>

Frankl, Viktor E. "Man's Search for Meaning." <u>Images from the Holocaust</u>. Ed. Jean Braun. NTC, 1997. 267-270.

Friedman, Lawrence S. <u>Understanding Cynthia Ozick</u>. Columbia: University of South Carolina Press, 1991.

Hampl, Patricia. "Memory and Imagination." <u>The Dolphin Reader</u>. Eds. Douglas Hunt and Carolyn Perry. Houghton Mifflin, 1999. 591-601.

Lowin, Joseph. <u>Cynthia Ozick</u>. Twayne' United States Authors Series 545. Boston: Twayne Publishers, 1988.

O'Brien, Tim. <u>The Things They Carried</u>. New York: Broadway Books, 1990.

Ozick, Cynthia. <u>The Shawl</u>. New York: Alfred A. Knopf, 1989.

Powers, Peter Kerry. "Disruptive Memories: Cynthia Ozick, Assimilation, and the Invented Past." <u>Melus</u> 20,3 (Autumn 1995): 79-97. JSTOR. Sojourner Truth Library. SUNY New Paltz. New Paltz, New York. 15 April 2003. http://Links.JSTOR.org/sici?sici.

Small, Brandla. "Brandla Small," <u>Mothers, Sisters, Resisters</u>. Ed. Brana Gurewitsch. Tuscaloosa: University Press of Alabama, 1998.

White, Hayden. "The Historical Text as Literary Artifact." <u>Critical Theory Since 1965</u>. Eds. Hazard Adams and Leroy Searle. Tallahassee: Florida State University Press, 1986. 395-407.

Wiesel, Elie. <u>Night</u>. New York: Bantam Books, 1986.

essay from JSTOR, full-text database

essay in edited volume

work by a single author

Visual Texts

Forms of Visual Texts

The practice of creating visuals to express oneself and convey meaning to others began as early as prehistoric man. The cave paintings in Lascaux, France, 17,000 years old, attest to the need of a primitive people to record, represent, and immortalize the rites, ceremonies, and life of their tribe. In addition, the appetite for beauty is in evidence in the graceful figures of the horses, bison, and deer that rush across the walls of the cave. The impulse to create art and the appreciation of the visual image is intrinsic to human nature and continues to drive us to develop new forms, styles, and technology.

A cave painting in the Lascaux Caves in France

Although the history of art is too expansive to offer an overview, it is important to note that every civilization has produced great art, sculpture, architecture, and design. Think of the pottery of the Anasazi, of Greek vases and statues, of the murals on the walls of the villas in Pompeii, of Persian miniatures, of frescoes in Romanesque and medieval churches, of the delicate beauty and mystery of Japanese landscape painting, of the awe-inspiring stone sculptures of Angkor Wat in Cambodia, and the intricate Bronze statues of Benin.

When we first think about art forms, painting and sculpture may immediately come to mind. We think of the great artists and art works of the Renaissance such as Leonardo da Vinci's "Mona Lisa" or Michelangelo's "David." Or we envision nineteenth century Impressionists such as Monet or Cezanne. Modern times have also produced groundbreaking works of fine art, such as Edward Hopper's stirring visions of American isolation or Andy Warhol's expressions of postmodern, irreverent sensibility in his pop art studies of Campbell soup cans and Marilyn Monroe.

Katsushika Hokusai (1760–1849) "South Wind and Clear Sky." Ca. 1823.
From "36 views of Mount Fuji."

Michelangelo Buonarroti (1475–1564) "David"

Other art forms besides painting, drawing, and sculpture emerged in the nineteenth century. Photography began with the work of Louis Daguerre who created images on silver-plated copper coated with silver iodide, and developed them with warmed mercury. Daguerreotypes led to the creation of images on glass or metal and, finally, to the development of what we now call the photograph. George Eastman created the first camera in the 1880s, popularizing this new art form. The development of the first motion picture is attributed to the Lumière brothers, who are credited with inventing the motion picture camera in 1895. However, even before that, in 1877, Eadweard Muybridge took the first step toward film when he made twelve photos of a horse and created an action sequence. In the twentieth century we saw the expansion of the film industry and the develop-

Eadweard Muybridge (1830–1904)
Transverse-Gallop, photograph, 1887. From
"Animals in Motion."

ment of television and video. Now in the twenty-first century we see the emergence of new genres: multi-genre texts that mix word and image (Japanese manga and the new expanded forms of graphic literature, for example) and interactive media such as increasingly complex and graphically realistic video games. Indeed, in our contemporary world, we are bombarded by the visual image: advertisement, Web sites, posters, graffiti, video, video games, and, of course, film and television. And as we start to download films and television programs onto our cell phones and iPods, we will have even more opportunities to experience visual media. All of these forms of the image continue to flourish side by side with the more traditional modes of visual representation and serve similar basic purposes as those ancient cave paintings and classical sculptures.

Elements of Visual Texts

As writers use language to convey meaning, artists work with the formal elements of a visual text and with their subject matter to create visions of reality. Although many different forms of visual texts exist, they do have some of the same formal elements. These elements exist in a framed and defined space, whether that space is a painting, photograph, or a shot in a film sequence (see Chapter 12 for a discussion of elements of film). Some of the formal elements include the following:

- placement of objects within the space and the relation of objects within the space
- use of perspective (depth and spatial relations)
- suggestion of foreground and background (details in the foreground appear larger, in the background more distant)
- focal point (the central part of the image to which the artist wants the viewer's eyes to be drawn)
- use of dark and light
- use of visual contrasts
- the color scheme (the use of color or black and white)
- the lines of the work or patterns of lines (horizontal or vertical lines, for example)
- the composition—the organization of the image (balance, symmetry, or asymmetry)
- proportion and scale (sometimes objects in the foreground of a picture are exaggerated for effect)

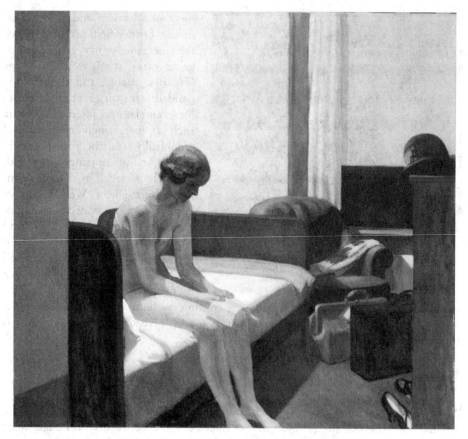

Hopper, Edward (1882–1967) Hotel Room. 1931.

- texture (the imagined "feel" of objects in a work—for example, rough as the surface of sandpaper or smooth as the texture of a silk dress)
- unity of all the elements
- choice of medium and effects (for example, the impact of particular techniques used only in film)

What can you learn about this painting by studying the visual elements? Consider the placement of the woman's figure in the foreground of the work, the pattern of light and dark, and the seeming isolation of her stance.

Visual Rhetoric

Other important aspects of the work include its **rhetorical situation;** that is, the particular purpose, audience, content, and context the artist had in mind when creating the piece. An artwork has a particular subject matter (details of the image) and context (political, historical, social, or cultural context). The artist also has a particular message that he or she wants to deliver through the subject matter, the details of the image, and its formal elements. As in literary works, the subject matter and formal elements together build the theme or main ideas of the work. Another aspect of the work is the

Homepage of the Environmental Defense Web site

particular genre or style; for example, a realistic photograph has a different sense and impact from a surreal one. Finally, an art object may incorporate textual elements (title, captions, headings, words) that add context within the body of the work.

This screenshot taken of the home page of the Environmental Defense Web site is a good example of the way images and words can be designed to convey information and elicit a response from viewers. The photograph of people being rescued from their flooded homes paired with the text about "Get the Facts on Global Warming" sends the message that global warming causes such disasters. The images of the flood and the cute polar bear cubs both make appeals to pathos, or the emotions of the audience by showing the negative effects global warming can have on the human and animal ways of life. The two sets of words and images taken together and their prominence on the Web page express to viewers the main purposes of the organization: to protect the environment through education and to help individuals, corporations, and policy makers develop practical solutions to environmental problems.

Sample Analysis of a Visual Text: Marjane Satrapi's "The Veil"

Let's look at a frame of *Persepolis*, the second frame in "The Veil," as an example of a visual text, and analyze the ways that the visual elements suggest meaning (for a complete version of "The Veil" see Chapter 5).

The central aspect of the work is that Marjane Satrapi's graphic memoir, an auto-biographical account of her coming of age during the Iranian Revolution, is designed to enlighten an audience about what it felt like to grow up as a young woman during those times. To orient the reader to those times, she begins with the description of the new ruling that all women must wear the veil. The first thing that a viewer may notice is the simplicity of the lines and of the black and white images of young girls wearing the veil and the confused and sad expressions on the girls' faces. The images in some ways resemble children's drawings. This simplicity reflects the child's perspective, rein-forced in the narrative point of view and the tone of the written text. These visual por-traits of the girls symbolically suggest the narrator's view of her world: the "black and white" world of traditional, Islamic fundamentalism that reinforces proscribed codes of rules, of behavior, for men and for women. In addition, the solid black of the veils contrasts with the more delicate lines of the girls' closed arms, suggesting their vul-nerability. The details—the pictures of the girls—are in the foreground of the frame, a position that intensifies their importance and suggests the radical change in young girls' and women's lives. Not only do the images reinforce this view of women's state in post-Revolutionary Iran, but the organization of the visual text also does this. The composition is unbalanced; it is asymmetrical. The narrator's face and body are almost outside of the frame, creating a sense of the chaos in the young girl's world, a world torn asunder by the Revolution. Her world is out of balance. The figure of the autobiographical persona, its placement, also suggests a larger message: the sense of invisibility that women in that culture experience as induced by repressive social codes. Thus, all the elements of this graphic text combine to suggest the larger themes and cultural contexts of the work: the denial of freedom to women after the Islamic Revolution. A sense of unity exists in the work; the subject matter and visual elements combine to create the messages of the text.

The Reading/Writing Process: Visual Texts

What follows is a checklist to help you to interpret, respond to, and write about visual texts. Consider using this checklist to help you analyze the graphic literature in each chapter of the thematic anthology.

Checklist of Questions for Reading and Writing about Visual Texts

1. What is the form of the work?
2. Does the title provide clues about the work?
3. What do you think the artist's purpose is? The imagined audience?
4. What is the subject matter of the work?
5. What is the genre of the work (i.e., painting, photograph, or graphic literature)? Does it break conventions of the genre? Mix genres? Mix visual and verbal modes?
6. How do you, as a reader, respond to the work? What strikes you as interesting, important, or emotionally moving? What associations do you make with the work? What experiences does it evoke? What story does it tell?
7. How do the visual elements (e.g., placement, perspective, line, color, composition, medium) work together to create the text?
8. Does the composition seem unified? How do all the elements combine to create the meaning of the work? For example, in a graphic literary text, how do the written and visual elements complement each other?
9. What are the political, historical, social, or cultural contexts of the work?
10. What is the significance of the work?

Critical Approaches to Literature

We approach literary texts with presuppositions, often undefined, about what literature is, about what it means, and about what determines its worth. Critical theories enable us to articulate assumptions and to devise methodologies for reading, for analyzing, for interpreting, for evaluating, and for writing about literary works. A number of theories offer sometimes complementary, often competing, views of the literary text, of language itself, of the meaning or meanings of the text, of the process of creating meaning, and of the question concerning who or what creates meaning—the work, the writer, the reader, the culture.

Some critics think of a work of literature as fixed—a thing in itself with little if any relationship to the author or to his or her purpose or experiences, with no relationship to the reader, or with no relationship to the culture of the writer. The work, according to such a view, is objective and, consequently, free from the subjectivity of the writer or the reader. We begin with these theories that focus on the text; then we move to critical approaches that center on the writer, the reader, or the culture.

Formalism/New Criticism

Formalism in English language literary criticism began with I. A. Richards's *Practical Criticism* (1929) in England. It was picked up and developed in the 1940s by a group of American literary critics including Cleanth Brooks, Robert Penn Warren, and Rene Wellek, who came to be known as the New Critics. Formalist criticism considers formal elements of literature (organization, structure, language, etc.) in order to determine meaning. Each work is independent, complete in itself, and everything external to the work is of secondary importance. The formalist is less concerned with the state of mind of the writer, with any biographical, economic, political, or social information than with such intrinsic features as plot, character, narrative technique, irony, and paradox.

Both the underlying assumptions and something of the methodology of formalism can be glimpsed in a quotation from Cleanth Brooks: "The language of poetry is the language of paradox." Brooks's use of the word "paradox" is key: a paradox is an apparent contradiction that is resolved on a deeper level. Perhaps the simplest example of this is the metaphor. Consider the statement, "my love is a red rose." Taken literally, such a statement is nonsensical: unless the speaker actually is in love with a flower, there is no way for it to be factually true. Taken nonliterally (as of course we do take it), the statement is easily understood: the speaker is comparing his beloved to a particular kind of flower. What seems contradiction is revealed to be coherent meaning. We find similar examples of such conflict and tension at the level of character and plot: consider the character of Hamlet, whose attitudes toward Ophelia include both callous indifference to her love for him and overwhelming grief at her death; or the conclusion of "The Story of an Hour," where we are told that Mrs. Mallard, who has spent the story awakening to the freedom her husband's death brings her, has died of "joy" at the sight of him still alive. For this reason, formalist critics are interested in irony, since irony is another means to reconcile seemingly contradictory meanings.

Formalist critics judge the use of language in a literary work as a special situation in which the way the substance of a work is conveyed is as important as the substance itself. For this reason, Cleanth Brooks writes of "the heresy of paraphrase," the mistaken belief that a summary of the literary work could be equivalent to the work itself. For the formalist, method and message are intimately connected—another example of formalism's concern with textual unity—and so there is no substitute for the literary text itself.

For the formalist critic, then, literature is an art form that always appears to be in tension with itself, but that ultimately resolves into a unified whole. It is the task of the formalist critic to demonstrate how that resolution is achieved, to identify the move from contradiction to coherence. To do so, the critic employs a strategy of "close reading," in which the work is subjected to close, even minute consideration and analysis, its moments of tension studied to reveal its underlying unity. A formalist reading of a literary work will attempt to demonstrate how its seemingly diverse components add up to a coherent whole.

In formalist criticism, the reader can make assumptions about the validity of interpretation and about the worth of the work of art; that is, some interpretations, based on evidence from the text, are better than others, while some works of art, based on their complexity, beauty, and depth, may be considered greater than others.

A formalist reading of "The Story of an Hour" by Kate Chopin (Chapter 10) might begin by focusing on the story's last line: "When the doctors came they said she had died of heart disease—of joy that kills." From having read the story, which has given us access to Mrs. Mallard's inner experience, we know that the doctors' assessment is incorrect. Mrs. Mallard has experienced "joy," but not the "joy" the doctors assume. Why, then, does the story conclude with their diagnosis? Is this ending a carefully planned, unifying culmination of the story's events, or is it merely a trick, a simple surprise? To answer this question, the formalist critic would seek to resolve the tension between what we know of Mrs. Mallard and the doctors' diagnosis. The critic would ask if there is a level of meaning on which the doctors' assessment could be true, if Mrs. Mallard could be described accurately as the victim "of joy that kills"? The critic might consider the descriptions of Mrs. Mallard's happiness at the freedom her husband's death brings her, of the way her "fancy . . . [runs] riot along those days ahead of her." The critic might hypothesize that it is this joy at her liberation from the constraints of marriage that stops her heart, as it turns to despair that she will not be free from marriage after all. Mrs. Mallard must be free, and if she cannot be free in life, then she will be free in death. Thus, the formalist critic would argue, the doctors are correct in their diagnosis, but they are so ironically. Through such an exploration, the formalist critic would begin to determine the unifying principle of the story's ending.

Although formalism has been superceded by more recent theories of literary criticism, its methodology of close reading remains the bedrock for beginning students of literary criticism and for most of the critical schools that come after it. If formalism has taught and continues to teach anything, it is that nothing substitutes for close attention to the literary text.

Structuralism

Like formalism, *structuralism* attempts to offer objective analysis of the meaning of literature. The structuralist critic also seeks to minimize considerations of history, economics, and politics. The theory aspires to scientific inquiry through ideas and methods borrowed from linguistics and from anthropology. Each work becomes a system, and the critic's task becomes the discovery of the laws that pertain to the interaction of elements in the system. The structuralist examines surface phenomena in order to uncover "a deep structure." For example, the structuralist attempts to define conventions of literary form, perhaps aspiring to understand the features or elements that identify a text as a poem or drama.

Because structuralism developed from linguistics, some critics apply linguistic approaches to literature. In *Course in General Linguistics* (1915), Ferdinand de Saussure, a French linguist, called the relationship between an object and the name by which the object is designated (i.e., a sign) arbitrary. A word makes sense only within the system of an entire language, and it signifies meaning only to those who know that particular language system. Saussure further assumes that signs or words are useful when they emphasize difference: a hand and a foot are both appendages, but a hand has fingers and a foot has toes. A hand is attached to an arm, a foot to a leg, and so on.

Saussure theorized about the rules that govern the complex system of signs in language. He claimed that a *semiotic* (a science of signs) principle, which enables humans to communicate through a system of signs, governs the structure of language. Literary critics who apply linguistics to texts assume that poems, fiction, and drama are part of a larger system. Any analysis of a work requires the comprehension of the system in which the work operates and of the difference between that system and other systems. Structuralism also requires readers to discover the way in which sign systems create meaning.

A structuralist approach, then, requires the critic to think about the way that a story functions as a story, as opposed to a poem or drama. Structuralism looks to establish categories: for kinds of plot, for occurrences within plots, for kinds of characters, and so on. In the case of "The Story of an Hour," a structuralist would seek to reduce the story to its essentials in order to understand how it functions. It begins with Mrs. Mallard's learning of the death of her husband. It has a middle that complicates the action—she uncharacteristically finds herself joyful because of her newly acquired freedom. The end, which has a surprising twist, is also Mrs. Mallard's end since she suffers a fatal coronary when she learns that her husband still lives. The structuralist would recognize conventions of plot, theme, and character that appear in similar stories: the surprise O. Henry ending, for example, which began as a device in mystery stories and remains a recognizable feature in short fiction. The structuralist would compare the story to others in which characters gain autonomy and happiness only to suffer a tragic reversal of fortune, a reversal both surprising and ironic. The structuralist would note that Mrs. Mallard is made happy by an event that should make her unhappy and made unhappy by an event that should make her happy. A scheme for the structure of this story, then, might be that a character undergoes a pair of reversals, each of which is received in a manner the reverse of what one might expect.

Structuralist criticism lost favor in the 1970s, and many new theories that borrowed from Saussure or that contradicted the objectivist approach appeared. Scholars often consider contemporary criticism to be "poststructuralism."

Deconstruction

Deconstruction contends that literary works do not contain unified or stable meanings. Unlike formalist critics, who seek to reconcile tensions in a text in order to establish the relation of the parts to the whole work, deconstructionists argue that any close reading of a text uncovers contradictions that inevitably "deconstruct" or dissolve the possibility of unity. Underlying and motivating deconstructive criticism is a belief that what we accept as truth, especially as it is conveyed through language, is nothing of the kind. Because they believe that language can never truly convey single, fixed messages, deconstructionists postulate that language creates endless meanings that destabilize a text and that create contradictions that cannot be reconciled.

Deconstruction begins with the assertion that there is nothing outside language, that language shapes and orders our perceptions. As described by its most prominent theorist, philosopher Jacques Derrida, language (and all linguistic constructions) operates through *différance*, a term that contains two meanings: "to be different" and "to defer." We do not understand a word, Derrida argues, because of any inherent qualities in it. Rather, we understand a word because of its difference from other words (e.g., "cat" is not the same as "cut" or "cap"). We also understand it in terms of other words (i.e., its dictionary definition), which we in turn understand in terms of other words (i.e., the dictionary definitions of the words that make up the dictionary definitions), and so on. Thus, meaning in language is always provisional and endlessly deferred. Deconstruction assumes that since the word that signifies an object is separate from that object, the word stands for the object in a metaphorical way, and so all language is metaphorical. Because words can only signify, they cannot serve as reality or truth. Because they cannot serve as truth, there is nothing to stop them from tangling and/or contradicting. If we read a text attentively, Derrida argues, we will see that this is exactly what happens. Every written text contains elements that will destabilize it. The appearance of stable, unitary meaning in a literary work is just that, an appearance: every work contains a multiplicity of meaning that undermines any notion of a stable, unitary literary text. Literary criticism that claims to find a single meaning in a text, deconstructionists argue, is, in fact, imposing that meaning onto it, choosing one of its competing meanings and focusing on it to the exclusion of all others.

Like formalists and structuralists, deconstructionists focus on the text. In deconstructing a work, however, the reader examines ambiguities, wordplay, competing meanings. The task of the critic becomes to expose the text's contradictions, to show the way that it does not add up to a unified achievement. One of deconstruction's favorite techniques is to take a text that has been understood as saying one thing and then to demonstrate how it can be read as saying exactly the opposite. The critic does so by examining the elements in the story that seem to be encouraging us to interpret it in one way and then demonstrating how those elements could as easily be understood as asking us to interpret it in exactly the opposite way. The purpose of such an interpretation is not to replace the old reading with the new, but to show how both readings exist within the text simultaneously, thus foreclosing any chance of achieving a unitary interpretation of it.

A deconstructive reading of "The Story of an Hour" might begin by considering the opposition the story appears to set up between freedom and captivity. Mrs. Mallard, it seems, moves from the captivity of marriage to the freedom of widowhood. The deconstructive critic might focus on the language the story uses to present that movement. After hearing the news of her husband's death, brought by "her sister Josephine," Mrs. Mallard sits facing an "open window." She is "reached" by the "notes of a distant song." She is "motionless, except when a sob . . . [shakes] her." Gradually, "something . . . [approaches] to possess her." Accepting her joy at her new freedom, Mrs. Mallard "[drinks] in a very elixir of life through that open window." The deconstructive critic would note that although these images ostensibly refer to Mrs. Mallard's becoming free, they do so using language that relentlessly emphasizes freedom as external to Mrs. Mallard. Freedom is something that is visited upon her, as much outside her control as was her marriage. Such language suggests that Mrs. Mallard still is not acting as an autonomous being and that she remains under the sway of external forces. Although, pragmatically speaking, Mrs. Mallard may be free of her marriage, at the level at which she experiences life she remains passive. Thus, the critic would argue, while the story appears to be telling us about Mrs. Mallard's moment of liberation, it does so in language that emphasizes her subjection. Mrs. Mallard is at once free and not free. The deconstructive critic would find another level of irony to the story's ending: namely, that Mrs. Mallard is killed by external forces, just as her entire life—even what has appeared to be her one moment of liberation—has been dominated by external forces.

Although not all critics accept deconstruction's insistence on the ultimate indeterminacy of meaning, a number of critical schools have employed deconstructive techniques in order to advance their own concerns. Feminist, gender, and postcolonial theorists, to name a few, have used deconstructive techniques to destabilize prevailing assumptions about sexuality and race.

Psychological Criticism

Psychological criticism applies the insights offered by such psychologists as Sigmund Freud, Jacques Lacan, and Julia Kristeva to the interpretation of literary works. Most psychological criticism has drawn on Freud's writing; although many of his insights into and assertions concerning consciousness have been superceded by more recent developments within the field, his ideas remain fruitful for the interpretation of literary works. A number of Freud's ideas—the Oedipus complex, the concept of repression, the significance of dreams—have entered popular discourse to the extent that we employ them unaware that they originated with him. We might find ourselves discussing the significance of Hamlet's attachment to his mother without being fully aware that our interpretation is informed by Freud's notion of the Oedipus complex. The responsible psychological critic makes an effort to understand Freud's (or Lacan's or Kristeva's) theories before attempting to apply them to a literary work. This is not to say that the psychological critic must be a practicing psychologist, only that a certain level of competency with the psychological concepts is necessary.

Psychological criticism tends to fall into one of three categories: the *biographical,* the *character oriented,* and the *structural.* In *biographical criticism,* the critic assumes a reasonably straightforward connection between events and forces in the author's personal life and the concerns, subject matter, and themes of her/his art. The artwork becomes a rather complex symptom through which the critic attempts to diagnose the writer. Such "psychobiographical" critics consider the connections they explore as being central to an understanding of the work.

Thus, in Kate Chopin's "Story of an Hour," the critic might assert similarities between Chopin's life and her heroine's existence: Chopin represented her own traditional marriage in which her role as a woman was restricted in her depiction of Mrs. Mallard's relationship to Brently. She recreated her genteel, bourgeois existence as the wife of a Creole cotton trader in her portrayal of Mrs. Mallard's domestic situation. The biographical critic might note that Chopin suppressed her own needs and desires until her husband died, as does Mrs. Mallard. Chopin subsequently chose to pursue a career as a writer to support her six children, a choice Mrs. Mallard never has. The biographical critic might suggest that Chopin created versions of her own life not only in this story, but again and again in her fiction.

Beyond psychobiography, the psychological critic may choose to *analyze the behavior of a character or characters in a literary work.* Such a critical approach assumes that since literary characters are meant to be representations of real people, they may be analyzed in the same manner as real people. The psychological critic approaching "The Story of an Hour" might notice the description of the "repression" in Mrs. Mallard's face. That same term is used in Freudian psychology to indicate the mechanism whereby the conscious mind suppresses unacceptable desires into the unconscious, whence they cannot arise directly without great trauma. Equipped with this definition, the critic might see that it describes Mrs. Mallard's character quite accurately: in order to fulfill her own expectations of what a good wife should be, Mrs. Mallard has repressed any feelings of dissatisfaction with her husband in particular and marriage in general. It is only through the unexpected shock of her husband's death that Mrs. Mallard's repressed feelings can surface, and their appearance is traumatic, heralded by "her bosom . . . [rising and falling] . . . tumultuously." The critic might note that Mrs. Mallard experiences the return of these repressed feelings as if they come from outside herself, as "something coming to her," as "this thing that was approaching to possess her," and that she struggles "to beat it back with her will." Her feelings are so unacceptable to Mrs. Mallard that she projects them outside herself and contests them to the end. The critic might note that it is not until Mrs. Mallard has accepted her feelings (or been overwhelmed by them) that she can articulate them: "free, free, free!" Having accepted what she had repressed, Mrs. Mallard achieves a new level of personal wholeness, indicated by her speaking of herself as free in "[b]ody and soul," that is, in a manner that emphasizes her integration physically and mentally. Like other critics, the psychological critic would recognize the irony of the story's ending: Mrs. Mallard integrates what she has so long repressed, and in so doing makes herself susceptible to the fatal shock of her husband's reappearance.

Finally, the psychological critic may choose to examine the way in which the literary work itself enacts psychological concepts. Such *structuralist psychological criticism* attempts to psychologize the literary text, treating it as a psychologist might treat a patient. The psychological critic looks to find the psychological principles at work in the construction of a given work. The critic approaching "The Story of an Hour" might find that, in addition to presenting a protagonist who represses information from herself, the story itself represses information from the reader. While the story wants to be about Mrs. Mallard's dawning realization of freedom, its language indicates that she is not free, that she is still acted upon by outside forces. It, therefore, contains a series of rhetorical Freudian slips. Mrs. Mallard is not in control of her own body: she sits "motionless, except when a sob . . . [shakes] her." Her awareness of her own freedom is "something . . . [approaching] to possess her." Even when she accepts her joy at her new freedom, Mrs. Mallard "[drinks] in a very elixir of life through that open window," taking it into herself from the outside. Such an interpretation has much in common with that offered by deconstruction; both critical approaches look to discover what other meanings may be present in the literary text than the seemingly obvious one.

The examples we have considered have employed principles drawn from Freudian psychology. They need not have: we could as easily have used the work of Lacan, Kristeva, or any number of other psychologists (and psychological critics) to analyze "The Story of an Hour." The benefit to psychological criticism is that it allows us to speak of dimensions of the work neglected by the critical schools we have considered thus far. As is always the case with literary criticism, however, the best psychological criticism is that which remains rooted in the text, drawing its insights from the words on the page.

Reader Response Criticism

Reader response criticism is grounded in certain assumptions about literary texts and their readers. The first is that texts have their existence in the reading: until a reader is engaged with the words on the page, we cannot speak of them as having meaning. Therefore, literary texts must be understood rhetorically, which is to say, for the effect they have on an audience. As Stanley Fish, one of the leading proponents of this school, has claimed, the critic should describe not what a poem is, but what it does. The reader response critic seeks to analyze the ways in which a given text arouses expectations that it then fulfills or frustrates. The emphasis is on understanding the text as a site where readers may produce meaning. Reader response critics differ in terms of how much independence they give to the text as a separate object of study. Louise Rosenblatt, for example, views the reading process as interactive, as "transitive," as an interaction between the world of the reader and the world of the text. Norman Holland envisions the reading process as a re-creation based on a dynamic interaction between a reader who has a particular "identity theme," a particular personality pattern, and a text that is re-created and shaped by the demands of the reader's identity theme. Holland theorizes that identity replicates itself—in all acts of living and of reading. David Bleich, another reader response theorist, contends in his early works, *Reading and Feeling* (1975) and *Subjective Criticism* (1978), that the reader response process primarily is individual and subjective and that the interpretation of a work is based on the reader's subjective response to it: the reader's "resymbolization" of that work. In his more recent work, *The Double Perspective: Language, Literacy, and Social Relations* (1988), Bleich acknowledges the role of gender and social context in shaping the reader's "resymbolization" of a work. What finally accounts for and governs response? Are there only totally idiosyncratic, subjective individual responses to works? For reader response critics, the reading process always will be personal; this is not to say, however, that such an approach must lapse into hopeless relativism and subjectivism. Reader response criticism is, as its name indicates, not only about the reader, but also about the response to a specific text. The best reader response criticism describes the reactions evoked by specific features of the text. In addition, the totality of response depends on what Stanley Fish labels "the interpretive community of readers." That is, part of the process is influenced by the intellectual community and concerns of readers. The community helps shape the intellectual background—the approach, views, and values—of the reader. Reader response critics also maintain that interpretation of a text may change depending on when a person reads a work. People read differently at different phases of their lives. Part of this process is determined by cultural context. The world of the 2000s in the United States, for example, contrasts drastically with the world of the 1950s in the United States.

The student's essay in Chapter 10 is a reader response to "The Story of an Hour." The writer compares Mrs. Mallard's entrapment and desire for freedom with her own situation: her own marriage and yearning for autonomy. Reader response criticism may begin with highly personal responses, as the freewrites that follow demonstrate. In them, the writer reflects on the changes in her view of "The Story of an Hour" at varying stages of her life.

> When I first read "The Story of an Hour," I thought about how entrapped Mrs. Mallard was and how limited her life and her options were. She seemed totally cowed by the authority figures in her life: her sister, her husband. She seemed spineless.

> I tasted her single delightful moment of freedom and felt sorry for her. I truly felt pity. As a young twenty-two year old, I couldn't imagine a life without infinite possibility.

> I reread the story in my thirties when I taught it in a creative writing class to a group of older, returning women students. I saw it as a story of awakenings. I saw it as a reflection of changing values. She recognized her own oppression. She realized a possibility for freedom. That opening up was vividly depicted in her looking out the window.

> That view of the story very much seemed to go with the times, with the burgeoning of the women's movement in the mid 1970s, with the faith that roles for women could be, as Adrienne Rich said, "reenvision(ed)." It was all in the recognition of oppression and the opening up. Writing was an act of consciousness. Mrs. Mallard's opening up of consciousness seemed the center of the work and her death—just at the point of dawning awareness—seemed tragic.

> As I reread the work to teach it again in my forties, what strikes me anew is imprisonment. Roles are still being redefined—but not as quickly or as easily. Women are still trapped. Women are still not able to let go of traditional roles. Many women are still caught in the same bind: the struggle between duty and responsibility and self-fulfillment.

> Mrs. Mallard's imprisonment and her only way out—death—seem more poignant—and even more realistic—now.

These responses represent the reader exploring her own changing response to the story. The next step in developing a critical essay would be for the writer to establish how her feelings are grounded in specific features of the text.

As criticism moves away from concentrating solely on the text and toward embracing both the writer and the reader, it also moves toward suggesting the place of the text within the larger social order. Sociological critics analyze the work within its cultural context. Treatment is given to the ways in which the text both mirrors and is defined by the social and cultural concerns of the age.

Feminist Criticism

One important form of sociological criticism is *feminist theory,* which views the work in terms of sexual politics. To talk about "sexual politics" is to talk about how the unequal distribution of power operates in male/female relationships and how this imbalance structures many unspoken assumptions about the roles that men and women are expected to play within society. That these roles have traditionally been oppressive for women is the basic foundation of feminist thought. Feminist critics assert that throughout history, men have exercised political, social, and economic authority in ways that have privileged their own needs and interests while making the needs and interests of women secondary. Women's roles have been defined in ways that tend to support the patriarchal system; moreover, the male perspective is presented as the norm for humankind while the female perspective is presented as being somehow intrinsically "feminine" rather than simply "human." Simone de Beauvoir describes this eloquently in "Woman as Other" (Chapter 7), where she says, "Thus humanity is male and man defines woman not in herself but as relative to him; she is not regarded as an autonomous being." Taking this unequal power dynamic as their basic starting point, feminist critics have raised many challenging questions about the ways in which literature is both written and read.

In the 1960s, feminist criticism sought to expose the patriarchal assumptions embedded in society by analyzing the representation of women in literary works written by men. In *Sexual Politics* (1970), Kate Millet took on the literary establishment by critiquing a number of canonical male novelists for the chauvinist assumptions underlying their characters. For instance, Millet claims that D. H. Lawrence associates activity and intellect with the masculine realm and sees any attempt by women to enter that realm as both unnatural and threatening to men. For Millet, literary criticism must address such chauvinism, because "sexual distinctions are political definitions." In *Thinking About Women* (1968), Mary Ellman considered the reader as well as the writer, noting that "the working rule is simple, basic: there must always be two literatures like two public toilets, one for Men and one for Women." The underlying claim in much feminist criticism of this period was that literature, no matter how "great" it might be, implicitly socializes men and women according to established categories of masculine and feminine.

In the 1970s, much feminist criticism was concerned with rediscovering and reevaluating women writers who had previously been excluded from the predominantly male canon of "great works." The Feminist Press in the United States and the Women's Press in Britain were committed to reprinting neglected works by women (for example, Rebecca Harding Davis's 1861 novel *Life in the Iron Mills*) and were instrumental in furthering feminist scholarship. One landmark study from this period is *A Literature of Their Own: British Women Novelists from Brontë to Lessing* (1977) by Elaine Showalter. Showalter charts the struggle of female writers to establish themselves in a predominantly male tradition. Bringing together famous and less well-known writers, Showalter describes an alternative female tradition that first imitated male models, then challenged them, and finally established its own agenda. Showalter also coined the term "gynocriticism," a new approach that would specifically address "the psychodynamics of female creativity; linguistics and the problem of a female language; the trajectory of the individual or collective female literary career; literary history; and, of course, studies of particular writers and works." By focusing on issues such as female creativity and female language, Showalter raised a question that preoccupied feminist critics of the 1980s: Is there a particularly female mode of writing?

In the 1980s, a number of poststructuralist feminists came to the forefront of literary theory. Influenced, like other poststructuralists, by the French philosopher Michel Foucault, these critics saw language not as a transparent medium that reflects reality, but as a system of meanings that partially construct what we understand as reality. And, like Foucault, these critics saw language as one of the fundamental means by which power relations are maintained in a society. Therefore, challenging the accepted ways of speaking and writing can be a means of challenging inequitable power relations. According to Luce Irigaray, feminists have to work within patriarchal discourses, whether literary, philosophical, or scientific, and challenge the assumptions of those discourses, in the process "leaving open the possibility of a different language." Similarly, Hélène Cixous advocated an *écriture féminine,* or "feminine writing," that would provide an alternative to the "phallocentric" language of Western culture—language that, in privileging reason and logic, privileged principles associated with the masculine intellect. Cixous sought a nonlinear, fluid form of writing that allowed for instability and excess of meaning; she also insisted on the connection between women's creativity and their sexuality: "Write your self. Your body must be heard." Other feminists, however, have critiqued this strong identification between feminine writing and the female body. For some, to define female writing as unstructured and diffuse is to revert to the biological essentialism that for so many centuries has categorized women as not intellectual, not logical, not coherent.

Current feminism continues to work with all of the preceding issues, but has also become more interested in race and class in relation to gender, resisting the idea of a universal female nature or experience. Postcolonial feminism, for instance, considers the assumptions at work within a predominantly white, middle-class, and academic feminist tradition, and whether the terms and concepts used by such feminists are relevant to those in minority or non-Western cultures. A woman can have multiple identities in terms of race, class, and sexual preference, and the tendency now is to talk about "feminisms" rather than simply "feminism."

A basic feminist reading of "The Story of an Hour" would foreground the tragedy inherent in the plot: that in order to feel empowered and emotionally connected, a woman must suffer the death of her husband. This is a harsh statement to make, but a feminist critic would argue that for the Victorian woman, marriage was such an oppressive institution that most women had to sacrifice their own needs and ambitions, even their identities as autonomous individuals. The pain of such sacrifice could be so acute that the death of a husband, while traumatic, could also represent tremendous freedom—the kind of freedom that would not be available to a young single woman whose sole purpose in life, in this era, was to marry and have children. By analyzing the process of change in Mrs. Mallard, the feminist critic might note the initial negativity of her portrayal: she is weak, emotionally and physically, even before the news of her husband's death. She sinks into a "comfortable, roomy armchair"—the symbol of her domestic entrapment—and is "pressed down by a physical exhaustion that seemed haunted her body and seemed to reach into her soul." Her dawning consciousness, however, is expressed positively in terms of the natural world, with images of spring and renewal: "the tops of the trees that were all aquiver with the new spring life." In this way, the text affirms Mrs. Mallard's process of self-empowerment, which becomes fully realized when she whispers, "Free! Body and soul free!" By encouraging the reader to empathize with Mrs. Mallard, this text communicates a powerful feminist message. But the feminist critic might also question the text's underlying assumption: that Mrs. Mallard is so much the victim of social institutions that only the death of her husband can free her. This is not, perhaps, such an inspiring message for women seeking to challenge those institutions.

Gender Criticism

Gender criticism is related to feminist criticism in that both are interested in how sexual difference functions socially and politically. However, gender criticism has several important differences. Firstly, gender criticism is not as woman-centered as feminist criticism. As Myra Jehlen puts it, "*The Adventures of Huckleberry Finn* is a man's book about a boy, and just as likely an object of gender criticism as writing by or about women." Jehlen focuses on the scene in which Huck, disguised as a girl, is discovered by the motherly Judith Loftus, who contrives a series of tests to prove that Huck is (as she suspects) actually a boy. By performing the tests of throwing, catching, and threading a needle like a boy, Huck shows that being a boy is largely a matter of performance—of playing a role according to certain learned behaviors. Jehlen describes this scene as "the reversal of feminity from nature to nurture—from sex to gender" and relates it to the broader themes of the novel: Huck learns through Jim that racial categories are also socially constructed, and he comes (however imperfectly) to learn another way of relating to Jim—as another person rather than as a black slave.

Secondly, gender criticism is also specifically interested in gay and lesbian issues, and many critics have adopted the term *queer theory* to describe their approach. Some of the issues they address are similar to those of feminist critics, but with a different emphasis. If there is a female tradition in literature, is there also a gay tradition? What happens when one rereads canonical authors from a perspective outside the category of heterosexual love? Are there identifiably gay strategies for reading and writing? How should a critic address homophobia in a literary text? How do we talk about these issues in the classroom? Such questions have motivated gender critics to reread such authors as Herman Melville, Emily Dickinson, Henry James, Willa Cather, and Virginia Woolf, writers whose conservative social contexts did not allow them to explore their sexual identities openly in their work. Other writers who were more open can now be appreciated for this openness. Walt Whitman, for instance, whose celebrations of male love were previously interpreted as asexual comradeship, can now be recognized as a great poet who was also a gay poet.

Within gender criticism there are those who wish to distinguish between male and female homosexuality. Some see women and men as essentially different regardless of their sexual preference. Some argue that society marginalizes the male homosexual differently from the female lesbian, and that, therefore, their lived experiences are different. Important questions are raised by this division. Is sexual preference or physiology the primary factor in identity formation? Are gay men psychologically more like women than other men? Does the biological fact of maternity create a distinctively feminine sensibility, regardless of whether the woman is straight or gay? Some critics, however, completely eschew the notion of innate male/female essences. According to Teresa de Lauretis, "sexuality, commonly thought to be a natural as well as a private matter, is in fact completely constructed in culture according to the political aims of the society's dominant class." But for all gender critics, the process of literary analysis is conceived of as a liberating project that can open up scholarly and classroom discussion to issues that have serious implications from all individuals and their communities. A readiness to explore the intersection of personal and social realities from the perspective of gender not only enriches the reading of literature, but also builds an understanding of the ways in which all cultures create categories of identification and difference that often need to be interrogated.

A gender critic would consider how individual characters in "The Story of an Hour" suggest particular things about the categories of "female" and "male" in Chopin's own social milieu. Several patterns emerge quite clearly: women are associated with the domestic sphere, with fragility and passivity, while men are associated with the public sphere, with control and activity. Thus, it is Richards who first learns about Brently Mallard's death in the newspaper office and brings that information back to Mrs. Mallard at home. She shuts herself away in her room and sinks into her "comfortable, roomy armchair," where, through the open window, she hears a peddler "crying his wares in the street below." The world through the open window is not one in which Mrs. Mallard can actively participate, but it calls to her powerfully as the implications of her husband's death begin to sink in: "she was drinking in a very elixir of life through that open window." When her husband appears at the end of the story, his entrance into the domestic sphere of the house is described so as to emphasize both his masculine activity and his self-control: "Somebody was opening the front door with a latchkey. It was Brently Mallard who entered, a little travel-stained, composedly carrying his gripsack and umbrella." The other male character, Richards, automatically moves to protect Mrs. Mallard—unsuccessfully, of course, but nonetheless reinforcing the role of men as active and women as passive. Such a reading need not undermine the effectiveness of the story, but would simply emphasize the extent to which all art, regardless of its aesthetic achievements, inevitably carries with it a sociological dimension.

New Historicism

The *new historicism* represents another variant of sociological criticism. By reading a literary work through its historical and social context, the new historicist seeks to reconnect the text with the complexity of lived experience during its own time. In doing so, the new historicist emphasizes issues of social power and considers how a particular text dramatizes the social and political struggles of certain groups. In this way new historicism is quite different from "old" or traditional historicism, which tended to explore the thematic unity of a work against the backdrop of "official" history—that is, the broad sweep of famous personages and noteworthy events. In contrast, new historicism is concerned less with thematic unity and more with the contesting voices in a work, voices that, when we allow ourselves to hear them, may destabilize thematic unity rather than reinforce it. The new historicist considers how a literary work speaks to the power struggles of its own time, struggles that often involve the ordinary people that traditional historicism had marginalized or silenced. This impulse to make the marginal the center of study arises from the assumption that all forms of writing embody cultural realities. The new historicist considers newspaper articles, legal documents, letters, advertisements, and popular entertainment in relation to literary texts, arguing that all are equally important as representations of social reality.

New historicism has been significantly influenced by French philosopher Michel Foucault and his ideas about power and language. For Foucault (and many other poststructural theorists), language and meaning are unstable and constantly being contested. When we learn language, we also learn the complex network of values and codes that maintain our culture. For although every society has concrete ways of maintaining order—such as police and prison systems—every society also uses religious, educational, and mass media systems to maintain its status quo. In this way, power is dispersed through a culture in innumerable subtle ways. One might ask, how is it that we don't all see the world in exactly the same way? Certain charismatic dictators have indeed striven for such uniformity. But in democracies, where freedom of speech is upheld, surely language cannot work to control us in the same way? Foucault would argue that the diversity in democratic systems often conceals the operations of power. For instance, advertising teaches us from an early age that material possessions equal social status, and hence we grow up into earning and spending citizens who participate in and support the capitalist economy. We might even say that the mass media produce desires in us that we satisfy through consumer goods. In this way, power is productive as well as repressive and says, "Yes, do this" as well as "No, don't do that." New historicists are interested in Foucault's claim that "Power is everywhere; not because it embraces everything, but because it comes from everywhere." Power is everywhere because language is everywhere, and new historicists want to read literary texts as cultural sites where meaning, and hence power, is contested. And like Foucault, new historicists favor an interdisciplinary approach that combines a variety of cultural documents in order to explore how a particular period constructs its own versions of "truth" and "reality."

The new historicist would read "The Story of an Hour," written in 1894, as articulating women's growing anger at their imprisonment within rigid social roles. Contemporaneous documents, such as articles from *Ladies Home Journal* or *Revolution*, the newspaper of the National Woman Suffrage Association, would be read alongside Chopin's story in order to illustrate the conflict for women of that time between a traditional marriage, in which the women belonged both sexually and economically to their husbands, and the independence advocated by such activists as Matilda Gage and Elizabeth Cady Stanton. In 1892 Stanton had given a speech, "The Solitude of Self," which argued for full civil rights for women, and other feminists of the time likewise argued that women should enjoy the privilege of "self-ownership" even within marriage, with the power to control their own reproductive destinies regardless of the marital "rights" of the husband. The new historicist might also look at the many medical documents of the time on the subject of female hysteria, at the dress and behavior codes that rendered women both fragile and nervous, and from such connections argue that Mrs. Mallard's "heart trouble" is a socially produced condition that manifests physically her mental suffering. In interpreting the text, a new historicist would consider how "The Story of an Hour" intersects with other cultural discourses on women and marriage, and how, in exposing the tyranny of a patriarchal social system, the story also demonstrates the seeming invincibility of that system. A new historicist might also be interested in the way that the medical discourse of the (undoubtedly) male doctors at the end fixes the meaning of Mrs. Mallard's death in a way that implicitly supports the existing patriarchy—she has died "of joy" at her husband's return.

Marxist Criticism

Marxist criticism resembles new historicism in its focus on how works mirror complex historical, social, and cultural realities and in its concentration on the plight of the marginalized in society. However, this school of literary critics examines works through the lens of Marxist social and economic theory. Karl Marx (*Das Kapital,* 1867–1891) proposed that the most important aspect of material reality was the economic realm, the means of production. In other words, the means by which a society produces both goods and services determines the relation of one class of people to another. Some are primarily producers, and others are primarily consumers—as was the case in slave and feudal systems. During the Industrial Revolution, a working class arose that was exploited by the middle class (or bourgeois) bosses who controlled the means of production (i.e., owned the mines and the factories). Marx argued that all social structures are primarily created by (i.e., determined by) the economic base. The economic base determines the superstructure (e.g., government, religious, educational, and family practices). For Marx, this economic determinism affects the way people think to such an extent that they cannot imagine living any other way. What keeps them in their place is ideology, a structured belief system, which Marx defines as "false consciousness." This ideology, which is circulated through educational, religious, and political systems, presents various justifications for the existing class structure and obscures the exploitation. For example, during Marx's time, and until quite recently, the prevailing opinion was that higher education was the right of a select, highly gifted few and that all others should "know their place" and remain manual laborers. When the workers were demystified, Marx argued, they would refuse to participate in the capitalist system, and this would trigger class warfare—a proletarian revolution that would overthrow the bourgeois exploiters, leading to a utopian, classless society in which the workers themselves owned the means of production.

Later Marxist critics argued that ideology was not simply the "false consciousness" of the proletariat but that all societies and all classes have their own set of structured beliefs that seem like common sense to them. Therefore, people have an "ideology" that provides a basis for their actions and the way they conduct themselves. Undoubtedly, though, societies have a ruling class—even in the supposedly classless society of the United States or those societies based on Marxism, in which the means of production are supposedly owned by the workers. How, then, does the ruling class remain in a dominant position? In totalitarian systems, force often is openly used through military, police, or judicial agencies, but democracies rely more on maintaining a dominant ideology through what the Italian theorist Antonio Gramsci in the 1930s called "hegemony." Direct force is not effective if used too often, because direct force may initiate direct resistance. Instead, if people can be persuaded to accept certain ideas, then they also will accept certain social and economic conditions and will consent to the dominant ideology and to the ruling class. This process of winning consent is what Gramsci calls hegemony; it can be understood as the maintenance of existing power relations not only through "official" channels but also through all aspects of lived experience, including family and marital relations and popular culture. Hegemony, however, is not unassailable—it can be challenged, sometimes successfully, and social conditions can change for the better. For Gramsci, it was important always to critique and to question reality and to work toward changing the hegemonic structure so that the marginalized and the exploited could achieve autonomy and more equitable living and working conditions.

Marxist critics often focus on works that overtly treat the fate of the working class or expose the underlying economic and social motifs in texts that are not necessarily considered to be political. For example, a Marxist film critic would explore the treatment of the autoworkers in filmmaker Michael Moore's *Roger and Me*. Or a Marxist critic would concentrate on the underlying treatment of the working class in Tillie Olsen's "I Stand Here Ironing" (Chapter 6), a short story more often studied in terms of the mother-daughter dynamic.

In Kate Chopin's "The Story of an Hour," a Marxist critic would concentrate on the pattern of economic domination and submission represented in the work, suggesting that Brently Mallard's power in the marriage results from his status as the provider while Mrs. Mallard's weakened physical state and her passivity suggest her economic disenfranchisement. In addition, her inability to imagine a way to live independently other than through the route of her husband's death arises from her "false consciousness"; that is, she sees no way to escape from the hegemonic structures—her economic subservience and her socialized gender role. That realization crushes her.

Postcolonial Criticism

Postcolonial criticism considers the legacy of European colonialism as it is represented in literature. Drawing its inspiration and methodologies from other schools of literary criticism including deconstruction, psychological criticism, feminism, new historicism, and Marxist criticism, postcolonial criticism focuses its attention in two directions: at literary texts currently being produced in former colonial regions, to discover the ways in which they respond to the impact of colonialism and its aftermath on their cultures, and at canonical texts to discover evidence of colonial themes. Postcolonial critics consider the ways in which such contemporary writers as Chinua Achebe, Gabriel García Márquez, and Nadine Gordimer represent the legacy of colonialism in their work; they also consider the ways in which such canonical texts as Defoe's *Robinson Crusoe* and Shakespeare's *The Tempest* represent colonial situations. Although the work of such writers as Aime Cesaire and Franz Fanon is important to the establishment of postcolonial criticism, probably the most important text to the movement is Edward Said's *Orientalism* (1978). Said extensively explores the link between English and French colonialism in the Middle East and the representation of the Middle East in scholarly and creative literature. Sometimes intentionally, sometimes unintentionally, Said concludes, scholarly and creative writers worked in collusion with colonial powers to construct an image of the Middle East as "the Orient," a decadent, culturally backward region in need of the steadying hand of European rule. Subsequent critics have built on Said's work, developing the connection between history and literature. Homi Bhabha, in particular, has sought to develop a critical language adequate to describing postcolonial literature. In *The Location of Culture* (1994), Bhabha offers a number of terms to describe postcolonial works, among them mimicry and hybridity. By mimicry, Bhabha refers to postcolonial writers' retelling of such canonical narratives as *Robinson Crusoe,* through their mimicry of those sources causing us to understand them in new ways. By hybridity, Bhabha refers to postcolonial literature's drawing on sources from both the indigenous culture and the culture of its former colonizers. Postcolonial critics might apply Bhabha's ideas to a story such as Adichie's "Half of a Yellow Sun," finding in the story a combination of fictional techniques drawn from European (and especially English-language) sources, and subject matter drawn from the history of Africa (Chapter 8).

Cultural Studies

Cultural studies critics focus on the social and cultural realities revealed in literary and nonliterary texts and the meanings that people ascribe to cultural phenomena. An eclectic school of critical theory, cultural studies draws on the perspectives of various disciplines—sociology, cultural anthropology, communication and media studies, film/video studies, philosophy, art history and criticism, and literary theory—to analyze cultural phenomena.

Cultural studies scholars examine modes of cultural production and consumption and relate these modes to matters of national identity, ethnicity, ideology, race, class, and/or gender. In this way cultural studies theorists employ a variety of critical lenses (poststructuralist, feminist, Marxist, New Historical, and postcolonial) to critique texts. The subjects of cultural studies are objects of cultural production, products of everyday life. They range from what are considered "high brow" literary texts to "low brow" objects of popular culture (rituals, festivals, such products as iPods or video games), or media texts (television programs, videos, films, advertisements, songs). Cultural studies critics also examine other products and practices of a culture such as fashion trends, food, fads, or hairstyles and the meanings people attach to them. These theorists explore the ways in which these texts have symbolic dimensions and suggest implied meanings about social, political, and cultural values. Cultural studies emerged as a field in Britain in the 1960s when such scholars as Raymond Williams and Stuart Hall studied the impact of class in British society and determined how certain hegemonic forces, particularly mass media, formidably shaped and reinforced the class structure in England.

In addition to analyzing the significance of cultural phenomena, cultural studies scholars, like Marxist or new historical critics, often concentrate on the ways that texts reveal and reify cultural hegemonies. A cultural studies perspective may expose patterns of domination (the workings of power) in a culture and critique prevailing hegemonic structures and values in order to bring about social change.

A cultural studies scholar might examine "The Story of an Hour," analyze the language used to describe Mrs. Mallard's heart disease, and suggest that it infantilizes her, reinforcing her passive, dependant position. Her sister treats her as a fragile being and presents the information of her husband's death in "veiled hints. . . ." Mrs. Mallard is described as a "child." The narrator explains, in addition, that "great care was taken to break to her as gently as possible the news. . . ." The cultural studies critic might then take a feminist perspective, make a leap, and suggest that the treatment reveals the way that the medical establishment (in its discourse and treatment of women) in the late nineteenth century pathologized certain women's illnesses such as hysteria and, thereby, kept women in a dependant position. This interpretation also might lead the critic to examine other pertinent documents such as medical textbooks, manuals, newspaper articles or advertisements, or other stories of that era that portray women's illnesses (see, for example, Charlotte Gilman Perkins's "The Yellow Wallpaper" in Chapter 7) to broaden the discussion.

Conclusion

If one views a work through the lenses of many critical interpretations, the work becomes kaleidoscopic. The fear may arise that the text will disintegrate and not bear the pressure of so many critical approaches. The work, however, is a pattern of many layers, and one may focus on one layer without hopelessly disrupting the whole design.

Moreover, not all works yield themselves to particular interpretations, and each framework for critical interpretation is not equally justified. In one class some years ago, for example, a student suggested that William Carlos Williams's "The Red Wheelbarrow" reveals the pervasive influence of a communist threat, foreshadowing the eventual takeover of the United States by communist forces. After all, the student contended, "the red wheelbarrow" was next to "the white chickens." This assertion was challenged by the other students, who argued that a political interpretation of the bucolic country scene seemed implausible, given what they knew of Williams's poetry, his motivations for writing, his artistic technique, and the relationship of that section of the poem to the themes of the work. In other words, this intellectual community of readers cited biographical, historical, and new critical bases for their response to the first student's interpretation. The community of readers pointed out more applicable interpretations of the poem. For this reason, it is also worth recognizing that the best critics tend to be eclectic, drawing on a variety of critical approaches in whatever combination seems most appropriate to the work at hand.

Critical interpretation leads ultimately to an enriched vision of the text: a pluralistic one in which many meanings coexist. Each interpretation must be contextualized. Each literary work is a particular confluence of linguistic, biographical, cultural realities—a single artifact of language that exhibits and represents those realities. This artifact has the power to sensitize a reader to the forces shaping values, to the ways in which interpretations of the world are based on these systems of values, and to prompt investigations of both the texts and the world in new and expansive ways.

Author Biographies

VIRGINIA HAMILTON ADAIR   Virginia Hamilton Adair (1913–2004) was born in New York City, was educated at Mt. Holyoke College and Radcliffe College, and did her postgraduate work at the University of Wisconsin, the University of Washington, and Claremont Graduate School. She was granted an Honorary Doctorate from Mt. Holyoke College. Adair has published three volumes of poetry and has contributed more than seventy poems to well-known periodicals, such as the *Atlantic Monthly* and *The New Yorker*. Adair, encouraged by her poet father, composed her first poem at the age of two. Her first book of poetry, *Ants on the Melon* (1996), was published when she was eighty-three and blind; she had previously been afraid that publishing would encourage her to write for someone other than herself.

CHIMAMANDA NGOZI ADICHIE   Chimamanda Ngozi Adichie (1977–) was born in the town of Nsukka in Southeast Nigeria. Both of her parents were employed by the University of Nigeria, and at the age of nineteen she moved to the United States. She attended both Drexel University in Pennsylvania and Eastern Connecticut State University where she studied communications and political science. She has since obtained her B.A. and is currently working on her M.A. in African Studies at Yale. She published her first novel, *Purple Hibiscus,* in 2003, and it was awarded the Commonwealth Writers' Prize for Best First Book (2005). Her second novel about the Biafran War, *Half of a Yellow Sun,* was released in 2006, and she is currently at work on a major literary project about the Nigerian immigrant experience in the United States.

MARJORIE AGOSÍN   Marjorie Agosín (1955–) was born in Bethesda, Maryland; lived in Santiago, Chile, as a child; and immigrated to the United States in 1969. Agosín was educated at Indiana University, where she received a Ph.D. in 1982. Agosín's many books include volumes of poetry, short fiction, autobiography, essays, longer works of nonfiction, and edited collections of other writers, totaling more than seventy publications. She was awarded a Fulbright fellowship to study in Argentina; the Good Neighbor Award for the National Association for Christians and Jews; the Latino Literature Prize, University of Miami North South Center (1995); the Letras de Oro Prize in Poetry; and the United Nations Leadership Award for Human Rights. Her bilingual collection of poetry, *Dear Anne Frank* (1994), is about the Holocaust, and *A Cross and a Star: Memoirs of a Jewish Girl in Chile* (1995), is the story of her mother's life in Chile, where, because she was Jewish, she was barred from the German, Catholic, and English schools. The poems, "Far Away" and "The Foreigner," from *At the Threshold of Memory* (2003), reflect on the complex relationship between an individual person and her homeland. Marjorie Agosín is currently a Professor of Spanish at Wellesley College where she teaches Spanish language and Latin American literature.

ANNA AKHMATOVA   Anna Akhmatova (1889–1966) was born in Odessa, Russia, and spent her childhood in St. Petersburg. In 1910, she married Nikolai Gumilev, a poet, who was killed by the Bolsheviks in 1921. Although the couple had been divorced since 1918, Akhmatova and her family were persecuted by the Communists for the next thirty years. None of her poetry was published until after Stalin's death, when she began visiting friends in the West and received a D. Lit. from Oxford University in 1965. Her volumes include *White Flock* (1914), *Anno Domini MCMXXI* (1922), and *Poem Without a Hero* (1940). Her great political work, "Requiem," published in 1957, protests the injustices of Stalinism by presenting one woman's endless waiting outside a prison for news of her son.

UWEM AKPAN   Father Uwem Akpan is a Jesuit priest from Nigeria who traveled to the University of Michigan in 2005 to complete his M.F.A. program in Creative Writing. His work, "My Parents' Bedroom," was originally presented in *The New Yorker* (2006). The piece is narrated by a nine-year-old child whose parents are murdered during the conflict in Rwanda. Fr. Akpan also has published another short story, "An Ex-Mas Feast" (2005), and received a fellowship from the University of Michigan's College of Literature, Science, and the Arts to produce his first book, *Fattening for Gabon* (TBA).

DANIEL ALARCÓN   Born in Peru, raised in Birmingham, Alabama, Daniel Alarcón (1977–) is a prolific Peruvian American writer whose works have been published in the pages of *The New Yorker, Harper's, Salon,* and many other magazines. From his home in Lima, Peru, Alarcón is the Associate Editor of *Etiqueta Negra,* an award-winning online magazine. *War By Candlelight* (2005), his short story collection, was a finalist for the 2006 PEN/Hemingway Foundation Award. His first novel, *Lost City Radio,* was published in 2007. His stories frequently depict a ravaged homeland whose people struggle between the impact of the awesome power of natural disaster versus the corrupt practices of authorities and rebels.

KIM ALLEN   Currently a "Ph.D. physicist by training," according to her personal Web site (http://kimallen.sheepdogdesign.net/), Kim Allen's personal interests have a technological bent: her prowess ranges from technical consultation to market analysis, with a focus on strategic planning as it relates to the production of new televisions. Besides her own Web site, she also helps to moderate the 3rd WW Wave, "Feminism for the New Millennium" site at www.3rdwwwwave.com.

JULIA ALVAREZ   Born in New York City, Julia Alvarez (1950–) was brought back to her parents' native Dominican Republic when she was a few months old. She stayed in the Dominican Republic until the age of ten, when her family returned to the United States, fleeing an oppressive military dictatorship. Her family expected Alvarez to assume the traditional role of housewife, yet her love of the printed page led her to an academic career. She read Jane Austen and Emily Dickinson in college, and eventually she came to realize that she could write in her own voice, as a powerful Latina woman. After receiving her M.A. in Creative Writing from Syracuse University, she began teaching in earnest and developed into a prolific writer. Among her many works are *Homecoming* (1984), *How the Garcia Girls Lost their Accents* (1990), *In the Time of the Butterflies* (1994), *The Other Side: El Otro Lado* (1996), *Homecoming: New and Collected Poems* (1996), *Yo!* (1997), *Something to Declare: Essays* (1998), *The Secret Footprints* (2000), *In the Name of Salome* (2000), *A Cafecito Story* (2001), *Before We Were Free* (2002), *The Woman I Kept to Myself: Poems* (2004), and *Saving the World* (2007).

SHERMAN ALEXIE   A Spokane/Coeur d'Alene Indian, Sherman Alexie (1966–) was born on the Spokane Indian Reservation in Wellpinit, Washington. He was educated at Washington State University. By the time his first novel, *Reservation Blues* (1995), was published, Alexie had published over three hundred poems, stories, essays, and reviews. His other works include the novel, *Indian Killer* (1996), and the short story collections, *The Lone Ranger and Tonto Fistfight in Heaven* (1993), which served as the basis for the 1998 film *Smoke Signals; The Toughest Indian in the World* (2000); and *Ten Little Indians* (2003). Alexie recently published his first new novel in ten years, *Flight* (2007).

AGHA SHAHID ALI   The English poet Agha Shahid Ali (1949–2001) was born in New Delhi and grew up Muslim in Kashmir. He pursued his education at the University of Kashmir, Srinagar, and the University of Delhi. He would eventually earn a Ph.D. from Pennsylvania State University (1984), and an M.F.A. from the University of Arizona (1985). His poetry, which exhibits many different metrical forms, investigates Indo-Muslim culture. His many volumes of poetry include *Bone Sculpture* (1972), *In Memory of Begum Akhtar and Other Poems* (1979), *The Half-Inch Himalayas* (1987), *A Walk Through the Yellow Pages* (1987), *A Nostalgist's Map of America* (1991), *The Beloved Witness: Selected Poems* (1992), *The Country Without a Post Office* (1997), *Rooms Are Never Finished* (2001), and *Call Me Ishmael Tonight: A Book of Ghazals* (2003–posthumous).

RUDOLFO ANAYA   Born in Pastura, Mexico, Rudolfo Anaya (1937–) and his family moved to Santa Rosa, New Mexico, when he was still a child. After a stab at business school, Anaya would eventually graduate from the University of New Mexico and then go on to teach public school for several years. Ever since the beginning of his undergraduate career, Anaya pursued writing and published his first and best known novel, *Bless Me, Ultima*, in 1972. The novel would go on to win the Premio Quinto Sol award, the national literary award given for best Chicano novel. Anaya is a prolific author, writing fiction, children's books, and nonfiction.

MAYA ANGELOU   Maya Angelou (1928–), born in St. Louis, Missouri, achieved fame at the age of forty-two with the publication of her first book, the autobiography *I Know Why the Caged Bird Sings* (1972). Before that, she lived a varied life, working as, among other things, a streetcar conductor in San Francisco and an on- and off-Broadway singer and dancer. Angelou has published four other volumes of autobiography, including *Gather Together in My Name* (1974), and *All God's Children Need Traveling Shoes* (1986), and several volumes of poetry, including *Just Give Me a Cool Drink of Water 'fore I Diiie* (1971), *And Still I Rise* (1978), and *I Shall Not Be Moved* (1990). She is Reynolds Professor of American Studies at Wake Forest University. Of her work, Angelou has said that she writes for "the Black voice and any ear which can hear it."

GLORIA ANZALDÚA   Gloria Anzaldúa (1942–2004) was born in Jesus Maria in the Rio Grande Valley of South Texas. She was educated at Pan American University and the University of Texas at Austin. Her first book, *This Bridge Called My Back: Writings by Radical Women of Color* (1981), co-edited by Cherrie Moraga, won the 1986 Before Columbus Foundation American Book Award. Anzaldúa has worked in the migrant farmer's movement, and she has taught at colleges including the University of Texas at Austin and Vermont College of Norwich University. Her other works include *Borderlands/La Frontera: The New Mestiza* (1987) and *Making Faces, Making Soul/Haciendo Caras* (1990). At the time of her death, she was close to completing her Ph.D. dissertation and receiving her doctorate from the University of California, Santa Cruz.

KWAME ANTHONY APPIAH   Kwame Anthony Akroma-Ampim Kusi Appiah (1954–) attended Bryanston School and then Clare College at the University of Cambridge, where he obtained a Ph.D. in philosophy. As a professor, Appiah taught philosophy, African studies, and African American studies at Yale University, Cornell University, Duke University, and Harvard University, ultimately joining the University Center for

Human Values at Princeton University in 2002. Appiah wrote about socio-political issues in *In My Father's House: Africa in the Philosophy of Culture* (1992). His next major
work, *Color Conscious: The Political Morality of Race* (1996), argues that the notion of
race is problematic. His latest work, *The Ethics of Identity* (2005) examines the idea of
group identity.

MATTHEW ARNOLD   Matthew Arnold (1822–1888), born at Laliham, Middlesex, England, attended Oxford University. He was professor of poetry at Oxford from 1857 to
1867, then an inspector of schools until 1886. His first volume of poetry, *The Strayed
Reveller and Other Poems,* appeared in 1849, to be followed by *Empedocles and Other
Poems* in 1852. In 1853, Arnold withdrew both volumes from circulation and replaced
them with *Poems*. Arnold's prose began to circulate after 1860. The most significant of
these works were *Essays in Criticism* and *Culture and Anarchy* (1869). He wrote religious
criticism as well as social and political analysis and attempted to improve education, in
particular secondary education.

MARGARET ATWOOD   Margaret Atwood (1939–) was born in Ottawa, Canada, and
was educated at the University of Toronto, Radcliffe College, and Harvard University.
Atwood is the author of twenty volumes of poetry, thirteen novels, and six short-story
collections. She has contributed to many anthologies and has edited numerous other
books, including *The Best American Short Stories* (1989). Atwood is best known for her
novel *The Handmaid's Tale* (1986), which won the Governor General's Award (1986),
the Los Angeles Times Book Award (1986), the Arthur C. Clarke Award for Best Science Fiction (1987), and the Commonwealth Literature Prize (1987). She is the recipient of numerous other Canadian, American, and international awards, and she has received honorary degrees from fourteen universities. Other novels include her first, *The
Edible Woman* (1969), *The Blind Assassin* (2000), and *Oryx and Crake* (2003). Atwood
is known as a feminist writer because her work analyzes the shortcomings of women's
lives in present-day society. She has said that the suffering of her female characters
reflects that of the women she meets.

W. H. AUDEN   W. H. Auden (1907–1973), born in York, England, received a scholarship to Oxford University, where he studied science and engineering before changing
his field of study to English. After immigrating to the United States and living there
for a number of years, Auden became a citizen in 1946. He taught at various colleges,
including Bryn Mawr and Barnard. Auden's work includes *Poems* (1928) and *Some Poems* (1940); and the plays, *The Dance of Death* (1934) and *No More Peace! A Thoughtful
Comedy* (1936). He also wrote introductions to many collections of verse and translated
a number of works. His many awards include the King's Gold Medal for poetry in 1937
and the Pulitzer Prize for poetry in 1948.

ULYSSES S. AWESOME   Ulysses S. Awesome is the pseudonym for Warren Burroughs
Warren, a product manager at an international financial corporation. Little is known
about Warren's background, since, according to his literary agent's website, he has obscured his identity in a cloak of changed names and events. It is known that he is the
founder of the Association of American Awesome and filmed a single episode of a
television program that was never aired. He is currently appearing at poetry readings
across the United States.

DEAN BAKOPOULOS   Born in Dearborn Heights, Michigan, to a Ukrainian mother and
Greek father, Dean Bakopoulos (1975–) was raised to speak both of his parents' lan-
guages. He wrote his first short story, "I Get Trapped," when he was seven years old.
After working at a horse farm, as a writer for a radio station, and as a book buyer, he

decided to join the University of Wisconsin M.F.A. Program and went on to write his first acclaimed novel, *Please Don't Come Back From the Moon* (2005). "Some memories of my father" is a chapter from the aforementioned novel.

JAMES BALDWIN   James Baldwin (1924–1987) was born and raised in Harlem. He grew up in a large family, and his stepfather was an evangelical preacher. An excellent student, Baldwin wrote from an early age. Although several well-known publications accepted his essays and short stories, and although Richard Wright helped him win a fellowship, it was not until he moved to Europe in 1948 that Baldwin's creative powers came to fruition. His first novel, *Go Tell It on the Mountain* (1953), is about a Harlem teenager's conflicts with a repressive father; his first play, *The Amen Corner* (1955), which deals with the Pentecostal faith, represents Baldwin's search for his racial heritage. These were followed by *Notes of a Native Son* (1955), the 1956 novel *Giovanni's Room, Nobody Knows My Name: More Notes of a Native Son* (1961), and *The Fire Next Time* (1963).

AMIRI BARAKA   Born Everett LeRoi Jones in Newark, New Jersey, Amiri Baraka (1934–) changed his name in 1967. He attended Rutgers and Howard Universities before serving two-and-a-half years in the U.S. Air Force. During the early 1960s, Baraka lived in Greenwich Village, obtained master's degrees in philosophy and German, and socialized with writers of the Beat movement. His first book of poetry, *Preface to a Twenty Volume Suicide Note,* was published in 1961. Famous for his poetry and his plays, Baraka has received the Obie Award; fellowships from the Guggenheim, Rockefeller, and John Whitney Foundations; an American Book Award; and prizes from the International Art Festival, the National Endowment of the Arts, and the New Jersey Council for the Arts. Baraka was named Poet Laureate of New Jersey in 2002. Most recently, in 2005, his poem, "Somebody Blew up America," was set to music in the multi-award-winning independent documentary *500 Years Later.*

LYNDA BARRY   Born in Richland Center, Wisconsin, Lynda Jean Barry (1956–) is one of the most popular non-mainstream American cartoonists, best known for her weekly comic strip *Ernie Pook's Comeek.* Barry's work is humorous, but often has serious undertones, delving into the reality of life, whether happy or tragic. She has published many collections of her cartoons, including *Girls and Boys* (1981), *Big Ideas* (1983), *Naked Ladies! Naked Ladies! Naked Ladies!* (1984), *Everything in the World* (1986), *The Fun House* (1987), *Down the Street* (1988), *Shake, Shake, Shake a Tail Feather* (1989), *Come Over, Come Over* (1990), *My Perfect Life* (1992), *It's So Magic* (1994), and is also a contributor of regular cartoon features to a number of different periodicals (including *The New York Times, Esquire,* and *Raw*). She is the author of the novel *The Good Times Are Killing Me* (1988).

ALISON BECHDEL   Alison Bechdel (1960–) is an American cartoonist best known for her work on the comic strip *Dykes to Watch Out For* (1983 to present), where she documents the life of a diverse group of comic strip characters, most of whom are lesbians. She was born in Lock Haven, Pennsylvania, graduated from college, and then moved to New York City. After working in a number of assistant-level jobs in the publishing industry, she crafted a single drawing that one of her friends recommended she send to the newspaper *WomanNews.* The strip caught on, and so *Dykes to Watch Out For* was printed in a number of other newspapers. In 2006, Bechdel published *Fun Home,* an autobiographical graphic novel that chronicled her childhood and the years that led up to the death of her father. The book received overwhelming critical praise, and *Time Magazine* named *Fun Home* number one of its 'Ten Best Books of the Year' in 2006.

EMILY BERNARD Emily Bernard (1967–) was born in Nashville, Tennessee. She received her Ph.D. in American Studies from Yale University. Bernard is the recipient of a Ford Foundation Fellowship, a National Endowment for the Humanities Fellowship, and an award from the W. E. B. Du Bois Institute for African and African-American Research at Harvard University. She currently teaches in the English Department and ALANA U.S. Ethnic Studies Program at the University of Vermont. Bernard is editor of *Remember Me to Harlem: The Letters of Langston Hughes and Carl Van Vechten, 1925–1964.*

BRUNO BETTELHEIM Born in Vienna, Austria, Bruno Bettelheim (1903–1990) received his Ph.D. in Psychology from the University of Vienna. Soon after, the Nazis annexed Austria, and Bettelheim was arrested and sent to concentration camps at Dachau and Buchenwald, an experience that influenced his study of human psychology. He moved to the United States in 1939 after having been released from Buchenwald. Bettelheim was an authority on childhood emotional disorders, especially autism and juvenile psychosis. He published more than twenty-five books, essays, and lectures on psychology and the survival of trauma. Bettelheim's writing brings psychological theory to laypeople in an accessible and interesting form.

WILLIAM BLAKE William Blake (1757–1827), born in London, began drawing at an early age; at fourteen, he was apprenticed to an engraver. Many of the poems he wrote during this period were eventually printed in *Poetical Sketches* (1783), his first book of poems. In 1789, Blake wrote and engraved his great poetic work, *Songs of Innocence,* which was followed in 1790 by the prose work *The Marriage of Heaven and Hell.* In 1804, he undertook the engravings of his final pieces, *Milton* (1808) and *Jerusalem* (1820). He also engraved his work on copper with the poems surrounded by illustrations that he painted, a process he called "illuminated printing."

SANDRA BLAKESLEE Sandra Blakeslee is an award-winning author and science writer for *The New York Times.* Blakeslee and Judith Wallerstein have coauthored the bestsellers *The Good Marriage* (1996) and *Second Chances: Men, Women and Children a Decade After Divorce* (2004).

LAURA ROSE BLUMENFELD Laura Rose Blumenfeld (1964–) received an M.A. in International Affairs from Columbia University. Since 1992 she has been a staff writer for *The Washington Post* and has contributed articles to periodicals such as *The New Yorker, The New York Times Magazine,* and the *Los Angeles Times.* The complete story of Blumenfeld's encounter with the Palestinian terrorist who shot her father is memorialized in her autobiographical work, *Revenge: A Story of Hope* (2002).

CARLEY REES BOGARAD Carley Rees Bogard (1936–1995) grew up in West Virginia's mining country, in the shadow of Appalachia. Bogard was a prize-winning poet, professor, and scholar who published in many journals, including *New Voices, Journal of Appalachian Women, Poetry Northwest, Valhalla,* and *The Soho Review.* She taught at the State University of New York at New Paltz for twenty-five years, where she was Chair of the Department of English. Bogard won many teaching awards during her tenure, including the Chancellor's Award for Excellence in Teaching, and Alumni Distinguished Teacher's Award, a Danforth Associateship, and the Woodrow Wilson Fellowship for Excellence in Teaching. "Kudzu" is from her 1995 poetry collection, *Outrageous Fortune.*

JORGE LUIS BORGES Born in Buenos Aires, Argentina, Jorge Francisco Isidoro Luis Borges Acevedo (1899–1986) spoke both Spanish and English at his home. Even at an early age, Borges was bilingual, reading untranslated Shakespeare at the age of 12. In

1914, his family moved to Geneva, Switzerland, where his father's failing eyesight (the same affliction that would impact Jorge Borges's life) required the attention of an eye specialist. In Geneva, Borges learned French and German and received his B.A. from the Collège de Genève in 1918. After World War I, the Borges family traveled considerably, and upon returning to Buenos Aires, Borges began his writing career in earnest. After the dictator Juan Perón came to power, Borges became disillusioned with the Argentinian government. Not long after, he began suffering from glaucoma and could write very little, so he switched to the occupation of public lecturer. Although he was politically persecuted, he became a very important public figure and obtained the position of President of the Argentine Society of Writers and then Professor of English and American Literature at the Argentine Association of English Culture. A poet, critic, and lecturer, Borges was one of the foremost literary figures of the twentieth century.

NEAL BOWERS   Residing in Ames, Iowa, with his wife Nancy (also a writer) and six cats, Neal Bowers (1948–) was originally born and raised in Clarksville, Tennessee. Long acclaimed for his poetry, Bowers has, in more recent years, turned to long-form fiction. He is the author of seven books, the most popular of these being *Night Vision* (1992), the nonfiction book *Words for the Taking: A Case of Plagiarism* (1997), the novel *Loose Ends* (2001), his poetry collection *Out of the South* (2003), the murder mystery *As Good As Dead* (2003), and his latest work, the true-crime novel *No Good Deed* (2006). Bowers currently teaches as a Distinguished Professor of English at Iowa State University.

T. C. BOYLE   Thomas John Boyle (1948–) was born in Peekskill, New York, where he spent most of his early life. At the age of seventeen he changed his middle name to "Coraghessen." After earning a B.A. in English and History from the State University of New York at Potsdam, he was accepted into the Iowa Writers Workshop (1972) and served as the fiction editor of the *Iowa Review*. Throughout his career as a writer, Boyle has received two prestigious fellowships, a Guggenheim and a National Endowment for the Arts, a Pen/Faulkner Award, a PEN/Malamud Prize, the PEN/West Literary Prize, the Commonwealth Gold Medal for Literature, a National Academy of Arts and Letters Award for prose excellence, six O. Henry Awards for short fiction, a number of Best American Short Story awards, and his 2003 book, *Drop City*, was a National Book Award Finalist. He has produced more than ten novels, eight short-story collections, and is currently at work on developing his latest novel, *Talk Talk* (2006), into a feature film at Universal Pictures.

KATE BRAVERMAN   Born in Los Angeles, California, Kate Braverman (1950–) received a B.A. in Anthropology from U.C. Berkeley and an M.A. in English from Sonoma State University. She helped to found the Venice Poetry Workshop, was a professor of Creative Writing at CSULA, a staff faculty member of the UCLA Writer's Program, and taught a private writer's workshop that included such talents as Janet Fitch, Cristina Garcia, and Donald Rawley. Braverman is an acclaimed writer, whose novels have been well-received, including *Lithium for Medea* (1979), *Palm Latitudes* (1988), *Wonders of the West* (1993), and *The Incantation of Frida K* (2001). Her poetry has been nominated for two Pulitzer Prizes, and she has published two books of short stories. Braverman has won three Best American Short Stories Awards, an O. Henry Award, a Carver Short Story Award, and the Economist Prize. She currently lives in San Francisco, where, in her spare time, she teaches and hosts a monthly literary talk show.

GWENDOLYN BROOKS   Gwendolyn Brooks (1917–2000) was born in Topeka, Kansas, and graduated from Wilson Junior College. A novelist and poet, she taught at a number of colleges and universities, including Columbia University and the University of

Wisconsin. Her many works include the novel *Maud Martha* (1953) and volumes of poetry, including *Annie Allen* (1949), which won the Pulitzer Prize for Poetry, *The Bean Eaters* (1960), and *To Disembark* (1981). She was the first African American poet to win the Pulitzer Prize, and she received numerous other awards and honors. She was Distinguished Professor of the Arts at the City College of New York in 1971.

ROBERT BROWNING   The English poet and playwright Robert Browning (1812–1889) was born in Camberwell, England, and he received most of his education at home. By his fourteenth birthday, he had learned Latin, Greek, Italian, and French. Although he enrolled in the University of London, he left the college to pursue education at his own pace. So inspired was he by Elizabeth Barrett's poetry, he corresponded with and married her in 1846. Although not recognized as a literary figure until his wife's death in 1861, Robert Browning became known for his technique of dramatic monologue. After failing to receive popularity in his earlier years, Browning went on to publish *Dramatis Personae* (1863) and *The Ring and the Book* (1868). The latter work was very well-received and garnered critical acclaim late in Browning's career. Further, Browning was awarded honorary degrees by Oxford University and the University of Edinburgh during the twilight of his life. Browning died on the day that his final volume of poetry (*Asolando*) was published in 1889.

FREDERICK BUSCH   Frederick Busch (1941–2006) was educated at Muhlenberg College and Columbia University. He served as the Fairchild Professor of Literature at Colgate University. His most popular novels include *The Mutual Friend* (1978), *Girls* (1997), *The Night Inspector* (1999), and *A Memory of War* (2003). Busch wrote twenty-seven books and was known in literary communities as a "writer's writer." His awards include Guggenheim and Ingram-Merrill Fellowships. In Busch's work, he explores the details of domestic life and the difficulties encountered by ordinary characters. "Ralph the Duck" is the second chapter of Busch's novel, *Girls: A Novel*. Busch died in 2006, the year his final work, *Rescue Missions,* was published.

ALBERT CAMUS   Albert Camus (1913–1960) was born in Algeria when it was still a French colony. While studying philosophy at the University of Algiers, he organized and directed a small theater company and became involved in political causes. During World War II, he was active in the French Resistance and also wrote *The Stranger* (1942), a novel, and *The Myth of Sisyphus* (1942), a philosophical essay, both important works in existential thought and the literature of the absurd. His other works include a novel, *The Plague* (1948), a short-story collection, *Exile and the Kingdom* (1958), and a collection of plays, *Caligula and Three Other Plays* (1958). Camus's work earned him the Nobel Prize for Literature in 1957.

LAURENCE CARR   Laurence Carr earned his B.F.A. at Ohio University in 1972 and his M.A. at New York University in 1995. He is an instructor at the State University of New York at New Paltz where he teaches Dramatic and Creative Writing. In 1998, he created the SUNY Playwrights' Project, which develops plays and theatre pieces created by students, alumni, faculty, and community writers that are then produced regionally and off-off Broadway in New York City. Carr has taught at The New School University, City University of New York, The Gotham Writers Workshop in New York City, and at Empire State College. Abroad, he has been a guest faculty member at The University of Linkoping, Sweden, the University of Gdansk, Poland, and DAMU, the State Theatre School in Prague, The Czech Republic. Carr is the recipient of playwriting grants from The National Endowment for the Humanities, The New York State Council on the Arts, and numerous regional commissions. His plays have been performed in the

United States and abroad. *36 Exposures* premiered in Prague and *Food for Bears* premiered in Warsaw. His poetry and prose have been published throughout the United States, and he has produced a book of microfiction, *The Wytheport Tales* (2006).

ANGELA CARTER   Born in Eastbourne, England, Angela Carter (1940–1992) first worked as a journalist but eventually became fascinated by oral storytelling from a matriarchal point of view. She would ultimately focus on reinvisioning fairy tales—a genre for which she would be well remembered, along with her devotion to the literary movement of "magical realism" (contemporary works that express surrealist visions through fantasy and mythology). "The Company of Wolves" is excerpted from Carter's short-story collection, *The Bloody Chamber* (1979). Apart from being a prolific fiction writer, Carter contributed articles to the *New Statesman* and also adapted two of her own works to the silver screen as a screenwriter: *The Company of Wolves* (1984) and *The Magic Toyshop* (1987).

RAYMOND CARVER   Raymond Carver (1938–1988) grew up in Oregon. He studied creative writing with John Gardner at Chico State College, earned his B.A. from Humboldt State College, and studied at the University of Iowa. He taught at a number of colleges, principally at Syracuse University. He achieved fame for his short stories, a form of which he was a master. His first collection of stories, *Will You Please Be Quiet, Please?* was nominated for the National Book Award in 1976. He subsequently published ten more collections of stories and poetry, including *What We Talk About When We Talk About Love* (1981), *Cathedral* (1984), and *Where I'm Calling From* (1988). With Richard Ford and Tobias Wolff, Carver was considered one of the leading members of the literary school of "dirty realism," fiction that focused on the minute, and frequently unpleasant, details of people's daily lives.

PAUL CELAN   One of the major poets of the post–World War II era, Paul Antschel (1920–1970) was born in Romania, the only child of a German-speaking Jewish family. He lived in France for most of his life, yet wrote in the German language. After the Nazis' rise to power, his parents were interred and died in a concentration camp while Celan was sent to a forced-labor camp. Although Celan managed to survive the Holocaust, he was imprisoned until 1943. After the Russian invasion of Romania, Celan fled to Bucharest where he immersed himself in writing and worked as an editor. After a brief stay in Vienna, Celan immigrated to Paris, eventually establishing his reputation as a poet in West Germany in the late 1940s. In his prolific works, Celan was known for minimalism, broken syntax, and his shattered perception of the world as a result of his experiences during World War II.

ANTON CHEKHOV   Anton Chekhov (1860–1904) was born in southern Russia. His short stories and plays were formative in the development of modern, realistic literature. His major plays are *The Sea Gull* (1898), *Uncle Vanya* (1899), *The Three Sisters* (1901), and *The Cherry Orchard* (1904). One theme dominates these plays: the protagonists' inabilities to change the circumstances of their lives—their imprisonment in the world of their failed dreams. During the last phase of his life, Chekhov also wrote several volumes of short stories: *Motley Stories* (1886), *Innocent Speeches* (1887), *In the Twilight* (1887), and *Stories* (1889).

MARILYN CHIN   Born in Hong Kong, Marilyn Chin (1957–) was raised in the United States and educated at the University of Massachusetts at Amherst and the University of Iowa, where she received an M.F.A. in poetry. Chin has published several collections of her own poems, has translated Chinese poems, and has edited anthologies of literature. She also has published her poems in prestigious anthologies, including *The Best*

American Poetry (1996) and the *Pushcart Press XX* (1996), and won several awards and fellowships for her writing. Chin's poems explore the often-difficult process of cultural assimilation into mainstream American society. Her latest work is *Rhapsody in Plain Yellow* (2002).

SANDRA CISNEROS Sandra Cisneros (1954–) was born in Chicago to a Mexican-American mother and a Mexican father. She has worked as an arts administrator and college recruiter and has taught both high school dropouts and university students. Her publications include *The House on Mango Street* (1984), which won the American Book Award and the Before Columbus Foundation Award (1985), as well as *Woman Hollering Creek and Other Stories* (1991), *Loose Woman* (1994), and *Caramelo* (2002). In spare, poetic language that resembles prose poetry, Cisneros explores issues of the Chicana/o community.

LUCILLE CLIFTON Born in Depew, New York, Lucille Clifton (1936–) attended Howard University and then graduated from the State University of New York at Fredonia in 1955. She has worked as a claims clerk, as the literature assistant in the Office of Education in Washington, D.C., and was poet-in-residence at Coppin State College in Baltimore. In 1979, she was named the Poet Laureate of the state of Maryland. Her first collection of poetry was titled *Good Times* (1969), and she published many other volumes, including *Good News About the Earth* (1972), *An Ordinary Woman* (1974), *Two-Headed Woman* (1980), *Good Woman: Poems and a Memoir: 1969–1980* (1987), *Next: New Poems* (1987), *Quilting: Poems 1987–1990* (1991), *The Book of Light* (1993), and *Blessing the Boats* (2000). Clifton also creates award-winning children's books written with an African-American audience in mind. She has been heavily anthologized, was the recipient of two creative writing fellowships from the National Endowment for the Arts, and received the Shelley Memorial Prize, the Charity Randall prize, the Shestack Prize, and even an Emmy Award for children's programming on public television. As of 1988, she is the only poet to have two different books of poetry appear as finalists for the Pulitzer Prize.

BILLY COLLINS William J. Collins (1941–) was born in New York City, and his poems have been featured in many anthologies, literature textbooks, and literary periodicals, including *American Scholar, Poetry, American Poetry Review, The New Yorker, Harper's,* and *The Paris Review.* His best-selling poetry collections include *Pokerface* (1977), *Video Poems* (1980), *The Apple That Astonished Paris* (1988), *Questions About Angels* (1991), *The Art of Drowning* (1995), *Picnic, Lightning* (1998), *Sailing Alone Around the Room: New and Selected Poems* (2001), *Nine Horses* (2002), and *The Trouble with Poetry* (2005). Collins was elected the 44th Poet Laureate of the United States, serving two terms from 2001 to 2003. His poetry is often humorous, unpretentious, accessible, and frequently rails against established convention. Collins is currently a Distinguished Professor of English at Lehman College, City University of New York.

BERNARD COOPER Bernard Cooper (1951–) was born in Oklahoma City and received an M.F.A. from the California Institute of the Arts (1975). Cooper's work has been printed in several magazines, including *Harper's, The New York Times Magazine,* and *The Paris Review,* and has been anthologized in *The Best American Essays* (1988) and *The O. Henry Prize Collection* (1995). He won the Ernest Hemingway Foundation/PEN Award for his collection of autobiographical essays and poems, *Maps to Anywhere* (1990). "Burl's," which is told from the perspective of a child whose view of the world broadens during a family outing, comes from Cooper's book, *Truth Serum: A Memoir* (1996).

SARAH CORBETT As a current contributing writer to the *New York Times Magazine* since 2000, Sara Corbett (1970–) has worked in Portland, Maine; Santa Fe; and Chicago; but (she states) never in a cubicle. She has been a freelance writer since 1994, after earning her M.A. in Creative Writing. She is a correspondent for *Outside*, is a contributing writer for *Skiing*, and was a contributor to the now-defunct *Sports Illustrated Women* (1997–2002). "The Lost Boys" (2001), a story about young African refugees, was originally presented in *The New York Times Upfront*.

COUNTEE CULLEN Born in New York City, Countee Cullen (1903–1946) was a central figure in the Harlem Renaissance. He published his first collection of poems, *Color*, in 1925 when he was a student at New York University. He received a Guggenheim Fellowship and published *Black Christ and Other Poems* in France in 1929. Cullen also wrote a novel and children's stories. He collaborated with his friend Arna Bontemps on a play, *St. Louis Woman*, which became a popular Broadway musical in 1946.

E. E. CUMMINGS Born Edward Estlin Cummings (1894–1962) in Cambridge, Massachusetts, cummings is known for the eccentric punctuation, yet traditional themes in his poetry. Cummings was educated at Cambridge High and Latin School and Harvard University. During the last few years of World War I, he was an ambulance driver in France, where an indiscretion led to his arrest and incarceration. He went on to divide his time between Paris and New York in the 1920s and 1930s, and he cultivated many famous literary friends during this period, supporting himself though painting portraits and writing for *Vanity Fair*. Cummings published more than 900 poems, two novels, several plays and essays, and numerous paintings throughout the course of his career. He was fascinated by the unconventional aspects of life and culture (jazz, cubism, slang), and his work endures as an example of the most unique and popular poetry of the twentieth century.

EDWIDGE DANTICAT Edwidge Danticat (1969–) was born in Haiti but has lived from the age of twelve in New York. Educated at Barnard College and Brown University, Danticat published her first collection of short stories, *Krik? Krak!*, in 1996. Her first novel, *Breath, Eyes, Memory*, appeared in 1994 and was followed by *The Farming of Bones* (1998), *Behind the Mountains* (2002), and *The Dew Breaker* (2004). Danticat's awards include a Granta Regional Award for Best Young American Novelist and a Pushcart Prize, while *The Dew Breaker* also won the 2005 Story Prize. In her writing, Danticat explores the history and lives of Haitians living in Haiti and in the United States.

SIMONE DE BEAUVOIR Simone de Beauvoir (1908–1986) had a strict, middle class, Catholic upbringing and traced the seeds of her feminism to her repugnance at that restricted social world. She studied philosophy at the Sorbonne, where she met Jean-Paul Sartre and began her career as a writer and as an existential philosopher. A prolific writer, a leftist, an intellectual, and an iconoclast, she wrote philosophical essays and memoirs, chronicling her personal, political, and intellectual development, as well as several novels, of which *The Mandarins* (1954) won the Prix Goncourt. Her most famous work is *The Second Sex* (1949), one of the most important works of twentieth-century feminism.

TOI DERRICOTTE Born in Michigan, Toi Derricotte (1941–) earned her B.A. in Special Education from Wayne State University and her M.A. in English Literature and Creative Writing at New York University. She is currently an associate professor at the University of Pittsburgh. Her poetry collections include *Tender* (1997), *Captivity* (1989), *Natural Birth* (1983), and *The Empress of the Death House* (1978). Her literary memoir, *The Black Notebooks* (1997), won the 1998 Annisfield-Wolf Book Award for Nonfiction. She is an acclaimed poet, who has been the recipient of two fellowships from the National Endowment for the Arts, the Distinguished Pioneering of the Arts Award from the United Black Artists, the Lucille Medwick Memorial Award from the Poetry Society of America, a Pushcart Prize, and the Folger Shakespeare Library Poetry Book Award. As a light-skinned black woman, Derricotte has suggested in interviews that: "[Her] skin causes certain problems continuously, problems that open the issue of racism over and over like a wound."

JARED DIAMOND   Jared Mason Diamond (1937–) was born in Boston to a physician and a teacher. He earned a B.A. at Harvard in 1958 and his Ph.D. in psychology and biophysics at Cambridge in 1961. He would return to Harvard on a teaching fellowship, and would move on to become Professor of Physiology at UCLA Medical School in 1966. An ambitious scientist, he developed a second career in ecology and currently acts as a Professor of Geography and the Environmental Health Sciences at UCLA. He has authored a number of popular science books, including *The Third Chimpanzee: The Evolution and Future of the Human Animal* (1992), *Why is Sex Fun? The Evolution of Human Sexuality* (1997), *Guns, Germs, and Steel Reader's Companion* (2003), and *Collapse: How Societies Choose to Fail or Succeed* (2005).

JUNOT DIAZ   Junot Diaz (1968–) was born in Santo Domingo, Dominican Republic, and educated at Rutgers and Cornell universities. He has published fiction in many magazines, including *The New Yorker, Story,* and *Paris Review.* His first collection of stories, *Drown,* was published in 1996. He is a professor in the Program of Writing and Humanistic Studies at Massachusetts Institute of Technology and is a fellow at Radcliffe Institute for Advanced Study at Harvard University. His first novel, *The Brief Wondrous Life of Oscar Wao,* was released in 2007.

EMILY DICKINSON   Born in Amherst, Massachusetts, Emily Dickinson (1830–1886) lived the life of a recluse. Although "The Belle of Amherst" wrote more than 1,700 poems, she only published ten during her lifetime. She was educated until eighteen, and then she returned home, where she spent the rest of her life, leaving "The Homestead" for only short trips to visit close relatives. The poetry Dickinson crafted during this period was unique because of its liberal use of dashes, unconventional capitalization, and unusual imagery and vocabulary. Although she never gained recognition during her lifetime, Dickinson's poems were collected and published by her editor, Mabel Loomis Todd. By the end of the nineteenth century, Dickinson's posthumously published verse was quite popular and continues to endure to this day. Along with Walt Whitman, she is regarded as one of the most important poets of the nineteenth century.

JOAN DIDION   Joan Didion (1934–) was born in Sacramento, California, and was educated at the University of California, Berkeley. Didion's work includes novels, essays, and screenplays, totaling more than twenty publications and has been published in *Vogue, The Saturday Evening Post, Holiday, Harper's Bazaar, The New York Times Book Review, The New Yorker,* and *The New York Review of Books.* Didion's first book of collected essays, *Slouching Toward Bethlehem* (1968), was widely acclaimed, as was her later volume, *The White Album* (1979); both works examine the confusing period of the 1960s and 1970s. Her book *Salvador,* which was based on a trip that Didion made to El Salvador in 1982, was nominated for a Pulitzer Prize. Didion's writing generally explores the social and political conditions within the United States; and two of her more recent books, *Where I Was From* (2003) and *Fixed Ideas: America Since 9.11* (2003), examine the myths and realities of her home state of California and criticize the political actions taken after September 11, 2001. Didion's latest work, *The Year of Magical Thinking* (2005), is a memoir that chronicles the year following her husband's death, a period during which her daughter was also taken ill. *The Year of Magical Thinking* went on to win the National Book Award for nonfiction in 2005.

JOHN DONNE   John Donne (1571–1631), born into a prominent Catholic family in London during a strongly anti-Catholic time, was educated at Oxford and Cambridge universities. After holding various jobs, Donne converted to Anglicanism, took Anglican orders in 1615 at the age of forty-two, and preached sermons that rank among the greatest of the seventeenth century. He was considered the greatest of the metaphysical poets, whose works combined passion and reason through highly innovative conceits or elaborate metaphors.

MARK DOTY   Mark Doty (1953–) was born in Maryville, Texas. He earned his B.A. at Drake University in Des Moines, Iowa, and his M.F.A. in Creative Writing from Goddard College in Vermont. In 1989, his partner Wally Roberts tested positive for HIV, which drastically influenced Doty's writing, and Roberts's death in 1994 inspired Doty to write *Atlantis: Poems* (1995). Doty is the winner of numerous awards, including the National Book Critics Circle Award, and he was the first American to win the T. S. Eliot Prize for his poetry collection, *My Alexandria* (1993). He has written other books of poetry as well, including *Turtle, Swan* (1987); *Bethlehem in Broad Daylight* (1991); *Sweet Machine* (1998); and *Source* (2002). In his writing, Doty explores his struggle with coming to terms with his sexual identity and with the pervasive impact of AIDS on the gay community.

RITA DOVE   Rita Dove (1952–) was born in Akron, Ohio. She began teaching at Arizona State University and is currently a professor at the University of Virginia. In 1987, she was awarded the Pulitzer Prize for poetry for *Thomas and Beulah* (1986), poems based loosely on the lives of Dove's maternal grandparents. In 1993, her *Selected Poems* was published, and she was appointed Poet Laureate of the United States, not only the first African American, but also the youngest person ever to receive this honor. Dove's book *On the Bus with Rosa Parks: Poems* (1999) received a National Book Critics Circle Award nomination (2000).

PAUL LAURENCE DUNBAR   Born to parents who had escaped from slavery, Paul Laurence Dunbar (1872–1906) was the only black student at Dayton Central High School, and he was an incredibly hard-working child, publishing articles in the Dayton Herald by fourteen. Financially unable to attend college, Dunbar took a job as an elevator operator where he continued writing in his spare time. Dunbar's skill attracted the attention of popular poet James Whitcomb Riley, who encouraged him to write. In 1893, Dunbar self-published a collection of his poems, *Oak and Ivy*. After moving to Chicago, Dunbar became close friends with Frederick Douglass, who touted him as "the most promising young colored man in America." By 1895, Dunbar's work began appearing in national newspapers and magazines, where his poems were well received, and he accepted a clerkship at the Library of Congress. While living in Washington, D.C., he married the writer Ruth Alice Moore, and then published another short story collection, *Folks from Dixie* (1898), a novel entitled *The Uncalled* (1901), and two more collections of poems, *Lyrics of the Hearthside* (1898) and *Poems of Cabin and Field* (1899). He would go on to publish three other short story collections and three more novels before passing away on February 9, 1906, at the age of thirty-three.

STEPHEN DUNN   Stephen Dunn (1939–) worked as a professional basketball player, editor, and advertising copywriter before settling on his profession as poet and Distinguished Professor of Creative Writing at the Richard Stockton College of New Jersey. Dunn has written fourteen collections of poetry, and he won the Pulitzer Prize for Poetry for his collection, *Different Hours* (2000). His poem, "The Sacred," is from *Between Angels,* his seventh poetry collection, praised for its ability to capture with wit and integrity the everyday life of average Americans.

BART EDELMAN   Bart Edelman (1951–) was born in Paterson, New Jersey, and spent his childhood in nearby Teaneck. Edelman moved to California after earning both his undergraduate and graduate degrees from Hofstra University. He has taught at Kingsborough Community College of the City University of New York, Santa Monica College, West Los Angeles College, Long Beach City College, and UCLA, and currently is a professor of English at Glendale College where he edits the literary journal, *Eclipse.* Edelman has won a number of grants and fellowships to conduct research in Egypt, Nigeria, India, and Poland. His first book of poetry, *Crossing the Hackensack* (1993), reflects the theme of living abroad. He followed that volume with *Under Damaris' Dress* (1996), *The Alphabet of Love* (1999), and *The Gentle Man* (2001). Edleman's work also has been frequently anthologized.

GRETEL EHRLICH   Gretel Ehrlich (1946–) was born in Santa Barbara, California, and was raised in Montecito on the California coast. She attended college in Bennington, Vermont, and at California's University of Los Angeles. She worked as an editor in New York while attending the New School for Social Research and then in California writing screenplays and directing documentaries for public television. Since then, Ehrlich has traveled to and written about China, Greenland, the Canadian Arctic, and Wyoming, the state she chose to make her home. When walking with her two dogs in 1991, Ehrlich was badly injured by a lightning strike, an event that is captured in her book, *A Match to the Heart: One Woman's Story of Being Struck by Lightning* (1994). Ehrlich's first published collection of poems, *Geode/Rock/Body* (1970), reflects the disintegration of boundaries between the landscape and the human, a theme that has solidified her reputation as a nature writer. She has written sixteen books and six scripts for television, has contributed numerous works to anthologies and periodicals, and has received several awards for her writing, including a Whiting Foundation grant and a Guggenheim fellowship. Her ten trips to Greenland resulted in the book, *This Cold Heaven: Seven Seasons in Greenland* (2001), a National Geographic story about the effect of climate change on the traditional hunting culture.

T. S. ELIOT   T. S. (Thomas Stearns) Eliot (1888–1965) was born in St. Louis, Missouri. After graduating from Harvard University, he moved in 1915 to England, where he lived for the rest of his life. Eliot published his first poem when he was a student, "The Love Song of J. Alfred Prufrock" when he was twenty-two, and continued to produce masterpieces including *The Waste Land* (1922) and *Four Quarters* (1943). He also wrote influential essays on poetry, gathered in *The Sacred Wood* (1920), and plays including *Murder in the Cathedral* (1935) and *The Cocktail Party* (1950). He was awarded the Nobel Prize for Literature in 1948. Eliot's poetry is noted for its evocative imagery, its range of form and style, and its allusions to myth, to legend, and to works from many traditions.

SHUSAKU ENDŌ   Born in Tokyo, Shusaku Endō (1923–1996) spent his early childhood in Manchuria, China, then returned to Japan after his parents separated, living with his mother in the home of a Roman Catholic aunt. He received his B.A. from Keio University and studied French Literature at Lyon University in France. A playwright, novelist, and short story writer, Endō frequently wrote about the clash between Eastern and Western morals and philosophy. His works include *Stained Glass Elegies* (1979), *The Samurai* (1980), *Deep River* (1994), and *The Girl I Left Behind* (1996).

LOUISE ERDRICH   Karen Louise Erdrich (1954–) was born in Little Falls, Minnesota. Erdrich grew up in North Dakota, where her parents were instructors at the Bureau of Indian Affairs School. She completed her undergraduate education at Dartmouth in anthropology and afterward engaged in a number of different professions: waitress, lifeguard, construction worker, and a poetry teacher at prisons. After acting as editor for the Boston Indian Council newspaper known as *The Circle,* she completed her M.A. in Creative Writing at Johns Hopkins (1979). The following year, she became a writer-in-residence at Dartmouth. Erdrich's works have appeared in the *New England Review, The Paris Review, The Prairie Schooner,* and *Redbook.* Some of her more popular novels are: *Love Medicine* (1984), *The Beet Queen* (1986), *Tracks* (1988), *Tales of Burning Love* (1996), and *The Antelope Wife* (1998), her children's book *The Birchbark House* (2000), and the collaborative *Crown of Thorn*s (1991). Her fiction and poetry reflect her Chippewa heritage and the complex issues that are intertwined with its tradition, and she is a foremost figure in the second wave of the Native American Renaissance of literature.

MARTIN ESPADA   Born in Brooklyn, New York, Martin Espada (1957–) has worked at jobs ranging from bouncer to tenant lawyer. Espada, a professor at the University of Massachusetts, Amherst, has won two National Endowment of the Arts Fellowships, a Massachusetts Artists' Fellowship, a PEN/Revson Fellowship, and the Paterson Poetry Prize. His volumes of poetry include *Immigrant Iceboy's Bolero* (1982), *Rebellion Is the Circle of a Lover's Hand* (1990), *Imagine the Angels of Bread* (1996), and *The Republic of Poetry* (2006). Espada's writing and life are devoted to improving the social conditions of Hispanic and other marginalized people.

WILLIAM FAULKNER   William Faulkner (1897–1962) lived most of his life in Oxford, Mississippi. His literary career began in New Orleans, where he wrote newspaper stories for the *Times-Picayune.* With the assistance of the writer Sherwood Anderson, whom he met in New Orleans, Faulkner published his first novel, *Soldier's Pay* (1926). In his major novels, considered among the greatest of the twentieth century, he created an imaginary region near Oxford called Yoknapatawpha County, chronicling its history in *The Sound and the Fury* (1929), *As I Lay Dying* (1930), *Light in August* (1932), *Absalom, Absalom!* (1936), *The Hamlet* (1940), and *Go Down, Moses* (1942). His short fiction can be found in *The Collected Stories of William Faulkner* (1951). Faulkner received the Nobel Prize for Literature in 1949.

HEINZ INSU FENKL   Heinz Insu Fenkl (1960–), born in Inchon, Korea, and raised in Korea, Germany, and the United States, is an internationally renowned author, editor, translator, and folklorist. His first book, *Memories of My Ghost Brother,* an autobiographical novel about growing up in Korea as a bi-racial child in the 1960s, was a Barnes and Noble "Discover Great New Writers" book in 1996 and a PEN/Hemingway finalist in 1997. He is also co-editor of two major collections of Korean American fiction: *Kori* and *Century of the Tiger.* Fenkl is currently the recipient of a fellowship from the Korean Literature Translation Institute to translate the seventeenth-century Korean Buddhist masterpiece, *Nine Cloud Dream.* He has also published short fiction in a variety of journals and magazines as well as numerous articles on folklore and myth. Fenkl teaches Creative Writing at the State University of New York at New Paltz.

CAROLYN FORCHÉ   Born in Detroit, Michigan, Carolyn Forché (1950–) attended Michigan State University and Bowling Green State University. Her publications include the volumes of poetry *Gathering the Tribes* (1976), which won the Yale University

Younger Poets Award; *The Country Between Us* (1981), which was named the Lamont Selection of the Academy of American Poets; *The Angel of History* (1994); and *Blue Hour* (2003). Forché lived in El Salvador from 1978 to 1980, working as a journalist and human rights activist, and she has translated the works of Salvadoran poets. She has edited an anthology of poetry of witness: *Against Forgetting* (1993).

ROBERT FROST Robert Frost (1874–1963) was born in California but moved to New England after his father died when Frost was eleven. He attended Dartmouth College and Harvard University. Frost attempted, among other things, to run his own farm before moving his family to England, where he published his first book of poems, *A Boy's Will* (1913), which drew favorable reviews from Ezra Pound. Pound assisted the publication of Frost's second book, *North of Boston* (1914), the success of which encouraged Frost to return to New England. For almost the next half-century, Frost enjoyed tremendous popular success. He also taught and lectured at colleges including Amherst, Dartmouth, and Harvard. His subsequent volumes include *New Hampshire* (1923) and *The Poetry of Robert Frost* (1969). Of poetry, Frost said that it should begin "in delight" and end "in wisdom."

MARY GAITSKILL Born in Lexington, Kentucky, in 1954, Mary Gaitskill's work largely deals with female protagonists coping with their own inner conflicts. Gaitskill used her own experience as a teenage runaway turned stripper turned prostitute to inject candid, realistic, and often taboo issues into her stories. Among her more famous works are *Because They Wanted To* (1988; nominated for the PEN/Faulkner Award), *Bad Behavior* (1988), *Two Girls, Fat and Thin* (1991), and *Veronica* (2005). Her many stories and essays have appeared in *Harper's Magazine, The New Yorker, Esquire, The Best American Short Stories* (1993), and *The O. Henry Prize Stories* (1998). Her story, "Secretary," contained in the collection *Bad Behavior,* was the impetus for the 2002 film. Gaitskill is the recipient of a Guggenheim Fellowship, and she currently teaches Creative Writing at Syracuse University.

DAGOBERTO GILB Toiling as a construction worker for sixteen years before he made his impact as a published writer, Dagoberto Gilb was born to a Mexican mother and a father of German descent. He went on to graduate from the University of California at Santa Barbara (1973) with a double major in Philosophy and Religious Studies, and he earned an M.A. in Religious Studies in 1976. After earning his degree he found it difficult to obtain a job and so sought employment at construction sites. During his tenure as construction worker, Gilb wrote in earnest, chronicling his life in journals without realizing that his working-class experience would influence his future writing. His first short story collection, *The Magic of Blood* (1994), received the PEN/Hemingway Award, and was a PEN/Faulkner finalist. Gilb has also written *The Last Known Residence of Mickey Acuña* (1995), and a collection of short fiction, *Woodcuts of Women* (2001). Gilb was the recipient of a Guggenheim Fellowship and a Whiting Writers' Award. He currently lives in Austin, Texas.

CHARLOTTE PERKINS GILMAN Charlotte Perkins Gilman (1860–1935), born in Hartford, Connecticut, was raised by her mother. After divorcing her first husband, Gilman began to write, lecture, and teach. "The Yellow Wallpaper," her most famous story, appeared in 1892 in *New England Magazine* and was based on her experience with treatment for postpartum depression. Gilman remarried in 1900. She wrote books about alternate social structures, including *The Home* (1903) and the feminist utopia, *Herland* (1915). She spoke at national and international women's conferences. Gilman committed suicide in 1935, stating that she preferred "chloroform to breast cancer" and that she felt it was her right to do so. Although she suffered from depression all her life, she was a remarkably productive writer and lecturer.

ALLEN GINSBERG   Allen Ginsberg (1926–1997) was born in Newark, New Jersey. After graduating from Columbia University, Ginsberg went to San Francisco, where he worked on his long poem, *Howl,* which was published in 1956 and distinguished him as a major Beat writer in the company of Jack Kerouac and William S. Burroughs. The Beat writers were characterized by their attempt to combine socially marginal behavior with the quest for spiritual enlightenment. During the early 1960s, he traveled extensively; in the late 1960s, he received a Guggenheim fellowship and visited many colleges and universities. Ginsberg taught at City College in New York and Naropa Institute in Colorado. His work, *Collected Poems* (1984), gives a view of American life over several decades, introducing readers to hundreds of personalities of the times.

NIKKI GIOVANNI   Nikki Giovanni (1943–) was born and educated in Tennessee, and has taught creative writing at Rutgers University and other colleges. Currently, she teaches at Virginia Polytechnic University as a Distinguished Professor of English. A prolific poet, her volumes of poetry include *Ego Tripping and Other Poems* (1973), *Cotton Candy on a Rainy Day* (1978), *Spin a Soft Black Song* (1985), *Sacred Cows and Other Edibles* (1988), *Blues: For All the Changes: New Poems* (1999), and *Quilting the Black-Eyed Pea: Poems and Not Quite Poems* (2002). Since college, Giovanni has been actively involved in the African-American struggle for equality, and in 2002 she was presented with the first Rosa Parks Woman of Courage Award.

SUSAN GLASPELL   Susan Glaspell (1882–1948), born in Davenport, Iowa, graduated from Drake University. In 1911, she moved to Greenwich Village; in 1913, she married George Cook; and in 1915, with her husband she founded the Provincetown Players on Cape Cod, Massachusetts. She wrote more than twenty plays as well as numerous short stories and novels. In 1930, her drama *Alison's House* won the Pulitzer Prize. Glaspell's most famous work is *Trifles* (1916), a one-act play she based on a trial that she covered as a reporter in Iowa and later transformed into a short story, "A Jury of Her Peers."

EUGENE GLORIA   Eugene Gloria was born in Manila, Philippines, and raised in San Francisco. He earned his B.A. from San Francisco State University, his M.A. from Miami University of Ohio, and his M.F.A. from the University of Oregon. Gloria is the author of two books of poems, *Hoodlum Birds* (2006) and *Drivers at the Short-Time Motel* (2000). The latter was selected for the 1999 National Poetry Series and the 2001 Asian American Literary Award. Gloria has also received a Fulbright Research Grant, another grant from the San Francisco Art Commission, a Poetry Society of America Award, and a Pushcart Prize. He is currently an associate professor of English and Chair in Creative Writing at DePauw University.

EMMA GOLDMAN   Born in Kovno, Lithuania, Emma Goldman (1869–1940) moved to the United States in 1885 to escape an arranged marriage. Goldman studied nursing and midwifery in Vienna, Austria, during the late 1890s, but she is known primarily for her work as a political activist. Goldman, an anarchist, was the founder and editor of *Mother Earth* magazine (1906–1917); lectured about social causes, including free speech and reproductive rights for women; and was deported to Russia in 1919 after being imprisoned for two years. Goldman wrote eleven books, including collections of essays, lectures, criticism, and memoirs. "Minorities vs. Majorities" is from *Anarchism and Other Essays* (1910), her first published collection.

ALLEGRA GOODMAN   Raised in the Jewish faith in Honolulu, Hawai'i, Allegra Goodman (1967–) wrote and illustrated her first novel at the age of seven. She graduated from Punahou School in 1985 and then pursued her higher education at Harvard University; she received her Ph.D. in English Literature at Stanford. Her writing career began with the publication of a poetry collection, *Total Immersion* (1989), and continued with another critically acclaimed collection, *The Family Markowitz* (1996). She also has produced three novels: *Kaaterskill Falls* (1998), *Paradise Park* (2001), and *Intuition* (2006). Her poems and fiction have appeared in *The New Yorker, Allure, Food and Wine, Vogue, Commentary,* and *Slate.* She is the recipient of a Whiting Award and the *Salon Magazine* award for fiction.

NADINE GORDIMER Born in Springs, South Africa, Nadine Gordimer (1923–) has published eleven short story collections and fourteen novels. Among these, her most famous books are *A Guest of Honour* (1970), *The Conservationist* (1974), *Burger's Daughter* (1979), *July's People* (1982), *A Sport of Nature* (1987), *My Son's Story* (1990), *None to Accompany Me* (1994), and *Get a Life* (2005)—the final novel written after the death of her husband as a result of cancer. Most of her works deal with the tensions sprouting from her racially divided place of birth, and in the past she wielded her pen as a political activist, protesting apartheid. Gordimer is a lauded writer, political activist, essayist, and novelist, and her writing prowess and ability to act as a narrative witness won her the Nobel Prize in Literature in 1991.

MARY GORDON Mary Catherine Gordon (1949–), born on Far Rockaway in Long Island, New York, has written six novels, including *Final Payments* (1978), *Men and Angels* (1985), *Spending* (1998), and *Pearl* (2005). Her shorter fiction has been collected in *Temporary Shelter* (1987) and *The Rest of Life* (1993). In a recent book, *The Stories of Mary Gordon* (2006), twenty-two previously unreleased stories and those from *Temporary Shelter* are collected together in one volume (along with "City Life"). Her nonfiction writings have been published in *Good Boys and Dead Girls* (1991) and *Seeing Through Places: Reflections on Geography and Identity* (1999). She has written two memoirs, *The Shadow Man* (1996) and *Circling My Mother* (2007). She also wrote a biography, *Joan of Arc* (2000). Winner of the Kafka Prize for fiction and the Short Story Prize, she holds the McIntosh Chair as Professor of English at Barnard College. Her writing is marked by its relentless scrutiny of experience.

DANUSHA VERONICA GOSKA Danusha Goska recently completed her Ph.D. at the University of Indiana's Folklore Department. She is the author of *Love Me More: An Addict's Diary* (2003), and her dissertation on Polish-Jewish relations will be published by Ohio University Press. Her writing has also appeared in *New York Folklore, Southern Folklore* and *2B, A Journal of Ideas.*

THOM GUNN Born in the town of Gravesend located in Kent, England, Thomson William Gunn (1929–2004) lived alone with his mother until she committed suicide when he was just fifteen. Some critics claim that the self-reliance and self-definition that is apparent in his poetry was a result of Gunn's early independence. He served in the army for a period of two years and then attended Cambridge, where he discovered John Donne and William Shakespeare. Gunn then moved to America and eventually settled in the San Francisco Bay area, teaching one term a year at Berkeley from 1958 to 1966. He was a prolific writer, most famous for the collections *Fighting Terms* (1954), *The Sense of Movement* (1957), *My Sad Captains and Other Poems* (1961), *Touch* (1967), *Jack Straw's Castle* (1976), *The Passages of Joy* (1982), *The Man With Night Sweats* (1992), *Frontiers of Gossip* (1998), *Boss Cupid* (2000), and his various tomes of collected poems. As a writer, critics commented that the restrictions of traditional verse form on Gunn often produced a remarkable imaginative tension in his poems.

JESSICA HAGEDORN Born in Manila in the Philippines, Jessica Hagedorn (1949–) moved to the United States in the 1960s and now resides in New York City. Hagedorn has published three books of poetry, three novels, and she has written or edited several other works, including *Charlie Chan Is Dead: An Anthology of Contemporary Asian American Fiction* (1993). In 1983 she won the National Book Award and the Before Columbus Foundation Award for her collection of poems, *Pet Food and Tropical Apparitions* (1981). In her writing, Hagedorn confronts disturbing subjects, many of which relate to her life in the Philippines or her experiences as an Asian American. "The Song of Bullets" is taken from her poetry collection, *Danger and Beauty* (1993).

BARBARA HAMBY Barbara Hamby (1952–) began writing poetry in grade school, but for many years her writing took a back seat to raising a family while pursuing a career as a secretary and legal assistant. Her poems have appeared in many magazines, including *The Paris Review, The Iowa Review, The Kenyon Review, The Harvard Review, the Southern Review,* and *The Yale Review.* Hamby's longer poetry collections have garnered critical acclaim from both writers and reviewers, with such standouts as *The Alphabet of Desire* (1999) and *Babel* (2004). Her 2003 poem "Ode to my 1977 Toyota" was originally published in *The Southern Review.* Hamby teaches in the Creative Writing Department at Florida State University,

JOY HARJO A member of the Creek Tribe, Joy Harjo (1951–) was born in Tulsa, Oklahoma. Educated at the University of New Mexico and the University of Iowa, Harjo has taught writing at Arizona State University, Tempe, and at the University of American Indian Arts in Santa Fe, New Mexico. Her volumes of poetry include *The Last Song* (1975), *She Has Some Horses* (1985), *In Mad Love and War* (1990), and *A Map to the Next World: Poetry and Tales* (2000). She has received numerous awards, including one from the American Academy of Poetry and two from the National Endowment of the Arts. In addition to writing poetry, Harjo's band, Joy Harjo and Poetic Justice, has released several recordings, including *The Woman Who Fell from the Sky* (1994) and *Letter from the End of the Twentieth Century* (1997).

FRANCES ELLEN WATKINS HARPER Although she was not born into a slave family in Baltimore, Maryland, Frances Harper (1825–1911) suffered from racial oppression. Her mother died when Harper was three, and the young girl then passed into the care of relatives who enrolled her in a "free school for colored children." Harper's gift for writing and natural academic curiosity made her a standout at school. Unfortunately, her formal education ended at age thirteen, when she obtained a job as a seamstress. In 1845 she published her first volume of poetry, the hugely popular *Forest Leaves,* of which no copies remain. A few years later, Harper joined the American Anti-Slavery Society as a lecturer. As a public speaker, she often read her poetry aloud, and her verse reflected her ideals: the abolition of slavery, the importance of women's rights, and her strong support of prohibition. She crafted one of the first books published by an African-American, a novel about a rescued black slave titled *Iola Leroy* (1892). Some of her more famous works are *Minnie's Sacrifice* (1869), *Sowing and Reaping* (1876–1877) and *Trial and Triumph* (1888–1889).

JASON HARTLEY Jason Hartley (1974–) was born in Provo, Utah, and lived in Salt Lake City until 1999, when he moved to New York City. Hartley was educated at Utah State University and the State University of New York at New Paltz, where he is majoring in English. Hartley joined the Army National Guard when he was seventeen and served in Iraq as an infantryman in the Sunni Triangle until January of 2005. He also served at Ground Zero from September 11 until September 22, 2001. Hartley's work has been published in the *Journal of Electronic Defense* (2003) and *Tokion Magazine* (2004). Hartley's essays began as Internet blog entries, but his penetrating perspective of Army life in Iraq has spread his popularity to offline readers as well. Hartley's *Just Another Soldier,* a compilation of posts from his blog, was published in 2005.

NATHANIEL HAWTHORNE Nathaniel Hawthorne (1804–1864) was born in Salem, Massachusetts, and educated at Bowdoin College. Twenty-two years separate his first novel, *Fanshawe* (1828), from his second, *The Scarlet Letter* (1850), time during which he honed his skills as a writer by working on the short stories that were collected in *Twice-Told Tales* (1837) and *Mosses from an Old Manse* (1846). Hawthorne wrote three other novels: *The House of the Seven Gables* (1851), *The Blithedale Romance* (1853), and *The Marble Faun* (1860). Hawthorne's fiction is marked by its use of symbol and allegory and its concern with sin.

ROBERT HAYDEN Robert Hayden (1913–1980) was born in Detroit, Michigan. He attended Detroit City College (now Wayne State University) and the University of Michigan. He garnered many honors and fellowships and in 1976 became the first African American poet to be chosen Consultant in Poetry to the Library of Congress. His works include *Heart-Shape in the Dust* (1940), *Words in Mourning Time* (1970), and *Robert Hayden: Collected Poems* (1982).

SEAMUS HEANEY Seamus Heaney (1939–) was born into a Roman Catholic family in predominantly Protestant Northern Ireland. Educated at Queen's University, Belfast, Heaney became part of a group of young, Northern Irish poets. His first book of poems, *Digging,* was published in 1966. Subsequent volumes include *North* (1975), *Station Island* (1984), *Seeing Things* (1991), and *Electric Light* (2001). Despite Heaney's commitment to the Catholic cause in Northern Island, he moved to the Republic of Ireland in 1972 and divides his time between there and the United States, where he teaches at Harvard University. He was awarded the Nobel Prize for Literature in 1995. His poetry is marked by its concern with the natural world, with Irish history, and with the language of everyday speech.

ANTHONY HECHT Born in New York City to German-Jewish parents, Anthony Hecht (1923–2004) showed little academic promise in his formative years. After deciding to turn to poetry, his university education came to an end when he was drafted to serve in World War II and was sent to Europe. The war was a profound experience for Hecht, who was involved in the liberation of a German concentration camp. Taking advantage of the G. I. Bill, upon his return to the States, Hecht studied under John Crowe Ransome at Kenyon College, Ohio, and published his first collection of poetry, *A Summoning of Stones* (1954). Hecht won many awards, including the Prix de Rome (1951) and the Pulitzer Prize for Poetry (1968). Despite his success as a poet, he eventually suffered a nervous breakdown because of his tragic experiences in World War II. After recovering from this breakdown Hecht went on to teach at many notable universities, with his longest term at the University of Rochester.

LILIANA HEKER Born in Argentina, Liliana Heker (1943–) published her first volume of short stories, *Those Who Beheld the Burning Bush* (1966), when she was still a teenager. She served as editor of the literary journal *The Platypus* during the years of Argentina's dictatorship, when many writers "disappeared" and many who objected to oppression were tortured and killed by death squads. Since then Heker has published several books, most recently a collection of essays entitled *Las hermanas de Shakespeare (The Sisters of Shakespeare,* 1999) and *La crueldad de la vida (The Cruelty of Life,* 2001).

ERNEST HEMINGWAY   Ernest Hemingway (1899–1961), born in Oak Park, Illinois, served as an ambulance driver during World War I and was severely wounded. After the war, he lived in Paris among many artists and intellectuals who comprised the "Lost Generation." In 1926, Hemingway published *The Sun Also Rises,* which made him famous. He was known for his condensed, allusive style, which was tremendously influential. Hemingway famously compared his writing to the movement of an iceberg, which, he noted, floated largely out of sight, hidden beneath the water but very much there. His subsequent works include *A Farewell to Arms* (1929), *For Whom the Bell Tolls* (1940), and *The Old Man and the Sea* (1952), for which he was awarded the Pulitzer Prize. In 1954, he was awarded the Nobel Prize for Literature.

BELL HOOKS   bell hooks (1952–), born Gloria Watkins in Kentucky and educated at Stanford University, published her first book, *Ain't I a Woman: Black Women and Feminism,* in 1981. A prolific writer, hooks has pursued the role of public intellectual, seeking to bring her concerns with matters of race and gender to a broad audience. Her books include *Talking Back: Thinking Feminist, Thinking Black* (1989), *Teaching to Transgress: Education as the Price of Freedom* (1994), *We Real Cool: Black Men and Masculinity* (2003), and *Teaching Community: A Pedagogy of Hope* (2003). In her latest collection of essays, *Outlaw Culture: Resisting Representations* (2006), hooks discusses gangsta rap, censorship, date rape, and Hollywood cinema.

MARIE HOWE   Marie Howe (1950–) was born in Rochester, New York, and was educated at the University of Windsor and Columbia University. She presently teaches writing at Sarah Lawrence College and is a visiting faculty member at New York University. The oldest of nine children, Howe entertained herself and her siblings by telling stories, an activity that she claims led to her career as a poet. Her publications include two books of poetry, *The Good Thief* (1988) and *What the Living Do* (1997). With Michael Klein, she edited a collection of writing about AIDS entitled *In the Company of My Solitude: American Writing from the AIDS Pandemic* (1994). Howe received both a Guggenheim and a National Endowment for the Arts fellowship, and her poems have appeared in *The New Yorker,* the *Atlantic, Agni, Harvard Review,* and the *New England Review.* "The Attic," written after her brother's death from AIDS, is from *What the Living Do,* a collection of poems about people who survive the death of those they love.

LANGSTON HUGHES   Born in Joplin, Missouri, Langston Hughes (1902–1967) wrote more than twenty books—poetry, fiction, drama, and nonfiction—becoming the best-known African American writer of his generation. Hughes, educated at Columbia University, published his first book of poems, *The Weary Blues,* in 1926. He was a member of the group of writers and artists known as the Harlem Renaissance, who celebrated African American experience and attempted to find literary forms more suited to it. In 1961, Hughes became a member of the National Academy of Arts and Letters. His works include *Shakespeare in Harlem* (1942), *One Way Ticket* (1949), and *Ask Your Mamma* (1961).

DAVID HENRY HWANG   David Henry Hwang (1957–) was born in Los Angeles, California, and was educated at Stanford and Yale Universities. Hwang has written close to twenty plays and has received awards for many of them, including an Obie Award for his first play, *F.O.B.* (1980), and for *Golden Child* (1998) as well as the Antoinette Perry "Tony" Award, the Outer Critics Circle Award, the John Gassner Award, the Drama Desk Award, and a Pulitzer Prize nomination for *M Butterfly* (1989). Although Hwang considers his ethnicity to be as insignificant as his hair color, many of his plays focus on the experiences of Asians living in the United States. As is clear in *M Butterfly* (1989), Hwang's work also examines Western attitudes toward gender and culture.

HENRIK IBSEN   Henrik Ibsen (1828–1906) was born in Norway and was educated at the University of Christiania (now Oslo). Noted for his many plays (more than twenty-five), Ibsen also published poetry and essays. Ibsen's drama writing is viewed as having had three stages—the romantic historical tragedies (*Love's Comedy*, 1862; *Peer Gynt*, 1867), those that portrayed social realism (*A Doll's House*, 1879; *Hedda Gabler*, 1890), and those that illustrated the conflict between life and art (*The Master Builder*, 1892; *When We Dead Awaken*, 1899). Ibsen is best known for having broken out of the Romantic mold of nineteenth-century drama to portray realistic characters in psychologically tense situations, offering at the end no clear moral solution to life's difficulties.

DAVID IVES   David Ives (1950–), born in Chicago, was educated at Northwestern University and the Yale School of Drama. His collection of one-act plays, *All in the Timing* (1995), which includes "Sure Thing," won an Outer Circle Award for playwriting and was nominated for a Drama Desk Award. He has written longer plays, including *Don Juan in Chicago* (1995), *The Land of Cockaigne* (1998), *English Made Simple* (1998), and *The Red Address* (1998), as well as two children's books, *Monsieur Eek* (2001) and *Scrib* (2005). He wrote the libretto for the opera *The Secret Garden*, which had its premier at the Pennsylvania Opera Theater. Ives's plays are marked by their wit and invention. In their play with language and their multiple interpretations of and variations on a single moment, Ives's plays exemplify postmodern literature.

HA JIN   Ha Jin (1956–) was born in a small rural town in the Liaoning province of China. From age fourteen to nineteen he volunteered in the People's Liberation Army, educating himself while in the service. He wanted to attend college after his army career was over, but colleges were closed during the Cultural Revolution. Therefore, he opted to work for the railroad. After colleges were reopened in 1977, Ha Jin was accepted at Heilongjiang University in Harbin, where he was assigned to study English. He received his B.A. and then went on to further his education by studying American literature and obtaining his M.A. He came to the United States to pursue his Ph.D., which he received at Brandeis University in 1993. After the Tiananmen Massacre, Ha Jin emigrated to the United States permanently, where he is currently an associate professor in English at Emory University. His award-winning works (two volumes of poetry, two books of short fiction, and a novella) eventually led Ha Jin to craft a full-length novel, *Waiting*, for which he won the 1999 National Book Award for Fiction and the 2000 PEN/Faulkner Award for Fiction and was a finalist for the *Los Angeles Times* Book Award for fiction.

JAMES JOYCE   James Joyce (1882–1941) was the eldest child of a poor, Catholic family in Dublin, Ireland. After graduating from University College, Dublin, he moved to Paris. Joyce lived on the Continent for the rest of his life, returning to Ireland only three times. In 1914, he published his famous collection of short stories, *Dubliners*. It was followed by *A Portrait of the Artist as a Young Man* (1916); *Ulysses* (1922), his masterpiece; and *Finnegans Wake* (1939). Joyce is considered one of the great literary innovators: developing the form of the modern short story and novel and experimenting with stream-of-consciousness, narrative form, language, myth, and symbol.

WENDI KAUFMAN   Wendi Kaufman (1964–) was born in Brooklyn, New York. Kaufman is a short story writer with work published in *The New Yorker* and many literary journals and magazines. Her stories have been anthologized in "Scribner's Best of the Fiction Workshops '98," *Elements of Literature*, and most recently, *Faultlines: Stories* *of Divorce.* Kaufman has won a Mary Roberts Rhinehart Award for Short Fiction and is a Breadloaf Writer's Conference Scholar in Fiction. She holds an M.F.A. in English/ Fiction Writing from George Mason University, is a frequent contributor and reviewer for *The Washington Post,* and teaches creative writing at Johns Hopkins University. Kaufman is finishing her first collection of short stories, *Life Above Sea Level.* She is also the creator and editor of The Happy Booker (thehappybooker.net), a prominent Washington, D.C.–based literary blog.

JOHN KEATS   John Keats (1795–1821) was born in London, the son of a livery-stable manager. After his father's death in 1804, his mother remarried, but the Keats family fell into misfortune when she died of tuberculosis in 1810. Keats was educated at Clarke's School, where his restless nature led to his fame for being a fighter. In 1811, Keats was apprenticed to a surgeon-apothecary, and he moved to London and resumed his surgical studies in 1815 as a student at Guy's Hospital. In 1816, Keats was licensed to practice surgery and, before devoting himself to poetry, worked as both a dresser and a junior house surgeon. While in London he met Leigh Hunt, editor of *The Examiner,* who introduced Keats to other young Romantic poets and published Keats's sonnet, "O Solitude." Keats's first book, *Poems,* was published in 1817, and sales were poor. When he was only twenty-one, Keats published his first long poem, *Endymion,* which was poorly received. This lack of reception did not daunt the young writer, and he went on to publish many other poems. His second volume of poetry gained critical success in 1820—when Keats was suffering from tuberculosis. To escape England's cold winter, Keats traveled to Rome, where he died at the age of 25 on February 23, 1821. His reputation grew after his death, and he is one of the best-known Romantic poets.

JANE KENYON   Born in Ann Arbor, Michigan, Jane Kenyon (1947–1995) received her B.A. from the University of Michigan in 1970 and her M.A. in 1972 after winning a major scholarship. While a student at the University of Michigan she met and eventually married the poet Donald Hall. After their marriage in 1972, the two moved to Wilmont, New Hampshire, where Kenyon eventually became the poet laureate of that state. Kenyon published four collections of poetry during her lifetime and became famous for translating the works of Anna Akhmatova into English. Her publications include *From Room to Room* (1978), *The Boat of Quiet Hours* (1986), *Let Evening Come* (1990), *Constance* (1993), *Otherwise: New and Selected Poems* (1996), *A Hundred White Daffodils* (1999), and her *Collected Poems* (2005).

JAMAICA KINCAID   Jamaica Kincaid (1949–) was born in Antigua in the West Indies. Kincaid emigrated to the United States to attend college, which she found "a dismal failure." She is now a naturalized citizen, living in New York City and in Burlington, Vermont. Her first collection of short stories, *At the Bottom of the River* (1983), won the Morton Dauwen Zabel Award of the American Academy and Institute of Arts and Letters. Her subsequent volumes have included *Annie John* (1985), *The Autobiography of My Mother* (1996), *My Brother* (1997), *Mr. Potter* (2002), and her latest work, *Among Flowers: A Walk in the Himalayas* (2005). "Girl" was Kincaid's first published piece of fiction (in *The New Yorker*), written in 1977 after reading Elizabeth Bishop's "In the Waiting Room." She drafted it in one rush of energy, and it consists of one long sentence.

BARBARA KINGSOLVER   Barbara Kingsolver (1955–) was born in Kentucky and was educated at DePauw University and the University of Arizona. She published her first novel, *The Bean Trees,* in 1989. Subsequent novels include *Animal Dreams* (1990), for which she was awarded the PEN fiction prize and the Edward Abbey Ecofiction Award in 1991, and *The Poisonwood Bible* (1998), winner of the National Humanities Medal in

2000. She has also published a collection of short stories, *Homeland and Other Stories* (1989); a collection of essays, *High Tide in Tuscon: Essays for Now and Never* (1995); a collection of poems, *Another America* (1992); a nonfiction book, *Holding the Line: Women in the Great Arizona Mine Strike of 1983* (1989); a collection of essays, *Small Wonder* (2002); and, most recently, the nonfiction narrative *Animal, Vegetable, Miracle: A Year of Food Life* (2007). Kingsolver has described the goal of her fiction as first to entertain and second to educate.

MAXINE HONG KINGSTON   Maxine Hong Kingston (1940–) was born in Stockton, California, to parents who immigrated from China. After graduating from the University of California, Kingston moved to Hawai'i and taught in secondary schools, colleges, and the University of Hawai'i. She is presently a Chancellor's Distinguished Professor at the University of California, Berkeley. *The Woman Warrior: Memoirs of a Girlhood Among Ghosts,* published in 1976, won the National Book Critics Circle Award. Her second autobiographical volume, *China Men,* was published in 1980. Kingston released her first novel, *Tripmaster Monkey,* in 1989; her second novel, *The Fifth Book of Peace,* was published in 2003. Kingston's writing interweaves her Chinese heritage with her American upbringing, transplanting the Chinese tradition to American soil. In 2007, Kingston was awarded the Northern California Book Award Special Award for her latest novel *Veterans of War, Veterans of Peace* (2006).

YUSEF KOMUNYAKAA   Yusef Komunyakaa (1947–) was born in Bogalusa, Louisiana, and was educated at the University of Colorado, Colorado State University, and the University of California, Irvine, where he received an M.F.A. Komunyakaa has published twelve collections of poetry and has edited several others, including the Best American Poetry 2003 and a translation of the work of the Vietnamese poet Nguyen Quang Thieu, *The Insomnia of Fire* (1995). His many awards include the 1994 Pulitzer Prize for poetry for his collection *Neon Vernacular* (1993). Komunyakaa's poems often reflect his experience as a soldier in Vietnam. His latest work, *Gilgamesh* (2006), was published by Wesleyan University Press.

TED KOOSER   Ted Kooser (1939–) was born in Ames, Iowa; he earned his B.A. at Iowa State University in 1962 and an M.A. at the University of Nebraska in 1968. Kooser has authored ten volumes of poetry. He has won two National Endowment for the Arts Literary Fellowships (1976, 1984), a Puschcart Prize, a Nebraska Book Award for Poetry (2001) and for Nonfiction (2004), and the Pulitzer Prize for Poetry for *Delights & Shadows* (2005). Kooser was the thirteenth Poet Laureate of the United States in 2004 and was reappointed for a second term in April, 2005.

GEETA KOTHARI   Geeta Kothari's (1963–) writing has appeared in the *Massachusetts Review, Best American Essays,* and the *Kenyon Review.* Kothari is a professor of English at the University of Pittsburgh. She was the recipient of a 2005 Fellowship in Literature from the Pennsylvania Council on the Arts, and she has published a novel, *Prayers in Another Language.* In "If You Are What You Eat, Then What Am I?," Kothari argues that longing for an American meal is integral for setting boundaries "between 'first-generationers' and the non-Indian community."

ETHERIDGE KNIGHT   Born to a poor family of seven children in Corinth, Mississippi, Etheridge Knight (1931–1991) dropped out of school at age fourteen. Overwhelmed by the limits of his education, Knight took on menial jobs until, in his emotional despair, he began to abuse drugs. Almost in reaction to this downward spiral, Knight then signed up for the Korean War, where he suffered a severe shrapnel wound. He used narcotics to treat the injury, was discharged, and promptly became a spinner of narratives. Knight's recurring drug abuse led him to a life of crime: after his arrest for steal-ing a woman's purse, he was sentenced to a lengthy prison term. In prison he turned to reading as a way of escaping the injustices heaped upon him in the prison system, developing his oral tales into poetry. Thus was born his collection of *Poems from Prison* (1968). He followed this with a new volume in 1970, *Black Voices from Prison,* and crafted *Belly Songs and Other Poems* (1973), written after his release. It was during the 1970s that Knight's popularity skyrocketed, launching his literary career and leading to his teaching positions at the University of Pittsburgh, the University of Hartford, and Lincoln University.

MAXINE KUMIN Maxine Kumin (1925–) was born in Philadelphia and educated at Radcliffe College. Kumin married, had three children, and then enrolled in writing workshops at the Boston Center for Adult Education. There she met Anne Sexton, with whom she had a celebrated friendship, collaborating on four children's books with her. In 1973, Kumin received the Pulitzer Prize for Poetry for her fourth volume, *Up Country: Poems of New England.* Her five other poetry collections include *Selected Poems: 1960–1990* (1997), *The Long Marriage* (2001), and her most recent volume, *Jack and Other New Poems* (2005). Kumin has published several novels, more than twenty children's books, a collection of short stories, and several volumes of essays. She has lectured at universities across the country and currently teaches poetry at New England College's Graduate M.F.A. Program.

ANDREW LAM Born in South Vietnam, Andrew Lam (1964–) is the son of General Lâm Quang Thi of the Republic of Vietnam. He and his family left Vietnam in 1975 in response to the Fall of Saigon. After pursuing his higher education in California, Andrew turned to writing. He is now a syndicated writer and editor with New America Media, a short story writer, and a regular commentator on NPR's *All Things Considered.* He is also the co-founder of New California Media. His essays have appeared in newspapers across the country, including *The New York Times, The L.A. Times, The San Francisco Chronicle, The Baltimore Sun, The Atlanta Journal,* and *The Chicago Tribune.* His essays have also been published in *Mother Jones, The Nation, San Francisco Focus, Proult Journal, In Context,* and *Earth Island Journal.* His book, *Perfume Dreams: Reflections on the Vietnamese Diaspora* (2005), won the Pen American "Beyond the Margins" Award.

JHUMPA LAHIRI Born Nilanjana Sudeshna in London and raised in Rhode Island, Jhumpa Lahiri Vourvoulias (1967–) was educated at Barnard College and Boston University. Her short stories have appeared in *The New Yorker, Story,* and *Salamander.* In 1999, she published her first collection of stories, *The Interpreter of Maladies,* which won a Pulitzer Prize; in 2003, she published her first novel, *The Namesake.* Lahiri, edu-cated in the United States and raised in England, has visited regularly with relatives in Calcutta, and her fiction captures the movement between these locations. Her book, *The Namesake,* was released as a film in 2007 in both the United States and the United Kingdom.

LAO-TZU Lao-tzu (570–490 B.C.) lived during the sixth century B.C. in the ancient state of Ch'u in China. The *Tao-te-Ching,* the major document of Taoism, is attributed to his authorship, although it may not be the work of a single person. Some of the *Tao-te-Ching*'s sayings may date from the time of Confucius, but others are certainly later, and the book as a whole may date from 300 B.C. Indeed, the name Lao-tzu may represent a type of sage and not a specific person, though the work attributed to him has continued to be respected in China and throughout the world. The *Tao-te-Ching* is a collection of eighty-one poems or segments that presents an eloquent expression of withdrawal from action, the way to virtue.

D. H. LAWRENCE D. H. (David Herbert) Lawrence (1885–1930) was born in Nottingham, England, the son of a coal miner and a former schoolteacher. He became a major literary figure with the publication of *Sons and Lovers* in 1913. Lawrence's best-known works include *The Rainbow* (1915), *Women in Love* (1920), and *Lady Chatterley's Lover* (1928). His shorter works and poems are found in *The Complete Stories* (1961), *Four Short Novels* (1965), and *Complete Poems* (1964). Suffering from tuberculosis and disgusted with his country's industrialism and commercialism, Lawrence spent much of his life traveling through Italy, France, Australia, the United States, and Mexico.

CHANG-RAE LEE Chang-rae Lee (1965–) was born in Seoul, Korea, and moved to the United States when he was three years old. Lee was educated at Yale University and the University of Oregon, where he received an M.F.A. in 1993. He has taught creative writing at the University of Oregon in Eugene, Hunter College, and Princeton University. Lee has published three books: *Native Speaker* (1995), *A Gesture of Life* (1999), and *Aloft* (2004). For *Native Speaker* he won the Hemingway Foundation/PEN award, the "New Voices" award from QPB, the Barnes & Noble Discover Great New Writers Award, the American Book Award from the Before Columbus Foundation, and the American Library Association Notable Book of the Year Award. In 1999, Lee was selected by *The New Yorker* as one of the twenty best writers under forty years old. Lee's work focuses on the complex search for identity in Asian-American immigrants who feel alienated from both the United States and the culture of their parents. "Coming Home Again" was first published in *The New Yorker* and was anthologized in *The Best American Essays, 1996.*

LI-YOUNG LEE Li-Young Lee (1957–) was born in Indonesia to Chinese parents. In 1957, his father was jailed by then-dictator Sukarno for nineteen months, sixteen of which he spent in a leper colony. After his father escaped, the family fled the country and settled in western Pennsylvania. Lee's culturally diverse background is evident in his love both of Chinese poetry and of Bible verses recited to him by his classically educated parents. His autobiography, *The Winged Seed* (1995), won the American Book Award and the Before Columbus Foundation Award. His first volume of poetry, *Rose,* was published in 1986; his second volume, *The City in Which I Love You,* won the Lamont Prize for Poetry in 1990; and his third, *Book of My Nights,* was published in 2001. In 2003, Li was awarded a fellowship in the Academy of American Poets.

ROBYN JOY LEFF Robyn Joy Leff (1964–) was born in Ohio and grew up in Cleveland, Chicago, California, and Tennessee before heading to Hampshire College in Massachusetts at age sixteen. She later received a degree in Media Studies from the University of California, Santa Cruz. Her short stories have appeared in such publications as *The Atlantic Monthly, Quarterly West,* and *Zyzzyva.* She currently lives in Los Angeles, where she writes marketing materials for motion pictures and is at work on a novel. Leff credits her physicist father and artistic mother as being polar influences in her life. "Burn Your Maps" appeared in the *Atlantic Monthly* in January 2002 and was anthologized in the *O. Henry Prize Stories, 2003.*

JONATHAN LETHEM Jonathan Allen Lethem (1964–) was born in Brooklyn, New York, where his mother was a political activist and his father was an avant-garde painter. He began his career as a painter and attended (and promptly dropped out of) Bennington College in Vermont. Lethem then hitchhiked to California, clerking in bookstores, and received his first big break when his novel *Gun, with Occasional Music* was published in

1994. The novel received critical praise and launched his literary career, leading Lethem to move back to Brooklyn. Among his most popular works are *As She Climbed Across the Table* (1997), *Girl in Landscape* (1998), *Motherless Brooklyn* (1999), *The Fortress of Solitude* (2003), and *You Don't Love Me Yet* (2007), along with an assortment of fiction collections. His works touch on pop culture and dystopian societies, among other ambitious themes.

JULIA M. LEWIS   is a co-principal investigator of the Children Divorce Project (a twenty-five-year study), and is a professor of psychology at San Francisco State University.

SHIRLEY GEOK-LIN LIM   Born in Meleka, Malaysia into a world of poverty and violence, Shirley Geok-Lin Lim (1944–) became an award-winning poet, critic, fiction writer, and one of Hong Kong's most famous authors. Although her formative teachers taunted Lim for favoring the American language over her native tongue, she pursued her love of poetry regardless. Among her more important works are *Crossing the Peninsula* (1980) and her memoir, *Among the White Room Faces: An Asian American Memoir of Homelands* (1996). Lim currently teaches in the English Department at the University of Santa Barbara.

AUDRE LORDE   Audre Lorde (1934–1992) was born in New York City to West Indian parents. She attended National University of Mexico, Hunter College, and Columbia University, where she received her M.L.S. Lorde subsequently worked as a librarian and taught school, and she spent a year at Tougaloo College, Mississippi, as poet-in-residence. Lorde taught writing and English at several colleges before becoming professor of English at Hunter College in 1980. Her volumes of poetry include *Cables to Rage* (1970), *Coal* (1976), and *The Black Unicorn* (1978). She also wrote an account of her struggle with breast cancer and mastectomy, *The Cancer Journals* (1980), and a prose autobiography, *Zami: A New Spelling of My Name* (1982).

MANNING MARABLE   Manning Marable (1950–) was born in Dayton, Ohio. Educated at Earlham College, the University of Wisconsin, and the University of Maryland, Marable was founding director of the Institute for Research in African American Studies at Columbia University from 1993 to 2003. He currently is professor of Public Affairs, History, and Political Science at Columbia University. Marable has pursued the role of public intellectual, and his weekly public affairs commentary, "Along the Color Line," is published in more than 280 journals and newspapers. His latest work is *The Great Wells of Democracy: The Meaning of Race in American Life* (2003), a book that offers a summary of America's history of race relations while surveying the current social/political climate.

GABRIEL GARCÍA MÁRQUEZ   Gabriel García Márquez (a.k.a. "Gabo"; 1928–) was born in the coastal village of Aracataca, Colombia. After studying at the University of Colombia at Bogota and the University of Cartagena, he traveled throughout South America, the United States, and Europe as a reporter and began writing short stories. Although he has lived in Mexico City for the past twenty years, García Márquez returns frequently to Colombia, the setting for most of his work. His most famous work is *One Hundred Years of Solitude* (1972); other works include *Chronicle of a Death Foretold* (1983), *Love in the Time of Cholera* (1987), and his most recent, *Memory of My Melancholy Whores* (2005). He was awarded the Nobel Prize for Literature in 1982. García Márquez is considered to be one of the leading practitioners of the school of fiction known as magical realism, which combines the fantastic with the realistic.

ANDREW MARVELL   Andrew Marvell (1621–1678) was born in Winchester, England, and was educated at Cambridge University. In 1659 he became a member of Parliament and wrote pamphlets and satires on politics. His lyric poetry speaks of love, nature, and God. Most of Marvell's poems were published posthumously in 1681, his satires in 1689. "To His Coy Mistress," Marvell's best-known poem, represents a common literary motif called *carpe diem,* which means "seize the day." The poet emphasizes that life is fleeting and urges the person addressed by the speaker—usually a virgin—to enjoy the pleasures of life and of love.

BOBBIE ANN MASON   Born in Mayfield, Kentucky, Bobbie Ann Mason (1940–) was educated at the University of Kentucky, the State University of New York at Binghamton, and the University of Connecticut. Her first collection of stories, *Shiloh and Other Stories* (1982), won the Ernest Hemingway Award for First Fiction. Subsequent works include *Love Life: Stories* (1988), *In Country* (1985), *Spence and Lila* (1988), *Feather Crowns* (1994), and *Zigzagging Down a Wild Trail* (2001). Mason has also written a memoir, *Clear Springs* (1999), a nonfiction book, *Elvis Presley* (2003), and her latest work, *An Atomic Romance* (2005). Mason is associated with so-called Kmart Realism— the use in fiction of icons of popular culture, particularly lower-class culture, to make serious points. She has been awarded fellowships by the National Endowment of the Arts and the Guggenheim Foundation.

HEATHER MCHUGH   Heather McHugh (1948–) was born in California and raised in rural Virginia. She was accepted into Harvard University at age sixteen, where she took a seminar course with Robert Lowell and at the same time published her very first poem in *The New Yorker.* She went on to earn her M.A. in English Literature at the University of Denver in 1972. McHugh has won many awards for her poetry from the National Endowment for the Arts, the Guggenheim Foundation, PEN (Voelcker Poetry Award), and Wellesley College (Sara Teasdale Award). She and her husband, translator Nikolai Popov, together won the 2001 Griffin Prize for Poetry in the International category. Her poetry collection, *Hinge & Sign (Poems: 1968–1993)* was a finalist for a National Book Award in 1994. Her other works are *Dangers* (1977), *A World of Difference* (1981), *To the Quick* (1987), *Shades* (1988), and *The Father of the Predicaments* (1999). Heather McHugh was named a Chancellor of the Academy of American Poets and a fellow of the American Academy of Arts and Sciences (2000).

GEORGE MEREDITH   Born in Portsmouth, England, George Meredith (1828–1909) was sent to Germany to pursue his education. He became a solicitor but, after marrying Mary Ellen Nichols at the age of twenty-one, pursued journalism and poetry. His early writings were collected into the well-received *Poems* (1851). Nichols left him in 1858; in response, he published *Modern Love* (1862), fifty connected poems that reflect his personal experience of the end of his marriage. In 1864, Meredith married Marie Vulliamy and settled in Surrey, a location that inspired many of his later poems. Meredith's most notable books include *Evan Harrington* (1860), *The Adventures of Harry Richmond* (1871), *The Egoist* (1879), and *Diana of the Crossways* (1885). His famous critical essay, *On the Idea of Comedy and the Uses of the Comic Spirit* (1897), was originally delivered as a lecture in 1877. Meredith is known for his cerebrally complex but comic works that contain detailed psychological character studies.

CZESLAW MILOSZ   Czeslaw Milosz (1911–2004) was born in Wilno, Poland. A leader in the Polish literary avant-garde in the 1930s, Milosz immigrated to the United States after the Second World War and settled in California, where he taught at the University of California, Berkeley. He has written essays, including *The Captive Mind* (1953) and *Beginning with My Streets: Essays and Recollections* (1992), as well as poetry, including

Facing the River (1995). His *Collected Poems* appeared in 1990. He received the Nobel Prize for Literature in 1980.

JANICE MIRIKITANI   Born in Stockton, California as a third-generation Japanese American, Janice Mirikitani (1941–) and her family were interred in Rowher, Arkansas, during World War II. After their release from this concentration camp, her family moved to Chicago. Her parents divorced soon thereafter, and Mirikitani found herself impoverished. After her mother remarried, Mirikitani was the victim of sexual abuse during the entirety of her adolescence. Her family moved to Los Angeles, where Mirikitani became the first family member to attend college. She graduated from UCLA with her B.A. in 1962 and then earned her teaching credentials from Berkeley. In the late 1960s Mirikitani became active in the Third World movement in San Francisco and eventually became involved in the Glide Memorial United Methodist Church; there she rose through the ranks and is currently Executive Director of Programs, whose focus is on social welfare and outreach. Mirikitani is the poet laureate of San Francisco and has published three volumes of poetry: *Awake in the River* (1978), *Shedding Silence* (1987), and *We, the Dangerous: New and Selected Poems* (1995). She is also the recipient of more than thirty prestigious literary awards.

GABRIELA MISTRAL   Gabriela Mistral (1889–1957), is the pseudonym of Lucila Godoy y Alcayaga. Born in Vicuña, Chile, she was involved in the educational systems of Mexico and Chile and in the cultural committees of the League of Nations; she was also Chilean consul in Naples, Madrid, and Lisbon. She taught Spanish literature in the United States at Columbia University, Middlebury College, Vassar College, and at the University of Puerto Rico. Her books of poetry include *Sonetos de la muerte* (1914), *Desolación* (1922), *Ternura* (1924), and *Tala* (1938). Her complete poetry was published in 1958. She won the Nobel Prize for Literature in 1945.

LESLI-JO MORIZONO   As a young girl, Lesli-Jo Morizono dreamed of being an actress, and at the age of fifteen she won an acting scholarship to the American Conservatory Theatre's Summer Congress Training Program. Morizono received a B.A. in psychology from the University of California. In 1992 she graduated with an M.F.A. in dramatic writing from New York University's Tisch School of the Arts. Her publications include *In the Valley of the Human Spirit* (1992), *Fried Rice* (1993), and *Now I Lie* (2003). In her most recent work, *In Freakish Times* (2002), characters respond to effects of the apocalypse.

TONI MORRISON   Toni Morrison (1931–) was born in Lorain, Ohio, and was educated at Harvard and Cornell. She published her first novel, *The Bluest Eye,* in 1970. Subsequent novels include *Sula* (1974); *Song of Solomon* (1977); *Beloved* (1987), which won the Pulitzer Prize; *Paradise* (1998); and *Love* (2003). Morrison also has co-written six children's books with her son, Slade Morrison. In 1993, Morrison was awarded the Nobel Prize for Literature, the first African American woman to receive it. She serves on the editorial board of *The Nation,* a U.S. periodical devoted to politics and culture. In 2006, Morrison announced she was retiring from her post at Princeton (where she was Goheen Professor of the Humanities, 1989–2006). In that same year, the *New York Times Book Review* named *Beloved* the best novel of the past twenty-five years.

BHARATI MUKHERJEE   Bharati Mukherjee (1940–) was born in Calcutta, India and lived in India and England before moving to the United States in 1961 and then to Canada in 1966. She is a naturalized citizen of both the United States and Canada. Mukherjee was educated at the universities of Calcutta and Baroda, and received her

M.F.A. and Ph.D. from the University of Iowa. She is presently a professor of English at the University of California, Berkeley. Mukherjee has published nearly ten novels—including *Wife* (1975), *Jasmine* (1989), and *Tree Bride* (2004)—as well as several collections of short stories, including *The Middleman and Other Stories* (1988), which received the 1988 National Book Critics Circle Award for Fiction.

SENADIN MUSABEGOVIĆ Bosnian Senadin Musabegović (1970–) was born in Sarajevo and served in the Army of Bosnia and Herzegovina. His first book of poetry, *Udarci tijela* (*Body Strikes*) was published in 1995 and was followed by *Odrastanje domovine* (*The Maturing of the Homeland*), which was published in 1999 and won the Planjax Prize for the Bosnian poetry collection and the Writers Association of Bosnia-Herzegovina Award for the best book published in Bosnia. His latest book is *Rajska Lopata* (*The Heavenly Sphere*), published in 2004.

AZAR NAFISI Born and raised in Tehran, Iran, Azar Nafisi (1955–) pursued her education in both England and the United States. In 1979 she returned to Iran, where she taught as a professor of English Literature at the University of Tehran for eighteen years. Nafisi witnessed the revolution in Iran firsthand (and the rise to power of Khomeini) and became disillusioned with the strict rules imposed upon women by the new leaders of her country. Since she had lived in the United States before the revolution in Iran, she placed a value on the freedom that women in other countries took for granted. In the mid-nineties, she eschewed teaching at the University of Tehran because she feared that authorities would scrutinize the ideology of her subject matter. Therefore, she and a select group of students had secret weekly meetings at her house, where they explicated literary texts considered too controversial for public forums. Nafisi left Iran in 1997 and moved to the United States, where she spoke on her experience as a woman living under the Islamic Regime. Nafisi is currently a Visiting Fellow and Lecturer at the Foreign Policy Institute of Johns Hopkins University's School of Advanced International Studies in Washington, D.C.

TASLIMA NASRIN Taslima Nasrin (1962–) was born in Mymensingh (the Djaka region of Bangladesh) where her father was a physician and professor at a government medical college. During the course of her early life, she was sexually assaulted by relatives and other men. Nasrin incorporated these and other experiences (regarding the treatment of women under Islam) into her award-winning and internationally acclaimed writing; and, as a result, her books were banned in Bangladesh. Her criticism of both the Islamic faith and the Koran (which Nasrin stated "should be revised thoroughly") led to her forced exile from Bangladesh for a period of ten years. In 2007, the All India Ibtehad Council offered 500,000 rupees for Nasrin's extermination and beheading, announcing that the bounty would be lifted only if Nasreen "apologizes, burns her books and leaves."

PABLO NERUDA Pablo Neruda (1904–1973) was born in Chile. He received an appointment to the consular service in his twenties, and he served in India and in other Asian countries. In 1934 he received a post in Spain, where he became deeply involved in the Spanish Civil War. As a result, his poetry, which had expressed a romantic view of life, explores concerns both personal and political. Among his works are *Selected Poems of Pablo Neruda* (1961), *The Heights of Macchu Picchu* (1966), and *Pablo Neruda: A New Decade* (1969). His *Collected Poems* has been translated into numerous languages, including English. Neruda was awarded the Nobel Prize for Literature in 1971.

SARA NOMBERG-PRZYTYK Born in Lublin, Poland, Sara Nomberg-Przytyk (1915–) attended the University of Warsaw. After spending several years in Polish jails for her leftist political activities, she moved east, near the Russian border, when the Germans invaded Poland in 1939. Nonetheless, she was caught in 1943 and transported first to a camp in Stutthof and then, in 1944, to Auschwitz. After her liberation in 1945, Nomberg-Przytyk worked as a journalist in Lublin and, in her free time, wrote about her experiences in Auschwitz. Nomberg-Przytyk's book, *Auschwitz: True Tales from a Grotesque Land,* was denied publication by Poland's communist government unless she agreed to eliminate all references to Jews. Nomberg-Przytyk moved to Israel in 1968, and her manuscript was published in English in 1985. "Natasha's Triumph" is taken from that book.

NAOMI SHIHAB NYE Naomi Shihab Nye (1952–) was born in St. Louis, Missouri, to a Palestinian father and American mother. While in high school she lived in both Jerusalem and Texas, and she obtained her B.A. from Trinity University in San Antonio, Texas. She is the author of numerous poetry collections, among them: *Hugging the Jukebox* (1982); *Red Suitcase* (1994), a collection of poems about the Middle East; *Fuel* (1998); *19 Varieties of Gazelle: Poems of the Middle East* (2002); and *You and Yours* (2005), recipient of the Isabella Gardner Poetry Award. Her poems and short stories have appeared in reviews or journals throughout Europe, North America, and the Far and Middle East.

JOYCE CAROL OATES Joyce Carol Oates (1938–), born in Lockport, New York, studied at Syracuse University and the University of Wisconsin. She became famous with the publication of *The Garden of Earthly Delights* (1967) and *Expensive People* (1968). In 1969, her novel, *them,* won the National Book Award. Known for her prolific and varied writing, Oates, the Roger S. Berlind Professor in the Humanities at Princeton University, has published more than seventy books: novels, short fiction, poetry collections, essays, and literary criticism. Recent works include Oates's novel *What I Lived For* (1994), a 1995 Pulitzer Prize finalist; *Blonde* (2000), a fictionalization of Marilyn Monroe's life that also won the National Book Award; *The Falls* (2004); *The Corn Maiden: A Love Story* (2005); and *The Gravedigger's Daughter* (2007). Oates based her most famous story, "Where Are You Going, Where Have You Been?" on an article in *Life* magazine about a murderer, Charles Schmid of Tucson, Arizona.

TIM O'BRIEN Born in Austin, Minnesota, Tim O'Brien (1946–) was educated at Macalester College and Harvard University. He served in the U.S. Army in Vietnam, ultimately attaining the rank of sergeant, and much of his fiction reflects his experiences of the Vietnam War. His work includes *Going After Cacciato* (1978), for which he was awarded the National Book Award; *The Things They Carried* (1990), which was nominated for the Pulitzer Prize; *In the Lake of the Woods* (1994); *Tomcat in Love* (1988); and *July, July* (2002). He is a frequent contributor to magazines and literary journals.

FLANNERY O'CONNOR Flannery O'Connor (1925–1964) was born in Savannah, Georgia. After being educated at Georgia State College for Women and the University of Iowa, O'Connor published her first novel, *Wise Blood,* in 1952. Afflicted by lupus, the same disease that killed her father, O'Connor lived most her life with her mother on the family farm in Milledgeville, Georgia. She is best known for short stories, collected in *A Good Man Is Hard to Find* (1955), the posthumous *Everything That Rises Must Converge* (1965), and *The Complete Stories* (1971), which won the National Book Award. Considered by many critics to be one of the finest American short story writers, O'Connor wrote stories distinguished by their violence, their use of the grotesque, and their deep spiritual concerns.

DWIGHT OKITA   Dwight Okita (1958–) was born in Chicago to a small family. He began writing poetry in first grade because "[He] had difficulty writing stories." He received his degree in Creative Writing from the University of Illinois at Chicago, and soon thereafter his first volume of poetry, *Crossing with the Light* (1992), was published. Okita is a Japanese American whose poetry reflects themes of homosexuality, ethnic identity, and Buddhist influences. His stage play, *The Rainy Season,* is contained in the collection *Asian American Drama: Nine Plays from the Multiethnic Landscape* (2000). He is currently at work on his first novel, *The Prospect of My Arrival.*

BEN OKRI   Born in Minna, northern Nigeria, to an Igbo mother and Urhobo father, Ben Okri (1959–) grew up in London before returning to Nigeria with his family in 1968. His early fiction explores the violence that he witnessed firsthand during the civil war in Nigeria. He left Nigeria when a government grant enabled him to study Comparative Literature at Essex University in England. During the mid-eighties, Okri was poetry editor for *West Africa* magazine and worked as a broadcaster for the BBC World Service. In 1991 he was appointed Fellow Commoner in Creative Arts at Trinity College Cambridge and also Fellow of the Royal Society of Literature; he was awarded honorary doctorates from the universities of Westminster (1997) and Essex (2002). His earliest works were two novels, *Flowers and Shadows* (1980) and *The Landscapes Within* (1981), followed by two short story collections: *Incidents at the Shrine* (1986) and *Stars of the New Curfew* (1988). His novel *The Famished Road* (1991) won the Booker Prize, and is the first in a trilogy of novels including *Songs of Enchantment* (1993) and *Infinite Riches* (1998). Some of his more recent works are *Astonishing the Gods* (1995), *Dangerous Love* (1996), *In Arcadia* (2002), and *Starbook* (2007).

SHARON OLDS   Born in San Francisco, Sharon Olds (1942–) established herself as a poet whose raw and honest approach to the themes of sexuality and power as wife, mother, and daughter resonate with women everywhere. She has published seven volumes of poetry and was New York Poet Laureate from 1998 to 2000. Among her more famous collections and books are *Satan Says* (1980), *The Dead and the Living* (1983), *The Gold Cell* (1987), *The Father* (1992), *The Wellspring* (1995), and *Blood, Tin, Straw* (1999). In September 2005, Olds made the national news when she declined a formal invitation to dine at the White House with First Lady Laura Bush and read from her works. Olds responded: "I thought of the clean linens at your table, the shining knives and the flames of the candles, and I could not stomach it."

MARY OLIVER   Mary Oliver (1935–) was born in Maple Heights, Ohio, and educated at Vassar College. Her first book of poems, *No Voyage and Other Poems,* was published in 1963. Subsequent volumes include *Twelve Moons* (1979); *American Primitive* (1983), which won a Pulitzer Prize; *New and Selected Poems* (1992), which won the National Book Award; and *West Wind* (1997). Oliver teaches at Bennington College and has received fellowships from the Guggenheim Foundation and the National Endowment for the Arts.

TILLIE OLSEN   Tillie Olsen (1913–2007), born in Omaha, Nebraska, is the daughter of blue-collar workers who fled czarist Russia after the 1905 revolution. She grew up in poverty and at fifteen quit high school to help support her family during the Depression. Celebrated as a crusader for the feminist movement and other causes, Olsen was presented the O. Henry Award in 1961 for *Tell Me a Riddle*. In 1934 she started work on her first novel, *Yonnondio*, which finally was published in 1974; *Silences*, a study exploring circumstances that interfere with women's creativity, appeared in 1978. Olsen received the Rea Award for the Short Story in 1994 for a lifetime of outstanding achievement in the field of short story writing.

SIMON ORTIZ   Simon Ortiz (1941–), an Acoma Pueblo Indian, was born in Albuquerque, New Mexico. Between 1961 and 1969 Ortiz attended college, interrupting his education to serve in the U.S. Army in Vietnam from 1963 to 1966. In 1969 he won a Discovery Award from the National Endowment for the Arts. In 1976, *Going for the Rain,* his first major collection of poems, was published. Subsequent volumes include *A Good Journey* (1977), *Fight Back: For the Sake of the People, For the Sake of the Land* (1980), *From Sand Creek: Rising in This House Which Is Our America* (1981), and *Out There Somewhere* (2002). Ortiz's work focuses on the intertwined destinies of the Native Americans and other cultures, alienation of human beings from their roots, and his dream for producing harmony between humans and nature.

WILFRED OWEN   Born in Shropshire, England, Wilfred Owen (1893–1918) attended the University of London. In 1915, he joined the British army and served in a rifle corps during World War I. After seven months, he was injured and sent to a war hospital in Scotland, where a fellow patient—poet Siegfried Sassoon—encouraged him to write. After recovering from his injury, Owen returned to the battlefield in France and was awarded the Military Cross for gallantry under fire. He was killed while leading troops across the Sombre Canal just a week before the Armistice. His work was collected and published by Sassoon in a volume titled *Poems* (1920).

CYNTHIA OZICK   Born in New York City, Cynthia Ozick's (1928–) writing shows the influence of her extensive reading in Jewish philosophy and the effects of anti-Semitism that she experienced as a child. Her work includes the novels *Trust* (1966), *The Puttermesser Papers* (1997), and *Heir to the Glimmering World: A Novel* (2004); a novella, *The Messiah of Stockholm* (1987); and the volumes of short fiction *The Pagan Rabbi and Other Stories* (1971) and *Bloodshed and Three Novellas* (1976). Several of Ozick's short stories have been chosen for The Best American Short Stories, notably "The Shawl" and its companion piece, the novella "Rosa." Her work also won first prize in the annual O. Henry Prize Stories collection in 1975, 1981, and 1984.

ZZ PACKER   ZZ Packer (1973–) was born in Chicago and raised in Atlanta and Louisville, Kentucky. Packer was named Zuwena—Swahili for "good"—but has been called ZZ by her family since childhood. Packer received a B.A. from Yale University (1994), an M.A. from Johns Hopkins University (1995), and an M.F.A. from the University of Iowa Writer's Workshop (1999). Packer's short stories have appeared in anthologies, magazines, and literary journals, including the *Best American Short Stories 2000, Harper's, Story,* and *The New Yorker.* The story is taken from her first book of the same name, *Drinking Coffee Elsewhere* (2003). Packer claims that her protagonists often struggle to understand their roles within their communities, and a recurring theme in her fiction is that of the outsider.

GRACE PALEY   Born Grace Goodside into a Jewish family in the Bronx, New York, Grace Paley (1922–2007) spoke English, Russian, and Yiddish as a young girl. After spending a few years as a typist and housewife, in the 1950s Paley turned her attention to poetry and fiction. Her first book of widely anthologized stories, *The Little Disturbances of Men* (1959), established her as a writer and eventually led to a career in teaching at Columbia

University, City College of New York, Sarah Lawrence College, and Syracuse University. In addition to being a teacher and writer, Paley is a political activist. Her other popular works include the short story collections *Enormous Changes at the Last Minute* (1974) and *Later the Same Day* (1985). All three aforementioned volumes were included in Paley's *Collected Stories* (1994), which was nominated for a National Book Award.

SUZAN-LORI PARKS Parks (1964–) was born in Fort Knox, Kentucky, attended high school in West Germany, and then graduated Phi Beta Kappa from Mount Holyoke College, Massachusetts (1985)—a college that Parks would later credit for her success. She has written screenplays for the film industry (including Spike Lee's *Girl 6* [1996]) and worked with Oprah Winfrey's Harpo Productions on *Their Eyes Were Watching God* (2005) and *The Great Debaters* (2008). Among her best-known plays are *Imperceptible Mutabilities in the Third Kingdom* (1995), *Death of the Last Black Man in the Whole Entire World* (1990), *The America Play* (1994), *In the Blood* (1999), and *Fucking A* (2000). Her play about the struggles of everyday African American life, *Topdog/Underdog* (2001), won the Pulitzer Prize for Drama in 2002. One of her most creative endeavours was writing *365 Days/365 Plays*, concocting one short play (a few pages at the most) every day for one full year (November 2002–November 2003).

LINDA PASTAN Linda Pastan (1932–) was born in New York City and attended Radcliffe College; in her senior year she won, as did her contemporary Sylvia Plath, the *Mademoiselle* poetry contest. She has published fifteen books of poetry, including her first, *A Perfect Circle of Sun* (1971), and more recently, *Carnival Evening* (1998) and *The Last Uncle: Poems* (2002). Her work appears in many periodicals, including *Atlantic Monthly*, *The New Yorker*, *The New Republic*, and *The Paris Review*. Beginning with the *Mademoiselle* Dylan Thomas Poetry Award in 1958, Pastan has been honored with several prestigious awards, including the role of Maryland's poet laureate from 1991 to 1995. Pastan's poetry frequently portrays the complexity of domestic life. "Secrets" was collected in Pastan's book, *Carnival Evening*.

MARGE PIERCY Marge Piercy (1936–) was born in Detroit, Michigan, and was educated at the University of Michigan and Northwestern University. She published her first novel, *Going Down Fast,* in 1969. She has written fiction, including *Woman on the Edge of Time* (1976), *Braided Lives* (1982), *He, She, and It* (1992), and *Three Women* (1999), as well as poetry, including the collections entitled *The Moon Is Always Female* (1980), *My Mother's Body* (1985), and *Available Light* (1988). In 1987, she edited *Early Ripening: American Women's Poetry Now.* In 2002 she published a memoir, *Sleeping with Cats,* and her latest works are *The Third Child* (2003) and *Sex Wars* (2005). Piercy, a feminist, writes about the oppression of people in society and desires her work to be, ultimately, "useful."

MARY PIPHER Dr. Mary Bray Pipher (1947–) received her B.A. in Anthropology in 1968 from the University of California, Berkeley, and a Ph.D. in Clinical Psychology in 1977 from the University of Nebraska–Lincoln. Dr. Pipher has appeared on numerous television programs and has received the American Psychological Association Presidential Citation (1988). Her most famous works are *Hunger Pains* (1997), *Another Country: Navigating the Emotional Terrain of Our Elders* (2000), *Letters to a Young Therapist* (2003), *The Middle of Everywhere: Helping Refugees Enter the American Community* (2003), *The Shelter of Each Other: Rebuilding Our Families to Enrich Our Lives* (1997), *Writing to Change the World* (2006), and *Reviving Ophelia: Saving the Selves of Adolescent Girls* (1994), which was number one on the *New York Times* best-seller list for twenty-seven weeks.

SYLVIA PLATH   Sylvia Plath (1932–1963) was born in Boston, Massachusetts, the daughter of German immigrants who taught at Boston University. Plath attended Smith College in Massachusetts, where she won a contest that sent her to work for a national magazine in New York—much like the protagonist of her novel, *The Bell Jar* (1963). Plath received a Fulbright Scholarship to Cambridge University in England, where she met the poet Ted Hughes. The two were married in 1956 and moved to Smith College, where Plath taught for a short time. The couple returned to England, where they had two children before separating. Plath's first volume of poems, *The Colossus,* appeared in 1960. She committed suicide in 1963 at the age of thirty, leaving the manuscript containing the highly acclaimed posthumous collection of poems, *Ariel* (1965). Like Anne Sexton and Robert Lowell, she is considered a Confessional poet. When Plath was eight years old her father died, an event from which she never seemed to recover. Biographical accounts show some connection between the man in "Daddy" and her father; however, Plath herself stated that the two should not be confused. When she read the poem for the BBC, she suggested that the poem's speaker suffers from an Electra complex.

WILLIAM POLLACK   Dr. William S. Pollack is the Director of the Centers for Men and Young Men as well as Director of Continuing Education at McLean Hospital (the major teaching facility of Harvard Medical School). He is also an Assistant Clinical Professor in the Department of Psychiatry at Harvard Medical School. He is past President of the Massachusetts Psychological Association, a member of the Boston Psychoanalytic Society, Diplomate in Clinical Psychology, and Founding Member (and Fellow) of The Society for the Psychological Study of Men and Masculinity. Dr. Pollack is internationally recognized as an authority on both boys and men, and he founded the REAL BOYS Educational Programs.

PLATO   Plato (428–347 B.C.) was born in Athens and studied with Socrates. After the latter's execution for heresy in 399 B.C., Plato left Athens for a number of years but returned to found the Academy, often considered the first university, where he taught philosophy and mathematics until his death. One of the world's great philosophers, Plato wrote many treatises in the form of dialogues among Socrates and other figures in which the philosopher and his circle debate central, metaphysical questions.

ALISSA QUART   Alissa Quart authored the acclaimed books *Branded: The Buying and Selling of Teenagers* (2003) and *Hothouse Kids: The Dilemma of the Gifted Child* (2006). The latter book acts as a cautionary tale against excessive parental expectation (Quart was herself a child prodigy). She writes opinion pieces and book reviews for *The New York Times* and has written for *The New York Times Magazine* and a number of other magazines and periodicals. In *Branded,* Quart charts the effect of corporations' marketing of products specifically to teenage consumers.

ADRIENNE RICH   Adrienne Rich (1929–), born in Baltimore, is one of America's finest poets and most influential feminists. She is also an essayist and teacher. Her works include the poetry collections *A Change of World* (1951), selected by W. H. Auden for the Yale Younger Poets Award; *Snapshots of a Daughter-in-Law* (1963); and *Facts of a Doorframe* (1984). She also wrote *On Lies, Secrets, and Silence—Selected Prose 1966–1978* (1979), *What Is Found There: Notebooks on Poetry and Politics* (1993), and *Fox: Poems, 1998–2000* (2001). Her awards include the 1974 National Book Award for *Diving into the Wreck.* In her latest work, *Poetry and Commitment* (2007), Rich reprints the essay that served as the basis for her acceptance speech for the 2006 National Book Foundation's Medal for Distinguished Contribution to American Letters.

RAINER MARIA RILKE   Born in Czechoslovakia, Rainer Maria Rilke (1875–1926) went to military school as a child and attended university in his native Prague, in Berlin, and in Munich. The work that first gained him recognition as a poet was *The Book of Images* (1902). Rilke wrote intermittently—in prolific bursts that he believed were periods of grace in which the poems were "dictated" to him. He composed *Sonnets to Orpheus* in 1923 while living alone in a tower in Switzerland, a work that was not published until eight years after his death from blood poisoning. Along with Rilke's *Duino Elegies,* the *Sonnets* are considered the greatest poems in modern German literature.

JOSÉ RIVERA   José Rivera (1955–) was born in San Juan, Puerto Rico; moved to Long Island, New York, in 1959; and attended Dennison College, where he began writing and producing plays. On a Fulbright fellowship, Rivera worked in London in 1989 and 1990 writing *Marisol* (1992), which in 1993 won an Obie Award for best play, a Susan Marton Award, a PEN West Dramatic Writing Award nomination, and the 1993 Joseph Kesselring Award Honorable Mention. After returning to the United States from London, Rivera moved to California to write screenplays. Rivera has written more than twenty plays and screenplays. "Gas" illustrates Rivera's sociopolitical perspective, which is presented with a touch of magical realism. Rivera recently wrote the screenplay for *The Motorcycle Diaries* (2004), a film based on Che Guevara's diary about a motorcycle trip that Guevara and his friend, Alberto Granado, took. In 2005, Rivera became the first Puerto Rican to be nominated for the "Best Adapted Screenplay" Academy Award.

THEODORE ROETHKE   Theodore Roethke (1908–1963) was born in Saginaw, Michigan. His father was a German immigrant whose death in 1923 profoundly affected Roethke's life, although he continued his studies at the University of Michigan and Harvard University and became a professor of English at the latter. He held teaching positions at Lafayette College, Penn State, Michigan State University, the University of Washington, and Bennington College. His works include *Open House* (1941); *The Lost Son and Other Poems* (1948); *Praise to the End!* (1951); *Words for the Wind* (1958); *I am! Says the Lamb* (1961); *Party at the Zoo* (1963); *The Far Field* (1964); the prose collection, *On Poetry & Craft* (1965); and *The Collected Poems of Theodore Roethke* (1966). His 1954 work, *The Waking,* was awarded the Pulitzer Prize for Poetry.

LIZ ROSENBERG   Liz Rosenberg (1955–) was educated at Bennington College and Johns Hopkins University. She is a frequent reviewer of poetry, prose, and children's books for publications that include the *Chicago Tribune* and the *Philadelphia Inquirer.* She was a Kellogg Foundation Fellow and in 1976 won the Atlantic First Award for her story "Memory." *The Angel Poems* (1984) was followed by *The Fire Music* (1986), which won the 1985 Agnes Lynch Stewart Award from the University of Pittsburgh Press, and *Children of Paradise* (1993). Rosenberg has edited a collection of poems, *Roots and Flowers: An Anthology of Poems about Family* (2001), that reflect her ongoing interest in children and family. Liz Rosenberg is also the author of more than twenty-five books for young readers. She teaches English and Creative Writing at the State University of New York at Binghamton and writes a monthly children's book review column for the *Boston Globe.*

CHRISTINA ROSSETTI   Born Christina Georgina Rossetti (1830–1894) in London, she was educated at home by her mother. Her family was impoverished by her father's failing physical and mental health; as a result, at fourteen, Rossetti suffered a nervous breakdown and other related illnesses. Her maladies led her as well as her mother and sister to the Anglo-Catholic movement of the Church of England. Her first work,

Goblin Market and Other Poems, was published in 1862. The collection was critically well-received, and she was considered to be the logical successor to Elizabeth Barrett Browning. Many other books followed: *The Prince's Progress and Other Poems* (1856), *Commonplace* (1870), *Sing-Song: a Nursery Rhyme Book* (1872), *A Pageant and Other Poems* (1881), *Verses* (1893), and *New Poems* (1895). Although she was not affiliated with the women's suffrage movement in her lifetime, many critics from the 1970s onward have identified feminist principles in her writing.

MARY JO SALTER   Mary Jo Salter (1954–), a graduate of Harvard University, teaches at Mount Holyoke College as the Emily Dickinson Senior Lecturer in the Humanities. She is a co-editor of the Norton Anthology of Poetry and is the author of five volumes of poetry and a children's book. Her volumes of poetry include *Henry Purcell in Japan* (1985) and *Unfinished Painting* (1989); recent works include *Sunday Skaters* (1994) and *Kiss in Space* (1999). In the early 1980s, Salter lived in Japan for three years. She also has lived in France, Italy, and Iceland. These locations all figure into her poetry, leading some to regard her as a first-rate travel writer.

SCOTT RUSSELL SANDERS   Scott Russell Sanders (1945–) was born in Memphis, Tennessee, received his Ph.D. from Cambridge University, and currently resides in Bloomington, Indiana, where he is a Distinguished Professor at Indiana University. Sanders is the author of twenty-six books as well as numerous essays and stories that have been anthologized in collections such as *The Best American Essays* (1987, 1993, 1999, and 2000) and many distinguished literary journals and magazines. He has won several fellowships and awards for his writing, including the National Endowment of the Arts (1983–1984), the PEN Syndicated Fiction Award (1988), the Great Lakes Book Award (1996) for *Writing from the Center* (1995), and the John Burroughs Award for best natural history essay (2000). Sanders is known as an environmentalist and a writer whose sense of wonder about the natural world is often expressed through his recognition of family ties as an instinctive and primitive human bond.

MARJANE SATRAPI   Marjane Satrapi (1969–) was born in Rasht, Iran, and witnessed Iranian politics firsthand as a child. At fourteen, Satrapi was sent by her parents to Vienna, Austria, in order to escape the Islamic regime. She returned to Iran to pursue her college education and (according to her own works) met, married, and divorced a man before moving to Strasbourg, France. Her career as an illustrator began when she met David Beauchard (a French comics artist) in Strasbourg. Imitating "David B." style in her early works, Satrapi became famous as a result of her autobiographical graphic novels *Persepolis* (2000) and *Persepolis 2* (2001). These works portray her childhood in Iran and her coming of age in Europe. *Persepolis* won France's highest comics honor: the Angoulême International Comics Festival's Prize for First Comic Book. A film adaptation of *Persepolis* was released in 2007.

ZACHARY SCOTT-SINGLEY   A sergeant in the 3rd Infantry Division (acting as an Arabic linguist) on his second tour of Iraq, Zachary Scott-Singley (1981–) started the online blog, "A Solider's Thoughts." In his blog, Scott-Singley is careful to note that "all opinions expressed on this blog are those of myself in my private capacity and not as a representative of the DoD, DA, or any particular element of the Army." The blog offers Scott-Singley's candid opinions about democracy, the war on terror, his children, and the "quagmire" of Iraq.

DAVID SEDARIS   Davis Sedaris (1957–) was born in Raleigh, North Carolina, and presently resides in New York City and Paris. In *Me Talk Pretty One Day* (2000), Sedaris claims he moved to France because in that country it is still socially acceptable to smoke in public. Sedaris was educated at the School of the Art Institute of Chicago, where he taught writing. He is known as an essayist, short-story writer, and radio commentator. He is the author of several books, many of which have hit #1 on the *New York Times* bestseller list for nonfiction: from his first, *Origins of the Underclass, and Other Stories* (1992), to his most recent, *Dress Your Family in Corduroy and Denim* (2004) and *Children Playing Before a Statue of Hercules* (2005). Sedaris's dry humor and quirky perspective of life have earned him popularity as a writer and humorist.

ANNE SEXTON Anne Sexton (1928–1974) was born in Newton, Massachusetts. She attended Garland Junior College in Massachusetts and taught high school and college. After suffering one of many nervous breakdowns, Sexton was urged by a psychiatrist to try writing poetry. She did so with immediate success: the poet Robert Lowell was one of her mentors. She published her first book of poems, *To Bedlam and Part Way Back,* in 1960. In 1967 she won the Pulitzer Prize for Poetry for *Live or Die.* With Lowell, Sexton is associated with the Confessional School of poetry, drawing on intensely personal subject matter for her poems. She committed suicide in 1974. Sexton's *Complete Poems* were published in 1981.

WILLIAM SHAKESPEARE William Shakespeare (1564–1616), the most widely known writer of English literature, was born in Stratford-on-Avon, England. By 1592, he had become an accomplished actor and playwright in London. Shakespeare and several other actors formed a syndicate to build a new playhouse, The Globe, which became one of the most famous theaters of its time. Shakespeare wrote nearly forty plays, sonnets, and narrative poems and is believed to have played supporting roles in many of his own plays. The dramas in the accepted canon—works authentically Shakespeare's—are usually arranged into four categories: comedies, histories, tragedies, and romances.

LESLIE MARMON SILKO Leslie Marmon Silko (1948–), born in Albuquerque, New Mexico, grew up on the Laguna Pueblo Reservation. Her heritage—Laguna, Mexican, European—provides the material and the inspiration for her writing. A graduate of the University of New Mexico, she taught until 1981 at the University of Arizona in Tucson, at which time a five-year MacArthur Foundation Grant allowed her to write full time. Silko published her first novel, *Ceremony,* in 1977. Subsequent works include *Storyteller* (1981), *Almanac of the Dead* (1991), *Yellow Woman and a Beauty of the Spirit: Essays on Native American Life Today* (1996), and *Gardens in the Dunes* (1999). Her fiction and poetry have earned her a grant from the National Endowment for the Arts, a poetry award from the Chicago Review and the Pushcart Prize for poetry.

CHARLES SIMIC Born in the Socialist Federal Republic of Yugoslavia, Charles Simic (1938–) emigrated with his family in 1953 and went on to graduate from Oak Park High School in Illinois. He gained fame in the 1970s for his terse and imagistic poems written in the vein of Romantic poet, William Blake. His current poems are immensely popular and exceedingly recognizable, and Simic was awarded a MacArthur "Genius" Grant as well as a Pulitzer Prize in 1990 for *The World Doesn't End.* He is currently a poetry editor for *The Paris Review* and was named U.S. Poet Laureate on August 2, 2007.

PETER SINGER Peter Singer (1946–) was born in Melbourne, Australia where his parents, Viennese Jews, had escaped to before Austria's annexation by the Third Reich in 1938. Singer was educated at Scotch College in South Australia; then studied law, history, and philosophy at the University of Melbourne; and earned his B.A. in 1967. After receiving his M.A. in 1969, he was awarded a scholarship to Oxford. Singer spent two years as a lecturer at Oxford and became a visiting professor at New York University for more than a year. He returned to Melbourne in 1977 but continued as a visiting professor until he moved to Princeton in 1999. His philosophical writings on animal rights (*Animal Liberation* [1975]), abortion, euthanasia, infanticide, evolution (*A Darwinian Left: Politics, Evolution, and Consideration* [1998]), and world poverty have brought him many fans and critics. His work is considered quite controversial.

LAUREN SLATER　Lauren Slater (1963–) is an American psychologist and writer who has authored six books, including *Welcome To My Country* (1996), *Prozac Diary* (1998), and *Lying: A Metaphorical Memoir* (2000). Her 2004 work, *Opening Skinner's Box: Great Psychological Experiments of the Twentieth Century,* describes psychological experiments and narrates them as stories; it was nominated for a *Los Angeles Times* Kirsch Award. Slater also won the New Letters Literary Award in creative non-fiction (1993) and the Missouri Review Award (1994); and she has twice been anthologized in *The Best American Essays* (1994 and 1997). She has contributed to many major magazines and periodicals, including *The New York Times, Harper's,* and *Elle.*

ANNA DEAVERE SMITH　Anna Deavere Smith (1950–) is an actress, playwright, and performance artist. A professor at New York University, Smith won an Obie award and was nominated for the 1992 Pulitzer Prize for Drama for *Fires in the Mirror: Crown Heights, Brooklyn, and Other Identities.* She also has written *Twilight Los Angeles 1992* (1994), which addresses the racial situation in Los Angeles after the police trials following the Rodney King beating, and *House Arrest: A Search for American Character in and Around the White House, Past and Present* (2003). Her work is concerned with representing the multiple perspectives of those experiencing contemporary American racial conflicts. According to Smith, "race and class are the big dividing lines in all society." Smith has appeared in several films, including *Philadelphia* (1993) and *The American President* (1995), and has performed in recurring television roles on *The West Wing* (2000–2004) and *The Practice* (2000).

LYNN SMITH　Lynn Smith is a staff writer for the *Los Angeles Times* and the *Washington Post,* where she covers entertainment, culture, and politics.

CATHY SONG　Born in Honolulu, Hawai'i, Cathy Song (1955–) is of Korean and Chinese descent. Song left the island to earn a baccalaureate degree from Wellesley and an M.A. in creative writing from Boston University. She returned to Hawai'i in 1983 and published her first collection of poetry, *Picture Bride,* in the same year. She has since published three other volumes: *Frameless Windows, Squares of Light* (1988), *School Figures* (1994), and *The Land of Bliss* (2001). She currently teaches at the University of Hawai'i at Manoa.

SOPHOCLES　Although he wrote more than one hundred and twenty dramas, only seven complete plays of Sophocles (496–406 B.C.) survive. Nonetheless, he is considered to be—with Aeschylus and Euripides—one of the great Greek tragic dramatists. In 468 B.C., his first play won the prize over Aeschylus. By 450 B.C., Sophocles had written at least twenty-four plays and had initiated significant changes in the form of tragedy, most notably that of introducing a third actor to the stage. He won more victories in the play competition than any other writer. In his *Poetics,* Aristotle praised Sophocles above all other dramatists.

GARY SOTO　Gary Soto (1952–), born in Fresno, California, won the Before Columbus Foundation 1985 American Book Award for his volume of autobiographical essays, *Living Up the Street* (1984). His volumes of poetry include *The Element of San Joaquin* (1977), *The Tale of Sunlight* (1978), *Black Hair* (1985), and *Shadow of the Plum: Poems* (2002), and he also has edited *Pieces of the Heart: New Chicano Fiction* (1993). Soto teaches Chicano Studies and English at the University of California at Berkeley. Among other honors, he has received a Guggenheim Fellowship and the Academy of American Poets Award. Soto now serves as Young People's Ambassador for the California Rural Legal Assistance (CRLA) and the United Farm Workers of America (UFW).

WOLE SOYINKA   Wole Soyinka (1943–) was born in Isara, Nigeria. He attended the University of Ibadan and received a B.A. with honors from the University of Leeds, England. Considered by many critics to be Africa's best writer, Soyinka has published drama, poetry, novels, and nonfiction. Among his works are a novel, *The Interpreters* (1965), and a nonfiction volume, *The Man Died: Prison Notes of Wole Soyinka* (1972). Among his many awards is the 1986 Nobel Prize for Literature. Soyinka's writing reflects contemporary Africa's political upheaval and efforts to blend traditional culture with technological advances.

ART SPIEGELMAN   The American comics artist and editor Art Spiegelman (1948–) was born in Stockholm, Sweden, to Polish-Jewish refugees. Spiegelman grew up in Rego Park (Queens) in New York City and graduated from the High School of Art and Design in Manhattan. He pursued his higher education at Binghamton University but did not graduate. In 1968, he suffered a nervous breakdown and, after his release from the hospital, his mother committed suicide. Spiegelman then became a pioneer in the underground comic book movement of the 1960s and 1970s and went on to edit the groundbreaking comics anthology, *RAW* (1980–1981). It was in *RAW* that he serialized his parents' story about surviving the Holocaust, the memoir known as *Maus*. In 1992, *Maus* won the Pulitzer Prize Special Award in Letters—a special and rare citation—among many other prestigious awards garnered by *Maus I: My Father Bleeds History* and *Maus II: A Survivor's Tale*.

ANDREW SULLIVAN   Born in Surry, England, Andrew Sullivan (1963–) is known as both an author and a political commentator. A former editor of *The New Republic* (1991–1996), he is a political conservative whose background (as an HIV-positive homosexual and practicing Catholic) often puts him at odds with other conservatives. He was one of the most popular bloggers at *Time Magazine* (with his blog, "The Daily Dish") and left *Time* in 2007 to pursue an opportunity at *Atlantic Monthly*. Sullivan has been featured on national news shows and has spoken at a number of universities across the United States.

WISLAWA SZYMBORSKA   Born in Kornik, Poland, Wislawa Szymborska (1923–) was educated at Jaigellonian University, where she studied Polish literature and sociology. From 1953 to 1981, she was poetry editor and a columnist for a literary weekly. She has published almost twenty volumes of poetry, including *Calling Out to Yeti* (1957), *No End of Fun* (1967), and *The People on the Bridge* (1986). In 1996, Szymborska was awarded the Nobel Prize for Literature.

RABINDRANATH TAGORE   Rabindranath Tagore (1861–1941) was born in Calcutta, India. A mystical experience in 1883 led him to a conception of God as intimate, a wellspring of inspiration that greatly influenced his work. He wrote nearly sixty volumes of verse, more than forty plays, fourteen novels, two hundred short stories, and thousands of songs in addition to numerous essays, journals, and religious and philosophical tracts. In 1913—shortly after he wrote *Gitanjali* ("Song Offerings"), a collection of serenely mystical poems inspired by the deaths of his father, wife, two daughters, and youngest son—Tagore became the first Indian writer to win the Nobel Prize for Literature.

AMY TAN   Amy Tan (1952–) was born Tán Ēnmĕi in Oakland, California, shortly after her parents emigrated from China to the United States. She was educated at San Francisco State University and San Jose University. In 1989 she published her first book of fiction, *The Joy Luck Club*. Her work includes several novels, *The Kitchen God's Wife* (1991), *The Hundred Secret Senses* (1996), and *The Bonesetter's Daughter* (2001) as well as a collection of essays, *The Opposite of Fate: A Book of Musings* (2003). In her work, Tan explores her Chinese heritage and the relationships between generations, especially those between Chinese immigrants and their American-born children.

DYLAN THOMAS   Born in Swansea, Wales, Dylan Marlais Thomas (1914–1953) attended an all-boys grammar school where his father taught English Literature. He was a neurotic child who was frequently ill and disliked school. After his first poem was published in the school's magazine, Thomas left school at sixteen to become a reporter for a brief time. He composed most of his poetry at his family's home, and his first volume, *18 Poems* (1934), was critically well received. However, not until his publication of *Deaths and Entrances* (1946) did he received international recognition. His powerful speaking voice resonated with American audiences during his speaking tours of the 1950s, and the content of his poems—with their charged emotion and lyricism—hypnotized audiences. He published ten volumes of poetry and twelve volumes of prose. Known for his boisterous public nature, Thomas drank heavily during his lifetime and collapsed at a tavern in Greenwich Village, Manhattan after a bout of heavy drinking. He died at St. Vincent's Hospital on November 9, 1953, after spending four days in a coma.

SOJOURNER TRUTH   Born into slavery in Ulster County, New York, Sojourner Truth (1797–1883) originally was named Isabella Van Wagener—after Isaac Van Wagener, who bought her and set her free just before New York State abolished slavery in 1827. In 1829 she traveled to New York City, where she preached in the streets. Taking the name Sojourner Truth in answer to a divine call, she left the city and began preaching and singing at camp meetings across the country. Although she never abandoned her message of God's goodness, she added to her speeches concern for the abolition of slavery and the rights of women. Her brilliant speeches attracted many listeners and made her famous. Sojourner Truth first gave the speech now referred to as "Ain't I a Woman?" at a women's rights convention in Akron, Ohio, in 1851. However, as Nell Painter (Truth's most recent biographer) has pointed out, the version of the speech that we associate with Truth was not transcribed until twelve years later by the activist Frances Dena Gage, who added to it considerably. For the popular consciousness, Gage's revision of Truth's speech has become the speech itself, inspiring countless people who have read it.

PAULINE POWERS UCHMANOWICZ   Born in Anchorage, Alaska, Pauline Uchmanowicz (1957–) earned an M.F.A. from the University of Iowa Writers' Workshop and a Ph.D. from the University of Rhode Island, where she held a dissertation fellowship. Her poems and essays have appeared in many publications, including *Ploughshares, Crazyhorse, Ohio Review, New American Writing, The Massachusetts Review,* and *Z Magazine*. She is the author of the poetry chapbook *Sand & Traffic* (2004) and editor of the textbook *Considering Cultural Difference* (2004). Uchmanowicz is an Associate Professor of English at the State University of New York, where she directs the Composition Program. She is also a food columnist for *Woodstock Times* and a regular contributor to the arts-and-culture magazine *Chronogram*.

JOHN UPDIKE   John Updike (1932–) was born in Shillington, Pennsylvania. In 1950, Updike attended Harvard University, where he wrote for and eventually edited the *Harvard Lampoon*. His first short story, "Friends from Philadelphia," was sold to *The New Yorker* the year he graduated from Harvard (1954); fifty years later, his stories, poems, and essays are still regularly printed in that magazine. Updike has published more than two hundred stories, dozens of novels, and a great number of poems and essays. Although he has won many awards for his short stories, Updike may be best known for his "Rabbit" novels—*Rabbit, Run* (1960), *Rabbit Redux* (1971), *Rabbit Is Rich* (1981), and *Rabbit at Rest* (1990)—which depict Rabbit Angstrom's life through youth, marriage, middle age, and death. He received a Pulitzer Prize and National Book Critics Circle Award for *Rabbit Is Rich* and for *Rabbit at Rest* as well as a National Book Critics Circle Award for *Hugging the Shore* (1983). Updike was elected to the National Institute of Arts and Letters in 1964 and the American Academy of Arts and Letters in 1977, and he was honored with the National Medal of the Arts in 1989. He was awarded the Harvard Arts First Medal and the 1998 National Book Foundation Medal for Distinguished Contribution to American Arts and Letters. Updike's stories depict the moral dilemmas that confront humans even in the most common of situations.

LUISA VALENZUELA   Born in Buenos Aires, Argentina, Luisa Valenzuela (1938–) attended the University of Buenos Aires. Since that time, Valenzuela has published nineteen books. Her work is considered to be experimental, going beyond the style of magical realism to convey life's nonlinear reality. Valenzuela left Argentina after the death of Juan Perón in 1974 to escape the subsequent military dictatorship that ruled until 1983. Before she fled she wrote: "Buenos Aires belonged then to violence and to state terrorism, and I could only sit in cafes and brood. Till I decided a book of short stories could be written in a month at those same cafe tables, overhearing scraps of scared conversations, seeping in the general paranoia. *Strange Things Happen Here* (1979) was born, and with it a new political awareness. And action."

LARA VAPNYAR   Lara Vapnyar (1971–) emigrated from Russia to New York in 1994 and began publishing short stories in English in 2002. She lives on Staten Island and is pursuing a Ph.D. in Comparative Literature at CUNY Graduate Center. Her most recent works have impressed critics; *Memoirs of a Muse* (2006) and *There Are Jews in My House* (2003) showcase her spare style, lucidity, and ability to show a post-*glasnost* Soviet Union from an insider's perspective.

ALMA LUZ VILLANUEVA   Born in Lompoc, California, Alma Villanueva (1944–) grew up in the mission district of San Francisco. She dropped out of high school in tenth grade to give birth to her first child, living on welfare while married to an abusive husband. Throughout this period of struggle, Villanueva wrote very little; it wasn't until her mid-twenties that she began her writing career and education in earnest (eventually earning an M.F.A. from Vermont College). She currently resides in San Miguel de Allende, Mexico, and she teaches in the M.F.A. in Creative Writing Program at Antioch University, Los Angeles. Her most popular publications include *Ultraviolet Sky* (1989, winner of the American Book Award), *Naked Ladies* (1994), *Vida* (2002), and *Weeping Woman: La Llorona and Other Stories* (1994). Her award-winning poetry collections—which include *Blood Root* (1977), *La Chingada* (1985), *Lifespan* (1984), and *Planet, With Mother, May I?* (1997)—echo the themes presented in her fiction: a childhood rooted in poverty, the strength of women, and the struggle to find a voice.

PAULA VOGEL   Paula Anne Vogel (1951–) was born to a Jewish father and a Christian mother in a Washington, D.C., working class family. After most of her early forays into playwriting were met with rejection (along with her dismissal from Bryn Mawr College), she recognized that approaching her craft in a unique way was necessary to success. She then focused on scatological humor and plain talk, and these aspects of her playwriting contributed to her success. Vogel is currently a renowned teacher of playwriting and is best known for the plays *How I Learned to Drive* (1998) and *The Baltimore Waltz* (1992), the latter written in response to the death of her brother from complications resulting from AIDS. *How I Learned to Drive* won many awards: an Obie, a Drama Desk Award, a New York Drama Critics' Award, an Outer Circle Critics Award, the Lucille Lortel Award, and the 1998 Pulitzer Prize for drama. Its (initial) off-Broadway run lasted for fourteen months, and it was produced in more than fifty different venues, regional and international, during the height of its popularity.

KURT VONNEGUT, JR.   Born in Indianapolis, Indiana, Kurt Vonnegut, Jr. (1922–2007) enlisted in the U.S. Army in World War II and was captured by the Germans in 1944. He survived the Allied firebombing of Dresden, after which he and his fellow prisoners were given the task of searching for corpses. This experience was the source for his best-known novel, *Slaughterhouse Five* (1969). His other novels include *Cat's Cradle* (1963), *Breakfast of Champions* (1973), *Galapagos* (1985), and *Timequake* (1997); his short stories are collected in *Canary in a Cathouse* (1961), *Welcome to the Monkey House* (1968), *Bagombo Snuff Box* (1999), *God Bless You, Dr. Kevorkian* (2000), and *A Man Without a Country* (2005), a collection of essays.

DIANE WAKOSKI   Diane Wakoski (1937–) was born in Whittier, California and educated at the University of California, Berkeley. Her volumes of poetry number more than twenty and include *Coins and Coffins* (1962), *The Man Who Shook Hands* (1978), *Medea the Sorceress* (1991), and *Argonaut Rose* (1998). Her collection entitled *Emerald Ice: Selected Poems, 1962–1987* won the William Carlos Williams Prize in 1989, and she was granted the Michigan Library Association's Author of the Year award in 2003. Much of Wakoski's poetry is concerned with creating a personal mythology for the writer. She currently teaches creative writing at Michigan State University.

DEREK WALCOTT   The first Caribbean writer to win the Nobel Prize for Literature (1992), Derek Walcott (1930–) was born on the island of St. Lucia. His first book appeared in 1948 when his mother gave him two hundred dollars to have *Twenty-Five Poems* published. His volumes of poetry include *Sea Grapes* (1976), *Midsummer* (1984), the epic *Omeros* (1990), *Tiepolo's Hound* (2000), and his *Selected Poems* (2007). Walcott's poetry celebrates the diversity of modern English, Creole pidgin, and slang.

ALICE WALKER   Alice Walker (1944–) was born in Eatonville, Georgia. After attending Spelman College and Sarah Lawrence College, Walker—influenced by her involvement in voter registration in Georgia and in welfare programs in Mississippi—began to write. Her first volume of poetry, *Once: Poems* (1968), contains accounts of her work and her travels to Africa. In 1979, she edited *I Love Myself When I Am Laughing*, a selection from the writings of Zora Neale Hurston that was responsible for new interest in and appreciation of Hurston's work. The author of more than ten books of fiction, Walker won the Pulitzer Prize and the National Book Award in 1982 for her third novel, *The Color Purple*. Her most recent novel is *Now Is the Time to Open Your Heart* (2004), and her latest nonfiction book is *We Are the Ones We Have Been Waiting For* (2006). Her essays have been collected in *In Search of Our Mother's Gardens* (1983) and *Living by the Word: Selected Writings 1973–1987* (1988). Walker, known as a "womanist" with a keen connection to nature, displays in her work a sense of hope even in the midst of despair.

JUDITH WALLERSTEIN   Judith Wallerstein (1921–) is a researcher and psychologist who has devoted twenty-five years to the study of divorce. She is considered one of the foremost authorities on the effects of divorce on children, having followed for a quarter century 131 children whose parents have divorced. Wallerstein and Sandra Blakeslee co-authored the bestsellers *The Good Marriage* (1996) and *Second Chances: Men, Women and Children a Decade After Divorce* (2004).

ANNA LEE WALTERS A member of the Pawnee and Otoe-Missouria tribes of Oklahoma, Anna Lee Walters (1946–) is a technical writer, an author of textbooks, and a poet. Her volumes of poetry include *The Man to Send Rain Clouds* (1974), *Warriors of the Rainbow* (1975), and *The Third Woman* (1978). She is director of the Navajo Community College Press, which publishes books about Native Americans past and present.

KATHERINE WAUGH Brought up in segregated Williamsburg, Virginia, in the forties and fifties, Katherine "Kappa" Waugh (1946–) and her family moved to California when she was eleven years old. She is a librarian, cartoonist, and jewelry maker who now lives in the Hudson Valley.

ROBERT WAUGH Robert Waugh (1944–) received his B.A. in Comparative Literature from Indiana University and his M.A. and Ph.D. in Comparative Literature from Harvard. On the faculty of the State University of New Paltz since 1968, he teaches creative writing and literature. He has published poems in various literary journals as well as essays on H. P. Lovecraft, David Lindsay, Olaf Stapledon, Arthur C. Clarke, Fritz Leiber, Michael Moorcock, Samuel R. Delany, and Vincent van Gogh. His book, *The Monster in the Mirror: Looking for H. P. Lovecraft* (2006), was recently published by Hippocampus Press.

WALT WHITMAN Walt Whitman (1819–1892) was born on Long Island. Until the early 1850s, he moved among printing, writing, and teaching jobs in New York. The first edition of his poetry, *Leaves of Grass*, was published in 1855 and consisted of twelve untitled poems, including the work eventually titled "Song of Myself." Whitman spent the rest of his life revising *Leaves of Grass*, editing the poems in it and adding new ones. The spacious, unconventional verse patterns in *Leaves of Grass* have had a profound and lasting effect on North and South American poetry.

ELIE WIESEL Elie Wiesel (1928–) was born in Sighet, Romania. His childhood world centered around Jewish tradition and the study of the Talmud, the Torah, and the teachings of the Hasidic masters. In 1944, he and his family were deported to Auschwitz, where three of his sisters and his parents were killed. After the war, Wiesel lived in France, eventually studying philosophy at the Sorbonne and writing for a French newspaper. In 1950 he became the chief foreign correspondent for the Tel Aviv daily newspaper *Yedioth Ahronot*. More than ten years after his liberation from the camps, he published several autobiographical novels based on his concentration camp and postwar experience: *Night* (1956), *Dawn* (1961), and *The Accident* (1962). Wiesel's other published works include a play, *Zalmen: or the Madness of God* (1968); *Legends of Our Time* (1966), a collection of short stories, autobiographical articles, and reflective essays; *A Beggar in Jerusalem* (1970), a novel that focuses on the 1967 Arab-Israeli conflict; a work of nonfiction, *After the Darkness: Reflections on the Holocaust* (2002); and his latest, *The Time of the Uprooted* (2005). Wiesel, who was awarded the Nobel Peace Prize in 1986, believes that he and other Holocaust survivors have a responsibility to tell their stories; "to remain silent and indifferent," he says, "is the greatest sin of all."

WILLIAM CARLOS WILLIAMS Dr. William Carlos Williams (1883–1963) was born in Rutherford, New Jersey, to an English immigrant father and a mother of Puerto Rican descent. He studied locally until he was sent to a variety of international institutions, arriving at the University of Pennsylvania Medical School in 1902. His circle of friends at Penn (such as Ezra Pound and Hilda Doolittle) led to a growing interest in poetry while he was engaged in a series of medical internships. He returned to Rutherford to practice pediatrics for nearly forty years, during which time he crafted poems, short stories, and even an autobiography. His most popular poem is the frequently anthologized Imagist piece, "The Red Wheelbarrow." He is frequently associated with both the Imagist and Modernist movements. In 1963, he was posthumously awarded the Pulitzer Prize.

AUGUST WILSON Born Frederick August Kittel in Pittsburg, Pennsylvania, August Wilson (1945–2005) was the fourth of six children born to a German immigrant baker and an African American cleaning woman. His parents divorced while he was young, and Wilson and his siblings were raised by their father in an economically disadvantaged neighborhood. The young Wilson encountered racism and discrimination at every turn, to the extent that threats forced him to leave one high school and to drop out of another. Wilson then had many vocations (short-order cook, porter, gardener, dishwasher, the Army), but he loved none more than that of writing. He began dramatic writing in earnest in the mid-1960s and never looked back, starting a repertory theater (The Black Horizon Theater) at which he served as a scriptwriter and director. However, Wilson's most prominent achievement is a cycle of ten plays known as "The Pittsburgh Cycle" (two of these won the Pulitzer Prize for Drama). Each of these ten plays is set in a different decade of the twentieth century and depicts the comedy and tragedy of the African American experience.

VIRGINIA WOOLF Virginia Woolf (1882–1941) was born in London. Largely self-educated, Woolf published her first novel, *The Voyage Out,* in 1915. She achieved fame with her experimental novels—which include *Mrs. Dalloway* (1925), *To the Lighthouse* (1927), and *The Waves* (1931)—and with her essays, which include shorter reviews and critical essays collected in *The Common Reader* (1925) and *The Second Common Reader* (1932) as well as longer essays about the position of women, *A Room of One's Own* (1929) and *Three Guineas* (1938). With her husband Leonard, Woolf founded the Hogarth Press in 1917, which published many of the leading writers of the time. Her posthumously published *Letters* (1975–1980) and *Diary* (1977–1984) give further evidence of her genius.

JAMES WRIGHT James Arlington Wright (1927–1980) was born in Martin's Ferry, Ohio, and attended Kenyon College, where he graduated cum laude. After traveling to Vienna on a Fulbright Fellowship, Wright returned to the United States and obtained a Ph.D. from the University of Washington, where he studied under the poets Theodore Roethke and Stanley Kunitz. The 1956 publication of his collection, *The Green Wall,* led to an invitation to join the faculty of the University of Minnesota; he then published in nearly every important literary journal before transferring to teach at nearby Macalester College. His poetry was initially conventional but became less so later in his career. Wright battled alcoholism and suffered dark moods throughout his life, but his poetry remained fairly optimistic. He was awarded the Pulitzer Prize for Poetry for his *Collected Poems* in 1972.

GENE LUEN YANG Gene Luen Yang was born in Alameda, California, and began drawing comics in the fifth grade. Yang began self-publishing comics in 1996 under the name Humble Comics and received the prestigious Xeric Grant in 1997 for *Gordon Yamamoto and the King of the Geeks*. He has since written and drawn a number of comic titles, including *Duncan's Kingdom* (with art by Derek Kirk Kim) and *The Rosary Comic Book*. In 2006, *American Born Chinese* became the first graphic novel to be nominated for a National Book Award; it is also the first graphic novel to win the American Library Association's Printz Award. His next project, a collaboration with Thien Pham, is entitled *Three Angels*.

W. B. YEATS William Butler Yeats (1865–1939) was born in Dublin, Ireland. The leader of the Irish Resistance, he helped found the Abbey Theater in 1904. In 1922 he was elected to a six-year term as senator after the Irish Free State was formed. Yeats's writing displays an imaginative, skillful blend of Eastern and Western cultures and of ancient and modern thought. Despite this impressive eclecticism, Yeats always remains an Irish poet. His works include the prose volumes *A Vision* (1925) and *Autobiographies* (1926) as well as the volumes of poetry *The Tower* (1928), *The Winding Stair* (1929), and *Collected Poems* (1933). Yeats was awarded the Nobel Prize for Literature in 1923.

ADAM ZAGAJEWSKI Born in Lwów, Poland, Adam Zagajewski (1945–) lived in Paris until 1991 before moving to Krakow, Poland, in 2002. He is currently a faculty member at the University of Houston Creative Writing Program. His collections of poetry include *Tremor* (1985), *Canvas* (1991), *Mysticism for Beginners* (1997), and *Without End: New and Selected Poems* (2002). He has also published three books of essays: *Solidarity, Solitude* (1990), *Two Cities* (1995), and *Another Beauty* (2000). His most famous (and frequently anthologized) poem is "Try To Praise The Mutilated World," printed in *The New Yorker* on September 24, 2001, in response to the 9/11 attacks.

HAROLD A. ZLOTNIK (1914–) is a poet who has been published in *The Saturday Review of Literature, The American Scholar, English Journal, Kaleidograph, The New York Times, The Herald Tribune, Washington Post,* and other periodicals. He is a retired educator, formerly with the New York City Board of Education where he served as Director of English, as Coordinator of High School English Curriculum, and as Coordinator of the landmark program, Poets in the Schools, developed through a collaboration between The Academy of American Poets and the Board of Education, City of New York. His latest volume, *Toys of Desperation* (1987), an epic poem about the Haymarket Affair, is a featured text at the Illinois History Society.

Glossary

abstract and concrete abstract language uses a high proportion of abstract nouns, which refer to concepts, qualities, or general conditions ("truth," "honesty," "poverty"). Concrete language, on the other hand, uses more concrete nouns, which refer to things perceptible through the senses ("house," "rain," "tree"). Effective writing balances the two, using specific details to illustrate abstract ideas.

act a major division in a play; each act normally is composed of several scenes.

aesthetic distance the emotional closeness of either writer or reader to a work of art.

affective responses the emotional responses, including feeling, remembering, and associating.

allegory a story in verse or prose that can be understood on both a literal and symbolic level. In *The Pilgrim's Progress* by John Bunyan (1678), Christian, the hero, embarks on a pilgrimage that takes him through the Slough of Despond, the Valley of the Shadow of Death, and so forth, until finally he reaches the Celestial City. Christian represents everyman, and his journey is an allegory of Christian salvation.

alliteration the repetition of consonant sounds for poetic effect, particularly at the beginnings of words.

allusion a reference to historical events or figures, used to develop and deepen the meaning of a work (e.g., Plath's "Daddy").

ambiguity the state that exists when there are several legitimate interpretations of a literary work.

anaphora repetition of a word at the beginning of successive clauses or verses (e.g., Whitman's "Out of the Cradle").

anecdote a brief account of a story about an individual or an incident.

antagonist the character or force opposing the protagonist in a play.

anthropomorphism the endowment of animals with human thoughts and feelings.

anticlimax a move—in a sentence, stanza, paragraph, or literary work—from a noble tone to a less elevated one.

antihero a protagonist who is deliberately unheroic, i.e., often passive, ineffectual, or self-interested.

apex the height of the action in a drama.

archetype a theme, emblem, or character that reoccurs so frequently in all literature that it is accepted as universal. Examples include the theme of the quest, in which the protagonist sets out on a journey of self-discovery; the character of the femme fatale, or deadly woman; and the emblem of the rose, the symbol for romantic love.

argument a basic rhetorical mode that seeks, through logic and reason, to convince an audience by providing factual evidence to support a certain point of view.

aside in drama, words spoken in an undertone to the audience that are assumed to be inaudible to the other characters on stage.

assonance the repetition of similar vowel sounds, usually close together, for poetic effect. The first lines of Keats's "Ode on a Grecian Urn" contain a number of long /i/ sounds, creating a sensual, unhurried effect: "Thou still unravished bride of quietness,/ Thou foster child of silence and slow time."

atmosphere the emotional ambience created by a writer through setting, action, and word choice (e.g., Hawthorne's "Rappaccinis Daughter").

authorial intrusion when the author of a narrative seems to step out of the story and address the reader directly.

autobiography a biography written by the subject about herself or himself.

ballad a narrative poem, usually arranged in quatrains, that employs the rhyme scheme ABCB. There are two types. The folk ballad, a form of great antiquity, is composed and transmitted orally. It tells a dramatic story vividly and is anonymous. A literary ballad is a conscious imitation of this form by a poet. Many of the most famous literary ballads were written during the Romantic period, such as Coleridge's *Rime of the Ancient Mariner* and Keats's "La Belle Dame sans Merci."

bathos a pejorative term that describes what happens when a writer describes an honestly tragic situation in such an overblown way that the situation becomes unintentionally comic.

Beat movement a literary movement centered in the United States in the 1950s and distinguished by its attempt to combine socially marginal behavior with the quest for spiritual enlightenment (e.g., Ginsberg's "America").

Bildungsroman a German term meaning "novel of education," in which the fortunes of the protagonist are traced from early years to adulthood.

blank verse unrhymed iambic pentameter.

canon the group of literary works a given culture judges to possess special merit.

caricature the exaggeration of aspects or features of a character, usually for humorous or satiric purposes.

catastrophe the tragic conclusion of action in a play.

catharsis Aristotle's term for the therapeutic sense of emotional release supposedly felt by an audience that witnesses the tragic or terrifying onstage.

cause and effect a form of process analysis that explains the factors creating a certain situation or the consequences of a particular event. The downfall of Creon, for example, can be analyzed in terms of cause and effect.

character any person represented in a literary work. Characters are commonly described as being *round* (psychologically complex and convincing), *flat* (simplistic and often stereotypical), or *foils* (existing only to highlight certain aspects of the protagonist). It is also useful to distinguish between *dynamic* characters (those undergoing change) and *static* characters (those remaining unchanged).

chorus a group of players in Greek drama who provide a collective commentary on the action and the main characters. Although an essential part of Greek tragedy, a full chorus has rarely been used in English or American drama; two notable exceptions to this are Milton's *Samson Agonistes* (1671) and T. S. Eliot's *Murder in the Cathedral* (1935).

classification the process of grouping items together based on their similarities. Thus, poetry can be classified according to such categories as the sonnet, the ballad, or the ode.

cliché an overused, and hence ineffective, figure of speech such as "pretty as a picture" or "white as snow." Since the purpose of figurative language is to surprise the reader into a new way of seeing, writers should avoid clichés.

climax the point in a narrative or play at which a crisis is reached and resolution achieved.

colloquial expressions informal words and phrases that are a normal part of everyday speech but that are inappropriate in formal writing.

comedy a term usually applied to drama, although any work may have comic elements. There are many types of comedy (high, low, romantic, satiric, etc.), but overall the genre is characterized by its use of humor and the "happy ending." The comedy moves from complication to resolution, frequently resolving individual and social problems through marriage.

comic relief the insertion of a comic scene or character into a serious or tragic work in order to temporarily release some of the work's tension.

commedia dell'arte a sixteenth-century form of drama with mimes, skits, buffoonery, and such stereotypical characters as the harlequin and the young lover.

comparison-contrast the process of analyzing and determining similarities and differences in objects, phenomena, literary works, and so forth; often essays on literature compare character, theme, style. For organization of essays, see Chapter 3.

conceit a figure of speech comparing two dissimilar things or states; an elaborate and extended metaphor. See Chapter 11.

Confessional poets a group of American poets of the 1950s and 1960s distinguished by their concern with intensely personal subject matter (e.g., Sexton's "My Little Girl").

conflict an aspect of plot that concerns the tensions between opposing forces. Conflicts exist within characters, between or among characters, and between characters and such forces as nature, society, and the cosmos.

connotation the meanings or emotional associations evoked by a word.

couplets in poetry, two-line stanzas.

denotation the dictionary definition(s) of a word.

denouement the part of a narrative that follows the climax, in which any remaining unresolved plot elements are resolved.

deus ex machina literally "god from the machine," this term from classical Greek drama is applied to plot complications that are resolved through unnatural or strained means.

dialect a manner of speaking peculiar to an individual, class, or region that may differ considerably from the standard language of the country. While perfectly acceptable within its own context, dialect should be avoided in most formal writing, as the writer cannot assume a knowing audience. Dialect is most frequently found in fiction or drama, where it is used to make individual characters more realistic.

dialogue the direct speech of characters in any literary context.

Dirty Realism an American school of fiction of the 1970s and 1980s that focused on the minute, and frequently unpleasant, details of people's daily lives (e.g., Carver's "Cathedral").

double plot a second story that becomes fascinating on its own merits and enlarges the meaning of the main plot.

drafting composing and concentrating on organization, development, and fluency in the early stages of the writing process.

drama any work meant to be performed on a stage by actors. Usually, the work is divided into acts and scenes.

dramatic irony see *irony*.

dramatic poetry poetry in which the speaker becomes an actor, as in a monologue or a soliloquy.

editing the stage of the writing process concerned with sharpening word choice and style to clarify meaning and to strengthen presentation of message.

elegy a poem that expresses mourning for the death of a particular person and/or for mortality in general.

Elizabethan or Shakespearean sonnet a fourteen-line poem comprising three quatrains and a final couplet. The quatrains express and develop a dilemma or proposition to which the couplet offers a response (e.g., Shakespeare's "Let Me Not to the Mariage of True Minds").

end rhymes rhymes that occur at the end of verse lines.

enjambment in poetry, a statement that runs on into the next line.

epic poetry poems derived from oral tradition that describe the adventures and accomplishments of great heroes.

epigram a short, pithy, generally humorous observation presented as a general truth.

epigraph the inscription on the title page of a book, which may be a quotation from another literary work or an original remark by the author and which calls attention to the book's theme.

epiphany in a short story, a sudden moment of insight when a character discovers a truth important to the story (e.g., Joyce's "Eveline").

essay a concise prose discussion of a limited topic for a general audience.

evidence the use of facts, statistics, personal experiences, or the opinions of authorities to support a writer's claims or conclusions.

explication the close reading of a text, usually involving line-by-line analysis.

exposition intended primarily to inform, this rhetorical mode can take a variety of forms, such as classification, definition, process analysis, comparison/contrast, and cause and effect.

extended metaphor see *conceit*.

fable a short tale told to illustrate a moral, in which the characters are animals whose character traits represent human traits.

figurative language language that includes figures of speech.

figures of speech expressions that are based on comparisons, either explicit or implied, and that are intended to be interpreted imaginatively rather than literally. Their purpose is to surprise the reader into a new way of seeing. Among the most common are *simile, metaphor, personification, hyperbole,* and *litotes.*

first person narrative point of view in which the narrator speaks as "I" and is a participant in the narrative (e.g., Baldwin's "Sonny's Blues").

flashback a term derived from cinema, referring to any scene inserted into a literary work in order to show an earlier event.

foreshadowing using the current action in a literary work to anticipate later events.

free verse verse with no regular meter or line length. Although it may appear haphazard at first, free verse can acquire rhythms and melodies of its own.

Freytag's Pyramid Gustav Freytag conceived of plot in drama as rising action, climax, and falling action that leads to a dénouement. His conception took the shape of a pyramid.

generalization a broad statement that may well be true but that is not supported by concrete evidence. Generalizations lack substance, and so essays should not rely on them.

genre a literary type or class. The major classical genres are *tragedy, comedy, satire, epic,* and *lyric.*

hamartia a tragic error in judgment in classical Greek drama (e.g., Sophocles's *Antigone*).

Harlem Renaissance a cultural movement of the 1920s centered in Harlem, New York, which celebrated African American experience and attempted to find literary forms suited to it (e.g., Hughes's "Let America Be America Again").

hubris in classical Greek drama, overweening pride (e.g., Sophocles's *Antigone*).

hyperbole a figure of speech that uses deliberate exaggeration, usually for comic effect.

iamb a poetic foot consisting of an unstressed syllable followed by a stressed syllable, as in "behóld."

illustration the use of concrete examples to support a generalization.

imagery concrete language that appeals to the senses. An image does not have to be interpreted literally; indeed, many are conveyed by figurative language. (See *figures of speech.*)

in media res literally "in the middle of things," beginning a story in the midst of the action.

inductive and deductive reasoning two forms of everyday thinking. Inductive reasoning uses specific examples to formulate a general truth; deductive reasoning takes a general truth and seeks to demonstrate it through examples.

interior monologue in a work of fiction, an extended passage relating a character's thoughts (e.g., Busch's "Ralph the Duck").

intrigue scheme in a drama in which a character entraps another person who is naïve, trusting, and vulnerable.

introduction the first section of a paper, which should get the reader's attention, state the thesis, and establish the tone and point of view. In most college writing assignments, one paragraph will be sufficient. In longer papers, the introductory material may consist of several paragraphs.

irony a complex attitude that relies on contrast for its effect. There are three basic types. *Verbal irony* occurs when what is said contrasts with what is meant (e.g., "You are really too kind" said with great bitterness). *Dramatic irony* contrasts what is expected with what actually happens (e.g., a character laughs at another's misfortune, unaware that the same misfortune is happening to her). *Structural irony* used a particular device to sustain irony throughout the entire work, i.e., the naïve hero who constantly misinterprets events.

jargon the specialized vocabulary of a particular field or trade, which the general reader is unlikely to understand.

journal a form of personal writing concerning the self. The presumed audience is the author.

Kmart Realism a school of American fiction during the 1980s distinguished by its use of the icons of popular culture to make serious points (e.g., Mason's "Shiloh").

komos revel in classical Greek drama, from which we derive the word *comedy.*

literary theory/criticism a conceptual framework for understanding and interpreting a work of art. (See Appendix C.)

litotes the opposite of *hyperbole,* this figure of speech uses understatement for humorous effect.

lyric any short, non-narrative poem that deals subjectively with the thoughts and feelings of a single speaker. Although written in the first person, its sentiments are not necessarily those of the poet, but may be those of an adopted *persona*.

Magical Realism a twentieth-century literary movement associated with Central and South America in which the fantastical and the everyday are presented as equally "real" (e.g., García Márquez's, "The Handsomest Drowned Man in the World").

meditation a reflection on a scene that moves from observation of the object to consideration of metaphysical ideas.

memoir the remembrances of a public figure and/or of an historical era; an autobiographical form.

metafiction fiction that reflects on the subject and writing of fiction.

metaphor an implied comparison that brings together two dissimilar things without the use of "like" or "as." For instance, the metaphorical equivalent of Burns's famous simile "My love is like a red, red rose" would be "My love is a red, red rose."

Metaphysical poets a seventeenth-century English literary movement, whose poetry combined passion and reason through highly innovative conceits (e.g., Donne's "The Flea"). (See *conceit*.)

meter the pattern of stressed and unstressed syllables in lines of verse, each unit being termed a foot. / denotes a long or *stressed* syllable; ˘ denotes a short or *unstressed* syllable. The most common feet in English verse are:

iamb:	˘ /	e.g., dĕsíre
trochee:	/ ˘	e.g., wómĕn
anapest:	˘ ˘ /	e.g., ĭn ă flásh
dactyl:	/ ˘ ˘	e.g., yéstĕrdăy
spondee:	/ /	e.g., outwíth

In addition, lines are named according to the number of feet they contain:

> monometer: one foot
> dimeter: two feet
> trimeter: three feet
> tetrameter: four feet
> pentameter: five feet

> hexameter: six feet
> heptameter: seven feet
> octameter: eight feet

metonymy the substitution of one thing for another with which it is closely associated, such as using "the White House" to refer to the president.

mimesis the literary process of attempting to create a convincing and uninterrupted illusion of real life.

miracle plays a dramatic genre presenting Christian saints' lives and miracles.

modernism A European and American literary movement of the first half of the twentieth century, distinguished by its use of experimental techniques, its concern with individual psychology, and its concern with the decay of civilization (e.g., Eliot's "Love Song of J. Alfred Prufrock").

monologue a sustained speech by a single character, either with or without a direct audience (e.g., Shakespeare's *Othello*).

mood the atmosphere or tone of a literary work, created not only by the characters and events but also by the author's style and choice of language.

morality plays a dramatic genre that allegorized Christian values.

motif a theme or image that occurs repeatedly within a literary work and thus acquires symbolic value.

motivation the reason a character performs an action.

multiculturalism the increasing emphasis on race, class, and gender in education. In recognition of the diversity of most classrooms, the traditional curriculum is being modified to encompass the achievements and experiences of many groups.

mystery plays dramas presenting biblical stories.

myth a story involving supernatural beings that usually explains the cosmos and the mysteries of life and death.

narration essay form that seeks to recreate a series of events (i.e., a "story") as vividly as possible using descriptive detail.

narrative poetry form of poetry that tells a story.

narrator person telling a story.

novel an extended work of prose fiction that, although traditionally realistic, can be highly experimental.

novella an extended work of fiction, longer and more expansive than a short story, but shorter than a novel.

objective and subjective terms used to describe the extent and type of the author's involvement with her or his work. *Objective* writing is primarily factual and maintains a detached, impersonal tone. *Subjective* writing reveals the author's feelings and attitudes and often seeks to involve the reader emotionally.

octave see *Petrarchan* sonnet.

ode a formal and elaborate lyric poem that praises either a person or a thing. The *Pindaric Ode*, named after the classical Greek poet Pindar, traditionally celebrates a noteworthy individual upon some public occasion. The *Horatian Ode*, named after the classical Roman poet Horace, is in contrast private and personal (e.g., Keats's "Ode on a Grecian Urn").

onomatopoeia the use of words that imitate the sounds they represent, such as "crash" and "buzz."

organization the way a writer chooses to develop ideas in both paragraphs and essays, according to the purpose and audience. The five main methods are: (1) *deductive*, from general statement to specific example, (2) *inductive*, from specific example to general statement, (3) *climactic*, from least to most important, (4) *chronological*, according to time sequence, (5) *spatial*, according to physical organization.

oxymoron a word or phrase composed of two words that apparently contradict each other, such as "bittersweet."

pageants the platforms used in productions of mystery, miracle, and morality plays.

parable a story with a moral, often religious, the purpose of which is instruction. See discussion of the prodigal son in Chapter 10.

paradox an apparent contradiction that resolves itself on a deeper level.

paragraph a group of logically related sentences that together develop a central idea. This idea is stated broadly in a topic sentence and illustrated with supporting detail. Paragraphs break information down into smaller units, which the reader can assimilate more easily.

paraphrase a detailed restatement of information in words other than those of the original source.

parody the imitation of a certain author's style, tone, or attitude with the intent to ridicule. The technique is one of exaggeration.

pastoral a poem celebrating the idyllic nature of country life.

pathetic fallacy the attribution of human emotions to the nonhuman, used particularly when the writing is clichéd or melodramatic.

pathos the aspect of a narrative that causes its reader to feel pity or sorrow for the various characters.

performance art a form of American art of the 1980s and 1990s, distinguished by its combination of aspects of drama and improvisation (e.g., Smith's *Twilight Los Angeles*).

persona from the Latin for "mask," this term originally referred to the false face of clay worn by actors. It now denotes the identity adopted by an author for any literary work.

personification the attribution of human qualities to inanimate things for poetic effect.

Petrarchan sonnet named for a famous Italian poet, Petrarch, this sonnet is composed of an eight-line *octave* (composed of two *quatrains*) and a six-line *sestet* (composed of two *tercets*). The octave states a problem or proposition to which the sestet replies; the shift from octave to sestet in the ninth line is called the *volta*.

philosophical treatise an extended formal meditation on a philosophical, religious, or political subject (see Chapter 13).

picture frame stage an innovation in European drama that created the effect of framing the stage.

plagiarism the representation of another's words or ideas as though they were the writer's own. This academic theft, whether conscious or unconscious, is a serious offense. To avoid plagiarism, document all outside information.

plot the arrangement of events in a narrative or dramatic work. When two story lines are developed in equal length, the work is said to have a *double plot*. When one story line dominates the other, the latter is said to be the *subplot.*

point of view the perspective from which a story is told. Events can be narrated in the *first person* (the narrator is part of the action), or the *third person* (the narrator is outside the action). Narration in the *second person* is rare. An *omniscient narrator* uses the third person and is all-knowing.

postmodernism A European and American literary movement of the second half of the twentieth century distinguished by its conspicuous irony and its self-conscious concern with the nature of art (e.g., Busch's "Ralph the Duck").

premises supporting statements.

prewriting the generating of ideas prior to the initial drafting of a paper. The common strategies are *freewriting* and *brainstorming.* Freewriting involves writing nonstop for a short period of time. The writer is not concerned with grammar or spelling but with the free association of ideas. Brainstorming involves quickly listing anything and everything related to the topic. Ideas can then be grouped or subdivided to establish what is relevant.

primary and secondary sources *primary sources* are original materials, whether novels, speeches, scientific reports, or government documents. *Secondary sources* are studies of those materials. Thus, Wilfred Owen's poem "Arms and the Boy" is a primary source; a critical analysis of its themes is a secondary source.

proofreading the final stage of the writing process, in which the writer rereads the finished draft carefully for grammatical, spelling, or mechanical errors.

proscenium arch a frame enclosing the stage area behind which the front curtain hangs.

protagonist the principal character in a work of drama or fiction.

purpose and audience a writer's purpose, generally speaking, can be to *entertain, to explain, to explore,* or *to persuade.* Often several purposes will overlap, but the writer's overall intention will be closely tied to the audience being addressed. This can be any individual or group, whether the self,

as in a journal entry, or the general public, as in a newspaper article.

quatrains in poetry, four-line stanzas.

realism although all literature is clearly artificial, certain works can be said to represent life more accurately than others. Such works attend to the minutiae of everyday experience and present characters and events realistically rather than romantically.

revision this stage of the writing process involves rewriting a rough draft to improve both form and content. *Purpose* and *audience* should be reconsidered, as should the overall focus and development of the paper. Material may be cut, expanded, or moved around, while the language itself should be reworked for clarity and conciseness.

rhetorical question a question to which no answer is expected, or to which the answer is assumed to be self-evident. Used primarily for stylistic effect, this device encourages an emotional response from the reader and, thus, is often used in persuasive writing.

rhetorical situation purpose, audience, occasion, and point of view for the generation of a piece of writing. It is mainly a term used for the analysis of nonfiction. See, for example, the speech by Sojourner Truth.

rhyme in English poetry, the repetition of the last accented vowel and all succeeding sounds (e.g., boy–joy).

rhyme scheme fixed pattern of rhymes characterizing a poem or its stanzas.

rhythm in poetry or prose, the patterns of beats that establish the rise and fall of sounds; cadence. See the analysis of rhythm in Shakespeare's sonnet, "My Mistress' Eyes Are Nothing Like the Sun" and the chanting patterns in Anna Lee Walters's "My Name Is 'I Am Living'"

Romanticism a European literary movement of the late eighteenth and early nineteenth centuries distinguished by its concern with the free and subjective expression of passion, pathos, and personal feelings (e.g., Keats's "Ode on a Grecian Urn").

satire literature that exposes folly and seeks to correct it through ridicule. While the irony employed in satire may be amusing, the intent is not simply to entertain but to enlighten an audience. Jonathan Swift's essay "A Modest Proposal" is a classic example.

scansion the process of measuring poetry, of marking accented and unaccented syllables, and of dividing lines into feet in order to discern the metrical pattern of the poem and to notice deviations from the pattern.

scene a unit of continuous action in a play in which the setting remains unchanged. Groups of interrelated scenes comprise larger units of the work, known as *acts*.

sestet see *Petrarchan sonnet*.

setting the time, place, and/or environment in which a literary work occurs.

sexist language the misrepresentation or exclusion of either sex. One of the most common forms of sexist language is the use of the male pronoun "he" for an individual of unknown gender.

Shakespearean sonnet see *Elizabethan sonnet*.

short story a fictional narrative of more limited scope than the novel, often focusing on a single incident or character. It is a challenging medium, as the theme must be developed and brought to a satisfactory conclusion within approximately thirty pages.

simile a figure of speech that compares two unlike things using "like" or "as." See *metaphor*.

slave narrative a form of nineteenth century autobiography that documents a slave's journey from bondage to freedom.

soliloquy a dramatic convention in which a character, alone on the stage, voices her or his private thoughts. It is generally assumed that the feelings expressed are sincere (e.g., *Hamlet*).

sonnet a lyric poem of fourteen lines, usually in iambic pentameter, that employs a highly formal pattern of organization. Although there are a great number of possible rhyme schemes, the two most common are the *English* (also known as the *Elizabethan* and the *Shakespearean*) and the Italian (also known as the *Petrarchan*). The English consists of three quatrains and a concluding couplet and deploys the rhyme scheme ABAB/ CDCD/EFEF/GG. The Italian consists of an octave and a sestet and deploys the rhyme scheme ABBA/ABBA/ CDC/CDC.

stanza the basic unit of structure in a poem. Each unit consists of a group of interrelated lines arranged in a pattern that is usually repeated throughout the poem.

stereotypes easily recognized types of characters, such as the fool.

stock characters see *stereotypes*.

subplots secondary plot or plots in drama or fiction.

summary a concise restatement of a longer piece of writing, containing only the essential information.

surprise essential element of plot that contradicts the audience's or reader's expectations.

Surrealism a European literary movement of the 1920s and 1930s that emphasizes the author's imaginative expression of dreams and other psychic states reached through the unconscious mind.

suspense element of plot that builds excitement and uncertainty about the resolution of events.

syllabic verse a method of composing poetry that disregards accentual feet and creates rhythm through a regularized pattern of counted syllables.

syllogism a deductive argument in three parts that moves from a major and minor premise to a logical conclusion. For example: a) water is wet; b) rain is water; therefore c) rain is wet.

symbol an object, character, or action that stands for something more than itself.

symbolist dramas form of drama that features many traditional poetic symbols, allegorical names, and a dreamlike atmosphere. All of the action would be interpreted symbolically.

synecdoche the use of a part of something to stand for its whole, i.e., saying "My heart belongs to you" to indicate that the entire self belongs to the beloved.

synonyms words that are close enough in meaning to be interchangeable. Exact synonyms are rare, however, since all words have slightly different connotations.

syntax the arrangement of words within a sentence and the way this arrangement can affect meaning.

tercets three-line stanzas.

Theater of the Absurd a form of drama prevalent in the 1950s and associated with such playwrights as Pinter, Ionesco, and Beckett. Although literature has always explored the potentially comic aspects of humankind, the Theater of the Absurd reflects explicitly the twentieth-century philosophical view of a meaningless universe in which there is no coherence and little dignity. The plays themselves are, therefore, intentionally meaningless.

theme the central idea or message in a work. It can be expressed either directly or indirectly.

thesis statement usually contained in the introduction, the thesis statement es tablishes the focus of the essay—what it is about—in one or two sentences. Experienced writers sometimes use an *implied thesis statement,* where the purpose of the essay is clear without being directly stated. Student writers, however, should ensure that the thesis statement is identifiable.

tone created by both word choice and syntax, tone reflects the author's attitude toward the subject matter, which can be humorous, sarcastic, and so forth.

topic sentence the concise statement of the idea being developed within a paragraph. The topic sentence focuses the paragraph in the same way that the thesis statement focuses the essay.

tragedy a term usually applied to drama, tragedy traditionally traces the downfall of an initially noble character in a serious and elevated manner. In classical Greek drama, this downfall is invariably attributed to some tragic flaw in the protagonist, a device also seen frequently in Shakespearean tragedy (e.g., *Othello*). Modern tragedy is often said to lack the grandeur of classical tragedy, perhaps because it aims at broader social commentary and deals more with ordinary people in everyday situations.

tragic flaw see *hamartia.*

tragic hero protagonist in a tragedy; a person of high moral stature whose downfall is, nonetheless, the result of some tragic flaw (e.g., Shakespeare's *Othello*).

tragicomedy a mixture of tragedy and comedy created by the classical Roman dramatist Plautus.

transitional expressions essential to effective writing, these signal connections between ideas, thus allowing fluency between sentences and paragraphs. Some common transitional expressions are *however, therefore, consequently,* and *on the other hand.*

triplets in poetry, three-line stanzas.

unity of action in the *Poetics,* the classical Greek philosopher Aristotle wrote that every part of the action in a play must be integral to the whole. Any missing or extraneous part destroys the play's integrity.

vignette a sketch or a short scene in a larger work written with great skill for the purpose of either creating a vivid, resonant picture or illuminating some larger aspect of a work's theme.

villanelle a poem consisting of five *tercets* and a *quatrain,* based on two rhymes and with systematic repetitions of lines one and three of the first tercet (e.g., Thomas's "Do Not Go Gentle into That Good Night").

voice the individual personality of the author. Although a work may have many characters and may shift in tone according to the subject matter, there will remain a distinct authorial presence beyond even a first-person narrator. Student writers should recognize the importance of allowing their own voices to develop in their writing.

Credits

This page constitutes an extension of the copyright page. We have made every effort to trace the ownership of all copyrighted material and to secure permission from copyright holders. In the event of any question arising as to the use of any material, we will be pleased to make the necessary corrections in future printings. Thanks are due to the following authors, publishers, and agents for permission to use the material indicated.

Chapter 1

Denise Levertov, "The Secret" from *Poems 1960-1967*. Copyright © 1964 by Denise Levertov. Reprinted by permission of New Directions Publishing Corp.

Theodore Roethke, "My Papa's Waltz" and "The Waking" from *The Collected Poems of Theodore Roethke*. Copyright 1953 by Theodore Roethke. Used by permission of Doubleday, a division of Random House, Inc.

Chapter 2

Gloria Anzaldua, "horse" from *Borderlands/ La Frontera: The New Mestiza*. Copyright © 1987, 1999 by Gloria Anzaldua. Reprinted by permission of Aunt Lute Books.

Chapter 5

Daniel Alarcon, "Flood" from *War by Candlelight*. Copyright © 2005 by Daniel Alarcon. Reprinted with the permission of HarperCollins Publishers.

Ulysses S. Awesome, "Who Places Things Exactly" Copyright © 2005 by Ulysses S. Awesome. Reprinted with the permission of the author.

Bruno Bettelheim, excerpt from *The Uses of Enchantment*. Copyright © 1976 by Bruno Bettelheim. Reprinted with the permission of Raines & Raines.

Neal Bowers, "Driving Lessons" from *Out of the South*. Originally published in *Shenandoah* 42.2 (Summer 1992). Copyright © 1992, 2002 by Neal Bowers. Reprinted with the permission of the author.

Angela Carter, "The Company of Wolves" from *The Bloody Chamber and Other Stories*. Copyright © 1979 by Angela Carter. Reproduced by permission of the author c/o Rogers, Coleridge & White Ud., 20 Powis Mews, London W11 1JN, England.

Raymond Carver, "Cathedral" from *Cathedral*. Copyright © 1983 by Raymond Carver. Used by permission of Alfred A. Knopf, a division of Random House, Inc.

Countee Cullen, "Incident" from *Color*. Copyright 1925 by Harper & Brothers; copyright renewed 1953 by Ida M. Cullen. Copyrights held by the Amistad Research Center, Tulane University, administered by Thompson and Thompson, Brooklyn, NY.

Joan Didion, "Goodbye to All That" from *Slouching Towards Bethlehem*. Copyright © 1967, 1968, and renewed 1996 by Joan Didion. Reprinted with the permission of Farrar, Straus & Giroux, LLC.

Rita Dove, "Adolescence I", "Adolescence II", and "Adolescence III" from *The Yellow House on the Corner,* Carnegie Mellon University Press, © 1980 by Rita Dove. Reprinted by permission of the author.

Stephen Dunn, "The Sacred" from *Between Angels*. Copyright © 1989 by Stephen Dunn. Reprinted with the permission of W. W. Norton & Company, Inc.

Gretel Ehrlich, "Looking for a Lost Dog." Copyright © 1995 by Gretel Ehrlich. Used courtesy of Darhansoff, Verrill, Feldman Literary Agents.

Louise Erdrich, "Indian Boarding School: The Runaways" from *Jacklight*. Copyright © 1984 by Louise Erdrich, reprinted with the permission of The Wylie Agency Inc.

Heinz Insu Fenkl, excerpt from *Memories of My Ghost Brother*. Copyright © 1996 by Heinz Insu Fenkl. Reprinted with the permission of the author and Bo-Leaf Books, boleafbooks.com.

Chapter 8

Chapter 9

Index of Authors, Titles, and First Lines of Poetry